ENCYCLOPAEDIA JUDAICA

ENCYCLOPAEDIA JUDAICA

SECOND EDITION

VOLUME 8
Gos–Hep

Fred Skolnik, *Editor in Chief*
Michael Berenbaum, *Executive Editor*

MACMILLAN REFERENCE USA
An imprint of Thomson Gale, a part of The Thomson Corporation

IN ASSOCIATION WITH
KETER PUBLISHING HOUSE LTD., JERUSALEM

Detroit • New York • San Francisco • New Haven, Conn. • Waterville, Maine • London

ENCYCLOPAEDIA JUDAICA, Second Edition

Fred Skolnik, *Editor in Chief*
Michael Berenbaum, *Executive Editor*
Shlomo S. (Yosh) Gafni, *Editorial Project Manager*
Rachel Gilon, *Editorial Project Planning and Control*

Thomson Gale
Gordon Macomber, *President*
Frank Menchaca, *Senior Vice President and Publisher*
Jay Flynn, *Publisher*
Hélène Potter, *Publishing Director*

Keter Publishing House
Yiphtach Dekel, *Chief Executive Officer*
Peter Tomkins, *Executive Project Director*

Complete staff listings appear in Volume 1

For more information, contact
Macmillan Reference USA
An imprint of Thomson Gale
27500 Drake Rd.
Farmington Hills, MI 48331-3535
Or you can visit our internet site at
http://www.gale.com

LIBRARY OF CONGRESS CATALOGING-IN-PUBLICATION DATA

Encyclopaedia Judaica / Fred Skolnik, editor-in-chief ; Michael Berenbaum, executive editor. -- 2nd ed.
v. cm.
Includes bibliographical references and index.
Contents: v.1. Aa-Alp.
ISBN 0-02-865928-7 (set hardcover : alk. paper) -- ISBN 0-02-865929-5 (vol. 1 hardcover : alk. paper) -- ISBN 0-02-865930-9 (vol. 2 hardcover : alk. paper) -- ISBN 0-02-865931-7 (vol. 3 hardcover : alk. paper) -- ISBN 0-02-865932-5 (vol. 4 hardcover : alk. paper) -- ISBN 0-02-865933-3 (vol. 5 hardcover : alk. paper) -- ISBN 0-02-865934-1 (vol. 6 hardcover : alk. paper) -- ISBN 0-02-865935-X (vol. 7 hardcover : alk. paper) -- ISBN 0-02-865936-8 (vol. 8 hardcover : alk. paper) -- ISBN 0-02-865937-6 (vol. 9 hardcover : alk. paper) -- ISBN 0-02-865938-4 (vol. 10 hardcover : alk. paper) -- ISBN 0-02-865939-2 (vol. 11 hardcover : alk. paper) -- ISBN 0-02-865940-6 (vol. 12 hardcover : alk. paper) -- ISBN 0-02-865941-4 (vol. 13 hardcover : alk. paper) -- ISBN 0-02-865942-2 (vol. 14 hardcover : alk. paper) -- ISBN 0-02-865943-0 (vol. 15: alk. paper) -- ISBN 0-02-865944-9 (vol. 16: alk. paper) -- ISBN 0-02-865945-7 (vol. 17: alk. paper) -- ISBN 0-02-865946-5 (vol. 18: alk. paper) -- ISBN 0-02-865947-3 (vol. 19: alk. paper) -- ISBN 0-02-865948-1 (vol. 20: alk. paper) -- ISBN 0-02-865949-X (vol. 21: alk. paper) -- ISBN 0-02-865950-3 (vol. 22: alk. paper)
1. Jews -- Encyclopedias. I. Skolnik, Fred. II. Berenbaum, Michael, 1945-
DS102.8.E496 2007
909'.04924 -- dc22

2006020426

ISBN-13:

978-0-02-865928-2 (set)
978-0-02-865929-9 (vol. 1)
978-0-02-865930-5 (vol. 2)
978-0-02-865931-2 (vol. 3)
978-0-02-865932-9 (vol. 4)
978-0-02-865933-6 (vol. 5)
978-0-02-865934-3 (vol. 6)
978-0-02-865935-0 (vol. 7)
978-0-02-865936-7 (vol. 8)
978-0-02-865937-4 (vol. 9)
978-0-02-865938-1 (vol. 10)
978-0-02-865939-8 (vol. 11)
978-0-02-865940-4 (vol. 12)
978-0-02-865941-1 (vol. 13)
978-0-02-865942-8 (vol. 14)
978-0-02-865943-5 (vol. 15)
978-0-02-865944-2 (vol. 16)
978-0-02-865945-9 (vol. 17)
978-0-02-865946-6 (vol. 18)
978-0-02-865947-3 (vol. 19)
978-0-02-865948-0 (vol. 20)
978-0-02-865949-7 (vol. 21)
978-0-02-865950-3 (vol. 22)

This title is also available as an e-book
ISBN-10: 0-02-866097-8
ISBN-13: 978-0-02-866097-4
Contact your Thomson Gale representative for ordering information.
Printed in the United States of America

10 9 8 7 6 5 4 3

TABLE OF CONTENTS

Initial letter "G" of the word "Ge" ("I" in old French) at the opening of a paraphrase of and commentary on I Sam. 19:11 in Old French and Latin. The historiated initial in this 13th-century manuscript depicts Saul sending messengers after David. Munich, Bayerische Staatsbibliothek, Cod. gall. 16, fol. 36r.

GOS–GY

GOSHEN (Heb. גֹּשֶׁן), a grazing area in the N.E. of lower Egypt, east of the delta. Goshen was the residence assigned to Jacob and his family, and it was there that the Israelites lived in Egypt (Gen. 45:10; Ex. 9:26). It is currently assumed that the name is derived from the Semitic root גוש, i.e., compact, solid, and fertile land, suitable for grazing and certain types of cultivation. In the Bible Goshen is described as "the best part of the land" of Egypt (Gen. 47:6). It is also called "the land of Rameses" (Gen. 47:11) and it was probably identical with or not far from the "field of *Zoan" (Tanis; Ps. 78:12, 43), the name of the Egyptian capital during the *Hyksos period. The Septuagint (Gen. 46:28) renders Goshen as Heroonpolis (i.e., *Pithom, Ex. 1:11), and once (Gen. 46:34) as "the Arab land of Gesem." Therefore it is generally assumed that Goshen is to be located in Wādi Tumeilāt, which stretches from the eastern arm of the Nile to the Great Bitter Lake and is known to be excellent pasture land. Support for this identification is found in a papyrus (Pritchard, Texts, 259) from the end of the 13th century B.C.E. which describes how nomadic shepherds moved from the land of Edom, past the Merneptah fortress in Teku to the wells of Pithom in order to keep themselves and their cattle alive (cf. Gen. 45:10; 47:4). Teku is Wādi Tumeilāt. The rulers of Egypt would therefore seem to have permitted nomadic Semitic tribes to come to Goshen and graze there.

BIBLIOGRAPHY: P. Montet, in: RB, 39 (1930), 5ff.; W.F. Albright, in: BASOR, 109 (1948), 15; 140 (1955), 30–31; idem, *Yahweh and the Gods of Canaan* (1968), 79, 134; H.H. Rowley, *From Joseph to Joshua* (1950), index; H. Kees, *Ancient Egypt* (1961), index, s.v. *Wadi Tumilat.*

[Pinhas Artzi]

GOSHEN-GOTTSTEIN, MOSHE (1925–1991), scholar of Semitic linguistics. Born in Berlin, Goshen-Gottstein immigrated to Palestine in 1939. He studied at the Hebrew University of Jerusalem and taught there from 1950 on, becoming professor of Semitic linguistics and biblical philology in 1967. He was also director of the lexicographical institute and biblical research institute of Bar-Ilan University. In 1988 he was awarded the Israel Prize in Jewish studies.

His three areas of research were biblical studies, Hebrew linguistics, and Semitic linguistics. His numerous articles and books included *Medieval Hebrew Syntax and Vocabulary as Influenced by Arabic, Introduction to the Lexicography of Modern Hebrew,* and *The Aleppo Codex.* He worked on a number of dictionaries, among them the *Millon ha-Ivrit ha-Hadashah* ("Dictionary of Modern Hebrew"), the first synchronic dictionary of Hebrew, of which only the introductory volume was published (1969).

GOSLAR, city in Lower Saxony, Germany. Jewish merchants from *Worms are mentioned there in 1074 and 1114. In 1252 the city demanded the rights to the taxes from its Jewish settlement for itself, opposing the royal prerogative on the Jews as *Servi camerae; royal taxes were levied on them through the municipality from 1274. In 1312 the community paid a direct tax identical to that paid by Christians. The city council intervened on behalf of the community against the exactions of Emperor Louis IV in 1336 and 1340. The community of Goslar did not suffer persecution even at the time of the *Black Death, and the local form of the Jewish *oath was relatively free of degrading formulas. Problems of residence rights (**ḥerem* *ha-yishuv*) gave rise to bitter quarrels between old and new settlers, which the municipal council was often called upon to arbitrate, and resulted in a split in the community in 1331 which lasted for seven years. At that time there were approximately 30 Jewish taxpayers.

From 1312 the city council issued an increasing number of *Judenbriefe* conferring rights and obligations on individual Jews, so that by 1340 at least half of the Jews in Goslar were not included in the community for taxation purposes. This process continued in the latter half of the 14th century, accompanied by increased taxation and decline of the community. By 1400 not even a *minyan* could be organized, and in 1414 several Jews secretly left for Brunswick to evade a heavy imperial tax. A *blood libel about 1440 contributed to the decline of the community. A community in Goslar is mentioned in 1615, when a *parnas* was installed and took the oath of office. The *pinkas* registering a community of nine members was begun in 1677. A synagogue was built in 1693.

The community numbered 43 persons in 1871 and 38 in 1933. On *Kristallnacht, Nov. 10, 1938, the synagogue (consecrated in 1802), and Jewish shops and homes were attacked and looted. The well-preserved community archives were destroyed. Twenty-two members of the community perished during the Holocaust. A new community was organized, with 46 members in 1948, but declined soon afterward.

BIBLIOGRAPHY: Germ Jud, 1 (1963), 117f.; 2 (1968), 283–95; M. Stern, in: *Israelitische Monatsschrift* (supplement to *Die Juedische Presse*), 40 (1909), 41–42, 45–47; 41 (1910), 6–7, 10–11; idem, in: *Israelitischer Lehrer und Cantor* (supplement to *Die Juedische Presse*), 31 (1900), 17–18; 32 (1901), 38–39; D. Loehr, in: *Friede ueber Israel*, 47 (1964), 147–9, 167–70; H. Fischer, in: *Zeitschrift der Savigny-Stiftung fuer Rechtsgeschichte, Germanistische Abteilung*, 56 (1936), 89–149; L. Rabinowitz, in: HJ, 2 (1940), 13–21.

[Henry Wasserman]

GOSLAR, HANS (1889–1945), a senior official of the Prussian government during the Weimar Republic and a leader of the *Mizrachi movement in Germany. Born in Hanover, Goslar wrote for periodicals, specializing in economic problems. He became an early adherent of Zionism and in 1911 published a book entitled *Die Krisis der juedischen Jugend Deutschlands* (1911). During World War I he served in Eastern Europe, where he came to know the Jewish masses and this profoundly revised his religious outlook. On his return to Germany in 1919, his activities in the German Social Democratic Party earned him the title of Ministerialrat and an appointment as director of the press section of the Prussian government, a post he retained until he resigned in 1932. In 1919 he published *Die Sexualethik der juedischen Wiedergeburt*, in which he urged a return to Jewish family ethics. He maintained his general Jewish, Zionist, and Mizrachi activities and published several books on Jewish as well as general themes. In 1933 Goslar immigrated to Amsterdam, where he continued his communal activities, especially on behalf of the rescue of Jews from Germany. He was a neighbor of Anne *Frank's family, and his daughter was Anne's friend, mentioned in Anne's diary on several occasions. In 1943 he was deported to the *Westerbork concentration camp and in 1944 was transferred to *Bergen-Belsen, where he died shortly before the liberation in 1945. He also wrote *Juedische Weltherrschaft: Phantasiegebilde oder Wirklichkeit?* (1919) and *Hygiene und Judentum* (1930).

BIBLIOGRAPHY: Pick, in: MB (July 12, 1957); Y. Aviad, *Deyokena'ot* (1962), 235–7. **ADD. BIBLIOGRAPHY:** T. Maurer, "Auch ein Weg Als Deutsche und Jude – Hans Goslar 1889–1945," in: J.H. Schoeps, *Juden als Traeger der buergerlichen Kultur in Deutschland* (1989), 192–239.

[Getzel Kressel]

GOSLAR, NAPHTALI HIRSCH BEN JACOB (c. 1700–?), rabbi and philosopher. Goslar acted as *dayyan* in his native *Halberstadt, but later moved to Amsterdam. Only in his 50th year did he begin to study Maimonides' *Guide* and religious philosophy in general. In his *Ma'amar Efsharut ha-Tivit* (Treatise on Natural Potentiality, Amsterdam, 1762), composed in dialogue form and partly in rhymed prose, he criticizes the doctrine of an uncreated prime matter and polemicizes against deism. The appendix to the *Ma'amar* contains talmudic novellae under the title *Meromei Sadeh*. Goslar addressed two letters, dealing with theological problems, to his son Samuel who too was *dayyan* at Halberstadt (published in German translation by B.H. Auerbach, *Geschichte der israelitischen Gemeinde Halberstadt* (1866), 100ff., 199ff.).

[Moshe Nahum Zobel]

GOSTYNIN, town in central Poland. The Jewish population numbered 157 in 1765, 634 in 1856, 1,849 in 1897, and 1,831 (27.5% of the total) in 1921. Between 1823 and 1862 there were special residential quarters for the Jews. The old synagogue, destroyed by fire, was rebuilt in 1899. It was situated in the former Jewish lane, and a side alley there was popularly known as the "alley of the dead," recalling the location of the old Jewish cemetery. The ḥasidic leader and rabbi Jehiel Meir *Lipschuetz lived in Gostynin in the 19th century. There were 2,269 Jews living in Gostynin on the eve of World War II.

Holocaust Period

Immediately after the German army entered the town in Sept. 1939, mass arrests and attacks on Jews began along with requisition and looting of Jewish property. Jews were ordered to hew the old wooden synagogue into pieces and carry them to German inhabitants for fuel. They were ordered to pay two "contributions" (fines) in succession; when the president of the community was unable to collect the second sum in time, he sent a delegation to the Warsaw Jewish community (on a German suggestion) and received the required amount.

A ghetto was set up in Gostynin which was at first open, but subsequently surrounded by barbed wire. Order was kept by Jewish police. Most of the Jews left the ghetto every morning for hard labor assignments. In August 1941 transports of men and women began to be sent to labor camps in the Warthegau. The ghetto was liquidated on April 16–17,

1942, when nearly 2,000 Jews were sent to the death camp at Chelmno.

By the end of the war all traces of Jewish life in the town had been obliterated. The cemetery had been desecrated and destroyed, the tombstones hauled away, and the tomb (*ohel*) of the local *ẓaddik* destroyed. The few Jews from Gostynin who survived the Holocaust subsequently emigrated.

BIBLIOGRAPHY: *Pinkes Gostynin: Yizkor Bukh* (1960); D. Dąbrowska, in: BŻIH, 13–14 (1955), 122–84 passim.

[Danuta Dombrowska]

GOTA, MOSES ZERAHIAH BEN SHNEUR (d. 1648), Turkish rabbi. Gota studied under Jehiel Basan and Joseph di Trani. After spending most of his life in Constantinople, he moved to Jerusalem and from there, to Hebron; financial difficulties compelled him to leave for Cairo, where he remained for the rest of his life. His contemporaries describe him as a great *posek* and as expert in Kabbalah. Apart from some responsa, all his works have remained in manuscript. They are: *Zeraḥ Ya'akov* on the *Beit Yosef* of Joseph *Caro; a commentary on Maimonides' *Mishneh Torah*; a supercommentary on Rashi's Pentateuch commentary; collected responsa and sermons. Some of his responsa are to be found in the Bodleian Library together with those of Eliezer Arḥa (rabbi in Hebron from 1634) and David *Habillo. Others appear in various works, among them in the collection of responsa *Zera Anashim* (1902). Gota's remains were interred on the Mount of Olives in 1650.

BIBLIOGRAPHY: Conforte, Kore, 51; Frumkin-Rivlin, 2 (1928), 31; Fuenn, Keneset, 337.

[Simon Marcus]

GÖTEBORG, city in S.W. Sweden. In 1780 a number of Jewish families were granted permission to enter the area, and by 1792, 20 Jews lived in the city. Though the first synagogue was built in 1808, the congregation was unable to secure the services of a rabbi, Carl Heinemann, until 1837. After an attempt to introduce radical reform measures, opposed by the rabbi, two members of the congregation secured Heinemann's resignation in 1851, replacing him with the liberal German rabbi, Moritz Wolff, who led the community until 1899. Numbers of Polish and Russian Jews settled in Göteborg between 1903 and 1920. During World War II the Göteborg community absorbed many Jewish refugees from Denmark and also from Poland and Russia (1943–45). The Jewish population increased steadily and in 1968 reached 1,450, making Göteborg the third largest Jewish community in Sweden. With the exodus of Jews from Poland in 1968, many Polish Jews settled in Göteborg as well as in Sweden's two other major cities of Stockholm and Malmö. Following the collapse of Soviet power and the dismantling of the Berlin Wall, a new wave of Jewish emigration saw a significant increase in the number of Jews arriving from Russia and its satellites. Now constituting the second largest Jewish community in Sweden, Göteborg's Jewish population stood at 1,600 in the early years of the 21st century, with another thousand or so living in and near the city who are not affiliated with the congregation.

BIBLIOGRAPHY: *Göteborgs mosaiska församling, 1780–1955* (1955); *Skrift till invigningen av mosaiska församlingens i Göteborg nya församlingshus...* (1962); H. Valentin, *Judarna i Sverige* (1964). **ADD. BIBLIOGRAPHY:** *Mosaiska församlingen i Göteborg 200 år* (1980).

GOTHA, city in Thuringia, Germany. Jews from Gotha are mentioned in *Cologne in 1250 and later in *Erfurt. Eight members of the community were killed in connection with a *blood libel in Weissensee in 1303. The community suffered during the *Black Death persecutions (1349) and again in 1391. Though the community disappeared after the persecutions of 1459–60, a *mikveh* (*Judenbad*) is mentioned in 1564 and 1614. Until 1848 no Jews were allowed to live in the duchy of Gotha but restricted trading was permitted. The community formed after 1848 increased from 95 in 1872/3, to 236 in 1880, and 372 in 1910 (0.9% of the total population). A synagogue was built in 1903. In 1932 the prosperous community of 350 members maintained a synagogue, school, cemetery, library, and six social and charitable organizations. On Nov. 10, 1938, the synagogue was burned down and 28 men of the community were sent to *Buchenwald. The 80 remaining Jews had been deported by 1939. The community was not reestablished after World War II.

BIBLIOGRAPHY: Germ Jud 1, 118–19; 2, 295–96; FJW, 372; PK.

GOTLIEB, ALLAN (1928–), Canadian lawyer, diplomat, public servant. Gotlieb was born in Winnipeg. His parents, David and Sarah Gotlieb, were very active in Jewish community and Israel support activities. Sarah Gotlieb was a leading figure in Canadian Hadassah and served as national president of the organization from 1951 to 1955.

Allan Gotlieb earned a B.A. at the University of California at Berkeley, his M.A. while a Rhodes' Scholar at Oxford, and a law degree from Harvard University. In 1957 he joined the Canadian Department of External Affairs, where in 1967 he became an assistant undersecretary and legal adviser. Gotlieb met Pierre Trudeau shortly after Trudeau was first elected to Parliament in 1965. While Trudeau was first parliamentary secretary to Prime Minister Lester Pearson and then minister of justice, the two men developed a close working relationship and consulted often on issues of federal-provincial relations and foreign affairs. When Trudeau became prime minister in 1968, Gotlieb was appointed deputy minister of the Department of Communication and in 1971 deputy minister of manpower and immigration. In 1977 he returned to External Affairs as an undersecretary and in 1981 Gotlieb was appointed Canadian ambassador to the United States, a post he held until 1989. While in Washington, Gotlieb, with the assistance of his wife, Sondra, was particularly effective in representing Canada's interests and raising Canada's profile.

From 1989 to 1994 Gotlieb was chairman of the Canadian Council for the Arts, a government-funded organization charged with fostering and promoting the study, enjoyment, and the production of art in Canada. He then became a senior adviser to a major Canadian law firm, specializing in areas of arbitration, government relations, and regulatory and public policy. In addition to his various professional and business interests, Gotlieb was also active in support of a number of arts foundations and research institutions. Among his many honors, he was a Companion of the Order of Canada.

[Harold Troper (2nd ed.)]

GOTS, Russian revolutionary family. ABRAM RAFAILOVICH GOTS (1882–1937 or 1940) was born in Moscow into the family of a wealthy tea merchant; from 1906 Gots was an active member of the fighting organization of the Socialist-Revolutionary (SR) party and a member of its central committee. For his participation in the planning of a terrorist act in 1907 he was sentenced to eight years imprisonment. After the February 1917 Revolution he led the SR faction in the Petrograd soviet. In June 1917 at the First Congress of Soviets he was elected chairman of the All-Russian Central Executive Committee. Following the October Revolution Gots joined the anti-Bolshevik Committee for Saving the Homeland and the Revolution. He was an organizer of the armed attack of the junkers (cadets) which took place in Petrograd. November 11–12, 1917. At the 4th Congress of SRS (November 1917) he defended the right to resort to terror against the forces which had usurped the rights of the Constituent Assembly. In 1920 he was arrested and in 1922 sentenced to execution, which was subsequently changed to five years imprisonment. In 1927 he was exiled, first to Simbirsk and then to Alma-Ata. In 1937 he was arrested again. According to some sources, he was shot together with Mark Liber in Alma-Ata. In Soviet political literature his name always appears as part of the trio "Gots-Liber-Dan" (see Fyodor *Dan) whom Lenin referred to as "social defenders," i.e. leaders of socialist parties who advocated the continuation of the war after the February Revolution.

His brother, MIKHAIL RAFAILOVICH GOTS (literary pseudonym, M. Rafailov; 1866–1906), entered Moscow University in 1885, but in the following year was arrested for revolutionary activities, and in 1888 was exiled to Eastern Siberia for 8 years. For armed resistance to the authorities in Yakutsk in 1889, during which he was wounded, he was sentenced to permanent exile, but in 1895 received amnesty. He lived in Kurgane, and then in Odessa where he took up literary activities. In 1901 Gots emigrated to Paris where, in collaboration with other revolutionaries, he published the journal *Vestnik russkoy revolyutsii*. From the establishment of the SR party (in late 1901) until his death, Gots was one of the heads of the party. In 1902 he moved to Geneva where he helped to publish the central organ of the SRS *Revollyutsionnaya Rossiya*. Gots' apartment in Geneva served as SR headquarters and he himself directed all party work. In 1903 when visiting Italy, Gots was arrested at the request of the Russian government but due to a campaign in the European socialist and radical press he was freed and deported to Switzerland. The money he received from rich relatives he used for party purposes. Apart from articles, he published a book: on criticism, dogma, theory, and practice.

[Mark Kipnis / *The Shorter Jewish Encyclopaedia in Russian*]

GOTSFELD, BESSIE (1888–1962), U.S. social worker and Zionist. Born Beilka Goldstein in Przemsyl, a middle-sized city in southeastern Poland, this daughter of a religiously Orthodox yet modern family was educated in a Polish gymnasium. In 1905, her family migrated to New York, where Beilka became Bessie. In 1909 she married Mendel Gotsfeld, her English tutor. A Zionist since her youth in Poland, Gotsfeld's interest in the movement was rekindled through contact with Mizrachi leaders Rabbis Wolf Gold and Meir Berlin. Thereafter she dedicated her life to religious Zionism. She cherished Mizrachi's objective, which was to secure "the land of Israel for the people of Israel, in accordance with the law of Israel."

In 1925 she founded a national organization, Mizrachi Women of America (which after 1982 became known as Amit). MWOA's double objective was to give voice to the inchoate desire of Orthodox women for a gendered connection to the new Zionist settlement in Palestine and to widen educational and vocational opportunities for the female Orthodox population of Ereẓ Israel.

To investigate the feasibility of starting a school, Gotsfeld traveled there in 1929–30 and selected a Jerusalem building to refurbish as a technical school. En route home, she contacted European women's groups and solicited their support. She convinced Orthodox women in Europe and America that this school would foster Zionism and religion. Skilled young women would contribute to the economy of the new settlement, put a new face on Orthodoxy, and assure continuity into the next generation.

In 1931 the Gotsfelds settled permanently in Tel Aviv and Bessie became the official (though unpaid) "Palestine representative of MWOA." At her suggestion and under her supervision MWOA founded three urban vocational schools for adolescent girls and two large farm villages that instructed girls and boys along similar lines. The largest, Kefar Batya in Ra'ananah, bears her Hebrew given name. MWOA also constructed children's homes in small settlements, supported day care centers in the cities, and funded youth programs. Gotsfeld kept the MWOA membership informed through letters, bulletins, and speaking tours in the United States.

Gotsfeld was caught up in the fierce battles between secular and Orthodox Jews over the education of child refugees who found their way to Palestine before, during, and after World War II. She found places in Orthodox institutions for Youth Aliyah children and immigrants from Arab countries. No other branch of Mizrachi matched MWOA's accomplishments during the pre-state years. Along with Hadassah and Pioneer Women, the other major American women's Zionist organizations, MWOA played a critical role in building the Yishuv.

Gotsfeld retired officially in 1948 but maintained a grip on organizational policy until her death in 1962. Her whirlwind activities over three decades is remarkable in light of illness and mounting disabilities suffered through most of her adult life. The institutions that she founded exemplify the process of modernization within 20th century Orthodox Judaism. They trained a generation of Orthodox female technicians and teachers competent in advanced methods of pedagogy, agriculture, and technology, and eager to assert their status as equal citizens of the new state.

BIBLIOGRAPHY: L.M. Goldfeld, "Bessie," Amit pamphlet (n.d.); B.R.Shargel, "American Jewish Women in Palestine: Bessie Gotsfeld, Henrietta Szold, and the Zionist Enterprise," in: *American Jewish History* (2002); idem, " 'Never a Rubber Stamp,' Bessie Gotsfeld, Founder of Mizrachi Women of America," in: *American Jewish Women and the Zionist Enterprise* (2005).

[Baila Round Shargel (2nd ed.)]

GOTTESFELD, CHONE (pseud. **Tuvye Shmeykhl**; 1890–1964), Yiddish humorist and writer of comedies. Born in Skala, Galicia, he attended gymnasium in Czernowitz, before immigrating at 18 to the U.S. From 1914 until his death he was on the editorial staff of the New York daily *Forverts*, editing for many years the news, as well as the humor section. Among his comedies, staged in the U.S. and Poland, the most successful were *Gevald, Ven Shtarbt Er?* ("Heavens, When Will He Die?"1926) and *Parnose* ("Livelihood"). Rudolph *Schildkraut and Maurice *Schwartz directed and acted in his plays. His humorous memoirs, *Vos Ikh Gedenk fun Mayn Lebn* ("What I Remember of My Life"), appeared in 1960 (Eng. 1965).

BIBLIOGRAPHY: LNYL, 2 (1958) 24–5; Z. Zylbercwejg, *Leksikon fun Yidishn Teater*, 1 (1931), 258–9. **ADD. BIBLIOGRAPHY:** M. Ravitch, *Mayn Leksikon*, 4 (1980), 108–10.

[Melech Ravitch]

GOTTESMAN, U.S. family of philanthropists. MENDEL GOTTESMAN (1859–1942), industrialist, banker, and philanthropist, was born in Munkacs, Hungary, and immigrated to the United States in the 1880s. He was a pioneer in the paper and pulp industry, and later founded and became president of an investment banking company. Gottesman founded and supported several *talmud torahs* on the Lower East Side of New York, particularly between the 1890s and 1915, during which time he became associated with the forerunner of Yeshiva University, the Isaac Elchanan Theological Seminary. In 1917 he organized the Gottesman Tree of Life Foundation, through which many of his charitable activities were carried out, including granting scholarships to Yeshiva University students. He served as treasurer of Yeshiva University for many years and as president of the Yeshiva Endowment Foundation, which he conceived and established, from 1928 to 1942. DAVID SAMUEL GOTTESMAN (1884–1956), merchant and financier, was born in Munkacs, Hungary, the son of Mendel Gottesman. He became his father's partner in the wood pulp industry and later developed his own companies in that business and in investment banking. In 1941 he established the D.S. and R.H. Gottesman Foundation to donate funds for higher education, local welfare, Jewish studies, and other causes. Among the foundation's charitable contributions were four Dead Sea Scrolls, purchased for the State of Israel in 1955, and the donations of funds in 1961 for the construction of the Shrine of the Book in Jerusalem to house the Dead Sea Scrolls; the building is now part of the Israel Museum.

BENJAMIN GOTTESMAN (1897–1979), born in New York City, the son of Mendel Gottesman, carried on his father's work in both business and philanthropic association with Yeshiva University. A trustee of the university, he was vice president and treasurer of the Gottesman Tree of Life Foundation, one of the founders of the Albert Einstein College of Medicine of Yeshiva University, president of the Yeshiva Foundation Endowment Inc., and chairman of the Investment and Endowment Committee. Gottesman also served on the Investment Advisory Committee of *Hadassah, of which his wife ESTHER GOTTESMAN (1899–1997), born in New York City, was national treasurer.

GOTTHEIL, GUSTAV (1827–1903), Reform rabbi, liturgist, and U.S. Zionist leader. Gottheil was born in Pinne, Posen. He was drawn to liberal Judaism at the University of Berlin, and studied with such scholars as Steinschneider and Zunz. During 1855–60 Gottheil was a teacher at the Reform Gemeinde in Berlin and preaching assistant to Samuel *Holdheim, who impressed him greatly. In Manchester, England, where he served the progressive Congregation of British Jews from 1869 to 1873, Gottheil mastered English, then joined Temple Emanu-El of New York City in 1873 as co-rabbi to the aging Samuel *Adler. Challenging the ethical culture theories of Felix Adler, son of Samuel Adler, Gottheil espoused a more traditional theistic Judaism, and was upheld by the congregation. He attempted to maintain a rabbinical school under Emanu-El's auspices during 1874–85, but it had very few students. Gottheil published a hymnal in 1886 and a devotional compilation *Sun and Shield* (1896). He voluntarily abandoned issuing his own prayer book in favor of the *Union Prayer Book*, which included a number of his translations and renderings. The most important American rabbi publicly to support Zionism during the First Zionist Congress in 1897, Gottheil, his son Richard *Gottheil, and Stephen S. *Wise were among the founders of the Federation of American Zionists. Gottheil was a teacher and friend to such young rabbis as Stephen S. Wise, Leon Harrison, and Samuel Schulman. In a sense he was a bridge from the German beginnings of Reform to its Eastern – as distinct from Midwestern – American flowering.

BIBLIOGRAPHY: R.J.H. Gottheil, *Life of Gustav Gottheil, Memoir of a Priest in Israel* (1936).

[Bertram Wallace Korn]

GOTTHEIL, RICHARD JAMES HORATIO (1862–1936), U.S. Orientalist. Gottheil was born in Manchester, England, the son of Gustav *Gottheil, and immigrated to New York with his parents in 1873. He taught Semitic languages at Columbia University from 1886 until his death, except for one year, 1920–21, at the University of Strasbourg; he was director of the Oriental Department of the New York Public Library from 1896 until his death and president of the American Oriental Society, 1933–34. Gottheil was an active Zionist and prominent in American Jewish life. Among other activities he served as president of the American Federation of Zionists, 1898–1904, president of the Society of Biblical Literature, 1902–03, and vice president of the American Jewish Historical Society from 1904 on. He founded the Zeta Beta Tau Fraternity, originally a Zionist society, and was one of the founders of the Jewish Institute of Religion (see *Hebrew Union College-Jewish Institute of Religion in New York). Among the works Gottheil published, in addition to numerous articles in scholarly and general periodicals and books, are *Zionism* (1914), *The Holy War* (1915), *The Belmont-Belmonte Family* (1917), and *The Life of Gustav Gottheil; Memoir of a Priest in Israel* (1936). Among the works he edited and translated are *A Treatise on Syriac Grammar by Mâr(i) Eliâ of Sôbhâ* (1887), and with W.H. Worrell, *Fragments from the Cairo Genizah in the Freer Collection* (1927). He was an editor of the *Jewish Encyclopedia* (1901–06) and the editor of the *Columbia University Oriental Series* (vols. 1–29, 1901–36).

BIBLIOGRAPHY: G.A. Kohut, *Professor Gottheil – an Appraisal at Seventy* (1933); J. Bloch, in: JAOS, 56 (1936), 472–9; S. Rosenblatt, in: BASOR (Dec. 1936), 2–3.

GOTTLIEB, ADOLPH (1903–1974), U.S. painter and sculptor. Best known for his abstract expressionist paintings, New York-born Gottlieb studied at the Art Students League with John Sloan and Robert Henri (1920–21). After traveling through Europe for two years, and attending life drawing class at the Académie de la Grande Chaumière in Paris, Gottlieb returned in 1923 to New York for additional art instruction. His first solo exhibition was held at the Dudensing Gallery in New York in 1930.

In 1935 Gottlieb cofounded "The Ten," a group of artists committed to progressive tendencies in art that also included Mark *Rothko. The Ten exhibited together regularly until 1939. Working under the Works Progress Administration's Federal Art Project since 1936, Gottlieb executed a mural for the Yerington, Nevada Post Office in 1939.

Influenced by European surrealists who settled in New York before World War II; primitive art; and Southwest Indian symbols, introduced to him in Arizona where he lived from 1937 to 1939; Gottlieb created his first pictograph in 1941. An amalgamation of abstraction and the subjectivity of Surrealist-inspired automatism, the Pictograph series is comprised of grid compartments in which Gottlieb placed stylized iconography that sometimes drew on his interest in ancient myths. Critics relate his art of the period to the distress of World War II. The Pictographs (1941–51) were followed by two other major series: Imaginary Landscapes (1951–57) and Bursts (1957–74). The Imaginary Landscapes, such as *The Frozen Sounds, No. 1* (1951, Whitney Museum of American Art, New York), are characterized by a horizontal line across the center of a canvas, above which he painted different geometric shapes reduced in color from the Pictographs. In the lower half of the canvas he applied a dense array of gestural marks. The Bursts marked the beginning of Gottlieb's work on oversized canvases. Gottlieb typically placed one or more disks floating on the top half of the canvas contrasting with an exploding mass of black gestures on the lower half. Similar shapes comprise sculptures executed in the 1960s.

In addition to painting, Gottlieb designed an ark curtain for Congregation B'nai Israel, Millburn, N.J. (1951), and a tapestry for the prayer hall as well as the valance of the ark curtain for Beth El in Springfield, Mass. (1953). He designed and supervised fabrication of a 35-foot-wide, four-story-high stained glass facade for the Milton Steinberg Center at New York's Park Avenue Synagogue (1954). Using compartmentalization similar to the Pictographs, 31 compositions are repeated and interspersed in 91 panels displaying partly abstracted Jewish symbols, biblical stories, religious rituals, and holidays. An arrow, for example, is meant to symbolize a Torah pointer, a serpent symbolizes phylacteries, and 12 calligraphic signs delineate the 12 tribes of Israel.

BIBLIOGRAPHY: M. Friedman, *Adolph Gottlieb* (1963); R. Doty and D. Waldman, *Adolph Gottlieb* (1968); A. Kampf, *Contemporary Synagogue Art: Developments in the United States, 1945–1965* (1966), 242–247; *Adolph Gottlieb: A Retrospective*, exh. cat. (1981).

[Samantha Baskind (2nd ed.)]

GOTTLIEB, BERNHARD (1885–1950), dental scientist. Born in Kuty, Slovakia, Gottlieb trained in Vienna, where he did research in diseases of the teeth, specializing in the cause of caries. He was the first to describe the epithelial tissue which joins the tooth surface to the gum. During World War I he served as a dental surgeon on the Russian-Romanian front. In 1921, he started to lecture at the University of Vienna, and was a pioneer in experimental animal studies which drew the attention of researchers in this field in Europe and the U.S. In 1938, under Nazi rule, Gottlieb was dismissed from his post at the university. With the help of some non-Jewish admirers he was able to leave Austria. Gottlieb was a keen talmudist, and identified with the cause and interests of a Jewish state in Ereẓ Israel. He went to Palestine where he spent two years teaching at the Hebrew University and helped to set up dental clinics. In 1940, Gottlieb emigrated to the United States, where he was visiting professor at the Kellogg Foundation Institute at Ann Arbor, Michigan.

[Jacob Yardeni]

GOTTLIEB, EDWARD (**"Eddie," "The Mogul"**; 1898–1979), pioneer innovator, administrator, and promoter of U.S. basketball; member of the Basketball Hall of Fame. Born in Kiev, Gottleib and his family immigrated to the U.S. when he was a child, first to New York and then Philadelphia, where he graduated from South Philadelphia High School in 1916. Gottlieb helped organize an amateur team under the Young Men's Hebrew Association in 1918, which was subsequently sponsored by the South Philadelphia Hebrew Association. That social club provided uniforms with the acronym SPHAS across the chest in the Hebrew letters *sameḥ*, *pe*, *he*, and *alef*, and the legendary team – considered one of the greatest early professional teams – won three league titles in the Philadelphia League, three out of four in the Eastern League, and eight of 13 in the American Basketball League, primarily with Jewish players. In 1946, Gottlieb helped establish the Basketball Association of America, winning the league's first championship, and was instrumental in merging the BAA with the National Basketball League to form the National Basketball Association in 1949. He coached the Philadelphia Warriors from 1947 to 1955, purchased the team in 1952, and led them to their first NBA title in 1956.

After selling the team in 1962 for a then-record price of $850,000, Gottlieb remained with the Warriors as general manager when they became the San Francisco Warriors, and stayed with the team until 1964. He served as chairman of the NBA Rules Committee for 25 years and was instrumental in the adoption of the 24-second clock, the rule against zone defenses, and the bonus penalty shot. For nearly 30 years he was the NBA's sole schedule maker. Gottlieb also helped organize overseas tours for the Harlem Globetrotters, and promoted professional doubleheaders. Upon his death, *The New York Times* wrote: "His mental powers were extraordinary and his memory almost faultless. He remembered the scores of games, the gate receipts, the attendance, and even the weather." The Eddie Gottlieb Trophy is awarded annually to the NBA's Rookie of the Year. Gottlieb was inducted into the Basketball Hall of Fame in 1971.

[Elli Wohlgelernter (2nd ed.)]

GOTTLIEB, EPHRAIM (1921–1973), historian of Kabbalah. Gottlieb was born in Munkács (Mukachevo), and received his education in Czech schools, yeshivot, and the Hebrew high school at Munkács, where he took part in Zionist activities. Immigrating to Ereẓ Israel in 1941, he first taught in the agricultural school at Mikveh Israel (until 1955). From 1945 to 1947 he was in Hungary on behalf of the *Beriḥah *("Aliyah Bet")*, organized by the Jewish Agency. From 1955 to 1965 he taught Jewish subjects in a municipal high school belonging to the religious trend in Tel Aviv. During the years 1952 to 1963 Gottlieb studied Talmud, Jewish philosophy, and Kabbalah (in which he specialized), becoming one of the foremost pupils of Gershom *Scholem and gaining his Ph.D. in 1963. From that year he lectured on Kabbalah at Bar-Ilan University, from 1964 at Tel Aviv University, and from 1965 at the Hebrew University of Jerusalem, where he became senior lecturer in 1966 and associate professor in 1970. Gottlieb's contributions (all in Hebrew) to the history of early Spanish and Italian Kabbalah, between the 13th and 16th centuries, are distinguished by profundity, wide knowledge of the sources, and philological precision. The history of Spanish kabbalistic literature, in particular, has benefited from this research. In his book *The Kabbalah in the Writings of R. Baḥya ben Asher ibn Ḥalawa* (1970), he analyzed the sources of Baḥya's famous commentary on the Torah and proved conclusively that the author used some parts of the Zohar extensively, translating, or paraphrasing them in Hebrew. His other studies, most of which appeared in *Tarbiz*, *Kirjath Sepher*, and the *Shenaton* of Bar-Ilan University, include research into the kabbalistic exegeses on Genesis 1 in the Gerona circle (*Tarbiz*, 37, 1968), into the works of (or attributed to) Joseph Gikatilla (*Tarbiz*, 39, 1969–70), and into the *Pekudin* section of the main body of the Zohar, later used by the author of the *Raaya Meheimna* portion of the Zohar and incorporated into this secondary work (KS, 48, 1973). Gottlieb studied the concepts of *devekut* and prophecy in an unpublished work by Isaac b. Samuel of Acre (*Papers of the Fourth World Congress of Jewish Studies*, 2, 1969) and some of the writings of R. Joseph from Ḥamadan which were first identified by him (KS, 48, 1973). He conclusively identified the hitherto anonymous author of the commentary on *Ma'arekhet ha-Elohut*, printed in the Ferrara edition of this work (*Memorial Volume for Prof. Benjamin de Vries*, 1969), and analyzed the discussion on the theory of transmigration, held in 1466 in Crete and preserved in two Vatican manuscripts (*Sefunot*, 11, 1974). He also disproved the authenticity, or in another case the lack of value, of kabbalistic texts which had been considered important by earlier scholars (the falsification of the work *Ginnat Bitan* and its commentaries ascribed to the early 14th century, in *Studies in Honour of G. Scholem*, 1968, and the construction of R. Elhanan the Blind's epistles, in *Michael*, 1, 1973). Gottlieb proved them to be plagiarisms based on Judah Ḥayyat's work *Minḥat Yehudah*. His lectures on the Kabbalah at the end of the 13th century, especially on Gikatilla and the book *Ma'arekhet ha-Elohut*, were published in mimeographed form (1969). Gottlieb died suddenly in October 1973, a month after his appointment as head of the Institute of Jewish Studies of the university.

[Gershom Scholem (2nd ed.)]

GOTTLIEB, FRANTIŠEK (1903–1974), Czech poet and author. Born in Klatovy, Bohemia, Gottlieb studied law and was influenced by Otokar *Fischer at Charles University in Prague. He was an active Zionist in his youth, and made Jewish nationalism the ideological basis of his first book of poetry, *Cesta do Kanaán* (The Way to Canaan, 1924), and of his earliest novel, *Životy Jiřího Kahna* (The Lives of George Kahn, 1930, 1947^2) a tragic story of the son of a Jewish merchant. In 1939, he emigrated to Palestine, but during World War II joined the Czechoslovak army in the Middle East. After the war, he returned to Prague, where he entered the Czechoslovak Foreign Ministry. His impressions of wartime Palestine are embodied in a volume of poems, *Dvojí nástup* (Double Ascent, 1942, 1946^2), and in two books of short sketches, *Čelem proti čelu* (Head On, 1947) and *Jaro a poušť'* (Spring and Desert, 1956, 1962^2). Eventually, he published a drama, *Golem* (1965), about Rabbi *Loew, in 1966 a volume of poems, *Rozpjatý den* (An

Extended Day), and a short story, "Z okna do okna" ("From Window to Window," 1973), a sorrowful tale of a Jewish family. Gottlieb was not deterred from dealing with Jewish themes after the Communist coup of 1948.

BIBLIOGRAPHY: O. Donath, *Židé a židovství v české literatuře 19. a 20. století*, 2 (1930), index; J. Kunc, *Slovnik českých spisovatelů beletristů 1945–56* (1957); R. Iltis, in: *Jewish Quarterly*, 13 (Summer 1965), 11. **ADD. BIBLIOGRAPHY:** *Lexikon české literatury* 1 (1985); A. Mikulášek et al., *Literatura s hvězdou Davidovou*, vol. 1 (1998).

[Avigdor Dagan / Milos Pojar (2nd ed.)]

GOTTLIEB, HEINRICH (1839–1905), lawyer, communal leader, and writer, born in Lvov. He practiced law in Kalisz and Lvov. As deputy chairman of the Lvov community, Gottlieb was responsible for its educational department and did much to develop its activities. His book *Schulbetrachtungen* (1872) deals with educational questions. He also wrote studies on pedagogy, law, philosophy, natural sciences, and history, including a series of articles on the Jewish Khazar kingdom (in *Oesterreichische Wochenschrift*, nos. 13, 17, 21, and 48, 1894). He was editor of the Polish periodical *Ekonomista* and contributed to *Izraelita*. Gottlieb also wrote literary essays and poetry (*Weltuntergang*, 1888).

BIBLIOGRAPHY: M. Bałaban, in: YE, 6 (c. 1910), 733–4.

GOTTLIEB, HINKO (1886–1948), Yugoslav author, translator, and Zionist leader. Born in a Croatian village, Gottlieb made his name as a Zionist poet and writer on Jewish themes while he was still a student in Zagreb. After graduating, he divided his activity between law practice and literary pursuits. His verse, which combined imagination and realism, reflected contemporary events and his whole output testified to his strong Jewish loyalties and his anti-Nazi sentiments. A prominent contributor to most Jewish publications in Yugoslavia between the world wars, Gottlieb founded the Jewish monthly *Ommanut*, which he edited from 1936 until 1941. He published Serbo-Croat translations of German, Yiddish, and Hebrew works, the latter for an anthology of modern Hebrew literature (1933), as well as translations from Heine (1936). A collection of his poems *Ijar, jevrejski maj* ("Iyyar, the Jewish May") appeared in 1935. As a lawyer, Gottlieb often defended Yugoslav communists and had contacts with Josip Broz, the World War II partisan leader who became President Tito. Following the Nazi invasion in 1941, Gottlieb was arrested and imprisoned in Vienna and then in Zagreb. He managed to escape and joined Tito's forces. In 1944 he was sent to Bari, Italy, where he organized the rescue of 1,500 Croatian Jews. In the following year he left Europe for Ereẓ Israel, where he completed and revised his stories of the Holocaust period. These later works include *Ključ od velikih vrata* (*The Key to the Great Gate*, 1947), a novel which later appeared in Hebrew (1950); and the short story *Kadiš u šumi* ("Kaddish in the Forest," 1944), which has been acclaimed as one of the outstanding products of Jewish underground literature.

BIBLIOGRAPHY: S. Radej, in: *Jevrejski Almanah 1954*; V. Dedijer, *Josip Broz Tito* (1953); C. Rotem, in: *Jevrejski Almanah 1957/8*; idem, in: *Davar* (June 14, 1945 and Oct. 31, 1958). **ADD. BIBLIOGRAPHY:** C. Rotem, "Hinko Gottlieb: Works," 2 vols. (Heb., 1980).

[Zdenko Lowenthal / Cvi Rotem]

GOTTLIEB, HIRSCH LEIB (1829–1930), Hebrew journalist. Born in Szigetvar, Hungary, Gottlieb translated works of Goethe, Schiller, and others into Hebrew. In 1878, in his native town, he began to publish *Ha-Shemesh*, the first Hebrew paper in Hungary. Among those who contributed to the paper were the Hebrew writers R.A. *Broides, G. *Bader, and D.I. Silberbusch. As a result of the opposition of the rabbi of Szigetvar the paper was moved for a time to Kolomea, Galicia, where it appeared once under the name *Ha-Shemesh* and once as *Ha-Ḥarsah*. Gottlieb ceased publishing it at the turn of the century, returned to Szigetvar, and began to publish Yiddish newspapers. Because of open advocacy of Zionism in his Yiddish paper *Zion* he was persecuted by religious extremists, but he nevertheless persevered until the eve of World War I. Gottlieb was also a well-known humorist whose anecdotes and light verse were published in his newspaper and in his book of Yiddish verse, published posthumously.

BIBLIOGRAPHY: *Tazlil*, 4 (1964), 44–65 (Hebrew translation of his autobiography); Yaari, in: KS, 35 (1959/60), 111–2.

[Getzel Kressel]

GOTTLIEB, JACOB (**Yankev**; 1911–1945), Yiddish and Hebrew poet, short story writer, and essayist. Born in Kovno, Lithuania, Gottlieb was a descendant of the ḥasidic rabbis of Nowy Sacz. He published his first poem at age 14 and contributed to numerous East European Yiddish periodicals. His first poetry collection, published at age 20, proved his mastery of various lyric styles as well as of blank verse. His poems were characterized by mystic imagery and treated universal themes such as love and nature, as well as social and national subjects. He envisaged a coming world decline and another Jewish catastrophe. Three additional volumes of lyrics appeared in 1933, 1936, and 1938, along with a study of H. *Leivick in 1939. With the outbreak of World War II, Gottlieb fled eastward from the Nazis, and survived the war years in Mari (Turkmenistan), where he died of typhus in 1945. A posthumous selection of his poems, *Geklibene Lider* ("Selected Poems"), was published in Montreal in 1959.

BIBLIOGRAPHY: LNYL, 2 (1958), 18; J. Leftwich (ed.), *The Golden Peacock* (1961).

[Melech Ravitch / Marc Miller (2nd ed.)]

GOTTLIEB, JEDIDIAH BEN ISRAEL (d. 1645), talmudic scholar and itinerant preacher in Poland. He visited the major Jewish communities, especially Lvov (Lemberg), Cracow, and Lublin. His biblical and talmudic homilies (*Ahavat ha-Shem*) were published in Cracow in 1641, and again in Lublin in 1645. This work includes 50 different explanations of Deuteronomy 10:12. His biblical commentaries, printed in Cracow in 1644 in three volumes under the title *Shir Yedidut*, reflect Jewish social, religious, and economic life in Poland in the first half of the 17th century, prior to the catastrophe of the *Chmielnicki uprising. As a prominent preacher, Gottlieb had the courage to castigate the rich members of the Jewish communities for being overzealous in their pursuit of worldly riches. He enjoined them to bequeath part of their fortunes for community needs and scholars, rather than leave everything to their children. From Gottlieb's homilies it also transpires that Jews with drive and initiative easily found economic opportunities in trade and tax farming, and acquired considerable wealth. He expressed his preference for "self-made" men over those who acquired wealth by inheritance, and supported their claim to social status. Gottlieb is representative of the itinerant preachers of that period who sensed the spirit of the times and often aroused delight by clever, humorous, or anecdotal explanations of the texts.

BIBLIOGRAPHY: Ḥ.D. Friedberg, *Ha-Defus ha-Ivri be-Krakov* (1900), 27; H.H. Ben-Sasson, *Hagut ve-Hanhagah* (1959), index.

GOTTLIEB, MAURYCY (1856–1879), Polish painter. Born in Drohobycz, in eastern Galicia, he was the son of a prosperous owner of an oil refinery. At the age of 13, he studied at the art school in Lemberg, and three years later at the Vienna Academy. Later, under the influence of his teacher at the Cracow Academy, professor Jan Matejko, an ardent champion of Polish nationalism, Gottlieb turned from German to Polish subject matter. Gottlieb was subjected to antisemitic taunts, and painted a self-portrait called "Ahasuerus," which referred to the legend of the Wandering Jew who was shunned by everyone. In 1876 he received a prize at Munich for his painting, "Shylock and Jessica." The noted publisher Bruckmann then commissioned him to make 12 illustrations for a deluxe edition of Lessing's drama *Nathan der Weise*. Yielding to antisemitic pressure, Bruckmann canceled the commission after seven of the illustrations had been finished. Gottlieb's next major work, "Jews Praying on the Day of Atonement," was stimulated by his studying Heinrich *Graetz's *History of the Jews*. The picture caused a sensation in Jewish circles, and the Jewish press hailed it as a genuinely Jewish masterpiece. With the aid of a Viennese patron, Gottlieb went to Rome, where he again met his teacher Matejko, who greeted him as "the most hopeful disciple of Polish art, whom I greet as my successor." After a few months in Rome, Gottlieb went back to Cracow, where he died at the age of 23. Considering the fact that Gottlieb's career covered only four or five years, his extant work is remarkable both in quality and quantity. "Shylock and Jessica" is so well and richly painted that the theatricality of the scene is overlooked, and "Jews Praying on the Day of Atonement" (which embodies a self-portrait) is an indisputable masterpiece. Gottlieb was also an excellent portraitist. His portraits are gems of psychological penetration in an era that often beautified and falsified its sitters. His portraits of girls and elderly women have delicacy, lightness of touch, and charm.

Maurycy's younger brother LEOPOLD GOTTLIEB (1883–1934), the 13th child of the Gottlieb family, studied in Cracow, Munich, and Paris, and for a while taught at the Bezalel School in Jerusalem. During World War I he was a lieutenant in the Polish Legion, and thereafter fought under Pilsudski in Poland's War of Independence. Among the numerous personalities who sat for him for portraits were Pilsudski and the writer Sholem Asch.

BIBLIOGRAPHY: M. Narkiss (ed.), *Maurycy Gottlieb, Iggerot ve-Divrei Yoman* (1955); *Polski Słownik Biograficzny*, 8 (1959–60), 386–7; Roth, Art, 556–62, 808–10.

[Alfred Werner]

GOTTLIEB, YEHOSHUA (1882–c. 1940–41), Zionist journalist and leader in Poland during the interwar period. Born in Pinsk, Gottlieb began his Zionist activities in 1913, becoming a member of the central committee of the Zionist Organization in Poland in 1916. He served the movement mainly as a journalist, writing for the great Warsaw Yiddish dailies *Haynt* (1919–35) and *Moment* (1935–39), and was one of the outstanding newsmen and essayists of his time. In 1935 he was elected to the Sejm (Polish parliament). From 1927 to 1934 he was chairman of the Warsaw Journalists' Association and from 1924 to 1939 was a member of the Warsaw Jewish Community Council, serving as its deputy chairman from 1926 to 1930. He was one of the founders of the Et Livnot ("Time to Build") faction of the *General Zionists, which supported *Weizmann's idea of an "enlarged" *Jewish Agency. On behalf of his faction, Gottlieb worked diligently in support of the Fourth Aliyah (from 1924 on), which consisted mostly of middle-class Jews from Poland. When World War II broke out, he fled to Pinsk, where he was arrested by the Soviets soon after their entry into the city. He died in prison in Poland, according to one version, while another version has it that he had been taken to northern Kazakhstan.

BIBLIOGRAPHY: LNYL, 2 (1958), 15–18; Kol, in: *Sefer Pinsk*, 2 (1966), 539–40; Remba, in: *Ḥerut* (Dec. 17, 1965). **ADD. BIBLIOGRAPHY:** Ch. Finkelstein, *Haynt, a Tsaitung baz Ziden 1908–1939* (1978), index.

[Getzel Kressel]

GOTTLOBER, ABRAHAM BAER (pseudonyms **Abag** and **Mahalalel**, 1810–1899), Hebrew and Yiddish writer and poet. Born in Staro-Konstantinov (Volhynia), Gottlober was taken to Tarnopol (now Ternopol), Galicia, by his father at the age of 17. In Galicia he came in contact with the Haskalah, of which he was a staunch advocate most of his life, and met Joseph *Perl in 1828. Upon his return to Volhynia, his pious father-in-law, violently opposed to his secular studies, compelled him to divorce his wife. Gottlober, embittered by the affair, developed a hostility toward orthodoxy and Ḥasidism which found satiric expression in his writings. At 19 he remarried and moved to Podolia where, under the influence of Menahem Mendel *Levin's works, he began writing in Yiddish and in Hebrew. He wandered from place to place, living between 1830 and 1850 in Bessarabia, Berdichev, and Kremenets. In

Kremenets he married for the third time and befriended I.B. *Levinsohn. Upon obtaining a government teaching license in 1850, he taught school until 1865 when he was appointed instructor of Talmud at the rabbinical seminary in Zhitomir. There he remained until the government closed down the seminary in 1873.

Hebrew Works

Gottlober's literary career extends over a 60-year period and though his writings are of a limited aesthetic value, they are a real, if modest, contribution to the development of the modern Hebrew language and literature and to Yiddish literature. During the 1830–50 period, he published two collections of Hebrew poems: *Pirḥei ha-Aviv* (1837) and *Ha-Nizẓanim* (1850). In 1874, on an extended sojourn in Vienna, he published his Hebrew translation of Lessing's *Nathan der Weise*, a number of nationalistic poems in Hebrew, and the short story *"Kol Rinnah vi-Yshu'ah be-Oholei Ẓaddikim" (Ha-Shaḥar,* 1874–75). When the editor of *Ha-Shaḥar*, Perez *Smolenskin, attacked the Berlin Haskalah and wrote disparagingly of Moses *Mendelssohn, Gottlober broke with him and founded the Hebrew monthly *Ha-Boker Or* which appeared intermittently in Lemberg and later in Warsaw (1876–86). The periodical, mainly a vehicle for Gottlober's attack on Smolenskin's views, published also many of his short stories and studies in biblical exegesis, and in 1886 the second part of his memoirs, *Zikhronot mi-Ymei Ne'urai*. (The first part had appeared separately in Warsaw in 1881, while supplementary material was published in *Ha-Asif*, 1885.) With the demise of his journal, Gottlober left Warsaw and lived first in Dubno, then in Rovno, spending the last years of his life in Bialystok. While the poet's longing for Ereẓ Israel found some poetic expression in the 1870s, the 1881 pogroms shocked him into further national realization: he joined the Ḥibbat Zion movement and most of his poetry was now imbued with yearning for the Land of Israel. *Kol Shirei Mahalalel* (1890) is a collection of his poetry, original and translated, that had not appeared in the previous collections. A scholar, Gottlober also published a number of research and critical works. Among these are *Bikkoret le-Toledot ha-Kara'im* (1865) a study of the history of the Karaites; *Iggeret Bikkoret* (1866), a critical work on modern Hebrew poetry; a translation of Moses Mendelssohn's *Jerusalem* (1867); and *Toledot ha-Kabbalah ve-ha-Ḥasidut* (1869), a history of the Kabbalah.

Yiddish Works

Gottlober's most productive period in Yiddish writing was between the years 1840 and 1870. One of his earliest works, *Feldblumen*, a collection of lyrics, and *Di Farkerte Welt*, a didactic poem, were lost, but most of the poems were recovered in the 1920s and 1930s. Many of Gottlober's Yiddish works were published long after they had been written: his three-act comedy *"Der Dektukh oder Tsvey Khupes in Eyn Nakht"* was written in 1838 and published in 1876, and the poem, *"Der Bidne Yisrolik,"* written in 1843, appeared in 1876. Often depicted against a ḥasidic background, the works are written in an everyday dramatic speech into which the author introduced a satirical note. Gottlober's attitude toward Yiddish was ambivalent: while he saw it as a language "without literature, without grammar, and without logic," he also felt that he could address the Jewish public only in its own language. Among his best Yiddish works are *Dos Lid finem Kugel* (1863), a parody on Schiller's poem *Lied von der Glocke; "Der Seim oder di Groyse Aseyfe in Vald, ven di Ḥayes Hoben Oysgekliben dem Layb far a Meylekh"* (1863, but written in 1842), a satiric fable in verse form; and *"Der Gilgul"* (1896), a sharp social satire which was first published in *Kol Mevasser* in 1871. *"Zikhroynes vegen Yudishe Shrayber"* (*Yudishe Folksbibliotek* 1, 1888) is his important nonfictional work in Yiddish. A collection of his Yiddish works appeared in 1927, *A.B. Gottlober's Yidishe Verk* (A. Fridkin and Z. Rejzen, eds.).

Initial Evaluation

Greatly overestimated in the prime of his career, Gottlober's writings have, nevertheless, left their mark on Hebrew and Yiddish letters. A facile writer, his style is fluent rather than compelling. Much of his writing is a direct attack on the obscurantism of the period and shows his firm support of the Haskalah. During the last 20 years of his life, however, he had become disappointed with the ideals of the Haskalah and had become one of the early champions of the nationalist movement and of the revival of Hebrew. While his poems are strongly marked by lyricism and often reflect his own experiences, his personal feelings were so closely interwoven with the public weal that much of his poetry bears a journalistic stamp. Its artistic value lies in the fact that it mirrors the aspirations and aesthetic criteria of his time. His incisive criticism influenced contemporary Hebrew poetry and led to greater metrical flexibility; his memoirs and short stories remain valuable for the interesting light they shed on many facets of Jewish life in Eastern Europe. Gottlober was also one of the first Hebrew writers to translate Russian poetry into Hebrew. His studies on the Karaites and on the Kabbalah, although highly imitative, served to draw attention to important but neglected areas of Jewish interest.

BIBLIOGRAPHY: Klausner, Sifrut, 5 (1955^2), 286–344 (includes bibliography); P. Shalev-Toren, *A.B. Gottlober vi-Yẓirato ha-Piyyutit* (1958); Rejzen, Leksikon, 1 (1926), 451–8; Waxman, Literature, 3 (1960^2), 255–8; A. Fridkin, *A.B. Gottlober un Zeyn Epokhe* (1925). **ADD. BIBLIOGRAPHY:** G. Kresel, *"Gottlober ha-Memu'arist,"* in: *Moznayim*, 44 (1977), 230–32; Y. Mazor, *"Sipporet ha-Haskalah,"* in: *Te'udah*, 5 (1986), 39–65; Z. Skodizki, *"Wejgen Falks Iberarbeitung fun Gottlobers Lider,"* in: *Die Yiddishe Literatur in 19. Jorhindert* (1993), 289–304.

[David Patterson]

GOTTSCHALK, ALFRED (1930–), chancellor emeritus of Hebrew Union College-Jewish Institute of Religion. Gottschalk was born in Oberwesel, Germany, and immigrated with his family to the United States in August 1939, just weeks prior to World War II. His parents had been comfortable in Germany as wine, grain, and hide dealers. His grandmother had been one of the first woman mayors in the Weimar Republic.

Upon arrival in the United States, his parents worked in the garment industry for seven dollars a week so young Alfred had to peddle newspapers. He entered school without speaking English. By the time he graduated high school, he was a football player, playing semi-pro. Though offered a scholarship to Brandeis and Brown, he chose to stay close to his recently widowed mother. After graduating from Brooklyn College he studied at the Hebrew Union College-Jewish Institute of Religion, first in New York and later in Cincinnati, where he was ordained in 1957. He was appointed dean of the newly established California School of HUCJIR in 1959, which served the rapidly expanding Jewish community of Los Angeles and all of California. Concurrently, he completed his Ph.D. at the University of Southern California (1965). Gottschalk served as dean until 1971, when he was appointed president of the Hebrew Union College-Jewish Institute of Religion, succeeding Nelson Gleuck, as the sixth president of the college, which had become a four campus facility. Headquartered in Cincinnati, the college has thriving programs in Los Angeles, New York and Jerusalem. He was also the John and Marianne Slade Professor of Jewish Intellectual History. Under his leadership, the college was set on firm financial footing. He ordained the first woman rabbi of the contemporary era in Sally Priesland and opened both the Rabbinical and Cantorial School to women. He established the first school of Jewish Communal Service and also was the first to train Israelis for the Reform rabbinate in Israel. The first Israeli woman Reform rabbi was ordained in 1992.

Leadership of the Reform movement is divided between the congregational arm, which was the Union of American Hebrew Congregations (now the Union of Reform Judaism) and The Hebrew Union College. Together with Rabbi Alexander Schindler, another German-Jewish refugee, Gottschalk provided stable and innovative leadership for Reform Jews, which has overtaken the Conservative movement as the allegiance of choice for a plurality of the American Jewish community.

Deeply sensitive to good fortune to be a refugee from Nazi Germany and thus to escape the Holocaust, Gottschalk was appointed in 1979 to the President's Commission on the Holocaust and then in 1980 to the United States Holocaust Memorial Council. He chaired the council's Academic Committee and stepped in as acting chairman of the council when Elie Wiesel suddenly resigned as chairman in 1986. He brought administrative skill and much needed stability to his brief service. After his retirement from Hebrew Union College in 1996, he served for a time as president of New York's Museum of Jewish Heritage: A Living Memorial to the Holocaust. He participated in the inauguration of President Ronald Reagan's second term but was not hesitant to criticize the President over the Bitburg issue.

Gottschalk's main interest is modern Jewish thought, particularly its relation to earlier Jewish sources. He was a leading authority on Aḥad Haam, the leader of cultural Zionism. He contributed articles on this subject to various publications. In addition, he has published *Your Future as a Rabbi – A Calling that Counts* (1967; 1989) and *Aḥad Ha-Am as Biblical Critic – A Profile* (1970).

GOTTSCHALK, LOUIS MOREAU (1829–1869), U.S. composer and pianist. Gottschalk grew up in New Orleans where he was exposed to the Creole music with its African-Caribbean rhythms that would later become a characteristic ingredient of his music. A child prodigy he went at 13 to Paris for piano and composition lessons and by 19, through the success of his "Creole" piano pieces, was hailed as the New World's first authentic musical spokesman, and his keyboard virtuosity was compared with Chopin's. After playing in Switzerland (1850) and Spain (1851) with spectacular success, he returned to the United States. His father's death (1853) proved to be a turning-point in his career; he was forced to increase the frequency of his concerts to earn enough money to support his family. For three years Gottschalk toured the country, his sentimental ballads ("The Last Hope," 1854, "The Dying Poet," 1863) proved immensely popular. He also contributed to the new "Western" idiom with his genre pieces *Le banjo* (1853, 1855). He spent the next five years in Puerto Rico, Guadeloupe, Martinique, and Cuba. There he found his musical roots and his vocation as a composer and wrote some of his finest works, including *Souvenir de Porto Rico, Ojos criollos* (four hands), a symphony and several operas. He also wrote for the American and French press. In 1862 Gottschalk had to resume his virtuoso career playing again for American audiences. In four and a half months he gave 85 recitals, a brutal pace which he maintained for more than three years, during which he did more than any other American musician to champion the Unionist cause and also to obliterate the line between high and popular art. In 1865, he had to leave the States after being unjustly accused in a scandal. The last four years of Gottschalk's life were spent in a triumphant tour of South America, where also he encouraged local talents, promoted classical music and championed public education. Gottschalk's own account of his troubled life was first published in 1881 as *Notes of a Pianist*.

BIBLIOGRAPHY: Grove; S.F. Starr, *Bamboula! The Life and Times of Louis Moreau Gottschalk* (1995); J.E. Perone, *Louis Moreau Gottschalk: A Bio-Bibliography* (2002).

[Naama Ramot (2nd ed.)]

GOTTSCHALK, LOUIS REICHENTHAL (1899–1975), U.S. historian. Born in Brooklyn, N.Y., Gottschalk taught at the University of Chicago from 1927 where he was professor from 1935. Gottschalk was assistant editor (1929–43) and acting editor (1943–45) of the *Journal of Modern History* and president of the American Historical Association (1953). Gottschalk's main historical interests were the era of the French Revolution, modern European history in general, and historiography. His major works include *Jean Paul Marat: a Study in Radicalism* (1927); *Era of the French Revolution* (1929); a multi-volumed study of Lafayette (5 vols., 1935–1969); and *Understand-*

ing History: A Primer of Historical Method (rev. ed., 1969). While maintaining exacting standards for the verification of past events, he recognized the influence of the historian's own environment on his interpretation. Gottschalk served on the International Commission for a Scientific and Cultural History of Mankind from 1956, becoming vice president in 1962. Gottschalk was active in Jewish affairs, and was president of the Chicago Board of Jewish Education (1942–45); council member of the Conference on Jewish Social Studies; and chairman of the Union of Chicago B'nai B'rith Hillel Foundation from 1963.

BIBLIOGRAPHY: R. Herr and H.T. Parker (eds.), *Ideas in History: Essays presented to Louis Gottschalk by his former students* (1965).

[Joseph I. Shulim]

GOTTSCHALK, MAX (1889–1976), Belgian social scientist and Jewish leader. Born in Liège, Gottschalk was a member of the bar at Liège and Brussels and joined the staff of the International Labor Office (1921–23). At the end of 1923, he was invited to join the Institute of Sociology of the Free University of Brussels as research professor, and was mostly occupied with problems of unemployment. The representative of the ILO for Belgium and Luxembourg (1923–40), Gottschalk became government commissioner for unemployment (1933–34) and president of the Social Security Board (1935–40). During World War II Gottschalk went to the United States, where he taught at the New School for Social Research in New York. After the war, he returned to the Institute of Sociology in Brussels, where he was president of the Center of Regional Economy and president of the International Council for Regional Economy (1958–68). On retiring from the Belgian and International Associations for Social Progress, he became honorary president of both these organizations.

His Jewish activities were religious, social, and intellectual. He presided over the Central Jewish Consistory of Belgium (1956–62). In the social field, he was vice president of the *Jewish Colonization Association, board member of *Alliance Israélite Universelle and ORT-Union, and a founder of the Centrale d'Oeuvres Sociales Juives (United Jewish Appeal) in Brussels. He directed the Research Institute for Peace and Postwar Problems of the American Jewish Committee (1940–49) and from 1959 the Centre National des Hautes Etudes Juives, financed by the Belgian government. As president of the Belgian Committee for Refugees from Nazi Germany (1933–40), he was instrumental in the rescue of the passengers from the ship *St. Louis*, which was sent back from Cuba and finally permitted to land in Antwerp (July 1939). Gottschalk wrote numerous publications in Jewish and non-Jewish fields.

GOTTSCHALL, MORTON (1894–1968), U.S. university teacher and administrator. Gottschall was born in New York City. He graduated from the City College of New York (1914), and became a tutor in history there. In 1919 he was named recorder of City College, a post he held for 15 years. During this period he also taught history and legal philosophy. In 1934 Gottschall was appointed professor and dean of the college, a capacity in which he served until his retirement in 1964. As dean, he was known for his consideration for the individual student. He was head of a large college whose enrollment was mostly Jewish and with whose needs and aspirations he deeply sympathized.

[Louis F. Sas]

GOUDCHAUX, MICHEL (1797–1862), French banker and politician. Born in Nancy, Goudchaux was a director of his father's bank there. In 1826 he became manager of the bank's Paris branch and helped found a working-class newspaper *Le National*. He participated in the revolution of July 1830 and was wounded when he placed himself at the head of an insurgent group. After the revolution, Goudchaux was made mayor of his district, member of the general council of the department of the Seine, and paymaster general in Strasbourg. In 1834, however, he returned to Paris and bitterly attacked the government's economic policies in a series of articles in *Le National*. Goudchaux became minister of finance in the Second Republic and in 1849, vice president of the National Assembly. He was defeated in the elections of 1852 and devoted his life to philanthropic work, founding Jewish schools in Nancy. In 1857 he was elected to the Legislative Assembly but refused to swear the oath of allegiance to Napoleon III and did not take his seat.

BIBLIOGRAPHY: R. Lazard, *Michel Goudchaux, son oeuvre et sa vie politique* (1907); Rabi (pseud.), *Anatomie du Judaïsme français* (1962), 65; JC (Jan. 9, 1863), 7.

[Shulamith Catane]

GOUDEKET, MAURITS (1912–1989), rabbi and leader of Progressive Judaism in the Netherlands and Curaçao. Dr. "Mau" Goudeket, who had been active in the Resistance, was a young physicist when he came out of hiding after the Holocaust. He immediately rode by bike to Levi Levisson, prewar Liberal Jewish leader in The Hague, and urged him to reestablish the Liberal Community. Goudeket had been an active member in prewar Amsterdam; he had great knowledge of Judaism and saw the reestablishment of the community as a crucial issue. In 1946 however, Mau, his wife Riek and their infant son moved to Willemstad, Curaçao, where he had accepted a job both as a teacher in physics at the local high school and as the new religious leader of the Reform congregation, Temple Emanu-El. This moribund community had lived in splendid isolation from mainstream developments in Reform and Liberal Judaism for about a century. Goudeket, functioning as its rabbi, revived the congregation and it became a member of the World Union for Progressive Judaism. In 1960 the Goudeket family returned to Amsterdam, where Goudeket became rector of the Spinoza Lyceum and, later on, advisor in educational affairs to the Amsterdam city council. He was soon chosen president of the Union of Liberal Religious Jews in the Netherlands and, two years later, president of the Liberal Congregation of Amsterdam after its first postwar leader Louis Jacobi stepped down. Goudeket rose to leading positions in the World Union for Progressive Judaism and, together with Rabbi Jacob *Soetendorp in Amsterdam and Robert A. *Levisson in The Hague, guided the Liberal Jewish community through a period of explosive growth during the 1960s and early 1970s. Three additional congregations were founded. Goudeket realized that a younger generation of rabbis had to be brought to the Netherlands and personally coached the young rabbi David Lilienthal. In the late 1970s Goudeket became president of Joods Maatschappelijk Werk (Jewish Social Work) in the Netherlands, the first Liberal Jew chosen for such a position. He played an important role in the European Council of Jewish Community Services.

BIBLIOGRAPHY: *Levend Joods Geloof*, 35:7 (1989); *ibid.*, 48:3 (2002).

[Chaya Brasz (2nd ed.)]

GOUDSMIT, JOEL EMANUEL (1813–1882), Dutch lawyer. Goudsmit was the first Jew to become a university professor in Holland and member of the Royal Netherlands Academy of Sciences. Goudsmit, who was born in Leiden, graduated in law in 1842. After a period in practice he was appointed professor of Roman law at Leiden in 1859. At the university he served as a secretary to the Senate in 1866 and became rector of the university in 1871. As a scholar he became famous through his *Pandecten-Systeem* (1866; *The Pandects*, 1873) which was translated into several languages. He was a member of the board of the first lawyers' association in the Netherlands. He was a member of the Leiden municipal council from 1861 until 1881. Also active in local and national Jewish affairs, he was for many years chairman of the Society for the Promotion of the Welfare of the Jews in Holland. He publicly protested against antisemitic publications in Holland and advocated the rights of the Jews in Romania.

[Henriette Boas / Bart Wallet (2nd ed.)]

°GOUGENOT DES MOUSSEAUX, HENRI (1805–1876), French antisemitic writer. A Catholic aristocrat who called himself "a soldier of Christ," Gougenot des Mousseaux was obsessed with demons and Jews. He is chiefly known for *Le Juif, le judaïsme et la judaïsation des peuples chrétiens* (1869). Published on the eve of the first Vatican council with the blessing of Pope *Pius IX, it was influential in Conservative circles in France before *Drumont's *France Juive*. The theme of the book is an alleged Jewish conspiracy to destroy Christianity and rule the world by means of 18th-century Liberalism and *Freemasonry. Translations appeared in 1876 in Austria and Romania, and a second edition was published in France in 1886.

BIBLIOGRAPHY: R.F. Byrnes, *Anti-semitism in Modern France*, 1 (1950), passim; L. Poliakov, *Histoire de l'antisémitisme*, 3 (1968), 348.

GOULD, ELLIOTT (1938–), U.S. actor. Born Elliott Goldstein in Brooklyn, New York, Gould was educated at the Professional Children's School and Columbia University and made his Broadway debut with *Rumple* at the Alvin Theater in 1957. Other Broadway performances include *Say, Darling; Irma La Douce;* and *I Can Get It for You Wholesale* (where he performed opposite Barbra *Streisand, whom he married in 1963). The 6′3″ curly-headed actor began his film career in 1964 with *The Confession*, but is best remembered for *Bob and Carol and Ted and Alice*, for which he received an Academy Award nomination. His memorable role as Trapper John in *M*A*S*H* made him a counterculture icon, as did appearances in such films as *Getting Straight*, *Move*, and *Little Murders*. He appeared in Ingmar Bergman's first English-language film *The Touch*, Robert Altman's *The Long Goodbye*, *California Split*, and *Nashville*, and Richard Attenborough's *A Bridge Too Far*. He is most recently remembered for his role as Jewish casino owner Reuben Tishkoff in *Ocean's Eleven* and *Ocean's Twelve*. His television series work includes *ER*, *Sessions*, *Getting Personal*, and the 1997 Stephen King mini-series *The Shining*. He also made appearances on *L.A. Law*, *Friends*, *Cybill*, *The Simpsons*, and *Alef-Bet Blast-Off*. Gould divorced Barbra Streisand in 1971. They had one child together, actor Jason Emanuel Gould.

[Adam Wills (2nd ed.)]

GOULD, MILTON S. (1909–1999), U.S. lawyer. Born in New York City, Gould graduated from Cornell University with a B.A. in 1930 and a law degree in 1933. He began practicing law at White & Case in the 1930s, a period in which predominantly Protestant firms tended to exclude Jewish lawyers. When Gould discovered that he would not be allowed to be in contact with clients but would be assigned only research duties, he quit that firm and joined the Jewish law firm Kaufman, Weitzner & Celler, with which he remained in private practice for many years.

In the 1930s he was legislative adviser to the Commissioner of Immigration and Naturalization and to the Assistant Attorney General in charge of the criminal division. From 1935 to 1937 he served under Federal Judge Samuel H. Kaufman as special attorney and special assistant in the U.S. Department of Justice.

In his private practice he specialized in corporate litigation arising under the Securities Exchange Act of 1934, the Investment Company Act of 1940, and the Public Utilities Holding Company Act. He was also active in litigation for utility companies.

In 1964 Gould's firm Gallop, Climenko & Gould merged with a Catholic firm run by William Shea, for whom New York City's baseball stadium was later named. Shea and Gould ran the firm together for 20 years, making a point of maintaining a balanced number of Christian and Jewish lawyers. From 1994 on, Gould was a partner at the law firm LeBoeuf, Lamb, Greene, & MacRae.

Gould also participated in the prosecution and defense of criminal cases in the federal courts. He especially attracted public notice internationally for his representation of Gen.

Ariel Sharon, who sued Time, Inc., for libel, arising out of the Israeli action in Lebanon in the early 1980s, in which the jury's finding was that Sharon had in fact been libeled, although no monetary damages were awarded. A powerful litigator, Gould represented many other high-profile clients, such as Donald Trump, Aristotle Onassis, Aldo Gucci, Abe Beame, David Dinkins, Leona Helmsley, and George Steinbrenner.

Gould served as an adjunct professor at Cornell Law School and at New York Law School, and lectured at the law school of the Hebrew University. He was active for the United Jewish Appeal. He was the author of two books: *The Witness Who Spoke with God and Other Tales from the Courthouse* (1979); and *A Cast of Hawks* (1985).

[Milton Ridvas Konvitz / Ruth Beloff (2nd ed.)]

GOULD, MORTON (1913–1996), composer, conductor, pianist. Born in Richmond Hill, New York, Gould was a precocious pianist and composer. He entered the Institute of Musical Art in New York at the age of eight. Later, he studied at New York University. By the time he was 18, his *3 Conservative Sketches* (1932) had been published by G. Schirmer. He worked as a pianist, arranger, composer, and conductor with various radio orchestras and at Radio City Music Hall in New York. He composed for television shows, including the educational World of Music series, the World War I and Holocaust broadcasts. Later he appeared as guest conductor with many of the major U.S. orchestras. In his compositions, Gould moved freely between the domains of light and serious music, often using American folk and popular idioms, and in many works adapting jazz resources to classical forms. In 1933 Stokowski and the Philadelphia Orchestra performed the premiere of his *Chorale and Fugue in Jazz*. Gould wrote for films (such as *Delightfully Dangerous* in 1945), stage, and ballet, and composed major works for concert bands (including two symphonies and orchestral works which he transcribed for band). His music is an important part of the American band repertory. In 1994 he received a Kennedy Center Honor for his contributions to American culture. His final orchestral work, *Stringmusic*, written for the farewell of Rostropovich from the National SO, won the Pulitzer Prize. Among his well-known pieces are: *Three American Symphonettes*, for orchestra (1933, 1935, 1937; the *Pavane* from the second symphonette became a popular light concert piece); *Spirituals*, for orchestra (1941, also frequently perfomed); *Chorale and Fugue in Jazz*, for two pianos and orchestra (1936); *Latin American Symphonette*, for orchestra (1941), *Of Time and the River*, for unaccompanied chorus (1946); *Concerto for Tap Dancer and Orchestra* (1952); Viola Concerto (1944).

BIBLIOGRAPHY: Grove online; L. Evans: *Morton Gould: his Life and Music*, diss., Columbia U. Teachers College (1978).

[Israela Stein (2nd ed.)]

GOULD, SAMUEL BROOKNER (1910–1997), U.S. educator and university administrator. Born in Shelton, Connecticut, Gould studied at Bates College and New York, Oxford, Cambridge, and Harvard Universities. He received his B.A. from Bates and his M.A. from New York University (1936). He converted to Christianity during his undergraduate years. He taught English at William Hall High School, West Hartford, Connecticut (1932–38). During World War II, he was a lieutenant commander in the U.S. Navy Pacific Theater, earning several medals for his service. He was head of the department of speech of the Brookline (Massachusetts) school system (1938–47). From 1947 to 1953, he served at Boston University, first as professor of radio and speech and director of the division of radio, speech, and theater, and then as assistant to the president. At BU he helped design the School of Public Relations and Communications and started Boston's first FM radio station as well as a TV studio and theater. Gould's major contribution to education was in college and university administration as president of Antioch College (1954–58) and chancellor of the University of California, Santa Barbara (1959–62). He also served as chancellor of the multi-campus State University of New York (1964–70), bringing the disparate SUNY campuses into one unified institution. As president of the Educational Broadcasting Corporation (1962–64), he took a leading role in raising the standards of American educational radio and television.

In 1970, Gould retired from SUNY and became chancellor emeritus. He served briefly as a director at McKinsey and Company. From 1971 to 1974, he was chairman of the Carnegie Commission on Non-Traditional Study, which attempted to modify and set new goals for education. During the 1970s, he worked periodically with the Venezuelan Ministry of Education in developing that country's university system, and in 1977 he accompanied his close friend Vice President Rockefeller on his tour of Latin America.

After he retired to Florida in 1974, Gould served for 10 years on the board of the University of Florida New College, helping draw up a master plan for higher education in the state. From 1976 to 1977, he served as interim chancellor for higher education for the State of Connecticut. He also served as a trustee of the Teachers Insurance and Annuity Association, and on the Commission for Post-Secondary Educational Planning in Florida.

Gould wrote *Knowledge Is Not Enough* (1959), *Today's Academic Condition* (1970), and *Diversity by Design* (1973). He edited *Explorations in Non-Traditional Study* (1972).

[William W. Brickman / Ruth Beloff (2nd ed.)]

GOULD, STEPHEN JAY (1941–2002), U.S. paleontologist and author. Born in New York City, Gould was educated at Antioch College, Yellow Springs, Ohio (A.B., 1963), and Columbia University (Ph.D., 1967). After a year of teaching geology at Antioch, Gould accepted an appointment at Harvard in 1967, where he remained for the rest of his life. At his death Gould was the Alexander Agassiz Professor of Zoology, with a concurrent appointment in the Department of the History of Science.

Gould was a leading evolutionary biologist who developed (with Niles Eldredge) a theory of evolutionary development called "punctuated equilibrium," which states that species do not evolve at a steady, even rate, but in sudden bursts over relatively short (in evolutionary time) periods during speciation, after which they remain stable in form – that is, in a state of "equilibrium" – until they become extinct. While this theory has not been wholly accepted, much of it has, and was in the 1970s a fruitful focus of ongoing scientific debate.

Gould became widely known, however, less for his academic work than for his prolific writing for a popular audience. As a columnist for *Natural History* magazine for 24 years and the author of many books (including several bestsellers), he was an eloquent popularizer of scientific discourse, educating the public about biology, geology, and evolution as well as issues such as scientific racism and the social context of science generally. He was a tireless advocate for good science and education and testified in a number of public hearings regarding the teaching of evolution in public schools. Probably his best-known work for a general audience is the classic *The Mismeasure of Man* (1981; revised edition 1996), an account of the fraudulent science and racist assumptions that lay at the origins of IQ testing. This instructive and realistic examination of how science is shaped by social values was a forceful intervention in an ongoing cultural and political debate in the 1980s that earned him the enmity of many on the political right. Gould's other works for general readers include collections of essays: *Ever Since Darwin* (1977), *The Panda's Thumb* (1980), *Hen's Teeth and Horse's Toes* (1983), *The Flamingo's Smile* (1985), *An Urchin in the Storm* (1987), *Bully for Brontosaurus* (1991); and *The Lying Stones of Marrakech* (2000); and books such as *Time's Arrow, Time's Cycle* (1987), and *Wonderful Life: The Burgess Shale and the Nature of History* (1989). His academic works, beside journal articles, include *Ontogeny and Philogeny* (1977) and his final, comprehensive statement of his understanding of evolution, published the year he died, *The Structure of Evolutionary Theory* (2002).

[Drew Silver (2nd ed.)]

GOURD (Heb. דְּלַעַת; pl. דְּלוּעִים), a plant. It occurs in the Bible only in the form of a place-name Dilan, a town in the inheritance of Judah (Josh. 15:38), but it is frequently mentioned in talmudic literature. In modern Hebrew the word is applied to the gourd of the genus *Cucurbita*, now grown extensively in Israel, but since this genus originates in America the word undoubtedly designated some other plant in ancient times. From its many descriptions in talmudic literature, the reference is clearly to the calabash gourd (*Lagenaria vulgaris*), then a most important crop in Ereẓ Israel. Its large fruit, usually shaped like a broad-bellied bottle, was used as a vegetable when soft and when hard its shell was used as a container for liquid and food (Kil. 7:1). Vessels made from the fruit have been found in ancient Egyptian graves. Talmudic literature has many descriptions of the gourd. Its extremely smooth skin gave rise to the expression "he shaves himself as smooth as a gourd" (Sot. 16a). Various dishes were prepared from the soft fruit (Shev. 2:10), but its dried seeds are not fit for eating (TJ, Shev. 2:10, 34a). The plant has leaves which are very large and hard, and which could be written on in an emergency (Tosef., Git. 2:3); it has tendrils by which it climbs any support (TJ, Er. 1:1, 18b). Various strains of the gourd were grown, among which the Mishnah mentions the Syrian, Egyptian, Remuẓian, and Greek gourds (Kil. 1:5; Ned. 51a). Of these the last strain was the most important and so vigorous that one plant could cover an entire field (Kil. 3:7). Also used in the Talmud to designate the gourd, *kara*, apparently an Aramaic word, is included among the food eaten on the New Year (Ker. 6a). (For the correct meaning of *kikayon* in Jonah 4:6 et al. (AV, JPS "gourd") see *castor plant.)

BIBLIOGRAPHY: Loew, Flora, 1 (1928), 542–8; J. Feliks, *Kilei Zera'im ve-Harkavah* (1967), 66–71.

[Jehuda Feliks]

GOURI, HAIM (1923–), Hebrew poet and novelist. Born in Tel Aviv, Gouri served in the *Palmaḥ from 1942 to 1947. He was sent on various missions by the Haganah to the displaced persons (DP) camps in Europe after World War II and was an officer in the Israeli forces during the War of Independence. From 1954, he wrote a weekly column in the daily *La-Merḥav*.

His first poems were light verses which appeared in various publications of the Palmah, and in 1943 he began to publish in literary magazines. *Pirḥei Esh* ("Flowers of Fire," 1949) was his first collection of poems. He published further volumes of poetry, as well as works of reportage, and a novel. He also translated French poetry and drama into Hebrew.

His early poetry, influenced by Natan Alterman, portrays a young boy's reactions to the newly discovered wonders of the world. Depicting mostly concrete situations where God, death, and time become tangible realities, most of these poems are void of abstractions. In *Pirḥei Esh* and *Ad Alot ha-Shaḥar* ("Till Dawn Breaks," 1950), the young maturing boy, in his first encounter with the adult world, assimilates the collective experiences of the Palmaḥ fighters, confronted by war and death, into an intimate personal experience. *Shirei Ḥotam* (1954) is marked by the poet's attempt to cling to the memory of distant experiences; he wishes to relive them, but, at the same time, emphasizes the gap existing between the original experience and life as now lived by his generation. His poetry became more cerebral; the early concrete grasp of reality was replaced by abstract expressions and conceptualizations.

Shoshannat ha-Ruhot ("The Wind Rose," 1960) portrays Gouri's poignant awareness of the sharp contrast between his lost world, alive only in memories – recalled through symbols and emotions which are rooted in the poet's strong ties to his homeland, in a collective responsibility, and in the demands of the times made on the individual – and the present in which the poet sees his homeland as an alien land. He is torn between two extremes: the desire to escape his past, to live anonymously in an "alien" land and cast off his heavy burdens; and his regret at his own alienation and isolation. The past, from which the poet finds no escape, is also revealed in the clear relation between these later poems and Gouri's early work. The early language patterns, imparting a new meaning, recur; these combine with the poet's longing to convert every visual phenomenon and inner mood into a lofty aesthetic experience.

Gouri's novel *Iskat ha-Shokolad* (1965; *The Chocolate Deal*, 1968) presents the Holocaust through the experience of its two heroes, whose physical survival and well-being belie their psychological deformity. The author, using allusive dialogue, interior monologue, and symbolic references, creates a mood where the dividing line between the real and the imagined, the believable and the unbelievable, becomes blurred, the whole melting into a painful reality. Another work, *Mul Ta ha-Zekhukhit* (1962; French *La cage de verre*, 1964), is a chronicle of the Eichmann trial in Jerusalem.

Two major books published after the Six-Day War were *Dappim Yerushalmiyyim* ("Jerusalem Pages," 1968), a miscellany, and *Tenu'ah le-Magga* ("Seek and Destroy," 1968), a collection of poems. The most important work in *Dappim Yerushalmiyyim* is a diary in which the author records his experiences as company commander of the Jerusalem brigade faced with the taking of Ammunition Hill, one of the strongest fortifications of Jerusalem. The work also includes feuilletons and sketches written before the war. The mood is strongly nationalistic. *Tenu'ah le-Magga* is a variation of the earlier theme, but the anguish of nostalgia for the past is relieved by a new element: personal youthful memories now search out the national collective reservoir on which the poet draws through his knowledge of the Bible. For the first time, biblical figures such as Joseph and his brothers Samson, Absalom, and Amos appear in his poetry, drawn intimately, as if they had risen out of the poet's childhood world. The experience in *Tenu'ah le-Magga*, reminiscent of *Pirḥei Esh*, is the poet's rediscovery, at a higher level, of his identification with the collective experience of his nation, meeting it for the first time on the ancient battlefields in the Bible. Gouri was awarded the Bialik Prize (1974) and the Israel Prize (1988) for literature. Other books of poems include *Marot Geḥazi* (1973), *Ad Kav Nesher* (1980), *Milim be-Dami Ḥoleh Ahavah* (1996; translated into English as *Words in My Lovesick Blood*, 1996). His later prose works include *Sefer ha-Meshugah* (1971), *Mi Makkir et Yosef G.* – (1980), and *Ha-Ḥakirah* (1981). Gouri has written and produced two movies related to Holocaust themes, *The Eighty-first Blow* (1974), on the Warsaw ghetto uprising, and *The Last Sea* (1978), on illegal immigration to Palestine. His poems, *Ha-Shirim*, appeared in two volumes in 1998. Later poems appeared as *Me'uḥarim* (2002). Poems by Gouri have been translated into a number of languages and are included, for instance, in T. Carmi (ed.), *The Penguin Book of Hebrew Verse* (1981) as well as in *The Modern Hebrew Poem Itself* (2003). A list of English translations of his work appears in Goell, Bibliography, 826–48.

BIBLIOGRAPHY: A. Huss, in: *Gazit*, 11 (1949), 63–5; S. Halkin, in: *Beḥinot be-Vikkoret ha-Sifrut...*, 1 (1952), 6–25; M. Brinker, in: *Massa*, 4 (1954); Ḥ. Bar-Yosef, in: *Eked*, 1 (1960/61), 136–8; G. Katznelson, in: *Moznayim*, 12 (1961), 277–81; G. Yardeni, *Tet Zayin Siḥot im Soferim* (1961), 167–81; A. Ukhmani, *Kolot Adam* (1967), 137–52. **ADD. BIBLIOGRAPHY:** S. Kramer, "*Ha-Meshorer ki-Ne'aro shel Navi*," in: *Moznayim*, 39 (1975), 393–99; Y. Orian, in: *Yedioth Aharonoth* (Mar. 13, 1981); M. Wilf, in: *Al ha-Mishmar* (May 15, 1981); W.J. Urbrock, "Sisera's Mother in Judges 5 and H. Gouri's '*Immo*,'" in: *Hebrew Annual Review*, 11 (1987), 423–34; Z. Shamir, "*Dor ha-Ma'avak le-Aẓma'ut u-Meshorero H. Gouri*," in: *Iton 77*, 100 (1988) 120–24; W.J. Urbrock, "Guarding the Walls in Psalm 48 and H. Gouri's '*Nidmeh li*,'" in: *Hebrew Annual Review*, 13 (1991), 107–17; H. Shaham, *Hedim shel Niggun: Shirat Dor ha-Palmaḥ be-Zikatah le-Shirat Alterman* (1997); R. Weisbrod, "*H.G. Shoshanat ha-Ruḥot*," in: *Meḥkarei Yerushalayim be-Sifrut Ivrit*,16 (1997), 157–82; R. Shoham, "From the Naïve to the Nostalgic in the Poetry of H. Gouri," in: *Prooftexts*, 18/1 (1998), 19–43; R. Shoham, "H. Gouri and 'The Jewish People Who Have Been Seriously Injured,'" in: *AJS Review*, 24/1 (1999), 73–100; A. Hirschfeld, "*Al Shir shel H. Gouri*," in: *Meshiv ha-Ruaḥ*, 9 (2001), 34–37.

[Matti Megged]

GOVERNMENT, PRAYER FOR THE, the prayer for the welfare of the government that forms part of the synagogue ritual on Sabbath mornings and on the festivals. Its inclusion in the service is based on the Mishnah: "R. Ḥanina, Segan ha-Kohanim said: Pray for the welfare of the government; since but for fear thereof, men would swallow each other alive" (Avot 3:2). The idea is found as early as Jeremiah; the prophet counseled the Jews who were taken into the Babylonian captivity: "Seek the peace of the city whither I [i.e., the Lord] have caused you to be carried away captive, and pray unto the Lord for it; for in the peace thereof shall ye have peace" (Jer. 29:7).

The prayer for the welfare of the ruling powers of the state (king, government, etc.) and petitions for the welfare of the congregation, belong to the morning service and are recited before the Scrolls of the Law are returned to the Ark. The Sephardim recite it on the Day of Atonement after *Kol Nidrei*. The traditional version of the prayer starts: "May He Who dispenseth salvation unto kings and dominion unto princes, Whose kingdom is an everlasting kingdom, Who delivereth His servant David from the destructive sword... [etc.]... may He bless, preserve, guard, assist, exalt, and highly aggrandize our Sovereign...," the titles following.

In non-monarchic countries the prayer is recited for the welfare of the head of the state (the president) and the government. In modern times the prayer is recited in most synagogues in the vernacular. The wording has frequently been modified in accordance with the circumstances.

In Israel a new version of this prayer was formulated and approved by the Chief Rabbinate after the establishment of the state in 1948; it also includes a prayer for the welfare of all Jews in the Diaspora. The prayer is also recited in the U.S. at public services on special occasions such as Thanksgiving Day, July 4, and Armistice Day.

For samples of prayers for the government in the different rituals, see P. Birnbaum (ed.), *Daily Prayer Book* (1949), 379 (Orthodox); Hertz, Prayer, 506–7 (Orthodox); Rabbinical Assembly of America and United Synagogue of America,

Sabbath and Festival Prayerbook (1946), 130 (Conservative); *Union Prayerbook*, 1 (1946), 148 (Reform).

BIBLIOGRAPHY: Abrahams, Companion, clx–clix.

GOZAN (Heb. גּוֹזָן; Akk. Guzana), an Aramaean city on the western shores of the Habor River, a tributary of the Euphrates. The site of Gozan, now Tell Halaf, was first excavated and explored by M. von Oppenheim (1911–19; 1929). Although Tell Halaf – from which is derived the name of the "Halaf Period," a period in the development of northeastern Mesopotamian polychrome pottery – is in itself a key site in the history of civilization, its chief historical importance lies in the fact that it was the site of Gozan, the capital city of the Aramaean kingdom of Bīt Baḫiāni (see *Aram) which was established between the 11th and 10th centuries B.C.E. The remains of the administrative and cultic center of Gozan disclosed by the excavations at Tell Halaf are of great importance for the understanding of the development of the mixed Hittite-Hurrian-Mesopotamian peripheric architecture, art, religion, and changing way of life in the first millennium B.C.E. On one of the orthostats there is the first depiction of an Aramaean camel rider. Bīt Baḫiāni and Gozan are first mentioned in the annals of Adad Nirari II, king of Assyria. It is recorded that in his seventh campaign, around 894 B.C.E., he gained the submission of Abisalamu (Heb. Absalom) son of the House/Tribe Baḫiāni. Although there is further evidence of this submission in the Assyrian annals, further archaeological evidence seems to indicate that there was a short independent period in the history of Bīt Baḫiāni and its capital Gozan. The central figure during this period was (according to this Aramean inscription) Kappara, son of Ḫadijānu (from a new dynasty). It was he who erected the monumental architecture of Gozan during the latter part of the second half of the ninth century B.C.E. which was a period of severe crisis in Assyria, especially between the end of the reign of Shalmaneser III and that of Shamshi Adad V (between 827–810). This period of independence ended in 808 B.C.E. when according to the Eponym Canon (Cb-1) Gozan was reconquered by Sammuramat (classical Semiramis), the queen mother, and her son Adad-Nirāri III. By 793 B.C.E. Gozan was already an organized Assyrian province. According to II Kings 17:6 inhabitants of Israel and Samaria were deported to the area along the "Habor River of Gozan." Assyrian documents discovered in Gozan and in other administrative centers contain information on the life of the inhabitants and deportees. Among these documents is a letter from Ḫabbishu of Samaria to the king (Waterman, no. 6331) which deals with various local affairs, mentioning several Hebrew-sounding names, such as *Ni-ri-ia-u* (Heb. Neriah), the *rab nikāsi*, overseer of income (*nekhasīm*) and *Pa-al-ti-ia-u* (Heb. Paltiah), and also a woman, all "servants" to the local governor. Another document (Waterman no. 167) speaks of moving inhabitants from Gozan, perhaps to Dūr-Sharrukîn, the new capital of Sargon II, king of Assyria, according to his policy of population mixing. The sender reports that some people mentioned in his list are missing, for example, Ḫūli the gardener with his family of five. Finally, a deed of slave sale discovered in Gozan (in AFO, supplement 6, no. 111) contains many other Hebrew names, such as *Da-a-na-a* (Heb. Dinah); *Isīʿa* (Heb. Hosea), *Milkirāme* (Heb. Malchiram), *Yasimēl* (Heb. Ishmael?); but one of the witnesses is Rīmanni-Ishtār, an Assyrian. The documents date from the late eighth and seventh centuries.

BIBLIOGRAPHY: E. Forrer, *Die Provinzeinteilung des assyrischen Reiches* (1920), index; L. Waterman, *The Royal Correspondence of the Assyrian Empire* (1930); E. Unger, in: *Reallexikon der Assyriologie* (1938), 37; J. Friedrich et al., *Die Inschriften von Tell Halaf* (1940); M. von Oppenheim, *Tell Halaf*, 2 vols. (1943–50); O. Callaghan, *Aram Naharaim* (1948); B. Maisler, in: BIES, 15 (1949/50), 83–85; A. Malamat, *ibid.*, 99–102; idem, *Ha-Aramim be-Aram Naharayim* (1952), 47ff.; H. Frankfort, *The Art and Architecture of the Ancient Orient* (1954), 172ff., passim; D.D. Luckenbill, *Ancient Records* (1968), index.

[Pinhas Artzi]

GOZHANSKY, SAMUEL (pseudonyms: **Ha-Moreh, "Lanu,"** 1867–1943) Bundist, born in Novovola, Belorussia. The son of a wagoner, Gozhansky graduated from the Teachers' Seminary in Vilna in 1888. He became a socialist and from 1891 to 1895 led the Jewish Social Democrats in Vilna, the pioneers of the *Bund. As almost their only writer in Yiddish, Gozhansky composed most of the explanatory pamphlets directed to the workers. The most important, the "Letter to Agitators" (1893–94; preserved in typescript in Russian, retranslated into Yiddish, 1939, and into Hebrew, 1967), primarily sets out the fundamentals of the ideology of the Jewish workers' movement. According to this, Jewish workers would obtain their social and political rights if they constituted "a recognizable force" of their own which would conduct "the national political struggle" for obtaining civil rights for all the Jews. The Jewish workers would join up with the general workers' movement as an independent body. Gozhansky was arrested for revolutionary activity in Bialystok in 1896 and exiled to Siberia. He returned in 1902. Subsequently he was active in the Bund in Warsaw, Vilna, and other places, standing as Bundist candidate in the elections for the second Duma, and contributing to the Bundist paper *Folkstseitung* during this period he was imprisoned several times. He was a member of the foreign committee of the Bund and as its delegate served as secretary of the Congress of the Russian Social Democratic Workers' Party in London in 1907. He wrote the pamphlets *Zionism* and *The Jewish Proletariat*. During World War I Gozhansky lived in Tula. After the 1917 Revolution he edited the Bund organ *Dos Profesionele Lebn* in Petrograd (Leningrad). He joined the Communist Party in 1919 but was not active in the *Yevsektsiya (Jewish section).

BIBLIOGRAPHY: *Revolyutsionnoye dvizheniye sredi yevreyev* (1930), index; LNYL, 3 (1958), 7–8; M. Mishkinsky, in: *Zion*, 31 (1966), 89–101.

[Moshe Mishkinsky]

GOZLAN, ELIE (1876–1964), Algerian pedagogue and journalist. Gozlan took part in the First Zionist Congress in Basle in 1897, was the secretary-general of the Algiers Jewish Consistory, and was one of the founders of the Algiers branch of the World Jewish Congress. He established and edited the *Bulletin de la Fédération des Sociétés Juives d'Algérie* (1936–47), which he courageously published during the Vichy regime. With the collaboration of outstanding Catholic and Muslim personalities, he helped found the Union des Croyants Monothéistes in Algiers. The Union was temporarily effective in establishing harmonious relations among all elements of the Algerian population.

BIBLIOGRAPHY: Elmaleh, in: *Maḥberet*, no. 15 (May 1961), 261–6 (French supplement).

[Robert Attal]

°GRABSKI, STANISLAW (1871–1949), Polish statesman and economist; he was the most prominent ideologist of the *Endecja (ND) Party and its leader for many years. Grabski held office as minister of education in 1923. In 1925–26, before the May Revolution, he played a prominent role in the conclusion of an agreement (*ugoda*) between the Jewish Parliamentary Club and the Polish government headed by his brother Wladyslaw. In 1926, he became alienated from Endecja because of his opposition to Fascist circles. Grabski was inconsistent in his political opinions during World War II in the government-in-exile in London, and in 1946 he returned to Warsaw, having reconciled himself with the new regime.

WLADYSLAW GRABSKI (1874–1938) was Stanislaw's brother. Before World War I he was a National Democrat (Endecja) deputy in the Russian *Duma. In independent Poland after the war, where he was a deputy of the Sejm (parliament), he left the party and took an independent position, serving as minister of finance in several governments. When the Red Army invaded Poland in 1920, Grabski became prime minister for a short while, and again headed the government from 1923 to 1925. The financial policy and taxation system introduced by Grabski became a severe financial burden to Jewish merchants and shopkeepers. The resulting crisis in the economic life of Polish Jewry served as an impetus to emigration on the "Fourth Aliyah" to Palestine of 1924–26, which became known as the "Grabski *aliyah*."

BIBLIOGRAPHY: *Polski Słownik Biograficzny*, 8 (1959–60), 519–28. **ADD. BIBLIOGRAPHY:** S. Rudnicki, *Zydzi w Parlamencie II Rzeczypospolitej* (2004), index; A. Ajnenkiel, *Od "Rzadow Ludowych" do Przewrotu majowego 1918–1926* (1964), index; S. Netzer, *"Medini'ut ha-Neẓigut ha-Yehudit (ha-'Kolo') be-Parlament ha-Polani be-1924,"* in: *Galed*, 12 (1991); idem, *"Ha-Antishemi'ut ha-Kalkalit be-Polin bi-Shenot ha-20 u-Ma'avaka shel ha-Neẓigut ha-Yehudit be-Beit ha-Nivḥarim Negdo,"* in: *Galed*, XIV; P. Korzec, *"Heskem Memshelet W. Grabski im ha-Neẓigut ha-Parlamentarit ha-Yehudit,"* in: *Galed*, I, 175–210.

[Moshe Landau]

GRACE AFTER MEALS (Heb. בִּרְכַּת הַמָּזוֹן, *Birkat ha-Mazon*), a central feature of the liturgical service in the Jewish home. It is considered to be a biblical ordinance, inferred from the verse "Thou shalt eat and be satisfied and bless the Lord thy God for the good land which He has given thee" (Deut. 8:10). If one is in doubt whether he has recited it it should be repeated rather than not said at all (Tur and Sh. Ar., OḤ 184; Maim., Yad, Berakhot 2:14; cf. Ber. 21a). Grace after Meals consists of four blessings and is recited only after a meal at which bread has been eaten. If bread is not eaten, a shorter form of grace is recited (for versions see below). The first blessing (*Birkat ha-Zan*) praises God for providing food for all His creatures. The second (*Birkat ha-Areẓ*) expresses Israel's particular gratitude for the "good land" God has given it, the redemption from Egypt, the covenant of circumcision, and the revelation of the Torah. The third benediction, called *Boneh Yerushalayim* and also *Neḥamah* (consolation), asks God to have mercy on Israel and to restore the Temple and the Kingdom of David. It includes a plea that He may always sustain and support Israel. To these three benedictions which form the core of the Grace a fourth (*Ha-tov ve-ha-metiv*) was added after the destruction of *Bethar. It combines thanks for God's goodness, with the prayer that He may fulfill specific desires (Ber. 48b–49b). It is followed by several petitions which begin with the word *Ha-Raḥaman* ("May the All-Merciful…"). Originally phrased to suit individual desires, the supplications have now become standardized. The number of these petitions varies greatly in different rites; the general Sephardi rite has some 15, while the Ashkenazi has nine.

According to the Talmud (Ber. 48b), the first benediction was instituted by Moses when the manna fell from heaven; the second by Joshua when he conquered Ereẓ Israel; the third by David and Solomon; and the fourth by the rabbis of *Jabneh in gratitude for the miracle that the corpses of the unburied dead of Bethar did not decay, and that permission was ultimately granted for their burial (see: *Bar Kokhba). Finkelstein, however, points out that the fourth blessing was known to *Eliezer b. Hyrcanus (Ber. 48b) who died before the fall of Bethar, and to *Yose the Galilean (Tosef., Ber. 1:9) and *Ishmael (TJ, Ber 7:1, 11a), who do not mention the incident. He, therefore, suggests that this blessing may have originated in the early years of the reign of *Hadrian. The Book of Jubilees (22:6–9) quotes the original threefold blessing, and attributes it to Abraham. Josephus (Wars, II:131) testifies to the custom of thanksgiving after meals, and traces it back to *Simeon b. Shetaḥ (also mentioned in TJ, Ber. 7:2, 11b). The Book of Ben Sira (Ecclus. 36:12–14, 17–19) clearly follows parts of the third benediction, and the Christian thanksgiving prayer in the *Didache* (a Christian work of the last decade of the first century) chapter 10, also bears strong resemblances to the Jewish formula. Among Portuguese Jews the Grace is known as *bençāo*, and among Ashkenazim by the Yiddish term *benshn*, a corruption of the Latin "benedictio" (by way of Old French).

According to the Talmud (BB 60b) it is forbidden to forget the destruction of the Temple even during meals, and thus the recitation of Grace should be preceded on weekdays by Psalm 137. The custom, however, is not often observed. More common is the practice to recite Psalm 126 on Sabbaths and festivals, its optimistic vision better fitting the spirit of these days. The rabbis ordained that whenever three or more have eaten bread together, one of them must summon the others to say Grace with him (Ber. 7:1–5). In reply to the invitation "Gentlemen, let us say Grace" (in Sephardi usage "with your permission"), the others reply "Blessed be the name of the Lord henceforth and forever." The leader repeats the statement and then continues, "With your consent (in Sephardi usage "with the permission of Heaven") let us now bless Him of whose food we have eaten." The others then respond: "Blessed be He whose food we have eaten and through whose goodness we live." This formula is known as *zimmun*, and according to the Talmud (Ber. 45b; Ar. 3a) must even be recited by three women who eat together. According to one opinion in the Mishnah, the *zimmun* formula becomes increasingly elaborate as the number of participants grows to ten, a hundred, a thousand, and ten thousand; more numerous and more solemn epithets of God are added every time (Ber. 7:3; Meg. 4:3). In modern times, the word *Elohenu* ("our God") is inserted in the third line of the formula when the number of participants is ten or more. The custom of communal grace, originally used only when the participants numbered at least ten, can be traced back to the custom of *ḥavurah (community) meals, held especially on the Sabbaths. The practice was widespread in the Second Temple period among the Pharisees, and certain sectarian groups such as the Essenes.

Grace may be recited in any language (Sot. 7:1), but must be said at the table from which one has eaten (Maim. Yad, Berakhot, 4:1) and on which some bread should be left until the conclusion of the benediction (Tos. to Ber. 42a and Sanh. 92a). It is followed by a blessing on a cup of wine. The codifiers differ as to whether the cup of wine is required only when Grace is recited with *zimmun* or even when it is recited individually (Sh. Ar., OḤ 182:1). It has become customary to have the cup of wine only at *zimmun* on Sabbaths, festivals, and other special occasions. Various changes are made in the grace to suit different circumstances. On Sabbaths and festivals a special section (*Reẓeh* and *Ya'aleh ve-Yavo* respectively) is inserted in the third blessing and an additional petition added in the series of *Ha-Raḥaman*; in the Ashkenazi rite the word *Magdil* (from Ps. 18:51) in the final *Ha-Raḥaman* is changed to *Migdol* (from II Samuel 22:51). The change probably originated through the confusion, by some early editors of the *siddur*, between בש"ב "B.SH.B." (meaning "in II Samuel"), and בשב' *be-Shabbat* ("on Sabbaths"). Special *Ha-Raḥaman* petitions are also inserted on New Moons, Rosh Ha-Shanah, Sukkot, and the Passover *seder*. On Ḥanukkah and Purim, Al *ha-Nissim is said during the second blessing which is devoted to thanksgiving (Shab. 24a; cf. Rashi *ibid.*). At a wedding banquet, the third line of the *zimmun* is changed to read "Blessed be our God in whose abode is joy, of whose food we have eaten and through whose goodness we live" (Ket. 8a; cf. Rashi *ibid.*), and the seven wedding benedictions are recited at the conclusion of Grace (Maim. Yad, Berakhot, 2:9, 5:5). At the house of a mourner, a special prayer is substituted for the end of the third benediction, a change is made in the text of the fourth, and the *zimmun* is slightly changed (Ber. 46b; Sh. Ar., YD 379, OḤ 189:2). At the meal which follows a circumcision ceremony, the wording of the *zimmun* is changed to suit the occasion. Among the several lines which begin with *Ha-Raḥaman* in the fourth blessing, a child, a guest (see Ber. 46a), and the master of the house may each insert passages to suit their particular circumstance (see Tur., OḤ 189). Since the establishment of the State of Israel, some families have also inserted a fourth *Ha-Raḥaman* "May the All-Merciful bless the State of Israel, and all who work for her."

Shorter Forms

Ever since the formulation of a "complete" *Birkat ha-Mazon*, there have been shorter versions for extraordinary occasions. The guiding principle has been that the *mitzvah* of reciting *Birkat ha-Mazon* is commanded by the Torah, but the actual content has developed over the ages. Workmen who eat during working hours, therefore, may recite a shortened form, consisting of the first *berakhah*, the "blessing for the land," and mention of Jerusalem (Sh. Ar., OḤ 191:1). Children are required to recite only small sections. In cases of extreme emergency, he who says, "Blessed be the Merciful One, the King, the Master of this land" has fulfilled his obligation. The *siddur* of Saadiah Gaon contains a highly abbreviated version of *Birkat ha-Mazon*. Another shortened form is found in the *Magen Avraham* commentary to the Shulḥan Arukh (OḤ 192:1). In general, shorter forms include the entire first *berakhah*, mention of the Covenant and the Torah as well as the blessing for the land in the second *berakhah*, and mention of Israel and the Davidic Kingdom in the third *berakhah*.

In the United States, the Conservative movement has evolved a shortened version based on this formula, used at public gatherings and summer camps (the traditional long form is usually recited on the Sabbath).

The Reform Prayer Book has a short version made up of two English paragraphs and concluding with the Hebrew ending of the traditional first *berakhah*.

When bread is not eaten there are two other forms of grace (known as *Berakhah Aḥaronah* – "final benediction") to be recited, depending on the nature of the food consumed. For food prepared from the five species of grain (wheat, barley, rye, oats, and spelt), wine, or the fruits of Ereẓ Israel (grapes, figs, olives, pomegranates, and dates) a short summary of the Grace after Meals is said. This is in the form of one benediction with insertions for the type of food eaten and for special occasions such as the Sabbath and festivals. This is called in the Talmud *Berakhah Me'ein Shalosh* – "the benediction summarizing the three" (benedictions of the regular grace). For any other food a short benediction (called in the Talmud *Ve-Lo-Khelum*, "Nothing," but popularly known by its first two words *(Bore Nefashot)* is recited (Ber. 37a–b; laws codified Sh. Ar., OḤ 207–8; texts Hertz, Prayer, 984, 988).

BIBLIOGRAPHY: Finkelstein, in: JQR, 19 (1928/29), 211–62; Abrahams, Companion, 207ff.; ET, 4 (1952), 475–511; Heinemann, in: JJS, 13 (1962), 23–29.

GRACE BEFORE MEALS. The rabbis required a blessing before partaking of food since they considered it sacrilegious to "enjoy of this world without a prior benediction" (Ber. 35a). They instituted separate blessings for the various species of food, of which those over bread and wine are considered the most important. The blessing for bread, "Who bringest forth bread from the earth" (*Ha-moẓi leḥem min ha-areẓ;* Ber. 6:1), is based upon Psalms 104:14, and, when recited at the start of a meal, exempts one from the obligation to recite most additional blessings for the remaining courses (Sh. Ar., OḤ 177). Since this blessing is often the only one recited before a meal, the popular term for the grace before meals is *Moẓi.* The blessing for wine, "Who createst the fruit of the vine ("*Bore peri ha-gafen*"; Ber. 6:1), is recited, even when the wine is drunk in the course of the repast and not at the beginning (Sh. Ar., OḤ 175, and see also 176).

Although the actual formulation of the blessings before meals was delineated during rabbinic times, the practice itself is of ancient origin. Thus in I Samuel 9:13 there is a reference to the people waiting for the prophet to bless the sacrifice before they would partake of its flesh. Josephus describes the grace before the meal recited by the *Essenes (Jos., Wars, 2:131). The rabbis attached great importance to the proper recitation of these blessings, and the father of R. Simeon b. Zevid was praised "as being a great man and well versed in the benedictions" (Ber. 38a).

BIBLIOGRAPHY: Hertz, Prayer, 984–95; Idelsohn, Liturgy, 122; E. Levy, *Yesodot ha-Tefillah* (1952^2), 279–81.

GRACIAN (Hen), SHEALTIEL BEN SOLOMON (14th century), Spanish rabbi, a contemporary of *Isaac b. Sheshet (Ribash), to whom he was related. Both apparently studied under R. Nissim Gerondi. After his marriage he lived in Fraga and was appointed rabbi of the community of Alcala in c. 1369, at which time he acceded to its request to affirm under oath that he would never leave this position. Later he regretted his hasty oath and requested Nissim Gerondi and Isaac b. Sheshet to absolve him of it, but they refused, and Isaac wrote him that "the truth is dearer to me – since both of us must respect it" (Ribash, no. 370). Around 1375 Shealtiel was appointed rabbi of Barcelona, in succession to Nissim who had died. R. Isaac b. Sheshet corresponded with him and mentions him in his responsa frequently and he states that, "he was a preeminent rabbinic authority… of outstanding scholarly attainments… and of foremost renown in Spain" (*ibid.*, no. 365). Isaac b. Sheshet asked him to mediate in a quarrel which arose between his daughter and her father-in-law. He urged him to lend his support, writing, "and should those in dispute with me, my enemies and their supporters, endeavor to incite you against me, do not listen to them" (*ibid.*, no. 415 end). However, Shealtiel disagreed with the stand which had been taken by Isaac b. Sheshet, and the outcome of the matter is unknown.

BIBLIOGRAPHY: Baer, Urkunden, 1 (1929), 499f., 543, 705; A.M. Hershman, *Rabbi Isaac ben Sheshet Perfet and His Times* (1943), 24n. 40, 66f., 87, 181f., 233, 242; Neubauer, Cat, no. 2218/4c.

[Yehoshua Horowitz]

GRADE, CHAIM (1910–1982), Yiddish poet and novelist. Born in Vilna, Grade became that city's most articulate literary interpreter. After his father's early death, his mother ran a market stall in order to provide him a traditional education; he attended several *yeshivot*, including seven years under the famed scholar-rabbi, the Ḥazon Ish, becoming attracted to the *Musar movement. He made his literary debut in *Dos Vort* (1932), became a member of Yung Vilne (1934), and soon was one of its staunchest pillars. The group sought both to synthesize secular Yiddish culture with new currents in world literature, and to bring the impoverished Jewish home into contact with the progressive forces of contemporary society. Grade's poems appeared in leading Yiddish periodicals in Europe and the U.S. His first book, *Yo* ("Yes," 1936), was acclaimed by critics for its stylistic elegance and its affirmation of faith in a synthesis of traditional and modern currents. His long poem "Ezekiel" demonstrated his understanding of the tragic nature of human and especially Jewish existence. Extremely important in his early period was *Geveyn fun Doyres* ("Weeping of the Generations," 1936), which treats the issues of Jewish identity and national history. His long poem "Musernikes" ("Musarists," 1939), describes the spiritual struggles of *yeshivah* students torn between the Musar traditions and worldly temptations. During World War II, Grade found refuge in Russia and continued to write, his next collection of poems, *Has* ("Hate," 1943), appearing in Moscow and following Soviet directives. After the war he dedicated a series of poems, "Mit Dayn Guf af mayne Hent" ("With Your Body in My Hands") to his wife who perished in the Holocaust. In his volumes *Doyres* ("Generations," 1945), *Pleytim* ("Refugees," 1947), and *Shayn fun Farloshene Shtern* ("Light of Extinguished Stars," 1950), he mourned the victims of the Holocaust and describes the survivors. With this attempt at confronting the national Jewish tragedy, Grade became in a sense the national Jewish poet, as Bialik had been in his day.

Grade's return to Vilna in 1946 was traumatic, as described in "Af di Khurbes" ("On Ruins," 1947), and he left for Poland but after the Kielce pogrom (July 1946) moved on to Paris, where he helped to revivify Yiddish cultural life among the surviving Jews, leading the Yiddish literary club. A collection of his poems from the years 1936 to 1939, *Farvoksene Vegn* ("Overgrown Paths," 1947) appeared. In 1948, he was sent to the U.S. as a delegate to the Jewish Culture Congress, settled in New York, and began his contributions to the *(Tog-) Morgn Zhurnal, Tsukunft, Yidisher Kemfer,* and *Di Goldene Keyt.* In 1950, he received a prize from the World Congress of Jewish Culture for *Der Mames Tsavoe* ("My Mother's Will," 1949), which includes some of the most outstanding lyrics in Yiddish, permeated with love and respect for his mother, who perished during the Holocaust. The dramatic dialogue "Mayn Krig mit Hersh Reseyner" (1951; Eng. trans. "My Quarrel with

Hersh Rasseyner"; *Commentary*, 1954; also in: I. Howe and E. Greenberg, *A Treasury of Yiddish Stories* (1954, 1989^2), 624–51) played an important role in Grade's artistic development. His mother is the central figure of his three-part *Der Mames Shabosim* (1955; Eng. trans. "My Mother's Sabbath Days," 1986), which describes his orphaned childhood in Vilna, his life as a refugee in Russia, and his return to postwar Vilna, decimated of its Jews and its Jewish institutions. Prewar Jewish Vilna comes to life in the collection *Der Shulhoyf* ("The Courtyard of the Synagogue," 1958), displaying some of the finest prose of the post-classical generation and including *Der Brunem* (Eng. trans. *The Well*, 1967). His novel, *Di Agune* ("The Abandoned Wife," 1961; Heb. trans. 1962; Eng. trans. 1974), depicts all segments of Jewish Vilna between the wars. *Der Mentsh fun Fayer* ("The Man of Fire," 1962) includes his poems on Israel and his elegy on martyred Soviet Yiddish writers. Two further volumes of poetry appeared: *Oyf Mayn Veg tsu Dir* ("On My Way to You," 1969) and *Parmetene Erd* ("Parchment Earth," 1968, with Heb. transl.). His poems in English translation appeared in J. Leftwich, *The Golden Peacock* (1961) and R. Whitman, *Anthology of Modern Yiddish Poetry* (1966).

Grade was one of the rare interpreters of yeshivah life in modern Yiddish literature, recreating the daily life of the yeshivah student with photographic accuracy, objectivity, and affection, and illustrating it with such scenes as rabbis discussing talmudic law, as in the novel *Tsemakh Atlas* (2 vols. 1967–8; Eng. trans. *The Yeshiva*, 1976–7; Heb. trans. 1968). Following that novel, he published two more collections of stories: *Di Kloyz un di Gas* ("The Small Synagogue and the Street," 1974; partial Eng. trans. *Rabbis and Wives*, 1983) and *Der Shtumer Minyan* ("The Silent Minyan," 1976), which again attempted to reconstruct the atmosphere of prewar Vilna. Grade's postwar poetry expressed, above all, the traumatic experience of the Holocaust and focused on the question of his own survival, while his prose works continued to reconstruct Jewish Vilna and the specific features of mind and piety of Lithuanian Jewry. From the beginning, his works possessed a distinct philosophical dimension.

BIBLIOGRAPHY: LNYL, 2 (1958), 335–8; E. Schulman, *Yung Vilne* (1946); I. Biletzky, *Essays on Yiddish Poetry and Prose* (1969), 233–42. **ADD. BIBLIOGRAPHY:** J. Cammy, in: K. Sorrel (ed.), *Yiddish Writing in the 20th Century* (2003); P. Sanford, in: *Yiddish*, 8 (1992); 55–8; R. Wisse, in: *New York Times* (Nov. 14, 1982), 3/18.

[Israel Ch. Biletzky / Joanna Lisek (2nd ed.)]

GRADE, LEW, BARON (1906–1998), British managing director of television networks. Born in Russia, son of Isaac Winogradsky, Grade grew up in England and went into the entertainment industry. He acquired interests in radio, television, and film companies, and in 1955 became deputy managing director (later managing director) of two leading companies in their field, Associated Television Ltd. and Incorporated Television Company Ltd. He also became chairman of AP Films Ltd., of ATV (France) and other companies associated with ATV in Australia, Canada, and the U.S. He was a brother of Lord Bernard *Delfont. At the time of the 1967 Arab-Israeli war, Grade and his brother Lord Bernard each gave £40,000 to Israel. In 1976, Grade was given a life peerage. Grade's later film-making career became noted for its expensive flops, such as his *Raise the Titanic!* (1980). In 1987, Grade published an interesting autobiography, *Still Dancing*. Grade's nephew, MICHAEL GRADE (1943–), the son of Lord Grade's brother and partner Leslie Grade, was appointed director-general of the BBC in 2004 after a controversial career in British television which included service as chief executive (1988–97) of Channel Four.

ADD. BIBLIOGRAPHY: ODNB online; Q. Falk and D. Prince, *Last of a Kind: The Sinking of Lew Grade* (1987).

[William D. Rubinstein (2nd ed.)

GRADENWITZ, PETER EMANUEL (1910–2001), musicologist, composer, and publisher. Born in Berlin, Gradenwitz studied musicology, sociology, and literature in Freiburg and Berlin with Wilibald Gurlitt, Arnold Schering, and Curt Sachs, and composition with Joef Rufer. In 1934 he pursued his research in Paris and Berlin, and in 1936 he received his doctorate with a thesis on the Stamitz family. In 1936 he joined the large migration of Jewish refugees from Germany and settled in Palestine, where he founded the first publishing house which specialized in concert music, Israeli Music Publications (IMP), in 1948. In 1968 Gradenwitz was appointed lecturer at Tel Aviv University. He regularly published concert reviews, mostly in *Das Orchester, Opernwelt* and the *Neue Zeitschrift fuer Musik*. In 1980 he was appointed honorary professor at Freiburg Universitiy.

One of his main fields of interest was music appreciation. He published three listening guides (in Hebrew) to symphonic (*Olam ha-Simfonyah* 1945, 1959), chamber (*Ha-Musikah ha-Kamerit*, 1948, 1953), and piano music (*Olam ha-Pesanteran*, 1952) which were widely read in Israel. He also studied the history of Jewish and especially Israeli music. His main publication in this field was *The Music of Israel* (1949, 1996^2). In 1954 he organized in Haifa the first Annual Music Festival of the International Society for Contemporary Music to be held outside Europe or the United States.

[Jehoash Hirshberg (2nd ed.)]

GRADIS, family of ship owners and community leaders, of Marrano extraction, which flourished in Bordeaux from the 17th century. DAVID GRADIS (1665–1751) founded an import-export firm (David Gradis et fils, 1696) whose trade relations extended to England, Canada, and the French West Indies. His nephew ABRAHAM (1699–1780) increased the firm's scope and prestige and was appointed royal purveyor in 1744. In 1748 he founded the Societé Gradis et fils under the auspices of the French government, and contracted to provide regular shipping services to Quebec for six years. For the entire period of the Seven Years' War (1756–63) his trade with Canada amounted to 9,000,000 livres. There were many losses, for more than half of the ships that he sent out were captured by the English, and he had trouble collecting from the state. Nevertheless, the Gradis House prospered greatly. In 1763 A. Gradis' friend Choiseul became the naval minister, and Gradis was given a contract to provision the French possessions in West Africa. In these transactions Gradis supplied spirits, gunpowder, knives, and cloth, taking his payment in slaves, whom he sold in San Domingo for sugar. In return for his services during the war, Gradis was praised by Louis XV through his minister Berryer, and later instanced by Abbé *Grégoire in support of arguments in favor of Jewish emancipation. MOSES GRADIS (1740–1788), a cousin of Abraham, inherited the firm after the latter's death. His brother, DAVID GRADIS (the Younger; 1742–1811), was a candidate for Bordeaux in the elections to the States General of 1789, and wrote several works on religion and philosophy. Similarly, his son BENJAMIN (1789–1858), and his grandson HENRI (1830–1905), divided their time between business, politics, and writing. Henri wrote *Histoire de la révolution de 1848* (2 vols. 1872), *Jérusalem* (1883), and *Le Peuple d'Israël* (1891). He was vice-mayor of Bordeaux and head of the Bordeaux *Consistory.

BIBLIOGRAPHY: J. de Maupassant, *Abraham Gradis* (Fr., 1931); A. Hertzberg, *French Enlightenment and the Jews* (1968), index; H. Graetz, in: MGWJ, 24 (1875), 447–59; 25 (1876), 78–85; A. Cahen, in: REJ, 4 (1882), 132–44; 5 (1882), 258–67; B.G. Sack, *History of the Jews in Canada* (1964), 13–31, 261; S. Rosenberg, *The Jewish Community of Canada*, 1 (1970), index.

°GRAEBE, HERMANN FRIEDRICH (1900–1986), non-Jew who saved Jews during the Holocaust. A native of Solingen, Germany, Graebe worked for the construction company, Jung. At one point he joined the Nazi Party, but after speaking out against them, he was sentenced to a short term in prison. The Jung company sent Graebe to Zdolbunov, Volhynia, in October 1941. There he was to be responsible for their undertakings for the German civil administration.

The Jung company employed thousands of Jews and Graebe did his best to ensure they were treated reasonably. In November 1941 and again in July 1942, he safeguarded his Jewish workers from being sent to their death, through contacts with the SD in Rovno. Sensing that the Jews who worked in the Jung head office in Zdolbunov were in danger, Graebe provided them with papers which represented them as Aryans and transferred them to Poltava. Ostensibly they were to work for Jung there, but in fact Graebe had moved them without the company's knowledge and supported them himself. In the fall, Graebe went to Dubno, where he saved the lives of several dozen Jews during the final *Aktion*. He described this incident at the Nuremberg Trial. After the trial, he immigrated to the United States. In 1966 he was officially recognized by *Yad Vashem for his courageous deeds.

[Robert Rozette]

GRAEBER, SCHEALTIEL EISIK (1856–?), Hebrew writer and publisher. Born in Galicia, he became involved in the Haskalah movement at an early age. He wrote for various Hebrew journals, but his major contribution in Hebrew letters was as a publisher. He published the periodical *Ha-Ohev Ammo ve-Ereẓ Moladeto* (1881), the annual *Beit Oẓar ha-Sifrut* (from 1887), and the works of Italian Jewish scholars, such as S.D. Luzzatto (*Iggerot Shadal*, 1882–94) and M.I. Tedeschi.

[Getzel Kressel]

°GRAES (Gratius), ORTWLN VAN DE (1480–1542), Dominican friar and fanatic anti-Jewish polemicist. He was co-author (or translator) of Victor von *Carben's *De vita et moribus Judaeorum* (1509) and translated into Latin some of the polemics of Johann *Pfefferkorn, to whose *Judenfeind* (1509) he wrote an introductory poem *De pertinatia Judaeorum* ("On the Obstinacy of the Jews"). In 1513 Johannes *Reuchlin directed his defense in his controversy with Pfefferkorn mainly against Graes who was also the principal target of *Epistolae obscurorum virorum* (1515 and 1517). Graes's wordy reply (*Lamentationes obscurorum virorum*, Cologne, 1518) was no match for this savage satire. The *Praenotamenta* (1514) and *Defensio* (1516) against Reuchlin's *Augenspiegel* are also considered Graes's work.

BIBLIOGRAPHY: Graetz, Hist, index; M. Brod, *Johannes Reuchlin und sein Kampf* (1965), 178ff.; J. Kracauer, *Geschichte der Juden in Frankfurt…*, 1 (1925), 247ff.; D. Reichling, *Ortwin Gratius…* (Germ., 1884).

GRAETZ, HEINRICH (Hirsch; 1817–1891), Jewish historian and Bible scholar. Graetz was born in Xions (Ksiaz Wielkopolski), Poznan, the son of a butcher. From 1831 to 1836 he went to the yeshivah in Wolstein (now Wolsztyn) near Poznan. At the same time, Graetz taught himself French and Latin and avidly read general literature. This brought him to a spiritual crisis, but reading S.R. *Hirsch's "Nineteen Letters on Judaism" in 1836 restored his faith. He accepted Hirsch's invitation to continue his studies in the latter's home and under his guidance. Eventually their relationship cooled; he left Oldenburg in 1840 and worked as a private tutor in Ostrow. In 1842 he obtained special permission to study at Breslau University. As no Jew could obtain a Ph.D. at Breslau, Graetz presented his thesis to the University of Jena. This work was later published under the title *Gnostizismus und Judenthum* (1846). By then Graetz had come under the influence of Z. *Frankel, and it was he who initiated a letter of congratulations to Frankel for leaving the second *Rabbinical Conference (Frankfurt, 1845) in protest, after the majority had decided against prayers in Hebrew. Graetz now became a contributor to Frankel's *Zeitschrift fuer die religioesen Interessen des Judenthums*, in which, among others, he published his programmatic "Construction der juedischen Geschichte" (1846).

Graetz failed to obtain a position as rabbi and preacher because of his lack of talent as an orator. After obtaining a teaching diploma, he was appointed head teacher of the orthodox religious school of the Breslau community, and in 1850, at Hirsch's recommendation, of the Jewish school of Lundenburg, Moravia. As a result of intrigues within the local community, he left Lundenburg in 1852 for Berlin, where during the following winter he lectured on Jewish history to theological students. He then began to contribute to the *Monatsschrift fuer Geschichte und Wissenschaft des Judentums*, which Frankel had founded in 1851 and which he later edited himself (1869–88). He also completed Volume IV (the first to be published, dealing with the talmudic period) of his *Geschichte der Juden von den aeltesten Zeiten bis zur Gegenwart* ("History of the Jews…," 1853). In 1853 Graetz was appointed lecturer in Jewish history and Bible at the newly founded Jewish Theological Seminary of Breslau, and in 1869 was made honorary professor at the University of Breslau.

The Historian and His Work

One of the major aspects of Graetz's outlook on the Jewish people and its history appear to have been laid during his association with S.R. Hirsch and under the influence of his ideas concerning the mission of the Jewish people. A second important source of his ideas can be found in his juvenile readings of Enlightenment authors as well as his studies in Breslau in philology and philosophy (the latter with Christlieb Julius Braniss (1792–1873)). In general, Graetz remained faithful to these ideas to the end of his days.

He set out his first comprehensive attempt at a concept of Jewish history in the two essays *Construction der juedischen Geschichte* (spring and autumn 1846; later editions as a continuous text, 1936, 2000; Heb. tr. *Darkhei ha-Historyah ha-Yehudit*, 1969; Engl. tr. *The Structure of Jewish History*, 1975). Proceeding from Hegelian ideas, he considered the basic ideas of Judaism as eternal, changing only their external forms. But as he failed to define such a basic idea, these two essays do not constitute a coherent text. In the first part, dealing with the history of the destruction of the Second Temple, the ideal form is harmony of the political and religious elements. Therefore Graetz regarded Judaism as a unique politico-religious organism, in which "the Law is the soul, the Holy Land the body." As for the second, the exilic part of Jewish history, however, Graetz agrees that theoretical-philosophical ideas have taken over: "Judaism becomes scientific scholarship," with the "talmudic system" instead of the Holy Land. He stated, however, that the process is not yet concluded and that "the task of Judaism's God-idea [seems to be] to found a religious state which is conscious of its activity, purpose, and connection with the world." Graetz's ideas on the nature of Jewish history underwent further development. In an essay titled *Die Verjuengung des juedischen Stammes* (in Wertheimer-Komperts' *Jahrbuch fuer Israeliten*, 1863; repr. with notes by Zlocisty in *Juedischer Volkskalender*, Brno, 1903; Eng. tr. in I. Lesser's *Occident* (1865), 193ff.) he rejected the belief in a personal Messiah, and maintained that the prophetic promises referred to the Jewish nation as a whole. In this period (1860s) Graetz under the influence of M. Hess' *Rome and Jerusalem* did not believe in the political revival of the Jews and in the possibility of the creation of a Jewish center in Ereẓ Israel (see letters to Hess and the conclusion of his pamphlet *Briefwechsel einer englischen Dame ueber Judentum und Semitismus*, which he published anonymously in 1883; also under the title *Gedanken einer Juedin ueber das Judentum…*, 1885). Both in this pamphlet and in his essay "The Significance of Judaism for the Present and the Future" (in JQR, 1–2, 1889/90), he emphasized the historical and religious significance of continuous Jewish existence. He saw the main importance of Judaism in the ethical values which it was its task to impart to the world. Judaism is the sole bearer of monotheism; it is the only rational religion. Its preservation and the propagation of the sublime ethical truths to be found in Judaism, these are the tasks of the Jews in the world and this is the importance of Judaism for human culture.

Graetz's life work is his *History of the Jews* and most of his other writings were merely preliminary studies or supplements to this gigantic structure. Even though attempts had been made before him by both Christians (Basnage) and Jews (Jost) to write a Jewish history, the work of Graetz was the first comprehensive attempt to write the history of the Jews as the history of a living people and from a Jewish point of view. With deep feeling, he describes the struggle of Jews and of Judaism for survival, their uniqueness, and their mission in world history. His approach has often been characterized as a history of suffering and intellectual achievement. Out of his appreciation of Judaism and his reaction against all that Christianity had perpetrated against Judaism, Graetz pointed out the failure of the Christian churches to provide a religion and ethics to serve as a basis for a healthy society. The writing of such a Jewish history in the midst of a society which in its vast majority identified itself with Christian culture was a daunting task.

After Volume 4 came out in 1853, eight further volumes of his *Geschichte der Juden* appeared between 1856 and 1870, leaving only the first two volumes – dealing with the biblical period and the early Second Temple period – to be completed. Volume 1 of the *History of the Jews* (to the death of Solomon) appeared in 1874, after Graetz had been able to travel to Palestine, and the two parts of the second volume (to the revolt of the Hasmoneans) followed in 1875–76.

From a historiographic point of view, the *History of the Jews* was a great and impressive achievement. Graetz made use of a vast number of hitherto neglected sources in several languages, though these were mainly literary sources; there was hardly any archival material on Jewish history available in his days. The same holds true for many social and economic aspects of history, though he recognized early the importance of coins as a historical source. In general, he adopted the philologic-critical method and succeeded in clarifying several obscure episodes in Jewish history. Having studied the works of outstanding personalities, especially those with whom he felt a spiritual affinity (such as Maimonides), Graetz succeeded in painting a series of particular figures as representatives of their respective epochs and the history of Judaism in general. His intuition as a historian was astonishing. Thus, for example, the documents discovered in the Cairo *Genizah* after the death of Graetz confirmed several of his surmises concerning the development of the *piyyut* and the period of the *geonim*. But Graetz the historiographer had his weaknesses as well, among which was his excessive and rather naive rationalism. He described everything which appeared to him understandable and logical in the history of his people and emphasized the forces and the ideals which had assured its survival throughout the centuries. Thus he stressed the importance of the universalist ethics of Judaism and showed little understanding for mystical forces and movements such as *Kabbalah and *Ḥasidism, which he despised and considered malignant growths in the body of Judaism. Graetz was not acquainted with and scarcely interested in the history of the Jews of Poland, Russia, and Turkey, and in his attachment to Haskalah expressed contempt bordering on hatred for "the fossilized Polish talmudists." To Yiddish he refers as a ridiculous gibberish ("jargon").

Nevertheless, Graetz wrote in a lively and captivating though sometimes partisan, style, which secured remarkable and long-lasting success for his work. Between 1887 and 1889 an abridged edition of his great work was published in three volumes under the title *Volkstuemliche Geschichte der Juden* (1887–89; 10 editions to 1930; Eng. tr. 1930[4]), which became one of the most widely read Jewish books in Central Europe. For several generations of Jews this work served as a very common bar mitzvah gift.

As to biblical research, Graetz's approach to the Pentateuch was traditional, but in his studies of Prophets and Hagiographa he occasionally adopted radical views. His commentaries on Song of Songs and Ecclesiastes (the latter written according to him in the time of Herod) were published in 1871 and his commentary to Psalms in 1882. These were generally not favorably received, though by making use of the old Bible versions and of talmudic Hebrew he was able to obtain some valuable results. Toward the end of his life it was Graetz's intention to publish a critical text on the Bible, but he left nothing more than emendations to the Prophets, Psalms, and Ecclesiastes which his student David Kaufmann published posthumously.

Critics and Legacy

Graetz's work had a tremendous effect on Jews everywhere, but he was not short of critics either. S.R. Hirsch voiced strong criticism as early as the publication of Volume 4 in the early years of his *Jeschurun* (1855–57), calling it "the phantasies of superficial combinations." The breach between teacher and pupil was now complete. From the opposite direction came Geiger's verdict that the work contained "stories but not history" (*Juedische Zeitschrift*, 4 (1866), 145ff.; cf. also Steinschneider's censure in HB, 3 (1860), 103f.; 4 (1861), 84; 6 (1863), 73ff.). Graetz replied to his contemporary critics in periodicals and in subsequent volumes of his history.

Beyond scholarly debates and throughout his life, Graetz was a pugnacious character. During his student years in Breslau, he fought ardent battles in Jewish and non-Jewish journals against Abraham *Geiger and the Reform movement. On his return from the Middle East, he published a memorandum which was highly critical of the social and educational conditions in Ereẓ Israel and of the system of **Ḥalukkah* in particular. He also played a role in the new wave of antisemitic attacks. In 1879 the nationalistic Prussian historian Heinrich von *Treitschke violently attacked the 11th volume of the *History of the Jews*, which dealt with recent times. He accused Graetz of hatred of Christianity, Jewish nationalism, and the lack of desire for the integration of Jews within the German nation ("Unsere Aussichten," in *Preussische Jahrbuecher*, 1879). This led to a public debate in which both Jewish and non-Jewish writers participated. While many of them rejected Treitschke's virulent antisemitism, even Jewish writers dissociated themselves, with few exceptions, from Graetz. That he was a controversial figure became once again evident when the Union of Jewish Communities set up in 1885 a Jewish Historical Commission with the purpose of publishing the sources for the history of the Jews in Germany. Despite his merits, Graetz was not invited to serve in any way. Thus in his later years, Graetz was cautious in his involvement in public affairs. He warmly welcomed the philanthropic program of the *Kattowitz Conference (1884), but withdrew immediately when the *Ḥovevei Zion movement took a political turn and tried to use his name for its purposes.

A wider Jewish public, and the world of Jewish scholarship in particular, honored Graetz on the occasion of his 70th birthday; a jubilee volume was published to celebrate the event. Graetz was invited to deliver the opening speech at the Anglo-Jewish Exhibition in London in 1887, which was published under the title of *Historic Parallels in Jewish History* (translated by J. Jacobs, 1887). In 1888 he was elected honorary member of the history department of the Academy of Madrid in honor of his description of medieval Jewish history in Spain up to the expulsion in 1492.

Graetz's *History* became the basis and the source for the further study of Jewish history, and in some fields of research its influence is felt to this day. It was translated into many languages. The great number of editions and translations (also of single volumes: cf. Brann, in MGWJ, 61 (1917), 481–91) of the *Geschichte* speak their own language of success. The various volumes were published in up to five editions until World War I. Several volumes of the last edition (11 vols., 1890–1909) were edited and annotated by M. Brann and others. The best known Hebrew version is an adaptation/translation by S.P. Rabinowitz (with A. Harkavy, 1890–99), which exerted much influence among the Hebrew-reading public of East European Jewry. Yiddish translations appeared in 1897–98, 1913, and 1915–17. The various English translations were influential as well: (1) without the notes and excurses, by Bella Loewy (5 vols., 1891–92), authorized and with an introduction and final retrospect by Graetz himself (1901); (2) the same with a sixth volume including P. Bloch's memoir, 1892–98; and (3) the "Popular History" (5 vols., 1919). As to French translations: volume 3 was translated by Moses *Hess under the title *Sinai et Golgotha* in 1867; and the whole work by M. Wogue and M.

Bloch (1882–97). The work was also translated into Russian, Polish, and Hungarian.

Most of Graetz's other published work was preparatory to the main "History," and appeared in the *Monatsschrift* and in the *Jahresberichte* of the Breslau Seminary. On the occasion of Graetz's 100th birthday anniversary the *Monatsschrift* (vol. 61 (1917), 321ff.) and the *Neue Juedische Monatshefte* (vol. 2, nos. 3–4, 1917–18) issued a series of memoirs and first biographical sketches on the life and works of the historian. A number of Graetz's essays and personal writings have been published in Hebrew (*Darkhei ha-Historyah ha-Yehudit* (1969), tr. by J. Tolkes), and an extensive selection of his diaries and letters was published by R. Michael (*Heinrich Graetz. Tagebuch und Briefe* (1977)). In more recent times, a few comprehensive studies of the life and work of Graetz have been finished.

BIBLIOGRAPHY: Kaufmann, Schriften, 1 (1908), 212–82; I. Abrahams, in: JQR, 4 (1892), 165–203; L. Graetz, in: *Ost und West*, 4 (1904), 755–64; P. Bloch, in Graetz, Hist, 6 (1949), 1–86; German original in: MGWJ, 48 (1904), 33–42, 87–97, 161–77, 22–241, 300–15, 346–60, 491–503; G. Deutsch, in: *Central Conference of American Rabbis Yearbook*, 27 (1917), 338–64; J. Meisl, *Heinrich Graetz… zu seinem 100. Geburtstage* (1917); M. Brann (ed.), *Heinrich Graetz: Abhandlhungen zu seinem 100. Geburtstage* (1917); idem, in: MGWJ, 62 (1918), 231–69; *ibid.*, 61 (1917), 212–5, 321–491 (various contributions, incl. bibls.); S. Baron, *History and Jewish Historians* (1964), 263–75 and 446–49; H. Liebeschuetz, *Das Judentum im deutschen Geschichtsbild* (1967), 132–56; S. Ettinger, in: *Darkhei ha-Historyah ha-Yehudit* (1969), 7–36. **ADD. BIBLIOGRAPHY:** I. Schorsch, in: *The Structure of Jewish History* (1975), 1–62; R. Michael, *Heinrich Graetz* (Hebrew, 2003); J. Blutinger, "Heinrich Graetz" (Ph.D. dissertation; UCLA, 2004); M. Pyka, in: Klaus Hoedl (ed.), *Historisches Bewusstsein* (2004), 109–18; M. Pyka, "Juedische Identitaet bei Heinrich Graetz" (Ph.D. dissertation, Munich, 2005).

[Shmuel Ettinger / Marcus Pyka (2nd ed.)]

GRAF, HERBERT (1904–1973), opera producer and administrator. Graf, who was born in Vienna, was the son of the critic Max Graf. He studied at the University of Vienna with Guido *Adler, graduating in 1925, after which he worked as stage director at the opera houses of Muenster, Breslau, Frankfurt on the Main, and Basle until 1934, when he left Germany. Thereafter he worked in the United States with the Philadelphia Opera and, from 1939 to 1960, at the Metropolitan (where he was general director of productions until 1949). He was head of the Curtis Institute of Music's opera department from 1949. As an opera producer, he worked at almost all the important world opera houses and festivals. Graf was director of the Zurich Opera (1960–63) and of the Grand Theatre, Geneva, from 1965 until his death. His many publications include *Opera for the People* (1951) and *Producing Opera for America* (1961).

[Max Loppert]

°**GRAF, KARL HEINRICH** (1815–1869), German Protestant Bible scholar. Graf was born in Mulhouse, Alsace, and died in Meissen, Saxony. He began as a teacher of French and Hebrew in Paris and Meissen, where, in 1852, he became a professor. The hypothesis of his teacher, E. Reuss, that the prophetic books preceded the literary formulations of the Pentateuchal laws led Graf to the further hypothesis (*Die geschichtlichen Buecher des Alten Testaments*, 1866) that the Priestly Code, i.e., the source which includes Leviticus, which had until then been considered the earliest source of the Pentateuch, was actually the latest of the Pentateuchal sources. This contribution to the reconstruction of the history of ancient Israel was later developed by J. *Wellhausen. He also wrote commentaries on Moses' blessing (1857) and the Book of Jeremiah (*Der Prophet Jeremia*, 1862).

ADD. BIBLIOGRAPHY: R. Smend, in: DBI, 1, 460–61.

GRAFFMAN, GARY (1928–), U.S. pianist. Graffman was born in New York City, and studied at the Curtis Institute of Music, Philadelphia, with Isabelle Vengerova (1936–46) and at Columbia University (1947–48). His debut as a soloist was with the Philadelphia Orchestra under *Ormandy (1947). Two years later he won the Leventritt Award, which marked the beginning of an important international career. Graffman, a typically brilliant virtuoso in the American style, made many recordings, in addition to numerous public appearances.

[Max Loppert]

GRAFSTEIN, JERAHMIEL S. (**Jerry**; 1935–), Canadian senator, lawyer, and businessman. Grafstein was born in London, Ontario, where his father, a Polish university-educated immigrant to Canada, was in business. Jerry Grafstein graduated with a B.A. from the University of Western Ontario and a law degree from the University of Toronto Law School. In 1960 he was admitted to the Ontario Bar and appointed Queen's Counsel in 1973. He founded and edited the *Journal of Liberal Thought* in 1965–66. Drawn to politics he was a Liberal Party fundraiser and political adviser who worked on numerous Liberal political campaigns. A skilled policy adviser, he worked in several important government ministries, including the Departments of Transportation, External Affairs, and Justice. He also served as a senior adviser to former Prime Minister Pierre Trudeau and in 1984 Trudeau appointed him to the Senate of Canada. Grafstein became a partner in the Toronto law firm of Minden, Gross, Grafstein and Greenstein specializing in communications and administrative law. He was also a financier and patron of many arts and health organizations. Among his business interests, Grafstein was one of the founders of CITYTV in Toronto in 1972, chaired the boards of media corporations, such as CUC Broadcasting Ltd., CITY TV, and Muchmusic, and served on the boards of other corporations such as the World Film Festival of Toronto and the Toronto Arts Awards. He served as co-chair of the Canada-U.S. Interparliamentary Group, the largest parliamentary group in Canada, and the Advisory Committee to the 1988 Toronto Economic Summit and as a member of the Executive of the 2008 Toronto Olympic Bid Committee. He published articles, delivered lectures, made panel appearances, and led conferences in the areas of technology, television, cable, film, broadcasting, and corporate and international finance.

[Andrea Knight (2nd ed.)]

GRAHAM, BILL (**Wulf Wolodia Grajonca, Wolfgang Grajonca**; 1931–1991), rock 'n' roll concert promoter and manager, member of the Rock and Roll Hall of Fame. Graham was born to Frieda (Sass) and Yankel, religious Russian Jews who had moved to Berlin before his birth. Jacob died from an accident two days after Graham was born, and his mother was forced to put her only son and the youngest of her five daughters in the Auerbach orphanage so that she could seek employment.

On July 4, 1939, Graham and 39 other children from the orphanage in Berlin left on a **Kindertransport* to France, arriving at Chateau de Quincy, 30 km southeast of Paris. Later Graham was placed in a baby orphanage in Paris, and then the group was spirited in the middle of the night into Free France, transported to Chateau de Chaumont, Creuse. In July 1941, Graham and his sister, Tolla, joined a group of children who took a train south to Marseille, and then to Spain and Portugal, not long before their mother was gassed by the Nazis. The children were severely malnourished, and Tolla fell ill with pneumonia in Lyon; Graham never saw her again. He left Lisbon with 55 other children on the Serpa Pinto on September 9, 1941, arriving in New York on September 24, 1941. Brought over by *HIAS as part of the One Thousand Children – the only group of unaccompanied children who were rescued from the Holocaust by the United States – Graham was sent to an orphanage at Pleasantville, N.J., and was subsequently adopted by Alfred and Pearl Ehrenreich. He changed his name to Graham and became an American citizen in 1949. Graham fought in the Korean War and was awarded a Bronze Star and a Purple Heart.

In 1955 he moved to San Francisco, joining two of his sisters who had emigrated there from Israel. After a few office jobs and acting gigs, he became the manager of the San Francisco Mime Troupe. Graham produced his first concert, a benefit for the Mime Troupe, on November 1, 1965, featuring the Jefferson Airplane, Lawrence Ferlinghetti, The Committee, The Fugs, Allen Ginsberg, and other elements of the San Francisco art scene and subculture. Four months later, on February 4, 1966, Graham promoted his first show under his new company, Bill Graham Presents, featuring the Jefferson Airplane at the Fillmore Auditorium, a dilapidated auditorium that Graham transformed into a tightly run concert hall. It was at the Fillmore that Graham helped launch the careers of some of the icons of rock: Janis Joplin, Otis Redding, Jefferson Airplane, Cream, Big Brother and the Holding Company, and the Grateful Dead.

"The Fillmore … was the church of rock 'n' roll, and Bill was the shepherd tending the flock," said Mickey Hart, the drummer for the Dead.

In 1968, Graham moved the Fillmore into the Carousel Ballroom, another old dance hall, and renamed it the Fillmore West to go with his opening the Fillmore East in New York City. He subsequently took over Winterland, another San Francisco concert venue. Graham also branched out into band management and tour promotion.

Considered the Barnum and Bailey of rock 'n' roll, Graham revolutionized concert promotion, bringing professionalism to the business of presenting rock shows. That included having great lighting, great sound, shows that started on time, making artists do encores, making sure artists showed up on time for shows – in short, Graham brought the rules, order, and concept of theater to rock 'n' roll, as well as setting the standard for well-produced large-scale rock concerts.

Graham, who lived by himself in a Marin County house he named "Masada," also devoted much time and energy to produce benefits, mobilizing musicians on behalf of a wide range of social issues. In 1975, Graham paid for Chabad's 22-foot-high "Mama Menorah," the first giant public menorah displayed outside Israel, which is now replicated around the world. After he was killed in a helicopter crash in California, the Bill Graham Foundation was formed as a supporting foundation of the Jewish Community Federation of San Francisco.

An unauthorized biography, *Rage & Roll: Bill Graham and the Selling of Rock*, was written by John Glatt in 1993, and Graham was in the middle of writing his own autobiography, *Bill Graham Presents: My Life Inside Rock and Out* (1992) with Robert Greenfield when he died. Graham was inducted into The Rock and Roll Hall of Fame in 1992.

[Elli Wohlgelernter (2nd ed.)]

GRAJEWO, small town in Bialystok province, Poland. Jews settled there at the beginning of the 18th century. According to the 1765 census, there were 83 Jews aged over one year (17 families), of whom six families resided in their own houses and eleven in leased dwellings; 336 Jews were living in 38 villages in the vicinity. They leased taverns or were occupied as small traders or artisans (tailors, tinsmiths). Until 1862 Grajewo was included in the towns of the Russian-German border zone, where Jewish residence was subjected to various restrictions. Jews organized a community in the late 18th century. They operated a number of factories and many owned stores. In the 19th century many Jews in Grajewo exported agricultural produce to Eastern Prussia. The community numbered 197 (39% of the total population) in 1808, 727 (57%) in 1827, 1,457 (76%) in 1857, 4,336 in 1897 and 2,834 (39% of a total 7,346) in 1921. There were anti-Jewish outbreaks in 1933. Under the Soviet occupation (September 1939–June 1941) Jewish businesses were nationalized.

The Germans captured the town on June 22, 1941, and instituted a reign of terror. In August 1941, 1,600–2,000 Jews were confined to a ghetto. In December 1942 most of the Jews in Grajewo were deported to Treblinka and the rest in January 1943 to Auschwitz.

BIBLIOGRAPHY: R. Mahler, *Yidn in Amolikn Poyln in Likht fun Tsifern* (1958), index; B. Wasiutyński, *Ludność Żydowska w Polsce…* (1930), 37

GRAJEWSKI, ARYEH LEIB (1896–1967), talmudic scholar, jurist, and journalist. Grajewski was born near Lomza in Poland and studied in the yeshivah of Israel Meir Ha-Kohen (the "Ḥafeẓ Ḥayyim"), in Radin and at Slobodka. At the age of 16 he was ordained rabbi by outstanding scholars. He left for Ereẓ Israel in 1913, but at the outbreak of World War I in 1914 he and his family were compelled to move to Egypt because of their Russian citizenship. On the initiative of Joseph Trumpeldor he participated in the founding of a school for the children of the refugees and exiles from Ereẓ Israel then in Alexandria. He assisted his father Simeon Ḥayyim, who was appointed Jewish chaplain to the British expeditionary force in the Near East. In 1919 he returned to Jerusalem where he taught Talmud in the Hebrew Gymnasium. In 1921 he went to Paris, completing his legal studies in the following year, taught Talmud at the Rabbinical Seminary of Paris, and was a member of the central council of the Federation of French Zionists, chairman of the Union of Jewish Students, director of a school preparing young refugees for teaching, president of the Paris union of Hebrew teachers, etc. He published poems, stories, and articles on Jewish and general topics in French newspapers (in *L'Intransigeant*, in which he ran a special section on Hebrew and Yiddish literature, in *Les Nouvelles Littéraires*, and in the *Revue du Levant*), in Jewish French-language newspapers, and in Hebrew papers in Ereẓ Israel and elsewhere; and he edited the French column of the Paris Yiddish paper, *Parizer Haynt*. He devoted himself mainly to research in Hebrew law and Talmud. His first articles in this field were published in Hebrew in *Ha-Toren* (no. 11, 1945), and in French in *Hamenora*. He was a regular contributor to the Jerusalem periodicals *Ha-Mishpat* and *Ha-Mishpat ha-Ivri*. In 1935 Grajewski returned to Ereẓ Israel and for two years was engaged in teaching, after which he devoted himself to law, practicing also as a rabbinic lawyer. He published a monograph on Joseph ibn Migash (1953, 1963[2]). He published *Dinei Perudin u-Ketatot ba-Mishpat ha-Ivri* (1948). He died in Jerusalem and bequeathed his library to the library of Hechal Shlomo in Jerusalem.

BIBLIOGRAPHY: Tidhar, 3 (1949), 1465f.

[Zvi Kaplan]

GRAJEWSKI, ELIEZER ZALMAN (1843–1899), rabbinic scholar, traveler, and journalist. Grajewski was born in Malyaty (Maletai), near Vilna. He served first as the rabbi of Kletsk and later of Orsha. In 1873, he visited Ereẓ Israel, where he became a strong supporter of the new settlers. Upon his return, he published reminiscences of his journey in *Ha-Ivri*. When the Mazkeret Moshe organization was founded to honor Sir Moses Montefiore, leading Russian rabbis advocated the appointment of Grajewski as its director in Ereẓ Israel, and for this purpose he went to England in 1876. He did not, however, obtain the appointment but instead was appointed rabbi in Liverpool in 1877. He also traveled extensively throughout the United States, where he lectured on the necessity of encouraging the upbuilding of Ereẓ Israel. In 1890 Grajewski settled in Jerusalem, where he lived for the remainder of his life, although he died in Rigrod, near the Prussian border, after having gone to Vienna for medical treatment. His published works include *Ginnat Egoz* (1887), consisting of sermons and talmudic novellae: *Ginzei Keneset Yisrael* (1877), and *Gevul Yam* (1889), two commentaries to the *Haggadah*; and *Si'aḥ Eli'ezer* (1896), explanations of *piyyutim* recited on special occasions.

BIBLIOGRAPHY: Tidhar, 2 (1947), 618f.

[Aaron Rothkoff]

GRAJEWSKY, PINCHAS (1873–1941), Ereẓ Israel historian. Grajewsky was born in Jerusalem, where he received a traditional yeshivah education. He was an official in the Bikkur Ḥolim Hospital in Jerusalem for 43 years. In 1895 he became a member of the Yishuv Ereẓ ha-Kodesh Association, which was founded to train yeshivah students for agricultural work. Grajewsky's main literary activity was in the publication of documents, letters, and memoirs, along with biographical sketches, relating to Jerusalem and Ereẓ Israel personalities, synagogues, and public institutions. Many of the 170 pamphlets published by Grajewsky were in series: *Mi-Ginzei Yerushalayim* (25) contained documents, memoirs, and Turkish *firmans; Avnei Zikkaron* (15) was on tombstones and inscriptions; *Zikhron ha-Ḥovevim ha-Rishonim* (20) on important individuals; *Benot Ẓiyyon* (10) on distinguished women of Jerusalem. Although his biographical material was not always accurate, it was because of him that many historical documents which might otherwise have been lost were preserved. He also published *Sefer ha-Yishuv* (1929) on the residential quarters of Jerusalem.

BIBLIOGRAPHY: *Enẓiklopedyah shel ha-Ẓiyyonut ha-Datit*, 1, 554–6; Kressel, 1, 504–5. M.D. Gaon, in: *Deyokena de-Yerushalayim* (1953).

[Benjamin Jaffe (2nd ed.)]

GRANACH, ALEXANDER (Isaiah Gronach; 1890–1945), German and Yiddish actor of proletarian types, who distinguished himself in expressionist portrayals. Granach, who was born in Werbowitz (Galicia), reached Berlin at the age of 15 while traveling with a Yiddish troupe. He was accepted at Max *Reinhardt's school and joined the Reinhardt Theater in 1908. He volunteered for the Austro-Hungarian Army during World War I and was sent to Galicia. After World War I, he specialized in modern plays, but also won acclaim for his Shylock and his Mephistopheles. He also played in Yiddish, appearing in Sholem Asch's *God of Vengeance*, and presented Yiddish plays in New York in 1931. After a period in Poland and Russia, he emigrated in the U.S. in 1938. Here he staged *Shylock* and other plays in Yiddish, and acted minor parts in Hollywood.

BIBLIOGRAPHY: A Zweig, *Juden auf der deutschen Buehne* (1928). **ADD. BIBLIOGRAPHY:** S. Hubach, "Das Krumme und das Gerade – Ueberlegungen zu Alexander Granachs Autobiographie 'Da geht ein Mensch,'" in: *The Jewish Self-Portrait in European and American Literature* (1996), 187–209; M. Schmidt, "The Shtetl's Curiosity and Style – Alexander Granach's Autobiographical Novel *Da geht ein Mensch*," in: A. Fuchs, R.E. Schade, and F. Krobb (eds.), *Ghetto Writing* (1999), 171–79 W. Huder, *Alexander Granach und das jiddische Theater des Ostens* (1971).

[Gershon K. Gershony / Bjoern Siegel (2nd ed.)]

GRANADA, city and province in Andalusia, S. Spain. According to tradition in the legends of Spanish Jewry, some of the Jews exiled by Nebuchadnezzar settled in Granada (Solomon ibn Verga, *Shevet Yehudah*, ed. by A. Shochat (1947), 33–34), which they called "the pomegranate of Spain." Even the Moors thought that the Jews had founded the city, which they called *Garnat al-Yahud* ("Granada of the Jews"). The earliest extant information on the Jewish community in Granada is that the garrison stationed in the city after its conquest by the Moors in 711 was composed of Jews and Moors. During the Umayyad period Granada was one of the most important communities in all Spain. In the 11th century as a result of the fragmentation of Andalusia – when Granada became an independent principality – Jews received a large share in its administration. *Samuel ha-Nagid was not only leader of his own people but also vizier and military commander in the state. Prominent Jews were also among his political opponents who fled from the principality after the victory of Samuel's faction (Ibn Daud, Tradition, 74). The Jewish position in the leadership of the state is explained by the conditions within the principality – controlled by a Berber military clique that did not strike roots within the state. In the many court intrigues the king could depend on a Jew who had no aspirations for the throne. At that time, the Jewish population of Granada was estimated at 5,000 people, constituting around 20% of the population, and Samuel led the Jews for the benefit of the state. Various libelous documents were issued against the position of the Jews, and were circulated through neighboring principalities. An anti-Jewish polemical tone was even voiced in their wars against Granada.

Samuel's son, Joseph ha-Nagid, fell victim to a mass revolt in 1066 in which the "[Jewish] community of Granada" perished along with him (*ibid.*, 76). According to a later testimony, "more than 1,500 householders" were killed (Ibn Verga, op. cit., 22). Soon afterward the Jews returned to a position of influence in Granada, however not for long. At the time of the conquest of the city by the Almoravid Ibn Tāshfin in 1090, the community was destroyed and the *Ibn Ezra family was among the refugees. During the Almohad regime (1148–1212), only Jews who had converted to Islam were permitted to live in the city. The attempt of Jews and Christians to overthrow Almohad rule in 1162 met with failure. At first, Jews, together with Christians, were expelled from the town during the wars of the Reconquest (1232). They returned to Granada when the kingdom of Granada was ruled by the Muslim Naṣrid dynasty (1232–1492). There is no available information on the Jews of Granada during the 13th–15th centuries, yet it is known that several of the kings of Aragon sent Jews as legates to Granada.

After 1391 *Conversos found shelter in Granada, where they openly returned to Judaism. In the agreement of surrender signed between the king of Granada and Ferdinand and Isabella in 1491 it was stated that Jews who were natives of Granada and its environs, and designated to be transferred to Spain, would be granted protection; those who wished to leave the country for North Africa would be given the opportunity to do so. Conversos who returned to Judaism were given a deadline to leave the country. It was also agreed that no Jew would have the right of judgment over the Moors, and that Jews would not serve as tax collectors.

On March 31, 1492, the edict of expulsion of the Jews from Spain was signed in the recently captured Granada. The traveler Hieronymus Muenzer, who visited Granada in 1494–1495, states that Ferdinand ordered the razing of the Jewish quarter in 1492, where, according to Muenzer, 20,000 Jews resided. Sources from the Archivo de Simancas prove this figure to be an exaggeration. According to Laredo Quesada the number of Jews in Granada in 1492 was around 550. In addition to the families of Samuel ha-Nagid and Ibn Ezra, natives of Granada included Judah ibn *Tibbon, Saadiah b. Maimon *Ibn Danān, Solomon b. Joseph ibn Ayyūb, and many other scholars and authors. The Jewish quarter in Granada was not located in a single place throughout the centuries of Muslim rule. It was moved, expanded, or contracted by the various dynasties which ruled the city. According to one source, *Garnat al-Yahud* (the City of the Jews) was on the hill by the *Alcazaba*, from the *Torres Bermejas* up to the Daro River, while according to Muenzer as far as the *Puerta Real*. The Jewish quarter was completely demolished, by order of King Ferdinand, and on its location a cathedral and a hospital were erected. In the Alhambra Palace, according to some scholars, the fountain in the Patio of the Lions was brought from the palace of Joseph ibn Nagrela. Ibn Nagrela's fountain is described in the contemporary Hebrew poetry. In the Alhambra, in the Ambassadors Hall the Catholic monarchs signed the Edict of Expulsion on March 31, 1492, three months after the fall of the Kingdom of Granada.

BIBLIOGRAPHY: Harkavy, in: *Me'assef*, ed. by L. Rabbinowitz, 1 (1902), 1–56; Baer, Urkunden, 2 (1936), 394, 413; Baer, Spain, index; S. Katz, *The Jews in the Visigothic and Frankish Kingdoms of Spain and Gaul* (1932), 116; H. Muenzer, *Viaje por España y Portugal 1494–1495* (1951), 44; J. de Mata Carriazo, in: *Al-Andalus*, 11 (1946), 69–130; L. Torres-Balbas, *ibid.*, 19 (1954), 193f.; Schirmann, Sefarad, 1 (1954), 74–78; Ashtor, in: *Zion*, 28 (1963), 51f.; Ashtor, Korot, 1 (1966²), 204ff.; 2 (1966), 84–120; L. del Marmol Carvajal, *Historia del rebelion y castigo de los moriscos del reyno de Granada* (1600). **ADD. BIBLIOGRAPHY:** S. Kibrick, *Por tierras de Sefarad*, vol. 3 (1975); J.M. García Fuentes, *La Inquisición en Granada en el siglo XVI; fuentes para su estudio* (1981); S. Gilman, in: *Nueva Revista de Filología Hispánica*, 30 (1981), 586–93; S. Katz, in: *Sinai*, 96 (1984–5), 114–34 (Hebrew); J. Edwards, in: *Renaissance and Modern Studies*, 21 (1987), 20–33; M.A. Ladero Quesada, *Granada después de la conquista; repobladores y mudéjares* (1988), 245–59; M.A. Bel Bravo, *El auto-de-fe de 1593* (1988); J. Blázques Miguel, in: *Hispania Sacra*, 40 (1988), 133–64; J.E. López de Coca Castañer, *El reino de Granada en la época de los Reyes Católicos*, vol. 1 (1989), 153–70; R. de Lera García, in: *Inquisição* (1990), 1087–1108; D. Gonzalo Maeso, *Garnata al-yahud, Granada en la historia del judaísmo español* (1990); F. García Ivars, *La represión en el tribunal inquisitorial de Granada, 1550–1819* (1991).

[Haim Beinart]

GRANADA, GABRIEL DE (b. 1629), Marrano, arrested for Judaizing by the Inquisition in Mexico in 1642. During his trial, although not under torture as is commonly supposed but under the frightening pressures of his surroundings, he implicated over 80 other people, including his mother, four aunts, grandmother, and brother. His father, Manuel de Granada, who had traveled to the Philippines, died before Gabriel's arrest; his mother, Maria de Rivera, starved herself to death in the Inquisition jail. The trial dragged on at least until September 1645 and Gabriel was not sentenced until April 16, 1646, when he was reconciled to the Church.

BIBLIOGRAPHY: C. Adler (ed.), *Trial of Gabriel de Granada by the Inquisition in Mexico 1642–1645*, tr. by D. Fergusson (1899 = AJHSP, 7 (1899), 1–134); AJHSP, index to vols. 1–20 (1914), and index to later volumes.

[Martin A. Cohen]

GRANDE, BENZION MOISEEVICH (1891–1974), Russian physician, Orientalist. Grande was born in Lithuania. On the eve of World War I he visited Ereẓ-Israel and the neighboring Arab countries and became interested in the Arabic language and culture. As a student in the medical faculty in Moscow he served as a medic in the Russian army during World War I. In 1918 he graduated as a physician and served in the Red Army. In 1922 he graduated from the Institut of Eastern Sciences and began his career teaching and studying Arabic. He did much to help develop the written languages of the small national groups in Russia, and from 1940 to 1960 held the Arabic chair at Moscow University. He published the results of his research on Semitic languages and after his retirement in 1960 devoted himself to studying the Hebrew language. In 1963 he edited F.L. Shapiro Hebrew–Russian Dictionary.

[Shmuel Spector (2nd ed.)]

GRANDITSKY, PALLE (1923–2001), Swedish actor and director. Granditsky worked at the City Theater of Uppsala and Gävle (1954–57) and was head of the City Theater of Borås (1957–64). Here he directed *Antigone* by Jean Anouilh and *The Three Sisters* by Chekhov. He then returned to Uppsala, where his outstanding productions were *The Dance of Death* by Strindberg and *Rhinoceros* (1964) by Ionesco.

GRANDVAL (Hirsch-Ollendorf), GILBERT YVES EDMOND (1904–1981), French statesman. Born in Paris, Grandval was director of a chemical production concern from 1917 to 1940 and after the fall of France joined the French Resistance, becoming one of its leaders. He was appointed military governor of the Saar region in 1945 and from 1948 to 1952 was French High Commissioner for the Saar. Grandval was later resident-general in Morocco (1953), secretary of state for foreign trade (1962), and from 1962 to 1966 was minister of labor.

GRANIN, DANIEL ALEKSANDROVICH (pseudonym of **D.A. German**; 1918–), Soviet author. Granin, who was born and raised in Petrograd, became an engineer and worked for a number of years at various industrial enterprises. After serving in the Red Army in World War II, he turned to literature. His favorite theme was the clash between the professional and personal integrity of a scientist or a technocrat and the powerful political pressures exercised by the Communist bureaucracy. Granin's early works include *Variant vtoroy* ("Second Version," 1949) and the novel *Iskateli* (1954; *Those Who Seek*, 1956). The publication of his story *Sobstvennoye mnenie* ("One's Own Opinion") in 1956 was one of the most significant events of the post-Stalin "thaw." He justified his advocacy of independent thought as serving, in the final analysis, the best interests of the Soviet state. But it provoked the anger of Party bureaucrats because it was taken, not unreasonably, as implying that the party's policy of thought control was harmful to the country. Granin's best-known novel is *Idu na grozu* (1962; *Bison*, 1990), which has been credited with providing the best portrait of the world of Soviet scientists. With Ales Adamovich he wrote *A Book of the Blockade* (1982) about the siege of Leningrad, and with William Styron he edited *The Human Experience: Contemporary American and Soviet Fiction and Poetry* (1989).

BIBLIOGRAPHY: V.M. Akimov et al. (eds.), *Russkiye sovetskiye pisateli prozaiki* (1959), 571–9, includes bibliography.

[Maurice Friedberg]

GRANOTT (Granovsky), ABRAHAM (1890–1962), Israeli economist, head of the *Jewish National Fund. Born in Folesti, Bessarabia, Granott was appointed secretary of the JNF in 1919. After the transfer of the JNF Head Office to Jerusalem in 1922, Granott settled in that city, becoming the Fund's managing director, chairman of its board of directors (1945), and president (1960). His plan for a joint land authority of the JNF and the State of Israel served as the basis for the land legislation passed by the *Knesset in 1960. In 1948 Granott was cofounder and chairman of the Progressive Party (see *Independent Liberal Party) and was elected to the first Knesset in 1949, serving as chairman of its finance committee. His main contribution to Israel's economy consisted of establishing the principles for a progressive agrarian policy, which he formulated in a number of works such as *Land System in Palestine* (1952) and *Agrarian Reform and the Record of Israel* (1956). For a full bibliography of Granott's writings (in Hebrew, English, French, Spanish, German, etc.) up to 1951, see the appendix to his book *Be-Hitnaḥel Am* (1951).

BIBLIOGRAPHY: Keren Kayemeth Leisrael, *Abraham Granott* (Heb., 1962); Y. Ronen (ed.), *Kalkalat Yisrael Halakhah le-Ma'aseh* (1963), 1–3.

[Theodore Hatalgui]

GRANOVSKY, ALEXANDER (pseudonym of **Abraham Azarch**; 1890–1937), Soviet theatrical director and founder of the post-Revolution Jewish State Theater. Born in Moscow, he studied at the Institute of Stage Arts in St. Petersburg and worked in Munich, where he was influenced by Rienhardt. Granovsky organized an amateur Yiddish drama group in 1918. In 1919 he was authorized to open a studio in Petrograd

(Leningrad), and after six months he presented Maeterlinck's *The Blind* followed by Sholem *Asch's *The Sinner* and *Amnon and Tamar.* Granovsky aimed at the creation of a new Jewish style which would break with the Yiddish "primitive" tradition. His studio grew into a repertory theater, and was finally called the "Jewish State Theater." It moved to Moscow and presented works mainly by Jewish authors, Shalom *Aleichem, Sholem *Asch, A. *Goldfaden, I.L. *Peretz, S. *Abramovitsh (Mendele Mokher Seforim), and L. *Reznik, and plays by non-Jewish authors such as *Uriel Acosta* by K.F. Gutzkow and *Trouhadec* by Jules Romains. His method of production was exemplified in his presentation of Peretz's *Night in the Old Market* (1925), which relied largely on music, movement, lighting, and the "art of silence." In 1928–29 he toured Western Europe. He did not return to Russia, but stayed in Berlin and directed Arnold Zweig's *Sergeant Grischa* in German and *Uriel Acosta* for *Habimah (1930). After the Nazis came to power, he moved to Paris, where he worked in the opera and cinema. Among his admirers and students were Solomon *Mikhoels and Benjamin Zuskin.

BIBLIOGRAPHY: *Das Moskauer juedische akademische Theater* (1928); M. Kohansky, *The Hebrew Theater* (1969), 123f.

[Gershon K. Gershony]

GRANT, BARON ALBERT (**Albert Gottheimer**; 1831–1889), British financier. Born in Dublin, educated in London and Paris, Grant introduced in Britain the Crédit-Foncier type of mobilizing small investments for large projects. Many of his enterprises lacked solidity, and he was often attacked and lampooned. His companies, 37 in all, included public utilities and financial institutions in Europe and overseas. Their issued capital totaled 25 million sterling ($125 million), but eventually were worth only 5 million ($25 million). Grant also initiated slum clearance and collected paintings. He was member of Parliament for Kidderminster, 1865–68 and 1874–80. He purchased Leicester Square (London), then a garbage dump, converted it into a public garden, and handed it over to the Metropolitan Board of Works in 1874. In 1868 he was ennobled by King Victor Emanuel of Italy. He died in comparatively poor circumstances at Bognor. One of the most visible and colorful Anglo-Jewish businessmen of his time, Grant is often said to have been the original of Auguste Melmotte in Anthony Trollope's famous novel *The Way We Live Now* (1875).

ADD. BIBLIOGRAPHY: ODNB online; DBB, II, 623–29.

[Joachim O. Ronall / William D. Rubinstein (2nd ed.)]

GRANT, LEE (**Lyova Rosenthal**; 1927–), U.S. actress. Born in New York, Grant was nominated for an Oscar in her first screen role as the young shoplifter in *Detective Story* (1951), but soon after was blacklisted because of her refusal to testify against her then-husband, TV/screenwriter Arnold Manoff (aka Joel Carpenter), before the House Un-American Activities Committee. After more than a decade, Grant returned to films and television, winning both an Oscar (Best Supporting Actress, *Shampoo*, 1975) and Emmy Awards (*Peyton Place*, 1966 and *Neon Ceiling*, 1971). Appearing in more than 70 films, she played diverse roles in such motion pictures as *Middle of the Night* (1959); *The Balcony* (1963); *In the Heat of the Night* (1967); *Valley of the Dolls* (1967); *The Landlord* (Oscar nomination for Best Supporting Actress, 1970); *Plaza Suite* (1971); *Portnoy's Complaint* (1972); *Voyage of the Damned* (Oscar nomination for Best Supporting Actress, 1976); *Little Miss Marker* (1980); *Teachers* (1984); *The Big Town* (1987); *It's My Party* (1996); *The Substance of Fire* (1996); *Under Heat* (1996); *Dr. T and the Women* (2000); *Mulholland Drive* (2001); and *Going Shopping* (2005).

She directed the films *Tell Me a Riddle* (1980); *What Sex Am I?* (1985); *Down and Out in America* (Academy Award for Best Documentary, 1986); and *Staying Together* (1989). In addition to directing several TV movies, such as *Nobody's Child* (1986) and *Seasons of the Heart* (1994), from 1998 Grant directed dozens of biographical TV documentaries entitled *Intimate Portrait*. The subjects of these personal profiles included such figures as Vanessa Redgrave, Gloria *Steinem, Bella *Abzug, Jessica Tandy, Betty *Friedan, Bo Derek – and herself (2001).

In 1983 she received the Congressional Arts Caucus Award for Outstanding Achievement in Acting and Independent Filmmaking; in 1989, Women in Film granted her their first-ever Lifetime Achievement Award.

Grant's daughter, Dinah Manoff, is also an actress (*Grease*; *Ordinary People; I Ought to Be in Pictures; Staying Together;* and the TV series *Soap*; *Celebrity*; *Empty Nest*; and *State of Grace*).

[Jonathan Licht / Ruth Beloff (2nd ed.)]

°**GRANT, ULYSSES SIMPSON** (1822–1885), victorious Union Army general of the Civil War and 18th president of the United States (1869–77). Grant's name has been linked irrevocably with anti-Jewish prejudice through his signature on General Order Number 11, issued at his headquarters of the Department of the Tennessee, located in Holly Springs, Miss., on December 17, 1862: "The Jews, as a class violating every regulation of trade established by the Treasury Department and also department orders, are hereby expelled from the department within twenty-four hours from the receipt of this order. Post commanders will see that all of this class of people be furnished passes and required to leave, and any one returning after such notification will be arrested and held in confinement until an opportunity occurs of sending them out as prisoners, unless furnished with permit from headquarters. No passes will be given these people to visit headquarters for the purpose of making personal application for trade permits." It cannot be proven indisputably whether this blanket condemnation and order of expulsion, executed in the area under Grant's military control in parts of the states of Kentucky, Tennessee, and Mississippi, was composed by Grant himself or by an underling, on the inspiration of an official of the War Department or in response to complaints by General W.T. Sherman, or in accordance with the wishes of gentile cotton-buyers in the area. Extensive research has uncovered much anti-Jewish prejudice on the part of military officers and civilian officials, but no conclusive key to the identity of the specific instigator of Grant's Order. The general himself had instructed one of his subordinates on Nov. 10, 1862, to insure that "no Jews are to be permitted to travel on the railroad south from any point… they are such an intolerable nuisance that the department must be purged of them." On the same day that he signed Order No. 11, he reported to an assistant secretary of war that "I instructed the commanding officer of Columbus [Mississippi] to refuse all permits to Jews to come South, and I have frequently had them expelled from the department…. The Jews seem to be a privileged class that can travel everywhere …" An explanation which Grant offered on September 14, 1868, in the thick of the presidential campaign, implied that reports to him from the field and a reprimand from Washington had led him to issue and publish the order "without reflection and without thinking of the Jews as a sect or race to themselves but simply as persons who had successfully … violated an order …" It is also possible that the fact that Grant's own father was involved in business dealings with Jews at this time had something to do with his frame of mind.

Lincoln insisted that the order be revoked, despite Grant's unique facility for winning battles. Debates about the order took place on the floor of both the House and Senate, but opinion was divided fairly closely along party lines. During Grant's victorious presidential campaigns of 1868 and 1872, discussion of the anti-Jewish order appeared in the public and Jewish press, and some Jews and non-Jews were torn between their admiration for General Grant and their detestation of Order Number 11.

No single act or word, let alone edict, of another president or federal official, in all of American history, compares with the Grant order for rank generalization, harshness, or physical consequences. Yet Grant did not previously, nor subsequently, reveal animus toward Jews or Judaism. He appointed a number of Jews to important office during his presidency, offering the secretaryship of the Treasury to Joseph *Seligman, whose family included long-term friends of Grant dating back as far as 1849. In 1870 Grant appointed the former head of the American B'nai B'rith, Benjamin Franklin *Peixotto, to the unsalaried position of consul at Bucharest as part of an effort to persuade the Romanian government to relent from its violent campaign of pogroms against its Jews. Simon *Wolf, a vigorous, albeit unofficial and unsupervised, representative of Jewish concerns in Washington, believed that Grant "did more on and in behalf of American citizens of Jewish faith, at home and abroad, than all the Presidents of the United States prior thereto or since." But Grant was a Republican, and so was Wolf, and Grant appointed Wolf recorder of deeds of the District of Columbia in 1869.

The Grant affair underlines the unconscious assimilation by many Americans of traditional anti-Jewish stereotypes, and the constant search for scapegoats which took place during the traumatic experience of the Civil War as it did in other periods of social and psychological crisis.

BIBLIOGRAPHY: S. Wolf, *Presidents I Have Known* (1918), 63–98; J. Isaacs, in: AJA, 17 (1965), 3–16; B. Korn, *American Jewry and the Civil War* (1951), ch. 6; L. Gartner, in: AJHQ, 58 (1968), 24–117. **ADD. BIBLIOGRAPHY:** J. Sarna, *American Judaism* (2004), 120–22.

[Bertram Wallace Korn]

GRANZ, NORMAN (1918–2001), U.S. jazz impresario. Born in Los Angeles to parents who owned a store that failed in the Depression, Granz grew up to make a fortune from the music he loved as a young man. After service in the Army Special Services in World War II, he attended the University of California at Los Angeles, where his major was philosophy. In 1944, he created Jazz at the Philharmonic, a touring group that took the jazz idiom out of the smoky, noisy bars and dance halls and tucked it into sumptuous concert halls, where it flourished. He also represented stars like Ella Fitzgerald and Oscar Peterson and sought to protect black musicians from the abuses of segregation, insisting that their concerts be open to blacks, no matter how segregated the city. He began Jazz at the Philharmonic in Los Angeles with Nat King Cole, then a jazz pianist who worked with a trio but was not yet a pop star. Granz persuaded him to appear in concert with the saxophonist Lester Young and Billie Holiday, the singer. Besides providing good music, the concert raised money for young Mexicans, whom Granz felt had been wrongly arrested in the Zoot Suit riots of 1944. The concert proved a smashing success and within a few years an ever-changing troupe of musicians and singers, including J.J. Johnson, Benny Carter, Illinois Jacquet, Duke Ellington, Count Basie, Buddy Rich, and others, were touring the country under the Jazz at the Philharmonic rubric. Granz paid them, regardless of color, equally and well. He also persuaded Fitzgerald to record her "songbooks" of the works of Cole Porter, George Gershwin, and other creators of American popular standards, recordings that kept selling well into the 21st century. Granz was also the founder, in 1955, of Verve Records, with which he recorded the artists whose appearances he sponsored. Under his leadership Verve captured some of the finest jazz performances ever recorded. He sold Verve to MGM in 1960; the label was subsequently taken over by Polygram. In 1974 Granz formed a record company he called Pablo, named after Picasso, whose work he admired and collected and whose friendship he cherished. From 1959 to the end of his life, Granz lived, mostly in retirement, in Geneva.

[Stewart Kampel (2nd ed.)]

GRASSHOPPER. Among the insects mentioned in the Bible as permitted for food are those "that go upon all fours, which have jointed legs above their feet, wherewith to leap upon the earth" (see *Animals of the Bible). These are "the *arbeh* ("*locust") after its kinds, and the *solam* (AV, JPS, "bald locust") after its kinds, and the *ḥargol* (AV, "beetle"; JPS, "cricket") after its kinds, and the *ḥagav* (AV, JPS, "grasshopper") after its kinds" (Lev. 11:21–22; and see *Dietary Laws). The last three, each followed by the expression "after its kinds," refer to numerous species of grasshopper, there being, according to an *amora*, as many as 800 (Ḥul. 63b). Although in the Bible *ḥagav* applies to the grasshopper and not to the locust, it may have the latter meaning in the verse, "if I command the *ḥagav* to devour the land" (II Chron. 7:13), as it has in the Mishnah, which speaks of it as being at times a countrywide plague. In Israel there are many species of grasshopper, some small, others up to 2 in. (5 cms.) and more in size. The small grasshopper hiding in the high grass symbolizes the puniness of man when viewed from above (Num. 13:33; Isa. 40:22). All species of the grasshopper in Israel develop (like the locust) by metamorphosis, that is, the larva (*zaḥal*) has no wings but the adult has wings covering most of its body, an essential characteristic of the permitted grasshopper (Ḥul. 65b). In mishnaic and talmudic times the grasshopper was widely used as food, being also preserved in salt (Av. Zar. 2:7; et al.). There are Yemenite Jews who, on the basis of tradition as to their *kashrut*, still eat locusts and species of grasshopper.

It is difficult to identify "the *solam* after its kinds." The word means "destroying, eating," and refers to the grass-eating grasshopper, said to have the characteristic of being *gabbaḥat*, that is, apparently, having an arched back and slender feelers; many such species are found in Israel. Some identify it with the long-headed grasshopper of the genus *Acridium* (but see Av. Zar. 37a), i.e., with a species known as *ayyal kamẓa* which is *kasher* according to evidence from Second Temple times (Eduy. 8:4). With regard to the next permitted group "the *ḥargol* after its kinds," the sages stated that the outstanding characteristic of the *ḥargol* is "that it has a tail." This applies to the long-horned grasshopper of the family Tettigoniidae, whose female has a long protuberance which is a tube for the laying of eggs. Most of these species do no damage to agriculture, since they feed on insects and not on grass. Among them are also species whose imago is wingless, such as the *Saga* species, the largest grasshopper in Israel, and prohibited as food (see Ḥul. 65b).

BIBLIOGRAPHY: Palmoni, in: EM, 1 (1950), 520 6, s.v. *Arbeh*; J. Feliks, *Animal World of the Bible* (1962), 116–8. **ADD BIBLIOGRAPHY:** Feliks, *Ha-Ẓome'aḥ*, 203, 209, 225, 234, 235.

[Jehuda Feliks]

°GRATIAN (Franciscus Gratianus; d. before 1179), monk of Bologna. He is known for his canonical compilation *Decretum Gratiani*, assembled about 1140. The other title of the compilation, *Concordantia discordantium canonum*, clearly indicates its purpose, to bring together a large number of patristic texts and decrees of Church councils and popes, arranged in order of content. Though never officially adopted by papal authority, it was used in schools and synods, and from around 1159 was the manual of the Roman Curia. Among the thousands of texts assembled in the compilation only a few isolated ones concern the Jews. They include canon 61 of the Fourth Council of Toledo held in 633 (see *Church Councils), securing for children who are true Christians the belongings of their parents who have returned to Judaism (E. Friedberg (ed.) *Corpus Juris Canonici*, 1 (1871), 419: c. 7, C. 1, qu. 4). Others are canon 34 of the Council of Agde held in 506, imposing an eight-month instruction period for Jewish candidates for baptism, and canon 56 of the Fourth Council of Toledo, compelling Jews converted by force to remain Christians (*ibid.*, 1392: c. 93–94, D. 4, De cons.). One small group of texts concerns mixed marriages, which must be dissolved and the children brought up by the Christian party; the converted Jews (of Spain) who have readopted Judaism, whose children must be given into the care of monasteries; converted Jews, who must avoid all contacts with their former coreligionists; and the prohibition on Christians eating the unleavened bread of Jews, living among them, consulting their physicians, bathing with them, or finally, sharing meals with them (various councils; *ibid.*, 1087: c. 10–14, C. 28, qu. 1).

BIBLIOGRAPHY: A. Villien and J. de Ghellinck, in: *Dictionnaire de théologie catholique*, 6 (1920), 1727–51; J. Forchielli and A.M. Stickler (eds.), *Studia Gratiana*, 1 (1953–); *New Catholic Encyclopedia*, 6 (1966), s.v.

[Bernhard Blumenkranz]

°GRATTENAUER, KARL WILHELM FRIEDRICH (1770–1838), German antisemitic pamphleteer. His first publication *Ueber die physische und moralische Verfassung der heutigen Juden* (1791) launched the idea of an unchangeably negative and corrupt "Jewish mentality." In another of his widely circulated tracts attempting to rouse public opinion against Jewish emancipation *Wider die Juden* (1803, running into five editions), Grattenauer suggested that the Berliners remove Moses *Mendelssohn's bust and replace it with Voltaire's. Following in the wake of the latter's allegedly rationalist arguments against the Jews, Grattenauer was among the first to introduce the concept of race, thus heralding a new and ominous tendency in antisemitism, based no longer on religious but on pseudo-scientific grounds. "That the Jews are a very singular race, no historian or anthropologist can contest," wrote Grattenauer.

ADD. BIBLIOGRAPHY: J. Katz, *From Prejudice to Destruction. Anti-Semitism 1700–1933* (1980).

GRATZ, U.S. family of merchants and community leaders in Philadelphia. The Gratz family was founded in the United States by BARNARD GRATZ (1738–1801), who was of Polish birth and who emigrated from London in 1754. After working in the mercantile house of David Franks, in 1757 he went into partnership with Michael Moses, and a few years later he and his younger brother MICHAEL (1740–1811) formed a long-lived partnership under the family name as shippers and traders operating on the east coast and inland. As part of their trading operation, the partners sold *kasher* meat to the West Indies and conducted an extensive and sometimes dangerous Indian trade. In the midst of a very busy social and business career Barnard, with other merchants, signed Non-Importation Agreements to boycott British goods during the Stamp

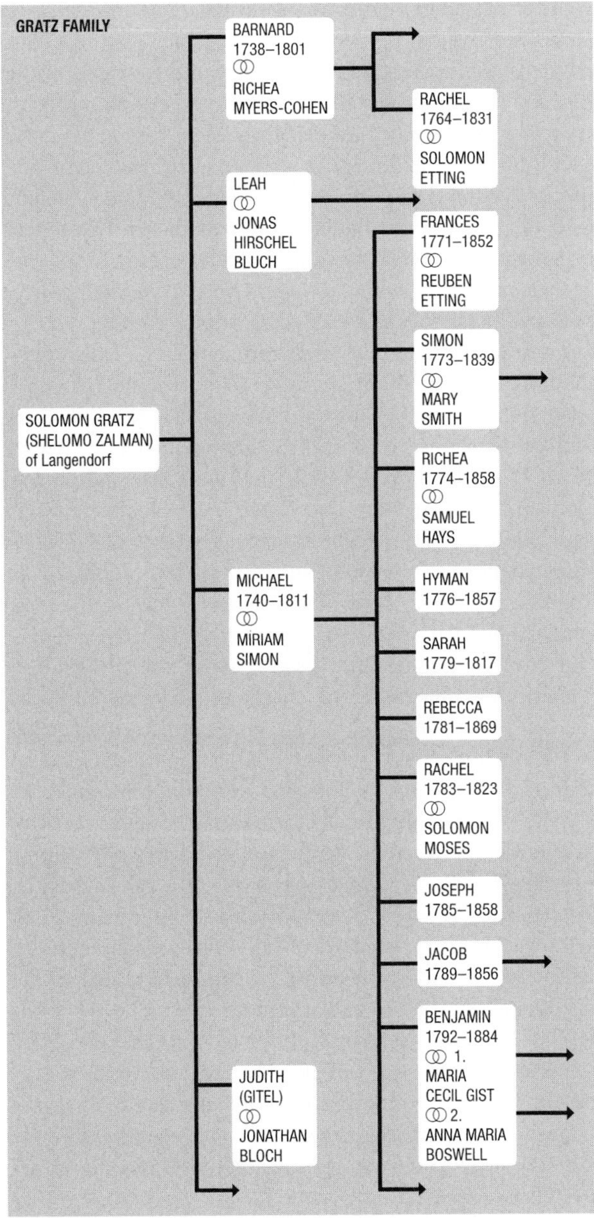

Act and Townshend Act crises prior to the Revolution. Always deeply involved with Jewish communal activities, the brothers helped found the first Philadelphia synagogue, which in 1773 evolved into Congregation Mikveh Israel. Barnard Gratz was named its first *parnas*, and Michael was on the board of directors. The Gratz family supported the Revolution, as did many Philadelphia Jews, and supplied goods to the Continental Army. After the war, the Gratzes became involved in a successful struggle for equal rights in Pennsylvania. Always interested in western lands, the Gratzes supplied money to the Indian trader and agent George Croghan and to George Rogers Clark in his Revolutionary expedition to capture Detroit, and in 1794 invested in real estate around Louisville, Kentucky. Michael founded Gratzburg, in Otsego County, New York, in 1793.

Two of Michael's sons, SIMON (1773–1839) and HYMAN (1776–1857), carried on the family business. Hyman was elected director of the Pennsylvania Company for Insurance in 1818 and president in 1838. He founded *Gratz College. Both brothers participated in the affairs of the Pennsylvania Academy of Fine Arts and the Pennsylvania Botanical Gardens. Though Simon and his younger brothers JACOB (1789–1856) and BENJAMIN (1792–1884) married gentiles, through their sisters' marriages the family was related to other prominent Jewish families. Their sister FRANCES (1771–1852) married Reuben *Etting; RACHEL (1783–1823) married Solomon Moses; and RICHEA (1774–1858) married Samuel *Hays. Richea is reputed to have been the first Jewish girl to attend college in the United States. Others of the Gratz family achieved considerable careers in law and politics as well as in business. Another of Michael's sons, JOSEPH (1785–1858), was an ardent Federalist, as was his brother Hyman. Joseph was a director of the Philadelphia Institution for the Instruction of the Deaf and Dumb, and of the Atlantic Insurance Company.

Jacob joined the family firm in 1806, but soon left to form his own dry goods firm. He received an M.A. degree (1811) from the University of Pennsylvania. In 1824 and 1839 he was elected to the state legislature. His younger brother Benjamin also joined the family firm and studied at the University of Pennsylvania. He was admitted to the bar in 1816. One of the early Jewish residents of Kentucky, where the family held land, he helped organize the Lexington and Ohio Railroad in 1830 and in 1835 helped found the Lexington branch of the Bank of Kentucky. Perhaps the best known of the Gratz family was Michael's daughter Rebecca *Gratz (1781–1869), who was active in various women's and children's organizations.

BIBLIOGRAPHY: E. Wolf and M. Whiteman, *History of the Jews of Philadelphia from Colonial Times to the Age of Jackson* (1957), index; W.V. Byars, *B. and M. Gratz Papers* (1916); D. Philipson (ed.), *Letters of Rebecca Gratz* (1929); R.G. Osterweis, *Rebecca Gratz: A Study in Charm* (1935).

[Leo Hershkowitz]

GRATZ, REBECCA (1781–1869), founder and leader of innovative organizations concerned with women and children. Gratz was born in Philadelphia, the middle child of ten in the family of Michael and Miriam Simon Gratz. She received an elite education at the Young Ladies Academy and at home, where she had access to an extensive library and learned about organizational life from her father, uncle, and brothers, who discussed their businesses, synagogue involvement, and philanthropic associations. Gratz, who never married, outlived all but her youngest sibling, and found meaningful social support and intellectual sustenance managing the organizations she established, in her study of Judaica available in English, and in her literary correspondence with luminaries such as Washington Irving, Maria Edgeworth, Fanny Kemble, and Grace *Aguilar.

In 1801 Gratz and her mother joined 20 Jewish and gentile women to found the Female Association for the Relief of

Women and Children in Reduced Circumstances, a women's mutual aid society which enabled married women to raise and dispense funds they could not legally control as individuals. Fourteen years later Gratz helped found the Philadelphia Orphan Asylum (1815). She served as secretary for both associations for more than two decades and advised her sister-in-law, Maria Gist Gratz, in establishing an orphanage in Lexington, Kentucky. Gratz lived with three bachelor brothers and her sister, Sarah, and raised six nephews and nieces following their mother's death in 1823. After Sarah's death, Gratz organized a short-lived and informal Hebrew school for her extensive family taught by an applicant for synagogue *ḥazzan*. She also developed close relationships with women of her Philadelphia synagogue, Mikveh Israel, and in 1819 organized the first non-synagogal Jewish charity in America, the Female Hebrew Benevolent Society, which remained active in the early 21st century. Gratz served as secretary, writing minutes, annual reports, and corresponding with donors, leaving more prestigious positions to others to ensure their commitment. Jewish women nationwide organized similarly named institutions throughout the 19th century.

To combat Christian evangelism, Gratz convinced the FHBS managers to open the Hebrew Sunday School in 1838. Educators Simha Peixotto and Rachel Peixotto Pyke supplied pedagogical expertise and wrote textbooks while Gratz served as superintendent. Isaac Leeser, *ḥazzan* at their synagogue, provided guidance and more advanced texts. Female graduates returned as volunteer faculty. Gratz assisted women in Charleston, Savannah, and Baltimore in establishing similar schools and due to her efforts Jewish Sunday schools staffed by female volunteers became the most popular Jewish educational institution in 19th century America. Gratz lived to see Philadelphia's Jewish Foster Home established in 1855. Much younger women shouldered most responsibilities but she assumed the vice presidency. She died with a reputation as the foremost Jewish woman in America. Some descendants thought her the inspiration for Rebecca of York in Sir Walter Scott's novel, *Ivanhoe*.

BIBLIOGRAPHY: ANB; D. Ashton, *Rebecca Gratz: Women and Judaism in Antebellum America*, (1997); E. Bodek, "Making Do: Jewish Women and Philanthropy," in: M. Friedman (ed.), *Jewish Life in Philadelphia, 1830–1940* (1983), 143–62; A. Braude, "The Jewish Woman's Encounter with American Culture," in: *Women and Religion in America*, vol 1 (1981).

[Dianne Ashton (2nd ed.)]

GRATZ COLLEGE, oldest independent college of Jewish studies in North America. In 1856 Hyman *Gratz, Philadelphia merchant, philanthropist, and scion of one of America's earliest Jewish families, established a trust indenture of approximately $150,000 to provide an annuity for his adopted son and, if the son died without issue, for a nephew. By 1893, both son and nephew had died childless. According to the deed of trust, the estate was then assigned to Congregation Mikveh Israel to establish "a college for the education of Jews residing in city and county of Philadelphia."

The limitations of the trust's income led Mikveh Israel to establish Gratz College for the more specific mission of educating Jewish teachers. Gratz's founders wanted it to serve the entire Philadelphia Jewish community and thus from its inception, Gratz accepted women, the first institution of higher Jewish education to do so. In that same spirit, even before the college opened classes, the Orthodox Mikveh Israel inaugurated the institution with public presentations by the leaders of Reform and Conservative Judaism.

Dedicated to the methodology of *Wissenschaft des Judentums and to being nondenominational, Gratz's mission was to teach Hebrew texts, train teachers for Jewish schools, and provide adult education. In 1909, it established a "school of observation practice" that allowed students to take college courses, while observing and practicing teaching in a Jewish elementary school. As Gratz's leaders were also dedicated to Zionism, the college introduced courses conducted in Modern Hebrew in 1922. As the Jewish community of Philadelphia expanded under the Jewish Federation model, Gratz College merged with the older Hebrew Education Society in 1928. Founded in 1848 by Isaac *Leeser, the Hebrew Education Society had received a state charter that allowed it to "furnish to graduates and others the usual degrees of Bachelor of Arts, Master of Arts and Doctor of Laws and Divinity." The merger thus conveyed to Gratz College the right to offer academic degrees, but despite faculty support, decisions of Gratz's governing board delayed Gratz's issuing of such degrees until 1952, when it awarded its first Bachelor of Hebrew Literature (BHL).

During the 1920s, Gratz's founding commitment to all streams of Judaism as well as to the Wissenschaft approach led to debates and compromises particularly regarding the training of Reform Jewish teachers. These concerns were ultimately resolved in 1960 by Gratz's establishment of the Isaac Mayer Wise program within its normal school, a unique development that produced educators specifically qualified to teach in Reform religious schools and recognized by the Union of American Hebrew Congregations (now the Union for Reform Judaism).

In 1967, Gratz College received full accreditation by the Middle States Commission on Higher Education. By 1987, Gratz had introduced master's degrees in Hebrew literature, Jewish music, Jewish education, Jewish studies, and Jewish liberal studies, as well as various graduate certificates. Self-study occasioned by the accreditation process more clearly defined Gratz's secondary school offerings eventually leading to the establishment of its Jewish Community High School (JCHS). Consolidating the Isaac M. Wise program with the large array of courses on topics ranging from intensive text and language to service learning to classes designed for Jewish students with special needs, the JCHS grew to 13 sites and almost 1,000 students by 2005.

As Gratz College developed, its funding by the local Jewish federation lessened. Thus, from the 1960s through 2005, the percentage of its funding from the Jewish Federation of

Greater Philadelphia declined from 78% to 12%. This reduction was both relative and absolute, yet it did not prevent Gratz from expanding its offerings and personnel.

Gratz's broad communal commitment extended to its academic resources. Its Tuttleman Library was opened to the public in 2003 and contains a research collection covering all areas of Judaic scholarship as well as specialized holdings such as rare Judaica beginning with the dawn of Hebrew printing, a major collection of Jewish music, and an archive of oral histories of the Holocaust that was among the first to be assembled in the United States. In the 1990s Gratz College inaugurated a Master of Arts in Education for teachers in public and private schools throughout eastern Pennsylvania. By 2005, some 900 graduate students had matriculated in that program.

From the 1990s Gratz College students had come from communities throughout the United States as well as from Israel, Europe, and occasionally East Asia. Building on its original mandate, Gratz College had become a transdenominational institution where Jews from all streams taught and studied together as members of its faculty, student body, and public audiences. In 2005 they pursued graduate certificates and professional degrees that provide advanced credentials for serving the Jewish community and general education and could also earn the baccalaureate. By 2005 Gratz's adoption of technology allowed it to offer more online courses in Jewish studies than any other institution as well as the first online Master of Arts in Jewish Studies. It also developed video conference courses and week-long intensive immersion courses while strengthening its on-campus offerings.

BIBLIOGRAPHY: D.A. King, "A History of Gratz College, 1893–1928" (Ph.D. diss., Dropsie University, 1976); J. Kutnick, "Serving the Jewish Community, Pursuing High Jewish Learning: Gratz College in Historical Perspective," in: R.M. Geffen and M.B. Edelman (eds.), *Freedom and Responsibility: Exploring the Challenges of Jewish Continuity* (1998), 321–48.

[Jonathan Rosenbaum (2nd ed.)]

GRAUBART, Y.L. (**Judah Leib**; 1861–1937), rabbi and halakhic authority. Judah Leib Graubart was born in Szrensk, Poland. One of at least eight children, he was raised with an appreciation of Talmud scholarship and ḥasidic piety even as he was exposed to Haskalah. His teachers included his father, elder brother Issachar Plock, the Kalisher rabbi, Ḥayyim Eliezer Wax, and Rabbi Nathan Leipziger of Szrensk. Graubart received *smicha* from both Wax and Leipziger.

Graubart went on to serve as rabbi in Yanov, Makov, and Stashov. In Makov he published the first volume of his five-volume collection of clarifications of talmudic texts and of responsa, the *Ḥavalim be-Ne'imim* (1901–39); volume 2 appeared while he was in Stashov. At the outbreak of World War I, the Russians accused Graubart (and others) of espionage, and imprisoned him in Siberia. By the time of the Bolshevik Revolution, Graubart was free in Moscow, where he led prayer services, taught, and collected funds for impoverished Jews. Graubart recorded his experiences in his memoir, *Sefer Zikaron* (Lodz, 1925/6).

Returning to Poland, Graubart supported Mizrachi Zionism against the Agudat Israel rabbis. Like prominent Polish Mizrachi Zionist, J.L. Zlotnik (Elzat), Graubart immigrated to Canada in the early 1920s. He became rabbi to Toronto's Polish Jews, while Jacob *Gordon served Russian-born Jews. Relations between the two soured when they sparred over supervision of kosher meat. In Toronto Graubart also spoke out against violators of the Sabbath, and even preached several outdoor Sabbath sermons in Toronto's bustling Jewish Kensington Market. A strong advocate of Jewish education, Graubart supported the *talmud torah* Eitz Chaim (est. 1918). He had complete disdain for the Reform rabbinate. He also acknowledged, with regret, that North American Orthodox rabbis fell short of an old-world level of learning. He nevertheless recognized that a new generation of North American-trained rabbis was needed and supported the modern Orthodox yeshivas in New York and Chicago.

Graubart continued writing in Canada. His last three volumes of *Ḥavalim be-Ne'imim* reflect New World concerns and show that he was now corresponding with other Orthodox rabbis in Canada. He published a collection of sermons in Hebrew, *Devarim Ki-Khetavam* (St. Louis, 1931/2) and a second collection of essays and sermons, *Yabi'a Omer* (Lodz, 1936). A number of shorter essays were published in the Yiddish press.

Despite misgivings about the state of Judaism, Graubart energetically worked to build Orthodox Jewish life in Toronto. He also fostered a tradition of advanced rabbinic scholarship in Toronto continued by Abraham *Price, Gedaliah *Felder, and others.

BIBLIOGRAPHY: S.A. Speisman, *The Jews of Toronto: A History to 1937* (1979); Ch.L. Fox *100 yor yidish un hebreyshe literature in kanade* (1980), 73–4.; M.D. Sherman, *Orthodox Judaism in American: A Biographical Dictionary and Sourcebook* (1996): 81–83.

[Richard Menkis (2nd ed.)]

GRAUMANN, SIR HARRY (1868–1938), South African mining magnate, industrialist, and financier. Born in England, Graumann went to South Africa at the age of 16 and engaged in mining in the Transvaal. He became a member of the Johannesburg Sanitary Board (forerunner of the town council) and was one of the city's four aldermen under the Kruger regime. During the Boer War (1899–1902), Graumann worked for Transvaal refugees in Capetown. After the war, he became the first Jewish mayor of Johannesburg. In 1912 he protested against the proposed restriction of Jewish immigration. He was elected to parliament in 1915. His memoirs, *Rand Riches and South Africa*, appeared in 1935.

GRAUR, ALEXANDRU (1900–1980), Romanian linguist. Born into the family of an accountant, Graur studied classical philology at the Bucharest University. Until 1946 he taught at various Bucharest high schools, with a few years off because of the racial laws that did not allow Jews to teach in non-Jewish schools (1939–44). In 1946 Graur became a university professor. At the University of Bucharest he taught general linguistics courses. He was interested both in the history of language and in its contemporary functioning (according to European descriptivists). In addition he was also interested in the popularization of his science, and he tried to explain how a natural language functions and its relationship to the culture it is called upon to serve (with special emphasis on the Romanian language). Graur's distinct theoretical orientation was a more traditional one (he never overstepped the theoretical frameworks of comparative-historical linguistics); he accepted very few, and those mostly critically, of the basic tenets of the different structuralist or post-structuralist trends in linguistics. Although never explicitly, he rejected from the very beginning generativism and all the other linguistic paradigms that appeared in the wake of Noam Chomsky's theories, starting from 1957.

Graur's attitude toward a culturally oriented Judaism was somewhat ambiguous: only in his old age did he start to show a certain interest in his forefathers' religion, culture, and language: he published in the Jewish community's newspaper several articles in which he demonstrated the Hebrew etymology of several Romanian words which entered this language through the intermediacy of the Greek and Latin languages, or through international use.

[Paul Schveiger (2nd ed.)]

GRAUR, CONSTANTIN (1877–1940), Romanian journalist. Born in Botosani, N. Moldavia, Graur started his career as a proofreader. In his youth he was a socialist. He began to publish in the Socialist journal *Munca* in 1894. In 1896 he was already a well-known socialist personality in the Bucharest party. He criticized the exodus of Romanian socialist intellectual leaders to the Liberal Party in 1900. He later edited newspapers in Galați and Ploesti, and went to Bucharest in 1919 to edit *Cuvîntul Liber* ("The Free World"). With other Romanian journalists, he founded the magazine *Facla* ("The Torch"), but continued writing for other papers, including the Jewish periodicals *Infratirea* ("Union") and *Adam*. In 1921, he became the chief manager of two daily papers *Dimineata* ("Morning") and *Adevârul* ("Truth"), which came to be regarded as "Judaized," because of the number of their Jewish contributors. During Nazi demonstrations, copies of these papers were burned on the streets. Graur had a democratic outlook and campaigned for Jewish emancipation and against antisemitism. His writings, many of them polemics embracing a socialist point of view, include *Manasse, cercetare critică* ("Manasse, Critical Research," 1904), *Din istoria socialismului Român* ("From the History of Romanian Socialism," 1912), *Socialiștii Români in slujba Germaniei* ("Romanian Socialists in Germany's service," 1914), *Cativa insi* ("Some People," 1931) and *Cu privine la Franz-Ferdinand* ("Concerning Franz Ferdinand," 1935). For his friend Dobrogeanu-Gherea, one of the founders of the Socialist movement in Romania, Graur wrote an obituary in the journal *Chemarea* (1920) in which he mentioned his Jewish origins.

BIBLIOGRAPHY: S. Podoleanu, *60 scriitori români de origine evreeasca*, 1 (1935), 137–42: T. Teodorescu-Braniște, Oameni și *paiațe* (1967), 355–9. **ADD. BIBLIOGRAPHY:** I.C. Atanasiu, *Miscarea socialista 1881–1900* (1932), 429 (index); C. Graur, in: Th. Loewenstein and N. Kittzler (eds.), *Israel in lume*, (1939), 75–96.

[Abraham Feller / Lucian-Zeev Herscovici (2nd ed.)]

GRAY, HERBERT ESER (**Herb**; 1931–), politician and Canada's first Jewish cabinet minister. Gray was born in Windsor, Ontario, graduated from the School of Commerce of McGill University and Osgoode Hall Law School in Toronto. He was admitted to the Ontario Bar in 1956. Gray practiced law in Windsor before entering politics in 1962 when he was elected the Liberal Party Member of Parliament for Windsor West. A strong advocate for human rights and freedom of conscience, Gray was returned to office in the next 12 consecutive elections, becoming the longest continuously serving Member of Parliament in Canadian history with close to 40 years of service in the House of Commons.

In October 1969, Gray was named minister without portfolio in Pierre Trudeau's first government, the first Jewish cabinet minister in Canadian history. He went on to hold a number of Liberal cabinet portfolios including National Revenue and Industry, Trade and Commerce, and president of the Treasury Board. When the Liberals were out of office, Gray served as Opposition House leader from 1984 to 1990, leader of the Opposition in 1990, and finance critic for the Official Opposition from 1991 to 1993. With the Liberal return to power in 1993, he was appointed leader of the Government in the House of Commons and solicitor general of Canada. From 1997 to 2002, he served as deputy prime minister, the first to turn this position into a full-time cabinet post. Following his retirement from the House of Commons in January 2002, he was appointed Canadian chair of the International Joint Commission, a Canadian-American bilateral organization dealing with transboundary issues.

Among his many honors, he received the title "Right Honourable," one of only six Canadians ever to hold the title usually reserved for current and former prime ministers, governors general, and chief justices of the Supreme Court of Canada. He was also a Companion of the Order of Canada. Gray's wife, SHARON SHOLZBERG-GRAY, served as president of the Canadian Healthcare Association.

[Judith E. Szaport (2nd ed.)]

GRAY, MARTIN (1925–), writer. As a Polish Jew from Warsaw, Gray was interned in the Warsaw ghetto and deported to the Treblinka extermination camp, from which he managed to escape, but left behind his entire family, of which he was the sole survivor. After his escape, he joined up with the Soviet Army advancing west towards Germany. After the war he settled in the United States, then in France where he published the bestselling *Au nom de tous les miens* (1971, written in collaboration with Max Gallo), which was adapted for the screen by Robert Enrico in 1983. Though some parts of the story may have been embellished and cannot therefore be considered historical documentation, Gray remains a valuable witness to the destruction of the Warsaw ghetto and the extermination process, and the publication of the book marked a crucial point in the development of Holocaust awareness in France, the specificity of the Jewish Holocaust having long been ignored in France because of the emphasis placed on the deportations of Resistance fighters.

[Dror Franck Sullaper (2nd ed.)]

GRAY, MORRIS ABRAHAM (**Moishe Guraryeh**; 1989–1966), Winnipeg community leader and politician. Gray was born near Gomel, Russia, to Abraham and Sara Guraryeh. He came to Canada in 1907 at age 18 and settled in Winnipeg. By 1917 he was a leader in the Winnipeg Jewish community, serving as secretary of the *Hilfs Farband*, an early mutual aid society, and of the Western Canada Jewish War Relief campaign to aid sufferers in World War I. He took a leading part in immigrant aid work and by 1923 was serving as secretary of the Jewish Immigrant Aid Society in Western Canada and served as president of the Jewish Children's Aid and Orphanage of Western Canada. Gray was a pioneer of the Labor Zionist movement in Western Canada and a founder of the Canadian Jewish Congress in 1919. First elected to public office in 1926, Gray served first as school trustee, then as Winnipeg city alderman for 16 years, endorsed by the Independent Labour Party. In 1941 he was elected as CCF member of the Manitoba Legislature, where he served for 25 years until his death.

In political office Gray campaigned for welfare for the unemployed, for increased old age pensions, and for antidiscrimination laws and a Bill of Rights, as well as for the establishment of a Manitoba Dental College. But his Jewish political engagement was also strong. During the Depression he worked with the Jewish Colonization Association to place unemployed Jews on farms, he was a founder of the Jewish Economic Bureau, which considered economic problems affecting Jews, he was president of the Jewish National Workers Alliance, and he was active in the reorganization of the Canadian Jewish Congress in 1934. He campaigned against antisemitism and was a leader in the anti-Nazi protest movement of the 1930s and 1940s. Gray was also a founder of the Labor Zionist's Histadrut Campaign in Western Canada. In 1957, he was honored at Winnipeg's annual Negev Dinner to mark the 50th anniversary of his arrival in Canada.

[Abraham Arnold (2nd ed.)]

GRAYZEL, SOLOMON (1896–1980), U.S. historian and communal leader. Grayzel was born in Minsk, Belorussia, but was educated in the United States. He received his B.A. from the City College of New York in 1917 and his M.A. in sociology from Columbia University in 1920. He was ordained by the Jewish Theological Seminary in 1921 and served as the first rabbi of Congregation Beth-El in Camden, N.J., continuing his studies at Dropsie College, where he earned a Ph.D. in history (1926). In 1929, upon his return from research studies abroad, he began teaching Jewish history at Gratz College in Philadelphia, continuing to teach there and serving as registrar until 1945. In 1939, he took an editorial position with the Jewish Publication Society of America, working under Isaac *Husik. At the latter's death in the same year he became the editor in chief, a position he held until 1966. He was elected to the presidency of the Jewish Book Council of America in 1945 and was connected with the *Jewish Book Annual* from its inception in 1942. From 1966, he taught Jewish history at Dropsie College.

Grayzel's major scholarly efforts centered on the relationship of Christians and Jews during the Middle Ages. His doctoral thesis, *The Church and the Jews in the Thirteenth Century* (1933, 1966^2), was followed by individual articles on related subjects, which appeared in the *Jewish Quarterly Review*, *Historia Judaica*, the *Hebrew Union College Annual*, and other publications. He also wrote a popular, one-volume *History of the Jews from the Babylonian Exile to the Present* (1947, 1968^2), widely used as a textbook, and *A History of the Contemporary Jews from 1900 to the Present* (1960).

BIBLIOGRAPHY: A.A. Steinbach, in: *Jewish Book Annual*, 28 (1970), 110–115.

[Simcha Berkowitz]

GRAZ, capital of *Styria, considered one of the oldest Jewish settlements in Austria. Although a gravestone, excavated in 1577 and erroneously dated to 70 B.C.E., long led to the belief that the community was much older, adjacent Judendorf was recorded in documents dating from 1147. In Graz itself there is reliable evidence of the presence of Jews only in the last decades of the 13th century. At that time they made their living mostly through moneylending, particularly to the local nobility. By 1398 a community had come into existence, located in a Jewish quarter, headed by a *Judenmeister* and a *iudex Judaeorum, and possessing a synagogue and a *mikveh*. Though expelled in 1439, the Jews returned by 1447. After the expulsion of the Jews from Styria in 1496, together with the rest of Austrian Jewry, almost four centuries passed before there was again a formal settlement of Jews in the town. Only in 1783 were they permitted to attend the yearly trade fairs then held in Graz. Individual families with special permits were allowed to settle in Graz after 1848. By 1863 a community had come into being and in 1868 the demand for special permits was rescinded; at that time an official organization of the community took place. From then on the community grew rapidly, partly because of economic factors. It numbered 566 in 1869 (0.7% of the total population), 1,238 in 1890, and 1,720 (1.1%) in 1934.

The community was able to finance its activities not only through the imposition of taxes on the Jews of Styria but on those of Carinthia and Carniola as well. Soon after its formal organization, a primary school was founded. By 1892 a large school was built; in 1895 an impressive synagogue was dedicated. The anti-Zionism of Graz's communal leaders was pronounced, but a large influx of refugees from Eastern Europe in the wake of World War I strengthened the Zionist movement considerably, and in 1919, the Zionists gained a majority in the community. The Jews in Graz were socially segregated, and in the later 1930s Graz was a center of Austrian National Socialism (known as the "capital of the insurrection" after 1938).

Immediately after the *Anschluss* (March 12, 1938), the Jewish cemetery was desecrated. The members of the community board were arrested and released only after prolonged negotiation. Local functionaries were anxious to make Graz the first town to be *Judenrein*. On the initiative of the head of the Jewish community, Elijah Gruenschlag, Adolf *Eichmann agreed to the transfer of 5,000,000 marks to facilitate the emigration of 600 Jews to Palestine, but the events of Nov. 10, 1938, put an end to the project. On the night of Nov. 9–10 (*Kristallnacht*), the synagogue was dynamited and burned to the ground. More than 300 Jews were taken to Dachau concentration camp, to be released in April 1939. Of the 1,600 Jews in Graz on *Kristallnacht*, 417 emigrated. In June 1939, only 300 were still in the city; most were sent to Vienna and then to the death camps. After World War II, 110 Jews settled in Graz. There were 420 in 1949 and 286 in 1950. A small synagogue in a communal center built on the site of the synagogue ruins was consecrated in 1968. A Jewish community of fewer than 100 members remained at the beginning of the 21st century. A new synagogue on the site of the one destroyed on *Kristallnacht* was consecrated in 2000.

The historian David *Herzog was rabbi of Graz (1908–38), and the Nobel Prize laureate Otto *Loewi taught pharmacology at Graz University from 1909 to 1938. Wilhelm Fischer-Graz (1846–1932), a writer popular at the time for many novels, mainly set in the town itself or in Styria, worked in Graz as a librarian.

BIBLIOGRAPHY: J.E. Scherer, *Die Rechtsverhaeltnisse der Juden…* (1901), 455–517; E. Baumgarten, *Die Juden in Steiermark* (1903), passim; A. Rosenberg, *Beitraege zur Geschichte der Juden in Steiermark* (1914), index; D. Herzog, *Die juedischen Friedhoefe in Graz* (1937); idem, in: MGWJ, 72 (1928), 159–67, 327; 75 (1931), 30–47; idem, in: ZGJT, 3 (1933), 172–90; F. Popelka, *Geschichte der Stadt Graz*, 2 (1935), 332–44; Rosenkranz, in: *Yad Vashem Bulletin*, 14 (1964), 40–41; Schwarz, in: J. Fraenkel (ed.), *The Jews of Austria* (1967), 391–4; Kosch, in: *Zeitschrift des Historischen Vereines fuer Steiermark*, 59 (1968), 33–43; Germ Jud, 1 (1963), 119; 2 (1968), 300–2; K. Hruby, in: *Judaica*, 25 (1969), 179–81; PK Germanyah.

[Meir Lamed]

GRAZER, BRIAN (1951–), U.S. producer-writer. Born in Los Angeles to a Jewish mother and Catholic father, Grazer graduated from USC with a bachelor's degree in psychology in 1974. He also attended the University of Southern California Law School for one year. He began his career in the entertainment industry as a legal intern with Warner Bros. and then joined Brut/Faberge Productions as a script reader. After joining the Edgar J. Scherick-Daniel Blatt Company, Grazer produced his first made-for-TV movies, *Zuma Beach* and *Thou Shalt Not Commit Adultery* in 1978. He signed a development deal with Paramount Pictures in 1980 and in 1982 he produced his first feature film, *Night Shift*, which also marked his first collaboration with director Ron Howard. In 1984, Grazer received an original screenplay Oscar nomination for his first turn as a writer on *Splash*, also directed by Howard. Grazer and Howard formed Imagine Entertainment in 1986, which developed such films as *Parenthood*, *Kindergarten Cop*, *The Doors*, *Backdraft*, and *Far and Away*. Grazer and Howard continued to work together on such feature films as *Apollo 13* and *A Beautiful Mind* (2001), which won the Academy Award for best picture. Grazer's other television work includes *From the Earth to the Moon*, *SportsNight*, *Felicity*, *24*, and *Arrested Development*.

[Adam Wills (2nd ed.)]

GRAZIANI, YITZHAK (1924–2003), Israeli conductor, arranger, and composer. Born in Russe, Bulgaria, Graziani studied composition and conduction at the Academy of Music in Sofia. In 1948, he immigrated to Israel and for 12 years was the conductor of the Zaddikoff Choir, founding its children's choir. He was instrumental in founding the Kol Israel Light Orchestra and, from 1961 to his death was the conductor of the Israel Defense Forces Orchestra. He also conducted performances of many musicals, the Israeli Opera, and Israeli song festivals. Besides his conducting, Graziani arranged more than a thousand pieces and composed music for a few Israeli films such as *Dalia ve-ha-Malakhim* and *Moishe Ventilator*.

[Uri (Erich) Toeplitz, Yohanan Boehm / Israela Stein (2nd ed.)]

GRAZIANO, ABRAHAM JOSEPH SOLOMON BEN MORDECAI (d. 1684), Italian rabbi. Graziano was born in Pesaro where he studied under Isaac Raphael Ventura. He lived for some time in Rome, proceeding from there to Modena where he studied under his grandfather, Nathaniel Trabot, who ordained him in 1647. He first served as a member of the *bet din* of Modena, where he was later appointed rabbi. His characteristic signature, *Ish Ger* ("a strange man") is a play on the first letters of his name and on his being a "stranger" in Modena. Abraham's leniency with regard to some local customs aroused the opposition of his contemporaries. He is known as the first collector of books and manuscripts among Italian Jews. He left no published works of his own; most of his rulings remain in manuscript and some are occasionally found in the work of his contemporaries. His commentary on the Shulḥan Arukh is mentioned in the *Zera Emet* (vols. 1,2) of Ishmael ha-Kohen. One of his responsa, from the year 1665, is written in Italian, interspersed with biblical verses and quotations in Hebrew. Of the 54 poems in his collected work, poems for festivals, births, weddings, and funerals, some have been published. His elegy on his brother, Aaron, who died in 1648, is of a high literary standard. Two elegies preserved at the beginning of *Ma'avar Yabbok* of Aaron of Modena are erroneously ascribed to him.

BIBLIOGRAPHY: Baron, in: *Studies... A.S. Freidus* (1929), 122–37 (Heb. part); Jona, in: REJ, 4 (1882), 112–26; Mortara, Indice, 28 n. 1; Ghirondi-Neppi, 3; Kaufmann, in: MGWJ, 39 (1895), 350–7.

[Simon Marcus]

GREAT POLAND (Pol. **Wielkopolska;** Heb. פּוֹלִין גָּדוֹל), historic administrative unit of Poland-Lithuania, and a Jewish historical geographical entity within the framework of the *Councils of the Lands. The region, which lay on both sides of the Warta River, consisted of the provinces of *Poznan, *Gniezno, *Kalisz, *Plock, Rawa, Sieradz, Leczyca, and Pomerania; in the Jewish organizational framework, it included 36 communities and mother communities, and over 60 small communities and subsidiary communities. Of the mother communities, the important communities of Poznan, Kalisz, *Leszno (Lissa), and *Krotoszyn attained a special status. The region was under Polish rule until the partitions of 1772 and 1793; largely under Prussian (later German) rule until 1918, with the interruption of the government of the grand duchy of Warsaw between 1807 and 1815; since World War I in independent Poland, with the interruption of Nazi German rule from 1939 to 1945.

The communities of Poznan, Gniezno, Kalisz, Plock, and others were founded in the 12th to 14th centuries, the legal basis for their development being laid down by the charter issued by Prince *Boleslav the Pious (1264). As throughout Poland-Lithuania, Jewish settlement in Great Poland developed considerably in the 16th to 17th centuries, while in the 18th century it underwent a decline. The Great Poland province (גָּלִיל, "circuit") in the Jewish autonomous framework was under the hegemony of the community of Poznan until the middle of the 17th century, passing to Kalisz until the beginning of the 18th century, and then to Leszno until the close of that century.

During the period under the hegemony of Poznan, rights of residence were obtained and preserved by means of a prolonged and stubborn struggle. The Jewish organizational framework was developed in the form of a Council for the Province of Great Poland, or the Council of the Province of Poznan, which acted on behalf of the Jews as regional spokesman in contact with external powers, such as the ecclesiastical authorities and the municipality, and with internal bodies, such as the local community leadership and the Council of Four Lands. Among the Jewry of Great Poland there thus developed an independent regional consciousness, having a specific social significance, collective responsibility, and spiritual authority and tradition (of the "Great Poland rite"). The foundations were therefore laid for the conservative pattern which successfully withstood the storms accompanying the religious-social movements which swept this Jewry during the 17th and 18th centuries. During the period of leadership of the communities of Kalisz and Leszno, a period of chaos in Poland when there was a third wave of Jewish settlement, both the local and central organs of the Jewry of Great Poland were weakened and the communities plunged into an increasing state of insolvency and "debts to the state." After the area passed to Prussia (by stages, in the late 18th century), severe restrictions were imposed on the Jews of Great Poland. In consequence of the limitations placed on their numbers, thousands of Jews were expelled from the communities. The ideas of Haskalah began to spread there owing to the proximity to Berlin and the influence of Solomon *Maimon. Under the government of the grand duchy of Warsaw from 1807 to 1815, the chances of emancipation for the Jews in Great Poland vanished, and new taxes were imposed on them (the recruiting tax and the kosher meat tax (see *Korobka). As a result, an increasing number of Jews immigrated to the German states. Following the renewal of Prussian rule in 1815, the struggle for emancipation was again taken up (1848–50), because the general regulations and the "temporary measures" (1833) had not granted emancipation to all the Jews of the province (with a distinction between citizens and "tolerated" persons). In accordance with the "temporary measures," changes were made in the structure of the communities (1833–47); attempts were made to reorganize the Jewish educational institutions, and germanization and Haskalah became of increasingly important influence in the lives of the Jews of the region. The Prussian authorities supported the Jewish communities, which made up about 15% of the total population, since they were useful in suppressing the Polish element, which formed about one-half of the total population of the region; as a result of the Jews' pro-German orientation, their relations with the Polish inhabitants became strained. On the other hand, tension arose between the German inhabitants and the Jews because of their economic success; these stresses resulted in increased waves of Jewish emigration to the West and overseas, so that a number of communities in Great Poland died out or were greatly reduced in size. When the region was incorporated into independent Poland after the end of World War I, the hostility of the Poles and Polish authorities toward the Jews was intensified in this area because of their pro-German tendencies. The social and economic ties of the communities there with Germany having been disrupted by the political changes, emigration appeared to many to be the best solution. After the Nazi occupation the community of Great Poland came to an end.

The Council of the Land (Province) of Great Poland

Great Poland is important in the history of Jewish *autonomy through this institution. The beginnings of the Council are obscure; its formation, however, preceded that of the councils of the communities of the other parts of Poland (see *Councils of the Lands). At the earliest, its creation is connected with the charter issued to the Jews by Boleslav the Pious in 1264. The history of the Council falls into two periods: the period of consolidation, which continued up to 1519, and its subsequent history until 1764. Its achievements during the first period include the extension of rights of residence and their renewed ratification (1364, 1453); defense against the slander of having introduced the *Black Death (1348), as well as many other negotiations accomplished successfully by *shtadlanut* (see *shtadlan); the appointment of a chief rabbi of the province or "provincial rabbi," the *Episcopus Judaeorum Posnaniae*; the extension of the area under his jurisdiction and the definition of the scope of his authority (1389–93, 1458, 1519). The Jewish leadership was also successful in its opposition to the officially appointed tax lessee, and was empowered to choose 11 assessors and five collectors (with the exception of Poznan and Kalisz) for estimating the amount of taxation (the *sekhum*, "sum"), its distribution and collection, and its transfer to the state treasury, the ministers, and the Council itself for its own internal requirements (1512–19). The history of the Council extends over a period of about 250 years (1519–1764). It met from once in three years to twice a year in various communities of the province of Rydzyna. During this period the Council extended its activities. A considerable part of these, of a general and standard nature, were drafted in the form of regulations, some of which have been preserved in the communal registers. The subjects it dealt with include livelihood, established claims, municipal affairs, disputes, loans, peddling, fairs, commerce in general and with non-Jews in particular, and Torah study. Responsibility for execution of the decisions was entrusted to the rabbi of the province and its communal leaders. The rabbi of the province was elected by 32 electors of the community of Poznan, in conjunction with (9–19) delegates from the province, by a majority vote for a period of three years. He acted as the rabbi of the community of Poznan and served as its *rosh yeshivah* (uninterruptedly from 1651). Until the middle of the 17th century he was assisted in his functions by one of the *dayyanim* of the province, chosen from the *dayyanim* of Poznan. Occasionally the influence of the rabbi of Great Poland extended beyond the borders of the province to the communities of Silesia (1540, 1583, 1626, 1637). The *parnasim* (leaders) of the communities usually acted as the *parnasim* of the province. The number of provincial *parnasim* varied between nine, six, and eleven (1668, 1677, 1685, 1754). Of these, two to three were delegates from Poznan. The *parnas* of the Council was assisted by the *ne'eman* (treasurer) of the province, the *sofer* (secretary) of the province (generally the same person), the *shammai* (assessor) of the province, the *shammash* (clerk) of the province, and the *shali'aḥ* (emissary) of the province. They were chosen by the *parnasim* of the Council during its sessions. The *parnas* of the Council was empowered to impose a series of punishments, such as imprisonment, expulsion, fines, and the *ḥerem* (ban) to ensure that these functions were fulfilled (1669). He was occasionally assisted by the influence and connections of the *shtadlan* of the Poznan community.

BIBLIOGRAPHY: A. Heppner-Herzberg, *Aus Vergangenheit und Gegenwart der Juden und der juedischen Gemeinden in den Posener Landen* (1902); B. Breslauer, *Die Auswanderung der Juden aus der Provinz Posen* (1909); R. Wassermann, in: *Zeitschrift fuer Demographie und Statistik der Juden*, 6 (1910), 65 76; L. Lewin, *Die Landessynode der grosspolnischen Judenschaft* (1926); U.U. Zarchin, *Jews in the Province of Posen* (1939).

[Dov Avron]

GREECE (Heb. יָוָן, *Yavan*), country in S.E. Europe.

SECOND TEMPLE PERIOD (TO 330 C.E.)

Although the earliest known Jews on the Greek mainland are to be found only from the third century B.C.E., it is highly probable that Jews traveled or were forcibly transported to Greece by way of Cyprus, Ionia, and the Greek isles by various enemies of Judah during the biblical period (cf. Joel 4:6; Isa. 66:19; see *Javan). The first Greek Jew known by name is "Moschos, son of Moschion the Jew," a slave mentioned in an inscription, dated approximately 300–250 B.C.E., at Oropus, a small state between Athens and Boeotia. This date coincides with the reign of the Spartan king *Areios I (309–265), who, according to later sources, corresponded with the Judean high priest Onias (I Macc. 12:20–1; Jos., Ant., 12:225). If this fact is to be accepted (cf. S. Schueller, in: JSS, 1 (1956), 268), one can assume that such a correspondence entailed a certain amount of Jewish travel to Greece and is thereby possibly connected with the establishment of a local Jewish community. Further growth of the Jewish community probably took place as a result of the Hasmonean uprising, when numbers of Jews were sold into slavery. At least two inscriptions from Delphi (Frey, Corpus, 1 (1936), nos. 709, 710) from the middle of the second century B.C.E. refer to Jewish slaves. Among those Jewish fugitives to reach Sparta during the reign of Antiochus IV Epiphanes was the high priest Jason (II Macc. 5:9).

During the Hasmonean period the Jewish community in Greece spread to the important centers of the country, and from the list of cities in I Maccabees 15:23 – probably dating to the year 142 B.C.E. – it appears that Jews already resided at *Sparta, Delos, Sicyon, Samos, *Rhodes, *Kos, Gortyna (on *Crete), Cnidus, and *Cyprus (cf. F.M. Abel, *Les Livres des Maccabées* (1949), 269). A similar list of Jewish communities in Greece is transmitted by Philo (*Legatio ad Gaium*, 281–2), and thus reflects the situation during the first century C.E.

Among those places containing Jews Philo lists "Thessaly, Boeotia, Macedonia, Aetolia, Attica, Argos, Corinth, and most of the best parts of the Peloponnesus. Not only are the mainlands full of Jewish colonies but also the most highly esteemed of the islands of Euboea, Cyprus, and Crete." That a sizable Jewish colony existed at Delos is further attested by the Jewish inscriptions in the area, including a number from the local synagogue (Frey, Corpus, 1 (1936), nos. 725–731; cf. Jos., Ant., 14:231–2, regarding Jews of Delos who are also Roman citizens). It may be assumed that the community at Rhodes was in close contact with the Judean king Herod, who is known to have generally supported the needs of the island (Jos., Wars, 1:424; 7:21; Ant., 16:147). The Jews of Crete are also mentioned by Josephus in reference to the imposter claiming to be the prince Alexander, who had been put to death by Herod (Jos., Wars, 2:103). The second wife of Josephus was also a resident of Crete (Jos., Life, 427). The Jewish population of Greece probably grew considerably during and after the Jewish War (66–70), and in one case Josephus relates that Vespasian sent

6,000 youths from Palestine to work for Nero at the Isthmus of Corinth (Wars, 3:540). An extremely large and powerful Jewish community also existed by the second century on Cyprus, for during the Jewish wars under *Trajan (115–7) the capital of Cyprus, Salamis, was laid waste by Jewish inhabitants and thousands of non-Jews were murdered. The consequence of this uprising, however, was a total ban on Jewish residence on the island, under pain of death (Dio Cassius 68:32; Eusebius, *Chronicon* 2:164). After Trajan, Hadrian (117–138) retorted with severe penal laws against the Jews, prohibiting circumcision, but these laws were allowed to lapse by Antoninus Pius (138–161), and henceforth the Jews were accorded a larger degree of tolerance. From the second century they were subject to the spiritual jurisdiction of a hereditary patriarch resident in Palestine. The Jews of the Diaspora early forgot Hebrew and adopted Greek (except for liturgical purposes), using a translation of the Bible – the Septuagint – which was begun at Alexandria under Ptolemy II. Apart from Cyprus, Greek Jews did not suffer any particular upheaval during the Roman period, and the ancient Jewish settlement served as a foundation for the Jewish settlement during the Byzantine period (from 330 C.E., see below) – when the capital of the Roman Empire was removed to Constantinople – and a basis for Jewish settlement in other Balkan countries (see individual countries).

[Isaiah Gafni]

EARLY AND MIDDLE BYZANTINE PERIODS (330–1204)

Byzantium's secular institutions, with the emperor at their head, gave her long periods of stability, while in the West the Church added to the feudal disorder. These characteristics had their bases in the seventh-century Heraclian dynasty, which brought agrarian reform and a reorganization of the provinces, producing an army from small landowners and controlling the capital of the empire. The Heraclians were not only able to preserve their domains after Syria, Palestine, and Egypt had fallen and Constantinople had been besieged, but were also able to maintain their own authority against incursions from the outside. The struggle against Islam and the internal and external threats to imperial sovereignty were the dangers, which faced Byzantium up to the First Crusade. Her successes in these realms shaped her external and internal policy. The emperor received and held the secular and ecclesiastical support of the people, enough so that this did not become a problem to the underlying unity of the empire. Religious conflicts which existed were largely resolved by the emperor, a believing Christian, who decided for the Church who was a heretic and who was not.

A far greater threat arose in the tenth century, when the Macedonian emperors had to fight against the attempts to destroy the foundations of Byzantine economic and military security through the acquisition of great estates, i.e., the liquidation of the smallholdings and the control of the soldiers settled upon them. Although the emperors were successful for a time, the end of the old order came in about the middle of the 11th century. Great landowners, partially independent from the emperor's influence, caused radical changes in the structure of Byzantine society. Additionally, the Normans in the western parts of the empire, the *Seljuks in Anatolia, and finally the Normans again – this time as Crusaders – succeeded in shattering the empire.

Byzantine Jewry in the seventh century is assumed to have continued in the status it held during the Roman period, as urban life was preserved and with it the main centers of Jewish population. Greece suffered greatly from Slavic incursions but the towns were hardly affected. *Salonika's Jewish history was unbroken and there were Jews in Rhodes and Cyprus.

The Middle Ages, for the Jew at least, begin with the advent to power of Constantine the Great (306–337). He was the first Roman emperor to issue laws which dramatically limited the rights of Jews as citizens of the Roman Empire, which were conferred upon them by Caracalla in 212. With the growth of Christianity the Roman emperors were influenced to further restrict the rights of the Jews. Constantine denied the Jews the right of proselytizing and prohibited intermarriage and Jewish possession of slaves. The legal status of the Jews was established by Christian Rome in the fifth century, when Theodosius II (408–450) introduced specific regulations into his codification of the laws, in his *Codex Theodosianus* (438). The Jewish community was recognized legally, even though not in a friendly manner, and religious worship was protected. In the sixth century, although more hostile and interfering, Justinian I (527–565) left the basic situation unaltered. It remained so in the seventh century also. Leo III (717–741), in the next imperial compilation of laws, the *Ecloga* ("Selections," 740), made no reference to the Jews. This preservation of legal status was very important to the Jewish community, as the Christian heretic had no legal status at all. Formal protection of the law minimally meant that the Jew had a place in the social structure.

Forced Conversion

In 632 Heraclius ordered the conversion of all Byzantine Jewry. This was a major point in his program of strengthening imperial unity, as he looked on the Jews as a political threat. Feeling that the Jews had shared in Persian military successes, he wanted to minimize their independence and influence within the empire. This policy of forced conversion was extended to Christian heretics but never took root for the Jews, who continued to be active in the civic life of the empire.

In 721 Leo III issued a decree, which later proved to be ineffectual, ordering all Jews to be baptized. In leading a new dynasty to power he, like Heraclius, wished to insure imperial unity and also may have suspected a lack of Jewish loyalty. The messianic movements to the East, having aroused fears in Leo's mind, had attracted Jewish support and may have caused the order to forcibly convert the Jews of the empire. In spite of these state actions Jewish prosperity still had

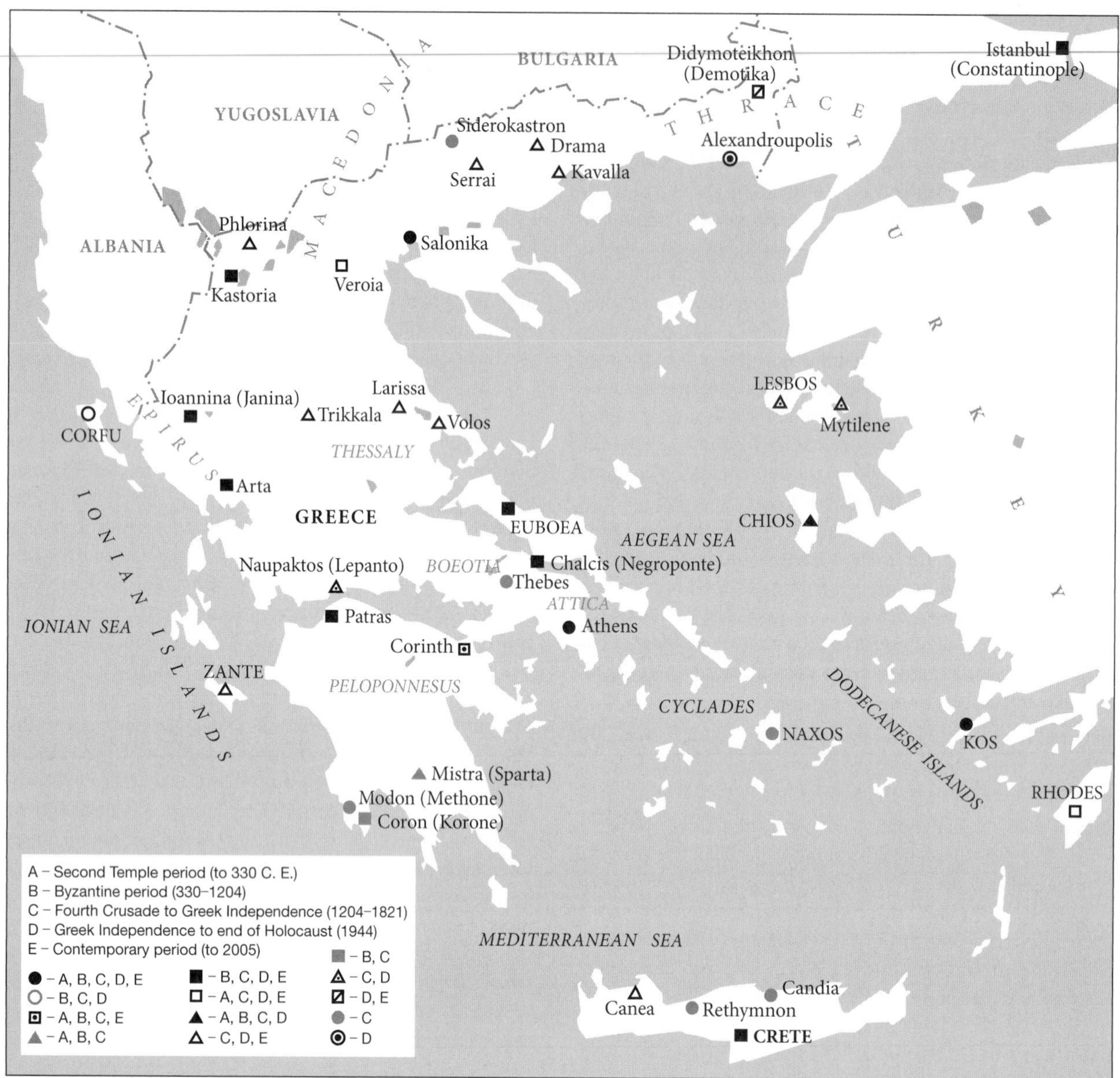

Major Jewish settlements in Greece. Jews are known to have settled in Greece in all the above periods, but in very few places was their settlement continuous, even within any specific period. Although there were Jews in many cities in the contemporary period, their numbers in the early 21st century were insignificant except in Athens (3,000) and Salonika (1,100).

room for existence in the empire and the results of the decree were as limited as they were in 632, even though some Jews left the empire and some converted outwardly. The termination of this decree seems to have been by 740.

The second Council of Nicaea in 787 reversed Leo's policy and criticized his handling of the Jews, proclaiming that Jews had to live openly according to their religion. According to Gregorios Asbestas, then metropolitan of Nicaea, the Jews who actually accepted Leo's inducements to convert were numerous enough to arouse this religious statement. Generally, these actions by Heraclius and Leo had little, if any, effect on the Jews of the empire.

Basil I (867–886), like his predecessors, also made an effort to convert the Jews forcibly, possibly to increase imperial unity but more probably to show his hand as a knowledgeable ruler in religious matters. Failing, where earlier Christians had, to persuade the Jews to convert, he issued a decree of forced conversion about 874. Like the Byzantine rulers before him, he failed in his efforts. The legal code of the period, the *Basilica*, made no basic changes in what Justinian had to say about the Jews, i.e., their legal status in religious and communal affairs continued to be recognized, and in some sense protected. Leo VI (886–912) apparently tried to follow in his father's policies but quickly gave it up.

Under Romanus I Lecapenus (920–944), who ruled in Constantine VII's (913–959) stead, further forced conversions, as well as persecutions, of the Jews were effected. This possibly happened by 932 and definitely by 943. His policy is known to have caused considerable migration to Khazaria. These acts may have been caused by Romanus' insecurity on the throne, as Constantine was the legitimate ruler and the former looked for ways to insure his position. In any event the persecutions were particularly severe, surpassing those of his predecessors. They were stopped quite suddenly when *Ḥisdai ibn Shaprut wrote to either Constantine or Helena, Romanus' daughter and the former's wife.

The last 250 years before the Fourth Crusade seem to have been a relatively quiet period for the Jews of the empire and it can be inferred that the situation actually improved and that no attempts were made by the authorities at coercing the Jews to convert. Further emphasis of this situation is provided by the fact that when the monk Nikon (tenth century) incited the inhabitants of Sparta to banish the Jews from their midst, his words were to no effect. In Chios an expulsion decree in 1062 was issued against those Jews who had recently settled there. There is no reason to believe that during the First Crusade in 1096, which took place during the reign of Emperor Alexius I Comnenus, the Jews were attacked when the Crusaders passed through the Balkans. The Jewish quarters, however, were looted. In the general panic which struck the Jewish world, a messianic effervescence also came to the surface in Salonika, Adrianople, and other cities. It is related that certain communities left their homes for Salonika in order to sail to Palestine from there. A tremendous emotion seized the community of Salonika, where both the authorities and the archbishop showed a positive attitude to the messianic spirit.

Social and Economic Conditions

The legal disabilities of the Jews during the period, known from the *Basilica*, were minimal and included exclusion from service in the armed forces and the government, even though Jews had been employed as tax collectors on Cyprus during the first two decades of the 12th century. Jews were forbidden to buy Christian slaves, but this had little effect on them. No other restrictions existed concerning economic matters which did not also affect Christians. The charging of interest in trade and the purchase of land, except Church land, were permitted, although the emperors tried to control these matters for themselves. The question as to whether there was a specific Jewish tax seems to be open to a great deal of debate, but J. Starr (see bibl. *The Jews in the Byzantine Empire*) felt that such taxes did exist but were little enforced after the seventh century. In short, the taxes provided for by Theodosius II in 429, Justinian's *Corpus*, and again three centuries later in the Nomocanon had little more effect on the Jewish community in the later period than on the Christian one. Such legal restrictions which did exist included the absence of the right of Jews to testify in cases involving Christians; the overriding imperial authority over religious matters between Jews; the right of Jewish testimony before Jewish judges only in civil litigation between Jews; the prohibition of Judaizing; and the necessity for Jews to take an oath in legal cases, which was contemptuous of the Jewish faith. Nevertheless, circumcision was officially permitted, the Sabbath and the Festivals were protected, synagogues were allowed, and even though the building of new ones was formally proscribed, the prohibition was not rigidly enforced. Although the Jew was restricted, he was in a much better position than Christian heretics. Jews were active as early as the seventh century as physicians and skilled artisans, particularly as finishers of woven cloth (e.g., in Sparta), dyers (in Corinth), and makers of silk garments (in Salonika and Thebes). Jews were also involved in commerce and farming and as owners of land.

In religious matters Hebrew remained the language of the Jews, although it was paralleled by the limited usage of Greek. Karaism began to appear in the empire in the tenth century (see Ankori, in bibl.) but only began to take root after the First Crusade. R. Tobiah b. Eliezer of Kastoria was an important Rabbanite spokesman. Aside from R. Tobiah little if any writing was apparently done in the areas of Midrash, Talmud, and *halakhah* during this entire period in Byzantium. There was literary activity in southern Italy, but then this area can only be included in the widest definition as to what was territorially part of Byzantine Greece. Additionally, about this time both Rabbanites and Karaites began to come to Byzantium from Muslim territory.

*Benjamin of Tudela, the 12th-century traveler, states that in his time there were Jews in Corfu, Arta, Aphilon (Achelous), Patras, Naupaktos, Corinth, Thebes, Chalcis, Salonika, Drama, and other localities. The Greek islands on which Jews lived were Lesbos, Chios, Samos, Rhodes, and Cyprus. He found the largest community in Thebes, where there were 2,000 Jews, while in Salonika there were 500, and in other towns from 20 to 400. The Jews of Greece engaged in dyeing, weaving, and the making of silk garments. After Roger II, the king of the Normans in Sicily, conquered some Greek towns in 1147, he transferred some Jewish weavers to his kingdom in order to develop the weaving of silk in his country. On Mount Parnassus Benjamin of Tudela found 200 farmers; there were also some serfs among the Jews. During the reign of the Byzantine emperor Constantine IX Monomachus (1042–1055), there were 15 Jewish families in Chios who were perpetual serfs to the Nea Moné monastery. The Jews of Chios paid a poll tax – in reality a family tax – which the emperor transferred to the monastery. The Jews of Salonika also paid this tax. The majority of the Jews conducted their trade on a small scale and with distant countries. The Greek merchants envied their Jewish rivals and sought to restrict their progress. *Pethahiah of Regensburg describes the bitter exile in which the Jews of Greece lived (see also *Byzantine Empire).

FOURTH CRUSADE AND LATE BYZANTINE PERIOD (1204–1453)

Greece from 1204 to 1821 was the subject of many conquests, divisions, reconquests, and redivisions at the hands of the Normans of Sicily, the Saracens, the Crusaders, the Venetians, the Genoese, the Seljuks, the Bulgars and the Slavs, the Byzantine emperors, the Cumans, the Ottoman Turks, and others.

Greek Rule

During this period Theodore Ducas Angelus, the Greek despot of *Epirus (?1215–30), who was defeated in 1230 by the czar of the Bulgars, John Asen II (1218–41), was notorious for his cruelty. Theodore added the kingdom of Salonika to his domain in 1223 or 1224, holding it until 1230. He initiated an anti-Jewish policy which other Greek rulers followed after him. Theodore apparently enriched himself by confiscating the wealth of the Jews, and refused them redress against his abuses. He is also charged with proscribing Judaism. After Theodore was defeated by John Asen, he was condemned to death and two Jews were ordered to put out his eyes. When they took pity on him and did not fulfill the emperor's order, they were thrown from the summit of a rock.

The Greek rulers of the Empire of Nicaea were also harsh in their policy toward the Jews. John III Ducas Vatatzes (1222–54) apparently continued Theodore's decree against the Jews. The motive for persecuting the Jews is conjectural, but it seems to reflect the upsurge of nationalism in the provinces which remained under Greek rule. Jewish presence in the Latin states and in the areas ruled by the ambitious John Asen apparently strengthened the distrust, which the Greek rulers had for their Jewish subjects in both Asia and Europe. Bulgaria's territorial expansion might have offered a degree of relief for the Jews, but the decline of the Latin Empire must have had a negative effect on them. By 1246 John III had entered Salonika and controlled the area from Adrianople to Stobi and Skopje, including the town of Kastoria.

With the restoration of Byzantine rule (in the guise of the Nicaean Empire) over a large part of the Balkans, various Jewish communities felt the weight of the rulers' anti-Jewish policy. Little information is available on this but it can be assumed that the communities of Kastoria, Salonika, and several others suffered from the Greek advances. Once the Greek "rump state" of Nicaea had recovered Constantinople under the leadership of Michael VIII Palaeologus (1258–82), the anti-Jewish policy became outdated. He then began to resettle and reconstruct the ravaged capital, evidently realizing that his program required the cooperation of all elements, other than those who were then hostile (notably the Venetians and the subjects of the kingdom of Naples). It is not known whether there were Jews in Constantinople when Michael captured it, but after his conquest he renounced the policy of John III and made it possible for Jews to return and live there quietly.

From the end of the Latin Empire the Byzantine emperors began to recover part of the Peloponnesus, nevertheless being frustrated in part in their attempts by Murad I, who held Salonika from 1387 to 1405, and Murad II, who secured Salonika for the Ottoman Empire (1430–1913). The disintegration of the Byzantine Empire and in a large part its seizure by the Ottoman Turks led to generally favorable conditions for the Jews living within the Turkish sphere (see *Ottoman Empire; Covenant of *Omar).

Jewish Immigrations into Greece

The important Jewish communities which existed after the Fourth Crusade were Crete, Corinth, Coron (*Korone), *Modon, *Patras, and *Chios. The *Romaniots (*Gregos*) – the acculturized Jewish inhabitants of Greece – were Greek-speaking. Until recently Greek was still spoken by the Jews of Epirus, Thessaly, Ioannina, Crete, and Chalcis (see also *Judeo-Greek). From the end of the 14th century refugees immigrated from Spain to Greece, and from the end of the 15th century from Portugal and Sicily. Jews who were also expelled from Navarre, Aragon, Naples, Provence, and elsewhere in the Iberian Peninsula and other Mediterranean Papal States in the late 15th and 16th centuries migrated to the Greek Peninsula. In towns such as Trikkala, Larissa, Volos, and above all in Salonika the Sephardim introduced their own language and customs. With the flight of the Jews from Hungaria in 1376 (probably connected with the Black Death and the persecution of Jews in Eastern Europe at the time) many Jews settled in the towns of Kavalla and Siderokastron; they brought their special customs with them. As a result of Sultan Suleiman's journey to Hungaria in 1525, a number of Jews emigrated from there to Greece (the Greek Peninsula), which was actually part of the Ottoman Empire then. The descendants of the Hungarian Jews were completely absorbed by the Sephardim after a few generations. A third group in Greek Jewry was that of the Italian-speaking Jews of Corfu, whose ancestors were expelled from Apulia in southern Italy.

During the 16th and 17th centuries the Jewish population increased with the addition of the Spanish Marranos, who fled to the countries dominated by the Turks, and after the persecutions of 1648, Polish refugees. The congregations (*kehalim*) were organized according to the regions of origin, and by generation and migratory waves. The Salonikan *kehalim* from Italy, Lisbon, Catalan, and Sicily were each divided into Yashan (old) and Ḥadash (new) based on migratory waves. Thus, during the 16th century in Patras there were the following *kehalim*: Kehillah Kedoshah Yevanim ("Greek Holy Community"), Kehillah Kedoshah Yashan ("Ancient Community," of Sicilian origin), Kehillah Kedoshah Ḥadash ("New Community," refugees from Naples and smaller Italian towns), and Kehillah Kedoshah Sephardim ("Sephardi Holy Community"). In Arta there were *kehalim* whose founders had come from Corfu, Calabria, Apulia, and Sicily.

OTTOMAN (AND LATE VENETIAN) RULE (1453–1821)

The important communities during the Turkish (and late Venetian) periods were, in the first place, Salonika, which was probably the largest Jewish community during the 16–18th centuries and which until the beginning of the 20th century was populated most of the time by a majority of Jews; Naupaktos; Patras, whose merchants were known as courageous travelers who went as far as Persia; Arta; Thebes, which was "renowned for its wisdom" (responsa of Elijah *Mizraḥi (Constantinople, 1559–61), No. 71); and *Ioannina (Janina), the largest Romaniot community. On Crete the Jews played an important part in the transit trade; the island was also known for its rabbis and scholars, notably the *Capsali family, *Delmedigo, and others. There were also some Jews on Cyprus. After the conquest of Rhodes by the Turks in 1552, Jews from Salonika arrived on the island, where their commercial role became an important one. The island also became a stopping place for pilgrims on their way to Palestine. It was widely known for its rabbis, especially the rabbinical dynasty of the *Israel family.

When Sigismondo Malatesta conquered Mistra (Sparta) in 1465, he burned down the Jewish quarter. In 1532 when the forces of Andrea Doria attacked the Greek towns which were in the hands of the Turks, the Jews of Coron, Modon, and Patras suffered greatly. Their property was confiscated and they were taken captive. During the reign of Selim II (1566–74) Don Joseph *Nasi was appointed duke of Naxos and the surrounding isles of the Cyclades. In 1669 the Venetian armies attacked the island of Chios. To commemorate the miraculous stand against their siege, the local Jews annually celebrated "Purim of Chios" on Iyyar 8. With the Venetian invasion of the Peleponnese in 1685, the Jews abandoned Patras in fear and fled to Larissa. They were also compelled to flee for their lives from the islands of the Aegean Sea. The Greek-Orthodox of the Peleponnese, who often rebelled against the Turks, massacred the Jews whom they considered allies of the Turks. During this period of confusion in the 18th century the communities of Patras, Thebes, Chalcis, and Naupaktos were greatly harmed and almost destroyed. In 1770, when Russia captured several sea towns of the Greek coast, the Ottoman Turks sent forces to the area. They did not differentiate between Greek-Orthodox and Jews and the Jewish communities of Patras, Thebes, Chalcis, and Lepanto (Naupaktos) were almost destroyed.

Religious Culture Under Ottoman Rule

The 16th century was the Golden Age of Salonikan Jewry, with religious figures like the decisors Rabbi Samuel de *Medina (Rashdam) and Isaac *Adarbi; Rabbi Joseph *Caro, who prepared a good part of his halakhic work *Beit Yosef* while residing 17 years in the city; the eminent Joseph Taitazak, *gadol ha-dor* (the foremost rabbi of his generation); Judah Abravanel; Moses *Alshekh; *Levi ben Habib (the Ralbaḥ); Jacob ibn Verga; Eliezer ha-Shimoni; Joseph ben Lev; the *paytan* Solomon Alkabeẓ, author of the Sabbath hymn "*Lekha Dodi*"; and the poet Saadiah ben Abraham Longo. The *talmud torah* was a mammoth center that not only was a school for over 10,000 pupils and 200 teachers but had a printing press, produced fabrics, and served as the bank for the community where members kept their money. It relieved the individual *kehalim* from the financial burden of maintaining their own schools. Salonika as a world Sephardi center hosted the Beit Midrash Le-Shirah ve-le-Zimrah, which approved *piyyutim* before they were accepted into prayer. Israel *Najara, a descendant of a Salonikan family, came to Salonika to develop and receive approval for his famous hymn "*Ẓur mi-Shello Akhalnu.*"

Anusim left the Iberian Peninsula in the 16th and 17th centuries and returned to Judaism when they reached Salonika and other Ottoman communities. The physician Lusitanus arrived in Salonika with a profound knowledge of religious Judaism. He was an expert on the menstrual cycle, published numerous treatises on the subject, and established both a medical school and yeshivah when he settled in Salonika. The newly arriving *anusim* and veteran former *anusim* also brought religious fervor, fanaticism, and an acute and active messianism, which created great turbulence within the Jewish communities of the northern Greek Peninsula. Salonika hosted the false messiahs Solomon Molcho and *Shabbetai Ẓevi; the latter causing a great decline among Salonikan Jewry after he was proclaimed messiah in 1666. The Jewish masses were swept up in the messianic frenzy and abandoned traditional Jewish law and religious customs and beliefs. While the core supporters converted to Islam after Shabbetai Ẓevi was exiled by the Sultan, forced to convert to Islam, and finally died in Montenegro, most Jews did not convert. Strict religious *takkanot* were enforced within the Salonikan Jewish community. This did not prevent the community from falling into spiritual and economic decay, but in the 18th century many more religious exegeses were published than previously, in the new spirit of religious conservatism.

Besides Salonika, which during the 16th and 17th centuries was a major Jewish center, there were also important rabbis and scholars in the smaller communities of Greece. During the 16th and 17th centuries these included Solomon Cohen (Mahar-SHa-KH) of Zante and the Peloponnesus; Samuel b. Moses *Kalai, the author of *Mishpetei Shemu'el*, of Arta; Moses *Alashkar of Patras, the author of responsa; during the 18th century: Isaac Algazi, the author of *Doresh Tov*; Isaac Frances of Kastoria, the author of *Penei Yiẓhak*; Ezra Malki of Rhodes, the author of *Malki ba-Kodesh* and other works; Jedidiah Tarikah of Rhodes, the author of *Ben Yadid* and other works; Isaac Obadiah of Patras, the author of *Iggeret Dofi ha-Zeman*; Eliezer b. Elijah ha-Rofeh ("the physician") Ashkenazi of Nicosia, Cyprus, the author of *Yosif Lekaḥ* on the Book of Esther.

Economic Situation of the Jews

During the Turkish period (1453–1821) the Jews of Greece were principally engaged in the crafts of spinning silk, weaving wool, and making cloth. They also controlled an important part of the commerce, money lending, and the lease of the taxes. In the Greek islands under Venetian rule the Jews only engaged in retail commerce, as the larger type of commerce was the monopoly of the Venetian nobility. Under Turkish rule, however, the wholesale trade was concentrated in Jewish hands. The Jews succeeded in developing connections in Italy, France, Amsterdam, Hamburg, London, and in the Orient with Constantinople, Izmir, and Alexandria. The merchants of Kastoria traded in hides, furs, cattle, metals, and broken silver vessels. The Jews of Naupaktos were engaged in the trade of palm branches. At a later stage the tobacco, grain, sesame, hashish, and raw hides trades became those of the Jews. However in Thessaly, the Peloponnesus, and the Balkans the Jews engaged in peddling and tinsmithing, living in extreme poverty. In Salonika all the port activities were in Jewish hands and the port was closed on Sabbaths and Jewish festivals.

GREEK INDEPENDENCE (1821)–WORLD WAR II (1940)

With the outbreak of the Greek revolt in 1821 Greek Jewry suffered intensively because of its support of and loyalty to Ottoman rule. In those towns where the rebels gained the upper hand, the Jews were murdered after various accusations had been leveled against them. In the massacre of the Peloponnesus 5,000 Jews lost their lives; the remainder fled to Corfu. From that time the condition of the Jews who lived among the Greeks, even within the boundaries of Turkish rule, began to deteriorate. From time to time there were blood libels, such as in Rhodes (Turkish until 1912; Italian until 1947) in 1840. In 1891 disorders broke out on the Greek islands; the Jews left in panic. During the same year there was also a blood libel in Corfu (Greek, from 1864). The Jews on the island, as well as on the neighboring island of Zante, were attacked. About 1,500 Jews left the Greek islands and settled in Italy, Turkey, and Egypt. The Jews of Corfu suffered a large-scale blood libel in 1891; for three weeks the Jews were locked into their ghetto during continual rioting, some 22 Jews died, and in light of apathy on the part of the Greek army, the Great Powers sent ships-of-war off the coast in order to pressure the government to restore order. Even the active participation of the Jewish citizens of Greece in the war against Turkey in 1897 was not mentioned in their favor; with the end of the hostilities in Thessaly, anti-Jewish riots broke out and an important part of the Jewish population was compelled to seek refuge in Salonika. At the beginning of the 20th century there were about 10,000 Jews in Greece. After the Balkan War (1912–13), with the annexation of further territories in 1912, which included Salonika, Chios, Crete, Epirus, Kavalla, and Phlorina, their numbers grew to 100,000.

After the population exchanges between Turkey and Greece as a result of the Treaty of Lausanne (1923) and the arrival in Salonika of 100,000 Greeks from Anatolia, the status of the Jews deteriorated because of the increased competition in commerce and the crafts. Many Jews were compelled to leave the city. The Asia Minor refugees introduced legislation in Salonika in 1924 forbidding work on Sunday, thus compelling Salonikan Jewry either to lose a day's work or break the Sabbath. When the legislation was promulgated nationally, Jews began leaving Ioannina for Ereẓ Israel. In the late 1920s, zealous elements amongst the Asian Minor refugee population continued to bait Salonikan Jewry and incited them in the Salonikan daily Greek newspaper *Makedonia*. In 1931, Isaak Cohen, a young Jew from Salonika and member of Maccabi who went to Sofia for a regional Maccabi meeting, was falsely accused on the front page of *Makedonia* of going to Bulgaria for Macedonian nationalist meetings and riots broke out against Salonikan Jewry in much of the eastern part of the city, which was heavily Jewish. The Campbell neighborhood, which housed Jewish fishermen and port workers, who had become homeless after the devastating 1917 fire, was burned to the ground by the student EEE (Nationalist Greek Union) and Jewish migration ensued to Ereẓ Israel. On the other hand, the economic position of the Jews in the provincial towns of Epirus, Thessaly, Macedonia, and the islands did not arouse the jealousy of their neighbors. Until World War II the situation of the Jews in Greece was satisfactory. They controlled the markets of paper, textiles, medicines, glassware, ironware, wood, and hides, and were also represented in heavy industry, international commerce, and banking. Many Jews were also employed in manual labor as stevedores, coachmen, and fishermen, as well as in various handicrafts. The number of Jews in Greece on the eve of World War II was 77,000.

Civic and Cultural Conditions of the Jews

Greece recognized the civic and political equality of the Jews from the time of its establishment as a modern state in 1821. In 1882 legal status was granted to the Jewish communities. This status was confirmed on various occasions when laws defining the privileges and obligations of the communities were passed. The community councils, which were elected by general suffrage, were responsible for the religious, educational, and social affairs.

At the beginning of the 20th century the Alliance Israélite Universelle still maintained a number of Jewish schools in Greece. The Jewish schools were attached to the communities and did not have any attachment to religious or political trends. Jewish children attended the state schools and the religious studies were entrusted to *ḥazzanim*, who were content to teach the prayers in their traditional tunes. It was only in Corfu that the religious studies were of a higher standard. In those regions, which were under Turkish rule until 1912, such as Thrace, Macedonia, and Epirus, there was a Jewish school in every community, which was supported by the Alliance. The greatest concentration of Jewish schools was in Salonika. In Salonika alone, at the beginning of the 20th century, there were some seven schools under the auspices of this Parisian-led Jewish school system. Between the two world wars there were 12 Jewish schools founded by the community, institutions of the Alliance, as well as private schools. In 1931 a law was passed which prohibited children of Greek nationality from attending foreign schools before they had completed their elementary education. This came as a fatal blow to the Alliance schools; the institutions of the Alliance amalgamated with the community schools in 1935. The Italians opened a seminary for the training of rabbis and teachers of Jewish subjects on the island of Rhodes, but it closed in 1938.

HOLOCAUST PERIOD

The Italian army attacked Greece on Oct. 28, 1940, and the Germans invaded on April 6, 1941. According to statistics of the *Salonika Jewish community, 12,898 Jews, among them 343 officers, served in the Greek army and several hundred Jews fell in battle. The entire country was occupied on June 2, 1941, and split up among the Axis (German, Italian, and Bulgarian) forces. Treatment of the Jews differed from one occupied zone to another.

German Zone

Salonika was taken by German troops on April 9, 1941. Anti-Jewish measures were at once instituted, beginning on April 12 when Jewish-owned apartments were confiscated and the Jewish inhabitants ordered to vacate them within a few hours. Three days later, the members of the Jewish community council and other prominent Jews were arrested. A "scientific" delegation arrived from Germany for the purpose of plundering the community of its valuable Hebrew books and manuscripts for transfer to the Nazi "Institute for Jewish Affairs" in Frankfurt. Before long, the impoverishment of the community became overwhelming and the community council was unable to extend aid to all those who were in need. Contagious diseases spread and the death rate rose steeply, especially among the children. In July 1942 the men were sent on forced labor; a short while later, however, the community council made an agreement with the Germans, whereby it undertook to pay them the sum of 2,500,000,000 old drachmas, due Dec. 15, 1942, in consideration of which the Germans would refrain from drafting Jews for forced labor. At the end of 1942 Jewish-owned factories and groceries were confiscated and the well-known Jewish cemetery was destroyed. On Feb. 6, 1943, racial restrictions were introduced; Jews were ordered to wear a yellow badge and confined to a ghetto, while special signs had to be posted above windows and establishments belonging to Jews. Jews were also prohibited from using public transport and had to be indoors by sundown. The transfer to the ghetto, set up in a specially designated area, had to be completed by March 25, 1943. On February 25, the trade unions were ordered to expel their Jewish members; on March 1 the Jews had to declare all the capital in their possession, and 104 hostages were seized to ensure full compliance with this order. At this time, a rumor spread that the Jewish population was about to be deported to *Poland. The recently established Jewish underground warned the Jews of the danger confronting them, but little heed was taken and only about 3,000 escaped to Athens. The first transport of Jewish deportees left Salonika for the gas chambers on March 15, 1943, followed by further transports of 3,000 Jews each at intervals of two to three days. Thus, various sectors of the ghetto were systematically cleared of their inhabitants. Five transports left in the last two weeks of March, nine in April, and two in May; in June 820 Jews were dispatched to Auschwitz, the transport consisting of members and employees of the community council and teachers. On Aug. 2, 1943, skilled workers, "privileged" Jews, and a group of 367 Spanish citizens were sent to *Bergen-Belsen, where they remained until Feb. 7, 1944. On Aug. 7, 1,800 starving Jewish forced laborers were brought to Salonika and deported from there in the 19th and final transport from Salonika to the death camps. In all 46,091 Salonika Jews were deported – 45,650 to Auschwitz and 441 to Bergen-Belsen – 95% of whom were killed. The renowned Salonika community, the great center of Sephardi Jewry, came to an end.

Other Districts under German Occupation

On Feb. 3, 1943, the chief rabbi of Salonika, Rabbi Ẓevi Koretz, was ordered to ensure adherence to the racial restrictions in the provincial towns under the jurisdiction of German headquarters in Salonika. These were the towns in East Thracia, near the Turkish border, as well as Veroia, Edessa, and Phlorina in central and eastern Macedonia. On May 9, 2,194 Jews from these towns were sent to Auschwitz. A few Jews were saved by the local population and the chief of police, e.g., in the town of Katherine. Prominent Greeks, among them the archbishop of Athens and labor leaders, tried to assist the Jews, and there were Greeks who offered shelter and helped the Jews escape to the mountains.

ITALIAN ZONE. The Italian forces controlled Athens and the Peloponnesus. As long as the zone was held by the Italians, the Jews were not persecuted, the racial laws were disregarded, and efforts were made to sabotage the Italian racial policy. After the Italian surrender (Sept. 3, 1943), however, the Germans occupied the entire country, and on Sept. 20, 1943, Eichmann's deputy, Dieter *Wisliceny, arrived in Athens with detailed plans for the destruction of the Jews. Elijah Barzilai, the rabbi of Athens, was ordered by Wisliceny to provide a list of all the members of the Jewish community. Instead of doing so, the rabbi warned the Jews of Athens and himself fled to a provincial town. This enabled a considerable number of Athenian Jews to escape. On Oct. 7, 1943, Juergen *Stroop, the *hoehere ss und Polizeifuehrer* in Greece, published an order in the newspapers, dated October 3, for all Jews to register, on penalty of death. Archbishop Damaskinos gave instructions to all monasteries and convents in Athens and the provincial towns to shelter all Jews who knocked on their doors. On March 24, 1944, the Athens synagogue was surrounded by the Nazis and 300 Jews were arrested; another 500 Jews were routed out of hiding. They were first interned in a temporary camp at Haídar and later sent to their death in Auschwitz on April 2, along with other Jews caught in Athens. The rest of Athenian Jewry hid with their Greek-Christian neighbors. The Jewish partisans supplied food to those in hiding in cellars and attics.

BULGARIAN ZONE. A large part of Thrace and Eastern Macedonia remained under Bulgarian occupation, including the towns of Kavalla, Serrai, Drama, Besanti, Komotine, and Alexandroupolis (Dedeagach). Over 4,000 Jews from Thrace and over 7,000 from Macedonia were deported by the Bulgarians (see *Bulgaria, Holocaust) to the gas chambers in Poland; about 2,200 Jews survived.

The total number of Jews in Greece sent to death in the extermination camps is estimated at 65,000 – about 85% of the entire Jewish population.

Jewish Resistance

The conquest of Athens by the Germans on April 27, 1941, marked the end of open warfare. Over 300 Jewish soldiers and 1,000 other Jews joined Greek partisan units. The Jewish partisans sabotaged German military centers and military factories, blew up German supply ships, and severed lines of communication. A group of 40 Jewish partisans took part in the blowing up of Gorgopotamo Bridge, causing a break in the rail link between northern and southern Greece. At the beginning of 1943 partisan units made up entirely or primarily of Jews were set up in Salonika, Athens, and Thessaly, under the command of Greek or British officers. The Salonika partisan units gathered information on troop movements in Macedonia and transmitted it to partisan headquarters in Athens. In Thessaly the national resistance organization, set up by the Jews in the towns of Volos, Larissa, and Trikkala, was under the command of an aged rabbi, Moses Pesaḥ, who roamed the mountains with a rifle in his hand. The courage and heroism displayed by the Jewish partisans earned them the praise of field marshal Wilson, the commanding officer of the Allied Forces in the Near East. Their main task was the establishment of contacts between the various parts of Greece and the Allied general headquarters in Cairo. The Jewish partisans also succeeded in hiding hundreds of Jews in the mountains and remote villages. Others worked for the Germans under assumed names in such places as the port of Piraeus and carried out acts of sabotage. The greatest single heroic act of the Greek-Jewish underground was the mutiny of 135 Greek Jews in Auschwitz; they were members of a *Sonderkommando*, charged with cremation of the corpses from the gas chambers. With the aid of a group of French and Hungarian Jews they blew up two crematoriums. Attacked by the SS guards and by five planes, the rebels held out for an hour until all 135 were killed.

CONTEMPORARY PERIOD

In the autumn of 1944, when Greece was liberated from Nazi occupation, over 10,000 Jews, almost all of them destitute, were in the country. A variety of factors (the general political instability, successive changes in the composition of the government, and the extended economic crisis) made the reconstruction of the Jewish community difficult. The Greek civil war also made emigration difficult for the Jews, as the majority of the men were obligated by the draft and could not receive emigration permits. After Greece's de facto recognition of the State of Israel a Greek cabinet committee decided (on Aug. 4, 1949) to permit Jews of draft age to go to Israel on condition that they renounce their Greek citizenship. Until the end of the 1950s about 3,500 Jews from Greece settled in Israel, 1,200 immigrated to the United States, and a few hundred others immigrated to Canada, Australia, South Africa, the Congo, and Latin American countries. In 1950 the number of Jews in Greece was about 8,000; in 1958 it was 5,209; and in 1967 about 6,500 Jews were scattered among 18 communities; 2,800 in Athens, 1,000 in Salonika (a number which rose to 1,300 by 1968), and 450 Jews in Larissa. As early as November 1944 a meeting of Athenian Jews elected a temporary council of 12 members that was recognized by the government as the representative of the Jewish community; in June 1945 the council was accorded legal status.

During the war, almost all of the synagogues had been destroyed or severely damaged; the synagogue in Athens was reconstructed, however, as were synagogues in other cities. A major obstacle to the reestablishment of Greek Jewry was the question of restitution of property that was confiscated during the occupation by the Nazis and compensation for the Nazi persecution. Although the anti-Jewish laws were repealed in most areas in 1944, they were canceled in Salonika only in June 1945. The question of compensation, however, involved a slower process. In 1949 the Organization for the Assistance and Rehabilitation of Greek Jews was established by official order to deal with this problem, but its work made no progress for a number of years. In spite of the lack of legal evidence as to who was deported to death camps, an agreement was signed in Bonn in March 1960 between the governments of West Germany and Greece on compensation to Nazi victims. About 62,000 claims for compensation were registered under this law; 7,200 of them were by Jews, of which about 6,000 were registered by Jews living outside Greece who had lost their Greek citizenship, and thus also their right to compensation.

During the first years after the liberation, Greek Jewry was materially supported by world Jewish organizations – the American Jewish *Joint Distribution Committee, the *Jewish Agency, etc. Only slowly did it rise above its state of poverty. As late as 1954 large numbers of survivors of the Holocaust continued to live in substandard conditions. Over the years the situation improved: unemployment decreased, and by the late 1960s the Jewish population included many artisans, merchants, retailers and wholesalers, industrialists (especially in clothing and textiles), free professionals, etc.

In spite of the stormy changes that passed over Greece after the war – and in spite of the influence of Nazi propaganda during the occupation – organized antisemitism was not evident in Greece, and the people generally refrained from activities motivated by hate against the Jews, except for some isolated incidents. Strong cultural contacts exist between the Jews and the Greeks, and the rate of intermarriage is on the rise.

A special problem arose from the fact that during the occupation a relatively large number of Jews participated in the struggle of the partisans and some of them afterward went over to the Communist camp. After the civil war the minister of defense issued a special order that clarified the position of the Jews who served in the ELAS brigades. He emphasized that these Jews were not to be viewed as "Communists," since during the Nazi occupation they had no choice but to flee to the mountains. Nonetheless, a number of Jewish partisans were executed. Five Jews who were condemned to death and 21 others who were deported to the islands were freed on the condition that they immigrate to Israel and renounce their Greek citizenship. When the situation in Greece became more stable, the Jews slowly returned to civilian life. They participated in elections – and were even candidates on various party lists – and a few were absorbed into government positions.

In 1964 a Jewish school existed in Athens with 150 pupils. Other areas were deprived of Jewish educational activities because of the small number of children and a shortage of teachers. The religious and communal life of Greek Jewry was very weak. Synagogues were empty except during the High Holidays. In the 1950s, in addition to the rabbi in Athens, there were rabbis in Volos, Ioannina, and Larissa; later there was only the one rabbi in Athens who also served as the chief rabbi of Greek Jewry. The Council of Jewish Communities was affiliated with the *World Jewish Congress and published a bimonthly; *WIZO carried on activities for women.

In the 1970s the Jewish population of Greece was approximately 5,000; 2,700 in Athens and about 1,000 in Salonika. The Council of Jewish Communities was affiliated with the World Jewish Congress and published a monthly magazine, *Chronika*. Other Jewish publications were *Jewish Review* (monthly) and *New Generation* published by the Jewish Youth Organization of Athens.

There were three rabbis in Athens, while Thessaloniki, Larissa, Volos, and Chalkis were served by *ḥazzanim*. The Athens Jewish school had 150 pupils, and there were educational facilities in Thessaloniki and Larissa. Women were particularly active in communal affairs and were organized in movements such as WIZO. There was also a chapter of B'nai B'rith and B'noth B'rith.

The 1980s can be characterized as the beginning of an active historical commemoration of the Judeo-Greek and the Sephardi heritages in Greece. Greek Jewry had aged, but a new generation of youth was being educated. Assimilation had taken a great toll and the legalization of civil marriages by the Papandreou government in the early 1980s greatly accelerated the process. Since then, most marriages were mixed and conducted outside of the synagogue, and there was no compelling need for the female to convert to Judaism. Jewish communities dwindled due to deaths in places such as Corfu, and Ioannina, and in Didamotiko, Zakynthos, and Cavalla deaths of influential leaders and the elderly brought Jewish communal life to an end. During the Lebanon War, Greek society was very critical of Israel and hostile to Israeli tourists and athletes. The press and the media vociferously condemned Israel for invading Lebanon, the course of the war, the bombing of civilian targets, and its treatment of Palestinian refugees in Lebanon. Greek Jewry was very uncomfortable during this period.

Until 1985, *Yad Vashem had only recognized 42 Greeks as Righteous Gentiles during the Holocaust. By 1994, 160 were recognized. In October 1992, at the dedication of Yad Vashem's Valley of the Communities, Greek Jewry was represented with stones for the communities of Salonika and Rhodes, and one general stone with the names of the other annihilated Greek Jewish communities by the Germans in the Holocaust. Yad Vashem established a room in their archive in memory of the annihilated Jewish community of Rhodes, and a foyer with an exhibit on the destroyed Salonikan Jewish community. In July 1994, Yad Vashem recognized the late Princess Alice as a Righteous Gentile for saving two Jewish families in Athens in WWII. Her son, Prince Philip of England, and daughter came to Jerusalem for the ceremony. Greek opposition leader Miltiadis Ebert came to Yad Vashem in 1995 for a ceremony honoring his father, Angelos Ebert, deceased Athens police chief, who had issued new identification cards with Greek names to thousands of Jews during WWII.

In 1999 at Yad Vashem, Bracha Rivlin, Yitzchak Kerem, and Leah Bornstein-Makovetsky published *Pinkas Kehillot Yavan*, a memorial volume on the history of the past Jewish communities of Greece destroyed in the Holocaust. The Holocaust Museum of Kibbutz Loḥamei ha-Gettao't established a permanent exhibition on Salonikan Jewry, the largest Jewish community of Greece annihilated in the Holocaust.

The Jewish Museum in Athens was founded in 1979 by the art historian Nikos Stavroulakis. After several years, it moved from Amalias Street to a new building purchased on Nikis Street. Stavrolakis in the late 1990s also restored the neglected synagogue of Chania, Crete, and turned it into a Jewish museum.

Greek Jewry, in particular in Athens, lost many of its elderly dynamic leaders. Owing to transportation problems in vast Athens, Jewish elementary school enrollment greatly decreased. The Jewish summer camp in Loutraki, operated by the Salonikan Jewish community, serving all the Jewish youth of Greece, increased its enrollment significantly in the latter half of the 1980s.

The retiree, Moshe Halegua officiated as rabbi in Salonika in the late 1980s. Rabbi Elie Shabetai left his position in Athens at KIS to serve in Larissa.

Several antisemitic events were passed over in the 1980s with little publicity and repercussions. During the Lebanon War, the doors of the Corfiote synagogue were damaged. In the 1989 Greek election campaign, the campaign staff of Prime Minister Andreas Papandreou fabricated a photo of opposition leader Mitsotakis embracing two Nazis, when the latter was a resistance officer in Crete. In Larissa, the Holocaust martyrs' memorial was defaced several times with antisemitic graffiti. In the 1980s Greek society shared identification with Jewish suffering in the Holocaust. Prime Minister Papandreou laid a wreath for Greek Jewry at Auschwitz in November 1984.

In the 1980s, 40 years after the Holocaust, Jewish survivors from Greece began to speak of their World War II experiences. By the early 1990s several books of Greek Jewish survivor testimonies were published. In 1985, "Dor Hemshech," the second generation of Greek Jewish Holocaust survivors in Tel Aviv, was founded. It publishes an annual publication on Greek Jewry and the Holocaust on Yom ha-Shoah.

The Salonikan Jewish community has been active in preserving its rich history. Local Jewish community historian Albertos Nar established the Salonikan Jewry Study Center in

1985. Salonikan Jewish academics founded the Society for the Study of the Jews of Greece, and organized a conference in fall 1991. Historian Yitzchak Kerem uncovered a rare photo collection of the Bulgarian deportation of Jews from Macedonia and Thrace in WWII to Treblinka.

At Cambridge University, England, the *Bulletin of Judeo-Greek Studies* was founded to advance the field of the study of Greek Jewry since classical times. David Recanati published in 1986 the second volume of *Zikhron Saloniki* ("Salonika Memoir").

Greek Jewry received growing exposure through the arts. Films on Greek Jewry in the 1980s and early 1990s included *Auschwitz-Saloniki, Ioannina, Athens, Jerusalem* (Yitzchak Kerem & Israeli Television Society), and *Because of that War* (Yehuda Polikar).

During the 1985–86 Austrian presidential election campaign, former UN secretary Kurt Waldheim was accused of WWII Wehrmacht activities in Yugoslavia and Greece as an intelligence officer outside of Salonika, and of connections to the deportations of the Jews of Ioannina, Crete, Corfu, and Rhodes. The Salonikan Buna (Auschwitz III) champion boxer Jacko Razon sued his former best friend and boxing apprentice Salomon Arouch and the producers for stealing his identity in the film *Triumph of the Spirit.* The problem of 700 Israeli Greek Holocaust survivors, who never received reparations from Germany, was aired on Israeli TV. The Israel government began to grant some of the survivors indemnities, but the Claims Conference, despite promises in writing in 1980 by its president Nahum Goldmann, did not recognize most Sephardi Holocaust survivors for German reparations. On May 7, 1995, Israeli Salonikan Auschwitz survivors appealed to the Israel High Court to upgrade their reparations payments parallel to German Jews.

Prominent Greek Jews include filmmaker and author Nestoros Matsas, radio interviewer Maria Rezan, radio music commentator Jak Menachem, play director Albert Ashkenazi, Post Office Director-General Moisis Kostantini, former Energy Ministry Director General Raphael Moissis, retired brigadier-general Marcos Moustakis, and retired military colonels Edgar Allalouf and Doctor Errikos Levi.

In the summer of 1993, the existing practice of listing one's religion on the identification card in Greece became a major news issue. A delegation of U.S. Jewish leaders met with Prime Minister Papandreou, and other officials, who promised to find a solution for the Jewish objections. The interior minister supported a change in the practice, but the political weight of the Greek-Orthodox Church was overwhelming. The European Parliament passed a decision noting that the obligation of entering one's religion on an identity card creates prejudice and is an infringement upon human rights. In the summer of 1991, there were anonymous threats to the Jewish summer camp in Loutraki.

Several changes occurred within the Greek Jewish leadership. In the unprecedented holding of communal elections in fall 1993, the Jewish community of Salonika elected Andreas Sephiha as president. The new regime was committed to Jewish education, Jewish renewal and continuity, and historical restoration and commemoration.

In Athens, Joseph Lovinger, Board of Greek Jewish Communities (KIS) chairman for many years, died and was succeeded by Nissim Mais, and later Mois Konstantini.

The Beit Loḥamei ha-Getta'ot Holocaust Museum established a permanent exhibition on Salonikan Jewry in September 1993. At Bar-Ilan University, Shmuel Refael produced a temporary exhibit on Jewish life in Salonika.

In New York in spring 1995, a Second Generation group of Salonikan Holocaust survivors was established by Dr. Joe Halio. For the Spielberg Foundation of the Shoah, Yitzchak Kerem filmed 99 Greek Jewish Holocaust survivors in the USA, France, and Israel, and Rena Molho interviewed several dozen survivors in Greece. Unfortunately, the Spielberg Shoah Foundation lacked the dedication to actively film Salonikan and other Greek Jewish survivors on a mass level in Tel Aviv.

After the revelation of the Secret Archives in Moscow of captured documents taken from Nazi Germany at the end of World War II, hundreds of Salonikan Jewish community files as well as several from the Jewish community of Athens were microfilmed for the U.S. Holocaust Museum in Washington, D.C.

The Jewish population of Salonika increased to some 1,100 in 2000 from about 800 in the 1980s.

Despite the establishment of numerous Holocaust memorials throughout Greece, media attention, and exposure to the Holocaust by both Jewish and non-Jewish Greek authors, the end of the 1990s marked a resurgence of Neo-Nazi activism and attacks on Jewish Holocaust targets in Greece.

Worrisome was the secret and spontaneous international gathering of 500 Neo-Nazis and Holocaust deniers in Thessaloniki in 1999. Neo-Nazi and Holocaust denial literature was still published in Greece by publishing houses like Nea Thesis, and Eleftheri Skepsis (Free Thought). General antisemitic literature still flowed freely. The Greek government and the Greek Jewish community did not combat this danger.

The small fascist Chryse Avge Party has been a very disturbing element. Remarks by antisemitic MP Yiorgos Karatzaferis about Greek Jewry or wild allegations about the Jewish roots of Greek politicians were generally not criticized by the government or Greek and Jewish organizations.

Attacks on most of the public memorial squares and statues took place in 1999 and 2000. Holocaust memorials for the annihilated Jewish communities were tainted by antisemitic graffiti and vandalized in Larissa, Athens, Thessaloniki, and Chalkis. Some of the messages called for the Jews to leave Greece. Also the Jewish cemeteries in Thessaloniki and Athens were vandalized by both far left and Neo-Nazi groups.

Opposed to Neo-Nazi activity in Greece, the Board of Jewish Communities (KIS) and general Greek-Orthodox groups have encouraged Holocaust education and commemoration. KIS encouraged students and authors to write essays on the Holocaust. In 1997, the Central Board of Jewish Communities began an active public Holocaust education campaign. The active role of Greek television in the production of documentary films on Greek Jewry in the Holocaust in Greece has increased public awareness.

The initiation of Jewish Holocaust squares and monuments in Athens, Salonika, Ioannina, Volos, Larisa, Castoria, Drama, Rhodes, and elsewhere has been a positive step in public Holocaust recognition in Greece.

In 2000–1 the Jewish Museum in Greece began an educational Holocaust project with Greek public schools. In Autumn 2004 the first Greek Holocaust conference for educators was held in Athens.

Following Neo-Nazi activity in the late 1990s and exacerbated by reactions to the second Palestinian Intifada, Greek antisemitism reached dangerous and unprecedented levels in the press, in desecration of cemeteries, synagogues, Holocaust memorials, and in threats and attempted attacks against Jewish institutions and individuals in Greece. Perturbing was the lack of condemnation by the Greek government and the Greek-Orthodox Church. Official revival and sponsorship by the Greek government and the Greek Orthodox Church of the Burning of Judas ceremony on Easter is equally heinous and surprising. Voices of Greek intellectuals and artists in support of Israel and Greek Jewry are rarely heard, and the singer Mikis Theodorakis created an international scandal with his pronouncements that the Jews and Israel are sources of all global evil and with his interview in *Haaretz* justifying his grandmother's belief in blood libel and Greek EON Fascist Youth Movement activities of the late 1930s. Neo-Nazi publications continue to be published actively in Greece, the Protocols of the Elders of Zion have been reprinted in Greek, and large segments of Greek society are influenced by conspiracy theories directed against world Jewry. In an October 2001 KAPA poll conducted amongst 622 households in greater Athens, 42% believed that 4,000 Jews intentionally did not go to the World Trade Center on September 11, 2001, while only 30% rejected the theory.

In Salonika, a Jewish museum opened and the community was strengthened by the hiring of young Rabbi Frezis, a native Greek-speaking Athenian ordained in Israel. In Athens, a Chabad center was opened at the beginning of the 21st century.

Relations with Israel

The relations between Greece and Israel have generally been cool. Greece was the only European country to vote against the UN partition plan for Palestine in 1947. After the establishment of the State of Israel, Greece recognized the new state de facto, but for a time did not establish diplomatic ties with it. Diplomatic representations were set up in Athens and Jerusalem only in 1952, but not on the level of an embassy or legation. Greece usually supports the Arab side in disputes brought before the UN. However, shipping, air, and trade ties exist between the two countries. After the *Six-Day War of 1967, Arab terrorists made Athens the scene of attacks on Israel air communications. In 1970 seven Arab terrorists were convicted by Greek courts and sentenced to various prison terms, from two to 18 years, for attacks on an El Al plane, throwing a bomb at the El Al office, killing a Greek child, and trying to hijack a TWA plane. In August 1970 when Arab terrorists hijacked an Olympic Air Lines plane and demanded the release of the seven convicted terrorists, the Greek government submitted to their blackmail and released them. After that incident, Greek authorities seem to have taken special precautions against the renewal of Arab terrorist activities on Greek territory.

The main event of the 1980s was the culmination of the process lasting throughout most of the decade in preparing the terms and the establishment of full *de jure* diplomatic relations between Greece and Israel, which was technically achieved on May 21, 1990. With the election of the Socialist Pasok Party in 1982 under the leadership of Andreas Papandreou, gradual preparations were made for eventual full diplomatic relations between Greece and Israel. When the moderate Nea Demokratia Party came into power in 1989, full diplomatic relations with Israel were established. In November 1991, Greek Prime Minister Constantinos Mitsotakis paid an official state visit to Israel. Israel Ambassador Moshe Gilboa toiled for the exit of over 300 Albanian Jews, most of whom were of Greek Ioanniote origin, to immigrate to Israel.

From the early 1990s relations between Greece and Israel have been cordial. Prime Minister Andreas Papandreou, returning to the premiership after sitting as opposition leader for four years, adopted a more moderate Israel policy than in the past. He apologized to Israel's deputy minister of foreign affairs, Yosi Beilin, for his past harsh policy toward Israel and his affinity for extremist Arab movements and countries. Following the Israeli-Palestinian peace accord Greek Defense Minister Gerasimos Ersenis visited Israel in December 1994. Greece and Israel signed a mutual military cooperation agreement.

[Simon Marcus / Yitzchak Kerem (2nd ed.)]

MUSICAL TRADITIONS OF GREECE AND THE BALKANS

The eastern migration of Jews expelled from the Iberian Peninsula, at the end of the 15th century, toward the main centers of the Ottoman Empire, led to a synthesis of musical traditions in the Balkan Peninsula in which Spanish elements – of Mozarabic or medieval Christian origin – were deeply fused with Greco-Byzantine, Turkish, and Slavic ones. Among the Balkan Jews, three distinct stylistic traditions could still be discerned at least up through the late decades of the 20th century: (1) the *Sephardi*, which was most evident until World War II among the Jewish cultural centers of Salonica, Larissa, and Volos (Greece) as well as in Sarajevo (Bosnia), Sofia (Bulgaria), Monastir (Bitolj, Yugoslavia), Bucharest, and Creiova (Romania). This Sephardi musical tradition differed from those of the dominant Arabic communities of the Near East, as well as the Andalusian in northern Morocco, and the Portuguese, which was more prominent in Western Europe (Amsterdam, Bayonne, Leghorn (Livorno), etc.). (2)

The *Romaniot*, evident in such isolated centers of continental Greece as Arta, Chalkis (Euboea, Negroponte), Ioannina, Patras, and Trikkala, and Crete, preserved remnants from the musical and liturgical traditions of the Byzantine period, in spite of the overwhelming influence of the Sephardi newcomers. The Romaniot Jews maintained a Judeo-Greek dialect in their hymnographic tradition, whose characteristic melodic conventions evolved independently during the 16th through 18th centuries. Even though they adopted the Sephardi rite in their liturgy, they did not entirely abandon their traditional music. (3) The *Italianate*, evident on the island of Corfu and neighboring centers – such as Zante – reflected the liturgical and musical influences of southern Italy which the Jews carried with them as early as the 14th and 15th centuries. A similar influence, traceable to Venice, was apparent in the now extinct Sephardi communities of Dalmatia – such as Dubrovnik, Split, and Vlona.

The chant of Balkan Sephardim, which was directly linked to that of the communities of Asia Minor (Izmir and Rhodes), integrated Greek and Turkish elements. The *Makam* scales of *ḥiijāz* and *ḥiijāz Kar* were widely used in secular songs; the Phrygian cadence (*a-g-f-e*) was frequent, while the *Makam Sika* (*Siga*) was preferred for the reading of the Torah. The stylistic differences between the men's and women's repertoire, however, was not as striking as one might surmise. The men's style, more Orientalized (microtonal) and ornamented, had been influenced by the florid *kontakionic* and *kalophonic* styles of Byzantine hymns and chants, respectively, and by the florid Muslim chant which was practiced mainly in the synagogue repertoire. The women, who preserved a domestic repertoire in Judeo-Spanish, sang in a more relaxed manner, yet with varied degrees of vocal ornamentation, microtonal inflection, and in a medium to high vocal register. Within the more predominantly Greek communities, the 15th-century Castilian ballads (*romances*) which had survived in their repertoire were stylistically different from ballads sung in other centers of the Balkans and northern Morocco. The predominant Greek traits included those that were found in Greek *klephtic* songs, wherein the textual hemistichs did not coordinate with the melody phrases, and the popular 7/8 *epitrite* dance meter. Even their texts varied greatly from those preserved in non-Greek centers. Like the folksongs of pre-World War II Greece, the varied Sephardi communities also assimilated elements from classical Greek and Byzantine church music. Chants, songs, and hymns in Judeo-Spanish played an important role during the varied liturgical and paraliturgical occasions. The chants, sung as vernacular translations of Hebrew texts, could be heard during the removal of the Torah scroll from the Ark, as well as the homiletic translations of Jonah, and the *haftarah* sung on the Ninth of Av. The songs were interspersed during the reading of the *Haggadah*; and the hymns were fervently rendered for Simḥat Torah.

The earlier Byzantine ("Romaniot") style flourished much more overtly in the areas where Judeo-Greek was spoken, particularly in Ioannina, Chalkis, and partly in Corfu. The men's synagogal chant was highly influenced by the Greek *kalophonia* and the microtonal intonations of the surrounding Greek and Muslim cults (as in Ioannina). Among the women, the style was plaintive, with minimal ornamentation and flourishes, and there existed the ancient practice of singing funeral lamentations mainly as distichs or quatrains bearing short verses that were sung responsorially or antiphonally. The women were also assigned the singing of paraliturgical hymns, like those on Purim, often based on midrashic traditions. These songs flourished during the 17th and 18th centuries, coinciding, more or less, with the post-Shabbatean period that also gave rise to the mystic brotherhoods. The traditional literature of liturgical music was performed in rhymed distichs or quatrains, often with refrains or intercalations in Hebrew, which revealed the existence of a more ancient homiletic tradition, preserved both orally and in manuscripts. It reached its highest level in the 17th century with the poet-composer Samuel Hanen.

Three distinct traditions coexisted and still exist to some degree among the Corfiote communities in Tel Aviv and Trieste: 1) the *Italian* or *Pugghiesi* (from Salento in Apulia-Puglia), which has remained the only important witness to the tradition of the medieval Jewish communities of southern Italy; 2) the *Greek* or "*Romaniot*," which was similar to that of Ioanina; and 3) the *Sephardi*. Some are sung alternatively in four languages (Judeo-Greek, Italian, Judeo-Spanish, and Hebrew) which confirm this symbiosis. A well-known bilingual folksong, which concerns a lubricious quarrel between mother and daughter, provides a good example of the differences of class and culture between the more bourgeois and assimilated Greeks, and the earthier Pugghiesi. However, the translations in the ancient Apulian dialect and the songs of this tradition, which are included in the Passover *Haggadah*, were the common property of all Corfiote Jews. A considerable number of manuscripts bear witness to the existence of a *Minhag Corfu*, rich in *piyyutim*, such as the elegy on the destruction of the Temple, for the Ninth of Av, in the Apulian-Venetian dialect. The chant of the Pugghiesi displays a singular persistence of medieval styles, also preserved in Greco-Italic church chants (mainly in those of the 8th mode). The more recent religious synagogue and domestic chants, Sabbath hymns, and popular poems in Hebrew, or in their Italian translation, are performed as polyphonic settings for three to six voices, similar to the folksongs sung among the gentile populations in the Adriatic-Dalmatic region.

[Leo Levi / Israel J. Katz (2nd ed.)]

BIBLIOGRAPHY: GENERAL: B.D. Mazur, *Studies on Jewry in Greece* (1935); *Joshua Starr Memorial Volume* (1953). SECOND TEMPLE AND ROMAN EMPIRE PERIOD: Schuerer, Gesch, 3 (1909⁴), 55–57; Lewis, in: JSS, 2 (1957), 264–6. BYZANTINE PERIOD: J. Starr, *The Jews in the Byzantine Empire, 641–1204* (1939); idem, *Romania – The Jewries of the Levant after the Fourth Crusade* (1949); idem, in: PAAJR, 11 (1942), 59–114; idem, in: JPOS, 15 (1935), 280–93; idem, in: *Byzantinisch-neugriechische Jahrbuecher*, 12 (1936), 42–49; idem, in: JQR, 38 (1947), 97–99; J. Parkes, *The Conflict of the Church and the Synagogue* (1934), index; J.R. Marcus, *The Jew in the Medieval World: A Source*

Book, 315–1791 (1938), 3–8; S. Krauss, *Studien zur byzantinisch-juedischen Geschichte* (1914); idem, in: *Recueil jubilaire en l'honneur de S.A. Rosanès* (1933), 53–67; M. Molho, *Histoire des Israélites de Castoria* (1938); E.S. Artom and M.D. Cassuto (eds.), *Takkanot Kandiyya ve-Zikhronoteha* (1943), passim; G. Ostrogorsky, *History of the Byzantine State* (1956, 1968²), index; Z. Ankori, *Karaites in Byzantium* (1959), 148–50; A. Sharf, in: *World History of the Jewish People*, second series, 2 (1966), 49–68; Perles, in: *Byzantinische Zeitschrift*, 2 (1893), 569–84; Kaufmann, *ibid.*, 7 (1898), 83–90; E. Csetényi, in: *Etudes orientales à la mémoire de Paul Hirschler* (1950), 16–20. OTTOMAN RULE AND INDEPENDENT GREECE UNTIL 1940: M. Molho, in: *Homenaje a Millás Vallicrosa*, 2 (1956), 73–107 (Fr.); Rosanes, Togarmah, passim; AZDJ, 54 (1890), 3–4. HOLOCAUST PERIOD: M. Molho and J. Nehama, *In memoriam: Hommage aux victimes juives des Nazis en Grèce*, 3 vols. (1948–53); idem, *Sho'at Yehudei Yavan 1941–1944* (1965); I. Kabeli, *La Contribution des juifs à la libération de la Grèce* (1946); idem, *Trois étapes de la tragédie juive en Europe* (1946); idem, in: YIVO *Bleter*, 37 (1953), 205–12; idem, in: YIVOA, 8 (1953), 281–8; Moissis, in: *Les Juifs en Europe (1939–1945)* (1949), 47–54; R. Hilberg, *Destruction of the European Jews* (1961), 442–53 and index; G. Reitlinger, *Final Solution* (1968²), 398–408; Melamed, in: *Cahiers de l'Alliance Israélite Universelle*, 95 (1956), 12–18; 96 (1956), 13–21; 97 (1956), 15–20; Roth, in: *Commentary*, 10 (1950), 49–55; Elk, in: *Yad Vashem Bulletin*, 17 (1965), 9–15; Sabille, in: *Le Monde Juif*, 6:49 (1951), 7–10; Neshamith, in: *Mi-Bifnim*, 22:4 (1960), 405–9; *Yedi'ot Beit Lohamei ha-Getta'ot*, 22 (1960), 109–16; P. Friedman, in: *Joshua Starr Memorial Volume* (1953), 241–8 (bibliographical survey on Holocaust period in Greece). CONTEMPORARY PERIOD: D.J. Elazar … [et al.] (ed.), *Balkan Jewish Communities: Yugoslavia, Bulgaria, Greece, and Turkey* (1984); J. Neḥama, in: *Cahiers Sefardis*, 1 (1946/47), 12–15; AJYB, 49 (1947/48), 434–6; S. Modiano, *ibid.*, 54 (1953), 294–300; M.G. Goldbloom, *ibid.*, 57 (1956), 359–65; V. Semah, *ibid.*, 61 (1960), 217–22; 66 (1965), 399–405; P.R. Argenti, *The Religious Minorities of Chios* (1971); M. Novitch, *Le Passage des Barbares*, Nice (no date). **ADD. BIBLIOGRAPHY:** B. Rivlin, Y. Kerem, and L. Matkovetski, *Pinkas Kehillot Yavan* (1999); Y. Kerem, "Rescue in Greece in the Second World War," in *Pe'amim*, 27 (1986), 77–109. MUSICAL TRADITIONS: S.G. Armistead, "Greek Elements in Judeo-Spanish Traditional Poetry," in: *Laografia*, 32 (1979–81), 134–64; R. Dalven and I.J. Katz, "Three Traditional Judeo-Greek Hymns and Their Tunes," in: *The Sephardic Scholar*, 4 (1979–82), 84–101; N. Kaufmann, "The Folk Songs of the Bulgarian Jews in the Past," in: *Annual of the Social Cultural and Educational Association of the Jews in Bulgaria*, 18 (1995), 184–209; A. Petrovic, "Sacred Sephardi Chants in Bosnia," in: *World of Music*, 24:3 (1982), 35–51; S. Weich-Shahak, "Childbirth Songs among Jews of Balkan Origin," in: *Orbis Musicae*, 8 (1982–83), 87–103; idem, "Wedding Songs of Sephardi Jews from Bulgaria," in: *Dukhan*, 12 (1989), 167–80; idem, "The Bosnian Judeo-Spanish Musical Repertoire in a Hundred Year Old Manuscript," in: *Jahrbuch fuer musikalische Volks- und Vokerkunde*, 14 (1990), 97–122; A. Shiloah, "Les chants de noce dans la tradition musicale des Juifs de Joannina," in: *Le Foklore Macédonien*, 5 (1972), 201–10; idem, *Greek-Jewish Musical Traditions* (Folkways Records, FE4201, 1978).

GREEK AND LATIN LANGUAGES, RABBINICAL KNOWLEDGE OF. The nature and extent of the knowledge of Greek and Latin on the part of the rabbis are subjects of scholarly controversy, differing opinions even being based on the same data, since they lend themselves to several interpretations. Such data are the Greek quotations in Talmud and Midrash, rabbinical knowledge of Greco-Roman institutions, written historical sources, archaeology, epigraphy, and certain changes in the Hebrew language. The problem is compounded by fluid historical situations prevailing in late antiquity, such as the varying policy of Rome as the protagonist of Hellenism in the Near East and the degree of native assertion which, in Jewish Palestine, led to sporadic condemnations (Meg. 9a) and supposed prohibitions of Greek. Among these, those after 66 C.E. (TJ Shab. 1:6, 3c) and during the "War of Quietus" (116 C.E.; Sot. 9:14, etc. – a prohibition of the use of Greek, which itself employed the Greek loanword *polemos* for "war"!) are probably real. However the ruling against the use of Greek in 65 B.C.E. because of an incident at the siege of Jerusalem, as cited in the Talmud (Sot. 49b; cf. Jos., Ant., 14:25–8) is probably legendary (although E. Wiesenberg argues that it was probably historical). The Tosefta (Av. Zar. 1:20) and *Menaḥot* 99b (c. 90 C.E. and before 135 C.E.) discourage the study of Greek wisdom. This very repetition of anti-Greek measures, however, and some endorsements (Yad. 4:6; TJ, Sanh. 10:1, 28a; Rabbi in: Sot. 49b; Meg. 1:8) and positive evaluations of Greek (Esth. R. 4:12; Gen. R. 16:4, 36:8) indicate the temporariness or ineffectiveness of prohibitions. The Talmud tries to harmonize these contradictions by declaring that Greek was permissible for foreign contacts only (Sot. 49b, et. al.) or as a social asset for girls (TJ, Sot. 9:16, 24c). Use of liturgical Greek is indicated in the Jerusalem Talmud (Sot. 7:1, 21b), possibly in *Sotah* 49b (Rabbi), et al.; and a sort of public or official instruction is reflected in the metaphorical "500" students of Greek of *Simeon b. Gamaliel II, c. 140 C.E. (Sot. 49b). Occasionally Greek wisdom is distinguished from Greek language but seems to be identical with it in the Hasmonean War report of Sot. 49b, etc. It may signify "sophistry" (Graetz) or the "rhetorical art" as preparation for administrators but hardly a full ephebic or philosophical-scientific education. Opinions as to rabbinic Greek thus differ widely: bilingualism or trilingualism (Hebrew, Aramaic, Greek), even a Palestinian version of the general Hellenistic vernacular (*koin*) and a Judeo-Greek have been surmised, in opposition, for example, to the view that the midrashic use of Greek stances is merely a device to impress non-understanding audiences!

There is, however, complete unanimity that Latin was little known (cf. Git. 80a, et al.), Greek being for nearly a millennium the language of Macedonian, Roman, and Byzantine administrations and many semi-independent cities in Palestine (332 B.C.E.–636 C.E.) and of importance even in Parthia. Moreover, "Latin" loanwords in Hebrew (*dux*, *matrona*, Caesar, "legion," "family," a.o.) were often loanwords already in the Greek from which they had been borrowed. Estimates as to the ratio of Greek to Latin loanwords in rabbinic literature have been as high as one hundred to one.

In view of this deadlock of opinions, the problem under review must be examined through fresh approaches.

Languages in Contact

Insufficient use has been made so far of the discipline of modern linguistics in solving this task. Both Aramaic and Hebrew of this period underwent transformation not only in lexicography – c. 3,000 Greco-Roman loanwords – (which is generally acknowledged) but also in phonology (e.g., the gradual weakening of laryngeals in some localities, cf. Meg. 24b; Ber. 32a; Er. 53b; cf. E.Y. Kutscher, in: JSS, 10 (1965), 21–51); in syntax (especially the dissolution of the construct case into a prepositional phrase); the frequency of an absolute nominative before conditional clauses (cf. M.H. Segal, *Grammar of Mishnaic Hebrew* (1927, repr. 1958), 213–4) resembling the Greek genitive absolute. According to Bendavid (see below) certain usages of the Palestinian sages indicate quasi-mechanical transfer from the Greek and can be found in phraseology (e.g., Heb. *lashon ha-ra*, Gr. *kakoglossia*, "evil tongue"); in semantics (Heb. *batlan*, "scholar," and Gr. *scholastikos* both allude to "leisure"; Heb. *yishuv*, Gr. *oikoumene*, "habitation"); change of gender (biblical *makkel*, "staff," becomes feminine after Greek *bakteria* and *rhabdos*); the increase of reflexive verbs; and new properties of the prepositions. The verb, according to linguists the most conservative element in language, was affected by a new tense system, notably a precise present tense and compound tenses (with auxiliary verb), and the creation of Hebraized roots from the Greek, among them such important verbs as *ḳ-l-s*, "praise"; *k-r-z*, "proclaim"; *h-g-n*, "be proper"; *p-y-s*, "pacify" and "cast lots"; *ṭ-g-n*, "fry"; *ṭ-k(ḳ)-s*, "arrange"; *s-m-n*, "signify"; *ḳ-ṭ-r-g*, "accuse"; and *p-r-s-m*, "publicize." The loanwords cover all aspects of life but are especially prominent in certain areas of material civilization (architecture, agriculture, fashion, commerce, and technology) and public life (government, taxation, law, and warfare). Apart from the salient keywords of Greco-Roman civilization, such as "circus," "theater," "stadium," "hippodrome," "column," "icon," "colony," "metropolis," "triumph," "emperor," "senator," "tyranny," "pedagogue," and "philosopher," even indispensable terms of daily life are loanwords, such as "air," "sandal," "tome," "collar," "sum," "salary," "mint," "nausea," "diarrhea," "character," "person," "type," et al. (all preceding English examples being approximately identical with the Greco-Hebraic terms). Even proper names of rabbis are affected: Alexander, Antigonus, Boethus, Dosa, Pa(p)pus, Symmachus, Tarphon, etc., alongside basic religious terms: Sanhedrin, *bimah, afikoman*, "angel" (Targum), *kairos*, "mystery," "blasphemy," et al. (Of course thousands of other Greco-Roman terms in modern Hebrew have been added in the modern technological era.) The orthography of actual Greek words and of loanwords is fairly systematic (though difficult to date and subject to error in scribal tradition and reveals Greek language change, e.g., the Greek *upsilon* in certain diphthongs is already given as v (or f) as in Byzantine and modern Greek (Selevcus for Seleucus, avto- for auto-). All these observations, however, do not yet give any information regarding the rabbinic knowledge of written Greek sources, especially since Krauss's views of the derivation (see below) of certain loanwords from Homeric or rare Greek poetry have not been generally accepted.

Greek as an Intercultural Representative Prestige Language

This was especially true of public display, including inscriptions in the Temple (even its ritual objects, cf. Shek. 3:2), and on synagogues, epitaphs, etc. Some of the Greek in Palestinian cemeteries may belong here and may not be diaspora Greek. To claim that all rabbis were excluded from this vast sector of public life through ignorance or hostility is manifestly absurd. It has been assumed, however, that the opposition to Greek was strongest among some popular preachers who continued earlier Zealot attitudes (see below, Avi-Yonah, 71).

Greek as Professional Expertise

There is much justification for the claim that Jewish mercenaries, slaves, tax collectors, and certain artisans, e.g., sculptors for idolatrous customers, and the rulers, courtiers, and diplomats of the Hasmoneans and Herodians had to resort to Greek because of their social-economic functions. It seems that the *tannaim* and many leading Palestinian *amoraim*, as well as their Pharisaic predecessors, belong to a group of "technocrat" experts who could administer, legislate, interpret, edit law and literature, theologize, moralize, and console – precisely the abilities and functions of their Greco-Roman counterparts, the rhetorician-scholar-bureaucrats, from Cicero to Seneca (once practically vice-emperor), from Dio Chrysostom to Plutarch (a priest-magistrate). The rabbis' idealization of the Sage – the characteristic ideology of hellenized bureaucracies – their popular ethics and their uses of Hellenic myth, literary forms, and *hermeneutics, their academic institutions and efforts at preserving tradition, suggest knowledge of their Greco-Roman colleagues. The presence of schools of law, philosophy, and exegesis in and near Palestine (Ashkelon, Beirut, Caesarea, Gederah, Gaza), the Roman administrative center in Caesarea, and wandering rhetors must have furthered the spread of "professional" Greek. True, most of the grecianized talmudic data could stem from audio-transmission of rhetorics, the expertise of Greco-Roman bureaucracy. Yet Greco-Hebrew legal terminology (*diatheke, hypotheke, epitropos, k(o)inonia*, cf. Prosbul, etc.), some talmudic science, and rabbinic use of isopsephy (**Gematria*) are more technical than the usual orations. Actual Greek halakhic documents (e.g., a marriage contract) and numerous Greek translations of Hebrew literature indicate some measure of literary experience. (Not for all the latter could the aid of proselytes be claimed. In any case, the semilegendary portrayals of the translator *Aquilas, a proselyte *Elisha b. Avuyah, the "heretic," and *Meir, a reputed descendant of proselytes, may belong to periods of native reassertion when it had become unthinkable that rabbis were fluent in Greek.) Moreover, the insistence on oral transmission may occasionally have been merely a literary pose in conformity with a general trend toward cynicism in rhetoric (cf. Diogenes Laertius, 6:2, 48). At this stage of history, Jewish tradition and its agents were probably highly literate and literacy-minded. The Greek knowledge of the Hillelite dynasty to *Rabbi, 200 C.E., and beyond of Joshua, Meir, and *Abbahu, must have been considerable, as their use of Hellenistic materials and disciplines, their friendliness toward Greek, and their contacts with the Roman government indicate. In later centuries, however, the increasing impoverishment of Palestine and the accompanying alienation from Christianized Rome may have modified this situation.

Comparative Studies of Other Hellenizing Cultures would further illustrate Judean situations: Cato the Elder, the Roman arch-conservative speaking excellent Greek; Roman senators outlawing Greek rhetoric; a similar mass of loanwords even within societies resisting Greek, such as the Western Roman Empire, the Syrian Church, and native Armenia and Egypt; and slaves, proselytes, and uprooted populations spreading the knowledge of Greek (in Judea: after the Maccabean wars, cf. E.E. Urbach's discussion of the "Canaanite slave," in: *Zion* 25 (1960), 141–89, Heb.).

All in all, the scarcity and ambiguity of talmudic sources and the problematics of the historical data do not lend themselves to generalizations. What type of "rabbi," for example, is mentioned in the Greek Leontius memorial of Bet She'arim (Frey, 1006). Did the rabbis debate with Christians in Aramaic or Greek? When they declared Greek as "suitable" for poetry and Latin for war (Est. R. 4:12), did they thereby evaluate languages or merely characterize these cultures in general? Do halakhic statements on Homeric books presuppose their intimate knowledge (TJ, Sanh. 10:1, 28a; Yad. 4:6)? Perhaps the true question is not whether the rabbis knew Greek slightly or in depth (even the rhetors used various aid books), but whether they knew it adequately for their purpose. Only additional finds, such as actual Greek literature or more Greek halakhic documents, will throw further light on these problems.

BIBLIOGRAPHY: Frey, Corpus; S. Lieberman, *Greek in Jewish Palestine* (1942); idem, *Hellenism in Jewish Palestine* (1962[2]); M. Avi-Yonah, *Bi-Ymei Roma u-Bizantyon* (1962[3]), 67ff.; S. Krauss, *Griechische und lateinische Lehnwoerter im Talmud, Midrasch und Targum* (1898–99) (to be used with reservation: see G. Zuntz, in: JSS, 1 (1956), 129–40; cf. however, H. Rosén, in: JSS, 8 (1963), 56–72); E. Wiesenberg: in: HUCA, 27 (1956), 213–33; A. Sperber, *ibid.*, 12–13 (1937–38), 103–274; M. Schwabe, in: *Sefer Zikkaron le-Asher Gulak ve-li-Shemu'el Klein* (1942), 187–200; idem, in: *Eshkolot*, 1 (1954), 73–85; A. Halevi, in: *Tarbiz*, 29 (1960), 47–55; 31 (1962), 157–69, 264–80; A. Bendavid, *Leshon Mikra u-Leshon Ḥakhamim* (1967[2]), 111–8, 135–52, 183–90; H.A. Fischel, in: *Semicentennial Volume of the Middle West Branch of the American Oriental Society* (1969), 59–88; J.N. Sevenster, *Do You Know Greek?* (1968).

[Henry Albert Fischel]

GREEK LITERATURE, ANCIENT. Greeks came into contact with the Land of Israel long before the Hellenistic period, but there is no information as to the impression made by Jews or Judaism upon them in the classical period. The only classical writings extant referring to the Jews are *Herodotus' *Histories*, but his acquaintance with them is at best highly superficial, and he considers them to be Syrians who practiced circumcision, which custom they had acquired from the Egyptians. Aristotle does mention a lake in Palestine, but without connecting it in any way with the Jewish people. Thus, although the ancient civilizations of Egypt, Babylon, and Persia were familiar to the Greek men of letters and philosophers – at least in their general outline even before the days of Alexander the Great – they were apparently completely ignorant of the specific religion and culture of Palestine.

This situation changed radically after Alexander the Great and the foundation of the various Macedonian kingdoms throughout the East. From earliest times descriptions of Jews and Judaism occur in the works of Greek authors, some of whom belonged to the school of Aristotle. Thus, Theophrastus, one of Aristotle's foremost pupils, in his work "On Piety" described the Jewish sacrificial rites as utterly different from those of the Greek, consisting entirely of holocausts, offered in the middle of the night. The Jews are described by him as philosophers whose custom it is to converse among themselves about theology at the time of the offering of the sacrifices and to gaze at the stars. His contemporary, Clearchus, who was also a member of the Peripatetic school, in his dialogue "On Sleep" gives the contents of a conversation supposedly held between Aristotle and a Jew in Asia Minor (see below). The Jews are also described as philosophers in the work of the traveler Megasthenes (see below).

More detailed, and in some respects more realistic, is the detailed description vouchsafed by *Hecataeus of Abdera, who spent a long time in Egypt at the beginning of the Hellenistic period. Hecataeus describes the origin of the Jewish people as resulting from an expulsion from Egypt of undesirable elements at the time of a plague. Their leader Moses, who excelled in ability and valor, conquered the land of Judea for the Jews, founded Jerusalem, erected the Temple there, and set down the constitution of the Jewish people. Hecataeus was familiar with the division into 12 tribes and was the first of the Greek writers whose works are still extant to note that the Jews make no images of their godhead, nor conceive Him to be of human form, since, according to him, the Jews equate their God with the heavens. Moses entrusted the keeping of the laws to the priests, whom he also appointed as judges. The Jewish constitution does not know the form of monarchy, and the high priest is described as the head of the Jewish nation. The position of high priest is filled by one of the priests, chosen from among the rest for his excellence of character and wisdom. Moses also commanded the Jews to raise all the children born to them, which is the reason for the rapid increase in their numbers.

At the beginning of the Hellenistic period, Judaism was known to Greek thinkers and men of letters only in the vaguest of outlines. Their impressions are not very different from those they had of other ancient civilized peoples of the East. Their tendency to consider the Jews to be the bearers of a philosophic religion is evident, and their descriptions are generally quite highly idealized. It should be noted that the descriptions of the Jews, not excluding that of Hecataeus, still lack any taint of that hostility which is characteristic of most of the later writers. This general attitude continues into the third century. Thus, Hermippus of Smyrna states that Pythagoras received some of his teachings from the Jews, and that his philosophy was influenced by Judaism.

From the third century B.C.E. on, however, with the crystallization of an anti-Jewish outlook, the Jews, their religion, customs, and origins, begin to be described in a definitely negative light. This new approach flourished in the anti-Jewish atmosphere of Egypt and was abetted not a little by the old tensions between Egyptians and Jews. As time passed, it continued to gather strength, fanned by the Greco-Jewish clash in Alexandria, particularly during the days of the early empire. Since the Greco-Alexandrian literature was one of the main cultural flowerings of the age, it was a very important instrument in the formation of informed public opinion throughout the Hellenistic world and the Roman Empire.

One of the most important authorities of this new, anti-Jewish spirit in Greek literature was the Egyptian priest, *Manetho. He seems already to have identified the Jews with the *Hyksos and Moses with the Egyptian priest Osarsiph, who was described by him as the leader of the lepers and the other unclean and defiling elements who had been harming the population of Egypt. It was probably at this time that the belief that the Jews worshiped an ass – the animal holy to the Egyptian god Seth-Typhon, Osiris' enemy – was evolved. Manetho was only one of the many mouthpieces for the anti-Jewish propaganda. Even more rabid than he was *Lysimachus of Alexandria. According to him also, the Jewish nation stems from the impure and undesirable elements who had been expelled from Egyptian society. Their leader, Moses, taught them to hate all mankind, and their opposition to the temples of other nations typifies their entire approach.

It was *Apion of Alexandria (first century C.E.) who collected this anti-Jewish material. Not only did he refine the literary form of the tradition concerning the Exodus, which was most derogatory to the Jews, but he also protested against the Alexandrian Jews' demands to be considered citizens of the city, spoke with contempt of the Jewish religious practices, repeated the statement that the Jews worshiped an ass, stressed their supposed hatred of foreigners, said that they had contributed nothing to human civilization, and saw in their lowly political status an expression of the worthlessness of their religion. Actually, Apion added little of his own, but in his works the anti-Jewish spirit was given free rein and his writings contain virtually the entire gamut of the anti-Jewish themes which formed the antisemitic stereotype in the ancient world, and they also left their mark on Latin literature.

In spite of the generally extreme anti-Jewish character of the Alexandrian Greek literature, which was not a little influenced by the national Egyptian tradition, one nevertheless finds at least one writer – Timagenes of Alexandria (second half of the first century C.E.) – who apparently preserved a more objective approach to the Jews and in his history even expressed admiration for the Hasmonean king Aristobulus I. Interest in Jews and Judaism was also shown by Greek writers outside Egypt, from Syria and other parts of the Greek world. Asia Minor was of first rank in the intellectual and cultural life of the Hellenistic-Roman period, and it was also liberally sprinkled with areas thickly populated by Jews. It is in the works of one of the writers from Asia Minor – the historian Agatharchides of Cnidus (second century B.C.E.) – that the first mention in Greek sources is found of the Sabbath rest. He notes with scorn that it was because of this superstition that Jerusalem, the capital of the Jews, was conquered by Ptolemy I.

In the wake of the conflict between the Jews and Rome and Pompey's conquest of Jerusalem, there was an increased interest in the history of the Jews and in their religious observances on the part of the Asia Minor writers. It found its expression, *inter alia*, in the writing of books devoted entirely to this subject. Among these, *Alexander Polyhistor's anthology is particularly interesting, consisting as it does largely of excerpts from other authors and particularly from Jewish-Hellenistic literature. Teucer of Cyzicus also wrote a special work on the Jews. *Apollonius Molon's book on the Jews enjoyed great influence. Apollonius was a rhetorician from Alabanda in Caria and some of the foremost men of Roman society were influenced by his works. He had some knowledge concerning Abraham, Isaac, Joseph, and Moses, and the biblical tradition is clearly reflected in his work. Nevertheless, his attitude toward the Jews was most negative, and he considered them to be the least capable of the barbarians (i.e., non-Greeks), a nation which had added nothing to the cultural store of mankind.

A different approach is to be found in the works of the historian and geographer *Strabo, from Amaseia in Pontus, who lived in the time of Augustus. In the 16th book of his geography he describes Moses as an Egyptian priest who rejected the Egyptian forms of divine worship which centered around the deification of animals, and likewise objected to the anthropomorphism of Greek theology. Moses' god was identified with the heavens and the natural world, and many people of discerning intellect were convinced by him and became his followers. Under Moses' leadership they gained control of what is now called Jerusalem and there he founded a polity in accord with his views. Strabo expresses his complete approval of this polity and adds that for some time Moses' successors continued to live according to his constitution and were truly just and God-fearing. However, in the course of time the priesthood – which among the Jews encompassed the political power as well – fell into the hands of superstitious men, and after them in the hands of those who had despotic leanings. The superstitions which were introduced gave rise to the Jewish laws concerning forbidden foods, circumcision, and the like. The tyranny engendered robbery and violence, and large portions of Syria and Phoenicia were subjugated by the Jews. In short, Strabo looked upon Judaism as a basically positive phenomenon, and lauds the pure belief in God which typified it in its early days, but according to him Judaism had in the course of time degenerated and become corrupt.

Among the representatives of Greek literature in Syria, the philosopher, historian, and polymath *Posidonius of Apamea is of importance. He also wrote concerning the Jews and undoubtedly influenced those who came after him, but his views concerning Jews and Judaism are still a mystery, since it is difficult to determine what is to be ascribed to him and what to his followers. An allusion to "the cold Sabbath" of the Jews is to be found in the works of the poet Meleager of Gadara (first century B.C.E.). More than any of the other Greco-Syrian writers, *Nicholas of Damascus was intimately connected with Jewish affairs. He wrote his "Universal History" under Herod's inspiration and spent many years in his court in Jerusalem. The history of Herod's reign and the events of contemporary Jewish history were assigned a very prominent place in his work. He also included biblical traditions in the earlier portions of the history. Unlike the other contemporary gentile authors, Nicholas dealt with the period of the Israelite monarchy, including such events as David's wars with the Arameans. Abraham is described by him as a king in Damascus.

Typical of the level of knowledge concerning Judaism current among the educated classes of the Hellenistic world in the first century B.C.E. is the material brought by the universal historian, Diodorus of Sicily. He mentions Moses among those lawgivers who ascribed their constitutions to divine inspiration, and he states that the God of the Jews was called Ἰάω. Elsewhere in his work – where he is apparently dependent upon Posidonius – he relates the origins of the Jewish people according to the version which grew up and became current in Greco-Egyptian circles; i.e., that the first Jews had been lepers who had been expelled for this reason from Egypt. The personality of Moses is also presented in a positive light by Pseudo-Longinus, a literary critic of first rank, in his excellent work "On the Sublime." The author, whose name has not come down, quotes the early part of the Book of Genesis ("...and there was light..." etc.) as an excellent example of lofty and exalted style and in this connection also expresses praise for the Jewish lawgiver.

*Plutarch is the only Hellenistic writer of the period of the early Roman Empire from Greece proper who is known to have written about Judaism. Most of his comments respecting the Jewish religion are to be found in his "Table-Talk," where the essence of the Jewish ritual is discussed as well as the nature of the Jewish godhead, and one of the participants even explains the supposedly close connection between the Dionysian rites and the Jewish festival of Tabernacles. At any rate, the tone is serious and does not reflect any innate animosity toward Jews or Judaism, and this is equally true in respect of the parts dealing with Jewish history which appear in his biographies of famous people, although in his work "On Superstition" the conduct of the Jews on the Sabbath during wartime is brought in as an illustration of superstitious conduct – just as it was already stressed by Agatharchides of Cnidus at the very beginning of the Hellenistic period.

In short, it may confidently be stated that Judaism as a phenomenon was familiar to the writers of the later Hellenistic period and to those who wrote during the early days of the Roman Empire. Their information concerning the history of the Jewish people is scanty and the influence of Jewish literature, even in translation (the Septuagint), is extremely meager. The attitude toward Judaism in Greek literature is not monolithic. Whereas particular hatred for the Jewish people and its religion is the hallmark of the representatives of the Greco-Egyptian literary school, definite sympathy is reflected in the writings of Pseudo-Longinus, and writers like Strabo or Plutarch express a relatively balanced view. In the descriptions of Judaism, stress is usually laid upon the origin of the Jewish nation and its religion, upon the personality of Moses on the one hand and on contemporary events on the other.

The attitude toward Judaism continued to be a live issue during the second half of the second century C.E., even after the rebellions during the reigns of Trajan and Hadrian had greatly weakened the Jewish people, and its religious influence diminished because of the competition posed by the spread of Christianity. *Numenius of Apamea, the forerunner of the neoplatonic school, may have been influenced in his philosophic thought by Philo of Alexandria. Be that as it may, his attitude to Moses was one of open admiration, and he even compared Moses to Plato. *Galen treats the Jewish philosophical conceptions seriously and critically. He is familiar with the cosmogony of Moses and specifically states his preference for the Greek conceptions in the form in which they are expressed by Plato. Whereas, he states, according to the Jewish view God's will is sufficient cause for anything and everything, according to the Greek view certain things are physically impossible and God chooses the best out of the possibilities of becoming. Moses is censured for having omitted the *causa materialis* and having thus postulated the *creatio ex nihilo.*

The historian *Dio Cassius also makes some interesting remarks touching upon Jewish history, in connection with his general survey of the history of Rome. Pompey's conquest of Jerusalem gave him the opportunity to describe the nature of the Jewish religion. He states that the Jews differ from all the rest of mankind in respect of their way of life, but in contrast to some of his predecessors he does not explain Jewish separatism on the grounds of misanthropy. He stresses the monotheistic and abstract nature of the Jewish belief, noting particularly the observance of the Sabbath, the Jew's loyalty to his faith, and the phenomenon of proselytization. As a contemporary of the Severi, he appreciates the fact that the Jews, in spite of their repression in the period immediately preceding, had nevertheless preserved and eventually won the right to live freely according to their customs.

The struggle between paganism and Christianity brought in its wake a pagan reappraisal of its attitude toward Judaism. The polemical works against Christianity of Celsus of Porphyry and of Julian, who had been raised as a Christian, reflect some accurate knowledge of the Bible. But to the extent that they come to grips with the Jewish outlook their attacks are in fact aimed mainly against Christianity, the roots of which are in the sanctified Jewish tradition. Hence, in spite of Judaism's particularistic and intolerant attitude toward paganism, they evince a sincere readiness to try to understand it as a national religion, anchored in an ancient tradition, contrasting it in this way to revolutionary Christianity. As the domination of Christianity became a fact, pagan writers like the Antiochene rhetor Libanius began to see Judaism as being in the same defensive camp as the pagan Hellenistic tradition.

No less than in the regular literary sources, the influence of Judaism is also clearly reflected in the syncretistic magical texts of the ancient world and in *Hermetic writings. Both these genres are replete with Jewish elements. The name of the Jewish godhead and the names of the angels are extremely common in magical papyri, and the thread of the biblical cosmogony is inextricably woven into the fabric of Hermetic tradition.

BIBLIOGRAPHY: Reinach, Textes (the basic source on the subject); Pauly-Wissowa; M. Radin, *The Jews Among the Greeks and Romans* (1915), 97ff.; O. Staehlin, in: W.V. Christ and W. Schmid, *Geschichte der griechischen Literatur*, 2, pt. 1 (1920[6]), 539ff.; I. Heinemann, in: Pauly-Wissowa, suppl. 5 (1931), 3–43; J. Lewy, *Olamot Nifgashim* (1960), 3–14; V. Tcherikover, *Hellenistic Civilization and the Jews* (1959), 287, 358ff.; M. Hadas, *Hellenistic Culture* (1959); F. Jacoby, *Die Fragmente der griechischen Historiker* (1958); S. Lieberman, *Greek in Jewish Palestine* (1942); E. Schwartz, *Griechische Geschichtschreiber* 1957), 36ff.; E. Gabba, *Appiano e la storia delle guerre civili* (1956); Y. Gutman, *Ha-Sifrut ha-Yehudit ha-Helenistit* (1958); L.G. Westerink (ed. and tr.), *Damascius, Lectures on the Philebus* (1959); W.N. Stearns (ed.), *Fragments from Graeco-Jewish Writers* (1908); B.Z. Wacholder, in: HTR, 61 (1968), 451–81, J.G. Gager, in: JTS, 20 (1969), 245–8 [on Helladius]. **ADD. BIBLIOGRAPHY:** M. Stern, *Greek and Latin Authors on Jews and Judaism*, 3 vols. (1974, 1980, 1984).

[Menahem Stern]

GREEK LITERATURE, MODERN. The literary image of the Jew was molded in Greece by the Jews themselves, by Greek non-Jews and, indirectly, by the Turks. In ancient Greece, Jews were referred to as a "community of philosophers." In the Hellenistic period there was some anti-Jewish writing; but, in the main, Jews and Greeks enjoyed a friendly cultural relationship (see *Hellenistic Jewish Literature; *Greek Literature, Ancient).

Influence of the Bible

Probably no work contributed more to the harmonious relationship between *Hellenism and Judaism than the *Septuagint. But in the *Byzantine Empire, fanatical rulers enacted anti-Jewish decrees which altered the image of the Jew and even threatened his survival, e.g., the anti-Jewish decrees of Constantine I, Novella 146 of *Justinian, as well as the anti-Jewish enactments of Basil I (867–886), as described in the *Chronicle* of *Ahimaaz b. Paltiel. The Greek Jews and the newly arrived Sephardi exiles from Spain, welcomed by Sultan Bajazet II, fared well under the *Ottoman Empire. Hebrew studies became popular and talmudic schools multiplied. Important achievements were an anonymous Polyglot Pentateuch (1547), the Book of Job (1576), and a medieval Greek translation of the Hebrew Bible in 1576 (see *Judeo-Greek). Jewish writing was revived again in the 18th and even more in the 19th centuries. Hebrew education was popularized in both synagogue and home by the Judeo-Greek translations. Among 20th-century Greek writers, G. Th. Vafopoulos wrote a tragedy based on the story of Esther (1934). Kosta Papapanayiotou published two dramas, one about Esther and the other about Rizpah, in 1963. Nikos Kazantzakis, in his *Sodhoma kye Ghomorra* (1956), relates the age of the Bible to the modern world which, in his view, has reverted to the corruption of the past. Despite his preference for the Old Testament over the New, Kazantzakis distorts rabbinic Judaism and the character of his own Jewish contemporaries. Ioanna Dhriva Maravelidhou, in her verse drama *Esther* (1967), pays homage to those Jews in the Persian Empire who were prepared for any sacrifice to preserve the idea of one God. In his book *Simon Bar Kochba*, published in 1966, Vassos Kaloyannis dealt with the epic Jewish struggle against Rome.

The Figure of the Jew in Modern Greek Literature

Contemporary prejudice marks the poetic "Story of the Little Jewess Marcada" (Venice, 1627), which tells of the heroine's abduction by her Christian lover and her subsequent apostasy. *I thisia tou Avraam* ("The Sacrifice of Abraham," 1696), a mystery play probably written in 1635 by the Cretan Kornaros (d. 1677), is the only masterpiece by a Greek of that time. The earliest surviving edition was printed in Venice in 1713. It may have been based on an earlier Italian drama and reveals both the influence of the Bible and a humanistic treatment of the Jew. In the *Thisia*, which continues to be revived in Greece almost annually and has been translated into all the major European languages, the author presents an anthropomorphic God and depicts Abraham not as a Hebrew patriarch but as a distraught father torn between love for his son and love of God.

For the next three centuries Greek writers devoted their efforts to liberating their country from the Turks. As a strategic measure against the revolutionary tide which finally led to the successful War of Greek Independence (1821–32), the Turks created a climate of covert hostility between Greek and Jew. It was not until almost all of Greece was liberated that a humanistic treatment of the Jew was again found in Greek literature. The novelist Gregorios Xenopoulos wrote a drama entitled *Rachel* (1909) on the expulsion of the Jews from Zante; Konstantinos Cavafy, the Alexandrian Greek poet, wrote a poem, in which he philosophized ironically on the dangers of Jewish assimilation; and Nikolaos D. Vizinos published several refutations of the *blood libel.

The one Greek writer to portray the Jew in universal terms was Nikos Kazantzakis who devotes a chapter to the Russian Jew in his travel book *Ti idha sti Rousia* ("What I Saw in Russia," 1928). Here he sees the Jew as a rebel and revolutionary by force of historical circumstance. In his autobiographical *Anafora ston Greko* (1961; *Report to Greco*, 1965) he shows profound sympathy for the suffering of the German Jewish students he met in Berlin. In Jerusalem, he longed not only for his own God but also for the Old Testament God, and he visited Mount Sinai to hear His voice as Moses heard it. Kazantzakis nevertheless remained bitterly opposed to Zionism, which he considered a reactionary delusion. Elsewhere, he showed admiration for Eliezer *Ben-Yehuda, the father of the Hebrew revival. In the novel with the Hebrew title *Todah Rabbah* (1934, English translation 1956), Kazantzakis portrays the Russian Jew as "one facet of a single consciousness that experienced and mirrored the complex, fluid, many-sided reality of the Soviet Union."

The playwright Spyros Melas turned to historical drama in *Judas*, first produced in Athens in 1934. In this play Judas is portrayed as a revolutionary leader who joins Jesus for the liberation of Judea. Manolis Georgiou Skoulidhis wrote *I ipothesis Dreyfus* ("The Dreyfus Case," 1960), in which he dramatized modern opinions about this famous trial. Pantelis Georgiou Prevelakyis, influenced by the ideology of his close friend Kazantzakis, wrote *O Lazaros* (1954), a drama in which he examined the attitude of an early Christian toward the new religion. A prose work by V. Ghazis on the Cain and Abel theme (1955) consists of seven allegorical accounts, the last of which predicts an eventual atomic war.

Several authors who were personally involved in World War II wrote works dealing with the Nazi occupation of Greece and their concentration camp experiences. One was Elias Venezis, whose play, *Block C*, was published in 1945. Venezis' novel *Okeanos* ("Ocean," 1956) gives a sympathetic portrait of a Jewish stowaway from Smyrna bound for the United States. Jacob Kampaneli, who spent the years 1943–45 in the Mauthausen concentration camp, wrote the first draft of a prose work on his experiences in 1947 and published a final version in 1965. His pro-Jewish sympathies are very evident, since after the liberation he remained in the camp until all the Jewish survivors who wished to had immigrated to Palestine. Other works on the concentration camp theme are the play *Epistrofi apo to Buchenwald* ("Return from Buchenwald," 1948) by Sotiris Patatzis and a long poem by Takis Olympios, *40382* (1965), inspired by the number branded on the arm of a girl who survived Auschwitz. A volume of poems by Sophia Mavroídhi Papadhaki (1905–), *To louloudhi tis tefras* ("The Flower of the Ashes," 1966), had its origin in a flower she saw growing among the ashes of Dachau. Papadhaki also wrote a life of David and short stories about Ruth and Jonah.

Vassos Kaloyannis was one of several non-Jewish authors to write about Jewish communities in Greece, which he did in his *Larissa, Madre d'Israel* ("Larissa, Mother of Israel," 1959). Demetrius Hatzis wrote about the Janina Jewish community in *I mikri mas polis* ("Our Small City") and the archimandrite Nikodemos Vafiadhis gave an account of the Jewish community of Didymotichon in his *I israilitikyi kyinotis Dhidhimotichou* (1954). The art critic Anghelos Georgios Procopiou, who spent a year in Israel, described his impressions of the country in his book *O Laos tis Vivlou* ("The People of the Bible"). The image of the Jew in Greek literature is still clearly identified with the history of Judaism and the Bible. In modern times, however, Greek authors are trying to create an emphatic, three-dimensional image of the Jew as a Greek citizen whose sufferings must not be forgotten. George Zoghrafakyis (1908–?), a non-Jewish writer from Salonika, who edited the works of Eliyia and published essays on modern Jewish figures such as *Herzl and *Agnon, should also be mentioned.

The Jewish Contribution to Greek Literature

Until World War II Salonika was the center of Greco-Jewish culture and Jewish authors wrote mainly in *Ladino, the language spoken by the majority of the Jewish community. Among the very few Jewish writers in Greek, who, between the two world wars, sought to interpret their background and traditions in terms of the contemporary world were the prominent journalist Moisis *Caïmis and the brilliant and prolific poet Joseph *Eliyia. After World War II Jewish writers in Greece showed a natural preoccupation with the tragic fate of their community during the Nazi occupation. J. Matarasso published the poignant *Kye omos oli tous dhen pethanan* ("Still They All have not Died," 1948); P. Chajidhimiou wrote a book of commemorative verse entitled *Bene Israel* (1957); and Joseph Matsas investigated the cultural achievements of the Jews in his native Janina. Although he wrote in French, Albert *Cohen, born in Corfu, used his native background as a setting for some of his novels.

Other Jewish writers returned to the path blazed earlier by Caïmis and Eliyia. They include the Zionist author Asher *Moissis; Raphael Konstantinis (1892–?), who edited two Jewish periodicals; Julius Caïmis; Joseph (Pepo) Sciaki; Baruch Schiby; and the outstandingly successful Nestoras *Matsas, who converted during World War II but retained a burning interest in his Jewish heritage and the tragedy of his people.

[Rachel Dalven]

The Jew in Modern Greek Literature

Frequent references are to be found in modern Greek literature to the Jewish people in general and more specifically to Greek Jews and the Holocaust. A number of the authors concerned emanate from or had close connections with Thessaloniki (Salonika) or Ioannina with their famed Jewish communities. The works are often inspired by personal experiences based on relations with Jewish friends annihilated in the Holocaust. Many of these appeared in the 1960s with the stimulation of public interest through the trial of the Nazi Dr. Merten in Greece and the *Eichmann trial in Israel.

Traditional Greek language and literature created a mass of negative stereotypes of the Jew, as found in proverbs, folksongs, and the shadow-theater. The figure of the Jew in this pre-modern literature has often no relation to reality. This has often passed into modern works. In the words of the outstanding writer Yiorgos Ioannou in 1979, "The still unstable modern Greek society does not even have the time and strength to collect its energy to combat the poisonous luxury of anti-semitism and racial discrimination."

However, other voices were heard also in the past. The national poet of Greece, Dionysios Solomos (1798–1857), published in 1822 a series of sonnets inspired by the Bible. In one of these he compared the revolutionary Greek nation to Zion reborn. The poet K.P. Kavafi (1863–1933) wrote two poems about the Jews of the Hellenistic period. In the poem "About the Jew – 50 B.C.E.," his protagonist is the imaginary Ianthis Antoniou who desires that "there always will be Jews, holy Jews." The second poem relates to Alexander Yannai and his wife, Hellenizing rulers of the Jewish state at the end of the Hasmonean era. Kostas Palamas (1852–1943) extravagantly praised the Zionist movement and was deeply impressed by Max Nordau. Alexander Papadiamantis (1851–1911) started from negative positions but revised his views, notably in his article "The Repercussion of Sense" where he reacted to the 1891 pogrom of the Jews in Corfu.

Of all the later writers, pride of place goes to Nikos Kazantzakis (1883–1957) who relates in his autobiography *Relation to Greco* that he persuaded his father to permit him to study Hebrew with the rabbi of Irakleon but was prevented due to the prejudices of the rest of his family. He also presents impressions of travelers from Jerusalem and Sinai who expound on the virtues of the Jewish people. In the memoirs of his mature age, he speaks of his bond with the German Jew, Rachel Lipstein, which is also indirectly reflected in his novels *Christ Recrucified* and *Captain Michael.*

Of later works, mention should be made of the fictional biography by M. Karagatsi (1908–1960) *King Laskos*, whose hero is in charge of a boatload of Jewish immigrants trying to beat the British blockade of Palestine, and the novel *Sergio and Bacchante* which pays tribute to the role of Jews in modern civilization. Ilia Venezi (1904–1973) wrote travel impressions from modern Israel as well as stories against the background of the 1948 Arab-Israel War. Yianni Berati (1904–1968) in his book *The Wide River* writes of the heroism of the Greek Jewish soldiers in the Greco-Italian War of 1940. Dimitri Yatha (1907–1979), the leading theatrical author, writer, and humorist, describes his recollections of a Jewish family of bankers in his *The Land of the Sea.* Strati Mirivili (1892–1963) also refers to Jewish soldiers in the anti-war chronicle *Life in a Grave.* Kosma Politi (1893–1974) preserved aspects of the Jewish community of Izmir in his book *To a Western European Pilgrim.* Dimitri Hatzi (1914–1981) described the Jewish community of Ionnina in his story "Shabetai Kabilli" in his book *The End of our Small City*, and Toli Kazantzi in his narrations sketches the coexistence of Greeks and Jews in pre-War Salonika.

A body of poetic work has been inspired by the Holocaust. Among the poets mention should be made of Manoli Anagnostaki (b. 1925), Taki Barvitsioti (b. 1916), Nino Kokkalidou-Nahmia (b. 1922), I.A. Nikolaidi (b. 1936), Marino Charalambous (b. 1937), Dino Christianopoulo (b. 1931), Yiorgos Ioannou (1927–1985), G. Th. Vafopoulou (b. 1903), the surrealistic Niko Engonopoulo (1910–1986), George Kaftantzi (b. 1920), Prodromo Markoglou (b. 1935), and Kimona Tzalla (1917–1988). Outstanding is the poem of Zoe Karelli (b. 1901), "Israel," which harks back to the sufferings of the Jews in biblical times and links them with the tragic fate of the Jews of Salonika. She seeks the causes of antisemitism and of the Holocaust, showing the common element throughout history, and also shows how Jews always maintained a discreet strength in their resistance to persecutions.

Among prose writers who have been affected by the Holocaust are G. Th. Vafopoulouy in his *Pages of Autobiographies*; Ilia Venezi (1904–1973) in the fictionalized biography *Archbishop Damaskinos*; the diary of Iakavou Kampanelli (b. 1922) *Mauthausen*; the tender novel *Tziokonta* of Nikou Kokantzi (b. 1927); Nikou Bakala (b. 1927) in his novel *The Big Square* and works by Vasili Vasilikou (b. 1934), Georgou Theotoka (1905–1966), Yianni Lambrinou (1909–1949), Nestoria Matsa (b. 1932), Kostoulas Mitropoulou (b. 1940), I.M. Papagiotopoulou (1901–1981), Yianni Starki (1919–1987), and Friksou Tzioba (b. 1919).

The major author who wrote of the Holocaust of Salonika Jewry is Yiorgos Ioannou. In his poems "Iliotropia" (1954) and "The Thousand Trees" (1963), he describes the last night of a Jewish family who lived in a nearby apartment and of his grief over their unbelievable disappearance. His book *For the Honor* (1964) describes the leveling of the old Jewish cemetery of Salonika. In *The Sarcophagus* (1971), *Our Own Blood* (1978), and *The Capital of the Refugees* (1984), he wonders at the persecution of the Jews in his neighborhood which culminated in the pillage of their homes and the testimony of his own father, a railroad worker, who experienced at first hand the songs sung on the journeys to the death camps from inside the sealed animal wagons.

All these works face the Jews with reverence and treat their suffering with the utmost respect and sympathy, emanating from the recognition of a longtime harmonious symbiosis.

[Albert Nar]

Noted Gentile Greek authors who wrote about Greek Jewry include Lily Zografos, who focuses on Jews in the Holocaust in *I Evrai Kapote* (*Mikael*) ("The Jews Once, Mikael," 1966) and elsewhere in *Antignosi, Ta thekanikia tou kapitalismou* ("Bad Sense, The Crutches of Capitalism," 1974); Yiorgos Zografakis, who published biographies of the military war hero Colonel Mordechai Frizis or the early 20th century Ioanniote poet and author Josep Eliyia; Dimitri Hatzi, who in the form of short stories colorfully depicted Ioanniote Jewry in the early 20th century several decades before its destruction in the Holocaust; or the literature professor Frangiski Ambatzopolou who wrote about Greek Jewish Holocaust survivors in modern Greek literature, *I Logotechnia Os Martitiria, Ellines Pezografi Yia to Yenoktonia Ton Evraion, Anthologia* ("The Literature of Testimonies, Greek Prose Writers on Horrific Events of the Jews, Anthology," 1995), and translated into Greek testimonies of Greek Holocaust survivors published in Hebrew in Israel and added a few testimonies of remaining survivors in Salonika.

Several Greek Jews can be included among popular Greek authors.

Nestoras *Matsas wrote a biography of Alexander the Great, *To Hirografo Tis Babilonas, Megalexandro Apomnimonevmata* ("The Manuscript of Babylon, the Memoirs of Alexander the Great," 1980), and about his experience hiding as a young boy in Athens during World War II in *Avto to paidi pethane avrio, Imerologio Katochis* ("That Boy Died Tomorrow, A Diary of the Occupation," 1987), and in *I Istoria Ton Hamenon Peristerion: Imerogio Enos Paidou Ston Emfilio* ("The History of the Lost Pigeon: Diary of a Boy in the Civil War," 1995). Michel Feis, born to a Jewish father in Cuomotini in 1957, wrote fictional accounts of Jewish life in Cuomotini through the centuries and generations, and published *Avtobiografia, enos vivliou, Mithistorima* ("The Autobiography of a Book, A Novel," 1995). He also wrote a book of short stories called *From the Same Glass and Other Stories* (1999), which won the State Short Story Award in 2000, and two works on Giulio Caimi, a Jewish artist: *Greek Landscapes* (1993) and *Giulio Caimi, A Man Suppressed. Recollections and Criticism. Selected Articles (1928–1976)*. Nina Kokkalidou-Nachmia has written over a dozen books since 1970 including the novel *Tilefoniko Kentro* ("Telephone Center," 1972), the children's book *Ti nea, kirie Gate* ("What's New, Sir Cat," 1984), *Otan I Ellines Iortazoun* ("When Greeks Celebrate," 1995), and *Palia Thessaloniki Kai Istoriki Diadromi Tis D.E.Th. 1926–1989* ("Old Thessaloniki and Historical Journey of the Municipality of Thessaloniki 1926–1989," 1996), which depicts the Old Salonika and its Jews, musicians, and modern postwar life. She also wrote a moving book related to the Holocaust entitled *Reina Zilberta, ena paidi sto geto tis Thessalonikis* ("Reina Zilberta, a Girl in the Ghetto of Thessaloniki," 1996).

[Yitzchak Kerem (2nd ed.)]

GREEN, ABEL (1900–1973), U.S. theatrical journalist, editor of *Variety*, the chief theatrical paper in the U.S. While at New York University, Green wrote theatrical interviews for the New York *Sunday World*. *Variety* was founded by Sime Silverman in 1905 and Green succeeded him as editor in 1933. A chronicler of theatrical news, Green added to English theatrical slang with coinages which he called "un-King's English." A shrewd critic, Green once capsuled a film review with the succinct phrase, "It went in one eye and out the other." He was the author of *Mr. Broadway*, a film script of *Variety's* founder-editor; coauthor with Joe Laurie, Jr. of *Show Biz from Vaude to Video* (1952); and editor of *Variety Music Cavalcade* (1952) and *The Spice of Variety* (1953).

[Jo Ranson]

GREEN, ADOLPH (1915–2002), U.S. theatrical writer. Born in the Bronx, New York, Green was educated at the City College of New York. He worked as a lyricist on many Broadway musicals. Among them were *On the Town* (and book, 1946); *Two on the Aisle* (1952); *Wonderful Town* (1953); *Peter Pan* (1954); *Bells Are Ringing* (and book, 1956); *Do Re Mi* (1960); *Subways Are for Sleeping* (and book, 1961); *A Doll's Life* (and book, 1982); *Singin' in the Rain*; (1985); and *The Will Rogers Follies* (1991). His main collaborator in lyrics, libretto, and screenplay work was Betty *Comden. His chief musical collaborators included Leonard *Bernstein, Jule *Styne, Andre *Previn, and Morton *Gould.

In the world of film, Green wrote the screenplay for such films as *Good News* (1947); *The Barkleys of Broadway* (1949); *On the Town* (1949); *Singin' in the Rain* (1952); *The Band Wagon* (1953); *It's Always Fair Weather* (1955); *Auntie Mame* (1958); *Bells Are Ringing* (1960); *What a Way to Go* (1964); and the TV movie *Applause* (1973).

Some of Green's best-known songs are "New York, New York," "The Party's Over," "Just in Time," "Make Someone Happy," "I Get Carried Away," "Lonely Town," "Lucky to Be Me," "Ohio," "Long Before I Knew You," "Something's Always Happening on the River," "Comes Once in a Lifetime," and "I'm Just Taking My Time."

In 1991 he won a Tony Award for Best Original Score for the Broadway musical *The Will Rogers Follies*. In 2001 the Writers Guild of America awarded Green and Comden the Laurel Award for Screen Writing Achievement. From 1960 Green was married to actress Phyllis Newman.

BIBLIOGRAPHY: A. Robinson, *Betty Comden and Adolph Green: A Bio-Bibliography* (1993).

[Ruth Beloff (2nd ed.)]

GREEN, ARTHUR (1941–), U.S. scholar, theologian, and rabbi. Born in Paterson, N.J., Green grew up in Newark. Raised in a non-observant Jewish home, he was educated as a child in public schools, a Conservative Hebrew school, and Camp Ramah.

After completing a B.A. at Brandeis University in 1961, Green trained for the rabbinate at the Jewish Theological Seminary (JTS) in New York. There, he was a close student of Abraham Joshua Heschel. Upon ordination from JTS in 1967 Green began doctoral studies at Brandeis under the direction of Alexander Altmann. The following year he co-founded *Havurat Shalom* in Somerville, Mass., a new informal religious community that wove together the insights of Jewish mysticism, Neo-Ḥasidism, and American counterculture. *Havurat Shalom* helped birth the national Ḥavurah and Jewish Renewal movements.

Green established himself as an academic with the publication of *Tormented Master: A Life of Rabbi Nahman of Bratslav* (1979). Widely read by scholars and general readers in the United States and Israel, it appeared in Hebrew translation in 1980. Green's other academic contributions include several essays and monographs on ḥasidic leadership and the history of kabbalistic symbolism, including *Keter: The Crown of God in Early Jewish Mysticism* (1997). Green has also translated several classical ḥasidic texts, including *The Language of Truth: The Torah Commentary of the Sefat Emet* (1998).

Green left *Havurat Shalom* in 1973 to join the department of religion at the University of Pennsylvania, where he remained for a decade. In 1984 he became dean and then president of the Reconstructionist Rabbinical College (RRC) in Philadelphia. Green's move to the RRC is indicative of his dual interests in academic and rabbinic education and his desire to serve as both a scholar and a religious leader. It was while at the RRC that Green wrote his major theological work, *Seek My Face, Speak My Name: A Contemporary Jewish Theology* (1992), a text that draws on an array of Jewish mystical sources in the construction of a modern Jewish spiritual vision. Green helped introduce a new appreciation for Jewish spirituality at the RRC, an institution founded upon Mordecai Kaplan's rationalistic program.

In 1990 Green left the RRC because of ongoing tensions with older Kaplan loyalists who were uncomfortable with his religious views, and because of his dissatisfaction with fundraising and administrative responsibilities. The following year Green returned to his alma mater, Brandeis University, assuming the Philip W. Lown Chair in Jewish thought, a position once held by his doctoral advisor, Alexander Altmann. In 2004 Green published *Eheyeh: A Kabbalah for Tomorrow*, an introduction to and contemporary interpretation of Kabbalah.

In 2004 Green was named founding dean of the Rabbinical School of Hebrew College in Newton, Mass. The Hebrew College Rabbinical School is a pluralistic Jewish seminary without any denominational affiliation. Green's turn to transdenominational rabbinic education represented the fulfillment of a dream from his time in *Havurat Shalom*, which he originally envisioned as a seminary/community. In 2005, Green retired from Brandeis to devote himself to the development of the Rabbinical School.

[Or N. Rose (2nd ed.)]

GREEN, DAVID EZRA (1910–1983), U.S. biochemist. Green was born in New York. He obtained a master's degree in biology (1932) from New York University, followed by a Ph.D. in biochemistry at Cambridge University, England (1934), before leaving for Harvard University Medical School (1940). He moved to Columbia University School of Medicine in New York (1941) until his appointment as professor and co-director of the Institute for Enzyme Research at the University of Wisconsin in Madison (1948), where he worked until his death. His lifelong interest in enzymes was stimulated in Cambridge. His major research achievement was to develop techniques for isolating and characterizing single enzymes initially, which contributed enormously to the characterization of multi-enzyme pathways and particularly those involved in fatty acid oxidation. In addition to his prodigious personal creativity, he directed highly successful programs which launched the careers of many young biochemists who achieved prominence in biochemistry. His honors included the first Paul-Lewis Award in Enzyme Chemistry (1946) and election to the National Academy of Sciences (1962).

[Michael Denman (2nd ed.)]

GREEN, GERALD (1922–2006), U.S. screenwriter, producer, author, and radio director. Three of Green's novels, *The Last Angry Man* (1956), *To Brooklyn with Love* (1967), and *The Brooklyn Boy* (1968), recreate life in New York City as remembered, stretching back to the 1930s. In *The Legion of Noble Christians* (1965), he satirized fanatical anti-Communism within a fictional framework of Christian efforts to save Jews during the Hitler era. Green also wrote *The Lotus Eaters* (1959), *The Heartless Light* (1961), *The Artists of Terezin* (1969), and *The Stones of Zion: A Novelist's Journal in Israel* (1971). He worked for NBC as a writer, director, and producer. Among his better-known screenplays are *The Last Angry Man* (1959; television, 1974) and *Holocaust*, a television miniseries (1978). In 1980 Green was awarded the Belgium Prix International Dag Hammerskjold for his novel *Holocaust* (1978) and his other literary work.

[Lewis Fried (2nd ed.)]

GREEN, PHILIP (1952–), British businessman. Born in London, the son of a property investor who died when he was 12, Green left school at 16 and worked for a shoe importer before starting a company which imported jeans from the Far East. Over a period of 20 years, starting in the mid-1980s, he built up one of greatest of contemporary British retailing fortunes. In the late 1990s he bought British Home Stores (BHS), a High Street retailing fixture with hundreds of branches, vastly increasing its profitability by a combination of hands-on direct management of all phases of BHS's operations and such counterintuitive means as not advertising. Green expanded his retailing empire to include such retailing giants as Arcadia, Top Shop, and Dorothy Perkins, although bids by him to purchase Safeway (2003) and Marks & Spencer (2005) were not successful. Green, who has lived in Monaco in recent years, was ranked in 2005 as Britain's fifth wealthiest man, worth £4.85 billion,.

[William D. Rubinstein (2nd ed.)]

GREEN, SHAWN DAVID (1972–), U.S. baseball player. Born in Des Plaines, Illinois to Ira and Judy, Green grew up in a non-practicing family in Tustin, California, did not attend Hebrew school, and did not have a bar mitzvah, but Green became a highly visible symbol for the Jewish community throughout his career. Green's father, a gym coach who later became the owner of a baseball training facility, worked closely with him to improve his baseball skills, and he became a standout player at Tustin High School. He made his Major League debut on September 28, 1993, and came up from the minors to stay in 1995. In 1998 Green became the first Jew to hit 30 home runs and steal 30 bases in one season. On May 23, 2002, Green had the most productive day in baseball history with the 19 total bases, hitting four home runs, a double and a single. The next day Green homered and singled, tying a two-game record with five HRs and 25 total bases. The following day Green hit two more HRs, and the seven home runs in three games was also a record. He had his best season in 2001, batting .297 with 49 HRs, 125 RBIs, and 20 SBs. He was voted to the All-Star team in 1999 and 2002, and won a Gold Glove Award in 1999. In 2005, Green hit his 300th career HR, the second Jew to ever do so.

Green was the most visible Jewish player during his career, in part because of his status as the best Jewish player of his generation. After the 1999 season with Toronto, he asked to be traded to a team in a city with a large Jewish population, and was sent to Los Angeles. In 2001, in the midst of a pennant race, Green opted not to play on Yom Kippur – while the other Jewish players did – which made news as it voluntarily stopped his 415 consecutive-game streak. Three years later, Green again made headlines when faced once more with a decision whether to play on Yom Kippur, in the midst of a crucial series in a late-season pennant race. This time he had games on Yom Kippur night and the following day, and decided to split the day, opting to play Kol Nidrei night but not the following afternoon. Green hit the game-winning home run that night, but the issue and his split decision was debated across the country, with many praising him for honoring the holiday and others criticizing him for his not fully observing Yom Kippur.

"Everyone approaches their worship in their own way and goes about it differently," Green said. "I'm not Orthodox. I am Jewish and I respect the customs, and I feel like this is the most consistent way for me to celebrate the holiday. I feel real good about my decision."

[Elli Wohlgelernter (2nd ed.)]

GREENACRE, PHYLLIS (1894–1989), U.S. psychiatrist. Greenacre, who was born in Chicago, received a B.S. from the University of Chicago in 1913, and graduated from Rush Medical College in 1916. She was appointed clinical professor of psychiatry at Cornell University Medical College in 1935. In 1942 she joined the faculty of the New York Psychoanalytic Institute and was its president from 1948 to 1950. She served as president of the New York Psychoanalytic Society from 1956 to 1957. She was also vice president, and later honorary vice president, of the International Psychoanalytical Association. She served on the editorial board of the influential annual *The Psychoanalytic Study of the Child*, from its inception in 1945.

One of her main interests was the subject of anxiety. In 1941 she published a paper in which she sought the roots of anxiety in the birth trauma of the fetus, as revealed in the newborn child and in the memory traces of the adult patient in psychoanalysis. Birth, with its enormous sensory stimulation after the relaxed fetal state, in her view, produced a strong narcissistic drive and a defensive organization of anxiety in the infant. Her book *Trauma, Growth and Personality* was published in 1952.

A further focus of Greenacre's interest was the sexual anomaly of fetishism. She stressed the magical value represented by the fetish in early life as a result of disturbed mother-child relationships. She wrote, too, on identity and its relation to body image, stressing the role of visual perception and perceptual distortion in the fetish image of the genitals and face. In 1953 she edited *Affective Disorders*. Her analysis of the creative personality and imagination was set out in her study of two lives, *Swift and Carroll* (1955). Her other publications include *The Quest for the Father: A Study of the Darwin-Butler Controversy as a Contribution to the Understanding of the Creative Individual* (1963); and *Emotional Growth: Psychoanalytic Studies of the Gifted and a Great Variety of Other Individuals* (1971).

BIBLIOGRAPHY: A. Grinstein, *Index of Psychoanalytic Writings*, 2 (1957), 6 (1964).

[Louis Miller / Ruth Beloff (2nd ed.)]

GREENBAUM, EDWARD SAMUEL (1890–1970), U.S. lawyer, soldier, and public servant. Greenbaum was born in New York, the son of Samuel, a Supreme Court Justice in New York, and Selina, president of the Jewish Working Girls Vacation Society. He entered law practice in 1915. A skillful attorney, Greenbaum dealt with diverse legal problems, and his clients included prominent public personalities. Greenbaum's public service career began in the 1920s when he participated in a study of U.S. legal practice. Reform of the courts became a lifelong interest: as a member of the Judicial Conference of the State of New York, he was a key campaigner for reorganization of the New York court system, finally achieved in 1960–61. Greenbaum enlisted in the army in World War I, retiring at its end as a major. Returning to active duty in 1940, he rose to brigadier general. During World War II he was a principal aide to the secretary of war and played a leading role in establishing War Department labor policy, for which he was awarded the Distinguished Service Medal in 1945. Public positions he held include Alcohol Control Commission chairman (1933); special assistant to the attorney general's office (1934–38); Long Island Railroad Commission counsel (1938); and alternate delegate to the United Nations (1957). He helped found the Jewish Big Brothers Organization; served on the executive committee of the Jewish Welfare Board, Armed Services Division; and was active on the American Jewish Committee and the Jewish Board of Guardians. He served as trustee of the Institute for Advanced Studies at Princeton. Greenbaum coauthored *King's Bench Masters*, a study of British pretrial practice (1932), and wrote an autobiography, *Lawyer's Job* (1967).

[Barton G. Lee]

GREENBERG, CLEMENT (1909–1994), U.S. art critic. After studying at the Art Students League (1924–25) and receiving a B.A. from Syracuse University (1930), Greenberg began contributing articles on art, literature, and politics to the left-wing journal *Partisan Review*, where he served as editor in 1940–42. Among other venues, his articles appeared in *The Nation*, a magazine for which he was the regular art critic (1942–49); *Contemporary Jewish Record*, where he served as managing editor from June 1944 until the final issue in June 1945; and *Commentary*, where he was associate editor (1945–57).

Greenberg was one of the most influential art critics of the 1950s and 1960s. Along with critic Harold *Rosenberg, Greenberg championed Abstract Expressionism. In particular, Greenberg was pivotal in the ascent of Jackson Pollock. After early consideration of social factors in his pivotal *Partisan*

Review article "Avant-Garde and Kitsch" (1939), Greenberg's formalist and often polemical mode of art analysis mostly ignored contextual considerations, a position largely rejected by subsequent art critics.

In addition to writing on Jewish themes and subjects, Greenberg also wrote about or discussed his own Jewish identity. In a 1944 contribution to a symposium on Jewish American literature Greenberg commented that he "has no more of a conscious position towards his Jewish heritage than the average American Jew – which is to say, hardly any." Unconsciously, however, Greenberg believed that "a quality of Jewishness is present in every word I write."

Along with his book *Art and Culture: Critical Essays* (1961), which includes "Avant-Garde and Kitsch," Greenberg wrote the monographs *Joan Miró* (1948), *Matisse* (1953), and *Hans Hoffman* (1961). His collected essays were published in four volumes (1986–93).

BIBLIOGRAPHY: D.B. Kuspit, *Clement Greenberg: Art Critic* (1979); J. O'Brien (ed.), *Clement Greenberg: The Collected Essays and Criticism*, 4 vols. (1986–93); F. Rubenfeld, *Clement Greenberg: A Life* (1997).

[Samantha Baskind (2nd ed.)]

GREENBERG, DAVID MORRIS (1895–1988), U.S. biochemist. Greenberg was born in Boston, obtained his doctorate at the University of California in 1924, and became professor of biochemistry at Berkeley in 1941. On his retirement in 1963, he worked as a research biochemist at the Oncologic Institute, University of California Medical School in San Francisco and played a key role in the development of biochemistry on the campus. He contributed broadly to studies on mineral metabolism, enzyme chemistry, and cancer research. Greenberg served on the U.S. Atomic Energy Commission and on the isotopes panel of the National Research Council. He was editor of the *Proceedings of the Society of Experimental Biology and Medicine*, and served as chairman of the California section of this society. Greenberg was a pioneer in the use of radioisotopes for biochemical investigations. He wrote *Aminoacids and Proteins* (1951), *Chemical Pathways of Metabolism* (1954), and *Metabolic Pathways* (1960). He published more than 400 scientific articles.

[Samuel Aaron Miller / Bracha Rager (2nd ed.)]

GREENBERG, ELIEZER (1896–1977), Yiddish poet and literary critic. Born in Bessarabia, at an early age he was influenced by the poets Eliezer *Steinbarg, Jacob *Sternberg, and Moshe *Altman, who were pioneers of Hebrew and Yiddish literature, and, later, by American English modernist poetry. In 1913, at the age of 17, Greenberg immigrated to the U.S., but impressions of his native town enriched his poetry throughout his life. His lyrics and essays began to appear in Yiddish periodicals and anthologies in 1919. He studied at the University of Michigan, before settling in New York. Together with Elihu Shulman, he edited *Getseltn* ("Tents," 1945–48), a periodical of verse and literary criticism. He and Irving *Howe edited important anthologies of translations from Yiddish into English: *A Treasury of Yiddish Stories* (1954), *Five Yiddish Poets* (1962), *A Treasury of Yiddish Poetry* (1969), *Voices From the Yiddish* (1972), *Yiddish Stories Old and New* (1974), *Selected Stories of I.L. Peretz* (1974), and *Ashes Out of Hope* (1977). His first volume of poetry, *Gasn un Evenyus* ("Streets and Avenues," 1928), portrays New York as the symbol of the modern ambition. It was followed by *Fun Umetum* ("From Everywhere," 1934), *Fisherdorf* ("Fishing Village," 1938), *Di Lange Nakht* ("The Long Night," 1946), "Baynakhtiker Dialog" ("Night Dialogue"), *Eybiker Dorsht* ("Eternal Thirst," 1968), and *Gedenkshaft* ("Memorabilia," 1974). The depression of the 1930s led to a more social proletarian tone in his poems. In the 1940s his verses became angrier and more despairing in response to unfolding events in Europe, later returning to calmer tones. As a critic, Greenberg wrote primarily about modernist Yiddish poets, including studies of Moyshe-Leyb *Halpern, H. *Leivick, and Jacob *Glatstein.

BIBLIOGRAPHY: LNYL, 2 (1958), 391–2; J. Glatstein, *In Tokh Genumen* (1956), 323–8; S. Bickel *Shrayber fun Mayn Dor* (1958), 144–7; S.D. Singer, *Dikhter un Prozaiker* (1959), 109–12. **ADD. BIBLIOGRAPHY:** "A Greenberg Portfolio," in: *Yiddish*, 3 (1978), 48–53.

[Sol Liptzin / Anita Norich (2nd ed.)]

GREENBERG, HAYIM (1889–1953), Zionist leader, essayist, and editor. Greenberg, born in the Bessarabian village of Todoristi in Russia, joined the Zionist movement while still a youngster and attracted immediate notice as a self-taught intellectual prodigy. In 1904 he attended the Zionist Congress in Helsinki as a correspondent, and while still in his teens moved to Odessa, where he emerged before long as a leading figure in Hebrew and Zionist letters, excelling as both an orator and an essayist on philosophical and political themes. With the outbreak of World War I, Greenberg moved to Moscow, where he edited the Russian-Jewish weekly *Razsvet* ("The Dawn"). After the Russian Revolution he served for a while as an instructor in medieval Jewish literature at the University of Kharkov and lectured at Kiev Academy. Arrested several times for Zionist activities by the Communist authorities, he left for Berlin in 1921, where he edited *Haolam* ("The World"), the official weekly of the World Zionist Organization.

Greenberg immigrated to the U.S. in 1924 to become editor of the Yiddish Zionist publication *Farn Folk* ("For the People"), which later became *Der *Yidisher Kempfer* ("The Jewish Warrior"), and in 1934 became editor of the Labor Zionist monthly *The Jewish Frontier*. From 1934 he was a permanent member of the Central Committee of the Labor Zionist Organization of America. During World War II he served as head of the American Zionist Emergency Council, and in 1946 he was appointed director of the Department of Education and Culture of the Jewish Agency Executive in America. Greenberg's influence on Zionist activities during these years was great. Particularly noteworthy were his accomplishments in winning the votes of several Latin-American delegations at the United Nations for the creation of a Jewish State, and later in helping to forge strong cultural ties between the new State of Israel and Jews the world over.

As an essayist in three languages, Yiddish, Hebrew, and English, Greenberg was distinguished by his breadth of knowledge, urbanity of approach, and deep moral earnestness. The core of his writings was devoted to expounding the philosophy of Zionism and attempting to demonstrate its consistency with the ideals of socialism, pacifism, and universalism to which he adhered. Collections of his essays have appeared in several volumes in Yiddish and in English, including: *The Inner Eye* (2 vols., 1953–64); *Yid un Velt* (1953); *Beytlakh fun a Tog-Bukh* (1954); *Mentshn un Vertn* (1954); and *Hayim Greenberg Anthology* (1968).

BIBLIOGRAPHY: Gordis, in: *Judaism*, 2 (1953), 99–100; LNYL, 2 (1958), 398–404; Kressel, Leksikon, 1 (1965), 509–10; S. Bickel, *Shreiber fun Mayn Dor* (1958), 256–66.

[Hillel Halkin]

GREENBERG, HENRY BENJAMIN (**"Hammerin' Hank"**; 1911–1986), U.S. baseball player, first Jewish sports superstar, first Jew inducted into the Hall of Fame. Greenberg was born in Greenwich Village, New York, the third of four children, to Orthodox Romanian immigrants Sarah (Schwartz) and David, who owned a textile factory. The family moved to the Bronx, kept a kosher home, and sent Greenberg to Hebrew school, but young Henry just wanted to play sports. He became an outstanding athlete in baseball, basketball, and soccer at James Monroe High School, leading the basketball team to a New York City title in 1929.

After graduation from high school in 1929, Greenberg signed with the Detroit Tigers, and played one game for them in 1930. He then played three seasons in the minors. At Raleigh, North Carolina, one of his teammates walked slowly around Greenberg staring at him, saying he had never seen a Jew before. "The way he said it, he might as well have said, 'I've never seen a giraffe before,'" said Greenberg. "I let him keep looking for a while, and then I said, 'See anything interesting?' "

Greenberg, a strong physical presence at 6′ 4″ and 215 pounds, joined the Tigers permanently in 1933. In 1934 he hit .339, and drove in 139 runs to lead Detroit to its first pennant since 1909, but not without some fanfare: Rosh Hashanah that year fell on September 10, in the middle of the pennant race. Greenberg, in a quandary whether to play, consulted a rabbi, who told him it was permissible. He hit two homers that day to win the game 2–1, and the next day the *Detroit Free Press* printed Greenberg's picture with Happy New Year in Hebrew captioned above the photo. However, Greenberg did not play on Yom Kippur, receiving instead a standing ovation when he showed up in synagogue.

Greenberg's Rosh Hashanah-Yom Kippur decisions stirred intense interest in the Jewish community, where second-generation Jews saw in Greenberg's refusal to play on Yom Kippur an example of how to balance loyalty to religion and tradition with the need to integrate fully in American life. Greenberg's resolution was echoed 31 years later, when Sandy *Koufax refused to play Yom Kippur in the first game of the World Series.

In 1935 Greenberg again helped guide the Tigers to the pennant, and a World Series win over the Chicago Cubs despite breaking his wrist in the second game. He led the league in RBI's, a statistic he valued above all others, with 170, and was named MVP. In 1936 Greenberg broke his left wrist again in the 12th game of the season, and sat out the remainder of the year. Well rested, he came back in 1937 to lead the league again in RBIs with 183, one shy of the American League record held by Lou Gehrig. It was Greenberg's biggest regret that he failed to break that record, more than Babe Ruth's record of 60 home runs that he chased the following season. Greenberg had 58 with five games left in 1938, and some claimed opponents prevented him from setting the record because of anti-Jewish sentiment, but Greenberg dismissed the notion as "crazy stories." He did, however, face constant reminders throughout his career from fans and other players on his ethnic background. "How the hell could you get up to home plate every day and have some son-of-a-bitch call you a Jew bastard and a kike and a sheenie and get on your ass without feeling the pressure?" he said. "If the ballplayers weren't doing it, the fans were. I used to get frustrated as hell. Sometimes I wanted to go into the stands and beat the shit out of them."

The following season Greenberg was moved to left field, and his hard work to master the position – and his ever-powerful bat – resulted in a second MVP, one of only three players to win MVP's at two different positions. He again took the Tigers to the American League pennant, slugging 41 homers and driving in 150 runs.

Greenberg was drafted into the army 19 games into the 1941 season, and missed the rest of that year and the next three and a half seasons. When Pearl Harbor was bombed two days after he was discharged, Greenberg immediately volunteered for more duty, and rose to the rank of captain serving in the Far East. Greenberg returned in the middle of the 1945 season and again led Detroit to the pennant, clinching it with a grand slam in the top of the 9th inning of the last game of the season. "The best part of that homer was hearing how the Washington Senators players responded," said Greenberg. "'Goddamn that dirty Jew bastard, he beat us again.'" His seven hits in the World Series helped the Tigers again beat the Cubs for the world championship. Greenberg returned to first base in 1946, and led the league with 44 HRs and 127 RBIs.

Greenberg played his final year for the Pittsburgh Pirates in 1947, the year Jackie Robinson became the first black to play baseball. Greenberg remembered the taunts he had to endure himself over the course of his career. Standing together at first base one game, Robinson recalled later, Greenberg "suddenly turned to me and said, 'A lot of people are pulling for you to make good. Don't ever forget it.' I never did."

Upon retiring Greenberg became a baseball executive, first as farm system director and general manager with the

Cleveland Indians, and then as part owner and vice president of the Chicago White Sox.

Despite his lost years to the war, Greenberg remains high on the career list of achievement nearly six decades after retiring: The five-time All-Star batted .313, with 331 home runs and 1,276 RBIs in 1,394 games. His .605 slugging percentage is sixth all-time, and his rate of .915 RBIs per game is third-best all time. Greenberg was the subject of a documentary, *The Life and Times of Hank Greenberg* (1998), and author of an autobiography, *The Story of My Life* (1989), with Ira Berkow. Greenberg was inducted into the Hall of Fame in 1956.

[Elli Wohlgelernter (2nd ed.)]

GREENBERG, IRVING (**Yitz**; 1933–), U.S. rabbi, author, and educator. Born in 1933 in Brooklyn, New York, Greenberg attended Yeshiva High School in Brooklyn and from there he attended the Yeshiva Bais Yosef, from which he received ordination as an Orthodox rabbi in 1953. At the same time he attended Brooklyn College, where he received a B.A. in history. He went on to obtain his M.A. and Ph.D. in American history from Harvard University. In 1959 he began teaching American history at Yeshiva University where he was among the first to introduce the teaching of Holocaust studies into a university curriculum. From 1965 to 1972 he was the communal rabbi of the Riverdale Jewish Center while he also taught at CCNY (1965–72). Shortly thereafter, he founded the organization that would later come to be known as the National Jewish Center for Learning and Leadership and served as its director from 1974 to 1997.

In 1975, along with Elie Wiesel, Greenberg founded the Holocaust memorial organization Zachor. In 1979 he was invited to serve as director of the President's Commission on the Holocaust and participated in the development of the initial recommendations for a center that later became the United States Holocaust Memorial Musuem. Twenty years later, from 2000 to 2002, he served as chairman of the museum's governing body, although his tenure was marred by controversy and internal dissension. From 1998 he also served as president of Jewish Life Network/Steinhardt Foundation, whose aim is to create and enrich the cultural and institutional life of American Jewry.

Rabbi Greenberg's thoughts and ideas have been disseminated through four decades of teaching and writing often in pamphlets and other popular articles. He has lectured in every American city with a fair-sized Jewish community and published his work in almost all major Jewish publications. He is the co-editor of a pioneering work, *Confronting the Holocaust*. Greenberg is also the author of *The Jewish Way: Living the Holidays* (1988) and *Living the Image of God: Jewish Teachings to Perfect the World* (1998), which presents his teachings on a wide range of subjects, including those central to his redemptive covenant theology.

Greenberg writes of the shattering of the covenant in the Holocaust. Following Elie Wiesel and Jacob Gladstein, he suggests a deep theological humility: "No statement, theological or otherwise, should be made that would not be credible in the presence of burning children." He states that the authority of the covenant was broken in the Holocaust, but the Jewish people, released from its obligations, chose voluntarily to renew it again. Greenberg writes, "We are in the age of the renewal of the covenant. God is no longer in a position to command, but the Jewish people are so in love with the dream of redemption that it volunteered to carry out the mission."

Greenberg is known for his thoughts on the issue of pluralism in Jewish life. His widely publicized essay "Will There Be One Jewish People in the Year 2000?" catapulted the issue of Jewish unity to the forefront of American Jewish concerns. He has often been accused of being the Conservative and Reform's Orthodox rabbi. A strong proponent of "centrist Orthodoxy" Greenberg has labored against its weakening from radical shifts, left and right. He has been a strong advocate of Orthodox Jews' full participation in American national life, seeking a synthesis between traditional Judaism and modernity. And as a strong champion of interfaith dialogue he has for four decades campaigned for Jewish and Christian reconciliation.

[Shalom Freedman and Michael Berenbaum (2nd ed.)]

GREENBERG, JOANNE (1932–), U.S. novelist. *The King's Persons* (1963) was a picture of Jewish life in medieval England. Her other works include *I Never Promised You a Rose Garden* (1964), written under the pseudonym Hannah Green; *The Monday Voices* (1965); *Summering* (1966); *In This Sign* (1970); *Season of Delight* (1981); and *Appearances* (2006).

GREENBERG, JOSEPH (1915–2001), U.S. anthropologist and linguist. Born on 28 May 1915, Joseph Greenberg was a gifted young pianist who had considered becoming a classical performer. He instead entered the academic world, graduating from Columbia University in 1936 and then earning his doctorate from Northwestern University in 1940. During World War II he served in the U.S. Army Signal Corps and Intelligence Corps. After the war he taught at the University of Minnesota, then at Columbia from 1948 to 1962. He was a professor of anthropology at Stanford University from 1962 to 1985; he served as chair of the Anthropology Department from 1971 to 1974, and from 1964 to 1981 also chaired the Committee on African Studies.

Greenberg's linguistic studies, which were concerned with both the structure of language and the similarities between languages, earned him an international reputation. His *Language Universals with Special References to Feature Hierarchies* (1966) established certain universal principles of language structure and attracted significant attention. His notion of the "implicational universal" influenced the work of many scholars in his field. His work on language families, however, sparked controversy. *The Languages of Africa* (1963), in which Greenberg determined that there were four basic groups of African languages, was considered speculative, though its premise was later accepted by many scholars. A similar theory presented in *Language in the Americas* (1987) found many in disagreement. Some critics took issue with Greenberg's data and methodology and dismissed this area of his research, though some contend that later discoveries of genetic similarities support Greenberg's groupings. In his last research, which he pursued until his death in 2001, Greenberg sought to prove links among what he called the "Eurasiatic" languages, claiming that most of the languages of Europe and Asia had commonalities.

Greenberg was a fellow of the National Academy of Sciences, the American Academy of the Arts and Sciences, and the American Philosophical Society. He served as president of the African Studies Association in 1964 and 1965, as president of the West African Linguistic Society from 1955 to 1970, and as president of the Linguistic Society of America in 1976. He was the recipient of many awards, including the Haile Selassie Prize for African Research in 1967 and the Talcott Parsons Prize for Social Science from the Academy of Arts and Sciences in 1977.

[Dorothy Bauhoff (2nd ed.)]

GREENBERG, LEOPOLD (1885–1964), South African judge, born in Calvinia, Cape Province. Raised to the bench at the age of 39, he became judge president of the Transvaal in 1938 and was elevated in 1943 to the Appellate Division of the Supreme Court, the highest judicial body in South Africa. He was acting chief justice in 1953 and served as officer administering the government in the absence of the governor-general. Known for his erudition, humanity, and caustic wit, he was acknowledged to be among South Africa's ablest judges. After his retirement in 1955, he sat on a judicial commission of inquiry into African disturbances in Johannesburg in 1957.

In Jewish life he was associated mainly with Zionist causes; for many years was honorary president of the Keren Hayesod, the Israel United Appeal, and the South African Friends of the Hebrew University. He was the first South African on the board of governors of the Hebrew University of Jerusalem, whose institute of forensic medicine, established from funds raised by South African Jewry, was named after him.

[Lewis Sowden]

GREENBERG, LEOPOLD JACOB (1861–1931), editor of the *Jewish Chronicle* and one of the first Zionists in Britain. Born in Birmingham, Greenberg was at first active in the non-Jewish press as a publisher and owner of a news agency. He became involved in Jewish affairs and began to attract notice as one of *Herzl's first adherents in Britain. He promoted Herzl's ideas before the general and Jewish public, and it was he who arranged for Herzl to appear before the Royal Commission on Alien Immigration in London in 1902 (through his close ties with Joseph *Chamberlain, secretary for the colonies, who also came from Birmingham). Herzl entrusted him with various political missions in England, such as those connected with the *El-Arish project and the *Uganda Scheme, and eventually Greenberg served as Herzl's official representative vis-à-vis the British government. Although he had supported the Uganda project, Greenberg did not join the *Territorialists. He became a leader of the British Zionist Federation and held various offices in the organization.

In 1907 he and his friends acquired the *Jewish Chronicle* in order to make it a Zionist organ and he was appointed editor in chief. He was a staunch fighter for Jewish rights and a particularly severe critic of the Czarist regime's attitude toward the Jews. Upon his appointment as editor, he gave up his official activities in the Zionist movement. Throughout the years, however, he persisted in his efforts to gain the support of various British circles for Zionism. After World War I, he opposed the official policy of the Zionist Organization, but his was a "loyal opposition." He was among the founders of *The Jewish Year Book* (1896–); *Young Israel*, a periodical for youth (1897); and other publications. Herzl described him as "the most able of all my helpers." In accordance with his last will, his ashes were taken to Deganyah and interred there (1932).

His son, IVAN MARION (1896–1966), joined the editorial board of the *Jewish Chronicle* in 1925 and served as its editor in chief from 1936 to 1946. During this period, he attacked the British government for its anti-Zionist policy in Palestine. He translated M. *Begin's book *Revolt* into English (1951). He was a leader of the *Revisionist Party in Britain.

BIBLIOGRAPHY: C. Roth, in: *The Jewish Chronicle 1841–1941* (1949), 124–40 and index; Rabinowitz, in: I. Cohen (ed.), *Rebirth of Israel* (1952), 77–97; T. Herzl, *Complete Diaries*, 5 (1960), index; L. Stein, *Balfour Declaration* (1961), index. **ADD. BIBLIOGRAPHY:** ODNB online; D. Cesarani, *The Jewish Chronicle and Anglo-Jewry, 1841–1991* (1994), index.

[Getzel Kressel]

GREENBERG, LOUIS (1894–1946), U.S. Conservative rabbi and scholar. Born in Russia, Greenberg immigrated to New York in 1913 and taught Hebrew and Bible while pursuing an American education. He graduated from the City College of New York in 1924 and was ordained by the Jewish Theological Seminary two years later. He then took a pulpit position at Temple Beth El in New Rochelle (1926–28) and moved to New Haven, where he became rabbi of B'nai Jacob Congregation. The congregation was already moving to the liberal wing of Conservative Judaism, with mixed seating, and late Friday evening services as well as a mixed choir. Greenberg introduced an organ. He developed the schools and the physical facilities of the congregation. While in New Haven, Greenberg pursued his Ph.D. at Yale University and wrote a major work on *The Jews in Russia: The Struggle for Emancipation*, two volumes being published in 1944 and 1951.

BIBLIOGRAPHY: *Bnai Jacob: One Hundred Years 1882–1982*; N. Zilberberg, *The George Street Synagogue of B'nai Jacob* (1961); *American Jewish Year Book*, vol. 48 (1946–47).

[Michael Berenbaum (2nd ed.)]

GREENBERG, MAURICE R. (1925–), U.S. insurance executive. Born in New York City, Greenberg was six when he moved to a dairy farm after his father's death and his mother's remarriage. After fighting in Europe, Greenberg went to college under the G.I. bill, graduating from the University of Miami and then from New York Law School. Recalled to fight in Korea, he came out as a captain at age 27 and won the Bronze Star. He got a job in the New York office of the Continental Casualty Company and became the protégé of Milburn Smith, an important executive at Continental, who brought Greenberg with him when he joined a predecessor of the American International Group in 1960. From 1967 to 1989, Greenberg, known as Hank, after the Jewish baseball star, was president and chief executive officer of AIG, which became the world's leading global insurance and financial services organization, operating in 130 countries. In 1989 be became chairman and chief executive officer. In 10 years under Greenberg, operating profits grew at a compound rate of 25 percent a year. A key to Greenberg's immense success was his concentration on giant commercial deals rather than cyclical car and home insurance business. During his tenure, he increased AIG's share of the life insurance business and supplied coverage on unusual risks: kidnap insurance and protection from suits against officers and directors of corporations. Known for his aggressiveness, Greenberg rarely lost money on underwriting, knowing which risks can be insured at a profit, how much to charge, and spreading the risk among others called reinsurers. AIG used brokers primarily as go-betweens, merely bringing business to the company, where AIG technicians examined the risk factors more closely. The reinsurers paid AIG a commission for the business they got, thus helping pay the cost of underwriting the whole risk.

Greenberg, whose company was founded in Shanghai but has had headquarters in New York since 1939, courted the Chinese market and won a major contract with the People's Insurance Company of China in 1980. He was active in a number of trade and cultural organizations, including the Asia Society, the U.S.-Philippine Business Committee, the U.S.-Korea Business Council and the Council of Foreign Relations. He served on the board of directors of the New York Stock Exchange and was a past chairman of the Federal Reserve Bank of New York. In New York City, he served on several hospital boards and museum boards.

Greenberg and his wife had four children, two of whom, Evan (1955–) and Jeffrey (1952–), became leaders of important insurance companies after they left AIG. Jeffrey joined the Marsh & McLennan Companies, an industry giant, as a partner in its investment unit. In November 1999 Jeffrey became chief executive of Marsh & McLennan and he added the title of chairman in 2002. In October 2004, New York's attorney general, Eliot *Spitzer, filed a civil suit against the brokerage, charging that Marsh & McLennan was rigging bids and fixing prices in the sale of property and casualty insurance to businesses. Jeffrey submitted his resignation as part of an agreement negotiated by the company and its directors that would keep Spitzer from bringing criminal charges against the company. At the time it was the largest insurance broker in the world. In 2004, Evan Greenberg became chief executive of Ace Ltd., a Bermuda-based insurer with worldwide reach. Ace did well in the insurance boom that followed the attacks on the World Trade Center. In November 2004 Ace was a subject of the New York attorney general's investigation into bid-rigging and price-fixing.

In March 2005, Maurice Greenberg stepped down as chief executive of AIG after a series of run-ins with regulators raised questions about the company's complex and often obscure operations. His exit appeared intended to avert a head-on collision with two regulators: the Securities and Exchange Commission and the New York attorney general, Spitzer. The departure of Greenberg after almost 40 years at the helm was a final chapter to one of corporate America's great rags-to-riches stories.

[Stewart Kampel (2nd ed.)]

GREENBERG, MOSHE (1928–), biblical scholar. Greenberg was born in Philadelphia, where after studying Bible and Assyriology with E.A. *Speiser, he obtained his Ph.D. in Oriental Studies from the University of Pennsylvania in 1954. The dissertation was published as *The Hab/piru* (1955). He received his rabbinical training at the Jewish Theological Seminary of America from which he also has a master's degree in Hebrew Literature.

He held various academic appointments at the University of Pennsylvania from 1954 to 1970, from assistant professor of Hebrew and Semitic languages and literature.

He became professor of Bible at the Hebrew University of Jerusalem in 1970. From 1971 to 1981 he served as academic advisor for Bible curriculum at the Israel Ministry of Education and Culture where he endeavored to place the study of Bible in the school system into a Jewish context.

Greenberg's grammar of Biblical Hebrew is widely used. In *The Religion of Israel* (1971) he made the work of Bible scholar Yehezkel *Kaufmann accessible to the international community in his one-volume abridgment and English translation of Kaufmann's monumental work. His holistic approach to biblical books, already seen in his commentary on Exodus (*Understanding Exodus*, 1969), was a harbinger of the "Bible as Literature" movement of the late 20th century. The same approach is evident in his commentaries on Ezekiel (Anchor Bible, *Ezekiel 1–20*; (1983), *Ezekiel 21–37* (1997)). A particular contribution of Greenberg's is to employ midrash in the service of plain-sense exegesis. He has sought to understand the value system underlying biblical literature and its relationship both to the Ancient Near East and Jewish thought.

Greenberg served as the divisional editor (law and society in the Bible) for the *Encyclopaedia Judaica*, 1968–71, and was a member of the Bible translation committee for the Jewish Publication Society of America (1966–82).

Greenberg was always committed to disseminating the results of professional scholarship to non-specialists. From

1982 he was a member of the academic council of the Open University of Israel and from 1985 served as editor for the critical but readable multi-volume Hebrew commentary series entitled *Mikra le-Yisrael* ("Bible for Israel").The range of Greenberg's interest may be seen in the essays collected in M. Greenberg, *Studies in the Bible and Jewish Thought* (1995).

ADD. BIBLIOGRAPHY: J. Tigay, in: DBI, 1:464–65.

[Elaine Hoter / S. David Sperling (2nd ed.)]

GREENBERG, NOAH (1919–1966), U.S. conductor and musicologist. Born in New York, Greenberg organized the Pro Musica Antiqua group (1952) which became known for its performances of medieval liturgical music drama and was in effect the first U.S. "Collegium Musicum" ensemble to achieve an international reputation. He took the group to Europe in 1960 and 1963, and recorded many of its performances, including the first recording of a selection of the sacred and secular works of Salamone de' *Rossi in musicologically valid versions. He also made arrangements of vocal works of the Renaissance period. The New York Pro Musica Antiqua continued its activities after his death.

GREENBERG, SAMUEL BERNARD (1893–1917), U.S. poet. Born in Vienna, Greenberg was taken to the U.S. in 1900; after a poverty-stricken life in New York City's ghetto he died from tuberculosis at the age of 24. Self-taught except for a few years in elementary school, he displayed remarkable precocity and power as a poet and was also a gifted artist. Influenced primarily by the American writers Emerson and Thoreau and by the English poets Keats, Shelley, and Browning, Greenberg wrote mystical poetry filled with vivid and strange imagery. His imperfect command of English grammar and vocabulary give his verse an unusual, surrealistic tone characteristic of some of the most sophisticated modernist poetry of the early 20th century. Greenberg might have remained unknown had not Hart Crane, the American poet, discovered his manuscripts in 1923. The poems had a profound effect on Crane and eventually, more than 20 years after Greenberg's death, a first selection (*Poems from the Greenberg Manuscripts*, 1939) was published, which helped to establish his important place in American literary history. A second selection, *Poems by Samuel Greenberg*, was published in 1947.

BIBLIOGRAPHY: M. Simon, *Samuel Greenberg, Hart Crane, and the Lost Manuscripts* (1978).

[Brom Weber]

GREENBERG, SIDNEY (1917–2002), U.S. Conservative rabbi, writer, and liturgist. Raised in New York, Greenberg was the product of Yeshiva elementary school and of the Talmudical Academy. He graduated cum laude from Yeshiva University in 1938 and then attended the Jewish Theological Seminary, where he was ordained in 1942 and subsequently earned his D.H.L. His first pulpit was also his last. He went to a small storefront synagogue in Philadelphia which was to remain his home for 53 years as Temple Sinai grew into a prominent Conservative congregation. (He served as a U.S. Air Force chaplain from 1944–46.)

Greenberg conducted Sermon Seminars and Pastoral Care Workshops at national and regional rabbinic conferences for four decades, and published numerous books based on his own sermons and on his widely read newspaper columns in the Jewish and general press. He also compiled several popular anthologies drawn from Jewish and world literature, and wrote inspirational volumes for both Jewish and general audiences.

During the 1960s he collaborated with Rabbi Morris Silverman, editor of the Prayer Book Press, whose edition of the *siddur* and the *maḥzor* dominated Conservative Judaism for several decades, in compiling instructional and worship texts for children. When the Prayer Book Press became part of Media Judaica in 1971, Greenberg was invited to serve as co-editor (with Rabbi Jonathan D. Levine) of a new series of innovative liturgical works. The series began with *Likrat Shabbat* – the *Kabbalat Shabbat* service when Friday evening was still the most widely attended service in a Conservative Congregation, and eventually included *Mahzor Hadash* for the High Holidays, *Siddur Hadash* for Sabbaths and Festivals, and *A Minyan of Comfort*. The series combined Hebrew liturgy with new gender-sensitive translations, inspirational notes and meditations, new reading elaborating on the themes of the traditional liturgy, alternative texts, passages from classical and contemporary Jewish sources, and extensive transliteration. During the last quarter of the 20th century and the early 21st century as successive volumes in the series were issued (and achieved record levels of distribution for independently published Jewish liturgy), the content and form of Greenberg's work increasingly influenced the publications of others, issued under a variety of auspices and in various sectors of North American Jewry.

[Jonathan D. Levine (2nd ed.)]

GREENBERG, SIMON (1901–1993), U.S. rabbi and educator. Greenberg, who was born in Russia, moved with his parents to the U.S. in 1905. He attended the Teacher's Institute of the Jewish Theological Seminary (1919) and earned his B.A. at City College of New York (1922). He was ordained by the Jewish Theological Seminary in 1925. From 1925 to 1946 Greenberg was rabbi of Har Zion Temple, Philadelphia, Pa., building it into one of the leading synagogues of the Conservative movement, a legacy that has endured. It was a point of pride at Har Zion that the lay leaders were knowledgeable and could lead services. He was also a leader in the Philadelphia community, a founder and director of the Philadelphia Psychiatric Hospital, president of the Philadelphia Zionist Organization of America, and a founder of the Akiva Day School, a Hebrew-speaking Jewish high school. He was president of the Rabbinical Assembly of America (1937–39), where he linked the three branches of the Conservative movement – the congregations, the Seminary, and the Rabbinical Assembly in joint fundraising efforts, which led to the Joint Campaign for Conservative Judaism.

All the while he taught at the Jewish Theological Seminary (1932–68). He then returned to the Seminary to serve as provost (1946–51), executive director of the United Synagogue (1950–53). He was appointed professor of homiletics and education in 1948 and vice chancellor in 1957, and was sent on behalf of the Seminary to establish the West Coast campus of the Jewish Theological Seminary, the University of Judaism in Los Angeles where he was president (1955–63), chancellor, and then chancellor emeritus. One of Conservative Judaism's most articulate spokesmen, Greenberg stressed the centrality of the Jewish people, the importance of Zionism and Hebrew, the religious character of American civilization, and the importance of Hebrew in Jewish education. He was also one of the movement's most important educators, working to shape its thought and educational goals. Greenberg was a member of the Jewish Agency Executive, president of the Rabbinical Assembly of America, and a leader of the World Council on Jewish Education. Greenberg's numerous writings include *Living as a Jew Today* (1940), *Ideals and Values of the Prayer Book* (1940), *The First Year in the Hebrew School: A Teacher's Guide* (1946), *Foundations of a Faith* (1967), *Words of Poetry* (1970), and a series of brochures on the Conservative movement in Judaism. He also compiled the Harishon series of Hebrew textbooks. In his eighties he made *aliyah* and served as the first executive director of the Conservative (Masorati) movement in Israel.

ADD. BIBLIOGRAPHY: M. Sklare, *Conservative Judaism* (1955), 144, 274–75; P.S. Nadell, *Conservative Judaism in America: A Biographical Dictionary and Sourcebook* (1988).

[Jack Reimer / Michael Berenbaum (2nd ed.)]

GREENBERG, URI ẒEVI (pseudonym **Tur Malka**; 1894–1981), Hebrew poet. He was born in Bialykamien, eastern Galicia, and was descended from ḥasidic leaders (Meir Przemyslany on his father's side and the *Saraf*, Uri Strelisk, on his mother's). In his infancy his parents moved to Lvov where Greenberg received a traditional ḥasidic upbringing and education. His earliest poems, both in Hebrew and Yiddish, were published in 1912 in leading periodicals of the day. In 1915 he was drafted into the Austrian army and, after serving on the Serbian front, he deserted in 1917, returning to Lvov where he witnessed the Polish pogroms against the Jews in 1918 – an event which made an indelible impression on him. After the war he published poems in both Yiddish and Hebrew and soon became a leader of a group of Yiddish expressionist poets (including Perez *Markish) and the editor of a short-lived avant-garde periodical, *Albatros* (1922–23). He spent a year in Berlin (1923) and then immigrated to Ereẓ Israel (1924).

In Ereẓ Israel, Greenberg stopped writing in Yiddish and published in Hebrew exclusively. When *Davar*, the Labor daily, was founded in 1925, he participated as one of its regular columnists. His columns were headed *Mi-Megillat ha-Yamim ha-Hem* and *Shomer Mah mi-Leyl* and expressed strong views against Zionist sloganeering and calling for self-realization through pioneering. Between 1925 and 1927 he edited the booklets *Sadan* and *Sadna Dar'ah* in which he contended that Hebrew artists must abandon "the fixed confines of art, join the Jewish collective, and wrestle with and think out the complex of problems of Jewish national life." Although during this period he was committed to the Labor Zionist movement, he already began to express extreme ultranationalistic ideas which contradicted the official line. In the wake of the Arab riots of 1929, he broke with the Labor movement, joined the ranks of the nationalist Zionist Revisionist Party, and denounced both the British government and the Zionist leadership of the *yishuv* for betraying the Zionist dream. He became active in political life and was elected as a Revisionist delegate to the *Asefat ha-Nivḥarim* (the legislative body of the *yishuv*) and to several Zionist Congresses. Between 1931 and 1934 he lived in Warsaw where he was sent by the Revisionist movement to edit its Yiddish weekly *Di Velt*. Returning to Ereẓ Israel in 1936, in his poetry and articles he attacked the moderate socialist Zionist leadership and warned of the imminent danger to European Jewry. During the final struggle against Great Britain for national independence, he identified with the *Irgun Ẓeva'i Le'ummi and following the establishment of the State of Israel was elected to Israel's Knesset as a member for the Ḥerut Party, serving from 1949 to 1951. He was awarded the Israel Prize for Hebrew literature in 1957. His 80th birthday was marked by a series of celebrations, most of which were held in 1976. He was awarded a doctorate *honoris causa* by Tel Aviv University in April 1976 and by Bar-Ilan University in June 1977. He was made a freeman of the cities of Tel Aviv and Ramat Gan, and a special session of the Knesset was held in his honor on November 1, 1977. In December he was awarded the Bialik Prize for the third time.

In contrast to most Hebrew writers who were committed to a secularist-humanist Zionism, Greenberg asserts a religious mystical view of Zionism as the fulfillment of the Jewish historical destiny. The Jew is, in his view, wholly other than the non-Jew, having been elected by God at the beginning of time as a holy instrument of His will. The covenant made with the Jewish Patriarch, Abraham, and renewed at Sinai, is a meta-historical event which cannot be altered by time nor ignored by Jew or gentile. The Jew exists outside of history in an eternal dimension in which mere rationality has no validity. "What shall be in the future, has already occurred in the past and what was not, shall never be. Therefore I put my trust in the future, for I hold the shape of the past before me: this is the vision and the melody. Selah, Hallelujah, and Amen" (*Reḥovot ha-Nahar*, 1951, p. 37). In Greenberg's scheme the future shall bring about the fulfillment of God's promise to establish Jewish sovereignty and the Messianic redemption. Any attempt by the Jew to shirk his cosmic role, either by default or by an attempt to imitate the value system of the unelected (Europe, the gentiles), leads him to disaster. The secular nationalism or socialism of most contemporary Jews is a superficial reading of the meaning of the Jewish destiny and can only lead to a holocaust. The call for the renewal of Jewish sovereignty is an imperative of the eternal mythos of

Judaism. It is neither a sociological nor historical solution of practical human needs, but an absolute value which may exact any price which its realization requires. Halfhearted attempts at Zionist fulfillment are doomed to failure whether they are inhibited by moral niceties, which are derived from alien value systems, or are diffused by human selfishness.

In his Yiddish phase, *In Malkhus fun Tselem* ("In the Kingdom of the Cross," 1922) Greenberg already foresaw the European Holocaust. His poetry from then on is obsessed with this vision of horror (*Migdal ha-Geviyyot*, "The Tower of Corpses," in *Sefer ha-Kitrug ve-ha-Emunah*, 1936). Greenberg in *Reḥovot ha-Nahar* wrote one of the most moving dirges composed about the Nazi Holocaust. The tragedy, in his view, is the logical culmination of the 2,000-year confrontation between the cross and the star of David and the six million dead are an insuperable barrier which shall eternally separate Christian from Jew. For Greenberg the Holocaust puts into question not only God's theodicy but appears as a horrible practical joke which God and history have played on the Jew: "You promised to come one day to gather and lead them proudly to Zion and to renew their kingdom, raise their king. But, behold you did not come, O God; the enemy came and gathered them all, an ingathering of exiles for annihilation. Now there is no need for redemption. Sit, sit, God, in your heavens" (*Reḥovot ha-Nahar*, p. 249). God, the Redeemer of Israel, has become "the keeper of the Jewish cemetery" (p. 250).

Greenberg's God however moves outside the rational dimension and in a sudden leap of faith the poet reasserts the vision of redemption: "Will the Messiah yet come? Amen, he shall surely come." Divine history, of which Jewish history is a part, is based on an irrational paradox. Thus, out of the ashes of the crematoria, redemption will come, and out of despair faith. The Holocaust and the vision of Jewish sovereignty are two sides of the same coin of history. Greenberg's personal poetry often sings of his agony as the suffering prophet-priest of the mythos of Jewish catastrophe and redemption. In the years preceding the Holocaust, he laments the tragic fact that the multitude did not heed his terrible message of the imminent massacres, reviling him as they had always spurned their prophets in the past. He is filled with revulsion at their obstinacy and their blind concern for material trivialities in the face of disaster: "God how did I ever get here, inside the swamps – a man of vision befouled by their mud?"

He associates his national poetry with his personal history which also turns into mythos. The Jewish home in Poland, its Eden-like security of faith, his mother and father, assume archetypal dimensions. His love poetry, too, is inhabited by these primordial symbols: mother and father, Adam and Eve, Eden, primeval forests, the sea, the moon, lakes, rivers; they form a mythical landscape not very different from that of much of his national verse.

In an age when poets were concerned with formal and aesthetic problems, Greenberg's poetry is one of engagement, his poetic energy is fired by his all-consuming ideological commitment. Often in his poetry the poetic line surrenders to the overwhelming force of his rhetoric with which he pounds his readers mercilessly. At other times his verse is terse and brilliantly lyrical. While philosophically he rejects European aesthetics and the European poetic tradition, in practice he sometimes uses its devices and forms. More frequently his formal resources are indigenously Jewish: the Bible, medieval dirges, and concepts and statements drawn from kabbalistic literature. His early commitment to expressionism is retained throughout and is evidenced by his rhetorical flourishes, changing rhythms within the poem and sometimes even in one single line, wild metaphors, free verse, and his frequently irregular rhyme patterns.

His anti-humanist approach and ultranationalism, although mitigated by a commitment to Jewish ethical values, are not representative of contemporary Jewish thought. But Hebrew literary criticism has recognized the poetic genius of Greenberg though it rarely shares his ideology. Not that Greenberg's views lack a genuine Jewish basis; they are often deeply rooted in the Jewish subconscious and when expressed expose the raw nerve of the Jewish historical experience. But Greenberg's ideology reflects only one aspect of the Jewish soul – the particularistic, aristocratic sense of election – and often ignores its universalistic humanist character.

U.Z. Greenberg's main works include:

In Yiddish: *Ergetz oyf Felder* (1915), *In Zaytens Roysh* (1919), *Krig oyf der Erd* (1921), *Farnakhtengold* (1921), *Mefisto* (1921, 1922^2).

In Hebrew: *Eimah Gedolah ve-Yare'aḥ* (1925), *Ha-Gavrut ha-Olah* (1926), *Ḥazon Aḥad ha-Ligyonot* (1928), *Anacreon al Kotev ha-Izzavon* (1928), *Kelappei Tishim ve-Tishah* (1928), *Kelev Bayit* (1919), *Ezor Magen u-Ne'um Ben ha-Dam* (1930), *Sefer ha-Kitrug ve-ha-Emunah* (1937), *Min ha-Ḥakhlil ve-El ha-Kaḥol* (in *Lu'aḥ Haaretz*, 1949), *Al Da'at ha-Nes ha-Nikhsaf* (1951), *Mi-Tokh Sefer he-Agol* (in *Lu'aḥ Haaretz*, 1950), *Menofim Reḥokei Mahut* (*ibid.*, 1951, 1952), *Reḥovot ha-Nahar – Sefer ha-Ilyot ve-ha-Ko'aḥ* (1951), *Massa ve-Nevel* (in *Lu'aḥ Haaretz*, 1953), *Shirei Aspaklar be-Hai Alma* (*ibid.*, 1955), *Massekhet ha-Matkonet ve-ha-Demut* (in *Moznayim*, 1954), *Be-Fisat ha-Arig u-ve-Ḥelkat ha-Ḥevel* (*ibid.*, 1965). Seventeen volumes of the Collected Works of U.Z. Greenberg (*Kol Kitvei*) were published up to 2004. A bibliography of his works is available in J. Arnon, *U.Z. Greenberg: Bibliografyah shel Mifalo ha-Sifruti u-Mah she-Nikhtav Alav*, 1980.

Poems by Greenberg have been translated into various languages. English translations are included, for instance, in T. Carmi (ed.) *The Penguin Book of Hebrew Verse* (1981) and in *The Modern Hebrew Poem Itself* (2003). For English translations, see Goell, Bibliography, 776–825, and ITHL at www.ithl.org.il.

BIBLIOGRAPHY: B. Kurzweil, *Bein he-Ḥazon le-vein ha-Absurdi* (1966) 3–99; J.H. Yeivin, *Uri Ẓevi Greenberg, Meshorer Meḥokek* (1938); idem (ed.), *Be-Ikkevei ha-Shir* (1949–50); J. Klausner, *Mi-Shenei Olamot* (1944), 209–15; idem, *Meshorerei Dorenu* (1956), 235–49; A. Liphshitz, *Uri Ẓevi Greenberg, Meshorer Adnut ha-Ummah* (1945); A. Ukhmani, *Le-Ever ha-Adam* (1953), 290–8; Y.T. Helman, *Hagut* *u-Demut* (1963), 124–41; S.Y. Penueli, *Demuyyot be-Sifrutenu ha-Ḥadashah* (1946), 124–30; idem, *Sifrut ki-Feshutah* (1963), 206–21; D.A. Friedman, *Iyyunei Shirah* (1964), 294–8; M. Ribalow, *Sefer ha-Massot* (1928), 146–59; Y. Rabinowitz, *Be-Ḥavlei Doram* (1959), 21–67; G. Katzenelson, *ibid.*, 21 (1966), 307–14; J. Friedlaender, *Iyyunim be-Shirat Uri Ẓevi Greenberg* (1966) (incl. bibl.); J.D. Abramsky, in: *Yad la-Kore*, 7 (1963–69), 79–86 (bibl.); Waxman, Literature, 4 (1960) 324–27. **ADD. BIBLIOGRAPHY:** Y. Friedlander, *U.Z. Greenberg: Mivḥar Ma'amrei Bikkoret al Yeẓirato* (1975); B. Harshav, *Ritmus ha-Raḥavut: Halakhah u-Ma'aseh be-Shirato shel U.Z. Greenberg* (1978); L. Yudkin, "Art in the Service of the People: On the Poetry of U.Z.Greenberg," in: *Jewish Affairs*, 36/8 (1981), 31–33; D. Landau, *U.Z. Greenberg: Shirei ha-Gavhut be-Ma'amake ha-Zeman* (1984); S. Lindenbaum, *Shirat U.Z. Greenberg ha-Ivrit ve-ha-Yidit* (1984); Y. Shavit, *U.Z. Greenberg:* "Conservative Revolutionarism and National Messianism," in: *Jerusalem Quarterly*, 48 (1988), 63–72; D. Miron, "U.Z. Greenberg's War Poetry," in: *The Jews of Poland between Two World Wars* (1989), 368–82; Z. Ben Porat, "Forms of Intertextuality and the Reading of Poetry: U.Z. Greenberg's *'Ba-Sha'ar,'*" in: *Prooftexts*, 10/2 (1990), 257–81; J. Arnon: *U.Z. Greenberg: Taḥanot be-Ḥayyav* (1991); Y.C. Biletzky, *U.Z. Greenberg der Yidish Dikhter* (1992); G. Kazenlson, *Golef ha-Kelim shel ha-Kosef: Masot al Shirat U.Z. Greenberg* (1993); A. Lipsker, "The Albatrosses of Young Yiddish Poetry," in: *Prooftexts*, 15/1 (1995), 89–108; H. Goldblatt, "From Back Street to Boulevard: Directions and Departures in the Scholarship of U.Z. Greenberg," in: *Prooftexts*, 16/2 (1996), 188–203; J. Winther, "U.Z. Greenberg – The Politics of the Avantgarde," in: *Nordisk Judaistik* 17/1–2 (1996), 24–60; S. Lindenbaum, "Between the Pole of Existence and the Pole of History: The Poetry of U.Z. Greenberg," in: *Jewish Affairs*, 52/3 (1997), 107–14; S. Wolitz, "U.Z. Greenberg's Ideological Conflict with Yiddish Culture," in: *Jewish Affairs*, 52/3 (1997), 99–106; D. Weinfeld, *U.Z. Greenberg* (1998); H. Weiss (ed.), *Ha-Matkonet ve-ha-Demut* (2000); A. Matalon, "Difference at War: S. Sassoon, I. Rosenberg, U.Z. Greenberg and the Poetry of the First World War," in: *Shofar*, 21/1 (2002), 25–43; D. Miron: *Akdamot le-U.Z.G.* (2002); R. Shoham, *Poetry and Prophecy: The Image of the Poet as a "Prophet," a Hero and an Artist in Modern Hebrew Poetry* (2003); A. Negev, *Close Encounters with Twenty Israeli Writers* (2003); Y. Eldad, *Dem'a ve-Nogah, Dam ve-Zahav: Iyyunim be-Shirat U.Z. Greenberg* (2003); H. Hever, *Moledet ha-Mavet Yafah: Estetikah u-Politikah be-Shirat U.Z. Greenberg* (2004).

[Ezra Spicehandler]

GREENBLATT, ALIZA WAITZMAN (1885–1975), U.S. Yiddish poet and Zionist leader. Born in Azarenits, Bessarabia, Greenblatt received a traditional *ḥeder* education. She came to the United States in 1900 and settled with her family in Philadelphia, where she was a garment worker. She married Isidor Greenblatt in 1907; the couple had five children. An active participant in Jewish organizations, Greenblatt became a successful fundraiser for the *Jewish National Fund, national president of *Pioneer Women, and an active member of *Hadassah. After a brief sojourn in Palestine in 1920, where Isidor attempted to establish a business, the Greenblatts settled in New York City, the center of Yiddish culture in the United States.

In her later years, Greenblatt collected five volumes of her poems which were widely published in the Yiddish press in the United States and Israel. These included *Ikh un Du* ("You and I," 1951); *Ikh Zing* ("I Sing," 1947); *In Sigate baym Yam* ("In Seagate by the Ocean," 1957); *Lebn Mayns* ("My Life," 1935); and *Tsen Lider mit Musik* ("Ten Poems with Music," 1939). Many of the poems were set to music and recorded. Greenblatt also wrote an autobiography, *Baym Fenster fun a Lebn* ("At the Window of a Life," 1966). She was a popular speaker at Jewish women's organizations across North America.

Greenblatt's collection of Yiddish books was donated by her daughter, dancer and medical activist Marjorie Mazia Guthrie, to the National Yiddish Book Center in Amherst, Mass., where the reading room was named in Greenblatt's memory.

BIBLIOGRAPHY: S.A. Shavelson, "Greenblatt, Aliza," in: P.E. Hyman and D.D. Moore (eds.), *Jewish Women In America*, vol. 1 (1998), 552–53; I. Commandav, "Guthrie, Marjorie," *ibid.*, 567–69.

[Judith R. Baskin (2nd ed.)]

GREENBLATT, ELIYAHU (1933–), *ḥazzan*. Born in Jerusalem, Greenblatt studied music at the Jerusalem Conservatory and trained as a *ḥazzan* under Shelomo Zalman *Rivlin. He conducted the Shirat Israel choir in Jerusalem and sang with the choir of Leib Glanz in Tel Aviv. He was *ḥazzan* of Tel Aviv's Bet El and Tiferet Ẓvi synagogues and of the Sydenham synagogue in Johannesburg. He is the possessor of a dramatic tenor voice and has performed on stage and synagogue worldwide. As a composer, he set many sections of the prayer services to music and arranged and re-edited compositions and recitatives of the *ḥazzanim* of earlier generations. This includes the compositions of Yehuda Srebnick, and his own working knowledge of the accentuation in Yossele *Rosenblatt's Hebrew singing has enabled him to revive a number of Rosenblatt's unpublished and unrecorded recitatives left in manuscript form at the time of Rosenblatt's untimely death. A cassette of Greenblatt's original compositions, among the last orchestrations done by Chanan Winternitz, is available on cassette (Musique Internationale).

[Akiva Zimmerman / Raymond Goldstein (2nd ed.)

GREENE, HAROLD H. (1923–2000), U.S. federal judge. Greene was born in Frankfurt, Germany. In 1939 the family fled, making their way to Belgium, Vichy France, Spain, and Portugal before arriving in New York in 1943. Greene already spoke fluent English; he entered the army and was sent back to Europe, where he was assigned to interrogate German prisoners. At the end of the war, Greene joined his parents in Washington, D.C., where he studied law and spent the rest of his life as a lawyer and judge. He was an active member of Congregation Beth El in Bethesda.

He earned his B.A. at George Washington University and after he graduated from GWU School of Law in 1952, he clerked for Circuit Judge Bennett Champ Clark in the U.S. Court of Appeals for the D.C. Circuit. His work as a lawyer was in the government: in the U.S. Attorney's office (1953–57) and then in the Justice Department, serving as the first head of the appeals and research section of the Civil Rights Division (1957–65). Greene is credited with being the principal legal architect of the two most significant statutes of 20th-century America, the Civil Rights Act of 1964 and the Voting Rights Act of 1965.

Greene's career as a trial judge in the nation's capital was equally distinguished. In 1965 President Lyndon B. Johnson nominated Greene to the D.C. Court of General Sessions, which dealt with essentially minor offenses and lesser civil matters. In 1966, Greene was named chief judge.

In 1968, after the assassination of the Rev. Martin Luther King, Jr., major rioting broke out in Washington. Hundreds of people were swept up and detained. In other cities, defendants were arraigned en masse. Greene refused to countenance that: to secure due process for each one who was arrested, he kept the judges of his court at work round-the-clock. Greene's administrative skills included not just efficiency, but also compassion for those accused.

In 1978 President Jimmy Carter nominated Judge Greene to serve on the U.S. District Court for the District of Columbia, where one of the first group of cases assigned to him was one of the most far-reaching cases in American history: the antitrust suit that broke up American Telephone & Telegraph Co. The Department of Justice view was that AT&T used profits from its monopoly on local telephone service to suppress competition in the emerging long-distance and telephone equipment industries. Greene took firm command of the litigation that broke the world's largest corporation into pieces. He thereby helped to reshape the entire telecommunications industry by creating the "Baby Bells" and ushering in a new world of competition.

In 1990 Judge Greene also presided over the criminal trial of Admiral John M. Poindexter, who was sentenced to six months in prison for his role in the "Iran-Contra" scandal. In 1991 the Court of Appeal for the D.C. Circuit reversed the convictions.

Greene became one of the best-known federal judges of his time and enhanced his reputation for fairness and hard work. A champion of equal dignity for citizens of all races and both genders, Greene was renowned for his commitment to due process and the independence of the judiciary. He stopped hearing cases in 1998, and died in 2000.

BIBLIOGRAPHY: The Historical Society of the District of Columbia Circuit, *The Honorable H. Greene: U.S. District Court for the District of Columbia* (1996); D.C. Bar, "A Conversation with Harold H. Greene," in: *Bar Report* (April/May 1996); Fred W. Henck and Bernard Strassburg, *A Slippery Slope: The Long Road to the Breakup of AT&T* (1988).

[Edward McGlynn Gaffney, Jr. (2nd ed.)]

GREENE, LORNE (1915–1987), actor. Born in Ottawa, Canada, Greene attended Queen's University in Kingston, Ontario. After he graduated, he began to work in radio broadcasting, rising to prominence as an accomplished newscaster. As chief radio announcer on the CBC during World War II (1939–42), he was known as the "Voice of Doom" because of his deep, resonant voice and the grim news it conveyed. In the late 1940s Greene formed the Academy of Radio Arts and the Jupiter Theatre in Toronto. For more than a dozen years, his school was a haven for Canadian actors.

In 1953 he left his native land and headed for Hollywood. Although he was best known for his long-standing starring role as the venerable Ben Cartwright on the popular TV western series *Bonanza* (1959–73), Greene performed on Broadway, on radio, in films, and on many other TV shows as well. In addition to his work in the U.S., he returned to Canada to participate in various projects.

On Broadway, Greene appeared in *The Prescott Proposals* (1954); *Speaking of Murder* (1957); and *Edwin Booth* (1958). His film roles include *The Silver Chalice* (1954); *Tight Spot* (1955); *Autumn Leaves* (1956); *Peyton Place* (1957); *The Hard Man* (1957); *The Last of the Fast Guns* (1958); *The Gift of Love* (1958); *The Buccaneer* (1958); and *Earthquake* (1974).

Greene's television credits include the title role in *Othello* (1953); the TV series *Sailor of Fortune* (1955); host of the series *To the Wild Country* (1972–75); the lead role in the series *Griff* (1973–74); host of *Lorne Greene's Last of the Wild* (1974); the lead roles in the series *Battlestar Galactica* (1978 and 1980) and *Code Red* (1981–82); and host of *Lorne Greene's New Wilderness* (1981–86). Greene's final film appearance was in the TV movie *The Alamo: Thirteen Days to Glory* (1987).

In 1980 he published *The Lorne Greene Book of Remarkable Animals*.

[Ruth Beloff (2nd ed.)]

GREENE, SHECKY (1926–), U.S. comedian-actor. Greene is known as the top of Las Vegas' tuxedo-wearing, rim-shot comedians, often compared to Don *Rickles and Buddy *Hackett. Born Fred Sheldon Greenfield in Chicago, Ill., Greene served in the Navy and was discharged in 1944. He enrolled in Wright Junior College and planned to become a gym teacher. Over the summer he took a job as social director at a resort near Milwaukee called Oakton Manor. With no budget for performers, Greene began developing a stand-up act to entertain guests. When he returned to college, he continued his act in Chicago nightclubs. By the late 1940s, he was working at a club in New Orleans and then opened for Martha Raye in Miami Beach, making $500 a week. In 1953, after signing to play Chez Paree in Chicago as Ann Sothern's opening act, Greene took an offer from the Golden Hotel in Reno, Nevada. Before long he was playing Las Vegas and his career as a stand-up comedian grew with the city. His comic style was as wild as the city he played in, using ad-libbing, barbs, impressions, and song parodies. His drinking and violent outbursts on the casino floor were tolerated, even encouraged, and became the stuff of legend. Greene played wisecracking Pvt. Braddock in the television series *Combat!* (1962–63) and appeared on such television shows as *Laverne and Shirley*, *The A-Team*, and *Northern Exposure*. His film roles include *History of the World: Part I* and *Splash*. He stopped drinking in the 1990s and his stand-up career was only slowed by throat surgery, cancer surgery, and a hip transplant.

[Adam Wills (2nd ed.)]

GREENEBAUM, Chicago family in second half of the 19th–20th centuries, originating in Eppelsheim, Germany; among the early Jewish settlers in Chicago. The brothers Michael and Jacob Greenebaum went to Chicago in 1846; the first of the family to arrive. Two other brothers, Elias and Henry, arrived in 1848. A few members of the family joined the California gold rush in 1849. However, the majority remained in Chicago and became involved in Jewish and civic affairs there.

Elias Greenebaum (1822–1919) worked for two years in a dry goods store after coming to Chicago and then became a clerk in the banking house of Richard K. Swift. In 1855 he and Henry founded the Greenebaum Brothers Banking House. In 1877 Elias organized the banking house under the firm name of Greenebaum Sons, which subsequently was incorporated as a state bank in 1911 under the name Greenebaum Sons Bank & Trust Company. The name was changed to Greenebaum Sons Investment Co. in 1921. Through consolidation with other companies it became successively the Bank of America, Central Trust Co. of Illinois, and Central-Republic Bank & Trust Co. Greenebaum and Associates and the Greenebaum Mortgage Co. still existed in 1970. Elias Greenebaum led the adherents of the Reform group when Chicago's only (at the time) congregation Kehilath Anshe Maarav split into Orthodox and Reform factions. He was a founder of the Juedischer Reformverein (1858), which founded Congregation Sinai, the first Reform congregation in Chicago (1861). He was director, treasurer, and vice president of this congregation at various times.

Michael Greenebaum (1824–94) became a tinner and plumber after his arrival in Chicago. Active in the Abolitionist movement, he led a crowd that freed a slave held prisoner by a U.S. marshall (1853). He founded and was the first president of the Hebrew Benevolent Society (1854), and a founder of the Chicago Public Library, the Chicago Historical Society, the Astronomical Society, the 82nd Illinois Volunteer Regiment of Veterans, and the Ramah Lodge of B'nai B'rith. Later, he was the first president of the District Grand Lodge 6 of B'nai B'rith. He also founded and served as first president of the Zion Literary Society (1877).

Henry Greenebaum (1833–1914) was a hardware salesman, and then a clerk in Richard K. Swift's banking house before founding the Greenebaum Brothers Banking House with Elias. He later became president of the German Savings Bank. Henry served as secretary and honorary member of Orthodox Congregation B'nai Sholom, was a founder and first president of the United Hebrew Relief Association in 1859, a founder of Congregation Sinai, first president of Congregation Zion (Reform), and later first president of Isaiah Congregation. He was the first Jew to serve on the City Council, as alderman from the Sixth Ward (1856), was a presidential elector on the Douglas ticket (1860), represented Cook County on the first Equalization Board (1856), and was a member of the West Chicago Park Commission. He was also a patron of the arts, the first president of the Beethoven Society (1876), and the first president of the Orpheus Maennerchor.

Henry Everett Greenebaum, Elias' elder son, was born in Chicago. A partner in the family banking business, he became treasurer of the first Chicago Home for Aged Jews, in 1893. Moses Ernst Greenebaum, Elias' second son, was also a partner in the family banking business. He was chairman of the Chicago Community branch of the Jewish Welfare Board, vice president of Michael Reese Hospital, treasurer of the Jewish Historical Society of Illinois, treasurer of the Citizens Association of Chicago, and president of Sinai Congregation (1906–29). JAMES E. GREENEBAUM (b. 1866) was treasurer of the Chicago Home for Jewish Orphans in 1893. EDGAR N. GREENEBAUM (b. 1890) served on the Chicago Board of Education.

[Morris A. Gutstein]

GREENFIELD, ALBERT MONROE (1887–1967), U.S. financier and civic leader. Greenfield, who was born in Kiev, Ukraine, was taken to the U.S. at the age of five. He worked at several jobs before he entered the real estate field, founding Albert M. Greenfield and Company. By the time he was 30, Greenfield had amassed a multi-million dollar fortune. Upon his retirement in 1956, his company was one of the largest real estate firms in the U.S. Greenfield lost much of his first fortune when his Bankers Trust Company was compelled to close in the early days of the Depression of the 1930s, and subsequently made another. In the 1950s and 1960s he took pride in his designation as "Mr. Philadelphia," because the Greenfield interests controlled so many department stores, hotels, and specialty shops, through his City Stores holding company, and because his participation was solicited for every conceivable philanthropic and civic cause. Greenfield was also extremely active politically and was considered a power in Philadelphia politics. He was a member of the Philadelphia Common Council (1917–20), and was extremely close to William S. Vare, the boss of the Philadelphia Republican machine. Although he seconded Herbert Hoover's nomination in 1928, from 1934 on he was identified with the Democratic Party (while continuing to give financial and other support to occasional Republican candidates). He served as a delegate to all the Democratic national conventions from 1948 through 1964. Greenfield was a member of the influential Jewish delegation which waited upon President Harry S. *Truman the night/morning he granted U.S. recognition to Israel. Greenfield was close to President Lyndon B. *Johnson, because he had been a member of the small group that supported Johnson for president in 1960. Greenfield was never wholly committed to a single Jewish cause or institution; he accepted the usual board memberships and honors, took pride in his early service as a trustee of the Jewish Institute of Religion, and in the decisive role which he played in the merger of three Jewish hospitals in Philadelphia in 1951. At one time, the National Conference of Christians and Jews briefly stimulated his interest, and through its agency he endowed a Center for Human Relations at the University of Pennsylvania.

[Bertram Wallace Korn]

GREENFIELD, JONAS CARL (1926–1995), U.S. Bible scholar, specializing in the languages and culture of the Ancient Near East. Born in New York, he received his early education from both public school and yeshivot. Greenfield showed early interest in Semitic Near Eastern Languages, learning both Arabic and Aramaic in his youth. He received his bachelor's degree from CCNY in English literature in 1949. In that same year he was ordained rabbi at Metivta Torah Vadaath. He entered the graduate school at Yale to study English, where he was required to study an early Indo-European language. Choosing Hittite taught by Albrecht Goetze the great cuneiformist, Greenfield soon realized that his heart was in the study of the ancient Near East. He received his doctorate from Yale University (1956) for his thesis "The Lexical Status of Mishnaic Hebrew," in which he applied his newer skills in Semitics to the texts originally learned in yeshivah.

Starting his teaching career in 1954 as instructor in Semitics at Brandeis University, he became assistant and later associate professor of Semitics at the University of California at Los Angeles (1956–65) and then professor of Semitics at the University of California at Berkeley (1965–71).

In 1971 Greenfield moved to Jerusalem where he became professor of Ancient Semitic languages at the Hebrew University. He also taught during the 1970s and early 1980s at Bar-Ilan University.

His interests within the field of Ancient Semitic languages were diverse. He was a known authority on comparative Semitic philology, Aramaic dialectology and lexicography, Ugaritic language and literature, Northwest Semitic epigraphy, and Canaanite and Aramaic religion, and was also interested in the social history of the period, legal matters, and Iranian studies.

He was a member of the publication supervisory committee for the Dead Sea Scrolls and was engaged in the publication of the papyri from Naḥal Ḥever and Naḥal Ẓe'elim.

From 1967 Greenfield was editor of the *Israel Exploration Journal* and associate editor of the *Bulletin of the American School of Oriental Research.* He was a member of the editorial committee of the Jewish Publication society of America and on the committee for the new JPS translation of the Hagiographia.

His works include *Jews of Elephantine and Arameans of Syene* (with B. Porten, 1974) and *The Bisitun Inscription* (with B. Porten, 1982). Most of his numerous English articles can be found in the two volumes edited by Paul (bibliography), and a full bibliography and biographical sketch in the Festschrift edited by Zevit (bibliography).

ADD. BIBLIOGRAPHY: Z. Zevit et al.(eds.), *Solving Riddles and Untying Knots...Studies...Greenfield* (1995); S. Paul et al. (eds.), *Al Kanfei Yonah: Collected Studies...Greenfield...Semitic Philology* (2001).

[Elaine Hoter]

GREENGARD, PAUL (1925–), U.S. neuroscientist and Nobel laureate. Greengard was born in New York City, where he received his primary education. After World War II service in the Navy, he graduated in mathematics and physics from Hamilton College (1948) and gained his Ph.D. (1953) from Johns Hopkins University, Baltimore, under the guidance of Frank Brink and Sidney Colowick. After postdoctoral studies at the universities of London, Cambridge, and Amsterdam, with Wilhelm Feldberg at the National Institute for Medical Research in Mill Hill, London, and with Sidney Udenfriend at the National Institutes of Health, Bethesda (1953–59), he became director of the Department of Biochemistry in Geigy's Research Laboratories in Ardsley, New York (1959–67). After one year as visiting professor during which he worked with Alfred Gilman and Earl Sutherland, he was appointed professor of pharmacology and psychiatry at Yale University (1968–83). In 1983 he became professor and head of the Laboratory of Molecular and Cellular Neuroscience at the Rockefeller University, New York. Greengard's research interest in neuroscience was inspired by Allen Hodgkin's lecture on nerve conduction at Johns Hopkins, where Greengard was a graduate student. Greengard's work addressed the process whereby signals are transmitted between nerve cells across the synapses which separate them and the role of fast and slow chemical neurotransmitters in neurotransmission. Novel findings were largely built on his entirely vindicated conviction that biochemical and biophysical events in the transmission across the synapses between nerve cells have to be analyzed in tandem. He and his colleagues concentrated on slow transmission by dopamine to analyze biochemical and physiological events on both sides of the synapse during neurotransmission and thereby discovered a key molecule in dopamine signaling called DARPP-32. These and other observations helped to build up a detailed picture of the mediators, structures, and signaling involved in trans-synaptic transmission whereby slow neurotransmitters serve to modulate fast transmission. His work has major implications for diseases involving the dopamine system such as Parkinson's disease, the adverse effects of drug abuse, and the design of therapeutic agents. He received the Nobel Prize in physiology or medicine jointly with Arvid Carlsson and Eric Kandel (1980). He continued to work on neurotransmission and the broader implications of his findings for other systems, diseases, and drug design. His many awards include the National Academy of Sciences Award in the Neurosciences (1991), the Goodman and Gilman Award in Receptor Pharmacology (1992), and the Lieber Prize for Outstanding Achievement in Schizophrenia Research (1996).

[Michael Denman (2nd ed.)]

GREENSPAN, ALAN (1926–), U.S. economist. Born in New York City, Greenspan received a B.S. in economics (summa cum laude) in 1948, an M.A. in economics in 1950, and a Ph.D. in economics in 1977, all from New York University. For many years Greenspan headed an independent economic consulting firm in New York, mainly for major corporations and institutions, including the United States Tresury and the Board of Governors of the Feeral Reserve System. He also served as a senior adviser to the Brookings Institution Panel on Economic Activity. In 1974 he was appointed by President Nixon to succeed Herbert Stein as chairman of the President's Council of Economic Advisers. He was chairman of the National Commission on Social Security Reform from 1981 to 1983. He also served as a member of President Reagan's Economic Policy Advisory Board, a member of *Time* magazine's Board of Economists, and a consultant to the Congressional Budget Office. Greenspan was known for his conservative economic views, which he developed partly under the influence of Ayn Rand.

[Joachim O. Ronall]

Greenspan also served as a corporate director for Aluminum Company of America (Alcoa); Automatic Data Processing, Inc.; Capital Cities/ABC, Inc; General Foods, Inc; J.P. Morgan & Co, Inc; Morgan Guaranty Trust Company of New York; Mobil Corporation; and The Pittston Company.

In 1987 he was nominated to the position of chairman of the Federal Reserve Board. Given the U.S.'s large budget deficit, which prevented the presidential and legislative arms of the administration from effectively utilizing tax and spending policies to influence the economy, this made him the most important economic policy-maker in the government, since he was able to exert a considerable influence over interest rates by controlling the money supply. Declaring his intention to "try to maintain the maximum sustainable long-term economic growth that is possible," he presided over a period of slow but steady economic growth until the summer of 1990, at which time recession hit the American economy. Despite critics' complaints that he first retarded economic expansion by keeping interest rates too high and then moved too slowly to end the recession, he was nominated to a second term by President George Bush in August 1991, and shortly thereafter he was also confirmed to his first full fourteen-year term on the Federal Reserve Board. In 1996 his third four-year term was confirmed. In 2004 he took office for a fifth term.

Greenspan also served as chairman of the Conference of Business Economists; president and fellow of the National Association of Business Economists; and director of the National Economists Club.

He received the Thomas Jefferson Award for the greatest public service performed by an elected or appointed official, presented by the American Institute for Public Service (1976); was elected a fellow of the American Statistical Association (1989); was decorated Legion of Honor (Commander) France (2000); was made honorary Knight Commander of the British Empire (2002); and was the first recipient of the Gerald R. Ford Medal for Distinguished Public Service (2003).

Among Greenspan's publications are *Income Inequality: Issues and Policy Options* (1998), *Changing Capital Markets: Implications for Monetary Policy* (2001), and *Achieving Price Stability* (2001).

[Rohan Saxena and Ruth Beloff (2nd ed.)]

ADD. BIBLIOGRAPHY: B. Woodward, *Maestro: Greenspan's Fed and the American Boom* (2000); J. Martin, *Greenspan: The Man behind Money* (2000); D. Jones, *The Politics of Money: The Fed under Alan Greenspan* (1991).

GREENSPAN, BUD (1926–), preeminent producer, writer and director of sports films, one of the world's leading sports historians, member of the U.S. Olympic Committee Hall of Fame. Born in New York City, Greenspan broke into sports at 16 as a radio announcer, and at 21 was promoted to sports director for station WMGM (WHN) in New York City, then the largest sports station in the country. Greenspan broadcast the pre- and post-game coverage of the Brooklyn Dodgers, and also covered hockey, basketball, track, and tennis events from Madison Square Garden. Greenspan went to the 1952 Olympic Games and made a documentary on weightlifter John Davis, and after selling the film for a huge profit decided there was a future in sports documentaries. In 1964 Greenspan took Jesse Owens to Berlin to shoot a one-hour film called *Jesse Owens Returns to Berlin*. It was an immediate success, playing in over 120 countries and earned Greenspan three Emmy Awards. The film was revolutionary, the beginning of telling the human story of sports instead of just the standard athletic story.

Greenspan was producer of the official films of the Olympic Games in 1984, 1988, 1992, and 1996, with his five-hour film on the '84 Olympics, *16 Days of Glory*, considered a classic. Greenspan produced numerous other Olympic-related films, including *Triumph and Tragedy: The 1972 Olympics*, *The Measure of Greatness*, *An Olympic Dream*, the television series *For the Honor of Their Country*, the two-hour docudrama, *Time Capsule: The 1936 Berlin Olympic Games*, and the 22-part TV series *The Olympiad* (1976–77), seen in more than 80 countries and which got him an Emmy Award. He also won Emmys for his *16 Days of Glory* films of the Winter Olympics at Calgary (1988) and Lillehammer (1994).

"There are some people who are very stylistic," Greenspan wrote. "They make films that are difficult to understand; yet some people find them genius. My approach is very simple. My stories have a beginning, a middle, and an end. The dumbest person in the world can understand my films."

Greenspan was awarded the Olympic Order in 1985, the 17th American to receive such an honor; the Directors Guild of America Lifetime Achievement Award in 1995; and the Peabody Award in 1996 for his outstanding service in chronicling the Olympic Games. He is the author of numerous books, including *Play It Again Bud* (1973), *We Wuz Robbed!* (1976), *Numero Uno* (1982), *100 Greatest Moments in Olympic History*

(1995), *Frozen in Time: The Greatest Moments at the Winter Olympics* (1997), and *The Olympians' Guide to Winning the Game of Life* (1997). Greenspan was elected to the U.S. Olympic Committee Hall of Fame in 2004.

[Elli Wohlgelernter (2nd ed.)]

GREENSTEIN, HARRY (1896–1971), U.S. social worker. Greenstein was born in Baltimore, Maryland. From 1928 until his retirement he served as executive director of the Associated Jewish Charities of Baltimore. Greenstein also served as State Relief administrator during 1933–36. He was director of welfare in the Middle East for the United Nations Relief and Rehabilitation Agency (UNRRA) from 1944–45 and in 1949 was the advisor to the American military governor on Jewish affairs in Germany. In the latter position, Greenstein was instrumental in the passage of the General Claims Law, which applied to reparations in the American zone and served as a basis for the 1952 Federal Supplementing and Coordinating Law in West Germany. He also helped to arrange for the care and resettlement of displaced persons. He was elected to the presidencies of the Baltimore Council of Social Agencies (1935–39), National Conference of Jewish Community Service (1937–38), and American Association of Social Workers (1939–40).

BIBLIOGRAPHY: L.L. Kaplan and T. Schuchat, *Justice, Not Charity* (1967).

[Kenneth D. Roseman]

GREENSTEIN, JESSE PHILIP (1902–1959), U.S. biochemist. Born in New York, Greenstein worked at Harvard, Kaiser Wilhelm Institute in Berlin, and the University of California before joining the National Cancer Institute, where from 1946 he was head of the biochemical laboratory. His most important fields of research were polypeptides and the biochemistry of cancer.

GREENSTONE, JULIUS HILLEL (1873–1955), U.S. educator and author. Greenstone was born in Mariampol, Lithuania, and immigrated to the United States in 1894. He studied at the City College of New York and the Jewish Theological Seminary of America, where he was ordained in 1900. In 1905 he joined the faculty of Gratz College, where he taught Jewish education and religion. He was principal of the college from 1933 to 1948. From 1902 on he maintained a modest Jewish bookshop in his home, toward which rabbis and everyone else interested in Jewish education gravitated to obtain books as well as advice and guidance. Greenstone was among the first American Jews to produce books of popular Jewish scholarship in English. His *The Religion of Israel* (1902) was later rewritten and expanded into *The Jewish Religion* (1920). *The Messiah Idea in Jewish History* (1906) was the first work in English to examine historically the messianic idea in Jewish literature. His commentaries on the biblical books Numbers and Proverbs appeared in the series *Holy Scriptures with Commentary*, published by the Jewish Publication Society (1939). He contributed articles to the *Jewish Encyclopedia* (1901). For some twenty years he contributed a popular though scholarly column to the Philadelphia weekly *Jewish Exponent*. Some of these essays were collected and republished in *Jewish Feasts and Fasts* (1945).

[Shulamith Catane]

GREENWALD (Grunwald), JEKUTHIEL JUDAH (Yekusiel Yehudah; Leopold; 1889–1955), U.S. rabbi and scholar. Greenwald, born in Hungary, studied in yeshivot in that country and in Frankfurt on the Main under Nehemiah *Nobel. In 1924 he settled in the United States, where he was the rabbi of Orthodox congregations in New York and of Congregation Beth Jacob in Columbus, Ohio, where he served for the last three decades of his life. Neither a great orator nor skilled pastor, Greenwald was a prolific writer and regarded as an authority on Jewish law and history. He wrote numerous monographs and articles in Hungarian, Yiddish, and Hebrew, was especially interested in rabbinic authorities and Jewish communities of Hungary, on which he wrote *Ha-Yehudim be-Ungarya* (1913) and *Toyznt Yor Idish Lebn in Ungarn* (1945). His work *Le-Toledot ha-Reformazyon ha-Datit be-Germanyah u-ve-Ungarya* (1948) is a history of the Reform movement in Germany and Hungary (this work contains a bibliography of Greenwald's work up to 1948 and an evaluation by C. Bloch, 1–28, second pagination). He also wrote works on the history of the Sanhedrin and biographies of leading rabbis, such as Joseph Caro and Moses Sofer. In the latter category are *Beit Yehonatan* (1908) about Jonathan *Eybeschuetz, and *Toledot Mishpaḥat Rosenthal* (1920) about the Rosenthal family, which included several rabbis. Greenwald compiled an important manual of traditional laws and rites of mourning, *Kol-Bo Avelut* (3 vols., 1947–52).

BIBLIOGRAPHY: N. Katzburg, in: *Sinai*, 37 (1955), 277–81; 40 (1957), 313–4; Kressel, Leksikon, 1 (1965), 511–2; EẒD, 1 (1958), 589–96. **ADD. BIBLIOGRAPHY:** M.L. Raphael, *Jews and Judaism in a Midwestern Jewish Community: Columbus, Ohio 1840–1953* (1979). M.D. Sherman, *Orthodox Judaism in America: A Biographical Dictionary and Sourcebook* (1996).

[Eisig Silberschlag / Michael Berenbaum (2nd ed.)]

GREETINGS AND CONGRATULATIONS. Although Jews have adopted the languages of the countries in which they live, they have always tended to retain traditional forms of greetings and congratulations either in Hebrew or Yiddish and occasionally in Aramaic, and some of these forms of greetings are adaptations of biblical verses while others are taken from the liturgy. Many are merely the expression of an emotion in Hebrew or Yiddish without any literary source. In the list below the most common forms of greetings are given; the list does not include the many variations which sometimes exist nor does it include simple translations such as *boker tov* (= good morning). (See Table: Greetings and Congratulations.)

Jewish Forms of Greetings and Congratulations

	Hebrew	Literal meaning	Occasions when said	Origin and/or reference
GREETINGS AND CONGRATULATIONS – GENERAL FORMS OF				
1. Shalom or Shalom lekha	שָׁלוֹם שָׁלוֹם לְךָ	Peace. Peace to you.	As a common greeting equivalent to "hello" or "goodbye" "Good day"	Gen. 29:6; 43:27; Ex. 18:7 Judg. 6:24 I Sam. 16:4
2. Shalom aleikhem	שָׁלוֹם עֲלֵיכֶם	Peace to you.	Same as above	
3. Aleikhem shalom	עֲלֵיכֶם שָׁלוֹם	To you, peace.	Response to greeting No. 2	
4. Barukh ha-ba	בָּרוּךְ הַבָּא	Blessed be the one who comes.	A common greeting, equivalent to "welcome." A child brought to the circumcision ceremony and a bride and groom approaching the wedding canopy are also greeted thus. The response to the greeting is No. 5 or 6.	
5. Barukh ha-nimẓa	בָּרוּךְ הַנִּמְצָא	Blessed be the one (already) present.	Response to greeting No. 4	Ps. 118:26
6. Barukh ha-yoshev	בָּרוּךְ הַיּוֹשֵׁב	Blessed be the one who is sitting.	Response to greeting No. 4. Used by a guest to the host sitting at the head of the table.	
7. Shalom berakhah ve-tovah	שָׁלוֹם בְּרָכָה וְטוֹבָה	Peace, blessing and (all) good (to you).	General blessing used by Sephardi Jews.	
8. Ḥazak u-varukh	חֲזַק וּבָרוּךְ	Be stong and blessed.	Same as above Also used in Sephardi synagogues to a person who returns to his seat after having performed liturgical functions.	
9. Yishar koḥakha or Yasher ko'akh	יִישַׁר כֹּחֲךָ	May your strength (increase) go straight.	Congratulations for success and achievement. In traditional synagogues also extended to a person who has been called up to the Torah reading.	
10. Ḥazak ve-emaẓ	חֲזַק וֶאֱמָץ	Be strong and of good courage.	Congratulations for success and achievement. Also extended to a bar mitzvah boy after he has finished reading the haftarah.	e.g., Deut 31:23
11. Biz hundert un tsvantsik	(Yiddish)	(May you live) until the age of 120.	A wish for long life.	
12. Tsu gezunt	(Yiddish)	Good health.	To a person who has sneezed; also to someone convalescing.	
13. a. Li-veri'ut	לִבְרִיאוּת	Good health.	Same as above	
b. Asuta	אָסוּתָא (Aramaic)	Good health.	Same as above	
14. Refu'ah shelemah	רְפוּאָה שְׁלֵמָה	(May you have) a complete recovery.	Wish to a sick person.	
SABBATH AND HOLIDAY GREETINGS				
15. a. Shabbat shalom	שַׁבָּת שָׁלוֹם	Good Sabbath.	The Sabbath greeting	
Gut shabes	(Yiddish)			
b. Shabbat hi mi-lizok u-refu'ah kerovah lavo	שַׁבָּת הִיא מִלִּזְעֹק וּרְפוּאָה קְרוֹבָה לָבוֹא	It is Sabbath and forbidden to make supplications but may you soon get well.	When visiting the sick on the Sabbath	Shab. 12a
16. a. Shavu'a tov	שָׁבוּעַ טוֹב	A good week.	Saturday night at the end of the Sabbath	
A gute vokh	(Yiddish)			
17. Gut khoydesh	(Yiddish)	A good new month.	On new moons	
18. Gut Yontev	(Yiddish) corrupted from the Hebrew Yom Tov	A good holiday (to you).	On holidays and festivals	
19. a. Mo'adim le-simḥah	מוֹעֲדִים לְשִׂמְחָה	Joyous holidays.	On festivals. The response to which is No. 20.	
b. Ḥag same'aḥ	חַג שָׂמֵחַ	Joyous holiday.		

Jewish Forms of Greetings and Congratulations (continued)

	Hebrew	Literal meaning	Occasions when said	Origin and/or reference
20. Ḥaggim u-zemannim lesason	חַגִּים וּזְמַנִּים לְשָׂשׂוֹן	Holidays and festivals for joy and gladness.	Response to No. 19a and 19b	This wording is from the prayer for the three festivals.
21. Ve-hayita akh same'aḥ	וְהָיִיתָ אַךְ שָׂמֵחַ	You shall have nothing but joy.	On Sukkot, when visiting a person in his sukkah	Deut. 16:15
		NEW YEAR AND DAY OF ATONEMENT		
22. a. Shanah tovah	שָׁנָה טוֹבָה	A good year (to you), or its more ample version:	During the Days of Penitence	
b. Le-shanah tovah tikkatevu (ve-tehatemu)	לְשָׁנָה טוֹבָה תִּכָּתֵבוּ (וְתֵחָתֵמוּ)	May you be inscribed (and sealed) for a good year (i.e. in the Book of Life), or its shorter form:		The wording is from the prayers *Amidah and *Avinu Malkenu
c. Ketivah tovah	כְּתִיבָה טוֹבָה	A good inscription (in the Book of Life).		
23. Gam le-mar	גַּם לְמַר	To you too.	Greetings in Nos. 22a, b, and c, as well as 24a and b	
			On the Day of Atonement, the day of "Sealing the book."	Wording from the prayer book.
24. a. Hatimah tovah	חֲתִימָה טוֹבָה	A sealing for good (to you), or its more ample version:		
b. Gemar hatimah tovah	גְּמַר חֲתִימָה טוֹבָה	A propitious final sealing (to you) (in the Book of Life).	As above. This form can be used until Hoshana Rabba.	
		ON JOYOUS OCCASIONS AND FAMILY EVENTS		
25. a. Mazzal tov	מַזָּל טוֹב	Good luck (i.e., may you enjoy a favorable zodiac constellation).	For joyous occasions, especially childbirth, betrothal, wedding, bar-mitzvah, etc.…	Ashkenazi custom.
b. Be-siman tov	בְּסִימָן טוֹב	Same as above	Same as above	Sephardi custom.
26. Barukh tihyeh	בָּרוּךְ תִּהְיֶה	Be you blessed (too), (i.e., the same to you).	Response to Mazzal tov wish	
27. Le-ḥayyim or	לְחַיִּים	To life.	On taking a drink, usually alcoholic.	Shab. 67b.
28. Le-ḥayyim tovim u-le-shalom	לְחַיִּים טוֹבִים וּלְשָׁלוֹם	Good life and peace (to you).	More ample form of No. 27.	
		DURING MOURNING		
29. Ha-Makom yenahem etkhem be-tokh avelei Ẓiyyon vi-Yrushalayim	הַמָּקוֹם יְנַחֵם אֶתְכֶם בְּתוֹךְ אֲבֵלֵי צִיּוֹן וִירוּשָׁלַיִם	May the Lord comfort you among all mourners for Zion and Jerusalem.	To a mourner during the week of mourning.	See: *Mourning
		ON YAHRZEIT		
30. Ad bi'at ha-go'el	עַד בִּיאַת הַגּוֹאֵל	(May you live) until the coming of the Messiah.	On the yearly anniversary of the death of a relative.	Among German Jews.
		IN WRITTEN FORM ONLY		
31. Ad me'ah shanah	עַד מֵאָה שָׁנָה (עמ"ש)	Until a hundred years.	In the heading of a private letter, after the addressee's name	
32. Zekhuto yagen aleinu	זְכוּתוֹ יָגֵן עָלֵינוּ (זי"ע)	May his merit protect us.	After name of distinguished deceased; usually ḥasidic.	

Jewish Forms of Greetings and Congratulations (continued)

	Hebrew	Literal meaning	Occasions when said	Origin and/or reference
33. Zikhrono li-verakhah or	זִכְרוֹנוֹ לִבְרָכָה (ז"ל)	May his memory be for a blessing.	After name of deceased; also in speech.	
Zekher ẓaddik li-verakhah	זֵכֶר צַדִּיק לִבְרָכָה (זצ"ל)	May the memory of the pious be for a blessing.		
34. Alav ha-shalom	עָלָיו הַשָּׁלוֹם (ע"ה)	Peace be on him.	As above.	
35. Natreih Raḥamana u-varkhei	נַטְרֵיה רַחֲמָנָא וּבַרְכֵיה (נר"ו) (Aramaic)	May God guard and bless him (you).	Written form of address.	
36. She-yiḥyeh le-orekh yamim tovim amen	שֶׁיִּחְיֶה לְאֹרֶךְ יָמִים טוֹבִים אָמֵן (שליט"א)	May he (you) live for many good days, Amen.	As above.	

°**GRÉGOIRE, HENRI BAPTISTE** (**Abbé Grégoire**; 1750–1831), Catholic clergyman, one of the activists of the *French Revolution. Grégoire led the campaign for the civic emancipation of the Jews before and during the Revolution. In the secular field, he held enlightened-revolutionary opinions, while in the religious field his outlook was neo-Jansenist. It was one of the principal expectations of the Jansenists that the Revolution would bring about the reform of the universe at the millennium and with it the return of Jews to the Christian religion and the Land of Israel. Grégoire adhered to these expectations, and the Jewish problem thus at first became the focal point upon which his secular activities and religious hopes converged. In 1785, Grégoire took part in a competition held by the Société Royale des Arts et Sciences of Metz on the question: "Are there possibilities of making the Jews more useful and happier in France?" His work, which shared the first prize, was published in 1789 under the title *Essai sur la régénération physique, morale, et politique des Juifs* (*Essay on the Physical, Moral and Political Reformation of the Jews*, London, c. 1791). In it Grégoire suggests that the Jews should be westernized and integrated within French society. He repeats the claim, which had already been voiced before him, that the main social and moral shortcomings of the Jews were due to the servitude to which they had been subjected. Amelioration of their status would also achieve reform of their character. Grégoire was, however, more extreme than C.W. *Dohm or *Mirabeau in pressing for the abolition of the fundamental causes of Jewish social and political separatism: communal autonomy, the Jewish quarters, Yiddish, and the "superstitious beliefs" to which the Jews adhered because they were misled by their rabbis. Grégoire however dismissed the traditional Christian claim that the Jews must suffer because of their sins as deicides. On this subject he said: "The oracles which announced the destruction of Jerusalem point out the distant moment at which the consequences of it are to end. The Deity directs every event in a manner agreeable to His supreme views; and perhaps He reserves for us the glory of realizing His designs in preparing by our humanity the revolution by which these people are to be reformed."

The opinions expressed in his work were the basis for his political and publicistic activities concerning the Jews from 1789 to 1806. Grégoire played an active and energetic role in raising the question of the Jews in the French National Assembly until emancipation was granted to them in September 1791. Among his other activities, he presented the delegation of Alsace-Lorraine Jews to the National Assembly on October 14, 1789, in connection with which he published a *Motion en faveur des Juifs*, which was a summary of his *Essai* drafted in a more revolutionary spirit. In 1802, while on a tour of Europe, he preached, advocating the emancipation of the Jews. In 1806, he published a pamphlet in answer to *Bonald's objections to the civic emancipation of French Jews. After *Napoleon Bonaparte's rise to power, Grégoire gradually withdrew from political activity and became increasingly engrossed in his religious and eschatological hopes, which centered on the expectation of the fall of Rome and the renewed establishment of a Jewish Jerusalem as the capital of a reconstituted Christian world. He organized a Franco-Italian circle which propagated these expectations. One of the members of this circle was A. Manzoni, a father of the Italian national movement. Later publications of his include *Observations nouvelles sur les Juifs, et spécialement sur ceux d'Allemagne* (2 vols., 1806), and *Histoire des sectes religieuses* (2 vols., 1810).

BIBLIOGRAPHY: H. Carnot (ed.), *Mémoires de H. Grégoire* (1838); P. Grunebaum-Ballin, *L'Abbé Grégoire et les Juifs* (1931); idem, in: REJ, 121 (1962), 383–96; F. Ruffini, *La vita religiosa di Alessandro Manzoni*, 2 (1931); M. Ginsburger, in: *Festschrift zu S. Dubnows 70ten Geburtstag* (1930), 201–6; A. Hertzberg, *French Enlightenment and the Jews* (1968), index.

[Baruch Mevorah]

°**GREGORY**, name of 16 popes.

GREGORY I (the Great), pope 590–604; the most important of the earlier popes from the point of view of Jewish history. It was he who formulated the Jewish policy of the papacy, faithfully followed in subsequent generations in both its favorable and its unfavorable aspects. Complaining bitterly in his sermons of the obduracy of the Jews and their stony hearts, he took care that the canonical restrictions against them should be obeyed in all their rigor. Twenty-eight of his 800 extant letters deal with Jewish matters. He strongly objected to the observance of any ceremonies that savored of Judaism or tended to obscure the boundaries between Church and Synagogue. Although approving of the initial stages of the reactions against the Jews in Spain under the Visigoths, nevertheless he insisted that the Jews should be treated with humanity and endeavored to have their legal rights confirmed and respected. The Jews of Italy and other countries frequently appealed to Gregory for protection. He was indignant when synagogues were destroyed and ordered them to be rebuilt. While condemning forced baptisms, he did not object to the offering of material benefits to prospective converts; although such actual converts might be insincere, their children would be brought up as faithful Christians. One of his epistles, beginning with the words *Sicut Judaeis*, emphasized that the Jews must be protected in the enjoyment of those rights guaranteed to them by law, and this phrase was prefixed (from the 12th century onward) to the traditional protective *bull generally issued by every pope on his accession.

[Cecil Roth]

GREGORY IX, pope 1227–41. Shortly after his election, Gregory granted the crusaders against the *Albigenses a moratorium on their debts to Jews and canceled the interest due. In 1229, he laid down that a Jewish child who had been baptized by his converted father was to be entrusted to the father and not to the mother, if she remained Jewish. During the same year, he also ordered that strong measures be taken against Jews who refused to pay the church tithes (which were due on houses acquired from Christians). Although the collection of decretals drawn up by *Raymond of Peñafort (as a continuation of the decree of Gratian) in 1230 and promulgated by Gregory in 1234 includes Gregory the Great's letter on the protection of synagogues, it also contains two texts from the Third Lateran Council which are unfavorable to the Jews (see *Church Councils). Intervening against the Jews of Hungary, Castile, and Portugal in 1231, he insisted on the observation of the canons relating to the Jewish *badge and the prohibition on the appointment of Jews to public office. In 1233, in Germany, he also condemned the employment of Christian servants by the Jews. However, during the same year, he issued the protective bull *Etsi Judaeorum* and in 1235 reminded all Christians of the terms of the bull *Sicut Judaeis*. Similarly, on Sept. 5, 1236, he issued orders to several archbishops and bishops of southwestern and western France to compel the crusaders to make good the losses the Jews had suffered at their hands. On several occasions from 1237 on Gregory replied to the anxieties expressed by King Louis IX of France over the use which should be made of the money paid by the Jews, inevitably derived from usury; the pope advised the king to employ this money for the relief of Constantinople or the Holy Land. Nicholas *Donin turned to Gregory with his denunciation of the Talmud; however, although he issued the order impounding the Talmud for an examination of its contents, its actual condemnation was pronounced by Pope *Innocent IV.

GREGORY X, pope 1271–76; one of the popes most kindly disposed toward the Jews. Renewing the bull of protection *Sicut Judaeis* in 1272, he added an important clause: an accusation against Jews based solely on the testimony of Christians was invalid; Jewish witnesses must also appear. Gregory vigorously combated the *blood libel, declaring that it was no more than an invention propagated in order to extort money from the Jews. He ordered that tribunals were not even to take such accusations into consideration: Jews who had been imprisoned on this charge were to be set free immediately, and in future a Jew was only to be arrested if actually caught in the act. At the Council of Lyons, in the summer of 1274, Gregory met Nathan b. Joseph *Official, with whom he had a lengthy discussion. In a memorandum drawn up for this council by Humbert of Romans in support of Gregory's policy, a long passage comes to the defense of the Jews against future attacks by crusaders. It should be noted, however, that Gregory also renewed the bull of Clement IV, *Turbato Corde*, which delivered the Jews (relapsed converts and their accomplices) into the hands of the Inquisition.

GREGORY XIII, pope 1572–85. It may be common knowledge that this pope reformed the calendar, but it is less well-known that Jews most probably contributed to this. Gregory's policy toward the Jews cannot be distinctly characterized, since it swayed between relative favor and severity. Soon after his election, he protected the Jews in the ghetto of Rome who were in danger of being attacked by the soldiers. Further, an order issued by his notary threatened with hanging any non-Jew found in the ghetto or its vicinity without a valid reason. Gregory authorized once more moneylending with a maximum interest rate of 24%. A warrant of June 10, 1577, confirmed the statutes of the Jewish community and permitted the collection of taxes. In 1581, he guaranteed the safe-conduct of Jews coming into Italy or passing through the country. Although Marranos were also able to benefit from this concession, Gregory nevertheless allowed the Marrano Joseph Saralbo, who had returned to Judaism in Ferrara, to be condemned to the stake in 1583. Gregory was also responsible for organizing regular compulsory missionary sermons, often with the collaboration of apostate preachers (see *Sermons to Jews). The Jewish community was compelled to defray the costs of this institution, as well as the expenses of the House of *Catechumens. In order that converts should not be defrauded of their share in the family fortune, Gregory ordered that an inventory of a family's belongings be drawn up immediately after the baptism of one of its members. The bull *Antiqua Judaeorum improbitas*, of June 1, 1581, authorized the Inquisition directly to handle cases involving Jews, especially those concerning blasphemies against Jesus or Mary, incitement to heresy or assistance to heretics, possession of forbidden books, or the employment of Christian wet nurses. During the same year, however, following the intervention by Avtalion *Modena, Gregory suspended the order which he had just issued confiscating the books of several Jewish communities of Italy. In 1581, he also exempted the Jews from wearing the badge on certain occasions (journeys, visits to fairs). The new prohibitions against Jewish physicians treating Christian patients contributed to the decline of medical science among Italian Jews. However, shortly before his death, Gregory intervened with the Knights of Malta to obtain the release of Jewish prisoners in their hands, even though the ransom he offered was lower than the sum demanded.

[Bernhard Blumenkranz]

BIBLIOGRAPHY: GREGORY I: S. Katz, in: JQR, 34 (1933/34), 113–36; B. Blumenkranz, *Juifs et chrétiens dans le monde occidental 430–1096* (1960), passim. GREGORY IX: S. Grayzel, *Church and the Jews in the XIII*[th] *Century* (1966[2]), passim; Vogelstein-Rieger, 211, 232–37; L. Auvray (ed.), *Les registres de Gregory IX*, 4 vols. (1890–1955); E. Friedberg (ed.), *Décrétales* (1881); A. Clerval, in: *Dictionnaire de Théologie Catholique*, 6 (1924), 1805–6. GREGORY X: S. Grayzel, *Church and the Jews in the XIII*[th] *Century* (1966[2]), index; Vogelstein-Rieger, 244f.; L. Gatto, *Il pontificato di Gregorio X* (1959), passim; P.A. Throop, *Criticism of the Crusade* (1940), 166ff. GREGORY XIII: Vogelstein-Rieger, 169–76; Roth, Italy, 315–7 and passim; Milano, Italia, 255–7 and passim; L. v. Pastor, *Storia dei Papi*, 9 (1955), passim.

GREGORY, SIR THEODORE (1890–1971), British economist. Gregory, who was born in London, taught at the London School of Economics from 1913 to 1919. He was professor of economics at the University of London from 1917 to 1937 and from 1929 to 1930 was dean of the faculty. In addition to his teaching activities, Gregory served from 1929 to 1931 on the Macmillan Committee on Industry and Finance which laid the basis for the renewal of Britain's financial system. At various times he also acted as an adviser to the governments of Australia, New Zealand, Greece, and the Irish Free State, and was the first economics adviser to the government of India. His main fields were general and monetary economics, and his numerous publications include *Gold, Unemployment, and Capitalism* (1933), *The Gold Standard and Its Future* (1932, 1935[3]), *India on the Eve of the Third Five-Year Plan* (1961), and *Ernest Oppenheimer and the Economic Development of Southern Africa* (1962). He was knighted in 1942.

[Joachim O. Ronall]

°GREGORY OF TOURS (Georgius Florentius; 538–594), bishop of Tours from 573. Most of the information on the Jews in Merovingian France during the second half of the sixth century comes from Gregory. He was present at – and later participated – in the disputation held between King Chilperic and the Jew *Priscus in 581, which he describes in his *Historia Francorum*. This same work contains a report on the forced conversion of Jews in *Clermont-Ferrand in 576 and Chilperic's forcible attempt to impose conversion throughout his whole kingdom in 582. Gregory is also the source testifying to the ancient presence of Jews in Tours, Marseilles, Orléans, Bourges, and other places. His works contain invaluable information on the economic and social conditions of the Jews. The manner in which he often introduces Jews into his tales of miracles is curious: their function is in a sense a guarantee to the authenticity of his narrative. It was Gregory who introduced into the West two legends of Oriental origin, concerning "the Jewish child of the blazing furnace" (who had taken communion and been punished by his father, but saved by the virgin Mary) and the desecrated icon (a painting representing Jesus, lacerated by the Jews, which had supposedly begun to bleed); these two legends are of grave significance because one was the distant source of the *blood libel and the other of the *Host desecration accusation.

BIBLIOGRAPHY: B. Blumenkranz, *Auteurs chrétiens latins* (1963), 67–73; idem, *Juifs et chrétiens…* (1960), index; F. Cayre, *Patrologie* (1945), 264–67.

[Bernhard Blumenkranz]

GRENOBLE, capital of the Isère department, France, formerly capital of Dauphiné. A lamentation on the martyrdom of ten Jews from Grenoble was incorporated in the Bourguignon *maḥzor* in the second half of the 13th century. After the Jews were expelled from France in 1306, Dauphin Humbert I allowed a number of them to settle in Grenoble, offering them relatively favorable privileges. However, at the time of the *Black Death in 1348, 74 Jews were arrested and, after a trial lasting three months, were burned at the stake. After the general expulsion of Jews from France in 1394, there were no Jews living in Grenoble until after the Revolution. In 1717, a group from Comtat Venaissin attempted to settle there, but the city *parlement* drove them out. A new community was formed after the Revolution. The arrival of Jews from Alsace in 1874 significantly increased the size and importance of the Grenoble community.

Holocaust and Postwar Periods

During World War II, Grenoble was first occupied by the Italians, and then later by the Germans. It was an important center for various forms of Jewish resistance, including armed struggle, the rescue of children, and the hiding and "camouflage" of adults. The *Gestapo became especially active in the area from 1943 on, arresting, torturing, and deporting hundreds of Jews and members of the Resistance. Marc Haguenau (for whom a Jewish group of the French underground was named) was tortured and killed in Grenoble. Léonce Bernheim, a noted Zionist leader, and his wife were arrested in the vicinity of Grenoble. In 1943 at a secret meeting in the city, Isaac *Schneersohn helped lay the groundwork for the creation of the *Centre de Documentation Juive Contemporaine to collect material on the Nazi genocide. After the war, many refugees stayed in Grenoble, and by 1960 the Jewish population numbered over 1,000. Beginning in 1962, the Jewish population increased rapidly, thanks to the influx of immigrants from North Africa. By the late 1960s, it numbered 5,000; by 1971, it had reached about 8,000, but by the turn of the century it had dropped to somewhat less than 7,000. The community has both an Ashkenazi and a Sephardi synagogue, and maintains a range of institutions, including kosher butchers, a *talmud torah,* various youth groups, and a community center. A Jewish radio station, Kol Hachalom (Voice of Peace), has been in operation in Grenoble since 1983.

BIBLIOGRAPHY: Gross, Gal Jud (1897), 143; Ḥ. Schirmann, in: *Zion*, 19 (1954), 66; Z. Szajkowski, *Franco-Judaica* (1962), no. 310; idem, *Analytical Franco-Jewish Gazetteer* (1966), 205–9; A. Prudhomme, Histoire de Grenoble (1888), 138ff., 198. **ADD. BIBLIOGRAPHY:** *Guide juif de France* (1971), 150.

[Georges Levitte / David Weinberg (2nd ed.)]

GRESH, ALAIN (1948–), French Egyptian-born historian, journalist, and political activist. Gresh was born in Cairo to a Coptic-Catholic father and a Jewish mother. Though an Egyptian citizen, he was raised and educated in French and studied at the French High School in Cairo. He remembers the war of 1956, after the nationalization of the Suez Canal by Nasser, when as a young boy he could not understand why French planes were bombing Egypt. After his high school was in turn nationalized, Gresh became aware of the growing anti-Jewish feeling in Egypt. Himself a declared atheist, he moved to France towards the end of the Algerian war of Independence, in 1962, and met in Paris Henri Curiel, who led a network of *"porteurs the valise"* – the French militants who provided help and weapons to supporters of Algerian independence. A left-wing, anti-colonialist militant, he grew closer to the left-wing Catholic activists of the CCFD and Témoignage Chrétien and to the *Monde Diplomatique* newspaper, a forerunner of the movement against globalization, and he eventually became one of the paper's chief editors together with fellow left-wing Jews Dominique Vidal and Serge Halimi. Still committed to atheism, he nevertheless advocated a dialogue between left-wing and grassroots religious movements, whether Christian (CCFD), Islamic, or Jewish. His sympathetic view of Islam is expressed in *L'Islam, la République et le monde* (2004), Gresh's contribution to the heated and passionate debate about Islam and French laicism. A relatively moderate anti-Zionist, accepting Israel as a given fact and advocating a two-state solution, Gresh got from his Egyptian childhood an understanding of the Arab cause, which he assimilated into his sincere adherence to French Republican values; his position on the Israeli-Palestinian conflict is summarized in a 2001 book, *Israël – Palestine, Vérités sur un conflit.*

[Dror Franck Sullaper (2nd ed.)]

°**GRESSMANN, HUGO** (1877–1927), German Protestant theologian, student of the Bible and the ancient Orient. His teachers included J. *Wellhausen, A. Eichhorn, and M. *Lidzbarski. Gressmann received his doctorate at Goettingen in 1900. In 1902–07 he taught in Kiel; from 1907 until his death he was professor of Bible at the University of Berlin. His main scholarly work was on the history of Israel's religion. A disciple of Gunkel, his approach was based on the analysis of literary genres and motifs. He acquired an interest in Palestinian archaeology after working with G. Dalman in Jerusalem and Petra. This led him to attempt to discover the influence of the Palestinian geographic milieu on the world view of Israel and on the way of life of the early inhabitants of Palestine. The same interest in realia led to the production of a monumental volume of translated ancient Near Eastern texts and an accompanying volume of illustrations relevant to biblical studies. Gressmann also created a scholarly institute in Berlin for research on post-biblical Judaism. His principal works are: *Der Ursprung der israelitisch-jüdischen Eschatologie* (1905), *Die aelteste Geschichtsschreibung und Prophetie Israels* (1910, 1921²), *Mose und seine Zeit* (1913), *Das Weihnachtsevangelium* (1914), and *Der Messias* (1929). He edited the *Altorientalische Texte zum Alten Testament* (1926²) and the *Altorientalische Bilder zum Alten Testament* (1927²); Gressman also edited the third edition of Bousset's *Die Religion des Judentums im spaethellenistischen Zeitalter* (1926³).

ADD. BIBLIOGRAPHY: W. Thiel, in: DBI, 1:467–68.

[Moshe Zevi (Moses Hirsch) Segal / S. David Sperling (2nd ed.)]

GREY, JOEL (**Joel Katz**, 1932–), U.S. musical-comedy actor. Born in Cleveland, Ohio, Grey went into vaudeville with his father, the bandleader Mickey Katz, and was helped by Eddie Cantor to secure nightclub engagements. He made his New York debut in *The Littlest Revue* (1956). He won critical acclaim for his Broadway performance in *Stop the World – I Want to Get Off* (1962) and gained further success in the role of Master of Ceremonies in *Cabaret* (1966), for which he won a Tony Award, and as George M. Cohan in *George M* (1968). Grey's other Broadway appearances include *Borscht Capades* (1951); *Come Blow Your Horn* (1961–62); *Goodtime Charlie* (1975); *The Grand Tour* (1979); and *Chicago* (1996). In 2003 he began his run as the Wizard of Oz in the musical *Wicked.*

Grey appeared in films as well, starting with *About Face* in 1952. His other films include *Come September* (1961); *Cabaret* (1972), for which he won an Academy Award for Best Supporting Actor; *Man on a Swing* (1974); *Buffalo Bill and the Indians* (1976); *The Seven Percent Solution* (1976); *Remo Williams* (1985); *Kafka* (1991); *The Music of Chance* (1993); *The Dangerous* (1994); *Venus Rising* (1995); *The Empty Mirror* (1996); *Reaching Normal* (1999); *Dancer in the Dark* (2000); and *The Fantasticks* (2000).

Grey is one of a handful of performers to win both a Tony and an Oscar for having portrayed the same role on stage and screen (in *Cabaret*). Others among that handful include Yul Brynner for *The King and I;* Rex Harrison for *My Fair Lady;* and Patty Duke for *The Miracle Worker.* He is the father of actress Jennifer Grey.

Grey published *Pictures I Had to Take* (2003), a book of photographs that he had taken over a span of 25 years during his travels to Southeast Asia, Europe, South and Central America, and throughout the United States.

[Ruth Beloff (2nd ed.)]

GRILICHES, AVENIR (1822–1905), Russian engraver. Griliches was born in Vilna. He was self-taught and attracted attention by engraving a striking resemblance of the czar. In 1871 he became one of the few Jews permitted to stay in St. Petersburg, where he was employed by the Imperial Mint. In 1889 and 1898 Griliches was listed officially as mint engraver at St. Petersburg. He is credited with engraving the state seals of Alexander III and Nicholas II, as well as the five ruble, one ruble, half ruble, and twenty kopeck coins. He produced some of the most distinguished Russian commemorative medals of the 1880s and 1890s. His son ABRAHAM (1852–c. 1916), also born in Vilna, graduated from the rabbinical school and painters studio there, and then from the St. Petersburg Academy of Fine Arts in 1876. He was employed as an engraver at the Imperial Mint. Raised to the position of senior engraver, he is credited with striking some dies of the coinage of Nicholas II, as well as the 1912 Alexander III commemorative medal. Abraham Griliches was even more noted for his medals, for which he received awards at the Paris Exposition in 1889 and 1900. He was also an excellent gem engraver. Many of his works are kept in the State Hermitage Museum and other museums in Russia.

[Daniel M. Friedenberg]

GRINBERG, ALEKSANDER ABRAMOVICH (1898–1966), Russian chemist. Grinberg graduated from the University of Leningrad and was appointed professor of chemistry at the Lensovet Leningrad Technological Institute (1936). He was an authority on the chemistry of complex compounds and especially platinum chemistry. He was awarded a Stalin Prize (1946) and was an academician of the U.S.S.R. Academy of Sciences (1958).

GRINKER, ROY RICHARD SR. (1900–1993), U.S. neuropsychiatrist and psychoanalyst. Born in Chicago, Grinker taught at the University of Chicago from 1927. During World War II he rose to the rank of colonel in the U.S. Army Medical Corps. From 1946 Grinker was director of the institute for psychosomatic and psychiatric research and training at the Michael Reese Hospital in Chicago, and supervisory analyst at the Chicago Institute for Psychoanalysis. From 1951 he was clinical professor of psychiatry at the University of Illinois and in 1969 became professor of psychiatry at the University of Chicago's medical school.

Grinker was chief editor of the *Archives of General Psychiatry* from 1956. He also wrote many books and articles in his professional field. After publishing the textbook *Neurology* (1934, 1966[6]), Grinker collaborated with J.P. Spiegel in writing *Men under Stress* (1945), an account of the treatment of war neuroses based on military personnel's experiences in North Africa. The two men developed the treatment of the emotionally traumatized soldier with a drug to promote a "catharsis" of his battle experiences. Grinker outlined the results of his research and therapeutic treatment of psychosomatic disturbances in two books: *Psychosomatic Research* (1953) and (with F.P. Robbins) *Psychosomatic Case Book* (1954). He also devoted much attention to the theory of an integrated approach to normal and disturbed human behavior. He tried to elicit the relations between the intrapersonal physical and psychological systems and those with which the person interacts in his environment. Grinker's views were elaborated in two published symposia: *Toward a Unified Theory of Human Behavior* (1956), which he edited, and *Integrating the Approaches to Mental Disease* (ed. by H.D. Kruse, 1957).

He was awarded the Distinguished Service Award by the American Psychiatric Association in 1972 and by the University of Chicago's Medical and Biological Sciences Alumni Association in 1974.

Other books by Grinker include *The Borderline Syndrome: A Behavioral Study of Ego Functions* (with B. Werble and R. Drye, 1968), *Psychosomatic Concepts* (1973), *Psychiatry in Broad Perspective* (1975), and *Fifty Years in Psychiatry: A Living History* (1979).

[Louis Miller / Ruth Beloff (2nd ed.)]

GRINSPUN, BERNARDO (1926–), Argentinian economist and statesman, specializing in international economic and foreign debt. He belongs to the outstanding Argentinian circle of economists of our time (Aldo Ferrer, Guido Di Tella, etc.) and was linked with the group that controlled economic affairs during the former Radical party's government of President Illia (1963–66) on whose staff Grinspun held the post of secretary of commerce. He is also connected with the enterprise group which led the Federation Economica de Buenos Aires and especially the medium-size entrepreneurs. When democratic rule was restored to Argentina in 1983, Grinspun was appointed minister of finance in the cabinet of President Raul Alfonsin, in which capacity he sought to extract the country from the serious economic plight in which it had been left by the military junta.

[José Luis Nachenson and Noemi Hervits de Najenson]

GRISHABER, ISAAC (d. 1815), Hungarian rabbi. Born in Cracow, Grishaber went in 1782 to Hungary and was appointed rabbi of Paks. For an unknown reason he left this community and went to serve the community of Baja, but toward the end of his life he returned to Paks. He was in halakhic correspondence with Ezekiel *Landau, author of the *Noda bi-Yehudah*, and studied under him for a while in Prague, as well as with Moses *Sofer. Grishaber was resolute in his views and fought for them stubbornly and courageously. He was involved in a violent controversy in 1798–99 because of his dispute with Rabbi Aaron *Chorin over whether sturgeon is *kasher*. He published a pamphlet on the subject, *Makel No'am* (Vienna 1799), giving his reasons for forbidding this fish, with supporting letters from contemporary rabbis in Hungary and elsewhere.

BIBLIOGRAPHY: P.Z. Schwartz, *Shem ha-Gedolim me-Ereẓ Hagar*, 1 (1913), 506 no. 227; A. Stern, *Meliẓei Esh al Ḥodshei Kislev-Adar* (1962[2]), 206 no. 67; D. Sofer, *Mazkeret Paks*, 1 (1962), 3–91.

[Samuel Weingarten-Hakohen]

GROBART, FABIO (**Avraham Simchovich**; 1905–1994), Cuban Communist leader. Grobart was born in Trzciany (Poland) as Avraham Moishe Grobard to an Orthodox family. His father cleaned hogs' skins and his mother was a servant. He was sent to school to Goniondz, where his uncle trained him to become a tailor. Attracted by Marxist ideals, he became an active member of the Communist Youth League in Bialystok. In 1922 he had to flee from the police and changed his name to Avraham Simchovich.

He reached Cuba in 1924, where he joined the small Sección Hebrea de la Agrupación Comunista de la Habana (Jewish Section of the Communist Organization of Havana), which had been founded shortly before. On August 16, 1925, he was one of the ten founders of the Cuban Communist Party, and was active in diffusing its doctrines among Jewish workers. After his arrest and deportation (1930) he reached Moscow, where he was probably trained to return to Cuba under a covert identity (as Otto Modley). He became a central figure in the Cuban Communist Party, although he acted mostly behind the scenes. From 1952 to 1960 he represented the Cuban workers in the World Labor Organization in Vienna and Prague.

In 1960, shortly after the outbreak of the Castro Revolution, he returned to Cuba, and in 1965 he was appointed director of the journal *Cuba Socialista*. He was considered the ideologist of the Cuban Communist Party. He founded the Institute of History of the Cuban Communist Party (1973) and was a deputy of the Cuban Parliament.

BIBLIOGRAPHY: M. Corrales, *The Chosen Island: Jews in Cuba* (2005).

[Margalit Bejarano (2nd ed.)]

GROCK (**Charles Adrien Wettach**; 1880–1959), Swiss clown. Born at Moulin de Loveresse, the son of a Jewish father and non-Jewish mother, Grock was first attached to a traveling circus. He performed on the stage in England from 1911 to 1924, and afterward throughout Europe. He specialized as a musical clown, playing a tiny violin at a grand piano and getting into trouble with both. He built his act into the world's most famous comic display. His German autobiography appeared in English in 1957 as *Grock, King of Clowns*.

GRODNO (**Horodno**), city in Belarus, formerly Poland-Lithuania. One of the oldest Jewish communities in the former grand duchy of *Lithuania (see *Poland-Lithuania), the Grodno community received a charter from Grand Duke Witold in 1389. This indicates the existence of a synagogue and cemetery and shows that Jews owned real property in the city and its environs and engaged in commerce, crafts, and agriculture. They were banished by the general decree of expulsion of the Jews from Lithuania in 1495 and their property was sequestered, but they were permitted to return and to claim their possessions in 1503. During the 16th century the townsmen of Grodno were consistently hostile to the Jews, the artisans in particular. Grodno, however, became noted as a center of Jewish learning. By the end of the century a number of *battei midrash* and yeshivot had been established and Horodno was written by the Jews as though it were *Har-Adonai* ("the holy mount" in Hebrew). The community was spared during the *Chmielnicki massacres in 1648–49 and gave asylum to fugitives from the south, but later suffered from the Russian invasions of 1655–57 and subsequent invasions by the Swedes. The fanaticism of the Jesuits was from 1616 an additional spur to frequent calumnies against the Jews, and the kidnapping of Jewish children for forced conversion. The community became heavily involved in debt to pay for the defense and ransom of those victims. A *blood libel in 1790 resulted in the death of R. Eleazar b. Solomon of Virbalis (Verzhbolow). Another ritual murder accusation was made in 1816. One of the three principal communities in Lithuania, Grodno was represented on the Council of Lithuania (see *Councils of the Lands). It thus assumed responsibility for the care of Jewish affairs in general, while undertaking Jewish defense in libel cases in particular, since it was the seat of the Lithuanian court of appeal. The first Hebrew book to be published in Lithuania was printed in Grodno in 1788 in the Royal press. A second Hebrew press, established in Grodno in 1793, formed the kernel of the celebrated publishing and printing house owned by the *Romm family, whose early publications were in "Vilna and Grodno" (subsequently in Vilna).

Population Figures

In 1549 the Jewish population formed 17% of the total; in 1560 it numbered 1,000 according to one estimate, in 1764, 2,418 and in 1793, some 4,000. When Grodno passed to Russia with the third partition of Poland in 1795, the Jewish community was the largest in Lithuania after Vilna. The Jewish population numbered 8,422 in 1816 (85.3% of the total); approximately 10,300 in 1856–57 (63.3%); 27,343 in 1887 (68.7%); 27,874 in 1904 (64.1%); 34,461 in 1912 (c. 60%); 15,504 in 1916 (64.4%); 18,697 in 1921 (53.4%); and 21,159 in 1931 (42.6%). The decrease in the Jewish population during World War I was partly due to their expulsion to inner Russia by the Russian military authorities in 1915. The decrease relative to the general population after the war was due both to Jewish emigration from Grodno and to the official encouragement given to Poles to settle there after its conquest by the Poles in 1919.

Occupations

The principal traditional sources of income of Grodno Jews were commerce (principally in agricultural and timber products) and crafts, and more recently, industry. In 1887, 88% of commercial undertakings, 76% of factories and workshops, and 65.2% of real estate in Grodno were Jewish owned. The situation did not alter appreciably before World War I, but after Grodno's reversion to Poland the Jews were systematically ousted from their economic positions and from the middle of the 1930s a stringent anti-Jewish economic boycott was imposed. In 1921 there were 1,273 industrial enterprises and workshops in Jewish ownership, employing 3,719 persons (2,341 of them hired workers, of whom 83.2% were Jews), 34.6% for food processing (and tobacco), and 29% garment manufacturing. In the 1930s there were 938 Jewish artisans: 364 were tailors and 168 cobblers. Jewish doctors and lawyers constituted half the professional people in Grodno. In 1937 there were 65 Jewish-owned large or medium-sized factories employing 2,181 workers, of whom 895 (41%) were Jews, as against 51 state-owned or non-Jewish enterprises employing 2,262 workers. Among the other main enterprises then owned by Jews were a large bicycle factory, a factory for artistic leather products, a glass factory, a lithographic plant, foundries, and breweries. Some of the plants proved good training grounds for potential immigrants to Palestine during the 1930s. The huge Y. Shereshevsky tobacco factory in Grodno employed, before World War I, some 1,800 workers and provided a livelihood for hundreds of families in subsidiary activities, nearly all Jewish. Work stopped on the Sabbath and Jewish festivals and it maintained a school for the children of the employees. The Polish government nationalized it in the 1920s, making it conform to the official pattern and the majority of the Jewish workers were forced out.

Rabbis and Authors

Among the notable rabbis serving in Grodno were Mordecai *Jaffe (16th century); Jonah b. Isaiah Te'omim, author of *Kikayon de-Yonah* (1630); Moses b. Abraham, author of *Tiferet le-Moshe* (1776); Joshua b. Joseph, author of *Meginnei Shelomo* (1715); Mordecai Suesskind of Rothenburg (17th century); and Simḥah b. Naḥman Rapoport of Dubno. The last to hold office was Benjamin Braudo (d. 1818). The dispute over the succession to the rabbinate after his death led to its abolition in Grodno and the appointment of *morei hora'ah* (decisors on law). The kabbalist and ethical pietist Alexander *Susskind, author of *Yesod ve-Shoresh ha-Avodah* and *Ẓavva'ah*, was a citizen of Grodno. Also renowned beyond Grodno in the 19th century was Nahum b. Uzziel – R. Noḥumke – a scholar who was famous for his devoted care of the poor.

Communal Institutions

In the 19th century, the Grodno community supported numerous *battei midrash* and societies formed by the **Mitnaggedim* for religious studies, which were attended regularly by people from all classes of the community. The famous scholar R. Shimon *Shkop headed the great "Sha'arei Hatorah" yeshivah in Grodno (1920–39). The Hebrew poet Abba Asher Constantin *Shapiro originated from Grodno. The Hebrew author Abraham Shalom *Friedberg and the Yiddish poet Leib Naidus lived there. The Jewish community made outstanding provision for benevolent and welfare institutions. From the 18th century there existed the society for care of the sick (Bikkur Ḥolim). Some wealthy members of the community contributed lavishly toward establishing orphanages, hospitals, old-age homes, and an excellent trade school. One of the first loan and savings cooperative funds in Russia was opened in 1900.

Labor and Socialist Movements

A Jewish Socialist circle already existed in Grodno in 1875–76 where the first Jewish Socialists turned their attention to the working man. From the end of the 1890s the various trends of Jewish labor movements became increasingly active in Grodno, in particular in the tobacco factory. Central to the movement was the *Bund. The labor movements played an important part in organizing Jewish self-defense in Grodno in 1903 and 1907, and some Jewish youngsters there also avenged the bloodshed that resulted from the pogroms at *Bialystok. In the years between the two world wars the working movement fought for the rights of the Jewish worker to obtain employment and against anti-Jewish discrimination by the Polish government.

Zionism

A legal document of 1539 which deals with a Jewish couple who intended to leave Grodno for Jerusalem is almost a symbol of the strong roots later struck by the Ḥibbat Zion and Zionist movements in Grodno. Among Grodno Jews joining the early settlements in Ereẓ Israel in the 19th century was Fischel *Lapin, who settled in Jerusalem in 1863 and was a prominent communal worker. A society for settling in Ereẓ Israel was founded in Grodno in 1872, and a second acquired land in *Petaḥ Tikvah on its foundation in 1880, where a pioneer settler from Grodno was Mordecai *Diskin. The society of *Ḥovevei Zion in Grodno in 1890 gave generous support in building the Girls' Hebrew school in Jaffa. Grodno was one of the most active centers of Ḥovevei Zion, as also subsequently of the Zionist movement in Russia, in which the two brothers Bezalel and Leib *Jaffe were prominent. Zionist shekels were printed clandestinely in Grodno. Grodno remained one of the important centers of the Zionist movement and its constituent parties and youth movements between 1916 and 1939. During World War II, when Grodno was under Soviet rule (1939–41), a clandestine Zionist center there transferred intending immigrants to Ereẓ Israel via Vilna, then the capital of Soviet Lithuania. In the educational sphere, the reformed *ḥeder* (*ḥeder metukkan*), founded in Grodno in 1900 and providing instruction in Hebrew, was among the first and most successful of its type in Russia. Hebrew teachers' preparatory groups were introduced in 1901 and the famous "Pedagogic Courses" which trained numerous pioneer Hebrew teachers in 1907. After World War I the Grodno Zionists, headed by Noah Bas, instituted the Hebrew educational system *Tarbut. Jewish pioneers from Grodno emigrated in the successive *aliyyot* from the beginning of the *Bilu movement, and Grodno youth were among the first to join the Second Aliyah. The Grodno *He-Ḥalutz association was among the first founded in Lithuania, and the Third Aliyah from Poland was initiated by Grodno pioneers.

Holocaust Period

Under Polish rule there were pogroms in Grodno as early as 1935. A large-scale pogrom took place between Sept. 18 and 20, 1939, during the Polish army's withdrawal from the town prior to the entry of the Soviet Army. The Nazis occupied Grodno on June 22, 1941, the day on which Germany attacked the Soviet Union. On July 7, around 100 Jews in the professions were arrested and executed by the Nazi authorities. Jews were banned from public transportation, from places of entertainment, and from using the sidewalks. A *Judenrat* was organized and forced labor was imposed. While Jews were evicted from their apartments, German soldiers looted Jewish homes. On Nov. 1, 1941, the Jews of Grodno were segregated into two ghettos: one for "skilled workers" housed 15,000 in the small, overcrowded "synagogue quarter" (*Shulhof*) and the fish market; the other, which was smaller and reserved for the "unproductive," held 10,000 in the suburb of Slobodka. On Nov. 2, 1942, the ghettos were surrounded and sealed off, and their liquidation began. The liquidation took place in several stages. On Nov. 14–22, the Slobodka ghetto was destroyed and its inhabitants were taken "to work places" but in fact to their death in Auschwitz. That same month 4,000 people were expelled from the ghetto in the *Shulhof* to the transit camp of Kelbasin, 4 mi. (6 km.) from Grodno. Some of them died there as a result of the inhuman conditions, and the rest were expelled after a short period together with the Jewish population of the villages in the Grodno region, who were then sent to either Auschwitz or Treblinka. In a big Nazi *Aktion* on Jan. 17–22, 1943, 11,600 Jews were sent to Auschwitz, where 9,851 were gassed immediately and 1,799 put to work. Another 5,000 from the skilled-worker ghetto remained in the city. In February 1943, 4,000 were deported to the Treblinka death camp, and the remaining 1,000 skilled workers were deported on March 12 to Bialystok. According to a Nazi source, 44,049 Grodno Jews were sent to the extermination camps, 20,577 Jews from Grodno itself, and 23,472 from neighboring townlets. Some 180 Jews remained in Grodno and the district, hidden among gentiles or otherwise concealed until the town was liberated by the Soviet Army on July 14, 1944. Early in 1942, a Jewish underground resistance and defense movement was formed; members of Zionist youth movements, like Bela Hazzan, set up a communications center in Grodno for contact with the ghettos in *Vilna, *Bialystok, and *Warsaw; there was also a workshop for forging "Aryan" papers and travel permits for members of the movement engaged in rescuing Jews and in armed defense. Before the big "*Aktion*," an unsuccessful attempt was made to assassinate Streblow, a chief executioner of Grodno Jewry. There was also an attempt to organize a mass escape from the Great Synagogue, which served as a collection center for deportation, and to assassinate Kurt Wiese, the other chief executioner of Grodno Jewry.

After World War II

Groups of Grodno Jewish partisans were active in forests. Some 2,000 Jews resettled in Grodno over a period of years following its liberation. By the 1960s Grodno had no synagogue. The "old" synagogue was a storehouse; the "new" one was used as a sports hall. In the mid-1950s the Jewish cemetery was plowed up. Tombstones were taken away and used for building a monument to Lenin. There are four mass graves of Jews near the city, on which monuments were erected after World War II. One of them was repeatedly desecrated and damaged and there were several cases of graves being similarly treated. In the 1990s the revived community started renovating the synagogue and in the early 2000s had a resident rabbi.

BIBLIOGRAPHY: Regesty, I–II; S.A. Friedenstein, *Ir Gibborim* (1880); Rabin, in: *He-Avar* (1957); *Grodno, dzieje w zarysie* (1936); Tenenbaum-Tamarof, *Dappim min ha-Deleikah* (1948); *Yedi'ot Beit Loḥamei ha-Getta'ot* (1957), no. 18–19, 53–62; H. Grosman, *Anshei ha-Maḥteret* (1965[2]), 172–84; *Grodner Opklangen*, no. 1–18 (Buenos Aires, 1949–1968).

[Dov Rabin]

GRODZINSKI, ḤAYYIM OZER (1863–1940), talmudic scholar and one of the spiritual leaders of Lithuanian Orthodox Jewry, son of the talmudic scholar, Solomon David Grodzinski (1831–c. 1908). Grodzinski studied in the yeshivot of Eisheshok and Volozhin, where he was known as an *illui* (prodigy). In 1887 he was appointed one of the *dayyanim* of the *bet din* of Vilna, and he came to be regarded as its leading *dayyan*. Grodzinski was one of the initiators of the Vilna Conference of 1909, which resulted in the formation of the Orthodox Keneset Israel organization. He also participated in the founding conference of the Agudat Israel at Katowice in 1914, served as a leading member of that party's Council of Sages, and was the prime force for spreading its influence in and around Vilna. An initiator of the conference of rabbis at Grodno in 1924 which founded the Va'ad ha-Yeshivot ("Council of the Yeshivot") for the spiritual and material support of yeshivot and their students, he was the moving spirit behind the Council.

Grodzinski was a vehement opponent of Zionism and of secular education for Jews, his aim being to preserve the Torah milieu of the Lithuanian yeshivot and townlets intact. In 1934 he prevented the transfer of the Hildesheimer rabbinical seminary from Berlin to Tel Aviv. Asked by an Agudat Israel kibbutz whether it was permitted to settle on Jewish National Fund land, he advised its members "Let him who is firm in spirit stay steadfast in his place and not hurry to join the swelling stream… until God has mercy on His people and hastens his redemption." In 1929, when Isaac Rubinstein was chosen as chief rabbi of Vilna, Grodzinski's supporters sparked a violent controversy in the community.

Grodzinski's responsa were published in three volumes under the title of *Aḥi'ezer* (1922, 1925, 1939). In the introduction to the last volume, written on the eve of the Holocaust, he spoke of the fear and dismay that was rapidly descending upon the entire Jewish people, both in the Diaspora and (in a reference to the 1936–39 riots) in Ereẓ Israel. He wrote about the spiritual disintegration of the Jewish community, and its laxity in the observance of the Sabbath, *kashrut*, and the laws of marital purity. All this he blamed on the Reform movement in the West and on secular education in the East. His sole consolation was in "the important work of preserving and strengthening Torah education" and in the fact that "the large and small yeshivot were the strongholds of Judaism… in Poland and Lithuania."

BIBLIOGRAPHY: S. Rothstein, *Aḥi'ezer* (1946[2]); O.Z. Rand (ed.), *Toledot Anshei Shem* (1950), 21–22; O. Feuchtwanger, *Righteous*

Lives (1965), 17–22; J.L. Kagan and H.B. Perlman, in: L. Jung (ed.), *Jewish Leaders* (1953), 433–56; A. Rothkoff, in: *Jewish Life* (May–June 1967).

[Haim Hillel Ben-Sasson]

GRODZINSKY, ZVI HIRSCH (1857/8–1947), Lithuanian-born U.S. rabbi and scholar. Grodzinsky, who served as chief rabbi of Omaha, Neb. (1891–1947), was a prolific rabbinic scholar and a leading organizer and framer of Orthodox Jewry and its rabbinate in America. Many of his works have become standard texts.

Born in Taurage, Lithuania, Grodzinsky received his early education in Ivye. In 1888, he came to Vilna to study in a *kollel* and probably received part of his education at the yeshivah of *Volozhin. By then, he had received *semikhah*, either from the rabbi of Taurage, Gershon Mendel Ziv, or Rabbi Isaac Elhanan *Spektor.

Grodzinsky gained an international reputation through his scholarly contributions. His published works include *Mikveh Yisrael*, a digest of the laws of *mikva'ot*; *Likutei Ẓvi* (1916), a reference work on the whole of *Orah Ḥayyim*; *Milei de-Berakhot* (1923, 1945) a commentary on the first 34 pages of Tractate *Berakhot*; and *Mikraei Kodesh* (1936, 1937, 1941), a three-volume examination of the laws of reading, writing, and qualifying Torah scrolls. He also authored articles in such leading rabbinic journals as *Ha-Meassef, Ha-Pardes*, and *Ha-Mesilah*.

Grodzinsky's published works comprise only a fraction of his written works. The bulk of his output remains in manuscripts, many in publishable form, housed at Oẓar ha-Poskim in Israel. They include *Tiferet Ẓvi*, 64 responsa; alphabetically arranged comments on Talmudic topics; a multi-volume commentary on Shulḥan Arukh, *Yoreh De'ah*; discussions of the laws of *stam yenam* and *niddah*; indexed comments on the responsa of R. *Asher Ben Jehiel (the Rosh); an alphabetical summary of the major Talmudic expressions and phrases; indexed sermons on the Babylonian Talmud and calendrical occasions; manuscripts of Grodzinsky's published works with corrections and addenda; loose responsa; and correspondence with American rabbinic leaders.

Arriving in Omaha in 1891, Grodzinsky sought to fulfill two roles: the communal responsibilities of the developing American rabbi and the halakhic duties of the East European *av beit din*. A founder of the *Agudat ha-Rabbonim, the first Orthodox rabbinical organization in North America, Grodzinsky personally encountered the pressure confronting European, Yiddish-speaking Orthodox rabbis in America. In 1916, before he had reached 60, the rise of Modern Orthodoxy and the Conservative movement compelled the two largest congregations he led in Omaha to seek an English-speaking rabbi.

Uncompromised by his Americanized congregants, Grodzinsky continued to serve as the halakhic decisor of his community and to write prolifically until his death. Yet, he also cautioned European Orthodoxy and its extensions in America to see the rabbi as an activist leader and halakhic authority rather than simply as a great scholar.

BIBLIOGRAPHY: J. Rosenbaum and M. Wakschlag, "Maintaining Tradition: A Survey of the Life and Writings of Rabbi Zvi Hirsch Grodzinsky," in: *American Jewish History*, 82 (1994); J. Rosenbaum, "Rabbinic Repartee: Rabbi Tsvi Hirsch Grodzinsky of Omaha and the Lights of the Land of Israel," in: *Eretz Israel, Israel and the Jewish Diaspora: Mutual Relations Through the Ages* (1991); M. Wakschlag, "*Mi-Toldotav*," in: M. Hirschler (ed.), *Halakhah u-Refu'ah* (1988).

[Jonathan Rosenbaum (2nd ed.)]

GRODZISK MAZOWIECKI, small town in Poland. It had 157 Jewish inhabitants in 1765, 790 in 1856, 2,154 in 1897, 2,756 in 1921 (out of 11,254), and 3,600 in September 1939. Grodzisk was the seat of a ḥasidic dynasty, founded by Elimelech of Grodzisk (d. 1892). His grandson R. Israel Shapiro, a scholar and writer of songs, who after World War I settled in Warsaw, perished in the Holocaust, as did Eliezer b. Abraham Ḥayyim of Falancz, rabbi in Grodzisk from 1913 to 1919. Members of the Grodzisk dynasty settled in Ereẓ Israel. During World War II, refugees swelled the local Jewish population to 6,000. In February 1941, the Germans transferred the Jews of Grodzisk to the Warsaw Ghetto, and subsequently to the death camp of Treblinka.

BIBLIOGRAPHY: *Bleter far Geshikhte*, 1 pt. 3–4 (1948), 146–8.

GRODZISK WIELKOPOLSKI (Ger. Graetz; Yid. גריידיץ), town in W. Poland, formerly in the province of Posen (Prussia). Jewish merchants frequented the town in the middle of 16th cantury and settled there at the end of the century The Jewish population numbered 374 in 1663, 812 in 1765, 1,156 (half the total population) in 1793, and 1,634 in 1820. In 1820 the existing synagogue collapsed and a new one was opened in 1822. Rabbis of Grodzisk include Judah Loeb b. Solomon of Prague, who had to flee during the Northern War (1700–21); Gershon b. Jehiel Landsberger (c. 1726–40); Ẓevi Hirsch b. Benjamin (c. 1768–70), author of *Tiferet Ẓevi* and rabbi in Brody and Hamburg; and Benjamin Schreiber (c. 1820–39). In the second half of the 19th century the noted talmudist and *ẓaddik* Elijah *Guttmacher, among the founders of Hovevei Zion, forerunner of Zionism, lived in Grodzisk and was famous as an *admor.* Many ḥasidim, mainly from Congress Poland, used to visit him and get his blessing. Kibbutz Sedeh Eliyahu is named for him. In 1898 a society for the study of Jewish history and literature was founded there. Toward the end of the 17th century Jews from Grodzisk visited the Leipzig fairs. Beginning from the 19th century Jewish merchants contributed to the economic development of the town, establishing business connections with various towns in Germany.

Toward the end of the 19th century the Jewish population declined, numbering 240 in 1905, and 61 in 1921 (out of a total population of 5,604), and 71 in neighboring Buk (out of 3,408). In 1922 the community ceased to exist. On the eve of World War II there were around 50 Jews in the town. Many fled, and on September 7, 1939, the last 13 Jews were expelled to Buk and from there to the General Gouvernement. In 1940 the synagogue and Jewish cemetery were destroyed and the site became a public garden. The communal archives (including Guttmacher's correspondence) were transferred to Jerusalem. Rudolph *Mosse, the well-known publisher of the *Berliner Tageblatt*, who was born in Grodzisk, founded a hospital there in the name of his father who practiced as physician in the town.

BIBLIOGRAPHY: A. Heppner and I. Herzberg, *Aus Vergangenheit und Gegenwart der Juden… in den Posener Landen* (1909), 420f.; Główny Urząd Staystyczny, *Skorowidz miejscowości Rzeczypospolitej Polski*, 10 (1926), s.v.; I.T. Eisenstadt et al., *Da'at Kedoshim* (1897–98), 45; D. Tollet, "Dzialalnosc gospodarcza Zydow w Grodzisku Wiekopolskim za panowania Wazow w latach 1558–1668," in: BŻIH 2:98 (1976).

[Shlomo Netzer (2nd ed.)]

GROJEC (Yid. **Gritse**), small town in Warsaw district. The privilege granted to the town in 1744 prohibited Jewish settlement there; nevertheless Jews began to settle there in the 18th century; they are mentioned there in 1754. The community numbered 1,719 in 1856 (68.7% of the total population), 3,737 in 1897 (61.9%), and 4,922 in 1921 (56.3%). On the eve of World War II there were approximately 5,200 Jews living in Grojec.

Holocaust Period

With the entry of the German army on Sept. 8, 1939, terrorization of the Jewish population began. The synagogue was burned. On Sept. 12, 1939, all men between the ages of 15 and 55 were forced to assemble at the market, and from there were marched on foot to Rawa Mazowiecka, about 37 mi. (60 km.) away. Many were shot on the way. During the spring of 1940 about 500 Jews from Lodz and the vicinity were forced to settle in Grojec. In July 1940 a ghetto was established and the plight of the Jewish inhabitants drastically deteriorated. They suffered from hunger, epidemics, and lack of fuel during the winter of 1940–41. About 1,000 fled to Bialobrzegi and were murdered there or deported to Treblinka in the fall of 1942. The Grojec ghetto was liquidated on February 28, 1942, when most of the remaining Jews were deported to the Warsaw ghetto to share the fate of the Jews there. Of those still in Grojec, 83 were deported after some time to a slave labor camp in Russia near Smolensk, where almost all were murdered. The last 250 Jews were executed in the summer of 1943 in a forest near Gora Kalwaria. After the war the Jewish community in Grojec was not reconstituted. Organizations of former Jewish residents of Grojec were established in Israel, France, the U.S., Canada, and Argentina.

[Stefan Krakowski]

BIBLIOGRAPHY: *Megillat Gritse* (Yid. and some Heb., 1956); *Bleter far Geshikhte*, 1 pt. 3–4 (1948), 146–8; *Megillat Polin*, 5 (1961), 278; Halpern, Pinkas, 399.

GRONEMANN, SAMUEL (**Sammy**; 1875–1952), German author and Zionist leader. Gronemann, who was born in Strasburg, West Prussia, was the son of Selig Gronemann (1845–1918), a rabbi and scholar who refused to endorse the anti-Zionist stand of the German "Protestrabbiner" in 1898. After studying at the Klaus in Halberstadt, the Hildesheimer Rabbinical Seminary, and the University of Berlin, Gronemann qualified as a lawyer and then embarked on a career as a journalist, playwright, and novelist. While serving on the eastern front in World War I, Gronemann came in touch with Jewish communities in the occupied territories, and after the war ended he personally helped many Jewish refugees. He also helped bring the Yiddish Theater from Vilna to Berlin. Gronemann served as legal adviser to the Union of German Actors and Playwrights. His novels include *Tohuwabohu* (1920); *Hawdoloh und Zapfenstreich* (1924), in which the East European milieu is prominently featured; and *Schalet* (1927). He also wrote a Purim play entitled *Haman's Flucht* (1926). A noted wit, Gronemann's most successful works were his comedies which were adapted for the Hebrew stage after he settled in Tel Aviv in 1936. These include *Jakob und Christian* (1936), which mocked Nazi race theories; *Der Prozess um des Esels Schatten* (1945), a political satire; *Heinrich Heine und sein Onkel* (1947), dealing with a debate about baptism in a Jewish family; and *Die Koenigin von Saba* (1951). He is perhaps best remembered, however, for *Der Weise und der Narr: Koenig Salomo und der Schuster* ("The King and the Cobbler," 1942), a comedy in a legendary biblical setting. The Hebrew version by Nathan *Alterman, *Shelomo ha-Melekh ve-Shalmai ha-Sandelar* (1942), was performed by the *Ohel Theater in Tel Aviv. In 1965 it was set to music by Alexander Argov and performed by the *Cameri theater. It became the first successful Hebrew musical comedy and was performed in various countries. A pioneer German Zionist, Gronemann was a delegate to the Zionist congresses from 1901 onward and was for many years a member of the Zionist Actions Committee. His reputation for political impartiality brought him the presidency of the Zionist Congress court. Gronemann's memoirs, *Erinnerungen eines Jecken* (published in Hebrew translation in 1947 and only in 2002/2004 in the original German), are an important contribution to the history of the Zionist Movement in Germany. A traditionally observant Jew, he was an outspoken critic of Diaspora assimilationism and also attacked certain aspects of ultra-Orthodoxy.

BIBLIOGRAPHY: Tidhar, 3 (1958), 1383–4; D. Stern, *Werke juedischer Autoren deutscher Sprache* (1969), 153. **ADD. BIBLIOGRAPHY:** S. Gronemann, *Erinnerungen. Aus dem Nachlass*, ed. J. Schlör (2002); S. Gronemann, *Erinnerungen an meine Jahre in Berlin. Aus dem Nachlass*, ed. J. Schlör (2004); R. Heuer, *Archiv Bibliographia Judaica – Lexikon deutsch-juedischer Autoren*, vol. 9 (2001), 315–23; H. Mittelmann, *Sammy Gronemann (1875–1952). Zionist, Schriftsteller und Satiriker in Deutschland und Palaestina* (2004).

[Manfred Moshe Geis / Joachim Schlör (2nd ed.)]

GRONER, DOVID YITZCHOK (1925–), Australian rabbi; leader of the Ḥabad movement in Australia. Groner was born in New York and settled in Melbourne in 1958. He had previously visited Australia as a student rabbi in 1947. He was probably the most important Lubavitcher rabbi in Australia, and was the principal of Yeshivah College, a Lubavitcher day school in Melbourne, from 1963. Under his leadership the Lubavitcher movement greatly expanded in Australia.

BIBLIOGRAPHY: W.D. Rubinstein, Australia II, index; D. Goldberg, "The Rebbe's Man Down Under," in: *Australian Jewish News* (July 23, 2004).

[William D. Rubinstein (2nd ed.)]

GROPER, JACOB (1890–1966), Yiddish poet. Born in Mihaileni, Romania, Groper was active in furthering Yiddish culture while studying law at the University of Jassy. After spending most of his life in Romania, mainly in Bucharest, he settled in Haifa in 1964. A participant in the 1908 *Czernowitz Yiddish Conference, he began to write in Romanian, German, and Yiddish, but from 1908 concentrated on Yiddish, his poems appearing from 1914 in periodicals in Vilna, Lemberg (Lvov), Jassy, Bucharest, and London, as well as in anthologies and in the volume *In Shotn fun a Shteyn* ("In the Shadow of a Stone," 1934). Some of his lyrics were printed in the Roman alphabet and in translation in various Romanian Jewish publications. While he was not a prolific writer, Groper's lyrics, romantic in tone, were orally transmitted among Jewish youth and contributed to raising the prestige of Yiddish in Romania. He was widely known and admired by Jews and Gentiles for his vast culture and brilliant mind as revealed in his improvised talks. By the terms of his will, his collected works were published in Yiddish in Israel with a parallel Hebrew translation (1975); another bilingual volume, of tributes to him, appeared the following year.

BIBLIOGRAPHY: Rejzen, Leksikon, 1 (1926), 623–5; LNYL, 2 (1958), 364; S. Bickel, *Inzikh un Arumzikh* (1936), 100–3; idem, *Rumenie* (1961), 193–204. **ADD. BIBLIOGRAPHY:** A. Spiegelblatt, in: *Di Goldene Keyt*, 58 (1967), 199–202; A.B. Yaffe, in: *Shevet Romania*, 4/5 (1979), 33–7.

[Sol Liptzin]

GROPPER, WILLIAM (1897–1977), U.S. cartoonist, painter, and printmaker. New York-born Gropper grew up in poverty on the Lower East Side. This early existence heightened Gropper's sensitivity to social inequality, and indeed he used his art to comment on the human condition. His studies with Robert Henri and George Bellows at the Ferrer School (1912–15) cemented the artist's desire to make art focusing on contemporary life, and by 1917 he regularly contributed incisive cartoons to the *New York Tribune*. He also created political satire for such left-wing publications as *The Liberator*, *New Masses*, and the Yiddish *Morning Freiheit* in the 1920s. Throughout these years Gropper also painted, but he did not have his first one-person show of oils until 1936. Paintings such as *The Senate* (1935, Museum of Modern Art) and *Hostages* (c. 1937, Newark Museum) address similar themes as Gropper's cartoons.

During the Depression, he was employed by the Works Progress Administration, for which he executed several murals, including one for the Department of the Interior in Washington, D.C. During the war he made cartoons, pamphlets, and war bond posters, often with overt anti-Nazi themes, as well as a few paintings expressing his horror at the incoming news of Nazi barbarism. In *De Profundis* (1943, collection unknown) he presents the Jew of Eastern Europe as the epitome of all human suffering. Gropper's 1948 visit to the ruins of the Warsaw Jewish Ghetto made a deep impression on him, and from that year on he made one painting annually in memory of those who died in the Warsaw Ghetto. Gropper also designed stained-glass windows for a Temple Har Zion in River Forest, Illinois (1965–67) and illustrated several books.

BIBLIOGRAPHY: A.L. Freundlich, *William Gropper: Retrospective* (1968); W. Gropper, *William Gropper: Fifty Years of Drawing, 1921–1971* (1971); L. Lozowick, *William Gropper* (1983).

[Samantha Baskind (2nd ed.)]

GROSMAN, LADISLAV (1921–1981), Slovak writer and scriptwriter. Born in Humenn, Slovakia, Grosman was deported to a forced labor camp during World War II. In 1945, he settled in Prague. He worked as an editor in Prague and Slovakia until 1963. From 1965 to 1968 he worked as a scriptwriter. In 1968 to immigrated to Israel, where he taught at Bar-Ilan University. Before then, more than 40 of his short stories and articles had been published in Czech cultural reviews and magazines. He rewrote his story *Past* ("The Trap," 1962), retitling it *Obchod na korze* ("The Shop on Main Street," 1965). The screen version of the story (directed by Jan Kadar and Elmar Klos) won an Academy Award in 1966 for Best Foreign Language Film. (The main protagonist of the story, the old shop owner played by Ida Kaminska, who is being "Aryanized," lives under the delusion that she cannot be harmed. The new owner respects her, and a special bond of esteem develops between the two.) A collection of stories *Nevěsta* ("The Bride," 1969) appeared just after Grosman left for Israel. It is comprised of seven stories from Slovakia's Jewish milieu. In Israel, Grosman wrote a screenplay for the TV movie *Dod David Holech Lirot Kala* (1972) and for an American TV movie *The Seventeenth Bride* (1986), based on his stories from the *Bride*. A new series of stories appeared in Zurich in Czech, entitled *Hlavou proti zdi* ("With a Head against the Wall," 1976); it was also published in Hebrew. His last work, a novel entitled *Z pekla těst* ("To Be a Lucky Dog," 1994), tells the story of a Jewish boy who was sent from Slovakia to Hungary to escape the Holocaust.

BIBLIOGRAPHY: *Slovník českch spisovatelů* (*Dictionary of Czech Writers*, 1982).

[Avigdor Dagan / Milos Pojar (2nd ed.)]

GROSS, ADOLF (1862–1937), lawyer, communal worker, and delegate in the Austrian parliament. Gross founded the Jewish Independent Party in Cracow, with the objectives of attaining equality of rights and a communal organization which would concern itself with the needs of the Jewish masses. In his profession Gross won a reputation as a jurist, and in public life as a political journalist and democratic mediator. He established a public company for the construction of cheap lodgings and founded consumer cooperatives. He achieved wide popularity as one of the most prominent members of the Cracow municipal council, on which he was active until 1897.

In the electoral campaign for the Austrian parliament of 1907 his opponent was Ḥayyim Hilfstein, a Zionist who exercised particular influence in assimilationist circles. However, Gross defeated him in the struggle for the Jewish vote. As a delegate, he joined the Polish Parliamentary Club in Vienna and collaborated with the Polish Socialist Party (PPS). Gross was a member of the public committee for the relief of poor Jews in Galicia founded on the initiative of philanthropic societies in England, Germany, and Austria. In the various institutions he upheld his opposition to Zionism and also opposed an attempt to establish a Jewish secondary school in Cracow.

BIBLIOGRAPHY: I. Tenenbaum, *Galitsye, mayn Alte Haym* (1952), 108, 127; I. Schwarzbart, *Tsvishn beyde Velt-Milkhomes* (1958), 170, 186; *Sefer Kraka* (1959), 123.

[Moshe Landau]

GROSS, CHAIM (1904–1991), U.S. sculptor. A native of Kolomea, Galicia, Gross went to the United States in 1921. Supporting himself by selling fruits and vegetables, he attended night classes at the Educational Alliance Art School in Manhattan, and then went on to study for four years at the Beaux-Arts Institute of Design. He supported himself by his art from the time he joined the New York Public Works of Art Project in 1933. Gross taught at the New School of Social Research for 40 years and at the Educational Alliance Art School for 68 years.

Gross made sculptures for public institutions, including the Hadassah Medical Center in Jerusalem. He wrote the book: *The Technique of Wood Sculpture* (1957). He produced a large number of works in different media – wood, stone, bronze, pen and ink, and water color – but his contributions to wood sculpture are the most outstanding. The forests of the Carpathian mountains near his birthplace first taught him the qualities and potentialities of wood. Gross used more than 80 exotic hardwoods in his work, his favorite being lignum vitae, an exceptionally hard South American wood. He never camouflaged or overpolished its surfaces and never disguised its colors but respected its texture and grain. Among his favorite themes were female acrobats and mothers playing with small children.

BIBLIOGRAPHY: J.V. Lombardo, *Chaim Gross, Sculptor* (1949); A.L. Chanin, in: C. Gross, *Fantasy Drawings* (1956), 716; L. Goodrich, in: *Four American Expressionists* (exhibition catalog; 1959).

[Alfred Werner / Rohan Saxena (2nd ed.)]

GROSS, CHARLES (1857–1909), U.S. historian. Born and educated in Troy, N.Y., Gross continued his studies in Europe. His doctoral dissertation was expanded into a classic two-volume work, *The Gild Merchant* (1890). In 1888 he was appointed an instructor at Harvard, and he was made a full professor in 1901. Gross took an active part in Jewish life. At the Anglo-Jewish Exhibition in London in 1887, he lectured on "The Exchequer of the Jews in England in the Middle Ages." In 1893 he translated into English Kayserling's volume on Christopher Columbus and the Jews. He was also vice president and a charter member of the American Jewish Historical Society. Among his most important works: *Select Cases from the Coroner's Rolls, 1265–1413* (1896), and *Select Cases Concerning the Law Merchant, A.D. 1270–1638* (1908–32), both of which he edited for the Selden Society; *Bibliography of British Municipal History* (1897); and *The Sources and Literature of English History from the Earliest Time to about 1485* (1900, 1915[2], 1951).

BIBLIOGRAPHY: Jacobs, in: AJHSP, 19 (1910), 189–93.

[Howard L. Adelson]

GROSS, DAVID J. (1941–), U.S. physicist and Nobel laureate. Gross was born in Washington, D.C. and educated in Jerusalem where his father established the School of Business Administration at the Hebrew University. He graduated B.Sc. in physics and mathematics from the Hebrew University of Jerusalem (1962). He returned to the U.S. and gained his Ph.D. in particle physics (1966) from the University of California at Berkeley under the direction of Geoffrey Chew. He was a research fellow of the Harvard Society of Fellows at Harvard University and visiting professor to CERN (1966–69) before joining Princeton University in 1969 where he became professor in 1973, Eugene Higgins Professor of Physics (1986–95), and Jones Professor of Physics (1995–97). From 1997 he was director of the Institute for Theoretical Physics and Frederick W. Gluck Professor of Theoretical Physics at the University of California at Santa Barbara. His research career was devoted to devising theoretical models to account for the accruing puzzling observations in particle physics. A particular problem is the observation that the force which attract quarks, the fundamental particles which comprise protons and neutrons, increases when quarks are separated and diminishes when they get closer to each other, a phenomenon termed "asymptotic freedom." With his colleagues H. David Politzer and Franz Wilczek, Gross devised the standard theoretical model of the strong interactive force between quarks and the gluons mediating this force and explaining this phenomenon. Because these particles carry a "color" charge, this field of study is termed "quantum chromodynamics." Their theory has been substantially validated experimentally. Gross, Politzer, and Wilczek shared the Nobel Prize in Physics (2004) for these discoveries. Gross was a major contributor to many key national and international organizations concerned with scientific policy and education. His many honors include election to the American Physical Society (1974), the American Academy of Arts and Sciences (1985), and the U.S. National Academy of Sciences (1986), the Dirac Medal (2000), and the Harvey Prize of the Haifa Technion (2000). He was visiting professor at the Hebrew University of Jerusalem (1984) and Weizmann lecturer at the Weizmann Institute (1996). He was director of the Jerusalem Winter School since 1999. He has two daughters, both academics, from his first marriage to Shulamith Toaff. He is now married to Jacquelyn Savani.

[Michael Denman (2nd ed.)]

GROSS, HEINRICH (**Henri**; 1835–1910), rabbi and scholar. Gross, who was born in Szenicze, Hungary, received his traditional rabbinical education as a student of Judah *Aszod, at the Breslau Jewish Theological Seminary, at Halle, at Berlin, and also with L. *Zunz. For a time, he was private tutor in the home of Baron Guenzburg in Paris. Gross served as rabbi in Gross-Strelitz (Strzelce, Poland), and from 1870 in Augsburg, Bavaria. He specialized in the study of the lives of leading French rabbis and their communities in the Middle Ages and published his researches in learned journals. Gross's lasting contribution to Jewish scholarship is his *Gallia Judaica* (1897), "a geographic dictionary of France according to rabbinic sources," which was translated into French from the German manuscript by M. Bloch and published by the Société des Etudes Juives. This standard work was reproduced in 1969 with additional notes by S. Schwarzfuchs.

BIBLIOGRAPHY: Wininger, Biog, 2 (1927), 525; 7 (1936), 34.

[Georges Weill]

GROSS, JOHN JACOB (1935–), English author and literary critic. Gross was born in London and studied at Cambridge, becoming a Fellow of King's College. After a distinguished literary career he was appointed literary editor of the *New Statesman* in 1972, and in 1974 became editor of the *Times Literary Supplement*, the authoritative and prestigious weekly magazine of literary criticism. He held this post for more than 15 years. He wrote widely on Jewish writers and Jewish themes in literature, and published *The Rise and Fall of the Man of Letters* (1973) and *James Joyce* (1970). Subsequently, Gross was theater critic of the London *Daily Telegraph*. Later works include an autobiography, *A Double Thread: Growing Up English and Jewish in London* (2002) and a study of *Shylock: Four Hundred Years in the Life of a Legend* (2002).

[Michael Wallach / William D. Rubinstein (2nd ed.)]

GROSS, MICHAEL (1920–2004), Israeli painter and sculptor. Born in Tiberias to a sixth generation Galilean family, the son of Leah Levi and Chaim Gross, Michael Gross had a very lonely childhood, as his father, a romantic pioneer, chose to live with his family in an isolated area near the shore of the Kinneret (Sea of Galilee). Surrounded by Arab villages, the family was in a precarious situation and Gross did not go to school until he was ten. In the 1936 riots, the family's house was burned down and they moved back to Tiberias. Three years later, in 1939, when the family returned to the ruined house, his father was stabbed to death by Arabs.

Gross studied art in Jerusalem at the Mizrachi Teacher's Seminar, followed by architectural studies at the Technion in Haifa. In 1951–54, he studied in Paris at the Ecole National Superieur des Beaux-Arts. When he returned he settled in Haifa and set up his studio at the artist's village of Ein Hod. Gross also taught art from 1960 to 1985 at the Oranim Kibbutz Teacher's Seminar. His artwork represented Israel in international exhibitions such as the Venice Biennial, the Sao Paulo Biennial, and the Documenta 9 in Kassel, and was very favorably received.

Many of Gross' works are an integral part of well-known collections such as at the Museum of Modern Art and the Guggenheim Museum in New York. In 2000 Gross received the Israel Prize.

The style of Gross' art is unique. He did not attach himself to any of the artist groups in Israel. His childhood loneliness was reflected in his solitary life as an artist, though many artists, such as Micha *Ullman and Belu Simon Fainaru, spoke of his great influence on them. His style is rooted in Minimalism and its various international languages. On the other hand, the style could be said to owe something to the local Israeli environment. His art always focuses on a certain landscape or a certain figure but its abstraction makes it difficult to identify. For example, Jerusalem is repeatedly symbolized with building motifs such as gates or windows. Later these became lines on a bright white background that suggested the sunlight typical of the Jerusalem area (*Untitled – Jerusalem*, 1975, Tel Aviv Museum of Art).

In the portrait genre Gross increasingly returned to his father. One of his first paintings was created shortly after he heard about his father's death and ever since then there was a bond between his art and his private feelings and perceptions of absence.

The motif of the house was repeatedly used in Gross' art. Over the years it became fragmented, so that only doors, walls, and shutters remained. Most of these fragments are readymade, and as the wooden constructions were painted and leaned against the museum's walls it seemed as if they had been left there by mistake (*Occurrence 11*, 1980, Israel Museum, Jerusalem). His public sculptures were also minimalist and in spite of their height they are almost invisible (*Tremor*, 1983, Independence Park, Jerusalem).

BIBLIOGRAPHY: Israel Museum, *Michael Gross: Outdoor and Indoor Works* (1977); O. Mordechai, *Michael Gross*, Genia Schrieber University Art Gallery, Tel Aviv University (1993).

[Ronit Steinberg (2nd ed.)]

GROSS, NAPHTALI (1896–1956), Yiddish poet, short story writer, essayist, and translator. Born in Kolomea (Galicia), he emigrated to the U.S. in 1913 and worked as a typesetter and as a teacher in Yiddish schools. His first published poems appeared in the Montreal daily, *Der Keneder Odler*. Gross was a talented translator of poetry from numerous languages into Yiddish. He published his works in Yiddish newspapers, such as *Der Yidisher Kemfer*, *Fraye Arbeter Shtime*, and *Der Tog*, and periodicals founded by Di Yunge, such as *Velt Oys-Velt Ayn*, *Der Groyser Kundes*, *Shriftn*. From 1946, he wrote a weekly column, "*Mayselekh un Mesholim*" ("Little Stories and Parables"), based on stories from readers for the New York *Forverts*, which appeared in book form (*Mayselekh un Mesholim*, 1955), illustrated by his brother, the artist Chaim *Gross. Naphtali Gross's major poetic works are *Psalmen* ("Psalms," 1919), *Der Vayser Rayter* ("The White Horseman," 1925), and

Yidn ("Jews," 2 vols., 1929 and 1938). In the 1920s, his neo-Romantic works deviated from the literary norm, and he was criticized by many for his preoccupation with religious motifs and with the idealization of the *shtetl* at a time of revolution. With Abraham Rejzen, he translated the poems of Solomon ibn *Gabirol. Gross's collected poems, *Lider* ("Poems," 1958), include a bibliography by E.H. Jeshurin.

ADD. BIBLIOGRAPHY: Rejzen, Leksikon, 1 (1927), 612–14; LNYL, 1 (1963), 349–52; Y. Botoshanski, *Portretn fun Yidishe Shrayber* (1933), 270–77; Z. Weinper, *Yidishe Shriftshteler*, 1 (1933), 40–45; Sh. Bickel, *Detaln un Sakhaklen* (1943), 242–44

[Shlomo Bickel / Marc Miller (2nd ed.)]

GROSS, NATHAN (1874–1922), a founder of *Po'alei Zion and general secretary of the *Jewish National Fund Head Office. Born in Tarnopol, Galicia, Gross moved to Vienna in his youth and worked as a clerk. At first he joined the Social Democrats, but when he became aware of the hostile attitude to Jews shown by the party's leaders (particularly those who were themselves Jews), he left the party. With the publication of Herzl's ideas of a Jewish state, Gross became a Zionist. He was among the organizers of the clerical union in Austria and in this manner contributed to the establishment of a Zionist labor movement. The first cells that he established in various places gradually coalesced into the Po'alei Zion movement, of which he and S. *Kaplansky became the chief spokesmen at Zionist Congresses and in the Zionist Movement. (As a consequence of new activities, *Merḥavyah was founded, thereby realizing Franz *Oppenheimer's plan for the establishment of agricultural cooperatives in Ereẓ Israel.) In 1908 Gross was appointed general secretary of the head office of the Jewish National Fund situated first in Cologne and, in 1914, moving to The Hague. He retained this post until his death.

BIBLIOGRAPHY: N. Agmon (Bistritsky, ed.), *Demuyyot*, 2 (1951), 277–9; M. Singer, *Be-Reshit ha-Ẓiyyonut ha-Sozyalistit* (1958), 444. **ADD. BIBLIOGRAPHY:** N.M. Gelber, *Toledot ha-Tenu'ah ha-Ẓiyyonit be-Galicia 1875–1918* (1958), index.

[Getzel Kressel]

GROSSBERG, MENASSEH (c. 1860–1927), rabbinical scholar. Born in Trestina, Russia, Grossberg led a wandering life, copying and publishing Hebrew manuscripts from libraries in Berlin, Paris, London, Amsterdam, Munich, and other cities. In the first decade of the 20th century he settled in London, copying manuscripts for European scholars at the British Museum and at Oxford. His many publications included a Pentateuch commentary by Jacob of Vienna (*Peshatim u-Ferushim*, 1888, repr. 1967) from a Munich manuscript; Meshullam b. Moses' *Sefer ha-Hashlamah* on tractates *Berakhot, Ta'anit*, and *Megillah* (from a Hamburg manuscript, the first with an introduction by H. Brody (1893, repr. 1967), and the last as an appendix to *Peshatim u-Ferushim); Ḥizzei Menasheh* (1901), a manuscript commentary on the Pentateuch by various medieval scholars also containing Jonathan of Lunel's novellae on *Horayot* (1901); *Sefer Yeẓirah* (1902); David b. Levi's *Sefer ha-Mikhtam on Megillah* (1904); *Megillat Ta'anit* (with an extensive introduction, 1906); and *Seder Olam Zuta* (also with introduction, 1910). Grossberg also published responsa and various halakhic treatises.

GROSSER, BRONISLAW (pseudonyms: **Slawek**; **Zelcer**; 1883–1912), lawyer born in Miechow, Poland; one of the second generation of *Bund leaders. The son of a lawyer, he became a leader of the Warsaw socialist youth while still at secondary school. His experience of antisemitism made him conscious of his Jewish identity, and influenced by Bundists from Lithuania, he joined the Bund. Grosser was among those who in 1906 consistently supported the independence of the Bund, being against its return to the Russian Social Democratic party. He was a member of the advisory committee of the Social Democratic group in the Fourth Duma (1912) and was elected to the central committee of the Bund. An incisive writer and fluent speaker, Grosser was outstanding among the relatively few intellectuals who joined the Bund in Poland at that time. He defined his task as "defense of the interests of the Jewish workers in Poland, and within this framework defense of the interests of the country."

BIBLIOGRAPHY: Rejzen, Leksikon, 1 (1926), 620–3; J.S. Hertz (ed.), *Doyres Bundistn*, 1 (1956), 319; *Polski Slownik Biograficzny*, 9 (1960–61), 6.

[Moshe Mishkinsky]

GROSSFELD, ABRAHAM ISRAEL (**"Abie"**; 1934–), U.S. gymnastic and coach; two-time Olympic competitor and five-time coach, World Championships and Pan American Games champion, winner of 17 medals at the Maccabiah, including 13 gold; member of the National Gymnastics Hall of Fame. Born on the Lower East Side of New York City to immigrant parents – his father was a window washer – Grossfeld spoke Yiddish until he was four. He began gymnastics at the age of 15 while at Samuel Gompers High School, training at the West Side YMCA. His first international competition was the 1953 Maccabiah, where he won six gold medals; four years later he won seven gold.

Grossfeld graduated from the University of Illinois in 1960, after finishing second in the individual all-around at the 1957 NCAA meet and first in 1958. He was also AAU national champion in the horizontal bars from 1955 to 1957.

Grossfeld competed internationally for the United States for 13 years, including in the 1956 and 1960 Olympic Games; the World Championships of 1958 and 1962; and the Pan American Games of 1955, 1959, and 1963. At the Pan Am Games he won 15 medals, including eight gold, and his record score in the 1955 Horizontal Bar stood until 1987. Grossfeld also won 17 medals at the Maccabiah Games of 1953, 1957, and 1965.

After retiring from competition, Grossfeld turned to coaching and became a legend. He was head coach of the U.S. Men's Olympic gymnastics teams of 1972, 1984, and 1988, with the 1984 squad winning the Combined Exercises championship. He was also assistant coach of the 1964 U.S. men's Olympic team, and the 1968 U.S. women's Olympic team. Grossfeld served as head coach of the U.S. men's gymnastics team at five World Championships (1966, 1981, 1983, 1985, and 1987); the U.S. men's team at the 1983 and 1987 Pan American Games; the U.S. men's team at the 1982 World Cup; the men's team at the 1986 Goodwill Games; and coached the U.S. gymnasts at the 1973, 1977 (men and women), 1981, and 1983 Maccabiah Games. During this time Grossfeld was head coach at Southern Connecticut State University for 40 years, helping the program become one of the best in the country.

Grossfeld was chosen NCAA National Coach of the Year three times, Gymnastics Federation Coach of the Year in 1984, was elected to the National Gymnastics Hall of Fame in 1979, and was named one of the 50 greatest New York sports figures by *Sports Illustrated* in 2004.

[Elli Wohlgelernter (2nd ed.)]

GROSSINGER, JENNIE (1892–1972), U.S. resort owner and manager. Grossinger, born in a small town in Galicia, was taken to America by her parents at the turn of the century. The Grossingers lived in extreme poverty on New York's Lower East Side, and Jennie went to work in a sweatshop after several years of public school. In 1912 she married her cousin Harry Grossinger (1890–1964), and the following year the entire family moved to a farm in the Catskill Mountains near Liberty, New York. The farm was converted into a kosher boardinghouse in 1914, and Grossinger's eventually grew under Jennie Grossinger's management into a giant resort of more than 1,000 acres, whose 800 employees served some 150,000 guests a year.

The grounds of Grossinger's Resort and Country Club included 35 buildings, a 27-hole golf course, a shopping arcade, bridle paths, a ski slope, indoor and outdoor swimming pools, tennis courts, a post office, two kosher kitchens, and a nightclub. Grossinger's attracted a host of well-known entertainers, who thrived in this area of the Catskills that was known as the "Borscht Belt." In addition to ordinary guests from all across the U.S. and Canada, the Grossinger roster included political figures, world-renowned scientists, movie stars, radio personalities, and sports figures.

Active in charities and dedicated to good causes, Grossinger received many awards for her philanthropy. During World War II she raised millions of dollars in war bonds at the hotel, and an Army airplane was named "Grossinger's" in her honor. On June 16, 1968, Governor Nelson Rockefeller made an official proclamation designating June 16 as Jennie Grossinger Day in New York State. That birthday tribute was the first time such a proclamation was issued to honor a living woman in New York State.

After her death, her son Paul and daughter Elaine took over the hotel, bringing the resort to even greater success and popularity. However, in 1985, Grossinger's was sold to a group of investors from New York City.

Jennie Grossinger wrote a cookbook entitled *The Art of Jewish Cooking* (1958).

BIBLIOGRAPHY: J. Pomerantz, *Jennie and the Story of Grossinger's* (1970).

[Hillel Halkin /Ruth Beloff (2nd ed.)]

GROSSMAN, ALLAN (1910–1991) and **LARRY** (1944–1997), Canadian father-and-son political team that, one after the other, represented a heavily Jewish inner-city Toronto riding in the provincial legislature for 32 consecutive years.

Allan Grossman was born in Toronto. His father, Morris, arrived in Canada from Poland in 1907 and two years later brought his wife, Sarah, and their six children to join him. Allan was their seventh child. As a young man Grossman developed an interest in Conservative Party politics. At 16 he was founder of the Junior Conservative Association. While he went into business and became a successful insurance agent he remained active in local politics. In 1951, Grossman entered municipal politics and won election to Toronto's municipal council and was reelected in the three following elections. In 1955 he shifted to provincial politics, running for the Progressive Conservatives. He won a hard-fought campaign against Communist Party incumbent Joseph Salsberg, taking the inner-city St. Andrews riding. Grossman was reelected in 1959 and in 1960 he was appointed to the provincial cabinet as minister without portfolio, becoming the first Jew appointed to a provincial cabinet. During 20 years in cabinet, Grossman often spoke out for stronger anti-discrimination and human rights legislation. He also went on to be the minister responsible for liquor sales in Ontario, a provincial government monopoly, then minister of reform institutions, overseeing administration of provincial correctional institutions. Under his leadership, Ontario initiated a long-overdue reform of the penal system. Before he retired from political life in 1971 Grossman held several other provincial cabinet posts, including minister of trade and development. In this capacity he led the first western trade mission to China.

Grossman was also active in many Jewish organizations, including the Jewish Immigrant Aid Society, the Canadian Jewish Congress, and the Zionist Organization of Canada.

Allan Grossman's son, Larry, was born in Toronto and studied law there. When his father retired from electoral politics, he gave up law for politics and ran in the same riding for the Progressive Conservatives and was elected. He held the seat through the next three elections. Considered among the more progressive members of his party – "a Tory with conscience" – he was appointed to the provincial Cabinet and held a number of different portfolios including Consumer and Corporate Relations, Education, Health, and Provincial Treasurer. In 1985, when then Premier William Davis announced his retirement, Grossman ran to replace him but lost to the much more conservative Frank Miller. Miller resigned after being soundly defeated by the Liberal Party in the 1985 provincial election and Grossman was chosen to lead a much divided provincial Progressive Conservative Party. The still popular Liberals went to the polls again in 1987 and the results relegated the Conservatives to third party in the legislature behind the NDP. Grossman lost his own seat and resigned. He returned to private legal practice but fell ill with brain cancer and died at 53.

BIBLIOGRAPHY: P. Oliver, *Unlikely Tory: The Life and Politics of Allan Grossman* (1985).

[Harold Troper (2nd ed.)]

GROSSMAN, ALLEN (1932–), U.S. poet. Grossman was born in Minneapolis and educated at Harvard and Brandeis, from which he received his Ph.D. in 1959. He received, among other awards, a MacArthur Fellowship and the Witter Bynner Prize. His poems often concern themselves not only with establishing the authority of the poet as the heir of perennial questions (such as the meaning and shaping powers of language and tradition), but also with reinvigorating the prophetic voice (as in seeking intimacy with, and invoking, the divine). His poetry is notable for its biblical resonance and moral aspiration. In this fashion, both individual and poetic situation are often liberated from sheer contingency. Among his works are *The Ether Dome and Other Poems: New and Selected, 1979–1991* (1991); *The Sighted Singer: Two Works on Poetry for Readers and Writers* (with Mark Halliday (1992); *The Long Schoolroom: Lessons in the Bitter Logic of the Poetic Principle* (1997); *How to Do Things With Tears* (2001); and *Sweet Youth: Poems by a Young Man and an Old Man, Old and New, 1953–2001* (2002).

BIBLIOGRAPHY: D. Morris, *Poetry's Poet: Essays on the Poetry, Pedagogy, and Poetics of Allen Grossman* (2004).

[Lewis Fried (2nd ed.)]

GROSSMAN, AVRAHAM (1936–), Israeli historian. Grossman focuses on the cultural, intellectual, and social world of the Ashkenazi and French rabbinical sages in the early Middle Ages. He was born in the moshavah of Mishmar ha-Yarden. In 1966 he graduated in Jewish history and Talmud from the Hebrew University of Jerusalem, receiving his M.A. in 1967 and his Ph.D. in 1974; he did postdoctoral work in London and Oxford in 1975. From 1969 to 1972 he taught Jewish history at the University of the Negev (now Ben-Gurion University) and in 1973–74 taught at the Hebrew University. In 1976 he became a lecturer there and in 1986 a professor. From 1991 to 1992 he was the head of the Department of Jewish History. Grossman was visiting professor at Harvard, Yale, and Ohio Universities. He was a member of numerous academic committees and editorial boards. He published more than 100 articles and books, among them, *The First Ashkenazi Wise Men* (1981); *The Jewish Community during the Middle Ages* (1988); *The First French Wise Men* (1995) and *Pious and Rebellious – Jewish Women in Medieval Europe* (2001). He received various awards for his work, including the Bialik Award. In 2003 he was awarded the Israel Prize for Jewish history.

[Shaked Gilboa (2nd ed.)]

GROSSMAN, DAVID (1954–), Israeli writer. Born in Jerusalem, Grossman studied philosophy and theater at the Hebrew University. He began a 25-year career at Kol Israel (Israel Broadcasting Authority) at the age of ten, as a correspondent for youth programs. He published his first book of prose, a collection of stories entitled *Raẓ* ("The Jogger"), in 1983. This was followed by the novel *Ḥiyukh ha-Gedi* (1983; *Smile of the Lamb*, 1990); *Ayen Erekh Ahavah* (1986; *See Under Love*, 1989); a non-fiction, politically oriented work *Ha-Zeman ha-Ẓahov* (1987; *Yellow Wind*, 1988); *Sefer ha-Dikduk ha-Penimi* (1991; *The Book of Intimate Grammar*, 1994); *Yesh Yeladim Zig Zag* (1994; *The Zigzag Kid*, 1997); *She-Tihiyi Li Sakkin* (1998; *You Shall be my Knife*, 2002); *Ba-Guf Ani Mevinah* (2002; *Her Body Knows*, 2005). One of the most prominent writers of his generation, Grossman also wrote a number of books for children and young readers, including *Du Krav* (1982; *Duel*, 1998) and *Itamar Mikhtav* ("The Itamar Letter," 1986). Among his works are also the play *Gan Riki* (1988; *Riki's Playground*) and non-fiction books such as *Mavet ke-Derekh Ḥayyim* (2003; "Death as a Way of Life").

Grossman is one of the leading heirs of the so-called "New Wave" in Israeli literature, whose oeuvre marks a turning point in Hebrew fiction. His writing correlates historically with the change in the political climate after the rise to power of the Likud Party. It addresses political and social issues, protesting time and again against the occupation of the territories, the use of violence, and the mentality of the new establishment.

His first novel, *Smile of the Lamb*, attempts to shed light on Israeli society following the Six-Day War and the Yom Kippur War. The story unfolds through a dual perspective, that of the Israeli Uri Leniado and, alternately, that of Hilmi, an old Arab. Interwoven in the narrative are essayistic sections, which give vent to Grossman's feelings about the occupation and the humiliation of the Arab population. Following this highly political prose work, Grossman published his most ambitious work of fiction, *Ayen Erekh Ahavah*. Bordering often on the grotesque, Grossman addresses the Holocaust while reflecting on the very (im-)possibilty of writing about it. Grossman uses sophisticated techniques: the first part of the novel is related from the point of view of Momik, a sensitive, imaginative child growing up in Jerusalem amid Holocaust survivors. Momik creates his own private myth about the Nazi beast, which he attempts to understand better and fight in his own little kingdom, in the cellar. The second part handles in a poetic-fantastic manner the fate of the well-known Polish-Jewish author Bruno *Schulz, who was murdered by the Germans. The third part relates Anschel Wasserman's (Momik's grandfather) strategy of survival in the camp, by telling the Nazi commander in charge stories after stories and keeping him in suspense. The fourth part, fragmentary and postmodernistic, is structured as an encyclopedia, listing and explaining a variety of words or concepts and omitting deliberately the entry "Love." Grossman attempts to blur the distinction between reality and fantasy and shatter the reader's illusion of certainty and knowledge.

The following novel, *The Book of Intimate Grammar*, is far more modest in its artistic aims: it does not seek to handle the metahistorical issues of a generation, neither the Holocaust nor the Arab-Israeli conflict. Grossman focuses on the childhood of Israelis who grew up in Jerusalem in the 1950s through an atypical but also typical Israeli family. The father survived the labor camp in Russia; the mother is an orphan who attended to the needs of her siblings. This historical-biographical background shaped their lives; Grossman is interested in the psychological effect of the past on their present lives, not – as in the previous novel – in a historiosophical account of a collective issue. From this point of view, the novel is closer to the earlier prose works of Yehoshua *Kenaz (for instance, *After the Holidays*) or to Yeshayahu Koren's novella *Levayah ba-Ẓohorayim* ("Funeral at Noon"). The familial context is seen through the eyes of Aharon, a 14-year-old boy, and it is his story of adolescence and growing up, oscillating between pain and humor, reality and fantasy.

She-Tihiyi Li Sakkin depicts a universal theme, that of a man's love for a woman whom he never meets. This epistolary novel deals, as it were, with the second phase of growing up, with the midlife crisis. The correspondence between Yair and Miriam pointedly disregards political-historical subjects. What matters more are the changes observed in nature, the blossoms of spring, the first rain. The letters exchanged by the protagonists, both belonging to the Ashkenazi elite, shed light on their lives, their dreams and passions, though ending in a rather anti-romantic manner. Grossman suggests that truth, art, and beauty exist in writing only. The protagonists prefer the narcissistic expedient of self-expression in writing to a physical encounter. The novel is an important milestone in Grossman's development as a writer; it is a highly introverted novel which is far from offering the reader shallow entertainment.

Grossman's novella *Ba-Guf Ani Mevinah* takes this process of introversion further: published during the second Intifada, when Israeli readers were expecting yet another political book from Grossman, author of the highly topical *Yellow Wind* (1987) and *Sleeping on a Wire* (1992), the story again deals with the relationship between imagination and reality, showing that the life of fantasy is perhaps more intense and rewarding than actual life. Sitting by the bedside of her dying mother, the daughter relates the mother's life-story: When you read it out to me, I have the feeling that these things really happened, says the mother. Many questions remain unanswered, others have the aura of mystery, suggesting that much in human existence remains inexplicable and perhaps unutterable.

Grossman's books have been translated into many languages, and he is undoubtedly one of the best known Israeli authors abroad.

BIBLIOGRAPHY: J. Lowin, "D. Grossman's Useful Fictions," in: *Jewish Book Annual*, 50 (1992), 114–27; N.B. Sokoloff, "D. Grossman: Translating the 'Other' in Momik," in: *Israeli Writers Consider the Outsider* (1993), 37–56; G. Morahg, "Creating Wasserman: The Quest for a New Holocaust Story," in: *Judaism* 51:1 (2002), 51–60; M.S. Bernstein, "The Child as Collective Subconsciousness," in: *Shofar*, 23:2 (2005), 65–79.

[Gershon Shaked (2nd ed.)]

GROSSMAN, LEONID PETROVICH (1888–1965), Russian literary historian and theater critic. Grossman was born in Odessa, graduated from Kiev university, and studied law in Sorbonne. He started writing criticism from 1903 and contributed to the *Jewish Encyclopedia* in the field of law. From 1910 to 1920 he produced poetry, mostly on biblical themes. From 1921 he lectured in various institutes in Moscow on the theory and history of literature, from 1945 as a professor. His works range from studies of Russo-Western cultural relations (e.g., on Balzac in Russia, 1937) to monographs on Russian literary masters such as Dostoyevski (1963). He also wrote comparative studies of literature and other creative arts, such as theater and painting. In *Ispoved yevreya* ("A Jew's Confession," 1925) Grossman dealt with A.U. Kovner, a picturesque Jewish convict, whose letters to Dostoyevski, published in 1903 some 30 years after their dispatch, accused the novelist of slandering the Jews in his *Diary of a Writer*.

[Shmuel Spector (2nd ed.)]

GROSSMAN, MEIR (1888–1964), Zionist leader. Born in Temryuk in the Krasnodar Territory, Russia, Grossman at an early age became a contributor to the Russian press. For a while he lived in Warsaw, where he began contributing to the Yiddish press. In 1913 he went to Berlin to study, becoming a member of the central committee of *He-Ḥaver, the Zionist students' society, and editing its Russian and Hebrew organs.

On the day that World War I broke out, Grossman left for Copenhagen, and worked there as a correspondent for the Russian daily *Russkoye Slovo*. A few months after his arrival he began the publication of a Yiddish daily, *Kopenhagener Togblat* (later renamed *Yidishe Folkstsaytung*). At *Jabotinsky's suggestion he published a Yiddish fortnightly, *Di Tribune*, dedicated to publicizing the cause of a Jewish Legion, a World Jewish Congress, and equal rights for Jews. Jabotinsky also persuaded him to move to London, which he did in the fall of 1916, publishing *Di Tribune* there as a daily. The campaign for a Jewish Legion did not, however, yield immediate results, and when the paper closed, Grossman returned to Copenhagen.

After the February 1917 Revolution in Russia, Grossman returned to Petrograd, where he became a contributor to *Petrograder Togblat*, the daily founded by Yiẓḥak *Gruenbaum. After the October Revolution he was asked to move to Kiev and there edited several periodicals: *Der Telegraf*, a daily, together with Naḥman *Syrkin; *Oyf der Vakh*, Zionist weekly; and *Die Velt*, another daily. He was a member of the executive committee of Ukrainian Zionists, took part in the National Jewish Assembly and in the work of the Provisional National Council, and was a deputy of the Rada, the national council of the independent Ukraine. When hostilities broke out and the Bolsheviks invaded the Ukraine, Grossman, together with Abraham Coralnik, was sent abroad to inform the world of the situation and appeal for help. In London and in the United

States, Grossman and Coralnik created aid organizations for Ukrainian Jews (1919).

At the end of 1919, Grossman joined Jacob *Landau, in establishing the Jewish Correspondence Bureau for the dissemination of news of Jewish interest. This bureau eventually became the *Jewish Telegraphic Agency (JTA). Grossman left the JTA in 1928 as a result of differences with Landau. In 1925 he had founded the *Palestine Bulletin*, an English-language daily in Jerusalem, which in 1932 became the *Palestine Post* (later the *Jerusalem Post*). After the 1920 riots in Palestine, Grossman criticized Weizmann's policies and called for his resignation. When Jabotinsky left the Zionist Executive and eventually founded the *Revisionist Party (in 1925), Grossman became one of his early supporters and was appointed deputy chairman of the new party's world center. In 1933 the party split on the issue of secession from the Zionist Organization; Grossman headed the minority, which opposed Jabotinsky and which was in favor of remaining in the *Zionist Organization. He then established the *Jewish State Party.

In 1934 he settled in Palestine, where he became the manager of Bank le-Hityashevut Amamit. In 1937 he caused a sensation at the Zionist Congress by reading from its rostrum confidential minutes of Weizmann's talks with the British colonial secretary, Ormsby-Gore, in which Weizmann promised to influence the Zionist movement in favor of the partition plan of Palestine, though the Zionist General Council had adopted a resolution against the plan. Grossman's "suspension from membership in the Zionist General Council" by the Zionist court, for having disclosed confidential Zionist documents, caused a stir in the Jewish press the world over, particularly in the London *Jewish Chronicle*. He spent the World War II years in the United States. After the war the two factions of the Revisionist Party were reunited, and Grossman attended the Zionist Congress as a representative of the united party. He did not, however, join the *Ḥerut Party, and preferred to join the *General Zionists, becoming one of its representatives in the Executive of the Zionist Organization (1954–60). When the General Zionist Party merged with the Progressive Party to form the Liberal Party, Grossman again did not follow his party's decision and resigned from the Zionist Executive. He continued his journalistic work and also participated in the activities of various public institutions. He took special interest in the situation of Soviet Jews and promoted the publication of Russian-language periodicals in Israel (*Vestnik Izraila*, and *Shalom*).

BIBLIOGRAPHY: Tidhar, 4 (1950), 1927–28; LNYL, 2 (1958), 359–60.

[Israel Klausner]

GROSSMAN, MORTON IRVIN (1919–1981), U.S. gastroenterologist. Born and educated in Ohio, he received his M.D. and Ph.D. in 1944 from Northwestern University. Grossman first served as assistant biochemist (1939–41) at Ohio State University Medical School and from 1950 to 1951 as professor of physiology in the Department of Clinical Sciences. From 1951 to 1955 he was chief of physiology in the Division of Medical Nutrition first in Chicago and then at Fitzsimons Army Hospital in Denver. In 1955 he joined the faculty of the University of California School of Medicine and was appointed chairman of the Department of Medicine in 1965. Grossman was consultant to the National Institutes of Health (1960–65) and a member of many professional societies. He was the father of modern gastrointestinal endocrine physiology. His most important contributions lay in defining the secretory mechanisms of the stomach and pancreas actions and of regulatory gastrointestinal peptides. He served as editor of *Gastroenterology* (1960–65) and wrote many papers on the physiology of the alimentary tract, gastrointestinal hormones, and the physiology of nutrition.

[Fred Rosner / Bracha Rager (2nd ed.)]

GROSSMAN, STEVEN, chair of national Democratic Party. Grossman was active in the American Jewish community and within Democratic politics. A graduate of Princeton and Harvard Business schools, he headed the Massachusetts Envelope Company that had been in his family since 1910. A leader of the Boston Jewish community, he served on the boards of Brandeis University, Beth Israel Hospital, and the Combined Jewish Philanthropies.

As a leader of the Democratic Party Grossman began his career within Massachusetts politics and was chairman of the Democratic Party in the state during the early 1990s, spearheading Bill Clinton's 20 point victory in 1992 and capturing enough Senate and House seats in Massachusetts to override the Republican governor's veto. His close association with Democratic politics and his relationship with the president was essential to his rise to leadership in the American Israel Public Affairs Committee (AIPAC), which had been increasingly moving to the right during the Reagan and George H.W. Bush presidencies and during Likud leadership in Israel. A Democratic and a strong supporter of the peace process, Grossman was named to head AIPAC, after his predecessor had committed the ultimate sin of American politics; he had been caught telling the truth about AIPAC's power, too directly and for attribution. Moderate but forceful, Grossman was a good choice, most especially during the Clinton-Rabin years where the organized Jewish community and their political supporters had to turn around their positions on the Palestinians and the Peace Process after the Oslo Accords.

He left AIPAC to serve as chair of the Democratic Party where his ties to the Clinton administration and his fundraising prowess served him in good stead. He made the transition successfully and seamlessly from Jewish leadership to national leadership of the Democratic Party, where Jewish support is a pillar of fundraising efforts.

Grossman was unsuccessful in his bid for the Democratic nomination for governor of Massachusetts in 2002 but became prominent again as chairman of the Howard Dean campaign for the U.S. presidency in 2004; Dean went from obscurity to front-runner status in near record time. Grossman was also instrumental in causing Dean to withdraw from actively pursuing the nomination when after deep losses, John Kerry's nomination became a foregone conclusion and Dean's chances were nil. Grossman held a press conference endorsing his home state candidate Kerry before Dean had formally withdrawn.

GROSSMAN, VASILI SEMYONOVICH (Joseph Solomonovich; 1905–1964), Soviet Russian writer. Born to a traditional Yiddish-speaking family in the intensely Jewish town of Berdichev, he moved to Moscow as a young man and, after graduating from the university, worked for a time as a chemical engineer in the coal mines of Donbas. His short story *V gorode Berdicheve* ("In the Town of Berdichev," 1934), which described the Civil War in and around his home town, earned the praise of Maxim Gorki. Grossman's most important early work is *Stepan Kolchugin* (1937–40), a three-volume novel describing the Communist underground before the Revolution. He became famous as the author of *Narod bessmerten* ("The People Is Immortal," 1942), the first important Soviet novel inspired by World War II. It was published in the Soviet army gazette *Red Star*, where he served as a war correspondent. The Holocaust of Soviet Jewry finds expression in the novels: *Staryi Uchitel* ("Old Teacher," 1943) and *Treblinskii Ad* ("The Inferno of Treblinka," 1945). His second war novel, *Za pravoye delo*, ("For the Just Cause"), the first part of which appeared in 1952, was never completed. It was found ideologically objectionable because of its underestimation of the Communist Party's role in the forging of victory over Nazism. Another cause of official displeasure probably was Grossman's emphasis on such "minor" traits of Nazism as the mass extermination of the Jews and its strong nationalism. Coming as they did at the height of Soviet antisemitic campaigns and the wave of glorification of everything Russian, Grossman's observations were against the official line. Somewhat earlier, fragments of the manuscript confiscated by the KGB were published in the West under the name *Zhizn I Sudba* ("Life and Fate," 1980). From 1956 until his death he worked on a book about the tragic Stalinist period, the anti-Jewish campaign, the persecution of intellectuals by the party apparatus, and the repression of any free thinking. It was published as *Vsio Techot* ("Everything Is Flawed") in the Samizdat in the 1960s and in Germany in 1970. Grossman and Ilya *Ehrenburg had tried to publish a "Black Book" of documentary evidence of Nazi crimes committed against the Jews on Soviet territory. The book was already set in type, but, as Ehrenburg pointed out in his memoirs, its publication was banned by the Soviet authorities, and the KGB destroyed the type frames. One volume was eventually published in Bucharest (1947) under the title *Cartea Neagr*, with a foreword by Grossman. A copy of the original manuscript is in the archive of Yad Vashem, Jerusalem and was published there in 1980.

BIBLIOGRAPHY: V.M. Akimov et al. (eds.), *Russkiye Sovetskiye pisateli prozaiki*, 1 (1959), 609–25; D. Litani, in: *Yedi'ot Yad Vashem*, 23/24 (1960), 24–26 (on the Black Book).

[Maurice Friedberg / Shmuel Spector (2nd ed.)]

GROSSMAN, YIZḤAK-DAVID (1946–), Israeli rabbi known for his unique activities in education and welfare, such as assistance to criminal youth and adults, immigration absorption, and the advancement of religious-secular relations. The crowning glory of his work is the Migdal Or educational system, with schools and dormitories in Israel and abroad. Grossman was born in Jerusalem, a sixth-generation Israeli. In 1966 he received his rabbinic ordination from R. Isser Yehuda *Unterman and R. Isaac *Nissim. In 1967 he was active in Jerusalem's slums, setting up three educational institutes there. In 1968 he moved to Migdal ha-Emek, a development town in northern Israel, and in 1970 he became its chief rabbi. In 1971 he founded the Or la-No'ar youth movement. In 1972 he established the Migdal Or educational complex in Migdal ha-Emek, which later became a national system. In 1991 he began to absorb immigrants from Ethiopia and the Former Soviet Union in Midgal Or. In the same year he founded Migdal Or institutes in Moscow and Leningrad. In 1993 he began to absorb new Yemenite immigrants at the institution. In 1995 he worked with French youth. Grossman received a number of awards, including the Aryeh Levin Father of Prisoners Award (1980), and the Love of Israel Award given by President Chaim Herzog and Prime Minister Menaḥem Begin (1983). In 2004 he was awarded the Israel Prize for his special contribution to Israeli society.

[Shaked Gilboa (2nd ed.)]

GROSSMANN, KURT RICHARD (1897–1972), German journalist. A pacifist after World War I, Grossmann became general secretary of the *Deutsche Liga fuer Menschenrechte* (German League for Human Rights) in his home town, Berlin (1926), and organized its fight against injustice in German law courts, which followed reactionary tendencies. Grossmann was active in cases such as that of the Russian war prisoner, Jacobowsky (executed and then adjudged innocent), and that of Walter Bullerjahn who had been imprisoned as the result of false witness. He wrote *Dreizehn Jahre "Republikanische" Justiz* (1932). Warned that the Nazis were about to arrest him, Grossmann escaped to Prague in 1933. There he established and directed the *Demokratische Fluechtlingsfuersorge* (Relief for Refugees by Democrats) and wrote brochures against Nazism. In 1938 he went to Paris and in 1939 to New York. In 1943 the World Jewish Congress entrusted Grossman with dealing with the European refugee problem. After World War II, Grossmann became a recognized spokesman on problems concerning Jewish refugees and *restitution and compensation. He was also involved in the Jewish-German process of reconciliation and lectured in Germany. Among the books written during his American years are *Die Unbesungenen Helden: Menschen in Deutschlands dunklen Tagen* (1957); *Ossietzky: ein deutscher Patriot* (1963), which won the Albert Schweitzer Prize; and a history of restitution, *Die Ehrenschuld: Kurzgeschichte der Wiedergutmachung* (1967); *Emigration, Geschichte der Hitler-Fluechtlinge 1933–45* (1969).

ADD. BIBLIOGRAPHY: L. Mertens, "Enttaeuschte Ambitionen – Kurt Grossmanns berufliche Erwartungen und politische Aktivitäten," in: *Exil. Forschung, Erkenntnisse, Ergebnisse*, 2 (1996), 40–49; idem, *Unermuedlicher Kaempfer fuer Frieden und Menschenrechte. Leben und Wirken von Kurt R. Grossmann* (1997).

[Frederick R. Lachman / Monika Halbinger (2nd ed.)]

GROSS-ZIMMERMANN, MOSHE (Gross; 1891–1974), Yiddish essayist. Born in Boryslav, Galicia, Gross-Zimmermann lived in Vienna from 1908 and there wrote German impressionistic lyrics, one-act plays, and aphorisms, and edited a Yiddish newspaper *Yidishe Morgenpost* (1918–20). His essays on Yiddish, French, and German writers appeared in the Viennese Yiddish monthly *Kritik*, as well as in leading periodicals in Warsaw and New York. In 1938 he settled in Palestine, joined the staff of the Hebrew daily *Davar*, and continued publishing literary essays in the Yiddish press in Israel and New York. From 1950 he headed the Yiddish department of Israel's overseas broadcasts program, and his weekly feuilletons were widely listened to. In his essays, collected in the volumes *Yidn Tsvishn Yidn* ("Jews among Jews," 1956), *Intimer Videranand* ("Intimate Contradiction,"1964), and *Dos Vort Vos Mir Shraybn* ("The Word We Write," 1971), he displayed a personal style with a Galician idiomatic flavor.

BIBLIOGRAPHY: LNYL, 2 (1958), 348–9; Sh. Bickel, *Shrayber fun Mayn Dor*, 3 (1970), 146–53; A. Spiegelblatt, *Di Goldene Keyt*, 115 (1985), 106–7

[Israel Ch. Biletzky]

°**GROTIUS, HUGO (Huig de Groot**; 1583–1645), Dutch statesman, jurist, theologian, and historian. Grotius' contacts with Jews and Judaism were concerned with both political and spiritual matters. As a result of the flight of Marranos from Spain and Portugal to the Netherlands in the late 16th and early 17th century, and the consequent formation, without a firm legal basis, of sizable Jewish communities in *Amsterdam and other cities, the estates of Holland appointed Grotius to a commission "to amend the regulations for protecting Jews living in these lands from all scandals, anxieties, and sanctions." Grotius' report, known as *Remonstrantie*, appeared in 1615, but was not published in full until 1949. In the report Grotius posed three questions: whether it is desirable to allow Jews to settle in the country; whether it is advisable to permit them to follow their religious traditions; and in what ways it is possible to prevent difficulties affecting either Christianity or the state, through the presence in the land of Jews observing their religion. Grotius answered the first question in the affirmative. On the second point, he advised that the Jews be granted freedom of worship subject to limitations to prevent certain religious and political hazards.

Though some of his replies were noteworthy for their tolerance, others were hardly agreeable to Jews. Grotius ruled that all Jews who entered the state should be obliged to register with the city authorities, declaring that they believed in one God and that the words of Moses and the prophets were true. They were to be allowed to live in urban areas only, and their number was to be limited to 200 families in the provinces of Holland and Friesland and to 300 families in Amsterdam. They were to be granted the privilege of engaging in commerce and industry. Mixed marriages between Jews and Christians were to be prohibited. Yet the Jews were neither to be compelled to conform to a particular style of dress nor to be separated from the rest of the residents in any other way. They must not be coerced to violate their Sabbath, nor should they desecrate Sundays and Christian holidays. Different penalties were fixed for those who might transgress these regulations. The *Remonstrantie* were accepted by the estates of Holland but were not adopted as a general law for the entire country.

Even more interesting are Grotius' intellectual contacts with Judaism. His conceptions of, and attacks on, Judaism were formed within the framework of Christian apologetics. He confesses his obligation to the Hebrew authors who, through their knowledge of the literature, language, and customs of their people, have revealed a special understanding of the Scriptures. Similar statements are found in the *Annotata ad Vetus Testamentum* (Paris, 1664). In his legal works Grotius quotes, in addition to the writings of Jewish authors who wrote in Greek (Philo and Josephus), the medieval Jewish commentators, as well as the Targum, Talmud, and Midrash. Occasionally his compositions contain Hebrew words and verses, and there can be no doubt that he had some knowledge of Hebrew and Aramaic; for example, he says in the *Annotata* that the beauty of the Song of Songs is marred in translations. His reported wide familiarity with Semitic languages nevertheless appears exaggerated. Many of his letters, especially to his friend Gerhard Johannes Vossius as well as to *Manasseh Ben Israel, indicate that he gained much of his information about Jews from the latter, whom he admired greatly. Because of the Jewish thread running through his works, which grew stronger in the course of time, Grotius was accused of leanings toward Judaism and of preferring Jewish to Christian biblical exegesis, accusations which, however, overlooked the spiritual ties between Protestantism and the Old Testament.

BIBLIOGRAPHY: J. Meijer (ed.), *Hugo de Groot. Remonstrantie nopende de ordre dije in de landen van Hollandt ende Westvrieslandt dijent gestelt op de Joden* (1949), introduction; J. Meijer, in: HJ, 14 (1952), 133–44; idem, in: JSOS, 17 (1955), 91–104; I. Husik, in: HUCA, 2 (1925), 381–417; A.K. Kuhn, in: AJHSP, 31 (1928), 173–80; A Loewenstamm, in: *Festschrift… des Juedisch-Theologischen Seminars*, 2 (1929), 295–302; M. Balaban, in: *Festschrift… Simon Dubnow* (1930), 87–112; J.M. van Eysinga, in: *Mededeelingen der Koninklijke Nederlandse Akademie van Wetenschappen, Afdeling Letterkunde*, 13 (1950), 1–8; C. Roth, *Life of Menasseh Ben Israel* (1934), 146–8.

[Shabtai Rosenne]

GROVE, ANDREW STEPHEN (Andros Grof; 1936–), U.S. engineer, technology executive. Born in Budapest, Hungary, to a middle-class secular family (his father was a dairy man), Grove almost died at four of scarlet fever, but he eventually become a founding father of the personal computer industry. Through foresight and good fortune, the family avoided the fate of many of their fellow Jews by successfully fleeing the Nazis, thanks to young Andris (as he was called) and his mother finding refuge with a Christian family on the outskirts of Budapest. They lived in a dark cellar in which "the sound of artillery was a continuous backdrop," Grove wrote in his memoir, as Russian bombs hit the area. Under the Communist regime that followed World War II, as his family rebuilt its business, Grove distinguished himself as a student of chemistry and was seemingly destined for a comfortable position in academia or industry, until revolution broke out in 1956 and he found himself in that cellar again. In June 1956 the popular Hungarian uprising was put down at gunpoint. Soviet troops occupied Budapest and randomly began rounding up young people. Grove and 200,000 others escaped to the West. In *Swimming Across*, his 2001 memoir, Grove re-created a Europe that has since disappeared, exploring the ways in which persecution and struggle helped shape his life. Grove went to the United States in 1957 knowing little English and with only a few dollars in his pocket. He earned a bachelor's degree in chemical engineering in 1960 from the City College of New York and a Ph.D. from the University of California, Berkeley, in 1963. He worked at Fairchild Semiconductor before participating in the founding of the Intel Corporation in 1968. In 1979 he was named president and in 1987, chief executive. Intel's microprocessor chips serve as the silicon "brains" in more than 90 percent of the world's personal computers. In 1987, the year Grove became chief executive, Intel reported profits of $248 million on sales of $1.9 billion. In 1998, the year he stepped down, Intel's profits reached nearly $6.95 billion on sales of $25 billion. Intel's popular Pentium II computer chip was developed at Intel's plant in Haifa, Israel.

Grove, who has written more than 40 technical papers and holds several patents on semiconductor devices and technology, was elected a fellow of the IEEE and a member of the National Academy of Engineering. In 1994 Grove was elected a fellow of the Academy of Arts and Sciences in the United States and *Time* magazine named him Man of the Year in 1997. His first book, *Physics and Technology of Semiconductor Devices*, published in 1967, has been used at leading universities in the United States. His *High Output Management* (1983) was translated into 11 languages. *One-on-One With Andy Grove* was published in 1987 and *Only the Paranoid Survive*, the blunt credo for which he was known, was issued in 1996.

Under Grove's stewardship, Intel thrived in the face of challenges, including up-and-down cycles in the technology industry, clone chip makers, and rival microprocessor designs. None proved an obstacle to Intel's progressive domination of the computer industry.

[Stewart Kampel (2nd ed.)]

GROVES, SACRED. The concept of sacred groves arose out of the traditional mistranslation of the Asherah as a sacred grove near the altar. The Asherah is now known to have been a man-made cult object that was placed near the altar. (For a fuller discussion see *Asherah.) There were, however, sacred *trees.

[Tikva S. Frymer]

GROZNY, capital of the Chechen Republic in Russia, formerly in S.W. European R.S.F.S.R. Situated on the Rostov-Baku railroad, it has been an oil-producing center since 1893. Until 1917 the city was outside the Pale of Settlement, but a community of *mountain (Tat) Jews existed there, which in 1866 numbered 928 persons living in 197 houses. In 1897 the Jewish population numbered 1,711 (11% of the total population) divided into two communities: mountain Jews and "Ashkenazim." In 1900 a synagogue built in Oriental style was opened. The community suffered heavily during the civil war of 1918–21 and many Jews left the city. There remained 1,274 in 1926 (1.7% of the population), but the Jewish population grew to 3,992 in 1939 (2.3% of the total), in 1939. In World War II, during the summer of 1942, the German advance was halted just before reaching Grozny and the Jews of the city were saved from annihilation. The Jewish population according to the 1959 census numbered 4,981 in the towns of the then Chechen-Ingush Autonomous Soviet Socialist Republic; it may be assumed that the majority lived in Grozny. By 1970 the number of Jews in Grozny was estimated at about 10,000. The only synagogue serving the "Tat" Jews, who reside in a Jewish quarter, was confiscated in 1962. In the 1990s almost all the Jews left, mostly for Israel.

[Yehuda Slutsky]

GRUBER, RUTH (1911–), U.S. journalist and writer on Jewish causes. Born in Brooklyn, Gruber completed her B.A. at New York University, an M.A. in German and English literature at the University of Wisconsin, and a Ph.D. from the University of Cologne in 1931, at the age of 20. Her prescient thesis, first published in Leipzig in 1935, was republished with additional material in 2005 (*Virginia Woolf: The Will to Create as a Woman*).

Returning to the U.S. during the Depression, Gruber found her academic ambitions thwarted and turned to journalism. In 1935, she returned to Europe with a Guggenheim Foundation Fellowship to study women's position under socialism, communism, and democracy. She was the first foreign correspondent allowed into Siberia, where she interviewed many of those living in the Gulag. U.S. Secretary of the Interior Harold I. Ickes hired her to do a social and economic study of Alaska in 1941 to determine its suitability for settlement of returning veterans.

In 1944, Ickes invited Gruber to participate in a secret mission to bring a thousand Jewish refugees from Italy to Oswego, N.Y. She was given the honorary rank of general so that, if captured, she would be treated as a prisoner of war rather than as a civilian spy. Gruber recorded the stories of the refugees, who called her "Mother Ruth," and was instrumental in persuading the U.S. government to allow them to apply for

American citizenship at war's end. This experience convinced her to devote her energies to Jewish causes.

Gruber's accomplishments include covering the Anglo-American Joint Committee of Inquiry on Palestine for the *New York Post*, where she encountered the Jews in Europe's displaced persons camps. She visited Palestine and the Arab countries as well. She also covered the UN Special Commission on Palestine for the *New York Herald.* While in Jerusalem, she learned that the ship *Exodus*, overflowing with 4,500 Jewish refugees, was illegally on its way to Haifa. As the only reporter permitted by the British to accompany the ship back to Germany, her articles furthered international support for Israel's foundation.

Gruber covered the Israeli War of Independence, immigration of Jews to Israel from Yemen, Iraq, North Africa, Romania, and the Former Soviet Union, as well as both mass *aliyot* of Ethiopian Jews to Israel. She also traveled to Korea and Vietnam to write about adopting Asian orphans.

Gruber's extraordinary life is chronicled in her many books, particularly a three-part autobiography, of which two volumes had appeared by 2005: *Ahead of Time* (2001) and *Inside of Time* (2004). *Haven* (2000), the story of the Jewish refugees in Oswego, was made into a television mini-series.

[Anne Lapidus Lerner (2nd ed.)]

GRUBY, DAVID (1810–1898), physician, born in Novi Sad, then Hungary; one of the pioneers of modern microbiology and parasitology. Gruby left home while young and moved to Budapest, where he worked in a Jewish restaurant. As a Jew, he could not be accepted in a high school, so he stood outside the classroom door and listened to lessons. Eventually one of the teachers took pity on him, and arranged his admittance. Gruby studied medicine in Vienna and received his degree in 1834. Despite his being a Jew, he was appointed a surgeon at the university medical school. The university proposed that he be made a professor, on condition that he would become converted to Christianity. Gruby rejected this proposal, left Vienna, and settled in Paris (1839). He was given a post at the Museum of Nature, and lectured there on normal and morbid pathology. From 1841 to 1852 he made a number of discoveries, from which evolved the new branch of mycology in both human and veterinary medicine, advancing the development of microbiology and parasitology. Gruby was the first to prove experimentally that a fungus was likely to be the cause of a specific disease in man. He was also one of the first to investigate parasitic worms and their life cycles. One of his most important discoveries, made in 1843, which represented a turning point in the history of microbiology, was the first description of the flagellate parasites of frogs' blood and tissues. Gruby called these parasites "trepanosomes." In the same year, working with the French veterinarian Delafond, he discovered microfilaria in the circulating blood of infested frogs, thus opening a new avenue for the investigation of filaria worms which constitute a widespread disease agent for man in tropical climates. He also did research on comparative anatomy, experimental physiology, experiments with chloroform and ether in anesthesia immediately after its introduction in Europe. In addition he investigated the composition of the lymph, the microscopic structure of the intestinal epithelium, and the treatment of war wounds. He was also one of the first to prepare microscopic photographs. From 1852 onward, he devoted his time to his large private practice. He was the private physician of Chopin, Liszt, Heine, and Dumas.

BIBLIOGRAPHY: Kisch, in: *Transactions of the American Philosophical Society,* 44 (1954), 193–226.

[Saul Aaron Adler]

°GRUEBER, HEINRICH (1891–1975), German pastor who saved Christians of Jewish extraction from Nazi persecution. Imprisoned in 1937 because of Christian religious opposition, he founded, after his release, the "Buero Grueber" for victims of the *Nuremberg Laws. The Buero aided non-Aryan Christians financially and helped them to emigrate. As a result of his protests in 1940 against the first deportations, Grueber was sent to the Sachsenhausen and later to the Dachau concentration camps. After his release in 1943, he secretly carried on with his work and at the end of the war set up an Evangelical Aid Society for Victims of Racial Persecution. In 1945 he became mayor of Berlin-Karlshorst and from 1949 was the representative of the Evangelical Church in the GDR, until he was forced to resign in 1958. He denounced all efforts to "whitewash" former Nazis and was a witness at the Eichmann trial held in Jerusalem in 1961. On his 70th birthday, the Grueber Grove was planted in Jerusalem. He wrote *Dona Nobis Pacem* (1957), *Leben an der Todeslinie: Dachauer Predigten* (1965^2), and *Erinnerungen aus sieben Jahrzehnten* (1968).

BIBLIOGRAPHY: *An der Stechbahn* (1957^2); *H. Grueber, Zeuge pro Israel* (1963). **ADD. BIBLIOGRAPHY:** H. Ludwig, "Als Zivilcourage selten war – Die evangelische Hilfsstelle 'Buero Pfarrer Grueber' 1838–1940," in: G.B. Ginzel (ed.), *Mut zur Menschlichkeit* (1993), 29–54; D. Winkler, *Heinrich Grueber – Protestierender Christ* (1993); J. Hildebrandt, *Bevollmächtigt zum Brueckenbau – Heinrich Grueber* (1991).

[C.C. Aronsfeld / Bjoern Siegel (2nd ed.)]

GRUEN, ADOLF (1877–1947), Austrian industrial organic chemist, born in Vienna. Gruen became chief chemist of Schicht Konzern at Aussig (Usti nad Labem), Bohemia, which eventually became part of Basle company, Hoffmann-La Roche A.G. His many patents and scientific publications were concerned mostly with fats, but he also did research in pharmaceutics. His books include *Analyse der Fette, Wachse und Erzeugnisse der Fettindustrie* (2 vols., 1925–28), *Fette, Wachse und aus diesen erzeugte Produkte* (1933), and *Synthese der Glyceride und Phosphatide* (1936).

GRUENBAUM, HENRY (1911–2006), Danish economist and politician. The son of a shoemaker, Gruenbaum was trained as an engraver but obtained a degree in economics. He joined the Labor Party, where he was active as an economist and statistician, and as editor of the party's paper *Socialdemokraten.*

During World War II Gruenbaum was a leading member of the Danish Resistance. After the war he was principally concerned with price control and vocational training. In 1964 he became minister of economics and Nordic affairs and from 1965 to 1968 finance minister, in which capacity he deputized for the prime minister in the latter's absence. His publications include *Industrielt demokrati* (1947).

[Joachim O. Ronall]

GRUENBAUM, MAX (1817–1898), German researcher in Jewish folklore and the popular languages of the Jews, one of the founders of Yiddish philology. He was born in Seligenstadt. In 1858 Gruenbaum was appointed director of the Hebrew Orphan Asylum in New York. In 1870 he returned to Europe, settled in Munich, and devoted himself to research. In the field of folklore, Gruenbaum investigated the history of aggadic themes and their influence on Islam. In the field of linguistics and literature Gruenbaum published his *Juedisch-deutsche Chrestomathie* (1882) and a selection from Yiddish literature. He was the first linguist to make a study of the structure and evolution of the Yiddish language. When he was 80 years old Gruenbaum published a chrestomathy of Judeo-Spanish which is important for the general research of Romance languages. Among his books were *Beitraege zur vergleichenden Mythologie aus der Haggadah* (1877); *Neue Beitraege zur semitischen Sagenkunde* (1893); *Die juedisch-deutsche Litteratur in Deutschland, Polen und Amerika* (1894) and *Juedisch-Spanische Chrestomathie* (1896).

BIBLIOGRAPHY: F. Perles, in: AZDJ (Dec. 25, 1898); idem, in: M. Gruenbaum, *Gesammelte Aufsaetze* (1901), introduction (repr. in: *Juedische Skizzen* (1912), 61–64); ADB, 49 (1904), 589–94; Rejzen, Leksikon, 1 (1926), 635.

[Martin Meir Plessner]

GRUENBAUM, YIẒḤAK (1879–1970), General Zionist leader, spokesman of Polish Jewry between the two World Wars, first minister of the interior in the Provisional Government of the State of Israel, and signatory of Israel's Declaration of Independence. Born in Warsaw, Gruenbaum grew up in Plonsk, and studied first in a *ḥeder*, then in a Jewish government school, and later a government gymnasium in Plotzk. He learned Hebrew from private teachers. Gruenbaum went to university in Warsaw, starting in medicine, but then switching to law. He became involved in Zionist activity and in publicist writing during his student days, frequenting the home of the writer Isaac Leib *Peretz; he later edited several newspapers in Polish, Yiddish, and Hebrew, inter alia serving on the editorial board of *Ha-Olam* and *Ha-Ẓefirah*. In later years he fought to close down the Jewish press in languages other than Yiddish and Hebrew. Gruenbaum was active in promoting Hebrew culture in Poland and in the *Tarbut organization. He tried to ensure that the struggle of the Jews in the Diaspora for their rights should be led by Zionists, and was a central figure at the conference of Russian Zionists at Helsingfors in 1906 (see *Helsingfors Program). In the years 1908–10 he lived in Vilna and was appointed secretary general of the Zionist Center in Russia. He participated in most of the Zionist Congresses from the Seventh Congress in 1905. Gruenbaum was politically active in Poland, struggling for the rights of the Jews there. In the elections to the Fourth Duma in 1912, he rallied support for the socialist candidate Jagiello, who supported equal rights for the Jews, and promised to fight against the antisemitic Polish nationalists. After the outbreak of World War I Gruenbaum settled in Petrograd, and upon the outbreak of the October Revolution became the editor of the Zionist daily *Petragrader Tageblatt*, advocating a secular community and official status for Yiddish in government institutions. In September 1918 he returned to Warsaw, becoming active in Zionist work while also participating in the establishment of the Polish Provisional National Council, which played an important role in the campaign for equal rights for the Jews during the first years of independent Poland. In 1919 Gruenbaum was elected to the Sejm (the Polish parliament) and was a member of the commission that prepared the Polish Constitution, advocating the inclusion of articles guaranteeing the rights of the national minorities. In order to overcome the distorted election regulations that sought to prejudice the chances of national minorities of being elected, he played an active role in the formation of a "National Minorities Bloc." In the 1922 elections this bloc, which included the Jews, obtained a considerable number of mandates. The policy of fighting for Jewish interests within the framework of the general struggle for minorities rights in Poland was controversial among the Polish Jews and was resented by many non-Jewish Poles. In the following elections the strength of the Minorities Bloc declined and in the course of the 1930s, upon the increase of overt antisemitism in Poland, it was abandoned. Gruenbaum remained a member of the Sejm until he left Poland in 1932. For much of time, he also served as the chairman of the Sejm's Jewish members club.

Gruenbaum first visited Palestine in 1925. Within the Zionist movement Gruenbaum opposed the enlargement of the Jewish Agency in 1929 through the cooperation of non-Zionists, and headed the radical Zionist faction known in Poland as Al ha-Mishmar. In 1932 he left for Paris. At the Zionist Congress of 1933 he was elected a member of the Jewish Agency Executive, following which he settled in Palestine. In the executive he headed the Aliyah Department in the years 1933–35 and the Labor Department 1935–48, and was also a member of the Organization Department (1935–46). In 1935–48 he headed the Mossad Bialik publishing house.

Gruenbaum was arrested by the British on "Black Saturday" in June 1946, and remained interned in Latrun until November. After the establishment of the State he was treasurer of the Jewish Agency until 1950 and served as its commissioner in 1950–51. On the eve of the establishment of the State of Israel, Gruenbaum was a member of the People's Administration, in charge of internal affairs, and in this capacity signed the Declaration of Independence. In the Provisional Government he was minister of the interior, in which position he was in charge of the elections to the Constituent Assembly in 1949. He ran in these elections in a personal list, but failed to pass the 1% qualifying threshold. In subsequent years Gruenbaum wrote on Zionist affairs and was a frequent contributor to the Mapam daily *Al ha-Mishmar.* He spent the last ten years of his life in kibbutz Gan Shemuel.

Gruenbaum's radical positions earned both admirers and enemies.

His principal writings are *Ha-Tenu'ah ha-Ẓiyyonit be-Hitpatteḥutah* (4 vols., 1942–54); *Milḥamot Yehudei Polin* (1922, 1941^2); *Bi-Ymei Ḥurban ve-Sho'ah* (1940–46); *Materjały w sprawie żydowskiej w Polsce* (2 vols., 1919–22); *Dor be-Mivḥan* (1951); *Penei ha-Dor* (2 vols., 1957–60); and *Ne'umim ba-Seim ha-Polani* (1963); he edited the first and sixth volumes of *Enẓiklopedyah shel Galuyyot* (1953, 1959).

[Haim Hillel Ben-Sasson / Susan Hattis Rolef (2nd ed.)]

GRUENBERG, KARL (1861–1940), economic and social historian. Gruenberg, who was born in Focsani, Romania, studied and practiced law from 1885. In 1900 he became an associate professor of economics and in 1909 full professor at the University of Vienna. He was director of the Institute of Social Research at the University of Frankfurt from 1924 until 1927 when he resigned because of ill health. Gruenberg wrote extensively on the agrarian history of the Austrian monarchy and the history of Socialism. Beginning in 1910 he published the *Archiv fuer die Geschichte des Sozialismus und der Arbeiterbewegung,* or *Episoden – Sechs Jahrzehnte Kampf um den Sozialismus.* Gruenberg was murdered by a Nazi in Frankfurt on the Main.

BIBLIOGRAPHY: *Oesterreichisches biographisches Lexikon*, 2 (1959), 88. **ADD. BIBLIOGRAPHY:** G. Nenning, *Carl Gruenberg und die Anfaenge des Austromarxismus* (1965).

GRUENBERG, LOUIS (1884–1964), U.S. composer. Born in Poland, near Brest Litovsk, Gruenberg was taken to the U.S. at the age of two. He studied in Berlin with Busoni, and made his debut as a pianist in 1912 at a concert of the Berlin Philharmonic, under Busoni's baton. In that year he composed a children's opera called *The Witch of the Brocken* which was followed by *The Bride of the Gods* (1913). After winning a prize for *The Hill of Dreams* (New York Symphony Society, 1919), Gruenberg devoted himself entirely to composition.

The League of Composers performed his *Daniel Jazz* in 1925. This was followed by *The Creation* (1923), into which he introduced Negro spirituals. In 1931 the Juilliard School of Music commissioned and produced his opera "Jack and the Beanstalk."

Gruenberg's most important work was his opera *Emperor Jones*, based on Eugene O'Neill's play of that name. Gruenberg was one of the first American composers to use elements of Negro spirituals and jazz in serious music. His opera *Green Mansions*, based on W.H. Hudson's novel, was commissioned by the Columbia Broadcasting System and broadcast in 1937. Moving to California, Gruenberg wrote background music for films, and composed two other operas, *Queen Helena* (1936) and *Volpone* (1945), five symphonies, and various chamber works. He was one of the organizers of the League of Composers.

BIBLIOGRAPHY: MGG, s.v.; Baker, Biog Dict, s.v. and suppl.; Grove, Dict, s.v.

[John W. Gassner]

GRUENBERG, SAMUEL (1879–1959), biblical scholar and communal worker. Gruenberg was born in Romania and in 1920 was appointed lecturer in Bible exegesis, history and geography of Palestine, and modern Hebrew at the Berlin rabbinical seminary. He was active in the Mizrachi movement and founded the Welt-Verband Shomre Shabbos, presiding over its founding congress in 1930. Gruenberg immigrated to Palestine in 1936 and then served as the chairman of the Mo'aẓah Datit ("religious council") of Tel Aviv.

With A.M. Silbermann he edited the *"Menorah"-Woerterbuch*, a modern Hebrew-German, German-modern Hebrew dictionary (1920). Gruenberg's exegetical work appeared mainly as articles in German (collected under the title *Exegetische Beitraege*, 5 vols., 1924–33) and Hebrew (collected under the title *Li-Feshuto shel Mikra*, 1945). He also wrote *Zur Geschichte der Bibelexegese I, Nordfranzoesische Klassiker der Bibelexegese* (1928). Among his Hebrew works is *Niẓẓanim* (1906), a book of poetry. Gruenberg was the editor of the Hebrew section of Joseph *Wohlgemuth's *Jeschurun*, to which he contributed many studies.

BIBLIOGRAPHY: I. Eisner, in: YLBI, 12 (1967), 46; Tidhar, 4 (1950), 1624–25.

GRUENBERG, SIDONIE MATSNER (1881–1974), U.S. educator, who exercised a dominant influence in advancing the study of guidance methods for parents and children. Sidonie Gruenberg was born in Austria and was educated in Germany and New York. In 1906 she joined the Child Study Association of America, became director (1923–1950), and served as consultant from 1950. Gruenberg wrote extensively for children and parents, and her books were translated into many languages. She was regarded as an authority on child-parent relationships and lectured in parent education, and was a member of the editorial boards of *Parents Magazine* and *Child Study.* She was chairman of the subcommittee of the White House Conference on Child Health and Protection (1930); a member of The White House Conference (1940) and The Mid-Century White House Conference (1950); director of the Public Affairs Commission (1947) and the Social Legislation Information Service (1947–61).

[Ronald E. Ohl]

GRUENEWALD, MAX (1899–1992), German rabbi and professor. Born in Koenigshuette, Upper Silesia, Germany, his father was a Jewish educator in the region. After service in World War I, he was ordained at the Breslau Rabbinical Seminary and received his doctorate in philosophy at the University of Breslau.

By 1938, Gruenewald served at the "Haupt" or "main" synagogue in Manheim for 12 years and had been elected president of the Jewish community (1933), the only rabbi to hold both offices in Germany. Owing to the rising tide of antisemitic legislation, he resigned these posts to accept a position in Berlin to work as a member of the inner council of all German Jewry. After several detentions and interrogations by the Gestapo, in discussion with Dr. Leo Baeck, he left for Palestine in late 1938 because "he saw and felt that no essential change could be effected in the fate of German Jews."

In 1939 Gruenewald accepted an invitation to teach at the Jewish Theological Seminary. The beginning of World War II left him stranded in New York and he accepted a weekend pulpit at Congregation Bnai Israel in Millburn, N.J. On May 13, 1945, Gruenewald left for Palestine to rejoin family, returning that December to accept what became a full time position in Millburn. Although offered other posts, both academic and congregational, his decision to stay in Millburn was in part prompted by his wish to build a new community fashioned with the values of his rabbinate in Manheim, rather than enter a more established congregation.

With the growth of the Millburn congregation, Gruenewald commissioned Percival Goodman to create a new form of synagogue architecture, highlighted by works of art from three "advance-guard U.S. abstractionists," according to *Time* magazine. Herbert Ferber designed an external burning bush sculpture, Robert Motherwell designed the lobby painting, and Adolph Gottlieb created the ark curtain, the original of which hangs at the Jewish Museum. Throughout his life Gruenewald dedicated himself to the preservation of the German Jewish cultural heritage. He died in Millburn.

BIBLIOGRAPHY: *Newark Sunday News* (July 23, 1950); Archives and letters of Rabbi Max Gruenewald; CBI, AJR information: December 1969; *Time* (November 19, 1951).

[Steve Bayar (2nd ed.)]

GRUENFELD, JUDAH (1837–1907), Hungarian rabbi. Gruenfeld was born in Satoraljaujhely. He was one of the most important pupils of Abraham Judah Ha-Kohen Schwartz, rabbi of Beregszasz-Mad, and like his teacher frequented the court of the Ḥasidic rabbi of Zanz. He lived for a time in Huszt, where Moses *Schick often consulted him on important problems. In 1883 he was appointed rabbi of Büdszentmihály, serving there until his death. His writings were not collected, but a substantial part of them were published by Joseph Schwartz in *Va-Yelakket Yosef* (1899–1917). Twenty-six important responsa were published in *Responsa Maharshag* (1961) by his son SIMEON (1881–1930), who served first as *dayyan* of Munkacs and then succeeded his father at Büdszentmihály. Simeon was the author of *Responsa Maharshag*, Pt. 1 (1931) on both *Oraḥ Ḥayyim* and *Yoreh De'ah*, Pt. 2 (1939) on *Oraḥ Ḥayyim* alone. In 1961 the work was republished in Jerusalem with his additional responsa on *Ḥoshen Mishpat* and *Even ha-Ezer*. His responsa are distinguished by their clarity, their penetration, and their great erudition. He also wrote *Zehav Sheva* (1933) on the Pentateuch. He left more than 2,000 responsa in manuscript, novellae on several tractates, a large work on the *halakhot* of *mikva'ot*, and a work on *ta'arovot* (mixtures containing forbidden food). It is doubtful if these works have survived.

[Naphtali Ben-Menahem]

GRUENHUT, DAVID BEN NATHAN (17th–18th centuries), German talmudist and kabbalist. In 1682 he printed Ḥayyim Vital's *Sefer ha-Gilgulim* ("On the Transmigration of Souls"), but was prevented from distributing it by the rabbinate of Frankfurt, which opposed kabbalistic works because of the danger of Shabbateanism. Two years later, however, while at Heimerdingen, he published it again, this time through a Christian printer in Frankfurt. After serving as rabbi for several years in neighboring towns (Idstein, Aue, and perhaps also Heimerdingen), he returned to Frankfurt, becoming one of the scholars in the *bet ha-midrash* founded by David *Oppenheim. Gruenhut published *Tov Ro'i* (Frankfurt, 1702), Jacob *Weil's work on the laws of ritual slaughter, to which he added his *Migdol David*, consisting of homilies and comments on Genesis. He published the *Sefer Ḥasidim* of *Judah he-Ḥasid with his own commentary (Frankfurt, 1712) and in the following year Samuel *Uceda's *Midrash Shemu'el* (Frankfurt, 1713). On friendly terms with *Eisenmenger and *Schudt before they published their antisemitic works, he wrote an adulatory preface to the former's edition of the Bible.

BIBLIOGRAPHY: Fuenn, Keneset, s.v.; M. Horovitz, *Frankfurter Rabbinen*, 2 (1883), 54–55.

[David Tamar]

GRUENHUT, ELEAZAR (**Lazar**; 1850–1913), rabbi and author. Gruenhut was born in Gerenda, Hungary, and in 1883 he was appointed rabbi of Temesvár. Impressed by the Haskalah and taking up the challenge he saw in it, he decided to augment his general education and acquire a scientific foundation for his Jewish studies. At the age of 40 he resigned his rabbinical post, left Temesvár, and moved to Berlin, where he studied at the Hildesheimer seminary and at the University of Berlin. He was especially influenced by Azriel *Hildesheimer and Abraham *Berliner. In 1892 he emigrated to Palestine and became head of the German-Jewish Orphanage. His introduction of secular studies there and his openly proclaimed Zionist views aroused the opposition of ultra-Orthodox circles in Jerusalem. Gruenhut was a prominent figure in the early Mizrachi. In addition to his communal and educational activities, Gruenhut continued his scholarly endeavors, mainly in Midrash and in Palestinian geography.

BIBLIOGRAPHY: S. Ha-Cohen Weingarten, in: *Lu'aḥ Yerushalayim*, 7 (1946/47), 168–77; 8 (1947/48), 211–4.

[Jacob Haberman]

GRUENHUT, MAX (1893–1964), criminologist and penal reformer. Gruenhut, who was born in Magdeburg, Germany, taught at Hamburg until 1922, when he went to Jena University. Later he went to Bonn as professor ordinarius. After the

Nazi accession to power he emigrated to Britain where he was appointed reader in criminology at Oxford. In 1948 he published his widely acclaimed work, *Penal Reform*. Gruenhut, who became a practicing Lutheran, took a special interest in the development of the probation system. He devoted several publications to this subject, stressing the extramural method of peno-correctional treatment as a possible alternative to imprisonment in many cases. The United Nations asked Gruenhut to undertake an investigation of certain problems relating to the efficacy of probation. The results were issued by the UN Social Affairs Department in 1964.

BIBLIOGRAPHY: Mannheim, in: *British Journal of Criminology*, 4 (1964), 313–5. **ADD. BIBLIOGRAPHY:** U. Fontaine, *Max Gruenhut (1893–1964) – Leben und wissenschaftliches Wirken eines deutschen Strafrechtlers juedischer Herkunft* (1998); H. Kaufmann, *Erinnerungsgabe an Max Gruenhut* (1965).

[Zvi Hermon]

GRUENING, ERNEST HENRY (1887–1974), U.S. journalist, administrator, and politician. Gruening was born in New York City to parents of German origin. He received a medical degree from Harvard in 1912, but decided on a career in journalism and joined the staff of the Boston *Evening Herald*. After serving as an artillery officer and on the War Trade Board's Bureau of Imports during World War I, Gruening edited *The Nation* from 1920 to 1923, winning fame for his crusades against U.S. economic exploitation of Latin America. In 1927 he moved to Maine and founded the muckraking Portland *Evening News*, which specialized in attacks on the power utilities. Gruening abandoned journalism as a profession in 1934 when he was appointed director of the Division of Territories and Island Possessions of the Department of the Interior, a post he held until 1939. From 1935 to 1937 he also served as relief and reconstruction administrator in Puerto Rico. Gruening became territorial governor of Alaska (1939–53), in which capacity he was a strong proponent of Alaskan statehood. When Alaska was admitted to the Union, Gruening was elected a U.S. senator (1958) and was reelected in 1962. He was defeated in his bid for a third term in the 1968 Democratic primary. Gruening's Senate career was marked by his vigorous opposition to American military intervention in Latin America and Vietnam and by his support for federal birth control programs and public power projects. His publications include: *Mexico and Its Heritage* (1928); *Public Pays and Still Pays* (1931, 1964); *State of Alaska* (1954); and *Vietnam Folly* (1968).

[Henry Sosland]

GRUENSTEIN, NATHAN (1877–1932?), German organic chemist. Gruenstein was born in Lithuania. Working for a chemical firm in Frankfurt on the Main, he developed a method of converting acetylene into acetaldehyde, with mercury salts as a catalyst, and thence into acetic acid, acetic anhydride, acetone, etc. His process, first used industrially in 1916, remained the chief method of producing these chemicals for nearly 50 years. Gruenstein was an active Zionist.

GRUENWALD, MORITZ (1853–1895), Czech rabbi and scholar. Gruenwald was born in Ungarisch-Hradisch, Moravia. He studied at the Breslau rabbinical seminary and served as rabbi in various cities, among them Pisek, Bohemia, 1887–93, before becoming chief rabbi of Bulgaria, residing in Sofia, in 1893. He also directed and taught at the Sofia rabbinical seminary.

In 1881 Gruenwald founded and edited until 1885 *Das Juedische Zentralblatt Zugleich Archiv… Boehmen* (1882–85), a periodical intended for the congregations in which he served. He published a number of books, including *Einfluss der Bibel auf die Bildung von Redensarten in europaeischen Sprachen* (1883); *Zur romanischen Dialektologie*, on Ladino and Rashi's *Lo'azim* (1883), and works on Czech Jewish history.

GRULËV, MIKHAIL VLADIMIROVICH (1857–?), Russian general, publicist, and military historian. In 1878 he volunteered for the Krasnoyarsk regiment and the following year converted to Russian Orthodoxy, after which he enrolled in the Warsaw Military Academy, from which he emerged as an officer in 1882. In 1889 he became a member of the General Staff. He served on missions to India, Egypt, China, and Japan and headed a scientific expedition to Manchuria which recommended a site for establishing the city of Harbin. During the Russo-Japanese War (1904–05) Grulëv commanded a regiment (and subsequently a division) during battles at the Shakhe River. A liberal by conviction, he refused to take part in the suppression of the revolutionary uprisings in 1905–07. From 1907 to 1909, when he had already attained the rank of general, he worked with the military-historical commission attached to the main directorate of the general staff in compiling the official history of the Russo-Japanese War (he was responsible for the two volumes on the operations at the Shakhe River). From 1910 he was commander of the Brest-Litovsk fortress. In 1912, following threats from the authorities, he was removed from his post in a disciplinary measure for the expression of radical views in the press. Grulëv handed in his resignation on grounds of "health" and retired to Nice (France), where he died.

His over 20 books and writings began with a poem written in Hebrew in the late 1870s and published in the newspaper *Ha-Ẓefirah* and included articles about the Dreyfus Affair, and a series of articles (1905–07) which revealed his interest in the position of the Jewish people. In the book *Zapiski generala-evreya* ("Notes of a Jewish General," Paris, 1930), Grulëv castigated antisemitism, and expressed his love and sympathy for the "long-suffering Jewish people." He donated the proceeds from this book to the *Jewish National Fund.

[Mark Kipnis / *The Shorter Jewish Encylopaedia in Russian*]

GRUMBACH, ANTOINE (1942–), French architect and town planner. Born in Oran, Algeria, Grumbach, a graduate of the Paris Ecole des Beaux-Arts (1967), focused mainly on public housing projects and public transportation (the Bibliothèque subway station of the Meteor line in Paris, transformation of the peripheral Paris boulevards for the creation of a new trolley line). Grumbach devoted his formative years mainly to writing, developing a theory of the influence of collective memory on urban landscape, leading to his social and humanistic approach to urbanism. His participation in the Roma Interrota exhibition in 1977 following his detailed study of the traditional urban fabric of Paris was a turning point in his theoretical development; from that time on he advocated the integration of new buildings in the existing urban matrix, as he views this integration as the unique means of connecting what is new to the social and collective memory of the city.

BIBLIOGRAPHY: A. Grumbach, "Figurer par la ruine l'espace de l'absence," in: *Travail de mémoire 1914–1998* (1999), 105–9; exhibition booklets: "Antoine Grumbach ou l'art de la mémoire collective"; A. Vidler, "Antoine Grumbach, le laboratoire de l'imaginaire," Centre Georges Pompidou; "Antoine Grumbach," Coll. Jalons, Centre Georges Pompidou.

[Dror Franck Sullaper (2nd ed.)]

GRUMBACH, SALOMON (1884–1952), French socialist. Born in an Alsatian village, Grumbach went to Paris as a young man to become editor of *L'Humanité* under Jean Jaurès. During World War I he was Swiss correspondent of the paper and wrote French propaganda tracts on such subjects as *Le Destin de l'Alsace-Lorraine* (Lausanne, 1916) and *Germany's Annexionist Aims* (Engl., 1918) in both German and French. Elected a member of the central committee of the French Socialist Party (SFIO), he represented it at the Third Socialist International and was elected on the Socialist ticket to the French Chamber of Deputies in 1928. Grumbach was a member of the Chamber almost continually until 1948 and was successively vice-chairman and then chairman of its Foreign Affairs Committee. Following the fall of France in 1940, he was imprisoned and later assigned a place of forced residence but escaped in 1942 and joined the French resistance movement. After the war, Grumbach was reelected to the Chamber of Deputies and concerned himself with aid for refugees. He exercised influence on France's recognition of the State of Israel. He was also active in the World Jewish Congress, especially on behalf of the Jews of North Africa and was secretary-general of the world executive of *ORT.

BIBLIOGRAPHY: JC (July 18, 1952), 19; *New York Times* (July 14, 1952), 17.

[Shulamith Catane]

GRUMBERG, JEAN-CLAUDE (1939–), French actor and playwright. When Jean-Claude Grumberg was three, his father was deported to Germany and never came back. Working first as a tailor after the war, Grumberg soon began acting, and wrote his first play, *Demain une fenêtre sur la rue*, in 1968. In 1974, he used some autobiographical material from his childhood and postwar memories to create *L'Atelier*, a tragi-comedy about women working in a Jewish-owned cloth factory immediately after the war, with the trauma of the Holocaust exposed in a very subtle manner. Other plays include *Rixe, Les Vacances, Amorphe d'Ottenburg, Dreyfus, Chez Pierrot, En r'venant d'l'Expo, L'Indien sous Babylone, Zone libre*. Grumberg was awarded numerous prizes, including the Theater Prize of the French Academy for *Zone Libre*, two "Molière" awards (best actor for *Zone libre* and best playwright for *L'Atelier*) and in 2000 the SACD Award for lifetime achivement. Grumberg also worked as a screenwriter for TV and film, assisting directors like Marcel Bluwal, François Truffaut, and Costa-Gavras.

[Dror Franck Sullaper (2nd ed.)]

GRÜNBAUM, ADOLF (1923–), U.S. philosopher of science. Grünbaum was born in Cologne, Germany, and immigrated to the United States in 1938. He received his M.S. in physics (1948) and his Ph.D. in philosophy (1951), both from Yale University. After rising through the ranks to an endowed chair at Lehigh University (1950–1960), he was appointed Andrew Mellon Professor of Philosophy in 1960 at the University of Pittsburgh, where he founded its leading Center for Philosophy of Science, of which he served as chairman. He also had an appointment there as research professor of psychiatry. Grünbaum's thorough knowledge of physical and mathematical problems enabled him to analyze some of the basic philosophical questions that arose in connection with space and time. His more than 375 publications range over the philosophy of physics, the theory of scientific rationality, the critique of Freudian psychoanalysis, and the discrediting of theism. His major books include *Philosophical Problems of Space and Time* (1973[2]), *The Foundations of Psychoanalysis: A Philosophical Critique* (1984), and *Philosophy of Science in Action* (2 vols., 2005). Grünbaum served as president of the American Philosophical Association, and president (twice) of the Philosophy of Science Association. He is a fellow of the American Academy of Arts and Sciences and a laureate of the International Academy of Humanism. His prestigious lectureships include the Gifford Lectures in Scotland, the Werner Heisenberg Lecture to the Bavarian Academy of Sciences in Munich, and the Leibniz Lectures in Hanover, Germany. He is the recipient of the Fregene Prize for science from the Italian Parliament, all four of whose prior recipients were Nobel laureates in one of the natural sciences. Yale University awarded him the Wilbur Lucius Cross Medal "for outstanding achievement." He received the Silver Medal from the venerable Italian University of Parma in recognition of his "prestigious career." His scholarship has also been recognized by the publication of three separate *Festschrift* (celebratory) volumes: (1) *Physics, Philosophy and Psychoanalysis: Essays in Honor of Adolf Grünbaum*, ed. R.S. Cohen and L. Laudan (1983, 1992); (2) *Philosophical Problems of the Internal and External Worlds: Essays on the Philosophy of Adolf Grünbaum*, ed. J. Earman et al. (1993); and (3) *Philosophy of Physics and Psychology: Essays in Honor of Adolf Grünbaum*, ed. A. Jokic (2005). Most recently, he was elected president (for 2006–7) of the International Union for History and Philosophy of Science, the worldwide umbrella organization of the various national societies in the philosophy of science and of history of science.

[Bracha Rager (2nd ed.)]

GRUNBERG (Grinberg), ABRAHAM (1841–1906), *Hibbat Zion leader. Born in Kishinev, Grunberg became a merchant and estate owner and one of the first wealthy Jews to join the Ḥibbat Zion movement. He lent his support to L. *Pinsker in Odessa. In 1889, at the Ḥovevei Zion Conference at Vilna, he was elected to the committee of trustees (the other members of which were S. *Mohilever and S.J. *Fuenn), which replaced Pinsker at the head of the movement. In 1890 he helped obtain from the Czarist authorities the authorization for the Society for the Support of Jewish Agriculturists and Artisans in Syria and Palestine (the official name of the Odessa Committee of Ḥovevei Zion), and upon Pinsker's death (1892) he was elected president of the society, a post which he retained until a few months before his death. Grunberg also headed a delegation that discussed with Baron *Rothschild in Paris the methods of agricultural settlement in Ereẓ Israel (1901). He frequently served as a Jewish representative before the Russian authorities.

BIBLIOGRAPHY: A. Druyanow (ed.), *Ketavim le-Toledot Ḥibbat-Ẓiyyon ve-Yishuv Ereẓ-Yisrael*, 2 (1925), index; 3 (1932), index.

[Yehuda Slutsky]

GRÜNBERG, CARLOS MOISÉS (1903–1968), Argentine poet born in Buenos Aires. He was among the most important and influential of Jewish authors of his generation in Argentina. Grünberg received his formal education from the University of Buenos Aires, earning advanced degrees in philosophy and law. In his early volumes of poetry – *Las cámaras del rey* (1922) and *El libro del tiempo* (1924) – Grünberg showed a close affiliation with the group of the 1920s avant-garde writers known as the *martínfierristas*, for their association with the literary journal *Martín Fierro*. He was also known for his translations of Heinrich Heine and H.N. Bialik into Spanish. He was active in the Zionist movement and was named a liaison between the State of Israel and Argentina in 1948.

Carlos Grünberg was unapologetic in his poetic expression of Jewish identity, which he especially sought to incorporate into his latter works. Much like his contemporary César Tiempo (Israel Zeitlin), Grünberg strove to define Argentine-Jewish identity in his poetry, a sometimes painful but always sincere project. His *Mester de juglaría* (1940) carried a laudatory preface by Jorge Luis Borges and consecrated him as a poet. Throughout the volume, emphasis is placed on forging a Jewish-Argentine identity. While many of the poems speak directly to the precarious and often dangerous situation for Jews in Argentina, Grünberg clearly posits his faith in the country as a hopeful new homeland. Since his perspective as a Jew was a secular one, in this book he rather forcefully and consistently denounces religiosity and declares his atheism. *Junto a un río de Babel* (1965), Grünberg's next volume of poetry, is marked by the significant historical events since the publication of *Mester*. The volume expresses the poet's frustration as a Diaspora Jew as he tries to negotiate his support for the formation of the State of Israel with his Argentine identity. Grünberg's complete works, along with a biography and critical study, are collected in Eliahu Toker (ed.), *Un diferente y su diferencia: vida y obra de Carlos M. Grünberg*. Carlos Grünberg continues to be considered one of the foremost of early Jewish poets in Argentina. His work has had a lasting impact on subsequent generations and remains as a testament to the poetic imagination as a foundry of cultural identity.

[Darrell B. Lockhart (2nd ed.)]

GRUNDIG, LEA (1906–1977) and **HANS** (1901–1958), German painters and graphic artists. Both were born in Dresden. Lea Grundig, born Lea Langer, began to study at the Dresden Academy of Arts in 1922. Already involved with the association of Communist students, she became a member of the German Communist Party (KPD) in 1926. Two years later, she married Hans Grundig, also a member of the Communist Party, and they both began to create posters and illustrations for Communist purposes. Lea Grundig focused on linolcuts, etchings, and drawings in a late-expressionist style describing the milieu of the lower classes, as in *Mutter und Kind vor der Fabrik* of 1933 ("Mother and Child in Front of the Factory"). Hans Grundig was recognized first for painted group portraits, like *KPD – Versammlung* ("Meeting of the German Communist Party," 1932, Neue Nationalgalerie, Berlin) in the neorealist style of the *Neue Sachlichkeit*, but soon turned to expressionist etching. In the mid-1930s, he created a series of allegories, human and brutish monsters in etching in which he denounced the National Socialist system as based on all-embracing terror. Both Hans und Lea Grundig were persecuted by the National Socialist authorities and had to give up working as artists. Lea was deported but managed to flee to Palestine in 1940, where she created several series of etchings related to the Holocaust. Hans Grundig was incarcerated and sent to the concentration camp of Sachsenhausen in 1940. He survived and met his wife again in 1949, when she returned to Dresden. She became a professor at the local Academy of Fine Arts. From the 1950s, they both adapted the style of socialist realism and took an active part in visualizing the ideology of the German Democratic Republic.

BIBLIOGRAPHY: G. Bruene, *Lea Grundig – Juedin, Kommunistin, Graphikerin* (Catalogue, Ladengalerie Berlin,1996); K. Mueller and D. Rose, *Lea Grundig – Werkverzeichnis der Radierungen 1933–1973* (1973); G. Feist, *Hans Grundig* (1979); R. Neugebauer: *Zeichnen im Exil-Zeichen des Exils, Handzeichnungen und Druckgraphik deutschsprachiger Emigranten ab 1933* (2003), 447–50; S. Weber, *Hans Grundig: Schaffen im Verborgenen* (2001).

[Philipp Zschommler (2nd ed.)]

GRUNDMAN, ZWI (1917–), Israel artist. Grundman was born in Poland into a family of artists (his father decorated synagogues and Holy Arks and painted biblical themes). In 1949 he settled in Israel. Much of his work is derived from Jewish philosophy. Grundman made series of oil paintings, gouaches, and lithographs based on the thought of the *Ḥasidim and of great East European rabbis. He also published an album of stoneblocks illustrating the ḥasidic story "The Seven Beggars" by R. Naḥman of Bratslav.

GRUNER, DOV (1912–1946), Jew executed by the British in Palestine. Gruner was born in Kisvarda and was one of a group of "illegal" Betar immigrants who came to Ereẓ Israel in 1940, when he joined IẒL. A year later he enlisted as a volunteer in the British army in which he served for five years. On April 23, 1946 he participated in an attack by IẒL on the Ramat Gan police station, and was wounded and captured. The desperate attempts of the *yishuv* to save his life extended over a year and were still in progress, when suddenly he was hanged together with Drezner and his two companions.

BIBLIOGRAPHY: Y. Nedava, *Olei-ha-Gardom* (1966); Y. Gurion, *Ha-Niẓẓaḥon Olei Gardom* (1971).

GRUNFELD, ERNIE (1955–), U.S. basketball player and administrator; considered one of the league's top general managers. Grunfeld was born to Holocaust survivors Alex and Livia (Samuel) in Satu Mare, Romania. During the war, Grunfeld's father – later a champion table tennis player, ranked 16th in the world in 1952 – spent time in a Romanian labor camp while his mother spent a year and a half hiding in basements in Budapest before obtaining false papers provided by Raoul *Wallenberg. Her parents and relatives were killed in Auschwitz. After waiting six years – and six months in Rome – they arrived in New York 11 days before Grunfeld's ninth birthday. Growing up in Forest Hills, New York, Grunfeld went to Hebrew school, was bar mitzvahed, went to synagogue with his parents on the holidays, and fasted on Yom Kippur, learning basketball in the schoolyard and playground courts. Grunfeld was a legend wherever he played, first at Russell Sage Junior High School and then Forest Hills High School, where he was All-American and All-City player his senior year, when he averaged 25.4 points and 16.6 rebounds per game. He was also named the outstanding student-athlete in New York City.

Grunfeld was picked to play on the 1973 U.S. Maccabiah team, the first high school player ever to play on a U.S. Maccabiah team. Grunfeld led the team – coached by Harry *Litwack – with 20 points per game and was named tournament MVP, though the team lost to Israel 86–80 in the final.

Grunfeld's star continued to shine as a celebrated guard at the University of Tennessee from 1973 to 1977, when he was featured on the cover of *Sports Illustrated* as a co-star of the "Bernie and Ernie Show" with his teammate Bernard King, a future NBA star. As a sophomore in 1975, Ernie was the second-leading scorer in the Southeast Conference with 23.8 points per game. He then played for the gold medal-winning basketball team in the 1975 Pan American Games. The following year, he led the conference in scoring with 25.3 points per game, and his 683 points was then a single-season record for Tennessee. Named captain his senior year, Grunfeld led them to a 22–6 record and the SEC championship, averaging 23.8. He was named Converse, Helms, and Sporting News (second team) All-America.

Grunfeld obtained his American citizenship in July 1976, in time to play for the U.S. at the Montreal Olympics, which netted Grunfeld a gold medal.

Grunfeld finished his career at Tennessee with 2,249 points, which set the school record, and 22.3 points per game, second in school history to Bernard King. Grunfeld was picked 11th by Milwaukee in the 1977 NBA draft, and enjoyed a nine-season career: two years with Milwaukee, three years with Kansas City, and four years with New York. Grunfeld retired following the 1985–86 season with 5,124 points, an average of 7.4 points per game in 693 career games played.

Grunfeld then worked as the Knicks radio analyst for the MSG Network from 1986 to 1989 before becoming assistant coach, vice president of player personnel, and president and general manager of the team. He led New York into the playoffs in all eight seasons of his tenure. In August 1999, Grunfeld became general manager of the Milwaukee Bucks, guiding that franchise to the postseason three times in four years. On June 29, 2003, Grunfeld was released from the final year of his contract with the Bucks, and the next day he was named president of Basketball Operations for the Washington Wizards, replacing Michael Jordan.

Grunfeld is a member of the New York City Basketball Hall of Fame.

[Elli Wohlgelernter (2nd ed.)]

GRUNFELD, ISIDOR (1900–1975), rabbi and author. Born in Tauberettersheim, Bavaria, Grunfeld studied law and philosophy at the universities of Frankfurt and Hamburg, and rabbinics at yeshivot there. After practicing law at Wuerzburg, Bavaria, he settled in England in 1933, where he studied for the rabbinate and was ordained in 1938. He was minister of the Finsbury Park synagogue (1936–38), and served first as registrar and later (from 1939) as *dayyan* of the London Beth Din, from which office he retired owing to ill health in 1965. Among his numerous communal activities were those for the Jewish War Orphans in Europe, and the British Council for Jewish Relief and Rehabilitation. He was also active in Amnesty International and various peace movements. Grunfeld's literary work is chiefly concerned with S.R. *Hirsch's writings, editing English translations of his work with extensive introductions and notes (*Judaism Eternal*, 2 vols., 1956; *Horeb*, 2 vols., 1962; introduction to I. Levy's English translation of S.R. Hirsch's Pentateuch commentary, 1959). He also wrote *The Sabbath* (1954) and *Three Generations* (on the history of neo-Orthodoxy, 1958). His wife Judith (née Rosenbaum) was active in the Beth Jacob movement (religious girls' schools) and in the Jewish secondary schools movement in England.

BIBLIOGRAPHY: JC (Oct. 28, 1960); *Jewish Review*, London (Nov. 4, 1961).

GRÜNVALD, PHILIP (Fülöp; 1887–1964), Hungarian historian. Grünvald was born in Sopron, the son of Mano Grünvald, rabbi of the Orthodox congregation there. In 1913 he started his teaching career at the Jewish secondary school in Budapest.

From 1919 to 1948 he taught at the Jewish High School and from 1948 to 1958 he was its principal. From the early 1950s until his death he taught Jewish history at the Jewish Theological Seminary in Budapest. As a teacher he was held in great esteem, especially because of his absolute integrity and deep religious commitment. Grünvald also served the Jewish Museum of that city for 30 years, first as curator and later as director.

In 1927 he presented an outline for a history of the Jews in Hungary (in: *A Zsidó Gimnázium Értesitője*, 8 (1927), 12–29). Later, he dealt with the history of the Jews in Buda, *A zsidók története Budán* (1938). His other works dealt with aspects of the history of Jews in Hungary. His major work was the continuation of *Monumenta Hungariae Judaica*, with A. *Scheiber, he edited volumes 5–7 (1959–63) of this important historical work.

BIBLIOGRAPHY: A. Scheiber, in: *Soproni Szemle*, 18 (1964), 187–8; idem, in: MHJ, 8 (1965), 11–17, incl. list of his works.

[Alexander Scheiber]

GRÜNWALD, AMRAM (d. 1870), Hungarian talmudist. Although he published no works he is extensively mentioned in the works of his contemporaries who referred difficult problems to him, e.g., Abraham S.B. Sofer in *Ketav Sofer* (OḤ, nos. 3, 94); Judah Aszod in *Teshuvot Maharia*, Pt. 2 (no. 236); David Neumann, in *Nir le-David* (nos. 105, 118). His ethical testament was published in the *Keren le-David* (1929) of his son Eliezer David Grünwald. Grünwald died in Csorna, Hungary.

[Naphtali Ben-Menahem]

His other son, MOSES (1853–1910), was a scholar and rabbi. He studied under Abraham Samuel *Sofer in Pressburg, but leaned to Ḥasidism and often visited R. Issachar Dov of *Belz. He served as rabbi in Homonna, Slovakia and Kisvarda, Hungary and from 1893 in Huszt, Carpatho-Russia, where he established one of the major Hungarian yeshivot. Grünwald wrote three works all with the title *Arugot ha-Bosem*: (1) responsa (1912); (2) a study of the talmudic principle of *Issur Ḥal al Issur* (more than one prohibition can apply to the same act; 1928); and (3) a commentary on the Pentateuch (1913). He also wrote *Mikveh Tohorah* on the laws of *mikveh* (1931). His will was published (1911) under the title *Hakhanah de-Rabbah*.

[Itzhak Alfassi]

BIBLIOGRAPHY: P.Z. Schwartz, *Shem ha-Gedolim me-Ereẓ Hagar*, 2 (1914), 256 no. 13; A. Stern, *Meliẓei Esh al Ḥodshei Adar* (1938), 77b (on Amram Grünwald). S.N. Gottlieb, *Oholei Shem* (1912), 234; P.Z. Schwartz, *Shem ha-Gedolim me-Ereẓ Hagar*, 2 (1914), 9a, no. 142 (on Moses b. Amram Grünwald).

GRUNWALD, HENRY ANATOLE (1922–2005), U.S. journalist and editor. Grunwald was born in Vienna, but immigrated to the U.S. at the age of 17. He studied at New York University and graduated in 1944. In the same year he began his career with Time Inc. as a copy boy and the following year as a writer for the publication, editing most of the sections of the news magazine. In 1968 he was appointed managing editor.

According to Grunwald, his most important contribution to *Time* was that of generating more original reporting. To that end, he introduced new departments and features, including guest essays by celebrated writers or experts; he added sections on the environment, behavior, and energy; and he created special issues devoted to a particular topic. He also introduced color photography to the magazine and granted bylines to the magazine's hitherto unnamed writers.

Grunwald relinquished the managing editor position in 1977 and in 1979 was appointed editor-in-chief in succession to Hedley Donovan. His appointment carried with it editorial responsibility for the journals *Time, Fortune, Life, Sports Illustrated, Money*, and *People*, in addition the international editions of *Time* and Time-Life Books Inc. He served in that capacity until he retired in 1987. In 1988 President *Reagan appointed Grunwald U.S. ambassador to Austria. Reappointed by President Bush, he maintained this post until 1990.

Among his many honors, Grunwald received the American Society of Magazine Editors Hall of Fame Award; the New York University Distinguished Alumni Award; and the International Rescue Committee Medallion. Among his published works, Grunwald wrote his autobiography, *One Man's America: A Journalist's Search for the Heart of His Country* (1998), and *Twilight: Losing Sight, Gaining Insight* (1999). His first novel, *A Saint, More or Less*, was published in 2003. He also compiled *Sex in America* (1964).

[Ruth Beloff (2nd ed.)]

GRÜNWALD, JUDAH (1845–1920), Hungarian rabbi. Grünwald was born in Brezó, and served as rabbi of Szobotisz for seven years, of Bonyhad a further seven years, of Surany for two and a half years, and of Szatmar (Satu-Mare) for 22 years. In Szatmar he founded a large yeshivah which achieved a wide reputation. After his death several of his works were published. The most important of them is the responsa *Zikhron Yehudah (Budapest-Satoraljaujhely*, 1923–28) in two parts. In part 1 (no. 187) he discusses whether one may associate with Zionists and expresses the fear that through Zionism "an opportunity will be given for us to be attacked and to make us disliked by the gentile countries." Another responsum (no. 200) to Joseph Ḥayyim Sonnenfeld in Jerusalem, dated 1913, on whether it is permitted to associate with the *Agudat Israel, was removed from the volume and replaced by a responsum on whether it is permitted to handle food and drink on the Day of Atonement in order to give it to children. Others of his published works are (1) *Shevet mi-Yhudah* (2 pts., 1922), on the Pentateuch; (2) *Ḥasdei Avot* (1925), on the tractate *Avot*; (3) *Olelot Yehudah*, a commentary on Psalms (1927); and (4) *She'erit Yehudah* (1938), on the Pentateuch.

BIBLIOGRAPHY: S.N. Gottlieb, *Oholei Shem* (1912), 425; P.Z. Schwartz, *Shem ha-Gedolim me-Ereẓ Hagar*, 1 (1914), 546 no. 292; A. Stern, *Meliẓei Esh al Ḥodshei Kislev-Adar* (1938), 526–36; *Sinai*, 5 (1939–40), 421–3; Weingarten, *ibid.*, 29 (1951), 98f.

[Naphtali Ben-Menahem]

GRUNWALD, MAX (1871–1953), rabbi, historian, and folklorist. Born at Hindenburg (now Zabrze, Silesia), Grunwald served as rabbi in Hamburg (1895–1903) and Vienna (1905–35). He settled in Jerusalem in 1938. Grunwald was a many-sided and productive scholar. He wrote on the history of the communities which he served (*Hamburgs deutsche Juden–1811*, 1904; *Portugiesengraeber auf deutscher Erde; Juden als Reeder und Seefahrer*, 1902; and on Vienna: *Geschichte der Juden in Wien* (for schools, 1926); *Wiener Ḥevra Kaddisha*, 1910; *Vienna*, 1936 (in the Jewish Communities series of the Jewish Publication Society of America)). Grunwald also wrote on such famous Viennese Jews as S. Oppenheimer (*Samuel Oppenheimer und sein Kreis*, 1913) and S. Wertheimer and his descendants (in: *Juedische Familienforschung*, 1926). Of more general historical interest is his anthology of the accounts of Jewish participants in Napoleon's campaigns (*Die Feldzuege Napoleons…*, 1913).

Grunwald's main interest, however, was Jewish folklore, and his contribution in this field is of lasting importance. In 1897 he founded the *Gesellschaft fuer juedische Volkskunde* and edited and largely wrote its organ, the *Mitteillungen* (1897–1922), which was succeeded by the *Jahrbuecher fuer juedische Volkskunde* (1923–25). In this area he contributed also to other periodicals as well as to a number of Festschriften (J. Lewy, 1911; *Gaster Anniversary Volume*,…) and published important studies such as *Hebraeische Frauennamen* (1894–), *Eigennamen des alten Testaments* (1895), and in the related field of Jewish art *Holzsynagogen in Polen* (with others, 1934). Among Grunwald's other interests were Spinoza, on whom he had written his dissertation (1892) and a prize-winning *Spinoza in Deutschland* (1897). On the occasion of the international exhibition on hygiene in Dresden in 1911 he published a book on that subject, *Hygiene der Juden* (1912). He also edited a German prayer book for women (*Beruria*, 1913^2) and one for serving soldiers (*Gebetbuch fuer israelitische Soldaten im Kriege*, 1914). On the occasion of Grunwald's 70th birthday *Omanut*, the publication of the Bezalel Museum in Jerusalem, issued his bibliography (1941).

His son, KURT (1901–1990), was a banker, economist, and public figure in Jerusalem. He wrote on aspects of Jewish economic history including *Tuerkenhirsch* (1966), a study of Baron de *Hirsch.

[Eliyahu Feldman]

GRUSENBERG, OSCAR OSIPOVICH (1866–1940), advocate in Russia also active in Jewish communal affairs, born in Yekaterinoslav. After completing his legal studies at the University of Kiev in 1889, he was invited to prepare for a professorship at the university on the condition, which he rejected, that he convert to Christianity. He settled in St. Petersburg and began to practice law, but as a Jew was only permitted to practice as an "assistant advocate." Although he soon won a reputation throughout Russia as a brilliant lawyer, it was only in 1905 that he was granted the title of a "certified lawyer." Grusenberg specialized in criminal cases and his appearance in political trials as the defender of liberals, revolutionaries, or representatives of minority groups always received wide publicity. He defended the writers Maxim Gorki, V. *Korolenko, and such political figures as P. Milyukov, and Leon *Trotsky as well as the group of representatives of the First *Duma after the Vyborg proclamation of 1906 protesting against the dissolution of the Duma by the government.

Grusenberg gained greatest renown, however, in specifically Jewish trials. Inspired with a national Jewish consciousness, and pride in the history of his people, he displayed great ability in defending the persecuted and obtaining justice for fellow Jews. In defending unjustly accused Jews, he was not content merely to obtain redress of wrongs done to them as individuals, but also tried to vindicate Jewish honor; and was called by Jews "the national defender." He disagreed with Jewish leaders who preferred that Jewish causes of public interest should be defended in court by Russian lawyers. Grusenberg appeared in the trials following the pogroms of *Kishinev and *Minsk; P. *Dashevski, who had made an attempt on the life of P. *Krushevan, the instigator of the Kishinev pogrom, and D. *Blondes in Vilna (1900–02) were defended by Grusenberg. In the Blondes case some Jews were inclined to accept the relatively light penalty imposed on the defendant by the lower court, but Grusenberg insisted on bringing the case before a higher court in order to clear the name of the Jews absolutely. The high point in his life and in his career as a lawyer was his appearance in the *Beilis trial in 1913, which he considered similar to the stand of the martyrs in the trials of the Inquisition. His success was the result not only of his brilliant forensic talents, his profound knowledge of criminal law, and mastery of court procedure, but also of his knowledge of the psychology of the common Russian, an important factor since the fate of the defendant in criminal cases was decided by a jury consisting, as a rule, of people from all walks of life.

As a member of the Russian Constitutional Democratic Party, Grusenberg was also active in Russian political life. In the elections to the Second *Duma he was a candidate in Vilna province, but was defeated by the Poles. He was later a member of the advisory council to the Jewish representatives in the Third and Fourth Dumas. After the *Balfour Declaration Grusenberg drew closer to Zionism and in 1917 joined the "Jewish Bloc" organized by the Zionists. That year he was made a senator by Kerensky's Provisional Government. In 1918–19 during the Russian civil war Grusenberg headed the Jewish Council for Self-Defense and the Council for Aiding the Victims of Pogroms. In 1919 he was chosen as one of the representatives of Ukrainian Jewry to the *Comité des Délégations Juives in Paris. After the Soviets came to power, Grusenberg left Russia. He stayed from 1921 to 1923 in Berlin and from 1926 to 1932 in Riga. In 1929 he served as the representative of the Jews of Latvia at the founding of the enlarged *Jewish Agency and was chosen a member of its council. Grusenberg spent the last years of his life in France.

Besides legal articles published in Russian professional journals, Grusenberg also wrote on Jewish subjects in *Voskhod* and in *Budushchnost*, edited by his brother Samuel. He wrote a book on his experiences as an advocate, and in 1938 his memoirs appeared under the title *Vchera* ("Yesterday"). A collection of his essays and speeches in Russian, including some critical appreciations, was published posthumously in 1944.

In 1950 his remains were brought to Israel in accordance with his will.

BIBLIOGRAPHY: S. Kucherov, in: *Russian Jewry 1860–1917* (1966), 219–52; A.A. Goldenweiser, *V zashchitu prava* (1952), 239–49; M. Samuel, *Blood Accusation* (1966), index.

[Simha Katz]

GRYDZEWSKI (Grytzhendler), MIECZYSLAW (1894–1970), Polish literary editor. Grydzewski played an important part in Polish literary and intellectual life between the world wars as editor of the weekly *Wiadomości Literackie* (1924–39) and of the monthly *Skamander* (1935–39). He also ran the French-language monthly *La Pologne littéraire* (1926–?). An exile after 1939, he edited (in London) the Polish émigré weekly *Wiadomości* and published literary essays such as *Henryk Dąbrowski* (1945).

GRYN, HUGO (1930–1996), British rabbi. Born in Berehovo, Czechoslovakia, Gryn was deported to Auschwitz at the age of 14. After the Holocaust he was taken to Britain and studied mathematics and biochemistry at Cambridge. Under the influence of Leo *Baeck, he studied for the Reform rabbinate at Hebrew Union College, Cincinnati. His first congregation was in Bombay. Returning to the U.S., he served as executive director of the World Union of Progressive Judaism and from 1962 to 1964 was a senior executive in the American Jewish Joint Distribution Committee. From 1964 he was rabbi at the West London synagogue. In 1990 he became president of the Reform Synagogues of Great Britain and from 1980 to 1991 was chairman of the European board of the World Union for Progressive Judaism. He became widely known throughout Britain among Jews and non-Jews for his frequent appearances and especially for his broadcasts. He was a leading figure in interfaith activities.

GRYNBERG, BERL (1906–1961), Yiddish writer. Grynberg grew up in Warsaw and emigrated to Argentina in 1923. He worked in Cordoba and Buenos Aires as a printer and, for decades, as linotypist for the Yiddish daily *Di Prese*, where his earliest stories appeared, arousing critical attention with their original combination of realistic and romantic characteristics. The stories often begin with actual happenings but soon become mystical and symbolic. The themes, landscapes, and characters of his six narrative volumes are both Argentinean and Jewish: *Morgnvint* ("Morning Wind," 1934), *Di Eybike Vokh* ("The Eternal Week," 1938), *Blut un Vayn* ("Blood and Wine," 1944), *Dos Bloe Shifele* ("The Blue Boat," 1948), *Libshaft* ("Love," 1952), *Dos Goldene Feygele* ("The Golden Bird," 1948). He was profoundly influenced by Sholem Asch and David Bergelson. He committed suicide in 1961.

BIBLIOGRAPHY: LNYL 2 (1958), 393–4; S. Bickel, *Shrayber fun Mayn Dor* (1965), 377–80. **ADD. BIBLIOGRAPHY:** Y. Horn, in: *Bay Zikh*, 13/14 (1979), 167–70.

[M. Rav / Tamar Lewinsky (2nd ed.)]

GRYNBERG, HENRYK (1936–), Polish author and actor. World War II memories and the European Holocaust dominate his *Ekipa "Antygona"* ("The Crew of the *Antigone*," 1963), collected stories, and the haunting *Żydowska wojna* (1965; *Child of the Shadows*, 1969). Grynberg's novella *Buszujący po drogach* ("The Catcher on the Roads," 1967) denounced officially inspired postwar antisemitism. A member of the Warsaw State Jewish Theater, he remained in the West after the company's 1967 season in New York.

GRYNSZPAN (Gruenspan), HERSCHEL (1921–?), assassin of a German diplomat in Paris. Grynszpan, who was born in Hanover, Germany, into a family of Polish Jews, moved to Paris early in 1938. When he learned that Polish Jews, including his parents, were being deported from Germany (Oct. 28, 1938), he decided to assault the German ambassador in Paris in order to arouse public opinion in the West regarding the Nazi persecution of Jews. Grynszpan shot at a German embassy official, Ernst vom Rath, who, mortally wounded, died two days later. His death served as a pretext for the November pogroms against Jews throughout Germany and Austria, termed **Kristallnacht*. Grynszpan was held for questioning by the French authorities, and the Germans accused him of being a tool of "world Jewry." When France capitulated, Grynszpan escaped to the Free Zone. However, he later returned to the Occupied Zone, where he was arrested and handed over to the Germans, who made elaborate preparations for a show trial. In the end, the whole affair was hushed up and Grynszpan disappeared without trace.

BIBLIOGRAPHY: F.K. Kaul, *Der Fall des Herschel Grynszpan* (1965). **ADD. BIBLIOGRAPHY:** R. Roizen, in: HGS, 1:2 (1986), 217–28; K. Jonca, in: SFZH, 10 (1987), 65–111; M.R. Marrus, in: *American Scholar*, 57:1 (1988), 69–79; L. van Dijk, *Der Attentäter Herschel Grynszpan und die Vorgänge um die "Kristallnacht"* (1988).

[Shaul Esh]

GUADALAJARA, city in Castile, central Spain. A Jewish community already existed there at the time of the *Visigoths, for the Jews are said to have been entrusted, by Ṭāriq ibn-Ziyād, with the defense of the town after the Arab conquest in 714. Joseph *Ferrizuel (Cidellus), the physician of Alfonso VI, was active on behalf of the Jews there after the Christian reconquest in 1085. Judah Halevi dedicated a poem to Ferrizuel on the occasion of the latter's visit in Guadalajara between 1091 and 1095. Further information on the Jews of Guadalajara is found in the charter granted to the Jews of the city by Alfonso VII in 1133. The Jews seemed to have occupied an important position there. One of the synagogues of the community was given to the monastery of Santa Clara in the 13th century. We have no information on the fate of the

Jewish community during the 1391 massacres. In 1414 a mass conversion of 122 Jews occurred after supposedly a cross appeared in the skies during the sermon of a Franciscan. In 1444 Juan II ordered that the New Christians be allowed to occupy public positions in the city. Most of the Guadalajara Jews earned their living from weaving, shoemaking, and tailoring. A tax of 11,000 maravedis, levied from the community as late as 1439, attests to its well-established financial situation. After the anti-Jewish persecutions of 1391, the order to confine the Jews and the Moors in separate sections of the city was rigorously enforced. Several Jews of Guadalajara acted as tax farmers even in the 15th century. The tax levied from the Jews of Guadalajara during the war against Granada was one of the highest paid by any Jewish community, amounting to 104,220 maravedis in 1488 and 90,620 maravedis in 1491.

Guadalajara was a foremost cultural center of Sephardi Jewry and the birthplace of the *Kabbalah in Castile. *Moses de León and other important scholars of the 13th century were active in Guadalajara. *Isaac ibn Sahula, author of the *Meshal ha-Kadmoni* and mystical commentaries on Job, Song of Songs and Psalms, was in practice there as a physician. In *Meshal ha-Kadmoni* we find for the first time a quotation from the Zohar. Moses de León lived 50 years in Guadalajara. Another Jewish resident of the city in the 13th century was Solomon ben Abraham ben Yaish who wrote on Ibn Ezra's commentary on the Torah. In the 15th century, Guadalajara continued to be an important Jewish cultural center. In Guadalajara between 1422 and 1430 Moses Arragel translated the Bible into Castilian at the request of Luiz de Guzmán, the Great Master of Calatrava. The translation and the notes show the high level of learning that the rabbi from Guadalajara had achieved. This Bible, known as *The Alba Bible*, is of great artistic, exegetical, and linguistic value. The earliest-recorded Hebrew printing press in Spain was established in 1482 in Guadalajara by Solomon *Alkabeẓ, famous for his poem *Lekha Dodi*, who produced there in that year the commentary of David *Kimḥi on the later prophets and the *Tur Even ha-Ezer* of *Jacob b. Asher (1480–82). During the years before the expulsion of the Jews from Spain, residents included Isaac *Abrabanel and Isaac *Aboab II who directed one of the most important yeshivot in Castile. A document of 1499, concerning Jewish property in Guadalajara at the time of the expulsion, lists three synagogues and 36 Jewish houseowners. The exiles from Guadalajara established their own synagogue in Algiers in the early 16th century.

Until 1412 the Jews of Guadalajara lived outside the walls, in what was known as *Castil de judíos*. From 1412 onwards, the Jews lived near San Adrés, the commercial center of the city, and near San Gil, Santa María de la Fuente, and San Miguel. The *judería* was not exclusively inhabited by Jews. Following the decision to segregate the Jews in 1480, attempts were made to move the Jews into an area where they could be isolated from the Christian inhabitants. On the eve of the Expulsion, four synagogues are mentioned: *Sinagoga mayor, Sinagoga de los Malutes, Sinoga del Midras,* and *Sinagoga de los Toledanos.*

BIBLIOGRAPHY: Baer, Spain, index; Baer, Urkunden, index; Suárez Fernández, Documentos, index; F. Cantera Burgos and C. Carrete Parrondo, *Las juderías medievales en la provincia de Guadalajara,* (1975) [rep. from *Sefarad,* 33–34 (1973–74); for Guadalajara, see *Sefarad,* 34 (1974), 43–78; 313–70]; F. Cantera Burgos, in: *Proceedings of 6th World Congress of Jewish Studies* (1976), 2:53–59; J.I. Alonso Campos and J.M. Calderón Ortega, in: *Wad al-Hayara,* 13 (1986), 401–4; J.E. Ávila Palet, in: *Actas del I Encuentro de Historiadores del Valle de Henares* (1988), 49–58.

[Haim Beinart]

GUADALUPE, town in Castile, W. Spain. Jewish landowners are recorded there in the second half of the 14th century. The community was annihilated in the wave of anti-Jewish riots which swept Spain in 1391, but was revived during the 15th century. In 1485, however, Jews were forbidden to live in Guadalupe by order of Nuño de Arévalo, the local inquisitor. In 1492, prior to the expulsion of the Jews from Spain, *veedores* (leaders) of the community sold the land of the old cemetery to the local bishop for 400 reals; a clause in the deed of sale states that the price was so low because of the kindnesses shown to the Jewish community by the bishop. The *Conversos in Guadalupe lived on a special street in the former Jewish quarter. Jews from Trujillo would stay at the homes of these Conversos, which became important centers for fulfilling the Jewish observances. Forty-six dossiers, almost all of 1485, are preserved concerning persons arraigned before a special tribunal sent by the Toledo Inquisition to uncover relapsed Conversos. Several Conversos who had entered the monastery of San Bartholomé de Lupiana near Guadalupe were tried there in 1489–90. The monks Diego de Marchena and García Çapata, whose conversion to Judaism caused a furor in the church in Spain, belonged to this monastery. They were burned at the stake as Jews.

BIBLIOGRAPHY: A. Sicroff, in: *Studies… U.J. Benardete* (1965), 89–125; H. Beinart, in: *Tarbiz,* 26 (1956/57), 78; idem, in: *Scripta Hierosolymitana,* 7 (1961), 167–92; F. Fita, in: *Boletín de la Academia de Historia,* 23 (1893), 283; E. Escobar, in: *El Monasterio de Guadalupe,* 1 (1916), 62; Suárez Fernández, Documentos, index; Baer, Urkunden, index; Baer, Spain, index.

[Haim Beinart]

GUASTALLA, ENRICO (1828–1903), Italian soldier and patriot. Born in Guastalla, central Italy, Guastalla gave up his career as a businessman in 1848 to volunteer for the Piedmontese army in the struggle for the unification of Italy. He fought against Austria in 1848 and participated in the abortive capture of Rome from the pope in the following year. For several years he was editor of *Libertà e Associazione*, but his radical views came into conflict with the authorities and in 1858 he fled to England, where he joined the radical patriot Giuseppe Mazzini. Guastalla returned to Italy in 1859 and joined Garibaldi in his campaigns of 1860, 1862, and 1866, being promoted major. In 1867 he married Sofia Weill-Schott and began to work in the bank of his father-in-law in Florence. In 1869 he moved finally to Milan where he was elected a member of the city council. He tried to be elected to the Italian parliament without success. He devoted the last years of his life to studies of the Italian Risorgimento, and in 1884 he founded and was president of the Museo del Risorgimento di Milano.

BIBLIOGRAPHY: F. Conti, "Guastalla, Enrico," in: *Dizionario Biografico degli Italiani*, v. 60 (2003), 483–85.

[Mordechai Kaplan / Federica Francesconi (2nd ed.)]

GUATEMALA, Central American republic, population 14,280,596 (2004); Jewish population 833 (1999).

Community History

Documents in the archives of the Mexican Inquisition attest to the presence of *Crypto-Jews in Guatemala during the colonial period. The first known immigrants to the country were German-speaking Jews entering Guatemala at the end of the 19th century. Most of them settled in Quetzaltenango and engaged in the sale of clothes and textiles in the coffee plantations. Following the earthquake of 1902 and the fall of coffee prices, the German Jews moved to Guatemala City, where they established in 1913 the Sociedad Israelita de Guatemala in order to provide for their religious and social needs. The community formed by these immigrants was small and isolated from the Jewish world, and its descendants are no longer Jews.

The origins of the present-day Jewish community date from the second decade of the 20th century. According to the data collected in the census survey made in 1999, the Jewish immigrants to Guatemala came from Syria, Iraq, Jerusalem, Panama, Jamaica (originally from England), and Turkey. The list extends also to Jews from Lebanon, Egypt, Poland, Russia, and the United States. The Sephardi Jews settled in Guatemala during the first and second decades of the 20th century. They started as poor peddlers in the provincial towns, and gradually moved to Guatemala City, where in 1923 they founded the Sociedad Israelita Maguén David. The East European Jews arrived in the 1920s following the restrictions on immigration imposed by the United States. Most of them were poor artisans, and they were assisted by the local Jews, particularly by the Maguén David. Jewish immigration in the 1930s consisted of Czechs and Germans as well as Jews from Jerusalem, Panama, and Poland.

At the beginning of the 20th century the liberal Guatemalan governments favored the immigration of foreigners who wished to settle in the country, allowing them to develop economically, socially, and culturally. This motivated the first groups of Jewish immigrants to Guatemala. Policy took a negative turn in 1944, when the president of the Republic, General Jorge Ubico, promulgated Decree No. 1241 of the Law of Foreigners, whose First Article prohibited "the entrance and permanent settlement in the country of foreigners occupied as peddlers" (para. 21–22), this being the trade of many of the Jews who had just arrived in the country.

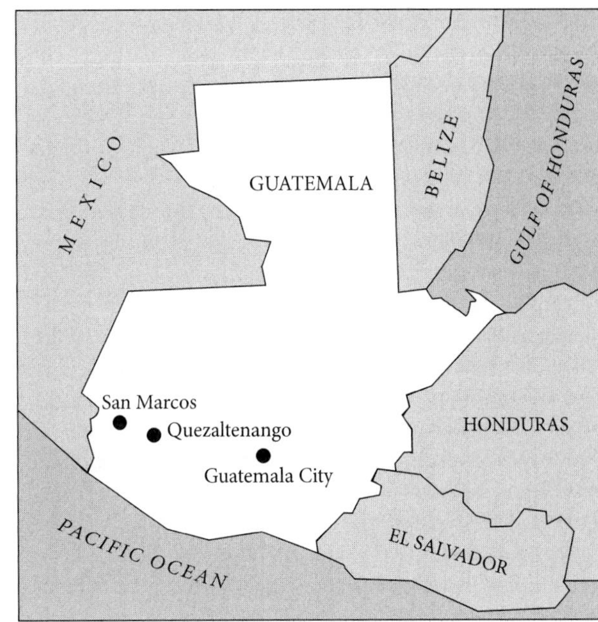

Centers of Jewish settlement in Guatemala.

Laws limiting immigration were rarely enforced after World War II, when Polish, Czech, and German Holocaust survivors entered the country. From the 1950s (through to the early 21st century) the Jews who immigrated to the country arrived from the most varied areas of the globe, with the main reason being marriage to members of the Jewish community of Guatemala or occupational mobility.

Demography

In 1999, there were 833 Jews in the country (400 women and 433 men), with a fertility rate of 2.7 children. The number of Jews in Guatemala never exceeded 1,200 (data calculated by the members of the community in the 1950s).

A singular characteristic is that 36% of Guatemalan Jews between 18 and 45 years live abroad (mainly in the United States). This is caused by two factors: (1) most of those who lived abroad for many years embarked on their professional careers in the country where they received their higher education, settling there permanently (66% of those who emigrated pointed to the lack of economic opportunity as the main cause of their emigration); (2) marriage: 38% of marriages with Jews from other countries resulted in immigration of the Guatemalan Jew to the country of residence of his or her spouse.

According to the 1965 census, the community had 74 mixed marriages, accounting for 27.2% of the Jewish population. In the 1999 census, only 6% of the members were married to non-Jews, while 12% were married to men and women who had converted to Judaism.

Communal Life

The first synagogue, inaugurated on August 11, 1938, was constructed by the Sephardi community Maguén David and provided for the religious needs of Sephardi and Ashkenazi Jews alike. In 1941 the Ashkenazi Jews founded their own organization, the Associacion Centro Hebreo, which opened its Shaaréi Biniamín synagogue (Orthodox) in 1968. Between 1969 and 1989 the Bet-El Synagogue (Conservative) operated, with a majority of members of West European origin. Centro Hebreo and Bet-El merged in 1989 under the name of the former.

The first organization that represented the Guatemalan Jews vis-à-vis the national and international authorities was the Sociedad Israelita de Guatemala (founded 1913). In 1968 it was replaced by the Comité Central de la Comunidad Judia de Guatemala. In 1981 the Comunidad Judía de Guatemala (called since 1994 Comunidad Judía Guatemalteca) or Guatemalan Jewish Community (GJC) was founded as the representative organ and the Jewish umbrella organization, responsible for the Jewish educational institutions (Gan Hillel, Tarbut, Talmud Torah, Mechon Noar, Maccabi ha-Ẓa'ir), social, sports, and cultural activities, the organization of groups of all the ages, the cemeteries, relations with local and international institutions (Jewish and general), and every matter related to the communal life of Guatemalan Jews.

Education, Culture, and Zionism

Between 1958 and 1976 there was a Jewish day school called the Albert Einstein (later Salomón Blenkitny). In the early 21st century there was a daily kindergarten, Gan Hillel, and supplementary schools that are open from one to three times a week. These are Tarbut, Talmud Torah, Mechon Noar, and the Machon leMadrijim.

A youth organization was founded in 1943 under the name of Young Centro Hebreo, and two years later it affiliated with the Maccabi World Union, creating Maccabi Ha-Ẓair Guatemala, active until the present.

Between 1994 and 2004 the GJC developed large building projects: the construction of a Jewish Community Center (finalized in 1995), which united all the educational, social, religious, and Zionist organizations, and the Har Carmel project, being an enormous stretch of land with 200 lots earmarked for housing for members of the GJC.

Most Zionist organizations have a representative in the country as well as in some of the international ones: Keren Hayesod, Keren Kayemet, WIZO, Zionist Federation, Maccabi World Union, B'nai B'rith, and others.

It should be emphasized that 69% of Guatemalan Jews declare themselves Zionists, and that all the members of the GJC are affiliated with the above-mentioned institutions.

The following periodicals were published by the community organizations: *Abucah* ("Torch"), 1943–45; *The Maccabee*, 1959–60; *Mabat*, 1978–86; *Kadima*, 1992–99; and *Beyajad*, from 1999.

GJC'S RELATIONS WITH GUATEMALAN ORGANIZATIONS. The number of affiliations of the Jewish community, as much on the individual level as on the institutional level, is very large. Guatemalan Jews are members, leaders, or cooperate in institutions such as Junkabal (Edgar Heinemann, chairman), the Guatemalan Red Cross (Max Russ, director), children's day care (Samuel Camhi, founder and benefactor; Enriqueta Engel, president), League against Cancer (Margot Halfon, deputy chairperson; Rosa Luchtan, director; Eduardo Halfon, director), volunteer and municipal fire departments (Max Russ, president; Max Trachtenberg, president; Moises Russ, director; Isaac Farchi, deputy chairman), Santa Lucia Orphanage (Sara Dreiffus, president), CACIF (Alberto Habie, president), Roosevelt Hospital (Irene Neumann and Sol Berkowitz, directors), Rotary Club (Tomas Rybar, president; Marcel Ruff, president), Municipality of Guatemala City (Roberto Stein, deputy mayor), Guatemalan Association of Journalism (Isidoro Zarco, president), Chamber of Commerce (Jaime Camhi, vice president; Moris Farchi, director), Chamber of Industry (Moises Russ, director; Alberto Habie, president; Joe Habie, director), National Congress (congressmen Isaac Farchi, Roberto Stein, Dr. Julio Sultán, Manfredo Lippman), ministries (Dr. Julio Sultán), embassies (Dr. Gert Rosenthal, ambassador at the UN; Moises Russ, ambassador in Israel), INCAP (Dr. Benjamin Torun, scientist, director of Research), Bricks for Guatemala City of Sanarate Reconstruction Committee (Margot Halfon, president; Marcel Ruff, general secretary), National Social Welfare Committee (Bella Russ, chairperson), YPO (Roberto Tenenbaum, president), Garden Club of Guatemala (Brenda de Rich, president), FUNDAP (Jaime Camhi, director), universities, volunteer groups in hospitals, FUNDESA (Manuel Yarhi, president; Jaime Camhi, president; Edgar Heinemann, president; Mario Nathusius, president), Cepal (Dr. Gert Rosenthal, secretary general), primary and secondary schools (Mario Nathusius, president; Saul Mishaan, president; Victor Cohen, director), National Bicycle Federation (Jaime Russ, president), as well as representing Guatemala in sports, science, chess, and more.

Four members of the Jewish community have been awarded the Vatican Order of Pope St. Sylvester: Moises Russ, Bella Russ, Margot Halfon, and Dr. Jacobo Sabbaj.

Relations with Israel

Guatemala had a crucial role in the vote on the partition of Palestine. The Guatemalan ambassador to the United Nations in 1947, Jorge García Granados, was a member of the UN Special Commission for Palestine (UNSCOP). Backed by the president of Guatemala, Dr. Juan José Arevalo, he worked tirelessly for the establishment of a Jewish state in a part of Palestine. His book *The Birth of Israel* was published in 1949. The two governments have engaged in various projects cooperatively. Guatemala demonstrated its support of the Jewish State in numerous votes in favor of Israel within the framework of the United Nations.

BIBLIOGRAPHY: F. Tenenbaum (ed.), *La comunidad Judía de Guatemala* (1963). **ADD. BIBLIOGRAPHY:** J. García Granados, *Así nació Israel* (2003²); C. Tapiero, *La Comunidad Jud ía de Guatemala: Estudio sociodemográfico, e identidad cultural y religiosa* (2000); S. Aldana and C. Siboni, *Historia de la Comunidad Judía Guatemalteca, Primera parte: 1898–1944* (1995); J. Russ, *Historia de la Comunidad Judía Guatemalteca, Segunda parte: 1945–2000* (2000).

[David Algaze / Carlos A. Tapiero (2nd ed.)]

GUBER, (Howard) PETER (1942–), U.S. film producer. Guber was born and raised in Boston, Massachusetts. His father, Samuel, operated a junk metal business in nearby Somerville. After receiving his B.A. from Syracuse and both business and law degrees from NYU, he was hired by Columbia Pictures in 1968. In a few short years, Guber ascended to head of worldwide production, one of the youngest studio chiefs, generating record-breaking profits with such films as *The Way We Were* (1973), *Shampoo* (1975), and *Taxi Driver* (1976). In 1976, Guber left Columbia to start producing films independently, winning critical and box office successes with *Midnight Express* (1978). Guber teamed with Jon Peters to form one of the most successful teams in Hollywood, producing such hits as *Flashdance* (1983), *The Color Purple* (1988), *Rain Man* (1988), and *Batman* (1989). In 1989, Guber and Peters became co-heads of Columbia Pictures Studio, which had been purchased by Sony. The rollercoaster ride of their free-spending ways and Sony's expensive education in the movie business is chronicled in detail in the book *Hit and Run* by Nancy Griffin and Kim Masters. Peters resigned in 1991. Nonetheless, Guber continued to deliver hits such as *Terminator 2* (1991) and *Groundhog Day* (1993) and developed Sony into a modern film and television studio powerhouse. In 1995, Guber left Sony and launched Mandalay, a multimedia entertainment company specializing in movies, television, and sports entertainment. The films Guber directly produced earned over $3 billion and 50 Academy Award nominations. In addition to producing, Guber taught at UCLA School of Theater, Film and Television for over 30 years. He appeared regularly on his own show, AMC's *Sunday Morning Shootout*, opposite Peter Bart, editor-in-chief of *Variety*.

[Max Joseph (2nd ed.)]

GUBER, RIVKA (1902–1981), Israel Prize winner for services in the absorption of immigrants, known as "the mother of sons." Born in Russia, Guber immigrated with her husband Mordecai in 1925. She lost her two sons in the War of Independence, and from then on devoted herself, together with her husband, to the absorption of immigrants. She organized the education system in the Kastina transit camp (*ma'abarah*), which later became Kiryat Malakhi, and assisted in immigrant absorption in the Lachish area. In her last years she devoted herself to writing and keeping up with her many "sons" all over the country. She received the Israel Prize in 1976. In 1979, she was part of the official Israeli delegation accompanying Prime Minister Menaḥem Begin to the United States to sign the Camp David Peace Treaty with Egypt.

GUEBWILLER, town in the Haut-Rhin department, E. France. In 1270 there was a community of at least 10 families in the town; from 1330 or earlier they owned a synagogue. However the community ceased to exist after the *Black Death persecutions (1348–49). Jews did not reappear in Guebwiller until the beginning of the 17th century. Their numbers did not grow to any extent until the 19th century (about 80 families in 1870), but subsequently declined once more. Several Jews from Guebwiller were deported by the Nazis. In 1969 a small community again existed. The present Rue des Tonneliers was formerly known as Rue des Juifs.

BIBLIOGRAPHY: E. Scheid, *Histoire des Juifs d'Alsace* (1887), 107, 136, 249; C. Wetterwald, *Strassennamen von Gebweiler* (1928), 32; Z. Szajkowski, *Analytical Franco-Jewish Gazetteer* (1966), 251; Germ Jud, 2 (1968) 270–1.

[Bernhard Blumenkranz]

GUEDALLA, HAIM (1815–1904), philanthropist and supporter of Jewish settlement in Ereẓ Israel. Born in London, Guedalla was descended from Moses Vita Montefiore and was a great-nephew of Sir Moses *Montefiore, whose niece he married. The Guedallas were originally Moroccan. Through his association with the Montefiore family he became interested in Ereẓ Israel. In the period 1876–80, he was the chairman of the Turkish Bondholders of the General Debt of Turkey, and in view of the size of the debt – £250,000,000 – he proposed that Ereẓ Israel be purchased from the Turks in exchange for the debt. George *Eliot, who was then taken up with the idea of the return of the Jews to their ancestral home, inspired this idea in him. There was considerable reaction to Guedalla's proposal in the Jewish world: some people treated it with amusement, while others (such as Y.M. *Pines) thought it worthy of consideration. Guedalla did in fact negotiate with Midhat Pasha, the grand vizier, but nothing came of the proposal. In 1863 Guedalla accompanied Moses Montefiore on a trip to Morocco to bring aid to its Jewish community, and on the way back he visited Spain. This trip was the beginning of his campaign designed to persuade the Spanish government to permit the return of the Jews, an aim which was in fact achieved in 1869. He also joined Montefiore on his fourth trip to Ereẓ Israel in 1855 and extended help to various institutions there. He published articles, pamphlets, and books dealing with Jewish affairs and supplied the funds for the English translation of *The Jewish Question of Russia* by Demidoff San Donato (1884). In the 1840s Guedalla was influential in establishing *The Voice of Jacob*, one of the earliest Anglo-Jewish newspapers.

BIBLIOGRAPHY: JC (Oct. 7, 1904).

[Getzel Kressel]

GUEDALLA, PHILIP (1889–1944), English biographer, historian, and essayist. A member of an old Sephardi family, and the son of David Guedalla, a pioneer English Zionist, Philip Guedalla was born in London and educated at Rugby school and at Oxford, where he excelled as a debater and actor, and later became a barrister. During World War I he was legal adviser to the ministry of munitions and the contracts department of the British War Office. After ten years at the bar, he retired in 1923 to devote himself to literature and politics. Guedalla's five attempts to secure election to Parliament as a Liberal MP failed; but his books on historical personalities and events, mostly of the 19th century, were an outstanding success. A witty speaker and writer, he developed a brilliant and highly individual style, often tinged with irony, in his works. These include *The Second Empire* (1922), on Napoleon III; *Palmerston* (1926); *Gladstone and Palmerston* (1928); a study of Wellington entitled *The Duke* (1931); *The Queen and Mr. Gladstone* (1933); *The Hundred Days* (1934), on Napoleon I's last campaign; *The Hundred Years* (1936), covering 1837–1936; *The Liberators* (1942); and *Middle East, 1940–42; A Study in Axis Power* (1944). He also wrote studies of famous personalities such as *Supers and Supermen* (1920) and *Masters and Men* (1923); two books of American interest, *Independence Day* (1926), which appeared in the U.S. as *Fathers of the Revolution* (1926), and *Conquistador* (1927); and published the works of Disraeli, to which he added his own introductory notes (1927). He was president of the British Zionist Federation, 1924–28, and in 1925 delivered his presidential address to the Jewish Historical Society of England on *Napoleon and Palestine*. Philip Guedalla was noted for his aphorisms, such as "Any stigma to beat a dogma," "History is the study of other people's mistakes," and "An Englishman is a man who lives on an island in the North Sea governed by Scotsmen." During World War II, at the age of 54, he became a squadron leader in the Royal Air Force. One of his last works was *Mr. Churchill: A Portrait* (1941).

BIBLIOGRAPHY: *The Times* (Dec. 18, 1944). **ADD. BIBLIOGRAPHY:** ODNB online.

[Godfrey Edmond Silverman]

GUEDEMANN, MORITZ (1835–1918), Austrian rabbi, historian, and apologete. Guedemann was born in Hildesheim, Prussia; he was ordained at the Breslau Jewish Theological Seminary, in 1862. Guedemann was appointed rabbi in Magdeburg in 1862. Four years later he went to Vienna as a *maggid* and in 1868 became a rabbi there. In matters of Jewish law and practice he took a conservative position, opposing, for example, the introduction of the organ and the omission of prayers relating to Zion, which contrasted with his liberal outlook in scholarly matters. In 1869 he was appointed head of the Vienna *bet din* and in 1891 became chief rabbi with Adolf *Jellinek and sole chief rabbi on the latter's death in 1894.

This period was one of rapid growth for the Vienna Jewish community and also of intensified political antisemitism. Guedemann played an active role in developing communal institutions. With Joseph Bloch he organized the Oesterreichisch-Israelitische Union (1886) and also helped found the *Israelitisch-Theologische Lehranstalt in 1893. Though Guedemann had not been trained as a historian, most of his numerous contributions to scholarship were in that field. His major work was *Die Geschichte des Erziehungswesens und der Cultur der abendlaendischen Juden* (3 vols., 1880–88), the first systematic attempt to examine some of the underlying trends and institutions of medieval Jewish life in terms of their non-Jewish milieu. Other works include *Das juedische Unterrichtswesen waehrend der spanisch-arabischen Periode* (1873) and *Quellenschriften zur Geschichte des Unterrichts und der Erziehung bei den deutschen Juden* (1892). During the final decades of his life Guedemann devoted an increasing amount of his scholarly output to the refutation of academic antisemitism. His *Juedische Apologetik* appeared in 1906.

[Ismar Schorsch]

Attitude to Zionism

When *Herzl was engaged in writing *Der Judenstaat*, he thought of three personages who would assist him in turning his idea into reality: Baron de *Hirsch, Baron *Rothschild, and Guedemann. It was to Guedemann that Herzl addressed one of his first letters (June 11, 1895) and his name appears frequently in Herzl's diary for the period in which Herzl began his preoccupation with political Zionism. In Herzl's eyes, Guedemann was not only Vienna's chief rabbi but one of the greatest authorities on Judaism, of which Herzl possessed only a very limited knowledge. But although opposed to the extreme Reform movement, Guedemann was in agreement with its attitude on the contemporary problem of the Jewish people. He could not understand why a Jew who had grown up among the German people and in the realm of its culture "should uproot himself by his own hands from the soil upon which he had grown," or, as he formulated it on one occasion, "Should I go from here, where the word Jew and all who bear that name are held up to shame, and leave the field to our enemies in order to form a majority in Palestine? No! A hundred thousand horses will not drag me from here, until I achieve revenge over the antisemites and joy over their downfall."

Over a period of many months, Herzl held meetings with Guedemann and exchanged letters with him. At the beginning, Guedemann was impressed by the idea of the *Judenstaat* and by its author; when the book came out, however, and caused a storm among the assimilationists, Guedemann's attitude underwent a decided change. For a while he wavered between support for Zionism and opposition to it; in the end, he published a book, *Nationaljudentum* (1897) in which he attacked Herzl's *Judenstaat*. In his book he sought to prove that not only was there no such thing as a Jewish people, but that it was the main task of the Jews to bring about the abolishment of nationalism. Both Herzl and *Nordau came out with sharp reactions to Guedemann's book.

[Getzel Kressel]

BIBLIOGRAPHY: B. Wachstein, *Bibliographie der Schriften Moritz Guedemanns* (1931); T. Herzl, *Complete Diaries*, 5 (1960), index; J. Fraenkel (ed.), *Jews of Austria* (1967), 111–29; Yerushalmi, in: S. Federbush (ed.), *Ḥokhmat Yisrael be-Ma'arav Eiropah* (1958), 187–98; I. Schorsch, in: YLBI, 11 (1966), 42–66; J. Fraenkel, *ibid.*, 67–82.

GUENZBURG (also **Guensburg**, **Guenzberg**, **Ginzburg**, **Ginsburg**, **Ginzberg**, **Ginsberg**, **Ginzburger**, **Ginsburger**), family name common among East European Jews, especially in Russia. The first known Jews to call themselves by this name (after the beginning of the 16th century) came from the town of Guenzburg in Bavaria. Relatives of this family from neighboring Ulm who settled in Guenzburg used the name Ulma-Guenzburg, or simply Ulma. Abbreviated forms of Guenzberg, such as Guenz or Gaunz were also used. Some branches of the

Guenzburg family later added Oettingen or Kliachko to form hyphenated names. When, early in the 19th century, the Russian authorities ordered the Jews to select family names, many in Poland, Lithuania, and Volhynia adopted the name Ginsburg, or a similar name, but these were not related to the emigrants from Guenzburg and their descendants in Bavaria.

The genealogy of the Guenzburg family has been traced back to Simeon Guenzburg (1506–1586), the grandson of Jeḥiel of Porto. The Guenzburg family produced numerous rabbis of note, including Aryeh *Gunzburg, author of *Sha'agat Aryeh*, in the 18th century, who, according to the family genealogy, was of the 11th generation to bear the name, and also the writer Mordecai Aaron *Guenzburg. The most celebrated branch of the family was that of the barons *Guenzburg.

BIBLIOGRAPHY: B. Friedberg, *Zur Genealogie der Familie Guenzburg* (1885); D. Maggid, *Sefer Toledot Mishpeḥot Ginzburg* (1899).

[Simha Katz]

GUENZBURG, distinguished Russian family of bankers, philanthropists, and communal workers, of whom three generations were active during the second half of the 19th and early 20th centuries in Russia and Paris. They gained a place in modern Jewish history for their efforts on behalf of Russian Jewry as semiofficial representatives before the czarist authorities as well as for their Jewish and general philanthropic activities. HORACE GUENZBURG was granted a baronetcy in 1871 by the archduke of Hesse-Darmstadt. In 1874 this title was also awarded to his father, JOSEPH YOZEL GUENZBURG. The title was made hereditary by Czar Alexander II. The most outstanding members of the family were: BARON JOSEPH YOZEL (YEVSEL) GUENZBURG (1812–1878), son of GABRIEL JACOB (1793–1853), who, according to the family genealogists, was of the 15th generation of the Guenzburg family. Born in Vitebsk, he received a traditional education, and acquired wealth in the 1840s as a lessee of the liquor monopoly and later as an army contractor. In 1857 he settled with his family in Paris but retained his enterprises in Russia. In 1859 he founded the Joseph Yevsel Guenzburg Bank, in St. Petersburg, which rapidly became one of the chief financial institutions in Russia and contributed significantly to the development of credit financing in that country. He participated in financing railroad construction and the development of gold mines in the Urals, Altai, and Trans-Baikal Siberia.

Guenzburg tried to utilize his contacts with influential Russian circles to improve the situation of the Jews, and especially to win rights of permanent Jewish residence outside the *Pale of Settlement for specific categories of Jews, such as merchants, craftsmen, or demobilized soldiers. In this he was successful. The first synagogue in St. Petersburg was built as a result of his efforts. He was one of the founders of the *Society for the Promotion of Culture among the Jews of Russia in 1863 and supported its activities. Guenzburg provided scholarships for Jewish youth to encourage higher education, especially in medicine, and donated substantial sums to encourage Jews to engage in agriculture, which he regarded as an important step toward improving their situation. In addition to awarding prizes for agriculture, he devoted the income from his extensive estates in southern Russia to settling Jews on these lands. He died in Paris and was buried in the family sepulcher there. He had one daughter and four sons, some of whom engaged in his enterprises.

His second son, the best known, was BARON HORACE (NAPHTALI HERZ) GUENZBURG (1833–1909), born in Zvenigorodka, in the province of Kiev. In addition to a general education, Horace received a Jewish education in his father's house. Among his teachers was the Hebrew writer Mordecai Sukhostaver, who for many years served as Joseph Yozel Guenzburg's secretary. Through him Horace became closely acquainted with the Hebrew poet Jacob *Eichenbaum who profoundly influenced him. While still a young man, Horace became his father's aide and principal partner in his financial enterprises as well as in his public activities. When his father established his bank in St. Petersburg, Horace became its acting director. His talents as well as his manners contributed to its success as one of the central financial institutions of Russia. His personal qualities gained him the respect and confidence of court circles. Among other activities he managed the financial affairs of the archduke of Hesse-Darmstadt, who appointed him consul-general in Russia (1868–72), the only instance when the Russian government consented to the appointment of a Jew as consul in its domains. The Russian government also showed its appreciation of Guenzburg's services by appointing him state councilor and awarding him orders of merit. Until 1892 he served as alderman in the St. Petersburg municipality. He was director of financial institutions, as well as a supporter and member of many non-Jewish social welfare institutions. In 1892 the Guenzburg bank suspended operations as a result of a crisis that was brought about by the suspension of credits by the Russian government.

Guenzburg's home in St. Petersburg was a meeting place for liberal scholars, authors, artists, and other intellectuals in the Russian capital. As well as a philanthropist, Horace was a generous patron of scientific, cultural, and social institutions, and of promising writers, artists, and musicians. Among others the sculptor Mark *Antokolski benefited from Guenzburg's assistance early in his career.

In Russian society Horace's position and his contacts with the authorities helped him continue with greater effect the activities of his father on behalf of Russian Jewry and as patron of its communal affairs. During the period of reaction in Russia, he had to keep vigilant watch to prevent the promulgation of an ever-increasing number of anti-Jewish decrees and to counteract the accusations against the Jews. When the new military service law was about to be passed in 1874, he succeeded in preventing the inclusion of special provisions directed against Jews. During the blood libel case in Kutais in 1878 he encouraged the celebrated scholar, the convert Daniel *Chwolson, to write a book tracing the history of the blood libel, which he subsidized. In 1881–82 he attempted to establish a countrywide organization of Russian Jews, and he convened and headed conferences of representatives of Jewish communities in St. Petersburg to plan action against the pogroms then taking place in southern Russia. Guenzburg also urged the government to rescind the "Temporary Regulations" of 1882 (*May Laws), which had been promulgated by the minister of the interior, *Ignatyev, and he actively participated in the work of the Pahlen Commission (1883–88) which had been empowered to review the laws pertaining to Jews.

After his father's death, Horace headed the Jewish community in St. Petersburg, and also the Society for the Promotion of Culture among the Jews of Russia. After the 1905 pogroms he organized and headed a committee to aid the victims. He opposed the emigration of Jews from Russia, and as chairman of the ICA (*Jewish Colonization Association) committee in Russia, he urged that the funds donated by Baron Hirsch be spent in Russia to encourage agriculture and crafts among Jews. He supported publications of historical interest, including the collection of Russian laws pertaining to Jews edited by V. Levanda, and other studies. Horace had 11 children.

His son, BARON DAVID GUENZBURG (1857–1910), was born in Kamenets-Podolski. He continued the family tradition of public and communal activity and philanthropy, but is mainly noted for his scholarly work in Judaic and Oriental studies. He specialized in Oriental subjects and linguistics, and medieval Arabic poetry, in the universities of St. Petersburg, Greifswald (Germany; 1879–80), and in Paris, and was a pupil of the Hebrew writer Ẓ. ha-Cohen *Rabinowitz, of A. *Neubauer, and of Senior *Sachs. The last, who was a tutor in the Guenzburg home in Paris, influenced David to study medieval Hebrew poetry. David gained a knowledge of most Semitic languages, and published a number of works. These include: the physician Isaac b. Todros of Avignon's *Be'er le-Ḥai* from the sole manuscript (1884); the first edition of *Sefer ha-Anak* (*Ha-Tarshish*) of Moses Ibn Ezra (1886); the diwan of the Spanish-Arab poet, Ibn Guzman (1896); studies of the foundations of Arabic poetry (in publications of the Oriental department of the Royal Archeological Society, 1892–97); a comprehensive work on ancient Jewish ornamentation, *L'Ornement Hébreu*, in collaboration with the Russian art critic, V.V. Stasov (1903), which contained examples of Jewish illuminations from medieval Hebrew manuscripts, among them illuminated Bible manuscripts of Oriental origin in a style which combined Byzantine and Arabic elements; a catalog and description of Arabic, Greek, and Coptic manuscripts in the Institute of Oriental Languages of the Russian Foreign Office; a book on the poetry of Lermontov (published posthumously in 1915; as a connoisseur of Russian poetry, Guenzburg was especially attracted by the Jewish and Oriental elements in Lermontov's works); a number of studies published in Russian, French, German, and Hebrew periodicals and in jubilee volumes honoring scholars of his day. He also coedited the jubilee volume honoring A. *Harkavy. His library, which had one of the most important collections of Judaica, was one of the largest in private ownership in the world, and contained a valuable collection of manuscripts and books, including incunabula (presently in the Lenin State Library in Moscow).

Although more interested in scholarly than public activity, David was active in the St. Petersburg community, which he headed after his father's death, in the Society for the Promotion of Culture among the Jews in Russia, in ICA, and in the society to encourage crafts and agriculture among Russian Jews. In 1910 he headed a conference of Russian Jews to solve religious problems. He was also active in areas that related to his academic interests, and was chairman of the Ḥovevei Sefat Ever ("Society of Lovers of Hebrew"), a member of the committee of *Mekiẓe Nirdamim, a founder of the Society for Oriental Studies, a member of the scientific council of the Ministry of Education, as well as a Founder member of other academic institutions in Russia and abroad, including the Société Asiatique of Paris. With Judah Leib Benjamin *Katzenelson (Buki ben Yogli) he was one of the editors in chief of the *Yevreyskaya Entsiklopediya* (Russian Jewish Encyclopedia), and responsible for the section dealing with geonic literature and the Arab period in Jewish history. The crowning achievement of his academic work was the creation of the Jewish Academy, officially named Higher Courses on Oriental Studies, which he established in St. Petersburg in 1908. This was a one-man project, for Guenzburg not only supported these courses with his funds, but was also its rector and lectured on Talmud, rabbinic literature, Semitic languages, Arabic literature, and medieval Jewish philosophy. Its lecturers included S. *Dubnow and J.L.B. Katzenelson, who headed it after Guenzburg's death. The academy, which continued until 1916, created a Russian school of Judaic scholarship, and was attended by Z. *Shazar, Joshua *Guttman, Y. *Kaufmann, and S. *Zeitlin, among other distinguished scholars and writers.

David's brother PIERRE (d. 1948), an industrialist living in Paris, left for the United States in 1940. His wife Yvonne de la Meurthe (d. 1969) served for 20 years as honorary president of ORT. Their daughter married Sir Isaiah *Berlin.

BIBLIOGRAPHY: D. Maggid, *Sefer Toledot Mishpeḥot Ginzburg* (1899); G.B. Slioberg, *Baron G.O. Guenzburg* (Rus., 1933); *He-Avar*, 6 (1958), 77–178.

[Simha Katz]

GUENZBURG, ILYA YAKOVLEVICH (1860?–1939), Russian sculptor. Born into a traditional family in Vilna, Guenzburg attracted the attention of Mark *Antokolski at the age of 11, and went with him to St. Petersburg where he studied under Antokolski himself. The art historian V.V. Stasov took an interest in his career. In 1878 he entered the St. Petersburg Academy of Arts where he received a gold medal for his "Lament of Jeremiah." After graduation in 1886, he traveled abroad for a year on a scholarship provided by Baron H. *Guenzburg, and returned to St. Petersburg, to continue his work. After the Russian Revolution he founded a Jewish Society at Petrograd for fostering art.

His work falls into three main groups: (1) scenes of children; (2) contemporary writers, artists, and scientists, e.g., Tolstoy, Tchaikovsky, Pasternak, and Mendeleyev; (3) abstract subjects, busts, and memorials (noted among them were those of Antokolski (in the Jewish cemetery of Leningrad) and that of V.V. Stasov). His sculptures were portrayed with realism, and included *A Child Before Bathing* and *The String* (depicting a child playing); both are in the Leningrad Museum. He published his memoirs, *Iz moyey zhizni* ("From My Life," 1908), which is also of historical value on Jewish life in Russia.

BIBLIOGRAPHY: *Ost und West* (March, 1904); YE, 6 (c. 1910), 534–6.

GUENZBURG, MORDECAI AARON (1795–1846), Hebrew author and founder of the first modern Jewish school in Lithuania. Guenzburg was born in Salantai and earned a living as an itinerant tutor until 1835 when he settled permanently in Vilna. In 1841 he and the poet Solomon *Salkind founded a modern Jewish school, which he directed as headmaster until his death. Guenzburg became one of the leading spokesmen for the Vilna Haskalah, though he was a moderate who opposed radical change. He observed the practical *mitzvot* which, under Moses *Mendelssohn's influence, he viewed as social regulations for the benefit of the Jewish community. He opposed the extremism of both the Orthodox and the secularists. When Max *Lilienthal was invited to Russia by the authorities, Guenzburg joined the Vilna *maskilim* in attacking Lilienthal's attempts to win over the Orthodox and ridiculed his German ways and superficiality.

Guenzburg's books in the area of French and Russian history enjoyed wide circulation and helped improve his financial condition. In 1844 and 1862 he published *Devir* (2 vols.), an anthology of letters, essays, and short stories, containing, among others, letters by Goethe, *Heine, and *Boerne, and a translation of the letters of Moses Montefiore's personal secretary, Eliezer Halevi (Louis *Loewe), who accompanied Montefiore on his first trip to Palestine. *Devir* also contained essays about the neglected Jewish communities in the Arab lands, China, and Ethiopia. *Devir* aroused in its readers a love for Palestine and influenced Abraham *Mapu and Kalman Shullmann. His autobiography *Avi'ezer*, his most original work, appeared in 1864 (reprint 1966). Written in the style of Rousseau's confessions, it portrays the inner world of the Jewish child, and is a ringing attack on the *ḥeder* system of education. Stylistically, Guenzburg surpasses his contemporaries by far. For the sake of accuracy he resorted to mishnaic Hebrew, introducing talmudic phrases and neologisms, many of which became commonly accepted and are still in use, for example, *milḥemet magen* ("defensive war"), *milḥemet tigrah* ("offensive war"), *rahitim* ("furniture"), *beit-do'ar* ("post office"), etc. Guenzburg was the literary forerunner of P. *Smolenskin, J.L. *Gordon, M.L. *Lilienblum, and R.A. *Broides. His other works include *Ittotei Rusyah Ha-Ẓarefatim be Rusyah* (1843), on the Franco-Russian War of 1812; *Pi-hahiroth* (1843), a history of the wars of 1813–1815.

BIBLIOGRAPHY: D. Maggid, R. *Mordecai Guenzburg 1795–1846*… (Heb., 1897), includes bibliography; J. Fichmann, in: M. Guenzburg, *Ketavim Nivḥarim* (1911); Klausner, Sifrut, 3 (1960^3), 120–70; J.S. Raisin, *The Haskalah Movement in Russia* (1913), 213–21; Waxman, Literature, index. **ADD. BIBLIOGRAPHY:** A.L. Mintz, "Guenzburg, Lilienblum and the Shape of Haskala Autobiography," in: *AJS Review*, 4 (1979), 71–110; M. Pelli, *"Iyyun be-Aviezer le-M.A. Guenburg,"* in: *Ha-Do'ar*, 62 (1983), 156–57; Y. Bartal, *"M.A. Guenzburg: Maskil Litai mul ha-Modernah,"* in: *Ha-Dat ve-ha-Ḥayyim* (1993), 109–25; M. Pelli, *"Ha-Otobiografyah ke-Zhaner Sifruti be-Sifrut ha-Haskalah: Ḥayyav shel ha-Maskit M.A. Guenzburg,"* in: *Ha-Do'ar*, 78 (1999), 19–20.

[Abba Ahimeir]

GUENZIG, EZRIEL (1868–1931), rabbi and scholar. Guenzig, who was born in Cracow, received the traditional talmudic education there. He later studied secular subjects in Berlin and philosophy and Semitics at Berne University. He served as rabbi in the Moravian communities of Dresnitz and Loschitz until 1918. After World War I, he settled in Antwerp, where he became head of the Taḥkemoni School and later was active as a bookseller. Guenzig's scholarly work was mainly concerned with the history of Haskalah in Galicia. However, he dealt with other subjects as well. He wrote on F. *Mieses (*Oẓar ha-Sifrut*, 3 pt. 5 (1890), 1–54), whose writing he prepared for publication. His other published works include *Der Commentar des Karaeers Jephet ben Ali* (1898); *Der Pessimismus im Judenthume* (1899); *Die Wundermaenner im juedischen Volke* (1921); and *Das juedische Schrifttum ueber den Wert des Lebens* (1924). Guenzig served as assistant editor of *Ha-Maggid, and edited the seven volumes of the literary journal *Ha-Eshkol* (1898–1913). The first two volumes of the latter were edited with J.S. Fuchs.

BIBLIOGRAPHY: G. Bader, *Medinah va-Ḥakhameha* (1934), 64–65; M. Mossler, in: *Haolam*, 19 (1931), 683–4; *Barkai* (Johannesburg; Feb.–March 1937), 7; (March–April 1937), 20; H. Gold (ed.), *Juden und Judengemeinden Maehrens* (1929), 319–20; Kressel, Leksikon, 1 (1965), 477–8.

[Getzel Kressel]

GUENZLER, ABRAHAM (1840–1910), Hungarian rabbinical publicist and polemicist. Born in Satoraljaujhely, Guenzler was gifted from youth with a talent for writing which he employed in defense of traditional Judaism. In 1868, he published a pamphlet, *Tokhaḥat Megullah*, in which he attacked Isaac Friedlieber's compilation *Divrei Shalom* and defended traditional Jewry against the Reform movement, then on the ascendant in Hungary.

Subsequently Guenzler moved to Sziget, a community of Ḥasidim and *maskilim*, where he began to publish a Hebrew weekly, *Ha-Tor*. It was the first Hebrew journal published in Hungary and exerted considerable influence. The revival of the Hebrew language was his main ambition, and in 1876 he published in Sziget a booklet, *Das Meter Moss*, most of which was in Hebrew because "there are people who understand Hebrew better than Yiddish." The journal was published in Sziget for three years (1874–76), but it seems that he could not maintain it there and moved with it to Kolomyya in Galicia and from there to Cracow. Meanwhile the pogroms against the Russian Jews broke out (1881). Guenzler accurately described them in *Ha-Tor*, with the result that the Russian government banned it from Russia. Since most of the journal's subscribers lived there (he had nearly 300 subscribers in Russia, and about 250 in Austria-Hungary), *Ha-Tor* ceased publication. Guenzler could not refrain, however, from commenting on contemporary and local issues. He published his articles in *Kol Maḥazike Hadas*, published fortnightly in Lemberg. Meanwhile R. Simeon Sofer of Cracow founded the weekly *Maḥazike Hadas* and Guenzler was appointed editor. The publishers of *Kol Maḥazike Hadas* sued Guenzler; eventually it was agreed that *Maḥazike Hadas* would stop publication and Guenzler would edit *Kol Maḥazike Hadas*, but he was later forced to resign.

BIBLIOGRAPHY: G. Bader, *Medinah va-Ḥakhameha (1934)*, 65–66.

[Naphtali Ben-Menahem]

°GUÉRIN, VICTOR (1821–1891), French explorer of the Near East. Guérin was professor of rhetoric at various French universities and finally at Paris. In 1852 he traveled extensively in Greece, Egypt, Tunisia, and Ereẓ Israel. His works include a seven-volume *Description géographique, historique et archéologique de la Palestine* (1869–80), containing three volumes on Judea and two each on Samaria and Galilee. Guérin's work combines historical information (especially from the church fathers and crusader authors) with topographical descriptions; although his work preceded the age of scientific archaeology, he noted many monuments which have since disappeared. He also wrote *La Terre sainte, son histoire, ses souvenirs* (2 vols., 1881–83) and *Jérusalem, son histoire, sa description, ses établissements religieux* (1889).

[Michael Avi-Yonah]

GUGGENHEIM, U.S. family. MEYER GUGGENHEIM (1828–1905), merchant and industrialist, was the progenitor of the American branch of the family. He was born in Lengnau, Switzerland, and immigrated to the United States in 1848 with his father Simon, settling in Philadelphia. After a period of peddling, Meyer established successful stove polish, lye, and lace-embroidery businesses. In the late 1870s he purchased an interest in the Leadville mines in Colorado. Leaving the embroidery business, the firm of M. Guggenheim's Sons rapidly acquired and built silver, lead, and copper mines and smelters in the western United States, Mexico, and other countries. In 1901 the firm merged with the American Smelting and Refining Company, in which the Guggenheims played a dominant role. At the height of the family's fortune, the company was estimated to be worth over $500,000,000. Meyer's seven sons continued the family's business operations as Guggenheim Brothers, expanding their holdings from Alaska to the Congo.

His eldest son, ISAAC (1854–1922), was born in Philadelphia. He promoted the family's enterprises, including the Guggenheim Exploration Company. He was a contributor to the New York Federation of Jewish Charities, Jewish Theological Seminary, and Hebrew Union College. Meyer's second son, DANIEL (1856–1930), became the leader of the Guggenheim Brothers' far-flung enterprises and was responsible for expansion and modernization. As president of American Smelting and Refining Company for nearly 20 years, he developed tin mines in Bolivia, diamonds in Africa, and nitrates in Chile. A progressive in labor relations, Daniel favored unionization and government economic legislation. With his brother Murry he endowed free music concerts in New York's Central Park; the Daniel and Florence Guggenheim Foundation; and the Daniel Guggenheim Fund for the Promotion of Aeronautics. He was a trustee of New York's Temple Emanu-El and one of the founders of the Jewish Theological Seminary. Meyer's third son, MURRY (1858–1939), participated actively in managing Guggenheim Brothers and the American Smelting and Refining Company. His philanthropies included a free dental clinic in New York. The fourth son, SOLOMON ROBERT (1861–1949), developed the family's interests in Mexican and Chilean mining. A benefactor of New York's Mt. Sinai and Montefiore Hospitals and the New York Public School Athletic League, he formed the Solomon R. Guggenheim Foundation, which encouraged nonobjective art. The Guggenheim Museum in New York, designed by Frank Lloyd Wright, commemorates this interest. A fifth son, BENJAMIN (1865–1912), entered the family mining business and then withdrew from the partnership in 1900 to head International Steam Pump. He died in the sinking of the *Titanic*. Meyer's sixth son, SIMON (1867–1941), was associated with the family's mining interests and, from 1907 to 1913, served as U.S. senator from Colorado. In 1925 he established the John Simon Guggenheim Foundation, which has provided fellowships to thousands of scholars, scientists, and artists. The seventh son, WILLIAM (1868–1941), managed company property until 1900, and then withdrew from the family firm. His subsequent activities were public affairs, writing, and philanthropy.

Daniel's son HARRY FRANK (1890–1971) served the family's mining enterprises and was senior partner of Guggenheim Brothers. As president of the Daniel Guggenheim Fund for the Promotion of Aeronautics from its inception in 1926, he did much to advance aviation. He established the Harry Frank Guggenheim Foundation, which supports scholarly research on problems of aggression, and violence. From 1929 to 1933 he served as United States ambassador to Cuba, and later founded and was president of the Long Island daily *Newsday*. Benjamin's daughter, MARGUERITE (Peggy; 1898–1979), spent most of her life in Europe, aiding the modern art movement, especially American abstract expressionism. Her home in Venice was a center for art display. In 1979 her memoir, *Out of This Century: Confessions of an Art Addict*, was published.

BIBLIOGRAPHY: H. O'Connor, *Guggenheims: The Making of an American Dynasty* (1937); M. Lomask, *Seed Money* (1964); E.P. Hoyt, *The Guggenheims and the American Dream* (1967). **ADD. BIBLIOGRAPHY:** R. Hallion, *Legacy of Flight: The Guggenheim Contribution to American Aviation* (1977); J. Davis, *The Guggenheims: An American*

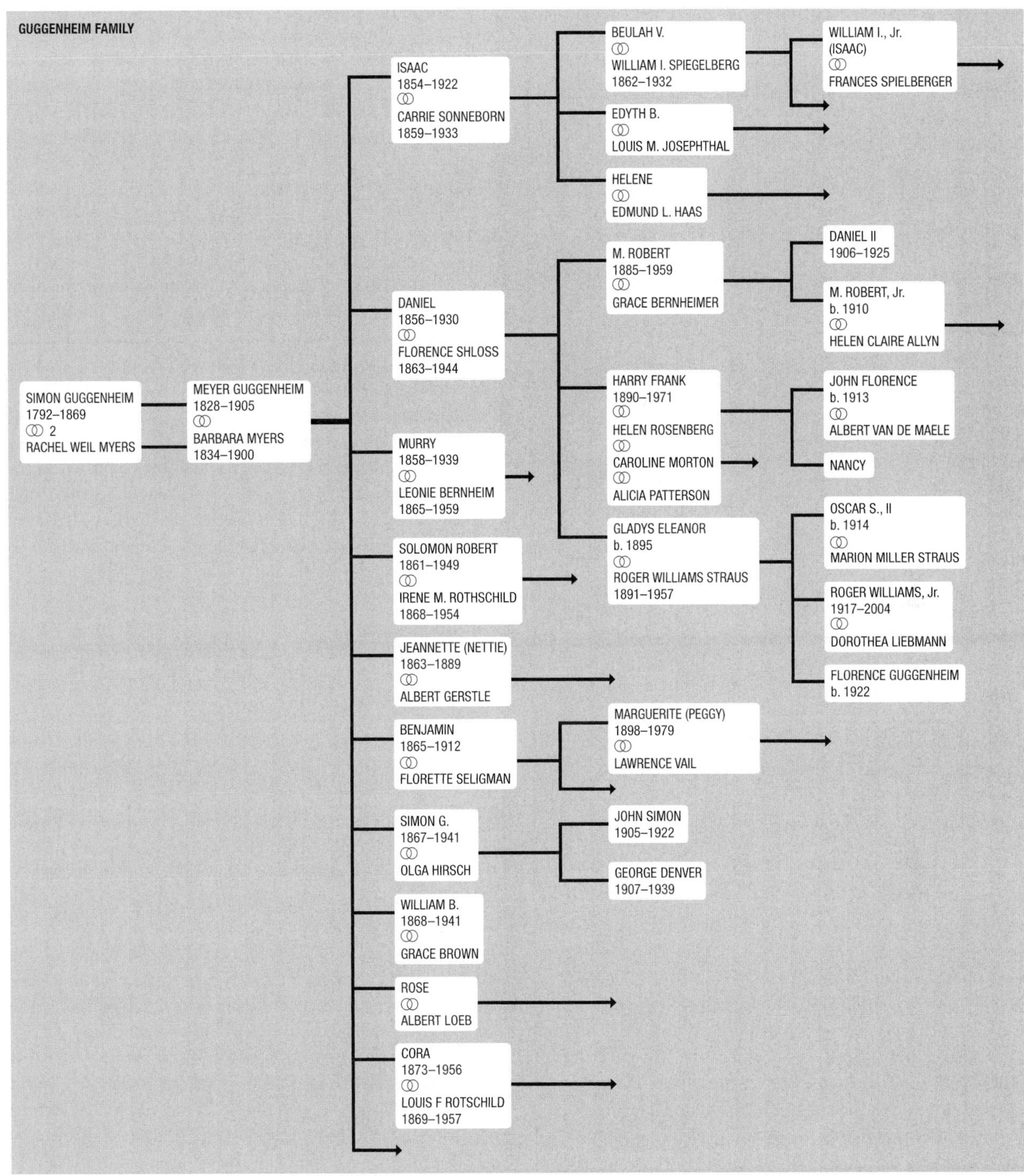

Epic (1978); J. Weld, *Peggy: The Wayward Guggenheim* (1986); A. Gill, *Art Lover: A Biography of Peggy Guggenheim* (2003).

[Morton Rosenstock]

GUGGENHEIM, CAMILLE (1863–1930), Swiss jurist and politician. Born in Zofingen, Guggenheim joined the Social Democratic Party in 1916 and later became Social Democratic member of the Great Council. He was member of the Swiss Federal Court (1929). Despite his short term in office, Swiss Fascists used his example after 1933 to prove the "Judaization" of Switzerland.

BIBLIOGRAPHY: A. Wyler, "Bundesrichter Camille Guggenheim. Der mensch und die Persönlichkeit," in: *Jüdische Presszentrale*, 616 (Oct. 10, 1930), 5; *Basler Nachrichten*, 268:2 (Oct. 1, 1930), obituary.

[Uri Kaufmann (2nd ed.)]

GUGGENHEIM, CHARLES (1924–2002), U.S. documentary film producer. Guggenheim was born in Cincinnati, Ohio, to German Jewish parents. His father and grandfather were furniture manufacturers. Guggenheim studied agriculture at the Colorado State College of Agriculture and Mechanical Arts before joining the U.S. Army in 1943. A foot infection kept him from shipping out overseas with his division, which took heavy losses during the Battle of the Bulge. After World War II, Guggenheim completed his undergraduate studies at the University of Iowa in 1948. After working for CBS Radio in New York, he moved to Chicago and worked behind the scenes for CBS children's shows and then to St. Louis, Missouri, to work in public television. In 1954, he founded his documentary production company, Charles Guggenheim and Associates. After producing the first political commercial aired on television for Democratic presidential candidate Adlai Stevenson in 1956, Guggenheim moved his company to Washington, D.C. He produced a variety of campaign ads for political figures, including the Kennedy brothers. The first documentary he directed, *A City Decides* (1956), earned Guggenheim the first of the 12 Oscar nominations he would receive throughout his career. Guggenheim's Oscar-winning documentaries are *Nine from Little Rock* (1964), about school desegregation in Arkansas; *Robert Kennedy Remembered* (1968), shown at the Democratic National Convention weeks after the senator was killed; *The Johnstown Flood* (1989); and *A Time for Justice* (1994). Guggenheim's final project was the documentary *Berga: Soldiers of Another War* (2002), about 350 American soldiers captured in the Battle of the Bulge who were sent to labor camps instead of POW camps because they were Jewish or thought to be Jewish. Guggenheim finished the film a few months before he died of pancreatic cancer in Washington, D.C.

[Adam Wills (2nd ed.)]

GUGGENHEIM, PAUL (1899–1977), Swiss jurist and authority on international law. Born in Zurich, Guggenheim became head of the Institute of International Law at the University of Kiel in 1927. Guggenheim became a member of the Permanent Court of Arbitration at The Hague in 1951 and judge ad hoc of the International Court of Justice in 1955. He represented a number of countries before The Hague court and also acted as arbitrator in many international disputes. He wrote extensively on subjects relating to international law. His books include *Lehrbuch des Voelkerrechts* (2 vols., 1948–51) and *Traité de Droit international public* (2 vols., 1953–54; second edition of the first volume, 1967). Guggenheim was president of the Central Committee of the Swiss community from 1944 to 1950. He wrote many scholarly articles on matters of Jewish interest such as Zionism, Palestine, Jewish postwar problems, minority rights, Swiss Jewish history (the first short history published), heirless property left in Switzerland, and the Jewish refugee problem. In 1960, he was elected president of the World Federation of the United Nations Association and in 1964 became its honorary president.

ADD. BIBLIOGRAPHY: J. Picard, *Die Schweiz und die Juden 1933–1945* (1994), index; P. Guggenheim, *Zur Geschichte der Schweizer Juden* (1934); idem, "Die erblosen Vermoegen in der Schweiz und das Voelkerrecht," in: Schweiz. Isr. Gemeindebund (ed.), *Festschrift zum 50-jährigen Bestehen* (1954), 107–120; *Israelitisches Wochenblatt*, 36 (Sept. 9, 1977), 71.

[Veit Wyler / Uri Kaufmann (2nd ed.)]

GUGGENHEIM-GRUENBERG, FLORENCE (1898–1989), pharmacist and historian, born in Berne, Switzerland. During the 1930s and 1940s she was active in Swiss Jewish national and international organizations, and from 1950 was president of the Juedische Vereinigung in Zurich. She was the editor of *Beitraege zur Geschichte und Volkskunde der Juden in der Schweiz*, a series devoted to the history and folklore of the Jews in Switzerland. She edited the typescript of Augusta Weldler-Steinberg and added chapters on the history of the communities of Lengnau and *Endingen in the two-volume *Geschichte der Juden in der Schweiz* (1966/1970), a history of the Jews in Switzerland from the 16th century to the period after emancipation. She was one of the first researchers of western Yiddish after 1945, providing ample oral documentation of a then nearly extinct dialect, and she fought for women's rights in Switzerland.

BIBLIOGRAPHY: D. Stern (ed.), *Buecher von Autoren juedischer Herkunft in deutscher Sprache* (1967), 106–7; H.P. Althaus, "In memoriam Florence Guggenheim-Grünberg," in: *Jiddistik-Mitteilungen* (Trier), 1 (April 1989), 11–16; U. Kaufmann, *Bibliographie zur Geschichte der Juden in der Schweiz* (1993), 120, 1382–1388; CD-ROM, *Surbtaler Jiddisch* (1994).

[Uri Kaufmann (2nd ed.)]

GUGLIELMO DA PESARO (known as **Guglielmo Ebreo**; 15th century), Italian dance master. He was a pupil of Domenichino da Piacenza, founder of the new school of dancing at the court of Ferrara, and taught in Florence, where he was apparently attached to the court of the Medici. Here he compiled (c. 1463) his "Treatise on the Art of Dancing," one of the most memorable works of the sort produced in Renaissance Italy. It includes two dances composed by the young Lorenzo de' Medici. In 1475 Guglielmo supervised the pageantry at a resplendent ducal wedding in Pesaro. After this he was apparently converted to Christianity under the name of Giovanni Ambrogio. He was then in the service of the Duchess of Milan who sent him to teach dancing at the Court of Naples. In 1481 he was dancing master to seven-year-old Isabella d'Este at Ferrara. Guglielmo introduced the fashion of the *moresche*, embodying both dance and mimicry, before the grand spectacle. He composed many *balletti* that were revolutionary for his time. His writing makes clear that he did not see as his final aim the mere compilation of dances. He attempted to explain the fundamentals of dancing, giving considerable thought to the relationship between dance and music. Guglielmo outlined six prerequisites for all dancers of which the first three were of enduring importance: *misura*, the dancer's ability to keep time to the musical rhythm; *memoria*, the ability to recollect steps in correct sequence; *partire del terreno*, the ability to do the right movement in space. Though he intended only to compose dances for courtly balls, Guglielmo outlined the requirements for the artistic dancer for all times.

BIBLIOGRAPHY: O. Kinkeldey, in: *Studies in Jewish Bibliography and Related Subjects – Freidus Memorial Volume* (1929), 329–72, includes bibliography; C. Roth, *The Jews in the Renaissance* (1959), 276–81, 363; F. Reyna, *Des origines du ballet* (1955), 42–49; A. Michel, in: *Medievalia et Humanistica*, 3 (1945), 121–4 (Eng.).

[Cecil Roth, Walter Sorell]

GUIANA (formerly **British Guiana**), state in N.E. South America, population: 650,000 (est. 2000); Jewish population: 40 persons (1990 estimate) living in the capital Georgetown. The earliest Jewish settlers in Guiana arrived during the Dutch rule which began in 1613. In 1657 an agreement was reached between Paulo Jacomo Pinto, acting on behalf of the Jews of Leghorn, and Phillipe de Fuentes, acting on behalf of the Jewish refugees from Dutch Brazil and Dutch cities of Middleburgh, Flushing, and Vere on the settling of Spanish-speaking Jews in the colony called Nova Zeelandia. Jews arrived from Amsterdam and Leghorn and were later joined by Jews from Hamburg and Salé (Morocco). The Jews settled in the town of New Middleburgh on the Pomeroon (Pauroma) river, and numbered 50 to 60 families, specializing in sugar cane plantations and vanilla. In 1666 an English attack destroyed the settlement, and the Jews dispersed in the Caribbean, mainly to Curaçao.

Before the outbreak of World War II there were a handful of Jews in the capital, Georgetown, but there was neither an organized community nor a synagogue. Early in 1939, 165 Jewish refugees from Europe, who arrived on the s.s. *Koenigstein*, were not permitted to disembark, and shortly thereafter the government barred immigration. However, 130 Jews found refuge in the country during the war years but most of these eventually emigrated.

In 1939, in the wake of the failure of the *Evian Conference on the German refugee problem and in view of Britain's intention to severely restrict Jewish immigration to Palestine (see *White Paper), Britain proposed her crown colony Guiana as a site for Jewish immigration and settlement. Thus, in February 1939, an international investigating committee under the auspices of the Inter-Governmental Commission on Refugees, formed at Evian, arrived in the country to explore the proposed area. The land under consideration consisted of approximately 42,000 sq. mi. in the forest and swamp region of the interior. Neither the coastal region, which comprises 4% of the area of British Guiana but holds 90% of the country's population, nor the open region adjacent to it, were included in the proposed area.

The committee stated that although the region was not ideal for the settlement of European immigrants, the quality of the soil, the availability of important minerals, and the climatic and health conditions did not preclude their settlement. The committee proposed a two-year trial period during which 3,000–5,000 sturdy young people with professional training would be sent to the region to test the practicality and the advisability of large-scale investment and development.

Many considered the British plan for Jewish settlement in British Guiana to be a political strategem. They pointed out that the same region was investigated in 1935 by an international commission and found unsuitable for the settlement of 20,000 Assyrians suffering persecution in Iraq. Not only had the commission stated unanimously that the region was unsuitable for settlement, but also its conclusion had been accepted by the British government itself.

However, in May 1939, before British policy on Palestine was officially proclaimed in the White Paper, the British government published the report of its own investigating committee which found British Guiana to be a place for possible settlement. Prime Minister Neville Chamberlain announced that Jewish settlement in British Guiana would bring the establishment of a new community which would enjoy a large measure of autonomy and representation in the government of the colony. The program was described in government circles as a "New Balfour Declaration" and as a plausible alternative to the Jewish National Home in Palestine.

The only Jewish organization which was seriously involved in the British Guiana scheme was the *American Jewish Joint Distribution Committee on whose behalf Joseph A. *Rosen participated in the inquiry commission.

Relations with Israel

Since April 1967 Israel's ambassador to Colombia has also been non-resident ambassador to Guiana. Out of a desire to mobilize the Arab and Soviet blocs in the international arena, for support of its own conflicts, Guiana formerly adopted a hostile line toward Israel. However, from 1969 relations between the two countries improved substantially. Israel has extended a certain amount of technical assistance to Guiana.

BIBLIOGRAPHY: M. Arbell, "The Jewish Settlement in Pomeroon/Pauroma (Guiana), 1657–1666," in: idem, *The Jewish Nation of the Caribbean* (2003); *Report of the British Guiana Refugee Commission…* (1939); E. Liebenstein (Livneh), *Ha-Teritoryalizm he-Ḥadash* (1944), 11–16.

[Aryeh Morgenstern / Mordecai Arbell (2nd ed.)]

°GUIDACERIO, AGACIO (**Agathius Guidacerius**; 1477–1540), Italian Hebraist. A priest from Calabria, Guidacerio began studying Hebrew at Rome under Jacob Gabbai, who was apparently a Portuguese refugee. Under the patronage of Pope Leo X, Guidacerio served as first professor of Hebrew at the University of Rome from 1514 onward. He published a pioneering *Grammatica hebraicae linguae* (Rome, c. 1514) and an annotated edition of Song of Songs (Rome, 1524; Paris, 1531). During the sack of Rome (1527), Guidacerio lost his library and subsequently fled to Avignon, from where he was called to Paris to become a royal reader at the College of the Three Languages. His other works include another Hebrew grammar, *Peculium Agathii-Mikneh Agathii* (Paris, 1537), and *Sefer* *ha-Diqduq – Grammaticae in sanctam Christi linguam institutiones* (Paris, 1539).

BIBLIOGRAPHY: H. Galliner, in: HJ, 2 (1940), 85–101; C. Roth, *Jews in the Renaissance* (1959), 145.

[Godfrey Edmond Silverman]

GUILDS.

In Antiquity

There is evidence in the Bible of a certain unity among craftsmen. This appears to have played a role similar to that of the unions of artisans which assisted their members in the economic and social spheres in ancient Babylonia at the time of Hammurapi. In this period, association among the artisans was confined to the framework of the family, most of whose members were employed in the same profession over the generations, and took the form of concentration of a given group of craftsmen in a certain site in the town for residence and work. The Bible mentions a valley of craftsmen (I Chron. 4:14). In Jerusalem, there was "the bakers' street" (Jer. 37:21). During the period of the Return to Zion, after the Babylonian Exile, the social cells of the professions had consolidated and were acknowledged to the extent that some are mentioned as a group when the walls of Jerusalem were rebuilt: "between the upper chamber of the corner and the sheep gate repaired the goldsmiths and the merchants" (Neh. 3:32). Distinctive indications of the existence of craftsmen's unions according to families, and their concentration in particular streets, are found during both the Second Temple era and the talmudic period in Ereẓ Israel, Egypt, and Babylonia. However, the forms of professional organization prevailing in the Hellenistic world gradually gained in influence and appear to have obscured the unifying role of the family in many professions. This was replaced by a special association (*ḥavurah*) of the members of a given profession for defined purposes: the synagogue was a unifying factor for these associations. The place of the hereditary craft is still evident in the tradition recorded in the Mishnah concerning the families of craftsmen in the Temple (Shek. 5:1; Yoma 3:11; 38a).

From the period preceding the Bar Kokhba revolt there is evidence on the organization of the Tarsians (weavers of flax, so called after the industry of Tarsus, the capital of Cilicia) around special synagogues in Tiberias and Lydda (Meg. 26a; Naz. 52a; TJ, Shek. 2:6, 27a), while during the period which followed the revolt there appeared the "master" of the Tarsians (Av. Zar. 17b) and the chief of the slaughterers in Sepphoris during the days of Judah ha-Nasi (Tosef., Ḥċýŏ 3:2). From the period of the *amoraim* there is mention of the studies of the "apprentice of the carpenter" (Mak. 8b) and the "apprentice of the smith" and his relations with "his master," the craftsman, who issues orders which he is expected to obey (BK 32b, see Shab. 96b). In a later Midrash there emerges the "company of donkey drivers" which, in partnership, engages in transportation; "they had a chief over the company" who directed its activities (Mid. Ps. 12:1). In Hierapolis, Phrygia, there were unions of dyers of purple stuff and carpet weavers, to whom someone bequeathed a sum of money in order to adorn his tomb on the festivals of Passover and Shavuot; presumably all, or the majority of, the members of these unions were Jews. In Alexandria there were found "the goldsmiths by themselves, the silversmiths by themselves, the weavers by themselves, and the Tarsians by themselves, so that a visitor could come and join his profession and thus earn his livelihood" (Tosef., Suk. 4:6).

Mutual assistance was then one of the declared objectives of the companies of craftsmen and there is a specification how "the woolworkers and dyers … the bakers … the donkey drivers … the sailors are authorized" to act and reach agreement among themselves for the benefit of their fellow craftsmen; they purchased their requirements in partnership; it was accepted to "observe a period of relaxation," i.e., an agreement to refrain from competition in the market and reduction of prices (see Tosef. BM, 11:24ff.; *Sefer ha-Shetarot* of Judah b. Barzillai al-Bargeloni, no. 57). Those whose work took them on the highways introduced a mutual insurance of their animals and implements employed in transportation (Tosef., *ibid.*). It is also known that Jews belonged to the general unions of craftsmen, though presumably they did not participate in their religious cults.

[Haim Hillel Ben-Sasson]

Middle Ages and Early Modern Era

The guilds of the Middle Ages in Europe were thoroughly Christian in character and the Jew had no place in them. Since few Jews in Ashkenaz practiced crafts, they did not organize their own guilds, while the Jewish merchants were restricted in their professions and arranged their affairs through the general communal regulations. In the Byzantine Empire, in the 12th century, an authorization was granted to Jewish craftsmen by Manuel I (1143–1180) to establish guilds in their towns. In Sicily there were Jewish guilds of silk weavers, dyers, and carpenters during the 12th to 15th centuries. In 1541 the tailors' guild of Rome reached an agreement with the Christian guild of the city. In Christian Spain the occupations of the Jews were highly diversified and many engaged in crafts. They established associations (*ḥavurot*) active in the economic, social, and religious spheres. Solomon b. Abraham *Adret clearly formulated the legal character of the guilds: "every company which has a common interest is to be regarded as a town apart … this was customary in all the holy communities and no one ever raised any doubts as to this" (Rashba, Resp., vol. 4, no. 185). The responsa of R. *Asher b. Jehiel, Solomon *Adret, and *Isaac b. Sheshet Perfet provide information on the structure and activities of the "companies" in Spain. The regulations presented to the king by the company of Jewish shoemakers in Saragossa in 1336 for ratification include arrangements for financial assistance to colleagues in times of sickness, a compulsory arrangement for the visiting of the sick and participation in the rejoicing and mourning of members modeled on the arrangements of the Christian guilds. Also recorded are institutions for charitable purposes and special prayer designed for craftsmen (such as in Perpignan and Saragossa) and the (*bet*) "*midrash* of the weavers" (in Calatayud) "which were set aside … for the individuals of the company, and were not consecrated for everyone that comes" (Ribash, Resp., no. 331). A main development in Jewish guilds among Ashkenazi Jewry took place in Eastern Europe, in Bohemia-Moravia, and in Poland-Lithuania, with the increasing number of Jewish craftsmen in those countries. The earliest information on these goes back to the 16th century. Despite the violent opposition of the Christian guilds, the number of Jewish artisans increased considerably and they organized themselves in guilds during the 16th to 18th centuries after the pattern of the Christian guilds, and in order to protect themselves from them. In Prague, there were Jewish guilds of butchers, tailors, furriers, embroiderers, shoemakers, goldsmiths, hairdressers, and pharmacists. In several towns of Poland and Lithuania, such as Brody, Cracow, Lublin, Lvov, Lissa (Leszno), and Vilna, there were numerous Jewish guilds, with up to ten in one community.

The regulations of the Jewish guilds in Eastern Europe followed the spirit of the general guilds, but their social-religious content was influenced by Jewish customs and modes of life. Since they were essentially economic organizations, the Jewish guilds established rules on the relations between their members, the status of the craftsmen, the trainees and the apprentices, and the standards and quotas of production authorized to every craftsman. The guilds were concerned to prevent unfair competition between their members and to protect them from local craftsmen who were not organized in a guild or from craftsmen not living in the town. They cared for their members' welfare, assisted those in difficulties, and provided relief to the widows and orphans of guild members. They developed organized activity for the religious education of members and their children. All the craftsmen, trainees, and apprentices were compelled to take part in public prayers and to observe the Sabbath and festivals. The guilds also formulated detailed rules for the election of committee members. Even though many guilds were first formed through the initiative of the communal administration, the relations between the two bodies gradually deteriorated until open clashes occurred during the 18th century between the guilds and the community leadership in Berdichev, Minsk, and Vitebsk. With the political and economic decline of Poland-Lithuania, the guilds lost their importance. In Russia, Austria, and Prussia, among which Poland was partitioned in the latter part of the 18th century, the guilds with their typical medieval structure were already on the verge of extinction. They ceded their place to modern forms of economic organization. Associations (*ḥavurot*) of craftsmen existing in many communities during the 19th century had slight economic influence and their function was confined to religious, cultural, and social activities. They continued until the 1930s. In Poland between the two world wars the *cechy* (guilds) legislation which limited the Jewish craftsmen was revived. As a result, the debate was renewed on the role and organization of the Jews in this modern reincarnation of the guilds.

[Mark Wischnitzer]

BIBLIOGRAPHY: M. Wischnitzer, *History of Jewish Crafts and Guilds* (1965); idem, in: HUCA, 23 pt. 2 (1950–51), 245–63; idem, in: JSOS, 16 (1954), 335–50: idem, in: *Zaytshrift far Yidisher Geshikhte, Demografie, un Ekonomik*, 2–3 (1928), 73–88; Juster, Juifs, 1 (1914), 486–7; T. Jacobovits, in: JJGJČ, 8 (1936), 57–145; M. Kremer, in: Zion, 295–325; idem, in: YIVOA, 11 (1956/57), 211–42; idem, in: *Bleter far Geshikhte*, 2 (1938), 3–32; I. Mendelsohn, in: BASOR (Dec. 1940), 17–21; Alon, Toledot, 1 (1953), 103–6; L. Frydman, in: *Yivo Bleter*, 12 (1937), 520–32; M. Hendel, in: *Oẓar Yehudei Sefarad*, 6 (1963), 77–84; I. Levitats, *The Jewish Community in Russia* (1943), index; I. Halpern, *Yehudim ve-Yahadut be-Mizraḥ Eiropah* (1969), 163–94.

GUINZBURG, HAROLD KLEINERT (1899–1961), U.S. publisher. Guinzburg, who was born in New York City, worked briefly as a journalist in Bridgeport and Boston. He later worked for the publishing house Simon & Schuster as a talent scout for new authors. In 1925 he and his friend George Oppenheim founded Viking Press, whose initial success resulted from the sale of quiz and "boner" books, though the firm later sponsored many prominent authors. A consistent innovator in the publishing field, Guinzburg founded the Literary Guild, one of America's first book clubs, in 1927; he sold his share in it in 1933, the same year that Viking again pioneered by establishing a special children's book department. During World War II he served both as chief of the Office of War Information's domestic bureau of publications (1943) and as head of its London publications division (1944). His armed forces anthology *As You Were* (1943), which was edited by Alexander Woollcott, was the start of the immensely popular Viking Portable Library series. After the war, Guinzburg launched Viking's own paperback line, Compass Books. A staunch civil libertarian and member of the New York Chapter Board of the American Civil Liberties Union, he strongly opposed literary censorship and contended that any limitation of free expression was incompatible with democracy. He also served as a director of the American Book Publishers Council and as its president from 1956 to 1958, and as vice president of the Jewish Telegraphic Agency. He contributed to *Books and the Mass Market* (1953).

GUKOVSKY, GRIGORY ALEKSANDROVICH (1902–1950), Russian literary scholar. Born in St. Petersburg into a Jewish family which had converted to Lutheranism, he graduated from the faculty of social sciences of Petrograd University in 1923. He worked at the Leningrad Institute of the History of Arts from the mid-1920s until 1929 and at the Institute of the Comparative History of Literature and Languages of the West and East associated with Leningrad University. In his scientific interests Gukovsky was close to the so-called "formal method." His works established the bases for the contemporary study of Russian literature of the 18th century. He wrote on the ideas of the Enlightenment and sentimentalism (*Orcherki po istorii russkoy literatury i obshchestvennoy mysli 18 veka* ["Essays on the History of Russian Literature and Social Thought of the 18th Century," 1938]), on romanticism (*Pushkin i russkie romantiki* ["Pushkin and Russian Romantics,"

1946]), and on realism (*Pushkin i problemy realisticheskogo stilya* ["Pushkin and Problems of Realistic Style," 1979]), *Realizm Gogolya* ["The Realism of Gogol," 1959]). Gukovsky was a pioneer of contemporary structural typology. While professor at Leningrad University (1936–49), he educated a whole constellation of Soviet literary scholars (Yu. M. Lotman, I.Z. Serman, and many others). In July 1949 Gukovsky and his brother Matvey (1898–1971), a historian of the Italian Renaissance and professor at Leningrad University, were arrested as "cosmopolitans." Gukovsky died under investigations in the KGB Lubyanka prison in Moscow.

Gukovsky's daughter, DOLININA NATAL'YA GRIGOR'EVNA (1928–1980), was a Russian writer. Her long story "*Otets*" ("Father," 1974) is devoted to the fate of her father.

[Mark Kipnis / *The Shorter Jewish Encylopaedia in Russian*]

GULAK, ASHER (1881–1940), historian of Jewish law. Gulak, who was born in Dackira, Latvia, obtained a diploma in law at Dorpat University in 1911, and pursued further legal study in Germany (1919–24). He returned briefly to Latvia, where he taught at government-sponsored courses for Jewish teachers, before settling in Palestine in 1925. Gulak was appointed lecturer (1926) and subsequently professor (1936) of Jewish law at the Hebrew University. He published books and numerous articles on talmudic and Jewish law, which were comparative studies on the Jewish, Greek, and Roman legal systems, as well as articles on current problems, particularly in the field of education. Gulak's pioneering four-volume work *Yesodei ha-Mishpat ha-Ivri* ("Foundations of Hebrew Law," 1922) was the first to present Jewish law systematically. This was followed in 1926 by an anthology of Jewish legal formularies and documents, *Oẓar ha-Shetarot ha-Nehugim be-Yisrael* (1926), later enlarged by his *Urkundenwesen im Talmud* (1935), *Le-Ḥeker Toledot ha-Mishpat ha-Ivri bi-Tekufat ha-Talmud* ("Research in the History of the Talmudic Law of Property," 1929), and *Toledot ha-Mishpat be-Yisrael bi-Tekufat ha-Talmud* (1939), a similar study of the law of obligations.

BIBLIOGRAPHY: Shochetman, in: KS, 17 (1940), 211–4; Alon, Meḥkarim, 2 (1958), 285–97; Kressel, Leksikon, 1 (1965), 436–7.

[Chaim Ivor Goldwater]

GULF WAR (1991).

Introduction

The Iraqi conquest of Kuwait on August 2, 1990, constituted an act of naked military aggression which, although distant from Israel, raised serious concern in Jerusalem. Since the Baghdad Arab Summit in 1978, through the enormous military build-up in the 1980s during the war with Iran, Iraq was seen as the linchpin of the threatening Eastern Front of Arab states dedicated to military confrontation with Israel, as opposed to Egypt's approach of political accommodation. There was a residue of deep acrimony between Iraq and Israel that went back to Israel's War of Independence of 1948 and the fact that Iraq, unlike other belligerent Arab states, had refused to sign an armistice agreement with Israel in 1949. Beyond Iraq's role in subsequent Arab-Israeli wars, Israel's air strike against the Iraqi nuclear reactor outside Baghdad on June 7, 1981, left its own mark on the animosity and conflict between the two countries. In April, just a few months prior to Iraq's invasion of Kuwait, Saddam Hussein had broadcast his vicious intention, minimally his blatant threat, "to burn half of Israel with chemical weapons."

Israel and the Gulf Crisis

Although Iraq had chosen in August to occupy a fellow-Arab state, and this for reasons of economic greed along with grandiose hegemonic aspirations in the Arab World as a whole, Israel had cause for caution and suspicion. Exactly a week after the Gulf crisis began, Prime Minister Yitẓhak Shamir addressed the army's National Defense College on the subject of aggression – that in the 1930s in Europe and that in the Middle East in 1990. He said:

> The great difference between those dark days of the 1930s and ours, is that this time the Jewish nation has the ability and means to deter, face, and defend itself from the threat, and if need be, to overthrow and defeat it.

The following day Defense Minister Moshe Arens reiterated the prime minister's confidence and warning. "Saddam Hussein," he remarked, "knows whom he will be dealing with if he starts anything with Israel." Relying specifically on the deterrent capacity of the Israel Defense Forces (IDF), its proven military strength and reputation for ingenious and determined strategic reach, the defense minister concluded that Saddam's threats would not materialize.

The Gulf crisis opened up possibilities to serve Israeli national interests in a fortuitous and dramatic fashion. Firstly, it deflected global attention away from the politically damaging Palestinian uprising (*Intifada*) that had besmirched Israel's standing in the world. Reduced coverage of Judea, Samaria, and Gaza could marginalize the Arab insurrection as a media scoop.

Secondly, the Gulf crisis diverted American attention from its focus on regional peace-making generally and the inauguration of a Palestinian-Israeli dialogue in particular. Secretary of State James Baker had exerted persistent efforts for many months to induce Israel's government to agree to America's formula for a Palestinian delegation that would negotiate with Jerusalem. The specifics of Baker's formula were unacceptable to Prime Minister Shamir and his markedly nationalist, and narrow, coalition government formed in the spring.

Thirdly, and most critically, the crisis evoked an immediate and resolute American response that portended military confrontation against Iraq. That reaction had the acceptable possibility, not necessarily explicit in the diplomatic language of official Jerusalem, that U.S. forces would defeat Israel's enemy to the east.

The United States moved with diplomatic and military alacrity to react to Iraq's occupation of Kuwait. The United

Nations Security Council convened on the very day of the invasion to condemn Iraqi aggression and demand an unconditional and immediate withdrawal. Under America's leadership, a coalition of military forces began to be organized to protect the Persian Gulf countries, Saudi Arabia particularly, from further aggressive moves that might emanate from Baghdad. President George H.W. Bush was explicit in identifying America's concerns and motives when he affirmed that Saudi independence "is of vital interest to the United States."

During subsequent months, an American-Arab alliance was fashioned that embodied the capacity and determination to impose the status quo ante in Kuwait and the Gulf. While the anti-Iraq purpose was fully compatible with Israeli interests, Operation Desert Storm reflected new political alignments and developments in the Middle East which could impinge negatively on Israel's future strategic standing and prospects. The crisis in the Gulf was an opportunity for Israel, but it was also a potential crisis as well.

America and Israel's Low Profile

The American-led Allied military coalition revolved specifically around three important Arab states. Egypt, a partner with the United States in the Camp David Accords, was a primary legitimizer for American intervention in the Gulf and against the Arab state of Iraq. In due course Washington not only coordinated its strategic planning with Egypt, but in October also canceled a $7.1 billion Egyptian debt to the United States. Saudi Arabia, stubbornly rejecting repeated American requests during the 1980s for the stationing of its troops or the establishment of bases on Saudi soil, was now not averse to the welcome protection by the U.S.-led coalition. In August the Saudis received $2 billion of American military assistance, including tanks, planes, and missiles. In November, following an initial Saudi request for a $21 billion arms sale, which apparently was supported – perhaps initiated – by the Bush administration, a first $7.5 billion deal was approved. The U.S. Congress expressed its opposition to a third installment in the arms deal, to the tune of $14 billion, that included AWACS, F-15s, Apache helicopters, Maverick missiles, and more. Yet that did not necessarily imply that the administration had capitulated to Capitol Hill.

Syria, erstwhile Soviet client and intrepid American foe, was a new Arab addition to the United States political network in the Middle East. Beyond lining up with Washington and against Baghdad, Syrian president Hafiz al-Assad actually flew to meet President Bush in Geneva in December, as the crisis slid closer to war. Syrian self-interest in rivalry with fellow-Ba'athist Iraq conformed effortlessly with America's search for a New Political Order in the region, in the wake of Iraqi aggression and the challenge to Saudi and Gulf integrity.

Israel's response to the crisis was bedeviled by the conflict between its desire to see Iraq stopped and defeated and by the constraint exercised by America to deny the Israeli army participation in this campaign. Israeli passivity would not enhance its regional reputation and strategic deterrence, but it could facilitate or uncomplicate an Allied triumph against Iraq. It was not unreasonable, though perhaps not necessarily correct, that Israeli involvement might upset the U.S.-Arab coalition. The Arab participants – Egypt, Saudi Arabia, Syria, Morocco, and others – would conceivably balk at fighting on the same side as Jewish troops against other Arab, viz. Iraqi, troops. Remaining on the military margins in the face of overt Iraqi threats was a painful political dilemma for Israel during the crisis period from August 1990 until January 1991, and then during the war itself from January 16 until the cease-fire on February 27.

Foreign Minister David Levy provided an early indication of his country's policy when he stated on September 6, that "Israel is maintaining a low profile." He would repeat this position throughout the succeeding months. In the heat of war, and just prior to the ground offensive in late February, he again articulated the policy of Israeli non-intervention, so as not to hamper the American-led coalition against Iraq.

Certainly the policy of a low profile became the hallmark of Israel's rhetorical and political quandary for the entire period of crisis and war. While the IDF was galvanized into military preparedness, it effectively carried out no offensive operations at all. The threats of painful punishment to Saddam Hussein, as in Shamir's statement of September 19, were left as a reminder of Israeli resolve although restraint actually colored policy-making. This was so even after Iraq's Scud missiles hit Israel beginning on January 17.

At that time, just a day after the attack, Army Chief-of-Staff Dan Shomron was forthright:

> First of all, I would like to state that the fact that missiles were fired at our civilian population is a very serious event, and, as all Israeli leaders have repeatedly said in the past, such an event demands a reaction.

Eliyahu Ben-Elissar, chairman of the Knesset Foreign Affairs and Defense Committee, conveyed a similar determination on January 25 after more Iraqi missiles had struck Israeli population centers. He said: "Our decision to respond was made as soon as the first missile fell on the Israeli population or entered our air space.…" But a growing and pervasive credibility gap clouded the rhetorical flourish reflected in such Israeli declarations. Saddam's threats from 1990 materialized, but Israeli policy statements did not.

Prime Minister Shamir gave voice to the cautionary element that intruded into Israel's traditionally activist military practice. In October he referred to the need not to be dragged into the maelstrom by Iraq and thereby derail the U.S.-Arab coalition. Even after more than 30 Scud missiles had hit Israel, having exacted a significant human and material toll, the prime minister stated laconically in an interview on Israeli television, on February 21, that "[t]here is no [state] interest that calls for automatic reaction always."

Problematics in Israeli-American Relations

The importance and sensitivity at the root of American-Israeli relations were severely tested during the period of crisis and war in the Persian Gulf. At the start, Jerusalem would have been satisfied to see the United States fulfill Israeli interests as Washington pursued its own global and regional goals against Iraq. Later, however, divergences surfaced in the pursuit of American and Israeli interests, and signs of tension seemed to grow over the months.

On August 10, just a few days after the Gulf crisis began, Foreign Minister Levy was questioned concerning U.S.-Israeli coordination. His rhetorical response – "Can anyone think for a second that we would be completely out of the circle of consultations and briefings?" – may have seemed reasonable at the time. After all, the two countries had engaged in an official strategic alliance since 1981 and had cooperated in a variety of military, weapons, and intelligence fields. The United States and Israel were moreover preoccupied on a nearly permanent basis in the search for a mechanism to consolidate and advance regional peace efforts. However, when tension arose, it went beyond the immediate question of Israel's role in the anti-Iraq military coalition. On that issue Israel was initially willing, as noted earlier, to maintain a low profile.

On September 6, it was reported that America had agreed to lease to Israel several Patriot missile batteries to provide air-defense capabilities, in the light of Saddam's blatant threats and Iraq's military capabilities. An agreement to this effect was signed in Washington, Israel represented by David Ivri, the Ministry of Defense director-general. But Patriot missiles were not delivered to Israel during the crisis period, and only arrived following two devastating Scud missile attacks against the region of Tel Aviv, on January 17 and 19.

In October 1990, an incident occurred on the Temple Mount in Jerusalem which strained relations between Israel and the United States. Near the Dome of the Rock and the Aqsa Mosque, Muslim rioters attacked Jewish worshipers praying below at the Western Wall during the Sukkot holiday festival. This precipitated the active intervention of the Israeli security forces who ended up killing 21 Arabs. This incident, alleged by some to be Arab provocation to catalyze an Israeli military response against Iraq, turned into a diplomatic imbroglio at the United Nations. The United States played an active role in supporting the Arab position which demanded censuring Israeli behavior, considered brutal and without due cause. The Security Council called for denouncing Israel and recommended sending an investigative commission to Jerusalem and the territories to examine Israeli policy, while providing security for the local Palestinian inhabitants. The Likud government was irrevocably unwilling to accede to the UN position and rejected the charges leveled against Israel regarding the Temple Mount incident itself. Throughout October and until December relations between America and Israel were sullied by this event in Jerusalem and its international repercussions emanating from United Nations headquarters in New York.

In an interview on October 19, Prime Minister Shamir took issue with the Bush administration on the general question of Jerusalem. Not only had the United States agreed that a United Nations delegation intervene in local Israeli affairs, but the very right of Jews to live in East Jerusalem was being challenged by Washington. The background to this lay in the delay of the State Department to grant approval for a $400,000,000 housing loan that Israel had requested for settling Soviet immigrants flooding into the country. The American administration had been pressuring Israel to commit in writing its formal agreement that no Soviet Jews would be settled anywhere across the 1967 "Green Line" borders, including East Jerusalem. The prime minister gave vent to his concern as follows:

> We cannot ignore this administration's attitude toward Israel. We are witnessing a process; the attitude toward us in the Temple Mount event is nothing but an illustration of this process. They want to teach us a lesson, to put it [Israel] in its place. I believe they have taken a mistaken approach…

The Israeli government felt virtually betrayed by the United States, for it considered the Temple Mount incident an act of Israeli self-defense against a violent Arab mob. In further violence perpetrated against innocent civilians, three Jews were stabbed to death in the Jerusalem Bakka neighborhood on October 21. There was no global outcry and no United Nations response. The reticence of the Security Council did little to enhance the status of the international organization in Israel's eyes. This point was confirmed when, as the world remained silent, Syria took advantage of the Gulf crisis to impose its will on Lebanon, removing General Aoun from power and killing some 700 people.

In late December, Foreign Minister Levy stated that Washington had shown weakness (perhaps rather than vindictiveness) in supporting the United Nations resolution. The Israeli government was by this time unconvinced that the Gulf military coalition would have collapsed had America adopted a different approach in the Security Council. The call by UN Secretary-General Javier Perez de Cuellar for the Security Council to protect the Palestinians in the Israeli-held areas was a transparent ruse, Israel considered, to undermine its authority without any political peace process in operation at all. Behind this development was an attempt by Saddam, Arafat, and others to link the withdrawal of Iraq from Kuwait with that of Israel from the territories. The United States officially and publicly rejected this linkage from the start of the crisis until the end of the war.

Nonetheless, despite the stressful U.S.-Israel relationship, or perhaps because of it, Secretary of State James Baker conveyed a desire, as in November, for political coordination with Jerusalem on the issue of the peace process in the Arab-Israeli conflict. Whether this was a calming measure or one likely to arouse Israel's nervousness could be debated. But Yitẓhak Shamir told the Likud Knesset faction on January 8, that "Once the Gulf crisis is over, we will have to face political threats." Military threats from the Iraqis and political threats from the Americans would, as suggested in Shamir's own words, provide Israel with more than enough problems once the war – not yet begun – was over.

From Crisis to War

On the domestic front, the crisis period beginning in August exacted a heavy price from the Israeli public. The possibility of war, in which Israel would somehow be involved, was considered likely by a majority of the population. The specific threat of chemical warfare became a weighty concern and, following a mini-national debate and some government hesitancy, the distribution of gas masks to the domestic population was begun in October. Other civil defense measures were undertaken and police readiness was maintained. In all, Israel wanted to be prepared for the possibility of war, but it did not want to convey the impression that its local defensive operations were a prelude to a preemptive tactical strike against Iraq. In the tense situation in the Gulf and beyond, Jerusalem had to act and speak with caution in order that it not inadvertently light the match in the explosive situation that Baghdad had prepared for the inevitable conflagration.

After Iraq's invasion of Kuwait, tourism to Israel fell by over 40 percent. Non-citizens in Israel began to leave the country as did foreign students and visitors. The State Department in Washington ordered United States citizens to leave the Middle East, Israel included. Later in January, Jewish solidarity missions from abroad offered compensation to the somewhat demoralized and economically suffering home front.

In contrast, the most satisfying and durable feature of 1990 was the astounding immigration from the Soviet Union: a monumental figure of 200,000 Jews arrived in Israel, despite Saddam's threats and the atmosphere of uncertainty in Israel that suggested the approach of war. Nonetheless, while an average of 1,000 Soviet immigrants had been arriving daily at the end of 1990, the figure dropped to 500 a day in the critical month of January 1991.

The United Nations had set January 15 as the final date for a complete Iraqi withdrawal from Kuwait. If not, then all measures including force would be employed to achieve this objective which international diplomacy, a remarkably tight embargo, and Arab censure could not achieve. The ultimatum date portended the start of war in the Persian Gulf. Israel was comforted by the fact that Iraqi aggression had been universally condemned and that America had stood firm – as in the Baker-Aziz Geneva meeting of January 9 – in rejecting the insidious attempt to link the Kuwaiti and Palestinian issues. In Israel it was felt that Washington had also come to realize more than before that, in essence, the broader Arab aspects of the conflict with Israel were more central than the Palestinian one.

Operation Desert Storm terminated the waiting period when Allied military forces led by the United States began operations on the night between January 16 and 17, with 1,200 air missions into Iraq and Kuwait in the first 36 hours of fighting. On the 17th Saddam carried out his word, and from the areas known as H2 and H3 in western Iraq, eight Scud missiles were fired at Israel and struck civilian centers in the Tel Aviv metropolitan district. A state of alert was declared throughout Israel as the nation began to face the damage and disorder. Apartment buildings were hit, their inhabitants were evacuated, and people were injured. Warning sirens, gas masks, and huddling in sealed rooms designed to provide protection from chemical attack became part of daily life. An evening curfew brought social life, entertainment activities, sports events, and parts of the economy to a virtual standstill.

During the initial three-week period of the war, many Tel Avivians abandoned their city which was Saddam's primary, though not sole, target. From the Mediterranean seashore they chose the safer environs of Jerusalem, the Dead Sea, and Elath. Local patriotism gave way to personal security. Meanwhile, all Israelis were advised to carry their gas mask with them all day long.

The final war tally on the civilian population, from January 17 until the last Scud attack in February, read as follows: 39 missiles hit Israel from Haifa in the North to the area of Beersheba in the South; 1,644 families were evacuated; and 4,095 buildings were damaged. Although only one person was killed due to a direct missile hit, several died resulting from misuse of their gas masks and from heart attacks. Considering the potential for havoc and ruin and death that the Scuds represented, many Israelis felt that the Jewish people had experienced a miracle. Saddam had been considerably less successful than his threats against Israel implied, while America, Britain, even Saudis, were fighting the war that defeated Israel's enemy.

The Israeli Cost-Benefit Ledger

The Gulf War witnessed two innovations in the chronicles of military confrontations that Israel has faced since 1948. At one and the same time, Israel suffered the danger and indignity of its civil population being victims of enemy attack, while unlike previous Arab-Israeli wars, the IDF this time remained outside the military fray.

The lack of an operative response by Israel in the face of Iraq's Scud missiles was tied directly to the exertion of American pressure. Jerusalem was brought to the point of acceding to Washington's request not to act, and thus leaving the Allied coalition to pursue the war without political complications. Prime Minister Shamir could not have been more explicit when he stated on January 28, that without consultations with the United States, Israel would not act. On the same occasion he commented that relations with Washington had improved.

It was the visit to Jerusalem by Deputy Secretary of State Lawrence Eagleburger following the initial missile attacks, and his remaining in the country for about a week, that dramatized Washington's grave concern regarding Israeli behavior. His mission was undoubtedly to restrain Jerusalem, assure that U.S. military forces would continue to search and destroy the Scud missile launchers in western Iraq, and offer sufficient aid and assistance to mollify Israel. A report from

January 21 divulged that President Bush was calling Prime Minister Shamir regularly (as was British Prime Minister John Major). Secretary Baker declared his appreciation on February 6 for Israel's restraint.

Yet the cost of Israel's restraint, in contrast to the praise earned, was cause for worry according to Israel's ambassador to Washington, Zalman Shoval. In a news report from February 11, Shoval suggested that the United States would not provide Israel with aid in the wake of the Gulf War on the pretext that Israel "is not part of it."

Three particularly irksome problems strained Israeli-U.S. relations during the war period. Intelligence information on the area of H3 in Iraq was apparently not generously supplied by the Americans to the Israelis. Warning time on incoming Scuds was initially very brief, though later extended to about five minutes due to a United States agreement to improve the transfer of needed data. Moreover, throughout the weeks of war, the Pentagon refused to provide Israel with the Friend-Or-Foe Code required to facilitate an Israeli aerial attack against Iraqi missile launchers. No air corridor was opened for the Israeli air force and no time slot was set aside by the Allied forces to allow Israel the opportunity to send its forces into action. The memory of the U.S. *Liberty* navy surveillance ship that was mistakenly attacked by Israel on June 7, 1967, during the Six-Day War, could not have been far from people's thoughts in January 1991. Certainly Israel would not want another accident to occur, and held its fire.

While suffering from Iraqi attacks and yet choosing to accommodate American wishes, or succumb to its enormous leverage, Israel became the beneficiary of global sympathy and support. The aggression and bellicosity of Saddam contrasted blatantly with Israel's peaceful and defensive demeanor. Patriot missile batteries arrived from Holland and German Foreign Minister Hans-Dietrich Genscher, during a visit to Israel on January 24, promised extensive assistance that would include Patriot missiles, German-financed Dolphin submarines, and other military equipment. Meanwhile, the European Economic Community announced on January 25, that it was revoking sanctions that had been imposed on Israel for its policies in the territories and would renew scientific cooperation between Israel and the Common Market countries. On January 28 a French Socialist Party delegation visited Israel to express its solidarity. However, the fact that French weapons and German chemicals had been sold to Iraq in the 1980s lent an air of coolness, perhaps hypocrisy, to the European gestures.

By the time the war ended in Israel, bombed-out streets in Tel Aviv and destroyed housing blocks in Ramat Gan became the visual symbols that this war, unlike most Arab wars against Israel, was conducted on Israel's own home front. Overall, from the start of the crisis to the termination of hostilities, Israel had suffered a $4 billion loss, in damages, tourism, sinking production, etc. The Patriot missile, originally designed basically as an anti-aircraft weapon, performed with only partial effectiveness against Iraq's Scuds. More often than not, the Patriot hit the Scud's engine and destroyed it, but the warhead continued on its trajectory on the path toward Israeli civilian targets. In this war unlike earlier ones, the skies over Israel were not clean of enemy activity, though on the ground Iraq was 340 kilometers from Israel's border.

Postwar Assessment

From Israel's perspective, the political balance-sheet by the end of the war in late February was mixed. A total American victory on the battlefield would serve Israel's immediate security concerns, yet provide Washington with the self-esteem and international acclaim to then pursue its version of peacemaking in the Middle East. Israel did not necessarily see eye-to-eye with America on the modalities of conflict-resolution, as when Jerusalem had for example questioned Baker's Five Point Plan of November 1989.

Another paradox inherent in Israel's strategic calculations related to Iraq's condition at the conclusion of the war. It would seem obvious that Jerusalem wanted Iraq totally defeated and militarily devastated, lacking any major conventional and certainly nonconventional lethal capabilities. Prime Minister Shamir added on February 26, that Israel is interested "in having this person, Saddam Hussein, disappear from the international arena." Nonetheless, a less than fully flattened Iraq, and one that expressed no regret or remorse for its illegalities and aggressions, would deny it the benefits of international assistance for national rehabilitation. A defeated Iraq – yes, but an absolutely destroyed Iraq was not necessarily the optimal solution for Israel.

During the course of the crisis and until the war's end, Jordan and the PLO were among the most dedicated and enthusiastic supporters of Saddam Hussein. The streets of Amman rocked with pro-Iraqi sentiments and mass vituperation against America and Israel. Yasser Arafat already early in August had gone on a political pilgrimage to Baghdad to embrace Saddam and line up the PLO behind his anti-Kuwait and pan-Arab ventures. In Judea and Samaria, and elsewhere, the Palestinians hailed Saddam as their savior and rejoiced on the roofs of their houses when Scud missiles tore apart buildings and terrified Jewish civilians in Tel Aviv.

But the war served to discredit Jordan's political reputation and to delegitimize the PLO's peace image. Support for Iraq was seen as advocacy of aggression and conquest by the sword. The United States would no doubt later be challenged to resurrect the role of these two Arab elements in the comprehensive approach to regional peace. In fact, it might be concluded that Washington's own decision to accord recognition of the PLO in December 1988, and then to open an official dialogue with it, was a discredited policy.

The implication of these developments for Israel under its Likud-led government was an affirmation of the policy of territorial retention of Judea and Samaria. The status quo based on Israeli control and Jewish settlement would presumably continue, a side gain from Arab misjudgments and Israeli good fortune. Although Israelis might endlessly debate the relationship between territories and missiles in the military sphere, the persistence of Israeli rule was the dominant theme in the political sphere.

Israelis would also debate whether the non-activation of the IDF irreparably harmed the army's deterrent capability, thereby contributing adversely to Israel's pre-eminent strategic standing in the Middle East. It was reasonable to conclude that while that question was subject to varied interpretation, the formidable loss to Arab esteem and dreams of glory and victory was a definite and glaring result of the crisis and Gulf War. Whether the Israelis had won was unclear, but the Arab nation had certainly lost. Another Arab myth, the Saddam myth like the earlier Nasser one, burst like a bubble in the fantasizing Orient.

The Gulf War represented an occasion when the United States would again attempt to mold a New Order in the Middle East. Its Arab partners would be Egypt and Saudi Arabia, and others. Its dynamic would be military success against Iraq and its purpose generating momentum for peace in the Arab-Israeli conflict. Secretary of State Baker declared before the United States House Foreign Affairs Committee on February 2, that it was important "to resume the search for a just peace and real reconciliation for Israel, the Arab states, and the Palestinians." In the same spirit, signs were visible or audible that some Arab spokesmen now considered that the time for peace with Israel had arrived. Prince Bandar, the Saudi ambassador to Washington, made unusually conciliatory statements about Israel during the crisis and war months.

It might seem that the Arab-Israeli framework had now been exposed as one of various alternative political frameworks or alignments in the Mideast. Certain unexpected developments had transpired in the region. Arabs had fought Arabs, Saudis against Iraqis, and this after one Arab country, Iraq, had brazenly gone ahead and swallowed up another Arab country, Kuwait. Then, Arabs had surprisingly agreed to cooperate openly with the United States and pursue their interest in conjunction with Islamically vilified America, traditionally portrayed in satanic colors in the religiously seething Muslim world. However, an American-Arab alliance formed in the sands of the Gulf and fought to victory.

In the aftermath of all this, it was perhaps possible to imagine the unimaginable: Arab-Israeli peace. Israel would be open to future political opportunities, aware as always of the dangers and risks, yet hopeful that a new realism and spirit of accommodation would come to the Middle East.

[Mordechai Nisan]

For the 2003 invasion of Iraq by the U.S. and its coalition partners, see *Arab World. For its part, Israel was content to sit on the sidelines. Gas masks were replenished among the civilian population and in what proved to be a very costly miscalculation the Israeli public was instructed to unseal the masks in anticipation of possible Iraqi action, thus shortening their shelf life. Otherwise Israel was not directly affected.

GULL (Heb. שַׁחַף; AV "cuckow," JPS "sea-mew"), bird mentioned in the Bible as prohibited as food (Lev. 11:16; Deut. 14:15), the Hebrew name means "thin" or "swift of movement" and, on the basis of its rendering as λάρος in the Septuagint, refers to the gull. Eight species of the genus *Larus* are found in Israel. Feeding on sea fish and scraps of food, they follow ships for the offal thrown overboard. The gull also penetrates to inland regions of the country (even to the Negev) where it lives on worms and snails. To the family of the gull (Laridae) belong the *Sterna*, a genus of which two species are found in Israel, distinguished from the gull by being web-footed along the entire length of their toes.

BIBLIOGRAPHY: J. Feliks, *Animal World of the Bible* (1962), 86; M. Dor, *Leksikon Zo'ologi* (1965), 330f.

[Jehuda Feliks]

GUMPERT, MARTIN (1897–1955), German author and physician. The son of a medical practitioner, Gumpert was born in Berlin and, after serving in the German Army Medical Corps during World War I, he began his medical studies at the university of Berlin, specializing in venereal and skin diseases. In 1927, he became the head of a Berlin clinic for the treatment of these complaints and the director of a center for the study of deformities, on which he published a manual, *Die gesamte Kosmetik* (1931). Between 1933 and 1936, when the Nazis forced him out of medical practice, Gumpert began to write the first of a series of works that were to make him famous: a biography of Samuel Hahnemann, the originator of homeopathy (1934); and *Das Leben fuer die Idee* (1935; *Trail-Blazers of Science*, 1936), portraits of outstanding scientists. Gumpert emigrated to New York in 1936, resumed his career as a dermatologist and became an American citizen in 1942. He soon moved to a new specialization, geriatrics, strongly maintaining that society was frittering away millions of useful lives through compulsory retirement at the age of 65. Gumpert rapidly achieved medical distinction, heading the geriatric clinic in New York's Jewish Memorial Hospital from 1951 and gaining many professional honors. Two medical works in English advocating a new approach to the treatment of the aged were *You Are Younger Than You Think* (1944) and *The Anatomy of Happiness* (1951).

In his youth, Gumpert had written two collections of lyrics, *Verkettung* (1916) and *Heimkehr des Herzens* (1921). Other literary works in German written after his move to the U.S. include *Berichte aus der Fremde* (1937), poems; *Dunant: Der Roman des Roten Kreuzes* (1938; *Dunant: The Story of the Red Cross*, 1938); *Hoelle im Paradies* (1939), an autobiography; and a novel, *Der Geburtstag* (1948). He also contributed a short article on his friend and fellow exile, Thomas *Mann, *The Stature of Thomas Mann* (1946). From 1952 until his death, Gumpert edited a New York medical journal, *Lifetime Living*.

BIBLIOGRAPHY: *Science Illustrated* (June 1946), 637–40; New Yorker (June 10 and 17, 1950); *Current Biography* (1951), 250–1; *New York Times* (April 19, 1955). **ADD. BIBLIOGRAPHY:** J. Ittner, "'Merkwürdig unjüdisch' – Identitaet und Antisemitismus in Martin Gumberts Autobiographien," in: *Exil*, 19:1 (1999), 5–22; D. Rosenberg, *Martin Gumpert – Arzt und Schriftsteller* (2000).

[Rudolf Kayser]

GUMPLOWICZ, LUDWIG (1838–1909), Austrian jurist and sociologist. He was born in Cracow, in Austrian Galicia (now Poland), and studied law at the University of Vienna. An ardent Polish patriot, he participated in the Polish insurrection against Russia in 1863, and as a consequence of the failure both of the rebellion and of subsequent nationalistic activities Gumplowicz had to leave Cracow and availed himself of an opportunity to become a *Privatdozent* in political science at the University of Graz. In 1862 he was appointed adjunct professor in political science, and 11 years later, in 1893, he received his full professorship. Gumplowicz was baptized, but retained a lively interest in Jewish affairs. Gumplowicz was a proponent of Jewish assimilation. He thought that the Jews, having no territorial basis and no common language, were lacking the prerequisite of a nationality. In a letter directed to Theodor Herzl and dated Dec. 12, 1899, he expressed this view in highly emotional language.

Academically, Gumplowicz remained isolated at a provincial university, but he had brilliant students, such as Franco Savorgnan and Franz Oppenheimer, and found himself recognized by early American sociologists. Gumplowicz was one of the first to achieve full emancipation for sociology from the nonsocial sciences by insisting that social phenomena and evolution are distinctive and can be understood only by reference to social causes. That which is unique about social phenomena arises from human groups in interaction rather than from the behavior of individuals abstracted from the influence of association and dissociation. According to Gumplowicz, social and cultural evolution is a product of the struggle between social groups. This struggle replaces individual struggle in his theory of evolution. Gumplowicz offers two basic hypotheses. One, the polygenetic hypothesis, asserting that the species man evolved from various older types at many different times and in many different places, so that between the races there is no blood bond; and two, the hypothesis that an unsurmountable antagonism exists between different groups and races. For Gumplowicz society was the sum total of conflicting ethnic groups, each group being centered around one or more common interests. Thus the struggle between these ethnic groups, which he called races, is relentless. Gumplowicz was pessimistic about progress. His polygenetic view precluded the possibility of unitary evolution. In every society and state partial evolution and progress have taken place; but in every society and state there have also been destruction and setbacks. Therefore, Gumplowicz holds that progress can be observed only in particular periods and particular countries.

Another important aspect of Gumplowicz's work includes the distinction he made between simple, limited groupings organized on the basis of consanguinity and community of culture, on the one hand, and compound groupings, such as the state, formed in the process of amalgamation of originally separate groups, such as masters and slaves or ethnic groups. In the state, ethnic groups merge into social classes, a common body of rights and obligations is developed, and internal conflict is toned down and possibly even composed. External conflict between states takes then the place of internal ethnic and class conflicts. Therefore, although Gumplowicz is classified often as a social Darwinist, he was actually one of the first social determinists. In his system, the individual and his motives were useless abstractions. The individual was the product of group experiences; his morals derived from his relations in the particular groups to whom he belonged, whereas his notions of rights could be traced to the accommodative norms developed by the struggle of interest groups in his society.

Gumplowicz's most important works include *Rasse und Staat* (1875), *Der Rassenkampf* (1893), and *Grundriss der Sociologie* (1885); the latter is his only work that has been translated into English by Frederick W. Moore, as *Outlines of Sociology* (1889) and reissued by Irving L. Horowitz (1962). An edition of all of Gumplowicz's writings, under the title *Ausgewaehlte Werke*, appeared in 1926. An evaluation of Gumplowicz as a Jew is contained in "Scholar and Visionary: the correspondence between Herzl and Ludwig Gumplowicz" (*Herzl Yearbook*, 1 (1958), 165–80).

BIBLIOGRAPHY: B. Zebowski, *Ludwig Gumplowicz: eine Bio-Bibliographie* (1926); *The Times* (London, Aug. 20, 1909), 10a.

[Werner J. Cahnman and Alvin Boskoff]

GUNDOLF, FRIEDRICH (pseudonym of **Friedrich Gundelfinger**, 1880–1931), German literary historian. Following Karl Wolfskehl, Gundolf was one of the earlier disciples of Stefan George and participated in his literary movement. Together with Wolfskehl, with whom he exchanged many letters from 1899 (published in 1977 in 2 vols.), Gundolf belonged to a group of Jewish intellectuals and writers who were strongly attracted by George's integrative cultural concept trying to unify Greek, Jewish, and German culture. But unlike Wolfskehl, Gundolf explicitly distanced himself from Judaism. Prior to his career as a university teacher he published poetry in the *Blaetter fuer die Kunst* (later also *Gedichte*, 1930) and worked from 1907 on the 10-volume German translation of Shakespeare's works which appeared under his editorship (1908–18). With his dissertation on Shakespeare in 1911 at the University of Heidelberg, Gundolf turned to an academic career. His scholarly studies covered a wide range. Starting with Shakespeare (*Shakespeare und der deutsche Geist*, 1911; *Shakespeare*, 2 vols., 1928), he published books on Goethe (1916), George (1920), Kleist (1922), Opitz (1923), Caesar (1924), Paracelsus (1927), Gryphius (1927), and the Romanticists (*Romantiker*, 2 vols., 1930–31), violating more and more the narrow normative canon of George, with whom he broke after his book on Kleist. In his decisive anti-positivist biographies of literary figures, Gundolf was not interested so much in the details of their daily lives as in the "spirit" revealed in their creative masterpieces, and he interpreted their unique *Gestalt* with a reverential awe. His publications still serve as examples of humanistic scholarship and literary style while Gundolf himself is understood as one of the important German-Jewish intellectuals of the beginning of the 20th century.

BIBLIOGRAPHY: V.A. Schmitz, *Gundolf, eine Einfuehrung in sein Werk* (1965); O. Heuschele, *Friedrich Gundolf, Werk und Wirken* (1947); E. Kahn, in: YLBI, 8 (1963), 171–83; W. Lewin, *ibid.*, 201–8 (Ger., with Eng. summary). **ADD. BIBLIOGRAPHY:** C. Sonino, in: G. Mattenklott et al. (ed.), *Verkannte Brueder?* (2001), 101–16; C. Blasberg: in: D. Hoffmann (ed.), *Handbuch zur deutsch-jüdischen Literatur des 20. Jahrhunderts* (2002), 81–102; M. Thimann, *Caesars Schatten. Die Bibliothek von Friedrich Gundolf* (2003).

[Andreas Kilcher (2nd ed.)]

°**GUNKEL, HERMANN** (1862–1932), German Bible scholar. Gunkel taught at the universities of Halle from 1888 to 1894 and 1920 to 1927, Berlin from 1894 to 1907, and Giessen from 1907 to 1920. The work of Gunkel has been a learned stimulant in biblical scholarship. His conviction that historical criticism, which seeks an ideal history of Israel based on the chronological and biographical terms and exemplified classically by the J. Wellhausen school, was inadequate in writing a history of Israel's literature led him to discover the importance of determining the oral prehistory of the written sources, and of classifying the source material into the appropriate categories of literary "forms." He thus pioneered the methods of form criticism to biblical studies, and introduced the traditional historical point of view in writing Israel's history. His first major work, *Schöpfung und Chaos in Urzeit und Endzeit* (1895, 1921), was a study into the mythology underlying the biblical ideas concerning the beginning and the end of the present world order. By piecing together the existing variants of the surviving texts, mainly in the poetic sections of the Bible, he made the first scholarly attempt to reconstruct the original myth of creation. His commentary on Genesis (1901, 1963[6]) argued for the great antiquity of the sagas, legends, and traditions of the first book of the Bible. The introduction, published separately and translated into English as *The Legends of Genesis* (1901, 1964[5]), was primarily interested in the characteristics of the story (German "Sagen" is better translated as "stories" than as "legends") as a genre and its historical development. His most successful attempt at a literary history of Israel, based primarily on an analysis of the types and forms of Israel's speech, appeared in the volume on *Die orientalschen Literaturen* (1906) in Hinneberg's series *Die Kultur der Gegenwart*. His approach has proved most fruitful in his studies on the Psalms: *Ausgewaehlte Psalmen* (1917[4]); *Die Psalmen uebersetzt und erklaert* (1926); and *Einleitung in die Psalmen* (published posthumously and under the joint authorship of J. Begrich, 1933), where the Psalms are classified according to their principle types (*Gattungen*) and each type is related to a characteristic life setting (*Sitz im Leben*). Gunkel's book on Esther (1916, 1958[2]) is fundamental for understanding the literary character of the book. A number of crucial studies related to form criticism are found in two series of published essays: *Reden und Aufsaetze* (1913) and *Was bleibt vom Alten Testament* (1916; *What Remains of the Old Testament? and Other Essays*, 1928). His *Das Maerchen im Alten Testament* (1917) historically traces the genre of the folktale in the Bible in light of Near Eastern culture. In addition to his many writings he served as an editor of *Die Religion in Geschichte und Gegenwart* (1909–13 and 1927–32[2]), and, with W. Bousset, of the series *Forschungen zur Religion und Literatur des Alten und Neuen Testaments*.

BIBLIOGRAPHY: *Festschrift... H. Gunkel* (1923), incl. bibl.; DB, s.v. (incl. bibl.); H.J. Kraus, *Geschichte der historisch-kritischen Erforschung des Alten Testaments* (1956), 309–34; H.F. Hahn, *The Old Testament in Modern Research* (1956), 119–28. **ADD. BIBLIOGRAPHY:** J. Scullion, in: DBI, 1:472–73.

[Zev Garber]

GUNSBERG, ISIDOR (1854–1930), British chess master and journalist. Gunsberg was born in Hungary and taken to England as a child. He was known as a master of attack and his name was particularly associated with the Allgaier gambit. Gunsberg defeated Bird and Blackburne, and drew with Tchigorin. In 1889 he lost the world championship match against *Steinitz by the surprisingly narrow score of 6–4 with 9 draws. He wrote *Chess Openings* (1896) and famous chess columns in the *Morning Post*. One of the strongest players of his time, by his death in 1930 he was one of the last survivors of the Victorian chess world, but has remained surprisingly neglected by chess historians since.

ADD. BIBLIOGRAPHY: D. Hooper and K. Wyld, *The Oxford Companion to Chess* (1992), 162–63.

[William D. Rubinstein (2nd ed.)]

GUNZBERG, ARYEH LEIB (Loeb) BEN ASHER (1695–1785), talmudist. Born in Lithuania, Aryeh became assistant to his father on his appointment about 1720 as rabbi of the upper district in Minsk, comprising at the time 40 small communities. In 1733 he founded a yeshivah, which soon attracted students from Belorussia and Lithuania. Differences over methods of instruction between Aryeh Leib and Jehiel Heilprin, author of *Seder ha-Dorot* and head of another yeshivah in Minsk, led to much friction between both the teachers and students, Heilprin being opposed to the pilpulistic method used by Aryeh Leib to stimulate the minds of his students. In the introduction to his famous volume of responsa, *Sha'agat Aryeh*, however, Aryeh Leib himself is critical of the role of *pilpul* in establishing the "truth of the Torah." Finally compelled in 1742 to leave Minsk, he settled in one of the nearby towns where he continued to help his aged father. In 1750 he was appointed rabbi in *Volozhin, where among some of his notable disciples were Ḥayyim *Volozhiner and his brother Simḥah. Here he prepared his halakhic work, *Sha'agat Aryeh* (Frankfurt on the Oder, 1755). He lived in poverty, became involved in disputes with the community leaders, and at the age of 69 wandered from city to city. He reached Germany and eventually accepted the position of *av bet din* in Metz (1765), becoming also head of a large yeshivah there. He remained in Metz until his death. Besides his *Sha'agat Aryeh*, Aryeh Leib published in his lifetime *Turei Even*, novellae on the tractates *Rosh Ha-Shanah*, *Ḥagigah*, and *Megillah* (Metz, 1781). His posthumously published works are *She'elot u-Teshuvot Sha'agat Aryeh ha-Ḥadashot* (1874); *Gevurot Ari*, novellae on *Ta'anit* (1862); and *Gevurot Ari*, on *Yoma* and *Makkot* (1907).

BIBLIOGRAPHY: *Ha-Me'assef*, 2 (1785), 161–8; Carmoly, in: *Israelische Annalen*, 2 (1840), 186, no. 15; Cahen, in: REJ, 12 (1886), 294ff.; B.Z. Eisenstadt, *Rabbanei Minsk ve-Ḥakhameha* (1898), 15ff.; D. Maggid, *Sefer Toledot Mishpeḥot Ginzburg* (1899), 35–52; S.J. Fuenn, *Kiryah Ne'emanah* (1915²), 163.

[Moshe Nahum Zobel]

GUNZBURG, NIKO (1882–1984), Belgian jurist and criminologist. Born in Riga, Latvia, his family settled in Belgium when he was a boy. In 1923 he was appointed lecturer in law at the University of Ghent where he later became the first Jew to be made a professor. He founded its Institute of Criminology in 1937 and headed it until 1952 except during World War II when he was attached to the Belgian embassy in Washington. From 1953 to 1956, he was professor of law at the University of Djakarta, Indonesia. His works on penal law and criminology earned him an international reputation. They include *Les transformations récentes du droit pénal* (1933) and *La trajectoire du crime; études sur le nouveau code Pénal du Brésil* (1941). A prominent figure in the Belgian Jewish community, Gunzburg was founder and president of the Central Committee for Jewish Welfare in Antwerp. He participated in the inaugural conference of the World Jewish Congress in 1936 and was chairman of the Council of Jewish Associations (1947–50). Gunzburg was also a passionate advocate of the use of the Flemish language and he was head of the society of Flemish Jurists.

[Zvi Hermon]

GUNZENHAUSER (Ashkenazi), JOSEPH BEN JACOB (d. 1490) and AZRIEL, his son, pioneers in Hebrew printing. The Gunzenhausers went to Naples from Gunzenhausen in southern Germany and set up a Hebrew press, which from 1487 to 1492 produced an impressive range of books (see *Incunabula), in all about 12 volumes. Among them were the Hagiographa with various rabbinical commentaries (1487); Avicenna's medical *Canon*, the first and only edition of the work in Hebrew (*Ha-Kanon*); and the first edition of Abraham Ibn Ezra's Pentateuch commentary (1488). After Joseph Gunzenhauser's death his wife (or daughter) and son continued his work. The Gunzenhausers assembled a team of distinguished typesetters and correctors from Italy. Joshua Solomon Soncino, who began printing at Naples about this time, issued a prayer book of the Spanish rite for Gunzenhauser in May 1490.

BIBLIOGRAPHY: D.W. Amram, *Makers of Hebrew Books in Italy* (1909), 63, 66; B. Friedberg, *Ha-Defus ha-Ivri be-Italyah…* (1956), 40ff.; A. Freimann (ed.), *Thesaurus Typographiae Hebraicae…* (1931), A57, 1ff.

GUR, BATYA (1947–2005), Israeli writer and literary critic. Gur was born in Tel Aviv, studied Hebrew literature and history at the Hebrew University of Jerusalem, and completed her M.A. in comparative studies. She worked as a high school teacher before moving to the United States and subsequently lived in Jerusalem, writing reviews and essays for the literary supplement of *Ha-aretz* and internationally known for her detective novels. The central figure in these novels is police detective Michael Ohayon, and the cases which he investigates lead to rather unusual domains such as literature, music, or psychotherapy while probing social and political aspects of current Israeli life. In *Ha-Merḥak ha-Nakhon* (1996; *Murder Duet: A Musical Case*, 1999), detective Ohayon investigates two murders in the world of classical music in Jerusalem, following the discovery of a requiem by Vivaldi; in *Reẓaḥ, Meẓalmim* (2004), Gur focuses on intrigues among the staff members of Israeli television. While her earlier thrillers seem to focus on social circles to be found anywhere in the world (a university department, the psychoanalytic society), her later novels consciously address local issues, turning the allegedly inferior genre of the detective story into a vehicle for reflecting on the erosion of the Zionist ethos and the maladies of Israeli society. Among her other books are *Reẓaḥ be-Shabbat ba-Boker* (1988; *The Saturday Morning Murder: A Psychoanalytic Case*, 1991), *Mavet ba-Ḥug le-Sifrut* (1989; *Literary Murder: A Critical* Case, 1993), *Linah Meshutefet* (1991; *Murder on a Kibbutz: A Communal Case*, 1994), and *Even Taḥat Even* ("Stone under Stone," 1998). Gur's novels have been translated into many languages.

BIBLIOGRAPHY: D. Gavrieli, *Konvenẓiyot bi-Sefat ha-Guf ba-Roman Reẓaḥ be-Shabbat ba-boker* (1996); N. Sokoloff, "Jewish Mysteries. Detective Fiction by Faye Kellerman and Batya Gur," in: *Shofar*, 15/3 (1997), 66–85; Ch. Bala, "*Kriminalistischer Postzionismus? Israel in den Romanen von Batya Gur und Shulamit Lapid*," in: *Zacher*, 10 (2000), 61–73; D. Abramovich, "Israeli Detective Fiction: The Case of Batya Gur and Shulamit Lapid," in: *Australian Journal of Jewish Studies*, 14 (2000), 147–79; G. Bronstein, "*Kulam Hayu Baneinu*" (on mourning and Gur's novel "Stone under Stone"), in: *Ha-Mishpat*, 13 (2002), 54–66; H. Hever, in: *Haaretz* (May 27, 2005); A. Hirschfeld, in: *Haaretz* (June 17, 2005).

[Anat Feinberg (2nd ed.)]

GUR (Gorban), MORDECAI (Motta; 1930–1995), Tenth Israeli chief of staff and politician; member of the Tenth to Thirteenth Knessets. Gur was born and grew up in Jerusalem. He joined the Haganah at an early age and held various positions of command. During the War of Independence he served in the ninth motorized special services battalion of the Negev Brigade of the Palmah. After the War of Independence, he served for two years in *Naḥal, later joining the paratroops and commanding numerous reprisal operations. In 1955 he was commended for his part in an operation across the border with Egypt in Khan Yunis, in the course of which he was wounded. During the 1956 Sinai Campaign he commanded an airborne Naḥal unit and in 1957 became deputy commander of the paratroops. In 1959–60 Gur studied at a military academy in Paris, and in 1961 was appointed commander of the Golani Brigade. In 1963 he was appointed to a senior post on the General Staff, and in 1966, after a year as commander of the Staff College, took charge of a brigade of airborne infantry. During the Six-Day War, Gur commanded the paratrooper brigade that captured the Old City of Jerusalem, and after the war was appointed commander of the forces in the Gaza Strip and Sinai Peninsula. In 1969 he was promoted to the rank of major general, and was appointed commander of the Northern Command, and in 1972–73 served as military attaché in Washington. After the Yom Kippur War, he was once again appointed commander of the Northern Command. In 1974, he succeeded Lieutenant General David *Elazar as chief of staff, serving in this capacity until 1978. As chief of staff he was responsible for the 1976 Entebbe Operation, in which the IDF freed Israeli and Jewish hostages hijacked to Uganda by terrorists, and for the 1978 Litani Operation, in which the IDF attacked Palestinian terrorist bases in Southern Lebanon. When Egyptian president Anwar *Sadat declared his intention to visit Jerusalem in November 1977, Gur reacted with suspicion.

After retiring from the IDF Gur, who had taken Oriental Studies at the Hebrew University of Jerusalem, attended Harvard Business School for a year, in 1979. He returned to Israel after being appointed director of the Histadrut-owned industrial enterprise of Koor Mechanics, a position he held until 1984. In these years he also became active in the *Israel Labor Party. In 1981 Gur was elected to the Tenth Knesset on the Alignment ticket. Reelected to the Eleventh Knesset he served as minister of health in the National Unity Government in 1984–86, when Shimon *Peres was prime minister. He resigned in 1986, refusing to serve under Yitẓhak *Shamir of the Likud after the rotation in the premiership. After his resignation from the government he continued to serve in the Knesset, but also became chairman of the Board of Directors of Solel Boneh, the Histadrut-owned construction company. He rejoined the government half a year before the elections to the Twelfth Knesset in 1988 as minister without portfolio. In the National Unity Government formed after the elections Gur continued to serve as minister without portfolio. In the course of these years Gur frequently met with Palestinian personalities in the West Bank, and even made an attempt to meet with PLO leader Yasser *Arafat. When Arafat expressed willingness to recognize Security Council Resolution 242 towards the end of 1988, Gur was inclined to admit that a certain change had taken place in the Palestinian position, but the following year he was disappointed by the positions of the Palestinians and adopted a more hawkish approach to the conflict with the Palestinians within the Labor Party.

Gur had planned to contend in the leadership contest in the Labor Party in 1992, and did not hide his ambition to be prime minister, but he finally withdrew when he was diagnosed with cancer. In the contest he supported Yitzhak *Rabin, and in the government formed by Rabin after the elections to the Thirteenth Knesset was appointed deputy minister of defense, with Rabin serving as minister. In July 1995, less than four months before the assassination of Rabin, when a turn for the worse occurred in his illness, he took his own life.

His *Azeet, Paratrooper Dog* became a successful series of children's books and he also wrote *The Battle for Jerusalem* (*Har ha-Bayit be-Yadeinu*, 1974) on the Six-Day War.

BIBLIOGRAPHY: Z. Ofer (ed.), *Rosh ha-Mateh ha-Kelali – Motta Gur* (1998).

[Misha Louvish / Rohan Saxen and Susan Hattis Rolef (2nd ed.)]

GURA-HUMORULUI, town in N. Romania, in the historic region of Bukovina. Frescos with a tableau of the "Day of Judgment" painted between 1547 and 1550 depicting among others Turkish and Jewish figures are found in the Voronet monastery there. A lone Jew lived in the town in 1788. Jewish settlement began in Gura-Humorului under Austrian rule in 1835, with five Jewish families (in a total population of 700). They increased to 20 by 1848 and formed an organized community. Prayers were first held in a private house. The first synagogue was erected in 1869, and the Great Synagogue in 1871. As in the other communities of Bukovina, the influence of Ḥasidism was strong. At first occupied as craftsmen, merchants, and purveyors to the Austrian army, Jews later established workshops for wood processing and lumber mills. At the close of the 19th century, they played an important role in the industrialization of the town. The community numbered 130 persons in 1856, 190 in 1867, 800 in 1869, 1,206 in 1890, 2,050 in 1910, and 1,951 in 1927. In 1880 it became possible to elect a community council and an executive board in accordance with Austrian law. The first rabbi, Meshulam Gebirer, was hired in 1860. Other rabbis were Menachem Mendel Babad and Meshulam Ginzberg. The cemetery was established in 1857. Many of the Jews were Sadagura *ḥasidim*; others were Vizhnitz *ḥasidim*. In 1894–1990, the *admor* of Vizhnitz, Moses Hager, lived in Gura-Humorului.

After the town passed to Romania at the end of World War I, and throughout the period between the two world wars, the authorities endeavored to restrict the Jews in their economic activities while there were also occasional antisemitic outbreaks. The Zionist movement, formed locally at the beginning of the 20th century, had a large following. *Aliyah* to Ereẓ Israel began during the 1930s. At the time of the persecutions by the Romanian Fascists, 2,954 local Jews and others who had gathered there from the surrounding area were deported in a single day (Oct. 10, 1941) to *Transnistria. In March 1944 around 1,500 were allowed to return. After the end of World War II, the survivors were joined by other Jewish inhabitants of the region who returned from their places of deportation, and numbered 1,158 in 1948. Nearly all the Jews there immigrated to Israel between 1948 and 1951. In 1997 only 10 Jews lived in Gura-Humorului, with a synagogue.

BIBLIOGRAPHY: H. Gold (ed.), *Geschichte der Juden in der Bukowina*, 2 (1962), 84–87. **ADD. BIBLIOGRAPHY:** S. Yeshurun (ed.), *Gura Humora* (1997).

[Yehouda Marton / Lucian-Zeev Herscovici (2nd ed.)]

GURALNIK, DAVID B. (1920–2000), U.S. lexicographer, one of the most influential figures in the 20th century in shaping the English language. Guralnik was the editor of the authoritative Webster's New World line of dictionaries from 1948 to 1985. He was born in Cleveland and had a passion for Yiddish, which he learned as a child. He intended to become a teacher but after graduating from Western Reserve University in 1941, he took the advice of one of his teachers and took a dictionary writing job at the World Publishing Company of Cleveland. After three years in the Army during World War II, where he was a translator, he said he could "manage" French, German, Russian, Greek, Latin, and Hebrew, languages he learned as a child and young man. He was the interpreter for his battalion, which called on him to speak four languages the day it liberated a German camp holding Russian and French soldiers as prisoners.

After the war, Guralnik returned to the publishing company and became editor in chief of its New World family of dictionaries. He was 28. Over the next 37 years he supervised works that carried his view of American English around the world. As the gatekeeper for words seeking admission to the literary mainstream, his definitions guided tens of millions of people who thumbed through the dictionaries he edited, and he wrote many of the definitions of new words himself. Among the works he edited, the best known is the College Edition of Webster's *New World Dictionary of the American Language*, a one-volume desktop popular not only among students but also with writers and other professionals. "Our emphasis is on the English language as spoken in America," he said, "and for that reason we chose to call it the dictionary of the American language. It does for the American language what the *Oxford English Dictionary* does for the language as a whole." The dictionary rules as the standard reference for the Associated Press, United Press International, *The New York Times*, and nearly every major news organization in the United States. The line has sold 85 million copies. The first edition appeared in 1953 and over the next decades the staff struggled to keep up with "not only a population explosion, but an information explosion of unprecedented proportions," Guralnik said in the foreword to the second edition. New words, new pronunciations, and new meanings were being born without the customary time for incubation.

He invariably had to answer questions as society's norms changed about which words, if any, to bar. He decided to eliminate racial epithets and to omit some common vulgar words. Some of these words were restored in the third edition, after his retirement. He later engaged in a war of words with the publisher of the 13-volume Oxford dictionary over parts of its treatment of the word "Jew," with a definition that referred to old stereotypes of usurious moneylenders.

Guralnik was a leader in the Jewish community of Cleveland, delivering a weekly radio commentary on words called *A Yiddish Vort*. And he spoke and wrote often on the subject. He was president of the Jewish Community Center, vice president of *The Cleveland Jewish News*, and a trustee of the Jewish Community Federation of Cleveland.

[Stewart Kampel (2nd ed.)]

GUREVICH, MIKHAIL IOSIFOVICH (1893–1976), Soviet aviation constructor. Gurevich was born in 1893 in the village of Rubanshchina which is in today's Kursk district, Russia. He graduated from the airplane construction faculty of the Kharkov Technological Institute in 1925. In 1929 he began working in the aviation industry and from 1938 to 1957 held the rank of deputy chief constructor and from 1957–1964 chief constructor. He received the degree of doctor of technological sciences in 1964. Together with Ar. I. Mikoyan in 1940 he planned and built the high-speed fighter plane the MiG-1 (the name being an abbreviation of Mikoyan and Gurevich). After being upgraded, as the MiG-3, this plane was widely employed during World War II. After the war, the same duo designed the first Soviet supersonic jet fighters (also part of the MiG series). Gurevich was awarded the order of the U.S.S.R., the Stalin Prize (in 1941, 1947, 1948, and 1953), and the Lenin Prize (in 1962). He was designated a Hero of Socialist Labor in 1957.

[*The Shorter Jewish Encylopaedia in Russian*]

GUREVICH, MOSHE (1874–1944), Bundist in Russia. Born in St. Petersburg, he came from a wealthy religious family. His grandfather Elhanan Cohen of Salant, a railroad contractor, carried on an independent struggle in St. Petersburg against the anti-Jewish czarist legislation. Many members of his family became revolutionaries. Gurevich studied at the universities of St. Petersburg and Berlin, joined the Social Democrats, and was active in St. Petersburg and Gomel. He later headed the *Bund in Vilna, and between 1901 and 1903 took a leading part in the Hirsh *Lekert affair and in opposing the *Independent Jewish Workers' Party. He was imprisoned for his socialist activities. After his release Gurevich went to the United States as an emissary of the Bund in 1905. He stayed there until his death and was a member of the educational committee of the *Workmen's Circle from 1920 to 1922.

BIBLIOGRAPHY: J.S. Hertz (ed.), *Doyres Bundistn*, 1 (1956), 269–73.

[Moshe Mishkinsky]

GURFEIN, RIVKA (1908–1983), Israeli author and literary critic. Born in Sanok, Poland, Gurfein graduated from the Cracow University. She joined Kibbutz Ein Shemer in 1932 and was appointed counselor of Youth Aliyah groups, and later cultural officer in the IDF. She was a lecturer in general literature and Hebrew poetry in the Ḥaderah Community College and in the Institute for Supplementary Education for Teachers in Haifa. As a member of the editorial board of *Devar ha-Po'elet*, she contributed articles on literature, culture, and society, and published essays and articles on general and Hebrew literature in various journals such as *Orlogin*, *Al ha-Mishmar*, and *Sedemot*.

Gurfein literary essays include "*Mi-karov u-me-Raḥok*" (1964), "*Im Shir*" (1967), "*Bi-Keriah Kashuvah*" (1969), and "*Le-Or ha-Katuv*" (1972). She is also the author of novels: *Ne'urim ba-Shemesh* (1954), *Kokhavim me-al ha-Gan* (1964) – for which she was awarded the Ussishkin Prize, and *Ta'am shel Beḥirah*

(1975). She received the Histadrut Y. Aharonovitch Prize and the Ḥayyim Greenberg Prize for her literary achievements and for her educational activities.

GURIAN (Gurfinckel), SORANA (1913–1956), Romanian novelist and journalist who later wrote in French. Sorana Gurian was born in Komrat, Bessarabia. After her university studies she spent three years in France, then returned to Bucharest on the eve of World War II and joined the anti-Fascist underground. After the war she became a journalist, but in 1947 her article calling for freedom of expression led to the suppression of her work. Early in 1949 she escaped from Romania and settled in Paris. Except for a two-year stay in Israel (1949–51), she spent the rest of her life in France, where she quickly established herself as a newspaper and radio political commentator as well as an author. Sorana Gurian's first novel, which made her famous, *Zilele nu se întorc niciodată* ("Never Do the Days Return," 1946), was the largely autobiographical story of an intellectual family in a Bessarabian town. *Intâmplări dintre amurg și noapte* ("Events Between Dawn and Night," 1946), a collection of stories, dealt with the sexual obsessions of lonely women. Her first book in French, *Les mailles du filet* (1950), a diary of the years 1947–49, had a factual authenticity which made it an important political document. She translated her first Romanian novel as *Les jours ne reviennent jamais* (1952), and wrote a sequel to it: *Les amours impitoyables*, which appeared in 1953, and which dealt with the political scene in pre-World War II Romania. Her last book, *Récit d'un combat* (1956), a record of her desperate search for treatment of the cancer from which she was dying, was enlivened by her thirst for life, her courage, and the support of her friends.

BIBLIOGRAPHY: C. Malraux, in: *Evidences* (Oct. 8, 1956), 48–49; G. Marcel, in: *Arts et Spectacles* (Feb.–March, 1956); Manès Sperber, in: *Preuves* (Feb. 1956), 45–46. **ADD. BIBLIOGRAPHY:** *Dicționarul scriitorilor români*, D-L (1998), 472–73; V. Durnea, in: *România literară* (2003), 20–21.

[Dora Litani-Littman]

GURLAND, ḤAYYIM JONAH (1843–1890), Russian rabbi and scholar. Gurland was born in Kletsk, Belorussia, and was educated at the Vilna rabbinical seminary and at the University of St. Petersburg, where he studied Oriental languages with D. *Chwolson. He wrote his dissertation on the influence of Islamic philosophy, in particular the Mutakallimūn, Muʿatazilites, and Ashʿarians, on Maimonides. While employed at the Imperial Library of St. Petersburg, Gurland worked on the *Firkovich manuscripts, being one of the first to discover his forgeries; he published the results of this research as *Ginzei Yisrael be – St. Petersburg* (1865–67). In 1873 he was appointed inspector of the Jewish teachers' seminary in Zhitomir; there he published a Yiddish and Russian calendar, entitled in Hebrew *Lu'aḥ Yisrael* (1878–81), which also contained scholarly articles. After three years in Western Europe, he returned to Russia and founded a Jewish high school in Odessa. In 1888 the government appointed him rabbi of Odessa. In addition to contributing articles to the leading Hebrew periodicals, Gurland published a Hebrew version of D. Chwolson's work on the Tammuz cult in ancient Babylonia, *Ma'amar ha-Tammuz* (1864), and a seven-volume work on the persecutions of Jews in Russia during the 17th and 18th centuries, *Le-Korot ha-Gezerot al Yisrael* (1887–89), with a posthumous addendum (1893) to the last volume containing a biography of the author by D. Cahana.

BIBLIOGRAPHY: Kressel, Leksikon, 1 (1965), 459–60; N. Sokolow, *Sefer Zikkaron le-Sofrei Yisrael…* (1899), 133–40.

GURS (near Pau, Basses-Pyrénées), one of France's largest concentration camps during World War II. Situated in southwestern France in what would later be the Unoccupied Zone, it was first used to intern Republican Spanish refugees, and then, later, refugees from Austria and Germany. After the Franco-German armistice in June 1940, Jews were brought to the camp. Food supply and sanitary conditions in Gurs were worse than in the camps of the Occcupied Zone. Some 800 Jews died there in the winter of 1940. In 1941 there were 15,000 internees, including 7,200 Jews who had been deported from the Palatinate and Baden in western Germany, and about 3,000 Jewish refugees who had been arrested in Belgium on May 10, 1940, and had been sent first to the French concentration camp Saint-Cyprien on the Spanish border. In the second half of July 1942, Theodor Dannecker, Adolf Eichmann's representative in France, inspected the Gurs camp. Shortly afterwards, most of the internees were sent to *Drancy, and from there to death camps. Deportations ended in the summer of 1943. Only 735 women, 250 men, and 215 children remained in Gurs when it was finally closed down. The cemetery near the camp contains the graves of 1,200 Jews.

BIBLIOGRAPHY: Z. Szajkowski, *Analytical Franco-Jewish Gazetteer* (1966), 214–2; J. Weill, *Contribution à l'histoire de camps d'internement dans l'Anti-France* (1946). **ADD. BIBLIOGRAPHY:** M.R. Marrus and R.O. Paxton, *Vichy France and the Jews* (1981), 172–3, 306–7.

[David Weinberg (2nd ed.)]

GURSHTEIN, AARON (1895–1941), Soviet Yiddish literary historian, critic, and editor. Born in Krolevets (Ukraine), Gurshtein attended a Jewish secondary school in Vilna and later studied Hebrew literature at the University of Petrograd. In 1920, he enlisted in the Red Army, in which he served for several years. In 1923, he published his first essay in *Emes*, the Yiddish organ of the Communist Party. He wrote Marxist treatments of 19th century Yiddish authors such as Sholem Yankev *Abramovitsh, I.L. *Peretz, and *Shalom Aleichem, and also analyzed the works of his contemporaries such as David *Bergelson, Der *Nister, Ezra *Finenberg and Shmuel *Halkin. During the thaw of the New Economic Policy (NEP), he welcomed the more liberal tendency to evaluate art aesthetically and not politically. His study *Vegn Undzer Kritik* ("About Our Criticism," 1925) was tolerant even of symbolism. By 1933, however, when with M. *Viner he wrote *Prob-*

lemes fun Kritik ("Problems of Criticism"), he retreated from his earlier tolerance and accepted socialist realism as the only desirable artistic approach. Gurshtein enlisted for service in World War II and in 1941 died in combat.

BIBLIOGRAPHY: LNYL, 2 (1958), 204f. **ADD. BIBLIOGRAPHY:** Y. Shatski, in: *YIVO Bleter*, 23 (1944), 125–39.

[Sol Liptzin / Marc Miller (2nd ed.)]

GURVITCH, GEORGES (1894–1966), French sociologist. Born in Russia, Gurvitch was educated at the universities of Petrograd and Paris. Gurvitch taught at the universities of Petrograd and Strasbourg, and from 1948 until his death at the University of Paris. He also was editor of the *Cahiers Internationaux de Sociologie* and the *Journal of Legal and Political Sociology*. He was profoundly influenced by the philosophers Hegel and Bergson, the socialists Petrajizhky and P.A. Sorokin, and especially by the phenomenological school in philosophy. Gurvitch worked on a highly analytical level, dealing particularly with the sociology of law, the nature of groups and social classes, and later the character of social time. Among his major sociological writings are *The Sociology of Law* (1942), *Essais de Sociologie* (1938), *Eléments de sociologie juridique* (1940), *La déclaration des droits sociaux* (1940), *La vocation actuelle de la sociologie* (1950), *Twentieth Century Sociology* (edited with W.E. More, 1945), *Traité de sociologie* (2 vols., 1958), *Industrialisation et technocratie* (edited with G. Friedmann, 1949), *Déterminismes sociaux et liberté humaine* (1955), *Dialectique et sociologie* (1962), and *The Spectrum of Social Time* (1964). He tried to increase awareness of (1) symbolic nuances in social life; (2) a series of conceptually distinct levels in human experience; (3) the importance of dialectical and oppositional mechanism in society; and (4) the relation between conceptions of time and human behavior. Gurvitch's distinction between microsociology and macrosociology has been widely accepted among sociologists, but his assertion that each uses distinct methods of investigation has been opposed by neo-positivists and functionalists.

BIBLIOGRAPHY: R. Toulemont, *Sociologie et pluralisme dialectique: introduction à l'oeuvre de Georges Gurvitch* (1955); P. Bosserman, *Dialectical Sociology* (1968).

[Alvin Boskoff]

GURWITSCH, AARON (1901–1973), U.S. philosopher and psychologist. Born in Vilna, he lectured at the Sorbonne from 1933. In 1940 he went to the U.S., where he taught at Brandeis University, Johns Hopkins University, and the New School for Social Research in New York. Gurwitsch was distinguished for his special philosophical approach to the problems of psychology. He sought to show the mutual relations which exist between the psychological image pattern, conceived in consciousness as an entity, and the conscious content which consciousness aims at when it knows or remembers it as conceived. He distinguished between the pattern and the content at which consciousness is aimed. This latter conception he called, after Husserl, "*noema*." The unity of the pattern and the *noema* are for Gurwitsch a "theme" (*thema*). The conscious horizon which surrounds the theme and which is liable to influence the shaping of its form in consciousness at every moment is called by him "the theoretical field." He tried to find phenomenological interpretations of other psychological theories such as those of W. James, J. Piaget, and Kurt *Goldstein. His writings include: "On the Intentionality of Consciousness," in *Philosophical Essays in Memory of E. Husserl* (1940), 65–83; *Théorie du champ de la conscience* (1957; *Field of Consciousness*, 1964); "Phenomenological and Psychological Approach to Consciousness," in *Philosophy and Phenomenological Research*, 15 (1955), 303–19; "Der Begriff des Bewusstseins bei Kant und Husserl," in: *Kantstudien*, 55 (1964), 410–27.

BIBLIOGRAPHY: H. Spiegelberg: *The Phenomenological Movement*, 2 (1960), 630.

[Aaron Gruenhut]

GURWITSCH (Gurvich), ALEXANDER GAVRILOVICH (1874–1954), Soviet Russian biologist. Gurwitsch was born in Poltava, Ukraine. After studying and teaching abroad he returned to Russia in 1906, and from 1907 until 1918 taught at the women's higher education courses in St. Petersburg. He was a professor at Simferopol University from 1918 to 1925 and at Moscow University from 1925 to 1930. For the next 18 years he worked at the All-Union Institute of Experimental Medicine in Leningrad. He was awarded a Stalin Prize in 1941.

Gurwitsch was one of the first scientists to study the effects of certain types of drugs on development. His concern with the problem of organization of embryonic growth led him to study the mechanics of cell division. In 1923 he began to publish a series of papers which aroused intense controversy. He claimed to have detected what he called "mitogenetic rays," a form of energy emitted by living cells, which he believed stimulated growth in other tissues. His original experiments were performed with onion roots. In a book published in 1937, *Mitogenetic Analysis of the Excitation of the Nervous System*, Gurwitsch attempted to extend his concept to explain the activity of the nervous system. The evidence on which these ideas were based was generally regarded as equivocal, and most biologists rejected his theories.

BIBLIOGRAPHY: Blyakher and Zalkind, in: *Byulleten Moskovskogo obshchestva ispytaniya prirody*, 60 (1955), 103–8.

[Norman Levin]

GUSEV, SERGEI IVANOVICH (formerly **Yakov Davidovich Drabkin**; 1874–1933), Soviet party and government official. Gusev was born in the settlement of Sapozhok, Riazan district, Russia. In 1896 he entered the St. Petersburg Technological Institute and in the same year joined the revolutionary movement. He was one of the leaders of the workers' uprisings in Rostov in 1902–03. At the second congress of the Russian Social Democratic Revolutionary Party he joined the Bolsheviks and was secretary of the bureau of the St. Petersburg committee of the Party (1904–05), of the Odessa committee (1906), and from 1906 to 1917 was engaged in Party work in Moscow and St. Petersburg. In 1917 he was secretary of the Petrograd military-revolutionary committee which organized the October armed uprising. From 1918 to 1920 Gusev was a member of the Revolutionary Military Soviet (RVS) of the 2nd and 5th Armies of the Eastern, Southeastern, and Southern Fronts, Commander of the Moscow defense sector, and member of the RVS of the republic. In 1921 he became head of the political directorate of the Red Army and in 1922 chairman of the Turkestan bureau of the Russian Communist Party. From 1923 he was secretary of the Party's Central Control Commission. In 1925–26 he headed the press department of the Control Committee of the All-Union Communist Party (Bolsheviks). From 1928 to 1933 Gusev was a member of the Comintern.

Gusev's daughter, ELIZAVETA YAKOVLEVNA DRABKINA (1901–1974) was a writer, who spent the years 1934–56 in forced labor camps and exile. She wrote novels and literary memoirs devoted to the revolution and civil war periods (written after her rehabilitation).

[*The Shorter Jewish Encylopaedia in Russian*]

GUSH EMUNIM ("The Bloc of the Faithful"), a spiritual-political movement established for the purpose of implementing its belief that the establishment of the State of Israel constitutes the "Beginning of the Redemption" which will lead to the ultimate complete Redemption by settling the entire area west of the Jordan. Although their program included Zionist education, political propaganda, *aliyah*, settlement, and social aims, in practice they confined themselves to the question of settlement in the areas liberated in the Six-Day War. Gush Emunim was formally founded in Kefar Etzyon at the beginning of 1974.

Its founders came from the *National Religious Party, the Land of Israel Movement, the religious settlements, the pupils of the Mercaz ha-Rav Yeshivah, the *Bnei Akiva yeshivot, and Orthodox academicians and the young Orthodox generation.

Their first practical step was taken in May 1974 to protest the intended return of Quneitra to Syria. They proceeded to establish a new settlement (Keshet) to serve as a barrier against withdrawal. During 1974 various attempts were made by the Elon Moreh group of Gush Emunim to establish a settlement in Samaria. At the first attempt, near the army camp at Ḥoron, Rabbi Ẓevi Judah Kook, whom they regard as their spiritual father, General Arik Sharon, and MKs Zevulun Hammer, Judah Ben Meir, and Geulah Cohen participated, but on the orders of the prime minister they were forcibly removed by the army. The same fate met six subsequent attempts. An eighth attempt to settle at the old railway station of Sebaste on Hanukkah of 1975 was attended by thousands of sympathizers who remained there for eight days. As a result of negotiations they were permitted to settle in the military camp at Kaddum near Sebaste.

At the same time, settlements were established at Ophra in May 1975 in an abandoned Jordanian military camp near Mt. Ba'al Ḥazor, which was declared a work camp, with the permission of the then Defense Minister Shimon Peres.

Immediately after his election victory in May 1977, Menaḥem Begin announced that henceforth there would be "many Kaddums," and it was officially declared a settlement. As a result Gush Emunim urged that 12 new settlements in Judea and Samaria – which had been approved in principle by the previous government – be established simultaneously.

The prime minister, however, postponed implementation of the plan after his visit with President Carter, and when on his return permission was not granted, Gush Emunim decided to act on their own on Sukkot 1977. As a result tension developed between the Gush and the new government. An agreement was subsequently reached whereby two sites would be established immediately and the other ten within five months, and from then until 1981, over 20 settlements were established by them. Some were established without government permission. The establishment of a settlement in the vicinity of Shechem was the subject of an appeal to the Supreme Court by Arabs as owners of the land and they won the case. The settlers were ordered to vacate the site. After heated discussions Gush Emunim decided to comply with the order and the settlement moved to Mt. Kabir, northeast of Shechem.

In order to further their aims the Gush established in 1980 an organization of all the settlements in Judea and Samaria, called Amanah.

During the visit of President Carter to Jerusalem in March 1979 the Gush mounted demonstrations and a number were arrested and held in detention until his departure.

Gush Emunim cooperated with the Teḥiyyah party founded in October 1979.

[Zvi Shiloah]

Developments in the 1980s and Early 1990s

Gush Emunim played a significant role in Israeli political life from 1977. Although the declared ideology of the movement continues to emphasize Zionist renewal in all spheres of life, in practice the Gush was concerned with the implementation of policies which will make impossible the return of any of the West Bank (Judea and Samaria) as a result of future peace treaties or negotiations. The retention of Israeli (Jewish) control over this region was viewed as being divinely ordained, and thus not to be negated by human or democratic decision, even if it is the elected government of the State of Israel. This element of fundamentalist belief underlies all of Gush Emunim's activities. However the activities themselves – the creation of irreversible settlement facts – were implemented through the most pragmatic of means.

Following the coming to power of the Likud government in 1977, the Gush presented a short-term "emergency" settlement plan to the new government, the objective of which was the establishment of 12 new settlements throughout the West Bank at locations previously rejected by the Labor government. The majority of these locations were indeed settled during the subsequent 18 months. In October 1978, Gush Emunim presented a more comprehensive blueprint for settlement in the region. This plan focused on the establishment of a widespread network of both rural and urban settlements as a means through which Israeli sovereignty over the region could be emphasized. This plan was similar in nature to parallel blueprints proposed by the joint head of the Settlement Department of the Jewish Agency, Ḥerut appointee Matityahu Drobles, and the minister of agriculture, Ariel Sharon. Despite the lack of any formal government or cabinet decision in favor of these plans, public resources were nevertheless made available for their gradual implementation.

The implementation of Gush Emunim settlement policy was carried out by its operational arm, the Amanah settlement movement. Formal government recognition of this movement, enabling it to become the recipient of government aid and funds, together with the legalization of the two existing Gush settlements at Ofrah and Camp Kaddum afforded legitimization to the Gush Emunim settlement objectives. Amanah included well over 50 settlements, of which nearly all are located in the West Bank (the minority were in *Gush Katif). The majority of these settlements were of the *yishuv kehillati* (community settlement) type, these being largely dormitory settlements wherein the settlers commute to the Israeli metropolitan centers for their employment. Despite their lack of domestic economic base, these settlements maintained a closed social unit and new or potential candidates must be approved by general vote. They ranged in size from around 15 to 20 families in the smaller newer settlements to over 500 families in the larger, more veteran units such as Kedumim, Bet Aryeh, and Elkanah.

Gush Emunim as such did not have any formal membership and it was therefore difficult to estimate its size or actual support. While the settlers themselves constituted the grass roots of power of the movement, the Gush also succeeded in obtaining support from a variety of Knesset members in the right-of-center political parties. Although the Gush did not transform itself into a political party as such, many of its members and activists became leading figures in other parties. Knesset members of the Teḥiyyah Party from 1981 and of the Matzad faction (a breakaway from the National Religious Party) between 1984 and 1986 were Gush Emunim activists. Such personalities included Gush Emunim founder Hanan Porat of Kefar Etzyon, Rabbi Chaim Druckman – a leading figure in the Bnei Akiva national religious youth movement – and Rabbi Eliezer Waldman, a head of the Kiryat Arba yeshivah.

Other leading activists became the administrators of the regional councils set up to provide municipal services to the new settlements. These regional councils received their budgets through Ministry of Interior grants as well as by means of local taxes. Thus the administrators became, de facto, public service workers, in a position to advance their political objectives through the control and allocation of municipal funds. Additional organizations, such as the Council of Settlements in Judea, Samaria, and Gaza (Mo'eẓet Yesha) and the Sheva finance company, established to promote Jewish settlement activity in the West Bank, were largely manned by Gush Emunim personalities. This gradual process of institutionalization did not include the charismatic figure of Rabbi Moshe Levinger, who continued to propound the mystical fundamental tenets of the Gush Emunim ideology. His position as the unofficial leader of Gush Emunim received a setback in 1984, following the appointment of an official general secretary for the movement, Daniella Weiss – a resident of Kedumim.

The Gush attempted to promote a populist image by means of an annual Independence Day Rally and hike through the West Bank as well as through organizing occasional demonstrations. The most significant rallying of ranks took place in the wake of the Camp David Accords and the subsequent withdrawal from Sinai. Gush Emunim and its leaders provided a focus for the Movement to Stop the Withdrawal from Sinai. Gush Emunim viewed the withdrawal from Sinai in general, and the destruction of Jewish settlements in particular, as a dangerous precedent for the West Bank. Many of their supporters remained in Yamit as a final protest before being forcibly removed by the Israeli army.

The discovery of a Jewish underground in the West Bank and its terrorist activities in 1984, and the subsequent arrest, trial, and imprisonment of 20 Jewish settlers, three of them for life terms, caused an ideological crisis amongst the Gush Emunim ranks. Their supporters were split into two, with one camp openly denouncing the underground activity as being outside the legitimate field of play, the other camp supporting the actions as being legitimate in the face of what they saw as non-action on the part of the Israeli government to safeguard their interests. The former viewpoint was put forward by many of the Gush Emunim founders and focused around the personality of Yoel Bin-Nun from the Ofrah settlement. In time, these two camps became largely reconciled around the question of clemency for the Jewish prisoners.

Opposition to Gush Emunim and their ideology remained intense, in both secular and religious sectors of the population. The *Peace Now Movement continued to protest against the establishment of settlements in the West Bank, which it viewed as obstacles in the achievement of any peace agreement between Israel and Palestinians. Religious opposition groups, Oz Ve Shalom and Netivot Shalom, which stress religious values of peace and the need for interethnic mutual respect, rather than the territorialism and nationalism preached by the Gush, have remained small and without influence, owing to the general identification of the religious population with the Gush Emunim viewpoint. The Gush derided the opposition movements as "speakers" only and points to their "doing" as proof of their commitment to their cause. Opponents tended to be labeled as "*yefei nefesh*" ("genteel souls") and as traitors to the cause of "Greater Israel."

The Gush Emunim ideology is expounded in the monthly magazine *Nekudah* (and its occasional English version, *Counterpoint*), published by Mo'eẓet Yesha. Recent years have witnessed a surprising amount of academic research into Gush Emunim, focusing on the group's origins, ideological viewpoints, and the functioning of the settlement network.

The change in government in 1992 had a major impact on the West Bank settler population. On the one hand, much of the Gush Emunim political lobby was lost when the Teḥiyyah party failed to gain any seats in the new Knesset.

The Teḥiyyah failure was attributed, by many, to the decision of Rabbi Levinger and Daniela Weiss to run as a separate party list. This resulted in a split in the traditional Gush Emunim vote, with neither party obtaining any seats.

With the intensification of the peace talks under the Rabin government, new groups were established among the West Bank settlers to replace the now defunct Gush Emunim. These included the "Emunim" movement, supposed to represent the next generation of ideologically inspired settlers, but free of the traditional Gush leadership. In addition, national-religious rabbis of the West Bank settlements formed their own organization, aimed at providing "halakhically" inspired answers to the new political dilemmas facing the settlers. Their basic message was uncompromising, returning to the traditional national-religious argument that the Divine Right to the Land of Israel cannot be voted away by government. They provided religious backing for opposition to the Rabin government peace initiatives.

By 1992, the West Bank settler population (excluding East Jerusalem) had increased to beyond 100,000. Most of these continued to live in the communities and townships of Western Samaria, close to the metropolitan center of Israel. Particular emphasis was placed along the new west-east highway connecting Tel Aviv to the Jordan Valley. Along this route lies the expanding town of Ariel, as well as the ultra Orthodox township of Emanuel. The *Gush Etzyon region, to the south of Jerusalem, also underwent internal growth, centered around the township of Efrat. The West Bank settlement network itself was greatly affected by the change in government. The new planning priorities redirected resources out of the Administered Territories and back into Israel itself – especially into the Negev and Galilee. Settlers who had previously been beneficiaries of tax concessions, easy-term mortgages, low-priced land, by virtue of their living beyond the green line, now found themselves facing conditions equal to any other region in the country. In the Gaza Strip, *Gush Katif formed a network of settlements that would become the focus of Israel's disengagement in 2005.

For subsequent political events, see *Israel, State of: Historical Survey.

[David Newman]

BIBLIOGRAPHY: M. Kohn, *Who Is Afraid of Gush Emunim?* (1976); M. Aronoff, in: *Political Anthropology*, 3 (1985); E. Don-Yihya, in: *Middle Eastern Studies*, 24 (1988), 215–34; G. Goldberg and E. Ben-Zadok, in: *Middle Eastern Studies*, 22 (1986), 52–73; D. Newman, "The Role of Gush Emunim and the Yishuv Kehillati in the West Bank" (Ph. D. diss., University of Durham; 1981); idem, in: *Jerusalem Quarterly*, 39 (1986); D. Newman (ed.), *The Impact of Gush Emunim* (1985); idem, in: *Middle Eastern Studies*, 28 (1992), 509–30; Z. Ra'anan, *Gush Emunim* (Hebrew; 1980); E. Sprinzak, in: *Jerusalem Quarterly*, 21 (1981), 28–47; L. Weissbrod, in: *Middle Eastern Studies*, 18 (1982), 265–75.

GUSH ETZYON (Heb. גוש עציון; Etzyon Bloc), group of 15 settlements in the Judean hills, located between Jerusalem and Hebron. The population of Gush Etzyon was about 17,000 in 2004.

In 1947, at the outset of Israel's *War of Independence, Gush Etzyon consisted of four settlements: *Kefar Etzyon (the first settlement in the area, founded in 1943), *Massu'ot Yitzḥak, *Ein Tzurim, and *Revadim. From the end of 1947, Gush defenders were able to fight off frequent Arab attacks. A unit of 35 *Haganah and *Palmaḥ fighters (known to posterity as the "Lamed-He") sent from Jerusalem as reinforcements was intercepted and wiped out by the Arabs on January 17, 1948, and a relief convoy suffered heavy losses on March 27. The Arab Legion and large numbers of Arab irregulars began the final assault on May 12. Many of the 500 defenders, men and women, were massacred by an Arab mob after surrendering to the Legion and the Gush was razed.

Jewish settlement in Gush Etzyon was renewed in 1967 after the *Six-Day War. In September 1967 Kefar Etzyon was reestablished by a *Ha-Kibbutz ha-Dati group that included children of former settlers. A year later, in 1968, Har Gilo was founded, in 1970 Allon Shevut and Rosh Tzurim were added, and the rest were established over the next 20 years. There has been a general consensus in Israel that Gush Etzyon will remain part of Israel in any peace settlement.

The settlements of Gush Etzyon are as follows:

ALLON SHEVUT (Heb. אלון שבות), established in 1970 near the lone oak tree for which the settlement is named. The nucleus of the community was the Har Etzyon Yeshivah. In 2002 the population of Allon Shevut was 3,030.

BAT AYIN (Heb. בת עין), established in 1989. In 2002 the population was 685. Residents earned their livelihoods in a variety of ways: raising sheep, organic farming, computers, etc. The settlement was home to many artists.

EFRAT (Heb. אפרת), urban community with municipal council, established in 1983. In 2002 the population was 6,810, mainly religious.

ELEAZAR (Heb. אלעזר), established in 1976 by a group of American immigrants. The settlement began as a *moshav shittufi, but became an ordinary community. In 2002 the population was 796. The name commemorates *Eleazar ben Mattathias, brother of *Judah Maccabi, who was killed during the war with the Greeks in nearby Bet Zekharyah.

HAR GILO (Heb. הר גילה), established in 1968, and located on a hill overlooking Bethlehem, 3,027 ft. (923 m.) above sea level. The nucleus of the settlement was a field school run by the Nature Preservation Authority, around which the community developed. The settlement had a hostel with 400 beds, an information center for the birds and plants of Eretz Israel, and a school for army commanders. The population in 2002 was 357, religious and secular. Residents worked in Jerusalem.

KADAR (Heb. קדר), established in 1985 by a group from the *Betar movement. The settlement is located on the north-

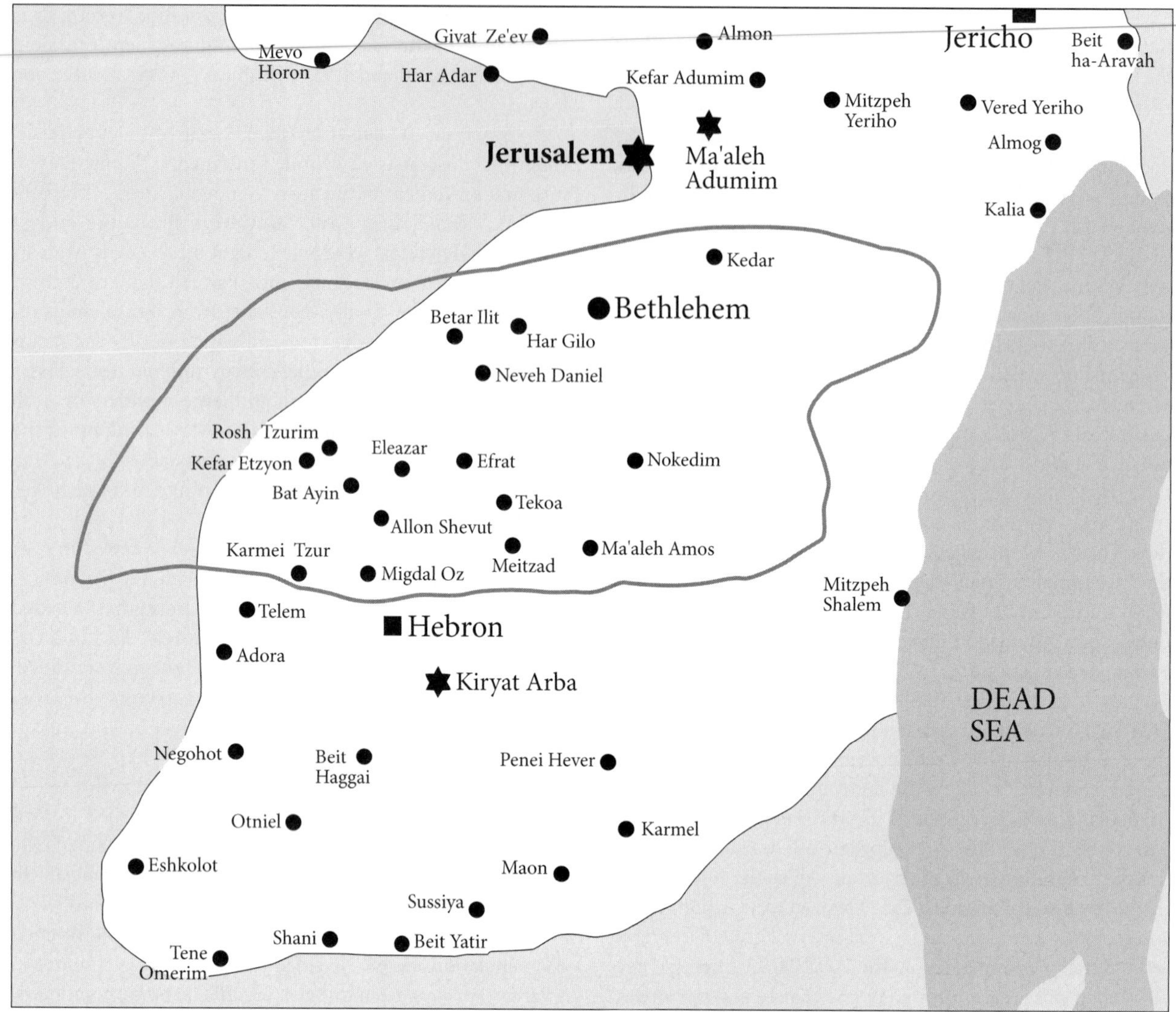

Gush Etzyon

eastern edge of the Gush, not far from *Ma'aleh Adumim. In 2002 the population was 585.

KARMEI TZUR (Heb. כרמי צור), established in 1984 by a group of Har Ezion yeshiva students. In 2002 the population was 579. The name of the settlement derives from the vineyards in its area and from nearby Tel Tzur, where the Hasmoneans fought against the Greeks.

KEFAR ETZYON (Heb. כפר עציון), religious kibbutz, reestablished in 1967. The kibbutz economy was based on farming and industry. In 2002 the population was 408.

MA'ALEH AMOS (Heb. מעלה עמוס), ultra-Orthodox community, established in 1982 by Esh ha-Torah yeshiva students. In 2002 the population was 258, mainly yeshivah students.

MEITZAD (Heb. מיצד) ultra-Orthodox community, established in 1984 with assistance from *Po'alei Agudat Israel. In 2002 the population was 218, many of them immigrants from the U.S., South Africa, France, and England. The men were mainly yeshivah students and the women worked in education.

MIGDAL OZ (Heb. מגדל עוז): religious kibbutz, established in 1977. In 2002 the population was 268. The kibbutz raised turkeys, dairy cattle, and field crops (together with the two other kibbutzim in Gush Etzyon) and had a packing house and a factory producing parts for airplanes.

NEVEH DANIEL (Heb. נווה דניאל), established in 1982. The settlement is located on the highest hill of the region, 3,254 ft. (992 m.) above sea level. In 2002 the population was 1,020. The majority of the population was employed outside the settlement.

NOKEDIM (Heb. נוקדים), established in 1982 by a group from nearby Tekoa. The settlement is located at the foot of *Herodium. In 2002 the population was 615. The name of the settlement derives from Amos 1:1 (*nokedim* = "herdsman"). Nearby there is an unauthorized settlement called Kefar Eldad (Heb. כפר אלדד), numbering 35 families.

ROSH TZURIM (Heb. ראש צורים), religious kibbutz, established in 1970 on the original site of Ein Tzurim (which was rebuilt in different location). In 2002 the population was 247. The main economic branches were field crops (together with the two other kibbutzim located in Gush Etzyon), dairy cattle, turkeys, and fruit orchards. The kibbutz owned the Mei Tzurim plant, which produced water filters.

TEKOA (Heb. תקוע), established in 1977 by a group of settlers affiliated with *Gush Emunim. In the 2002 the population was 1,040, religious and secular. Some residents worked outside the settlement, while others were employed in agriculture (mushrooms, dairy) inside Tekoa.

WEBSITE: www.gush-etzion-region.muni.il.

[Shaked Gilboa (2nd ed.)]

GUSH KATIF (Heb. גוש קטיף; Katif Bloc), group of 18 settlements in the *Gaza Strip. Their combined population in 2004 was about 7,800.

The Jewish settlement of Gush Katif aimed at creating a buffer zone in the face of terrorist attacks originating in the Gaza Strip following the *Six-Day War and at tactically controlling communications between the densely populated Arab sections of the Strip. The plan called for five "fingers" extending into the Strip. The first was located in northern Gaza and aimed at creating a belt of Jewish settlement from Ashkelon to the outskirts of Gaza city. The settlements Nisanit and Elei Sinai were established there. The second was located between Gaza city and Deir al-Balaḥ and included Netzarim. The third was located between Deir al-Balaḥ and Khan Yunis, and included the settlements Netzer Ḥazani, Katif, Kefar Darom, and Ganei Tal. The fourth "finger" was located between Khan Yunis and Rafa and included the settlements Gan Or, Gadid, Bedolaḥ, Atzmonah, Morag, Pe'at Sadeh, and Rafiaḥ Yam. The fifth finger, which was planned to connect the Rafa region with Sinai was not implemented. The plan was approved by the government and on October 11, 1970, Kefar Darom was established by a *Naḥal group. In February 1972 another Naḥal settlement was founded in Netzarim, and in September 1972 a third was established in Morag. Eight months later a fourth Nahal settlement was founded in Katif. In 1976 Katif became a civilian moshav. A year later, the name Katif was changed to Netzer Ḥazani, to commemorate Michael Ḥazani, the father of religious settlement. In 1978 a group of settlers established a new moshav, also called Katif. In 1979 Atzmonah and Ganei Tal were established. The remaining settlements were established in the 1980s, with Dugit the last in 1990. Netzarim became a civilian settlement in 1984, Bedolaḥ in 1986. Most residents earned their livelihoods from farming, with the area gaining fame for its hydroponically grown vegetables. Near Neveh Dekalim, an industrial area was established which included a garage, carpentry shop, press, etc.

During the years 1987–92, the years of the first Intifada, Gush Katif settlers suffered from Arab attacks, mainly stone throwing on the roads. Two Kefar Darom residents were killed. During these years all the settlements were expanded

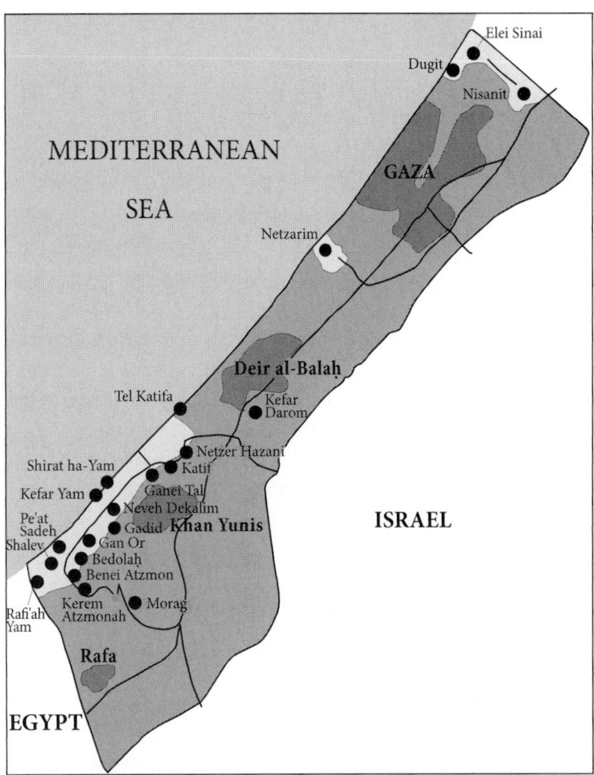

Gush Katif

and absorbed new residents. From October 2000, the start of the second, "al-Aqsa" Intifada, the settlements of Gush Katif came under constant terrorist attacks: gunfire, suicide bombers, and Kassam rockets. In this period, 4,000 shells hit the settlements and 12 people were killed. In 2003 Prime Minister Ariel *Sharon announced his intention to evacuate the settlements in the Gaza Strip, perceived by many as a drain on Israel's defense resources and serving no ostensible purpose. Following his declaration, the settlers began an intensive campaign to reverse the decision but to no avail. All Gush Katif settlements were evacuated in August 2005 and subsequently dismantled.

The Gush Katif settlements were as follows:

ATZMONAH (Benei Atzmon) (Heb. עצמונה), religious agricultural community, established in 1978. In the 2002 the population was 566. The main farming branches were dairy cattle, poultry, field crops, and plant nurseries.

BEDOLAḤ (Heb. בדולח), religious moshav, established in 1986 in affiliation with *Ha-Po'el ha-Mizrachi. In 2002 the population was 189, earning its livelihood in advanced greenhouse farming.

DUGIT (Heb. דוגית), established in 1990 in the northern Gaza strip, near the seashore. In 2002 the population was 65 inhabitants. Residents earned their livelihoods in various occupations connected with the sea.

ELEI SINAI (Heb. אלי סיני), established in 1983 by former *Yammit residents. Located in the northern Gaza Strip, 9 mi. (15 km.) south of Ashkelon, near the seashore. In 2002 the population was 347. Most of the residents were professional people.

GADID (Heb. גדיד), religious moshav, established in 1982. In 2002 the population was 298. Farming was mainly of the greenhouse variety.

GAN OR (Heb. גן אור), religious moshav, established in 1983 in affiliation with Ha-Po'el ha-Mizrachi. In 2002 the population was 274. Farming was based on greenhouses.

GANEI TAL (Heb. גני טל), religious moshav, established in 1979. In 2002 the population was 273. The main farming branches were organic and nonorganic vegetables, flowers, nursery plants, and herbs.

KATIF (Heb. קטיף), religious moshav, established in 1985. In 2002 the population was 338. The main farming branches were nursery plants, dairy, and organic vegetables.

KEFAR DAROM (Heb. כפר דרום), established in 1970. In 2002 the population was 324. Residents earned a living in farming, education, and various professions.

KEFAR YAM (Heb. כפר ים), established in 1983 on the remains of a holiday village operated by the Egyptian army. The settlement numbered just four families, who earned their living as greenhouse farmers and professionals.

MORAG (Heb. מורג), religious moshav, established in 1972 as a Naḥal settlement, became a civilian settlement in 1983. Affiliated with Ha-Po'el ha-Mizrachi. In 2002 the population was 170. Farming was mainly of the greenhouse variety.

NEVEH DEKALIM (Heb. נווה דקלים), religious community, established in 1983. Neveh Dekalim was the largest settlement in Gush Katif and served as an urban center for the rest of the settlements. In 2002 its population was 2,470.

NETZER ḤAZANI (Heb. נצר חזני), religious moshav, established in 1973. In 2002 the population was 316. Farming mainly took place in greenhouses.

NETZARIM (Heb. נצרים), established in 1972 as a Naḥal settlement, became a civilian community in 1984. Located in the center of the Gaza Strip. In 2002 the population was 409 inhabitants. Residents earned their livelihoods in farming, education, and the professions.

NISANIT (Heb. ניסנית), established in 1980 as a Naḥal settlement, became a civilian community in 1993. In 2002 the population was 1,000, working in the region's settlements.

PE'AT SADEH (Heb. פאת שדה), established in 1989. In 2002 the population was 110, religious and secular, most employed in farming.

RAFI'AḤ YAM (Heb. רפיח ים), established in 1984. In 2002 the population was 128 inhabitants, most employed in advanced greenhouse farming.

SHALEV (Heb. שליו), established in 1980 as a Naḥal settlement. In 2002 the population was composed of ten families of former Yammit residents.

In addition there were a number of unauthorized settlements in Gush Katif: Tel Katifa (Heb. תל קטיפא), established 1992, 15 families; Shirat ha-Yam (Heb. שירת הים), established 2001, six families; Kerem Atzmonah (Heb. כרם עצמונה), established 2001; five families.

BIBLIOGRAPHY: E. Buhadana and U. Yablonka, "*Mish'al Ḥayeikhem*" ("The Opinion Poll of Their Lives"), in: *Ma'ariv* (April 16, 2004); M. Friedman, "Life Goes on in Gaza," in: *The Jerusalem Report* (April 5, 2004). **WEBSITE:** www.katif.net.

[Shaked Gilboa (2nd ed.)]

GUSIKOW, JOSEPH MICHAEL (1802–1837), musician. Descendant of a long line of *klezmerim*, Gusikow, who was born in Shklov, Belorussia, first took up the flute but had to abandon it because of incipient consumption. He then constructed an improved xylophone consisting of 15 (later 29) tuned wooden staves, with a chromatic range of two-and-a-half octaves laid upon supports of tied straw and beaten with two thin sticks, which he called "Holz und Stroh." With this instrument he began to tour Russia and in the mid-1830s Austria, when he appeared before the emperor. His repertoire by now included many virtuoso and salon pieces originally written for the piano (including concertos), operatic arias, and – his specialty – extempore variations on arias, Jewish and gentile folk tunes, and even national anthems, all without having had a single music lesson. Society lionized him, and his orthodox earlocks became a ladies' fashion – the coiffure à la Gusikow. Concerts in Germany, France, and Belgium followed. In Leipzig, a Hebrew ode was published in his praise (1836). In Brussels his instrument and manner of playing were analyzed by the musicologist Fétis. Gusikow's illness had in the meantime grown worse. He died at Aachen. Lamartine, Félix *Mendelssohn-Bartholdy and his sister Fanny, as well as numerous other musicians of discernment, all attested to his virtuosity and creative power. The English writer Sacheverell Sitwell was therefore not exaggerating when he described Gusikow as "the greatest untaught or impromptu musician there had ever been." One of his tunes was published by Abraham Moses *Bernstein in *Muzikalisher Pinkes* (1927), p. 114.

BIBLIOGRAPHY: S. Sitwell, *Splendours and Miseries* (1943), 143–66; D. Sadan, *Ha-Menaggen ha-Mufla* (1947); Sendrey, Music, nos. 3529, 4098–98a, 5812–17.

[Bathja Bayer]

GUSINSKY, VLADIMIR ALEXANDROVICH (1952–), Russian businessman and Jewish communal figure. Gusinsky's grandfather was a victim of Stalinist terror (executed in 1937) and his grandmother spent nine years in Stalinist camps. Gusinsky graduated from the Gubkin Institute of the Oil and Gas Industry and the A. Lunacharsky State Institute of Theatrical Art. He then worked as a theater director in Tula and other cities. In the early 1980s he moved to Moscow, where he founded his first company in 1986. In 1988 Gusinsky created the Infax consulting firm, specializing in legal and financial counseling as well as providing political analysis to mostly foreign clients. In 1989 Infax and the Arnold and Potter law firm became partners, starting up the Most Bank in 1989 and the Most Group (Gruppa Most) holding company in 1992. In 1994 Gusinsky became vice president of the Russian Bank Association and in 1995 a member of the presidium of the Coordinating Council of the All-Russian Business Roundtable Union.

Gusinsky took an active part in the revival of Jewish communal life in post-Communist Russia. In January 1996 he was elected president of Russia's Jewish Congress (see *Russia) and in 2000 he became vice president of the World Jewish Congress for Eastern Europe and Russia.

In 1997 Gusinsky resigned as president of the Most Bank and became head of Media Most, embracing several TV companies (including NTV, the country's first privately owned station), the *Segodnia* newspaper, and some magazines. The media controlled by Gusinsky took an opposition stand during Putin's election campaign, vigorously criticizing his policy in the Chechnya conflict and his authoritarian tendencies. Gusinsky was promptly accused of economic crimes and in June 2000 was arrested, but he was released within a month and left for Spain. There he was placed under house arrest after the Russians requested his extradition, but was released in February 2001. Gusinsky resigned from the presidency of Russia's Jewish Congress and sold his shares in NTV to foreign investors (including Ted Turner). In August 2003, again accused of laundering money by the Russians, Gusinsky was arrested at Athens airport, but was released after a court hearing. The prolonged legal embroilments of the former media tycoon are typical of the misadventures of Russia's new "oligarchs."

[Naftali Prat (2nd ed.)]

GUSTON, PHILIP (1913–1980), U.S. painter. Born Philip Goldstein in Montreal, Canada, Guston moved with his Russian immigrant parents to Los Angeles when he was seven years old. At 14 he became interested in art and by 17 he began formal art training at the Otis Art Institute (1930), where he remained for three months.

Amalgamating the influences of the Mexican muralists, Italian Renaissance painters, and ultimately Cubism, Guston executed several murals for the Works Progress Administration's Federal Art Project. His murals include works for the 1939 World's Fair, the Queensbridge Housing Project in New York City (1940), and the Social Security Building in Washington, D.C. (1942).

In 1941–45 Guston was artist-in-residence at the State University of Iowa in Iowa City, followed by two years teaching at the School of Fine Arts at Washington University at Saint Louis. During this time, Guston assimilated aspects of abstraction and mythology, making gestural paintings comprised of short brushstrokes often in hatched configurations. By the 1950s Guston's entirely non-objective paintings were characterized by critics as "Abstract Impressionist" based on his heavily laid paint and lyrical use of color. After retrospectives at the Guggenheim (1962) and New York's Jewish Museum (1966), Guston boldly returned to figuration. Expressing a desire "to tell stories," Guston made blocky, cartoon-inspired narratives using a limited palette of pale colors, particularly salmon pink, white, black, and gray. In several of these paintings Guston included a hooded figure, often employed as a surrogate self-portrait. While he painted hooded Ku Klux Klan members in social realist works of the 1930s, the hooded figures that emerged in the late 1960s were influenced by the legend of the clay-sculpted Golem. Guston's noted body of work as both an abstract and a figurative artist makes him unique among 20th century painters.

BIBLIOGRAPHY: D. Ashton, *Yes, But ... A Critical Study of Philip Guston* (1976); R. Storr, *Philip Guston* (1986); J. Weber, *Philip Guston: A New Alphabet, The Late Transition* (2000); M. Auping, *Philip Guston: Retrospective* (2003).

[Samantha Baskind (2nd ed.)]

GUTENBERG, BENO (1889–1960), geophysicist. Born in Darmstadt, from 1912 to 1923 Gutenberg was assistant at the International Seismological Bureau at Strasbourg. He was then appointed teacher at Frankfurt University, where he became professor in 1926. In 1930 he emigrated to the U.S. to take up the position of professor of geophysics and meteorology at the California Institute of Technology, Pasedena, where in 1946 he became director of the Seismological Laboratory. Gutenberg was the president of the International Association for Seismology (1951–54) and a member of the National Academy of Sciences in Washington. As one of the outstanding seismologists of the last decades, he confirmed the occurrence of earthquakes down to depths of 375 mi. (600 km.) and was the originator of the hypothesis of continental spreading (Fliess theory). He carefully analyzed the available information on the earth's interior and made the first exact determination of the earth's core at 1812 mi. (2,900 km.) below the surface and detected the "asthenosphere channel" at a depth of 62–124 mi. (100–200 km.). This discovery had a critical influence on identifying elastic waves produced by large artificial explosions. He also investigated the nature of the atmosphere. On the basis of the research of Lindemann and Dobson, Gutenberg revolutionized existing conceptions. He maintained that at the height of 31 mi. (50 km.) the temperature was probably as high as on the earth's surface, and that the composition of the atmosphere remained unchanged up to a height of 94 mi. (150 km.). He contributed a lot to modern geophysical ideas on the earth's crust and mantle. Among his works are *Seismische Bodenunruhe* (1924), *Der Aufbau der Erde* (1925), *Grundlagen der Erdbebenkunde* (1927), *Lehrbuch der Geophysik* (1929), the important *Handbuch der Geophysik* (1930), *Seismicity of the Earth* (with C.F. Richter, 1941), *Internal Constitution of the Earth* (1939), and *Physics of the Earth's Interior* (1959).

BIBLIOGRAPHY: P. Byerly, in: *Science*, 131 (April 1960), 965–6; R. Stoneley, in: *Nature*, 186 (May 7, 1960), 433–4.

GUTFREUND, OTTO (1889–1927), Czech sculptor. Born in eastern Bohemia, Gutfreund was sent in his youth to study in Paris, and became a pioneer of cubism in sculpture. During World War I he joined the French Foreign Legion. His war experiences left a deep impression on his human and artistic development. Returning to Prague in 1920, he abandoned all earlier formalism and turned to simplified, stylized reality, choosing scenes from everyday life. Among his best work from the cubist period are *Anxiety* (1911), *Don Quixote* (1911), and *Hamlet* (1912). The period of his artistic maturity is best represented by the monumental group *Grandmother* (1922), the allegoric groups *Industry and Commerce* (1923), and the life-size statue of President Masaryk in Hradec Králové, which was removed when the Communists came to power in 1948. Gutfreund had probably a more profound influence on modern Czech sculpture than any other of his contemporaries.

BIBLIOGRAPHY: Wander, in: *Das Zelt*, 1 (1924–25), 244–7; V. Kramář et al., *Gutfreund* (Cz., 1927); *Otto Gutfreund* (Cz., 1948), includes reproductions; *Příruční slovník naučný*, 1 (1962), plate opp. p. 305, no. 8; 2 (1963), 66, s.v.

[Avigdor Dagan]

°**GUTHE, HERMANN** (1849–1936), German Old Testament scholar and researcher of Palestine. Born in May 1849 in Westerlinde (Braunschweig), he conducted his gymnasium studies at Wolffenbuettel, with theology studies between 1867 and 1870 at the universities of Goettingen and Erlangen. First working as a tutor, in 1877 he began his academic teaching at Leipzig, where he lived until his death. He served as the professor for Old Testament at the university from 1884 until his retirement in 1922.

Guthe was one of the most important and influential figures within German Palestine studies for more than 50 years. In 1877 he was one of the founders of the Deutscher Verein zur Erforschung Palaestinas (DPV), together with Albert Socin, Emil Kautzsch, Otto Kersten, and Conrad Fuerrer, serving from the beginning as its secretary and librarian. He was the founder and first editor of its periodical, the *Zeitschrift des deutschen Palaestina-Vereins* (ZDPV), until 1896, when he started editing for ten more years the Society's second publication, the *Mittheilungen und Nachrichten des Deutschen Palaestina-Vereins*. Always a member of the committee, he served between 1911 and 1925 as chairman. He was also responsible for recruiting some of the other prominent figures in the society, notably Peter Thomsen, a student of his who undertook the difficult bibliographical work.

Guthe gave the society its archaeological direction and he initiated most of its excavations. He visited Palestine three times, in 1881, 1904, and 1912, and there he made the acquaintance of the leading resident German scholars, Conrad Schick and Gottlieb Schumacher, recruiting them into the service of the Society. As a first step in a long partnership, Schick drew a map which was added to Guthe's first paper on Palestine dealing with the ruins of Ascalon, which was published in the first volume of the ZDPV. On his first visit he participated in excavations, mainly those in the Ophel. The 1904 visit gave him the opportunity to observe the works in Megiddo and to visit Madaba and copy the mosaic map.

His studies dealt mainly with questions and places of antiquity, concerning historical, geographic-topographical, and archaeological themes. He also wrote highly critical book reviews. Many of his papers were devoted to the results of new research. He was also lucky to be a witness to the sensational discovery of the Siloam inscription and was the only one to prepare a gypsum (plaster?) cast and to make a good drawing of it before it was removed, broken, and then taken to Constantinople.

Guthe published a number of geographical books, among them *Palaestina in Wort und Bild* (with Georg Ebers, 1883) and a monograph titled *Palaestina* (1908). He was also involved in the production of many maps of the country, historical as well as recent, mainly with Hans Fischer, the cartographer of the Society. Many of his contributions described processes, events, organizations, etc., existing in the country at that time. He wrote exegeses on various books of the Bible, issued a biblical atlas, and cooperated with Kautzsch on a biblical dictionary.

BIBLIOGRAPHY: For obituaries, see: A. Alt, "Hermann Guthe," in: ZDPV, 59 (1936), 177–80; C. Steuernagel, "Ein Rueckblick auf 50 Jahre der ZDPV," in: ZDPV, 51 (1928), 1–4; P. Thomsen, "Dt. theol. et phil. Hermann Guthe zum 10. Mai 1919," in: ZDPV, 42 (1919), 117–31; H. Bardtke, in: NDB, vol. 7, 343f.; F.W. Bautz, in: *Biographisch-Bibliographisches Kirchenlexikon*, 2 (1990).

[Haim Goren (2nd ed.)]

GUTHEIM, JAMES KOPPEL (1817–1886), U.S. Reform rabbi. Gutheim, trained in his native Westphalia as a teacher, immigrated to the United States around 1843. In 1846 he went to Cincinnati to become rabbi of B'nai Yeshurun Congregation (today the Isaac M. Wise Temple), then in 1850 accepted an invitation to become the leader of Shaare Chesed Congregation of New Orleans. In 1853 he became *ḥazzan* of the New Orleans Spanish-Portuguese Congregation, the Dispersed of Judah. After New Orleans was captured from the Confederacy, Gutheim refused to take the oath of allegiance to the Union and went into voluntary exile, serving the Jews of Montgomery, Alabama, and Columbus, Georgia, from 1863 to 1865. He returned to New Orleans after the war, and from 1868 preached in English at Temple Emanu-El of New York City. He was highly regarded as a pulpiteer in New York, and many of his sermons and addresses were printed in the *Jewish Times*, which published a volume of his efforts entitled *Temple Pulpit* (1872). Gutheim was the author of many hymns in English. He also prepared a translation of the fourth volume of Heinrich *Graetz's *History of the Jews*, of which the first five chapters were printed in the *Jewish Times* as early as 1869. The volume itself was published by the American Jewish Publication Society in 1874, marking the first appearance in America of Graetz's epoch-making book. Meanwhile, Gutheim had decided to return to New Orleans in 1872 to serve a new Reform congregation, Temple Sinai, which had been organized in 1870 and had already built a new synagogue, probably in order to attract Gutheim back to the city. Gutheim became the acknowledged leader of the Jews of New Orleans, and held important civic posts as well. He was a close friend and faithful supporter of Isaac Mayer *Wise in the development of the Union of American Hebrew Congregations and Hebrew Union College.

BIBLIOGRAPHY: B.W. Korn, *American Jewry and the Civil War* (1951), 47–50; *Early Jews of New Orleans* (1969), 251–4; L.C. Littman, *Stages in the Development of a Jewish Publication Society* (unpubl. M.A.H.L. thesis, Hebrew Union College - Jewish Institute of Religion, N.Y.C.), 75, 78–93; J.G. Heller, *As Yesterday When It Is Past* (1942), 32–41; M. Heller, *Jubilee Souvenir of Temple Sinai* (1922), 48–52; L. Shpall, in: *Louisiana Historical Quarterly*, 12 (1929), 461–7.

[Bertram Wallace Korn]

GUTHRIE, ARLO DAVY (1947–), U.S. folk singer. Guthrie was born in Coney Island, New York, to legendary songwriter and singer Woody Guthrie and Marjorie (Mazia), a professional dancer with the Martha Graham Company whose parents were Isidore and Aliza Greenblatt. Aliza was a Yiddish poet and songwriter, and took to her new son-in-law and became close with her grandson Arlo. "We would go to her home on Friday night for Shabbat dinner and she was a great cook," Guthrie said in a 2004 interview. "Nobody ever came close to her blintzes." In preparation for Guthrie's "hootenanny bar mitzvah" in 1960, his parents hired a "sweet young rabbi" as a tutor, Guthrie recalled, named Meir *Kahane, later the founder of the Jewish Defense League and the Kach political party in Israel.

Surrounded by his father's musician friends, including Pete Seeger, Leadbelly, and Jewish folk musician Ramblin' Jack Elliott (Elliot Adnopoz), and then by the burgeoning New York folk-rock crowd of Bob *Dylan, Joan Baez, and Phil *Ochs, Guthrie learned to play the guitar at age six and grew up naturally influenced toward a musical career. In December 1967, two months after his father died, Guthrie released the album *Alice's Restaurant Massacre*, an 18-minute 20-second narrative song about his getting arrested for littering on Thanksgiving Day two years earlier, and how his police record and court appearance for dumping garbage in Great Barrington, Massachusetts, prevented him from being drafted by the army. The album was the only one of 19 he produced that went gold. Guthrie went on to star in the 1969 film version of *Alice's Restaurant*, which was released a week after he appeared at the Woodstock Music Festival on August 15. At Woodstock, he sang and subsequently released a recording of "Coming into Los Angeles," about smuggling marijuana, which became another hit. His other noteworthy songs were a 1972 cover version of Jewish country-folksinger Steve Goodman's song "City of New Orleans," Guthrie's only hit single, and "The Motorcycle Song."

Like his father, Guthrie carved out a career as a folksinger and songwriter with a social conscience, touring 10 months of the year and working for causes such as environmentalism. Guthrie launched his own record label, Rising Son Records, in 1983. He has also acted, and wrote successful children's books.

In 1991, Guthrie bought the church building that served as the centerpiece of *Alice's Restaurant* and converted it to the Guthrie Center and the Guthrie Foundation, named for his parents. It is an interfaith foundation and meeting place that provides a wide range of local and international services.

Guthrie also performed Hanukkah, Holocaust, and Jewish children's songs that were written by his father and discovered after his death, and were set to music by the Klezmatics.

[Elli Wohlgelernter (2nd ed.)]

GUTMAN, ALEXANDER B. (1902–1973), U.S. physician. Born in New York City, he was educated in the U.S. and Austria. From 1951 he served as director of the department of medicine and physician in chief of New York's Mount Sinai Hospital. On his retirement in 1968 he was appointed professor of medicine at the Mount Sinai School of Medicine. Gutman was editor in chief of the *American Journal of Medicine* which he founded in 1946. He was also associate editor of the classic Cecil-Loeb *Textbook of Medicine* (1950–60). He served on many advisory boards and professional societies.

Gutman introduced the acid phosphatase test for prostatic cancer. He became one of the world's authorities on gout and his research into its cause and treatment resulted in new insights into this disease and brought him many honors, prizes, and awards. He made major contributions toward the understanding of the pathophysiology of purine metabolism.

BIBLIOGRAPHY: *National Cyclopaedia of American Biography*, 1 (1960), 190.

[Fred Rosner]

GUTMAN, CHAIM ("Der Lebediker"/"The Lively One"; 1887–1961), Yiddish humorist and theater critic. Born in Petrikov (Belorussia), he immigrated to the U.S. in 1905, where he became successful as a writer of epigrams and sketches for numerous periodicals, particularly the humorous journals *Der Kibetser* and *Der Kundes* (which he later edited), and wrote humor columns, as well as theater reviews, for New York Yiddish dailies. His language was rich, vivid, and colloquial, an American East-Side Yiddish employing some Anglicisms for local color. His sketches *Azoy hot geret Pompadur* ("Thus Spake Pompadour," 1918), were followed by seven more humorous collections. A two-act comedy *Meshiekh oyf Ist Brodvey* ("Messiah on East Broadway") was occasionally staged. His sketches enriched the repertoire of Yiddish comedians for several decades.

BIBLIOGRAPHY: Rejzen, Leksikon, 1 (1926), 544–9; LNYL, 2 (1958), 177–80; A. Mukdoni (ed.), *Zamelbukh... Der Lebediker* (1938).

[M.Rav./ Jerold C. Frakes (2nd ed.)]

GUTMAN, ISRAEL (1923–), historian of the Holocaust. Gutman was born in Warsaw, Poland. He was a member of the Ha-Shomer ha-Ẓa'ir Zionist youth movement, active in the Jewish underground in the Warsaw ghetto, and fought in the Warsaw Ghetto Uprising. In the aftermath of the uprising he was imprisoned in Majdanek and then in Auschwitz-Birkenau and Mauthausen. He immigrated to Palestine in 1947, where he settled on kibbutz Lehavot ha-Bashan. In 1961 he testified at the trial of Adolf Eichmann in Jerusalem. Gutman studied at the Hebrew University of Jerusalem, receiving his Ph.D. in 1975 with a dissertation on the Warsaw ghetto. He served as director of research at Yad Vashem (1975–83), and headed its Academic Committee for many years. He is professor emeritus of the Institute of Contemporary Jewry of the Hebrew University, where he also served as head (1983–85). Gutman was a founder of Moreshet, Anielewicz Memorial Center, academic advisor to the United States Holocaust Memorial Council, a member of the Academic Committee of the United States Holocaust Memorial Museum, founding head of the International Institute for Holocaust Research at Yad Vashem (1993–96), chief historian of Yad Vashem (1996–2002), academic advisor to Yad Vashem (2002–), a member of the International Auschwitz Council (2000–), the initiator and editor of the *Encyclopedia of the Holocaust* (1990), and chief historical consultant to the new Holocaust History Museum at Yad Vashem. In 2002 Gutman received the prestigious Landau Award for Science and Research for his work in the field of the Holocaust and Israeli history.

Gutman was one of the most influential historians of the Holocaust in the world. He was part of the small group of survivor historians of the subject, but stood out as one of the most prominent and significant among them. His meticulous and thorough research, sharp analytical skills, deep insight, and lucid writing made him one of the most sought-after scholars to participate actively in advisory committees, editorial boards, research groups, and conferences. He played a seminal role in laying the foundations and building the edifice for Holocaust studies in Israel. It can be said that Gutman had a major influence in the articulation of what might be called the "Jerusalem School" of Holocaust scholarship, which sees the Jews as a subject of history and not only as a victim of Nazi actions, and therefore sets out to identify, find, and utilize Jewish documentation in order to tell the story of the Jews during the Holocaust. His research reflects this approach, and indeed, his book, *The Jews of Warsaw 1939–1943*, is a prime example of this historical school's approach. The book is the standard text for anyone wishing to study or teach about the Jews of Warsaw during the Holocaust.

Gutman had a profound influence on the study of the day-to-day lives of the Jews under Nazi rule; the ghettos; the Judenraete and their varied policies regarding the Jewish communities and labor under the Nazis; the concept of *Amidah*, which might be loosely translated as resilience and unarmed resistance; understanding the changes in roles between the traditional Jewish leadership and the youth movement activists in many places, and hence the significant role of youth movements in Jewish underground activity; the understanding of the centrality of antisemitism to the Nazis and to Nazi planning of anti-Jewish policy; and more.

One of Gutman's contributions to Holocaust scholarship was to articulate the uniqueness of the Holocaust, which he saw in the singular combination of factors that enabled the Holocaust to happen: historical antisemitism; the demonic view of the Jews in Europe; the Jews' prolonged exilic existence and their protracted and persistent persecution by Christianity; the biological racial view the Nazis had of the Jews, which saw the Jews as an immutable danger of cosmic significance; and Germany's defeated and weak status in the aftermath of World War I.

Gutman has advocated and taught meticulous empirical research in all relevant languages, both of official German documentation and of Jewish documents from the period and later, as well as documentation from local non-Jewish populations. According to Gutman, oral history is an important source which, although it needs to be read carefully and critically as well as corroborated in the same way as other documentation, is integral to trying to gain a fuller picture and understanding of events. Many scholars who began as his students have gained prominence in their own right in various universities and research institutes.

After the collapse of communism in Poland, Gutman became a celebrity there, sought after for advice, articles, conferences, committees, public lectures, and awards. In 1995 he received an honorary doctorate from Warsaw University, an event that he saw as bearing great symbolic significance, as this was a place, as he put it, into whose hallowed halls he could not have wished to enter when he was a Jewish citizen of Poland.

Gutman published numerous books and articles. Among his major books are *The Jews of Warsaw 1939–1943: Ghetto, Underground, Revolt* (1977; Eng., 1982); *The Catastrophe of European Jewry* (edited with Livia Rothkirchen, 1976); *Documents on the Holocaust* (edited with Yitzhak Arad and Avraham Margaliot, 1978; Eng., 1981); *The Nazi Concentration Camps* (edited with Avital Saf, 1984); *The Jews in Poland After the Second World War* (Heb., 1985); *Unequal Victims: Poles and Jews During World War Two* (with Shmuel Krakowski, 1986); *Encyclopedia of the Holocaust* (editor, 1990); Emanuel Ringelblum's *Diary and Notes from the Warsaw Ghetto: September 1939–December 1942* and *Last Writings: Polish-Jewish Relations; January 1943–April 1944* (Heb.; edited with Joseph Kermish and Israel Shaham, 1992 and 1994); *Anatomy of the Auschwitz Death Camp* (edited with Michael Berenbaum, 1994); *Resistance: The Warsaw Ghetto Uprising* (1994); and *Holocaust and Memory*, a textbook (Heb., 1999).

BIBLIOGRAPHY: Y. Sheleg, "Being There," in: *Haaretz* (April 25, 2003); "Yisrael Gutman Talks to Daniel Blatman: Youth and Resistance Movements in Historical Perspective," in: *Yad Vashem Studies*, 23 (1993), 1–71.

[David Silberklang (2nd ed.)]

GUTMAN, NAHUM (1898–1980), Israeli painter and sculptor. Gutman was born in Telenshty, Bessarabia. In 1905 the Gutman family immigrated to Ereẓ Israel, settling in Aḥuzat Bayit (on the site of modern Tel Aviv). He began his art studies in 1913 at the Bezalel School of Arts and Crafts in Jerusalem and in 1920 continued in Vienna at the School of Arts and Crafts. In 1926–28 Gutman participated in two exhibitions that were of great significance in Israeli art history: the Tower of David exhibition, which expressed the Bezalel spirit, and the Modern Artists' Exhibition at the Ohel Theater in Tel Aviv, which proclaimed a new direction in art.

Gutman was one of Israel's best-known artists and a well-known writer. In 1939 he began to publish his own books, which he wrote as well as illustrated. He was chosen to represent Israel in the Venice Biennial and participated in many exhibitions all over the world. Gutman had a great influence on Israeli children through his books and the articles he published in the children's newspaper *Davar Li-Yeladim*. In 1962 one of his books, *Path of Orange Peels*, was awarded the Hans Christian Andersen Literary Prize on behalf of UNESCO. The link between his art and the child's world can be seen in his art style, which integrates a Naive method of drawing with colorful compositions. Gutman made a great impression on the city of Tel Aviv. Many of the monumental buildings of the city are decorated with his mosaic walls (*Homage to Tel Aviv*, Shalom Tower, Tel Aviv).

Gutman was among those artists who painted the Arab figures that peopled their surroundings in the 1920s. In some of his paintings he depicted scenes of daily life in a rural landscape or in Jaffa's orchards, painting Arabs in their daily occupations, as in *The Goatherd* (1926, Israel Museum, Jerusalem) or *The Bearer of Sheaves* (1927, Israel Museum, Jerusalem). In these paintings the Arab workers were greatly magnified: their bodies extended over the entire canvas, their postures recalled old Egyptian figures, their clothes were painted in graceful colors, and they came off looking very admirable. It is clear that Gutman saw them as models for the new pioneer immigrants who were novice farmers in their old-new land. After the riots of 1929, his manner of depiction changed and the drawings became more realistic.

Gutman's small clay sculptures look as if they stepped out of his paintings. Although in sculpture it is difficult to capture the look of a moment or create a living expression, Gutman succeeded in this, producing humoristic figures (*Neighbor's Quarrel*, 1970, Gutman Museum, Tel Aviv).

BIBLIOGRAPHY: Gutman Museum, *Nahum Gutman 1898–1980* (2003); idem, *Gutman Visits the Realms of Evil* (2000).

[Ronit Steinberg (2nd ed.)]

GUTMANN, AMY (1949–), political philosopher and educator. Gutmann was born in Brooklyn, New York, and earned her bachelor's degree from Harvard University (Radcliffe College, 1971), her master's degree from the London School of Economics and Political Science (1972), and her doctorate from Harvard (1976). She taught at Princeton University from 1976, entering as an assistant professor; she became an associate professor in 1981 and professor of politics in 1987. She was the Laurance S. Rockefeller University Professor of Politics and the University Center for Human Values from 1990 to 2004, and she was provost at Princeton from 2001 until 2004. Her appointment as provost under Princeton president Shirley Tilghman marked the second time in the history of the Ivy League that two women had served simultaneously as president and provost. Gutmann was the founding director of the University Center for Human Values at Princeton, and she chaired the executive committee of Princeton University Press. In 2004 she was named president of the University of Pennsylvania.

Gutmann's scholarly work centers on moral and political philosophy, practical ethics, liberalism, and the moral challenges of democracy. Her widely cited *Democratic Education* (1987) discusses the potential incompatibilities of the principles of democracy with a belief in the rights of the individual. Her other works include *Liberal Equality* (1980), *Color Conscious: The Political Morality of Race* (with Anthony Appiahand, 1996), *Democracy and Disagreement* (with Dennis Thompson, 1996), and *Identity in Democracy: A Humanist View* (2003). *Color Conscious*, which explores ethnic and cultural pluralism, was praised as a significant contribution to social philosophy. In *Democracy and Disagreement*, Gutmann and Thompson present the concept of "deliberative democracy" as a moral alternative to discord. Her books have been translated into numerous languages, including French, Italian, Japanese, Swedish, and Hebrew. Her many essays have appeared in such journals as *Ethics*, *Philosophy and Public Affairs*, and *Political Theory*.

Gutmann served as president of the American Society of Political and Legal Philosophy from 2001 to 2004. She was a fellow of the American Academy of Arts and Sciences, the W.E.B. DuBois Fellow of the American Academy of Political and Social Science, and a fellow of the National Academy of Education. In 2000 she received the President's Distinguished Teaching Award from Princeton University, and in 2003 she was awarded Harvard's Centennial Medal for "exceptional contributions to society." Her numerous awards and honors also include the Ralph J. Bunche Award and the North American Society for Social Philosophy Book Award (both in 1997, for *Color Conscious*), the Gustavus Myers Human Rights Award (1997), and the Bertram Mott Award from the American Association of University Professors (1998).

[Dorothy Bauhoff (2nd ed.)]

GUTMANN, DAVID MEIR (1827–1894), Ereẓ Israel pioneer. Born in Hungary in 1827, Gutmann fought in the Hungarian War of Independence in 1848, but was disillusioned by the Hungarian attitude toward Jews. In 1876 he sold his property and settled with his wife in Ereẓ Israel. In Jerusalem he was influenced by the visionary ideas of his friend Akiva Yosef *Schlesinger, gave large donations to charitable institutions, took part in land purchase and the establishment of new quarters outside the walls of the Old City, and also searched for land for agricultural settlement, despite the objection of several rabbis. He joined a group of Jerusalemites who, when they failed in attempts to purchase land near Jericho, acquired the Mullabis lands by the Yarkon River in 1878 and established

Petaḥ Tikvah there. Gutmann was one of the founders of the settlement and suffered greatly on its behalf. He sold all his property in Jerusalem to pay the settlement's debts and conduct its law cases with the previous landowners. In his old age he was greatly impoverished. He died in Jaffa and was buried in Jerusalem.

BIBLIOGRAPHY: Tidhar, 1 (1947), 304; EẒD, 1 (1958), 457–9; G. Kressel, *Em ha-Moshavot Petaḥ Tikvah* (1953), ch. 5.

[Galia Yardeni-Agmon]

GUTMANN, EUGEN (1840–1925), German banker. Born in Dresden, the son of an old-established banking family, Gutmann, together with several partners, took over the banking house of Michael *Kaskel and formed the Dresdner Bank. After initial difficulties a branch which had been opened in Berlin came under Gutmann's guidance. He developed it into a leading national and international financial institution with worldwide interests that included railways in Turkey, mining in Bohemia, and banking in Latin America. Gutmann directed the bank for more than 40 years. Germany's defeat in 1918 and the subsequent economic collapse broke Gutmann's health, and in 1920 he retired.

BIBLIOGRAPHY: S. Kaznelson, *Juden im deutschen Kulturbereich* (1959), 743–5; NDB, 7 (1966).

[Joachim O. Ronall]

GUTMANN, JOSEPH (1923–2004), U.S. art historian. Gutmann, who was born in Wuerzburg, Germany, immigrated to Philadelphia with his parents in 1936 after the rise of the Nazis. He served in the army as a chaplain and interpreter from 1943 to 1946. Gutmann earned a B.A. from Temple University and an M.A. from New York University's Institute of Fine Arts. At Hebrew Union College in Cincinnati he received a doctorate in Jewish history and a rabbinical degree.

After teaching at Hebrew Union College and the University of Cincinnati, he was appointed professor of art history at Wayne State University, Detroit, in 1969. A pioneer in the field of Jewish art, he wrote or edited 19 books, including *Images of the Jewish Past: An Introduction to Medieval Hebrew Miniatures* (1965), *Beauty in Holiness: Studies in Jewish Customs and Ceremonial Art* (1970), and *Hebrew Manuscript Painting* (1978).

[Samantha Baskind (2nd ed.)]

GUTMANN, JOSHUA (1890–1963), scholar of Jewish Hellenism. Born in Belorussia, Gutmann studied with Chaim *Tchernowitz (Rav Ẓa'ir) in Odessa at the Slobodka Yeshivah, at Baron Guenzburg's Institute of Oriental (i.e., Jewish) Studies, and at the universities of St. Petersburg, Odessa, and Berlin. From 1916 to 1921 he taught in Odessa, and from 1921 to 1923 he was principal of the Hebrew Teachers' Seminary in Vilna. He settled in Berlin in 1923 and in 1925 joined the editorial board of the German *Encyclopaedia Judaica* and that of the Hebrew encyclopedia *Eshkol*, contributing hundreds of articles in a wide range of Jewish subjects; he also lectured at the Hochschule (Lehranstalt) fuer die Wissenschaft des Judentums. Gutmann emigrated to Palestine in 1933, at first teaching in the Reali school in Haifa and later becoming head of the Hebrew Teachers' Seminary in Jerusalem. From 1942 to 1953 Gutmann served on the editorial staff of the biblical encyclopedia *Enẓiklopedyah Mikra'it* and from 1946 to 1961 on that of the *Encyclopaedia Hebraica*. In 1949 he began teaching Jewish-Hellenistic studies at the Hebrew University. In 1954 with M. *Schwabe he founded *Eshkolot*, a periodical for classical studies, serving as its sole editor from 1956.

Gutmann's main work in Jewish Hellenism was the first two volumes of *Ha-Sifrut ha-Yehudit ha-Hellenistit* (1958, 1963), which deal with the beginnings of that literature. He also contributed to Hebrew, Russian, and English periodicals and to several Festschriften; he edited with M. Schwabe the Hans Lewy memorial volume, *Sefer Yoḥanan Levi* (1949). Gutmann's wide-ranging scholarship in both Judaism and the classics enabled him to make significant contributions to the understanding of the Hellenistic period in Jewish history and literature. He gave fresh insight into the Greek philosophers' interest in Judaism, which was an important element in the growth of Jewish Hellenism.

BIBLIOGRAPHY: A. Fuks, S. Safrai, and M. Stern, *Al Profesor Yehoshu'a Gutmann* (1964), includes bibliography.

[Moshe David Herr]

GUTMANN, WILHELM, RITTER VON (1825–1895), Austrian industrialist and philanthropist. Born in Lipnik (Leipnik, Moravia) and a pupil of the yeshivah there, he began his career as a commission agent in the coal business. Subsequently, in partnership with his brother DAVID (1834–1912), he founded the firm of Gebrueder Gutmann (1853) which eventually controlled the bulk of the Austro-Hungarian coal trade, at first selling imported coal and later acquiring and developing coal seams in the Ostrava basin and in Galicia, thereby improving considerably the monarchy's trade balance. The Witkowitz Steel Works, which they established, developed into one of the outstanding firms on the continent, numbering the Viennese *Rothschilds and members of the nobility among its partners; after 1918 it became a joint-stock company. Following the Munich agreement (1938), lengthy negotiations took place between the Nazis and the Gutmann and Rothschild families; a price of £10,000,000 was offered but the deal was never concluded. The company became part of the Hermann Goering concern without being owned by it. After World War II, it became a Czechoslovakian state-owned enterprise.

Founder of the Oesterreichischer Industriellenklub and a member of the board of the Creditanstalt, Wilhelm was a member of the Lower Austrian Diet, where he supported German liberalism. Both brothers were knighted, Wilhelm in 1878 and David a year later. The Gutmanns were also active in Jewish affairs, Wilhelm as president of the Vienna Jewish community (1891–92) and David as head of the Israelitische Allianz in Vienna and the Baron de *Hirsch school fund for Galicia. They were cofounders of the *Israelitisch-Theologische Lehranstalt. Both gave generous support to Jewish and non-Jewish philanthropic institutions: among the Jewish foundations they established and supported were an orphanage for girls at Doebling, a childrens' hospital in Vienna, an institution for the crippled at Krems, and an old-age home in Lipnik. They defrayed Joseph *Bloch's expenses in the Bloch-*Rohling trial. In 1891 Ritter published his autobiography, *Aus meinem Leben.*

MAX GUTMANN (1857–1930), Wilhelm's son, studied mining engineering at Leoben Academy (Austria), gaining a worldwide reputation in the field and publishing several books on it. He was also an authority on labor relations and a pioneer in social insurance.

BIBLIOGRAPHY: H. Gold, *Geschichte der Juden in Maehren* (1929), index; *Neue deutsche Biographie*, 7 (1966), 347–8; R. Hilberg, *The Destruction of the European Jews* (1967[2]), 66–72; K. Kratochvil, *Banki* (1962), index.

[Meir Lamed]

GUTNICK, family of Australian rabbis. Rabbi CHAIM GUTNICK (1921–2003) was probably the best-known Orthodox rabbi in Australia during the last third of the 20th century. Born in Palestine, Gutnick's family fled to England after the 1929 riots, and then lived in Eastern Europe, managing to escape to Australia during World War II. Gutnick was for many years head of the Elwood Orthodox synagogue in Melbourne and was president of the Orthodox Rabbinical Association of Australia. He was close to the Lubavitcher movement, although never directly associated with a Lubavitcher synagogue. Several of his relatives became well-known Australian rabbis, including Sholem Gutnick, head of the Caulfield Hebrew Congregation in Melbourne. Gutnick's last years were marked by a dispute over the Melbourne Orthodox *Beth Din* and demands for its reconstitution. Chaim Gutnick's younger son JOSEPH (1953–), also an Orthodox rabbi, became internationally prominent in the 1990s after amassing a fortune in diamond mining. Joseph Gutnick appeared in the annual Australian "Rich Lists" from the 1990s, being credited with a fortune of A$100 million (U.S. $60 million) in 2000. He became noted for his generous donations to Israel's *Likud political party and, most unusually, was also president of the Melbourne Australian Rules Football club. In the early 2000s he was widely publicized in the Australian Jewish and general press when he sued his sister and brother-in-law, the heads of Sydney's Yeshiva College, to recover funds he allegedly lent them.

BIBLIOGRAPHY: D.H. Bernstein, *Diamonds and Demons: The Joseph Gutnick Story* (2000).

[William D. Rubinstein (2nd ed.)]

GUTT, CAMILLE (1884–1971), Belgian statesman. Born in Brussels, Gutt qualified as a lawyer and joined the Liberal Party. At the end of World War I he was appointed secretary-general to the Belgian delegation to the Reparations Commission and from 1920 to 1924 was chief secretary to the minister of finance. Gutt himself was minister of finance from 1934 to 1935 and from 1939 to 1940 when Belgium was overrun by the Germans. He escaped with the rest of the Belgian cabinet to Britain and held various ministerial posts in the Belgian government in exile until the Liberation. From 1946 to 1951 he was managing director of the International Monetary Fund.

GUTTMACHER, ALAN F. (1898–1974), U.S. professor of obstetrics and proponent of world population control. Born and educated in Baltimore, Maryland, he served as clinical professor of obstetrics and gynecology at Columbia University's College of Physicians and director of the department of obstetrics and gynecology at New York's Mount Sinai Hospital until 1962 when he became president of the Planned Parenthood Federation of America, and in 1964 chairman of the medical committee of the International Planned Parenthood Federation (1964–68).

Guttmacher lectured and wrote extensively on the subject of world population control. His later books on the subject include *Babies by Choice or by Chance* (1959); *Pregnancy and Birth* (1962); *Planning your Family* (1965); and *Birth Control and Love* (1969).

[Fred Rosner]

GUTTMACHER, ELIJAH (1795–1874), rabbi and forerunner of the Ḥibbat Zion movement. Born in Borek, district of Posen, Guttmacher studied at various yeshivot, the most outstanding of which was that of R. Akiva *Eger in Posen. He also studied Kabbalah and acquired a good knowledge of German and general subjects. From 1822 he was the rabbi of Pleschen, and from 1841 until his death he served as rabbi in Grodzisk Wielkopolski (Graetz). His great erudition and his way of life, which was akin to that of the Ḥasidim in Eastern Europe, made his name famous in the Jewish world, and a stream of visitors made their pilgrimage to him, as to a ḥasidic *rebbe*, to obtain amulets for the cure of diseases and the solution of personal problems. To end this kind of veneration, he published a request asking people to refrain from approaching him on such matters; these appeals, however, were of no avail and he acquired the unsought position of the *rebbe* of West European Ḥasidim.

Guttmacher's inclination to mysticism and his preoccupation with problems affecting the Jews of his time led him to ponder the idea of redemption and its practical realization as a solution to the misery of the Jews. He was one of a small minority of rabbis who, despite their belief in the Messiah, did not think that the Jewish people should wait for the coming of redemption passively, but rather should do all in their power to hasten redemption by engaging in constructive work in Ereẓ Israel. Thus Guttmacher lent his support to Ẓ.H. *Kalischer's efforts to organize potential settlers for Ereẓ Israel and propagated the idea in his letters and articles. He wrote,

> It is an error to believe that everyone will live his life in the usual manner and suddenly, one day, the gates of mercy will open, miracles will happen on heaven and earth, all the proph-

> ecies will be fulfilled, and all will be called from their dwelling places. This is not so, I say, and I add, that settling in the Holy Land – making a beginning, redeeming the sleeping land from the Arabs, observing there the commandments that can be observed in our day – making the land bear fruit, purchasing land in Ereẓ Israel to settle the poor of our people there – this is an indispensable foundation stone for complete redemption.

He reiterated this theme, or variations thereof, repeatedly and this provided invaluable support to the budding Ḥibbat Zion movement, which was opposed by both Orthodox and assimilationist rabbis. Guttmacher left behind many works on talmudic and kabbalistic subjects, only a small portion of which have appeared in print (many of the manuscripts are stored in Jerusalem archives). Among his works are novellae on the *mishnayot* and the *Gemara* contained in the Talmud edition published by Romm; *Ẓafenat Pa'ne'aḥ* (1875), a book devoted to the tales of Rabbah b. Ḥana as told in *Bava Batra; Sukkat Shalom* (1883); and *Shenot Eliyahu* (1879); the latter two books are linked to the study groups established in Jerusalem at his inspiration.

BIBLIOGRAPHY: N. Sokolow, *Hibbath Zion* (Eng., 1934), 17–28; A.I. Bromberg, *Ha-Rav Eliyahu Guttmacher* (1969); EẒD, 1 (1958), 448–56.

[Getzel Kressel]

GUTTMACHER, MANFRED (1898–1966), U.S. criminologist and psychiatrist. His career was devoted to the study of the mentally disturbed, maladjusted offender. Born in Baltimore, he graduated from Johns Hopkins University in 1923. From 1930 to 1960 he was chief medical officer of the Supreme Court of Baltimore. He held the rank of colonel in the U.S. Army Medical Corps during World War II (1942–46), and served as chief psychiatric consultant to the Second Army. During 1948 he served as scientific adviser to the United Nations Social Commission dealing with the causes and prevention of crime and the treatment of offenders. He taught at Johns Hopkins University, the University of Maryland, and at a number of other universities. His works include *Sex Offenses* (1961), *Psychiatry and the Law* (1952), and *Mind of the Murderer* (1960).

[Zvi Hermon]

GUTTMAN, LOUIS (Eliahu; 1916–1987), sociologist. Born in New York, he was educated at the University of Minnesota, where he taught from 1936 to 1940. From 1941 to 1950 he taught at Cornell University; during the years 1941–45 he also served as an expert consultant to the U.S. War Department in the information and education division. A member of the Labor Zionist movement from his early youth, Guttman moved to Israel in 1947, where he founded and became the director of the Israel Institute of Applied Social Research, a position he held throughout his life. The institute was later renamed the Louis Guttman Institute of Applied Social Research. He was appointed professor at the Hebrew University in 1954, where he taught social and psychological assessment. Guttman's reputation rests on his work in methodology. The Guttman scale, which is described in "A Revision of Chapin's Social Status Scale," *American Sociological Review* (1942), ranks items in such a way that the statements appearing at the top of the scale must also check all the preceding ones. This is done by taking a number of random samples of population and then ranking the statements in the order in which they are consistently chosen by the respondents. Other contributions by Guttman appeared in P. Horst (ed.), *Prediction of Personal Adjustment* (1941); S.A. Stouffer (ed.), *Measurement and Prediction* (1949); and in P.L. Lazarsfeld (ed.), *Mathematical Thinking in the Social Sciences* (1954). The last contains Guttman's original approach to testing-factor analysis, the radex. The major difference between the radex and older forms of factor analysis is that it deals with the order of the factors, not just the common factors. The radex involves the notion that there is a difference in kind and a difference in degree between the tests used for analysis.

In 1971, Guttman was listed in the journal *Science* as one of the 62 most important contributors to scientific research in the social sciences since the beginning of the 20th century. He was a fellow of the Center for Advanced Study in the Behavioral Sciences (Stanford, 1955–56). Awards he received include the Rothschild Prize (1962); the Outstanding Achievement Award from the Regents of the University of Minnesota (1974); the Israel Prize in the social sciences (1978); and the Educational Testing Service Measurement Award from Princeton (1984).

Guttman wrote *What Is Not in Statistics* (1976); *The Impact of Sadat in Jerusalem on the Israeli Jew* (1977); and *Theory Construction and Data Analysis in the Behavioral Sciences* (with S. Shye, 1978).

ADD. BIBLIOGRAPHY: *Louis Guttman on Theory and Methodology: Selected Writings* (1994); *Louis Guttman in Memoriam: Chapters from an Unfinished Textbook on Facet Theory* (1997).

[Werner J. Cahnman / Ruth Beloff (2nd ed.)]

GUTTMANN, ALEXANDER (1904–1994), talmudic scholar, son of Michael *Guttmann. Guttmann was born in Budapest. He received both his rabbinical diploma and his doctorate in Breslau. Guttmann taught Talmud and was the rabbi authorized to grant ordination at the Hochschule fuer die Wissenschaft des Judentums in Berlin (1935–40). From 1940 he taught Talmud at the Hebrew Union College in Cincinnati, Ohio, Guttmann published several works and numerous scholarly articles, including *Das redaktionelle und sachliche Verhaeltnis zwischen Mischna und Tosephta* (1928) and *Rabbinic Judaism in the Making* (1970).

[Eugene Mihaly]

GUTTMANN, JACOB (1845–1919), historian of Jewish philosophy. Born in Beuther (Bytom), Silesia, Guttmann studied at the University of Breslau, and at the Jewish Theological Seminary of that city. His doctoral thesis dealt with the relation between Spinoza and Descartes (*De Cartesii Spinozaeque philosophiis*, 1868). He served as a rabbi in Hildesheim from

1874 to 1892, and in Breslau from 1892 until his death. From 1910 he was president of the German Rabbinical Assembly (*Rabbinerverband*). Guttmann published a number of monographs, each of which gives a detailed exposition of the doctrine and sometimes of the sources of some medieval Jewish philosophers. These monographs are *Die Religionsphilosophie des Abraham Ibn Daud aus Toledo* (1879); *Die Religionsphilosophie des Saadja* (1882); and *Die Philosophie des Salomo Ibn Gabirol* (1889). His study of Isaac Israeli appeared in Baumker's *Beitraege zur Geschichte der Philosophie des Mittelalters* (vol. 10 no. 4, 1991). He also published important works dealing with the relation between Christian scholasticism and medieval Jewish philosophy. One of these, entitled *Das Verhaeltnis des Thomas zum Judentum und zur juedischen Literatur* (1891), studies the extent of the influence of Maimonides on Thomas Aquinas. In *Die Scholastik des 13. Jahrhunderts in ihrem Beziehungen zum Judentum und zur juedischen Literatur* (1902), Guttmann discussed the influence of Maimonides, Gabirol, and Isaac Israeli upon William of Aurenge, Albertus Magnus, Duns Scotus, Roger Bacon, and others. Maimonides' influence on Christian thought is also discussed in "Der Einfluss der maimonidischen Philosophie auf das christliche Abendland," one of the two articles contributed by Guttmann to the volume *Moses ben Maimon* (1914), of which he was coeditor; the other one, entitled "Die Beziehungen des Religionsphilosophie des Maimonides zu den Lehren seiner juedischen Vorgaenger," dealt with the relation between Maimonides and earlier Jewish philosophers.

ADD. BIBLIOGRAPHY: J. Guttmann (ed.), *Fest- und Sabbath-Predigten von Prof. Dr. Jacob Guttmann* (1926); M. Brann, in: MGWJ, 64 (1920), 1–7; I. Heinemann, *ibid.*, 250–72; *Festschrift zum siebzigsten Geburtstag Jacob Guttmanns* (1915), incl. bibl. to date; G. Hasselhoff, "The Rediscovery of Maimonidean Influence on Christianity in the Works of Moritz Steinschneider, Manuel Joel, Joseph Perles and Jacob Guttmann," in: G. Hasselhoff and O. Fraise (eds.), *Moses Maimonides (1138–1204) – His Religious, Scientific, and Philosophical Wirkungsgeschichte in Different Cultural Contexts* (2004), 449–78.

[Shlomo Pines / Yehoyada Amir (2nd ed.)]

GUTTMANN, JULIUS (**Yitzhak**; 1880–1950), philosopher of religion and historian of Jewish philosophy; son of *Jacob Guttmann. In 1903 he received his Ph.D. at the University of Breslau and in 1906 he was ordained as rabbi by the Juedisch-Theologisches Seminar of that town. From 1911 he lectured as *Privatdozent* in general philosophy at the University of Breslau. In 1919, a year after the death of Hermann *Cohen, he received a call from the Hochschule fuer die Wissenschaft des Judentums in Berlin to serve as Cohen's successor. He was a professor of Jewish philosophy at that institute until 1934. In 1922 he was also nominated as the principal of the Akademie fuer die Wissenschaft des Judentums in that city. A year after National Socialism took power in Germany, Guttmann fled from the country and immigrated to Jerusalem, where he became professor of Jewish philosophy at the Hebrew University. In Jerusalem Guttmann could shape the philosophical and scholarly groundings for the research of Jewish philosophy in the new Zionist, Hebrew environment and worked hand in hand with Gershom *Scholem, the founder of modern research in Kabbalah and Jewish mysticism.

Guttmann's literary activity focused solely almost from its very first steps on the philosophy of monotheism in general and the philosophy of Jewish religion in particular. Guttmann was a close student of Hermann Cohen and his neo-Kantian school, though he never studied with him personally. Some of his early works deal directly with the Kantian philosophy (among others: *Der Gottesbegriff Kants* (dissertation), Breslau, 1903; "Kant und das Judentum," in: Schriften, Hrsg. Gesellschaft zur Forderung der Wissenschaft des Judentums, Leipzig, 1908, pp. 41–61 (Hebrew: "*Kant ve-ha-Yahadut*," in: *Dat u-Madda* [see below], pp. 218–29); *Kants Begriff der objektiven Erkentniss*, 1911). Guttmann's attachment to the philosophy of Cohen is evident in all his writing. He followed his master's philosophy of religion and ethics in his early stages (see for example his: "Hermann Cohens Ethik," MGWJ, Jahrg. 29, Neue Folge 13 (1905), pp. 385–404) and was heavily influenced by the new notions developed by Cohen in his *Religion der Vernunft aus den Quellen des Judentums* (1919; *Religion of Reason out of the Sources of Judaism*). These notions and the new discourse they open are at the bases of Guttmann's fundamental article *Religion und Wissenschaft im mittelalterlichen und im modernen Denken* (Berlin, 1922; English: "Religion and Science in Medieval and Modern Thought," in: A. Jospe [ed.], *Studies in Jewish Thought* (1981), pp. 281–339). In that article Guttmann formulated explicitly the task of the philosophy of religion and its rootedness in the medieval encounter between monotheistic religions and Greek philosophy: "These religions, by the virtue of the strength of their claims to truth and to the profundity of their spiritual content, confront philosophy as an autonomous spiritual power. They believe that they possess the ultimate and unconditional truth that needs no validation by science, and that they provide a consistent and conclusive answer to the questions with whose solution philosophy is wrestling. The meeting between these two spiritual worlds that differ so completely in their origins creates the philosophy of religion." The examination of the philosophic account of religion and its truth-claims was Guttmann's main object in his research and philosophy, foremost in regards to Jewish religion. Guttmann's approach rests on two basic presuppositions: (a) philosophy and religion, especially philosophy and Jewish religion, are anchored in two – totally different and alien – spiritual environments. Philosophy of religion is hence an expression of the encounter between these two and is, therefore, apologetic in nature; (b) the philosopher of religion – in particular, the Jewish philosopher of Judaism – must have a clear well established notion, not only of the philosophy he adheres to, but also of the nature and content of (Jewish) religion. This notion is rooted in the non-philosophic reading of the formative writings of (Jewish) religion as well as in the personal evidence of religion that the philosopher shares as a religious person. This notion of religion serves as a methodological basis for the philosophical analysis of (Jewish) religion and the defense of religion from philosophic conceptions that counter its nature and teachings. These two presuppositions dominate Guttmann's entire work and especially his magnum opus *Die Philosophie des Judentums* (1933; Heb. trans. with corrections and additions by the author, *Ha-Filosofiyah shel ha-Yahadut*, 1951; English: *Philosophies of Judaism* (from Heb. version), 1964; *The Philosophy of Judaism*, 1988). In this as yet unrivaled book Guttmann attempts to give an account of the various ways Jewish philosophers – from Philo to modern times – tried to deal with that fundamental question. The book opens with an analysis of formative biblical (and to a lesser extent rabbinic) religious notions. The diversity of such efforts – grounded in the diversity of philosophical and cultural contexts in which those Jewish philosophers worked – does not contradict, in Guttmann's eyes, the fact that all those attempts are stages in one coherent journey of a "Jewish philosophy" that will serve as a theoretical grounding and defense of those biblical notions.

Though Guttmann's entire work is anchored in a clear notion of the nature and content of religion, it is important to note that throughout his life this notion was gradually developed. At his early stage he fully adopted Kant's and the young Cohen's notion that religion was no more than popular ethics and that its uniqueness is only of a psychological-sociological nature. Following Cohen's late philosophy Guttmann started in the early 1920s (see above: *Religion und Wissenschaft*) to search for a deeper understanding of religion and its particularity. Under the influence of Schleiermacher's philosophy, that can easily also be traced to Cohen's late work, he gradually moved in the last 30 years of his life towards a dialogical notion of God and His relationship with the human as the center of the teaching of religion. Though ethics remained a highly important component in Guttmann's account of religion, it was seen now only as one sphere of the religious being, accompanied by the notion of holiness and mystery. This new notion reaches its full expression in Guttmann's *Devarim al ha-Filosophyah shel ha-Dat* (1959, ed, by Nathan Rotenstreich; English: *On Philosophy of Religion*, 1976), where he examines a wide range of borderlines between religion and various philosophic dimensions. Such an examination could not cover, to his mind, religion in its full meaning, but could only locate the question of religion from an external point of view.

In the early 1940s Guttmann was active in the "religious circle," an intellectual group that aimed at a renewal of religious Jewish life in Israel in line with the notions of Liberal Judaism in Central Europe. Among the lectures he gave in this frameworks are "*Al Yesodot ha-Yahadut*" (*Dat u-Madda*, pp. 259–280; English trans. in *Conservative Judaism*, 14:4 (1960), pp. 1–23) and "*Ha-Muḥlat ve-ha-Yaḥasi be-Ḥayyenu*" (1942). A full account of his critique of (Heidigerian) existentialism is given in his "*Existenẓia ve-Ide'ah*" (*Dat u-Madda*, pp. 281–304). A close analysis of this article reveals, that though Guttmann wishes to stick to idealistic notions, he basically adopts not only the semi-idealistic notions of the late Cohen but also some clear dialogical notions, that place him in a close relationship with the philosophy of Franz *Rosenzweig.

Guttmann's *Philosophie des Judentums* was heavily criticized, from a fundamentally different approach, by *Leo Strauss in his *Philosophie und Gesetz* (1933; *Philosophy and Law*, 1987). Guttmann responded to this critique in an article titled, "Philosophie der Religion oder Philosophie des Gesetzes." It is not clear why he never published this article, which appeared posthumously (in: *Proceedings of the Israeli Academy of Science and Humanities*, 5 (1971–76), pp. 146–173; Hebrew: "*Filosofiya shel ha-Dat o filosofiya shel ha-Ḥok*," *Divrei ha-Akademya ha-Le'ummit ha-Yisra'elit le-Madda'im*, 5, pp. 190–207).

BIBLIOGRAPHY: J. Guttmann, *Dat u-Madda* (1955); *ibid.*, "Establishing Norms for Jewish Belief," in: A. Jospe (ed.), *Studies in Jewish Thought* (1981), 54–69. BIBLIOGRAPHIES OF J. GUTTMANN: Iyyun, 2 (1951), 11–19 and 182–84; M. Schwarcz, "*Ha-Haskalah ve-Hashlakhoteha al ha-Filosofya ha-Yehudit ba-Et ha-Ḥadashah (le-Divrei ha-Pulmus bein L. Strauss le-J. Guttmann)*," in: *Daat*, 1 (1978), 7–16; E. Schweid, "Religion and Philosophy – the Scholarly-Theological Debate between Julius Guttmann and Leo Strauss," in: *Maimonidean Studies* 1 (1990), 163–95; *ibid., Toledot Filosofyat ha-Dat ha-Yehudit ba-Zeman he-Ḥadash*, vol. 3, 2 (2005), 199–238; Y. Amir, "*Yitzhak Julius Guttmann ve-Ḥeker ha-Filosofyah ha-Yehudit*," in: H. Lavski (ed.), *Toledot ha-Universitah ha-Ivrit bi-Yrushalayim – Hitbassesut u-Ẓemiḥah* (1) (2005), 219–55; J. Cohen, "*Yesodot Shitatiyyim be-Ḥeker ha-Filosofyah ha-Yehudit bi-Zemanenu*," in: *Daat*, 38 (1997), 105–12.

[Yehoyada Amir (2nd ed.)]

GUTTMANN, SIR LUDWIG (1899–1980), founder and former director of the National Spinal Injuries Centre at Stoke Mandeville in Buckinghamshire, England. Born in Upper Silesia, Germany, Guttmann was an accomplished neurosurgeon and medical director of the Jewish Hospital in Breslau when he was invited in 1939 to do research work at Oxford on his highly original – and at the time controversial – ideas on rehabilitating persons suffering from irreversible spinal injuries that resulted in paraplegia. He made England his home and acquired world fame with his treatment and rehabilitation of paraplegics.

In 1944, when the impending Allied invasion of Hitler's Europe was expected to lead to large numbers of serious injuries, Guttmann was invited by the British government to put his ideas into practice at Stoke Mandeville. His single-minded determination produced remarkable results; through his methods of treatment, coupled with a deep humanity and understanding (he was known by his patients as "Poppa Guttmann"), many of the wounded were able to live useful lives, which previously would have been denied them. He reduced the death rate of paraplegics from over 80% to under 10% within three years of injury, and after an average stay at Stoke Mandeville of less than one year, 75% of those released were gainfully employed. His establishment of the increasingly successful annual Stoke Mandeville Games was a practical expression of his determination that paraplegics lead normal lives in all respects. Guttmann was consulted by many countries throughout the world on the establishment of paraplegic centers, and as a result of his visit to Israel in 1949 the paraplegic center at Tel Ha-Shomer was opened in 1953. Probably his most lasting legacy was the establishment of the Paralympic Games, which grew out of his Stoke Mandeville games. These began as an international event in 1948 to coincide with the Olympic Games held that year in London. These are now a major, mainstream international event.

The many honors bestowed upon him include the Rehabilitation Prize of the World Veterans' Association in 1953 (he was the first recipient). He was awarded successively the O.B.E., the C.B.E., and in 1966 a Knighthood by Britain, and the minister of pensions said in 1945: "Thank you, Hitler, for sending us men like these." In 1972 President Heinemann bestowed upon him the Star of the Grand Cross of the Order of Merit of the Federal Republic, West Germany's highest award, at the 21st international Stoke Mandeville Games for the paralyzed held in Heidelberg, Germany.

Both Sir Ludwig and Lady Guttmann were active in the local Jewish community and supported Israel's cause in many ways.

ADD. BIBLIOGRAPHY: ODNB online.

[Michael Wallach]

GUTTMANN, MICHAEL (1872–1942), Hungarian talmudic scholar. Guttmann was born in Hungary and studied at the Budapest rabbinical seminary and at the University of Budapest. From 1903, the year of his ordination at the Budapest rabbinical seminary, to 1907 he was rabbi at Csongrád. He lectured on Jewish law from 1907 to 1921 at the Budapest seminary. From 1921 to 1933 he was rabbi and professor of Talmud and *halakhah* at the Breslau Jewish theological seminary and in 1925 he was visiting professor of Talmud at the Hebrew University of Jerusalem. In 1933 he was appointed head of the Budapest seminary. Guttmann combined a wide knowledge of the sources with an acute modern, critical approach. Among his publications in this field were *Einleitung in die Halacha* (Budapest Seminary *Jahresberichte*, 1909, 1913); *Asmakhta* (Breslau Seminary *Jahresberichte*, 1924), on talmudic methodology; and *Beḥinat ha-Mitzvot* (*ibid.*, 1928) and *Beḥinat Kiyyum ha-Mitzvot* (*ibid.*, 1931), on the reasons for the observance of the commandments. He edited *Abraham b. Ḥiyya's textbook of geometry, *Ḥibbur ha-Meshiḥah ve-ha Tishboret* (introduction, 1903; the work itself 1912–13). Guttmann was one of the editors of *Ha-Ẓofeh le-Ḥokhmat Yisrael* (1911–14), editor of *Ha-Soker* (from 1933), and of *Magyar Zsidó Szemle* and published articles in these and other periodicals in Hebrew, Hungarian, French, and German. He was also an editor of and contributor to the *Oẓar Yisrael* encyclopedia and the Eshkol *Encyclopedia Judaica*, in both the German and Hebrew editions. His *Das Judentum und seine Umwelt* (part 1, 1927) deals with the attitude of Judaism to the non-Jewish world. Written against the background of rising nationalism and antisemitism in Germany in the 1920s, when everything Jewish, and the Talmud in particular, was under virulent attack, it is completely apologetic. Guttmann planned as his major life work a vast talmudic encyclopedia, which would have been beyond the talents of most other scholars working alone. Only four volumes of Guttmann's *Mafte'aḥ ha-Talmud*, covering the letter *alef*, appeared (1910–30); the rest of the material was lost after his death when the Nazis occupied Hungary in 1944. Even this small installment is of major importance as a talmudic reference work.

BIBLIOGRAPHY: D.S. Loewinger, in: S. Federbush (ed.), *Ḥokhmat Yisrael be-Ma'arav Eiropah*, 1 (1959), 130–47; idem (ed.), *Jewish Studies in Memory of M. Guttmann* (1946), incl. bibl.; A. Guttmann, in: *Bitzaron*, 8 (1943), 46–48.

[Moshe David Herr]

GUTTMANN, ROBERT (1880–1942), Czech primitive painter. During his life, Guttmann was better known for his unusual personality than for his paintings. He was a familiar figure of the Jewish scene in Prague as he walked from one coffeehouse to another, his work rolled up under his arm, arranging impromptu exhibitions of his drawings and watercolor paintings. His subjects were mainly people, landscapes, and street scenes. However, his work was not taken seriously until after his death in the Lodz ghetto in 1942. It was only when his work was exhibited after World War II, that he was recognized as an original, genuine Naive artist whose works – most of them now in the Jewish Museum in Prague – were widely admired at a number of posthumous exhibitions. He was a lifelong Zionist. At the age of 17 he walked from Prague to Basle to attend the First Zionist Congress, and he made his way on foot to all subsequent Congresses held during his lifetime.

BIBLIOGRAPHY: A. Heller, *Guttmann: eine psychologische Studie ueber den Maler Robert Guttmann* (1932).

[Avigdor Dagan]

°GUTZKOW, KARL FERDINAND (1811–1878), German nationalist author. Gutzkow, born in Berlin, was a prominent figure in the "Young Germany" literary movement where he led the reactionary wing, in contrast to the liberal trend influenced by Rahel Varnhagen von *Ense, *Heine, and *Boerne. Like *Goethe, Schlegel, and Brentano, Gutzkow expanded the theme of the *Wandering Jew in German literature, as for instance in his "Julius Moses Ahasver" (in: *Vermischte Schriften*, 2, 1842). His books, such as *Wally, die Zweiflerin* (1835), *Zopf und Schwert* (1844), and *Urbild des Tartueff* (1844) brought him fame but criticism as well. Gutzkow also wrote a historical drama, *Uriel Acosta* (1846), in which the author's own emotional experiences and inner conflicts are echoed. Gutzkow had already treated this story in a tale, *Der Sadduzaeer von Amsterdam* (1833). Discrepancies between the drama and Acosta's actual life roused protests from H. *Jellinek and induced him to write a monograph on Spinoza's forerunner, *Uriel Acosta's Leben und Lehre* (1847).

See also Image of the Jew in *German Literature.

BIBLIOGRAPHY: L. Poliakov, *Histoire de l'antisémitisme*, 3 (1968), index; G. Brandes, *Main Currents in Nineteenth Century Liter-*

ature, 6 (1923), index, J.G. Robertson, *A History of German Literature* (1959), index; V. Eichstaedt, *Bibliographie zur Geschichte der Judenfrage* (1938), index. **ADD. BIBLIOGRAPHY:** H. Steinecke, "Gutzkow, die Juden und das Judentum," in: *Conditio Judaica*, 11 (1989), 118–29; J.S. Skolnik, "Writing Jewish History between Gutzkow and Goethe; Auerbach's 'Spinoza' and the Birth of Modern Jewish Historical Fiction," in: *Prooftexts*, 19, 2 (1999), 101–25; T.C. Kinney, *Challenging the Myth of "Young Germany" – Conflict and Consensus in Karl Gutzkow, Heinrich Laube, Theodor Mundt and Ludolf Weinbarg* (1997).

°**GUY, PHILIP LANGSTAFFE ORD** (1885–1952), archaeologist. Born in Scotland, he joined the excavations at Carchemish and el-Amarna after World War I. From 1922 to 1925 he was chief inspector of antiquities in Palestine and excavated an Iron Age cemetery in Haifa. He directed the excavations at Megiddo (1925–35) where he introduced a method of balloon photography and cleared the mound to stratum V (Iron Age). As director of the British School of Archaeology in Jerusalem from 1938 to 1939 he began a survey of the Negev. He served in the British Army in World War II and rejoined the department of antiquities in 1947. He remained in Israel as chief of its division of excavations and survey until his death. He directed excavations at Bet Yeraḥ, Jaffa, and Ayyelet ha-Shaḥar. His publications include excavation reports of Tell el-Amarna and Megiddo, including the large volume *Meggido Tombs* (1938). He married a daughter of Eliezer *Ben-Yehuda.

[Michael Avi-Yonah]

GUZIK, HANNA (1909–), actress. She began to act in 1924 in the theatrical group of her father, Jacob Guzik. She played in Yiddish in the plays of Goldfaden, Shalom Aleichem and others. In 1932–1933 she played in musical comedies in the Russian theaters in the big cities of the Soviet Union, and afterwards she performed with a Jewish theatrical ensemble in many cities. Her particular talent was in playing various roles on stage, even in the same play, and to sing in various styles. In 1973 she immigrated to Israel.

[Shmuel Spector (2nd ed.)]

GUZIK, JACOB (Jack, Jake, "Greasy Thumb"; 1886–1956), U.S. gangster, the trusted treasurer, financial wizard, and legal advisor to Al Capone. He was born in Moscow to Max and Fannie, an Orthodox couple who raised 10 children. The family immigrated to the U.S. when Guzik was a year old and settled in Chicago, where Max supported the family by running a small cigar store. Guzik became a bartender and pimp in the whorehouse run by his older brother, Harry. In the early 1920s Guzik supposedly overheard a plan to murder Capone, informed him, and the two became lifelong allies. Guzik became a powerful political "fixer" operating out of a restaurant, where he received district police captains and sergeants who collected graft for themselves and their superiors. Also stopping by were bagmen sent over from City Hall. His nickname "Greasy Thumb" derived from the green stain earned from counting the money of mobster kingpin Capone, who once called Guzik "the only friend I can really trust." Guzik was convicted of tax evasion and went to prison in 1932, serving three years of his five-year sentence. Upon his release, Guzik assumed total control over the finances of Capone's Chicago Outfit for the next 20 years. Guzik brought numerous lawsuits against newspapers for portraying him as a gangster, dismissing the wisdom of such suits saying, "I'm paying these judges, so why shouldn't I use them." Guzik received an Orthodox Jewish funeral, and a lavish one, his bronze coffin alone costing $5,000. Rabbi Noah Ganz of the Chicago Loop Synagogue eulogized Guzik as a man "who never lost faith in his God. Hundreds benefited by his kindness and generosity. His charities were performed quietly. And he made frequent and vast contributions to my congregation."

[Elli Wohlgelernter (2nd ed.)]

GVATI, CHAIM (1901–1990), Israeli pioneer and politician. Chaim Gvati was born in Poland and immigrated to Eretz Israel in 1924. One of the founders of kibbutz Gevat in 1926, he later helped found kibbutz Yifat where he remained. Gvati was minister of agriculture from 1964 to 1974 in Labor governments. In 1982 he was awarded the Israel Prize for his contribution to the development of the state as a *ḥalutz* ("pioneer") and for his role in the establishment and development of agricultural settlements.

[Fern Lee Seckbach (2nd ed.)]

GYMNASIUM, ancient Greek institution devoted to physical education and development of the body (γυμνός, "naked"). Although originally established for functions of a purely athletic and competitive nature, the gymnasium eventually became dedicated to the furthering of intellectual, as well as physical, aspects of Greek culture. During the Hellenistic period attendance at the gymnasium was recognized as the standard educational prerequisite for Greek youths wishing to attain citizenship in the *polis*. Thus, with the establishment of a Hellenistic administration in Jerusalem during the reign of *Antiochus IV Epiphanes, the high priest *Jason was given permission "to set up a gymnasium and ephebeum" (II Macc. 4:9). This act was abhorred by the vast majority of Palestinian Jews, who rightly considered the gymnasium a symbol of the Greek heathen culture chosen to supplant ancient Jewish law in Jerusalem (cf. I Macc. 1:13–15). The author of II Maccabees stresses that the gymnasium was erected adjacent to the Temple, and describes the priests abandoning their service at the altar "to participate in the unlawful exercises of the palaestra as soon as the summons came for the discus throwing" (I Macc. 4:14). Opposition to participation in the gymnasium was not as vehement among the Jews of Ptolemaic Egypt, and it may be assumed that the upper classes of Alexandrian Jewry were interested in obtaining this training for their youth. This interest was enhanced with the Roman conquest of Egypt, for Roman policy identified the graduates of the gymnasium as legitimate Greek "citizens," and only these might serve as the basis for local administration. It is therefore understandable that the Greek population of Alexandria was violently opposed to the enrollment of "non-Greeks" (i.e., Egyptians and Jews) among the *epheboi* (cf. the "Boule Papyrus," Tcherikover, Corpus 2 (1960), 25–29 no. 150). The Greek demands were eventually supported by the emperor Claudius (41 C.E.), who decreed, according to another papyrus (*ibid.*, no. 153), that the Jews "are not to intrude themselves into the games presided over by the gymnasiarchs."

BIBLIOGRAPHY: E. Bickerman, *From Ezra to the Last of the Maccabees* (1962), 104ff.; A.H.M. Jones, *The Greek City* (1940), 220ff.; Tcherikover, Corpus, 1 (1957), 38ff., 73, 76; idem, *Hellenistic Civilization and the Jews* (1959).

[Isaiah Gafni]

GYONGYOS (Hung. **Gyöngyös**), city in N. Hungary. Jews are first recorded there in the 15th century, and in 1735 there was an organized community. The synagogue, built before the end of the 18th century, was destroyed in the great fire which devastated the city in 1917. The community always remained a *status quo ante community, though a separate Orthodox community was established in 1870. The first rabbi of the community was Feivel b. Asher Boskovitz; he was succeeded by Wolf Lippe (officiated 1840–50), a noted bibliophile. Eleazar Fuerst (1853–1893) founded a yeshivah in the town. The Jewish population numbered 2,250 in 1920, and 2,429 in 1941. In June 1944 they were deported to Auschwitz; of these only 461 survived the Holocaust. There were 300 Jews in Gyongyos in 1946 and 414 in 1949. Most left in 1956.

BIBLIOGRAPHY: R.L. Braham, *Hungarian-Jewish Studies*, 2 (1969), 143, 160, 180; *Magyar Zsidó Lexikon* (1929), 331–2; MHJ, index.

[Baruch Yaron]

GYÖR (Ger. **Raab**), city in northwest Hungary, near the Austrian border. The earliest information on Jewish settlement there dates from the last third of the 14th century, though it is probable that an organized community had existed earlier. A Jews' Street is recorded in the municipal land register of 1567, and a synagogue is mentioned in the municipality's accounts. The Church, which would permit only Catholics to reside in the city, compelled the Jews to settle on the nearby Györ-Sziget Island on the Danube River. A community was organized there in 1791 and a synagogue established in 1795. Jews did not settle in the city proper until 1840. In 1851 they formed a single community with the island Jews. A new synagogue was built in 1870. In 1871 a separate Orthodox community was organized. Noted rabbis of Györ were S. Ranschburg, J. Fischer, and E. Roth. The last stimulated the ideology of Jewish nationalism in the community; he was deported to Auschwitz in 1944.

The Jews of Györ, mainly manufacturers, artisans, and merchants, numbered 5,904 in 1920, and 4,688 in 1941. Between 1942 and 1944 the majority of male Jews were sent to labor camps. The Nazis occupied Hungary in March 1944, and on June 11, they were deported to Auschwitz. After the war 700 survivors returned. In 1946 there were 950 Jews in Györ but in 1970 only 200 remained. The synagogue was sold in 1969.

BIBLIOGRAPHY: J. Kemény, *Vázlatok a györi zsidóság történetéböl* (1930); A. Scheiber, *Hebraeische Kódex-Ueberreste in ungarlaendischen Einbandstaefeln* (1969), 95–99; MHJ, 12 (1969), 10 (1967); 9 (1966); 8 (1965); 7 (1963); 6 (1961); 5 (2 pts., 1959–60), index locorum, s.v.; 4 (1938), index locorum s.v. *Rab*; 3 (1937), index s.v. *Györ megye, györi zsidók*; R.L. Braham, *The Hungarian Jewish Catastrophe; a selected and annotated bibliography* (1962), geographic index, s.v.

[Alexander Scheiber]

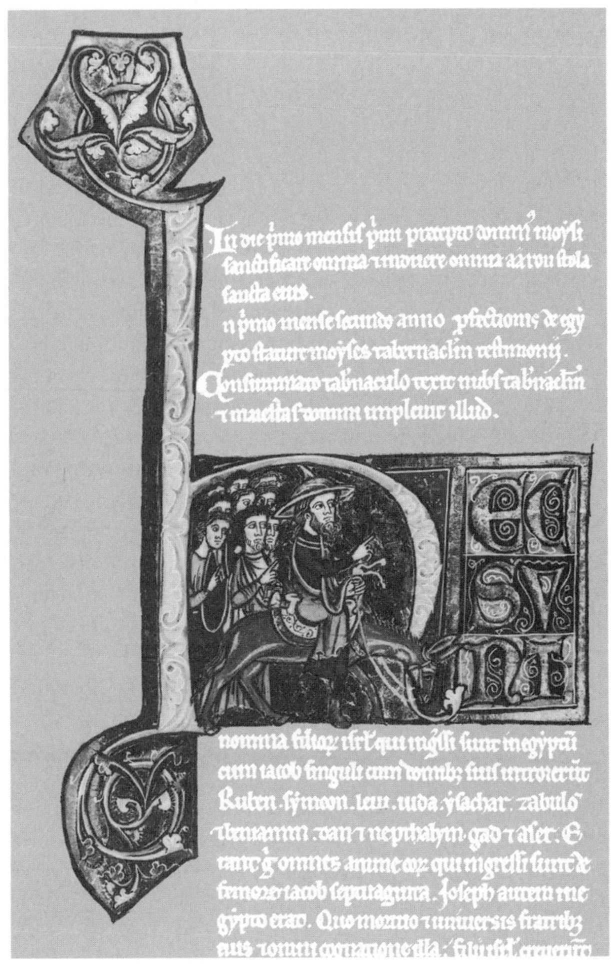

Initial letter "H" from the beginning of Exodus in a Latin Bible, France, 12th century. The illumination shows Jacob and his sons going down to Egypt. Amiens, Bibliothèque Municipale, Ms. 21, fol. 27.

HA–HEP

HAAN, JACOB ISRAËL DE (1881–1924), Dutch poet and novelist, international jurist, and journalist, politically active in Palestine during the early years of the Mandate until assassinated. Born in Smilde, De Haan was the son of a cantor and the younger brother of the authoress Carry van *Bruggen. Marked by a complex personality, his life was full of contradictions: extreme generosity opposing cruelty and downright meanness, a lucid rationality versus a strong inclination towards mysticism. A remarkable constancy in his life on the other hand lies in an emotional and at the same time practical sense of justice. A further complicating factor was De Haan's homosexuality.

De Haan started his career as a teacher and editor of the children's page of *Het Volk*, the leading Dutch Socialist newspaper. Having abandoned the Jewish faith he became active in the Socialist movement. In 1904 he published the novel *Pijpelijntjes*, which depicted candidly and without apology the homosexual relationship between two young men. Its publication led to a scandal and to his dismissal as teacher and editor. Although the turmoil caused a severe physical and psychological crisis, he published another novel, *Pathologieën* (1908), in which the homosexual theme was extended into an essentially sadomasochistic relationship. This novel is still considered the only Dutch work in the genre of Decadent Symbolism. In the meantime he began to study law and married a non-Jewish woman. A few years after his marriage he returned to the Orthodox faith and Judaism became the main theme in his poetry. At a time when the Jewish contribution to Dutch literature was significant, De Haan became its main protagonist as a self-styled Poet of the Jewish Song. Meanwhile, social and political abuses remained uppermost in his mind. When international indignation about the fate of political prisoners in Czarist Russia was strong, De Haan visited extensively both political and criminal prisons in Russia and published a moving account of his experiences (*In Russische gevangenissen*, 1913). He was successful in interceding with the Russian authorities in favor of some political prisoners. In the course of his law studies he associated himself with the new international school of Significs, which dedicated itself to probing the meaning of words and terms. According to the Significs, analyzing language and purifying it from false meanings could solve many social problems. De Haan specialized in legal terminology and in 1916 published his thesis *Rechtskundige significa en hare toepassing op de begrippen: "aansprakelijk, verantwoordelijk, toerekeningsvatbaar."* Though he surprised the Dutch legal world by his original, intelligent analysis and by the colorful style of his articles, in the end he failed through an apparent inability to formulate a consistent theory of significs. In 1917 he was passed over for an appointment as professor in criminal law at the Municipal University of Amsterdam.

During these years, as De Haan developed his Jewish poetry, he took to Zionism and became a member of the Mizrachi movement. Disappointment in his legal career, compounded by the spiritual conflict into which his marriage to a non-Jewish woman had brought him, and his growing Jewish-national consciousness persuaded him to go to Palestine to witness and take part in the Zionist experiment. He was appointed Palestinian correspondent for the leading Dutch newspaper *Het Algemeen Handelsblad*, receiving a handsome salary. Covering thousands of pages, he wrote perhaps the most vivid, humorous and moving chronicle of life in Palestine in the years following World War I. In January 1919 he arrived in Jerusalem an ardent Zionist, watched by the Mandatory government because of his anti-Arab utterances. He also played a part in the legal defense of Zionists who were prosecuted for defending themselves in the anti-Zionist riots in the spring of 1920. Together with *Jabotinsky he became lector at the Law School that had been established by the British. But in about a year and a half he became appalled at what he considered the aggressive and tactless nationalism of the young Zionist movement. De Haan often expressed his sympathy for the Arab-Palestinian cause. Yet his main grievance was the subordination of non-Zionist orthodoxy to a Zionist, partly layman, rabbinical organization. He became the most formidable spokesman for the Jerusalem Agudat Israel, led by Rabbi Chaim *Sonnenfeld. He acquired for this Orthodox group access to leading non-Jewish politicians and opinion leaders, e.g., the. press magnate Lord Northcliffe, who appointed him correspondent for *The Daily Express*. He also led an Agudist delegation to King Hussein of the Hejaz on the occasion of the latter's visit to his son Abdallah, king of Trans-Jordan in 1924.

However, the question remains as to how effective De Haan's actions were: At the end of his life he was considered deranged by friends and enemies alike. His diplomatic success lay mainly in the fact that he – though only for the time while – had a part in thwarting Herbert Samuel's efforts to establish a kind of public legal status for Palestine Jewry, including the authority to raise taxes in religious matters. The still vulnerable Zionist movement felt discredited by De Haan's criticism, which was shared by a number of Zionists but never systematically brought to the non-Jewish world as he did. Besides, in exposing misleading Zionist pretensions, De Haan was a master in ridiculing his opponents. In the last two years of his life he was repeatedly menaced by death threats. It is still not clear if these were merely meant to frighten him away from the Palestinian scene. What prompted the actual murder is not known. Evidently, at the end of his life De Haan was planning to expose more embarrassing failings in the National Home, e.g., the embezzlement of Zionist funds by Chaim *Kalvarisky, who administered a program for Arab-Jewish rapprochement. Whatever the real reasons, the highest echelons of militant Palestine Zionism had decided to eliminate him and on June 30, 1924, he was shot to death on the orders of the Haganah, the first known political assassination in the Zionist movement. The news of his death drew worldwide attention, including in the Arab countries. After the hate-campaign against De Haan, his murder deeply embarrassed the Zionist organization, but at the time it could divert suspicion to the Arabs because of the well-known fondness of the deceased for Arab boys. Only in the 1960s was the Zionist responsibility gradually revealed. The enigmas in De Haan's life can be perceived to resonate posthumously. At present he is still regarded as the champion of both Dutch homosexual liberation and international anti-Zionist Jewish Orthodoxy.

BIBLIOGRAPHY: J. Meijer, *De zoon van een gazzen. Het leven van Jacob Israël de Haan, 1881–1924* (1967). **ADD. BIBLIOGRAPHY:** E. Marmorstein, *A Martyr's Message. To Commemorate the Fiftieth Anniversary of the Murder of Professor De Haan* (1975); L. Giebels, in: *Studia Rosenthaliana*, 13 (1979), 194–219; 14 (1980), 44–79; 15 (1981), 111–42; 188–216; idem, in: *Exquisite Corpse*, nos. 5 and 6, at: www.corpse.org; R.H. Delvigne and L. Ross, *Brieven van en aan Jacob Israël de Haan 1899–1908* (1994); G.C.J.J. van den Bergh (ed.), *De taal zegt meer dan zij verantwoorden kan* (1994); M. Berkowitz, in: A.T. Alt and J. Berhard, *Arnold Zweig. Sein Werk im Kontext der deutschsprachigen Exilliteratur. Jahrbuch fuer internationale Germanistik* (1999), 111–24.

[Henriette Boas / Ludy Giebels (2nd ed.)]

HAAN, MEIJER DE (also **Meijer Jacob, Meijer Isaac**; 1852–1895), Dutch painter. De Haan was born in Amsterdam, where his father ran a flourishing biscuit factory. After having initially joined his two brothers in the family business, Meijer started studying painting under the Dutch academician Petrus Franciscus Greive from 1870 on. Because of his poor health, he was not able to complete his artistic education. During this period he worked in a somewhat academic style, painting portraits and choosing some Jewish subjects as well, as in *The Talmudic Dispute* (1878) and *Dietary Laws* (1880; also referred to as *Is This Chicken Kosher?*). Deeply disappointed by the poor response to his major opus, *Uriel d'Acosta*, on which he struggled for 10 years, he left for Paris in 1888 together with his student J.J. Isaacson. Through Vincent van Gogh's brother, Theo, Meijer de Haan met Gauguin, whom he accompanied to Brittany in 1889, where they worked together for almost two years in Le Pouldu and Pont Aven. De Haan became Gauguin's faithful student, making it possible for his idol to carry out his artistic experiments without disturbance by supporting him financially. Although he himself was influenced by Gauguin's synthetic style and incorporated some of his motifs and arrangements, De Haan adhered to his own inclination towards contrast of light and darkness and true-to-nature colors. When Gauguin wanted to take his friend on a journey of adventure to Tahiti, De Haan's family intervened and threatened to stop his allowance if he continued his association with Gauguin. In 1890 De Haan returned to Amsterdam and, after a short stay in Paris eventually settled in Hattem, Netherlands, in 1891. Until recently little attention was paid to De Haan beyond noting that his pathetic likeness appears in several of Gauguin's works, but research has revealed De Haan as one of Gauguin's most talented disciples. His works figure in several museum collections, e.g., the Jewish Historical Museum, Amsterdam; the Van Gogh Museum, Amsterdam; The Kröller Möller Museum, Otterlo, Netherlands; Musée de Beaux-Arts, Quimper, France; and several important private collections.

BIBLIOGRAPHY: J. Zürcher, *Meijer de Haan's Uriël Acosta* (1888); W. Jaworska, in: *Nederlands Kunsthistorisch Jaarboek*, 18 (1967), 197–225; E. Zafran (ed.), *Gauguin's Nirvana, Painters at Le Pouldu, 1889–1890* (2001).

[Jelka Kröger (2nd ed.)]

HA'ANAKAH (Heb. הַעֲנָקָה), the gratuity which the master was enjoined to pay his Hebrew bound servant when the latter was set free. This institution is the source, in Jewish law, of the laws of severance pay, i.e., payment of compensation to employees on their dismissal. The term *ha'anakah* has been interpreted as deriving from the word *anak* (עֲנָק) in the sense of an ornament (around the neck, Prov. 1:9), i.e., that the bondsman must be "ornamented" with the gratuity, or in the sense of "loading on his neck" (Rashi and Ibn Ezra to Deut. 15:14).

Scriptural References

The duty of *ha'anakah* is enjoined in the Bible as both a negative and a positive precept – "when thou lettest him go free from thee, thou shalt not let him go empty," and "thou shalt furnish him liberally out of thy flock, and out of thy threshing floor, and out of thy winepress of that wherewith the Lord thy God hath blessed thee" (Deut. 15:13, 14) – and in this twofold manner has been included in the enumeration of the precepts (Maim., *Sefer ha-Mitzvot*, pos. comm. 196 and neg. comm. 233; *Semag, lavin* 178 and *asayin* 84; *Sefer ha-Ḥinnukh*, nos. 450, 484). The duty of *ha'anakah* arose upon completion of the six-year period of service (Deut. 15:12) and the grant was to be made out of the things with which the master's house had been blessed by virtue of the bondsman's service (Deut. 15:14; Kid. 17b; see statement of Eleazar b. Azariah). The duty of *ha'anakah* was enjoined as a reminder of the bondage in Egypt and exodus to freedom (Deut. 15:15), when the Israelites were "furnished" with property of their Egyptian masters (Sif. Deut. 120; Rashi and Rashbam, ad loc.). The institution of *ha'anakah*, unique to Jewish law as opposed to other ancient legal systems, was rooted in the special attitude toward a Hebrew bondsman, whose position was compared to that of a worker hired for a fixed term: "… for to the double of the hire of a hireling hath he served thee six years" (Deut. 15:18).

The Right to the Gratuity

It was laid down that the servant became entitled to the gratuity upon expiry of his term of service, or termination thereof on account of the Jubilee or his master's death, but not for reasons attributable to the servant himself, as, for example, when he gained his freedom by "deduction from the purchase price" (i.e., by refunding his master part of the price paid for himself, pro rata to the uncompleted term of his service): "You shall furnish to whomever you set free, but not to anyone who sets himself free" (Sif. Deut. 119; Kid. 16b). For this reason, the gratuity right was forfeited by a runaway, notwithstanding intervention of the Jubilee. In the opinion of R. Meir, one who was freed by deduction from the purchase price remained entitled to the gratuity since it took place with the master's approval (Kid. 16b); on the other hand, some of the *tannaim* denied the gratuity right to one who was set free on account of his master's death (TJ, Kid. 1:2, 59c).

In the *Midrash Halakhah* the gratuity right was extended both to the one sold into bondage through the court on account of his theft (Ex. 22:2) and to one who sold himself into bondage on account of utter poverty (Lev. 25:39), nor were these cases distinguished in the Mishnah (see Ḥ. Albeck, *Shishah Sidrei Mishnah, Seder Nashim*, 409f.). In a *baraita* disputing opinions were expressed on this matter, some scholars holding that only one sold into bondage through the court and not one selling himself was entitled to gratuity, with R. Eliezer (Kid. 14b) holding that both were entitled thereto; this dispute was carried over into the codes (Yad, Avadim, 3:12; Tos. Kid. 15a, s.v. *idakh*; and commentaries). One of the grounds for the view that one who sold himself into bondage was not entitled to the gratuity was that in doing so voluntarily, he transgressed the prohibition, "For unto Me the children of Israel are servants; they are My servants" (Lev. 25:55) "and not the servants of servants" (Kid. 22b; *Yam shel Shelomo*, Kid. 1:22).

Substance of the Gratuity Right

In tannaitic times the gratuity was looked upon as a personal right of the freed servant which was not transferable on death (Sif. Deut. 119), but the *amoraim* held it to be part of his remuneration and therefore transmissible "… just as the wages of a hired servant belong to his heirs, so here too…" (Kid. 15a; cf. also the version of Elijah Gaon, loc. cit. and see *Minḥat Ḥinnukh* no. 482). Contrary to the principle of "R. Nathan's Lien" (see *Shi'buda de-Rabbi Natan) with regard to the general right to recover a claim from a third party indebted to the debtor, the gratuity right was not attachable by the servant's creditor (Kid. 15a–16b) and, according to the majority of the *posekim*, the creditor could not recover his debt from the amount of the gratuity – not even when the servant was already released and in possession of the gratuity payment (Maim. comm. to Kid. 1:2; cf. Nov. *Penei Yehoshu'a* Kid., final collection).

The duty of furnishing a gratuity was, according to the majority view of the scholars, independent of the measure of gain derived by the master from his servant's labor (Sif. *ibid.*;

Kid. 17a/b and cf. contrary opinion of Eleazar b. Azariah), but all the scholars accepted that a minimum was payable (although disagreeing on the amount: Kid. 17a), together with an increment according to the measure with which the master has been "blessed," such increment being payable by the master with a "generous hand" (Sif. Deut., 119–20).

Two opposing views concerning the legal substance of the gratuity were expressed in the codes. According to some scholars it was not part of the servant's remuneration for his labor but derived from the institution of charity (*ẓedakah*; Shakh. to ḤM 86:3) or of waiver and gift (*Sema*, ḤM, 86:2 and see *Giddulei Terumah* to *Sefer ha-Terumot*, 51:1:5); other *posekim*, following the *halakhah* of the *amoraim* concerning transmissibility at death, of the gratuity took the view that the gratuity was mainly to reward the servant for services rendered "beyond his wages" (Beit ha-Beḥirah, Kid. 15a) and therefore it had to be considered as part of his remuneration (*Penei Yehoshu'a* Kid. 16b; *Mishneh la-Melekh*, to Yad. *ibid.*).

Severance Pay

Adaptation of the gratuity institution to one of general compensation for employees upon dismissal was first mentioned toward the end of the 13th century, when it was stated that notwithstanding the abolition of Hebrew bound service, which was linked with observance of the Jubilee year, the employer still had to pay a gratuity to his departing worker regardless of the period of service (*Sefer ha-Ḥinnukh*, 450). Although this was phrased at that time as a moral obligation only, later scholars found it possible to recognize this duty of the employer as legally binding. In recent times this development has been acknowledged in the decisions of various scholars, and particularly in the judgments of the rabbinical courts in Israel, in three different ways:

(a) In accordance with the principle of the bound servant's gratuity, in pursuance of the statements in the *Sefer ha-Ḥinnukh* (*ibid.*), it was held that "… the intention of the Torah was to make it the employer's duty to be concerned about the worker's future so that the latter should not depart from his work empty-handed" (PDR, 3:286 f.). Because Jewish law compared the position of a bound servant to that of a hired worker, it was concluded that the latter "certainly enjoys all the former's privileges… the more so since he does not transgress a prohibition" (i.e., that of selling himself into bondage – see above; resp. Maharam of Rothenburg, ed. Prague, no. 85: see also *Yam ha-Gadol*, no. 22).

(b) A different approach was adopted by Benẓion *Ouziel (see his responsum quoted in *Teḥukat Avodah* (see bibl.) 132 f.). Holding that the law of the gratuity could not properly be relied upon to support the existence of a full legal duty to compensate an employee upon his dismissal, he preferred to base this duty on the scriptural admonition, "That thou mayest walk in the way of good men, and keep the paths of the righteous" (Prov. 2:20) in the same way as it was relied upon in the Talmud with reference to exempting the hired worker in certain circumstances from liability for damage negligently caused to his employer (BM 83a). Although conceding that this talmudic principle was a matter of equity (*li-fenim mi-shurat ha-din*) rather than binding law, R. Ouziel followed the opinion of numerous *posekim* that it was nevertheless enforceable by the court (*Mordekhai* BM 257; Sh. Ar., ḤM 12:2, and *Rema* in loc.; also *Baḥ* ḤM 12), and therefore decided that the court, "having due regard to the respective positions of the parties and reasons for the worker's dismissal or for his own departure," was empowered to order an employer to compensate his worker.

(c) Since it was not generally accepted that an obligation solely *li-fenim mi-shurat ha-din* is enforceable by the court, some scholars preferred to base the principle of severance pay on the Jewish legal source of custom (see **Minhag*; PDR, 1:330 f.). Thus the rabbinical courts, applying the rule that "custom overrides the law" has special reference to labor law (TJ, BM 7:1; 11b) and recognizing "the spread in our time of a usage to pay severance pay," have laid down that severance pay "is not a matter of grace but a claim under law" which is payable even if the employer be a charitable institution. In arriving at this decision the rabbinical courts incorporate also the principle of the gratuity, holding that particular significance attaches to custom in this instance, since "we find a basis for it in the Torah and *halakhah*," and since this custom is founded on the Torah, "the gratuity payable to the Hebrew bound servant is therefore fit and proper" (PDR, 1:330 f., 3:286 f.; 4:120).

It may be noted that R. Ouziel, in giving his above-mentioned decision (in 1945), specifically refrained from basing the severance pay obligation on custom – for the reason that such a usage was not yet sufficiently known and widespread. A mere 10 years later the court, seeking a basis for full legal recognition of the severance pay duty, had reason to find as follows: "Now that the custom has spread and become accepted in the whole country, and is common and practiced daily, it must be followed and the above-mentioned statements [of R. Ouziel] no longer apply." This is an illustration of great flexibility in recognizing the establishment of a custom.

In the years since the establishment of the State of Israel, the rabbinical courts have laid down a number of rules concerning the matter of severance pay, including the following provisions: compensation is to be paid at the customarily accepted rate, or if this be uncertain, as determined by the court (PDR, 1:332 f.); it is payable also to a temporary employee – if he has worked for a period approximating two years (*ibid.*), and also to a part-time employee (4: 129), but an independent contractor is not entitled to severance pay (3:272). An innovation was the rule that the employer is obliged to provide his worker with one month's prior notice of dismissal, or a month's remuneration in lieu thereof. This was deduced by the analogy of the landlord's duty, in Jewish law, to provide the tenant with a month's notice of eviction, in order that the latter be not deprived of a roof over his head; *a fortiori* in the case of a worker, so that he be given an opportunity to find an alternative source of livelihood. (Sh. Ar., ḤM 312:5; PDR, 4:130

and 3:281–3, where disputing opinions are quoted on the aptness of the analogy.)

In the State of Israel

In Mandatory times the obligation of severance pay was upheld in numerous judgments of the Mishpat ha-Shalom ha-Ivri. This fact contributed toward entrenchment of the usage, which came to be recognized as legally binding in a decision of the Mandatory High Court (Cohen v. Capun, in: *Palestine Law Reports* 7 (1940), 80, 88) and until 1963, custom alone formed the legal basis for the payment of severance pay under the general law. Thus the Supreme Court of Israel, in considering the antiquity of the above custom, stated: "It is common cause that the principle of severance pay is rooted in the scriptural duty of *ha'anakah*" (PDR, 5:275; 17, pt. 2:1255). The lack of statutory guidance led to many difficulties in the application of the custom. In 1963 the Severance Pay Law was enacted by the Knesset, with emphasis on the fact that the fundamental idea of this law derived from traditional Jewish law. The following are some of the law's main provisions:

A person dismissed by his employer after having been continuously employed for one year or – in the case of a seasonal employee – for two seasons in two consecutive years, is entitled to severance pay at the rate of a month's wages per year of employment for a "salaried employee" and two week's wages per year for employment for a "wage earner" (i.e., one whose remuneration is paid on the basis of a lesser period than one month; secs. 1, 12); in certain circumstances the employee is entitled to severance pay following his own resignation, i.e., by reason of an appreciable deterioration of his conditions of employment, or on account of his or a member of his family's state of health, or the transfer of his residence (secs. 6–8, 11). The employee is also entitled to severance pay if his employment has ceased owing to the death of his employer, and for certain other reasons (sec. 4) and upon the employee's own death, severance pay is payable to his survivors (sec. 5). A person employed under a contract for a fixed period is entitled to severance pay at the end of the period, as if dismissed, unless the employer has offered to renew the contract (sec. 9). Severance pay is deemed to be wages payable in precedence to all other debts (sec. 27) and a composition and acknowledgment of discharge as to severance pay are invalid unless reduced to writing and expressly state that they relate to severance pay (sec. 29).

[Menachem Elon]

SEVERANCE PAY – SOCIAL OBLIGATION, NOT SALARY The question of how to characterize severance pay – whether as a social right given to an employee who has been dismissed, irrespective of his salary, or as part of the salary – arose in the Israel Supreme Court in the case of *Ben Moshe* (CA 293/73, *Ben Moshe v. Ben Moshe*, 28(2) PD 29). In that case, the question arose in the context of divorce proceedings, regarding the scope of the husband's obligation to pay maintenance to the wife. The woman was entitled to receive a certain amount of money as severance pay from her employer. Classifying that severance pay as salary would result in it being regarded as money earned through her handiwork (*ma'asei yadeha*); consequently, her husband would be entitled to deduct the sum received as severance pay from his obligation to pay maintenance, inasmuch as her maintenance was offset by her income earned through her own handiwork (see *Maintenance). If, on the other hand, severance pay is classified as a social right unrelated to salary, it would not affect the husband's obligation to make maintenance payments.

The Court (Justice Kister) examined the one-time grant of severance pay by analogy to the laws of *ha'anakah* paid to a Jewish slave under Jewish law, in accordance with the aforementioned explanation of *Sefer ha-Ḥinukh*, (§482), on the basis of which he drew his conclusion regarding the nature of severance pay. Rambam rules that *ha'anakah* is given to the slave himself and not to his creditor (Yad, Avad. 3.15; p. 33 of the decision). *Me'irat Einayim* stresses that, unlike salary, which may be subject to a lien, *ha'anakah* is not subject to lien because "*ha'anakah* is not given to the Jewish slave under the rubric of a debt, but rather under the rubric of waiver and gift, according to the principles of amnesty" (*Me'irat Einayim*, Sh. Ar, ḤM, 86.2), while the *Shakh* rules that "it is known that *ha'anakah* is derived from the laws of *ẓedakah* (alms) (*Shakh*, ad loc., 3; p.34 of decision).

This was the basis for the Court's conclusion that severance pay is in the order of a social obligation imposed on the employer who fired his employee and is not a component of the employee's salary. (The Court noted that the term "laws of *ẓedakah*" does not imply that this is a purely moral obligation that cannot be imposed through coercion, inasmuch as the term *ẓedakah* derives from the same root as *ẓedek* (justice) and there are cases in which the giving of *ẓedakah* may be legally coerced. The term "laws of *ẓedakah*" should therefore be imputed the same meaning as the modern term "social obligations," which are also imposed by coercion). Accordingly, severance pay is not viewed as the wife's "handiwork" and should not be offset against the maintenance payments (decision, *supra*, pp. 33–35).

The Jerusalem Rabbinical Court (File 51/569, 18 PDR 346) dealt with a similar case, in which the provisions of a divorce agreement compelled the husband to pay his wife a specified percentage of his salary. The husband was fired from his job, and the question was whether his severance payment should be regarded as salary, in which case the husband would be obligated to pay his wife part of it pursuant to the agreement, or whether it should be regarded as a grant that is not regarded as salary. The minority opinion (Rav Kilav) was that, as law of the state requires severance payment, the employment contract between the employee and the employer was concluded in reliance upon the existence of this obligation, and therefore it should be viewed as part of the salary. On the other hand, if the employee and employer had agreed upon severance pay in excess of the statutorily mandated sum prior to the employee's dismissal, then the balance in excess of the statutory requirement should be viewed as a grant that is not part of the salary.

However, the majority opinion (Rabbi S. Fisher) was that severance pay is to be regarded as additional payment for years of service, similar to manager's insurance, and therefore should not be regarded as part of the salary but rather as a separate grant. Nonetheless, the majority concurred that severance pay not be regarded as "*ha'anakah*" within the meaning of that term in Jewish law, but rather as money paid by force of custom.

For a further discussion of the obligation to pay severance pay as a matter of the custom of the State and not as an obligation derived from the law of *ha-anaka*, see the opinion of the High Rabbinical Court in Case 59/734, PDR 21 188.

THE LEGAL POSITION IN THE STATE OF ISRAEL. As stated, the Rabbinical Court held that there are halakhic grounds for the duty of giving advance notice prior to an employee's dismissal or, alternatively, to provide compensation for dismissing an employee without prior notice (19/2535, 3 PDR 272; 4 PDR 126). In 2001, the Prior Notice of Dismissal or Resignation Law 2001, was enacted. This law establishes the employer's duty to give an employee prior notice of his/her impending dismissal within a certain prescribed period of time, as well as the employee's duty to give his employer prior notice a certain period of time prior to resigning. The law also provides that an employer dismissing an employee without prior notice is required to pay the employee an amount equivalent to his regular salary for the period of time prescribed, and that an employee who resigned without prior notice must pay his employer a penalty for the period during which the notice was not given.

[Menachem Elon (2nd ed.)]

BIBLIOGRAPHY: H. Baker, *Legal System of Israel* (1968), 189–94; M. Wager and P. Dickstein, *Pizzuyei Pitturin* (1940); S.B. Bar-Adon, *Dinei Avodah* (1942), 51–63; M. Finding, *Teḥukat ha-Avodah* (1945), 49f., 132f.; ET, 9 (1959), 673–87; Sh. Warhaftig, *Dinei Avodah ba-Mishpat ha-Ivri*, 2 (1969), 643–53, 1090–1100; M. Elon, in: ILR, 4 (1969), 87–89. **ADD. BIBLIOGRAPHY:** M. Elon, *Ha-Mishpat ha-Ivri* (1988), 1:140, 749f., 754, 765; 3:1367f, 1422, 1533; *ibid, Jewish Law* (1994), 1:158; 2:924, 929, 942; 4:1631, 1694, 1823; M. Elon and B. Lifshitz, *Mafte'aḥ ha-She'elot ve-ha-Teshuvot shel Ḥakhmei Sefarad u-Ẓefon Afrikah* (legal digest), 1 (1986), 84–85; B. Lifshitz and E. Shochetman, *Mafte'aḥ ha-She'elot ve-ha-Teshuvot shel Ḥakhmei Ashkenaz, Ẓarefat ve-Italyah* (legal digest) (1997), 55; B. Lifshitz, *Oved ve-Kablan – Bein Kinyan le-vein Hitḥayyevut* (1993).

HAARETZ (Heb. הָאָרֶץ), Israeli daily newspaper published in Tel Aviv. Established on June 18, 1919, by a group of businessmen headed by Isaac Leib *Goldberg and S. Salzmann, it was originally named *Hadashot Haaretz*. Edited by N. *Touroff, the contributors were Hebrew writers and journalists, recent immigrants from Russia. Its name was subsequently changed to *Haaretz*. The newspaper has since then had four editors. Dr. Moshe Gluecksohn was appointed editor in 1922, serving until 1939, a period during which the paper moved from Jerusalem to Tel Aviv. Gluecksohn's influence as editor was paramount, and during his editorship the paper acquired its liberal orientation. It was noted for its quality of writing, including its literary supplement. Its weak financial base made the newspaper dependent partly on philanthropists, including subsidies from Zionist institutions. In 1939 Salman *Schocken, a German immigrant, acquired the paper, appointing his son Gershom *Schocken as editor and publisher, a post he held for 51 years, and one characterized by absolute freedom of expression. Becoming an elitist highbrow newspaper, *Haaretz* was identified with the liberal wing of the Zionist movement. Its editorial policy was characterized by a minimalist stance on the Arab-Israeli conflict, and supported territorial withdrawal from territories captured in the 1967 war. Economically, the newspaper championed free enterprise in the face of the country's socialist ethos. It saw human rights as a supreme value. It supported separation of religion and state. While he saw the newspaper as an ideological vehicle, Schocken succeeded in strengthening its weak economic base, partly through establishing a chain of local newspapers in the 1980s. Upon his death in 1990, his son, Amos, became publisher, and Hanoch Marmori, editor. A graphic artist, and previously editor of *Ha-Ir*, the Schocken chain's local Tel Aviv newspaper, Marmori shook off the stuffy German heritage of the newspaper and attracted younger and non-Ashkenazi readers. In addition to the two main sections for news and for features and editorial comment, Marmori introducted a lifestyle section called "Galley," featuring culture and entertainment pieces, and a midweek Books Supplement. Noteworthy was its coverage of developments in the Palestinian Authority created after the 1993 Oslo Accords. The Palestinian Intifada beginning in 2000 brought to the surface sharp divisions inside the editorial board between a left of center stance, identified with Marmori, and the more extreme left-wing position of other editorial board members and the publisher, Amos Schocken, whose views reflected a "post-Zionism" outlook. Marmori resigned in 2004 after Schocken separated the newspaper's economic section from the main paper and made it an editorially independent supplement called "The Marker." David *Landau was appointed as Marmori's replacement. In 2005 the newspaper's circulation was 70,000 daily and 90,000 on weekends. *Haaretz*'s influence broadened with the establishment in 1997 of an English edition, of which Landau was the founding editor, which included the local printing of the *International Herald Tribune* and which had a daily circulation in 2005 of 12,000 and 20,000 on weekends. According to *Haaretz*, the newspaper's Internet websites in Hebrew and English had, respectively 700,000 and 1 million monthly users in 2005.

BIBLIOGRAPHY: O. Elyada, "*Haaretz* 1918–1937: From an Establishment-Sponsored Newspaper to a Commercial Newspaper," in: *Kesher*, 29 (2001) (Heb.); A. Katzman, "In the Liberal Tradition: *Haaretz*," in: *Kesher*, 25 (1999) (Heb.); G. Kressel, *Toledot ha-Ittonut ha-Ivrit be-ErezYisrael* (1964), 118–52.

[Yoel Cohen (2nd ed.)]

HAAS, FRITZ (1886–1969), German zoologist. Born in Frankfurt, Haas was the youngest of four children in a banker's family. His early interest in zoology was focused on mollusks, and his entire scientific career was devoted to a study of these animals. In 1911 he was appointed assistant keeper of invertebrate zoology at the Naturmuseum Senckenberg, Frankfurt. In 1914 Haas was on a collecting visit to the Pyrenees and was stranded in Spain for the duration of World War I. He put these years to productive use, and did extensive investigations with Spanish mollusks, which resulted in more than a score of papers on the molluscan fauna of Spain. On returning to Germany after the war, he became editor of the *Archiv fuer Molluskenkunde* and in 1922 was promoted to keeper of invertebrate zoology. With the advent of the Nazi regime, Haas was removed from his posts in 1936, and fled to the U.S. In 1938 he was appointed curator of lower invertebrates at the Field Museum of Natural History, Chicago. Though officially retired, from 1959 Haas continued his scientific activity with vigor, publishing a number of important monographs during the following decade, including the definitive monograph on freshwater clams in *Das Tierreich*.

BIBLIOGRAPHY: A. Solem, in: *Fieldiana: Zoology*, 53 no. 2 (1967), 71–144, includes bibliography of his writings.

[Mordecai L. Gabriel]

HAAS, GEORG (1905–1981), Israel zoologist. Born in Vienna, Haas studied zoology and paleontology. From 1931 to 1932 he was a visiting investigator at the Kaiser Wilhelm Institute in Berlin, where he did research on protozoan cytology. In 1933 he immigrated to Israel and joined the staff of the Hebrew University of Jerusalem. He was appointed professor in 1954.

Although Haas chief interest was the functional anatomy and evolution of reptiles, he also published extensively on the mollusks of Israel and on fossil reptiles and mammals of the region. A dedicated teacher, he had a seminal influence on the growth of zoological science in Israel, and many of Israel's outstanding zoologists were trained in his laboratory.

[Mordecai L. Gabriel]

HAAS, HUGO (1901–1968), Czechoslovakian actor and film director. Haas was with the National Theater in Prague before World War II and also acted in many Czech films. In 1939 he escaped from Nazi-occupied Prague and went to the United States. On Broadway, he appeared in Čapek's *R.U.R.* and in a dramatization of Tolstoy's *War and Peace*. He eventually formed his own company in Hollywood. Among his pictures were *Pick-up* (1951) and *Edge of Hell* (1956). He also played the title role in the TV series *Rabbi on Wheels*. In 1963, Haas settled in Vienna.

HAAS, LEO (1901–1983), Czech painter and cartoonist. His most important works were his drawings in the concentration camps of Nisko and Theresienstadt (Terezin) during World War II. In tortured lines and a grotesque expressionism, they captured the squalor and misery of human beings awaiting death. He hid the drawings in Terezin, but later recovered them, having survived Auschwitz, Sachsenhausen, and Mauthausen. Haas studied in Berlin and Vienna, and became director of a lithographic printing house in his birthplace, Opava. After the war, he returned to Czechoslovakia to become one of the leading political cartoonists of the Communist press. In 1955 he left for East Germany. He is represented in museums in Prague and East Berlin.

BIBLIOGRAPHY: F. Hermann, et al. (eds.), *Terezin* (Eng., 1965), 156–61, 319.

[Avigdor Dagan]

HAAS, LUDWIG (1875–1930), German politician. Born in Freiburg, Baden, Haas practiced law in Karlsruhe, where he was a city councilor from 1908 to 1919. In 1912 he entered the Reichstag as a member of the Progressive People's (later Democratic) Party. On the outbreak of World War I Haas volunteered for the army and was decorated for distinguished service on the Western front. At the end of 1915 he was seconded to the German military government of occupied Poland as head of the Jewish department, where he worked in close contact with Emanuel Carlebach and Pinchas *Kohn in an attempt to reorganize Polish Jewry. The Jewish community statute, which was the fruit of this collaboration, regulated the life of Polish Jewry until the end of the Polish republic in 1939. During the war he protested against the census of the Jewish soldiers in the German army (1916) because of its antisemitic connotation. After the 1918 revolution in Germany, Haas became minister of the interior in the first republican government of Baden. He continued to represent his party in the Reichstag, and became its chairman in 1929. Haas founded the *K-C Jewish student society at Freiburg, supported the Reichsbanner Schwarz-Rot-Gold (1924), and was active in the *Central-Verein deutscher Staatsbuerger juedischen Glaubens (Central Union of German Citizens of the Jewish Faith).

BIBLIOGRAPHY: Schrag-Haas, in: BLBI, 4 (1961), 73ff.; Carlebach, in: YLBI, 6 (1961), 62ff. **ADD. BIBLIOGRAPHY:** L. Luckemeyer, "Ludwig Haas als Reichstagsabgeordneter der Fortschrittlichen Volkspartei und der Deutschen Demokratischen Partei," in: G. Schulz (ed.), *Kritische Solidaritaet – Betrachtungen zum deutsch-juedischen Selbstverstaendnis* (1971), 119–74.

HAAS, SOLOMON BEN JEKUTHIEL KAUFMANN (d. 1847), Moravian rabbi and author. Haas studied under Benjamin Wolf Loew, rabbi of Kolin, then became a member of the *bet din* of Holleschau and later rabbi of Strassnitz (Moravia). Haas is the author of glosses to all four parts of the Shulḥan Arukh. Those to *Yoreh De'ah, Oraḥ Ḥayyim*, and *Even ha-Ezer* were published under the title *Kerem Shelomo* (Pressburg, 1840, 1843, and 1846 respectively), which was highly praised by Moses *Sofer, Nehemiah *Trebitsch, and Haas's teacher Benjamin Wolf Loew. He later made extensive additions to it. Those to *Ḥoshen Mishpat* were published in the *Likkutei Ḥaver ben Ḥayyim* of F. Plaut (Munkács, 1855). Other works, still in manuscript, include a volume of sermons of considerable interest for the cultural history of the time, and a collection of poems, *Benot ha-Shir* (completed in 1820), consisting of secular songs and plays, some of them translated from German into Hebrew.

BIBLIOGRAPHY: S. Wiener, *Kohelet Moshe* (1893–1918), 648, no. 5384; H. Gold, *Juden und Judengemeinden Maehrens* (1929), 520 f.

[Joseph Elijah Heller]

HAAS, WILLY (1891–1973), German essayist, critic, and translator. Born in Prague, where he studied law, Haas belonged to the literary circle of Franz *Werfel, Paul *Kornfeld, Max *Brod, and Franz *Kafka. While still a student he published in the *Herder-Blaetter* (1911–12), which was an early organ of the young German-Jewish poets of Prague. Moving to Berlin after the war, in which he served as officer, Haas pursued his career as a journalist, writing film reviews and screenplays and publishing among other things an essay in 1922 on his spiritual teacher Hugo von *Hofmannsthal emphasizing his Jewishness (in: *Juden in der deutschen Literatur*, ed. G. Krojanker), for which he was criticized by Hofmannsthal himself. Haas founded and edited the weekly, *Die literarische Welt*, from 1925 to 1933, which soon turned out to be one of the most important intellectual platforms in the Weimar Republic. With the rise of Nazism Haas went back to Prague trying to continue his weekly under the title *Die Welt im Wort*, and in 1939 to India working for a British film company. He returned to Germany in 1947 and joined the editorial staff of *Die Welt* in Hamburg. Haas dealt with the more profound problems of contemporary literary and cultural life and became one of postwar Germany's leading critics and essayists. He published books on Brecht (1958), Hofmannsthal (1964), the Belle Époque (1967), and his autobiography, *Die literarische Welt* (1957), where he gives a detailed account of his life in three countries.

ADD. BIBLIOGRAPHY: L. Valentini, *Willy Haas* (1986); P. Avenel, *Willy Haas et le périodique Die literarische Welt* (1995).

[Rudolf Kayser / Andreas Kilcher (2nd ed.)]

HAASE, HUGO (1863–1919), German socialist leader. Born in Allenstein, East Prussia, and a lawyer by profession, Haase became a socialist with a deeply humanitarian approach. He was first elected to the Reichstag as a Social Democrat in 1897 and after August Bebel's death in 1912 led the socialist faction. As a lawyer and attorney he defended the Social Democrats Karl Liebknecht and Otto Braun. At the second Socialist International, Haase worked for Franco-German friendship and the prevention of a European war. On the outbreak of World War I in August 1914 he was persuaded by the majority of the party that this was a war of self-defense and supported the German government, saying: "In the hour of danger we will not leave the Fatherland in the lurch." In 1915, however, he joined Karl Kautski and Eduard *Bernstein in a plea to stop the war, and left the Social Democrats to form the Independent Social Democrat Party which fought against the government's annexationist policies. In 1918, on the defeat of Germany and the outbreak of revolution, Haase became one of six members of the provisional government and for a time shared the presidency of the Council of the People's Deputies. He soon resigned, on the ground that the majority Socialist Party had deviated from the strict socialist line toward the bourgeois democratic establishment, and he formed his own left-wing opposition group in the Weimar National Assembly. After the foundation of the Communist Party he supported the reunion of the left-wing opposition with the Social Democratic Party. Haase was attacked by a German nationalist in October 1919 and died later as a result of his injuries.

BIBLIOGRAPHY: E. Haase (ed.), *Hugo Haase, sein Leben und Wirken* (1929). **ADD. BIBLIOGRAPHY:** L Heid, "'…das ich mit vielen Banden an Königsberg fest und gern hänge' – Hugo Haase eine Skizze," in: M. Brocke (ed.), *Zur Geschichte und Kultur der Juden in Ost- und Westpreussen* (2000), 485–509; K.R. Calkins, *Hugo Haase – Democrat and Revolutionary* (1979); D. Engelmann, *Hugo Haase – Lebensweg und politisches Vermächtnis eines streitbaren Sozialisten* (1999).

HA-ASIF (Heb. הָאָסִיף), six literary annuals, published in Warsaw intermittently from 1884 to 1894 and edited by Nahum *Sokolow. *Ha-Asif* was the first attempt to bring Hebrew literature to the masses at a popular price: volume 1 reached a circulation of 12,000, an unusual achievement for the period. Editorial policy, which favored cultural Zionism, considered Ereẓ Israel as one of the solutions to the Jewish problem, "however, to put all our trust in one suggestion is a great danger." Consequently *Ha-Asif* favored constructive action on behalf of Diaspora Jewry mainly in the cultural and intellectual realms. *Ha-Asif*'s ample volumes were filled with a variety of materials. The earlier volumes featured a practical, almanac-type section, which was dropped in the later issues, completely literary in content. Sokolow wrote the annual review in which literary matters were stressed. Among his colleagues were D. Frischmann, M. Weber, and I.Ḥ. Zagorodski. The contributors to the literary section included the leading authors of the period. Shalom Aleichem first published his original stories in Hebrew in *Ha-Asif*. In the Jewish studies section, which also occupied a prominent position, almost all Jewish scholars of note participated. Some published complete books (S. Bernfeld, translation of M. Kayserling's book on the Spanish and Portuguese Jews; *Ha-Asif* 4 (1887)). Others published ancient manuscripts. Sokolow's detailed reviews of new books and journals in Jewish studies dominated the criticism section. E. Atlas, another critic, published a series of sharp critical articles which are still of some relevance to contemporary criticism. Criticism of rabbinical literature – which, in general, was ignored by Hebrew periodicals – was published by I. Suwalski (vol. 4). *Ha-Asif* also contained articles about the Jews of Ereẓ Israel in the 19th century (J. Goldman, vols. 1–4 and Z. Wissotsky, vols. 4 and 7). J.D. Eisenstein published a survey of Jewish life in the United States (vol. 2). It also contained a section devoted to general sciences, including medical, scientific, and technical materials. The first Hebrew article on the flora of Ereẓ Israel also appeared in *Ha-Asif*. The success of *Ha-Asif* brought about the appearance of similar annuals. According to Sokolow, the mass circulation of *Ha-Asif* was a main cause of the creation of the Hebrew press (1886).

BIBLIOGRAPHY: G. Kressel (ed.), *Mivḥar Kitvei N. Sokolow*, 1–3 (1958–61), index; Waxman, Literature, 4 (1960) 452–4.

[Getzel Kressel]

HAAVARA, a company for the transfer of Jewish property from Nazi Germany to Palestine. The Trust and Transfer Office Haavara Ltd., was established in Tel Aviv, following an agreement with the German government in August 1933, to facilitate the emigration of Jews to Palestine by allowing the transfer of their capital in the form of German export goods. The Haavara Agreement is an instance where the question of Jewish rights, Zionist needs and individual rescue were in deep tension. Jewish organizations outside of Germany had declared a boycott against German goods and hoped to delegitimate the Nazi regime. The Zionists saw this agreement as a way of attracting Jews to Palestine and thus rescuing them from the Nazi universe even if that meant cooperation with Hitler. For a time the Nazi program of making Germany Judenrein and the Zionist policy of seeking *olim* coincided. The amounts to be transferred were paid by prospective emigrants into the account of a Jewish trust company (PALTREU – Palestina Treuhandstelle zur Beratung deutscher Juden) in Germany and used for the purchase of goods, which the Haavara then sold in Palestine. The proceeds, in Palestine currency, were paid to the emigrants living in Palestine. The rate of exchange was adjusted from time to time by the Haavara according to the disagio, necessitated by the subsidy which the Haavara granted the Palestinian importers, to make up for the steadily deteriorating value of the Reich mark, so the German goods could compete with other imports. The ensuing disagio, borne by the emigrants, accordingly increased from 6% in 1934 to 50% in 1938. The major part of the transfer proceeds provided the 1,000 Palestine Pounds (then $4,990) necessary for a "capitalist" immigration certificate of the Mandatory administration, but also for other categories of immigration, such as Youth Aliyah, students, and artisans as well as for the transfer of public funds. The transfer weakened the boycott of German goods declared by many Jewish organizations around the world, and thus met with considerable opposition. The controversy was settled at the Zionist Congress in Lucerne (1935) which decided by a vast majority in favor of the transfer and placed the Haavara under the supervision of the *Jewish Agency. The Zionists sought to attract immigrants to Palestine, most especially the affluent German Jewish immigrants and the Germans sought to get rid of their Jews, increase their exports and a propaganda victory by dividing the Jews regarding the boycott. The Haavara continued to function until World War II, in spite of vigorous attempts by the Nazi Party to stop or curtail its activities. The total transfer amounted to LP 8,100,000 (Palestine Pounds; then $40,419,000) including LP 2,600,000 (then $13,774,000) provided by the German Reichsbank in coordination with Haavara. The Haavara transfer was a major factor in making possible the immigration of approximately 60,000 German Jews to Palestine in the years 1933–1939, and together with the money invested by the immigrants themselves, in providing an incentive for the expansion of agricultural settlement and for general economic development. It also served as a model for a similar arrangement with the Czech government and the immigration of several thousand Jews on the eve of World War II.

BIBLIOGRAPHY: E. Marcus, in: *Yad Vashem Studies*, 2 (1958), 179–204; S. Esh. in: *Am Yisrael be-Dorenu* (1964), 330–43; L. Pinner, in: *In zwei Welten* (1962), 133–66. **ADD. BIBLIOGRAPHY:** E. Black, *The Transfer Agreement: The Dramatic Story of the Pact between Nazi Germany and Jewish Palestine* (2001).

[Ludwig Pinner]

HABAKKUK (Heb. חֲבַקּוּק; cf, Akk. *ḫambaququ* or *ḫabbaququ*, a fragrant herb), prophet at the time of the *Chaldeans' ascent to power in the early seventh century B.C.E. (Hab. 1:6), a time apparently after the Egyptian defeat at Carchemish (Jer. 46:2) and Hamath, when the Babylonian forces under Nebuchadnezzar occupied the area. The Book of Habakkuk is the eighth unit within the book of *tere ʿasar*, "the twelve," and consistently follows *Nahum in all textual witnesses. Habakkuk contains only three chapters (totaling 56 verses) and is traditionally divided into two parts according to content: narrative (chapters 1 and 2) and prayer (chapter 3). In many places the text is either enigmatic or corrupt. The Pesher Habakkuk from Qumran comments only on the first two chapters of our biblical book, thus supporting the view that the third chapter was not part of the original book (see below). The narrative consists of a series of five short prophetic utterances. The first (1:2–4) is a complaint (reminiscent of Jeremiah 12:1–2 and much of the book of Job) against God for allowing violence and injustice to prevail unchecked in the land, one of the great theological problems in biblical thought. The second utterance (1:5–12) is a divine oracle prophesying that the instrument of judgment – the Chaldeans – is near at hand. The depiction of the Chaldeans is ambivalent and its precise sense is debated. On the one hand, the Chaldeans are God's instrument; on the other hand, their description fits the typical biblical description of "the enemy" (e.g., Deut. 28:49–53; Isa. 5:26–30; Jer. 4:13; 5:15–17; 6:22–23). In 1:10 the prophet speaks of the Chaldeans' power in language usually reserved for describing the power of God: "And they scoff at kings, and princes are a derision to them" (cf. "who brings princes to nought, and makes the rulers of the earth as nothing" Isa. 40:23) and in the last words of verse 11: "guilty men, whose own might is their god" (in 1QpHab it is written "he makes his own might to be his god"). Thus, the instrument of justice is none other than the wicked enemy. The ambivalent description of the Chaldeans and the reiteration of the original question about divine justice have brought scholars to conclude that the Chaldeans are not the answer to the prophet's complaint but a heightened form of that complaint. When he speaks of the injustice in the world, Habakkuk is referring to the Chaldeans and their deeds. Like others who asked why the unjust thrive, Habakkuk relates the question to a specific historical situation. The third utterance (1:13–17) asks why God allows the wicked to devour the righteous, to which the fourth utterance (2:1–5) responds: eventually the wicked shall fail, but the righteous shall live by their faithfulness. The first biblical appearance of *qeẓ* ("end") in its apocalyptic sense is in Habakkuk, and subsequently in the Bible this usage is found exclusively in Daniel (8:19; 11:13, 27, 35; 12:4–13). Indeed, Dan. 10:14 looks like a "fulfillment" of Hab. 2:3.

The fifth utterance (2:6ff.) takes the form of five parables that begin with "woe to him" and stresses the punishment that the wicked will receive (some of the parables are found differently phrased in other books of the Bible, e.g., Isa. 14, 51; Jer. 22:13, which indicates their popularity among the people of Judah). The fifth parable contrasts idols – brilliantly ornamented, but utterly lifeless and dumb – to the divine glory of God, which strikes the whole world dumb.

The prayer comprising chapter 3 is divided into four sections (3:1–2, 3–7, 8–15, 16–19), the second and third sections recalling God's deeds, and the first and fourth constituting the essence of the prayer. Most scholars hold that chapter 3 was not part of the original Book of Habakkuk and bears no connection to the first two chapters. Other scholars, however, believe the entire book to be a single, continuous literary piece, and view chapter 3, which describes the punishment of the wicked, as a response to the questions raised in chapter 1. The prayer opens with "Upon Shigionoth" (3:1). The term *šiggāyôn* also occurs in the rubric of Ps. 7:1, and is probably borrowed from Akkadian *šigû* ("lamentation," "type of prayer"). The closing, in the manner of the Psalms with "For the Leader with string music" (*la-menaẓẓe'aḥ bi-neginotai*; 3:19), seems to be the introduction to another composition, now lost. In a spirit similar to that found in the beginning of the Blessing of *Moses, the Song of *Deborah, and Psalm 77 (17ff.), the prophet entreats the return of God's compassion. The prayer cites as precedent God's actions at the time of the Creation (Isa. 51:9; Hab. 3:2). Just as in other poetry in the Bible and in Ugaritic and Mesopotamian sources, the creator god had to fight off the forces of chaos such as the sea (Hab. 3:8, 9). References to historical battles combine with mythic ones. The sun and moon are personified and the ancient plague god *Resheph (3:5) brings pestilence. There may be a reference to the horned god Haby known from Ugaritic texts in Habakkuk 3:4. In the historical past, God delivered His people and His anointed one, smiting the wicked and "laying him bare from thigh to the neck" (Hab. 3:13). After recounting the past, the prophet looks to the future and prays: "May I be relieved on the day of trouble, when the [Chaldean?] people invade with their troops" (3:16). Habakkuk concludes by describing the effects of drought (3:17), a symbol of evil, but nevertheless his hope and faith: "yet I will rejoice in the Lord, I will exult in the God of my salvation" (verse 18).

The language of Habakkuk in general, and especially in the two middle sections of the prayer, is vigorous and rich, and abounds in ancient poetic and rhetorical forms, of which analogous examples appear in early biblical poetry (Blessing of Moses, Song of Deborah, etc.). It occasionally resembles Ugaritic poetry in construction, and at times also in the use of rhetoric (as in the use of climactic parallelism, 3:2, 8, 13), and archaic diction. Linguistic features that once argued for a late dating of the book (such as the absence of the definite article) might also be taken as signs of antiquity.

According to *Seder Olam Rabbah* 20, Habakkuk lived at the time of Manasseh (698–642 B.C.E.). Critical scholars now contend that he lived in the time of Jehoiakim (608–598 B.C.E.), and some place him earlier, at the end of Josiah's reign (639–609 B.C.E.), when the Assyrian kingdom was destroyed. However, Y. Kaufmann dates the prayer to the brief reign of Jehoiachin (597 B.C.E.). The hypothesis of B. Duhm that the word *Kasdim* (Chaldeans, 1:6) is to be emended to Kittim (Heb. כִּתִּים), and that it refers to the campaigns of Alexander the Great, has not been found acceptable. The *Dead Sea Scrolls show that as early as the time of the Second Temple the word "Chaldeans" was interpreted as referring to the Roman campaigns in the Orient in the sixties of the first century B.C.E. (see *Pesher).

According to legend, Habakkuk was the son of the Shunammite woman (Zohar, 1:7; 2:44–45). This identification is apparently based on his name, for the verb *ḥbq* ("to embrace") is employed in connection with the annunciation of the birth of the woman's son in II Kings 4:16. In the apocryphal story of Bel and the Dragon, which tells of Daniel's exploits against Babylonian idolatry, Habakkuk is presented as a contemporary of Daniel, probably because both mention the arrival of the Chaldeans (Hab. 1:6; Dan. 1:1). In the same story he is considered to be the son of Jeshua the Levite (Bel, 1). This reference is apparently to a levite family called Jeshua, which is mentioned in Ezra 2:40, et al. According to Rabbi Simlai (2nd generation *amora*), Habakkuk based all the 613 commandments received by Moses on the single principle that "the righteous shall live by his faith" (Hab. 2:4; Mak. 23b–24a). This may be a response to the Christian use of the verse by Paul as a prooftext for the doctrine of justification by faith rather than by works (Rom. 1:17; Gal. 3:11).

[Yehoshua M. Grintz and Dvora Briskin-Nadiv / S. David Sperling (2nd ed.)]

In the Arts

The prophet Habakkuk has inspired no literary works of major importance but is of some significance in art and music. He is identified with the prophet brought by an angel to nourish Daniel in the lions' den, and thus his attributes are an angel and a basket of bread. In Christian typography he is one of the prophets who foresaw the Nativity. He appears alone on the wooden doors of Santa Sabina, Rome (fifth century); in the 12th-century *Christian Typography* of Kosmas Indicopleustes (Vatican); and on the door of the Vierge Dorée (Amiens Cathedral, 13th century). The famous 15th-century statue by Donatello known as *Lo Zuccone* ("The Bald One") represents

Habakkuk. Formerly in the Florence Campanile, it is now in the Museo dell' Opera del Duomo, Florence. A 17th-century statue by Bernini in the Chigi Chapel at Santa Maria del Popolo, Rome, shows the angel lifting Habakkuk by his hair. He is frequently seen in company with Daniel. There are examples on fourth-century sarcophagi; on a sixth-century Coptic textile; again in the Kosmas Indicopleustes manuscripts; on a 13th-century bas-relief from the portal of the Virgin, Laon Cathedral; and on stained-glass windows in Auch (16th century) and Cambridge (17th century).

The psalm-like third chapter of Habakkuk is included among the *cantica* in the liturgy of all Christian denominations, and is generally sung to a simple psalmodic formula. There are a few art-music settings of this section, such as F. Giroust's *Domine quidvi auditionem* for chorus (1779) and, in the 20th century, cantatas entitled *Habakkuk* by György Kósa (1954) and Jacques Berlinski (b. 1913).

BIBLIOGRAPHY: B. Duhm, *Das Buch Habakuk* (1906); E. Sellin, *Das Zwölfprophetenbuch* (1930); M.D. Cassuto, in: *Keneset*, 8 (1943), 121–42; W.H. Ward, *Habakkuk* (ICC, 1911, 1948³); W.F. Albright, in: H.H. Rowley (ed.), *Studies in Old Testament Prophecy Presented to T.H. Robinson* (1950), 1–18; Kaufmann Y., Toledot, 3 (1960), 360–8; O. Eissfeldt, *The Old Testament, an Introduction* (1965), 416–23 (incl. bibl.); Ginzberg, Legends, index; M.H. Segal, *Mevo ha-Mikra*, 2 (1967⁴), 488–90. **ADD. BIBLIOGRAPHY:** Y. Avishur. *Enẓiklopediyah Olam ha-Tanakh*, vol. 15b (1993), 88–115; M. Graham, in: DBI, 1:475–78 (with bibliography); J.J.M. Roberts, *Nahum, Habakkuk and Zephaniah* (1991); M. Sweeney, in: VT, 41 (1991), 63–83; idem, in: ABD, 3:1–6; CAD 17/2, 413–14; P. Xella, in: DDD, 377; F. Andersen, *Habakkuk* (AB; 2001).

HABAKKUK, PROPHECY OF, book attributed to Habakkuk, in an appendix to the sixth-century lists of Apocrypha, the Stichometry of Nicephorus and that of Pseudo-Athanasius. It is mentioned together with works of Baruch, Ezekiel, and Daniel. Further, the title of **Bel and the Dragon* in the Septuagint (but not Theodotion) reads: "From the prophecy of Habakkuk son of Jesus of the tribe of Levi." This story tells how Daniel was cast into a lion's den. On the sixth day of his imprisonment Habakkuk was taking food to the reapers in the field in Judea, when he was seized by the hair and miraculously transported to Babylon, where he gave the food to Daniel. This story appears in the *Life of Habakkuk* in the Pseudo-Epiphanian *Lives of the Prophets* (ed. Torrey, 28 ff.) in a somewhat different version. The *Life* also ascribes to Habakkuk inter alia visions of the destruction, restoration, and subsequent destruction of the Temple. These might perhaps also reflect the Habakkuk apocryphon. The story is also known (apparently from Christian sources) in later Jewish works such as *Josippon*, *Chronicle of Jerahmeel* (ed. Gaster, 220 ff.), and *Sefer Yuḥasin* (1925), 238.

BIBLIOGRAPHY: M.R. James, *Lost Apocrypha* (1920); Charles, Apocrypha, 1 (1913), 652; A. Kahana, *Ha-Sefarim ha-Ḥiẓoniyyyim*, 1 (1936), 554–5.

[Michael E. Stone]

HABAS, BRACHA (1900–1968), Hebrew writer and editor; wife of David *Hacohen. Born in Alytus, Lithuania, she was taken to Palestine in 1907. After a period of teaching she turned to journalism, serving on the editorial board of the newspaper *Davar* (1935–53) and of the Am Oved publishing house. Among other publications she edited *Davar li-Yladim* and *Devar ha-Shavu'a*. Her books include: *Ḥomah u-Migdal* ("Stockade and Tower," 1939); *Korot Ma'pil Ẓa'ir* ("Story of a Young Immigrant," 1942): *Derakhim Avelot* ("Paths of Mourning," on the DP camps and the Jewish Brigade, 1946); *David Ben-Gurion ve-Doro* (1952); *Pagodot ha-Zahav* ("Golden Pagodas," Burmese legends, 1959); *Benot Ḥayil* (on Palestinian ATS volunteers, 1964); *Ḥayyav u-Moto shel Joop Westerweel* ("The Life and Death of Joop Westerweel," 1964); *Tenu'ah le-Lo Shem* ("Movement without a Name," on volunteer work by veteran settlers among new immigrants, 1965); *He-Ḥaẓer ve-ha-Givah* ("The Yard and the Hill," the story of kevuẓat *Kinneret, 1968). A list of her works translated into English appears in Goell, Bibliography, 28, 88, 96.

BIBLIOGRAPHY: J. Harari, *Ishah va-Em be-Yisrael* (1958), 470 f.; R. Katznelson, *Massot u-Reshimot* (1947), 207: *Kol Kitvei... G. Schoffmann*, 5 (1960), 130 f.: Tidhar, 3 (1949), 1128 f.; 16 (1967), 5001 f.

[Getzel Kressel]

ḤABBĀN, a town on the western border of *Ḥaḍramawt, formerly in the Wāḥidī Sultanate, an important junction and post on the incense way. It was the extreme southeastern settlement with a Jewish community. During the last generation of their life in *Yemen the Jews of Ḥabbān lived under the protection of Sulṭān Nāṣir ibn 'Abd Allah ibn Muḥsin. The community of Ḥabbān was the religious and social center for the Jewish communities around it. It numbered about 450 people, most of them divided into five main families: Maʿṭūf, Hillel, Shammākh, Maifa'ī, and 'Adanī. All of them were silversmiths and goldsmiths who wandered from one place to another to provide the Muslims with weapons and jewelry. In their wanderings they reached as far to the east at Mukallā, moving all over Ḥaḍramawt where Jews had not been allowed to dwell since the end of the 16th century. Some of them used to come home only for the High Holidays and Passover. With their leaving the country in 1949, however, the Jews of Ḥabbān carried with them the knowledge of working silver and gold which they had made their specialty.

Ḥabbāni Jews, like their Bayḍani coreligionists, lived in their own quarter (Ḥārat al-Yahūd), located on the down slopes of a hill. The sultan's palace separated the Jewish quarter from the Muslim quarter. The Jews lived in tall houses, two to five stories high, a situation against the ruling regulations throughout Yemen and other Muslim countries. There were two synagogues practicing a combination of the local old rite (*baladī*) and the newly imported Sephardi rite (*shāmī*). The synagogues also functioned as religious courts. The Jews of Ḥabbān were very different in their appearance and behavior from most other Yemenite Jews, as most of the discriminatory anti-Jewish Muslim regulations were not in force there.

They had long hair reaching down over their shoulders but no sidelocks, and did not wear black dresses but covered their bodies with multi-colored fabrics with a decorated belt, just like their Muslim tribal neighbors. The women tied nets decorated with silver jewelry around their heads and also wore wide silver belts. A few generations ago they apparently even used to carry weapons and took part in inter-tribal battles of the Muslims. There were no priests (Kohanim) and Levites among them. They were distinctive as well in terms of Jewish daily life. A few of them had already immigrarted to the land of Israel in the 1940s, but it was only after the establishment of the State of Israel that the community as a whole submitted their house keys to the local sultan and prepared themselves to immigrate to the new-born Jewish state. But the sultan did not give them permission and only after his unexpected death and the messengers of the State of Israel having paid a ransom for each of them were they allowed to leave for the British colony of *Aden and from there to fly to Israel. Most of them settled in their own settlement – moshav Bareket – where they could preserve their distinctive communal and religious life. Since their immigration they have attracted scholars in various fields and were the subject of many studies on communal life, folklore, music, health, and liturgy.

BIBLIOGRAPHY: S. Maʿtūf, *Yahadut Ḥabbān* (1987); K. Blady, *Jewish Communities in Exotic Places* (2000), Y. Tobi, *Moreshet Yehudei Teman* (1977), M. Rodionov, in: TEMA, 8 (2004), 153–68; S. Jawnieli, *Massa le-Teiman* (1952), 36–37, 222–8; J. Sha'ir, in: *Harel, Kovez Zikkaron… Rephael Alshekh* (1962), 231–5; T. Ashkenazi, in: *Sinai*, 22 (1947/48), 248–57; idem, in: JQR, 38 (1947/48), 93–96; Y. Shai, *Traditional Songs of the Habbani Women and Their Role in the Wedding* (1985).

[Yosef Tobi (2nd ed.)]

ḤABBAR, ḤABBAREI, persecutors of the Jews in Babylon, mentioned in the Babylonian Talmud. They created hardships for Jews, forbidding them to light lamps on their (the Ḥabbareis') festive days (Shab. 45a; Git. 17a), to perform burials and slaughter of animals (Yev. 63b) in accordance with Jewish law, and interfering with the proper observance of the festivals by the Jews (Beẓah 6a; see Rashi *ibid.*). The rise of the Ḥabbarei in Babylon may be established as occurring between the death of R. Ḥiyya the Great and that of Rabbah Bar Bar Ḥana, i.e., at the end of the first quarter of the third century C.E. (Yev. 63b). It is possible that the Ḥabbarei were Zoroastrian priests, fire worshipers, whose influence increased in Babylon in the course of that century after the rise to power of the Sassanid dynasty.

BIBLIOGRAPHY: Kohut, Arukh, 3 (1926), 339f.; S. Krauss, *Tosefot Arukh ha-Shalem* (1937), 178f.; J. Obermeyer, *Landschaft Babylonien* (1929), 262f.

[Moshe Beer]

HABE, HANS (pseudonym of **János Békessy**; 1911–1977), Budapest-born German novelist whose works reflect fierce opposition to the Nazis. Habe became the League of Nations correspondent of the *Prager Tagblatt* in 1935. On the outbreak of World War II he enlisted in the French army. He escaped from a German POW camp in 1940, and served in the U.S. forces for the rest of the war. In 1945 he founded the American-backed Munich *Neue Zeitung*. Habe's novels include *Drei ueber die Grenze* (1937: *Three over the Frontier*, 1939), *Weg ins Dunkel* (1951; first published as *Walk in Darkness*, 1949), and *Im Namen des Teufels* (1956; *Agent of the Devil*, 1959). The autobiographical *Ob Tausend Fallen* (1943; first published as *A Thousand Shall Fall*, 1941) describes the ordeal of foreign volunteers and loyal French troops deprived of arms and encouragement by the incompetent and defeatist French high command. His book on the assassination of President John F. Kennedy, *Der Tod in Texas* (1964), appeared in the U.S. as *The Wounded Land*. Habe also wrote an autobiography, *All My Sins* (1957); *Die Mission* (1965; *The Mission*, 1966), based on the *Evian Conference of 1938; and *Christopher and His Father* (1967), which deals with the question of Federal Germany's remorse. His autobiography was published under the title *Ich stelle mich – Meine Lebensgeschichte*.

ADD. BIBLIOGRAPHY: R.K. Zachau, "Hans Habe als Herausgeber der '*Neuen Zeitung*,'" in: W. Benz and M. Neiss, *Deutsch-Juedisches Exil – Das Ende der Assimilation?* (1994), 151–64.

HABER, family of German bankers. SALOMON (SAMUEL) HABER (1764–1839), born in Breslau, moved to Karlsruhe toward the end of the 18th century, and set up a banking and finance house. He and his sons were prominent in the early industrial development of Baden and Wuerttemberg, and from about 1820 S. Haber and Sons became one of Europe's leading bankers. In 1829 hereditary nobility was bestowed on Salomon's son LOUIS (LUDWIG; 1804–1892). Frequent marriages with other Jewish moneyed families fortified the Habers' financial and social status, but when in 1847 the bank experienced difficulties it was the government of Baden which came to the rescue, and not the family connections. Louis' brother MORITZ (1798–1874) took part in the formation of the Bank fuer Handel und Industrie in Darmstadt, the forerunner of the Darmstaedter Bank. Together with his brother Louis he was also among the founders of the Vienna Kreditanstalt (1855), and in 1863 of the Bodenkreditanstalt. The youngest of the brothers, SAMUEL (1812–1892), settled in Paris where Moritz had to take refuge after he had killed his opponent in a duel in Karlsruhe.

BIBLIOGRAPHY: H. Schnee, *Die Hoffinanz und der moderne Staat*, 4 (1963), 68–86.

[Joachim O. Ronall]

HABER, FRITZ (1868–1934), German physical chemist and Nobel laureate. Haber was born in Breslau, the son of a prosperous chemical and dye merchant and an alderman of the city. After a period in industry and business, he went in 1893 to the Technische Hochschule at Karlsruhe, and in 1906 became professor of physical and electrochemistry. His work on carbon bonds led to a rule bearing his name. Turning to electrochemistry, he wrote *Grundriss der technischen Electroche-*

mie auf theoretische Grundlage (1898) and was a co-developer of the glass electrode. In 1905 he wrote *Thermodynamics of Technical Gas Reactions*. His most important work, started in 1904, was the synthesis of ammonia from hydrogen and nitrogen. His laboratory demonstration interested Bosch, Bergius, and the Badische Anilin-und Sodafabrik companies, and they eventually developed the process into a commercial operation. Haber was awarded the Nobel Prize in chemistry in 1918 "for the synthesis of ammonia from its elements"; this work of Haber was to be invaluable to the German military effort in World War I. In 1911 he was made director of the new Kaiser Wilhelm Research Institute in Berlin-Dahlem, and in 1914 this was turned over to war work, particularly gas warfare, starting with chlorine and ending with mustard gas. After Germany's defeat, he reconstituted his Institute, and in the 1920s it became probably the leading center of physical chemistry in the world. Haber was president of the German Chemical Society, and of the Verband deutscher chemischer Vereine (which he created), and after some months spent in Japan he created the Japan Institute in Berlin and Tokyo.

Haber left the Jewish faith, and with the Nazi accession to power in 1933 was not immediately threatened but he was ordered to dismiss all the Jews on the staff of his institute. He refused and resigned. His health, already poor, deteriorated. He went to a sanatorium in Switzerland, where he died. In 1952 a tablet was unveiled in Haber's memory at the Kaiser Wilhelm Institute.

BIBLIOGRAPHY: M.H. Goran, *The Story of Fritz Haber* (1967), incl. bibl.; R. Stern, in: YLBI, 8 (1963), 70–102.

[Samuel Aaron Miller]

HABER, SAMUEL L. (1903–1984), U.S. economist and organization executive. Haber, who was born in Harlau, Romania, was taken to the U.S. in 1911. He received a B.A. from the University of Wisconsin in 1924. He worked as a researcher on labor and economic problems (1925–43), and then served in the U.S. Army, 1943–46. In 1947 Haber became director for Germany of the American Jewish Joint Distribution Committee, where he headed an extensive program for approximately 200,000 displaced persons (DPs). He developed and directed programs to assist in their rehabilitation and immigration to Israel, the United States, and other amenable countries. In 1954 Haber was sent to Morocco to organize a comprehensive Jewish welfare program for more than 50,000 of the country's 240,000 Jews. In 1957 he established a welfare program for Jews in Poland, becoming the first JDC representative permitted to function in that country since 1950. After serving as assistant director general of JDC's European headquarters in Geneva (1958–64) and assistant executive vice-chairman in New York (1964–67), Haber was appointed to succeed the murdered Charles *Jordan as Joint executive vice-chairman in 1967. Although Haber retired from the JDC at the end of 1975, his co-workers honored him by electing him honorary executive vice president of the organization.

From the 1960s to the early 1980s Haber was also a frequent speaker at fundraising campaigns in American Jewish communities; he served as vice chairman of the American Council of Agencies; vice president of the Israel Education Fund of the United Jewish Agency; national chairman of the Associates Division of the American Friends of Hebrew University; chairman of the executive committee of the Institute of Contemporary Jewry of Hebrew University; consultant for the Jewish Studies program of Columbia University; and trustee of the interfaith Hunger Appeal, which he helped establish in 1978.

[Ruth Beloff (2nd ed.)]

HABER, SHAMAI (1922–1995), Israel sculptor. He was born in Lodz, Poland, and in 1935 emigrated to Palestine where he studied in Tel Aviv and fought in the War of Independence. From 1949 he lived in Paris. He worked close to nature, and created portraits under the influence of such French masters as Charles Despiau. In 1954 he turned to abstraction. In 1962 he produced his first monumental work for the atomic reactor building at Naḥal Sorek (Nebi Rubin) in Israel. In 1965, together with Yitshak *Danziger, he created a monumental composition for the Israel Museum, Jerusalem. When he turned to abstraction Haber worked in stone. He used large blocks and assembled them in such a manner as to create a static relationship between the volumes and the spaces between them. The solitary presence of his sculpture in its surroundings has an archaic quality which is increased by his method of working the stone.

[Yona Fischer]

HABER, WILLIAM (1899–1988), economist and communal worker. Haber was born in Romania but immigrated to the U.S. in 1909. In 1937 he was appointed professor of economics at the University of Michigan in Ann Arbor, was chairman of the Department of Economics in 1962–63, and from 1963 to 1968 was dean of the College of Literature, Science, and the Arts.

Haber held important posts in U.S. government bodies, including that of chairman of the National Committee on Long Range Work and Relief Policy (1941); chief of the Planning Division of the Conference on Post War Relief Readjustment (1942); adviser on Manpower to the Director of War Mobilization (1945–46); and chairman of the Federal Advisory Council on Employment Security (1948–58). He was adviser on Jewish Affairs to Gen. Lucius Clay, Commander in Chief in Germany (1948–49).

Haber played a prominent role in Jewish organizations. He was chairman of the National Hillel Commission of B'nai Brith (1955–63) and of the Academic Council of the American Friends of the Hebrew University (1967). His main interest, however, was the *ORT organization. He was appointed president of the American ORT Federation in 1950, and continued in that office after his appointment as president of the Central Board of the World ORT Union in 1955. He retired from the ORT presidency in 1980, although he remained honorary president of the federation and the international group until his death. ORT created an award in Haber's honor in 1984, presented annually to people who have contributed to the federation's work or aims.

The University of Michigan also established an award in his honor. The William Haber Award is bestowed upon applicants who have created high-quality programs for the Jewish campus community.

Haber published some 20 books, including *Unemployment Relief and Economic Security* (1936), *The Michigan Economy* (1960), *Social Security: Programs, Problems and Policies* (1954, reprinted 1966), and *Unemployment Insurance in the American Economy* (with Merrill G. Murray, 1966). He also edited the book *Labor in a Changing America* (1966).

[Rohan Saxena (2nd ed.)]

HABERLANDT, GOTTLIEB (1854–1945), German plant physiologist. Born in Ungarisch-Altenberg, Hungary, Haberlandt rose to a professorship first at the University of Graz (Austria) and later at the University of Berlin. His contributions in the field of plant responses to environmental stimuli helped to establish plant physiology as a significant separate discipline within the biological sciences. In 1884 Haberlandt described the important relationship between the anatomy of plants and their physiological capacities in a classic volume, *Physiologische Pflanzenanatomie* (1884; *Physiological Plant Anatomy*, 1914). In utilizing function as a basis for establishing structural categories he anticipated 20th-century interest in physiological plant ecology. Later works include *Das Reizleitende Gewebesystem der Sinnpflanze* ("Stimuli Transmitting Tissue System of the Mimosa," 1890) and *Sinnesorgane im Pflanzenreich* ("Sense Organs of the Plant Kingdom," 1901) as well as numerous research reports dealing with the mechanism of plant tropisms, the significance of transpiration in the migration of nutrients, and the general functions of the vascular system.

BIBLIOGRAPHY: *Neue Deutsche Biographie*, 7 (1966), includes bibliography.

[George H. Fried]

HABERMAN, JOSHUA O. (1919–), U.S. Reform rabbi. Haberman was born in Vienna, where his education was interrupted by the German invasion of Austria in 1938. Fleeing to the United States, he earned his B.A. from the University of Cincinnati (1940) and M.H.L. from Hebrew Union College-Jewish Institute of Religion, where he was ordained in 1945. HUC-JIR awarded him an honorary Doctor of Divinity in 1970. His first pulpit was in Mobile, Alabama (1944–46), where he worked to bring the Reform and Conservative communities closer together as rabbi of Congregation Shaarei Shamayim (the Government Street Temple). While serving as rabbi of Temple Beth Zion in Buffalo, New York (1946–51), Haberman founded the *Hillel Center at the University of Buffalo, acting as its first director (1946–47). In 1951, he became rabbi of Har Sinai Temple in Trenton, New Jersey, whose membership quadrupled under his leadership. Haberman chaired both the Trenton Board of Rabbis and the local Israel Bonds Drive; coauthored *Encounter for Reconciliation: Guidelines for Inter-religious Dialogue*, published jointly by the *Union of American Hebrew Congregations and the United Presbyterian Church of America; and continued to foster mutual understanding within the Jewish community. He also lectured at Rutgers University and served on the Executive Committee of the Central Conference of American Rabbis (1967–69).

In 1969, Haberman was appointed rabbi of Washington Hebrew Congregation. His predecessor had been a classical Reform rabbi who was the son of an Orthodox *rosh yeshivah*. Haberman was far more traditional and far more oriented toward Israel. He developed a dialogue with the Roman Catholic diocese of Washington, D.C., with evangelical Christian leaders, and with Imam Wallace D. Muhammad of the World Community of Islam in the West. He served as president of the Washington Board of Rabbis (1982–84), as well as on the Advisory Committee on Ethical Values of the United States Information Agency (1982–83) and on the boards of directors of the Ethics and Public Policy Center (1983–89) and the Jewish Institute for National Security Affairs (1985). In 1984, in anticipation of retiring from the pulpit, he founded the Foundation for Jewish Studies, which sponsors cultural and educational programs for the entire Washington Jewish community as well as interested adherents of other faiths. In 1986, Haberman became rabbi emeritus of Washington Hebrew Congregation and assumed the active presidency of the FJS. On a national level, he was a member of the board of alumni overseers of the HUC-JIR and served as president of the National Association of Retired Reform Rabbis (NAORR, 1999–2000). In 2001, he was the representative of Jewish participation in the National Cathedral's memorial service marking 9/11.

Haberman contributed articles to English and German publications and wrote three books, *Philosopher of Revelation: The Life and Thought of S.L. Steinheim* (1990); *The God I Believe In: Conversations about Judaism with 14 Prominent Jewish Intellectuals* (1994), and *Healing Psalms: The Dialogues with God that Help You Cope with Life* (2000). In addition, he taught at Georgetown University, Wesley Theological Seminary, and American University. He received the Brotherhood Award of the National Conference of Christians and Jews (1978) and the Elie Wiesel Holocaust Remembrance Award, conferred by the State of Israel Bonds (1992). Haberman's son is an Orthodox rabbi.

[Bezalel Gordon (2nd ed.)]

HABERMANN, ABRAHAM MEIR (1901–1980), bibliographer and scholar of medieval Hebrew literature. Born at Zurawno (Galicia), Habermann from 1928 was librarian at the Schocken Library in Berlin. He immigrated to Palestine in 1934 and served as director of the Schocken Library in Jerusalem until 1967. From 1957 he taught medieval literature at Tel Aviv University (professor, 1969) and taught at the

Graduate Library School of the Hebrew University. He was editor of the department of bibliography (Jewish printers) for the *Encyclopaedia Hebraica* and the department of medieval Hebrew poetry for the first edition of the *Encyclopaedia Judaica*. Habermann began his study of medieval literature in 1925, specializing in the Ashkenazi *piyyut* from the time of R. Ephraim ben Jacob of Bonn. A prolific writer, his books include *Ha-Madpisim Benei Soncino* (1933): *Gevilim; Me'ah Sippurei Aggadah* (1942); *Ha-Genizah* (1944); *Toledot ha-Sefer ha-Ivri* (1945); *Ha-Piyyut* (1946); *Ateret Renanim, piyyutim* and songs for Sabbath and festivals (1967); *Ha-Sefer ha-Ivri be-Hitpatteḥuto* (1968); *Sha'arei Sefarim Ivriyyim* (1969); and *Toledot ha-Piyyut ve-ha-Shirah* (1970), which is the first attempt at a survey of the history of Hebrew *piyyut* and poetry and its development in various cultural centers from post-biblical times to the Haskalah period. Habermann edited and compiled such diverse medieval works as: *Piyyutei Rashi* (1941); *Seliḥot u-Fizmonim* of R. Gershom Me'or ha-Golah (1944; new printing, 2004); *Gezerot Ashkenaz ve-Ẓarefat* (1946); *Niẓoẓot Ge'ullah*, an anthology of redemption and messianism (1949); *Maḥberot Immanu'el ha-Romi* (1950); *Even Boḥan* of Kalonymus ben Kalonymus (1956); Studies of the Dead Sea Scrolls, *Edah ve-Edut* (1952), and *Megillot Midbar Yehudah* (1959). Shortly after his death, the Habermann Institute for Literary Research was created in Lod (Lydda), Israel. In 1983 Z. Malachi published *Yad le-Heman*, a memorial volume in his honor.

BIBLIOGRAPHY: Kressel, Leksikon, 1 (1965), 568f.

[Yehoshua Horowitz]

ḤABIB, ḤAYYIM BEN MOSES BEN SHEM TOV (16th century), rabbinical author. Among the Jews exiled from Portugal in 1497, he escaped to Fez. In 1505 he compiled over 3,000 responsa of Solomon b. Abraham *Adret, in *Sefer ha-Battim*. Ḥ.J.D. *Azulai heard of the existence of the manuscript in Fez. Joseph Samon, the author of *Edut Bi-Yhosef*, eventually took it to Jerusalem, where it came into the possession of Sussman Jawitz (1813–1881), father of the historian Ze'ev *Jawitz who had emigrated to Jerusalem from Warsaw (see introduction to *Berakhah Meshulleshet*, Warsaw, 1863). *Sefer ha-Battim* was published by Sussman's son Abraham, together with the glosses of Isaac Goldman who had also published Adret's novellae on tractate *Menaḥot*. Ḥabib's characteristic signature: "Ḥayyim b. Moses ibn Ḥabib whose knees did not kneel to Baal, nor to fire and wood," is probably an allusion to his flight from Portugal.

BIBLIOGRAPHY: Fuenn, Keneset, 355; J.M. Toledano, *Ner ha-Ma'arav* (1911), 86; Azulai, 2 (1852), 21 no. 131.

[Simon Marcus]

ḤABIB, MOSES BEN SOLOMON IBN (c. 1654–1696), Turkish rabbi and author. He was born in *Salonika, a descendant of *Levi ben Ḥabib, and went to Jerusalem in his youth. He studied in the yeshivah of Jacob *Ḥagiz and from c. 1677 to 1679 he traveled as an emissary of Jerusalem, reaching as far as Budapest. In 1688 Ḥabib was appointed head of the yeshivah in Jerusalem maintained by the philanthropist Moses ibn Ya'ish, of Constantinople. In the following year, on the death of Moses Galante, Ḥabib was appointed to succeed him as chief rabbi of Jerusalem (1689). His grandson, Jacob *Culi, who published most of his grandfather's works, also had in his possession a number of other manuscripts which he used in his own work *Me-'Am Lo'ez* (Constantinople, 1733). A manuscript of his sermons is in the National Library in Jerusalem. The ascription to him of the *Eẓ ha-Da'at* (printed in *Or Ẓaddikim*, Salonika, 1799) has been questioned by S. Ḥazzan.

He wrote the following works: *Get Pashut* (Ortakoi, 1719), on the laws of divorce and *ḥaliẓah; Shammot ba-Areẓ* (Constantinople, 1727), consisting of "*Yom Teru'ah*," on the tractate *Rosh Ha-Shanah*, "*Tosafot Yom ha-Kippurim*," on the tractate *Yoma*, and "*Kappot Temarim*," on the tractate *Sukkah* (Constantinople, 1731); and *Ezrat Nashim* (*ibid.*, 1731), on the laws of *agunah*. Ḥ.J.D. *Azulai states that most of Ḥabib's responsa were lost at sea; however some have survived, and have been published, part in *Kol Gadol* (Jerusalem, 1907), and part in the works of contemporary scholars (*Devar Sha'ul*, 1927). Moses also wrote a commentary on the Jerusalem Talmud entitled *Penei Moshe* of which tractates *Berakhot, Pe'ah*, and *Demai* are extant in manuscript (Sassoon Ms. 592).

BIBLIOGRAPHY: S. Ḥazzan, *Ha-Ma'alot li-Shelomo* (1859); Rosanes, Togarmah, 4 (1935), 326–8; 5 (1938), 14; Frumkin-Rivlin, 2 (1928), 89–91; M.D. Gaon, *Yehudei ha-Mizraḥ be-Ereẓ Yisrael*, 2 (1938), 241; Yaari, Sheluḥei, 298f.; J. Molcho, in: *Oẓar Yehudei Sefarad*, 5 (1962), 81ff.; Scholem, *Shabbetai Ẓevi*, 1 (1959), 200f.; D.S. Sassoon, *Ohel Dawid*, 1 (1932), 104–6; Lieberman, in: *Sefer ha-Yovel… A. Marx* (1950), 313–5; Benayahu, in: *Tarbiz*, 21 (1950), 58–60.

[Simon Marcus]

ḤABIBA, JOSEPH (beginning of the 15th century), Spanish talmudic scholar. Virtually no biographical details are known of Ḥabiba. His teachers were *Nissim b. Reuben (the Ran) and Ḥasdai *Crescas. Author of novellae to the Talmud and a commentary on Isaac *Alfasi known as the *Nimmukei Yosef*, he is regarded as the last of the *rishonim to comment on the Talmud and the *Hilkhot ha-Rif*. It was previously thought that Ḥabiba wrote commentaries only to those tractates of Alfasi on which Nissim b. Reuben did not comment, but it is now believed that his commentary covered the whole work. Only his commentaries to tractates *Mo'ed Katan, Yevamot, Bava Kamma, Bava Meẓia, Bava Batra, Sanhedrin*, and *Makkot* have been published in editions of the Talmud, but his commentaries to the tractates *Megillah* and *Pesaḥim* (1960) and to *Gittin* (1963) and *Avodah Zarah* in M.J. Blau (ed.), *Shitat ha-Kadmonim al Massekhet Avodah Zarah* (1969) have been published. His commentaries on *Berakhot, Shabbat, Ta'anit*, and *Ḥullin*, are still in manuscript. Of his novellae to the Talmud there have been published *Shevuot* (in *Beit ha-Beḥirah* of Menahem ha-Meiri; Leghorn, 1795), and *Ketubbot* and *Nedarim* (in the *Ishei ha-Shem, ibid.*, 1795, new ed. 1960).

In his commentary Ḥabiba usually quotes the *geonim*, the

Spanish *posekim until *Jacob b. Asher, and Yom Tov *Vidal of Tolosa. According to Malachi ha-Kohen (in his *Yad Malakhi*), Ḥabiba differs from Nissim in that he quotes the aforementioned authors and Yom Tov b. Abraham *Ishbili, and in that he commences each of the novellae with "the author says" and concludes with "thus far the words of the author," something not found in the works of other *rishonim*. It is this characteristic, as well as the numerous quotations from the works of Yom Tov Ishbili and Asher b. Jehiel, which serve as indubitable indications of the author of the *Nimmukei Yosef*. Ḥabiba's style is direct and succinct. Some see his commentaries as aimed at encouraging the study of Talmud rather than the *Hilkhot ha-Rif*, which, through its wide circulation, tended to displace the study of the Talmud. Consequently *Nimmukei Yosef* is regarded as a supplement rather than a commentary, the addition of passages of the Talmud omitted by Alfasi making the talmudic text readily available to the student. The *Nimmukei Yosef* is a valuable source for clarifying the opinions and approach of various *rishonim*, since in addition to quoting from their actual works he also gives oral traditions handed down by their pupils. He was highly regarded in later generations as an authoritative *posek*.

BIBLIOGRAPHY: Malachi b. Jacob ha-Kohen, *Yad Malakhi* (Przemysl, 1888 ed.), 154d; Weiss, Dor, 5 (1904[4]), 760f.; H. Tchernowitz, *Toledot ha-Posekim*, 1 (1946), 163f.; M.J. Blau (ed.), in: J. Ḥabiba, *Nimmukei Yosef al Massekhtot Megillah u-Fesaḥim* (1960), introd.; M. Margalioth (ed.), *Hilkhot ha-Nagid* (1962), 79; Waxman, Literature, 2 (1960), 112.

[Yehoshua Horowitz]

°HABIBI, EMIL (1922–1996), Israeli Arab poet and Knesset member. A Christian Arab born in Haifa, after 1948 he was a founder of the Israel Communist Party and a Knesset member on its behalf. He left the Knesset in 1972 to devote himself to editing *Al-Ittihad* and to his literary work. In 1983 he founded the Committee of Israeli and Palestinian Writers, Artists and Academics, on which he served as chairman until he died. In 1990 he founded the Arabesque Publishing House. In 1991 he withdrew from active political life. In 1992 he received the Israel Prize for literature and poetry. In 1995 he began publishing *Masharef*, a periodical of Palestinian literature. He wrote several novels as well as shorter items, many of which have been translated from Arabic into Hebrew. His writings, which opened a window to the Palestinian experience in general and in Israel in particular, express his special feeling for Haifa, the city of his birth, where he also chose to be buried. The inscription on his tombstone sums up this emotional and political connection: "I Stayed in Haifa."

[Shaked Gilboa (2nd ed.)]

ḤABIL, the name of four places inhabited by Jews at the time of their emigration from Yemen (1948–49). All four are located in the southernmost regions of present-day Yemen, or close to its border. Among the *genizah* fragments there is a letter of appointment from a *gaon* to a person, whose name has not been preserved, requesting that the latter undertake the collection of funds for the Babylonian Academy. A letter was sent to the inhabitants of al-Ṣawīl and al-Ḥabil, which was to be read to them so that they would make their contributions; these were to be sent to the head of the academy in San'a or the emissaries of the academies in Yaman and Yamāma.

BIBLIOGRAPHY: S.D. Goitein, in: *Tarbiz*, 31 (1961/62), 360–1.

[Haïm Z'ew Hirschberg]

HABILLO, DAVID (d. 1661), kabbalist of Safed and Jerusalem and emissary from Jerusalem. Habillo was the outstanding pupil of the kabbalist Benjamin b. Meir ha-Levi of Safed, whom he accompanied when he moved to Jerusalem. Ḥ.J.D. Azulai relates that the veteran rabbis of Jerusalem told him that Habillo lived there in 1652 and had a heavenly mentor (*maggid*). Habillo wrote a commentary on *Sefer Yeẓirah* which has remained in manuscript. During the 1650s he went to Turkey as an emissary from Jerusalem. He met Abraham Yakhini in Constantinople before 1660 and also the youthful *Shabbetai Ẓevi, who almost certainly learned Kabbalah from Habillo. When Shabbetai Ẓevi was subsequently compelled to leave Constantinople, he proceeded to Smyrna with Habillo, who died there on the ninth of Av. After his death a dispute arose between his son, JUDAH HABILLO, who claimed the inheritance left in Smyrna by his father, and the heads of the Jerusalem community, who claimed the money as the proceeds of the mission on their behalf. Ḥayyim *Benveniste, the *av bet din* of Smyrna, decided in favor of the son.

BIBLIOGRAPHY: Azulai, 1 (1852), 23a no. 17; A. Freimann, *Inyanei Shabbetai Ẓevi* (1912), 141 no. 9; Frumkin-Rivlin, 2 (1928), 29, 34, 69f.; Yaari, Sheluḥei, 154, 283, 287; G. Scholem, in: *Zion*, 13–14 (1948–49), 61f.; Scholem, Shabbetai Ẓevi, 1 (1957), 138–40, 154.

[Avraham Yaari]

HABILLO (Xabillo), ELIJAH BEN JOSEPH (Maestro Manoel; second half 15th cent.), Spanish philosopher and translator of philosophical writings. Habillo was an admirer of Christian scholasticism, and translated some of the works of the Christian scholastics from Latin into Hebrew, including: Thomas *Aquinas' *Quaestiones disputatae, Quaestio de anima* (*"She'elot ba-Nefesh"*), *De animae facultatibus* (*"Ma'amar be-Koḥot ha-Nefesh,"* published by A. Jellinek in *Philosophie und Kabbala*, 1854), *De universalibus* (*"Be-Inyan ha-Kolel"*), and questions on Aquinas' treatise *De ente de essentia* (*"She'elot Ma'amar be-Nimẓa u-ve-Mahut"*); William of Occam's three treatises entitled *Summa totius logicae* (*"Perakim be-Kolel"*), to which he added an appendix, and *Quaestiones Philosophicae*; and the pseudo-Aristotelian *Liber de causis* (*"Sefer ha-Sibbot"*). It is also supposed that Habillo translated anonymously Vincenz of Beauvais' *De universalibus* under the title *Ma'amar Nikhbad be-'Kelal'* (see M. Steinschneider, Parma Ms. no. 457[7]).

BIBLIOGRAPHY: S. Munk, in: OLZ, 7 (1904), 725; Munk, Mélanges, 303; Steinschneider, Uebersetzungen, 265, 470, 477, 483.

HABILLO, ELISHA (called **Mercado**; 1719–1792), rabbi of Sarajevo. Habillo studied under David *Pardo, author of *Shoshannim le-David*. He wrote *Avodat ha-Tamid* (Sarajevo, 1788), a commentary on the Sephardi liturgy for the whole year, together with the order of service for weekdays, with brief laws and explanations. In this work the author at times cites the explanations of Nehemiah *Ḥayon, only to dissociate himself from them at the end. He published his teacher's book of prayers for festivals, *Shifat Revivim* (Leghorn, 1787), including in the original his elegy on the ill-treatment by the Turks of the Sarajevo Jews who fled from the Austrians, and added a number of his poems. Habillo also wrote a commentary on the Passover *Haggadah* and on the Grace after Meals.

BIBLIOGRAPHY: M.D. Gaon, *Yehudei ha-Mizraḥ be-Ereẓ Yisrael*, 2 (1938), 242; Frumkin-Rivlin, 3 (1929), 97; Rosanes, Togarmah, 5 (1938), 177.

[Simon Marcus]

HABIMAH (Heb. הבימה; "the Stage"), repertory theater company; founded in Moscow in 1917 as the first professional Hebrew theater in the world, and now the National Theater of Israel. Its initiator was Nahum David *Zemach, who was joined by Menahem Gnessin and the actress Ḥannah *Rovina in Warsaw, but World War I halted their efforts. They met again in Moscow in 1917 and were soon joined by a number of young Jewish actors. Their idea was not simply to found a theater but to give expression to the revolutionary change in the situation of the Jewish people and especially to the revival of Hebrew. Zemach turned to the great Russian theater director Konstantin Stanislavski and adopted his famous "method." It was, in fact, their idealism which enabled the Habimah actors to overcome the great initial difficulties, first of all the economic problem of the revolutionary period. David Vardi, one of its founding members, wrote in his diary in September, 1918: "Today we held a meeting… On the agenda was the food problem. It was decided to send two members out to the country, to look for potatoes and flour… We were each allotted a [role]. Mine was to bring potatoes from the he-Ḥalutz farm to the Habimah cooperative kitchen…."

There were also political problems. The Yevsektsiya, the Jewish section of the Communist Party, lodged a protest with Stalin, the People's Commissar of Nationalities, against Habimah's very existence. Stalin, however, overruled their intervention (1920). In this struggle Zemach succeeded in enlisting the support of leading artists, writers, and political personalities, such as Lunacharski, the commissar for education and culture, who proved a true friend of Habimah. Maxim *Gorki was also an enthusiastic supporter. Habimah introduced plays of a type that had never been staged by Jewish troupes, and they were directed by great teachers, all of them non-Jewish disciples of Stanislavski.

Habimah first performed in 1918, presenting four one-act plays by Jewish writers. It became one of the four studios of the Moscow Art Theater. Habimah scored its greatest triumph with S. *An-Ski's *The Dybbuk*, which was the third play it staged. Bialik translated it into Hebrew and Joel Engel composed its musical score. Its first performance took place on Jan. 31, 1922, and it established Habimah's reputation, as well as that of Yevgeni Vakhtangov, a young director of Armenian origin who had been delegated to Habimah by Stanislavski.

The Dybbuk owed its triumph to its outstanding orchestration, its forceful symbolism, and its glaring contrasts, but mainly to the boundless enthusiasm of the company in its acting and singing. Even in the mass scenes, every person on the stage gave his individual, distinct contribution; every Ḥasid and every beggar stood for something different, and yet together they formed a team. Vakhtangov's method, which was an endless process of refining, came to its perfect expression in the beggars' dance in Act II. In 1926 Habimah left Soviet Russia and went on a tour abroad. *The Dybbuk* was hailed as an unusual phenomenon. In 1927, when Habimah arrived in the United States, the company split. Zemach and several actors decided to stay in the country. According to David Vardi, "differences arose between Zemach and some of the younger actors, who had taken a giant step forward, of which Zemach hardly took note."

Habimah visited Palestine in 1928–29 and presented two productions, *Ha-Oẓar* ("The Treasure") by *Shalom Aleichem and *Keter David* ("David's Crown") by Calderon, both under the direction of the Russian Alexander Diki. In 1930 the company went to Berlin, where it performed *Twelfth Night*, directed by Michael Chekhov, and *Uriel da Costa*, under the direction of Alexander Granovski. It finally settled in Palestine in 1931. In the course of time it added to its repertoire a great variety of plays derived both from Jewish literature (of messianic and biblical content) and from world literature. It sought to foster dramas depicting Jewish life in the Diaspora, which it succeeded in presenting with extraordinary authenticity. Its aim was to present all phases of Jewish historical experience.

For the next 17 years Habimah was under the direction of its own members, mainly Barukh Chemerinsky and Ẓevi Friedland, the former concentrating on Diaspora dramas and original Hebrew plays, and the latter on world drama. Eventually Habimah also invited foreign directors, such as Leopold Lindberg, Leopold Jessner, and Tyrone Guthrie. It was Guthrie's 1948 production of *Oedipus Rex* which inaugurated a new era in the life of the company.

In the period in which Habimah relied mainly on its own directors, progress was slow. Each new performance became a festive occasion and Habimah had its admirers, a Habimah "circle," and a youth studio, as well as its own periodical (*Bamah*); but the company failed to keep pace with the cultural and social transformation of the *yishuv*. It did not rid itself of expressionistic oddities, and young people, as well as immigrants from the West, kept away. It also did not absorb the young talent which was crying out for a chance to prove its mettle. The graduates of the company's school for the most part joined the *Cameri, whose founding caused a crisis for Habimah.

In April 1948, Habimah went on a tour of the United States, presenting four productions (*The Dybbuk, The Golem, Keter David,* and *Oedipus Rex*). Although acclaimed by the critics, Habimah failed to attract audiences. When the company returned to Israel in July, it had nothing in its repertoire to express the heroic period of the national struggle. There was also conflict over the company's organization. For years there had been opposition to the continued existence of Habimah as a "collective," for it was argued that such a structure had become an obstacle to the company's progress because of the undue protection that it provided to members who had failed to attain the required artistic standard. This conflict was to remain unresolved for another two decades. Relief came from an unexpected quarter, the "generation of 1948." Yigal Mossinsohn's play *Be-Arvot ha-Negev* ("In the Negev Desert") had its premiere in February 1949 and met with an enthusiastic response. It expressed the spirit of the times, the highlights being Aharon Meskin's masterful acting and the play's portrayal of the new Israel-born generation.

In the following years Habimah enlisted directors of world renown: André Barsac from France, Alexander Bardini from Poland, Sven Malmquist from Sweden, John Hirsch from Canada, and Lee Strasberg and Harold Clurman from the United States. Under their direction, Habimah successfully mounted high-quality productions. At the same time, it continued to employ its own directors – Ẓevi Friedland, Israel Becker, Shimon Finkel, Shraga Friedman, and Avraham Ninio.

In 1958, on the 40th anniversary of its first performance in Moscow, Habimah was awarded the title of "National Theater of Israel." The honorific award could not, however, conceal the company's shortcomings. There was neither an artistic authority nor a true collective, and conflicts between various factions, as well as financial difficulties, threatened the theater's very existence. Finally, in 1969, the members decided to dissolve the "collective." The Ministry of Education and Culture appointed its representatives to the management of Habimah, and a new administering director, Gavriel Zifroni, took over. In 1970 Habimah dedicated its beautiful renovated hall in the center of Tel Aviv. In the same year the veteran actor Shimon Finkel was appointed artistic director. In 1972 it opened the Bamartef small hall for experimental productions. In 1975, Yossi Yisraeli was named artistic director. In 1976, Ḥannah Rovina played her last role as the queen mother in Shakespeare's *Richard III*. In the same year, Shlomo Bar Shavit became artistic director. In 1978, Shmuel Omer was named general director and David Levin artistic director, replaced in 1985 by Omri Nizan. In 1986 Habimah went on tour to Moscow. In 1992, Shmuel Omer became both general and artistic director. In 1995 Yaakov Agmon replaced him, remaining at the helm until 2004. In 1995 Ilan Ronen established the Habimah's youth group, which aimed at advancing young actors. In 1997 Habimah produced *The Dybbuk,* its most popular play, to celebrate the theater's 80th birthday. Under Agmon's management, the theater began to produce successful musicals, such as *Bustan Sefaradi* ("Spanish Orchard") and *Mary Lou* (based on songs of the pop composer-singer Zvika Pick). In 2004 Habimah employed 80 actors performing in 33 productions.

BIBLIOGRAPHY: M. Kohansky, *The Hebrew Theatre* (1969), 76–85, 113–26 and index; N. Zemach, *Be-Reshit ha-Bimah* (1966); Y. Bertonov, *Orot mi-be ad la-Masakh* (1969); M. Gnessin, *Darki im ha-Te'atron ha-Ivri* (1946). **WEBSITE:** www.habima.org.il.

ḪABIRU (or better: **Ḫapiru**), an element of society in the Fertile Crescent during the greater part of the second millennium B.C.E. They are mentioned in more than 250 texts. From their earliest appearance in documents of the 18th century B.C.E., the Ḫabiru constitute a class of dependents, displaced people who originated from both urban and tribal sedentary populations, not from nomadic groups. In the early Assyrian and Babylonian period (18th–17th centuries) they appear in Cappadocia and in the kingdoms of Larsa, Babylon, Mari and the surrounding areas as bands of warriors attached to, and maintained by, the local rulers. Fifteenth-century documents of Alalakh (northern Syria) list the members of the Ḫabiru military units belonging to the adjacent towns. Nuzi documents of the same periods mention Ḫabiru units and individuals as receiving protection from the state. However, what is unique in these Nuzi documents is the number of contracts entered into between individual Ḫabiru men and women and wealthy citizens in which the relationship partakes of the character of both slavery and adoption. Hittite documents of the 14th and 13th centuries B.C.E. list the gods of the Ḫabiru among others who are signatories to international alliances. Hittite cult documents place the Ḫabiru (Ḫapiri) at the head of a list of subject and enslaved peoples or classes. Akkadian documents from Ugarit mention "the Ḫabiru [= SA. GAZ] of the Sun [= king of Heth]" and in Ugaritic alphabetic script *Ḫlb ʿprm* i.e., the Ḫabiru quarter of the city of Ḫalbu (not identical with the great city of Ḥalab). From the 15th to the 12th centuries the *ʿpr.w* appear in Egyptian documents as captives from Palestine-Syria, and as slaves of the state.

Along with their appearance as dependents and protégés in lands of stable government, independent groups of Ḫabiru appear in times of disintegrating rule and lack of central control. In the Mari period of clashes between nations and cities, the Ḫabiru appear as robber bands, which attacked and plundered settlements, either on their own or together with residents of nearby settlements. Similarly in Palestine-Syria during the *el-Amarna period (15th–14th centuries B.C.E.), the confusion that resulted from the clashes between the local princes and the Egyptian governors provided an opportune time for the bands of Ḫabiru to run wild. On their own, together with local people, or as mercenaries helping either the city princes or the Egyptians they contributed greatly to the general confusion that was characteristic of the period.

The Ḫabiru were of varied origin. In Mari, a band of auxiliary soldiers was called Iamutbalian Ḫabiru ("i̯amutbalāju

Ḫa-bi-ru"), the former being the name of a western Semitic tribe and of the territory west of Baghdad. Documents from Mari and Alalakh cite cities as the origin of most of the Ḫabiru listed. Some of the Ḫabiru in Nuzi came from Akkad, Assyria, etc. A significant element among the Ḫabiru of the El-Amarna period was mutineers against the local kinglets. Their names also testify to a varied ethnic makeup: an early Babylonian list includes Akkadian and Western Semitic names; in Alalakh the names are principally non-Semitic (which corresponds with the surroundings); and in Nuzi there is a mixture of Akkadian and non-Semitic names. The ease with which they absorbed everyone who wished "to be a Ḫabiru" (in the language of the documents) indicates that they were not distinguished by ethnic unity.

All those called Ḫabiru shared a common inferior status. Almost all were fugitives from their original societies, and, as strangers without rights, they made themselves dependent on lords. For a few it is specifically noted that they were fugitives from authority or from personal calamities, or ordinary scoundrels (cf. similar bands in Israel during the biblical period: Judg. 9:4, 26ff.; 11:3; and especially David's band, I Sam. 22:2). The circumstances in which the Ḫabiru emerged are unclear. There are vague indications of a western-Semitic origin: their name; a settlement of Amorite (= MAR.TU; see *Amorites) soldiers of the early Babylonian period, named *Ḫa-bi-ri* (KI); the fact that the documents about them begin to appear at the height of Amorite migration to Mesopotamia. It is possible that Amorite unfortunates, stripped of land and possessions, formed the original core to which a rabble of paupers, refugees, and criminals was attracted in the course of time, without consideration of ethnic origin.

Ugaritic and Egyptian writings indicate that the root of the word Ḫabiru is *ʿapiru* (noun form). The existence of the *ʿayin* in the cuneiform, in the sign *ḪA*, points to a western-Semitic origin, since ordinarily the initial *ʿayin* becomes an *ʾalef* in Akkadian which is not the present case. These writings also establish the pronunciation of the second syllable – *BI* in cuneiform must in this case represent *pi*, which makes it highly unlikely that the word is to be derived from *ʿBR*.

In many sources the ideogram SA.GAZ is interchangeable with the term "Ḫabiru." This ideogram is translated in late lexicographical lists by the word *ḫa-ba-tu*, meaning "robber," but also migratory workers, who in El-Amarna letter no. 318:11–12 are kept apart from the Ḫabiru. (The later lexical identifications are not conclusive evidence.) It is probable that in many places the ideogram was pronounced Ḫabiru, but there is no definite proof for this. Some read the ideogram as *ša-ga-šu* based on the variants SA.GA.AZ, SAG.GAZ, meaning "murderer" (as in Akkadian) or "restless, foul" (as in Aramaic and Arabic). In any event, it is clear that both SA.GAZ and Ḫabiru had a negative connotation, to the extent that at times (and many such instances appear in the El-Amarna letters) the terms were used as synonyms for mutineers and paupers.

[Moshe Greenberg]

Habiru and the Hebrews

The problem of the connection between the Ḫabiru and the Hebrews has been discussed for almost 150 years. The earlier stages of the problem are summarized by M. Greenberg (in bibl., 4–12, esp., 91–96; see R. de Vaux, W.F. Albright, M.P. Gray, J. Weingreen, J. Bottéro and E.F. Campbell in bibl.; see also *el-Amarna). For more recent discussion, see Additional Bibliography.

One cannot simply equate Ḫabiru with the "Hebrews" because it is clear that the Ḫabiru are always a social element, while "Hebrew" is at least sometimes equivalent to the ethnicon "Israel" (Gen. 40:15; 43:32; Ex. 1:18; 2:11; 3:18; 5:3) if not always (I Sam. 14:21; Na'aman 1986). Abraham was called *ʿivri* (Gen. 14:13) because he is a descendant of Eber (Gen. 10:25). Yet as a leader of an armed band able to form local alliances he fits certain social structural identifications with the Ḫabiru; other parts of the Israelites also could fulfill, for a short time, this traditional identification based on this structure (cf. Campbell, in bibl., 14). It is possible that a reminiscence of the negative connotation of Ḫabiru survives in the designation *eved ivri* (Ex. 21:2) or in the *ʿivrim* mentioned in connection with Saul in I Samuel 13–14 (although they may not be Israelites at all; see above).

BIBLIOGRAPHY: J. Bottéro *Le problème des Ḫabiru…* (1954); K.M. Kenyon, *The Bible and Recent Archaeology* (1978); R. de Vaux, *The Early History of Israel* (French, 1971; English, 1978); M. Greenberg, *The Ḫab/piru* (1955); idem, in: *Tarbiz*, 24 (1955), 369–79; M.P. Gray, in: HUCA, 29 (1958), 180–2; W.F. Albright, in: BASOR, 163 (1961), 53–54: E.F. Campbell, BA, 23 (1960), 10, 13–16; J. Weingreen, in: *Fourth World Congress of Jewish Studies, Papers*, 1 (1967), 63–66 (Eng. section); P. Artzi, in: JNES, 27 (1968), 166–7; R. de Vaux, *ibid.*, 221–8 (incl. bibl.). **ADD. BIBLIOGRAPHY:** N. Na'aman, in: JNES, 45 (1986), 271–88 (extensive bibliography); idem, in: JNES, 47 (1988), 192–94; JAOS, 120 (2000), 62–74; W. Moran, in: D. Golomb (ed.), *Working with No Data… Studies… Lambdin* (1987), 209–12; A. Rainey, in: JAOS, 107 (1987), 539–41; N. Lemche, in: ABD, 3:6–10 (with bibliography); idem, ibid., 95; R. Biggs, in: JNES, 58 (1999), 294–95.

HA-BOKER (Heb. הַבֹּקֶר "The Morning").

(1) Daily Hebrew newspaper, published in Warsaw under the editorship of David *Frischmann from Jan. 14, 1909, until Aug. 20, 1909 (180 editions). Published with the Yiddish daily *Haynt*, to which Frischmann was a regular contributor, *Ha-Boker* was politically non-aligned. The editor was very exacting in the stylistic standard of the paper and intent upon attracting as contributors the best Hebrew writers and intellects of the day. Translations from world literature were also published in *Ha-Boker*. The paper had regular writers in London (Asher *Beilin), and in the United States (A. Fleishman), and occasional contributors elsewhere. Two current events filled up entire editions: the discovery of the *agent provocateur*, *Azeff, and the rebellion of the Young Turks in Turkey. Especially through the treatment of the latter, *Ha-Boker* took the stand, opposed to the official Zionist opinion, namely that the Young Turks would aggravate the already negative Turkish position on the Zionist undertaking (which indeed

proved the case). Extensive debates were conducted, too, on the topic of Yiddish-Hebrew, and the "Hebrew in Hebrew" teaching method.

(2) Daily Hebrew newspaper published in Tel Aviv, 1935–65. Right-wing circles of the *yishuv* founded *Ha-Boker* as their organ for General Zionism. The orientation of the paper was formulated in the first edition by M. *Dizengoff. A brief period of groping was followed by consolidation in the editorial staff, especially after J.H. Heftman became editor in chief (he served intermittently as sole editor or as coeditor with Perez *Bernstein). *Ha-Boker* is credited with several journalistic innovations in the country, especially with vivid reporting, then in its pioneering stages. The literary supplement was edited for years by Baruch *Karu (Krupnik). After Heftman's death, Y. Gruman served as the paper's editor, followed by P. Bernstein and G. Ẓifroni. With the formation of the Liberal Party (1961), which consolidated the two branches of General Zionism, this paper served as its organ, and as a forum for publicists and writers in sympathy with the party. Finally, with the formation of the Ḥerut Liberal Party bloc (*Gaḥal) in 1965, the two party newspapers, *Ḥerut* and *Ha-Boker,* were replaced by a new paper, *Ha-Yom.*

BIBLIOGRAPHY: G. Kressel, *Toledot ha-Ittonut ha-Ivrit be-Ereẓ Yisrael* (1964^2), 162–6.

[Getzel Kressel]

HA-BONIM (Heb. הַבּוֹנִים), moshav shittufi in central Israel, by the seacoast, 6 mi. (10 km.) northwest of *Zikhron Ya'akov, affiliated with Tenu'at ha-Moshavim, founded in 1949 by graduates of the Iḥud Habonim youth movement from South Africa and other English-speaking countries. They were later joined by Israeli-born youth and new immigrants from other countries. The economy was based on citriculture, livestock, etc. Ha-Bonim beach, a nature resort with marine species and unique plants, lies near the moshav. In 1968 Ha-Bonim had 150 inhabitants, rising to 249 in 2002.

[Efraim Orni /Shaked Gilboa (2nd ed.)]

HABOR (Heb. חָבוֹר), a river flowing through Mesopotamia for 218 mi. (350 km.) from north to south in the region of el-Jazira, the area between the Euphrates and Tigris rivers. It rises from Mt. Kharagah, and is joined by five tributary streams, emptying into the Euphrates north of Mari. The surrounding region was productive in antiquity; grain was raised mainly in the north while in the southern Habor Valley sheep and cattle, and later also horses, were raised. Beyond the northern Habor lay an important trade route, which started at Nineveh, the Assyrian metropolis, and ran by way of Nisibis, Gozan, and Haran to Carchemish on the Euphrates. This route was apparently used in the days of Abraham and even before. On the evidence of the remains excavated at Chagar Bazar, the Habor Valley was first settled in the Neolithic period. In the 18th century B.C.E., many attempts were made to channel the river's waters by means of dams and canals, as is known from the Mari letters of that period. In the 16th-14th centuries B.C.E. the region of the Habor was in the center of the mighty kingdom of Mitanni, and the area was reduced to ruins until it was revived in the 10th century B.C.E. The city of Gozan (Tell Halaf) became especially important, and according to the Bible the river was apparently named after it. The Assyrian conquest of the Habor district began in the ninth and eighth centuries. When insurrections in the conquered cities increased, one city after another was destroyed and the inhabitants deported. In their place Tiglath-Pileser III settled the Israelite exiles from Transjordan (I Chron. 5:26), and later Sargon II settled the exiles from Samaria there (II Kings 17:6; 18:11; cf. Pritchard, Texts, 284–5). Documents found in the excavations of Gozan prove the presence of Israelite exiles in this city (see *Gozan and Assyrian *Exile).

BIBLIOGRAPHY: F. Sarre and E.E. Hertzfeld, *Archaeologische Reise im Euphrat-und Tigris-Gebiet*, 1 (1911); J. Seidmann, *Die Inschriften Adadniraris II* (1935); C.J. Gadd, in: *Iraq*, 7 (1940), 22ff.; J. Kupper, in: *Archives Royales de Mari*, 3 (1950), 2, 5, 80; J. Lewy, in: *Orientalia*, 21 (1952), 265–92, 393–425.

[Michael Avi-Yonah]

ḤABSHUSH, SHALOM BEN YAḤYA (c. 1825–1905), head of a yeshivah in San'a, Yemen, *dayyan*, and author. A goldsmith by profession, he kept aloof from public office and communal affairs, and devoted himself to the study of the Torah. He was the last head of the San'a yeshivah, which closed down in 1905 during a siege and famine. He wrote two works, which were published together (Aden, 1893): *Korban Todah*, explanations and novellae on the *Mekor Ḥayyim* of R. Yaḥyā Ṣāliḥ b. Jacob, dealing with the laws of ritual slaughter and *terefot*; and *Shoshannat ha-Melekh*, an abridged version of the responsa *Pe'ulat Ẓaddik* of R. Yaḥyā Ṣāliḥ. It was written and possibly copied by the author himself in 1862. The abridged responsa are presented in the form of *halakhot* and verdicts. In the margins he added the *Gan Shoshannim*, which indicates the source of the *halakhah*. The part on *Oraḥ Ḥayyim* and *Yoreh De'ah* was published together with R. David Mizraḥi's commentary on the Shulḥan Arukh, *Shetilei Zeitim* (2 vols. 1886–96).

BIBLIOGRAPHY: S. Gridi (ed.), *Shoshannat ha-Melekh* (1967), introduction.

[Yehuda Ratzaby]

HACKENBURG, WILLIAM BOWER (1837–1918), U.S. silk manufacturer and philanthropist. After becoming secretary of the Hebrew Relief Society in 1858, Hackenburg devoted a great deal of his time to doing philanthropic work in his native Philadelphia. He was a founder of the Jewish Hospital, being largely responsible for its development into a major public institution, a trustee of both the Baron de Hirsch Fund and Dropsie College, and a vice president of the Board of Delegates of American Israelites. In 1878 he supervised the latter organization's compilation of a statistical survey of American Jewry. He was also active in Russo-Jewish refugee relief work.

[Sefton D. Temkin]

HACKETT, BUDDY (**Leonard Hacker**; 1924–2003), U.S. comedian. Born in Brooklyn, New York, Hackett's wit and story-telling ability won him success on television in the 1960s. Previously he had performed in nightclubs and appeared in the Broadway farce *Lunatics and Lovers* (1954) and the comedy *I Had a Ball* (1965). In 1960 he won attention in David Susskind's television program *Open End*. This was followed by roles in such films as *All Hands on Deck* (1961); *Everything's Ducky* (1961); *The Music Man* (1962); *The Wonderful World of the Brothers Grimm* (1962); *It's a Mad, Mad, Mad, Mad World* (1963); and *The Love Bug* (1968). His distinctive voice also earned him a variety of vocal roles in animated films, such as the TV movie *Jack Frost* (1979); *The Little Mermaid* (1989); *Mouse Soup* (1992); and *The Little Mermaid II* (2000), as well as the 1992 TV series *Fish Police*.

Hackett's TV career encompassed frequent appearances on such shows as *What's My Line?*; *The Dean Martin Show*; *Rowan and Martin's Laugh-In*; and *The Tonight Show Starring Johnny Carson*, as well as a recurring role in the 1999 sitcom *Action*. He also played Lou Costello in the 1978 TV movie *Bud and Lou*.

Despite his success in movies and on television, Hackett preferred his nightclub work. He performed in clubs around the country, particularly in Las Vegas, where he ultimately became one of the top headliners in Vegas history. One of the pioneers of "blue" comedy, Hackett was noted for his risqué material and off-color language. But among his fellow comedians, he was regarded as an ingenious ad-libber and a comic who knew just how long to keep a joke or a routine in his act before it became stale.

Hackett devoted much time to a foundation combating Tay-Sachs disease, a malady that occurs mostly among Jewish children of Middle European background. He wrote *The Truth about Golf, and Other Lies* (1968) and *The Naked Mind of Buddy Hackett* (1974).

[Ruth Beloff (2nd ed.)]

HACOHEN, DAVID (1898–1984), Israeli politician and diplomat; member of the First to Sixth Knessets. Hacohen was born in Gomel, Russia, the son of Mordecai ben Hillel *Hacohen, who immigrated to Ereẓ Israel with his family in 1907. In Gomel he went to a reformed *ḥeder*, and in Tel Aviv went to the Herzlia Gymnasium. Hacohen enlisted to the Turkish Army in 1916 and served in Anatolia. In 1919–23 he studied economics at the London School of Economics. Upon his return to Palestine in 1923 he was appointed manager of the Office for Public Works and Planning in the *Histadrut, which eventually became *Solel Boneh. During World War II he was *Haganah liaison officer to the British Army and British Intelligence. His house in Haifa served as the center of Free French Forces radio transmission to the Vichy-occupied Levant. For many years during the British Mandate, Hacohen served as a member of the mixed Arab-Jewish Haifa Municipality. Together with other *yishuv* leaders, he was arrested by the British on "Black Saturday," June 29, 1946, and interned at Latrun. After being a member of *Aḥdut ha-Avodah, Hacohen was elected to the First Knesset on the *Mapai list, and remained a member of the Knesset for 20 years until 1969, with a break in 1953–55, when he served as Israel's first ambassador to Burma. In the Second to Sixth Knessets he was chairman of the Knesset Foreign Affairs and Defense Committee. He led many of the Knesset delegations to the Inter-Parliamentary Union in Geneva, and was twice a member of its Executive.

David Hacohen's second wife was Bracha *Habas.

[Benjamin Jaffe / Susan Hattis Rolef (2nd ed.)]

HACOHEN, MORDECAI (1906–1972), rabbi and scholar. Born in the old city of Jerusalem, where his father, Rabbi Ḥaim, a well-known kabbalist who immigrated to Ereẓ Israel at the turn of the century, was leader of the service at the Western Wall for more than 50 years.

Rabbi Hacohen was educated at Jerusalem yeshivot and was ordained by Rabbis Abraham Isaac Kook, Joseph Ḥayyim Sonnenfeld and Abraham Ẓvi Schorr, head of the Ḥasidic Beth Din, whose daughter he married. With the establishment of the Hebrew University in Jerusalem in 1925 he enrolled as one of its first students.

He spearheaded and directed the Maḥzike Hadas network of institutions in Jerusalem with the aim of "bringing back" from among the secular population the "children who strayed away" – especially in the kibbutzim – to a renewed positive relationship with Jewish tradition. In line with these efforts, he published and edited (1943–49) a biweekly, *Nerot Shabbat* ("The Lights of Shabbat"), which was dedicated solely to the Shabbat, its content, meaning and beauty.

His literary works, which cover a wide range of topics, deal not only with academic subjects and theoretical halakhic problems, but also with relevant contemporary issues, and include *Al ha-Torah* (5 vols., 1956) and *Min ha-Torah* (5 vols., 1973), the popular and oft-reprinted collection of his original commentaries on the weekly portions of the Torah; *Midrash Bereshit Zuta* (1957); *Erke Midot be-Torat ha-Rambam* (1956; "Ethical Values in the Teachings of Maimonides"); *Kotel Maʿaravi* (1968); *Meʿarat ha-Makhpelah* (1970).

After his death, Yad Ramah – a research and publication institute, commemorating his name and ideas – was established. Among the Yad Ramah publications are the following volumes of his collected essays: *Halakhot ve-Halikhot* ("Contemporary Issues in Halakhah"), *Mikdash Meʿat* ("On Synagogue and Prayer"), *Ḥiddush va-Ḥeker* ("Talmudic Studies"), *Ishim u-Tekufot* ("Historical and Biographical Studies"), *Be-Einei Ḥazal* ("The World of the Sages"), and *Ha-Bayit ve-ha-Aliyah* ("Studies Concerning the Temple and Pilgrimage").

BIBLIOGRAPHY: Tidhar, 3, 1229; Kressel, Leksikon, 2 (1967), 123; Y.Z. Wasserman, *Mi-Yekirei Yerushalayim* (1973), 99.

HACOHEN, MORDECAI BEN HILLEL (1856–1936), Hebrew writer and Zionist. At the age of 18 he began publishing in Hebrew periodicals, such as *Ha-Levanon, Ha-Ẓefirah*, and *Ha-Kol*, and, from 1876, was on the editorial staff of *Ha-*

Shaḥar. In 1878–9 Hacohen, who was influenced by *Smolenskin's nationalism, published a long article sharply criticizing the Haskalah movement for having caused a spiritual crisis among the Jewish youth of Eastern Europe. No less effective was his article in **Ha-Meliẓ* (1879), depicting the dire economic plight of Russian Jewry. In 1878 he moved to St. Petersburg. In 1880 he wrote a comprehensive survey of Jewish agriculturalists in modern Russia for the Russo-Jewish periodicals. Hacohen joined the *Ḥibbat Zion movement in 1881 and, in the same year, published in **Ha-Maggid* his article "*Kumu ve-Na'aleh Ẓiyyon*" ("Arise and Let Us Go to Zion"), the first of a series on the new movement. In 1886 he wrote from a Jewish nationalist standpoint the first comprehensive survey of Smolenskin's career. He visited Palestine at the end of 1889 and published his impressions in *Ha-Meliẓ*. In 1891, in his native town of Mogilev, Hacohen founded two societies for promoting settlement in Palestine, visiting the country again on their behalf in that year. He reported on his journey in *Lu'aḥ Aḥi'asaf* 9 (1901) and 11 (1903) criticizing the colonizing activities of the Ḥovevei Zion and of their agent, Ze'ev Tiomkin. A delegate to the first Zionist Congress (1897), he was the first to deliver a speech in Hebrew. In 1907 he settled in Palestine. Hacohen, who was one of the founders of Tel Aviv, played an active part in the economic and cultural life of the *yishuv*. He helped to start the monthly youth magazine *Moledet*, of which he later became an editor. He was also one of the organizers of the Association of Hebrew Writers. Hacohen's articles are characterized by their practical approach to contemporary problems, as exemplified by his demand that Jewish nationalism be given a sound economic basis. Especially noteworthy is his essay on "The Literary Vision of Israel and Its Land," as expressed in the works of Smolenskin, George Eliot, Disraeli, and Baharav (*Ha-Shilo'aḥ*, vols. 2, 6, 11). His memoirs and diaries are also of historical and cultural importance.

His Hebrew works include a collection of articles and stories (2 vols., 1904); *Kevar*, memoirs (1923); *Olami*, memoirs (5 vols., 1927–29); *Milḥemet ha-'Ammim*, a diary of World War I (5 vols., 1929–30); *Athalta* (2 vols., 1931–42), a collection of articles on Ereẓ Israel in the years 1917–20; *Ḥayyim Naḥman Bialik* (1933); *Be-Sivkhei ha-Ya'ar ve-'od Sippurim* (1934); and *Sefer Shemot*, biographical sketches of Hebrew writers and Zionist workers (1938). A selection of Hacohen's Yiddish writings was published in the miscellany *In Mame Loshen* (1935). Two of Hacohen's articles in Russian, "Jerusalem and its Region" (1909) and "On the Balance of Trade of Jaffa Harbor" (1913), were reprinted in pamphlet form. On the 50th and 60th anniversaries of the beginning of his literary work, miscellanies were published in his honor, *Me-Erev ad Erev* (2 vols., 1904) and *Mi-Boker ad Erev* (1925), which also contain biographical and bibliographical material about him.

[Gedalyah Elkoshi]

HACOHEN, RAPHAEL ḤAYYIM (1883–1954), rabbi and communal leader. Born in Shiraz, Persia, he was taken by his parents to Jerusalem in 1890. After a thorough rabbinical education, he began to take an active part in all communal affairs of the *yishuv* and the then small settlement of Persian Jews. He founded an organization, Agudat Ohavei Zion, which aimed to improve the economic and cultural situation of the Persian Jews in Jerusalem. A devoted Zionist, he was a delegate to the Convention (Kenesiyyah) in Zikhron Ya'akov, organized by M. *Ussishkin in 1903. In 1922 he signed a memorandum to the Zionist Congress, outlining the conditions and requirements of the Persian Jewish colony in Jerusalem. In 1912 he established a Hebrew printing press in Jerusalem, which published many works of *Judeo-Persian literature. He himself was the author of *Shir u-Shevaḥah* (1905; 1921²), a collection of songs and *pizmonim* of his family and of the Jews of Shiraz, and of an *Autobiography*.

BIBLIOGRAPHY: M.D. Gaon, *Yehudei ha-Mizraḥ be-Ereẓ Yisrael*, 2 (1938), 303–4.

[Walter Joseph Fischel]

HADAD, an early Semitic god, first appears in texts written in the Old Akkadian dialect and in Eblaite (third millennium). He was one of the chief gods of the *Amorites and, later, the *Canaanites and Arameans. In Akkadian documents Hadad appears as Adad / Addu and in Ugaritic as "Hd." He also appears at *Emar in Syria. The name Hadad probably means "thunderer," and as god of the storm he is responsible for fertility as well as destruction. He appears together with the sun goddess as guarantor of the treaty between Ebla and Abarsal. A letter found at Mari (A. Roberts, 1968, 166–68, 18th century B.C.E.) refers to a prophet of Adad, reminding King Zimri-Lim of Mari that it was Adad who returned Zimri-Lim to his ancestral throne and who gave the king the divine weapons with which he had defeated the sea god. This ancient myth is echoed in Ugaritic sources in which Baal, also called Hd, defeats Yam the sea god, as well as in Ps. 89:21–6. The cult of Hadad persisted in Syria from the earliest period up to Roman times. By the ninth century B.C.E. Baal and Hadad had bifurcated, with Baal, the biblical rival of Yahweh, worshipped in Israel, the Phoenician homeland in Lebanon, and the Phoenician diaspora, and Hadad among the Arameans, where he headed the pantheon. The bullock was sacred to him, and the sheaf of wheat, symbol of fertility, was one of his symbols. His consort was Atarʿata (called Atargatis, "the Syrian goddess," in Greek sources).

The centers of the Hadad cult were Damascus and Baalbek, where he was identified with the sun god. There were temples of Hadad in Gozan-Sikanu, Sefire, Aleppo, Sam'al, and elsewhere. He was depicted on Syrian reliefs as a bearded man standing astride a bullock, holding shafts of lightning in his hands. In a later period he was depicted as a tall man wrapped in a tight garment decorated with emblems of the heavenly bodies, holding a threshing board in one hand and ears of grain in the other; next to him stand two bullocks. The Baal-Hadad cult was denounced by Elijah the prophet (I Kings 18) and by *Hosea. In Palestine Hadad was known by the epithet Rimmon (properly, Ramman, "thunderer"), and was worshiped in the Valley of Megiddo (cf. "…as the mourning of Hadadrimmon in the plain of Megiddon," Zech. 12:11). In the Aramaic Tel Dan Inscription (COS II, 162–63) the victorious Aramean king credits Hadad with preceding him and giving him victory over Israel.

In the Hellenistic period an altar was erected to Hadad near Acre. He and Atarʿata were also the chief gods of Hierapolis in Syria, but during the Hellenistic-Roman period the cult of the goddess gained in importance. When the Syrian cult spread west to the Greek and Roman cities, Hadad played only a secondary role.

Hadad appears in the Bible as the name of Edomite kings (Gen. 36:35; I Kings 11:14–25; I Chron. 1:46, 50) and is also a component of the names of Aramean kings Bar-Hadad, i.e., "Son of Hadad," hebraized as *Ben-Hadad (I Kgs. 20:1) and Hadadezer (II Sam. 8:3).

BIBLIOGRAPHY: A. Deimel, *Pantheon Babylonicum* (1914), 43ff.; G. Dossin, in: *Syria*, 20 (1939), 171–2; Albright, Stone, 160, 176, 187–8, 332; S. Moscati (ed.), *Le Antiche Divinitá Semitiche* (1958). **ADD. BIBLIOGRAPHY:** J. Greenfield, in: DDD, 377–82; J. Roberts, *The Bible and the Ancient Near East* (2002), 159–60, 166–68.

[Michael Avi-Yonah / S. David Sperling (2nd ed.)]

HADAMARD, JACQUES SALOMON (1865–1963), French mathematician. Born in Versailles, Hadamard held chairs of mathematics at the Collège de France from 1897 and the Ecole Polytechnique from 1912 until his retirement in 1935. He was elected a member of the Academy of Sciences in 1912 and was the first to be awarded the Feltrinelli Prize founded by the Italians in 1955 to compensate for the absence of a Nobel Prize for mathematicians. A brother-in-law of Alfred *Dreyfus, Hadamard took an active interest in the Dreyfus case, and for 60 years was a member of the central committee of the Ligue des Droits de l'Homme founded at the time of the Zola trial in 1898. The dangers of Hitlerism were recognized by Hadamard at an early stage. He was a free-thinker, but worked to alleviate the plight of German Jewry. He was a member of the French Palestine Committee and of the administrative board of the Hebrew University of Jerusalem. He escaped from France in 1941 to the United States, and moved to England to engage in operational research with the Royal Air Force. Hadamard produced important work in analysis, number theory, differential geometry, calculus of variations, functional analysis, partial differential equations, and hydrodynamics, and inspired research among successive generations of mathematicians. He published numerous papers and books. His *An Essay on the Psychology of Invention in the Mathematical Field* (1945; *Essai sur la psychologie de l'invention dans le domaine mathématique*, 1959) was published many years after his retirement.

BIBLIOGRAPHY: Mandelbrojt and Schwartz, in: *Bulletin of the American Mathematical Society*, 71 (1965), 107–29; Cartwright, in: *Journal of the London Mathematical Society*, 40 (1965), 722–48.

[Barry Spain]

HADAS, MOSES (1900–1966), U.S. classical scholar and humanist. After graduating from Emory University, Hadas proceeded to Columbia University, at the same time pursuing studies at the Jewish Theological Seminary of America, from which he received his rabbinical diploma. Appointed instructor in Greek at the former institution in 1925, he became associate professor in 1946 and full professor in 1953. Three years later he was elected to the prestigious John Jay Chair in Greek, which he occupied until his death. During World War II he served with the Office of Strategic Services in North Africa and Greece.

Hadas' cardinal contribution to classical studies in the United States was to bring them out of the narrower confines of textual criticism into the broad area of general humanistic interest. This he did through a series of spirited and elegant renderings of the Greek dramatists and romances (e.g., Heliodorus) and of Caesar, Tacitus, Seneca, and other writers. He also wrote popular histories of Greek and Latin literature (1950, 1952); a broad, if sometimes controversial, survey of the Greco-Roman age, entitled *Hellenistic Culture: Fusion and Diffusion* (1959); a study (with Morton Smith) of classical aretalogy; and, in a lighter vein, an entertaining ancilla to classical reading. Many of these works appeared in inexpensive paperback editions, and thus introduced the ancient masterpieces to the general reader.

Hadas was a major figure at Columbia University. Through the humanity of his writings and the urbane temper of his character and outlook, he left an indelible impression on several generations of students and readers alike, and he was among the foremost to remove the traditional fustian from classical studies.

Outside of the classical field, Hadas produced, among other works, a delightful rendering of Joseph ben Meir *Ibn Zabara's *Book of Delight* (1932) and *Fables of a Jewish Aesop* (1966), a translation of the fox fables of the 12th century *Berechiah ha-Nakdan. In his earlier years he was prominently identified with the Menorah movement in American universities.

[Theodor H. Gaster]

HADASSAH, THE WOMEN'S ZIONIST ORGANIZATION OF AMERICA, largest Zionist, Jewish, and women's organization in the United States, with 300,000 members. Hadassah first sent public health nurses to Palestine in 1912 and in the decades following played a leading role in developing the social welfare infrastructure of pre-State Israel. With a program budget of $125 million by 2005, Hadassah now provides vital funding for Israel's medical facilities and supports many health, educational, and vocational programs in Israel and the United States. Hadassah also offers its medical expertise and assistance in countries throughout the developing world.

Early History

Hadassah has its origins in a turn-of-the-century visit to Palestine by two American Jewish women. In 1909, soon after joining a New York City "Daughters of Zion" study group, the writer and editor Henrietta *Szold, along with her mother, visited the Holy Land for the first time. They were both shocked by what Szold described as the "misery, poverty, filth, disease" they saw there. Upon returning to New York, Szold proposed to her study group that they take up the practical work of relieving Jewish suffering in Palestine.

In 1912, 30 women attended a meeting at New York City's Temple Emanu-El to discuss this idea and agreed to form a new organization called "Daughters of Zion, Hadassah Chapter." The group elected Szold as president, drew up a constitution, and adopted a motto: "The healing of the daughter of my people." The group's first priority would be to provide health care to women and children in the *yishuv* (Jewish community of Palestine). Less than a year later, Hadassah's Alice *Seligsberg accompanied the first two Hadassah nurses, Rose Kaplan and Rachel Landy, on their voyage to Palestine. In 1913, the nurses opened a small clinic in Jerusalem, called a Nurse's Settlement, to deal primarily with maternity care and trachoma cases. The model for this project was the system of visiting nurses set up by Lillian *Wald at the Henry Street Settlement House in New York City's impoverished Lower East Side neighborhood.

The new organization changed its name to "Hadassah, the Women's Zionist Organization of America" at its first annual convention in 1914, declaring that its mandate was "to promote Jewish institutions and enterprises in Palestine and to foster Zionist ideals in America." Policy would be decided at future annual conventions with a central committee making decisions between conventions. Hadassah pledged to develop modern, American-style health and social welfare services in the *yishuv*, and promised members that their donations would go directly to support projects in Palestine.

After the outbreak of World War I, the Nurse's Settlement in Jerusalem was forced to close down in 1915. But the World Zionist Organization issued an urgent appeal for an emergency medical force to be sent to war-stricken Palestine. In 1918, Hadassah sent a 45-member medical team, the American Zionist Medical Unit (AZMU), to establish hospitals and clinics across Palestine. Hadassah established a Nurses Training School in Jerusalem and a School Hygiene Department and launched campaigns to eradicate malaria, cholera, trachoma, and other infectious diseases. Szold herself moved to Palestine in 1920 to administer Hadassah's ever-expanding network of health facilities and social welfare programs. The following year, the AZMU was renamed the Hadassah Medical Organization or HMO.

At a time when most Zionist organizations concentrated on political lobbying and land development to advance the Zionist cause, Hadassah's focus on health care, and on women and children, was sometimes criticized as frivolous charity work. But Hadassah's leaders replied that they were doing the nation-building work of creating a public health system. Indeed, Hadassah regarded its social welfare activities as women's distinctive contribution to the Zionist state-building effort. "It is the woman's part in constructive national work that Hadassah seeks to stress – the mother tasks," explained the organization.

Hadassah adopted a succession of projects pioneered by Progressive activists in the United States and adapted them for local use in the *yishuv*. First, Hadassah created a system of visiting nurses, infant welfare stations, pasteurized milk depots, and the *Tippat Ḥalav* or Drop of Milk program, which used donkeys to deliver containers of pasteurized milk to mothers and babies. Other projects included school hygiene programs, maternity education, nutrition education, domestic science programs, school lunches, and supervised playgrounds.

These types of community-based public health initiatives emphasizing the role of health education in preventive medicine had a measurable effect. Hadassah helped reduce maternal deaths as well as infant mortality rates, prevented the spread of infectious disease, and taught adults and children the importance of hygiene, sanitation, recreation, and nutrition.

Among Zionist organizations working in Palestine, Hadassah was also distinguished by its interest in creating a pluralistic and tolerant Jewish society in which Arabs and Jews lived harmoniously. A strictly nonsectarian policy meant that from the start Hadassah's services were available to all residents of Palestine regardless of nationality or religion. Hadassah leaders often claimed that this helped to reduce tensions between Arabs and Jews.

Women's equality was also central to Hadassah's Zionist vision. In the 1920s, as Jewish women in the *yishuv* organized to fight for their social and political rights, including property rights and the right to vote in local elections, Hadassah supported their cause.

The services and institutions that Hadassah established in Palestine were designed to promote the development of a modern, egalitarian, and cohesive Jewish society. But Hadassah's larger goal was the creation of an independent Jewish state which could survive without Diaspora assistance. Thus Szold and Hadassah demanded that Hadassah-initiated projects be transferred to local control and management as soon as it was feasible.

In the United States, Hadassah resisted enormous pressure from the Zionist federations to join in national fundraising campaigns and pool its donations with those of other organizations. Persevering through acrimonious and well-publicized clashes with other Zionist organizations, Hadassah fought to preserve its organizational autonomy and the right to fund and administer its own projects. These battles cemented Hadassah's reputation for organizational and financial integrity and won it the loyalty of growing numbers of American Jewish women. An expanding membership base made Hadassah – with 66,000 members in 1939 – the largest single Zionist organization in the United States in the interwar period. This support, in conjunction with a well-developed fundraising apparatus, allowed Hadassah to accomplish its goals in the *yishuv*.

The needs of American Jewish women were also high on Hadassah's agenda. The organization aimed to educate these women "not only to Judaism but to a realization of their civic and national responsibilities." Szold insisted that Hadassah establish only one chapter in each city so that it could include both immigrant and native-born women from all social and educational backgrounds. In an era when few women had access to higher education or professional opportunities, Hadassah membership gave women a chance to learn new skills and an opportunity to participate in public life. Many women were transformed by their Hadassah work, taking up public speaking, organizing and running chapters of the organization, writing publicity materials and, for some, getting involved at the national and even international level.

Szold formally resigned as Hadassah president in 1926 when the World Zionist Congress asked her to join its Palestine Executive with responsibility for the health and welfare portfolio. Nevertheless, Szold remained in close contact with Hadassah's leadership over the years, effectively giving the organization a supporting role in the Jewish self-government of pre-State Israel. At the same time, Szold left her imprint on Hadassah for the future: an emphasis on health, social welfare, and education; a concern with organizational efficiency and financial transparency; faith in women's abilities; and a commitment to developing Jewish community life in the United States as well as in Palestine (later Israel).

Throughout the 1920s and 1930s, Hadassah continued to expand its programs in the *yishuv*. With Jewish immigrants constantly arriving from all over the world, Hadassah's health care workers tried to inculcate modern, Western ideas of health and preventive medicine. These immigrants, wherever they came from, were considered superstitious and backward. Hadassah's workers combated poor nutrition, high rates of illiteracy, patriarchal (and in some cases polygamous) family structures, child labor, and child marriage.

By the 1930s, Hadassah had created a countrywide network of maternity and child welfare programs, as well as many hospitals and clinics. In keeping with its policy of devolution, Hadassah handed over many of its programs to local authorities, and was soon looking for a new focus. When Recha *Freier, a German Jewish Zionist, asked for Szold's help to get Jewish youth out of Germany, Hadassah found its new purpose. In 1935, Hadassah became the sole American sponsor of the Youth Aliyah movement which rescued Jewish children from Nazi Europe and brought them to Palestine to be raised communally on kibbutzim. During World War II and in the years following, Hadassah helped Youth Aliyah to rescue, house, and educate thousands of young European Jewish refugees. This work, in turn, prepared Hadassah for its later role in helping the new State of Israel absorb the children of the Middle Eastern and North African Jews who arrived, en masse, during the first decade of statehood.

Despite wartime stresses, and the burden of helping to care for Youth Aliyah children, Hadassah's attention to building facilities for health and education never flagged. In 1939, the Rothschild-Hadassah University Hospital, the first teaching hospital and medical center in the country, opened on Mount Scopus. In 1942, Hadassah established the Alice L. Seligsberg Trade School for Girls, the first such school in Palestine, followed in 1944 by a Vocational Guidance Bureau in Jerusalem, the forerunner of the still active Hadassah Career Counseling Institute.

In 1948, after an ambush killed 77 of its medical staff, Hadassah evacuated its medical facilities on Mount Scopus, and set up five temporary hospitals around Jerusalem. The new Hadassah-Hebrew University Medical Center in Ein Kerem was dedicated in 1960. In 1962, as part of Hadassah's Golden Anniversary celebration, a synagogue was dedicated at the Ein Kerem facility. The synagogue's 12 stunning stained glass windows depicting the 12 tribes of Israel were designed by artist Marc *Chagall and draw visitors from all over the world.

In 1967, after the Six-Day War, Hadassah returned to Mount Scopus and began to rebuild. Hailed as a milestone event for Hadassah as well as for Israel, thousands of people attended the rededication ceremony in 1975 when the new Hadassah-Mount Scopus Hospital was finally reopened.

In 1983 Hadassah jettisoned the unwritten agreement limiting its membership to the United States, and promptly began setting up Hadassah affiliates worldwide. The Hadassah International Medical Relief Association (now called Hadassah International) opened membership to all who wished to fundraise for, and otherwise support, Hadassah's medical work. Hadassah International groups in more than 30 countries are generating support for the Hadassah Medical Organization, as well as coordinating international professional exchanges and symposiums.

Modern Challenges

In the 1980s and 1990s Hadassah faced fresh challenges at home. While the economic pressure of supporting programs in Israel was mounting, Hadassah's membership was aging. With career and family pressures competing for their attention, fewer young women were joining the organization. To appeal to this younger generation, Hadassah developed new and expanded domestic programming, including more involvement in American social policy issues. The organization is now deeply engaged in advocacy at the state and national levels in the areas of health care, education, equality, and social justice, including everything from reproductive choice to gun control, environmental protection, immigration policy, and stem-cell research.

On other fronts, Hadassah training programs cultivate women's leadership and organizational skills. Groups like Educators' Councils, Nurses' Councils, and Attorneys' Councils give professional women both a forum for networking and a vehicle for contributing their professional skills to Hadassah. Organized "missions" or trips to Israel for Hadassah members show them what the organization has accomplished on the ground and make connections between American Jewish women and Israelis. On the local level, hands-on programs such as helping a women's shelter, or literacy tutoring, offer tangible results as well as a sense of community and connection with other Jewish women. Hadassah's Department of Women's Health promotes self-education to detect and prevent diseases which affect women and raises awareness of other pertinent health issues like genetics testing and counseling, and organ and tissue donation.

Young people are drawn into the orbit of Jewish community through Hadassah programs like the Training Wheels-*Al Galgalim* program which teaches parents and toddlers about Jewish traditions. Other programs for American Jewish youngsters include Young Judea clubs, summer camps, summer and year abroad programs in Israel, and campus-based programs.

In 1997, Hadassah established the first university-based research center devoted to the study of Jewish women – the International Research Institute on Jewish Women at Brandeis University – now renamed the Hadassah-Brandeis Institute.

In Israel, new immigrants and native-born Israelis alike still rely on many Hadassah-initiated and supported services. Hadassah's vocational education and career counseling programs help tens of thousands of adults each year to retrain and find employment. With Hadassah's continued financial and logistical support, Youth Aliyah has helped more than 300,000 children since 1935 and now serves over 12,000 youngsters yearly.

The Hadassah Medical Organization (HMO) is now a state-of-the-art diagnostic, research, and teaching center serving nearly a million patients from Israel, across the Middle East, and around the world each year. Cutting-edge medical research has led to breakthroughs and medical advances in areas such as Alzheimer's disease, cancer, cystic fibrosis, "cold" laser eye surgery, Post Traumatic Stress Disorder, Mad Cow disease, and more. The HMO also runs an extensive network of community-based health care programs and specialized outpatient clinics in locales across Israel.

The Hadassah University Medical Center – a tertiary care referral facility, teaching hospital, and research center where new medical techniques have been pioneered – consists of two hospitals in Jerusalem, one on Mount Scopus and the other in Ein Kerem, and five schools of the medical professions. All these institutions are run jointly by Hadassah and the Hebrew University. In 2004, a Center for Emergency Medicine was added to the hospital in Ein Kerem with the capacity to treat up to 120,000 trauma patients annually.

Hadassah's international programs have expanded dramatically over the years. Since 1980, more than 500 people from 70 countries have received an International Masters Degree in Public Health from Hadassah's Braun School of Public Health and Community Medicine – the newest of the HMO's five schools of professional medicine in Israel. The Hadassah Medical Organization runs cooperative projects in 112 countries throughout the developing world, including Asia, Africa, and Latin America, sending doctors and nurses to build and staff clinics, and offering medical training. Hadassah's medical personnel also offer emergency relief and assistance in response to catastrophes all over the world.

Hadassah's humanitarian work and commitment to the United Nations was recognized in 2001 when the United Nations Economic and Social Council (ECOSOC) conferred on Hadassah special consultative status as a non-governmental organization (NGO). In 2005, the Hadassah Medical Organization, described as "an example to the world that hatred and suspicion can be overcome by people of goodwill," was nominated for the Nobel Peace Prize.

BIBLIOGRAPHY: J. Dash, *Summoned to Jerusalem: The Life of Henrietta Szold, Founder of Hadassah* (1979); A. Gal, "Hadassah and the American Jewish Political Tradition," in: J.S. Furock and M.L. Raphael (eds.), *An Inventory of Promises: Essays in Honor of Moses Rischin* (1995); M. Levin, *It Takes a Dream: The Story of Hadassah* (1997); M. McCune, "Social Workers in the *Muskeljudentum*: 'Hadassah Ladies,' 'Manly Men' and the Significance of Gender in the American Zionist Movement, 1912–1928," in: *American Jewish History*, 86:2 (June 1998), 135–65; E.B. Simmons, *Hadassah and the Zionist Project* (2005).

[Erica Simmons (2nd ed.)]

HADASSI, JUDAH (ha-Avel) BEN ELIJAH (12th century), *Karaite scholar of Constantinople. His greatest work is the *Eshkol ha-Kofer* (or *Sefer ha-Peles*), which according to his own testimony he began in 1148. The work is arranged according to the Ten Commandments and alphabetically. Written partly in verse, it explains the *mitzvot* and the *halakhot* and the reasons for their observance in accordance with the specific commandment on which they depend. It represents an encyclopedic corpus of Karaite belief and knowledge as it existed in the author's time. According to Hadassi, Karaite doctrine derives and may be learned from the Torah and the Prophets by way of a complete system of homiletical exposition, which he specifies in detail. The discussion on the *mitzvot* is preceded by a comprehensive treatment of the rules of vocalization and grammar in the Bible. Hadassi believed in man's free will in matters of faith and methods of Torah study. The rationalist trend in Karaism is recognizable in his attacks on the legends in the Talmud and the customs and interpretations of the *Rabbanites. There is also a certain measure of social criticism in his argument that the Rabbanites circumvent the prohibition against lending money on interest. Hadassi sharply attacked Christianity and Islam, but, like his Karaite predecessors, he attributed the corruption of Christianity to the Apostles, especially St. Paul; he stated that "Jesus was an exemplary, wise, and righteous man from the first ... the scholars encompassed him ... and killed him as they killed other pious men who criticized them."

The description given of the world and nature by Hadassi evidently reflected the current beliefs of the Jews living in the Byzantine Empire. He had an unqualified belief in astronomy and accepted demons and sorcerers. He knew of strange creatures in distant lands – a mixture of images from rabbinic legends, ancient mythology, and Eastern tales – and also of "the tribes of Jeshurun hidden beyond the Sambatyon River."

Hadassi was thus a compiler rather than an original thinker, and in spite of his anti-Rabbanite bias he drew much of his material from Rabbanite sources. His Hebrew style, however, unlike that of his Rabbanite contemporaries, is awkward and not easily understandable and the rhymed arrangement often makes it obscure. *Eshkol ha-Kofer* was published by the Karaite press in Eupatoria, Crimea (1836). A few hymns by Hadassi are included in the official Karaite prayer book.

BIBLIOGRAPHY: S. Pinsker, *Likkutei Kadmoniyyot* (1860), 223–5 (first pagination); B. Frankl, in: MGWJ, 31 (1882), 1–13, 72–85, 268ff.; W. Bacher, *ibid.*, 40 (1896), 14ff.; idem, in: JQR, 8 (1895/96), 431–44; L. Nemoy, *Karaite Anthology* (1952), 235–377; Z. Ankori, *Karaites in Byzantium* (1959), index s.v. *Yehudah Hadassi.*

[Haim Hillel Ben-Sasson]

HADAYAH, OVADIAH (1893–1969), rabbi. Hadayah was born in *Aleppo, Syria. In 1898 he was brought to Ereẓ Israel and settled in Jerusalem. He studied in Sephardi schools and yeshivot, including Yeshivat Porat Yosef, where from 1923 he taught both Talmud and Kabbalah. He was a member of the *bet din* of the Sephardi community of Jerusalem. From 1939 to 1950 he was chief rabbi of the Sephardi community in Petaḥ Tikvah, and from 1951 chairman of the rabbinical high court of appeals and a member of the chief rabbinate council. He revived the kabbalist yeshivah Kehal Ḥasidim Bet El in Jerusalem, previously housed in the Old City but destroyed in 1948 during the War of Independence. Attached to the yeshivah was a department for the training of rabbis, His works include *ʿEved ha-Melekh* on Maimonides; *ʿAvda de-Rabbanan*, on the Mishnah and Talmud; and the responsa *Va-Yikaḥ Ovadyahu*, *Yisrael ʿAvdi*, and *Deʿah ve-Haskel.* He was awarded the Israel Prize for Rabbinical Literature in 1968.

ḤADDAD, EZRA (1903–1972), educator, author, and journalist. Ḥaddad mastered several languages, including Hebrew. He published Hebrew poems in the Jewish weekly *Yeshurun* (Baghdad, 1920) and from 1926 to 1951 he directed the Jewish schools al-Waṭaniyya and Shammāsh in Baghdad. After his immigration to Israel in 1951, he held leading executive positions in the Histadrut. In addition to his Hebrew poems, Ḥaddad published an Arabic translation of the *Travels of Benjamin of Tudela* (1945) together with notes and an introduction. He also wrote a textbook for the study of Hebrew.

BIBLIOGRAPHY: A. Ben-Jacob, *Yehudei Bavel* (1965), 307f.

[Haim J. Cohen]

HADDAD, SARIT (1978–), Israeli pop singer. When Haddad first made a name for herself in the mid-1990s with her first album, *Niẓoẓ ha-Ḥayyim* ("Spark of Life"), she was on the well-trodden path of so-called Mediterranean, or Eastern, pop music. She did not offer anything new in terms of musical style, but her vocals set a new standard which numerous singers have since tried to emulate.

Haddad was born in Afulah as the youngest of eight children. When she was eight years old she taught herself to play the guitar, organ, and various percussion instruments, and, without her parents' knowledge soon began performing at local clubs. When she was 16 Haddad was discovered by impresario Avi Gaute when she performed in a beach show. Gaute took Haddad under his wing and began to develop her career, initially targeting the Sephardi community. On *Niẓoẓ ha-Ḥayyim* Haddad joined forces with well-known young Druze male vocalist Sharif and the album sold well. By now Haddad had become a star on the national Eastern music club circuit.

In 1997, Haddad broke into the international market after a Jordanian television director caught her act. A tour of Jordan was soon arranged, with Haddad performing under the assumed identity of a Palestinian singer. The tour was a success and was followed by the release of *Sarit Haddad Shara be-Aravit* ("Sarit Haddad Sings in Arabic"), which was also sold in Arabic-speaking countries.

In the same year Haddad's Israeli market presence grew significantly when she teamed up with top ethnorock group Teapacks (Tipex), and with her 1998 record *Ḥok ha-Ḥayyim* ("The Law of Life") she broke into mainstream Israeli culture.

Since then Haddad has achieved, and maintains, megastar status in Israel, and has performed in Europe and the United States. Every record she released was an immediate success; she was voted Singer of the Year several times and represented Israel at the Eurovision Song Contest in 2002, placing 12th.

[Barry Davis (2nd ed.)]

ḤADERAH (Heb. חֲדֵרָה), town in central Israel, in the northern Sharon, founded in 1890 by members of Ḥovevei Zion from Vilna, Kovno, and Riga who had bought the land a few months earlier. The area was swampy and infested with malaria, and the settlers underwent great suffering, with more than half dying of malaria in the first 20 years of Ḥaderah's existence. In 1895 Baron Edmond de *Rothschild began aiding the village, sending Egyptian workers to lay out the first drainage network and planting large eucalyptus groves; the eucalyptus tree soon became Ḥaderah's symbol. Dr. Hillel *Joffe worked indefatigably in combating the malaria in Ḥaderah. Although the disease ceased to constitute a problem from the late 1920s, the last vestiges of the swamps disappeared only in 1945, when a larger canal leading to the sea was dug. Whereas field and vegetable garden crops initially constituted main farm branches, citrus groves began to be planted before World War I and were greatly enlarged in the 1920s and 1930s. With the construction of the Lydda-Haifa railway in 1918–19, Ḥaderah became a railway station, and with the completion of the Ḥaderah–Petaḥ Tikvah highway in 1937, it also became an important crossroads, connected with Haifa in the north and the Jezreel Valley in the east. The number of inhabitants increased from 152 in 1898 to 320 in 1914, 450 in 1922, 3,372 in 1931, and 11,819 in 1948. Ḥaderah became a regional center, receiving municipal council status in 1936 and municipal status in 1952. During the first years of Israel's independence, after 1948, Ḥaderah doubled its population. In 1961 it had 26,000 and, in 1968, 31,100 inhabitants; of the latter, 40% were Israeli-born, 33% hailed from Europe and America, and 27% from Asia and Africa. In the mid-1990s, the population was approximately 56,100 and by the end of 2002 it was already 74,000. Although agriculture (carp ponds, bananas, cattle, poultry, beehives, flowers, etc., in addition to citrus and various field and garden crops) continued to develop, industry became the main element in the town's economy. Concentrated on a dune area in the northwest, it included the American Israel Paper Mills and Alliance Tire and Rubber Company (each with over 1,000 employed in 1970), food-preserve plants, and other enterprises. Near the estuary of the Haderah River there is a large electric power station run by Israel's Electric Company. As the center of a sub-district, Ḥaderah fulfills administrative functions and has the Hillel Joffe hospital and educational institutions. The large municipal area of 20 sq. mi. (50 sq. km.), extending over the sand dunes west to the seashore, provides ample space for expansion of residential and industrial quarters. During the al-Aqsa Intifada, commencing in 2001, Ḥaderah came under a number of terrorist attacks, including a suicide bombing at a bar mitzvah, which killed six and wounded 35.

The name Ḥaderah is derived from the Arabic *al-Khaḍrā'* ("the Green"), referring to the color of the former swamp vegetation and to the algae-covered water of Naḥal Ḥaderah. The area around Ḥaderah was first settled in the Chalcolithic period; house-shaped pottery ossuaries with painted decorations from this time were found in excavations there in 1936. Bronze Age remains, as well as ruins of buildings, mosaics, and a Roman bridge, were also discovered. In the Crusader period the city was called Lictera after the Arabic name al-Khuḍayra. Because of the many swamps in its vicinity, the site was abandoned after the Crusades.

BIBLIOGRAPHY: L.I. Shneorson, *Mi-Pi Rishonim* (1963); E. Hadani, *Ḥaderah, 1891–1951* (Heb., 1951); *Yedi'ot Ḥaderah*, nos. 1–3 (1965–68); M. Smilansky, *Ḥaderah* (Heb. 1930, 1936[2]); *Histadrut ha-Ovedim ha-Ivrim ha-Kelalit be-Ereẓ-Yisrael, Ḥaderah ha-Ovedet-le-Yovlah 1891–1941* (1941).

[Shlomo Hasson / Shaked Gilboa (2nd ed.)]

ḤAD GADYA (Aram. חַד גַּדְיָא; "An Only Kid"), initial phrase and name of a popular Aramaic song chanted at the conclusion of the Passover *seder. Composed of ten stanzas, the verse runs as follows: A father bought a kid for two *zuzim*; a cat came and ate the kid; a dog then bit the cat; the dog was beaten by a stick; the stick was burned by fire; water quenched the fire; an ox drank the water; a *shoḥet* slaughtered the ox; the *shoḥet* was killed by the Angel of Death who in punishment was destroyed by God. Each stanza repeats the previous verses closing with the refrain: "*ḥad gadya, ḥad gadya*." Jewish commentators have invested "*Ḥad Gadya*" with a hidden allegorical meaning in which the kid symbolizes the oppressed Jewish people. It was bought by the father (God) for two coins (Moses and Aaron). The devouring cat stands for Assyria; the dog is Babylon; the stick represents Persia; the fire Macedonia; the water is Rome; the ox, the Saracens; the *shoḥet*, the Crusaders; and the Angel of Death, the Turks who in those days ruled Palestine. The end of the song expresses the hope for messianic redemption: God destroys the foreign rulers of the Holy Land and vindicates Israel, "the only kid." Other commentators have tried to interpret "*Ḥad Gadya*" as an allegorization of the *Joseph legend or of the relationship between body and soul as reflected in Jewish mysticism. The best-known Jewish interpretations of "*Ḥad Gadya*" are (1) *Kerem Ein Gedi*, by Judah b. Mordecai Horowitz (Koenigsberg, 1764); (2) a commentary by Jonathan *Eybeschuetz (Neubauer Cat Bodl. 1 (1886), no. 2246); (3) two commentaries by the Gaon of Vilna (e.g., in the *Haggadah Migdal Eder*, Vilna, 1923); (4) and a commentary by R. Moses *Sofer (*ibid.*). Most scholars agree, however, that the song was borrowed from a German folk song of the Hobelbanklied type ("*Der Herr der schickt den Jokel aus*") which, in turn, is based on an old French nursery song. Joseph *Jacobs (in notes to his *English Fairy Tales*, London, 1893) points to the analogy of "*Ḥad Gadya*" with Don Quixote and with certain Persian and Indian poems. The riddle of the motif and meaning of "*Ḥad Gadya*" was also dealt with by Christian writers, notably by Hermann von der Hardt, in his *Ḥad Gadia Historia Universalis Judaeorum in aenigmate* (Helmstadt, n.d.) and also by J.C. *Wagenseil, and by J.C.G. *Bodenschatz. The song seems to have originated in the 16th century and appears for the first time in a *Haggadah* printed in Prague (1590). It was never part of the Sephardi and the Yemenite rituals. It was incorporated into the *Haggadah (like the other concluding songs; see "*Eḥad Mi *Yode'a*") for the amusement of the children so that they might not fall asleep before the end of the *seder.*

BIBLIOGRAPHY: Kohler, in: ZGDJ, 3 (1889), 234–6; D. Goldschmidt, *Haggadah shel Pesaḥ, Mekoroteha ve-Toledoteha* (1960), 96–98; M. Kasher, *Haggadah Shelemah* (1961), 190f.; A.M. Habermann, in: *Maḥanayim*, 55 (1961), 140–3; D. Sadan, *ibid.*, 144–50; For detailed bibl. see Kohut, in: JE, 6 (1904), 128, and Davidson, Oẓar, 2 (1929), 224 no. 39.

HADID (Heb. חָדִיד), city in the northern Shephelah, in the western part of the territory of *Benjamin. It is mentioned together with *Lydda and *Ono among the cities to which the Babylonian exiles returned (Ezra 2:33; Neh. 7:37; 11:34). The city had strategic importance; it was fortified by the Hasmonean *Simeon who camped nearby during Tryphon's invasion (I Macc. 12:38; 13:13 – Adida). The battle between the Nabatean King Aretas and Alexander *Yannai took place near Hadid, and Vespasian later conquered it (Jos., Ant. 13:392; Wars 4:486). According to the Mishnah, it was already fortified in Joshua's time (Ar. 9:6). Eusebius describes it as being east of Lydda (Onom. 24:24 – Aditha) and it also appears on the *Madaba Map (no. 59). A mosaic pavement with figurative nilotic scenes was found there in 1940. The ancient town was situated on a hill northwest of the abandoned Arab village of al-Ḥadītha, 3½ mi. (6 km.) east of Lydda. In 1951, 60 Yemenite immigrant families founded a settlement called Ḥadid near the village. They were joined later on by immigrants from Romania. In the mid-1990s, the population was approximately 480 and in 2002 it numbered 555.

BIBLIOGRAPHY: Yeivin, in: *Eretz Israel*, 3 (1954), 35; Avi-Yonah, *ibid.*, 2 (1953), 49; Alt, in: PJB, 24 (1928), 71–72; M. Noth, *Das Buch Joshua* (1938), 93ff.; Abel, in: RB, 35 (1926), 218; Beyer, in: ZDPV, 56 (1933), 233. **ADD. BIBLIOGRAPHY:** Y. Tsafrir, L. Di Segni, and J. Green, *Tabula Imperii Romani. Iudaea – Palaestina. Maps and Gazetteer.* (1994), 138. **WEBSITE:** www.calcalit.co.il/moatzot.asp.

[Michael Avi-Yonah]

HADITH, the science of Islamic tradition, applying particularly to the *sunna* (actions, sayings, virtues, opinions, and ways of life of *Muhammad). The hadith is one of the four fundamentals which form the background of **fiqh* (Islamic jurisprudence). It encompasses all the relationships between man and God and between man and man, including methods of prayer, fasting, pilgrimage, marital laws, and commercial affairs. The believer must be acquainted with the *sunna* of the Prophet and model his life in accordance with it; any deviation from the traditional path is a *bidʿa* ("a harmful innovation").

The first to hand down the hadith were the companions (*ṣaḥāba*) of Muhammad, who followed the course of Muhammad's life and heeded his words. After his death, masses of believers went to the companions in order to hear the *sunna* of the Prophet. The men of the second generation continued to propagate the tradition which they had received from the *ṣaḥāba*, handing it down to their followers. Thus, a chain of traditionalists was formed, the *isnād* ("support"), which preceded the texts (*matn*) themselves or the main part (of the teaching). At first, the hadith was handed down orally. A few of the traditionalists, however, wrote down the traditions for their personal use; these lists (*ṣaḥīfa*, "sheet") aided subsequent traditionalists, as well as the editors of the hadith. The editing of collections of the hadith began at the end of the *Umayyad period; the editors adopted two different methods: *musnad*, the classification of traditions according to the names of the traditionalists and *muṣannaf*, their classification according to subject, and editing according to the content. The oldest extant documents are a fragment on papyrus of the *ṣaḥīfa* by Ibn Lahīʿa (d. 790), found in Egypt and containing traditions which are mainly of an eschatological nature; the collection by Mālik ibn Anas (d. 795), *al-Muwaṭṭa*: a section of the collection of ʿAbdallah ibn Wahb (d. 812), also written on papyrus, which contains the sayings of the Prophet, the first caliphs, and the men of the second generation, mainly on ways of behavior and virtues; and the *musnad* of Aḥmad ibn Ḥanbal, which contains about 30,000 hadiths.

From the beginning of *Islam the believers attributed great importance to the hadiths as complementary and explanatory material to the *Koran. The principle that certain traditions of the Prophet were nullified by later sayings of the Prophet was accepted; many works were written on the subject. The most eminent Muslim scholars dedicated their efforts to the clarification of the unusual words which are found in the hadith.

The struggle between social movements, political parties, and various religious trends within Islam gave rise to an abundance of hadiths which were attributed to the Prophet. Some contradicted others, thus confusing the Muslim scholars of tradition. A special science was established which is concerned with meticulous investigation into the reliability of the men of the *isnād*, as to character, talent, propriety, and ideological attachment to the various social and political groups. The hadiths were classified as "genuine" (*ṣaḥīḥ*, the best category), "fair" (*ḥasan*, the middle category), and "weak" (*ḍaʿīf*) and were divided accurately and systematically according to their frequency, the number of authorities in the *isnād*, the relationship which existed among them (oral or written tradition), etc. During the ninth century six collections of hadiths (*muṣannaf*, see above) were written and accepted as reliable by Muslims: al-Bukhārī (d. 870), Muslim (d. 875), Abu Dāʾūd (d. 888), al-Tirmidhī (d. 892), al-Nasaʾī (d. 915), and Ibn Māja (d. 886). The works of al-Bukhārī and Muslim were particularly esteemed: the former contains 7,275 hadiths selected by the author from about 200,000 hadiths after a most meticulous examination. In the course of time many collections of hadiths were compiled; some are more comprehensive but not as esteemed as the six aforementioned works, which have been edited and commented upon in detail by Muslim scholars. The great interest in the hadith gave rise to a special movement of "searchers of knowledge" *(ṭullūb al-ʿilm)*, who wandered around the world in search of the scholars of the hadith in order to listen to their teachings. The influence of Judaism on the development of the *ḥadith* is evident not only in their content (see *Qiṣaṣ al-Anbiyāʾ* ("The Legends of the Prophets") and *Bible in Islam) but also in the form in which they have been handed down. There is a striking similarity between the *isnād* and the chain of masoretes in tannaitic and amoraic literature in the *halakhah* and the *aggadah* (cf. also the concept of "a ruling received by Moses at Sinai" and the opening of the tractate *Avot*: "Moses received the Torah at Sinai and handed it down to Joshua, Joshua to the Elders, the Elders to the prophets,…"). Judaism has also influenced the hadiths which deal with the daily conduct of man, man's relationship to God, ethics, piety, various customs, as well as legal affairs, marital laws, and rites. The influence of Christianity on the hadith is not as apparent.

[Meir Jacob Kister and Haïm Z'ew Hirschberg]

While the Jews and their religion, and the Israelites and their history, receive relatively scant attention in the hadith literature proper (especially in the aforementioned six canonical collections), other Islamo-classical genres composed primarily of hadith reports – including *sīra* (prophetic biography), *maghāzī* (chronicles of military campaigns) and above all *tafsīr* (Koran commentary) – devote considerable space to subjects Jewish. This distinction may be attributed to the central purpose of the *muṣannaf* hadith compilations – namely, to inculcate legal and behavioral norms as opposed to relating anecdotes of solely historical or anthropological interest – as well as to an increasing distaste on the part of medieval Muslim purists for the reservoir of Jewish material (known as *Isrā'īliyyāt*) that had infiltrated Islamic discourse since the faith's inception. Hadith reports as expressed in these various other frameworks (*sīra, maghāzī, tafsīr*) dwell at length on matters pertaining to the Jews, who are referred to with a certain rough interchangeability as *Yahūd, Banū Isrā'īl* or *ahl al-kitāb* (people of the book). They delve into issues such as ancient Israelite history; tales of the biblical prophets; the rocky relationship between the Children of Israel and their God (Allāh); Arabian Jews and their interaction with the fledgling Muslim community; Jewish theology, law, custom and ritual; the role and fate of the Jewish community in the Eschaton; the character of the Jews and the correct Muslim attitudes toward them; and more.

The information obtained by Muslims concerning Jewish norms and historiography and reflected in the hadith ranges from the impressively accurate (including near verbatim recapitulations of biblical and midrashic passages and relatively sophisticated rehearsals of Talmudic *sugyot*) to the confused, propagandistic and fantastic: Jews excise urine-splattered flesh, pluck each other's eyes out in retribution, are enjoined by the Torah to forego booty in war, and believe Ezra is the son of God as the Christians believe Jesus is the son of God; Jewish law forbids the consumption of geese and ducks, prohibits the use of sand for purification if water cannot be found, commands its adherents to slaughter a yellow heifer if an unidentified corpse is found in a field, etc. While ancient Israelites are on some rare occasions portrayed positively in the hadith literature, for the most part Jews of all periods are presented in a highly negative light. They are *Muḥammad's (as they were Jesus', as well as their own prophets') most intractable adversaries, who lost no opportunity to try and trip up the Arabian apostle and mock his message. They are conceived as the historical epitome of excess and evil and – having been abandoned by God as a result of such noxious traits – now also the model of misery. The Jews may be said to function as the emblem of all that Muslims should not be, a kind of *sunna* (exemplary tradition) in reverse.

[Z.A. Maghen (2nd ed.)]

BIBLIOGRAPHY: I. Goldziher, *Muslim Studies* (trans. Barber and Stern), 2 (1970), 15–250; A.J. Wensinck, *Handbook of Early Mohammedan Tradition* (1927); E.I.J. Rosenthal, *Judaism and Islam* (1961), index; **ADD. BIBLIOGRAPHY:** F. Rahman, *Islamic Methodology in History* (1965); A. Jeffery, *A Reader on Islam* (1962), 79–248; A. Guillaume, *The Traditions of Islam* (1924); J. Schacht, *The Origins of Muhammadan Jurisprudence* (1950); M.M. Azmi, *Studies in Early Hadith Literature* (1968). Most of the canonical collections of hadith have been translated – with varying accuracy and eloquence – into English, and are available in book form and online. There are many scholarly studies on Jews in, and the influence of Judaism on, hadith-based Islamic literature. Among the most accessible are A. Geiger, *Judaism and Islam* (trans. F.M. Young) (1970); S.D. Goitein, *Jews and Arabs: Their Contacts through the Ages* (1955), esp. chap. 4; C. Adang, *Muslim Writers on Judaism and the Hebrew Bible* (1996); H. Lazarus-Yafeh, *Intertwined Worlds* (1992); B. Wheeler, *Prophets in the Qur'an: An Introduction to the Qur'an and Muslim Exegesis* (2002); U. Rubin, *Between Bible and Qur'an: The Children of Israel and the Islamic Self-Image* (1999); G. Newby, *The Making of the Last Prophet: A Reconstruction of the Earliest Biography of Muhammad* (1989).

HADRACH (Heb. חַדְרָךְ), city in Syria. Its identification is established by the biblical reference to the "land of Hadrach" in context with Damascus, Hamath, Tyre, and Sidon (Zech. 9:1). Some scholars also emend Ezekiel's description of the country's northern border from "the way of [Heb. *ha-derekh*] Hethlon" to "Hadrach-Hethlon," and accordingly locate it between the Mediterranean and Zedad (Ezek. 47:15). The city Hazrak is mentioned in an inscription of Zakir, king of Hamath and Lu'at (L's; c. 780 B.C.E.), who captured the city and resisted its invasion by a coalition of kings from northern Syria and southern Anatolia. In the eighth century, the Assyrians stormed the city three times before Tiglath-Pileser III succeeded in conquering it in c. 738 B.C.E. He reduced it to an Assyrian province, bearing its name; an Assyrian governor is still found there in 689 B.C.E.

Since Hadrach appears in Assyrian documents together with Mt. Saua (apparently Mt. al-Zāwiya), scholars locate the land of Hadrach between the valley of Unqi (Antiochia) in the north, Hamath in the south, and the Orontes in the west. The location of the city Hadrach, however, is disputed; it is most likely Kharake, near Mu'arat e-Nu'aman.

A note from R. Joseph b. Dormaskit to R. Judah indicates that in talmudic times Hadrach was thought to be located in the vicinity of Damascus (Sif. Deut. 1). In the Middle Ages, the seat of Gaon Solomon b. Elijah and his yeshivah was called Hadrach; this is possibly the city Javbar, two miles (3 km.) northeast of Damascus, where remains of an ancient synagogue have been found. Hadrach was still mentioned by the travelers of the 16th and 17th centuries, as the place where the "Synagogue of the Prophet Elijah" whose ruins subsist to this day, was situated.

BIBLIOGRAPHY: M. Noth, in: ZDPV, 52 (1929), 124–41; A. Dupont-Sommer, *Les Araméens* (1949), 51, 55, 62 f.; Mann, Texts, 2 (1935), 230 n. 215; A. Malamat, in: *Eretz Israel*, 1 (1951), 81ff.; B.Z. Luria, *Ha-Yehudim be-Suryah* (1957), 214, 243; I. Ben-Zvi, *She'ar Yashuv* (1965), 484ff.; Luckenbill, Records, index.

[Michael Avi-Yonah]

ḤADRAMAWT. A province of *Yemen, a coastal region of the south Arabian peninsula on the Gulf of Aden in the Arabian Sea, extending eastward from Yemen to Oman. Historically, the name refers to the Ḥadramawt sultanates, a collective term for the Qu'aiṭī and Kāthirī sultanates, which were loosely under a British protectorate of South Arabia, guided by the British resident at *Aden, until 1957. Society is still highly tribal, with the old Sayyid aristocracy descended from *Muhammad, traditionally educated and strict in their Shāfi'ī Islamic observance. Though Bible dictionaries derive Ḥadramawt from Hazarmaweth, a son of Joktan (Genesis 10:26–8), it actually derives from Greek *hudreumata* or enclosed watering stations at wadis. The frankincense trees that supplied the "Incense Road" grew to the east of the Ḥaḍramawt, in the Dhofar. Ḥaḍramawt was the country of two separate pre-Islamic kingdoms in south Arabia: Kathabān and Ḥaḍramawt. In pre-Islamic time Ḥaḍramawt was almost completely Jewish as local tribes such as the Kindah judaicized, but most of them became Muslim after the country was conquered by the army sent by Muḥammad. Jews, however, continued to live there under the end of the 15th century, when they were killed or expelled as a result of a Jewish messianic uprising. Since then the country was considered as a holy land where the tomb of the mythological prophet Hūd was found, so Jews were not permitted to reside there. Only in the western part were there in modern times some Jewish settlements, such as *Ḥabbān and Bayḥān. But the Jewish silversmiths and goldsmiths were allowed to wander all over the country to make a living. Some of them converted to Islam, probably at the end of the 19th century.

BIBLIOGRAPHY: R.B. Serjeant, BSOAS, 1953, 117–31; M. Rodionov, TEMA, 8 (2004), 153–68; Lawrence Loeb, in: E. Isaac and Y. Tobi, *Proceedings of the Second International Congress of Judeo-Yemenite Studies* (1999), 71–99; R. Meissner, TEMA, 7 (2003), iii–xix.

[Yosef Tobi (2nd ed.)]

HADRAN (Heb. הַדְרָן; Aram. "we returned"), a term indicating both the celebration held on the completion of the study of a tractate of the Talmud (*siyyum*) and the type of discourse delivered on that occasion. The origin of the term is the formula found at the end of the chapters of the tractates of the Talmud – "*hadran alakh* chapter so-and-so" (at a later date the words "*ve-hadrakh alan*" were added). Two explanations of the term have been given: "We shall return to thee"; and indicating "beauty" or "splendor," a form of farewell salutation to the tractate comparable to "Homage to thee, O Altar!" (Suk. 4:5, see Lieberman, in: *Alei Ayin, Minḥat Devarim... S. Schocken* (1948–52), 81 n.33). The celebration and feasting held on such an occasion are mentioned in the Talmud (Shab. 118b–119a), and it is laid down that the meal ranks as a religious one (Sh. Ar., YD 246:26). As a result it can exempt a person from the obligation of fasting, as for instance on the Fast of the *Firstborn on the eve of Passover (*Mishnah Berurah*, OḤ 470:10), or exempt those who have adopted the custom of fasting on the anniversary of their parents' death. On it one may partake of meat and wine during the days of mourning between the First of *Av until the Ninth of Av (Isserles to Sh. Ar., OḤ 551:10). The essential elements of prayer recited at the conclusion of the study of a tractate (printed at the end of each tractate in most editions of the Talmud), which includes the enumeration of the ten sons of Rav Papa as a kind of incantation, is already mentioned by *Abraham b. Isaac of Narbonne in the *Sefer ha-Eshkol* (Z.B. Auerbach's edition, 2 (1968), 49, Sefer Torah no. 14; = S. Albeck's edition, 1 (1935), 159) in the name of *Hai Gaon, who observes that they refer to scholars from different eras and that they were not all the sons of the same Rav Papa. It also includes the expanded version of the *Kaddish de-Rabbanan*. The discourse delivered at this celebration took on a special character. By recourse to ingenious *pilpul* it aimed at connecting the end of the tractate with its beginning or with the beginning of the next tractate to be studied. A special literature of this type thus developed, which began to appear mainly at the beginning of the 18th century (the first discourse of this class is perhaps the one at the end of the novellae on *Bava Kamma* (1631) of Meir *Schiff (published Hamburg, 1747)). Because of their pilpulistic character they gave rise to opposition and criticism.

BIBLIOGRAPHY: J. Widler, *Hadar Yiẓḥak* (1940); S.K. Mirsky, *Siyyumei ha-Massekhtot ba-Mishnah u-va-Talmud ha-Bavli* (1961); Preshel, *ibid.*, 265–94 (listing 282 *hadranim*); Leiter, in: *Sinai*, 33 (1953), 56–61; Margaliot, in: *Ba-Mishor*, 7 (1945), 8 no. 277; Y.Z. Stern, in: TB, Ber. 236 (Third pagination).

[Shlomoh Zalman Havlin]

°**HADRIAN (Adrian) I**, pope (772–95). Under Hadrian's papacy the Second Council of Nicaea, which condemned iconoclasm, was held in 787. On several occasions when Hadrian intervened personally in the controversy over graven images, and again in letters to Empress Irene and to Charlemagne, he fulminated against the Jewish respect for the biblical command against images; finally he compared the iconoclasts – whom the Council of Nicaea eventually declared heretics – with the Jews. In several edicts attempting to regulate relations between Christians and Jews he forbade Christians to celebrate Passover with the Jews, to accept unleavened bread from the Jews, and to rest on the Sabbath "after the Jewish fashion." In a letter addressed in 794 to the bishops of Spain, Hadrian complained in passing that he had learned that "many people who claim to be Catholics live freely with Jews and unbaptized pagans, sharing both food and drink with them." He urged the bishops to see that nothing of the sort occurred again and that the regulations laid down by Church Fathers were followed.

BIBLIOGRAPHY: B. Blumenkranz, *Les auteurs chrétiens latins...* (1966), 142ff.

[Bernhard Blumenkranz]

°**HADRIAN, PUBLIUS AELIUS**, Roman emperor, 117–138 C.E. According to all the indications, Hadrian did not entertain any hostility toward the Jews at the beginning of his reign. On the contrary, it would appear that the Jews hoped for an improvement in their situation. Hadrian's first act, the execution of Lusius *Quietus, the governor of Judea, certainly appealed to the Jews. There is apparently an echo of the hopes raised by Hadrian's accession in the *Sibylline Oracles, which state that the man whose name is like that of the sea (H-adrian–Adriatic) will act favorably toward the Jews (5:46–50). There may also have been contacts between the Jews and the Roman government. Although there is no explicit information to that effect, it would appear that rumors began to spread that the Temple was to be rebuilt (cf. Gen. R. 64:10), but nothing practical resulted. It is not certain whether Hadrian issued decrees against Jewish observance before the

*Bar-Kokhba War (132–135). One opinion holds that the Jews were affected, even if unintentionally, by a decree issued by Hadrian forbidding castration, which was interpreted as including a prohibition of circumcision. Others reject any connection between this decree and circumcision, and are of the opinion that the decrees against circumcision and other observances were enacted after the war.

The emperor also decided to erect a gentile city on the site of destroyed Jerusalem to be named *Aelia Capitolina after himself. According to Dio Cassius this decision was made about two years before the Bar-Kokhba War and it is regarded by many as one of the chief causes of the Jewish revolt, even though the project was implemented only after the revolt had been crushed. Hadrian frequently visited parts of the empire. He visited Judea in 130 C.E., but there is no knowledge of any contact between him and the Jews during this visit, although in talmudic literature many conversations of Hadrian with R. *Joshua b. Ḥananiah are reported. According to those who date Hadrian's anti-Jewish decrees, especially with regard to Aelia Capitolina, before the revolt, the visit resulted in fanning the flames of discontent. A reference to the visit has been preserved in a coin which shows the province of Judea, in the guise of a woman, greeting the emperor on his arrival. It should be borne in mind, however, that the official view represented on the coin in no way reflects the attitude of the Jews. From Judea Hadrian proceeded to Egypt, returning in 131. During his sojourn in Judea and the neighboring countries the Jews outwardly kept the peace, but in 132 the revolt broke out in full force. Despite some initial successes of the rebels, Hadrian's commander, Julius Severus, succeeded eventually in crushing the revolt (see *Bar Kokhba). It was then, most probably, that Hadrian issued the harsh restrictive edicts against the study of the Torah and the practice of Judaism, including circumcision, making their observance capital offenses. Presumably it was in the subsequent persecutions that R. *Akiva and other rabbis were martyred (see the *Ten Martyrs). It was then also that Aelia Capitolina was constructed on the ruins of Jerusalem. A temple to Jupiter Capitolinus and an equestrian statue of the emperor were erected on the site of the Temple. These edicts of Hadrian remained in force until the time of his heir, Antoninus Pius, and in cruelty and scope they recall the decrees of Antiochus 300 years earlier. Hadrian's decrees give eloquent expression to the detestation felt by the emperor, "the friend of culture and enlightenment," for Judaism and his complete inability to understand it, as well as to the gulf between Judaism and the world of the Roman Empire.

[Uriel Rappaport]

In the Aggadah

To the rabbis, Hadrian was a symbol of wickedness and cruelty. His name is usually accompanied by the epithet "the wicked" or by the imprecation "may his bones rot" in Hebrew or Aramaic. In addition the appellation "the wicked kingdom" refers very frequently to Rome in the days of Hadrian. All manner of stories are related about the murder of Jews at the command of Hadrian after the fall of *Bethar. On the verse "the voice is the voice of Jacob" (Gen. 27:22) R. Johanan states that it refers to the voice of Emperor Hadrian, who "killed 80,000 myriads of people in Bethar" (Gen. R. 65:21; Lam. R. 1:16; 45). Nevertheless Hadrian appears in the *aggadah* in a more genial role which tends to emphasize his contacts with Jews, both scholars and the common people. He is said to have had discussions with Joshua ben Ḥananiah on the creation of the world (Gen. R. 10:3), and on resurrection, in which there appears the legend of the **luz*, the indestructible nut (coccyx) of the spinal column (*ibid.*, 28:3). Similarly, stories are told of him walking through Ereẓ Israel before the Bar Kokhba War and conversing with farmers. One of them describes him asking a centenarian who was planting fig trees whether he expected to eat of its fruits. The old man answered that as he had found fruit trees when he was born, so he was planting them for his children. Three years later, after the war, the man presented him with a basket of figs from that planting and Hadrian filled the basket with gold pieces (Lev. R. 25:5). These stories seem to be connected with the devastation caused by the war and the subsequent restoration of the previous fertility of the land, a fact specifically mentioned in connection with the aftermath of the war (TJ, Pe'ah 7:1, 20a).

[Louis Isaac Rabinowitz]

BIBLIOGRAPHY: Weber, in: cah, 11 (1936), 294–324. For Hadrian and the Jews, see bibliography on Bar Kokhba. IN THE AGGADAH: Ginzberg, Legends, index; M. Radin, *Jews among the Greeks and Romans* (1915), 343–4. **ADD. BIBLIOGRAPHY:** S. Perowne, *Hadrian* (1960); G. Foerster, "A Cuirassed Bronze Statue of Hadrian," in: *Atiqot*, 17 (1985), 139–60.

HADUTA (also known as **Hedvata**) **BEN ABRAHAM** (c. 6th century), one of the early *paytanim* in Ereẓ Israel. His *piyyutim form a distinct group in *piyyut* literature because of their special subject material: a series of hymns commemorating the 24 watches (*mishmarot) of priests (cf. I Chron. 24:7–18), practiced in the time of the Second Temple. One *kerovah* is dedicated to each watch. A prayer commemorating the watches dated 1034, found in the Cairo *Genizah*, gives evidence of the custom of the Palestinian Jews, whereby on each Sabbath the name of the division belonging to that Sabbath was proclaimed. It thus emerged that Haduta's *kerovot* were not *kinot* ("dirges") for the Ninth of *Av, as had been supposed, but were recited in the Palestinian synagogues each Sabbath.

The hymns mention many details concerning the names and the dwelling places of the watches. They are thus an important source of information for research of Palestinian topography. Possibly the priests were still concentrated in certain defined localities in Haduta's time.

Haduta (הֶדְוָתָא, הֲדוּתָא) sometimes signed his name חֲדוּתָה, חֶדְוָתָה (with ח and ה instead of ה and א), and it is unlikely that there were two or three hymnologists of the same name.

BIBLIOGRAPHY: Epstein, in: *Tarbiz*, 12 (1940/41), 78; Habermann, in: YMḤSI, 5 (1939), 80 n.; J.H. Schirmann, *Shirim Ḥadashim min ha-Genizah* (1965), 13–22; Zulay, in: *Ginzei Kaufmann*, 1 (1949),

36–38; idem, in: *Tarbiz* 22 (1950/51), 28–42; P. Kahle, *Masoreten des Westens*, 1 (1927), texts; YMḤSI, 5 (1939), 111–20, texts.

[Menahem Zulay]

HA-EFRATI (Tropplowitz), JOSEPH (c. 1770–1804), Hebrew poet and dramatist. Born in Tropplowitz, Silesia, he was a tutor for several years, during which he wrote the first acts of *Melukhat Sha'ul* ("Saul's Kingdom"), a drama that was completed in Prague in 1793. Although many of his poems were published in the first issues of *Ha-Me'assef*, his principal work remains *Melukhat Sha'ul*. The Yiddish translation became part of the traditional *Purimshpil ("Purim play") in many Lithuanian and Polish towns. *Melukhat Sha'ul*, the first modern Hebrew drama of the Haskalah period, is noteworthy for its new egalitarian and humanistic ideas. Evidently influenced by Shakespeare, Goethe, Schiller, and von Haller, as well as M.Ḥ. *Luzzatto, Ha-Efrati was particularly successful in his depiction of a man in the grip of irrational forces. Yet critics have argued that the play's weakness lies in its flat characterizations of all personages except Saul. David, Jonathan, and Michal represent abstract ideas rather than lifelike characters. Ha-Efrati, however, improved upon all the numerous attempts throughout the Middle Ages to dramatize the tragedy of Saul. He portrayed the pathos of a suffering hero, ridden with envy and guilt, torn by fears and loneliness, and not merely a proud and jealous king. The drama very likely influenced J.L. *Gordon's *David u-Varzillai* and *Ahavat David u-Mikhal* (1857). Parts of a newly discovered book of Ha-Efrati's Hebrew poems were published by A.Z. Ben-Yishai (*Beḥinot*, 11 (Fall 1957), 59–71).

BIBLIOGRAPHY: Klausner, Sifrut, 1 (1952), 193–9; J.L. Landau, *Short Lectures on Modern Hebrew Literature* (1938^2), 86–95; *Melukhat Sha'ul* (1968), introd. by G. Shaked; A. Yaari, in: KS, 12 (1935/36), 384–8; Kressel, Leksikon, 2 (1967), 32–33. **ADD. BIBLIOGRAPHY:** Ch. Shmeruk, *Sifrut Yiddish, Perakim le-Toledoteha* (1978); M. Granot, "*Elokim u-Malakhim bi-Yeẓirot Mikraiyot mi-Tekufat ha-Haskalah*," in: *Ben Yehuda* (1981), 274–82; S. Werses, "*Mi-Ḥilufei Lashon le-Ḥilufei Mashma'ut: Al Melukhat Sha'ul be-Tirgumo le-Yiddish*," in: *Ḥulliyot* 6 (2000), 55–78.

HA-EMET (Heb. הָאֶמֶת, "The Truth"), the first Hebrew socialist periodical, published in Vienna during the summer of 1877. The idea of issuing a socialist organ for Jews originated in the revolutionary circles of Vilna. The editor and publisher (under the pseudonym Arthur Freeman) was Aaron Samuel *Liebermann. After he fled from Russia in 1875, Liebermann had at first attempted, unsuccessfully, to establish a bilingual periodical, *Ha-Pattish* ("The Hammer"), in Yiddish and in Hebrew, for both the Jewish masses and the *maskilim*. He received the support of the Jewish students' circle in Berlin, as well as Jewish revolutionaries such as Lazar *Goldenberg, Aaron *Zundelevich, and non-Jewish revolutionary leaders like P. Lavrov and V. Smirnov, editors of the periodical *Vperyod*. In its prospectus Liebermann announced that *Ha-Emet* would not concern itself with "religious and national issues" but with "the necessities of life" – "bread and work" and "the spoon and the fork question," which "took precedence over all other contemporary problems." The publication of the newspaper was motivated by "our love for our people solely in their capacity of human beings" and by a particular responsibility felt toward them "being conscious of their lives and their afflictions." As a newspaper issued legally, *Ha-Emet* maintained a cautious tone. Liebermann himself wrote almost all the articles (which were unsigned). It included poems by J.L. *Levin (Yahalal), who with M. Kamyonski actively promoted the newspaper in Russia. Its agent in Galicia and Ukraine was Rabbi A. Eisner. The publication of *Ha-Emet* provoked wide controversy in the Jewish press. The newspaper closed down after three issues through lack of funds and the prohibition on its entry into Russia. Its direct successor was **Asefat Ḥakhamim*, whose editor M. *Winchevsky was influenced by Liebermann. Photographic editions of *Ha-Emet* were published by Ẓ. Krol with appendixes (1938), and in Jerusalem (1967).

[Moshe Mishkinsky]

HAENDEL, IDA (1928–), violinist. Born in Chelm, Haendel studied as a child prodigy with Michałowicz in Warsaw, and in 1933 won the conservatory gold medal and the first Huberman Prize with Beethoven's Violin Concerto. She then pursued her training in Paris and London with Flesch and Enesco, making her London debut in 1937. Her wartime activities included many concerts for Allied troops, National Gallery appearances, and a performance of Dvořák's Concerto at the composer's centenary Prom. She began her international concert career after World War II and came to be regarded as one of the leading soloists of her generation. She made tours in America, Russia, Europe, South America, and Asia. In 1973 she was the first Western soloist (with the London Philharmonic) invited to perform in China. Haendel's virtuoso technique won her admirers in both the concerto and recital repertoires. Among her first performances were Dallapiccola's *Tartiniana seconda*, (1957) and Alan Pettersson's Violin Concerto no.2 (1980), which was dedicated to her. Haendel was awarded the Sibelius Medal (1982), created a CBE (1991), and appointed Fellow of the Royal College of Music (2000). She published her autobiography, *Woman with Violin* (1970), and her career was the subject of a CBC-TV documentary (1988).

ADD. BIBLIOGRAPHY: Grove online; MGG^2.

[Naama Ramot (2nd ed.)]

HAEZRAḤI (originally **Brisker**), **YEHUDA** (1920–1974), Hebrew novelist and playwright. Born in Jerusalem, he served in the British Army during World War II. He wrote several novels and plays, as well as numerous articles and sketches. Haezraḥi's works include *Ke-Ẓel Over* (1946), a novel; *Ananim ba-Sa'ar* (1947), a collection of stories; *Im Shaḥar* (1959), two novellas; a collection of three plays (1960) – *Ha-Te'omim, Ha-Mishtammet*, and *Ha-Seruv*; a novel, *Panim u-Massekhah* (1963); *Beit ha-Sefarim ha-Le'ummi ve-ha-Universita'i* (1967), a history of the national library at the Hebrew University;

and *Ir Even ve-Shamayim* (1968), a belletristic description of Jerusalem. He edited albums of the paintings of *Alva (1954), Nahum *Gutman (1965), and Yossi Stern (1965). (A list of his works translated into English appears in Goell, Bibliography, 67.)

His wife, PEPITA HAEZRAḤI (1921–1963), taught philosophy at the Hebrew University of Jerusalem. She published works in English and in Hebrew in the fields of philosophy, aesthetics, and ethics.

[Getzel Kressel]

Following the reunification of Jerusalem after the Six-Day War, Haezraḥi played a leading part in the campaign to preserve the beauty of Jerusalem. He founded and became chairman of the Jerusalem Committee of the Council for a Beautiful Israel, and the works he published after 1967 reflected his absorption with this subject. They include *Yerushalayim Asher Baḥarti* (caricatures by S. Katz, 1970) and the text of the Sound and Light Program on the Tower of David, "A Stone in David's Tower."

BIBLIOGRAPHY: M. Avishai, *Bein ha-Olamot* (1962), 157–73; A. Cohen, *Soferim Ivriyyim Benei Zemannenu* (1964), 109–18; Kressel, Leksikon, 1 (1965), 58. **ADD. BIBLIOGRAPHY:** M. Avishai, "*Olamo shel Y. Haezrahi*," in: *Al ha-Mishmar* (Elul 12, 1974); G. Shaked, *Ha-Sipporet ha-Ivrit*, 3 (1988), 240.

ḤAFEẒ ḤAYYIM (Heb. חָפֵץ חַיִּים), kibbutz in the southern Coastal Plain of Israel, 3 mi. (5 km.) S.E. of Gederah, affiliated with *Po'alei Agudat Israel. In 1937 Ha-Kibbutz ha-Me'uḥad members founded a village there, Sha'ar ha-Negev, but later moved north to establish their permanent settlement, *Kefar Szold. Afterward an Orthodox group, graduates of the Ezra youth movement in Germany, who previously worked on land near *Afulah, took over the site (1944). The kibbutz has intensive farming and also developed hydroponics to permit the literal observance of the *shemittah precepts. Ḥafeẓ Ḥayyim runs a guest house, recreation home, and water park geared to the needs of Orthodox Jews. Its farming includes field crops, citrus groves, dairy cattle, and poultry. The kibbutz used to own a towel factory, now in private hands. The kibbutz is named after Rabbi Israel Meir *ha-Kohen (Ḥafeẓ Ḥayyim). In 1968 its population was 360, and in the mid-1990s it grew to approximately 585. However, by 2002 it had dropped sharply to 382, as many of the young left the kibbutz.

[Efraim Orni]

HAFFKINE, WALDEMAR MORDECAI (1860–1930), bacteriologist. Born and educated in Odessa, Haffkine studied under the Nobel prizewinner Elie *Metchnikoff. He was offered a teaching post provided he converted to the Russian Orthodox Church, which he refused to do. Invited in 1889 by Metchnikoff, then at the Pasteur Institute, Paris, to become its librarian, he was later made assistant to the director. In 1892 Haffkine developed the first effective vaccine against cholera. Lord Dufferin, British ambassador to France, formerly viceroy in India, persuaded him to substitute India for Siam as the field-test area to combat cholera. In 1893, with a group of doctors and laboratory workers, Haffkine went through India inoculating, with excellent results, villagers who had volunteered for treatment. In 1896, when plague struck Bombay, the government sent him there to develop a vaccine against the plague. He succeeded within three months. Germany, Russia, China, and France sent scientists to study his methods and demands for his vaccine flooded his laboratory. In 1897, Queen Victoria named him Companion of the Order of the Indian Empire and in 1899 he was granted British citizenship.

In 1902 plague struck the Punjab, which received large quantities of vaccine. Nineteen of the tens of thousands inoculated contracted tetanus and died. Haffkine was charged with sending contaminated vaccine. An inquiry was launched as a result of which Haffkine was suspended and his pay forfeited. In 1904 he presented evidence in his defense at the Lister Institute, London, and the Pasteur Institute. Although Haffkine defended himself in the official inquiry and, subsequently, in scientific circles, it was only after the *London Times*, on July 29, 1907, published a long scientific defense of Haffkine that the government exonerated him. Haffkine returned to Calcutta with neither the promotion nor the salary increase he had been promised, to continue laboratory research until compulsory retirement at the age of 55.

Later Haffkine settled in Paris, where he participated actively in various Jewish organizations' efforts to create an independent Jewish state in Palestine. In 1919, with others, he presented a petition to the Peace Conference in Versailles, stressing minority rights for Jews in Eastern Europe.

In 1925 the Plague Research Laboratory he had founded in Bombay was renamed the Haffkine Institute in his honor. An observant Jew most of his life, in 1929 he created the Haffkine Foundation in Lausanne, bequeathing to it his fortune of $500,000, and stipulating that the interest be used to foster religious, scientific, and vocational education in yeshivot in Eastern Europe.

[Edythe Lutzker]

On August 17, 1971, V.V. Giri, president of India, unveiled a plaque at the entrance to the Petit Laboratory, Bombay, in memory of Haffkine. Another plaque in his honor was unveiled on September 21, 1972, at the Pasteur Institute in Paris.

BIBLIOGRAPHY: S.A. Waksman, *Brilliant and Tragic Life of W.M. Haffkine, Bacteriologist* (1964), incl. bibl.; M.A. Popovsky, *Fate of Dr. Haffkine* (Rus. 1963); E. Lutzker, in: *Actes du XI*[e] *Congrès International d'Histoire des Sciences* (1965), 214–9, (Eng.) incl. bib.; idem, in: *Acts of the XXI*[st] *International Congress of the History of Medicine* (1968); M. Einhorn, in: *Harofé Haivri*, 38 (1965), 362–334 (Eng.).

HAFKA'AT SHE'ARIM (Heb. הַפְקָעַת שְׁעָרִים), raising the price of a commodity beyond the accepted level, or that fixed by a competent authority.

Profiteering and Overreaching

The law of *Hafka'at She'arim* ("profiteering") is analogous to that of overreaching (**ona'ah*, "misrepresentation"), it being the object of the law in both cases to preserve a fair and just price. However, the law of overreaching – fraudulent or innocent (i.e., mistaken) – stems from a biblical prohibition (Lev. 25:14): the law was fixed that if the price exceeded the value by one-sixth, the seller must return this part to the purchaser; if the price was higher yet, the purchaser might demand cancellation of the transaction; conversely, if the price was too low, the law applies *mutatis mutandis* in favor of the seller. The law of profiteering on the other hand has its source in rabbinic enactment designed to prohibit the setting of prices in excess of the customarily accepted ones, even if the purchaser is aware of and agrees to the inflated price; "… even when he [the seller] says 'it cost me one *sela* and I want to earn two on it,' he has not transgressed the law of *ona'ah* but he is prohibited by rabbinic enactment from making a profit of more than one-sixth in essential commodities" (*Beit ha-Beḥirah*, BM 51b).

Price-fixing and Control; Prohibition against Profiteering

It would seem that in the mishnaic period there were fixed prices, apparently determined by a competent authority (BM 4:12, 5:7). There is evidence that in Jerusalem – prior to the destruction of the Temple – the market commissioners "did not supervise prices but measures only" (Tosef., BM 6:14); in Babylonia (at the commencement of the third century C.E.) there was supervision of prices at the instigation of the *exilarch (TJ, BB 5:11, 15a; TB, BB 89a). The sages of that period were divided, however, on this matter. Some expressed the opinion that "price inspectors do not need to be appointed" and that competition between merchants would suffice to stabilize the price while others were of the opinion that it was incumbent on the court to supervise the prices because of the "swindlers" who hoarded commodities toward a time when they might be in short supply in order to sell them at a high price (TJ and TB, BB 89a). Over the course of time the view favoring price supervision apparently became generally accepted (BB 89a; Yoma 9a) and thus it was decided in the codes: "But the court is obliged to determine prices and to appoint commissioners for this purpose, to prevent everyone from charging what he likes …" (Yad, Mekhirah 14:1; Tur and Sh. Ar., ḤM 231:20).

The scholars compared profiteering to the transgressions of "giving short measure of the ephah" (deceit with regard to *weights and measures) and to that of charging interest on loans (BB 90b; and see *Usury). In their opinion, the profiteer transgresses the biblical injunction "that thy brother may live with thee" (Lev. 25:36; *Sma* ḤM 231:43) and they regarded profiteers as "bandits who prey on the poor … on whom they concentrate their attention" (Meg. 17b and Rashi, *ibid.*). The prescribed punishment for them: "flagellation and they are compelled to sell at the market price" (Yad, Genevah, 8:20; Tur and Sh. Ar., ḤM 231:21). Authority to determine prices was given not only to the court, but also to local communal representatives: "and the townspeople are authorized to fix prices" (of wheat and wine, so as to maintain the price in a particular year – Rashi) "and measures and workers' wages, which they may enforce by means of punishment" (i.e., fines; cf. BB 89a and Rashi; Tosef. BM 11:23; BB 8b; see also **takkanot ha-Kahal*). It appears that already in the talmudic period, the law of profiteering was only applied to essential commodities such as wheat, oil, and wine, and this was confirmed in the codes: "Prices [of nonessentials] are not determined but everyone may charge what he likes" (Yad, Mekhirah 14:2 and standard commentaries ad loc.; Tur and Sh. Ar., ḤM 231:20).

The maximum profit generally permitted to the seller was one-sixth (BB 90a). Some of the authorities took the view that this rate applied to one selling his merchandise in bulk, without toil (a wholesaler); a shopkeeper, however, "selling his merchandise little by little, might have his toil and overheads accounted for in addition to a profit of one-sixth" (Tur and Sh. Ar., ḤM 231:20). They also decided that the rules concerning profiteering were only to take effect if imposed as measures of general application to all vendors, otherwise the individual could not be obliged to adhere to the permitted maximum rate of profit (*ibid.*).

Stringent Supervision in Ereẓ Israel

Particular care was taken to maintain a cheap supply of essential products in Ereẓ Israel, where no middleman between producer and consumer was tolerated: "It is forbidden to speculate in essential commodities in Ereẓ Israel but everyone shall bring from his barn and sell so that these [commodities] may be sold cheaply" (Tosef. Av. Zar. 4:1; BB 91a, Yad, Mekhirah 14:4; Sh. Ar. ḤM 231:23); however, it was decided that in the case of a commodity in free supply or where a middleman worked to prepare and process the product, such as baking bread from wheat, profit-making was permitted, even in Ereẓ Israel (Tosef. Av. Zar. 4:1; BB 91a and *Rashbam, Yad Ramah* and *Beit ha-Beḥirah ibid.*; Yad, Mekhirah 14:4; Sh. Ar., ḤM 231:23).

Measures to Prevent Profiteering

The sages sought in various ways to eliminate the factors which made for a climate for profiteering. Thus it was forbidden to hoard produce bought on the market, lest this cause prices to rise and bring losses to the poor, and in a year of famine no hoarding at all was permitted (not as much as a "cab of carobs"), not even of the produce harvested from one's own field (BB 90b; Yad, Mekhirah 14:5–7). In later *halakhah* storing of produce from the producer's own field was permitted, even in a famine year, for the sustenance of his family (Tur., ḤM 231:29) for a period of one year (Sh. Ar., ḤM 231:24). Produce hoarders, like profiteers, were compared to those who charged interest on loans (BB, 90b). In order to prevent profiteering, it was not permitted to export essential products from Ereẓ Israel, since this might cause a shortage and a consequent rise in prices (BB 90b–91a, Yad, Mekhirah 14:8; Sh. Ar., ḤM 231:26). With the same object in mind the rabbis laid down that the proclamation of a public fast (on account of drought) should not be announced for the first time on a Thursday as this would cause panic (out of fear of famine) at a time when everyone was preparing for the Sabbath, and this might lead to profiteering (Ta'an. 2:9).

In their war against profiteers the scholars made use of a deliberate *interpretation of the law. At a time when the numerous sacrifices required to be brought by a woman who had given birth caused the price of a pair of sacrificial birds (two doves) to be raised to a golden dinar (25 silver dinars), Simeon b. Gamaliel the Elder vowed: "I shall not sleep this night until a pair sells for a dinar" (i.e., silver; Ker. 1:7). He entered the court and taught that a woman who had had five definite births (and thus should bring five sacrifices) need bring one sacrifice only and might eat of the *zevaḥim* ("sacrificial animals"), i.e. is ritually pure, and that "the remainder is not obligatory upon her; that same day the price of sacrificial birds stood at a quarter [of a silver dinar per pair]." (*ibid.*); Rashi (Ker. 8a) comments: "though he interpreted the word of the law leniently, it was a time to campaign for the Lord (*et la'asot la-shem*) for if no remedy had been found, not even one [sacrifice] would have been brought." Some 1,600 years later, when the fishmongers of Nikolsburg, Moravia, greatly raised the price of fish, "having seen that the Jews were not deterred by expensive prices from buying fish for the Sabbath," the Nikolsburg community enacted a *takkanah* which prohibited everyone from buying fish for a period of two months. Asked whether this *takkanah* did not in some measure slight the honor of the Sabbath, M.M. *Krochmal, chief rabbi of Moravia, replied that in order to enable also the poor "to honor the Sabbath by [eating] fish" it were better not to buy fish for a few Sabbaths so as to bring down the prices, and he quoted the statements of Simeon b. Gamaliel (above), as a clear practical illustration of the saying: "It is well to desecrate one Sabbath, so that many Sabbaths be observed" (*Ẓemaḥ Ẓedek*, no. 28).

In the State of Israel

In the State of Israel there are a number of laws designed to combat profiteering in essential commodities. The Commodities and Services (Control) Law, 5718 – 1957, provides for various means of supervision over commodities declared to be subject to control by the minister charged with implementation of the law, enforcible on pain of imprisonment, fine, and closing down of a business, etc. The Tenants' Protection Laws, 5714 – 1954 and 5715 – 1955, control maximum rentals for residential and business premises and also limit the right of ejectment to grounds specified in these laws only. These laws are supplemented by the provisions of the Key Money Law, 5718 – 1958. The Restrictive Trade Practices Law, 5719 – 1959, restricts, among others, the artificial manipulation of price levels at the hands of a monopoly or cartel. In the Knesset debates preceding the passing of these laws, some members relied on Jewish law in support of their arguments (*Divrei ha-Keneset* vol. 7, p. 564; vol. 14, p. 1822; vol. 18, p. 2176; vol. 21, p. 169; vols. 23, pp. 372, 374, 383; vol. 24, pp. 2478, 2514).

BIBLIOGRAPHY: Gulak, Yesodei, 1 (1922), 64–66; P. Dickstein, in: *Ha-Mishpat ha-Ivri*, 1 (1925/26), 15–55; ET, 10 (1961), 41–49.

[Menachem Elon]

HAFSIDS (also known as **Banu Hafs**), *Berber dynasty of the 13th through 16th centuries in Ifriqiyah (*Tunisia and eastern Algeria of today), founded by the *Almohad leader Abu Zakariyya Yaḥya in 1230. Under his rule local Berber tribal disputes and unrest were pacified and economic activity through trade accords with Spain and Italy brought on prosperity. One of his sons, al-Mustansir, assumed the title of caliph in the 1250s, increasing the power of the dynasty to its zenith. By then the Hafsids had extended their influence to the borders of northern Morocco and Spain. Hafsid unity was interrupted by dissension under several of al-Mustansir's successors but was largely restored under the leadership of Uthmān in the 1430s. The dynasty came to an end when the *Ottoman Turks occupied parts of *Algeria and transformed Tunis into a *paşalik* in 1574.

With minor exceptions, the Jews under Hafsid domination benefited from the prevalence of cultural and commercial florescence. They traded in the Mediterranean with their co-religionists, notably in Italy, as well as with local merchants who constituted part of the Christian minority. Ifriqiyah's Jewry had been reinforced in the late 15th and early 16th centuries by an influx of Jews who were expelled from Spain. The military incursion of the Spaniards and Portuguese – the former oppressors of the Jews – into Ifriqiyah in the mid-16th century sowed panic among the members of the Jewish community, prompting many of them to flee from the larger cities into the desert. Their anxieties were short-lived, however. The conquest of the region by the Ottoman Turks in the latter half of the 16th century significantly improved their socio-economic and political status once again.

BIBLIOGRAPHY: H.Z. Hirschberg, *A History of the Jews in North Africa*, vol. 1 (Eng. tr., 1974); J.M. Abun-Nasr, *A History of the Maghrib in the Islamic Period* (1987); D. Larguèche, "The *Mahalla*: The Origins of the Beylical Sovereignty in Ottoman Tunisia during the Early Modern Period," in: J. Clancy-Smith (ed.), *North Africa, Islam and the Mediterranean World* (2001).

[Michael M. Laskier (2nd ed.)]

HAFTARAH (Heb. הַפְטָרָה), a portion from the Prophets read after the reading from the Torah (see Torah, Reading of) on Sabbaths, festivals, and fast days. On Sabbaths and festivals it is read during the morning service, on fast days at the *Minḥah service only (with the exception of the Day of *Atonement and the Ninth of *Av when there is a *haftarah* after the Torah reading in both the morning and the afternoon service). There is, however, evidence that during the talmudic period a *haftarah* was read at *Minḥah* on Sabbaths (see Shab. 116b and 24a, and Rashi and Tos. ad loc.) and in some places the custom continued until the end of the geonic period (Sefer ha-Ittim, para. 181), but it is unknown today.

Unlike the Sabbath reading from the Pentateuch, which consists of a continuous reading of successive portions of the Five Books of Moses without any omission, the *haftarah* is a portion from a book of the Former or Latter Prophets. Only two prophetic books are read completely as *haftarot*: the Book of Obadiah, which consists of only 21 verses (for the portion *Va-Yishlaḥ* (Gen. 32:4–36:43), according to the Sephardi custom and that of Frankfurt on the Main), and the Book of Jonah, which is the *haftarah* for the *Minḥah* service of the Day of Atonement. There were two criteria which determined the selection of a particular *haftarah*. When no other considerations prevailed, the choice was determined by the similarity of the contents of the prophetic portion to those of the portion of the Pentateuch read. Thus the *haftarah* to the portion *Be-Shallaḥ* (Ex. 13:17–17:16), containing the Song of Moses, includes the Song of Deborah (Judg. 4:4–5:31); and to *Shelaḥ* (Num. 13:1–15:41), describing the incident of the 12 spies sent by Moses, it is Joshua 2:1–24, concerning the spies sent by Joshua; and so on.

For about one-third of the *haftarot*, however, this criterion is abandoned, and the choice for those Sabbaths is determined either by the calendar or by historical circumstances. For ten successive weeks, from the Sabbath before the 17th of Tammuz until the Sabbath before Rosh Ha-Shanah, the *haftarot* consist of the three *haftarot* of tribulation (*pur'anut*) and the seven of consolation (those from Isaiah 40–66). Special *haftarot* are read on a Sabbath which is also Rosh Ḥodesh, on the Sabbath which falls on the day before Rosh Ḥodesh, on the Sabbath before Passover, on the Sabbath of the *Ten Days of Penitence, and on the Sabbath (or Sabbaths) of Ḥanukkah. The choice of the *haftarot* for the Four Special *Sabbaths depends on the special additional portion read on these days, and not on the ordinary Sabbath portion.

On festivals and fast days the *haftarah*, like the Torah reading, consists of a portion appropriate to the festival. For *Minḥah* on fast days (apart from the Day of Atonement) it is always Isaiah 55:6–56:7. In a few cases the *haftarah* is not a continuous portion (cf. Meg. 4:4).

History

The origin of the custom of reading a portion of the prophets after the Torah reading is unknown. The most plausible suggestion (dating from not earlier than the 14th century) is that the custom was instituted during the persecutions by *Antiochus Epiphanes which preceded the Hasmonean revolt. According to this theory, when the reading of the Torah was proscribed, a substitute was found by reading a corresponding portion from the Prophets; and the custom was retained after the decree was repealed (Abudarham; see also *David in the Liturgy). Buechler, however, was of the opinion that it was instituted against the Samaritans, who denied the canonicity of the Prophets (except for Joshua), and later against the Sadducees.

The earliest reference to the actual reading of a *haftarah* is found in the New Testament. Acts 13:15 states that "after the reading of the law and the prophets" Paul was invited to deliver an exhortation. Another reference (Luke 4:17) states that during the Sabbath service in Nazareth the Book of Isaiah was handed to Jesus, "and when he had opened the book, he found the place where it was written," the passage being Isaiah 61:1–2. Unfortunately, the Greek word used there meaning "found" does not make it clear whether the passage read was fixed beforehand or whether it was chosen at random.

The earliest reference in talmudic literature to the specific selection of a *haftarah* is in Tosefta, *Megillah*, 4 (3): 1, which gives the *haftarot* for the Four Special Sabbaths. A *baraita* in *Megillah* 31a, which has later additions by the Babylonian *amoraim* who add the *haftarot* for the second days of the festivals (and who sometimes change the order of the *haftarot* as a result) – gives the *haftarot* for every one of the festivals, including their intermediate Sabbaths, as well as a Sabbath which is also Rosh Ḥodesh, the Sabbath which immediately precedes Rosh Ḥodesh, and Ḥanukkah. However, nowhere in the Talmud are the *haftarot* given for ordinary Sabbaths, which were not fixed until after the talmudic period. The only other mention of the matter in tannaitic literature is the prohibition against the reading of certain prophetic passages: the *haftarah* on the *Merkavah* (Ezekiel 1) according to the anonymous Mishnah (but permitted by R. Judah, and in fact it is at present the *haftarah* for Shavuot; cf. Meg. 31a), and Ezekiel 16:1ff. according to R. Eliezer (Meg. 4:10), which, despite his strong disapproval, was read in his presence (Meg. 25b). The same Mishnah (Meg. 4:10) permits the reading of II Sam. 11:1–17 ("the story of David," i.e., and Bath-Sheba), and the "story of Amnon" (*ibid.* 13:1ff.) providing the Targum is not read (see below). These passages would seem to indicate that in mishnaic times the choice of the *haftarah* was generally not determined, and as late as geonic times different *haftarot* were in vogue in different localities. Even some of the *haftarot* mentioned in the Talmud are not those established at the present time, and to this day there are certain variations of choice, mostly between Sephardim and Ashkenazim, but also between different Ashkenazi rites (particularly that of Frankfurt on the Main).

The most interesting is the *haftarah* for *Simḥat Torah. According to the above-quoted passage in Megillah 31a, the *haftarah* for Shemini Aẓeret (which in Israel is also Simḥat Torah) was I Kings 8:54ff. and for the next day (Simḥat Torah in the Diaspora) I Kings 8:22. The universal custom today, to read Joshua I on Simḥat Torah, is attributed either to Hai Gaon (Tos. ad loc.) or the *savoraim (Or Zaru'a, II 293). When the *Triennial cycle was in vogue in Ereẓ Israel, there was naturally a *haftarah* to each portion, and the number must therefore have been about 150. They are, to some extent, reflected in the **Pesikta Midrashim*. Similarly, there are *haftarot* for the second day of each festival in the Diaspora which are not read in Ereẓ Israel, where the second day is not observed.

Various suggestions have been made as to the connotation of the word *haftarah*. One opinion is that it corresponds to the Latin word *demissio*, since in Temple times the service ended with the *haftarah*. Abudarham regards it as meaning "taking leave of," i.e., of *Shaḥarit, when one, so to speak, "takes one's leave" of the scriptural reading.

Regulations and Customs

The person who reads the *haftarah* is called the *maftir* since he is also called to the reading of the last part of the weekly portion from the Torah. As he is not included in the minimum obligatory number of seven persons who have to be called up on the Sabbath (Meg. 32a), the custom later arose for the concluding passage of the portion to be read a second time for the *maftir* (see Tos. ad loc.). On festivals, Rosh Ḥodesh, and the Four Special Sabbaths, however, the *maftir* is called to the reading of the special additional portion for those days from the second scroll. With the completion of that reading, the *Sefer Torah* is raised and rolled up (see *Hagbahah and Gelilah) and only then the *maftir* reads the *haftarah*, preceding it with two blessings and concluding the reading with three blessings, to which, on Sabbaths and festivals, a fourth blessing is added, the formula of which is changed according to the nature of the day. The text is given in *Soferim* 13:9–14, with slight variations from the text as established today. The *haftarah* is sung with a special cantillation, and the custom has developed for the introductory blessings to be chanted with the same cantillation. The Sabbath *haftarah* has to consist of a minimum of 21 verses (Meg. 23a), but for the festivals 15 suffice (Rema, OḤ 284:1).

It is not obligatory for the *haftarah* to be read from a manuscript scroll, but may be read from a printed book. In some congregations, however, especially in Israel, the *haftarah* is read from a scroll of the Prophets. Despite the general prohibition against committing to scroll writing only sections of the Prophets, in contrast to the complete Book of the Prophets, an exception was made in the case of a book containing only the *haftarot*; such a book is, in fact, mentioned in the Talmud (Git. 60a). Since the *maftir* was not included in the seven called to the reading of the Torah, a minor is permitted to be called to that portion (Meg. 4:5). The custom has become almost universal, however, to reserve the reading of the *haftarah* for a *bar mitzvah boy, but this is largely in order to provide him with an opportunity to show his prowess. Some *haftarot*, however, are regarded as being of such importance that a minor, and in some places even a bar mitzvah, is precluded from reading them. They include the *Merkavah* (Ezek. 1) on Shavuot, the Song of David on the seventh day of Passover, the *haftarah* on the Sabbath of the Ten Days of Penitence, and the *haftarah* of *Shabbat Zakhor* (see Special *Sabbaths), in this last case because the Torah reading of the *maftir* is considered obligatory by biblical law.

During the talmudic period, when the biblical reading was accompanied by its translation into Aramaic, the translation of the Torah reading was given verse by verse, but that of the *haftarah* after every three verses (Meg. 4:4), unless each verse constituted a separate "paragraph." Isaiah 52:3, 4, 5 is quoted as an example (Meg. 24a). The person who read the *haftarah* was invited to *"pores al shema"* (Meg. 4:5), a phrase to which different interpretations are given, but in the context it appears to mean to continue as the reader of the service which follows.

[Note: The order of chapters three and four in the Mishnah Megillah is reversed in the Babylonian Talmud. The mishnaic references given are therefore to be changed accordingly when their discussion in the Talmud is given.

BIBLIOGRAPHY: A. Buechler, in: JQR, 6 (1893), 1–73; Elbogen, Gottesdienst, 174–84; L. Rabinowitz, in: T.W. Manson (ed.), *Companion to the Bible* (1939), 14–16; J. Mann, *The Bible as Read and Preached in the Old Synagogue*, 2 vols. (1940–66), introduction and passim; ET, 10 (1961), 1–32; J. Heinemann, *Ha-Tefillah bi-Tekufat ha-Tanna'im veha-Amora'im* (1966[2]), 143ff.

[Louis Isaac Rabinowitz]

HAGAI, BARUCH (1944–), Israeli athlete in handicapped sports. Hagai is the only athlete in the world to win four consecutive gold medals in the Paralympic Games. He was born in Tripoli, Libya, and immigrated to Israel in 1951 at the age of seven. At the age of two he was stricken by polio. He began his career in 1960 in two sports: basketball and table tennis. In the 1964 Handicapped Olympics held in Tokyo he won a gold medal in table tennis and in the 50 meter breast stroke in swimming, as well as in the slalom race. In 1971 he won a gold medal in basketball in the World and European Championships for the handicapped. In 1972 he won a gold medal in table tennis in the Handicapped Olympics held in Heidelberg. In 1975 he won a gold medal in basketball in the World Championship for the handicapped. In 1976 he won a gold medal in table tennis in the Handicapped Olympics held in Toronto. In 1978 he won a gold medal in basketball in the European Championship. In 1980 he won a gold medal in basketball in the Handicapped Olympics held in Arnhem, The Netherlands. In 1981 he won a gold medal in basketball in the European Championship. In 1997 he received a special gold medal for his special contribution to national and international sport. He was named Sportsman of the Year in Israel on the 40th and 50th anniversaries of its independence. In 2001 he was awarded the Israel Prize for his contribution to handicapped sports in Israel. From the 1980s he coached other handicapped athletes.

WEBSITE: www.education.gov.il/pras-israel.

[Shaked Gilboa (2nd ed.)]

HAGANAH (Heb. הֲגָנָה), the underground military organization of the *yishuv* in Ereẓ Israel from 1920 to 1948. The idea of establishing a defense organization that would protect the *yishuv* throughout Ereẓ Israel was born during the Ottoman period. The head of *Ha-Shomer, Israel *Shoḥat, sent a memorandum to the Executive of the Zionist Organization at the end of 1912, suggesting the establishment of a country-wide organization for self-defense around Ha-Shomer.

Initial Organization

With the British conquest of Ereẓ Israel, it seemed that there would be no need for a Jewish defense organization, for a European power had assumed responsibility for the preservation of civil order with the aid of legally constituted forces from the *yishuv*. Especially in favor of this position was Vladimir *Jabotinsky. He viewed the perpetuation of the *Jewish Legion, which was established in the framework of the British army during World War I as a garrison in Palestine, as the best assurance of the peace and security of the *yishuv*. The Arab assault on the Jewish settlements in Upper Galilee in March 1920 (see *Tel Ḥai), the imminent danger to the settlements in Lower Galilee in the summer of 1920, and, above all, the failure of the self-defense activities openly organized by Jabotinsky during the Passover riots in Jerusalem in 1920 destroyed these illusions. Those who regarded themselves responsible for the defense of the *yishuv*, members of Ha-Shomer and soldiers of the Jewish Legion, came to realize that it was impossible to depend upon the British authorities and that the *yishuv* must create an independent defense force, completely free of foreign authority – in a word, an underground – for both security and political considerations. In contrast to Ha-Shomer, this organization should encompass masses of people and be subordinate to a public Jewish authority. The *Aḥdut ha-Avodah (A) conference at Kinneret in June 1920 accepted Ha-Shomer's resolution to disband and declared its own responsibility "to concern itself with the arrangement of defense matters." A committee was chosen "to organize a defense organization," and among its members were Shoḥat and Eliahu *Golomb. In September 1920 the *Gedud ha-Avodah (the "Joseph Trumpeldor Labor and Defense Legion") was established with the participation of ex-members of Ha-Shomer. In addition to their tasks as workers and guards, the members of the Gedud were to serve as a reserve force for the Haganah. In December 1920, the *Histadrut accepted responsibility for guard and defense matters at its founding convention, and at the first Histadrut council in March 1921, a defense committee was set up, consisting of Israel Shoḥat, Eliahu Golomb, Joseph *Baratz, Ḥayyim *Sturmann, and Levi Shkolnik (*Eshkol), and the first steps were taken toward training members and purchasing arms.

The riots of May 1921 caught the new defense organization unprepared, but they proved the necessity for its existence. Members were sent to Vienna to begin organizing the consignment of arms (revolvers and ammunition) to Palestine by various means (in beehives, refrigerators, steamrollers, etc.). In addition, the first course for Haganah instructors was run under the command of an ex-Legionnaire, Elimelekh Zelikovich ("Avner"). On Nov. 2, 1921 ("Balfour Day"), an organized group of defenders repelled an attack of an Arab mob on the Jewish quarter of the Old City of Jerusalem and prevented the slaughter of its inhabitants.

During the 1920s

At the outset of Haganah activities, there was friction in the organization's leadership, originating in disagreement over defense systems between ex-Ha-Shomer people and Golomb's group. The Histadrut leadership supported Golomb's group, and the friction finally led to the disassociation of the Ha-Shomer people from the activities of the Haganah and their concentration in the Gedud ha-Avodah, in which they created an underground within an underground by developing an independent network to acquire arms, providing training courses, and pursuing an unsuccessful attempt to develop ties with the Soviet Union (1926). Their major achievement was the arms' cache at Kefar Giladi.

When the ex-Ha-Shomer members left the Haganah framework, the leadership of defense affairs remained, in effect, in the hands of an ex-Legionnaire, Yosef Hecht, who received his salary from the Histadrut Executive and maintained loose contact with the secretary of the Histadrut, David *Ben-Gurion. He was aided in his work, especially in the northern areas, by Shaul Meirov (*Avigur) of kevuẓat Kinneret. In the 1920s the Haganah was composed of separate branches in the major cities, a few moshavot, and a few kevuẓot and kibbutzim. In the cities there were also local committees composed of people who collected money for defense purposes. Each city had a Haganah commander who received a salary from the local Haganah committee. All the rest of the members, whose number did not exceed a few hundred, served as volunteers, training on Saturdays and in the evenings – mostly with revolvers and hand grenades – and being mobilized for guard duty on the border line between the *yishuv* and the Arab population during critical days (the anniversary of the *Balfour Declaration – November 2, the Ninth of Av, the festival of al-Nabī Mūsā in Jerusalem, etc.). A national officers' course, which was held on Mount Carmel near Haifa (1925), strengthened the contact among the handful of commanders. From time to time, meetings were held among the chief commanders, who formulated the "Constitution of the Haganah" in 1924. Primitive arms caches were set up in Shekhunat Borochov near Tel Aviv, in Geva, Kinneret, and Ayyelet ha-Shaḥar. In reality, the Haganah in the 1920s was an underground of such limited scope that it was not necessary to subject its activities to civilian control. Characteristic of the spirit of this period were activities such as the assassination of Jacob Israel de *Haan in June 1924 or the blowing up of a house near the Western Wall in September 1927 in response to Arab provocation of Jewish worshipers.

The riots of August 1929 brought about a complete change in the Haganah position. During the first days of the riots, when there were almost no British security forces in the country and the Arab police force did not carry out its tasks, the meager number of Haganah volunteers with their limited supply of arms filled the gap and saved the Jewish communities of Jerusalem, Tel Aviv, and Haifa from mass slaughter. In contrast, massacre and destruction of property were rampant in those places in which the Haganah was absent or in which its organization was deficient (Hebron, Safed, Moẓa). A deep impression was made by the defense of Ḥuldah, in which a handful of Haganah members fought against thousands of Arab attackers until British forces evacuated them. Old rivalries were forgotten during the riots, and ex-members of Ha-Shomer joined the Haganah fighters and took part in organizing the defense of the cities and the settlements. They also turned their central arms cache in Kefar Giladi over to the Haganah.

1931–1935

After 1929, the need to maintain, expand, and strengthen the Haganah was recognized by all parts of the *yishuv*. Its central command, i.e., Hecht, was ordered to broaden the framework of the Haganah and facilitate greater public control over the organization and its activities, and the civil institutions of the *yishuv* were also called upon to provide full cooperation with the Haganah command. Hecht, who objected to these changes because they went against his concept of the clandestine nature of the Haganah, was relieved of his command. The crisis of command led to the secession of a group of commanders in Jerusalem, led by Avraham Tehomi, that joined together with Revisionist groups to form the *Irgun Ẓeva'i Le'ummi (IẒL) in 1931. In the same year civil institutions of the *yishuv* arrived at an agreement, by which the national command of the Haganah was established on the basis of equal representation – three representatives of the Histadrut (Golomb, Dov *Hos, and Meir Rutberg) and three non-labor representatives (Dov Gefen, Issachar Sitkov, and Sa'adyah Shoshani). The moving spirit in the command was Golomb, whose personal influence was greater than his position as one of the six members of the command and whose modest apartment on Rothschild Boulevard in Tel Aviv was open night and day to people of the Haganah and served as a kind of headquarters of the organization.

The years 1931–35 were a period of quiet development for the Haganah. The structure of the organization hardly changed, and the major administrative work was centered in the three urban branches, whose commanders were Ya'akov Pat (Jerusalem), Elimelekh Zelikovich (alias Avner, Tel Aviv), and Ya'akov Dostrovsky (*Dori, Haifa). These branches constituted the mainstay of the organization, and the membership in each branch numbered in the hundreds. Training methods, however, did not change and were concentrated, as before, in the study of the revolver and hand grenade in the cities and the use of the rifle in the villages. The influence of the national command strengthened with the institution of systematic annual officers' courses (in Ḥuldah and Gevat) and the development of the communications branch (consisting basically of visual communication – flags, lanterns, heliographs) and intelligence. The national command also handled the acquisition of arms, especially from abroad. In 1935 rifles and rifle ammunition began to be sent in barrels of white cement from Belgium. On Nov. 18, 1935, the British authorities confiscated 537 barrels containing arms in Jaffa port, and the incident aroused substantial excitement among the Arabs of Palestine. The Haganah also began to develop workshops to produce hand grenades. The rural settlements began to organize into "blocs," and by 1936 about 20 of these blocs were in existence. At the head of each was a bloc commander who was responsible for the training of its members, acquiring arms and protecting them, and gathering intelligence on the security situation in the area. The position of the Haganah in each bloc was largely dependent upon the initiative of its commander.

During this period, the basic principles of the Haganah consolidated as follows: to maintain complete independence of any non-Jewish factor; to accept the authority of the Jewish national institutions – especially the Political Department of the *Jewish Agency; to maintain a national framework independent of political parties; and to shun militarism for its own sake. The organization was built upon the devotion and voluntary service of thousands of members. The British authorities were aware of the existence of the Haganah, but initially took no serious steps to follow its activities, arrest its commanders or members, or find its arms caches.

The Policy of Restraint

The years 1936–39, those of Arab rebellion, in which the *yishuv* in both the cities and the countryside was under a perpetual siege and was attacked by Arab guerilla bands, were the years in which the Haganah matured and developed from a militia into a military body. It confronted riots by using methods learned from the previous disturbances. The Jewish quarters and settlements in the cities and countryside were surrounded by defense devices: wire fences, concrete positions, trenches, communication trenches, and floodlights. The Arabs made practically no attempts to attack these fortified areas, but they destroyed the harvests in the fields, chopped down orchards and forests, tried to disrupt Jewish transportation on the roads, and set out on a terrorist campaign that affected casual passersby, women, and children.

With the outbreak of the riots, the Jewish Agency declared that the *yishuv*'s response to Arab acts of terror would be "restraint" (*havlagah*). In addition to the moral side of the question, the Jewish Agency believed that a policy of restraint would lead to a positive response from the British authorities who would provide the beleaguered Jews with arms. In fact, the authorities cooperated with the Jewish Agency by establishing a broad formation of Jewish auxiliary police (*ghafirs*) dressed in special police uniforms and provided with arms (rifles, and, after a time, light machine guns). During the period of the riots, this formation developed, and its members were formed into the Jewish Settlement Police (JSP), whose stations were placed in all agricultural settlements and in many urban quarters in the country. This force served as a cover for the activities and training of members of the Haganah. Later the members of the Haganah began to "go beyond the fence" and to develop forms of active fighting; escorts and reconnaissance units went into the fields and roads and other groups set ambushes for Arab terrorists. In 1937 field squads (Peluggot Sadeh) were established under the command of Yiẓḥak *Sadeh and Elijah Ben-Ḥur, trained specifically for war against terrorist gangs. These units gained battle experience with the establishment of the Special Night Squads (SNS) under the command of Orde *Wingate, a British captain who was a proven friend of the Jewish cause. During the years of the riots, the Haganah protected the establishment of over 50 new settlements in new areas of the country (the *Stockade and Watchtower settlements). All attacks of Arab gangs that came to uproot these settlements (the largest of these were the attacks on Tirat Ẓevi, Ḥanitah, and Ma'oz) were repulsed.

In 1937 IẒL split and part of its members, together with its commander, Tehomi, returned to the Haganah. Only the Revisionist members continued the independent existence of the organization. It did not engage particularly in defending the *yishuv*, but in 1937–38 it carried out counter-terrorist acts against Arab civilians on the roads and in markets, from which the Haganah disassociated itself for moral and political reasons. Unofficial cooperation with the British authorities did not deflect the Haganah from its independent course. The demand of the authorities that the Haganah be disbanded and its arms be turned in was rejected, and the Haganah even increased its efforts to enlarge its supply of arms. The underground industry for the production of arms was enlarged. In 1937 an agreement was reached between the emissary of the Haganah, Yehudah *Arazi, and the Polish government whereby the Poles would supply the Haganah with arms (rifles, ammunition, and machine guns) that would be transported to Palestine in steamrollers and various types of machinery. Haganah instructors in Poland were also allowed to utilize Polish arms in training young Jews who were going to settle in Palestine. The Haganah was active in organizing the clandestine emigration of Zionist youth from Europe that began in 1934, and until the outbreak of World War II, it assisted the landing of close to 6,000 "illegal" immigrants on the shores of Palestine.

At the end of the riots in Palestine, the number of men and women in the 20 branches of the Haganah reached 25,000. Its arms stores contained about 6,000 rifles and more than 220 machine guns (in addition to the arms of the JSP). Changes were made in its high command. In 1937, Yoḥanan *Ratner was appointed head of the national command by the Executive of the Jewish Agency, and at the end of 1939 a general staff was established, headed by Ya'akov Dostrovsky (Dori). To finance the activities of the Haganah, a special system of donations and taxes, called Kofer ha-Yishuv, was organized, which continued to exist until the establishment of the State of Israel.

During World War II

With the anti-Zionist turn in British policy (White Paper of May 1939), a clash of opinion broke out in the *yishuv* in relation to the Haganah's main task. Non-labor circles wished to limit its activities to guarding settlements and urban quarters against Arab attackers. The Jewish Agency, however, wanted to turn the Haganah into the military arm of the *yishuv*'s struggle against the British White Paper policy, which was also the desire of most members of the Haganah. In 1941 the crisis was settled with the establishment of a security committee composed of representatives of all circles in the *yishuv* and given control over the Haganah.

With the outbreak of World War II, the Haganah was faced with new problems. On the one hand, it actively supported the volunteering to the Jewish units that were established in the framework of the British army. Many of the founders and members of the Haganah joined these units and did much to foster Jewish leadership in them and preserve their Zionist character. The members of the Haganah also developed networks for the clandestine acquisition of arms within the British army, and they cared for Jewish survivors and refugees in the countries of Europe in which they were stationed at the close of the war.

At the same time, the general staff continued its activities in Palestine and developed the defense forces of the Haganah itself. Its members were divided into a "Guard Force," based on older members, for the static defense of the settlements, and a "Field Force," based on younger members (up to the age of 35), who were trained for active defense activities. A special paramilitary youth movement (*Gadna) was established to train youth between the ages of 14 and 18. In addition, courses were held for commanders of all ranks, among which the most important was the annual course for platoon leaders at Ju'āra near Ein ha-Shofet. The secret arms industry also expanded and produced mortars, shells, and submachine guns. National general defense programs were formulated in the *yishuv* (Program A in 1941, Program B in 1945). Finally the intelligence service of the Haganah (Shay – short for *sherut yedi'ot*) was developed and reached a very high level of effectiveness.

In 1941, a mobilized formation of the Haganah – the *Palmaḥ (short for *Peluggot Maḥaẓ* – "crack units") – was established. It was a regular underground army whose units were located in kibbutzim in all parts of the country. The members of the Palmah earned a substantial amount of their living expenses by agricultural labor (14 days a month), and they received excellent training. When the German army stood at the gates of Egypt, contact was reestablished between the Haganah and the British military authorities and joint efforts were carried out in which hundreds of Palmaḥ members received commando training by British officers. At a later time, a paratroop unit was established in this cooperative framework, and 32 of its members parachuted in Europe into enemy territory to organize Jewish youth in Nazi-occupied territory for resistance against the Nazis. From the end of 1939, the Haganah legally published a monthly entitled *Ma'arakhot* that was devoted to military thought and studies of military planning.

In general, however, the British authorities were hostile to the Haganah and saw it as an obstacle to their anti-Jewish policy. In 1939–40 many members of the Haganah were imprisoned and searches were carried out to locate the arms caches. The British military forces met with opposition that gradually reached the stage of bloodshed (Ramat ha-Kovesh, 1943), and show trials were held against Haganah members accused of stealing arms from British military depots. In 1944 the dissident underground organizations (IẒL and *Loḥamei

Ḥerut Israel – Leḥi) began attacking the British, against the established policy of the Jewish Agency. The Haganah was charged with stopping the activities of IẒL after the latter refused to heed the warnings of the Jewish Agency. This task (called the "saison") was carried out mainly by volunteers from the Palmaḥ. This mission aroused bitter feelings, even in the ranks of those who carried it out, mainly because some of the imprisoned members of IẒL were turned over to the British authorities.

The Policy of Resistance

A short time after the end of World War II, when it became clear that the British government would not abandon its anti-Zionist policy of the 1939 White Paper, the Jewish Agency charged the Haganah with leading the "Jewish resistance movement" against this policy. A special committee (Committee X) was established to control the activities of this movement. The implementation of the resistance plan was entrusted to Moshe *Sneh, then head of the national command, and Yiẓḥak Sadeh, acting chief of staff. In order to coordinate all underground activities, an agreement was arrived at with IẒL and Leḥi. The insurgent activities in this common framework began on Nov. 1–2, 1945, with the coordinated attack on rail lines and equipment. At the center of the resistance activities was the "illegal" mass immigration from Europe and North Africa, whose organization on land and sea devolved on the Haganah and its various arms: the *Beriḥah and the Organization ("Mosad") for "Illegal *Immigration." In Palestine, units of the Palmah destroyed army and police equipment, and the Haganah organized mass demonstrations that clashed with the British police and army. In addition to these, IẒL and Leḥi carried out their activities with the approval of the Haganah. The activities were accompanied by illegal written and oral propaganda (the *Ḥomah* wall newspaper and the clandestine broadcasts of the "*Kol ha-Haganah*"). On June 17, 1946, these activities reached their height with the blowing up of all the bridges on the borders of Palestine by the Haganah forces. About two weeks later, on June 29 ("Black Saturday"), the British authorities responded by imprisoning the members of the Jewish Agency Executive and the Va'ad Le'ummi and by vigorous searches in the kibbutzim in order to catch members of the Palmaḥ and uncover the arms caches of the Haganah (a large store was uncovered at Yagur).

After "Black Saturday," the Executive of the Jewish Agency called for a pause in the resistance, but IẒL and Leḥi refused to obey this order and continued their armed attacks. The Haganah limited its armed struggle to attempts to score direct hits against the operational devices installed to interfere with "illegal" immigration (radar devices, boats that deported immigrants to Cyprus, etc.). The "illegal" immigration also increased and reached new heights with the refugee ship *Exodus 1947* (summer 1947) and the two giant ships, *Pan Crescent* and *Pan York*, which set sail at the end of 1947 with 15,000 immigrants on their decks. These actions were greatly aided by the Haganah delegation to Europe, headed by Naḥum Kramer (Shadmi), that organized Haganah units in the Jewish DP camps in Central Europe and Italy and in other Jewish population centers (France, Romania, Hungary, etc.). In Palestine the Haganah concerned itself with the security of settlements in new areas of the country, such as the northern Negev (11 settlements were established simultaneously at the close of the Day of Atonement, 1946), the Judean Mountains, and Upper Galilee. A substantial number of these settlers received military training in the Palmaḥ.

The commissions of inquiry that visited Palestine at the time (the Anglo-American Commission and the UN Special Commission on Palestine) met with representatives of the Haganah and drew conclusions that substantially affected the formulation of policy in 1947, namely, that in the event that a political solution desired by the Jews was arrived at, the Haganah would be able to withstand any attack, whether by the Arabs of Palestine or those of the neighboring states, without outside aid. In the spring of 1947, when a political solution began to be worked out (namely the UN plan for the partition of Palestine), David Ben-Gurion took it upon himself to direct the general policy of the Haganah, especially its preparation for the impending Arab attack, and appointed Israel *Galili head of the national command. The Haganah budget was substantially increased, and the purchase of arms was expanded by the emissary of the Haganah, Ḥayyim Slavin, who concentrated upon the acquisition of machinery to manufacture arms and ammunition from the United States. Preparations were made for the formation of new services and first and foremost an air force, which was initiated in the framework of the Haganah before the outbreak of World War II. By the eve of the War of Independence there were 45,000 members in the Haganah, about 10,000 of whom were in the Field Force and more than 3,000 in the Palmaḥ.

The War of Independence

At the outbreak of the War of Independence, the Haganah was prepared for its defense tasks. The Jewish settlements were fortified, and in accordance with a Haganah tradition from the days of Tel Ḥai, even settlements completely cut off from the main areas of Jewish settlement were not abandoned (such as the Eẓyon Bloc, the settlements of the Negev, and Yeḥi'am), although holding them cost the Haganah great efforts. The Haganah also increased its retaliatory actions against the attacks of Arab gangs on Jewish traffic, and the movement of vehicles was guarded by armed escorts. A general mobilization was declared in the *yishuv*, but the first major blows of the war fell on the mobilized formations of the Haganah, the JSP, and units of the Palmah, which in a short period of time comprised three brigades (Yiftaḥ, Harel, and Negev). At the same time the quick mobilization and training of the Field Force began, and it was divided into seven brigades (Golani, Karmeli, Alexandroni, Kiryati, Givati, Eẓyoni, and the Seventh Brigade). Superhuman efforts were made to purchase arms of every type, including heavy arms and planes in America and Europe.

In the first four months of the war the Haganah engaged mainly in defending the positions of the *yishuv*. One of the reasons for its defensive stance was the presence of the British army, which, during its evacuation from the country, interfered in battles, usually to the advantage of the Arabs. Great achievements were made in these defensive actions, such as repulsing an attack on Tirat Ẓevi, the Eẓyon Bloc, and convoys to Jerusalem and other places, but losses were very heavy (about 1,200 civilians and soldiers, including the 35 fighters, called the "Lamed He," on a mission to the Eẓyon Bloc and 42 people in a convoy to Yeḥi'am). The feeling in the *yishuv* and in the world at large was that the Haganah had overrated its ability to withstand the attacking forces, and this feeling made itself felt in the international attitude to the Jewish prospects in the Palestine conflict.

In the beginning of April 1948, however, a great change took place in the activity of the Haganah, that was connected with the completion of the organization of the new brigades and the first large shipments of arms that had arrived from Europe. The beginning of this turn came with Operation Naḥshon, in which the road to besieged Jerusalem was broken through and the major fortifications on the hills on both sides of the road were captured. During the same period, the attacks of semi-regular Arab forces on Mishmar ha-Emek and Ramat Yoḥanan, whose purpose was to break through to Haifa, were repulsed. A series of conquests began, starting with the capture of Tiberias (April 18) and followed by the battle for Haifa, which ended with Haganah forces holding the entire city. Safed was captured on May 12, and the next day Arab Jaffa surrendered to the Haganah command. With the evacuation of British forces from Jerusalem, Haganah forces controlled the new city, but the Jewish quarter of the Old City was forced to surrender to the Arab Legion of Transjordan on May 28. The Eẓyon Bloc also fell to the Arab Legion.

On May 15, 1948, Haganah forces faced the armies of the surrounding Arab states that had invaded Palestine. These were large armies whose equipment, including cannons and tanks, outweighed that of the Haganah. The assault of the Syrian army on the northern Jordan Valley was halted in a series of desperate battles, in which the Haganah used its first cannons. Forces of the Iraqi army were stopped at the borders of the hills of Samaria. The assault of the Arab Legion and the Egyptian army on Jerusalem, accompanied by indiscriminate cannon bombardment on the city, was repulsed. Heavy battles were waged in the Latrun area on the highway to Jerusalem. When the Haganah proved unable to occupy the Latrun area it paved a temporary road to the city, south of Latrun (the "Burma Road"), and thus ensured communication with Jerusalem. In the south, the advance of the Egyptian army was halted by the Palmaḥ, the Givati Brigade, and members of the settlements in the area, including Yad Mordekhai and Negbah.

In the midst of these battles, the provisional government of Israel decided to turn the Haganah into the army of the state. The transition was basically a formality, but it symbolized the end of an era. In the Order of the Day of May 31, 1948, the minister of defense, David Ben-Gurion, announced that with the establishment of the State of Israel, the Haganah abandoned its underground character and became the regular army of the state. The name of the Haganah was incorporated into the official name of the army of the new state: Ẓeva Haganah le-Israel (Israel Defense Forces).

BIBLIOGRAPHY: Dinur, Haganah; Z. Gilad and M. Meged (eds.), *Sefer ha-Palmaḥ*, 2 vols. (1955); *Ha-Haganah be-Tel-Aviv* (1956); Y. Avidar, *Ba-Derekh le-Ẓahal* (1970); Y. Bauer, *From Diplomacy to Resistance* (1970); N. Lorch, *The Edge of the Sword* (1968^2); M. Mardor, *Strictly Illegal* (1964); Y. Allon, *Shield of David* (1970); idem, *The Making of Israel's Army* (1970).

[Yehuda Slutsky]

HAGAR (Heb. הָגָר), Egyptian maidservant of *Sarah (Sarai). The tradition involving Hagar is preserved in two narrative cycles. The passage in Genesis 16:1–16 records how Hagar was given to Sarai's husband Abram as a concubine (1–13). When Hagar conceived, she became contemptuous of Sarai, who, in turn, abused her until she fled into the desert (4–6). There, by a spring, Hagar encountered an angel, who exhorted her to return (7–9) and gave her a favorable oracle concerning her future son to be named *Ishmael (10–12). Hagar named the place in honor of the event (13–14). Finally, she bore Ishmael (15). The second tradition (Gen. 21:8–21) records that after Sarai – now Sarah – had borne Isaac, she demanded the expulsion of Hagar and her son. According to the Septuagint, she was distressed to see Ishmael playing "with her son Isaac." Upon receiving divine reassurance (12–13), Abraham reluctantly banished Hagar (14ff.) to the desert, where she and Ishmael were saved from death by divine intervention (17ff.).

The problem of surrogate motherhood arises elsewhere in the Bible (Gen. 30:3) as well as in Hammurapi's code and in legal documents from the ancient Near East and Egypt spanning over a millennium. While there is as yet no exact parallel to the Hagar stories, these documents attest to the possibility of a slave's son becoming an heir, the slave woman's lack of deference to her mistress after bearing children (Hammurapi, 146), and the mistreatment of the slave by the mistress.

Contemporary critical scholarship regards the first tradition about Hagar as predominantly J (Jahwist), with P (Priestly) inserts comprising verses 1a, 3, 15–16; the second is agreed to be entirely E (Elohist). As a whole, however, the literary transmission of these narratives has long presented difficulties. The problems are both literary and chronological. The literary problems arise from the fact that both accounts involve the banishment of Hagar (16:6; 21:14), the encountering of an angel who provided an oracle (16:7–12; 21:17–18), and the presence of a well (16:14; 21:19). It has been suggested that two independent versions of Hagar's banishment originally existed, the first referring to her pregnancy and the second to the time after Isaac's birth. Consequently, some scholars resolve the assumed conflation by judging 16:9 to be a late redaction whose purpose was to give sequence to the narratives; others assume that the naming of Ishmael was deleted in the second tradition. These difficulties are lessened if the narratives are considered separate crystallizations of the Hagar-Ishmael saga, each one limited and both integrated by the root *šmʿ* (שמע; 16:2, 11; 21:12, 17). Each would serve both as an independent version of the etiology of the Ishmaelite-Hagarite tribes and a literary foil for the Isaac theme interwoven through it. However, the combination has introduced a chronological problem which did not exist when these traditions stood alone. According to Genesis 16:16, Abraham was 86 years old when Ishmael was born and 100 when Isaac was born (21:5), which would make Ishmael more than 14 years old at the time of his banishment (21:10ff.). This difficulty has resulted in various attempts to account for the conflation, as, e.g., the view that an account of the banishment of Hagar and her young son was combined with an account of the birth of Isaac in Abraham's old age.

As a female name Hagar is well attested in ancient Arabia in Palmyrene and Safaitic. There is probably no connection between Hagar and the Hagrites (Knauf), an ethnic group named in Chronicles (I Chr. 5:10, 19, 20; II Chr. 5:20). The etymology of Hagar is obscure, but some scholars have connected it with an Old South Arabic word meaning "city, area."

[Maurice Friedberg / S. David Sperling (2nd ed.)]

In the Aggadah

Hagar was the daughter of Pharaoh. When "Pharaoh saw the deeds performed on Sarah's behalf in his house, he gave Hagar to Sarah, saying; 'Better let my daughter be a handmaid in this house than a mistress in another's'" (Gen. R. 45:1). According to Philo (Abr., 251), Sarah testified about Hagar her handmaid, not only that she was a free woman of noble disposition, but also that she was a Hebrew in her way of life. Hagar was given to Abraham after he had dwelt ten years in the land of Canaan (Gen. 16:3) since a man having no children from his wife for ten years may not abstain any longer from the duty of propagation (Yev. 6:6). As soon as Hagar was with child she began to slander Sarah, saying to the ladies who came to visit her mistress, "My mistress Sarah is not inwardly as she appears outwardly. She pretends to be a woman of piety, but she is not, as she has prevented conception in order to preserve her beauty" (Gen. R. 45:4). When this came to the notice of Sarah she took Abraham to task for remaining silent at these taunts and she also made Hagar do servile work despite the fact that Abraham objected to any burden being added to that of childbearing (Gen. R. 45:6). Four or five angels visited her after she fled from Sarah but Hagar, who was quite accustomed to the appearance of these celestial beings in Abraham's household, was not at all startled (Gen. R. 45:7). When Hagar came to the wilderness, she took up the idol-worship of the house of her father Pharaoh (*ibid.*; PdRE. 30). However, she gave it up when it proved worthless (Targ. Yer. Gen. 21:16). Hagar is identical with Keturah, whom Abraham married after the death of Sarah (Gen. 25:1). She was so called, because after having gone astray after idols, she again attached herself to a life of virtue (*keturah*, lit. "attached"; Zohar, Gen. 133b; Gen. R. 61:4).

For the figure of Hagar in Islam see *Abraham; *Ishmael, sections on Islam.

[Elimelech Epstein Halevy]

BIBLIOGRAPHY: D.H. Mueller, *Die Gesetze Hammurabis* (1903), 139–41; J. Skinner, *Genesis* (ICC, 1910); F. Dornseiff, in: ZAW, 52 (1934), 67; R. de Vaux, in: RB, 56 (1949), 26ff.; E.A. Speiser, *Genesis* (1964); N.M. Sarna, *Understanding Genesis* (1966), 127–9; Ginzberg, Legends, 1 (1909), 223, 231–2, 237–9. **ADD. BIBLIOGRAPHY:** J. van Seters, in: JBL, 87 (1968), 401–8; T. Frymer- Kensky, in: BA, 44 (1981), 209–17; N. Sarna, in: *JPS Torah Commentary Genesis* (1989), 119; E. Knauf, in: ABD, 3:18–19; D. Graf, ibid., 24.

HA-GASHASH HA-ḤIVER (Heb. הגשש החיוור), Israeli comedy trio, including SHAIKE LEVI (1948–); GAVRI BANAI (1940–); and ISRAEL POLIAKOV (1941–). Ha-Gashash is the longest-running and most successful comedy team in the history of Israeli entertainment. Over the years the threesome have built up an audience from across the entire spectrum of Israeli society and all age groups. Their vast range of material, sketches, and songs has appealed to the highbrow and the lowbrow, and their language has spawned numerous expressions that have found their way into everyday speech.

Ha-Gashash was created in 1963 by promoter Avraham "Pashanel" *Desheh. Levi, Banai, and Poliakov had previously worked under Desheh as part of the *Tarnegolim* ("Roosters") singing troupe and when it disbanded Desheh suggested that they form a trio performing comic sketches and songs. Ha-Gashash's first show, entitled *Simḥat Zekinti*, premiered in 1964 with material written by actor-comedian Shaike *Ophir. The show was a great success and Levi, Banai, and Poliakov decided to keep the team together. Ophir also wrote material for the next production, *Tokhnit Dalet* ("Plan D"), which came out in 1966 and included songs written and arranged by Aryeh Levanon, some of which became hits.

In 1969 the threesome decided to try their luck in the mainstream music arena by entering that year's Israel Song Festival with a song called *Mayim le-David ha-Melekh* ("Water for King David"). True to their comic bent, Levi, Banai, and Poliakov added a comic visual effect to their singing by wearing overly short biblical-style tunics. By now Ha-Gashash ha-Ḥiver had become the most popular comedy team in the country.

In the early 1970s the group used material written by Yossi *Banai, who doubled as director, as well as sketches derived from the works of world-renowned satirist Ephraim *Kishon. The group also furthered its across-the-board musical appeal with a string of hits, such as Naomi *Shemer's *Yesh Li Ḥag* ("I Have A Holiday"). Ha-Gashash later released an entire album of Shemer numbers, including *Lu Yehi* ("If Only") and *Orḥim La-Kayiẓ* ("Summer Guests"), which sold well.

In 1984 the threesome contributed sketches to the Labor Party's political broadcasts for that year's general elections, some of which formed the basis of subsequent productions, such as 1985's *For a Fistful of Dollars* directed by Motti *Kirschenbaum. In 1990 Levi, Banai, and Poliakov decided to further their solo careers but temporarily regrouped after being awarded the 2000 Israel Prize. All three continued to work separately, both as actors and singers, but periodically appeared with new Ha-Gashash material.

[Barry Davis (2nd ed.)]

HAGBAHAH, GELILAH (Heb. הַגְבָּהָה וּגְלִילָה; "lifting and rolling" of the Torah scroll), the elevation and subsequent rolling together of the Scroll of the Law in the synagogue. *Hagbahah* is the raising of the open Torah scroll, so that the congregation may see the writing and testify: "And this is the Law which Moses set before the children of Israel" (Deut. 4:44); "According to the word of the Lord by Moses" (Num. 9:23). In the Sephardi ritual, Deuteronomy 4:24, 33:4 is immediately followed by Psalms 18:31. In the Reform ritual, "This Torah is a tree of life to those who hold fast to it; and of them that uphold it everyone is rendered happy" (Prov. 3:18) is recited instead. In the Ashkenazi ritual, this rite is performed after the reading from the Pentateuch and before the reading from the Prophets (*haftarah*). One person lifts up the Torah scroll in such a way that the congregation can see three columns of the writing. He then sits down and another person rolls the scroll, binds it, dresses it with a mantle, and replaces its various ornaments. This part of the rite is called *gelilah* ("rolling together"). In many ḥasidic synagogues *hagbahah* is made with an open scroll before the reading from the Torah and again after the reading, with a closed scroll which is then bound. In the Sephardi ritual, *hagbahah* is performed before the reading from the Pentateuch. The person who takes the Torah scroll from the ark opens it and carries it open to the reading platform. According to the Talmud, the person who performs the *gelilah* ceremony is honored even more than those who are called to the actual reading of the Pentateuch (Meg. 32a, see also: Sh. Ar., OḤ 134). In some places, it has become the custom to let the *gelilah* be performed even by minors (under the age of bar mitzvah) who are not qualified to be called to the Pentateuch reading. In the Western Sephardi rite, however, *hagbahah* is performed only by an honorary official or members of an honorary brotherhood (levantadores).

BIBLIOGRAPHY: ET, s.v., *Gelilah* and *Hagbahah*; Eisenstein, Dinim, s.v.; E. Munk, *The World of Prayer*, 1 (1961), 175.

HAGEN, town in North Rhine-Westphalia, Germany. A small Jewish community came into existence in Hagen during the early years of the 18th century. Among the town's 675 inhabitants in 1722 were four Jewish families, two of them glassmakers and two animal butchers. Little is known of the community in the following decades, but in 1799 there is evidence of a significant settlement of 23 Jews, mostly engaged in peddling. During the 19th century their numbers increased, and they were particularly prominent in the development of the textile industry. In this period they established a school and finally built a synagogue in 1859. By 1897 there were 470 Jews among the population. On the eve of the Nazi regime in 1930, there were 679 Jews in Hagen. The synagogue was set on fire in 1938, Jewish stores and homes were destroyed, and all Jewish men were deported to Sachsenhausen-Oranienberg and Dachau. Over the next year emigration intensified, with around 300 managing to leave during the entire Nazi period. The remaining Jews were deported between 1942 and 1943 via Dortmund to Theresienstadt and Zamosc and from there to Belzec, and later to Auschwitz directly. In all, 153 perished. By 1956 there were again 20 Jews living in Hagen. The synagogue in Hagen-Hohenlimburg (Hohenlimburg was incorporated into Hagen in 1975), which was damaged in 1938, was bought and restored by the city of Hagen in 1960. In 1986 it was opened as a memorial site (Alte Synagoge Hohenlimburg). The Jewish community numbered 38 in 1989 and 338 in 2004. Most of the members are immigrants from the former Soviet Union, who came to Germany after 1990.

BIBLIOGRAPHY: Hagen Municipality, *Gedenkbuch zum tragischen Schicksal unserer juedischen Mitbuerger* (1961). **ADD. BIBLIOGRAPHY:** H. Zabel (ed.), *Mit Schimpf und Schande aus der Stadt, die ihnen Heimat war. Beitraege zur Geschichte der juedischen Gemeinde Hagen*. vols. 1, 2 (1994; Beitraege zur Foerderung des christlich-juedischen Dialogs, volume 11); idem (ed.), *Adolf Nassau – Mann des Glaubens und der Gerechtigkeit. Ein Beitrag zur Geschichte der juedischen Gemeinde Hagen* (1989; Beitraege zur Foerderung des christlich-juedischen Dialogs, volume 4); A. Boening (ed.), *Der juedische Friedhof in Hohenlimburg* (1986; Beitraege zur Foerderung des christlich-juedischen Dialogs, vol. 3); B. Gase, *Geschichte der Juden in Hagen* (1986; Hagener Hefte, vol. 14).

[Ze'ev Wilhem Falk / Michael Berenbaum and Larissa Daemmig (2nd ed.)]

HAGENBACH, village in Bavaria, Germany. The existence of a Jewish community in Hagenbach was first noted through its suffering during the *Rindfleisch massacres (1298). Nothing more is known of it until 1478, when the expulsion of Jews from nearby *Bamberg increased the numbers and importance of the Jewish communities in Hagenbach and the neighboring villages. The various communities lived under the protection of the country gentry and formed an association to provide common rabbinic leadership and to represent their shared interests before the governmental authorities. The local *Memorbuch, an important historical document, records that a synagogue and cemetery were consecrated in 1737. In 1813 an independent rabbinate was established, with its seat in Hagenbach, embracing 14 other small communities. In 1867 the community (totaling 126 persons) was united with that of *Baiersdorf, while in 1894 both were included in the rabbinate of Bamberg. The Jewish population numbered 88 in 1900 and only 24 in 1933. All left by November 1938. The community was not reestablished after World War II.

BIBLIOGRAPHY: PK Bavaria; M. Weinberg, in: JJLG, 18 (1927), 203–16; A. Eckstein, *Geschichte der Juden im ehemaligen Fuerstbistum Bamberg* (1898), 48, 51.

HAGGADAH, PASSOVER (Heb. הַגָּדָה; "telling"), a set form of benedictions, prayers, midrashic comments and psalms recited at the *seder* ritual on the eve of *Passover.

INTRODUCTION

The *Haggadah* is based on the *seder* service prescribed by the Mishnah (Pes. 10), which had apparently been conducted in the form of a banquet. The observance of the precepts at the *seder* – the eating of the *pesaḥ* (the *paschal sacrifice), *matzah ("unleavened bread"), and **maror* ("bitter herbs"); the drinking of arba *kosot ("four cups of wine"); and the recital of the story of the exodus from Egypt (the narrative of the *Haggadah*) were integrated into this banquet celebration. Essentially, the *Haggadah* is an account of the Egyptian bondage, a thanksgiving to God for the redemption, and, in Temple times, a thanksgiving for the acquisition of the Land of Israel. After the destruction of the Second Temple, the latter was replaced by a prayer for the ultimate redemption. The purpose of the *Haggadah* ("*Ve-higgadta le-vinkha*" – "And thou shalt tell thy son," Ex. 13:8), one of the central commandments of the day, is represented by the narrative itself. Not written by any particular author, or group of authors, the *Haggadah* is not a "literary composition" in the accepted sense of the term. Its narrative is a collection of excerpts from the Bible, Mishnah, and Midrash, interpolated with the ritual performances: the **Kiddush*, the benedictions recited on the performance of precepts, and for food, *Grace after Meals, and the **Hallel*. Gradually, stories, psalms, and songs were added. Many recensions of the *Haggadah*, differing from one another to a greater or lesser degree, have been preserved in various manuscripts, mostly dating from the 13th to the 15th century, and also in fragments from the Cairo **Genizah*. Some halakhic works also contain the text of, and commentaries on, the *Haggadah* (see below: Manuscripts and Editions). In keeping with its compilatory character and the varied nature of its sources, the literary or logical nexus between the different sections of the *Haggadah* is not always discernible. The quotations, derived from a multiplicity of sources, have mostly been adapted to the needs of the *seder* service.

COMPONENT PARTS

(1) The **Kiddush*. It is not specific to the *seder* service but is prescribed for all the festivals.

(2) *Ha Laḥma Anya ("This is the bread of affliction") are the opening words of a declaration in Aramaic, designating the *matzah* as the bread of affliction and inviting the needy to join the meal. It ends with "This year we are here, next year may we be in the Land of Israel. This year we are slaves, next year may we be free men." There seems to be no clear connection between the three statements of the declaration. It appears to be a folk composition which was added to the *seder* liturgy after the destruction of the Temple.

(3) *Mah Nishtannah ("How is this night different"), popularly known as "the four questions," is according to the Mishnah (Pes. 10:4) apparently a formula with which the father can instruct his son. This formula passed through a number of stages till it assumed the forms which are to be found in the different recensions that are in use today.

(4) *Avadim Hayinu* ("We were bondmen") is an introduction to the formal narration of the exodus from Egypt, based on the views of Samuel (Pes. 116a). Passages of unknown origin supplement the narration stressing its importance.

(5) *Ma'aseh be-Rabbi Eli'ezer… Amar Rabbi Elazar* ("It is told of R. Eliezer… R. Eleazar b. Azariah said") is a story concerning the leading *tannaim*, followed by a discussion between them, whose purpose it is to emphasize the importance of the narration. While the story is preserved only in the *Haggadah*, the debate is cited in the Mishnah (Ber. 1:5) and in halakhic Midrashim (Sif. Deut. 130; Mekh., Pisḥa 16).

(6) The *baraita* of the Four Sons, also preserved in a halakhic Midrash (Mekh., Pisḥa 18) and in the Talmud (TJ, Pes. 10:4, 37d), but in a recension differing considerably from *Haggadot* in use today, incorporates all the biblical verses enjoining the narration of the exodus (Deut. 6:20; Ex. 12:26; 13:8; 13:14). It adapts them to four different types of "sons": the wise, the wicked, the simple, and the disinterested, who should be instructed according to the *halakhah* "that according to the understanding of the son the father instructs him" (Pes. 10:4).

(7) *Yakhol me-Rosh Ḥodesh* ("It might be thought that [this exposition should begin] from the New Moon [of Nisan]") is a tannaitic commentary on Exodus 13:8 (Mekh., Pisḥa 17), adducing exegetical proof that the narration of the exodus story is obligatory on the eve of Passover.

(8) *Mi-Teḥillah Ovedei Avodah Zarah Hayu Avoteinu* ("In the beginning, our fathers worshiped idols") is an introduction to the narration of the exodus story based on Rav as opposed to Samuel's view (see above *Avadim Hayinu*).

(9) A tannaitic Midrash on *Arami oved avi* (Deut. 26:5–8) – "An Aramean would have destroyed my father" (usually rendered: "A wandering Aramean was my father") which, according to the Mishnah (Pes. 10:4), everyone is obliged "to expound." This commentary, also preserved in the Midrashim based on the *Sifrei* (Sif. Deut. 26:5 (301), especially Mid. Lek. Tov, and Mid. Hag., ad loc.), is a haphazard selection of aggadic interpretations. In the *seder* ritual, it is prefaced with "Blessed be He who observes His promise… Go and learn what Laban the Aramean sought…," a passage not found in the Midrashim and apparently composed in the post-talmudic period.

(10) Commentaries of the *tannaim* on the miracle of the plagues and the division of the Red Sea during the exodus from Egypt are recited. In most Jewish communities these have been seen as a continuation of the preceding Midrash; their source is the *Mekhilta* (*Va-Yehi be-Shallaḥ* 6).

(11) *Kammah Ma'alot Tovot la-Makom Aleinu* ("How many goodly favors has the Almighty bestowed upon us") is a poem in two versions which is preserved only in the Passover *Haggadah*. The poem was composed during the Second Temple period and seems to have no direct connection with the *seder* service.

(12) The Mishnah of Rabban Gamaliel. It explains the significance of the Passover sacrifice, the unleavened bread, and the bitter herbs. Taken from the Mishnah (Pes. 10:5), it

was reworded (in a question-and-answer form) during the post-talmudic period.

(13) *Be-Khol Dor va-Dor* ("In every single generation") is a passage from the Mishnah (Pes. 10:5), or from an expanded Mishnah (*baraita*), which had been supplemented by a statement of Rava (Pes. 116b).

(14) The first two chapters of *Hallel* are recited, as prescribed in the Mishnah following Bet Hillel (Pes. 10:6).

(15) The benediction for redemption "Who redeemed us" is based on the ruling of R. Tarfon and R. Akiva in the Mishnah. After observing the commandments to eat unleavened bread and bitter herbs, the meal is eaten, followed by Grace after Meals. (According to the opinion of scholars such as Elbogen, Ginzberg, and Finkelstein, etc. it is obvious from the text of the *Mah Nishtannah* that at some stage in the development of the *seder* service this part of the ritual followed rather than preceded the meal.) The company then continues with the second part of the *Haggadah*.

(16) *Shefokh Ḥamatkha* ("Pour out Thy wrath") is a collection of verses whose theme is a supplication for vengeance on the nations that have oppressed Israel. The custom to recite these verses is attested since medieval times; their number and order differ according to the various rites.

(17) The last part of the *Hallel* is recited, as specified in the Mishnah (Pes. 10:7).

(18) *Yehallelukha Adonai Eloheinu al Kol Ma'asekha* ("All Thy works shall praise Thee") is a benediction of praise ("*Birkat ha-Shir*") in accordance with R. Judah's view (Pes. 118a).

(19) The Great *Hallel* (Ps. 136). Its recital became obligatory at a later date. (It is based on the *baraita* of R. Tarfon (*ibid.*).)

(20) *Nishmat Kol Ḥai* ("The breath of all that lives"), another version of the *Birkat ha-Shir* ("Benediction over the Song") is recited, in accordance with the view of R. Johanan (*ibid.*).

RITUAL ACTS

The text of the *Haggadah* is also divided according to the prescribed ritualistic acts of the *seder* service. Each textual section is headed by a descriptive phrase which, in some rites, is chanted as a separate litany. The sections are *kaddesh* (the Kiddush), *u-reḥaẓ* ("washing" of the hands), *karpas* (eating the "herbs" dipped in saltwater), *yaḥaẓ* ("dividing" the middle *matzah*), *maggid* (the "narration"), *raḥaẓ* ("washing" the hands for the meal), *moẓi-matzah* (the "benediction" over the *matzah*), *maror* (eating the "bitter herbs"), *korekh* (eating "bitter herbs with *matzah*"), *shulḥan orekh* (the "meal"), *ẓafun* (eating of the *fikoman* – the "last *maẓẓah*"), *barekh* ("Grace after Meals"), *hallel* (recitation of the second part of *Hallel*), and *nirẓah* (the closing formula). This Passover *Haggadah* and *seder* ritual follows the practice of the Pumbedita and Sura academies of Babylonia and was adopted by all the Jewish communities in the Diaspora. It completely superseded the ancient Palestinian recension which differed from it in certain respects (such as the omission of sections 4–7 listed above.

TEXTUAL ELABORATIONS

A tendency, however, existed to elaborate on the text of the *Haggadah* with midrashic and poetic sections. These additions are neither obligatory nor universally accepted: e.g., the tannaitic exposition *Ani Adonai ve-lo Aḥer* ("I the Lord and no other"; *Maḥzor Vitry*, 293) and an interpretation of *ve-natan lanu et mamonam* ("and gave us their substance"; the *siddur* of Saadiah Gaon, 143), the latter is derived from the *Mekhilta de-R. Simeon b. Yoḥai*, and was adapted to the *seder* ritual. Similarly, certain benedictions were expanded through the interpolation of *piyyutim* (e.g., in the *siddur* of Saadiah Gaon, 144). Among Oriental communities it is customary to recite in the first part of the *seder* service the hymn "And ye shall say: This is the offering of the Passover." In later times, hymns and roundelays were gradually incorporated into the *Haggadah*, and sung at the end of the *seder: *Az Rov Nissim* ("Of old, Thou didst Perform most Miracles at Night"; from a *kerovah* by *Yannai); *Omeẓ Gevurotekha* ("The Strength of Thy Might"; from a *kerovah* by R. Eleazar *Kallir); *Ki Lo Na'eh* ("For to Him Is it Becoming"; by an anonymous *paytan*); and *Ḥasal Seder Pesaḥ* ("Accomplished is the Order of the Passover"; from a *kerovah* by R. Joseph Tov Elem *Bonfils). Other hymns introduced are just folk songs composed for the entertainment of children, e.g., *Addir Hu ("Strong is He"); *Eḥad Mi *Yode'a ("Who Knows One?"); *Ḥad Gadya ("One Only Kid"). In other communities different *piyyutim* have been adopted: e.g., "On Passover in Egypt my Captives went forth Free"; "From the House of Iniquity, Seat of my Strifes" or "Home of my Medanite [captors]" (both are in the *Maḥzor Carpentras*); or "Who Wrought Wonders in Egypt" (*Maḥzor Romania*, Constantinople, 1510). In northern France it was customary to sing at the end of the *seder* "The Lovers Sing with Ringing Voice" (*Maḥzor Vitry*, 298).

COMMENTARIES

Textual difficulties in the *Haggadah* called for the annotation of the text. The earliest commentaries were written in a talmudic style and can be found in the halakhic works of the school of Rashi and his disciples (e.g., in *Maḥzor Vitry; Ha-Orah*, ed. by S. Buber, 1905; *Siddur Rashi*, ed. by S. Buber and J. Freimann, 1911; *Ha-Pardes*, ed. by D. Ehrenreich, 1824). The commentary attributed to R. *Samuel b. Meir is written in the same style. A more comprehensive and profound exposition is found in *Shibbolei ha-Leket* by R. Zedekiah b. Abraham *Anav (13th century; ed. by S. Buber, 1886), in which are incorporated some annotations by Isaiah di *Trani, as well as interesting novellae, by the author's brother. The two important commentaries composed in the 14th century were by R. Aaron b. Jacob ha-Kohen of *Lunel (in *Orḥot Ḥayyim*; it also appeared in Kol *bo) and by R. David b. Joseph *Abudarham (in his commentary on the prayer book; Venice, 1566). These early commentators merely annotated the text. They were not concerned with the investigation of the historical aspect of the *Haggadah* and did not refer to the sources of its different texts. This simple explanatory type of commentary came to a close in the 15th century with *Afikoman* by R. Simeon b. Ẓemaḥ *Duran, which until that time was the only commentary published as a separate book. After the 15th century, the commentators included material of their own in their expositions, both as an elaboration on the narrative and as a discussion of philosophical and theological concepts. R. Isaac *Abrabanel in *Zevaḥ Pesaḥ* (Venice, 1545; figure 3) poses 100 questions which he answers at length. With reference to the verse "Know thou of a surety…" (Gen. 15:13), he asks: "What benefit have we derived from the exodus from Egypt, in view of the fact that we are once again in exile?" In his reply he discusses the significance of the exile and the ways of Providence at great length, without establishing any direct connection with the text. The commentary thus becomes a separate discourse. Subsequent commentators, who followed his style, mostly annotated in an aggadic vein, while a few gave mystical interpretations, e.g., R. Eliezer *Ashkenazi in *Ma'asei Adonai* (Venice, 1583); R. *Judah Loew b. Bezalel (the Maharal) of Prague in *Gevurot Adonai* (Cracow, 1582), in which he also expounds halakhic matters; and the kabbalists R. Moses *Alshekh and R. Isaiah *Horowitz. The best known later commentators are: R. Jacob *Emden, R. *Elijah b. Solomon Zalman of Vilna, *Jacob of Dubno, Jacob b. Jacob Moses *Lorberbaum (of Lissa), and Moses *Sofer (Schreiber) who wove their homiletic compositions round and into the Passover *Haggadah*. R. Ḥayyim Joseph David *Azulai (18th century), known for his critical approach, also follows the above method in his commentaries on the *Haggadah*, though occasionally the critical view is discernible. Only in the 19th century did scholars begin to analyze the text, to clarify its sources, and to determine the original wording. This method was adopted by H. Edelman, E. *Landshuth, D. *Cassel, M. Friedmann, and D. Goldschmidt, whose commentaries were published in articles or in book form.

MANUSCRIPTS AND EDITIONS

Through the generations the Passover *Haggadah* has been one of the most popular works – perhaps the most popular – in Jewish religious literature. Many recensions, differing from one another to a greater or lesser degree, have been preserved in various manuscripts mostly dating from the 13th to the 15th century, and also in fragments from the Cairo *Genizah*. These manuscripts originate from all countries in which Jews have lived. Some halakhic works also contain the text of and commentaries on the *Haggadah*. Others are found in daily or festival prayer books; the majority, however, are separate works for use on the eve of Passover only. These manuscripts have not yet been adequately investigated; only a selected few, particularly the illuminated copies, have engaged the attention of scholars. In the seventh or eighth century the *Haggadah* was apparently compiled as a separate work by the *geonim*. The oldest extant version however is in the prayer book (*siddur*) of Saadiah Gaon (10th century; ed. by I. Davidson, S. Assaf and B.I. Joel, 1941); other early versions are found in Maimonides' *Mishneh Torah* (12th century) and in *Maḥzor Vitry* (11th century). Since the 15th century, the *Haggadah* has had more than 2,700 editions, either with or without commentaries. Later editions have included as many as 200 commentaries. The Haggadah has been translated into vernaculars used by Jews, e.g., Yiddish, Ladino, Judeo-Greek, Judeo-Arabic (in its various dialects), and Judeo-Persian, which are often printed together with the *Haggadah*. Oral vernacular renderings are traditional in those communities which have no printed literature in their spoken idiom (e.g., in modern Aramaic). The *Haggadah* has been rendered into a number of languages, and the translation, whether with or without commentary, is often included in the editions. "Emended" editions, which do not give the traditional but a substitute version, are customary in certain communities, e.g., the *Haggadah* of S. *Maybaum (1891), Caesar *Seligmann (Frankfurt, 1913), Guggenheim (Offenbach, 1927), the Central Conference of American *Rabbis (from 1905 onward), the Union of Liberal and Progressive Synagogues in London (1953), and the *Reconstructionist movement in the U.S. The tendency to "reform" the *Haggadah* exists also in Israel, especially in nonreligious kibbutzim which tend to emend the text of the *Haggadah* from year to year; as a rule, these editions do not appear in print, but in cyclostyled form only. The Karaites have composed a Passover *Haggadah* of their own, which is completely different from that of the Rabbanites, and consists of biblical verses and a few benedictions. It has been printed several times (Pressburg, 1879; Odessa, 1883; Vilna, 1900; Ramleh, 1953). *Haggadah* editions based on scientific analysis and research are by: H. Edelman (1845); E.L. Landshuth (*Maggid me-Reshit*, with an introduction, 1855); J.D. *Eisenstein (*Oẓar Perushim ve-Ẓiyyurim al Haggadah shel Pesaḥ*, 1920); C. *Roth (in English, 1939); D. Goldschmidt (with a commentary in Hebrew; 1947) and with an introduction on the history of the *Haggadah* and the texts of all the midrashic and paytanic additions in 1960; and M.M. *Kasher (containing Mss. recensions, *genizah* fragments, and a collection of commentaries, as well as a lengthy introduction, 1955).

[Ernst Daniel Goldschmidt]

ILLUMINATED MANUSCRIPTS

Introduction

During the 13th to 15th centuries the Passover *Haggadah* was one of the most popular Hebrew illuminated manuscripts in Sephardi as well as Ashkenazi or Italian communities.

The popularity of the *Haggadah* for embellishment at that time was the result of the fusion of several factors. To begin with, the crystallization of its text into a single received and authoritative version made it easier to extract the Passover *Haggadah* from the complete annual cycle of prayers contained in the *siddur* and to copy it as a separate book. Such a book, the record of the most important private, domestic ritual, performed with the entire family gathered around the Passover table, was a much more personal object, less subject to communal prescription and prohibition, and so lent itself to the expression of personal taste in enrichment more than any other sacred codex. Being instructive in nature, the illustrations may have served as a means of holding the interest of the children through the long Passover eve ceremony. Because of its comparatively small size, it was not too expensive for the head of a family to commission or purchase, nor too laborious for scribe to write and artist to illuminate. Nor is it a coincidence that, just at the time when illuminated *Haggadah* manuscripts began to appear as separate books, that is to say during the 13th century, new developments were coming to the fore in European manuscript production. The social and economic growth of town life at this period fostered an increase in the number of secular workshops concerned with the manufacture of books. Interest in learning and need for the written means of its transmission coincided with a feeling of freedom and security in the more established towns. At the same time, new techniques in the preparation of parchment, inks, colors, gold leaf, and other materials brought the acquisition of illuminated manuscripts within the reach of many citizens.

Even so, not every household in the Jewish community could afford to possess an illuminated *Haggadah*. Only the richer Jews, who, especially in Spain, were employed by princes or their courtiers and were therefore better acquainted with beautifully illuminated codices, would have the means to attempt the imitation of the fashion for such objects by commissioning the illumination of Hebrew books. Such commissions would present the artist with the problem of a subject matter which was new to him, and the problem was met by the fusion of traditional Jewish themes, motifs, and iconography, with the more fashionable styles and layout of contemporary Christian illumination, according to the style of the artist and the taste of his patron. In the 14th and 15th centuries, especially in Germany, a more popular type of illuminated *Haggadah* was developed which could reach many more patrons and more easily satisfy the growing demand. The pattern, system, and choice of subject in the illuminated *Haggadot* were influenced by Greek and Latin illuminated manuscripts, chiefly psalters, of a type common in the princely courts of Europe.

Types of Illustration

The range of *Haggadah* illumination was obviously dependent in the first place on the contents of the book, which can be roughly divided into four categories: textual, ritual, biblical, and eschatological. These four categories may be applied to all illuminated *Haggadot* of the 13th to the 15th centuries, whether Ashkenazi, Sephardi, or Italian. The most common textual illustrations are of the main elements of the Passover ritual according to Rabban *Gamaliel: *pesaḥ* (paschal lamb), *matzah* (unleavened bread), and *maror* (bitter herb). In fact, the *matzah* and *maror* may have been the earliest textual illustrations in the *Haggadot* of the ninth and tenth centuries and, judging from the fact that an example was found in the Cairo **Genizha*, may have derived from Egypt, Palestine, or Mesopotamia. Decorated initial words were common to most Hebrew illuminated manuscripts, though some were peculiar to the *Haggadot*. One example is the decorative construction of bold initial words, written one under the other on either side of the page, for the poem *Dayyeinu* ("It would have sufficed us"). This construction exists in eastern *Haggadot*, as well as in those included in the prayer book. In some *Haggadot* Rabban Gamaliel himself and his pupils are illustrated, as well as other rabbis mentioned in the text. Other textual illustrations include the "four sons," described in the narrative; the wise son was depicted as a rabbi, the wicked son as a soldier, the simple one as a boy, and the one who "does not know how to ask" as a jester. Some of the decorations are pictorial witticisms, such as the one of the man pointing at his wife while reciting *maror zeh* – "this bitter herb" or literal representations of the text, like the man leaving prison as an illustration to Psalm 118:3–7 in the *Sassoon Spanish Haggadah*. In Italian and Ashkenazi *Haggadot* there are even more literal illustrations of the Hebrew text, such as that of a man dressed for travel coming out of a town gate placed beside the text which begins, "Come out and learn what Laban the Aramite sought to do to Jacob"; or the picture of a naked woman to illustrate Ezekiel 16:7 as in the *Joel b. Simeon *Haggadah* in the British Museum.

The ritual illustrations are for the most part didactic, beginning with the preparations for Passover – the baking of the *matzot*, the killing of the paschal lamb, and the cleansing of the house and the dishes. Other illustrations show people reciting the *Haggadah* in the synagogue – a custom which was known in Spain – or leaving the synagogue; the family sitting round the *seder* table; the washing of the hands; the pouring, lifting, or drinking of the four cups of wine; the hiding and finding of the *afikoman*; and the eating of the various herbs. These genre scenes of medieval Jewish life depict the customs of various European communities by portraying their daily and festive dress, household utensils, furniture, and buildings and may have been invented at the time by the Jewish artists themselves for use in the *Haggadah*. Most interesting of all the categories are the biblical pictures. They begin as illustrations of the biblical and midrashic texts contained in the *Haggadah*, with the chief emphasis on the story of the Exodus, preceded by the history of the Patriarchs. The cycle was sometimes broadened to include other episodes ranging from the Creation, as in the Spanish *Sarajevo Haggadah* (see below), to Jonah under his gourd in the *Yahuda Haggadah* (Israel Museum, Jerusalem) and the *Second Nuremberg Haggadah* (Schocken Library, Jerusalem. Sometimes these biblical illustrations and the ritual pictures are intermingled. For example, the smearing of the lintel with blood is incorporated into a cycle of the preparations for Passover in the *Rylands Spanish Haggadah* (John Rylands Library, Manchester, England); and the baking of *matzot* is introduced into the Exodus story in the *Birds' Head Haggadah* (see below).

Many legendary episodes from early Midrashim are depicted along with the biblical illustrations, some being found in Sephardi as well as Ashkenazi *Haggadot*. Only a few can be mentioned here: Abraham cast into the fire by Nimrod; Joseph's meeting with the angel on his way to his brothers in Dothan, as in the *Golden Haggadah* (see below); Joseph's coffin thrown into the Nile by the Egyptians in the *Sarajevo Haggadah*; the testing of Moses by means of gold and a live coal in the *Kaufmann Haggadah* (see below); Zipporah feeding Moses in prison for seven years in the *Yahudah Haggadah*; and Moses receiving two tablets of the Law and passing on five – the Pentateuch – in the *Birds' Head Haggadah*. Some biblical illustrations are quite literal, such as a tongueless dog barking at the Israelites coming out of Egypt to illustrate Exodus 11:7 in the *Kaufmann Haggadah*.

The eschatological illustrations refer to the ultimate destiny of the Jewish nation and the fate of the individual Jew. One such representation is the entry of the righteous into paradise (Psalm 118:19), which is depicted in the *Birds' Head Haggadah*, for example, as the three Patriarchs led by an angel. In many *Haggadot* the passage "Pour out Thy wrath upon the nations that know Thee not" (Psalm 79:6) is an invitation to eschatological illustration. In the *Kaufmann Haggadah* an angel is seen pouring the contents of a cup over a group of people.

More common in Ashkenazi *Haggadot* is an illustration associated with the prophet Elijah, the traditional harbinger of the Messiah, who is to come riding on an ass, bringing vengeance on the unbelievers who have destroyed Israel and redeeming the Jewish nation. The custom of opening the door to Elijah during the recital of "Pour out Thy wrath" is illustrated in the *Washington Haggadah*. The final verse of the *Haggadah*, "Next year in Jerusalem," is illustrated in the *Birds' Head Haggadah* by a rendering of the newly built Jerusalem and its Temple, with Jews adoring it, while in the *Sarajevo Haggadah* the facade of the Temple is depicted. In the *Second Nuremberg Haggadah* the prophet Elijah is seen riding a donkey with the Israelites following him to Jerusalem.

Regional Schools

Three types of *Haggadot* are distinguishable on the basis of their illustrations and the way these are placed: Ashkenazi, Sephardi, and Italian. While some features are common to all schools, each regional school has some local trait peculiar to its *Haggadah*.

The rich Spanish *Haggadah* is usually composed of three parts: the text; full-page biblical miniatures; and a collection of the *piyyutim* recited in the synagogue during Passover week and on the Sabbath before Passover. The text of the Spanish *Haggadah* is very sparsely illustrated, mainly with textual and ritual representations, and the *piyyutim* section is barely decorated. The most significant artistic section is that of the full-page miniatures. The best known of about a dozen surviving specimens of this rich type of Spanish *Haggadah* are the *Sarajevo*, the *Kaufmann*, and the *Golden Haggadah*.

The full-page biblical miniatures that preceded the Spanish *Haggadot* may have been derived from the manner of illuminating the Latin psalter in England and France during the later Middle Ages, which in its turn was based on the "aristocratic" type of Greek psalter illumination of earlier Byzantine schools.

The Ashkenazi *Haggadot*, from France and Germany, are all decorated with illustrations in the margins surrounding the text. There are two main groups; the earlier one places ritual and biblical illustrations, literal representations of the text, adjoining the passages they interpret. Good examples are the 13th-century *Dragon Haggadah* from France, now in Hamburg, Germany, and the *Birds' Head Haggadah* of about 1300. The later group contains a consecutive cycle of pictures from any of the books of the Bible, placed with no direct relation to the *Haggadah* text. Examples of this decoration can be found in Jerusalem in the Schocken Library and in the *Yahuda Haggadah*. The famous *Darmstadt Haggadah*, of the first half of the 15th century, has very few textual and ritual illustrations, and none is biblical. Equally few appear in the *Erna Michael Haggadah* in the Israel Museum. Joel b. Simeon of Bonn was responsible for many illuminated *Haggadot*, both in Germany and in Italy; his best in the German style is the one in the British Museum. A crude but expressive example of his transition period is the *First Nuremberg Haggadah* in the Schocken Library. The *Washington Haggadah* illuminated in the Florentine style is one of his best.

The third type of *Haggadah*, the Italian, may have been the earliest of the three and the model for the others. Since no early Italian *Haggadah* has survived, however, the type must be reconstructed from later examples which have already been subject to other influences. In the 15th century, the Italian *Haggadot* must have been influenced mainly by the Ashkenazi type, since they contain marginal illustrations only. In the first half of the century the Ashkenazi influence is apparent chiefly in the general overall design. Following an influx of Jews expelled from Germany, a new group of Italo-Ashkenazi *Haggadot* emerged in which, though the style is Italian, the script and layout are Ashkenazi. In this group are the numerous manuscripts executed in the workshops of Joel b. Simeon, and those influenced by him. The *Haggadah* in the sumptuous *Rothschild Miscellany* in the Israel Museum is illustrated on traditional Ashkenazi lines in the Ferrarese style of about 1470.

The most outstanding examples of the illuminated *Haggadot* are discussed in greater detail below.

[Bezalel Narkiss]

Examples of Illuminated Haggadot

BIRDS' HEAD HAGGADAH (Israel Museum, Jerusalem, Ms. 180/57). So named because many of the human figures are depicted with birds' heads, this is probably the oldest surviving Ashkenazi illuminated *Haggadah* manuscript. It was discovered in 1946 by Mordekhai *Narkiss. It was copied in the south of Germany late in the 13th century by a scribe named Isaac who also copied the first volume of the *Leipzig Maḥzor*. Its illumination consists mainly of marginal text illustrations, depicting historical scenes from Exodus, and ritual as well as eschatological scenes. The style of the illumination, the bright colors, and the decorative motifs, though somewhat primitive, indicate its Upper Rhenish origin. Its name is imprecise because the artist uses other methods of human distortion, such as a boy with a bulbous nose, angels with blank faces, and Egyptians in helmets with lowered visors. The manuscript was reproduced in facsimile in 1967 accompanied by an introductory volume of essays.

[Bezalel Narkiss]

CINCINNATI HAGGADAH is a 15th-century illuminated script in the library of the Hebrew Union College, Cincinnati. It was copied in square Ashkenazi script on 69 vellum leaves by the scribe Meir b. Israel Jaffe of Heidelberg. It is decorated with painted initial-word panels, a decorative border, and miniatures in the margin illustrating the Passover ceremony and the text. The style of the miniatures and decorations indicate that the manuscript was executed in the late 15th century in southern Germany. Landsberger suggested that the scribe was also the artist of the *Haggadah*. This theory however has been challenged on the grounds that more than one artist seems to have worked on this manuscript. Moreover, it is unlikely that a scribe-artist would paint miniatures which obliterate his own script, as happens on several folios.

[Joseph Gutmann]

DARMSTADT HAGGADAH is an early 15th-century manuscript preserved in the Darmstadt Landesbibliothek (Cod. Or. 8). Its richly decorated folios are unusual for *Haggadot*. It was copied about 1430 by Israel b. Meir of Heidelberg in two full-page miniatures. The illustrations consist mainly of teachers, with male and female students, some in small frames and others in many-storied gothic frames, an unusual iconographic feature. The origin of these types must have been on contemporary "Heroes and square Ashkenazi script. Its decoration contained initial-word panels, a few fully framed borders, and Heroines tapestries" or frescoes showing Hebrew, pagan, and Christian worthies. The miniatures depict a hunting scene and a spring of youth. Little room is left in the manuscript for the text. Though the artist of the miniatures is unknown, the fact that the 15th-century art was not wholly dependent on church and court workshops made the emergence of an outstanding Jewish illustrator among the expert Jewish calligraphers possible. A facsimile reproduction was produced in 1927 in Leipzig.

[Robert Weltsch]

GOLDEN HAGGADAH (British Museum Add. Ms. 27210) is the earliest and most sumptuous of the illuminated Sephardi *Haggadot*. It contains the text of the *Haggadah*, a collection of 100 *piyyutim*, and 15 full-page miniatures illustrating the biblical story from Adam naming the animals up to the exodus from Egypt. The style of the miniatures and the text illustrations suggest that it was executed in Barcelona in the first quarter of the 14th century. It is based on the northern French gothic style of the late 13th century. The full-page miniatures, divided into four compartments each painted on a burnished gold background, were executed by two artists. The *iconography of the scenes derives from the illustrations of contemporary Latin manuscripts and from Jewish aggadic iconography which may go back to early Jewish Bible illumination. There is a companion manuscript of the second half of the 14th century in the British Museum (Or. Ms. 2884). A facsimile reproduction was produced in 1970 in London and New York (figure 7).

KAUFMANN HAGGADAH (Budapest, Library of the Hungarian Academy of Sciences, Kaufmann Collection, Ms. A422) is a 14th-century Spanish manuscript composed of two parts: 14 full page miniatures (fols. 1v–10, 57v–60) and an illustrated *Haggadah* (fols. 11v–56). The *Kaufmann Haggadah* has an incomplete miniature cycle of Exodus. The manuscript is incorrectly bound, as the entire group of full-page miniatures is dispersed, with some attached to the beginning of the manuscript (fols. 1v–10) and others to the end (fols. 57v–60). The facsimile edition of the manuscript, by the Hungarian Academy of Sciences in 1954, did even more to hinder an understanding of the cycle by printing the miniatures on both sides of the pages and omitting alternate blank pages, thus preventing a correct reconstruction of the sequence. The episodes represented in the extant miniatures begin with the discovery of the infant Moses and end with Miriam's song after crossing the Red Sea, with one miniature of the preparations for Passover eve (fol. 2). Among the biblical illustrations are many midrashic ones such as Moses removing Pharaoh's crown from his head. In most cases these illustrations are within the large, painted, initial-word panels, but sometimes they appear in the margins between the extended foliage scrolls. The *Haggadah* also contains some red, green, and purple filigree-work panels. The text illustrations are elaborate and contain, besides the usual rabbis, four sons, *matzah*, and *maror*, some repetitions of the biblical episodes depicted in the full-page miniatures, such as the labor of the Israelites (fol. 15v), the throwing of the male children into the river (fol. 27v), and the Israelites coming out of Egypt (fol. 43).

The Italianate style of the illumination is pronounced. In describing this *Haggadah* in the introductory volume of *Die Haggadah von Sarajevo*, J. von Schlosser attributed the style to northern Italy. In fact, it is Castilian of the late 14th century, characterized by many Italian stylistic elements. The Byzantine-Bolognese figure style and the very colorful, fleshy leaves support this assumption, as does the triple-towered castle – the emblem of the Kingdom of Castile – which is depicted in the center of the round, decorated *matzah* surrounded by four naked personifications of the winds blowing trumpets.

Sarajevo Haggadah (Sarajevo National Museum) is a 14th-century Spanish illuminated manuscript composed of the traditional three parts: 34 full-page miniatures (fols. 1v–34); illuminated *Haggadah* text (fols. 1*–50*); and *piyyutim* and Torah readings for Passover week (fols. 53*–131*). It is by far the best-known Hebrew illuminated manuscript, and has been reproduced in part twice during the last 70 years with scholarly introductions by H. Mueller and J. von Schlosser, and by C. Roth. The full-page miniatures in the *Sarajevo Haggadah* display the widest range of subjects even among the rich

Spanish *Haggadot*, from the Creation of the World to Moses blessing the Israelites and Joshua before his death, followed by illustrations of the Temple, preparations for Passover, and the interior of a Spanish synagogue. There are few full-page miniatures; most are divided horizontally into two framed sections, with some in four sections. Although the greater part of the iconography of the miniatures is derived from Latin Bible illumination of the Franco-Spanish school, some Jewish elements can be detected, as in the abstention from representation of God or any heavenly beings. Other Jewish aspects can be found in the text illustrations of the *Haggadah*, such as a miniature of Rabban Gamaliel and his students, and the *matzah* and *maror*. Stylistically, the illuminations are related to the Italian-gothic school prevailing in Catalonia in the 14th century. That the *Sarajevo Haggadah* originates from the Kingdom of Aragon can be inferred from three coats of arms displayed in the manuscript. The *Haggadah* reached the Sarajevo Museum when in 1894 a child of the city's Sephardi Jewish community brought it to school to be sold, after his father had died leaving the family destitute.

[Bezalel Narkiss]

WASHINGTON HAGGADAH (Library of Congress in Washington, D.C.) consists of 39 vellum leaves, 6 by 9 in. (15 × 22.5 cm.), written in square Ashkenazi script, completed by Joel b. Simeon in 1478. It has painted initial-word panels, and many marginal illustrations of the Passover ceremonies and the Exodus story. Although the illustrations depict German customs, their stylistic features and decorative elements indicate a late 15th-century northern Italian origin. The illustrations are closely related to those in other manuscripts believed to have been executed in the northern Italian workshop of the same scribe-illustrator. A facsimile was produced in 1965 with a preface by Lawrence Marwick.

[Joseph Gutmann]

PRINTED EDITIONS OF ILLUSTRATED HAGGADOT

Introduction

The earliest known edition of the *Haggadah* to be printed separately was produced in Spain at Guadalajara about 1482, on 12 pages in double column. Only a single copy is known to exist, and it may well be that other, perhaps earlier, editions have disappeared. The bibliography of the Passover *Haggadot* published by A. Yaari in 1960 includes 2,717 entries, but taking into account omissions and later editions, there can be no doubt that the total to the present date is at least 3,000. In the text of the *Haggadah* included in the prayer book according to the Italian rite (Casalmaggiore, 1486), there is a conventional representation of the *mazzah*, as in some of the earliest *Haggadah* manuscripts, and these may be considered the earliest known illustrations to the printed *Haggadah*. The crudely executed but by no means ignorant illustrations in the Latin *Ritus et celebratio Paschae* (Frankfurt, 1512) by the Christian Hebraist Thomas Murner, drawn by his brother Beatus, may have been inspired by a Jewish model. In the extremely rare *Seder Zemirot u-Virkat ha-Mazon* (Prague, 1514) there are figure woodcuts on the same subjects which appear later in illustrated *Haggadot*, and may derive from some lost edition. Of the earliest known illustrated edition, hypothetically attributed to Constantinople about 1515, only fragments remain. From the worn state of some of the blocks it may have been a reprint. From these fragments it is obvious that the whole work must have been lavishly illustrated.

Prague Edition (1526)

The continuous record of the illustrated printed *Haggadah* begins with the *Prague edition of 1526. This magnificent work, with its profuse marginal cuts and decorations and its superb borders, is among the finest productions of the 16th-century press. The beauty of the work lies above all in the disposition of the type and the exquisite balance of the pages. Its most remarkable feature is three pages with engraved borders in monumental gothic style. The printers and publishers were Gershom Solomon Kohen Katz and his brother Gronem (Geronim). The artistic work was apparently executed partly by Ḥayyim Shaḥor (Schwartz), Gershom Kohen's collaborator, who sometimes signed his initials, and partly by a gentile assistant. Some of the decorative features were derived from non-Jewish works, including the Nuremberg chronicle of 1484. In recent years the Prague *Haggadah* has been reproduced repeatedly in facsimile. The cuts and illustrations in the publication were long imitated, deteriorating progressively as the years went by. The Prague edition of 1556 retained some of the original elements but this was not the case with the one published in 1590 or with other commonplace editions that continued to appear in Prague and elsewhere down to the mid-18th century. An interesting new edition, apparently by Ḥayyim Shaḥor, appeared in Augsburg in 1534. This, however, had little influence and only one complete copy is preserved.

Mantua Edition (1560, 1568)

The next important step in the record of the illustrated *Haggadah* was the Mantua edition of 1560, published by the *shammash*, Isaac b. Samuel. This reproduced the text of the Prague edition page for page and letter for letter in facsimile, but introduced new illustrations and marginal decorations which had already been used in non-Jewish publications and were in conformity with Italian taste. The format was repeated with remarkable success in another edition published in Mantua in 1568 by a non-Jewish firm which concealed its identity under the name Filipponi. The marginal decorations were specially recut for this production, which rivals the Prague edition of 1526.

Venice Editions

The Mantua editions served as precise models for a group of illustrated *Haggadot* in smaller format produced in rapid succession at the turn of the century (1599, 1601, 1603, and 1604) in Venice, which had become the great center of Jewish publishing. These converted the hybrid but impressive Mantua editions into a cohesive but unimpressive unity, reproducing every accidental decoration and copying every accidental marginal detail. The major illustrations at the foot of the pages were expanded into an entirely fresh series of 17 engravings, some of them appearing more than once. These illustrated the *seder* service, the subject matter, and the story of the Exodus. Thus, this is the first *Haggadah* which is consistently and systematically illustrated.

In 1609 the veteran printer Israel ha-Zifroni of Guastalla planned an edition with completely new illustrations. Printed for him by Giovanni da Gara, it was set in bold type, each page within an engraved architectural border. The illustrations were placed at the top or foot of almost every page in the early part of the volume, and more sparsely toward the end. There was one important innovation in this edition: in a series of small panels on an introductory page, the various stages in the Passover celebration are illustrated with men and women dressed in contemporary fashion; a later page similarly illustrates the ten plagues. These features were henceforth to become usual in illustrated *Haggadot*.

The illustrations of the first part of the service (before the meal) are almost wholly devoted to the exodus, while those in the second part (after the meal) deal with the biblical story in general and with the messianic deliverance. In 1629 a further edition based on ha-Zifroni's with a similar format was published in Venice by the Bragadini press. This continued to be reproduced, without any basic change but with increasingly worn types and indistinct blocks, until late in the 18th century. The illustrations continued to be copied in *Haggadot* printed in the Mediterranean area, especially in Leghorn, almost to the present day. Thus the pattern of the traditional illustrated *Haggadah* was established.

Amsterdam Editions

In 1695 there appeared in Amsterdam a new edition of the illustrated *Haggadah* which followed closely, in its general layout as well as in detail, the example of the now accepted Venetian prototype. The illustrations were, however, much improved by being engraved on copper. The artist was *Abraham b. Jacob, a former Protestant preacher. He chose many of the same incidental scenes as had appeared in the Venice *Haggadot*, but he drew them afresh, basing his work on the biblical pictures in the *Icones Biblicae* by Matthew Merian the Elder; he probably used the second edition of the work which had appeared in Amsterdam in c. 1655–62. Abraham b. Jacob also used miscellaneous scenes taken from other works by Merian. Thus the four sons of the *Haggadah* text (depicted together for the first time in one illustration) are miscellaneous figures brought together from various publications of Merian, without any attempt at grouping. The "wise son" and the "son who could not ask," for example, come from an engraving of Hannibal sacrificing before the altar, while the scene of the sages celebrating at Bene-Berak is reproduced – with some alterations – from Merian's picture of the feast given by Joseph to his brethren. The first map of Ereẓ Israel known in a Jewish publication was added on a folding page at the end of the book. A further edition of the work was produced in Amsterdam in 1712, with minor differences, and the name of the artist was omitted from the title page.

As the Venice *Haggadah* of 1609/29 was widely imitated in southern Europe, so the Amsterdam editions had an enduring influence on the *Haggadot* produced in the Ashkenazi world. The pictures were imitated, if not copied, time after time with increasing indistinctness in innumerable editions illustrated with woodcuts or steel engravings. Such editions appeared in Frankfurt in 1710 and 1775, in Offenbach in 1721, and in Amsterdam in 1765 and 1781. Throughout the 19th century and down to the present day the illustrations, including the four sons and the Passover at Bene-Berak, continued to be reproduced in ever-decreasing quality in hundreds of cheap *Haggadot* published on both sides of the Atlantic. The Amsterdam editions also inspired a number of illustrated *Haggadot* by 18th-century German Jewish manuscript artists, some of whom even improved on the original.

Some Later Editions

A few independently conceived *Haggadot* of the later period may be mentioned: the Trieste edition of 1864 with 58 original copper engravings of considerable artistic merit by K. Kirchmayer; the Prague edition of 1889 with illustrations by the Slovak artist Cyril Kulik; and the curious lithograph edition published in Poona in 1874 for the benefit of the Bene *Israel community. In the 20th century, editions have appeared illustrated (or in some cases entirely executed) by artists of the caliber of Joseph *Budko, Jakob Steinhardt, Arthur *Szyk, Albert Rothenstein, and Ben *Shahn, and in Israel by J. Zimberknopf and David Gilboa (d. 1976), the last being written in scroll form. The modified *Haggadot* produced for the kibbutzim are also almost always illustrated, sometimes by local artists.

[Cecil Roth]

MUSICAL RENDITION

Chanting and singing the texts of the *Haggadah* is generally observed in all Jewish communities, each one according to its peculiar style and custom. Although the celebration of the *seder* night is a family affair in which nobody is obliged to sing, it is customary to do so according to the example set by one's parents. From a musical point of view, the *Haggadah* text offers opportunities for solo chant as well as for responsorial and community singing. The scope of singing styles encompasses the simple chant (of the narrative and didactic sections), a more developed and melodious recitation that blends well with the responses of the company (for psalms and the old-style hymns), and melodies sung by all those present (for the more recent songs). The melodic recitations often come close to the simpler forms of synagogue chant; the Ashkenazi reader, for instance, largely uses the *Adonai Malakh Shteyger*, while the Jews of Iraq employ their *Tefillah* mode for some chapters. The psalms of the **Hallel* are usually intoned to the ancient patterns of psalmody (see Jewish *Music), and sung with great enthusiasm; already in the *Gemara* a proverb is quoted which says that singing the *Hallel* "cracks the ceiling" (TJ and TB, Pes. 7:12). The stanzas of the medieval poems that conclude the *Haggadah*, however, are given veritable song tunes in contemporary and past popular styles. These tunes vary from family to family and constitute a still unexplored treasure of folklore. Melodies in the folk style are normally attached to the poems *Addir Hu, Ki Lo Na'eh* (*Addir bi-Melukhah*), *Eḥad Mi Yode'a*, belonging to the widely disseminated category of "counting songs," and *Ḥad Gadya*. Less frequent are *Ḥasal Seder Pesaḥ* and the two acrostical hymns following it, as well as certain psalm verses and responsorial refrains in the earlier sections. The homelike atmosphere of *Haggadah* reading also permitted singing these poems in the vernacular. In the Ashkenazi community, this custom is not attested later than the 18th century, when it appears to have been abandoned. The Sephardim, however, not only continue singing the poems in the Ladino vernacular, but extend this even to more formal chapters such as *Ha Laḥma Anya*. There is an example from Bulgaria in which every Ladino verse is repeated immediately in Bulgarian and Turkish; the Bulgarian version was to serve the young generation, the Turkish text was meant for the older one, while Ladino was for all.

At some places it is regarded as a merit and even a duty to extend the celebration of the *seder* night by joyful singing, eventually accompanied by dance steps, for as long as possible. This custom, of course, has its roots in mystical concepts, but it did not remain confined to such circles and is honored by eastern and western communities as well. Ḥasidic *niggunim* ("melodies") are most often inserted by Ashkenazi celebrants. The *Haggadah* was also adapted by the Reform tendencies; there were several additions of music in rather dull style, but the substance was not touched. Kibbutzim in Israel have either designed their own tunes out of old and new elements or embellished tradition by additional songs and melodies. Israel songs (in the "classical" style of the 1940s and 1950s) are largely employed for stressing the national and seasonal aspects of Passover, and these tunes display their full charm in the traditional setting. A widely used "Kibbutz *Haggadah*" setting is that by Yehudah *Sharett. Another side-development was the use of the *Haggadah* for an oratorio, jointly undertaken by Max *Brod and the composer Paul *Dessau in 1933–35. There the traditional text has been expanded by selected scenes from the Bible and Midrash, and the music combines a declamatory style with the harsh harmonies of that period and full orchestral accompaniment.

[Hanoch Avenary]

FEMINIST HAGGADOT

Feminist *Haggadot* create a format for women's communal celebration of Passover by giving prominence to the experiences of women in the narrative of the exodus from Egypt and by acknowledging women's efforts to achieve full participation in Jewish communal and religious life. Inspired by the liberation and exodus imagery used by Civil Rights and New Left political activists, American Jewish women designed the first feminist *Haggadah* in 1971 for use in private women-only Passover *seders*. The growth of Jewish feminism and new forms of religious expression during the 1970s and 1980s fostered the production of innovative rituals and liturgy among non-Orthodox religious Jews. A number of feminist *Haggadot* circulated and were adapted to fit the distinct concerns of each *seder*'s attendees. These *Haggadot* share many features in structure and content. Relying on classical midrashic texts, they give significant attention to female leadership in the exodus narrative. Miriam takes a central role in the *magid* and other sections of the *seder*, supplanting Elijah in portending redemption. The *Haggadot* present girls and women with historic Jewish female role models who struggled against oppression, including sexism within the Jewish community. Feminine or gender-neutral God language and feminine liturgical language are the norm.

In these *Haggadot*, the rituals and symbols of the traditional *seder* are revised or reinterpreted to relate to women's lives. Common features include: (1) modifications of the Four Questions to fit a *seder* consisting only of women and inclusion of questions about the need for female separatism, the reasons for the bitterness of women's oppression, and the potential for liberation; (2) the Four Sons are transformed into Four Daughters; (3) the Four Cups are presented as stages in women's emancipation or as representative of Jewish heroines; (4) the Ten Plagues are re-named as the plagues cast upon women in Jewish life, for example, blood represents the myriad ways that women's menses and reproductive capacity are blamed for excluding women from Torah study and communal privileges; (5) the *Dayyenu* song is altered to acknowledge advances in women's status and to voice dissatisfaction with incomplete emancipation; and (6) the *seder* foods and rituals are given multiple symbolic meanings relating to women's lives. New features include the Passover-themed songs of Debbie *Friedman; the use of *Kos Miryam* (Miriam's Cup), a goblet of water signifying Miriam's sustaining guidance in the wilderness; and the placing of an orange on the *seder* plate to acknowledge the contributions of gays and lesbians in the Jewish community. Most feminist *Haggadot* exist only in photocopied form. Hebrew Union College Library and Ma'yan: The Jewish Women's Project have archived many for research purposes.

[Jody Myers (2nd ed.)]

BIBLIOGRAPHY: Haggadah: E. Baneth, *Der Sederabend* (1904); A. Berlinere, *Randbemerkungen zum taeglichen Gebetbuche*, 2 (1912), 47ff.; Finkelstein, in: HUCA, 23 (1950–51), pt. 2, pp. 319–37; idem, in: HTR, 31 (1938), 291–317; 35 (1942), 291–332; 36 (1943), 1–18; M. Friedmann (Ish-Shalom), *Me'ir Ayin al Seder ve-Haggadah shel Levlei Pesaḥ* (1895); D. Goldschmidt, *Haggadah shel Pesaḥ ve-Toledoteha* (1960), introduction (cf. reviews by E.E. Urbach in KS, 36 (1961), 143ff., and J. Heinemann in *Tarbiz*, 30 (1960/61), 405ff.); Z. Carl, *Mishnayot im Be'ur Ḥadash: Pesaḥim* (1927), introduction; J. Lewy, *Ein Vortrag ueber das Ritual des Pessachabends* (1904); Marx, in: JQR, 19 (1927/28), 1ff.; Stein, in: *Jewish Studies*, 8 (1957), 13–44; Zunz, Vortraege, 133–5; ET, 8 (1957), 177–93. **Illuminated Manuscripts:** Mayer, Art, index; B. Narkiss, *Hebrew Illuminated Manuscripts* (1969), index. BIRDS' HEAD

HAGGADAH: M. Spitzer (ed.), *The Birds' Head Haggadah of the Bezalel National Art Museum in Jerusalem* (1967), bibliography in introductory volume, pp. 123–4. CINCINNATI HAGGADAH: Landsberger, in: HUCA, 15 (1940), 529–58. DARMSTADT HAGGADAH: B. Italianer, *Die Darmstaedter Pessach-Haggadah* (1927–28); R. Wischnitzer, in: P. Goodman (ed.), *Passover Anthology* (1961), 295–324. GOLDEN HAGGADAH: Margoliouth, Cat, no. 607; Gutmann, in: SBB, 7 (1965); Mayer, Art, no. 1792 (102–4, 106–7); B. Narkiss, *The Golden Haggadah* (1970). KAUFMANN HAGGADAH: Mayer, Art, no. 1792 (187–99, pls. xxxi–xxxv); no. 2061; no. 2302; B. Narkiss, in: KS, 34 (1958/59), 71–79; 4 (1966/67), 104–7. SARAJEVO HAGGADAH: Mayer, Art, index and nos. 1792, 2235–7; no. 2969 (nos. 30, 41). WASHINGTON HAGGADAH: Landsberger, in: HUCA, 21 (1948), 73–103; Gutmann, in: SBB, 7 (1965), 3–25. **Printed Editions:** Mayer, Art, index; S. Wiener, *Bibliographie der Oster-Haggadah* (19492), contains a list of 884 editions between 1500 and 1900; idem, in: SBB, 7 (1965), 90–125 (addenda of 330 editions); A. Yaari, *Bibliografyah shel Haggadot Pesaḥ* (1960). **Music:** E. Werner, in: SBB, 7 (1965), 57–83; M. Brod, in: *Musica Hebraica*, 1–2 (1938), 21–23; B. Bayer, in: *Dukhan*, 8 (1966), 89–98; Idelsohn, Melodien, 2 (1922), nos. 16–26; 3 (1922), nos. 14–16; 4 (1923), nos. 76, 78, 79; L. Algazi, *Chants Sephardis* (1958), nos. 23–28; Levy, Antología, 3 (1968), nos. 189–316; A. Schoenfeld, *Recitative und Gesaenge… am ersten und zweiten Abende des Ueberschreitungsfestes* (1884); E. Piattelli, *Canti liturgici ebraici di rito italiano* (1967), 168–9. **ADD. BIBLIOGRAPHY: Feminist Haggadot:** *The San Diego Women's Haggadah* (1980, 1986); E.M. Broner with N. Nimrod, *The Women's Haggadah* (1993); *The Journey Continues: The Ma'yan Passover Haggadah* (2000); S.C. Anisfeld, T. Mohr, and C. Spector (eds.), *The Women's Passover Companion* (2003); idem, *The Women's Seder Sourcebook* (2003).

HAGGAHOT (Heb. הַגָּהוֹת "glosses"; "corrections"), a term used both to mean the examination of manuscript and printed works in order to correct errors and in the sense of "glosses," i.e., notes and brief comments on the text.

This entry is arranged according to the following outline:

In the Bible, the verb, *haggiha* means to enlighten (cf. Ps. 18:29), and Kutscher conjectures that originally it had the same meaning when applied to books, since the main task of the *maggiha* (person making the *haggahah*) in the early period was to go over faded writing in order to "brighten" it.

Correction of Errors

Haggahah has been an integral element of writing and printing from the beginning since it is humanly impossible to avoid error. The types of error (both the authors' and the copyists') and correspondingly the categories of *haggahot* can be classified in two main groups.

CORRECTION IN THE CONTENT. This type of correction was mostly done by the author himself. In early literature with a large circulation the *haggahah* was done by scholars and experts. It was reported of Isaac Ruba, a *tanna* in the school of Judah ha-Nasi, that he had a corrected text of the Mishnah (TJ, Ma'as. Sh. 5:1, 55d). At a later period the *amora* Zeira complained that contemporary scholars did not correct the Mishnah in their possession in accordance with the version of R. Isaac (*ibid*). *Haggahot* of this type were done both on the basis of original and established texts, but at times they were also made at the discretion of the *maggiha*. Various scholars have pointed out *haggahot* of this later type which have found their way into the text of the Mishnah. Fragments of the *Mishneh Torah* of Maimonides in the author's own handwriting were discovered in the Cairo *Genizah* by M. Lutzki (d. 1976), who published them at the end of the Schulsinger edition (1947), and from them it is possible to trace the process of corrections and emendations whereby the final work was created. Manuscripts of Maimonides' commentary to the Mishnah, likewise thought to be in his own hand, have also been discovered and contain many of the author's *haggahot*; in some of them he changes his mind and gives a different opinion. The text of the *Ba'alei ha-Nefesh* of Abraham b. David of Posquières in the edition of Y. Kafaḥ (1965), a text emended by the author following the *hassagot* ("criticisms") of Zerahiah b. Isaac ha-Levi Gerondi, is a similar example. From this type of correction the "*Haggahot* literature" (see below) later developed.

CORRECTION OF STYLISTIC OR GRAPHIC ERRORS. This category consists essentially of technical mistakes resulting from such common copyists' errors as repeating the same word twice (dittography), omitting one of two similar adjacent letters or words (haplography), and missing words or lines because the same word occurs further on in a passage (homoioteleuton). In early times (and in Yemen until quite recently) there was also a class of errors which resulted from the practice of the "publishers" of those days of appointing a group of people (mainly slaves), skilled writers who wrote from dictation exactly what they heard (to this type belong such errors as *eilav*, "unto him," for *el av*, "unto father"). This type of error was obviated in copying the text of the Bible because of the prohibition against copying from dictation. The correction of such errors, made by others than the author himself, was done by comparing the text with an early or authoritative copy which adhered closely to the original text.

In early days a checked, original copy was deposited in the Temple, library, or archives, and whenever necessary the correct text was determined by it. The Midrash (Deut. R. 9:9) reports a tradition of a special **Sefer Torah* written by Moses and placed in the ark so that the correct text could be established (see S. Lieberman, *Hellenism in Jewish Palestine* (1950), 85f.). There are also reports of *Sifrei Torah* that were preserved in the Temple for the same purpose, and from them the *Sefer Torah* of the king was checked by the supreme *bet din*. The scroll was called "the Temple scroll," and texts were examined by a group of "book correctors" in the Temple, whose wages were paid from the public funds of the Temple treasury (Ket. 106a, Lieberman op. cit., 22); according to some commentators these correctors also examined the scrolls belonging to individuals and were also paid from the communal treasury. Similar scrolls were known which were regarded as especially accurate because they had been written by an expert scribe and had been meticulously checked; such a scroll was called "a checked (*muggah*) scroll." Examples were those written by Assi (Lieberman op. cit., 25). A medieval manuscript of the *Mishneh Torah* exists (Neubauer, Bod. Cat, no. 577) which was corrected on the basis of the author's text, and Maimonides confirms this by his signature at the end of the manuscript. Later this manuscript was kept at the *bet din*, and it was forbidden to use it for any purpose other than correcting later copies (according to the instructions in the colophon).

Uncorrected Torah scrolls were regarded as unauthoritative, and it was forbidden not only to use them but even to keep them (Ket. 19b); at a later period this prohibition was extended to include halakhic works (Sh. Ar., YD, 279). A complete set of halakhic rules was laid down for the correction of *Sifrei Torah* – their fitness for public reading being conditional on many details, including accurate *haggahah*. A scroll containing a certain number of errors was disqualified, and it was forbidden to correct it since the *haggahah* would spoil its appearance. If the errors were less numerous, an added letter could be erased or a missing one inserted. In the event of an error in the Divine Name, which it is forbidden to erase, it was sometimes the practice to peel off a layer from the parchment (Pitḥei Teshuvah to Sh. Ar., YD 276:2). The *haggahah* of *Sifrei Torah* is a purely technical task, as the text itself is naturally never emended and no discussion on the text of the Bible is found in talmudic literature (Lieberman, op. cit. 47). In some places, the scribe was made responsible for the *haggahah* (Resp. Rashba, pt. 1. no. 1056). There is evidence of the existence of corrected manuscripts of the Mishnah, such as "in an accurate Mishnah corrected from that of R. Ephraim" (*Maḥzor Vitry*, ed. by S. Hurwitz (1923²), 536). The following correctors of the Mishnah are known from the era of printing: Joseph Ashkenazi; the "*tanna* of Safed," Samuel Lerma; Soliman Ohana; Menahem de Lonzano; Bezalel Ashkenazi; and his pupil Solomon Adani.

INFLUENCE OF HAGGAHOT ON TEXT. The failure to distinguish between the two types of *haggahah*, as well as between corrections based on accurate texts and sources and those based on the judgment of the scribe, together with an exceptional caution against changing the actual text, caused the *haggahot* to be relegated to the margin instead of the text itself being corrected. As various copyists failed to appreciate this, the *haggahot* were subsequently incorporated into the body of the text. A critical examination in later ages revealed and indicated places where external *haggahot* had been arbitrarily and artificially included in the text (the question of the different sources of the material of the Babylonian Talmud and its transmission, which are known to have influenced the text, belongs to a different category). The *geonim* already pointed out this phenomenon (see M.M. Kasher, in *Gemara Shelemah*, Pesaḥim pt. 1 (1960), introd.). Despite this, it should be noted that in the main the text of the authoritative halakhic literature was meticulously preserved because of its importance in legal decisions and in leading a life in accordance with *halakhah*. The Jerusalem Talmud and the various halakhic and aggadic Midrashim were not preserved in a sufficiently corrected form, however, because the attitude to them was less punctilious. An example of how such *haggahot* creep into a text is found in the following story. Rabbi Ḥayyim of Volozhin once asked his teacher, the Gaon of Vilna, about the word, *ḥesed*, that appeared in a particular line of the *Zohar. The word seemed out of place. The Vilna Gaon answered that a number of lines were missing in the manuscript on which Rabbi Ḥayyim's printed edition was based. In the manuscript, the word, *ḥaser*, appears, implying that some lines were missing. The typesetter misread the word, replacing the letter, *resh*, with a *dalet* and inserting the word into the text. (see Y.D. Rubin (ed.), *Nefesh ha-Ḥayyim*, 1989, 461).

The *haggahot* of various scholars affected the text of the Talmud, and this custom apparently became so widespread that *Gershom b. Judah of Mainz (who is stated to have copied books, among them the Bible) found it necessary to impose a ban on those who emended books, although it seems that this step was unsuccessful in completely eradicating the practice. A few generations later Jacob *Tam came out sharply against the emendation of books (introduction to *Sefer ha-Yashar*). He described the method of his grandfather, Rashi, stating that he did not emend the text itself but noted his emendations in the margin. It was Rashi's pupils who corrected the text in conformity with these notes, and Tam criticizes them for it. He also differentiates between *haggahah* which consisted of erasing words and that which was merely addition. Among other things he reveals that his brother Samuel b. Meir (Rashbam) also frequently made *haggahot* in the body of the text. It is important to note that the present text of the Babylonian Talmud is considerably influenced by Rashi's emendations, in contrast to the *haggahot* of the tosafists and other scholars. Perhaps this fact is to be attributed to the attitude of Tam. In the age of printing this same process is encountered. Many of the *haggahot* of Solomon Luria have been introduced into the printed text of the Talmud, though he noted them in a special book and they were originally published in this form. In later editions of the Talmud, however, the text was already emended according to his notes (see below). The *haggahot* of Samuel Edels (the Maharsha), who was opposed to *haggahot* of the text (see his introduction), were nevertheless incorporated in the text.

PROOFREADERS. During the age of printing the influence of proofreaders and printers on the texts of books became increasingly important, and today it is occasionally possible to trace the methods of different proofreaders. After it had been established beyond doubt that the Leiden manuscript of the Jerusalem Talmud is the one from which the first edition was published in Venice (1523, by Bomberg), Lieberman showed in his essay on the tractate *Horayot* in the Jerusalem Talmud how great a share the proofreader – Cornelius Adelkind – had in establishing the present text (*Sefer ha-Yovel*... C. Albeck, 1963, 283–305). The research of R.N.N. Rabbinovicz on the text of the Babylonian Talmud provides a great deal of information on the activities of its first proofreaders. The most prominent of them was Ḥiyya Meir b. David, one of the rabbis of Venice, who was given the responsibility of correcting the whole Talmud edition by Bomberg in the course of three years (1520–23), as well as the commentary of Asher b. Jehiel. The proofreader of the first tractates of the Soncino Talmud (1484) was Gabriel b. Aaron Strasburg, and Rabbinovicz shows that his work is very faulty.

Gradually notes and corrections in the margins of books increased until they at times assumed the character of a textual apparatus. Still later these notes were even collected and issued in the form of independent works in which the word *haggahot* generally appeared in the title. The word is applied to many books, though their contents and character differ from one another.

Haggahot Literature

In the *haggahot* literature which developed, two main groups can be distinguished, the first constituting additions and supplements to the contents of the work – glosses – and the other consisting of emendations and notes to the text. The most prominent and best known of the first group were compiled on works of codification. An additional characteristic common to books of this category is that they lack formal structure and, since they were not authoritative, they were subjected to later adaptation and editing.

GLOSSES ON THE CODES. Such glosses were added to the great halakhic code, *Hilkhot ha-Rif*, of Isaac *Alfasi. Only fragments remain of the earliest gloss, the *haggahot* of his pupil, Ephraim (Abraham b. David, *Temim De'im* no. 68 and citations in the *Ha-Ma'or* of Zerahyah ha-Levi). One of the important motives for such works is the tendency to make the code reflect the views of the scholars of a particular country, and also apply to other spheres of the *halakhah*. It was with this aim that the great halakhic compilation, the *Mordekhai* of Mordecai b. Hillel, consisting of the rulings and responsa of German and French scholars, was compiled on the *Hilkhot ha-Rif*. In the manuscripts, however, the *Mordekhai* appears as a gloss to the work itself. The *Mordekhai* was not edited by its compiler and there are different versions and editions. In the 13th century Meir ha-Kohen, Mordecai's colleague and according to some his brother-in-law (both were pupils of Meir b. Baruch of Rothenburg), wrote his *haggahot*, called **Haggahot Maimuniyyot*, on the *Mishneh Torah*. It attempted to add to Maimonides' rulings the opinions and decisions of the scholars of Germany and France, and the views and responsa of Meir of Rothenburg occupy a prominent part of the work. As a result of this amalgamation of halakhic rulings there emerged a work which could serve as an authoritative halakhic code in different centers.

The *haggahot* of the tosafist *Perez b. Elijah of Corbeil to the *Tashbeẓ* of Samson b. Zadok was written for a similar purpose. Perez noted the customs and halakhic decisions of his teacher, Meir of Rothenburg, and added the customs and rulings of the French scholars. He also wrote *haggahot* to the *Sefer Mitzvot Katan* (*Semak*) of *Isaac b. Joseph of Corbeil, which are mainly a summation of the views of the early scholars. Because of the succinctness and brevity of the *Semak*, *haggahot* were added to it by many scholars from different localities. The best known are the as yet unpublished *haggahot* of Moses of Zurich (see Urbach, Tosafot, 450). To the comprehensive *Piskei ha-Rosh* of Asher b. Jehiel, who moved from Germany to Spain at the beginning of the 14th century, was added the *Haggahot Asheri* of Israel of Krems (14th century). In the main this consists of summarized quotations from the *Or Zaru'a* of Isaac b. Moses of Vienna and of the rulings of Hezekiah b. Jacob of Magdeburg (13th century) from whom he collected the rulings of Isaac b. Samuel.

The best-known *haggahot*, which had a decisive influence on the establishment of the *halakhah*, are those of Moses *Isserles of Cracow to the Shulḥan Arukh. Their purpose was both to supplement the rulings of Joseph Caro, who based himself upon the three *posekim*, Isaac Alfasi, Maimonides, and Asher b. Jehiel, with the rulings of the scholars of Germany, France, and Poland, and also to note the customs and decisions which were accepted by Ashkenazi Jewry where they differed from those accepted by the Sephardim. The *haggahot* of Isserles were noted on the margins of the Shulḥan Arukh and are based upon his *Darkhei Moshe* (Resp. Rema 131:3), and were copied and circularized by his pupils (on Sh. Ar. OḤ, Hilkhot Niddah, Cracow, 1570, on the whole Sh. Ar., *ibid.*, 1578). The notes and source references to the *Haggahot ha-Rema* were added later by others (first in the Cracow, 1607 edition). Isserles also compiled *haggahot* to other works such as *The Guide of the Perplexed* of Maimonides and the *Mordekhai*. With a similar purpose, Jacob Castro, chief rabbi of Egypt, also wrote *haggahot* to the Shulḥan Arukh – *Erekh Leḥem* (Constantinople, 1718) – which reveal many similarities with those of Isserles, but were not widely used.

This category of *haggahot* had several consequences, both positive and negative. On the one hand, they preserved fragments of large works which have been lost, apparently because of their size and the difficulties of transporting and copying them, or because they were superseded by the codes. On the other hand, it is possible that the abridgments and summaries actually contributed to the original works being forgotten (some were later rediscovered, e.g., the *Or Zaru'a*, *Ravyah*, and others).

TEXTUAL NOTES AND EMENDATIONS. In the *haggahot* literature of the second category, those of Solomon b. Jehiel *Luria of Lublin to the Babylonian Talmud are outstanding in their scope and importance. According to his sons, who published them separately under the title *Ḥokhmat Shelomo* (Cracow, 1581–82), he had no intention of committing his *haggahot* and comments to book form, but they served him as "notes and a prolegomenon to his major work, the *Yam shel Shelomo*." These *haggahot* were written in the margin to the Bomberg edition of the Talmud in which he studied. Although the proofreaders of this publishing house were noted scholars (see above), this edition contains many mistakes and errors. The *haggahot* were made by comparing the text with sources and parallels, and according to his sons, Luria made use of manuscripts of the Talmud, of Rashi, and of the *tosafot* in his possession. In the Talmud published at that time in Constantinople by the brothers Yavetz, these *haggahot* were appended to the various tractates, and sometimes corrections were made according to the *haggahot* in the body of the work and indicated in the margin. In the later editions they were incorporated into the text and cannot be detected without special investigation (numerous examples are to be found in the *Dikdukei Soferim* of R.N.N. Rabbinovicz). Luria also wrote *haggahot* to many other halakhic works. A. Berliner saw his *haggahot* to Maimonides in the town of Sokol (see Assaf in bibl.).

Also known are the *Haggahot ha-Baḥ* of Joel *Sirkes of Cracow, which he also inscribed on the margins of the first editions of the Talmud in which he studied. They were first published in Warsaw in 1824 as a separate work and thenceforth in the later editions of the Talmud. Like those of Luria, these *haggahot* greatly affect the understanding of the text of the Talmud and its commentaries, but in contrast to those *haggahot* which in many cases were based upon manuscripts, Sirkes' corrections were mainly according to linguistic considerations and internal comparisons within the Talmud itself. Among the outstanding scholars who devoted themselves to *haggahot* and emendations in this sense was *Elijah the Gaon of Vilna. According to tradition, his corrections and amendments covered the whole range of talmudic, midrashic, and kabbalistic literature. Although he himself published none of his *haggahot*, some were printed later, but not all have survived in an accurate and original form. Among his published *haggahot* are some of those on the Babylonian Talmud (in late editions starting Vienna, 1816–26), on the *Mekhilta* (Vilna, 1844), the order *Zera'im* of the Jerusalem Talmud (Koenigsberg, 1858), *Sifrei* (1866), Tosefta (firstly independently and later in the Vilna edition of the Talmud), and the *Sifra* (1959). Scholars have concerned themselves with the question whether Elijah of Vilna's *haggahot* are also based upon manuscripts and early versions or are the outcome of his own discretion. With regard to the Tosefta, S. Lieberman (*Tosefet Rishonim*, 3 (1939), introd.) has established that in essence they are derived from quotations of the text in the works of the *rishonim*, and apparently those on the Jerusalem Talmud also belong to this category.

In this category of *haggahot* are works which are less well known but of considerable importance, since through them the original readings of manuscripts and early printed works, from which the *haggahot* were taken, have been preserved. This phenomenon is especially notable in the works of Sephardi rabbis of recent centuries, who had access to manuscripts which they used frequently. Among them are *Haggahot Tummat Yesharim* (Venice, 1622) on *Avot de-Rabbi Nathan*, the *Sifra*, Alfasi, etc. Many such *haggahot* are also enshrined in the works of Ḥ.J.D. Azulai, who saw and used more manuscripts and early printed editions than any other author. In his first work, compiled in his youth, the *Sha'ar Yosef* (Leghorn, 1757) on *Horayot*, he made extensive use for the first time of the well-known manuscript of the Babylonian Talmud (now Ms. Munich no. 95, issued in photographed facsimile by H.L. Strack in Leiden in 1912), from which he corrected texts of the Talmud. His other works (see Benayahu's lists, p. 185–252) constitute a rich source of knowledge on the nature and existence of manuscripts in talmudic literature and of *haggahot* from them. This category of *haggahot* contained in the works of the Oriental scholars, which has scarcely been investigated, contains a considerable amount of material both on texts and contents of the works and is a fruitful field for historical and literary research into the history of talmudic literature.

BIBLIOGRAPHY: Y. Kutscher, *Ha-Lashon ve-ha-Reka ha-Leshoni shel Megillat Yeshayahu ha-Shelemah mi-Megillot Yam ha-Melaḥ* (1959), 462f.; S. Lieberman, *Hellenism in Jewish Palestine* (1950), 20–27, 83–99; idem (ed.), Maimonides, *Hilkhot ha-Yerushalmi* (1947), introd.; Y. Kafaḥ (ed.), Abraham b. David, *Ba'aleiha-Nefesh* (1965), introd.; Epstein, Mishnah (1948), 168ff., 201, 352, 424–595, 1269–75, 1284–90; E.S. Rosenthal; in: PAAJR, 31 (1963), 1–71 (Heb. pt.); idem, in: *Sefer Ḥ Yalon* (1963) 281–337; R.N.N. Rabbinovicz, *Ma'amar al Hadpasat ha-Talmud*, ed. by A.M. Habermann (1952); M. Kasher, in: *Gemara Shelemah*, Pesaḥim pt. 1 (1960), introd.; E.M. Lipschuetz, in: *Sefer Rashi* (1956), 190–3, 236; B. Benedikt, in: KS, 26 (1949/50), 322–38 (on *Haggahot* of R. Ephraim); S. Kohen, in: *Sinai*, 9–16 (1941–45), esp. 9 (1941), 265f., 12 (1943), 99–106 (on the *Mordekhai*); idem, *ibid.*, 11 (1942), 60f. (on *Haggahot Maimuniyyot*); Urbach, Tosafot, 436f. (on the *Mordekhai*), 437f. (on *Haggahot Maimuniyyot*), 439, 453ff. (on *Haggahot* of Perez of Corbeil), and index 590 s.v. *nusḥa'ot*: I. Nissim, in: *Sefunot*, 2 (1958), 89–102 (on *Haggahot* of J. Castro and J. Ẓemaḥ); idem, in: *Sinai-Sefer Yovel* (1958), 29–39 (on *Haggahot* of Isserles); A. Sier, *Ha-Rema* (1957), 59ff. (ditto); S. Assaf, in: *L. Ginzberg Jubilee Volume*, Heb. pt. (1946), 455–61 (on S. Luria's *Ḥokhmat Shelomo*); S.K. Mirsky, in: *Horeb*, 6 (1942), 51–55 (on Joel Sirkes' *Bayit Ḥadash*); J.H. Levin, *Aliyyot Eliyahu* (1963), 79ff. (on *Haggahot* of Elijah of Vilna); K. Kahana, in: *Ha-Ma'ayan*, 2 no. 1 (1955), 24–41 (ditto); S. Goren, in: J.L. Maimon (ed.), *Sefer ha-Gra*, 4 (1954), 45–107 (ditto); M. Vogelmann, *ibid.*, 108–10 (ditto); M. Benayahu, *Rabbi Ḥ.Y.D. Azulai* (Heb., 1959), 81ff. **ADD. BIBLIOGRAPHY:** E.Z. Melamed in: *Tarbiz*, 50 (1981), 107–27; Y.S. Spiegel in: *Avi'ad* (1986), 395–98; Y. Buxbaum, in: *Mori'ah*, 6:10–11 (1976), 19–25; M.Z. Fuchs in: *Sidra*, 15 (1999), 111–17; A. Berger in: *Zekhor le-Avraham* (1992) 83–91; idem, in: *ibid.* (1993), 118–137; D. Metzger in: *Mori'ah* 8:8–9 (1979) 14–28; S. Luria in: ibid. (1982) 10–11; S.E. Stern, in: *Esh Tamid* (1989), 173–177; Y.M. Peles, in: *Zekhor Le-Avraham* (1990) 19–25; A. Eisenbach in: *Zefunot*, 2:3 (1991) 22–26; D. Kaminetsky, in: *Yeshurun*, 4 (1999) 245–254; Z.M. Koren in: ibid. 4 (1999) 43–77; D.Z. Rotstein in: *Sefer ha-Zikaron Le-Rabbi Moshe Lipschitz* (1996) 355–460; D. Divlitsky in: *Zefunot* 1:1 (1989), 49–59; idem, in: *ibid.*, 1:2 (1989), 86–87; Y.M. Peles, in: *Yeshurun*, 9 (2001) 756–767; idem, in: *ibid.*, 13 (2003) 744–87; D. Heiman, in: *Mi-Peri ha-Aretz*, 4

(1991), 30–63; S.E. Stern, in: *Zefunot*, 1:3 (1989) 15–20; M. Benayahu, in: *Sinai*, 100:1 (1987) 135–42; *Mori'ah*, 9:11–12 (1980), 20–23, 24–27; *ibid.*, 17:11–12 (1991), 17–23; M. Lehman, in: *Sinai*, 85:1–2 (1979), 42–47; S. Bamberger, in: *Ha-Ma'ayan*, 24:1 (1984), 57–77; 24:2, 55–64; 24:3, 65–80; 24:4, 85–96, 25:1 (1985), 61–79; A. Mirsky in: *Sinai*, 102 (1988) 161–82; Y.Z., in: *Kiryat Sefer*, 52:1 (1977) 173–86; A. Grossman, in: *Tarbiz*, 60:1 (1993), 67–98; S. Zuker, in: *Mori'ah*, 20:3–4, 107–18; E. Siegal, in: *Alei Sefer*, 9 (1981), 130–139; Y. Katan, in: *Ha-Ma'ayan*, 37:3 (1997), 69–75; Y.H. Frankel in: *Ha-Gra u-Beit Midrasho* (2003), 29–61; S.Y. Friedman, in: *Rashi: Iyyunim li-Yeẓirato* (1993),147–5; Y. Avivi, in: *Mori'ah*, 13:1–2 (1984), 34–37; L. Fogel, in: *ibid.*, 23:6–9 (2000), 50–60; Y. Mondshein, in: *ibid.*, 21:5–6 (1997), 101–103.

[Shlomoh Zalman Havlin]

HAGGAHOT MAIMUNIYYOT, a comprehensive halakhic work which is one of the most important sources for the halakhic rulings of the scholars of Germany and France. The author, Meir ha-Kohen of Rothenburg (end of the 13th century), was the distinguished pupil of *Meir b. Baruch of Rothenburg. He compiled it as a supplement and notes (see **Haggahot*) to the *Mishneh Torah* of Maimonides, and its first part was published in the Constantinople edition of the *Mishneh Torah* (1509), and has appeared in all subsequent editions. Of it, Levi ibn Ḥabib writes (Responsa, ed. Lemberg No. 130): "If the author of the *Haggahot* is a small man in your eyes, he is great in the eyes of all Israel." It may originally have been written on the margins of the *Mishneh Torah*, as it appears in early manuscripts, and as seems to be the case from the passages to which the words "written in the margin" are appended. Of the 14 books of the *Mishneh Torah*, the only books to which there are no *Haggahot* are *Hafla'ah*, *Zera'im* (save for a fragment at its end), *Avodah*, *Korbanot*, and *Tohorah*. The chief aim of the author was to attach the rulings of the scholars of Germany and France to the work of Maimonides, whose decisions and conclusions are in the main based upon the traditions and rulings of the scholars of Spain. This aim was the result of the great preoccupation with Maimonides' work in the school of Meir of Rothenburg (who also compiled works connected with Maimonides – see Urbach, 434ff.), as well as the need felt to adapt the work of Maimonides, which was spreading more and more as a comprehensive halakhic work, for use also in Germany and France.

The work is divided into two sections, one of glosses and notes attached to the *Mishneh Torah*, and the other – also called *Teshuvot Maimuniyyot* (first published in the Venice ed. of 1524) – appended at the end of each book of the *Mishneh Torah* and containing responsa by German and French scholars relevant to the topics dealt with in the body of the work. It is difficult to determine whether this division is the work of the author himself or was the work of a later editor, although it is early and already appears in early manuscripts of the work. This division is not absolute, however, and in the section of glosses one can still find responsa which, apparently in view of their brevity and direct connection with the *halakhah* under discussion, were not given separately (for examples see Urbach, 436 n. 20). On the other hand, the section of responsa contains non-responsa material (*ibid.*, n. 21).

There are differences between the editions of 1509 and 1524, some of which are material. The wording of the glosses in the Venice edition (from which the later editions were printed) is more original and the author generally speaks in the first person, while the wording of the 1509 edition shows signs of being a later version, and has obviously passed through adaptation and abbreviation at the hands of a later editor. In many places in the 1509 edition the passages end with the words: "thus far the language of R.M.K." (= R. Meir ha-Kohen); the editor even comments on the words of Meir ha-Kohen (see Hilkhot Zekhiyyah u-Mattanah 11:19; "however may the All-Merciful pardon Meir ha-Kohen…"). Certain passages appear in the Constantinople version which are absent from the Venice version, and vice versa. The Constantinople edition contains additions that may have been added by the editor, most of them taken from the *Sefer Mitzvot Gadol* (*Semag*) of Moses of Coucy, the *Sefer Mitzvot Katan* (*Semak*) of Isaac of Corbeil, the *Sefer ha-Terumah* of Baruch b. Samuel of Mainz, the *Ha-Roke'aḥ* of Eleazar of Worms, the *Seder Olam* of Simḥah of Speyer, etc.

From Urbach's comparison of the two editions there can be no doubt about the identification of Meir ha-Kohen as the author of the glosses, nor is there any reason to assume that other authors participated in it, as was assumed by S. Cohen and J. Wellesz. The close connection between the sections of the book is also beyond doubt, and there is no need to assume that Meir ha-Kohen made use of a preexisting collection of responsa. The section of glosses (Venice edition) contains references in many places to the section of responsa (see the list in Wellesz, p. 52, to which many additions can be made). It is difficult to determine whether these references are the author's own or the editor's. They do not, however, seem to replace responsa included in the glosses of the original work, which when taken out were left as mere references (see, e.g., the *Haggahot* Sheluḥin ve-Shutafin, 5 no. 6). The section of responsa is on the books *Nashim* (37 items), *Kedushah* (27), *Hafla'ah* (7), *Nezikin* (22), *Kinyan* (40), *Mishpatim* (71), and *Shofetim* (20), and contains a valuable collection of the responsa of the author's teacher Meir of Rothenburg, which in some cases gives a reading of greater value than other sources, while others are unknown from any other source. Also cited in it are responsa by Jacob Tam, Isaac b. Samuel ha-Zaken, Samson of Sens (copied from the *Nimmukim* of his pupil Jacob of Courson, who collected them into a book – see Resp. to Ma'akhalot Asurot, no. 13), and his brother Isaac b. Abraham, Simḥah b. Samuel of Speyer, Baruch b. Samuel of Mainz, etc.

No biographical details of Meir ha-Kohen are known other than that he was the pupil of Meir of Rothenburg; Mordecai b. Hillel ha-Kohen was his colleague and, according to some, his brother-in-law and colleague (Ishut 9, no. 1); and he lived in Rothenburg (Responsa to Shofetim, no. 16, where the reading should be "here Rothenburg" and not "in it, in Rothenburg"; see *Sefer ha-Parnas* (1891), no. 269). He attended upon his teacher when the latter was imprisoned in Wasserburg (Shab. 6 n. 6) and later in the fortress of Ensisheim (to Tefillah 14:5, according to the Constantinople ed.), and there discussed halakhic matters with him. His teacher sent halakhic responsa to him (Sefer Torah 7 n. 7; Tefillah 15 n. 1; Ishut 3 n. 15). In one responsum (Resp. Maharam of Rothenburg, ed. Prague, no. 78) he addressed him thus: "the lips of the priest preserve decisive Torah opinion [cf. Mal. 2:7], my intimate associate R. Meir ha-Kohen."

The supplements and variants of the Constantinople edition, which is now rare, were published in the El ha-Mekorot edition of the *Mishneh Torah* (1954–56), and in the Po'alei Agudat Israel edition (1944) to the books *Madda* through *Nashim*. A substantial number of manuscripts are known (in Jerusalem, Oxford, British Museum, Cambridge, Sassoon, and other libraries), but they have not yet been investigated and examined. The attempt of Allony to fix the date of the writing of the Cambridge manuscript (13.1) of the *Mishneh Torah* as 1230 instead of 1170 is a mistake, for he did not notice that it contains the *Haggahot Maimuniyyot*. I.Z. Kahana, who began to issue a critical edition of the rulings and responsa of Meir of Rothenburg (vols. 1–3, 1957–63), drew a great deal from the *Haggahot Maimuniyyot*, utilizing four manuscripts of the work.

BIBLIOGRAPHY: Azulai, 2 (1852), 33 no. 23; Weiss, Dor, 5 (1904[4]), 77f.; S. Kohen, in: *Sinai*, 10 (1942), 10; Wellesz, in: *Ha-Goren*, 7 (1908), 35–59; N. Allony, in: *Aresheth*, 3 (1961), 410; Urbach, Tosafot, 434–6. **ADD. BIBLIOGRAPHY:** D. Divlitsky, in: *Zefunot*, 1:1 (1989), 49–59; Y.M. Peles, in: *Yeshurun*, 13 (2003), 744–87.

[Shlomoh Zalman Havlin]

HAGGAI (Heb. חַגַּי; "born on a festival"), prophet who lived in the post-Exilic period and whose book is the tenth in the Minor Prophets. The book of Haggai and chapters 1–8 of Zechariah appear to be part of the same redactional effort. Considering the small size of Haggai, there are numerous differences between the received Hebrew text and the Septuagint. Haggai's extant prophecies, never narrated in the first person, consist altogether of 38 verses, dating from the second year of the reign of Darius I, king of Persia, i.e., 520 B.C.E., between the first of Elul and the 24th of Kislev. It appears, however, that the prophet was previously well-known to the people and that his words carried weight (1:12). He is referred to (Hag. 1:13) as *malak* YHWH, often used of non-human messengers of YHWH. The author of Ezra-Nehemiah notes the important role he played in the rebuilding of the Temple (Ezra 5:1; 6:14).

His prophecies deal mainly with the construction of the Temple, and with the great events that the nation will experience in the future as a result. Haggai turns first to *Zerubbabel, son of Shealtiel, governor of Judah, and to Joshua, son of Jehozadak, the high priest (1:1–2), and then to the people (1:3–11), encouraging them not to postpone the construction of the Temple, but to begin immediately. He claimed that all the mishaps of poverty, famine, and drought which befell the nation were caused by the delay in the work. The people listened to Haggai's words despite their fears (1:13) and, led by Zerubbabel and Joshua, they began work on the temple. Although the new temple seemed poor in their eyes (2:3) Haggai assured the people that the second temple would be more richly adorned than the first temple (2:7–9; see below).

Three months later, on the 24th of Kislev (2:10–19), when the Temple's foundations were laid, Haggai proclaimed two new prophecies. He turned to the priests to seek guidance from them (cf. Jer. 18:18 "instruction from the priest"). He asked what the law is concerning a man who carries hallowed meat in the skirt of his garment which touches any food. They replied that the food does not become holy, but if a man made unclean by a dead body touches the food, the food does become unclean. From the fact that holiness is far less contagious than impurity, Haggai deduces that the achievement of holiness demands hard work: as long as the Temple was not built, despite the fact that sacrifices were being offered on the altar, the people were unclean. Only when the Temple is rebuilt will the Lord's blessing (Hag. 2:19) return. That very day (2:20ff.) the prophet uttered an oracle about Zerubbabel. He announced that God was about to shake the heavens and earth and overthrow the "throne of kingdoms and destroy the strength of the nations, overthrow the chariot and those who ride in it. The horses and their riders will come down, everyone by the sword of his brother" (Hag. 3:22). Haggai's words probably reflect the great disturbances that shook the Persian Empire in 522–21 until Darius I took full control as successor to Cambyses. As for Zerubabel, says Haggai, his time will come. Whereas Jeremiah had prophesied about Jehoiakim (22:24), "though Coniah the son of Jehoiakim king of Judah were the signet ring on My right hand, yet I would pluck thee thence," Haggai turned the curse into a blessing for his grandson Zerubbabel: "I will take you… and make you like a signet ring" (2:23). With Talshir, it is probably inaccurate to regard this vision as messianic in any utopian sense. It is rather about the restoration of the earthly Davidic monarchy and the rebuilding of the Jerusalem temple, for both of which there were still living eyewitnesses (Hag. 2:3). Haggai agrees with Isaiah 60:5 that "the wealth (*ḥayil*) of nations" will come to the temple (Hag. 2:7–9; the terms *ḥayil*, *kavod* and *ḥemdah* all mean "wealth"). But in contrast to Isaiah 60 and Zechariah 8:20–23, the nations themselves will not come to the Jewish temple. Israel's earthly kingdom will be renewed, the second temple will be richer than the first, but the gentiles will not be converted. The language of the book is difficult to classify as either prose or poetry (see e.g. 1:5–11; 2:6–9, 21–23). It is apparent that Haggai had recourse to earlier writings that would become "biblical." The prophet uses phrases from the Torah (cf. Haggai 2:5 with Ex. 24:8; Haggai 2:12 with Lev. 6:20; etc.). He alludes to Jeremiah's words (Jer. 22:24) which he reinterprets; and to the prophecies of Ezekiel (Ezek. 37:27) about the holy spirit resting upon the new Temple. He is similar to Zechariah, his contemporary, with regard to the greatness of Zerubbabel (*ibid.*, 3:8). The prophecies of Haggai were probably assembled not long after they were delivered. Fragments of Haggai are found in the *tere asar* (book of the 12 minor prophets) scroll written probably in the second century C.E. and unearthed in cave 5 at Wadi Murabbat. Probably encouraged by Haggai's legal questions to the priests (Hag. 2:12–13), rabbinic tradition credited Haggai with halakhic (legal) decisions (Yev. 16a; Kid. 43a). The sages (BB 15a) attributed the editing of the book to the elders of the Great Assembly.

BIBLIOGRAPHY: GENERAL: Ackroyd, in: JJS, 2 (1951), 163–76; 3 (1952), 1–13, 151–6; idem, in: JNES, 17 (1958), 13–27; Bentzen, in: RHPR, 10 (1930), 493–503; H.W. Wolff, *Haggai* (1951); K. Galling, *Studien zur Geschichte Israels im persischen Zeitalter* (1964); Hess, in: *Rudolph Festschrift* (1961), 109–34; Kaufmann, Y., Toledot, 4 (1956), 215, 225. SPECIAL STUDIES: Bloomhardt, in: HUCA, 5 (1928), 153–95; Budde, in: ZAW, 26 (1906), 1–28; James, in: JBL, 53 (1934), 229–35; Kittel, Gesch, 3 pt. 2 (1929), 441–57; Noth, in: ZAW, 68 (1956), 25–46; Siebeneck, in: CBQ, 19 (1957), 312–28; Waterman, in: JNES, 13 (1954), 73–78; J.W. Rothstein, *Juden und Samaritaner* (1908). **ADD. BIBLIOGRAPHY:** D. Petersen, *Haggai and Zechariah 1–8* (1984); C. Meyers and E. Meyers, *Haggai, Zechariah 1–8* (1990); idem, in: ABD, 3:20–23; Z. Talshir, *Enẓiklopedyah Olam ha-Tanakh*, vol.15b (1993), 138–66; R. Albertz, in: R. Albertz and B. Becking (eds.), *Yahwism after the Exile* (2003), 1–17.

[Yehoshua M. Grintz / S. David Sperling (2nd ed.)]

HAGGAI (or **Ḥagga**; fl. c. 300 C.E.), Palestinian *amora*. Probably born in Babylon (TJ, Or 3:1, 63a; TJ, Av. Zar. 3:14, 43c), he went to Palestine, where after initial difficulties (Av. Zar. 68a) he became a prominent member of the academy of Tiberias and one of the principal pupils of *Zeira whom he often accompanied (TJ, Dem. 3:2, 23b) and in whose name he transmitted sayings (TJ, Kid. 3:2, 63d). In a dispute with *Ḥanina in a case of marital law, Haggai was praised by R. Hilla as a scholar of sound judgment (*ibid.*). Because of his important position in the academy he opened each study session while *Yose and Jonah closed them (TJ, RH 2:6, 58b). Haggai was also the pupil (according to Frankel, *Mevo ha-Yerushalmi*, 79b–80b, the associate) of Yose (BB 19b; TJ, Pes. 4:3, 31a; TJ, Kid. 3:3, 64a; see TJ, Shab. 1:5, 4a, where Yose calls him "rabbi"; cf. TJ, RH 2:6, 58b). In a case brought before *Aḥa he supported the view of his teacher Yose by an oath "By Moses," a formula often employed by him (TJ, Naz. 5:1, 54a; TJ, 4:3, 24a, etc.). Like Yose he held the view that the reason for the interdiction against looking at the kohanim while they are reciting the Priestly Benedictions is because it may distract them from proper concentration (TJ, Ta'an. 4:1, 67b).

His close pupil and associate was *Mana, the head of the academy in Sepphoris, who participated in Haggai's scholarly discussions (*ibid.*). Once Mana visited his sick teacher on the Day of Atonement and gave him permission to drink, but Haggai declined to avail himself of it (TJ, Yoma 6:4, 43d). His daughter was involved in lawsuits because she squandered her property (TJ, BB 10:15, 17d). His son Eleazar was a pupil of Mana's academy in Sepphoris (TJ, Shek. 7:3, 50c). Haggai appears to have lived for a while in Tyre (TJ, Ket. 2:6, 4a) and some sources hint at the fact that he migrated to Babylonia in the days of *Abbaye and *Rabbah since he is quoted in the Babylonian Talmud as having had discussions with them (e.g., BM 113b but see Dik. Sof. BM 169b, n. 100). The Haggai who ordered Jacob of Kefar Nibburaya to be punished by flagellation for falsely interpreting Scripture to the effect that fish must be slaughtered in the same way as animals and that the son of a gentile mother may be circumcised on the Sabbath is probably this Haggai and not *Haggai of Sepphoris.

BIBLIOGRAPHY: Bacher, Pal Amor, 3; Hyman, Toledot, s.v.; J.L. Maimon, *Yiḥusei Tanna'im ve-Amora'im* (1963), 229–30; Ḥ. Albeck, *Mavo la-Talmudim* (1969), 323–5.

HAGGAI OF SEPPHORIS (third century C.E.), Palestinian *amora*. Born in Babylonia, one of the principle pupils of *Huna (the exilarch), he emigrated to Palestine where he joined the pupils of R. *Johanan. There is considerable confusion between him and another *amora* of the same name (see preceding entry). In fact, most authorities, including the classical ones (*Yiḥusei Tanna'im ve-Amora'im*, s.v. *Haggai*), do not distinguish between the two. Even accepting that there were two distinct men called Haggai (and there were more, see Albeck, *Mavo la-Talmudim*, 391), it remains difficult to determine which events recorded apply to the one and which to the other. Haggai transmitted halakhic rules in the names of Abba b. Avda, Abbahu, Isaac, Johanan b. Lakhish, Joshua b. Levi, Samuel b. Naḥamani, etc. When the coffin of his teacher Huna (probably the exilarch mentioned above, see Tos. to MK 25a; and TJ, Kil. 9:4, 32b–c) was brought (in 297 C.E.) to Palestine to be placed in a cave (sepulcher) at the side of *Ḥiyya's remains, Haggai was chosen to place his teacher's coffin there, a special honor and privilege (MK 25a). According to another version (TJ, Ket. 12:3, 35a) he was at that time an old man of over 80 and people suspected that he wished to enter the cave only to die at that chosen spot. Thus he asked that a rope be attached to his feet so that he might be pulled out from the cave after the burial of Huna.

In *Genesis Rabbah* (9:3) he quotes, in R. Isaac's name, an interpretation of I Chronicles 28:9 to teach that "even before thought is born in a man's heart, it is already revealed to God." Further (Gen. R. 60:2), based upon Genesis 24:12, he states that everybody needs God's grace, since even Abraham, in whose merit favor is granted to the whole world, was in need of divine grace for the success of the choice of a bride for Isaac. It is stated that when he appointed officials (*parnasim*) he handed them a Torah scroll to symbolize that authority comes only from the Law, as it is written, "By me kings reign… by me princes rule" (Prov. 8:15–16).

BIBLIOGRAPHY: Bacher, Pal Amor; Hyman, Toledot, s.v.; J.L. Maimon, *Yiḥusei Tanna'im ve-Amora'im* (1963), 229–30; Ḥ. Albeck, *Mavo la-Talmudim* (1969), 287.

ḤAGIGAH (Heb. חֲגִיגָה); the last tractate – according to the customary arrangement – of the order **Mo'ed* in the Mishnah, Tosefta, and the Babylonian and Jerusalem Talmuds. It is also called *Re'iyyah* (so in the Zuckermandel edition of the Tosefta). The Mishnah contains three chapters. Chapters

1:1–2:4 deal with the laws of peace-offerings which were offered during the festivals (hence the name of the tractate) and with kindred subjects such as the duty of *pilgrimage (*re'iyyah*, "appearance," hence the alternative name of the tractate), and the laws of sacrifices during the festival in general. From 2:5 until the end of the tractate it deals with the laws of ritual purity and impurity connected with sacred objects and the Temple. The *mishnayot* 1:8–2:1 are entirely different from the rest of the tractate and have a character of their own. Nachman *Krochmal suggested that the original tractate *Ḥagigah* may have commenced with these two *mishnayot* (cf. Epstein, Tannaim, 46–47), which are a kind of introduction to the different categories of *halakhah* (which include laws of *Ḥagigah*) whose purpose is to emphasize the relationship of the Midrash to the *halakhah* and the tendency to depart from the previous method of deriving *halakhot* from direct exposition of Scripture (see *Midreshei Halakhah*). Chapter 1:7 is an addition from the Tosefta (Epstein, Tannaim, 48). Mishnah *Ḥagigah* preserves many traditions deriving from the Temple period and most of the scholars mentioned in it belong to that period. The Tosefta similarly contains three chapters and deals with similar themes, and the same applies to the two Talmuds. The Tosefta contains a series of aggadic traditions (2: 1–7) – including the famous story of the four "who entered *pardes*" – which expand upon the *ma'aseh bereshit* and Merkabah themes already mentioned in the Mishnah (2:1). These themes are further expanded and elaborated in the Babylonian (Ḥag. 11b–16a) and Jerusalem Talmuds (TJ Ḥag. 2:1, 77a–77d). This material, which forms a continuous and self-contained "mystical midrash" (cf. Weiss, Literary, 260–261), provided the foundation for much of the later literature of the *Merkabah mysticism, and the four "who entered paradise" (TJ, Ḥag. 2:1; Ḥag. 13b–15a) and even the medieval Kabbalah. *Ḥagigah* is currently available in various translations and editions.

BIBLIOGRAPHY: Ḥ. Albeck, *Shishah Sidrei Mishnah* 2 (1958), 387–90; Epstein, Tanna'im, 46–52; (1952), 75; E.E. Urbach, in: *Beḥinot*, 3 (1952), 75. **ADD. BIBLIOGRAPHY:** A. Weiss, *On the Literary Creation of the Amoraim* (Hebrew; 1962), 260–261.

[Stephen G. Wald (2nd ed.)]

HAGIOGRAPHY. Although hagiographies, embellished accounts of biblical worthies, are not unknown in previous ages, particularly in the apocrypha (e.g., Lives of the *Prophets and Martyrdom of *Isaiah), in the Middle Ages they developed as a specific genre of literature, of which they constitute a major type (see *Fiction, Hebrew). These may be divided into two main categories according to the protagonist portrayed: (a) hagiographies whose heroes are ancient Jewish sages and martyrs (biblical and talmudic characters); (b) hagiographies whose heroes are medieval scholars, rabbis, and martyrs.

Different fields of medieval literature have adapted the hagiography to their specific needs. Ethical literature used it to exhort in the footsteps of the hero (see *Exemplum); Hebrew historical writings usually substituted the hagiography for the biography of medieval and ancient Jewish scholars. Medieval collections of Hebrew stories abound with hagiographic material; while in kabbalistic and ḥasidic literature, the hagiography was a formal literary device to convince the reader of the veracity of the Jewish mystics' visions.

Use of Biblical and Talmudic Material

Biblical and talmudic stories were freely adapted. In *Midrash Va-Yissa'u* (in A. Jellinek, *Beit ha-Midrash*, 3 (1938²), 1–5), a narrative about Jacob and his sons, the characters are portrayed as medieval knights who fight over Shechem and other cities, in the same way as the Crusaders had fought in the capture of a city. Abraham and Moses were also subjects of individual works, embellished by hagiographic additions. So were the lives of talmudic sages; the medieval Midrash *Pirkei Rabbi Eliezer*, for instance, opens with a hagiographic account of *Eliezer b. Hyrkanus. One of the most typical examples of medieval hagiography is the story of the *Ten Martyrs, known also as *Midrash Elleh Ezkerah* (ed. by A. Jellinek, 1853). Some of the material is drawn from talmudic sources, but most of its treatment is within the framework of medieval themes and literary conventions. It is an account of the tortures inflicted by the Romans on 10 martyrs, most of them *tannaim* (the 10 martyrs had not been contemporaries and could not have been executed together); the story also inspired the composition of prayers and *piyyutim*, and became the cornerstone of Hebrew medieval martyrologic hagiography.

Use of Contemporary Stories and Personages

Hagiography of the Middle Ages which centered around medieval characters contains historical and biographical details, as well as fiction. Some of the legends included are entirely original, while others thematically belong to international hagiographic motifs. The miracle associated with Rashi when still in his mother's womb (that a wall opened to let his pregnant mother hide from a group of soldiers) is told about many other sages, and has nothing whatsoever to do with Rashi's personality or biography. Sometimes the heroes of such legends are purely fictional, and the hagiography thus is not even related to a historical personality.

The development of the hagiography in the Middle Ages is perhaps best exemplified by the evolvement of cycles of hagiographies centered around the leaders of the Ḥasidei Askhenaz: *Samuel he-Ḥasid, R. *Judah he-Ḥasid, his son, and *Eleazar ben Judah of Worms. The earliest known versions were found (in manuscript) and published by N. *Bruell (*Jahrbuecher fuer Juedische Geschichte und Literatur*, 9 (1889), 1–71). Different versions are extant in many later Hebrew and Yiddish collections. There are no hagiographies about these rabbis from their own time (12th and 13th centuries); the stories begin to appear in the 14th and 15th centuries. However, many of the hagiographies from these cycles point to the fact that the elaborate narrative about one of these rabbis sprang from a much simpler story that was told and written by that writer himself. In the simple narrative, the hero's name is not mentioned nor did he see himself as the hero. In one of his theological works, R. Judah he-Ḥasid has a five-line story about a rabbi who miraculously discovered some clothes that had been stolen from one of his pupils. A hagiography written in the 15th century, about R. Judah, contains a long and well-developed legend about the rabbi's discovery of a treasure which had been entrusted to a Jew and stolen from him, thus endangering the lives of a whole Jewish community. The core of the narrative is the same, but the plot was elaborated upon, many details were added, and the anonymous hero became R. Judah he-Ḥasid himself. Short descriptions, such as the one by R. Judah he-Ḥasid in Ḥasidei Ashkenaz literature of sorcerers and demons, were later expanded into hagiographies describing contests between the pietist sages and gentile sorcerers in the working of miracles and sorcery. While these early theological works receded into oblivion, the stories to which they gave birth survived and evolved into the fully developed genre of hagiography.

IBN EZRA AND OTHER SPANISH JEWISH SCHOLARS. One of the most prominent heroes of medieval Hebrew hagiography was R. Abraham *Ibn Ezra. Nothing in his actual biography justifies the stories told about him, except that he was a traveler, and visited many countries in the East and in the West. Abraham ibn Ezra became the "traveling hero" of a cycle of hagiographic legends. Disguised so that nobody would recognize him, in a dramatic moment he would reveal his true identity. In these tales, Ibn Ezra pokes fun at proud rich men, helps Jews in danger, and is the hero of both popular jokes and tragic legends. Ibn Ezra was a hero of fiction up to modern times, and in the 19th century, stories describing his miraculous adventures were still being printed.

Other Spanish Jewish scholars also became central figures of hagiographies. The beginnings of the Jewish center of learning in Spain were described by Abraham *Ibn Daud in his *Seder ha-Kabbalah* by means of the hagiographical story "The Four Captives." *Judah Halevi's pilgrimage to Jerusalem was the focus of a cycle of hagiographical stories; and this most rationalistic of Spanish Jewish scholars did not escape legends which told about his later adherence to the Kabbalah.

MARTYROLOGIC HAGIOGRAPHY. The martyrologic hagiography developed especially in Germany during the Crusades of the 11th–13th centuries. Thousands of Jewish martyrs became subjects of legends. The best known revolves about R. *Amnon, the alleged author of the prayer *U-Netanneh Tokef. Many other martyrs were described in a similar hagiographic manner in collections of historical writings and stories.

HAGIOGRAPHY AND KABBALAH. The most powerful creative force of Jewish hagiography in the Middle Ages was the Kabbalah. Kabbalists of the 12th and 13th centuries told legends about their teachers and mystical mentors. The first kabbalistic scholar in Provence, head of a school of kabbalists, Rabbi *Isaac Sagi Nahor ("the blind"), was described by his disciples as capable of distinguishing between a "new" and an "old" soul, i.e., between persons whose souls had entered the human form for the first time and souls that had transmigrated from previous existences (see *Gilgul*). In Spain, there were kabbalists who wove wonderful tales about the mystics of Germany. R. Isaac ha-Kohen of Segovia (the second half of the 13th century) told about the powers of Eleazar of Worms who, according to him, traveled on a cloud whenever he had an urgent trip to make.

THE ZOHAR AND LATER KABBALISTIC WRITINGS. The Zohar is full of hagiographic references to R. *Simeon b. Yoḥai, his son *Eleazar, and his disciples. Their wondrous deeds are incorporated into the homiletics that make up the whole work. When R. Simeon b. Yoḥai studied, for example, birds stopped flying all around, fire encircled him, and wonderful events happened to people in his vicinity. Among the many miracles attributed to him and his disciples by the author of the Zohar, some are founded solely on myth, e.g., the legends about his contradicting God's will and his prevalence, or his fight with the powers of darkness, the *Sitra Aḥra* ("The Other Side," i.e., Satan). The Zohar influenced later kabbalistic writings in which the same approach toward the mystics is adopted. Two anonymous 14th-century Spanish works, *Sefer ha-Kaneh* (Prague, 1610) and *Sefer ha-Peli'ah* (Korets, 1784), have for their central characters members of the family of the *tanna* R. *Neḥuna b. ha-Kaneh. A whole set of hagiographical stories is woven around each member of the family. Many of these stories describe a meeting of the heroes with heavenly powers.

The deterioration of the situation of the Jews in Spain (at the end of the 14th and during the 15th century) gave birth to a new kind of hagiography, also associated with the Kabbalah: stories about sages who had attempted to hasten the redemption in one way or the other. Some of these include much historical data, like the stories about the martyr Solomon *Molcho; others are purely fictional, like the story about *Joseph Della Reina, who almost succeeded in overcoming and enslaving Satan and *Lilith, but at the last moment, failed and became enslaved by them instead. From this period onward, Jewish hagiography is mostly concerned with messianic expectations and activity.

ISAAC LURIA AND OTHER SAGES OF SAFED. The hagiographic cycle of stories about Isaac *Luria, who lived in Safed in the years 1570–72, were the first to be compiled into a book. His disciples preserved and wrote legends describing his superhuman powers. There are two main versions of the cycle of stories about him: *Shivḥei ha-Ari*, a collection of letters written by R. Solomon Shlumil of Dreznitz, who described not only Luria, but other sages in Safed, and a later work, *Toledot ha-Ari which was dedicated to Luria almost exclusively. It includes more than 50 stories. Some of them describe mostly his supernatural knowledge, his ability to know the past and the future, what was happening at great distances and in heaven, and his power to read the thoughts and the hearts of other people. The other stories, which seem to be later additions to the original cycle, describe miracles which he was said to have performed. Even when taking into consideration these later additions, the dominant hagiographic motif in these cycles is the supernatural knowledge of Luria, and not the miracles he performed. Luria's greatest pupil, R. Ḥayyim *Vital, unlike his teacher, did not leave it to later generations to write and to compile the hagiographic stories about him. He did it himself. He kept a diary which was published under the title *Sefer ha-Ḥezyonot* (1866) and previously, in a shorter version, as *Shivḥei Rav Ḥayyim Vital* (1826). Like his teacher Luria, Vital also had messianic aspirations. Basing himself on the conjurations of witches, sorcerers, his own visionary dreams and his teacher's sayings, he saw himself destined for great deeds. Luria and Vital are also connected with the first famous version of "The Dibbuk" story (told in different versions in *Sefer ha-Ḥezyonot* and in *Shivḥei Rav Ḥayyim Vital*). The theme of the **dibbuk* later became one of the standard motifs in Jewish hagiography: the ability to drive out evil powers or strange souls which had taken hold of a human body.

The stories about the great sages of Safed spread throughout the Jewish world. Their development varied in form and according to geographic locales. In the east, hagiographic cycles had for their central figures especially R. Ḥayyim Joseph David *Azulai and R. Ḥayyim b. Moses *Attar; in the west and in Eastern Europe R. *Judah b. Bezalel Loew and R. Joel Ba'al Shem became the heroes of such legends. In the 18th and 19th centuries up to the beginning of the 20th century hagiographic stories about sages of later ages (after Luria) were still being collected and published.

Modern Jewish Hagiography

Modern Jewish hagiography is connected with the ḥasidic movement which began in Eastern Europe in the second half of the 18th century. With the publication of *Shivḥei ha-Besht* (Berdichev, 1815) the genre was brought to its highest artistic expression. The book is a compilation of hagiographic stories about the founder of the ḥasidic movement and his disciples, collected from manuscripts. The stories, written both in Hebrew and in Yiddish (since the 16th century, Yiddish being the main medium of expression for hagiographic stories in Eastern Europe), had circulated among the Ḥasidim since the *Baal Shem Tov's death in 1760.

Later ḥasidic leaders and their followers used the *Shivḥei ha-Besht* as a model for the writing of hagiographic stories about later ḥasidic sages. Consequently, there are hagiographic collections about almost every major ḥasidic rabbi, even those who lived in the early 20th century. The stories in these compilations are often about several sages and may be arranged according to a main theme, e.g., *The Revelation of the Ẓaddikim*, a collection of stories about the ways in which the greatness of the ḥasidic sages was revealed (see, e.g., S. Gavriel, *Hitgallut ha-Ẓaddikim* (1905)).

Side by side with the development of ḥasidic hagiography, another kind of hagiography came into being. These were hagiographies about the **Lamed-Vav Ẓaddikim*, the thirty-six anonymous and mysterious holy men, because of whose humble manner, just deeds, and virtue the world continues to exist. Many of the motifs of this cycle of legends are taken from older tales and hagiographies. Together with the ḥasidic stories, they take Hebrew hagiography into the 20th century.

BIBLIOGRAPHY: J. Meitlis, *Das Ma'assebuch* (1933); idem, in: *Di Goldene Keyt*, 23 (1955), 218–234; G. Scholem, in: *Tarbiz*, 6 (1935), no. 2, 90–98; idem, *Judaica* (Ger., 1963), 216–25; *Mishnat ha-Zohar*, ed. by F. Lachover and J. Tishby, 1 (19572), introd.

[Joseph Dan]

ḤAGIZ, family of Spanish origin which immigrated to Morocco after the expulsion decrees of 1492, and settled in Fez, where some of its representatives were at the head of the Castilian community of *Megorashim* ("the exiled"). ABRAHAM ḤAGIZ (I) (d. before 1563) arrived in Fez with the Spanish exiles when still very young. He was brought up and educated there and is the signatory of a *takkanah* of 1545. SAMUEL ḤAGIZ (I) (d. c. 1570) was probably the younger brother of Abraham; his grandson, Samuel Ḥagiz (II), in his *Mevakkesh ha-Shem* mentions some of his grandfather's biblical commentaries and credits him with directing an important yeshivah, as is also confirmed by his disciple, Samuel b. Saadiah ibn Danan. In the *takkanot* of Fez, Samuel's signature is almost always found together with those of the other Castilian rabbis and it also appears on ordinances and decisions of the years 1545, 1559, and 1568. JACOB ḤAGIZ (d. 1634), a signatory of the Castilian *takkanot* of Fez between 1588 and 1608 (cf. *Kerem Ḥemed*; s.v. *Malkhei Rabbanan*), is probably the son of Samuel Ḥagiz (I) and not the grandfather of Jacob *Ḥagiz, the author of *Halakhot Ketannot*. There is a controversy about this relationship which has not been resolved (J. Ben-Naim in his *Malkhei Rabbanan* completely confuses the two). SAMUEL ḤAGIZ (II) left Fez, his birthplace, about 1590, remained for some time in Tripoli, North Africa, then traveled to Venice where, in 1597, he published *Mevakkesh ha-Shem*, sermons on the Pentateuch, and *Devar Shemu'el*, a homiletic commentary on Deuteronomy. He then immigrated to Ereẓ Israel and settled in Jerusalem. ABRAHAM ḤAGIZ (II), signatory of decisions in Fez dated 1638, 1640, and 1647, remained in Morocco after the departure of Samuel (II), probably his older brother. Members of the family also settled in Ereẓ Israel.

BIBLIOGRAPHY: J. Ben-Naim, *Malkhei Rabbanan* (1931), 10b, 16b, 65b, 72a, 123a; J.M. Toledano, *Ner ha-Ma'arav* (1911), 80, 83, 102–4, 110, 134.

[Haim Zafrani]

ḤAGIZ, JACOB (Israel; 1620–1674), Jerusalem scholar. He was the son of Samuel Ḥagiz, who was rabbi of Fez, and son-in-law of Moses *Galante. During his youth he resided in various communities in Italy. In 1658 he emigrated to Jerusalem, where he headed a yeshivah founded and maintained by the Vega brothers of Leghorn, in which secular subjects and Spanish were also studied. Jacob himself, in addition to his Torah study, occupied himself with philosophy, astronomy, medicine, and grammar. He instituted several **takkanot* in Jerusalem, mainly in the field of divorce procedure. In contrast to his father-in-law, Jacob was a vehement opponent of *Shabbetai Ẓevi from the beginning, being one of the first to regard him as a false messiah, and he was one of those who excommunicated him in 1665. In 1673, he went to Constantinople, in order to publish his *Leḥem ha-Panim* but died before achieving this.

He was also the author of *Eẓ ha-Ḥayyim*, a commentary to the Mishnah (*Mishnayot*, Leghorn, 1652–56); *Halakhot Ketannot* (Venice, 1704), responsa; *Teḥillat Ḥokhmah*, a talmudic methodology, published with the *Sefer Keritot* of *Samson of Chinon (Verona, 1647); *Ein Yisrael*, an adapted edition of the *Ein Ya'akov* of Jacob ibn Habib with the additions of Leone Modena (Verona, 1645); *Petil Tekhelet* (Venice, 1652) a commentary on the *azharot* of Solomon ibn Gabirol; *Dinei Birkat ha-Shaḥar, Keri'at Shema u-Tefillah*, laws of the morning blessings, of the reading of the *shema* and of the *amidah* (Verona, 1648); *Almenara de la Luz* (Leghorn, 1656), a Spanish translation of the *Menorat ha-Ma'or* of Isaac *Aboab.

BIBLIOGRAPHY: Scholem, Shabbetai Ẓevi, index; M. Benayahu, in: HUCA, 21 (1948), 1–28 (Heb. sect.); idem, in: *Sinai*, 34 (1954), 172ff.; Frumkin-Rivlin, 2 (1928), 61–64.

[David Tamar]

ḤAGIZ, MOSES (1672–c. 1751), scholar, kabbalist, and opponent of Shabbateanism; son of Jacob *Ḥagiz. He was born in Jerusalem and studied with his grandfather, Moses *Galante. He appears to have quarreled in his youth with the rabbis and lay leaders of Jerusalem, for when in 1694 he left Ereẓ Israel to collect money to found a yeshivah in Jerusalem, damaging letters were sent after him to the communities to which he turned. Moses visited Egypt and then Italy, where in 1704 he published his father's *Halakhot Ketannot*. He traveled by way of Prague to Amsterdam where he made contact with Ẓevi Hirsch *Ashkenazi, then rabbi of the Ashkenazi community, and collaborated with him in an energetic struggle against Shabbateanism and its secret adherents. When in 1713 Ashkenazi and Moses refused to retract the excommunication of the Shabbatean Nehemiah *Ḥayon, a fierce quarrel broke out between them and the elders of the Portuguese community. In 1714 when Ashkenazi resigned his rabbinical office and left Amsterdam, Moses was compelled to leave with him. He went first to London with Ashkenazi, there continuing the fight against Ḥayon and his allies, and then to Altona, home of Jacob *Emden, Ashkenazi's son, where he resumed the struggle against Shabbateanism. Among those he attacked were Michael Abraham *Cardoso and even Jonathan *Eybeschuetz, and he took the offensive against Moses Ḥayyim *Luzzatto, inducing the rabbis of Venice to excommunicate him. In 1738 Moses returned to Ereẓ Israel and settled in Safed. He died in Beirut and was taken to Sidon for burial.

A talmudic scholar of the first rank and a prolific writer, Moses was assisted by a good grounding in secular knowledge and by a command of several foreign languages. In Altona he was friendly with Johann Christopher *Wolf, who mentions him in his *Bibliotheca Hebraica*.

His works include *Leket ha-Kemaḥ*, novellae on the Shulḥan Arukh, *Oraḥ Ḥayyim* and *Yoreh De'ah* (Amsterdam, 1697), and *Even ha-Ezer* (Hamburg, 1711); responsa *Shetei ha-Leḥem* (Wandsbeck, 1733); the ethical treatises *Ẓerror ha-Ḥayyim* and *Mishnat Ḥakhamim* (*ibid.*, 1728–31 and 1733 respectively); *Elleh ha-Mitzvot* (Amsterdam, 1713), on the numeration of precepts in Maimonides' *Sefer ha-Mitzvot*, on the Oral Law, and on Kabbalah; *Sefat Emet* (Amsterdam, 1697); and *Parashat Elleh Masei* (Altona, 1738), on the sanctity of the land of Israel. His literary activity also included the editing of many early books.

BIBLIOGRAPHY: Scholem, Shabbetai Ẓevi, index; M. Benayahu, in: HUCA, 21 (1948), 1–28 (Heb. sect.); Frumkin-Rivlin, 2 (1928), 124–34; A.M. Luncz, in: *Yerushalayim*, 1 (1882), 119f.; M.D. Gaon, *Yehudei ha-Mizraḥ be-Ereẓ Yisrael*, 2 (1938), 243–5; Yaari, Sheluḥei, 363–71; Y. Nadav, in: *Sefunot*, 3–4 (1960), 303, 307–10, 326; M. Friedmann, *ibid.*, 10 (1966), 483–619, passim.

[David Tamar]

HA-GOSHERIM (Heb. הַגּוֹשְׁרִים), kibbutz in the Ḥuleh Valley, Israel, affiliated with Ha-Kibbutz ha-Me'uḥad, first founded in 1943 as a Ha-Po'el ha-Mizrachi moshav called Neḥalim, the fourth of the "Ussishkin Fortresses" (see *Stockade and Watchtower). It was taken over in the summer of 1948 by the present group, whose nucleus is composed of settlers from Turkey. The settlers of Neḥalim meanwhile established themselves at the former *Templer colony of Wilhelma near Lydda. The 1951–52 split in Ha-Kibbutz ha-Me'uḥad brought new settlers – veteran members of *Kefar Giladi and other kibbutzim – to Ha-Gosherim in order to remain within their movement's framework. The kibbutz developed intensive farming (fruit plantations, field crops, and poultry) and operated a guest house. In the late 1980s it developed a depilatory device for women called Soft and Easy (later marketed as Epilady), selling over 25 million throughout the world, but the local company subsequently ran into financial difficulties and passed into private hands. Ha-Gosherim's population was 412 in 1968 and 526 in 2002. It is located near the Ḥurshat Tal Nature Reserve with its giant Tabor oaks, lawns, and pools fed by the Dan River. Ha-Gosherim, meaning "Bridge Builders," refers to the local topography – the Jordan headstreams, Iyyon (*Ijon), Senir, and Dan, spanned by a number of bridges.

WEBSITE: www.hagoshrim.org.il.

[Efraim Orni / Shaked Gilboa (2nd ed.)]

HAGOZER, JACOB and **GERSHOM** (first half of the 13th century), father and son, *mohalim* (practitioners of circumcision, hence the name *Gozer*, a synonym for *mohel*) in Germany. Little is known of Jacob except that he composed a book on the laws of circumcision which served as the basis for a more comprehensive work on the same subject by Gershom, who also made use of the work of his uncle *Jacob b. Yakar of Worms. Gershom's works covered every aspect of the subject. Large sections from it were copied word for word and incorporated into two works by two anonymous *mohalim*. All that is known of the author of the first is that he was a nephew of *Ephraim of *Bonn and that he knew Jacob personally, received oral traditions from him, and quoted his customs and conduct. This author added many aggadic passages in praise of the precept of circumcision and its virtues, many local customs and medical details concerning circumcision, and various sermons delivered at such ceremonies. The book is of considerable value for its picture of the life of the Jews of Germany at that time and also contains important quotations from earlier literature for which there is no other source.

This *mohel*, like Gershom, introduced hygienic improvements into the circumcision ceremony and brought about the abolition of many unsound practices of ultra-conservative *mohalim*. The author of the second work was a pupil of *Eliezer b. Joel ha-Levi, himself a *mohel*, and quotes him and Gershom freely. At the end of the book is appended a collection of relevant passages from other works. The two books were published by Jacob Glassberg in his *Zikhron Berit la-Rishonim* (1892). They were the first books in the rabbinic literature of Germany wholly devoted to the laws of circumcision, and probably the first works in the whole of German rabbinic literature dealing with one specific subject.

BIBLIOGRAPHY: Mueller, in: J. Glassberg, *Zikhron Berit la-Rishonim* (1892), introd.

[Israel Moses Ta-Shma]

HAGRONIA (Lat. **Agranium**), town on the Euphrates. It served as a kind of citadel for the town of *Nehardea, as its name Akra ("fort") di Hagronia (BB 73b) testifies. After Nahardea declined as a religious center following its partial destruction by Papa bar Nazar in 259 C.E. (see *Odenathus), most of its Jews settled in Hagronia. Its Jewish community, though not large (BB 73b), was of considerable importance. Rava, head of the Pumbedita academy from 338 to 52, went from Maḥoza to Hagronia to proclaim a public fast (Ta'an. 24b) and it is reported that the exilarch lectured there during the second half of the fourth century (Yoma 78a). Its scholars were termed "the elders of Hagronia" (Shab. 11a). Many talmudic scholars are known to have been born there – Avimi (BM 77b), Judah (Av. Zar. 39a), Samuel b. Abba (BK 88a), Hilkiah (Yev. 9a), Eleazar (Ta'an. 24b), and Mordecai (Sot. 46b).

BIBLIOGRAPHY: Neubauer, Géog., 347f.; A. Berliner, *Beitraege zur Geographie und Ethnographie Babyloniens im Talmud und Midrasch* (1883), 31f.; J. Obermeyer, *Die Landschaft Babylonien im Zeitalter des Talmuds und des Gaonats* (1929), 265–70; Neusner, Babylonia, 2 (1966), 248. **ADD. BIBLIOGRAPHY:** B. Eshel, *Jewish Settlements in Babylonia during Talmudic Times* (1979), 102–03.

[Moshe Beer]

HAGUE, THE (Dutch: **'s Gravenhage, Den Haag**), seat of the government of the Netherlands and capital of South Holland province. Jewish settlement in The Hague dates to the last decades of the 17th century. By that time two Portuguese Jewish congregations, Beth Jacob and Honen Dal, had been founded in The Hague. The two congregations joined together in 1743 under the latter and used the synagogue on the Princessegracht dating from 1726. The Ashkenazi community opened its own synagogue on the Voldersgracht in 1723. In 1694, Ashkenazi Jews purchased land for a cemetery on the present-day Scheveningseweg, where Portuguese Jews also buried their dead. By 1710 the cemetery was divided into two separate burial grounds. By the 18th century, growing wealth and international connections gave local Portuguese Jews a large measure of influence in all segments of Dutch society. The Portuguese community of The Hague also produced several important rabbis. By the late 18th century, however, general economic conditions worsened and reduced many members of the Portuguese community to penury.

Over the course of the 18th century, the Ashkenazi population of The Hague grew to surpass that of the Portuguese. Most Ashkenazi Jews still resided in the poor Jewish neighborhood near the center of the city.

The Emancipation Decree of 1796 totally transformed the legal and social status of Jews and the structure of the communities. As a result many Dutch Jews from the provinces migrated to The Hague, attracted by the importance of The Hague as the country's center of government.

The Jewish population of The Hague continued to increase throughout the 19th and early 20th centuries. Despite social changes, most of the Jews in The Hague continued to live in poverty in the large Jewish neighborhood. The relatively small population of well-off Jews, however, produced a steady stream of bankers, parliamentarians, painters, poets, and writers, as well as the first Jew to become a minister in the national government. The community also continued to produce prominent rabbis.

In 1844, a new Ashkenazi synagogue was consecrated at the Wagenstraat. Another Ashkenazi synagogue, located at the Voldersgracht, was completed in 1887. Smaller synagogues were scattered throughout the city. Despite the emancipation Jews continued to prefer Jewish schools for their children. Yiddish remained the language of instruction in Ashkenazi schools until the mid-19th century. Following the educational reform of 1857, The Hague's Jewish schools continued to operate as purely religious institutions. In 1920, all independent Jewish schools were closed and replaced by secular schools with optional religious instruction.

In 1836, a council was established to administer aid to the poor. The community maintained an old age home, orphanage, and hospital. Community members also formed all kinds of voluntary charitable organizations.

From the end of the 19th century until the eve of the World War II, the Jewish population of The Hague grew threefold. Jews settled throughout the growing city, leading to the establishment of additional prayer houses and voluntary organizations. A vibrant Jewish community also arose in The Hague's fishing village, Scheveningen, in part due to its popularity as a seaside vacation resort amongst the Jews of Antwerp. Polish Jews who settled in Scheveningen during and after World War I formed their own community and consecrated a synagogue on the Harstenhoekweg in 1926. In the same year, the Jewish community of the wealthy suburb of Wassenaar merged with that of The Hague.

The secularization of The Hague community, begun in the 19th century, continued in the 20th. New Jewish social, cultural, and sports organizations arose. In addition organizations aimed at Jewish youth were founded to counter a rising trend towards assimilation. Between the two world wars, Zionist and anti-Zionist organizations came to play a central role in Jewish life in The Hague. The wave of East European Jews who settled in Scheveningen following their expulsion from Germany after the Nazi takeover in 1933 became enthusiastic participants in local cultural, religious, and Zionist activities.

The 1930s saw the rise of Liberal (Reform) Judaism in The Hague, aided in part by the arrival of Liberal Jewish refugees from Germany. Despite strong opposition from the local Orthodox Jewish establishment, a Liberal Jewish community was founded in The Hague on the very eve of World War II.

Holocaust Period

The wartime occupation of the Netherlands by the Germans affected the Jews of The Hague just as it did Jews elsewhere. In May of 1940, the Germans established their central occupational administration for the Netherlands in The Hague. A significant number of Jews committed suicide.

In September 1940 all Jews not holding Dutch nationality were forced to leave the coastal regions of the Netherlands. Almost 2,000 Jews were expelled from The Hague and Scheveningen as a result. The Jews who remained in The Hague were subject to registration of person and property, dismissal from the civil service, and a ban on the practice of professions.

Late in 1940, the Jewish Coordination Commission was founded to represent Jewish interests. It was superseded a year later by the German-controlled Jewish Council (*Joodse Raad*). After the expulsion of Jewish children from public education in September 1941, a number of Jewish elementary schools, high schools, and vocational schools were established. These functioned until the very last deportations of Jews from The Hague in September 1943.

Between May 1940 and August 1942, anti-Jewish measures were implemented one after another. The situation worsened when a member of the Dutch Nazi Party (NSB) was appointed mayor of The Hague.

During the early months of the deportations, which began in August 1942, Jews were confined at the Scheveningen prison prior to being transported out of the city. The former Jewish orphanage on the Paviljoensgracht later fulfilled this function. Despite protests from the Council of Churches and, sometimes, aid from several quarters of the population, deportations continued until the last day of September 1943, the eve of Rosh ha-Shanah, the Jewish New Year. Approximately 80% of the 10,000 Jews of The Hague were deported. Most were murdered. Of the remaining 2,000, most survived the war in hiding.

During the war, almost all of The Hague's many synagogues were plundered, heavily damaged, or destroyed. Only the Portuguese synagogue survived the war undamaged.

Following the war, religious services were resumed at several locations. Eventually, the synagogues on the Wagenstraat and De Carpentierstraat were closed and their buildings sold. The former synagogue on the Wagenstraat today serves as a mosque. The present-day synagogue of The Hague's Orthodox Jewish Community is located on the Cornelis Houtmanstraat.

The Portuguese Jewish Community of The Hague was officially dissolved in the aftermath of the war and its synagogue on the Princessegracht sold to the Liberal Jewish Community, which has used the building since 1976. An extensive restoration of the building was completed in 1997.

The Jewish cemetery on the Scheveningseweg was restored during the late 1980s.

Today, almost all of the Netherlands' Jewish organizations have branches or offices in The Hague. The Hague is the seat of the Embassy of the State of Israel and of the Dutch-Jewish CIDI organization (Center for Information and Documentation Israel).

Throughout The Hague, plaques, monuments, and names of streets and institutions commemorate aspects of the Jewish past. In 1994, the L.E. Visserhuis Jewish old age home was opened on the Doorniksestraat in Scheveningen. The home commemorates *Visser, a famed Dutch Jewish jurist who, during the war, was expelled from his position as minister of justice.

In 2003 the remains of the archive of The Hague's Jewish community was returned to The Hague from Russia. The documents are now kept at The Hague's Municipal Archive.

BIBLIOGRAPHY: J. Michman, H. Beem, and D. Michman, *Pinkas: geschiedenis van de joodse gemeenschap in Nederland* (1999).

[Jelka Kröger (2nd ed.)]

HAGUENAU, Alsatian town in the Bas-Rhin department, E. France. The earliest information on the presence of Jews in Haguenau dates from 1235; in that year a blood libel was perpetrated against the Jews of the town, but thanks to the protection of the emperor, whose *servi camerae they were, they escaped harm. The Jews had to pay taxes to both the emperor and the municipality. The latter also protected them effectively, especially in 1338 against the *Armleder bands, but unsuccessfully at the time of the *Black Death: by February 16, 1349, the Jewish community had been destroyed. The first synagogue (the courtyard of which was used in 1352 for the wheat market) stood on the former Rathausplaetzel, later the Place de la Republique; the *mikveh* was situated on the bank of the Moder, on the site of the present municipal hospital. In 1354, the Jews returned to Haguenau and formed a new community. A house (number 8 of the present Rue du Sel) was then used as a synagogue. A good deal of Hebrew type was used in books printed in Haguenau between 1517 and 1520, among them works by

*Reuchlin and *Melanchthon. In 1528, *Joseph (Josel) b. Gershom of Rosheim obtained from the emperor the abrogation of an expulsion order issued by the town. Haguenau subsequently became a refuge for the Jews of the surrounding district on various occasions. During the second half of the 17th century, several Jews who had fled from Poland settled there. From 1660, there has been a rabbi in Haguenau. Notable rabbis included Meyer Jaïs, later chief rabbi of Paris, who held office in Haguenau between 1933 and 1938.

The community of Haguenau consisted of 34 families in 1735, 64 in 1784, and 600 souls on the eve of World War II. Of these, 148 persons died in deportation or on the battlefield. In 1968, the community numbered about 300 and at the outset of the 21st century around 700. The present synagogue on the Rue des Juifs (plundered by the Nazis and later renovated) was erected in 1821. The cemetery is known to have existed from the 16th century, but it was probably established during the Middle Ages. For a long time, it also served all the Jews of the region. The oldest epitaph preserved there dates from 1654.

BIBLIOGRAPHY: M. Ginsburger, in: Germ Jud, 1 pt. 2 (1963), 121ff., 2 pt. 1 (1968), 318ff.; E. Scheid, in: REJ, 2 (1881), 73–92, 3 (1881), 58–74, 4 (1882), 98–112, 5 (1882), 230–9, 8 (1884), 243–54, 10 (1885), 204–31; A. Marx, *Studies in Jewish History and Booklore* (1944), 326f.; J. Bloch, *Historique de la Communauté Juive de Haguenau…* (1968); Z. Szajkowski, *Analytical Franco-Jewish Gazetteer 1939–1945* (1966), index.

[Bernhard Blumenkranz]

HA-ḤINNUKH (Heb. הַחִנּוּךְ; "the Education"), an anonymous work on the 613 precepts (see *Commandments, 613) in the order of their appearance in Scripture, giving their reasons and their laws in detail. The various attempts to identify the author have proved unsuccessful; the most widely held view is that he was *Aaron b. Joseph ha-Levi of Barcelona, the identification being based on an obscure allusion in the introduction: "A Jew of the house of Levi of Barcelona." From certain references in the book (precept 400) it has been concluded that the author was a pupil of Solomon b. Abraham *Adret. The first edition (Venice, 1523) gives "Rabbi Aaron" as the author. In the opinion of S.H. Kook the basis for this identification lies in the introduction to precept 95: "out of fear of drawing near to the tabernacle of the Lord, the levites my brethren [*aḥai*] were purified and Aaron offered them." The proofreader of the second edition (*ibid.*, 1600–01) in fact based himself on this passage but he is mistaken because it is the biblical Aaron who is referred to and the text should read: "and the levites after [*aḥar*] being purified" (cf. Num. 8:21). This identification was already questioned by Ḥ.J.D. Azulai and other scholars, who have shown it to be completely without foundation. Elsewhere the name of the author is given as Baruch (David ibn Zimra, *Meẓudat David*, precept 206). The book was compiled at the end of the 13th century. Some deduced the date of its composition from the date 1257 mentioned in precept 326 with reference to the sabbatical years, but the passage in question is taken from the novella of Solomon b. Abraham Adret to *Avodah Zarah* 9a. The Vatican library contains a manuscript written in 1313.

The name of the book is taken by some as referring to its educational aim, to which in fact the author alludes at the end of the introduction: "To touch the heart of my young son and his companions in that each week they will learn the precepts that are included in the weekly portion of the Law" (see also *Meẓudat David*, precept 397). This is the reason both for the order in which the commandments are given, and its contents, which are mainly for the purpose of study and not to give the *halakhah*. The work follows a definite pattern: (1) a definition of the essence of the precept; (2) its source in the Written Law and the connection with its development in the Oral Law; (3) the principles of the precept and its reasons; (4) its main details.

The book is mainly based on the *Sefer ha-Mitzvot* and the *Mishneh Torah* of Maimonides, at times whole sections being copied verbatim (precepts 173, 485). The author used Ibn Ḥasdai's Hebrew translation of the *Sefer ha-Mitzvot*. He also used the works of other authors, including those of Alfasi and chiefly of Adret and Naḥmanides. The uniqueness of the work lies in the section dealing with the explanation of the principles of the precepts, especially "the simple description" (precept 98). His explanations are based on common sense. His style and presentation are clear and understandable befitting its educational aim for youth and ordinary people. Many editions of the work have appeared. The best known is that containing the commentary *Minḥat Ḥinnukh* of Joseph *Babad. Other well-known authors to devote compositions to it include Judah *Rosanes and Isaiah *Pick. It has been issued according to the first edition with notes, variant readings, and an introduction by C.B. Chavel (1962[5]).

BIBLIOGRAPHY: C.B. Chavel (ed.), *Sefer ha-Ḥinnukh* (1962[5]), introd., and 797–806; H. Heller (ed.), *Sefer ha-Mitzvot le-Rabbenu Moshe ben-Rabbi Maimon* (1914), 8f. (introd.); S.H. Kook, *Iyyunim u-Meḥkarim*, 2 (1963), 316–20; Munk, in: ZHB, 11 (1907), 186–8; D. Rosin, *Ein Compendium der juedischen Gesetzeskunde aus dem vierzehnten Jahrhundert* (1871); J. Rubinstein, in: J. Babad, *Sefer Minḥat Ḥinnukh ha-Shalem*, pt. 3 (1952), 151ff. (bibliographical list of editions of *Sefer ha-Ḥinnukh*).

[Shlomoh Zalman Havlin]

HAHN, ALBERT L. (1889–1968), German banker and economist. Hahn was born in Frankfurt and during the 1920s joined the Deutsche Effekten-und Wechselbank, in which his family had a sizable interest. In 1929 he became professor of economics at the University of Frankfurt. In 1939 he went to the U.S. and taught at the New School for Social Research in New York. He left the U.S. in 1950 and eventually returned to his teaching career at Frankfurt University. Hahn's main concern was the theory of money and credit. He consistently advocated a stable currency as a prime social safeguard. His many publications include *Volkswirtschaftliche Theorie des Bankkredits* (1920), *Common Sense Economics* (1956), *Fuenfzig Jahre zwischen Inflation und Deflation* (1963), *Ein Traktat ueber Waeh-*

rungsreform (1964), and *Nationale und internationale Aspekte der amerikanischen Währungspolitik* (1966).

[Joachim O. Ronall]

HAHN, JOSEPH BEN MOSES (c. 1730–1803), German talmudic scholar. Hahn was *dayyan* of the *bet din* of the combined communities of Hamburg, Altona, and Wandsbeck and was beloved as the preacher in the old as well as in the new *klaus* in Hamburg which was renamed after him. In the *Emden-*Eybeschuetz controversy he sided with the latter. In 1789, Saul *Berlin, the ill-famed son of R. Ẓevi Hirsch Berlin, published under the nom de plume Obadiah b. Baruch, *Mizpeh Yokte'el*, a criticism of the *Torat Yekuti'el* (Berlin, 1772) of Raphael *Kohen, the famous rabbi of the three communities. Hahn presided over the *bet din* which excommunicated the author on the grounds of his having libeled ha-Kohen. In another case he ruled that the body of a Jewish woman, executed by the civil authorities for poisoning her mother-in-law and sister-in-law, should be reburied in a Jewish cemetery without religious qualification or restriction, as she had been mentally disturbed at the time. He was said to have had an encyclopedic mind and memory.

BIBLIOGRAPHY: E. Duckesz, *Chachme AHW* (1908), Germ. pt. 34, Heb. pt. 97f.; idem, *IVOH Lemoschaw* (1903), 66f.; E.L. Landshuth, *Toledot Anshei ha-Shem u-Fe'ulatam ba-Adat Berlin* (1884), 90.

[Marvin Tokayer]

HAHN (Nordlingen), JOSEPH YUSPA BEN PHINEHAS SELIGMANN (1570–1637), German rabbi and author. Hahn spent all his life in Frankfurt. He was present during the *Fettmilch riots, the subsequent expulsion of the Jews from the city in 1614, and their triumphant return two years later after Fettmilch was hanged. Hahn was head of the Frankfurt *bet din* and of the local yeshivah. When there was no other incumbent, he also filled the office of communal rabbi. Hahn was a contemporary and colleague of Isaiah *Horowitz (Shelah). Hahn is best known for his book *Yosif Omeẓ* (Frankfurt, 1723). In 1718, Joseph Kosman, one of Hahn's descendants, published his own *Noheg Ka-Ẓon Yosef* in Hanau, in which he quoted freely from his kinsman's work, sometimes without indicating his source. Hahn's *Yosif Omeẓ* deals mainly with the laws and customs of the Jewish calendar and liturgy, particularly those prevalent in contemporary Frankfurt. He quotes the custom of reciting the hymn "*Lekhah Dodi" on Friday evenings as a "new" one, recently introduced. Hahn deliberately substitutes his own phrases for those which, in the original, refer to "going out" to meet the Sabbath, since this custom obtained only in Ereẓ Israel, where the hymn was composed; the words he substituted retain the acrostic of the author's name. Hahn also voiced his displeasure at the new custom of delaying the commencement of the evening service on the first night of *Shavuot until a late hour.

The *Yosif Omeẓ* is a valuable source book for the history of the contemporary Frankfurt Jewish community. Hahn mentions, for instance, the local Purim (Adar 20), instituted to commemorate the hanging of Fettmilch (no. 1107–09). He also records the comparatively slight damage suffered by the community as a result of the passage of soldiers through the area during the Thirty Years' War. The *Yosif Omeẓ* is written in a pious vein, and the concluding chapters are devoted to ethics. In the sections on pedagogy, Hahn deplored the ignorance of the Bible prevalent among rabbis of his day. He suggested that a boy who showed no sign of progress in the study of the Talmud by the age of 13 be withdrawn from its study and taught Bible instead.

BIBLIOGRAPHY: M. Horovitz, *Frankfurter Rabbinen*, 2 (1883), 6–18; J. Horovitz, in: *Festschrift… A. Freimann* (1935), 35–50; idem, in: *Festschrift… J. Freimann* (1937), 78–93; S. Esh (ed.), *Koveẓ le-Zikhro shel Eli'ezer Shamir* (1957), 155–62.

[Alexander Tobias]

HAHN, KURT (1886–1974), German-British educator. Hahn was born in Berlin and educated at both German universities and Oxford. While in Germany he conceived the idea of a coeducational boarding school which would emphasise self-discipline, enterprise, and physical fitness. In the 1920s Hahn founded Salem school, in Germany near Lake Constance, to put his ideas into practice. Hahn was a conservative close to monarchist circles in Weimar Germany; through them, Hahn met relatives of the boy who would later become Britain's Prince Philip. Arrested by the Nazis just after they came to power, as a Jew Hahn quickly emigrated to Britain and, with influential backing, founded Gordonstoun school in Scotland, run along lines similar to Salem school. Prince Philip (b. 1923) and, later, Prince Charles (b. 1948) and his two brothers received parts of their education at Gordonstoun. Hahn's influence on British public (i.e., exclusive private) schools was considerable. After 1953 Hahn returned to Germany, where he died.

BIBLIOGRAPHY: ODNB online; D.A. Byatt (ed.), *Kurt Hahn, 1886–1974, An Appreciation of His Life and Work* (1976).

[William D. Rubinstein (2nd ed.)]

HAHN, MICHAEL (1830–1886), governor of the state of Louisiana. Born in Bavaria, Germany, Hahn was brought to New Orleans, La., as a child and was admitted to the bar in 1851. During the Civil War he supported the Unionist cause and was elected to Congress in 1863. He became governor of Louisiana in the following year – the first Jewish governor in the U.S. Hahn resigned the governorship in 1865 following his election to the Senate but never took his seat. He returned to Congress as a Republican in 1884 and served until his death.

HAHN, REYNALDO (1875–1947), composer and conductor. Born in Caracas, Venezuela, Hahn studied under Massenet at the Paris Conservatory. He wrote several light operas and songs which recall Massenet's melodic charm. His compositions include eight operas and light operas, incidental music to plays, pantomimes, ballets (notably *Le Dieu bleu* (1912) for the Diaghilev Ballet), two symphonic poems, chamber music, songs, an oratorio *La Reine de Sheba* (1926), and a Christmas mystery *Pastorale de Noël* (1908). From 1935 Hahn was music critic of *Le Figaro*. In 1945 he was appointed director of the Paris Opera. His book of recollections, *Thèmes variés*, appeared in 1946.

HAI BAR RAV DAVID GAON, head of the *Pumbedita academy from 890 to 898. Hai was *dayyan* in Baghdad for many years before he became *gaon*; he transferred the academy of Pumbedita to Baghdad (*Sha'arei Simḥah* of R. Isaac *Ibn Ghayyat, 1 (1861), 63–64). None of his responsa has been preserved, but some of those attributed to R. "Hai" without further definition, may be his. Harkavy attributes the *Sefer ha-Shetarot* ("Book of Documents") to him, but Wertheimer, L. Ginzberg, and Assaf hold more plausibly that the author of the *Sefer ha-Shetarot* was the famous *Hai b. Sherira. Several early Karaite scholars attributed to Hai a book of polemics against the Karaites on the subject of the intercalation of the month and the arrangement of the calendar; many scholars believe that this was Hai b. David.

BIBLIOGRAPHY: Mann, in: JQR, 11 (1920/21), 434–5; S. Assaf, *Sefer ha-Shetarot de-Rav Hai Ga'on* (1930), 7–8; Ibn Daud, Tradition, 52, 37, 129; Abramson, Merkazim, 911.

[Mordecai Margaliot]

HAI BEN NAHSHON, *gaon* of *Sura from 885–896. Both Hai's father and paternal grandfather, Zadok, had preceded him as *geonim* of Sura. In one of the few of his responsa which have been preserved he opposes the recitation of *Kol Nidrei on the eve of the Day of Atonement, since in his opinion authority for the granting of absolution from vows is no longer to be obtained. It seems that the Karaite al-*Kirkisani was referring to Hai b. Nahshon when he wrote that the *gaon* Hai and his father translated the *Sefer ha-Mitzvot* of Anan from Aramaic to Hebrew. If any credence can be given to this statement it can only mean that they subjected the work to a critical examination, or that they translated it in order to dispute with him and challenge his views.

BIBLIOGRAPHY: S.J.L. Rapoport, *Teshuvot Ge'onim Kadmonim* (1848), 9a–b; J. Mueller, *Mafte'aḥ Teshuvot ha-Ge'onim* (1891), 151–7; Lewin, in: *Ginzei Kedem*, 2 (1923), 1–3; S. Assaf, in: *Tarbiz*, 4 (1933), 36, 199f.

[Mordecai Margaliot]

HAI BEN SHERIRA (939–1038), *gaon* of Pumbedita and molder of the *halakhah* and the most prominent figure of his time. Of his youth nothing is known. From 986 he was the *av bet din* in the academy of *Pumbedita, acting as the deputy to his father Sherira *gaon*; in this role he left his mark upon the mode of studies and general orientation of the academy. According to some, he had a share in composing the *Iggeret Rav Sherira* (see *Sherira). Some time after he and his father had been released from prison, where they had been kept on a false charge, he became the *gaon* of Pumbedita, while his father was still alive, a position which he held for 40 years (998–1038). Although his position had been vied for by Samuel b. Hophni the latter withdrew his claim to the gaonate when Hai married his daughter. Students came to Hai's academy from Byzantium and from western Christian countries, from where queries were also sent to Hai. His ties with Spain and his influence upon *Samuel ha-Nagid in particular are well known.

Aside from his preeminence in rabbinic knowledge, he was well acquainted with the Persian and Arabic languages and with Arabic literature. While he permitted children to be taught Arabic writing and arithmetic, he warned against the study of philosophy (from a letter ascribed to him and addressed to Samuel ha-Nagid). He criticized his father-in-law, Samuel b. Hophni, "and others like him, who frequently read the works of non-Jews."

Hai occupies a central position in the history of the *halakhah*. Later generations regarded him as the supreme authority, declaring that "he, more than all the *geonim*, propagated the Torah in Israel … both in the east and in the west.… No one among his predecessors can be compared to him, who was the last of the *geonim*" (Abraham *Ibn Daud, *Sefer ha-Kabbalah*). The measure of his influence and the volume of his responsa, decisions, and comments can be gauged from the fact that approximately a third of all extant geonic responsa are his (some of them in conjunction with his father).

In his writings Hai set out in detail his approach to the principles of faith and to the requirements of community leadership. In his *piyyutim* he expressed with much bitterness his sense of living in exile from Ereẓ Israel. He was a mystic, who ascribed sanctity to the **heikhalot* literature, believing that whoever studied it in holiness and purity could ascend to the world of the angels and of the divine chariot (*merkavah*). Contrary to the view of his father-in-law, he believed "that God performs signs and awe-inspiring acts through the righteous, even as He did through the prophets." But he vigorously opposed those who believed that the divine names and charms were efficacious in changing the course of nature, declaring emphatically that its laws cannot be modified by such means. Vehemently antagonistic to any tendency toward anthropomorphism, he maintained that anthropomorphic passages in the *aggadah* were to be interpreted metaphorically. In his formulation of the ideals and values of the complete Jew, he described the rewards for observing divine precepts. These rewards greet the righteous and form "groups that go to meet the Divine Presence" and say to the righteous: "Ascend to your grade, stand in your division (in heaven), you who have conquered your evil inclination … who have borne the yoke of the commandments, and in your fear of Him have endured suffering."

Hai drew special attention to the duty of the *dayyanim* to guide and admonish the people, to take responsibility for people's conduct and to be accountable for their sins. He demanded that strong measures be taken against dissenters and thieves, and under certain circumstances even permitted recourse to Jewish courts of law. He was opposed to the absolute annulment of vows on the eve of the Day of Atonement, his formulation of the **Kol Nidrei* prayer being: "Of all vows…

which we have vowed… and have omitted to fulfill either through neglect or under constraint we pray that the Lord of heaven may absolve and pardon us." He adopted a tolerant attitude towards traditional local liturgical practices, but was opposed to delving into the reasons for them, insisting on "the observance of institutions introduced by those superior to our generations in learning and in caliber" (lit. "number"). He retained his physical and mental energies to the end. At the age of 99, a few months before his death, he replied with remarkable vigor to questions submitted to him. After his death, Samuel ha-Nagid eulogized him, saying: "During his lifetime he acquired all the choicest wisdom," and though "he left no child, he has, in every land, both east and west, children whom he reared in the Torah" (*Ben Tehillim*, 11).

[Haim Hillel Ben-Sasson]

Of Hai's works the following are extant: (1) fragments of the Arabic original of *Sefer Shevu'ot* (*Kitāb al-Aymān*; "A Treatise on Oaths"), and a Hebrew rendering by an unknown translator of the entire work entitled *Mishpetei Shevu'ot* (Venice, 1602; Hamburg, 1782); (2) fragments of the Arabic original of *Sefer ha-Mikkaḥ ve-ha-Mimkar* (*Kitāb al-Shirā wa-al-Baye*; "Treatise on Commercial Transactions"). This, his chief literary production, was translated into Hebrew by Isaac *Al-Bargeloni (Venice, 1602; Vienna, 1800), and another version is extant in manuscript; (3) *Sefer ha-Shetarot* ("Treatise on Documents"), containing the texts of various documents, such as a *ketubbah*, a *get*, etc. (published by Assaf in *Tarbiz*, 1 (1930), supplement). Fragments of Hai's commentary on several tractates of the Babylonian Talmud have also been preserved. The ascription of certain other works to Hai has, in recent years, been rejected. (4) Hai wrote numerous responsa. In 1986, T. Groner published a complete bibliography of Hai's responsa and his other works as well (see *Alei Sefer* 13, 1986). (5) To aid the study of Arabic, Hai wrote *Kitab Al-Hawi*, a comprehensive Hebrew/Aramaic-Arabic anagrammatic dictionary. It was very popular and in use through the end of the 13th century. A. Maman published 10 of the 32 folios of the dictionary. Only three folios had been previously published. The rest was extant only in manuscript (see *Tarbiz* 69, 3 (2000), 341–422).

To Hai are ascribed some 25 poems, most of which are prayers, *seliḥot*, and *piyyutim*, a few of them didactic poems on laws and etiquette and eulogies of contemporary personalities. Most of these are in meter and rhyme, but in form and content reveal very little similarity to Arabic poetry. For poetic power, pride of place should be given to a group of five *seliḥot* (not *kinot*) for the Ninth of *Av; these are without meter and rhyme and voice a bitter and vehement complaint in the manner of Job against the suffering endured by the Jewish people in exile in the face of its great faith in God. Hai's authorship of several poems, and even the fact of his having written poetry at all, which was questioned in modern times (from the beginning of research into the poetry of the Middle Ages) has now been confirmed.

[Jacob S. Levinger / David Derovan (2nd ed.)]

BIBLIOGRAPHY: S. Naschér, *Der Gaon Haia und seine geistige Thaetigkeit* (1867?); Weiss, Dor, 4 (19044), 155–71; J.N. Epstein, *Der gaonaeische Kommentar zur Ordnung Tohorot* (1915), 1–36; Assaf, in: *Ha-Ẓofeh le-Ḥokhmat Yisrael*, 7 (1923), 277–87; idem, in: *Tarbiz*, 17 (1945/46), 28–31; Assaf, Ge'onim, 198–202; Kroll, in: *Mizraḥ u-Ma'arav*, 4 (1929/30), 347–51; E.E. Hildesheimer, *Mystik und Agada im Urteile der Gaonen R. Scherira und R. Hai* (1931); H. Brody, *Piyyutim ve-Shirei Tehillah me-Rav Hai* (1937); J.L. Fishman (Maimon; ed.), *Rav Hai Ga'on* (1938); H. Tchernowitz, *Toledot ha-Posekim*, 1 (1946), 95–105; Abramson, in: *Sefer Yovel J.N. Epstein* (1950), 296–315; idem, in: *Talpioth*, 5 (1952), 773–80; Weill, in: *Sefer Assaf* (1953), 261–79; Baron, Social[2], index. **ADD. BIBLIOGRAPHY:** T. Groner, *The Legal Methodology of Hai Gaon* (1985); idem, in: *Alei Sefer*, 13 (1986); R. Brody, in: JQR, 76:3 (1986), 237–45; A. Maman, in: *Tarbiz*, 69:3 (2000), 341–422.

HAIDAMACKS, paramilitary bands that disrupted the social order in Polish Ukraine during the 18th century. The name originated from the Turkish word *haida* meaning "move on!" The Haidamack movement was mainly the outcome of the social ferment which had already developed in the Ukraine toward the end of the 16th century and reached a peak in the Cossack uprising led by *Chmielnicki in 1648. The Haidamacks were mainly peasant serfs who had fled from the Polish landowners to the steppes beyond the River Dnieper. They were joined by poorer elements among the townsmen, sons of the impoverished nobility and clergy, members of heretical sects who had fled from Russia, and even Jewish renegades. The Haidamacks ambushed travelers or attacked small settlements, not for political reasons but principally for robbery accompanied by murder. However, they unwittingly served the political ends of the Russian administrators and the Russian Orthodox clergy since their persistent attacks helped to erode the position of the Polish kingdom in this period.

The Haidamack bands are first mentioned in documents dating from the beginning of the 18th century, but received a strong impetus in 1734, when dissensions broke out among the Polish nobility over the election of a new king. In 1768 the most violent Haidamack outbreak took place, known as Koliivshchina or (in Polish) Kolizczyzna, headed by Maxim Zhelesnyak (see below), in which religious, national, and social elements combined. The expulsion of the Jews or their destruction had long been the avowed purpose of insurgents in the Ukraine in the period of Chmielnicki and even earlier. The monks, who were the chroniclers of the period and the recorders of popular tales, glorified murder of the Jews and confiscation of their property as if they were deeds of piety. In addition, the Jews were a convenient target to attack because the competition in trade and commerce with the townsmen was so keen that the latter showed no disposition to defend Jews and would even divulge the movements of Jewish merchants to the Haidamacks. Most of the Jews were helpless against the brigands, and the Polish state authorities were not always able to defend them. The propaganda of the Russian Orthodox priests only intensified the hatred against the Jews. In this area the rivalry between the clergy of the Orthodox and Catholic churches accounts for the sharp rise in the number of *blood libels against the Jews from the fourth to sixth decades of the 18th century precisely in the region where the Haidamacks were active.

Most of the attacks made by the Haidamacks against the Jews took the form of robbery and murder of merchants traveling on the highway and assaults on Jewish tenant farmers living in isolated places and on inhabitants of small defenseless towns. During the years when the revolts increased (1734, 1750, 1768) even heavily fortified places were attacked, claiming large numbers of Jewish victims: 27 Jews were slaughtered in Korsun in 1734; 35 were murdered in Pavoloch in 1736. In the same year the Haidamacks captured the town of Pogrebishche and murdered 14 Jews; many others were wounded and their property stolen. Massacres of Jews took place in various towns in 1738 and 1742. A wave of attacks was perpetrated in 1750: Jews were killed in Vinnitsa, Volodarka, and in other cities. But these calamities were overshadowed by the wholesale massacres that took place in 1768 (known as the persecutions of Ukraine or of *Uman). Initially, about 700 people were killed in the city of Fastov including many scores of Jews. In the townlet of Lysyanka a Jew, a Polish priest, and a dog were hanged side by side to indicate the equality of their respective religions.

Zheleznyak, an active leader of the gangs, massacred the Jews who had been unable to escape from Zhabotin, Kanyev, and Korsun before going on to the fortified city of Uman, to which many thousands of Poles and Jews had streamed from other places out of terror of the Haidamacks. The treachery of the Cossack commander Gonta led to the surrender of the city on June 19, 1768, and there ensued a frightful massacre of its inhabitants. The Jews attempted to hide but were unsuccessful. Some fought heroically until slain by the enemy. The majority of Jews were murdered in the synagogue. A number of prominent Jews, required to pay a ransom, were brutally murdered after they had complied. The number of Jewish victims ran into thousands, the slayers sparing neither women nor children. The synagogues were razed and the Torah scrolls desecrated and burned. According to some records the number of victims reached 20,000, both Poles and Jews. Some of the Jews in the surrounding districts who attempted to flee to the border city of Balta, half of which was situated in Turkish territory, were caught by brigands, who laid waste to the city. The Jews in the entire southeastern portion of Poland were seized with terror. They placed their hopes on the commander of the Polish army, Branicki, and a special prayer was composed in his honor. Although Branicki himself did not take part in the war against the Haidamacks, he had severely punished their leaders and was for this reason regarded by the Jews as the savior of Polish Jewry. The revolt was suppressed by the Russian and Polish troops. The rebels were tried by Polish punitive units and the Haidamack movement came to an end. The memory of the Haidamacks lingered in Ukrainian lore and entered the national literature (*Haydamaky* (1841), by Taras Shevchenko). It became a legacy of the Ukrainian national movement, and the Ukrainian partisan bands that perpetrated pogroms on the Jewish population in 1919–20 and 1941–44 were referred to as Haidamacks.

BIBLIOGRAPHY: F. Rawita-Gawroński, *Historya ruchów hajdamackich*, 2 vols. (1913²); idem, *Żydzi w historji i literatur ze ludowej na Rusi* (1923); A.A. Skalkovski, *Nayezdy gaydamak na zapadnuyu Ukraynu v xviii stoletii, 1733–1768* (1845); *Arkhiv yugo-zapadnoy Rossii*, pt. 3, vol. 3 (1876); Ḥ.J. Gurland, *Le-Korot ha-Gezeirot al Yisrael*, 3 (1888), 7 (1892); Dubnow, Hist Russ, index.

[Shmuel Ettinger]

HAIFA (Heb. חֵיפָה), port in Israel and commercial and administrative center of the north of the country. The city extends over the northwest side of Mt. Carmel and the coastal strip at its northern slope, and over the southern end of the Zebulun Valley and the northern edge of the Carmel Coast. Its total area is about 23 sq. mi. (60 sq. km.).

Early History

The earliest settlement in Haifa's vicinity was located at Tell Abu Hawam, a small port town founded at the beginning of the 14th century B.C.E. (Late Bronze Age) and was in existence until the Hellenistic period. The city was not a part of the area regarded as sanctified by the exiles returning from Babylon (see *Israel, Historical Boundaries). Haifa is possibly mentioned in the Persian period in the list of cities attributed to the geographer Scylax, between the bay and the "Promontory of Zeus," i.e., the Carmel. In the Hellenistic period the city moved to a new site, south of Bat Gallim (the old port had apparently become blocked by sand). Tombs from the Roman period, including Jewish burial caves, have been found in the vicinity. The major city in the region was Shikmonah, which Eusebius even identifies with Haifa (*Onomastikon*, ed. by E. Klostermann (1904), 108:31). Haifa is mentioned in Jewish sources as the home of R. Avdimos (Avdimi, Dimi) and other scholars (Tosef., Yev. 6:8). It was a fishing village whose inhabitants, like the people of Beth-Shean and Tivon, could not distinguish between the pronunciation of the gutturals *ḥet* and *ayin* (TJ, Ber. 2:4). According to the Talmud, the murex (shellfish yielding purple dye used for the *tallit*) was caught along the coast from Haifa to the Ladder of Tyre (Shab. 26a). Politically Haifa throughout this period belonged to the district of *Acre. Its Jewish inhabitants were on hostile terms with the Samaritans in neighboring Castra, a fortress built by the Romans. A *kinah* speaks of the destruction of the Jewish community, along with other communities, when the Byzantines reconquered the country from the Persians in 628. Haifa is not mentioned in the sources dealing with the first 400 years of Muslim rule in Ereẓ Israel. It appears again only in the mid-11th century: in 1046 the Persian traveler Nasir-i Khusrau relates that large sailing ships were built there. He also mentions date palms that he found there and the sand used by goldsmiths. In 1084, the *gaon* *Elijah ben Solomon ha-Kohen went from Tyre to Haifa to proclaim the New Year on the soil of Ereẓ Israel and to renew the ordination of rabbis and the gaonate there.

On the eve of the First Crusade Haifa is described as an important and well-fortified city. The Crusaders pushing southward initially spared the city but later laid siege and conquered it with the help of the Venetian navy (summer 1100). All Haifa's Jewish defenders (who comprised the majority of the city's population) and its Egyptian garrison were slaughtered, bringing to an end another brief but flourishing chapter in Haifa's history. During the Crusader era Jews apparently did not resettle in Haifa. The city remained a small fortress and an insignificant port under the shadow of its mighty neighbors, *Acre and *Caesarea; during this period it was the capital of a seigniory held by a Crusader family, Garcia Alvarez. The fortress of Haifa was destroyed in 1187 when Saladin dealt a crushing blow to Crusader rule. It was returned under the peace treaty of 1192 to the Franks during the Third Crusade (1192–1265). In the mid-13th century the city's fortifications were rebuilt by Louis IX, king of France, but in 1265 Haifa again fell, this time to the Mamluk Sultan Baybars who drove the remaining Crusaders from the country. During Baybars' systematic destruction of the coastal cities of Ereẓ Israel and Syria (to prevent their reoccupation by the Franks), Haifa was also razed (1291) and did not revive throughout the period of *Mamluk rule. The Carmelite Order was founded on Mt. Carmel in 1156, but the monastery was destroyed by the Muslims in 1291. From the time of its conquest by the Muslims until the 15th century, Haifa was either uninhabited or an unfortified small village. At various times there were a few Jews living there, and both Jews and Christians made pilgrimages to Elijah's cave on Mt. Carmel.

Ottoman Rule

Haifa was apparently deserted at the time of the *Ottoman conquest (1516). The first indication of its resettlement is contained in a description by the German traveler Raowulf who visited Ereẓ Israel in 1575. Haifa is subsequently mentioned in accounts of travelers as a half-ruined, impoverished village with few inhabitants. The expansion of commercial trade between Europe and Ereẓ Israel from the beginning of the 17th century improved Haifa's position. More and more boats began anchoring at the safer Haifa port in preference to the plugged-up bay at Acre. Haifa's revival as a flourishing port city is also to be credited to the emirs of the Turabay family, who ruled part of Ereẓ Israel at that time, and also Haifa. These local rulers also gave permission to the Carmelite monks to reestablish themselves in 1631, but only four years later the Muslims turned their church into a mosque. Later the monastery was rebuilt; in 1775 it was ransacked, and in 1821 it was destroyed by Abdullah, pasha of Acre. It was reestablished in 1828 and exists to this day.

At the beginning of the 18th century a new local ruler Zahir al-ʿUmar gained control of northern Ereẓ Israel and set up his capital in Acre. In 1742 Haifa again came into existence as a village or a small town located at the foot of Mt. Carmel near the present-day Bat Gallim quarter. It had a small Jewish community and a synagogue. In the middle of the century Zahir annexed Haifa as well. Unfortified and spread over a wide and vulnerable plain, Haifa was almost captured in 1761 by the Turks. To prevent its falling into his enemies' hands, Zahir ordered his soldiers to raze the city to the ground and scatter boulders in the anchorage; thus the ancient city of Haifa was demolished. Zahir provided his growing capital with a safe alternative port of call 1⅓ mi. (2 km.) southeast of ancient Haifa, on a strip of coast at the foot of the Carmel at an easily defensible point. Unlike the ancient city of Haifa, the new port was situated on the crossroad from Acre to *Jaffa. Zahir walled in the area and built another fortress on the slope above (known as the Burj, located on the site of Castrum Samaritanorum). The new city of Haifa grew up within these walls – retaining its old name.

18th–19th Centuries

Haifa gradually recovered and increased from an estimated 250 settlers in old Haifa at the beginning of the 18th century to 4,000 a century later. R. Naḥman of Bratslav spent Rosh Ha-Shanah of 5559 (1798) with the small Jewish community of Haifa. The composition of the population changed, mainly due to the growing influence of the Carmelite monks, so that in 1840 about 40% of the city's inhabitants were Christian Arabs living alongside the Muslim majority. Despite severe difficulties and opposition from the local inhabitants and the authorities, the Carmelite monks, with the aid of France, managed to hold on to the dark crypts above "Elijah's Cave" and also erected nearby the Stella Maris monastery. Its cornerstone was laid in 1827 and construction was carried out without incident under the Egyptian rule in force in Ereẓ Israel at that time (1831–40) which was well-disposed to Christians in general and especially to those under French protection.

The Egyptian conquest of Ereẓ Israel lent much impetus to Haifa's development, which was especially to the disadvantage of its rival Acre. The steamboats, which made their appearance at this time in eastern Mediterranean ports and contributed to the economic rebirth of Ereẓ Israel, used Haifa rather than Acre as their port of call. The consular representatives therefore began leaving Acre (which was also dominated by Muslim extremism) to settle in Haifa, with its large Christian population and better climate; the latter took over more and more of Acre's export trade, which had consisted largely of grain, cotton, and sesame seeds. In 1858 the walled city of Haifa was already overcrowded and the first houses began to be built outside the ancient city on the mountain slope. Ten years later the first German Templers arrived in the country from Wuerttemberg and built a colony, which became a model residential suburb, just west of Haifa. The members of this sect made important contributions to Haifa's development – they introduced the stagecoach, paved roads, and set up a regular coach service to Acre and Nazareth. The Templers also established Haifa's first industrial enterprises and applied modern methods in agriculture, crafts, and commerce. Toward the end of the century the Germans enlarged their settlement and built the first residential quarter on the top of the Carmel (near the present-day Merkaz ha-Carmel). In 1905 Haifa's position and importance was further strengthened when it was connected up with the Hejaz railroad which was then being laid between Damascus and the Arabian Peninsula; most of the exports from the fertile lands of the Hauran now passed through Haifa.

Revival of Jewish Settlement

Haifa's Jewish community expanded gradually. Very few Jews had apparently settled there when the ancient city was rebuilt at the beginning of Turkish rule. In 1742 it contained a small Jewish community, composed mainly of immigrants from Morocco and Algeria. In 1839 there were 124 Jews in Haifa; in 1864, 384; in 1871, 760; and in 1901, 1,041. Up to this time North African Jews still comprised the majority of the community, which also contained some Sephardi Jews from Turkey and a few Ashkenazim. (In 1917 the number of Jews rose to 1,400 of whom a third were of North African origin, a third Sephardi, and a third Ashkenazi.) In the last quarter of the century, the Jews comprised about one-eighth of the total population. They lived in the *Ḥarat al-Yahūd* ("Jewish quarter") inside the poor Muslim district in the eastern part of the lower city. Most of them barely subsisted by petty trade and peddling in Haifa or nearby villages. The importance of the Jewish community in the city increased with the arrival of members of the First and Second Aliyah from Eastern Europe, mostly from Russia. From the 1880s onward, and especially in the early 20th century, extensive Jewish commercial and industrial activity sprang up. During his visit to Ereẓ Israel in 1898–99, Theodor Herzl recognized Haifa's numerous potentialities as the future chief port and an important inland road junction. In his *Altneuland* (1902), the description of Haifa occupies a central place in his vision of rebuilt Israel. The laying of the cornerstone of the *Technion in 1912 marked the high point of the intensified Jewish activities and was a signal for further development projects.

On the eve of World War I, Haifa, with more than 20,000 inhabitants and a constantly expanding export-import trade, was the key city of northern Ereẓ Israel. A progressive European minority added to its cosmopolitan character and an extensive network of schools, most of them Catholic, provided a high standard of education. New residential quarters were added in the east and west and on the southern slopes of the Carmel and eventually embraced the ancient site of the city.

British Mandate Period

On September 23, 1918, after four centuries of Ottoman rule, Haifa was captured in fierce battles by the British forces. During the British Mandate, Haifa rapidly grew into a large modern city in which the Jewish population played an increasingly predominant role. In 1919 the Haifa-Lydda railroad was added to the narrow gauge Haifa-Ẓemaḥ-Dara line. In the 1920s and 1930s the road network which linked up the various parts of Haifa was greatly improved and extended.

The 1922 census recorded a population of 25,000 in Haifa, of whom more than 9,000 were Muslims, slightly fewer Christian Arabs, and more than 6,000 Jews. According to the 1931 census, it contained 50,403 residents, including about 20,000 Muslims, 15,923 Jews, and about 14,000 Christians. By 1944 the number of inhabitants had grown to 128,000 of whom 66,000 were Jewish, 35,940 Muslim, 26,570 Christian, and 3,000 Bahais. At the end of the Mandate (1948) the Jews comprised nearly two-thirds of the population (about 100,000 out of 150,000). The completion of the large harbor in 1934 produced a great burst of prosperity and Haifa became the main and practically only port of international repute in Ereẓ Israel, taking precedence over Jaffa. Haifa's economy was further strengthened by the completion in 1939 of the oil pipeline from Iraq to its Mediterranean terminus at Haifa and the large oil refineries near the city. At this time the port facilities encouraged many new industries, some of them the largest in the country (textiles, glass, bricks, petroleum products, cement, metal, ceramics, etc.), in Haifa and the vicinity, especially in the Zebulun Valley. Tension between the city's Arab and Jewish residents, in the Mandate period, however, impeded Haifa's development. The riots of 1936–39 in particular adversely affected the city's economy and business dwindled between the conflicting sides as well as trade with Syria and Lebanon. The Arab population, mainly concentrated in the lower city, obstructed the Jews on their way to the adjoining industrial areas and to the port and services adjacent to it (marine shipping companies, banks, transport, insurance, etc.), as more and more Jews from the 1920s onward settled in the Hadar ha-Carmel section (the continuation of the Herzliyyah district founded before World War I). Hadar ha-Carmel developed rapidly around the Technion, which was inaugurated in 1925. The Mandate authorities granted some municipal autonomy to the new Jewish quarter. The Jewish settlement in this period also climbed higher up the slope around Merkaz ha-Carmel, in the Aḥuzzat Herbert Samuel quarter, and in Neveh Sha'anan. When the land in the Zebulun Valley on the coast of the bay was purchased in 1928, the Zionist movement made its first venture into comprehensive urban planning, for which it engaged the British city planner Patrick Abercrombie. The area stretching from the southeast corner of the bay up to Acre was divided into functional regions – an industrial zone in the south near the port; a residential area in the center in which from 1930 onward the Kerayot were built (Kiryat Ḥayyim, Kiryat Bialik, Kiryat Motzkin, Kiryat Yam); and an agricultural belt in the north.

Toward the end of the British Mandate, both the Jews and the Arabs attempted to gain control over the city. The hostilities which broke out at the end of 1947 reached a peak on April 21–22, 1948, when the British suddenly decided to evacuate the city. In a lightning military action, the Haganah captured the Arab quarters and took over the city. Only about 3,000 of Haifa's 50,000 Arab residents chose to remain in the city; the rest, in response to the Arab High Command's orders, refused to accept Jewish rule and abandoned their homes.

In the State of Israel

Late in 1948 Haifa's population numbered 97,544, of whom 96% were Jews. At the end of 1950 there were 140,000 inhabitants; at the end of 1952, 150,600; at the end of 1955, 158,700; in 1961, 183,021; and at the end of 1967, 209,900. In the mid-1990s, the population was approximately 246,500, including 35,000 new immigrants. At the end of 2002 the population of was Haifa 270,800, making it the third largest city in Israel after Jerusalem and Tel Aviv. Of Haifa's non-Jewish population, 10% are Arabs, 60% of them Christian and 30% Muslim.

The built-up area of Haifa continued to expand along the shore area and on the slopes and ridges of the Carmel. The lower city (whose former nucleus had been largely left in ruins in 1948) was rebuilt as the "City" – Haifa's main business section. The population density on Hadar ha-Carmel (also a center for retail trade, services, and entertainment) increased until residents started moving to the upper Carmel. Housing projects on a large scale were erected, including extensive suburbs such as Kiryat Eliezer on the coast and southern Romemah on a ridge of the Carmel. Later, other neighborhoods sprung up on the upper Carmel, including Aḥuza, Carmelia, Vardia, and Denia (private homes on the southern slopes of the Carmel).

In the 1950s and 1960s a number of changes were made in the functional arrangement of the city with Haifa and Acre being conceived as the axes of a comprehensive regional scheme. In the Haifa Bay area the industrial zone extended north along the coastal dune strip up to Acre and included "Steel City." Residential quarters were built east of this zone. On Mt. Carmel the crest and narrow spurs branching off to the west and east were reserved for building and parks and orchards fill the gorges. Downtown Haifa extended westward, spilling over southward into the Carmel Coast area. After the establishment of the State of Israel, the port was greatly expanded and modernized and became the home port of Israel's fast-growing navy. The piers were tripled in number, the water level deepened, and many port facilities added, such as the Dagon storage silos with a 75,000 ton capacity. In 1954 an auxiliary port was built at the Kishon River outlet, its pier was lengthened in 1964 to 2,099 ft. (640 m.). A shipyard for building and repairing ships, a floating dock, and a jetty for Israel's fishing fleet were also built in the Kishon area (1959). Haifa continued to be almost the exclusive embarkation and debarkation sea point in Israel

Haifa's industry continued expanding in this period, especially in the bay area. Two factories in Israel for the production and assembly of cars were set up there, as well as large chemical and petrochemical industries, an industrial and craft center, a plant for producing organic fertilizers from waste, a plant for purifying sewage water, and numerous other industrial enterprises. Also located in Haifa are the national offices of the Israel Railways (including their large workshops), the Israel Electric Company, Solel Boneh (Israel's largest contracting company), Zim (the largest shipping company), and others. Employment in the port area, which provided work for a tenth of the city's population, and in Haifa's varied industry, drew a very large labor force to the city, which is the best organized in the country. From the 1980s, the southern outskirts of the city began to be developed as an economic center for hi-tech companies, including branches of some the world's largest corporations, such as Intel, Microsoft, and Elbit (an Israeli firm manufacturing weapons systems). Nearby there is a transportation center, including both a railroad station and main bus terminal. From 1951 until his death in 1969, the mayor of Haifa was Abba *Khoushi, formerly the secretary of the Haifa labor council. He did much to develop and beautify the city.

The *Bahai sect, with its world center in Haifa, built a gold-domed sanctuary and cultivated one of the finest and largest gardens in the country. In 1987 the Bahais begin to enlarge the gardens, added 18 hanging gardens running for a kilometer along the slopes of the mountain and thus linking the upper part of the mountain with the lower part. In addition, the Bahais built other buildings, among them a library and administrative building. Another unique feature of the city is the Carmelit, Israel's only subway, which was set up in 1959.

The educational system has received particular attention. Haifa University College (see *Haifa, University of) was founded in 1963 by the municipality under the academic supervision of the *Hebrew University. It was granted independent status and in 1970 it offered courses in the humanities and social sciences and had a department for training high school teachers. Enrollment in 1969/70 totaled 3,600 and the academic staff numbered 340. In 1967 the college was transferred to the university campus (designed by the architect Oscar Niemeyer) on the summit of the Carmel. In the early years of the 21st century Haifa University had approximately 13,000 students. The university is under continuous expansion, adding new departments each year. The *Technion has another 13,000 students, studying engineering and the exact and life sciences. Various cultural and social centers, public buildings, and museums have been built to house among other things the National Science Museum, the Railroad Museum, the Naval Museum, the Museum of Modern Art, the Japanese Art Pavilion, the *Haifa Municipal Theater, and the Haifa Symphony Orchestra. In addition, Haifa has a zoo and nature and prehistoric museum. One of the best-known community centers is the James de Rothschild Center. In 1963 a Jewish-Arab youth center, Bet Gefen, was opened through the efforts of Abba Khoushi, to help integrate the minority youth. The city of Haifa hosts three yearly festivals: an international film festival during the Sukkot holiday, a children's theater festival on Passover, and the Holiday of Holidays in December corresponding to the three religions holidays of the season: the Jewish Hanukkah, the Muslim Ramadan, and the Christian Christmas.

Haifa has not been immune to terrorist attacks. Four suicide bombings in 2001–2003 claimed dozens of lives and injured nearly 200 people.

BIBLIOGRAPHY: R. Hecht, *Sippurah shel Ḥeifah* (1968); Z. Vilnay, in: *Sefer ha-Shanah shel Ereẓ Yisrael*, 1 (1923), 125–9; idem, *Ḥeifah be-Avar u-va-Hoveh* (1936); J. Schattner, in: IEJ, 4 (1954), 26ff.; Hamilton, in: QDAP, 4 (1935), 1ff.; J. Braslavski (Braslavi), in: BJPES,

12 (1945/6), 166–7; idem, *Le-Ḥeker Arẓenu* (1954), index; E.G. Rey, *Les colonies franques de Syrie…* (1883), 431; Prawer, *Ẓalbanim*, index; V. Guérin, *Description géographique… Samarie*, 2 (1875), 252 ff.; Mann, Egypt, index; EIS, s.v.; L. Oliphant, *Haifa, or Life in Modern Palestine* (1887); A. Carmel, *Toledot Ḥeifah bi-Ymei ha-Turkim* (1969); S. Klein, *Toledot ha-Yishuv ha-Yehudi be-Ereẓ Yisrael* (1935), index; *Ḥeifah ba-Asor le-Yisrael* (1959). **WEBSITE:** www.haifa.muni.il.

[Alex Carmel / Shaked Gilboa (2nd ed.)]

HAIFA, UNIVERSITY OF. In 1970, the name of Haifa University College, founded in 1963, was officially changed to "University of Haifa" and in 1972 the Council for Higher Education granted the university full academic accreditation, including the right to award a B.A. degree in 24 departments and an M.A. in 12. The university, which is located on the Carmel Mountains, high above the city of Haifa, has faculties of Humanities and Social Sciences, Law, Science and Science Education, Social Welfare and Health Studies, Education, a graduate school for Business Administration, and a Center for Maritime Studies. It has about 13,000 students and 40 research centers in various fields. The Oranim Teachers' College and the Ohel Sarah College of the Emek became branches of the university. Subsequently the Ohel Sarah College became the independent Emek Jezreel College while the Oranim Teachers College continued partially to cooperate with the university in various fields of study. In 1984 the Hecht Museum, named for Reuven and Edith Hecht, was established on the campus. The museum exhibits Reuven Hecht's collections of Ereẓ Israel archeology and modern art. The university also runs an overseas study program for students from all over the world who wish to study in Israel. The library, which is situated in a specially designed modernistic unit, includes 700,000 volumes and has pioneered the use of computers for preparation of bibliographies and bibliographic data. It also includes material for psychological tests and audio-visual material. The Haifa campus houses the IBM building, thus enabling the university to cooperate with the high-tech industry.

WEBSITE: www.haifa.ac.il.

[Shaked Gilboa (2nd ed.)]

HAIFA MUNICIPAL THEATER, Haifa repertory company, founded in 1961 by the Haifa Municipality. It was the first theater in Israel to be initiated by a public body, as well as the first with a paying membership (subscribers were guaranteed five new productions each season). The theater was warmly welcomed by residents of Haifa, and from its inception had 12,000 subscribers. Unlike other theaters in Israel, the Haifa Municipal Theater began in a magnificent building with up-to-date stage equipment and a municipal subsidy which guaranteed its solvency. Its budget in 1967 was IL2 million, of which IL420,000 was subsidy. However, since there had never been a theater in Haifa before, it had difficulty in recruiting actors. Despite this handicap, it succeeded in presenting several excellent productions, among them Berthold Brecht's *The Caucasian Chalk Circle*, which was performed with great success in Israel in 1962 and at the Venice Festival in 1963, and Shakespeare's *Richard III* (1966), both staged by the Haifa Municipal Theater's first artistic director, Yosef *Millo. The repertoire of the Haifa Municipal Theater consists of classical, contemporary, and original Hebrew plays. In 1970 it recruited the avant-garde group of young actors and directors, led by Oded Kotler, who constituted *Bimat ha-Saḥkanim*. The 1970s were the golden age of Israeli theater, and the theater preformed plays by Yehosuha *Sobol, Hanoch *Levin, Hillel *Mittelpunkt, Yosef Bar-Yosef, Yaakov *Shabtai, and others. During these years Nola Chelton and a group of actors called the Project Group joined the theater and preformed several major plays. After Kotler, the theater was led by Amnon Maskin and later by Omri Nizzan and Noam Semel. Under their management the theater focused on Jewish-Israeli plays, the best-known being Sobol's *Ghetto* and *Jewish Soul*. *Jewish Soul* was the first Israeli play to participate in the Edinburgh Festival. *Ghetto* was shown at the Berlin Festival in the presence of the president of Germany. Later, both plays were shown at other international festivals. In 1987 the theater established a stage for plays in Arabic. In 1988 the theater found itself in the midst of public controversy over Sobol's politically charged *Jerusalem Syndrome*, a play written for Israel's 40th anniversary. The controversy led to the resignation of Sobol and Gedaliah Besser, the artistic directors. In 1990 Oded Kotler was reappointed to head the theater, a position he held until 1997. The theater continued to perform Israeli plays alongside foreign ones, but later faced financial problems, lost many subscribers, and failed to perform significant plays.

WEBSITE: www.haifa-theatre.co.il/mainPage.html

[Mendel Kohansky / Shaked Gilboa (2nd ed.)]

HAILPERIN, HERMAN (1899–1973). U.S. Conservative rabbi and author. Hailperin was born in Newark, New Jersey, and educated in New York City, where he earned his B.A. from New York University (1919) and was ordained at the *Jewish Theological Seminary (1922). In 1933, he received his Ph.D. from the University of Pittsburgh, where he had arrived in 1922 to become the rabbi of the Tree of Life Congregation. Hailperin transformed the venerable synagogue (founded in the 1860s) into a model Conservative synagogue-center, while instituting a number of innovations more in line with Reform practice, such as the playing of an organ during worship services and abolishing the observance of the second day of festivals. His actions – which were rewarded by his congregation with a life contract – represented a challenge to the authority of the *Rabbinical Assembly, which had decreed that Conservative Judaism would attempt to revitalize the custom of *Yom Tov Sheni* (observing two days of major festivals in the Diaspora). Faced with the alternatives of either disciplining Hailperin – a former member of the RA's Executive Committee and Committee on Jewish Law and Standards – or abandoning its policy that decisions were binding on all members, the RA elected to relax its policy of binding decisions.

A scholar in the field of medieval philosophy and theology, Hailperin also taught Jewish history at the University of Pittsburgh and Duquesne University. He wrote three books: *A Rabbi Teaches: A Collection of Addresses and Sermons* (1939, commemorating the octocentennial of the birth of Maimonides); *Rashi and the Christian Scholars* (1963), an analysis of the influence of the Jewish sage's biblical commentary on medieval Christian scholars; and *The Three Great Religions: Their Theological and Cultural Affinities* (1978, posthumously).

[Bezalel Gordon (2nd ed.)]

BIBLIOGRAPHY: P.S. Nadell, *Conservative Judaism in America: A Biographical Dictionary and Sourcebook*, 1988.

HAIMOVICI, MENDEL (1906–1973), Romanian mathematician. Born in Jassy, he completed his mathematical studies at the University in Jassy (1930). In 1932–33 he studied for his doctorate at the University of Rome, completing his thesis in 1933 in the field of the mechanics of fluids: "Sur l'écoulement des liquides pesants dans un plan vertical," presented in French to a committee headed by Tulio Levi-Civita. Upon his return to Jassy, Haimovici was appointed assistant lecturer at the Mathematical Seminary of the local university headed by Alexandru Myller, in the field of analytical geometry (1933–40). Excluded from the university by the racial laws during the Holocaust period, he returned to his position only after the collapse of the pro-Nazi regime, on August 23, 1944. In 1945 he became assistant professor, in 1946 full professor, and in 1948 chairman of the theoretical mechanics department at the university. In 1949 he became a corresponding member and in 1963 a full member of the Romanian Academy of Sciences, mathematical sciences section. In 1949 he became the director of the Mathematical Institute of the Jassy branch of the Romanian Academy of Sciences. Haimovici was a specialist in differential geometry and mathematical analysis. He made contributions to Finsler spaces, mechanics, theory of outer differential systems, and Pfaff systems of equations. He published numerous studies – books and articles – in these fields. His brother, ADOLF HAIMOVICI (1912–1993), was also a well-known mathematician, a specialist in geometry and professor of mathematical analysis at Jassy University.

BIBLIOGRAPHY: G.S. Aandonie, *Istoria matematicii in Romaniai*, 3 (1967), 106–12, 147–55; S. Marcus and C. Roman, in: N. Cajal and H. Kuller (eds.), *Contributia evreilor din Romania la cultura si civilizatie* (1996), 116–17.

[Lucian-Zeev Herscovici (2nd ed)]

HAIMOWITZ, MORRIS JONAH (1881–1958), Yiddish writer. Born in Mir (Belorussia), where he studied at the yeshivah, he immigrated to the United States in 1902, spending the rest of his life in New York. He published his first story, "Blondzhendik" ("Erring," 1905) in the *Fraye Arbeter Shtime*, joined the literary group, Di *Yunge, and coedited their anthology *Yugend* (1907–8), in which he published his stories and essays. Later, he co-edited the miscellany *Literatur* (1910) and the almanac *Di Naye Heym* (1914). His novels about Jewish life in the U.S., and historical novels about Jesus and Shabbetai Ẓevi (*Yor 1666/426: Shabtay Tsvi in Shtambul*, "The Year 1666: Shabbetai Ẓevi in Istanbul," 1946), display a deep understanding of human nature and of historical events. In *Arum dem Man fun Natseres* ("Concerning the Man from Nazareth," 1924), he presented a novel interpretation and characterization of the early Christian movement and its leading personalities. He portrayed himself in the character of Levin in the novel *Oyfn Veg* ("En route," 1914).

BIBLIOGRAPHY: Rejzen, Leksikon, 1 (1926), 1137–9; LNYL, 3 (1960), 717–9. **ADD. BIBLIOGRAPHY:** M. Krutikov, *Yiddish Fiction and the Crisis of Modernity* (2001), 145, 155–7.

[Elias Schulman / Jerold C. Frakes (2nd ed.)]

HAINDORF, ALEXANDER (Zwi Hirsch ben Nessannel; 1784–1862), German educator and physician. In 1825 he founded at Muenster, Westphalia, an institution for the advancement of crafts among Jews and the training of teachers for Jewish elementary schools. An endowment by Haindorf's father-in-law enabled the school to train about 350 artisans in 50 years. The school had such an excellent reputation that the Prussian government permitted Christian pupils to attend it; in 1830 they outnumbered the Jews. One of Haindorf's aims was to promote the amalgamation of Judaism and Christianity, and in "slow and cautious imparting of Christian education" he saw a step in this direction.

BIBLIOGRAPHY: Steinberg, in: JZWL, 2 (1863), 1–11; M. Eliav, *Ha-Ḥinnukh ha-Yehudi be-Germanyah* (1960), 285, 295–6, 310. **ADD. BIBLIOGRAPHY:** S. Freund, "Alexander Haindorf – Grenzgaenge zwischen juedischer und christlicher Kultur," in: F. Siegert (ed.), *Grenzgänge – Festschrift fuer Diethard Aschhoff* (2002), 175–93; *Biographisches-Bibliographisches Kirchenlexikon*, 20 (2000), 693–706.

[Meir Lamed]

HAINOVITZ, ASHER (1939–), *hazzan*. Hainovitz was born in Jerusalem and studied *ḥazzanut* under Shelomo Zalman *Rivlin. He studied at the Jerusalem Rubin Academy of Music and later received his L.R.S.M. degree from the Royal Academy of Music of London. After serving as cantor in Bulawayo, Zimbabwe, Pretoria, and London he was appointed to the Central Yeshurun Synagogue in Jerusalem. He is the possessor of a sweet lyric tenor voice and has made the performance of Yiddish *lid* a specialty. Hainovitz is equally at home on stage and at the pulpit, both in Israel and abroad. He prides himself on being a *ba'al tefillah* ("master of prayer") at the pulpit. For the Rennanot Institute for Sacred Liturgical Music, he has recorded the entire *Ha-Yamim Ha-Nora'im nusaḥ* with organ accompaniment by Raymond *Goldstein. Other recordings include Yiddish song in *Ḥazzonim Zingt Yiddish*.

[Akiva Zimmerman / Raymond Goldstein (2nd ed.)]

HAITI, republic on the Caribbean island of Hispaniola, with a Jewish population of less than 30 persons (2002). Columbus landed there during his first voyage in 1492. In the second half of the 17th century the French gained control of the western part of the island of Hispaniola. By the treaty of Ryswich in 1607, Spain officially ceded this part of the Hispaniola to France which named it Saint Domingue or Haiti.

Individual Jews who left Dutch Brazil in 1654 used their expertise in sugar growing and settled on French plantations but never founded a congregation. The "Black Code" of 1685 ordering the expulsion of the Jews from the French islands caused them to leave Hispaniola. Only Jews holding special "Lettres patentes" could settle there. Most prominent were the members of the Jewish Gradis company, which had offices in Cap Francois (today's Cap Haitien), Sain Louis, Fond de l'isle a Vache, and Leogan. With the required permission, Jews arrived from Bayonne and Bordeaux (including the distinguished Mendes France family). They were joined by Jews from Curaçao, who settled mainly in Cap Francais (where they employed a cantor and a circumciser), Jeremie, Les Cayes, and in smaller numbers in Port au Prince. Jews also came from Jamaica and St. Thomas of the Virgin Islands. All of them were either Dutch, English, or Danish citizens. With the nomination of Jean Baptiste Charles Henry Hector Comte d'Estaing as governor of the French Windward Islands (Isles de Vent), the tolerable, semi-legal existence of the Jews in Haiti was put under the yoke of heavy taxation. Jews had to pay for the financing of infrastructure projects and for the maintenance of the army. An attempt was made to expel the Jews from Cap Francais.

In day-to-day life there was no real discrimination. Dr. Michel Lopez de Pas of Leogan was nominated as "Medecin du Roy" (Royal Physician), others were named as judges and to other public functions. Moron, a town of 12,000 in habitants, is named after the Curaçao Jew Simon Isaac Henriquez Moron, who owned a plantation there.

The Haitian slave rebellion at the end of the 18th century caused the exodus of the Jews to New Orleans, to other Caribbean islands, or to France. It is almost impossible to estimate the exact number of Jews residing legally or illegally in Haiti in the 18th century.

In the 1920s Jews from Syria and Lebanon, later joined by Jews from Germany and Eastern Europe, settled in Haiti. In time they numbered some 30 to 40 families, but no congregation was formed. With the unstable political and economic situation, in the 1990s only five or six families remained.

Relations of Haiti with Israel are usually friendly. In the 1970s Israel maintained an embassy in Port au Prince, which was later closed for financial reasons. In the early 21st century relations between the two countries were governed by non-resident ambassadors.

Israel's technical cooperation with Haiti is fruitful; Israel helped develop several regions in Haiti.

BIBLIOGRAPHY: Z. Loker, "Were there Jewish Communities in Saint Domingue (Haiti)," in: *Jewish Social Studies*, 45/2 (1983: 135–46); Z. Loker, "Un Juif portugals: fondateur de Moron?," in: *Conjonction: Revue Franco-Haitienne*, 139 (1978): 85–91; A. Cahen, "Les Juifs dans les colonies francaises au XVII siecle," in: REJ, 4 (1882): 127–45, 238–72; M. Arbell, *The Jewish Nation of the Caribbean* (2003).

[Mordechai Arbell (2nd ed.)]

HAJDU, ANDRÉ (1932–), Israeli composer, pianist, and ethnomusicologist. Born in Budapest, Hajdu studied composition and ethnomusicology with Kódaly at the Franz Liszt Academy. He spent two years among Hungarian gypsies collecting their songs. After the failure of the Hungarian uprising in 1956 he escaped to Paris, where he studied with *Milhaud and Messiaen. In the 1950s, Hajdu became acquainted with avant-garde music at the Darmstadt festivals, but preferred to compose in more traditional styles. In 1966, he immigrated to Israel, where he conducted research into ḥasidic music and taught composition at the Jerusalem Academy of Music and Dance, and later in the Department of Musicology at Bar-Ilan University, where he became a professor. In 2000 Hajdu was awarded the Israel Prize for his achievements in composition.

Hajdu composed in all major genres, including orchestral, chamber, and vocal music. His output includes many educational works, such as *The Milky Way* (1975–76), *Merry Feet* (1977), and *The Book of Challenges* (1991–99). Hajdu's style is pluralistic, and combines various tonal, modal, and post-tonal influences, with frequent use of humor and wit. This pluralism reflects Hajdu's personality, which he himself describes as full of contradictions, and his diverse background, as a religious Jew who grew up in an assimilated family.

Many of Hajdu's works are based on Jewish themes or texts, e.g, *Mishnayot* ("The Floating Tower"; 56 songs and choral pieces, 1971–73); *Teru'at Melekh* (for clarinet and strings, 1974) composed for Giora *Feldman; *The Prophet of Truth and the Prophet of Deceit* (for narrator and string orchestra, 1977); *Jonas* ("biblical opera," 1985–87); *Dreams of Spain* (cantata, 1991); *Kohelet* (for cello solo with three cellos, 1994). Among his other works are *Ludus Paschalis* (miniature opera, 1970), *Stories about Mischievous Children* (orchestra, 1976), *Instants suspendus* (for violin, 1978), *On Light and Depth* (for chamber orchestra, 1983–84), and *B.A.C.H.D.I.E.S.* (for instrumental ensemble, 2000). Hajdu published with M. Zakai, *Dialogue* (1999); and an essay: "Le théâtre intérieur: Eléments de mise en scène dans ma musique," in *Perspectives* (2003).

BIBLIOGRAPHY: Grove online.

[Yossi Goldenberg (2nd ed.)]

HAJDU, MIKLÓS (1879–1956), Hungarian journalist and author. Born in Gölle, Hajdu studied in Budapest. From 1897, he was on the editorial boards of *Budapesti Napló* ("Budapest Daily") and *A Nap* ("The Day"), later becoming editor of the latter. Bright in style, *A Nap* was the first "boulevard" type paper in Hungary. Hajdu had a keen interest in Jewish communal life and was one of the leaders of the liberal Isaiah Religious Society. He supported the Zionist cause before World War I and after the revolution of 1918 continued the struggle against assimilation within the framework of the Pest Neolog community. His literary works describe Jewish village life in western Hungary, and include *Gilead* (1914) and *Szeniczei Savuot* ("The Shavuot of Szenice," 1939). In 1939 he emigrated to Ereẓ Israel and settled in Tel Aviv.

BIBLIOGRAPHY: *Magyar Zsidó Lexikon* (1929), 337–8; *Magyar Életrajzi Lexikon* (1964), 657.

[Baruch Yaron]

HAJEK, MARKUS (1861–1941), laryngologist. Hajek, who was born in Yugoslavia, served in Vienna as assistant in the Rudolf Hospital and the University Polyclinic, and then became professor of laryngology at the University of Vienna. Hajek made fundamental contributions to anatomic, pathological, and clinical subjects in rhinolaryngology. He developed a systematic and scientific approach in the diagnosis and therapy of sinus ailments based on anatomical and pathological studies. He conducted studies on tuberculosis of the upper respiratory tract. He devised many practical instruments, suggested a new method of operation on frontal sinusitis, and improved the technique of extralaryngeal operations for cancer of the larynx. Hajek had to emigrate when the Nazis annexed Austria and died a destitute refugee in London. Among his publications are *Pathologie und Therapie der entzuendlichen Erkrankungen der Nebenhoehlen der Nase* (1899) which was translated into English in 1926, and *Syphilis of the Oral Cavity, Pharynx and Nasopharyngeal Cavity* (1928).

BIBLIOGRAPHY: S.R. Kagan, *Jewish Medicine* (1952).

[Suessmann Muntner]

HAJIM, JISRAEL (**Bohor**, also known as **Davico**; 1800–1880), author and printer; scion of a Sephardi family in Belgrade. Hajim lived in Vienna as well as Belgrade, where he belonged to the "Turkish" (i.e., Sephardi) Synagogue as *gabbai* and was also employed in the printing shops of Holzinger and Schmid, writing, editing, and typesetting Hebrew prayer books along with his own Ladino translations of the Psalms and other Biblical texts. He also produced an alphabetical guide for Jewish students called *Ḥinukh le-No'ar*. In the late 1830s he returned to Belgrade and worked for some 20 years as a Hebrew printer and editor in the print shop of the Serbian Prince Milosh. Hajim composed Judeo-Spanish or Ladino (sometimes referred to as Judesmo) introductions, translations, and commentaries on Hebrew texts. He is considered a pioneer in the literary usage of Ladino. He is credited with having declared: "*Byen avinturado sira il ki travajera nil ladinu*" ("Happy is he who writes in Ladino").

BIBLIOGRAPHY: M. Kayserling, *Bibliotheca espanola-portuguesa-judaica*, 2:4 (1890), 51; Y. Eventov, *Toledot Yehudei Yugoslavia*, vol. 1 (1971), 151; Z. Lebl, *Jevrejske knjige stampane u Beogradu 1837–1905*, (1990), 27–29; M. Mihailovic, "Dve stotine godina porodice Hajim - Davico u Beogradu," in: *Zbornik*, 6, (1992), 249–76; D. Bunis, "Yisrael Haim of Belgrade and the History of Judesmo Linguistics," in: *Histoire, epistémologie, langage*, 18:1, 151–66.

[Zvi Loker (2nd ed.)]

HAJJĀJ (Hagège), DANIEL (1892–?), *Tunis-born publicist and Judeo-Arabic writer who immigrated to Paris in 1959. Hajjāj published, translated, adapted, and edited over 30 novels and worked on several local papers, while at the same time being employed in a series of professions – including pharmacist and typographer. Among his writings in Judeo-Arabic are "The Barber's Assistant" (1930), a short story followed by a collection of 1,000 Tunisian, Judeo-Arabic proverbs (*Mille proverbes tunisiens*), arranged in alphabetical order and "Tunisian Judeo-Arabic Literature" (1939), a survey of Judeo-Arabic literature and writers. He also founded and edited the scientific and artistic periodical *La Gaieté Tunisienne* (1913–15, 1933).

BIBLIOGRAPHY: Attal, in: *Studies and Reports of the Ben Zvi Institute*, 3 (1960), 56–59, 46–48 (Heb. part).

[Robert Attal]

HAJNAL, ANNA (1907–1978), Hungarian poetess, writer, and translator, wife of I. *Keszi. Hajnal was born in Gyepűfűzes. In 1937–38 she was one of the editors of the literary journal *Argonauták* ("Argonaut"). Her poems are marked by perfection of form and metaphysical feeling. Her lyrical poems cover a wide area and include Jewish, especially biblical, themes, such as "*Tánc a frigyláda kõrű*" ("Dance Around the Ark of the Covenant") and "Job." The greatest of her Jewish poems, if not of all her poems, is certainly her long poem "Tiszta, tiszta, tiszta" ("Pure, Pure, Pure"), which she terms "a Jewish Dirge." It is a paraphrase of the ritual of **tohorah* (the traditional washing of the dead before burial). Both in form and in translation the poem is a masterpiece; the lyrical elements of the text, particularly of the Song of Songs and the thoughts of the mourners, are interwoven with unconventional inner dialogue. Among her published works mention should be made of her collected poems (1948); *Ébredj fel bennem álom* ("Wake Up My Innermost Dreams," 1935–48), and *Esõ esik-versek gyermekekenek* ("It Is Raining – Poems for Children," 1954).

[Baruch Yaron]

HAJÓS, ALFRÉD (1878–1955), architect and first Hungarian Olympic swimming champion (1896), designer of sports stadiums. His main project was the roofed swimming pool (1930) on Margaret Island in Budapest. Hajós was a convert to Christianity.

[Eva Kondor]

ḤAKAM AL, Baghdad family, members of which were rabbis of the community from the 18th to the 20th centuries. Moses Ḥayyim (1756–1837), rabbi and halakhic authority, was born in Baghdad. He served as rabbi of Basra for several years, and then—from 1787 until his death – as rabbi of Baghdad. The Jews of Baghdad continued to follow his decisions and takkanot. His novellae and sermons are scattered in the works of his contemporaries. ELIJAH BEN ḤAYYIM MOSES (1807–1859) was a rabbi, preacher, and kabbalist, and the author of *Midrash Eliyahu* (1862), a work on kabbalistic explanations of biblical and talmudic passages. He was also a wealthy and generous merchant. His son, JOSEPH ḤAYYIM (1833 (or 1835)–1909) was an outstanding scholar. His son JACOB (1854–1920), rabbi, kabbalist and preacher, succeeded his father (1909). He wrote: *Ẓiẓim u-Feraḥim* (1904), homilies on the Pentateuch and *Ze-*

khut Avot, which he appended to his father's work *Ḥasdei Avot* (1904). Several of his works, including responsa, and novellae on *aggadah*, are still in manuscript. Many of his novellae are scattered throughout his father's works. He was succeeded in turn by his son, DAVID.

BIBLIOGRAPHY: A. Ben-Jacob, Yehudei Bavel (1965), 127, 192.

[Avraham David]

HA-KARMEL (Heb. הַכַּרְמֶל), Hebrew periodical published in Vilna under the editorship of S.J. *Fuenn. It first appeared as a weekly (1860–70) and later as a monthly (1871–80). *Ha-Karmel* was required by terms of its license to publish a Russian supplement. This supplement was a more extreme advocate of the enlightenment than its Hebrew equivalent. Fuenn was a moderate *maskil* who tried to bridge the gap between the traditionalist and liberal elements. He supported the policy of the Russian government toward the Jews, closer association of the Jews with the Russian nation and its culture, and advocated the transition to labor, especially agriculture. Among the contributors to *Ha-Karmel* were A.B. Lebensohn, Ẓ.H. Katzenellenbogen, M. Plungian, E. Zweifel, J. Eichenbaum, A.B. Gottlober, J.L. Gordon, Kalman Schulmann, J. Reifmann, A. Harkavy, Solomon Buber, S. Rubin, R.A. Braudes, and J.M. Pines. For a short time (1866–68), *Ha-Karmel's* editorial policy became more liberal and a number of articles by more radical authors appeared (A.U. Kovner, A.J. Paperna, and L. Kantor). Editorials came out in support of M.L. Lilienblum who also began to contribute to it. However, it soon resumed its more moderate course. The number of subscribers fluctuated between 300 and 500. *Ḥevrat Mefiẓei ha-Haskalah*, to which the periodical devoted much space from the time of the founding of that society (1863), supported *Ha-Karmel*, although not pleased with its moderate position. The literary level of the periodical was generally low, its language flowery, the poems (with the exception of those of J.L. Gordon) and stories few and poor, and the articles written in a cumbersome style. Permeated with a spirit of Russian patriotism, *Ha-Karmel* supported the Russification policy in the regions of Lithuania and Poland. The paper devoted much space to news of Jewish life in Vilna and its surroundings.

BIBLIOGRAPHY: S.J. Fuenn, in: *Ha-Karmel*, 1 (1860), 372–3; Klausner, Sifrut, 4 (1954), 11–20; G. Elkoshi, in: *He-Avar*, 13 (1966), 66–97; 14 (1967), 105–42; Y. Slutsky, *ibid.*, 14 (1967) 153–8.

[Yehuda Slutsky]

HAKDAMAH (Heb. הַקְדָּמָה), introduction to a book. The first known *hakdamah* is the introduction to the **Halakhot Gedolot*. In effect it is a sermon in praise of the Torah which its author saw fit to place at the beginning of his book as a preface. In medieval literature the *hakdamah* served as a literary genre and halakhic authors regarded themselves duty bound to attach a *hakdamah* to their works. Generally speaking the author in his *hakdamah* gives his motives for writing the book, and says something about its contents, but very often the *hakdamah* has important literary value of its own. Spanish and Italian authors also gave their *hakdamot* an aesthetic form by means of rhyme, meter, and even verses and complete poems, and some of them are literary gems. Especially noteworthy are those of Naḥmanides who wrote many fine *hakdamot*, of especial merit being those to his *Milḥamot ha-Shem* and his *Torat ha-Adam*. Some *hakdamot* are complete works, both in scope and in quality, and of these the introduction of Menahem b. Solomon *Meiri to his commentary *Beit ha-Beḥirah* on *Avot* is especially noteworthy. Occasionally the contents, purpose, and scope of the book cannot be fathomed without the *hakdamah*. Because the ordinary reader usually omits the reading of the *hakdamah*, some authors literally adjured copyists not to copy their works without the introduction, as did, for example, the author of **Ha-Ḥinukh*. So important was the *hakdamah* regarded that a popular proverb has it that "a book without a *hakdamah* is like a body without a *neshamah*" ("soul").

[Israel Moses Ta-Shma]

The *hakdamah* attained full development with Saadiah Gaon, in the tenth century. A systematic thinker, he found it necessary to explain what had motivated him to treat the particular subject he had chosen, thus laying the foundation of his thesis as well as apprising the reader of the content of the book he was presenting. He followed this pattern in his *siddur* and particularly in his philosophical work, the *Sefer ha-Emunot ve-ha-De'ot*. In his rather lengthy introduction he states that he wrote this book in order to resolve the doubts and confusions of his contemporaries concerning their traditional faith. The method followed by Saadiah Gaon was further developed and perfected by Moses Maimonides. He used his prefaces to certain orders, tractates, and chapters of the Mishnah, to sections of his great code, the *Mishneh Torah*, to expound his own philosophical ideas, in addition to elucidating such recondite subjects as the various degrees of ritual impurity dealt with in the order of *Tohorot* or the plants mentioned in the order of *Zera'im*. Thus, in the "Eight Chapters" prefacing his commentary on the tractate *Avot*, he unfolds a complete system of ethics, while in his introduction to the tenth chapter of the tractate *Sanhedrin*, where the afterlife is mentioned, he discusses resurrection, listing what he regards as the fundamentals of Jewish belief, the 13 "principles" of Judaism. Maimonides' philosophical magnum opus, the *Guide of the Perplexed*, has both a short dedicatory preface addressed to his favorite pupil for whom it was written, as well as a fairly extensive general introduction, outlining his understanding of the text of Scripture, which, according to him, cannot always be taken literally. He also cautions the reader not to judge the merit of his book by a few isolated statements but to consider it in its totality and with the same seriousness with which it was written. Among the medieval Jewish scholars whose prefaces to their works are worthy of note, Abraham ibn Ezra stands high on the list. In a rhymed introduction to his commentary on the Pentateuch, after dismissing as worthless four other methods of interpretation, he summarizes his own approach, namely that of a critical understanding of the biblical text, making use of all the aids of philology available, regardless of the conclusions to which such an approach may lead.

The prefaces of books by medieval Jewish authors started out, like those of the Muslim writers of the time, with praise of God. With the introduction of printing it became customary for publishers, editors, and even proofreaders to write prefaces asking the indulgence of the readers for typographical errors and mistakes due to other causes.

[Samuel Rosenblatt]

ḤAKETÍA, the Judeo-Spanish of North Africa. The Judeo-Spanish dialect spoken until two or three generations ago in the Jewish North African communities of *Morocco and *Algeria, and also the city Gibraltar, is known as Ḥaketía, Jaquetía, or Ḥakitíya. It is based on the language spoken by the Jews in *Spain before their expulsion. Ḥaketía is distinct from Judesmo, spoken in *Turkey and in the Balkans, hence its distinct name, the etymology of which is unknown – the root may be Arabic *ḥky* or *ḥkt* in the sense of speaking or conversing. The term thus applies only to the spoken dialect, which has borrowed many words from the neighboring Maghreb dialects, both Jewish and Muslim, and even from Spanish Arabic. This use of Arabic decreases with the rise in register, and may become negligible. So while the term Ḥaketía may be applied for convenience to the dialect as a whole, it must be remembered that the dialect also contains literary registers which use the general Judeo-Spanish koiné, namely Ladino, although Ḥaketía has its own distinct features. The most prominent is the high incidence of a velar-fricative realization [x] of the phoneme spelled in Hispanic Spanish with the letter "j" (*jota*) alongside the alternants characteristic of Judeo-Spanish, namely a voiced or voiceless post-alveolar sibilant [ʒ] or [ʃ].

In contrast with the Eastern Judesmo, Ḥaketía retained links with the Spanish of the Iberian Peninsula throughout the ages following the Expulsion because of its geographical proximity as well as Spanish and Portuguese presence in various North African coast cities: Ceuta, Melilla, Oran, Tangier, Arcila, and Larache. Its decline was greatly accelerated by the massive Spanish presence in Northern Morocco since 1860 when the city of Tetuan was conquered by Spain for two years, and more so since the establishment of the Protectorate in 1912. The intensive daily interaction between the entire Jewish population (not just merchants and the like) and the Spaniards greatly accelerated the transition from a "Hispanicized" form of Ḥaketía to almost pure Spanish. Sons of Ḥaketía speakers began to restrict their dialect to domestic circles (home and community) and to defined functions. In the resulting diglossia, Ḥaketía was the Low variety. This state of affairs was due to the threat, perceived by the young generation, of Ḥaketía to their linguistic image, as they were aspiring for education, progress, and cultural emancipation. Most of them did indeed achieve this goal, and modern Spanish, with all its assets, became their primary language. Today Ḥaketía remains in partial usage, limited to certain registers in the speech of these community members, most of whom have since emigrated from Morocco to Israel or to various Western countries. At this distance it seems Ḥaketía no longer poses a threat; it is no longer regarded as broken Spanish but rather as a language in its own right, with its own merits and history. Now people have begun to relive it, reconstruct some of its usages, and compose and act plays in it, albeit restricted to humoristic genres; Ḥaketía will probably never again be used in serious contexts.

The first to write a detailed, scientific account of the dialect was Joseph Benoliel in the 1920s. Most of what we know about Ḥaketía today is based on this account. Benoliel has salvaged much material belonging to the cultural tradition (oral texts, proverbs, etc.), grammar (phonology and morphology), and lexicon. He remembered the dialect as he had heard it in the second half of the 19th century, when it was still in current, spontaneous use. Respanification was already in progress, as was later verified with the discovery of the 1861–1875 protocols of the Tangier community committee, which showed many influences from Standard Spanish. Admittedly, these protocols represent an official register, but Spanish influence was also found in manuscripts of folktales and chronicles from the beginning of the 19th century.

Judeo-Arabic was also current in these communities. Judeo-Spanish/Judeo-Arabic bilingualism may explain the high portion of Arabic words in Ḥaketía. Further research could ascertain whether bilingualism was a communal or individual phenomenon, whether it was limited to men or included women, to what extent and what purposes each dialect served, whether a certain kind of diglossia emerged, and what part was played by *forasteros* ("strangers," i.e., immigrants from other Moroccan communities). The massive shift to modern Spanish in these communities can only be explained if we assume that the Arabic element was secondary in their speech. Further proof of that is the suppression of any Arabic elements as soon as the register was raised. High-register Ḥaketía is not represented in literary works, which are nonexistent in this dialect; it occurs rather in religious sermons, miscellaneous manuscripts, and prescriptive essays, such as *Dat Yehudit* ("Jewish Religion"), introducing women to their specific observance practices, by Abraham Laredo and Isaac Halevy, first printed in Livorno in 1827.

Scholars of both Spanish and non-Spanish origin have shown an interest in Ḥaketía (see bibliography). Important research has been conducted in academic institutions such as the Arias Montano Institute in Madrid, subsequently the CSIC (Consejo Superior de Investigaciones Científicas). Most of the researchers, of cultural-historical orientation, were keen to collect documentation of the oral-literary tradition, romances, coplas, elegies, wedding songs, etc. These collections represent a high linguistic register, inclining towards "pure" Spanish, both old and new. Therefore the picture they supply of vernacular Ḥaketía is only partial. Most of the dialectal research conducted so far has concentrated on its description as a Romance language. The Arabic element is still unexplored, and the Hebrew element only partially studied. One major advantage of Benoliel's works is his concept of the dialect as a living vernacular, not just a literary language. Similarly, Iacob Hassan, who has dedicated a large number of studies to revision and analysis of literary texts, shows a keen interest in aspects of the vernacular. Both these scholars are also distinguished in their study of the Hebrew element in Ḥaketía.

Noteworthy fieldwork has been conducted by Alegria Bendelac, who interviewed and recorded hundreds of informants, publishing her studies in three volumes. Bendelac's *Los Nuestros…* (1987) is a book aspiring to sketch a portrait of the Ḥaketiphonic community in its native land by means of scores of transcribed texts acquired at recorded interviews. These texts reflect the spoken, everyday dialect in its diversity and registers. Bendelac's *Voces Jaquetiescas* (1990) is a kind of glossary of Ḥaketian expressions, where the writer notes that, despite its far-reaching overlap with Standard Spanish, it is still "alive and kicking," especially by virtue of its distinct intonation, phraseology, and connotations. In 1995 Bendelac published a dictionary that comprises not only what the writer found in Benoliel's book, but also material she collected in her recordings, including authentic quotations that demonstrate actual linguistic usage.

As stated, some of the current scholarly activity in the domain of Ḥaketía is conducted by both scholars and laymen who thereby express their longing for the past of the community, a past which looms up in the distance and projects its glory over the present. Of note is "Centro de estudios sefardíes de Caracas," which publishes books and a periodical called *Maghen*. Some individuals took the initiative to actively collect texts, such as Benazeraf's 1978 collection of Ḥaketía proverbs, while others continue to do so. This endeavor is most prominent in the field of modern artistic creativity: humoristic sketches, such as those written and performed by Solly Levy and the tapes recorded by the brothers Esther Aflalo and Mozi Cohen. These writers display an impressive mastery of the dialect. Although the Ḥaketía in their writings is reconstructed, their memory and praiseworthy talent can be relied upon, and the authenticity of their materials is convincing. The protocols of the Tangier community committee and other written documents may now be found on scholars' desks. As this work progresses, so will our state of knowledge in this field.

BIBLIOGRAPHY: M. Alvar, *Endechas judéo-españolas. Estudio léxico y vocabulario* (1969); idem, *Cantos de boda judeo-españoles* (1971); T. Alexander & Y. Bentolila, "Elementos hispánicos y jaquéticos en los refranes judeo-españoles de Marruecos," in: *Jewish Studies at the Turn of the 20th Century*, vol. 2, *Judaism from the Renaissance to Modern Times*, 421–29 (1998); O. Anahory-Librowicz, *Florilegio de romances sefardíes de la Diáspora (una colección malagueña)* (1980); S.G. Armistead, "El cancionero judeo-español de Marruecos en el siglo 18 (Incipits de los Ben-Çûr)," in: *Nueva Revista de Filología Hispánica*, 22 (1973), 280–90; idem, "La colección Nahón de romances judeo-españoles de Tánger," in: *La Coronica*, 5:1 (1976), 7–16; S.G. Armistead & J.H. Silverman, "Four Moroccan Judeo-Spanish Folksongs," in: *Incipit (1824–1825)*; idem, in: *Hispanic Review*, 42:1 (1974), 83–87; idem, *Judeo-Spanish Ballads from New York* (1981); idem, with the collaboration of O.A. Librowicz, *Romances judeo-españoles de Tanger recogidos por Zarita Nahón* (1977); R. Benazeraf, *Recueil de "Refranes" (proverbes) judéo-espagnols du Maroc (Hakitía)* (1978); A. Bendayan de Bendelac, *Los Nuestros: Sejiná, Letuarios, Jaquetía y Fraja. Un retrato de los sefardíes del norte de Marruecos a través de sus recuerdos y de su lengua (1860–1984)* (1987); idem, *Voces Jaquetiescas* (1990); idem, *Diccionario del Judeoespañol de los Safardíes del Norte de Marruecos* (1995); Y. Bentolila, "Le composant hébraïque dans le judéo-espagnol marocain," in: I. Benabu & J. Sermoneta (eds.), *Judeo-Romance Languages* (1985), 27–40; idem, "Alternances d'hébreu et de judéo-espagnol dans un Daroush marocain," in: S. Morag, M. Bar-Asher & M. Mayer Modena (eds.), *Vena Hebraica* (1999), 203–19; P. Bénichou, "Observaciones sobre el judeo-español de Marruecos," in: *Revista de Filología Hispánica*, 7 (1945), 209–58; idem, *Romances Judeo-españoles de Marruecos* (1946, 1968²); idem, "Notas sobre el judeo-español de Marruecos," in: *Nueva Revista de Filología Hispánica*, 14 (1960), 307–12; J. Benoliel, "Dialecto judeo-hispano-marroquí o hakitía," in: *Boletín de la Real Academia Española*, 13 (1926), 209–33, 342–63, 507–38; 14 (1927), 137–68, 196–234, 357–73, 566–80; 15 (1928), 47–61, 188–223; 22 (1952), 255–89 (also as *Dialecto judeo-hispano-marroquí o hakitia*, edited by R. Benazeraf (1977)); F. Cantera, "Hebraísmos en la poesía sefardí," in: *Estudios dedicados a Menéndez Pidal*, vol. 5 (1954), 67–68; J. Chetrit, "Judeo-Arabic and Judeo-Spanish in Morocco and their Sociolinguistic Interaction," in: J. Fishman (ed.), *Readings in the Sociology of Jewish Languages*, 261–79 (1985); I. Hassán, "De los restos dejados por el judeo-español en el español de los judíos del norte de Africa," in: *Actas del XI Congreso Internacional de Lingüística y Filología Románica*, vol. 4 (1968), 2127–40; idem, "Más hebraísmos en la poesía sefardí de Marruecos: Realidad y ficción léxicas," in: *Sefarad*, 37 (1977), 373–428; idem, "Testimonios antiguos de la jaquetía," in: C. Casado-Fresnillo (ed.), *La lengua y la literatura españolas en Africa…* (1998), 147–69; A. de Larrea Palacín, *Cuentos populares de los judíos del norte de Marruecos* (1943); idem, *Cancionero del Norte de Marruecos: Romances de Tetuán*, vols. 1–2 (1952); idem, *Cancionero judío del norte de Marruecos: Canciones rituales hispano-judías*, vol. 3 (1954); S. Lévy, *YA ASRA – Escenas †aquetiescas* (1992); J. Martínez Ruiz, "Morfólogía del judeo-español de Alcazarquivir," in: *Miscelanea Filológica dedicada a Mons. A. Griera*, vol. 2 (1960), 103–28; "La poesía tradicional sefardita de Alcazarquivir," in: *Archivum*, 12 (1962), 79–215; idem, "Textos judeo-españoles de Alcazarquivir," in: *Revista de Dialectología y Tradiciones populares*, 19 (1963), 78–115; "Arabismos en el judeo-español de Alcazarquivir (Marruecos) 1948–51," in: *Revista de Filología Española*, 49 (1966), 39–71; "Lenguas en contacto: judeo-español y árabe marroquí: interferencias léxicas, fonéticas y sintácticas," in: *Cuarto Congreso Internacional de Hispanistas* (1982), 2:237–49; S. Pimienta, *Libro de Actas de lamina selecta de la Comunidad Hebrea de Tanger, desde 5621 hasta 5635* (1992); H.V. Sephiha, "Extinction du judéo-espagnol vernaculaire du Maroc ou Hakitía," in: *Yod*, 2 (1976), 83–88; idem, "Vestiges du judéo-espagnol vernaculaire du Maroc (hakitía), parmi les juifs de l'Oranie," in: *Actes du 1er Colloque International sur les Juifs d'Afrique du Nord* (1977); idem, "Le judéo-espagnol au Maroc," in: *Juifs du Maroc, Identité et Dialogue* (1980), 85–97; idem, "Le judéo-espagnol du Maroc ou Haketiya," in: *Combat pour la Diaspora*, 6 (1981), 77–80; S. Weich-Shahak. *Judeo-Spanish Moroccan Songs for the Life Style: Cantartes Judeo Españoles de Marruecos para el Ciclo de la Vida* (1989); idem, *Romancero sefardí de Marruecos: antología de tradición oral* (1997).

[Yaakov Bentolila (2nd ed.)]

ḤAKHAM (Heb. חָכָם; lit. "wise" or "sage"), title given to rabbinic scholars. Originally, it was inferior to the title "rabbi" since a scholar who possessed *semikhah* was called "rabbi" while the lesser savant was called *ḥakham*, or "sage" (BM 67bf.). Afterward it was also utilized for ordained scholars (Tosef., Yev. 4:6). Another talmudic distinction was between *ḥakham* and *talmid* ("disciple"). The disciple was only expected to answer inquiries that pertained directly to his studies, while the sage was required to respond to questions in all areas of rabbinic scholarship (Kid. 49b). The title *ḥakham* was also used as a formal designation of the third in rank after the *nasi* and *av bet din* of the Sanhedrin (Hor. 13b).

Sephardi Jews later used the title *ḥakham* for their local rabbis (in London and Amsterdam, applied to the rabbi of the Spanish and Portuguese congregations, it is written Haham), and reserved the more honorable designation of rabbi for preeminent scholars (David Messer Leon, *Kevod Ḥakhamim*, ed. by S. Bernfeld (1899), 63f.). Turkish Jewry designated its chief rabbi as **ḥakham bashi.*

ḤAKHAM, SIMON (1843–1910), author and Bible translator. Ḥakham was born in Bukhara, the son of a scholarly Baghdad emissary. He emigrated to Jerusalem in 1890. During his years in Jerusalem, he was active as editor, publisher, translator, and author. Among his major publications are *Shir ha-Shirim* (1904²), *Midrash Petirat Moshe* (1897), prayers and *piyyutim* for holidays (1902), *Pitron Ḥalomot* (1901), the Passover *Haggadah* (1904), and *Targum Sheni* to *Megillat Esther* (1905). He edited and published *Sefer Shahzadeh we-Sufi ve-hu Sharḥ al ha-Sefer *Ben ha-Melekh ve-ha-Nazir* (1907) by Abraham ben Samuel ha-Levi (ibn) *Ḥasdai, which Elijah b. Samuel had translated into Judeo-Persian in 1684. He also published a Judeo-Persian translation of parts of the Shulḥan Arukh under the title *Likkutei Dinim* (1901–03), prepared by Abraham Aminoff, the leading rabbi of the Jerusalem Bukharan colony. He translated Abraham Mapu's biblical novel *Ahavat Ẓiyyon* (1912²), and brought out part of the famous *Sefer Sharḥ Shahin al ha-Torah* (1902–4) by the 14th-century Judeo-Persian epic poet Maulana *Shahin of Shiraz, along with some of his own poetry.

His translation of the Bible into the Judeo-Persian of the Bukharan Jews was a monumental achievement which ranks him with the great Bible translators. He began his *tafsir* in 1906, and it appeared in successive volumes along with the Hebrew text, *Targum Onkelos*, and Rashi. By the time of his death he had completed the Pentateuch and the Prophets up to Isaiah 41:9; his collaborators completed the translation of the whole Bible.

BIBLIOGRAPHY: Yaari, in: *Moznayim*, 3 pt. 48 (1932), 10–12; idem, in: KS, 18 (1941/42), 382–93; 19 (1942/43), 33–55, 116–39; Fischel, in: L. Finkelstein (ed.), *The Jews* (1960³), 1180–82; Fischel, in: L. Jung (ed.), *Jewish Leaders* (1964²), 535–47.

[Walter Joseph Fischel]

ḤAKHAM BASHI, the title of chief rabbi in the *Ottoman Empire, composed of the Hebrew work *ḥakham* ("sage," "wise man") and the Turkish word *bashi* ("head," or "chief"). At the end of 1836 or the beginning of 1837 the Ottoman authorities confirmed the first *ḥakham bashi*, Rabbi Abraham Levi, in Constantinople (see *Istanbul). According to a report in the official gazette of the empire this gesture was made at the request of those members of the community in the capital who were subjects of the sultan. They had no Christian-European powers behind them and were jealous of the honor of official confirmation that the government accorded to the Greek and Armenian patriarchs. Current research attributes the Ottoman authorities with imposing the *ḥakham bashi* on the Jewish community. The motivation for such a change in their policy regarding the Jews was the recent Greek war of independence that resulted in the establishment of a Greek state in 1832. As a result, the Ottoman Empire began a series of reforms that changed their relationship with various minority communities. Another factor was the improved relations with Great Britain, which was expressing increased interest in "Jewish Emancipation." Since European intervention assisted the Greeks in their war of independence, the Ottoman authorities were careful not to alienate other minority communities. This interpretation of events explains the fact that for over 30 years, the Ottoman Jewish communities regarded the *ḥakham bashi* with suspicion, to a great extent ignoring the rabbis who occupied the office. Thus, the *rav ha-kolel* was regarded as the religious leader. In 1864, when Rabbi Jacob Avigdor was appointed *ḥakham bashi*, his prestige as an esteemed scholar finally won over the Jewish community. His successor, also a scholar of great repute, Rabbi Yakir Geron (*ḥakham bashi* from 1863 to 1872), helped cement the communities positive attitude toward the *ḥakham bashi*. In any event, this was in fact a turning point in the policy of the Ottoman authorities, who hitherto had not interfered in the internal affairs of the Jewish community and for centuries past had given no official status to its representatives. The original copies or authentic texts of the *berat hümayun* (imperial confirmation of appointments) occurring from 1836 onward, which were also granted to chief rabbis in *Adrianople, *Salonika, *Izmir (Smyrna), Broussa (now *Bursa), and *Jerusalem, show that there was indeed a policy, the significance and consequences of which went beyond mere confirmation or appointments. Implicitly contained was an official recognition of the Jewish *millet (a religious communal organization of non-Muslims in the Ottoman Empire).

A *berat* was concerned with three interrelated matters: the religious powers of the *ḥakham bashi*, his powers as representative of the government, and the permission to read the Torah. Within his area of jurisdiction the *ḥakham bashi* was the supreme authority in all religious matters and in charge of all *ḥakhamim* and heads of the community. He alone was authorized to ban and excommunicate offenders and to prohibit their religious burial. The person and official residence of the *ḥakham bashi* enjoyed immunity which extended also to the *ḥakhamim* and officials subordinate to him. Disagreements on religious questions between *ḥakhamim* and the local

Muslim authorities were to be settled before the supreme authorities of the empire in Constantinople. As representative of the government the *ḥakham bashi* was responsible for the collection of government taxes. Government officials had to lend the *ḥakham bashi*'s officials every assistance in performing this task and place guards at their disposal. To protect his officials from molestation and restrictions when traveling, they were excused from wearing distinctive Jewish clothing and permitted to carry arms. They were thus exempt from two important provisions of the Covenant of *Omar. By an order of 1850 the religious heads of the four millets were required to collect the poll tax. Regarding the permission to read the Torah, the intention to grant rights to the community as a whole is conspicuous in a clause figuring in all *berat* texts; it declared that the reading of the Torah in the *ḥakham's* house and in other houses is permitted in the Jewish religion, as is hanging veils and candelabra where such reading takes place. This declaration was tantamount to the permission to establish permanent synagogues, and it constituted an ingenious circumvention of a prohibition contained in the Covenant of Omar, which was a source of many difficulties and an occasion for incessant extortion. The *berats* issued in provincial towns to the *ḥakham bashi* state expressly that they were granted upon the recommendation of the *ḥakham bashi* of Constantinople, who was thus the head of all the rabbis in the empire. This was why, in the event of a disagreement among the members of a community concerning the appointment of the local *ḥakham bashi*, the disputants would try to influence the *ḥakham bashi* of Constantinople. His decision not infrequently was based on other than objective considerations. From certain (especially Tripolitanian and Iraqi) sources it appears that a *ḥakham bashi* was sometimes sent from the capital without the local community having been consulted. The provincial *ḥakham bashis* were technically on an equal footing with the *ḥakham bashi* in Constantinople. However, the central Ottoman authorities viewed the *ḥakham bashi* in Constantinople as the leader of the Jews throughout the empire.

It is clear that while the *ḥakham bashi*'s official functions enhanced his importance and prestige, they were not in themselves sufficient to grant him supremacy in the field of *halakhah* and religious jurisdiction. In fact, this post was sometimes assigned to a simple schoolteacher. Besides the *ḥakham bashi* who was described in French as temporal head (a translation of the Arabic-Turkish term *shaykh zamani*), there were *ḥakhamim* bearing the designation *rav ha-kolel* (chief rabbi) or spiritual head (*shaykh rūḥī*). It happened sometimes that a *ḥakham bashi* who had resigned or been deposed subsequently served as *rav ha-kolel*, just as *rav ha-kolel* (see *Kolel) was occasionally appointed *ḥakham bashi*. The powers vested in the *ḥakham bashi* show that he was regarded by the Ottoman authorities as their representative vis-à-vis the Jewish population, performing official functions on behalf of the Jews, and he was so regarded by the Jews themselves. His situation was further complicated by dissension between strictly traditionalist, anti-modernist members of the community and those favoring a general education and reforms in communal affairs. This situation accounts for the fact that of the five such chief rabbis officiating in the years 1836–63, three were deposed by the community and one was dismissed by the government because of his non-Turkish nationality. Three continued in office in the post of *rav ha-kolel*, which seems to indicate that they had been deposed as a result of clashes between the different factions within the community.

The first *ḥakham bashi* in Jerusalem was appointed by imperial firman in 1841. His Hebrew title **rishon le-Ziọn* was used by the Sephardi chief rabbis of Jerusalem. The "Organizational Regulations of the Rabbinate," confirmed by imperial firman in 1865 (see *Millet and *Community), describe in the first 15 clauses the status and powers of the *ḥakham bashi* as the head of the Jewish millet in the empire. The powers of the provincial chief rabbis have always been defined in the firmans issued on their appointment. In 1835 *Tripolitania again came under the direct rule of the Sublime Porte who introduced there the same order that existed throughout the empire. The first *ḥakham bashi* was appointed by imperial firman in 1874 and therefore Tripoli is not mentioned in the "Organizational Regulations of the Rabbinate" of 1865. The title became so common that it referred to the head of every small community. The title *ḥakham bashi* is still in use in the Turkish republic, which has in Istanbul the largest Jewish community of the territories which once belonged to the empire, except Israel. After *Iraq's separation from the *Ottoman Empire and the establishment of the British Mandate, *Baghdad Jewry was presided over by the deputy *ḥakham bashi* and spiritual head of Baghdad. This title was abolished in Iraq in 1932 and the title *raʾīs al ḥakhāmīm* came into use.

Holders of the office of ḥakham bashi

Abraham Levi Pasha	1836–1839
Samuel Hayim	1839–1841
Moiz Fresko	1841–1854
Jacob Avigdor	1854–1870
Yakir Geron	1870–1872
Moses Levi	1872–1909
Chaim Nahum Effendi	1909–1920
Shabbetai Levi	1920–1922
Isaac Ariel	1922–1926
Chaim Bejerano	1926–1931
Chaim Isaac Saki	1931–1940
Raphael David Saban	1940–1960
David Asseo	1961–2002
Isak Haleva	2002–

BIBLIOGRAPHY: M. Franco, *Essai sur l'histoire des Israëlites de l'Empire Ottoman…* (1897), 151–2; A. Galanté (ed.), *Documents officiels turcs concernant les Juifs…* (1931), 32–50; *Appendice…* (1941), 4–8; H.Z. Hirschberg, in: A.J. Arberry (ed.), *Religion in the Middle East*, 1 (1969), 187, 196–201. **ADD. BIBLIOGRAPHY:** A. Levy, in: *The Jews of the Ottoman Empire* (1994), 425–38; S.J. Shaw, *The Jews of the Ottoman Empire and the Turkish Republic* (1991), index; J.M. Landau, *Exploring Ottoman and Turkish History* (2004), index; Y. Harel, in:

Pe'amim, 44 (1990), 110–31; idem, in: *Asufot*, 11 (1998), 211–43; idem, in: *Zion*, 66 (2001), 201–25; A. Ha-Levi, in: *Pe'amim*, 55 (1993), 38–56; idem, in: *Yemei ha-Sahar: Perakim be-Toledot ha-Yehudim ba-Imperiyah ha-Otomanit* (1996), 237–71.

[Haïm Z'ew Hirschberg / David Derovan (2nd ed.)]

HAKHEL (Heb. הַקְהֵל; "assemble"). The Bible enjoins that "At the end of every seven years, at the time of the year of release, at the Feast of Tabernacles" there is to take place an assembly of the whole people, "men, women, children, and the stranger that is within your gates." The purpose of this assembly is "that they may hear and so learn to revere the Lord your God and to observe faithfully every word of this Teaching" (Deut. 31:10–13). This ceremony, called *Hakhel* ("assemble") after the opening word of verse 12, is mentioned only once in the Talmud (Sot. 7:8), but in great detail and includes an interesting historical incident. The Mishnah lays it down (*ibid.*) that the date referred to is on the first day of the festival of Sukkot after the close of the seven-year period of *shemittah, i.e., on the 15th day of the first month of the eighth year.

The Mishnah connects this ceremony with another passage which deals with an entirely different subject, namely the duties of the king as laid down in Deuteronomy 17:14–20 and which it calls "the Chapter of the King." According to the Mishnah it was at the *Hakhel* ceremony that the king read that and other passages. It is possible that the coalescing of these passages is due to the similarity of wording between the two, the passage quoted above, and the passage with regard to the king "that he may learn to fear the Lord his God to keep all the words of this law and these statutes to do them" (*ibid.*, 17:19).

The Mishnah states that a wooden platform was set up in the Temple court upon which the king sat. "The minister (*ḥazzan*) of the synagogue used to take a scroll of the Torah and hand it to the chief of the synagogue, and the chief of the synagogue gave it to the deputy high priest who handed it to the high priest who handed it to the king. The king received it standing and read it while seated." The passages read were not "all the words of the Torah" but selected passages from Deuteronomy; from the beginning to 6:19, the last verses of which are the first paragraph of the *Shema, the second paragraph of the *Shema* (11:13–21), 14; 22–27; 26:12–15; 17:14–20 ("the Chapter of the King"), and 27:15–26. He concluded the reading with eight benedictions, of which seven were identical with those pronounced by the high priest on the Day of Atonement (see Sot. 7:6) and the eighth (the fourth in number) for the festival instead of the one for pardon of sin pronounced by the high priest.

The continuity of the description of the ceremony in the Mishnah is interrupted by the information that despite the rule that the king read the passages while seated, "King Agrippa read it standing, for which he was praised by the rabbis," and continues with the moving story of the king, conscious of his mixed descent, bursting into tears when he read "thou mayest not put a foreigner over thee who is not thy brother" (Deut. 17:15) and the assembled people called out "thou art our brother." Most scholars identify this Agrippa who was so beloved of the people with *Agrippa I, who reigned from 41–44 C.E., the first of which years coincides with the year of *shemittah*. Others, however, ascribe it to *Agrippa II. In recent years in Israel an attempt has been made to revive a symbolical form of the *Hakhel* ceremony.

BIBLIOGRAPHY: ET, 10 (1961), 443–52; A. Beuchler, in: *11. Jahresbericht der Israelitisch-Theologischen Lehranstalt in Wien* (1895), 11–14; S. Goren, *Torat ha-Mo'adim* (1964), 127–38; S.J. Zevin, *Le-Or ha-Halakhah* (1957^2), 135–45.

[Louis Isaac Rabinowitz]

HAKHNASAT KALLAH (Heb. הַכְנָסַת כַּלָּה; "bringing in the bride," i.e., under the wedding canopy), a rabbinic commandment to provide a dowry for brides and to rejoice at their weddings (Maim. Yad., Avelim 14:1). The term is popularly applied to the provision of dowry for the poor brides. The precept is of such importance that it is permissible to interrupt even the (public) study of Torah in order to fulfill it (Meg. 3b and Tos. ad loc.). It is reckoned in the prayer book as among those deeds "for which a man enjoys the fruits in this world, while the stock remains for him for the world to come." (Hertz, Prayer, 17, version of Pe'ah 1:1 and Shab. 127a). A man who raises an orphan and enables her to marry is considered as continually doing acts of righteousness and justice (Ps. 106:3; Ket. 50a).

Communal charity collectors are permitted to use the funds they collected for other purposes for the dowry of poor brides (Sh. Ar., YD 249:15, and Siftei Kohen ad loc.). The Mishnah specified the minimum sum of 50 *zuz* to be given to a bride, but "if there was more in the poor funds they should provide for her according to the honor due to her" (Ket. 6:5). This minimal sum of "50 *zuz*" must be reassessed in every generation in accordance with its own economic conditions (Turei Zahav to Sh. Ar. YD 250:2). As in other aspects of communal Jewish charity, specific organizations were formed to supervise the collection and distribution of funds for the dowries and trousseaux of poor girls and orphans. These groups were often called Hakhnasat Kallah societies. In the ghetto of Rome, during the 17th century, for example such a society functioned actively (Roth, Italy, 364). Samuel Portaleone, an Italian preacher, in his description of seven charity boxes which existed in Mantua, Italy, in 1630, lists among them *hakhnasat kallah* (JQR, 5 (1893), 510). Hakhnasat Kallah societies have continued to function throughout the Jewish world.

In addition to aiding poor brides, the precept also demands that a person attend and rejoice at the marriage of any bride. It was considered meritorious to accompany the bride from her father's home to where the wedding ceremony was to take place (Rashi to Meg. 29a). This aspect of *hakhnasat kallah* may also be fulfilled by accompanying the bridegroom to the *bedekin* ("covering" the face) of the bride (Beit Shemu'el to Sh. Ar. EH 65:1). While it is also customary to dance before the bride and to praise her, Bet Shammai held that the virtues of the bride are not to be exaggerated, and that she is only to be praised "as she truly is." Bet Hillel, on the other hand, ruled that every bride should be regarded and praised as "beautiful and graceful" (Ket. 16b–17a).

The fulfillment of the precept of *hakhnasat kallah* should be performed humbly, modestly and in privacy, thus complying with the dictum "to walk humbly with thy God" (Micah 6:8; Suk. 49b).

BIBLIOGRAPHY: ET, 9 (1959), 136–43; Baron, Community, 1 (1942), 362ff., 2 (1942), 332f., 3 (1942), 212f.; I. Abrahams, *Jewish Life in the Middle Ages* (1920), 326; I. Levitats, *Jewish Community in Russia* (1943), 252; H.H. Ben-Sasson, *Hagut ve-Hanhagah* (1959), index.

HA-KIBBUTZ HA-ARẒI HA-SHOMER HA-ẒA'IR, a union of kibbutzim in Israel, founded in 1927 by the first collective settlements of *Ha-Shomer ha-Ẓa'ir pioneers. It regards itself as an avant-garde nucleus of the future socialist society in Israel and adheres strictly to the principles of collective life of its members and the collective education of their children. The first settlers arrived in Israel in 1919, and in 1922 established Bet Alfa, the first kibbutz of the movement. In 1936 the movement joined forces with the Socialist League and the two founded Mifleget Po'alim-Ha-Shomer ha-Ẓair in 1946. In 1948 the new party united with *Aḥdut ha-Avodah-Po'alei Zion to form *Mapam. New kibbutzim continued to be established into the statehood period. In 1970, Ha-Kibbutz ha-Arẓi comprised 75 kibbutzim with a population of about 30,000, while in the mid-1990s it numbered 85 kibbutzim. In 2000 it united with the second secular kibbutz movement, Ha-Tenu'ah ha-Kibbutzit ha-Me'uḥedet (Takam) to create the *Kibbutz Movement, now comprising 244 kibbutzim with a population of 115,600. Ha-Kibbutz ha-Arẓi ha-Shomer ha-Ẓa'ir emphasized ideological unity and mutual economic aid among its member kibbutzim. It established the Kibbutz Arẓi Choir, the Sifriat Hapoalim press, and the daily *Mishmar*, which later became **Al-ha-Mishmar* and continued to appear until 1995.

For further details see *Kibbutz Movement, Ha-Kibbutz ha-Arẓi ha-Shomer ha-Ẓa'ir.

[Shaked Gilboa (2nd ed.)]

HA-KIBBUTZ HA-DATI, a union of 16 religious kibbutzim in Israel, established in 1935 by members of *Ha-Po'el ha-Mizrachi. It combines religious practice with collective life and labor and exerted a political influence in the *National Religious Party by strengthening its left-wing faction, "La-Mifneh." The movement saw itself as a bridge between religious and secular people in Israel, and initiated projects to enhance understanding between these two groups. Eleven of the kibbutzim were founded before the establishment of the State of Israel, of which five were destroyed during the War of Independence (those of the *Eẓyon Bloc were overrun and destroyed by Arab forces) and were reestablished later. Three other kibbutzim became moshavim shittufiyyim, and left the movement, while eight additional kibbutzim were founded after 1948. Many of the religious kibbutzim are located in dangerous border areas, in settlements clusters aimed to assist one another. The founders of the kibbutzim were mainly Europeans, while over the years Bnei Akiva graduates from Israel and abroad joined them. In 1970 Ha-Kibbutz ha-Dati comprised 13 settlements with a population of about 4,000, while in 2004 it included 16 kibbutzim with a population of 8,000. The kibbutzim of Ha-Kibbutz Ha-dati base their economy on agriculture, industry, and tourism. The organizational structure of the movement is based on a council with 100 representatives from all the kibbutzim. The council, as the highest institution of the movement, meets every few years to discuss important issues. It appoints a secretariat with authority to make decisions between the council meetings. The secretariat, composed of 35 members, meets a few times a year. Day-to-day affairs are in the hands of an executive committee under a secretary-general chosen every four years.

For further details see *Kibbutz Movement, Ha-Kibbutz ha-Dati.

WEBSITE: www.kdati.org.il.

[Shaked Gilboa (2nd ed.)]

HA-KIBBUTZ HA-ME'UḤAD, a union of kibbutzim in Israel founded at a conference in Petaḥ Tikvah in 1927 by the first "large" kevuẓot, established primarily by pioneers of the Third Aliyah, including previous groups of *Gedud ha-Avodah ("Labor Legion"). In 1951 a split occurred in its ranks due to political and ideological tensions between *Mapai and the left-wing *Aḥdut ha-Avodah. The split led to the breakup of kibbutzim, the establishment of new kibbutzim, and large-scale population movement between kibbutzim. The Mapai-oriented members seceded, eventually founding the *Iḥud ha-Kevuẓot ve-ha-Kibbutzim. During the 1960s and the 1970s, the two movements became politically closer, until their reunion in "Takam" (the united kibbutz movement) in 1980. In 1970, Ha-Kibbutz ha-Me'uḥad numbered about 60 kibbutzim with a population of about 25,000–30,000. In 1980, Takam included 154 settlements with a population of 73,370. Its kibbutzim owned 206 industries and accounted for 40% of agricultural production in Israel. In 1996 the movement numbered 173 settlements with a population of 80,000. In 2000 it united with Kibbutz ha-Arẓi ha-Shomer ha-Ẓa'ir to form the *Kibbutz Movement. The movement had close connections with two youth movements – Ha-Maḥanot ha-Olim and *Ha-No'ar ha-Oved ve-ha-Lomed. Day-to-day activity in Takam was in the hands of an executive committee. The highest institution of the movement is the general assembly, where each kibbutz has at least one representative. The movement sponsored a wide range of social and cultural activities.

For further details see *Kibbutz Movement, Ha-Kibbutz Ha-Me'uḥad.

[Shaked Gilboa (2nd ed.)]

ḤAKIM, ELIAHU (1925–1945), Jew executed in *Egypt in the Mandate Period. Ḥakim was born in *Beirut, and was brought to Ereẓ Israel by his parents at the age of seven. At the age of 17 he joined Leḥi. Together with Eliahu Bet-Ẓuri he was sent by his organization to *Cairo to assassinate Lord Moyne, then British Minister of State for the Middle East, whose seat was in Cairo. The attempt was successful, but Bet-Ẓuri and Ḥakim were apprehended. They were sentenced to death by a military court in Cairo on Jan. 1, 1945, and executed on Mar. 22. Their remains were interred in the Jewish cemetery of Cairo.

BIBLIOGRAPHY: Y. Nedava, *Olei-ha-Gardom* (1966); Y. Gurion, *Ha-Nizzaḥon Olei Gardom* (1971).

ḤAKIM, SAMUEL BEN MOSES HA-LEVI IBN (?1480–after 1547), rabbi in *Egypt and *Turkey. Samuel came from a distinguished family of Spanish origin which had settled in Egypt. His father, Moses, was a personal friend of the governor of Egypt and, when difficulties arose, intervened on behalf of the Jews. Samuel studied in Egypt under the *nagid*, Jonathan ha-Kohen *Sholal, and at the beginning of the 16th century he was already regarded as one of the eminent Egyptian rabbis. He later left Egypt for Constantinople, where he also occupied an important position in the Jewish community, but it is difficult to ascertain in which year he made this move. According to a responsum it was c. 1517, but this seems to be a mistake for c. 1527, since there is extant a *haskamah* signed by Samuel and R. *David b. Solomon ibn Abi Zimra in Egypt in the year 1527 (Neubauer, Chronicles, 1 (1887), 158), a date confirmed by two manuscripts. His departure for Constantinople could not therefore have taken place before 1527, unless it be supposed that two scholars of the same name lived in Cairo at the same time, which is very difficult to accept. The problem of two Samuel b. Moses ha-Levi ibn Ḥakim (Hakam) is further complicated by the existence of Samuel Hakan who is definitely not identical with Samuel Ḥakim. Samuel was a friend of Moses *Hamon, physician to Sultan *Suleiman. He frequently engaged in sharp polemics with the important rabbis of his time and even strongly criticized a halakhic ruling made by Shalom *Shakhna b. Joseph of Lublin on the laws of *sivlonot* (the gifts given by the bridegroom to his bride on the occasion of their engagement) which appeared at the end of the novellae of *Aaron ha-Levi of Barcelona (?) to *Kiddushin* (1904), which perhaps points to contacts between the rabbis of Constantinople and Poland. In 1547 he published a collection of responsa of *Isaac b. Sheshet Perfet (Ribash) in Constantinople. The book was published in sections and Samuel followed the accepted Constantinople custom of distributing the sections to purchasers on the Sabbath, in the synagogue. Isaac ibn Lev complained that this custom was tantamount to engaging in business on the Sabbath. Samuel pointed to the precedent of the similar sale of such books as *Toledot Adam ve-Ḥavvah* (1516) of *Jeroham b. Meshullam and *Toledot Yiẓḥak* (1518) of Isaac *Caro. Furthermore, he said, the greatest rabbis had not protested against it.

Only a small number of Samuel's many responsa have survived; some are preserved in the works of his contemporaries such as the responsa of Joseph *Caro and *Levi ibn Ḥabib, and a few responsa are still extant in manuscript. He is frequently mentioned in contemporary and later responsa. Ḥakim was on friendly terms with the *Karaites of Constantinople and was well acquainted with their customs. In one of his responsa written before 1533 (still in manuscript) he expresses the opinion that they sin inadvertently, not deliberately, and should not be treated as apostates or the illegitimate offspring of forbidden marriages. It is therefore permitted to intermarry with them, to drink their wine, to eat of their *sheḥitah*, and to accept them as witnesses in matters of personal status. This original opinion, for which no parallel or supporting view could be found either in his own or in succeeding generations, aroused the most vehement opposition of the other authorities. Among them were David b. Solomon ibn Abi Zimra (Responsa, pt. 2, no. 796), Moses di *Trani (Responsa, pt. 1, no. 37), and Bezalel Ashkenazi (Responsa, no. 3). There are extant glosses by Ḥakim to the novellae of Solomon b. Abraham *Adret on the tractate *Shabbat*, as well as a short introduction to the *Masoret Seyag la-Torah* of Meir ha-Levi *Abulafia. The place and date of Ḥakim's death are unknown.

BIBLIOGRAPHY: C. Bernheimer, in: REJ, 66 (1913), 102; S. Assaf, in: *Alim*, 1 (1934–35), 73–75; idem, in: *Minḥah le-David* (1935), 223, 236–7; idem, in: *Zion*, 1 (1936), 213–4; idem, *Be-Ohalei Ya'akov* (1943), 185–6; Assaf, Mekorot, 220, 221, 255–6; idem, in: *Sinai*, 4 (1939), 532–50; Ashtor, Toledot, 2 (1951), 481–4; A. Yaari, *Ha-Defus ha-Ivri be-Kushta* (1967), 14, 103.

[Abraham David]

°**ḤĀKIM BI-AMR ALLAH, AL-**, the sixth caliph (996–1021) of the Ismāʿīlī *Fatimid dynasty, which ruled in North Africa, Egypt, Palestine, Syria, and wide areas of the Arabian Peninsula. In the year 400 A.H. (1009–10 C.E.) a major change took place in al-Ḥākim's attitude toward the Muslim and Ismāʿīlī traditions and he issued proclamations which were decisive for the development of the *Druze faith and community, of which he was the founder. The harassment of Christians, which had begun several years previously, was intensified, and the Church of the Holy Sepulcher in Jerusalem was burned down. According to Christian and Muslim sources these persecutions also included the Jews, but these reports should be treated with caution. A *Megillat Miẓrayim* ("Egyptian Scroll") from 1012, which is extant in two versions, mentions al-Ḥākim as the protector of the Jews, who allegedly assembled in the Great Synagogue of Fustat to thank God that the caliph had saved them from a rioting mob. This favorable appraisal is confirmed in letters written by the heads of the Palestinian and the Fustat yeshivot which mention that al-Ḥākim subsidized their institutions. After 1012 the persecution also included the Jews; synagogues were burned, and there were instances of forced conversion to Islam. The difficulties ceased only in the last years of al-Ḥākim (1017–20). Christians and Jews were permitted to rebuild their places of worship and forced converts were allowed to return to their former religion. At that time al-Ḥākim openly presented himself as the incarnation of the deity. The two above-mentioned events undoubtedly were related. Early in 1021 al-Ḥākim disappeared, and it is believed that he was murdered. A rumor spread among his followers that he was hiding on Mount al-Muqaṭṭam (near Cairo) and would appear again in the fullness of time (after a thousand years). The first article of the Druze faith is that al-Ḥākim was the last incarnation of the deity; he cannot have died, and his followers, therefore, are awaiting his return *(raj'a)*. Al-Ḥākim's personality and Druze doctrines influenced later Jewish mystic movements. Joseph *Sambari (17th cent.) recounts in his chronicle *Divrei Yosef* (Paris, Alliance Israélite Universelle, Hebrew manuscript no. 22–23) the story of al-Ḥākim's persecutions. According to this version, the persecution of the Jews was caused by the Arabic translation of the Passover *Haggadah*, which tells of the drowning of the Egyptian king. Al-Ḥākim thought that this referred to him and forbade further translations of the *Haggadah*. Sambari further states that al-Ḥākim was murdered by his sister in the year 411 A.H., i.e., 1021.

BIBLIOGRAPHY: S. de Sacy, *Exposé de la religion des Druzes*, 2 vols. (1838); Mann, Egypt, 1 (1920), 30–7; 2 (1922), 35–6, 70; H.Z. Hirschberg, in: A.J. Arberry (ed.), *Religion in the Middle East*, 2 (1969), 332–5; EIS², 2 (1965), S.V. Durūz. **ADD. BIBLIOGRAPHY:** S.D. Goitein, *A Mediterranean Society*, vol. 6, index; Y. Lev, in: *Asian and African Studies* (Haifa), 22 (1988), 73–91.

[Haim Z'ew Hirschberg]

HAKKAFOT (Heb. הַקָּפוֹת), term used to designate ceremonial processional circuits both in the synagogue and outside it, on various occasions.

Such circuits are mentioned in the Bible. There were, for instance, seven circuits around Jericho (once a day for six days, and seven times on the seventh day; Josh. 6:14–15). The Mishnah records that the *lulav* was carried around the Temple altar during the seven days of *Sukkot (Suk. 3:12). Although the *Gemara* makes no mention of similar circuits during Sukkot in the post-Temple period, both Hai Gaon (B.M. Lewin, *Oẓar ha-Ge'onim* (1934), Sukkah, 60, no. 151), and Saadiah Gaon (in his *Siddur*) mention the custom of making a circuit around the synagogue with the *lulav* and *etrog* on Sukkot. Nowadays a single circuit is made around the *bimah* on each of the first six days of Sukkot (except for the Sabbath) during the chanting of **hoshanot* at the close of the *Musaf* service. On *Hoshana Rabba, the seventh day of Sukkot, the procession around the *bimah* is repeated seven times. It is related that on this day, Hai Gaon used to make a pilgrimage to Jerusalem, and there make seven processional circuits around the Mount of Olives (*Sefer Ḥasidim*, ed. by J. Wistinetzki (1924²), no. 630). The Torah scrolls are carried around the synagogue in processional circuits during both the *Ma'ariv* and *Shaḥarit* services on *Simḥat Torah (a custom first mentioned by Rabbi Isaac Tyrnau, 14th–15th century; *Minhagim* (Lunéville (1806), 51a). The Ḥasidim perform these *hakkafot* also at the conclusion of the *Ma'ariv* service on *Shemini Aẓeret. In Reform congregations, these *hakkafot* are performed on Shemini Aẓeret. In Israel where Simḥat Torah coincides with Shemini Aẓeret, many congregations perform *hakkafot* again after *Ma'ariv* at the completion of the festival. With the advent of the Jewish women's movement in the 1970s, particularly in the United States, there was an on-going attempt to include women above the age of bat mitzvah in traditional synagogue ritual. This effort has had an impact across the spectrum of contemporary Jewish life. By the beginning of the 21st century, it was not unusual in modern/centrist Orthodox circles to give women one or more of the congregational Torah scrolls with which to make *hakkafot* and with which to dance. In most Conservative/masorti and in all Reconstructionist and Reform congregations, women and men participate in the same *hakkafot* and dance together with the Torah scrolls.

Hakkafot are also performed on a number of other occasions. For instance, Torah scrolls are carried around in a processional circuit during the dedication of both synagogues and cemeteries. In a number of communities, it is customary for the bride to make either three or seven *hakkafot* around the bridegroom during the wedding ceremony. The Sephardim and Ḥasidim walk around a coffin seven times prior to burial. It is also customary to walk around the cemetery when praying for the sick.

On all of these occasions one may note the juxtaposition of the "magic circle" with the mystical figure of seven, and the implied attempt to dissuade *shedim* ("evil spirits") from intruding upon the object of attention. With regard to the funerary *hakkafot* it has been suggested that the purpose is to ward off the spirits of the dead man's unborn children and to appease them with symbolic gifts of money. It is also significant that *Ḥoni ha-Me'aggel's miracles were performed after he had made a circuit (in the form of a drawn circle), around the place on which he stood (Ta'an. 19a, 23a).

BIBLIOGRAPHY: ET, 10 (1961), 539; Eisenstein, Dinim, 105.

[Harry Rabinowicz / Rela M. Geffen (2nd ed.)]

ḤALAFTA (early second century C.E.), *tanna*, father of the well-known *tanna* *Yose. Ḥalafta lived in *Sepphoris where he was a leader of the community (Tosef., Ta'an. 1:14; RH 27a). His colleague was *Johanan b. Nuri who discussed *halakhah* with him; seemingly among his associates were also *Akiva (BB 56b, where Ḥalafta is called Abba Ḥalafta as also in Shab. 115a; Tosef., BB 2:10; Tosef., Kelim, BM 1:5), *Ḥanina b. Teradyon (Ta'an. 2:5), and *Eleazar b. Azariah (Tosef., Kelim, BB 2:2). It is possible that in the last years of the Temple he was living in Jerusalem since he transmitted an incident about Gamaliel the Elder (Tosef., Shab. 13:2). Several statements by him in *halakhah* and *aggadah* have been preserved, some by his son Yose (Kelim 26:6; Tosef., Bek. 2:19, et al.).

BIBLIOGRAPHY: Hyman, Toledot, s.v.; J. Kanowitz, *Ma'arekhot Tanna'im*, 2 (1967), 107–9.

[Zvi Kaplan]

ḤALAFTA BEN SAUL (early third century C.E.), Palestinian *amora*. Ḥalafta taught *beraitot* which are cited both in the Jerusalem Talmud (Ber. 1:8, 3c; Pe'ah 2:6, 17a; Shev. 2:7, 34a;

Hag. 3:7, 79d, et al.) and in the Babylonian (Zev. 93b; MK 10a; see Dik. Sof. *ibid.*). It is possible that he is to be identified with the Taḥlifa b. Saul who taught a *baraita* quoted in the Babylonian Talmud (Men. 7b, et al.). An *aggadah* is also cited in his name (Ber. 29a). It has been suggested by some that he was the brother of Johanan b. Saul, and Yose b. Saul, a pupil of *Judah ha-Nasi.

BIBLIOGRAPHY: Judah b. Kalonymos, *Yiḥusei Tanna'im ve-Amora'im*, ed. by J.L. Maimon (1963), 311f.; Hyman, Toledot, 454, s.v.; Margalioth, Ḥakhmei, 313f., s.v.

[Zvi Kaplan]

HA LAḤMA ANYA (Aram. הָא לַחְמָא עַנְיָא; lit. "Behold the poor bread"), opening words of an introductory paragraph of the Passover **Haggadah*. The announcement is in Aramaic, and is proclaimed at the **seder* service immediately after the conclusion of the *karpas* ceremony (in which greens are dipped in salt water; see *Passover *seder*).

The announcement is composed of three unrelated sentences. The first reads, "Behold this poor bread (or, 'bread of poverty'), which our fathers ate in the land of Egypt." This points to the centrality of the *maẓẓah* ("the unleavened bread") in the Festival of Passover. The second sentence invites the poor to the Passover meal: "Let anyone who is hungry come in and eat; let anyone who is needy come in and make Passover." The third sentence reads, "This year we are here; next year we shall be in the land of Israel; this year we are slaves, next year we shall be free men."

The origins and exact purport of the *Ha Laḥma Anya* are obscure. Most early portions of the *Haggadah* were written in Hebrew and are mentioned in the Mishnah. The language and content of this announcement, however, suggest that it was composed in Babylon after the destruction of the Temple. The second sentence does find an almost exact analogy in the Talmud (Ta'an., 20b), where R. Huna is said to have exclaimed before his meals "Let every needy person come and eat." Mattathias Gaon, in the ninth century, claimed that this sentence of *Ha Laḥma Anya* had always been a *minhag avoteinu* ("custom of our fathers"; B.M. Lewin, *Oẓar ha-Ge'onim*, 3 (1930), *Pesaḥim* 112). Had this sentence been the central feature of the announcement, however, the *Ha Laḥma Anya* would be expected to open the *Haggadah*, and to precede the **kiddush* and *karpas*.

The present version of the announcement is probably a combination of several texts which date from the talmudic and post-talmudic periods. It has undergone several modifications. *Maimonides (Yad, appendix to *Ḥameẓ u-Matzah*) cites the present version with minor changes and a small addition. *Saadiah Gaon's text opens with the third sentence, and is followed by the second. He omits the first sentence altogether. In certain late medieval manuscripts, the first sentence reads, "Behold like this poor bread…." Most texts, including those of Maimonides and *Judah Loew b. Bezalel, have the simple version in use today, "Behold the poor bread."

BIBLIOGRAPHY: Davidson, Oẓar, 2 (1929), 116, no. 2; Liber, in: REJ, 82 (1926), 217–9; E.D. Goldschmidt, *Haggadah shel Pesaḥ ve-Toledoteha* (1960), 7–9; M.M. Kasher, *Haggadah Shelemah* (1955), 5–8 (Hebrew pagination).

[H. Elchanan Blumenthal]

HALAKHAH.

DEFINITION

The word "*halakhah*" (from the root *halakh*, "to go"), the legal side of Judaism (as distinct from *aggadah*, the name given to the nonlegal material, particularly of the rabbinic literature), embraces personal, social, national, and international relationships, and all the other practices and observances of Judaism. In the Bible the good life is frequently spoken of as a way in which men are "to go," e.g., "and shalt show them the way wherein they are to go and the work that they must do" (Ex. 18:20). Originally the term *halakhah* (pl. *halakhot*) had the meaning of the particular law or decision in a given instance, as in the frequent expression "this is a law given to Moses on Sinai" (*Halakhah le-Moshe mi-Sinai). This usage persisted, but side by side with it there developed the use of *halakhah* as a generic term for the whole legal system of Judaism, embracing all the detailed laws and observances. For instance, the Talmud (Shab. 138b) comments on "the word of the Lord" (Amos 8:12) that this means the *halakhah*.

The study of the *halakhah* in the rabbinic period and beyond it became the supreme religious duty. Because of its difficult subject matter and its importance for practical Judaism this study took precedence over that of any other aspect of Jewish teaching. Typical is the rabbinic saying that after the destruction of the Temple, God has nothing else in His world than the four cubits of the *halakhah* (Ber. 8a). The superiority of halakhic study over aggadic was expressed in the parable of the two merchants, one selling precious stones, the other small ware. Only the connoisseur comes to buy from the former (Sot. 40a).

The general assumption in the classical Jewish sources is that the *halakhah* in its entirety goes back to Moses, except for various later elaborations, extensions, applications, and innovations in accordance with new circumstances. Thus Maimonides (Yad, intro.) counts 40 generations backward from R. Ashi, the traditional editor of the Babylonian Talmud, to Moses and concludes: "In the two Talmuds and the Tosefta, the *Sifra* and the *Sifrei*, in all these are explained the permitted and the forbidden, the clean and the unclean, the liabilities and lack of liability, the unfit and the fit, as handed down from person to person from the mouth of Moses our teacher at Sinai." But the verdict of modern scholarship is that the *halakhah* has had a history and that it is possible to trace the stages in its development with a considerable degree of success (see below).

[Louis Jacobs]

DOGMATICS OF THE HALAKHAH

Sources of Authority

Like other legal systems, the *halakhah* is composed of different elements, not all of equal value, since some are regarded as of Sinaitic origin and others of rabbinical. Five sources can be differentiated:

THE WRITTEN LAW. According to the traditional concept of halakhic Judaism, the Written Law is not a collection of legal, religious, ethical statutes and the like deriving from separate sources, but a law uniform in nature and content and a revelation of the will of God – a revelation that was a single nonrecurring historical event (at Sinai). This law is considered to be a book of commandments, positive and negative, numbering 613 (see *Commandments, the 613).

STATEMENTS HANDED DOWN BY TRADITION (KABBALAH). On the verse "These are the commandments" (Lev. 27:34), the *Sifra* (*Be-Ḥukkotai*, 13:7) comments, "Henceforth no prophet may make innovations." Thus such commandments or injunctions the source of which is in the words of the prophets or the Hagiographa (referred to as Kabbalah) are generally regarded as of Sinaitic force, on the assumption that the prophets received them as an interpretation or as a *halakhah* given to Moses at Sinai. Thus, e.g., it is inferred from Jeremiah 32:44; "and subscribe the deeds, and seal them, and call witnesses," that the signature by witnesses to a document is a Sinaitic law (Git. 36a). At times, however, the *amoraim* conclude that the verse is to be regarded as a mere support (**asmakhta*), and the matter does not come within the definition of Torah law. An ambivalent attitude on their part toward traditional statements can be discerned; there is even in the Babylonian Talmud a rule: inferences concerning statements of the Torah may not be drawn from statements contained in Kabbalah (Ḥag. 10b; BK 2b; Nid. 23a).

From the dogmatic point of view, however, the statement of Naḥmanides (on principle 2 of Maimonides' *Sefer ha-Mitzvot*) and his differentiation seem correct; namely that wherever in the prophets and Hagiographa statements are made as commands and injunctions, they are merely an explanation of the Torah and have the same authority as the Oral Law, as tradition, while where statements are made by way of narrative, as "relating some event" (e.g., the case of sale in the Book of Jeremiah) they are of rabbinic status. The same applies to those laws designated in the Talmud as **takkanot* ("regulations") of the prophets, even if attributed to Moses himself. For the concept *de-rabbanan* ("of rabbinical authority") is not chronological but qualitative, so that such statements can be *de-orayta* (of Sinaitic authority) even if first revealed in the words of a late prophet, and *de-rabbanan* even if attributed to Moses, if they were transmitted as a *takkanah* or the confirmation of an ancient custom (e.g., the seven days of bridal festivity, the seven days of mourning).

THE ORAL LAW. The *Oral Law includes: the interpretation of the Written Law transmitted, according to the sages, in its entirety with its details and minutiae at Sinai; *halakhah*, e.g., given to Moses at Sinai in the restricted sense; and logical deduction.

Interpretation of the Written Law. This interpretation consists of two elements: that regarded as certainly handed down at Sinai; that intrinsically inherent in the written word, but made manifest through the interpretation of Scripture by means of the accepted hermeneutical rules (see *hermeneutics). According to talmudic tradition anything transmitted directly by tradition counts as *de-orayta* and is in every way equivalent to the Written Law, while difference of opinion is found with regard to *halakhah* inferred only by means of interpretation since the Talmud itself has no systematic dogma on the subject.

Maimonides and Naḥmanides differ on this. According to the former (*Sefer ha-Mitzvot*, principle 2), anything inferred by interpretation is *de-orayta* only if supported by a tradition. If the Talmud does not clearly testify to its having been transmitted, then it is "the words of the *soferim*" or *de-rabbanan*.

On the other hand Naḥmanides holds (gloss, ad loc.) that anything derived by interpretation is also *de-orayta* whether or not supported by a talmudic tradition, unless the Talmud states explicitly that this is *de-rabbanan* (in the language of the Babylonian Talmud: "It is *de-rabbanan*, the verse being a mere support"). Both from the statements of Maimonides, as well as from those of Naḥmanides, it follows that *halakhot* inferred by interpretation of Scripture may be divided into three categories: *halakhah* received from Sinai where the purpose of the interpretation is to explain it and to connect it with the scriptural verse; in these cases there is no dispute as to the content of the *halakhah* since the interpretation at times merely serves a mnemotechnical purpose; *halakhah* not received from Sinai, but deduced by the sages from the scriptural verse, where the interpretation is in most cases to the point and included in the meaning of the verse; *halakhah* which all agree to be an innovation and *de-rabbanan*, the purpose of the interpretation being to find a support for it in Scripture (e.g., the rabbinic injunction against marrying relatives of the second degree, derived from Lev. 18:30: "Therefore shall ye keep My charge" (Yev. 21a)).

Halakhah Given to Moses at Sinai. This designation is given to ancient *halakhot* for which there is no scriptural support (or at the most very faint support). Examples are quantities (in connection with **issur ve-hetter* and things ritually unclean and clean, such as an olive's bulk, a quarter of a log, etc., Er. 4a), or that **tefillin* must be square (Meg. 24b) and written on parchment (Shab. 79b). It is difficult to decide whether in the early tannaitic period they actually regarded such *halakhot* as having been given at Sinai or whether the term "at Sinai" is employed merely to indicate their antiquity in order to increase their holiness and thus to immunize them against challenge (see the commentaries of Samson of Sens and Asher b. Jehiel to Yad. 4:3; Jair Ḥayyim Bacharach, in his *Ḥavvot Ya'ir* (no. 192) enumerates about 70 such *halakhot*). See also *Halakhah le-Moshe mi-Sinai.

Logical Deduction. Sometimes the authors of the Talmud say of a certain *halakhah*, "it is self-evident," and as such it does not require scriptural proof since it is regarded as axiomatic; such as "whoever wishes to claim anything in the possession of his fellow must bring proof." To this category belong, strictly speaking, also fundamental concepts such as *ḥazakah, the majority *rule, etc., since the scriptural verse adduced is only intended to provide a support for the *halakhah*. It is not the verse which is the source but logical reasoning and analogy.

SAYINGS OF THE SCRIBES (ELDERS). In talmudic literature, the expression *mi-divrei soferim* (of scribal origin) has two meanings: a statement in principle from the Torah but whose explanation is of scribal origin (see above, and e.g., Sanh. 88b); a statement decreed or enacted originally by the *soferim*, like "the second degrees of forbidden marriages are of scribal origin" (Yev. 2:4). What follows applies to the second meaning. Everything whose source is in statements of the scholars throughout the generations, from Moses to the present time, is called *de-rabbanan*. These teachings include: positive enactments (*takkanot*) made to protect the principles of religion and Torah, and negative enactments (*gezerot*) decreed to prevent breaches. From the verse "According to the law which they shall teach thee… thou shalt not turn aside from the sentence which they shall declare unto thee, to the right hand, nor to the left" (Deut. 17:11) it was inferred that it is a positive precept to obey the great *bet din* not only in everything applying to the text of the Torah, but also in everything that they found necessary to enact, and a warning is issued to anyone disregarding it.

The Authority of the Sages. In the Talmud the authority of the sages was defined as follows:

The sages have the power to abolish a biblical injunction (Yev. 89b–90b) in certain circumstances, such as: in monetary matters, on the basis of the rule that "deprivation of ownership by the *bet din* is valid"; in cases of the passive act of "refraining from an action" (*shev ve-al ta'aseh*), in which they forbade the *lulav and *shofar to be handled and used on the Sabbath, lest they be carried in a public domain (thus the rabbinic prohibition is the cause of the biblical precept being ignored!).

The *bet din* has the power to temporarily disregard a biblical precept in order to reinforce observance. Similarly the court "may inflict flagellation and other punishment not in accordance with Torah law, in order to erect a protective fence round the Torah," but such acts may not be defined as *halakhah* – which would imply that the ruling is of a permanent character. So too, if it saw a temporary need to suspend a positive precept, or to transgress an injunction, in order to bring many back to religion, or to save the community from being ensnared in a transgression, all in accordance with the need of the time but not for future generations (Maim. Yad, Sanhedrin 24:4; Mamrim 2:4). The classical example is Elijah offering sacrifice on Mt. Carmel at the time when the Temple existed (and sacrifice outside it was prohibited, Zev. 4b).

No restriction may be imposed upon the congregation if the majority cannot abide by it (BB 60b). So too no restriction may be imposed that would cause substantial loss (see, e.g., MK 2a) or excessive trouble. "It is preferable for them to transgress inadvertently rather than deliberately" (Beẓah 30a).

No court can abolish the decision of another contemporary court unless it be greater in wisdom and in number. The possibility of abolishing a restriction thus depends upon an important limitation: "It must be greater in wisdom and number" (Eduy. 1:5; for the meaning of this rule, which apparently prevents all possiblity of abolishing a *bet din* ruling, see Weiss, Dor, pt. 2, sec. 7 and Albeck in the supplements to Mishnah *Nezikin*).

At times the sages gave their pronouncements the same, and at times even greater, validity than those of the Torah. For example: "These days, enumerated in Megillat Ta'anit, are forbidden [for fasting], along with both the preceding and the following day. As to Sabbaths and New Moons, fasting on them is forbidden, but it is permitted on the preceding and following days. What is the difference between them? The latter are of biblical origin and words of the Torah require no reinforcement, whereas the former are of scribal authority and the words of the scribes require reinforcement" (RH 19a). Thus they were more stringent about the fulfillment of their *takkanot* than about the enactment of the Torah itself, because for the latter no danger of negligence was anticipated, as it was with their regulations. Many of the edicts and *takkanot* are anonymous, just as the early *halakhah* in general is anonymous: according to dogmatic conception they were all enacted and accepted by a vote of the great *bet din* in which, too, all disputed matters were decided. The modern historical approach, too, is close to this view, even though the concept "the great *bet din*" was not identical in all periods (see Ḥ. Albeck, in: *Zion*, 8 (1942–43), 85–93, 165–78; L. Finkelstein, *The Pharisees*, 1962[3]). Notwithstanding, many *takkanot* and edicts are mentioned that are connected with the names of definite persons or places, such as Joshua b. Gamla, Simeon b. Shetaḥ, Bet Shammai and Bet Hillel, Gamaliel the Elder, Johanan b. Zakkai, Gamaliel of Jabneh, the scholars of Usha, Judah ha-Nasi, etc. There are also many *halakhot* that are attributed to biblical personalities such as Moses, Joshua, Samuel, David, Solomon, Hezekiah, Daniel, the prophets (and the men of the *Great Synagogue). The individuals enumerated appear as heads of *batei din*.

The distinction between the concepts *de-orayta* and *de-rabbanan* in the whole field of *halakhah* actually derives from the *amoraim*, but it already existed in the time of the *tannaim* and is recognizable by the penalties fixed for transgressions of the different categories, and there is also found the explicit expression "statements of the scribes" in contrast to "statements of the Torah" (e.g., Yev. 2:4; Par. 11:5–6; Yad. 3:2; Zev. 99b). But the views of the *tannaim* and *amoraim* on this matter do not completely coincide, and at times a matter which according to tannaitic sources appears to be *de-orayta* becomes in the era of the *amoraim de-rabbanan*. The difference between the two concepts *de-orayta* and *de-rabbanan* not only expresses itself in penalties (thus, e.g., the sacrifices which one who transgresses the words of the Torah must bring as an atonement for his iniquity are not imposed as an obligation on one transgressing a prohibition of the sages, but on the other hand the sages have the right to flog one transgressing their words with "stripes of correction" in order to punish and reform him); there is also a difference in the halakhic consideration: "In the case of doubt with regard to a biblical injunction the stringent view is accepted, in the case of rabbinical, the lenient" (Beẓah 3b; TJ, Er. 3:4).

CUSTOM. The word custom (Heb. *minhag*) has various meanings in talmudic literature, and not all have the same force, even though all serve as sources of *halakhah*.

Religious custom which can be relied upon where the *halakhah* is unclear: "Every *halakhah* that is unclear in the *bet din* and you do not know its nature, go and see how the community conducts itself and conduct yourself accordingly" (TJ, Pe'ah 7:5). Here the concept of custom is close to the concept of "consensus" in Muslim law in its original stage: the people as a whole do not err, and therefore custom decides the matter; its nature is as the nature of the *halakhah*. In the Babylonian Talmud this idea is expressed in the words "Go and see how the public are accustomed to act" (Ber. 45a), and this too is certainly what Hillel meant when he said: "Leave it to Israel; if they are not prophets, they are the children of prophets" (Pes. 66a).

Religious custom that is not publicly proclaimed as the official *halakhah* (see Ta'an 26b): here too, as in the previous section, the reference is not to a new custom but to fixing the norm in a *halakhah* concerning which there is a dispute, in accordance with the existing custom.

A custom that is in contradiction to the theoretical *halakhah* but by virtue of being a public custom, and that of conscientious people, has the power to cancel the *halakhah* (TJ, Yev, 12:1; Sof. 14, ed. Higger, 270f.): in these cases, the custom replaces the *halakhah*.

A custom introduced by a definite group – such as the citizens of a town, a group of pious men, women, professional groups, etc. – in some area of religious, social, or legal life, additional to the existing *halakhah*: such a custom serves as a source of *halakhah* which may not be altered and has the same authority as the words of the sages (see, e.g., Pes. 4:1; BM 7:1; et al.).

[Benjamin De Vries]

See also *Minhag*.

DEVELOPMENT OF HALAKHAH

The Early Period

Codes of law are found in the Pentateuch (Ex. 21–23:19; Lev. 19; Deut. 21–25) together with smaller collections and numerous individual laws. Biblical criticism explains the differences in style and the contradictions between one collection and another on the grounds that these groups of laws were produced in different circles at diverse times, e.g., in one collection the tithe is given to the levite (Num. 18:20–32) whereas in Deuteronomy it is retained by the farmer himself to be eaten in the place of the central sanctuary (Deut. 14:22–26). This kind of solution was not open to the Pharisaic teachers so that the early *halakhah* reconciles the two passages by postulating two tithes, the first (*ma'aser rishon*) to be given to the Levite and the second (*ma'aser sheni*) to be eaten in the place of the central sanctuary. Moreover, according to the traditional view, God conveyed to Moses together with the Written Law (*torah she-bi-khetav*) an Oral Law (*torah she be-al peh*). This latter embraced both the specific "laws given to Moses at Sinai" and the many interpretations of the written text now found in the rabbinic literature.

One of the main points at issue between the Sadducees and the Pharisees was the validity of this doctrine of the Oral Law, the Pharisees affirming and the Sadducees denying it. But this is to oversimplify the problem. It is obvious that some process of interpretation of the written texts must have begun at the earliest period since many of the texts are unintelligible as they stand (though this is very different from the affirmation that the interpretation was uniform and handed down unimpaired from generation to generation). Buying and selling, for example, are mentioned in the Pentateuch without any indication of how the transfer of property was to be effected. The law of divorce (Deut. 24:1–4) speaks of a "bill of divorcement," but gives no information on how this is to be written. Ezekiel 44:31 would seem to be an interpretation of the laws found in Exodus 22:30 and Deuteronomy 14:21 (Weiss, Dor, 1 (1904[4]), 44–45). Jeremiah 17:21 is an interpretation of what is involved in Sabbath "work." It would appear certain that by about 400 B.C.E., after the return from Babylon and the establishment of the Second Temple, the Pentateuch had become the Torah (the Written Law) and there had begun to develop an oral interpretation of the Pentateuchal texts.

The identity of the men of the Great Synagogue, who are said to have flourished immediately after the return, is still a major problem, as is the relationship of this body to the "Scribes" (*soferim*; according to Frankel, *Darkhei ha-Mishnah* (1923), 3–7 et al.). The men of the Great Synagogue were the executive of a movement of Pentateuchal interpretation of which the "Scribes" formed the general body. However, more recent studies have demonstrated that the *soferim* were simply a class of biblical exegetes inferior in status to the "sages" so that it is illegitimate to speak of the period of the "Scribes" (Kaufmann, Y., Toledot, 4 (1960), 481–5; E. Urbach, in: *Tarbiz*, 27 (1957/58), 166–82). The Midrash process, in which the texts were carefully examined for their wider meaning and application, no doubt had its origin in this period. Another vexed question is whether the Midrash of a particular text is the real source of the law said to be derived from it or whether the law came first with the Midrash no more than a peg on which to hang it. The most convincing way of coping with the evidence on this matter is to suggest that the earliest Midrashim were in the nature of a real derivative process by means of which the deeper meaning and wider application of the texts were uncovered (although this must not be taken to exclude the existence of actual traditions for which texts were subsequently found). In the later Midrash the process is reversed.

The whole period down to the age of the Maccabees – on any showing the formative period in the history of the *halakhah* – is shrouded in obscurity. Y. Baer (in *Zion*, 17 (1951–52), 1–55) has argued that there was little pure academic legal activity at this period and that many of the laws originating at this time were produced by a kind of rule of thumb in which pious farmers in a comparatively simple form of society worked out basic rules of neighborly conduct, much in the same way as this was done among the Greeks in the age of Solon. Some of these rules can possibly still be detected among the earliest strata of the Mishnah, e.g., in the first chapter of *Bava Kamma*, which includes a formulation of the law of torts worded in the first person.

There are references in the sources to five pairs of teachers – the *zugot* ("pairs," *duumviri*) – beginning with Yose b. Joezer and Yose b. Johanan in the time of the Maccabees and ending with Hillel and Shammai in the time of Herod. The ethical maxims of these teachers are recorded in the Mishnah (Avot 1:4–5) but little legal material has been transmitted in their name. At this time, it was said, there was no legal debate in Israel (Tosef., Ḥ¦vŏ 2:9), i.e., the law was known or where in doubt was decided by the "great court" in Jerusalem.

Historically considered there is no question, however, of a uniform *halakhah*, even at this early period, handed down from generation to generation in the form the *halakhah* assumes in the tannaitic period. Apart from the great debates on legal matters between the Sadducees and the Pharisees, the *halakhah* in the books of the Apocrypha (and the writings of the Qumran sect) is not infrequently at variance with the *halakhah* as recorded in the Mishnah and the other tannaitic sources (e.g., the law of false witnesses in Susannah conflicts with the Pharisaic law as recorded in the Mishnah, Mak. 1:4). Even in the Pharisaic party itself the schools of Hillel and Shammai at the beginning of the present era differed on hundreds of laws, so that it was said that there was a danger of the Torah becoming two *torot* (Sanh. 88b).

A major problem here is the motivation behind the approaches of the two rival schools. The theory associated with L. Ginzberg (*On Jewish Law and Lore* (1955), 102–18) and L. Finkelstein (op. cit.) finds the differences in the different social strata to which the schools belonged. The school of Shammai, it is argued, was legislating for the upper classes, the wealthy landowners and aristocrats, while the school of Hillel was legislating for the poorer urban workers and artisans. Thus according to the school of Hillel the legal definition of a "meal" is one dish, whereas according to the school of Shammai it is at least two dishes (Beẓah 2:1). In most societies the woman has a much more significant role among the upper classes than among the lower. Hence the school of Hillel rules that a valid marriage can be effected by the delivery to the woman of the smallest coin – a *perutah* – whereas the school of Shammai demands the much larger minimum amount of a *dinar* (Kid. 1:1). The school of Shammai only permits the divorce of a wife if she is unfaithful whereas the school of Hillel permits it on other grounds (Git. 9:10). While there is undoubtedly some truth in the theory of social motivation it is too sweeping to be entirely adequate. Other motives, such as different exegetical methods, were also at work (see Alon, *Meḥkarim*, 2 (1958), 181–222).

The Tannaitic Period (c. 1–220 C.E.).

The debates between the schools of Hillel and Shammai set in motion new debating processes among the rabbinic teachers of first- and second-century Palestine, the *tannaim*. Prominent in the second century were the rival schools of R. Akiva and R. Ishmael, who differed in their concept of the Torah revelation and, as a result, in their attitude toward the scope of the *halakhah* (see A.J. Heschel, *Torah min ha-Shamayim* (first 2 vols., 1962, 1965). According to R. Ishmael's school "the Torah speaks in the language of men" (Sif. Num. 15:31) and it is therefore not permissible to derive new laws from such linguistic usages as the infinitive absolute before the verb. According to the school of R. Akiva it is legitimate to do this and to derive laws from the use of the particles *gam* ("also") and *et* (the sign of the accusative), for example in Pesaḥim 22b, since in the view of this school no word or letter of the Torah can be considered superfluous or merely for the purpose of literary effect. A later teacher characterized the methods of the Akiva school by telling of Moses on high asking God why He had affixed the decorative "crowns" to some of the letters of the Torah. God replies that after many generations there will arise a man, Akiva b. Joseph by name, "who will expound upon each tittle heaps and heaps of laws." Moses then asks permission to see Akiva and is transported across time to enter Akiva's academy where he is unable to follow the arguments! Moses is distressed but is later comforted when Akiva replies to the question of his disciples: "Whence do you know this?" by stating: "It is a law given to Moses at Sinai" (Men. 29b).

At the end of the second century R. Judah ha-Nasi edited the Mishnah, in which were summarized all the legal debates and decisions of the *tannaim*. Judah ha-Nasi is better spoken of as the editor of the Mishnah, not its author, since it is clear that his compilation is based on earlier formulations, particularly those of R. Akiva and his disciple R. Meir. Indeed it is possible to detect various early strata embedded in the final form the Mishnah has assumed. For instance, the Mishnah (Pes. 1:1) records a rule that a wine cellar requires to be searched for leaven on the eve of Passover and then records a debate between the schools of Hillel and Shammai on how this rule is to be defined.

The Amoraic Period (c. 220–470 C.E.)

Once the Mishnah had been compiled it became a sacred text second only to the Bible. The word of the post-mishnaic teachers in both Palestine and Babylon (the *amoraim*) was confined chiefly to discussion and comment on the Mishnah and to the application of its laws (and those found in the other tannaitic sources). It became axiomatic that no *amora* had the right to disagree with a *tanna* in matters of law unless he was able to adduce tannaitic support for his view. It must not be thought, however, that the *amoraim* were only concerned with practical application of the *halakhah*. A good deal of their work was in the field of abstract legal theory in which purely academic questions were examined and debated (see M. Guttmann, in *Devir*, 1 (1923), 38–87; 2 (1923), 101–64).

The *halakhah* of the Palestinian *amoraim* was eventually collected in the Jerusalem Talmud, that of the Babylonian *amoraim* in the Babylonian Talmud. With the "closing" of the Talmud this work virtually became the infallible source of the *halakhah*. Occasionally in the Middle Ages, as Weiss (Dor, 3 (1904[4]) 216–30) has demonstrated, authorities would disagree with talmudic rulings. Maimonides, for example, disregards in his code any laws based on a belief in the efficacy of magic even though the laws are found in the Talmud and are not disputed there. Some of the *geonim* tended to adopt a more lenient attitude toward the talmudic laws governing the relations between Jews and gentiles on the grounds that the gentiles in their milieu (the Muslims) were not idolaters. But such exceptions were few. The history of post-talmudic *halakhah* is founded on the appeal to the Talmud as the final and overriding authority. "To it [the Talmud] one must not add and from it one must not subtract" (Maim., Comm. to Mishnah, intro.). Of the two Talmuds the Babylonian became the more authoritative for a number of reasons. The *halakhah* of the Babylonian Talmud is more highly developed and more comprehensive; the Babylonian Talmud is later than the Jerusalem and hence able to override the decisions of the latter; the textual condition of the Babylonian Talmud is in a more satisfactory state; the Babylonian *geonim* at Sura and Pumbedita were in direct succession to the Babylonian *amoraim* (so that the Babylonian Talmud became "our Talmud") and the hegemony of the teachings of Babylonia was considerably strengthened as a result of political developments, including the emergence of Baghdad as the seat of the caliphate. Maimonides (Yad, intro.) states the accepted view: "All Israel is obliged to follow the matters stated in the Babylonian Talmud. Every city and every province are to be coerced to follow all the customs which the sages of the Talmud followed and to obey their decisions and follow their enactments since all the matters in the Talmud have been accepted by all Israel. And those sages who made the enactments or introduced the decrees or ordained the customs or decided the laws, teaching that the decision was so, were all the sages of Israel or the majority of them. And they heard by tradition the main principles of the whole Torah generation after generation reaching back to the generation of Moses our teacher on whom be peace."

Rules for determining the actual decision in law from the labyrinth of legal debate and discussion that is the Talmud are provided by the Talmud itself and by the savoraic additions to the Talmud, and other rules were widely accepted by the post-talmudic authorities. The following, in addition to those mentioned above, are some of the more important of these rules which enabled the Talmud to serve as the final authority in *halakhah* even though it is not itself a code of law.

Where there is a debate between an individual sage and his colleagues the view of the majority is adopted (Ber. 9a). The school of Hillel is always followed against the school of Shammai (Er. 6b). In the many matters debated by Rav and Samuel the view of Rav is followed in religious matters and that of Samuel in civil law (Bek. 49b). Except in three specified cases the opinion of R. Johanan is followed against that of R. Simeon b. Lakish (Yev. 36a). Similarly, except in three specified cases the opinion of Rabbah is followed against that of R. Joseph (BB 114b). The decision of Rava is followed against that of Abbaye except in six specified cases (Kid. 52a). Wherever a talmudic debate concludes with the statement "the law is…" (*ve-hilkheta*) this ruling is adopted. The lenient opinion is adopted when there is a debate regarding the laws of mourning for near relatives (MK 26b). The rulings of later authorities are generally preferred to those of earlier ones (from Rava onward) on the grounds that the later scholars, though aware of the opinions of the others, still saw fit to disagree with them (*Sefer Keritut*, 4:3, 6). It is generally accepted that where a ruling is conveyed in a talmudic passage anonymously (*setama*) this implies unanimity among the final editors and is to be followed even if elsewhere in the Talmud the matter is a subject of debate (see Tos. to Ber. 20b and Yev. 116a). Halakhic decisions are not generally to be derived from aggadic statements (based on TJ, Peʿah 2:4; see ET, 1 (1951[3]), 62). This rule was not applied consistently and was occasionally departed from, particularly in the French and German schools in the Middle Ages for whom the entire talmudic material, including the *aggadah*, tended to be invested with infallible authority.

In spite of the "closing" of the Talmud (occasioned chiefly by the disturbed conditions at the end of the fifth century when the great Babylonian schools were closed for a fairly long period) and its acceptance as the final authority, new legislation could still be introduced under the heading of *takkanah* ("enactment"), of which there are many examples in the Talmud itself. By means of the *takkanah* it was possible to cope with new circumstances not covered by the talmudic law. From time to time the principle, found in the Talmud, was resorted to that "a court can inflict penalties even when these run counter to the Torah" if the times require it (Yev. 90b; see above). In Spain, for example, in the Middle Ages, the courts assumed the power to inflict capital and corporal punishment even though this right had long been taken from them according to the strict letter of the law (see Baron, Community, 1 (1942), 168–9 and notes).

Codification of the Halakhah

Teachers of the *halakhah* in the Middle Ages and afterward were of two main types. Firstly there were the legal theoreticians such as Rashi and the tosafists, whose main activity consisted of exposition of the classical legal texts of the Talmud and other early rabbinic works. These were known as the *mefareshim* ("commentators") and their writings were naturally utilized to determine the practical law even though this was not their own province. Secondly there were the *posekim* ("decision-makers") whose opinions in practical legal matters were accepted because of their acknowledged expertise in this field. The activity of the *posekim* was of two kinds: responsa and codification. Questions of law on which direct guidance from the Talmud was not forthcoming were addressed to the great legal luminaries and from time to time these responsa were collected, helping to form the basis for new codifications of the *halakhah*. Both the new and older laws were frequently classified and codified. The process of responsa and subsequent *codification has continued down to the present.

One of the earliest codes was the **Halakhot Gedolot* of Simeon Kayyara (ninth century). Isaac *Alfasi compiled an abbreviated, and with regard to some texts an expanded, version of the Babylonian Talmud in which only the conclusions of the talmudic discussions were recorded so as to provide a digest of talmudic *halakhah* in its practical application. Where the Babylonian Talmud has no rulings Alfasi followed decisions found in the Jerusalem Talmud. *Maimonides compiled his gigantic code, the *Mishneh Torah* (called, after his death, the *Yad ha-Ḥazakah*), in which he presented the final decisions in all matters of *halakhah*, including those laws which no longer obtained in his day, such as the laws of the sacrificial cult. *Asher b. Jehiel, known as the Rosh (Rabbenu Asher), compiled a code in which due weight was given to the opinions of the French and German authorities which frequently differed from those of the Spanish authorities as recorded by Maimonides. Asher's son, *Jacob b. Asher, followed in his father's footsteps in his code known as the *Tur* ("row," pl. *Turim*, properly the "Four Rows," so called because the work is divided into four parts).

By the time of Joseph *Caro there was much confusion in the whole realm of practical *halakhah*. In addition to the many differences between the codes, Jewish communities tended to differ in their application of the laws so that, as Caro remarks (*Beit Yosef*, Intro.), the Torah had become not two *torot* but many *torot*. In his great commentary to the *Tur*, called *Beit Yosef*, Caro sought to remedy the situation by working out a practical guide for a uniform application of the *halakhah*. His method was to follow a majority opinion whenever the three earlier codes of Alfasi, Maimonides, and the *Tur* disagreed and to rely on other authorities whenever this method of deciding was not possible. Caro's *Shulḥan Arukh contains the gist of his decisions as worked out in the *Beit Yosef*. Unfortunately, however, Caro's method weighted the scales in favor of the Spanish schools, since these were generally in accord with the views of Alfasi and Maimonides, against the German views as represented by Asher b. Jehiel and the *Tur*. The Shulḥan Arukh was thus incapable of serving as a practical guide to the German Jews and their followers in Poland, which from the 16th century became a foremost center of Jewish life. The remedy was provided by Moses *Isserles of Cracow who added notes to the Shulḥan Arukh, known as the MAPPAH, in which the German-Polish practices were recorded where these differed from the opinions of the Shulḥan Arukh. The Shulḥan Arukh, together with the *Mappah*, became the most authoritative code in the history of the *halakhah*, partly, at least, because it was the first code to be compiled after the invention of printing and was therefore sure of the widest dissemination.

The Shulḥan Arukh marked a turning point in the history of the *halakhah*. Even when later authorities departed from its rulings they did so reluctantly. Adherence to the Shulḥan Arukh became the test of Jewish fidelity. The "Shulḥan Arukh Jew" became the supreme type of Jewish piety. Earlier rabbinical authorities were known as **rishonim* while later ones were known as **aḥaronim*. Rabbinic authority even in modern times is much more reluctant to disagree with the *rishonim* than the *aḥaronim*.

The Authority of the Halakhah

Halakhah is the distinctive feature of Judaism as a religion of obedience to the word of God. It united Jews of many different temperaments, origins, and theological opinions, though the view ("pan-halakhism" as A.J. Heschel called it) that submission to the *halakhah* is all that is demanded of the Jew is a travesty of traditional Judaism. The major practical differences between Orthodox and Reform Judaism depend on the different attitudes of these groups to the *halakhah*. Orthodoxy considers the *halakhah*, in its traditional form, to be absolutely binding, whereas Reform, while prepared to be guided by the legal decisions of the past in some areas, rejects the absolute binding force of the traditional *halakhah*. Conservative Judaism adopts a midway position, treating the traditional *halakhah* as binding but feeling freer to interpret it and attempting to preserve the dynamic principle of legal development which, it claims, is typical of the talmudic period. The Orthodox rabbi, when faced with new halakhic problems raised, for instance, by the invention of printing and the use of electricity, will try to arrive at a decision by applying directly the ancient halakhic principles in the new circumstances. The Reform rabbi will be more inclined to consider the religious demands of the new age and will tend to operate within nonhalakhic categories. The Conservative rabbi will try to utilize these latter in working out a fresh interpretation of the traditional *halakhah*.

[Louis Jacobs]

BIBLIOGRAPHY: Weiss, Dor; Frankel, Mishnah; Halevy, Dorot; G.F. Moore, *Judaism in the First Centuries of the Christian Era*, 3 vols. (1927–30); J. Kaplan, *The Redaction of the Talmud* (1933); Ḥ. Tchernowitz, *Toledot ha-Halakhah*, 4 vols. (1934–50); idem, *Toledot ha-Posekim*, 3 vols. (1946–47); J.Z. Lauterbach, "Midrash and Mishnah," in his *Rabbinic Essays* (1951), 163–256; B. Cohen, *Law and Ethics in the Light of Jewish Tradition* (1957); idem, *Law and Tradition in Judaism* (1959); ET, 9 (1959), 241–339; M. Kadushin, *The Rabbinic Mind* (1965^2), includes bibliography; Z.H. Chajes, *The Student's Guide Through the Talmud* (1960^2); B. Herring, *Jewish Ethics and Halakhah for Our Times: Sources and Commentary*, 2 vols. (1984–1989). Conservative: On Zacharias Frankel, see M. Krakauer, *Zacharias Frankel's prinzipieller Standpunkt in der Reformfrage des Judentums* (1883); L. Ginzberg, *Students, Scholars, Saints* (1958), 195–216; M. Brann, *Geschichte des juedisch-theologischen Seminars in Breslau* (1904); I. Heinemann, in: G. Kisch (ed.), *Das Breslauer Seminar* (1963), 85–109. On changes in Judaism, see M. Waxman (ed.), *Tradition and Change*

(1964), 43–50. On philosophy of Jewish law, see L. Ginzberg, "Tradition and Change," *op. cit.*, 129–138; M. Arzt, in: *ibid.*, 139–51; R. Gordis, in: *ibid.*, 375–91; E. Dorf, in: CJ, 27, 3 (1973), 65–77; S. Siegel, in: CJ, 24, 3 (1971), 33–40; R. Gordis, in: *ibid.*, 49–55; *idem.*, in: CJ, 26, 3 (1972), 70–74; J. Agus, in: PRA, 31 (1967), 81–89; I. Klein, in: *ibid.*, 22 (1958), 102–7; M. Higger, in: CJ, 5, 4 (1949), 20–22; S. Simon, in: *Judaism*, 3 (1954), 48–53; S. Greenberg, in: CJ, 24, 3 (1970), 75–141. On responsa and decisions of the Committee on Jewish Laws and Standards, see: B.Z. Kreitman, in: PRA, 22 (1958), 68–80; J. Segal, in: PRA, 31 (1967), 195–208; I. Klein, in: CJ, 24, 3 (1970), 26–33; I. Silverman, in: CJ, 18, 2 (1964), 1–5; I. Klein, in: CJ, 28, 2 (1974), 34–46. Reconstructionist: I. Eisenstein, *Judaism under Freedom* (1956), 180–88; idem, *Tradition and Change*, ed. M. Waxman (1958), 447–53; M.M. Kaplan, *The Future of the American Jew* (1967), 187–401; idem, *Judaism as a Civilization* (1957), 431–78; idem, *The Meaning of God in Modern Jewish Religion* (1937), 315–20; idem, *A New Zionism* (1959), idem, *Questions Jews Ask* (1959); E. Kohn, *Religious Humanism* (1953); J.J. Cohen and E. Kohn, "Jewish Law and Ritual" (undated pamphlet); H.M. Schulweiss, "Democracy and Jewish Religion" (undated pamphlet). **ADD. BIBLIOGRAPHY:** M. Elon, *Ha-Mishpat ha-Ivri*, 3 vols. (1973; *Jewish Law, History, Sources, Principles*, 4 vols., 1994); N. Hecht et al., *An Introduction to the History and Sources of Jewish Law* (1996); N. Rakover, *A Bibliography of Jewish Law*, 2 vols. (1975–90); B.S. Jackson et al., "Halacha and Law," in: M. Goodman (ed.), *Oxford Handbook of Jewish Studies* (2002), 643–79, incl. bibl. For periodical literature, see *Halakhic Periodicals.

HALAKHAH LE-MOSHE MI-SINAI (Heb. הֲלָכָה לְמֹשֶׁה מִסִּינַי; "a law given to Moses at Sinai"). As part of the *Oral Law, a number of laws, possessing biblical authority but neither stated in Scripture nor derived by hermeneutical principles, are stated in rabbinic literature to be "laws given to Moses at Sinai." The term occurs only three times in the Mishnah (Pe'ah 2:6; Eduy. 8:7; Yad. 4:3) but is found frequently together with terms of similar import, in the other sources of rabbinic Judaism, particularly in the Talmud (such as – "there is a received *halakhah*"; "there is a received tradition"; or simply "received"). Similarly, according to the Jerusalem Talmud (Shab. 1:4, 3b) the expression "in truth they said" also belongs to this category (however, see BM 60a and Rashi s.v. *be-emet*).

Among the laws said to have been given to Moses at Sinai are the 18 defects which render an animal *terefah (Ḥul. 42a); the duty of walking round the altar with willows and the feast of water drawing, both on the festival of Tabernacles (Suk. 34a); the underside and duct of the *tefillin*, the parchment of the *tefillin*, that the straps of the *tefillin* be black and the *tefillin* themselves square (Men. 35a), and that they should have a knot (Er. 97a); the minimum quantities of forbidden foods to constitute an offense and the rules regarding interpositions on the body which invalidate a ritual immersion (Er. 4a); that only half the damage is to be paid when damage is done by pebbles flying from under an animal's feet (BK 3b); and that doubtful cases of levitical defilement, if occurring in the public domain, are to be treated as pure (Ḥul. 9b). It will be seen that all these refer to long-established rules which could not have been known without a tradition to that effect. The medieval commentators point out that on occasion the term, *halakhah le-Moshe mi-Sinai*, is used of much later enactments and is not always to be taken literally, but refers to a *halakhah* which is so certain and beyond doubt that it is as though it were a *halakhah* given to Moses at Sinai (Asher ben Jehiel *Hilkhot Mikva'ot*, 1 (at the end of his *Piskei ha-Rosh* to *Niddah*) and his *Commentary to Mishnah*, Yad. 4:3). In most cases, however, they explain it literally, i.e., that these *halakhot* were transmitted by God to Moses at Sinai. Modern scholarship is skeptical about the whole question, but it is clear that the rabbis themselves did believe in the existence of laws transmitted verbally to Moses.

BIBLIOGRAPHY: Weiss, Dor, 1 (1904[4]), index; W. Bacher, in: *Studies in Jewish Literature… K. Kohler* (1913), 56–70 (Ger.); Ḥ. Tchernowitz, *Toledot ha-Halakhah*, 1 (1934), 29–36; L. Strack, *Introduction to the Talmud* (1945), 9; J. Levinger, *Darkhei ha-Maḥashavah ha-Hilkhatit shel ha-Rambam* (1965), 50–65.

[Louis Jacobs]

HALAKHIC PERIODICALS. The first Jewish periodical to appear was the **Peri Eẓ-Ḥayyim* which first appeared in 1691. This journal consisted primarily of responsa to halakhic queries sent from all parts of the Dutch empire of its day; 13 volumes were published during the 116 years of its existence, until 1807.

Halakhic periodical literature continued to develop through the years. Noteworthy is the *Shomer Ẓiyyon ha-Ne'eman*, which appeared in Germany during the years 1846–56, under the guidance of Rabbi Jacob Ettlinger, containing, *inter alia*, responsa. The turn of the 20th century saw the growth of rabbinic halakhic periodicals in Eastern Europe, and eventually in America; e.g., *Ha-Pardes* which was originally founded in Poland in 1913, still appears in New York. Among the European periodicals, *Tel Talpiot* (Vac, Hungary), appeared from 1812–1938, and *Yagdil Torah* (Slutsk, Belorussia, 1908–28) are especially worthy of mention.

After World War II the center of halakhic activity naturally shifted to Israel, with the United States taking second place. *Sinai*, which was founded even before the war (Jerusalem, 1937–) includes contemporary and historical responsa.

The establishment of the State of Israel has generated an intensification of activity in applying *halakhah* to all facets of modern life – its technology, society and economy have all been the subject of halakhic research. It gave rise to *Ha-Torah ve-ha-Medinah*, published by the Rabbinical Association of Ha-Po'el Ha-Mizrachi (1949–62), which dealt with such topics as security, medical ethics, legislation, law applying to the Land of Israel and Family Law. Thus, among topics discussed in vol. 1 are: the right to grant clemency to those sentenced by the courts of Israel, the authority of the president and the institutions of elected government, and the legal status of spoils of war. Vol. 4 (1952) included articles on the rights of women according to the *halakhah*, and women's service in the armed forces; vols. 5–6, security measures in the State on the Sabbath and Festivals; vols. 7–8, the powers of municipal authorities according to the *halakhah*; vols. 11–13 (1960–62), the religious duty of *aliyah*, the prohibition against leaving Israel, and the liability of rabbis to taxation. *Or ha-Mizraḥ* (1959–), issued by the Ha-Po'el Ha-Mizrachi of the United States, is essentially a Diaspora equivalent of *Ha-Torah ve-ha-Medinah*.

Unlike the above two works, which appear under the aegis of a public body, *No'am* (1959–), "A platform for the clarification of halakhic problems," is a venture of the Torah Shelemah Institute of Jerusalem, and its scope is much wider. Among the practical problems dealt with are the use of the birth control pill (11:167), heart transplants (13:1), the transplanting of kidneys and artificial kidneys (14:308), artificial insemination (10:314), and even whether the laws of the Torah are applicable to a Jew on the moon (13:196). Among the other contemporary Israeli journals containing responsa, noteworthy are *Assia*, published in Jerusalem by the Dr. F. Schlesinger Institute for Medical Halakhic Research at Shaare Zedek Hospital (1969–), which acts as a forum for modern medical ethical problems; *Ha-Ma'yan*, published in Jerusalem by the Y. Breuer Institute (1952–); *Kol Torah* (Jerusalem, 1930–); *Torah She-be-al Peh*, published in Jerusalem by Mosad Ha-Rav Kook, consisting of the proceedings of the annual Oral Law Conferences devoted to various fields of current interest (1958–); *Moriah*, published in Jerusalem (1969–), and *Shma'atin* (1964–), a forum for dealing with problems in religious education. Devoted to Jewish Law (*Mishpat Ivri*) are *Diné Israel* (1969–), an annual published by the Faculty of Law of Tel Aviv University, and *Shenaton ha-Mishpat ha-Ivri* (1974–), published by the Institute for Research in Jewish Law at the Hebrew University Law School.

In America, *Ha-Darom* (1957–), published in New York by the Rabbinical Council of America, discusses a broad spectrum of modern halakhic questions. The English language *Tradition* (1958–), also published in New York by the RCA, includes a section, a "Survey of Recent Halakhic Periodical Literature" as well as halakhic articles and essays. *Talpiot* (1943–63), which was published in New York by Yeshiva University, is also worthy of mention.

[Menahem Slae]

HALAKHOT GEDOLOT (Heb. הֲלָכוֹת גְּדוֹלוֹת), halakhic code belonging to the geonic period.

Nature of the Code

The *Halakhot Gedolot* gives a systematic and comprehensive summary of all the talmudic laws. Although in general it follows the order of the tractates of the Talmud, it groups together the various *halakhot* scattered in the Talmud according to their logical order, and, contrary to the procedure adopted in the Mishnah and *Gemara*, first states the general principle before giving the details. It also assigns new names to certain groups of *halakhot*, and embodies laws (such as those dealing with sacrifices and some of those applicable to the priests) which were no longer observed after the destruction of the Temple. The decisions are founded on those of the Talmud and on the halakhic principles laid down by its sages. The work is based on the Babylonian Talmud but the author also makes use to some extent of the Jerusalem Talmud, which he refers to as "the Talmud of the West." Other sources are the responsa of Babylonian *geonim* and the halakhic work of the same period *Sefer ha-Ma'asim shel Benei Ereẓ Yisrael*. *Halakhot Gedolot* spread throughout Jewry, and in the course of time decisions of *Yehudai Gaon and those of a later date were incorporated into it. The earlier authorities often quote excerpts from it which are different, or entirely absent, from the extant work.

The *Halakhot Gedolot* has an introduction – it is the first rabbinic work to have one – and it is generally held that it was directed against the *Karaites and others who rejected the Oral Law. It is in two parts, the one comprising aggadic statements in praise of the Torah and its students; the other enumerating, for the first time, the 613 *commandments mentioned in the Talmud (Mak. 23b). They are classified according to the degree of punishment incurred in transgressing them and according to their common character. This list of 365 negative and 248 positive commandments, which provided the basis for similar elaborations in various *azharot, was severely criticized by Maimonides in his *Sefer ha-Mitzvot*, and defended by Naḥmanides.

Recensions of the Work

The work is extant in two recensions. The one (*Halakhot Gedolot 1*), published in Venice in 1548, is the Babylonian recension, which is the earlier and which preserves the original version. It was this recension that was used by the French and German scholars. The other (*Halakhot Gedolot* 2) was published by A. Hildesheimer on the basis of the Vatican manuscript (1892) and is, in the opinion of scholars, identical with *Halakhot Gedolot shel Ispamya* ("Spain"; Tos. to Yev. 48a, see below), the version used by the scholars of Spain, southern France, and Italy. Various excerpts from this Spanish recension are not found in *Halakhot Gedolot 1*, having been omitted by copyists. Moreover, the former contains later additions, commentaries, and supercommentaries, and also the names of *geonim* who lived after Simeon Kayyara (see below), the last *gaon* to be mentioned in it being Ẓemaḥ b. Paltoi (890 C.E.). This recension, which may have been compiled in North Africa (Kairouan), was called by the northern French scholars *Halakhot Gedolot shel Ispamya*, having reached them from Spain by way of southern France. There may also have been other recensions of the work, for a southern French author mentions "our *halakhot* of Simeon Kayyara that came from Ereẓ Israel" (*Ha-Ittur*, pt. 2 (1874), 22c), while various excerpts from *Halakhot Gedolot*, not contained in the other recensions, have been found in the Cairo *Genizah*.

Date and Authorship

The authorship and date of the *Halakhot Gedolot* have been the subject of many studies and given rise to conflicting views. The work has been variously ascribed to Sherira Gaon (A.E.

Harkavy (ed.), *Teshuvot ha-Ge'onim*, no. 376; *Zikkaron la-Rishonim ve-gam la-Aḥaronim*, 1/4 (1887)), Hai Gaon (D. Cassel (ed.) *Teshuvot Ge'onim Kadmonim* (1848) no. 87, et al.), by the scholars of Spain and Provence to Simeon Kayyara and to Yehudai Gaon by those of northern France and Germany. In his *Sefer ha-Kabbalah*, Abraham ibn Daud states that Simeon Kayyara lived before Yehudai Gaon and that the latter was the author of *Halakhot Pesukot, written in 741 C.E., which "he compiled from *Halakhot Gedolot*" (Ibn Daud, Tradition, 47f., see also 127, n. 18–19). S.J. Rapoport, following Abraham ibn Daud, held that *Halakhot Gedolot* is composed of two parts: the original *Halakhot Gedolot* of Simeon Kayyara and *Halakhot Pesukot* of Yehudai Gaon, which the latter's pupils incorporated into the former work. According to Rapoport, Yehudai Gaon's statements in *Halakhot Gedolot* can be recognized in two ways: by the Aramaic in which various passages are written, and by the word *pesak* ("legal decision"), which is associated with several statements and which, according to him, derive from *Halakhot Pesukot*. This, however, has been controverted by S.D. Luzzatto (*Beit ha-Oẓar*, 1 (1847), 53af.). Graetz maintained that the work was written by Simeon Kayyara who lived at the end of the ninth or the beginning of the 10th century, some 150 years after Yehudai Gaon had composed *Halakhot Pesukot*. I. Halevy held that the author of *Halakhot Gedolot* was a younger contemporary of the writer of *Halakhot Pesukot*, the latter work being a compilation of Yehudai Gaon's practical decisions, while the former, more theoretical work has its source in the Talmud. A. Epstein contended that *Halakhot Gedolot* was written in Sura by Simeon Kayyara about 825 and that its main sources were Aḥa of Shabḥa's *She'eltot* and Yehudai Gaon's *Halakhot Pesukot*. Seventy years later there was compiled the second recension of the work, the *Halakhot Gedolot shel Ispamya*, the first recension being ascribed by them to Yehudai Gaon.

Simeon Kayyara came from Bozrah in Babylonia, as is attested by Hai Gaon. The city of Bozrah is mentioned twice in *Halakhot Gedolot* (in *Hilkhot Ḥallah* and in *Hilkhot Eruvin*) and was under the spiritual authority of Sura. Indeed, many of the laws and customs mentioned in the work conform to those of Sura, and several of its legal decisions are cited in the name of *geonim* of Sura.

The work has been reprinted several times: Venice (1548), Lemberg (1804), Vienna (1811), Berlin (1888–92, ed. by A. Hildesheimer). The various editions include comments by Solomon Salem (Amsterdam, 1764), notes by S.A. Traub (1875), and the commentary *Sefat Emet* by A. Margalioth (1894).

Halakhot Gedolot-Halakhot Pesukot

A new edition of the *Halakhot Gedolot* is being published by Azriel Hildesheimer through the Mekiẓei Nirdamim publishers, Jerusalem, two parts of which have already appeared (part 1, 1972; part 2, 1980). This edition is based on manuscripts found in the Ambrosiana Library in Milan (henceforth M). Besides this manuscript there are two others which include the entire *Halakhot Gedolot* or most of it, both in the Vatican Library: the first (Ebr. 142) served as the basis of the edition of the *Halakhot Gedolot* (Berlin 1888–92), published by Azriel Hildesheimer, grandfather of the current editor, the other is (Ebr. 136, referred to as R). The *Halakhot Gedolot* published in Warsaw (1875) is based upon the Venice (V) ms. and the Paris (P). Other manuscripts from the *Genizah* are incomplete. Part of this latest Hildesheimer edition includes *halakhot* for the Seder Moed; part 2, Seder Nashim and the three Bavot of the order Nezikin.

Rabbi Isaac *Ibn Ghayyat and *Judah ben Barzillai, author of *Sefer ha-Ittim*, are among the first Spanish sages who quote extensively from the *Halakhot Gedolot* using the text B and the early Ashkenazi sages also rely on it and only rarely cite *halakhot* and variant readings from M.

According to Hildesheimer the author of the *Halakhot Gedolot* wrote only one edition and the many textual variants resulted from adaptations by various other parties, and it is difficult to determine which version is the original one. The M edition was not written in Kairouan and is not identical to the *Halakhot Gedolot shel Ispamya* as A. Epstein thought (*Kitvei A. Epstein*, 2 (1968), 399) though his opinion has been accepted by scholars dealing with the Geonic period. *Halakhot Gedolot* includes many citations from the Talmud which are of importance for the study of the talmudical text itself, since they include many textual variants, some of which, however, are derived from the explanations and commentaries of the author of *Halakhot Gedolot* which he interwove into the text of the Talmud. Hildesheimer's edition gives cross references to the Talmud which were missing in edition B. He has also noted the variances between the text of M and all the other versions of *Halakhot Gedolot*.

THE RELATION OF HALAKHOT GEDOLOT TO HALAKHOT PESUKOT. In contrast to the opinion of various scholars that Rabbi Yehudai Gaon was the author of the *Halakhot Pesukot* published by Sassoon from a manuscript entitled *Halakhot Pesukot of Rabbi Yehudai* (Jerusalem, 1951), Hildesheimer is convinced that *Halakhot Pesukot* is one of the versions of *Halakhot Gedolot* and that it is not identical with the *Halakhot Pesukot* of Rabbi Yehudai; the *Halakhot Pesukot* of the Sassoon manuscript was not written by Rabbi Yehudai Gaon but in a later period, making it impossible for the *Halakhot Pesukot* of the Sassoon manuscript to have served as the source of the *Halakhot Gedolot*. On the contrary, it is based on the *Halakhot Gedolot*. He reached this conclusion on the basis of the following: (1) the arrangement of the *Halakhot Pesukot* as a book divided into chapters according to subjects and topics in contrast to that of the *Halakhot Gedolot* which is based on the order of occurrence the *Halakhot* on the pages of the *Gemara* (especially in the three *Bavot* of *Nezikin*); (2) the citation of *halakhot* in the *Halakhot Pesukot* without noting their source and the deletion of long passages of the *Gemarot* which are given in the *Halakhot Gedolot*. In addition to this, *halakhot* are written out in full in the *Halakhot Gedolot*. In the introduction to the second part of the *Halakhot Gedolot* Hildesheimer cites other proofs to buttress his argument about the connection of the *Halakhot Gedolot* to the *Halakhot Pesukot*. S. Morell, on the other hand, maintains "that the *Halakhot Pesukot* is not an abridged edition of the *Halakhot Gedolot* but an independent work relying on early sources. The two works drew upon the same material and not from each other, the result being that the *Halakhot Pesukot* and *Halakhot Gedolot* are neither an abridgment or expansion but rather the same items arranged according to different systems." Morell is of the opinion that the *Halakhot Pesukot* of the Sassoon manuscript is one of the editions of the *Halakhot* of Rabbi Yehudai which served as a source for the author of the *Halakhot Gedolot*.

With regard to the talmudic topics (*sugyot*) in the *Halakhot Pesukot*, Morell tries to prove that there were other *beraitot* and statements available to the Talmudic sages which were not available to the author of the *Halakhot Pesukot* and vice versa. There are topics in the *Halakhot Pesukot* which are missing in the Talmud and there are intricate discussions in the Talmud which are missing prior to the *Halakhot Pesukot*. There is even an instance in which the Talmudic version is an abridgment of a longer original version retained in the *Halakhot Pesukot*. The sages of the talmudic *sugyot* and those of the *Halakhot Pesukot* used the same raw material which included *beraitot* and received texts of questions and answers, and they edited this material in different ways.

Note should also be taken of the linguistic research concerning the Babylonian Aramaic forms of language as evidenced by the *Halakhot Gedolot* (the Paris manuscript of 1402) which includes words vocalized according to the Babylonian system. Kutscher established the fact that the *Halakhot Pesukot* is the prototype of Babylonian Aramaic, the Aramaic of which is remarkably precise. In the *Halakhot Pesukot* examples of various Aramaic dialects are found: (1) the Aramaic of the texts of contracts in the *Halakhot Pesukot*, (2) Babylonian Aramaic of the quotations from the Babylonian Talmud, (3) Gaonic Aramaic. Some scholars feel that there is linguistic similarity between Babylonian Aramaic and Mandaic.

BIBLIOGRAPHY: Rapoport, in: *Kerem Ḥemed*, 6 (1841), 236ff.; Graetz, in: MGWJ, 7 (1858), 217, 228; Halberstamm, *ibid.*, 8 (1859), 379–86; 31 (1882), 472–5; Graetz-Rabbinowitz, 3 (1893), 261; Reifmann, in: *Ha-Maggid*, 5 (1862), 293f.; Gottheil, in: MGWJ, 36 (1887), 457–61; Weiss, Dor, 4 (1904[4]), 29–37; Schorr, in: *Jubelschrift… L. Zunz* (1884), 127–41 (Heb. pt.); A. Hildesheimer, in: *Jahresbericht des Rabbiner-Seminars zu Berlin 5646* (1885/86); idem (ed.), *Halakhot Gedolot al pi Ketav Yad Romi* (1892), introd.; Halevy, Dorot, 3 (1923), 200f.; A. Epstein, in: *Ha-Goren*, 3 (1902), 46–81f. (*Kitvei A. Epstein*, 2 (1957), 378–409); L. Ginzberg, *Ginzei Schechter*, 2 (1929), 48–101, 110f., 201f.; L. Ginzberg, *Geonica*, 1 (1909), 95–111; Epstein, in: MGWJ, 61 (1917), 127–32; idem, in: *Tarbiz*, 10 (1939), 119–34; 283–308; 13 (1942), 25–36; 16(1945), 79–82; Marx, in: ZHB, 13 (1909), 70–73; H. Tchernowitz, in: *Ha-Tekufah*, 5 (1923), 240–79; idem, *Toledot ha-Posekim*, 1 (1946), 70–78; Frankl, in: JJLG, 14 (1921), 208–16; V. Aptowitzer, *Mavo le-Sefer Ravyah* (1938), 230–3; idem, *Meḥkarim be-Sifrut ha-Ge'onim* (1941), 28, 30f., 78, 82; Waxman, Literature, 1 (1938[2]), 284–6; S. Assaf, *Teshuvot ha-Ge'onim* (1942), 39, 44; idem, *Tekufat ha-Ge'onim ve-Sifrutah* (1955), 168–70; H.L. Strack, *Introduction to the Talmud and Midrash* (1945), 163f.; S.K. Mirsky (ed.), *She'iltot de-Rav Aḥai Ga'on*, 1 (1960), 12–16 (introd.). **ADD. BIBLIOGRAPHY:** A. Hildesheimer, in: *Sefer ha-Yovel shel "Sinai"* (1958), 563–572; idem, in *Sefer Zikkaron le-Rav Y.Y. Vainberg* (1970), 303–312; idem, *Mavo le-Halakhot Gedolot*, 1 (1972), 15–45; 2 (1980), 11–36; idem, *Le-Mivneh ha-Sefer Halakhot Pesukot* (1978), 153–171; S. Morell, in: HUCA, 46 (1975), 510–532; idem, HUCA, 50 (1979), Hebrew section, 11–32; Y. Ta-Shema, in KS, 55 (1980), 197–200. LINGUISTIC STUDIES: Y. Kutscher, in: *Leshonenu*, 26 (1962), 153, 173–174; S. Morag, in: *Leshonenu*, 32 (1968), 67–88; M. Bar-Asher, in: *Leshonenu*, 34 (1970), 278–286; 35 (1971), 20–35; A. Sokolof, in: *Leshonenu*, 35 (1971), 235–242; Y. Melon, in *Leshonenu*, 37 (1973), 161–164.

[Yehoshua Horowitz]

HALAKHOT KEẒUVOT (Heb. הֲלָכוֹת קְצוּבוֹת), a collection of *halakhot* belonging to the geonic era, attributed to *Yehudai Gaon. *Halakhot Keẓuvot* contains *halakhot* pertaining to the mishnaic order *Mo'ed* and also laws of divorce, wine of gentiles, mourning, *tefillin, ẓiẓit, mezuzah, terefot*, and a special chapter entitled *Shimmush Bet Din* dealing with legislation coming within the jurisdiction of the *bet din*, such as matrimonial and civil laws. The work, written for the most part in fluent simple Hebrew, does not give the sources of the *halakhah* and confines itself to laws of practical application. It is clear now that the *Halakhot Keẓuvot* is not by Yehudai. Some suppose the book to have been written in Ereẓ Israel, but in the opinion of M. Margalioth, it was composed in southern Italy during the second half of the ninth century, shortly before 863. The author draws on the one hand on *Halakhot Pesukot* (as he did not have in his possession the *Halakhot Gedolot), and on the other on a Palestinian halakhic work similar to *Sefer ha-Ma'asim*. Many of the customs cited in the work are contrary to those of the *geonim* but conform with those prevailing in Italy, and the redemption money of a firstborn (see *Pidyon ha-Ben) is given in Italian currency. Likewise, many of its linguistic forms are found only in the works of Italian scholars and the book was known and accepted in Italy for centuries, Italian scholars making extensive use of it. Differences in traditional *halakhot* are attributable to special traditions existing in the place of composition.

Although the book was hardly recognized in Babylonia, the *geonim* paying no attention to it and ignoring it as a source in their decisions, in the European countries it came to be regarded as authoritative. Among those making use of it are *Gershom b. Judah, *Hananel, Judah al-Bargeloni, and Melchizedek of Siponto, and whole sections from it are quoted in works emanating from the school of Rashi, e.g., *Sefer ha-Pardes, Sefer ha-Oraḥ, Siddur Rashi, Maḥzor Vitry, Ma'aseh ha-Ge'onim*, and others. The chief importance of the book is historical, since it is the first halakhic work composed in Europe, and reflects the customs, methods of study, and style of the Jews of southern Italy, the first Torah center in the West. *Halakhot Keẓuvot* was first published by C.M. Horowitz in the collection *Beit Nekhot ha-Halakhot* (*Toratan shel Rishonim*, 1881).

BIBLIOGRAPHY: V. Aptowitzer, *Meḥkarim be-Sifrut ha-Ge'onim* (1941), 27, 84, 91–95; M. Margalioth (ed.), *Halakhot Keẓuvot* (1942), 1–60; Hartom, in: KS, 19 (1942/43), 84–86; Hildesheimer, in: *Sinai*, 13 (1944), 271–87; 14 (1944), 21–32, 82–94; H. Tchernowitz, *Toledot ha-Posekim*, 1 (1946), 112–6; idem, in: *Melilah*, 2 (1946), 238–42; Assaf, Ge'onim, 170.

[Mordecai Margaliot]

HALAKHOT PESUKOT (Heb. הֲלָכוֹת פְּסוּקוֹת; "Decided Laws"), the first known halakhic work of the *geonim*, written in the eighth century and attributed to *Yehudai Gaon or to his pupils. It confines itself to those *halakhot* which are of practical application, arranging them according to subject matter: laws of *eruvin*, Sabbath, Passover, etc. Its language is the Aramaic of the Talmud (for the most part giving the actual wording of the Talmud) and it generally follows the order of the Talmud, only occasionally combining isolated or scattered *halakhot*. The author makes use of the halakhic Midrashim and the Tosefta and there are a few quotations from the Jerusalem Talmud and the *Sefer ha-Ma'asim*. In addition there are cited many explanations and traditions of the *savoraim* handed down by the *geonim*, and mention is made of some of the scholars belonging to the period of the *savoraim*.

Although much of the material in the *Pesukot Halakhot* corresponds to that of the *She'iltot* of R. *Aḥa and it is therefore probable that the author utilized it, it is also possible that both drew upon a common source, a collection of early interpretations available in the academy. Although the *geonim* ascribe the work to Yehudai Gaon, it should not be assumed that he compiled it himself. To explain away the fact that many of the *halakhot* in the *Halakhot Pesukot* differed from the accepted *halakhah*, the *geonim* and *rishonim* propagated the tradition that Yehudai was blind and that his disciples wrote the work ascribed to him. Yehudai is in fact frequently mentioned in the work, generally as *rosh metivta*, and his son, Joseph, is also mentioned once in the *Hilkhot Re'u*, the Hebrew translation of the work. Further evidence of the work not being wholly that of Yehudai may be seen in its inclusion of *Terefot de-Ereẓ Yisrael*, to which Yehudai was vehemently opposed (see Margalioth, in *Talpioth*, 8, 1963), although it may be that an early copyist added to the Babylonian work a section dealing with the *halakhot* in Ereẓ Israel to provide a parallel between the Babylonian and the Ereẓ Israel laws.

In consequence of this work, Yehudai achieved a reputation enjoyed by few in his time. *Pirkoi b. Baboi, his pupil, says of his master, "for many years there has been none like him… and he never said anything that he had not heard from his teacher… and Mar Yehudai of blessed memory added, 'I have never given any answer to a question for which there was no proof from the Talmud and I learned the law from my teacher, who had it from his own teacher.'" The intent of the above is apparently to emphasize the fact that the work is based on the two pillars of Talmud and tradition and, indeed, it contains no independent views, giving only the words of the talmudic sages or the traditions of the *savoraim* and early *geonim*.

Halakhot Pesukot filled a great need. Yehudai was in constant contact with the communities outside Babylon which turned to him with halakhic problems, and his realization that not everyone could find his way in the Talmud, and that it was impossible to turn to the *geonim* with every problem, led him to take on himself the task of giving the essence of the Talmud, the halakhic conclusion without the involved discussion. The work became indispensable almost as soon as it appeared, "most people turning to the digested *halakhot* saying, 'what concern have we with the Talmud?'" Paltoi, the *gaon* of Pumbedita, opposed this practice, fearing it would cause people to abandon the study of Torah (*Ḥemdah Genuzah*, no. 110).

Many adaptations and abridgments of the book were made, of which fragments have been found in the *genizah*. The scholars who published them gave them the names which were common among the *rishonim*, e.g., *Halakhot Ketu'ot, Halakhot Ketannot*, etc. One of these adaptations is the *Halakhot Keẓuvot, compiled in southern Italy during the first half of the ninth century.

The most important adaptation, which became even more widespread than the original, eventually displacing it, is the *Halakhot Gedolot (Venice, 1548) which absorbed most of the *Halakhot Pesukot*, and added to it a great deal of material from the sources. The *Halakhot Pesukot* was translated into Hebrew and Arabic shortly after it was written. The Hebrew translation (published from an Oxford Ms. by A.L. Schlossberg with an introduction by S.Z.H. Halberstamm in Versailles in 1886) was given the name *Hilkhot Re'u*, since it begins with Exodus 16:29, of which "*Re'u*" is the first word. The translation, executed in Ereẓ Israel, is the first of halakhic material from Aramaic into Hebrew to survive. Its literary standard is not high and many passages which it was difficult to translate were left in the original Aramaic. The translation contains many of the peculiarities of the style and script characteristic of the Jerusalem Talmud and the *Sefer ha-Ma'asim*. The beginning and end of the manuscript are defective, although the Cairo *Genizah* contains many excerpts from which the missing portions could be restored. In general, there is a need for a new scientific edition, since that of Schlossberg is defective and full of errors.

Many fragments of the Arabic translation have also come down, most containing a section of the Aramaic original, followed by the translation, although there are also fragments of a consecutive translation. In all probability there were a number of Arabic translations, testimony to the great popularity of this first halakhic code after the compilation of the Talmud.

Until 1911 *Halakhot Pesukot* was known only through quotations in the books of the early scholars. In that year, however, a manuscript of the work was found by David Sassoon in San'a, the capital of Yemen, and was published by his son Solomon (1951). This unique manuscript is in a fragmentary state; both the beginning and the end are lacking, as well as portions in the body of the text. (Many individual pages of the missing section, however, have been found in the Cairo

Genizah.) *Hilkhot Terefot* from the *Halakhot Pesukot* have been published recently from several remnants.

BIBLIOGRAPHY: Azulai, 1 (1852), 63 no. 8, s.v. *Yehudai Ga'on*; Epstein, in: *Tarbiz*, 8 (1937), 16–31; 10 (1939), 283–308; idem, in: JQR, 4 (1913/14), 423–33; 5 (1914/15), 97–8; V. Aptowitzer, *Meḥkarim be-Sifrut ha-Ge'onim* (1941), 27–28; Ḥ. Tchernowitz, *Toledot ha-Posekim*, 1 (1946), 78–84; Assaf, Ge'onim, 167–8; Hildesheimer, in: *Sefer ha-Yovel shel "Sinai"* (1958), 566–72; Abramson, in: Sinai, 23 (1948), 75 n. 19; idem, in: *Tarbiz*, 18 (1946/47), 42 n.12; Margalioth, in: *Talpioth*, 8 (1963), 307–30 (text of *Hilkhot Terefot*); Bruell, Jahrbuecher, 9 (1889), 128–33; 232–44; Poznański, in: REJ, 63 (1912), 232–44; Waxman, Literature, (1960^2), 28 1ff.

[Mordecai Margaliot]

HALBERSTADT, city in Germany. The earliest document testifying to the presence of Jews in Halberstadt dates from 1261; in it the city promises its protection to the Jews "as in the past." It is probable that Jews were already settled in the city in 1189. A Jewish community (*Judendorf*) possessing a synagogue was first mentioned in 1364; it comprised 11 families in 1456, mainly occupied in moneylending. The Jews were expelled from Halberstadt in 1493; although some returned in the 16th century, they were expelled once more in 1595. Shortly afterward, several Jews again settled in the city and built a synagogue, which was destroyed during the Thirty Years War. In 1650 ten Jewish families were granted privileges allowing them to engage in business and moneylending, but forbidding them to build a synagogue. They were permitted to elect a rabbi in 1661. The authorities protected the Jews from the jealousy of Christian merchants and as a result the community had grown to 118 families (639 persons) by 1699. In 1689 Behrend *Lehmann, the powerful *Court Jew of Saxony and protector of the community, established a *bet midrash*, the renowned *klaus* (1707), and in 1712 permission was granted to build a new synagogue. Halberstadt then served as a center for the smaller communities in its environs (e.g., *Halle and *Magdeburg) and was the largest Jewish community in Prussia. Occupations of Jews in this period ranged from simple handicraft to finance and industry. The community was world renowned as a center for Torah study and philanthropy in the 17th and 18th centuries. In 1795 a school for children of poor families, called Hazkarat Ẓevi, was opened. It existed until shortly before the destruction of German Jewry. In the 1850s and 1860s some Hebrew works were printed in Halberstadt. A beautiful *maḥzor* was issued by H. Meyer: J.Z. *Jolles' *Melo ha-Ro'im* was edited by Y.F. Hirsch and printed at the press of J. Hoerling's widow (1859); B.H. *Auerbach's controversial *Sefer ha-Eshkol* appeared in 1867–79; and Elijah of Vilna's *Adderet Eliyahu* was published there. In the 19th and early 20th century the Hirsch family was outstanding in the industrial sphere and for its philanthropic activities.

Halberstadt was the center of Orthodox Jewry in Germany and until 1930 the central organizations of German Orthodox congregations and other Orthodox bodies were situated there. Several famous rabbis served in Halberstadt, including Ẓevi Hirsch *Bialeh, Hirschel *Levin, and members of the *Auerbach family. In 1933 there were 706 Jews in Halberstadt (1.4% of the total population). With the rise of Nazism, and its consequent economic and social pressure, many Jews began to leave. The community reacted to persecution by developing a complex of cultural and educational institutions, and formal relationships were retained with the governmental authorities. In October 1938, some 100 Polish Jews were expelled. On Nov. 10, 1938 the synagogue was first set on fire. Ninety Torah scrolls were desecrated in the streets; the synagogue was subsequently demolished. Some 40 Jewish men were arrested and sent to Buchenwald. Stores were looted and homes were wrecked. The Jewish school was closed in 1941. Between 1939 and 1942, 186 persons were deported; none returned. The only Jews who remained were intermarried.

In 1995 the Moses Mendessohn Academy was founded which is financed by the Federal State of Saxony-Anhalt, the city of Halberstadt, and private donors. It is located in a complex of buildings: the renovated former Klaus synagogue, the site of the former baroque synagogue, the former house of the cantor, and the renovated former bathhouse. The latter houses the Berend Lehmann Museum on Jewish history and culture, which was opened in 2001. It focused on the history of the Jews in Halberstadt as a model for Jewish history in Prussia. In 2005, 30 Jewish families from the former Soviet Union founded a new Jewish community.

BIBLIOGRAPHY: Germ Jud, I (1963), 123–4; 2 (1968), 317–9; B.H. Auerbach, *Geschichte der israelitischen Gemeinde Halberstadt* (1866); E. Lehmann, *Der polnische Resident Behrend Lehmann* (1885); S. Stern, *Der preussische staat und die Juden*, 1 (1962), Akten, no. 104–35, 54a–370, p. 531ff.; 2 (1962), Akten, no. 454–95; idem, *The Court Jew* (1950), index; M. Koehler, *Beitraege zur neueren juedischen Wirtschaftsgeschichte. Die Juden in Halberstadt und Umgebung bis zur Emanzipation* (1927); Y. Levinsky, in: *Reshumot*, new series, 1 (1945), 142–50; J. Meisl, *ibid.*, 3 (1947), 181–205; H.B. Auerbach, in: BLBI, 10 (1967), 124–58, 309–35; idem, in: *Zeitschrift fuer Geschichte der Juden*, 6 (1969), 11f., 19f., 151f., 155f.; PKG. **ADD. BIBLIOGRAPHY:** W. Hartmann, "Halberstadt," in: J. Dick (ed.), *Wegweiser durch das juedische Sachsen-Anhalt*, (1998; Beitraege zur Geschichte und Kultur der Juden in Brandenburg, Mecklenburg-Vorpommern, Sachsen-Anhalt, Sachsen und Thueringen, vol. 3), 72–91; M. Schmidt, "Issachar Baermann-ben-Jehuda ha-Levi, sonst Berend Lehmann genannt, Hoffaktor in Halberstadt," in: J. Dick (ed.), *Wegweiser durch das juedische Sachsen-Anhalt* (1998; Beitraege zur Geschichte und Kultur der Juden in Brandenburg, Mecklenburg-Vorpommern, Sachsen-Anhalt, Sachsen und Thueringen, vol. 3), 198–211; W. Hartmann (ed.), *Juden in Halberstadt. Geschichte, Ende und Spuren einer ausgelieferten Minderheit. Belege und Beitraege*, vol. 1–6 (1991–96); A. Maimon, M. Breuer, and Y. Guggenheim (eds.), *Germania Judaica*, vol. 3: 1350–1514 (1987), 493–7.

[Zvi Avneri / Larissa Daemmig (2nd ed.)]

HALBERSTADT, ABRAHAM BEN MENAHEM MENKE (d. 1782), German rabbi. Halberstadt studied under his father who was *dayyan* of Halberstadt, as well as under Jonathan *Eybeschuetz. In 1733 he published the Shulḥan Arukh, *Yoreh De'ah* in Amsterdam. In addition to his talmudic learning he acquired a profound knowledge of grammar, mathematics, and astronomy. In his interesting correspondence with his Berlin friend Jeremiah (who has been identified either with Jeremiah b. Naphtali Hirsch of Halberstadt or with Jeremiah b. Ephraim Segal who died in 1788), he expresses his views on the problems of contemporary German Jewry. In a letter written in 1774 he stresses the importance of the study of grammar and the Bible, and in another letter the next year he expresses his admiration for Moses *Mendelssohn and N.H. *Wessely, and suggests that the latter's *Yein Levanon* be used by rabbis as a basis for their sermons. He affirmed that the ignorance of grammar and secular subjects by many rabbis was the cause for their inability to understand correctly certain passages of the Talmud. In a letter in 1770, while emphasizing that all the accusations against Eybeschuetz were baseless, he nevertheless severely censured Eybeschuetz' careless conduct, and condemned the negative character of many of his pupils. His glosses to the Talmud, *Penei Avraham*, have remained in manuscript. He published the *Ba'alei Nefesh* (Berlin 1762) of *Abraham b. David (Rabad), adding to it glosses published in Venice (1741). He died in Berlin.

BIBLIOGRAPHY: B.H. Auerbach, *Geschichte der israelitischen Gemeinde Halberstadt* (1866), 78, 98ff., 187–97; L. Landshuth, *Toledot Anshei ha-Shem*, 1 (1883), 120.

[Yehoshua Horowitz]

HALBERSTADT, MORDECAI (also known as Mordecai of Duesseldorf; d. 1770), rabbi and grammarian. Born in the town of Halberstadt at the beginning of the 18th century, Mordecai studied under Abraham b. Judah Berlin, the local rabbi, and Ẓevi Hirsch Ashkenazi, the head of its yeshivah. He proceeded to Frankfurt in 1730 where he studied under Jacob ha-Kohen, author of *Shav Ya'akov*, whose rulings and responsa he quotes in his *Ma'amar Mordekhai* (nos. 10, 69, 70, et al.). He taught at the Halberstadt yeshivah and, on the recommendation of Jacob ha-Kohen, was appointed *av bet din* of Griesheim near Frankfurt (*Ma'amar Mordekhai*, nos. 2, 8, 14). He later served as rabbi of Darmstadt, and then at Duesseldorf (no. 23), where he remained until the end of his life. Requested by Samuel Heilmann of Metz and Joshua *Falk of Frankfurt to join in the ban against Jonathan *Eybeschuetz and to give his opinion about the amulets, Halberstadt was reluctant to attack Eybeschuetz personally and instead recommended that they content themselves with adverse criticism of the activities of the circles close to Shabbateanism. He was the author of the responsa, *Ma'amar Mordekhai* (Bruenn, 1790). Responsum no. 30 deals with the case of an animal in whose stomach was found a needle adhering to the midriff. The scholars of the Rhineland regarded such an animal *kasher* on the basis of responsa by Ephraim Solomon *Luntschitz and Isaiah *Horowitz (*ibid.*, 41b). Halberstadt proved with profound acumen that these alleged responsa were forgeries by the Bonn informer, Krauss, "who forged and testified falsely in the names of those great scholars." *Leḥem Eden*, a pamphlet containing the glosses of Halberstadt's son, MENAHEM MENDEL HALBERSTADT, is appended to the book. Mordecai Halberstadt also compiled a work on grammar that has remained in manuscript. His grandson, who published the *Ma'amar Mordekhai*, refers to him as "Mordecai *Balshan* [the 'linguist'], because of his profound knowledge of the holy tongue and Hebrew grammar."

BIBLIOGRAPHY: B.H. Auerbach, *Geschichte der israelitischen Gemeinde Halberstadt* (1866), 74–76, no. 11; idem (Ẓevi Binyamin), *Berit Avraham* (1860), 24f.; P. Frankl, in: *Nachlath Zvi*, 8 (1937), 79.

[Yehoshua Horowitz]

HALBERSTAEDTER, LUDWIG (1876–1949), Israel radiologist. Born at Beuthen (Bytom), Silesia, he was appointed head of the department of radiotherapy at the Cancer Institute at the University of Berlin in 1919, becoming professor there in 1929. When the Nazis came to power in 1933, he settled in Ereẓ Israel, where two years later he was made professor of radiology and radiotherapy at the Hebrew University, Jerusalem. He was also head of the radiobiology department of the university and director of the cancer department at the Hadassah University Hospital.

Halberstaedter was a radiobiologist and radiotherapist of international reputation. A pioneer in several fields, he investigated the nature of monkey malaria and together with von Prowazek discovered the Halberstaedter-Prowazek bodies widely believed to present a stage in the life history of the causal virus of trachoma.

BIBLIOGRAPHY: S.R. Kagan, *Jewish Medicine* (1952), 537–8.

HALBERSTAM, ḥasidic dynasty, originating in western Galicia in the mid-19th century. The most important personality in the dynasty was its founder, ḤAYYIM BEN LEIBUSH (1793–1876). Born in Tarnogrod, on his mother's side Ḥayyim was a descendant of Ḥakham Ẓevi (Ẓevi Hirsch *Ashkenazi). Ḥayyim's father directed a *ḥeder*. In 1830 he was appointed rabbi of Nowy Sacz (Zanz). As a youth Ḥayyim was brought to *Jacob Isaac the ḥozeh ("seer") of *Lublin who strongly influenced him and he became a Ḥasid; he studied under Naphtali of *Ropczyce and Ẓevi Hirsch of *Zhidachov. Ḥayyim also studied with Ẓevi Hirsch of *Rymanow, Shalom Rokeaḥ of *Belz, and Israel of *Ruzhin. Ḥayyim administered his yeshivah in the best scholarly tradition of the old-style yeshivot in Poland. He would not permit his pupils to cultivate Ḥasidism until a late stage. Thus both Ḥasidim and *mitnaggedim* were attracted to his yeshivah. Known as strict in matters of learning and observance, he conducted his "court" modestly and discreetly and avoided the splendor and luxury customary at the "courts" of other *ẓaddikim* in that period. The main event in his public life was the dispute between the Ḥasidim of Zanz and Sadagora, which aroused a controversy that spread beyond Galicia and also involved the leading non-ḥasidic rabbis. The principal cause of the dispute lay in the basic difference between the Zanz pattern of Ḥasidism with its stress on traditional learning and ecstatic expression in religious life and the manner of life adopted by Israel of Ruzhin and followed by his descendants. They lived in almost literally royal style, in the utmost luxury and splendor, which aroused resentment and opposition particularly of the Ḥasidim of Zanz, and also of the conservative Ḥasidim of Galicia generally. The publication of Dov Baer of Lyova, the youngest son of Israel of Ruzhin, in which he renounced Ḥasidism and expressed his support of the Haskalah, gave the Ḥasidim of Zanz a weapon against the dynasty of Ruzhin. Ḥayyim issued a letter in which he openly expressed his strong reservations about the way of life of the Sadagora Ḥasidim. It was circulated throughout Galicia, and a stormy debate between the two ḥasidic groups ensued. A rabbinical convention in the Ukraine called for Ḥayyim's excommunication and even demanded that he should be handed over to the authorities. The dispute reached Ereẓ Israel, where it took on an added dimension in affecting the financial arrangements of the *ḥalukkah*, and apportionment of the money from Poland, to support the community in Ereẓ Israel. A number of rabbis, including Joseph Saul *Nathanson of Lvov and Dov Berush *Meisels, rabbi of Warsaw, Ḥayyim's brother-in-law, attempted to reconcile the opposing parties. The Hungarian rabbis intervened without success. After several months the dispute died down, but Ḥayyim remained consistent in his opinions on the matter. Ḥayyim wrote: *Divrei Ḥayyim* (Zolkiew, 1864), on ritual purity and divorce laws; responsa *Divrei Ḥayyim* (Lemberg, 1875), and *Divrei Ḥayyim* (Munkacz, 1877), ḥasidic sermons on Torah and the festivals. His works reveal a profound knowledge of the Talmud and commentaries, the *midrashim*, and medieval philosophical literature. He quotes widely from Judah Halevi's *Kuzari*, Maimonides, Naḥmanides, and Abraham ibn Daud. From later literature, he cites Isaiah Horowitz, Judah Loew of Prague, the prayer book of Jacob Emden, and his teachers in Kabbalah and Ḥasidism. An opponent of asceticism, Ḥayyim was an exponent of the ecstatic mode of prayer and developed the ḥasidic melody. In his writings he emphasized the duty of charity and criticized *ẓaddikim* who lived luxuriously.

Ḥayyim had eight sons. The most important was EZEKIEL SHRAGA OF SIENIAWA (1811–1899), considered a scholar and strict in matters of *halakhah*. He was responsible for the transcription and publication of Abraham b. Mordecai *Azulai's commentaries on the *Zohar, *Or ha-Ḥammah* (1896–98) and *Zohorei Ḥammah* (1881–82), and Ḥayyim *Vital's *Sefer ha-Gilgulim* (1875). In 1878 Akiva ha-Kohen Lieber of Yasienica studied with him and edited his posthumous work *Divrei Yeḥezkel* (Sieniawa, 1906), novellae, sermons on the Torah and for the holidays, and a few responsa. Other influential sons were BARUCH of Gorlice (1826–1906), DAVID of Kshanow (1821–1894), AARON of Zanz (d. 1906), *ẓaddik* and rabbi of Zanz and later of the region. SOLOMON BEN MEYER NATHAN OF BOBOVA (1847–1906), grandson of Ḥayyim, founded a large yeshivah, attracting youth and many Ḥasidim. His son BEN ZION (1873–1941) became celebrated for the beautiful melodies he composed and also attracted many Ḥasidim. He perished in the Holocaust. Ben Zion's son, SOLOMON (d. 2000), found refuge in the United States where he established a ḥasidic center in the Boro Park section of Brooklyn. In December 1959 he also founded the small settlement of Bobova, near Bat Yam, which has subsequently become a center for Bobova Ḥasidim in Israel. Solomon was replaced by his son NAFTALI, who died in 2005. Several descendants of Ḥayyim Halberstam moved to Slovakia where they served as rabbis. One of them, JACOB SAMSON OF CZHOW, settled in Klausenburg (Cluj), Transylvania, in 1917. Another descendant is JEKUTHIEL JUDAH (1904–1994), who later became the Klausenburg Rebbe. Although his wife and 11 children perished in the Holocaust, Jekuthiel survived and reestablished his court in the Williamsburg section of Brooklyn. In 1956 he founded Kiryat Zanz near *Netanyah in Israel. He later permanently settled in Kiryat Zanz, along with many of his Ḥasidim. His two sons succeeded him.

BIBLIOGRAPHY: R. Mahler, in: *Proceedings of the Fourth World Congress of Jewish Studies*, 2 (1968), 223–5; A. Marcus, *Ha-Ḥasidut* (1953), 266–74, 277; Horodezky, Ḥasidut, index; I. Even, in: *Ha-Ivri*, 6 (1916), no. 1–no. 28; E. Roth, in: *Talpioth*, ed. by S.K. Mirsky, 6 (1953), 346–58; M. Zailikovitz (ed.), *Yalkut ha-Ro'im* (1896); *Keneset ha-Gedolah* (1869); W. Ehrenkranz, *Makkel Ḥovelim* (1869); M. Buber, *Tales of the Hasidim*, 2 (1966[3]), 208–15; H. Rabinowicz, *The World of Hasidim* (1970), 227; G. Kranzler, *Williamsburg* (1964), 150, 178, 209.

[Pnina Meislish]

HALBERSTAM, DAVID (1934–), U.S. writer. Halberstam was the younger of two sons born in the Bronx to Charles, a military surgeon whose parents had immigrated from Poland, and Blanche (Levy), a schoolteacher whose parents had come from Lithuania. His father's work took him to Winsted, Connecticut, El Paso and Austin, Texas, and Rochester, Minn. In 1951 Halberstam graduated from Roosevelt High School in Yonkers, N.Y., where he wrote for the school newspaper, and he then attended Harvard College, where he became managing editor of the *Crimson*. Upon graduation in 1955, Halberstam chose to work in the South, his first job coming at *The Daily Times Leader* in West Point, Mississippi, the state's smallest daily newspaper, and seven months later he moved to *The Tennessean* in Nashville, where he covered the early Civil Rights movement. Halberstam joined the *New York Times* in 1960, working first in Washington before being assigned to the Congo, and then in September 1962 to the paper's bureau in Saigon. It was there that Halberstam became a legend as one of a small group of reporters who began to question and speak out against the official administration version of the war in Vietnam, which led U.S. president John F. Kennedy to request that Halberstam be transferred to another bureau. Halberstam's reporting earned him the George Polk Award in 1963 and the Pulitzer Prize in 1964 for international reporting. In January 1965 he was sent to Poland, where his reporting on the repressive and antisemitic policies of the Communist regime led to his being ordered to leave the country. Halberstam then reported from Paris, and in 1967 he left the *Times* to become a contributing editor for *Harper's*. He started writing books, including *The Making of a Quagmire: America and Vietnam During the Kennedy Era* (1965), *The Unfinished Od-*

yssey of Robert Kennedy (1969); and *Ho* (1971), a biography of Vietnamese revolutionary leader Ho Chi Minh. But it was his bestselling book, *The Best and the Brightest* (1972), a critical history of America's involvement in the Vietnamese conflict, which established Halberstam as an important commentator on American politics and power.

The enormous success of *The Best and the Brightest* led to a career in writing on a wide range of topics filled with anecdotes, metaphors, and a narrative tone usually seen in fiction. It included *The Powers That Be* (1979), which examined the influence of the news media on American society; *The Reckoning: The Challenge to America's Greatness* (1986), a comparative history of the Japanese and U.S. automobile industry; *The Next Century* (1991), on the diminishing educational standards and decline in economic productivity in the U.S.; *The Fifties* (1993), a look at the decade, embracing social change, politics, and technology and their impact on each other and the world, which was made into an eight-part television series; *The Children* (1998), about the youth who were part of the Civil Rights movement; *War in the Time of Peace: Bush, Clinton, and the Generals* (2001), a look at how U.S. domestic politics came to dictate foreign policy, which was a runner-up for the Pulitzer Prize; and *Firehouse* (2002), the story of the firefighters who sacrificed their lives on September 11, 2001. Halberstam also wrote fiction: *The Noblest Roman* (1961) and *One Very Hot Day* (1968).

Halberstam is also a leading sportswriter, beginning with *The Breaks of the Game* (1981), an account of his year spent with the Portland Trailblazers, considered among the best books ever written on professional basketball. He also wrote *The Amateurs: The Story of Four Young Men and Their Quest for an Olympic Gold Medal* (1985), a study of the world of sculling; *Summer of '49* (1989), a look at the drama of the 1949 pennant race; *October 1964* (1994), chronicling the season and World Series that was to become the last year of the New York Yankees dynasty; *Playing for Keeps: Michael Jordan and the World That He Made* (1999), documenting the making of a legend; *The Teammates: A Portrait of Friendship* (2003), about the 60-year friendships of baseball players Ted Williams, Dominic DiMaggio, Johnny Pesky, and Bobby Doerr; and *The Education of a Coach* (2005), an in-depth look at the life and career of NFL coach Bill Belichick of the New England Patriots. Halberstam also edited the anthology *Best American Sports Writing of the Century* (1999).

[Elli Wohlgelernter (2nd ed.)]

HALBERSTAM, ISAAC BEN ḤAYYIM (1810–1880), talmudist and author. Halberstam was born in Brody and belonged to a distinguished rabbinical family. He was a brother-in-law of Dov Berush *Meisels, rabbi in Cracow and Warsaw, in partnership with whom he directed a banking establishment in Cracow. After losing his fortune, Halberstam devoted himself exclusively to study. His novella to the Pentateuch, arranged in the order of the weekly portions, were published by his son, Solomon Zalman Ḥayyim, under the title *Si'aḥ Yiẓḥak* (1882).

BIBLIOGRAPHY: I. Halberstam, *Si'aḥ Yiẓḥak* (1882), preface; Z. Horowitz, *Kitvei ha-Ge'onim* (1928), 90.

HALBERSTAM, SOLOMON (Zalman) ḤAYYIM (known from his acronym as **ShaZHaH**; 1832–1900), Polish scholar and bibliophile. Halberstam was born in Cracow and studied with his father, Isaac Halberstam, an eminent talmudist. During his years as a successful merchant in Bielsko (Bielitz), Poland, he collected rare books and manuscripts. He studied some and lent others to Jewish scholars. Halberstam was one of the founders of the *Mekiẓe Nirdamim society. In addition to scholarly articles and notes to the works of other scholars, he published with introductions and notes some of the manuscripts from his library, among them being *Yom Tov b. Abraham's novellae on tractate *Niddah, Ḥiddushei ha-Ritba* (1868); Abraham *Ibn Ezra's *Sefer ha-Ibbur* (1874); and *Judah b. Barzillai's *Sefer ha-Shetarot* (1898) and *Perush Sefer Yeẓirah* (1885). In 1890 he published *Kohelet Shelomo*, a catalog of his manuscripts which listed 411 items. After Halberstam's death most of his manuscripts were sold to the Judith Montefiore College in Ramsgate, England, and are now at Jews' College, London. The majority of the printed books in his library and a small part of his manuscript collection were acquired by the Jewish Theological Seminary in New York and the library of the Vienna community. Most of his correspondence is preserved in the library of the Jewish Theological Seminary. Halberstam also wrote notes to H. Michael's bibliographical work *Or ha-Ḥayyim* (in the Mosad ha-Rav Kook edition, 1965).

BIBLIOGRAPHY: N. Sokolow (ed.), *Sefer Zikkaron le-Soferei Yisrael ha-Ḥayyim Ittanu ha-Yom*, (1889), 28; G. Bader, *Medinah ve-Ḥakhameha* (1934), 76–77; Davidson, in: *Yad va-Shem… A.S. Freidus* (1929), 1–14 (Heb. sect.); Zeitlin, Bibliotheca, index; B. Wachstein et al. (eds.) *Hebraeische Publizistik in Wien*, 2 (1930), 17; Shunami, Bibl., 890.

[Abraham Meir Habermann]

HALBWACHS, MAURICE (1877–1945), French sociologist. In social psychology he investigated the problems of memory considered as a social fact and the influence of collective memory and tradition on beliefs, and traced the delicate interconnections between psychology and sociology. He combined an avid concern with sociographic investigation in various fields with his strong bent for theorizing in works on demographical statistics, on which subject he contributed to the *Encyclopédie Française*. He taught at the universities of Caen, Strasbourg, and Paris (after 1935), and a few months before his deportation and murder by the Nazis he was nominated to occupy the chair of social psychology at the College de France. He perished in the Buchenwald concentration camp. Among his works were *La théorie de l'homme moyen: Essai sur Quetelet et la statistique morale* (1913), *Les cadres sociaux de la mémoire* (1925, 1952[2]), *L'évolution des besoins dans les classes ouvrières* (1933), *Morphologie sociale* (1934), *Esquisse d'une psychologie des classes sociales* (in *Enquêtes Sociologiques…*, 1938; repub. posthum., 1955; *The Psychology of Social Class*, 1958), *La topographie légendaire des Evangiles en Terre Sainte* (1941),

Psychologie collective (1942), and *Mémoire et Société* (1949), posthumous.

BIBLIOGRAPHY: Alexandre, in: *Année Sociologique*, 1 (1949), 3–10; Cuvielier, in: J.S. Roucek, *Contemporary Sociology* (1958), 716 ff.; G. Gurvitch and E. Moore (eds.), *Twentieth Century Sociology* (1945). **ADD. BIBLIOGRAPHY:** C. Baudelot and R. Establet, *Maurice Halbwachs: consommation et société* (1994); G. Namer, *Halbwachs et la mémoire sociale* (2000); A. Becker, *Maurice Halbwachs: un intellectuel en guerres mondiales, 1914–1945* (2003).

[Ephraim Fischoff]

HALEVA, ISAK (1940–), chief rabbi of Turkey from October 2002. Born in Istanbul, Haleva graduated from the Jewish high school there and continued his higher education at Jerusalem's Porat Yosef Yeshivah, from which he graduated with the title of rabbi in 1961. He served as a member of the Bet Din of Turkey's Chief Rabbinate and taught religion and ethics at the Jewish high school from 1963 until 2000. He also taught Hebrew and Jewish religion at Marmara and Sakarya universities in the faculty of theology. He was a member of the European Rabbis Conference. His son Naftali Haleva was a rabbi and member of the Bet Din.

[Rifat Bali (2nd ed.)]

HA-LEVANON (Heb. הַלְּבָנוֹן, "Lebanon"), the first Hebrew newspaper in Ereẓ Israel. *Ha-Levanon*, edited by Jehiel *Brill, Joel Moses *Salomon, and Michael Cohen, first appeared in Jerusalem in March 1863. The paper was established as the organ of the *ḥalukkah trustees at a time of strife within the Jerusalem Ashkenazi community.

Throughout the paper's career, Brill, the editor in chief and the paper's moving spirit, consistently held that Jews living in the old city of Jerusalem should found suburbs outside the city's walls in which to live. Further, the *yishuv* living on the *ḥalukkah* should turn to productive occupations, particularly farming. At the same time, however, Brill objected to Ḥovevei Zion's fervent advocacy of the settlement of Ereẓ Israel, claiming that the movement's plans were impracticable, fired as they were by imagination rather than by a thorough knowledge of conditions in the country. He did approve of feasible programs of settlement and throughout the years urged Ḥovevei Zion to adopt a realistic attitude. Among the settlement programs supported by *Ha-Levanon* were *Moẓa and Petaḥ Tikvah.

Contributors to the paper included journalists and scholars from abroad as well as from Jerusalem. *Ha-Levanon* engaged in a bitter controversy with the rival paper, *Ḥavaẓẓelet*, established in Jerusalem during the summer of 1863. As a result both papers closed down in 1864. After a year's interval, Brill revived *Ha-Levanon* in Paris, where it appeared as a biweekly until 1868 when it became a weekly. Although published in Europe, the paper appeared in Jerusalem on a monthly basis and continued to print much news of Ereẓ Israel, most of its articles, in fact, being devoted to *yishuv* affairs. The paper, especially in its literary supplement (*Kevod ha-Levanon*), printed diverse studies on Judaism and belles lettres (mostly translations), with leading local and foreign writers as contributors. Trapped in the siege of Paris during the Franco-Prussian War (1870–71) and the Commune, Brill depicted the latter for *Ha-Levanon*, and eventually he left for Germany where he revived *Ha-Levanon* in Mainz (1872) as a supplement of the German Orthodox paper *Israelit*. Becoming the Hebrew organ of Orthodoxy, it provided the forum for a bitter controversy with the religious Reform movement of M.L. *Lilienblum, J.L. *Gordon, and others. Concurrently, Brill continued to support every constructive plan relating to the *yishuv*. The Russian pogroms of the early 1880s brought about an ideological reorientation in *Ha-Levanon*. Brill severed his connection with the Orthodox circles and became a zealous advocate of the settlement of Ereẓ Israel. He conducted propaganda campaigns in Russia, and was responsible for the immigration to Ereẓ Israel of Jewish farmers who later founded the village of Ekron. At the end of 1882 *Ha-Levanon* ceased publication. In 1884 Brill settled in London, where he revived *Ha-Levanon* in 1886, but the paper closed on Brill's death that same year. A pioneer of the modern press in Ereẓ Israel, *Ha-Levanon* provided during its 20 years of existence the first opportunity for Hebrew journalists in Ereẓ Israel.

BIBLIOGRAPHY: G. Kressel, *Ha-Levanon ve-ha-Ḥavaẓẓelet* (1943); idem, *Toledot ha-Ittonut ha-Ivrit be-Ereẓ Yisrael* (1964), 27–41: S.L. Zitron, in: *Ha-Olam*, 6 (1912), nos. 28, 30, 31, 33, 35, 36, 38; R. Malachi, in: *Meyer Waxman Jubilee Volume* (1967), 70–142; G. Yardeni, *Ha-Ittonut ha-Ivrit be-Ereẓ Yisrael ba-Shanim 1863–1904* (1969), 17–29; Z. Ravid, in: *Hadoar*, 42 (1963), 18–22.

[Getzel Kressel]

HALEVI, EZEKIEL EZRA BEN JOSHUA (1852–1942), one of the most prominent scholars and poets of Iraqi Jewry in recent generations; born in Baghdad and died in Jerusalem. In 1897 Halevi emigrated to Ereẓ Israel and settled in Jerusalem. He earned his livelihood as a preacher; he was also a communal worker, president of the committee of the Iraqi community, and one of the founders of the yeshivah Shoshannim le-David. Of the more than 10 books which he wrote, five were published, including *Arugat ha-Bosem* (1905), on the *aggadah*; *Tehillah ve-Tiferet* (1914), a commentary on the Book of Psalms; and also his *Simḥat Yom Tov* (c. 1934), which was a commentary on the Passover *Haggadah*.

BIBLIOGRAPHY: A. Ben-Jacob, *Yehudei Bavel* (1965), 133, 194, 205; Tidhar, 11 (1961), 3843.

[Abraham Ben-Yaacob]

HALEVI, ḤAYYIM DAVID (1924–1998), Israeli rabbi and halakhist. Born in Jerusalem, Halevi studied in the Porat Yosef Yeshivah. He received his rabbinic ordination from the head of Porat Yosef, Rabbi Atiah, and from Chief Rabbi Ben-Zion Meir Ḥai Ouziel. During the War of Independence, he served in the "yeshivah" brigade, Tuvia. In 1948 he was appointed a neighborhood rabbi in Jerusalem and was Rabbi Ouziel's personal secretary. At the same time, he taught in Yeshivat

Sha'arei Zion. In 1951 Halevi became the Sephardi chief rabbi of Rishon Le-Zion. He served on the Rabbinic Council of the Israeli Chief Rabbinate and the Rabbinic Council of the Mizrachi Party from the mid-1960s. From 1974 to 1997 he served as the chief rabbi and head of the rabbinical court of Tel Aviv-Jaffa. In 1992 he campaigned for the post of chief rabbi of Israel, but lost. In 1996 he received the Israel Prize for Torah literature.

Throughout his life, Halevi's main concern was Jewish law. His numerous halakhic works are free of arcane terminology and rely more on straightforward logic than numerous quotes from halakhic literature. His works include *Bein Yisrael la-Ammim*, a treatise on the spiritual and political stature of Israel among the nations (1954); *Devar Mishpat*, three volumes on the laws of the Sanhedrin in Maimonides' code (1963–65); *Mekor Ḥayyim ha-Shalem*, a five-volume synopsis of Jewish law (1967–74); *Dat u-Medinah*, religion in modern Israel (1969); *Mekor Ḥayyim le-Ḥatan, le-Kallah u-le-Mishpaḥah* (1972) on marriage law; *Kiẓẓur Shulḥan Arukh Mekor Ḥayyim*, a summary of Jewish law widely used in schools in Israel; *Mekor Ḥayyim le-Banot* (1977); *She'elot u-Teshuvot Aseh Lekha Rav*, responsa, many of which deal with modern issues (1976–89); *Mayim Ḥayyim*, responsa (1991–98). Halevi also published a three-volume work on the weekly Torah readings, *Torat Ḥayyim* (1992–93), as well as a topical index to the Zohar, *Mafteḥot ha-Zohar ve-Ra'ayonotav* (1971).

Halevi was a courageous halakhist. He tackled many modern-day issues and was the first to issue a rabbinic prohibition against smoking.

[David Derovan (2nd ed.)]

HALEVI, JOSEPH ẒEVI BEN ABRAHAM (1874–1960), Israeli rabbi and halakhic authority. Halevi was born in Slobodka and studied in its famous yeshivah. In 1891 he settled in Ereẓ Israel, where in 1897 he was appointed *dayyan* and assistant to his father-in-law, Naphtali Herz ha-Levi, the first Ashkenazi rabbi of Jaffa. In 1902 on the death of his father-in-law, he served for a time as rabbi of Jaffa, but when A.I. *Kook was appointed rabbi of Jaffa, Halevi was appointed head of the first permanent *bet din* established there. During Kook's absence from Ereẓ Israel in World War I he took over his functions as rabbi of the Ashkenazi community and together with Ben Zion *Ouziel represented the Jewish community of Jaffa-Tel Aviv before the Turkish government. Following the expulsion of Jews from Jaffa-Tel Aviv by the Turks, Halevi went to Petaḥ Tikvah and to Rishon le-Zion, returning to Jaffa after the entry of the British into Ereẓ Israel. He continued to fill the office of *av bet din* also during the rabbinates of Aaronson (1923–1935), Amiel (1936–1945), and Unterman (from 1947).

Halevi was a prolific author. Most of the 17 books he wrote deal with the *halakhot* and precepts applying to the land of Israel, maintaining that with the beginning of the "ingathering of the exiles" attention should again be paid to these laws. The following are some of his works: *Hora'at Sha'ah* (1909), an exposition of the principles permitting the working of the land in the Sabbatical year by selling it to a gentile; *Hashkafah li-Verakhah* (1930), on the laws of the separation of the tithes; *Aser Te'asser* (1935), on *terumot and ma'aserot ("tithes"); *Neta ha-Areẓ* (1939), *Zera ha-Areẓ* (1941), *Kerem ha-Areẓ* (1943), *Leḥem ha-Areẓ* (1950); *Ḥovat Giddulei ha-Areẓ* (1953), dealing with the laws of **orlah, *kilayim* (mixed species) of seeds and trees, *kilayim* of the vineyard, the law of *ḥallah and the laws of *leket, shikhḥah and pe'ah; *Amirah Ne'imah* (1948; second series 1955 in two parts), halakhic expositions and novella; *Va-Tomer Ẓiyyon*, 2 pts. (1950–58), homilies on the Pentateuch; *Torat ha-Korbanot* (1959), an exposition of 288 *halakhot* in Maimonides' laws of the sacrifices. Most of his works follow a standard pattern. The basis is the text from Maimonides' *Mishneh Torah*, to which he adds the decisions of *rishonim* and the decisions based upon new developments. Although there is an element of casuistry in his works, in the main he aims at giving the practical *halakhah*. In 1958 he was awarded the Israel Prize.

BIBLIOGRAPHY: *Ha-Ẓofeh* (March 3–4, 1960, Apr. 1960); Tidhar, 1 (1947), 354f.; S.J. Zevin, *Soferim u-Sefarim*, 1 (1959), 59–70; I. Goldschlag, in: *Shanah be-Shanah* (1961), 361–63; *Yahadut Lita*, 3 (1967), 84.

[Yehoshua Horowitz]

HA-LEVI, SASSON BEN ELIJAH BEN MOSES (also known as R. Sasson Smuha; 1820–1910), Baghdad rabbi and disciple of R. Abdullah *Somekh. Ha-Levi held the position of *dayyan* from 1841 to 1876. In 1860 he intervened to prevent the expropriation from Jewish hands of the traditional tomb of the prophet Ezekiel in the village of Kifl. From 1876 to 1879 he was *ḥakham bashi* of Baghdad. A controversy then broke out between him and several members of the community, who deposed him and appointed R. Elisha Dangoor in his place. A dispute ensued between the two during the years 1880 to 1885. The majority of the rabbis supported Dangoor, while some of the wealthy sided with Ha-Levi. The matter reached the chief rabbi of Constantinople, who decided in favor of the former. Ha-Levi composed two *piyyutim*, which have been included in books of liturgical hymns.

BIBLIOGRAPHY: A. Ben-Jacob, *Yehudei Bavel* (1965), 162f.

[Abraham Ben-Yaacob]

HALÉVY (19th–20th centuries), French family of authors. LÉON HALÉVY (1802–1883) was born in Paris. He was the younger son of Elie Halfon *Halévy and younger brother of the composer Jacques François Fromental *Halévy. A scholar of distinction, Léon Halévy became assistant professor of French literature at the Ecole Polytechnique in 1831 and head of the antiquities department in the Ministry of Education six years later. Although his connection with the community was intermittent and he married a non-Jewess, he never abandoned Judaism. He evidently found official prejudice strong enough to prevent his advancement, and in 1853 retired from public life and became a writer. Doctrinally a Saint-Simonian, he was critical of the development of post-biblical Judaism, favoring a reformist return to the "primitive faith" on semi-Christian lines. Halévy's works include *Résumé de l'histoire des juifs anciens* (1825) and its sequel, *Résumé de l'histoire des juifs modernes* (1828). He also wrote two volumes of verse, rhymed translations and plays, which included tragedies and dramas such as *Luther* (1834) and *Electre* (1864) and some popular vaudeville comedies.

Léon's son, LUDOVIC HALÉVY (1834–1908), was a writer whose comedies, librettos, novels, and stories dealt with the gay life of the French during the Second Empire. In collaboration with Henri Meilhac he wrote the text for Bizet's opera *Carmen* (1875), and librettos for several operettas by Jacques *Offenbach, including *La belle Hélène* (1865), *La Vie parisienne* (1866), *La Grande-Duchesse de Gérolstein* (1867), and *La Périchole* (1868). Their play *Le Réveillon* (1872), based on a German drama, was later adapted for Johann Strauss' *Die Fledermaus*. Their greatest success was the comedy *Frou-Frou* (1870). With H. Crémieux, Halévy wrote the libretto for Offenbach's *Orphée aux enfers* (1858). His other works include the novels *Un Mariage d'amour* (1881) and *L'Abbé Constantin* (1882), and several volumes of memoirs, notably *L'Invasion* (1872). He was elected to the Académie Française in 1884. In his later years he revealed a consciousness of his Jewish heritage. Ludovic Halévy's two sons were the philosopher and historian Elie *Halévy (1870–1937), and the historian and essayist DANIEL HALÉVY (1872–1962). Although the latter graduated in Semitics and at first supported *Dreyfus, he became a reactionary and a convert to Catholicism. In later years Daniel Halévy even betrayed antisemitic tendencies, defending Marshal Pétain and the arch-antisemite Charles *Maurras. His ideological break with his old Dreyfusard friend Charles *Péguy provoked the latter's indignant criticism in *Notre jeunesse* (1910). Daniel Halévy's works include *Apologie pour notre passé* (1910), polemics with Péguy; *Charles Péguy et les cahiers de la quinzaine* (1918, 1941); *Cahiers verts* (1921–27); *La Fin des notables*, a history of the Third Republic (2 vols., 1930–37); and *Nietzsche* (1944).

BIBLIOGRAPHY: Catane, in: *Evidences*, 46 (1955), 7–13; Szajkowski, in: JSOS, 9 (1947), 35, 43–44; A. Silvera, *Daniel Halévy and his Times* (1966); G. Weill, in: REJ, 31 (1895), 261–73.

[Moshe Catane]

HALEVY, ABRAHAM H. (1927–), Israeli botanist. Halevy, a 10th-generation Israeli, was born in Tel Aviv and completed his undergraduate and graduate studies in biology and agriculture at the Hebrew University of Jerusalem. After receiving his Ph.D. at the university in 1958, he went on to teach there, establishing the Department of Ornamental Horticulture in 1964 and serving as its chairman until 1985. He became a full professor in 1970 and was named Wolfson Family Professor of Ornamental Horticulture in 1982. He retired officially in 1995 but continued his research and supervision of doctoral and postdoctoral candidates as professor emeritus.

Halevy was a research fellow at the Plant Industry Station in Beltsville, Maryland, and served as visiting professor at Michigan State University in East Lansing and, on a regular basis, at the University of California at Davis. He is a renowned international expert on floriculture and horticulture. His research has contributed significantly to the advancement of commercial floriculture in Israel and throughout the world. The department he founded and developed has long been considered one of the leading horticultural research and teaching groups in the world. The research has centered on the growth, development, and physiology of florist crops, with specific interest in the physiology of flowering (including the development of ways to control and time flowering), senescence and post-harvest physiology of flowering, and the development of new floriculture crops.

Halevy was named a fellow of the American Society of Horticultural Science in 1983. In 1986 he founded the International Working Group on Flowering and its publication, *Flowering Newsletter*, and in 1999 he was elected to the Norwegian Academy of Science and Letters.

He received numerous citations and awards during his career. In 1990 the president of Israel honored him with the title "Maker of a Beautiful Israel." He was also the recipient of the Israel Prize for agriculture (2002). He was a prolific writer, with over 350 publications appearing in international refereed journals. His six-volume *Handbook of Flowering* is considered the most comprehensive treatise published to date on the topic.

[Ruth Rossing (2nd ed.)]

HALÉVY, ÉLIE (1870–1937), French philosopher and historian. He was the son of Ludovic and brother of Daniel (see *Halévy family). He was raised as a Protestant (his mother's religion). He became professor at the Ecole libre des Sciences politiques where he taught English history and European socialism. A Dreyfusard and a secular rationalist, he was a founder of the *Revue de Métaphysique et de Morale* and the Société française de Philosophie. His first work, *La Théorie platonicienne des sciences* (1896), dealt with Plato's negative dialectic as a way to positive construction. He applied this theory in a basic study of the Benthamite movement, *La formation du radicalisme philosophique*, 3 vols. (1901–04; *The Growth of Philosophic Radicalism*, 1928). His important *Histoire du peuple anglais au XIXe siècle*, 5 vols. (1912–32; *A History of the English People in the 19th Century*, 1924–34) covering the periods 1815–41, and 1895–1914 (he died before completing the rest), was an anti-Marxist interpretation of English history, stressing the role of religious factors in English political stability. He also wrote *The World Crisis of 1914–18* (1930), *L'ère des tyrannies* (1938) against fascism and communism, and *Histoire du socialisme européen* (1948; from his notes). Halévy favored transforming collective belief through compromise rather than fanaticism as the means to international peace. At the end of his life he was pessimistic, convinced that war was inevitable and that the fascist and communist tyrannies would be perpetuated. He played an important role in English as well as in French intellectual life.

BIBLIOGRAPHY: Brunschvicg, in: *Revue de Métaphysique et de Morale*, 44 (1937), 679–91; C.C. Gillispie, *Journal of Modern History*, 22 (1950), 232–49; M. Richter, *International Encyclopedia of the Social Sciences*, 6 (1968), 307–10.

[Richard H. Popkin]

HALÉVY, ELIE HALFON (1760–1826), writer and poet in Hebrew and French. Born into an illustrious Jewish family in Fuerth, Bavaria, he received an Orthodox upbringing. As a young man he moved to Paris where he served as cantor, secretary of the community, and teacher. In Paris he acquired a broad general education and was greatly influenced by classical French literature. From 1817 to 1819 he edited and published a weekly journal in French, *L'Israélite Français*, which called for "Jewish enlightenment," and was animated by strong French patriotism. His only published book, *Limmudei Dat u-Musar* ("Teachings of Religion and Ethics," 1829), was a catechism for Jewish religious instruction. The tract is written in the spirit of the Haskalah and includes the decisions of the *Sanhedrin convened by Napoleon in 1807. His most important literary work, the poem "*Ha-Shalom*" ("Peace"), commemorated the cease-fire between France and England in 1802, when it was sung as a hymn, in both Hebrew and French, in the Great Synagogue of Paris. The poem was printed with a French and German translation by the imperial printing press in Paris, and reprinted in R. Fuerstenthal's *Ha-Me'assef* (1829, pp. 216–26). Written in the form of a classic Greco-Roman ode, it reflects the stormy period of the French Revolution and the subsequent wars and mirrors both the patriotic mood and the atmosphere of fear prevalent at the time. It remains a classic of the early period of modern Hebrew literature. Halévy was the father of the composer Jacques François Fromental *Halévy and the author and playwright Léon *Halévy.

BIBLIOGRAPHY: Klausner, Sifrut, 1 (1950²), 322–5; I. Zinberg, Sifrut, 5 (1959), 260–2.

[Gedalyah Elkoshi]

HALEVY (Rabinowitz), ISAAC (1847–1914), Polish rabbinical scholar and historian. Halevy was born in Ivenets, now Belorussia. After studying at the Volozhin yeshivah, he settled in Vilna as a businessman, later turning to scholarship. Interested in Jewish education, he tried to find a way to reconcile the character of religious schools with the demands of the Russian government for reform. He lived in various cities, including Pressburg (Bratislava), Homburg, and Hamburg, in the last serving as *Klausrabbiner*. It was Halevy's idea of a world organization for Orthodox Jewry that led to the founding of *Agudat Israel in 1912. He took the initiative in founding the Juedisch-Literarisch Gesellschaft in Frankfurt, whose yearbook (JJLG) appeared from 1903 to 1933. Halevy's major work, *Dorot ha-Rishonim* (6 vols., 1897–1939; repr. 1967), is a grandly conceived history of the Oral Law, the talmudic-rabbinic tradition from biblical times to the *geonim*. Halevy brought a vast talmudic erudition, ingenuity, and originality to his work, but in extra-rabbinic studies he was self-taught; he knew neither Latin nor Greek and quoted classical sources from their translations into German. Halevy worked "backward." Commencing with the savoraic and geonic period, he proceeded to that of the *amoraim* and the *tannaim*, and then to that of the *soferim* and the "men of the Great *Synagogue." The last volume deals with the biblical period and is a sustained attack on the critical school and attempts, following D.Z. *Hoffmann, to prove the validity of the traditional view. The main purpose of the work was to demolish the historical theories advanced by such scholars as N. *Krochmal, S.J. *Rapoport, Z. *Frankel, H. *Graetz, and I.H. Weiss on the development of *halakhah* from earliest times. For Halevy, trained as he was in the old school, the Oral Law was revealed on Mount Sinai and was handed down unchanged; rabbinic controversies and the Palestinian-Babylonian differences in law and custom concern only the details of rabbinic enactments and extensions of the laws of the Torah. In his criticism of the historical school, which he accuses of tendentious misinterpretation, he writes with animosity and invective, and critics were not slow to point to the obvious shortcomings, both scholarly and literary, of *Dorot ha-Rishonim*. Nevertheless, it remains a major contribution to Jewish historical research.

[Yehoshua Horowitz]

O. Asher Reichel has now published the letters of Halevy, *Igrot R. Yiẓhak Aizik Halevi* (Heb., 1972). The letters throw new light on Halevy. They reveal that he was not opposed to Haskalah or rabbis having secular knowledge and that he took an active part in halakhic questions of his time.

BIBLIOGRAPHY: O. Asher Reichel, *Isaac Halevy: Spokesman and Historian of Jewish Tradition* (1969); M. Auerbach (ed.), *Sefer ha-Zikkaron le-Y.I. Halevy* (1964); H. Schwab, *Chachme Ashkenaz* (Eng., 1964), 62f.

HALÉVY, JACQUES (François) FROMENTAL ÉLIE (1799–1862), French operatic composer. He was born in Paris, the son of Elie Halfon *Halévy. He entered the Paris Conservatory at the age of ten, studied composition with Cherubini, and won the Rome Prize in 1819 for his cantata "Herminie." He taught at the conservatory from 1816, becoming professor of counterpoint and fugue in 1833, and of composition in 1840. His students included Bizet (who later became his son-in-law) and Gounod. Halévy's fame rests primarily on his grand opera *La Juive* (1835), and his comic opera *L'Eclair* of the same year, achievements which he never equaled. He composed about 20 operas (among them *Le Juif errant*; 1852), five cantatas, and ballets. His writings include memoirs of his activity in the Académie des Beaux Arts, of which he became permanent secretary in 1854.

Halévy's operatic style was greatly influenced by Meyerbeer, especially in the dazzling orchestration that was much in favor at the time. In *La Juive*, a renaissance story of a prince in love with a Jewess (libretto by Scribe), he portrayed effective characters in situations of dramatic tension: Eleazar's aria "Rachel, quand du Seigneur" has remained one of the star items in the repertoire of dramatic tenors.

Halévy's attitude to Judaism seems to have been consciously neutral. In 1820 he composed a "Marche Funèbre et De Profundis" for three voices (text: Ps. 130 in Hebrew), for the memorial service to the Duc de Berry in the synagogue in the Rue Saint-Avoye, now Rue du Temple. His cantata "Noé" (Noah) was completed post-humously by Bizet. Richard Wagner wrote in praise of Halévy's works, and also arranged a potpourri for two violins from his *La Reine de Chypre* (1841).

Halévy's brother Léon (*Halévy family) wrote one of the first biographies of Halévy, *F. Halévy, ses œuvres* (1863).

BIBLIOGRAPHY: MGG, s.v.; Grove, Dict., s.v.; M. Curtis, in: *Musical Quarterly*, 39 (1953); Sendrey, Music, index.

[Josef Tal]

HALÉVY, JOSEPH (1827–1917), French Orientalist and Hebrew writer. Halévy began his career as a Hebrew teacher in his native Adrianople, Turkey, and later taught in Bucharest, Romania. In 1868 he visited Ethiopia under the auspices of the Alliance Israélite Universelle to study the Falashas (*Beta Israel). His report (not published), affirming the Jewishness of that forgotten tribe, led to a widespread philanthropic campaign on their behalf. The scientific results of his journey on the Beta Israel's language, literature, and customs, important in themselves, interested the French Académie des Inscriptions et Belles Lettres, which subsequently commissioned Halevy to explore Southern Arabia for Sabean inscriptions. For self-protection he traveled in the guise of a Jerusalem rabbi collecting alms for the poor. Ḥayyim *Ḥabshush, a Yemenite Jew who acted as Halevy's guide, described this expedition in *Travels in Yemen* (Arabic text, ed. and summarized in Eng. by S.D. Goitein, 1941; Heb. tr., *Mas'ot Ḥabshush*, 1939).

The rich scientific harvest was 686 inscriptions, which were partly in Minean, a sister language of Sabean. Halévy published them under the title *Études Sabéennes* (1875; = *Journal Asiatique*, 1 (1873), 305–365; 2 (1874), 497–585). He also wrote reports of his journeys, *Rapport sur une Mission Archéologique dans le Yémen* (1872), and *Voyage au Nadjran* (1873). The researches were of importance not only for the knowledge of Sabean language and culture but for biblical studies as well. In 1879 Halévy began teaching Ethiopic at the Ecole Pratique des Hautes Etudes in Paris and became the librarian of the Société Asiatique. In 1893 he founded the *Revue Sémitique d'Epigraphique et d'Histoire Ancienne*, to which he contributed a great many articles on Semitic epigraphy and Bible studies. In the latter, published separately as *Recherches Bibliques* (5 vols., 1895–1914), he interpreted the first 25 chapters of Genesis on the basis of Babylonian-Assyrian discoveries, rejecting the Graf-Wellhausen documentary hypothesis (see *Bible: biblical criticism). He also discussed problems in the Bible in the *Revue des Etudes Juives, Revue Critique*, and *Revue de l'Histoire des Religions*. Halévy dealt with recently discovered parts of the Hebrew texts of Ben Sira in *Le nouveau fragment hébreu de l'Ecclésiastique* (1902); with the origins of Christianity in *Etudes évangéliques* (1903); and with Ethiopian, particularly Beta Israel, literature in *Seder Tefillot ha-Falashim* (1876), *Te'ezaza Sanbat* ("Sabbath laws"; 1902), *La guerre de Sarsa-Dengel contre les Falachas* (1907), and others.

Prompted by his "Semitic" pride, Halévy argued obstinately against the view that Sumerian was a non-Semitic language, which with Sumerian culture and cuneiform scripts preceded its Semitic successors. Halévy rejected this now accepted view, believing Sumerian to be not a language but a hieratic, artificial script invented by the Assyrian-Babylonian priesthood for its own purposes. One of his works on this subject is his *Le Sumérisme et l'histoire babylonienne* (1900). In contrast to the assimilationist trend among French Jewry, Halévy was an ardent Hebraist and *Ḥovev Zion*. In his youth he was a regular contributor to Hebrew periodicals, such as *Ha-Maggid, Ha-Levanon*, and *Yerushalayim*, both in prose and in poetry, which were later collected and published under the title *Maḥberet Meliẓah va-Shir* (1894). The titles of his poems, such as "*Admat Avotai*" ("Land of My Fathers"), "*Al ha-Yarden*" ("By the Jordan,") and "*Tikvati*" ("My Hope") revealed his strong attachment to Ereẓ Israel. Halévy translated into Hebrew poems by Schiller, Byron, Victor Hugo, and others. In an article in *Ha-Maggid* of 1861 he proposed the establishment of a society, Marpei Lashon, for the development of the Hebrew language, an idea later realized in the Va'ad ha-Lashon ha-Ivrit and its successor, the Academy of Hebrew Language.

BIBLIOGRAPHY: N. Sokolow, *Ishim*, 4 (1935), 144–92; F. Perles, in: *Ost und West*, 17 (1917), 105–10; M. Schorr, in: *Deutsche Literaturzeitung*, nos. 19–20 (May 12, and 19, 1918), 595–601, 627–33; D. Sidersky, *Quelques portraits de nos maîtres des études sémitiques* (1937), 59–63; M. Eliav, in: *Tarbiz*, 35 (1966), 61–67; T.B. Jones, *Sumerian Problem* (1969), 22–47. **ADD. BIBLIOGRAPHY:** Y. Tobi, "*Yosef Halevi ve-Ḥeker Yehudei Teiman*," in: *Pe'amim*, 100 (2005), 23–71.

[Hans Jacob Polotsky]

HALEVY, MEYER ABRAHAM (1900–1972), Romanian and French rabbi and scholar. Halevy was born in Piatra Neamt, Romania and studied at the Sorbonne, receiving his doctorate and his rabbinical diploma from the Seminaire Israélite de France in 1925. He was also a Diplomate at the Ecole des Hautes Etudes. In the same year he was appointed rabbi of Jassy, and in the following year to the Sephardi Community of Bucharest, and subsequently to the following congregations in the capital: Great Synagogue Jewish Center, 1925–35; Holy Unity Temple, 1935–40; Choral Temple, 1940–45; and Spiritual Union Congregation, 1946–63. From 1950 to 1963 he was Research Professor of Oriental, Classical and Numismatic Studies at the Romanian Academy and Lecturer on the History of Medicine at the Romanian Society of History of Medicine from 1955 to 1963.

During World War II he was continuously harassed by the authorities and arrested on a number of occasions because of the sympathy and spiritual care he extended to political prisoners during the German occupation. After the intervention of a number of important personalities, including

Pastor Martin Niemöller, and the payment of a ransom, he was permitted to leave Romania and settled in Paris, where he acquired French citizenship. He was appointed professor of Jewish history at the Seminaire Israelite de France, and Consistorial Grand Rabbi at the Tournelles Jewish Center, Paris. Halevy wrote numerous works in French and Romanian, including the Commentary of Joseph Bekhor-Schor on Leviticus (1924), *Le problème des Khazares* (1935), *Science et Conscience dans l'Histoire de la Médicine juive au* XV*e Siècle* (1957), and *La Médicine des Rabbins-thaumaturges au* XVIII*e Siècle* (1955).

HALEVY, MOSHE (1895–1974), Israeli theatrical director and founder of the *Ohel Theater. He studied engineering in Moscow before joining the newly formed Habimah Studio as assistant director (1917). He left the company early, however, to found his own theater in Palestine and in 1925 established Ohel, a workers' theater under the auspices of the Histadrut. His first production, based on stories by I.L. *Peretz, was a great success, especially in the kibbutzim which, for many years, were to provide Ohel's main audiences. In his production of *Fishermen* (*Op Hoop van Zegen*) by Heijermans, he demonstrated his belief in the theater as an instrument for social betterment. For 25 years he directed almost all Ohel's productions, but left the company after disagreements in 1951. He engaged in other ventures, among them a small traveling Moshe Halevy Theater (1960), which continued until 1967. His autobiography *Darki Alei Bamot* ("My Stage Career") appeared in 1954.

BIBLIOGRAPHY: Tidhar, 2 (1947), 953–4.

[Mendel Kohansky]

HALEVY, YOSEF (1924–), Israeli painter. Halevy was born in Tel Aviv and graduated from the Painting Teachers' School there. Of Yemenite origin and deeply imbued with Yemenite folklore, he chose as subjects for his early paintings his memories and his inner world, and in this period one sees wide brushstrokes, forming color planes and contoured patterns, with a clear development toward abstraction. In his second stage, the Yemenite background almost entirely disappears, and his painting is based more on color and form, the colors on the canvas being more spontaneous and expressive. In his third phase, the forms become smaller and Halevy gives expression to mythological and lyrical forms, suggesting figures that intermingle with each other, sometimes creating almost completely abstract patterns.

[Judith Spitzer]

ḤALFAN, ELIJAH MENAHEM (16th century), Italian physician, rabbi, and kabbalist. Elijah was the son of the astronomer Abba Mari Ḥalfan and grandson of Joseph *Colon. He was one of the Italian rabbis approached to express his view of Henry VIII's divorce from Catherine of Aragon, on which he gave an affirmative opinion. He was also a supporter of Solomon *Molcho. Both these facts aroused the opposition of the physician Jacob *Mantino who feared that the close relationship with the English king as well as with the messianic agitation of Molcho would render the pope unfavorably disposed toward the Jews. Ḥalfan wrote responsa (including one in which he favored instructing non-Jews in the Torah; Ms. Kaufmann, no. 156:1 from 1545) and Hebrew poems (several verses are extant in Ms.; Neubauer, Cat, no. 948: 1, 6). In a halakhic decision dated 1550, Elijah's name appears together with that of Meir Katzenellenbogen of Padua among others (Resp. Rema 56). He owned a valuable library in Venice, a catalog of which was published by A.Z. Schwarz (*Die Hebraeischen Handschriften der Nationalbibliothek in Wien* (1925), 145ff.).

An important epistle has been preserved in Ms. New York, JTS 1822, where Halfan describes the history of Kabbalah and the openness to this lore among Christians in the Renaissance. He envisioned this openness as a sign of messianism.

BIBLIOGRAPHY: Carmoly, in: *Revue Orientale*, 2 (1842), 133f.; K. Lieben, *Gal Ed* (1856), German section, 171 no. 168, Hebrew section, xlv no. 17; Michael, Or, no. 394; Kaufmann, in: JQR, 9 (1896/97), 500–8; idem, in: REJ, 27 (1893), 51–58; Vogelstein-Rieger, 2 (1895), 51–53; U. Cassuto, *Gli Ebrei a Firenze* (1918), 272; A.Z. Aescoly, *Ha-Tenu'ot ha-Meshiḥiyyot be-Yisrael* (1956), 271–3; Tishby, in: *Perakim*, 1 (1967–68), 135–7. **ADD. BIBLIOGRAPHY:** M. Idel, "The Magical and Neoplatonic Interpretations of Kabbalah in the Renaissance," in: B.D. Cooperman (ed.), *Jewish Thought in the Sixteenth Century* (1983), 186–89.

[Umberto (Moses David) Cassuto]

HALFANUS (Halfan, Chalfan), family that migrated from Provence to Italy after 1394 and later moved to Prague and Vienna. The family was linked with the famous *Kalonymus family which was prominent in the Middle Ages. Most of its members were physicians and were well known for their scholarship in science and literature. ABBA MARI, a son-in-law of Joseph *Colon, lived in Italy and published in 1490 an elegy and a work on astronomy. His son was Elijah Menahem *Halfan. Another ABBA MARI (d. 1586) was a physician in Prague. His son ELIAS (1561–1624) lived first in Prague and was granted his licence as a physician by Rudolph II (1598). With Aaron *Maor Katan (Lucerna) he later achieved prominence as a physician and *dayyan* in Vienna, and was also known as a book collector. He was even proposed as an army surgeon.

A second Ḥalfan family living in Vienna later changed its name to Wechsler. Its members included ELIEZER BEN URI SHRAGA PHOEBUS (d. 1670), who was head of the community and was apparently the last person to be buried before the 1670 expulsion. His son URI SHRAGA PHOEBUS (c. 1640–1707) headed a yeshivah in Prague. His *Dat Esh*, responsa and novellae on Maimonides' *Yad Hilkhot Kilayim*, was published in Berlin in 1743.

BIBLIOGRAPHY: B. Wachstein, *Die Inschriften des alten Judenfriedhofes in Wien*, 1 (1912), index s.v. *Chalfan*; Kisch, in: JGGJC, 6 (1934), 15; Engelmann, in: *Juedische Familienforschung*, no. 44 (1937), 803–5; Bruck, in: HJ, 9 (1947), 161–70.

[Meir Lamed]

ḤALFON (Khalfon), ABRAHAM (late 18th century), rabbi in *Tripoli. Information about Ḥalfon is limited to the fact that his book, *Ḥayyei Avraham* (Leghorn, 1826), was published posthumously by his son Raḥamim. The *haskamot* (recommendations) for the book were written by two emissaries from Tiberias, Joseph ibn Samon and Samuel Shoshanah, indicating Ḥalfon's ties to that town. The book contains traditional explanations of the commandments in the Shulḥan Arukh (*Oraḥ Ḥayyim* and *Yoreh De'ah*). The explanations, based on the Talmud, the *Zohar, Ketem Paz* (a commentary on the Zohar), *Sefer Ḥasidim*, and *Penei David* by Ḥayyim Joseph David *Azulai, are lucidly and attractively presented and avoid wearying casuistry. The book was published in several succeeding editions: 1844, 1857, 1861. Several other works by him, halakhic and homiletical, are still in manuscript.

ḤALFON BEN NETHANEL HA-LEVI ABU SAʿĪD (12th century), wealthy businessman in Egypt. Ḥalfon's affairs extended from India and Yemen to Spain. Numerous letters, addressed to him from furthest parts of the Jewish Diaspora, which bear evidence of his generosity and wealth, have been found in the Cairo *Genizah. He was a close friend of *Judah Halevi, who also appears to have been his relative. Some of the letters which were sent by the latter to Ḥalfon have been preserved. It seems that the contacts between them dated from the time of Ḥalfon's visit to Spain in order to arrange personal affairs. Halevi then wrote poems and letters in the former's honor which were published by H. *Brody. When on his way to Ereẓ Israel, Halevi stayed at Ḥalfon's home in Cairo from 1140 to 1141. One of Ḥalfon's brothers was R. Moses b. Nethanel, the *av bet din* of the tribunal of the *gaon* *Maẓli'aḥ b. Solomon Ha-Kohen.

BIBLIOGRAPHY: S.D. Goitein, *A Mediterranean Society*; vol. 1–4, index (vol. 6) idem, in: *Sinai*, 33 (1953), 228–30; idem, in: *Tarbiz*, 24 (1955), 21–47, 134–49; 25 (1956), 393–412; 28 (1959), 346–61; 31 (1962), 366–8; 35 (1966), 274–7; Schirmann, *ibid.*, 9 (1938), 295; Strauss, in: *Zion*, 7 (1941/42), 145–51; Abramson, in: KS, 29 (1953/54), 136–7, 142; **ADD. BIBLIOGRAPHY:** M. Gil and E. Fleischer, *Yehudah ha-Levi u-Benei Hugo.* (2001), 27–80, 91–92, 100, 156–57, 210–12, 224–26, 236–38.

[Abraham David]

HALHUL (Heb. חַלְחוּל), town in the territory of Judah mentioned once in the Bible together with Beth-Zur and Gedor (Josh. 15:58). An Idumean village called Aluros (identical with Halhul) is referred to by Josephus (Wars, 4:522) as a fortified city which was destroyed by Simeon b. Giora along with Hebron during the Jewish War (66–70/73). Jerome mentions the city Alula belonging to Jerusalem near Hebron (Eusebius, Onom., 87:11–12). The "tomb of Jonah" was shown there. In the 14th century Jews were living in Halhul and according to tombstone lists compiled by medieval Jewish travelers, the grave of the prophet Gad was located there. Today, the Muslim Arab village Ḥalḥūl is located at the highest spot of the Judean Hills about 3,347 ft. (1020 m.) above sea level, 2.5 mi. (4 km.) north of Hebron. As a result of the proximity of Hebron, Ḥalḥūl expanded in the 1950s and 1960s; in 1968 the village had over 6,000 inhabitants. Fruit orchards and particularly vineyards constituted its principal farming branch. In 2005, including the surrounding villages, the population exceeded 50,000.

BIBLIOGRAPHY: Nestle, in: ZDPV, 34 (1911), 79; E. Mader, *Altchristliche Basiliken und Lokaltraditionen in Suedjudaea* (1918), 35ff.

[Michael Avi-Yonah]

HALICZ (Russ. **Galich**), small town formerly in Poland, now in Stanislaw district, Ukraine. The earliest information relating to Jews in Halicz dates from 1488. In 1506, the Jews there were granted a remission of their taxes because of hardship caused by war. Halicz had one of the few organized *Karaite communities to exist continuously in Eastern Europe. It was founded by Karaites from Lvov. They were accorded the same rights "as other Jews" by the Polish monarch in 1578. Until the close of the 18th century the Karaites formed the majority of the Halicz community. Records of 1627 show that 24 houses there were owned by Karaites and only a few by Rabbanites. Subsequently the Rabbanite community increased. In 1765 it numbered 258, while there were 99 Karaites, and in 1900 there were 1,450 Rabbanites and 160 Karaites. By 1921 the combined population was only 582 as a result of emigration. The Karaites lived in a separate street and worshiped in their own synagogue, built at the end of the 16th century.

The Karaite community looked for cultural guidance to their spiritual center in the East, since the forefathers of the founders came from Crimea and their native language was Tatar. When the links with the parent center became attenuated, the cultural level of the Karaites in Halicz became so poor that by the first half of the 17th century there was no one in the community qualified to serve as *ḥakham* (or *ḥazzan*). The situation improved with the arrival of an emissary from Jerusalem, David Ḥazzan, around 1640. He was followed (c. 1670) by two brothers, Joseph and Joshua. Joseph, who earned the encomium "Ha-Mashbir" ("the provider"), discharged the duties of *ḥakham* and composed *piyyutim* which were included in the Karaite prayer book. His descendants served as *ḥakhamim-ḥazzanim* of the Halicz Karaite congregation until the beginning of the 19th century, when the office was held by members of the Leonovich family. Karaite autonomy was recognized by the Austrian government during the period when Halicz was administered by Austria. Abraham, the first of the Leonovich *ḥakhamim*, was one of the Karaites to be influenced by the ideas of *Haskalah. He corresponded with some of the luminaries of the movement, including Naḥman *Krochmal and Abraham *Geiger, who on their part took an interest in Karaism. Later, around the beginning of the 20th century, with the strengthening of the Polish cultural influence, most of the Karaites tended toward assimilation while a few drew closer to the Rabbanites.

The community was destroyed by the Germans in 1942, when the Jews were deported to Stanislawow and Belzec.

BIBLIOGRAPHY: M. Balaban, in: *Studya historyczne* (1927),

1–93; R. Fahn, *Le-Korot ha-Kara'im be-Galizyah* (1870), 2–16. **ADD. BIBLIOGRAPHY:** PK.

[Simha Katz]

HALICZ (Heb. הָעֶלִיץ, **Helicz, Halic, Helic**), family of printers in Cracow in the 16th century. Three brothers, Samuel, Asher, and Elyakim, sons of Ḥayyim Halicz, established Poland's first Jewish press there in about 1530. Their name indicates that the family originally came from the small town of Halicz on the Dniester in eastern Galicia. Their type and page arrangements show they learned their craft (and probably obtained type and equipment) in Prague. It is likely that they left Prague because a royal order of 1527 designated Gershom Kohen as Bohemia's sole Hebrew printer; all other Hebrew print shops closed, and the brothers probably could find no further work there. The decorative borders for their opening pages were certainly brought by them from Prague. Three works listed by *Zunz as being from Cracow in 1530 were probably the earliest products of their press. These were a Pentateuch; Tur, *Yoreh De'ah*; and a Passover *Haggadah* (all otherwise unknown). Their earliest surviving works, both dating from 1534, were *Issur ve-Hetter* by R. Isaac Dueren and *Mirkevet ha-Mishneh*, a Hebrew-Yiddish Bible dictionary by a R. Anshel. Yet evidently they did not prosper, and Asher dropped out.

In 1535 Samuel and Elyakim produced R. David Cohen's *Azharot Nashim* in Yiddish, a work dealing with religious laws for women. Then Elyakim alone issued a Yiddish version of Asher b. Jehiel's *Oraḥ Ḥayyim*. Samuel spent 1536 in Oels, Silesia, where he and his brother-in-law printed a book of *Tefillot mi-Kol ha-Shanah* (Prayers for All Year) in large type. However, his books and equipment were destroyed in a fire and he returned to Cracow.

It was probably economic misery or possibly excessive pressure from the Polish church that made the three undergo baptism in 1537; they became Andreas (Samuel), Johannes (Elyakim), and Paul (Asher; or perhaps Asher became Andreas, and Samuel was Paul). Repelled by their act, the Jews boycotted them and would not even pay their debts. At the brothers' plea, King Sigismund I issued a decree dated March 28, 1537, commanding that Poland's Jews might buy only their books; no others were to print or sell Jewish works, and none might be brought in from other countries, on pain of a stiff fine. Yet, under tacit excommunication by the Jews, their plight only worsened. Believing, though, that the royal decree must improve matters, Johannes resumed printing in 1538–39, issuing mainly books for popular use.

Through their bishop, the desperate Halicz brothers sought and obtained a new royal decree on December 31, 1539, ordering the Jews of Cracow and Posen to buy their entire stock of some 3,350 volumes, valued at 1,600 florins. Pleading poverty, the two Jewish communities had their coreligionists in Lemberg (Lvov) included in the order. The complete stock of books was paid for in three years and destroyed. The Halicz firm went out of existence. In 1540 Johannes began printing Latin and Polish theological works. Paul, who became a Catholic missionary among the Polish Jews, printed a New Testament (Cracow, 1540–41), in a Judeo-German transcription of Luther's translation. He also produced *Elemental oder Lesebuechlein* (Hundsfeld, 1543), an instruction book in Hebrew for gentiles. Lukasz Halicz, a printer in Posen (1578–93), was apparently his son. Samuel returned to Judaism. After working as a bookbinder in Breslau, he went to Constantinople (c. 1550) and resumed Hebrew printing. He subsequently printed the Scriptures (1551–52; repenting of his conversion in the colophon); the "Story of Judith" (1552–53); and R. Isaac Dueren's *Issur ve-Hetter*, retitled *Sha'arei Dura* (1553). In 1561–62, when Samuel was no longer living, the name of Ḥayyim b. Samuel Ashkenazi, apparently his son, appears as the printer of the responsa of R. Joseph ibn Lev in part 2.

BIBLIOGRAPHY: M. Balaban, in: *Soncino-Blaetter*, 3 (1929/30), 1–9, 36–44; idem, *Yidn in Polyn* (1930), 183–95; Ḥ.D. Friedberg, *Toledot ha-Defus ha-Ivri be-Polanyah* (1950), 1–4; A.M. Habermann, in: KS, 33 (1957/58), 509–20; B. Schlossberg, in: *Yivo Bletter*, 13 (1938), 313–24.

[Charles Wengrov]

HALIVNI, DAVID WEISS (1927–), U.S. talmud scholar. Born in Poljana Kobielecka, Czechoslovakia (now Ukraine), Halivni was raised in Sighet, Romania, by his mother and his maternal grandfather, Isaiah Weiss, a prominent rabbinic scholar. Recognized as a talmudic prodigy (*ilui*), Halivni was ordained a rabbi in Sighet before reaching the age of 17. Upon the occupation of the Carpathian region by Germany, the family was confined to the ghetto of Sighet, and thence deported to Auschwitz, Halivni being transferred to forced labor in Silesia. The sole survivor of his family, Halivni was liberated from the concentration camp of Ebensee, in Upper Austria, in May 1945, and came to the U.S. in 1947. Through the coincidence of a relative of Saul *Lieberman being employed in the Bronx orphanage where Halivni was billeted, he soon met that scholar, and so was taken under the wing of the leading academician in the field of rabbinic literature. Following undergraduate studies at Brooklyn College, in tandem with residence in the Yeshivat Rav Chaim Berlin, and graduate study at New York University, Halivni pursued a doctorate of Hebrew letters under Lieberman at the *Jewish Theological Seminary of America (JTSA) where he joined the faculty as professor of Talmud and Rabbinics.

Halivni's early work included a study of the pseudo-Rashi commentary on the Babylonian Talmud's tractate *Ta'anit*, the misattribution of whose opening segment he first suggested on the basis of literary comparison and then confirmed by means of an early manuscript that he identified in the Seminary's library collection. In 1968, Halivni completed the first volume of his ongoing talmudic commentary, *Mekorot u-Mesorot* ("Sources and Traditions"). In the first stages of this work, often starting with difficulties noted by traditional commentators, Halivni developed a source-critical approach to the talmudic page, aiming to uncover earlier, variant readings and textual substrates altered in transmission. (This methodology, and aspects of Halivni's personality, provided a basis for characters and for a paradigm of critical talmudic study dramatized in the first two novels of Chaim *Potok.)

Halivni's great achievement was a complete re-conceptualization of the redaction of the Babylonian Talmud.

Appointed to the American Academy of Arts and Sciences, Halivni was awarded Israel's Bialik Prize in 1985 for his ongoing talmudic research; he also received honorary doctorates from a number of Israeli universities, as well as the University of Lund, Sweden, and JTSA. Halivni was also a charter participant in the Institute for Advanced Studies of Tel Aviv University.

In the mid-1980s, Halivni left the Seminary for a professorship at Columbia University and also participated in the founding of the *Union for Traditional Judaism and its rabbinical academy, the Institute of Traditional Judaism, where he served as rector. He also became the de facto and then official rabbinic adviser of a small group, which initially met for Sabbath services in the home of the infirm Louis Finkelstein and subsequently burgeoned into a large community on Manhattan's Upper West Side.

Halivni's books in English include *Midrash, Mishnah and Gemara: The Jewish Predilection for Justified Law* (1986), *Peshat and Derash: Plain and Applied Meaning in Rabbinic Exegesis* (1991), and *Revelation Restored: Divine Writ and Critical Responses* (1996).

In his later years, Halivni confessed something of a return to the mysticism of the ḥasidic milieu of his youth, expressed through a certain ecstasy in prayer (especially on days including memorial prayers), and also, most notably with regard to his scholarship, in terms of the doctrine of *ẓimẓum* – that is, divine contraction or withdrawal from the world.

Halivni is also the author of a memoir, *The Book and the Sword: A Life of Learning in the Shadow of Destruction* (1996). Reticent for decades about his personal experience of the Holocaust, Halivni had said, with reference to Sighet *ḥeder*-mate, fellow survivor, and long-time friend, Elie Wiesel, "He speaks [about the Holocaust], and I am silent; but when we are together, I shout, and he listens." With his often poignant and thoroughly frank autobiography, Halivni broke his silence to speak of the transfiguring impact of the devastation on the course of his life.

[Jonah C. Steinberg (2nd ed.)]

HALKIN, ABRAHAM SOLOMON (1903–1990), Orientalist and educator; brother of Simon *Halkin. Born in Novo-Bykhov, Russia, Halkin was taken to the U.S. in 1914. He was lecturer in Semitic languages from 1928 to 1950, and from 1950 to 1970 professor of Hebrew at the City College of New York. He also taught at the Jewish Theological Seminary from 1929 to 1970. In 1970 he settled in Jerusalem. Halkin edited part two of al-Baghdādī's *Muslim Schisms and Sects* (*al-Farq bayna al-Firaq*, 1935); the Arabic original and three Hebrew versions of Maimonides' *Iggeret Teiman* (1952); Ibn Aknin's Arabic commentary on the Song of Songs with a Hebrew translation, *Hitgallut ha-Sodot* (1964); and *Zion in Jewish Literature* (1964). He also worked on a new critical edition and Hebrew translation of Moses Ibn Ezra's *Kitāb al-Muḥāḍara wa-al-Mudhākara*, a classic work on Hebrew poetics, and wrote the introduction to a new edition of J.A. Montgomery's *The Samaritans: The Earliest Jewish Sect* (1968). He was editor of the *Encyclopaedia Judaica's* department of Judeo-Arabic literature and medieval translations. He also compiled *201 Hebrew Verbs* (1970) and translated *Crisis and Leadership: Epistles of Maimonides* (with D. Hartman, 1985).

ADD. BIBLIOGRAPHY: L. Schwarz (ed.), *Great Ages and Ideas of the Jewish People* (1956).

[Jacob Lassner / Ruth Beloff (2nd ed.)]

HALKIN, SHMUEL (1897–1960), Soviet Yiddish poet. Born in Rogachev, Belorussia, Halkin grew up in a ḥasidic home and early came under the influence of Hebrew poetry and wrote Hebrew lyrics. He dreamed of becoming an artist, but ultimately turned to Yiddish poetry and was encouraged by Peretz *Markish in Ekaterinoslav (now Dnepropetrovsk, Ukraine) and by David *Hofstein in Moscow. His first book of lyrics, *Lider* ("Poems"), appeared in 1922. Other volumes of poems and plays followed between 1929 and 1948. Until 1924, Halkin belonged to a Zionist circle and contemplated settling in Palestine, as is evident from a Hebrew song, *Shir ha-Ḥaluẓah*, written at this time and published in Israel after his death. In his autobiography, he acknowledged the influence of Judah Halevi and Solomon ibn Gabirol in the shaping of his lyric personality. Attacked for his Jewish nationalism, his nostalgic despair, and his deviation from the Communist party line on literature, he was compelled to recant his literary heresies. Thereafter, he avoided controversial themes and, in his 1932 poetic collection *Far dem Nayem Fundament* ("For the New Foundation"), formulated the Soviet writers' credo: "We write what we want to-/we write what we have to." He fruitfully worked with Yiddish theater: *Shulamis* (1940), a dramatic poem, based on *Goldfaden, and a verse drama, *Bar Kokhva* (1939), were staged in Moscow and by other theater troupes. In the latter he describes in a communist-ideological spirit the social and class differences between Bar Kokhba and R. Akiva on the one hand and the rich classes of Judea on the other. In 1939 he was decorated with the Order of the Sign of Honor. He translated some of Shakespeare's plays (most notably *King Lear*) and some of the works of Pushkin, Gorki, and other Russian authors into Yiddish.

His dramatic poem *Ghettograd* on the Warsaw Ghetto Uprising was scheduled for the Moscow Yiddish Theater in 1948, but the theater was closed when the Jewish *Anti-Fascist Committee was liquidated that year and Halkin was arrested as one of its prominent members and sent to a labor camp. He was released in 1955, rehabilitated, and, in 1958, decorated with the Order of the Red Banner. After his death in 1960, his native city named a street after him, and in 1966 a selection of his Yiddish lyrics was issued in Moscow. He was a cousin of Simon and Abraham S. *Halkin. His *Lider fun Tfise un La-*

ger ("Poems from Prison and Camp") was published in Tel Aviv in 1988.

BIBLIOGRAPHY: LNYL, 3 (1960), 41ff.; J. Glatstein, *In Tokh Genumen* (1947), 350–8; C. Madison, *Yiddish Literature* (1968), 409–11. **ADD. BIBLIOGRAPHY:** Ch. Shmeruk (ed.), *A Shpigl oyf a Shteyn* (1987), 567–627, 759–61; J. Veidlinger, *The Moscow State Yiddish Theater* (2000), index.

[Sol Liptzin / Gennady Estraikh (2nd ed.)]

HALKIN, SIMON (1898–1987), Hebrew poet, novelist, and educator. Born in Dobsk near Mohilev, Russia, he immigrated to the United States in 1914. He taught at the Hebrew Union College School for Teachers in New York City (1925–32), and after settling in Ereẓ Israel in 1932, he taught English at a Tel Aviv high school. In 1939, he returned to America and became professor of Hebrew literature at the Jewish Institute of Religion in New York. He was appointed professor of Modern Hebrew Literature at the Hebrew University in 1949.

In Halkin's works, metaphysical flights coalesce with earthly desires. This dichotomy already appears in his first novel *Yeḥi'el ha-Hagri* (1928) whose main character is torn between love of God and love of woman. It receives a more mature expression in *Be-Yamim Shishah ve-Leilot Shivah* (1929), a cycle of 36 sonnets; in *"Al Ḥof Santa Barbara"* (1928); and in *"Tarshishah."* These and other poems were collected in *Al ha-I* ("On the Island," 1945). Other motifs in Halkin's poetry are the tension between the death wish and the will to live, the loss of religious faith and the consolation which comes with the acceptance of the agony of living. In *Ma'avar Yabbok* ("The Ford of the Jabbok," 1965), Halkin deals in depth with the death motif. The speaker, obsessed with the love of his dead lover, discovers that the memory of love alone is able to sustain him through the agony of living. *"Ya'akov Rabinowitz be-Yarmouth"* is Halkin's maturest treatment of this theme. The poem depicts an encounter with a dead friend and writer and the ensuing dialogue across the chasm of death is punctuated by the knowledgeable irony of two men who have lived long and have learned the secret of resignation.

Halkin's works in literary criticism include *Arai va-Keva* ("Transient and Permanent," 1942), his unedited lectures on the history of modern Hebrew literature (mimeographed), and his English *Trends in Modern Hebrew Literature* (1950; 1970). The latter is a socio-historical appraisal of Hebrew writing during the last 200 years. Halkin also wrote *Zeramim ve-Ẓurot ba-Sifrut ha-Ivrit ha-Ḥadashah* (1984) and a volume of essays entitled *Ẓiyyonut le-lo Tenai* (1985). Though a long-time resident of the United States, he expresses a negative attitude toward American Judaism and insists that its spiritual resources are limited, a view which permeates his unfinished novel *Ad Mashber* (1945) and his monograph *Yehudim ve-Yahadut ba-Amerikah* (1946).

Of his numerous translations, that of Walt Whitman's *Leaves of Grass* (1952) is outstanding. He also translated Shakespeare's *Merchant of Venice* (1929) and *King John* (1947); Jack London's *Before Adam* (1921) and *The Sea Wolf* (1924); and Shelley's *A Defense of Poetry* (1928).

Nekhar, a collection of 11 short stories written over 40 years, appeared in 1972, and in 1981 the volume of poems *Ulai*. In 1975 Halkin was awarded the Israel Prize for Hebrew literature, and in 1977 there appeared his *Shirim*, consisting of his collected works. He has also translated George Seferis' early verse into Hebrew. In 1984 there appeared three volumes of his collected poems. A volume entitled *Sefer ha-Yovel*, with essays on Halkin on the occasion of his 75th birthday, was edited by B. Shahevitch. R. Weiser prepared a bibliography of Halkin's works (1975).

A list of English translations of his work appears in Goell, Bibliography, index.

BIBLIOGRAPHY: D. Laor, *Mivḥar Ma'amarei Bikkoret al Yeẓirato shel Shimon Halkin*, 1978; Malachi, in: *Yad la-Kore*, 3 (1951–53), 32–38; A. Epstein, *Soferim Ivrim ba-Amerikah*, 1 (1952), 172–208; *Gilyonot*, 23 (1949), 133–44; Kressel, Leksikon, 1 (1965), 617f.; Waxman, Literature, 4 (1960^2), 1073f.; R. Wallenrod, *Literature of Modern Israel* (1956), index. **ADD. BIBLIOGRAPHY:** B. Shahevitch, *Ye'arot Metoḥamim: Episodot be-Biografiyah Literariyah shel Shimon Halkin* (1982); M. Dror, *Shirat Shimon Halkin* (1983); Y. Shofet, *Shimon Halkin, Pegishah* (1993); A. Arye, *Ideologiyah u-Vikoret Sifrutit: Halkin ve-Kurzweil* (1997).

[Eisig Silberschlag

HALL, MONTY (Maurice Halperin; 1924–), Canadian game-show host, producer. The son of a poor butcher, Hall was born in Winnipeg, Manitoba. Receiving a loan from a local businessman, he was able to attend the University of Manitoba, where he exhibited talent in both musical and dramatic productions and was elected president of the student body. After earning his B.S. in 1945, Hall served in the Canadian Army during World War II, where he emceed a number of army shows. In 1955, he moved to New York, where he worked as an anchor on NBC's radio and television program *Monitor.* In 1960, CBS brought Hall to Hollywood to become the emcee of their show *Video Village* and in 1963 Hall partnered with writer-producer Stefan Hatos to create *Let's Make a Deal.* The show turned out to be a wild success and ran for the next 23 years on all three major American networks, evolving into a pop-culture phenomenon and rendering Hall one of the most famous persons of his era. Throughout the 1970s, Hall emceed his own variety show specials and appeared as a guest on countless television shows such as *The Odd Couple* and *Love Boat.* On August 24th, 1973, Hall was immortalized when he received his own star on Hollywood's Walk of Fame. Beyond his television career, Hall's work in philanthropy has earned him over 500 awards, the most prestigious being the Order of Canada Award (the highest award Canada offers) bestowed upon him in 1988 for his humanitarian endeavors. For years, Hall was among the most, if not the most, prominent Hollywood entertainer to be directly involved in the organized Jewish community, contributing generously to the Jewish Federation and participating in synagogue life. Many attributed his unique participation to the education he had received in the close-knit Jewish community of Manitoba.

[Max Joseph (2nd ed.)]

HALL, OWEN (**James Davis**; 1848–1907), English playwright and journalist. Owner-editor of *The Bat* (1885–87), he chose his pen name as a result of gambling losses which led to his "owing all." Davis is mainly remembered as the writer of successful musical comedies, notably *A Gaiety Girl* (1894), *The Geisha* (1897), and *Florodora* (1899). He later edited a weekly, *The Phoenix*.

ḤALLAH (Heb. חַלָּה), a form of bread (II Sam. 6:19). The term also applies to the portion of dough set aside and given to the priest (Num. 15:19–20). The etymology of the word is traced either to the Hebrew root for "hollow" and "pierce" (Heb. חלל, *ḥll*), suggesting a perforated and/or rounded loaf, or to the Akkadian *ellu* ("pure"), referring to the bread's sacral use. Until new evidence allows more precision, however, *ḥallah* must be rendered "loaf" (parallel to the Hebrew word *kikkar*, cf. Ex. 29:23; Lev. 8:26). In the Bible, *ḥallah* is a bread offering subsumed under *minḥah*, the grain sacrifice. Commonly used in an unleavened form, and only rarely in a leavened form (Lev. 7:13; probably Num. 15:20), the bread is made with or without oil (Ex. 29:2, 23; Lev. 2:4; 7:12; 8:26; 24:5; Num. 6:15, 19).

[Jacob Milgrom]

Post-Biblical

According to the rabbis, the precept of setting aside *ḥallah* applies to dough kneaded from one of the *five species of grain (Ḥal. 1:1), since only from them can the bread (referred to in Num. 15:19: "when you eat of the bread of the land" etc.) be made, although Philo (Spec. 132) limits it to wheat and barley alone. The time of setting aside the *ḥallah* was derived by the sages from the words, "Of the first of your dough" – which they interpreted as meaning "as soon as it becomes dough" – hence one may eat casually of dough before it forms a ball in the case of wheat, and a lump in the case of barley (Sif. Num. 110), i.e., when the kneading is finished. If, however, it had not been set aside from the dough it must be set aside from the baked bread (*ibid.*). The Septuagint translates the word *ḥallah* as baked bread, and both Philo and Josephus (Ant. 4:71) also imply that the precept of setting aside the *ḥallah* applies to baked bread. The quantity of dough from which *ḥallah* must be taken is not explicitly stated in the Bible, and Shammai and Hillel already differed on the quantity (Eduy. 1:2). In later generations, however, the quantity was fixed, based on the words "Of the first of your dough," which was taken to mean "as much as your dough was," viz, "the dough of the wilderness." How much was this? It is written (Ex. 16:36): "Now an *omer* is the tenth part of an *ephah*" (Er. 83a–b). It was accordingly laid down that dough is liable for *ḥallah* if it is kneaded from a bulk of at least 43⅕ medium-size eggs (approximately 1¾ kg.; Maim. Yad, Bikkurim 6:15; Sh. Ar., YD 324:1), and as a mnemonic the sages pointed out that the numerical value of the word *ḥallah* is 43. Since the Bible does not specify the amount of *ḥallah* to be given, according to the letter of the law even a single barley corn exempts the whole dough, but the sages fixed a quantity in accordance with the size of the whole dough: "a householder whose dough is usually small sets aside 1/24; a baker sets aside 1/48." According to biblical law the obligation to separate *ḥallah* applies only to Ereẓ Israel, and "even in Israel there is no Torah obligation except when all Israel [i.e., the majority] are there" (cf. Ket. 25a). So that the obligation of *ḥallah* should not be forgotten, however, the rabbis made it obligatory to separate it nowadays too, and even outside Ereẓ Israel.

Ḥallah is one of the 24 perquisites of the priest (cf. Ezek. 44:30): "in order that the priests, who are always occupied with Divine service, should live without any exertion" (*Sefer ha-Ḥinnukh*, no. 385). *Ḥallah* must be eaten by priests in a state of ritual purity; the commoner who eats it deliberately is liable to the penalty of **karet*, and if eaten inadvertently must pay its value plus an added fifth to the priest, in the same way as a commoner who eats **terumah*. Nowadays since the obligation to give *ḥallah* is rabbinic and the priests are unable to eat it because of ritual uncleanness, it is customary to set aside an olive's bulk from any dough liable for *ḥallah* and to burn it. The precept of *ḥallah* is the subject of a special tractate of the Mishnah in the order *Zera'im* that bears its name and the Jerusalem Talmud also has a *Gemara* to it. The word *ḥallah* is popularly employed for the special Sabbath loaves.

[Israel Burgansky]

Women and Ḥallah

Domestic bread production has always been a largely female task. From the early rabbinic period, "taking *ḥallah*" was considered one of three *mitzvot* (commandments), together with *hadlakah* (kindling Sabbath *candles) and **niddah*, which women were obligated to perform. These three commandments are known as the *ḤaNaH* mitzvot, an acronym of *Ḥallah, Niddah*, and *Hadlakat ha-Ner*, which, in a play on words also evokes Hannah, the mother of the biblical Samuel, considered a model of female piety. A number of midrashic sources declare that these obligations are female punishments or atonement for the disobedience of the first woman in the Garden of Eden and her responsibility for human mortality (e. g. ARN² 9, 42; Gen. R. 17:8; TJ, Shab. 2:6, 8b). According to the Mishnah (Shab. 2:6), women who neglect these commandments risk death in childbirth (also ARN² 42). Popular vernacular *teḥinnot* or **tkhines*, supplicatory prayers for women from the early modern period, offer positive interpretations of this tradition. *Tkhines* to be recited while separating *ḥallah* recalled the ancient bringing of tithes, thus making women participants in ancient Temple worship and invoking the messianic era when the Temple rites would be restored.

[Judith R. Baskin (2nd ed.)]

BIBLIOGRAPHY: IN THE BIBLE: D.Z. Hoffman, *Sefer Va-Yikra*, 1 (1953), 107; Ben-Yehuda, Millon, 2 (1960), 1559; K. Elliger, *Leviticus* (Ger., 1966), 46. POST-BIBLICAL: Mishnah, *Ḥallah*; Maim.,

Yad, Bikkurim, 5–8; Sh. Ar., YD 322–30; Epstein, Tanna'im, 269–75; Ḥ Albeck (ed.), Shishah Sidrei Mishnah, 1 (1958), 271–3. **ADD. BIBLIOGRAPHY:** J.R. Baskin, *Midrashic Women* (2002), 66–73; C. Meyers, "Having Their Space and Eating There Too: Bread Production and Female Power in Ancient Israelite Households," in: *Nashim*, 5 (2002), 14–44; C. Weissler, *Voices of the Matriarchs* (1998), 29–35, 68–75.

ḤALLAH (Heb. חַלָּה), the name of a tractate in the Mishnah, Tosefta, and Jerusalem Talmud dealing with portions that are to be removed from bread for the support of the priesthood. Although the original meanings of some key terms in Numbers 15:17–21, including *ḥallah* itself, are not entirely certain, the Jewish oral tradition interpreted the passage as a requirement to set aside a portion of the bread or dough to be consumed by the priests under conditions similar to the *terumah* that is taken from other produce, and which is commanded in similar phrasing. Nehemiah 10:38 demonstrates that the Torah's formula, "a portion for a gift unto the Lord," was understood as a stipulation that the *ḥallah* is directed to the priests, and is not a sacrificial offering.

An early tradition, attested in the Septuagint, rendered *arisoteikhem* in Numbers 15:20 as "your kneading troughs," implying that the obligation of *ḥallah* falls on the unbaked dough; however, the verse also makes reference to the "bread of the land," leading some early authorities (including Philo, Josephus, and Rabbi Akiva) to apply the precept to baked bread. The developed tannaitic *halakhah* determined that the *ḥallah* should initially be separated from the dough, but if one has not done so, the obligation remains in force after baking.

Out of the laconic and ambiguous biblical sources, the rabbinic treatises formulated an elaborate framework of precise rules and measures governing the separation of *ḥallah*. Several of the laws for *ḥallah* were derived through analogies with comparable areas of religious law, especially *terumah*. The definition of "bread" is equated with *five species of grain, employing the same criteria that apply to the leavened or unleavened bread for purposes of Passover, *eruv*, or vows. In most matters, the restrictions arising from *ḥallah's* sacred status are derived from those of standard *terumah*; i.e., it must be kept in a state of purity, and can be consumed only by priests and their household members when they themselves are in a state of purity. As with *terumah*, consumption of the *ḥallah* by a non-priest incurs a divinely executed death penalty or (if done inadvertently) restoration with an additional fifth. Also like *terumah*, *ḥallah* is not incumbent upon dough that is ownerless or that is part of the Torah's entitlement to the poor. The fact that the Torah introduces the precept with the words "When ye come into the land whither I bring you" was understood to imply that *ḥallah* is required only from bread from the Land of Israel; and the Mishnah discusses the halakhic borders of the land, instances where the grain crossed the borders during the process, etc.

The rabbis discuss several types of dough products whose function as bread is questionable or borderline. An ancient mishnah in *Eduyot* (1:2) records a disagreement between Shammai, Hillel, and the sages over the minimum quantity of dough that is subject to *ḥallah*. The Mishnah presupposes the view of the sages, as adapted by Rabbi Yosé: five quarter-*kavs*. Although it was understood that (as with *terumah*) the Torah stipulated no minimum proportion for the *ḥallah* vis à vis the whole loaf, the rabbis determined that it should be one twenty-fourth (or one twenty-eighth for professional bakers).

Because the bread was usually *ḥallah* by women in their homes, the sources dealing with *ḥallah* provide some valuable glimpses into the domestic lives of Jewish women in antiquity. From the halakhic discussions, we learn that they often prepared bread in shared facilities, about their state of dress during the process, about difficulties in maintaining the requisite purity standards during their menstrual periods and the stratagems that were adopted to avoid defilement (e.g., by working with amounts smaller than the legal minimum).

BIBLIOGRAPHY: J.N. Epstein, *Prolegomena ad Litteras Tannaiticas* (1957), 270–5; S. Krauss, *Kadmoniyyot ha-Talmud*, vol. 2, 1 (1929), 153–206; H.W. Guggenheimer, *The Jerusalem Talmud: First Order: Zeraim: Tractates Ma'aser Šeni, Hallah, 'Orlah, and Bikkurim: Edition, Translation, and Commentary*, Studia Judaica, ed. E.L. Ehrlich (2003).

[Stephen G. Wald (2nd ed.)]

HALLE, city in Germany. Although Jews may well have been present in Halle at the end of the 11th century, the first definite information on their settlement in the city comes from the second half of the 12th century. Then under the protection of the archbishop of Magdeburg, they were hated by the burghers: in 1206 their houses were burned or looted – some Jews were killed and the rest expelled from the city. However, in the mid-13th century there were again Jews in Halle, living in a special quarter, and mainly engaged in moneylending. in 1261, most of their property was confiscated by the archbishop, serving as a cause for a two-year war between the archbishop and the burghers. During persecutions accompanying the *Black Death (1350) the community was destroyed, but in the 14th and 15th centuries Jews returned once more to Halle. The renewed community existed until 1493, when the expulsion of the Jews was decreed. It possessed both a synagogue and a *mikveh*, and a cemetery existed long before 1350. Toward the end of the 17th century the elector of Brandenburg allowed several Jews to settle in Halle, to the dismay of the burghers. In 1693 a Jewish cemetery was officially designated and a synagogue dedicated in 1700. The government recognized the community in 1704. About 1708 a Hebrew printing press was set up in Halle by J.H. Michaelis, for whom the wandering proselyte printer Moses b. Abraham and his son Israel (of Amsterdam) printed a Hebrew Bible (1720). With the help of generous patrons, in 1709 Moses himself began to print some Talmud tractates.

The number of Jews in Halle increased from 12 families in 1700 to 50 in the middle of the 18th century. They were emancipated in 1808 and the community, numbering 150 persons, was given a constitution. In 1840 there were 167 members of the community, 443 in 1864, 660 in 1900, 1,902 in 1920, and 1,300 in 1933 (0.5% of the total population). The April 7, 1933, expulsion of Jews from the civil service resulted in the dismissal of 6 Jewish professors, 13 lawyers, and 41 Jews in public service. Zionist activities increased. After the Nazi rise to power; they won 4 of 10 seats on the community council. On Nov. 10, 1938, the synagogue and communal center were demolished. Two hundred men were arrested and sent to *Buchenwald; three of them lost their lives. In all, 584 Jews emigrated; 17 committed suicide. The rest were concentrated in "Jew houses" and used for forced labor. In 1942, 262 Jews were deported to the East; only 43 survived. On July 1, 1944, 92 were still living there protected by their non-Jewish spouses. The community was renewed after World War II and numbered 50 in 1966 (.02% of the population). A new synagogue was consecrated in 1953. Between 1953 and 1962 Halle was the seat of the Association of Jewish Communities in the GDR. After 1990 the membership, which had fallen to just five in 1989, increased due to the immigration of Jews from the former Soviet Union. In 2004 it numbered 731. In 1996 a liberal Jewish community was founded in Halle. It numbered 32 in 1996 and 200 in 2005. It is a member of the Union of Progressive Jews in Germany.

BIBLIOGRAPHY: Germ Jud, 1 (1963), 124–30, 508–12; 2 (1968), 319–22; S. Neufeld, *Die Halleschen Juden im Mittelalter* (1915); S. Schultze-Gallera, *Die Juden zu Halle im Mittelalter…* (1922); G. Kisch, in: *Sachsen und Anhalt; Jahrbuch der historischen Kommission fuer die Provinz Sachsen und fuer Anhalt*, 4 (1928), 132–66; 5 (1929), 332–46; 6 (1930), 306–36; idem, in: ZGJD, 2 (1930), 166–8; Ḥ.D. Friedberg, *Toledot ha-Defus ha-Ivri…* (1937), 74–75; T. Tykocinski, in: MGWJ, 57 (1908), 32–43; S. Stern, *Der preussische Staat und die Juden*, 1 (1962), index; 2 (1962), no. 513–67. **ADD. BIBLIOGRAPHY:** C. Zimmermann, "Juden im Wirtschaftleben der Stadt Halle im 19. und 20. Jahrhundert," in: *Menora. Jahrbuch fuer deutsch-juedische Geschichte* (2000), 369–376; V. Dietzel (ed.), *300 Jahre Juden in Halle. Leben, Leistung, Leiden, Lohn* (1992; Dokumente und Beitraege, vol. 1); S. Spector (ed.), *The Encyclopedia of Jewish Life Before and During the Holocaust* (2001).

[Zvi Avneri / Michael Berenbaum and Larissa Daemmig (2nd ed.)]

HALLE, MORRIS (**Pinkowitz**; 1923–), U.S. linguist. Born in Liepaja, Latvia, Halle was educated in American universities, receiving his M.A. in linguistics from the University of Chicago in 1948 and his Ph.D. from Harvard in 1955. He began his teaching career as an instructor of Russian at North Park College, Chicago. Thereafter he lectured at Chicago and at Harvard. In 1951 he joined the faculty of the Massachusetts Institute of Technology, where he became professor of modern languages in 1961. In the same year, he founded the university's doctoral program in linguistics. Halle taught linguistics, phonology, morphology, phonetics, and Slavic languages. Over the years he held positions at MIT ranging from assistant professor and department head to institute professor. He retired from MIT in 1996 and became institute professor emeritus.

Halle was renowned for his research in linguistic science. Russian, Slavic, and English were the languages most often involved in his linguistic studies. He also focused on the linguistic aspects of Swedish, Arabic, German, Polish, Old and American English, the dialects of southern Russia, and – in one case – Hebrew ("The Term *Canaan* in Medieval Hebrew," by R. Jakobson and M. Halle, in *For Max Weinreich on his 70th Birthday* (1964), pages 147–172). Halle noted the implications of the computer for linguistics, and co-authored "On the Recognition of Speech by Machine" (in *Proceedings of the International Conference on Information Processing 1959* (1960), 252–6). He received recognition for his book *The Sound Pattern of Russian* (1959), and for two books he co-authored, *The Sound Pattern of English* (with N. Chomsky, 1968) and *Preliminaries to Speech Analysis* (1952, 5th repr. 1963).

Regarded by many as the father of the modern study of speech sounds (phonological and phonetic theory), Halle also wrote *Fundamentals of Language* (with R. Jakobson, 1956), *English Stress* (with S. Keyser, 1971), *Problem Book in Phonology* (with G. Clements, 1983), *Language Sound and Structure* (1984), *Handbook of Phonological Theory* (with W. Idsardi, 1994), and *From Memory to Speech and Back* (2002). He edited, among other books, *Roman Jakobson: What He Taught Us* (1983).

Halle served as vice president of the Linguistic Society of America in 1973 and as president in 1974. For decades he was a member of the Linguistic Society of America, a fellow of the American Academy of Arts and Sciences, and a member of the National Academy of Sciences.

[Ruth Beloff (2nd ed.)]

HALLEGUA, family of White Jews in *Cochin. Originally from Aleppo, Syria, the family provided communal leaders from the 17th century until the present day. One of the first recorded members was MOSES HALLEGUA (Aleguo), whose tombstone is dated 1666. The title and office of the *mudaliar* (head of the autonomous Jewish community in Cochin) fell to the Hallegua family when this hereditary position became vacant. When Anquetil-Duperron visited Cochin in 1757, JOSEPH HALLEGUA held the office. ḤAYYIM JOSEPH HALLEGUA, who moved to Bombay, was instrumental in publishing in 1846 the Marathi translation of the Passover *Haggadah* of the *Bene Israel.

BIBLIOGRAPHY: J.H. Lord, *Jews in India* (1907), 97; Fischel, in: *Herzl Yearbook*, 4 (1961–62), 316–8; J.J. Cotton, *List of Inscriptions… in Madras* (1905), 274, no. 1550. **ADD. BIBLIOGRAPHY:** J.B. Segal, *A History of the Jews of Cochin* (1993).

[Walter Joseph Fischel]

HALLEL (Heb. הַלֵּל), the general term designating Psalms 113–118 when these form a unit in the liturgy. These psalms are essentially expressions of thanksgiving and joy for divine redemption. *Hallel* is recited in two forms: (a) The "full" *Hallel*, consisting of Psalms 113–118. It is chanted in the synagogue on *Sukkot, *Ḥanukkah, the first day of *Passover (the first two days in the Diaspora), *Shavuot (Tosef., Suk. 3:2, Ta'an. 28b), and (in many synagogues) *Israel Independence Day. *Hallel* is also recited during the Passover *seder service (Tosef., Suk. 3:2), when it is known as *Hallel Mizri* ("Egyptian *Hallel*") because of the exodus from Egypt which the *seder* commemorates (Ber. 56a; cf. Rashi ad loc.). On this occasion it is recited in two parts (Pes. 10:5–7; Maim. Yad, Ḥamez u-Mazzah 8:5). (b) The "half" *Hallel*, consisting of the "full" *Hallel*, excepting Psalms 115:1–11, and 116:1–11. According to the Yemenite rite, the order is slightly different, based on Maimonides (Yad, Ḥanukkah 3:8). It is recited in the synagogue on the *New Moon (Ta'an. 28b; but see also Ar. 10a–b) and on the last six days of Passover (Ar. 10b).

The term *Hallel ha-Gadol* ("Great *Hallel*") refers only to Psalm 136 (Tosef. Ta'an. 3:5) which is recited during *Pesukei de-Zimra at the morning service on Sabbaths and on festivals (Tos. to Ta'an 26a). It is the daily psalm on the last day of Passover (Sof. 18:2), and is added to the *seder Hallel* (Pes. 118a; TJ, Pes. 5:7, 32c). According to the Mishnah (Ta'an 3:9), this psalm was sung on joyous communal occasions, e.g., the long-awaited rain after a period of severe drought.

In the Talmud, various origins are attributed to the custom of chanting *Hallel*. R. Eleazar claims that it was Moses and the people of Israel who first recited *Hallel*; R. Judah states that it was the Prophets who instituted its recitation for every occasion that the people of Israel should be redeemed from potential misfortune (Pes. 117a). The Talmud relates that *Hallel* was recited by the levites in the Temple (Tos. to Pes. 95b), and it was also chanted on Passover eve while the paschal lambs were being slaughtered (Pes. 5:7). *Hallel* became part of the synagogue service at an early stage, and in talmudic times, communities in Erez Israel added it to the end of the evening service for Passover (TJ, Pes. 10:1, 37c). This practice later spread to the Diaspora (Sof. 20:9), and is still the custom among Oriental Jews and Ḥasidim (Sh. Ar., OḤ 487:4; but see Isserles ad loc.) and in most synagogues in Israel.

Hallel is recited on all major biblical festivals, with the exception of *Rosh ha-Shanah and the Day of Atonement; the solemnity of those occasions, when each mortal's destiny and fate is being decided, is deemed unsuitable for psalms of joy (Ar. 10b). Similar considerations caused these psalms to be omitted in a house of mourning on the New Moon and Ḥanukkah (Magen Avraham to Sh. Ar., OḤ 131:4). *Hallel* is not recited on *Purim, since the scroll of Esther is considered the festival's *Hallel* (Ar. 10b; Meg. 14a). One rabbinic tradition is that only the "half" *Hallel* is recited on the last six days of Passover because joy is mitigated by the calamity that then befell the Egyptian host when pursuing the Israelites (see Meg. 10b); another reason given is because no different sacrifice was offered each day (At. 10b). On Sukkot the *lulav* is waved during the refrains of Psalm 118:1–4, 25, and 29 (Suk. 3:9). *Hallel* may be recited at any time during the day (Meg. 2:5), although in the synagogue it is recited immediately after the morning service (RH 4:7). Special benedictions are recited before and after *Hallel* except at the *seder* service when no benediction is recited before it.

There is a difference of opinion among the early authorities as to whether the obligation to recite the *Hallel* is to be considered biblical or rabbinical (see *Sefer Mitzvot Katan* 146, *Yere'im ha-Shalem* 262; Maim. Yad, Ḥanukkah 3:6; *Sefer ha-Mitzvot*, ch. 1). The recitation on the New Moon is considered to be a custom (Ta'an. 28b), and there are some opinions that it is only recited in congregational prayers on that day. Similarly there are authorities who ruled that for the full *Hallel* the benediction should read "Blessed art Thou… who hast commanded us to finish (*ligmor*) the Hallel" instead of the customary "to read (*likro*) the Hallel." According to the *tosafot* (Sot. 32a, s.v. *Keri'at Shema*), *Hallel* may be recited in any language (see also Tosef., Sot. 7:7). It should be read standing (*Shibbolei ha-Leket* 173; Sh. Ar., OḤ 322:7), except at the *seder* service. Various traditions are related to the manner in which the *Hallel* is chanted. In some communities, it was sung antiphonally (Tosef., Sot. 6:2); in others (as is still the practice among Yemenite Jews) the congregation responded with *hallelujah* after each half of a verse (Suk. 3:10; TJ, Shab. 16:1, 16c). Among Ashkenazi Jews, it is customary to repeat Psalm 118:1, 21–29 (see Suk. 3:10 and 39a). Opinions and customs differ regarding the recital of Hallel on Israel Independence Day.

For musical rendition see *Psalms.

BIBLIOGRAPHY: Abrahams, Companion, 184ff.; Zeitlin, in: JQR, 53 (1962/63), 22–29; Finkelstein, in: HUCA, 23 (1950–51), part 2, 319–37; E. Levy, *Yesodot ha-Tefillah* (1952[2]), 209–13; ET, 9 (1959), 390–432; Idelsohn, Liturgy, 134, 158–9.

HALLELUJAH (Heb. הַלְלוּיָהּ), liturgical expression occurring 23 times, exclusively in the Book of Psalms. Apart from 135:3, it invariably appears as either the opening (106, 111–3, 135, 146–50) or closing word of a psalm (104–6, 113, 115–7, 135, 146–50) or in both positions (106, 113, 135, 146–50). In all cases, with the exception of 135:3 and 147:1, the term is not part of the body of the psalm. This fact, together with its total nonappearance in those psalms cited in other biblical books (cf. Ps. 106:48 with I Chron. 16:36) and its restriction to the last divisions of the Psalter (cf. Ber. 9b), suggest a late coinage.

It is generally agreed that Hallelujah means, "praise [ye] the Lord." The plural imperative form of the verb would indicate that the term was a directive to the worshiping congregation in the Temple by the presiding functionary which was meant to evoke a public response. In the course of time it became an independent cultic exclamation so that the Greek-speaking Jews simply transliterated it (70, Ἀλληούϊα). On the other hand, a consciousness of its composite nature is preserved in amoraic discussions as to whether the Hebrew should be rendered by the scribes as one word or two. (Pes. 117a; Sof. 5:10, TJ, Suk. 3:12, 53d;TJ, Meg. 1:11, 72a). A novel explanation is given by Joshua b. Levi who regards the final syllable as a superlative suffix and who translates the term, "praise Him with many praises" (Pes. 117a).

[Nahum M. Sarna]

In Music.

The tradition of rendering the word Hallelujah at the beginning and/or end of a psalm, by a special melodic phrase is certainly very old, judging by its survival in the usages of many Jewish communities. In some of them, the word is even added at the end of each verse on some occasions. The Yemenites prefix "Hallelujah" or "Ve-Hallelujah" to certain frestive *piyyutim*, which are therefore called *Halleluyot.* Christian tradition attests the practice of "Hallelujah-singing" from the earliest periods, especially in a form which may or may not have been taken over from Jewish practice: songs on the single word, in which the "lu" and "jah" syllables were drawn out as long flourishes, until they became the so-called *Jubilus* – a wordless ecstatic outpouring. In the Middle Ages these long Hallelujahs began to serve as the basis, in the lower or middle voice, of elaborate compositions in which the upper voices uttered a poetic expression of praise. Sometimes the word itself was split – as in the 13th-century three-voiced "*Alle*-psallite-cum-*luja*" (see A.T. Davison and W. Apel (eds.). *Historical Anthology of Music*, I (19642), 35). During the Renaissance and Baroque periods the *Jubilus*-like setting of the word *Alleluia* is found again, of course in the form of elaborate polyphonic compositions. The word also became a favorite vehicle for canons. The tradition continues until today, for example: the "Hallelujah chorus" in Handel's *Messiah,* Mozart's *Alleluja* for soprano and orchestra (actually the second part of his motet *Exsultate, jubilate*, K. 165), and the great *Alleluja* pieces in William Walton's *Belshazzar's Feast* (1929–31) and Arthur Honegger's *Le Roi David* (1921).

[Bathja Bayer]

BIBLIOGRAPHY: IN MUSIC: G. Reese, *Music in the Middle Ages* (1940), index, s.v. *Alleluia;* B. Staeblein, in: MGG 1 (1949), 331–50; E. Gerson-Kiwi, in: *Festschrift Heinrich Besseler* (1961), 43–49 (Eng).

HALLER'S ARMY (**"Blue Army"**), force of Polish volunteers organized in France during the last year of World War I, responsible for the murder of Jews and anti-Jewish pogroms in Galicia and the Ukraine. The group was organized on the initiative of the Polish National Council (KNP), achieved French recognition in June 1917, and with the appearance in Paris in July 1918 of General Józef Haller (1873–1960) known for his struggles for Polish freedom within the framework of the Polish legions, command was transferred to him. The political direction lent by the National Council in Paris, headed by Roman *Dmowski, gave the group an extreme nationalistic character. The army had about 50,000 men who moved to the southeast front in Poland during the months of April, May, and June 1919. The addition of Haller's substantial forces to the regular Polish army enabled the Poles to conquer eastern Galicia. Foreign officers and the ties with France kept Haller's forces independent of the official Polish command, a fact exploited by Haller's soldiers (called the "Hallerczycy") for undisciplined and unbridled excesses against Jewish communities in Galicia. Attacks on individual Jews on the streets and highways, murderous pogroms on Jewish settlements, and deliberate provocative acts became commonplace. While these may have been on the initiative of individual soldiers, they were known to their officers, if not openly supported by them. In 1920, during the Polish offensive toward Kiev resulting from the Pilsudski-Petlyura alliance, anti-Jewish pogroms occurred in the region.

Haller, who was a member of the Sejm (parliament) in 1922–23, became a member of the Polish government-in-exile during World War II.

BIBLIOGRAPHY: A. Micewski, *Z geografii… politycznej II Rzeczypospolitej* (1964), index. **ADD. BIBLIOGRAPHY:** J. Majchrowski (ed.), *Kto byl kim w drugiej Rzeczypospolitej* (1994), 125; A. Ajnenkiel, *Polska po przewrocie Majowym* (1980), index.

[Moshe Landau]

HALLGARTEN, family of U.S. bankers. LAZARUS HALLGARTEN (d. 1875), a native of Frankfurt, Germany, arrived in New York in 1848 and in 1850 opened an office for exchanging immigrants' currency. By establishing connections with Frankfurt and other European banking centers, he and his partners developed a successful foreign exchange business. During the 1860s the firm became prominent as one of the largest gold bullion dealers in the United States. For its role on "Black Friday" (September 24, 1869) in stabilizing the price of gold that had been skyrocketed by the speculations of Jay Gould, the firm received official recognition by the United States Treasury. During the latter part of the 19th century the firm was engaged in the reorganization of the country's major railroads, and expanded its trading in bonds and stocks. In 1881 it became a member of the New York Stock Exchange. Meanwhile, Lazarus' sons CHARLES (1838–1908) and JULIUS (d. 1884) had joined the firm, and the financing of industrial combines became a major field for Hallgarten & Co. World War I saw an intensification of the firm's domestic business, and between the two world wars the firm acted as fiscal agents for many foreign governments, and established offices and representations in almost all the European financial centers. With the passing of the 1934 Securities and Exchange Act it limited itself to underwriting and general brokerage business. As late as 1950 the majority of the firm's active members were direct descendants of a partner of Lazarus Hallgarten. Most of the Hallgartens were interested in community activities as well as in the arts. Lazarus' son, Charles, who moved to Frankfurt and conducted the firm's banking affairs there, was especially active in philanthropic work. He held a leading position in the *Alliance Israélite Universelle, the Hilfsverein der Deutschen Juden, and the Jewish Colonization Association, and helped to organize efforts for the relief and emigration of the Jewish victims of the Russian pogroms. He was the founder of the Gesellschaft zur Erforschung Juedischer Kunstdenkmaeler (Society for Research of Monuments of Jewish Art). He also helped to found an association for public education and a legal aid office for women.

BIBLIOGRAPHY: R. Hallgarten, *Charles L. Hallgarten* (Ger., 1915); *Reden gehalten bei der Beerdigung des Herrn Charles L. Hall-*

garten (1908); W. Emrich, *Bildnisse Frankfurter Demokraten* (1956), 22–25; NDB, 7 (1966).

[Joachim O. Ronall]

HALLO, RUDOLF (1896–1933), German art historian, friend and successor of Franz Rosenzweig as head of the Freies Juedisches Lehrhaus in Frankfurt. Hallo was born in Kassel to a prominent family of court Jews and artisans, which included Israel Aron Hammerschlag of Prague and his grandson and namesake, who was made a Court Jew in 1657 by Frederick William of Brandenburg. The family tradition of painting, gilding, and synagogue decoration began in 1816, when Simon Hallo became an apprentice housepainter, the medieval painters' guild having opened to Jews in the wake of the Emancipation. The firm Gebrueder Hallo was founded in 1891 and moved to Tel Aviv in 1935.

Trained in classical art at the University of Goettingen, Rudolf Hallo contributed significantly to the founding of Jewish art history as a discipline and also wrote on biblical and archaeological subjects. His interest in art history, especially Jewish and Hessian provincial art and handiwork, carried on the family tradition on an academic level.

Franz Rosenzweig was the son of his mother's closest friend. Hallo married Gertrude Rubensohn, also a friend of Rosenzweig and one of his circle (see Rosenzweig's *Briefe*, 285, 288). Upon his incapacitation Rosenzweig designated Hallo to succeed him as head of the Lehrhaus (*Briefe*, 354). Because of differences between the two men concerning educational policy, which stemmed from deeper disagreements in philosophical outlook (cf. *Briefe*, 364, 365), Hallo resigned at the end of the summer trimester of 1923 (Briefe, 373). He returned to his native Kassel, and there became curator at a state museum, where he created a department of Jewish art. He continued writing and lecturing. Among Hallo's works are *Juedische Kunst aus Hessen und Nassau* (1933), *Juedische Volkskunst in Hessen* (1928), *Rudolph Erich Raspe* (1934, posthumously), *Geschichte der juedischen Gemeinde Kassel* (1931), and *Judaica* (1932, separate printing from *Religioese Kunst aus Hessen und Nassau*).

His son, WILLIAM W. HALLO, Assyriologist, was born in Kassel in 1928. He immigrated to the United States in 1940. Hallo taught Bible and Semitic languages at Hebrew Union College in Cincinnati (1956–62), and from 1962 taught Assyriology at Yale University, serving as curator of the Babylonian collection there. He published extensively on ancient Near Eastern and biblical subjects.

ADD. BIBLIOGRAPHY: G. Schweikhart (ed.), *Rudolf Hallo. Schriften zur Kunstgeschichte Kassel. Sammlungen Denkmaeler Judaica* (1983).

[Joel Kraemer]

HALLO, WILLIAM (1928–), Assyriologist and Bible scholar. Hallo was born into a prominent Jewish family in Kassel, Germany. His father Rudolf *Hallo was one of the founders of the discipline of Jewish art history, and successor to Franz *Rosenzweig at the Franfurt Lehrhaus. His mother was Dr. Gertrude Rubensohn Hallo. William Hallo and his sisters were among a group of Jewish children who were sent out of Nazi Germany and other Nazi-held areas in 1939 to England as part of the *Kindertransport* program. Rejoined by their mother (his father had died in 1933), Hallo and his sisters came to the United States in 1940. He earned his B.A. at Harvard in 1950 and spent 1950–51 at Leiden University, Netherlands, on a Fulbright scholarship studying the languages of ancient Mesopotamia with F.R. Kraus, among others. He came to the Oriental Institute of the University of Chicago, where he earned his Ph.D. in 1955 under Ignace *Gelb. He was also an assistant to Benno *Landsberger. Between 1956 and 1962, Hallo taught at Hebrew Union College in Cincinnati. He left for Yale in 1962, where he was appointed curator of the Yale Babylonian Collection and professor of Assyriology, and spent the next 40 years at Yale. Within Assyriology, Hallo specialized in Sumerian literature, history, and language. Applying his work in Assyriology to biblical studies, Hallo pioneered in a "contextual" approach that shows the importance of comparing and contrasting the respective literatures. With K.L. Younger, Hallo edited the three-volume *The Context of Scripture* (1997–2002), a collection of ancient Near Eastern documents. A highly prolific professional scholar, Hallo brought some of the results of his scholarship before larger audiences through his contributions to the Torah Commentaries published by the Reform movement. He also translated Rosenzweig's *Star of Redemption* (1990).

BIBLIOGRAPHY: S.D. Sperling, *Students of the Covenant* (1992), 90–92; D. Weisberg, in: M. Cohen et al. (eds.), *The Tablet and the Scroll … Studies Hallo* (1993), 9–10; L. Pearce, bibliography of Hallo's publications, ibid., 11–16; W. Hallo, in: *Vergegenwärtigen des zerstoerten juedischen Erbes* (1997), 147–57.

[S. David Sperling (2nd ed.)]

HALMI, ROBERT (1924–), U.S. executive producer. The legendary and prolific television producer Robert Halmi was born in Budapest, Hungary, the son of a playwright and a photographer. In 1944, he joined the Hungarian Resistance to hold off the Nazis in Poland. He was captured and sentenced to death but released when the Russians liberated Poland in 1945. In 1952 he emigrated to the U.S. and became a writer-photographer for *Life* magazine, specializing in exotic and dangerous places. His exploits included being stranded for three days on an Alaskan glacier, spending three months with a tribe of African pygmies, and flying hot-air balloons professionally. Halmi's film career began in 1962 when he started producing documentaries on outdoor subjects. By the mid-1970s Halmi had crossed over to producing feature films but he soon shifted his attention to television. He quickly established himself as the king of the mini-series, producing lavish, star-studded productions of classics. Halmi's credits include *Svengali* (1983), *Gulliver's Travels* (1996 Emmy Award), *20,000 Leagues Under The Sea* (1997), *The Odyssey* (1997), *Robinson Crusoe* (1997), *Moby Dick* (1998), *Merlin* (1998) and perhaps his most acclaimed achievement, *Lonesome Dove* (1989), which received seven Emmy Awards. In 1994 Hallmark Entertainment purchased Halmi's production company, RHI Entertainment, and promoted Halmi to chairman of the board. He went on to work with his son, Robert Halmi, Jr., who became president and CEO of Hallmark. Halmi, Sr. continued to produce two or more projects a season, such as *Animal Farm* (1999), *The Lion in Winter* (2003), and *The Five People You Meet in Heaven* (2004).

[Max Joseph (2nd ed.)]

HALPER, ALBERT (1904–1984), U.S. novelist. His first novel, *Union Square* (1933), on a radical theme, was an immediate success. His experiences in a mail order house in his native Chicago and in the Chicago central post office found expression in his novels *The Chute* (1937), *The Little People* (1942), and *The Golden Watch* (1953), a story of a West Side Chicago Jewish family. *The Chute* showed Halper in retreat from the Jewishness of his immigrant parents, presenting a wholly negative picture of American Jewish life. In *Sons of the Fathers* (1940), however, he portrayed Jewish customs and ceremonies with objectivity and even sympathy. *Atlantic Avenue* (1956) is a story of violence in New York City. He recounted his struggle as a writer in *Good-bye, Union Square, A Writer's Memoir of the Thirties* (1970).

BIBLIOGRAPHY: F. Champney, in: *Antioch Review*, 2 (1942), 628–34; S. Liptzin, *Jew in American Literature* (1966), 183–6. **ADD. BIBLIOGRAPHY:** J. Hart, *Albert Halper* (1980).

[Sol Liptzin]

HALPER, BENZION (1884–1924), Hebraist, Arabist, and editor. Halper was born in Zhosli (Zasliai), Lithuania. He emigrated to Germany and from there to England. In 1907 he began studying Semitics at the University of London. While at the university he also studied at Jews' College. In 1910 he spent a year in Egypt under university auspices. During this period he contributed regularly to the Hebrew periodical *Ha-Yehudi*. In 1911 Halper went to New York and worked as classifier and copyist of *genizah* fragments in the library of the Jewish Theological Seminary of America. In 1912 he became a Fellow at Dropsie College in Philadelphia, and from 1913 taught there in the departments of rabbinics and cognate (Semitic) languages. In 1923 he was advanced to the rank of associate professor of cognate languages. He also served the college as custodian of manuscripts. From 1916 to 1924 Halper was editor of the Jewish Publication Society of America.

Among the *genizah* fragments brought to Dropsie College by Cyrus Adler, Halper discovered a portion of *Sefer ha-Mitzvot* ("Book of Precepts") by the 10th-century halakhist and philosopher *Ḥefeẓ b. Yaẓli'aḥ. He translated it into Hebrew and published both the original Arabic text and the translation with an introduction and critical notes as *The Book of Precepts* (1915). His scholarly and at the same time popular anthology, *Post-Biblical Hebrew Literature* (Hebrew and English, 2 vols., 1921), presented some previously unpublished texts as well as critical notes and a glossary. Under the title *Shirat Yisrael* (1924), he published an edition and Hebrew translation of *Kitab al-Muḥadara wal-Mudhakara* (Book of Discussions and Remembrances) by the 12th-century Hebrew poet, Moses *Ibn Ezra, dealing with Hebrew prosody and, more generally, with Jewish life and literature. Halper's last important work was the *Descriptive Catalogue of Geniza Fragments in Philadelphia* (1924), which identifies and describes in detail nearly 500 fragments. Halper's first major essay, entitled "The Participle Formations of Geminate Verbs" (in ZAW, 30 (1910), 42–57, 99–126, 201–28), discussed Hebrew roots from אבב to תפץ. His major studies included "The Scansion of Medieval Hebrew Poetry" (in JQR, 4 (1914), 153–224), "An Autograph Responsum of Maimonides" (*ibid.*, 6 (1916), 225–9), "A Dirge on the Death of Daniel Gaon" (*ibid.*, 10 (1920), 411–20), and analyses of *genizah* discoveries and Jewish literature in Arabic (in *Ha-Tekufah*, 1923, 1924, 1928).

BIBLIOGRAPHY: C. Adler, in: AJYB, 26 (1924), 459–71; J.N. Simchoni, in: *Ha-Tekufah*, 23 (1927), 490–500; I.M. Elbogen, *ibid.*, 24 (1928), 541–2.

[Meir Ben-Horin]

HALPERIN, HAIM (1895–1973), agronomist. Halperin was born in Russia and studied agriculture at the University of Kharkov, immigrating to Ereẓ Israel in 1924. He was a delegate to several Zionist congresses and founded the Ruppin Agricultural College and the Israel Agricultural Bank. On the foundation of the State he was appointed the first director-general of the Ministry of Agriculture. He was professor of agricultural economics at the Hebrew University and was for a time dean of the faculty. His *Agrendum* was translated into Japanese, among other languages. Halperin was the husband of Beba *Idelson. He was awarded the Israel Prize in 1973 and died shortly after.

HALPERIN, YEḤIEL (1880–1942), Hebrew educator. Born in Priluki, Ukraine, Halperin taught in Y. Adler's "progressive *ḥeder*" in Gomel and later in S.L. *Gordon's in Warsaw. In 1909 he established the first Hebrew kindergarten in Warsaw, and, in 1910, a Hebrew seminary for kindergarten teachers. At the outbreak of World War I (1914) Halperin moved to Odessa where he established a similar seminary. Emigrating to Palestine in 1920, he served as a supervisor of Hebrew kindergartens from 1922 to 1925, and was appointed head of the Kindergarten Department of the Lewinsky Teachers' Seminary in Tel Aviv (1926). In 1936 he founded a special college for kindergarten teaching in Tel Aviv, which continued to function until 1941. Halperin published a journal devoted to the Hebrew kindergarten, *Ha-Ginnah* (in Odessa, from 1918; then in Jerusalem from 1922). His collected works were published in three volumes: *Shi'urim be-Torat Ḥinnukh ha-Tinokot* (1944): *Be-Keren Zavit* (1945), kindergarten play songs; and *Mah Sipper Yare'aḥ Li* (1952), eight legends. His sons were the poet Yonathan *Ratosh and the philologist Uzzi Ornan.

BIBLIOGRAPHY: Epstein, in: *Hed ha-Ḥinnukh*, 17 (1943), 59–62; 1. Gruenbaum, *Penei ha-Dor*, 1 (1957), 316–9; Spivak, in: D. Levin (ed.), *Al ha-Rishonim* (1959), 63–68.

[Gedalyah Elkoshi]

HALPERN, BENJAMIN (Ben, 1912–1990), U.S. sociologist, educator, and Zionist. Halpern, who was born in Boston, Massachusetts, was active in the Zionist movement and Jewish affairs from his youth. He served as national secretary of the He-Ḥalutz Organization of America (1936–37), managing editor of the *Jewish Frontier* magazine (1943–49), and associate director of the departments of culture, education, and publications of the Jewish Agency (1949–56). In 1956 Halpern became research associate in Middle Eastern studies at Harvard University. He began his association with Brandeis University in 1962 and was subsequently appointed professor of Near Eastern studies there, retiring in 1981. He was a member of the Jewish Agency Executive from 1968 to 1972. Halpern's scholarly work was closely associated with his Jewish and Labor Zionist commitments and interests. His numerous publications, many of which were published in *Jewish Frontier* and *Midstream* magazines, deal chiefly with problems of Zionism, Israeli society, and the role of the Jews in U.S. society. In his *The American Jew: A Zionist Analysis* (1956), which deals with both the implications and realities of assimilation and differences and similarities between U.S. Jews and other Jewish communities, Halpern contends that Jews will never be completely accepted into U.S. life as long as they remain Jews. Halpern's most important book is *The Idea of the Jewish State* (1969[2]), which traces the development of Zionism both as an ideology and a movement. He also wrote *Clash of Heroes: Brandeis, Weizmann, and American Zionism* (1987).

[Werner J. Cahnman]

HALPERN, GEORG GAD (1878–1962), economist and leading figure in the economic activities of the Zionist Organization. Born in Pinsk, Halpern studied economics in Germany (his doctoral dissertation was entitled *Die juedischen Arbeiter in London*, 1903). He became active in Zionist affairs in his youth and, beginning in 1903, he attended all Zionist Congresses. During the period of the *Democratic Fraction, he became a close associate of Chaim Weizmann and throughout the years served as an adviser for and administrator of the financial affairs and economic institutions of the Zionist Organization. He also wrote on economic affairs for the German press and was the director of an oil company. From 1921 to 1928 he was a director of the *Jewish Colonial Trust in London. Halpern was the moving force behind various economic institutions sponsored by the Zionist Organization: the Anglo-Palestine Bank, the Palestine Electric Corporation, *Keren Hayesod, the Land Development Co., etc. He settled in Palestine in 1933, founded the Migdal Insurance Co. (1934), and was a member of the board of Bank Leumi.

BIBLIOGRAPHY: Tidhar, 10 (1959), 3613; *Sefer Pinsk* (1966), 508–9.

[Getzel Kressel]

HALPERN, HARRY (1899–1981), U.S. Conservative rabbi. Halpern was born in New York City and earned his B.A. at City College (1919) and his Orthodox ordination from Yeshiva University's Rabbi Yitzhak Elchanan Theological Seminary (1922). While serving as rabbi of the Jewish Communal Center of Flatbush (1922–29), he earned his L.L.B. (1925) and J.D. from Brooklyn Law School (1926). He was ordained a second time, in 1929, at the *Jewish Theological Seminary, where he earned a D.H.L. in 1951. That year, he became rabbi of the East Midwood Jewish Center, one of the largest synagogue-centers in Brooklyn, where he was to spend his entire 48-year career. An early champion of intensive Jewish day school education, he founded the Rabbi Harry Halpern Day School, housed in his congregation's building, and was a guiding force behind the expansion of the Yeshivah of Flatbush, chairing its Board of Education. He was also president of the Brooklyn region of the *Zionist Organization of America (1947–49) and a member of its National Executive (1954–56).

Halpern rose to the highest positions of rabbinic leadership in metropolitan New York and nationally. He was a director of the Rabbinic Cabinet of the United Jewish Appeal of Greater New York, a founder and life trustee of the Commission on Synagogue Relations of the Federation of Jewish Philanthropies, and president of the New York Board of Rabbis (1961). He also served on the executive committee of the New York Division of the National Conference of Christians and Jews and was instrumental in organizing the Metropolitan New York Region of the *Rabbinical Assembly. His efforts led to his election as national president of the RA (1945–6), where he revived the quarterly *Conservative Judaism*, oversaw the publication of the Rabbinical Assembly *ketubbah* (as amended by Saul *Lieberman), and established a Committee on Tenure and Related Matters. His ambitious attempt at establishing a national *bet din* together with the Orthodox Rabbinical Council of America was rebuffed, however. Upon leaving office, Halpern became an activist chairman of the Joint Commission on Social Action of the Rabbinical Assembly and the United Synagogue (1956–61), lobbying against federal aid to private and parochial schools.

Halpern remained deeply connected with the Jewish Theological Seminary, as chairman of the Rabbinic Cabinet (1951–53), co-chairman of the Seminary Planning Commission, and a member of the Seminary's Board of Directors (1951–53). One of the founders of the institution's pastoral counseling program, he taught pastoral psychology and homiletics at the Seminary. In 1974, Halpern published *From Where I Stand*, a collection of columns he had written for the synagogue bulletin.

BIBLIOGRAPHY: P.S. Nadell, *Conservative Judaism in America: A Biographical Dictionary and Sourcebook* (1988).

[Bezalel Gordon (2nd ed.)]

HALPERN (Halperin), ISRAEL (1910–1971), Israel historian. Halpern was born in Bialystok, Poland, emigrated to Ereẓ Israel in 1934, began his teaching career at the Hebrew University in 1949, and became professor in 1963. His main interest was the history of East European Jewry, particularly *pinkasim* ("registers"). His publications include *Pinkas Va'ad Arba Araẓot*

("Minutes of the Council of the Four Lands," 1945); *Ha-Aliyyot ha-Rishonot shel ha-Ḥasidim le-Ereẓ Israel* ("Early Ḥasidic Immigration to Palestine," 1956); and *Takkanot Medinat Mehrin* ("Moravian Community Enactments," 1952). He also edited *Sefer ha-Gevurah* (3 vols., 1941, 1951²), a historical-literary anthology of Jewish self-defense and martyrdom, and *Beit Yisrael be-Polin* (2 vols., 1948–54), a collection of essays on Polish-Jewish history. Halpern took a leading part in the work of the Israel Historical Society, and was coeditor of the journals *Zion* and *Shivat Ẓiyyon*, publications devoted to the history of Zionism. He was the brother of Lipman *Halpern, the neurologist.

HALPERN, JACK (1925–), Canadian inorganic and physical chemist. Born in Poland, he received his B.S. in 1946 and his Ph.D. in 1949 from McGill University. He joined the University of British Columbia (1950) and became professor of chemistry there in 1956, and later at University of Chicago (1962). Throughout his long and distinguished career, he conducted research on kinetics and mechanisms of inorganic reactions, catalysis, fast reactions, electron transfer processes, and coordination and organometallic chemistry. Among his many awards, he was named co-recipient of the 1994 Robert Welch Award in chemistry, which recognizes outstanding contributions to the field of chemistry for the betterment of mankind.

[Bracha Rager (2nd ed.)]

HALPERN, LIPMAN (1902–1968), Israeli neurologist, brother of the historian Israel *Halpern. Born in Bialystok, Poland, Halpern settled in Ereẓ Israel in 1934. In 1938 he was invited to start a neuropsychic outpatient clinic at the Hadassah University Hospital, Jerusalem and became head of the newly formed department of neurology in 1941. He was appointed to the faculty of medicine being formed at the Hebrew University-Hadassah Medical School in 1946, becoming dean of the faculty in 1965 and playing an active part in the development of medical education in Israel. In 1953 he was awarded the Israel Prize for medicine. Halpern won an international reputation for his research on extrapyramidal diseases, the sensory functions, functions of the frontal brain, and the dynamics of aphasia of polyglots. His major work was a study of posture and its relations to the functions of the organism and the influence of sensory stimuli on posture. He also drew attention to the influence of color on the organism. Among his publications is *Le Syndrome d'induction sensorimotrice* (1951).

HALPERN, MOYSHE-LEYB (1886–1932), Yiddish poet. Born in Galicia, Halpern emigrated to the United States in 1908, after participating in the Czernowitz Yiddish Language Conference, and lived mainly in New York. He associated with *Di Yunge*, but his style was at odds with their aestheticism. Early influenced by German literature, especially Heine and Expressionism, his first collection of poems, *In Nyu York* ("In New York," 1919) brought him recognition as a major Yiddish poet, followed by *Di Goldene Pave* ("The Golden Peacock," 1924). Two volumes entitled *Moyshe-Leyb Halpern* were published posthumously in 1934. Halpern was a rebel who, refusing to compromise his art, lived in poverty, earning some money by writing for satirical and left-wing Yiddish journals. In his poetry, Halpern invented a series of personae through which he expresses the conflicting ideas inherent in his work: social engagement and political skepticism, nostalgia for his heritage and brutal rejection of it, a tormented relationship to America, lyricism juxtaposed with self-mockery and disturbing language and imagery. His writing expresses his rejection of social injustice, his sympathy for the underprivileged, and his horror of war.

BIBLIOGRAPHY: Reyzen, Leksikon, 1 (1926), 769–72; Z. Weinper, *Moyshe-Leyb Halpern* (1940); E. Greenberg, *Moyshe Leyb Halpern* (1942); lnyl, 3 (1960), 31–38. **ADD. BIBLIOGRAPHY:** R. Wisse, *A Little Love in Big Manhattan* (1988); C. Kronfeld, *On the Margins of Modernism* (1996); J. Cammy, in: S. Kerbel (ed.), *Jewish Writers of the Twentieth Century* (2003), 218–20.

[Sol Liptzin and Shlomo Bickel / Heather Valencia (2nd ed.)]

HALPHEN, family of Alsatian origin. They included ACHILLE-EDMOND HALPHEN, who compiled the standard collection of documents on French Jewish history *Recueil des lois, décrets, ordonnances… concernant les Israélites depuis la Révolution de 1789* (1851); FERNAND HALPHEN (1872–1918), Parisian composer, who was a pupil of Massenet and Fauré, and composed several orchestral pieces and songs, a one-act opera, and a sonata for violin and piano; GEORGES-HENRI HALPHEN (1844–1889), mathematician, born in Rouen, who taught at the Ecole Polytechnique in Paris and became a member of the Académie des Sciences: in 1881 his work on the classification of curves was granted an award by the Berlin Academy; ALICE FERNAND-HALPHEN (d. 1963) author of a monograph on Gracia Mendes *Nasi (1929); and LOUIS *HALPHEN, historian.

BIBLIOGRAPHY: Sendrey, Music, nos. 7889–90 (on F. Halphen); H. Poincaré, *Savants et écrivains* (1910), 125–40; E. Picard, *Mélanges de mathématiques et de physiques* (1924), 1–11.

HALPHEN, LOUIS (1880–1950), French historian. Born in Paris, he taught medieval history at the University of Bordeaux from 1910 until 1928 when he became a lecturer in the Paris Ecole des Hautes Etudes and later professor of medieval history at the University of Paris. In 1940 he fled to unoccupied France and taught at the University of Grenoble from 1941 until 1943, after which the Nazis took the city and he went into hiding. In 1944 he returned to Paris and resumed his teaching career at the Sorbonne. Halphen first gained importance as a medieval historian through two publications, *Le Comté d'Anjou au XIe siècle* (1906) and *Etudes sur l'administration de Rome au Moyen Age 751–1252* (1907). He adhered strictly to the sources, of which he had full command. In his *Initiation aux études d'histoire du Moyen Age* (1940, 1952³), he provided an exposition of his methodology as a guide for young scholars. Among his works of broader scope are *L'essor de l'Europe,* xɪ^e–xɪɪɪ^e siècles* (1932, 1948³), and *Les Barbares* (1926; 1948⁵) which he wrote for the series *Peuples et Civilisations.* In these books he emphasized the importance of relating European history to Asian and Islamic history. He also wrote *Charlemagne et l'empire Carolingien* (1947).

BIBLIOGRAPHY: *Mélanges d'histoire du Moyen Age dédiés à la mémoire de Louis Halphen* (1951), xv–xxiii (list of his publications).

[Joseph Baruch Sermoneta]

HALPRIN, ANN (**Anna**; 1920–), U.S. dancer, choreographer, and teacher. Halprin distinguished herself as an exponent of dance related to environment. She founded and ran the Dancers' Workshop in San Francisco (1948–55). Her first "environmental" work, *Birds of America* (1960), led to *Four-Legged Stool* (1961), *Esposizione* (1963), and *Parades and Changes* (1964). From the late 1970s Halprin organized events conceived as "rituals" in which males and females from the audience as well as performers are united in a single process. Her *Circle the Earth* (1981) was a call for peace and also served as a healing ritual; her *Planetary Dance: A Prayer for Peace*, performed in Berlin (1995) in commemoration of the 50th anniversary of the end of World War II, involved hundreds of participants. In 1997, she received the Samuel H. Scripps/American Dance Festival Award, honoring lifetime achievement in modern dance.

ADD. BIBLIOGRAPHY: IED, 3, 336.

[Amnon Shiloah (2nd ed.)]

HALPRIN, ROSE LURIA (c. 1895–1978), U.S. Zionist leader, born in New York City of a traditional Jewish family. She studied Hebrew and attended the Teachers' Institute of the Jewish Theological Seminary of America, Hunter College, and Columbia University. Rose Halprin served as president of Hadassah during 1932–34 and 1947–51. During 1934–39 she lived in Palestine, where she was Hadassah's Palestine correspondent. She was Hadassah's first representative to the Zionist General Council from 1939 to 1946. In 1946 she was elected to the Executive of the Jewish Agency for Palestine and continued in that office for more than 20 years. In 1955 she became acting chairman and from 1960 to 1968 she was chairman of the American Section of the Jewish Agency. During her Hadassah career, Rose Halprin served in many capacities. She was a member of the Board of Governors of the United Jewish Appeal and of the Hebrew University in Jerusalem.

[Gladys Rosen]

HALSMAN, PHILIPPE (1906–1979), U.S. photographer. Born in Riga, Latvia, Halsman became interested in photography at 15 when his father, a dentist, gave him an old camera. He studied engineering but gave it up and moved to Paris. When German troops were approaching in 1940, Halsman, after a decade as a successful portraitist, left for New York with an emergency visa, obtained through the intervention of Albert *Einstein, whom he photographed frequently. The first picture Halsman made in the United States, of an unknown model, Connie Ford, lying on an American flag fashioned from paper, was bought by the cosmetics company Elizabeth Arden for display, making the model, and photographer, famous. Halsman made a photograph of Salvador Dali with a ballerina on a city rooftop. It became the Picture of the Week for *Life* magazine. The two men became close friends, working together on a number of surreal images. Their successful collaboration resulted in 1954 in a book entitled *Dali's Mustache*, a light-hearted look at the artist's famous mustache. Halsman was responsible for more than 100 covers for *Life* magazine, then a weekly picture magazine. He achieved international acclaim for his portraits of Churchill and John F. Kennedy and the actresses Ingrid Bergman, Elizabeth *Taylor, and Marilyn *Monroe. In 1966 the United States engraved two of Halsman's portraits, of Adlai E. Stevenson and of Einstein, on postage stamps. One of Halsman's most famous series shows the rich and famous jumping for the camera. Marilyn Monroe jumps exuberantly, the Duke and Duchess of Windsor do so demurely and Richard M. Nixon does it rather prudishly. The *Jump Book* was published in 1959. Halsman was the first president of the American Society of Magazine Photographers.

[Stewart Kampel (2nd ed.)]

HALTER, MAREK (1934–), painter and writer. Halter was born in Warsaw but during World War II was exiled to Uzbekistan. After returning to Poland in 1945, he decided to study art in Paris. After a short period at the Ecole des Beaux-Arts, he preferred to study alone and undertook a long series of journeys in Latin America, the Middle East, Israel, and the United States. Halter was a particularly gifted draftsman, working in a free, speedy manner, linking delicate linear definitions with heavy areas of black paint. He illustrated a number of publications, including *Proverbs* and *Song of Songs* issued by Oved, Tel Aviv, and the poems of Perl Halter, edited by Massada, Tel Aviv. Albums of his drawings and screenprints were published in Paris, where a film was also made about his work. Halter also worked for the theater, in France and Spain, and designed stained-glass windows for the Great Neck Synagogue, New York. In addition to these diverse talents, Halter paints principally in oils. Much of his life and art is motivated by political ideals, not of a revolutionary nature, but idealistic objectives of a moralistic and democratic nature. His first one-man exhibition was at the Galerie Cimaise, Paris (1953); he also held exhibitions throughout Europe, in Argentina, Canada, and the United States, and at both the Tchemerinski and Gordon galleries in Tel Aviv. In 1976, Halter published his first book, *Le fou et les rois* (*The Jester and the Kings*, 1989), an autobiography with a marked political dimension. Then began a rich literary career, mainly consisting of historical sagas combining reflections on the fate of the Jewish people with a humanistic outlook: *La mémoire d'Abraham* (1983; *The Book of Abraham*, 1986) and its contemporarily focused sequel *Les fils d'Abraham* (1989; *The Children of Abraham*, 1986); *Le Messie* (1996); *Les mystères de Jérusalem* (1999); and *Le vent des Khazars* (2001; *The Wind of the Khazars*, 2003). In 1994, he directed a documentary on the *Righteous Among the Nations, *Tzedek*, whose principal interviews were collected in his 1995 book *La force du bien* (*Stories of Deliverance: Speaking with Men and Women Who Rescued Jews from the Holocaust*, 1998).

In 2003 Halter began publishing a trilogy devoted to biblical women: *La Bible au feminin: Sarah* (tr. 2004), *Tsippora* (tr. 2005), and *Lilah* (tr. 2006).

Besides his artistic activities, Halter was very active in promoting human rights, the fight against racism, and peace in the Middle East. He was chairman of the Andrei Sakharov Institute and the International Institute for Jewish Culture, co-founder of the French anti-racist movement "S.O.S. racisme," and involved in the first encounters between Israelis and PLO representatives.

[Charles Samuel Spencer / Dror Franck Sullaper (2nd ed.)]

ḤALUKKAH (Heb. חֲלֻקָּה), financial allowance for the support of the inhabitants of Ereẓ Israel from the contributions of their coreligionists in the Diaspora. In a wider sense, *ḥalukkah* denotes the organized method of this support and the institutions responsible for it, especially after the end of the 18th century. The support given by the Jews of the Diaspora to their brothers in Ereẓ Israel was customary even in ancient times and there are references to it in the periods of the Mishnah and the Talmud. Rabbis left Ereẓ Israel to seek contributions abroad for the support of Torah scholars. During the Middle Ages and especially during the following centuries, this method of support for the inhabitants of Palestine became widespread and encompassed the whole of the Jewish world. The fundamental idea on which the *ḥalukkah* is based is the conviction that Ereẓ Israel held the central position in the religious and national consciousness of the people, hence the special importance accorded to the population residing there. This population is not to be considered as any other entity of Jews, but rather as the representative of the whole Jewish people, the guardian of all that is sacred in the Holy Land; in this role it merits the support of the whole people. The Jews, in the lands of their dispersion, both communities and individuals, were conscious of their duty toward the *yishuv* and considered their support of it as an act of identification with it.

In the 16th century organized methods for the collection of contributions were established in large Jewish centers; the charity-boxes named for R. Meir Ba'al ha-Nes ("The Miracle-Worker") were a popular instrument for the collection of contributions. Communities and national communal organizations urged the public to fulfill its duty and contribute toward the *yishuv*. The communal organizations of Poland, Lithuania, Moravia, and elsewhere included special clauses in their regulations concerning the Palestinian funds and their collection, and even appointed officials for this purpose. The contributions were usually transferred to Palestine through commercial centers and harbor towns which maintained relations with the Orient. From the beginning of the 17th century, Venice was such a center and funds from Poland and Germany passed through there. In the 17th–18th centuries Leghorn also served this purpose. Amsterdam became a center for the contributions of Western Europe from the 17th century onwards. The most important center for the Palestinian funds was Constantinople; it was near Palestine and the capital of the Turkish government. There was also a spiritual affinity between its rabbis and those of Palestine. Contributions from Eastern Europe also passed through there. The Constantinople center not only handled contributions but also intensively encouraged their collection. During the first quarter of the 18th century, the community in Constantinople undertook the improvement of the financial position of the Jerusalem community and tried to extricate it from its heavy debts. A special tax was levied for this purpose and the expenses of Jerusalem were subject to the control of Constantinople.

From the beginning of the 19th century, Vilna attained a special importance as the center for the collection of contributions from Russia, and the Ashkenazi *Perushim* (followers of the Gaon R. Elijah of Vilna) community in Jerusalem depended on this center. In accordance with the (internal) Jewish regulations of 1823, this center had exclusive authority for the collection of all contributions in Russia; its decisions on the distribution of funds to beneficiaries and general expenses were binding. The Amsterdam center, which was reorganized at the beginning of the 19th century under the leadership of Ẓevi Hirsch *Lehren (1784–1853), was also of great importance. It appointed collectors in the important communities of Western Europe and received annual pledges from them. These funds were then distributed between the various communities of Palestine, according to a fixed scale and with the consent of the leaders of the *yishuv*. Besides these centers, which in their time served several countries, there were similar national centers at Frankfurt, Vienna, Prague, Pressburg, etc. The collection of contributions was made more efficient by special emissaries who left Palestine for the Diaspora and who described the difficulties in Ereẓ Israel in order to encourage the public in their duty toward the *yishuv*. These missions from Palestine, together with the support of the *yishuv*, were an ancient institution and played an important part in the mutual relationship and binding ties between the Diaspora and the Holy Land. The emissaries of Palestine reached the most far-flung areas of the Jewish world. Apart from this main object, they also gave religious and spiritual guidance, some of these emissaries being prominent scholars.

After the beginning of the 17th century, objections were raised against these missions in order to reduce the expenses involved in them. It was suggested that the collection of funds and their transfer be carried out by the communities themselves. The leaders of the *yishuv* opposed this plan for fear that the living relationship between Palestine and the Diaspora would be ruined, and with the absence of personal contacts, the needs of Palestine Jewry would not be satisfied. In spite of the objections, emissaries continued to visit the Oriental countries. On the other hand, the objections of the Amsterdam center were more determined and these missions were stopped in 1824. The leaders of the *yishuv* agreed to this arrangement but tried to circumvent it periodically by sending emissaries to Western Europe for special needs. Lehren was, however, adamant in his decision. At first, the contributions collected were destined for the scholars and the needy, without any distinction as to their land of origin. With time, however, especially during the last third of the 18th century, a tendency to allocate contributions to a defined section of the *yishuv* came into existence. This development was connected with the new Ashkenazi settlement in the country, and from then onward became a characteristic of the *ḥalukkah*. The first *Ḥasidim to emigrate to Palestine during the last quarter of the 18th century regularly received support from their colleagues in their country of origin. Similar arrangements existed for the *Perushim* who emigrated to Palestine and formed their own community at the beginning of the 19th century. As the Ashkenazim were a small minority and the funds contributed, according to prolonged tradition, were remitted to the Sephardi community, the former felt the necessity to assign the incomes from Eastern Europe for themselves alone. Once their numbers increased, the Ashkenazim requested that a portion of the contributions from the rest of Europe also be given to them. After the 1820s these demands were accepted and from that time regular arrangements were made between the two communities concerning ratios for dividing the income from Western Europe and other countries where Ashkenazi and Sephardi communities existed.

Until the end of the first third of the 19th century, there were two principal sections within the Ashkenazi community, the Ḥasidim and the *Perushim*. In the late 1830s, the Ashkenazi community began to break up into organizations based on the countries and regions of origin in Europe. One such organization, known as **kolel*, was characteristic and exclusively confined to the Ashkenazi *yishuv* in Palestine of the 19th and early 20th centuries. This sub-division into *kolelim* was due to economic factors, especially the desire of the emigrants of a given country to ensure themselves the incomes from their country of origin. The sub-division into *kolelim* was almost nonexistent among the Sephardim because they were not dependent on the *ḥalukkah* to the same extent as the Ashkenazim. However, even among them there were some who considered themselves to be discriminated against. Thus, the Georgians and the North Africans broke away from the general Sephardi community. The breaking-up process began in the 1830s when the immigrants from Germany and Holland formed their own *kolel*, the *kolel Hod* (abbreviation for Holland ve-Deutschland). In 1845 the *kolel Varsha* (Warsaw) was established and consisted of members of Polish origin who were dissatisfied with the leadership of the *Perushim* and who felt themselves discriminated against.

The fragmentation process was especially intensified in the 1850s when six *kolelim* were founded by emigrants of Eastern and Central European countries and regions. In 1858 the *kolel Hungaryah* (Hungary; *Kolel Shomerei ha-Ḥomot*, "*Kolel* of the Guardians of the Walls"), the most important one of the period, was established. The pupils of R. Moses Sofer, who had immigrated to Palestine, and those immigrants who had come from the countries of the Austro-Hungarian Empire during the 19th century belonged to this *kolel*. It was one of the largest *kolelim*, both numerically (about 2,500 souls in 1913), and in its real estate holdings; as such it was an influential factor in Jerusalem's communal life. Many of the members of this *kolel* stood out because of their religious zealotry and their opposition to any innovation. The *Neturei Karta* ("Guardians of the City"), the zealous faction of Jerusalem's religious Jews, emerged from this group. On the other hand, the first agricultural pioneers also came from this *kolel*. A further wave of subdivisions occurred in the 1870s, when another five *kolelim* were established. All of these, except one, separated themselves from the ḥasidic *kolel*, whereas those of the 1840s and 1850s had broken away from the old Ashkenazi community. In 1913 there were 26 Ashkenazi *kolelim* in Jerusalem.

The leadership of the *kolelim* was composed of rabbinical personalities. Abroad, a president, who was generally the most prominent rabbi of that country, was the head of the *kolel*. With the ḥasidic *kolelim*, it was the *rebbe* of that trend. Wealthy volunteers worked under the guidance of the president; the *kolel* leaders in Palestine, also prominent rabbis, were appointed by the leaders abroad, as were the communal workers and officials. The *kolel*, which functioned according to set regulations, was in close relationship with the country of origin of its members. The Sephardi *kolel* was led by the Sephardi chief rabbi, assisted by a council of rabbis.

The *ḥalukkah* arrangements were different with the Sephardim and the Ashkenazim. With the former *ḥalukkah* was only distributed to such scholars whose study was their profession, in accordance with the principle that the purpose of *ḥalukkah* was to support those who studied the Torah. The poor of the community only benefited from the *ḥalukkah* indirectly. The justification for this system was that the Sephardim were integrated in the country. They could earn their livelihood and were not dependent solely on *ḥalukkah*. In practice, with the absence of regular support, there were many poor in the community. In addition to the *ḥalukkah* for individuals, the Sephardi *kolel* also set aside a part of its income for general community expenditure. The *ḥalukkah* of the Ashkenazim was divided on the basis of a fixed sum per head. In addition to this, scholars received an additional allocation in accordance with their status. Occasionally, there were supplementary allocations derived from special contributions which the *kolel* received apart from its regular income. The *ḥalukkah* allocations differed from *kolel* to *kolel*, according to the income and the number of members. In 1913 the *ḥalukkah* of the Hungarian *kolel* was 100 francs for every person each year, while that of the Holland-German *kolel* was 360 francs for a couple with a further 80 francs for a child. These were the two most firmly established *kolelim*. Generally, the *ḥalukkah* allocation was far from sufficient to provide for the requirements of those who received it, and as the possibilities of gaining a livelihood were extremely limited in Jerusalem, most of the *ḥalukkah* beneficiaries lived in poverty. They and their *kolelim* were generally in debt. In light of this, there was a great deal of friction between the individual members of *kolelim* and between the *kolelim* themselves. Furthermore, the *kolel* leaders were targets for attack. The echoes of these *kolel* and *ḥalukkah* controversies were also heard abroad; there were many discussions in halakhic literature over these questions.

The division within the Ashkenazi community required the establishment of a body which would concern itself with the general interests of the community and deal with such matters the *kolelim* were not involved in. Consequently, the Va'ad ha-Kelali ("General Committee") of the Ashkenazi *kolelim*, on which each *kolel* had a representative, was established in 1866. The committee preoccupied itself with the general requirements of the community, such as the rabbinate, religious education, welfare, taxes, payments to the government, and the support of scholars. The committee also distributed *ḥalukkah* to persons who were not members of any *kolel*. Later its income came principally from America but also from other regions in accordance with arrangements made with various *kolelim*, though these were not always honored by the *kolelim*, who generally gave preference to their own particular interests.

The *ḥalukkah* was a decisive factor in the existence and the development of the Jewish population in Palestine. Its importance grew during the 19th century, when immigration reached serious proportions. At that time Palestine was economically poor and was ruled by a backward and corrupt government. Under these circumstances the *yishuv* could not have existed, much less have grown, had it not been organized within the framework of the *kolelim*, who provided for their people and gathered money from abroad. (The other non-Muslim communities in Palestine were also supported to a large extent from abroad.) The *kolelim*, which were responsible for the *ḥalukkah* distributions, played an important role in the development of urban settlement, especially outside the walls of the Old City in Jerusalem. The Jewish quarters, which were built after 1869 on the initiative of the *kolel* leaders, were an important factor in the territorial expansion of the Jewish population of Jerusalem. The Jewish population in the other three "holy cities" – Hebron, Safed, and Tiberias – also was essentially reliant on the *ḥalukkah*.

From the middle of the 18th century, criticism of the way and manners of life of the *yishuv* increased in the Jewish world of Western Europe. The *ḥalukkah* and its arrangements were the center of criticism in the writings of L.A. *Frankl, who visited Palestine in 1856, the historian *Graetz (1872), and Samuel *Montagu, in his report in 1875. The principal objection was that the *ḥalukkah* was also distributed to those who were neither scholars nor needy.

The criticism of the *ḥalukkah* intensified when the Ḥibbat Zion movement, which sought to build a society based on its own labor, was established. It challenged the very system of *ḥalukkah* and belittled its importance. The heads of the *kolelim* rejected this criticism and explained the necessity of the *ḥalukkah* in the prevailing social and economical situation. They also stressed its merits for the maintenance of the *yishuv*, the integration of immigrants, and the construction of new quarters. Even so, the deficiencies of the *ḥalukkah* were not unknown to members of the old *yishuv*, and calls for reform were voiced. The public discussion of this matter became one of the principal topics of the Hebrew writers in Palestine and abroad. The negative attitude toward *ḥalukkah* held by the Ḥovevei Zion was passed on to Zionist ideology, which regarded the old *yishuv* unfavorably. Current historical literature has been more favorable toward the old *yishuv* in light of its place as an important link in the renewal and revival of Ereẓ Israel. Consequently, the *ḥalukkah* is also looked upon with less criticism. With the beginning of the new *yishuv*, the importance of the *ḥalukkah* decreased continually, and after World War I it was limited to the circles of the old *yishuv*. In these circles, some *kolelim* still exist, but they have lost their former public importance. In practice, they have become charitable societies and their principal income is derived from their property and contributions given out of traditional sympathy.

[Nathaniel Katzburg]

Ḥalukkah and Women

Ḥalukkah payments were originally intended to enable Jewish men in the old *yishuv* to devote their lives to Torah study and prayer. Yet demographic data demonstrate that women, who were the majority of the Jewish population of Jerusalem (by far the largest Jewish community in the Holy Land) in the 19th century, also benefited significantly from *ḥalukkah*. Many of the Jewish women in the old *yishuv* were widows, poor and wealthy, who had come to the Holy Land to spend their remaining days visiting sacred sites and preparing themselves for the next world.

Ḥalukkah was distributed separately by the Ashkenazi and Sephardi authorities. All members of the Ashkenazi community, men and women, infants and children, received *ḥalukkah*; men who devoted themselves to Torah study were entitled to an extra allowance. In the Sephardi community *ḥalukkah* was distributed only to learned men and the impoverished. Thus, poor Ashkenazi women who had immigrated to the Holy Land could rely on this income.

In the course of the 19th century, an effort was made to link *ḥalukkah* to pious behavior by the enforcement of bylaws (*Takkanot Yerushalayim*) that applied to men and women alike. Transgressions meant loss of *ḥalukkah*. A number of these bylaws were directed at women; they prescribed certain forms of dress and forbade unchaperoned women from using the communal oven. Women were forbidden to attend synagogue at night and were forbidden to stay in synagogue courtyards after the Sabbath morning prayers. Any mingling between men and women was looked upon as a sin. A betrothed girl was forbidden to meet her fiancé, and a woman was not allowed to sell anything to gentile men. Husbands and fathers were expected to supervise the women of the family to preserve the sanctity of the community and to ensure that the family received its allotted share of *ḥalukkah*. According to these regulations every grown male was instructed to marry, and, if not, he was expelled from the city. Thus, *ḥalukkah* money not only provided for the material existence of the community, it was also used to regiment the behavior of all Jewish residents of the Holy Cities who relied on it for their daily needs.

[Margalit Shilo (2nd ed.)]

BIBLIOGRAPHY: Luncz, in: *Yerushalayim*, 7 (1906), 25–40, 181–201; 8 (1907), 306–21; 9 (1911), 1–62, 187–213; Malachi, in: *Lu'aḥ Ereẓ Yisrael*, 18 (1912/13), 81–102; Yaari, Sheluḥei, passim; L.A. Frankl, *Nach Jerusalem*, 2 (1858), 43–51, 58–60; S. Montagu, *Report… to the Sir Moses Montefiore Testimonial Fund* (1875); Eberhard, in: *Mitteilungen und Nachrichten des Deutschen Palaestina Vereins*, 14 (1908), 17–29; A.M. Hirsch, in: *Historia Judaica*, 14 (1952), 119–32; Rivlin, in: *Zion*, 2 (1927), 149–72; Frumkin-Rivlin, 138–57; Baron, in: *Sefer ha-Shanah li-Yhudei Amerikah*, 6 (1942), 167–79; idem, in: JSOS, 5 (1943), 115–62, 225–92; E. Hurwitz (ed.), *Mosad ha-Yesod* (1958[2]); Y.Z. Kahana, in: *Sinai*, 43 (1958), 125–44; B. Gat, *Ha-Yishuv ha-Yehudi be-Ereẓ Yisrael, 1840–1881* (1953), passim; Rivlin, in: *Yad Yosef Yiẓḥak Rivlin* (1964), 108–50; J.J. Rivlin and B. Rivlin (eds.), *Iggerot ha-Pekidim ve-ha-Amarkalim me-Amsterdam* (1965); J. Rivlin, *Megillat Yosef* (1966), 149–216; Weinstein, in: *Bar Ilan Yearbook*, 6 (1968), 339–56 (Heb.); M.M. Rothschild, *Ḥalukkah* (1969); J. Meisel, *Heinrich Graetz* (1917), 142–51. **ADD. BIBLIOGRAPHY:** M. Shilo. *Princess or Prisoner? Jewish Women in Jerusalem, 1840–1914* (2005).

HAM (Heb. הָם), biblical city in Transjordan where Chedorlaomer, king of Elam, and his allies defeated the Zuzim in their campaign against the rebellious Canaanite kings (Gen. 14:5). In this biblical reference, Ham appears between Ashteroth-Karnaim and Kiriathaim, both of which are located in Transjordan, and it has therefore been identified with Tel Ham, 4½ mi. (7 km.) south of Arbel (Irbid) in Gilead. The identification of Ham with a place of the same name in the list of Thutmose III (no. 118) is doubtful. At Tel Ham three megalithic walls and pottery from the Early Canaanite period have been found but no remains from the Patriarchal (Middle Bronze) Age have been uncovered there so far.

BIBLIOGRAPHY: Maisler (Mazar), in: *Koveẓ ha-Ḥevrah la-Ḥakirat Ereẓ Yisrael va-Attikoteha*, 4 (1945), 68; Bergman, in: JPOS, 16 (1936), 237ff.; Glueck, Explorations, 1 (1951), 165f.; Aharoni, Land, index.

[Michael Avi-Yonah]

HAM (Heb. חָם), one of the three sons of Noah. Although he is always placed between Shem and Japheth (Gen. 5:32; 6:10, et al.), he appears to have been the youngest of the three (9:24). The Bible relates how Ham observed Noah drunk and naked in his tent. He "saw his father's nakedness," implying in the biblical Hebrew a sexual act or even rape, i.e., sodomized him (cf. "see the nakedness" in Lev. 20:17, and see Sanh. 70a). In contrast, when he told his brothers of the incident, they at once covered Noah, doing so with the utmost delicacy (9:22–23). When Noah became aware of what had transpired, he cursed Canaan for his action: "Cursed be Canaan; the lowest of slaves to his brothers" (9:24–25). The reason for Noah cursing Canaan, and not Ham, is not clear. Actually "Ham the father of" in verses 18b and 22 seems to be a somewhat crude link between verses 18–19 and 20ff., in which Noah's sons are Shem, Japheth, and Canaan. Ugaritic epic poetry makes it clear that a son had the obligation to take special care of his drunken father, and not to disgrace him (cf. Isa. 51:17–18). Accordingly, the biblical depiction of Ham-Canaan's depravity is probably to be taken as an ethnic slur rather than as a reflection of Canaanite reality (see *Canaan, Curse of), a tendency continued in Jewish Midrash (see below). Ham had four sons, Cush, Mizraim, Put, and Canaan, who became the progenitors of numerous nations (Gen. 10:6–20). As the home of the most important nation descended from Ham, Egypt is poetically called "Ham" in one psalm whose date is controversial (Ps. 78:51), and "the land of Ham" in two late psalms (Ps. 105:23, 27; 106:22; cf. Genesis Apocryphon, 19:13). Egypt is apparently the nucleus of the Hamite genealogy, the others having been added because of geographical proximity or political ties.

[Max Wurmbrand / S. David Sperling (2nd ed.)]

In the Aggadah

Ham's descendant (Cush) is black skinned as a punishment for Ham's having had sexual intercourse in the ark (Sanh. 108b). When Ham saw his drunken father exposed, he emasculated him, saying, "Adam had but two sons, and one slew the other; this man Noah has three sons, yet he desires to beget a fourth" (Gen. R. 36:5). Noah therefore cursed Canaan (Gen. 9:25), Ham's fourth son, since through this act he was deprived of a fourth son (Gen. R. 36:7). According to another opinion, Ham committed sodomy with his father (Sanh. 70a) and Noah cursed Canaan because Ham, together with his father and two brothers, had previously been blessed by God (Gen. R. loc. cit.). Another tradition attributes the curse to the fact that it was Canaan who castrated Noah. Ham was nevertheless to blame because he informed his brothers of their father's nakedness (PdRE 23). Canaan was so wicked that his last will and testament to his children was: "Love one another, love robbery, love lewdness, hate your masters, and do not speak the truth" (Pes. 113b). Ham was also punished in that his descendants, the Egyptians and Ethiopians, were taken captive and led into exile with their buttocks uncovered (Isa. 20:4; Gen. R. 36:6). Ham was responsible for the ultimate transfer to Nimrod of the garments which God had made for Adam and Eve before their expulsion from the Garden of Eden. From Adam and Eve these garments went to Enoch, and from him to Methuselah, and finally to Noah, who took them into the ark with him. When the inmates of the ark were about to leave their refuge, Ham stole the garments and kept them concealed for many years. Finally, he passed them on to his firstborn son, Cush, who eventually gave them to his son, Nimrod, when he reached his 20th year (PdRE 24; *Sefer ha-Yashar*, Noaḥ, 22).

[Aaron Rothkoff]

BIBLIOGRAPHY: A. Reubeni, *Shem, Ḥam ve-Yafet…* (1932), 71–182; J. Skinner, *A Critical and Exegetical Commentary on Genesis* (1912), 181–7, 200–4: Jeremias, Alte Test; Maisler (Mazar), in: *Eretz*

Israel, 3 (1954), 18–32; U. Cassuto, *A Commentary on the Book of Genesis* (1964); Ginzberg, Legends, 1 (1942), 166–73, 177; 5 (1947), 188–95. **ADD. BIBLIOGRAPHY:** N. Sarna, *JPS Torah Commentary Genesis* (1989), 63–72; E. Isaac, in: ABD, 3, 31–2.

ḤAMA (**of Nehardea**; fourth century), Babylonian *amora* and head of the *Pumbedita academy from 356–377 C.E., in succession to *Naḥman b. Isaac. Ḥama was a native of *Nehardea (BB 7b and Rashi *ibid.*) and the term "*amora* of Nehardea" is stated to apply specifically to him (Sanh. 17b). He was evidently a disciple of Rabbah, whose teachings he transmitted (Ket. 86a). Ḥama's teachings and practices are referred to in several places in the Talmud (Ber. 22b; MK 12a, et al.). His legal decisions were approved by later generations as the authoritative law (BB 7b; Shevu. 48b). Ḥama made a living by selling goods where they were cheap at the higher cost prevailing in other markets, the purchaser transporting the goods there at Ḥama's risk (BM 65a; cf. 69b). It is stated that King Shapur of Persia asked Ḥama about the biblical source of Jewish burial rites (Sanh. 46b), which being quite different from those of the Persians seemed strange to him. Ḥama did not know. When Aḥa b. Jacob heard of this, he said "The world is run by fools! Why did he not cite the verse [Deut. 21:23] 'Thou shalt surely bury him the same day'?" However, since Shapur I – it is unlikely that Shapur II (310–379) is being referred to, since he was not on close terms with the Jews – reigned from 241 to 272, the reference is probably to another, earlier, Ḥama.

BIBLIOGRAPHY: Hyman, Toledot, 456–8, s.v.; Margalioth, Ḥakhmei, 316, s.v.; Ḥ. Albeck, *Mavo la-Talmudim* (1969), 408f.

[Zvi Kaplan]

ḤAMA BAR BISA (end of second century C.E. to third century), Palestinian scholar, contemporary of *Judah ha-Nasi. He was the father of Oshaiah, and at times is referred to simply as "Father of Oshaiah" (MK 24a). He lived in the southern part of the country (TJ, Nid. 3:2). Judah ha-Nasi praised him before Ishmael b. Yose b. Ḥalafta (Nid. 14b; TJ, Nid. 2:1). Ḥama b. Bisa was a judge, and his halakhic teachings are mentioned in the Jerusalem Talmud in his name, as they were transmitted by Yose b. Ḥanina (TJ, Shev. 2:2, 33d.) and Judah b. Pazzi (TJ, Suk. 1:1, 52b), and there is also a reference to a question Ḥama posed before Ḥiyya pertaining to a halakhic matter (TJ, Nid. 3:2). In the Babylonian Talmud too, there is a quotation in his name on a question of *halakhah* (MK 24a). It is related that he had left his home and city for 12 years in order to devote his time to the study of Torah. Upon his return he did not wish to startle his family by his sudden reappearance. He stopped at the *bet ha-midrash* and sent word to his family, informing them of his arrival. His son Oshaiah came to welcome him but was unrecognized by the father. They engaged in scholarly discourse, and R. Ḥama was deeply impressed with the young man's erudition, regretting his failure to give his son an adequate education because of his long absence from home. To his great surprise he finally learned the identity of his son (Ket. 62b). Bisa, Ḥama's father, was also a prominent scholar. To these three generations of scholars, Bisa, Ḥama, and Oshaiah, Rami b. Ḥama applied the verse (Eccles. 4:12): "A threefold cord is not quickly burst asunder" (Ket. 62b; BB 59a). Opinion is divided as to whether this Oshaiah is identical with *Oshaiah Rabbah, the compiler of the *beraitot* (cf. Tos. to BB. 59a).

BIBLIOGRAPHY: Bacher, Pal Amor; Frankel, Mevo, 85b; Hyman, Toledot, 458; Ḥ. Albeck, *Mavo la-Talmudim* (1969), 160.

[Zvi Kaplan]

ḤAMA BAR ḤANINA (third century), Palestinian *amora*. He lived in the period of Judah Nesi'ah (Shab. 38a), the grandson of Judah Ha-Nasi (but cf. TJ, Shab. 3:1, 5d for a different reading), and may have headed an academy at *Sepphoris as his father *Ḥanina b. *Ḥama had done (TJ, Shab. 6:2, 8a). Like his ancestors Ḥama was wealthy and built a synagogue in Sepphoris (TJ, Pe'ah 8:9, 21b). One of his close friends was *Oshaiah, and once, while visiting the synagogues of Lydda with him, Ḥama exclaimed: "What vast treasures have my ancestors sunk here [in erecting the synagogue]." Oshaiah responded: "How many lives have your ancestors sunk here! For were there not many needy people here who studied Torah in great poverty?" (TJ, Pe'ah 8:9, 21b; Shek. 21a). Although often mentioned as participating in halakhic discussions (Shab. 147b; TJ, Shab. 5:3,7c et al.), he distinguished himself particularly in the field of *aggadah*. Many of his homilies are quoted in his name by the aggadist R. Levi II, especially in *Midrash *Tanḥuma*. He explained the curtailed form of the Divine name and the word for "throne" in Exodus 17:16 to teach that as long as Amalek's offspring exist, God's name and throne are not complete (Tanḥ. B., Deut. 45), and Psalms 29:4, to the effect that at the Revelation at Mount Sinai, God spoke to the young and strong with power, whereas to the old and weak with majesty (Song R. 5:16).

Commenting on Deuteronomy 13:5, "Ye shall walk after the Lord your God," he asked: "How can man walk after God, of whom it is written 'The Lord thy God is a consuming fire'?" (Deut. 4:24) and explained that it comes to teach that "as God clothed the naked [i.e., Adam], visited the sick [i.e., Abraham after his circumcision], comforted the mourning [i.e., Isaac after the death of his father], and buried the dead [i.e., Moses], so should man pursue similar deeds of lovingkindness in imitation of God's ways" (Sot. 14a). Among his many other beautiful statements in the *aggadah* may be mentioned, "If a man sees that he prays and is not answered, he should pray again" (Ber. 32b) and "Great is penitence for it brings healing to the world" (Yoma 86a). He expounded Proverbs 18:21, "death and life are in the power of the tongue," to teach that by the power of speech a man can kill another man even at a distance (Ar. 15b). Hyman distinguishes between two scholars by the same name, the second one being the pupil of R. *Ḥiyya b. Abba (an *amora* of the third generation, c. 290–320).

BIBLIOGRAPHY: Bacher, Pal Amor; Hyman, Toledot, 460–1; Ḥ. Albeck, *Mavo la-Talmudim* (1969), 237f.

HAMADAN, a city situated in the western part of *Iran. Hamadan is Ahmatha of the Bible (Ezra 6:2) which was the capital city of the Medes (708–550 B.C.E.). It is probable that Jews who were deported from Samaria to Media (II Kings 18:11) in about 722 B.C.E. by the Assyrian king Shalmaneser also settled in Hamadan. The city was called by the Achemenian kings, who replaced the Medes around 550 B.C.E., Hangmatana, Agbatana or Akbatana – probably meaning "gathering place." The biblical name "Ahmatha" does not occur in the Talmud, instead we find there the name as ḤMDN (Kid. 72a). The Persian Jews identify Hamadan with "Shushan ha-Bira," which obviously is a mistake.

The 10th-century *Karaite historian, Qirqisani (Kirkisani), mentions a rebellious Jewish individual by the name of Yudghan (perhaps Yehuda) of Hamadan who headed a movement in the eighth century against the Arab authorities of his time. In about 1167, Benjamin of Tudela estimated the number of Jews in Hamadan from 30,000 to 50,000. Around that time there probably existed there a yeshivah which functioned in connection with the Jewish authorities in Baghdad (see *Iggerot* of Samuel ben Ali).

Benjamin's travelogue (p. 57) is, so far, the earliest Jewish record which mentions the tradition held by the Persian Jews regarding the tombs of Esther and Mordecai in Hamadan. The tombs are also mentioned by the Judeo-Persian poet of the 14th century, Shāhīn, and about 300 years later by *Bābāi ben Lutf. The archeologist Ernst Herzfeld (pp. 104–107) suggested that the Queen Shushandokht, the wife of the Sasanian king Yazdegerd I (399–420), is buried under the mausoleum. However, Jews and Muslims alike regard these tombs as a holy site. The tombs are visited especially during Purim, in the month of Adar, by Jews from all over *Persia (Netzer, 1984, 177–184).

Rashid al-Dawlah, a great Jewish scholar, historian, and the first vizier to the Ilkhanids, was born in Hamadan (about 1247). He was accused of plotting to murder the Ilkhan and executed in 1318. The Jews of Hamadan, like Jews of many towns all over Iran, suffered mortal persecutions and forced conversions during the Safavid period (1501–1736). Their suffering is recorded in the Chronicle of Bābāi ben Lutf (JTS Ms 401, fols 55–60).

According to David de-Beth Hillel (pp. 102–103), who visited Hamadan around 1827, there were 200 Jewish families living among 100,000 Muslim inhabitants. Some Jews were physicians, others goldsmiths or wealthy merchants. The city also had about 1,000 Armenian families. Benjamin II was in Hamadan in 1850 and reported that the city had 500 Jewish families that had three synagogues and three rabbis (pp. 248–253). Two years later, the missionary Stern visited Hamadan for the purpose of converting its Jews to Christianity. He claimed that the Jews of Hamadan were enthusiastic to purchase and read the New Testament. He, too, reported that 500 Jewish families lived in the city in their own separate Mahalleh. He complained about the harsh treatment of the Jews by the Muslim clergy (244ff.). Rabbi Yehiel Fischel Castleman visited Hamadan in 1860 and described most of the Jews of the city as wealthy but hated by the Muslims (71).

Ephraim Neumark visited Hamadan in 1884 and wrote of the Jewish poor. He also described the solicitous efforts of the Christian mission in Hamadan, which opened a school in the city that the Jewish children attended free of charge and also helped the poor families materially and financially. Then he says: "There is not a family [in Hamadan] that has not been touched by the blight of the Bahāis bearing the banner of their mission. And what will happen when the faithful [Jewish] boys grow up in the Missionary School? God alone knows!" (pp. 80–81). The beginning of this blight was evidenced among the Jews first in Hamadan from which it spread to *Teheran, Kashan, and elsewhere. "Those who left the Jewish faith for this creed found refuge from [the] wrath of the king, Nāser al-Dīn Shah, in the shadow of the Christian mission, which lay in wait for their souls, for in their terror of the king, it served as a [sheltering] wall" (80–81). According to Neumark, there were about 800 Jewish families in Hamadan, approximately 150 of whom were Jews who had converted to the Bahāi religion (p. 81).

In 1892 there rose a fanatic, Mulla ʿAbdallah, in Hamadan who issued a *fatwā* to kill the Jews of the city if they refused to abide by restrictions imposed upon Jews, such as wearing the "Jewish patch." Later they were ordered to embrace *Islam or face the death penalty. For about 40 days Jews were afraid to leave their Mahalleh. The intervention of the central government together with the British consulate prevented a brutal massacre (BAIU, 18, (1892), 48; Levy, 756–762). Narrating the event, Levy argues that if one recalls the severe persecutions led by Mulla ʿAbdallah and the warm, friendly, supportive attitude of the Bahāi inhabitants towards the persecuted Jews, who were on the verge of annihilation, one can also understand the mutual affection evinced by believers of both these religions in Hamadan. Levy points out that during this time, about 30 Jews from the community's elite in Hamadan were forced to convert to Islam. Later, some of the converts turned to the Bahāi religion. According to Levy, the positive approach demonstrated by some of Hamadan Jews toward the Bahāi religion also rubbed off on Teheran's Jewish community and the other provincial towns.

Yehudah Kopeliovitz (Almog) visited Iran in 1928. Referring to the Jewish women's organization in Hamadan, which was founded around 1910, Kopeliovitz mentions that one paragraph (#12) in the charter of the "Hadassah Society for Jewish Women in Iran – Hamadan" stated that the society endeavors to influence the Jewish women not to take part in Bahāi meetings (handwritten papers are kept in the Ben-Zvi Institute, Jerusalem).

The geographer Dr. Abraham Jacob Brawer visited Iran in 1935 and during his visit to Hamadan, he was given an estimated number of 8,000 Jews out of a total population of 100,000. He felt that because of the government's closure of the city's Bahāi schools, Bahāi children were attending Jewish schools. He writes:

> As I was told, approximately one quarter of Hamadans Jews were converted to the Bahāi religion. The conversion movement was only halted 12 years ago during the new regime [of Reza Shah]. The return to Zion [Land of Israel] and the country's modernization put an end to the Jews' fascination with Bahāism. (p. 22).

According to the *Bulletin de Alliance Israélite Universelle* (BAIU, 1904, 169) there were about 5,900 Jews in Hamadan. This figure decreased to 3,000 in 1948, on the eve of the independence of Israel (Landshut, 63). It was reported that about 15 individual Jews lived in Hamadan at the end of the 20th century.

BIBLIOGRAPHY: M.D. Adler (ed.), *The Itinerary of Benjamin of Tudela* (1907); *ʿAlam-e Yahud*, a Jewish monthly in Persian published in Teheran, 21 (1946), 362; BAIU; J.J. Benjamin II, *Eight Years in Asia and Africa from 1846 to 1855* (1863); A.J. Brawer, "*Mi-Parashat Massʿotay be-Paras*," in: *Sinai*, 1–2 (1938), 1–38; Y.F. Castleman, *Massaʿot Shaliʾaḥ Ẓefat be-Arẓot ha-Mizraḥ* (1942); David d'Beth Hillel, *Unknown Jews in Unknown Lands (1824–1832)*, ed. W.J. Fischel, (1973); S. Landshut, *Jewish Communities in the Muslim Countries of the Middle East* (1950), 61–66; H. Levy, *History of the Jews of Iran*, 3. *Teheran* (1960); A. Netzer, "*Kivrot Esther u-Mordekhai ba-Ir Hamadan she-be-Iran*," in: *Yisrael: Am ve-Ereẓ* (1984), 177–84; idem, "*Redifot u-Shemadot be-Toledot Yehudei Iran ba-Meʾah ha-17*," in: *Peʿamim*, 6 (1980), 32–56; idem, "*Yahudiyānei Iran dar avāset-e qarn-e bistom*," in: *Shofar* (a Jewish monthly in Persian), 244 (June 2001), 23; E. Neumark, *Massa be-Ereẓ ha-Kedem*, ed. A. Yaari, (1947); H. Sarshar, "Hamadan: Jewish Community," in: *Encyclopedia Iranica*, ed. Ehsan Yarshater, 11 (2003), 615–23; J.B. Schechtman, *On Wings of Eagles* (1961); H.A. Stern, *Dawning of Light in the East* (1854).

[Amnon Netzer (2nd ed.)]

ḤAMADYAH (Heb. חֲמַדְיָה), kibbutz in the Beth-Shean Valley, affiliated with Iḥud ha-Kibbutzim. It was first founded as a *Stockade and Watchtower settlement by a moshav group in 1939, but was taken over by kibbutz Ḥermonim in 1942. Their initial difficulties were considerable due to the hot and dry climate and their proximity to the then Arab town Beth-Shean. A security problem again arose after the Six-Day *War (1967) when Ḥamadyah underwent frequent artillery barrages from Transjordan. The kibbutz developed various agricultural branches, and opened two industrial enterprises for furniture (mainly doors) and plastics. Ḥamadyah was also co-owner of Ganei Huga, a water and recreation park located nearby. Ḥamadyah's name, meaning "God-cherished," was adapted from an adjacent Arab village named after the Turkish sultan ʾAbd al-Ḥamīd. Its population was 260 in 1968 and 347 in 2002.

[Efraim Orni / Shaked Gilboa (2nd ed.)]

HA-MAGGID (Heb. הַמַּגִּיד, "The Declarer"), the first Hebrew newspaper. *Ha-Maggid* began publication in 1856 in Lyck, eastern Prussia, under the editorship of Eliezer Lipmann Silbermann. Silbermann, whose writing talents were limited, was nevertheless a genuine pioneer in Hebrew journalism. Although periodicals had existed for a hundred years prior to the founding of *Ha-Maggid*, the problems of running a newspaper were different from those of running a literary, scientific, and social journal. The paper lacked journalists, publishers, and a news agency. Because the rhetorical biblical Hebrew of the time was not adapted to reporting news and making comments on current affairs, a new journalistic idiom had to be developed.

Ha-Maggid appeared as a weekly (except during its first few months) until it ceased publication in 1903. Until 1890 it was published in Lyck, then in Berlin, and from 1892 in Cracow. The paper grew in importance under David *Gordon, editor from 1858 to 1886, who made the paper of interest to all Jews by reporting both Jewish and general news. *Ha-Maggid* became a fount of information on Jewish life throughout the world during the second half of the 19th century. In a series of articles in 1863 and 1869, a time when the Hebrew press was either opposed or indifferent to nationalist ideas, Gordon took a strong stand in favor of Jewish settlement in Palestine. After the 1881 pogroms in Russia, *Ha-Maggid* fervently advocated Jewish nationalism and settlement in Ereẓ Israel. In this respect it served as a precedent for many of the Hebrew papers that followed.

Throughout the years the paper devoted a special section to Judaic studies, in which the greatest scholars of the day participated. Like most other papers of that period, *Ha-Maggid* espoused moderate Haskalah, i.e., accommodating the religious and traditional heritage to the needs of the time, insofar as the accommodation was not in violation of Jewish law. *Ha-Maggid's* contributors included representatives of all trends of thought. The paper also developed popular sections for science and technology (e.g., a medical section) thereby making Hebrew richer and more adaptable. After Gordon's death (1886) the paper began to decline, a process accelerated by the establishment that year of the Hebrew daily, **Ha-Yom*. In its later years *Ha-Maggid* was moved to Galicia and became the organ of the local Ḥovevei Zion movement. The paper's last editor, S.M. Laser, founded the weekly **Ha-Miẓpeh* (1904) after *Ha-Maggid* ceased publication in 1903.

BIBLIOGRAPHY: S.L. Zitron, in: *Ha-Olam*, 6, no. 1–2 (1912), 4, 6, 8, 10–12; D. Gordon, *Mivḥar Maʾamarim*, ed. by G. Kressel (1942); Posner, in: *Yad la-Kore*, 4–5 (1958–59), 89–94; J. Barzilai, in: *Bitzaron*, 37 (1957/58), 78–88, 178–90; H. Toren, in: *Anakh*, 1 (1954), 232–41.

[Getzel Kressel]

HAMAN (Heb. הָמָן), son of Hammedatha, the Agagite, according to the *Scroll of Esther, an official in the court of Ahasuerus who was superior to all the king's other officials. Resentful of *Mordecai the Jew, who was the only one among the servants of the king in the royal court who would not bow down to him, Haman decided to exterminate all the Jews, "the people of Mordecai" (3:6). To determine the day of the destruction he cast a lot (*pur*), and then received the consent of the king to publish a royal decree throughout the entire Persian kingdom proclaiming the extermination. Through Mordecai, however, the news reached Esther, who immediately set about saving her people. She invited Haman and the king to feasts on two consecutive nights, and at the second feast revealed to the king, in Haman's presence, the evil designs that the latter harbored against her people. In his anger, the king ordered that Haman be hanged on "the tree which Haman has prepared for Mordecai" (Esth. 7:10), and that his hanging be followed by that of his sons. The king then issued a decree permitting the Jews "to gather and defend themselves" on the day that had been set aside for their extermination (Esth. 8:11). This decree and the victory of the Jews over their enemies were the reasons for the establishment of the holiday of *Purim.

Various explanations have been offered to explain the name and designation of the would-be exterminator of the Jews. Among other suggestions, the name has been connected to the Elamite high god Huban/Humman. The name of Haman's father is clearer, appearing in almost identical form in the Elephantine Papyri as Haumadatha, "Given- by-Haōma" (= [Sanskrit *soma*], the deified sacred drug) (הומדת; Cowley, Aramaic, 8:2 = TAD B2.3:2; Cowley, Aramaic 9:2 = TAD B2.4:2), the name of a Persian military commander in the Jewish colony at Elephantine. The author of Esther traces Mordecai's line back to the Benjaminite Kish, father of Saul (2:5). The clear implication of Esther 3:2–4 is that anyone who was told that Mordecai was a Jew would immediately understand that it would be degrading for him to do obeisance to Haman. As such, the author must have intended the designation of Haman as "the Agagite" to indicate descent from Saul's opponent *Agag, king of Amalek (Deut. 25: 17–19; I Sam. 15; cf. Jos., Ant., 11:209). He was less interested in making ethnic connections between Persians and Amalekites than in connecting the present enemy with its traditional one. Although Saul displayed leniency toward Agag (I Sam. 15:9), the latter's distant descendant was not only a personal rival of Mordecai but an inveterate "enemy of the Jews" (Esth. 3:10, 8:1, 9:10; cf. 7:6) who had to be destroyed along with his 10 sons (7:10, 9:6–10; cf. Ex. 17:8–16 and Deut. 25:17–19).

In the Septuagint and the apocryphal *Additions to Esther*, the designation Agagite is replaced by the inexplicable terms Bugaean (LXX 3:1; 9:10; Add. Esth. 12:6) or Macedonian (LXX 9:24; Add. Esth. 16:10). The *Additions to Esther* describes Haman as bent upon delivering the Persian kingdom to the Macedonians (16: 14).

[Bezalel Porten / S. David Sperling (2nd ed.)]

In the Aggadah

In the Midrashim (Esth. R. 7–8; *Targum Sheni; Midrash Abba Guryon* and others) Haman is depicted as a foe of Israel typical of the times in which these writers of the Midrashim lived. The enemies of Israel maintained that the Jews were ungrateful to their benefactors and mocked the faithful of the nations in whose midst they dwelt. The feast that Ahasuerus prepared at the beginning of his reign is attributed by these same Midrashim to the evil designs of Haman, whose purpose was to undermine Israel with exotic foods and incestuous orgies, so that the Jews who attended this feast, against Mordecai's advice, would bring down upon themselves the destruction ordained by Heaven (Esth. R. 7:13). However, the decree was annulled as a result of the cries of the schoolchildren who were studying with Mordecai because they also were involved in the decree of extermination. A humorous piece of folklore relates that Haman was a barber for 22 years in the town of Kefar Karzum (Kefar Karnayim in Transjordan, or Kerazim), and his father was a bath attendant in the town of Koranis and these professions stood them in good stead later when Mordecai had to be dressed and bathed after he had been weakened by fasting. There is an interesting *aggadah* to the effect that all the various trees put forward a claim, on the basis of their virtues, that Haman should be hanged on them. The thornbush was chosen, however, since because it had no virtues, the wicked Haman should be hanged on it (Esth. R. 9:2).

Haman continued to be regarded as the prototype of the enemy of the Jews throughout the ages. It became customary to make a loud noise in the synagogues to drown out his name whenever mentioned in the Purim reading of the Book of Esther. Ironically, the custom has served to perpetuate Haman's memory.

[Yehoshua M. Grintz]

In Islam

Hāmān, according to the Koran, was one of the foremost advisers of Pharaoh-Firʿawn. He built a tower for his master, who planned to climb up to the God of Moses (Sura 28:5, 7, 38; 40; 38; 51:38–39). In Suras 29:38 and 40:25–26 Hāmān appears together with Firʿawn and Qārūn (Korah), who was also Moses' enemy.

[Haïm Z'ew Hirschberg]

BIBLIOGRAPHY: I.Scheftelowitz, *Arisches im Alten Testament* (1901–03); L.B. Paton, *The Book of Esther* (ICC, 1908); P. Renard, in: DBI, 1 (1912), 433ff.; H.H. Schaeder, *Iranische Beitraege*, 1 (1930); J. Lewy, in: HUCA, 14 (1939), 127ff. IN THE AGGADAH: Ginzberg, Legends. IN ISLAM: Vajda, in: EL2; Kisā'ī, *Qiṣaṣ* ed. by I. Eisenberg (1922), 202; H. Speyer, *Biblische Erzaehlungen…* (1961), 412. **ADD. BIBLIOGRAPHY:** P. Grelot, *Documents Araméens d'Égypte* (1972), 472; P. Jensen apud R. Zadok, in: ZAW, 98 (1986), 268; A. Berlin, *JPS Bible Commentary Esther* (2001).

HA-MA'PIL (Heb. הַמַּעְפִּיל), kibbutz in central Israel in the Ḥefer Plain, affiliated with Ha-Kibbutz ha-Arẓi Ha-Shomer ha-Ẓa'ir, founded in 1945 by pioneers from Eastern and Central Europe, some of whom were veterans of World War II. It engaged in intensive farming, including field crops, citrus groves, fruit plantations, fishery, poultry, beehives, and dairy cattle. The kibbutz also operated a stocking and plastics factories. In 2002 the population was 465. The name, meaning "ascender," alludes to the *ha'palah* (see *Illegal Immigration).

[Efraim Orni / Shaked Gilboa (2nd ed.)]

HAMAS (Arab. "zeal"; abbreviation of *harakat muqawama al-islamiyya* – Islamic Resistance Movement), Palestinian Islamic movement engaged in community activity and armed struggle against Israel; from 2006 the majority party in the Palestinian parliament and government. Hamas was officially founded during the first *intifada* in 1988 under the leadership of Sheikh

Ahmad Yasin (later assassinated by Israel) as a branch of the Muslim Brotherhood, operating both in the Gaza Strip and the West Bank. From its establishment it remained the main opposition to the *Palestine Liberation Organization and, from 1993, to the peace process. Throughout this period it launched particularly violent terrorist attacks against Israeli civilians while expanding its civil base through wide-ranging social services to the Palestinian population, including schools, hospitals, mosques, family centers, and welfare. Establishing its political bureau abroad to protect it against Israeli crackdowns, it also sought legitimacy by running in Palestinian elections. With increasing popular support and charges of corruption being leveled against the *Palestinian Authority, it scored an upset victory in the January 2006 parliamentary elections and formed a new government replacing the Palestine Liberation Organization in power. Attacks against Israel continued, however, until Israel again entered Gaza in summer 2006. For a summary of the latter events, see *Israel, State of: Historical Survey; for a detailed review of Israel's war against terrorism, see *Israel, State of: Israel Defense Forces ("The War against Terrorism"). See also *Palestine Authority; *Palestine Liberation Organization.

HAMASHBIR HAMERKAZI, the main wholesale supplier for consumers' cooperatives and labor settlements in Israel; the first economic agency to be established by the labor movement in Ereẓ Israel. It was founded (as Hamashbir) in 1916, during the economic crisis of World War I, to supply the working population with reasonably priced goods, and was reorganized as Hamashbir Hamerkazi in 1930. In addition to its wholesaling activities, it developed the consumers' cooperative movement all over the country, opened large stores in the main towns, and established factories, mainly in the textiles and food-processing industries, which were transferred to a separate company, Hamashbir Hamerkazi Le-Taasia. Hamashbir was affiliated to the *Histadrut, whose economic arm, Ḥevrat ha-Ovedim, was entitled to appoint a representative on its general management and intervene in matters of principle. Its general conference, consisting of delegates from collective and cooperative villages and of cooperative societies, elected a 71-member council, which appointed a general management of 21, which, in turn, chose the 10-man active management. Its turnover in 1968 was IL376 million ($107 million) and it supplied 800 cooperative stores in town and country. In the 1990s, as the Histadrut sold off its assets, it passed into private hands. Hamashbir Hamerkazi Le-Taasia ceased to exist.

BIBLIOGRAPHY: Histadrut, Makhon le-Meḥkar Kalkali ve-Ḥevrati, *Meshek ha-Ovedim 1960–1965* (1967); I. Avineri (ed.), *Ha-Lu'aḥ ha-Ko'operativi shel Medinat Yisrael* (1968).

[Leon Aryeh Szeskin]

HA-MAVDIL (Heb. הַמַּבְדִּיל; "who distinguishes"), name of a hymn sung in the *Havdalah ceremony at the close of the Sabbath. The acrostic yields the name of the author Isaac the Younger (probably Isaac b. Judah *Ibn Ghayyat of Spain (1030–1089)). There are two versions of the hymn; in both the refrain starts: "May He who maketh a distinction between holy and profane pardon our sins (in most versions: "and our wealth"); may he multiply our offspring as the sand and as the stars in the night." The hymn was probably composed for the concluding service (*Ne'ilah*) of the Day of Atonement. One version is still recited as a *seliḥah piyyut* in the *Ne'ilah* service of some of the Sephardi rites (e.g., Algeria); the other, and better known version, has become the standard hymn for the *Havdalah* service in all Jewish rites, including the Karaite one.

BIBLIOGRAPHY: Zunz, Poesie, 14ff.; Hertz, Prayer, 750ff.; Davidson, Oẓar, 2 (1929), 147ff., nos. 741ff.

HAMBRO, JOSEPH (1780–1848), merchant and financier. Born in Copenhagen, the son of Joachim Hambro (1747–1806), a silk and cloth merchant, Joseph started his career as a peddler in the streets of his native city. At the age of 13 he went to Hamburg to be trained in a commercial firm and after his return prospered as a wholesale dealer. Hambro was the first in Denmark to run a steam mill, and he traded with the Danish West Indies. The government commissioned him to arrange a Danish-English public loan and to regulate economic relations between Denmark and Norway after the peace treaty of 1814. In 1820 Hambro was appointed court banker by the king of Denmark. At the age of 60 he settled in London, where later he was buried as a Jew in the presence of the chief rabbi although he had married a gentile. In his bequest Hambro left considerable sums to the community in Copenhagen. His son, CARL JOACHIM HAMBRO (1808–1877), was baptized with his father's consent at the age of 15. He established the great banking firm of Hambros (1839), which also negotiated public loans and was active in the financing of Danish railways and in the founding of the Great Northern Telegraphic Company. Neither father nor son forgot the community of Copenhagen although they remained aloof from the London Jewish community.

BIBLIOGRAPHY: J. Wechsberg, *Merchant Bankers* (1966), 21–98; H. Faber, *Danske og Norske i London* (1915); *Dansk Biografisk Leksikon*, 9 (1936), 13–15.

[Julius Margolinsky]

HAMBURG, city and state in Germany, including the cities of *Altona and *Wandsbek from 1937.

The Sephardi Community

The first Jews to settle in Hamburg were Portuguese and Spanish Marranos, who arrived via the Netherlands at the end of the 16th century and at first sought to conceal their religion. When it was discovered that they had been observing Jewish customs, some of the inhabitants demanded their expulsion, but the city council, pointing to the economic benefits accruing from their presence, opposed the measure. Among the Jews were financiers (some of whom took part in the founding of the Bank of Hamburg in 1619), shipbuilders, importers (especially of *sugar, coffee, and *tobacco from the Spanish and Portuguese colonies), weavers, and goldsmiths. In 1612 the Jews of Hamburg paid an annual tax of 1,000 marks and by 1617 this sum was doubled. The kingdoms of Sweden, Poland, and Portugal appointed Jews as their ambassadors in Hamburg. Those who had come to Hamburg from Spain and Portugal continued to speak the languages of their native lands for two centuries and about 15 books in Portuguese and Spanish were printed in Hamburg from 1618 to 1756. (From 1586 Hebrew books, especially the books of the Bible, had been published in Hamburg by Christian printers, mostly with the help of Jewish personnel.)

As early as 1611 Hamburg had three synagogues, whose congregations jointly owned burial grounds in nearby Altona. In 1652 the three congregations combined under the name of Beth Israel. Uriel da *Costa lived in Hamburg in 1616–17; the local physician Samuel da *Silva wrote a pamphlet attacking him; the excommunication of da Costa by R. Leone *Modena was read publicly in the Hamburg synagogue. Shabbateanism swept the community in 1666; so certain were they of the imminence of the Messiah that the governing board of the community announced that the communal buildings were for sale. The rabbi, Jacob b. Aaron *Sasportas, was one of the few not carried away by the prevailing enthusiasm. At that time the Sephardi community, consisting of about 120 families, was still the only acknowledged Jewish community in Hamburg. When in 1697 the city unexpectedly raised the annual tax levied against the Jews to 6,000 marks, the majority of the rich Jews of Hamburg (most of whom belonged to the Spanish-Portuguese congregation) moved to Altona and Amsterdam.

Among the prominent Jews of Spanish and Portuguese origin who lived in Hamburg were the physician and author Rodrigo de Castro (1550–1627), R. Joseph Solomon *Delmedigo (1622–25 in Hamburg), the physician and lexicographer Benjamin *Mussafia (1609–1672), the grammarian and writer Moses Gideon Abudiente (1602–1688), the rabbi and writer Abraham de Fonseca (d. 1651), and the poet Joseph *Ẓarefati (d. 1680).

The Ashkenazi Community

From about 1600, German Jews were admitted to Wandsbek and in 1611 some of them settled in Altona, both cities under Danish rule. By 1627 German Jews began to settle in Hamburg itself, although on festivals they continued to worship at Altona, where the Danish king had permitted the official establishment of a congregation and the building of a synagogue in 1641. They submitted their disputes to the jurisdiction of the rabbi of the Altona congregation. Many Jews, fleeing from persecutions in Ukraine and Poland in 1648 arrived in Hamburg where they were helped by the resident Jews. However, most of these refugees soon left for Amsterdam since at that time the Christian clergy in Hamburg was inciting the inhabitants to expel the Ashkenazi Jews from the city, an expulsion which took place in 1649. Most went to Altona and a number to Wandsbek; only a few remained in Hamburg, residing in the homes of the Spanish-Portuguese Jews. Within a few years many of those who had been driven out returned to Hamburg, and in 1656 a number of refugees from *Vilna also found asylum there.

Most Ashkenazi Jews in Hamburg at that time were Danish subjects and officially belonged to the Jewish community of either Altona or Wandsbek, while others had officially registered as servants in one of Hamburg's Sephardi households to obtain legal status in the city. These "*Tudescos*" formed a congregation of their own. In 1671 the three Ashkenazi congregations – Altona, Hamburg, and Wandsbek – united to form the AHW congregation, with the seat of their rabbinate in Altona. One of the most famous rabbis of the merged congregation was Jonathan *Eybeschuetz who was appointed to the post in 1750. His equally famous adversary, Jacob *Emden, lived in Altona. R. Raphael b. Jekuthiel *Kohen, who served the community for 23 years, was one of the fiercest opponents of *Mendelssohn's translation of the Pentateuch (1783). The AHW congregation ceased to exist in 1811 when the French authorities imposed a single consistorial organization; the Ashkenazim and Sephardim united to form one congregation, the Altona community retaining its own rabbinate which was also recognized by the Jews of Wandsbek until 1864.

Around 1800, about 6,300 Ashkenazi and 130 Portuguese Jews lived in Hamburg, accounting for around 6 percent of the population. During the French occupation (1811–14), the Jews officially enjoyed full equality but suffered greatly under Marshal Davoust's reign of terror. In 1814, when the city had regained its independence, the Jews were again denied civil rights. The *Hep! Hep! riots of 1819 were especially severe in Hamburg, and similar outbreaks occurred in 1830 and 1835. While no ghetto or Jewish quarter existed in Hamburg, the Jews' right of residence was effectively limited to two areas until 1842, when large parts of the city were destroyed by fire. By 1850 they were granted citizenship, due in large measure to the efforts of Gabriel *Riesser, a native of Hamburg.

The Reform movement, which began in Berlin, eventually reached Hamburg. A Reform temple was dedicated in 1818, and in 1819 a new prayerbook was published to accord with the liturgical ritual of the new congregation. The rabbinate in Hamburg published the opinions of noted Jewish scholars to discredit the temple (titled *Elleh Divrei ha-Berit*, Altona, 1819) and prohibited the use of its prayer book. Isaac *Bernays, leader of the community from 1821 to 1849, espoused the cause of "modern Orthodoxy" and sought to endow the traditional divine service with greater beauty. In his day controversy flared up again when the Reform congregation occupied a new building and the more radically abridged and revised version of its prayerbook *Siddur ha-Tefillah* was issued (1844). At the time the Orthodox rabbi was Jacob *Ettlinger, founder of an anti-Reform journal.

Other German Jews who lived in Hamburg included Glueckel of *Hameln, the merchant and philanthropist Salomon *Heine (the uncle of Heinrich Heine), Moses Mendelssohn, the poets Naphtali Herz *Wessely and Shalom b. Jacob ha-Kohen, Isaac *Halevy, the author of *Dorot ha-Rishonim*, the art historian A. *Warburg, the philosopher Ernst *Cassirer, the psychologist William *Stern, Albert *Ballin, and the financiers Max *Warburg and Karl *Melchior. Among Orthodox rabbis of recent times worthy of note is Nehemiah *Nobel and among the Reform, C. *Seligmann and P. *Rieger. In 1884 the fortnightly *Laubhuette* and in 1900 the weekly **Israelitisches Familienblatt* began to be issued in Hamburg. The municipal library and the library of the University of Hamburg contain a large number of Hebrew manuscripts, listed by M. *Steinschneider. Nearly 400 Hebrew books were printed in Hamburg in the 17th–19th centuries. In the 19th century, the Jewish printers issued mainly prayer books, the Pentateuch, mystic lore, and popular literature.

The Jewish congregation of greater Hamburg was the fourth largest community in Germany. In 1866 there were 12,550 Jews at Hamburg and in 1933 about 19,900 (1.7% of the general population), including more than 2,000 at Altona. The last rabbi was Joseph *Carlebach, who was deported in 1942 and killed by the Nazis.

Holocaust Period

In the years 1933–37 more than 5,000 Jews emigrated; on Oct. 28, 1938, about 1,000 Polish citizens were expelled. The pogrom of *Kristallnacht* (Nov. 9–10, 1938), in which most synagogues were looted and closed down, caused an upsurge of emigration. In 1941, 3,148 Jews were deported to Riga, Lodz, and Minsk. In July 1942, 1,997 Jews were deported to *Auschwitz and *Theresienstadt. Nearly 8,900 Hamburg Jews lost their lives in the Nazi era (153 mentally ill were executed and 308 committed suicide), including those deported from places of refuge in Western Europe after the Nazi occupation. In this period the community was led by Max Plaut and Leo Lippmann (who committed suicide in 1943). A few hundred Jews, privileged or of mixed marriage, outlived the war. A concentration camp, Neuengamme, was situated near the city. A total of 106,000 inmates passed through its gates and more than half of them perished.

Since World War II

On May 3, 1945, Hamburg was liberated by British troops who offered aid to the few hundred Jewish survivors. On September 18 a Jewish community was organized, which reopened the cemetery, old age home, *mikveh*, and hospital soon after. By March 18, 1947 the community totaled 1,268, its numbers changing due to emigration, immigration, and a high mortality rate. In January 1970 there were 1,532 Jews in Hamburg, two-thirds of whom were above 40 years old. In 1960 a 190-bed hospital was opened and a large modern synagogue consecrated. Herbert Weichmann (b. 1896) was elected Buergermeister in 1965. An institute for German-Jewish history was founded in 1966. Within the Jewish community, several hundred Iranian Jews have formed a distinctive element during the last decades. As a result of the immigration of Jews from the former Soviet Union, the number of community members rose from 1,344 in 1989 to 5,019 in 2003.

BIBLIOGRAPHY: H. Kellenbenz, *Sephardim an der unteren Elbe…* (1958); A. Cassuto, *Gedenkschrift anlaesslich des 275-jaehrigen Bestehens der portugiesisch-juedischen Gemeinde in Hamburg…* (1927); M. Grunwald, *Portugiesengraeber auf deutscher Erde…* (1902); M. Grunwald, *Hamburgs deutsche Juden bis zur Aufloesung der Dreigemeinden…* (1904); O. Wolfsberg et al., *Die Drei-Gemeinde… Altona-Hamburg-Wandsbeck* (1960); H. Gonsierowski, *Die Berufe der Juden Hamburgs von der Einwanderung bis zur Emanzipation* (1927); L. Dukes, *Uebersicht aller… Anstalten… Vereine… Stiftungen der Deutsch-und der Portugiesisch-israelitischen Gemeinde in Hamburg* (1841); J.S. Schwabacher, *Geschichte und rechtliche Gestaltung der portugiesisch-juedischen und der Deutsch-israelitischen Gemeinde zu Hamburg* (1914); Glueckel von Hameln, *Life of Glueckel of Hameln…* (1962); E. Lueth, *Hamburgs Juden in der Heine-Zeit* (1961); H. Krohn, *Die Juden in Hamburg, 1800–1850…* (1967); E. Duckesz, *Iwoh lemoschaw…* (1903); H. Goldstein (ed.), *Die juedischen Opfer des Nationalsozialismus in Hamburg* (1965); B. Brilling in: *Zeitschrift des Vereins fuer Hamburgische Geschichte* 55 (1969), 219–44. **ADD. BIBLIOGRAPHY:** M. Studemund-Halévy, *Bibliographie zur Geschichte der Juden in Hamburg* (1994); H. Krohn, *Die Juden in Hamburg … 1848–1918* (1974); I. Stein, *Juedische Baudenkmaeler in Hamburg* (1984); I. Lorenz, *Die Juden in Hamburg zur Zeit der Weimarer Republik*, 2 vols. (1987); P. Freimark and A. Herzig (ed.), *Die Hamburger Juden in der Emanzipationsphase* (1989); *Die Juden in Hamburg 1590–1990* (1991); I. Lorenz and J. Berkemann, *Streitfall juedischer Friedhof Ottensen*, 2 vols. (1995); M. Studemund-Halévy, *Biographisches Lexikon der Hamburger Sefarden* (2000); J. Braden, *Hamburger Judenpolitik im Zeitalter lutherischer Orthodoxie* (2001); F. Bajohr, *Die Deportation der Hamburger Juden* (2002[2]); A. Buettner, *Hoffnungen einer Minderheit* (2003).

[Zvi Avneri / Stefan Rohrbacher (2nd ed.)]

HAMBURG, ABRAHAM BENJAMIN (**Wolf**; 1770–1850), German talmudic scholar. Hamburg was born in Fuerth and studied at the yeshivah of R. Meshullam-Solomon Kohn, the chief rabbi of Fuerth. He succeeded his teacher as head of the yeshivah, and in 1820 was appointed *moreh-ẓedek* ("spiritual leader") of the congregation, serving also as cantor and *mohel*. The appointment of a new chief rabbi, however, was indefinitely postponed and Hamburg was hard put to combat the inroads of the Reform movement into the community. In his correspondence with Moses *Sofer, who describes Hamburg as a "great man of high stature," he talks of his difficulties in building a communal *mikveh* (see M. Sofer, *Ḥatam Sofer, Yoreh De'ah* (1958[2]), no. 214; *Even ha-Ezer*, 1 (1958[2]), no. 82). By 1830, the adherents of the Reform movement had obtained a majority in the communal administration and had him removed from all his positions, except from that in the Klaus synagogue in which he had vested rights (it had been founded by one of his ancestors, Baermann Fraenkel). His yeshivah was closed and his opponents enlisted the help of the police in expelling his students, who numbered more than 100, from Fuerth. Ultimately, Hamburg himself was driven from the city and died heartbroken.

Hamburg's published works include sermons, responsa, talmudic novellae, and memorial addresses. *Sha'ar Zekenim* (Sulzbach, 1830) consists of sermons, eulogies, and ethical tracts. The latter half of the work also contains responsa addressed to former pupils and rabbinical contemporaries. *Simlat Binyamin* (Fuerth, 1840–41), Hamburg's other major work, is in three parts. The first contains responsa on *Oraḥ Ḥayyim* and *Yoreh De'ah*, and the second under the title *Naḥlat Binyamin* on *Even ha-Ezer* and *Ḥoshen Mishpat*, as well as *aggadot*; this section deals at length with the laws of circumcision. In the third section under the title *Sha'ar Binyamin* (unpublished) the author includes his own interpretations, additions, and novellae. One of his eulogies is in honor of his teacher, Solomon Kohn (*Kol Bokhim…*, Fuerth, 1820). He also paid homage to Sir Moses *Montefiore in a poem on his visit to Fuerth in 1841 together with Adolphe *Crémieux, on their return from the Orient. Hamburg taught and inspired a number of eminent disciples, among them Seligmann-Baer *Bamberger, and Moses Sofer.

BIBLIOGRAPHY: Fuenn, Keneset, 304–5; Loewenstein, in: ZGJD, 2 (1888), 90; idem, in: JJLG, 6 (1909), 209–14, 225.

HAMBURGER, JACOB (1826–1911), German rabbi and scholar. Hamburger, who was born in Loslaw (Wodzislaw, Poland), served as rabbi in Neustadt (near Pinne, Poland) and Mecklenburg-Strelitz (Prussia). His most important work was his two-volume *Real-Encyklopaedie fuer Bibel und Talmud*, the first such work ever published in the German language (1874–83) dealing with the Bible and Talmud respectively. This he later extended into a three-volume *Real-Encyklopaedie des Judentums* (1874–1900, 1904–05³), the third volume dealing with post-talmudic Judaism. Hamburger also began to write *Geist der Hagada*, an alphabetical anthology of talmudic and midrashic sayings, but only completed the letter A (1857). He also contributed the section on the Karaites and other matters to Winter and Wuensche's standard work on post-biblical literature, *Juedische Litteratur seit Abschluss des Kanons* (1894–96).

BIBLIOGRAPHY: N. Sokolow (ed.), *Zikkaron le-Soferei Yisrael…* (1889), 29.

[Alexander Carlebach]

HAMBURGER, MICHAEL (1924–), German-born English poet, translator and critic. Hamburger was born in Berlin and, with his family, settled in London in 1933. He was educated at Westminster School and at Oxford. At the age of 19, he translated a volume of Hoelderlin's verse into English. Hamburger held a variety of academic posts in Britain and the United States. While lecturing in German (1952–64), Hamburger wrote poems that dealt with increasingly somber themes, such as the *Eichmann trial. Among them are *Poems 1950–1951* (1952), *The Dual Site* (1957), *Weather and Season* (1963), and *In Flashlight* (1965). His other works include critical studies: a bilingual edition of Hoelderlin's poems (1967) and some of the translations in *O The Chimneys* (1967), poems on the Holocaust by Nelly *Sachs. His *Collected Poems,1941–1994* appeared in 1995.

[William D. Rubinstein (2nd ed.)]

HAMBURGER, SIR SIDNEY (1914–2001), British communal leader. Hamburger was probably the most prominent leader of the Jewish community in Manchester in the last decades of the 20th century. He served as mayor of Salford (a part of Greater Manchester) in 1968–69 and was concerned with a wide variety of Jewish and public causes in Manchester. For many London Jews, he was the public face of Jewish Manchester during the latter part of the 20th century. Hamburger was a member of British Mizrachi and was closely associated with fundraising for Bar-Ilan University. He was knighted in 1981. He was seen as perhaps the last in a long line of leading Jews resident in Manchester with a local power base independent of London Jewry.

BIBLIOGRAPHY: B. Williams, *Sir Sidney Hamburger and Manchester Jewry: Religion, City, and Community* (1999).

[William D. Rubinstein (2nd ed.)]

ḤAMDĪ, LEVI BEN YESHU'AH (1861–1930), hymnologist, *ḥazzan*, and preacher. Ḥamdī was born in *San'a, Yemen, and emigrated to Palestine in 1891; he died in Jerusalem. In Yemen he was a Hebrew teacher, and his *ḥeder* was renowned for its progressive educational methods. In Jerusalem he became a Torah scribe, and also wrote amulets, charms, and lots. Many came to him believing that he was a man of great powers and a miracle worker. His strange behavior, possibly connected to his chronic illness and the deaths of his children in infancy, included self-mortification and fasts. He even exiled himself to Egypt in order to achieve the remission of his sins. Ḥamdī is generally known as a poet and *ḥazzan*. As a kabbalist, he thought that the poetry of Yemen was mystical and holy. He assisted A.Z. *Idelsohn in his research into Jewish melodies, and sang many Yemenite melodies for the latter to record. Ḥamdī composed hymns and prayers of supplication on such themes as the exile, the redemption, and Ereẓ Israel. In Yemen, he wrote prayers expressing his yearning for Ereẓ Israel. *Koveẓ Shirim*, a collection of his hymns and prayers, was published in Jerusalem in 1966.

BIBLIOGRAPHY: Idelsohn, in: *Reshumot*, 1 (1925), 3–68; M.D. Gaon, *Yehudei ha-Mizraḥ be-Ereẓ Yisrael*, 2 (1938), 257–8; Geshuri, in: *Ha-Ẓofeh* (1939), no. 270.

[Yehuda Ratzaby]

HAME'ASSEF (Heb. הַמְּאַסֵּף; lit. "the collector"), first Hebrew organ of the *Haskalah. Founded in 1783 in Koenigsberg by pupils of Moses Mendelssohn, *Hame'assef* was devoted to the education of youth, the increased use of the Hebrew language, and raising the general cultural level of the people. Although the organ was planned as a monthly, it actually appeared as a quarterly whose numbers were collected into annual volumes. The first three volumes were published in Koenigsberg from 1783 to 1786; the next three in Berlin, 1788–90; four issues of the seventh volume in Breslau, 1794–97; and three volumes of the renewed *Hame'assef* in Berlin, Altona, and Dessau (1809–11), after which it ceased publication. The editors in

Koenigsberg were Isaac *Euchel (who also participated during the first period in Berlin) and Mendel Bresslau; in Berlin and Breslau they were Aaron *Wolfsohn-Halle and Joel *Loewe (Brill). The renewed *Hame'assef* was edited by the poet, Shalom *Cohen. Many of the articles published in the periodical were unsigned. Mendelssohn's occasional contributions, for instance, do not bear his name. However, Naphtali Herz *Wessely, who was adviser to the organ, was an exception to this practice and signed his many poems and articles. In addition to Haskalah writers, a number of moderate rabbis also contributed to the periodical. The radicalism of Wolfsohn-Halle not only led religious Jews to shun *Hame'assef*, but also caused Wessely to cease writing for it. The organ's moderate Haskalah policy, which avoided breaking with tradition, was restored only when publication was renewed under Cohen. In the spirit of Haskalah, *Hame'assef*'s literary section published poems in praise of wisdom and nature, in denigration of obscurantism and idleness; festive poems, ethical parables, and hymns of praise to notable persons and kings. It also published linguistic articles, biblical exegesis, historical studies, biographies of famous Jews, reviews, news relevant to the Jewish world, translations of works from world literature, and supplements in German, which were occasionally printed in Hebrew letters. In its support of Hebrew, *Hame'assef* sometimes criticized East European Jews for their use of Yiddish. In its advocacy of pure language, the periodical sought to remain faithful to the language and metaphorical style of the Bible. Yet, despite this, it quoted rabbinical sayings and Aramaic expressions. Although its reportage of news and its educational articles were of immediate practical value, *Hame'assef* was mainly literary in character and somewhat detached from the concerns of daily life. The periodical hoped, perhaps naively, to prepare Jews for emancipation. Nevertheless, there occasionally appeared writings of a Jewish nationalist nature, such as Judah Halevi's *Ẓiyyon ha-Lo Tishali* printed in the 1789 volume, and the yearnings for Zion expressed in a number of the poems published in the renewed *Hame'assef*. *Hame'assef* became the symbol of the Haskalah movement, and Haskalah writers were called the "generation of *Me'assefim*." *Maskilim* of this time long lamented its demise and for many years the *Bikkurei ha-Ittim* (1821–32) of Vienna reprinted "the best of *Hame'assef*." Raphael Fuerstenthal's publication appeared in Breslau in 1829. Even beyond the borders of Germany, *Hame'assef*'s content and form were, for generations, the prototype for Haskalah organs.

BIBLIOGRAPHY: S. Bernfeld, *Dor Tahpukhot* (1914); M. Eliav, *Ha-Ḥinnukh ha-Yehudi be-Germanyah* (1960); B.Z. Katz, *Rabbanut, Ḥasidut, Haskalah* (1956), 248–66; Klausner, Sifrut, 1 (1952); Kressel, Leksikon, 1 (1965), 87–89, 346, 378f., 645–8, 697f.; 2 (1967), 126–8, 391–401, 632f.; Waxman, Literature, index. **ADD. BIBLIOGRAPHY:** M. Pelli, *The Gate to Haskalah* (2000).

[Tsemah Tsamriyon]

HAMEIRI (Feuerstein), AVIGDOR (1890–1970), Hebrew poet, novelist, and translator. Hameiri was born in Dávidháza, Carpatho-Ukraine (then Hungary). His first Hebrew poem "*Ben he-Atid*," which appeared in the weekly *Ha-Mizpeh* (1907), was followed by others in various Hebrew journals. His first volume of verse, entitled *Mi-Shirei Avigdor Feuerstein*, was published in 1912. In 1916 he was captured by the Russians while serving as an Austrian officer on the Russian front, imprisoned in Siberia, and released in 1917 after the October Revolution. In 1921 he immigrated to Palestine, joined the staff of the daily *Haaretz*, and edited several critical journals. In Tel Aviv, he founded the first Hebrew social satirical theater, Ha-Kumkum (1932). Hameiri published various novels, short stories, and poetry collections that gave literary expression to his war experiences, the Third Aliyah, and later, the Holocaust. He also translated into Hebrew works of Heine, Schiller, Arnold Zweig, Stefan Zweig, and others.

Hameiri belongs to the earliest exponents of expressionism in Hebrew poetry. Sustained pathos, and strained and occasional exaggerated figures of speech characterize his work. He attacked the stagnation of Jewish life, described the gruesomeness and the frenzy of hatred that engulfed all of humanity during World War I and particularly the vulnerability of Jews to its consequences. After he settled in Palestine, he castigated the new Jewish society for not realizing its declared ideals. The key figures in his poetry are his mother, whom he lost in his childhood, and his grandfather, who raised him; the former becomes the symbol of Jewish motherhood and the latter – age-old Israel. Hameiri's power as a storyteller is revealed mainly in his realistic war stories. Their central theme is the peculiarly tragic fate of the Jewish soldier fighting wars which are not his. He loathes the bloodshed and the bestiality of combat, and yet, since he is an outsider, is unable to find comfort in the companionship of his fellow soldiers. In 1968 he was awarded the Israel Prize.

Sefer ha-Shirim ("The Book of Poems," 1933) contains his complete poetry up to its publication. His subsequent works of poetry included *Ha-Moked ha-Ran* ("The Singing Pyre," 1944), collected poems from 1933 to 1944; *Ḥalomot shel Beit-Rabban* ("Schoolboy Dreams," 1945), and *Be-Livnat ha-Sappir* ("In a Pavement of Sapphire," 1962). His works of fiction include the novel *Ha-Shigga'on ha-Gadol* (1950; *The Great Madness*, 1952; 1985; 1989); *Be-Geihinnom shel Mattah* ("In Lower Hell," novel, 1932; 1989); *Tenuvah* ("Produce," 1947^2); *Ha-Mashi'aḥ ha-Lavan* ("The White Messiah," novel, 1948); *Bein Laylah le-Laylah* ("Between the Nights," short stories, 1944); and *Sodo shel Socrates* ("Socrates' Secret," historical novel, 1955). A list of his works translated into English appears in Goell, Bibliography, 861–81, 2123–34.

BIBLIOGRAPHY: S. Streit, *Penei ha-Sifrut*, 2 (1939), 280–91; Waxman, Literature, 4 (1960), 174–8, 320–4; R. Wallenrod, *The Literature of Modern Israel* (1956), index; S. Halkin, *Modern Hebrew Literature* (1950), 121, 154; S. Samet, *Eifoh Hem ha-Yom?* (1970), 21–27. **ADD. BIBLIOGRAPHY:** Y. Rabikov, "*A. Hemiri – Meshorer ha-Yahadut ha-Loḥemet*," in: *Hara'ayon*, 17–18 (1970), 58–62; G. Shaked, *Ha-Sipporet ha-Ivrit*, 2 (1983), 313–18; H. Yaoz, "*Livetei Zehut ve-Livetei Kiyumiyut Yehudit bi-Yeẓirat Hameiri*," in: *Zehut*, 3 (1983), 217–24;

A. Holtzman, *Avigdor Hameiri ve-Sifrut ha-Milḥamah* (1986); A. Holtzman, *Ha-Zahav ve-Sigav: Bein Bialik le-A. Hameir,*" in: *Halel le-Bialik* (1989), 337–48.

[Gedalyah Elkoshi]

HAMEIRI (Ostrovsky), MOSHE (1886–1947), rabbi and Mizrachi leader in Ereẓ Israel. Born in Karlin, Belorussia, Hameiri settled in Ereẓ Israel in 1897. He studied at yeshivot in Jerusalem and was ordained by Ḥayyim Berlin and A.I. Kook, becoming rabbi of the *Ekron settlement in 1912. Active from his youth in the Mizrachi movement, in 1919 he became one of the chief planners and organizers of the religious school system in Palestine. Hameiri taught Talmud at the Mizrachi Teachers' Seminary in Jerusalem. He was a member of the Va'ad Le'ummi executive, heading its department of local religious communities. Hameiri helped to organize the Chief Rabbinate in Palestine and was one of the founders of the Kiryat Moshe quarter in west Jerusalem. His books include *Ha-Middot she-ha-Torah Nidreshet Bahen* ("The Principles by Which the Torah is Expounded," 1924); *Mevo ha-Talmud* ("Introduction to the Talmud," 1935), a textbook for schools and teachers' seminaries; *Toledot ha-Mizrachi be-Ereẓ Yisrael* ("The History of Mizrachi in Ereẓ Israel," 1944); and *Irgun ha-Yishuv ha-Yehudi be-Ereẓ Yisrael* ("The Organization of the Jewish Yishuv in Ereẓ Israel," 1942).

BIBLIOGRAPHY: EẒD, 2 (1960), 122–5; *Sefer Ish ha-Torah ve-ha-Ma'aseh* (1946), for his 60th birthday, includes bibliography.

HA-MELIẒ (Heb. הַמֵּלִיץ, "The Advocate"), the first Hebrew paper in Russia. *Ha-Meliẓ* was founded in Odessa in 1860 by Alexander *Zederbaum with the assistance of his son-in-law, A.J. Goldenblum. Zederbaum obtained the license to publish the paper through his connections with the czarist authorities. *Ha-Meliẓ* was long the organ of the moderate Haskalah movement in Russia, although at times it served the extreme wing of the Haskalah, publishing the writings of M.L. *Lilienblum and J.L. *Gordon, advocates of religious reform. In the literary sphere, *Ha-Meliẓ* was involved in a bitter controversy concerning A.U. *Kovner and his destructive criticism of Hebrew literature (Kovner also sharply criticized *Ha-Meliẓ* in his *Ẓeror Peraḥim*, 1868). Appearing in Russia, where censorship was severe, *Ha-Meliẓ* defended the czarist regime, but also criticized it surreptitiously. Zederbaum introduced into *Ha-Meliẓ* the Hebrew journalistic article with all its virtues and defects and attracted contributors from among the best authors in Russia, such as *Mendele Mokher Seforim. After 10 years in Odessa, *Ha-Meliẓ* was transferred to St. Petersburg (1871) where it appeared until it ceased publication in 1904. As *Ha-Meliẓ* was pro-Russian, it advocated Haskalah, Jewish agricultural settlement in Russia, occupation in trades, and improving education while fostering traditional and religious values. Accordingly, it held a reserved attitude toward nationalist and Zionist ideals which were gaining impetus in the early 1880s. Only as Zionism grew stronger, and under the influence of A.S. *Friedberg, one of the paper's editorial assistants, did *Ha-Meliẓ* become the organ of the Ḥibbat Zion movement in Russia. In response to the growing interest in Zionism in the 1880s, *Ha-Meliẓ*, which had been a weekly, became a semiweekly in 1883 and a daily from 1886, until it ceased publication. For different reasons the paper did not appear for periods of various lengths, from a few months in 1871–72 and in 1879, to a few years, from 1874 to 1877. *Ha-Meliẓ* flourished in the 1880s and 1890s, particularly under the editorship of the poet Judah Leib *Gordon (1880–83, 1885–88). Promoting Hebrew literature in Russia during the second half of the 19th century, *Ha-Meliẓ* published the earliest writings of Aḥad Ha-Am, Bialik, and scores of other Hebrew authors and scholars in Russia and abroad. *Ha-Meliẓ* also published controversy which, descending to the personal level, bore negative consequences. When *Ha-Meliẓ* became the organ of the Ḥibbat Zion movement in Russia it published the best nationalist-Zionist journalism. For many years *Ha-Meliẓ* published various literary collections, introducing writers of all political and religious factions. On Zederbaum's death in 1893, the paper ceased to appear for a few months until it was taken over by Yehudah Leib *Rabinovich, who served as its last editor.

BIBLIOGRAPHY: S.L. Zitron, in: *Ha-Olam*, 7 (1913), passim; 8 (1914), passim; S. Bernstein, *Be-Ḥazon ha-Dorot* (1928), 74–102; R. Malachi, in: *Hadoar*, 40 (1961), no. 13–27, passim; Kressel, Leksikon, 2 (1967), 703f.

[Getzel Kressel]

HAMELN (Hamelin), city near Hanover, Germany. Jews are first mentioned in the privileges granted to the town in 1277. The formula of the Jewish oath of Hameln, almost identical with the earlier formula of Dortmund, was recorded in the municipal ledger. In the early years of Jewish settlement there were no more than about 10 Jewish families, engaged mostly in moneylending under the protection of the municipal authorities. By the middle of the 14th century the number of Jews had grown significantly, and in 1344 they opened a synagogue. Shortly thereafter however, during the *Black Death persecutions (1349–50), the community ceased to exist. For the next two centuries only individual Jews settled in Hameln. By the middle of the 16th century their members had increased and a "Jewish Street" is mentioned in 1552. In 1590 Duke Henry Julius banished all the Jews from his provinces, but the Hameln town council, claiming its traditional right to control the fate of the Jews in the town, determined to ignore the order. Nevertheless, most of the Jews left. In her memoirs, Glueckel of *Hameln indicates that only two Jewish families lived there in 1660.

By the end of the 17th century the Hameln community had increased and a number of its members were among those attending the Leipzig fairs (1691–1763). A new cemetery was consecrated in 1743. Resident rabbis were appointed in the city until 1782. The 12 Jewish families in Hameln in 1777 had declined to five families in 1814 and risen again to 10 only in 1830. In 1832 the community was put under the jurisdiction of the rabbinate of Hanover and a school was established. A new synagogue was dedicated in 1879. The Jewish population numbered 86 in 1845; 149 in 1875; and 170 (0.6% of the total) in 1931. In 1933, when the Nazis took power, the Jewish population was 136. Jewish businesses were vandalized and the synagogue subject to arson. Jews emigrated or left for larger cities. There were only 86 Jews left by 1935. The synagogue was destroyed in 1938, the cemetery was desecrated and 10 Jews were sent to Buchenwald, two of them died there. The remainder of the community (44 in 1939) was deported in 1942. In 1963 a memorial to the Jews of Hameln was erected in the city. In 1997 a liberal Jewish community was founded. It is a member of the Union of Progressive Jews in Germany. It numbered 18 in 1997 and 200 in 2004. In 1998 another Jewish community was founded which is affiliated with the Central Council of Jewish Communities in Germany, the main Jewish organization in Germany. It numbered 331 in 2003. Almost all of the members of both communities are immigrants from the former Soviet Union. In 1999 the Jewish cemetery, desecrated during World War II, was reopened for use. In 2001 a new Jewish cemetery was opened.

BIBLIOGRAPHY: Germ Jud, 2 (1968), 323–34; A. Neukirch, *Hamelner Renaissance...* (1950); A. Reimer, *Juden in niedersaechsischen Staedten des Mittelalters* (1907), passim; H. Spanuth and R. Feige (eds.), *Geschichte der Stadt Hameln* (1963). Part of the communal archives (1709–1844) are in the Central Archives for the History of the Jewish People in Jerusalem. **ADD. BIBLIOGRAPHY:** B. Gelderblom, *Sie waren Buerger dieser Stadt. Die Geschichte der juedischen Einwohner Hamelns im Dritten Reich* (1996); idem, *Der juedische Friedhof in Hameln* (1988); S. Spector (ed), *The Encyclopedia of Jewish Life Before and During the Holocaust* (2001).

[Zvi Avneri and Ze'ev Wilhem Falk / Larissa Daemmig (2nd ed.)]

HAMENAḤEM, EZRA (1907–1993), Hebrew writer. Born in Skoplje, Serbia, he settled with his family in Ereẓ Israel in 1914. After receiving a religious education in the Old City of Jerusalem, he worked in a Jerusalem bank and then at Mosad Bialik, the Am Oved publishing house, and as editor of literary programs on the Israel radio. In the late 1930s, he began writing about the old and new cities of Jerusalem, particularly about their Oriental Jewish community. His collections of short stories include *Bein ha-Ḥomot* (1941), *Afar ha-Areẓ* (1948), *Be-Ẓel ha-Yamim* (1956), *Sippurei ha-Ir ha-Attikah* (1968), and *Mi-Sippurei Na'ar Yerushalmi* (1988).

BIBLIOGRAPHY: A. Cohen, *Soferim Ivriyyim Benei Zemannenu* (1964), 144–6; Y. Keshet, *Maskiyyot* (1953), 261–72; R. Wallenrod, *Literature of Modern Israel* (1956), 188. **ADD. BIBLIOGRAPHY:** M. Lipshitz, "*E. Hamenaḥem: Romantikan Yerushalmi*," in: *Moznayim*, 48/4 (1979), 285–88; N. Govrin, "*Tokheḥah mi-Golah*," in: *Yeda Am*, 20 (1981), 15–28; G. Shaked, *Ha-Sipporet ha-Ivrit*, 2 (1983), 301–3.

[Getzel Kressel]

HA-ME'ORER (Heb. הַמְעוֹרֵר; "the Awakener"), a Hebrew monthly published in London in 1906–07 and edited by J.Ḥ. *Brenner. *Ha-Me'orer* began publication after the failure of the Russian revolution of 1905. While living in London, Brenner was involved in the Jewish and general labor movements there. Through this monthly, dominated by his sharp and nonconformist thinking, Brenner hoped to establish a Hebrew center in England at a time when there were few Hebrew papers in Russia. He was severely critical of complacency in Hebrew literature, which resisted original thought, and of the Jewish labor movement in Russia, which promoted Yiddish instead of Hebrew. In particular, Brenner denounced what he considered hollow verbiage current in the Jewish workers' movement on the one hand, and in the Zionist movement and its literature on the other.

Ha-Me'orer was the periodical in which Brenner first crystallized the approach characterizing the periodicals he later edited. His reactions to current affairs and to literature were a model of original, non-conventional thinking. In addition to printing stories and plays of his own and others, he also published poems, essays, and translations of Ibsen, Wilde, and Maeterlinck. Contributors to *Ha-Me'orer* were authors, old and young, who appreciated the editor's attempts to maintain a Hebrew paper single-handedly. After appearing for less than two years, however, the paper could no longer maintain itself and ceased publication. *Ha-Me'orer* greatly influenced young Jews and particularly the generation of the Second *Aliyah*.

BIBLIOGRAPHY: Kressel, Leksikon, 1 (1965), 369–72; idem, in: *La-Merḥav* (Sept. 26, 1969). **ADD. BIBLIOGRAPHY:** Y. Bakon, *Brenner in London* (Hebrew, 1990).

[Getzel Kressel]

HAMEROW, THEODORE STEPHEN (1920–), U.S. historian. Born in Warsaw, Hamerow spent his childhood in Poland, where his parents were members of the well-known Yiddish theater ensemble, the Vilna Company. He lived in Germany from 1921 to 1924 and then returned to Poland (1924–30). After emigrating to the United States in 1930, he studied at the City College of New York, Columbia University, and Yale University. He received his Ph.D. in 1951. He taught European, particularly German, history at the University of Illinois from 1952 to 1958 and was then appointed professor of history at the University of Wisconsin–Madison in 1958. He conducted research in Germany and was a Fulbright Research Scholar in 1962–63. From 1973 to 1976 he served as chairman of the history department at Wisconsin. Hamerow retired in 1991 as G.P. Gooch Professor of History.

His main studies, relating to 19th and 20th-century Germany, are *Restoration, Revolution, Reaction: Economics and Politics in Germany, 1815–1871* (1958); and *Otto von Bismarck, a Historical Assessment* (1962), which he edited. Other books by Hamerow include *The Birth of a New Europe* (1983), *Reflections on History and Historians* (1991), *On the Road to the Wolf's Lair: German Resistance to Hitler* (1997), and *Remembering a Vanished World: A Jewish Childhood in Interwar Poland* (2001).

[Ruth Beloff (2nd ed.)]

ḤAMEẒ (Heb. חָמֵץ; "fermented dough"; cf. Ex. 12:39). *Ḥameẓ* is prohibited in Jewish religious usage in two instances, one of which has a purely theoretical application at the present day, while the other is of topical application. The first was the prohibition against offering up *ḥameẓ* of any kind (or honey) on the altar as a concomitant of sacrifices (Lev. 2:11, where it is referred to as *se'or*). *Se'or* and *ḥameẓ* are by no means synonymous. *Se'or* refers to the leavening agent, while *ḥameẓ* is the new dough to which the *se'or* is added, and it is expressly called *leḥem ḥameẓ* ("leavened bread"; Lev. 7: 13). This distinction is clearly shown by Exodus 12: 15: "Seven days you shall eat unleavened bread (*mazzot*); on the first day you shall remove leaven (*se'or*) from your houses, for whoever eats leavened bread (*ḥameẓ*) from the first day to the seventh day that person shall be cut off from Israel." Further corroboration of this distinction is furnished by a linguistic criterion: *se'or* is never used with the verb *akhal* ("eat"), since it is too sour to be edible. The leavened bread mentioned with regard to the sacrifices is given directly to the priest or is consumed by the worshiper (cf. Lev. 2: 12, 7: 13; 23: 17, 20). The instructions for the making of shewbread contain no prohibition of the use of leaven (Lev. 24:5–9) since it was not consumed but merely displayed. Post-biblical tradition, however, prohibits it (Jos., Ant. 3: 142, 255ff.; cf. Men. 5:1). It was permitted, however, as part of the sacrificial meal (Lev. 7: 13). The other is the complete prohibition of *ḥameẓ* (or anything containing it) during *Passover, which includes its consumption, deriving any benefit from it, and retaining it in one's possession (Ex. 12: 19). To this the rabbis added the prohibition after Passover of leaven which had been in one's possession during the festival (Pes. 2:2; 28b; Sh. Ar., OḤ 448). However, the author of the "Passover Papyrus" of Elephantine (Cowley, Aramaic, 21, p. 60ff.) felt that it sufficed to keep the leaven out of sight, i.e., stored away. Nonetheless he did follow the *halakhah*, in opposition to the stricter Samaritan view (a restored text), in maintaining that only fermented grain but not fermented fruit (wine) was included under the definition of leaven (H.L. Ginsberg, in: Pritchard, Texts, 491, esp. n. 6).

The criterion for rendering grain *ḥameẓ* is that on decomposition it ferments. This characteristic was stated to apply only to the five species of grain, usually translated as "wheat, barley, spelt, rye, and oats" (but see *Five Species). Other grains which, instead of fermenting, "rotted," were not regarded as coming within the prohibition of *ḥameẓ*; in this class, as is specifically stated, belong rice and millet (Pes. 35a). Despite this fact, Ashkenazi authorities, in contrast to Sephardi, not only forbid the use of rice (and millet) on Passover, but extend the prohibition to include a whole additional range of products which they regard as belonging to the category of *kitniyyot* ("pulse") or even "doubtful *kitniyyot*," including such foods as beans, peas, maize, and peanuts, since flour is made from them and thus people might come to use ordinary flour in such a way as to make it *ḥameẓ*. In practice, among Ashkenazi Jews the only flour used on Passover is "*maẓẓah* meal" (i.e., ground *maẓẓah*) and potato flour, while the Sephardim use rice.

Prohibited *ḥameẓ* is divided into three categories of descending stringency: *ḥameẓ gamur*, that which is "completely" *ḥameẓ*, i.e., one of the above fermented doughs and such derivatives as whisky; *ta'arovet ḥameẓ*, that which has in it an admixture of even the smallest amount of *ḥameẓ;* and *ḥameẓ nuksheh*, roughly, *ḥameẓ* which is unsuitable for food, such as writer's paste (Pes. 3:1). It is only for the first that the penalty of *karet is involved, although Maimonides (Yad, introd., negative commandment no. 198) regards the word *maḥmeẓet* (Ex. 12:19) as referring to *ta'arovet* which is therefore, according to him, forbidden by the Bible. The penalty of *karet* is involved, and the minimum amount for which liability is incurred is an olive's bulk.

Whereas the prohibition of most forbidden food is nullified if it is accidentally mixed in more than 60 times its volume of permitted food and this applies even to leaven mixed in permitted food being prepared for Passover prior to the festival – during Passover *ḥameẓ* can never be nullified in this way; the most minute admixture renders everything with which it has been mixed forbidden as *ta'arovet.* As a result, practically every food product which has not been specially prepared under supervision in order to ensure the complete absence of *ḥameẓ* is regarded as belonging to this category. For the same reason all vessels which have been used during the year are forbidden for use during the festival, unless they have been cleansed in accordance with halakhic requirements (see *Passover).

The period which it takes for flour mixed with water to begin fermenting is stated as the time it takes to walk a (Roman) mile (Pes. 46a); the authorities have established this as 18 minutes. This, however, applies to normal conditions and varies according to the circumstances. Thus, on the one hand, if the temperature of the water is above normal the process is accelerated; on the other hand, the continuous manipulation of the dough delays, and even prevents, fermentation (OḤ 459; for details see *Maẓẓah).

Ḥasidim, believing that there is a possibility that some of the flour in the *maẓẓah* may have remained unbaked, take up the extreme attitude of not eating *maẓẓah* or *maẓẓah* meal which has been soaked in water during the whole of the seven days of Passover; they permit it only on the eighth day (which obtains in the Diaspora).

The prohibition of *ḥameẓ* commences from the time that the paschal sacrifice used to be offered, at midday on the 14th of Nisan, but the period has been extended to two hours earlier (Pes. 28b).

Leaven in Jewish Thought

Leaven is regarded as the symbol of corruption and impurity. The "yeast in the dough" is one of the things which "prevents us from performing the will of God" (Ber. 17a). The idea was greatly developed in the Kabbalah. The New Testament also refers to "the leaven of malice and wickedness" which is contrasted with "the unleavened bread of sincerity and truth" (1 Cor. 5:8). Similarly the word is applied to what was regarded as the corrupt doctrine of the Pharisees and Sadducees (Matt. 16: 12; Mark 8: 15).

It was applied particularly to the admixture of elements of impure descent in a family. (Fermented) "dough" was contrasted in this context with "pure sifted flour." Thus, with regard to purity of family descent, "All the countries are regarded as dough compared to Ereẓ Israel, while Ereẓ Israel is regarded as dough compared to Babylonia" (Kid. 71a). Ezra did not leave Babylonia until he had made its "Jewish population pure sifted flour" (by bringing up those of doubtful descent to Ereẓ Israel, *ibid.* 69b). The widow of a man of doubtful descent is referred to as a "dough widow" (Ket. 14b).

BIBLIOGRAPHY: S. Zevin, *Ha-Mo'adim ba-Halakhah* (1959[7]), 231ff.

[Louis Isaac Rabinowitz]

ḤAMEẒ, SALE OF (Heb. מְכִירַת חָמֵץ). No **ḥameẓ* (leaven) may be present, or seen, in the house of a Jew during Passover. In addition to the prohibition against eating *ḥameẓ* or deriving any benefit from it, the Pentateuch explicitly states: "Seven days shall there be no leaven found in your houses" (Ex. 12: 19), "neither shall there be leaven seen with thee, in all thy borders" (Ex. 13:7). Any *ḥameẓ* which a Jew has kept over Passover becomes forbidden forever (Pes. 2:2 and 29a; Sh. Ar. OḤ, 448:3).

Disposal of Hamez

The disposal of all ḥameẓ which is in the possession of a Jew is carried out after the **bedikat ḥameẓ* ("search for leaven") has taken place on the eve of the 14th of Nisan. According to the *halakhah*, the *ḥameẓ* may be disposed of in three ways. It may be burnt (which must be done before 10 o'clock on the morning of the 14th of Nisan). It may be annulled by declaring, "May all leaven in my possession, whether I have seen it or not, whether I have removed it or not, be annulled and considered as the dust of the earth." It may also be sold. Since the first method might involve hardship, especially where large quantities of foodstuffs are involved, or where the *ḥameẓ* is used for business purposes, the *ḥameẓ* is sold to a non-Jew. This applies only to foodstuffs; utensils which have been used for ḥameẓ need only be washed and stored separately.

The Legal Character of the Sale

The transaction by which the *ḥameẓ* is sold must be of a legal character, carried out by means of a bill of sale. The purchaser must both lease the place in which the *ḥameẓ* is stored, and buy the *ḥameẓ* itself. The gentile thus becomes the legal owner of the *ḥameẓ* which the Jew, if he so desires, may buy back after Passover. The completion of the sale is effected by the signing of the contract and by the transfer of money, usually in the form of a down payment (see Modes of *Acquisition). The rabbinic insistence that such a bill of sale be in accordance with the requirements of the *halakhah*, and the inconvenience which would result were every Jew to attempt to sell his own *ḥameẓ* gave rise to the formal sale of the *ḥameẓ*. The Jewish vendor merely appends his signature to a composite document which grants power of attorney to sell his *ḥameẓ* to an agent (usually the local rabbi) who, in turn, arranges the contract with the non-Jewish buyer. The agent buys the *ḥameẓ* back after Passover, and restores it to its original owners. All the contracts are written in Hebrew although it has been suggested that the vernacular be used for the bill of sale so as to ensure the Gentile's understanding of the contract.

Stages of Development of the Transaction

Four distinct stages in the evolution of the transaction whereby *ḥameẓ* is sold can be traced in rabbinic literature. The first sales, referred to in the Talmud (Pes. 2:1; Tosef., Pes. 1:7; Shab. 18b; Pes. 13a, 21a), were clearly of a simple nature. Although the *Gemara* does not discuss any details, such a sale presumably involved the physical transfer of *ḥameẓ* from Jew to non-Jew "in the market place" (Pes. 13a). The beginning of the second stage, by which it became common practice to sell *ḥameẓ* to a non-Jew with the mutual understanding that the Jew would buy it back after Passover, is hinted at in the Tosefta (Pes. 1:24, also in TJ, Pes. 2:2, 28d). Although the author of *Halakhot Gedolot* (ed. by I. Hildesheimer (1892), 136) stipulated that there must be no suggestion of such an intention, the practice had clearly earned rabbinic consent by the time of the compilation of the Shulḥan Arukh (OḤ 448:3). The condition that the *ḥameẓ* must be physically transferred from the property of the Jew to that of the non-Jew still remained (*Magen Avraham*, Sh. Ar., OḤ 448:3). It was the observation of Joel *Sirkes (*Bayit Ḥadash*, OḤ 448) – that this caused considerable inconvenience to merchants – which initiated a new chapter in the history of the sale of *ḥameẓ*. He suggested that such inconvenience might be avoided by selling (or later leasing) the room in which the *ḥameẓ* was stored to the non-Jew, a transaction which involved a small down payment and the physical transfer only of the key to the room. In later times the official nature of the transaction was stressed by the writing of a bill of sale. A copy of such a document (in Judeo-German) written by R. Ezekiel *Landau of Prague is preserved in his son Samuel Landau's responsa (*Shivat Ẓiyyon* 11); others were sometimes printed in *Haggadot*. The final stage in the evolution of the sale of *ḥameẓ* was introduced by R. *Shneur Zalman of Lyady. Objecting to the blatant legal fiction involved in Sirkes' method, he proposed the idea of a "general" sale, with an agent acting on behalf of the Jewish vendor. Despite the opposition of numerous rabbis, including Solomon b. Judah Aaron *Kluger of Brody and R. Joseph Saul *Nathanson, this proposal has generally been accepted as the form of the sale of *ḥameẓ*.

BIBLIOGRAPHY: S.J. Zevin, *Ha-Mo'adim ba-Halakhah* (196310), 245–55.

[Harry Rabinowicz]

HAMILTON, city in southern Ontario (total pop. 495,000 in 2001), with the eighth largest Jewish community in Canada (4,765). Hamilton Jewry comprised 1.3% of the Canadian Jewish population in 2001 compared with 1.4% in 1991, and 1.5% in 1981. Despite its small numbers, the community enjoyed an impressive array of institutions, including, for example, three active synagogues, a *mikveh* (ritual bath), a retirement and nursing home for the Jewish elderly (Shalom Village), a community center, and day and afternoon schools.

The community's Jewish population has reflected the larger Canadian experience. By 1941, Jews in Hamilton numbered some 2,600, with half identifying Yiddish as their mother tongue; by 1951, the number had risen to 3,000. Little population expansion occurred over the following two decades. However, this changed in the late 1960s and 1970s when the expansion of McMaster University attracted Jewish academics and medical professionals. In addition, between 1975 and 1980, some 300 Russian Jews settled in Hamilton, though the vast majority eventually left for Toronto. By 1981, the Canadian census listed 4,250 Jews in the Hamilton area.

The Jewish presence in Hamilton reaches back more than 150 years. In 1853 the city record identified 13 Jewish families. They formed the Hebrew Benevolent Society Anshe Sholom Hamilton. They were soon renamed the Jewish Congregation Anshe Sholom of Hamilton, constituting the first Jewish congregation in Hamilton and the first Reform congregation in Canada. All charter members were of German origin and the records were recorded in German. In 1874 Anshe Sholom women formed the Deborah Ladies Aid Society, the first Jewish women's charity society in Canada. Initially Orthodox in orientation, it aligned with Reform following changes to traditional liturgical practices and rituals.

Finding these changes unacceptable, a number of Orthodox Jews who had immigrated to Hamilton in the 1870s established the Beth Jacob congregation in 1883. In 1901 the congregation organized its Talmud Torah, and in 1908 the women formed a Ladies Aid Society. Its Orthodox orientation changed to Conservative in 1954. Membership peaked in the 1960s and 1970s. The congregation later proclaimed that it offered a fully egalitarian religious service. Immigrants from central Poland and Galicia founded the Adas Israel that served as the community's Orthodox congregation. In 1914 they adopted the name "Adas Israel Anshe Poilen." Known informally by its street designation, Cannon Street shul, its members formed a Loan Society in 1930 followed by a Ladies Auxiliary two years later.

For the community's first 75 years, Jews concentrated around the city's core. This area housed the synagogues (a total of five at one time), other communal institutions, and the vast majority of Jewish-owned commercial enterprises. As the Jewish population moved into west and southwest Hamilton, and to neighboring Dundas and Ancaster, there remained hardly any trace of this former institutional presence. Ironically, but hardly unique to Hamilton, Jews now reside in areas from which they were formerly barred owing to the presence of restrictive covenant practices.

The need to look after its own being understood, the number of institutions established to service the Jewish community was both impressive and extensive. Four organizations – the Hamilton Hebrew Institute, the Hamilton Jewish Relief Society, the Hamilton Free Loan Society, and the Israelitish Benevolent Society – attended to matters of financial assistance, immigration, and communal and civic affairs. They amalgamated in 1916 under the United Hebrew Association, which assumed responsibility for most philanthropic work. Other institutions helped shape the community's rich diversity. For example, the Grand Order of Israel Benefit Society was coordinated in 1907, and the Viceroy Reading Lodge of B'nai B'rith and the Council of Jewish Women were established in the city in 1921 and 1922, respectively. Formal participation in Zionist activity began with the formation of the Daughters of Zion in 1914 and the second Hadassah chapter in Canada in 1917. Shortly thereafter chapters of Pioneer Women and Mizrachi also organized. Organizations evolved and new ones were established to coordinate the integration of immigrants who arrived following World War II. The Council of Jewish Organizations was established in 1955 and represented the Jewish community locally and nationally, coordinating and overseeing matters pertaining to education, recreation, and culture. Renamed the Hamilton Jewish Federation in 1975, it served as the community's central Jewish organization.

While Jews in Hamilton endured antisemitism in the decades leading to and immediately following World War II, they successfully integrated into the mainstream. Several played prominent roles in the wider community as patrons of the arts and charitable campaigns. Their integration was also reflected in the community's changed occupational structure. While the earliest generations of immigrants were peddlers, storekeepers, and salespersons in the manufacturing trades (notably in steel, scrap, and auto parts), subsequent generations, university-educated, were active in various commercial enterprises and, not unexpectedly, proliferated the professions – accounting, education, law, dentistry, and medicine.

Demographically, the 2001 number of census-identified Jews in Hamilton represents a loss from the 5,165 recorded in 1991, the highest number ever. Indeed, the recent decrease reversed a trend of steady population growth during the preceding several decades. A closer examination of the available demographic figures reveals several features certain to impact on the community's ongoing organization, including the number of elderly, a decrease in school-age youth, and a steady increase in numbers living below the poverty line. In addition, with fewer family-based businesses where offspring are expected to succeed their parents, there is a greater tendency for younger persons to leave the community for larger urban centers. This out-migration will inevitably impact on the community's abilities to sustain the educational and cultural institutions it currently enjoys.

Despite the outflow of native Hamiltonians to larger centers, the community continued to support a vibrant institutional base and could experience growth in the foreseeable future. While university-age Jews may continue to leave, this movement could be more than offset by the arrival of newcomers attracted to the city for occupational opportunities, more affordable housing and other cost-of-living considerations, and the availability of a sound and potentially expanding Jewish infrastructure to cater to their religious, ethnic, and other requirements.

[William Shaffir (2nd ed.)]

ḤAMIẒ, JOSEPH BEN JUDAH (d. c. 1676), physician, philosopher, kabbalist, and communal leader. Born in Venice, from his youth Ḥamiẓ devoted himself to Torah and scholarship and was one of the outstanding pupils of Leone *Modena. In 1624 he received the degree of doctor of medicine and philosophy at the University of Padua. At the same time the rabbis of Venice decided to ordain him as rabbi. In honor of his graduation, his teacher and colleagues published a "collection of eulogies and poems" under the title *Belil Ḥamiẓ* (Venice, 1624; also in: *Seridim*, 1938). To Modena's distress, Ḥamiẓ came under the influence of esoteric teachings and joined the kabbalistic circles of Moses *Zacuto and *Aaron Berechiah b. Moses of Modena. In 1658 he and Zacuto published an expanded edition of the *Zohar Ḥadash* with glosses on the *Zohar, titled *Derekh Emet*. During the same period Ḥamiẓ began to write a commentary on the Zohar but ceased this work because he decided to move to Jerusalem. Thereafter all traces of him are lost.

During recent years two collections of his works have been found. I. Tishby discovered that a manuscript in Oxford University Library (Ms. Bod. 2239) is a collection of Ḥamiẓ's works written during the years 1667–75. From its contents it is clear that he was associated with Shabbatean circles and was active in the movement. E. Kupfer discovered that Ms. Parma 1283 was written by Ḥamiẓ in the town of Zante, where he stayed around 1666 on his way from Venice to Ereẓ Israel with his family. Apparently he delayed there because of the troubles that befell him: His wife and many members of his family who had accompanied him from Venice died in Zante. While staying there, he practiced as a physician, devoted much of his time to Torah, and was active in the life of the Jewish community. In 1674 he promoted the conference for the union of the communities in Zante, and was chosen to introduce *takkanot* for the united community.

From his writings in the Parma manuscript, it is clear that despite his devotion to Kabbalah and his association with Shabbatean activists he continued to be in doubt and disturbed. Even in his later years, side by side with kabbalist writings there are philosophical ideas and studies based on the school of Maimonides. Among the works in this collection is the *Pirkei ha-Musar u-Middot*, which he wrote as a kind of testament for his children.

Hamiẓ collected material from a variety of early kabbalistic material, including several books of Abraham *Abulafia and even earlier Kabbalah, and thus preserved material that is hardly known from other sources.

BIBLIOGRAPHY: M. Benayahu, *Iggerot R. Shemu'el Abohav ve-R. Moshe Zakut u-Venei Ḥugam*, 2, 8 (1955); I. Tishby, in: *Sefunot*, 1 (1956), 80–117; Scholem, Shabbetai Ẓevi, 2 (1957), index; E. Kupfer, in: KS, 40 (1965), 118–23; idem, in: *Sefunot* (in print).

[Ephraim Kupfer]

HA-MIẒPEH (Heb. הַמִּצְפֶּה; "the Watchtower"), a Hebrew weekly newspaper. Appearing in Cracow from 1904 to 1921 (with intervals during World War I), *Ha-Mizpeh* was edited by Simon Menahem Laser. Laser, the last editor of *Ha-Maggid*, which ceased publication in 1903, wanted to maintain the Hebrew press in Galicia. His new paper had a religious Zionist orientation and was the faithful organ, without official status, of the *Mizrachi movement. At the same time it fought the opponents of Zionism, including both Ḥasidim and assimilationists. *Ha-Mizpeh* reached its highest popularity at the time of the elections for the Austrian parliament, when it fought with extraordinary vigor the government-approved anti-Zionist pact between assimilationists and the ḥasidic rabbis. The paper also combated negative manifestations in the Zionist movement. Laser encouraged literary talents in Galicia. He discovered S.Y. *Agnon (then still known as Czaczkes), Avigdor *Hameiri, U.Z. *Greenberg, and many others who later became famous in Hebrew literature. Apart from Laser's journalistic pieces, the paper published studies, poems, stories, essays, feuilletons, and a humorous section for Purim. It was maintained throughout the years by Laser's efforts and without any subvention, even during World War I when he revived the paper after it had been forced to close. Laser was among the few who understood the nature of the Bolshevik regime's attitude toward the Jews, the problematic nature of the Balfour Declaration, and other political issues.

BIBLIOGRAPHY: G. Kressel (ed.), *Al ha-Mizpeh, Mivḥar Kitvei Shimon Menaḥem Laser* (1969).

[Getzel Kressel]

HAMLISCH, MARVIN (1944–), U.S. composer and arranger. Born in New York City, Hamlisch was the youngest student (at age seven) ever admitted to the Juilliard School of Music (which he attended until 1964). He is the composer and/or arranger of music scores for such films as *The Swimmer* (1968), *Take the Money and Run* (1969), *Bananas* (1971), *Save The Tiger* (1973) and *Kotch* (1971). In 1974 Hamlisch became the first individual to receive three Academy Awards in one night – one for best scoring of *The Sting*, one for best original dramatic score for the film *The Way We Were*, and one for best original song, "The Way We Were." He also received four Grammys for his work on *The Sting*. Hamlisch also won a Pulitzer Prize and a Tony Award for writing the script and composing the score of the Broadway musical *A Chorus Line* (1975).

His musical scores for other Broadway productions include *They're Playing Our Song* (1979), *Shirley Maclaine on Broadway* (1984), *Smile* (1987), *The Goodbye Girl* (1993), *Sweet Smell of Success* (2002), and *Imaginary Friends* (2003). Written by Neil Simon, *They're Playing Our Song* was based on the personal and professional relationship between Hamlisch and his long-time collaborator, lyricist Carole Bayer Sager. It was nominated for four Tony Awards, among them Best Musical.

Hamlisch also wrote the music for such films as *The Prisoner of Second Avenue* (1975), *The Spy Who Loved Me*

(1977), *Ice Castles* (1978), *Starting Over* (1979), *Chapter Two* (1979), *Gilda Live* (1980), *Ordinary People* (1980), *Seems Like Old Times* (1980), *Pennies from Heaven* (1981), *Sophie's Choice* (1982), *Three Men and a Baby* (1987), *January Man* (1989), *Shirley Valentine* (1989), *Missing Pieces* (1991), *Open Season* (1996), and *The Mirror Has Two Faces* (1996).

In addition to his work as a composer, Hamlisch is the principal pops conductor with the Pittsburgh Symphony Orchestra and the National Symphony Orchestra in Washington, D.C. He is the first person to hold such a position with either of those orchestras. In 1992 Hamlisch published his memoirs, *The Way I Was* (with G. Gardner).

ADD. BIBLIOGRAPHY: D. Flinn, *What They Did for Love* (1989); G. Stevens and A. George, *The Longest Line: Broadway's Most Singular Sensation – A Chorus Line* (1995).

[Jonathan Licht / Ruth Beloff (2nd ed.)]

HAMLYN, PAUL, BARON (1926–2001), British publisher. Born Paul Hamburger in Vienna, the son of a professor of pediatrics, Hamlyn came to England with his family in 1933. He left school at 15 and changed his name to "Hamlyn," unlike his brother, the poet and translator Michael *Hamburger (1926–). After a series of odd jobs, including a period of work as a coal miner, Hamlyn became a book remainder merchant and then a publisher. By the late 1960s he was the head of a large-scale publishing conglomerate, IPC. He later became a partner with Rupert Murdoch in News International and Octopus Books. By the 1980s he had become one of the richest men in England, while his original firm, Paul Hamlyn Ltd., had absorbed such old-established publishers as Heinemann and Butterworth. A longstanding supporter of the Labour Party, Hamlyn was given a life peerage in 1998.

BIBLIOGRAPHY: ODNB Supplement for 2001.

[William D. Rubinstein (2nd ed.)]

ḤAMMAT GADER (Heb. חַמַּת גָּדֵר; **Emmatha, El Hamme**), ancient site on the right bank of the Yarmuk Valley, north of *Gadara (Umm Qeis) and to the southeast of the Sea of Galilee. It was a Jewish town in the Roman and Byzantine periods. Ḥammat contained several hot springs and these attracted settlers from earliest times. In talmudic times it was included in the territory of *Gadara, and the Talmud thus refers to it as "Ḥammat of Gadara." It was heavily populated in this period, and many visitors from the south, the Golan, and Galilee, including Judah ha-Nasi and his pupils, came to bathe in the springs. The Romans also used the springs during the bathing season. The ruins include a temple, a theater, a synagogue, and a large complex of baths.

[E. Cindof / Shimon Gibson (2nd ed.)]

In the Modern Period

The five thermal springs of Ḥammat Gader (the waters of the hottest and richest in minerals have a temperature of 124° F (51° C)) intermittently served local inhabitants for healing purposes. The place became a station on the narrow-gauge railway branch that connected Haifa through Ẓemaḥ with the Hejaz railway (traffic on the line was finally halted in 1946 when the Palmaḥ blew up a bridge crossing the Yarmuk near Ḥammat Gader). The border of the British Mandate of Palestine protruded eastward into the narrow Yarmuk gorge for 3 mi. (5 km.), thus creating a wedge, including Ḥammat Gader, of a few hundred meters width only, between Transjordanian and Syrian territory. In Israel's War of Independence (1948), the Syrians occupied the place when advancing toward Lake Kinneret; in the 1949 Armistice Agreement, the Ḥammat Gader tongue returned to Israel sovereignty, although it was declared a demilitarized zone where only the previous (i.e., Arab) inhabitants were permitted to return. Nevertheless in 1951, Syrian forces occupied Ḥammat Gader and held it until 1967. The Syrians turned the spot into a rest center for their officers and officials, building a mosque, hotel, bathhouses, and other installations. In the Six-Day War (1967), Ḥammat Gader returned to Israeli control. In the ensuing years, it was repeatedly shelled from Jordanian positions on the steep slope directly above it, and mines planted by terrorists caused a number of losses to Israel civilians. Because of the security situation, plans for developing Ḥammat Gader as a farming, tourist, and recreation center had to be postponed, and the group preparing to settle there had to erect its collective village, Mevo Ḥammat, 3 mi. (5 km.) to the northwest on the Golan plateau. Subsequently, however, it was developed into one of Israel's leading tourist sites with water sports, a crocodile farm, and other attractions in addition to the baths.

[Efraim Orni]

BIBLIOGRAPHY: Albright, in: BASOR, 35 (1932), 12; Glueck, *ibid.*, 49 (1933), 22; E.L. Sukenik, *The Ancient Synagogue of el-Ḥammeh "Hammath-by-Gadara"* (1935); idem, in: JPOS, 15 (1935), 101–80. **ADD. BIBLIOGRAPHY:** Y. Hirschfeld, "The History and Town-Plan of Ancient Hammat Gader," in: ZDPV 103 (1987), 101–16; Z. Ilan, *Ancient Synagogues in Israel* (1991), 91–93; Y. Hirschfeld, *The Roman Baths of Hammat Gader* (1997).

HAMMATH (Heb. חַמַּת), city in the territory of Naphtali mentioned in the Bible together with Rakkath and Chinnereth (Josh. 19:35). Its name indicates the presence of hot springs. Most scholars identify Hammath with Hammath-Dor, a city of refuge and a levitical city (Josh. 21:32), which is generally located at Hammath Tiberias, south of Tiberias. No remains from the biblical period, however, have thus far been uncovered there, and the site of the ancient town should probably be identified with the early remains within the confines of Roman Tiberias. Hammath was famous for its hot baths in the Second Temple period (Jos., Wars 4:11; Jos., Ant. 18:36); when Tiberias rose to prominence in talmudic times, Hammath, one mile away and joined to Tiberias for halakhic purposes, also became well known (Meg. 2b; Tosef., Er. 7:2; TJ, Er. 6 (5); 13). After the destruction of the Second Temple, priests of the Maziah course settled there (*Baraita of the Twenty-Four Mishmarot*, 24); the Emmaus mentioned in the Mishnah *Arakhin* 2:4 may refer to the place. R. Meir was one of the many talmudic scholars who lived there. A Jewish community is attested there up to the time of the Cairo *Genizah*.

During the excavation of the foundations of bathhouses, two synagogues were discovered; the first was excavated by N. Slouschz in 1920 and the other by M. Dothan in 1961–63. The first, belonging to the transitional type of synagogue, consisted of a basilica-shaped hall without an apse. The facade oriented to Jerusalem contained four small marble columns which apparently supported a marble lintel above the Ark of the Law. The synagogue was paved with mosaics; fragments of the "seat of Moses" (cathedra) were found there, as well as a stone seven-branched *menorah*, carved in relief and decorated with a "button and leaf" pattern in the form of pomegranates. In the second synagogue four building phases were distinguished. (1) The earliest structure consisted of a public building (probably not a synagogue) with rooms surrounding a central courtyard. (2) A synagogue from the third century C.E. (3) Directly above this synagogue and using its columns was another synagogue built in the form of a basilica with an outstanding mosaic pavement which contained (from north to south): a dedicatory inscription flanked by two lions; a zodiac of a high artistic standard with the sun god Helios on his chariot in the center and representations of the four seasons in the corners; the Ark of the Law with *menorot* and other ritual articles. Inscriptions in Greek and one in Aramaic commemorate several builders, especially a certain "Severus, the pupil of the most illustrious patriarchs." The building, 47½ ft. (14½ m.) wide, contains a nave with two aisles east of it and to the west of it, an aisle, and a hall (women's gallery?). The synagogue is attributed to the beginning of the fourth century C.E.; in a later period a stationary *bamah* ("platform") was installed and the entrance was moved from the southern to the northern side. (4) Above the site of this synagogue another one was built in the sixth century with a slightly different orientation. It was basilica in shape, 62 × 49 ft. (19 × 15 m.) with an apse and a mosaic pavement with geometric designs.

Bathhouses have again been built at Hammath Tiberias in modern times. They are fed by five springs whose waters reach a temperature of 140°–144° F (60°–62° C) and contain graphite, iron, and magnesium chloride. Of curative value, they are widely used, especially in the winter seasons. The grave of R. *Meir Ba'al ha-Nes is reputed to be near Hammath Tiberias, and a large synagogue is situated on the site. The grave site became famous in the Jewish world beginning in the 18th century because of the collection boxes, named after R. Meir, widely distributed by emissaries of charitable institutions. It is an ancient custom to hold festivities and build bonfires near the grave on the 14th of Iyyar.

BIBLIOGRAPHY: Slouschz, in: JPESJ, 1 (1921), 5–39, 49–52; W.F. Albright, in: BASOR, 19 (1925), 10; M. Dothan, in: IEJ, 12 (1962), 153–4; idem, in: *Qadmoniot*, 1 (1968), 116–23; A. Saarisalo, *Boundary between Issachar and Naphtali* (1927), 128 n. 1; M. Noth, *Das Buch Josua* (1938), 90–91; D.W. Thomas, in: PEFQS, 65 (1933), 205; 66 (1934), 147–8. **ADD. BIBLIOGRAPHY:** Z. Ilan, *Ancient Synagogues in Israel* (1991), 139–43; Y. Tsafrir, L. Di Segni, and J. Green, *Tabula Imperii Romani. Iudaea – Palaestina. Maps and Gazetteer.* (1994), 138–39.

[Michael Avi-Yonah]

HAMMER, ARMAND (1898–1990), U.S. industrialist and art collector. When studying at Columbia Medical School in his native New York in 1918, he joined his father's business, a chain of drug stores which was about to go bankrupt. Hammer demonstrated his business acumen when he bought quantities of medicine cheaply at the end of World War I and sold them as the price rose quickly, making $1 million.

After graduating medical school in 1921, he took off six months before beginning his internship and went to the U.S.S.R. His father was a member of the Communist party of America and a strong supporter of the Russian Revolution. Hammer went to help set up medical clinics in Moscow and other Russian cities. In the aftermath of the Revolution, the health-care system no longer existed and he made a significant contribution.

A businessman by nature, Hammer began arranging business deals for the Soviet Union. The first major one was an American wheat purchase in exchange for Russian furs and caviar. When Lenin saw Hammer's capabilities, the Russian leader gave the young man mining rights in Siberia. To show his appreciation, Hammer engineered deals involving Ford, U.S. Rubber, and other large companies with the Soviet Union.

Remaining in Russia for nine years until 1930, he and his brother, who had joined him, bought up Russian art treasures which were available for needed cash. He made another $1 million when Lenin granted him the exclusive rights to manufacture wooden pencils in the Soviet Union.

On his return to the United States with an enormous horde of art treasures, many from the royal Romanov family, he had trouble selling the works because of the Depression. To be innovative, he merchandized the paintings and other art objects through major department stores such as Macy's and Gimbels. His first book dealt with his adventures collecting art in Russia and was entitled *The Quest for the Romanoff Treasure.* During the next 25 years, he earned a major fortune buying and selling distilleries. He retired in California in 1956, but within a short time he bought the controlling interest in Occidental Petroleum Company, a company about to fail. He struck oil with several new leases, soon registering major profits amounting to $300 million a year. This company, under his leadership, became the largest oil company in the world under private ownership.

In the early 1970s his close relationship with the Soviet government resulted in his negotiating a major fertilizer purchase by the Russians from an American company worth $8 billion. His ties with Russia helped to reawaken his Jewish roots. Although secret at the time, it is now clear that Hammer intervened to seek to persuade Russian leaders to permit Soviet Jews to leave the U.S.S.R. in the 1970s – ultimately almost 200,000 then emigrated.

Although publicly non-committal about Israel and his Judaism until the 1980s, he visited the country secretly and also tried to help develop certain business ties for Israel with various countries, which had no relations with her. From the mid-1980s, he was active in getting refuseniks released and he flew Ida Nudel to Israel in his own plane when she was finally freed. He also invested in oil explorations in Israel and in offshore sites nearby, none of which produced any marketable finds. He died in his sleep only a few days before he was to have had a belated bar mitzvah.

[David Geffen (2nd ed.)]

HAMMER, REUVEN (**Robert A.**; 1933–), American-Israeli scholar, leader of Masorti/Conservative Judaism, and advocate for special needs students in Jewish schools.

Hammer received rabbinic ordination and a D.H.L. from the Jewish Theological Seminary and a Ph.D. in Communicative Disorders from Northwestern University. After serving as a chaplain in the U.S. Air Force and as a congregational rabbi, Hammer was prominent among the young Conservative rabbis and educators who made *aliyah* from North America in the early 1970s and created many of the institutions of what became Israel's Masorti (Conservative) movement.

He headed the Israel campus of the Jewish Theological Seminary in Jerusalem, and after taking part in the planning process that led to the creation of a Conservative seminary in Jerusalem, in 1984 he took on an additional role as director of the Seminary of Judaic Studies, which later grew into the Schechter Rabbinical Seminary and an academic institution, the Schechter Institute of Jewish Studies.

A decade later he served as his movement's representative on the Ne'eman Commission appointed to avert a crisis over "who is a Jew" in Israeli law after the courts insisted on government recognition of non-Orthodox conversions – the Conservative rabbi to serve in an official position vis-à-vis the government of Israel. He later represented the Masorti movement on the board of the Joint Conversion Institute whose establishment was sparked by the Ne'eman Commission's discussions.

In Israel's Masorti movement, Hammer served as the head of the Rabbinical Court for Conversion and chairman of the movement's Public Affairs Committee. Hammer also worked to further the interests of Masorti/Conservative Judaism in Israel and elsewhere through the Rabbinical Assembly, which he served as president of its Israel Region and later as president of the worldwide body.

Hammer's wide-ranging scholarly endeavors included teaching at the institutions mentioned above as well as the Hebrew University of Jerusalem, the David Yellin College of Education, and other academic institutions in Israel, Argentina, and Russia. His voluminous writings include *Sifre, A Tannaitic Commentary on Deuteronomy* (an English translation and commentary, 1986) and many works that brought Jewish scholarship to a wide audience: *Entering Jewish Prayer* (1994), *Entering the High Holy Days* (1998), and a collection of his own annotated translations of passages from midrash, *The Classic Midrash* (1994). He edited *The Jerusalem Anthology* (1995), a collection of documents and belles-lettres about Jerusalem over the ages. His magnum opus on the literary and theological appreciation of Jewish liturgy, *Or Hadash* (2003), takes the form of a commentary to the Conservative *Sim Shalom* prayerbook. The first of two volumes appeared in 2003.

Hammer was among the first vocal proponents of providing instruction and support designed to take into account learning disabilities and differences of learning style in North American Jewish education. While still living in the U.S., he undertook his doctoral studies in that field in order to be able to start programs for special education in synagogue schools, which were then non-existent. His book, *The Other Child in Jewish Education*, enjoyed decades of use and influence.

[Peretz Rodman (2nd ed.)]

HAMMER, ZEVULUN (1936–1998), Israeli political leader; member of the Seventh to Fourteenth Knesset. Hammer was born in Haifa, studied at the religious Yavneh high school, and joined *Bnei Akiva in 1945, later becoming a member of its national council, and a leader in many of its branches. He served in the IDF within the framework of *Nahal, and attended the National Security College. Hammer graduated from Bar-Ilan University in Jewish and Bible studies. From 1961 he headed the Students Association, and was a member of the presidium of the National Students Association, in which capacity he was in charge of the World Union of Jewish Students. After graduation he entered the teaching profession.

In the course of the 1960s he became leader of the *National Religious Party young guard. After the Six-Day War he acted to transform the NRP from a party whose focus was on religious affairs to a movement whose main concern was the preservation of the integrity of Ereẓ Israel and security. In 1974 he actively supported the establishment of the *Gush Emunim settlement movement. Hammer was first elected to the Seventh Knesset in 1969. From January 1973 to January 1974 he served as deputy minister of education and culture and in 1975–76 as minister of welfare in the first government formed by Yitzhak *Rabin. In 1976 he was largely responsible, with his colleague MK Dr. Judah Ben-Meir, for ending the "historical coalition" between the NRP and the *Israel Labor Party. In 1977–84 he served as minister of education and culture, introducing free education in high schools and pre-compulsory kindergartens. He introduced Holocaust studies in 10th grade, made an effort to enhance Jewish studies in non-religious schools, and established a Supreme Committee for Scientific and Technological Education. Despite sincere efforts, he failed to close the educational gap between the Ashkenazi and Sephardi Jewish sectors of the population, on the one hand, and between the Jewish and Arab sectors, on the other. In 1986–90 he served as minister for religious affairs, returning to the Ministry of Education and Culture after the Labor Party left the National Unity Government in March 1990. The

NRP did not join the government formed by Yitzhak *Rabin in 1992. After Joseph *Burg, whom he had helped get elected as leader of the NRP in 1977, resigned the leadership in 1986, Hammer was elected secretary general of the NRP. As leader of the NRP he tried to move away from extreme positions and acted to try to build bridges between the religious and secular communities in Israel. Following Rabin's assassination Hammer was one of the national religious leaders who called for serious soul searching in the national-religious movement. In the elections to the Fourteenth Knesset the NRP under Hammer's leadership managed to regain some of its lost strength, going up from its 4–6 seats in the Tenth to Thirteenth Knessets to nine.

In the government formed by Binyamin *Netanyahu in 1996 he was once again appointed minister of education and culture, as well as deputy prime minister, in which capacity he served until his death in 1998 after an illness.

[Susan Hattis Rolef (2nd ed.)]

HAMMERSTEIN, U.S. family closely associated with the development of opera and the popular musical theater in U.S. Its two most famous members were Oscar Hammerstein I (1847–1919) and his grandson, Oscar II (1895–1960). Born in Berlin, OSCAR HAMMERSTEIN I ran away from home, reached New York in 1863, and worked in a cigar factory. He soon became an important and wealthy figure in the industry. His passion, however, was for building opera houses. The Harlem Opera House, built in the 1880s, was his first. The Victoria (1899) was a successful vaudeville theater managed by his son WILLIAM. Altogether he built 10 opera houses and theaters in New York, in addition to an opera house in Philadelphia (1908) and one in London (1911). His Manhattan Opera House (1906), a venture in which his son ARTHUR (1873–1955) was closely involved, competed with the dominant Metropolitan Opera House until 1910, when the Metropolitan bought it out for $1.2 million. In its time the Manhattan helped to make grand opera exciting by bringing new talent and works to American audiences. His later ventures were less successful. OSCAR HAMMERSTEIN II, librettist, was born in New York, the son of William Hammerstein. He played an important role in developing the "musical play" into an integrated dramatic form. He worked for his uncle Arthur as a stage manager. By 1920 he had produced the books for three musicals. *Wildflower* (1923) was his first real success. Subsequently he collaborated on such Broadway musicals as *Rose Marie* (1924), *Desert Song* (1926), and *Show Boat* (1927). After some years in Hollywood, he formed his partnership with the composer Richard *Rodgers in 1943. Together they produced a series of successful musicals with a style and form of their own. These included *Oklahoma* (1943), *Carousel* (1945), *South Pacific* (1949), which won a Pulitzer Prize, *The King and I* (1951), and *The Sound of Music* (1959). The Rodgers and Hammerstein Foundation, New York, established a fund for cancer research in 1963, at the Hebrew University Hadassah Medical School, Jerusalem.

BIBLIOGRAPHY: J.F. Cone, *Oscar Hammerstein's Manhattan Opera Company* (1966); *Fact Book Concerning the Plays of Richard Rodgers and Oscar Hammerstein* (1954).

[Harvey A. Cooper]

HAMMURAPI (the spelling of the name with a "p" rather than a "b" seems assured by the writing *ʿmrpʾ* in Ugaritic apparently "the [divine] kinsman is a healer," but interpreted by post-Kassite Babylonian tradition as *kimta rapaštu*, "widespread kinfolk"), the sixth king (1792–50 B.C.E.) of the first dynasty of Babylon, one of several Amorite kingdoms which rose in southern Babylonia in the aftermath of the fall of the third dynasty of Ur. Amorites spoke a West Semitic language with similarities to Aramaic and Hebrew. Because the cuneiform system lacks *ayin*, ḪA served as its approximation, the *ḫammu-*, corresponding to Hebrew *ʿam*, "people," "kin." As such the king's name is of the same type as Am-ram; Ammi-el etc. Sources for the reign of Hammurapi are his own inscriptions, including the lengthy prologue to the code which bears his name; year names in date formulas which, in keeping with established tradition, list an outstanding military, political, or domestic event by which the year is known; letters, both from Hammurapi's own chancellery, and from other centers, especially the large political archive from *Mari in the upper Euphrates valley; business documents; and legal texts. Since Hammurapi's Babylon has not been excavated, his own diplomatic archive has not been uncovered.

When Hammurapi assumed the throne, Babylon was a small city-state, his predecessors having limited themselves to maintaining their local rule against the ambitions of similar states in the vicinity and against the incursions of nomads. As seen from a document written in the generation before Hammurapi, and from the contemporaneous Mari letters, the situation in southern Babylonia during the early Old Babylonian period was such that each ruler managed to govern within the limited confines of his city-state, while the open interurban spaces were given over to the control of nomadic and seminomadic tribes who roamed the area. It was Hammurapi's accomplishment to weld these several city-states into a cohesive base from which to embark on the wider conquest of the rest of Mesopotamia.

To his contemporaries, Hammurapi was a somewhat lesser figure than he is thought to be today – a minor king in comparison to others, according to a Mari letter. Indeed, for the first 10 years or so of his reign, Babylon seems to have been at least partially subservient to Assyria, then ruled by Shamshi-Adad I. After the death of the latter during, or just after, Hammurapi's 10th year, Assyria began to decline, and a complicated political and military maze took form in Babylonia, expressing itself in a system of ephemeral alliances and counter alliances and reciprocal demands for military aid, each king continually jockeying for a more advantageous position. The serious rivals of Hammurapi were then Yarim-Lim of Yamhad (Aleppo), Zimri-Lim of Mari, Rim-Sin of Larsa,

Amut-pi-el of Qatana, and Ibal-pi-El of Eshnunna, together with his Elamite allies.

For the middle 20 years or so of Hammurapi's reign, nothing militarily or politically decisive occurred and the year names of this period reflect in the main a time of intensive civic building and canal making. By the 29th year of his reign Babylon must have been strong enough to take on its rivals. That year initiated 10 years of intensive campaigning, which gave Hammurapi control of all of Mesopotamia. After a long period of seemingly friendly relations, Rim-Sin of Larsa was defeated in the 30th year of Hammurapi's reign; a coalition of forces from Assyria, Eshnunna, and Elam was defeated in the 31st year; Mari, in the 32nd; and Assyria was finally subdued in the 36th and 38th years. This seems to be the limit of Hammurapi's conquests, and there is no reason to identify him with *Amraphel of Genesis 14.

Hammurapi is best known for the so-called Code of Hammurapi (see *Mesopotamia). This is a misnomer, at least to the extent that it is not comprehensive. Modern scholarship tends to view the code as an abstract formulation of actual precedents in the form of ad hoc decisions of the king gathered from the state archives, plus an undetermined smaller element of deliberate, reforming legislation, all this cast in the traditional form of law codes consisting of a prologue, body of law, and epilogue. The actual function, if any, of this code is unknown, and it is never referred to in contemporary legal texts. The code reflects a tripartite division of society: an upper level of free men (*awīlum*), a class of state dependents (*muškēnum*, cf. Heb. *misken*, "poor"), and a slave caste (male *wardum*; female *amtum*), with no social mobility between classes. In other basic aspects, the code shows fundamental points of contact with the slightly older Eshnunna code, as well as with the Book of the *Covenant in Exodus 20ff.

The small amount of Old Babylonian literature preserved shows that this was a period of great and original creativity in Akkadian literature. It produced, furthermore, the last reliable formulation of the Sumerian traditions, and present knowledge of Sumerian language and literature is based, to a large extent, on the products of the contemporary scribal school. In religion, the rise of Marduk, the local god of Babylon, to the status of a great god, concomitant with the political rise of Babylon, should be noted.

BIBLIOGRAPHY: C.J. Gadd, in: CAH², vol. 2, ch. 5 (1965; incl. bibl., 55–62); J.J. Finkelstein, in: JCS, 20 (1966), 95–118. **ADD. BIBLIOGRAPHY:** S. Meier, in: ABD, 3, 39–42; M. Roth, *Law Collections from Mesopotamia and Asia Minor* (1995), 71–142; A. Kuhrt, *The Ancient Near East c. 3000–330 BC* (1995), 108–16; J. Sasson, in: CANE, 2, 901–15; M. van de Mierop, *King Hammurabi of Babylon: A Biography* (2004).

[Aaron Shaffer]

HAMNUNA, the name of several Babylonian *amoraim*.

HAMNUNA SABA ("the elder"), a pupil of Rav (BK 106a), mid-third century C.E. He transmitted his teacher's sayings (Er. 16b; et al.). Rav was fond of Hamnuna and taught him a number of apothegms (Er. 54a). He succeeded Rav as the head of the academy of Sura. According to the Talmud, statements of "the school of Rav" emanated from Hamnuna (Sanh. 17b). There are both halakhic and aggadic statements in his name, and many of the latter emphasize the duty of study of the Torah and the gravity of its neglect, e.g., "Jerusalem was destroyed only because they neglected the teaching of schoolchildren" (Shab. 119b); "Man is judged first in respect of study of Torah alone" (Kid. 40b). The Talmud also cites formulae of prayers uttered by him, some apparently composed by him (Ber. 11b; 17a; 58a; et al.). Hamnuna was an associate of Ḥisda (Shab. 97a; et al.) and Ḥisda once became so enthusiastic at his exposition that he said: "Would that we had feet of iron so that we could always run and listen to you" (see Ber. 41b and Rashi *ibid.*). It is stated that his body was transported for burial to Ereẓ Israel where miraculous events occurred on that occasion (MK 25a–b).

HAMNUNA, an *amora* of the beginning of the fourth century C.E. A native of Harpania in Babylonia (Yev. 17a), he resided in Harta of Argiz in the vicinity of Baghdad where he taught (Er. 63a; Shab. 19b). He was a pupil and colleague of Ḥisda (Er. 63a) who praised him highly to *Huna (Kid. 29b). He also studied under R. Judah (Shevu. 34a) and Ulla (Yev. 17a).

HAMNUNA ZUTA ("the younger"), fourth century C.E. The formula of the Confession of Sin, which he was accustomed to recite on the Day of Atonement, the opening words of which are "O my God! Before I was formed, I was not worthy," is included in the liturgy of that day. When requested to sing a song at the wedding of Mar, the son of Ravina, he sang: "Woe to us, that we must die!" asking his colleagues to join in with the refrain: "Where is the Torah and where is the Commandment that they may shield us?" (Ber. 31a).

Other *amoraim* of the same name, some with and some without appellations, who lived in the third and fourth centuries and whom it is difficult to identify, are referred to in the talmudic sources.

BIBLIOGRAPHY: Hyman, Toledot, 376–9; Ḥ. Albeck, *Mavo la-Talmudim* (1969), 281–3, 197f.

[Zvi Kaplan]

HA-MODI'A (Heb. הַמּוֹדִיעַ), daily newspaper published in Jerusalem by the *Agudat Israel Party. Established in 1949 by Yitzhak Meir Levin, son-in-law of the Gur Rebbe, and edited by his son Yehudah Leib Levin, *Ha-Modi'a* ("The Herald") represented three streams in the **ḥaredi* world. In addition to the Gur Rebbe's own ḥasidic or "central" stream, there was the so-called "young" Agudat Yisrael identified with the Lithuanian (or "Litvak") stream, and the Shomrei Emunim (Guardians of the Faith) or Jerusalem stream.

When Yehudah Leib Levin died in 1981 he was replaced by a troika of three editors, Ḥayyim Knopf, Moshe Akiva Druck, and Yisroel Spiegel, representing the ḥasidic, Shomrei Emunim, and Lithuanian streams, respectively. In practice, while Knopf formally had the title of editor he handled the newspaper's business side, the editing being done by Druck and Spiegel on a rotation basis.

During the Levin period, the newspaper included four pages daily and six–eight pages on Sabbath and holiday eves. Content comprised mostly political news, including the full texts of speeches by its Knesset representatives, as well as news about the ḥaredi community. Supplements occasionally appeared such as to mark the death of a famous sage. Under the "troika," news coverage expanded to include national, financial, and foreign news.

The Lithuanian stream withdrew to form its own paper, *Yated Ne'eman*, in 1985 after Rabbi Eliezer *Shach resigned from the Council of Torah Sages over the question of the construction of a hotel in Tiberias on the site of Jewish graves. Shach was affronted by the newspaper's preference in 1982 for the Gur Rebbe's lenient ruling in the face of Shach's more stringent one in the matter. *Ha-Modi'a* subsequenlty became identified publicly with the ḥasidic stream of ḥaredim.

On Druck's death in 1992, he was replaced by Itzhak Tennenbaum. By 2000, Yisroel Schneider (of the ḥasidic or "central" stream) had become Knopf's right-hand man as acting editor. News coverage was expanded with special correspondents covering politics in addition to the Knesset, the military, economics, Jerusalem, and Bene Berak. A weekly economics supplement was introduced.

In addition to party journalism, *Ha-Modi'a* acts as an educational instrument in both an active and passive or filtering sense. The newspaper is controlled by a spiritual committee, whose censors examine the contents – editorial and advertisements – of each issue prior to publication. Sex-related matters and pictures of women are not printed in order to comply with ḥaredi strictures about modesty (*ẓeniyyut*). The names of women journalists on the newspaper are abbreviated. Crime is barely covered, entertainment and sport not at all. In aspiring to build the model Jewish society, the ḥaredi newspaper is also a channel for conditioning readers in the hisorical haredi view of Zionism as premature vis-à-vis the arrival of the Messiah, and for attacking state institutions like the Knesset and the Supreme Court for making decisions regarded as running counter to Torah values.

In the face of competition from a commercial ḥaredi press in the 1980s and 1990s the newspaper expanded. On Sabbath eve the newspaper has two supplements: one for general news features and a religious section containing articles by rabbis on the week's Bible reading, halakhic issues, and Jewish history. The separate religious section allows the ḥaredi Jew to avoid reading about non-religious matters on the Sabbath. Also added was a 16-page children's supplement. *Ha-Modi'a's* layout was conservative, with small print and headlines, though it added color.

In 2005, 25% of ḥaredim saw *Ha-Modi'a* daily and 26% on weekends. A 1995 survey found that 65% of *Ha-Modi'a* readers were ḥasidim, 31% were "uncommitted" ḥaredim (only 9% of Lithuanian ḥaredim saw the paper). Its influence was particularly wide given the fact that ḥaredim are not exposed to television or to secular newspapers. Economically, *Ha-Modi'a* was strapped financially, but the demographic trend toward large families in the ḥaredi community suggested that the newspaper's long-term chances for success were good.

Ha-Modi'a introduced three English-language daily and weekly editions, in Israel, the U.S., and Britain. The estimated circulation of the U.S. edition was 40,000. In accordance with the ḥaredi rabbinical ban on Internet, the newspaper does not maintain a website.

BIBLIOGRAPHY: M. Micholson, "Haredi Newspapers in Israel," in: *Kesher*, 8 (1990); Y. Cohen, "Mass Media in the Jewish Tradition," in: D. Stout and J Buddenbaum, *Religion and Popular Culture* (2001); idem, "Religion News in Israel," in: *Journal of Media and Religion*, 3 (2005); Israel Advertisers Association, *Seker Ḥasifah le-Emẓa'ei Tikshoret: Ḥaredim* (1995).

[Yoel Cohen (2nd ed.)]

HAMON, family of Spanish and Portuguese origin which lived in *Turkey. ISAAC HAMON (second half of 15th century) was a physician in the court of King Abdallah of Granada. Following the Spanish expulsion the family settled in the *Ottoman Empire, where its members rapidly achieved fame as physicians of considerable influence in the courts of the sultans. JOSEPH HAMON "THE ELDER" (c. 1450–1518), a native of Granada, was the son of Isaac Hamon and settled in *Istanbul in 1492/93, just after the expulsion from Spain. He was court physician to the sultans *Byazid II (1481–1512) and Selim I (1512–20), and it seems that he was also the latter's counselor. Hamon accompanied the latter in his military expedition to *Egypt from 1516 to 1517 and died of disease in *Damascus during the return journey in 1518. According to Rabbi Joseph Garcon, Joseph served the two sultans for 25 years. His influence at the court of the sultan enabled him to assist his coreligionists when they were in danger. The best known and most important member of the Hamon family was his son MOSES (c. 1490–1554), who succeeded his father as the physician of the sultan Selim I and was also physician to *Suleiman the Magnificent (1520–1566). Moses soon became the leading court physician. He also wielded extensive influence as a result of his connections with the powerful court party, led by Roxolana-Khūrram, the favorite wife of Suleiman, and her son-in-law, the chief vizier Rustum Pasha. Shortly before his death, he was dismissed as a result of court intrigues. In times of need Moses employed his influence to help his brother Jews. For example, he obtained a firman from Suleiman the Magnificent protecting the Jews from *blood libels. According to this decree, all such libels were to be brought by the accusers before the Royal Dīwān instead of before an ordinary judge. Hamon also intervened with Sultan Suleiman in the affair of the properties of Gracia Mendes *Nasi, which had been confiscated in *Venice. When the community of *Salonica appealed to him (between 1539 and 1545) for assistance in dealing with powerful members who had disturbed the communal discipline by flouting new regulations, he had them brought to Constantinople where they were penalized by the government, which upon his request also sent a judge and an official to supervise the execution of the regulations.

Moses and his descendants (who are referred to as Evlad-i Musa, "children of Moses," in official documents) were exempted from the payment of certain taxes in recognition of their services to the country. Moses, who accompanied Suleiman in his campaign against *Persia in 1534, returned from *Baghdad with R. Jacob b. Joseph *Tavus, who, with the financial support of Moses, published the Torah, together with his own Persian translation and the Arabic translation of *Saadiah Gaon in 1546. In the synagogue, which was named after him, Moses maintained a yeshivah which was headed by R. Joseph *Taitaẓak of Salonica. He owned a valuable and rare collection of manuscripts, which included the *Codex Dioscorides* (a famous pharmaceutical work) of the sixth century which is now in Vienna. He also wrote several works on medicine, including an important one on dental cure, which is to be found in the Istanbul University Library.

JUDAH HAMON (d. 1578) was a court physician who settled in Adrianople and died there when he was 74 years old.

ABRAHAM YESHA HAMON (17th century), a descendant of Moses Hamon, was one of the Istanbul community's wealthy figures. He was known as a philanthropist and traveled to Venice in order to help the captives there. His name is mentioned in a letter from Istanbul's rabbis to Venice in 1675.

JOSEPH (d. 1577) son of Moses, was the physician of Suleiman the Magnificent and Selim II (1566–74). From the latter, he obtained the renewal of the rights of the Jews of Salonica in 1568. It appears that between 1559 and 1560, he maintained relations with the renowned Jewish physician in Salonica, *Amatus Lusitanus. Joseph belonged to the literary circle of Istanbul, which was led by Gedaliah *Ibn Yaḥia and which included the poets Saadiah Longo and Judah Zarko. Like his father, he also acted as a patron of Hebrew poets. His widow, Korshi, wrote a letter to Rabbi Judah *Abrabanel in 1578 in which she mentioned her children Judah and Av Hamon and her daughter and her son-in-law David.

JUDAH (d. 1644) was listed among the Jewish physicians serving Sultan Murad IV in 1618. He died childless and his will was discussed by the rabbis of Istanbul in 1644.

AV HAMON (d. c. 1650) was one of the renowned scholars of Istanbul in the 17th century who was involved in 1641 in the dispute about the rabbinate in the Sephardi congregation Neve Shalom. At that time he was old. In 1644 he requested the nullification of his brother Judah Hamon's will. His brother had bequeathed his property to scholars. The rabbis of Istanbul objected to Rabbi Av Hamon's request.

ISAAC (16th–17th century), another son of Joseph, also a physician. He declined a proposal of the Spanish government, which offered him a sum of money if he influenced the Ottoman government in negotiating a peace treaty with Spain. He was the father of the poet Aaron ben Isaac *Hamon.

In Istanbul there existed in the years 1603 and 1649 a so-called Hamon congregation.

BIBLIOGRAPHY: Solomon Ibn Verga, *Shevet Yehudah*, ed. by A. Shochat (1947), 56, 92, 144; H. Gross, in: REJ, 56 (1908), 1–26; 57 (1909), 56–78 Rosanes, Togarmah, 1 (1930²), 93, 126; 2 (1938), 4, 56–57, 286–98; 3 (1938), 354–6; A.H. Freimann, in: *Zion*, 1 (1936), 192, 205; S. Krauss, *Geschichte der juedischen Aerzte* (1930), 4, 55; A. Galanté, *Histoire des Juifs d'Istanbul* (1941), 10; U. Heyd, in: *Oriens*, 16 (1963), 152–70; B. Lewis, in: *Bulletin of the School of Oriental and African Studies*, 14 (1952), 550–63. **ADD. BIBLIOGRAPHY:** T.F. Jones, in: AHA *Annual Report for 1914*, 1, 159–67; A. Danon, in: JQR, n.s. 17 (1926), 242; U. Heyd, in: *Sefunot*, 5 (1961), 135–50; C. Roth, in: *Oxford Slavonic Papers*, 2 (1960), 8–20; M. Benayahu, *Haskamah u-Reshut bi-Defusei Venezia* (1971), 311; idem, in: *Sefunot*, 12 (1971–78), 46; Terzioğlu, in: RHMH, 112 (1975), 39–45 (repr. in: *Mélanges d'histoire de la Médecine hébraïque* (2003)); M.A. Epstein, *The Ottoman Jewish Communities and their Role in the Fifteenth and Sixteenth Centuries* (1980), 84–88, 188; E. Bashan, *Sheviya u-Pedut* (1980), 195; M. Benayahu, in: *Michael*, 7 (1982), 124–34; L. Bornstein-Makovetsky, in: S. Trigano (ed.), *La Société Juive à travers l'Histoire*, 3 (1994), 433 f.; A. Levy, in: A. Levy (ed.), *The Jews of the Ottoman Empire* (1994), 31, 133; L. Bornstein-Makovetsky, in: *Michael*, 9 (1985), 27–54; Baron, Social 13 (1983), 74–75; M. Rozen, *Bi-Netivei ha-Yam ha-Tikhon* (1993), 164.

[Simon Marcus / Leah Bornstein-Makovetsky (2nd ed.)]

HAMON, AARON BEN ISAAC (early 18th century), Hebrew poet. Hamon, who lived in Constantinople and Adrianople, wrote a preface to Reuben Mizraḥi's *Ma'yan Gannim* (Constantinople, 1721): a poem published in Isaac Cheleby's *Semol Yisrael* (Constantinople, 1723), in which all the words begin with the letter ש (*sin*); and a considerable number of devotional poems. The latter are included in the poetry collections of Turkish Jews, and some of them even in the Karaite liturgy. He was influenced by the poetry of Israel *Najara and the latter's contemporaries. Hamon's poetry was popular and widely read.

BIBLIOGRAPHY: Zunz, Poesie, 358; Michael, Or, 135 no. 283; S. Landauer, *Katalog… Strassburg* (1881), 63 no. 41; Gross, in: REJ, 56 (1908), 26; 57 (1909), 78; Benjamin Raphael b. Joseph (ed.), *Shirei Yisrael be-Ereẓ ha-Kedem* (1926), 81, 86, 177, 191, 204, 208; Davidson, Oẓar, 4 (1933), 359.

[Jefim (Hayyim) Schirmann]

HAMON, LEO (Goldenberg; 1908–1993), French lawyer and politician. Born in Paris to a family of Polish immigrants, Hamon practiced as a lawyer and following the fall of France in 1940 joined the Resistance. He was a member of the French Provisional Assembly (1944–45) and sat as a senator for the Seine department from 1945 to 1958. Hamon was a founding member of the Movement Republicain Populaire (MRP) but in 1954 joined the pro-Gaullist Jeune République. He continued to support de Gaulle after the latter became president of France in 1958 and in June 1969 was appointed spokesman of the French cabinet. Hamon was a professor of law at the University of Dijon from 1959 to 1960 and for the next four years at the Institut des Hautes Etudes d'Outre-mer. He served as vice chairman of the national television planning committee from 1965 to 1969 and was later a member of the Research Center in Constitutional Law of Paris 1 University. In June 1972 Hamon was appointed to a special post as secretary of state for "participation," i.e., the process of the participation of workers in the running of factories, in the government of Chaban Delmas, but held the position for only seven weeks, ceasing to be a minister when a reshuffle took place in July. His writings include *Le Conseil d'Etat juge du fait* (thesis, 1932), *De Gaulle dans la République* (1958), *La France et la guerre de demain…* (1967), *Une République présidentielle?: institutions et vie politique de la France actuelle* (with X. Delcros, 1975), *Socialisme et pluralité* (1976), *Acteurs et données de l'Histoire* (1979), *Juges de la loi: naissance et rôle d'un contre-pouvoir: le Conseil Constitutionnel* (1987), and *Lettre au Président de la République nouvellement élu* (1988). In 1991 he published his autobiography, *Vivre ses choix*, and a year later, in collaboration with R. Poznanski, an historical work on the life of Parisian Jews during the first months of the Nazi occupation: *Avant les premières grandes rafle: les juifs à Paris sous l'Occupation, juin 1940–avril 1941.*

HAMOR (Heb. חֲמוֹר; "ass"), the leading citizen of the town of Shechem in the time of the patriarch Jacob; his son was called Shechem (see *Dinah). Jacob bought a parcel of land from the sons of Hamor and built an altar upon it (Gen. 33:19–20). Joseph's bones were buried on this ground by the children of Israel when they returned from Egypt (Josh. 24:32). There are mutually contradictory data on the ethnic character of Hamor. In Genesis 34:2 he is called a Hivite, prince of the land. In the Alexandrine Septuagint he is called the Horite; while Genesis 48:22 indicates that the Amorites ruled in Shechem.

Hamor and his son were killed by Simeon and Levi in revenge for Shechem's dishonoring of their sister Dinah, after which the city was plundered and destroyed (Gen. 34). This deed aroused the anger of their father, Jacob (Gen. 34:30), and echoes of this linger in his deathbed blessings (Gen. 49:5–6). In S. Yeivin's view, this story would appear to be an early description of the domination by two of the Israelite tribes over a region of the land; therefore there is no mention of wars of conquest in the region of the hills of Ephraim in connection with the settlement of the land by the tribes (but see Bibliography for *Dinah).

The name Hamor is associated with the dwellers of Shechem in the days of *Abimelech: "Who is Abimelech and who is Shechem that we should serve him? Did not the son of Jerubbaal and his officer, Zebul, once serve the men of Hamor, the father of Shechem?" (Judg. 9:28). W.F. Albright believed, on the basis of Mari documents in which the phrase "to kill an ass" means "to conclude an alliance," that the phrase "the men of Hamor" as applied to the Shechemites during this period designates them as "allies." F. Willesen found further evidence for this hypothesis in a South Arabian inscription in which the word *ḥmrn* seems to mean entering into an alliance. The temple of the Shechemites is called Beth-El-Berith ("house of the god of the covenant or alliance"; Judg. 9:46). On the basis of the Arslan Tash (between Carchemish and Harran) plaques, Albright tried to identify the god bearing this epithet as the Canaanite Horon (see *Beth-Horon), god of treaties. The name Hamor (Himār) also occurs as a proper name among the early Arabs.

BIBLIOGRAPHY: S. Yeivin, *Meḥkarim be-Toledot Yisrael ve-Arẓo* (1960), 143–4; E. Meyer, *Die Israeliten und ihre Nachbarstaemme* (1906), 416; G. Ryckmans, *Les noms propres sud-sémitiques*, 1 (1934), 105; Albright, Arch Rel, 113; Von Soden, in: *Die Welt des Orients*, 3 (1948), 187, 213; Willesen, in: VT, 4 (1954), 216–7; W. Robertson-Smith, *The Religion of the Semites* (1956), 468; E. Nielsen, *Schechem* (Eng., 1959²), passim. **ADD. BIBLIOGRAPHY:** N. Sarna, *JPS Torah Commentary Genesis* (1989), 233.

[Ephraim Stern]

ḤANA BAR ḤANILAI (end of the third century C.E.), Babylonian *amora*. Ḥana belonged to the circle of R. *Huna (Meg. 27a), for whom he showed great respect, regarding himself as his pupil. When he saw R. Huna carrying his tools on his shoulder, he took them from him to relieve him of his burden (Meg. 28a). Ḥana was, apparently, a leader of the community in his city (Meg. 27a). He was well known for his wealth and famed for his charity. R. *Ḥisda states that there were 60 bakers working in his house during the day and a similar number during the night to provide bread for the poor; that his hand was always in his purse, ready to extend help to any deserving poor, sparing them the embarrassment of waiting; that the house had entrances on all four sides to facilitate their entry and anyone who entered the house hungry left it sated; also, that when there was famine in the land, he left food outside, in order that the poor who were ashamed to take it during daylight could help themselves in the darkness (Ber. 58b). Very little is known of his halakhic views; only once is he mentioned in a discussion with Ḥisda.

BIBLIOGRAPHY: Judah b. Kalonymus, *Yiḥusei Tanna'im ve-Amora'im*, ed. by J.L. Maimon (1963), 330f.; Margalioth, Ḥakhmei, 323 f., Hyman, Toledot, 464f.

[Zvi Kaplan]

ḤANA BEN BIZNA (third–fourth century C.E.), Babylonian *amora*. Ḥana was primarily an aggadist, most of his statements being quoted in the name of Simeon Ḥasida (Ber. 7a; 43b; Yoma 77a, et al.), whose name is otherwise unknown. One of them is, "Better that a man throw himself into a fiery furnace than put his neighbor to shame in public" (BM 59a, et al.). His contemporary, *Sheshet, admitted that Ḥana was his superior in the field of *aggadah* (Suk. 52b). Ḥana was judge in Pumbedita in *Naḥman b. Isaac's time (Ket. 50b; BK 12a) but he is also mentioned as being in Nehardea where, in spite of criticism he allowed himself to frequent pagan barber shops (Av. Zar. 29a). The *amora* *Joseph relied on his judgment in matters of *halakhah* (Suk. 47a).

BIBLIOGRAPHY: Judah b. Kalonymus, *Yiḥusei Tanna'im ve-Amora'im*, ed. by J.L. Maimon (1963), 327–30; Hyman, Toledot, 463f., s.v.

[Zvi Kaplan]

HANAMEL (or **Hananel**; Heb. חֲנַנְאֵל ,חֲנַמְאֵל), high priest in 37/36 B.C.E., reappointed in 34. According to the Mishnah (Par. 3:5) Hanamel was an Egyptian. However, Josephus states that he was a Babylonian. He was appointed high priest by Herod, who deliberately disregarded the obvious choice, Aristobulus, the younger brother of Mariamne. Herod's choice was dictated by his desire to withhold this office from any member of the Hasmonean family. In face of the protests of Alexandra and Mariamne, Herod was obliged to depose Hanamel and appoint Aristobulus in his stead, but Hanamel was restored to office after the murder of Aristobulus on Herod's instructions. The Mishnah mentions Hanamel as one of the high priests during whose term of office the *red heifer was burned.

BIBLIOGRAPHY: Schuerer, Gesch, 2 (1907[4]), 269; Halevy, Dorot, 1 pt. 3 (1923), 114ff.; Klausner, Bayit Sheni, 4 (1950[2]), 12–14, 42; A. Schalit, *Hordos ha-Melekh* (1964[3]), 62–64, 363, 376, 379, 512.

[Abraham Schalit]

HANAN THE EGYPTIAN (second century C.E.), *tanna*. He is mentioned in a *baraita* brought a number of times in the Babylonian Talmud (Yoma 63b, Zevahim 34b and 74a, Menaḥot 59b, Temurah 6b; cf. Tosefta Zevahim 3:6). The other two references to him in talmudic sources are contradictory, and one of them is uncertain. He is mentioned together with ben Azai and ben Zoma, as one of "those who argued before the sages" in *Jabneh (TB Sanh. 17b). On the other hand he is placed in Jerusalem before the destruction of the Second Temple, but only as an alternative reading in the text of a *baraita* in TB Ket. 105a.

BIBLIOGRAPHY: Hyman, Toledot, 471.

[Zvi Kaplan]

HANANEL BEN ḤUSHI'EL (d. 1055/56), scholar, *posek*, and commentator. Hananel was born in *Kairouan, the son of *Ḥushi'el b. Elhanan. The early authorities refer to him as "of Rome," lending credence to the suggestion of Italian origin. Like his father, he was accorded the title *resh bei rabbanan* ("chief among the rabbis") by the Babylonian academies. After his death in Kairouan the title passed to *Nissim Gaon, his pupil. Hananel's most important work, which has not been completely preserved, was his commentary on the Talmud. Unlike Rashi, he limited himself to the subject matter only and did not give a running commentary, his main intention being to sum up the discussion and decide the *halakhah*. He relied greatly on the *geonim*, and in particular upon *Hai Gaon to whom he refers as "the *gaon*" without further qualification. In many places the commentary of Hananel is simply a word for word copy of Hai's commentary, sometime without acknowledgment. When he writes "we have received" a certain explanation – which contradicts the opinion of the *geonim* – the reference is to traditions received from his father or earlier Italian scholars, upon whose teaching he drew. The commentary contains explanations of many difficult words, chiefly in Arabic or Greek, most of which found their way into the *Arukh* of *Nathan b. Jehiel of Rome. Hananel was the first to make frequent use of the Jerusalem *Talmud, and he regularly compares it with discussions in the Babylonian Talmud. In consequence some scholars have exaggerated the importance of his influence upon the spreading of the study of the Jerusalem Talmud in particular. In addition to the Jerusalem Talmud, he also includes much from the Tosefta and the halakhic Midrashim in his commentary. It is not certain whether the commentary covered all the six orders of the Talmud, and in particular whether he wrote commentaries to those tractates whose subjects have no practical application. The following of his commentaries are extant: *Berakhot* (collected from published books and manuscripts in B. Lewin, *Oẓar ha-Ge'onim*, 1 (1928), appendix; the whole of the order *Mo'ed* (published in the standard editions of the Talmud); most of the order *Nashim* (also in *Oẓar ha-Ge'onim*, 7–11 (1936–42)); most of the order *Nezikin* (in the standard Talmud); and a fragment to tractate *Ḥullin* (ed. by B. Lewin, in: *Sefer ha-Yovel – J.L. Fishman* (1926), 72–79). The commentaries to *Horayot* (in standard Talmud edition) and *Zevaḥim* (the last three chapters, ed. by I.M. Ben-Menahem (1942)) attributed to him are not by him. This list shows that he also wrote commentaries to sections not of practical application (e.g., the second half of tractate *Pesaḥim* and the fragment of *Ḥullin* which includes chapter 11).

Hananel's commentary gained wide circulation soon after its appearance, and served as the main bridge between the teaching of the Babylonian *geonim* and the scholars of North Africa and that of the scholars of Europe and Ereẓ Israel. *Eliezer b. Nathan was the first of the scholars of France and Germany to make use of and disseminate it, and Nathan b. Jehiel of Rome was the first of the Italian scholars. In Ereẓ Israel it was used first by *Nathan (*Av ha-yeshivah*) and in Spain by the author of *Sha'arei Shavu'ot* (see Isaac b. Reuben). Among the scholars of North Africa, extensive use was made of it by Isaac *Alfasi who copied very many of his rulings, both in his name and anonymously; in fact, the whole of Alfasi's work is based upon it. From Alfasi it passed to the scholars of Spain after him, such as *Joseph ibn Migash, *Maimonides, Meir ha-Levi *Abulafia, and others. In Germany and France the tosafists based themselves to a considerable extent on Hananel, and he is frequently quoted by them. All the *rishonim* laid great store on the readings of the Talmud embedded in his commentary, and he himself several times emphasized his readings. In addition to his commentary he wrote a *Sefer Dinim* whose nature is not known (see S. Assaf, *Teshuvot ha-Ge'onim* (1942), 51), and there are a number of citations from a book in *Hilkhot Terefot*. The *rishonim* quote his commentary to the Pentateuch and fragments of it have been collected by A. Berliner (in *Migdal Ḥananel*, 1876) and by J. Gad (*Sheloshah Me'orot ha-Gedolim*, 1950). Some of the *rishonim* erroneously attributed to Hananel the anonymous *Sefer Mikẓo'ot*.

BIBLIOGRAPHY: S.J.L. Rapoport, in: *Bikkurei ha-Ittim*, 12 (1831), 11–33; *Migdal Ḥananel* (1876), includes biography; S. Poznański, in: *Festschrift… A. Harkavy* (1908), 194–8 (Heb. pt.); Kohut, Arukh, 1 (1926[2]), 12–13 (introd.); V. Aptowitzer, in: *Jahresbericht der Israelitisch-*

Theologischen Lehranstalt in Wien, 37–39 (1933), 3–50; (= *Sinai*, 12 (1943), 106–19); S. Abramson, in: *Sinai*, 23 (1948), 57–86; idem, *Rav Nissim Ga'on* (1965), index; Urbach, Tosafot, index.

[Israel Moses Ta-Shma]

HANANEL BEN SAMUEL (first half of 13th century), Egyptian (?) talmudist. There are no biographical details of Hananel, but he is known to have composed commentaries, which Ḥ.J.D. Azulai saw in manuscript, to the *Halakhot* of Isaac *Alfasi on several tractates of the Talmud. The commentaries to *Eruvin* (Margoliouth, Cat, no. 479) and *Kiddushin* (Neubauer, Cat, no. 438/7) are extant, but they have not yet been published. S. Abramson in his *Rav Nissim Ga'on* (1965) excerpted from the commentary to *Eruvin* many of the quotations there from Nissim Gaon's commentary on that tractate. According to one view Hananel was head of the academy of Fostat in Egypt and Peraḥyah b. Nissim was his pupil. According to Steinschneider, his father was the *nagid* Abu Manzur, Samuel b. Hananiah, but in the opinion of Mann this is impossible.

BIBLIOGRAPHY: Steinschneider, Arab Lit, 227 nos. 166–7; S.D. Luzzatto, in: *Ha-Levanon*, 3 (1866), 285f.; idem, in: *Literaturblatt des Orients*, 11 (1850), 242–5; Carmoly, in: *Ha-Karmel*, 6 (1867), 94; J. Horovitz, in: ZHB, 4 (1900), 155–8; S. Poznański, *ibid.*, 186; Mann, Egypt, 1 (1920), 195 n. 2; S. Assaf, in: KS, 23 (1946/47), 237f.

[Shlomoh Zalman Havlin]

HANANI, ḤAIM (1912–1991), Israeli mathematician. Hanani was born in Slupca, Poland, and studied at the universities of Vienna (1929–31) and Warsaw (1931–34), where he received his M.A. Immigrating to Ereẓ Israel in 1935, he obtained his doctorate in mathematics from the Hebrew University in 1938. On his arrival in Ereẓ Israel, Hanani joined the Betar movement and later the Irgun Ẓeva'i Le'ummi, playing a central role in its activities in Jerusalem. As a result, he was arrested by the British in 1944 and, after a period of imprisonment at Latrun, was sent to detainee camps in Eritrea and Kenya. Returning to Israel after his release in 1948, he held various teaching posts, and was appointed associate professor of mathematics at the Technion, Israel Institute of Technology in 1955 and full professor in 1962. He was also dean of the faculty of mathematics. As adviser to the Ministry of Education from 1964 to 1967, Hanani urged the establishment of an institute of higher learning in the Negev, and when it became the University of the Negev in 1969 he was appointed its first rector. He has published numerous articles in the field of mathematics in Hebrew, German, French, and English.

HANANIAH (Hanina), nephew of Joshua b. Hananiah (second century C.E.), *tanna*. Some are of the opinion that Hananiah was the son of Judah b. Hananiah who is mentioned in a single source as the author of an aggadic statement (Sif. Deut. 306), but there is no doubt that his teacher was his uncle *Joshua b. Hananiah (Nid. 24b), and probably for this reason he is usually referred to as "Hananiah, nephew of Joshua b. Hananiah." The Talmud tells that when in Simonia, he gave a ruling without having authority to do so. R. Gamaliel expressed his displeasure until Joshua sent him a message, "It was on my instructions that Hananiah gave the ruling" (Nid. 24b). It also relates that on one occasion Hananiah went to Babylon during the lifetime of his uncle and then returned to Ereẓ Israel (Suk. 20b). This tradition may be connected to the incident described in a tannaitic Midrash, which states that while on their journey: "they remembered Israel … and they burst into tears and rent their garments… and returned to their place, saying: 'Dwelling in Israel is equivalent to all the precepts of the Torah'"(Sif. Deut. 80). For a reason that is not clear (Eccles. R. 1:8, 4), it seems that he returned to Babylonia where he remained until his death. In the well-known *baraita* that enumerates those scholars to whose locality it is worth going to study, he is mentioned: "After Hananiah, the nephew of Joshua, to the exile" (Sanh. 32b). According to the Talmud, Hananiah was the greatest of the scholars in Ereẓ Israel at the time of the Hadrianic persecutions which followed the failure of the Bar Kokhba revolt in 135, and with his departure the power of the Sanhedrin was diminished. As a result Hananiah permitted himself "to intercalate the years and to fix the new moons" in exile, in conformity with the *halakhah* that the greatest among the ordained scholars of the generation may do so outside Ereẓ Israel if he has not left his equal in the land. He continued to do so after the persecutions abated and Ereẓ Israel again became the center of Torah, because he regarded himself as the outstanding scholar of the generation and the scholars of Ereẓ Israel as inferior to him. The Jews of Babylonia followed his calendar, and in consequence the scholars of Ereẓ Israel took vigorous steps against him. Representatives were sent from Ereẓ Israel to Babylonia, but even after *Judah b. Bathyra of Nisibis demanded that the authority of the center in Ereẓ Israel be accepted, Hananiah refused to obey (TJ, Ned. 6:8; TB, Ber. 63a–b). Probably the most famous *halakhah* associated with the name Hananiah is the dictum quoted in TB Shab. 12a, 20a, et al. However, it has recently been questioned whether this *halakhah*, in the form in which it is brought in the Babylonian Talmud, can be of tannaitic origin (Friedman). In line with this, it has been suggested that behind this *halakhah*, ascribed in the Babylonian Talmud to the *tanna* Hananiah, lies a tradition ascribed in the Jerusalem Talmud to the *amora* Hananiah (Hanina) "comrade of the Rabbis" (Wald).

BIBLIOGRAPHY: Halevy, Dorot, pt. 2 (1923), 190–205; Hyman, Toledot, s.v.; Allon, Toledot, 1 (1958), 151–2; 2 (1961), 75–6; A. Burstein, in: *Sinai*, 38 (1956), 32–7; 40 (1957), 387–8. **ADD. BIBLIOGRAPHY:** S. Friedman, in: *Sidra*, 14 (1998), 77–91 (Heb.); S. Wald, in: *Sidra*, 19 (2004), 47–75 (Heb.).

[Zvi Kaplan]

HANANIAH (Hanina) BEN ḤAKHINAI (sometimes referred to simply as **Ben Hakhinai**; middle of the second century C.E.), *tanna* in Ereẓ Israel. Ḥananiah was "one of those who debated before the sages" in *Jabneh (Sanh. 17b). He was one of the distinguished pupils of *Akiva (Tosef. Ber. 4:18), who also taught him mystic lore (Tosef., Ḥag. 2:2; Ḥag. 14b).

He studied with Akiva in Bene-Berak for 12 years without once returning home (Ket. 62b), and his wife was held up as an example of a "helpmeet for him" because of her forbearance (Gen. R. 17:3). He then dwelt apparently in Sidon from where he sent a query to Akiva (Nid. 52b). He is quoted three times in the Mishnah, *Kilayim* 4:8, *Makkot* 3:9, and in *Avot* 3:4, where he states: "He who wakes up at night, or he who goes on his way alone, and turns his heart to idle thoughts, sins against himself." He is also mentioned several times in the Tosefta, one of his dicta there being: "He who deals falsely with his fellow denies God" (Shevu. 3:6). He also knew many languages (TJ, Shek. 5:1, 48d). According to one version in a late Midrash he was one of the *Ten Martyrs.

BIBLIOGRAPHY: Hyman, Toledot, s.v.

[Zvi Kaplan]

HANANIAH (Hanina) BEN TERADYON (second century C.E.), *tanna* during the *Jabneh era, and martyr. Two halakhic precedents are brought in his name (Ta'an. 2:5; Tosef. Ta'anit 1:13), and a small number of explicit dicta in *halakhah* and *aggadah* are ascribed to him (Tosef. Mik. 6:3, cf. Men. 54a; Avot 3:2). A halakhic dispute between his son and his daughter is mentioned in the Tosefta (Kel. BK 4:17), and Sifre Deut. 307 briefly relates the story of his martyrdom, mentioning also his daughter. These traditions concerning his life, his family, and his martyrdom are further elaborated in the later talmudic aggadah. According to tradition, Hananiah was head of the yeshivah of *Sikhnin in Galilee (Sanh. 32b). When the news of the martyrdom of Akiva at Caesarea reached *Judah b. Bava and Hananiah, they said that his death was an omen that the land of Israel would soon be filled with corpses and the city councils (*Boule) of Judea abrogated (cf. Sem. 8:9, Higger's edition p. 154–5). This was apparently a reference to the destruction of Judea which followed the crushing of the *Bar Kokhba revolt and to the ensuing religious persecution by Hadrian. Hananiah's martyrdom was apparently also a part of these persecutions. He was sentenced to death for teaching the Torah and holding public gatherings in defiance of the prohibition against it, in order to foster Judaism. Unlike *Eleazar b. Parta who was arrested with him, Hananiah, when interrogated, admitted that he had been teaching Torah, since it was a divine command. He was sentenced to be burnt at the stake, his wife to be executed, and his daughter sold to a brothel. All three accepted their fate with equanimity, justifying the way of God, except that Hananiah was distressed that he had devoted himself only to study and not to philanthropic activity. He was burnt at the stake wrapped in the *Sefer Torah* (which he had been holding when arrested). To prolong his agony tufts of wool soaked in water were placed over his heart so that he should not die quickly. In answer to the wonder of his daughter at the fortitude with which he bore his sufferings, he answered, "He who will have regard for the plight of the *Sefer Torah*, will also have regard for my plight." It is stated that the executioner (*quaestionarius*), moved by his sufferings, removed the tufts and increased the heat of the fire, and when Hananiah expired he too jumped into the flames, whereupon a heavenly voice proclaimed that the two "are assigned to the world to come" (Av. Zar. 17b–18a; Sem. 8:12, D.T. Higger's edition p. 157–9). His daughter, who had been consigned to a brothel, preserved her virtue, and was eventually ransomed by *Meir who had married her sister, the learned *Beruryah. It is also related that one of Hananiah's sons associated with robbers (possibly the reference is to a group of political rebels) and when he was put to death, Hananiah would not permit him to be eulogized but applied to him censorious verses from the Bible (Lam. R. 3:16, No. 6; Sem. 12:13, Higger's edition p. 199–200). In the stories of the *Ten Martyrs in the **heikhalot* literature, the account of Hananiah's martyrdom is further embellished with mystical additions.

BIBLIOGRAPHY: Bacher, Tann; E.E. Urbach, in: *Sefer Yovel le-Yiẓhak Baer* (1960), 61–64.

[Moshe David Herr]

HANANIAH (Hanina) OF SEPPHORIS, Palestinian *amora* (late fourth century. C.E.). Probably a disciple of R. Phinehas, many of whose teachings he transmitted (TJ, Ma'as. 3:3, 50c; TJ, Or. 1:8, 61c, et al.), he is mentioned frequently in halakhic and aggadic conflict with his friend and contemporary Mana b. Jonah (TJ, Ḥal. 2:2, 58c; TJ, Pes. 3:1, 30a, et al.; also, TJ, Ber. 3:1, 6a; TJ, Ket. 1:2, 25b) who may have been his brother (TJ, MK 3:5, 82d). After the death of R. Jonah, Hananiah was head of the academy of Sepphoris but later resigned from his post in favor of Mana, and assumed the position of student under him (TJ, Ma'as. Sh. 3:9, 54c; TJ, Yev. 3:4, 4d, et al.). Because of this R. Hananiah was listed among those "who have relinquished their crown in this world, to inherit the glory of the world to come" (TJ, Pes. 6:33a). There is a geonic tradition to the effect that Hananiah emigrated to Babylonia (*Teshuvot ha-Ge'onim* Harkavy, §248), where he joined the circle of Rav Ashi (BB 25b; Ḥul. 139b); however it is obvious that, for chronological reasons, it is necessary to differentiate between the two Hananiahs.

BIBLIOGRAPHY: Hyman, Toledot, s.v.; Z.W. Rabinowitz, *Sha'arei Torat Bavel* (1961), 406–7; Ḥ. Albeck, *Mavo la-Talmudim* (1969), 393–4.

[Zvi Kaplan]

HANANIAH SON OF AZZUR (Heb. חֲנַנְיָה בֶּן עַזּוּר), of Gibeon, prophet, contemporary of the prophet *Jeremiah (Jer. 28:1) and opposed to his teachings. Hananiah prophesied that Judah would be freed of the yoke of Babylon, that the Temple vessels would be returned, and that Jeconiah (i.e., Jehoiachin), the son of *Jehoiakim, king of Judah, would be restored as king in Jerusalem. The setting of his prophecy, as proclaimed in the fourth year of Zedekiah's reign of Judah (593 B.C.E.; Jer. 28:2–4), was the gathering of the representatives of Edom, Moab, Ammon, Tyre, and Sidon in Jerusalem to plan a coordinated activity against *Nebuchadnezzar. Jeremiah argued against this treaty in the name of God, for it would not succeed. He put a yoke on his neck to symbolize the yoke of Nebuchadnezzar and the kingdom of Babylon imposed by God for three generations (*ibid.* 27:1ff.). Thus, the prophets in Judah who predicted that all the Temple vessels and Jeconiah would be returned from Babylon were speaking false prophecies. It is not known whether Hananiah prophesied together with those prophets, or separately, though his prophecy coincided with theirs. To Hananiah Jeremiah responded "Amen" in bitter irony, but he added that a true prophet can only be one whose prophecies for good are fulfilled (cf. Deut. 18:18–22). Thus, in two years they would know if Hananiah spoke the truth. Hananiah, to give credence to his words, broke the yoke off Jeremiah's neck in public, as a sign of the breaking of the yoke of Nebuchadnezzar (Jer. 28:lo–11). Jeremiah proclaimed that the act was, on the contrary, not a symbol of the breaking of the yoke, but of the replacement of the wooden yoke by an iron one. He also predicted that Hananiah would die in that same year, and three months later Hananiah died (28:16–17).

[Yehoshua M. Grintz]

In the Aggadah

Hananiah was one of the prophets who misused the gifts with which he had been divinely endowed (Sif. Deut. 84). He is particularly criticized for using Jeremiah's prophecy of the defeat of Elam (Jer. 49:35) as the basis of his own forecast that a similar fate would befall the Babylonians (Jer. 28:2). He reached this conclusion, not as a result of prophecy, but by reasoning, arguing: "If Elam, which only came to assist Babylon, will be broken; how much more certain is it that Babylon itself will be destroyed" (Sanh. 89a). Jeremiah then challenged Hananiah to give some sign to indicate the validity of his prophecy that God would perform this miracle "within two full years" (Jer. 28:3). Hananiah retorted that Jeremiah first had to give some sign that his prophecies of gloom would be fulfilled. Initially reluctant to do so (because God's evil decrees can always be averted by repentance), Jeremiah eventually prophesied that Hananiah would die that same year. This prophecy was fulfilled; the reference to his death in the "seventh month" (which commences a new year), indicates that he died on the eve of Rosh Ha-Shanah, but commanded his family to keep the death secret for a few days in an attempt to discredit Jeremiah (TJ, Sanh. 11:5).

BIBLIOGRAPHY: W. Rudolph, *Jeremia* (Ger., 1947), index. IN THE AGGADAH: Ginzberg, Legends, 4 (1947), 297–8; 6 (1946), 389; I. Ḥasida, *Ishei ha-Tanakh* (1964), 158. **ADD. BIBLIOGRAPHY:** T. Overholt, in: JAAR, 35 (1967), 241–49; J. Crenshaw, *Prophetic Conflict* (1971); R. Carroll, *Jeremiah* (1986), 440–50; H. Sun, in: BASOR, 275 (1989), 81–3; W. Holladay, *Jeremiah 2* (1989), 455.

HANAU, city near Frankfurt, Germany. The earliest documentary evidence for the presence of Jews in Hanau dates from 1313. During the *Black Death persecutions in 1349 the Jewish community of Hanau was destroyed and its synagogue confiscated. There were no more Jews in the city until 1429 when there were again two Jewish families living there. In 1603 Count Philip Ludwig II granted 10 Jewish families a privilege (*Judenstaettigkeit*) allowing them to settle in Hanau, build a special quarter (*Judengasse*), and erect a synagogue, which was dedicated in 1608. Previously, Jewish families had brought their dead to Frankfurt and then Windecken for burial, but a cemetery was consecrated in Hanau itself in 1603. By 1607 the community had grown to 159; 100 years later there were 111 families, or 600 to 700 individuals, resident in the city. In 1659 a conference of notables representing five Jewish communities took place in Hanau. Among the many talmudic scholars active in Hanau in the 17th and 18th centuries, best known was R. Tuviah Sontheim (1755–1830), *Landrabbiner* from 1798, and chief rabbi for the whole province of Hanau from 1824 to 1830. He was followed in office by Samson Felsenstein (1835–82).

In the 17th and 18th centuries Hanau developed into an important center of Hebrew printing. From Hans Jacob Hena's press, which was established in 1610, issued such important works as responsa by Jacob *Weil, Solomon b. Abraham *Adret, and Judah *Minz as well as Jacob b. Asher's *Arba'ah Turim*. Employing both Jews and gentiles, this press produced a great number of rabbinic, kabbalistic, and liturgical items within about 20 years. A hundred years later Hebrew printing was resumed in the city by H.J. Bashuysen, who published Isaac Abrabanel's Pentateuch commentary (1709). In 1714 Bashuysen's press was taken over by J.J. Beausang and was active until 1797.

During the last quarter of the 18th century several Court Jews lived in Hanau, mainly occupied as suppliers of the army. From 1806 the Jews were allowed to live in any part of the town, but full emancipation was not granted until 1866. The community numbered 540 persons in 1805, 80 families in 1830, 447 persons in 1871, and 657 at the turn of the century. In 1925 there were 568 Jews in Hanau and 447 in 1933. At that time there existed a synagogue, a cemetery, three charitable societies, and a religious school attended by 75 children.

Jews were active in many aspects of the commercial and industrial life of the town. However, Nazi economic boycotts had a telling effect so that the number of Jews had dwindled by May 1939 to 107. On Nov. 9/10, 1938, the synagogue was burned to the ground; the site was later cleared and title to it transferred to the city. The teachers' quarters owned by the community were demolished and many gravestones at the Jewish cemetery were overturned. The last 26 Jews of Hanau were deported in 1942 to Auschwitz and Theresienstadt. Another five Jews, partners of mixed marriages, remained in the town. In 1968, a few Jews resided in Hanau. In 2005 a Jewish community with about 130 members was refounded. The majority of the members were immigrants from the former Soviet Union.

BIBLIOGRAPHY: L. Loewenstein, *Das Rabbinat in Hanau nebst Beitraegen zur Geschichte der dortigen Juden* (1921: = JJLG, 14 (1921), 1–84); Germ Jud, 2 (1968), 336–7; H. Schnee, *Die Hoffinanz und der moderne Staat*, 2 (1954), 352–60: E.J. Zimmermann, *Hanau Stadt und Land...* (1903), 476–521; L. Rosenthal, *Zur Geschichte der Juden im Gebiet der ehemaligen Grafschaft Hanau...* (1963); FJW, 187–8; L. Una, in: *Juedisches Litteratur-Blatt*, 20 (1891), 10–11, 14–15, 19, 23, 80–81; E.J. Zimmermann, in: *Hanauisches Magazin (Hanauer Anzeiger*, June 1, 1924). **ADD. BIBLIOGRAPHY:** R. Schaffer-Hartmann, *700 Jahre Stadtrechte, 400 Jahre Judenstaettigkeit* (2003; Stadtzeit, volume 6); *Fuer einen Gulden Bede ... Von Hanaus juedischem Totenhof* (1999);

M.I. Pfeiffer, M. Kingreen, *Hanauer Juden 1933–1945. Entrechtung, Verfolgung, Deportation* (1998).

[Chasia Turtel]

HANAU, SOLOMON ZALMAN BEN JUDAH LOEB HA-KOHEN (1687–1746), Hebrew grammarian. Born in *Hanau where his father served as cantor, Solomon Hanau taught at Frankfurt. There, in 1708, he published *Binyan Shelomo*, a Hebrew grammar written in the form of casuistic criticism of earlier grammarians. The criticism led to resentment, and the leaders of the Frankfurt community demanded that he add to his work an apology to those whom he had "offended." Hanau moved to Hamburg. There he taught for a number of years and continued his linguistic research. He published *Sha'arei Torah* (Hamburg, 1718). The book was based on "natural inquiry" (i.e., on independent investigation of the language, deviating from traditional grammar wherever the author deemed it necessary). A brief essay on the scriptural accents, "*Sha'arei Zimrah*," was added to the book. *Yesod ha-Nikkud* (Amsterdam, 1730) is another minor work on the subject. His most famous work, *Ẓohar ha-Tevah* (Berlin, 1733), published in at least 12 editions, includes all his grammatical innovations. It influenced numerous grammarians of the Haskalah and the Revival period of the Hebrew language and was the book which set *Ben Yehuda (according to the latter's own statement) on the course which made him revive spoken Hebrew. Hanau answered the attacks of his adversaries in *Kurei Akkavish* (Fuerth, 1744).

In *Binyan Shelomo*, Hanau had already mentioned the linguistic "errors" (i.e., non-biblical-forms) contained in contemporaneous prayer books, and in *Sha'arei Tefillah* (Jessnitz, 1725, and three other editions) he recorded a number of these errors with his corrections. Apparently the book aroused the anger of the conservatives, and Hanau was compelled to leave Hamburg. He went to Amsterdam; a few years later he returned to Germany where he wandered from city to city (among others, Fuerth and Berlin), and died in Hanover. In 1735, while in Copenhagen, Hanau was engaged as a private tutor to Naphtali Herz *Wessely, then aged 10; Hanau, it seems instilled in his pupil an affection for the Bible and the study of the Hebrew language. Several essays by Hanau have survived in manuscript form, including *Ma'aseh Oreg*, an explanation of the grammatical passages in Rashi's commentary on the Torah, *Mishpat Leshon ha-Kodesh*, philosophical writings and commentaries on the Bible, and *Shivah Kokhevei Lekhet*, a work in Yiddish on the calendar.

[Chaim M. Rabin]

HANBURY, LILY (1874–1908), British actress, member of the Davis family which also included Julia *Neilson. She made her debut at the Savoy Theatre, London, in 1888, in a revival of W.S. Gilbert's *Pygmalion and Galatea*. Thereafter she acted under the management of Wilson Barrett and later Beerbohm Tree at His Majesty's Theatre, appearing in Shakespeare, Sheridan, and Ibsen. Her most successful roles were Ophelia, Portia, and Calpurnia. She married Herbert Guedalla in 1905.

HANDALI, ESTHER (d. ca. 1590), most famous among several Jewish women, known as **kieras*, who performed various services for the women of the royal harems in Istanbul. Handali, of Sephardi origin, worked with her merchant husband, Eliyah Handali, as an intermediary with the royal harem, buying and selling cosmetics, clothing, and jewelry. After her husband's death, and probably after the death of a previous *kiera*, the Karaite Strongilah, she began her independent activities in the harem of Sultan *Suleiman the Magnificent (1520–66). After the accession of Sultan Selim II to the throne Esther became the *kiera* of Nur Banu, Selim's beloved Venetian consort. This powerful and influential lady trusted and relied on her *kiera*, even when she became mother of a reigning sultan, following the accession of her son, Murad III (1574–95). Besides her services as supplier of luxury goods, Handali acted as a reliable intermediary, personal emissary, translator, and trustee at the highest levels, accumulating, during her many years at the court, a great fortune. Esther took part in Nur Banu's correspondence with the doge and senate of Venice. In a letter of December 18, 1582, written in Spanish, she mentioned some of her negotiating skills and discreet services on behalf of both sides. Nur Banu's two letters of September 1583 requested the Venetians to grant her *kiera*'s son, Salamon, a permit to conduct a lottery in Venice of "certain jewels which are suitable for Franks" (Skilliter, *The Letters*, p. 526).

Hebrew sources emphasize Esther's generosity and her acts of charity both covert and public. She used her money and connections to assist the needy in the Jewish community of *Istanbul, supporting widows and orphans as well as destitute merchants, sponsoring scholars, and subsidizing publications of Hebrew books. Following the great fire in Istanbul (1569) many refugees found shelter in her house. Esther Handali probably died around the year 1590, at a time when another well-known *kiera*, *Esperanza Malchi, was at the peak of her power. Due to the inconsistency of the sources and the fact that *kieras* were not always mentioned by name, Malchi's murder in 1600 has been wrongly connected with Handali.

BIBLIOGRAPHY: S.A. Skilliter, "The Letters of the Venetian 'Sultana' Nur Banu and her Kira to Venice," in: A. Gallotta and U. Marazzi (eds.), *Studia Turcologica Memoriae Alexii Bombaci Dicata* (1982), 515–36; M. Rozen, *A History of the Jewish Community in Istanbul: The Formative Years (1453–1566)* (2002), 205–7.

[Ruth Lamdan (2nd ed.)]

HANDALI, JOSHUA BEN JOSEPH (17th century), Turkish rabbi. Handali was born in Skopje in Yugoslavia. In his youth he moved to Salonika, where he studied under Ḥayyim Shabbetai. His first work, written in 1613, was a pamphlet on the laws pertaining to gifts from a groom to his bride (*sivlonot*). He was recognized as a halakhic authority and various Balkan communities turned to him with their problems. In 1621 he moved to Safed, where he was one of the pioneers of the Jewish resettlement. He later settled in Jerusalem where he is mentioned as being involved in the Shabbetai Ẓevi controversy. Toward the end of his life he interested himself in Kabbalah. Some of his responsa are included in his *Penei Yehoshu'a* (included in the collection *Me'orot ha-Gedolim*, Constantinople, 1739), and others in the *Benei Aharon* by Aaron Lapapa (Smyrna, 1674).

BIBLIOGRAPHY: Frumkin-Rivlin, 2 (1928), 32.

[Simon Marcus]

HANDELSMAN, MARCELI (1882–1945), Polish historiographer. Born in Warsaw, Handelsman served as professor of general history at Warsaw University from 1915. He was head of the Warsaw Institute for History, and a member of the Académie des Sciences Morales et Politiques in Paris. Handelsman's historical research covered several fields. His first study dealt with punishment in early Polish law (*Kara w najdawniejszym prawie polskim*, 1907). His main areas of interest were the history of Poland from the time of its first partition in 1772, the Napoleonic era, and Franco-Polish relations. In these fields he published the following books: *Napoléon et la Pologne, 1806–07* (1909); *Francja-Polska 1795–1845* (1926); *Les Idées françaises et la mentalité politique en Pologne au XIXe siècle* (1927). Handelsman also wrote essays of general historiographical importance, on the development of the present-day nationalism, and on methodology and the interpretation of history. He had a progressive-realistic attitude to historical research and opposed the romantic-conservative school. Although he had converted to Christianity Handelsman was sent by the Germans to the Nordhausen concentration camp where he died.

BIBLIOGRAPHY: W. Moszczenska, in: *Kwartalnik Historyczny*, 63, no. 3 (1956), 111–50; Polska Akademia Nauk, *Polski Slownik Biograficzny* (1960–61); A.B. Boswell, in: *Slavonic and East European Review*, 25 (1946), 247–9.

HANDLER, MILTON (1903–1998), U.S. attorney. Handler was born in New York City. He graduated from Columbia Law School (1926) and served on its faculty from 1927. A specialist in trademarks and antitrust law in both private and public practice, Handler held posts on the National Labor Board, serving as special adviser to the Department of Agriculture (1933–34), U.S. Treasury Department (1938–40), Lend-Lease Administration (1942–43), Foreign Economic Administration, of which he was special counsel, and the U.S. attorney general's national committee to study antitrust laws (1953–55). In 1955–56 he was the chairman of the Special Commission to Study N.Y. State Antitrust Legislation.

During the movement for Israel's independence, Handler was chairman of the American Jewish Conference's Palestine Committee, member of the American Zionist Emergency Council (1944–48), and co-author of a report on Palestine submitted to the United Nations in 1947. In 1969 he was appointed chairman of the American Friends of the Hebrew University.

He retired from teaching at Columbia in 1972 and was named professor emeritus. In his honor, the Milton Handler Chair in Trade Regulation was established in 1974 at the Columbia University School of Law. Other honors accorded Handler include the Scopus Award from the American Friends of the Hebrew University (1963), the Medal of Excellence awarded by Columbia Law Alumni (1976), the Outstanding Research in Law and Government Award from the Fellows of the American Bar Association (1977), the Human Relations Award of the Lawyers' Division of the Anti-Defamation League Appeal (1979), and the John Sherman Award from the Antitrust Division of the U.S Justice Department (1988).

Handler's books and articles include *Antitrust in Perspective* (1957), *Cases and Materials on Trade Regulation* (ed., 1967^4), and *Twenty-five Years of Antitrust* (1973).

His wife, MIRIAM HANDLER, was active in American Jewish support for Israel. She served on the U.S. Manpower Commission Training within Industry (1943–45), was a member of the Hadassah National Board from 1947, and held other leadership positions with the American Friends of the Hebrew University and the American-Israel Cultural Foundation. In 1975 the Handler Auditorium on Mount Scopus at the Hebrew University in Jerusalem was dedicated in their name.

[Ruth Beloff (2nd ed.)]

HANDLER, PHILIP (1917–1981), U.S. biochemist. Born on a New Jersey farm, Handler taught at Duke University, North Carolina, from 1939. He was a professor of biochemistry there from 1950 and in 1960 assumed the chair of biochemistry at the university. Handler's early research dealt with pellagra, a dietary deficiency disease. He and his collaborators showed that the vitamin nicotinic acid was a component of NAD and NADP, two coenzymes important in electron transfer in cells. Handler's later research was concerned with niacin and choline deficiency, purine metabolism, hypertension, and parathyroid tumors. Handler served at various times as president of the American Society of Biochemists and of the Federation of American Societies for Experimental Biology. He held leading positions in the National Science Foundation, including the chairmanship of the National Science Board, its policy-making body. In 1964 Handler was appointed to the President's Science Advisory Committee. In the same year he was elected to membership of the National Academy of Sciences and in 1969 became president of the Academy, a position he held until June 1981. In October 1981 he was awarded the National Medal of Science by President Reagan. He died in December of that year.

He was coauthor of *Principles of Biochemistry* (1954) and from 1957 was the editor of *Geriatrics*.

BIBLIOGRAPHY: *Current Biography Yearbook* (1964), 174–6.

[Samuel Aaron Miller]

HANDLER, RUTH MOSKO (1916–2002), U.S. entrepreneur, toy manufacturer, inventor of the Barbie doll and the Nearly Me breast prosthesis. Handler was born in Denver to first generation Polish immigrants, Jacob Joseph Mosko and his wife, née Ida Rubenstein. She married her high school boyfriend, Elliott Handler, and the two moved to Los Angeles in 1938.

The Handlers started their first business, plastic furniture, in their garage and Ruth sold products to Douglas Aircraft. During World War II a partner, Harold "Matt" Matson, and Elliot combined letters in their names to form another company, Mattel. They originally sold miniature picture frames but found dollhouse furniture to be more profitable. After Matson sold out to his partner, Elliot and Ruth Handler concentrated on manufacturing toys. In 1955 the Handlers pioneered a new way to market products directly to children by buying a year's worth of advertising on the new *Mickey Mouse Club* television show for which they created "Mouseguitar." Still it was the Barbie doll that would be their most successful product. During a trip to Europe Ruth bought a German doll, Lilli, for her daughter, Barbara. After buying the rights to market Lilli, Ruth made a few changes and put the Barbie doll on the market in 1959. Although Ruth Handler believed it was important for girls' self-esteem to play with a doll with breasts, critics have said that the doll's unrealistic measurements, translated to human size, 39″-18″-33″, could have the opposite effect. Mattel did adjust the doll's measurements over the years, but the proportions remained out of reach for most women. The enormous appeal of Barbie, her ever-changing wardrobe pieces and her entourage, including boyfriend Ken (named for the Handlers' son Kenneth), Midge, Barbie's best friend, and Allan, Ken's pal and Midge's beau, led Mattel to become a publicly owned company in 1960, and by 1965 Mattel was on the Fortune 500 list. Ruth Handler, who became Mattel's president in 1967, was indicted in 1978 for fraud and securities violations from the early 1970s. Handler, who was diagnosed with breast cancer and had a mastectomy in 1970, pled no contest, saying she wanted to work on her new business, based on the breast prosthesis she designed and called Nearly Me. She did public service to serve her sentence. Handler published an autobiography, *Dream Doll: The Ruth Handler Story* in 1995. She died in 2002 at the age of 86, at which time more than a billion Barbies had been sold in 250 countries. The phenomenal success of Barbie found the doll among items buried in the official Bicentennial time capsule.

BIBLIOGRAPHY: M.G. Lord. *Forever Barbie: The Unauthorized Biography of a Real Doll* (1994).

[Sara Alpern (2nd ed.)]

HANDLIN, OSCAR (1915–), U.S. historian. Handlin, who was born in Brooklyn, New York, graduated from Brooklyn College in 1934 and a year later earned his master's degree at Harvard University. He received his Ph.D. from Harvard in 1940 and taught history there from 1939. He directed the Center for the Study of Liberty at Cambridge, Massachusetts (1958–66), and in 1966 assumed the directorship of the Charles Warren Center for the Study of American History. After his retirement, he became the Carl M. Loeb University Emeritus Professor of History at Harvard.

A prolific writer, Handlin produced almost a book a year during his prodigious career. His works include the Pulitzer Prize-winning study of American immigrants, *The Uprooted* (1951), *Boston's Immigrants* (1941), *Chance or Destiny* (1955), *Al Smith and His America* (1958), *The Newcomers: Negroes and Puerto Ricans in a Changing Metropolis* (1959), *The Americans* (1963), *Children of the Uprooted* (1966), *Statue of Liberty* (1971), *A Pictorial History of Immigration* (1972), *The Wealth of the American People* (with his wife, Mary Handlin, 1975), *Truth in History* (1979), and *The Distortion of America* (1981).

By applying sociological insights to historical research, Handlin brought new evidence to bear on many controversial issues in American history, such as the nature of the Populists, the origins of antisemitism, the economic foundations of colonial slavery, and the conservatism of American immigrants. A vice president of the American Jewish Historical Society, his contributions to American Jewish history include *Danger in Discord: Origins of Anti-Semitism in the United States* (with M. Handlin, 1948); *Adventure in Freedom: Three Hundred Years of Jewish Life in America* (1954); "A Century of Jewish Immigration to the United States" (with M. Handlin), in AJYB, 50 (1948), 1–84; and *American Jews: Their Story* (1972).

[Hans L. Trefousse / Ruth Beloff (2nd ed.)]

HANFMANN, GEORGE MAXIM ANOSSOV (1911–1986), U.S. archaeologist. Hanfmann was born in St. Petersburg, Russia, and was educated at the University of Berlin. With the advent of the Nazis he was forced to leave Germany and went to Harvard. He became curator of classical art at the Fogg Art Museum in 1946 and professor of fine arts at Harvard in 1956. From 1958 he excavated at *Sardis as field director of the excavations in Turkey. He was largely responsible for the discoveries of the ruins and partial reconstruction of the Sardis synagogue. His earlier work specialized in Etruscan sculpture, but he extended his work by dealing with the interrelation between Greek and neighboring Near Eastern cultures in the Homeric and post-Homeric archaic age. Hanfmann's expertise ultimately encompassed Etruscan sculpture, Roman sarcophagi, Anatolian city planning, Hellenistic survivals in Byzantine art, Near Eastern narrative, and ancient technology, especially metallurgy.

In honor of Hanfmann and his contributions to classical archaeology and Greek and Roman art, the Hanfmann Lectureship was established in 1988 by the Archaeological Institute of America. Scholars who hold the position specialize in one or more of the subjects to which Hanfmann was dedicated.

Hanfmann's publications include *Season Sarcophagus in Dumbarton Oaks*, 2 vols. (1951), *Etruskische Plastik* (1956), *Roman Art* (1964), *Classical Sculpture* (1967), *Letters from Sardis* (1972), *From Croesus to Constantine* (1975), *Sculpture from Sardis* (1978), and *Sardis from Prehistoric to Roman Times* (with W. Mierse, 1983).

[Penuel P. Kahane / Ruth Beloff (2nd ed.)]

HANGCHOW, coastal capital of Chekiang province, E. China. It was the one of the largest cities in the world during the 14th century. At that time, it is generally believed, a Jewish community with a synagogue existed there. The Arab traveler Ibn Baṭṭūṭa in the first half of the 14th century described Hangchow as consisting of six cities, each with its own wall, and an outer wall surrounding the whole. Ibn Baṭṭūṭa "entered the second city through a gate called the Jews' Gate. In this city live the Jews, Christians, and sun-worshiping Turks, a large number in all." The Chinese Jew, *Ai T'ien, during a visit to Peking (Beijing) in 1605, told Matteo Ricci, the Jesuit missionary, about the presence of numerous Jews and the existence of a synagogue in Hangchow. Nothing is known of the further history of the community.

BIBLIOGRAPHY: H.A.R. Gibb, *Ibn Baṭṭūṭa, Travels in Asia and Africa 1325–1354* (1929), 293; A.C. Moule, *Christians in China before the Year 1550* (1930), 3.

[Rudolf Loewenthal]

ḤANĪF (pl. **Ḥunafā**), Arabic term which occurs many times in the *Koran in connection with true monotheism. The primary meaning and the origin of the word is still to be determined. In pre-Islamic times it seems to have been used for adherents of Hellenistic culture. *Muhammad uses it as a term for the God-fearing, righteous men in the pre-Islamic period, who followed the original and true religion. Abraham was one of them, Muhammad is his true follower, and Islam is the reappearance of the true faith distorted by Judaism and Christianity (e.g., Sura 10:105; 16:121, 124; 30:29). According to Muhammad's biographers, many such God-seekers who lived in Arabia during his lifetime, such as *Umayya ibn Abī al-Ṣalt, did not accept his prophetic mission to the Arabs. In later usage *ḥanīf* means Muslim.

BIBLIOGRAPHY: V.V. Bartold, *Muzulmanskiy mir* (1917), 48 (*Mussulman Culture*, 1934); Wensinck, in: *Acta Orientalia*, 2 (1924), 191; K. Ahrens, *Muḥammad als Religionsstifter* (1935), 17, n. 3; J.W. Hirschberg, *Juedische und christliche Lehren* (1939), index; N.A. Faris and H.W. Glidden, in: JPOS, 19 (1941), 1–13; W. Montgomery Watt, in: EIS², 3 (1966), s.v.

[Haïm Z'ew Hirschberg]

ḤANINA (**Hananiah**; **Comrade of the Rabbis**; end of the third-beginning of the fourth century), Palestinian *amora*. Ḥanina was born in Babylonia; in his youth he migrated to Ereẓ Israel and studied under Johanan among others (Men. 79b; Ber. 5b; et al.). Johanan was greatly distressed because he was unable to ordain him, but Ḥanina comforted him, saying: "It is because we are descendants of Eli the Priest; we have a tradition that none of this family is destined to be ordained" (Sanh. 14a). For this reason he was called *ḥaver* ("comrade") of the rabbis. He is frequently mentioned together with Oshaya, who was also a priest of the family of Eli that emigrated to Ereẓ Israel; they may have been brothers (*Yiḥusei Tanna'im re-Amora'im* (1963, 388)). Both earned their living by sandal-making. In illustration of their great piety, the Talmud relates that their workshop was in the market of the harlots for whom they made shoes, yet they never raised their eyes to look at them. The harlots, recognizing their piety, used to swear "by the lives of the holy rabbis of Israel" (Pes. 113b). Ḥanina's halakhic sayings are cited in the Talmud. Problems were directed to him (TJ, Ber., 1:1, 2b; MK 3:5, 82b), and in reply to a query about abolishing an accepted custom, he replied: "Since your ancestors were accustomed to forbid this, do not change the custom of your ancestors, that they may rest in peace" (TJ, Pes. 4:1, 30d). He sent *halakhot* in the name of Johanan from Ereẓ Israel to Babylonia (Yev. 58b). He disputed with Ilai in *halakhah* (Shab. 84b), and had discussions with Zeira (RH 13a). He also had connections with Rabbah and repeated *beraitot* before him (BM 6b; et al.). Some are of the opinion that Rabbah (b. Naḥamani) was his brother (see *Yuḥasin*. s.v. Rabbah bar Naḥamani). It has recently been suggested that behind the well-known *halakhah* ascribed in the Bavli (Shab. 12a, 20a, et al) to the *tanna* Hananiah, lies a tradition properly ascribed in the Yerushalmi to Hanina (Hananiah) "comrade of the Rabbis" (Wald).

BIBLIOGRAPHY: Bacher, Pal Amor; Hyman, Toledot, s.v.; Ḥ. Albeck, *Mavo la-Talmudim* (1969), 241–3; S. Wald, in: Sidra 19 (Hebr.) (2004), 47–75.

[Yitzhak Dov Gilat]

ḤANINA BAR ḤAMA (early third century C.E.), Palestinian scholar of the transitional generation from *tannaim* to *amoraim*. Ḥanina was born in Babylon (TJ, Pe'ah 7:4, 20a), and studied there under a scholar called Hamnuna (TJ, Ta'an. 4:2, 68a). He went to Ereẓ Israel and lived in Sepphoris where he was a distinguished pupil of Judah ha-Nasi (TJ, Nid. 2:7, 50b). He transmitted information about the rulings and customs of his teacher (TJ, Ber. 3:5, 6d) who greatly admired him (Av. Zar. 10b). He was friendly with Ishmael b. Yose, with Bar Kappara, and with Ḥiyya, in whose presence Ḥanina boasted of the sharpness of his intellect, saying, "Were the Torah, God forbid, to be forgotten in Israel, I would restore it by means of my dialectics" (Ket. 103b; BM 85b). Ḥanina's colleagues were Rav, Jonathan, and Joshua b. Levi, and he went with the last to visit the Roman proconsul in Sepphoris (TJ, Ber. 5:1, 9a). According to the Jerusalem Talmud Ḥanina was not ordained by Judah ha-Nasi during the latter's lifetime, because he was vexed with him over a certain matter, but he ordered his son Gamaliel who succeeded him to ordain him (TJ, Ta'an. 4:2). According to a *baraita* quoted in the Babylonian Talmud, however (Ket. 103b), Judah ha-Nasi ordered before his death: "Ḥanina b. Ḥama shall preside," which Rashi explains as meaning to preside over the college. This indeed seems to be the meaning of the phrase in its context which deals with the appointments to be made in the college after Judah's death. Further it is stated that Ḥanina refused to accept this appointment "because R. Afes was two and a half years older than he." Afes was appointed, and only after his death did Ḥanina accept the office. Among his most prominent pupils were Johanan and Simeon b. Lakish and also Eleazar, who frequently transmits in his name. Eleazar's statement in the name of Ḥanina: "The disciples of the wise increase peace in the world, as it says [Isa. 54:13]: and all thy children shall be taught of the Lord, and great shall be the peace of thy children. Read not *banayikh* ['thy children'] but *bonayikh* ['thy builders']" (Ber. 64a; et al.) has become famous and is incorporated in the daily prayer book.

Ḥanina lived to a very advanced age (Ḥul. 24b). He earned a living by trading in honey (TJ, Pe'ah 7:4, 20b) and also practiced medicine, in which he was regarded as an expert (Yoma 49a). He harshly rebuked his fellow citizens of Sepphoris and bemoaned their hardheartedness (TJ, Ta'an, 3:4, 66c). He emphasized the value of rebuke in his statement: "Jerusalem was destroyed only because they did not rebuke each other" (Shab. 119b). He frequently spoke in praise of Ereẓ Israel (TJ, Pe'ah 7:4, 20b) and explained the description of Ereẓ Israel as *ereẓ ẓevi* (lit. "land of the hind," JPS "beauteous," AV "glorious"; Dan. 11:41) as follows: "Just as the skin of the hind cannot hold its flesh; so the land of Israel when it is inhabited can provide space for everyone, but when it is not inhabited it contracts" (Git. 57a). Ḥanina was strongly opposed to anyone leaving the land of Israel, and said of him, "He has abandoned the bosom of his mother, and embraced the bosom of a stranger" (TJ, MK 3:1, 81c). He was especially opposed to a priest leaving the country, even for religious reasons (*ibid.*).

Ḥanina's aggadic statements are numerous. He was of the opinion that the planets influence Israel too, and that "the constellation of the hour is the determining influence" (Shab. 156a). This influence, however, does not limit the activity of divine providence, since both witchcraft and constellations are subject to the providence of the creator "for if there be no decree from Him, they can do him no harm" (Rashi to Ḥul. 7b; cf. Sanh. 67b). The overall power of providence is stressed in his saying: "No man bruises his finger here on earth, unless it was so decreed against him in heaven" (Ḥul. 7b). But this emphasis does not nullify the value of man's freedom of will: "Everything is from heaven, excepting cold draughts, as it is written [Prov. 22:5]. Cold draughts [thus he understands the words usually rendered "thorns and snares"] are in the way of the froward; he that keepeth his soul holdeth himself far from them" (BM 107b). Moreover it is certain that no one should rely upon his constellation or upon providence in all that pertains to his character, since "Everything is in the hand of heaven except the fear of heaven" (Ber. 33b), but the attainment of the fear of heaven is not given to all men equally and for the same effort (*ibid.*). Ḥanina stressed the heinousness of profaning the Divine Name: "The Holy One was indulgent of idolatry – but He was not indulgent of the profanation of the Name" (Lev. R. 22:6); "It is better for a man to commit a transgression in secret – and not profane the Name of Heaven in public" (Kid. 40a). Among his other noteworthy sayings are, "He who lifts a hand against his fellow, even without smiting him, is called a sinner" (Sanh. 58b); "Let not the blessing of a common person be light in your eyes" (Meg. 15a); "The son of David will not come until the haughty in Israel are extinct" (Sanh. 98a).

BIBLIOGRAPHY: Bacher, Pal Amor; Hyman, Toledot, s.v.; E.E. Urbach, in: *Sefer ha-Yovel le-Yeḥezkel Kaufmann* (1960), 141–6.

[Zvi Kaplan]

ḤANINA (Hinena) BAR PAPA (Pappi; end of third and beginning of fourth century C.E.), Palestinian *amora.* Ḥanina belonged to the circle of R. Johanan's pupils, Abbahu, Isaac Nappaḥa, Ammi, etc., though he only once actually quotes R. Johanan himself (TJ, BK 10:2, 71b.). He was renowned in the field of *aggadah*, and was considered an excellent preacher (Sot. 9a, et al.). He may have learned his *aggadah* from Samuel b. Naḥman whom he calls "rabbi" (TJ, Shev. 4:3, 35b). He was considered a paradigm of holiness (Kid. 81a) and even the night spirits feared him. It is related of him that he distributed alms at night (TJ, Pe'ah 8:9, 21b). When the Angel of Death came to take him, he requested another 30 days in which to revise his learning. The Angel of Death, who respected him deeply, granted this request, and when he died a pillar of fire separated him from the people (Ket. 77b).

BIBLIOGRAPHY: Judah b. Kalonymus, *Yiḥusei Tanna'im ve-Amora'im*, ed. by J.L. Maimon (1963), 376–8; Margalioth, Ḥakhmei, 346–8, s.v.; Hyman, Toledot, 494–7, s.v.; Ḥ. Albeck, *Mavo la-Talmudim* (1969), 239f.

[Zvi Kaplan]

ḤANINA BEN ABBAHU (c. 300), Palestinian *amora.* Ḥanina was the son of the famous *Abbahu who lived in Caesarea. He studied under his father and transmitted teachings in his name, as well as about him (Kid. 33b; TJ, Bik. 3:7, 65d; et al.), but later his father sent him to study at the yeshivah of Tiberias. When his father heard that instead of devoting himself to study there he was engaging in works of benevolence, he sent him a message: "Is it because there are no graves in Caesarea [cf. Ex. 14:11; the reverential interment of the dead being one of the highest of benevolent activities] that I sent you to Tiberias? For it has already been decided that study takes precedence over good deeds" (TJ, Pes. 3:7, 30b). Ḥanina apparently returned to Caesarea (TJ, Ket. 4:15, 29b) where he was a *dayyan* (TJ, Yev. 2:4, 3d) and is referred to also as "Ḥanina of Caesarea" (Song R. 1:20, no. 3). In addition to *halakhah*, aggadic sayings were transmitted in his name (TJ, Shab. 6:9, 8d; Lam. R., Proem 34; *ibid.* 2:1, no, 2; et al.).

BIBLIOGRAPHY: Frankel, Mevo, 87b–88a; Hyman, Toledot, s.v.; Ḥ. Albeck, *Mavo la-Talmudim* (1969), 327–8.

[Zvi Kaplan]

ḤANINA BEN ANTIGONUS (first half of second century C.E.), *tanna.* According to the Talmud Ḥanina was a kohen (Bek. 30b), and it is seems that in his youth he lived in Jerusalem before the destruction of the Temple and was able to report certain details of that period (Tosef., Ar. 1:15; see also Kid. 4:5). Similarly, many of the teachings quoted in his name are on the subject of the Temple and its vessels (Bek. 6:3, 4, 10; Tosef., Shek. 3:15; Tosef., Suk. 4:15; et al.), which is the main subject matter of his quoted statements. He also transmitted a halakhic tradition in the name of R. Eleazar Ḥisma (Tosef., Tem. 4:10). It is told of his son that R. Judah and R. Yose sought his judgment on questions of ritual purity (Bek. 30b).

BIBLIOGRAPHY: Hyman, Toledot, 479–80.

[Zvi Kaplan]

ḤANINA BEN DOSA (first century C.E.), *tanna*. Ḥanina lived in Arav in lower Galilee (north of the valley of Bet Netofah) and was a disciple-colleague of *Johanan b. Zakkai. More has been transmitted about his pious deeds and his wonders than about his dicta, and the little preserved is in the field of *aggadah*, confining itself to emphasis on the importance of good deeds: "He whose deeds exceed his wisdom, his wisdom shall endure; but he whose wisdom exceeds his deed, his wisdom will not endure. He in whom the spirit of his fellow creatures takes delight, in him the spirit of the All-present takes delight; and he in whom the spirit of his fellow creatures takes not delight, in him the spirit of the All-present takes not delight" (Avot 3:9–10). It was said of him "that he was praying when a scorpion bit him, but he did not interrupt his prayer. His pupils went and found it dead at the entrance to its hole. They said: Woe to the man bitten by a scorpion, but woe to the scorpion that bites Ben Dosa" (Tosef., Ber. 3:20; and cf. Ber. 5:5, TJ, Ber. 5:1 and Ber. 33a). Similarly it was said of him: "When Ḥanina b. Dosa died, men of deeds ceased and piety came to an end" (Sot. 9:15; cf. Tosef. Sot. 15:5). Of his wife too it was said that she resembled her husband in piety (BB 74b) and like him was "accustomed to miracles" (Ta'an. 25a). He was also praised for his integrity. The sages applied to him the phrase (Ex. 18:21) "men of truth" (Mekh., Malek 2). In the Talmud he was held up as an example of a completely righteous man (Ber. 61b), and described him as "one for whose sake God shows favor to his entire generation" (Ḥag. 14a). He refused to benefit from the property of others though he was destitute, and such remarkable things are related about this conduct that it was stated, "Every day a divine voice proclaims from Mt. Horeb: The whole world is sustained by the merit of my son Ḥanina, and Ḥanina my son subsists on a *kav* of carobs from one week to the next" (Ber. 17b). He was zealous in observing precepts: e.g., in the observance of the Sabbath, which he kept from midday on Friday (Gen. R. 10:8); in separating tithes (TJ, Dem. 1:3); and in returning lost property to its owner (Ta'an. 25a). His prayers were regarded as being specially accepted, and as a result he was frequently requested to pray for the sick and those in trouble (Ber. 34b; Yev. 121b). When the son of Johanan b. Zakkai fell ill, Ḥanina prayed for him and he recovered. Johanan b. Zakkai claimed that he himself would not have succeeded in achieving this and when his wife asked, "Is Ḥanina greater than you?" he replied, "No! but he is like a servant before the king, and I am like a courtier before the king" (Ber. 34b). The *aggadah* speaks extensively of the miracles that happened for him (Ta'an. 24b–25a; ARN[1] 8, 38). On one Sabbath eve at twilight he saw his daughter sad. He said to her: "Why are you sad?" She replied: "I exchanged my vinegar can for my oil can, and I kindled the Sabbath light with vinegar (and it will be extinguished)." He said to her: "My daughter, why should this trouble you? He who commanded the oil to burn will also command the vinegar to burn" (Ta'an. 25a).

BIBLIOGRAPHY: Bacher, Tann; Hyman, Toledot, s.v.; G.B. Zarfati, in: *Tarbiz*, 26 (1956/57), 130ff.; E.E. Urbach, *Ḥazal* (1969) index.

[Zvi Kaplan]

ḤANINA BEN GAMALIEL (mid-second century C.E.), *tanna*. He was a son of Rabban *Gamaliel of Jabneh, and an older brother of the patriarch (*nasi*) *Simeon b. Gamaliel, who quotes his teachings (Tosef., Nid. 7:5). Ḥanina was apparently a disciple of *Tarfon (see Ned. 62a; Kid. 81b). He differed on *halakhah* with *Akiva (Nid. 8a) and with Yose ha-Gelili (Men. 5:8), and engaged in halakhic discussions with the disciples of Akiva (Tosef., Av. Zar. 4 (5): 12; Tosef., Nid. 4:5; et al.). He was also well-versed in the *aggadah* (MK 23a) and many *aggadot* are quoted in his name. He apparently died young, and because of this his younger brother was appointed to the position of *nasi*.

BIBLIOGRAPHY: Hyman, Toledot, s.v.

[Zvi Kaplan]

ḤANINA (Ahonai) KAHANA BEN HUNA (the second half eighth century), *gaon* of Sura (769–774). A priest belonging to a significant priestly family, he let his nails grow, saying "the Temple will soon be rebuilt and they will require a priest qualified for *melikah*" (slaughtering the sacrificial bird by pinching the back of its neck; Yev. 1:15). Ḥanina was a student of *Yehudai b. Naḥman Gaon. His interpretations and rulings, found in the *Halakhot Gedolot*, were highly regarded by succeeding *geonim*. The value of the *sela* coin as determined by him has been incorporated in the text of the Talmud (Bek. 50a). Ḥanina was the teacher of Jacob b. Mordecai ha-Kohen, who was known among the *geonim* for his independent views, and also of Samuel, the first portion of whose *Midrash Asefah* has been included in the *Halakhot Gedolot*, in collections of geonic responsa, and also in the Midrashim of Yemen. Some passages of Ḥanina's works have been included in the Yalkut Shimoni.

BIBLIOGRAPHY: B.M. Lewin (ed.), *Iggeret R. Sherira Ga'on* (1921), 108; idem, *Oẓar ha-Ge'onim (Ta'anit)*, pt. 2 (1932), 30; L. Ginzberg, *Geonica*, 2 (Eng., 1909), 31, 94, 113; Baron, Social[2], 7 (1958), 259f.; J. Mueller, *Mafte'aḥ li-Teshuvot ha-Ge'onim* (1891), 72.

[Meir Havazelet]

ḤANINA SEGAN HA-KOHANIM (first century C.E.), *tanna* living in the last years of the Second Temple, the designation *Segan ha-Kohanim* referring to the fact that he was deputy high priest (cf. Yoma 39a). He transmitted details about the Temple service both from his knowledge of his father's customs (Zev. 9:3) and from those of the other priests (Pes. 1:6; Eduy. 2:1–2), and about other customs prevalent in Temple times (Eduy. 2:3; Men 10:1; et al.). On the basis of his testimony cited in *Pesaḥim* 1:6, an extensive and ramified discussion is developed in the Babylonian Talmud (Pes. 14a–21a). The Mishnah also gives information about the customs of his family in the Temple (Shek. 6:1). His intense love of the Temple is expressed by a remark in connection with the prohibition against bathing on the Ninth of Av: "The house of our God merits that for its sake a man should forego an immersion once a year" (Ta'an. 13a). Two *halakhot* in his name are found in the Tosefta (Ter. 9:10; Neg. 8:6), both dealing with the laws of ritual purity. His aggadic sayings extol the virtue of peace: "Great is peace which is equal to the whole act of creation." He says that the word "peace" in the priestly blessing refers to domestic peace (Sif. Num. 42), and he enjoins, "Pray for the peace of the ruling power, since but for fear of it men would have swallowed up each other alive" (Avot 3:2), and in praise of Torah: "Everyone who takes the words of the Torah to heart… will have removed from him fear of the sword, fear of famine, foolish thoughts… fear of the yoke of human beings" (ARN[1] 20, 70). According to Maimonides (Commentary to Mishnah, introd.), Simeon b. ha-Segan (cf. Shek. 8:5; Ket. 2:8) was the son of Ḥanina.

BIBLIOGRAPHY: Hyman, Toledot, s.v.

[Zvi Kaplan]

ḤANITAH (Heb. חֲנִיתָה), kibbutz situated on the Israel-Lebanese frontier in western Upper Galilee, 4½ mi. (7 km.) E. of Rosh ha-Nikrah. Ḥanitah, affiliated with Iḥud ha-Kevuẓot ve-ha-Kibbutzim, was founded in 1938, at the height of the Arab riots, as a stockade and watchtower outpost, with the aim of gaining a foothold in a region until then devoid of Jewish settlement, and of closing the border gap through which armed gangs used to infiltrate from Lebanon. Ḥanitah became the epitome of the defense settlement and its foundation was the subject of the Hebrew opera *Dan ha-Shomer* by Shin *Shalom and Marc *Lavry (1945). First established by a *Haganah unit at a site known as "lower Ḥanitah," the settlement had to repel incessant attacks, two defenders falling the very night it was founded. A month later, "upper Ḥanitah" was set up on the permanent site at the top of the ridge. In 1939, a group of settlers from Eastern Europe took over. Arduous reclamation work was required to carve cultivable land (mainly for deciduous fruit orchards and vineyards) out of the rocky terrain overgrown with wild brush. Forests were planted and ancient woodlands in the vicinity restored. Ḥanitah established a large rest resort, which went out of business though guest rooms were still rented, a lens-making factory, and a factory for coating, laminating and metallicizing polyester film. Farming included fruit plantations, citrus groves, and field crops. Its population in 1968 was 390, rising to 610 in the mid-1990s and then dropping to 465 by 2002. Its name dates back to the second and third centuries C.E. and is preserved in the form Ḥanita (חניתא; Tosef., Shev. 4:9 and TJ, Dem. 2:1, 22b), today Khirbat Ḥānūtā at the site of the kibbutz.

WEBSITE: www.hanita.co.il.

[Efraim Orni]

HANKIN, YEHOSHUA (1864–1945), Ereẓ Israel pioneer, instrumental in acquiring large tracts of land for Jewish settlement. Born in Kremenchug, Ukraine, Hankin went to Ereẓ Israel in 1882 with his father, who was one of the founders of Rishon le-Zion. In 1887 the family moved to Gederah where he established friendly relations with the Arab *felaḥeen* and landowners, which helped him in negotiating for the purchase of land for the expansion of Jewish settlement. His first purchase, in 1890, was of the lands on which Reḥovot was established, and a year later he bought the land on which Ḥaderah was founded; he also purchased the lands on which the *Jewish Colonization Association (ICA) settlements in the Galilee and elsewhere were set up. In 1908, when the Zionist Organization began to engage in practical work in Ereẓ Israel and established the Palestine Land Development Corporation (for the purchase and cultivation of land for the *Jewish National Fund and private purchasers), Hankin joined this company. As early as 1897 he had negotiated for the purchase of the Jezreel Valley lands, but the first sale there was delayed until 1909, when Hankin at last succeeded in buying the lands of Kafr Fūla (10,000 dunams), on which Merḥavyah, the first Jewish settlement in the valley, was established. In 1915 he was exiled to Anatolia, Turkey, by the Turkish authorities, returning to Palestine three years later. In 1920 he purchased a large tract of land (51,000 dunams) in the Jezreel Valley, on which many agricultural settlements were later established (En-Harod, Tel Yosef, Nahalal, and others), and as a result he became known as "The Redeemer of the Valley." Seven years later he submitted to the Zionist leadership a daring 20-year plan for the acquisition of Palestinian lands; from 1932 he served as director of the Palestine Land Development Corporation. Hankin wrote *Jewish Colonization in Palestine* (1940, ed. and tr. by E. Koenig). He died in Tel Aviv and was buried on Mt. Gilboa opposite the land he redeemed in the Jezreel Valley, near the Harod spring. During his lifetime, he purchased more than 600,000 dunams of land, most of which passed into the possession of the Jewish National Fund. The moshav Kefar Yehoshu'a in the Jezreel Valley is named after him.

BIBLIOGRAPHY: Y. Ya'ari-Poleskin, *Yehoshu'a Hankin ha-Ish u-Mifalo* (1933); M. Smilansky, *Mishpaḥat ha-Adamah*, 3 (1951), 207–81; Tidhar, 2 (1947), 752–5; M. Sharett, *Orot she-Kavu* (1969), 102–8; A. Ashbel (ed.), *Shishim Shenot Hakhsharat ha-Yishuv* (1970).

[Gedalyah Elkoshi]

HANNAH (Heb. חַנָּה; "graciousness, favor"), wife of Elkanah, of the family of Zuph from Ramathaim-Zophim in the hill country of Ephraim; mother of the prophet *Samuel. Hannah appears in the Bible in connection with the birth of Samuel. Together with Elkanah and her co-wife Peninnah, she used to make the pilgrimage annually to the Temple in Shiloh to offer sacrifices (I Sam. 1:2–7; 2:19; the Septuagint and a fragment from Cave 4 at Qumran in 1:24). Though the favored wife of her husband, she was unhappy because she was childless for many years and taunted about it by her co-wife. As she once stood in the Temple, pouring out her bitter anguish inaudibly, with only her lips moving, and vowing to dedicate any son born to her to the Temple and the service of God, *Eli the high priest at Shiloh observed her and chided her for her apparently drunken behavior. On ascertaining its true cause, however, he added his blessing to her pleas. Hannah gave birth to a son, Samuel, and after weaning him brought him to the Temple, offered a sacrifice and a song of thanksgiving, and left him with Eli to serve in the Temple for life. Each year she would return to bring him a small cloak, when she went up with her husband to offer the yearly sacrifice. Eli blessed her and Hannah bore three more sons and two daughters (I Sam. 2:21).

The story of Hannah and the birth of Samuel is one of the most charming in the Bible. It is similar to other stories of barren mothers who late in life bore sons destined to be leaders of the nation, and to the story of *Rachel who was also the favored wife of her husband. Hannah's pledging her son before his birth is similar to the action of Samson's mother (Judg. 13), who pledged him as a *nazirite. This was a common practice of the period (although it was later forbidden – "a woman shall not pledge her son as a nazirite," Naz. 4:6). Amos 2:11–12 refers to prophets and nazirites jointly. It is worth noting that according to the Septuagint and the fragment from Qumran, 4QSama, Hannah dedicates her son specifically "as a nazirite for all time" who is forbidden to partake of wine and spirits (similarly in Ecclus. 46:13; Jos., Ant., 5:347). According to R. Nehorai (Naz. 9:5; Maim. Yad, Nezirut, 3:16) Samuel was a nazirite like Samson. Hannah's prayer served as the model for Mary's prayer in the New Testament (Luke 1:46–55), famously referred to as "Magnificat," its opening Latin word.

[Yehoshua M. Grintz]

In the Aggadah

Hannah was one of the seven prophetesses (Meg. 14a). It was at her instigation that Elkanah took a second wife after 10 years of marriage without children (PR 43, 181b). Once Peninnah had given birth, however, she ceaselessly taunted Hannah (cf. I Sam. 1:6), constantly reminding her of her childlessness (PR 43, 182a–b). The expression "O Lord of hosts" (I Sam. 1:11), which she was the first to use, implies: "Of all the hosts You have created, is it so hard to give me one son" (Ber. 31b), and to have contained the suggested criticism of God: "To which host do I belong? If the heavenly, then I will never die; if the mortal, then I should be able to give birth" (PR 43, 179b). The triple repetition of the phrase "thy handmaid" refers to her contention that she had not transgressed any of the three transgressions for which women die in childbirth (Ber. *ibid.*, cf. Shab. 2:6). Hannah was so assured of the righteousness of her case that not only did she "hurl words at God" (*ibid.*) but she even volunteered to feign adultery, so that she would have to undergo the ordeal of water, after which, according to the Bible, "she will be cleansed and shall conceive seed" (Num. 5:28; Ber. *ibid.*).

BIBLIOGRAPHY: H.P. Smith, *Critical and Exegetical Commentary of the Books of Samuel* (ICC, 1899), 3–19; M.Z. Segal, *Sifrei Shemu'el* (1964[2]), 1–20; Cross, in: BASOR, 132 (1953), 15–26. **ADD. BIBLIOGRAPHY:** S. Bar-Efrat, I *Samuel* (1996), 53.

HANNAH AND HER SEVEN SONS, a story told in II *Maccabees, Chapter 7, of seven brothers who were seized along with their mother by *Antiochus IV Epiphanes, presumably shortly after the beginning of the religious persecutions in 167/166 B.C.E., and commanded to prove their obedience to the king by partaking of swine's flesh. The brothers defiantly refused to do so. Encouraged in their resolve by their mother, they were executed after being put to frightful tortures. When the mother was appealed to by the king to spare the youngest child's life by prevailing upon him to comply, she urged the child instead to follow in the path of his brothers, and she herself died shortly thereafter.

The accounts of the manner in which she met her death differ. According to IV Maccabees, she threw herself into the fire. The Midrash states that she lost her reason and threw herself to her death from a roof, while according to *Josippon* she fell dead on the corpses of her children. The story, along with that of the martyrdom of the aged priest Eleazar (II Macc. 6:18–31), became the subject of the book known as the Fourth Book of Maccabees. In rabbinic literature the story is recounted as an instance of martyrdom during the Hadrianic persecution (Lam. R. 1:16, no. 50; Git. 57b; PR 43:180; SER 30:151). The martyrs were venerated in the Roman Catholic calendar of saints (Aug. 1) as the "Seven Maccabee Brothers," although the mother is also mentioned with them, their martyrdom being considered a prefiguration of later Christian martyrdoms. According to Antiochene Christian tradition, the relics of the mother and sons were interred on the site of a synagogue (later converted into a church) in the Kerateion quarter of Antioch. On this and other grounds, it has been suggested that the scene of the martyrdom was Antioch rather than Jerusalem.

Whatever its historical substratum, the story in II Maccabees and in all subsequent sources is doubtless an adaptation of a stock form of a terrible tragedy (cf. I Sam. 2:5 and Isaiah di Trani's commentary; Job 1:2, 19; Ass. Mos. 9; Jos., Ant., 14:429; BB 11a; Sem. 8:13). Drawing directly on II Maccabees, *Sefer Josippon* (c. 953) restored the story to its original Epiphanian setting. Although in II Maccabees and *Gittin* the name of the mother is not given, in other rabbinic accounts she is called Miriam bat Tanḥum, while in Syriac Christian accounts she is called Shamone and/or Maryam. However, the obvious association with I Samuel 2:5 impelled a Spanish reviser of the *Josippon* (ed. Constantinople, 1510, 4:19) to name the anonymous mother of II Maccabees "Hannah," by which name she has become famous, thanks to the dissemination of the longer (Spanish) version of *Josippon* and the medieval *piyyutim* in Hebrew, Arabic, and Judeo-Persian which are based on it. The shorter recension of the work (ed. Mantua, c. 1480, 126f.) and the literature based on it continued to refer to her anonymously. The story has inspired many legends on the place of the martyrs' burial, as well as works of art, poetry, and drama on their martyrdom, down to modern times.

BIBLIOGRAPHY: G.D. Cohen, in: *Sefer ha-Yovel… Kaplan* (1953), 109–22; H.M. Michlin, in: *Mizraḥ u-Ma'arav*, 3 (1928/29), 194–9; J. Gutman, in: *Sefer Yoḥanan Levi* (1949), 25–37; F.M. Abel, *Les Livres des Maccabées* (1949), 370–84; E.J. Bickerman, in: *Byzantion*, 21 (1951), 63–83 (Fr.); M. Hadas (ed.), *The Third and Fourth Books of Maccabees* (1953), 91ff.; Nissim b. Jacob, *Ḥibbur Yafeh me-ha-Yeshu'ah*, ed. and tr. by H.Z. Hirschberg (1954), 58ff., introduction; T.W. Manson, in: BJRL, 39 (1956/57), 479–84.

[Gerson D. Cohen]

HANNATHON (Heb. חַנָּתֹן), city in the territory of Zebulun between Rimmon and Iphtahel (Wadi al-Malik) in Lower Galilee (Josh. 19:13–14). It is mentioned in two el-Amarna letters as Ḥinnatuni or Ḥinnatuna (ed. Knudtzon, 8, 245); in one it is referred to as the place where the kings of Shimron and Acre attacked a Babylonian caravan which was on its way to Egypt, and in the other, as the place where the king of Acre freed Labayu, king of Shechem, after he had been captured at Megiddo. Tiglath-Pileser III mentions Hannathon (Ḥinatuna) among the cities captured during his Galilean campaign in 733 B.C.E., together with Kanah and Jotbah. The site is generally identified with Tell al-Badaywiyya at the western end of the Bet Netofah Valley, on an important road near Rammun, Kanah, and Jotapata. Pottery dating from the Middle Bronze, Late Bronze, and Iron Ages has been found there. An alternative identification locates Hannathon at Khirbat al-Ḥarbaj in the southern end of the plain of Acre (but see *Achshaph).

BIBLIOGRAPHY: Alt, in: PJB, 21 (1925), 62ff.; Y. Aharoni, *Hitnaḥalut Shivtei Yisrael ba-Galil ha-Elyon* (1957), index; Aharoni, Land, index; Albright, in: BASOR, no. 11 (1923), 11; idem, in: AASOR, 2–3 (1923), 23f.

[Michael Avi-Yonah]

ḤANNELES, JUDAH LEIB BEN MEIR (d. 1596), rabbi and author, probably from Posen; known by the initials of his name, as "Maharlaḥ" (**M**orenu **ha**-**R**av **L**eib **Ḥ**anneles). Judah, the son of Meir of Tannhauser, was one of nine brothers, among them *Eliakim Goetz b. Meir, a leading scholar of Posen, Jacob *Temerls, and Akiva of Hotzenplatz. He is the author of *Va-Yiggash Yehudah*, a commentary on the *Arba'ah Turim* of *Jacob b. Asher, which he explains word by word, noting each halakhic ruling, giving its source and citing the various opinions. In his commentary Judah sought to complete the *Beit Yosef* of Joseph *Caro; he disagrees with Caro in several instances and also gives more accurate versions of the *Arba'ah Turim*, of which Caro was not aware. At times he even disagrees with Jacob b. Asher. He began the publication of his work toward the end of his life, and died before it was completed. His brother, Jacob Temerls, continued with the publication of *Oraḥ Ḥayyim* (Lublin, 1596–99). In the later editions of the *Arba'ah Turim*, beginning with that of Dyhernfurth (1791–96), a second corrected edition of *Va-Yiggash Yehudah* on *Oraḥ Ḥayyim* was published, in which the sources were omitted. Although the *Ḥiddushei ha-Ga'on Leib Ḥanneles* on *Oraḥ Ḥayyim* printed in the standard text of the *Arba'ah Turim* have been wrongly ascribed to him (being a selection of glosses from commentators compiled by the brothers Michael Simon and Joseph Maya the sons of the printer, Jehiel Maya), they nevertheless include many selections from Ḥanneles' work.

BIBLIOGRAPHY: Eliakim Goetz ben Meir, *Even ha-Shoham u-Me'irat Einayim* (Dyhernfurth, 1733), 5 (introd.); Hoffman, in: *Magazin fuer juedische Geschichte und Literatur*, 1 (1874), 8; H.D. Friedberg, *Toledot Mishpaḥat Shor* (1901), 14–15; S. Wiener, *Kohelet Moshe*, 5 (1904), 549, no. 4512; H. Tchernowitz, *Toledot ha-Posekim*, 2 (1947), 299–300.

HANNEMANN, PABLO (1906–?), Argentine sculptor. Born in Germany, Hannemann designed and illustrated several books for Jewish publishing companies before he immigrated to Argentina in 1937. In 1955 he founded an Argentine art school. He organized, together with two architects, the first Israeli industrial exhibition in Argentina. Besides carving in wood, he worked in concrete and made large sculptures, as he considered concrete to be the only true link with architecture. His sculpture is filled with Jewish content.

HANNOVER, ADOLPH (1814–1894), Danish scientist and physician, known for his experimental studies in histology and microscopic technique. Hannover's detection of a plant parasite on the salamander was of vital importance to medicine for it proved for the first time the significance of vegetative contagious matter in the transmission of infectious diseases. Hannover's use of chromium acid as a hardening agent contributed to microscopic technique. His treatises on the microscopy of the nervous system, on the construction of microscopes, on the retina, and on the nature of cancer were translated into many languages.

BIBLIOGRAPHY: M.A. Hannover: *Adolph Hannovers fédrene og mødrene Slérgt* (1914).

[Julius Margolinsky]

HANNOVER, NATHAN NATA (d. 1683), preacher, kabbalist, lexicographer, and chronicler. During the *Chmielnicki massacres which started at the end of 1648, he had to leave his birthplace in Volhynia and he wandered through Poland, Germany, and Holland for several years. His sermons, delivered during those years of wandering, were compiled into a book covering the entire Pentateuch. In 1653 he went to Italy. In the same year in Venice, he published *Yeven Meẓulah* (Miry Pit), dealing with the Chmielnicki persecutions. He associated with the great kabbalists of the period: Samuel Aboab and Moses Zacuto of Italy; and those who had come from Ereẓ Israel – Ḥayyim Cohen, Nathan Shapira, and Benjamin ha-Levi of Safed. He studied the Kabbalah doctrines of the school of Isaac Luria for a number of years and enjoyed the munificence of patrons in Leghorn in 1654 and in Venice in 1655–56.

In 1660 in Prague, Hannover published *Safah Berurah* (Clear Language), a Hebrew-German-Latin-Italian conversation lexicon, text, and guidebook for travelers, and in 1662, *Sha'arei Ẓiyyon* (The Gates of Zion), a collection of prayers for *tikkun ḥaẓot* (midnight prayers), and for other kabbalistic rituals of the Lurianic school. These two books were the result of his studies in Italy. In 1662, he was appointed president of the *bet din* and head of the yeshivah in Jassy, Walachia, which was then a Turkish province. He was still in Jassy in 1666, the "year of redemption," when the Messiah was due, according to the beliefs of the Shabbatean movement. He is mentioned among those who wrote to Lithuania to announce the event. He spent about ten years in Jassy, and according to tradition, in Pascani too. He then moved to Ungarisch Brod, Moravia, on the Hungarian border, where he was preacher and religious judge. He was killed, while praying with the community, by Turkish soldiers who raided the town.

Hannover was a prolific writer, but most of his works, sermons and writings on the Kabbalah, were lost. Apart from the sermon *Ta'amei Sukkah*, printed in Amsterdam, 1652, and a kabbalistic writing on Purim, preserved in manuscript, only the three books published in his lifetime are extant. The subject matter and the style of these works are diverse, yet each had considerable influence for a long time. The prayer book, *Sha'arei Ẓiyyon*, was reprinted over 50 times, chiefly in Italy, Holland, and Central and Eastern Europe. The book served as a channel for introducing into the ordinary prayer book certain elements of the Lurianic Kabbalah, such as the *Berikh Shemei* prayer. *Safah Berurah* also had several editions, being published both under its own title and other titles in its original form and in a modified version. Up to the 19th century, it was used for the study of foreign languages in Central and Eastern Europe. It is still an important source for research into the Yiddish and the Hebrew used in the author's time.

The small book *Yeven Meẓulah*, on the Chmielnicki pogroms of 1648–52, has relatively few personal experiences of the author. It is mainly based on eyewitness accounts of others and hearsay evidence (including information Hannover found in print). This was the manner of writing of chroniclers of the period. Hannover's broader vision, lucid language, and simple and graceful manner of relating events gave the book an appeal it still retains. Among the Ashkenazi Jews, it was reprinted in the original version and in Yiddish translation, in almost every generation (including a Hebrew edition, 1945; a Yiddish edition, 1938), It was translated into French (1855), German (1863), Russian (1878), Polish (1912), and English (*Abyss of Despair*, 1950). The book has also been a source of information on the massacres of the Chmielnicki period to modern writers and poets like S. Asch and Minsky. Some historians have followed the narrative uncritically, without submitting it to historical analysis.

BIBLIOGRAPHY: I. Israelson, in: YIVO, *Historishe Shriftn*, 1 (1929), 1–26 (cf. 2 (1937), 684–5, notes by Halevy); M. Weinreich, in: *Tsaytshrift far Yidishe Geshikhte, Demografye...*, 2–3 (1928), 706–16; I. Nacht, in: *Reshumot*, 1 (1946), 164–7; N. Prylucki, in: *YIVO Bleter*, 1 (1931), 414ff.; I. Shatzky, in: *Gezerot Taḥ* (1938), 9–159; Elbogen, Gottesdienst, 200, 390.

[Israel Halpern]

HANNOVER, RAPHAEL LEVI (1685–1779), mathematician and astronomer. Born in Weikersheim, he worked as a bookkeeper in the house of Oppenheimer in Hanover, where he met the philosopher Leibniz and became his devoted pupil, studying mathematics, astronomy, and natural philosophy. He wrote two books in Hebrew on astronomy: *Luḥot ha-Ibbur*, astronomical tables for the Jewish calendar (Leiden-Hanover, 1756–7; Dessau, 1831) and *Tekhunat ha-Shamayim ve-Khol Ẓeva'am u-Mahalakham* (Amsterdam, 1756). He left several unpublished manuscripts.

BIBLIOGRAPHY: Zinberg, Sifrut 3 (1957), 306.

[Getzel Kressel]

HA-NO'AR HA-IVRI-AKIBA, pioneering and scouting Zionist youth movement with special attachment to the traditional values of Judaism. The movement was founded in Cracow as an organization of Jewish students in non-Jewish high schools. In 1924 Akiba united with similar youth organizations in western Galicia and assumed the character of a pioneering Zionist youth movement. A group that left the movement constituted the nucleus of the youth movement of the *General Zionists, Ha-No'ar ha-Ẓiyyoni. Akiba was active in Poland and to a lesser degree in Austria, Czechoslovakia, Greece, Yugoslavia, Bulgaria, and Palestine between the two World Wars, during the Holocaust, and almost until the establishment of the State of Israel. Its pioneering members began to settle collectively in Palestine in 1930. They were among those who fought for Jewish labor in Petaḥ Tikvah, Be'er Ya'akov, Ekron, and Ḥaderah and were among the founders of Neveh Eitan, Usha, Bet Yehoshu'a, Bustan ha-Galil, Benei Zion, and elsewhere.

Before the Holocaust, the membership of the movement reached 30,000. At the 21st Zionist Congress (1939), the last before the war, the movement was represented by six delegates. The ideological foundation of Akiba was based on the following principles: both assimilation – as a pragmatic means to solve the Jewish problem – and the leftist movements – especially Communism – lead to the destruction of Judaism. The efforts of assimilationists for generations have ended in failure, and the same is true of leftist movements, which denied Jewish national identity. Akiba advanced the desire to create an original Jewish experience through a pioneering way of life in Ereẓ Israel and viewed Zionism as the perpetuation of Jewish history.

Akiba educated its members toward a positive attitude to the traditional Jewish way of life. This emphasis was important among semi-assimilated youth who had been drawn away from Judaism. Its guiding principle was that even those who doubted the values of faith must agree that the traditionally religious way of life embodies the original creation of the Jewish people and its unifying quality was still valid in the present. Therefore behavior in public and in Jewish institutions should not contradict the traditional way of life. During the Holocaust, the leaders of Akiba were among the heads of the Jewish fighting organizations and participated in the armed revolts in the Cracow ghetto (1942) and the Warsaw ghetto (1943). The ideological leader of the movement was Yoel Dreiblatt.

BIBLIOGRAPHY: *Ha-Tenu'ah ha-Ḥalutzit be-Aguddat ha-No'ar ha-Ivri Akiva* (1940); Y. Dreiblatt, *Ziv Mo'adei Yisrael* (1946); G. Davidson, *Yomanah shel Yustinah* (1953); *Sefer Cracow* (1953), 263–70, 286–9; *Cracow Memorial Journal* (1968), 939–45. **ADD. BIBLIOGRAPHY:** J. Orenstein et al. (eds.), *Mishnat ha-Ẓiyyonut shel Agudat ha-No'ar ha-Ivri "Akiva"* (1986); B. Jehieli, *Akivah, Ẓemikhata, Hitpatḥuta u-Leḥimata bi-Shenot ha-Sho'ah* (1988).

[Moshe Singer]

HA-NO'AR HA-OVED VE-HA-LOMED (Heb. "Working and Student Youth"), Israel youth movement for boys and girls aged 9–18. It is an integral part of the *Histadrut. It was founded as Ha-No'ar ha-Oved in 1926 to conduct educational activities among working youth aged 13–18 and improve their wages and working conditions. Its founder and mentor was David *Cohen (d. 1976). The movement ran evening classes, which were taken over by the state in 1955; labor exchanges, taken over by the State Employment Service in 1959; and youth groups for ages 10–12, 13–15, and 16–18. Most of the instructors came from the kibbutzim of *Iḥud ha-Kevuẓot ve-ha-Kibbutzim and *Ha-Kibbutz ha-Me-'uḥad. In 1933 a group of members founded its first kibbutz, *Na'an, and it has provided founding members for about 40 kibbutzim in all. In 1959 Ha-No'ar ha-Oved merged with Habonim-Ha-Tenu'ah ha-Me'uḥedet to form the present organization. In 1970 it had about 100,000 members; somewhat more than one-third were working boys and girls and belonged to the trade sections, and the rest, most of them still at school, belonged to the educational groups. While it had no formal party affiliation, most of its youth leaders belonged to the *Israel Labor Party. At the outset of the 21st century the movement had hundreds of branches, centers, and clubhouses throughout Israel, used by Jewish, Arab, and Druze youth; including young people who work and study in the cities, development towns, kibbutzim, and young immigrants. The movement runs the Labor Union for Youth, which is the organization that acts as the legal representative of young working people in Israel. The movement focuses on involvement in Israeli society and initiates such educational activities as seminars, camps, and daily meetings. The counselors are movement graduates who postpone their military service for one year and work voluntarily in the movement centers or live as a group in development towns. The movement also has activities in the former Soviet Union in order to encourage and prepare young people to immigrate to Israel. At the end of the 1980s, a group of graduates established Merḥav, a movement of people aged 22–30 who live cooperatively in cities and villages and are active in educational work. Members of Merḥav established two new kibbutzim: Ravid and Eshbal, located in Galilee.

BIBLIOGRAPHY: *Ba-Ma'aleh, Itton ha-No'ar ha-Oved* (1926–); *Ittim, Ḥoveret Ezer la-Madrikh* (1966–); *Aleh, Itton Ḥativat No'ar ha-Iḥud* (1966–). **WEBSITE**: www.noal.co.il.

[Shaked Gilboa (2nd ed.)]

HANOKH, SHALOM (1946–), Israeli rock singer-songwriter, among the most influential figures in Israeli rock since the 1970s. After teaming up with iconographic singer Arik *Einstein in 1967 he produced an extensive volume of work, ranging from blues-inflected songs to high-energy rock and gentle ballads.

Hanokh was born in kibbutz Mishmarot and spent much of his formative musical years writing songs with fellow kibbutz member singer-songwriter Meir Ariel. After being brought up on classical music, musicals, gospel, blues, folk music, and French chansons, Hanokh discovered the Beatles. When he was 18 a song he wrote called *Stav* ("Fall") was recorded by top singing duo of the time, Hedva and David.

Hanokh joined the IDF at the age of 19 and was eventually accepted into the Naḥal army band, although not as a soloist. During his military service Hanokh also found time to appear in civilian shows with performers such as Ḥanan Yovel, Menaḥem Silverman, and Eli Magen. In 1967, Hanokh wrote a satirical number called *Jacques Aboutboul*, together with Yossi Pollak. It was this effort that brought him to the attention of Einstein, already an established star in the Israeli pop world. Shortly after hearing Hanokh perform *Jacques Aboutboul* Einstein recorded four Hanokh compositions and one of the important duos in the annals of Israeli rock was born.

After his release from the army in 1968, Hanokh left his kibbutz, moved to Tel Aviv, and began a highly productive period during which he wrote the music for hits by numerous top performers, such as Yossi *Banai, Ili Gurelitzki, and Ḥanan Yovel. More importantly, he also wrote the music for *Prague* with which Einstein won the 1969 Israeli Song Festival. Between 1969 and 1970 Hanokh collaborated with Einstein on two albums, *Shablul* and *Plastelina*, appeared in the movie *Shablul*, and took part alongside Einstein in two episodes of the satirical program *Lul*. Hanokh then spent three years trying to develop an international career in London but failed and returned to Israel in 1973. He resumed his partnership with Einstein before his Israeli rock career took off in earnest with the formation of the country's first rock band, Tammuz.

In 1977 Hanokh released a melancholy album called *Adam Betokh Atzmo*, before returning to his original high-energy rock style. Further collaborations with Einstein ensued and, by the end of the 1970s, Hanokh was the top rock performer in Israel. In 1984 Hanokh released *Meḥakim le-Mashi'aḥ* ("Waiting for the Messiah"), his most successful album to date, and although his career had a few ups and downs in the interim, Hanokh remained the premier rock artist in Israel.

[Barry Davis (2nd ed.)]

ḤANOKH BEN MOSES (d. 1014), Spanish talmudist. The biography of Ḥanokh the son of *Moses b. Ḥanokh, is told in Abraham *Ibn Daud's *Sefer ha-Kabbalah* (*The Book of Traditions*, ed. by G.D. Cohen (1967), 65–71). On the death of his father in about 965, Ḥanokh was appointed rabbi of Córdoba and as a result was virtually chief rabbi of the whole of Muslim Spain. Joseph *Ibn Abitur, who was his equal in knowledge of Torah and excelled him in secular knowledge, competed with him for the post, but Ḥ *Ḥisdai ibn Shaprut decided in Ḥanokh's favor. When Ḥisdai died, the struggle was renewed, and on this occasion the caliph, al-Ḥakam II al-Mustanóir (961–76), confirmed the appointment of Ḥanokh; whereupon Ibn Abitur was put under the ban and left Spain. However, when the caliph died and the vizier al-*Manṣūr took control of the kingdom in Spain, a Jewish merchant, Jacob *Ibn Jau rose in power. The latter supported Ibn Abitur, Ḥanokh was dismissed from office, and Ibn Abitur was invited to return to

Spain. Ibn Abitur did not accept the invitation. Subsequently, Ibn Jau was imprisoned by al-Manṣūr and Ḥanokh was restored to office, serving until his death. From all the information that is available, it appears that Ḥanokh followed his father in all matters. He was an outstanding talmudic scholar, some of whose responsa were included in the contemporary gaonic responsa. Like his father, he worked to establish an independent Torah center in Spain. R. *Hai Gaon complains bitterly that Ḥanokh did not answer his letters. He had important disciples, the greatest of whom was *Samuel ha-Nagid.

BIBLIOGRAPHY: Abramson, Merkazim, 84–90; idem, in: *Tarbiz*, 31 (1961/62), 196ff.; Ashtor, Korot, 1 (1966²), 233–48; M. Margalioth, *Hilkhot ha-Nagid* (1962), index.

[Eliyahu Ashtor]

ḤANOKH OF ALEKSANDROW (1798–1870), ḥasidic *ẓaddik* and leader; son of Phinehas ha-Kohen of Lutomirsk. He became a disciple of *Simḥah Bunim of Przysucha (Pshiskhah) and Menahem Mendel of *Kotsk, and served as rabbi in *Aleksandrow near Lodz, and later in Nowy Dwor, and in Pressnitz. Ḥanokh spent most of his life in the circles of the Ḥasidim of Przysucha and their successors in Kotsk and Gur, and in 1866 Ḥanokh succeeded Isaac Meir *Alter as leader of Gur Ḥasidism (see *Gora Kalwaria). He settled in Aleksandrow which had become a center for Kotsk-Gur Ḥasidism. Ḥanokh continued the Kotsk trend in a mystical religious interpretation. He emphasized the value of Torah study which he termed "internal worship." Ḥanokh taught that every *mitzvah* must be performed from within and not merely externally. Man should dedicate his entire being to the performance of a *mitzvah* and in turn shall receive the strength of his being from the *mitzvah* he performs. His devotion effects a transformation in the world order and causes a divine emanation. Ḥanokh taught that while a man should occupy himself with the entire Torah and all the *mitzvot*, he should select one *mitzvah* for his particular attention. Of himself Ḥanokh states: "I have chosen the quality of humility."

Ḥanokh believed that everyone could follow the path of Ḥasidism by his own efforts, and that the *ẓaddik* was merely a guide. However, a compelling attachment exists between the *ẓaddik* and his community: "The true leader successfully serves God with the aid of the Ḥasidim who gather round him." Ḥanokh emphasized joy and happiness in life, but his joviality concealed a serious thinker. His teachings are distinguished by brevity and acuity. Only a few of his writings – responsa on halakhic questions, letters and sermons, poems and riddles – have survived in manuscript. Most of his teachings were recorded by his disciples and are published in *Ḥashavah le-Tovah* (1929); his stories and sayings are collected in *Si'aḥ Sarfei Kodesh* (1923).

BIBLIOGRAPHY: P.Z. Gliksman, *Tiferet Adam* (1923), 56–58; L. Grossman, *Shem u-She'erit* (1943), 12; A.Y. Bromberg, *Mi-Gedolei ha-Torah ve-ha-Ḥasidut*, 14 (1958); L.I. Newman, *Hasidic Anthology* (1963), index; M. Buber, *Tales of the Hasidim*, 2 (1966³), 312–8.

[Esther (Zweig) Liebes]

ḤANOKH ZUNDEL BEN JOSEPH (d. 1867), commentator on the Midrash. Ḥanokh lived in Bialystok (Poland), and devoted himself to writing commentaries on the Midrash. They are largely based upon the earlier commentators such as the *Mattenot Kehunnah* of Berman Ashkenazi, the *Yefeh To'ar* of Samuel Jaffe Ashkenazi, and the *Yedei Moshe* of Abraham Heller Ashkenazi, but he adds original comments. In the *Eẓ Yosef* he strives to give the plain meaning of the text and establish the correct readings, while the *Anaf Yosef* is largely homiletical (published together as *Yalkut al Petirat Aharon u-Moshe*, Warsaw, 1874). In addition to his commentaries on the classical Midrashim, the *Rabbah* (1829–34), and the *Tanḥuma* (1833), he also wrote commentaries on other midrashic works, such as the *Seder Olam Rabbah* (1845), *Midrash Shemu'el* (1860), *Aggadat Bereshit* (1876), and the *aggadot* in the *Ein Ya'akov* of Jacob ibn Ḥabib (1883). He also wrote a commentary on *Pirkei Avot* (1892), and *Olat ha-Ḥodesh* (1859), consisting of the prayers for the new moon, with a commentary. His commentaries on *Yalkut Shimoni* and the *Mekhilta* are still in manuscript.

BIBLIOGRAPHY: Fuenn, Keneset, 312; Joel, in: KS, 13 (1936/37), 513 no. 1, 519 no. 19.

[Yehoshua Horowitz]

HANOVER (Ger. **Hannover**), city in Germany. Sources dating from 1292 note the presence of Jews in Hanover's "old city" (Altstadt). The period was one of significant expansion for the city and, therefore, Jewish moneylenders were welcomed and promised protection by the city council. A municipal law of 1303 prohibited anyone from molesting the Jews "by word or deed." The Jewish community grew significantly, and by 1340 ritual slaughter was permitted in the city. During the *Black Death persecutions the Jews were driven from the city. In 1369–71 only one Jew lived in Hanover until he, too, was expelled by the council, with the permission of the duke. In 1375 the dukes yielded to the city the privilege of admitting Jews and retaining their taxes. Shortly thereafter historical records again attest to the presence of Jews in the city. By 1500 several Jews also lived in the "new city" (in 1540, there were three families in the old city, and five in the new). During this period the Jews maintained a synagogue and a rabbi. In 1451 the bishop of Muenden forced the Jews of Hanover to wear the distinguishing *badge, and in 1553 the Jews were compelled to listen to the court preacher Urbanus Rhegius in the synagogue. Between 1553 and 1601 the dukes issued six orders of expulsion against the Jews, but they were either canceled or not carried out. Apparently the Jews who were under the protection of the city were not affected by these orders. In 1588 the council forbade all business connections with Jews, and for a long time Jews did not live in the "old city."

In 1608 the residence of six Jewish families in the "new city" is mentioned, but when they opened a synagogue it was destroyed by the burghers (1613). In the 17th century the dukes permitted the settlement of several wealthy Jews in the "new city." At the request of the Court Jew Leffmann *Behrens, a resident of Hanover, a rabbinate was founded for the Duchy of Hanover. In 1704 a synagogue was established in Behrens' home. In 1710 only seven Jewish families lived in the city, but subsequently their numbers increased considerably, reaching 537 in 1833. Hanover became an important center of Jewish learning and increasingly the residence for important Jewish figures in the financial world. A larger synagogue was built in 1870 and expanded in 1900. From 1848 to 1880 Solomon *Frensdorff, the masoretic scholar, headed a teachers seminary. Hebrew printing took place in Hanover during the 18th and 19th centuries. Among the more significant works produced was Jacob b. Asher's commentary on the Pentateuch (1838). Prominent rabbis of Hanover include Nathan *Adler (1831–45) and Selig Gronemann (1844–1918). The Jewish population numbered 1,120 in 1861 (1.9% of the total population), 3,450 in 1880 (2.8%), 5,130 in 1910 (1.7%), 4,839 in 1933 (1.1%), and 2,271 in 1939 (0.5%). On the eve of World War II Hanover had one of the 10 largest Jewish communities in Germany, with over 20 cultural and welfare institutions. The anti-Jewish boycott started even before the nationwide boycott of April 1, 1933, when the Karstadt Department story fired all its Jewish employees. There was anti-Jewish rioting in May 1933 and the attacks continued the next year. Jews understood their perilous plight; many left and others closed their business and professional practices. By 1938, 552 Jewish business and legal and medical practices in Hanover were no longer operating. As their public life as Germans narrowed, Jewish communal life became more intense. In October 1938, 484 Jews of Polish origin were expelled to Poland. On *Kristallnacht* the synagogue was burned, Jewish stores were looted and homes ransacked. The mortuary was also destroyed and the *mikveh* was wrecked. Three hundred and thirty-four men were arrested and sent to Buchenwald. In a rapid operation on September 3–4, 1941, 1,200 Jews were evicted from their homes and consigned to 15 "Jew houses." Deportations began in December 1941 and continued in March and July 1942, when the Jewish population was reduced to some 300. In February 1945 Jews married to non-Jews were deported. At least 2,200 Jews from Hanover died in the Holocaust. Some 100 survived within the city.

After the war 66 survivors of the prewar community returned. In 1963 a new synagogue was opened; in 1966 there were 450 Jews in Hanover (0.03% of the total population). In 1988 the European Center for Jewish Music was established at the University for Music and Theatre. It is devoted to the reconstruction and documentation of liturgical music. The Jewish community numbered 379 in 1989 and 3,898 in 2004. The membership increased due to the immigration of Jews from the former Soviet Union. Since 1997 the community has employed a rabbi. In 1995 a liberal community was established which had more than 450 members in 2005. It is a member of the Union of Progressive Jews in Germany. Hanover is the seat of two associations of Jewish communities in Lower Saxony: the association which is affiliated with the Central Council of Jews in Germany with nine communities (founded in 1953) and the association of liberal Jewish communities (founded in 1997) with seven members (2005).

Former German State

The Duchy of Hanover was formed out of the former territories of *Brunswick and Lueneburg in the 17th century. Duke Ernst August (1679–98) obtained the title of elector through the services of Leffmann Behrens, whose descendants continued in the service of the crown till the middle of the 19th century. Other prominent families of Court Jews were David, Cohen, and Gans. The dukes established their rights of taxation and guardianship over the Jews, expressed in the *Judenordnung* of 1723, in force until 1842, which severely restricted the number of Jews there. In 1808 the Jews of Hanover received civil rights either through annexation of the territory to France or its incorporation in the newly created Kingdom of Westphalia. These rights were abolished in 1815, and the basic 1842 legislation concerning the Jews confirmed discrimination against them by expressly excluding Jews from state posts. The Jewish oath was rescinded only in 1850. The Jews finally achieved emancipation three years after Hanover passed to Prussia (1866).

BIBLIOGRAPHY: H. Bodemeyer, *Die Juden: ein Beitrag zur Hannoverschen Rechtsgeschichte* (1855); Wiener, in: *Jahrbuch fuer die Geschichte der Juden und des Judenthums,* 1 (1860), 167–216; idem in: MGWJ, 10 (1861), 121–36, 161–75, 241–58, 281–97; 13 (1864), 161–84; M. Zuckerman, *Dokumente zur Geschichte der Juden in Hannover* (1908); S. Gronemann, *Genealogische Studien ueber die alten juedischen Familien Hannovers* (1913); Blau, in: *Zeitschrift fuer Demographie und Statistik der Juden,* 8 (1912), 70–75; 10 (1914), 110–6; S. Stern, *The Court Jew* (1950), index; *Leben und Schicksal: zur Einweihung der Synagoge in Hannover* (1963); Germ Jud, 2 (1968), 337–40; A. Loeb, *Die Rechtsverhaeltnisse der Juden im... Hannover* (1908); *Pinkas ha-Kehillot* (1963); S. Freund, *Ein Vierteljahrtausend Hannoversches Landrabbinat 1687–1937* (1937); H. Schnee, *Die Hoffinanz und der moderne Staat,* 2 (1954), 11–85; BJCE. **ADD. BIBLIOGRAPHY:** A. Quast, *Nach der Befreiung. Juedische Gemeinden in Niedersachsen seit 1945. Das Beispiel Hannover* Goettingen (2001; Veroeffentlichungen des Arbeitskreises Geschichte des Landes Niedersachsen (nach 1945), volume 17); R. Roehrbein, Waldemar, *Juedische Persoenlichkeiten in Hannovers Geschichte* Hanover (1998); P. Schulze, *Beitraege zur Geschichte der Juden in Hannover* (1998; Hannoversche Studien, volume 6); P. Schulze (ed), *Juden in Hannover. Beitraege zur Geschichte und Kultur einer Minderheit* (1989; Kulturinformation, volume 19); C. Ochwadt, *Die Kristallnacht in Hannover. Erinnerungen eines damals 15jaehrigen* (1988); M. Buchholz, *Die hannoverschen Judenhaeuser. Zur Situation der Juden in der Zeit der Ghettoisierung und Verfolgung 1941 bis 1945* (1987; Quellen und Darstellungen zur Geschichte Niedersachsens, volume 101); P. Schulze (ed.), *"... dass die Juden in unseren Landen einen Rabbinen erwehlen ..." Beitraege zum 300. Jahrestag der Errichtung des Landesrabbinats Hannover am 10. Maerz 1987* (1987); F. Homeyer, *Gestern und heute. Juden im Landkreis Hannover* (1984); S. Spector (ed), *Encyclopedia of Jewish Life Before and During the Holocaust* (2001).

[Zvi Avneri / Larissa Daemmig (2nd ed.)]

HANRAY, LAWRENCE (1874–1947), British actor. Born in London, Hanray directed the Liverpool Repertory Company from 1913 and took the company to London. In 1920 he joined

Everyman Theater, Hampstead, and played in the original production of *Loyalities*, 1922, and later revivals of this and other Galsworthy plays. He also acted in Chekhov, Ibsen, and Euripides and did a season in New York, 1927–28. From 1932 until his death he appeared in supporting roles in many British films, especially historical costume dramas produced by Sir Alexander *Korda such as *The Private Life of Henry VIII* (1933) and *Nicholas Nickleby* (1946).

HANSON, NORMAN LEONARD (1909–), South African architect. Hanson made a major contribution to the town planning of Ashkelon in Israel, designed the national headquarters of the South African Zionist Federation in Johannesburg (his birthplace) and the mining and geology block at the Witwatersrand University. He served on its faculty of architecture for many years. Hanson was president of the Institute of South African Architects in 1947. In 1963, he left South Africa to take up the chair of architecture at Manchester University.

[Louis Hotz]

HANTKE, ARTHUR (**Menahem**; 1874–1955), Zionist leader. Born in Berlin, the son of a religious family from the district of Posen, Hantke was in 1893 a founding member of the Juedische Humanitaetsgesellschaft, a society of Jewish students in Berlin, which in the course of time adopted a Jewish national outlook. He joined the Zionist Organization soon after it was founded in 1897. In 1905 he became a member of the Zionist General Council of the World Zionist Organization and was appointed director of the office of the Zionist Federation in Germany. From 1910 to 1920 he served as president of this organization. At the Tenth Zionist Congress held in Basle (1911) he was elected to the Zionist Executive, a post in which he was responsible for financial and organizational affairs. During World War I he was charged with important political tasks, one of which was to establish contact with the German Foreign Ministry on behalf of the Zionist Organization. After the publication of the *Balfour Declaration in London he attempted to obtain similar declarations from the Central Powers and succeeded in obtaining a pro-Zionist statement from the Austro-Hungarian foreign minister, Count Czernin (Nov. 17, 1917). After the war he lived for a time in London, where he continued to deal with organizational affairs of the Zionist Organization. In 1920 he was put in charge of the Central European department of the *Keren Hayesod and of the Berlin office of the Zionist Organization. In 1926 Hantke settled in Palestine, and from then he served (with L. *Jaffe until 1948) as the managing director of the head office of the Keren Hayesod in Jerusalem. The moshav Even Menaḥem on the Israel-Lebanese border is named after him.

BIBLIOGRAPHY: K. Blumenfeld, *Erlebte Judenfrage* (1962), index; R. Lichtheim, *Toledot ha-Ẓiyyonut be-Germanyah* (n.d.), index; I. Gruenbaum, *Penei ha-Dor*, 2 (1960), index; Z. Shazar, *Or Ishim*, 1 (1963^2), 108–18.

[Michael Heymann]

ḤANUKKAH (Heb. חֲנֻכָּה; "dedication"), an annual eight-day festival commencing on the 25th of Kislev. According to a well-founded tradition it was instituted by *Judah Maccabee and his followers. The term *ḥanukkah* is found in Hebrew and in Aramaic (ḥanukta) in rabbinic literature, while in Greek it is ὁ ἐγκαινισμὸς τοῦ θυσιαστηρίου, "dedication of the altar," (I Maccabees 4:59) and τά ἐγκαίνια, "feast of the dedication" (John 10:22, where it is an abbreviation of *ḥanukkat ha-mizbe'aḥ*, "dedication of the altar," of I Maccabees, and of *ḥanukkat beit Ḥashmonai*, "dedication of the Hasmonean Temple" in rabbinic literature). The sources which refer to Ḥanukkah yield little information on the institution of the festival. They were composed long (perhaps even generations) after its establishment; legends seem to be inextricably interwoven with the historical traditions. I Maccabees (4:36–59) states that Judah Maccabee, after defeating Lysias, entered Jerusalem and purified the Temple. The altar that had been defiled was demolished and a new one was built. Judah then made new holy vessels (among them a candelabrum, an altar for incense, a table, and curtains) and set the 25th of Kislev as the date for the rededication of the Temple. The day coincided with the third anniversary of the proclamation of the restrictive edicts of Antiochus Epiphanes in which he had decreed that idolatrous sacrifices should be offered on a platform erected upon the altar. The altar was to be consecrated with the renewal of the daily sacrificial service, accompanied by song, the playing of musical instruments, the chanting of **Hallel*, and the offering of sacrifices (no mention of any special festival customs is made). The celebrations lasted for eight days and Judah decreed that they be designated as days of rejoicing for future generations. Ḥanukkah, as the festival that commemorates the dedication of the altar, is also mentioned in the scholium of **Megillat Ta'anit*, as well as in the traditional **Al ha-Nissim* ("We thank Thee for the miracles") prayer for Ḥanukkah.

In II Maccabees (1:8; 10:1–5), the main aspects of Ḥanukkah are related as in I Maccabees. The book adds, however, that the eight-day dedication ceremony was performed on an analogy with *Solomon's consecration of the Temple (2:12). The eight days were celebrated "with gladness like the Feast of Tabernacles remembering how, not long before, during the Feast of Tabernacles, they had been wandering like wild beasts in the mountains and the caves. So, bearing wands wreathed with leaves and fair boughs and palms, they offered hymns of praise" (10:6–8). Ḥanukkah is, therefore, called *Tabernacles (1:9), or Tabernacles and Fire (1:18). Fire had descended from heaven at the dedication of the altar in the days of Moses and at the sanctification of the Temple of Solomon; at the consecration of the altar in the time of *Nehemiah there was also a miracle of fire, and so in the days of Judah Maccabee (1:18–36, 2:8–12, 14; 10:3).

Josephus, whose history of Ḥanukkah is based on I Maccabees, does not mention the term Ḥanukkah and concludes: "From that time onward unto this day we celebrate the festival, calling it 'Lights'" (Φῶτα, Ant. 12:325). He explains that the festival acquired this name because the right to serve God came to the people unexpectedly, like a sudden light (*ibid.*).

None of these writings mentions the kindling of lights on Ḥanukkah. Reference is first made in a *baraita*: "The precept of light on Ḥanukkah requires that one light be kindled in each house; the zealous require one light for each person; the extremely zealous add a light for each person each night. According to Bet *Shammai: 'On the first day, eight lights should be kindled, thereafter they should be progressively reduced' while *Hillel held that: 'On the first night one light should be kindled, thereafter they should be progressively increased'" (Scholium to *Megillat Ta'anit*; Shab. 21b). Another *baraita* states that the Hasmoneans could not use the candelabrum in the Temple since the Greeks had defiled it. They, therefore, took seven iron spits, covered them with zinc, and used them as a candelabrum (Scholium to *Megillat Ta'anit*). Indeed the sages of the second century C.E. observe that the candelabrum of the early Hasmoneans was not made of gold (Men. 28b; et al.). This tradition forms the core of the story, a later version of which relates that the Hasmoneans found in the Temple "eight iron bars, erected them, and kindled lights in them" (PR 2:5). Another *baraita* ascribes the eight-day celebration of Ḥanukkah to the kindling of the Temple candelabrum. It states that on entering the Temple, the Hasmoneans discovered that the Greeks had defiled all the oil, except for one cruse, which contained enough oil to keep the candelabrum burning for only one day. A miracle, however, happened and they kindled from it for eight days; in its commemoration a festival lasting eight days was instituted for future generations (Scholium to *Megillat Ta'anit*; Shab. 21b; cf. also *Scroll of Antiochus). All these stories seem to be nothing but legends, and the authenticity of the "oil cruse" story was already questioned in the Middle Ages.

Certain critics conjectured that the origin of Ḥanukkah was either a festival of the hellenized Jews or even an idolatrous festival that had occurred on the 25th of Kislev. Antiochus had, therefore, chosen the day to commence the idolatrous worship in the Temple. No allusion can be found in the sources to bear out this surmise. Ḥanukkah is also not connected in any way, except in calendrical coincidence, with the celebrations of the shortest day of the year (the birthday of the sun), or with the feasts of the Greek god Dionysius.

Most of the Ḥanukkah traditions complement one another, and what is lacking in one may be found in the other. Probably, during the eight-day dedication of the altar by Judah Maccabee, a second Tabernacles (analogous to the Second *Passover) was held because the festival had not been celebrated at its proper time. They observed the precept of taking the **lulav* in the Temple though not the precept of sitting in tents, for this was done at its proper time even by the partisans in the mountains. The custom of Simḥat Bet ha-Sho'evah ("the water-drawing festival"), with its kindling of torches and lamps in the courts of the Temple and the city of Jerusalem, seems likely to have been transferred as well from *Sukkot to Ḥanukkah. This was the general pattern of the festival as Judah instituted it. Before long, however, the custom of taking the *lulav* during Ḥanukkah was abolished and forgotten in time. The author of I Maccabees, who lived in Alexander Yannai's time, was unaware of the custom although it was still remembered in the Diaspora and is recorded by Jason of Cyrene and by the author of II Maccabees. Hints of a connection between Ḥanukkah and Sukkot are also preserved in rabbinic literature. The rejoicing with lights and illuminations in the Temple (after which Ḥanukkah came to be called Urim, "Lights") also became less common after a time so that Josephus no longer knew why the name "Lights" was given to the festival. By then, however, the custom of kindling lights on Ḥanukkah had spread to places outside Jerusalem, lights being kindled in the streets or in the homes. This variety of customs associated with Ḥanukkah is reflected in the *baraita* which discusses the controversy between the schools of Shammai and Hillel (see above) seemingly about the second half of the first century C.E. The custom of kindling the Ḥanukkah lights was then fixed by the sages as a rule for each man; thus it spread throughout Israel, and when other festive days mentioned in *Megillat Ta'anit* were revoked, Ḥanukkah remained as a holiday (RH 18b–19b). Consequently, Ḥanukkah evolved from a distinct Temple festival into a popular family one.

The *halakhah* prescribes that lighting the Ḥanukkah lamp should take place between "sunset and until there is no wayfarer left in the street. The lamp should be placed outside the entrance of the house. If a person lives on an upper story, it should be set on the window, nearest to the street. If he is in fear of the gentiles, the lamp may be placed inside the inner entrance of the house, and in times of danger, the precept is fulfilled by setting it on the table" (Scholium to *Megillat Ta'anit*; Shab. 21b). "Danger" not only existed in Ereẓ Israel during the Hadrianic persecution, but also in Babylonia, where Jews feared the *Habbarei who were fire worshipers (Shab. 45a). Perhaps because of the danger involved, Jews in Babylonia were most particular in the observance of the Ḥanukkah precepts; they decided that "because its purpose is to publicize the miracle," it takes precedence over the purchase of wine for *Kiddush* on the Sabbath (Shab. 23b). "Women are also obliged to kindle the Ḥanukkah lamp since they were also included in the miracle" (Shab. 23a). The precept is best fulfilled by kindling with olive oil; however, any oil may be used (*ibid.*). The Ḥanukkah lamp and the Ḥanukkah light may not serve any practical purpose (Shab. 21b). On kindling the lights, two benedictions are recited, one is a blessing on the lights and the other for the miracle; on the first night, "*She-Heḥeyanu*" (the blessing for the season) is added. The kindling of the light is followed by a short prayer which begins with the words "*Ha-Nerot Hallalu*" ("these lamps"; Sof. 20:4). A summary of the event, i.e., *Al ha-Nissim… Bi-Ymei Mattityahu* ("In the days of Mattathias") is recited in the **Amidah* prayer and in the Grace after Meals. The entire *Hallel* is said on each of the eight days. The reading of the law is from the portion of the Torah which describes the sacrifices brought by the princes at the dedication of the sanctuary, and the kindling of the candelabrum

(Num. 7:1–8:4); special *haftarot* are prescribed for the Sabbaths of Ḥanukkah. **Taḥanun* is not said and it is forbidden to eulogize the dead or to fast.

In medieval times, Ḥanukkah became such a popular festival it was said "Even he who draws his sustenance from charity, should borrow, or sell his cloak to purchase oil and lamps, and kindle" the Ḥanukkah light (Maim. Yad, Megillah va-Ḥanukkah, 4:12). In some communities, women did not work while the lights were burning, and often even during the whole of Ḥanukkah. It became the custom to feast on Ḥanukkah and, relying upon late Midrashim which associate the story of *Judith with Ḥanukkah, cheese was customarily eaten. Pancakes (*latkes*) are eaten in many Ashkenazi communities, and in Israel doughnuts (*sufganiyyot*) have become customary food for the festival. "**Ma'oz Ẓur Yeshu'ati*" ("Mighty Rock of my Salvation"), a hymn composed in Germany by a 13th-century poet about whom nothing is known except his name Mordecai, is usually sung in the Ashkenazi ritual after the kindling of the lights. The Sephardim recite Psalm 30. The origin of the custom to have an additional light, the *shammash* ("servant") with which the Ḥanukkah lights are kindled, is based on two injunctions: not to kindle one Ḥanukkah light with another; and not to use the Ḥanukkah lights for illumination.

Ḥanukkah celebrations were also expressed in ways of which the halakhists disapproved, e.g., in card playing which became traditional from the end of the Middle Ages. On Ḥanukkah, children play with a *dreidel* or *sevivon* ("spinning top"), and also receive gifts of "Ḥanukkah money." Among Sephardim, special feasts for the children and competitions for youths are arranged. In countries where Christmas became a popular family festival, Ḥanukkah, particularly among Reform Jews, assumed a similar form. In modern Israel, Ḥanukkah symbolizes mainly the victory of the few over the many, and the courage of the Jews to assert themselves as a people, which was the impetus of the national renaissance. This view found literary and artistic expression and is also reflected in such customs as the torch relay race which sets out from *Modi'in where the revolt broke out and the Hasmoneans are buried.

In Israel giant Ḥanukkah lamps, visible for great distances, are kindled during the feast atop public buildings, such as the Knesset building in Jerusalem.

BIBLIOGRAPHY: O.S. Rankin, *The Origins of the Festival of Hanukkah…* (1930); idem, in: *The Labyrinth*, ed. by S.H. Hooke (1935), 161–209; E. Bickerman, *The Maccabees* (1947), 42–44; S.J. Zevin, *Ha-Mo'adim ba-Halakhah* (1963[10]), 156–81; T.H. Gaster, *Purim and Hanukkah in Custom and Tradition* (1950); idem, *Festivals of the Jewish Year* (1955); V. Tcherikover, *Hellenistic Civilization and the Jews* (1959), index; E. Solis-Cohen Jr., *Hanukkah* (1960); Krauss, in: REJ, 30 (1895), 24–43, 204–19; 32 (1896), 39–50; Lévi, in: REJ, 30 (1895), 220–31; 31 (1895), 119–20; Hochfeld, in: ZAW, 22 (1902), 264–84; Leszynsky, in: MGWJ, 55 (1911), 400–18; Liber, in: REJ, 63 (1912), 20–29; Hoepfel, in: *Biblica*, 3 (1922), 165ff.; R. Marcus, *Law in the Apocrypha* (1927), 90–93; Finkelstein, in: JQR, 22 (1931/32), 169–73; Lichtenstein, in: HUCA, 8–9 (1931/32), 275f.; Zeitlin, in: JQR, 29 (1938/39), 1–36; Alon, Meḥkarim, 1 (1957), 15–25; Petuchowski, in: *Commentary*, 29 (1960), 38–43.

[Moshe David Herr]

ḤANUKKAH LAMP (also known as **ḥanukkiyyah** and Ḥanukkah **menorah**). The central ritual of the eight-day Festival of *Ḥanukkah is the kindling of a lamp that has receptacles for eight lights, one for each night. A ninth receptacle, called the servitor or *shammash*, is often included in the lamp as well. The festival began in 164 B.C.E., when *Judah Maccabee liberated the Jerusalem Temple from Greek control, resanctified it, and declared an eight-day celebration of "joy and gladness" (I Macc. 4:26–59). Yet, there is no record of exactly how Jews commemorated the holiday in the years following the rededication of the Temple. By the late first or early second century C.E., it was already the custom to kindle eight lights, as recorded in the Talmud. There was a disagreement between two important rabbinic schools in ancient Israel over how to light the lamps. Bet Shammai argued that one should light eight lights on the first night and decrease each night to one, while *Bet Hillel, which soon prevailed, preferred to light one lamp on the first night and increase it to eight (Shab. 21b).

No lamps survive from antiquity that can be identified definitively as Ḥanukkah lamps. It is likely that any of the secular oil lamp types known from the Greco-Roman and Byzantine Periods were used, including single- or multi-wick lamps of clay or metal, sometimes set on a stand, and hanging lamps. The Talmud describes two lamp types that could be used on Ḥanukkah: single dishes with eight wicks arranged around the edge (and covered with another vessel), and lamps with more than one spout (Shab. 23b).

It is not until the Middle Ages that the first lamps clearly designated for Ḥanukkah appear or are illustrated in Hebrew manuscripts. Many of these lamps were in bench form, characterized by a row of light receptacles on a strip or block, usually with an attached backplate. Among the earliest is a stone block with oil wells across the top, which bears the Hebrew inscription "For the commandment is a lamp, and the teaching is light" (Prov. 6:23). Found in Avigon, it has been variously dated between the 10th and 13th centuries. Metal lamps with triangular backplates for suspension on the wall and an openwork arcade of interlace arches, also with a Hebrew inscription, were made in Germany or northern France in the 13th century. Another type of wall lamp with a crenellated rectangular backplate is depicted in an Italian Hebrew manuscript of 1374 in the British Library.

While the form of the stone block lamp might have been derived from similar secular lighting devices called cresset stones, that of the sconce-form metal lamps seems to have been an innovation developed for Jewish ritual use. The secular sconces of the medieval period consisted of single brackets for candles that projected out from the wall; backplates were unknown until the 16th century. The development of a wall lamp for Ḥanukkah is based on the talmudic injunction to hang the lamp outside one's home, since its purpose is to publicize the miracle commemorated on the holiday. If one lived on an upper floor, one could place it in the window, and in times of persecution, on a table (Shab. 21b, 23b). These exceptions led to the addition of feet to backplate lamps, so they could stand on a table. Perhaps the earliest datable example of this custom is a German metal lamp created by Meir Heilprin in 1573–74.

The second basic form of the Ḥanukkah lamp is that of the candelabrum: a central shaft with four arms rising upward from each side, all in a single row. This shape is certainly based on that of the seven-branch candelabrum, or *menorah*, that was designed for the Tabernacle in the desert (Ex. 25:31–40); later versions illuminated the First and Second Temples. *Menorah*-form lamps probably were originally confined to synagogue use. The Rothschild Miscellany, written in Ferrara, Italy around 1470, contains the earliest depiction of a large standing synagogue lamp, consisting of a tall square column that widens at the top to hold eight candles. A 15th- to 16th-century synagogue lamp from Padua is in true *menorah* shape and has leaves projecting from the arms. Smaller *menorah*-form lamps probably for home use appeared in Frankfurt in the late 17th century.

A third lamp type kindled on Ḥanukkah in Europe during the medieval period consisted of a metal star-shaped oil receptacle with eight projecting spouts arranged in a circle. Suspended from the ceiling, it could serve as ordinary room illumination, Sabbath light, and Ḥanukkah lamp (if it had eight spouts). It continued in use for the festival at least until the 16th century, when it is mentioned in Moses *Isserles' notes to the Shulḥan Arukh, called the *Mappah*.

Rabbinic proscriptions governed certain developments in Ḥanukkah lamp form. One is the inclusion of a ninth light, the *shammash*. The basis for this light lies in the talmudic instruction that the lights of the Ḥanukkah lamp were sacred, and that one could not use them for ordinary illumination. Thus, in situations where there was no other light source, an additional lamp had to be kindled so one could see to perform other tasks. By the Middle Ages, Sephardi Jews developed the tradition of always placing a light next to the Ḥanukkah lamp. Ashkenazi Jews had a different custom, of kindling the eight lights with a ninth light, called a *shammash*, which they then set next to the Ḥanukkah lamp. This ninth light eventually became incorporated into the lamp itself, as exemplified by the 13th-century triangular metal lamps from Germany or northern France described above. This custom appears to have been widely adopted, since a *shammash* is found on the vast majority of lamps from subsequent periods and among all three traditions: Sephardi, Ashkenazi, or Mizraḥi.

Another aspect of form dictated by rabbinical rulings is the placement of all eight lights in a single row and on the same level. Talmudic sages required that each light had to be perceived as distinct from the others, in order to count as one of the eight. Lights in the round, such as eight lights around the rim of a dish, were acceptable as long as the dish was covered and the lights did not appear to be a single bonfire. The tradition of lights in the round was accepted by later Sephardi rabbis, for example Joseph *Caro in his early 16th-century authoritative code, the Shulḥan Arukh. However, for medieval Ashkenazi rabbis, the lights had to be placed in a single row and on the same level, with the exception of hanging star-shaped lamps. This position is reflected in Moses Isserles' Ashkenazi modification of the Shulhan Arukh in the later 16th century. To judge from the Ḥanukkah lamps produced since then, Isserles' injunction was followed by most Jewish communities around the world. However, lamps in the round or with semi-circular lights continued in use in the Netherlands in the 17th to early 18th century, and in Iraq, Yemen, and India in the 19th and 20th centuries. In addition, *menorah*-form lamps with arms of uneven heights continued to be made sporadically in Eastern Europe, Germany, and France into the 18th and 19th centuries, primarily for synagogues.

Since the earliest documented examples, Ḥanukkah lamps have generally borne some form of decorative element or imagery, whether on the backplates of bench lamps, the arms and shafts of *menorah*-form lamps, or on bases and supporting legs. Motifs include floral designs and scrollwork, animal and human figures, and architectural elements.

The centrality of Judah Maccabee and his military victory in the events of Ḥanukkah would suggest that he would often be depicted on the lamps used for the festival. However, he appears rarely until the 20th century. Instead, one of the most common motifs on bench lamps is the seven-branch *menorah* (sometimes represented as a nine-branch Ḥanukkah lamp). Its popularity began at least by the 18th century, and it was especially favored in Germany, Italy, and Eastern Europe through the 19th century. The explanation for the preference of the seven-branch *menorah* on Ḥanukkah lamps lies in the Talmud. In answer to the question of why Ḥanukkah is celebrated, the sages related a story not included in the earlier apocryphal books of the Maccabees of how, when it came to rekindle the Temple *menorah*, only one vial of sanctified oil could be found, enough for one day. But a miracle occurred, and the oil burned for eight full days (Shab. 21b). It is this later story that is cited as the reason for the holiday, and is referred to as the miracle of Ḥanukkah. When the Jerusalem Temple was destroyed in 70 C.E. and the Jews came under Roman rule, it is possible that rabbinic leaders chose to emphasize the spiritual aspects of the holiday and the hope for divine redemption of Zion, symbolized since antiquity by the *menorah*.

Many Ḥanukkah lamp backplates take the form of an actual building, or are ornamented with such architectural elements as columns, gables, and arches. The explanation for this usage is more complex, lying both in the vocabulary of general decorative arts throughout time and place, and in Jewish religious iconography. The suggestion that the use of architectural imagery on Ḥanukkah lamps symbolizes the ancient Temple may have some merit, based on the popularity of images of the Temple *menorah*. More explicitly Jewish references are found in East European lamps of the 18th and 19th centuries, whose backplates take the form of Torah arks.

The use of human imagery on Ḥanukkah lamps is quite circumscribed. Biblical or mythological figures were favored in Western and Central Europe, and later in the United States and Israel, but human representations appear to be absent in

Eastern Europe, North Africa, and the Middle East. This is understandable in Islamic lands, where iconoclasm was often predominant on ritual objects. However, this pattern may also represent varying attitudes on the part of different Jewish communities toward depicting living things, as proscribed in the Second Commandment. One popular figure was the biblical heroine, *Judith, who was found on lamps from Italy, Germany, and the Netherlands through the 18th century (and on later copies). While the original story of Judith contained no connection to the events or personages of Ḥanukkah, medieval rabbinical sources recounted a different version, in which Judith lived many centuries later than the apocryphal account, and was a descendant of Judah Maccabee's Hasmonean family. Judith's inclusion on lamps may also be related to her popularity in European art in general, where she symbolized a number of positive and negative traits, including civic and religious virtue.

Many of these motifs continued throughout the 20th century alongside newer developments in lamp design. One was the appearance of Judah Maccabee. In the early part of the century, his military victory reflected the Zionists' call for Jews to return to farm the land of Israel and defend it. Later, in the mid-20th century, Israel's struggle for independence with its miraculous victories echoed those of Judah Maccabee, and representations of Judah and of modern soldiers on lamps intensified. A second 20th century development was the outgrowth of modern design movements such as the Bauhaus, which eschewed surface ornamentation in favor of the purity of functional form. European artists such as David Heinz Gumbel and Ludwig Y. Wolpert brought this modern aesthetic to Israel in the 1930s, where they taught in the New Bezalel School; Wolpert later served as a stimulus for modernism in the United States upon his immigration to New York in 1956. Subsequent art and design movements influenced Ḥanukkah lamp form and decoration as well, as exemplified by the Abstract Expressionist synagogue pieces by Ibram Lassaw, and the Memphis-style lamps of Peter Shire.

Geographically, a number of distinctions can be seen in the materials, techniques, or forms favored from country to country. Wall-hung bench lamps were predominant in the Netherlands, Italy, North Africa, Iraq, and India, and probably represent Sephardi and Mizraḥi traditions. On the other hand, standing bench lamps were highly characteristic of Ashkenazi lands such as Germany, Austria, and Eastern Europe. Large *menorah*-form lamps were used in European synagogues, but were rare in Islamic lands and may be a late introduction. Smaller *menorah*-form lamps were used in homes primarily in Germany, the Netherlands, Austria, and Eastern Europe through the 19th century, becoming widespread during the course of the 20th century.

Silver, the most expensive material, was highly favored in Germany, Austria, and Eastern Europe, and rarer among other Jewish communities. Various rabbis over the centuries had recommended that Ḥanukkah lamps be made of gold and silver in order to celebrate the ritual in as magnificent way as possible. For example, Moses Makhir in the Land of Israel advocated in the 15th century that one should have a silver lamp even if only one light holder each night was of that material, an opinion echoed by Joseph Yuspa Hahn Noerdlingen of Germany in the 17th century. It is possible that economic circumstances and proximity to silversmithing centers influenced the ability of Jews to obtain silver lamps for Ḥanukkah.

Lamps of copper alloy (i.e., bronze or brass) are common in a number of countries, but can be distinguished from place to place by their materials and techniques. For example, sheet metal backplates were widely found in the Netherlands, Italy, and North Africa. However, Dutch backplates were executed in repoussé with reflective bosses, while those from North Africa were more often flat and covered with incised designs. In Italy, sheet metal backplates were flat with appliqué decoration. Bench-form lamps of copper alloy were also made by casting and were characteristic of Italy, Eastern Europe, the Netherlands, and North Africa. By contrast, cast *menorah*-form lamps for synagogue and home use were most common in Germany, the Netherlands, and Eastern Europe, but rare in Italy and absent in North Africa.

A large number of standing bench lamps of pewter were produced in southern Germany from c. 1750 to 1850, possibly as a less costly version of silver. Their forms resemble those of German inkstands of the same period. Wall-hung pewter lamps were also produced in the Netherlands in the 18th century. Lamps made of tin were characteristic of the Upper Rhine region of southern Germany, Alsace, and the Basel area.

Stone lamps are known from only three regions: France (where the unique medieval example was found), Morocco, and Yemen. Most are in block form with oil wells carved out along the top, although occasionally Yemenite Jews lit a star-shaped lamp more often used on the Sabbath.

A number of Jewish communities throughout the world did not use permanent lamps for Ḥanukkah. In Turkey, for example, Jews favored simple tin lamps that were discarded at the end of the festival. Jews in eastern lands such as Iran, Afghanistan, and Central Asia were known to use eight ordinary cups of metal or ceramic. Finally, in many countries the indigent would use more ephemeral materials such as egg shells, walnut shells, or even potatoes scooped out to hold the oil.

BIBLIOGRAPHY: S.L. Braunstein, *Five Centuries of Hanukkah Lamps from The Jewish Museum: A Catalogue Raisonné* (2004); M. Narkiss, *Menorat ha-Hanukkah* (with English summary, 1939); S. Landau, *Architecture in the Hanukkah Lamp* (1978); R. Eis, *Hanukkah Lamps of the Judah L. Magnes Museum* (1977); C. Benjamin, *North African Lights: Hanukkah Lamps from the Zeyde Schulmann Collection of the Israel Museum* (2002).

[Susan L. Braunstein (2nd ed.)]

HA-OGEN (Heb. הָעֹגֶן; "the anchor"), kibbutz in central Israel in the Ḥefer Plain, affiliated with Kibbutz Arẓi Ha-Shomer ha-Ẓa'ir, founded in 1947. The founding settlers from Czechoslovakia and Austria were later joined by new members from other countries. In 1969 Ha-Ogen had 500 inhabitants and engaged in intensive farming, ran a plastic-tube factory, and was a partner in a rubber factory. The kibbutz also operated a recording studio, serving leading Israeli singers. In the mid-1990s, the population was approximately 600, dropping to 542 in 2002.

[Efraim Orni / Shaked Gilboa (2nd ed.)]

HAOLAM, the central organ of the World Zionist Organization, published as a weekly from 1907 to 1950 (except for short intervals). Established on the initiative of N. *Sokolow during his service as general secretary of the World Zionist Organization, *Haolam* was a Hebrew counterpart of Die *Welt, the German-language official organ of the Zionist Organization. Like *Die Welt*, for most of the years of its existence *Haolam* also had a yellow cover, which, according to *Herzl, symbolized the transformation of the shameful "yellow badge" to a color of pride and respect. At first *Haolam* was edited in Cologne – the residence of David *Wolffsohn, then president of the Zionist Organization – and printed in Berlin. Sokolow, who was preoccupied with other affairs, left most of the editing to his assistant, A. Ḥermoni. It soon became clear that Western Europe was not the appropriate place to publish a Hebrew paper; moreover, most of the members of the Zionist Executive regarded the paper as a burden upon the budget. As a result, at the end of its second year of publication (December 1908), the paper was moved to Vilna, where it became the organ of the Zionist Organization in Russia, under the editorship of A. *Druyanow. In the spring of 1912, upon the initiative of M.M. *Ussishkin, *Haolam* was moved to Odessa and continued its publication there until the outbreak of World War I.

Publication was resumed in 1919, in London, which had by then become the seat of the Zionist leadership, with Abraham *Idelson as editor (until 1921). Idelson planned to transfer the paper to Berlin, which had become a center of Hebrew literary activity in the early postwar period, but he died before achieving his aim. It was not until 1923 that Idelson's plan was realized, and H. *Greenberg, S. *Perlman, and M. *Kleinmann became the new editors. The former two soon left the editorial board, leaving Kleinmann as the sole editor until his death in 1948. In 1924, when conditions in Germany took a turn for the worse, *Haolam's* editorial offices were again moved to London. For several years the printing was done in Paris. Its final move took place in 1936, when the paper was transferred to Jerusalem, which by then had also become the headquarters of the World Zionist Organization. Upon Kleinmann's death, his two assistants, M. Chartiner and M. Cohen, became its editors until February 1950, when the paper ceased to exist.

For two generations, *Haolam* served as a faithful reporter of events and developments in Zionist and Jewish affairs. It also had a literary section, which published articles and the complete works in installments of outstanding Hebrew authors and scholars (such as Sokolow's book on *Spinoza, A.A. *Kabak's work on Solomon *Molcho, S.L. *Zitron's history of Hebrew journalism, stories by *Abramovitsh (Mendele Mokher Seforim), etc.). The paper carried excellent informational columns, and A. Litai's column on events taking place in the *yishuv* has retained its value as an important historical source.

BIBLIOGRAPHY: A. Ḥermoni, *Be-Ikkevot ha-Bilu'im* (1952), 128–66; *Haolam* (Feb. 21, 1950), last issue, includes its history.

[Getzel Kressel]

HA-ON (Heb. הָאוֹן; "strength"), kibbutz on the eastern shore of Lake Kinneret, Israel, south of *Ein Gev, affiliated with Iḥud ha-Kevuẓot ve-ha-Kibbutzim, founded in 1949. Some of its members are Israel-born, and others came from Eastern Europe and other countries. Until the *Six-Day War (June 1967) the kibbutz was constantly exposed to the Syrian gun emplacements directly above it on the Golan Plateau. Its farming included bananas, date palms, fruit orchards, field crops, carp ponds, and dairy farming. Ha-On was also a partner in the Lake Kinneret fishing cooperative and ran a metal factory. One of its economic mainstays was a holiday village with 96 guest rooms, a private beach, and special attractions like an ostrich farm, bird center, and paintball. In 2002 its population was 191.

WEBSITE: sites.tzofit.co.il/haoneng.

[Efraim Orni]

HA-OVED HA-ẒIYYONI (Heb. הָעוֹבֵד הַצִּיּוֹנִי "The Zionist Worker"), Israel labor movement founded as a *Histadrut faction at Ra'anannah on Nov. 22–23, 1935, by pioneer immigrants of General Zionist Youth from Eastern Europe, many of them members of kibbutzim. In Ereẓ Israel, these pioneers belonged to the General Zionist Organization but opposed its policy of boycotting the Histadrut. They worked inside the General Zionist movement to ensure its classless character and inside the Histadrut, which they regarded as the home of all trends in Jewish labor, to oppose class tendencies and the adoption of socialist symbols. There was much controversy on this subject inside the General Zionist movement, especially during the five years between a first gathering at Petaḥ Tikvah in 1930 and the foundation conference in 1935. Ha-Oved ha-Ẓiyyoni worked for the implementation of the principle of Jewish labor as an essential element in the upbuilding of the nation but not as a matter for class conflict. It established and built kibbutzim and moshavim for the implementation of the pioneering Zionist idea but not as instruments for socialism and demanded the establishment of nonparty labor exchanges allocating work on the basis of individual rights and qualifications.

After 1948, Ha-Oved ha-Ẓiyyoni helped to establish the Progressive Party and became part of its successor, the *Independent Liberal Party. It established six kibbutzim (in the framework of the movement of Ha-No'ar ha-Ẓiyyoni), 13 moshavim, five moshavim shittufiyyim, and five youth villages. In the Histadrut, it favored workers' participation in management and profits. It supported the maintenance of a pluralistic economy, with encouragement for all sectors. In the

1969 Histadrut elections it received 5.69% of the vote. Later on the movement was united with Ḥever ha-Kevuẓut.

[Moshe Kol]

HA-PARNAS, SEFER (Heb. סֵפֶר הַפַּרְנָס), work by Moses Parnas, one of the pupils of *Meir b. Baruch of Rothenburg, who lived in the first half of the 14th century. Almost nothing is known of its author. His work was well known to the scholars of Germany in the 15th century, such as Jacob *Moellin, Joseph *Colon, Israel *Isserlein, and Israel *Bruna. It was afterward lost, but was published in 1891 with notes by David *Luria as far as section 17, as well as those of its publisher, Moses Samuel Horowitz. This book is very typical of the works belonging to "the school of Meir of Rothenburg," and its author cites traditions, customs, rulings, and teachings of his master based both upon what he himself had seen, as well as culled and abridged from other collections, such as *Tashbeẓ* by Samson b. Zadok.

BIBLIOGRAPHY: Urbach, Tosafot, 439.

[Israel Moses Ta-Shma]

HAPAX LEGOMENA (Gr. "once said"), words which are only once recorded in a certain kind of literature. Since the interest in Middle Hebrew lexicography arose comparatively late, Middle Hebrew texts are frequently not well-established philologically and new texts are often discovered, the interest in hapax legomena in Hebrew is, for all practical purposes, limited to the Bible or, more precisely, to biblical Hebrew. There are in biblical Hebrew about 1,300 hapax legomena (yet their precise number cannot be stated, since the exact definition is not clear as to whether or not they include homonymic hapax legomena). Most of them (about 900) are not too difficult to interpret, being derived from well-known biblical roots (as *ʿemdah*, Micah 1:11, *moʿomad*, Ps. 69:3, both denoting "standing ground," being derived from the well-known root עמד, "to stand"). About 400, however, cannot be derived from known biblical roots and are therefore more difficult to interpret. Occurring only once, their exact meaning is more difficult to establish from context than that of words attested more often. Except for this fact and the possibility that hapax legomena may have arisen through error in transmission, the philological treatment of hapax legomena does not differ from that of words occurring more often. The meaning of both is elucidated by comparison with other Semitic languages, which often makes it possible to establish the etymology of the word treated. Middle Hebrew has, of course, a special standing in this matter. Since the Bible, because of its small size and limited topics, has preserved only a small part of Hebrew vocabulary, it is often due to mere chance that a word occurs only once in the Bible, though there may be ample examples of it in Middle Hebrew (as in the case with *sullam* "ladder," Gen. 28:12). Even the sages of the Mishnah did not understand the hapax legomenon *we-teʾteʾtiha*, "and I will sweep it" (Isa. 14:23), except with the help of vernacular speech, as used by Rabbi's handmaid (RH 26b). Hapax legomena sometimes belong to removed subject matters (as Isa. 3:18 ff., describing the ornaments of Zion's daughters), and there are relatively many hapax legomena denoting animals, plants, and diseases (as *letaʾah* "lizard," Lev. 11:30; *luz*, "almond tree," Gen. 30:37; *ḥarḥur*, "fever," Deut. 28:22) and loan words (as *ʾappiryon*, "litter," Song 3:9). The Book of Job, with its special style and many Aramaisms, contains a relatively large proportion of hapax legomena, 145 in number, among them 60 without derivation from known biblical roots. The (much larger) Book of Isaiah has 201 hapax legomena, among them, again, 60 without derivation.

In Hebrew literature hapax legomena are called *ʾen lo ʾaḥ, ʾen lo ḥaver, ʾen lo reʿa ba-Miqraʾ*, "it has nothing alike, no brother, no fellow, no comrade in the Bible," or *millim boddedot*, "isolated words." *Saadiah Gaon wrote in Arabic *Kitāb al-Sabʿīn Lafẓa min Mufradāt al-Qurʾan* ("The Book of Seventy Hapax Legomena in the Bible"), dealing with over 90 (!) hapax legomena, which he explains by means of mishnaic words. It stands to reason that this book originally contained 70 words, and was expanded later, either by Saadiah himself or by others, yet preserving its original name. Although it is one of the oldest and most important philological works in the history of Hebrew linguistics, it is in its intention a polemic work against Karaites, endeavoring to prove the value of tradition from the linguistic point of view: without mishnaic Hebrew even the linguistic interpretation of the Bible is impossible.

BIBLIOGRAPHY: I.M. Casanowicz, in: JE, 6 (1904), s.v.; B. Klar, in: *Meḥkarim ve-Iyyunim* (1954), 159–75; N. Allony, in: *Goldziher Memorial Volume*, 2 (1958), 1–48 (Heb. section); idem, in: HUCA, 30 (1959), 1–14 (Heb. section); Ch. Rabin, in: EM, 4 (1962), 1066–70. **ADD. BIBLIOGRAPHY:** H.R. Cohen, *Biblical Hapax Legomena in the Light of Akkadian and Ugaritic* (1978); P. Daniels, in: JAOS, 101 (1981), 440–41; J. Huehnergard, in: BASOR, 264 (1986), 286–90; F. Greenspahn, *Hapax Legomena in Biblical Hebrew* (1984); idem, in: ABD, 3:54–5; E. Greenstein, in: JAOS, 107 (1987), 538–39.

[Joshua Blau]

HAPHARAIM (Heb. חֲפָרַיִם), town in the territory of Issachar (Josh. 19:19), located between Chesulloth and Shunem on one side and Shion and Anaharath on the other. A place with the same name is mentioned in the Mishnah (Men. 8:1) as the source of fine wheat supplied to the Second Temple. Eusebius (Onom. 28:26) identified it with Aphraia, 6 mi. (10 km.) north of Legio (al-Lajjūn near Megiddo), which may point to the vicinity of Afulah. Recent scholars, relying on the spelling Afarayim in talmudic literature (Tosef., Men. 9:2; TB, Men. 83b), have proposed its identification with *Ophrah of Gideon (Judg. 6:11), and perhaps the *fr* in the list of Thutmose III. The site of Hapharaim is possibly at al-Tayyiba in the hills north of the Jezreel Valley. Another suggested identification, with Khirbat al-Farriyya near Megiddo, is less probable.

BIBLIOGRAPHY: G. Dalman, *Sacred Sites and Ways* (1935), 219; Abel, Geog, 2 (1938), 343, 402; Albright, in: JBL, 58 (1939), 183; M. Noth, *Das Buch Josua* (1953[3]), 117; EM, s.v.

[Michael Avi-Yonah]

HAPOEL (Heb. הַפּוֹעֵל "The Worker"), Israel workers' sports organization, affiliated with the *Histadrut. It had its beginnings in a Haifa soccer team in 1924. The countrywide association was organized in 1926 with a twofold aim: to provide opportunities for physical education and sport for the masses of Palestinian youth and to involve them in the labor movement. Hapoel members pioneered in naval and other activities in order to assist "illegal" immigration into Palestine. They also helped to establish settlements and were active in the *Haganah, the pre-state Jewish defense organization. Through Hapoel's efforts the number of swimming pools in the country increased and floodlit playing fields were opened making possible nighttime basketball and volleyball. Hapoel organized the Lake Kinneret swims in which some 10,000 swimmers participate annually, road marches, and long-distance foot races as well as sports conventions (*Poeliad*) with international participation. Hapoel's teams and individual contestants won championships in most of the fields of Israel sport. The organization also encourages sports activities in various places of work, such as factories, shops, etc. From 1927 Hapoel was affiliated with the International Labor Sports Organization. After the establishment of the state it played an important role in encouraging and organizing sports activities in the underdeveloped African countries. In 1968 there were more than 85,000 members of Hapoel in 600 branches throughout the State of Israel. In 2004 Hapoel supported 980 youth groups, 325 adult groups, and 765 sports associations in 28 different competitive sports branches, among them successful athletes who represent Israel in the Olympic Games and other international competitions. In addition, Hapoel was also affiliated with workplace teams, competing in 15 sports in the framework of workplace leagues.

BIBLIOGRAPHY: Paz and A. Lahav, *Alafim ve-Allufim* (1961), with notes in Eng. **WEBSITE**: www.hapoel.org.il.

[Yehoshua Alouf / Shaked Gilboa (2nd ed.)]

HA-PO'EL HA-MIZRACHI, religious pioneering and labor movement in Ereẓ Israel. Religious pioneers who settled in Ereẓ Israel in 1920–21 banded together and in April 1922 founded Ha-Po'el ha-Mizrachi, whose program stated that it "aspires to build the land according to the Torah and tradition and on the basis of labor, to create a material and spiritual basis for its members, strengthen religious feeling among the workers, and enable them to live as religious workers." The new framework was a product of the Third *Aliyah, which included many young people marked by their religious consciousness. They were pioneers and workers who viewed settling in Ereẓ Israel as a *mitzvah*, a religious commandment and task, but did not find a place in the existing labor community, despite the fact that socially they belonged to it. They opposed the prevalent view among workers in the 1920s that regarded religion as obsolete and adherence to the *mitzvot* as an obstacle to the building of the land according to socialist principles. The ideology of the new religious labor group was developed for the most part by Shemuel Ḥayyim *Landau, Isaiah *Shapira, Nehemiah Aminoaḥ, Isaiah Bernstein, Shelomo Zalman *Shragai, and Shimon Geshuri. It was called Torah va-Avodah (Torah and Labor), after the saying: "The world stands on three things: Torah, divine service (*avodah* – literally, work), and deeds of loving-kindness" (Avot 1:2). The sources of this ideology also included ideas from Polish Ḥasidism and from the system of "Torah with *Derekh Ereẓ*" of Samson Raphael *Hirsch.

The concept of Torah va-Avodah emphasized the demand for social justice and a productive life as an essential condition of the return to the homeland and as an integral part of a full religious life in Judaism. In view of the desiccation of Jewish life in the Diaspora, even greater emphasis should be placed on those elements which were practically excluded from Jewish existence outside Ereẓ Israel. The ideology proclaimed that complete Judaism is a synthesis of religious, social, moral, national, and political elements, realized mainly through personal commitment and creativity. All these aspects of national life must be inspired by the Written and Oral Law. Special emphasis was placed on the demand for social justice. "Only he who earns his living by his own labor is certain that his livelihood is free from the labor of others, from exploitation and fraud." "Morality and justice are links in a long chain of sanctification and purification of life, which originates in the acceptance of the rule of God." This outlook led its followers along the path of productivization and especially toward cooperative and collective agricultural settlement.

From its earliest appearance there were conflicts between Ha-Po'el ha-Mizrachi and *Mizrachi because of the former's socialist trends, though technically it was an organizational part of Mizrachi. On the other hand, it had differences with the *Histadrut, because of Ha-Po'el ha-Mizrachi's religious concept of the Jewish people, its opposition to the class struggle, and its demand for obligatory arbitration in labor disputes. In practice, it appeared as an independent element in the labor market. After an unsuccessful attempt to join the Histadrut in the 1920s, Ha-Po'el ha-Mizrachi acted as a part of the world Mizrachi movement. In 1925, however, it created a special body of its own in the Diaspora called Ha-Berit ha-Olamit shel Tenu'at Torah va-Avodah, which included Mizrachi youth groups and the pioneering Mizrachi movements in different countries. Thus Ha-Po'el ha-Mizrachi united an ideological movement, a labor federation, and a political party in one body.

As an ideological movement, Ha-Po'el ha-Mizrachi propagated its ideas and opinions in its organ *Netivah* (edited by Geshuri), in pamphlets and books in the Torah va-Avodah Library, and later on in *Moreshet*. It attracted to its ranks the religious kevuẓot united in *Ha-Kibbutz ha-Dati and established the pioneering youth movement *Bnei Akiva, which later on founded the yeshivah high school under the initiative of Moshe Ẓevi *Neriah. As a labor federation, Ha-Po'el ha-Mizrachi was active in the same areas as the Histadrut. It established employment bureaus and welfare institutions and was active developing Jewish labor, the *Haganah, and the organization of pioneering and "illegal" immigration. It founded economic enterprises such as Bank Ha-Po'el ha-Mizrachi; a mortgage bank, Adanim; the financial tool of the settlements, Yaniv; the construction company for housing, Mash'hav; and several cooperatives, united under one roof, Merkaz ha-Mosedot ve-ha-Mifalim ha-Kalkaliyyim shel ha-Po'el ha-Mizrachi. It also organized young religious workers in Ha-No'ar ha-Dati ha-Oved and established the sports organization, Eliẓur. In 1935 its women members organized the Women's League of Ha-Po'el ha-Mizrachi and later united with the Women's Mizrachi Organization of the *National Religious Party.

As early as the 1920s the movement started its settlement activity. At first, the common form was the *moshav ovedim, which seemed more suitable for the members of Ha-Po'el ha-Mizrachi than the kevuẓah or kibbutz. Sedeh Ya'akov, established in 1927 in the western Jezreel Valley, was the movement's first moshav. Ha-Po'el ha-Mizrachi had to overcome the opposition of the Histadrut and of the official Zionist institutions before it was recognized as an independent factor in settlement. Before 1948 eight moshevei ovedim were established, all in areas of regional settlement projects of the Zionist Organization. During the great immigration of the 1950s, Ha-Po'el ha-Mizrachi was allocated 20% of the settlement. In the course of five years, 40 moshavim of new immigrants, and later on, another 10, were added. In addition, four moshavim shittufiyyim were founded. All these were organized in the Iggud ha-Moshavim shel Ha-Po'el ha-Mizrachi, whose organ is *Ma'anit* (established in 1951).

From the early 1930s groups for collective settlement sprang up within Ha-Po'el ha-Mizrachi. These first religious kevuẓot or kibbutzim were formed by members of *Berit Ḥalutzim Datiyyim* (Baḥad) in Germany, the trainees of the Mizrachi youth *hakhsharah* ("training") in Poland, and later on, by the Ha-Shomer ha-Dati in Poland and in Galicia. They established Ha-Kibbutz ha-Dati in 1935. It established settlements from 1937, the first being *Tirat Ẓevi (after Ẓevi Hirsch *Kalischer) in the Beth-Shean Valley. Ha-Kibbutz ha-Dati followed a policy of *hityashevut gushit* ("bloc settlement"), concentrating a number of settlements in one area in order to develop fully its social-religious ideas and its strength as a religious factor in society. This policy forced it to go to the farthest frontiers of the existing settlement areas. A bloc of religious kibbutzim was created in the Beth-Shean Valley, the Eẓyon bloc in the Hebron mountains, and another bloc in the vicinity of Gaza. Before the establishment of the state (1948) Ha-Kibbutz ha-Dati movement numbered 16 settlements, 10 already set up and the rest about to be settled. Because of their location on the borders of the *yishuv*, the *War of Independence dealt them a severe blow. The Eẓyon bloc (including the three religious kibbutzim Kefar Eẓyon, Massu'ot Yiẓḥak, and Ein Ẓurim) was completely wiped out, most of the settlements at the approach to Gaza were destroyed (Be'erot Yiẓḥak and Kefar Darom), and the movement lost seven percent of its adult population. After the war, 12 of these settlements remained, and three became moshavim shittufiyyim.

The relations of Ha-Po'el ha-Mizrachi with the Histadrut developed after some violent conflicts in the late 1920s and the early 1930s concerning labor, settlement, and cooperation. In 1928 an agreement was reached on the distribution of labor and participation in Kuppat Ḥolim. The agreement did not fulfill the anticipated hopes, and Ha-Po'el ha-Mizrachi abrogated it in 1941. Despite the friction, more cooperation was achieved between the two federations after the establishment of general labor bureaus in the early 1940s. In the course of time, Ha-Po'el ha-Mizrachi joined the agricultural center of the Histadrut, its trade union department, and the teachers organization. However, the trend for a complete merger was never realized though its demand became even greater in light of the great religious *aliyah* after the establishment of the state. The majority in Ha-Po'el ha-Mizrachi preferred an independent framework. Ha-Kibbutz ha-Dati organized in the 1930s the religious sector of *Youth Aliyah. It directs the activities of Bnei Akiva, absorbs *Naḥal groups, and maintains *ulpanim* for new immigrants.

Ha-Po'el ha-Mizrachi entered politics almost from its inception, at first mostly as a function of its labor activity and of its affiliation with Mizrachi. In the Zionist Organization it acted as a part of Mizrachi. However, gradually Ha-Po'el ha-Mizrachi developed independent activity in the *yishuv* institutions and also in the Zionist Organization. From the 19th Congress in 1935, it was represented on the Zionist Executive by Moshe Ḥayyim *Shapira, who from that time served as head of Ha-Po'el ha-Mizrachi. It was represented on the Va'ad Le'ummi Executive by Shragai and later on by Zerah *Wahrhaftig. In the last elections of the Asefat ha-Nivḥarim in 1944, Ha-Po'el ha-Mizrachi received 9.5% of the total vote. It became a major factor in the religious community of the *yishuv*. The relations between Ha-Po'el ha-Mizrachi and Mizrachi were tense throughout their existence as separate organizations, while they were united only in the world center of the body called Mizrachi-Ha-Po'el ha-Mizrachi. The antagonism between the two was particularly bitter in Ereẓ Israel, where Mizrachi belonged to the non-labor camp and Ha-Po'el ha-Mizrachi had an agreement with the Histadrut. But the increasing strength of Ha-Po'el ha-Mizrachi in Ereẓ Israel led it more and more to a takeover of Mizrachi instead of separating from it. This trend eventually led to their merger and the establishment of the National Religious Party.

From the 1930s, when political activity began to occupy a prominent place in Ha-Po'el ha-Mizrachi, three main factions emerged in it. The El ha-Makor group leaned to the right, supporting the strengthening of ties with Mizrachi (as opposed to attachment to the labor movement) and advocating political activism against the Mandatory regime. La-Mifneh constituted the left wing, demanding the strengthening of links with the labor camp, joining the Histadrut, and seceding from the Mizrachi organization. It demanded political moderation, in the spirit of Chaim *Weizmann's policy, and more concern for settlement and movement activity. In the middle was the "centrist" faction, which took a compromising stand on political questions in the *yishuv* and Zionist policy. The main struggle for leadership in Ha-Po'el ha-Mizrachi took place between the "centrist" faction and the faction of the left-wing La-Mifneh.

In 1937 Ha-Po'el ha-Mizrachi was among the opponents of the partition plan, though, on the whole, it was closer than Mizrachi to Weizmann's leadership, stressing its loyalty to the Zionist and *yishuv* institutions and supporting the unification of all the forces of the country, including the dissident underground organizations (*Irgun Ẓeva'i Le'ummi and *Loḥamei Ḥerut Israel). Though its demands concerning religious matters, such as observance of the Sabbath and *kashrut* in public institutions, etc., were its political raison d'être, it took also an active stand on general questions, such as labor problems, immigration, defense, settlement, and social matters. With the establishment of the state, political matters came to the fore. Despite the foundation of the United Religious Front in the First Knesset, in which all religious parties took part (with the exception of Ha-Oved ha-Dati, which was represented by *Mapai), Ha-Po'el ha-Mizrachi maintained a certain independence, as, e.g., on the question of the conscription of women who were released from military service for religious reasons. In 1949 it defined its position by demanding to change the law of compulsory conscription of religious women to that of compulsory national service for them, and, as long as the law was not changed, it called on every observant young woman to be drafted into the religious units of the Naḥal.

Ha-Po'el ha-Mizrachi emphasized the need for religious Jews to participate actively in public life and deal with the general objectives of the people and the state, thus preserving a live connection between the religious tradition and public life, especially in legislation. Hence its approach to topical political questions (as, e.g., the integrity of the area of Ereẓ Israel after the *Six-Day War), appropriate legal arrangements affecting the entire nation (marriage and divorce), the public way of life (Sabbath law, observances of Sabbath and *kashrut* in the Israel Defense Forces), official religious institutions (the rabbinate, religious councils), and especially the securing of religious education for all who wish it. In the Knesset and the government, Ha-Po'el ha-Mizrachi acted as a compromising and unifying element both on foreign and domestic policy. It participated in practically all governments, twice causing a government crisis, first regarding religious education in immigrant camps, and again on the question of the items "religion" and "nationality" in the registration of population (known colloquially as the "Who is a Jew?" problem).

In 1956 Ha-Po'el ha-Mizrachi decided to merge with Mizrachi, both in Israel and in the Zionist Organization, and in July 1956 the *National Religious Party was established. The unified party acted in accordance with Ha-Po'el ha-Mizrachi principles. Thus, it was an initiator of the Government of National Unity prior to the Six-Day War in 1967. It also demanded action on the Arab refugee problem by settling them in Judea and Samaria and flexibility in negotiations with Arab states.

BIBLIOGRAPHY: J. Salmon, *Ha-Po'el ha-Mizrachi be-Ereẓ Yisrael, Kronologyah u-Bibliografyah 1920–28* (1968); Y. Raphael, *Madrikh Bibliografi le-Sifrut Ẓiyyonit Datit* (1960); N. Ammino'aḥ, *Al ha-Mabbu'a* (1968); S. Don-Jechia, *Admor-Ḥalutz* (1961); idem, *Ha-Mered ha-Kadosh* (1960); S.Z. Shragai, *Ḥazon ve-Hagshamah* (1956); Y. Bernstein, *Ye'ud va-Derekh* (1956).

[Moshe Unna]

HA-PO'EL HA-ẒA'IR (Heb. הַפּוֹעֵל הַצָּעִיר; "The Young Worker"), first newspaper of the labor movement in Ereẓ Israel; founded in 1907. After five years as a biweekly, *Ha-Po'el ha-Ẓa'ir* became a weekly, which it remained until it ceased publication in 1970. During its lifespan, the paper attained a continuity of publication enjoyed by no other Hebrew periodical. There were, however, periods during which the paper did not appear: it was discontinued in 1915 and renewed in the fall of 1918. *Ha-Po'el ha-Ẓa'ir* was edited by Yosef *Aharonovitch until 1923, and then by Yiẓḥak *Laufbahn until his death in 1948, and finally by Israel *Cohen. It was the organ of the Ha-Po'el ha-Ẓa'ir Party. When that party merged with *Aḥdut ha-Avodah to become Mifleget Po'alei Ereẓ Israel (*Mapai), the paper became the organ of Mapai (1930), and from 1968 of Mifleget ha-Avodah ha-Yisre'elit (*Israel Labor Party). *Ha-Po'el ha-Ẓa'ir* reflected the development of the Israel labor movement. The pioneers of this movement could not identify with the existing Hebrew papers, and established *Ha-Po'el ha-Ẓa'ir* with the meager resources at their disposal. The paper's ideology, expressed in its motto: "An indispensable condition for the realization of Zionism is the conquest of all branches of labor in Ereẓ Israel by the Jews," attracted all Second Aliyah workers until the founding of the Po'alei Zion paper *Ha-Aḥdut* in 1910. *Ha-Po'el ha-Ẓa'ir* expressed the party's persistent demand that the Zionist Organization implement practical Zionism, and also encouraged the use of Hebrew as the common language of the *yishuv*. *Ha-Po'el ha-Ẓa'ir* became the most distinguished paper in Ereẓ Israel during the Second Aliyah. Its contributors were among the best Hebrew authors and journalists, some of whom first appeared in print in this paper. Among the early regular contributors were: A.D. Gordon, J.Ḥ. Brenner, Ya'akov Rabinowitz, Rabbi Binyamin, S.Y. Agnon, Yiẓḥak Elazari-Volcani (then Wilkanski), and Moshe Smilanski. Its excellent literary supplement was edited during its first years by Devorah *Baron. A complete index of authors and subjects in *Ha-Po'el ha-Ẓa'ir* during the 50 years 1907–57 was compiled by Isa and G. Kressel in 1968.

BIBLIOGRAPHY: Y. Laufbahn (ed.), *Arba'im Shanah* (1947); *Ha-Po'el ha-Ẓa'ir* (June 12, 1957; Sept. 26, 1967); G. Kressel, in: *Asuppot*, 4 (1954), 44–65, 5 (1957), 108–20.

[Getzel Kressel]

HA-PO'EL HA-ẒA'IR (Heb. הַפּוֹעֵל הַצָּעִיר; "The Young Worker"), Ereẓ Israel labor party founded by the first pioneers of the Second Aliyah. Its full name was Histadrut ha-Po'alim ha-Ẓe'irim be-Ereẓ Israel – and it was called Ha-Po'el ha-Ẓa'ir for short. Ha-Po'el ha-Ẓa'ir was founded in Petaḥ Tikvah in the autumn of 1905 on the initiative of Shelomo *Ẓemaḥ and Eliezer *Shoḥat, who were among the first arrivals of the Second Aliyah in 1904. Its name symbolized the new character of the Jewish worker of the Second Aliyah, to be distinguished from that of the earlier workers (who had been organized since the beginning of the 1890s) and from *Po'alei Zion (the first of whose members began to arrive in the country at the same time). The new idea was expressed in the words carried as a motto on its newspaper for years: "An indispensable condition for the realization of Zionism is the conquest of all branches of labor in Ereẓ Israel by the Jews." Certain modifications were made in this definition after the revolution of the Young Turks (1908) because of the misunderstanding that might be aroused by the word "conquest." The wording was then changed to "the increase of Jewish workers in Ereẓ Israel and their consolidation in all branches of labor."

The uniqueness of this party was in its being the first indigenous workers' party in Ereẓ Israel. It groped to formulate an exact program for its activities, but its direction was clear to its founders and its members, and it was formulated a few years after the party's foundation by one of its first ideologists and the editor of its paper, Yosef *Aharonovitch. These were: to introduce the principle of labor into the official work program of Zionism; to spread the idea of the "conquest of labor" among the farmers and employers in Ereẓ Israel; to win over Jewish youth and inspire them to join the ranks of the "conquerors of labor"; and to pave the way for and assist the workers in Ereẓ Israel, who would set out to establish their place in labor.

From its foundation, Ha-Po'el ha-Ẓa'ir opposed Po'alei Zion because of the latter's acceptance of international socialism and the theory of the class struggle, which Ha-Po'el ha-Ẓa'ir felt were incongruous with the situation in Ereẓ Israel. There were also disagreements between the two movements over the relationship to Yiddish; Po'alei Zion began to publish its paper, *Onfang*, in Yiddish in 1907 (but later changed over to Hebrew) and fought for the use of Yiddish abroad. Nonetheless, there was complete cooperation between the two parties in almost every sphere of practical activity, in spite of the perpetual polemics in their newspapers. The idea of labor, which was the fundamental principle of Ha-Po'el ha-Ẓa'ir and its great innovation in Ereẓ Israel, was exalted a few years later by A.D. *Gordon (who never formally joined the party, but maintained strong ties with it and its press throughout his life) as an absolute and cosmic value in the life of man and in his inner and spiritual worlds. Labor was transformed from a means of livelihood into a supreme value, as an answer to the moral demand of the Jews.

At the time, the "conquest of labor" meant basically the competition of Jewish workers in the Jewish villages with Arab laborers who were willing to accept lower wages. There were members of the party who wished to propose other means of rooting the Jewish worker in the soil of Ereẓ Israel, e.g., by settlement on the land, and also requested the inclusion of city workers in the party's program. Eventually, a compromise was reached between the "conquest of labor" in the villages and the establishment of independent agricultural-workers' settlements. The members of Ha-Po'el ha-Ẓa'ir were among the founders of the "mother of kevuẓto," *Deganyah; among the initiators of the idea of the moshav ovedim (e.g., E.L. Joffe); and the founders of the first moshav, *Nahalal, after World War I. Politically the party was able to express its ideas only after the revolution of the Young Turks. It formulated them as "a Jewish majority, healthy in the economic and cultural sense." This political article was also connected with the "conquest of labor" and with rooting the Jewish laborer in Ereẓ Israel by perpetual encouragement of immigration (the party even published a manifesto which called for *aliyah*). The constitutional freedom afforded by the Turkish revolution was not regarded as valuable in itself, except as a means of reaching a Jewish majority in Ereẓ Israel.

The members of Ha-Po'el ha-Ẓa'ir participated in guarding the settlements and self-defense activities, but their relationship to *Ha-Shomer, which was established by members of Po'alei Zion, was one of reserve. The same is true of participation in volunteering for the *Jewish Legion at the end of World War I. However, there were those who supported enlistment in the Legion, and when the supporters eventually constituted a majority, the minority (which included A.D. *Gordon and other leaders) continued to oppose it. The party participated in Zionist congresses, beginning with the Eighth Congress in 1907, and maintained ties with the Ẓe'irei *Zion movement abroad. Before World War I, the party took steps to establish a world organization, an aspiration that was realized after the war at the Prague Conference (1920), which created the *Hitaḥadut from Ha-Po'el ha-Ẓa'ir in Palestine and Ẓe'irei Zion abroad.

Ha-Po'el ha-Ẓa'ir did not join *Aḥdut ha-Avodah (A) when it was formed in 1919 to unite all the workers of Ereẓ Israel because it regarded Aḥdut ha-Avodah as a branch of the world movement of Po'alei Zion. On the other hand, it participated in the establishment of the *Histadrut in 1920. In it Ha-Po'el ha-Ẓa'ir was a minority party, facing an Aḥdut ha-Avodah majority (26 delegates to 37 from Aḥdut ha-Avodah at the first conference, 36 to 69 at the second conference, 54 to 108 at the third conference) and struggling against it. A representative of Ha-Po'el ha-Ẓa'ir, Joseph *Sprinzak, was the first workers' representative from Ereẓ Israel to become a member of the Zionist Executive (1921). Members of Ha-Po'el ha-Ẓa'ir were also among the leaders of the Agricultural Workers' Organization in Galilee and Judea (Ha-Histadrut ha-Ḥakla'it ba-Galil u-vi-Yhudah) before World War I, which was the first nucleus of a roof organization for Second Aliyah workers, and were also the founders of the agricultural press in Hebrew, which reflected the agricultural experience of Jewish laborers (the editor was E.L. Joffe and among the first contributors was Berl *Katznelson).

The ideological evolution of Ha-Po'el ha-Ẓa'ir did not cease after World War I, especially with the rise of Chaim *Arlosoroff, who coined the term "popular Socialism," as distinct from the class struggle. Arlosoroff was influenced by the ideas of Gustav *Landauer and Martin *Buber (also a member of the party and among the participants in the Prague Conference) and the practical experience of his party in Ereẓ Israel. With the first consolidation of the kibbutz federations in the 1920s (*Ha-Kibbutz ha-Me'uḥad), the bloc of small kevuẓot was consolidated into Ḥever ha-Kevuẓot with ties to Ha-Po'el ha-Ẓa'ir (see *Iḥud ha-Kevuẓot ve-ha-Kibbutzim). In the controversy over forms of collective settlement (between the kibbutz and moshav), the party's stand was equally in favor of both forms. Ha-Po'el ha-Ẓa'ir adopted *Gordonia abroad, the first of whose members settled in Palestine in 1929 during the discussions over the merger with Aḥdut ha-Avodah. The pioneers of *Ha-Shomer ha-Ẓa'ir who arrived in Palestine with the Third Aliyah were also close to Ha-Po'el ha-Ẓa'ir, and only later did they part ways.

Ha-Po'el ha-Ẓa'ir had extensions in a number of countries, the most outstanding of which was in Germany. This branch was created after World War I, and its outstanding figures were Martin Buber, Georg *Landauer, Arlosoroff, and others. Ha-Po'el ha-Ẓa'ir's *aliyah* bureau in Vienna was a very impressive instrument after World War I; it was created by members of the party in Palestine and assisted and directed the first immigrants of the Third Aliyah. Ha-Po'el ha-Ẓa'ir created the first labor newspaper in Ereẓ Israel, called *Ha-Po'el ha-Ẓa'ir* (1907 in stencil and printed from 1908). With the cessation of publication during World War I, it was replaced by several journals until it could resume publication in 1918 (until 1970). The party also had a publishing house during the Second Aliyah called La-Am, which published tens of popular scientific pamphlets (in Hebrew translation), and after the war it published a social-literary monthly, *Ma'abarot*, edited by Jacob *Fichmann (1919–21). Ha-Po'el ha-Ẓa'ir laid the groundwork for the new Hebrew literature in Ereẓ Israel, and the best of its authors contributed to the party's periodicals and publications.

During its existence, the party held 21 conferences. At the last one (1929), it was decided by a large majority to merge with Aḥdut ha-Avodah. The union was carried out in the following year through the creation of a common party: Mifleget Po'alei Ereẓ Israel (Ereẓ Israel Workers' Party) – *Mapai. The most outstanding personalities in Ha-Po'el ha-Ẓa'ir, throughout its existence, were A.D. Gordon, Joseph *Vitkin, Joseph Aharonovitch, Yiẓḥak *Elazari-Volcani, E.L. Joffe, Joseph Sprinzak, Shelomo *Shiller, Eliezer *Kaplan, Shemuel *Dayan, Ẓevi Yehudah, Joseph *Baratz, and others.

BIBLIOGRAPHY: J. Shapira, *Ha-Po'el ha-Ẓa'ir* (1967), detailed bibl. 492–6; I. and G. Kressel, *Mafte'aḥ le-ha-Po'el ha-Ẓa'ir (5668–5717)* (1968).

[Getzel Kressel]

HAPSBURG (Habsburg) MONARCHY, multi-national empire in Central Europe under the rule of the Hapsburg dynasty from 1273 until 1918; from 1867 known as Austro-Hungary. Its nucleus was *Austria and it included at different times countries with considerable Jewish populations (*Bohemia and *Moravia, and *Hungary from 1526), parts of Italy between 1713 and 1866. With the annexation of *Galicia (1772) and *Bukovina (1775) it became the state with the largest Jewish population in Europe. As the Hapsburgs were also Holy Roman Emperors, they were the supreme lords of the empire's *servi camerae regis (servants of the treasury), the Jews. The legal position of the Jewish communities varied, according to the differing legal status of the Hapsburgs in their hereditary lands (Austria, *Carinthia, *Syria, etc.), the countries of the Bohemian crown, the countries of the crown of St. Stephen (Hungary, *Transylvania, Croatia-Slavonia, and the Banat), Galicia, Bukovina, and from 1908 Bosnia and Herzegovina. However, it was based in principle on juridical and religious autonomy. After the marriage of *Maria Theresa to Francis Stephen, duke of Lorraine (1736), the Hapsburgs also bore the title of "King of Jerusalem."

During the period of the Counter-Reformation the Hapsburgs, protagonists of militant Catholicism, were influenced by the spirit of religious intolerance. Still, they tended to protect the Jews in their domains, in part because of Jewish fiscal contributions at a time of domestic and foreign war. They frequently sided with the Jews against the Estates, who were, as a rule, unfriendly to the Jews. However, it was the declared policy of the Hapsburgs to limit the number of Jews in their domains (see *Familiants Laws). Nevertheless Jewish communities often turned to the monarch with considerable success to annul decrees of banishment legislated by local authorities. The Hapsburg Empire was the first to conscript Jews for *military service, and *Joseph II's Toleranzpatents were the first laws to lift humiliating restrictions. From 1848 enjoyment of civil rights was made independent of religious affiliation, and from 1867 Jews enjoyed full civic equality in the empire. Jewish participation in the economic life of the empire was significant, particularly in its industrialization.

At the beginning of the 19th century developing nationalist ideologies of peoples within the empire were seeking expression with centrifugal effect. Jews were one of the elements, besides the army, bureaucracy, nobility, and the Catholic Church, to support the dynasty in preserving the empire's unity. Jews throughout the empire developed their own particular brand of patriotism and on the emperor's birthday synagogues were crowded. Both the emperor and the Jews recognized their mutual interest, with the Jews considering the sovereign to be their sole recourse against the antisemitic tendencies of nascent nationalisms. *Francis Joseph I in particular won the gratitude of the Jews for his frequent statements against antisemitism (see *Christian Social Party, Austria; Karl *Lueger; Georg von *Schoenerer; Karl Hermann Wolf; Ernst Schneider). Jewish politicians such as Adolf *Fischhof and Otto *Bauer were particularly aware of the danger to the monarchy in the conflicts between the nationalities, and they suggested remedies. Joseph Samuel *Bloch created an ideological foundation for Jewish patriotism. Theodor *Herzl's ideas were influenced by the monarchy's problem of contending with its competing nationalities. The dismemberment of the Hapsburg Empire brought into being successor states with nationalistic policies that indeed often proved to be disadvantageous for their Jewish minorities.

Alleged Jewish Descent

Antisemitic propaganda claimed that the Hapsburgs were contaminated with Jewish blood, the protruding lower lip characteristic of many of them being considered a racial mark! The allegation was based on the assertion that Roger II of Sicily (1095–1154), whose offspring intermarried with the Hapsburgs, had married a *Pierleoni, a sister of the Jewish antipope *Anacletus II. The claim became notorious when the Austrian noble Adalbert von Sternberg declared around 1900 that he could have Jewish blood only through his kinship to the Hapsburgs. Modern research dismisses the allegation.

BIBLIOGRAPHY: R.A. Kann, *The Habsburg Empire* (1957); idem, *The Multinational Empire…, 1848–1918* (1950); J.E. Scherer, *Die Rechtsverhaeltnisse der Juden in den deutsch-oesterreichischen Laendern* (1901), 339–452; A. Sternberg, *Paepste, Kaiser, Koenige und Juden* (1926); A. Czelitzer, in: *Juedische Familien-Forschung*, 23 (1930), 282–3; J. Prinz, *Popes from the Ghetto* (1966), 248 n. 83; G. Schimmer, *Statistik des Judentums in den im Reichsrathe vertretenen Koenigreichen und Laendern* (1873); idem, *Die Juden in Oesterreich nach der Zaehlung vom 31. December 1880* (1881); Baron, Social², 9 (1965), 194ff.; 332–4; 14 (1969), 147–223; Z. von Weisel, in: J. Slutsky and M. Kaplan, *Ḥayyalim Yehudim be-Ẓivot Eiropah* (1967), 17–29. **ADD. BIBLIOGRAPHY:** W.O. McCagg, *A History of Habsburg Jews 1670–1918* (1989). See also bibl. for *Austria.

[Meir Lamed]

HARAN (Harran) (Heb. חָרָן; Akk. *Harrāni(m)*, "caravan station").

Name and Location

Haran is located some 10 miles north of the Syrian border, at the confluence of the wadis which in winter join the Balikh River just below its source. It is strategically located about halfway between Guzana (Gozan) and Carchemish on the east-west road which links the Tigris and the Mediterranean, at the very point where the north-south route along the Balikh links the Euphrates to Anatolia. It is thus the traditional crossroads of the major routes from Mesopotamia to the west and the northwest (cf. Ezek. 27:23), and its very name in Akkadian (and Sumerian) implies as much. The biblical name Paddan-aram (Gen. 25:20 et al.), "the Aramean highway," seems to identify the same site by a synonym reflecting its later role as a center of Aramean settlement.

In the "Patriarchal Age"

Written sources first mention Haran in an Old Babylonian itinerary as an important crossroads and in a letter addressed to Yasmaḫ-Addu (= Adad), the Assyrian viceroy at Mari (c. 1790 B.C.E.). Another letter shows that Haran was an important center of the semi-nomadic "Benjamites." It alerts the king of Mari to the conclusion of a formal alliance between Asdi-takim, who was then king of Haran, and the (other) kings of Zalmaqum on the one hand, and the sheikhs and elders of the "Benjamites" on the other hand. This alliance was concluded in the temple of the moon-god Sin at Haran. The land of Zalmaqum was the object of an extended campaign by Šamši-Addu (= Shamshi-Adad) I of Assyria (c. 1815–1782 B.C.E.) and probably became subject to him together with Haran. With his death, however, the Old Assyrian Empire broke up and Haran was thus, apparently, an independent principality at the very time when, presumably, the biblical traditions reflect the sojourn of the Terahides in the area (Gen. 11:25). The migration of the Terahides parallels what appears to have been the movement of the moon cult from Ur to Haran, and the personal names of the Terahides reflect the geographical names of the Haran area. Specifically Serug, the grandfather of Terah, may be compared with the town of Sarugi (modern Seruj), some 35 miles west of Haran, and Nahor, his father (and second son) with the town of Nahur, probably located on the Upper Habor River due east of Haran. Terah's own name has been identified with Til (-sha)-Turahi on the Balikh south of Haran and his third son, Haran, recalls the name of the town, although the two names are spelled differently in Hebrew. At all events, the Mari letters document a political, social, and economic state of affairs in the latitude of Haran which makes entirely plausible the settlement there of at least five generations of pastoral Terahides. Albright has further suggested that they took advantage of the strategic position of Haran to engage in a far-flung trade, based on donkey caravans, in conjunction with Abraham and Lot, the son of his brother Nahor, who, he suggests, journeyed onward to Damascus, Canaan, and Sinai.

In the Late Second Millennium

Haran is not mentioned in the cuneiform sources of the Mitannian period. However, it probably belonged to that Hurrian state and was captured by the Hittites along with other Mitannian centers when it is first heard of again in the 15th century. Matiwaza, son-in-law of Shuppiluliuma, conquered the legitimate Mitannian ruler, Shuttarna III, with the help of Shuppiluliuma's son Piyashilli of Carchemish and presently had to cede Haran and his other conquests west of the Habor River to the latter. The first mention of Haran in Middle Assyrian documents occurs under Adad-Nirari I (c. 1304–1273 B.C.E.), who briefly conquered the Hittite vassal states as far as the Euphrates. His son Shalmaneser I (c. 1272–1243 B.C.E.) repeated these feats, as did his grandson Tukulti-Ninurta I (c. 1242–1206 B.C.E.), but in the 12th century newly entrenched waves of Aramean settlers began to make the region their own and the invasions of the Sea Peoples (c. 1200 B.C.E.) upset all of the traditional balance of power in the Near East. By the end of the 12th century, Haran was a center of Aramean settlement ruled by pretended or actual successors of the early Hittite royal houses. Hence the biblical names of this region, Aram Naharaim and Paddan-aram.

As Assyrian Crownland

While it is uncertain precisely when Haran passed under direct Assyrian rule, it is clear that it was one of the first of the more distant provinces to do so, for it always enjoyed a special status within the empire; was loyal to the king when other provinces revolted; never the object of a recorded Assyrian campaign in the first millennium; and even harbored the last Assyrian defenders when the cities of Assyria proper had already collapsed. In the years 615–12 B.C.E., the last king of Assyria, Ashur-uballit II, made a final desperate attempt at Haran to save the empire, and it was not until he fled Haran in 609 B.C.E. that the fate of Assyria was finally sealed. In the Neo-Babylonian period Haran was one of the centers of Nabonidus' religious-political activity.

Haran is identified with Sultan Tepe. An important library from the Babylonian period has been uncovered nearby.

BIBLIOGRAPHY: CHW. Johns, *An Assyrian Doomsday Book* (1901); W.F. Albright, in: JBL, 43 (1924), 385–93; idem, in: BASOR, 163 (1961), 36–55; G. Dossin, in: *Mélanges Syriens... R. Dussaud* (1939); J. Levy, in: HUCA, 19 (1945–46), 405–89; B. Maisler (Mazar), in: *Zion*, 11 (1946), 1–16; R.T. O'Callaghan, *Aram Naharaim* (1948); Seton Lloyd and W. Brice, in: *Anatolian Studies*, 1 (1951), 77–112; D.S. Rice, *ibid.*, 2 (1952), 36–84; C.J. Gadd, *ibid.*, 8 (1958), 35–92; D.J. Wiseman, *Chronicles of Chaldaean Kings* (1961); H. Tadmor, in: *Assyriological Studies*, 16 (1965), 351–63.

[William W. Hallo]

HARAN, MENAHEM (1924–), Bible scholar. Haran was born in Soviet Russia, where his father had him secretly taught the Bible by a tutor. Brought by his family to Palestine in 1933, Haran grew up in Tel Aviv and served in the Israeli army during the War of Independence. He earned his B.A., M.A., and Ph.D. at the Hebrew University of Jerusalem and, aside from visiting professorships in the United States and Europe, spent his entire academic career there. A student of Yehezkel *Kaufmann, much of Haran's work concentrates on biblical religion and cult, attempting to uncover the underlying conceptions of the Bible's detailed rituals. His studies of the cultic appurtenances, the cherubs, the ark, incense, and priestly garments compare the biblical material with the cultic realia of the larger ancient Near East. With Kaufmann, Haran dates the P(riestly) source of the Torah earlier than the D(euteronomic) source, but argues that P was made public at a later time. Against Kaufmann, Haran sees the E(lohistic) source as distinct, and views it as the inspiration of many of D's concepts. Haran believes that the four documentary sources identified by classical critics, J, E, P, and D extend beyond the Pentateuch, through Joshua to Kings. Beginning in the 1980s Haran began to study the physical form of the Bible, including writing materials, scribal practices, and codicology. Yet another significant area of Haran's interest is study of canon and the process of canonization. His publications include *Libraries in Antiquity* (1996); *The Biblical Collection* (1996); and with M. Sæbø (eds.), *Hebrew Bible/Old Testament ... Interpretation* (1996).

BIBLIOGRAPHY: V.A. Hurowitz, in: M. Fox, V.A. Hurowitz et al. (eds.), *Texts, Temples and Traditions ... Tribute Haran* (1996), 13–22. For Haran bibliography through 1995, see ibid, 23–35.

[S. David Sperling (2nd ed.)]

HARARI, family of rabbis from *Aleppo. The founder of the family was MOSES (d. 1649). ISAAC BEN MOSES (d. 1810), rabbi of Aleppo and author of *Zekhor le-Yiẓhak* (Leghorn, 1818), died in Safed. NISSIM BEN ISAIAH (d. 1830), referred to as Rafoul, was the author of *Alei Nahar* (Jerusalem, 1903). He died in Aleppo. MOSES BEN ISAAC (d. 1816) was *dayyan* in Aleppo, emigrated to Ereẓ Israel, and died in Jerusalem. R. ḤAYYIM SOLOMON (d. 1888) held the position of *Ḥakham Bashi* in *Damascus at the end of the 19th century. During the 20th century SHALOM (SELIM; d. 1938), who was born in *Jaffa, achieved distinction. He studied law in Constantinople and after the revolution of the Young Turks, he was appointed judge in *Beirut and later was member of the Court of Appeals in Jerusalem. After the occupation of *Lebanon by the French, he lived there and practiced law. In the 1930s he became president of the Jewish community of Beirut, where he died.

[Haim J. Cohen]

HARARI (Blumberg), ḤAYYIM (1883–1940), educator and author in Ereẓ Israel. Born in Dvinsk (then Russia), he began teaching at the Herzlia High School in Tel Aviv in 1906. One of the pioneers of the Hebrew theater, he established an amateur group called Ḥovevei ha-Bamah ha-Ivrit, in which he participated as a director, actor, and translator of plays. He contributed to the Hebrew press in Russia and Ereẓ Israel and edited two volumes on the festivals entitled *Sefer ha-Ḥanukkah* (1937) and *Sefer Tevet, Shevat, Adar* (1941). His articles and stories were collected in an anthology entitled *Kitvei Ḥayyim Harari* (2 vols., 1941–42).

His wife, YEHUDIT (1885–1979), educator and public figure in Ereẓ Israel, was the daughter of Aaron *Eisenberg, a founder of Reḥovot. In 1903 she founded the second Hebrew kindergarten in Ereẓ Israel in Reḥovot. She also taught at the Herzlia High School and the Levinsky Teachers Training College in Tel Aviv and was headmistress of the model school attached to the college. She published articles in the Hebrew press, and her books include *Bein ha-Keramim* (1947) and *Ishah va-Em be-Yisrael* (1959).

Their son, IZHAR (1908–1978), parliamentarian and lawyer, was born in Jaffa. He was active in the *Haganah and Ẓahal (*Israel, State of: Defense Forces) and was a member of the Knesset for the Progressive (later Liberal and *Independent Liberal) Party from 1949. He joined the *Israel Labor Party in 1968. He was the founder and chairman of the Israel Foreign Policy Association.

BIBLIOGRAPHY: Tidhar, 1 (1947), 497f.; 2 (1947), 831f.; 4 (1950), 1717f.

[Abraham Aharoni/Benjamin Jaffe]

HARARI, ḤAYYIM (1940–), physicist. Born in Jerusalem, Harari completed his doctorate at the Hebrew University in 1965. From 1970 he held the Annenberg Chair in High Energy Physics at the Weizmann Institute of Science in Reḥovot, of which he served as president from 1988 until 2001. From 1978 he has been a member of the Israeli Academy of Sciences. He has published more than 100 articles on particle physics. In 1989 he was awarded the Israel Prize for exact sciences. He also served (1979–85) as chairman of the Planning and Budgeting Committee (VATAT) of the Council for Higher Education and chairman of the Supreme Committee of Science and Technology Education in israel ("MAHAR 98," 1991–92). In 2001 he became chairman of the Davidson Institute of Science Education at the Weizmann Institute and chairman of the Management Committee of the Weizmann Global Endowment Management Trust (New York).

[Bracha Rager (2nd ed.)

HARARI, OVADIAH (1943–), Israeli aeronautical engineer. Harari was born in Cairo and came with his family to Israel in 1957. He studied aeronautical engineering at the Technion in Haifa where he recived his B.Sc. (1964) and his M.Sc. (1967). In 1966–70 he served as a project officer in the Israel Air Force in his profession. In 1978 he was appointed head of the Lavi fighter airplane project which employed about 1,800 people, half of whom were engineers. Subsequently he worked in executive and managerial capacities on various projects for Israel's Aircraft Industry (IAI). From 1997 he was executive vice president and chief operations officer for IAI. Harari was twice the recipient of the Israel Defense Prize, in 1969 and 1975. In 1987 he received the Israel Prize for technology and engineering.

[Gali Rotstein (2nd ed.)]

HARARI, SIR VICTOR RAPHAEL (1857–1945), Egyptian Jewish financier from Cairo. He began his career at the Egyptian ministry of finance, where he rose to the position of director general of the accounts department. In 1929 he was elected to the board of directors of the Egyptian National Bank and headed the boards of directors of many economic enterprises. He was knighted by King George V in 1928.

BIBLIOGRAPHY: J.M. Landau, *Ha-Yehudim be-Miẓrayim* (1967), 17, 174–5. **ADD. BIBLIOGRAPHY:** idem, *Jews in Nineteenth-Century Egypt* (1969), index.

[Haim J. Cohen]

HARBIN (Chinese: **Ha örl pin**), the capital of Heilung Kiang Province, in N. Manchuria, China. The modern development of Harbin began at the close of the 19th century, with the beginning of the Russian penetration of Manchuria. When Russia was granted the concession to build the Chinese Eastern Railway under the Russo-Manchurian treaty of 1898, Harbin became its administrative center with a 30-mi. (50 km.)-wide zone along the railway. In the same year, a number of Russian Jewish families went to Harbin with the official consent of the czarist government, which was interested in speedily populating the area, and which, consequently, granted them a better status than that of the Jews in Russia. Among the first Jews were F.I. Rif, the brothers Samsonovich, and E.I. Dobisov. Along with other minority groups (such as Karaites), the Jews were granted plots of land on the outskirts of the town. Not being allowed to work directly on the railway, they were active as shopkeepers and contractors.

By 1903 a self-administered Jewish community existed in Harbin, numbering 500 Jews. After the Russo-Japanese War of 1905, many demobilized Jewish soldiers settled in Harbin, followed by refugees from the 1905–07 pogroms. By 1908 there were 8,000 Jews in the city, and a central synagogue was built in 1909. Several institutions came into being within the community, including clubs, a home for the aged, and a hospital providing care for all other nationalities as well. A *ḥeder* was established in Harbin in 1907 and a Jewish secondary school (Yevreyskaya Gimnaziya) in 1909, which had 100 pupils in 1910. However, 70% of the Jewish pupils attended non-Jewish schools, because a numerus clausus did not exist for Jews in Harbin. The influx of Jewish refugees during World War I, the Russian Revolution (1917), and the Russian civil war sharply increased the Jewish community, which reached its peak – 10,000–15,000 – in the early 1930s. It numbered about 5,000 in 1939. A Jewish National Bank was established in Harbin in 1923 as well as a Jewish library. Between 1918 and 1930 about 20 Jewish newspapers and periodicals were also established. All were in Russian except the Yiddish *Der Vayter Mizrekh,* appearing three times a week with a circulation of 300 in 1921–22. The Russian-language weekly *Yevreyskaya Zhizn* ("Jewish Life", which until 1926 was called *Sibir-Palestina*) appeared from 1920 to 1940 with a circulation throughout Manchuria and North China. The Zionist movement, led by Abraham Kaufman, and several youth clubs played a major part in the life of the community. Until 1921 Harbin Zionists were affiliated to the Russian and Siberian Zionist Organization and participated in their conferences. When Zionism was outlawed in the Soviet Union, Harbin became an island of Russian-language Zionism. In the years from 1924 to 1931 the Soviet regime, largely preoccupied with internal problems, exercised only limited influence on Manchurian territory. During this time the Jews of Harbin enjoyed the same rights as all other foreigners, and were left alone to prosper. However, in 1928, when the Chinese Eastern Railway was handed over to the Chinese, an economic crisis broke out and many Jews left Harbin, some to the Soviet Union, others to Shanghai, Tientsin, etc. This situation changed drastically for the worse when Manchuria came under Japanese occupation (1931–45). The treatment of Jews became even more oppressive in World War II when the Japanese now allied with Nazi Germany and somewhat influenced by Russian right-wing emigrés adopted an antisemitic policy in some respects. Under Japanese rule, Jewish national life was kept alive by Zionist youth movements, particularly *Betar and *Maccabi, which organized Jewish cultural activities. Betar, which was the strongest Zionist youth organization, published a Russian-language magazine, *Ha-Degel* ("The Flag"). Until 1950 four synagogues existed in Harbin. Many Jews left Manchuria before the outbreak of World War II, for the U.S., Australia, Brazil, and other countries. During 1945–47, Harbin was under Soviet occupation, and Jewish community leaders were then arrested and sent to the Soviet interior. About 3,500 of the former "Chinese" Jews, most of them from Harbin, live in Israel, where they play an active role in all walks of life.

BIBLIOGRAPHY: I. Cohen, *Journal of a Jewish Traveller* (1928), 160–81; H. Dicker, *Wanderers and Settlers in the Far East* (1962), index; *Yevreyskaya zhizn*, nos. 3–4 (1939); N. Robinson, *Oyfleyzing fun di Yidishe Kehiles in Khine* (1954); S. Rabinowitz, in: *Gesher*, 2 (1957), 121–68. **ADD. BIBLIOGRAPHY:** Z. Schickman-Bowman, "The Construction of the Chinese Eastern Railway and the Origins of the Harbin Jewish Community 1898–1931," in; J. Goldstein (ed.), *The Jews of China: Historical and Comparative Perspectives* (1999).

[Rudolf Loewenthal and Noah W. Dragoon]

HARBURG, E.Y. (Edgar "Yip"; Isidore Hochberg; 1898–1981), U.S. songwriter. Born in New York to Orthodox Jewish parents, Harburg graduated from City College in 1921. After traveling through Latin America working for newspapers, Harburg turned to writing lyrics for Broadway musicals, such as *Walk a Little Faster* (1932), *Life Begins at 8:40* (1934), *The Show Is On* (1936), *Hold on to Your Hats* (1940), and *Bloomer Girl* (1944). His particular vein was the so-called "socially conscious," and his "Brother Can You Spare a Dime?" which he wrote during the Depression of the 1930s became a classic. He wrote the lyrics and co-authored the book for the witty Broadway musical *Finian's Rainbow* (1947) and wrote lyrics for *The Wizard of Oz* (1939), *Cabin in the Sky*, and other popular films. His songs "Over the Rainbow" and "Happiness Is a Thing Called Joe" won Academy Awards. A victim of the Hollywood blacklist, he returned to Broadway and wrote songs for such musicals as *Flahooley* (1951), *Jamaica* (1957), and *The Happiest Girl in the World* (1961). Among his other well-known songs are "April in Paris," "Home on the Range," "It's Only a Paper Moon," and "That Old Devil Moon." Harburg was inducted into the Songwriters' Hall of Fame in 1972. He wrote *Rhymes for the Irreverent* (1965) and *At This Point in Rhyme* (1976).

ADD. BIBLIOGRAPHY: H. Meyerson, *Who Put the Rainbow in The Wizard of Oz?: Yip Harburg, Lyricist* (1995).

[Jo Ranson / Ruth Beloff (2nd ed.)]

HARBY, ISAAC (1788–1828), U.S. author, journalist, teacher, and pioneer of Reform Judaism. Harby was born in Charleston, South Carolina. He became both teacher and journalist at the age of 16. He then began to study law, but the death of his father in 1805 left him the main support of a large family. He returned to teaching, opening a school at Edisto Island and then at Charleston. Finding journalism more profitable, Harby worked on various Charleston newspapers, editing several of his own not too successfully. A play, *Alberti*, was successful in Charleston in 1819, but Harby soon returned to teaching. After his wife's death in 1827, he left Charleston to establish a school in the more prospering metropolis of New York, but died soon after. Many tributes were paid him, including the publication of a memorial volume by his friend Abraham *Moise. A man of rare literary taste, and author of excellent dramatic criticisms, Harby played an important role in the establishment of the Reformed Society of the Israelites, the pioneer effort of Jewish religious reform in the United States. In 1824 a group of 47 members of Charleston's Congregation Beth Elohim unsuccessfully petitioned the congregation's board to modify the ritual, remove the Spanish and Portuguese archaisms and permit explanatory discourses in English. Later that year the Reformed Society of Israelites was organized. On its first anniversary, Harby delivered a discourse outlining the Society's aims; in 1827 he was elected president. His departure for New York and subsequent death left a void. Other leaders left Charleston, also for economic reasons, and by 1833 the Society dissolved. A number of Harby's literary, political, and religious essays appear in J. Blau and S. Baron (ed.), *Jews of the United States*, 3 (1963).

BIBLIOGRAPHY: L.C. Moise, *Biography of Isaac Harby* (1931); Kohler, in: AJHSP, 32 (1931), 35–53; Fagin, in: AJA, 8 (1956), 3–13.

[Malcolm H. Stern]

HARBY, LEVI MYERS (1793–1870), U.S. naval officer. Born in Georgetown, South Carolina, Harby joined the navy as a boy and was captured by the British during the war of 1812. He was cashiered from the navy in 1836 for siding with the secessionist Texans but was later reinstated. Promoted to captain, he fought in the Mexican War (1846) and the Bolivian War of Independence. Harby fought on the Confederate side in the American Civil War and distinguished himself in the defense of Galveston.

HARDEN, MAXIMILIAN (originally **Felix Ernst Witkowski**; 1861–1927), German journalist and polemist. He edited his periodical *Die Zukunft*, founded in 1892, with vigor, erudition, and an eye for intrigue that often exposed society and government circles. Born Witkowski in Berlin, he reacted violently against his Jewish origin, was baptized at 16, and changed his name. But he could not escape his ancestry, and among his German contemporaries he was the symbol of Jewish arrogance which they said was undermining Prussian militarism. His political articles written under the pen name "Keut" revealed a talent for satire. Two collections were published, *Apostata* (1892) and *Literatur und Theater* (1896). With irony and courage, Harden attacked William II and the neo-Byzantinism which surrounded him, championing the cause of the aging ex-chancellor Bismarck. *Die Zukunft* became the most influential German weekly of its time and the mouthpiece of liberal opposition to the Kaiser. For subjecting the monarch to ridicule, Harden was twice imprisoned. In 1906–07 he brought about the downfall of Prince zu Eulenburg, the Kaiser's most influential adviser, with revelations about his private life that scandalized the monarchy. During World War I he criticized the German high command and, after the abdication of the Kaiser, the revolutionary regime. In his later years he showed an interest in Jewish affairs. In 1900 he published Walter Rathenau's article "*Hoere Israel*" in *Die Zukunft*, and later expressed appreciation of the Zionist movement. *Die Zukunft* ceased publication in 1922; and an attempt was made on Harden's life that same year. Harden collected his articles in four volumes, *Koepfe* (1910–24). He also published in two volumes *Krieg und Friede* (1918). In 1983 an edition of

Harden's correspondence with Walter *Rathenau came out as *Briefwechsel 1897–1920*, ed. by. H.D. Heilige. In 1984 another edition of his correspondence with Björnsterne Björnson *Briefwechsel*, ed. by A. Keel, appeared, and in 1996 an edition of *Briefwechsel mit Maximilian Harden* with Frank Wedekind and Thomas and Heinrich Mann, ed. by A. Martin.

GEORG WITKOWSKI (1863–1939), his younger brother, was a leading German literary historian. He also embraced Lutheranism, but his abandonment of Judaism did not protect him from Nazi persecution. Witkowski lectured at the University of Leipzig, specializing in literature of the era of Goethe. His works include the *Geschichte des literarischen Lebens in Leipzig* (1909), and *Das deutsche Drama des neunzehnten Jahrhunderts* (1923). Between 1909 and 1933 Witkowski edited the *Zeitschrift fuer Buecherfreunde*.

BIBLIOGRAPHY: H.F. Young, *Maximilian Harden, Censor Germaniae* (1959); Gottgetreu, in: YLBI, 7 (1962), 215–46. **ADD. BIBLIOGRAPHY:** J. Le Rider, "Die Dreyfus-Affaere in den Augen der assimilierten Juden Wiens und Berlins: Karl Kraus' 'Die Fackel' und Maximilian Hardens *'Die Zukunft*,'" in: J.H. Schoeps (ed.), *Dreyfus und die Folgen*, (1995), 139–55; K. Hecht, *Die Harden-Prozesse. Strafverfahren, Oeffentlichkeit und Politik im Kaiserreich* (1997); S. Armbrecht, *Verkannte Liebe. Maximilian Hardens Haltung zu Deutschtum und Judentum* (1999); M. Sabrow, *Walther Rathenau und Maximilian Harden. Facetten einer intellektuellen Freund-Feindschaft* (2000); H. and M. Neumann, *Maximilian Harden (1861–1927). Ein unerschrockener deutsch-juedischer Kritiker und Publizist* (2003).

[Sol Liptzin / Konrad Feilchenfeldt (2nd ed.)]

°HARDENBERG, KARL AUGUST VON (1750–1822), Prussian chancellor from 1810, instrumental in enacting the edict concerning the civil status of the Jews (March 3, 1812). While administrating the principality of *Bayreuth-Ansbach for the Prussian king (1790/92–97), he had already dealt with the problem of Jewish rights and was in social contact with David *Friedlander and other members of the Berlin community. Considering that Jewish emancipation was a vital part of the general Prussian reforms, he stated that he was not prepared to approve any law which was based on more than four words: equal rights, equal duties. He did not, therefore, approve of the restrictions still contained in the edict. At the Congress of Vienna (1815) he once more advocated Jewish rights. While there, he was a frequent guest in Fanny von *Arnstein's house. He tried unsuccessfully to have Eduard *Gans appointed to Berlin University while Gans was still Jewish. D.F. *Koreff was his personal physician, adviser, and protégé. After 1815 Hardenberg continuously opposed the Prussian king and his reactionary ministers, who repudiated their promises of justice and equality for the Jews made during the Napoleonic wars, but since he remained in a minority in the cabinet his support was ineffectual. His diaries were published in 2000.

BIBLIOGRAPHY: S.W. Baron, *Die Juden-Frage auf dem Wiener Kongress* (1920), index; H. Fischer, *Judentum, Staat und Heer in Preussen* (1968), index; F. Morgenstern, in: JSOS, 15 (1953), 253–75. **ADD. BIBLIOGRAPHY:** Th. Stamm-Kuhlmann, in: *Vierteljahreshefte fuer Sozial- und Wirtschaftsgeschichte*, 83 (1996), 334–46; H.-W. Hahn, in: Th. Stamm-Kuhlmann (ed.), *Bestandsaufnahme der Hardenbergforschung* (2001), 141–62; I. Hermann, *Hardenberg* (2003).

[Meir Lamed]

HARDMAN (Salutski), JACOB BENJAMIN (1882–1968), U.S. labor leader and writer. Hardman, born Jacob Benjamin Salutski in Vilna, joined the Marxist Social Democratic Party as a young man, working as an organizer in Vilna in 1906 and in Kiev in 1907. After several arrests, he was exiled in 1908 by the czarist government for illegal political activities. Arriving in the United States in 1909, Hardman was elected secretary of the Jewish Language Federation of the Socialist Party at its founding in 1912. From 1914 to 1920 he edited *Naye Welt*, the federation's Yiddish weekly. Hardman joined the national executive of the Communist Worker's Party in 1921, but was expelled in 1923 for his criticism of the Jewish left's pro-Bolshevik line and its nihilistic approach to Jewish problems. From 1925 to 1944 he edited *The Advance*, organ of the Amalgamated Clothing Workers Union, and was a member of the executive of the Conference for Progressive Labor Action (1927–34). During World War II Hardman helped organize the American Labor Press Association, of which he became president, and from 1945 to 1953 he was editor of the periodical *Labor and Nation*. He was also editor of *American Labor Dynamics in the Light of Post-War Developments* (1928), *Clothing Workers in Philadelphia* (1940), and *House of Labor* (1951), and during the 1950s was director of research of the Columbia University project "Trends in Union Leadership."

BIBLIOGRAPHY: M. Epstein, *Jews and Communism* (1959), passim; *New York Times* (Jan. 31, 1968), 38.

HARE (Heb. אַרְנֶבֶת, *arnevet*), according to the Pentateuch one of the prohibited animals (Lev. 11:6; Deut. 14:7). The Hebrew word is connected with the Akkadian *annabu* ("the jumper"). The Vulgate translates it from the Greek λαγώς ("a hare") as *lepus*. In spite of this the Septuagint gives the translation δασύπους, that is, "the hairy-legged." The Talmud explains that the wife of *Ptolemy Philadelphus, who according to tradition appointed 72 elders to translate the Pentateuch, was named Λαγώς and the translators made the change, apprehensive that the king might say: "The Jews have mocked at me and put my wife's name [as an unclean animal] in the Pentateuch" (Meg. 9b; TJ, Meg. 1:11, 71d).

The description in the Pentateuch of the *arnevet* as a ruminant raises a difficulty since the hare is not one, and hence some cast doubt on this identification. The reference, however, is apparently to the movement of its jaws when it eats and perhaps also to its habit of regurgitating the food it eats in the early morning hours and of later chewing it again, as in rumination.

In Israel there are three species of hare: in the coastal lowland, in the mountains, and in the Negev. It is extensively hunted, but its rapid propagation prevents its extermination. The *halakhah* mentions "the wool of hares" among those to which the law of *sha'atnez* ("the prohibition of wearing material containing wool and linen") does not apply (Shab. 27a), the reference here being apparently to the rabbit – *Dryctolagus cuniculus* – which the Romans bred extensively and which may have been introduced into Ereẓ Israel in mishnaic times. Some mistakenly identify the *shafan* (AV "coney"; JPS "rock-badger"), coney, mentioned in the Pentateuch alongside the hare, with the rabbit, and this is its common usage in modern Hebrew.

BIBLIOGRAPHY: J. Feliks, *Animal World of the Bible* (1962), 41; M. Dor, *Leksikon Zo'ologi* (1965), 46f.

[Jehuda Feliks]

ḤAREDIM (lit. "reverently fearful," from Hebrew *ḥared*, "fearful, trembling, pious"; common definition, ultra-Orthodox Jews).

Introduction

Orthodox Jews constitute the smallest major Jewish religious denomination. Although found in all principal areas of Jewish settlement, they are primarily resident in the United States and Israel. Numbering about 500,000 in the United States, the Orthodox constituted nearly 10% of American Jewry. About three-quarters of these are those called "Centrist Orthodox," Jews who choose a middle-way between whole-hearted acculturation to America and strict insulation from it. These are Jews who, although attached to *halakhah* (Jewish law, literally "the way"), value and receive a general education in addition to their intensive Jewish one (commonly by means of attendance at a Jewish day school), attend university, and embrace middle class aspirations of a professional career and material comforts. They share high concern for Israel, accept the idea of modern Zionism, and more than any other Jewish denomination, entertain the idea of moving to Israel, often but not always settling in the territories. While practicing birth control, American Centrist Orthodox Jews tend to have just under three children per family, giving them about a 33% greater fertility rate than the rest of American Jewry. Located mostly along the northeast corridor of the Eastern United States and in metropolitan Toronto and Montreal in Canada, they are also established in Los Angeles, Southern Florida, Cleveland, and Chicago.

In addition to Centrists, about a quarter of American Orthodox Jews qualify as *ḥaredim*, sometimes called "ultra-Orthodox." In Israel, conservative estimates have put the number of those qualifying as *ḥaredim* at between 250,000 and 300,000. Included here are not only Jews of Ashkenazi origins but also some of those of Sephardi, North African, and Middle-Eastern origins who are affiliated with Orthodox lifestyles and commitments, though not always in as consistent a way as their Ashkenazi counterparts. These latter Jews often effect a folk-religious attachment to *ḥaredi* rabbis and customs even as they sometimes deviate from some of the strict rules and regulations of the rabbis.

Definition

The term "*ḥaredim*" – once used to simply denote the religious – is today commonly reserved for those most extreme of Orthodox Jews who, although they have changed over time, claim to have made no compromises with contemporary secular culture or essential changes in the way they practice their Judaism from what the tradition and *halakhah* have sanctified throughout the ages. Yet *ḥaredim* are not simply pristine Jews who quiescently live a traditional Jewish life but rather culturally combative proponents of tradition who often seek to aggressively assert their connection to the ways of the past in the precincts of modernity, most often contemporary U.S. and Israel.

On the surface, they have used some relatively simple mechanisms to establish and maintain their traditional quasi-ethnic identity and the separation or insularity it demands. These include dressing (and grooming themselves) in ways that make them clearly stand apart from those in the surrounding culture. For men this means wearing a beard and long earlocks as well as black caftans and black hats (fur hats or *shtreimels* on the Sabbath for married or adult men), and often some form of knee pants and black shoes. For women it means dressing in modest clothing which covers most of the body and for the married among them, a head covering that may range from a kerchief over a shorn head for the most extreme to a wig for those less so. Variations are determined by sectarian affiliation within the *ḥaredi* world.

Ḥaredim also distinguish themselves by speaking Yiddish, a Jewish language that increasingly is limited only to them. In addition they have created environmental and residential barriers – segregated neighborhoods, for example – behind which they build their relatively insular neighborhoods and communities. They also send their children to private schools in which only those who share their values and lifestyle are included.

Beyond these relatively passive aspects of their identity, *ḥaredim* struggle actively against the influences of secular culture. Often this has led to their fighting to keep the contemporary lifestyle of permissiveness and sexual openness from entering their domains. In Israel this has taken the form of forcing the secular out of *ḥaredi* neighborhoods, demonstrating and militating against vehicular traffic on the Sabbath, fighting against what are viewed as the culturally corrosive effects of television, newspapers, or the posting of immodest advertisements in public, or against archeological digs in areas where they claim Jewish graves are to be found. In America, this has taken the form of struggling against legitimating non-Orthodox definitions of Judaism and Jews as well as trying to keep non-*ḥaredim* at a distance.

Groupings

Although to outsiders *ḥaredim* often appear to constitute a single ultra-Orthodox group, they are in fact subdivided into Ḥasidim who are organized around their fidelity to a particular charismatic rabbi-leader or *rebbe* on the one hand and *benei yeshivah*, those who identify with a particular academy of Jewish learning and its leading scholar (*rosh yeshivah*), students and interpretive traditions on the other. Within each of these two subcultures, there are divisions. Hence one group of Ḥasidim may clearly distinguish itself from another while those who are attached to one *yeshivah* may have little to do with those associated with another. Thus a *ḥaredi* is either a particular kind of Ḥasid, or a member of a particular *yeshivah* community, follower of a particular rabbi's interpretation of Jewish law. The divisions, supported by customs and quasi kin-group ties, may be so great as to erupt in conflict and even violence. Yet what divides these *ḥaredim* from one another pales in comparison with what divides *ḥaredim* in general from the rest of society. *Ḥaredi* identities take on a quasi-ethnic dimension as they become increasingly taken for granted because of common residence, endogamy, and a host of other instrumental links. They transcend time, place, and generation, precisely as does ethnicity.

Psycho-Social Worldview

Like ethnics, *ḥaredim* share a psycho-social worldview. This is their common (often hostile) perception of a world that opposes them and seeks to undermine their attachments to one another and to the tradition. They see themselves as an often lonely force endlessly combating obstacles, convinced that catastrophes of existence come as the inevitable culmination of past choices and experiences, which most contemporary members of secular society have made and had. While a few *ḥaredim* – most prominently Lubavitcher/Chabad Ḥasidim – have tried to engage and reach out to this world in order to try to bring it in line with their image of what is authentic, most *ḥaredim* are content to try to struggle against it by demanding it provide protection for their way of life or at the very least leave them alone. They view the culture of yesterday (as imagined nostalgically) as inherently more authoritative than today and as a genuine guide for tomorrow. They consider their lives as a service to God and Jewish tradition and the only true merit that which is prescribed by the Torah and its accepted rabbinic interpretations. In general, in the *ḥaredi* worldview, conformity to group norms and collective solidarity holds greater importance than individual self-actualization and personal liberty. Individuals only have merit insofar as they serve God and follow the dictates of tradition; that is their primary *raison dêtre*. To know precisely how to go about this, they must be guided by those who know the law and whose understanding is informed by the tradition – the rabbis.

The modern world may be used as an instrumentality to improve this service to God, but there is nothing about modernity – including science, medicine, and technology, all of which *ḥaredi* Jews utilize and exploit – which has ontological value in and of itself. The modern world is only to be valued insofar as it makes it more possible to serve God, continue Jewish tradition, and enhance Torah values. Studying Torah for as long as possible is thus the ideal for men, while women are expected to give birth to and rear children who will serve God and grow to be Torah scholars or the wives and mothers of scholars.

Although there are many other elements that distinguish *ḥaredim* from other contemporaries, Jews and even other Orthodox Jews, perhaps the most outstanding has to do with their attitude toward sexuality. Unlike mainstream and so-called modern Orthodox Jews who allow for the free mixing of males and females in social and educational settings, *ḥaredim* are scrupulous about separating the sexes from the earliest years of life. Not only do they offer separate education of males and females, they also discourage dating and the free selection of marital partners but rely instead on arranged marriages, usually accomplished by the very early twenties or late teens, and commonly to other *ḥaredim*. Although there are variations within the *ḥaredim* world, for the most part sexual relations between husband and wife are strictly regulated by Jewish law, custom, and habit. The aim of sexual relations is procreation, and *ḥaredi* men and women are expected to be fruitful and multiply; a childless *ḥaredi* couple is a rarity, their situation invariably the result of fertility problems. While pleasure plays a part in these relations between husband and wife, it is not expected to become central to the relationship. In some groups, for example followers of the Ger ḥasidic dynasty, sexual relations between a married couple are to be as brief and unemotional as possible. Thus for a Ger Ḥasid, almost any desire for extended sexual experience would be viewed as excessive and hence sinful. But even in the most liberal of *ḥaredi* groups, sexuality is to be rigorously regulated. Even husband and wife may only have sexual contact at certain times of the month (specifically, seven days after the end of the woman's menstrual period and after she has immersed herself in a ritual bath or *mikveh*) and even within the permitted period there are those *ḥaredim* who consider some times superior to others (the Sabbath, for example).

Hasidism, the Yeshivah World, and the Ḥaredim

Among Jews of Ashkenazi origin, most *ḥaredim* affiliate with Ḥasidism. There are many ḥasidic courts. In Israel the Gerrer Ḥasidim are probably the most numerous, followed by the Belzers, Vizhnitzers, and Lubavitchers. However, there are also other important groups who, although smaller in number, have had an impact on the character of hasidic life. These include Klausenbeger, Karliner, Lalover, Bobover, and Satmar Ḥasidim. In addition small sub-groupings, like the Toldos Aharon *ḥaredim*, who share many traditions with Satmar and distinguish themselves by their fellowship and attachment to traditions begun by Rabbi Aharon *Roth, play an important role through their activism on behalf of their customs and world view.

The *yeshivah* world, as distinguished from Ḥasidism, is populated by those who identify with a particular academy of Jewish learning and its leading scholars, students and interpretive traditions. These often see themselves as heirs of the *Mitnaggedim*, those who opposed the religious excesses of Ḥasidism and its cult of personality. In general, these *ḥaredim* represent the most liberal group within the *ḥaredi* world. They tend to allow for greater individual initiative as well as more extensive contact with the outside world.

While the differences between these two categories of *ḥaredim* are significant, when compared with other American Jews the similarities between them are striking. Over time, Hasidim have embraced the idea of *yeshivah* study over the pietism and zealotry that first shaped them during their emergence in Eastern Europe in the 18th and 19th centuries. On the other hand, the *yeshiva* world, which traces its primary origins to the same era in Lithuania, has transformed its attachment to its scholar-rabbis into a charismatic attachment to them in personality cults not altogether unlike those characteristic of Hasidim. Moreover, both Ḥasidim and the heirs of the Lithuanian-style *yeshivah* society today are both the most noticeable of Orthodox Jews and share a common goal of eschewing the values and many of the lifestyles of contemporary secular society and emphasizing instead a punctiliousness in religious ritual, a cultural separation from what they view as the corrupting influences of the outside world, and an attachment to the idea of preserving tradition, seen as a sacred order containing venerable truths and customs that may not be abrogated. Externally, they look and dress similarly, the men embracing black hats and coats and the women modest dress and head-coverings, and the use of Yiddish among themselves as their *lingua franca* and linguistic vehicle for keeping themselves separate from general society and bonded to one another. Although continuing to be attentive to what distinguishes them from one another, all share a common sense of being engaged in a culture war against contemporary secular culture in general and the principles of secular Zionism which has sought to redefine Jewish identity in particular. Zionism is also regarded as an expression of religious hubris and rebellion for it assumes that Jews can act to end a divinely imposed exile which, according to most *ḥaredim*, can only be ended when God acts.

Confrontation with Modernity

Because the inherent attraction of contemporary culture is so powerful, many Orthodox Jews have managed to find ways of entering the situation of modernity and the spirit of the times while still keeping strictly within the letter of the law. This has led *ḥaredim* to become partisans of the stringent rather than the lenient interpretations of Jewish law. The espousal of stringencies led *ḥaredim* to take on customs that were often beyond the demands of the Jewish law; another group – in order to demonstrate its greater piety – would find an even stricter interpretation. Thus there are repeated calls by *ḥaredim* to oppose any inroad of contemporary culture, whether this be acceding to the passing of cars through their neighborhoods on the Sabbath, allowing for archeological digs that "desecrate" Jewish graves, or countenancing immodest dress in their neighborhoods or even approving the wearing of wigs by married women rather than their shaving their heads and covering them with kerchiefs. Moreover, the requirements of the Jewish law are always enlarged in scope to include custom and folkway, and there are frequent efforts to shun material pleasures and insert an ascetic strain into Judaism.

The American *ḥaredim* could not and for a long time did not want to fight America, their new diaspora haven. They tried instead to ignore its culture whenever possible – even to the extent of some of the most extreme traveling through it inside their own buses – and saved their most active battling in the struggle to keep other, non-Orthodox Jews at bay. In America, the *ḥaredim* withdrew themselves from intra-Jewish organizations as much as possible, maintaining only the ties they needed to get money coming into their institutions. They vilified the Reform and Conservative Jews and were privately contemptuous of those who called themselves modern Orthodox. They refused to join most intra-communal Jewish organizations and even organized their own rabbinical association ("Agudas Ha-Rabonnim") that was made up of Orthodox rabbis who were not affiliated with the more mainstream Orthodox Rabbinical Council of America.

In America, the contra-acculturative Orthodox thus paid much attention to making money, the ultimate American power, and limiting the influence of non-Orthodox Jews in Jewish life, particularly in determining matters of personal status (deciding who was a Jew or who was married and divorced). The money, the result of an open society which provided many economic opportunities never before available to those who remained Orthodox, would give independence and help support the Orthodox way of life. For some this meant developing strength in the diamond trade, for others real estate, the garment industry, and in the last 25 years, the electronics business. Based on a community of people who trust one another and a no-nonsense approach to business which – somewhat akin to the Protestant ethic – reinvests profits and limits spending to necessities and charitable giving, seeing nothing inherently valuable in money except in what it can do to help maintain the Jewish way of life, these Jews succeeded in this goal.

Moreover, to keep America responsive to their needs, these Jews (like their other co-religionists) were careful to vote at election time, making increasingly certain that the parties and candidates knew that they voted in high numbers and en bloc. In this last regard, they allowed themselves to be publicly identified as Jewish voters – so much so that candidates seeking Jewish votes often have themselves photographed with *ḥaredim*, hoping that this will symbolize their attraction for all Jewish voters.

In Ereẓ Israel and later in the new Zionist state, *ḥaredim* also tried to recreate and resurrect their traditional experience. To these Orthodox Jews – even those who shared similar ḥasidic or *mitnagged* affiliations – their American counterparts were not really "*ḥaredim*"; they were "Americans." They read American newspapers, worked with Americans, spoke English, and had subtly been swept up by America and the ways of the gentile society. They could not really overcome so powerful a cultural giant as the American way of life. True *ḥaredim*, the Israelis maintained, fought relentlessly against all outside influences – including the host society – and did not allow themselves to be assimilated by the modern world even in the quest for funds for the institutions.

For Israeli *ḥaredim* this meant not serving in the Israel Defense Forces, viewed as a secular institution that would undermine the insularity and authoritative order of *ḥaredi* society. As part of an agreement made during the early years of the state, all male students studying in a *yeshivah* were exempted from the universal Israeli military draft while Orthodox girls were likewise exempted. For the men, this served to encourage increased *yeshivah* study for longer periods. Thus insulated in the *yeshivah* in order to remain free of the draft, *ḥaredi* men tended to become more extreme and stringent, and less compromising with the demands of contemporary secular society than did their American counterpart who went to work in the outside world and learned to yield and adjust to it more easily. It also made the Israelis more dependent on financial stipends from *ḥaredi* political parties who in turn drew funds from the government in return for their political support. Over time, *ḥaredi* educational institutions have absorbed increasing amounts of money devoted solely to maintaining the *ḥaredim* who spend their time in study in place of gainful employment. In addition, *ḥaredi* society depends heavily on "*gemaḥim*," communal charity organizations and philanthropic donations from abroad. This economic precariousness of a society that absorbs more money than it generates remains among the most severe crises confronting contemporary *ḥaredim*.

Outreach

While most *ḥaredim* remain inward-looking, concerned only with maintaining their own members, Lubavitcher Ḥasidim, at the urging of their late leader, Menachem Mendel *Schneersohn (d. 1995), have established a large outreach program serviced by emissaries who travel the world and try to bring back wayward Jews to a more stringent and Orthodox Jewish way of life. This large outreach effort has made the Lubavitcher Ḥasidim often the only *ḥaredim* with whom outsiders have had any sort of extended contact. In contrast to the disregard that most *ḥaredim* seem to have for those unlike themselves, the Lubavitcher attitude seems to have made friends for the *ḥaredi* way of life. The actual numbers that Lubavitcher *ḥaredim* have recruited to their version of Judaism, however, by most counts remains relatively small.

[Samuel C. Heilman]

The Challenge of Material Subsistence

While the *ḥaredi* population in Israel has maintained its coherence and single-mindedness, it has not been unaffected by the winds of change. Exposure to the ethos of a consumer society and a steadily worsening economic situation have created pressures from within, often coming from the woman of the house, on whose shoulders the financial burden of earning a living often falls in the absence of a working husband. Two factors have contributed to the increasing impoverishment of the *ḥaredim* in Israel: the mushrooming of the nonworking yeshivah population, which embraced some 80,000 men in the early 2000s, about half of them married, and the drastic cutback in welfare spending by the Israeli government in the face of the deep recession brought on by the second intifada and global factors. The system of army deferment and state support for "professional yeshivah scholars" has a long history in Israel. Originally the number of such scholars qualifying for support in the new state was just 400, earmarked to revive the lost yeshivah world of Europe. In 1968 their number was doubled. In 1977, as part of Menaḥem Begin's coalition agreement with the religious political parties, the quota was abolished and virtually all *ḥaredi* men who wished to do so could engage in protracted full-time yeshivah study. The inducements to remain in the yeshivah were great: a government stipend and perpetual draft deferment. In the United States, where such inducements did not exist, a different kind of yeshivah world had evolved. Ḥasidim, who lacked a strong scholarly tradition, would leave the yeshivah at around the age of 21 and enter the labor market, usually in low-paying, unskilled jobs, which indeed caused many with their large families to subsist beneath the poverty line. However, the "Lithuanian" *ḥaredim*, while prolonging their studies in a flourishing yeshivah world, though rarely beyond the age of 30, often combined vocational and even academic studies in suitable frameworks, like the *Touro college system, with yeshivah study, and consequently were able to get well-paid jobs in high-tech industries and other professions. In Israel no such socio-economic differentiation existed as between ḥasidim and "Lithuanians" in the United States. All stayed in the yeshivot under the Israeli system, including "Eastern" *ḥaredim* who had adopted the lifestyle of Ashkenazi *ḥaredim* under the influence of R. Eleazar *Shach, the mentor of their leader, R. Ovadiah *Yosef. Ironically, unlike the Lithuanian Jews of Europe, who had closed themselves in against the temptations of the outside world, Eastern Jews had never feared assimilation in the surrounding Muslim population and had therefore lived in a more open society in which working to earn one's keep was a natural part of life. It was only in Israel that they became "Ashkenazim."

Starting in the mid-1990s, bending to the pressure from within to raise the standard of living among *ḥaredim* and alleviate their traditional "voluntary poverty," *ḥaredi* rabbis began to show a certain measure of flexibility with regard to the subject of vocational training. However, their attitude has been ambiguous and they have often wavered in determining what is permissible. Nonetheless a number of frameworks were established permitting such study, like the Ḥaredi Center for Technological Studies in Bene Berak and Jerusalem, and thousands of men and women have enrolled over the years, though fewer than might have been expected. It is clear, however, that a new direction is tentatively being explored in keeping with economic and social realities. Though political realities could very well reinstitute a regime of government largesse and reverse the trend, it would seem that the *ḥaredi* world, too, is being affected by modern life.

[Fred Skolnik (2nd ed.)]

ADD. BIBLIOGRAPHY: A. Gonen, *From Yeshiva to Work: The American Experience and Lessons for Israel* (2001); J. Lupu, *A Shift in Haredi Society: Vocational Training and Academic Studies* (2004).

HAREL (Heb. הַרְאֵל), kibbutz in the Jerusalem corridor, east of Ḥuldah, affiliated with Kibbutz Arẓi ha-Shomer ha-Ẓa'ir, founded in October 1948. Harel was established on a site where hard battles had been fought four months earlier (see Israel *War of Independence). The first settlers were *Palmaḥ veterans of the Harel Brigade who had fought in the area and in Jerusalem; they were later joined by immigrants from various countries. Farming was based on deciduous fruit orchards, field crops, grapevines, etc. In more recent years the kibbutz set up a winery together with private investor, producing wines from the kibbutz's grapes. In addition, Harel owns a guesthouse with 33 rooms. Carob plantations and large forests have been planted in the vicinity, in the middle of which stands the Harel panorama tower. In the mid-1990s, the population was approximately 70, doubling in size to 145 by 2002.

[Efraim Orni / Shaked Gilboa (2nd ed.)]

HAREL, DAVID (1950–), Israeli mathematician and computer scientist. Harel was born in London and immigrated to Israel in 1957. After service in the Israel Defense Forces (1968–71), he graduated with a B.Sc. in mathematics and computer science from Bar-Ilan University (1974), followed by an M.Sc. in computer science from Tel Aviv University (1976), and a Ph.D. from the Massachusetts Institute of Technology (1978). He joined the faculty of the Department of Computer Science and Applied Mathematics of the Weizmann Institute of Science, Reḥovot, in 1980 and was appointed professor (1989), William Sussman Professor of Mathematics (1990), department chairman (1989–95), and dean of the Faculty of Mathematics and Computer Science (1998–2004). His past research interests include computability theory, program logic, and database and automata theory. His later interests were software and systems engineering, visual languages, synthesis and communication of smell, and modeling and analysis of biological systems.

He invented the language of statecharts and co-designed Statemate and Rhapsody, LSCs, and the play in/out methodology. One of his long-term goals was to adapt the language and tools of computer systems to model and simulate a complete multi-cellular animal such as the C. elegans worm. His national and international reputation is reflected by his many plenary and keynote lectures to conferences worldwide, membership on editorial boards, visiting professorships, and membership on international review committees. His awards include the Association of Computing Machinery's Karl V. Karlstrom Outstanding Educator Award (1992), the Israel Prime Minister's Prize for Software and Software Methods (1997), and the Israel Prize in computer science (2004). Harel has a major interest in education in his field and in science in general. He was a member of Israel's Higher Education Committee (1988–89) and of the Ministry for Education's High School Committee for Computer Science (1990–97). He also gave a series of lectures and organized programs on computer science for Israeli radio and television. His books, such as *Computers Ltd.: What They Really Can't Do* (2000) and *Algorithmics: The Spirit of Computing* (1987, 1992, 2004), are acclaimed as readable, outstanding computer science texts for specialists and general readers alike.

[Michael Denman (2nd ed.)]

HAREL, MENASHE (1917–), Israeli scholar in Ereẓ Israel studies. Harel is known for his field trips throughout Israel combining academic pursuits with hiking. Harel was born in Samarkand and immigrated to Israel in 1921. In 1941 he served as a Palmaḥ instructor in kibbutz Mismar ha-Emek. From 1943 until 1945 he was the Palmaḥ representative in Syria, engaged in education, teaching, and assisting Jews to immigrate to Israel. In 1948 he joined the IDF, serving until 1952. Among his missions in the IDF was the establishment of the Naḥal patrol. In 1955 he graduated in geography and historical geography of Ereẓ Israel from the Hebrew University of Jerusalem. In 1957 he received his M.A. degree in historical geography and archaeology from the Hebrew University. In 1963 he received his Ph.D. from New York University. From 1952 until 1961 he was a teacher at the David Yellin teachers seminary. From 1964 until 1969 he taught the methodology of geography at the Hebrew University and the Technion, and the historical geography of Ereẓ Israel at the Technion. From 1969 until 1981 he served as senior lecturer for geographical history in the Department of Geography and the School of Education at Tel Aviv University. From 1982 until 1987 he served as professor in the Department of Geography at Tel Aviv University, becoming professor emeritus in 1987. During these years he was a visiting professor at New York University, Clark University, and Hebrew Union College. Harel was a member of various public institutions and produced 12 books and six monographs among other publications, including *Travels in Israel* (1960), *Geography of Ereẓ Israel* (1960); *Sinai Journeys* (1963); *This is Jerusalem* (1969); *Journeys and Battles in Ancient Times* (1980); *Landscape, Nature and Man in the Bible* (1984); and *The Historical Geography of Ereẓ Israel* (1997). In 2002 he was awarded the Israel Prize for historical geography.

[Shaked Gilboa (2nd ed.)]

HAREL, YISRAEL (1938–), Israeli journalist and settlement leader. Born in Chernowitz, near Kovina, Ukraine, Harel emigrated to Palestine in 1947. He fought in the 1967 and 1973 wars, participating in the capture of the Old City of Jerusalem. In 1968 he was appointed managing editor of the revisionist daily *Ha-Yom*, and the following year joined *Maariv* as deputy editor of its weekend section. His employment was interrupted after he moved to the then illegal settlement of Ofra in 1976, and he subsequently joined *Yedioth Aharonoth* as a writer-at-large. A founding member of the Greater Israel movement, in 1980 he established the Council of Settlements of Judea, Samaria, and Gaza, acting as its secretary-general for the first seven years, and its chairman for the next eight years, to 1995. Harel's period at the council was characterized by intensive settlement activity (the number of settlements increasing from 20 in 1980 to 140 by the time he left) and by a pragmatic approach in the council's dealings with successive Labor and Likud governments.

Harel also founded and edited *Nekudah*, the council's monthly journal. Originally a magazine reporting the manifold activities of different settlements, it evolved into an intellectual journal campaigning for Jewish settlement, often featuring controversial writing, its voice influencing the nationalist agenda. While many of its contributors and readers were within the religious strata of the settlement movement, they also extended to the mainstream Israeli populations, including people identified with the Left. Never making a profit, its circulation hovered around 7,000.

Against the background of the Rabin assassination, Harel established the Forum for National Responsibility as a framework for dialogue between religious and secular Jews, which produced the so-called Kinneret memorandum. He wrote a book on religious Zionism.

[Yoel Cohen (2nd ed.)]

HARENDORF, SAMUEL JACOB (1900–1969), Yiddish playwright and journalist. Born in Chenzin, Poland, Harendorf worked on Jewish papers in Vienna and Prague, moving to England before World II. In 1940 he founded the Yiddish World News Agency and edited it until his death. Harendorf was author of *The King of Lampedusa* (1944), a play based on an incident in World War II, when a Jewish RAF pilot accepted the surrender of an Italian island in the Mediterranean. The play had the longest run in the history of the London Yiddish stage. He also wrote a play called *Hanna Senesh*.

ADD. BIBLIOGRAPHY: D. Mazower, *Yiddish Theatre in London* (1996), index; S.J. Harendorf, *The King of Lampedusa* (ed. and trans. H. Valencia, 2003).

HA-REUBENI (Rubinowitz), EPHRAIM (1881–1953), botanist and pioneer in Ereẓ Israel. Born in Novo-Moskovsk, Ukraine, Ha-Reubeni settled in Ereẓ Israel in 1906 and worked as teacher of natural science in various high schools. In 1907 he founded the first museum of botany in Ereẓ Israel. Together with his wife Hannah (d. 1956) he founded in 1912 the Museum of Flora of the Bible and Talmud, in Rishon le-Zion. In 1936 they were transferred to the Hebrew University. He joined the academic staff of the Hebrew University in 1926 and in 1935 was appointed lecturer in botany of the Bible and Talmud. Ha-Reubeni contributed much to the investigation of plants in Ereẓ Israel, their uses and associated folklore. On the basis of their research, together with linguistic studies of plant names in Hebrew, Aramaic, Arabic, and other languages, the Ha-Reubenis did much to explain the ancient Hebrew botanical terms and to identify the plants mentioned in the Bible and Talmud. They wrote *Meḥkarim bi-Shemot Ẓimḥei Ereẓ Yisrael* (1930) and *Oẓar Ẓimḥei Ereẓ Yisrael* (1941).

BIBLIOGRAPHY: C. Tartakower, in: *Menorah*, 2 no. 3 (Ger., 1924), 1–2; Tidhar, 12 (1962), 3946–47; *Ha-Teva re-ha-Areẓ*, 7 (1947), 303 (bibliography).

[Frederick Simon Bodenheimer]

HAREVEN, SHULAMITH (1930–2003), Israel author. Hareven was born in Warsaw, Poland; she arrived in Ereẓ Israel in 1940 and lived in Jerusalem. She served in the Haganah underground and was a combat-medic during the War of Independence. Later she worked with refugees and immigrants from various Arab countries and was one of the initiators of the Army Broadcasting Station for which she worked as correspondent during the Yom Kippur War. She began her literary career with a poetry collection, *Yerushalayim dorsanit* ("Predatory Jerusalem") in 1962, and later published novels, stories, books for children, and essays. Among these are the impressionistic novel *Ir Yamim Rabbim* (1972; *City of Many Days*, 1977), depicting life in Jerusalem under British Mandate, with Jews, Christians and Muslims sharing experiences and pleading tolerance. The story *Bedidut* ("Loneliness," 1980) tells about the desolate life of Dolly Jacobus, a Holocaust survivor, who marries into a veteran Jerusalemite family, yet fails to integrate and remains frustrated as a woman. Other books by Hareven include the novella *Sone ha-Nissim* ("The Miracle Hater," 1983), a historic miniature about the Exodus in the Sinai desert and the emergence of monotheism; *Navi* (1989; *Prophet*, 1990), and a collection of essays on political and socio-cultural issues which was translated into English under *The Vocabulary of Peace* (1995). A lifelong member of the Israeli Peace Movement "Shalom Akhshav," Hareven reported from Arab villages during the Intifada. She was the first woman to be elected as a member of the Hebrew Language Academy and was known for her rich, idiomatic Hebrew. A year before she died, her autobiography was published under *Yamim Rabbim* ("Many Days," 2002). Other translations into English include *Twilight and Other Stories* (1991) and the story "My Straw Chairs" is included in *The Oxford Book of Hebrew Short Stories* (1996). For translations into various languages see the ITHL website, www.ithl.org.il.

Her daughter GAIL HAREVEN (1959–), is one of the original voices among the younger Israeli prose writers. Born in Jerusalem, she studied behavioral sciences at Ben-Gurion University as well as Talmud and Jewish Philosophy at the Shalom Hartman Institute. She teaches creative writing and feminist theory and has published collections of stories, children books as well as plays. Among these are *Aruḥat Ẓohorayim im Ima* ("Lunch with Mother," 1993) and *Ha-Derekh le-Gan Eden* ("The Way to Heaven," 1998). In 2002, she received the prestigious Sapir Prize for her novel *My True Love* (2000).

BIBLIOGRAPHY: Y. Granach, "*Gevulot ha-Muda'ut ha-Aẓmit*," in: *Biẓaron*, 5, 19/20 (1983), 92–95; Y. Fischer-Nave, *Motivim Mikra'iyyim ke-Bavuah la-Ani ha-Liri* (1987); R. Feldhay Brenner, "Discourses on Mourning and Rebirth in Post-Holocaust Israeli Literature: Leah Goldberg's 'Lady of the Castle' and Shulamith Hareven's 'The Witness,'" in: *Hebrew Studies*, 31 (1990) 71–85; A. Holtzman, "*Mekomot Nifradim: Bein Sippur le-Massah bi-Yeẓirat S. Hareven*," in: *Shenaton ha-Sefer ha-Yehudi*, 49 (1992), 133–39; I. Scheinfeld, "*Ketivah el he-Avar*," in: *Apiryon*, 20/21 (1991), 27–30; Y. Nave, "In Those Days and this Time: Lyric and Ideology in S. Hareven's Short Stories," in: *Hebrew Annual Review*, 13 (1991), 77–87; Y. Feldman, *No Room of Their Own: Gender and Nation in Israeli Women's Fiction* (1999); idem, "Our Primary Myth of Violence: Hareven's Peace Politics," in: *Midstream*, 51:3 (2005), 26–30; E. Bar-Eshel, in: *Alei Si'aḥ*, 48 (2002), 64–76; Y. Berlovitz, "*Likro et Yerushalayim ke-Tekst Nashi*," in: T. Cohen and Y. Schwartz (eds.) *Isha bi-Yerushalayim* (2002), 158–91.

[Anat Feinberg (2nd ed.)]

HARF, HANNS (1914–2004), founder and rabbi of the Nueva Comunidad Israelita – NCI (Jews of German origin) in Buenos Aires, Argentina. Born in Monchengladbach, Germany, he studied in the University of Berlin Law School and learned theology, also in Berlin, at the Conservative rabbinical seminary from which he received rabbinical ordination and a Ph.D. On **Kristallnacht* (November 9–10, 1938) he was taken to the Oranienburg concentration camp. After his liberation he married Dr. Suse Hallenstein and immigrated to Argentina. He founded the NCI and the "Lamroth Hakol" communities in Buenos Aires and was active rabbi of the former for 60 years. He was also co-founder of the Seminario Rabínico Latinoamericano "Marshall T. Meyer" (Conservative rabbinical seminary) and professor there for homiletics. He was also active in Interfaith Christian-Jewish Associations and was well known for his liberal ideas. He participated in religious-oriented television programs. Until his last days, he dedicated his life to the members of his community.

HARF, SUSE HALLENSTEIN (1912–2002), librarian of Jewish Studies. Born in Hamburg, she studied theology and philosophy at the University of Berlin and was one of the last Jewish students permitted to receive a Ph.D. there. Later she worked as a librarian in the local rabbinical Conservative seminary. In 1962 she founded, together with Rabbi Marshall T. Meyer, the library of the Seminario Rabínico Latinoamericano, which became one of the best libraries of Jewish Studies in Latin America. She became head librarian, working in the library until her retirement in 1988.

HAR HA-MELEKH (Heb. הַר הַמֶּלֶךְ; "king's mountain"; Aramaic *Tor Malka*), a hilly district in Judah. It should probably be identified with the toparchy of Orine (Latin for "the hilly one," Pliny, *Natural History*, 5, 14:70), i.e., the district of Jerusalem in Hasmonean times (Josephus, War 3, 3:5 (54–55); Antiq. 12, I:I (7)) and this may very well be the same as the "hill country" mentioned in Luke (1:39–40, 65). The Protevangelium of James (c. 150 C.E.) also mentions Mary and Joseph going into "the hill country." According to the Talmud, "any mountain that is in Judah is Har ha-Melekh" (TJ, Shev 9:2, 38d). Its original borders thus extended from Gibeah of Saul (Tell el-Ful) in the north to Solomon's Pools in the south and from Kiriath-Jearim in the west to the ascent of Adummim in the east. The word *melekh* ("king") apparently indicates the Hasmonean kings beginning with Alexander Yannai. Har ha-Melekh, according to rabbinic sources, was very fertile and contained fields and vegetable gardens, olives, and grapes, and its fowls were sent to the Temple. After the destruction of the settlements in the district during the Bar Kokhba War (132–135), Har ha-Melekh was attached to the territory of *Aelia Capitolina. Its Jewish inhabitants were expelled and its produce, which continued to be supplied to Caesarea, was considered gentile produce and thus exempt from tithes. In later talmudic literature the true extent of its area was forgotten and villages in the Bet Guvrin district (e.g., Kefar Bish, Kefar Shiḥlayim) were erroneously attributed to Har ha-Melekh. The alleged number of its villages reached fantastic proportions ("60,000 myriads") and their populations are also highly exaggerated (TB, Git. 57a; Lam. R. 2:2, no. 4). B.Z. Luria proposed to locate Har ha-Melekh in the Mt. Ephraim range, in the direction of the Carmel, between Kefar Otenai and Narbata.

BIBLIOGRAPHY: S. Klein, *Ereẓ Yehudah* (1939), 239ff.; B.Z. Luria, *Yannai ha-Melekh* (1961), 38ff.; Press, Ereẓ, s.v. **ADD. BIBLIOGRAPHY:** G. Dalman, *Sacred Sites and Ways: Studies in the Topography of the Gospels* (1935), 52–53; E. Schurer, *The History of the Jewish People in the Age of Jesus Christ (175 BC–AD 135)*, rev. and ed. by G. Vermes, F. Millar, and M. Black, vol. 2 (1979), 191; S. Gibson, *The Cave of John the Baptist* (2004), 25–26.

[Michael Avi-Yonah / Shimon Gibson (2nd ed.)]

ḤARIF, family, many of whose members were rabbis in Poland from the 16th to the 19th centuries. Some regard the family as descended from *Shalom Shakhna b. Joseph of Lublin. They included MOSES HA-ZAKEN ("the elder") BEN ISRAEL (16th–17th centuries) – the first to be given the epithet *ḥarif* ("sharp-witted") – who served as rabbi of Kremienec, Lvov, and Uleynov. He was the author of *Seder Gittin* (still in mss.) which was in the possession of Ephraim Zalman Margolioth. ISRAEL, his son, headed a yeshivah in Lvov and was *av bet din* of Uleynov. MOSES PHINEHAS (1625–1702), son of Israel, was chief rabbi of Lvov, and presided over the Council of Four Lands in 1685. He was an opponent of the Shabbateans, and added supplements to his grandfather's *Seder Gittin*. ISRAEL, second son of Israel b. Moses, was born on the day his father died, and was given his name. He was *av bet din* of Alik. Of the sons of Moses Phinehas, ẒEVI HIRSCH (d. 1737) was the *av bet din* of Jaworow, and Jacob was *av bet din* of Leszniow and the province of Podolia. One son of Jacob, JUDAH LEIB, was *av bet din* of Korow, and another, SAUL (first half of 18th century), *av bet din* of Olesko, and later of Brody where he founded a *bet midrash* called after him. MOSES ḤAYYIM BEN ELEAZAR (1690–1760), grandson of Moses Phinehas, was rabbi of Komarno, Zloczow (1719), and Lvov (1724). After a violent controversy between him and Jacob Joshua *Falk concerning the rabbinate of Lvov, which arose out of an allegation by a proselyte that Moses Ḥayyim had influenced him to become a Jew, he was compelled to flee to Khotin, which was under Turkish rule, and he died there. JACOB ISAAC (?1710–1771), son of Moses Ḥayyim, changed his name to Hochgelerter, and in 1740 was appointed rabbi of Zamosc. His son JOSEPH (1740–1807) was rabbi of Jampol and Zamosc. His halakhic glosses, *Ḥiddushei Mahari*, were published in the *Zera Aharon* (Zolkiew, 1757). *Mishnat Ḥakhamim* (Lvov, 1792), the first part of his commentary to Maimonides' *Mishneh Torah*, was also published. His sons were ḤAYYIM BEN JOSEPH (1770–1809), rabbi of Ostrowiec, Hrubieszow, and Grabowiec, author of halakhic novellae entitled *Ḥut ha-Meshullash*, appended to his father's *Mishnat Ḥakhamim*, and ISAAC BEN JOSEPH (1771–1825), rabbi of Tarnograd, Chelm, and Zamosc, author of *Zikhron Yiẓḥak* (c. 1822), consisting of responsa and homilies.

BIBLIOGRAPHY: G. Sochestow, *Maẓẓevat Kodesh*, 4 (1869), 73b–74b; Ḥ.N. Dembitzer, *Kelilat Yofi*, 1 (1888), 86a–88a; S. Buber, *Anshei Shem* (1895), 130, 158–62, 195f.; J. Cohen-Ẓedek, *Shem u-She'erit* (1895), 58f.; idem, in: *Ha-Goren*, 1 (1898), 28–31; Ẓ.(H.) Horowitz, in: *Ha-Ivri*, 11 no. 13 (1921), 8–10; 11 no.14 (1921), 8f.; idem, *Kitvei ha-Ge'onim* (1928), 28–30, 59–61; idem, *Toledot Mishpaḥat Horowitz* (n.d.), 21 n.41; idem, in: MGWJ, 72 (1928), 494ff.; M. Bersohn, *Słownik biograficzny uczonych żydów polskich XVI, XVII, i XVIII wieku* (1905), 68f.

[Yehoshua Horowitz]

ḤARIF HA-LEVI, family of rabbis and scholars in Poland in the 17th and 18th centuries. The founder of the family was SOLOMON BEN ISAAC ABRAHAM of Przemysl (d. 1638), a pupil of Joshua *Falk, and son-in-law of Joseph ha-Kohen. He was rabbi of Lemberg when he died. His elder son, ISAAC SEGAL, was the son-in-law of Samuel *Edels, and rabbi of Rymanow. He was the ancestor of many generations of rabbis and scholars including Ephraim Zalman *Margalioth of Brody and Samuel Kamnitzer, great-grandfather of Eisik Segal of Lemberg. Solomon's second son, MOSES SEGAL, was rabbi of Polna and later head of a yeshivah in Lemberg. Moses' son, JOSEPH SEGAL (d. 1702), was rabbi of Przemysl, and the Ḥakham Ẓevi (Ẓevi Hirsch *Ashkenazi) said of him that his only transgression was his disobedience of the *takkanah* of Usha which laid it down that one should not give more than one fifth of one's income to charity. JEKUTHIEL ZALMAN SEGAL, son of Joseph, was the first rabbi of Drohobycz, appointed in 1670. Of his six sons, all of whom were rabbis, the most distinguished was ISAAC HA-LEVI. NATHAN NETA, another son of Jekuthiel, was rabbi and *av bet din* of Lemberg. He died apparently in 1776.

BIBLIOGRAPHY: Ḥ.N. Dembitzer, *Kelilat Yofi*, 1 (1888), 41–42b; S. Buber, *Anshei Shem* (1895), 203f.; J. Cohen-Ẓedek, in: *Ha-Goren*, 1 (1898), 24, 26, 28 (second pagination); E.Z. Margaliot, *Ma'alot ha-Yuḥasin* (1900), 34–36; Margaliot, in: *Sinai*, 31 (1952), 92; Z. Horowitz, *Kitvei ha-Ge'onim* (1928), 47, 69f.

[Yehoshua Horowitz]

ḤARIRI, family of kabbalists of the village of Ḥarir, in the district of Irbil, Kurdistan. ISAAC BEN MOSES (17th century), the founder of the family, lived in this village during the first half of the 17th century. He wrote the kabbalistic work *Naḥalat ha-Shem* and a number of religious *piyyutim*. His son PHINEHAS, who was attracted to Shabbateanism, was also a *paytan* and author. The sons of Phinehas, ḤAYYIM and ISAAC, were rabbis in the townlet of Rawanduz, in the district of Irbil. ABRAHAM BEN PHINEHAS (19th century) left six works in manuscript. His son MOSES was a teacher for beginners in Köi in the district of Irbil and owned a large library of religious books. He wrote at least three works, of which *Va-Yivḥar Moshe* was published in Baghdad in 1930. Moses' son Isaac was rabbi in Rawanduz.

BIBLIOGRAPHY: A. Ben-Jacob, *Kehillot Yehudei Kurdistan* (1961); index.

[Haim J. Cohen]

ḤARIZI, ABU ISAAC ABRAHAM (fl. c. 1100), Hebrew poet of Toledo, Spain. Moses Ibn Ezra mentions him in his poetics (tr. by A. Halkin, *Kitab al-Muhadara wal-Mudhakara* (1975), 40b) as being a contemporary of Abu Harun ibn Abi al-'Aysh. Judah *Al-Ḥarizi praises Abraham's verses in two passages in the *Taḥkemoni* (ed. by Kaminka (1899), 39, 41). It is uncertain whether he belonged to the same family as Judah al-Ḥarizi, being probably two generations older. A number of poems, known to have been composed by a "Ḥarizi" (*Maḥzor Aleppo*, *Siftei Renanot*, Karaite Rite and Ms.), may be Abraham's. There were, however, also other Ḥarizis (Ms. Adler 135 contains poems by a Simḥah Ḥarizi).

BIBLIOGRAPHY: Sachs, in: *Oẓar Ḥokhmah*, 2 (1861), 37; Brody, in: A. Berliner, *Aus meiner Bibliothek* (1898), 6 (Heb. sect.); Habermann, in: *Mizraḥ u-Ma'arav*, 4 (1930), 18–21; J.H. Schirmann, *Shirim Ḥadashim min ha-Genizah* (1965), 284.

[Jefim (Ḥayyim) Schirmann]

HARKAVI, YITZHAK (**Isaac**; 1915–2001), Zionist leader and educator. Born in Bialystok, Poland, he emigrated to Moisesville, Argentina, in 1926. He studied law in Santa Fe and was a teacher in the Hebrew schools of Moisesville and Santa Fe. In 1939 he moved to Buenos Aires where he worked as a teacher in the Jewish schools of the Cursos Religiosos network, and when Natan Bistritzky arrived in Argentina (1942), Harkavi directed the JNF office. An activist in the Poa'lei Zion Hitaḥdut party (connected to *Mapai – Labor Party in Ereẓ Israel) during the 1930s, he emerged as one of the key leaders of the Zionist Movement in Argentina. Harkavi promoted democratization of the Zionist Movement and addressing the youth, including direct elections and representation. He represented his Zionist party at the Central Zionist Council in Argentina from 1943, in DAIA, and in Vaad Hachinuḥ – Board of Jewish Education of AMIA (Jewish Ashkenazi Community of Buenos Aires). Harkavi was general secretary of the first Latin American Zionist Congress, held in Montevideo in 1945, and in the early 1950s was appointed president of the Central Zionist Council.

As teacher and director (from 1946) of the Buenos Aires Bialik Hebraist school, one of the most important Zionist schools in Argentina, Harkavi contributed enormously to the increasing influence of the young State of Israel in Jewish schools and communities in South America through the promotion of the Hebrew language. He also established the ICAI – Cultural Institute Argentina-Israel (in 1952) – under the sponsorship of the Israeli diplomatic representation. In 1950 he was appointed representative of the Jewish Agency for Latin America. Before moving to Israel in 1954 he succeeded in bringing an Israeli *shali'aḥ* as director for the Bialik school.

In Israel Harkavi was appointed the general secretary of the Mapai-Ichud Olami Party (1954–60) and Israeli ambassador to Uruguay (1960–63) and to Brazil (1968–73). He also served as a member of the Zionist Executive Council and head of the Department for Jewish Education and Culture in the Diaspora of the World Zionist Organization (1963–68).

[Yossi (Jorge) Goldstein (2nd ed.)]

HARKAVY, ALBERT (**Abraham Elijah**; 1835–1919), Russian Orientalist, scholar of Jewish history and literature. Harkavy was born in Novogrudok, Belorussia. He studied at Lithuanian yeshivot and at the universities of St. Petersburg, Berlin, and Paris. On his return to Russia in 1870 he began teaching ancient Oriental history. The opposition in certain circles to the appointment of a Jew to a university lectureship prompted the Russian government to cancel his post, and he was transferred to the department of Jewish literature and Oriental manuscripts at the Imperial Library in St. Petersburg. In 1877 he was made head of that department, remaining in that position for the rest of his life.

Harkavy started his literary and scientific work in 1861, publishing articles mainly in *Ha-Karmel* and *Ha-Meliẓ* on the natural and physical sciences and on current problems in education and literature. At about that time Harkavy started his research on the origin of the Jewish community in Russia. His efforts were part of the general efforts of the Wissenschaft des Judentums school to secure equality for Russian Jews. They based their claims on the ancient Jewish heritage in Russian language. Harkavy argued his theories in several essays and articles, and especially in his first Russian book, *O yazyke yevreyev,… i o slavyanskikh slovakh, vstrechayemykh u yevreyskikh pisateley* (1865), which also appeared in Hebrew as *Ha-Yehudim u-Sefat ha-Slavim* ("The Jews and the Slavic Language," 1867).

Harkavy claimed that the Jewish community in Russia was formed by Jews who migrated from the region of the Black Sea and Caucasia, where their ancestors had settled after the Assyrian and Babylonian exiles. These people, who preserved an ancient Jewish heritage, which they spread among the *Khazars, expanded through the Khazar kingdom westward to Czechoslovakia. Their spoken language was Slavic, at least from the ninth century on; not until the 17th century did it change to Yiddish, and that was because many Ukrainian Jews fled the 1648–49 pogroms to Poland, where Yiddish was spoken. This theory concerning the origins of Russian Jewry led to Harkavy's research into the history of the Khazars, the most important of which is his essay *Skazaniya yevreyskikh pisateley o khazarakh i khazarskom tsarstve* ("Jewish Authors' Reports on the Khazars and the Khazar Kingdom," 1874). The reports were few and sketchy but Harkavy showed uncanny knowledge and acumen in their interpretation.

An important part of his work was publishing Jewish manuscripts by Jewish authors that were in the possession of the St. Petersburg library, with his comments and critical notes. Among them were works by the later *geonim*, including Saadiah Gaon, Samuel b. Hophni, and Hai Gaon; and the Spanish sages, including Samuel ha-Nagid, Joseph ha-Nagid, Judah Halevi, and Abraham ibn Ezra. He also published manuscripts in the journals *Me'assef Niddaḥim* (16 issues, 1878–80) and *Ḥadashim Gam Yeshanim* (20 issues, 1886–1907); in the series of monographs he edited, *Zikkaron le-Rishonim ve-gam le-Aḥaronim* (7 issues, 1879–82), and in other publications.

Significant information in Jewish history is included in his comments on volumes three to eight of H. Graetz's *Geschichte der Juden*. Among the manuscripts he published were geonic responsa and the long version of "The Letter of King Joseph of the Khazars to R. Ḥisdai ibn Shaprut" and other manuscripts that the library acquired from the Karaite scholar Abraham Firkovich.

While working on Karaite documents it occurred to Harkavy that Firkovich had forged many of the manuscripts and tombstone epitaphs. He proved this claim in a series of articles and essays, of which the most significant were *Altjuedische Denkmaeler aus der Krim mitgetheilt von Abraham Firkowitsch 1839–1872* ("Ancient Jewish Monuments from Crimea…," 1876) and *"Po voprosu o iudeyskikh drevnostyakh naydennykh Firkovichem v Krymu"* ("On Jewish Antiquities Found by Firkovich in Crimea," in *Zhurnal Ministerstva narodnago prosveshcheniya*, 1877). Harkavy's keen, systematic analysis in this controversy placed him in the first rank of Jewish scholars of his time. Since Firkovich used his forgeries to obtain equality for the Karaites (but not for all the Jews) in Russia, Harkavy felt he was fighting for the whole of Jewry. The controversy escalated when the learned apostate Daniel *Chwolson of the University of St. Petersburg took Firkovich's side and defended his theories. Of his many articles about the Karaites the most significant are the one on Anan (in *Voskhod*, 1900) and his extensive research in *Ocherki istorii karaimstva* ("Notes on the History of the Karaites," 1896–1900).

Harkavy published in Russian a description of Samaritan scrolls of the Torah found in the St. Petersburg public library (1874), and with H.L. Strack a description in German of the Bibles found in Firkovich's collection (1875). He devoted a special essay in German, *"Neuaufgefundene hebraeische Bibelhandschriften"* (1884), to biblical manuscripts he acquired later. These descriptions are important from both paleographic and historical points of view, as the manuscripts contain various notes and comments added by the authors and copyists. Harkavy was esteemed by the czarist regime, and in the 1890s he was awarded a hereditary noble title and made an honorary member of several scientific societies in various countries. He was active in the Jewish community of St. Petersburg as the *gabbai* of the central synagogue and as a member of Mefiẓei

Haskalah be-Yisrael and Mekiẓei Nirdamim societies. A listing of his entire work through 1907, including 392 titles, was published by D. Magid with corrections and supplements by S.A. Poznański in a Festschrift published on the occasion of Harkavy's 70th birthday, *Zikkaron le-Avraham Eliyahu* (1908).

BIBLIOGRAPHY: Y. Guttman, in: *Ha-Shilo'aḥ*, 24 (1871), 161–70; S. Assaf, in: *Kobez al Jad*, 11 (1936), 191–243; Z. Harkavy, in: S.K. Mirsky (ed.), *Ishim u-Demuyyot be-Ḥokhmat Yisrael…* (1959), 116–36.

[Abraham N. Poliak]

HARKAVY, ALEXANDER (1863–1939), Yiddish lexicographer. A relative of the Orientalist and historian Albert *Harkavy and grandson of the rabbi of Novogrodek (Yid. Navaredok), Harkavy was born in that Belorussian town. He had a traditional Jewish education, showed an early interest in languages, and acquired some knowledge of Hebrew, Russian, Syriac, German, and Yiddish in his teens. In 1878 Harkavy went to Vilna, where he was befriended by the Yiddish author Isaac Meir *Dik and wrote his first work, in Yiddish. He earned a living as a bookkeeper for *Romm, the Hebrew-Yiddish publishing house. After the pogroms of 1881 Harkavy moved to Warsaw and joined the *Am Olam movement, before immigrating to the United States, intending to settle in a Jewish collective agricultural colony. When the project did not materialize, he worked as a stevedore, farm laborer, and dishwasher, studying English intensively and then tutoring English and Hebrew privately.

Harkavy's love of Yiddish soon crystallized into a vocation, but for about ten years his search for a steady income sent him wandering. He was in Paris in 1885, returned to New York in 1886, taught Hebrew at a *talmud torah* in Montreal in 1887, where he published the first Yiddish newspaper (*Di Tsayt*), went to Baltimore in 1889 and there founded the short-lived periodical *Der Yidisher Progres*, before returning once more to New York in 1890. A year later his first popular textbook, *Der Englisher Lerer* ("The English Teacher"), was published, of which almost 100,000 copies were sold. Through this and other books in the "English self-taught" genre, such as his guide to writing letters, *Der Englisher Brivnshteler* ("The English Letter-Writer," 1892), Yiddish translations of classics, classroom lectures and popular expositions of American history and culture, New York Yiddish literary anthologies (*Der Nayer Gayst*, "The New Spirit," 1897–98; *Der Tsvantsikster Yorhundert*, "The Twentieth Century," 1900), and above all his Yiddish dictionaries, he became the teacher par excellence of two generations of immigrants. He translated *Don Quijote* into Yiddish (1910) and revised the King James English Bible and translated it into Yiddish for a dual-language edition (1926). His popular expositions included *Columbus, Entdeker fun Amerike* ("Columbus, Discoverer of America," 1892). He taught U.S. history and politics for the New York Board of Education and Yiddish literature and grammar at the Jewish Teachers' Seminary in New York, while also lecturing for the Workmen's Circle. He wrote a column called "Kol-Boy" ("Everything in It") for the *Abend-Post* and occasional articles for many Yiddish, Hebrew, and English papers and journals. In 1935 he published *Perakim me-Ḥayyai* ("Autobiographic Chapters"). His most lasting achievements were, however, in lexicography. His English-Yiddish and Yiddish-English dictionaries, encompassing about 40,000 Yiddish words, went through two dozen editions and reprints. His crowning work was the *Yiddish-English-Hebrew Dictionary* (1925; suppl. 1928; fifth reprint 1988), which played a significant role in educating East European Jewish immigrants in English and is still an outstanding example of a multilingual dictionary used by Yiddish speakers and lexicographers.

BIBLIOGRAPHY: B.G. Richards, in: AJYB, 42 (1941), 153–64; Y. Mark, in: JBA, 26 (1968/69); I. Shatzky, *Harkavis bio-bibliografye* (1933); LNYL, 3 (1960). **ADD. BIBLIOGRAPHY:** A. Harkavy, *Yidish-Eynglish-Hebreisher Verterbukh*, ed. with introd. by D. Katz (1988).

[Mordkhe Schaechter / Jean Baumgarten (2nd ed.)]

HARKAVY, MINNA B. (1887–1987), U.S. sculptor, active in artistic and political circles. She is recognized for figurative sculptures with Expressionist tendencies that often address social issues in bronze, wood, and stone.

One of 10 surviving children born in Estonia to Yoel and Hannah Rothenberg, Harkavy immigrated to the United States in her early teens. She studied art in America and Europe, most notably with French sculptor Antoine Bourdelle, and showed her work at the Salon d'Automne and the Jeu de Paume in Paris. She graduated from Hunter College in Manhattan and married Louis Harkavy, a pharmacist who also published in Yiddish-language periodicals. Some of the artist's subjects were friends like art collector Leo Stein, singer Paul Robeson, and anarchist (and lover) Carlo Tresca. A copy of Harkavy's bust of Tresca was installed in his birthplace of Sulmona, Italy, after his 1943 assassination. Other works immortalize downtrodden or oppressed people, such as coalminers in the American Midwest and European Jews threatened by Hitler. Harkavy's celebrated bronze *American Miner's Family* (1931), owned by the Museum of Modern Art, features heads of the miner, his wife and children in a tableau of stoic resolve. The elongated terra cotta head of her *New England Woman*, displayed at the 1939 New York World's Fair, is reminiscent of African art and Modigliani. Harkavy's large stone sculpture *Two Men*, a comment on human communication, won first prize in a 1951 national sculpture competition held by the Metropolitan Museum of Art.

Harkavy was heavily involved in political advocacy and in organizing other artists. She was a founder of the New York Society of Women Artists in 1920, the American Artists' Congress, and the Sculptors' Guild, both in the 1930s. An activist in two languages, Harkavy represented the John Reed Club at a Communist anti-war conference in Amsterdam in 1932, and served on the Art Committee of the American Section of the Yidisher Kultur Farband (YKUF), the World Alliance for Yiddish Culture. Harkavy was deeply concerned with the fate of European Jewry. Her entry in the 1939 Sculptors' Guild Exhibition, *Lamentations: My Children Are Desolate Because the Enemy Prevailed*, portrays a mother with arms wrapped protectively around her child.

The artist participated in a variety of group exhibitions, including those organized by the Jewish Art Center in the 1920s and the John Reed Club in the 1930s, as well as at the Whitney Studio Club and, later, the Whitney Museum, from the 1920s to the 1950s. In the 1930s, she worked under the aegis of the WPA Fine Arts Program. A one-woman show was devoted to Harkavy at the Rhode Island School of Design in 1956. Her work is included in numerous prominent collections, including the Whitney and the Museum of Modern Art in New York, the Tel Aviv Museum, the Pushkin Museum in Moscow, the Hermitage in St. Petersburg, and several university museums. During her last decades, she taught students in her studio at the Ansonia Hotel in Manhattan. Harkavy died in New York, three months before her 100th birthday.

[Lauren B. Strauss (2nd ed.)]

ḤARLAP, JACOB MOSES BEN ZEBULUN (1883–1951), Ereẓ Israel rabbi. Ḥarlap was born in Jerusalem, where his father, who had emigrated from Poland, was a *dayyan* in the *bet din* of Moses Joshua Judah Leib Diskin. His main teacher was the Jerusalem scholar, Ẓevi Michael Shapira and under his influence Ḥarlap engaged in *Kabbalah and practiced asceticism. After Shapira's death, Ḥarlap published *Ẓevi la-Ẓaddik* (1907) in his memory, and arranged his writings for publication, publishing his halakhic work *Ẓiẓ ha-Kodesh* (two parts, 1920–51) with his own additions. When Rabbi A.I. *Kook arrived in Ereẓ Israel in 1904, Ḥarlap immediately came under his influence, and a bond of unusual intimacy developed between them which was strengthened by their common interest in Kabbalah and their leaning toward mysticism and poetic meditation. Ḥarlap was particularly attracted by Kook's thought which stressed the special role of the Jewish people as a whole, the sanctity of the Land of Israel, and the Zionist movement and its upbuilding of Ereẓ Israel – a first stage in the future messianic redemption.

When in 1908 the Sha'arei Ḥesed district of Jerusalem was established outside the Old City, Ḥarlap was appointed its rabbi. In 1912 he was appointed to the Eẓ Hayyim yeshivah. In 1918 he was one of the chief speakers at the meeting of the rabbis of Jerusalem with Chaim *Weizmann demanding that the Zionist movement confine itself to the political field, but he refused Weizmann's offer that he undertake the conduct of religious affairs in the *yishuv.* When the Merkaz ha-Rav yeshivah was founded in Jerusalem by Kook, Ḥarlap was invited to serve as head of the yeshivah and he continued in this post until his death. After the death of Rabbi Kook in 1935, many expected Ḥarlap to be chosen as chief rabbi, and in any case he was later regarded by many as his natural successor. On the establishment of the State of Israel Ḥarlap expressed orally and in writing his belief in "the beginning of the redemption"; at the same time he demanded an amelioration of religious standards. Ḥarlap never left Ereẓ Israel during his life and regarded it as a merit "that I never departed from holy confines and never [breathed] the air [or trod the] ground of the land of the gentiles."

Ḥarlap's main halakhic work is *Bet Zevul*, comprising his halakhic discourses, novellae on the Talmud and on Maimonides' *Mishneh Torah*, and halakhic responsa, in six parts, of which two were published in his lifetime (1942 and 1948) and the others between 1957 and 1966. His books on Jewish thought and religious meditation bear the general title *Mei Merom*. Seven volumes were published (1945 ff.), among them a discussion of Maimonides' *Shemonah Perakim*, tractate *Avot*, the High Holidays, and repentance. The central idea of these works is the need to purify one's heart, and sanctify one's life. The aim of the Torah is the perfection of man in thought and in action, the penetration of "the light and spark of holiness that dwells within the people of Israel" into "the depth of the nation's soul which will bring about the redemption." Among his other works are: *Hed ha-Ḥayyim ha-Yisre'eliyyim* (1912); *Tovim me-Orot* (1920), a defense of A.I. Kook's *Orot; El Am ha-Shem* (1943), some of his sermons and articles; *Imrei No'am* (1947), "words of comfort, and encouragement to the people of Israel"; and *Hed Harim* (1953), a collection of his letters to A.I. Kook.

BIBLIOGRAPHY: J.S. Rabinson, *Ha-Rav Rabbi Ya'akov Moshe Ḥarlap* (1936); S. Daniel, in: *Miẓpeh, Shenaton "Ha-Ẓofeh"* (1953), 645–70; J. Rubinstein, in: *Hadoar*, 32 (1953), 93; J. Gershony, *ibid.*, 40 (1961), 53–55; H. Lifschitz, in: *Sinai*, 32 (1953), 246–52; idem, in: S. Federbush (ed.), *Ḥazon Torah ve-Ẓiyyon* (1960), 287–303; S. Bornstein, in: *Sinai*, 43 (1958), 418–28; EZD, 2 (1960), 371–90; *Or ha-Mizraḥ*, 10 no. 3–4 (1962), 1–22; K.P. Tchursh, *ibid.*, 17 (1968), 77–80.

[Zvi Kaplan]

HARLAU (Rom. **Hârlău**), town in Moldavia, N.E. Romania. A Jewish settlement is known from 1742. In 1768 a Jew was authorized to establish a factory for window glass and a paper mill in Harlau. From 1751 the documents mention the "Jews' Guild," which in 1834 became the local community organization. The oldest of the five synagogues in Harlau was built in the 18th century. The community had a primary school (founded c. 1900), which was erected with the assistance of the *Jewish Colonization Association. There were also a *talmud torah*, a *mikveh*, and two Jewish cemeteries. Many Jews were *ḥasidim* of the *admor* of Pascani.

Antisemitic persecutions led half of the Jewish population of Harlau to immigrate to the United States during 1899–1900. However, at the same time Jews expelled from the villages settled in Harlau, so the Jewish population did not decrease. The community numbered 784 in 1803, 2,254 (56.6% of the total) in 1886, 2,718 (59%) in 1899, and 2,032 (22.3%) in 1930. The majority of both craftsmen and merchants enumerated in Harlau in 1913 were Jews. Following emancipation in 1919 the Jews took an active part in the municipal council. A small cooperative credit bank was founded in Harlau with the aid of the American Jewish Joint Distribution Committee. Rabbis of Harlau included Israel Isaacson (b. 1895), a deputy in the Romanian parliament, who settled in Israel.

The Zionist movement was also strong in the 1920s and 1930s. Three local Zionist leaders, Sami Stern-Kochavi, Michael Landau, and Valter Abeles (three brothers-in-law) became Jewish-Romanian political leaders in Israel in the 1950s. During World War II some of the Jews in Harlau were deported to Botosani, and others to Jassy. There were 1,936 Jews living in Harlau in 1947. In 1969 approximately 60 Jewish families were living there and they maintained a synagogue. In 2005, 22 elderly Jews lived in Harlau.

BIBLIOGRAPHY: M. Schwarzfeld, *Ochire asupra evreilor din România…* (1887), 38; E. Schwarzfeld, *Impopularea, reîmpopularea și întemeierea tîrgurilor și tîrgușoarelor in Moldova* (1914), 21, 22; S. Savin, in: *Revista cultului mozaic*, 19 (1965), no. 119; M. Carp, *Cartea Neagră* 1 (1946), 66, 158, 200, 202; PK Romanyah, 1 (1970), 112–4. **ADD. BIBLIOGRAPHY:** *Izvoare și marturi*, 2:1 (1998), 46; I. Bar-Avi, *Emigrarile anului, 1900* (1961), 117–8; Ch. Zaidman, *Der hob fun zikhron* (1982); M. Marcovici-Meridan, *Hirlau* (1993); FEDROM-*Comunitati evreiești din Romania* (Internet, 2005).

[Theodor Lavi / Lucian-Zeev Herscovici (2nd ed.)]

HARLOW, JULIUS (1931–), rabbi, liturgist, and editor. Born in Sioux City, Iowa, Harlow received his B.A. from Morningside College in Sioux City and then entered the Jewish Theological Seminary, where he was ordained in 1959. He then became associate director of the Rabbinical Assembly, the organization of Conservative rabbis.

Harlow carved out a unique place at the Rabbinical Assembly, working as the editor and chief liturgist for the Conservative movement for some four decades. He began as the secretary of a committee charged with editing a weekday prayer book. The project had lingered until the newly ordained Rabbi Harlow, working with the senior rabbis of the movement, brought it out within two years. It bore the marks of all his other liturgical work; a clarity of language and a crispness of style. By 1965 he had become the editor of the Rabbinical Assembly publications. Among his first project was a *Rabbi's Manual, Likute Tefiilah,* a small black book that rabbis brought with them to religious occasions, that contained the traditional liturgy. It won near universal acceptance in the movement and was used well beyond Conservative Judaism.

Harlow was sensitive to the twin revolutions of modern Jewish life: the Holocaust and the State of Israel, and the necessity of giving religious expression to both. This was clearly reflected in the *Maḥzor for Rosh Hashanah and Yom Kippur* (1972), in which he wove into the traditional matryology of *Eleh Ezkerah* themes of the Shoah, and composed the moving *Kaddish*, which used the dissonance between the well known words of the doxology and interspersed 17 – one less than *ḥai* (Heb. "life") – concentration camps and killing centers, the ghettoes and other sites of Jewish catastrophe, into the prayer. The insertion of these words and the places and experiences they represent means that even the most learned cannot recite the prayer by rote, and the magnification of the Divine name is brought down to earth, shattered by the painful reality of Jewish victimization.

His major project for the next decade was *Siddur Sim Shalom* (1985), which, unlike the widely used Silverman edition, could be used for weekdays as well as Sabbaths, and included many additional texts and readings. It is a complete *siddur* with readings and with *Pirkei Avot*. By 1994 a new version included a choice in the *Amidah* between including the Matriarchs or not, as the Conservative Movement became more egalitarian, more inclusive of women. Harlow was not pleased with some of the changes introduced into the *siddur* in the intervening decade. He objected in an essay published in the journal *Conservative Judaism*; Harlow noted that "changes based upon gender language referring to God disrupt the integrity of the classic texts of Jewish prayer, drive a wedge between the language of the Bible and the language of the prayerbook, and often misrepresent biblical and rabbinic tradition." A recent work, *Pray Tell: A Hadassah Guide to Prayer,* offers a wonderful guide to Jewish prayer representing many denominations. Even in retirement, Harlow continued his life calling, translating *Megilat Shoah* written by Avigdor Shinan of the Hebrew University, that seeks to formalize a text for reading on Yom Hashoah, primarily in the Conservative synagogue.

[Michael Berenbaum (2nd ed.)]

HARMAN (Herman), AVRAHAM (1914–1992), Israel diplomat and president of the Hebrew University. Born in London, Harman, who studied law at Oxford, settled in Palestine in 1938. From 1939 to 1940 he was in Johannesburg as a staff member of the South African Zionist Federation and then returned to Jerusalem to head the English Section of the Youth Department of the Jewish Agency. From 1942 to 1948 he was the head of the Information Department of the Agency, and after the establishment of the State of Israel Harman became deputy director of the Press and Information Division of the Israel Foreign Ministry. In 1949 he was appointed Israel consul-general in Montreal, Canada, and then became the director of the Israel Office of Information and counselor to the Israel delegation to the United Nations (1950–53). After a two-year period as the Israel consul-general in New York, Harman returned to Jerusalem in 1955 and was appointed a member of the Jewish Agency Executive, heading its Information Department. In 1959 he was appointed Israel ambassador to the United States, a post he held until 1968. His warm identification with the Jewish community and its problems brought him personal popularity wherever he served. Upon his return to Israel, Harman was appointed president of the Hebrew University, Jerusalem. He held that position until 1983, when he became university chancellor. The Institute for Contemporary Judaism and the chair of the Department of the History of the Jewish People at the Hebrew University are named for him. His wife, ZENA (1914–), was born in London and educated at the London School of Economics and Political Science. She served on several Israel delegations to the UN. In 1964 she was elected chairman of UNICEF (the United Nations Children's Emergency Fund). In 1969 she was elected to the Seventh Knesset on behalf of the Israel Labor Party.

HARMAN, JANE (1945–), U.S. politician, attorney, and college professor. Born in New York City to Adolph N. and Lucille (Geier) Lakes, Harman graduated from the Los Angeles public schools, Smith College (1966), and Harvard University Law School (1969). She married twice, to Richard Frank and to Sidney Harman, and had four children. The Harman family's wealth enabled her to mount costly campaigns. A six-term Democratic congresswoman, who represented the 36th congressional district of California in the United States House of Representatives, Harman was first elected to Congress in 1992. She gave up her seat in Congress in 1998 in an unsuccessful bid for governor of California. In 2002, upon her return, the House Democratic leadership appointed Harman to serve as ranking member on the Permanent Select Committee on Intelligence for the 108th Congress. As ranking member on the panel's Subcommittee on Terrorism and Homeland Security, Harman was at the forefront of all House actions made in response to the terrorist attack on the World Trade Center on September 11, 2001. Harman also served as a member of the House Select Committee on Homeland Security. Before her re-election to Congress in 2000, Harman was on the 10-member panel of the congressionally mandated National Council on Terrorism. Harman was fiscally moderate, but supported defense spending, thereby aiding defense and aerospace contractors in her district. She was a liberal on social issues, supporting abortion rights and pro-female and pro-child legislation.

Prior to being elected to the U.S. Congress, Harman was a lawyer, a staff member for California Senator John V. Tunney (1972–73), chief counsel and staff director of the U.S. Senate Judiciary Subcommittee on Constitutional Rights (1975–77), deputy secretary to the cabinet at the White House under President Jimmy Carter (1977–78), and special counsel to the Department of Defense (1979). An adjunct professor at Georgetown University Law Center (1974–75), Harman taught public policy and international relations at the University of California, Los Angeles where she was named Regents Professor in 1999.

BIBLIOGRAPHY: "Harman, Jane," in: K.F. Stone, *The Congressional Minyan: The Jews of Capitol Hill* (2000), 195–97; "Harman, Jane," in: P.E. Hyman and D. Dash Moore (eds.), *Jewish Women in America: An Historical Encyclopedia*, vol. 1 (1997), 594–95; "Harman, Jane," in: *Who's Who in America 2004*, vol. 1, 2158; *The Almanac of American Politics 2004*, 257–59. **WEBSITES:** www.house.gov/harman; www.congress.org/congressorg/bio.

[Peggy K. Pearlstein (2nd ed.)]

HARMATZ, WILLIAM ("**Willie**," "**Bill**"; 1931–), U.S. jockey, winner of the 1959 Preakness Stakes. Born in Wilkes Barre, Pa., the youngest of nine children and the son of a cattle buyer, Harmatz grew up in California, where he excelled as a gymnast and was a member of the Los Angeles All-City team. After graduating from high school, Harmatz started working at a racetrack, and a career was born. He won 1,770 races between 1953 and 1971, including 12 $100,000 events, and won six consecutive races on April 23, 1954. In 1959 Harmatz won the Preakness aboard Royal Orbit, after finishing fourth at the Kentucky Derby and before finishing third at the Belmont Stakes. He received the Jockey's Guild Meritorious Award in 1957 and the George Woolf Sportsmanship Award in 1960. Harmatz co-founded the Jockey's Association in 1968 and was its executive director from 1972 to 1978.

[Elli Wohlgelernter (2nd ed.)]

HARNICK, SHELDON (1924–), U.S. songwriter. Born and raised in Chicago, Harnick began studying the violin while in grammar school. After service in the army for three years, he enrolled in the Northwestern University School of Music and earned a bachelor of music degree in 1949. Though his focus had been on the violin, Harnick developed skills as a writer of comedy sketches, songs, and parody lyrics. By the early 1950s, Harnick had moved to New York to try his skill on Broadway. His first song in a Broadway show, "The Boston Beguine," for *New Faces of 1952*, introduced theatergoers to the wry, subtle humor and deft wordplay indicative of a Harnick lyric. For the next few years, he contributed lyrics and songs to several Broadway shows before he joined up with Jerry *Bock to write their own musicals. Their first, *The Body Beautiful*, was a moderate success, and in 1959 they wrote *Fiorello!*, about the legendary, half-Jewish, combative former mayor of New York City. It won the Pulitzer Prize, the Tony award, and Drama Critics' Circle award as best musical of the year. Next was *Tenderloin* in 1960, set in the seamy Tenderloin district of late 19th-century New York. That was followed in 1963 by *She Loves Me*, a musical set in a pre-World War II ice cream parlor in Budapest whose songs like "Vanilla Ice Cream" and "She Loves Me" became classics.

These shows were a prelude to Harnick and Bock's greatest success, *Fiddler on the Roof*, in 1964, starring Zero *Mostel as Tevya the dairyman with five daughters. Working with the director-choreographer Jerome *Robbins and the book writer, Joseph Stein, they created a musical masterpiece that vividly evoked a vanished community while telling a story with universal and timeless appeal. *Fiddler*, based on a series of short stories by *Shalom Aleichem, earned the Tony award and a gold record for both its Broadway cast album and film soundtrack recordings. In 1971, with the Broadway production still running, the film version, starring Chaim *Topol, was released and played worldwide. The following year the stage production, with such songs as "Tradition," "Sunrise, Sunset," Do You Love Me?," and "Matchmaker, Matchmaker, Find Me a Match," became the longest-running show in Broadway history with more than 3,000 performances, until that record was eclipsed in 1979. Over the years, the show has been performed thousands of times all over the world in dozens of languages, common and obscure.

After *Fiddler*, Bock and Harnick collaborated on *The Apple Tree* in 1966, three one-act musicals, and *The Rothschilds* (1970), a musical based on the founding of the banking dynasty. The partnership foundered at that point, but Harnick went on to collaborate with a number of well-known Broadway and film figures, including Richard *Rodgers, Mary *Rodgers, Michel Legrand, and Joe Raposo. Harnick also provided English-language librettos for classical operas and oratorios, including works by Stravinsky, Ravel, Mozart, Bach, and Verdi. He also wrote the theme songs for two films, both with music by Cy *Coleman: *The Heartbreak Kid* in 1972 and *Blame It on Rio* in 1984.

[Stewart Kampel (2nd ed.)]

HARO (**Faro**), city in Castile, northern Spain. A charter (*fuero*) given to the city by Alfonso VIII (1158–1214) granted the Jews in Haro, who had aided him during the war against Navarre, a series of privileges which included arrangements concerning their security, the indemnity to be paid for the murder of a Jew, and release from various taxes. In the 13th century the community of Haro was the largest in the region of La Rioja. Around 1,000 Jews lived then in the town. Jews were permitted to fish in the river, to establish mills, and to engage in dyeing. Many Jews owned land, particularly vineyards. The *fuero* was later endorsed by Sancho IV (1284–95) and Ferdinand IV (1295–1312). Alfonso settled some Jews in the fortress but they also lived in the unwalled sections of the city. In 1305 they were authorized to choose their own judges in suits involving members of different faiths. The Jews of Haro were not directly hit by the 1391 massacres, but following the persecutions and the war of succession between Pedro I and Enrique of Trastámara the community declined drastically. An organized community continued to exist throughout the 15th century. In the second half of the 15th century some 250–300 Jews lived in Haro constituting no less than 10% of the general population. Jews owned lands and vineyards which they leased to Christians and Muslims. Some were potters. Prominent in the 15th century were the tax farmer Don Solomon Zadik and Samuel Cubo who represented the community in 1476 in a dispute with the town council regarding pasture land and the slaughterhouse. A census in 1492 at the time of the expulsion of the Jews from Spain showed that the community numbered 48 taxpayers who possessed 55 houses in the Mota quarter.

From the 12th century the Jews lived in the castle called "de la Mota." In the course of time it expanded and included adjacent areas. There are no remains of the Jewish quarter.

BIBLIOGRAPHY: Baer, Spain, index; Baer, Urkunden, index; D. Hergueta, *Noticias históricas de la Ciudad de Haro* (1906), 61, 208, 242, 267; Cantera, in: *Sefarad*, 2 (1942), 327; 22 (1962), 87ff.; León Tello, *ibid.*, 15 (1955), 157–69; Suárez Fernández, Documentos, 68, 76. G. Martínez Díez, ed. "Fueros de la Rioja," in: *Anuario de historia del derecho español*, 49 (1979), 373–74; 437–39.

[Haim Beinart]

ḤAROSET (Heb. חֲרוֹסֶת), paste made of fruit, spices, nuts, and wine which forms part of the *seder* rite on *Passover eve. It is symbolic of the mortar that the Jews made when they were slaves in Egypt. The word is of unknown origin. It has been suggested that it may stem from *ḥeres* (חֶרֶס, "clay"), because of the color resemblance. The ingredients vary in different communities; in most western countries, it is made of apples, chopped almonds, cinnamon, and red wine. In many Sephardi communities, however, the fruits, etc. that grew in Ereẓ Israel in Bible times – grapes, wheat (*maẓẓah* meal), dates, figs, olives, apricots, pomegranates, and almonds – are used. North Africans also include pine-nuts and hardboiled eggs, flavoring the paste with piquant and often pungent spices, such as ginger. Yemenites add other seasoning: e.g., chili pepper. In Israel, the bland occidental mixture is turned into a dessert by adding bananas, dates, candied peel, orange juice, and sugar. It is often served as a course of the meal.

BIBLIOGRAPHY: M. Kasher, *Haggadah Shelemah* (1955), 62–64.

[Molly Lyons Bar-David]

HAROSHETH-GOIIM (Heb. חֲרֹשֶׁת הַגּוֹיִם), biblical locality, the seat of *Sisera, commander of the army of Jabin king of Canaan (Judg. 4:2). When Sisera heard that *Barak was assembling his army at Mount Tabor, he advanced from Harosheth-Goiim to the brook of Kishon, where Barak defeated him and drove his army back to Harosheth-Goiim (*ibid.* 4: 12–16). Various scholars have proposed to identify the site with either Khirbat al-Harbaj or Tell al-ʾAmar near al-Ḥārithiyya. These identifications, however, are disputed by B. Mazar, who argues that Harosheth-Goiim is not the name of a city but a general term designating the forested regions of central Galilee (cf. *Gelil ha-goyim*, "Galilee of the nations," Isa. 8:23), over which Sisera attempted to impose his rule. The root חרש in Hebrew and related languages means "forest"; the Septuagint also translates Harosheth as *drymos*, "forest" (Judg. 4: 16).

BIBLIOGRAPHY: Abel Geog, 2 (1938), 343f.; Maisler (Mazar), in: HUCA, 24 (1953), 81–84; Y. Aharoni, *Hitnaḥalut Shivtei Yisrael ba-Galil ha-Elyon* (1957), 101f.; Aharoni, Land, index.

[Michael Avi-Yonah]

HARRAN (**Hirsch**), **DON** (1936–), Israeli musicologist. Born in the United States, Harran received his B.A. degree at Yale University in Romance languages, and then gained his M.A. and Ph.D. in musicology at Berkeley. In 1965 he settled in Israel and was among the small group of founders of the Musicology Department at the Hebrew University of Jerusalem, the first in the country, and became full professor in 1979. He was chair of the department, president of the Israeli Musicological Society, and vice president of the International Musicological Society. Harran earned a high international reputation as a meticulous, prolific, and original researcher. His primary area of specialization was the music of the Renaissance and early Baroque. His publications include more than a hundred articles and editions of late Italian madrigals and books on humanism in Italy, most importantly, *Word-Tone Relations in Musical Thought: From Antiquity to the Seventeenth Century* (Musicological Studies & Documents, 40, Neuhausen-Stuttgart: Hänssler-Verlag for the American Institute of Musicology, 1986). His life-long project has been the monumental critical edition of the music of Salamone Rossi (c. 1570–c. 1628), the great Jewish composer, on whom he also published an extensive monograph: *Salamone Rossi, Jewish Musician in Late Renaissance* (Mantua, Oxford University Press, 1999). In recent years he has focused on the research of Jewish music in later periods, as well as on studies of the setting of Psalm verses.

[Jehoash Hirshberg (2nd ed.)]

HARRIS, BARBARA (**Sandra Markowitz**; 1937–), U.S. actress. Born in Evanston, Illinois, Harris attended the Goodman Theater School and the University of Chicago. Generally acknowledged as one of the pioneering women in the field of improvisational theater, Harris began her career with the famous Second City improvisation troupe. She moved from there to Broadway, where she won a Tony Award for Best Actress for her performance in the musical *The Apple Tree* (1967). Her other Broadway performances were *From the Second City* (1961); *Mother Courage and Her Children* (1963); and *On a Clear Day You Can See Forever* (1965). She also starred in a stage production of *Oh Dad, Poor Dad ...*, for which she won a Theater World Award in 1962.

Harris made her film debut in the bittersweet comedy *A Thousand Clowns* (1965) and went on to star in such films as *Oh Dad, Poor Dad...* (1967), *Plaza Suite* (1971), *Who Is Harry Kellerman and Why Is He Saying Those Terrible Things About Me?* (1971), *The War between Men and Women* (1972), *Mixed Company* (1974), *Nashville* (1976), *Freaky Friday* (1976), *Movie Movie* (1978), *The Seduction of Joe Tynan* (1979), *The North Avenue Irregulars* (1979), *Second-Hand Hearts* (1981), *Peggy Sue Got Married* (1986), *Dirty Rotten Scoundrels* (1988), and *Grosse Pointe Blank* (1997).

[Jonathan Licht / Ruth Beloff (2nd ed.)]

HARRIS, CYRIL KITCHENER (1936–), chief rabbi of the Union of Orthodox Synagogues, South Africa, 1988–2004. Born in Glasgow, Harris served as a rabbi in London (1958–87) before moving to South Africa. During his U.K. period, he also served as senior Jewish chaplain to Her Majesty's Forces (1966–71), as national director of the B'nai B'rith Hillel Foundation (1972–75), as chairman of the Rabbinical Association of the United Synagogue (1978–82) and as joint chairman of Mizrachi, Great Britain (1984–85). As South African chief rabbi, he was prominently involved in speaking out against the country's then racial policies and, with the commencement of the process of political reform, was at the forefront of Jewish leaders encouraging the Jewish community to identify with the new democratic dispensation. He was the co-founder of MaAfrika Tikkun, the Jewish community's initiative in respect of uplifting the disadvantaged in South Africa. Awards received included the Distinguished Leadership Award of the South African Jewish Board of Deputies (1997), the Commonwealth Jewish Council Award (2000, awarded jointly with his wife, Ann), the Jerusalem Prize for Communal Leadership (2002), and the International Keren Hayesod IUA & UCF Honorary Award (2004). Publications include *The Jewish Obligation to the Non-Jew* (1996) and *For Heaven's Sake: The Chief Rabbi's Diary* (autobiography, 2000).

[David Saks (2nd ed.)]

HARRIS, SIR DAVID (1852–1942), South African mining magnate, soldier, and politician. A cousin of Barney *Barnato, Harris went to South Africa from London in 1871, and made on foot the 600-mile journey from Durban to the diamond mines at Kimberley, where he worked for a time as a digger. His marriage to Rosa Gabriel in 1873 was the first Jewish wedding to take place in Kimberley. He became associated with Cecil Rhodes, and from 1897 to 1931 was a director of De Beers Consolidated Mines, founded by Rhodes and Barnato. On Barnato's death in 1897, Harris was elected to his seat in Parliament, where for 32 years he was esteemed as an authority on the diamond industry. Harris fought in several frontier wars in the Cape Colony, rising to the rank of lieutenant colonel. In the Boer War (1899–1902) he commanded the town guard of Kimberley during the historic 125-day siege. He was mentioned in dispatches and decorated for his services. Later he was knighted. Harris was one of the founders of the Griqualand West Hebrew Congregation and was its president for many years. His benefactions to the community included the site on which the Kimberley synagogue was built in 1875. In Parliament he frequently spoke on immigration and other matters of Jewish concern. Known as the "grand old man" of Kimberley, Harris told the story of his life in *Pioneer, Soldier and Politician* (1931). His Anglo-Boer War career is described in "Sir David Harris – Hero of the Siege of Kimberley," in: *Jewish Affairs*, vol. 54, no. 3 (1999).

[Louis Hotz]

HARRIS, JED (**Jacob Horowitz**; 1900–1979), U.S. theatrical producer. Born in Vienna, Harris was taken to the U.S. as a child. His first big success, *Broadway* (1926), had a three-year run. Other productions included *The Front Page* (1928), *Uncle Vanya* (1930), *The Inspector General* (1930), *Our Town* (1938), *A Doll's House* (1938), *The Heiress* (1948), and *The Crucible* (1953). At one period he had four successes running on Broadway and was reputed to have amassed and lost more than five million dollars. Regarded as an "irascible genius," Harris was the hero in Ben Hecht's novel *A Jew in Love* (1931) and Frederic Wakeman's *The Saxon Charm* (1947). Harris wrote *Watchman, What of the Night?* (1963) and *A Dance on the High Wire: Recollections of a Time and a Temperament* (1979).

ADD. BIBLIOGRAPHY: M. Gottfried, *Jed Harris: The Curse of Genius* (1984)

HARRIS, LOUIS (1921–), U.S. pollster and author. Harris was born in New Haven, Connecticut. He was educated at the University of North Carolina where he received his B.A. in economics (1942) and then entered the Navy. He was later trained in polling by Elmo Roper of Roper Poll fame, drafting columns and newspaper articles and learning the craft of the then emerging science. Harris formed his own firm, Louis Harris and Associates in 1956 and served as the pollster and political advisor for John F. Kennedy's presidential bid of 1960. In the next few years his influence broadened as he became the chief pollster for CBS News, later switching to ABC News. He simultaneously served as a newspaper columnist for such publications as the *Washington Post*, *Newsweek*, the *Chicago Tribune*, and New York's *Daily News*. The Harris poll became widely recognized, while polling itself became an indispensable and increasingly precise part of every political campaign and essential to business planning and marketing. With the advent of the computer, the processing of information became easier and the availability of information to process ever greater. Louis Harris and Associates advised candidates for public office at every level; both Democrats and Republicans are among clients who made use of their marketing services.

Harris left Louis Harris and Associates in 1992 and formed his own research firm, LH Research. He wrote many books and countless studies, some public and some quite private. From his publications one can note a particular interest in the racial issues that gripped the United States in the 1960s and the strained ties between the African American community and the Jews.

[Michael Berenbaum (2nd ed.)]

HARRIS, MARK (1922–), U.S. novelist and critic. Harris received a Ph.D. in 1957 from the University of Minnesota. He is best known for his books about baseball players, notably the Henry Wiggen novels: *The Southpaw* (1953); *Bang the Drum Slowly* (1956), which was made into a film in 1973; A *Ticket for a Seamstitch* (1957); and *It Looked Like For Ever* (1979). Harris also wrote "problem" novels such as *Trumpet to the World* (1946), *Something About a Soldier* (1957), and *Wake Up, Stupid* (1959). *City of Discontent* (1952) dealt with Vachel Lindsay, and *Friedman and Son* (1963) was a play about the conflicts of Jewish life. His novel *The Goy*, about a gentile professor grappling with the meaning of historical writing as well as the meaning of his own life, including his response to Jews, was published in 1970. His study of Bellow, *Saul Bellow, Drumlin Woodchuck*, was published in 1980. His autobiographical reflections can be found in *Mark the Glove Boy, or the Last Days of Richard Nixon* (1964), *Twentyone Twice: A Journal* (1966) and *Best Father Ever Invented: The Autobiography of Mark Harris* (1976). His novel *Speed* was published in 1990, followed by *Diamond: Baseball Writings of Mark Harris* (1994). He also edited *The Heart of Boswell* (1981).

[Lewis Fried (2nd ed.)]

HARRIS, MARVIN (1927–2001), U.S. anthropologist. Born in New York City, educated at Columbia University (A.B., 1949; Ph.D., 1953), Harris taught at Columbia from 1952 to 1981 and was graduate research professor at the University of Florida from 1981 until his retirement in 2000.

Marvin Harris was one of the originators of the anthropological theory known as cultural materialism and is perhaps the scholar most closely associated with it. He first proposed this approach in his book *The Rise of Anthropological Theory* (1968), which rejected the then dominant structuralist approaches associated with *Durkheim and *Levi-Strauss and their followers, which attribute changes in cultural development to changes in ideas rather than to material necessity. Cultural materialism, in attempting to account for the evolution of sociocultural systems, holds that the values and practices of a culture develop from the interaction of technology, the environment, population levels, and basic biological needs. Institutions like religion, law, or kinship systems – or human sacrifice, or the prohibition against eating cows or pigs – must have some function that gives a society a material advantage in its environment, or they would not have developed. Critics claim that cultural materialism is too deterministic and reductive, trying to explain too many diverse cultural phenomena too simply, but its fundamental insight – that societies are shaped by their material needs – has been incorporated into anthropological discourse, though the theory as a whole remains somewhat controversial. Its primary intellectual ancestors are Marx and Malthus, but it draws upon other sources as well.

Harris was concerned to participate in public debate, and most of his books were in fact written for a nonscholarly audience. Among his works for the general public are *Cows, Pigs, Wars, and Witches: The Riddles of Culture* (1974), *Cannibals and Kings: The Origins of Cultures* (1977), *Cultural Materialism: The Struggle for a Science of Culture* (1979), *Why Nothing Works: The Anthropology of Daily Life* (1983), *Good to Eat: Riddles of Food and Culture* (1986), and *The Sacred Cow and the Abominable Pig* (1987). His more scholarly work includes *Town and Country in Brazil* (1956), *Portugal's "Wards": A First-Hand Report on Labor and Education in Moçambique* (1958), *Minorities in the New World: Six Case Studies* (1958), *The Nature of Cultural Things* (1964), *Patterns of Race in the Americas* (1964), *The Rise of Anthropological Theory: A History of Theories of Culture* (1968), *Death, Sex, and Fertility: Population Regulation in Preindustrial and Developing Societies* (1987, with Eric B. Ross), *Food and Evolution: Toward a Theory of Human Food Habits* (1987, with Eric B. Ross), and *Theories of Culture in Postmodern Times* (1999).

[Drew Silver (2nd ed.)]

HARRIS, MAURICE (1859–1939), U.S. rabbi and communal worker. Born in London, he came to the United States at 10 and entered the business world. He studied at Columbia University earning his B.A. (1887), M.A. (1888), and Ph.D. (1889). He was ordained at Temple Emanu-El Theological Seminary, a short-lived affiliate of the famed New York Congregation (1884) and became the rabbi of Temple Israel in Harlem. His most important work was with the immigrant population. He was a founder of the Jewish Board of Guardians, the New York Society for the Prevention of Crime and a founder and president of the Federation Settlement and the Jewish Projectory, an organization designed to facilitate the successful absorption of the immigrants who flooded New York beginning in 1881. He was the author of several books, among them *History of the Medieval Jews* (1924), *The People of the Book*, 3 volumes (1929–1933), *Modern Jewish History* (1910, 1924, 1928), *Modern Jewish History from the Renaissance to the World War* (1922), *The Story of the Jew* (1919), *The Story of the Jew in America* (1921); and *A Thousand Years of Jewish History* (1927).

BIBLIOGRAPHY: K.M. Olitzsky, L.J. Sussman and M.H. Stern *Reform Judaism in America: A Biographical Dictionary and Sourcebook* (1993).

HARRIS, MILTON (1906–1991), U.S. polymer and textile chemist. Born in Portland, Oregon, at the age of 16 Harris received his B.S. from Oregon State University (OSU) in chemical engineering and his Ph.D. in chemistry from Yale University in 1929. Harris spent a large part of his career in commercial research. In 1931 Harris was one of the founders of the institute for the study of textiles at the National Bureau of Standards. Their work resulted in fibers that were water-repellent, flameproof, and rotproof. He helped develop processes for permanent press in woolen goods and wash-and-wear cotton finishing. His work led ultimately to the development of synthetic polymers such as nylon, polyester, and plastics. He was director of research at the Textile Research Institute in 1938–44. In 1945 he founded his own research laboratory, which later became a subsidiary of the Gillette Company. He was director of research and vice president of Gillette from 1956 until his retirement in 1966. He was chairman of the American Institute of Chemists (1961–62) and later chairman of its board of directors. He edited *Handbook of Textile Fibers* (1954), and the dyes and textile section of *Chemical Abstracts* (1949–61). In addition to the Milton Harris Chair at OSU, his gifts have supported three scholarships, two teaching grants, and awards in chemistry, biochemistry, and basic research. His last major financial gift to OSU was a trust fund that will provide an endowment of roughly $2 million for the Department of Chemistry.

[Bracha Rager (2nd ed.)]

HARRIS, SIR PERCY ALFRED (1876–1952), English politician. Born in London and educated at Harrow and Cambridge, Harris was admitted to the bar in 1899, although by profession he was engaged in his father's mercantile business which traded with New Zealand. Harris retained a lifelong interest in that country, and published *New Zealand and Its Politics* in 1909. He traveled around the world three times and lived in New Zealand for three years. From 1907 to 1934 and from 1946 until his death he was a member of the London County Council and served as its deputy chairman from 1915 to 1916. In that year he returned to parliament as Liberal member for Harborough. Harris was elected for a second time in 1922 and sat continuously until 1945 when he retired. He was made a baronet in 1932 and from 1940 to 1945 was deputy leader of the Liberal Party in the House of Commons. His publications include *London and Its Government* (originally written in 1913 and rewritten in 1931) and an autobiography, *Forty Years In and Out of Parliament* (1947).

BIBLIOGRAPHY: ODNB online.

[William D. Rubinstein (2nd ed.)]

HARRIS, SAM HENRY (1872–1941), U.S. theatrical manager. Born in New York, Harris produced many successful plays. Several of them won Pulitzer Prizes, such as *Icebound* (1923) by Owen Davis and *Of Thee I Sing* (1931) by George S. *Kaufman. His partnership with playwright George M. Cohan lasted 15 years and resulted in the production of about 50 plays. Among them were the Broadway successes *The Music Box Revue* (1921), *Rain* (1922), and *The Jazz Singer* (1925). In 1929 Harris lost a considerable fortune but managed to recoup it with *Once in a Lifetime* (1930) and Moss *Hart's Pulitzer Prize-winning *You Can't Take It with You* (1936).

Harris was considered one of the great gentlemen of the theater, renowned for his fairness and kindness to actors, writers, and others involved in show business. One of the Great White Way's most prolific independent producers, Harris presented more than 130 Broadway plays and musicals. They include *The Talk of New York* (1908), *The Little Millionaire* (1911), *Hamlet* (1922), *The Cocoanuts* (starring the Marx Brothers, 1925), *Chicago* (1926), *Animal Crackers* (starring the Marx Brothers, 1928), *Dinner at Eight* (1932), *Of Mice and Men* (1937), and *The Man Who Came to Dinner* (1939). Later productions performed in the theater owned and operated by the Estate of Sam H. Harris include *I Remember Mama* (1944), *Lost in the Stars* (1949), and *Five Finger Exercise* (1959).

[Ruth Beloff (2nd ed.)]

HARRIS, SYDNEY (1917–), Canadian jurist, Jewish community leader. Harris was born in Toronto in 1917. He received his B.A. from the University of Toronto in 1939 and a law degree from Osgoode Law School in 1942. He was called to the Bar that same year. For 34 years Harris was a leading criminal lawyer appearing in courts at every level of the judicial system, including the Supreme Court of Canada. He was then appointed a judge in the Ontario Provincial Court. Among his more controversial cases was the 1978 trial of a gay Toronto newspaper charged with two different obscenity violations under the Canadian Criminal Code. In a decision still hailed as a major step in the struggle for gay rights and freedom of the press in Canada, Harris found the newspaper not guilty on both charges. After retiring from the bench in 1992, he served as a deputy judge, a member of the Ontario Assessment Review Board, and a member of the Council of Ontario Land Surveyors.

Harris was one of Canada's foremost postwar Canadian Jewish community leaders. As a member of the Canadian Jewish Congress for 60 years, Harris served as chair of Community Relations in the 1960s and as national president from 1974 to 1977. He was instrumental in lobbying the Canadian government on behalf of Soviet Jews and was a major proponent of hate propaganda legislation and active in the anti-Nazi campaign in Toronto in the 1960s. Harris also served as president of several other organizations, including the Jewish Vocational Service, Upper Canada Lodge of B'nai B'rith Canada, and the Canadian Council of Reform Congregations. In later years, he provided counsel to the leadership of the Canadian Jewish Congress. Harris was honored with the 1967 Confederation Centennial Medal and the 1973 Queen's Jubilee Medal.

[Frank Bialystok (2nd ed.)]

HARRIS, ZELLIG SABBETAI (1909–1992), U.S. linguist. Harris was born in Russia and was taken to the United States as a child of four. He graduated from the University of Pennsylvania and joined the faculty there in 1931. In 1946 he founded the first linguistics department in the country and in 1947 was appointed professor of linguistics. One of his best-known students was Noam *Chomsky.

In the late 1930s his interests shifted from Semitics to general linguistics. His early work was devoted primarily to the development of procedures of linguistic analysis. At the time, he wrote *Development of the Canaanite Dialects* (1939). His purpose was to devise a set of precisely formulated methods which, applied to data of a particular language, would yield a grammatical description of this language. This was completed in the late 1940s, and Harris then turned his attention to the study of connected discourse. He observed that formal operations of a general nature could be applied to the utterances of a discourse, reducing it to a "normalized" form. Procedures analogous to those of structural linguistics could then be applied, finally yielding a structural analysis of the discourse. This work led to an intensive investigation of the properties of the formal operations ("transformations"). Other investigations resulted in the development of computer programs for the analysis of language structure, many studies of the detailed properties of English syntax, and more abstract investigation of the formal properties of linguistic structures.

Harris helped to develop the adult education program for Israeli kibbutzim centered in Givat Ḥavivah.

Harris' major publications on his work are *Methods in Structural Linguistics* (1951), *String Analysis of Sentence Structure* (1962), *Discourse Analysis Reprints* (1963), *Mathematical Structures of Language* (1968), *The Form of Information in Science* (1989), and *A Theory of Language and Information* (1992). His book *The Transformation of Capitalist Society* was produced posthumously from a completed manuscript prepared for publication by M. Eden, W. Evan, and S. Melman (1997).

ADD. BIBLIOGRAPHY: B. Nevin and S. Johnson (eds.), *The Legacy of Zellig Harris: Language and Information into the 21st Century* (2002).

[Noam Chomsky / Ruth Beloff (2nd ed.)]

HARRISBURG, capital city of Pennsylvania. Of a total population of 251,798 in Harrisburg City (48,950) and the surrounding Dauphin County, there were an estimated 5,164 Jews (according to a 1994 demographic survey). Cumberland County, across the Susquehanna River, had an estimated 1,821 Jews out of a population of 213,674. The first Jewish settlers in Harrisburg were immigrants from Germany and England; they arrived in the 1840s and assembled regularly for Sabbath and holiday services under the leadership of Lazarus Bernhard. In 1853, this group drew up the constitution for the first synagogue, Ohev Sholom, which was Orthodox until 1867, when it adopted Reform. Rabbi Philip David Bookstaber, spiritual head of the congregation from 1924 to 1962, was a leader of the Boy Scouts of America. Other congregations that formed since then were Chisuk Emuna (1884), now Traditional Conservative; Cong. Kesher Israel (1902), the leading Orthodox institution in central Pennsylvania; Temple Beth El (1926), egalitarian Conservative; and Machzike Hadas (1904), now known as Chabad-Lubavitch (ḥasidic). Other area synagogues include B'nai Jacob Synagogue, Conservative (on the National Registry of Historic Places), founded in 1906 in nearby Middletown (Dauphin County); Cong. Beth Shalom (1970), Reconstructionist, in Mechanicsburg; and Cong. Beth Tikvah, egalitarian, Carlisle, both in Cumberland County. Eliezer *Silver, who served as rabbi of Kesher Israel from 1907 to 1925, founded many of the community's services, including the Harrisburg Hebrew School, a *talmud torah*; the Hebrew Free Loan Society; and the Transient Home. Yeshiva Academy, providing secular and Jewish education to children from preschool through eighth grade, was one of the first Jewish day schools in the country outside a major metropolitan area. It was established (and renamed for) Rabbi David L. Silver, rabbi of Kesher Israel, and Aaron S. Feinerman. The Jewish Community Center was founded in 1915 as a YMHA, by Leon Lowengard; its name was changed in 1941, and it has occupied its current building since 1956. The Jewish Federation of Greater Harrisburg was formed in 2002 through the consolidation of the United Jewish Community (founded in 1933) and the Jewish Community Center. The Federation serves as the central fundraising agency, speaks officially for the community on both Jewish matters and Jewish-gentile community relations, promotes the quality and values of Jewish life, and publishes the biweekly newspaper *Community Review*. Agencies supported by the Federation include the Jewish Family Service, the Jewish Group Home (for the developmentally disabled), the Jewish Home, and The Residence, a senior living community on the campus of the Home. David Silver, rabbi of Kesher Israel from 1932 to 1983, was the driving force (with Horace Goldberger) of the Jewish Home. In addition to afternoon schools at a few area congregations, the Federation sponsors the Harrisburg Hebrew High School for public school students. The Harrisburg Jewish community had the highest per capita donation in the country to the UJA emergency fund during Israel's Six-Day War. For decades its leading philanthropist was businesswoman Mary Sachs, known as the "Merchant Princess." The late David Javitch founded the Giant Food Stores chain with one meat market in Carlisle in 1923; in 1968 his son Lee (now retired) took over as president of the chain, now a part of Ahold U.S.A. Companies.

Other community leaders have included Albert Hursh (d. 2004), who served the JCC and Federation professionally for eight decades; Rite Aid Corporation founder Alex Grass, who has served as chair of the Board of Governors of the Hebrew University of Jerusalem, member of the board of United Jewish Appeal, and member and past chair of the Board of Governors of the Jewish Agency for Israel; and Lois Lehrman Grass, philanthropist and patron of the arts.

Until the 1940s most Jews were engaged in the merchandising of food, clothing, and furniture; the scrap business; and peddling. In the 1960s, many were engaged in manufacturing clothing, food distribution, retail merchandising, the professions, and state government positions. In 1958 attorney Gilbert Nurick was the first Jew to head the State Bar Association. The first community college in the state, Harrisburg Area Community College, was established mainly because of the efforts of Bruce E. Cooper, chairman of its board. In 1969, William Lipsitt became the first Jewish judge of a county court. By the 1990s, most Jews were found in the professions and state government positions.

[Barbara Trainin Blank (2nd ed.)]

HARRISON, LEON (1866–1928), U.S. rabbi. Born in Liverpool England, Harrison immigrated to the United States with his parents and studied in public schools, the City College of New York, and Columbia University. He then attended the Congregation Emanu-El Theological Seminary and was ordained by Kaufmann Kohler and Gustav Gottheil. His first pulpit was in Brooklyn and later he officiated in St. Louis. He first introduced Sunday services in St. Louis and later abandoned them for late Friday evening services. Deeply concerned socially, he was vice president of the Anti-Tuberculosis Society, director of the Tenement House Improvement Association, and a founder of the Social Settlement League and the Fresh Air Society in St. Louis. A wonderful preacher he delivered a eulogy at the funeral of Henry Ward Beecher and also gave the McKinley memorial address at the St. Louis Coliseum. He was the co-editor of the Semitics section of the *Editor's Encyclopedia*. A posthumous publication of his sermons was titled *The Religion of the Modern Liberal.*

BIBLIOGRAPHY: American Jewish Year Book, 5 (1903); *Universal Jewish Encyclopedia*; K. Olitzsky, I. Sussman, and M.H. Stern, *Reform Judaism in American: A Biographical Dictionary and Sourcebook* (1993).

[Michael Berenbaum (2nd ed.)]

HARRISON, LESTER ("**Les**"; 1904–1997), U.S. basketball coach, owner, and organizer; member of the Basketball Hall of Fame. Born and raised in Rochester, New York, "Laizer" Harrison began a lifelong involvement with basketball as a player at East High School and in the inaugural New York State Section V Basketball tournament in 1922, Harrison scored 18 points in his team's 22–18 victory over West High. Harrison played, coached, organized, and promoted professional basketball in New York State for the Rochester Seagrams, Ebers, and Pros from the 1920s through the 1940s, before forming a semi-pro team, the Rochester Pros, with his brother Jack in 1944. The next year the team – renamed the Rochester Royals – began playing in the National Basketball League, where Harrison coached the team to a 99–39 record and three straight NBL finals, winning the championship as well as being named Coach of the Year in 1946. Harrison led the way for a merger of professional basketball leagues by joining the Basketball Association of America for the 1948–49 season, leading the Royals to a 45–15 record, going 33–1 at home and getting to the finals. After the season the NBL merged into the BAA to form one league, the National Basketball Association. The Royals won the NBA championship in 1951, making Harrison the first of five Jewish coaches to win the NBA title. He stepped down as coach after the 1954–55 season, leaving with a six-season NBA record of 250–166, and a 10-season coaching career record of 394–220, along with five divisional titles. Harrison moved the Royals to Cincinnati before the 1957–58 season and sold the team the following year. Harrison was a member of the NBA's Rules Committee and Board of Directors, and was elected to the Hall of Fame in 1980.

[Elli Wohlgelernter (2nd ed.)]

HARRISSE, HENRY (1829–1910), U.S. historiographer. Born in Paris, Harrisse immigrated to the United States in 1849. After teaching in South Carolina, he became professor of French at the University of North Carolina and simultaneously prepared for the bar at its Law School. In 1857, he settled in Chicago and four years later in New York, dividing his time between the practice of law and writing on philosophy, French literature, and historiography. In New York, he met Samuel Barlow, the eminent attorney and Americana bibliophile, who stimulated his interest in the period of discovery. Together they published *Notes on Columbus* (1866). Harrisse's *Bibliotheca Americana Vetustissima*, which evaluated every book referring to America from 1493 to 1551 (1866; repr. 1922, 1958), established his reputation and, when he returned to Paris (1866) to practice law, he was acknowledged as an authority in American studies.

Among his other books on the period of discovery are: *Notes pour servir à l'histoire, à la bibliographie et à la cartographie de la Nouvelle-France et des pays adjacents, 1545–1700* (1872); *Ferdnand Colomb, sa vie, ses œuvres…* (1872); *Christophe Colomb, son origine, sa vie, ses voyages, sa famille et ses descendants* (2 vols., 1884–85); *The Discovery of North America* (1892); *Americus* (Eng., 1895); *John Cabot, the Discoverer of North America…* (1896); and *The Diplomatic History of America. Its First Chapter…* (1897).

BIBLIOGRAPHY: H. Cordier, *Henry Harrisse* (Fr., 1912); R.G. Adams, *Three Americanists* (1939).

[Maury A. Bromsen]

HARRY, MYRIAM, pen name of Mme. **Emile Perrault**, née Shapira (1875–1958), French author. She was born in Jerusalem, the daughter of Moses William Shapira; her mother was a former Protestant deaconess. Myriam was educated in

Berlin and Paris, where she became secretary to the French critic, Jules Lemaître. She led an active life and many of her experiences found their way into her stories. Her sensitivity to human suffering lent depth and color to such works as *La Conquête de Jérusalem* (1903), *La Divine chanson* (1911), *La petite fille de Jérusalem* (1914), *Siona chez les Barbares* (1918), *Siona à Paris* (1919), and *Le Tendre cantique de Siona* (1922). Myriam Harry also wrote accounts of her travels in Tunisia, Egypt, the Levant, Madagascar, Persia, Indochina, and Palestine. Three of these, *Les Amants de Sion* (1923), *La Nuit de Jérusalem* (1928), and *La Jérusalem retrouvée* (1930), show clearly her sympathy for the Zionist movement.

BIBLIOGRAPHY: A. Mailloux, *Myriam Harry* (Fr., 1920); *Le Monde* (March 12, 1958).

[Moshe Catane]

HARSHAV, BENJAMIN (Hrushovski; H. Binyomin/Binyamin; 1928–), literary theorist, scholar, and poet. Born in Vilna, Harshav studied in the U.S.S.R. during World War II and was active in the Zionist-Socialist movement in Germany before immigrating to Palestine in May 1948, serving in combat in the Israeli War of Independence and studying at the Hebrew University of Jerusalem and at Yale. He founded the Porter Institute for Poetics and Semiotics at Tel Aviv University, developing the approach of "constructive poetics." In the fields of literary theory, poetics, cultural semiotics, prosody, and comparative and Hebrew literature he published over 30 monographs, in addition to numerous edited and translated volumes (especially of poetry into Hebrew and, with Barbara Harshav, into English), among them: *American Yiddish Poetry* (1986), *The Meaning of Yiddish* (1990), *Language in Time of Revolution* (1993), *Shirat ha-Tekhiya ha-Ivrit* ("Poetry of the Hebrew Revival," 2 vols., 2000), *Marc Chagall and His Times: A Documentary Narrative* (2004), *Marc Chagall / The Lost Jewish World: The Nature of his Art and Iconography* (2006), and five volumes of his selected works in Hebrew (his important theoretical work especially in vols. 1–2; 2000). Beyond his long tenure at Hebrew University (1954–65), Tel Aviv University (1965–87), and Yale (from 1987), he held guest professorships and research fellowships at several universities in Europe and the U.S., and was a fellow of the American Academy of Arts and Sciences. He founded and edited the scholarly journals *HaSifrut*, PTL *(Poetics and Theory of Literature)*, and *Poetics Today*, and the monograph series *Sifrut, Mashma'ut, Tarbut*. Harshav wrote poetry in both Hebrew (*Shirei Gabi Daniel*, 2000) and Yiddish (under the name [H.] Binyomin): *Shtoybn* ("Dust," 1948) and *Take oyf Tshikaves: Geblibene Lider* ("For the Sake of Curiosity: Remnant Poems," 1994).

BIBLIOGRAPHY: Z. Ben-Porat (ed.), *Aderet le-Vinyamin*, 2 vols. (1999–2001); idem, in: *Poetics Today*, 22 (2001), 245–51.

[Jerold C. Frakes (2nd ed.)]

HART, English family, sons of Hartwig (Naphtali Hertz) Moses, formerly of Breslau, later of Hamburg. The elder son AARON HART (Uri Phoebus; 1670–1756) first studied and taught in Poland. After 1705 he was appointed rabbi of the Ashkenazi community in London in succession to Judah Loeb b. Ephraim Anschel. The appointment was largely due to the influence of his wealthy brother Moses. Aaron was implicated in a dispute concerning the divorce of a member of the community, in defense of which he published his *Urim ve-Tummin* (1707), the first book printed entirely in Hebrew in London and his only literary production. He continued as rabbi of the Great Synagogue until his death. His authority was recognized in the Jewish communities that were springing up in the provincial towns, and he may be regarded as being informally the first chief rabbi of Great Britain. Edward Goldney, an English conversionist, engaged in a disputation with him in the last years of his life. His brother MOSES (1675–1756) emigrated to England about 1697. Partly through the assistance and support of his cousin, the magnate Benjamin Levi, he amassed a fortune as a broker. In 1722 he rebuilt the Ashkenazi synagogue (later the Great Synagogue) at his own expense and continued to control it until his death. He was highly regarded in government circles and was partly responsible for British diplomatic efforts at intervention at the time of the expulsion of the Jews from *Prague in 1745.

BIBLIOGRAPHY: C. Roth, *History of the Great Synagogue* (1950), index; Busse, in: JHSET, 21 (1968), 138–47; Kaufmann, *ibid.*, 3 (1899), 105ff.; Adler, in: *Papers... Anglo-Jewish Historical Exhibition* (1888), 230–78; E. Goldney, *Friendly Epistle to Deists and Jews* (1759). **ADD. BIBLIOGRAPHY:** ODNB online for Aaron Hart and Moses Hart; Katz, England, 205–22, index; T. Endelman, *Jews of Georgian England*, index.

[Cecil Roth]

HART, AARON (1724–1800), early settler in Canada. Hart was a native of London of Bavarian-born parents. He immigrated to New York via Jamaica about 1752. At the time of General Jeffrey Amherst's capture of Montreal in 1760, Hart was a civilian supplier to the British troops. He stayed in Canada, settling in Trois Rivières, where he acquired considerable property and engaged in the fur trade and other commercial pursuits. As seigneur of Becancour, Hart recruited a militia battalion which bore his name. The second post office established in British Canada was located in his home, with Hart as postmaster. He played a leading role in the public life of Trois Rivières and was considered responsible for developing the town into an important trading center. The Hart family was identified with this city for more than a century. To avoid marrying outside his faith, Hart sailed to England and married his cousin Dorothea Catherine Judah, whose brothers had also settled in Trois Rivières. His prayer book reveals that he was an Ashkenazi Jew and kept his family records in Yiddish. By the time he died, Hart was reputed to be the wealthiest man in the British colonies.

BIBLIOGRAPHY: Rosenbloom, Biogr Dict; R. Douville, *Aaron Hart* (Fr., 1938); A. Tessier, in: *Cahiers des Dix*, 3 (1938), 217–42; S. Rosenberg, *Jewish Community in Canada* (1970), index.

[Ben G. Kayfetz]

HART, ABRAHAM (1810–1885), first important U.S. Jewish publishing executive and leading Philadelphia Jew of his generation. Hart was born in Philadelphia of German Dutch parents. On the death of his father in 1823, he secured a job with Carey and Lea, the prominent publishing house founded by Matthew Carey. In 1829 he and Edward L. Carey established their own firm, E.L. Carey & A. Hart, which was soon in the first rank of American publishers. Among the authors they published were Macaulay, Thackeray, Longfellow, and James Fenimore Cooper. Although Carey died in 1845, Hart continued to use the name Carey and Hart until 1850, when his publications began to appear under the imprint A. Hart which he used until he retired in 1854. With his fortune made, Hart gave his time to civic activities and to investments in such fields as mining and sewing machines. He served as president of Mikveh Israel Congregation of Philadelphia for more than 30 years (1841–64 and 1867–76). Hart presided at the 1845 meeting that inaugurated the *Jewish Publication Society and was its president until a fire in his own building in 1851 wiped out almost the entire stock of the society's books. He was active in the agitation for a presidential pronouncement on the *Mortara Case in 1858. For three years beginning in 1866 he was president of the *Board of Delegates of American Israelites. Hart was treasurer of the Hebrew Education Society in the years 1848–75 and was the first president of *Maimonides College. During his time no Jewish development of note in Philadelphia, and virtually none nationally, took place without his support.

BIBLIOGRAPHY: H.S. Morais, *Jews of Philadelphia* (1894), 53–58 and index; E. Wolf and M. Whiteman, *History of the Jews of Philadelphia* (1957), 352–3.

[Bertram Wallace Korn]

HART, BENJAMIN (1779–1855), early Canadian army officer and magistrate. Hart was born in Trois Rivières, the third son of Aaron *Hart. In February 1811 he applied for a commission in the Lower Canada militia. Thomas Coffin, commander of the district, responded a year later advising against it on the grounds that Christian soldiers would not tolerate Jews in their midst. In August 1812 he wrote the governor refuting the objection with letters from a Catholic officer and a Protestant chaplain and pointing out Coffin's "private resentment" at being defeated by Benjamin's brother Ezekiel in the 1807 election. Nothing came of this exchange but despite this snub Benjamin Hart provided the sum of £1,000 to assist the paymaster in his needs. Shortly afterward Hart enlisted and saw active service in the War of 1812. Hart was justice of the peace in Montreal in 1837, and in the rebellion of that year and the following, he read the Riot Act and took an active role in quelling the disturbances, both as an army officer and magistrate. In 1826 he was president of the Shearith Israel Synagogue in Montreal.

BIBLIOGRAPHY: Rosenbloom, Biogr Dict; J.J. Price, in AJHSP, 23 (1915), 137–40; S. Rosenberg, *Jewish Community in Canada* (1970), index.

[Ben G. Kayfetz]

HART, BERNARD (1763–1855), American merchant, father of Congressman Emanuel B. *Hart. Hart was born in London to a family which probably originated in Fuerth. He had immigrated to Canada by 1776–77 and appears to have lived and traded in both Montreal and New York City until about 1800. In 1799 he was married to a non-Jewess, Catherine Brett, ei-

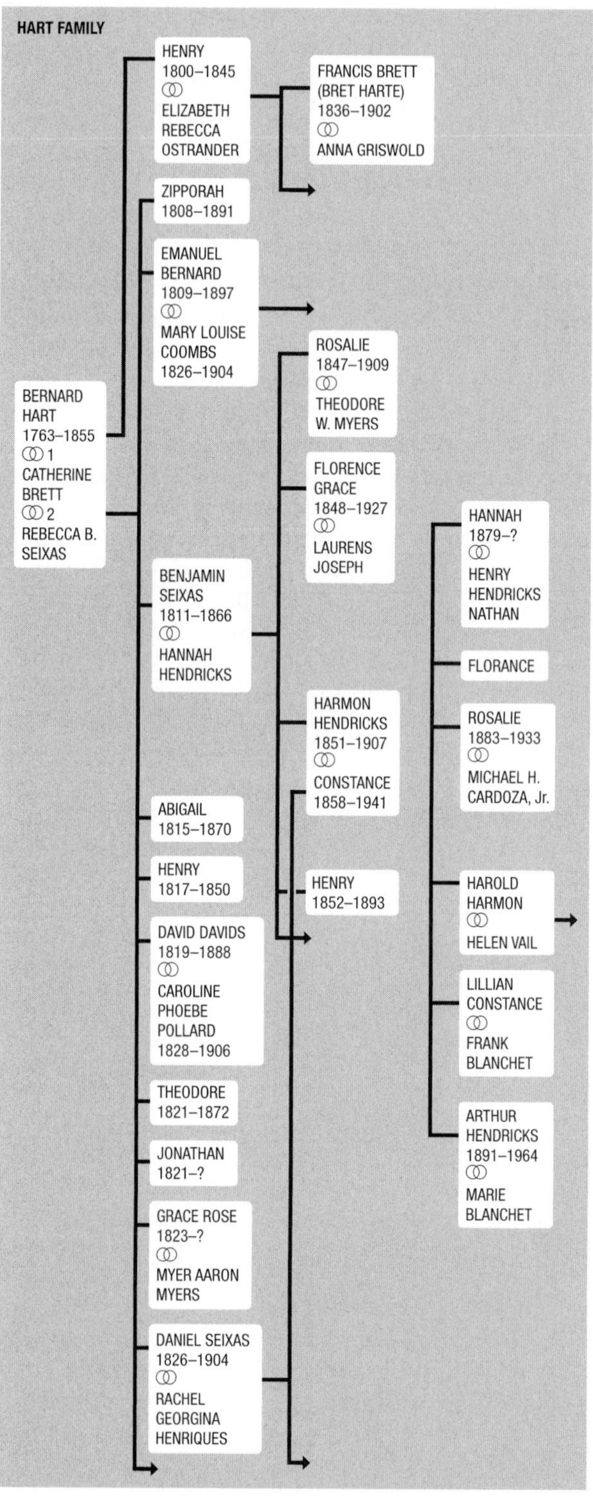

ther in Canada or New York, but the marriage was a brief one. Catherine bore him one son, Henry, in whom Bernard took no interest aside from financial support. Henry's son was the literary figure Bret Harte. By the time of Bernard Hart's second marriage, in 1806, to Rebecca Seixas, niece of *ḥazzan* Gershom Mendes *Seixas, Hart had become *parnas* of Shearith Israel Congregation in New York, a post which he held for three years. He was active in the affairs of the congregation for many years, especially in its burial society. Hart is reported to have served as a quartermaster in the New York State Militia in 1787, and as a major during the War of 1812. He was a member of the committees that established the first New York Exchange office in 1792, and the New York Stock and Exchange Board in 1817, serving as secretary of the latter 1831–53.

BIBLIOGRAPHY: Rosenbloom, Biogr Dict, s.v.; D. Pool, *Portraits Etched in Stone* (1952), index; H. Simonhoff, *Jewish Notables in America* (1956), 239–42.

[Bertram Wallace Korn]

HART, CECIL M. (1883–1940), Canadian ice hockey pioneer. Born in Bedford, Quebec, a direct descendant of Aaron *Hart, Canada's first Jewish settler, Cecil Hart organized, managed, and played for the Star Hockey Club from 1900 to 1922. In 1910 he formed the Montreal City Hockey League, and his Stars became champions in 1914–15 and 1916–17. Hart organized the first international amateur hockey series between Canada and the United States. Entering professional hockey in 1921, Hart secured the Montreal Canadiens of the National Hockey League for a group of businessmen and became manager. For six straight seasons they reached the championship playoffs. The Canadiens won the Stanley Cup (emblematic of the world professional championship) in 1929–30 and 1930–31.

BIBLIOGRAPHY: B. Postal et al. (eds.), *Encyclopedia of Jews in Sports* (1965), 333–4.

[Jesse Harold Silver]

HART, DANIEL (1800–1852), Jamaican lawyer and politician. A merchant in Kingston for over 30 years, Hart was the first Jew to be granted civil and political privileges in Jamaica. He was the senior representative for the Parish of St. Mary in the Jamaican House of Assembly and in 1851 was appointed *custos rotulorum* (parish registrar). For many years, he was an alderman and a member of the assembly for the city and parish of Kingston, as well as a justice of the peace and assistant judge of the Court of Common Pleas.

[Bernard Hooker]

HART, EMANUEL BERNARD (1809–1897), New York City Democratic politician and leader of Jewish institutions. Hart was born in New York City, son of Bernard Hart, a New York Stock Exchange member, and Rebecca Seixas Hart. He began his political activity in 1832 as a Jacksonian Democrat, and became a member of the Tammany Society. He served for two terms as an alderman in New York City (1845–46). Defeated in his first campaign for the federal Congress, Hart won on the second try and served from 1851 to 1853. Among many other positions which he held throughout a long, but not particularly distinguished career of office-holding were surveyor of the Port of New York (1857–62); a commissioner of Immigration (1870–73); a New York Excise commissioner (1880–83); disbursing agent at the New York custom house (1885–89); and cashier in the New York County sheriff's office (1889–93). He was also an officer in the New York State Militia. In earlier years when he was not on the public payroll, Hart was a stock and bond broker, and in later years he was a merchant. Hart was a member of Shearith Israel Congregation, as was his father, and served as president of the Mount Sinai Hospital (1870–76), when the hospital's new structure on Lexington Avenue was dedicated. He was also president of the Hebrew Home for the Aged and Infirm.

BIBLIOGRAPHY: Davis, in: AJHSP, 32 (1931), 99–111; M.U. Schappes (ed.), *Documentary History of the Jews in the United States* (1950), 285–6, 641.

[Bertram Wallace Korn]

HART, EPHRAIM (1747–1825), U.S. communal leader and stockbroker. Hart, who was born in Fuerth, Bavaria, went to New York before the outbreak of the American Revolution. After the British captured New York (1776), Hart moved to Philadelphia. He was one of the first members of the Spanish and Portuguese Synagogue in Philadelphia, dedicated in 1782. He returned to New York in 1787, became a stockbroker, and also speculated successfully in real estate. Hart was a charter member of the Board of Stock Brokers (1792). He served as an elector of Congregation Shearith Israel (1787) and was a founder of its burial society Hebra Hesed ve Emet (1802). Hart sat in the New York State Senate (1810) and was a business associate of John Jacob Astor.

HART, ERNEST ABRAHAM (1836–1898), British physician, medical editor, and humanitarian. Born and educated in London, during the Crimean War (1854) Hart led his fellow students in a successful appeal to the Admiralty to improve the status of the naval doctors aboard ship. At 20 he qualified as a specialist in opththalmology and in 1864 became an ophthalmologic surgeon and lecturer at St. Mary's Hospital in London. He introduced new methods in dealing with eye diseases, particularly in the treatment of aneurysm. Later he was appointed aural surgeon and dean of the medical school.

In 1858 he had begun writing for the medical journal, *Lancet*, and shortly thereafter was named coeditor. In 1866 he accepted the editorship of the *British Medical Journal*, the official publication of the British Medical Association. He expanded and improved the journal and through his efforts the membership of the Association increased rapidly. As chairman of its Parliamentary Bills Committee, he undertook a number of projects to eliminate the ills which militated against public health and sound social conditions in Britain. His exposure of the deplorable state of the London workhouse infirmaries led to the establishment of the Metropolitan Asylums Board and to better treatment of the sick among the poor. He campaigned against the evil of baby farming, and it was largely through his efforts that the Infant Protection Act was passed in 1872. Hart had a large part in securing legislation ensuring the quality of the milk supply in cities, in abating the smoke nuisance, bettering working conditions in factories, and safeguarding the health of workers. He worked for the amelioration of the plight of Irish peasants and for reclaiming of wasteland in Ireland. He attacked the Indian Government for its neglect in eliminating the conditions which produced cholera. He denounced the fraud of hypnotism and mesmerism in a series of articles, which appeared under the title of "The Eternal Gullible."

As a young man he had advocated the granting of equal rights to Jews in the columns of *Frazier's* magazine and in 1877 he published *The Mosaic Code*, which dealt with the hygienic laws of the Bible.

HART, EZEKIEL (1767–1843), early Canadian political figure. Hart was born in Trois Rivières, the second son of Aaron *Hart. He succeeded his father as seigneur of Becancour. In 1807 he was elected to the legislature of Lower Canada for Trois Rivières. Because of the sharp rivalry between the French and English camps he was prevented from taking his seat at the following session of the legislature in 1808. Regarding him as a member of the English faction the French-speaking deputies pointed out that as a Jew he could not take the oath "on the true faith of a Christian." He was reelected in May 1808, and in April 1809, he was again prevented from being seated.

BIBLIOGRAPHY: Rosenbloom, Biogr Dict, 52; J.J. Price, in: AJHSP, 23 (1915), 43–53; S. Rosenberg, *Jewish Community of Canada* (1970), index.

[Ben G. Kayfetz]

HART, HERBERT LIONEL ADOLPHUS (1907–1992), British philosopher of law, generally known as H.L.A. Hart. Born at Harrogate and educated at Cheltenham, Bradford Grammar School, and New College, Oxford, in 1932 Hart became a barrister. From 1932 to 1940 he practiced at the Chancery Bar, and from 1939 to 1945 served in the British War Office. He returned to Oxford in 1945, becoming a fellow of University College, and professor of jurisprudence in 1952–68. His major writings include *Causation in the Law* (with A.M. Honoré, 1959), *The Concept of Law* (1961), *Punishment and the Elimination of Responsibility* (1962), *Law, Liberty and Morality* (1963), and *The Morality of the Criminal Law* (1964). Each of these works is characterized by the application of the techniques of contemporary philosophy to areas of serious legal and moral contention. In general, Hart's work stands in opposition to philosophical determinism, the notion that nobody can act differently from the way he does, and therefore cannot be held responsible for what he does. To accept this point of view would risk blurring the general recognition that a man's fate should depend upon his choice, and with it the whole way of conceiving human relationships. Not only in the law or in morally crucial situations, but also in our everyday transactions, we view one another as responsible and not "merely as alterable, predictable, curable, or manipulable things." From 1973 to 1978 he was principal of Brasenose College, Oxford. Hart visited Israel in 1964, giving the Lionel Cohen lectures in Jerusalem. He is regarded as one of the foremost exponents of the theory of "legal positivism."

ADD. BIBLIOGRAPHY: ODNB online; J. Hart, *Ask Me No More* (1998); N. Lacey, *A Life of H.L.A. Hart* (2004).

[Avrum Stroll / Williiam D. Rubinstein (2nd ed.)]

HART, ISAAC (d. 1780), U.S. merchant. Hart, a Loyalist, left England about 1750, and established himself in Rhode Island. He soon became one of the wealthiest merchants in the colony, and his prominent position made Hart a leader of *Newport's Jewish community. He served on the committee which raised funds for the building of Newport's Touro synagogue, was one of the purchasers of the land it stands on, and his firm, Naphthali Hart and Company, erected the building. In 1780 the revolutionary government of Rhode Island exiled him with other Loyalists, and in December he was killed, supposedly during an American raid on Fort George in New York.

BIBLIOGRAPHY: Rosenbloom, Biogr Dict, s.v.

[Neil Ovadia]

HART, JACOB (1745–1814), kabbalist and grammarian. He was the first native-born English scholar of this type in the modern period. A jeweler by profession, Hart took an active part in communal affairs in London and received rabbinical ordination in Europe some time between 1800 and 1804. Under his Hebrew name of Eliakim b. Abraham he published various works in Hebrew on religion, Kabbalah, and grammar. They include *Asarah Ma'amarot*, of which five treatises only were published, three of them in England (1794–99); *Milḥamot Adonai*, a polemic in defense of religion against science and philosophy, sharply criticizing Voltaire and other rationalist writers; *Binah la-Ittim*, a computation of the date of the end of the world (*keẓ*) according to the Book of *Daniel, predicting it for 1843; *Ẓuf Novelot* on kabbalistic subjects; an abridgment of *Novelot Ḥokhmah* by Joseph Solomon *Delmedigo with notes and a commentary in which Hart attempted to prove *creatio ex nihilo*. Two of his works were published in Berlin in 1803, *Ma'yan Gannim*, an abridgment of *Ginnat Egoz* by Joseph b. Abraham *Gikatilla, and *Ein ha-Kore* on the Hebrew vowels, which contends that the Ashkenazi pronunciation is correct. In the same year Hart published in Roedelheim the grammatical treatise *Ein ha-Mishpat*. His works indicate that Hart was a man of broad general education.

BIBLIOGRAPHY: A. Barnett and S. Brodetsky, in: JHSET, 14 (1940), 207–23; A. Barnett, *The Western Synagogue through Two Centuries* (1961), index.

[Cecil Roth]

HART, JOEL (1784–1842), U.S. doctor. Hart was born in Philadelphia and educated at the Royal College of Surgeons in London. Establishing himself in New York, Hart became a leader of the city's medical community. He was one of the charter members of the Medical Society of the County of New York (1806) and was among the group that founded the College of Physicians and Surgeons in 1807. Hart gave up his practice in 1817 to become United States consul at Leith, Scotland, a position he held until 1832. He then returned to New York where he practiced medicine until his death.

BIBLIOGRAPHY: Rosenbloom, Biogr Dict, s.v.

[Neil Ovadia]

HART, KITTY CARLISLE (1910–), U.S. entertainer, arts administrator. Born in New Orleans, La., as Catherine Conn, she was brought up in Paris and in Switzerland. She was educated at the Sorbonne, the London School of Economics, and the Royal Academy of Dramatic Art in London. A singer and actress, she appeared in the *Marx Brothers' farcical film *A Night at the Opera* in 1935 after appearing in three films the previous year: *Here Is My Heart, She Loves Me Not*, and *Murder at the Vanities*. Known for her gracious manners and personal elegance, she dated George *Gershwin and married the playwright Moss *Hart in 1946. As Kitty Carlisle, she became a household name in the United States through appearances on the panel of the television program *To Tell the Truth*, in which three contestants aver to having the same secret. She also was a guest panelist for many years on the popular series *What's My Line?*, in which panelists try to guess the contestant's occupation. Both programs gave her an opportunity to showcase her wit and intelligence.

Taking on the real-life role of arts administrator, she headed the New York State Council on the Arts, a statewide agency, for many years and raised countless thousands to support cultural institutions large and small. She proved a tireless champion of the arts, and traveled throughout the state to see performances by professional and amateur organizations. She resumed her acting and singing career in the mid-1980s and appeared both in acting roles and as herself in film and television series. She retained her singing voice well into her nineties and her one-woman shows, played in various parts of the United States, included memories of her career, anecdotes of her experiences with the Marx Brothers and Gershwin, and theatrical stories about her late husband.

[Stewart Kampel (2nd ed.)]

HART, LORENZ (1895–1943), U.S. musical comedy lyricist. Born to immigrant parents, Larry Hart traced his descent through his mother from the German poet Heinrich *Heine. Hart graduated from the Columbia University School of Journalism in 1916. Although indifferent to academic studies outside literature and drama, Hart single-handedly changed the craft of lyric writing. He became the expressive bard of the urban generation that matured between the wars after he was introduced to a 16-year-old Richard *Rodgers by a mutual friend. Together the team of Rodgers and Hart created some of the greatest musicals of the first half of the 20th century. Hart was working in the theater for the *Shuberts, translating German plays, and Rodgers was writing variety shows at Columbia. The pair contributed to the Broadway musical *Poor Little Ritz Girl* in 1920 and by 1925 they had their own success on Broadway, *The Garrick Gaieties*, an intimate revue that was a counter to huge, flossy "girlie" productions. Rodgers and Hart believed that monotony was killing the musical and that songwriters had to integrate libretto, lyrics, and music. The two men were diametrically opposed in temperament, but not in artistic spirit. Rodgers was reserved, disciplined, and stern. Hart was emotional and earthy, quick with a joke, and effusively warm. Hart suffered from a mild dwarfism and was a homosexual at a time of great social repression. In his songs, Hart was interested in exploring a single moment of pure emotion. The pair's songs were written to work on two levels: they had to function within the plotline of the show and they had to transcend the show so that people could listen at home and appreciate the music. Hart's songs often worked on a third level. Unable to find a mate, Hart rarely wrote a requited love song. His output is dominated by dreams and fantasies, lovers dancing on the ceiling, funny, ugly valentines.

Nevertheless, the partners had a string of successes on Broadway, including *A Connecticut Yankee* in 1927, *The Boys From Syracuse* in 1938, *On Your Toes* in 1936, *Pal Joey* in 1940, and *By Jupiter* in 1943. Their songs became American classics: "The Girl Friend, Manhattan" ("We'll have Manhattan, the Bronx and Staten Island, too"), "Thou Swell," "You Took Advantage of Me," "I'd Rather Be Right," "Little Girl Blue," and "I Married an Angel," to mention a few. In the 1930s Hart wrote the lyrics for "Have You Met Miss Jones?," "The Most Beautiful Girl in the World," "The Lady Is a Tramp," "Blue Moon," "My Romance," "Where or When," and "Falling in Love With Love" from *The Boys From Syracuse*. The latter, based on *A Comedy of Errors*, was the pioneer adaptation of Shakespeare for musical comedy. Most of these songs were delicately oblique for a Depression-era audience that did not embrace sentimentality, but Hart penned the poignant "My Funny Valentine," a tribute to a homely lover; it became a classic American torch song.

By 1940 Hart and Rodgers decided that more of the naturalism of contemporary literature and drama had to be infused in musical comedy. In collaboration with the celebrated novelist John O'Hara they adapted his *Pal Joey*. The theme of a nice-looking young white song-and-dance man who could flirt and have sex with women was not easily digested by the American public. Most of the songs in the production were harshly witty. An older woman sings, "Take him, but don't ever let him take you." The show had a mixed reception but a decade later it was revived to enthusiastic audiences.

When wartime came, Hart was out of step with a patriotic public absorbed with traditional American values. The folksy *Oklahoma!* held no interest for him as he sank deeper into alcohol and depression, and Rodgers turned to Oscar *Hammerstein for a collaborator. But in 1943 Hart and Rodgers reunited for a revival of *A Connecticut Yankee*. On opening night, Hart slipped away and vanished for two days. He died a few days later of pneumonia.

[Stewart Kampel (2nd ed.)]

HART, MOSS (1904–1961), U.S. playwright. Born and raised on New York's East Side, Hart wrote his first play when he was 12 and gained early experience as a producer in Jewish clubs. His first success was *Once in a Lifetime* (1930), a satire on Hollywood written in collaboration with George S. *Kaufman. With Kaufman he went on to write *Face the Music* (1932), a satire on New York municipal government which became an Irving *Berlin revue; *As Thousands Cheer* (1933), a revue with music by Irving Berlin; *Merrily We Roll Along* (1934), a satire on Broadway; and two famous comedies, *You Can't Take It With You* (1936), which won a Pulitzer Prize, and *The Man Who Came To Dinner* (1939). On his own, Hart wrote the satirical *George Washington Slept Here* (1940); the libretto for the musical *Lady in the Dark* (1941); and *The Climate of Eden* (1952). Hart's direction of *My Fair Lady*, the 1956 musical based on Shaw's *Pygmalion*, was widely acclaimed. Hart's autobiography, *Act One* (1959), a modest but moving story, was filmed shortly after his death. He was married to Kitty Carlisle *Hart.

BIBLIOGRAPHY: J. Gould, *Modern American Playwrights* (1966), 154–67. **ADD. BIBLIOGRAPHY:** Steven Bach, *Dazzler: The Life and Times of Moss Hart* (2001).

[Bernard Grebanier]

HART, MYER (d. 1797), early American merchant, and a founder of the town of Easton, Pennsylvania, in 1752. Hart, an immigrant to the colonies, prospered with the town, and by 1763 was Easton's largest taxpayer and civic leader. Although he became a British subject in 1764, he actively supported the American Revolution. Hart was appointed to the Pennsylvania State Commission charged with the care of British prisoners of war, and in 1778 he testified that, despite contradictory reports, the Englishmen were well treated. In 1782 he moved to Philadelphia; his business there failed some years later.

BIBLIOGRAPHY: E. Wolf and M. Whiteman, *History of the Jews of Philadelphia* (1957), index; Rosenbloom, Biogr Dict, s.v. incl. bibl.

[Neil Ovadia]

HART, SAMUEL (c. 1747–1810), Nova Scotia merchant and politician. Hart is known to have settled in the British colony of Nova Scotia, to have been a dry goods merchant in Halifax in the 1780s, and to have lived at Maroon Hall, in Preston. He was a member of the small Jewish community which existed in Nova Scotia in the second half of the 18th century and which dwindled and expired by the mid-19th century. From 1793 to 1799 Hart was a member of the Nova Scotia House of Assembly for Liverpool Township, thus becoming the first Jew to sit in a legislative body in territory that was later to become Canada.

[Ben G. Kayfetz]

HART, SOLOMON ALEXANDER (1806–1881), English painter. Hart was the son of a Plymouth engraver and Hebrew teacher and moved with his family to London in 1820. First apprenticed to an engraver, Hart entered the Royal Academy as a student in 1823; three years later he exhibited a miniature portrait of his father. He continued for a time to paint miniatures for a livelihood. In 1828 he showed his first oil at the British Institute, and, two years later, *Elevation of the Law* (now in the Tate Gallery, London), also called *Interior of a Jewish Synagogue at the Time of the Reading of the Law* (depicting the interior of the former Polish synagogue in London). An associate of the Royal Academy in 1835 and a full member five years later, he was professor of painting at the Royal Academy from 1854 to 1863. In his last eighteen years he served there as librarian. Hart's crowded canvases usually illustrate famous episodes of English history, and are done in the formal, dignified academic style that matured in the Regency period. Paintings on Jewish themes are also frequent. His *Rejoicing of the Law in the Ancient Synagogue at Leghorn* represents the procession of the Scrolls on Simḥat Torah. His painting *Manasseh ben Israel* was destroyed in the London Blitz during World War II. His *Reminiscences of Solomon Alexander Hart, R.A.*, edited by Alexander Brodie, was published in 1882.

ADD. BIBLIOGRAPHY: ODNB online.

[Alfred Werner]

HARTFORD, capital of Connecticut. Population of greater Hartford County, 870,000; Jewish population, 34,000 (2001).

Early History

Hartford's town records reveal an early Jewish presence in colonial times. General court proceedings in 1659 mention a certain "David the Jew," an itinerant peddler; in 1661 a party of Jews in the city was given permission "to sojourn in Hartford seven months"; in 1667 "Jacob the Jew" transported horses to New York; in 1669 "David Jew" and "Jacob Jew" were among the 721 inhabitants listed in the town records. Advertisements in *The Hartford Courant* in 1788 and 1801 contain references to a thoroughfare known as "Jew Street," but whether it was actually inhabited at the time by Jews or Jewish merchants is unknown.

Jewish settlement in Hartford did not begin in earnest, however, until the 1840s with the first wave of immigrants from Germany. In 1847 Congregation Beth Israel was formed with an initial membership of six; four years later it had 150 members "of thriving business and good standing in society." A B'nai B'rith lodge was established in 1851, and in 1854 a *Frauen Verein* was organized to provide mutual aid and serve as a center of social activities. In 1856 Beth Israel acquired its first permanent structure, a refurbished Baptist church, and engaged Rabbi Isaac Mayer (1809–1898), who served for 12 years. With growing affluence and acculturation, the congregation erected a new synagogue in 1876, and in 1878 dropped its traditional orientation to join the Reform Union of American Hebrew Congregations.

East European Immigration

As a result of the great East European immigration to America, Hartford's Jewish population increased from 1,500 in 1880 to over 7,000 in 1910 and to almost 20,000 by 1920. The new immigrants founded the Adas Israel Synagogue in 1884, the Agudas Achim Synagogue in 1887, and six other Orthodox synagogues in the ensuing years. Two East European rabbis, Isaac S. Hurewitz, who served in Hartford from 1893 to 1935, and Zemach Hoffenberg, who served from 1899 to 1938, ministered to these congregations. They were among the many rabbis who served for more than four decades. Other Jewish institutions and organizations sprang up: the Hartford Sick Benefit Association and the Hebrew Ladies Benevolent Society in 1898; the B'nai Zion Society, which sponsored a group of 12 Zionist clubs, also in 1898; the Hebrew Institute Talmud Torah in 1901; the Hebrew Home for the Aged in 1907; the Hebrew Home for Children in 1907; a *mikveh* in 1907; the Council of Jewish Women in 1910; and a chapter of the Labor Zionist Farband in 1914. In 1912 some 30 of these organizations merged to form the United Jewish Charities. A Hadassah chapter was set up by Henrietta Szold in 1914, and in 1918, through the joint efforts of five local branches of the Workmen's Circle, the Labor Lyceum opened its doors. Among the immigrants were some who added new dimensions to Hartford's economic life. Expert furriers from Russia helped make Hartford a center of the fur trade, and skilled Jewish carpenters and cabinetmakers introduced the reproduction of antique furniture.

Post-World War I

Between the two world wars, with the cutoff of mass immigration, Hartford's Jewish community grew at a slower pace; this period was primarily one of further consolidation and integration into the general life of the city. Hartford's first Conservative congregation, the Emanuel Synagogue, was organized in 1919. Its first Jewish country club, the Tumble Brook Country and Golf Club, was opened in 1922. Mount Sinai Hospital, the first and only Jewish hospital in the state, was established in 1923. The weekly *Jewish Ledger*, founded by Samuel Neusner in 1929, with Rabbi Abraham J. Feldman as editor, has chronicled Jewish activity in the city. In 1935 a Jewish Community Council was formed, and in 1937, the Jewish Welfare Fund; the merger of these two organizations into a single Federation in 1945 united all Jewish communal and philanthropic endeavors under one roof. A Yeshiva Day School, established in 1940 and later renamed the Bess and Paul Sigel Hebrew Academy of Greater Hartford, had nine grades, with several hundred students, in 1970. An eight grade Solomon Schechter Day School affiliated with the Conservative movement opened in 1971 and a Hebrew High School, supported by the communities of Springfield, MA, New Haven, and Hartford opened in 1996. By the mid 1990s more than 400 youngsters in the Greater Hartford area were receiving an intensive Jewish day school education.

During the post-World War II period, Jewish community life in Greater Hartford centered around the city's synagogues – 11 Conservative, eight Orthodox, and three Reform – and around its Jewish Community Center, built in 1955, with over 7,000 members. Prominent rabbis in the community have included Morris *Silverman (1923–1961), who edited and translated the standard *siddur* that was used in Conservative Congregations for half a century or more, Abraham J. Feldman (1925–1968), Abraham AvRutick (1946–1982), and William Cohen (1946–1994). In all, Greater Hartford had 132 Jewish philanthropic, religious, cultural, and social organizations (1970). During the post-war years, Hartford's religious leadership was unusually stable with many rabbis serving in their congregations for more than three decades including Rabbis Stanley Kessler (Beth El, 1954–1994); Hans Bodenheimer (Tikvoh Chadoshoh, 1942–1996); Henry Okolica (Tifereth Israel, New Britain, 1960–1993); Philip Lazowski (Beth Hillel, 1962–1995); Isaac Avigdor (United Synagogues, 1954–1993); Haskel Lindenthal (Teferes Israel, 1956–1993); Harry Zwelling (B'nai Israel, New Britain, 1936–1971); and Leon Wind (Beth Shalom, Manchester, 1946–1979).

The economic life of the Jewish population is concentrated in the professions and in business. Over one-fifth of Hartford's doctors, approximately one-third of its dentists and attorneys, and one-half of its certified public accountants are Jews. Jews own over half of Hartford's retail businesses, although, in the 1960s, fewer than 2% of the city's commercial bank executives and barely 1% of the executives in the 10 largest insurance companies were Jewish. In the last quarter of the 20th century those percentages changed dramatically as Jewish professional life increased, obstacles to Jews entering banking and insurance ended, and large chain stores replaced small retailers on many Main Streets in the United States. At the University of Hartford Jews comprise roughly 20% of the faculty and 33% of the student body. As is the tendency elsewhere, Hartford's Jews moved in increasing numbers to the suburbs, so that in 1970 the majority lived outside the city proper. There was a great white flight to the suburbs in the 1950s and 1960s and many of the synagogues and Jewish institutions were relocated from Hartford to West Hartford. In the 1990s Jews moved further into other surrounding communities including Glastonbury and the Farmington Valley towns of Farmington, Avon, and Simsbury.

Jews in Public Life

Between 1860 and 1969, 102 Jews were elected to city and town councils; 34 served in the state legislature since 1919. In 1933 Herman P. *Kopplemann became the first Jew from Hartford to be elected to Congress, where he served four terms. Some Hartfordites holding public office were Morris Silverman, chairman and member of the Connecticut State Commission on Human Rights and Opportunities from 1943; Bernard Shapiro, state welfare commissioner during 1959–70; Elisha Freedman, city manager, from 1963; M. Joseph Blumenfield, U.S. District Court judge from 1964; and Louis Shapiro and Abraham S. Bordon on the state judiciary. Annie Fisher was the first Jewish district superintendent of schools. During the mid to late 20th century, Hartford's best-known Jewish citizen was Abraham A. *Ribicoff, who was governor of Connecticut, served in the Cabinet of John F. Kennedy, and was then elected to the Senate.

Jews have played an active role in Hartford's educational and cultural life. They are prominent in the University of Hartford, Trinity College, and the Hartford Symphony. A Jewish president, Stephen J. Tractenberg significantly improved the University of Hartford and during his tenure the Maurice Greenberg Center for Judaic Studies was established. Trinity College also has a Judaic Studies program that adds to the intellectual life of the community.

BIBLIOGRAPHY: M. Silverman, *Hartford Jews: 1659–1969* (1970). **ADD. BIBLIOGRAPHY:** D.G. Dalin, J. Rosenbaum, and D.C. Dalin, *Making a Life, Building a Community: A History of the Jews of Hartford* (1997).

[Morris Silverman / Leon Chameides (2nd ed.)]

HARTGLAS, MAXIMILIAN MEIR APOLINARY (1883–1953), Zionist leader in Poland during the interwar period. Born in Biala Podlaska, Hartglas studied law at Warsaw University and from 1907 to 1919 practiced his profession in Siedlce. As a young student he joined the Zionist academic circle, beginning a long friendship with I. *Gruenbaum. At an early age he took part in the struggle for Polish independence, in Jewish defense, and in Zionist activities. He was among those who formulated the "work in the present" (Gegenwartsarbeit) program for Zionism at the *Helsingfors Conference (1906). In 1917 at the Third Zionist Convention in Warsaw he laid out "the foundations of the Zionist Organization in Poland," published in Polish in 1918.

In 1919 he was elected together with 10 others on the list of the Union of Jewish Members of the Sejm (Polish parliament). The Union demanded the recognition of Polish Jewry as a national community with the rights of a national minority, entitled to organize themselves as an autonomous entity. They opposed the Polish government's discriminatory policy toward the Jews. Hartglas served as defense attorney in several famous Polish trials in which the reason for the indictment was the fact that the accused were Jews. He was instrumental in obtaining the repeal in 1931 of antisemitic czarist laws in Poland's former Russian provinces. Hartglas served as chairman of the Polish Zionist Organization and was a member of the "Jewish Club" (Kolo Zydowskie) in parliament. He settled in Palestine in 1940 and joined the staff of the *Jewish Agency. Upon the establishment of the state (1948), he became director general and later legal adviser of the Ministry of the Interior headed by Gruenbaum. Throughout his life he published articles in various Jewish newspapers on the problems of Polish Jewry and Zionism in various languages, to which he added Hebrew after his settlement in Israel.

BIBLIOGRAPHY: A. Harglas, *Na pograniczu dwoch swiatow* (ed. J. Zyndul, 1996); I. Schiper et al. (eds.), *Zydzi w Polsce odrodzonej*, vol. 1.(1933), 313–59; M. Landau, *Mi'ut Yehudi Loḥem 1918–1928*, index; S. Netzer, *Ma'avak Yehudei Polin al Zekhuyoteihem ha-Ezraḥiyot ve-ha-Le'ummiyot be-Polin* (1980), index.

[Shlomo Netzer (2nd ed.)]

HARTMAN, DAVID (1931–), rabbi and contemporary Jewish thinker in Jerusalem. Born in the United States to a family that had emigrated from the old *yishuv* in Jerusalem, Hartman received a traditional education in Jewish day schools, and then in the prestigious Lakewood yeshivah. His transfer to the Isaac Elhanan Seminary of Yeshiva University resulted in a major shift in his life, as he came under the influence of Rabbi Joseph B. *Soloveitchik, whose teachings would become the focus of much of Hartman's intellectual and spiritual quest. Soloveitchik represented, for the young Hartman, an exemplary combination of profound religious commitment and openness to the modern, Western intellectual world, a combination appropriate for the committed modern Jew. This combination of two worlds would become a central axis of Hartman's thought.

Following his rabbinic ordination by Soloveitchik, Hartman served several congregations in the U.S. and Canada, while completing his graduate studies at Fordham University, a Jesuit institution. This exposure to believing Christians, deeply committed to their religion but open to the world outside of religion, and to other religions, left an indelible impression on Hartman, and is clearly reflected in his thought. After receiving his Ph.D. he began his academic career, in addition to continuing his rabbinical work, and became professor of philosophy at McGill University. After his immigration to Israel in 1971 he joined the faculty of the Hebrew University of Jerusalem, and was promoted to professor of Jewish thought.

Hartman regarded his immigration as having religious-theological significance. Only in the Land of Israel, he believed, can one realize a full Jewish life. In the Diaspora, Jewish life is limited to the private realm and to the synagogue, and does not encompass the entire person. By contrast, in Israel, and only in Israel, the Jew is obligated to comprehensive political responsibility; this responsibility, in turn, bears religious and theological significance. Hartman is thus prominent among contemporary Jewish thinkers in emphasizing the religious significance of Zionism, climaxing in the establishment of the State of Israel and reflecting the theological imprint of the covenant at Sinai. In that covenant, the Jewish people received exclusive and absolute responsibility for interpreting the Torah and implementing it in the world, and the return to Zion expands that covenant into history. God, who gradually withdrew from direct control of history, entrusted it to human responsibility. Today, with the return to Zion, the Jewish people has realized its responsibility by reestablishing Jewish life in all areas of life. For Hartman, the importance of the State of Israel thus lies in the very possibility of establishing Jewish life, and not in its being a metaphysical program of redemption. In this regard, Hartman was close to such other thinkers as Yeshayahu *Leibowitz, Eliezer *Berkovits, and his friend Eliezer *Goldman, each of whom, in his own way, pointed out the necessity of the state for Jewish life, without attributing to the state any metaphysical significance. In adopting this position, Hartman distanced himself from the view of his teacher Soloveitchik, who did not draw a metaphysical, theological map of Israel's redemption, yet regarded the establishment of the State as the Jewish people's response to the direct metaphysical challenge posed by God in history. For Soloveitchik, historical events are the voice of the "lover" who is knocking (Song of Songs 5:2) and who awaits his people's response. Hartman, on the other hand, regarded the Zionist enterprise as an exclusively human endeavor, which is the culmination of the historic covenant at Sinai.

This sense of responsibility led Hartman to accept the challenge of restoring the possibility of a new Jewish dialogue, integrating commitment to Jewish tradition with openness to the present, and took upon himself the task of establishing a new *bet midrash* to serve this vision. In 1976 a group of young men and women joined Hartman in this search for a new way to express their connection to tradition. Most of them were graduates of religious Zionist education, who felt basically uncomfortable regarding the relation of the present to the past. Hartman offered them a new way of studying, which in cultural terms is a dialogue with tradition, and which in religious terms is the realization of the covenant at Sinai and the implementation of the Torah in human life. This group of young men and women became the foundation stone of the Shalom Hartman Institute in Jerusalem, which has since then become a leading institution of Jewish research, frequented by scholars from diverse disciplines and different fields of Jewish studies, but sharing the recognition of the need to shape a new dialogue between present and past. Hartman's approach has become a recognized school of thought in Jewish studies, combining the best of classical scientific research with contemporary inter-disciplinary approaches, thus making possible a new approach to Jewish tradition. This school of thought is a realization of Hartman's religious-theological vision, even if not all its members share his theological presuppositions.

The Shalom Hartman Institute is not merely a theoretical *bet midrash* for a scholarly elite. It promotes a wide range of educational activities, including training teachers for Jewish studies in Israel and the world; seminars for Jewish communal and intellectual leaders from Israel and abroad; and, more recently, training senior officers in the Israel Defense Forces in Jewish identity and values. Hartman himself remains active in all these diverse areas of the Institute's program.

Beyond his institutional and educational activity, Hartman is among the leading Jewish theologians today. While always remaining indebted to his teacher Soloveitchik, Hartman continually rejects Soloveitchik's strict existential stance and refuses to adopt the philosophy of fracture and contradiction which typifies Soloveitchik's later thought. For the same reason, he rejects Leibowitz's conclusions. Although, like Leibowitz, Hartman recognizes the decisive role played by the believer in shaping the religious world, he rejects Leibowitz's idea that at the essence of Judaism lie a rupture and contradiction with the world of moral values. To the contrary, for Hartman this is the very meaning of the covenant at Sinai: God establishes a covenant with people as they are, with the totality of their values and conceptions. The believer is not required to withdraw from his human world, but to locate the covenant in the heart of human life itself. In this respect, Hartman is close to Eliezer Goldman. Both Hartman and Goldman emphasized, in different contexts, the fact that the realm of religious life is not located outside the totality of human life, but at its center. The difference between them is that Goldman regarded religious decisions as nourished by a cultural and social understanding of human existence, and by an analysis of the meaning of the *halakhah*, whereas Hartman regarded these decisions as founded on the theological significance of the covenant at Sinai.

Hartman may be considered an *a priori* modernist, for whom modern values are accepted as a matter of principle, and make possible a renewed and more mature encounter with Jewish tradition, as opposed to an *a posteriori* position, such as we find in Soloveitchik's later thought, according to which Judaism develops internally, as a closed system, independently of the external world, but is forced by circumstances to participate in the external world. Hartman's position thus reflects a Hegelian view of history, in which a later stage is more important and decisive. Unlike Hegel, however, in Hartman's view the later historical stage permits a renewed return to the beginning and a more profound insight into what is latently present in earlier formative stages. For instance, in Hartman's view, the neutralization of God in the world, which post-Nietzschean modernists expressed imperfectly as the death of God, is not opposed to Judaism. To the contrary, the neutralization of God is the profoundest significance of the covenant at Sinai. In contrast with the creation of the world and the exodus from Egypt, in which God acts alone, at Sinai God turns to people. The belief in the covenant at Sinai, therefore, is for Hartman not grounded on a past historical event, but on the partnership between people and God. Jewish history is a continual expression of the historic imprint in which people take on an ever-increasingly active role. This imprint began in the period of the Talmud, with the cognition that God does not act in history: "The world behaves in its customary way" (*olam ke-minhago noheg*). Whereas in the biblical period the encounter with God was immediate and direct, for the rabbis the relationship with God was intermediated by halakhic norms. Hartman's preference for the talmudic over the biblical period is based not only on his Hegelian orientation, but is also a matter of principle, in two regards. First, whereas the biblical period was theocentric, seeing God as the exclusive agent in nature and history, the talmudic period was more anthropocentric, shifting attention away from the divine drama of creation to the real history of people, who are now responsible for God's presence in the world, by studying Torah, observing the commandments, and prayer. The talmudic approach is thus more responsive to the modern insistence on retaining autonomy and personal freedom. Hartman's later thought regards the formation of a sovereign Jewish community in the State of Israel as an additional stage in this process of increasing human responsibility for the divine presence in the world. Second, biblical thought makes the material status of the human being dependent on human actions. This dependence, however, opens the way for the belief in "other gods" who also are capable of assuring material blessings. In Hartman's opinion, the talmudic world-view, and especially Maimonides' subsequent revolution, saved Judaism from such idolatrous belief.

The struggle against idolatry, which was thus a major factor in Hartman's preference for the talmudic period, also points to the great proximity between Hartman's thought and that of Leibowitz: they both maintain a transcendent conception of God and both understand the struggle against idolatry in terms of rejecting the contingent and immanent roles attributed to God. They also share the view that the subject of idolatry is not necessarily another, foreign god, but an erroneous conception of God's status in the world.

The transcendent conception of God, together with the emphasis on the centrality of human religious activity, enabled Hartman to develop a type of religious pluralism, based on the idea that revelation reflects the divine desire to encounter people in their finitude and historical context, and to develop a dialogue with them in their own language. This approach enabled Hartman to a universalization of the covenant, to include not only Jews but also believers from other religions. This radical interpretation, in turn, enabled Hartman to reinterpret religious commitment. Instead of the classical understanding of religious commitment in terms of objective truth which is universally valid, Hartman's theology posits religious commitment as the believer's loyalty to his or her faith. Different believers have diverse religious commitments, and none can claim exclusivity of commitment; yet their commitments are not thereby harmed.

Hartman's emphasis on the autonomous, human dimension could have led him to conclude that belief is an entirely private and voluntary affair. In opposition to this view, he repeatedly emphasized the decisive role of community. The believer does not encounter God alone and isolated from the experience of the real and historic Jewish community; the believer is thus a partner in a historical covenant with God, and is not a founder of a new covenant.

Hartman's thought may thus be characterized both as continued interpretation of Maimonides and Soloveitchik, the two thinkers who had greatest impact on him, and as constructive dialogue with such modern and post-modern thinkers as Charles Taylor, Alastair MacIntyre, Richard Rorty, and others.

Hartman's works include *Maimonides: Torah and Philosophic Quest* (1976); *Joy and Responsibility: Israel, Modernity and the Renewal of Judaism* (1978); *A Living Covenant, The Innovative Spirit in Traditional Judaism* (1985); *Crisis and Leadership: Epistles of Maimonides* (Eng. tr., 1985); *Conflicting Visions, Spiritual Possibilities of Modern Israel* (1990); *A Heart of Many Rooms, Celebrating the Many Voices within Judaism* (1999); *Israelis and the Jewish Tradition, An Ancient People Debating its Future*, (2000); *Love and Terror in God Encounter, The Theological Legacy of Rabbi Joseph B. Soloveitchik*, vol. 1 (2001).

BIBLIOGRAPHY: A. Sagi and Z. Zohar (eds.), *Renewing Jewish Commitment, The Work and Thought of David Hartman*, 2 vols. (Heb., 2001); J. Malino (ed.), *Judaism and Modernity, The Religious Philosophy of David Hartman* (2004).

[Avi Sagi (2nd ed.)]

HARTMAN, GEOFFREY (1929–), child survivor of the Holocaust and scholar. Born in Frankfurt, Germany, Hartman was sent on a Kindertransport to England in 1939. He spent the war years in Waddeston with 19 other boys, on the estate of James Rothschild. In 1945, he came to the United States where he was reunited with his mother. Hartman attended Queens College in New York City and earned his Ph.D. at Yale where he taught for almost 40 years. He was the Sterling Professor Emeritus of English and Comparative Literature at Yale and project director and faculty advisor to the Fortunoff Video Archive.

Hartman became acquainted with the Holocaust Survivors Film Project in 1979 through his wife's participation. When the project's founders decided to expand to include survivors' testimonies from around the country, Hartman, both a project board and Yale faculty member, urged the university to assist the effort. He recognized the importance and urgency of preserving Holocaust testimony and believed the university's expertise in collections and cataloguing would make it an ideal home for the project. With his encouragement and Yale's president, A. Bartlett Giamatti's support, almost 200 testimonies were deposited at the Sterling Memorial Library in 1981. Professor Hartman became faculty advisor and was actively involved in directing the project's development and growth. "The original thought about the archive was that when we reached a collection of 1,000 testimonies, we'd close shop," said Hartman. "But our feeling changed, and we decided that any survivor who wanted to tell his or her story should be heard." The project became the Fortunoff Video Archive in 1987. The Archive now houses over 4,300 testimonies recorded in more than 20 languages.

Hartman is an iconoclastic scholar of international repute in the field of contemporary criticism. Trained at Yale as a comparatist, and part of "The Yale School" in the 1970s and 1980s, his name is associated with the theory of deconstruction. His range of thinking, however, cannot be confined to one school of thought. Hartman's ideas regarding the synergy of the theoretical and the practical and the relationship between the text and its reader have shaped the field of criticism. This profound approach also underlies his reading of Holocaust testimony.

In addition to his large body of works in literary criticism, Hartman has written extensively on Holocaust memory. Both his own experiences and those recorded in the Archive, have informed Hartman's work, which includes *Holocaust Remembrance: The Shapes of Memory*; *The Longest Shadow: In the Aftermath of the Holocaust*; and *Scars of the Spirit: The Struggle Against Inauthenticity*. He is also the author of and has co-authored numerous related articles. In his writing he probes the subject of Holocaust memory in all of its complexities; finding a balance between authentic remembering and meaningful representation; the effect of and integration of trauma and Holocaust memory in survivors' lives; and how traumatic memories play out in the consciousness of the larger society as well.

[Beth Cohen (2nd ed.)]

HARTMANN, HEINZ (1894–1970), psychoanalyst. Hartmann, who was born in Vienna, was a leading theoretician in psychoanalysis and a pioneer in the field of psychoanalytic ego psychology. In 1939 he published his paper *Ich-Psychologie und Anpassungsproblem*, translated into English in 1958 as *Ego Psychology and the Problem of Adaptation*. Like Anna *Freud, he emphasized the activities of that psychic construct, the ego, as no less important than that of the drives, the id. He pointed out the importance of man's adapting to an "average expectable environment" as a function of the ego. In the same paper, he defined the "conflict-free sphere of the ego" – where patterns of behavior develop independently of unconscious intrapsychic conflict; they do so either, primarily, through inborn autonomous ego functions or, secondarily, by gaining autonomy from the conflicts which helped bring them about. A student of Freud, Hartmann amplified and elaborated numerous aspects of psychoanalytic theory, including the relation of intrapsychic events and of psychoanalysis to the environment, to society, and to the social sciences. He emigrated to Switzerland in 1938 and in 1941 settled in the United States. He served as president of the International and New York Psychoanalytic Associations (1951–57 and 1952–54 respectively). In 1959 he was made honorary president of the International Association.

BIBLIOGRAPHY: L. Eidelberg (ed.), *Encyclopedia of Psychoanalysis* (1968), index; A. Grinstein, *Index of Psychoanalytic Writings*, 2 (1957) 7 (1964); R.M. Loewenstein, in: F. Alexander et al., *Psychoanalytic Pioneers* (1966), 469–83, includes bibliography.

[Rafael Moses]

HARTMANN, MORITZ (1821–1872), German author and revolutionary. Hartmann was born in Dušniky, near Přibram, Bohemia. One of the first Jewish youngsters in Bohemia to receive a general high school education, Hartmann demonstratively abandoned Judaism as a youth, although he never formally converted to Christianity. Extolling the Hussites and the revived Czech national feeling of his time in *Ein Tage aus der Böhmischen Geschichte* (1845) and *Kelch und Schwert* (1845), he transferred the Jewish yearning for Zion to the Czech longing for independence and spoke of Prague as the "Slavic Jerusalem." Austrian objections to Hartmann's pro-German sympathies resulted in his flight to Leipzig and eventually to Paris, where he met *Heine and George Sand. Returning to Prague in 1847, he was briefly imprisoned and then became the central figure in "Young Bohemia," a group of German writers which included Siegfried *Kapper (later Hartmann's brother-in-law) and Friedrich Hirsch-Szarvady, later a Hungarian nationalist. Faced with the anti-Jewish excesses of the 1840s, Hartmann blamed the Czech people for the Prague disturbances and for the antisemitic tendencies of Czech nationalist leaders such as Karel Havliček-Borovský. He turned to German liberalism, and in 1848 he was elected delegate to the revolutionary German national assembly in Frankfurt, where he was a popular idol of the extreme left and was made a member of the assembly's delegation to Vienna.

Following Windischgraetz's suppression of the revolution, Hartmann became a fugitive and expressed his disappointment and anger with the liberals in his satirical *Reimchronik des Pfaffen Mauritius* (1849). His experiences during the 1848 Revolution and abortive Baden uprising were summarized in *Bruchstuecke revolutionaerer Erinnerungen* (1861), edited by H.H. Houben as *Revolutionaere Erinnerungen* (1919). Hartmann earned his living as a foreign correspondent, particularly during the Crimean War (1854), after which he moved first to Paris and then to Geneva, where he taught German literature from 1860 onward and married a Protestant. Following the general amnesty of 1868 he returned to Vienna and joined the editorial staff of the *Neue Freie Presse*. The many novellas which Hartmann published during the 1850s–1860s include a few stories on Jewish themes. His collected works in 10 volumes (ed. W. Vollmer) appeared posthumously in 1873–74 and a selection of his letters (ed. R. Wolkan) in 1921.

His son, LUDO MORITZ HARTMANN (1865–1924), was a prominent Austrian Social Democrat and, as a result of his atheism and political activities, was denied a chair in history at the University of Vienna until after the fall of the Hapsburgs in 1918. Ludo Hartmann founded the *Vierteljahresschrift fuer Sozial- und Wirtschaftsgeschichte*, his major work being a comprehensive *Geschichte Italiens im Mittelalter* (4 vols., 1897–1915). He was the Austrian republic's ambassador in Berlin from 1918 until 1921.

BIBLIOGRAPHY: O. Donath, in: JGGJČ, 6 (1934), 323–442 passim; M. Grunwald, *Vienna* (1936), index; J. Goldmark, *Pilgrims of '48* (1930), index; H. Bergmann, in: G. Kisch (ed.), *Czechoslovak Jewry, Past and Future* (1943), 22–24; G. Kisch, *In Search of Freedom* (1949), index; A. Hofman, *Die Prager Zeitschrift "Ost und West"* (1957), index; *The Jews of Czechoslovakia* (1968), index. **ADD. BIBLIOGRAPHY:** O. Wittner, *Moritz Hartmanns Jugend* (1903); idem, *Moritz Hartmanns Leben und Werke*; vols. 1–2 (1906–7); St. Hoehne, "Moritz Hartmanns 'Krieg um den Wald': zur literarischen Verarbeitung von Vormaerz und 48er Revolution," in: *Bruecken* 4 (1996), 171–88; H. Blaukopf, "Moritz Hartmann (1821–1872)," in: *Literatur und Kritik*, 315/316 (1997), 99–106; E. Kleinschmidt, "Revolutionäre Spiegelungen: zu Moritz Hartmanns 'Reimchronik des Pfaffen Maurizius' (1849)," in: H. Kircher and M. Klanska (eds.), *Literatur und Politik in der Heine-Zeit. Die 48er Revolution in Texten zwischen Vormaerz und Nachmaerz* (1998), 185–203; S.P. Scheichl, "Zur Freundschaftskultur von Prager und Wiener Juden im Vormaerz: Briefe aus dem Umfeld von Moritz Hartmann," in: H. Denkler (ed.), *Juden und juedische Kultur* *im Vormärz* (1999), 165–80 (Forum Vormaerz-Forschung: Jahrbuch; 1998 = 4. Jg.); H. Beutin, "'Der ich komm' aus dem Hussitenlande': Tradition, Revolution und Demokratie in der Gedankenwelt Moritz Hartmanns," in: J. Dvorák (ed.), *Radikalismus, demokratische Strömungen und die Moderne in der oesterreichischen Literatur* (2003), 87–105; E. Bourke, "Moritz Hartmann, Bohemia and the Metternich System," in: D. Kopp (ed.), *Goethe im Vormaerz* (2004) 353–71 (Forum Vormaerz-Forschung: Jahrbuch; 2003 = 9. Jg.)

HARTOG, LEVIE DE (1835–1918), jurist and Orientalist. Born at Gorinchem, Holland, he was professor of public law at the University of Amsterdam from 1877 to 1906, and served from 1887 on the board of trustees of the Nederlands Israëlietisch Seminarium, the Jewish theological seminary of Amsterdam. Hartog published a textbook on Dutch public law, collated the Leiden manuscripts for M. Steinschneider's *Alfabeta de-Ben-Sira* (Berlin, 1858), and wrote a biography in Dutch of his teacher of Oriental languages, R.P. Dozy.

[Frederik Jacob Hirsch]

HARTOG, SIR PHILIP JOSEPH (1864–1947), British educator. His mother was Marion Moss (1821–97), who with her sister Celia had published pioneer sketches of Jewish history in English. Hartog, who was born in London, began his career as lecturer in chemistry at Owens College, Manchester (1891). He served as academic registrar of the University of London from 1904 to 1920. Hartog did extensive chemical research and published the results of his investigations on the thermochemistry of the sulphites, the flame spectrum of nickel compounds, and the latent heat of steam. He was associated with the founding of the School of Oriental and African Studies in London. He was a member of the Viceroy's Commission on the University of Calcutta, India, in 1917. From 1920 to 1925 Hartog served as the first vice chancellor of the University of Dacca, Bengal. He was instrumental in the creation of the National Foundation for Educational Research, London, to study the nature and purpose of school examinations. He played a leading role in the improvement of school and college examinations. In 1930 Hartog was knighted for distinguished public service. In 1933 he went to Palestine as chairman of the committee of inquiry on the organization of the Hebrew University in Jerusalem. In the same year he became chairman of the Jewish Professional Committee to assist refugees from Germany. He was chairman of the Liberal Jewish Synagogue and active in the Anglo-Jewish Association and Board of Deputies of British Jews. Hartog's works include: *The Writing of English* (1907), *Blaise Pascal* (1927), *Joseph Priestley and his Place in the History of Science* (1931), *Some Aspects of Indian Education, Past and Present* (1939), and *Words in Action* (1947).

Hartog's brother, NUMA EDWARD (1846–1871), was a mathematician who had attracted attention when in 1869 he had graduated as Senior Wrangler and Smith's Prizeman at Cambridge University but as a Jew had not been admitted to a fellowship. It is generally believed that Hartog's case led to the passage by Parliament of the Test Act, 1871, which removed religious barriers to holding fellowships at Oxford and Cambridge. Numa Hartog died of smallpox at the age of only 25. Their cousin was the philosopher H. *Bergson.

BIBLIOGRAPHY: M.H. Hartog. P.J. Hartog: *a Memoir by his Wife Mabel Hartog* (1949). **ADD. BIBLIOGRAPHY:** ODNB online for both; Jolles, *Distinguished British Jews,* index; I. Finestein, "Religious Disabilities at Oxford and Cambridge and the Movement for Abolition, 1771–1871," in: idem., *Anglo-Jewry in Changing Times* (1999), 102–39.

[Ernest Schwarcz]

HARTOGENSIS, BENJAMIN HENRY (1865–1939), U.S. jurist, historian, and civic leader. Hartogensis, born in Baltimore, was a lifelong resident there, practicing law from 1893. He wrote for the Baltimore *Sun* and *Baltimore American*, and for Jewish publications, including the (Philadelphia) *Jewish Exponent*, of which he was an associate editor, and the *Publications of the American Jewish Historical Society.* Hartogensis' major interests were legal and historical, particularly the history of religious liberty in America, including Jewish law (especially marital) and biblical influences on American law. A leader in civic and Jewish organizations, Hartogensis was a founder of Baltimore's night schools and the Baltimore branch of the Alliance Israélite Universelle. He established the Jewish legal section of the Baltimore Law Library.

[Robert S. Goldman]

HARVEY, LAURENCE (1928–1973), British actor. Born Hirsch Moses Skikne in Lithuania, Harvey was brought up in South Africa, the son of a building contractor. He went to England after World War II and achieved his first big success at Stratford-on-Avon in *Romeo and Juliet* (1954), which he also played on the screen. Starring roles followed in the musical *Camelot* (1964) and in many feature films. He was at his best in cynical roles of the British realistic school such as in *Room at the Top* (1959), for which he received a "Best Actor" Oscar nomination, and *Darling* (1966), as well as in *The Manchurian Candidate* (1962).

BIBLIOGRAPHY: ODNB online.

HARZFELD (Postrelko), AVRAHAM (1888–1973), labor leader in Ereẓ Israel. Born in Stavishche, Ukraine, he studied at the yeshivot of Berdichev and Telz, receiving a rabbinical diploma. In 1906 he joined the Russian Socialist Zionist Party (SS), for which he was twice arrested and imprisoned for two years in Vilna. In 1910 he was sentenced to life imprisonment with hard labor in Siberia, but in 1914 escaped from Siberia and reached Ereẓ Israel, where he worked as an agricultural laborer in Petaḥ Tikvah and was active in the labor movement. During World War I he played an important role in helping Jews who had been arrested by the Turks, including members of the secret *Nili group. Harzfeld was a member of *Po'alei Zion (1914–19), *Aḥdut ha-Avodah (1919–30), and *Mapai (from 1930) and was one of the founders of the *Histadrut in 1920. From 1919 he was a prominent member of the Histadrut's earlier Central Agricultural Council (Ha-Merkaz ha-Ḥakla'i) and in over 40 years of office played an important role in planning agricultural settlement in Palestine. He initiated many settlement projects and followed with dedication and diligence the development of new settlements throughout the country. For more than 40 years, including the difficult *Stockade and Watchtower period, there was hardly an establishment of a new settlement at which Harzfeld was not personally present. He was a member of the Zionist General Council from 1921, a member of the directorate of the Jewish National Fund from 1949, and a Mapai Knesset member in the first, second, and third Knesset. Harzfeld was awarded a special Israel Prize in 1972, in appreciation of his lifelong service to the State. He became known for the "ḥasidic" atmosphere of enthusiastic group singing, which he introduced in intervals at the meetings of Zionist and *yishuv* bodies.

BIBLIOGRAPHY: S. Kushnir, *The Village Builder: biography of A. Hartzfeld* (1967).

[Gedalyah Elkoshi]

ḤASAN, ABU ALI JEPHETH IBN BUNDĀR (second half of 11th century), thought to be one of the first of the Yemenite *negidim* who lived in *Aden between the 11th and early 14th centuries. His name indicates he was of Persian origin. According to *genizah fragments and tombstone inscriptions, Jewish leadership was transferred from *San'a to Aden, because of the rising importance of the latter's port as a center of trade between *Egypt and *India. According to documents connected with Ḥasan's name, he was active during the second half of the 11th century until approximately its close. One of the documents contains the date 1409 of the Seleucid era (1097/98 C.E.).

As a wealthy man who engaged in trade with India and served as a "traders' official" in Aden, i.e., a colleague and representative of the traders, Ḥasan was also a public leader. He was called "the head of the communities," meaning that he had authority over the Jewish communities of southern *Yemen. His title **nagid* is found in the eulogy of the Tunisian trader Abraham b. Peraḥyah b. Yajo for his son Maḍmūm: "And all the community called him *nagid* the son [*nin*] of a *nagid*" (*nin* being son according to Targ. Onk., Gen. 21: 23). Ḥasan's descendants were also wealthy traders who signed agreements with tribal chiefs and pirates in control of the sea routes from Egypt, by way of the Red Sea, to India, thus assuring freedom of navigation and trade. They were also called *negidim* and were active in public life in Yemen. They had connections mainly with the Palestinian academy in Egypt.

BIBLIOGRAPHY: E. Strauss, in: *Zion*, 4 (1939), 217–31; S.D. Goitein, in: *Sinai*, 33 (1953), 225–37; idem, in: Jewish Theological Seminary, N.Y., *Sefer ha-Yovel... M.M. Kaplan* (1953), 45, 51–53; idem, in: *Tarbiz*, 31 (1961/62), 357–70; idem, in: Y. Ratzaby (ed.), *Bo'i Teiman* (1967), 15–25; idem, in: JQR, 53 (1962/63), 97: E. Subar, *ibid.*, 49 (1958/59), 301–9; J. Mann, in: HUCA, 3 (1926), 301–3.

[Eliezer Bashan (Sternberg)]

ḤASAN (Hussein) BEN MASHI'AḤ (tenth century), Karaite scholar. According to *Ibn al-Hītī he lived in Baghdad, where he held religious *disputations with the Christian scholar Abu Ali ʿIsā ibn Zarʿa. *Sahl b. Maẓli'aḥ states that Ḥasan had disputations with *Saadiah Gaon (d. 942), which seems chronologically unlikely. Ḥasan also wrote a polemical treatise against Saadiah, passages of which are incorporated in the *Eshkol ha-Kofer* of Judah *Hadassi and in a manuscript in Leningrad. A remark of *Ibn Ezra in the introduction to his commentary on the Pentateuch suggests that Ḥasan wrote biblical commentaries.

BIBLIOGRAPHY: S. Poznański, *Karaite Literary Opponents of Saadiah Gaon* (1908), 15f.; Mann, Texts, 2 (1935), index.

[Leon Nemoy]

ḤASDAI (Ḥisdai), name of four Babylonian exilarchs. ḤASDAI BEN BUSTANAI lived in the 7th century. Both he and his brother Baradoi served as exilarchs following the death of their father, *Bustanai, in about 670. The two brothers attempted to undermine the position of the sons of their father's Persian wife, alleging that she had the status of a female prisoner of war who had not been manumitted.

ḤASDAI BEN BARADOI (d. 733?) was exilarch at the beginning of the 8th century. He was the father-in-law of R. Natronai b. Nehemiah, the head of the Pumbedita academy. Various legends are told about him in Arab chronicles. His son Solomon was exilarch from 733 to 759, if not later. His second son, David, was the father of *Anan, founder of the Karaite sect. ḤASDAI BEN NATRONAI was exilarch during the first half of the 9th century.

ḤASDAI BEN DAVID BEN HEZEKIAH (the Second) was exilarch in the 12th century (d. before 1135). During this period the office of exilarch gained in prestige, and its bearers had great influence at the court of the caliph Muhammad al-Muktafi, who appointed him as exilarch. Benjamin of Tudela, the 12th-century traveler, reports that Ḥasdai was one of the teachers of David *Alroy, the false Messiah. His son Daniel took his place as exilarch. Abraham *Ibn Ezra may have met him during his visit to Baghdad in 1139. He died a year before *Pethahiah of Regensburg's visit to Baghdad in about 1175.

BIBLIOGRAPHY: M.N. Adler (ed.), *Masot Binyamin mi-Tudela*, (1907), 54 (Eng. pt.); Pethahiah of Regensburg, *Sibbuv*, ed. by L. Gruenhut (1905), 9; S. Poznański, *Babylonische Geonim im nachgaonaeischen Zeitalter* (1914), 115–8; Ch. Tykocinski, in: *Devir*, 1 (1923), 145–79; J. Mann, in: *Sefer... S.A. Poznański* (1927), 23; Mann, Texts, 1 (1931), 208–9, 211, 228; S. Abramson, in: KS, 26 (1950), 93–94. **ADD. BIBLIOGRAPHY:** Y. Gil, *Be-Malkhut Ishma'el*, vol. 1, 95–97, 307, 433–35.

[Abraham David]

HASEFER, official publishing house of the Federation of Jewish Communities in Romania. Founded in 1990 in Bucharest for the purpose of publishing Rabbi Moses *Rosen's works, it was expanded after his death (1994). The president of the Federation, Nicolae Cajal, aimed to build a spiritual bridge between Jews and Romanians in order to fight antisemitism by presenting Jewish spirituality, history, and contribution to civilization to people who would not know of them in the Communist period. It was also a period of growing interest in Jewish studies in Romania. The publishing house was enlarged and created in a way similar to that of Judaica publishing houses in other countries. The philosopher, social scientist, and literary critic Zigu Ornea was appointed director in 1995 because of his experience as director of the Minerva publishing house in Bucharest. Funding came from the Federation of Jewish Communities and from the Romanian government department for minorities. The name Hasefer ("The Book") was taken from the former bookshop of the same name that had existed in Bucharest between the two world wars, owned by Henry (Herman) Steinberg. After Zigu Ornea's death, the assistant director, Alexandru Singer, took over as director (2003). By April 2005, Hasefer had published 260 books, mainly in Romanian on the subjects of Judaism, Jewish philosophy and history, Romanian Jewish history, Holocaust, Yiddish literature, and Israeli literature. Among the well-known authors published in Romanian translation are Isaac Bashevis *Singer, Andre *Neher, Saul *Bellow, Primo *Levi, Moshe *Idel, Nava Semel, Moses *Mendelsohn, *Josephus Flavius, and *Philo of Alexandria.

BIBLIOGRAPHY: Hasefer Publishing House, catalog on CD (2005); B. Tercatin (ed.), *Calendar Luah 5766/2005–2006*; A. Mirodan, *Dicționar neoconvențional*, 2 (1997), 218–19.

[Lucian-Zeev Herșcovici (2nd ed.)]

HASENCLEVER, WALTER (1890–1940), German poet and playwright. Born in Aachen of a Jewish mother and a non-Jewish father, Hasenclever served in the German army during World War I but his experiences made him a pacifist. After 1918 he worked for a time as a foreign correspondent in Paris and the U.S. Leaving Germany in 1933, he eventually settled in France. After the French collapse in 1940, Hasenclever was twice interned and, fearing the arrival of the Nazis, committed suicide in a detention camp near Aix-en-Provence. A friend of the critic Kurt Pinthus and of Franz *Werfel, Hasenclever was an early expressionist who became famous with his revolutionary drama, *Der Sohn* (1914). This dealt with the conflict between the generations and preached resistance to blind authority. Three verse collections were *Der Juengling* (1913), *Tod und Auferstehung* (1917), and *Gedichte an Frauen* (1922). His pacifist ideas were expressed in the plays *Der Retter* (1916), and *Antigone* (1917), while satire and pathos distinguished such later dramas as *Die Menschen* (1918), *Gobseck* (1922) and *Mord* (1926). In *Jenseits* (1920) Hasenclever briefly turned to the occult. From the late 1920s he wrote plays in a more comic or ironic spirit, such as *Ehen werden im Himmel geschlossen* (1928) and *Napoleon greift ein* (1929). He also wrote German versions of foreign plays and films, one of his collaborators being Ernst *Toller. His drama *Muenchhausen*, written in 1934, appeared posthumously in 1952. His collected works in five volumes (ed. D. Breuer and B. Witte) appeared in 1990–97 and a selection of his letters in two volumes (ed. D. Breuer and B. Kasties) appeared in 1994.

BIBLIOGRAPHY: K. Pinthus, in: W. Hasenclever, *Gedichte, Dramen, Prosa* (1963), 6–62; H. Kesten, *Meine Freunde, die Poeten* (1959), 229–36; A. Soergel and C. Hohoff, *Dichtung und Dichter der Zeit*, 2 (1963), 274–81. **ADD. BIBLIOGRAPHY:** H. Denkler, in: B. Poll, *Rheinische Lebensbilder*, 4 (1970), 251–72; M. Raggam, *Walter Hasenclever, Leben und Werk* (1973); D. Breuer, *Walter Hasenclever (1890–1940)* (1990, 1996[2]); B. Kasties, *Walter Hasenclever, eine Biographie der deutschen Moderne*, (1994); C. Spreitzer, *From Expressionism to Exile: The Works of Walter Hasenclever (1890–1940)* (1999); B. Schommers-Kretschmer, *Philosophie und Poetologie im Werk von Walter Hasenclever* (2000); K. Schuhmann, *Walter Hasenclever, Kurt Pinthus uns Frant Werfel im Leipziger Kurt-Wolff-Verlag (1913–1919)* (2000).

HA-SHAḤAR (Heb. הַשַּׁחַר), Hebrew journal which was published and edited in Vienna by Peretz *Smolenskin from 1868 to 1884. During these 16 years, 12 volumes of *Ha-Shaḥar* were published. In theory *Ha-Shaḥar* was a monthly; in practice, however, the financial and organizational difficulties caused prolonged interruptions in its regular appearances. In his first article "*Petaḥ Davar*" ("Preface") Smolenskin describes its aims: the diffusion of *Haskalah; war against its Orthodox opponents, especially the Ḥasidim: war against assimilationists and religious reformers; and defense of the national values of the nation and the Hebrew language. Smolenskin molded the image of *Ha-Shaḥar* as an independent and militant journal. *Ha-Shaḥar* was initially designed mainly for Russian Jews. Because of Russian restrictions against the Hebrew press, however, it was published in Vienna, from where copies were sent to the offices of the censor in Russia before distribution through agents in Russia. Sometimes, an article which the censor was liable to reject was published in a special supplement, and sent to the subscribers in Russia in sealed envelopes separately from the regular copy. Outside Russia as well, *Ha-Shaḥar* acquired a large audience of readers, especially in Austria, Galicia, and Romania. The number of subscribers to the annual fluctuated between 800 to 1,300.

Subscriptions covered only a part of the expenses even though the publisher did not pay fees to his writers and carried out himself a large part of the proofreading and the distribution of the copies to the subscribers. Smolenskin invested his own money in *Ha-Shaḥar* and was supported by contributors from among the well-to-do *maskilim*, and subsidies from the *Alliance Israélite Universelle in Paris and the Ḥevrat Mefiẓei ha-Haskalah ("Society for the Dissemination of the Haskalah") in St. Petersburg.

Ha-Shaḥar published belles lettres and articles dealing with Jewish scholarly matters and current affairs. Among the Hebrew writers of the generation who contributed were M.D. *Brandstadter, R.A. Broides, the poets J.L. *Gordon, A.B. *Gottlober, J.L. *Levin (Yehalel), I. *Kaminer, S. *Mandelkern, and M.M. *Dolitzki. There, too, Smolenskin published his novels (*Ha-To'eh be-Darkhei ha-Ḥayyim, Simḥat Ḥanef, Kevurat Ḥamor, Ha-Yerushah, Nekam Berit*). The works are written mainly in the flowery *maskil* style. Most condemn the rabbinical orthodoxy of the time and especially the Ḥasidim, but at the same time assail the assimilationist *maskilim*. Socialistic undertones are heard especially in Yehalel's poetry ("*Kishron ha-Ma'aseh*," and others).

In the area of Judaic studies *Ha-Shaḥar* published works of scholars from Western and Eastern Europe, including Solomon *Rubin, David *Kahana, Y. *Reifman, S. *Buber I.H. *Weiss, S. *Sachs, Meir *Ish-Shalom (Friedmann), A. *Jellinek, J.H. *Gurland, A.E. *Harkavy, Ḥ.Z. *Lerner, A. *Krochmal, E. Shulman, and D. Holub. *Ha-Shaḥar* also published letters of Jewish scholars and authors of the early Haskalah: S.J. *Rapoport, S. *Luzzatto, and J. *Perl. Most of the book reviews were written by Smolenskin.

Of prime historical importance were the articles which dealt with current problems. Smolenskin himself published his major articles on Jewish problems in which he introduced his nationalist ideology. These views, and especially his attack on *Mendelssohn, the cultural hero of the Haskalah, alienated many of his supporters, and by the end of 1880 Smolenskin was forced to discontinue publication. With the rise of the Ḥibbat Zion movement in the wake of the pogroms of 1881, Smolenskin renewed the publication of *Ha-Shaḥar* which now openly advocated the Ḥibbat Zion program for Jewish settlement in Ereẓ Israel. Smolenskin filled *Ha-Shaḥar* with dozens of articles on the new movement. He attacked the Alliance Israélite Universelle, which had once supported him, for their opposition to Jewish settlement in Ereẓ Israel. E. *Ben-Yehuda, M.L. *Lilienblum, A.S. *Friedberg, A.A. Sirotkin, and others now wrote in *Ha-Shaḥar*. In spite of his weakening state of health, Smolenskin continued to publish *Ha-Shaḥar* until his death, after which his brother, Y.L. Smolenskin, published the last four copies, completing the 12th volume.

BIBLIOGRAPHY: Klausner, Sifrut, 5 (1955[2]), index; A. Sha'anan, *Ha-Sifrut ha-Ivrit ha-Ḥadashah li-Zerameha*, 2 (1962), 44–47; A. Kristianpoller, *Die hebraeische Publizistik in Wien*, abt. 3 (1930).

[Yehuda Slutsky]

HA-SHILO'AḤ (Ha-Shillo'ah; Heb. הַשִּׁלֹחַ). Hebrew literary, social, and scientific monthly in Russia until World War I. Founded in 1896, *Ha-Shilo'aḥ* was first edited by *Aḥad Ha-Am in Odessa and Warsaw and printed in Berlin and Cracow until after the Russian revolution of 1905. From 1907 to 1919 it was edited and printed in Odessa, while from 1920 until it ceased publication in 1926, it was edited and printed in Jerusalem. Altogether 46 volumes appeared in 23 years of publication (there were intervals during which the monthly did not publish, e.g., the Russian revolution of 1905, in 1915 under the czarist regime, in 1919 under the Soviet regime).

Aḥad Ha-Am intended *Ha-Shilo'aḥ* to be a journal devoted to Zionism, Jewish scholarship, and belles lettres in a style accessible to the general reader. Not believing in art for art's sake, he was interested in making literature serve the monthly's general objectives of Zionism and "usefulness" to the people. This approach was attacked by young authors (*Berdyczewski, in particular) and the controversy helped determine the course of Hebrew literature in the early 20th century. *Ha-Shilo'aḥ* expressed Aḥad Ha-Am's bitter antagonism to Herzl and political Zionism, which elicited a strong reaction from the Zionist movement. The writing in *Ha-Shilo'aḥ* was free of rhetoric, the result of the great effort Aḥad Ha-Am spent, as his letters testify, in guiding the writers and editing their work. Thus the monthly, which only printed material of high quality, was from its inception a novelty in Hebrew periodicals. Aḥad Ha-Am's successor, Joseph *Klausner, who edited the monthly from 1903 until it ceased publication, followed a similar policy, but devoted more space to belles lettres and the works of such authors as J.Ḥ. *Brenner, I.L. *Peretz, S. *Asch, Z. *Shneour, and S. *Tchernichowsky. Ḥ.N. *Bialik, many of whose works were printed in *Ha-Shilo'aḥ*, coedited volumes 13–21. Most of Aḥad Ha-Am's essays also appeared in *Ha-Shilo'aḥ*, both while he was editor and after.

Ha-Shilo'aḥ revolutionized all genres of Hebrew literature and journalism. It became a model of Hebrew writing, both in form and content, and authors regarded it as an honor to publish in the journal. Indeed, the writings in *Ha-Shilo'aḥ* remain of interest and value today both for the subject matter and the style they introduced into Hebrew literature. Unlike Aḥad Ha-Am, Klausner was an adherent of political Zionism, yet *Ha-Shilo'aḥ* reflected all the trends within Zionism. When Klausner immigrated to Ereẓ Israel in 1920, *Ha-Shilo'aḥ* resumed publication in Jerusalem, and from 1925, Jacob *Fichmann, editor of the literary section, coedited the monthly. In Jerusalem the journal did not enjoy the same importance as it had in Russia. There were already a number of newspapers and periodicals in Ereẓ Israel where, in addition, the atmosphere in which *Ha-Shilo'aḥ* had thrived in Russia was lacking. A bibliography of the writings and authors printed in *Ha-Shilo'aḥ* was compiled by Joshua Barzilai-Folman (1964).

BIBLIOGRAPHY: Aḥad Ha-Am, *Iggerot*, 1–6 (1956–60[2]); Ḥ.N. Bialik, *Iggerot*, 1–5 (1937–39); J. Klausner, *Darki li-kerat ha-Teḥiyyah ve-ha-Ge'ullah*, 1–2 (1955[2]); B. Shoḥetman, in: *Sefer Klausner* (1937), 525f.; idem, in: *Gilyonot*, 21 (1947), 101–7; Waxman, Literature, 4 (1960), 404ff.

[Getzel Kressel]

HASHKIVENU (Heb. הַשְׁכִּיבֵנוּ; "cause us to lie down"), initial word of the second benediction after the *Shema of the daily evening prayer. This prayer for protection during the night is mentioned in the Talmud (Ber. 4b) and is considered as an extension of the **Ge'ullah* benediction which precedes it. There are two versions of this prayer, the Sephardi liturgy employing a shorter version for Friday evenings in view of the discouragement of supplication on the Sabbath (TJ, Ber. 4:5, 8c; also I. Davidson et al. (eds.), *Siddur Rav Sa'adyah Ga'on* (1941), 27 and iii). The prayer closes on weekdays with the benediction: "Blessed art thou, O Lord, who guardest thy people Israel for ever" (which uses the Babylonian text), whereas on Friday evening it ends: "Blessed art thou, O Lord, who spreadest the tabernacle of peace over us, over Israel and over Jerusalem" (which was the Palestinian text). The Midrash to Ps. 6:1 attributes the inclusion of the prayer in the evening service to the fact that the *ẓiẓit*, which perform a protective function, are not worn during the night.

BIBLIOGRAPHY: Elbogen, Gottesdienst, 99–109.

HA-SHOMER (Heb. הַשּׁוֹמֵר, "The Watchman"), association of Jewish watchmen in Ereẓ Israel, which was active between 1909 and 1920. It was founded by pioneers of the Second *Aliyah, many of whom had been active in revolutionary movements and Jewish self-defense in Russia, and were critical of the methods used to protect life and property in the Jewish settlements based upon non-Jewish guards (Bedouin, Circassian, Mughrebim, etc.). Most of them were members or sympathizers of the *Po'alei Zion Party. On the initiative of Israel Shoḥat, about 10 of them, including Izhak *Ben-Zvi and Alexander *Zeid, met in Jaffa in 1907 and founded a secret society called Bar-Giora, which aimed at winning the right to work and keep guard in the settlements and develop Jewish settlement in new areas. It adopted as its watchword a line from Ya'akov *Cahan's poem "*Biryonim*" ("Zealots"): "*Be-dam va-esh Yehudah naflah, be-dam va-esh Yehudah takum*" ("By blood and fire Judea fell; by blood and fire Judea shall rise"). The members of Bar-Giora were given responsibility for the protection of Sejera (now Ilaniyyah) in lower Galilee, and, in 1908, of Mesḥa (Kefar Tavor). On the initiative of Bar-Giora a wider organization, called Ha-Shomer, was established in April 1909 at a meeting in Mesḥa. It was headed by a committee of three: Shoḥat, Israel *Giladi, and Mendel Portugali. Bar-Giora, in effect, merged with the new body. Within three years, Ha-Shomer assumed responsibility for the protection of seven villages, among them Ḥaderah, Reḥovot, and Rishon le-Zion. Other settlements passed also to an all-Jewish guard system. Within a short time the Jews in Ereẓ Israel no longer relied on the protection of foreign consuls and powerful neighbors, but were capable of defending their lives and property. Ha-Shomer based its methods on a close study of the conditions in the country, the ways of the Ottoman authorities, and the character of the Arab bedouin and peasants. The *shomerim* spoke Arabic, wore a mixture of Arab and Circassian dress, and carried modern weapons; some of them became expert horsemen. In 1914 they numbered about 40, with another 50–60 candidates for membership and temporary auxiliaries; at harvest time, they could deploy some 300 men. Candidates had to undergo a year's trial and take a ceremonial oath after being approved by a two-thirds majority at the annual general meeting. The *shomerim*, with their picturesque dress and armament, were prominent in the life of the new *yishuv* and played an important part in settling new and disputed land. They were widely known in the Zionist movement, which supported them. *Yizkor*, a memorial volume in honor of their casualties, in Hebrew, Yiddish and German, had a great influence after World War I on Diaspora Jewish youth. Ha-Shomer was criticized by some circles, especially the supporters of the *Ha-Po'el ha-Ẓa'ir party, because of its independence and the fear that it might anger the Arabs. On the outbreak of World War I, Ha-Shomer had to go underground, and two of its leaders, Manya and Israel Shoḥat, were exiled in 1915 to Anatolia. Its difficulties were intensified by internecine dissensions, as a result of which a group of members, headed by Israel Giladi, left and founded southwest of Metulah the settlement of Kefar Giladi. In 1916 it started to recover: its members collected and stored arms, and organized the protection of Jewish property. Ha-Shomer opposed the espionage activities of *Nili because it endangered the Jewish community, and decided to execute Yosef *Lishanski, one of the Nili group who had escaped, in case he fell into the hands of the Turkish authorities and betrayed the secrets of the defenders. Lishanski was caught by the Turks, however, and told them all he knew. As a result, 12 *shomerim* were interrogated in Damascus and four of them imprisoned. During the British campaign in Palestine, members of Ha-Shomer joined the *Jewish Legion, while others joined the mounted police, which kept order in Galilee, and played a prominent part in the defense of *Tel Ḥai and Jerusalem. However, new elements in the *yishuv*'s leadership demanded the reorganization of defense on a broader basis under the discipline of the recognized Jewish authorities, public and political bodies. On the proposal of some of its new members, led by Eliyahu *Golomb and Yiẓḥak *Tabenkin, it was decided that the organization should disband and its members serve as the basis for a new defense system. On June 15, 1920, *Aḥdut ha-Avodah accepted the responsibility for the reorganization of defense, and Ha-Shomer ceased to exist as a separate body. Its members continued, however, to maintain contact and made an important contribution to the *yishuv*'s defense and its constructive efforts. Ha-Shomer was the first body in the Zionist movement and the Jewish *yishuv* which believed that the existence of an organized Jewish armed force would be a decisive factor in the realization of Zionism, and its example was an inspiration to the *Haganah and the pioneering youth movements.

BIBLIOGRAPHY: *Koveẓ Ha-Shomer* (1937), Sefer Ha-Shomer (1957); Dinur, Haganah, 1 pt. 2 (1956), index; Y. Ya'ari-Poleskin, *Ḥolemim ve-Loḥamim* (1964[3]); S. Sheva, *Shevet ha-No'azim* (1969), passim; Z. Nadav, *Mi-Ymei Shemirah ve-Haganah* (1955); Y. Allon, *The Making of Israel's Army* (1970).

[Yehuda Slutsky]

HA-SHOMER HA-ẒA'IR, Zionist-socialist pioneering youth movement whose aim is to educate Jewish youth for kibbutz life in Israel. Ha-Shomer ha-Ẓa'ir had its roots in two youth movements that came into being in Galicia (then a province of the Austro-Hungarian Empire) before World War I: Ẓe'irei Zion, which emphasized cultural activities; and Ha-Shomer, primarily a scouting movement (based on the British model). During the war, when many thousands of Jews from the eastern part of the empire took refuge in Vienna, the two movements merged and took on the name Ha-Shomer ha-Ẓa'ir (1916). At the same time a similar development took place among the Jewish youth movements in the Russian part of Poland.

The early years of the movement coincided with the immediate postwar period, which was marked by a national and social awakening among the peoples of Europe, the October Revolution in Russia, and the great hope of standing on the threshold of an era of peace and progress. The ideology of the new movement was also profoundly affected by the persecutions to which East European Jewry was exposed at the time (the Petlura pogroms in the Ukraine, the pogrom in Lvov, etc.). On a spiritual level, Ha-Shomer ha-Ẓa'ir drew its inspiration from the *Ha-Shomer in Ereẓ Israel; the writings of A.D. *Gordon, J.Ḥ. *Brenner, J. *Trumpeldor; as well as from the romantic aura surrounding the revolutionary anticzarist underground and its heroes. Other influences on the movement are to be found in the Free Youth Movement (the Wandervogel) as it was first developed in Germany before World War I and in the new philosophy, literature, psychology, and pedagogy of the time, which called for a reevaluation of existing modes of life and thought. Thus, Ha-Shomer ha-Ẓa'ir sought to create a synthesis between Jewish culture and the rebuilding and defending of Ereẓ Israel, on the one hand, and universal cultural and philosophical values, on the other, and this was to become a characteristic aspect of the movement's ideology.

Educational Method

Another characteristic of Ha-Shomer ha-Ẓa'ir is its educational method, which provides for an organic combination of "training and study groups" with the independent culture and life of youth as practiced by the Free Youth Movement, and also utilizing the symbols and the discipline of scouting. The movement puts special emphasis on the training of the individual and the development of the personality (in its early years Nietzsche's *Thus Spake Zarathustra* was very popular in the ranks of the movement). The basic pedagogic unit of Ha-Shomer ha-Ẓa'ir is the *kevuẓah* (in which the sexes are not mixed), several of which, of the same age groups, combine for certain activities to form larger, coeducational units, such as the *peluggah* ("company") and *gedud* ("batallion"). There are three age groups – the young level (age 11–14), known as *kefirim* ("cubs"), *benei midbar* ("sons of the desert"), or *benei Massada* (sons of Massadah); the intermediate level (15–16), known as *ẓofim* ("scouts"); and the adult level (from 17 upward) known as *bogerim* ("adults"), as well as *keshishim* ("oldsters") and *magshimim* ("implementers, those who fulfill"). Each level has its own program, which is adapted to its emotional needs and intellectual capacity. A local branch is a *ken* ("nest"), and it is headed by *hanhagat ha-ken* ("ken leadership"); a district branch is *ha-galil* and is headed by *hanhagat ha-galil*; while a national federation is headed by *ha-hanhagah ha-rashit* ("chief leadership") and the entire world movement is headed by *ha-hanhagah ha-elyonah* ("supreme leadership").

Before World War II, the Warsaw headquarters of the movement published two periodicals, both in Hebrew: *Ha-Shomer ha-Ẓa'ir*, which served as the organ of the movement as a whole and its adult level, and *Ha-Mizpeh*, which was the organ of the intermediate level. There was also a Ha-Shomer ha-Ẓa'ir publishing house in Warsaw, which put out books of educational content. The various national branches also had their own organs, either in Hebrew or the local languages.

Personal Fulfillment

Ha-Shomer ha-Ẓa'ir is also noted for its application of the principle of personally fulfilling the ideals of the movement. It fosters among its adherents radicalism in the original sense of the term – the search for the root of things and the demand for consistency of thought, analysis, and action; this leads to the principal obligation of the individual – that of personal fulfillment of ideals and conclusions. As a result, the movement took up the struggle against assimilation (including "Red" assimilation, i.e., the widespread phenomenon of Jewish youth and intellectuals being drawn entirely into communist or socialist movements, denying their Jewish identity, and abandoning Jewish values and their responsibility for the fate of the Jewish people). It fostered the use of Hebrew – as opposed to the local language – and created a pioneering Jewish atmosphere in its groups, a pedagogic measure culminating in the paramount obligation of its members – *aliyah* and life in a kibbutz. The strict application of the principle of personal fulfillment resulted in tens of thousands of young people passing through the ranks of Ha-Shomer ha-Ẓa'ir and being forced to leave the movement for failing to settle in Israel, failing to join a kibbutz, or failing to fulfill other demands put upon them by the movement. There were, of course, thousands who stood the test and settled in Ereẓ Israel in kibbutzim of Ha-Shomer ha-Ẓa'ir.

Ha-Shomer ha-Ẓa'ir insists on the organic continuity of its program, from the youngest level up to the personal fulfillment by its adult members in the form of membership in a kibbutz in Israel. The principle of personal fulfillment also accounts for the profound educational influence exerted by the *kevuẓah* leader. This derives not only from his way of life and the quality of his performance as their instructor, but also from the conviction on the part of the young members that whatever their leader demands of them, he is about to fulfill himself – settling in Israel and joining a kibbutz.

Beginnings in Ereẓ Israel

During the Third Aliyah, (1919–23) some 600 members of Ha-Shomer ha-Ẓa'ir settled in Ereẓ Israel. There was no institutional link between the various groups of these settlers or between them and the movement abroad. As a result, the strength of this first wave of Ha-Shomer ha-Ẓa'ir settlers was dissipated. They were dispersed all over the country and, to some degree, were not absorbed in kibbutz life. Furthermore, the removal of the most mature and most active members from the tasks they had fulfilled as instructors and guides caused a general slackening in the activities of the movement abroad. A severe crisis of "individualism" set in, known in the annals of the movement as "the great drift." It was not until 1927, when the Kibbutz Arẓi Ha-Shomer ha-Ẓa'ir was founded, that a permanent framework was established for the organized absorption of Ha-Shomer ha-Ẓa'ir settlers in

Ereẓ Israel and for the guidance of the movement abroad. In the period of the Third and Fourth Aliyah (up to 1926), Ha-Shomer ha-Ẓa'ir evolved its ideology. Slanted toward Marxism, it represented a synthesis between Zionism and socialism, between pioneering construction and class war. When the *Histadrut was founded (1920), the Ha-Shomer ha-Ẓa'ir kibbutzim failed to find a common language with any of the existing parties, and, instead of joining any of them, they declared themselves an independent group. Apart from its tasks in the kibbutzim, in the settlement of newcomers, and in education, the Kibbutz Arẓi also became a framework for the joint development of political ideology ("ideological collectivism") and for joint political action in the Histadrut and the Zionist Movement.

The World Movement

The World Federation of Ha-Shomer ha-Ẓa'ir was founded in Danzig in 1924. It had been preceded by the establishment of Ha-Shomer ha-Ẓa'ir movements in Romania, Lithuania, Latvia, the U.S.S.R. (in addition to the existing movements in Galicia, Poland, and Austria), and by the initiation of efforts on the part of the kibbutzim in Ereẓ Israel to cooperate in the organized and concentrated guidance of the movement abroad. More branches were founded in the period between the First and Second World Convention (the latter also held at Danzig in 1927) in Czechoslovakia, the U.S., Canada, Belgium, and Bulgaria. The founding of the Kibbutz Arẓi greatly enhanced the influence of Ha-Shomer ha-Ẓa'ir in Ereẓ Israel upon the movement abroad. Ha-Shomer ha-Ẓa'ir in the U.S.S.R., Latvia, and, to some degree, in Lithuania, however, did not accept the independent political orientation of the majority of the movement, and members of the movement in these countries who settled in Israel found their way to the *Aḥdut ha-Avodah Party (which in 1930 merged with *Ha-Po'el ha-Ẓa'ir to become *Mapai), and did not join the Kibbutz Arẓi upon its establishment. When the Kibbutz Arẓi was in its early stage, there was still hope that the split in the ranks of the movement would eventually heal, and thus the Second Convention decided to regard the Kibbutz Arẓi only as the "principal path for the movement." The Russian-Latvian minority in Israel, however, not only failed to join Kibbutz Arẓi, but became one of the founders of *Ha-Kibbutz ha-Me'uḥad (linked to Aḥdut ha-Avodah and later to Mapai); disappointed in its expectations, the Third Convention (held in Vrutky, Czechoslovakia in 1930) decided that the Kibbutz Arẓi was now the only correct path for Ha-Shomer ha-Ẓa'ir. The Russian-Latvian minority responded by seceding from the movement and forming "Neẓaḥ" (No'ar Ẓofi-Ḥalutzi – Ha-Shomer ha-Ẓa'ir – Scouting Pioneering Youth, see below).

On the Eve of World War II and the Holocaust

At the time of the Fourth World Convention (Poprad, Czechoslovakia, 1935), Ha-Shomer ha-Ẓa'ir had reached the height of its strength and achievements: groups in Hungary, Germany, Yugoslavia, France, Britain, Switzerland, Tunisia, Egypt, and South Africa had joined the movement, and there were encouraging beginnings in Latin America; membership totaled 70,000, with the majority about to go to Palestine or undergoing agricultural training, and with the adult members active in *He-Ḥalutz, the League for Labor Ereẓ Israel, the elections to the Zionist Congress, etc. The rising tide of fascism in Eastern and Central Europe forced the movement to organize itself for self-defense and for the continuation of its activities under conditions of semilegality or, if this should become necessary, as an underground movement.

When World War II broke out, large numbers of members seeking to escape from the invading German forces converged upon Vilna. A part of this Vilna group eventually joined other refugees in fleeing to the Soviet Union, where they fought in the ranks of the Red Army. Some succeeded in reaching Ereẓ Israel before the German-Russian war broke out (June 1941). Others, however, were ordered by the movement to return to Nazi-occupied territory, where they became outstanding activists of the Jewish resistance, the Jewish partisans, and the ghetto fighters. Mordecai *Anielewicz, the commander of the revolt in the *Warsaw ghetto, was a member of the Ha-Shomer ha-Ẓa'ir movement, and elsewhere in the Polish ghettos and in other countries under Nazi occupation the movement's members were among the leaders of the uprisings.

The Postwar Period

After the war, the surviving members of the movement prepared for *aliyah* and took an active part in the organization of the "illegal" immigration to Ereẓ Israel and the rehabilitation and reeducation of the surviving refugee children in the displaced persons camps in Germany and Italy. In the wake of the political developments in Eastern and Central Europe, the little that had remained of the movement soon dissolved. Henceforth, Ha-shomer ha-Ẓa'ir centered its activities particularly upon Latin America, and members from this area are to be found in most of the movement's kibbutzim in Israel. Branches of the movement continue to exist also in North America, Western Europe, South Africa, and Australia. The Fifth World Convention, held in 1958, was the first to meet in Israel, which had by then become the seat of the headquarters of the movement. Branch offices also existed in Paris, New York, and Buenos Aires. Their task was to direct the work of the emissaries of Kibbutz Arẓi dispatched to the various countries.

Ha-Shomer ha-Ẓa'ir in Israel

The Israel Federation of Ha-Shomer ha-Ẓa'ir naturally occupied a special place among the various branches. When the federation was first established (in 1930), the principles and methods applied by the movement in its work in the Diaspora had to be adapted to the conditions prevailing in Ereẓ Israel, where the problems of Jewish youth were radically different and where the kibbutz was not far away. The relative importance of the Israel movement in the World Federation and as a reservoir of manpower for the Kibbutz Arẓi grew from year to year, and it also played an ever-increasing role in the establishment of new Ha-Shomer ha-Ẓa'ir kibbutzim and the consolidation of existing kibbutzim. The first kibbutz founded by graduates of the movement in Ereẓ Israel was Nir David in the Beth-Shean Valley, established in 1936. (See also *Mapam.)

U.S.-Canada

The movement was founded in North America in 1923. Ha-Shomer ha-Ẓa'ir has found it difficult to make headway in the American Jewish community, with its economic prosperity, its lack of a youth-movement tradition, and the philanthropic character of its Zionist movement. Nevertheless, there are a number of kibbutzim in Israel in which U.S. Ha-Shomer ha-Ẓa'ir graduates predominate (such as Ein ha-Shofet, Kefar Menahem, Hazor, Galon, Sasa, and Barkai). In the course of time, the American movement was also instrumental in the establishment of adult groups (Americans for Progressive Israel, linked to Mapam in Israel), made up of people who were attracted by the Zionist-socialist orientation of Ha-Shomer ha-Ẓa'ir. In the U.S. the movement had its own organ, *Young Guard* and maintained branches in Detroit, Boston, New York, Los Angeles, and, in Canada, in Montreal and Toronto, as well as training farms for the specific purpose of preparing for *aliyah* and kibbutz life. In the early 21st century it had a few hundred members and ran camps in Liberty, New York, and Perth, Ontario.

Great Britain

The movement was founded in Great Britain in the late 1930s, by Ha-Shomer ha-Ẓa'ir members among the refugees from the continent, and by members of He-Ḥalutz and Habonim, who were attracted by Ha-Shomer ha-Ẓa'ir ideology. While it made progress during the war and the immediate postwar period, the movement has not succeeded in recovering the losses in its ranks caused by the *aliyah* of its founders and leading members (in the period 1946–1950), nor has it yet been able to reach the second generation, British-born Jewish youth. Branches exist in Manchester and in London. In Israel, Ha-Shomer ha-Ẓa'ir settlers from Britain are found primarily in the kibbutzim Ha-Ma'pil, Ha-Zore'a, Yasur and Zikim.

South Africa

Founded in 1935, the movement has branches in Johannesburg and Capetown. In Israel, South African *ḥalutzim* of the movement have settled in Shuval, Barkai, Naḥshon, and Zikim.

Australia

Australian Ha-Shomer ha-Ẓa'ir was founded in 1953, with branches in Melbourne and Sydney. Its settlers in Israel are concentrated mainly in Nirim.

[Peretz Merhav]

Neẓaḥ

Neẓaḥ was established in 1930 as the result of a split in Ha-shomer ha-Ẓa'ir, and was disbanded during World War II. The origins of Neẓaḥ are in the Ha-Shomer ha-Ẓa'ir in Russia at the beginning of the Soviet regime. During this period many groups of Jewish scouts existed in Russia; some were affiliated with *Maccabi, while others had no affiliations.

Ha-Shomer Ha-Ẓa'ir in Russia held its clandestine founding convention in Moscow in 1922 and established itself as a country-wide movement. During David *Ben-Gurion's visit to Russia in 1923 the movement's basic ideology became personal fulfillment through *aliyah* and pioneering in Ereẓ Israel. Although illegal and persecuted by the authorities, Ha-Shomer ha-Ẓa'ir grew in size and had as many as 20,000 adherents throughout Soviet Russia. Its last "Information Page" was circulated as late as 1932, and there is evidence that some of its groups continued to exist even after that date.

The first *ḥalutzim* of this movement went to Palestine in 1924 and founded a Ha-Shomer ha-Ẓa'ir kibbutz from the U.S.S.R. on the shores of Lake Kinneret (now kibbutz Afikim). Their underground existence in Russia had prevented their attending the founding convention of the world movement of Ha-Shomer ha-Ẓa'ir and upon their arrival in Ereẓ Israel they discovered that there were substantial differences between them and the movement that developed outside Russia. They advocated membership in one of the existing labor parties (from 1930 this party was Mapai). They also opposed the creation of Ha-Kibbutz ha-Arẓi as a separate federation of kibbutzim of Ha-Shomer ha-Ẓa'ir and proposed joining kibbutzim from other movements in a single federation (which later became ha-Kibbutz ha-Me'uḥad); they disagreed with the ideological transformation which took place in Ha-Shomer ha-Ẓa'ir, and turned it from a pioneering youth movement into a political body advocating, in one of its planks, the "socialist revolution" in the leftist meaning of the term.

The struggle inside Ha-Shomer ha-Ẓa'ir went on for six years, ending in the secession of the Russian Ha-Shomer ha-Ẓa'ir from the movement and the creation of Neẓaḥ, which adhered to the original ideology of the Russian Ha-Shomer ha-Ẓa'ir. The new movement was composed of the Ha-Shomer ha-Ẓa'ir from Russia, Latvia, Estonia, and Lithuania, and was later joined by the *Blau-Weiss (or Tekhelet Lavan) movement, in Austria, Czechoslovakia, and Yugoslavia. It also maintained close ties with the Borissia movement of Transylvania, and, in its last years, with the *Iḥud Habonim in England and America. Members of Neẓaḥ may be found in Afikim, Kefar Giladi, Ein Gev, Kinneret, Ne'ot Mordekhai, and other kibbutzim. Most of them became members of Mapai (from 1968, the Israel Labor Party).

[Joseph Israeli]

BIBLIOGRAPHY: D. Leon, *The Kibbutz* (1964); A. Ben-Shalom, *Deep Furrows* (1939); I.L. Lindheim, *Parallel Quest* (1962); *Israel Horizons* (1953–); *Young Guard* (1934; title varies); *Hashomer Hatzair* (Johannesburg, 1936–56); *Labour Israel* (1948–59); *Sefer Ha-Shomer ha-Ẓa'ir*, 3 vols. (1956–64); *Sefer Ha-Shomer ha-Ẓa'ir*, 3 vols. (1956–1964); *Sefer Ha-Shomerim 1913–1933* (1934); P. Merḥav, *Toledot Tenu'at ha-Po'alim be-Ereẓ-Yisrael* (1967); A. Ophir, *Afikim be-Maḥaẓit Yovelah* (1951); D. Horowitz, *Ha-Etmol Shelli* (1970), 73–152; A. Margalit, *Ha-Shomer ha-Ẓair me-Adat Ne'urim le-Marxism Mahpkhani* 1971).

ḤASIDEI ASHKENAZ, a social and ideological circle, with a particular religious outlook, in medieval German Jewry. The first centers of the movement were Regensburg in southern Germany and the communities of Speyer, Worms, and Mainz on the Rhine; from there, its influence spread over most of Germany and, to a certain extent, to France also. Its main literature was composed during the first half of the 13th century. This movement developed in the spiritual and social atmosphere of the Jewish communities in German towns of the 12th and 13th centuries. **Kiddush ha-Shem* (martyrdom) was an extremely important factor in its formation. Another significant factor was the challenge of the Christian pietist movements. It reacted against the pressure from these trends in Christianity and was also influenced by them. Added to these was the movement's feeling of spiritual supremacy derived from its own strength and duties to God and the nation.

The Literature of the Circle

The literature of the Ḥasidei Ashkenaz developed in two different directions. The movement produced some ethical works, intended to influence the mass of the Jews and direct them toward rigorous observance of the commandments and the moral values of Judaism (see *Ethical Literature). Most important of these works was the *Sefer *Ḥasidim*, which continued to influence Jewish ethical thought throughout the centuries, and remained an active force in shaping Jewish ethics until modern times.

The second direction in which the Ḥasidei Ashkenaz developed was the writing of a vast body of esoteric works, some containing mystical elements. According to the traditions of the Ḥasidim themselves, this esoteric lore reached them through a long chain of verbal tradition, beginning in Italy in the eighth century. This tradition was carried mainly by the *Kalonymus family, which was transferred in the ninth century from Italy to Germany by one of the Carolingian emperors. Most of the prominent leaders of the Ḥasidei Ashkenaz were members of this family, notably *Samuel b. Kalonymus he-Ḥasid ("the Pious") in the second half of the 12th century, his son *Judah b. Samuel he-Ḥasid (d. 1217), and his pupil, *Eleazar b. Judah b. Kalonymus of Worms (d. c. 1230). The tradition continued to flourish in this family, and prominent among its bearers are some of the descendants of Judah he-Ḥasid: Moses, his son; *Eleazar b. Moses ha-Darshan; and Moses b. Eleazar, Judah's great-grandson. Other writers belonging to this circle were disciples of Eleazar of Worms, among them *Abraham b. Azriel, author of *Arugat ha-Bosem* and *Isaac b. Moses of Vienna, author of *Or Zaru'a*. The Kalonymus family represents the central group of the Ḥasidei Ashkenaz, authors of esoteric literature. There were, however, other groups or individuals who wrote such works without being in close touch with the core. Most of these works remained anonymous and very little is known about the place and time in which they were written. One of the most important is the **Sefer ha-Ḥayyim*, written about the turn of the 13th century by a ḥasidic scholar who was deeply influenced by Abraham *Ibn Ezra in formulating his theology, which also includes elements similar to some kabbalistic ideas. Another anonymous writer was the author of *Sefer ha-Navon*, a commentary on the verse "*Shema Israel*"; the author had no direct connection with the main group of the Kalonymus family, though apparently he had access to at least one work written by Judah he-Ḥasid.

Besides these scattered, anonymous writers it seems that there existed a group of mystical writers in the 12th and 13th centuries who are distinguished by their use of a pseudepigraphic *baraita* attributed to *Joseph b. Uzziel, known in Hebrew literature as the grandson of Ben Sira, the legendary son of the prophet Jeremiah (see *Ben Sira, Alphabet of). The *baraita* is mainly cosmological, closely related to *Sefer *Yeẓirah*. One of the earliest commentaries on this *baraita* is attributed to a scholar called Avigdor ha-Ẓarefati. Among the works which originated in this group was the commentary on *Sefer Yeẓirah* attributed to *Saadiah Gaon (not to be confused with Saadiah's true commentary on that work). The best-known writer of this group is *Elḥanan b. Yakar, who lived in the first half of the 13th century in England and France and wrote two commentaries on *Sefer Yeẓirah* and a theological work, *Sod ha-Sodot*.

The theology of the Ḥasidei Ashkenaz aroused some controversy in Ashkenazi Jewry; in *Ketav Tamim* Moses *Taku attacked their ideas as expressed in Judah he-Ḥasid's *Sefer ha-Kavod*, in the *Sefer ha-Ḥayyim*, which Taku erroneously attributed to Abraham *ibn Ezra, and in the sources of these ideas, especially the works of Saadiah Gaon, *Emunot ve-De'ot* and the commentary on the *Sefer Yeẓirah*.

Various sources were used in the formulation of Ashkenazi ḥasidic esoteric thought. There were, undoubtedly, some external, Christian influences, especially some of the neoplatonic medieval writings. In most cases these sources are unknown; only in one case, that of Elhanan b. Yakar, has it been established that he made use of material included in medieval Christian theological works. It is possible that some ideas came to the Ḥasidei Ashkenaz through verbal, not written, sources. As for the Jewish sources, the Ḥasidim made extensive use of *heikhalot* and *Merkabah literature, which they copied and quoted extensively, thus preserving some texts which might otherwise have been lost. They also made use of the works of some of the first medieval theological writers in Hebrew: Shabbetai *Donnolo, *Abraham b. Ḥiyya, and *Judah ha-Nasi of Barcelona; of special significance was the influence of Abraham ibn Ezra and there is hardly a ḥasidic work which does not, directly or indirectly, reflect his influence. However, the basic ideas of the Ashkenazi ḥasidic thinkers came from Saadiah Gaon, whose writings were known to them not in the 12th-century translation by Judah ibn *Tibbon, but from an earlier, poetic paraphrase in which the discursive, philosophical character of the works had been obliterated. No wonder, therefore, that the Ḥasidei Ashkenaz saw Saadiah as a mystic, similar to the ninth-century *Aaron of Baghdad (Abu Aharon) who came from Babylonia to Italy, and on whom they relied for some mystical knowledge, especially in the interpretation of prayer.

Theology

The basic idea which the Ḥasidei Ashkenaz tried to teach was the unity and incorporeality of God, opposing all anthropomorphic descriptions of God. In this their teachings were similar to those of the Jewish philosophers in Spain. The difference, however, lies in their concept of the intermediary powers between God and man. The Ḥasidei Ashkenaz accepted from Saadiah Gaon the idea that a supreme power, the *Kavod* ("Divine Glory"), also called the **Shekhinah*, is the subject of all the anthropomorphic descriptions of God in the Bible, but they differ from him in their concept of the essence of the *Kavod*. According to Saadiah the *Kavod* was created and was one of the angels, though supreme above all. Most of the Ḥasidei Ashkenaz described the *Kavod* as a divine being, emanating from God himself (though they did not have a special word for the concept of emanation, as did the kabbalists). Some writers even described a whole world of many *Kevodot*, thus using the neoplatonic concept of a ladder of emanated beings descending from the Godhead toward the created world. *Kavod* plays a prominent part in the doctrines of the Ḥasidei Ashkenaz: the soul is connected with the *Kavod*, or even emanates from it, and receives its spiritual sustenance from it. Some of the many writings on prayer, prayer exegesis, and instructions on the right way to pray, emphasize that prayer should be directed toward the Godhead itself and not the *Kavod*, thereby suggesting that there were tendencies in the circles of the Ḥasidei Ashkenaz to consider the *Kavod* as a divine entity toward whom prayers should be directed. However, all of them regarded the *Kavod* as the major divine entity exerting influence on events in the lower world.

The theology of the Ḥasidei Ashkenaz is deeply grounded in the idea of divine immanence, and they emphatically state that the Godhead is itself present within all created things, and not the *Kavod*. In this, Saadiah's influence is again paramount. The immanence of God is clearly expressed in the oldest remaining work of the Ḥasidei Ashkenaz, the **Shir ha-Yiḥud*, which was probably composed at the end of the 12th century. The idea of immanence was so central to their theology, that it was questioned why a man should turn toward heaven while praying when God was present everywhere. The answer was that in heaven dwelt the *Kavod*, and this was the revealed part of God, a sign toward which man should turn, though not one toward which he should direct his prayers.

The Ḥasidei Ashkenaz did not regard the regular laws of nature, man, and society as revealing God's true nature. These laws were arbitrary, and sometimes their purpose was adverse to God's intentions; that is, they were created in order to serve as a trial (*nissayon*) for the just and pious who must overcome them. Wonders and unusual happenings, however, and certainly the miracles which occur in the world, do reveal God's true nature, and the pious and learned scholar can interpret them in order to understand better the ways and nature of God. In this connection the Ḥasidim made extensive use of demonological phenomena, regarding them as a kind of miracle and trying to divine some theological moral from the analysis of such phenomena. Thus their literature contains probably the largest extant body of demonological and magical information in medieval Hebrew literature.

Secretly the Ḥasidei Ashkenaz also dealt in messianic speculation, though they tried to conceal this (thus it is almost unmentioned in *Sefer Ḥasidim*). Believing that the messianic age was about to dawn, probably around 1240, they expected retribution to be meted out to the gentiles for all the sufferings undergone by German Jewry in the dreadful age of the Crusades.

[Joseph Dan]

The followers of Ḥasidut Ashkenaz regarded themselves as bearers of a religious consciousness deeper than that generally prevailing and subject to religious duties severer than the accepted ones. The maximum was asked of the person able and willing to take upon himself the "restrictions of Ḥasidut," while a lesser standard sufficed for those who had not entered its circle. From the *tovim* (the "good"), the Ḥasidim (the "pious"), and the *ẓaddikim* (the "righteous"), a maximum of emotional fervor and utmost purification of soul and thought were demanded, together with exact attention to the details of both major and minor precepts. The other members of the community at large were divided into the *ra'im* ("evil ones") and the despotic ones – whom the Ḥasidim fought against – and the *peshutim* ("simple ones") – whom the Ḥasidim guided inasmuch as they were capable of observing and feeling. In its relations with the community and its institutions, the Ḥasidei Ashkenaz therefore fluctuated between two contrasting attitudes: between the desire for leadership and service, and the tendency among its members to seclude themselves in order to live their exalted individual lives.

Their Symbolism

The array of symbols of Ḥasidei Ashkenaz is based to a considerable extent on faith in the strength of the Holy Names and the mystic power of the letters of the Holy Language (Hebrew) and their combinations; these are the channels of man's communication with the celestial worlds, through study and prayer: "Every blessing and prayer … everything … according to its measure and its weight, its letters and its words; if it were not so, then our prayers would, God forbid, be comparable to the song of the uncircumcised nations." Love of the Creator played a dominant role in the doctrine of the Ḥasidei Ashkenaz and among the duties of the Ḥasid; this love must saturate all his senses and resources; its strength must lead him toward joy so that no void remained in his instincts through which sin or the thought of it might penetrate. In the writings of the Ḥasidim the fervor of their emotional love and joy is expressed in symbols and parables drawn from the experiences and emotions of sexual relationships.

"Prayer is called a service like the service on the altar; when the Temple existed, the angels rose heavenward in the flame of the sacrifices … and today … they rise in the prayer which issues from the heart; for prayer is like a ladder. If there is no devotion behind the words of any blessing, the ladder stops there." The perfection of the "ladder" is so conceived that "the pronunciation of every word must be prolonged, so that there is devotion in a man's heart for every word that issues from his mouth" (*Sefer Ḥasidim* no. 11). Inner devotion is achieved through external methods: the letters should be counted. Melodies should be appropriate: "For supplications and demands, a melody which causes the heart to weep; for words of praise, a melody which causes the heart to rejoice." However, he who is not a Ḥasid may be content with general devotion; simple men and women may be exempted from reciting the prayers in Hebrew, and in certain cases even exempted from saying them in their established form, as long as they devote their hearts to their Father in Heaven.

The supreme manifestation of love for God is *Kiddush ha-Shem* ("the sanctification of the Holy Name," i.e., martyrdom), a glory for which the Ḥasid yearns. In this act, he wages the war of the people of God against Christian heresy and serves the Creator by sacrificing his body. The Ḥasidim were among "the first of the martyrs" during periods of persecution. Their courage, their service of the *Kavod* and the Lord, and their self-sacrifice became an example for others.

In ḥasidic doctrine concerning the world and man, there are numerous occult elements. The Jew lives in a world and in a community in which, to a certain extent, the dead continue their association with the living; demons and spirits also encompass man from all sides and Judah he-Ḥasid even believed that they obeyed the *halakhah*. Sorcery is a concrete factor and a common occurrence in people's lives, and the teachings of the Ḥasidim contain many instructions and rules of conduct which serve as a protection against these powers. In these conceptions can be discerned the imprint of Christian superstitions current in their surroundings.

Ethical Views

The Ḥasidim make no reference to two inclinations in man – toward the "good" and the "evil" – and it appears that man is regarded as having only "one inclination"; the way in which this is used determines whether a deed is good or evil. The Ḥasidim therefore taught that the instincts, desires, and longings of the heart were to be turned toward the good side. According to them, mortification of the body was a method of repentance. They taught "commensurate repentance," that is, the acceptance, measure for measure, of affliction and degradation in return for the pleasure and the reward gained from sin; in some details these ideas show the influence of the notions and practices of repentance current among Christian monks. Mortification, however, had a merit of its own: the sufferings of the righteous vindicate the masses: "the Messiah bears the sins" of the nation and it is incumbent upon the Ḥasidim to adhere to this principle. In this approach there is undoubted evidence of Christian influence.

In relations between man and man, they demanded of themselves a mode of behavior according to "the law of Heaven," the application of absolute justice in the fullest sense of its spiritual significance and content; the "law of the Torah" was sufficient only for the man who was not a Ḥasid. There were some Ḥasidim who decided: "When two people come before the rabbi for him to dispense justice, if these two are of a quarrelsome disposition, the rabbi will apply the law of the Torah, even though a contrary decision would be reached according to the law of Heaven; if, however, these two are good and God-fearing men and heedful of the words of the rabbi, he must apply the law of Heaven, even if the law of the Torah requires the opposite." A practical example of this was their willingness to admit the testimony of "honest women." In their statements on the "two laws" lie occasional criticisms of the *halakhah* because of their demand for perfection of the soul. Some said that the punishments detailed in the Torah "corresponded to man's conception of what is unlawful" – that is, in respect of social codes of behavior, but "do not correspond to instinctive awareness" – that is, they do not accord with the standard by which the Ḥasid assesses sin, which gives due consideration to temptations and the difficulty of overcoming them.

From the words of the Ḥasidim there emerges a kind of cynical indifference toward those who mock them; to bear insult in this fashion they regarded as a pious virtue. In this they reveal the reaction of a minority which is resolute in its opinion and convinced of its uniqueness in the face of possible attacks from the majority and a clash with accepted habits. Their place in society can thus be deduced from this aspect of their doctrine. In the eyes of the Ḥasidim "humility for the sake of Heaven" is a virtue which elevates the soul of the individual, and through this the public attains stability and unity. Their extreme candor and their belief in the single uniform instinct in man brought them to realize the dialectic tension which is entailed when the way of life of the minority becomes known and honored by the many. They describe how "others honor themselves with their humility… they are greater than us and yet do not want to take precedence over anyone, as if to say, we are humble."

Social Doctrine

The social doctrine of the Ḥasidim assumes that the original and desirable situation is complete equality in respect of property and social status; inequality is the result of sin. However, they attributed moral significance to the unequal distribution of riches: wealth is given to the rich so that they may sustain the poor. In accordance with this, they were accustomed to give a tenth of their money to charity. Because of this outlook, the Ḥasidim were troubled by the problem of the criterion of uniformity – which does not draw any distinction between rich and poor – in the imposition of taxes and public obligations on individuals. They justified the prevalence of this system in public life through the fear that if individual considerations were taken into account, the "evil ones" would attempt to evade their responsibilities. However, they required that "good ones" judge for themselves, after the general imposition, their ability and duty to see whether they were capable of making restitution to the poor for that which had unjustly been taken from them. R. Judah b. Samuel he-Ḥasid and his colleagues even advised a man to forgo the public honor of a *mitzvah* purchased in the synagogue if someone was prepared to acquire it for a higher price; the reward for this *mitzvah* would belong to him who had relinquished it if he secretly gave to the poor the sum he had previously paid in public for the *mitzvah*.

This outlook resulted in some tension between the circle of the Ḥasidim and the community leaders on several occasions. The writings of the Ḥasidim contain a critical account of these leaders and their deeds; clashes between the leaders of the Ḥasidim and the community are also mentioned. It is evident that the Ḥasidim disapproved of several principles of the leadership, while many others in the community objected to the attempt at practical application of the doctrines of the Ḥasidim within the communities.

To the Ḥasidim family life is the basis and framework of piety. Love between man and woman is legitimate as long as it does not lead to sin; they also considered that this love had a definite spiritual content. A man fasts and prays in order to win the woman he loves. In their writings, they gave considerable thought to matchmaking, believing that love and family descent were commendable and desirable factors and considerations. Family descent was also regarded as a basic element in the preservation of the proper way of life of the community. However, they considered money as a negative factor and consideration in matchmaking, although they did not ignore its importance in practice.

Along with their emotional depth and mysticism, the Ḥasidim also preserved the tradition of meditation and study. Their respect for books is profound: in the *Sefer Ḥasidim*, the "righteous" bewail the fact that their libraries are scattered after their deaths. They believed that it was commendable not to haggle over the price of a book.

The attitude of the Ḥasidim to the non-Jewish world is imbued with the bitterness of those who battle against a successful foe and suffer cruel oppression. But even here, in several instances, it is possible to recognize the influence of the spiritual environment of Christianity and current ideas.

The Ḥasidei Ashkenaz became influential in the Jewish world, while at the same time they adapted many and profound elements foreign to that world. They were marked by a refinement of feeling and simplicity of thought, and were woven together by bonds of personal honesty and responsibility before the Creator. Even at its height, the movement comprised only a small group within German Jewry, but as a result of the example of its leading personalities and its growth from the spiritual climate of the time, it succeeded in leaving its imprint. The testaments and customs of the leading Ḥasidim greatly influenced the general way of life, as well as specific details, conceptions of *halakhah*, and the versions of prayers. From the second half of the 13th century onward they even exerted some influence over Spanish Jewry. The Jews of Poland-Lithuania of the late Middle Ages also pointed out with pride that "we are of the lineage of the Ḥasidei Ashkenaz," although the atmosphere of their social and religious life had undergone many changes since the time of the Ḥasidim.

BIBLIOGRAPHY: J. Dan, *Torat ha-Sod shel Ḥasidei Ashkenaz* (1967); idem, in: JJS, 17 (1966), 73–82; M. Guedemann, *Ha-Torah ve-ha-Ḥayyim*, 1 (1897); Scholem, Mysticism, 80–118; idem, *Ursprung und Anfaenge der Kabbala* (1962), s.v. *Chasidim, deutsche*; A. Cronbach, in: HUCA, 22 (1949), 1–147; J. Trachtenberg, *Jewish Magic and Superstition* (1939), index; M. Harris, in: JQR, 50 (1959), 13–44; Y. Baer, in: *Zion*, 3 (1938), 1–50; 18 (1953), 91–108; 32 (1967), 129–36; idem, in: *Meḥkarim… le-Gershom Scholem* (1968), 47–62; J.N. Simhoni, in: *Ha-Ẓefirah* 42 (1917); E.E. Urbach, in: *Zion*, 12 (1947), 149–59; Urbach, Tosafot, 141–94, 285–370; idem, *Sefer Arugat ha-Bosem…* (1963), 177–85; H.H. Ben-Sasson (ed.), *Toledot Am Yisrael*, 2 (1969) index.

ḤASIDEI UMMOT HA-OLAM (Heb. חֲסִידֵי אֻמּוֹת הָעוֹלָם, lit., "The pious ones of the nations of the world"), a rabbinic term denoting righteous gentiles. The concept is first found (albeit in a limited form) in the Midrash. The *Yalkut Shimoni*, for instance, explains that the verse "Let thy priests be clothed with righteousness…" (Ps. 132:9) refers to "the righteous of other nations who are priests to the Holy One in this world, like Antoninus and his type" (Yal. Isa. 429). The notion that the *ḥasidei ummot ha-olam* also merit a place in the world to come (a true sign of their worthiness) is found in the Tosefta, which teaches that they are as eligible as any member of the House of Israel to a share in the hereafter (Tosef., Sanh. 13:2). This dictum is twice codified by Maimonides (Yad, Teshuvah 3:5), who also defines the concept (Yad, Melakhim 8:11): "All who observe the Seven Commandments"—obligatory to the descendants of Noah (see Noachide *laws) are *ḥasidei ummot ha-olam*, provided that they are motivated by belief in the divine origin and the authenticity of Moses' prophecy, and not by mere intellectual cogency. In the latter case they are to be considered only as "wise ones of the other nations" (*ḥakhmeihem*, according to some versions). Without specifically naming the righteous gentiles, Maimonides also equates "all human beings who ardently seek God… desire to worship Him, to know Him, and to walk uprightly in His ways…", with priests and levites (Yad, Shemittah 13:13). The concept of *ḥasidei ummot ha-olam* was elaborated and embellished in medieval Jewish literature. It is mentioned by such philosophers as Hasdai *Crescas (*Or Adonai* no. 364:4) and *Abrabanel (introduction to commentary to Isaiah), R. Isaac *Arama states, "Every true pious gentile is equal to a 'son of Israel'" (*Akedat Yiẓḥak*, ed. Venice, ch. 60). The concept is mentioned in a legal context in the Shulḥan Arukh (YD 367:1, Be'er ha-Golah). The Zohar states that all gentiles who do not hate Israel, and who deal justly with the Jews, qualify as *ḥasidei ummot ha-olam* (Exodus, 268a).

Since World War II the term has been used for those non-Jews who helped Jews to escape the Nazi persecutions. (See *Righteous Among the Nations.)

BIBLIOGRAPHY: Zunz, Gesch, 388; M. Guttmann, *Das Judentum und seine Umwelt*, 1 (1927), 171.

[H. Elchanan Blumenthal]

ḤASIDIM (Heb. חֲסִידִים, "pietists"), term used in rabbinic literature to designate those who maintained a higher standard in observing the religious and moral commandments. The various definitions in rabbinic literature of the *ḥasid*, and the more numerous accounts given there of them and their actions, clearly indicate that the image of the *ḥasid* was not identical at all times and in all circles. The sources reflect a broad spectrum of religious types, each distinguished in its own way, but common to all is a divergence from what was regarded as conventional behavior and the normal standard that was deemed praiseworthy, as is evident from the appellation *ḥasid*.

The precise period of the *ḥasidim ha-rishonim* ("first ḥasidim") mentioned in rabbinic literature cannot be determined. Statements about them recount their virtues, which were utter devotion to fulfilling the *mitzvot* with a total disregard of any danger, extreme solicitude for human relations to the extent of transcending the strict requirements of the law, a fear of sin expressed by avoiding anything that might possibly lead astray or to the commission of sin, and by a constant readiness to undergo purification and to seek atonement for any doubtful sin by offering sacrifices. Before praying the early *ḥasidim* would meditate for an hour in order to direct their hearts to God (Ber. 5:1), nor did they interrupt their prayers even in the face of possible danger (Tosef., Ber. 3:20; TB, Ber. 32b). They refrained on a weekday from doing anything that involved the slightest apprehension of ultimately desecrating the Sabbath (Nid. 38a). They would bury thorns and broken glass deep in their fields, "placing them three handbreaths deep in the ground so that the plow might not displace them" and people stumble over them (Tosef., BK 2:6). The *tanna* R. Judah stated that "the early *ḥasidim* were eager to bring a sin offering," but since they did not inadvertently commit sins "they made a free-will vow of naziriteship that they might bring a sin offering" (Tosef., Ned. 1:1; TB, Ned. 10a). They were accustomed to making a free-will offering of a suspensive guilt offering (*asham talui*), and this type of sacrifice "became known as the guilt-offering of the *ḥasidim*" (Ker. 6:3; Tosef., Ker. 4:4).

Akin to the *ḥasidim ha-rishonim* are the "*ḥasidim* and men of action" (*ḥasidim ve-anshei ma'aseh*). This phrase does not indicate two distinct groups of people – the *ḥasidim* were so called on account of the special good deeds which they performed and the miracles vouchsafed them by virtue of these good deeds. The only extant tradition states that during the "Rejoicing of the Water-drawing" (*simḥat bet ha-sho'evah*) "they used to dance with lighted torches and sing songs and praises." Some of them used to say, "Happy my youth, that has not put to shame my old age"; others, "Happy my old age, that has atoned for my youth" (Suk. 5:4; Tosef., Suk. 4:2). Outstanding representatives of the "*ḥasidim* and men of action" were *Ḥoni ha-Me'aggel, his grandsons *Abba Hilkiah and Ḥanan ha-Neḥba (Ta'an. 23a), and *Ḥanina b. Dosa who lived at the end of the Second Temple period and whom the Mishnah regards as the last of the "men of action" (Sot. 9:15; the reading in TJ is "*ḥasidim*"). These men did not belong to the class of the halakhists, and there was even certain opposition to them (cf. Ta'an. 23a; Ber. 34b). Expressive of their deep faith and implicit belief in God's omnipotence are the deeds of the "*ḥasidim* and men of action" and the remarks that accompanied them on various occasions. Thus Ḥanina b. Dosa entertained no doubts when he said, "He who commanded oil to burn will also command vinegar to burn" (Ta'an 25a), for to them the miraculous was regarded as quite natural. When a poisonous lizard bit Ḥanina b. Dosa and died, he brought it on his shoulder to the *bet ha-midrash*, commenting simply: "See, my sons, it is not the lizard that kills, it is sin that kills" (Ber. 33a). The contents, motifs, and form of several stories related in the sources about "a certain *ḥasid*" (e.g., Tosef., Pe'ah 3:8; TJ, Shab. 15:3, 15a; BK 50b, 80a) indicate that the stories refer to these early ones (BK 103b). A difficulty is posed by the statement that "wherever the Talmud speaks of a certain *ḥasid* it refers either to Judah b. Bava or Judah b. Ilai" (Tem. 15b). However, this may mean no more than that these *tannaim* were the ones who reported such stories.

Despite the differences in time and conditions, the conduct and deeds of the *ḥasidim* and men of action bear a certain resemblance to the stories in the Bible about the earlier prophets, in that their influence derived not from the power of their exhortations but from the force of their deeds, courage, and sense of dedication. The rabbis gave expression to this in their homiletical interpretation of Genesis 2:5, "And there was not man to till the ground," on which they commented: "There was no man to cultivate people's allegiance to God, such as Elijah and Ḥoni ha-Me'aggel" (Gen. R. 7; and see Theodor-Albeck, 117, n. 5).

The early *ḥasidim* created no organization or sect but were active as individuals, each in his own vicinity and time. Nor can they be identified with the *Essenes, as various scholars from the 19th century onward (Frankel, Geiger, Derenboug, Kohler) have sought to do, for what is known about them does not accord with the descriptions of the Essenes in Philo, Josephus, Pliny, and others. Y. Baer has assigned to the "early *ḥasidim*" a central place in the history of Second Temple times, identifying them with the sages who flourished in the pre-Hasmonean period. Thus he contends that the Great Synagogue was a development of *ḥasidim* and sages, that its continuity was preserved by the *zugot, and that these *ḥasidim* are to be identified with the Essenes and with Philo's *Therapeutae. He believes that they were the first exponents of the *halakhah* as embedded in the earliest layers of the Mishnah, and that they laid the foundations of the entire structure of faith as reflected in the ascetic-spiritual-martyrological aspects of statements in the *aggadah*, Midrash, and Philo's writings. This account of them does not, however, accord with what is reported in rabbinic sources about the early *ḥasidim* and their activities. They were not the creators of the ancient *halakhah*, nor the initiators of a philosophic and mystical teaching. The fact that they lived a simple and modest life with a minimum of material needs – "Ḥanina my son is satisfied with a *kav* of carobs from one Sabbath eve to another" (Ta'an. 24b) – does not constitute asceticism. Manifestations of abstinence among talmudic scholars are not remnants of outworn ancient ascetic teaching of the early *ḥasidim*, but are connected with the circumstances of a much later period. Moreover, the tannaitic period preserved a memory of them as being specifically distinguished and separated from the sages as a whole. Furthermore, the type of *ḥasid* of that period differed in outlook from the early *ḥasidim*. Thus *Hillel, who in his teachings incorporated ideas inherited from the early *ḥasidim*, is the author of the aphorism that "an ignorant person cannot be a *ḥasid*" (Avot 2:5). Nor could there be any piety without the study and knowledge of the Torah (see ARN[1] 12, 56; ARN[2] 27, 56). When Hillel died, they said of him: "Alas, the humble man, alas the *ḥasid* [is no more]" (Tosef., Sot. 13:4), his eminence in the Torah having been combined with humility (Lev. R. 1:5), and with implicit trust in the Almighty (Ber. 60a), and "all his actions were for the sake of Heaven." But Hillel, whose personality comprised many other aspects as well, was not regarded as one of the early *ḥasidim*, and yet precisely he and those who followed in his footsteps represent the *ḥasid*-sage.

Generally the term *ḥasid* came later to refer to ideal and exemplary behavior in some sphere of life. A *ḥasid* is one who declares "what is mine is yours, and what is yours is yours" (Avot 5:10) and "he whom it is hard to provoke and easy to pacify" (*ibid.* 5:11). This and other definitions are far removed from the ways of the early *ḥasidim*. There was moreover a definite line of abstinence and of extreme asceticism which reached full maturity and became a characteristic feature of the *ḥasid* only in the amoraic period. This trend started after the destruction of the Second Temple "when the abstinent ones increased in Israel" (Tosef., Sot. 14:11), seeking in fasts a substitute for atonement, now denied to them with the cessation of sacrifices. At the beginning of the second century these expressions of abstinence vanished but reappeared to spread with greater force during the persecutions following the Bar Kokhba revolt. Ben Azzai, of whom it was said that "whoever sees Ben Azzai in a dream can hope to attain piety" (Ber. 57b), proclaimed extreme abstinence from all earthly pursuits, declaring, "Let the world be sustained by others" (Tosef., Yev. 8:4; Yev. 63b). A similar circumstance is reflected in R. Meir's homiletical interpretation that "Adam was a great *ḥasid*" (see Er. 18b; Gen. R. 20, ed. Theodor-Albeck, 195). At the end of the tannaitic period there once again appear sages who, in their extreme demands, spontaneous reactions, and miraculous deeds, are reminiscent of the early *ḥasidim* and the men of action. Of such a type was *Phinehas b. Jair who defined and enumerated the steps leading to *ḥasidut* regarded by him as a stage in the attainment of the holy spirit (Sot. 9:15).

In the amoraic period extreme conclusions were drawn from Akiva's principle that suffering is to be lovingly accepted as the ultimate goal of anyone who serves God, the same interpretation being applied to man's normal suffering – and not only to times of persecution – as a punishment for sins. But while a *ḥasid* therefore prays that he may suffer, not everyone is privileged to have such prayers answered, and accordingly some pious *amoraim*, instead of awaiting suffering, deliberately afflicted and mortified themselves. This was done by Ḥiyya b. Ashi (Kid. 81b), Zera (BM 85a), Mar b. Ravina (Pes. 68b). Not that all the *amoraim* agreed that self-denial entitled one to be called a *ḥasid* (Ta'an. 11b), Simeon b. Lakish declaring that "a scholar may not afflict himself by fasting because thereby he lessens his heavenly work" (*ibid*). There were also *amoraim* called "*ḥasid*," such as Ameram the Ḥasid (Kid. 81a; Git. 67b), Simeon the Ḥasid (Ber. 43b) and Mar Zutra (Ned. 7b), who acquired this title not on account of acts of mortification but of other virtues and deeds. The Ḥasid Huna declared anyone who has a fixed place for prayer to be a *ḥasid* (Ber. 6b), R. Alexandri that "whoever hears someone curse him and keeps silent is called a *ḥasid*" (Mid. Ps. to 16:11). A certain criticism was leveled against "the *ḥasidim* of Babylonia" – the *amoraim* Huna, Ḥisda, and Naḥman – in the Babylonian Talmud itself, which disparagingly contrasted their humility and courtesy with those of the Ereẓ Israel sages, although the latter were known for their hardness (Meg. 28b; and see Ḥul. 122a). In principle, the *ḥasid* is one who does more than is required of him by the letter of the law, and *halakhot* which go beyond the strict legal requirements are termed by the *amoraim* "the Mishnah of the *ḥasidim*" (TJ, Ter. 8:10, 46b; or "the measure of the *ḥasidim*" (BM 52b). The popular test of a *ḥasid* was if his prayer for rain was answered (Ta'an. 23b). In the days of both the *tannaim* and the *amoraim* the sages were displeased with ignorant people who adopted the standards of the *ḥasid* (Shab. 121b; and see TJ, Av. Zar 2:3, 41a). Simeon b. Lakish even maintained that "if an ignorant man is a *ḥasid*, do not dwell in his vicinity" (Shab. 63a). On R. Joshua's statement in the Mishnah that a foolish *ḥasid* is to be included among those who bring destruction upon the world, the two Talmuds quote instances of the *ḥasid* who, on account of his rigid observance of the *mitzvot* and of his abstinence, refrains from saving his fellow from death (TJ, Sot. 3:4, 19a; TB Sot., 21b).

Colloquially, the term "*ḥasid*" was used to designate a just, upright, and good person, this inexact usage being sometimes found also in literary sources: "it fits him to become just, *ḥasid*, upright, and faithful" (Avot 6:1); "even as the earlier righteous men were *ḥasidim*" (ARN[1] 8, 38; and see TJ, Sanh. 6:9, 23c, where *Simeon b. Shetaḥ and someone who flourished in the days of King David are referred to as *ḥasidim*). Inscriptions on Jewish epitaphs at Bet She'arim and in Italy contain, alongside δίκαιος ("righteous"), the term ὅσιος which is found in the Septuagint both for *ḥasid* and for *yashar*, an upright man.

BIBLIOGRAPHY: Frankel, Mishnah (1923[2]), 14, 42; idem, in: *Zeitschrift fuer die religioesen Interessen des Judenthums*, 3 (1846), 441–61; idem, in: MGWJ, 2 (1853), 30–40, 61–73; A. Buechler, *Types of Jewish-Palestinian Piety* (1922); L. Gulkowitsch, *Die Bildung des Be-*

griffes Ḥasid (1935); S. Lieberman, *Greek in Jewish Palestine* (1942), 69–78; Y.F. Baer, in: *Zion*, 18 (1953), 91–108; idem, *Yisrael ba-Ammim* (1955); Sarfatti, in: *Tarbiẓ*, 26 (1957), 126–48; Avigad, in: *Eretz Israel*, 5 (1959), 182; E. Urbach, in: *Sefer Yovel le-Y. Baer*, 48–68; idem, *Ḥazal, Pirkei Emunot re-De'ot* (1969), index; Jacobs, in: JJS, 8 (1957), 143–54; Safrai, *ibid.*, 16 (1965), 15–33; Falk, in: *Sefer Zikkaron… B. De Vries* (1969), 62–69. **ADD. BIBLIOGRAPHY:** S.A. Singer, *The Hasid in Qumran and in the Talmud* (1974).

[*Encyclopaedia Hebraica*]

ḤASIDIM, SEFER (Heb. סֵפֶר חֲסִידִים, "Book of the Pious"), major work in the field of ethics, produced by the Jews of medieval Germany. It comprises the ethical teachings of the *Ḥasidei Ashkenaz movement in the 12th and early 13th centuries. Two versions of the book have survived, one printed in Bologna and the other found in manuscript in Parma.

Tradition attributes the entire *Sefer Ḥasidim* to R. *Judah he-Ḥasid (the Pious) of Regensburg (d. 1217), the great teacher of Ashkenazi Ḥasidism. There is some proof, however, that the first two "*maḥbarot*" (groups into which the book is divided) of the Parma version were written by Judah's father, R. Samuel b. Kalonymus he-Ḥasid. This is substantiated by a study of their style. These two "*maḥbarot*" discuss the fear of God and repentance. Some of the passages in *Sefer Ḥasidim* bear close similarity, in language and ideas, to the ethical introductions to the *Roke'aḥ*, the halakhic work by R. Eleazar of Worms. A number of scholars, therefore, conclude that R. Eleazar, R. Judah's most prominent disciple, was the author of some of the passages in *Sefer Ḥasidim*, and probably its editor. It is equally possible, however, that R. Eleazar used portions of the *Sefer Ḥasidim* in his writings, as he did with other mystical works of his teacher. No conclusive proof is to be found as to what extent R. Eleazar participated in the authorship of the work; whereas there is a clear statement by R. Judah's son, Moses, describing how R. Judah wrote two pages of *Sefer Ḥasidim* (Ms. Guenzburg 82, 64b) in the last week of his life. It can be concluded that *Sefer Ḥasidim* was written by R. Judah he-Ḥasid, and that some material was added to it from the writings of his father R. Samuel. A problem nevertheless exists regarding the origin and development of the work. Some of the earliest quotations from the *Sefer Ḥasidim* found in the Ashkenazi ḥasidic writings of the first half of the 13th century are in neither of the two known versions. It is possible that parts of the original *Sefer Ḥasidim* were lost early in the development of the two versions that survived.

Many of the passages in *Sefer Ḥasidim* are homiletic and exegetic in nature, explaining the ethical, and sometimes the philosophical or mystical, meanings of biblical verses or talmudic sayings. Most of the passages, however, discuss only ethics, and do so in direct connection with everyday life. *Sefer Ḥasidim* is the prime example of pragmatic and realistic ethical teachings in Jewish ethical literature; it takes into account the special characteristic of every case, the psychology of the person discussed, the historical and economic situation, and the person's special relationship to other people. This approach renders *Sefer Ḥasidim* the most important historical source for the study of everyday Jewish life in medieval Germany; it throws light especially on economic and religious relations of Jews with gentiles. The book has some descriptions of actual incidents, clarifying the situation in Germany during and after the disasters brought by the crusaders on Jews in Germany and France. Later Jewish ethical works influenced by *Sefer Ḥasidim* retained its strict and uncompromising adherence not only to the commandments, but to the entire body of religious ethics. The book instructs the pious man how to resist temptation and avoid any situation which may lead to sin. It teaches how to dress, to speak, to pray, to work, and to sleep; how to choose a wife and to select friends; how to harmonize between the necessities of existence and the requirements of religious life; which city is suitable for a pious person to live in and which is not; the right relationship between teacher and pupil; how to choose a righteous teacher; in what fields one may have commercial contact with gentiles and how to treat them, and many other subjects. No other Hebrew work in ethics covers so much ground and devotes such close attention to realistic detail. All later writers in the field of ethics in Ashkenazi literature used *Sefer Ḥasidim* as a basis; many of them added very little to what they had taken from it. After the 15th century, writers of *halakhah* used the work as an authority, sometimes the final authority, on the Jewish way of life.

The Bologna version was printed in 1538 and later in numerous other places (including Jerusalem 1957, edited by R. Margaliot). The Parma manuscript was published by J. Wistinetzky (Berlin, 1891–94) and in 1924 at Frankfurt, with an introduction by J. Freimann. The manuscripts found in a number of libraries are incomplete, each containing only a tenth of the whole work. Scholars who have compared the two versions reached the conclusion that the Parma one was the earlier and more reliable. It comprises more than 1,900 passages, whereas the Bologna version has less than 1,200. The Parma version has many duplications and inconsistencies, which were either omitted or harmonized in the Bologna edition. There the passages are better arranged and a system is apparent, whereas the Parma manuscript seems, in places, unedited and chaotic. The Bologna edition was probably edited and changed later by an editor who may have lived in France, probably before 1300. In the Parma version the transliterated vernacular words are in "German," whereas in the Bologna edition they are in "French."

The book is compiled from independent passages (*simanim*), arranged in groups (*maḥbarot*), sometimes under titles describing the subject of the single group (*maḥberet*), e.g., "witchcraft," "books," "prayer," etc. Titles such as "This is the Book of the Just" (*Sefer Ḥasidim*), "*Sefer Ḥasidim* on the Book of Proverbs," or "This also is *Sefer Ḥasidim*" are to be found in the Parma version as well. It is evident that the book was compiled from smaller collections which themselves were compiled from independent passages.

BIBLIOGRAPHY: J. Wistinetzki and J. Freimann (eds.), *Sefer Ḥasidim* (1924²), 1–73; Simḥoni, in: *Ha-Ẓefirah* (1917), passim; Scholem, Mysticism, 80–99; Harris, in: JQR, 50 (1959), 13–44; idem, in:

PAAJR, 31 (1963), 51–80; Cronbach, in: HUCA, 22 (1949), 1–147; Baer, in: *Zion*, 3 (1938), 1–50; S.G. Kramer, *God and Man in the Sefer Ḥasidim* (1966).

[Joseph Dan]

ḤASIDISM, a popular religious movement giving rise to a pattern of communal life and leadership as well as a particular social outlook which emerged in Judaism and Jewry in the second half of the 18th century. Ecstasy, mass enthusiasm, close-knit group cohesion, and charismatic leadership of one kind or another are the distinguishing socioreligious marks of Ḥasidism.

This article is arranged according to the following outline:

HISTORY

Beginnings and Development

The movement began in the extreme southeast of *Poland-Lithuania, and was shaped and conditioned by the tension prevailing in Jewish society in the difficult circumstances created by the breakup of Poland-Lithuania in the late 18th century and the three partitions of the country. This combined with the problems inherited as a result of both the *Chmielnicki massacres and the *Haidamack massacres. The framework of Jewish leadership was shaken, and the authority and methods of Jewish leaders were further undermined and questioned in the wake of the upheaval brought about by the false messianic and kabbalistic movements of *Shabbetai Ẓevi and Jacob *Frank, the shadow of the latter lying on Ḥasidism from its inception. As well as furnishing an ideological background, *Kabbalah, combined with popular traditions of ecstasy and mass enthusiasm, provided constructive elements for a new outlook in religious and social behavior. The earlier messianic movements and authoritarianism of the community leaders prevailing at that time, combined with the necessarily individualistic leadership of the opposition to such authoritarianism, coalesced to accustom the Jewish masses to charismatic as well as authoritative leadership. Mystic circles in Poland-Lithuania in the 18th century combined to create ḥasidic groups (*ḥavurot*) with a distinct pattern of life, mostly ascetic, sometimes with their own synagogue (for example, the so-called *kloyz* of the ascetic Ḥasidim of *Brody). These circles were noted for their special behavior during prayer, for their meticulous observance of the commandments, and also by their daily life. Their prayers were arranged for the most part according to the Sephardi version of Isaac *Luria. They were not looked upon favorably by the official institutions of the community because of the danger of separatism and because of their deviation from the accepted religious customs. Some among them secluded themselves, and spent their days fasting and undergoing self-mortification. Others were ecstatic – "serving the Lord with joy." These groups were quite small and closed; their influence upon the general public was very small.

At first, *Israel b. Eliezer Ba'al Shem Tov (the Besht) appears to have been one of a number of leaders characterized

Main centers of Ḥasidism in Europe. Alternative names in Yiddish, Polish, Russian, and German are given in parentheses.

by ecstatic behavior and an anti-ascetic outlook. A popular healer who worked with magic formulas, amulets, and spells, he attracted to his court, first at Tolstoye and then at Medzibozh, people who came to be cured, to join him in ecstatic prayer, and to receive guidance from him. Israel also undertook journeys, spreading his influence as far as Lithuania. After his "revelation" in the 1730s, which marked the beginning of his public mission, he gradually became the leader of ḥasidic circles; drawn by his personality and visions, more and more people were attracted to the ḥasidic groups, first in Podolia, then in adjacent districts in southeast Poland-Lithuania. Unfortunately it is not possible to fix their number but more than 30 are known by name. Both Israel himself and his whole circle were deeply convinced of his supernatural powers and believed in his visions. Some who came within his orbit continued to oppose him to some degree (see *Abraham Gershon of Kutow, *Naḥman of Horodenko, and *Naḥman of Kosov); under his influence others turned away from ascetic talmudic scholarship to become the theoreticians and leaders of Ḥasidism and Israel's disciples (see *Dov Baer of Mezhirech and *Jacob Joseph of Polonnoye). At his death (1760) Israel left, if not a closely knit group, then at least a highly admiring and deeply convinced inner circle of disciples, surrounded by an outer fringe of former leaders of other ḥasidic groups who adhered to him while dissenting from his views to some extent, and a broad base of devout admirers in the townships and villages of southeast Poland-Lithuania. His outlook and vision attracted simple people as well as great talmudic scholars, established rabbis, and influential **maggidim*.

After a brief period of uncertainty (c. 1760–66), the leadership of the second generation of the movement passed to Dov Baer of Mezhirech (known as the great *maggid* of Mezhirech), although he was opposed by many of Israel's most prominent disciples (e.g., Phinehas Shapiro of Korets and Jacob Joseph of Polonnoye), and many of this inner circle of his opponents withdrew from active leadership, a fact of great significance for the history of Ḥasidism. Nevertheless, Ḥasidism continued to propagate and spread. *Toledot Ya'akov Yosef* (1780), by Jacob Joseph of Polonnoye, embodied the first written theoretical formulation of Ḥasidism, transmitting many of the sayings, interpretations, and traditions of Israel Ba'al Shem Tov, and Jacob Joseph continued with these expositions in subsequent works. From Dov Baer's court missionaries went forth who were successful in attracting many scholars to Ḥasidism and sending them to the master at Mezhirech to absorb his teaching. Due to illness he did not often meet with his disciples. Unlike the Ba'al Shem Tov he was not a man of the people, and favored young scholars whose intellectual foundation did not dampen their ecstatic tendencies. From the new center at Volhynia, Ḥasidism thus spread northward into Belorussia and Lithuania and westward into Galicia and central Poland (see *Shneur Zalman of Lyady, *Levi Isaac of Berdichev, Aaron (the Great) of *Karlin, and Samuel Shmelke *Horowitz). At this time Ḥasidism even penetrated into the center of opposition to it, in Vilna. Many local ḥasidic leaders became influential as communal leaders and local rabbis.

Ḥasidic groups went to Ereẓ Israel creating a far-flung and influential center of ḥasidic activity, notably in Tiberias. Israel Ba'al Shem Tov intended to go to Ereẓ Israel, but for some unknown reason turned back in the middle of the journey. His brother-in-law Abraham Gershon of Kutow went there in 1747, settled in Hebron, and six years later moved to Jerusalem where he established contact with the mystical group "Beth El," which had been founded by the Yemenite kabbalist Sar Shalom *Sharabi. Other Ḥasidim went to Ereẓ Israel, some settling in Tiberias. The newcomers made no notable impression on the Jews settled there. In 1777 a group of Ḥasidim of Ryzhin emigrated to the Holy Land under the leadership of *Menahem Mendel of Vitebsk. There were many who joined the caravan who were not members of the ḥasidic camp, and it numbered at the time of its arrival in Ereẓ Israel about 300 people. The newcomers settled in Safed but after a short while Menahem Mendel and some of his followers moved to Tiberias. Some remained in Safed, others moved to Peki'in, and so it was that the Ḥasidim spread over Jewish Galilee. Even in the very year of their immigration persecution against the Ḥasidim began in Galilee, for **Mitnaggedim* in Lithuania sent collections of "evidence" against the Ḥasidim after they had left. The Sephardim in Safed participated in the controversy and sided with the *Mitnaggedim*. In 1784 Menahem Mendel built a house for himself and in it there was a synagogue. The Ḥasidim sent emissaries to collect money on their behalf and laid the foundation in Ryzhin, Lithuania, and in other places for the permanent support of the Ḥasidim of the Galilee.

The basic pattern of ḥasidic leadership and succession emerged in the third generation of the movement (c. 1773–1815). The spread and growth of Ḥasidism, both geographically and in numbers, the diversified and illustrious leadership of charismatic individuals who became heads of local centers, each developing his own style of teaching and interpretation of the ḥasidic way of life, the breakup of former lines of communication and of cultural ties caused by the partitions of Poland-Lithuania (1772, 1793, and 1795), and last but not least the pressures brought to bear on ḥasidic communities by the struggle against Ḥasidism – all these factors contributed to the decentralization of leadership of the ḥasidic world and consequently to an ever-growing diversification of ḥasidic thought and variation in the ḥasidic way of life. From this generation onward, there were always a number of contemporaneous leaders, each claiming the allegiance of his followers. In the main, both leadership and allegiance were handed down from generation to generation and thus arose both the dynasties of ḥasidic *ẓaddikim* and the hereditary camps of their followers. At times the living charismatic force reasserted itself anew, as in the case of *Jacob Isaac ha-Ḥozeh ("the seer") of Lublin, who began to lead a community in the lifetime of his master, *Elimelech of Lyzhansk, without his blessing, or Jacob Isaac *Przysucha who led a community in the lifetime of his master, though without leaving him. Descent from the first leaders of Ḥasidism did not inevitably guarantee preeminence (see *Abraham b. Dov of Mezhirech) nor was it a defense against bitter attacks on unconventional leadership (see *Naḥman of Bratslav, the great-grandson of the Ba'al Shem Tov).

In this third generation, the new pattern of leadership assured the victory of Ḥasidism over its opponents and its increasing spread throughout Eastern Europe. With the inclusion of Galicia in the Austrian Empire, Ḥasidism also gained adherents among Hungarian Jewry (see *Teitelbaum family, *Mukachevo). At this time Ḥasidism also developed systematic schools of theology, such as the more intellectual and study-centered *Ḥabad Ḥasidism. Some ḥasidic personalities, like Levi Isaac of Berdichev, were venerated by all Jewry as models of piety and love of humanity. The spiritual outlook and pattern of leadership of the practical *ẓaddik* (see below) also crystallized in this generation. Clearly, with such diversification in leadership and attitudes, from this generation on there was considerable and open tension between the various dynasties and courts of Ḥasidism, which sometimes flared up into bitter and prolonged conflicts (see, for example, *Naḥman of Bratslav, *Belz, *Gora Kalwaria (Gur), *Mukachevo, *Kotsk).

By the 1830s the main surge of the spread of Ḥasidism was over. From a persecuted sect it had become the way of life and leadership structure of the majority of Jews in the Ukraine, Galicia, and central Poland, and had sizable groups of followers in Belorussia-Lithuania and Hungary. With the great waves of emigration to the West from 1881, Ḥasidism was carried into Western Europe and especially to the United States. In the West its character was gradually, but ever more rapidly, diluted and its influence became more external and formal. With the abatement of the struggle against Ḥasidism by the end of its third generation and its acceptance as part of the Orthodox camp, Ḥasidism attained the distinction of being the first religious trend in Judaism since the days of the Second Temple which had a self-defined way of life and recognizable rite of worship, but yet was acknowledged (albeit somewhat grudgingly) by those who differed from it as a legitimate Jewish phenomenon.

Opposition to Ḥasidism

This recognition came only after a bitter struggle. However, only in Lithuania and possibly Ryzhin in the last 30 years of the

18th century did this struggle show clear signs of an organized movement. Except for this period, the opposition to Ḥasidism was confined to local controversies. The anti-ḥasidic camp was inspired by the ideas, fears, and personality of *Elijah b. Solomon Zalman, the Gaon of Vilna, who influenced the communal leadership to follow him in his opposition to Ḥasidism. To the Gaon, Ḥasidism's ecstasy, the visions seen and miracles wrought by its leaders, and its enthusiastic way of life were so many delusions, dangerous lies, and idolatrous worship of human beings. Ḥasidic stress on prayer seemed to him to overturn the Jewish scale of values in which study of the Torah and intellectual endeavor in this field were the main path to God. Aspersions were also cast on Ḥasidism because of the supposed hidden influence of the secret teachings of Shabbateanism and in particular of the almost contemporaneous Jacob Frank. Various ḥasidic changes in the knives for *sheḥitah, and even more so in their change from the Ashkenazi to the Sephardi prayer rite, were seen as a challenge to Orthodoxy and a revolutionary rejection of traditional authority.

Writings of rabbis contemporaneous with the Besht reveal some suspicion and derision (Moses b. Jacob of Satanov in his *Mishmeret ha-Kodesh*, Solomon b. Moses *Chelm in his *Mirkevet ha-Mishneh*, and Ḥayyim ha-Kohen *Rapoport). In 1772 the first and second *ḥerem* were proclaimed against the Ḥasidim, ḥasidic works were burned, and the first pamphlet against Ḥasidism, *Zemir Ariẓim ve-Ḥorvot Ẓurim*, was published. The Ḥasidim countered with a *ḥerem* of their own and with burning the *Zemir Ariẓim*; at the same time Menahem Mendel of Vitebsk and Shneur Zalman of Lyady tried to approach Elijah of Vilna, but to no avail. In 1781 another harsh *ḥerem* was proclaimed against the Ḥasidim: "They must leave our communities with their wives and children… and they should not be given a night's lodging; their *sheḥitah* is forbidden; it is forbidden to do business with them and to intermarry with them, or to assist at their burial."

The struggle sharpened during the 1780s and in particular in the 1790s. Not infrequently both Ḥasidim and their opponents denounced each other to the secular authorities (see *Avigdor b. Joseph Ḥayyim, *Shneur Zalman of Lyady), leading to arrests of various ḥasidic leaders and mutual calumnies of a grave nature. With the crystallization of the movement of the *Mitnaggedim* in Jewish Lithuania on the one hand and the appearance of the *Haskalah as an enemy common to all Orthodoxy on the other, the bitterness and ferocity of the struggle between Ḥasidism and its opponents abated, though basic differences remained on estimation of the Jewish scale of values, the place of the leadership of *ẓaddikim*, and the permissibility of certain ecstatic traits of the ḥasidic way of life; sometimes latent and sometimes active, these differences never wholly subsided. The code for the Jews which came out in Russia in 1804 permitted each Jewish sect to build special synagogues for itself and to choose special rabbis for itself, and thus legalization was given to the Ḥasidim in Russia. In the conflict between the *Mitnaggedim* and the Ḥasidim, it was the Ḥasidim who were eventually victorious.

The wars of Napoleon and especially his Russian campaign (1812) aroused a strong reaction among the Jewish community. The Jews of Poland and Russia were located on opposite sides of the front. These wars gave birth to many ḥasidic traditions, whose degree of trustworthiness is unknown. According to them *ẓaddikim* "participated" in the battles, giving their magical thrust for one side or the other. In addition to the legendary material, there are two tested facts. Levi Isaac of Berdichev was at the top of the list of Jewish contributors to the war effort of the Russians against Napoleon (1807). Shneur Zalman of Lyady ordered his Ḥasidim to spy on behalf of Russia, by explaining that "if Bonaparte wins, the wealthy among Israel would increase and the greatness of Israel would be raised, but they would leave and take the heart of Israel far from Father in Heaven" (*Beit Rabbi*).

Modern Period

In the late 19th century and up to World War II various ḥasidic dynasties and camps entered the political life of modern parties and states. Ḥasidim were the mainstay of *Agudat Israel (and see also *Maḥzike Hadas).

This change constituted a new stage in the development of the ḥasidic movement. Alongside the spiritual leaders a growing class of secular activists developed. The expansion of the ḥasidic camp and its penetration to positions of authority and public responsibility in the communities gained influence for the activists who recognized the authority of the *ẓaddik* and submitted to his leadership. Yet, sometimes the *ẓaddik* was only a tool in their skillful hands. Through all of this Ḥasidism finally lost more and more of its spiritual character; it was eventually cut off from its kabbalistic sources and turned instead to organization.

To be sure, this process did not take place without sharp battles, and even in later generations there were *ẓaddikim* who tried to raise anew the foundations of the Ḥasidism of the Ba'al Shem Tov. Generally, the institutionalization of Ḥasidism continued to a greater degree and notable changes took place in its content. Spontaneity gave way to routine forms.

In the second half of the 19th century the expansion of Ḥasidism stopped. With the greater – albeit moderate – tendencies toward the secularization of Jewish life, Ḥasidism shut itself in and passed from a position of attack to one of defense. The ideas of the Enlightenment, national and socialist ideals, and the Zionist movements shook the traditional Jewish way of life. Ḥasidism strongly opposed any change in the way of life and in spiritual values and alienated itself from the new forces which rose up among the Jews. The movement of Ḥibbat Zion was not welcomed in the courts of the *ẓaddikim*. At the end of the 19th and the beginning of the 20th centuries, the Jewish workers' movements were outside the ḥasidic camp. The numbers of Ḥasidim did not decline, but its power of attraction was failing. Only in one area did Ḥasidism produce something new: namely, a strong emphasis on Torah study. The first ḥasidic yeshivah was founded, apparently, by Abraham Bornstein of Sochaczew in the 1860s. At the end of the century the *ẓaddikim* of Lubavitch founded yeshivot of "Tomekhei Temimim." An attempt was also made to establish a yeshivah at Gur in Poland. It seems that by the study of Torah the ḥasidic leaders sought to immunize the ḥasidic youth from the "harmful influences" from outside. With this they repeated, in essence, the attempt of the *Mitnaggedim* of Lithuania, who were defending themselves from Ḥasidism.

In World War I (1914–18) and the first few years following it, the distribution of Ḥasidism changed. Many of the *ẓaddikim* who lived in the area of the battles were driven out of their towns or were forced to leave because of economic difficulties and threats to security. The vast majority of them escaped to the big cities and some of them remained there after the war. The collapse of the Austro-Hungarian Empire and the formation of new countries sometimes cut off masses of Ḥasidim from their leaders and they found themselves politically in Romania or Czechoslovakia. However, the most important and most tragic event in the lives of the Ḥasidim was the cutting off of the Russian branch, as the result of the Bolshevik regime.

The changes which took place in Jewish society in Eastern Europe in the period between the two World Wars (1918–39), and the problems which then faced the Jews, left their imprint upon the Ḥasidim of those countries. Ḥasidism continued in its conservatism. It was the main sector, and at times the only part of the Jewish population, which carefully maintained the tradition of dress, language, and education. The majority of Ḥasidim strongly opposed the Zionist movement and especially religious Zionism; they did not even encourage emigration to Ereẓ Israel which was growing during those years, although they did not interfere with it. However, many Ḥasidim did join the waves of emigration to Ereẓ Israel. Some of them founded Bene Berak, Kefar Ḥasidim, etc., and others settled in cities and concentrated themselves in special ḥasidic *minyanim*. They remained loyal to the *ẓaddikim* abroad, naming themselves after them, and maintained their connections.

During the Holocaust the ḥasidic centers of Eastern Europe were destroyed. The masses of Ḥasidim perished and, together with them, most of the ḥasidic leaders. *Ẓaddikim* who survived moved to Israel or went to America and established new ḥasidic centers there. Although many Ḥasidim were active in Ereẓ Israel and were enthusiastic supporters of the foundation of the State of Israel (see e.g., *Kozienice, *Gur, Lubavitch-*Schneersohn), for some of them this was a very late development, while others retained a bitter and active hostility to everything modern in Jewish life and culture and in particular to the State of Israel (see Joel *Teitelbaum of Satmar).

In the 20th century the philosophy of Martin *Buber and A.J. *Heschel and the works of such writers as Isaac Leib *Peretz helped to mold neo-Ḥasidism, which consequently had a considerable influence on modern Jewish culture and youth.

[Avraham Rubinstein]

United States

Ḥasidim emigrated to the U.S. within the great Jewish migration of 1880–1925, where they generally formed part of the larger body of pious immigrant Jews while frequently establishing *shtiblekh* of their own. They seem to have been less successful than non-ḥasidic immigrant Jews in transmitting their style of religious life to the next generation, because, apart from their *ẓaddikim*, who had remained in Europe, they apparently felt a fatalistic impotence to perpetuate the Judaism they knew. After World War I several *ẓaddikim* went to the U.S., including the Twersky dynasties from the Ukraine and the Monastritsh *ẓaddik*. They gathered followers but lacked the means and the sectarian fervor to establish a ḥasidic movement. This enervation ended with the arrival in 1940 of R. Joseph Isaac *Schneersohn, the *Lubavicher rebbe*, and the general revival of Orthodox Judaism in the U.S. from that date. A network of yeshivot and religious institutions was founded under the control of R. Joseph Isaac Schneersohn and his successor R. Menahem Mendel Schneersohn, and the unprecedented practice was initiated by Lubavitch Ḥasidim of vigorously evangelizing Jews to return to Orthodoxy. The Lubavitch Ḥasidic movement achieved wide attention and exercised some influence on the U.S. Jewish community.

Following World War II, surviving Polish and especially Hungarian Ḥasidim came to the U.S., including the *ẓaddikim* of Satmar (R. Joel Teitelbaum), Klausenburg-Sandz (Halberstam), and Telem (R. Levi Isaac Greenwald). The Hungarian Ḥasidim exhibited no interest in winning over other Jews and remained self-segregated. A small community of Ḥasidim, followers of the *ẓaddik* of Skver, established the suburban township of New Square, Rockland County, near New York City. Most Hungarian Ḥasidim concentrated in a few neighborhoods of New York City, shunned the daily press and the mass media, and rejected secular education with grudging acceptance of the state's minimum standards. Most controversial was the relentless hostility toward the State of Israel, especially of Satmar Ḥasidim, who published tracts and conducted public demonstrations against it.

[Lloyd P. Gartner]

Women and Ḥasidism

Ḥasidism brought no significant changes in women's legal or social status, and in some ways intensified negative views of women already present in traditional rabbinic Judaism and Jewish mystical traditions. Ḥasidic lore preserves descriptions of daughters, mothers, and sisters of rabbinic leaders who were renowned for their rigorous standards of personal piety; a few are reputed to have become leaders of ḥasidic communities. Among them are Sarah Frankel *Sternberg (1838–1937), daughter of ḥasidic Rabbi Joshua Heschel Teomim Frankel and wife of the *ẓaddik* Ḥayyim Samuel Sternberg of Chenciny, a disciple of the famed Seer of Lublin. After her husband's death, she is said to have functioned successfully as a *rebbe* in Chenciny and was highly regarded for her piety and asceticism. Her daughter, Hannah Brakhah, the wife of R.

Elimelekh of Grodzinsk, was an active participant in the life of her husband's court. A. Rapoport-Albert has pointed out that there is little written documentation about most of these women. She suggests that their authority was based on their connection to revered male leaders, writing that "Hasidism did not evolve an ideology of female leadership, any more than it improved the position of women within the family or set out to educate them in Yiddish" (Rapoport-Albert, 501–2). It is most likely that these "holy women" achieved their reputations for leadership because many important ḥasidic leaders refused to meet with women who sought their spiritual presence and advice. Female supplicants were directed, instead, to the rebbe's female relatives.

The only apparent instance of a woman who crossed gender boundaries to achieve religious leadership in a ḥasidic sect on her own was the well-educated, pious, and wealthy Hannah Rochel Werbermacher (1806–1888?), known as "The Maid of *Ludomir." Werbermacher acquired a reputation for saintliness and miracle-working, attracting both men and women to her own *shtibl* (small prayerhouse), where she lectured from behind a closed door. Reaction from the male ḥasidic leaders of her region was uniformly negative, and pressure was successfully applied on Werbermacher to resume an appropriate female role through an arranged marriage. Although her marriage was unsuccessful, it had the intended result of ending her career as a religious leader in Poland. Around 1860, she immigrated to Ereẓ Israel, where she again attracted a following of ḥasidic women and men, built her own study house, and presided at a variety of religious gatherings. After her death, her grave on the Mount of Olives became a site of devotion. While many other women throughout Jewish history have undoubtedly shared Werbermacher's piety and spiritual charisma, it was her inheritance and independent control of significant financial resources that allowed her to construct settings in which she could exercise these qualities despite male disapproval.

In its emphasis on mystical transcendence and male attendance on the *rebbe* during the Sabbath and festivals, to the exclusion of the family unit, Ḥasidism contributed significantly to the breakdown of the Jewish social life in 19th-century Eastern Europe. Similar tensions between family responsibility and devotion to Torah were also present among the non-ḥasidic learned elite of this milieu, where wives tended to assume the responsibility for supporting their families while husbands were studying away from home. The sexual ascetism of the homosocial ḥasidic courts and rabbinic yeshivot of the 18th and 19th centuries offered young men a welcome withdrawal from family tensions, economic struggles, and the threats of modernity. Similarly, the negative attitudes toward human sexuality endemic in these environments were often openly misogynistic, incorporating many demonic images of women from rabbinic, kabbalistic, and Jewish folklore traditions.

[Judith R. Baskin (2nd ed.)]

AFTER WORLD WAR II. The displacement of surviving ḥasidic communities after the genocide of the Holocaust created multiple diasporas with new roles and opportunities for women. While numerous ḥasidic dynasties reestablished yeshivot and religious governance in the new State of Israel, small communities also resettled and flourished throughout the English-speaking world, in South Africa, Australia, England, and Canada. Since the United States had already offered safe harbor to the Lubavitcher Rebbe in the prewar 1930s, assuring the centralization of the Chabad outreach wing of Ḥasidism in New York, Lubavitcher Chabad outposts expanded rapidly across North America. This movement offered a greatly expanded role for women and girls, due to the sixth and seventh Rebbes' emphasis on female education and missionary work.

Women served as important agents of faith and family life in the transmission of ḥasidic belief to new generations of followers, the *ba'alei teshuvah* of the postwar era. Where the ultra-Orthodox Satmar and Belz communities limited women's education to the minimum required by state law and, in the case of the Satmar communities of Monsey and Kiryas Joel, actively sought public accommodation of gender segregation customs, the Lubavitcher movement aggressively expanded female activism beyond the neighborhood sphere. This activism dovetailed with the emerging and secular women's movement in the U.S., transforming traditional ḥasidic women into advocates for a return to religious observance in an era of shifting gender roles. The proliferation of Chabad houses and outreach workers adjacent to secular college campuses made Lubavitcher women the most visible representatives of Ḥasidism for students curious about Jewish observance, while the number of Crown Heights women sent to lonely Chabad outposts served as a reminder of the Rebbe's trust in their religious values.

Lubavitcher educational institutions offering both English- and Yiddish-language studies for women grew far beyond the first Bais Rivkah girls schools of the 1940s to include a teacher-training seminary, an adult-education school called Machon Chana, and the *ba'al teshuvah* seminary Bais Chana in Minneapolis. Beginning in the mid-1960s, under the auspices of the N'shei Chabad women's organization, regular publications such as *Di Yiddishe Heim* and books on women's issues were produced from Crown Heights and circulated globally, permitting a number of women to attain public roles as authors and editors. Biannual conferences also brought together female activists, who enjoyed audiences with the Rebbe until his passing in 1994. Much of the focus in Lubavitcher women's campaigns involved urging more assimilated Jewish women to light candles and to observe the laws of family purity; attaining a greater level of observance by all Jews is thought to hasten the arrival of the Messiah.

[Bonnie J. Morris (2nd ed.)]

Ḥasidic Way of Life

LEADERSHIP PATTERNS. The personality and activities of Israel Ba'al Shem Tov, and the theories and traditions transmitted in his name and developed and augmented by his followers and disciples, shaped the pattern of leadership in Ḥasidism:

The leader was the *ẓaddik*, whose charismatic personality made him the paramount authority in the community of his followers. Tensions already evident at the time Dov Baer of Mezhirech assumed the leadership of the Ḥasidim, and the splintering of the leadership after his death, caused variations and sometimes deviations in this pattern, but in its essentials it remained unchanged.

All ḥasidic leadership is characterized by an extraordinary magnetism, given expression through various activities and symbols. The *ẓaddik* is believed in, devoutly admired, and obediently followed. From the end of the third generation of Ḥasidism, a dynastic style of leadership often developed, with generation after generation of a certain dynasty of *ẓaddikim* following in the main its own specific interpretation of the ḥasidic way of life and communal cohesion (e.g., the more intellectual and theoretical pattern with the Lubavitch-Schneersohn dynasty at the head of the Chabad wing; the enthusiastic and revolutionary teachings, style of leadership, and communal pattern of the Kotsk dynasty).

Laying differing stress on the various elements of ḥasidic belief and life-style, the *ẓaddik* provides the spiritual illumination for the individual Ḥasid and the ḥasidic community from his own all-pervasive radiance, attained through his mystic union with God. This union and the ensuing enrichment of his soul are used for the sake of the people, to lead them lovingly to their creator. The *ẓaddik* is a mystic who employs his power within the social community and for its sake. A wonder-healer and miracleworker, in the eyes of his followers he is a combination of confessor, moral instructor, and practical adviser. Also a theoretical teacher and exegetical preacher, with a style of preaching peculiar to *ẓaddikim*, he expounds his ḥasidic *torah* (Hebrew for the teaching of the *ẓaddikim*) at his table (in Ḥasidic parlance *der tish*) surrounded by his followers, generally during the third meal on the Sabbath (*se'udah shelishit*). For the individual Ḥasid, joining the court of his *ẓaddik* is both a pilgrimage and a revitalizing unification with the brotherhood gathered at the court, united around and through the *ẓaddik*. The Ḥasid journeyed to his *ẓaddik's* court at least for the High Holidays (although this practice later weakened) to seek his blessing, which was also entreated from afar. He submitted a written account of his problems (known as a *kvitl*), usually accompanying this with a monetary contribution (*pidyon*, short for *pidyon nefesh*, "redemption of the soul"). The money went toward the upkeep of the *ẓaddik* and his court (who were not dependent on or supported by any single community) and was also used to provide for the needs of the poor in the ḥasidic community. Serving as intermediaries between the *ẓaddik* and the Ḥasidim were the *gabbai* (the administrative head of the court) or the *meshammesh* (the *ẓaddik's* chamberlain), who from the first generation onward mediated between the *ẓaddik* and the Ḥasid in matters of *kvitl* or *pidyon*. In Ḥasidism the *ẓaddik* is conceived of as the ladder between heaven and earth, his mystic contemplation linking him with the Divinity, and his concern for the people and loving leadership tying him to earth. Hence his absolute authority, as well as the belief of most ḥasidic dynasties that the *ẓaddik* must dwell in visible affluence.

THE PRAYER RITE AND OTHER CUSTOMS. From its beginnings Ḥasidism developed its own prayer rite. In fact, the ḥasidic version of the prayers, though called *Sefarad*, is not identical with the Sephardi rite, nor with the Ashkenazi, but is a combination of (1) the Polish Ashkenazi rite; (2) changes made by Isaac Luria; and (3) the Sephardi rite of Palestine upon which Luria based his changes.

The result is a patchwork and was a source of great confusion. The ḥasidic version itself is not uniform, and there are many differences between the various ḥasidic prayer books. The first ḥasidic prayer book was that of Shneur Zalman of Lyady (Shklov, 1803). The main differences in ḥasidic prayer are: the recitation of the collection of verses beginning with I Chronicles 16:8 ("*hodu*") before **Pesukei de-Zimra*; in the *Kedushah*, they recite *Nakdishkha* in *Shaḥarit* and in *Minḥah*, *Keter* in *Musaf* (see **Kedushah*). Prayer for the Ḥasid is ecstatic and loud, involving song, body movements, shaking, and clapping.

In the first generations of Ḥasidism, while it was still a minority belief in most communities and under bitter attack, the Ḥasidim opened their own small prayer houses, called *shtiblekh*, a name which continued to be used. The separateness of the ḥasidic community was aggravated by their insistence on a specific type of highly sharpened (*geshlifene*) *sheḥitah* knife, a demand which both necessitated and permitted a separate ḥasidic *sheḥitah* with its own income and organization. The reason for this custom has not been sufficiently explained.

As by the mid-19th century Ḥasidism prevailed in most communities of the Ukraine, Volhynia, central Poland, Galicia, and in many in Hungary and Belorussia, the pattern of leadership based on the *ẓaddik* changed the character of local community leadership to a considerable extent. Local leaders and rabbis became subject to the authority of the *ẓaddik* whose followers were the most influential ḥasidic group in a given community.

The image and memory of past and present *ẓaddikim* are shaped and kept alive through the ḥasidic tale (*ma'aseh*), which is recounted as an act of homage to the living link between the Ḥasid and his God. As well as embodying the sayings of such teachers as Israel Ba'al Shem Tov, Levi Isaac of Berdichev, Naḥman of Bratslav, and Menahem Mendel of Kotsk, these tales reflect popular philosophy to a great extent.

The insistence of Ḥasidism from its inception on joy (*simḥah*) as the prime factor in the good Jewish life and the essential element of divine worship led to the importance of the ḥasidic dance and song as expressions of piety and group cohesion, whether in the *shtiblekh* in the individual community or when united together at the *ẓaddik*'s court and table. Ḥasidic influence was spread, but was also further splintered, by the widespread custom of giving support and something approaching the status of *ẓaddik* to descendants of a dynasty

ḤASIDIM (chart of the relationships of the leading ḥasidic dynasties, from the Ba'al Shem Tov to the 20th century)

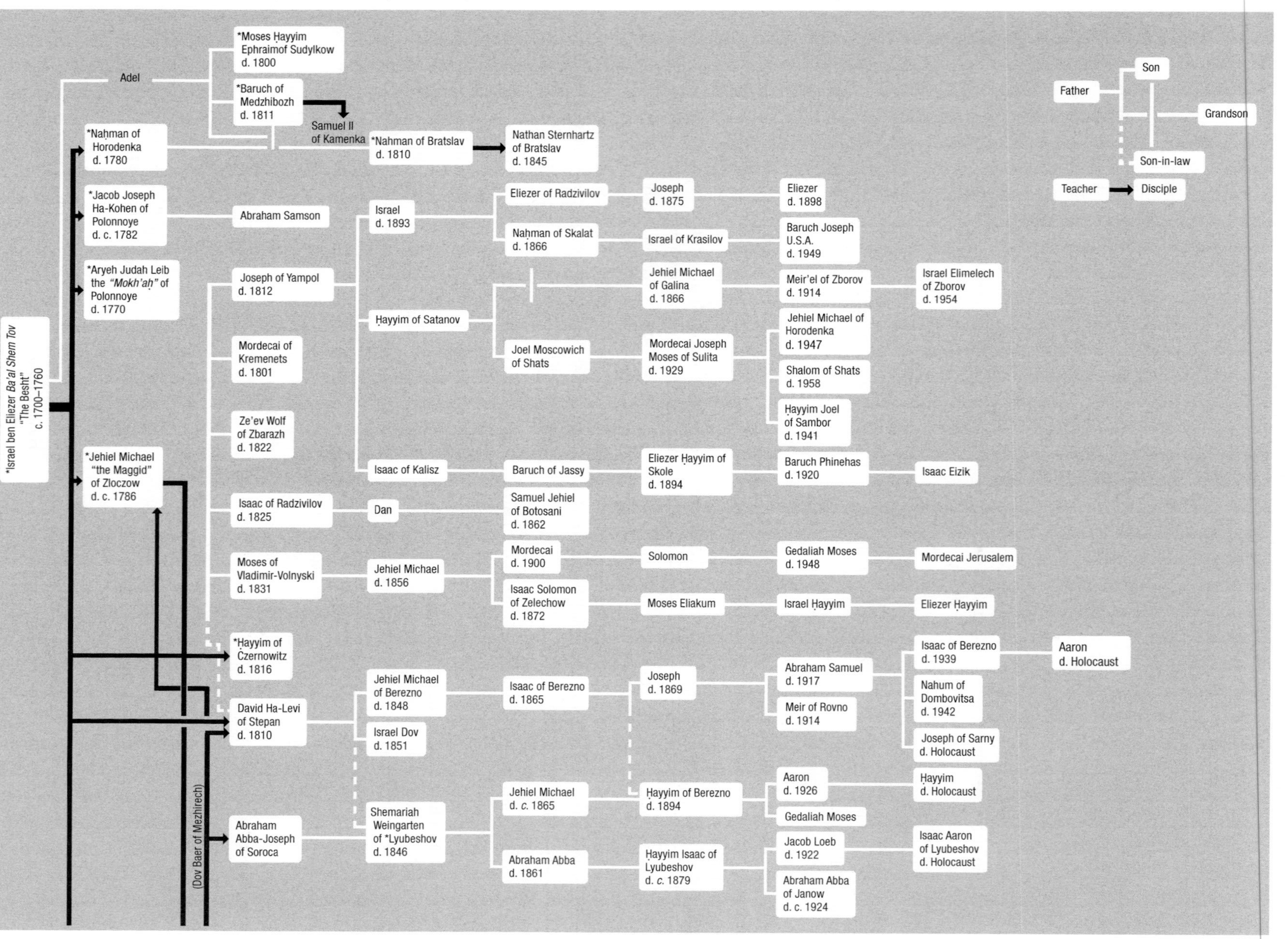

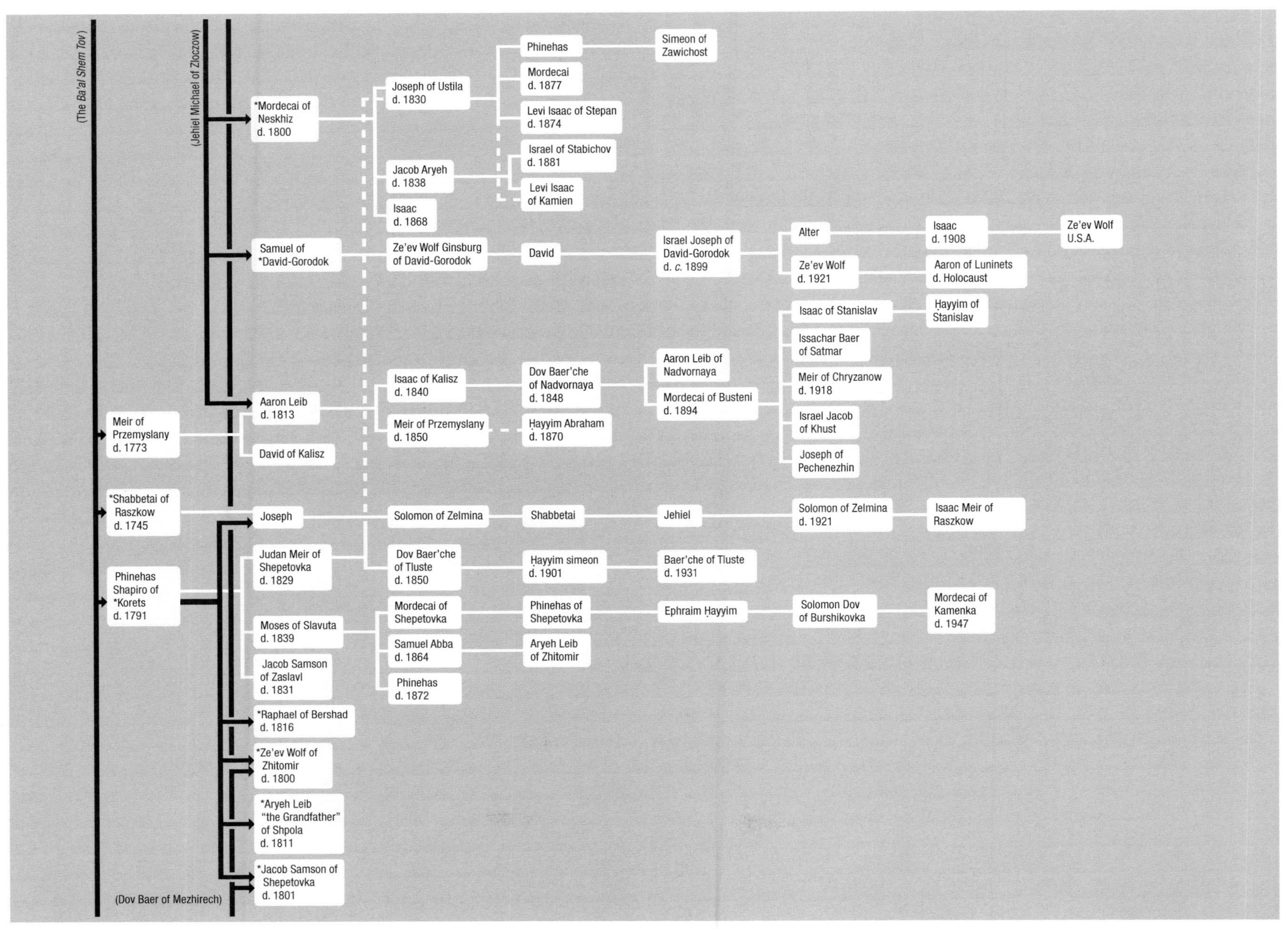
(The Ba'al Shem Tov)
(Jehiel Michael of Zloczow)
(Dov Baer of Mezhirech)
Meir of Przemyslany d. 1773
*Shabbetai of Raszkow d. 1745
Phinehas Shapiro of *Korets d. 1791
*Mordecai of Neskhiz d. 1800
Samuel of *David-Gorodok
Aaron Leib d. 1813
David of Kalisz
Joseph
Judan Meir of Shepetovka d. 1829
Moses of Slavuta d. 1839
Jacob Samson of Zaslavl d. 1831
*Raphael of Bershad d. 1816
*Ze'ev Wolf of Zhitomir d. 1800
*Aryeh Leib "the Grandfather" of Shpola d. 1811
*Jacob Samson of Shepetovka d. 1801
Joseph of Ustila d. 1830
Jacob Aryeh d. 1838
Isaac d. 1868
Ze'ev Wolf Ginsburg of David-Gorodok
Isaac of Kalisz d. 1840
Meir of Przemyslany d. 1850
Solomon of Zelmina
Dov Baer'che of Tluste d. 1850
Mordecai of Shepetovka
Samuel Abba d. 1864
Phinehas d. 1872
Phinehas
Mordecai d. 1877
Levi Isaac of Stepan d. 1874
Israel of Stabichov d. 1881
Levi Isaac of Kamien
David
Dov Baer'che of Nadvornaya d. 1848
Ḥayyim Abraham d. 1870
Shabbetai
Ḥayyim simeon d. 1901
Phinehas of Shepetovka
Aryeh Leib of Zhitomir
Simeon of Zawichost
Israel Joseph of David-Gorodok d. c. 1899
Aaron Leib of Nadvornaya
Mordecai of Busteni d. 1894
Jehiel
Baer'che of Tluste d. 1931
Ephraim Ḥayyim
Alter
Ze'ev Wolf d. 1921
Isaac of Stanislav
Issachar Baer of Satmar
Meir of Chryzanow d. 1918
Israel Jacob of Khust
Joseph of Pechenezhin
Solomon of Zelmina d. 1921
Solomon Dov of Burshikovka
Isaac d. 1908
Aaron of Luninets d. Holocaust
Ḥayyim of Stanislav
Isaac Meir of Raszkow
Mordecai of Kamenka d. 1947
Ze'ev Wolf U.S.A.

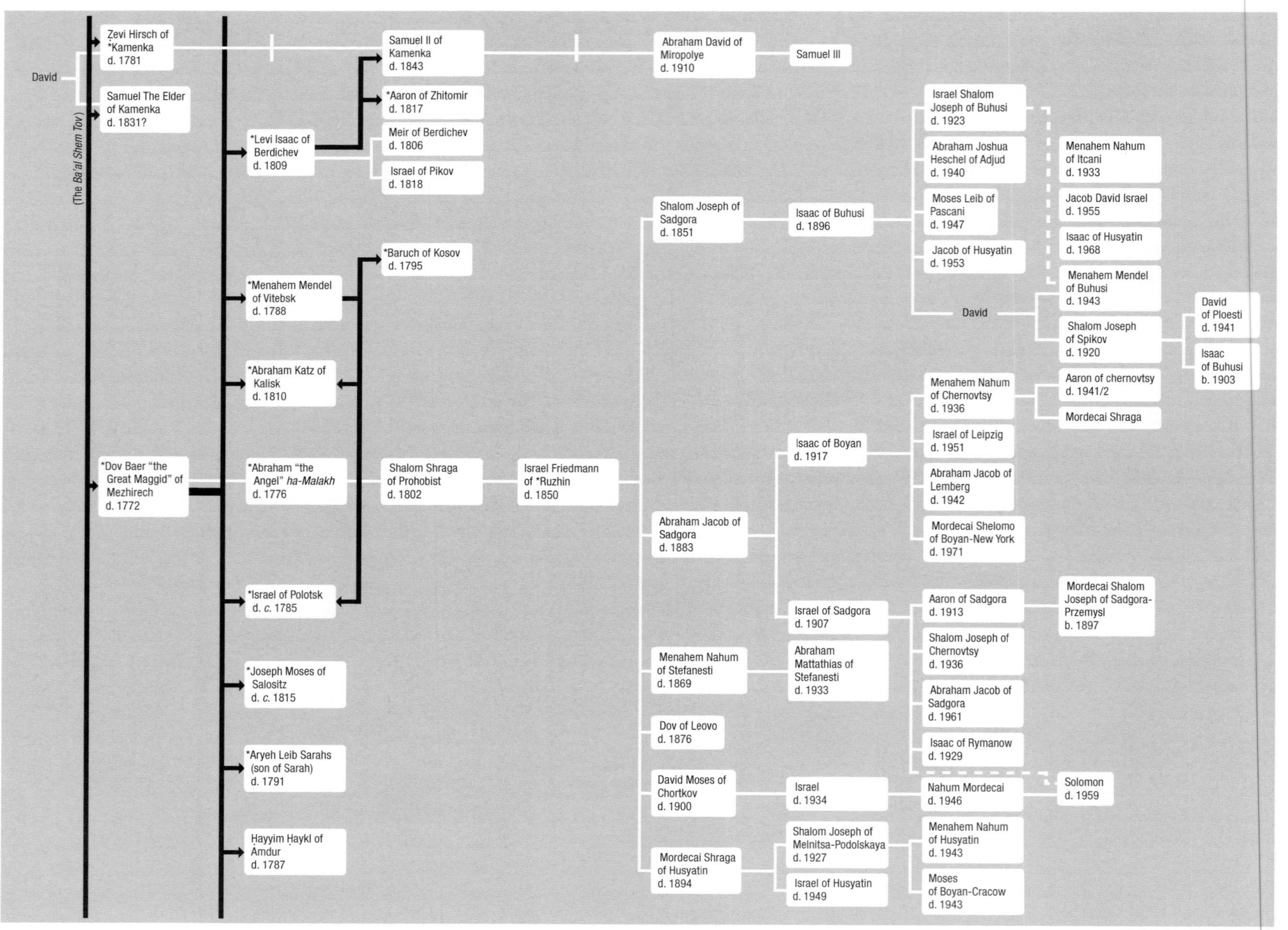
ḤASIDIM (continued)
David
(The Ba'al Shem Tov)
Ẓevi Hirsch of *Kamenka d. 1781
Samuel The Elder of Kamenka d. 1831?
*Levi Isaac of Berdichev d. 1809
*Menahem Mendel of Vitebsk d. 1788
*Abraham Katz of Kalisk d. 1810
*Dov Baer "the Great Maggid" of Mezhirech d. 1772
*Abraham "the Angel" ha-Malakh d. 1776
*Israel of Polotsk d. c. 1785
*Joseph Moses of Salositz d. c. 1815
*Aryeh Leib Sarahs (son of Sarah) d. 1791
Ḥayyim Ḥaykl of Amdur d. 1787
Samuel II of Kamenka d. 1843
*Aaron of Zhitomir d. 1817
Meir of Berdichev d. 1806
Israel of Pikov d. 1818
*Baruch of Kosov d. 1795
Shalom Shraga of Prohobist d. 1802
Israel Friedmann of *Ruzhin d. 1850
Abraham David of Miropolye d. 1910
Samuel III
Shalom Joseph of Sadgora d. 1851
Abraham Jacob of Sadgora d. 1883
Menahem Nahum of Stefanesti d. 1869
Dov of Leovo d. 1876
David Moses of Chortkov d. 1900
Mordecai Shraga of Husyatin d. 1894
Isaac of Buhusi d. 1896
Isaac of Boyan d. 1917
Israel of Sadgora d. 1907
Abraham Mattathias of Stefanesti d. 1933
Israel d. 1934
Shalom Joseph of Melnitsa-Podolskaya d. 1927
Israel of Husyatin d. 1949
Israel Shalom Joseph of Buhusi d. 1923
Abraham Joshua Heschel of Adjud d. 1940
Moses Leib of Pascani d. 1947
Jacob of Husyatin d. 1953
David
Menahem Nahum of Chernovtsy d. 1936
Israel of Leipzig d. 1951
Abraham Jacob of Lemberg d. 1942
Mordecai Shelomo of Boyan-New York d. 1971
Aaron of Sadgora d. 1913
Shalom Joseph of Chernovtsy d. 1936
Abraham Jacob of Sadgora d. 1961
Isaac of Rymanow d. 1929
Nahum Mordecai d. 1946
Menahem Nahum of Husyatin d. 1943
Moses of Boyan-Cracow d. 1943
Menahem Nahum of Itcani d. 1933
Jacob David Israel d. 1955
Isaac of Husyatin d. 1968
Menahem Mendel of Buhusi d. 1943
Shalom Joseph of Spikov d. 1920
Aaron of chernovtsy d. 1941/2
Mordecai Shraga
Mordecai Shalom Joseph of Sadgora-Przemysl b. 1897
Solomon d. 1959
David of Ploesti d. 1941
Isaac of Buhusi b. 1903

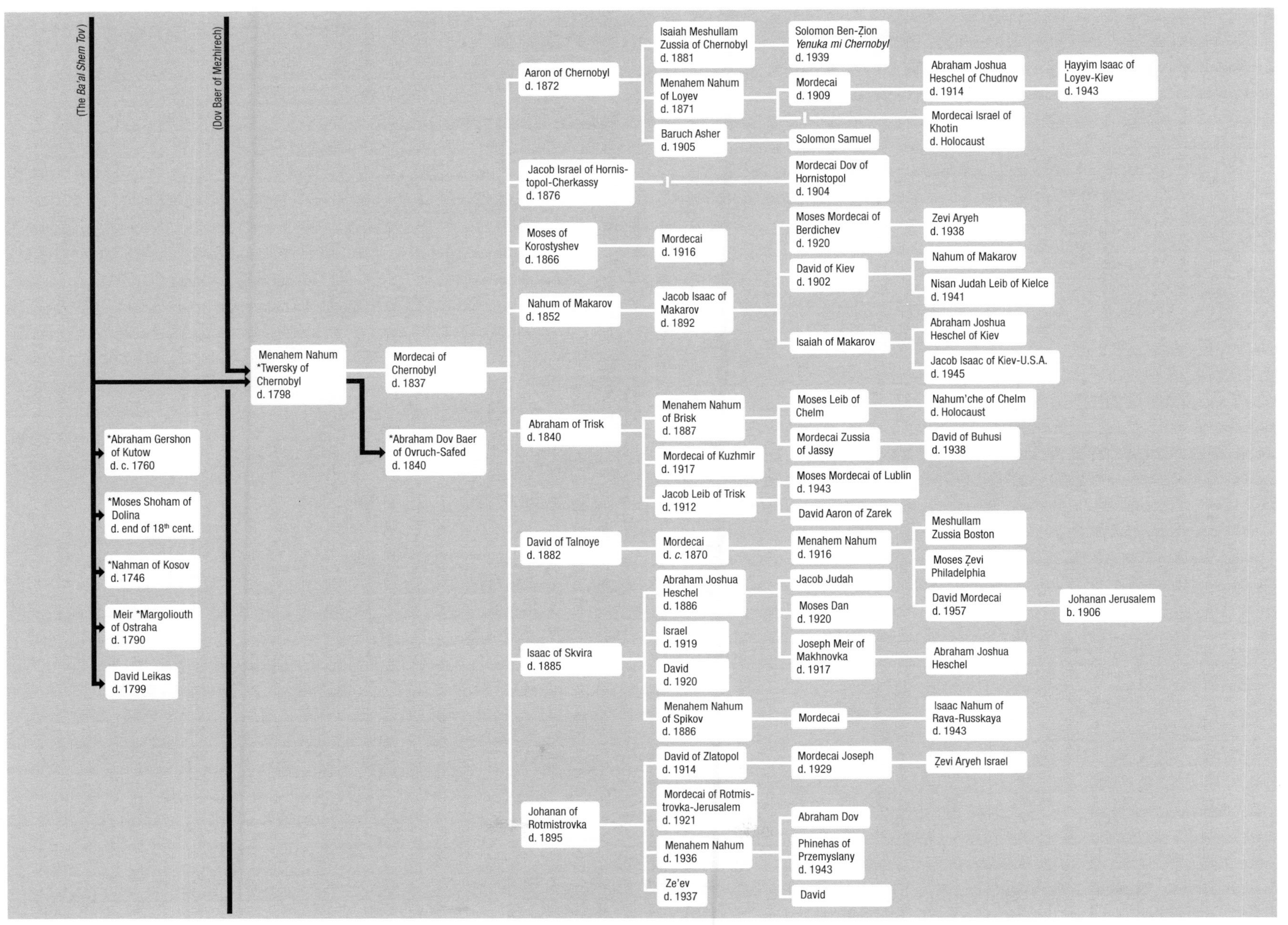
(The Ba'al Shem Tov)
(Dov Baer of Mezhirech)
*Abraham Gershon of Kutow d. c. 1760
*Moses Shoham of Dolina d. end of 18th cent.
*Nahman of Kosov d. 1746
Meir *Margoliouth of Ostraha d. 1790
David Leikas d. 1799
Menahem Nahum *Twersky of Chernobyl d. 1798
Mordecai of Chernobyl d. 1837
*Abraham Dov Baer of Ovruch-Safed d. 1840
Aaron of Chernobyl d. 1872
Jacob Israel of Hornis-topol-Cherkassy d. 1876
Moses of Korostyshev d. 1866
Nahum of Makarov d. 1852
Abraham of Trisk d. 1840
David of Talnoye d. 1882
Isaac of Skvira d. 1885
Johanan of Rotmistrovka d. 1895
Isaiah Meshullam Zussia of Chernobyl d. 1881
Menahem Nahum of Loyev d. 1871
Baruch Asher d. 1905
Mordecai d. 1916
Jacob Isaac of Makarov d. 1892
Menahem Nahum of Brisk d. 1887
Mordecai of Kuzhmir d. 1917
Jacob Leib of Trisk d. 1912
Mordecai d. c. 1870
Abraham Joshua Heschel d. 1886
Israel d. 1919
David d. 1920
Menahem Nahum of Spikov d. 1886
David of Zlatopol d. 1914
Mordecai of Rotmis-trovka-Jerusalem d. 1921
Menahem Nahum d. 1936
Ze'ev d. 1937
Solomon Ben-Ẓion Yenuka mi Chernobyl d. 1939
Mordecai d. 1909
Solomon Samuel
Mordecai Dov of Hornistopol d. 1904
Moses Mordecai of Berdichev d. 1920
David of Kiev d. 1902
Isaiah of Makarov
Moses Leib of Chelm
Mordecai Zussia of Jassy
Moses Mordecai of Lublin d. 1943
David Aaron of Zarek
Menahem Nahum d. 1916
Jacob Judah
Moses Dan d. 1920
Joseph Meir of Makhnovka d. 1917
Mordecai
Mordecai Joseph d. 1929
Abraham Dov
Phinehas of Przemyslany d. 1943
David
Abraham Joshua Heschel of Chudnov d. 1914
Mordecai Israel of Khotin d. Holocaust
Ḥayyim Isaac of Loyev-Kiev d. 1943
Ẓevi Aryeh d. 1938
Nahum of Makarov
Nisan Judah Leib of Kielce d. 1941
Abraham Joshua Heschel of Kiev
Jacob Isaac of Kiev-U.S.A. d. 1945
Nahum'che of Chelm d. Holocaust
David of Buhusi d. 1938
Meshullam Zussia Boston
Moses Ẓevi Philadelphia
David Mordecai d. 1957
Johanan Jerusalem b. 1906
Abraham Joshua Heschel
Isaac Nahum of Rava-Russkaya d. 1943
Ẓevi Aryeh Israel

ḤASIDIM (continued)

(Dov Baer of Mezhirech)

Aaron Perlov "the Great" of *Karlin d. 1772

Solomon Ha-Levi of *Karlin d. 1792

*Shneur Zalman *Ba'al ha-Tanya* of Lyady d. 1813

Abraham Ḥayyim of Zloczow d. 1816

Samuel Shmelke *Horowitz of Nikolsburg d. 1778

Jacob Isaac of Lublin

Asher of Karlin-Stolin d. 1826

Mordecai of *Lachowicze d. 1810

Moses of Ludmir d. 1829

Uri *ha-Saraf* of *Strelisk d. 1826

*Aaron Ha-Levi of Starosielce d. 1828

Dov Baer of Lubavich d. 1827

Menahem Mendel of Kosov d. 1825

*Moses Leib of Sasov d. 1807

Yizhak Isaac Taub of *Kallo d. 1821

Aaron the Second of Karlin-Stolin d. 1872

Aaron d. 1796

Noah of Lachowicze d. 1832

Solomon of Ludmir

Judah Ẓevi Hirsch of *Stretyn d. 1854

Moses of *Kobrin d. 1858

Menahem Mendel Schneersohn *Ẓemah Ẓedek* of Lubavich d. 1866

Ḥayyim Hager of Kosov d. 1844

Jekuthiel Samuel Shmelke of Sasov d. 1861

Moses Ḥayyim of Rozdol d. 1831

Asher the Second of Stolin d. 1873

Solomon Ḥayyim of *Koidanov d. 1862

Mordecai II of Lachwicze

Nahum of Ludmir

Abraham of Stretyn d. 1865

Samuel Zanvil d. 1887

Abraham Weinberg of Slonim d. 1883

Samuel of Lubavich d. 1882

Abraham David *Lawat d. 1890

Menahem Mendel Hager of *Vizhnitz d. 1884

Jacob of Sasov

Solomon d. 1879

Israel of Stolin *Yenuka mi-Stolin* d. 1922

Abraham Aaron of Pukhovichi

Noah of Gorodishche d. 1904

Baruch Mordecai of Koidanov d. 1870

Aaron d. 1881

Gedaliah

Noah Naphtali of Kobrin d. 1889

Shalom Dov Baer of Lubavich d. 1920

Baruch of Vizhnitz d. 1893

Israel Leib of Krimlov

Judan Ẓevi d. 1888

Aaron d. 1942

Moses of Stolin d. 1942

Abraham Elimelech of Karlin d. 1942

Johanan of Lutsk d. 1955

Jacob Ḥayyim U.S.A. d. 1946

Aaron of Koidanov d. 1897

Shalom of Bragin d. 1925

Noah II d. 1920

Uri Aaron of Kalisz d. 1943

Moses of Stanislav d. 1943

Samuel of Slonim d. 1916

Noah Tiberias d. 1927

David Solomon of Kobrin d. 1918

Aaron of Damachevo d. 1907

Joseph Isaac U.S.A. d. 1950

Israel of Grosswardein d. 1938

Ḥayyim of Itinia d. 1935

Phinehas of Borsa d. 1941

Abraham of Zawiercie d. 1915

Phinehas Ḥayyim of Rozdol d. 1935

Joseph of Koidanov d. 1915

Nehemiah of Baranovichi d. 1927

Johanan d. Holocaust

Abraham II of Baranovichi d. 1933

Issachar Aryeh of Slonim d. 1928

Abraham III Jerusalem b. 1890

Moses Aaron d. 1942

Baruch Joseph Zak "Rabbi of Kobrin" d. 1949

Ḥayyim Meir of Vizhnitz-Bene-Berak b. 1881

Menahem Mendel d. 1941

Eliezer Jerusalem d. 1946

Baruch b. 1895

Jehiel Judah d. 1937

Baruch Meir Jacob Shoḥet b. 1955

Shalom Alter of Baranovichi d. 1941

Solomon David Joshua of Baranovichi d. 1943

Menahem Mendel Schneersohn U.S.A. 1902–1994

Ḥayyim Judah Meir

Menahem Mendel b. 1922

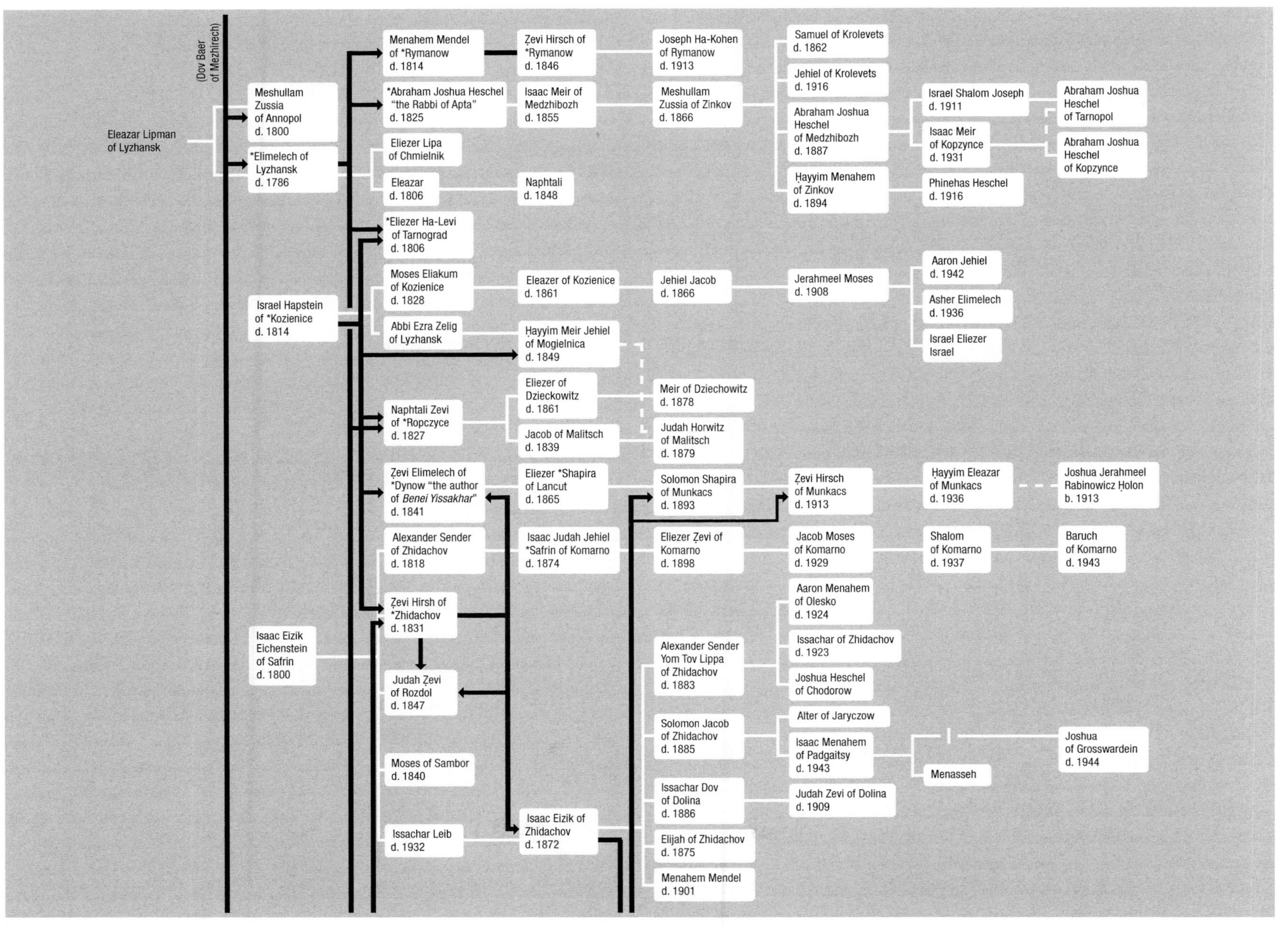
Eleazar Lipman of Lyzhansk
(Dov Baer of Mezhirech)
Meshullam Zussia of Annopol d. 1800
*Elimelech of Lyzhansk d. 1786
Israel Hapstein of *Kozienice d. 1814
Isaac Eizik Eichenstein of Safrin d. 1800
Menahem Mendel of *Rymanow d. 1814
*Abraham Joshua Heschel "the Rabbi of Apta" d. 1825
Eliezer Lipa of Chmielnik
Eleazar d. 1806
*Eliezer Ha-Levi of Tarnograd d. 1806
Moses Eliakum of Kozienice d. 1828
Abbi Ezra Zelig of Lyzhansk
Naphtali Zevi of *Ropczyce d. 1827
Ẓevi Elimelech of *Dynow "the author of *Benei Yissakhar*" d. 1841
Alexander Sender of Zhidachov d. 1818
Ẓevi Hirsh of *Zhidachov d. 1831
Judah Ẓevi of Rozdol d. 1847
Moses of Sambor d. 1840
Issachar Leib d. 1932
Ẓevi Hirsch of *Rymanow d. 1846
Isaac Meir of Medzhibozh d. 1855
Naphtali d. 1848
Eleazer of Kozienice d. 1861
Ḥayyim Meir Jehiel of Mogielnica d. 1849
Eliezer of Dzieckowitz d. 1861
Jacob of Malitsch d. 1839
Eliezer *Shapira of Lancut d. 1865
Isaac Judah Jehiel *Safrin of Komarno d. 1874
Isaac Eizik of Zhidachov d. 1872
Joseph Ha-Kohen of Rymanow d. 1913
Meshullam Zussia of Zinkov d. 1866
Jehiel Jacob d. 1866
Meir of Dziechowitz d. 1878
Judah Horwitz of Malitsch d. 1879
Solomon Shapira of Munkacs d. 1893
Eliezer Ẓevi of Komarno d. 1898
Alexander Sender Yom Tov Lippa of Zhidachov d. 1883
Solomon Jacob of Zhidachov d. 1885
Issachar Dov of Dolina d. 1886
Elijah of Zhidachov d. 1875
Menahem Mendel d. 1901
Samuel of Krolevets d. 1862
Jehiel of Krolevets d. 1916
Abraham Joshua Heschel of Medzhibozh d. 1887
Ḥayyim Menahem of Zinkov d. 1894
Jerahmeel Moses d. 1908
Ẓevi Hirsch of Munkacs d. 1913
Jacob Moses of Komarno d. 1929
Aaron Menahem of Olesko d. 1924
Issachar of Zhidachov d. 1923
Joshua Heschel of Chodorow
Alter of Jaryczow
Isaac Menahem of Padgaitsy d. 1943
Judah Zevi of Dolina d. 1909
Israel Shalom Joseph d. 1911
Isaac Meir of Kopzynce d. 1931
Phinehas Heschel d. 1916
Aaron Jehiel d. 1942
Asher Elimelech d. 1936
Israel Eliezer Israel
Ḥayyim Eleazar of Munkacs d. 1936
Shalom of Komarno d. 1937
Menasseh
Abraham Joshua Heschel of Tarnopol
Abraham Joshua Heschel of Kopzynce
Joshua Jerahmeel Rabinowicz Ḥolon b. 1913
Baruch of Komarno d. 1943
Joshua of Grosswardein d. 1944

ḤASIDIM (continued)

- (Dov Baer of Mezhirech) → *Jacob Isaac *ha-Ḥozeh mi-Lublin* "the Seer of Lublin" d. 1815
- (Samuel Shmelke, of Nikolsburg) → *Jacob Isaac *ha-Ḥozeh mi-Lublin* "the Seer of Lublin" d. 1815
- (Elimelech of Lyzhansk) → Kalonymus Kalman *Epstein of Cracow d. 1823; *Jacob Isaac *ha-Ḥozeh mi-Lublin* "the Seer of Lublin" d. 1815

*Jacob Isaac *ha-Ḥozeh mi-Lublin* "the Seer of Lublin" d. 1815

- Kalonymus Kalman *Epstein of Cracow d. 1823
  - Aaron of Cracow d. 1883
  - Joseph Baruch "the good Jew" of Neustadt d. 1867
- Shaiom Roke'aḥ of *Belz d. 1855
  - Joshua d. 1894
    - Issachar Dov d. 1927
      - Aaron d. 1957
      - Issachar Dov b. 1948
  - Joseph Meir Weiss of *Spinka d. 1909 (also from (Isaac of Zhidachov) and from Ḥayyim *Halberstam of Zanz)
    - Joseph Meir Kahana Jerusalem b. 1910
    - Naḥman Bene-Berak b. 1905
    - Isaac Eizik of Spinka d. 1944
      - Samuel Ẓevi Horowitz U.S.A. b. 1920
      - Jacob Joseph Weiss U.S.A. b. 1917
- Moses *Teitelbaum of Ujhely d. 1841
  - Eleazar Nisan of Drogobych d. 1855
    - Samuel of Gorlice
    - Nahum Ẓevi of Drogobych
    - Jekuthiel Judah of Sighet d. 1883
      - Abraham Aaron of Kolbuszowa d. 1910
      - Moses Joseph of Uphely d. 1897
      - Elyah Bezalel of Havasmezo and Tecso d. 1918
      - Hananiah Yom Tov Lipa of Sighet d. 1904
        - Ḥayyim Ẓevi of Sighet d. 1926
          - Jekuthiel Judah of Sighet d. 1944
        - Joel of Satmar b. 1887
- Ḥayyim *Halberstam of Zanz d. 1876
  - Ezekiel Shraga of Sieniawa d. 1899
    - Moses of Sieniawa
      - Aryeh Leibush of Sieniawa
      - Jacob Samson Kaner of Czchow-Klausenburg d. 1941
        - Baruch of Czchow-Zanz d. 1953
  - Baruch of Gorlice d. 1906
    - Ẓevi Hirsch of Rudnik d. 1918
      - Jekuthiel Judah of Klausenburg-Israel b. 1904
  - David of Kshanow d. 1894
  - Solomon of Bobova d. 1906
    - Ben-Zion of Bobova d. 1941
      - Solomon of Bobova
  - Aaron of Zanz d. 1906
    - Shalom of Zanz d. 1925
  - *Ẓevi Hirsch Friedman of Lesko d. 1874
    - Yozefa Goldberger d. 1908
    - Ḥayyim Friedlander of Lesko d. 1904
- Isaiah of *Przedborz d. 1830
  - Emmanuel Weltfreid d. 1865
    - Abraham Moses of Rozprze d. 1918
      - Emmanuel of Lodz d. 1939
      - Isaiah of Kalisz d. 1939
      - Solomon of Tomaszow d. Holocaust

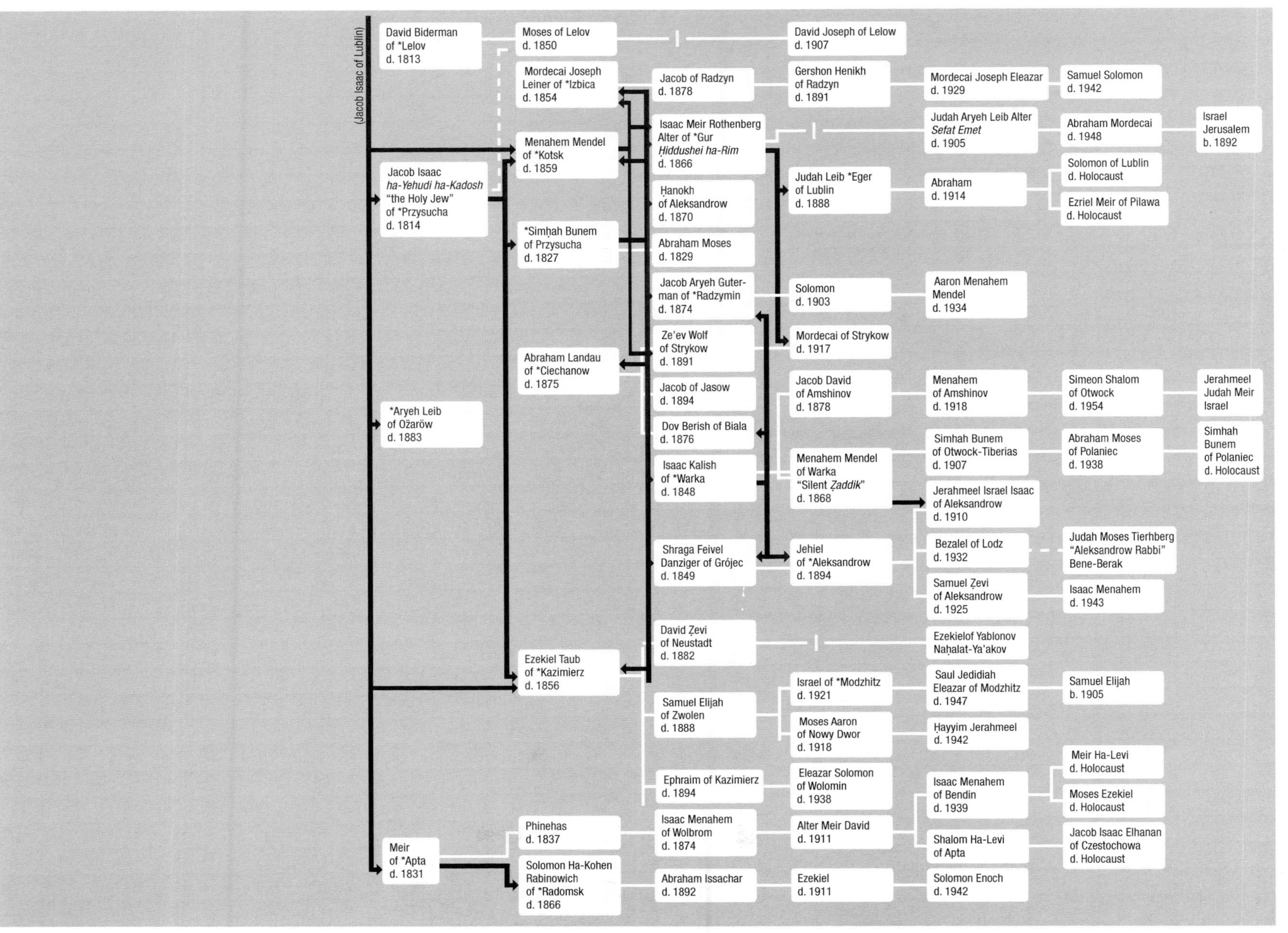
(Jacob Isaac of Lublin)
David Biderman of *Lelov d. 1813
Jacob Isaac ha-Yehudi ha-Kadosh "the Holy Jew" of *Przysucha d. 1814
*Aryeh Leib of Ožarów d. 1883
Meir of *Apta d. 1831
Moses of Lelov d. 1850
Mordecai Joseph Leiner of *Izbica d. 1854
Menahem Mendel of *Kotsk d. 1859
*Simḥah Bunem of Przysucha d. 1827
Abraham Landau of *Ciechanow d. 1875
Ezekiel Taub of *Kazimierz d. 1856
Phinehas d. 1837
Solomon Ha-Kohen Rabinowich of *Radomsk d. 1866
Jacob of Radzyn d. 1878
Isaac Meir Rothenberg Alter of *Gur Ḥiddushei ha-Rim d. 1866
Ḥanokh of Aleksandrow d. 1870
Abraham Moses d. 1829
Jacob Aryeh Guter-man of *Radzymin d. 1874
Ze'ev Wolf of Strykow d. 1891
Jacob of Jasow d. 1894
Dov Berish of Biala d. 1876
Isaac Kalish of *Warka d. 1848
Shraga Feivel Danziger of Grójec d. 1849
David Ẓevi of Neustadt d. 1882
Samuel Elijah of Zwolen d. 1888
Ephraim of Kazimierz d. 1894
Isaac Menahem of Wolbrom d. 1874
Abraham Issachar d. 1892
David Joseph of Lelow d. 1907
Gershon Henikh of Radzyn d. 1891
Judah Leib *Eger of Lublin d. 1888
Solomon d. 1903
Mordecai of Strykow d. 1917
Jacob David of Amshinov d. 1878
Menahem Mendel of Warka "Silent Ẓaddik" d. 1868
Jehiel of *Aleksandrow d. 1894
Israel of *Modzhitz d. 1921
Moses Aaron of Nowy Dwor d. 1918
Eleazar Solomon of Wolomin d. 1938
Alter Meir David d. 1911
Ezekiel d. 1911
Mordecai Joseph Eleazar d. 1929
Judah Aryeh Leib Alter Sefat Emet d. 1905
Abraham d. 1914
Aaron Menahem Mendel d. 1934
Menahem of Amshinov d. 1918
Simhah Bunem of Otwock-Tiberias d. 1907
Jerahmeel Israel Isaac of Aleksandrow d. 1910
Bezalel of Lodz d. 1932
Samuel Ẓevi of Aleksandrow d. 1925
Ezekielof Yablonov Naḥalat-Ya'akov
Saul Jedidiah Eleazar of Modzhitz d. 1947
Ḥayyim Jerahmeel d. 1942
Isaac Menahem of Bendin d. 1939
Shalom Ha-Levi of Apta
Solomon Enoch d. 1942
Samuel Solomon d. 1942
Abraham Mordecai d. 1948
Solomon of Lublin d. Holocaust
Ezriel Meir of Pilawa d. Holocaust
Simeon Shalom of Otwock d. 1954
Abraham Moses of Polaniec d. 1938
Judah Moses Tierhberg "Aleksandrow Rabbi" Bene-Berak
Isaac Menahem d. 1943
Samuel Elijah b. 1905
Meir Ha-Levi d. Holocaust
Moses Ezekiel d. Holocaust
Jacob Isaac Elhanan of Czestochowa d. Holocaust
Israel Jerusalem b. 1892
Jerahmeel Judah Meir Israel
Simhah Bunem of Polaniec d. Holocaust

who did not become *ẓaddikim* (the so-called *einiklakh*, "the grandsons"). Various other specific ḥasidic customs (e.g., the rushing to the *ẓaddik*'s table to obtain a portion of the remnants (*shirayim*) of the food he had touched) were contributing factors to the closeness of the ḥasidic group. The ecstatic prayer of the *ẓaddik* – mostly when reciting the Song of Songs or the *Lekhu Nerannenah* prayer on the entry of the Sabbath – which figures frequently in ḥasidic tales, was a powerful element in holding the group together.

The elements of ḥasidic song, dance, and tale later became influential in modern Jewish youth movements and helped to shape neo-Ḥasidism. From the end of World War I, the Ḥabad-Lubavitch movement led the underground struggle to maintain Jewish religious life and culture under communist regimes (see *Russia). Some ḥasidic dynasties took part in the creation of agricultural settlements in Israel (*Kefar Ḥasidim, *Kefar Ḥabad). In recent times, groups of young Jews in the United States have demonstrated their allegiance to protest movements through turning to ḥasidic modes of expression to embody their enthusiasm, specific cohesion, and adherence to Jewish identity.

[Avraham Rubinstein]

BASIC IDEAS OF ḤASIDISM

Creator and Universe

While it is true that many of the basic ideas of Ḥasidism are grounded in earlier Jewish sources, the Ḥasidim did produce much that was new if only by emphasis. With few exceptions, ḥasidic ideas are not presented systematically in the ḥasidic writings, but an examination of these writings reveals certain patterns common to all the ḥasidic masters. Central to ḥasidic thought is an elaboration of the idea, found in the Lurianic Kabbalah, that God "withdrew from Himself into Himself" in order to leave the primordial "empty space" into which the finite world could eventually emerge after a long process of emanations. This "withdrawal" (*ẓimẓum*), according to Chabad thought especially and to a considerable degree also to ḥasidic thought in general, does not really take place but only appears to do so. The infinite divine light is progressively screened so as not to engulf all in its tremendous glory so that creatures can appear to enjoy an independent existence. The whole universe is, then, a "garment" of God, emerging from Him "like the snail whose shell is formed of itself."

In a parable attributed to the Ba'al Shem Tov a mighty king sits on his throne, situated in the center of a huge palace with many halls, all of them filled with gold, silver, and precious stones. Those servants of the king who are far more interested in acquiring wealth than in gazing at the king's splendor spend all their time, when they are admitted to the palace, in the outer halls, gathering the treasures they find there. So engrossed are they in this that they never see the countenance of the king. But the wise servants, refusing to be distracted by the treasures in the halls, press on until they come to the king on his throne in the center of the palace. To their astonishment, once they reach the king's presence, they discover that the palace, its halls, and their treasures are really only an illusion, created by the king's magical powers. In the same way God hides Himself in the "garments" and "barriers" of the cosmos and the "upper worlds." When man recognizes that this is so, when he acknowledges that all is created out of God's essence and that, in reality, there are no barriers between man and his God, "all the workers of iniquity" are dispersed (*Keter Shem Tov*, I, 5a–b). In its context this parable refers to prayer. Man should persist in his devotions and refuse to be distracted by extraneous thoughts. But the idea that all is in God is clearly implied. The verse: "Know this day, and lay it to thy heart, that the Lord He is God in heaven above and in the earth beneath; there is none else" (Deut. 4:39) is read as: "There is nothing else." In reality there is nothing but God, for otherwise the world would be "separate" from God and this would imply limitation in Him (*Keter Shem Tov*, I, 8b).

The ḥasidic leader R. Menahem Mendel of Lubavich observes (*Derekh Mitzvotekha* (1911), 123) that the disciples of the Ba'al Shem Tov gave the "very profound" turn to the doctrine of the oneness of God so that it means not only that He is unique, as the medieval thinkers said, but that He is all that is: "That there is no reality in created things. This is to say that in truth all creatures are not in the category of 'something' [*yesh*] or a 'thing' [*davar*] as we see them with our eyes. For this is only from our point of view since we cannot perceive the divine vitality. But from the point of view of the divine vitality which sustains us we have no existence and we are in the category of complete nothingness [*efes*] like the rays of the sun in the sun itself… From which it follows that there is no other existence whatsoever apart from His existence, blessed be He. This is true unification. As the saying has it: 'Thou art before the world was created and now that it is created' – in exactly the same manner. Namely, just as there was no existence apart from Him before the world was created so it is even now."

As a corollary of ḥasidic pantheism (more correctly, panentheism) is the understanding in its most extreme form of the doctrine of divine providence. The medieval thinkers limited special providence to the human species and allowed only general providence so far as the rest of creation is concerned. It is purely by chance that this spider catches that fly, that this ox survives, the other dies. For the Ḥasidim there is nothing random in a universe that is God's "garment." No stone lies where it does, no leaf falls from the tree, unless it has been so arranged by divine wisdom.

Particularly during prayer but also at other times man has to try to overcome the limitations of his finite being to see only the divine light into which, from the standpoint of ultimate reality, he and the cosmos are absorbed. This transcendence of the ego is known in ḥasidic thought as *bittul ha-yesh*, "the annihilation of selfhood." Humility (*shiflut*) does not mean for Ḥasidism that man thinks little of himself but that he does not think of himself at all. Only through humility can man be the recipient of God's grace. He must empty himself so that he might be filled with God's gifts.

Optimism, Joy, and Hitlahavut

Ḥasidic optimism and joy (*simḥah*) are also based on the notion that all is in God. If the world and its sorrows do not enjoy true existence and the divine light and vitality pervade all, what cause is there for despair or despondency? When man rejoices that he has been called to serve God, he bestirs the divine joy above and blessing flows through all creation. A melancholy attitude of mind is anathema to Ḥasidism, serving only to create a barrier between man and his Maker. Even over his sins a man should not grieve overmuch: "At times the evil inclination misleads man into supposing that he has committed a serious sin when it was actually no more than a mere peccadillo or no sin at all, the intention being to bring man into a state of melancholy [*aẓvut*]. But melancholy is a great hindrance to God's service. Even if a man has stumbled and sinned he should not become too sad because this will prevent him from worshiping God" (*Ẓavva'at Ribash* (1913),9). Some ḥasidic teachers, however, draw a distinction between man's "bitterness" (*merirut*) at his remoteness from God and "sadness." The former is commendable in that it is lively and piercing whereas the latter denotes deadness of soul. A further result of the basic ḥasidic philosophy is *hitlahavut*, "burning enthusiasm," in which the soul is aflame with ardor for God whose presence is everywhere. Man's thought can cleave to God, to see only the divine light, and this state of attachment (*devekut*), of always being with God, is the true aim of all worship.

Love and Fear

The study of the Torah, prayer, and other religious duties must be carried out in love and fear. The bare deed without the love and fear of God is like a bird without wings. A ḥasidic tale relates that the Ba'al Shem Tov was unable to enter a certain synagogue because it was full of lifeless prayers, which, lacking the wings of love and fear, were unable to ascend to God. As observant Jews the Ḥasidim did not seek to deny the value of the deed but they taught repeatedly that the deed could only be elevated when carried out in a spirit of devotion. R. Ḥayyim of Czernowitz writes (*Sha'ar ha-Tefillah* (1813), 7b): "There is a man whose love for his God is so strong and faithful that he carries out each *mitzvah* with superlative excellence, strength and marvelous power, waiting in longing to perform the *mitzvah*, his soul expiring in yearning. For, in accordance with his spiritual rank, his heart and soul know the gracious value of the *mitzvot* and the splendor of their tremendous glory and beauty, infinitely higher than all values. And how much more so the dread and fear, the terror and trembling, which fall on such a man when he performs a *mitzvah*, knowing as he does with certainty that he stands before the name of the Holy One, blessed be He, the great and terrible King, before Whom 'all the inhabitants of the earth are reputed as nothing; and He doeth according to His will in the host of heaven' [Dan. 4:32], who stands over him always, seeing his deeds, for His glory fills the earth. Such a man is always in a state of shame and lowliness so intense that the world cannot contain it, especially when he carries out the *mitzvot*. Such a man's *mitzvot* are those which fly ever upward in joy and satisfaction to draw down from there every kind of blessing and flow of grace to all worlds."

This idea was applied to all man's deeds, not only to his religious obligations. In all things there are "holy sparks" (*niẓoẓot*) waiting to be redeemed and rescued for sanctity through man using his appetites to serve God. The very taste of food is a pale reflection of the spiritual force which brings the food into being. Man should be led on by it to contemplate the divine vitality in the food and so to God Himself. In the words of the highly charged mythology of the Lurianic Kabbalah, the "holy sparks" released by man provide the *Shekhinah* with her "Female Waters" which, in turn, cause the flow of the "Male Waters" and so assist "the unification of the Holy One, blessed be He, and His *Shekhinah*" to produce cosmic harmony. Because of the importance of man's role for the sacred marriage and its importance in the ḥasidic scheme, the Ḥasidim adopted from the kabbalists the formula: "For the sake of the unification of the Holy One, blessed be He, and His *Shekhinah*" (*le-shem yiḥud*) before the performance of every good deed, for which they were vehemently attacked by R. Ezekiel Landau of Prague (*Noda bi-Yhudah*, YD no. 93). (The redemption of the "holy sparks" was one of the reasons given for ḥasidic fondness for tobacco. Smoking a pipe served to release subtle "sparks" not otherwise accessible.)

***Kavvanah* and Ẓaddikism**

Is a program of sustained contemplation, attachment, and utter devotion to God (**Kavvanah*) really possible for all men? The ḥasidic answer is generally in the negative. This is why the doctrine of ẓaddikism is so important for Ḥasidism. The holy man, his thoughts constantly on God, raises the prayers of his followers and all their other thoughts and actions. In the comprehensive work on ẓaddikism, R. Elimelech of Lyzhansk's *No'am Elimelekh*, the *ẓaddik* appears as a spiritual superman, with the power to work miracles. He is the channel through which the divine grace flows, the man to whom God has given control of the universe by his prayers. The *ẓaddik* performs a double task: he brings man nearer to God and he brings down God's bounty to man. The *ẓaddik* must be supported by his followers. This financial assistance is not for the sake of the *ẓaddik* but for the sake of those privileged to help him. By supporting the *ẓaddik* with their worldly goods his followers become attached to him through his dependence on them, which he readily accepts in his love for them. Their welfare thus becomes his and his prayers on their behalf can the more readily be answered. The *ẓaddik* even has powers over life and death. God may have decreed that a person should die but the prayers of the *ẓaddik* can nullify this decree. This is because the *ẓaddik*'s soul is so pure and elevated that it can reach to those worlds in which no decree has been promulgated since there only mercy reigns.

But if such powers were evidently denied to the great ones of the past how does the *ẓaddik* come to have them? The rationale is contained in a parable attributed to the Maggid of Mezhirech (*No'am Elimelekh* to Gen. 37: 1). When a king is on his travels he will be prepared to enter the most humble dwelling if he can find rest there but when the king is at home he will refuse to leave his palace unless he is invited by a great lord who knows how to pay him full regal honors. In earlier generations only the greatest of Jews could attain to the holy spirit. Now that the *Shekhinah* is in exile, God is ready to dwell in every soul free from sin.

Social Involvement

The social implications of ḥasidic thought should not be underestimated. The sorry conditions of the Jews in the lands in which Ḥasidism was born were keenly felt by the ḥasidic masters who considered it a duty of the highest order to alleviate their sufferings. In the ḥasidic court the wealthy were instructed to help their poorer brethren, the learned not to look down on their untutored fellows. The unity of the Jewish people and the need for Jews to participate in one another's joys and sorrows was repeatedly stressed. The preachers who seemed to take a perverse delight in ruthlessly exposing Jewish shortcomings were taken to task by the Ba'al Shem Tov and his followers. The *ẓaddik* was always on the lookout for excuses for Jewish faults. R. Levi Isaac of Berdichev is the supreme example of the *ẓaddik* who challenges God Himself to show mercy to His people.

From the numerous anti-ḥasidic polemics (collected e.g., by M. Wilensky, *Ḥasidim u-Mitnaggedim*, 1970) we learn which of the ḥasidic ideas were especially offensive to their opponents. The doctrine that all is in God was treated as sheer blasphemy. The doctrine, it was said, would lead to "thinking on the Torah in unclean places" i.e., it would obliterate the distinction between the clean and the unclean, the licit and the illicit. The alleged arrogance of the claims made for the *ẓaddik* were similarly a cause of offense. The ḥasidic elevation of contemplative prayer over all other obligations, especially over the study of the Torah, seemed to be a complete reversal of the traditional scale of values. The doctrine of *bittul ha-yesh* was criticized as leading to moral irresponsibility. The bizarre practice of turning somersaults in prayer, followed by a number of the early Ḥasidim as an expression of self-abnegation, was held up to ridicule, as was ḥasidic indulgence in alcoholic stimulants and tobacco. The resort of the Ḥasidim to prayer in special conventicles (the *shtiblekh*), their adoption of the Lurianic prayer book, their encouragement of young men to leave their families for long periods to stay at the court of the *ẓaddik*, were all anathema to the *Mitnaggedim* who saw in the whole process a determined revolt against the established order.

[Louis Jacobs]

TEACHINGS OF ḤASIDISM

Origins of Ḥasidic Teachings

The teachings of Ḥasidism are as notable for their striking content as they are for the colorful literary form in which they are cast. Their sources, however, are readily traceable to kabbalistic literature and to the *musar* literature of Safed deriving from it. The first generation of ḥasidic teachers usually embodied their teachings in terse aphorisms. These, too, reflect the influence of the aforementioned literature. The first evidence of the spread of ḥasidic teaching dates from the 1750s and comes from the anti-ḥasidic polemical writings of the *Mitnaggedim*, their implacable opponents. Authentic ḥasidic teachings appeared in print only at the beginning of the 1780s. These published teachings of the Ḥasidim make no reference to the doctrines ascribed to them by their mitnaggedic opponents. For this curious fact, two possible explanations suggest themselves. Either the *Mitnaggedim* were guilty of exaggeration and distortion in their hostile description of ḥasidic doctrine or, in the interim, a process of internal criticism had moderated original ḥasidic teachings in the decades preceding their publication. The likelihood is that both factors were at work. This does not mean to imply, however, that the teachings of Israel b. Eliezer (the Ba'al Shem Tov) recorded by his disciples are to be regarded as having been censored, thus casting doubt on their authenticity. What is to be inferred is that the antinomian and anarchistic doctrines taught by certain circles were not incorporated into classical Ḥasidism. While no evidence of the specific character of such teachings is available, there can be no doubt of the existence of such groups.

The teachings of the earliest circles of Ḥasidim were transmitted in the name of Israel Ba'al Shem Tov, Judah Leib Piestanyer, Naḥman of Kosov, Naḥman of Horodenko (Gorodenka), and others. This was a group of decided spiritual (pneumatic) cast which also fashioned for itself a particular communal life-style, a community built not on family units but rather on meetings organized around prayer circles. As a matter of principle, this pattern served as the basis for the development of the classic ḥasidic community.

It may be said that for the first time in the history of Jewish mysticism, ḥasidic thought reflects certain social concerns. There is present a confrontation with distinctly societal phenomena and their transformation into legitimate problems in mysticism as such. This concern is expressed not in the establishment of specific liturgical norms or formulas devised for the convenience of the congregation but in such doctrines as the worship of God through every material act, and the "uplifting of the sparks" (*niẓoẓot*). In the teachings of the Ba'al Shem Tov and his circles these doctrines involved a sense of social mission.

Worship through Corporeality (Avodah be-Gashmiyyut)

One of the most widespread teachings of Ḥasidism from the very beginnings of the movement is the doctrine calling for man's worship of God by means of his physical acts. In other words, the human physical dimension is regarded as an area capable of religious behavior and value. From this assumption, a variety of religious tendencies followed. To be especially noted is the extraordinary emphasis placed on the value of such worship and the subsequent attempt to limit it to a devotional practice suitable only for spiritually superior individuals. In the teachings of the Ba'al Shem Tov, this doctrine developed in uncontrolled fashion, culminating in the tenet that man must worship God with both the good and the evil in his nature.

The ideological background of worshiping God through such physical acts as eating, drinking, and sexual relations was suggested by the verse "in all thy ways shalt thou know Him" (Prov. 3:6). For if it is incumbent upon man to worship God with all his natural impulses by transforming them into good, then obviously the realization of such an idea demands involvement in that very area in which these impulses are made manifest – the concrete, material world. In addition, the revolutionary views concealed within the interstices of the teachings of the Ba'al Shem Tov make it clear that corporeal worship (*avodah be-gashmiyyut*) saves man from the dangers of an overwrought spiritualism and retreat from the real world. This is expressed by Jacob Joseph of Polonnoye, a disciple of the Ba'al Shem Tov, in the name of his teacher: "I have heard from my teacher that the soul, having been hewn from its holy quarry, ever ought to long for its place of origin, and, lest its reality be extinguished as a result of its yearning, it has been surrounded with matter, so that it may also perform material acts such as eating, drinking, conduct of business and the like, in order that it [the soul] may not be perpetually inflamed by the worship of the Holy One blessed be He, through the principle of the perfection [*tikkun*] and maintenance of body and soul" (*Toledot Ya'akov Yosef*, portion *Tazri'a*). The point made here in advocacy of corporeal worship is largely psychological and not theological.

The theological concept designed to reinforce the affirmation of corporeal worship is grounded in the dialectical relationship that operates between matter and spirit. In order to reach the spiritual goal, man must pass through the material stage, for the spiritual is only a higher level of the material. The parables of the Ba'al Shem Tov of the "lost son" point to the theological function served by the concept of "corporeal worship." The son, in foreign captivity, enters the local tavern with his captors, all the time guarding within him a hidden secret which is none other than the key to his redemption. While his captors drink only for the sake of drinking, he drinks in order to disguise his true happiness which consists not in drinking but rather in his "father's letter" – his secret – informing him of his impending release from captivity. In other words, there is no way to be liberated from the captivity of matter except by ostensibly cooperating with it. This ambivalent relation to reality forms a supreme religious imperative.

Social Consequences of the Doctrine of "Corporeal Worship"

The dialectic tension between matter and spirit or between form and matter – the conventional formulation in Ḥasidism – assumes social significance and the polar terms come to denote the relationship between the *ẓaddik* and his congregation. In this context, the opposition between spirit and matter is conceived so as to create a seeming tension between the inner content of the mystical act and the forms of social activity. It is within the community, however, that mystical activity should be achieved though, of course, in hidden fashion. Those who surround the *ẓaddik* are incapable of individually discerning the moment in which the transformation of the secular into the holy occurs. This indispensable transformation can be experienced only communally. Therefore, the community of Ḥasidim becomes a necessary condition for the individual's realization of the mystical experience. It became the imperative of Ḥasidism to live both in society and beyond its bounds at one and the same time. The social and psychological conditions necessary for fulfillment of "corporeal worship" are rooted not alone in the disparity between form and matter, i.e., between the masses and the *ẓaddik*, but rather in the inner spiritual connection between the two. Only the presence of a basic common denominator makes possible the appearance of a mystical personality which grows dialectically out of otherwise disparate elements. The *ẓaddik* represents the "particular amid the general." The absence of such integration precludes the consequent growth of the spiritual element.

In the teachings of the Ba'al Shem Tov, little stress is placed on the theories of the Lurianic Kabbalah centering on the "uplifting of the sparks." Nevertheless, these theories later served as the theoretical justification for the necessity of *avodah be-gashmiyyut*. The Lurianic theory, as interpreted by the Ḥasidim, maintains that through contact with the concrete material world by means of *devekut* ("communion" with God), and *kavvanah* ("devotional intent"), man uplifts the sparks imprisoned in matter. In this context, the concept of *avodah be-gashmiyyut* carries with it a distinct polemical note, since it is asserted that its validity has particular application to the sphere of social life. Thus, a major religious transvaluation finds expression in the creation of a new system of social relations. This is exemplified in the instructions given by the Ba'al Shem Tov granting permission to desist from *devekut* during prayer in order to respond to some social need. He indicates that should a man be approached during a period of *devekut* by a person wishing to talk to him or seeking his assistance he is permitted to stop praying since in this latter action (i.e., in directing his attention from prayer to his fellow) "God is present." Here, the temporary abandonment of the study of Torah (*bittul Torah*) and of *devekut* is justified by the fact that this encounter too constitutes part of the spiritual experience of the "spiritually perfect man." As a result, the meaning of religious "perfection" is determined by a new system of values.

In the teachings of the Ba'al Shem Tov's disciple, Dov Baer, the Maggid of Mezhirech, these motives disappear. The direction of thinking assumes a completely typical spiritualistic character. *Avodah be-gashmiyyut* is conceived of as an indispensable necessity although it is covertly questioned whether every man is permitted to engage in it. A pupil of one of the Maggid's disciples, Meshullam Feivush of Zbarazh, specifically states that it was not the Maggid's intention to proclaim *avodah be-gashmiyyut* as a general practice but rather as a practice intended for an elite immune to the danger of the concept's vulgarization. One of the Maggid's most important disciples, Shneur Zalman of Lyady, mentions the practice with a touch of derision. Nevertheless, it came to occupy a central place in the literature of Ḥasidism. The meaning and limits of the concept served as a focal point of an ongoing controversy among the movement's proponents.

The Ethos of Ḥasidism

From the moment that the formula *yeridah le-ẓorekh aliyyah* ("the descent in behalf of the ascent") became established in the context of the emphasis placed upon it by the Ba'al Shem Tov, a certain perturbation of the traditional system of ethical values in Judaism was imminent. Although the precise limits of the descent into the region of evil were still open to debate, the acceptance in principle of man's mandate to "transform" evil into good, through an actual confrontation of evil in its own domain, was an idea definitely unwelcome in any institutionalized religion. The classical example of dealing with this problem propounded in the teachings of the Ba'al Shem Tov was that of the encounter with evil in the sphere of human impulses: "A man should desire a woman to so great an extent that he refines away his material existence, in virtue of the strength of his desire." The significance of this statement lies in its granting a warrant to exhaust the primordial desires without actually realizing them; it is not a dispensation for the release of bodily desires through physical actualization but through their transformation. This concept is of great importance to an understanding of the significance of confronting evil, as it points to the peculiar inner logic implicit in the idea of *avodah be-gashmiyyut* as found expression in the ethical sphere.

Within the framework of the concept of "descent" (*yeridah*) – a concept over which Ḥasidism wavered a great deal – can be included the idea of the "descent" of the *ẓaddik* toward the sinner in order to uplift him. This "descent" carries with it bold ethical implications in that it justifies the "descent" into the sphere of evil and demands the consequent "ascent" from the domain of sin. A moral danger is of course implicit in the real possibility that a man may "descend" and thereafter find himself unable to achieve the consequent ascent. Here again, the very act of confronting evil requires an independent valuation, admitting of no previous criticism or censorship, although such confrontation was regarded as the special prerogative of men of "spirit," i.e., the *ẓaddikim*. Thus, out of the teachings of the Ba'al Shem Tov arose a primary imperative to turn toward material reality and the worldly inferior sphere. If only in moral terms, this demand grew from a basic ethical-religious claim that man is not at liberty to abstain from the task of transfiguring the material world through good.

The teachings of the Maggid of Mezhirech reveal a more restrained doctrine on the one hand, and an interiorization of spiritual problems on the other, evidenced by the greater degree of introspection and inwardness characteristic of the mystic. In the Maggid can be discerned a tendency toward an increasing spiritualization, accompanied by greater moral restraint. Among the followers of the Maggid, however, developments took place in very different directions. In the courts of some *ẓaddikim* the influence of the thinking of the Ba'al Shem Tov was apparent in the doctrines they broadcast, propagating social responsibility and a communal mysticism. These centers of teaching developed primarily in Galicia, the Ukraine, and also in Poland at the court of the rabbi of Lublin. This last school reached a crisis point during the period of its heirs in *Przysucha, *Kotsk, and *Izbica, when it began to cast doubt on the large majority of accepted ḥasidic doctrines, especially on their moral significance. At the same time Chabad Ḥasidism in Belorussia developed in the direction of a rationalized religious life by preserving pre-ḥasidic moral biases, and by shunning the mystical adventurism of the Ba'al Shem Tov and even the Maggid of Mezhirech, which in its attempt to spiritualize reality, had propounded as necessary the confrontation with evil and laid down the conditions for this conflict, while seeing in the "uplift of the sparks" its great mission. Nevertheless in the person of Dov Baer, son of Shneur Zalman of Lyady, the founder of Chabad Ḥasidism, can be discerned a thinker with a tendency toward a pure and aristocratic mysticism, a fact which establishes his affinity to the views of the Maggid of Mezhirech, although this holds true only in terms of this aristocratic bent. In terms of an "ethical mentality," as it were, Dov Baer is a representative of his father's line of thought.

Prayer

In the second and third generation of Ḥasidism, some Ḥasidim testified to the fact that, in their view, the major innovation of the Ba'al Shem Tov lay in his introducing in prayer a fundamentally new significance as well as new modes of praying. The author of *Ma'or va-Shemesh*, a disciple of Elimelech of Lyzhansk, writes, "Ever since the time of the holy Ba'al Shem Tov, of blessed and sanctified memory, the light of the exertion of the holiness of prayer has looked out and shone down upon the world, and into everybody who desires to approach the Lord, blessed be He…" This can be understood to mean that the Ḥasidim saw in the doctrine of the Ba'al Shem Tov two things as essentially one: the radiance (of the light of holiness) and new hope, and the revived exertion (involved in the holiness of prayer). These dual motifs began to function as guidelines for ḥasidic prayer, in the following senses:

(1) The origins of prayer lie in the conflict with the external world, known as "evil thoughts." Prayer requires a great effort of concentration if man is to overcome the tendency of the plenitude of exterior reality to permeate his consciousness. This quite natural permeation to which man responds instinctively is considered in Ḥasidism as the "wayfaring" of thought and as such is the very opposite of its concentration, which requires a negation of the world, a turning away from it, and is based on man's ability to achieve pure introspection devoid of all content. The function of this introspection is to achieve the utter voiding ("annihilation") of human thought

and to uplift the element of divinity latent in man's soul. The transformation of this element from a latent to an active condition is understood as true union with God, the state marking the climax of *devekut* ("clinging to God," "communion with God"). Prayer, then, is regarded as the most accessible foundation for the technique of *devekut* with God. The spiritual effort involved in prayer was considered so strenuous as to give rise to the ḥasidic dictum "I give thanks to God that I remain alive after praying."

(2) The two stages described as constituting the process of prayer are: *dibbur* ("speech") and *maḥashavah* ("thought"). In passing through the first of these stages man contemplates the words of the prayer through visualizing their letters. Concentrated attention on these objects before his eyes gradually depletes the letters of their contours and voids thought of content, and speech, the reciting of the prayers, becomes automatic. Man continues to recite the prayers until an awesome stillness descends upon him, and his thought ceases to function in particulars; he establishes a connection with the divine "World of Thought" which functions on transcendent and immanent perceptible levels at one and the same time. This immanent activity is identical with the revelation of the "apex," the inner "I." In the wordplay of the Ḥasidim: "The I (אני) becomes Nought" (אין); in the "flash of an eye" a condition of utter annulment is established, and this is the state of nothingness the mystic seeks to achieve.

(3) For Ḥasidism the significance of prayer lies neither in beseeching the Creator and supplicating Him, nor in focusing attention on the contents of prayer. Rather, prayer is primarily a ladder by means of which a man can ascend to *devekut* and union with the Divinity. Ḥasidism did not embrace the Lurianic doctrine of *kavvanot* since it failed to accord with the primary intent of *devekut*. However, in spite of all the individualistic tendencies inherent in prayer through *devekut*, the Ḥasidim did not belittle the importance of communal worship, nor did they demand of the Ḥasid that he achieve *devekut* outside the bounds of the community and the halakhic framework of prayer. When there arose problems of prayer through *devekut* within the framework of the time sequence conventionally set for prayer, there were those Ḥasidim who chose to dispense with the framework, and even allowed a man to worship outside of the time limits set for prayer, provided that he infused his prayer with *devekut*. However, as a result, the Ḥasidim quite rapidly felt themselves in danger of jeopardizing the framework of the *halakhah*, and, for the most part, they recanted and accepted the authority of the existing frameworks.

(4) *Devekut*, which became the banner under which Ḥasidism went forth to revitalize religious life and modify the traditional hierarchy of values in Judaism, quickly led to a confrontation between it and the daily pattern of existence of the Ḥasid. Not only was traditional worship and its significance brought face to face with new problems, the same held true for *talmud torah*. The reason for this lay not in a fundamental revolt against the study of the Torah as such, but rather in the fact that *devekut* laid claim to the greater part of man's day and left little time for learning. In this confrontation *devekut* gained the ascendency, though there can be discerned in ḥasidic sources a tendency to strike a balance with the problematic nature of prayer, in order to prevent the study of Torah being swallowed up in mysticism. In the 19th century a distinct reaction in the direction of scholarship at the expense of *devekut* took place in certain ḥasidic "courts."

The performance of the *mitzvot*, too, and all man's actions attendant upon them, was overshadowed by *devekut*, as the fulfilling of the *mitzvot* was assessed in terms of the *devekut* achieved by man. In the new hierarchy of values the *mitzvah* itself became a means – and only one of several – to *devekut*. The widespread ḥasidic slogan "Performance of the *mitzvah* without *devekut* is meaningless" bears supreme testimony to the fact that the new mystical morality came to terms with traditional Jewish patterns on a new plane.

The existential status of man was conceived anew in Ḥasidism, and an attitude of resignation toward the world was emphasized. The Ḥasid was asked to rejoice in order to obviate any possibility of self-oriented introspection which might lead him to substitute, as his initial goal, personal satisfaction for the worship of God. The Ḥasidim went to great lengths to crystallize the primary awareness that they were first and foremost "sons of the higher world."

ḤASIDIC LITERATURE

Ḥasidic literature comprises approximately 3,000 works. No comprehensive bibliography is as yet available, although partial bibliographies exist, mostly as part of the general catalog of Hebrew literature. These include such works as *Seder ha-Dorot, Shem ha-Gedolim he-Ḥadash, Oẓar ha-Sefarim*, and *Beit Eked Sefarim*, in which ḥasidic works are listed. In more detailed fashion, the literature of Ḥasidism has been catalogued by G. *Scholem in his *Bibliographia Kabbalistica* (1933). A detailed bibliography of Bratslav Ḥasidism can be found in the pamphlet known as *Kunteres Elleh Shemot* (1928), also edited by G. Scholem. In addition, there is a detailed bibliography of Chabad Ḥasidism, compiled by A.M. Habermann, called *Sha'arei Ḥabad*, which can be found in the Salman Schocken jubilee volume *Alei Ayin* (1952).

Ḥasidic literature began to appear in print in 1780; the first published work was *Toledot Ya'akov Yosef* (Korets, 1780) by Jacob Joseph of Polonnoye. The following year saw the publication of *Maggid Devarav le-Ya'akov* (Korets, 1781), a work of the teachings of Dov Baer of Mezhirech. The earliest works of Ḥasidism were printed at Korets (Korzec), Slavuta, Zhitomir, Kopust, Zolkiew, Przemysl, Leszno, Josefov, and at several other places. Speculative works were the first type of ḥasidic literature published; it was only in the 19th century that anthologies of ḥasidic tales came into their own, and successive anthologies began to appear in print. Several manuscripts of major importance in the canon of speculative writings, which were composed in the 18th century, were first published in the 19th century. As they gradually acquired authoritative standing among the Ḥasidim, these works were frequently reprinted.

Speculative Literature

The great bulk of Ḥasidism's speculative literature was compiled in the manner of homiletic discourses (*derashot*) on selected passages from the weekly Torah readings as well as from other portions of Scripture. For the most part, it consists of recorded literature and not original writings. The homiletic framework, traditionally used for expository purposes throughout the literature of Judaism, served as background for ḥasidic ideas as well. The reader can immediately feel the ḥasidic "pulse" in each and every homiletic sermon, which reveals the presence of a distinct type of propaganda designed to spread the aims and ideas of its authors. The associative context underlying these homiletic sermons is highly complex, for it relies not only upon exegesis of scriptural passages but also on the vast range of rabbinic literature throughout the ages, on the literature of the *halakhah* from the *rishonim* to the *aḥaronim*, on the early and Lurianic Kabbalah, and on the *musar* literature of Spain and Safed. The language of these writings is influenced by the oral nature of the *derash*, in which scant attention is paid to either syntax or to artifices of style, and the idiomatic characteristics of Yiddish have left their mark on the sentence structure of the Hebrew.

Expository Pamphlets and Letters

Conscious of the need to clarify the complexities of their teachings, in order to define them with as great a degree of precision as possible, the Ḥasidim adopted a special form of writing, the expository pamphlet. This was not done with the intention of creating a new literary genre, but as a way of replying to contemporary problems over which opinion was divided. Among the important literature of this class are the *Tanya* (Slavuta, 1796) by Shneur Zalman of Lyady and *Kunteres ha-Hitpa'alut* by his son, Dov Baer. In this class, too, fall Dov Baer's prefaces to several other works. In addition, the prefaces to the writings of *Aaron of Starosielce, Shneur Zalman's foremost disciple, should be classified as belonging to this genre, although they can stand in a class of their own. Similarly, the *Derekh Emet* (1855) by Meshullam Feivush of Zbarazh, is close to an expository pamphlet in its content, while in form it is epistolary. Treatises of the explanatory type, shorter and more compressed, appear in several well-known letters, such as those of *Ḥayyim Ḥaikel of Amdur, Menaḥem Mendel of Vitebsk, and *Abraham b. Alexander Katz of Kalisk, and a type of epistolary literature, known as the "*Iggerot ha-Kodesh*" of Shneur Zalman of Lyady and Elimelech of Lyzhansk, was widely dispersed; among the richest of these collections of letters is the *Alim li-Terufah* (1896) by Nathan Sternherz of Nemirov, a disciple of Naḥman of Bratslav. Apart from this category of writing there exists a wealth of epistolary literature dealing with both current affairs and with the social problems of the Jewish communities of the time; these letters are primarily of historical importance.

Kabbalistic Writings

Notwithstanding the differences of opinion within the ḥasidic community over the relative importance of close study of the Lurianic Kabbalah – differences resulting from a variety of factors – Ḥasidism counted among its adherents several of the leading kabbalists of the age. While Elijah b. Solomon, the Gaon of Vilna, expressed particular interest in the Kabbalah of the Zohar, ḥasidic kabbalists were largely influenced by Cordoverianic and Lurianic Kabbalah. Outstanding among ḥasidic writers of kabbalistic texts were the *maggid* Israel of *Kozienice, Ẓevi Hirsch of Zhidachov, and Jacob Ẓevi Jolles, author of a lexicon of Lurianic Kabbalah entitled *Kehillat Ya'akov* (1870). It is noticeable that the kabbalistic commentaries of these Ḥasidim are not always integrated within the framework of their ḥasidic teachings, but here and there it is possible to discern traces of ḥasidic thought in their commentaries on the Zohar and on the *Ez Ḥayyim* of Ḥayyim *Vital. A more pronounced attempt at integrating the two trends of thought, though in the direction of Kabbalah, becomes evident when the works in question are ḥasidic writings which attempt to locate their origins and sources of continuity in the Kabbalah.

Halakhic Writings

Eighteenth-century Ḥasidism did not give rise to many halakhic treatises; the best-known works of this type are the *Shulḥan Arukh* (Kopust, 1814) by Shneur Zalman of Lyady, and the writings of his grandson, the Ẓemaḥ Ẓedek. Polish Ḥasidism revitalized the scholastic tradition; prominent scholars among them were Isaac Meir of *Gur, author of *Ḥiddushei ha-Rim*, and Gershon Ḥanokh of Radzyn (see *Izbica-Radzyn), who reinstituted the custom of wearing a blue-fringed garment, or *ẓiẓit tekhelet*. Galician Ḥasidism, too, had outstanding men of learning like Ḥayyim *Halberstam of Zanz, author of *Divrei Ḥayyim* (1864), and Isaac Judah Jehiel of Komarno.

Liturgy

Although it was not ḥasidic practice to create a new liturgy, nevertheless exceptional cases are known in which Ḥasidim composed and instituted novel prayers. There were those Ḥasidim who were accustomed to add Yiddish words to their prayers, and there were also prayers which were composed and recited as additions to the conventional liturgy. Typical examples of these additional and spontaneous prayers are found in Bratslav Ḥasidism. Phinehas of Korets paid particular attention to modifications in the liturgy and even added changes of his own, which have come down in manuscript only. The *Siddur ha-Rav* of Shneur Zalman of Lyady did much to establish specific liturgical norms for the adherents of Chabad Ḥasidism.

Vision Literature

Visions were favorably regarded by the Ḥasidim, but they were allowed scant publicity and their publication was limited. In spite of this there remain a few writings which hint at the ex-

The solemn Tisha Be-Av prayer. Men are sitting on the floor and women are standing in the women's section, while the rabbi is blowing the shofar. From the *Rothschild Miscellany*, northern Italy, c. 1470. *Collection, The Israel Museum, Jerusalem. Photo: Z. Radovan, Jerusalem.*

Though the illumination of Hebrew manuscripts conceivably began in the Hellenistic period (330–63 b.c.e) and continued into the 20th century, it is essentially an art of the Middle Ages. Styles varied by region and period but the main inspiration was the Bible.

ILLUMINATED MANUSCRIPTS

Judaeo Persian Manuscript, Iran, 1686. 180/54 Fol. 38 r. *Collection, The Israel Museum, Jerusalem. Photo © The Israel Museum, Jerusalem.*

Different stages of ritual in the Kosher preparation of meat. From the "Golden Haggadah," an illuminated Hebrew manuscript, Spain, 1320. *British Library, London. Photo: Z. Radovan, Jerusalem.*

TOP LEFT: Noah's Ark. The dove is returning with a branch in its beak, a sign that the flood water has receded. Hebrew Manuscript from northern France, c. 1280. *British Library, London. Photo: Z. Radovan, Jerusalem.*

BOTTOM LEFT: "Sacrifice of Isaac." Abraham holding the knife to sacrifice his son Isaac, with the angel holding his hand from striking the fatal blow. Hebrew Manuscript from northern France, c. 1280. *British Library, London. Photo: Z. Radovan, Jerusalem.*

BELOW: Moses receiving the Tablets of the Law and bringing them to God's people on Mt. Sinai. Page from the *Birds' Heads Haggadah*, the earliest illuminated manuscript from Germany, c. 1300. Ms. I 80/52. Parchment. *Collection, The Israel Museum, Jerusalem. Photo: Z. Radovan, Jerusalem.*

Al Hakol Yitgadal—"Magnificent above all." The prayer preceding the Torah reading on Sabbaths and festivals. A man wearing a *tallit* (prayer shawl), holding a covered Torah, standing before a closed Torah ark covered by a *parokhet* (Torah ark curtain). From the *Rothschild Miscellany*, northern Italy, c. 1470. *Collection, The Israel Museum, Jerusalem. Photo: Z. Radovan, Jerusalem.*

Erna Michael Haggadah. Haggadah of German rite, Passover rules with commentary on the text and rules, Middle Rhine, c. 1400. Passover Eve table with seated men reading the Haggadah. A gold Sabbath oil-lamp hangs in the middle of the room. Pen and ink, tempera and gold leaf on parchment, handwritten, 35 X 25.5 cm. 181/18 M549-3-66, Fol. 40. *Collection, The Israel Museum, Jerusalem. Gift of Jakob Michael, New York, in memory of his wife, Erna Sondheimer-Michael, 1966. Photo © The Israel Museum, Jerusalem, by Moshe Caine.*

A carpet page from the *Damascus Keter*. Bible with masoretic notes, Spain, Burgos, 1260.
The scrolls and leaves are outlined by micrographic Masorah (the traditional textual apparatus of the Bible) and this in turn is surrounded by a frame of Masorah in large letters. This Bible was written by Menahem bar Abraham Ibn Malik in 1260. It was for many centuries the pride of the Damascus synagogue.
Jewish National and University Library, Jerusalem, Ms. Heb. 4°790. Photo: Z. Radovan, Jerusalem.

Illuminated Hebrew Manuscript of Avicenna's Canon of Medicine—Ibn Sinna's Canon (medical treatise), Italy, Ferrara, 15th century. The first chapter of each book contains a page with a decorative framed border illustrating the contents of that particular book. The style of the illustrations is Ferrarese of the late 15th century. *Bologna, University Library, Ms. 2197. Photo: Z. Radovan, Jerusalem.*

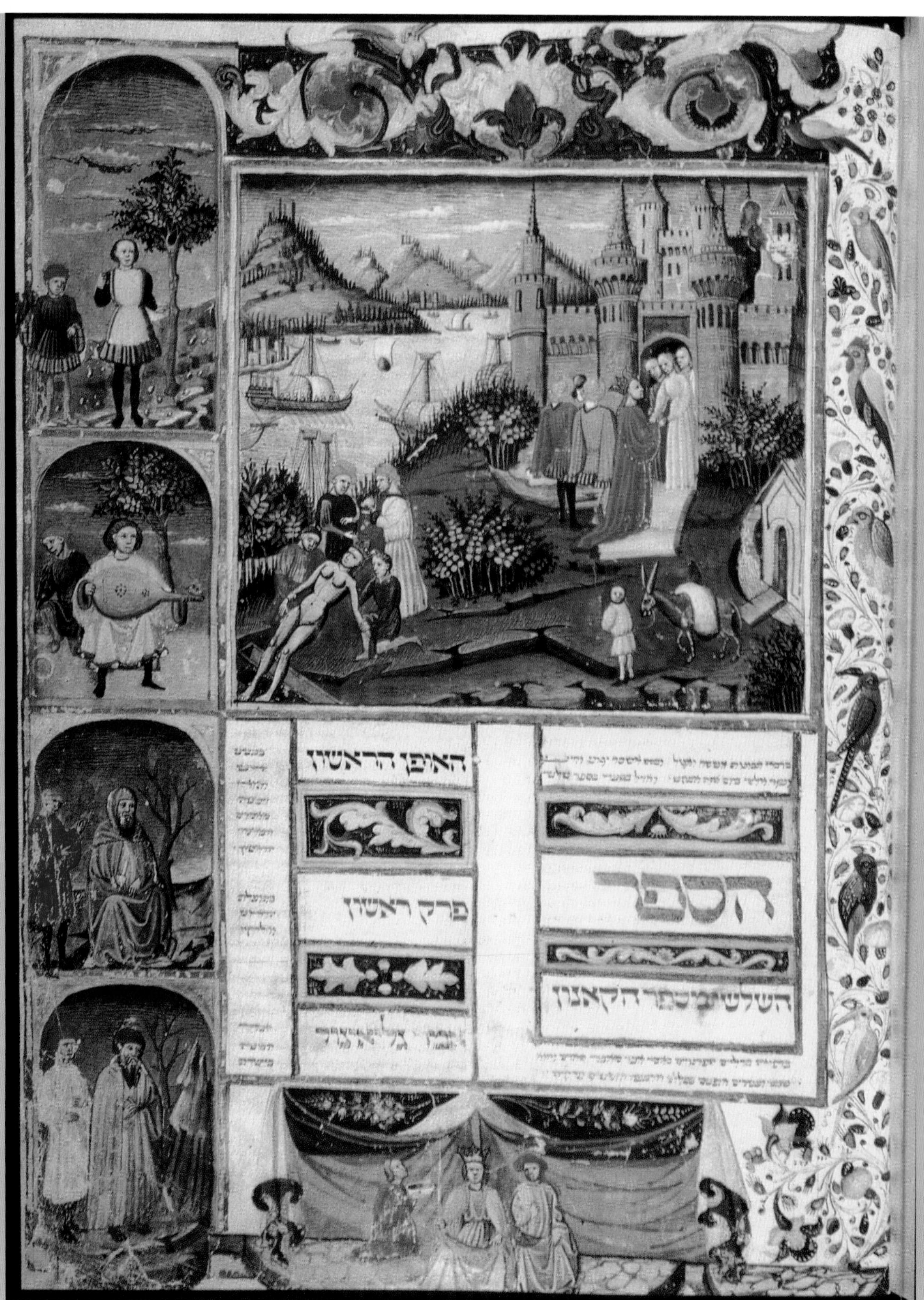

istence of visionaries. Writings by one of them, Isaac Eizik of Komarno, were widely circulated; a selection appeared in print: *Megillat Setarim* (1944).

Narrative Literature

The literature of the ḥasidic movement is generally known largely through its treasury of tales and legends. The first collections appeared in the early 19th century; the earliest of these was the *Shivḥei ha-Besht* ("Praises of the Ba'al Shem Tov"), edited by the *shoḥet* of Luniets, and published in 1805 in Kopust. This purported to be a documentary monograph, but there is no doubt that it is simply a collection of stories which, however, contain a measure of historical fact. To some extent the *Shivḥei ha-Besht* is an imitation of the *Shivḥei ha-Ari* (Constantinople, 1766); however, there are few examples of this *shevaḥim* genre in ḥasidic literature. Few biographies or autobiographies appear in ḥasidic writings; exceptions are Nathan Sternherz of Nemirov on Naḥman of Bratslav and the works of some 20th-century biographers.

From the mid-19th century, hundreds of story anthologies began to appear. These early anthologies should not be seen as truly documentary; rather they are stories reflecting the ethos of Ḥasidism. Each story consists of a specific lesson embedded in a social or historical situation, narrating a single event and expressed in the conventional manner of "once upon a time…" From this point, the narrative situation evolves into a moral homily. The stories have a simple narrative basis; the time element is insignificant and there are no epic descriptions. The events of the story serve only as a framework for the lesson it contains, and the situation is of a spiritual and not a historical nature. In this manner, the epigrammatic element is also highlighted. It is characteristic of this type of story to recount events in the first person, thus lending the narrative a touch of authenticity, that is, the air of having been passed down by word of mouth from generation to generation. At times the stories are told in the name of some famous person, mentioned by name; at others, they are presented in the name of "a certain Ḥasid." Every ḥasidic dynasty saw to it that collections of its own stories were compiled. Fairly frequently, collections were published containing stories belonging to several dynasties, originating in the same geographical region, such as Poland, Galicia, and Ukraine.

The tradition of collecting and publishing ḥasidic tales continued down to the present century, still deriving its authority from the oral tradition. Some better-known collections are: *Sefer Ba'al Shem Tov* (1938), *Mifalot Ẓaddikim* (1856), *Teshu'ot Ḥen* (Berdichev, 1816), *Nifla'ot ha-Sabba Kaddisha* (2 vols., 1936–37), *Irin Kaddishin* (1885), *Nifla'ot ha-Rabbi* (1911), *Si'aḥ-Sarfei Kodesh* (1923), *Ramatayim Ẓofim* (1881), *Abbir ha-Ro'im* (1935), *Heikhal ha-Berakhah Iggera de-Pirka* (1858), *Kehal Ḥasidim* and *Siftei Ẓaddikim* (1924). Several 20th-century men of letters have compiled collections of ḥasidic tales, notably *Berdyczewski, Martin Buber, Eliezer *Steinman, and Judah Kaufman (Even Shemuel). Buber's anthology was published in English as *Tales of the Ḥasidim*.

INTERPRETATIONS OF ḤASIDISM

From its beginnings the ḥasidic movement has attracted the attention of both supporters and opponents in each succeeding generation. Anti-ḥasidic polemics were in print even before the movement's own writings were first published. Although in the main, complaints were voiced against the eccentric practices of the sect, among the accusations can be discerned matters of principle which were destined to figure prominently on both sides in the modern debate over Ḥasidism.

Early Opposition

The earliest opponents of Ḥasidism, such as Moses b. Jacob of Satanov, author of *Mishmeret ha-Kodesh* (Zolkiew, 1746), charged the Ḥasidim with avarice, boorishness, and contempt of the *halakhah*. In the 1770s, more adverse testimony began to accumulate; among the more important of these are the works of Israel Loebel, *Ozer Yisrael* (Shklov, 1786) and *Sefer ha-Vikku'aḥ* (Warsaw, 1798). Loebel accused the Ḥasidim of changing the liturgical conventions from the Ashkenazi to the Sephardi; of praying according to Isaac *Luria's doctrine of *kavvanot*; of praying with exaggerated joy when proper devotion demands tears and repentance; and of praying with wild abandon and with accompanying bodily movements. Solomon of Dubna, a follower of Moses *Mendelssohn, reproached the Ḥasidim for pride and high-handedness, and for a propensity to drunkenness. A more inclusive attack, embracing a wide range of accusations dealing mainly with the Ḥasidism's changes in traditional Jewish ways and practices, was made by Mendelssohn's teacher, Israel of Zamosc, author of *Nezed ha-Dema* (Dyhernfurth, 1773). Inveighing against both the spiritualism of their religious demands and the "moral corruption" of *ẓaddik* and Ḥasid alike, Israel of Zamosc pointed to evidence of the movement's bias toward separatism revealed in their changes in customs, such as the wearing of white and the adoption of the blue-fringed garment (*ẓiẓit tekhelet*) with the fringes worn on the outside. Among the ritual and spiritual claims of the Ḥasidim he denounced: the pretension to a profound religiosity; the practice of ritual bathing prior to morning and evening prayers in order to become worthy of the Divine Spirit; abstinence and fasting; spiritual arrogance; the claim to be "visionary" seers; breaking down the "walls of the Torah"; advocating the doctrine of "uplifting the sparks" (niẓoẓot) in the act of eating according to the doctrine of *tikkun*; and introducing a "new liturgy of raucousness." Among their immoral practices he counted cupidity, hypocrisy and abomination, gluttony, and inebriation.

Israel of Zamosc did not assemble his charges into an ordered exposition of the nature of Ḥasidism; nevertheless, they served as the basis for an interpretation of Ḥasidism which found expression in the writings of the most profound, systematic, and recondite of Ḥasidism's opponents – Ḥayyim of Volozhin (*Volozhiner), a disciple of Elijah b. Solomon Zalman, the Gaon of Vilna. In his book *Nefesh ha-Ḥayyim* (Vilna, 1824), in which the term Ḥasid is discreetly omitted, the principles of an interpretation of Ḥasidism as a novel religious phenomenon are first adumbrated. Ḥayyim of Volozhin presented Ḥasidism as a spiritual movement which ignores a cardinal principle in Judaism, namely that where the very nature of a *mitzvah*, as well as its fulfillment, is jeopardized by an idea, the latter should be set aside. Equally, where new values – lofty though they may be – threaten to come into conflict with tradition, the latter should be upheld. He rarely voiced an objection to specific ḥasidic practices but objected on a theoretical basis to matters of fundamental belief in Ḥasidism which appeared to him as dangerous. In so doing, he managed to detach his polemic from its historical context. Ḥayyim of Volozhin saw the spiritual uniqueness of Ḥasidism as follows:

(1) Ḥasidic teachings imparted a new significance to the concept of "Torah for its own sake," an idea which Ḥasidism understood as "Torah for the sake of *devekut*" ("communion") with God. According to Ḥayyim the study of the Torah for itself alone (and not for the sake of *devekut*) had a value transcending the fulfillment of the *mitzvot* themselves.

(2) Ḥayyim objected to the centrality in ḥasidic thought of the necessity for "purity of thought," since in his opinion the essence of the Torah and *mitzvot* did not necessarily lie in their being performed with "great *kavvanah* and true *devekut*." Here, Ḥayyim of Volozhin pointed out the opposition between mysticism and the *halakhah*. He emphasizes the dialectic process by which the performance of a *mitzvah* with excessive *kavvanah* leads to the destruction of the *mitzvah*. The very act of fulfilling the *mitzvah* is the fundamental principle and not the *kavvanah* accompanying its performance. He therefore challenged Ḥasidism on a matter of basic principle: performing *mitzvot* for the sake of heaven, he stated, is not a value in itself.

(3) He regarded the ḥasidic attempt to throw off the yoke of communal authority as social amoralism.

(4) He objected to the practice of praying outside the specified times set for prayer and to the consequent creation of a new pattern of life.

Ḥasidism and Haskalah

By the 1770s Ḥasidism had already come under the fire of the Haskalah. In Warsaw Jacques Kalmansohn published a scathing criticism of the social nature of Ḥasidism, as did Judah Leib Mises in his *Kinat ha-Emet* (Vienna, 1828). However, the writer who displayed the most striking talent for caricature and pointed satire sarcasm was Joseph *Perl of Tarnopol in his booklet *Ueber das Wesen der Sekte Chassidim aus ihren eigenen Schriften gezogen im Jahre 1816* ("On the Essence of the Ḥasidic Sect, Drawn from their own Writings in the Year 1816"; Jerusalem, National Library, Ms. Var. 293). The intent of his essay was to portray the material and spiritual conditions of the Ḥasidim in the lowest terms and to exert pressure on the Austrian authorities to force all the Ḥasidim to receive a compulsory education within the state-run school system. Perl's major contention was that as a socio-religious phenomenon Ḥasidism was an anti-progressive factor owing to its spiritual insularity and its social separatism: in spirit it was idle and passive and as a social group it was unproductive.

A more ambivalent view of Ḥasidism appears in the memoirs of Abraham Baer *Gottlober (*Abraham Baer Gottlober un Zayn Epokhe*, Vilna, 1828), who, when he later adopted the principles of the Haskalah, became convinced that it was Ḥasidism which had facilitated the spread of the Haskalah movement, in that it constituted a critical stage in the life of Judaism. Ḥasidism, according to Gottlober, threw off the yoke of rabbinical authority and in so doing opened the first sluicegate for the advance of the Haskalah. He also believed that Ḥasidism lay at the root of the crisis involving the Shulḥan Arukh. It displaced Shabbateanism and the Frankist movement, and tarnished the glory of "rabbinism." Gottlober evinced a particular admiration for the Chabad Ḥasidism because of their affinity to the Haskalah. However, Ḥasidism itself he regarded as a social movement which was disintegrating in its very essence because its criticism was internally directed.

Toward the end of the 1860s and the beginning of the 1870s there began to appear in print selections of the writings of E.Z. *Zweifel, under the title *Shalom al Yisrael*, a work which came to the defense of Ḥasidism, attempting to interpret its teachings on the basis of Ḥasidism's own authentic sources. In his balanced and informed argument, the author undertook an analysis of fundamental ḥasidic sayings and teachings, pointing out their significance and underlining, too, their uniqueness in comparison with Kabbalah. As a *maskil*, he had, of course, reservations about the "popular" elements of Ḥasidism, and about a number of its social aspects. Among the *maskilim* most influenced by *Shalom al Yisrael* was Micha Josef Berdyczewski, whose interpretation of Ḥasidism in his book *Nishmat Ḥasidim* (1899) was couched in romantic terms. Viewing the movement as a Jewish renaissance, an attempt to break down the barriers between man and the world, he saw in Ḥasidism "joy and inner happiness" and the opportunity to worship the Lord in many different ways.

Martin Buber and His Successors

Martin Buber was influenced by Berdyczewski, and in principle adopted his opinions, but his thesis was far more profound. Buber's first works on Ḥasidism are written in the spirit of mysticism, such as *Die Geschichten des Rabbi Nachman* (1906; *Tales of Rabbi Nachman*, 1962²) and *Die Legende des Baalschem* (1908; *Legend of the Baal-Shem*, 1969²). From his existentialist teachings, which he developed and consolidated during the 1930s and 1940s, Buber utilized the principle of dialogue as a criterion for understanding the essence of Ḥasidism, which he saw as giving support to the direct encounter, active and creative, between man and the world surrounding him. According to Buber, especially in his mature work *Be-Fardes ha-Ḥasidut* (1945), the dialogue of encounter reveals the reality of God; the cosmos is potentially holy, the encounter with man makes it actually holy. Buber sought to locate the origin of this fundamental concept, which he called pan-sacramentalism, in the ḥasidic doctrine of the worship of God through the corporeal and worldly dimensions of man's being, and attempted to view through this aspect the revival of Judaism that found expression in Ḥasidism as opposed to the *halakhah*. The ḥasidic renaissance was seen by Buber as a fresh and living religious phenomenon, and also as a process of social and communal consolidation of novel educational importance. He believed that the *ẓaddikim* gave expression to this new educational and religious meaning, for every *ẓaddik* represented a special experience acquired as a result of the encounter through dialogue. Particularly emphasizing the concrete and historical import of Ḥasidism, Buber placed little value on the abstract ideas of Ḥasidism, the intellectual games of the Kabbalah, and its millenarian hopes and expectations, being convinced that Ḥasidism had liberated itself from these elements and constructed a realistic experience of life. Buber understood the ḥasidic imperative "Know Him in all thy ways" as transcending the bounds of the *mitzvot* as religious experience over and above the *halakhah*. The element of mystery in Ḥasidism has been studied by Hillel Zeitlin.

A scathing attack on Berdyczewski and Buber was made by the Zionist *maskil* Samuel Joseph Ish-Horowitz, who, early in the 20th century, brought out a series of articles which later appeared in booklet form under the title of *Ha-Ḥasidut ve-ha-Haskalah* (Berlin, 1909). "Modern" Ḥasidism, known as neo-Ḥasidism, was taken to be that of Berdyczewski and Buber. In his work, the Ḥasidism of the Ba'al Shem Tov is depicted as a wild, undisciplined movement, while the Ba'al Shem Tov himself is shown as a charlatan influenced by his rustic surroundings and by the Haidamak movement. According to Horowitz, Ḥasidism contributed no new truths or ways of looking at the world: it simply appropriated to itself the vocabulary of the Kabbalah without fully understanding its implications, and colored it with quasi-philosophical notions "belonging to the household mentality and chronic psychology of the ghetto." Modern or neo-Ḥasidim (specifically Berdyczewski and Buber) attempted to discover in Ḥasidism ethical values and a positive popular force, in particular in the ḥasidic "joy," which they interpreted as a protest against the dejection produced by the conditions of the Diaspora, but for Horowitz the Shabbatean movement was to be preferred to Ḥasidism, as it took an upright stand, advocating a breaking free of the bonds of the Diaspora and the ghetto. Horowitz dismissed the claims that Ḥasidism was a movement of revival and revolt as little more than arrant nonsense; Ḥasidim, far from rebelling against the rabbinate, kept the *mitzvot*, minor as well as major. He contended that the neo-Ḥasidim were deceiving themselves by interpreting the values of Ḥasidism in secular terms, which he regarded a perversion of history in the spirit of a new humanism. He believed that Ḥasidism was continuity and not revolt, and that the neo-Ḥasidim did violence to its true nature by viewing it as a revolutionary movement in Jewish history.

In recent years a criticism of Buber's views of Ḥasidism has been put forward by Gershom Scholem and Rivka Schatz. Opinion is also divided on the messianic significance of Ḥasidism, between Benzion Dinur and Isaiah Tishby, on the one hand, and Scholem on the other. J.G. Weiss (1918–1969) did remarkable work on Ḥasidism in many of his essays, most of which appeared in the *Journal of Jewish Studies*. He contributed much to the understanding of Bratslav Ḥasidism. Rivka Schatz's *Ha-Ḥasidut ke-Mistikah* ("Ḥasidism as Mysticism," 1968), a phenomenological analysis of Ḥasidism on the basis of available texts, attempts to answer certain fundamental questions concerning the spiritual aims of Ḥasidism and assesses the value attaching to ḥasidic innovations.

[Rivka Shatz-Uffenheimer]

DEVELOPMENTS IN ḤASIDISM AFTER 1970

Ḥasidism maintained a period of expansion and development. Not only did all existing ḥasidic dynasties continue to exist, in many instances they introduced new branches. There even came into being dynasties which linked themselves in the vaguest of manners to ones which had existed in Eastern Europe. Groups which had not been directly affiliated with Ḥasidism took upon themselves ḥasidic garb and recognized ḥasidic leadership, accepting a dynasty's *rebbe* as their own. This is especially noticeable among Hungarian emigrés. In this way R. Joseph Greenwald, the rabbi of Papa, became the *admor* (ḥasidic rabbi) of Papa, and his sons, R. Jacob Hezekiah and R. Israel Menaḥem have also become *admorim*. R. Johanan Sofer became the *admor* of Erlau, and R. Israel Moses Duschinsky, a member of the *bet din* (rabbinic court) of the ultra-Orthodox community (*edah ḥaredit*) became an *admor*. R. Raphael Blum of Kashoi – New York also became an *admor*.

This period of dynamic growth included the widespread building of housing for Ḥasidim and even led to competition – who builds more, whose *bet midrash* (study hall) is larger, with the erection of *talmudei torah, yeshivot, kollelim*, girls' schools, and even kindergartens. The networks of the *admorim* keeps on growing. The various ḥasidic groups establish new centers in addition to the area in which the *admor* himself lives. In Israel the Gur Ḥasidim set up centers in Ashdod, Arad, Ḥazor ha-Gelilit, and Immanuel – with the senior leadership in Jerusalem sending people to live in the new centers. The Vizhnitz group established new centers in Jerusalem and Reḥovot, the Belz established a new center in Ashdod, the Boyan Ḥasidim in the new town of Betar, the Lubavitch in Kefar Chabad, Kiryat Malakhi, and Safed.

The large ḥasidic groups have garnered great political influence which has led to friction. The Belz Ḥasidim left Agudat Israel, feeling that they had not been given the political weight they felt they deserved, and joined the "Lithuanians."

Later Ḥasidic Literature

Original ḥasidic literature has continued to be widely distributed. The most astounding range is that of the Lubavitcher group. Scores of basic books on and by the *ẓaddikim* of the dynasty, particularly by the current *admor*, are printed one after the other. Of the letters of the leader, R. Menaḥem Mendel Schneersohn, 18 volumes had been published by 1990.

Of the basic works of the *ẓaddikim* of the current generation (the past 20 years), we can cite *Imrei Emet* by R. Abraham Mordecai Alter of Gur (4 volumes) and *Beit Yisrael* by his son, R. Israel (5 volumes); *Imrei Ḥayyim* by R. Ḥayyim Meir of Vizhnitz and *She'erit Menaḥem* by R. Menaḥem Mendel of Vishiva; *Be'er Avraham, Divrei Shemu'el, Zikhron Kadosh, Netivot Shalom, Torat Avot* by the *admor* of Slonim; *Divrei Yo'el*, in 14 volumes by R. Joel Teitelbaum of Satmar, and another number of volumes on his teachings; *Ginzei Yisrael, Oholei Ya'akov, Pe'er Yisrael, Naḥalat Ya'akov, Abir Ya'akov* by the *ẓaddik* of the Rozhin line; *Ne'ot ha-Deshe* by the Sochaczew *ẓaddikim; Kol Menaḥem* by R. Menaḥem Mendel Taub of Kalov; *Avodat Elazar* by R. Israel Eleazar Hofstein of Kozienice; *Emunat Moshe* by R. Judah Moses Tiehberg of Aleksandrow; *Kedushat Mordekhai* by R. Moses Mordecai Biederman of Lelov; *Avodat Yeḥi'el* by R. Jehiel Joshua Rabinowitz of Biale; *Ẓidkat ha-Ẓaddik* by R. Joseph Leifer of Pittsburgh; *Yikra de-Malka* by R. Mordecai Goldman of Zweihl; *Zekher Ḥayyim* by R. Ḥayyim Judah Meir Hager of Vishiva.

Additional works are *Shefa Ḥayyim*, 5 volumes by R. Jekutiel Judah Halberstam of Zanz–Klausenberg *Birkat Moshe* by R. Moses Leib of Pascani *Or ha-Yashar ve-ha-Tov* by R. Ẓevi Hirsch of Liska *Divrei Yeḥezke'el Sheraga* by R. Ezekiel Shraga Lifshitz of Strupkov; and *Esh Da'at* and *Be'er Moshe* by R. Moses Jehiel of Izirov, in 10 volumes.

Dozens of anthologies on the early ḥasidic ẓaddikim have been published. Among them are *Avnei Zikkaron*, the Seer of Lublin; *Imrei Pinḥas*, R. Phineas of Korets; *Yalkut Menaḥem*, R. Menaḥem Mendel of Riminow; *Likkutei Shoshanim* of R. Moses Ẓevi of Savran; *Midbar Kadesh* by R. Shalom of Belz; and *Ner Yisrael*, by the *ẓaddikim* of the Rozhin dynasty. A specialist in preparing these anthologies is R. Elisha Hakohen Faksher.

There have been several new luxury editions of ḥasidic works with added information, and institutions devoted to publishing them have been set up. Most prominent are the Ginzei Maharitz Institute which produces the works of the *admor* of Biale and that of R. Abraham Isaac Kahn of Shomerei Emunim.

Among these fresh editions are *Ohev Yisrael* by the rabbi of Apta; *Me'or Einei Ḥakhamim* by R. Meir of Korotsyshev; *No'am Elimelekh* by R. Elimelech of Lyzhansk; *Avodat Yisrael* of the *maggid* of Kozienice; *Amud Avodah* by R. Baruch of Kosov; *Panim Yafot* of R. Phineas of Frankfort; and *Peri ha-Arez; Ẓidkat ha-Ẓaddik; Ẓemah Ẓaddik; Kedushat Levi; Kol Simḥah*; and many others. There is almost no ḥasidic work which has not been reproduced in the United States and Israel; they are simply too numerous to mention all.

From later ḥasidic interpretive literature, there have been editions of *Netiv le-Tanya* by Prof. Moshe Halamish, and *Torat ha-Ḥasidim ha-Rishonim* by Menaḥem Mendel Wischnitzer. The teachings of R. Menaḥem Mendel of Kotsk were the subject of three new books by Israel Ehrlich, Simḥa Raz, and Saul Maislish. New editions of *Shivḥei ha-Besht* were prepared by S.Y. Agnon and Pinḥas Sade. *Orot Yismaḥ Yisrael* by M.H. Tiehberg also appeared.

Biographical literature devoted to Ḥasidim has also been prominent. Among the works are *Enẓiklopedyah shel ha-Ḥasidut*, vol. 1; *Tiferet she-be-Malkhut; Ha-Ḥasidut be-Romanyah*, and *Be-Sedei ha-Ḥasidut* by Yiẓḥak Alfassi; *Rebbi Levi Yiẓḥak mi-Berditchev* by Yisrael Ehrlich; *Rebbi Ẓevi Elimelekh mi-Dinov* by Nathan Ortner; *Raza de-Uvda* by R. Ẓevi Hirsch Rosenbaum; *Arzei Levanon* by R. Eleazar Arenberg; *Abirei ha-Ro'im* by Israel Ehrlich; *Ẓaddikim vi-Yrelim* by Isser Kliger; *Ẓaddik Yesod Olam* by D. Werner; *Ba'al Shem Tov* by M. Eidelbaum; *Ha-Shevil ve-ha-Derekh, Ẓaddikei ha-Ḥasidim be-Ereẓ Yisrael, Hod u-Gevurah*; and *Ereẓ Yisrael shel Ma'alah* by Jehiel Greenstein; *Kedosh Yisrael* by Nathan Elijah Roth; *Ish ha-Pele* by Menashe Miller; *Ha-Mufla be-Doro* by A.Y. Tykozki; *Ha-Tekhelet* by Menaḥem Burstein; *Ohel Yosef* by R. David Halachmi (Weisbrod); *Merbiẓei Torah be-Olam ha-Ḥasidut*, 3 pts., by Aaron Sorasky; *Perakim be-Mishnat ha-Ḥasidut* by M.S. Kasher; *Admorei Tchernobyl* by Israel Jacob Klapholz; and *Kotsk* by Prof. Abraham Joshua Heschel. There have also appeared a series of biographies on Lubavitch *ẓaddikim* by Abraham Ḥanoch Glitzstein; five books on the R. Menahem Mendel Schneersohn, the Lubavitch *admor; Bi-Netivei Ḥasidut Izbica-Radzin* by S.Z. Shragai; *Enẓiklopedyah le-Ḥakhmei Galiẓiyyah* ("Encyclopaedia of the Sages of Galicia") – most of whom were ḥasidim – by Meir Wender who also wrote *Ohel Shimon; Tal Orot* by Aaron Jacob Brandwein; *Tehillot Eliezer*, the story of R. Eliezer Zusya Portugal of Skolen; *Ha-Rav mi-Apta* by H.Y. Berl and Yiẓḥak Alfassi (two books on the same subject); *Be-Libbat Esh* by Aaron Sorasky; *Bet Karlin-Stolin* by Jacob Israel; and *Or ha-Galil* by Jacob Shalom Gefner.

With regard to scholarly literature on Ḥasidism, one should note the scientific edition of the *Maggid Devarav ke-Ya'akov* by Rivka Shatz; editions of *Toldot Ya'akov Yosef* and *No'am Elimelekh* by Gedaliah Nigal; *Shivḥei ha-Besht*, a photographed manuscript edition with annotations by Joshua Mundshein; *Ḥasidim u-Mitnaggedim*, 2 pts., by Mordecai Wiliensky; *Sifrut ha-Hanhagot – Toldotehah u-Mekomah be-Ḥayei Ḥasidei ha-Besht* by Ze'ev Gross; *Bi-Ymei Ẓemiḥat Ha-Ḥasidut* and *Ḥasidut Polin – Megamot bein Shetei Milḥamot ha-Olam u-vi-Gezerot 1940–1945*, both by Mendel Pikarsh; *Ha-Ḥasidut ve-Shivat Ẓiyyon* by Yiẓḥak Alfassi; a scientific edition of *Shalom al Yisrael* by A.Z. Zweifel prepared by A. Rubenstein; *Mishnat ha-Ḥasidut bi-Khtavei Rebbi Elimelekh mi-Lizhansk*, a dissertation by Gedaliah Nigal; *Rebbi Naḥman mi-Breslav: Iyyunim bi-Sfarav* by Judith Kook; *Meḥkarim Be-Ḥasidut Breslav* by Joseph Weiss; *Ha-Sippur ha-Ḥasidi* by Joseph Dan; *Torat ha-Elohut ve-Avodat ha-Shem be-Dor ha-Sheni shel Ḥabad* by Rahel Elior; *Mishnato ha-Iyyunit shel R. Shne'ur Zalman mi-Lyady* by Moses Halamish; *Ma'aseh Ḥoshev*, studies on the ḥasidic story by Joel Elstein; *Ba'al ha-Yesurim* by Avraham Isaac Green; and *Ha-Sipporet ha-Ḥasidit, Toldotehah u-Noseḥah* by Gedaliah Nigal.

Publications of Chabad or Breslav are the majority of those which appear in languages other than Hebrew. A few of the English-language works available are *The Ẓaddik: R. Levi of Berdichev* by Samuel Dresner; *Ideas and Ideals of the Ḥassidim* by Aaron Milton; *Ḥassidic Celebration* by Elie Wiesel; *Legends of the Ḥassidim* by J.R. Mintz; *Maggid* by J.J. Shochet; *Until the Mashiach – R. Nachman's Biography* and *The Ḥasidic Masters and their Teachings* by Arie Kaplan; and *Ḥassidism and the State of Israel* by Harry Rabinowicz.

A special type of ḥasidic literature is the publication of letters by *ẓaddikim*. The letters of the Lubavitcher *rebbe* Menaḥem Mendel Schneersohn were mentioned above. The letters of Israeli *ẓaddikim* were reprinted by Y. Bernai. Munkacs *ẓaddikim* have had their letters published in *Igrot Shappirin*. There have also appeared a collection of the letters of the author of *Sefat Emet* from Gur; letters of Chabad ḥasidim; and *Igrot Ohavei Yisrael*.

One should also mention the discovery of hitherto unknown manuscripts by *ẓaddikim* which were first published in the period under discussion, such as *Or Yehoshua* by R. Abraham Joshua Heschel Kopzynce, *Mishkenot ha-Ro'im* by R. Menaḥem Nahum Friedman of Boyan, and *Zikhron Moshe* by R. Moses Eichenstein. There are many more examples.

[Yitzhak Alfasi]

Publications

Ḥasidic publications are very influential. Besides the ongoing first-rate, general ḥasidic series, such as *Kerem ha-Ḥasidut, Naḥalat Ẓevi*, and *Siftei Ẓaddikim*, every self-respecting branch in Ḥasidism has its own publications. The Gur Ḥasidim find their voice for general representation in the daily newspaper, *Ha-Modia* in Israel, which always has at least one ḥasid of Gur on its editorial board. The other Gur publication, *Koveẓ Torani Mercazi Gur*, is devoted to Torah learning. The Lubavitch movement produces countless materials, including the weekly *Siḥat ha-Shavu'a* and *Kefar Ḥabad* in Israel and the *Morgen Journal* in New York, which is a general weekly with strong Lubavitch influence.

Other weeklies of the same type as *Siḥat ha-Shavu'a* appear in various countries. Belz Ḥasidim publish *Ha-Maḥaneh ha-Ḥaredi*: the Satmar group in the United States has the weekly *Der Yid*. Monthlies are also produced: *Az Nedaberu* by Vizhnitz Ḥasidim, *Tiferet Yisrael* for the Boyan Ḥasidim, *Bet Aharon ve-Yisrael* of Karlin Ḥasidim, and *Kerem Shelomoh* by Bobover Ḥasidim in the U.S.

Other regularly appearing periodicals are *Mesillot* of the Sadigora group; *Shevil ba-Pardes* from followers of R. Ashlag; *Naḥalatenu* by the Biale Ḥasidim in Bene Berak and *Ma'ayanei ha-Yeshu'ah* from the Biale-Lugano-Jerusalem group; *Or Kaliv* from the Kaliv Ḥasidim. The Nadvoznaya (Nadwozna) group publishes *Si'aḥ Sarfei Kodesh*, and the Klausenberg Ḥasidim produce *Zanz*. *Or ha-Ganuz* is by the Lelov (Lelow) Ḥasidim of Bene Berak. *Torah Or* is published by the Seret-Vizhnitz group in Haifa. The followers of R. Alter of Lelov produce *Or Yahel* and Breslav Ḥasidim publish *Or ha-Ẓaddik*. Skvira Ḥasidim have *Be-Oholei Ya'akov* and Aleksandrow Ḥasidim produce *Karmenu*. *Kol Emunim* is the organ of followers of Reb Ahrele, while *Mayyim Ḥayyim* is a Torah anthology published by Nadwozna Ḥasidim. *Bet Yisrael* is produced by Kuznitz Ḥasidim and *Ohel Moshe* belongs to Schotz-Vizhnitz Ḥasidim. Most of these works are written in modern Hebrew and are well-designed, employing many photographs.

SURVEY OF ḤASIDIC DYNASTIES

Descendants of First Generation

There are no direct descendants of the founder of Ḥasidism, the Ba'al Shem Tov, but there are people directly related to R. Dov Baer of Mezhirech, the second leader of the movement. Among those named Friedman, the most senior rabbi as well as one of the most revered was R. Isaac Friedman of Bohush–Tel Aviv. His followers established an important center for him in Bene Berak. During the Holocaust, Friedman was well known for saving many refugees and for helping the Zionist underground in Romania. R. Avraham Jacob Friedman of Sadigora, a member of the Council of Great Torah Scholars of Agudat Israel, was well versed in all facets of Jewish culture and knew several languages. He succeeded his father, R. Mordecai Shalom Joseph, in Tel Aviv in 1978.

Other descendants of R. Dov Baer of Mezhirech were R. Nahum Dov Breuer, who was made *rebbe* after the death of his maternal grandfather, R. Mordecai Solomon Friedman of Boyan (1971). His style of leadership was characterized by moderation, modesty, and exemplary demeanor. This vibrant group has hundreds of followers and is centered in Jerusalem. In 1985, R. Samson Dov Halperin of Vaslui carried on in place of his father, R. Jacob Joseph Solomon of Vaslui, in Tel Aviv.

Another dynasty harking back to the first generation of Ḥasidism is that of Peremyshlyany, from which the Nadwozna dynasty headed by the Leifer-Rosenbaum family branched off. In this family, the sons became *admorim* while their father was still living, so that the "Old Admor," Rabbi Itamar of Nadwozna–New York–Tel Aviv, saw a fourth generation of his family's ḥasidic leadership in 1972.

R. Itamar's sons were:

(1) R. Ḥayyim Mordecai of Nadwozna–Bene Berak, the only *admor* who succeeded in turning this branch into a group with a large, significant following. He lived in Jaffa and then moved from there to Bene Berak. His son, R. Jacob Issachar Ber, the only one to use the name Nadwozna explicitly, continued the expansion begun by his father.

(2) R. Issachar Ber Rosenbaum of Strezhnitz–New York (1981) – all of his sons became *admorim*. These included R. Asher Mordecai of Strezhnitz–New York, R. Meir of Mosholow–New York, R. Yiẓḥak Isaac of Cleveland–Ra'ananah, R. Joseph of Kalush–New York; R. Yiẓḥak Isaac of Zutchka–Bene Berak, a great Torah scholar who published widely on current issues, and who relinquished his father's Tel Aviv locale in favor of Bene Berak, while his son R. Israel was an *admor* in New York.

(3) R. Asher Isaiah Rosenbaum, the *admor* of Bucharest–Ḥaderah–Bene Berak, a very captivating figure.

Additional members of this dynasty were the *admorim* R. Shalom Leifer of Brighton–New York; R. Meir Isaacson of Philadelphia; R. Aaron Moses of Khust–New York, and his son

R. Barukh Pinḥas Leifer in Jerusalem; R. Jacob Joseph Leifer of Ungvar (Uzhgorad)–New York; R. Joseph Leifer of Petah Tikvah; R. Yeḥiel Leifer of Jerusalem; R. Meshullam Zalman Leifer of Brooklyn; R. Levi Isaac Leifer of Jerusalem (the last four are the sons of R. Aaron Aryeh of Timisoara–Jerusalem.); R. Meir Leifer of Cleveland; R. Issachar Ber Leifer of Bania–New York; R. Aaron Yeḥiel of Bania–Safed; R. Joseph Meir, the son of R. Meshullam Zalman of Brooklyn.

The Kretchnif (Crachuneşti) family is a particularly important branch of this group. R. David Moses Rosenbaum settled in Reḥovot and developed, at his own initiative, a large ḥasidic following. His son, R. Menaḥem Eliezer Ze'ev, who took over from his father at an early age, firmly established and expanded this dynasty. His brothers, who spread out throughout Israel and set up local *batei midrash* (Talmudic learning centers), were R. Israel Nisan (who went to New York) in Kiryat Gat; R. Meir of Bene Berak who took on the name Peremyshlyany; R. Samuel Shmelka in Jaffa whose family name is that of the city Bitschkov. The *admor* R. Ẓevi, who moved from Kiryat Ata to Jerusalem, also belongs to this family. A significant place in this group is held by the *admor* R. Abraham Abba Leifer of Pittsburgh–Ashdod, who was succeeded by his son R. Mordecai in 1990.

The descendants of R. Yeḥiel Mikhal of Zlotchow, also a member of the first generation of Ḥasidism, continued to hold direct positions of leadership through the *admorim* of the Zweihl family, which has lived in Jerusalem for four generations. The *admor*, R. Abraham Goldman, the son of R. Mordecai, was very involved in public affairs and was one of the few *admorim* in a position of leadership who did not come from the yeshivah world but through public life.

The Moscowitz family, to which many *admorim* belonged, mainly in Romania, was also part of this dynasty. In recent times, among the *admorim* of this family were R. Joel Moscowitz of Schotz (Suczawa)–Manchester, Montreal, London, and Jerusalem; R. Jacob Isaac of Jerusalem; R. Naftali of Ashdod; R. Jacob of Bene Berak; R. Israel David of New York; R. Moses Meir of Schotz–Har Nof (Jerusalem); R. Joseph Ḥayyim of Flatbush; and R. Isaac Eleazar in the United States.

Another link to this clan is through the Rabinowitz family of *admorim* from Skole. R. Israel Rabinowitz lived in New York and at the end of his life moved to Tel Aviv. After his death in 1971, no one took his place. His brother, R. David Isaac, lived in Brooklyn and was followed by his grandchildren, R. Abraham Moses Rabinowitz, who was the oldest, and R. Raphael Goldstein, his son's son-in-law.

Of this dynasty, there were also R. Shalom Michaelowitz of Rishon le-Zion–New York, R. Samuel Halevi Josephov of Haifa, and R. Yeḥiel Mikhal of Zlotchow–Netanyah, who was part preacher, part *rebbe*.

Of the descendants from Chernobyl belonging to the Twersky family there are scores of *admorim*. Exceptionally successful were the ẓaddikim from Skvira: R. Isaac of Skvira–New York who moved to Tel Aviv in 1978 towards the end of his life; R. Eleazar of Skvira Flushing, New York, who was followed by his son, R. Abraham, in 1984. R. Abraham's son, R. Solomon, was the *admor* in New York. R. David of Skvira, following his father R. Jacob Joseph, established a large ḥasidic center, New Square in New York, with branches in London and Israel. R. David the second of Skvira–Boro Park was very well versed in medicine and had connections to hospitals in New York. His brother, R. Mordecai, was in Flatbush.

Of the house of Skvira, although not bearing the name, was R. Abraham Joshua Heshel of Machnovka, who continued as *admor* in Russia as well. In his old age he immigrated to Israel and settled in Bene Berak, where he established an important center. His sister's grandson, R. Joshua Rokach, replaced him.

The name Chernobyl itself was used by R. Jacob Israel in New York and by his son R. Solomon who took over from him, as well by as R. Meshullam Zusha of Chernobyl (1988). His sons were R. Nahum of Bene Berak and R. Isaiah in New York.

The *admorim* of the Ratmistrovka family immigrated to Palestine before the Holocaust. The latest *admor* was R. Johanan. His sons continued the dynasty: R. Israel Mordecai of Jerusalem and R. Hai Isaac in the U.S. Another member of this family was R. Ẓevi Aryeh of Zlatpol, who settled in Tel Aviv in 1968.

Of the Talnoye family, R. Moses Ẓevi of Philadelphia (1972) and R. Meshullam Zusha (1972) of Boston were *admorim*. The only one active in the late 20th century was R. Johanan of Montreal–Jerusalem.

The *admor* of Korostyshev was R. Isaac Abraham Moses, who succeeded in emigrating from Russia and settled in Bene Berak (1985).

The sixth Chernobyl dynasty was that of Cherkassy. The original founder of this line, R. Jacob Israel, had no sons and was succeeded by his daughter's son, R. Mordecai Dov in Hornistopol, who changed his surname to Twersky. The *admor* in the third quarter of the 20th century was R. Jacob Israel, who settled in Milwaukee, Wisconsin (1973). All of his sons had academic degrees and were very effective ḥasidic leaders. His sons were R. Solomon Meshullam Zalman, who established himself as an *admor* in Denver (1982), and R. Jeḥiel-Michal, who took his father's place in Milwaukee.

Of the seventh dynasty of Chernobyl, that of Trisk, in recent times was R. Jacob Leib of Trisk–London–Bene Berak. His sons were R. Ḥayyim of London and R. Isaac of Bene Berak. Also related to the Trisk family was the *admor* R. Ḥanokh Henikh of Radomyshl–Jerusalem. His grandson established institutions in Jerusalem in the name of Trisk.

There is no continuation of the eighth line, Makarov.

Of the other dynasties devolving from the first generation of Ḥasidism – Korets, Rashkov, Kaminka – there are a few remnants. R. Abraham Shapiro of Tluste (Tolstoye)–New York (1972) left no descendants in the position of *admor*. The only one left of the Korets-Shapiro family was R. Salomon Dov Shapiro of Shipitovka–New York, who managed to escape from Russia.

Descendants of Second Generation

Karlin Ḥasidism was represented after the Holocaust by R. Johanan Perlov, who lived in New York and Jerusalem. After his death, a segment of his followers looked to R. Moses Mordecai Biderman of Lelov as their leader, giving him – against his wishes – the title of the *admor* of Lelov–Karlin. Following his death, these Karliners made the Lelover rabbi's son, R. Simon Nathan Neta, their new *admor*. When R. Simon refused to add the term Karlin to his title, the Karliner Ḥasidim broke away from him and made R. Aaron ha-Kohen Rosenfeld their *admor*. Most of the Karlin Ḥasidim, mainly the younger members, designated R. Johanan's grandson, R. Baruch Jacob Halevi Shohat, as the *admor* of Karlin–Stolin. He was the second *yanuka* (very young person chosen as *admor*) in the history of this branch of Ḥasidism, and when he grew up he displayed excellent characteristics of leadership. He lived in New York, visited Jerusalem regularly, and planned to settle there. Karlin-Stolin operated a network of educational institutions.

The Ostrog (Ostraha) Ḥasidim had no one to replace R. Abraham Pinḥas Sepharad of New York upon his death in 1950.

The Lyzhansk Ḥasidim were led by the *admorim* R. Moses Isaac Gevirtzman of Antwerp (1977) and his replacement, R. Jacob Leizer of Antwerp. In the late 20th century, another descendant, R. Elimelech Schiff of Lyzhansk–Jerusalem, began to act as *admor* of Lyzhansk.

Lubavitch Ḥasidism was led by R. Menahem Mendel *Schneersohn of Lubavitch–New York until his death in 1994. He had great influence among all circles of Torah Judaism and was noted for his superb organizational abilities, his literary capabilities, and his religious and political activities the world over. This combination is a rarity in ḥasidic circles. His literary output is unparalleled in the ḥasidic world. For over 40 years he was a dynamic, creative leader.

The descendants of R. Ḥayyim Tyrer of Chernovtsy (Czernowitz) included R. Moses Lupowitz of Bucharest–Tel Aviv (1985).

The Zbarzh-Brezhen dynasty included R. Ẓevi Hirsh Halperin of Brezhin–New York, whose children perished in the Holocaust. A relative, R. Elḥanan Heilperin, lived in London.

Of the Linitz-Rabinowitz dynasty there were two *admorim*: R. Jacob Meshullam of Monastritsh–Philadelphia–Ramat Gan (1971), and R. Ben Zion Joseph Rabinowitz of Orel–United States–Givatayim (1968). The only *admor* of this line in the late 20th century was R. Gedalyahu Aaron Rabinowitz of New York–Jerusalem. He spent a long period in Moscow as an emissary from Israel.

Descendants of Third Generation

Of the Neskhiz dynasty, the *admor* was R. Nahum Mordecai Perlow of Novominsk. His son, R. Jacob, who replaced him, was well learned in Torah and active in charitable works. He occupied a central role in Agudat Israel and lived in Brooklyn.

The Olyky dynasty ended upon the death of R. Ẓevi Aryeh Landa in New York in 1966.

The Kalov dynasty had two successors. One was R. Menaḥem Mendel Taub of Rishon le-Zion-Bene Berak, a very energetic, active *admor* who frequently appeared before Sephardi audiences. Among his important projects was "Bar bei Rav," a day of concentrated studies. The other was R. Moses ben R. Menaḥem Mendel of New York, who came from a different branch of the family.

Descendants of the *maggid* of Kozienice were R. Moses David Shapira of Gwozdiek and R. Abraham Elimelech Shapira of Grodzisk, who left no successors. In the early 21st century, there was Rabbi Elimelech Shapiro of Piaseczno-Grodzisk, who lived in Bet Shemesh, the only *admor* who considered himself an official Zionist. He was the son of Yeshayahu Shapira, a founder of Ha-Po'el ha-Mizrachi. The other *admor* was Samson Moses Sternberg, his grandson, the son of his daughter and the *admor* Rabbi Israel Eliezer Holstein of Kozienice, who lived in Kefar Ḥasidim-New York-Tel Aviv. He attracted many followers at his Tel Aviv base.

This period saw the deaths of all of the *admorim* deriving from R. Abraham Joshua Heschel of Apta. R. Moses Mordecai Heschel of Kopzynce–New York passed away at a young age in 1976, after having been appointed to replace his father – R. Abraham Joshua Heschel. R. David Mordecai Heschel of New York died in 1964, and R. Isaac Me'ir Heschel of Medzhibozh–New York–Haifa died in 1985. There was a center named in honor of the founder in Jerusalem directed by R. Isaac Meir Feinstein, the son of R. Abraham Joshua Heschel. He did not bear the title *admor*.

An exceptionally successful ḥasidic dynasty was that of the family named Hager, which originated with R. Menaḥem Mendel of Kosov – the author of *Ahavat Shalom*. The most outstanding of them was R. Moses Joshua Hager of Vizhnitz–Bene Berak, who headed the Mo'eẓet Gedolei ha-Torah of Agudat Israel. He had thousands of Ḥasidim the world over. His brother, R. Mordecai, lived in Monsey, New York, and he also enlarged the circle of his followers. R. Eliezer Hager of Seret-Vizhnitz was the leader of a large group in Haifa. In addition to gathering many more followers around him, he established branches in Jerusalem and Bene Berak. R. Naftali Hager was the leader of the Vishiva (Viseul de Sus)–Bene Berak Ḥasidim, but he did not take upon himself the title of *admor*. R. Moses Hager was the *admor* of Itnia in Bene Berak, but he had a limited circle of followers. A member of this family was R. Menaḥem Mendel Chodorov of Talnoye–Vizhnitz, who settled in New York. He was the author of *Be-Mo'ado*. A new Vizhnitz group, called Vizhnitz Ḥasidim, was established in Haifa and was led by R. Menaḥem David Hager.

Descendants of Fourth Generation

In the last quarter of the 20th century, the Lelov dynasty had three *admorim*: R. Abraham Solomon, who was centered in Jerusalem; R. Simon Natan-Neta, who was located in Bene Berak and was followed, as stated above, by a large section of the Karlin Ḥasidim; and R. Alter, who lived in Bene Berak. They succeeded their father, R. Moses Mordecai Biederman of Lelov–Jerusalem–Tel Aviv–Bene Berak, who had died in 1988. He was the last of the special personages in Ḥasidism and the only one about whom "wonder-making" stories were told. His leadership was unusual and unique. Other descendants of the founder of this line were members of the Horowitz family of Boston. R. Moses Horowitz of Boston lived in New York, and when he died in 1985 his son R. Ḥayyim-Abraham took his place.

R. Moses' brother, R. Levi Isaac of Boston, was one of the most outstanding figures among all current *admorim*. Most of his Ḥasidim were American-born, and he was the only *admor* who preached in English as well as Yiddish. He had excellent relations with physicians and hospitals and his generosity was legendary.

Admorim of the Zhidachov-Komarno dynasty of the Eichenstein-Safrin families were R. Ḥayyim Jacob Safrin of Komarno–New York–Jerusalem, whose son R. Shalom succeeded him, and his son R. Menaḥem Monish (d. 1990) in Bene Berak, where he established a yeshivah and large *bet midrash*. R. Menaḥem Monish was succeeded by his son.

Admorim of the Eichenstein family were R. Menashe Isaac Me'ir Eichenstein of Klausenberg-Petah Tikvah, he was succeeded by R. Dov Berish Eichenstein, who was in turn followed by his son, R. Joshua. R. Matityahu Eichenstein, who lived in New York, and R. Nathan Eichenstein who lived in Tel Aviv. Neither have successors as *admorim*.

An established line is the Zhidachov dynasty of Chicago. The current *admor* is R. Joshua Heshel, the son of R. Abraham Eichenstein, who is a third-generation Chicagoan. More distant members of the Zhidachov-Komarno line were R. Yeḥiel Ḥayyim Laavin of Makova and R. Moses Kleinberg of Cracow, who lived in Antwerp. This group had no significant center.

The Ropshitz dynasty of the Horowitz and Rubin families had dozens of *admorim*. R. Judah Horowitz of Dzikow-Tarnobrzeg refused to become an *admor* and only accepted the role at an advanced age, when he moved to London. Upon his death (1990), leaving no sons, the line ceased. His nephew, R. Joshua, was the *admor* of Dzikow in New York. A Dzikow center in Jerusalem was run by R. Yeḥezkel Horowitz, the grandson of another brother of R. Judah, who was not an *admor*.

R. Abraham Ẓevi Horowitz of Ozikow settled in New York, and his son, R. Shalom, succeeded him. R. Raphael Horowitz of Kolomea also settled in New York, as did R. Judah Horowitz of Stettin; R. Israel David Horowitz of Schotz (Suczawa); R. Isaac Horowitz of Melitz, the author of *Kevod Shabbat* and *Birkat Yizḥak*; and R. Ḥayyim Shlomo Horowitz of Stryzov, whose son, R. Israel-Jacob-Joel, succeeded him. R. Abraham Simḥah Horowitz of Melitz settled in Jerusalem (1973).

The *admorim* of the Rubin family were R. Abraham David Rubin of Lancut–New York (1963) and his son, R. Shlomo, who succeeded him; R. Joseph David Rubin of Sasov-New York; R. Sender Lipa Rubin of Roman–Romania; R. Issachar Berish Rubin of Dombrova – New York; R. Isaac Rubin of Jawozow–Jerusalem; R. Issachar Berish Rubin of Dolina–New York; R. Sender Lipa Rubin of Wolbrow-New York; R. Shalom Yeḥezkel Shraga Rubin of Zeshinov-New York, (one of the greatest bibliographers of modern times, who was well versed in many fields and the author of *Pinnat Yikrat* on the Tomashov community written under the pseudonym Shalom Lavi. After his death, his son R. Aryeh Leibush Ben-Ẓiyyon was given the title *admor*); R. Simḥah Issachar of Tomashov – New York; the brothers, R. Menaḥem Mendel of Muzaly, R. Samuel Shmelka of Sulyca; R. Mordecai David Rubin of Szaszregen – all of whom lived in New York; R. Abraham Joshua Heschel Tubin of Los Angeles; R. Naftali Ẓevi Rubin of Dombrowa – New York; and R. Simḥah Rubin of London.

Of the dynasty of R. Me'ir of Apta, the *admor* was R. Issachar Ber Rottenberg of Vyadislov–New York, who was an able leader of the rabbinic association founded by the Satmar Ḥasidim. His son succeeded him.

Of the dynasty of R. Uri of Strelisk were the rabbis of the Landman family, most of whom lived in Romania. In recent times there were R. Levi Isaac Landman of Tarnopol–New York, R. Ẓevi Landman of Baku–Nahariyyah (1965) and R. David Landman of Bucharest, who lived in Netanyah.

Of the line of "ha-Yehudi ha-Kadosh" ("The Holy Jew") there remained only the *admorim* of the Biale family. The *admor* R. Yeḥiel Joshua Rabinowitz survived the Holocaust and reestablished Biale Ḥasidism in Tel Aviv and later on in Jerusalem and Bene Berak. Upon his death, four of his sons were recognized as *admorim*. The youngest, R. Ben-Ẓiyyon, who was a rabbi in Lugano, used the family name Biale and his center was in Jerusalem. His brother, R. David Mattityahu, who was responsible for the group's institutions during his father's tenure, established an important center in Bene Berak, with a branch in Jerusalem. The third brother, R. Ẓevi Hirsh, called himself the *admor* of Przysucha. The fourth son, R. Jacob Isaac, also lived in Bene Berak.

Of the dynasty of R. Moses Teitelbaum of Ujhely, considered to be Hungarian Ḥasidism, the one who occupied the central position in the entire world of Ḥasidism was R. Joel Teitelbaum of Satmar, an exceptionally brilliant scholar. He established a very solid organization with dozens of institutions. He was the most extreme of the ḥasidic *ẓaddikim*, and in addition to a number of books on Jewish learning he published two books against Zionism and the State of Israel. He had no sons, and upon his death his nephew, R. Moses Teitelbaum, became the group's leader. Previously he had been the *admor* of Sighet, but he then changed his title to the *admor* of Satmar. His appointment led to the formation of factions within Satmar Ḥasidism. The group calling itself Benei Yoel ("the sons of Joel"), inspired by his widow, Feige, was vociferous in its opposition to him. Another segment gave the title *admor* to his disciple, R. Yeḥiel Michal Leibowitz, and they were called the Ḥasidim of the rabbi of Nikolsburg. R. Yeḥiel Michal was a scholarly young man who modified the extremism of his mentor to a significant degree. A further faction which studied in the yeshivah, headed by Rabbi Menaḥem Mendel Wachter who was considered a Satmar ḥasid – left with the head of the *yeshivah* to Lubavitch Ḥasidism. All of this internal friction was widely publicized, with acrimonious mutual recriminations, and even various incidents.

Other *admorim* in the Teitelbaum family were R. Naftali of Ecsed; R. Yekutiel Judah of Lados–Zanz–New York; R. Alexander Samuel of Kolbuszowa–New York; R. Joshua Ḥayyim of Tscenjowic–New York, and his sons, R. Aaron and R. Samuel; R. Hananyah Yom Tov Lipa of Volove–New York; and R. Mordecai David of Hussakow–Beersheba.

Of the lineage of R. Ẓevi Elimelech of Dynov–Shapira, the following were *admorim* in recent times: R. Israel Shapira of Blazowa (a Holocaust survivor who lived to the age of 100, the oldest *admor* of this generation) his stepson, R. Levi Judah, who took on the surname of Shapiraand who was his successor; R. Eliezer Shapira of Kovesd–New York (1973); the *admor* of the Munkacs line, R. Baruch Rabinowitz, who inherited the title from his father-in-law, R. Ḥayyim Eleazar Shapira. R. Baruch, who was able to draw thousands of Ḥasidim, relinquished the position of Munkacs *admor*, although he did establish his own *bet midrash* (school) in Petaḥ Tikvah. Of his sons, R. Moses-Leib was the very successful *admor* of Munkacs in New York and established a Ḥasidic empire; R. Jacob was the *admor* of Dynov in New York.

Of the Ozarow-Epstein line, there remained only the *admor* R. Moses Jehiel, author of *Esh Dat* and *Be'er Moshe* (1971). An exceptionally talented scholar, he was awarded the Israel Prize in 1967. His daughter's son, R. Tanḥum Benjamin Becker, who succeeded him, had his *bet midrash* in Tel Aviv.

The *admorim* of the Dombrova-Ungar line were R. Jacob Isaac of Dombrova–New York and R. Israel Aaron of Kaschau (Kosice)–Montreal. Affiliated with this lineage were the *admorim* of the Spiegel family: three brothers, R. Elḥanan Johanan of the Bronx; R. Moses of Brooklyn; and R. Phineas Elijah of Long Beach. Belonging to the generation following them were R. Jacob Isaac of Boro Park, R. Moses, and R. David, who were sons of R. Phineas Elijah.

Of the Wisnicz-Lifshitz family line, the *admorim* were R. Moses Lifshitz of Philadelphia–Jerusalem (1975) and R. Ezekel Shragai Lifshitz, whose title was *admor* of Strupkov after his mother's father, who was R. Abraham Shalom Halberstam of Strupkov. He lived in Jerusalem and earned a reputation as a scholar. His son, R. Abraham Shalom, was the *admor* of Sieniawa.

There was no continuation of the Buczacz (Wahrman) and Radoshitz (Baron, Finkler) dynasties. A young man, R. Aharontchik, attempted to reestablish the Radoshitz line, and it was named after him.

The *admoriut* of the Belz Ḥasidim is still one of the largest dynasties in Ḥasidism. The *admor*, R. Issachar Ber who received the title at a very young age, replacing his uncle – R. Aaron of Belz – displayed excellent leadership qualities, although his uncommon resoluteness made him opponents. He turned out to be a true nonconformist. His followers numbered in the thousands and his center in Jerusalem was one of the largest in the ḥasidic world.

The importance of the other *admorim* of the Rokach family was limited to their own circles. Among them were R. Moses Rokach of Kozlov, who had a huge library in New York and who was succeeded by his son-in-law, R. Jehiel Michal Rottenberg; R. David of Montreal, and R. Hanina of Turkow; and R. Baruch Rokach of Skahl who lived in New York.

Descendants of the founder of the line, R. Shalom of Belz, include R. Hananiah Yom Tov Lipa Teitelbaum of Sasov, the founder of Kiryat Yismaḥ Moshe in Ganei Tikvah; his son, R. Joseph David, who was his successor; R. Joel of Kiralhaza–New York; R. Ḥayyim Meir Jehiel Shapira of Narol–Bene Berak; R. Ḥanokh Ḥenikh Ashkenazi of Rzeszoz-Jerusalem; R. Abraham Alter Pollak of Petaḥ Tikvah, who was also a descendant of R. Joseph Meir of Spinka but was raised by his stepfather, R. Aaron of Belz.

Of the Stretyn-Langner-Brandwein family, the following served as *admorim*: R. Uri Langner of Krihynicze–New York who was a prolific scholar; R. Solomon Langner of Toronto; R. David Flam of Montreal; R. Yiẓḥak Isaac Langer of Toronto; R. Abraham Brandwein of Piatra–Neamt–Haifa; R. Judah Ẓevi Brandwein of Tel Aviv–Jerusalem, who was known as the "rabbi of the Histadrut." In the late 20th century those bearing the name Stretyn were R. Shalom Flam of New York, whose mother belonged to the Langner family, and R. Aaron Jacob Brandwein of New York who refused to take any money from his followers or members of his *bet midrash*. A very talented scholar, he owned a large, significant private library.

Of the descendants of R. Ezekiel Panet there were three *admorim*, brothers who lived in New York, and bore the name Dej in their title. They were R. Ẓevi Meir of Dej, who also had a *bet midrash* in Bene Berak, and Rabbis Judah and Elimelech Alter.

Of the line of R. Joseph of Tomaszow (Frishman), there remained only R. Joshua of Tomaszow, who survived the Holocaust while losing all of his family. After he died in 1974, there was no successor.

Descendants of Fifth Generation

The Kazimierz (Kuzhmir)–Modzhitz dynasty was continued through R. Israel Dan Taub, who succeeded his father as the *admor* of Modzhitz, and replaced him on Mo'eẓet Gedolei ha-Torah of Agudat Israel. He was a renowned Torah scholar. A cousin of his in America also became an *admor* and caused a split among the Modzhitz Ḥasidim in America.

Of the descendants of R. Isaac of Warka – the Kalish family – only the Amshinov branch still exists. The last member of the Warka family, R. Jacob-David-Baruch, died in 1983. The Amshinov group had two *admorim*: R. Isaac who lived in New York and was one of the oldest and most senior of the *admorim* since he had held the title since before the Holocaust, and R. Jacob Aryeh Isaiah Milikovsky who replaced his grandfather, R. Jerahmiel Judah, who died in 1976. This young *admor* gained a group of followers despite unusual practices, such as, for example, making *havdalah* (separation of the Sabbath from the weekday) on Sunday afternoon.

The famous Kotsk dynasty was represented by R. Menaḥem Mendel Morgenstern, whose *bet midrash* was in Tel Aviv. He was not an official *admor*, since he earned a living from business. He printed the Torah teachings of his father and his grandfather. Another *admor*, R. Yeḥiel Meir Morgenstern, lived in New York but died with no successor.

The dynasty with the largest number of *admorim* is Zanz of the Halberstam family. Prior to the Holocaust, hundreds of its members had founded dynasties and even now they are very numerous.

The most important sectors of this group are the Bobov Ḥasidim, under the dynamic leadership of R. Salomon of Bobov, who had thousands of Ḥasidim and educational institutions as well as other projects, and the Zanz-Klausenberg Ḥasidim, led by R. Jekutiel Judah Halberstam, an exceptional Torah scholar, which had centers throughout the world, specifically in Netanyah, where they had also established the modern Laniado hospital.

Other, active Zanz descendants were R. Ḥayyim of Czchow–New York, R. David of Kashanov–New York, R. Ezekiel David of Parkrzwice–New York, and his son R. Jehiel, R. Jekutiel Judah of Sieniawa, R. Moses Aryeh of Nasoid–New York, R. Jacob of Szczakowa–Jerusalem, and his son R. Naftali. His son, R. Meir, who had been an office worker, began to serve as *admor* with the title of the *admor* Ropczyce. R. Jacob's son-in-law, R. Joshua Wagshal, was the *admor* of Lancut. Also included were R. Israel of Zhimgorod–New York, R. Aryeh Leibush of Zhimgorod–New York, R. Naftali of Gribov–New York, R. David Moses of Dinov and R. Abraham Abish Kanner of Chekhov–Haifa, whose *bet midrash* continued to function without an official *admor*.

Other Zanz ḥasidic groups were led by R. Shalom Ezekiel Shragai Rubin and R. Ezekiel Shragai Lipshitz of Stropkov who were mentioned above with their families. These two men added the name Halberstam to their family names.

The Radomsk (Rabinowitz), Kaminka (Rosenfeld), Kobrin (Palier), and Radzymin (Gutterman) dynasties had no continuation.

The Izbica-Radzyn dynasty found no direct successor from the Leiner family, and R. Abraham Issachar Engelrad, a Holocaust survivor and brother-in-law of the last *admor* of Radzyn, R. Samuel Solomon Leiner, was chosen *admor*. A large center was established for him in Bene Berak. A Radzyn center was also set up in the United States, directed by the *admor* R. Mordecai Joseph Leiner (d. 1991), the son of R. Jeruham of Radzyn.

The Gur dynasty is focal in Polish Ḥasidism. Before the Holocaust it was the largest ḥasidic group in Poland and since its leader, R. Abraham Mordecai Alter, looked favorably upon settlement in the Land of Israel, many of his followers immigrated to Palestine. The dynamic leadership of his son, R. Israel, the author of *Beit Yisrael* (1977) brought new vitality to the Gerer Ḥasidism, making it the largest ḥasidic group in Israel. Continuing the leadership, in his own distinctive manner, was the *admor*, R. Simḥah Bunim Alter.

The Ciechanow line of the Landa family was another Polish ḥasidic group, and was led by R. Abraham Landa, the *admor* of Strykow (a branch of this ḥasidic division), who first lived in Tel Aviv and then in Bene Berak. He had a fine reputation as a scholar.

The Lithuanian Slonim Ḥasidism was led by R. Shalom Noah Brazovsky, well-versed in Torah learning, who directed the Slonim yeshivah and was the son-in-law of the last *admor* R. Abraham Weinberg of Tiberias–Jerusalem. R. Abraham was chosen since there was no direct descendant of the Slonim *admor* and R. Abraham was related to the founder of the line. A number of Ḥasidim did not accept the choice of R. Shalom Noah and gave the title to R. Abraham Weinberg, a young Torah scholar, who belonged to the family of the Slonim *admor*. He settled in Bene Berak, established a yeshivah, and gained the fierce loyalty of his followers. R. Abraham Joshua Heschel Weinberg, an *admor* who had been in business and who was a direct descendant of the Slonim family, died in 1978 and his sons did not succeed him.

Of the Wielopole–Frankel family, the only ones to serve as *admor* in this period were R. Solomon-Zalman, and R. Ben Ẓiyyon. R. Solomon Zalman's nephew, R. Joseph, was an *admor* in Flatbush, New York.

Descendants of Sixth Generation

Those ḥasidic groups established in the sixth generation of Ḥasidism continue to function.

The Lublin dynasty of the Eiger family is represented by the *admor* R. Abraham Eiger, a Holocaust survivor, who lives in New York.

The Sochaczew dynasty of the Bornstein family, reestablished after the Holocaust, was hard hit by the tragic death in 1969 in a traffic accident of R. Menaḥem Solomon, for whom a great future had been expected. His son, R. Samuel, was appointed to take his place.

The Aleksandrow dynasty, led by the Danziger family, which had been the second largest ḥasidic group in Poland with thousands of members, found it very difficult to reconstitute itself after the Holocaust. The survivors appointed as *admor* R. Judah Moses Tiehberg, the son-in-law of R. Bezalel Yair Danziger of Aleksandrow, who had not been the main *admor* of the group. The selection was not accepted by everyone and internal friction prevented the expansion of Aleksandrow Ḥasidism. R. Judah Moses' son, R. Abraham Menaḥem, was given the title *admor* in 1973 and gave new vitality to the group, establishing new branches and institutions. He changed his surname to that of the dynasty, Danziger. He, too, however, could not do away with the internal strife. An opposition group appointed R. Jehiel Menaḥem Singer of New York as *admor* and upon his death his son succeeded him.

The Wolborz dynasty was reconstituted only recently

with the arrival in Israel of R. Ẓevi Turnheim from Brazil. He set up a *bet midrash* in Bene Berak which was very active.

The Sambor court of the Ulis family was led by R. Eleazar of Montreal. Another descendant, R. Efraim Eliezer, who served as a rabbi in Philadelphia and lived to a very advanced age, did not fill the role of *admor*, but after his death his grandson became the Sambor *admor* in Jerusalem.

The Tash (Tass) dynasty of the Lowey-Rotenberg family continued along its two lines. Tash was represented by R. Meshullam Feish Lowey, who established a large, very successful ḥasidic neighborhood in Montreal and by R. Ḥayyim Solomon of Khust in New York. For the Rotenberg family, the *admorim* of the Kason line were R. Menaḥem Israel of Boro Park and R. Meshullam of Boro Park, who were the sons of R. Moses Samuel of Kosoni, R. Jacob of Monsey and R. Joel Ẓevi of Williamsburg, the sons of R. Mordecai Rotenberg of Salka–Kosoni, and R. Asher Isaiah, the son of R. Moses (the second) of Kosoni.

R. Ẓevi Elimelech Panet, a descendant of this line on his mother's side, established his own *bet midrash*, in the name of Kason, in Bene Berak.

Of the Liska-Friedlander line, the *admorim* were R. Solomon of Liska, R. Moses David of Borgopzund and R. Yoska of Lisk, and the latter's son, R. Ẓevi, succeeded him.

Of the Spinka dynasty of the Weiss-Kahana families, there were several *admorim*: R. Jacob Joseph Weiss was the most outstanding of the Spinka *admorim*. He conducted a large network of institutions centered in New York, where he lived. After his death in 1989, the line was carried on by his three sons, R. Naftali Ḥayyim in Los Angeles, R. Israel in Bene Berak, and R. Meir in Boro Park. Two other sons died while their father was still alive. R. Naḥman Kahana was the Spinka *admor* in Bene Berak until his death in 1977, when his sons were chosen as *admorim*, with R. Moses Eliyakim in Bene Berak and R. Baruch, the *admor* of Karlsburg, in Jerusalem. R. Joseph Meir Kahana was the *admor* of Spinka in Jerusalem. In 1978 his title was divided between his sons, R. Mordecai David and R. Alter, the *admor* of Zhidachov, in Jerusalem. R. Ẓevi Kahane was the *admor* of Spinka in Los Angeles and R. Ẓevi Hirsch Horowitz was the Spinka-Kareli *admor* in Williamsburg.

Of the B'kerestur dynasty, the *admorim* were R. Issachar Dov Rubin and R. Naftali Gross.

The *admor* of the Hadas court was R. Eliezer Fish of Williamsburg.

The dynasty of "Rebbe Aharele," an independent dynasty in Beregszaz and Jerusalem, was continued by his son, R. Abraham Ḥayyim Rata in Bene Berak, a unique personality, and his son-in-law, R. Abraham Isaac Kahn, who greatly increased the number of his followers. His *bet midrash* was a center of Jerusalem zealousness in content and in form.

Of the dynasty of R. Judah Leib Ashlag, another independent line which did not bear the name of a city, there were three *admorim*, the son, R. Baruch Shalom in Bene Berak, and two grandsons, R. Ezekiel Joseph and R. Simḥah Abraham. They were sons of R. Solomon Benjamin Ashlag, the son of the founder of the dynasty. The uniqueness of these *admorim* is in their teaching of Kabbalah in public and in disseminating information about it.

The Entradam-Naszod line of the Freund family was represented by a non-direct descendant, R. Moses Aryeh Halberstam, who lived in New York. The rabbi of the Edah Ḥaredit in Jerusalem, R. Moses Aryeh Freund, was a direct descendant of the line and therefore functioned, to a great degree, like an *admor*.

Of the Bikszad dynasty, the successors were R. Nahum Ẓevi Fish and R. Moses Aryeh Lev, both of whom are in the United States.

In the post-Holocaust generation, new *admorim* became effective. R. Eliezer Zusya Portugal, the Skolener *rebbe*, gained his reputation for rescuing children and educating them after the Holocaust. Following his death his son, R. Israel Abraham, replaced him as *admor*. The father and son established a network of institutions in Israel under the name of "Ḥesed le-Avraham." Others are R. Isaac Huberman of Ra'anannah (1978); R. Zavel Abramowitz of Rimnitz, who was in the United States; R. Avraham Fish in Jaffa; R. Asher Freind in Jerusalem. All of them gained reputations as "wonder-workers" and attracted followers.

Sometimes a name comes up as a "wonder-worker." A noted example is R. Eleazar Abu-Ḥazeira of Beersheba. The phenomenon of recognizing an *admor* has been developing among Sephardi communities and deserves its own study.

The Braslav Ḥasidism, which had been exceptional ever since it was founded, continued to expand greatly. The increase in followers led to the establishment of different groups in Jerusalem, Safed, and a group revolving around R. Eliezer Solomon Shick. He was also a "new" Braslaver, who set up a ḥasidic center in Jabne'el in Galilee. He was considered the greatest disseminator of Braslav teachings, with his publication of hundreds of booklets of the teachings of R. Naḥman of Braslav. Braslav Ḥasidism has dozens of books of various types in distribution spreading its teachings.

THE MUSICAL TRADITION OF ḤASIDISM

Problems of Definition and Research

By one definition, the field of ḥasidic music would include all music practiced in ḥasidic society. By another, and related, definition, any music performed in "ḥasidic style" is ḥasidic. A further possibility could be to define ḥasidic music by its content, i.e., by those musical elements and forms, which distinguish it from any other music. So far, such distinctions have not been formulated according to the norms of musical scholarship. The Ḥasidim themselves also possess criteria – formulated in their own traditional terms – according to which they judge whether a melody is "ḥasidic" or not, and to which dynasty-style and genre it belongs. These, too, have not yet been translated into ethnomusicological terms. Moreover, none of the existing studies of ḥasidic music has as yet managed to furnish a systematic description of the ḥasidic repertoire or even part of it. First steps in this direction were made by by Y. Mazor and A. Hajdu from 1974. A pioneer effort was made by A.Z.I *Idelsohn, the tenth volume of whose *Thesaurus* is devoted to ḥasidic music. Idelsohn based his analyses on very loosely defined form and scale types – criteria, which are not sufficient for an exclusive and thorough definition. The fundamental difficulty lies in the anthologist character of the body of material, which he assembled as a base for his analysis. Idelsohn's 250 items include vocal music, instrumental music, liturgical pieces, dance tunes, folk songs in Yiddish, etc., and are taken from various and often distant dynastic repertoires. A systematic description requires analyzing the material first by sub-units, such as dynastic repertoires or genres (dance tunes, prayer melodies, or instrumental music, etc.). A comparative summary of these would then reveal the basic aspects of ḥasidic music. Nowadays the location of these units has itself become difficult, because of the far-reaching changes, which have occurred during the last 70 years in the ḥasidic communities, especially as a result of the Holocaust. The original communal frameworks were for the most part destroyed, although attempts were made to reconstruct them in other places (chiefly in Israel and the U.S.). For some dynasties this proved impossible, since all that remained of them were a number of survivors living in various countries that could, at best, try to preserve the remnants of the tradition in their personal memory. Other dynasties did achieve a renascence around new geographical centers but the interference of new external and internal factors could not but cause radical changes in the traditional patterns, including all aspects of the musical repertoire.

Two opposing tendencies can be discerned in the present-day repertoire. On the one hand, there is the attempt to preserve the traditional functions with their traditional melodies as strictly as possible such as Sabbath and festival prayer customs and, to a certain extent, the *tish* (i.e., rabbi's table assemblies). However, the desire to preserve tradition could paradoxically lead to major or minor changes, as happened with the Vizhnitz and Karlin ḥasidim, who made a special effort to collect forgotten *niggunim* and to reincorporate them into the pertinent ritual occasions. These changes often affected the repertoire of ritual events that up until then had maintained their distinctive traditional character. Furthermore, original elements appear in, and are stimulated by, those occasions on which both the adherents of diverse dynasties and non-ḥasidic Jews come together and influence each other, such as weddings, *Simḥat Torah celebrations, and the *hillulot* of *Lag ba-Omer and the Seventh of Adar. These events have created a distinctive repertoire, which arose mainly in Israel and the U.S. after World War II; it is made up chiefly of dance and "rejoicing tunes," which were originally linked with specific functions and dynasties and have now been detached from their earlier framework and adopted by this "pan-ḥasidic" public. Here, many melodies have been furnished with new words; individual dynastic traits have been eroded, and the repertoire has absorbed a number of recently composed melodies. This repertoire, however, has not accepted melodies, which are too exclusively associated with a specific dynasty, nor the slow *tish* tunes. This "pan-ḥasidic" phenomenon is found even among those ḥasidim whose communities did achieve a renaissance after the Holocaust, such as Boyan, Gur, Vizhnitz (see mus. Ex. 8).

The historical dimension of ḥasidic music poses problems of its own. In fact, we still do not know whether ḥasidic music developed out of an existing tradition and repertoire or was created as a new style in response to the new social and spiritual conditions established by the rise and development of ḥasidic society. Without this knowledge any historical theory about ḥasidic music would be farfetched. In any case one must take into account the dynastic filiations and interrelations, geographical proximity or isolation, and the importance of the "court musicians" and *klezmerim* as transmitters of musical elements from one dynastic center to another.

The Place of Music in Ḥasidic Thought

Joy and its principal means of expression – song and dance – have been important values of the ḥasidic movement since its inception in the second half of the 18th century and the ḥasidic leaders devoted increasing attention to music and dance in their writings. This signified an innovation in Jewish culture, in contrast to the general attitude of the Ashkenazi rabbinical establishment to music. A thorough survey of the musical evidence in the literary sources, and their interaction with oral traditions, is not yet available, but a beginning has been made at the Jewish Music Research Center at the Hebrew University of Jerusalem (see Mazor 2002). The literary evidence has been expressed in different ways:

(1) Sayings of *ẓaddikim* and their disciples about the virtues of music: They appear either as part of a story or as independent maxims and discourses in their writings. They also include kabbalistic interpretations of the **shofar*, its tones and its liturgical functions (see, e.g., the writings of Jacob Joseph of Polonnoye, *Nahman of Bratslav).

(2) The musical activities of the *ẓaddikim*: Stories about these activities began with *Israel ben Eliezer Baal Shem Tov himself (see, e.g., *Shivḥei ha-Besht*). These also include stories about the creation of particular melodies by *ẓaddikim* or their "court musicians," and descriptions of the miraculous properties were sometimes attributed to such melodies.

(3) Musical elements in the ḥasidic tales: The most fascinating of these can be found in the tales of R. Naḥman of Bratslav (see especially the "Tale of the Seven Beggars").

(4) Miscellaneous stories and descriptions by the opponents of Ḥasidism: a most valuable contribution is furnished by the polemic writings of those who, from the beginning, constantly poured their scorn on the Ḥasidic predilection for singing and dancing. Their very vehemence and undoubted exaggerations demonstrate the difference between the two cultures, and the importance they accorded to music. Because of the lack of explicit descriptions in the early Ḥasidic literature

(for reasons which are as yet unclear), these anti-Ḥasidic writings are all the more important as historical sources.

The central place of music in ḥasidic life is anchored in their musical ideology. Ideological differences between the various streams of Ḥasidism as well as recurring conceptual changes throughout the generations are reflected in their attitude to music. In their approach to music, a prominent conceptual change involves the movement of ḥasidic thought from the theosophical sphere to the psychological one, e.g., from the divine to the human soul. In the early ḥasidic writings, magical and theurgical conceptions prevailed that were rooted in the theosophical kabbalistic doctrine, in particular that of the Lurianic Kabbalah. These conceptions affirm human deeds, including musical activity, as having the power to affect the *sefirot* (Godhead) and, as a result, the entire world. Naḥman of Bratslav (1772–1810), for example, discusses the power of the tune of the prayer in *Likkutei Moharan*. Later generations abandoned the view that one can influence the divine world with music and ascribed this power only to the *ẓaddik*.

This change occurred under the leadership of R. *Dov Baer, the Maggid of Mezhirech (1704–1772) and especially through the teachings of some of his disciples. According to this view music was part of contemplation, of the soul-seeking required to reveal its divine source, and allowing communion with God, *devekut*, to take place. One witnesses, then, a drift from the emphasis put on music in textual context to the belief that music can act in its own right, whether connected to a text or not. In the opinion of some *ẓaddikim* and their adherents, music and singing were ranked even higher than explicit prayer. In consequence, ḥasidic melodies are mostly sung without words, though some are adapted to brief verses from the prayer book or *piyyutim*. However, some *niggunim* remained with a fixed text, such as the recitative *niggunim* of the Sabbath **zemirot*, *Kol Mekaddesh* and *Barukh Adonai Yom Yom*, and dance songs of Lag ba-Omer (see Hajdu-Mazor. *101 Ḥasidic Dance Niggunim*, nos. 8–10). In addition, a drift took place from the performance of music in the individual, meditative sphere towards a predominant collective expression of the entire congregation. Today only the Lubavitch (Chabad) and Bratslav movements engage in both individual and collective performance. Yet, in some dynasties certain *niggunim* are performed by the Rebbe himself.

Since most ḥasidic songs are textless, such a predominance of the melodic element over the textual aspect may well be directly linked with this doctrine. The primacy of the melody characterizes even the sung parts of ḥasidic prayer: instead of rendering the text, the ḥasidim actually perform the melody into which the words are freely interpolated. Some of these renditions often sound as if the text did not exist at all. An extreme example is the singing of the Sabbath *zemirot* by the Slonim ḥasidim, which is entirely textless: they have the words well in mind without uttering a single syllable.

The *niggun* as an expression of innermost emotions that cannot be expressed through words is considered as a means for the *ẓaddik* to plumb the depths of a person's soul, and to discover whether that person is evil or pious. It also enables him to refine that person's soul and raise it to a higher level of existence. As for simple people, who have not achieved the level of the *ẓaddik*, the *niggun* can help them to attain spiritual elevation, either through singing, or passively, by listening. Hearing the *ẓaddik* singing a *niggun*, provides the ordinary person with a foothold at the edge of the world of the Sacred.

Musical Acculturation

Adopting tunes from surrounding non-Jewish cultures is a hallmark of ḥasidic music. Leading ḥasidic sages tried to explain this phenomenon of musical acculturation and even gave to it the force of a religious duty. For example, R. Naḥman of Bratslav approved of singing gentile music as a way to attract God's increased attention to His people's sufferings at gentile hands and to induce Him to redeem them. A more typical view holds that sacred melodies in gentile music have been, as it were, taken captive by evil forces in the constant struggle between divine forces and the forces of evil. The "divine sparks" (*niẓẓoẓot*) hidden in them, await redemption. *Ẓaddikim* and their emissaries, wherever they lived, were constantly seeking out melodies with a "sacred flavor" in order to redeem the sparks and restore them to their heavenly source. Thus, local gentile, folk and popular melodies (Russian, Polish, Ukrainian, Romanian, Hungarian, Turkish, and Arabic) left a strong stamp on ḥasidic music. The plurality of melodic styles has brought about the opinion that ḥasidic music could not be considered as an autonomous ethnomusical unit. But such an attitude disregards the obvious processes of transformation and re-creation, which occurred in these tunes through their adoption by ḥasidim

Occasionally, ḥasidim borrowed gentile folksongs with the original texts, but endowed them with a new meaning in the spirit of Ḥasidism, justifying the texts as being allegorical (see mus. ex. 1). Some of the original songs or melodies, were preserved together with the story (apocryphal or real) of how it came to be "lifted up" from the "sphere of impurity," and by whom. Such are, for instance, the songs attributed to R. Yitzhak Eizik Taub of Kalov (one of which is illustrated in example 2).

Dynastic Styles

Which dynasties have a characteristic musical style and which dynasties share a common style? Ḥasidim with a musical ear insist that they can identify the dynastic origin of a tune at first hearing and claim that the *niggunim* of certain dynasties have a unique musical flavor. There are indeed a few characteristic features that can be associated with specific dynasties. For example, in dynasties closer to the West – Bobov, Gur, and Modzhitz – there is a strong Western influence, which finds expressions through a harmonic-tonal conception traceable to operatic melodies, modern cantorial compositions, and polyphonic elaboration (see mus. ex. 3). Romanian and Hungarian influences appear in dynasties in Transylvania, Hungary, and the Carpathian Ukraine such as Vizhnitz, Satmar, Munkacs, and Kalov without the tonal-harmonic thinking.

The melodic framework shows the traits found in the surrounding ethnic cultures: modes, pentatonic, and some scales with the augmented second. The *tish niggunim* of the Gur, Vizhnitz, and Modzhitz ḥasidim, whether sung to *zemirot* or with liturgical texts, are distinguished by their length. Some *niggunim* of the Vizhnitz ḥasidim resemble cantorial compositions and are sung by the *kapelye* (choral group) in a variety of polyphonic textures, such as parallel thirds, canons, and other imitative techniques, sometimes over an ostinato (see mus. ex. 4).

Ḥasidic marches can be found mainly in the repertoires of Gur, Vizhnitz, and Modzhitz ḥasidim; they are less frequent in other dynasties.

Dance niggunim of the Bratslav ḥasidism show the influence of their Ukrainian surroundings. The melodies are mostly short, simple in form, and in general do not exceed the range of one octave. Their melodic elements do not differ significantly from those of the Carpathian and Transylvanian dynasties described above (see: Hajdu-Mazor, *101 Hasidic Dance Niggunim*, nos. 23–26). The northern area – Belorussia and Lithuania – comprises the centers of Chabad, Karlin, and Slonim Ḥasidism. Russian motives and traits of performance are found in the Chabad repertoire, although part of it is also influenced by the Romanian *doina* style (see: Zalmanoff, no 303–304). The singing of the Karlin ḥasidim is distinguished by a strong rhythmic emphasis on every beat, while the melodic range is limited and often does not exceed the fifth. The melodies are built on progression by seconds and on the variation repetition of brief motifs (see. mus. ex. 11). Since the Karlin ḥasidim are now concentrated in Israel, and this style is closely related to several styles found in the Near East, the question arises whether these traits were already present in the original Karlin repertoire, or whether they entered and dominated it only after the reconstitution of the community in Palestine and Israel; but in the absence of older recordings and notations it must remain unanswered.

There is another specific phenomenon in the singing of some ḥasidic communities. We can define it as a gradual but continuous rise of pitch, sometimes to impressive proportions, as among the ḥasidim of Boyan, Lubavitch, and Slonim. The latter have an even more peculiar way of singing which has no parallel in other dynasties: the constant and somewhat irregular shifting of the melodic phrases upwards, through chromatic and even microtonal displacement, resulting in a continuous shifting of the tonal center. The impression it gives is one of a wide-ranging melody, though the motifs and phrases themselves (without the shifting) should give only a very small range. The upward shift can be also found in other dynasties, such as Chabad, but appear there only as an imperceptible "creeping."

The Place of Music in Ḥasidic Life

The role of music in Ḥasidic life is intrinsically different from that of other communities. The latter distinguishes between music sung in the synagogue – which is the center of community's religious life – and music belonging to everyday life. In Ḥasidic society the house of the *ẓaddik*, as well as the *shtibl*, is the spiritual and religious center for prayer and for events where much singing was involved, such as the *tish*. The aura of sanctity, which enveloped everything that took place in the *ẓaddik*'s house, therefore extended itself also to those musical activities of the Ḥasidic community, which were not strictly speaking a liturgical activity. In consequence, the boundary between sacred and secular music became blurred: secular forms such as marches and waltzes could be taken over for prayer tunes, and tunes used for dances could be furnished with texts from the liturgy. Since the dance was also considered a sanctified action it was and still is found even in the synagogue, before, between, and after certain prayer services.

THE REBBE AS MUSICAL LEADER. Many ḥasidic leaders were highly musical; some also earned fame as gifted *ba'alei tefillah* (prayer-leaders) or composers. Such leaders cultivated their communities' musical repertoire and encouraged original creativity, or drew gifted composer-*ḥazanim*, together with their *kapelyes*, to their "courts." Very famous were the *ḥazanim* Nissan Spivak ("Nissi Belzer," 1824–1906) in Sadgora, Yosef Volynetz ("Yosl Tolner," 1838–1902) in Talnoye and Rakhmistrivke (Rotmistrovka), Jacob Samuel Morogovski ("Zeydl Rovner," 1856–1942) in Makarov and Rovno, Pinḥas Spector ("Pinye Khazn," 1872–1951) in Boyan and its branches, and the *menagnim* (musicians) Yankl Telekhaner in Koidanov, Stolin, Lechovitch, and probably Slonim, and Jacob Dov (Yankl) Talmud (1886–1963) in Gur.

A new type of leadership emerged after the Holocaust, stemming from the danger that the musical tradition would disappear with the annihilation of entire communities. The late *rebbe* of Vizhnitz (Ḥayyim Meir Hager, 1888–1972), who reestablished his community in Israel, felt this danger, and took steps to revive the musical tradition, and at the same time encouraged the inclusion of *niggunim* of other ḥasidic sources. He also established a *kapelye* that would sing in the polyphonic style, and would perform works of *ḥazzanim* from the past.

The musical leadership of the *rebbe* also finds expression during the *tish*. Some *rebbes* sing all the *niggunim* on their own, while the congregation joins in only at specified places. Other *rebbes* conduct the *tish* through subtle cues – they signal to the congregation, or the *kapelye*, with a hand gesture or even with a glance. The late Vizhnitz *rebbe* used to conduct the singing of his congregation, correcting the congregation when the *niggun* was sung inaccurately. In some communities, the *rebbe* has a special sign to bring about greater excitement in the singing. Among the Vizhnitz, the excitement reaches its peak when the *rebbe* stands up; among the Boyan, this happens when the *rebbe* claps his hands. The latter also try to affect the tempo and as a result, a *niggun* may be rendered with unusual changes of tempo (Mazor 2004).

Among the Belz ḥasidim, who were known as "not musical," a veritable revolution took place when the current Vizhnitz *rebbe*'s son-in-law, Yissachar Dov Rokach, became the *rebbe* of Belz. The encouragement of original musical creations, together with the establishment of a *kapelye*, modeled on that of Vizhnitz, brought about a new and unique repertoire in addition to the traditional *niggunim*. The current *rebbe* of Karlin has directed the collection of Karlin traditional *niggunin* from all possible sources, even from the National Library in Jerusalem, in order to revive them. The guarding of the tradition included the prohibition to take the *niggunim* out of the congregation, whether through publication, recording, or handing over the scores to individuals from outside the community.

THE MUSICAL GENRES. *Niggun* (Yid. *nign*, from *nagen*, which probably meant "singing" in biblical Hebrew) is the ḥasidic term for a musical unit, i.e., a "tune," be it sung (with or without words) or played. All this is opposed to the current meaning of the term in modern Hebrew, which uses it for playing only. The *niggun* is the central musical manifestation of ḥasidic life. The term is not applied to the prayer **nusaḥ*, or the cantillation of the *masoretic accents, or other types of popular songs. While the latter are conditioned by the textual factor, the *niggun*, even when sung with words, is conceived as a completely autonomous musical entity. Most *niggunim* are sung without any words, with the frequent use of carrier syllables such as *Ah, Ay, Oy, Hey, Bam, Ya-ba-bam, ti-di-ram*, etc. Others have a partial text underlay. One *niggun* may also be sung to various texts. Where a *niggun* has a fixed text, the setting shows that the melody came first and the words were fitted to it afterward; even where it is known that a *niggun* was composed specifically for a certain text, the result sounds as if the text had been adapted to the melody.

Of all the dynasties, Lubavitch alone has successfully evolved a kind of "*niggun*-theory," through which it tries to explain ḥasidic musical activity, and to distinguish between different genres. Hasidic musicians ("*menagnim*") of various dynasties use different terms to classify *niggunim*, and as a result some genres are referred to with more than one term.

1) *Tish* ("table") *nigunim*. These make up the core of the ḥasidic repertoire, and constitute the major part of melodies sung at the assembly of the *rebbe*'s table. Most have stylistic similarities to the Lubavitch genre of *devekut* (adhesion) *niggunim*, also called *hitva'adut* (gathering) tunes. In other dynasties they are known as *hisorerus* (awakening), *makhshove* (meditation), *moralishe* (moral), *hartsi* (hearty), or bet (begging) *niggunim*. All are characterized by slow tempi, expressing serious, meditative and even sad moods and by metrical or free rhythm (see: mus. ex. 5). Sometimes this free rhythm is combined with metrical sections resulting in a variable tempo. One of the most widespread types resembles a slowed-down *mazurka*, with the first beat changing, perhaps under the influence of the well-known Hungarian metric formula (see mus. ex. 6). In some dynasties, such as Chabad and Vizhnitz, these *niggunim* show the impact of East European folk forms, such as the Romanian *doina* (called by them "*a volach*" or "*vulechl*"); in others, such as Modzhitz and Bobov, they are influenced by West European art music (e.g., operatic melodies). The length of such a *niggun* may vary. It is divided into sections, called "*fal*" in Yiddish or designated by the Aramaic term *bava* ("gate"). Their number can go from two to seven and in exceptional cases can reach 32, as in the *Ezkerah* of R. Israel Taub of Modzhitz (M.S. Geshuri, *Neginah ve-Ḥasidut be-Veit Kuzmir u-Venoteha*, pt. 2 (1952), pp. 9–18). Most *tish niggunim* are textless. The texts of the others are generally taken from the Sabbath and **zemirot* or from the liturgy (see mus. ex. 6–7).

2) Dance *niggunim* – called also *tentsl* or *freylekhs*. Other terms used by Polish ḥasidim are *hopke, dreidl*, or *redele*. Many dance *niggunim* have the following characteristics: duple meter; fast tempi; a periodic or symmetric structure in multiples of four bars; few sections – between one to five (the structure a-b-c-b being the most frequent); a small range, generally not more than one octave – sometimes only a fifth or a sixth; and a small number of motives (see Hajdu-Mazor, *101 Hasidic Dance Niggunim*, no 87–92). Some tunes consist of one or two motives and their developments (see mus. ex. 8). The most common tonal framework is that of the minor hexachord (aeolian mode), extended sometimes by a lower or higher second. Others of these *niggunim* use different scales characterized by the augmented second (see mus. ex. 9). Dance tunes are performed mainly at weddings and rejoicing festivals such as Simḥat Torah and Lag ba-Omer, but have an important role at the ḥasidic *tish* and synagogue prayers. About a third of these niggunim has fixed texts, mostly short, taken from biblical verses or from the liturgy, and fitted to the melody through the repetition of words or parts of sentences. A related category is called "tunes of rejoicing," which possess all the above characteristics but is sung in a slower tempo and mostly without dancing (see mus. ex. 10).

3) March and waltz. These joyful tunes were adopted from, or influenced by, non-Jewish cultures from Central Europe (mostly Polish and Austro-Hungarian). They are mostly used at the *tish* or for prayer but not used for dancing or marching; they are generally sung slower than their gentile counterpart. Most *niggunim* of these types are sung without text. They can be used in Sabbath and holiday services and applied to poetical texts such as *Lekha Dodi, El Adon, Ki Anu Amekha, Ki Hine ka-Ḥomer, Ha-Yom Te'amẓenu*, etc. The Vizhnitz repertoire includes *niggunim* having some characteristics of a march despite their triple meter. They call them "marsh" but they could be better called "marsh-vals".

4) Other genres. In addition to the types of *niggunim*, the ḥasidic repertoire includes *badkhones* (jester's tunes sung with Yiddish rhymed verses), bilingual songs, and compositions in the style of choral music composed by cantors.

Tradition and Renewal in Ḥasidic Music

The main way to determine whether music in ḥasidic society grew from an existing tradition or mapped out new paths is to look for parallels in the music of non-ḥasidic communities in and after the 18th century. Two dominant musical elements are common to the ḥasidic and non-ḥasidic prayer of the communities of Eastern Europe: The modality (in Yiddish, *shtayger*) and the recitative style. The extensive use among ḥasidim of the term "*Velts Nusakh*" for the style of liturgical recitative common to both ḥasidim and *mitnaggedim* applies also in this sense. The specific character of prayer among Karlin ḥasidim, as well as certain characteristic elements in the so-called "Volhynia *Nusakh*" (which has survived among offshoots of Ruzhin Ḥasidism – Boyan, Sadegora, Czortków, etc.) and in the *nusah* of such communities as Vizhnitz, Zydaczów and its offshoots (Spinka, Kosoni, Tass), may be attributed to the preservation of old local traditions. One can see in the polyphonic practice of certain communities (such as Boyan and Vizhnitz), a continuation of polyphonic practice before the rise of Ḥasidism.

Research and Collections

Toward the end of the 19th century, Yoel Engel (1898), Sussmann Kisselgof (1912), and the former Jewish Historical Ethnographic Museum (1912–14) took in Russia the first steps in collecting and transcribing ḥasidic music (as a part of Jewish music). As for Moshe *Beregovski (1927–46), he was mainly devoted to instrumental and wordless vocal genres. The collection of ḥasidic melodies, their analysis and classification in the context of ḥasidic social life and religious thought, has been a major focus of documentation and research work at the Jewish Music Research Center in Jerusalem since its inception in 1964. This recorded material is cataloged at the National Sound Archives (NSA) of the JNUL. Recently some ḥasidic communities felt the need to produce documentation of their own. This led to the establishment of the archives of the Lubavitch, Modzhitz, and Karlin-Stolin heritage including recordings and notations of music as well as comments.

[A. Hajdu and Y. Mazor (2nd ed.)]

BIBLIOGRAPHY: Horodetzky, Ḥasidut; idem, *Leaders of Ḥassidism* (1928); Dubnow, Ḥasidut; idem, in: *Ha-Shiloʾaḥ*, 7 (1901), 314–20; A. Walden, *Shem ha-Gedolim he-Ḥadash* (1864); M. Bodek, *Seder ha-Dorot He-Ḥadash* (1865); A.Z. Zweifel, *Shalom al Yisrael*. 4 vols. (1868–73); S. Shechter, *Studies in Judaism*, 1 (1896), 1–45; A. Markus ("Verus"), *Der Chassidismus* (1901); I. Berger, *Zekhut Yisrael*, 4 vols. (1902–10); M. Ben-Yehezkel (Halpern), in: *Ha-Shiloʾaḥ*, 17–22 (1907–10); idem, *Sefer ha-Maʿasiyyot*, 6 vols. (1968³); S.J. Horowitz, *Ha-Ḥasidut ve-ha-Haskalah* (1909); C. Bloch, *Die Gemeinde der Chassidim: ihr Werden und ihre Lehre* (1920); A. Kahana, *Sefer ha-Ḥasidut* (1922); A.Z. Aescoly, *Le Hassidisme* (1928); idem, in: *Beit Yisrael be-Polin*, 2 (1954), 86–141; Y.A. Kamelhaar, *Dor Deʿah* (1933); T. Ysander, *Studien zum best'schen Hasidismus in seiner religionsgeschichtlichen Sonderart* (1933); Z. Fefer, in: *Sefer ha-Shanah li-Yhudei Polanyah*, 1 (1938), 233–47; Y. Raphael, *Ha-Ḥasidut ve-Ereẓ Yisrael* (1940); idem, *Sefer ha-Ḥasidut* (1955²); Scholem, Mysticism; idem, in: *Zion*, 6 (1941), 89–93; 20 (1955), 73–81; idem, in: *Hagut... S.H. Bergman* (1944), 145–51; idem, in: *Review of Religion*, 14 (1949/50), 115–39; idem, in: *Molad*, 18 (1960), 335–56; idem, in: *Commentary*, 32 (1961), 305–16; I. Tishby, in: *Keneset*, 9 (1945), 238–68; Y.Y. Grunwald, *Toyzent Yor Yidish Leybn in Ungarn* (1945); I. Halpern, *Ha-Aliyyot ha-Rishonot shel ha-Ḥasidim le-Ereẓ Yisrael* (1946); idem, in: *Zion*, 22 (1957), 194–213; M. Buber, *Ḥasidism* (1948); idem, *Origin and Meaning of Hasidism* (1960); A.I. Bromberg, *Mi-Gedolei ha-Ḥasidut*, 24 vols. (1949–69); J.G. Weiss, in: *Zion*, 16 (1951), 46–105 (second pagination); idem, in: *Alei Ayin* (1952), 245–91; idem, in: *Erkhei ha-Yahadut* (1953), 81–90; idem, in: JJS, 4 (1953), 19–29; 8 (1957), 199–213; 9 (1958), 163–92; 11 (1960), 137–55; idem, in: *Tarbiz*, 27 (1957/58), 358–71; idem, in: HUCA, 31 (1960), 137–47; idem, in: *Meḥkarim... Gershom Scholem* (1968), 101–13; E. Steinman, *Beʾer ha-Ḥasidut*, 10 vols. (1951–62); idem, *Garden of Hasidism* (1961); A. Shochat, in: *Zion*, 16 (1951), 30–43; M. Gutman, *Mi-Gibborei ha-Ḥasidut* (1953²); J.S. Minkin, *Romance of Hasidism* (1955²); B. Dinur, *Be-Mifneh ha-Dorot* (1955), 83–227; idem, in: *Zion*, 8–10 (1942–45); H.M. Rabinowicz, *Guide to Hassidism* (1960); idem, *World of Hasidism* (1970); S.H. Dresner, *The Zaddik* (1960); S. Werses, in: *Molad*, 18 (1960), 379–91; A. Wertheim, *Halakhot ve-Halikhot be-Ḥasidut* (1960); H. Zeitlin, *Be-Fardes ha-Ḥasidut ve-ha-Kabbalah* (1960); Y.L. Maimon (ed.), *Sefer ha-Besht* (1960); R. Mahler, *Ha-Ḥasidut ve-ha-Haskalah* (1961); A. Rubinstein, in: *Areshet*, 3 (1961), 193–230; idem, in: KS, 38 (1962/63), 263–72, 415–24; 39 (1963/64), 117–36; idem, in: *Tarbiz*, 35 (1965/66), 174–91; idem, in: *Sefer ha-Shana shel Bar-Ilan*, 4–5 (1967), 324–39; S. Poll, *Hasidic Community of Williamsburg* (1962); L.I. Newman, *Hasidic Anthology* (1963); S. Federbush (ed.), *Ha-Ḥasidut ve-Ẓiyyon* (1963); A. Yaari, in: KS, 39 (1963/64), 249–72, 394–407, 552–62; M.A. Lipschitz, *Faith of a Hassid* (1967); R.S. Uffenheimer, *Ha-Ḥasidut ke-Mistikah* (1968), with Eng. summary; S. Ettinger, *Toledot Yisrael ba-Et ha-Ḥadasha*, ed. by H.H. Ben-Sasson (1969), index s.v. *Ḥasidim and Ḥasidut*; M. Wilensky, *Ḥasidim u-Mitnaggedim* (1970); W.Z. Rabinowitsch, *Lithuanian Ḥasidism* (1970). **ADD. BIBLIOGRAPHY:** M. Altschuler, *The Messianic Secret of Hasidism* (Heb., 2002); J. Dan, *Jewish Mysticism*, vol. 3: *The Modern Times* (1999); idem, *The Hasidic Story – Its History and Development* (Heb., 1975); R. Elior "The Affinity between Kabbalah and Hasidism – Continuity or Changes," in: *Ninth World Congress of Jewish Studies Division C* (1986), 107–14 (Heb.); idem, *The Paradoxical Ascent to God*, tr. Jeffrey Green (1993); idem, *The Theory of Divinity of Hasidut Habad, Second Generation* (Heb., 1982); Y. Elstein, *The Ecstasy Story in Hasidic Literature* (Heb., 1998); Z. Gries, *The Book in Early Hasidism* (Heb., 1992); M. Idel, *Hasidism: Between Ecstasy and Magic* (1995); L. Jacobs, *Hasidic Prayer* (1978); M. *Uniter of Heaven and Earth, Rabbi Meshullam Feibush of Zbarazh and the Rise of Hasidism in Eastern Galicia* (1998); N. *Communicating the Infinite: The Emergence of the Habad School* (1990); S. Magid, *Hasidism on the Margin, Reconciliation, Antinomianism and Messianism in Izbica/Radzin Hasidism* (2003); R. Margolin, *The Human Temple, Religious Interiorization and the Inner Life in Early Hasidism* (Heb., 2004); H. Pedaya, "The Mystical Experience and the Religious World in Hasidism," in: *Daat*, 55 (2005), 73–108 (Heb.); M. Piekarz, *Ideological Trends of Hasidism in Poland During the Interwar Period and the Holocaust* (1990); idem, *Studies in Braslav Hasidism* (Heb., 1995); idem, *The Beginning of Hasidism – Ideological Trends in Derush and Musar Literature* (Heb., 1978); idem, "The Devekuth as Reflecting the Socio-Religious Character of the Hasidic Movement," *Daat*, 24 (1990), 127–44 (Heb.); A. Rapoport-Albert, "God and the Zaddik as the Two Focal Points of Hasidic Worship," in: *History of Religions*, 18 (1979), 296–325; idem, "The Hasidic Movement," in: *Zion*, 55 (1990), 183–245 (Heb.); idem (ed.), *Hasidism Reappraised* (1996); A. Rubinstein (ed.), *Studies in Hasidism* (Heb., 1977); I. Tourov, "Hasidism and Christianity of the Eastern Territory of the Polish-Lithuanian Commonwealth: Possible Contacts and Mutual Influences," in: *Kabbalah*, 10 (2004), 73–105; J. Weiss, *Studies in Eastern European Jewish Mysticism* (1985). WOMAN AND HASIDISM: D. Biale, *Eros and the Jews* (1992); A. Rapoport-Albert. "On Women in Hasidism...," in: A. Rapoport-Albert and S. Zipperstein (eds.), *Jewish History* (1988),

495–525; N. Deutsch, *The Maiden of Ludmir* (2003); E. Taitz, S. Henry, and C. Tallan, *The JPS Guide to Jewish Women* (2003); J. Belcove-Shalin. *New World Hasidism* (1994); L. Davidman, *Tradition in a Rootless World* (1991); S.Fishkoff, *The Rebbe's Army* (2002); D. Kaufman, *Rachel's Daughters* (1991); S. Levine. *Mystics, Mavericks and Merrymakers* (2004); B. Morris. *Lubavitcher Women in America* (1998). MUSICAL TRADITION: Sendrey, Music, nos. 2700–30, 6913, 7414, 7824, 7995, 8024, 9121, 9129, 9138–39, 9176, 9189, 9404–79, 9536; A.Z. Idelsohn, *Thesaurus of Hebrew Oriental Melodies*, 10 (1932); M.S. Geshuri (ed.), *La-Ḥasidim Mizmor* (1936), incl. bibl.; idem, *Neginah ve-Ḥasidut be-Veit Kuzmir u-Venoteha* (1952); idem, *Ha-Niggun ve-ha-Rikkud be-Ḥasidut*, 3 vols. (1956–59); H. Mayerowitsch, *Oneg Shabbos, Anthology of Ancient Hebrew Table Songs (Zemiroth)* (1937); V. Pasternak, *Songs of the Chassidim* (1968); J. Stutschewsky (ed.), *Rikkudei Ḥasidim* (1947); idem, *Niggunei Ḥasidim*, nos. 1–7 (1944–46); idem, *Me'ah ve-Esrim Niggunei Ḥasidim* (1950); idem, *Niggunim Ḥasiydyyim, Shabbat* (1970); S.Y.E. Taub, *Kunteres Ma'amarim (Kunteres Tiferet Yisrael)*, nos. 1–8 (1941–48), includes music supplement in each issue; J. Talmud, *Rikkudei Ḥasidim Yisre'eliyyim* (1956); M. Unger, *Khasides un Yontev* (1958); idem, *Di Khasidishe Velt* (1955); C. Vinaver, *Anthology of Jewish Music* (1953); S. Zalmanov (ed.), *Sefer ha-Niggunim* (1949).

Musical Examples

Example 1. Ḥabad. Nie Zhuristi Khloptsi. *"Rejoicing" and dance niggun for a devotional gathering (hitva'adut) and festive occasions, derived from a Ukrainian song. Said to have been sung by the followers of the "Middle Admor," Dov Ber b. Shneur Zalman of Lyady, on their pilgrimages to his court. The second and third sections are probably an original ḥasidic development of the basic tune. This is also sung to a Yiddish text,* Gits nit kayn Nekhten. *Recorded by Y. Mazor at Kefar Ḥabad, 1969 (Jerusalem,* J.N.U.L.*, National Sound Archives, Yc 121/16–17). Transcription Y. Mazor.*

Example 2. Kalov. Vald, Vald, *attributed to R. Isaac of Kalov. Present distribution not ascertained. Recorded by Y. Mazor in Jerusalem, 1967, from a descendant of a family of Zhikiv Hasidim (Jerusalem, Israel Institute for Sacred Music, M72/943). Transcription Y. Mazor. R. Isaac is said to have taken the tune from a shepherd's love song, changing the words in the second part to demonstrate the allegorical meaning: "Forest (Diaspora), how enormous thou art / Rose /*(Shekhinah)*, how far thou art./ Were the forest (Diaspora) not so great/then were the rose / *(Shekhinah)* not so far.*

Example 3. Dance Nigun. *Sung by Gur and Modzhitz Hasidim. Recorded by Y. Mazor, at Jerusalem 1966, from Rahmistrovka Hasid and his sons (Jerusalem,* J.N.U.L.*, National Sound Archives, Y 3678/1). Transcription Y. Mazor.*

Example 4. Vizhnitz. Part from Shira la-Shem *("Song to the Lord") for choir, sung at devotional gatherings. Recorded by Y. Mazor, at the wedding of the Rebbe's son, Bene-Berak, 1976 (Jerusalem, J.N.U.L., National Sound Archives, Yc 1007/8). Transcription Y. Mazor.*

Example 5. Ḥabad. Hitva'adut *(gathering)* niggun *for devotional gatherings and festive occasions. Transcribed by E. Avitzur from S. Zalmanoff, Jerusalem 1980. From S. Zalmanoff (ed.)* Sefer ha-Niggunim, *3rd volume, 1980.*

Example 6. Karlin. Textless niggun, *sometimes also sung to the words of* Yah Ekhesor. *Believed to be old. Recorded by Y. Mazor in Jerusalem, 1970, when sung at a Karlin wedding before the entry of the bridegroom (Jerusalem, Israel Institute for Sacred Music, M74/962). Transcription A. Hajdu.*

Example 7. Ḥabad. Avinu Malkenu *("Our Father, our King"),* niggun *for a devotional gathering, sometimes also sung during the* Avinu Malkenu *prayer. Attributed to R. Shneur Zalman of Lyady. From S. Zalmonoff (ed.),* Sefer ha-Niggunim, *1949.*

Example 8. Pan-ḥasidic. Dance niggun, *of unknown provenance, nonspecific in function. Recorded by Y. Mazor in Bene-Berak, 1957, as played by a Jerusalem* klezmer *group (Jerusalem, Israel Institute for Sacred Music, M39/490). Transcription A. Hajdu.*

Example 9. Ḥabad. "Rejoicing" and dance niggun *for a devotional gatherings and festive occasions. Recorded by Y. Mazor at Kefar Ḥabad, 1967, on the "Feast of redemption" (19th Kislev), at the devotional meeting in the yeshivah (Jerusalem, Israel Institute for Sacred Music, M33/514). Transcription A. Hajdu.*

Example 10. "Rejoicing" niggun *for various occasions. Sometimes sung to the text* Ashrenu mah tov helkenu *("Blessed are we, how goodly is our portion"). From S. Zalmonoff (ed.),* Sefer ha-Niggunim, *1949.*

Example 11. Karlin. Opening niggun *for the* hakkafot. *At present sung also in many other ḥasidic communities. Recorded by Y. Mazor, In the* Yeshivat ha-Matmidim, *Jerusalem on Simhat Torah night 1966 (Jerusalem, Israel Institute for Sacred Music, M33/514). Transcription A. Hajdu. In Israel the tune was used by the pioneers of the Fourth Aliyah (1924–1931) as a wordless dance-song, and adapted by M. Ravina to the text of* Kol Dikhfin *in the Passover* seder.

HASKALAH (Heb. הַשְׂכָּלָה), Hebrew term for the Enlightenment movement and ideology which began within Jewish society in the 1770s. An adherent of Haskalah became known as a *maskil* (pl. *maskilim*). The movement continued to be influential and spread, with fluctuations, until the early 1880s. Haskalah had its roots in the general Enlightenment movement in Europe of the 18th century but the specific conditions and problems of Jewish society in the period, and hence the objectives to which Haskalah aspired in particular, all largely differed from those of the general Enlightenment movement. Haskalah continued along new and more radical lines the old contention upheld by the Maimonidean party in the *Maimonidean Controversy that secular studies should be recognized as a legitimate part of the curriculum in the education of a Jew. For Jewish society in Central Europe, and even more so in Eastern Europe, this demand conflicted with the deeply ingrained ideal of Torah study that left no place for other subjects. As in medieval times, secular studies were also rejected as tending to alienate youth from the observance of the precepts and even from loyalty to Judaism.

The Haskalah movement contributed toward *assimilation in language, dress, and manners by condemning Jewish feelings of alienation in the **galut* and fostering loyalty toward the modern centralized state. It regarded this assimilation as a precondition to and integral element in *emancipation, which Haskalah upheld as an objective. The *maskilim* also advocated the productivization of Jewish occupation through entering *crafts and *agriculture. The emphasis placed on these common objectives naturally varied within Jewish society in different countries and with changing conditions. Greater emphasis was placed on assimilation, and it became more widespread in Western and Central Europe than in Eastern Europe. Here the struggle for secular education and productivization was continuous and strong (see also Haskalah in Russia, below).

Beginning and Background of Haskalah

Moses *Mendelssohn is generally considered to be the originator of the Haskalah movement (the "father of the Haskalah"). However, this opinion has to be corrected in that a desire for secular education had already been evinced among the preceding generation of German Jews, and some individual Jews in Poland and Lithuania, during the 1740s. Knowledge of European languages could be found among members of the upper strata of Jewish society there many years before. Mendelssohn considered that a Jewish translation of the Bible into German was "a first step toward culture" for Jews. It seems, however, that he was doubtful about encouraging the spread of Haskalah among Jewry. When in the early 1780s it was proposed to translate certain works into Hebrew so as to lead the Jewish people to abandon "its ignorance and the opposition to every sensible reform," Mendelssohn "thought that any enterprise of this sort would indeed not be harmful, but neither would it be very beneficial" (see Solomon Maimon, *An Autobiography* (1947; repr. 1967), 97). Mendelssohn was opposed to *education of Jewish and non-Jewish children together; he was also against the *Toleranzpatent* issued by Emperor Joseph II, fearing that the method of education proposed there would lead Jews to *apostasy.

The birth and growth of the Haskalah movement were considerably facilitated by the policies of the absolutist regimes of Germany, Austria, and Russia during the 18th century, which deprived the Jewish community leadership of its coercive authority, such as exercise of the right of *herem* ("ban"). Large-scale commercial transactions undertaken by the *Court Jews at this time brought the upper classes of Jewish society in contact with non-Jewish circles, and as a result there formed a section of the Jewish community which diverged from the traditional way of life. Others open to influence by Haskalah were individual Jews, frequently Jewish peddlers who often migrated to new localities without a communal organization or rabbis, where the individual was consequently left to himself.

Haskalah had a positive impact on the status of Jewish women. Many wealthy Jews hired tutors to teach their daughters modern European languages and other accomplishments. Elite women who acquired German and French language and culture played a significant role in transmitting the ideas and literature of the Enlightenment into the Jewish community. In traditional Jewish society girls had received only minimal religious training; now, instruction in music and modern languages together with exposure to a new world of secular novels, poetry, and plays distanced young women from brothers and husbands whose lives were restricted narrowly to commerce and finance. It is not surprising that many of these wealthy and accomplished women found success in a *salon society where gentiles and Jews mixed socially. Sometimes, these social contacts led to divorces from Jewish husbands, conversions to Christianity, and marriage to gentile suitors, often from the nobility. The number of Jewish women who followed this course was small and their motives in doing so were complex. However, some of the women who abandoned Judaism were integrated into the dominant upper-class culture and society. In making the choices they did these women experienced "at an early date and in a gender-specific way the basic conflict between group loyalty and individual emancipation that would torment so many European Jews in the two centuries to follow" (Hertz, *Jewish High Society*, 198).

The experience of the "salon Jewesses" was not typical for most Western and Central European Jewish women as Haskalah rapidly transformed Jewish life. Generally, gender tended to limit the assimilation of Jewish women since most had few contacts with the non-Jewish world. Confined to the domestic scene, restricted in their educational opportunities, and prevented from participating in the public realms of economic and civic life, women's progress to integration was halting and incomplete in comparison to Jewish men. Nevertheless, Haskalah had a far reaching impact on gender relations, following the lead of Mendelssohn, himself, who opposed arranged marriages and advocated love matches (Biale, *Eros and the Jews*, 153–58).

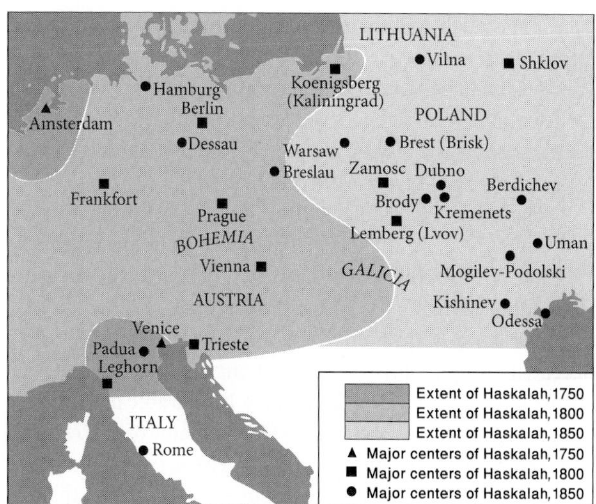

The spread and main centers of the Haskalah in Europe. From H.H. Ben-Sasson (ed.), History of the Jewish People, *Tel Aviv, 1969.*

Haskalah operated as an active trend within German Jewry in the space of one generation. Its influence first spread in *Galicia (which passed to Austria with the partition of Poland) and later in Lithuania and other provinces of the Russian *Pale of Settlement.

There were also countries where attitudes similar to those adopted by the Haskalah circles in Germany had been manifest among Jews earlier, where they were unaccompanied by disintegration of Jewish tradition. In Italy, men who had studied medicine and were well acquainted with philosophy and the classics, as well as Christian theological literature, held rabbinical positions. The prestige won by Jewish physicians of note was generally considered an asset and encouragement to the Jewish community (see Isaac Cantarini, *Et Keẓ* (Amsterdam, 1710) 1b). In Italy also, study of Kabbalah was compatible with secular studies (see Jacob Frances, in: I. Frances, *Metek Sefatayim*, ed. by H. Brody (1892), 74; Moses Hayyim *Luzzatto).

Early stirrings of a positive appreciation of secular culture among Jews had even appeared in Germany by the first half of the 18th century and were manifest earlier among some traditional scholars and leaders like *Tobias b. Moses Cohn the physician, author of *Ma'aseh Tuviyyah*, Jonathan *Eybeschuetz, or Jacob *Emden. More positive and active participation in general culture still combined with a traditional outlook is reflected in Israel *Zamosc and Aaron Elias Gomperz, who wrote his *Ma'amar ha-Madda* (1765) to point out the importance of the sciences (see also below).

The specific approach characterizing Haskalah was expressed by those to whom secular culture and philosophy became a central value which raises man to the highest spiritual level, possibly not below that of religious meditation, and for whom it symbolized the sublime aspect of man, who by his initiative can achieve progress in and dominate nature. They considered that such culture would elevate both the human and social stature of the Jew. The new spirit prompted a number of Haskalah writers to compose works popularizing science in Hebrew, like Mordecai Gumpel b. Judah Leib Schnaber (d. 1797; published under the name Marcus George Levisohn). Articles on natural sciences were published in the first Hebrew secular monthly *Ha-Me'assef* (see below) by Baruch Lindau (1759–1849) and Aaron Wolfsohn Halle.

Haskalah, like its parent the European Enlightenment movement, was rationalistic. It accepted only one truth: the rational-philosophical truth in which reason is the measure of all things. During the 1740s some of the youth had already begun to study Maimonides' *Guide of the Perplexed*. Haskalah accepted Enlightenment *Deism, giving it a specifically Jewish turn. Gotthold Ephraim *Lessing, in the parable of the Three Rings in *Nathan der Weise*, rejected the claim of any religion to represent the absolute truth. Mendelssohn held that there was nothing in the Jewish faith opposed to reason and that the revelation on Mount Sinai did not take place to impart faith but to give laws to a nation, because faith cannot be achieved by decree, while the laws which were given on that occasion were designed to serve as the laws of a unique Jewish theocratic state. Mendelssohn thus attempted to remove Judaism from the struggle between Enlightenment and revealed religion. The attitude of such Jews toward tradition underwent a radical change. The conception of Divine Providence in favor of Israel, the belief in the election of Israel, and the religious reasons advanced for the exile of Israel were weakened and the anticipation of Israel's future redemption began to wane.

While Mendelssohn and Naphtali Herz *Wessely, the pioneer of Haskalah education, did not doubt the sanctity and the authority of the Oral Law, they tried to demote the study of Talmud from its supreme position in Jewish education. Mendelssohn, in his letter to Naphtali Herz *Homberg, stressed the importance of actions and the study of the Bible in order to preserve the society of "true theists" (i.e., Judaism), while the Talmud is not mentioned there at all. This anti-talmudic mood was widespread. Study of the Talmud was not included in the curriculum of the "Free School" founded in Berlin in 1778 (see below). Wessely expressed this approach in the words: "We were not all created to become talmudists." Representing the most radical wing of Haskalah, David *Friedlaender was openly glad that the yeshivot were declining. The Talmud was also criticized in Russia. Abraham *Buchner, a teacher in the rabbinical seminary of Warsaw, even wrote a book entitled *Der Talmud in seiner Nichtigkeit* ("The Talmud in its Emptiness," 2 vols., 1848). In Galicia, Joshua Heschel *Schorr claimed that although the Talmud was historically important, its legal decisions were outdated socially and spiritually and hence no longer binding. Later Moses Leib *Lilienblum, too, considered the Talmud important but demanded from the rabbis, in the name of the "spirit of life," reform in *halakhah*.

In Western Europe and the German states, especially the northern German states, observance of *halakhah* was already being neglected before the advent of the Haskalah movement. Mendelssohn reacted sharply against the tendency to ignore the burden of the precepts found among persons close to him, some of whom even denied Divine Revelation to Moses. Among the *maskilim* who frequented Mendelssohn's home there were, according to Solomon Dubno, "a group of men who were to be suspected of having discarded the yoke of the Torah." This negation of halakhic precepts, which was often coupled with contempt toward the whole of Judaism, also served as a factor leading to mass apostasy among the Jewish bourgeoisie of *Berlin and its surroundings.

Linguistic Assimilation

Linguistic assimilation increasingly became a hallmark of Haskalah. In Germany, as well as in Alsace-Lorraine, wealthy Jews had begun to have their children taught German and French at the close of the 17th century to facilitate both their business and social contacts with non-Jews. French became the language of the "elite" in Jewish circles, where the reading of general literature became widespread. In the 1780s there were "the daughters of Israel, who are all able to speak the language of the gentiles with eloquence, but cannot converse in Yiddish" (*Ha-Me'assef* (1786), 139). By the 1790s the younger generation of the Jewish bourgeoisie of Berlin had begun to adopt German as their spoken language. A negative attitude toward Yiddish developed. German writers had claimed in the past that the Jews had been able to deceive non-Jews by the use of Yiddish in business transactions, and as a result decrees had been issued compelling Jews to write their commercial documents and keep their books in German.

Apparently Mendelssohn was influenced by these claims and even thought that Yiddish was ridiculous, ungrammatical, and a cause of moral corruption. He initiated translation of the Pentateuch into German, in order to induce Jews to use this language (see *Bible: Translations, German). Wessely approved wholeheartedly of the measures which Joseph II introduced against the use of Yiddish (*Ha-Me'assef* (1784), 178). David Friedlaender called for the removal of Yiddish as the language of instruction in the *heder* and Jewish schools; in his opinion the use of Yiddish was responsible for unethical conduct and corruption of religion. He translated the prayers into German, "the language spoken by the inhabitants of these regions," because the Yiddish translations "were repulsive to the reader in their style and contents" (*Ha-Me'assef* (1786), 139). The *maskil* Zalkind *Hourwitz also suggested that the Jews be prohibited from employing either Yiddish or Hebrew for bookkeeping and business contracts, not only for transactions between Jews and Christians but also between Jews themselves, in order to prevent fraud.

A move against Yiddish in favor of the "mother tongue" (in this case, Dutch) was initiated by the *maskilim* in the *Netherlands during the period of French rule there. A Jewish weekly began to appear in Dutch in 1806. In 1808 a society was formed in Amsterdam for translation of the Bible and the prayer book into Dutch, as well as for the publication of textbooks in Hebrew and Dutch, the establishment of new schools, and the training of suitable teachers for them.

King Louis Bonaparte issued a decree in February 1809, in force from Jan. 1, 1811, prohibiting the use of Yiddish in documents. Sermons in the synagogues were to be delivered in Dutch, while Dutch was to be the language of instruction for Jewish youth. The *consistory of the Netherlands ordered that notices in the synagogues be published in Dutch only, and all correspondence between the communities and the consistory was to be conducted in Dutch only. In France, the *maskilim* encountered no difficulties in their struggle against Yiddish in favor of French. French had been widely spoken among Jews before the Haskalah period. *Berr Isaac Berr preferred Mendelssohn's German translation of the Pentateuch to the one existing in Yiddish until a proper Jewish-French translation had been made. In Hungary, the *maskilim* were active in substituting Hungarian for the Yiddish vernacular during the 1840s. Hungarian became the language of instruction in the Jewish schools of several communities and preachers even began to employ this language in synagogues.

Development of Hebrew

Hebrew was not only of central importance to people like Jacob Emden and Jonathan Eybeschuetz, who apparently wished that Jews should be able to speak fluent Hebrew; Mendelssohn also considered the Hebrew language a national treasure. In his *Kohelet Musar*, 3 issues (1750), he called for an extension of its frontiers, on the example of other living languages. Cultivation of Hebrew was also one of the aims of the *Biur*, the commentary on the Pentateuch initiated by Mendelssohn. For these scholars Hebrew meant biblical Hebrew. Study of the Bible held a central position in the educational program of the Haskalah movement, whereas both the content of the Talmud and even more so the style of Hebrew used in the 18th century, and by earlier Ashkenazi rabbis, drove Haskalah scholars to reject the post-biblical layers in the Hebrew language. The interest shown by German gentile scholars in the Bible and its language also contributed to a certain extent to the preference of Haskalah circles for biblical Hebrew, though from the beginning some voices expressed reservations toward this extremist approach (see also *Ha-Me'assef* (1784), 185).

Ha-Me'assef served as the organ of the Haskalah in its Hebrew aspect. It was published regularly between 1783 and 1790, with difficulties until 1797, and revived from 1809 to 1811. It was published by the Doreshei Leshon Ever ("Friends of the Hebrew Language") in Koenigsberg founded in 1783, and renamed in 1786 Shoharei ha-Tov ve-ha-Tushiyyah ve-Doreshei Leshon Ever ("Seekers of Good and Wisdom and Friends of the Hebrew Language"). Even *Ha-Me'assef* published articles in German; its publication ceased through extreme assimilation of the adherents of Haskalah, in particular in Germany and Austria. German attracted younger and progressive circles. The literary contribution by the so-called **Me'assefim* generation was an important stage in the development of Hebrew language and literature. Hebrew became a vehicle for secular and professional scientific expression. *Maskilim* also contributed much to research in grammar and purity of expression. In Eastern Europe Hebrew remained the language of Haskalah literature for a longer period, appealing to a much wider public with deeper roots in Jewish culture than in Central and Western Europe. The *maskilim* there further developed and enlivened Hebrew (see Haskalah in Russia, below).

Education

The adherents of Haskalah shared the rationalist belief in the boundless efficacy of a rational education. They therefore turned to a change in the curriculum and methods of teaching as the main means of shaping a new mode of Jewish life. The first school to be guided by this ideal was founded in Berlin in 1778 and named both Freischule ("Free School") and Hinnukh Ne'arim ("Youth Education"). It was primarily designed for children of the poor and was without fee. The curriculum included study of German and French, arithmetic, geography, history, natural sciences, art, some Bible studies, and Hebrew. The school had a revolutionary effect on Jewish education, for it heralded the transfer of the center of gravity from Jewish studies to general subjects. The school was successful from the beginning; only half of its 70 first pupils came from poor homes. Wessely's welcome of Joseph II's educational proposals for Jews (*Divrei Shalom ve-Emet*, 4 pts. (1782–85)) and his call to the Jews of Austria to establish schools on this pattern were an outcome both of the success of the Freischule as well as the fear that if Jews themselves did not take the initiative, Jewish children would be compelled to attend the state schools. In this work Wessely set out both a detailed program and a basic philosophy for Haskalah education. German Jews of the upper social strata were ready for this program, though it aroused much rabbinical opposition, influenced from outside Germany.

In the same year (1785), the bishop of Mainz admitted 19 Jewish boys to the general school without difficulties. Many programs for Haskalah education were proposed, some drawing on the experience of Italian Jewish and Sephardi schools, whose curricula were considered near to Haskalah aims. The question of education was widely discussed in *Ha-Me'assef*. Some radical *maskilim* demanded that German and arithmetic should be taught to begin with and Hebrew reading and writing be added at a later stage. David Friedlaender sought to introduce German as the language of instruction in all subjects and the teaching of selected chapters of the Bible of ethical value to both boys and girls. In regard to religious instruction, he also suggested that only the ethical precepts be taught.

The *maskilim*, who despised the old-style Polish teachers, the *melammedim*, whom they considered uncouth and uncultured, were not satisfied with criticism alone. On their initiative new schools sprang up in Berlin, Dessau, and Frankfurt on the Main, among other places, in which Hebrew and general studies were taught. A limited number of hours were usually devoted to Hebrew studies, while study of the Talmud was almost completely abandoned. Several educators wrote textbooks where the educational aims of the Haskalah movement found expression. The first to be written were the *Toledot*

Yisrael (Prague, 1796), on Jewish history by Peter *Beer; *Imrei Shefer* (Vienna, 1816) and *Bne-Zion* (Ger., *ibid.*, 1812), religious and moral readers for young people by Naphtali Herz Homberg. In 1807 a confirmation ceremony for boys in German, in imitation of the Christian custom, was introduced in the school at Wolfenbuettel, whence it spread to the other Jewish schools in Germany.

The influence of Haskalah also penetrated to Orthodox circles who were compelled to respond to the demands of the times. Even R. Ezekiel *Landau agreed that it was necessary "to know language and writing"; although "Torah is the main thing," "one should grasp both." R. *David Tevele of Lissa conceded to the emperor's request "to teach the children to speak and write the German language for an hour or two." The first "integral" schools (in which Jewish and general subjects were taught) were opened by the Orthodox in Halberstadt and Hamburg (see also Samson Raphael *Hirsch; *Neo-Orthodoxy).

Haskalah brought a considerable change in the education of girls. The daughters of the wealthy elite, who generally studied under private teachers, were taught European languages and music and played an important role in introducing European culture and Enlightenment ideas into Jewish life. The *maskilim* also began to show concern for the education of the daughters of the poor. Schools for girls were established in the 1790s in Breslau, Dessau, Koenigsberg, and Hamburg. The curriculum generally included some Hebrew, German, the fundamentals of religion and ethics, prayers, and arithmetic; there were also schools where the writing of Yiddish, handiwork, art, and singing were taught.

Schools with curricula based on the educational ideals of Haskalah were also established in France and other Western European countries. On the example of the "integral" schools in Germany, similar schools were also founded in East European countries. In 1813 a school was founded by Josef *Perl in Tarnopol (Galicia), where in addition to Bible, Mishnah, *Gemara*, and Hebrew grammar, the subjects of Polish, French, arithmetic, history, and geography were also taught; the language of instruction was German and there were also classes for girls. A similar school was established in Lvov in 1845. In Warsaw, three schools in which the language of instruction was Polish were established by Jacob *Tugendhold in 1819; two schools for girls were also established here.

With the foundation of the new schools, the problem of training teachers arose. Isaac *Euchel, David Friedlaender, and Judah Loeb *Jeiteles were among the first *maskilim* to raise this problem. Special institutions were established, but on many occasions the rabbinical seminaries also served this purpose. The first teachers' training seminary was opened in Kassel in 1810 by the consistory of the kingdom of Westphalia, followed by others through the first half of the 19th century. A seminary for teachers and rabbis was opened in Amsterdam in 1836 and a seminary for teachers in Budapest in 1857. Secondary schools did not develop anywhere. Only the Philanthropin school at Frankfurt extended its curriculum in 1813 to include a secondary science-orientated section providing six years' studies after the four years of elementary classes. Some private institutions of a commercial-science orientation were established in Berlin. Those who went on to secondary studies generally attended non-Jewish institutions.

GOVERNMENT INTERVENTION IN JEWISH EDUCATION. The educational ideals of Haskalah largely coincided with the aims set out for "improvement of the Jews" (see *emancipation) and their education as conceived by "enlightened" absolutist rulers. Typical were the edicts issued by Joseph II for the Jews of Bohemia (1781), Moravia (1782), Hungary (1783), and Galicia (1789). The Jews were ordered to establish "normal" schools or to send their children to the state schools; Jews were also permitted to enter secondary schools and universities. Anyone who studied Talmud before completing the school curriculum was liable to be sentenced to a term of imprisonment; marriage was prohibited without a certificate of school attendance.

As a result of these edicts, 42 schools were opened in Moravian communities by 1784, 25 in Bohemia by 1787, and about 30 in Hungary by the end of the 1780s. In Galicia 104 schools were established but were closed down in 1806 during the period of reaction for fear of the "harmful" influence of the "anti-religious" Jewish teachers. Naphtali Herz Homberg was appointed to supervise the program in Galicia. In most German states the process of government intervention in the education of the Jews occurred at the beginning of the 19th century. Usually the Jews were ordered to establish secular schools for the education of their children or to send them to the general schools. There were also some states in Germany which at first did not authorize the Jews to establish separate schools and preferred that education be given to the Jewish children in the *ḥeder* or the public schools. In Prussia the general schools were opened to Jewish children in 1803; until 1847 the separate Jewish schools were recognized only as private schools. The trend toward Germanization was especially marked among the large Jewish population in the Polish region of former *Great Poland.

Some states also intervened in regard to yeshivot. They began to demand that the rabbis should have a general education and especially instruction in philosophy. In 1820 Francis I of Austria issued a decree obliging rabbis to acquire secular education and employ the language of the country in prayers and sermons. A rabbinical seminary, the first of its kind was opened in Padua in 1829. This was followed up in many states and in different forms through the first half of the 19th century (see: *Rabbinical Seminaries).

The advocates of "improvement of the Jews" (see *emancipation; C.W. von *Dohm) considered the restructuring of their occupations from moneylending and trade to productivization through taking up crafts and agriculture to be an essential element in and precondition for accomplishing both betterment of their character and their position. In the main the *maskilim* accepted this social and economic program as well as the criticism of Jewish life it implied. They hoped that productivization would bring a moral regeneration as well as change the image of the Jew for enlightened Christians. In the new schools established by the *maskilim* in Germany (see above), instruction in crafts was also introduced and some also took care that their graduates should be apprenticed to Christian craftsmen. In various German states, societies to care for the interests of Jewish apprentices were organized. In Berlin a society for the Promotion of Industry was established in 1812 following the emancipation law issued in Prussia that year. Its objective was "to awaken and promote as much as possible the creative spirit among members of the Jewish religion by means of support and encouragement" and to "courageously refute the old-established opinion that we supposedly have an exclusive tendency to commerce" (see also *Joseph II; *Crafts). Naphtali Herz Homberg advocated manual work which he considered was necessary from the moral as well as economic aspect. Homberg based his opinion on sayings of the rabbis in the Talmud in praise of labor and condemned the prevailing attitude of contempt toward the "worker" within Jewish society. Like Mendelssohn, he did not completely reject commerce from the aspect of its utility for society, but considered that the creativity of manual labor surpassed commerce from the aspect of social morality. Phinehas Elijah *Hurwitz complained that "the majority of our people do not want their sons to be taught crafts because they say with pride and arrogance that the occupation of crafts is shameful for us." He considered that commerce contributed to hatred of the Jews and to the allegation widespread among non-Jews that the Talmud teaches the Jews how to deceive them.

Cooperating with the authorities of the enlightened absolutist states and other regimes to promote general education and productivization among Jews, with the majority agreeing on the need for improvement of the Jews and the desirability of their assimilation, Haskalah circles found it natural to emphasize the complete loyalty which Jews acknowledged to the secular rulers as their protectors, and to the country and state as the framework for their security of life and autonomy. The *maskilim* did not content themselves with the traditional prayers for the king. Laudatory poems were written in honor of Frederick the Great of Prussia, noted for his "love" of the Jews. The Austrian emperor, Joseph II, was also honored with enthusiastic poems of praise and thanksgiving. Their enthusiasm for reform led a number of *maskilim* to advise the authorities how to "improve" the Jews without paying attention to whether these improvements were desired by them or not. Some collaborated with the authorities and bypassed the regular heads of the Orthodox communities not hesitating to slander them, a method used by Naphtali Herz Homberg and his staff of teachers in Galicia.

Trends in Ideology

An ahistoric stand, inclination to assimilation, and desire for emancipation helped to erode messianic hopes in Jewish society, at the close of the 17th and the first half of the 18th century, a trend apparent in Amsterdam, Italy, and Germany. The general anti-messianic position taken by *maskilim* was aided by the failure of the *Shabbetai Zevi movement. Jacob Emden quoted Jonathan Eybeschuetz as having preached that the main achievement of the Messiah for the Jews would be that "they would find clemency among the nations" – a traditional expression for attainment of a better legal and social status. The messianism of Jacob *Frank was oriented to nihilistic religious experience and to the conditions of contemporary Jewish existence in Poland. Some have regarded these attitudes as the catalysts of the anti-halakhic movement and the weakening of messianic hopes in Haskalah. Mendelssohn adhered in principle to the messianic hope, though he considered that it did not have "any influence on our civic behavior" – at least not in places where "they have treated the Jews with tolerance"; in his view the redemption would come through the Divine Will alone, though he once gave his opinion that the return of the Jewish people to Erez Israel could be a political-secular event, during a world war. A few *maskilim*, according to Mordecai Schnaber, equated the Messiah with the reign of universal peace and toleration. Zalkind Hourwitz in his *Apologie des Juifs* (Paris, 1789) thought like Mendelssohn that the effect of messianic faith on the actual behavior of Jews was similar to the influence of the certainty of death on human activity; "this does not prevent them… from building, sowing, and planting in every place where they are permitted to do so."

After emancipation was attained a further weakening of messianic faith set in. When latter-day *maskilim* began to combine Haskalah ideology with a nationalist Jewish attitude their anti-messianic stand became a starting point for aspirations for redemption by natural agency (see *Hibbat Zion; *Zionism). Mendelssohn, however, regarded the Torah as a kind of divine legislation intended for the Jewish society and state only; but he saw this type of Jewish unity as a society of theists; nationalism per se was absent in his theory regarding the Jews.

Many *maskilim* identified themselves emotionally and expressly as "Germans." In his German writings, Mendelssohn repeatedly uses the phrase "we Germans," and he criticized use of the expression "Germans and Jews" instead of "Christians and Jews" by Johann David *Michaelis. After Jewish emancipation had been attained in France in 1791, Berr Isaac Berr proclaimed: "By Divine Mercy and the government of the people, we have now become not only men, not only citizens, but also Frenchmen." The *Assembly of Jewish Notables convened by Napoleon in 1806 coined the term "Frenchmen of the Mosaic religion." It also declared that "the Jews are no longer a nation" and that "France is our fatherland." From 1807 the appellation "*israélite*" in France (in German "*Israelit*") also spread to the German states. The change expressed trends to assimilation as well as a tendency to efface former appellations for Jews that had become connected with an odious image. Both fitted in with Haskalah ideology.

Haskalah ideology was one of the foundations of the *Reform movement in the Jewish religion. The idea of reform had already been conceived by David Friedlaender in 1799. Through his influence the first steps in reform were taken by Israel *Jacobson, in the state of Westphalia. Friedlaender himself began to introduce reform in religion in Berlin after the Jews of Prussia had obtained their emancipation in 1812. He called for exclusion from the prayer book of all prayers for the return to Zion and the dirges on the destruction of the Temple, and demanded that prayers be recited in German; with this he also desired that the "society of true theists," after the expression of Mendelssohn, continue to exist. Haskalah ideology was also the basis for the efforts and achievements of the founders of the *Wissenschaft des Judentums in 1819 (see also Zacharias *Frankel; Abraham *Geiger; Marcus *Jost; Moritz *Steinschneider; Solomon Judah *Rapoport; Nachman *Krochmal; Samuel David *Luzzatto; Leopold *Zunz).

The beginnings of a renewed modern interest in Jewish history are already found in the generation of Mendelssohn and Wessely. In *Ha-Me'assef*, a special section was set aside for "biographies of eminent Jewish personalities" in which popular articles were written on Maimonides, Don Isaac Abrabanel, Moses Raphael de Aguilar, Isaac Orobio de Castro, and others. In these articles the first efforts were also made to bring to light ancient sources. The program of *Ha-Me'assef* also included the publication of works on the biographies of "living Jewish scholars." Accordingly Isaac *Euchel wrote a biography of Mendelssohn, and David *Friedrichsfeld a biography of Wessely (the two works were however published after the deaths of Mendelssohn and Wessely). In addition, a section of *Ha-Me'assef* was to deal with "the innovations taking place among our people which concern all the Jews, on their freedom in some countries, and the education of their youth… for the utility of youth with a quest for knowledge." Biographies of eminent Jewish personalities were also published in *Shulamit*. However, serious research into Jewish history on a wide scale was taken up by Haskalah circles when the poet and scholar Solomon *Loewisohn published his work *Vorlesungen ueber die neuere Geschichte der Juden* in Vienna in 1820, the first Haskalah attempt to present a general view of Jewish history from the earlier Diaspora period down to the time of the author.

Haskalah thus became one of the mainsprings of a renewed study of the nature of Judaism and the fate of the Jewish people. Mendelssohn attempted to demonstrate the superiority of Judaism over Christianity in his description of Judaism as a rational religion and of the practical precepts as the laws of the former Jewish state (and possibly also a future state) and as symbols of the ideals of the rational faith. Mendelssohn apparently thought that even at the millennium, when the whole world would submit to the "yoke of the Kingdom of Heaven," the Jews would still be obliged to observe the precepts because their function as "symbols," as educational factors, would never be abrogated. This was because Mendelssohn did not believe in the entire perfectibility of mankind in any period, seeing that "the whole of humanity is in constant motion, either in ascent or decline." Even though Mendelssohn did not say so explicitly, it may be assumed that his references to the election of Israel and its mission were not only intended to explain the past but also to indicate the situation in the future.

During the 19th century further attempts were made in the Haskalah camp to define the nature of Judaism. Some regarded Judaism as a "spiritual religion" in contrast to the idolatrous religions which were "religions of nature" and in contrast to Christianity, which served as the battleground between the elements in the Jewish "spiritual religion" and the idolatrous elements (Solomon *Formstecher). Others regarded Judaism as a moral religion, a religion of the heart and the emotions, in contrast to Hellenism, the religion of cold reason (S.D. Luzzatto, and others). N. Krochmal defined the faith of Israel as belief in the Infinite "Absolute Spiritual One" and considered this to be the secret of the eternity of the Jewish people. The growing development of historical consciousness supplanted traditional views on the fate of Israel in Haskalah thought. Exile was no longer conceived as a chastisement meted out by Providence, but the result of natural historical factors. In the West, emancipation was generally regarded as the end of the Exile (see *Galut*). However, the difficult struggle for emancipation, which in Germany extended over several decades, awakened some doubts on the future of the Jews in Europe and here and there some far-reaching conclusions, such as emigration to America or a return to Palestine (Mordecai Manuel *Noah; *Salvador; Moses *Hess).

[Azriel Shochat/Judith R. Baskin (2nd ed.)]

Haskalah in Russia

Haskalah was introduced into Russia from Western Europe, particularly Germany. It was brought to the communities of Lithuania and Ukraine by merchants, physicians, and itinerant Jewish scholars from the close of the 18th century. As early as the 1780s some Jews in towns of Lithuania and Poland were subscribers to the *Biur* of Moses Mendelssohn and *Ha-Me'assef* of the German *maskilim*. The earliest *maskilim* in Eastern Europe were Israel Zamosc, Solomon Dubno, Judah *Hurwitz, Judah Loeb *Margolioth, Baruch *Schick, and Mendel *Lefin. They maintained direct relations with the *maskilim* of Berlin, but when spreading Haskalah in their own environment they based themselves formally on the views of *Elijah b. Solomon Zalman, the Gaon of Vilna, and regarded themselves as his disciples. Baruch Schick, who published several works on mathematics and astronomy, wrote in his introduction to his translation of Euclid (Amsterdam, 1780) that he had heard the Gaon state that "in proportion to a man's ignorance of the other sciences, he will be ignorant of one hundred measures of the science of the Torah." Solomon Dubno contributed to the *Biur*, Mendelssohn's commentary on the Bible. Phinehas Hurwitz published the *Sefer ha-Berit* (Bruenn, 1797), a type of encyclopedia of various sciences, combining ethical observations and research in the spirit of moderate Haskalah. *Manasseh b. Joseph of Ilya, who was persecuted by the zealots for his free ideas, also belonged to this circle. As customary at this time, all these authors sought and obtained the written approval of outstanding rabbis for their works.

At the close of the 18th century the wealthy *maskil* Joshua Zeitlin established a center for *maskilim* and traditional Torah scholars on his estate near Shklov. In his large library they were able to dedicate themselves to their studies and religious perfection. Included in this group were Baruch Schick and Mendel Lefin of Satanov. These *maskilim* made use of their relations with the Russian authorities as merchants, purveyors, and physicians, and submitted proposals to the administration for the improvement of the situation of the Jews by admitting them to various crafts, by the encouragement of agricultural settlement, and by the opening of modern schools for the Jews (memoranda of Jacob Hirsch of Mogilev, 1783; of Nathan Note *Notkin of Shklov, 1797; of the physician Jacob Elijah Frank of Kreslavka (Kraslava), 1800). The *maskilim* already concerned themselves with spreading education among the masses during this period. While having reservations against the use of Yiddish, they wrote works in that language for the education of the people. The physician Moses Markuse published *Sefer Refu'ot* in Poritsk, Volhynia, in 1790 in which he offered, as well as medical advice, guidance on the education of children. In 1817 the merchant Chaim Haykl *Hurwitz of Uman published his *Tsofnas Paneakh*, an adaption of the work of J. Campe, *Die Entdeckung von Amerika*.

A small group of *maskilim* organized themselves in the new community which was established in St. Petersburg at the close of the 18th century. Their outlook was expressed in the Russian pamphlet *Vopl docheri iudeyskoy* (1802), published in a Hebrew version, *Kol Shavat Bat Yehudah*, in Shklov a year later. Written on the occasion of the debate on the Jewish problem which then took place within the Russian government, it took up the defense of the Jewish people, and included a plea that kindness and mercy be shown to it. A few years later its author, Judah Leib *Nevakhovich, became an apostate, as did his patron, the merchant Abraham *Peretz, the son-in-law of Nathan Note Notkin. These conversions, as well as the information concerning the epidemic of conversions among the *maskilim* of Germany, stiffened the hostility and suspicions felt by the mass of Jews in Russia toward the *maskilim*. They became a considerable obstacle in the spread of Haskalah there.

During the 1820s the Haskalah movement was revived in Lithuania and Southern Russia. Its promoters were emigrants from Galicia, such as the "Brodysts" in Odessa, as well as Jews from Courland, influenced by German culture, and the inhabitants of the townlets bordering upon Prussia and Courland (Raseiniai; Zagare). During this period the *maskilim* gained a hold in Vilna, one of the centers of commerce with Western Europe. The *maskilim*, who dressed in German style and insisted on speaking pure German among themselves instead of Yiddish, which they regarded as a corrupted German dialect, were referred to by the masses as "Deytshen" or "Berliners." One of their main aims was to establish modern Jewish schools in which the pupils would be taught general subjects and Jewish studies in the German language. In 1822, Hirsch Hurwitz (son of the above-mentioned Chaim Haykl Hurwitz) founded a school in Uman based on the "Mendelssohnian system." Of even greater importance was the foundation of a Jewish school in Odessa under the direction of Bezalel *Stern (1826). Similar schools were subsequently founded in Riga, Kishinev, and Vilna. During those years, the program of the *maskilim* was elaborated by Isaac Dov (Baer) *Levinsohn (Ribal) of Kremenets in his *Te'udah be-Yisrael* (Vilna, 1828) and *Beit Yehudah* (*ibid.*, 1839). The essence of this program was the establishment of a network of elementary schools for boys and girls in which the pupils would study Jewish and general subjects, as well as some kind of a profession; it also included the foundation of high schools for the more talented children, the promotion of productivization, particularly agriculture, among the Jewish masses, and departure from Yiddish in favor of "the pure German or Russian language."

The *maskilim* endeavored to organize themselves under the difficult conditions for free organization in general and for the Jews in particular during the reign of Czar Nicholas I. In many towns small groups of *maskilim* were established, among them the Shoharei Or ve-Haskalah ("Seekers of Light and Education") society founded by Israel Rothenberg in Berdichev, the Maskilim Society in Raseiniai, and the Maskilim Group led by the author Mordecai Aaron Guenzburg in Vilna, which established its own synagogue, Taharat ha-Kodesh, in 1846. Harassed by censorship, they struggled to publish their works, which included the first Hebrew literary periodical there, *Pirhei Zafon* (Vilna, 1841). Among them a modern Hebrew literature began to emerge. Mordecai Aaron Guenzburg wrote stories based on Jewish, general, and Russian history, adapted from non-Jewish sources or collected from other authors in this period. During the following years, Kalman *Schulmann proceeded with this enterprise. A number of poets wrote on secular subjects in lyrical Hebrew, many expressing the ideas of Haskalah. The most prominent in this group were Abraham *Dov Lebensohn (Adam ha-Kohen), whose first collection of poems, *Shirei Sefat Kodesh*, was published in Leipzig in 1842, his son Micah Joseph *Lebensohn (Mikhal), and the leading Haskalah poet, Judah Leib *Gordon. Abraham *Mapu created the Hebrew novel, and his *Ahavat Ziyyon* (Vilna, 1853) has become a landmark in the history of Hebrew literature. Despite their opposition to Yiddish, the Haskalah authors wrote works in this language in order to propagate their ideas among the masses by means of stories and works of popular science. The most outstanding of these authors, Isaac Meir *Dick, wrote hundreds of stories which were published in Vilna and Warsaw. Israel *Axenfeld and Solomon *Ettinger wrote stories and plays in the Haskalah spirit. Many of their works could not be published because of the censorship and were circulated in manuscript.

Even in the period of oppression and anti-Jewish legislation during the reign of Nicholas I, the *maskilim* looked upon the Russian government as a supporting force in their struggle for the realization of their ideas. In memoranda submitted to the authorities, they called for the imposition of reforms on the masses, such as change of their traditional dress for the European clothes of the period, and the strict supervision of Hebrew printing presses which were to be reduced to two or three in the whole country in order to make this possible. The government accepted these proposals and had them enforced. The *maskilim* found particular satisfaction in the government's program to establish a network of governmental Jewish schools in which the language of instruction would be German (later Russian). During the early 1840s the government entrusted Max *Lilienthal, the principal of the Jewish school of Riga, with the execution of this program. He was assisted by the local *maskilim* in every town. During the 1840s and 1850s many such schools were founded in the towns of the Pale of Settlement. Their Jewish teachers were drawn from *maskilim* circles who were granted the status of government functionaries. In Vilna and Zhitomir, government rabbinical seminaries were established. Their students were exempted from military service and were trained with the aim of becoming the future teachers and rabbis of the Jewish communities. In these schools and seminaries, which were financed by special taxes imposed on the masses (*candle tax), a new class of *maskilim* was educated. They received their education in Russian, and their ties with the Hebrew language and Jewish tradition were flimsy.

Haskalah received considerable stimulus through economic changes, particularly when a wide class of Jews engaged in liquor contracting emerged. As a result of their contracts with government officials, they and their employees required a knowledge of the Russian language, arithmetic, and other sciences. There thus arose a whole class of thousands of families who were no longer dependent on Jewish society from the economic and social point of view. These Jews wore the non-Jewish dress, neglected the observance of the religious precepts, shaved their beards, and were drawn closer to the Russian language and culture. The *maskil* of the former generation had been self-taught, familiar with Jewish literature, whose principal education was drawn from German literature, as well as from the *Hokhmat Yisrael* ("Jewish Science") literature. In contrast, the new *maskil* received his education in a Russian-Jewish school or in a general Russian school and was conspicuous for his considerable alienation from Jewish tradition.

The period of the important reforms at the beginning of the reign of Alexander II and the suppression of the Polish uprising in 1863 gave a strong impetus to the spread of Haskalah among the masses of Jewish youth. The Jewish press, whose founders, journalists, and publishers were essentially *maskilim*, played a decisive role in this development. Among newspapers outstanding for their struggle in favor of Haskalah were the Hebrew **Ha-Meliẓ* (founded in 1860) and the Yiddish **Kol Mevasser* (1862), issued by A. *Zederbaum and first published in Odessa. The first newspapers issued by the Russian-oriented *maskilim* also appeared in Odessa, **Razsvet* and *Sion* (in 1860/61) and *Den* (1869–71), to which the leading Russian *maskilim* contributed. The older authors were joined by new ones, among them S.J. *Abramovitsh (later Mendele Mokher Seforim), who wrote in Hebrew and Yiddish, I.J. *Linetzky (Yiddish), L. *Levanda, and G. Bogrov (Russian). Their writings produced a more advanced stage in Haskalah ideology, which found its expression in the saying of the poet J.L. Gordon: "Be a man when you go out and a Jew in your home." This press called for an alliance between the Jewish *maskilim* and the Russian government in order to fight "those in darkness" from within, especially the Hasidim and their *ẓaddikim*, and to support the governmental Russification policy throughout the Pale of Settlement. During the 1860s the institution of *kazyonny ravvin* ("government-appointed rabbi") was introduced. Its candidates were drawn from the ranks of the *maskilim* who had been educated in the Russian-Jewish schools.

In 1863, on the initiative of the richest Jews of the capital (the *Guenzburg, *Polyakov, and *Rosenthal families), the Hevrat Mefizei ha-Haskalah ("*Society for the Promotion of Culture among the Jews of Russia") was founded in St. Petersburg. This society came to the assistance of *maskilim* in the provincial towns, particularly high-school students, and encouraged the publication of Haskalah literature in Hebrew, Yiddish, and Russian.

Most of the *maskilim* believed the general assumption that Russia, in the wake of the other European states, was about to declare the emancipation of the Jews. The rights which had been granted to certain Jewish circles, such as the large-scale merchants (1859), intellectuals (1861), craftsmen (1865), and members of the medical profession (physicians, pharmacists, male nurses, midwives, etc.), seemed to point in that direction. The introduction of the general obligation of military service (1874), which included important concessions in the conditions and period of service for those with a Russian education, prompted many parents to send their children to the Russian schools. While in 1870 only 2,045 Jewish children studied in Russian secondary schools, by 1880 their numbers had increased to 8,000.

During this period there were two marked trends among the *maskilim*. One called for a rapid association with the Russian nation, even to the point of assimilation. The Hebrew language (and all the more so Yiddish) was merely regarded as a temporary instrument for spreading Haskalah among the retarded masses. At most, adherents to this trend recognized the need for the promotion of *Wissenschaft des Judentums* in the Russian language. This was the path which had been adopted by West European Jewry and along which Russian Judaism was also to be led. On the other hand, the standard-bearers of a nationalist ideology which called for the fostering of the Hebrew language and loyalty to Jewish nationalism also raised their voices. The voice of this trend was the newspaper –**Ha-Shahar* (1868–84), published by Peretz *Smolenskin in Vienna but particularly addressed to Russian Jewry. Smolenskin sharply criticized the Mendelssohnian Haskalah and called for the promotion of Jewish nationalist values. During this period, however, he was a lone voice. To the majority of the *maskilim* it appeared that the historical evolution which had taken place in Western Europe would also overtake Russian Jewry. Some opinions considered this evolution to be natural and desirable, even drawing some far-reaching conclusions from it (A.U. *Kovner), while others expressed their regrets with regard to it (J.L. Gordon, in *Le-Mi Ani Amel*, 1871).

A significant change, however, occurred in the lives of the Russian Jews during the 1870s. The breakthrough into the general economy and Russian culture by the Jews resulted in the emergence of a powerful anti-Jewish movement, whose spokesmen included leading Russian intellectuals (Aksakov; Dostoyevski). A press inciting the Russian masses against the Jews and warning them of "domination" by the Jews, especially intellectuals, over the country was created. The reaction that set in in Russia in the wake of Alexander II's assassination at first resulted in anti-Jewish pogroms (1881–83) and later in severe restrictions of Jewish rights. One of these, the *numerus clausus, was especially designed to bar the way of the Jewish youth to the Russian schools.

The *maskilim* reacted to this situation in various ways. Those of the older generation attempted to adhere to their policies and placed their faith in "progress" which would eventually be victorious and bring the anticipated emancipation. This circle of Jewish-Russian intelligentsia centered around the newspaper **Voskhod* (St. Petersburg, 1881–1906). A considerable section of Jewish youth joined the Russian revolutionary movement with the hope that the fall of the czarist regime would eliminate all restrictions, and that the Jews would be assimilated and rapidly absorbed within the Russian people so that the Jewish problem would automatically disappear. Another section of the older generation and the intellectual Jewish youth resorted to Jewish nationalism. They established the *Ḥibbat Zion movement which considered that the solution of the Jewish problem in Russia lay in the emigration of the Jews to Ereẓ Israel where they would engage in productive occupations. They called for an alliance with the Jewish masses who were attached to their traditions and language in order to realize this project. The organ of this sector was the Jewish-Russian newspaper *Razsvet* (1879–83) and later *Ha-Meliẓ*. Haskalah, as an ideological trend on the Jewish scene, now ceded its place to the new trends, all of which – even if they violently criticized Haskalah from various directions – had received many of their ideas from it.

Even if from the historical point of view Russian Haskalah was a continuation of the Central European it nevertheless possessed an originality stemming from the particular character of Russian Jewry. The large number of Jews in that country and their great concentrations in the towns and townlets of the Pale of Settlement prevented the Haskalah movement from degenerating into a rapid course of assimilation and disintegration, as had occurred in Western Europe. In Russia the new Hebrew literature became a permanent fact and not an ephemeral phenomenon as in the West. Haskalah produced, even if in opposition to its own ideology, a secular literature in Yiddish, especially of Yiddish fiction. It gave rise to an alert Jewish press in three languages, Hebrew, Yiddish, and Russian. It also bequeathed to the nationalist movement, and particularly to the Zionist movement, the idea of productivization of the Jewish masses and their transition to labor in general and agricultural work in particular.

In the last three decades of the 19th century, the Haskalah in Eastern Europe had a significant literary impact on Jewish women as both readers and writers. As in Western and Central Europe, women preceded men in their knowledge of European languages and culture and as readers of secular Jewish literature in both Yiddish and Hebrew, particularly fiction and poetry. Often, women readers introduced new ideas into their families which contributed to the undermining of the values of traditional society. Reading of worlds and opportunities previously unimagined, they exerted a strong influence against the cultural constraints of their restricted society, sometimes encouraging the men in their circles to defect from the limitations of the yeshivah world (I. Parush, *Reading Jewish Women*).

Numerous female authors wrote and published poetry and prose in Hebrew, Yiddish, and particularly Russian periodicals between 1870 and 1914. Some came from the shtetl; others, the daughters of prosperous middle-class urban Jews, attended gymnasia, learned European languages, and earned university degrees. Among women writing in Hebrew was Sarah Feiga Meinkin Foner (1855–1936) of Dvinsk, Latvia, the first woman to publish a Hebrew novel (*The Love of the Honest* (Vilna, 1881–83)). She went on to write children's stories, a novella, and a memoir (C. Balin, *"To Reveal Our Hearts,"* 22–23). Miriam Markel-Mosessohn (1839–1920), an excellent Hebraist who became a protégée of Judah Leib Gordon, mainly devoted herself to translating European literature into Hebrew and journalism, apparently believing it was inappropriate for a woman to write original works in Hebrew.

[Yehuda Slutsky / Judith R. Baskin (2nd ed.)]

BIBLIOGRAPHY: Z. Yavetz, n: *Keneset Yisrael*, 1 (1896), 89–152; S. Bernfeld, *Dor Hakham* (1896); idem, *Dor Tahppukhot*, 2 vols. (1897); Graetz, Hist, 5 (1895); Dubnow, Weltgesch, 8 (1928); 9 (1929); Y. Kaufmann, *Golah ve-Nekhar*, 2 (1930); B. Offenburg, *Das Erwachen des deutschen Nationalbewusstseins in der preussischen Judenheit* (1933); M. Wiener, *Juedische Religion im Zeitalter der Emanzipation* (1933); J. Katz, *Die Entstehung der Judenassimilation in Deutschland und deren Ideologie* (1935); idem, *Tradition and Crisis* (1961), 260–74; A. Orinovsky, in: *Rishonim: Kovez Mukdash la-"Kursim ha-Pedagogiyyim ha-Grodna'iyyim"* (1936), 174–89; Baron, Social, 3 (1937); P. Sandler, *Ha-Be'ur la-Torah shel Moshe Mendelssohn* (1941); G. Scholem, *Mi-Tokh Hirhurim al Hokhmat Yisrael* (1945; repr. from: *Lu'ah ha-Arez* (1945), 94ff.); Y. Fleishman, in: *Erkhei ha-Yahadut* (1953); E. Simon, in: *Sefer ha-Yovel…Mordekhai Menahem Kaplan* (1953), 149–87; R. Mahler, *Divrei Yemei Yisrael, Dorot Aharonim*, 2 (1954), 57–88, 223–43; 3 (1955), 34–94, 169–72; 4 (1956), 9–90; idem, *Ha-Hasidut ve-ha-Haskalah* (1961); B. Dinur, *Be-Mifneh ha-Dorot* (1955), 231–54; idem, in: *Tarbiz*, 20 (1959), 241–64; B. Katz, *Rabbanut, Hasidut, Haskalah*, 1 (1956), 140–266; 2 (1958), 122–251; Zinberg, Sifrut, 3 (1958), 260–335; 5 (1959), 13–143, 258–99; 6 (1960); J. Klausner, in: *Yahadut*

Lita, 1 (1960), 405–12; M. Eliav, *Ha-Hinnukh ha-Yehudi be-Germanyah bi-Ymei ha-Haskalah ve-ha-Emanzipazyah* (1960); Y. Slutski, in: *Zion*, 25 (1960), 212–37; A. Schochat, *Im Hillufei Tekufot* (1960); idem, in: *Ha-Molad*, 23 (1965/66), 328–34; I.E. Barzilay, *Shelomo Yehudah Rapoport (Shir) 1790–1867* (Eng. 1969); idem, in: PAAJR, 24 (1955), 39–68; 25 (1956), 1–38; idem, in: JSOS, 21 (1959), 165–92; S. Ettinger, in: H.H. Ben-Sasson (ed.), *Toledot Am Yisrael*, 3 (1969); Z. Rejzen, *Fun Mendelssohn bis Mendele* (1923); M. Erik, *Etyudn tsu der Geshikhte fun der Haskole* (1934); H.S. Kazdan, *Fun Heder un Shkoles bis* CYSH-O (1956), 19–64. HASKALAH IN RUSSIA: J.S. Raisin, *The Haskalah Movement in Russia* (1913); S. Spiegel, *Hebrew Reborn* (1930); D. Patterson, *The Hebrew Novel in Czarist Russia* (1964); J. Meisel, *Haskala, Geschichte der Aufklaerungsbewegung unter den Juden in Russland* (1919); S. Tsinberg (Zinberg), *Istoriya yevreyskoy pechati v Rossii* (1915); E. Tcherikower, *Istoriya Obshchestva dlya rasprostraneniya prasveshcheniya mezhdu yevreyami v Rossii* (1913); P. Marek, *Ocherki po istorii Prosveshcheniya* (1909); 9 (1958^{2}), 130–4, 225–38; Klausner, Sifrut, 3–4 (1953–54); R. Mahler, *Divrei Yemei Yisrael, Dorot Aharonim*, 4 (1956), 53–68; Y. Slutski, *Ha-Ittonut ha Yehudit-Rusit ba-Me'ah ha-19* (1970); J. Shatzky, *Kultur Geshikhte fun der Haskole in Lite* (1950); I. Sosis, *Di Geshikhte fun di Yidishe Gezelshaftlekhe Shtremungen in Rusland in 19th Yorhundert* (1929); M. Erik, *Etyudn tsu der Geshikhte fun der Haskole* (1934). **ADD. BIBLIOGRAPHY:** D. Biale, *Eros and the Jews* (1992); D. Hertz, *Jewish High Society in Old Regime Berlin* (1988); C.B. Balin, *"To Reveal Our Hearts": Jewish Women Writers in Tsarist Russia* (2000); I. Parush, *Reading Jewish Women: Marginality and Modernization in Nineteenth-Century European Jewish Society* (2004).

HASKAMAH (**Askamah**; Heb. הַסְכָּמָה, אַסְכָּמָה; "agreement," "approbation"), in Jewish literature, a term with several meanings: (1) Rabbinic approval and approbation of the legal decisions of colleagues, usually attached to the original legal decision and circulated with it. These *haskamot* sometimes amplify the original, by including additional sources and pointing out implications. (2) In the Spanish and later also in the Italian and Oriental communities, the term was used for the statutes and ordinances enacted by the communities (see **Ascama*). (3) In the philosophical literature of the Middle Ages, "consensus," "harmony between entities," "pre-established harmony" (see Klatzkin, Thesaurus Philosophicus 1, 185–6). (4) More commonly, the recommendation of a scholar or rabbi to a book or treatise.

This entry deals with the last meaning.

ORIGINS AND HISTORY. Various opinions have been offered on the origin or development of the *haskamah* for books. Some see the influence of the *approbatio* of the Church, others see it as resulting from the papal action of 1553 in the dispute between the publishing houses of *Bragadini and Giustiniani which resulted in the burning of the Talmud (see *Censorship). The first *haskamah* appeared in the 15th century, in the *Agur* by Jacob Landau (Naples, c. 1490), the first Hebrew book printed during its author's lifetime; it was signed by seven rabbis. The *haskamah* for Elijah Levita's *Sefer ha-Baḥur* (Rome, 1518) signed by the rabbi of Rome, threatens excommunication for republication within 10 years. Thus the *haskamah* fulfilled the function of a copyright, the period of protection extending from five to 25 years. The *haskamah* in Joseph Caro's *Bedek ha-Bayit* (Venice, 1606) is signed by three rabbis (the number of *haskamot* varied from book to book); and it concluded with a declaration by the sexton that he has read it in all the synagogues of Venice. With the introduction of title pages in the 16th century, *haskamot* came to be printed at the beginning rather than at the end of a book.

Thus, the *haskamah* developed from a recommendation to an expression of approval to a method of protecting the author's rights and finally to a form of self-censorship to protect the Jewish community against the church censorship and later to counteract kabbalistic, pseudo-messianic, and Haskalah tendencies. Thus, at the Rabbinical Synod of Ferrara of 1554, it was enacted that no book should receive its first printing without prior approbation of three rabbis of the particular region. Similar *takkanot* were issued in Poland in 1594 and 1682. Such restrictions were used to prevent the spread of the heretical Shabbatean doctrines, or to protect the printers of the expensive Talmud editions. This led to many disputes and litigations. The majority of *haskamot* issued in the 17th and 18th centuries originated in the centers of Hebrew printing, such as Venice, Amsterdam, and Constantinople. *Haskamot* were usually written in a combination of Hebrew and Aramaic, frequently using the florid style of rabbinic writings. They sometimes contain bibliographic, biographic, and geographic data, which, though not always exact, are an important source for historians and scholars, and bibliographers like Roest, Wachstein and Wiener utilized this source.

Abuses

Haskamot have been much abused. Often their place and date were intentionally altered. Some writers, eager to have *haskamot* appended to their works, forged signatures and *haskamot*, as was the case in Nehemiah Ḥayon's *Ha-Kolot Yeḥdalun* (Amsterdam, 1725). Earlier *maskilim* used forged approbations to their works in order to deceive the pious reader. Others printed only part of the book which had received the *haskamah*, and some authors published their books on inferior paper with unclear type. As a result some *haskamot* included such specifications as "the condition of this *haskamah* that the printing of this book should be completed within two years" or "on condition that the printer should print the book on white paper with black ink." These factors, and others as well, made many rabbis reluctant to write *haskamot*. Samson *Wertheimer was ready to approve only the works of relatives or scholars who were poor. Some writers of approbations made no secret of the fact that they had been given to help the author financially (see Abraham ha-Kohen's *Beit Ya'akov*, Leghorn, 1792). Some rabbis denied *haskamot* to any book which dealt with Jewish law; others were ready to add their names only if a well-known rabbi had already given his *haskamah*. Still others protested that they had no time to read the entire book, or that they were not sufficiently acquainted with the subject; which did not prevent some from granting their approbation merely on the reputation of the author.

Some authors were not eager to obtain the *haskamah* of rabbis who could not read the work; thus Moses Mendelssohn did not request *haskamot* for his books, nor did Raphael ha-Kohen for his *Torat Yekuti'el* (Berlin, 1772); other authorities disapproved of them altogether (Responsa *Ḥatam Sofer* HM 41); Ezekiel Landau used his *haskamah* to the Prague Pentateuch of 1785 to express his disapproval of Mendelssohn's Pentateuch edition. Between 1499 and 1850, 3,662 haskamot were issued, the majority in Eastern Europe. Authors of religious books are still anxious to print a *haskamah* by a prominent rabbi or authority. In secular works the worldwide custom of using a preface or an introduction by a well-known authority fulfills the same role.

BIBLIOGRAPHY: L. Loewenstein, *Index Approbationum* (1923); I.S. Reggio, *Iggerot Yashar* (1834–36); B. Wachstein, in: MGWJ, 71 (1927), 123–33; I. Halperin (ed.), *Pinkas Va'ad Arba Araẓot* (1945), index; M. Carmilly-Weinberger, *Sefer ve-Sayif* (1966), xii–xiv, 177–85; Shunami, Bibl., 501

[Moshe Carmilly-Weinberger]

HASKELL, ARNOLD LIONEL (1903–1980), British ballet critic and author. In 1927 Haskell started his career with a firm of London publishers, devoted himself to ballet and in 1930 was joint founder of the Camargo Society, which was influential in the revival of ballet in England. For three years Haskell was critic of the *Daily Telegraph* (1935–38). He was director of the Royal Ballet School from 1946 and a governor of the Royal Ballet from 1957. In 1954 he advised the Dutch government on the formation of a National Ballet. His books on ballet were important in the cultivation of popular taste. Among them were *Balletomania* (1934), a word he introduced into the English language; *Diaghileff* (1935); *The Making of a Dancer* (1946); *In His True Centre* (1951), his autobiography; *The Russian Genius in Ballet* (1963); *What is Ballet?* (1965); and *Heroes and Roses* (1966).

HASKIL, CLARA (1895–1960), Romanian pianist, of Sephardi background. Born in Bucharest, Haskil studied at the Conservatory in 1901 and made her debut in Vienna 1902 as a child prodigy. She studied with Richard Robert and later in Paris with Cortot.

Her technique and capacity for poetic expression won her a great reputation. Though a muscular disorder severely impeded her career, she continued playing concerts during periods of remission, making numerous appearances with Ysaÿe, Enesco, Casals, and Grumiaux and appearing as a soloist with major symphony orchestras in Europe and America. She lived in Paris from 1927 until 1940, when the German invasion forced her to flee the city. In 1949 she acquired Swiss nationality.

Haskil was made a Chevalier of the Legion d'Honneur in belated recognition of the inimitable clarity and eloquence of her playing. Her interpretation of Beethoven, Schumann, Schubert, and especially Mozart was profoundly sensitive and unique. She made memorable recordings of the complete Beethoven sonatas for violin and piano with Grumiaux as well as of several Mozart concertos. A Clara Haskil Prize was established at the International Music Festival in Lucerne.

BIBLIOGRAPHY: NG^2; MGG^2; Melkonian, Martin. *Clara Haskil: Portrait* (1995)

[Naama Ramot (2nd ed.)]

HASMONEAN BET DIN (Heb. בֵּית דִּין שֶׁל חַשְׁמוֹנָאִים); according to a talmudic source (Sanh. 82a; Av. Zar. 36b) "the court of the Hasmoneans decreed that an Israelite who had intercourse with a heathen woman is liable to punishment on account of "נשג"א" (NShGA), a mnemonic designating four counts of liability: נִדָּה (*niddah*; "a menstruating woman"), שִׁפְחָה (*shifḥah*; "a maidservant"), גּוֹיָה (*goyah*; "a gentile"), and אֵשֶׁת אִישׁ (*eshet ish*; "a married woman"). A second tradition in the Talmud has Z instead of A, designating *zonah*, "harlot." There is no further mention of this Hasmonean court, and it has therefore been suggested, that the reference is to a temporary court set up early in the Hasmonean revolt, to fill the void created by the death of the religious leaders of the period. If this is so, it would appear that this court was responsible for the ruling that defensive battle is permissible on the Sabbath (I Macc. 2:39–41). However, it is more likely that the court was created after the establishment of Hasmonean rule in Palestine following the early successes of Judah and his brothers. Derenbourg claims that the court existed toward the end of the second century B.C.E., during the reign of Simeon and the first years of John *Hyrcanus. He further suggests that Hyrcanus changed the name of the court from *Bet Din shel Ḥashmona'im* to *Sanhedrin during the last years of his rule, following the schism with the Pharisees. Other scholars tend to identify the Hasmonean court with the "sons of the Hasmoneans" mentioned in the Mishnah (Mid. 1:6; in Yoma 16a, Av. Zar. 52b the reading is "house of Hasmoneans") as having "hidden away the stones of the altar which the Greek kings had defiled," but there is insufficient proof of this. Likewise, there is no reason to identify, as does I.H. Weiss, the Hasmonean *bet din* with the "Great Synagogue" of priests and elders that officially appointed Simeon high priest and leader of the nation (I Macc. 14:28; see *Asaramel). The most likely solution of the problem is that the Hasmonean court "was the private council of the Hasmoneans at the peak of their power." If this is so, the Hasmonean court was established by John Hyrcanus toward the end of his reign, or by his son Alexander Yannai during his struggle against his Pharisaic enemies. This court may have been responsible for the harsh treatment of the Pharisaic rebels. It was composed of Sadducean followers of the Hasmonean king (cf. Jos., Ant., 13:408ff., which relates how the Pharisees avenged their martyrs in the days of Queen Alexandra).

BIBLIOGRAPHY: Derenbourg, Hist, 84ff.; Weiss, Dor, 1 (1904^4), 102f.; Frankel, Mishnah, 43.

[Isaiah Gafni]

HASMONEANS (Gr. Ἀσαμωναίος; Heb. חַשְׁמוֹנָאִים), title for Maccabees in Josephus (Ant., 12:263), Mishnah (Mid. 1:6), and Talmud (Shab. 21b), but nowhere occurring in the Book of Maccabees. Josephus derives the name from the great-grandfather of Mattathias, Asamonaios. Probably the name is to be connected with the village of Heshmon (Josh. 15:27). It has also been suggested to connect the name with Hushim (I Chron. 8:11) or the place Hashmonah (Num. 33:29, 30). The Hasmoneans headed the rebellion against the Seleucid kingdom, established an autonomous Jewish state, annexed the most important regions of Ereẓ Israel, and absorbed a number of neighboring Semitic peoples into the Jewish people. These achievements were not only of major importance to Jewish history, but also left their impact on humanity as a whole. The successful rebellion of the Hasmoneans assured the continued existence of the Jewish religion and contributed to the decisive influence of monotheism in Western culture and history. Through the policy of the Hasmoneans, initiated after the rebellion, the Jewish people ceased to play a marginal role in history and exercised influence for generations to come.

The Hasmoneans were a priestly family, probably one of those which had moved from the territory of Benjamin to the lowlands of Lydda in the last days of the First Temple. They belonged to the Jehoiarib division of priests, who lived in *Modi'in on the border of Samaria and Judea. When the restrictive edicts of Antiochus were extended to the country towns and villages of Jewish Palestine, *Mattathias b. Johanan, then the head of the family, raised the banner of revolt in Modi'in, uniting under his leadership all those who were opposed to Antiochus' policy. After Mattathias' death in 167/166 B.C.E., his son *Judah Maccabee, a military genius, succeeded him as leader of the revolt. He scored a number of victories against the Seleucid army, and achieved the conquest of Jerusalem and the purification and rededication of the Temple in 164 B.C.E. (see: *Ḥanukkah). Judah continued to strive for the autonomy of Judea. He won additional victories against the Seleucid forces and in 161 B.C.E. established an alliance with Rome. Though Judah's death in battle slowed down somewhat Judea's progress toward independence, his brothers Jonathan and *Simeon continued his policy, taking advantage of the waning political star of the Seleucid dynasty to strengthen their own influence and to extend the borders of Judea. They annexed the districts of Lydda, Ramathaim, Ephraim, and the Ekron region, conquered Jaffa port, and seized control of the fortresses of the Acra in Jerusalem and Beth-Zur. The appointment of *Jonathan Apphus, the youngest son of Mattathias, to the high priesthood in 152 B.C.E., made this office one of the Hasmoneans' main sources of power. In 143–142 B.C.E., Demetrius II recognized the independence of Judea, and in 140 B.C.E. a decree was passed by the Great Assembly in Jerusalem confirming Simeon as high priest, ruler, and commander of the Jewish people and making these offices hereditary. Simeon's son, John *Hyrcanus (134–104 B.C.E.), continued the territorial expansion. He conquered Idumea, Samaria, and portions of Transjordan, and forcibly converted the Idumeans to Judaism. The internal crisis produced by a rift between the Hasmoneans and the Pharisees began during his reign. John's heir, *Aristobulus I (104–103 B.C.E.), was the first Hasmonean to arrogate to himself the title of king. Aristobulus continued the policy of conquest, compelling the Itureans in the north to become proselytes. During the reign of his brother, Alexander Yannai (103–76 B.C.E.), who succeeded him, the Hasmonean state reached the zenith of its power. The whole of the sea coast, from the Egyptian border to the Carmel, with the exception of Ashkelon, was annexed to Judea. Yannai also extended his rule over some of the Greek cities of Transjordan and strove to establish absolute authority as king and as high priest. It was his latter capacity which brought him into open conflict with the Pharisees. Yannai's wife, Salome Alexandra (76–67 B.C.E.), continued her husband's foreign policy, but reached an understanding with the Pharisees on internal affairs. Pompey's annexation brought the independence of the Hasmonean state to an end. Though the Romans allowed *Hyrcanus II, the oldest son of Alexander Yannai, to remain high priest and ethnarch, they abolished the monarchy and also detached large areas from Judea. Much had been gained, however – Judea proper, as well as Galilee, Idumea, many parts of Transjordan, the coastal plain and the coastal belt remained Jewish in character and culture for a long time as a result of the Hasmoneans' policy. The last to attempt to restore the former glory of the Hasmonean dynasty was *Antigonus Mattathias, with the help of the Parthians. His defeat and death in 37 B.C.E. at the hands of the Romans brought the Hasmonean rule to

Expansion of the Hasmonean kingdom, 167-76 B.C.E. After Zev Vilnay (ed.), New Israel Atlas, *Jerusalem.*

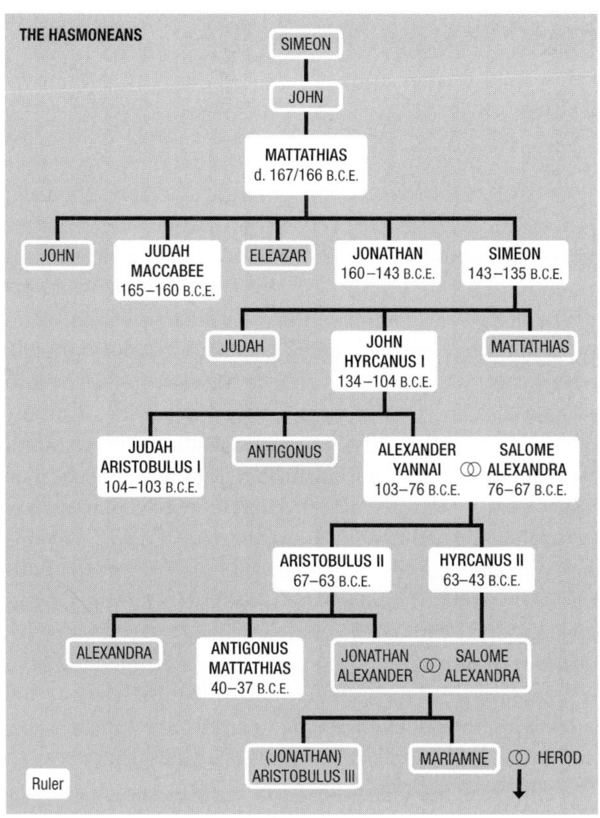

a close, and prepared the way for Herod. Herod, however, at the height of military success had strengthened his position by betrothal to the granddaughter of Hyrcanus II, Mariamne, whom he subsequently married. The popularity of his sons by her, Alexander and Aristobulus, and of their grandson (Herod Agrippa I) was due to their Hasmonean descent. (See Chart: Hasmonean Family).

[Menahem Stern]

In the Arts

A vast number of literary works have been inspired by the heroism of Mattathias and the embattled Maccabees and by the martyrdom of Hannah and her Seven Sons, as recounted in the Apocrypha. In 1722 Antoine Houdar de La Motte published his French lyrical tragedy *Les Machabées*, but it was not until the 19th century that the subject achieved wider popularity among writers. I.B. Schlesinger's Hebrew epic *Ha-Ḥashmona'im* (1816) was followed by *Die Mutter der Makkabaeer* (Vienna, 1820), a late historical drama by the German visionary Zacharias Werner, and by a more conventional tragedy, Alexandre Guiraud's *Les Machabées, ou le Martyre…* (Paris, 1822). Interest in the theme first reached a peak in the mid-19th century with dramas including *Die Makkabaeer* (1854) by Otto Ludwig, J. Michael's *Die Hasmonaeer* (1856; with music by V. Lachner), and a traditional Jewish interpretation of the story by Leopold Stein (1810–1882), also entitled *Die Hasmonaeer* (1859). Three later treatments of the subject were poems by Seligmann *Heller entitled *Die letzten Hasmonaeer* (1865); *The First of the Maccabees* (1860), a historical novel by the U.S. Reform pioneer Isaac Mayer *Wise; and Minnie Dessau Louis' *Hannah and Her Seven Sons* (1902). In the Far East, Joseph *David (Penker) produced *The Maccabeans* (1921), a drama in Marathi. Between the world wars, the Brazilian novelist Antonio Castro published *A Judéa e os Macabeus* (1930) and Izak *Goller wrote *Modin Women* (1931), one of his plays on biblical themes. Under the impact of Nazism, the Holocaust, and the birth of the State of Israel, several Jewish writers returned to the heroic theme of the Hasmonean revolt. Abraham Lavsky published a Yiddish historical novel, *Di Khashmonayim Helden oder di Makkabeyer* (1941); the U.S. author Howard *Fast wrote the novel *My Glorious Brothers* (1948). Of these, Fast's was easily the outstanding and best-known work. A work on a related theme was the Israel author Moshe *Shamir's historical novel *Melekh Basar va-Dam* (1954; *The King of Flesh and Blood*, 1958), which dealt with the career of the later Hasmonean ruler Alexander Yannai. Innumerable plays and stories devoted to the Ḥanukkah festival have been written for children, including many by Jewish authors and religious leaders in the United States.

The Maccabean wars have proved somewhat less attractive to artists. *Maccabeans*, a painting by the Austrian artist Jehuda Epstein, shows the beginning of the Jewish revolt. Boris *Schatz sculptured a heroic figure of Mattathias, formerly in the Royal collection, Sofia, Bulgaria. Gustave Doré produced dramatic engravings of Mattathias' call to arms and of the heroic death of Eleazar, brother of Judah, who was crushed by an elephant which he slew in battle (I Macc. 6). Another episode (I Macc. 9) – the battle of Jonathan and Simeon against Bacchides, a friend of the Syrian king, as transmitted by Josephus – was treated by the 15th-century French artist Jean Fouquet in his illuminations to the *Jewish War* and *Antiquities of the Jews*. Jonathan Maccabee appears on tapestries woven in Brussels in the 15th century, of which three portions have been preserved, showing Jonathan's coronation and receipt of gifts from other kings. A subject more commonly treated was the story of the seven martyred brothers, "Maccabees" only by association with the Apocryphal books (II Macc. 7), who preferred torture and death to being compelled to eat the flesh of swine. This became very popular in medieval Europe: the seven "Maccabean Martyrs" were canonized, Christians holding them to represent the Church Militant, while Antiochus symbolized the Antichrist. A church of the Seven Holy Maccabees stood in Lyons, France, and there was a chapel of the Maccabees in the cathedral of Saint Pierre, Geneva. Artists represented the Martyrs with amputated hands, together with Hannah, their mother. The Virgin with seven swords sometimes appears beside the figure of the latter. The theme also occurs in an eighth-century fresco at Santa Maria Antiqua, Rome, in medieval illuminated manuscripts, on the 13th-century southern portal of Chartres Cathedral, and in a 15th-century painting attributed to the Maître de Saint-Gilles (Amiens Museum). In the late Renaissance Jacopo Bassano painted the same subject.

In music there were a few compositions about the Hasmoneans dating from the late 18th and early 19th centuries, of which only Ignaz Seyfried's melodrama *Die Makkabaeer* (c. 1835) was of significance. Anton *Rubinstein's opera *Die Makkabaeer* (première in Berlin, 1875), for which Solomon *Mosenthal wrote the libretto after Otto Ludwig's drama, had only a brief stage career, yet it became a source of pride for East European Jewry. The aria *Leas Gesang* became a favorite at musical recitals and it was also arranged for instrumental combinations. Together with *Der heilige Sabbath* it can be found in the *Lider-Zamelbukh* edited by S. Kisselgoff (1911), with the text translated into Yiddish by A. Rivesman and into Hebrew by Saul *Tchernichowsky (no. 83–4). A comparison with the ḥasidic dance *Ladier Chabadnitze* (no. 62) in the same collection shows where the roots of the melody lie. Michael *Gnessin's *Makkavei*, a Russian "symphonic movement" for soloists, choir, and orchestra, was written after the composer's visit to Ereẓ Israel in 1922 and was first performed in 1925. Handel's oratorio *Alexander Balus* (1777; première in 1748), with libretto by Thomas Morrell, touches on the Maccabean theme.

The theme of the Seven "Maccabean" Martyrs also achieved a degree of popularity from the end of the 17th century and throughout the 18th, inspiring an opera by Johann Wolfgang Franck (1679) and oratorios by various composers, including Attilio Ariosti (1704), Francesco Conti (1732), and Antonio Sacchini (1770). In Johann Heinrich Rolle's *Thirza und ihre Soehne* (1781), the story is ostensibly about Christian martyrs, but the characters and content are identical with the history of the Maccabees. A later example is Vittorio Trento's opera *I sette Maccabei* (1818).

The "Story of Hannah" has a permanent and honored place in the religious folksong traditions of Mediterranean and Near Eastern Jewry and it is generally sung by women on the Ninth of Av. The songs are in the vernacular and their poetical and musical form resembles the historical ballads of the various surrounding gentile cultures; only the tradition as such is the common "Jewish" element. The poems are not infrequently found in manuscripts or printed booklets of *kinot*, but the tradition is basically oral and it probably occurs throughout the vast area from North Africa to Persia and from the Ladino-speaking communities of Greece and Turkey to the Yemen.

See also *Judah Maccabee in the Arts.

[Bathja Bayer]

BIBLIOGRAPHY: E.J. Bickerman, *The Maccabees* (1947); R.H. Pfeiffer, *History of New Testament Times* (1949), 5–45; W.R. Farmer, *Maccabees, Zealots, and Josephus* (1956); V. Tcherikover, *Hellenistic Civilization and the Jews* (1959); M. Stern, *Ha-Te'udot le-Mered ha-Ḥashmona'im* (1965); Schuerer, Hist, index, s.v. *Asmoneans*; Meyer, Ursp, 2 (1921), 205–78; B. Maisler (Mazar), in: *Yedi'ot ha-Ḥevrah ha-Ivrit la-Ḥakirat Ereẓ Yisrael ve-Attikoteha*, 8 (1941), 105–7. **ADD. BIBLIOGRAPHY:** E.J. Bickerman, "The Maccabean Uprising: An Interpretation," in: J. Goldin (ed.), *The Jewish Expression* (1976), 66–86; M. Hengel, *Jews, Greeks and Barbarians* (1980); F. Millar, "The Background to the Maccabean Revolution…," in: *Journal of Jewish Studies*, 29 (1978), 1–12; I. Shatzman, *The Armies of the Hasmoneans and Herod* (1991); D. Mendels, *The Land of Israel as a Political Concept in Hasmonean Literature* (1987); idem, *The Rise and Fall of Jewish Nationalism* (1992); D. Amit and H. Eshel, *The Days of the Hasmonean Dynasty* (1995).

HA-SOLELIM (Heb. הַסּוֹלְלִים; "the Trail Blazers"), kibbutz in Lower Galilee, Israel, 5 mi. (8 km.) northwest of *Nazareth, affiliated with Iḥud ha-Kevuẓot ve-ha-Kibbutzim and aligned politically to Ha-No'ar ha-Ẓiyyoni (Independent Liberals) movement. It was founded in 1949 as the first Jewish settlement in the region. The original settlers were Israel-born and other veterans of World War II, who were later joined by new immigrants from North America. In 1969 various fruit orchards, beef cattle, and field crops constituted its principal farm branches. The *Bet Netofah Storage Lake for the National Water Carrier is located near the kibbutz. Ha-Solelim was one of the first kibbutzim to introduce peripheral neighborhoods for nonmember residents who wished to enjoy rural life without being part of the collective. The kibbutz now operates as an association with cooperative activities in the fields of education, culture, welfare, and security. It also operates guest rooms and an art gallery. In 1968 it had 216 inhabitants. By the mid-1990s, the population had grown to approximately 305, and at the end of 2002, after expansion, it stood at 557.

WEBSITE: www.hasolelim.org.il.

[Efraim Orni / Shaked Gilboa (2nd ed.)]

HASSAGAT GEVUL (Heb. הַסָּגַת גְּבוּל), a concept which originally had specific reference to the unlawful taking of another's land; later it was extended to embrace encroachment on various economic, commercial, and incorporeal rights of others.

Encroachment on Land

IN SCRIPTURE. The original meaning of the term *hassagat gevul* was the moving (cf. *nasogu aḥor*, Isa. 42:17) of boundary stones or other landmarks from their resting places into the bounds of another's adjoining area of land, for the purpose of annexing a portion of the latter to one's own land. Naḥmanides' comment on the passage, "Thou shalt not remove thy neighbor's landmark, which they of old time have set, in thine inheritance which thou shalt inherit in the land that the Lord thy God giveth thee to possess it" (Deut. 19:14), is that Scripture speaks here "in terms of the present," i.e., of the usual situation, since it is common for landmark removal to take place in respect of ancient landmarks set up "of old time" which are not generally known and familiar. The prohibition against removal of the landmark is repeated in the enumeration of curses for recital on Mount Ebal (Deut. 27:17). The exact marking of land boundaries was already emphasized in patriarchal times, as may be gathered from the description of the field in *Machpelah bought by Abraham from Ephron the Hittite (Gen. 23:17), and this was also the case in other countries of the ancient East. Many boundary stones, engraved with invocations and curses against their removal, have been found in ancient Babylonia.

Removal of the landmark is exhorted against and castigated in the books of the prophets and the hagiographa (Hos. 5:10; Prov. 22:28, 23:10). In Proverbs too the reference is to the "present" and usual situation, namely removal of ancient landmarks set by earlier generations. In the Book of Hosea the castigation is directed against the princes, the strong, and in Proverbs it is hinted that the weak, the fatherless, were the main sufferers. In Job too removal of the landmark is mentioned among other injustices perpetrated on orphans, widows, and the poor (24:2–4).

IN THE TALMUD. In the talmudic period the abovementioned passage from Deuteronomy 19:14 was given a literal interpretation and the special prohibition against landmark removal was held to be applicable to land in Ereẓ Israel only. The fact that the enjoinder, "Thou shalt not remove the landmark," appears after it is already stated that "Thou shalt not rob," was held to teach that anyone who uproots his neighbor's boundaries breaks two prohibitions, robbery and removal of the landmark, but that this was the case in Ereẓ Israel only, since it is written "… in thine inheritance which thou shalt inherit in the land…" (*ibid.*), and outside Ereẓ Israel only one prohibition (robbery) is transgressed (Sif. Deut. 188). The *halakhah* was likewise determined in later times (Maim. Yad, Genevah 7:11; Sh. Ar., ḤM 376:1).

Land robbery, even outside Ereẓ Israel, has been regarded with great severity in Jewish law. The Talmud speaks of persons specially engaged in land measuring and the fixing of precise boundaries; surveyors are specifically instructed to make accurate calculations – down to the last fingerbreadth – and not to measure for one in summer and for the other in winter, since the measuring cord shrinks in summer (and expands in winter; BM 107b and Rashi *ibid.*; 61b; BB 89a; Maim. Yad, Genevah 8:1–3; Sh. Ar., ḤM 231:16–18).

IN THE CODES. It is explained that the general distinction made in Jewish law between *genevah* and *gezelah* (see *Theft and Robbery) – the former taking unlawfully by stealth and the latter openly with violence – applies also to the matter of trespass on land: "A person who removes his neighbor's landmark and encloses within his own domain even as much as a fingerbreadth from his neighbor's domain is a robber if he does so with violence and a thief if he does so stealthily" (Yad, Genevah 7: 11; Sh. Ar., ḤM 376; from the *Semag, Lavin*, 153 it also appears that this was understood to be the version of Sif. Deut. 188). The opinion was expressed by some of the *posekim* that the prohibition against robbery or theft – in relation to trespass on land – forms part of the *de-rabbanan* (Oral Law) and not the *de-oraita* (Written Law) law, since land is never stolen but always remains in its owner's possession; this opinion is however contrary to the plain meaning of the abovementioned statements in *Sifrei* (Tur, ḤM 371:10, 376; *Perishah, ibid., Sma.* to YD 371:2).

The great severity with which trespass on land has been regarded in Jewish law is illustrated in a responsum of Solomon b. Abraham *Adret (Rashba) concerning the following matter: "A person trespassed and built a wall within his neighbor's yard, thereby appropriating therefrom a cubit of land to his own, and then built a big house supported on this wall; now the owner of the yard comes to demolish the other's whole building." Asked whether in terms of the *takkanat ha-shavim* ("*takkanah* of restitution," see *Theft and Robbery) the trespasser might pay for the value of the land taken without having to demolish the building in order to restore the land to its owner, Rashba replied in the negative: "The *takkanat ha-shavim* was instituted in respect of movable property only, and in respect of land it was not stated that he [the injured party] should sell his property and break up his inheritance" (Resp. vol. 3, no. 188).

Widening of the Concept

The first manifestations of a widening in the doctrine of *hassagat gevul* are traceable back to talmudic times, when various *halakhot* were derived from the doctrine by way of *asmakhta*. Thus the doctrine was cited in support of the prohibition against withholding from the poor (all or anyone of them) their gleanings from the produce of the field (Pe'ah 5:6; on the meaning of the term *olim* and *al tasseg gevul olim*, see Albeck, *Mishnah, ibid.*). The prohibition against *hassagat gevul* was similarly invoked to lend a quasi-legal recognition to an individual's right (copyright) in respect of his own spiritual or intellectual creations: "Whence can it be said of one who interchanges the statements of Eliezer with those of Joshua and vice versa, so as to say of pure that it is unclean and of unclean that it is pure, that he transgresses a prohibition? It is taught: 'you shall not remove your neighbor's landmark'" (Sif. Deut. 188). Even the prohibition against marrying a pregnant woman or one weaning a child (i.e., by another man, for reasons of the possible threat to the welfare of the embryo or child), is supported by the doctrine of *hassagat gevul* (Tosef. Nid. 2:7; see also Mid. Tan., Deut. 19: 14; Comm. R. Hillel, Sif. Deut. 188).

Trespass on Economic, Commercial, and Incorporeal Rights

Post-talmudic economic and social developments fostered the need to give legal recognition and protection to rights which had not become crystallized within any accepted legal framework during the talmudic period. Some of these rights found legal expression and protection through an extension of the prohibition against landmark removal, so as to embrace also encroachment on another's economic, commercial, and spiritual confines.

TENANCY RIGHTS. Jewish places of settlement in the Middle Ages were restricted – at times voluntarily, at other times by force – to particular streets or quarters. Hence the demand by Jews for dwellings in these particular places frequently exceeded the available supply, and sometimes a prospective Jewish tenant would offer a landlord a higher than customary rental in order to have the existing tenant evicted, the more so since the *halakhah* excluded neither an offer to pay a high rental nor eviction of a tenant upon termination of his lease. In order to fill the breach against this undesirable social phenomenon, various *takkanot* were enacted in the different centers of Jewish life. These *takkanot*, aimed at protecting tenants from eviction, were reconciled with the principles of Jewish law through a widening of the doctrine of *hassagat gevul* to take in also the tenant's right to remain in occupation of the premises hired by him. The earliest of these *takkanot*, akin in content to the tenants' protection laws found in many modern legal systems, are attributed to the time of *Gershom b. Judah (tenth century; for the text, see Finkelstein, Middle Ages, 31).

In a 13th-century *takkanah* of the community of Crete (Candia) it was laid down that: "A person shall not encroach on his neighbor's boundaries by evicting him from his home… from today onward no Jew shall be permitted… to offer an excessive payment or rental to any landlord in order to gain occupation of his house… and thereby cause him to evict the existing Jewish tenant, for this is a transgression against 'cursed be he that removes his neighbor's landmark,'" not only was the offender to be fined, but the *takkanah* also prohibited anyone to hire the house in question for a full year from the date of its being vacated (*Takkanot Kandyah*, ed. Mekiẓe Nirdamim, p. 16). Similar *takkanot* were customary in different Jewish centers during the Middle Ages (see, e.g., Ferrara *takkanot* of 1554, in: Finkelstein, Middle Ages 93f., 302, 305).

TRESPASS IN MATTERS OF COMMERCE AND THE CRAFTS. In tannaitic times the opinions of most sages inclined in favor of free commercial and occupational competition (BM 4: 12, 60a–b; BB 21b). In the third century C.E., moral censure of someone setting up in competition with a fellow-artisan was expressed by some of the Palestinian *amoraim*, although without any legal sanction (Kid. 59a; Mak. 24a; Sanh. 81a). In the same century, in Babylonia, *Huna laid down the legal principle that a resident of a particular alley operating a handmill could stop a fellow-resident from setting up in competition next to him, because this involved an interference with his source of livelihood (BB 21b). This view was not, however, accepted as *halakhah*, and at the end of the fourth century it was decided by Huna b. Joshua that one craftsman could not restrain a fellow craftsman and resident of the same alley from setting up business (in the same alley), nor even the resident of another town from setting up in the same town, as long as the latter paid taxes to the town in which he sought to ply his craft (BB 21b). Even so, however, there was no definition of the legal nature and substance of even this limited right of restraint, nor was it enforced by any sanctions upon infringement, such as the payment of compensation.

With the restriction of Jewish sources of livelihood in the Middle Ages, and the resulting intensified competition, the whole question once more came to the fore. A Jew who with much effort and money had succeeded in acquiring a monopoly in a particular commercial field stood to lose his investment and livelihood through the competition of a fellow-Jew. From the tenth century onward, the question of a right of monopoly, its scope and sanctions, came to be widely discussed in the literature of the responsa and the codes. This discussion took in the *ma'arufyah* (a form of private monopoly) *takkanah*, which prohibited encroachment on the *ma'arufyah* of a fellow-Jew (*Or Zaru'a*, BM 10a, no. 28). Legally, the *ma'arufyah* right was a full-fledged right, capable of being sold (Resp. *Ge'onim Kadmoniyyim* 151) and was even discussed in relation to whether it passed on inheritance (Resp. *Ḥakhmei Ẓarefat va-Loter* 87). The law of the *ma'arufyah* was not free of dispute, and as late as the 16th century Solomon *Luria differed thereon in a number of material respects (Resp. Maharshal, 35, 36; *Yam shel Shelomo*, Kid. 3:2); yet he too recognized extension of the doctrine of *hassagat gevul* to include a prohibition against infringement of another's livelihood, and the majority of the *posekim* accepted the overall law of the *ma'arufyah* (Sh. Ar., ḤM 156:5 and standard commentaries; *Ir Shushan*, ḤM 156:5; *She'erit Yosef* 17).

Various *takkanot* have come down concerning the restriction of competition, particularly with reference to the acquisition of a right of lease or concession. In medieval times, particularly in Poland, a substantial proportion of the tax-collection concessions granted in respect of the wine trade, mints, border-customs, salt-mines, distilleries and saloons, etc., were concentrated in the hands of Jews, and various *takkanot* were enacted to restrict the competition in this field that had led to higher rentals and reduced profits (Halpern, Pinkas, 11f.; *Pinkas Medinat Lita*, nos. 46, 73, 87, 104; Resp. Bah., Yeshanot 60; *Masot Binyamin* 27; Resp. Maharam of Lublin 62; *Takkanot Medinat Mehrin*, p. 86, no. 259; *Ḥavvot Ya'ir*, 42).

Setting up in competition with a fellow-artisan or professional was similarly restricted in various fields. Thus a *melammed* ("teacher") was prohibited from encroaching on a colleague's confines by taking one of the latter's pupils into his own *ḥeder* (Takk. Cracow of 1551 and 1638, quoted by P.H. Wettstein, in: *Oẓar ha-Sifrut*, 4 (1892), 580 (second pagination) and it was likewise decided with reference to ritual slaughterers (*Ba'ei Ḥayyei*, ḤM pt. 2, 80; *Naḥalah li-Yhoshu'a*, 29; *Mishpat Ẓedek*, vol. 3, no. 14), the offender in this case being regarded as a robber who could be deprived of the remuneration received for such *sheḥitah* (Resp. *Divrei Ḥayyim*, pt. 2, YD 20) which might possibly even be declared ritually unfit (Resp. Shneur Zalman of Lyady, 9; see also Meshullam Roth, *Kol Mavasser*, pt. 1, no. 17).

An interesting development in this field is related to the office of rabbi. As late as the 15th century, it was decided by Israel *Isserlein and Jacob *Weil that a scholar holding the office of rabbi in a particular town could not restrain another from holding a similar office there, even though the latter would interfere with the former's prospects of earning remuneration in return for services such as arranging weddings, divorces, and the like. This decision was based on the reasoning that accepting a remuneration for such services was essentially contrary to the *halakhah* and its permissibility was not easily justifiable, and therefore it could hardly be recognized as an occupation or source of livelihood to be protected from the encroachment of competitors (*Terumat ha-Deshen, Pesakim u-Khetavim* 128; Resp. Maharyu, 151; *Rema*, YD 245:22). This *halakhah*, however, underwent a change in the light of new economic and social realities. Already in the mid-17th century it was stated that even if competition of this kind was not prohibited in law, "perhaps there is reason for protesting against it on the grounds of custom" (*Siftei Kohen* to Sh. Ar., YD 245:22, n.15); and at the commencement of the 19th century the change was also given legal recognition when Moses *Sofer (Resp. *Ḥatam Sofer*, ḤM 21) explained that the rule which held the law of *hassagat gevul* to be inappropriate to the rabbinate was only applicable "to that particular period when a rabbi was not engaged in the same way as a worker… but every scholar led the community in whose midst he lived and as such remuneration for *gittin* and *kiddushin* came to him naturally… but nowadays a rabbi is engaged – sometimes from another town – for remuneration, in the same way as any other worker and the community is obliged to provide him with his livelihood; we are not deterred from the acceptance of such reward, and therefore any one encroaching on the rabbi's confines is in the position of a craftsman setting up in competition with his neighbor." and "a rabbi who does so is disqualified from his position" (Resp. *Shem Aryeh*, OḤ 7).

The legal basis for the restriction of competition, with imposition of sanctions, was found in an extension of the legal doctrine of *hassagat gevul* to include encroachment on the confines of another's trade and source of livelihood. An interesting insight into the manner in which the said extension was arrived at is offered in the method of interpretation adopted by Solomon *Luria (despite his advocacy of greater freedom of competition). In the case of a person ousted by his neighbor from a concession to a customs post, Luria reasoned that the defendant might be held liable for the pecuniary loss suffered by the other party even though it was decided law that there is no liability for **gerama* (a form of indirect damage) in tort. Luria relied on Roke'aḥ's statement that anyone interfering with another's source of livelihood falls within the enjoinder, "Cursed is he who removes his neighbor's landmark," a statement Luria explained on the basis that this passage seemed to be redundant in the light of the prior scriptural injunction, "You shall not remove your neighbor's landmark," unless it was accepted that this passage related to trespass in the field of bargaining. Luria's decision accordingly was that the customs post be restored to the first concessionary without cost, or the defendant compensate him for the damage caused (Resp. Maharshal 89). Other scholars regarded trespass on a neighbor's trading interests as an integral part of the prohibition against trespass on another's right of tenancy (see Resp. Maharam of Padua 41).

COPYRIGHT. The first hints at recognition in Jewish law of the ownership of incorporeal property were given as early as tannaitic times. Thus it was stated, "a person who eavesdrops on his neighbor to reproduce his teachings, even though he is called a thief, acquires for himself" (Tosef., BK 7:13), and support for the prohibition against interchanging one scholar's statements with another's was found (Sif. Deut. 188) in the passage, "Thou shalt not remove thy neighbor's landmark." At the end of the 12th century the same passage was quoted by Judah he-Ḥasid in warning an heir against complying with a direction in the will of his deceased father to inscribe the latter's name as the author of a book, even though it was known to have been written by someone else (*Sefer ha-Ḥasidim*, ed. Mekize Nirdamim, nos. 17–32). It was nevertheless only from the 16th century onward that copyright became a defined legal right, protected by sanctions and partially based on the extended doctrine of *hassagat gevul*.

As in other legal systems, this development arose from the spread of printing and a need for the protection of printers' rights. As early as 1518 an approbation (*haskamah*) to the *Sefer ha-Baḥur* of Elijah *Levita contained a warning, on pain of ban, against anyone reprinting the book within the following 10 years. In the mid-15th century, when Meir *Katzenellenbogen complained to Moses Isserles about the appearance of a rival edition of Maimonides' *Mishneh Torah* (shortly after his work had been printed by Katzenellenbogen), Isserles responded by imposing a ban on anyone purchasing the *Mishneh Torah* from Katzenellenbogen's competitor (Resp. Rema 10). Thereafter it became customary to preface books with approbations containing a warning against trespass in the form of any unauthorized reprint of the particular book within a specified period. Halakhic literature contains detailed discussions on various aspects of encroachment on printers' rights. Thus Isserles imposed his abovementioned ban on anyone purchasing the *Mishneh Torah*, because in that instance it would not have availed against the printer, a non-Jew. Other scholars held the opinion that the ban should be imposed, not on the purchasers of the book – as this would cause study of the Torah to be neglected – but on the printer instead, except if he be a non-Jew (*Zikhron Yosef*, ḤM 2; Resp. *Ḥatam Sofer*, ḤM 89). Unlike Isserles, who confined the operation of his ban (to purchasers) within the country concerned only, other scholars extended operation of the ban to printers everywhere (Resp. *Ḥatam Sofer*, ḤM 41 and 79). In most cases the period of the prohibition varied from three to 15 years, but was sometimes imposed for as long as 25 years. Some of the scholars held that a prohibition imposed against trespass on a printing right takes effect from the date of the approbation in which it has been formulated, but other scholars held the prohibition to come into effect upon commencement of the printing (Halpern, Pinkas 486; Resp. *Shem Aryeh*, ḤM, 20; *Mayim Ḥayyim*, YD 44; Resp. *Sho'el u-Meshiv*, pt. 1, no. 44).

The above prohibition was mainly justified on grounds of the printer's need for an opportunity to recover his heavy outlay through the subsequent sale of the printed product, since reluctance to undertake any printing in the absence of such protection was likely to send up the price of books and cause study of the Torah to be neglected by the public. In this regard there was a fundamental difference of opinion among scholars concerning the fate of the prohibition once the printer had sold the whole of his edition, i.e., prior to expiry of the period of his protection. According to some scholars the prohibition remained fully effective against all other printers, but others held that continuation of the printer's protection, after he had already obtained his remuneration, was itself likely to cause the price of books to rise and to contribute to the neglect of study (*Ḥatam Sofer*, ḤM 79; *ibid.* Addenda no. 57; *Parashat Mordekhai*, ḤM 7; *Tiferet Ẓevi*, YD 62; *Mayim Ḥayyim*, YD 44; *Pitḥei Teshuvah*, YD 236:1; *Ateret Ḥakhamim*, YD 25). This was the central halakhic issue in the dispute, at the beginning of the 19th century, between the respective printers of the Slavuta edition of the Talmud (the brothers Shapiro) and the Vilna-Grodno edition (the widow and brothers Romm).

Out of this discussion grew the recognition given, in later generations, of the existence in Jewish law of a full legal right in respect of one's own spiritual creation. Thus Joseph Saul *Nathanson, rabbi of Lvov, distinguished between printing the work of others, e.g., the Talmud, and printing one's own work, stating that in the latter event "it is clear that he has the right thereto for all time… for with regard to his own [work] a person is entitled to decree that it shall never be printed without his permission or authority… and this right avails him against the world at large" (*Sho'el u-Meshiv*, pt. 1, no. 44). In support of this opinion, Nathanson had reference to the copyright offered the patent-holder of an invention under general Polish law, adding that the effect of an author's restriction against any reprint of his work within a specified period was not to prohibit what would otherwise be permissible, but, on the contrary, to authorize others to reprint his work upon expiry of the period specified because "even if no express restriction is imposed… this remains prohibited as *hassagat gevul* by the law of the Torah" (*ibid.*). A similar view was expressed by Naphtali Ẓevi Judah *Berlin concerning the individual's right in respect of his own teachings; he held that the individual might treat these as he would his own property – save for its total destruction, because it was a *mitzvah* to study and to teach others (*Meshiv Davar*, pt. 1, no. 24).

This view was not, however, generally accepted by the halakhic scholars. Thus Isaac *Schmelkes saw no reason why others might not reprint a book – even if first printed by the author himself – once the original edition had been completely sold; "everyone retains the right to study and to teach… why should another not be able to benefit his fellow men and print and sell cheaply?" (*Beit Yiẓḥak*, YD, pt. 2 no. 75). In his opinion Nathanson's analogy of a patent-right offered no real support for the correctness of his view, since in that case the perpetuity of the right derived from royal charter, without which others might freely copy the inventor's model, and furthermore, a work relating to the Torah was to be distinguished from any other work of the spirit inasmuch as "the Torah was given to all free of charge… not to be used with a view to gaining remuneration" (*ibid.*). At the same time Schmelkes conceded the validity of a restriction imposed against reprint of a book within a specified period, not as a matter of *halakhah*, but in pursuance of the general law of the land, by virtue of the rule of **dina de-malkhuta dina* ("the law of the land is law").

The doctrine of *hassagat gevul* strikingly illustrates one of the paths for the development of Jewish law, namely extension of the content of a legal principle beyond its original confines, in a search for solutions to problems arising through changes in social and economic conditions.

[Menachem Elon]

Hassagat Gevul (Trespass) in the Publishing of Manuscripts

The Jerusalem Rabbinical court (5715 / 861, PDR I 276) heard a case involving a claim of *hassagat gevul* by a person who engaged in the business of publishing manuscripts and who had published R. Isaiah di-Trani's commentary on various books of the Bible. As he was about to publish di Trani's commentary on other books of the Bible, it was brought to his attention that another person intended to publish the same manuscript with the commentary on those books. He therefore petitioned the court for an injunction to prevent him from doing so, on the grounds that he had already given public notification of his intention to publish the commentary on those additional works, and hence it was a case of trespass.

The court discussed various aspects of the limits of business competition (see *Business Ethics) and, at the end of its decision, cited R. Hayyim Halberstam of Zanz (*Resp. Divrei Hayyim*, ḤM 56), who states that the custom of prohibiting the purchase of books from any printer who encroached on the rights of another printer "was based on the words of the *geonim* who preceded us," and was conditional upon a significant rabbinical figure having agreed to the publication by the first printer. He added that this prohibition had acquired the status of a custom (*minhag*), and was therefore valid even if it was contrary to the laws of the Torah.

The court ruled that there was no difference in this regard between a person who had invested funds in the printing of books and one who had invested resources in the preparation of manuscripts for printing. However, in the case in question, the plaintiff, i.e., the first printer, had not only failed to obtain an approbation from a rabbinical authority warning anyone against encroaching on his rights in this work but, according to the court, had not even given due notice of the fact that he was about to publish the commentary on the other books as well. Moreover, the defendant had not used the original invention of the plaintiff or his work, and therefore should not be forbidden to publish the commentary on those books.

Trespass by Infringement on a Monopoly

In the *Atlantic* case (CA 6126/92 *Atlantic v. Doug Frost*, PD 50(4) 471), the Supreme Court of the State of Israel relied on the prohibition against *hassagat gevul* in the context of encroachment upon commercial competition. A fishing company, which for many years had been the only entity operating in a particular part of the fishing sector, had gone bankrupt. This collapse was the result of competition from another company that had begun operating in the same line of business.

The competitor imported much larger quantities of merchandise into Israel without tax than was permitted by the authorities, resulting in a steep drop in prices and the plaintiff's bankruptcy. The court (Justice Z. Tal) examined the issue against the background of the Unjust Enrichment Law, 5738 – 1978 (see *Unjust Enrichment). This law, as is apparent from the preamble to the draft bill, derives from Jewish legal sources (pp. 482–83 of the judgment); hence, in this case as well Justice Tal based his ruling on the provisions of Jewish Law. The Court likened the case to the above-cited law of *ma'arufyah*, establishing the right of a person who had received a permit to engage in a particular area as a legally recognized monopolist, and determined that the plaintiff had grounds to prevent the defendant from engaging in competition with him, and possibly even to restore any profit which the defendant had earned as a result of his unfair competition.

The Law in the State of Israel

The Copyright Act (1911) and the Copyright Ordinance (1924), both of which originated in ordinances from the time of the British Mandate, determine the scope of the prohibition against publication and reproduction of works, including translating, processing, recording or copying such works, and the remedies – both civil and criminal – available for a breach of copyright.

The Performers' Rights Law 5744 – 1984 determines the entitlement of an artist performing artistic, literary, dramatic or musical works, not to have copies made of his performances without his consent, and his right to royalties for the use of his works.

LEGAL PROTECTION OF "MORAL RIGHTS" IN THE STATE OF ISRAEL. In a 1981 amendment, the Copyright Ordinance (1924) was amended, and section 4A was added, bearing the title "Moral Rights." This section established an author's right to have his name applied to his works and to object to any modification to his works liable to prejudice his honor or reputation. A violation of this right constitutes a civil wrong, according to Israeli torts law (see *Torts). The explanation of the draft bill states that

> In contrast to the belated recognition… by other countries of an author's intellectual property rights, the talmudic Sages were cognizant of such rights even in earliest times. An author's right to have his name applied to his own work is established both in the Sages' praise for "one who reports a saying in the name of the person who said it" [of whom it is stated that he "brings redemption to the world" – (TB, Meg. 15a ME). and the comparison drawn between a person who does not credit the author of a composition and a thief: One who attributes other people's ideas to himself is even worse than one who steals a tangible asset. By prohibiting "theft of words," the Sages demonstrated the value attached to wisdom in general, because someone who "wears another person's prayer shawl" causes a situation in which there is "no advantage to the wise person over the fool." The obligation to report a statement in the name of its maker is not merely moral in character: some authorities regarded a "stealer of words" as a "thief" to all intents and purposes, and even applied penal sanctions against those who published other people's works in their own name…" (Draft Bill 5741, p. 238).

In a similar vein, in the *Qimron* case the Supreme Court addressed the Jewish legal perspective on the protection of copyright and intellectual property (CA 2790/93 *Eisenman v. Qimron*, PD 54(3) 817). A U.S. researcher published, without permission, parts of a study conducted by an Israeli scholar, who had devoted 11 years to reconstructing fragments of a scroll from the Second Temple period found in the Qumran caves. The court (Justice Y. Turkel) stated that "The roots of this important principle also derive from Jewish legal sources, which emphasizes the magnitude of the sin of a person who fails to report statements in the name of those who made them." Justice Turkel cites the words of R. Isaiah ha-Levi Horowitz, who states: "It is a great principle to report sayings in the name of those who said them, and not to steal sayings from those who said them, for such theft is worse than stealing money… How great, in my eyes, is the sin of a person who cites an interpretation that has been published in a book, or which he has heard, and fails to mention the name of the original maker or writer of the interpretation" (*Shnei Luḥot ha-Brit, Shavuot*, 183:2).

Regarding encroachment on the business and commercial rights of others, see *Business Ethics.

[Menachem Elon (2nd ed.)]

BIBLIOGRAPHY: Gulak, Yesodei, 1 (1922), 172–5; Gulak, Oẓar, 355, 359f.; S. Funk, in: JJLG, 18 (1927), 289–304; Z. Markon, in: *Ha-Mishpat*, 2 (1927), 192–201; Herzog, Instit, 1 (1936), 127–36; L. Rabinowitz, *Ḥerem Hayyishub* (Eng., 1945), 122–6; Z. Falk, *Ha-Kinyan ha-Ruḥani be-Dinei Yisrael* (1947); E. Rivlin, in: *Emet le-Ya'akov… Freimann* (1937), 149–62; F. Baer, in: *Zion*, 15 (1949/50), 35f.; ET, 9 (1959), 542–6; J. Katz, *Tradition and Crisis* (1961), 59f. **ADD. BIBLIOGRAPHY:** M. Elon, *Ha-Mishpat ha-Ivri* (1988), 1:66, 329f, 553, 555, 653; 3:1420; idem, *ibid., Jewish Law* (1994), 1:74, 394f.; 2:673, 674f, 808; 4:1691; idem, M. Elon, "Profiteering and Overreaching in Jewish Law," in:, *Maḥanayim*, 2 (5752), 8–19 (Heb.); N. Rakover, *Copyright in Jewish Sources* (Heb., 1991); A. Sheinfeld, "*Torts*," in: N. Ravkover (ed.), *Ḥok le-Yisrael* (Heb., 1991/92), 143–54; A. Hacohen, *Law and Economics in the Responsa Literature* (Heb.), 62–77.

HASSAGOT (Heb. הַשָּׂגוֹת), name given to rabbinic works wholly devoted to the criticism, usually negative, of earlier books. *Hassagot* literature is a part of a much wider literary genre, including *tosafot on the one hand, and on the other, supplements in the style of the *Sefer ha-Hashlamah* of *Meshullam b. Moses. They appeared initially in the time of *Saadiah Gaon, when rabbinical "books" in the modern sense were first written, the first book of *hassagot* apparently being one by Mevasser against Saadiah. *Hassagot* literature reached its peak in the 12th century, especially in Provence, the best known author of such works undoubtedly being *Abraham b David of Posquières (*ba'al ha-hassagot*). From the 14th century onward this class of literature began to decline, taking more and more the form of *haggahot, limited in content and generally relegated to the margins of the books.

Only a small number of *hassagot* works were thus termed by their authors. The first such is Jonah *Ibn Janaḥ's work against the grammatical works of Judah *Ḥayyuj. It was translated from the original Arabic into Hebrew by Judah ibn *Tibbon, and given the title *Sefer ha-Hassagah*, thus giving the word *hassagah* its present meaning. *Zerahiah ha-Levi, a friend of Ibn Tibbon, also uses this term with the same meaning in the introduction to his *Sefer ha-Ma'or*. Some *hassagot* works (such as the above-mentioned book of Mevasser) confine themselves to exposing the errors of the text under review, but most offer alternative views and opinions, and sometimes as in the case of Abraham b. David, even defend, explain, and supplement the text in question. *Hassagot* literature embraces a wide range of subjects, including *halakhah*, theology, and grammar. Likewise, writers of *hassagot* differ in their aims, from Mevasser who attacked, apparently on a personal background, the whole of Saadiah's literary work, classifying his *hassagot* according to chapter headings, through *Dunash b. Labrat who wrote *hassagot* on the works of his teacher Saadiah with pure academic interest on linguistic and biblical subjects alone, to Naḥmanides, who was prolific as a writer of *hassagot* (on the *Sefer ha-Mitzvot* of Maimonides, the *Sefer ha-Ma'or* of Zerahiah ha-Levi, and on the *hassagot* of Abraham b. David on *Alfasi). The *hassagot* of Naḥmanides were all written with the sole purpose of defending his predecessors, Alfasi and the author of the *Halakhot Gedolot, against the criticisms which had been leveled against them.

Some *hassagot* were written in order to justify local customs, such as those of Zerahiah on Alfasi, and some in order to undermine a scholar's authority, such as those of Meir *Abulafia on Maimonides. Most writers of *hassagot* confine themselves to important and prominent personalities, such as those mentioned above. Of the critics of Alfasi, mention should be made of his pupils, Ephraim and Joseph *Ibn Migash, whose books are not extant. Particularly noteworthy are the scholars of *Lunel, whose *hassagot* of Maimonides were written for their own instruction and were sent by them to Maimonides in order to elicit replies from him.

The *hassagot* have a style of their own. They are brief, pungent, and provocative. Their sometimes astonishing brusqueness is merely external and, in practice, was not taken amiss. The brevity of style was designed to strike a chord of decisiveness.

BIBLIOGRAPHY: Jonah ibn Janaḥ, *Sefer ha-Rikmah*, ed. by M. Wilensky, 1 (1964^2), 19 n. 7; M. Zucker (ed. and tr.), *Hassagot al Rav Sa'adyah Ga'on* (introd.); I. Twersky, *Rabad of Posquières* (1962), 128–98; B.Z. Benedikt, in: *Sefer Zikkaron… B. de Vries* (1969), 160–7.

[Israel Moses Ta-Shma]

HASSAN, Spanish-Moroccan family whose most famous member in Spain was JAHUDA ABEN HAÇEN, the ambassador of Aragon to Granada in 1287. A refugee in Morocco, SHEMAYYAH HASSAN countersigned *takkanot* ("regulations") in Fez (c. 1575). During the 17th century, his family settled in Salé and Tetuán. Shem Tov and DAVID HASSAN extended their affairs to Gibraltar, where SIR JOSHUA *HASSAN was the first head of government (1964–69). In 1790, the Spanish consul in Tetuán, SOLOMON HASSAN, was hanged upon the order of the sultan Moulay Yazd. A branch of the family then settled in Mogador, whence RAPHAEL HASSAN (d. after 1825), author of *Leḥem Oni* (1834), left for London. In Tetuán, the financier SALVADOR HASSAN (d. after 1879) represented Spain and Italy, and his sons represented Portugal in Tangier, where they founded an important banking company.

BIBLIOGRAPHY: S. Romanelli, *Ketavim Nivḥarim* (*Massa ba-Arav*), ed. by H. Schirmann (1968), 135 f.; A. Leared, *A Visit to the Court of Morocco* (1879), 84–86; I. Laredo, *Memórias de un viejo Tangerino* (1935), 425f.

[David Corcos]

HASSAN, SIR JOSHUA (**Abraham**; 1915–1997), Gibraltar lawyer and politician. Born in the British colony of Gibraltar to a Sephardi family of North African origin, Hassan was admitted to the bar in 1939. Mayor of Gibraltar from 1945 to 1950 and again from 1953, he was chief member of the Legislative Council from 1950 to 1964. In that year he became chief minister, a post equivalent to that of premier, and championed the right of the colony to remain under British rule and not to be transferred to Spain. He lost the position as a result of the elections in 1969. Hassan was a devoted and observant Jew and president of the management board of the Jewish community. He was also active in Zionist affairs and was president of the Jewish National Fund Commission for many years. Even while holding the highest offices, Hassan continued to go from house to house collecting the contents of the J.N.F. boxes. He became a queen's counsel in 1954 and in 1963 received a knighthood. Hassan again served as chief minister of the Gibraltar legislative council from 1972 to 1987.

BIBLIOGRAPHY: ODNB online.

ḤASSĀN IBN ḤASSĀN (second half of tenth century), Spanish astronomer, who was called by some Ḥassān ibn Mar Ḥassān and by others Ali ibn Mar Ḥassān It seems that Ḥassān was not his father's personal name but his family name. Ḥassān was a *dayyan* in Cordoba. That he lived in the tenth century can be inferred from the date 972 C.E., which he used in his calculations. He was an astronomer who followed the system of al-Battānī, writing three works which were in the possession of Jewish astronomers in *Spain and in Eastern countries during the Middle Ages but were later lost.

BIBLIOGRAPHY: Ashtor, Korot, 1 (1966^2), 197, 297.

[Eliyahu Ashtor]

HASSENFELD, SYLVIA KAY, U.S. philanthropist, community activist. Hassenfeld was born in Philadelphia, Pennsylvania, after World War I, the daughter of Sophie and Joseph Kay. After marrying Merrill Hassenfeld, she moved to Providence, Rhode Island, and joined his family members in their extensive service to the Jewish and local community. As the Hassenfeld's family business expanded from pencil manufacturing to the Hasbro Corporation, one of the foremost global manufacturers of toys and games, Sylvia Hassenfeld became involved with the Hasbro Children's Foundation, Hasbro Children's Hospital in Providence, and other philanthropic initiatives. She also occupied Jewish communal positions of increasing responsibility and influence, chairing the National Women's Division of United Jewish Appeal, serving as a member of the Board of Governors of the Jewish Agency for Israel, and becoming the first female president of the American Jewish Joint Distribution Committee (JDC). During Hassenfeld's tenure as president of the JDC from 1988 to 1992, she worked to protect the Jewish populations of Eastern Europe as the communist Soviet Union dissolved. She also supported the Israeli government's efforts to airlift Ethiopian Jews to Israel. After her term as president of the JDC was over, she became the chairman of the board of the JDC. Hassenfeld was a longtime advocate for Israel and a major figure in the Jerusalem Foundation. Other Jewish communal activities included sitting on the boards of the United Israel Appeal, the Memorial Foundation for Jewish Culture, and the Council of Jewish Federations. She was on the boards of the New York University Medical Center, the Paul Nitze School of Advanced International Studies at Johns Hopkins University as well as the Hasbro Children's Foundation. She was also appointed a member of the United States Holocaust Memorial Council. In 1994 the American Jewish Historical Society honored her with the Emma Lazarus Statue of Liberty Award, an award that was noted in the Senate of the United States. As one of the few women to achieve such stature in the world of Jewish philanthropy, Hassenfeld was an important and effective member of the American Jewish community.

[Melissa Klapper (2nd ed.)]

HASSID, WILLIAM ZEV (1897–1974), U.S. biochemist. Born in Jaffa, Hassid served in the British Army in World War I, then went to the U.S. in 1920. He became professor of plant biochemistry at Berkeley, California, 1950, and of biochemistry, 1959. His field of research was in structural carbohydrate chemistry and on carbohydrate metabolism in plants. He was the chairman of the Carbohydrate Division of the American Chemical Society and a member of the National Academy of Sciences.

HASSIDEANS (**Assideans**; Greek form of Hebrew *Ḥasidim*; "pious ones"), religious group or sect which originated in about the third or fourth century B.C.E. It centered around the revival and promotion of Jewish rites, study of the Law, and the uprooting of paganism from the land. The date of origin cannot be known with certainty. The Hassideans are first mentioned by name during the persecutions of Antiochus IV (Ephiphanes), king of Syria (175–164 B.C.E.), when its members joined the Maccabean opposition led by Mattathias in his revolt against the Syrians. They formed the nucleus of the Maccabean revolt and refused to compromise in any way with the Hellenizing policy of the Syrians. The Hassideans were exposed to torture and death for their refusal to desecrate the Sabbath and other Jewish observances. In I Maccabees 2:41 it is recorded that they were "mighty men in Israel… such as were devoted to the Law." In I Maccabees 4 they are described as welcoming peace with the Syrians when the latter offered them assurances of religious liberty. The Hassideans ceased to cooperate with the Hasmoneans (the successors of Judah the Maccabee) in their fight for political independence.

Certain references to the **Ḥasidim* are found in the Psalms (12:2, 30:5, 31:24, 38:28, et al.), but it is doubtful that these accounts refer to the *Ḥasidim*. The passages speak of the efforts of the Ḥasidim to observe the Law, their persecutions by their adversaries, and their struggles against their enemies. References to *Ḥasidim* in the Mishnah and the Talmud (Ber. 5:1, Hag. 2:7, Sot. 3:4, Avot 5:10, and Nid. 17a) may refer to the Hassideans or merely to pious individuals of a later period. The Talmud refers to the strict observance of the commandments by *Ḥasidim*, to their ardent prayers, which they would not renounce even at the risk of their lives, and to their rigid observance of the Sabbath. Because of their meticulous observances the Hassideans have been linked with the *Essenes, but scholarly consensus places them as the spiritual forerunners of the *Pharisees.

BIBLIOGRAPHY: J.W. Lightly, *Jewish Sects and Parties in the Time of Jesus* (1925); R.T. Herford, *Judaism in the New Testament Period* (1928); S. Zeitlin, *History of the Second Jewish Commonwealth: Prolegomena* (1933); idem, *Rise and Fall of the Judean State*, 2 vols. (1962–67); Baron, Social[2], 1–2 (1952); N.H. Snaith, *Jews from Cyrus to Herod* (1956); Schuerer, Hist, index, s.v. *Pious*; R. Kaufman, *Great Sects and Schisms in Judaism* (1967).

[Menahem Mansoor]

HAST, MARCUS (**Mordechai**; 1840–1911), *ḥazzan* and composer. Born in Praga, near Warsaw, Hast served as *ḥazzan* in Warsaw, Torun, and Breslau, and from 1871 in the Great Synagogue in Duke's Place in London. He published the traditional repertoire of the London synagogue, together with some of his own compositions, in *Oẓar ha-Rinnah ve-ha-Tefillah* (1874, with Michael *Bergson), *Seder ha-Avodah* (1879), and *Avodat ha-Kodesh* (1910). He also composed some cantatas and oratorios on Jewish subjects (*Bostanai, Azariah, The Death of Moses, The Destruction of Jerusalem*), conducted the Amateur Choral Society, and founded the Association of Cantors of Great Britain. Some of his synagogal compositions were included in the collections edited by his son-in-law Francis Lyon *Cohen.

HATCHWELL, SOL (or **Suleika**; 1820–1834), Jewish martyr of Morocco, where she is known as "Sol ha-Ẓaddikah." After Sol Hatchwell had visited Muslim friends in her native Tangier, two Moors testified that she had recited the *Shahāda* (Muslim declaration of faith). In spite of her vigorous protests, she was henceforth, according to Muslim law, considered a Muslim. Her case was brought before the sultan of Morocco, who ordered that she be brought from Tangier to Fez. Despite alternating offers of honor and threats, she refused to renounce

Judaism. Condemned to death, she was publicly beheaded in Fez. For a long time, her martyrdom remained a historical topic, inspiring numerous Jewish and non-Jewish authors. The authors of legends, novels, plays, and *kinot* adopted the story of the "Jewish heroine" as their theme; the painter Dehodencq depicted her in his painting known as "The Torment of the Jewess." Her tomb in the cemetery of Fez became the site of pilgrimages of both Jews and Muslims.

BIBLIOGRAPHY: H. de la Martinière, *Souvenirs du Maroc* (1919), 8; L. Godard, *Description et histoire du Maroc* (1860), 83–84; L. Voinot, *Pèlerinages judéo-musulmans au Maroc* (1948), 50–51; L. Brunot and E. Malka, *Textes judéo-arabes de Fès* (1939), 213–7; Attal, in: *Sefunot*, 5 (1961), 507; D. Corcos, in: JQR, 55 (1964/65), 56; Hirschberg, Afrikah, 2 (1965), 304f.

[David Corcos]

HA-TEKUFAH (Heb. הַתְּקוּפָה; "The Season"), Hebrew periodical devoted to literary, scientific, and social subjects which appeared (first as a quarterly, then as an annual) intermittently between 1918 and 1950. *Ha-Tekufah* received the financial backing of Abraham Joseph *Stybel, a philanthropist who had placed David *Frischmann in charge of launching Hebrew literary projects on an unprecedented large scale. Accordingly, Frischmann established both the Stybel publishing house, and launched *Ha-Tekufah*, serving as the editor of both projects. The first volume of *Ha-Tekufah* appeared in Moscow early in 1918, before the Bolshevik regime had decided to suppress Hebrew literature. Frischmann published the works of the world's best authors and scholars. The literary standards of the periodical were high. Frischmann encouraged young authors, for example Eliezer *Steinman. In all respects and not least for its beautiful graphic work, *Ha-Tekufah* was a rare phenomenon in Hebrew literature. Following the suppression of Hebrew in Russia, Frischmann moved to Warsaw where he published issues 5–15. After his death in 1922, he was succeeded by Ya'akov *Cahan and F. *Lachower. When Stybel's publishing house underwent a crisis, *Ha-Tekufah* was moved to Germany and volumes 24–27 (1928–30) were edited in Berlin by Benzion *Katz, S. *Tchernichowsky, and S. *Rawidowicz. The twin volume 26/27 (1930) lists Berlin–Tel Aviv as its places of publication. Volumes 28–29 (1936) were edited by Ya'akov Cahan and published in Tel Aviv. Finally, *Ha-Tekufah* moved to the United States, volumes 30–35 (1946–1950) appearing in New York, edited by E. *Silberschlag and Aaron *Zeitlin (the last volume by Zeitlin alone).

Ha-Tekufah is a treasure trove of Hebrew literature of all genres, including belles lettres by many of the leading writers of the time. Its scholarly articles and translations were also by the leading figures in their field. The contributors to *Ha-Tekufah* are listed in an index appended to volume 25 (author's name only), and in an index (authors and subjects) to all the volumes prepared by J. Barzilai-Folman (1961).

BIBLIOGRAPHY: B.Z. Katz, in: *Ha-Ẓefirah*, no. 24 (1927), 36, 42, 54, 60; idem and A. Zeitlin, in: *Hadoar* (1956), no. 37; P. Birnbaum, *ibid.* (1968), no. 36.

[Getzel Kressel]

HA-TENU'AH LE-MA'AN EREẒ ISRAEL HA-SHELEMAH (The Land of Israel Movement), a nation-wide grouping founded in the immediate aftermath of the Six-Day War, which aimed at ensuring the permanent retention by Israel of the territories occupied in that war. Its membership embraced political elements of the Right and Left, including a particularly strong group of the left-wing *Ha-Kibbutz ha-Me'uḥad as well as most of the Young Guard of the *National Religious Party. Its first manifesto, published in September 1967, was signed by leading writers, including S.Y. *Agnon, Ḥayyim *Hazaz, Nathan *Alterman, and U.Z. *Greenberg, high-ranking army officers of the IDF Reserve, and leaders of commerce and industry, as well as university teachers, rabbis, and members of the various kibbutz movements. The manifesto laid down three basic propositions: first, that the Jewish people was bound both by its history and by its responsibility to the future to retain possession of the entire area of the Land of Israel as circumscribed by the cease-fire lines of June 1967, which were to become the permanent borders of the State; second, that no Israeli government had a mandate for surrendering any part of this inalienable trust; third, that the key to the integration of the new areas lay in immigration and intensive settlement.

The movement campaigned by means of mass meetings throughout the country, as well as by political lobbying among all the partners to the government coalition. From April 1968, it began publishing its own bi-weekly paper, *Zot ha-Areẓ*. It was directly involved in the resettlement of Jews in *Hebron in 1968, and less directly in other settlement projects on the West Bank and the Golan Heights. In 1970, a group sympathetic to the ideas of the Land of Israel Movement was formed in the U.S. under the name of "Americans for a Secure Israel." This group publishes a periodical, *Outpost*, which appears at irregular intervals.

After the adherence of the Israeli government to the U.S. peace proposals (associated with the so-called "Rogers Plan") in the summer of 1970 and the subsequent withdrawal of Gaḥal from the government coalition, the Land of Israel Movement spearheaded a "National Committee to Oppose Withdrawal," which included leading members of the main political parties both of the government and the opposition, with Dr. Chaim Yaḥil as chairman.

In 1973, a group of leading members of the Land of Israel Movement joined the new Center Block (Likud) under the leadership of Menaḥem *Begin. The group was represented in the Likud list by General (Res.) Avraham Yoffe and by the writer Moshe *Shamir, and Yoffe was elected to the Eighth Knesset as a result of the elections held on December 31, 1973.

In March 1976 this group joined with the Independent Center and the State List (led by Yigael Hurvitz) to form a new party, La'am ("For the People"), which became the third largest component of the Likud. In the elections to the Ninth Knesset in May 1977, La'am gained eight seats with Moshe Shamir representing the Land of Israel group. The Likud was now in power and the Land of Israel group was at the center of the political map with the majority of La'am supporting its position.

Throughout this period, the original Land of Israel Movement, led by Zvi Shiloaḥ, remained in existence as a non-party forum. In September 1977 it formed an association with Gush Emunim and with the En Vered Circle (a group of Labor veterans from the moshavim). All these elements were united in a common determination to develop and extend Israeli settlements beyond the Green Line, and in particular in Judea and Samaria. They withdrew their support from the Begin administration after the signing of the Camp David accords in September 1978, and finally found a means of expressing their radical opposition to the government peace plans through a new formation, the Land of Israel Loyalists (Berit Ne'emanei Ereẓ Israel) set up at the end of 1978. This body had a wide political base both within and outside the government coalition. Led by such personalities as Professor Yuval Ne'eman, Yigael Hurvitz, Moshe Shamir and Moshe Tabenkin, it aimed at rallying mass opposition to the proposed autonomy plan and the peace agreements with Egypt.

A significant development came in October 1979 with the establishment of Tnu'at ha-Teḥiyah ("The Movement for Revival") consisting of the chief elements of Berit Ne'emane Ereẓ Israel with the exception of a group led by Yigael Hurvitz which remained in the government coalition resuming the name of Rafi. Teḥiyah was set up as a full-fledged political party inexorably opposed to the autonomy plan and to further concessions to Egypt. Prominent in its leadership were two members of the Ninth Knesset, Geulah Cohen and Moshe Shamir, who withdrew from the Likud in order to identify with the new party as a right-wing opposition. Professor Yuval Ne'eman had a central role in a collective leadership which included Gershon Shafat and Rabbi Eliezer Waldman (central figures in Gush Emunim) as well as Dr. Israel Eldad, Professor Yair Sprinzak, Israel Shenkar and Zvi Shiloah. Teḥiyah mounted a public campaign in 1980 prior to the elections for the Tenth Knesset (in those elections, held in June 1981, Teḥiyah won three seats). The effect of this political challenge was widely felt, especially among the Likud factions and in the National Religious Party. Whilst some were inclined to rejoice at the removal from their midst of the "Land of Israel Loyalists," thinking this would free them for a more moderate political line, others felt that the new development dictated a firmer stand on the part of the older established parties in all that concerned concessions to Egypt, autonomy and settlement on the West Bank. A major feature in Teḥiyah's platform was the emphasis on the need to combine religious and secular elements of the country in a single political framework.

With the electoral success of Teḥiyah and the rise of the more aggressive *Gush Emunim the movement gradually lost its attraction for the younger generation.

BIBLIOGRAPHY: R.J. Isaac, *Israel Divided. Ideological Politics in the Jewish State* (1976); M. Ben Ami (ed.), *Sefer Eretz Israel Hashelemah* (1977); H. Fisch, *The Zionist Revolution: A New Perspective* (1978).

[Harold Harel Fisch]

HA-TIKVAH (Heb. הַתִּקְוָה; "The Hope"), anthem of the Zionist movement, and national anthem of the State of Israel. The poem was written by Naphtali Herz *Imber, probably in Jassy in 1878, and first published as *"Tikvatenu"* ("Our Hope") in his *Barkai*, 1886 (with the misleading note "Jerusalem 1884"). Its inspiration seems to have been the news of the founding of *Petaḥ Tikvah; the themes of the poem, together with those of Imber's *"Mishmar ha-Yarden"* ("Guarding the Jordan"), show the influence of the German *"Die Wacht am Rhein"* and *"Der Deutsche Rhein"* (the "River" and "As long as" motives) and the Polish patriots' song which became the national anthem of the Polish republic ("Poland is not lost yet, while we still live"). In 1882 Imber read the poem to the farmers of *Rishon le-Zion, who received it with enthusiasm. Soon afterward – probably in the same year – Samuel Cohen, who had come to Palestine from Moldavia in 1878 and settled in Rishon le-Zion, set the poem to a melody which he consciously based on a Moldavian-Romanian folk song, *"Carul cu Boi"* ("Cart and Oxen"). In an atmosphere in which new songs and adaptations became folk songs almost overnight because folk songs were needed, and at a time when no one thought of copyright, the melody became anonymous in an astonishingly swift process of collective amnesia. Thus even Abraham Zvi *Idelsohn, who settled in Jerusalem in 1906, approached it as a purely folkloric phenomenon; in his *Thesaurus* (vol. 4, 1923) he published the first of his comparative analyses of the melody, which have been widely accepted and copied since, not always with the proper credit. The true history of *"Ha-Tikvah"* was rediscovered independently by Menashe *Ravina and by an Israel amateur musicologist, Eliahu Hacohen. The Moldavian *"Carul cu Boi"* is itself only one of the innumerable incarnations of a certain well-known melodic type (or pattern) found throughout Europe in both major and minor scale versions. Probably the earliest printed version of *"Ha-Tikvah"* with its melody is found in S.T. Friedland, *Vier Lieder mit Benutzung syrischer Melodien*… (Breslau, 1895).

Many, but not all, of the changes which intervened between the original text and early forms of the melody of *"Ha-Tikvah"* and the current version can still be retraced through songbooks, memoirs, etc. Some of these arose spontaneously; others were made on purpose, either to modify the text according to contemporary opinion or literary criteria, or to achieve the Sephardi syllable-stress instead of the old-fashioned Ashkenazi stress of the original. The standard harmonization is the one established in 1948 by the Italian conductor Bernardino Molinari, who orchestrated *"Ha-Tikvah"* for the *Israel Philharmonic Orchestra; another orchestration by Paul *Ben-Haim is also current. The first English translation of the poem was made by Israel *Zangwill, the first German one by Heinrich *Loewe. In religious Zionist families there is a tradition of singing Psalm 126 (*Be-Shuv Adonai et Shivat-Ẓiyyon*) with the *zemirot to the melody of *"Ha-Tikvah."* The words can be found in several of the traditional collections of religious poetry published in Near Eastern communities during the past 50 years, and "*Ha-Tikvah*" was therefore entered by Israel *Davidson in his *Ozar*.

Two competitions for a Zionist anthem, the first proclaimed in *Die Welt* in 1898 and the second by the Fourth Zionist Congress in 1900, came to nothing because of the unsatisfactory quality of the songs composed or suggested. At the Fifth Zionist Congress in Basle in 1901 one of the sessions concluded with the singing of what was still called "*Tikvatenu*." During the Sixth Zionist Congress (Basle, 1903), it was sung by dissenting factions. The Seventh Zionist Congress (Basle, 1905) ended with an "enormously moving singing of '*Ha-Tikvah*' by all present," a moment which can be said to have confirmed its status. Although already proposed by David *Wolffsohn, the formal declaration of "*Ha-Tikvah*" as the Zionist anthem was only made at the 18th Zionist Congress in Prague in 1933. Under the Mandate, "*Ha-Tikvah*" was the unofficial anthem of Jewish Palestine. At the Declaration of the State on May 14th, 1948, it was sung by the assembly at the opening of the ceremony and played by members of the Palestine Symphony Orchestra at its conclusion. However, "*Ha-Tikvah*" has not been given official status as a national anthem by a proclamation of the Knesset.

BIBLIOGRAPHY: JC (Jan. 3, 1902), 32; (Aug. 28, 1903), viii and passim; (Aug. 4, 1905), 24; (Aug. 11, 1905), 19; Idelsohn, Melodien, 4 (1923), 116; 9 (1932), xix; Idelsohn, Music, 222–3; E. Hacohen, in: *Gittit*, no. 37 (June 1968), 4–5; M. Ravina, *Ha-Tikvah* (Heb., 1969), incl. bibl.; Goell, Bibliography, 895–900.

[Bathja Bayer]

HATOKAI, ALDIN (1944–), Israel laborer. Hatokai was awarded the Israel Prize in 1986 for managing a work crew of Jews, Muslims, Druze, and Circassians in an exemplary manner and setting an outstanding example as an employee of the American-Israeli Paper Mills in Ḥaderah.

HATRED (Heb. שִׂנְאָה), overt or covert ill will. The Torah explicitly prohibits hatred of one's fellow in the verse "Thou shall not hate thy brother in thine heart" (Lev. 19:17). Hatred is understood by the rabbis as essentially a matter of mental disposition, as implied in the phrase "in thine heart." One who expresses hostility to his fellow through word or deed, although he violates the commandment "love thy neighbor" and injunctions against injury, insult, vengeance, etc., is not, according to most rabbinic authorities, guilty of the specific sin of hatred referred to in Lev. 19:17 (Sifra, Kedoshim; Ar. 16b; Maim. Yad, De'ot 4:5, *Sefer ha-Mitzvot*, prohib. 302; *Ḥinnukh* 238). The reasons are, apparently, that covert hatred is the more vicious form (*ibid.*) and that a person can defend himself against open hostility (I.M. Kagan, *Ḥafeẓ Ḥayyim* (Vilna, 1873), 13, n. 7). The Talmud is emphatic in its denunciation of hatred. Hillel taught that the essence of the entire Torah is, "What is hateful to you, do not do to others," all else being "commentary" (Shab. 31a). Hatred of one's fellow creatures "drives a man out of this world" (Avot 2:16). One who hates his fellow is considered a murderer (DER, 11).

Gratuitous Hatred

(Heb. שִׂנְאַת חִנָּם). According to the Talmud gratuitous hatred is the most vicious form of hatred, and the rabbis denounce it in the most extreme terms. In their view the Second Temple was destroyed as punishment for this sin (Yoma 9b; cf. Story of Kamẓa and Bar Kamẓa, Git. 95b). It is equal to the three paramount sins of idolatry, fornication, and murder (Yoma 9b).

Halakhic Implications of Hatred

According to all rabbinic authorities one who hates (that is, one who, out of enmity, has not spoken to his fellow for three days) is ineligible to serve as a judge in cases involving his enemy; according to some he may not even be a witness (Sanh. 27b). Certain relatives of a woman (e.g., mother-in-law, stepdaughter) may not testify concerning the death of her husband, for fear they may harbor hidden enmity (Yev. 117a).

Permissible Hatred

It is proper to hate the wicked. "Do not I hate them, O Lord that hate Thee?" (Ps. 139:21); "The fear of the Lord is to hate evil" (Prov. 8:13). The same thought is expressed in the Talmud (Pes. 113b). Exhortations to hate all manner of evil abound in the Bible (e.g, Ex. 18:21; Ps. 26:4). God Himself hates every form of immorality (e.g., Deut. 12:31; Isa. 1:14; Ps. 5:6) because of its harm to mankind, since God Himself cannot be affected (Saadiah Gaon, *Beliefs and Opinions*, 4:4). The enjoinder to hate evildoers applies, however, only to impenitent and inveterate sinners, those who pay no heed to correction (Maim. Yad, Roẓe'aḥ 13:14; *Ḥinnukh*, 238).

The Bible, nevertheless, distinguishes between the person as such and the sinner in him, "As I live, saith the Lord, I have no pleasure in the death of the wicked, but that the wicked turn from his way and live" (Ezek. 33:11). One must assist even one's enemy in transporting his burden (Ex. 13:5) for otherwise "he may tarry [by the wayside]" and endanger his life (BM 32b; Pes. 113b). Furthermore, in order to learn to subdue one's baser inclinations, one must give priority to aiding the wicked over the good (BM 32b; Maim. Yad, Roẓe'aḥ 13:13). Thus, the true object of proper hatred is the sin, not the sinner, whose life must be respected and whose repentance effected. Beruryah, wife of Rabbi Meir, offered her interpretation of Psalm 104:35, "Let sins [*in loco* – sinners] cease out of the earth," and thereby admonished her husband to pray not for the destruction of sinners but for their regeneration (Ber. 10a). It is forbidden to rejoice at the downfall of even those sinners whom it is proper to hate: "Rejoice not when thine enemy falleth" (Prop. 24:17). Thus, since one can never be certain of one's motives, of the absolute wickedness of the sinner, and of whether one has discharged or is indeed even capable of completely discharging his obligation to reform the sinner, the rabbis stress the obligation of loving all men: "Be of the disciples of Aaron, loving peace and pursuing peace, loving your fellow creatures and drawing them near to the Torah" (Avot 1:12).

BIBLIOGRAPHY: J.D. Kranz, *Sefer ha-Middot* (1967), 202–27; G.F. Moore, *Judaism in the First Centuries of the Christian Era*, 2 (1946), 89ff.; M. Lazarus, *Ethics of Judaism*, 2 vols. (1900), passim;

A. Cohen, *Everyman's Talmud* (1949), 210ff.; E. Bar-Shaul, *Mitzvah ve-Lev* (1966), 167–77.

[Joshua H. Shmidman]

HATRY, CLARENCE CHARLES (1888–1965), British company promoter. Born in London, the son of a silk merchant, Hatry was educated at St. Paul's. In 1910 he took over his father's silk business and promptly went bankrupt. Notwithstanding this setback, he emerged within a few years as a successful insurance broker. With the temporary boom created by the end of the World War I, Hatry developed into probably the best-known company promoter in Britain, buying, consolidating, and then selling virtually any company he could find, often amalgamating them into poorly conceived trusts and making and losing several fortunes. Just before the 1929 Wall Street crash, when rumors of a large-scale swindle involving Hatry began to circulate in the City of London, he voluntarily confessed to fraud and, in 1930, was sentenced to 14 years' imprisonment for defrauding his customers of an estimated £15 million. Released in 1939, Hatry reemerged in the post-1945 period as a reformed businessman, owning London's famous Hatchard's Bookshop and other firms. Just after his release from prison he also managed to write an intelligent book on immigration and minority groups, *Light Out of Darkness* (1939). He is said to have been depicted in numerous detective stories of the time in which a swindler is murdered, including Ngaio Marsh's *Death at the Bar* (1939).

BIBLIOGRAPHY: ODNB; DBB, III, 110–14.

[William D. Rubinstein (2nd ed.)]

HATVANY-DEUTSCH, a 19th-century family of Hungarian industrialists and landowners, originally from the province of Arad. In the 20th century members of the family achieved distinction as painters, writers, and patrons of the arts. Its founder was IGNAC DEUTSCH (1803–1873), who established Hungary's first sugar refinery in the 1820s. Under his sons, BERNÁT and JÓZSEF (I) DEUTSCH, the business expanded and made an immense contribution to the Hungarian national economy. As a reward the brothers were raised to the nobility in 1879 and authorized to add "de Hatvan" ("Hatvany") to their surname, the town of Hatvan, east to Budapest, having become the center of their industrial operations.

József I's son, SÁNDOR HATVANY-DEUTSCH (1852–1913), was, like his father and grandfather, born in Arad. He continued the development of the family business and founded the Hungarian manufacturers' association, but he was also a noted patron of the arts. He helped to establish various charitable institutions and received a barony in 1908. Sándor's sons gained distinction in Hungarian cultural life. The elder, LAJOS HATVANY (1880–1961), author, literary critic, and journalist, wrote in Hungarian and German. Born in Budapest, he entered the literary life of the Hungarian capital and, as a young man, was a founder of the literary periodical *Nyugat*. A generous supporter of aspiring writers, he was a prominent champion of Endre Ady (1877–1919), the great Hungarian poet. Among the journals which Lajos Hatvany edited before and during World War I was *Pesti Napló* ("Pest Journal"). His political outlook was radical and he took an active part in the democratic October Revolution of 1918. At the outbreak of the Communist Revolution of 1919 he went to Vienna, but returned to Budapest in 1927 and gave himself up for trial. He was found guilty of treason and libeling the Hungarian people, and sentenced to a short term in prison. On his release he resumed his writing career, but with the advent of the Hitler regime, he was again forced to leave the country in 1938. He spent World War II in England and returned to Hungary in 1947. During the 1950s he was condemned to silence, and was only granted recognition after 1959.

Lajos Hatvany's studies and criticisms were thorough. A convinced assimilationist and himself converted, he never ceased to deal with the problem of the Hungarian attitude toward Jews, and of Jewish assimilation and nationalism. His great trilogy, *Urak és emberek* ("Gentlemen and People," vol. I, 1927; complete, 1963^2), depicts the history of a Jewish family at the turn of the century and is a clear reflection of his own internal struggle. An English version of the first part appeared in New York as *Bondy Jr.* (1931). His other works include *Die Wissenschaft des Nichtwissenswerten* (1908), a satire on philological exaggerations; *Die Beruehmten* (1913), a drama; *Das verwundete Land* (1921); *Gyulai Pál estéje* ("The Sunset of Paul Gyulai," 1911, 1960^2); and *Ady – cikkek, emlékezések, levelek* (1959^2).

The second son of Sándor was the painter FERENC HATVANY (1881–1958). Like his brother Lajos, he was born in Budapest and converted to Christianity. As a student he came under the influence of Adolf *Fényes. He acquired a fine collection of 19th-century French paintings and some of his own nudes and still lifes are displayed in the Budapest Museum of Fine Arts. He settled in Paris about 1947 and died in Lausanne.

The descendants of Ignac Deutsch's other son, Bernát, also attained importance in Hungarian public life and a few of them remained within the Jewish fold. Bernát's son, JÓZSEF (II) HATVANY-DEUTSCH (1858–1913), collaborated with his cousin Sándor in the development of the sugar industry, and his banking and other financial interests made him one of the wealthiest Jews in Hungary. Active in Jewish communal affairs, he was a trustee and benefactor of the Budapest rabbinical seminary and a generous supporter of the Hungarian Jewish Literary Society (IMIT). He also established pioneering welfare and sickness benefit schemes for workers in his factories. In 1908 József II, like Sándor, was created a baron and became a member of the Hungarian parliament's upper house. He died in Germany. József II's children were the author LILI HATVANY (1890–1967), the political writer ANTONIA HATVANY-DEUTSCH (b. 1894), and the industrialist and writer BERTALAN HATVANY (1900–1980). Born in Budapest, Bertalan was a successful businessman, and a patron of literature, one of the writers whom he supported being the great Hungarian poet, Attila József (1905–1937). An active

Zionist and a generous contributor to the movement, he held views similar to those of the *Berit Shalom on the problem of peace between Jews and Arabs. Bertalan Hatvany left Hungary in 1939, spent some time in Australia, and then settled in Paris. His early travels are reflected in books such as *Ázsia és a nacionalizmus* ("Asia and Nationalism," 1931); *Ázsia lelke* ("The Soul of Asia," 1935, which includes much of Jewish interest, including impressions of Ereẓ Israel); *Konfuciustól Nehemiásig* ("From Confucius to Nehemiah," 1936); *A kínai kérdés története* ("History of the Chinese Question," 1938); and *Az út és az ige könyve* ("The Book of the Way and the World," a translation of Tao-te Ching, 1957).

BIBLIOGRAPHY: B. Kempelen, *Magyarországi zsidó és zsidó eredetü családok*, 2 (1938), 61–64; A. Szerb, *Magyar irodalomtörténet* (1943); *Magyar Zsidó Lexikon* (1929), s.v.; *Magyar Irodalmi Lexikon*, 1 (1963), s.v.; UJE, 5 (1941), 249–50.

[Baruch Yaron]

HAUBENSTOCK-RAMATI, ROMAN (1919–1994), composer. Haubenstock-Ramati was born in Cracow, where he worked as a radio conductor from 1947 until 1950. He then spent some years in Israel, heading the Central Music Library, Tel Aviv, and teaching composition at the Rubin Academy of Music there. In 1957 he settled in Vienna, where he directed the reading of modern scores for the Universal Edition (1957–68). Later he was appointed professor of composition at the Vienna Musikhochschule (1973–89), where he continued the Schoenberg tradition in his teaching, being himself a late representative of the Second Viennese School. In the 1950s Haubenstock-Ramati was impressed by the mobile sculptures of Alexander Calder and strove to express their kinetic energy in his music series of *Mobiles* (1957–58). The composer created variable forms in which components can be varied, repeated, or combined; he also developed his own system of graphic notation. The combination and confrontation of mobile and stable forms dominate his compositions of the 1960s, especially the opera *Amerika*, 1962–64, based on the novel by *Kafka.

ADD. BIBLIOGRAPHY: NG²; MGG²; *Festschrift R. Haubenstock-Ramati* (1989).

[Yulia Kreinin (2nd ed.)]

°**HAUPT, PAUL** (1858–1926), U.S. Orientalist and Bible scholar. He taught from 1880 at the University of Goettingen. In 1885 he was appointed to head the incipient Oriental Seminary in Johns Hopkins University in Baltimore, Maryland, U.S., but he continued to lecture at Goettingen each summer until the outbreak of World War I. His more than 500 publications in German and English (as well as one Hebrew article on the Pentateuchal sources, 1895) and his training of several generations of Semitic philologists significantly influenced American biblical and Oriental studies.

The scholarly writings of Haupt are governed by the empirical historical method with full employment of linguistic and philological data. His first essay, "The Oldest Semitic Verb Form" (in JRAS, 1878), showed that the Akkadian present is probably the most archaic verb form preserved in the extant Semitic languages. His biblical commentaries on the Song of Songs (1902), Ecclesiastes (1905), Nahum (1907), Esther (1908), and Micah (1910) emphasize Hebrew metrics. In *Purim* (1906) he discussed the origin of the Purim festival, tracing it to the Persian Nauroz feast, and in *Midian and Sinai* (1909; = ZDMG, 63 (1909), 506–30) he argued for the historical and cultural maturity of the Mosaic era. In his semipopular writings, Haupt was very productive, but whimsical and pontifical. Influenced by the writings of E. Burnouf, he wrote two learned articles on the Aryan ancestry of Jesus, which were later used by the Nazis as propaganda against the Jews. His original writings were supplemented by his editorial work on important series of Orientalia and Biblica. He edited with W.R. Harper the early volumes of *Hebraica* and with Friedrich Delitzsch the *Assyriologische Bibliothek* and *Beitraege zur Assyriologie und semitischen Sprachwissenschaft*. Three series of Oriental studies published by Johns Hopkins University were under his supervision. He also edited the *Polychrome Bible* (1893, 1896–1904) and with H.H. Furness edited the English translation of selected portions.

BIBLIOGRAPHY: *Oriental Studies Dedicated to P. Haupt* (1926), includes bibliography; Albright, in: *Beitraege zur Assyriologie und semitischen Sprachwissenschaft*, 10 no. 2 (1928), xiii–xxii.

[Zev Garber]

HAUPTMAN, HERBERT AARON (1917–), U.S. mathematician and Nobel laureate in chemistry. Hauptman was born in New York City and received his B.S. at City College (1937), M.A. at Columbia University (1939), and Ph.D. from the University of Maryland (1954) in mathematics after serving in the U.S. Navy in World War II from 1942. He was a staff member of the Naval Research Laboratory in Washington, D.C. (1947–70), before joining the crystallography group of the Medical Foundation of Buffalo (now the Hauptman-Woodward Medical Research Institute), where he became research director in 1972 and then president. He was also research professor in the departments of biophysical sciences and computer science of the University of Buffalo. Hauptman's research work stems from his collaboration with the physicist Jerome Karle starting in 1947. They developed mathematical methods for establishing the structure of complex molecules which could previously only be determined by time-consuming, classical crystallographic techniques of more limited scope and accuracy. He was awarded the Nobel Prize jointly with Jerome Karle (1985), the only mathematician to have received the award in chemistry. His Nobel lecture discusses the integration of direct and mathematical techniques for establishing molecular structure. Subsequently he continued to refine these methods, which are in universal use in basic and medical research and in drug design. He remained actively involved in the work of the institute named after him, which studies protein structure, protein interactions, and the alterations predisposing to disease. His many honors include the Gold Plate Award of the American Academy of Achievement (1986), election to the U.S. National

Academy of Sciences (1988), and an honorary degree from Bar-Ilan University (1990).

[Michael Denman (2nd ed.)]

HAUPTMAN, JUDITH (1943–), U.S. scholar of rabbinics, rabbi. Born in Brooklyn, New York, Hauptman was a graduate of the Yeshivah of Flatbush in 1961. She then enrolled in Barnard College. After a year there, she moved to Jerusalem and spent three years studying at the Hebrew University; she then returned to Barnard College and received her bachelor's degree in economics in 1967. At the same time, she also earned a bachelor's of Hebrew literature in Talmud from the Seminary College of Jewish Studies. Hauptman continued her studies by entering the graduate program in rabbinics at JTS, receiving her masters degree in Talmud in 1973 and pursuing her doctorate under the supervision of David *Weiss Halivni. When she completed her graduate studies in 1982, she became the first woman to ever be awarded a Ph.D. in the field of Talmud and Rabbinics.

Hauptman then joined the faculty of the Jewish Theological Seminary, where she served as the assistant dean of the Seminary College of Jewish Studies, held the Rabbi Philip R. Alstat Professorship in Talmud, and was appointed the E. Billie Ivry Professor of Talmudic and Rabbinic Culture.

One of the major focuses of Hauptman's scholarly work has been in the synoptic study of rabbinic texts: the study of parallel and related texts found in different documents as a means of exploring the historical development of laws, traditions, and documents in rabbinic culture and writing. Her first book, published in 1988, was *Development of the Talmudic Sugya: Relationship Between Tannaitic and Amoraic Sources*, which addresses the place of early, "tannaitic" literature in the rabbinic culture of study that ultimately produced the two Talmuds. Hauptman became a pioneer in a growing new approach, one that sees in the Tosefta materials which predate the Mishnah and out of which mishnaic material was developed.

A second prominent focus of both Hauptman's scholarly and other work has been Jewish feminism. In the early 1970s she was a member of Ezrat Nashim, a group advocating for the greater inclusion of women in Jewish ritual in the Conservative movement, including the ordination of women as rabbis. In 1972, she published "An Assessment of Women's Liberation in the Talmud" in the journal *Conservative Judaism*, and two years later her essay "Images of Women in the Talmud" appeared in the collection *Religion and Sexism*, edited by Rosemary Ruether; she went on to publish numerous works analyzing rabbinic attitudes and legislation regarding women. This aspect of Hauptman's work is exemplified by her book *Rereading the Rabbis: A Woman's Voice*, published in 1998. In this work, Hauptman examines the historic development of rabbinic legislation in a number of areas relating to women and women's lives – marriage and divorce, social relations between the sexes, dowry and inheritance, etc. – in order to demonstrate a consistent trend toward greater (though still unequal) rights and protections for women over time. Her 1993 articles "Some Thoughts on the Nature of Halakhic Adjudication: Women and Minyan" and "Women and Prayer: An Attempt to Dispel Some Fallacies," both in *Judaism*, became the basis on which JTS Chancellor Ismar *Schorsch revised JTS policy to allow full participation for all women in egalitarian services at the seminary.

Having trained rabbis for more than a decade and having advocated the ordination of women, Hauptman applied to the rabbinical school of the JTS. The result was quite surprising. Citing concerns about the potential conflicts that might arise if Hauptman were to sit in classes with those who were her students on other occasions, Chancellor Schorsch denied her application. Undeterred, she subsequently enrolled in the Academy for Jewish Religion, and was ordained as a rabbi in 2003.

[Gail Laibovitz (2nd ed.)]

HAURAN (Heb. חַוְרָן), region in northeastern Transjordan, today part of Syria. The name occurs for the first time – as *Hauranu* – in the account of Shalmaneser III's expedition against Hazael of Aram-Damascus in 841 B.C.E. Tiglath-Pileser III in 733/2 B.C.E. turned it into an Assyrian province called Haurina. This is apparently the Hauran mentioned by Ezekiel in the only biblical reference to the place (47:15–18). In describing the ideal boundaries of Ereẓ Israel, Ezekiel cites on the north "Hazer-Haticcon [probably Hazer-Inum] which is by the border of Hauran" and on the east "between Hauran and Damascus." The Septuagint reads here "Auranitis"; the suffix *-itis* indicates that it was a Ptolemaic administrative district. In 198 B.C.E the district of Hauran was taken from the Ptolemies by the Seleucids and with the decline of that kingdom it became the possession of the Itureans who held it also at the beginning of Roman rule. In order to restrain the inhabitants of adjacent *Trachonitis who were in the habit of raiding the convoys of Damascus, Augustus in 23 B.C.E. assigned the Hauran (together with Trachonitis and Batanaea) to Herod who settled Jews there in military colonies (Jos., Ant., 15:343; Wars, 1:398). It remained in the domain of the Herodian dynasty, passing from Herod's son Philip to Agrippa I and Agrippa II and with the death of the latter it was attached to Syria. At the end of the third century the Hauran was transferred to Provincia Arabia of which it remained a part until the end of Byzantine rule. The Hauran flourished during the Roman period when many cities were founded there including Canatha and Dionysias-Soada. As it was located in Jewish territory, the Hauran was one of the places in the Second Temple period where beacons were lit to announce the approach of Rosh Ha-Shanah and the festivals. After the signals were received at the Hauran from Agrippina (Grapina)-Kawkab al-Hawā they were transmitted to Bet Bitlin (RH, 2:4). The Hauran's border with the Nabatean kingdom in the Roman period can be very precisely established by inscriptions and eras used for dating purposes. The border included al-Mushannaf, Bosana (Būsān), Ḥabrān, Dionysias-al-Suwayda, and Karak in the Hauran. In Roman times it is therefore apparent that the concept of the Hauran had expanded and also included the fertile valley known today as al-Nuqra. The borders of Hauran thus reached Arabia along Wadi al-Dhahab in the south, the slopes of the Jebel el-Druze (Druze Mountain) in the east, Trachonitis in the north, and the Bashan (in the limited sense) and the city of Dion in the west.

Jewish settlement in the Hauran continued in talmudic times; several rabbis bore its name (e.g., Ḥunya de-Berat Huran; TJ, Shek. 1:1, 46a). In the fourth and fifth centuries Christianity became deeply rooted in the Hauran as is indicated by the participation of bishops from the Hauran in church councils and the many ruins of churches found there. These churches inherited the independent style of the Eastern tradition which had evolved in the architecture and ornament of the buildings of the Hauran as early as Roman times and which also influenced synagogues in the Galilee. As in other border districts, Arabic influence increased in the Hauran in the Byzantine period. It was incorporated in the kingdom of Benu Ghassān under Byzantine protection but in 634 the Arabs conquered it without undue effort. The Hauran thereafter declined until *Druze from Lebanon began settling there in the 18th century. Following the riots in Lebanon between Druze and Christians in 1860, Druze settlement in the Hauran increased considerably and the region today is called Jebel el-Druze (Mount of the Druzes). Geographically the term Hauran comprises three separate concepts: (1) Mt. Druze itself, 5,900 ft. (1,800 m.) high; (2) the mountain, its slopes, and the el-Nuqra valley; and (3) all of the eastern part of northern Transjordan from Damascus to the Yarmuk. About 80,000 Druze live in the region.

BIBLIOGRAPHY: S. Klein, *Ever ha-Yarden* (1925), 19–21; Tcherikover, in: *Tarbiz*, 4 (1933), 233, 361; Avi-Yonah, Geog, index; E. Fouer, *Die Provinzeinteilung des assyrischen Reiches* (1920), 52, 63; Elliger, in: PJB, 32 (1936), 68–69; Noth, *ibid.*, 33 (1937), 37–40; Epstein (Elath), in: PEFQS (1940), 13ff.; D. Sourdel, *Les cultes de Hauran à l'époque romaine* (1952); M. Dunand, *Le Musée de Soueida* (1934).

[Michael Avi-Yonah]

HAURWITZ, BERNARD (1905–1986), U.S. physical scientist. Haurwitz was born in Glogau, Germany, and studied mathematics and science at the Universities of Breslau and Gottingen before getting his Ph.D. in geophysics at the University of Leipzig under the supervision of Ludwig Weickmann (1931). After a lectureship in Leipzig (1931–32), he visited the Massachusetts Institute of Technology (MIT) and the California Institute of Technology. Electing not to return to Nazi Germany, he worked at the University of Toronto as a Carnegie Institution fellow (1935–37) and with the Canadian Meteorological Service (1937–41). He returned to MIT as associate professor (1941–47) before moving to New York University as professor and chairman of the newly formed meteorology department and research associate at the Woods Hole Oceanographic Institution. He moved to Boulder, Colorado, initially as professor of geophysics at the University of Colorado and research associate at the High Altitude Observatory (1959–64), and then to the National Center for Atmospheric Research to direct the Advanced Study Program (1964–67). On retirement (1976) he became senior research associate. During the period 1964–85 he was also research associate and then visiting professor at the Geophysical Institute of the University of Alaska in Fairbanks. Haurwitz's research interests centered on dynamic meteorology, defined as the application of mathematics and physics to studying the atmosphere and ocean tides. He was a theoretician who also excelled in precise observation and analysis. He made major contributions to analyzing the physical state of the upper atmosphere and its effects on ocean tides, the influence of solar activity on the atmosphere, and the nature of noctilucent clouds which form at very high altitudes and usually at high latitudes. His work had practical applications to weather forecasting, of particular importance during World War II. Haurwitz was a renowned teacher and his papers and books are models of clarity. His honors included election to the U.S. National Academy of Sciences (1960), the Carl-Gustaf-Rossby Award of the American Meteorological Society (1962), and the Bowie Medal of the American Geophysical Union (1972). He served on the Board of Governors of the Hebrew University of Jerusalem. Haurwitz was twice married, the second time to the scientist Marion Wood. He was passionate about hiking and skiing, activities that largely influenced his choice of working location. He died in Fort Collins, Colorado.

[Michael Denman (2nd ed.)]

HAUSDORF, AZRIEL ZELIG (1823–1905), a precursor of the *Ḥibbat Zion movement and pioneer of Jewish settlement in Ereẓ Israel. Born in Myslowice, Silesia, Hausdorf attended a yeshivah until the age of 20, when he went to London. He left in 1847, to settle in Jerusalem. He was a translator and expert on Jewish subjects for the Austrian consul and also represented the Jews at the Prussian consulate. He thus helped to protect the rights of refugees from Russia and Poland who did not enjoy the protection of a foreign power. When Baron Gustave de *Rothschild visited Ereẓ Israel, Hausdorf assisted him in founding the Misgav la-Dakh Hospital in the Old City of Jerusalem. He was a founder of the Ḥevrat Ahavat Zion, formed by members of Kolel Hod (Holland-Deutschland community), which bought a plot of land in the vicinity of the Temple Mount (1858), in order to found the Battei Maḥaseh quarter for the poor. The *kolel* sent him to Holland and Germany, where he acquired the support of Ẓevi Hirsch *Kalischer. He helped to acquire various plots of lands (near Jaffa and at Moẓa).

BIBLIOGRAPHY: E. Hausdorf, *Zelig Hausdorf u-Fe'ulotav le-Hatavat ve-Haramat Maẓẓav Eḥav* (1905); P. Grajewsky, *Zikkaron la-Ḥovevim ha-Rishonim*, 1 (1927), 24–26; 2 (1929), 45–47; Yaari, Sheluḥei, 805–7; Eliav, in: *Sinai*, 61 (1967), 298–315.

[Geulah Bat Yehuda (Raphael)]

HAUSDORFF, FELIX (1868–1942), German mathematician. Hausdorff was born in Breslau, and was professor of mathematics at Greifswald from 1913 to 1921 and at Bonn from 1921 until his retirement in 1935. Together with his wife he committed suicide in 1942 in order to avoid the deportation order of the Gestapo. Hausdorff was an authority on set theory and its applications to sets of points and real analysis. His textbook *Mengenlehre* (Leipzig, 1935) is recognized as one of the great classics of set theory. The depth and simplicity of his research into fundamental problems was a source of inspiration in the rapid development of modern mathematics. Hausdorff was devoted to music and literature and published belles lettres under the pen name of Paul Mongré.

BIBLIOGRAPHY: *Poggendorff's biographisch-literarisches Handwoerterbuch der exakten Naturwissenschaften*, 7a (1958), 402.

[Barry Spain]

HAUSER, EMIL (1893–1978), violinist and teacher. Born in Budapest, Hauser became a teacher at the Hoch Conservatory, Frankfurt, in 1913, and joined the Adolph Busch Quartet. In 1917 he formed the Budapest String Quartet, in which he played first violin, until emigrating to Palestine in 1932. He founded the Palestine Music Conservatory, Jerusalem, in 1933, which was the first professionally oriented music school in the country with a comprehensive program for all instruments, theory, composition, history, and Arab music. Hauser headed the chamber music class at the Juilliard School of Music, New York, from 1947 until 1959 and Pablo Casals' master courses in Zermatt, Switzerland, for four years. His *Interpretation of Music for Ensemble* was published in 1952.

[Jehoash Hirschberg (2nd ed.)]

HAUSER, HENRI (1866–1946), French historian. Hauser was born and educated in Oran, Algeria, but made his career in France. He was professor of ancient and medieval history at the University of Clermont-Ferrand (1893), taught modern history at the University of Dijon (1903), and after 1921 economic history at the University of Paris. Hauser's works include *L'enseignement des sciences sociales* (1903), *Travailleurs et marchands dans l'ancienne France* (1920), and *Les débuts du capitalisme* (1927). In *L'impérialisme américain* (1905), he prophesied the decline of Europe and dominance of the United States, and his *Méthodes allemandes d'expansion économique* (1915) pertained largely to the role German industry had upon the outbreak of World War I. When the Nazis occupied France in 1940, he fled to the south where, in hiding and despite failing eyesight, he completed a study on the economic thought of Richelieu.

BIBLIOGRAPHY: *American Historical Review*, 52 (1946), 221f., obituary.

[George Schwab]

HAUSER, PHILIP MORRIS (1909–1994), U.S. sociologist. Hauser was born in Chicago, where he also studied, receiving his Ph.D. from the University of Chicago in 1938. From 1938 until 1947 he was deputy director at the U.S. Bureau of the Census; in 1947 he was appointed professor of sociology at the University of Chicago. He was president of the American Sociological Association (1967–68) as well as the American Statistical Association and the Population Association of America.

Hauser worked on various studies of population, urban problems, and city planning. He continued the ecological emphasis of the Chicago School of Sociology, and channeled it demographically. He founded the University of Chicago's Population Research Center, a leading center for the study of demographic processes. He served as its director until 1979. Hauser became the Lucy Flower Professor Emeritus of Urban Sociology at the University of Chicago in 1974.

An internationally known demographer, Hauser was an active proponent of population control in the United States and elsewhere. He also took an active interest in the civil rights movement. Especially concerned with the consequences of racial segregation and overpopulation, Hauser was a member of Chicago's board of governors of the Metropolitan Housing and Planning Council (1958 to 1970) and served as a consultant for the city's Department of Development & Planning and the Department of Health. In 1963 he became chairman of the Advisory Panel for the Desegregation of the Chicago public schools

His works include *Government Statistics for Business Use* (1946), *Population and World Politics* (1958), *Housing a Metropolis* (1960), *The Population Dilemma* (1963), *Handbook for Social Research in Urban Areas* (1967), *Differential Mortality in the United States* (with E. Kitagawa, 1973), *Social Statistics in Use* (1975), and *The Challenge of America's Metropolitan Population Outlook, 1960 to 1985* (with P. Hodge).

[Werner J. Cahnman / Ruth Beloff (2nd ed.)]

HAUSER, RITA ELEANOR (1934–), U.S. lawyer and U.N. representative known for her interests in world peace, human rights, and philanthropic ideals. The elder of two daughters of Nathan and Frieda Abrams, Hauser received her B.A. from Hunter College in 1954, did graduate work in France on a Fulbright Scholarship, and attended Harvard Law School where she was one of the first women students. Hauser's advanced degrees included a Ph.D. in political economy from the University of Strasbourg in France; an LL.B. from New York University Law School, and the French equivalent of an LL.B. (a License en droit) from the University of Paris Law Faculty. An international lawyer, Hauser was senior partner and counsel in the New York City law firm Strook, Strook, and Lavan for more than 20 years. Raised in a Republican family, Hauser became involved in high-level Republican politics, where she was recognized as a distinguished strategist and speech writer. Hauser was appointed as the U.S. Representative to the United Nations Commission on Human Rights from the late 1960s to the early 1970s and was also a member of the United States delegation to the United Nations General Assembly. While serving at the U.N. Hauser met Golda *Meir, who encouraged her engagement with Jewish issues and Middle East politics. As head of the International Center for Peace (1984–91) Hauser was instrumental within the team brokering the Oslo Accords between the Palestine Liberation Organization and the State of Israel. In her capacity as chair of the International Peace Academy (which is affiliated with the United Nations), Hauser was also invited by the Palestine Elections Committee to serve as an official observer of the 1996 Palestinian elections. Hauser and her husband, Gustave, the parents of two children, created the Hauser Foundation, a philanthropic organization "that aims to illuminate the vital role that the nonprofit sector and nongovernmental organizations play in aiding societies to discover and accomplish important public purpose." The Hauser Foundation also focused specifically on conflict resolution in the Middle East. Hauser was the founding chair of the Advisory Board of the RAND Center for the Middle East Public Policy (an acronym, RAND, was derived from the contraction of research and development). Hauser was director of the International Institute for Strategic Studies in London and served on the boards of the New York Philanthropic Society and the Lincoln Center for Performing Arts. She also served as vice chair of the Dean's Advisory Board of Harvard Law School, as national co-chair of the Harvard University Campaign, and on commissions of the U.S. Department of State and at the Brookings Institution. In 2001 President Bush appointed her to the U.S. President's Foreign Advisory Board and to the U.S. President's Intelligence Oversight Board.

BIBLIOGRAPHY: R. Gursky, "Hauser, Rita Eleanor," in: P.E. Hyman and D. Dash Moore (eds.), *Jewish Women in America: An Historical Encyclopedia*, vol. 2 (1997), 602–4. **WEBSITE:** www.afgw.libraries.psu.edu/profiles/hauser.html.

[Marla Brettschneider (2nd ed.)]

HAUSNER, BERNARD (1874–1938), rabbi, Polish Zionist leader, and representative of Poland in Palestine. Born in Czortkow, Galicia, he studied at the University of Vienna and at the rabbinical seminary there, graduating in 1901. He taught religion at the secondary schools of Lemberg (1899–1914) and was rabbi and spiritual leader of the Lemberg Jewish community for the two years that the city was occupied by the Russians (1914–16). He also served as military chaplain in the Austrian army on various fronts (1916–18). After the war he became a leader of the Zionist movement, particularly of Mizrachi, in Poland. He served as a member of the Sejm (Polish parliament) from 1922 to 1927, when he settled in Palestine. In 1926 Hausner published a treatise in Polish on the financial rehabilitation of Poland, which earned him the reputation of an economic expert. In Palestine, he served first as economic adviser to the Polish government and later (1932–34) as Polish consul in Tel Aviv. Both in Poland and Palestine, Hausner took an active part in public affairs and published essays on Jewish subjects (in Polish), as well as a Polish translation of the *maḥzor.*

His son was GIDEON *HAUSNER (1915–1990), chief prosecutor in the *Eichmann trial.

BIBLIOGRAPHY: Tidhar, 9 (1958), 3316–17; EẒD, 2 (1960), 19–23. **ADD. BIBLIOGRAPHY:** J. Majchrowski et al. (eds.), *Kto byl kim wdrugiej Rzeczypospolitej* (1994), 293.

[Getzel Kressel]

HAUSNER, GIDEON (1915–1990), Israeli lawyer. Hausner was born in Lvov (Lemberg) where his father Bernard *Hausner was rabbi. He came to Ereẓ Israel in 1927 and after graduating from the Hebrew University in 1941 and from the Law School in 1943 entered private practice. He was lecturer in Commercial Law at the Hebrew University from 1954 to 1960, when he was appointed Attorney General, serving until 1963. In this capacity he served as chief prosecutor in the *Eichmann Trial, about which he wrote *Justice in Jerusalem* (1966, 1967²). Speaking in the name of the Jewish people in a powerful opening statement and telling the story of the Holocaust with the aid of over 100 witnesses and 1,600 documents, Hausner became the voice most clearly identified with the trial and the achievement of a final reckoning with one of the most monstrous figures of the Nazi era. Hausner was a member of the Knesset from 1965 to 1981, representing the Independent Liberal Party and was chairman of its parliamentary group from 1967 to 1974. He was a minister without portfolio in the Israeli cabinet from 1974 to 1977. He was chairman of the Israel Association for Human Rights since 1965 and of the Council of Yad Vashem from 1969.

°HAUTVAL, ADELAÏDE (1906–1988), French psychiatrist and Righteous Among the Nations. Born in Hohwald (Bas Rhin), France, to a Protestant family, Hautval studied medicine in Strasbourg and after her qualification worked in several psychiatric wards. In April 1942, traveling to her mother's funeral, she was arrested trying to cross the demarcation line separating the two zones of France without a permit. Awaiting her trial in Bourges prison, she vehemently protested the harsh treatment of Jewish prisoners who were incarcerated there. The reply she received was, "As you wish to defend them, you will follow their fate." Sent to Auschwitz with a convoy of women prisoners, she arrived there in January 1943. She reportedly bore a sign, stitched on her overcoat, with the inscription: "A friend of the Jews." At Auschwitz, she helped hide a group of women afflicted with typhus and looked after them as best as she could. She was then asked by the SS garrison doctor, Eduard Wirths, to participate in the sterilization experiments practiced on the bodies of Jewish women in the infamous Block 10, which involved removing their ovaries either surgically or by means of radiation in order to produce sterility. Hautval told Wirths that she was completely opposed to these experiments. Wirths was surprised that she would object to a program whose ultimate purpose was the preservation of a superior race. Wirths asked her, "Cannot you see that these people are different from you?" and she answered him that there were several other people different from her, starting with him. After her confrontation with Dr. Wirths, she was advised to stay out of sight; she feared retribution but was not punished. Moved to the nearby Birkenau camp, she continued to practice medicine and heal the prisoners as much as possible, considering the circumstances, until August 1944, when she was transferred to the Ravensbrueck women's camp in Germany. She survived and was liberated in April 1945. In 1963, she appeared in London at the trial of Leon Uris vs. Wladyslaw Dering. Uris, in his book *Exodus*, had mentioned the experiments perpetrated by Dering and others on bodies of prisoners in Auschwitz, without the use of anesthesia, and Dering had consequently sued Uris for libel. A witness for the defense, Hautval refuted Dering's claim that it was futile to disobey orders in Auschwitz, since in Dering's words, "to refuse would be sabotage," adding that in Auschwitz "all law, normal, human, and God's law were finished." Hautval, by contrast, maintained that SS orders to remove women's ovaries could be gotten around in such ways as to avoid punishment. Justice Lawton in his summing up of the evidence to the jury described Dr. Hautval as "perhaps one of the most impressive and courageous women who has ever given evidence in the courts of this country [England]." Years later, recalling the Holocaust, she stated: "This unspeakable horror could have been avoided. If only this organized contempt of humanity, this megalomaniac insanity, had been confronted by a civilized world – lucid, courageous, and determined to safeguard its primary values." On a visit to Israel in 1966, to plant a tree in the Garden of the Righteous at Yad Vashem, after being honored the previous year with the title of Righteous Among the Nations, she stated, "The return of the people of Israel to their own country is an accomplishment concerning not only itself but the world at large.… Israel has always played a gestative, fermentative role, due to which it was hated or respected. Its mission in the world continues. May Israel remain faithful to it. The entire history of the Jewish people demonstrates the primacy of spiritual forces. Hence, its undertaking cannot but be successful."

BIBLIOGRAPHY: Yad Vashem Archives M31–100; A. Hautval and H. Tennyson, "Who Shall live, Who Shall Die?" in: *Intellectual Digest*, Vol II, No. 7 (March 1972), 52–54; M. Hill and N. Williams, *Auschwitz in England* (1965); M. Paldiel, *The Path of the Righteous* (1993), 62–64; "Auschwitz in an English Court: The Dossier on Dr. Dering," in: *World Jewry: Review of the World Jewish Congress*, Vol. VII, No. 3 (May/June 1964); I. Gutman (ed.), *Encyclopedia of the Righteous Among the Nations: France* (2003), 298–99.

[Mordecai Paldiel (2nd ed.)]

HAVANA, capital of Cuba; general population: 2,180,000 (2001); estimated Jewish population 1,000 (82% of the Jews in the country).

During colonial times Havana was considered by Spain as "the key to the Americas" for its important strategic location. It was the meeting point of the treasure fleet on its return to Spain. Historians assume that *Crypto-Jews were present among the inhabitants of Havana as well as among the merchants from non-Catholic countries who were involved in illegal commerce with the Spaniards.

The first Jewish group to settle in Havana after Cuban independence (1902) came from the United States. They founded the United Hebrew Congregation in 1906. They were followed by Sephardim, mainly from Turkey, whose communal congregation, Shevet Ahim, was founded in 1914. In the 1920s thousands of Jews from Eastern Europe arrived in Cuba, hoping to use it as a stepping stone to the U.S. Many of them settled in Havana, where they founded the Centro Israelita (Jewish Center) in 1925, together with a large number of social, religious, cultural, and political organizations. In the late 1930s and during World War II Havana became a temporary haven for thousands of Jews fleeing Nazi Germany, using loopholes in Cuba's immigration laws. In May 1939, however, Havana was the scene of the tragic episode of the S.S. **St. Louis*, whose passengers were refused landing and were compelled to return to Europe, where many of them perished in extermination camps.

Following World War II the Havana community prospered both economically and socially. In 1951 the Ashkenazi community laid the cornerstone for the Patronato, a magnificent building that symbolized the social mobility and prosperity of Havana Jews. When the Sephardim inaugurated their Sephardi Center, Fidel Castro was already in power.

The Cuban revolution of 1959 marked the decline of Havana Jews. Following the nationalization of private business, around 90% of them emigrated from Cuba, most of them to the United States. The government respected the right of the Jewish community to continue its religious life, but the demographic decline, the emigration of lay and religious leaders, and the influence of the atheistic policy of the state had a growing impact on Jewish life. In 1973 Cuba severed its diplomatic relations with Israel, and the isolation of Havana Jews increased. The deterioration of communal life continued until the late 1980s, when 752 Jews (82% of the total in Cuba) were registered in the community's records for the distribution of products for Passover, sent annually by the Canadian Jewish Congress.

Since 1990 the community in Havana experienced a great revival. The collapse of Communism in the Soviet Union forced the Castro government to look for new sources of hard currency, and Cuba was opened to tourists and foreign investors. The community in Havana receives moral and material support from Jewish organizations, especially from the *Joint Distribution Committe. Today there are three religious congregations functioning in Havana – the Patronato (with a Conservative synagogue), Adath Israel (Orthodox), and the Sephardi Center. In addition there are several other groups, including the B'nai B'rith, the Women's Organization, and ORT. For a detailed history of Havana Jews (including bibliography) see *Cuba.

[Margalit Bejarano (2nd ed.)]

HAVA (also known as **Hana** or **Fava**) **OF MANOSQUE**, surgeon in early 14th century Provence. Hava was one of many Jewish women active in medicine during the Middle Ages. She belonged to a prominent medical family; her husband and son were also surgeons and she probably apprenticed with a relative. In late 1321 or early 1322 Hava faced court charges over her treatment of a Christian who had injured his testicles; the court wanted to know if Hava had palpated the wound. She answered in the negative because her son, Bonafos, had assisted in the treatment. Hava gave the instructions and designated the necessary medicines, while her son had physical contact with the patient.

BIBLIOGRAPHY: J. Shatzmiller, "No 47," in: *Médecine et Justice en Provence Médiévale: Documents de Manosque, 1262–1348*. Aix-en-Provence: Publications de l'Université de Provence, (1989), 150–51; "Hava/Hana of Manosque," in: E. Taitz, S. Henry, and C. Tallan, *The JPS Guide to Jewish Women, 600 B.C.E.–1900 C.E.* (2003), 79.

[Cheryl Tallan (2nd ed.)]

HAVAS, GÉZA (pen name, **K. Havas Géza**; 1905–1945), Hungarian journalist, born in Nagykanizsa. In 1936 he joined the review *Szép szó*, whose editor was the poet Attila József. He chose the Nazi economists as his target and wrote incisive articles against them. He also edited collections of essays on socialism and wrote a study on Magyar lyrics of the 20th century, *Új magyar lira* (1940). From 1941 he was interned in labor camps and in 1944 was deported to Germany. He died in the concentration camp of Guenskirchen, near *Mauthausen, a few hours before the arrival of the U.S. Army.

ḤAVAẒẒELET (Heb. חֲבַצֶּלֶת), Hebrew newspaper, first published in Jerusalem in 1863, discontinued after approximately one year, revived at the end of 1870, and continued until close to the outbreak of World War I. Founded by Israel Bak, a pioneer of the Hebrew press, *Ḥavaẓẓelet* began publication after **Ha-Levanon* on July 13, 1863 in the wake of a controversy which broke out in Jerusalem concerning the affairs of the Eẓ Ḥayyim school. It opposed the position taken by *Ha-Levanon*, its journalistic rival. So fierce was the dispute that both papers were forced to discontinue publication in 1864. When *Ḥavaẓẓelet* resumed publication in 1870, Bak's son-in-law, I.D. Frumkin, gradually moved into the editorial staff, and soon became its editor. In the last years of the paper his son Gad Frumkin also served as editor.

The paper was the organ of the Ḥasidim, who were a minority among the general Ashkenazi *yishuv* in Jerusalem, mainly composed of *Mitnaggedim*. *Ḥavaẓẓelet* opposed the leadership of the Ashkenazi *yishuv* and supported the programs for the settlement of Israel (see S. *Berman, Rabbi J. *Alkalai) which were opposed by Ashkenazi rabbis of Jerusalem. In 1873 it launched an attack against the controllers of the *ḥalukkah* funds and those countered with a boycott against *Ḥavaẓẓelet* and its editor. Frumkin advocated the "productivization" of the Jewish community in Israel, especially by means of agriculture, and opposed Sir Moses Montefiore's programs because of his excessive sympathy for those in charge of the *ḥalukkah*. He encouraged young forces from among the members of the *yishuv* to participate in the newspaper.

Ḥavaẓẓelet appeared originally as a monthly, and from the second copy of the second year as a weekly, continuing as such for several decades. Only in its last years was the format enlarged, and the paper was published three times a week (1908–10); in the end it was printed again as a weekly. In 1870–71 a Yiddish supplement (*Die Roze*) came out. The literary supplement was called *Pirḥei Ḥavaẓẓelet*. In 1882, under the editorship of A.M. Luncz, there was published a foreign language supplement called *Gazette de Jerusalem*, and in 1884, the supplement *Mevasseret Ẓiyyon* appeared under the editorship of Eliezer Ben-Yehuda.

After the pogroms in Russia in the beginning of the 1880s the paper advocated *aliyah* and encouraged the first immigrants to settle on the land of Petaḥ Tikvah. With the arrival of the first wave of *aliyah* from Russia and from Yemen, the paper endeavored to ease their absorption both in agricultural work and in Jerusalem. Frumkin invited Ben-Yehuda to Jerusalem from Paris to work on the *Ḥavaẓẓelet*. Ben-Yehuda's publication of his own independent newspaper, *Ha-Ẓevi* in the autumn of 1884, gave rise to an antagonism between *Ha-Ẓevi* and *Ḥavaẓẓelet*. *Ḥavaẓẓelet* soon became the mouthpiece of the older generation of the *yishuv* in Jerusalem, while *Ha-Ẓevi* supported the new *yishuv*, especially the agricultural villages. The former, which in the beginning had been in opposition to the *ḥalukkah*, now became its loyal supporter. It now rejected the program of enlightenment that it had advocated in the 1870s, turned against the modernists of the *yishuv*, and later opposed political Zionism.

Gad Frumkin tried to revive the flagging spirit of the *Ḥavaẓẓelet* at the beginning of the present century, but his energy was curbed by his father. While this newspaper died out, a new press with an entirely different direction rose in its place. *Ḥavaẓẓelet* nevertheless raised a generation of writers and scholars, mainly from the old *yishuv*, who later filled distinguished positions in literature, science, and public life in Jerusalem and Ereẓ Israel. In 1954 a selection of the writings of I.D. Frumkin from the volumes of the *Ḥavaẓẓelet*, together with a comprehensive introduction and comments, was published in Jerusalem.

BIBLIOGRAPHY: G. Kressel, *"Ha-Levanon" ve-"Ha-Ḥavaẓẓelet"* (1943); idem, *Toledot ha-Ittonut ha-Ivrit be-Ereẓ Yisrael* (1964; see cap. 1); G. Yardeni, *Ha-Ittonut ha-Ivrit be-Ereẓ Yisrael bi-Shenot 1863–1904* (1969), 17–81, 107–162; A. Frumkin, *In Friling fun Idishn Sotsialism* (1940); G. Frumkin, *Derekh Shofet bi-Yrushalayim* (1955); D. Idelovitch (ed.), *Kovez Ma'amarim le-Divrei Yemei ha-Ittonut be-Ereẓ Yisrael*, 2 (1936), 28–38; S. Ha-Levi, *Ha-Sefarim ha-Ivriyyim she-Nidpesu bi-Yrushalayim* (1963).

[Getzel Kressel]

HAVDALAH (Heb. הַבְדָּלָה; "distinction"), blessing recited at the termination of Sabbaths and festivals, in order to emphasize the distinction between the sacred and the ordinary, with regard to the Sabbath (or festival) that is departing and the ordinary weekday. *Havdalah* is one of the most ancient blessings: according to the Talmud "the men of the *Great Synagogue instituted blessings and prayers, sanctifications and *Havdalot* for Israel" (Ber. 33a). Some authorities hold that the obligation to recite the *Havdalah* derives from the Pentateuch. According to the Babylonian Talmud, it was originally inserted in the *Amidah*, but subsequently "when they became richer – they instituted that it should be said over the cup of wine; when they became poor again – they inserted it again into the prayer" (*ibid.*). Three views are mentioned in the Jerusalem Talmud (Ber. 5:2, 9b): (1) *Havdalah* was originally inserted in the *Amidah* and then also transferred to the cup of wine "for the benefit of the children"; (2) it was originally instituted over the cup of wine; (3) it was instituted in both places at the same time. Because of these variations, there were four opinions, already in the time of the *tannaim*, on the place of *Havdalah* in the *Amidah*. Moreover, in accordance with most of the *tannaim*, the present practice is to recite the proper *Havdalah* blessing over the cup of wine, while in the *Amidah* only mention of it should be made. At a much later date, in the middle of the medieval period, the custom began to develop of reciting *Havdalah* over a cup of wine in the synagogue as well, in order to exempt those who had no wine (cf. Ta'an. 24a).

The text of the *Havdalah* ceremony over a cup of wine developed over a long period of time and, in the Ashkenazi version, a number of verses were added at the beginning as "a good omen" (Tur, OḤ 296:1). These usually commence with, "Behold, God is my salvation," etc. (Isa. 12:2–3). This introduction is followed by three blessings – over wine, spices, and light – inserted in the *Havdalah* arrangement much before the time of *Bet Hillel and Bet Shammai, who already differed about their text and order (Ber. 8:5), even though R. Judah ha-Nasi instituted the last two over the cup of wine merely for the benefit of his household (Pes. 54a). The purpose of the blessing over light – "Who createst the light of the fire" – is to show that work is now permitted and to stress the departure of the Sabbath. The blessing over the wine itself stems from the duty to recite *Havdalah* over a cup of wine, as in the case of *Kiddush. The reason for the blessing over spices has not been clarified. The *rishonim* explained it as compensation to the Jew for the loss of the "additional soul" which traditionally accompanied the Jew throughout the Sabbath (see Ta'an. 27b; Sof. 17:5; and see Tos. to Pes. 102b); other reasons have also been suggested (Tur, OḤ 296).

The *Havdalah* blessing itself, the fourth and final, according to the order of the prayer, was known from early times in various versions, differing primarily in the number of distinctions (e.g. "between the Sabbath and the other days of the week") they contained. In the Talmud (Pes. 103b; TJ, Ber. 5:2, 9b) it is laid down that "He who would recite but few distinctions, must recite not less than three, but he who would proliferate must not recite more than seven." R. Judah ha-Nasi, however, recited only one, the distinction "between the holy and the profane" (Pes. loc. cit.). Poetic versions containing seven distinctions have been preserved in the *Genizah* fragments (see Zulay in bibl.). Similarly with its wording in the *Amidah* of which various versions are known in the liturgies, of the different communities and in the *Genizah* fragments (see Zulay, bibl.).

Havdalah over a cup of wine is customary also when the Sabbath is immediately followed by a festival, since the festival's stringency is less than that of the Sabbath (Ḥul. 26b). Combined in this case with the *Kiddush*, its wording is: "Who makest a distinction between holy and holy." The order of this *Kiddush-Havdalah* is indicated by the well-known acrostic *yaknehaz (*yayin* ("wine"), *Kiddush, ner* ("candle"), *Havdalah, zeman* ("season" = *she-heḥeyanu*)). This *Havdalah* is mentioned in the evening blessing for the sanctification of the day and the combined formula, fixed by *Rav and *Samuel in Babylonia, is known as "the pearl of Rav and Samuel" (Ber. 33b). When the termination of the festival is followed by a working day, *Havdalah* is recited without candle or spices.

There are many customs connected with *Havdalah*: the pouring of some of the wine on the ground as an omen of blessing (cf. Er. 65a), and hence the custom of overfilling the cup (Turei Zahav to OḤ 296:1); passing the last drop of wine in the cup over the eyes (cf. PdRE 20), and extinguishing the lamp with the remaining drops; when saying the blessing over the light, some look at their fingernails and some at the lines on their palms (S. Assaf, *Sifran shel Rishonim* (1935), 177). After *Havdalah* it is customary to chant special hymns, the best known being: "May He who sets the holy and the ordinary apart," originally instituted for the termination of the Day of Atonement, and "Elijah the prophet." Other songs and hymns said before or after *Havdalah* are mostly based upon the Jerusalem Talmud (loc. cit.).

[Israel Moses Ta-Shma]

The Spice Box (Hadas)

In the ceremony of *Havdalah*, it is customary for a box of aromatic *spices to be handed round accompanied with an appropriate blessing. In medieval Europe, sweet-smelling herbs such as myrtle (Heb. *hadas*) were generally used for this purpose. For this reason, the spice box came to be known as a "*hadas*" when spices were substituted for herbs. The moment of transition is marked by Rabbi Ephraim of Regensburg in the 12th century, who recorded that he said the blessing not over a branch of myrtle, but over spices contained in a special glass receptacle. This is probably the earliest mention of a special spice box. The earliest extant example, however, dates from about 1550. It originated from the synagogue at Friedberg, Germany and is now in the Jewish Museum, New York. Another example, dated 1543, was formerly in the Landes museum at Kassel but was lost when the museum was destroyed by the Nazis. The spice box has taken a large variety of forms and has inspired craftsmen to fantasy and often to whimsy. Among the Ashkenazi Jews it often took the form of a fortified tower. It has been suggested that this form was adopted because spices, which came from the Orient, were so valuable that they had to be stored in the castle or city hall. It is also thought to have been derived from the ritual implements of the Church, such as the monstrance and thurible, which also took this form, as the implements of the Church were executed by the same gentile craftsmen as those of the synagogue. A "Jewish monstrance" commissioned from a Frankfurt silversmith in 1550 is thus probably a spice box. The tower form could be imitated from a local tower or church steeple, surrounded by a balustrade, surmounted with a pennant and carrying a clock face indicating the conclusion of the Sabbath. It was executed in silver, sometimes engraved to resemble masonry, and later in filigree. Human and animal figures were placed around the tower: biblical worthies, soldiers, musicians, various synagogal officials such as the *shoḥet* (ritual slaughterer) with his knife, the scribe with his pen and inkwell, the *Schulklopfer* with his hammer (who woke worshipers for morning prayers), or sometimes a Jew holding a beaker of wine and performing *Havdalah*. A variant of the tower form was executed in northern Italy in the 18th century, where it was covered with delicate filigree work, studded with semiprecious stones and adorned with enamel plaques depicting scenes from the Bible. Spice boxes were also made in many other forms, such as animals, fish, birds, flowers and fruit, and even windmills. There was also the simpler form of round, square, or rectangular boxes. On occasion the spice box was combined with the taperholder used in the *Havdalah* ceremony. The spices were contained in a drawer beneath the taper, which was sometimes supported by a figure. In the East small jars and boxes were used to keep the herbs. In Persia these were jars with elongated necks, sometimes filled with rose water. As a result of the revival of Jewish ritual and synagogal art in Israel and the United States after World War II, spice boxes have been designed and executed by eminent artists in a contemporary manner.

BIBLIOGRAPHY: M. Brueck, *Pharisaeische Volkssitten und Ritualien* (1840), 108–25; A. Jawitz, *Mekor ha-Berakhot* (1910), 44–47; Abrahams, Companion 172f., 145, 190f.; I. Elbogen, in: *Festschrift... I. Lewy* (1911), 173–87; Mann, in: HUCA, 2 (1925), 318f.; Finesingen, *ibid.*, 12–13 (1937–38), 347–65; Zulay, in: *Sefer Assaf* (1953), 303–6; ET, 8 (1957), 67–102; Narkiss, in: *Eretz Israel*, 6 (1960), 189–98.

ḤAVER, 16th-century family of rabbis, originally from Damascus. The best-known members of the family are Isaac and his son Ḥayyim. ISAAC (d. 1541) was a rabbi and *posek*. According to Moses *Basola, before 1522 he was the head of the Sicilian community of Damascus and a physician. He discussed halakhic problems with Jacob *Berab I. He died in Damascus and in 1564 his remains were taken by his son ḤAYYIM, to Safed for burial. Ḥayyim was already an important rabbi of Safed before his father's death, since his signature appears on a ruling of 1536 together with those of other great Safed halakhists (see Responsa *Avkat Rokhel*, of Joseph Caro, no. 124). He was apparently called to Damascus to succeed his father. In 1546, in accordance with his father's custom, Ḥayyim sent to Safed from Damascus the yearly calendar of the Sicilian community. He appears to have returned to Safed after a number of years and to have become one of the members of the *bet din* of Moses di *Trani, his signature appearing on a halakhic ruling of 1557 together with that of Di Trani and Shem Tov Bibas (Moses di Trani, Responsa *Mabit*, 1:287). A ruling by Ḥayyim from his Damascus period appears in *Avkat Rokhel* (no. 114). He died in Safed. ISAAC, one of his sons, is mentioned in a responsum of 1567 (*Mabbit*, 2:88). Apparently JOSHUA ḤAVER, the friend of Israel *Najara and a merchant in Syria, was also a member of this family.

BIBLIOGRAPHY: Ashtor, Toledot, 2 (1951), 494; Assaf, in: KS, 22 (1945/46), 244; Frumkin-Rivlin, 1 (1929), 82; R.J.Z. Werblowsky, *Joseph Karo, Lawyer and Mystic* (1962), 92 n. 6. **ADD. BIBLIOGRAPHY:** A. David, in: *Zion and Jerusalem, The Itinerary of Rabbi Moses Basola (1521–1523)* (1999), 87.

[Abraham David]

ḤAVER, ḤAVERIM (Heb. חָבֵר, pl. חֲבֵרִים; "member"), the name for those belonging to a group that undertook to observe meticulously both the laws of **terumah* ("heave-offering") and **ma'aser* ("tithing") as well as the regulations of impurity and purity. The regulations binding the obligations of the *ḥaver* were already laid down in the time of Hillel and Shammai, since Bet Hillel and Bet Shammai differ about the details. A candidate for membership of the group was not immediately accepted as a full *ḥaver*, but was subjected to a period of education and probation. The candidate declared his readiness "to accept the obligations of a *ḥaver* in the presence of three *ḥaverim*" (Bek. 30b). He was first accepted "for wings" (Tosef., Dem. 2:11), according to S. Lieberman, one who washed his hands before eating and before touching ritually clean food (*Tosefta ki-Feshutah* (see bibliography), pt. 1, 214). In the next stage he undertook more stringent obligations of ritual purity, undertaking "that he would not give *terumah* or *ma'aser* to an **am ha-areẓ*, nor prepare ritually clean food for him, and that he would eat ordinary food in a state of ritual purity" (Tosef., *ibid.*, 2:2; Lieberman, *ibid.*, 210; see Dem. 2:3). After undertaking to observe all the obligations of a *ḥaver* he underwent a period of probation – 30 days according to Bet Hillel and 12 months according to Bet Shammai – before being accepted as a full *ḥaver*. Anyone could join the group, including women and slaves (Tosef., Dem. 2:16–17), on condition that they undertook to fulfill the aforementioned obligations. No candidate was exempted from the conditions of acceptance ("even a scholar had to undertake them," *ibid.*, 2:13). Joining the group of *ḥaverim* meant separation from those who were not *ḥaverim* – from the *am ha-areẓ* – raising many problems in daily life, even in the life of the family, when some members were *ḥaverim* while others were not. In pursuit of their aims the *ḥaverim* did not isolate themselves from society or create special centers for themselves, nor did they form an organized group with officeholders having particular functions. Detailed *halakhot* were evolved to regulate relations between them and their environment in all spheres of life.

It is not possible to determine the exact period of the group's first emergence. The fact that the *halakhot* dealing with the *ḥaver* were mainly transmitted in the names of the *tannaim who lived after the Bar Kokhba revolt does not suffice to support the opinion of A. Buechler (see bibliography) who ascribed them to the era of Usha and even assigned them to the priests of Galilee. Not only is this contradicted by some sources, as stated, that Bet Shammai and Bet Hillel differed on details of these *halakhot* (see Tosef., Av. Zar. 3:9–10 for the period of Rabban Gamaliel), but other evidence also conflicts with Buechler's opinion. It has long been recognized that the arrangement for accepting *ḥaverim* is reminiscent of the description given by Josephus (Wars, 2:137) of the acceptance into the fold of the Essenes, and parallels have been pointed out with the school of the Pythagoreans. The discovery of the Scroll of the *Manual of Discipline in the Judean desert throws new and important light on the subject. It is a document of a society in Ereẓ Israel, describing its life and regulations. There are indeed differences between the two; the Dead Sea group was a fraternity whose members lived communally and shared their possessions. Nevertheless the regulations with regard to ritual purity and many of the arrangements for initiation were common to both, and the same phrases and expressions occur in both. It seems reasonable to suppose that the various groups of *ḥaverim* among the Pharisees too were not all of one character and certainly did not always conduct themselves in all matters with the same degree of stringency. The differences are still reflected in those tannaitic statements which incorporate earlier *halakhot*.

It seems that originally when the *ḥaverim* were few in number their regulations were more stringent, but as they came to be accepted by wider circles a more lenient tendency developed. There are explicit references to this effect. "At first they said that a *ḥaver* who becomes a tax collector is to be expelled. Later they said that as long as he is a tax collector, he is not trusted, but if he withdraws from it, he is to be trusted" (Tosef., Dem. 3:4). It would also appear that *halakhot* which are quoted as disputes between *tannaim* are in actual fact merely transmissions of *halakhot* from different times, as for instance: if they regret becoming *ḥaverim*, they can never again be accepted, so claims R. Meir; R. Judah says: If they regret it publicly they can be accepted, but if clandestinely (i.e., they disregarded the regulations in private, but behaved in public as *ḥaverim*) they are not to be accepted (because of their hypocrisy); R. Simeon and R. Joshua b. Korḥa say: They may be accepted in both cases (*ibid.* 2:9). Meir's view represents the remnant of the strict rules of a group of *ḥaverim*, which, by the way, have a parallel in the scroll of the Manual of Discipline 7:1: "And if he cursed… then he shall be set apart and never again return."

The fact that most of the *halakhot* of the *ḥaverim* were taught during the era of Usha does not point to the time they came into existence but to the fact that at that time the regulations were renewed with the purpose of making *halakhot*, which at one time were of concern to small groups of *ḥaverim*, into the *halakhot* of the community as a whole. Meir took a stringent view while his colleagues favored a more lenient one. The renewal of these *halakhot* after the Bar Kokhba revolt can be ascribed to the general tendency towards asceticism then prevailing. However, it seems that, in practice, these stringencies were confined to scholars and their disciples, so that in the time of the *amoraim* "*ḥaver*" became a synonym for a scholar, so that it was said "The *ḥaverim* are none other than the scholars" (BB 75a; cf. the expression "*ḥaverim* of Torah" TJ, Ber. 1:1, 2d; Tanh., Niẓẓavim, 4; Lieberman in: *Tarbiz*, 2 (1930/31), 106), and it seems that in Babylon the Palestinian *amoraim* were called "*ḥavurah*" ("group of *ḥaverim*"; Shab. 111b; "the lion of the *ḥavurah*"; Pes. 64a).

The Post-Talmudic Period

In the academies of Babylon during the geonic period the three scholars sitting in the first row after the seven heads of the *kallah called *allufim ("chiefs") were known as *ḥaverim*. At the close of the geonic period this title was also bestowed upon important scholars outside the academy, such as Jacob b. Nissim and Saadiah b. Ephraim of Kairouan. In the academies of Ereẓ Israel, an ordained scholar was called "*ḥaver* of the Great Sanhedrin," and the 70 members of the academy were called collectively "*ḥavurta kadishta*" ("holy association"). The five *ḥaverim* after the *gaon* and the head of the academy were referred to by number, "third of the *ḥavurah*," "fourth of the *ḥavurah*," etc. A candidate for the *ḥavurah* was called *me'uttad la-ḥavurah* ("destined for the *ḥavurah*"). The designation was also widened figuratively into "the most eminent *ḥaver* of the *ḥavurah*," "the splendor of the *ḥaverim*," and "the glory of the *ḥaverim*," etc. In the 11th century the title *ḥaver* was added to the names of the *dayyanim* heading the communities of Ereẓ Israel, Syria, and Egypt, who were apparently ordained by the yeshivah of Ereẓ Israel. The title was also current in the academy of Fostat (a letter of 1441 mentions "our teacher and master, R. Pethahiah Kohen, the *ḥaver* of the Great Sanhedrin"). In Arabic-speaking countries the term "*ḥaver*" became a synonym for an educated man and a scholar and found its way into the Arabic language. The Jewish scholar in Judah Halevi's *Kuzari* is called in the Arabic original "Al-Ḥibr." In France, Italy, and Germany, it was used as a designation for young scholars, *benei ḥavurah* (*Or Zarua*, pt. 2, nos. 91 and 329; see Urbach, in: *Tarbiz* 10 (1938/39) 32 n.17). Only in the 14th century when the appointment of a rabbi in Germany depended upon ordination and the granting of the title *morenu*, did the title *ḥaver* become an indication of official recognition of exceptional merit in Torah learning. Its attainment was bound up with the fulfillment of certain conditions which varied from country to country and from one period to another. In the *takkanot* of the communities and regional councils of Poland, Lithuania, and Moravia, the conditions of the right to bear this title, together with a preferred status in the community, concessions in taxation, and other privileges, were laid down. The additional privileges granted to the bearers of the title brought the communal leaders to lay down the conditions for attaining the titles, even though they were granted by rabbis. The decline of the institutions for Torah study at the end of the 17th century in Poland and Lithuania brought with it also a modification of the requirements for the title of *ḥaver*, and it tended to become a mere title of respect.

BIBLIOGRAPHY: A. Buechler, *Der galilaeische ʿAm-ha ʾAreṣ des zweiten Jahrhunderts* (1906); J. Lévy, *La légende de Pythagore de Grèce en Palestine* (1927), 236–63; Allon, in: *Tarbiz*, 9 (1937/38), 1–10, 179–95 (= Alon, Meḥkarim, 1 (1957), 148–76); Geiger, Mikra, 80–87; Lieberman, in: JBL, 71 (1952), 199–206; idem, *Tosefta ki-Feshutah*, 1 (1955), 209–33; Ch. Rabin, *Qumran Studies* (1957); Urbach, in: *Sefer Yovel le-Y. Baer* (1960), 68; Neusner, in: HTR, 53 (1960), 125–42; Zunz, Lit Poesie, 284f.; S. Poznański, *Inyanim Shonim ha-Noge'im li-Tekufat ha-Ge'onim* (1909), 46, 59, 62; idem, *Babylonische Geonim im nachgaonaeischen Zeitalter* (1914), 103 n. 1; Mann, Egypt, 1 (1920), 54, 182, 264, 272, 277f.; 2 (1922), 348; Assaf, Geonim, 99; J. Katz, *Masoret u-Mashber* (1958), 227f., 267.

[*Encyclopaedia Hebraica*]

ḤAVER IR or **Ḥever Ir** (Heb. חֲבֵר עִיר; חֶבֶר עִיר), a phrase whose exact vocalization and therefore meaning is uncertain. If the reading is *ḥaver ir* (lit. "an associate of the city"), it refers to an individual; if it is *ḥever ir* (lit. "a town association") the reference is to a specific association or organization. The latter reading could also imply a congregation or the religious quorum (*minyan*) required for public worship. The Mishnah (Ber. 4:7) records a difference of opinion as to whether the individual may himself recite the *Musaf* prayers or whether they may only be said publicly by the *ḥever ir*. In this context the phrase seems to mean a *minyan*. A similar conclusion is reached from the discussion concerning the differences between the order of the sounding of the *shofar* during private worship and public *ḥever ir* (RH 34b).

The rules regarding deportment at a funeral and in a house of mourning seem to indicate that the phrase refers to a specific communal fraternal society. The *ḥever ir* must participate in a man's funeral but not a woman's (Sem. 11:2). Neither was the *ḥever ir* obligated to extend condolences on the day that people gather the bones of relatives for reburial in ossuaries (Sem. 12:4). When the *ḥever ir* was present at the house of mourning, visitors were permitted to bring less costly food, since there were then many people to be fed (Ḥul. 94a; Sem. 14:13). In Jerusalem, there originally were *ḥavurot* ("associations") for participating in joyful events such as marriage and circumcision and in gathering the remains of the dead and comforting mourners (Tosef. Meg. 4 (3):15; Sem. 12:5). It may be that these *ḥavurot* were the precursors of the *ḥever ir*, or that they functioned together with it. They differed in that the *ḥavurot* were voluntary organizations whereas the *ḥever ir* was officially appointed by the townspeople as their representatives in performing these meritorious deeds.

Nevertheless, there are also instances where *ḥaver ir* seems to be the correct reading. After transient visitors to a town are assessed for charity, they may demand reimbursement for distribution to the poor in their own communities before their departure. However, when a *ḥaver ir* is in charge of the communal charity, no refund is granted and the *ḥever ir* uses it at his discretion (Meg. 25a–b, Rashi ad loc.). Likewise, the poor man's tithe could be given to the *ḥaver ir* who used it at his discretion (Tosef., Pe'ah 4:16). A kohen who had a disqualifying blemish was not permitted to utter the Priestly Benediction publicly, since the people would be distracted by it. If he is also a *ḥaver ir*, however, he may recite the benediction, since he is so well known that they will pay no attention to his disability (Tosef., Meg. 4 (3):29).

BIBLIOGRAPHY: Geiger, Mikra; T. Horowitz, in: *Festschrift zum Geburstage Jacob Guttmanns* (1915), 125–42; idem, in: JJLG, 17 (1926), 241–314; S. Krauss, *ibid.*, 125–42; S. Ginsburg, *Perushim ve-Ḥiddushim ba-Yerushalmi*, 3 (1941), 410–32; S. Lieberman, *Tosefta ki-Feshuta*, 1 (1955), 190.

[Harry Freedman]

HAVILAH (Heb. חֲוִילָה), name mentioned five times in the Bible, both as a personal and place name. The name Havilah was applied to the territory watered by the Pishon River (Gen. 2:11), which was noted for choice gold, bdellium, and lapis lazuli (Gen. 2:12). Josephus and most Church Fathers identified the land of Havilah with the Ganges Valley. While the proper identification is still unknown, there are various theories concerning its location. The association of the land of Havilah with the products mentioned above supports Y.M. Grintz's identification of Havilah with Aualis, an Abyssinian district mentioned in Greek and Latin sources. This Havilah, or Aualis, is perhaps the Meluḥḥa referred to in cuneiform records and identified as the Egypt of the period of the Cushite dynasty; however, this latter point is especially questionable in relation to Havilah. Friedrich Delitzsch located the land of Havilah in the Syrian Desert, west and south of the Euphrates. P. Haupt, who regarded the Pishon as the belt of water formed by the Kerkha, Persian Gulf, and Red Sea, identified Havilah with Arabia. In E.A. Speiser's view, the identification of the whole geographic background revolves around the proper location of the biblical Cush, which is identified either as an African kingdom (Ethiopia) or as the Mesopotamian kingdom of the Kassites (Akk. Kaššû). Speiser prefers the latter identification. Thus the background of Havilah remains that of the Garden of *Eden in Babylonia (Persian Gulf). According to Cassuto, the common element in all five references to Havilah is the ethnic ties between the various peoples located on either bank of the Red Sea. The Bible, however, distinguishes the Havilah that serves as one of the boundaries of Ishmaelite territory from all other places named Havilah, with the qualifying phrase "by Shur, which is close to Egypt" (Gen. 25:18). It was in the area between this Havilah and Shur that Saul defeated the Amalekites and captured Agag, their king (I Sam. 15:7). The personal name Havilah appears in the Table of Nations (Gen. 10:7 = I Chron. 1:9) and in Abrahamic genealogies (Gen. 10:29 = I Chron. 1:23). In the former, Havilah is one of the five sons of *Cush the son of Ham. In the latter, Havilah is the sixth generation in lineal descent from Shem. The latter Havilah, the son of Joktan, apparently stands for a locality in South Arabia, as do Hadoram (Gen. 10:27), Sheba (Gen. 10:28), and Ophir (Gen. 10:29).

BIBLIOGRAPHY: F. Delitzsch, *Wo lag das Paradies?* (1881), 301;

W.F. Albright, in: JAOS, 42 (1922), 317ff.; idem, in: AJSLL, 39 (1922), 15ff.; J.A. Knudtzon, *Die El-Amarna Tafeln* (1915); F. Hommel, *Grundriss der Geographie und Geschichte des alten Orients* (1926), 272 n. 1, 556 n. 4, 570; D.D. Luckenbill, *Ancient Records of Assyria and Babylonia*, 1 (1925), 170; J. Skinner, *Genesis* (ICC, 1930), 62–66: S.A. Montgomery, *Arabia and the Bible* (1939), 39; E.A. Speiser, *Oriental and Biblical Studies* (1967), 23–34; Y.M. Grintz, *Moẓa'ei Dorot* (1969), 35–50.

[Mayer Irwin Gruber]

ḤAVIV, AVSHALOM (1926–1947), Jew executed by the British in Palestine. Ḥaviv was born in Haifa and when he was two years old his parents moved to Jerusalem. While still a secondary pupil in Bet ha-Kerem he joined the IẒL. After serving in the *Palmaḥ in En-Ḥarod under the "year of service" program, he returned to Jerusalem where he renewed his activity in IẒL, relinquishing studies at the Hebrew University. Together with Meir Nakar and Yaacov Weiss he was a member of the group which was given the task of ensuring the retreat of the members of IẒL who performed the daring break into the prison of Acre in 1946, but failing to hear the agreed signal for retreat, they remained there too long and were captured. They were sentenced to death on May 16, 1947, and were hanged in Acre prison on the 12th of Av of that year, together with Eliezer Kashani and Mordekhai Alkaḥi.

BIBLIOGRAPHY: Y. Nedava, *Olei-ha-Gardom* (1966); Y. Gurion, *Ha-Nizzaḥon Olei Gardom* (1971).

ḤAVIV-LUBMAN, AVRAHAM DOV (1864–1951), pioneer of Jewish settlement in Ereẓ Israel. Born on a Jewish agricultural settlement, Graitzevo, near Mogilev, Ḥaviv-Lubman joined the Ḥovevei Zion movement and, in 1885, moved to Ereẓ Israel. He went to live in Petaḥ Tikvah with his uncle, Mordekhai Lubman, who worked as a land surveyor for Baron Edmond de *Rothschild. He disliked the settlement's traditional way of life and moved to Rishon le-Zion, where he struggled together with others against the baron's paternalistic management of the new agricultural settlement. He was a founder of the Aguddat ha-Koremim ("The Vintners' Association"), which took over the supervision of the baron's wine cellars. For 16 years he was at intervals head of the local council of Rishon le-Zion. He wrote memoirs of his childhood and the early days of settlement in Ereẓ Israel entitled *Mi-Sippurei ha-Rishonim le-Ẓiyyon* (1934) and *Benei Dori* (1946), as well as a monograph on Rishon le-Zion (1929).

BIBLIOGRAPHY: J. Ḥurgin, *Dov Ḥaviv-Lubman* (Heb., 1942); D.A. Yanovsky, in: *Mi-Sippurei ha-Rishonim le-Ẓiyyon* (1934), 3–8; D. Idelovitch, *Rishon le-Ẓiyyon* (1941), 419–21.

[Yehuda Slutsky]

HAVRE, LE, major port, N. France. From about the beginning of the 18th century, Jews, especially from *Bordeaux and its environs, wished to settle in Le Havre. In 1714, *Louis XIV ordered the town to expel all foreign Jews except "those who call themselves 'Portuguese.'" Around 1725, however, two Jewish families of German origin, the Hombergs (who were converted after a while) and the Lallemends, settled in Le Havre and obtained letters of naturalization. In 1776 the town once more refused several Jews permission to reside there in spite of their "royal passports" (actually valid for Paris). An organized community was founded in the mid-19th century. A new community, reconstituted after World War II, had a population of about 1,000 in 1969 and possessed a synagogue and community center.

BIBLIOGRAPHY: A.-E. Borely, *Histoire de la ville du Havre*…, 3 (1881), 441ff.

[Bernhard Blumenkranz]

HAVURAH. The havurah, or Jewish fellowship group, encompasses "a wide range of approaches in which relatively small groups of Jews come together regularly for programs which include Jewish study, celebration, and personal association" (Reisman, 1977). Use of the Hebrew term *ḥavurah* (pl. *ḥavurot*) as a social institution has its origins in the small communities of Pharasaic Jews from which emerged rabbinical Judaism over 2,000 years ago. In contemporary usage, the havurah refers to an attempt to restore a sense of Jewish community to North American Jewish life. In contrast to the synagogue, the havurah is distinguished by the personal responsibility assumed by members for their religious and social activities, rather than delegating them to the rabbi or other institutional officials.

Contemporary havurot emerged through two different and unrelated avenues. In the early 1960s, the Reconstructionist movement, which had espoused fellowship groups since its inception in the 1930s, established havurot to give substance to the teachings of Rabbi Mordecai Kaplan to transform the Jewish community. After becoming an independent denomination in 1968, Reconstructionists continued to create havurot as a substitute for, or adjunct to, its synagogues.

In the late 1960s, inspired by the counterculture of that period, many havurot were created predominantly by Jewish students who combined their Jewish seeking with political activism and opposition to the Vietnam War. Notable among these havurot were Chavurat Shalom in Somerville, Massachusetts (1968), the New York Havurah (1969), and Fabrangen in Washington, D.C. (1970). Havurot in this period also often adapted Ḥasidic motifs such as communalism, mysticism, ecstatic singing, and transcendence, both to restore what members felt was missing from Jewish life, and to emphasize their rejection of the conventional "corporate" synagogue.

The havurah may thus be considered a postmodern institution in that it celebrates the "cultural, and social transformations that have come together in the contemporary period and that include a movement away from the modern idea of a universalistic rational culture and toward a multicultural reality that celebrates the value of the local and the particular and attempts a new openness to premodern forms and motifs" (Kepnes 1996).

By the early 1970s the havurah had become an accepted part of the American Jewish scene, and were divided between independent and synagogue-affiliated havurot. Research conducted at that time found that most havurah members were young families with young children, closely resembling the demographics of synagogue members. However, they demonstrated a higher level of personal observance than synagogue members and were more likely to espouse liberal or radical political opinions. Since 1974, an annual summer retreat has been sponsored by the National Havurah Committee, the organizing body of independent havurot; by 1982 it was estimated that 20% of Reform congregations had one or more havurot.

Today there are several hundred independent havurot, primarily in the U.S., although the idea has spread to Canada, Israel, and several European countries. Approximately one-third of all Conservative and Reform congregations have one or more havurot, and some 40 havurot are affiliated with the Reconstructionist movement. While their loose organization makes it impossible to gather precise statistics about havurot, their influence on American Jewish life far exceeds their modest numbers. Havurah members occupy positions in academic Jewish studies, cultural organizations, Jewish federations, Jewish education, and the rabbinate. The egalitarianism of the havurah has become a fixture in American Jewish life, especially with regard to Jewish feminism. Other innovations inspired by the havurah and adopted by many Jewish organizations include retreats, the exercise of creating imaginative, non-rational midrash, the use of Hasidic *niggunim* (melodies), Jewish folk music, and the revival of Jewish crafts.

Indeed, the havurah example has stimulated the creation of new Jewish institutions such as the Elay Hayyim Jewish Retreat Center in New York State, and the proliferation of *minyanin* (prayer and study groups) in cities across the United States. As the havurah continues to evolve, the children of havurah members of the 1960s have themselves founded second-generation havurot, and National Havurah Conference's annual retreat has become a multi-generational event.

In addition, unaffiliated and highly mobile young Jews increasingly incorporate computer communications into their creation of postmodern Jewish fellowships and communities. An example of this is Kehillat Hadar in New York, founded in 2001 with seed money from the Jewish Federation of New York, a trans-denominational egalitarian community with members in their 20s and 30s who use a World Wide Web site and electronic mailing list to organize and schedule study, celebration, and social action in rented facilities. Similarly, Mishpacha, funded by the Memorial Foundation for Jewish Culture, is an online havurah providing interaction and Jewish learning for young Jewish parents.

The havurah has not become as stable and self-sustaining a Jewish institution as the synagogue. However, for four decades it has provided an avenue of involvement for Jews who seek to express their Judaism in a small, self-directed group, while stimulating innovation in the larger Jewish community. It is still too soon to determine if the recent experiments influenced by the havurah will have similar influence and longevity.

BIBLIOGRAPHY: S. Kepnes (Editor), "Introduction" in *Interpreting Judaism in a Postmodern Age* (1996); B. Reisman, *The Chavurah: A Contemporary Jewish Experience* (1977); G. Bubis/H. Wasserman, *Synagogue Havurot: A Comparative Study* (1983); R. Prell, *Prayer and Community: The Havurah in American Judaism* (1989); J. Neusner, *Contemporary Judaic Fellowship in Theory and Practice* (1972).

[Peter Margolis (2nd ed.)]

HAVVOTH-JAIR (Heb. חַוֹּת יָאִיר), an area in northern *Gilead (Num. 32:41; I Kings 4:13; I Chron. 2:22), also ascribed to the *Bashan and to the *Argob district, that was part of the kingdom of *Og of Bashan (Deut. 3:14; Josh. 13:30). According to A. Bergman (Biran), the city of *Ham was originally the center of the region. After Og's defeat at *Edrei, the region was occupied by *Jair, son of Manasseh, and named after him (Num. 32:41). A nomadic population called Ya'uri, Yari, or Yaḥiri, is known from Assyrian documents to have been in the area of the Euphrates beginning with the 13th century B.C.E., and some scholars assume that groups of these nomads reached Gilead and were gradually incorporated into the Israelite tribes. The meaning of *havvoth* is apparently "villages," i.e., groups of tent camps of nomads or seminomads surrounded by loose stone walls (in the *Nuzi documents, the word *khawu* designates a stone wall around a field). The half-tribe of Manasseh, cattle breeders who had settled in Transjordan, probably had many such camps and moved with their herds from one to another in search of pasture (Num. 32). According to Judges 10:3–5, Havvoth-Jair was named for *Jair, the Gileadite, who judged Israel for 22 years and was buried at Kamon (modern Qamm) in Gilead. According to I Chronicles 2:22, however, it may have received its name from Jair, son of Segub, of the tribe of Judah. The villages of Jair are again mentioned in Solomon's sixth administrative district under the son of Geber from Ramoth-Gilead; the villages were joined to Argob in Bashan (I Kings 4:13). The area was later lost to Aram and annexed by Geshur (I Chron. 2:23). *Jeroboam II seems to have retaken it for a short time (I Chron. 5:11–17), but it was finally conquered and depopulated by *Tiglath-Pileser *III (I Chron. 5:26).

BIBLIOGRAPHY: G.A. Smith, *Historical Geography of the Holy Land* (18964), 551–2; Abel, Geog, 2 (1938), 71–80; Bergman, in: JPOS, 16 (1936), 235–7; EM, S.V.

[Michael Avi-Yonah]

HAWAII, the 50th state of the United States; admitted in August 1959. Jewish beginnings in Hawaii are shrouded in myth. Ebenezer Townsend, Jr., a sailor on the whaling ship *Neptune*, wrote in the ship's log on Aug. 19, 1798, that the king came aboard ship and brought "a Jew cook with him." This may or may not be true, but it is the first mention of Jews in connection with Hawaii.

A Torah scroll and *yad* ("pointer") owned by the royal family of Hawaii show a connection between it and the early

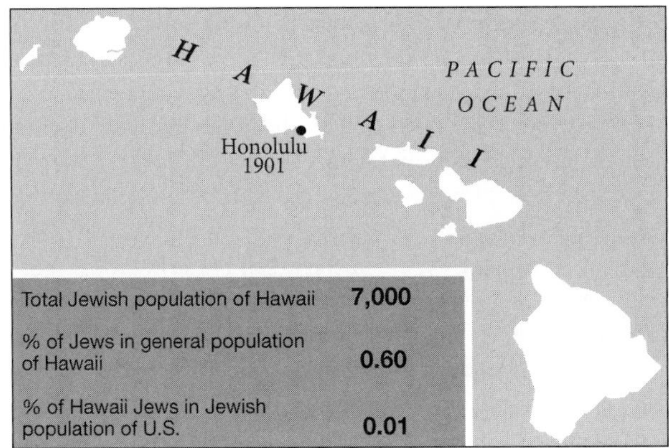

Jewish population of Hawaii, 2001.

Jewish community. How the scroll and *yad* came into the possession of King David Kalakaua is not clear. The *Daily Pacific Commercial Advertiser* of Dec. 24, 1888, states that Queen Liliuokalani, Kalakaua's successor, had the scroll draped around the inside of the tent at Her Majesty's bazaar. As late as 1930, the Jewish community borrowed the scroll from the descendants of the royal family for use on holidays. The *yad* and the scroll have recently been donated to Temple Emanuel, a Reform congregation. Because of its condition, it is no longer used for ritual purposes, but can be seen on display.

It is believed that Jewish traders from England and Germany first came to Hawaii in the 1840s. A few American Jews came from California at the end of the 19th century, but there was no organized Jewish community until the founding of the Hebrew Benevolent Society in 1901. The same year marked the consecration of a Jewish cemetery at Pearl City Junction. In 1923 the National Jewish Welfare Board (JWB) established the Aloha Center for Jewish military personnel. In 1938 the Honolulu Jewish community was established. Temple Emanuel was organized in 1951. The temple had a membership of 300 families in the early 21st century. In 1971 Congregation Sof Ma'arav, a Conservative synagogue, was founded. In 1975 the Aloha Jewish Chapel, a synagogue for military and ex-military, was built at Pearl Harbor. Chabad of Hawaii was established in 1990 and maintained regular services and a small presence. During the 1990s Jewish synagogues were established on Maui, the island of Hawaii, and Kauai.

The total Jewish population probably numbered about 10,000 in 2005, with the majority in Honolulu on the island of Oahu. This is out of a state population of 1,236,100. Because of the large number of unaffiliated Jews, this number is only an approximation. The population is both youthful and largely transient. Most of the Jews arrived since World War II; some were stationed there during the war and after the war returned with their families. A few have been there for 40 years or more. Since statehood in 1959 the population of the state has almost doubled. The influx of new people included many Jews and many in the professions, such as medicine, law, university teaching, government services, both federal and state. A number went into real estate and other businesses. As of 2005, three of the last four attorneys-general of the state were Jewish. The governor, Linda *Lingle, was also Jewish. She was a member of all three congregations. A men's club and sisterhood were affiliated with Temple Emanuel. A B'nai B'rith Lodge and a Hadassah Chapter were organized. In 2004 a Hillel chapter was established at the University of Hawaii at Manoa in Honolulu. Religious services were held regularly by all three congregations. There were no specific Jewish neighborhoods; Jews lived everywhere and were active in all aspects of Hawaiian life, feeling very much at ease in Hawaii's multiracial society.

[Gertrude C. Serata / Robert Littman (2nd ed.)]

HAWK, bird of prey. Two genera of hawk are found in Israel, the *Accipiter* and the *Falco*, these being referred to respectively in the Bible as *neẓ* (AV, JPS = hawk) and *taḥmas* (AV, JPS = "nighthawk"), mentioned among the unclean birds that are prohibited as food (Lev. 11:16; Deut. 14:15). The *neẓ* is generally identified with the sparrow hawk (*Accipiter nisus*), which nests on trees in various places in Israel, pounces in flight on its victims, particularly small birds, and is recognizable by its bright abdomen streaked with dark lateral stripes. It winters in Israel and some migrate to southern lands, as mentioned in Job (39:26). The Pentateuch refers to "the *neẓ* after its kinds." In Israel there are two other transmigratory species that belong to this genus. But the expression *neẓ* may also include other genera of birds of prey. Thus, for example, the *aggadah* says that Israel is like a dove which the *neẓ* seeks to devour (Song R. 2:14, no. 2), the reference here being to a bird of prey larger than the hawk, such as the *buzzard which preys upon doves (the *Accipiter* hunts only small birds: see Ḥul. 3:1) or the saker falcon (*Falco cherrug*) which in certain countries is trained to pursue birds and animals. Of the genus *Falco* there are several species in Israel, the most common being the non-migratory kestrel (*Falco tinnunculus*) which preys upon birds and field mice and is apparently the biblical *taḥmas*, a word meaning "robber, bandit."

BIBLIOGRAPHY: E. Smolly, *Ẓipporim be-Yisrael* (1959^2), 85; R. Meinertzhagen, *Birds of Arabia* (1954), 366ff.; J. Feliks, *Animal World of the Bible* (1962), 64f. **ADD BIBLIOGRAPHY:** Feliks, Ha-Ẓome'aḥ, 255.

[Jehuda Feliks]

HAWN, GOLDIE (1945–), U.S. actress. Hawn, whose mother was Jewish and father Presbyterian, was born in Washington, D.C. She first found work on the short-lived television series *Good Morning, World* and then achieved almost instant stardom on the successful television comedy-variety show *Laugh-In* (1968–70). Hawn left the cast for motion pictures and achieved major status immediately in her first film, *Cactus Flower*, winning an Oscar for Best Supporting Actress (1970). She has since starred in such films as *There's a Girl in My Soup* (1970); *Dollars* (1971); *Butterflies Are Free* (1972); *The Sugarland Express* (1974); *The Girl from Petrovka* (1974); *Shampoo* (1975); *Foul Play* (1978); the hugely successful *Private Ben-*

jamin, for which she was nominated for a Best Actress Oscar (1980); *Seems Like Old Times* (1980); *Bird on a Wire* (1990); *Best Friends* (1982); *Swing Shift* (1984); *Protocol (1984); Wildcats (1986); Overboard (1987); Deceived* (1991); *Housesitter* (1992); *Crisscross* (1992); *Death Becomes Her* (1992); *The First Wives Club* (1996); *Everyone Says I Love You* (1996); *The Out-of-Towners* (1999); *Town and Country* (2001); and *The Banger Sisters* (2002). Nominated for eight Golden Globe Awards, she won one in 1970, along with her Oscar, for Best Supporting Actress in *Cactus Flower.* Hawn is the mother of actress Kate Hudson.

ADD. BIBLIOGRAPHY: M. Shapiro, *Pure Goldie, the Life and Career of Goldie Hawn* (1998)

[Jonathan Licht / Ruth Beloff (2nd ed.)]

HÁY, GYULA (**Julius**; 1900–1975), Hungarian and German playwright. From 1919 Háy lived in Germany but after 1933 moved to the U.S.S.R., returning to Hungary in 1945. While *Isten, császár, paraszt* ("God, Emperor, Peasant," 1940) was popular in Hungary, a number of Háy's Marxist dramas were successful in pre-Nazi Germany and later in East Berlin. These include *Haben* (1938) and *Gerichtstag* (1946). Jailed after the 1956 revolution, Háy moved to West Germany in 1966.

His autobiography, *Born 1900*, appeared in English in 1974.

°**HAY, JOHN MILTON** (1838–1905), U.S. statesman who supported Romanian and Russian Jewish rights. Hay was a secretary of state under presidents William McKinley and Theodore Roosevelt from 1898 to 1905. He was involved in U.S. diplomatic representations during this period on behalf of Romanian and Russian Jews. In 1902, at the urging of American Jewish leaders including Oscar S. Straus and Jacob H. Schiff, Hay addressed a note to the signatories of the Berlin Treaty of 1878 protesting Romania's violation of that treaty by its restrictions on Jews. Following the *Kishinev pogrom of 1903, again after Jewish pressure and with an eye to domestic political considerations, Hay publicized a protest petition drawn up by B'nai B'rith.

BIBLIOGRAPHY: T. Denett, *John Hay: From Poetry to Politics* (1933), 395–400; N.W. Cohen, *Dual Heritage* (1969), 83–131.

[Morton Rosenstock]

ḤAYDĀN. A town and a region in north *Yemen, after which all Jews living there were called Ḥayādinah, in about 40 small communities such as Ṣa'dah, Baraṭ, Qal'ah, Ghālib, Harāḍ, and Mashhad. Known also as Ḥaydān al-Shām (in the north), to distinguish it from another Ḥaydān in the south-west. The earliest information about the Jews of Ḥaydān is a document from 1670, dealing with the division of a house in Ṣanʿā (*Sanʿa) among three brothers of the Ḥaydānī family. The existence of the Jews of north Yemen among the Muslim majority was not based on the Muslim discriminatory rules (*ghiyār*) as in other places in Yemen and other Muslim countries, but on the tribal pre-Islamic system, where the Jews, as other weak segments of the society, were *jārs* (neighbors) whom the Sheikhs had to protect on behalf of their honor. There are many testmonies about wars waged by an Arab tribe, in consequence of killing or hurting a Jew protected by that tribe, against another tribe from which the killer came. As a result of their special status, the Jews of north Yemen did not wear sidelocks, the most distinctive sign in the appearance of the Yemenite Jew. Many of them were expert in the art of repairing the Arabs' weapons and could even carry weapons and sometimes took part in tribal wars. They also could live among the Muslims in more than two-story houses in contrast to the rule in other places. Another of their major occupations was silversmithing. Although we have scant information about the Jews of north Yemen in some sources like the account of the traveler R. Baruch b. Samuel of Pinsk (1833), they were first exposed to scholars only after Joseph Halévy and Ḥayyim Ḥibshūsh wrote the accounts of their travel to that area in 1870. Subsequently some of the Jews emigrated from N. Yemen, such as A. Tabib, Z. Glusqa, and M. Kappara, and published books about the Jews living there. These Jews began to immigrate to the Land of Israel in 1907, and two personalities later became prominent leaders of the Yemenite community: Abraham Tabib and Zekharyah Glusqa. They settled in Reḥovot and Rishon le-Zion and engaged in agriculture, playing a leading role in the promotion of Jewish labor. Another movement of *aliyah* took place in the mid-1940s, led by R. David Ẓadok ha-Levi. They wandered in Yemen for two years until they reached *Aden and later arrived in Israel on the "Magic Carpet" in 1949 with their countrymen. They settled in nearby Kiryat Ekron and Kefar Gevirol (near Reḥovot).

BIBLIOGRAPHY: Y. Tobi, *Jews of Yemen* (1999), 142–156; idem, "The Jews in Ḥaydān and North Yemen," in: ʿA. Zindani, *Yalkut Ovadia*, 15–39; A. Tabib, *Golat Teman* (1931); idem, *Shavei Teman* (1932); Z. Glusqa, *Le-Ma'an Yehudei Teman* (1974); M. Kappara, *Minni Teman U-ve-Sha'arayim* (1978).

[Yosef Tobi (2nd ed.)]

HAYDEN, HENRI (1883–1970), painter. Hayden was born in Warsaw, and arrived in Paris in 1907 to join a compatriot, *Marcoussis. Hayden's first major influence was Gauguin, but he soon came under the spell of Cezanne, notably in his first major painting "The Chess Players at La Rotunde," exhibited in 1914. Through the poet and critic André Salmon he met Juan Gris and Jacques *Lipchitz, who introduced him to Cubism. In due course he became a colleague of Picasso, Metzinger, Andre Lhote and Robert de la Fresnaye. The dealer Leonce Rosenberg put him under contract and bought his entire studio. His Cubist masterpiece "The Three Musicians" (1920) is now in the National Museum of Modern Art, Paris. From 1922 he adopted a more figurative style and returned to landscape. In 1939 he was forced to leave Paris and went to live in the remote French countryside, where he became a close friend of the writer Samuel Beckett. On his return to Paris in 1944 Hayden found his studio ransacked and most of his Cubist paintings missing. In the last 20 years of his life Hayden enjoyed renewed fame and popularity. His landscapes and still lifes combine a simplified Cubism with a new lyrical sense of color.

[Charles Samuel Spencer]

HAYDEN, MELISSA (1928–), U.S. ballerina. Hayden's dramatic power and virtuoso technique marked her as one of the outstanding dancers in America. Born Mildred Herman in Toronto, Canada, she trained early to be a dancer and at 17 went to New York, where she attended the School of American Ballet. After dancing in the ballet corps of Radio City Music Hall, she joined Ballet Theater in 1945, became a soloist, and joined the New York City Ballet in 1950, where she was named principal dancer in 1955. During her first season there she danced leading roles in *Illuminations, The Duel*, and *Age of Anxiety*. She also created roles in George Balanchine's *Agon, Firebird, Midsummer Night's Dream*, and other works of the repertoire. In 1963, she danced *Swan Lake* and *Coppélia* with the National Ballet of Canada. In her book *Melissa Hayden – Offstage and On* (1963) she explained her approach to dancing for the benefit of young people. From 1977 to 1983 she directed her own ballet school and from 1983 taught ballet at North Carolina School of the Arts. Hayden was awarded the Handel Medallion, New York's highest award for cultural achievement. She wrote *Off Stage and On* (1963), *Ballet Exercises* (1969), and *Dancer to Dancer* (1981).

BIBLIOGRAPHY: IED, 3, 351–52.

[Marcia B. Siegel / Amnon Shiloah (2nd ed.)]

HAYES, ISAAC ISRAEL (1832–1881), U.S. explorer. Born in Chester, Pennsylvania, Hayes volunteered in 1853 as ship's surgeon on Kane's expedition to the North Pole in search of Sir John Franklin. His ship was icebound in Kane's Basin for two years, during which time Hayes took part in many sledge expeditions, on one of which he discovered and explored Grinnell Land. With nine of the ship's crew he also attempted to reach Opernavik (Greenland), and get help for the stranded ship (1854). Although he was forced to return to the ship, the following summer the whole crew made use of the route he had taken to make their escape. In 1860 Hayes sailed from Boston in command of the schooner *United States* in an attempt to discover the open water which he maintained surrounded the North Pole. After wintering in Kane's Basin, he continued north by sledge. He finally observed what he thought was the open polar sea but which in fact was the Kennedy Channel, which opens into the Arctic via the Mall Basin. He returned to Boston in 1861. He made his last trip to the Arctic in 1869, when he was accompanied by the American artist, William Bradford. Later in life he became a member of the New York Assembly.

The careful notes made by Hayes on his expeditions were a valuable contribution to natural history, meteorology, glaciology, and hydrology, and were included in the annals of the exploration society. He also took the first photographs of the Arctic. His writings include *An Arctic Boat Journey* (1860), *Physical Observations in the Arctic Seas 1860 and 1861* (1867), *The Open Polar Sea* (1867), *Cast Away in the Cold* (1868), and *The Land of Desolation* (1871).

BIBLIOGRAPHY: E.K. Kane, *Arctic Explorations: The Second Grinell Expedition* (1856); G.W. Cullum, in: *Journal of the American Geographic Society*, 12 (1881), 110–24.

HAYES, SAUL (1906–1980), Canadian Jewish community official, lawyer. Born in Montreal, Hayes was the voice of the Jewish community of Canada from the late 1930s through the 1960s. A graduate of McGill University and a lawyer, Hayes' first job was as a lecturer in the university's School of Social Work in 1934. He soon joined a prominent Montreal law firm.

But law was not Hayes' primary interest; Jewish community service was. And so when industrialist Samuel *Bronfman became president of a struggling and ineffective Canadian Jewish Congress in January of 1938, Hayes eagerly accepted his invitation to become its director. Through the CJC's United Jewish Refugee Committee, which he headed for many years, Hayes led the battle against the antisemitsm that permeated Canada in the 1930s and 1940s. As well, and perhaps more importantly, he organized Canadian Jewry – along with a very small number of non-Jewish organizations – to lobby a hostile government to let in some of the desperate Jews of Europe looking for a haven from Nazi persecution.

Hayes was the Jewish community's first native-born civil servant. He was a passionate and eloquent spokesman for its interests. For almost 40 years he appeared before parliamentary committees, met with hundreds of cabinet ministers, legislators, and bureaucrats, wrote countless speeches and articles, and represented Canadian Jewry at international meetings, including the founding conference of the United Nations in San Francisco in 1945 and the Paris Conference on Post-War Peace Treaties in 1946. He well deserved the description of him by Yaacov Herzog, Israel's ambassador to Canada in the 1960s, as "the foremost civil servant of the Jewish people."

What Hayes was most proud of were his contributions to the modernization of a highly restrictive Canadian society. He was instrumental in forcing federal and provincial governments in the postwar period to adopt laws against racial and religious discrimination in housing and employment, was an early proponent of multiculturalism, was highly influential in persuading dubious Canadian authorities to allow into the country thousands of Jewish immigrants following the war, and was a member of an innovative royal commission which crafted legislation against hate-mongers. He also lobbied successfully to create a Jewish education system in Quebec largely funded by the provincial government.

A lifelong Zionist, Hayes created the Israel Bond Association in Canada, paved the way for Canadian investment in Israel, and led the fight against the *Arab boycott of the Jewish state. In representing Israeli interests in Canada, Hayes often played a more important role than Israel's ambassador in Ottawa.

Hayes retired from the Canadian Jewish Congress in 1974, the same year he was appointed to the Order of Canada, the nation's highest honor.

[Irving Abella (2nd ed.)]

HAYNT (הײַנט), leading Yiddish daily in Warsaw before World War II. It was founded in 1908 by the Hebrew-Yiddish journalist Samuel Jacob Jackan and two Zionists, the brothers Noah and Nehemiah *Finkelstein, as a continuation of the daily *Yidishes Tagblat*, which they had published from 1906. Its first issue appeared on Jan. 22, 1908, with Jackan as editor and a staff that included David *Frischmann, Hillel *Zeitlin, Hirsch David *Nomberg, and Moshe Bunem *Justman ("B. Yeushzon"). *Haynt* supported Zionist ideology and in 1909 reached the unprecedented circulation of 70,000. In 1910 another Yiddish daily *Der Moment* was founded in Warsaw, edited by Ẓevi *Prylucki, which attracted some members of *Haynt's* staff. In the ensuing continuous competition *Haynt* maintained its lead. It attracted readers by publishing stimulating articles and thrilling novels in serial form, and also offering prizes (among them a trip to Ereẓ Israel). By 1914 its circulation had risen to more than 100,000. Its staff at that time included Sholem *Asch, Menahem *Boraisha, Abraham *Goldberg, Shemarya *Gorelik, Z. Wendroff, A.L. Jacobowitz, J.A. Leizerowicz, H.D. Nomberg, David Frischmann, Isaac Leib *Peretz, and *Shalom Aleichem. *Haynt* took a firm Jewish national stand in the elections to the fourth *Duma in 1912. It also fought the assimilationists in Warsaw in the Jewish communal elections of that year. In 1915, *Haynt* was closed down by the Russian authorities but reopened a few months later, when Warsaw was captured by the Germans. In independent Poland *Haynt* was deprived of many readers in the Ukraine and other regions not included in Poland's boundaries. It reached an agreement with the daily *Dos Yidishe Folk*, published from 1919 by the Zionist Organization of Poland, becoming an organ of the Zionist Organization and replacing Jackan with Yehoshua *Gottlieb as editor. From 1921 Abraham Goldberg was the editor, but the paper's basic policy was determined by Yiẓḥak *Gruenbaum. In 1932 *Haynt* passed to the ownership of a cooperative composed of members of the editorial board and employees. After Goldberg's death in 1933, Aaron Einhorn and Moshe Indelmann edited the paper until its last issue on Sept. 22, 1939, on the eve of the German occupation of Warsaw. Leading contributors of *Haynt* included Vladimir *Jabotinsky (until 1933), B. Singer, I.J. Singer, Osias *Thon, Gershon Levin, Jacob *Lestschinsky, Z. *Segalowitch, Nahum *Sokolow, Ephraim *Kaganowsky, Ezriel *Carlebach, Z. *Shneour, and M. *Kipnis. It also issued periodicals in Yiddish and Polish, as well as two newspapers in Hebrew: the daily *Ha-Boker* (1909), edited by David Frischmann, and the weekly *Ba-Derekh* (1932–37).

BIBLIOGRAPHY: *Haynt, 1908–1928, Yubiley Bukh* (1928); *Haynt, Yubiley Bukh 1908–1938* (1938); *Fun Noentn Over*, 2 (1956), 1–237. **ADD. BIBLIOGRAPHY:** M. Fuks, *Prasa zydowska w Warszawie 1823–1939* (1979), index; Ch. Finkelstein, *Haynt, a Tsaytung bayYidden, 1908–1939* (1978).

[Gedalyah Elkoshi]

HA-YOM (Heb. הַיּוֹם, "the Day"), the first Hebrew daily newspaper. Published in St. Petersburg for 25 months, Feb. 12, 1886, to March 12, 1888, *Ha-Yom* was edited by Judah Leib *Kantor, who enjoyed the regular help of David *Frischmann and Judah Leib *Katzenelson. The Hebrew press had existed for 30 years when *Ha-Yom* appeared, and the Hebrew newspapermen of that time regarded the venture with skepticism and even derision. But Kantor's persistence overcame all obstacles and the paper appeared daily, in large format, with news gathered by telegrams received directly from the Russian telegraphic agency.

Another innovation was *Ha-Yom*'s simple and clear style, by means of which Kantor hoped to dislodge the stilted Hebrew still dominant in the press. The editor proved that a Hebrew paper could report on political and social events as efficiently as a paper in any other language and *Ha-Yom* actually became a European-style daily. The editorials and political articles were usually written by Kantor, while Frischmann regularly published feuilletons as well as the first of his famous literary letters, and Katzenelson contributed articles on science. Reporters from London, the U.S., and other Jewish centers contributed to the paper, which also printed substantial reports from Ereẓ Israel. However, the paper could not hold its ground owing to the rivalry with *Ha-Meliẓ* and *Ha-Ẓefirah*, which by the admission of its editors, Judah Leib *Gordon and Nahum *Sokolow respectively, reluctantly became dailies in order to compete with *Ha-Yom*. Another cause for its failure was its reserved and even cool attitude toward the Ḥibbat Zion movement. The paper proved, as Kantor said in his introduction to the first issue, that "the Hebrew language had the resources to discuss everyday life as it did in the old days."

BIBLIOGRAPHY: N. Sokolow, *Ishim* (1958), 153–91; R. Malachi, in: *Ḥerut* (Dec. 31, 1965); Kressel, Leksikon, 2 (1967), 781; J.S. Geffen, in: AJHSQ, 51 (1961/62), 149–67.

[Getzel Kressel]

ḤAYON, NEHEMIAH ḤIYYA BEN MOSES (c. 1655–c. 1730), kabbalist with Shabbatean tendencies. Because of the bitter dispute which centered around Ḥayon, the information about his life is full of contradictions and must be sifted critically. His ancestors came from Sarajevo, Bosnia. From there, his father moved to Ereẓ Israel after spending several years in Egypt where, according to his own testimony, Ḥayon was born. As a child, he was taken to Jerusalem, grew up in Shechem (Nablus) and in Jerusalem, and studied under Ḥayyim Abulafia. At the age of 18 he returned to Sarajevo with his father and married there. His enemies claimed that from that time on he was known for his adventures. He traveled widely throughout the Balkans and spent several years in Belgrade until its occupation by Austria in 1688. He may have joined his father as an emissary to Italy for the ransoming of captives from Belgrade. According to the testimony of Judah Brieli, Ḥayon was in Leghorn in 1691. Later he served for a short time in the rabbinate of Skoplje (Üsküb), Macedonia, at the recommendation of one of the great rabbis of Salonika.

He returned to Ereẓ Israel c. 1695 and lived for several years in Shechem (Nablus). After his first wife's death, Ḥayon married the daughter of one of the scholars of Safed. Ḥayon was well versed in exoteric and esoteric lore. From his youth, he was attracted to Kabbalah and he knew the Shabbatean groups intimately. His kabbalistic doctrine evades the issue of Shabbetai Ẓevi's messianic claims, but is based on principles common to Shabbateanism. When Ḥayon received the pamphlet *Raza de-Meheimanuta* ("The Mystery of the True Faith"), attributed to Shabbetai Ẓevi by his sectarians, he claimed that he himself wrote it and that it was revealed to him by Elijah or by the angel *Metatron. Changing its name to *Meheimanuta de-Khula* he began to write a detailed commentary. In the meanwhile, he lived briefly in Rosetta, Egypt, and from that time he became known as one who engaged in practical Kabbalah. When he returned to Jerusalem (c. 1702–05), hostility developed between him and R. Abraham Yiẓḥaki who for several years leveled many accusations against Ḥayon (but never directly accused him of Shabbateanism). Later, he returned to Safed and from there he went to Smyrna, apparently intending to publish his long commentary to *Meheimanuta de-Khula* and to find supporters for a yeshivah, which he wished to establish in Jerusalem. On his return to Jerusalem, the rabbis began to harass him and he was forced to leave Ereẓ Israel. He went to Italy via Egypt (1710–11). According to the testimony of Joseph *Ergas, in Leghorn, Ḥayon disclosed to him his belief in Shabbetai Ẓevi. In 1711, in Venice, he published his small book *Raza de-Yiḥuda* on the meaning of the verse on the unity of God, *Shema Yisrael*, as an abridgment of his larger work to which he added, in the meantime, a second commentary. The rabbis of Venice gave approbations to this booklet without understanding its intent. The book did not arouse controversy. Later, Ḥayon moved to Prague where he was received with great honor in scholarly circles and gained approval for *Oz le-Elohim*, his main work, and *Divrei Neḥemyah*, a book of sermons. David Oppenheim approbated *Divrei Neḥemyah* and Ḥayon altered the approbation to include the kabbalistic *Oz le-Elohim* as well. R. Naphtali Cohen, who at first befriended Ḥayon, kept him at a distance after a rumor got about that connected him with the *Doenmeh in Salonika. Ḥayon traveled via Moravia and Silesia to Berlin where, in 1713, supported by the wealthy members of the community, he succeeded in publishing *Oz le-Elohim*. It was daring of Ḥayon to publish a text which in many manuscripts was circulated then as a work of Shabbetai Ẓevi. With great acumen, he tried to prove in his two commentaries that this doctrine was firmly based in the classical texts of the Kabbalah. In some passages, he criticized the works of *Nathan of Gaza and Abraham Miguel *Cardozo, in spite of his doctrine being basically close to Cardozo's. Ḥayon's innovations were a new formulation of the principles of the beginning of Emanation and the difference between the First Cause which he calls "*Nishmata de-Kol Ḥayyei*" ("Soul of All Living Beings") and the **Ein-Sof* ("The Infinite Being"). What the kabbalists call *Ein-Sof* is in his opinion only the extension of the Essence (of God) or the *Shoresh ha-Ne'lam* ("the Hidden Root," i.e., God), but paradoxically enough this Essence is finite and it possesses a definite structure, **Shi'ur Komah* ("Measure of the Body of God"). Ḥayon thought that Isaac Luria's doctrine of *Ẓimẓum* ("withdrawal") must be understood literally and not allegorically. His doctrine of the three superior *parẓufim* ("aspects of God"), *attika kaddisha, malka kaddisha*, and *Shekhinah*, differs from the theories of other Shabbateans only in details and in terminology. His book may by defined as a strange mixture of basically Shabbatean theology and exegetical acumen by which he read the new theses into the *Zohar and the Lurianic writings. He prefaced his book with a long essay in which he argued, apparently hinting at the unorthodox sources of his thought, that it is lawful to learn Kabbalah from everyone, not only from those who conform to traditional Orthodox criteria. *Divrei Neḥemyah* contained a long sermon in which it was possible to see an indirect defense of the apostasy of the Doenmeh sect in Salonika, but which could also be interpreted as criticism of them. In June 1713 Ḥayon left Berlin for Amsterdam. Apparently he knew of the hidden Shabbatean tendency of Solomon *Ayllon, rabbi of the Sephardi congregation. Indeed, Ḥayon received the patronage of Ayllon, his *bet din*, and the *parnasim* of the community. However, a bitter and complex struggle developed between the supporters of Ḥayon and those of Ẓevi *Ashkenazi, the rabbi of the Ashkenazi community, and of Moses *Ḥagiz who knew of Ḥayon's early quarrels in Ereẓ Israel and recognized the Shabbatean "heresy" in his opinions, when they investigated his book. In this controversy, relevant factors (the true views of Ḥayon and his Shabbateanism) and personal factors (the arrogant behavior of Ẓevi Ashkenazi, personal antagonisms) are mingled. Essentially, the accusers of Ḥayon were right but from a formal and procedural point of view the Sephardi *bet din* was right. The quarrel aroused strong emotions, at first in Amsterdam, in the summer and the winter of 1713, and it swiftly spread to other countries. Naphtali Cohen apologized for his previous approval of Ḥayon and excommunicated him. So did Italian rabbis to whom both sides turned for support. The leaders were Judah Brieli of Mantua and Samson Morpurgo of Ancona. Most of the participants in the controversy had not actually seen the books of Ḥayon and depended only on the letters from both sides. The major pamphlets against Ḥayon are: *Le-Einei Kol Yisrael* (the judicial decision of Ẓevi Ashkenazi and letters from him and from Naphtali Cohen; Amsterdam, 1713); *Edut le-Yisrael* (*ibid.*, 1714); works by Moses Ḥagiz including *Milḥamah la-Adonai ve-Ḥerev la-Adonai*, also including the letters of many Italian rabbis (Amsterdam,

1714); *Shever Poshe'im* (London, 1714); *Iggeret ha-Kena'ot* (Berlin, 1714); *Tokhaḥat Megullah ve-ha-Ẓad Naḥash* by Joseph Ergas (London, 1715); and *Esh Dat* by David Nieto (London, 1715). This book and several leaflets also appeared in Spanish. The *bet din* of the Sephardim published in Hebrew and in Spanish *Kosht Imrei Emet* (Amsterdam, 1713; in Spanish, *Manifesto*). Ḥayon answered his critics in several books and pamphlets in which he defended his views but denied that they contain any Shabbatean doctrine. They include *Ha-Ẓad Ẓevi Ashkenazi*; (Amsterdam, 1714); *Moda'a Rabba* (1714, including his biography); *Shalhevet Yah* (against Ergas), also including the pamphlets *Pitkah min Shemaya, Ketovet Ka'aka*, and *Iggeret Shevukin* (1714). His polemics against Ergas' *Ha-Ẓad Naḥash*, called *Naḥash Neḥoshet*, is found in Ḥayon's handwriting (Oxford, Ms. 1900). Because of the controversy he had aroused, Ḥayon did not succeed in publishing his second comprehensive work on Kabbalah, *Sefer Ta'aẓumot*. A complete manuscript of the work is preserved in the library of the *bet din*, formerly that of the *bet ha-midrash*, in London (62).

Ẓevi Ashkenazi and Moses Ḥagiz were forced to leave Amsterdam. However, the intervention of the rabbis of Smyrna and Constantinople, who excommunicated Ḥayon and condemned his works in 1714, decided the struggle against Ḥayon, whose supporters advised him to return to Turkey in order to obtain the annulment of the excommunication. Ḥayon returned and attempted to achieve this but he succeeded only partially. In his old age, he went back to Europe where in the pamphlet *Ha-Kolot Yeḥdalun* (1725) he published some documents in his favor. His journey was unsuccessful because Moses Ḥagiz again came out against him in the booklet *Leḥishat Saraf* (Hanau, 1726) where he threw suspicion on several of the documents, or on the circumstances under which they were signed. Most of the communities did not allow him access and even Ayllon refused to receive him in Amsterdam. Ḥayon wandered to North Africa and apparently died there before 1730. According to Ḥagiz, his son converted to Catholicism in order to take revenge on his father's persecutors and was active in Italy.

BIBLIOGRAPHY: Graetz, Hist, 5 (1949), 215–31; D. Kahana (Kogan), *Toledot ha-Mekubbalim, Shabbeta'im, ve-ha-Ḥasidim* (1913), 123–7; Kauffmann, in: *Ha-Ḥoker*, 2 (1894), 11–15; Scholem, in: *Zion*, 3 (1929), 172–9; Sonne, in: *Kobez al jad*, 2 (1937), 157–96; Herling, in: *Amanah*, 1 (1939), 259–74; idem, in: KS, 15 (1939), 130–5; Kahana, in: *Sinai*, 21 (1947), 328–34; A. Freimann (ed.), *Inyanei Shabbetai Ẓevi* (1912), 117–38; Friedmann, in: *Sefunot*, 10 (1966) 489–618; Levi, in: RI, 8 (1911), 169–85; 9 (1912), 5–29.

[Gershom Scholem]

HAYS, family established in the New World in the first quarter of the 18th century, when MICHAEL HAYS (d. 1740) emigrated from Holland to New York. Michael's sons JACOB (d. 1760), SOLOMON, ISAAC (d. 1765), and JUDAH (1703–1764) and their descendants flourished in the American colonies. Jacob was active in building Congregation Shearith Israel in New York City in 1730. Jacob's sons BENJAMIN (d. 1816), MICHAEL (1753–1799), and DAVID (1732–1812) became farmers in Westchester County, and all actively supported the American cause during the Revolution, Benjamin by fighting in the army, Michael by permitting colonial troops to use his farm to store supplies. To keep the rebel army from utilizing the stores, the British army seized Michael's farm in 1776 and did not restore it until 1782. After the war Michael served in the New York State Constitutional Convention. The youngest brother, David, operated a store in Bedford in addition to his farm. He married into the *Etting family. While he was serving with the American army, Loyalists, who were attempting to keep supplies from reaching the colonial forces, burned his home, his store, and the rest of Bedford on the night of July 9, 1779. David's eldest son, JACOB (1772–1850), converted to Christianity and in 1802 was appointed high constable (chief of police) of the City of New York, a position he held until a year before his death.

BIBLIOGRAPHY: Rosenbloom, Biogr Dict.

[Neil Ovadia]

HAYS, ARTHUR GARFIELD (1881–1954), U.S. lawyer and civil liberties advocate. Hays, who was born in Rochester, New York, practiced law in New York for 20 years. In 1925 he abandoned his private practice to become general counsel of the American Civil Liberties Union. He represented clients without remuneration in numerous cases involving the violation of freedoms guaranteed by the Bill of Rights. Hays served as co-counsel with Clarence Darrow in 1925 in the celebrated Scopes anti-evolution case which became known as the "monkey trial." Although Scopes was convicted for violating a state law which prohibited the teaching of any theory that denied divine creation, the trial compelled the State of Tennessee to abandon the enforcement of this law. Hays was involved in the defense of Sacco and Vanzetti, and the Scottsboro Boys whose death sentence for alleged rape was reversed by the U.S. Supreme Court. He also defended Dmitrov and other Communists tried in Germany for the Reichstag fire, pleading through a German as the Nazis would not permit Hays, a Jew, to plead himself. After World War II, he helped the occupation forces to re-create democratic institutions in Germany. Hays was never prepared to confine his defense of liberty only to the causes for which he had sympathy. Thus, although he detested Nazism, he joined the attorney of Friends of New Germany in seeking an injunction against a police commissioner in New Jersey who had closed all halls to Nazi meetings (1937). He wrote several books, among them *Trial by Prejudice* (1933), *Democracy Works* (1939), and his autobiography, *City Lawyer* (1942).

[Alan Reitman]

HAYS, DANIEL PEIXOTTO (1854–1923), U.S. lawyer. Hays who was born in Westchester County, New York, received his LL.B. from Columbia University Law School in 1875. A member of an old and prominent New York Jewish family, he was the grandson of Benjamin Etting Hays (1779–1858) and a descendant of Jacob Hays (see *Hays family), who went to the New York Colony in the 1720s. Active in New York City and Westchester County politics for many years, Hays served as president of the Harlem Democratic Club, as delegate to several New York State Democratic conventions, and was appointed head of New York City's Municipal Civil Service Commission by Mayor Gilroy. Hays vigorously supported the presidential candidacy of Grover Cleveland in *City and Country*, a Nyack, New York, newspaper owned by him. Hays was also extremely active in Jewish communal affairs, serving on the executive committee of the Union of American Hebrew Congregations, as trustee and secretary of the Jewish Publication Society, and president of the Young Men's Hebrew Association. He was also a founder of the *American Hebrew*. His *Collected Poems* appeared in 1905.

[Abram Kanof]

HAYS, ISAAC (1796–1879), U.S. physician. Hays, a descendant of Michael Hays' son Isaac (see *Hays family), was born in Philadelphia. He graduated from the University of Pennsylvania (1816) and received an M.D. there (1820). An oculist, he was one of the pioneers in the study of astigmatism and color blindness, and he invented a scalpel for use in cataract surgery. Hays's contribution extended beyond his specialty. He was the editor of several important journals, one of the founding members of the American Medical Association (1847), and wrote the code of medical ethics which has been adopted throughout the United States.

BIBLIOGRAPHY: Rosenbloom, Biogr Dict, s.v. *Hays, Isaac*[3].

[Neil Ovadia]

ḤAYYAT, JUDAH BEN JACOB (c. 1450–c. 1510), kabbalist. Ḥayyat was born in Spain and studied Kabbalah under Samuel ibn Shraga. Around 1482 he addressed basic questions on Kabbalah to Joseph *Alcastil, who answered him at length. After the expulsion of the Jews from Spain in 1492 he suffered many hardships on sea voyages and in North Africa. In 1494 he reached Italy and for several years lived in Mantua where at the request of Joseph *Jabez he wrote in the early 16th century a detailed commentary on *Ma'arekhet ha-Elohut*, an early kabbalistic work that was widely circulated among contemporary kabbalists in Italy. The commentary, titled *Minḥat Yehudah*, was published together with the *Ma'arekhet* in Ferrara in 1558 and in several later editions. It is considered one of the outstanding works of Kabbalah in the generation of the Spanish Expulsion. More than a commentary on the *Ma'arekhet* it is an independent, systematic work whose intention and major views differ greatly from those in the book which it supposedly intends to expound.

Ḥayyat was a radical representative of the Kabbalah of the *Zohar, in contrast to the Kabbalah of Abraham *Abulafia, which was accepted in Italy, and to the semi-philosophical Kabbalah of Isaac b. Abraham ibn *Latif, which Ḥayyat harshly criticized. He was one of the first to quote at length passages of the Zohar and the *Tikkunim* and based his kabbalistic theory on their sayings. He had reservations about philosophical commentaries on the Kabbalah which circulated in Italy. He also disputed against the *Iggeret Ḥamudot* of Elijah of *Genazzano which identified the **Ein Sof* ("the Infinite") with the first *Sefirah* ("emanation"). Concerning the essence of the *Sefirot*, Ḥayyat mainly concurred with the view of Menahem *Recanati. The process of creation is explained, according to him, by the double movement of expansion and contraction of the divine will. Creation is nothing but a realization into actuality through the divine will of the potential hidden unity of the *Ein-Sof*. Ḥayyat had a recognizable influence on all 16th–17th century Kabbalah. Even those who falsely wrote under names of earlier authors used his works at length. His supercommentary on Recanati's commentary to the Pentateuch has not been preserved.

[Gershom Scholem]

Ḥayyat was probably acquainted with the Italian Kabbalah as represented by Johanan Alemanno with his penchant for a more philosophical understanding of this lore and for Abraham *Abulafia's Kabbalah. Ḥayyat's book represents a successful attempt to establish the Spanish Kabbalah in a center in which other forms of this lore had been studied.

[Moshe Idel (2nd ed.)]

BIBLIOGRAPHY: G. Scholem, in: *Tarbiz*, 24 (1954/55), 174–206; E. Gottlieb, in: *Studies in Mysticism and Religion Presented to G. Scholem* (1968), 63–86 (Heb. section). **ADD. BIBLIOGRAPHY:** M. Idel, "Encounters between Spanish and Italian Kabbalists in the Generation of the Expulsion," in: B. Gampel (ed.), *Crisis and Creativity in the Sephardic World* (1997), 189–222.

ḤAYYIM ABRAHAM RAPHAEL BEN ASHER (d. 1772), Jerusalem rabbi and kabbalist. Ḥayyim was a member of the *bet din* of Raphael *Meyuḥas, and later *av bet din* in Jerusalem. Toward the end of his life, in 1771, he was appointed *rishon le-Zion* (Sephardi chief rabbi). In 1731 (or 1734) he published in Constantinople the *Sha'arei Kedushah* of Ḥayyim *Vital. Between the years 1734 and 1765 he traveled as an emissary of Jerusalem, seeking contributions in Constantinople, Italy, France, and Egypt. Ḥayyim was a signatory of the *Shetar Hitkasherut* ("articles of association") of the society of kabbalists. Head of the yeshivah Yefa'er Anavim in Jerusalem, he cosigned the *takkanah* forbidding bachelors between the ages of 20 and 60 from residing in Jerusalem. He gave approbations to many works, among them the *Zivḥei Shelamim* of Judah Diwan (Constantinople 1728), and the *Shulḥan Gavoha* of Joseph Molkho, Salonika, OḤ 1756; YD 1764. He died during a famine and plague that raged in Jerusalem.

BIBLIOGRAPHY: Frumkin-Rivlin, 3 (1929), 98f.; Yaari, Sheluḥei, 289–91; Rosanes, Togarmah, 5 (1938), 240, 243; Katsh, in: *Sefunot*, 9 (1964), 323–35.

[Simon Marcus]

ḤAYYIM BEN ABRAHAM HA-KOHEN (c. 1585–1655), kabbalist, born in Aleppo. His ancestors went to Ereẓ Israel after the expulsion from Spain (1492) and later settled in

Aleppo. Ḥayyim was the disciple of Ḥayyim *Vital during his last years in Damascus, and he left an interesting story about his growing attachment to the study of Kabbalah under his teacher. Later, he was one of the rabbis of Aleppo. Ḥayyim wrote numerous works in the course of a 20-year period, which are listed in the introduction to his book *Torat Ḥakham*. During a long sea voyage, which he undertook in order to bring these manuscripts to print, the ship was attacked by pirates off Malta. He saved himself by jumping into the sea near the coast, but all his manuscripts were lost. He states that he decided to write them again. Around 1650 he set out again for Constantinople where he stayed two to three years. The first part of his book *Mekor Ḥayyim*, a detailed kabbalistic commentary on the rules of the Shulḥan Arukh, was published here. At the end of 1652 he was in Smyrna; later he went to Venice and returned through Zante to Aleppo. Through the mediation of Samuel *Aboab of Verona he had published in Venice the large volume of sermons, *Torat Ḥakham* (1654), with the kabbalist Moses *Zacuto acting as proofreader. Another part of *Mekor Ḥayyim*, called *Tur Bareket*, was published by the brothers Raphael and Abraham b. Danan in Amsterdam in 1654. In the same year Ḥayyim set out again for Italy where he published two additional parts, *Tur Piteda* and *Tur Yahalom* (Leghorn, 1655). He died in Leghorn during the publication of his last book which thus remained incomplete, and only single sections have survived as pamphlets. All his commentaries on the Shulḥan Arukh have been published in two volumes (1878). In Leghorn, he introduced Nathan *Hannover to Isaac *Luria's Kabbalah. Hannover included in his *Sha'arei Ẓiyyon* a lament by Ḥayyim for the *Tikkun Ḥaẓot* (midnight prayer), *Kol be-Ramah Nishma*, which has since become part of every edition of this midnight liturgy. Among his commentaries on the Five Scrolls, only *Ateret Zahav* on Esther, explained both according to the literal meaning (*peshat*) and the Kabbalah, in the author's handwriting (Jerusalem, JNUL, Ms. 8° 1581), and *Torat Ḥesed* on Ruth, have been preserved. The last, however, was published by the kabbalist David Lida as his own, under the title *Migdal David* (Amsterdam, 1680). This plagiarism was known in kabbalist circles even before it was made public by Ḥ.J.D. *Azulai in *Shem ha-Gedolim*. In his books Ḥayyim quotes only portions from throughout the *Zohar, and sometimes also the sayings of his teacher Vital, but most of his presentation is not based on other sources "and all his words are as if written from Sinai" (Nathan Hannover, introduction to *Sha'arei Ẓiyyon*). A prayer book with kabbalistic meditations by Ḥayyim is extant in several manuscripts (two at the Ben-Zvi Institute in Jerusalem). Ḥayyim "was very careful not to write amulets," and was also opposed to those who spent too much time in prayer, wasting thus the whole day upon mystical meditations. Among kabbalists he was considered more of a theoretical scholar than a practical mystic.

BIBLIOGRAPHY: Michael, Or, no. 844; M. Benayahu in: *Sinai*, 34 (1953), 162–64, 194–7; idem, *Sefer Toledot ha-Ari* (1967), index.

[Gershom Scholem]

ḤAYYIM BEN BEZALEL (c. 1520–1588), talmudic scholar. Ḥayyim was born in Posen, and was the eldest of four brothers, all rabbis, the most famous being *Judah Loew b. Bezalel of Prague (the Maharal) who mentions him in his responsa (no. 12). Ḥayyim studied first with Rabbi Isaac Sepharadi in Posen. From him, Ḥayyim acquired his abiding love for Bible study and the in-depth study of Rashi's commentary. As a young man he studied in the yeshivah of *Shalom Shakhna at Lublin where he was a contemporary of Moses *Isserles. His final teacher was Rabbi Solomon Luria, the Maharshal. From him, Ḥayyim acquired a method for studying *halakhah* as well as a dislike for halakhic codes (see below), Ḥayyim settled in Worms in 1549 where he lived in the home of his uncle, Jacob b. Ḥayyim, the local rabbi, succeeding him in 1563. He subsequently left to become rabbi of Friedberg, remaining there until his death.

When Isserles published his *Torat Ḥattat* on *issur ve-hetter* (on the dietary laws), Ḥayyim published a vigorous polemic against it in his *Vikku'aḥ Mayim Ḥayyim*. The introduction to the work was couched in such strong language both against Isserles and Joseph *Caro that it was omitted from editions after the first (Amsterdam, 1712), but has been reproduced in full by Tchernowitz (see bibl.). Ḥayyim's criticism was a general one against all those who presumed to publish halakhic codes which purported to give the final definitive *halakhah*, since they lead to neglect of the early authorities and can be used with disastrous results by the unlearned. Of Joseph Caro he comments that after saying "who am I to decide between the opposing views of the great authorities?" he then proceeds to do so. "It is like a man who says, 'I have the greatest respect for what you say, but you are lying'!" The main target of his criticism, however, is Isserles' work. The *Torat Ḥattat* ("Law of the Sin-Offering") was rightly named, he said, since it, albeit unwillingly, causes people to sin, and it "even borders on *ḥillul ha-Shem* (Profanation of the Name of God)." In the same way as Moses set up the Copper Serpent with the best of intentions, yet when it became an object of idolatry Hezekiah did not hesitate to destroy it, so would he act with regard to this work of the "later Moses." He felt that Isserles should at least have stated that his work was only to be used by qualified scholars. (He himself had spent 16 years in composing a similar work, but only for his private use, and when one of his students purloined it and copied it, he sternly reproved him and destroyed the copy.) In addition to his general criticism he specified three reasons for his opposition: (1) Isserles had amended the code of Caro which reflected the Sephardi *minhag* to make it accord with the Polish *minhag*, but he had completely ignored the differences between the Polish and the German *minhag*, which was more authoritative and ancient. (2) He had introduced a new element of leniency when "considerable (financial) loss" or "exceptional circumstances" (*she'at ha-deḥak*) were involved. (3) He abolished the *halakhah* in favor of unsubstantiated custom.

Ḥayyim wrote a number of other works. His *Sefer ha-Ḥayyim*, which he wrote in two months while he was confined to his house on account of a plague in 1578, is a moral and ethical dissertation. In style and language it is reminiscent of the pietistic works, and in fact his brother refers to him as "he-Ḥasid." In general, Ḥayyim was not in favor of the study of philosophy. He thought that only advanced students should study philosophy, even Jewish philosophy. As for the study of Kabbalah, Ḥayyim praised the *mekubbalim* (Kabbalah practitioners) for their ability to enter God's palace, yet he was critical of their abandoning the "small interests of the King," namely the study of Talmud and Halakhah. His *Eẓ Ḥayyim* on Hebrew grammar (written in 1579) is still in manuscript. He was inspired to write it because of the criticism of Christian Hebrew scholars who accused the Jews not only of neglecting the study of Hebrew in favor of the Talmud, but even of forbidding it. He admits that he used the grammatical works of these detractors as one of his sources. He attributes the neglect of the study of Hebrew grammar to the fact that in the "bitter and long exile … it was impossible to encompass all subjects in the curriculum, for which reason alone the early authorities, especially the Ḥasidei Ashkenaz, confined their instruction to the Talmud" (Introduction). He also wrote *Be'er Mayim Ḥayyim*, a supercommentary on Rashi's Pentateuch commentary in response to the great popularity enjoyed by Rashi's commentary but the lack of true comprehension of Rashi's work. Ḥayyim's work focuses on the correct translation of the Torah text, the grammatical comments made by Rashi, and those aspects of his commentary that are unique. In addition, Ḥayyim wrote *Iggeret ha-Tiyyul* (Prague, 1605) consisting of explanations of talmudic passages using the methods of **Pardes*, (*peshat, remez, derash, sod*) in alphabetical order.

BIBLIOGRAPHY: A. Gottesdiener, in: *Azkarah… A.I. Kook*, 4 (1937), 265f.; Ḥ. Tchernowitz, *Toledot ha-Posekim*, 3 (1947), 91–100; A. Siev, *Ha-Rema* (1957), 47–49; H.H. Ben Sasson, *Hagut ve-Hanhagah* (1959), 15, 35 n. 3. **ADD. BIBLIOGRAPHY:** E. Zimmer, *Rabbi Chaim ben Bezalel of Friedberg* (Heb., 1987); **WEBSITES:** http://www.torah.org; http://chareidi.shemayisrael.com.

[Alexander Tobias / David Derovan (2nd ed.)]

ḤAYYIM BEN HANANEL HA-KOHEN (second half of the 12th century), French tosafist. Ḥayyim lived in Paris and was a distinguished disciple and admirer of Jacob *Tam about whom he said that he would have defiled himself (referring to the prohibition against defilement of a kohen through contact with the dead) had he been present at his death (cf. Tos. to Ket. 103b). Ḥayyim wrote *tosafot* to several talmudic tractates and is quoted in the printed *tosafot* and in many other *rishonim*. "On him" said Isaac the Elder, "rested the honor of the entire generation." Ḥayyim opposed immigration to Palestine, stating that "in our generation the commandment to live in Palestine does not apply," as it was impossible to observe many commandments connected with the land (*ibid.*, 110b). However, he considered Jewish existence in the Diaspora as temporary. Ḥayyim was the grandfather of *Moses b. Jacob of Coucy, author of the *Semag*, and among his most prominent disciples was *Samson b. Abraham of Sens.

BIBLIOGRAPHY: Urbach, Tosafot, 107–10; V. Aptowitzer, *Mavo le-Sefer Ravyah* (1938), 250.

[Zvi Meir Rabinowitz]

ḤAYYIM (Eliezer) BEN ISAAC "OR ZARU'A" (late 13th century), German rabbi and halakhic authority, called "Or Zaru'a" after the famous work composed by his father, *Isaac b. Moses of Vienna. Ḥayyim was orphaned in his early youth. His principal teacher was Meir b. Baruch of Rothenburg, whose opinions he frequently cited. He also studied under such eminent scholars as Asher b. Jehiel and Ḥayyim b. Moses of Wiener-Neustadt. His permanent places of residence were Regensburg, Neustadt, or Cologne and he is said to have spent some years in France. Ḥayyim is considered one of the last of the tosafists. While his father, Isaac b. Moses, the author of the *Or Zaru'a*, is mentioned numerous times throughout the **tosafot* commentaries, Ḥayyim is only mentioned in the *Tosafot Yeshanim*, a variant version of the *tosafot* commentaries.

Ḥayyim's responsa (Leipzig, 1865; repr. Jerusalem, 2002, with commentary) are especially valuable for the light they shed on the people, places, and events of his time. Thus he mentions (no. 110) a rabbinical synod which he attended at Mainz in about 1288, in which one of the matters discussed was the taxes imposed on the Jews by Rudolf of Hapsburg. In the same responsum he refers in passing to R. Meir of Rothenburg's imprisonment (see also no. 164). Some of the responsa provide important source material on Jewish-Christian relations in the 13th century. Most of Ḥayyim's decisions are based on those of the French and German halakhic authorities, particularly on his father's *Or Zaru'a*. His abridged version of that codification, which he entitled *Kiẓẓur Or Zaru'a* (or *Simanei Or Zaru'a*), summarized each section of the original work, omitted the legal discussions, and included his own views together with those of other scholars. From the many references to the *Kiẓẓur Or Zaru'a* in German rabbinic literature of the 14th and 15th centuries it is clear that his abridgment enjoyed long popularity. An important aspect of Ḥayyim's work is the lively correspondence he conducted with many of his contemporaries. It is believed that he addressed inquiries even to the Spanish scholar Solomon b. Abraham *Adret (Resp. Rashba, pt. 1, no. 572).

Knowledge about the life and teaching of Ḥayyim "Or Zaru'a" derives from a book of responsa of which he was the author and a book of homiletic sermons (*derashot*) which was published under the title *Derashot MHR"H, Halakhic Decisions of Rabbi Ḥayyim Or Zaru'a*, first ed. according to Parma MS Moscow by Yitzḥak Shimshon Lange (Jerusalem, 1973).

The book of *Derashot* contains homiletic treatises on 25 portions of the Torah, summing up various laws and customs. Both his responsa and homiletic treatises contain a wealth of material throwing light on relations between Jews and their gentile surroundings. He endeavors throughout to provide the Jews of Ashkenaz with guidance in their dealings with the hostile gentile environment. From the copious historical material found in his responsa, much can be learned about the Jewish communities (*Kehillot*), their internal organization, leadership, rights, and obligations. We also learn how he grappled with the challenges and dangers of living as a Jew in the midst of a medieval, gentile society.

BIBLIOGRAPHY: Wellesz, in: MGWJ, 48 (1904), 211–3; idem, in: REJ, 53 (1907), 67–84; 54 (1907), 102–6; Freimann, in: JJLG, 12 (1918), 314 (index), s.v. *Chajim Elieser b. Isak Or Sarua*; M. Pollak, *Juden in Wiener-Neustadt* (1927), 8, 35, 39; Urbach, Tosafot, index, s.v. *Ḥayyim b. Yiẓḥak*; Y. Horowitz, "Rabbi Ḥayyim Or Zaru'a and his Relationship to Gentiles" (Hebrew), in: *Proceedings of the 9th World Congress of Jewish Studies*, Division B, vol. 1 (Jerus., 1986), 107–112. **ADD. BIBLIOGRAPHY:** M.M. Rozner, in: *Piskei Rabbenu Asher: Mesekhet Megillah* (1999); Y. Horowitz, in: *Hevrah ve-Historiyah* (1980), 93–102; Y. Ta-Shema, in: *Sinai*, 66 (1970), 339–46.

[Shlomo Eidelberg / Yehoshua Horowitz / David Derovan (2nd ed.)]

ḤAYYIM BEN JEHIEL ḤEFEẒ ZAHAV (13th century), German talmudist. Ḥayyim studied under his father and under *Samuel of Evreux. Many of his responsa are included in the responsa of *Meir b. Baruch of Rothenburg (ed. by M. Bloch, 1895, nos. 188–9, 209, 241, 249, 296–8, 339–41, 355–6, 382–3, 461–3). In a responsum (no. 241) he affirms that he filled the post of "emissary of Kolonia," probably Cologne. It has been therefore assumed by some that he was a member of the Cologne *bet din* and represented the community before the government. He was probably given the appellation "*Ḥefeẓ Zahav*" because of his book bearing this title, but from the endings of many of the responsa (nos. 189, 241, 339) it can also be deduced that his father was the author of the book. It appears that Ḥayyim was a colleague of Samuel b. Menahem, the teacher of Meir of Rothenburg, since in one responsum (no. 188) he refers to him as "my associate." This Ḥayyim is not to be identified with Ḥayyim b. Jehiel, the brother of *Asher b. Jehiel.

BIBLIOGRAPHY: Michael, Or, no. 876; H. Gross, in: MGWJ, 34 (1885), 313f.; Germ Jud, 1 (1934), 151, 484; 2 (1968), index; I. Agus, *Rabbi Meir of Rothenburg*, 1 (1947), xxvi, 106, 129, 131, 146–8, 160f.

[Yehoshua Horowitz]

ḤAYYIM BEN SAMUEL BEN DAVID OF TUDELA (14th century), talmudic scholar of Tudela, Spain. Ḥayyim was a pupil of Solomon b. Abraham *Adret, and the latter's responsa contain a number addressed to Ḥayyim. For some time Ḥayyim was in France, where he studied under *Perez b. Elijah. His main work is the *Ẓeror ha-Ḥayyim* (published in 1966), consisting of the laws appertaining to blessings, prayer, Sabbaths, and festivals, arranged according to the order of the calendar; it is based on views of various French, Provençal, and Spanish scholars but chiefly upon his teachers, Adret and Perez, though he does not mention them by name. His other work, *Ẓeror ha-Kesef*, on topics in *Ḥoshen Mishpat*, is still in manuscript. These books (referred to by the *rishonim* as the *ẓerorot*, "bundles") were in the possession of later scholars (but cf. Resp. Ribash, no. 396), who made use of and quoted them. This was particularly so in the case of the 16th-century Safed scholars, including Joseph *Caro. In this work, Ḥayyim alludes to a book of sermons he wrote, and Masud Ḥai Roke'aḥ, at the beginning of his *Ma'aseh Roke'aḥ* (Venice, 1742), quotes Ḥayyim's commentary to the tractate *Mo'ed Katan*, which is also cited by Bezalel *Ashkenazi in *Kelalei ha-Shas* (in Ms.). Among Ḥayyim's relations was Joseph ha-Dayyan, referred to respectfully several times in the responsa of Isaac b. Sheshet (Ribash).

BIBLIOGRAPHY: Michael, Or, no. 904; S.H. Yerushalmi, *Mavo le-Sefer Ẓeror ha-Ḥayyim* (1966).

[Israel Moses Ta-Shma]

ḤAYYIM BEN SOLOMON TYRER OF CZERNOWITZ (c. 1760–1816), rabbi and ḥasidic leader; born near *Buchach, Galicia. A disciple of *Jehiel Michael of Zloczów, he later served as rabbi in Mogilev, Kishinev, Czernowitz and district, and Botoșani. He had a profound knowledge of rabbinical literature and mysticism, was an eloquent preacher and a talented writer. He did much to spread Ḥasidism and opposed the spread of *Haskalah in Romania. His resistance to certain government decrees forced him to relinquish his office in Czernowitz in 1807. In 1813 he immigrated to Ereẓ Israel and settled in Safed. He wrote the following works, which were published in many editions: *Siddur shel Shabbat* (Mogilev, 1813); *Be'er Mayim Ḥayyim* (Sudilkov, 1820, with Pentateuch; Czernowitz, 1849); *Sha'ar ha-Tefillah* (Sudilkov, 1825); and *Ereẓ ha-Ḥayyim* (Czernowitz, 1861).

BIBLIOGRAPHY: Frumkin-Rivlin, 3 (1929), 78; S.J. Schulsohn, in: *Jeschurun*, 15 (1928), 419–26.

[Avraham Rubinstein]

ḤAYYIM ḤAYKL BEN SAMUEL OF AMDUR (d. 1787), ḥasidic leader in Lithuania. At first *ḥazzan* in Karlin, and a teacher in the little town of Amdur (Indura), near Grodno, he was attracted to *Ḥasidism through Aaron the Great of *Karlin. Ḥasidic sources relate that he subjected himself to excessive fasting and self-mortifications before he made the acquaintance of Dov Baer, the Maggid of Mezhirech. Becoming one of Dov Baer's most prominent disciples he founded a ḥasidic center in Amdur after the death of his teacher in 1773. A profound thinker and an enthusiastic and fearless propagandist of Ḥasidism, Ḥayyim was the ḥasidic personality most hated by the *Mitnaggedim* in Lithuania in the 1780s, and was a considerable factor in the outbreak of a second round of polemics between the two factions in 1781. He is described in somber tones in the literature of the *Mitnaggedim*, especially in the writings of *David of Makow. In *Shever Poshe'im* (in M. Wilensky, *Ḥasidim u-Mitnaggedim*, vol. 2, 1970) he and his associates are discussed with scorn. The *Mitnaggedim* persecuted him to such an extent that Ḥayyim was compelled to leave Amdur for a while and to stay in a village. He was undeterred by these persecutions, however, and continued to lead his congregation as *ẓaddik* until his death, bequeathing his position to his son Samuel.

Ḥayyim taught that God is infinite and men cannot comprehend Him. However, there is much latent power in man's intellect and by losing his own sense of being, he can be drawn nearer to and be united with his source. Ḥayyim therefore preached a complete negation of the human will before the divine will. The observance of a *mitzvah* was interpreted as an act desired by God, and it is only this desire of God's which imparts validity to the *mitzvah*. It is also forbidden to serve God for the purpose of attaining the World to Come or other rewards. Ḥayyim is revealed as an extreme spiritualist: "We should forget ourselves as a result of our adhesion to Him." One should despise this world: "He who prays for his sustenance should be ashamed for doing so." If "I have set the Lord always before me, then I have no time to consider the events which befall me, for God surely knows of my needs better than I do myself." When a man stands before the Creator, all his limbs should tremble for fear of the Lord so that he does not know where he is standing, so much has he meditated on His essence. If, at that time, evil thoughts enter his mind, he should not repel them. On the contrary, this gives him the opportunity to elevate these thoughts to their source. If a man has sinned, he should rather endeavor to unite himself to the soul of the *ẓaddik*, as a result of which he will adhere to God.

His sermons were collected in *Ḥayyim va-Ḥesed* (1891, 1953^2), including "rules of behavior" and letters to his followers, some of which had been previously published in *Iggeret ha-Kodesh* (Warsaw, 1850).

BIBLIOGRAPHY: M. Wilensky, *Ḥasidim u-Mitnaggedim* (1970), index; M.H. Kleinemann, *Mazkeret Shem ha-Gedolim* (1967^2), 49–55; W. Rabinowitsch, *Lithuanian Ḥasidism* (1970), index; R. Schatz, *Ha-Ḥasidut ke-Mistikah* (1968), index; A. Rubinstein, in: *Aresheth*, 3 (1961), 193–230

[Moshe Hallamish]

ḤAYYIM JUDAH BEN ḤAYYIM (17th–18th century), talmudist, rabbi of Janina (Ioannina), Greece. Ḥayyim Judah was born in Salonika, where he studied under Solomon *Amarillo, whose daughter he married. Toward the end of his life he emigrated to Jerusalem, where he had many disciples, among them Solomon Havdalah, a member of the *bet din* of Abraham Yiẓḥaki and in his old age rabbi of Jerusalem. Ḥ.J.D. *Azulai speaks of having seen a volume of Ḥayyim's responsa in manuscript. He carried on a halakhic correspondence with Samuel Florentin, author of the responsa *Me'il Shemu'el*, and others. His responsa are found in the works of others, e.g., *Kerem Shelomo* (Salonika, 1719) and *Zera Avraham* (Constantinople, 1732).

BIBLIOGRAPHY: Fuenn, Keneset, 356; Azulai, 1 (1852), 58, no. 28; Rosanes, Togarmah, 4 (1935), 329; 5 (1938), 287.

[Simon Marcus]

ḤAYYIM PALTIEL BEN JACOB (late 13th–early 14th century), German talmudic scholar. Ḥayyim Paltiel was a pupil of *Eliezer of Touques, and also, apparently, of *Meir b. Baruch of Rothenburg. He traveled through the cities of Bohemia and served as rabbi of Magdeburg. His questions to Meir of Rothenburg are included in the Cremona (1557, nos. 32–34), Prague (1608, no. 226), and Lemberg (1860, no. 507, et al.) editions of the latter's responsa and a number of his responsa to other scholars are also included in these collections. Of great historical importance is the responsum (Lemberg ed. no. 476) he wrote in 1291 from Magdeburg on the subject of the **Ḥerem ha-Yishuv*. He was one of the first – if not the first – to add the self-effacing epithet *tola'at* ("worm") to his formal signature, Ḥayyim Paltiel Tola'at (abbreviated to *Ḥapat*). One of his responsa to two of his pupils was forwarded by them to *Asher b. Jehiel for his opinion (Resp. Rosh, Kelal 30, no. 4). Ḥayyim Paltiel's chief importance lies in his *Sefer ha-Minhagim*, which contains the customs for the whole year, referring to benedictions, prayers, and festivals, according to the Ashkenazi rite. The work was later used by Abraham *Klausner, who adapted and amended it, and added other customs and explanations. The connection between the work of Klausner and that of Ḥayyim Paltiel was first suggested by H.J. Ehrenreich in the introduction to his edition of Klausner's *Minhagim* (1929), and was proved beyond doubt when Paltiel's work was discovered and published in *Kirjath Sepher* by D. Goldschmidt (see bibliography). Ḥayyim Paltiel thus emerges as one of the first authors of the *Minhagim books, which gained wide popularity in 14th-century Germany and which laid the foundation for the spread of the version known in essence as *nosaḥ Ashkenaz* ("the Ashkenazi rite"). It is probable that he is identical with the Ḥayyim Paltiel whose biblical explanations are extensively quoted in a still unpublished manuscript of a Bible commentary by a 14th-century French scholar.

BIBLIOGRAPHY: Ziemlich, in: MGWJ, 30 (1881), 305–16; Abraham Klauser, *Sefer ha-Minhagim*, ed. by H.J. Ehrenreich (1929), introd.; D. Goldschmidt, in: KS, 23 (1946/47), 324–30; 24 (1947/48), 73–83; Urbach, Tosafot, 456.

[Israel Moses Ta-Shma]

ḤAYYIM (Ben) SHABBETAI (known as **Maharhash – Morenu Ha-Rav Ḥayyim Shabbetai**; before 1555–1647), rabbi in Salonika. He studied under Aaron Sason, and subsequently became head of the yeshivah of the "Shalom" community. Many of his pupils became leading authorities such as Solomon ha-Levi, Isaac Barki, Ḥasdai ha-Kohen *Peraḥyah, and David *Conforte. It is not clear whether Jacob Ruvio or Ḥayyim Shabbetai was appointed to the post of chief rabbi by the leaders of the Salonikan communities in 1638, but certainly after Ruvio's death in 1640, Ḥayyim Shabbetai served as chief rabbi. In point of fact, he had been referred to as "the great rabbi" as early as 1622. He devoted himself assiduously to congregational matters, introducing many important regulations, and was regarded as the outstanding halakhic authority of his time, questions being addressed to him from communities near and far. Only part of his works have been published. These include novellae on the tractate *Ta'anit* and on the last chapter of tractate *Yoma*, published in the *Torat Moshe* of his son Moses (Salonika, 1797); responsa on *Even ha-Ezer* (Salonika, 1651); and *Torat Ḥayyim* (3 parts, Salonika,

1713, 1715, 1722), responsa. The second part of this last work is preceded by a *Kunteres ha-Moda'ah re-ha-Ones*, on contracts entered into under duress, which was published separately (Lemberg, 1798) with a commentary by Jeremiah of Mattersdorf and his son Joab. Ḥayyim also wrote *Torat ha-Zevaḥ*, on the laws of slaughtering and inspection and *Seder Gittin* (unpublished). Many additional responsa are to be found in the works of his contemporaries and disciples. He was also rabbi of Kahal Shalom Synagogue in Salonika in which position he was succeeded by his son Moses.

BIBLIOGRAPHY: Conforte, Kore, index; Michael, Or, 412; Toiber, in: KS, 8 (1932), 275f.; Rosanes, Togarmah, 3 (1938), 175–8; I.S. Emmanuel, *Gedolei Saloniki le-Dorotam*, 1 (1936), 294–6, no. 448; idem, *Maẓẓevot Saloniki*, 1 (1963), 298–301, no. 685; Benayahu, in: *Sinai*, 34 (1954), 164f.

[Abraham David]

ḤAYYOT, MENAHEM MANISH BEN ISAAC (d. 1636), Polish and Lithuanian rabbi. Ḥayyot's father served as rabbi of Prague. He himself was rabbi of Turobin, Moravia, apparently while very young, and later became a rabbi in Vilna. No biographical details of him are known but he is quoted in the works of many of his great contemporaries, such as Ephraim of Vilna in his *Sha'ar Efrayim* (Sulzbach, 1688) and Samuel Bacharach of Worms in his *Ḥut ha-Shani* (Frankfurt, 1679). His son-in-law was Joseph Josefa *Horowitz. His tombstone was the oldest in Vilna. Of his works the following have been published: *Kabbalat Shabbat*, also entitled *Zemirot le-Shabbat* (Prague, 1621), Sabbath songs; an elegy, *Kinah le-Ḥurban*, on the fire in Posen in 1590 (Prague, 1590?); and a fragment of his supercommentary to Abraham ibn Ezra to Exodus 3:15 (see Herschkowitz, bibliography). In the catalogue of David *Oppenheimer there is mention also of a manuscript of *Derekh Temimim* (no. 375) by Ḥayyot, a commentary to the weekly portion of the Law, *Balak*, giving the plain meaning as well as homiletical and kabbalistic interpretations.

BIBLIOGRAPHY: S.J. Fuenn, *Kiryah Ne'emanah* (1915^2), 67–70; H.N. Maggid-Steinschneider, *Ir Vilna* (1900), 1f.; M. Herschkowitz, in: *Sinai*, 59 (1966), 97–127.

[Itzhak Alfassi]

ḤAYYUJ, JUDAH BEN DAVID (c. 945–c. 1000), the most important Hebrew grammarian towards the turn of the 10th century. About his life little is known. He was born in Fez and arrived at Córdoba in 960 when the dispute between *Menahem b. Jacob ibn Saruq and *Dunash b. Labrat was at its height. It is doubtful whether he should be identified with Judah b. David, one of the three students of Menahem who composed *Teshuvot al Dunash ben Labrat,* the two others being Isaac ibn Kapron and Isaac ibn *Gikatilla (ed. by Z. Stern in 1870).

His works include (1) *Kitāb al-Tanqīṭ* or *Kitāb al-Nuqat* ("Book of Vocalization") was translated into Hebrew by Abraham Ibn Ezra. It includes grammatical and masoretic matters, dealing mainly with nouns. (2) *Kitāb al-'Af 'āl Dhawāt Ḥurūf al-Līn* ("The Book of Weak Letter Verbs"), translated into Hebrew by Moses ha-Kohen ibn Gikatilla, by Ibn Ezra, and by Isaac b. Eliezer ha-Levi (1458); parts of an anonymous translation have been found. (3) *Kitāb al-'Af 'āl Dhawāt al-Mithlayn* ("The Book of Geminate Verbs"), translated into Hebrew by Moses ha-Kohen ibn Gikatilla and Ibn Ezra (entitled *Po'ole ha-Kefel*).

(4) *Kitāb al-Nutaf* ("Book of Plucked Feathers"); Ibn Ezra called the book *Sefer ha-Korḥah* ("Book of Baldness"), and this later became corrupted to *Sefer ha-Rokḥah.* In this book he intended to explain the difficult verses in the eight books of the Prophets by linguistic method. There are extant parts on Joshua, Judges, Kings, Isaiah, Jeremiah, and Ezekiel, which include discussions of individual words, as well as a discussion on the importance of the *meteg* and other accents for understanding the Hebrew language.

The originals and the Hebrew translations of (1) (2) and (3) were published by J.L. Dukes (1844), G.W. Nutt (1870), and M. Jastrow (1897). Remnants of the Arabic original of (4) and their translation into modern Hebrew were published by P. Kokovtsov (see bibl.), S. Abramson, I. Eldar, and N. Allony. Recently, all these and other remnants were republished by N. Basal in *Kitāb al-Nutaf* (2001).

In his two works on the verb, Ḥayyuj developed the view that all Hebrew roots are made up of three letters, one of which, however, may be interchanged when conjugated with a weak letter, and may be elided or assimilated to a letter with a *dagesh.* This is a departure from the earlier view which recognized two-letter roots (בל, רע, קם, תם) and even some one-letter roots (the ז and the ט of ויז and ויט). According to G. Goldenberg (*Leshonenu* 44 (1980), 281–292), however, Ḥayyuj's major invention was not the tri-literality of the Hebrew verb but rather his concept of *s?sin layyin.*

His works spread rapidly throughout the Eastern countries and even became popular in Germany. Jonah ibn Janāḥ completed in his *Kitāb al-Mustalḥaq* the material missing in Ḥayyuj's works. Based on Ḥayyuj's theory, Ibn Janāḥ also wrote a comprehensive biblical Hebrew grammar and lexicon. Moses ha-Kohen ibn Gikatilla (?) prepared a synopsis in *Mukhtaṣar Ḥayyuj* (synopsis of Ḥayyuj's works); copies of these books were found in the Cairo *Genizah.* Several works following Ḥayyuj's footsteps were written, including *Sefer ha-Shoham*, by Moses b. ha-Nesi'a, and *Sefat Yeter* by Isaac b. Eliezer ha-Levi. All the work on Hebrew language and biblical exegesis since Ḥayyuj has been based on his ideas, and much of what he said, as well as his terminology (coined later on in Hebrew), is used to this day.

See also *Linguistic Literature, Hebrew.

BIBLIOGRAPHY: W. Bacher, *Die grammatische Terminologie des Jehuda b. Dawid Hajjug* (1882); idem, in: J. Winter and A. Wuensche, *Die juedische Litteratur,* 2 (1894), 159–61; B. Drachman, *Die Stellung und Bedeutung des Jehuda Hajjug* (1885); M. Jastrow (ed.), *The Weak and Geminative Verbs in Hebrew by Abu Zakariyya Yahya ibn Dawud of Fez* (1897); Steinschneider, Arab Lit, 119; S. Poznański, in: JQR, 16 (1925/26), 237–66; H. Hirschfeld, *Literary History of Hebrew Grammarians and Lexicographers* (1926), 35–40; P. Kokovtsov, *Novye materialy…*, 2 (1916), 1–74 (Russ. pt.), 1–58; S. Pinsker, *Likkutei Kadmoniyyot* (1860), index; D. Yellin, *Toledot Hitpatteḥut ha-Dikduk ha-Ivri* (1945), 113 f., Abraham b. Azriel, *Arugat ha-Bosem*, ed. by E.E. Urbach, 2 (1947), 140; N. Allony, in: *Minḥah li-Yhudah [Zlotnick]* (1950), 67–83; idem, in: BM, 16 (1963), 90–105; P. Kokovtsov, *Mi-Sifrei ha-Balshanut ha-Ivrit* ed. by N. Allony (1970).

[Nehemya Allony / Aharon Maman (2nd ed.)]

ḤAYYUN, ABRAHAM BEN NISSIM (d. 1500), Portuguese scholar; a pupil of Joseph b. Abraham *Ḥayyun, rabbi of Lisbon. He was among the Jews who left Portugal after the decree of expulsion was issued in 1496, settling in Constantinople. He wrote *Imrot Tehorot*, an ethical work (Constantinople, 1515–20; Salonika, 1595; and Jerusalem, 1876), and *Ma'amar be-Mofetim*, on miracles described in the Bible (mentioned by Abraham b. Solomon Ḥayyun at the end of Joseph Ḥayyun's *Millei de-Avot*).

BIBLIOGRAPHY: M. Kayserling, *Geschichte der Juden in Portugal* (1867), 74; Benjacob, Oẓar, 41 no. 786; A. Yaari, *Ha-Defus ha-Ivri be-Kushta* (1967), 79, 128.

ḤAYYUN, JOSEPH BEN ABRAHAM (d. 1497), last rabbi of the Jewish community of Lisbon before the expulsion. Among his distinguished disciples were Abraham b. Nissim *Ḥayyun and Joseph *Jabez. While Ḥayyun was still in Lisbon, Isaac *Abrabanel consulted him on various halakhic questions, concerning one of which he composed a tract, *Maggid Mishneh*. After the decree of expulsion from Portugal was issued in 1496, Ḥayyun went to Constantinople, where he died shortly afterward. His published works are a commentary on the Book of Psalms (Salonika, 1523), and *Millei de-Avot*, a commentary on *Avot* (Constantinople, 1578; republ. Venice, 1606); a number of his notes on the order of the *haftarot* are included in *Likkutei Man* (Amsterdam, 1764). Other works remain in manuscript.

BIBLIOGRAPHY: Benjacob, Oẓar, 324 no. 1106, 641 no. 380; Ben-Sasson, in: *Sefer Yovel le-Y. Baer* (1960), 217 ff., 220; idem, in: *Zion*, 28 (1961), 56 ff., 60; A. Yaari, *Ha-Defus ha-Ivri be-Kushta* (1967), 128.

HAZA, OFRA (1957–2000), Israeli singer. Haza was born in the Hatikva quarter of Tel Aviv to parents who had come from Yemen. She started singing as a child and at the age of 12 was accepted into the "Hatikva Quarter workshop" under the direction of Bezalel Aloni. Having completed her army service, she took part in 1979 in the movie *Shlager* where she sang the "freiha" song (lyrics, Assi Dayan, music, Zvika Pik), which became a huge hit and send her to the top of all the charts. She was crowned "singer of the year" four years in a row (1980–1983) and in 1983 represented Israel at the Eurovision song contest. She soared to international fame when her song *Galbi* ("My Heart"; 1984) was reworked for the European market and became a best seller. Another Hebrew Yemenite wedding song of the famous poet Shalem Shabazi, *Im Nin'alu*, went through a similar process and sold two million copies in Europe alone. After her performances in New York in 1989 she recorded the album "Desert Wind" (1989) and noted singers such as Paul Anka and Cliff Richards recorded duets with her. In 1998 the producer Steven Spielberg invited her to perform the theme song in his animated epic *Prince of Egypt* and she did this in the 29 languages the film was translated into. She also gave her voice to the character of Yokhebed. In spite of her international success she remained faithful to the Israeli public and her performances drew huge crowds. She participated and won first prizes in the music festival and the festival of children music. Her repertoire was based in great part on Yemenite singing.

She was asked to come to Oslo to sing when Yitzhak Rabin, Shimon Peres, and Yasser Arafat received the Nobel Peace Prize. She received second prize at the Eurovision contest.

Ofra Haza recorded 25 albums, including seven in foreign languages recorded in Europe and in the United States.

[Nathan Shahar (2nd ed.)]

HAZAEL (Heb. חֲזָאֵל; "God has taken note"), king of Aram-Damascus (c. 842–798 B.C.E.). According to an inscription of Shalmaneser III, King of Assyria (858–24), Hazael was the "son of a nobody" – who took the throne after Hadad-ezer (Adad-Idri) disappeared or died following his defeat by Shalmaneser (RIMA 3, p. 118). He founded a dynasty in Damascus during the unsettled period that also witnessed the accession of *Jehu in Israel and *Athaliah in Judah.

According to I Kings 19:15–16, Hazael was to be anointed king of Damascus by *Elijah, as Jehu was to be anointed king of Israel. When, thereafter, Ben-Hadad (= Hadad-ezer) lay ill, *Elisha directed Hazael, a royal servant, to tell Ben-Hadad that his illness was not fatal, but that in fact Ben-Hadad would not survive, and that Hazael would be king. The unclear text of II Kings 8:7–15 has usually been understood to mean that Hazael smothered Ben-Hadad in order to usurp the throne of his master (see, e.g., *Ben-Hadad and Pitard in Bibliography, but contrast Rashi and Gersonides a.l. as well as Lemaire). Hazael immediately began the attacks on Israel predicted by Elisha, attacking *Ramoth-Gilead and seriously injuring Joram of Israel (II Kings 8:28–29).

During the campaigns of Shalmaneser III in the West, Aram, under Ben-Hadad (or Hadadezer), had stood at the head of a southern Syrian coalition which effectively repulsed the Assyrian armies under Shalmaneser at the battle of *Karkar in 853, and thereafter in 848 and 845. In 841, when Shalmaneser again campaigned in the West, Hazael alone resisted, withstanding a siege of Damascus, while Tyre, Sidon, and Israel became vassals of Assyria. A punitive campaign by Shalmaneser in 838 again failed to subdue Damascus, and the Assyrians withdrew, leaving Hazael the undisputed power in southern Syria. Hazael then began a series of attacks on Israel which resulted in the period of Aram's greatest territorial control and Israel's greatest weakness. At the end of the reign of Jehu, Hazael conquered all the Israelite lands east of the Jordan, and took possession of the highlands of Galilee (II Kings 10:32–33; Amos 1:3). After Jehu's death he overran the entire territory of Israel, proceeding south along the coast to Gath on the border of Judah (II Kings 12:18–19). Hazael completely humbled the kingdom of Israel throughout the reign of Jehoahaz (II Kings 13:1–3, 7, 22), dominated the trade routes to Arabia, probably conquered all of Philistia, and even threatened Jerusalem, retreating from the city only upon the payment of a heavy tribute by Joash, king of Judah (II Kings 12:19; cf. II Chron. 24:23–24). So great was Hazael's power and domination over Israel and Judah that the resumed expeditions of Assyria under Adad-Nirari III in 805 were viewed as a liberation, and Adad-Nirari was acclaimed a deliverer (II Kings 13:5). As Dion has observed, the Aramean king who claimed victory over Israel and "the house of David" in the Tel Dan Inscription (COS II, 161–62) was most likely Hazael. The mention of the victorious king's father in that inscription would seem to conflict with the biblical characterization of Hazael as a royal servant and the Assyrian "son of a nobody," but both accounts may be "enemy propaganda" (Dion: 1999, 153–54).

Some interesting artifacts remain from Hazael's reign, of note is the ivory bed plaque inscribed as "belonging to our Lord Hazael" (*lmr'n ḥz'l*) that was discovered at Arslan Tash (the Assyrian provincial capital Hadattu). A horse's nose piece found in Samos, Greece, in 1984 and inscribed in Aramaic marks the year that Hazael "crossed the river" (COS II, 163).

BIBLIOGRAPHY: E. Kraeling, *Aram and Israel* (1918); R. de Vaux, in: RB, 43 (1934), 512–8; B. Maisler [Mazar], in: JPOS, 18 (1938), 282–3; idem, in: D.N. Freedman and E.F. Campbell (ed.), *The Biblical Archaeologist Reader*, 2 (1964), 144–5; W.W. Hallo, *ibid.*, 160–4; M.F. Unger, *Israel and the Arameans of Damascus* (1957), 75–82, 160–3. ASSYRIAN SOURCES: Luckenbill, Records, 1 (1926), nos. 575, 578, 664, 672, 681; E. Michel, in: *Die Welt des Orients*, 2 (1947), 57–58; 3 (1948), 265–6, 268–9. **ADD. BIBLIOGRAPHY:** A. Lemaire, in: D. Charpin and F. Joannès (eds.), *Marchands, diplomates... Études... Garelli* (1991), 91–108; W. Pitard, in: ABD, 3:83–4; P. Dion, *Les Araméens...* (1997) 191–204; idem, in: Y. Avishur and R. Deutsch (eds.), *Michael... Studies... Heltzer* (1999), 145–56.

[Tikva S. Frymer / S. David Sperling (2nd ed.)]

HAZAI, SAMU (1851–1942), Hungarian army officer and minister. Born in Rimazombat, Hazai graduated from the military academy in Vienna. He taught at the Ludovika Military Academy of Budapest and at the officers' school, of which he later became director. He was made Hungarian minister of defense in 1910 and was later given a barony and raised to the rank of fieldmarshal-lieutenant. During World War I, Hazai instituted several emergency laws, and later was in charge of recruitment for the entire Austro-Hungarian army. After the collapse of the empire in 1918 he was arrested for a short time by the Hungarian revolutionary government, and later played no further part in public affairs. Hazai converted to Christianity in his youth and had no interest in Jewish matters.

ḤAZAK (Heb. חֲזַק; "be strong"), a salutation of well-wishing based on Moses' address to Joshua "Be strong and of good courage" (Deut. 31:7; 31:23; cf. II Sam. 10:12; Haggai 2:4). A fuller version, *Ḥazak, ḥazak venitḥazzak* ("Be strong, be strong, and let us be strengthened"), is recited at the Torah reading in the synagogue when one of the five books of the Pentateuch is completed (Isserles to Sh. Ar., OḤ 139:11). In the Sephardi ritual, the person who returns to his seat after having been called up to the Reading of the *Torah is greeted by his neighbors with *Ḥazak u-varukh* ("Be strong and blessed"); he replies *Barukh tihyeh* ("Be blessed"), or *Kulkhem berukhim* ("Be you all blessed").

BIBLIOGRAPHY: Eisenstein, Dinim, 129.

ḤAZAKAH (Heb. חֲזָקָה; lit. "possession," "taking possession"), a term expressing three main concepts in Jewish law: (1) a mode of acquiring ownership; (2) a means of proving ownership or rights in property; (3) a factual-legal presumption (*praesumptio juris*) as to the existence of a particular fact or state of affairs. In its first connotation *ḥazakah* creates a new legal reality, unlike the latter two cases where it is merely instrumental in proving or presuming an existing one. For *ḥazakah* in its connotation of possession see also *Evidence, *Ownership, *Property. For (1) see *Acquisition, Modes of.

HAZAKAH AS PROOF OF OWNERSHIP

Immovable Property

Possession per se of immovable property (*karka* or *mekarke'in*, lit. "land," as opposed to *metaltelin*, "movable property") known to have belonged to another does not displace the title of the legal owner (*mara kamma*, "first owner") thereto, for "land is never stolen" (*karka einah nigzelet*; BK 95a; TJ, BK 10:6, 7c) and "is always in the possession of its owner" (BM 102b). The possessor is accordingly required to prove that he acquired the property in a legally recognized way. If, however, he has held undisturbed possession in the manner of an owner for a period of three consecutive years, without protest from the previous owner, the possessor's plea that he purchased the property or received it as a gift (from the first owner or his father) and that the deed thereto has been lost, is believed. Where his possession is not accompanied by such a claim of right (*she-ein immah ta'anah*) but merely with the contention that "no one ever said anything to me," the *ḥazakah* is not established (BB 3:3). Where the property is purchased or inherited from another, the holder's mere plea (some scholars require proof on his part) that the deceased or seller held possession of the property in the manner of an owner, for even one day, will validate the occupier's *ḥazakah*, for "he cannot be expected to know how his father came by the property" (Rashbam, BB 41a). For this reason the court would "plead the cause" of the heir or purchaser (BB 23a), to the effect that he came by the property in a lawful manner.

In Jewish law *ḥazakah* is part of procedural law B 170a; for this reason the laws of *ḥazakah* are treated by Maimonides in *hilkhot To'en ve-Nitan* and not in the book on *Kinyan*), in contrast with the Roman law *usucapio* of the Twelve Tables, which is a matter of the substantive law whereby ownership is created by virtue of possession for a period of two years. The *ḥazakah* of Jewish law is somewhat akin to the possession in the Roman *praescriptio longi temporis* of the end of the second century C.E., according to which possession of property for 10 or 20 years effectively established title, if accompanied by *iusta causa*. There, however, possession is equally effective even if it transpires that ownership was acquired in a defective manner *ab initio*, in contrast with the Jewish law, where "he who possesses a field by virtue of a deed which is found to be defective, his *ḥazakah* is not established" (Tosef., BB 2:2; BB 32b; cf. TJ, Shevu. 6:2, 37a, where a contrary opinion is expressed).

PERIOD OF POSSESSION. According to some *tannaim* (BB 36b and BB 3:1; *Tanna Kamma*) *ḥazakah* always requires possession for a period of three full years (this period is mentioned already in the Hammurapi code, sec. 30–31). Rava, a Babylonian *amora* of the first half of the fourth century, explains the length of this period on the ground that it is not customary for a purchaser to preserve his title deed for longer than three years, and that thereafter the first owner is not entitled to demand production of the purchaser's deed (BB 29a). In the case of a field producing one annual crop only, the period is 18 months according to Ishmael and 14 months according to Akiva, i.e., a period sufficient for the cultivation and enjoyment of three crops; a period covering the production of three crops – even if enjoyed in one year – is sufficient, according to Ishmael, in the case of a field of diverse trees whose fruits are harvested in different seasons (BB 3:1). According to Judah, a *tanna* of the second century, the period of three years applies in the case of an absent (abroad, "in Spain") owner (BB 3:2), but one year suffices where both the first owner and the occupier are present in the same country (Tosef., BB 2:1; according to BB 41 a *ḥazakah* is immediately effective in the latter case). An analogous distinction is made in the Roman *praescriptio longi temporis*, between possession *inter absentes* (20 years) and *inter praesentes* (10 years). Some scholars (Gulak, Karl) are of the opinion (based on BB 3:2) that in ancient *halakhah* the law of *ḥazakah* was applicable only when both parties were in the same country; at the commencement of the amoraic period, this *halakhah* was interpreted as having been instituted because of "conditions of emergency" (BB 38a–b), whereby there was no means of travel between various districts within Ereẓ Israel; in times of peace, however, *ḥazakah* is effective even in the absence of the first owner. However, the question of the operation of *ḥazakah* between parties in different countries remained a disputed one even during the early amoraic period (TJ, BB 3:3, 14a).

MANNER OF EXERCISING POSSESSION. Possession must be held "in the manner in which people normally use the particular property" (Yad, To'en ve-Nitan 11:2); it must therefore be held for an uninterrupted period, unless it is local custom to cultivate the field one year and leave it fallow the next (BB 29a). It is a requirement that the possessor not only cultivate the field, but that he also enjoy its fruits, "for the essence of *ḥazakah* is the gathering of fruit…," without which evidence of all his other activities on the land will not avail (TJ, BB 3:3, 14a; BB 36b).

PROTEST. Protest on the part of the first owner within the period of three years interrupts the occupier's *ḥazakah*, because it has the effect of warning the occupier to preserve his title deed as proof of ownership. In ancient *halakhah* this protest (variously called עֲרָר or עִרְעָר (*arar*; Tosef., BB 2:4; TJ, BB 3:3; BB 39b) and מְחָאָה (*meḥa'ah*; BB 29a, 39a et al.) by the *amoraim* of Ereẓ Israel and Babylonia respectively), served the procedural function of commencing litigation (analogous to the Roman *litis contestatio*) and was accordingly required to be made before the court. Doubt was already cast on this requirement by the *amoraim* of Ereẓ Israel (TJ, BB 3:3), and according to the Babylonian *amoraim* protest requires no more than that it should be made known to the public (*gillui milta le-rabbim*) by the first owner, or that he make a statement before witnesses that he maintains his interest in the property (BB 39b). In the fourth century the Babylonian *amoraim* prescribed a formula for the protest: "*Peloni* is a robber who occupies my land by robbery and on the morrow I shall bring suit against him," but an unqualified statement: "*Peloni* is a robber" is not an effective protest (BB 38b–39a), lest the occupier plead that "he merely insulted me and therefore I did not look to my deed" (Yad, To'en 11:7). Protest before two witnesses – not necessarily in the presence of the occupier – suffices, for the fact thereof is bound to come to the occupier's notice one way or another (BB 38b, 39b; Yad, To'en 11:5).

Any reasonable explanation for the lack of protest is a bar to effective *ḥazakah*. For this reason *ḥazakah* does not operate between husband and wife or parent and child, each in respect of the other's property, for in these cases the one party is not fastidious about the other's use of the property (BB 3:3; *Teshuvot ha-Rashba ha-Meyuḥasot le-ha-Ramban*, no. 93). In suits between other related parties, the issue of *ḥazakah* is decided by the court on the merits of the evidence in each case, depending on "whether one brother relied on the other in the running of his affairs," etc. (Resp. Rashba, pt. 1, no. 950; Tur and Sh. Ar., ḤM 149:6–8). Nor is *ḥazakah* gained by artisans (building contractors), *partners, metayers (אריסין – tenants receiving a share of the crop; see *Hiring and Letting), and guardians (see *Apotropos; BB 3:3), for they occupy by license (*reshut*; BB 42b; TJ, BB 3:5) and there is therefore no purpose in making protest against them. Possession will also not lead to *ḥazakah* when the first owner is unable to make protest, whether for lack of communication with the occupier because of emergency conditions (BB 38a–b; see above) or because the occupier came on the property by the use of force, "like those of a certain family who are prepared to commit murder for monetary gain" (BB 47a). The exilarchs ("of that time") were also barred from gaining *ḥazakah* because the property owners "stood in awe of them" (i.e., of making protest; Yad, To'en

13:2; BB 36a; Rashbam ad loc.; Joseph b. Samuel *Tov Elem, *Teshuvot Ge'onim Kadmonim* no. 48, ascribes the lack of protest to the pleasure derived by the owners from the exilarch's use of their property). Nor could others gain *ḥazakah* over the property of the exilarchs, for the latter did not "hasten" to protest, because they were able to take forcible possession of their property or because they were not particular, on account of their wealth, about others using their property (BB 36a and Rashbam *ibid.*; *Ge'onim Kadmonim*, no. 48; *Bet ha-Beḥirah*, BB 36a). A non-Jew who acquires forcible possession and a Jew who derives his title through him do not gain *ḥazakah* over the property of a Jew (BB 35b), though in the time of R. Joseph, in Babylonia, it was decided otherwise, for there was a "judicial system which permitted no person to exercise duress against any other person" (*Beit ha-Beḥirah*, BB 36a and Git. 58b).

PLURALITY OF OCCUPIERS AND SUCCESSIVE OWNERS. *Ḥazakah* may be gained through someone occupying on behalf of the person claiming *ḥazakah*, as in the case of the tenant to whom the claimant lets the dwelling (BB 29a); and possession by one partner on behalf of another is similarly effective if each of them has occupied the property for part of the three-year period, provided that this partnership arrangement between them was publicly known (BB 29b; *Beit ha-Beḥirah*, BB 29b; Yad, To'en 12:5 – "since they are partners, they are as one"). The required period for *ḥazakah* is cumulative both as against successive "first owners" and in favor of successive possessors, who respectively derive title from their predecessors (Tosef., BB 2:7–8). At the commencement of the amoraic period, Rav determined that the combined period for which possession was held by both the seller and the purchaser would only be cumulative in the case of a sale by deed, as in this manner the matter would become public and the "first owner" aware that a cumulative *ḥazakah* was challenging his ownership.

ASPECTS OF HAZAKAH IN POST-TALMUDIC TIMES. Aspects of *ḥazakah* were discussed by the *posekim* against the prevailing social and communal background. One matter discussed was the application of *ḥazakah* to a permanent seating place in the synagogue, which became an asset capable of being alienated and inherited (Sh. Ar., ḤM 162:7; Rema and *Pitḥei Teshuvah* ad loc.). Some of the scholars recognized the application of *ḥazakah* thereto (Meir ha-Levi Abulafia and others), but stress was laid on the difficulty of establishing uninterrupted synagogue attendance at all appointed services for three years – a requirement for effective *ḥazakah (Shitah Mekubbeẓet* and Nov. Ritba to BB 29b). Some scholars excused absence on account of illness or mourning (*Beit ha-Beḥirah* BB 29a) and even occasional absence for pressing business reasons (Responsa Rashba pt. 1, no. 943; Tur, ḤM 140:16; *Beit ha-Beḥirah* BB 29a differs), and the latter view prevailed (*Beit Yosef* ḤM 141:2; Rema ḤM 140:8). On the other hand, *ḥazakah* was generally not recognized as extending to public and communal property such as consecrated property, *talmud torahs*, charitable institutions, and the like, for "who shall make protest?" (Rashba, pt. 1 no. 642), and when recognized, *ḥazakah* was held to be effective only under special circumstances and in respect of property in the care of appointed officials or seven representative citizens (Tur and Sh. Ar., ḤM 149 end).

Many of the discussions of this period centered on relationships between Jews of different social status and between Jews and their gentile neighbors. The talmudic *halakhah* precluding others from gaining *ḥazakah* of the property of exilarchs and vice versa was discussed by Solomon b. Abraham *Adret and *Asher b. Jehiel in relation to the property of Jews who held official positions and exercised authority. Both decided that the cases were not analogous, for the exilarchs functioned as "quasi-royalty" and "… in these generations a Jew who should find favor with the king does not impose such awe…" as would deter the owner of property from protesting (Resp. Rosh 18:17; Resp. Rashba, pt. 1, no. 941; Tur, ḤM 149:13; *Sma* ḤM 149, no. 18; *Siftei Kohen* ḤM 149, n. 12). The question of *ḥazakah* in relation to a non-Jew or a Jew deriving title through him was frequently treated and the decision made dependent on the prevailing attitude of the central government toward the particular Jewish community: "In a case where the Jew can bring the non-Jew before the court of the land, a Jew deriving title through a non-Jew has *ḥazakah*" (Ravyah, quoted in *Mordekhai* BB 3:553; Rah quoted in the Nov. Ritba, BB 35 and see Ha-Ittur's dissenting opinion; cf. also Tur and Sh. Ar., ḤM 149:14 and 236:9; BB 55a and commentators ad loc.). Some of the *halakhot* of *ḥazakah* relating to immovable property were applied also in the matter of *Ḥezkat ha-Yishuv* ("the right of domicile").

Movable Property

Contrary to the rule in the case of immovable property, "movables" are in the *ḥazakah* of the person having the physical possession thereof even if the plaintiff brings witnesses that the movables are known to belong to him, and the former's plea that he acquired them according to law is accepted (Yad, To'en 8:1; Tur, ḤM 133:1; source of the rule: BB 3:3; Tosef., BB 2:6; only "the launderer has no *ḥazakah*"), except when the chattels are known to be stolen property (BK 68b, 94b; Sh. Ar., ḤM 354:2). The authorities were in dispute on the requirement of a plea of right on the part of the possessor in the case of movables (*Shitah Mekubbeẓet* BB 28b). *Ḥazakah* of movables is gained forthwith, possession for a period of two or three days and sometimes even one hour – depending upon the subject matter – being sufficient (BB 36a and Rabbenu Gershom ad loc.; also Rashbam BB 42a). However, not every *tefisah* ("taking of possession," "seizure") establishes valid *ḥazakah*, thus "… if they saw him hiding articles under his garments and he came out and said 'these are mine' he is not believed," unless there is a reasonable explanation for this type of behavior, as in the case of articles which are habitually concealed and the like (Shevu. 46a–b).

The rule excluding the operation of *ḥazakah* as between "first owners" and possessors standing in a special relationship toward each other (see above) applies also to movables, e.g., in the case of the artisan, the bailee, etc. (BB 3:3; Tosef., BB 2:5–6). Similarly it does not operate in respect of "articles which are made to be given on loan or hire" (Shevu. 46a–b), where the first owner may account for the fact that movables of this type are found in the hands of the possessor on these grounds. On the other hand, the first owner's claim that these movables were stolen from him is not believed, for this is an admission that they were not lent and "we do not presume a man to be a thief" (Shevu. 46b; Rosh and Ran ad loc.). Most commentators include in the category of "articles which are made to be given on loan or hire," all chattels "which are likely to be lent by their owners" (Rif and Ran to Shevu. 46b). According to this view, only chattels which their owners fear may be damaged, such as certain types of books (Rashi to Shevu. 46b), or those which are particularly valuable, such as articles of silver and gold (*Terumat ha-Deshen*, no. 335), are not to be considered as made to be given on loan or hire. This view is opposed by Maimonides, who holds that such a view in effect invalidates in respect of most movables – the principle that a thing must be considered to be the property of the person in whose possession it is found. Maimonides distinguishes between articles which are "likely to be given on loan or hire" – in which category he places all movables – and things which are "made to be given on loan or hire," defined by him as articles which in a particular locality are specifically made with a view to their being borrowed or hired for a fee and not for sale or home use, such as "large copper kettles for cooking at celebrations," *ḥazakah* being included in the latter case only (Yad, To'en 8:9); other articles may also come within the latter category but only where their owner has witnesses to prove that he has constantly lent or hired them out and that he holds them for such purpose (To'en 8:9 and 10 and Rabad's stricture thereon).

SPECIAL CATEGORIES OF MOVABLES. In the case of slaves, a period of three years is required for effective *ḥazakah* (BB 3:1). Animals (livestock) were apparently deemed to be like other movables in the tannaitic period, i.e., *ḥazakah* was effective immediately; this may be deduced from the existence of a special ruling precluding shepherds from acquiring *ḥazakah*, as in the case of the artisan and bailee (Tosef., BB 2:5). At the commencement of the amoraic period, Simeon b. Lakish determined that the normal rule of *ḥazakah* did not apply in respect of livestock (BB 36a), for they "stray from place to place" (TJ, BB 3:1, 13d) and therefore "the fact of detaining it under his hand does not constitute proof, for it went of its own accord into his *reshut*" (i.e., domain; Yad, To'en 10:1). Differing opinions were expressed with regard to establishing *ḥazakah* in respect of chattels not falling within the normal rule, e.g., articles made to be given on loan or hire and livestock; some of the *posekim* expressed the opinion that in these cases *ḥazakah* is never established; others held that it is established after a period of three years; and some held that there is no fixed period for effective *ḥazakah*, the court having the discretion to decide the matter in each case (*Yad Ramah* BB 36a; Rashbam BB 36a; Nov. Ritba BB 36a; Nov. Rashba BB 46a; Tur, ḤM 133:10 and 138:1–2; Resp. Maharam of Rothenburg, ed. Prague, no. 180).

See also *Limitation of Actions. For *ḥazakah* in relation to servitudes (*ḥezkat tashmishim*) and torts see *Servitudes.

ḤAZAKAH AS A LEGAL-FACTUAL PRESUMPTION

This occurs in a number of forms:

(1) A legal presumption of the continued existence of a once-ascertained state of affairs, until the contrary be proved – "an object is presumed to possess its usual status" (Nid. 2a), e.g., that the flesh of an animal is presumed to be forbidden as having been cut from a living animal until it is ascertained that it was ritually slaughtered; once slaughtered, the animal's flesh is presumed to be permitted unless the manner in which it became *terefah* becomes known (Ḥul. 9a); that the husband is alive at the time that the bill of divorce is handed to the wife, even though he was old or ill when the agent or *shali'aḥ* left him (Git. 3:3); similarly the presumptions of normal health and fitness, referred to variously as *ḥezkat ha-guf* (Ket. 75b), *ḥezkat bari* (Kid. 79b; BB 153b), and *ḥezkat kashrut* (BB 31b).

(2) A legal presumption of the existence of a fixed and accepted custom or of the psychological nature of man, such as the following: that an agent fulfills his mandate (Er. 31b); that a woman does not have the impudence to declare (falsely) in her husband's presence that he has divorced her (Yev. 116a) and she is therefore believed; that a debtor does not settle his debt before due date, therefore his plea (without proof) that he repaid the debt before due date is not believed (BB 5a–b); that a **ḥaver* does not allow anything which is untithed to leave his hands and therefore if he dies leaving a silo full of produce, this is presumed to have been tithed (Pes. 9a); that no man affixes his signature to a document unless he knows the contents thereof, and he cannot therefore plead that he did not read or understand its contents (PDR 1:293–5).

(3) Legal presumptions permitting a conclusion of fact to be inferred from particular surrounding circumstances. Presumptions of this kind were relied upon even in cases of capital punishment, as if the conclusion had been proved by the evidence of witnesses: "we flog … stone and burn on the strength of presumption" (Kid. 80, and examples there quoted), "even where there is no testimony on the matter" (Rashi ad loc.). Similarly, in certain circumstances a woman reputed to be married to a particular man was held to be his wife (Yad, Issurei Bi'ah, 1:21, as per TJ, Kid. 4:10).

Support for the validity of the latter presumptions was found in the law of the Torah that the penalty for "one who curses or smites his father" is death: "how do we know for sure that he is his father? Only by way of presumption" (Yad and TJ, loc. cit.; in Ḥul 11b, the aforesaid *halakhah* concerning "one who smites his father" serves as a basis for deduction of the *majority rule).

[Menachem Elon]

IN THE MIDDLE AGES AND EARLY MODERN TIMES

Hazakah was one of the main normative concepts of Jewish economic and social life. In the course of time it was applied to the most varied rights and objects: e.g., right of settlement in a given community, rights over a certain clientele, as well as rights to seats in a synagogue, and the right to exercise certain honorific functions at religious services.

Since it fitted into the structure and spirit of the guilds and civic economy and social morality, *ḥazakah* developed and proliferated. Based in principle on talmudic law (see above), its widening application came through communal authorities enacting new *takkanot to meet new circumstances (see *Arenda, Councils of the *Lands, *Ḥerem *ha-Yishuv*, **Ma'arufyah*, and *Poland-Lithuania). For that reason it was mainly the lay leaders of the communal administration (*kahal*), not the rabbi, who passed final judgment on the protection of tenancy and other acquired rights. The dispensation of *ḥazakah* ultimately rested upon the goodwill of the community and its leaders. As a result, practices varied in different communities, from town to town, and certainly from country to country. The prohibition on settling in a community without permission (*ḥerem ha-yishuv*) was the source of one of the main forms of *ḥazakah*. *Ḥazakah* proper generally applied to tenant protection, whereby no Jew was permitted to rent from a gentile owner a house occupied by another Jewish tenant without the latter's consent, a right the latter usually acquired after three years of occupancy. The purpose of the prohibition was to prevent raising the rents of old or new tenants. An ordinance attributed to Gershom b. *Judah stated that the house of a gentile from which a Jew had been evicted might not be leased by another Jew for an entire year. Even houses owned by Jews were included in similar decisions by the conference of Candia in 1238 and by some halakhists. At a meeting of elders in Ferrara in 1554 it was resolved:

> Whereas there are some who infringe the *takkanah* of R. Gershom, which forbids any Jew from ousting another Jew from a house rented from a Christian landlord, and whereas such offenders claim that when the landlord sells his house the Jewish tenant thereby also loses his *ḥazakah*, we therefore decree that though the Christian owner sell his house, the right of the Jewish tenant to retain possession is unchanged; any Jew who ousts him is disobeying the *takkanah* of R. Gershom and also this *takkanah*, now newly enacted."

In Italy this law, which was recognized by the authorities, was called *jus gazaga* or *casaca*. The Lithuanian Council of the communities adopted a rule in 1623 that a house owned by a gentile and rented to a Jew who had a *ḥazakah* on it might be sold to another Jew by permission of the head of the *bet din*. The buyer thereby also acquired the *ḥazakah*. However, if he did not move into the house himself, he had to grant the tenant priority in occupying the house. The same ordinance was made to apply to a store in the market-place which was also governed by the three-year *ḥazakah* rule; in this case the buyer had to recompense the tenant for his *ḥazakah* costs. Although few *ḥazakah* records remain for Polish Jewry in the days when its council functioned, the communal law was enforced in Poland also. The practice was particularly prevalent in countries where Jews could not own lands, or were restricted to crowded ghettos or voluntarily inhabited Jewish quarters. The rule was a necessity to prevent exorbitant rent. In Spain, where Jews could own land, the *ḥazakah*, or *praescription*, applied to ownership of land as well as to rentals. Since *ḥazakah* was an important property right, it was negotiable, testable, and used as a dowry. The *kahal* made it an important source of income.

In Russia *ḥazakah* persisted long after the abolition of the *kahal* in 1844. The leaders of the Minsk community sold possession of a gentile's store to a Jew and bound every future *kahal* to protect this man's right to the acquired option on the property. The same enforcement of acquired rights was practiced with equal stringency within the Jewish community: merchants were shielded against outside competition; there were rules against the importation of meat and wine and many other protectionist regulations; artisans could acquire a form of *ḥazakah* on a customer, *ma'arufyah*, whereby no other craftsman was permitted to do work for him; a person could acquire rights to a seat in the synagogue, to a Torah Scroll, or to ornaments loaned to the congregation for its use. The term *ḥazakah* also applied to tenure of communal workers. In Moravia a law was passed that a rabbi who refused to appear in court to be tried, or engaged in trade, could lose his tenure and be dismissed.

[Isaac Levitats]

Ḥazakah as a Legal-Factual Presumption

The second category mentioned above – i.e., reliance on the presumed nature and behavior of human beings – also includes another form of legal presumption, pertaining to a will written by a person in a life-threatening situations. The context may either be that of a *shekhiv me-ra* (a person presumed to be dying), or that of a healthy person who regards himself as being in a life-threatening situation. In both cases the assumption is that the will reflects the testator's full and binding intention. Moreover, in the case of a deathbed will (i.e., the will of a *shekhiv mera*) the will is valid even without a *kinyan*, because we assume that, due to the unique circumstances of its making, it reflected the person's final decision (Maimonides, Yad, Zekhiyah u-Matanah 8.2, 4, 24, 26.)

In an Israeli Supreme Court decision in the *Koenig* case (FH 80/40 *Koenig v. Cohen*, 36(3) PD 701), Justice Menachem Elon held that this halakhic rule should determine the interpretation of Section 23 of the Succession Law, 5725 – 1964. Section 23 utilizes the term *shekhiv me-ra*. Justice Elon ruled that the use of this talmudic term indicates its origin in Jewish law regarding a deathbed will, and hence the applicability of the Jewish law to such a case. The decision in the *Koenig* case related to a case in which a woman left a will on a piece of paper without a date or signature just before she killed herself. The justices disputed the legal validity of the will, and Justice Elon contended that the will should be seen as a deathbed will and therefore valid, notwithstanding its deficiencies and flaws, on the basis of the aforementioned legal presumption. (*ibid*, pp. 733–738.; cf. *Acquisition, *Succession)

Another legal presumption is that "a son does not dishonor his father" (*Resp. Zikhron Yehudah* § 92; R. Judah b. R. Asher [Asheri]). In the *Hager* case the Supreme Court based its ruling on this presumption (CA 1482/92 *Hager v. Hager* judgment 47(2) 793; per Justice Elon, p. 806). The case concerned a disagreement between the widow and the parents of the deceased. The widow had unilaterally erected a tombstone on the grave. The parents applied to the Court, requesting it to order that the engraving on the tombstone be changed, inter alia, because it did not include the names of the deceased's parents. On the basis of the aforementioned legal presumption the Court ruled in the parents' favor, determining that the deceased would not have wished to distress his parents by omitting their names from his tombstone.

[Menachem Elon (2nd ed.)]

BIBLIOGRAPHY: Z. Frankel, *Der gerichtliche Beweis nach mosaisch-talmudischem Rechte* (1846), 437–74; M. Bloch, *Das mosaisch-talmudische Besitzrecht* (1897), 13–48; J. Lewin, in: *Zeitschrift fuer vergleichende Rechtswissenschaft*, 29 (1913), 151–298; J. Kohler, *ibid.*, 31 (1914), 312–5; J.S. Zuri, *Mishpat ha-Talmud*, 4 (1921), 19–28; Gulak, Yesodei, 1 (1922), 16f., 168–75; 4 (1922), 99f., 105, 114–28; A. Gulak, *Le-Ḥeker Toledot ha-Mishpat ha-Ivri bi-Tekufat ha-Talmud*, 1 (1929) *(Dinei Karka'ot)*, 95–108; J.L. Kroch, *Ḥazakah Rabbah* (1927–63); Z. Karl, in: *Ha-Mishpat ha-Ivri*, 4 (1932/33), 93–112; Herzog, Instit, 1 (1936), 225–73; A. Karlin, in: *Sinai*, 22 (1947/48), 223–34; J.N. Epstein, *Mevo'ot le-Sifrut ha-Amora'im* (1962), 246–8; ET, 1 (1951³), passim (articles beginning with *"Ein Adam…"*); J. Unterman, in: *Sinai*, 54 (1964), 4–10; Z. Warhaftig, *Ha-Ḥazakah ba-Mishpat ha-Ivri* (1964); Elon, Mafte'aḥ, 72–79; J. Algazi, *Kehillat Ya'akov*, 2 (1898), 64a–87b (*"Kunteres Middot Ḥakhamim"*). IN THE MIDDLE AGES AND EARLY MODERN TIMES: I. Abrahams, *Jewish Life in the Middle Ages* (1920); Baron, Community, 3 (1942); Newman, Spain; I. Levitats, *Jewish Community in Russia* (1943); S. Dubnow, *Pinkas Medinat Lita* (1925); I. Halpern, *Pinkas Va'ad Arba Araẓot* (1945); idem, *Takkanot Medinat Mehrin* (1952); H.H. Ben-Sasson, *Hagut ve-Hanhagah* (1959), index. **ADD. BIBLIOGRAPHY:** M. Elon, *Ha-Mishpat ha-Ivri* (1988), 1:71, 221, 305, 364, 432, 502, 509, 586, 596f., 720, 733, 735, 753, 754f., 807, 810, 812f., 822f., 827; 2:881, 993, 1107f., 1110f., 3:1465, 1551f.; idem, *Jewish Law* (1994), 1:79, 249, 365, 440; 2:527, 611, 620, 721f., 737f., 888f., 903f., 906, 928, 930f., 989, 992, 995f., 1007f., 1013; 3:1074f., 1201, 1331f., 1335f., 4:1739, 1843.

ḤAZAN, YA'AKOV (1899–1992), Israeli political leader and leading figure in the *Mapam socialist party; member of the First to Seventh Knessets. Born in Brest Litovsk in Russia. Ḥazan studied in a reformed *ḥeder*, then later at a Hebrew high school and the Warsaw Politechnicum. In 1915 he was one of the founders of the Hebrew Scout movement in Poland, which developed into *Ha-Shomer ha-Ẓa'ir, and of the *He-Ḥalutz movement in Poland. In 1923 he immigrated to Palestine, where he worked as a farm laborer and in the draining of swamps before settling in kibbutz Mishmar ha-Emek and participating in the foundation of *Ha-Kibbutz ha-Arẓi, the kibbutz movement of Ha-Shomer ha-Ẓa'ir in 1927. For many years he was a member of the *Histadrut Executive. Together with Meir *Ya'ari he headed Ha-Kibbutz ha-Arẓi, and later Mapam. While Ya'ari was more of an ideologue and writer, Ḥazan was a brilliant orator and charismatic leader. Until the mid-1950s he supported, together with Ya'ari, a pro-Soviet line. In the Knesset he was Mapam's main spokesman on foreign and defense issues. In the Third, Fourth, Sixth, and Seventh Knessets, when Mapam had representatives in the government, neither he nor Ya'ari accepted ministerial positions. Prior to the elections to the Ninth Knesset in 1969 he was one of the architects of the establishment of the Alignment between Mapam and the *Israel Labor Party, and fought against those who wished to dissolve it. Within Mapam he was considered to be relatively hawkish in his positions. However, in 1984 those within Mapam who objected to the establishment of the National Unity Government between the Alignment and the *Likud gained the upper hand, and Mapam returned to being an Independent parliamentary group in the Knesset. In 1989 Hazan received the Israel Prize for exemplary lifelong service to Israeli society. Among other writings he published the autobiographical *Yaledut u-Ne'urim* on his childhood and youth.

BIBLIOGRAPHY: *Optimist le-Lo Takanah: Ḥayyim Guri Meso-ḥe'aḥ im Ya'akov Ḥazan* (1989); Z. Ẓaḥor, *Ḥazan Tenu'at Ḥayyim: Ha-Shomer ha-Ẓa'ir, Ha-Kibbutz ha-Me'uḥad, Mapam* (1997).

[Susan Hattis Rolef (2nd ed.)]

ḤAZANI, MIKHA'EL YA'AKOV (1913–1975), Israeli politician; one of the leaders of the *National Religious Party. Ḥazani was born in Bedzin, Poland, and studied at a rabbinical seminary. Immigrating to Ereẓ Israel in 1931, he became a prominent member of the Lamifneh faction of *Ha-Po'el ha-Mizrachi. He was one of the pioneers settling Kefar Jawitz and a supporter of Jewish settlement in the Lower Galilee. Considered one of the founding fathers of religious settlement, he was an enthusiastic supporter of the development of Gush Katif. The name of Moshav Katif was changed in 1975 to Neẓer Ḥazani in commemoration of him; it was evacuated in 2005 along with the other settlements in Gush Katif.

Ḥazani was elected to the Knesset in 1951. Specializing in economic affairs he was appointed vice chairman of the boards of the Bank of Israel and the Mizrachi Bank. He was appointed deputy minister of education in 1969 and succeeded Yosef Burg as minister of social welfare in 1970. He was reappointed in the short-lived government of Golda Meir, formed on March 10, 1974, but submitted his resignation on April 2 as a result of his disagreement with his party's attitude on the question of "Who is a Jew?"

On October 30, 1974 Ḥazani was again given the portfolio of social services when the National Religious Party rejoined the coalition and he served in this capacity until his death in 1975.

HAZAZ, ḤAYYIM (1898–1973), Hebrew writer. Born in Sidorovichi (Kiev province), Hazaz received a traditional and secular education, studying Hebrew and Russian literature. From the age of 16 (1914), when he left home, to 1921 he moved from one large Russian city to another. During and after the Russian Revolution he worked in Moscow on the Hebrew daily *Ha-Am* and at the time of the *Denikin and Wrangel pogroms he was in the Ukraine from where he escaped to the Crimean Mountains (1920). Hazaz went to Constantinople in 1921 where he lived about a year and a half and then moved to Western Europe, spending nine years in Paris and Berlin. The German capital had for a short time in the early 1920s become the Hebrew literary center after the Russian one had been destroyed by the revolution. Early in 1931 he left for Ereẓ Israel and settled in Jerusalem. Hazaz was politically active much of his life. He was the president of the Israel-Africa Friendship Association from 1965 (when it was founded) until 1969. After the Six-Day War (1967) Hazaz was prominent in the Land of Israel movement calling for settlement in the territories occupied during the war and for their permanent inclusion in the State of Israel.

Early Period – Russia

Hazaz began his literary career in Russia, publishing in *Ha-Shilo'aḥ* (1918, 274–84) under the pseudonym Ḥ. Ẓevi *"Ke-Vo ha-Shemesh,"* a sketch, followed half a year later by his only short poem, *"Al ha-Mishmar,"* dedicated to Saul Tchernichowsky. *"Meri"* and *"Ma'amar Moshe Rabbenu"* also appeared in *Ha-Shilo'aḥ* (1925, 1926), but under his own name. Hazaz published much during this period; his stories were well received and he gained wide acclaim. Many of his stories are set against the background of the Russian Revolution, among these are: *"Mi-Zeh u-mi-Zeh"* ("From This and That," in *Ha-Tekufah*, 21 (1924), 1–32); *"Pirkei Mahpekhah"* ("Chapters of the Revolution," *ibid.*, 22 (1924), 69–97); and *"Shemu'el Frankfurter"* (*ibid.*, 23 (1925), 81–184). The overall theme is the fate of the Jewish *shtetl* and the chaos and destruction wrought in its traditional way of life by the revolution whose impact is however only implicitly expressed. It is reflected in the interaction of forces from within and from without rather than directly represented by any single character. In all three stories only one non-Jewish revolutionary appears. Hazaz' fundamental interest in the revolution is thus on the level of human relations and understanding where it sowed bewilderment and confusion. The brief and concise description of events, trends, emotions, and characters and the fragmentary dialogue lend reality and immediacy to the narrative. However, the division of characters into the young revolutionary generation on the one hand and the anti-revolutionary older generation on the other is somewhat schematic. The general pervading mood is one of destruction in which the old world is wrenched from its axis while the new world is as yet not clearly focused. Thus the older generation, in the throes of tragedy, gains the sympathy of the reader. The young, however, are neither accused nor derided and even the irony directed against them is mild. Hazaz rewrote two of the stories: *"Mi-Zeh u-mi-Zeh"* became *"Nahar Shotef"* ("Flowing River," 1955, 1958, 1968), and *"Pirkei Mahpekhah"* became *Daltot Neḥoshet* ("Copper Doors," 1 vol., 1956; 2 vols., 1968). Best among the revolutionary stories, *"Shemu'el Frankfurte,"* has as a protagonist a revolutionary idealist, a Jesus-like figure, whose noble character leads him to a martyr's death. The story was excluded from his collected works and the author has stated that it needs rewriting (*Ma'ariv*, Sept. 26, 1969). At this time Hazaz also wrote a number of works not on the *shtetl* theme. *"Ḥatan Damim"* ("Bridegroom of Blood," in *Ha-Tekufah*, 23 (1925), 149–72), a prose poem, unfolds against the stark Midian desert. Zipporah, the wife of Moses, is portrayed as a tragic figure abandoned by her husband who had become a man of God. Modern in tone, the work is a lyrical masterpiece. It appeared in all of Hazaz' editions (in four slightly different versions) including a bibliophilic edition. *Be-Yishuv shel Ya'ar* ("In a Forest Settlement," 1930), Hazaz' first novel, is set in the early 1900s during the Russo-Japanese war. The plot centers around a Jewish family living among gentiles "in a forest settlement" and evolves against a background of revolutionary ideas and the disintegration of tradition. The gentile characters are tall strong woodcutters closely tied to their native soil. On the surface the members of the Jewish family seem to be living peacefully but beneath the apparent calm lurks the reality of the Jew's rootlessness. This alienation casts him simultaneously in a derisive and in a tragic light. The Jewish characters seem to be haunted by a fatalistic pessimism which affects everything they do. Thus they view their moving to the countryside and their abandoning of traditional values as determined by fate. The parodic and satiric figure of the young *melammed*, a revolutionary who expounds Marxian theories, also believes that his failure to be active in political affairs is predetermined by fate. The underlying symbol of cutting down the trees is imbued with Jewish characteristics. *Be-Yishuv shel Ya'ar* has not been included in any edition of Hazaz' works. He called it "a book full of printing errors and sown with some wild oats. This book does not exist for me" (*Ma'ariv*, Dec. 29, 1967), and yet he thought of rewriting it (*Ma'ariv*, Sept. 26, 1969).

Ereẓ Israel

Reḥayim Shevurim ("Broken Millstones," 1942) marks the beginning of Hazaz' Ereẓ Israel period. Six stories are still set in the Jewish *shtetl* while the remaining three depict life in Ereẓ Israel. The themes of the Diaspora stories – poverty, the *bet ha-midrash* and Torah study, interest on loans, loafers' banter, *maskilim* and gentiles, and riots – were also treated by his predecessors, but his individualistic outlook and style invested them with new meaning, originality, and verve. In *"Shelulit Genuzah"* ("The Hidden Puddle"), the protagonist, Eliah Kotlik, a pauper, runs away from his ever-nagging wife. The story is built upon a series of "flights" which reach their climax in his escape from Reb Kamatzel, who owes him money. Kotlik's last flight is of a moral nature motivated by the precept of the Torah not to harass an impoverished debtor. The contrast between the first and last flights points up the spiritual growth of the hero: the fleeing victim of the first flight turns into the fleeing persecutor of the last. On another level, the last flight reveals the shortcomings of the value system of modern society in contrast to that of traditional Judaism. Despite its debased material conditions, the Judaism of the *shtetl* was imbued with a great humanitarian spirit. Kotlik's jump into the muddy puddle is thus a symbolic act: he disturbed "… the stagnant puddle which had been contemplating the heavens." *"Adam mi-Yisrael"* ("A Jew") is a story episodic in structure whose narrator, the protagonist's son, relates the wanderings of his father from *bet midrash* to *bet midrash* and his death at the hand of rioters. A *shtetl's* mute cry on the day of a riot permeates *"Ashamnu"* ("We Have Sinned"), an ideational story. The quelled attempt at rebelling against the conventional behavior of the *galut* Jew in the face of danger serves but to heighten the anguish of the writhing *shtetl*. The tone, bitter and hostile, carries a note of choked helplessness. The structural framework of *"Dorot Rishonim"* ("First Generations") is a retrospective view of the destroyed *shtetl* on which Hazaz lavishes praise. The aura of stability and spiritual harmony of the *shtetl* is however disturbed by a sense of imminent danger. Ereẓ Israel is the locale of *"Ha-Tayyar ha-Gadol"* ("The Big Tourist"). The protagonist, a grotesque character, is drawn against the background of a satiric-humoristic description of the numerous holy historical sites that seem to spring up all over Ereẓ Israel. Hazaz' second major work, *Ha-Yoshevet ba-Gannim* ("Thou That Dwellest in the Gardens," 1944), is a novel which narrates the experiences of three generations of Yemenites living in Ereẓ Israel. The generation of elders is represented by an old man who dreams of the Messiah and tries to calculate his advent. Moving in a visionary world of his own, his sanity at times is doubted. His son represents the second generation that has thrown off the burden of the traditions of Yemenite-Jewish culture, but at the same time has not adapted to the cultural milieu of Israel. The third generation, the young daughter, though alive to the new environment, is unable to strike deep roots in the new culture and her integration remains superficial. *Avanim Roteḥot* ("Boiling Stones," 1946), his third book, is comprised of 10 stories, the first of which is the second edition of *"Ḥatan Damim." "Galgal ha-Ḥozer," "Ba'alei Terisin,"* and *"Yeraḥem ha-Shem"* are sketches of Yemenite life. *"Harat Olam"* and *"Ḥavit Akhurah"* depict the life of German-Jewish immigrants in Ereẓ Israel. Humor and tragedy become inextricably intertwined especially when a ludicrous, grotesque, and mixed-up Israeli intrudes upon their life and creates even greater confusion. *"Esh Bo'eret"* and *"Drabkin"* are insights into the lives of immigrants from Eastern Europe. The former describes the naive devotion of *ḥalutzim* who, despite overwhelming hardships, escaped from Russia. In the latter the protagonist, Drabkin, is an embittered Zionist who in the Diaspora had dedicated his life to the rebuilding of the homeland but in Ereẓ Israel was unable to find a significant role to play in its life. Drabkin's rejection is psychological. Having been badly received on arrival he projects his frustrations onto his ideals. The gap between ideals and their practical realization is questioned by a number of Hazaz' heroes. In *"Ha-Derashah"* ("The Sermon"), perhaps the most famous of his works, the hero, Yudke, strongly criticizes the accepted notions of Zionism. He objects to Jewish history which he describes as a boring chronicle of massacre and futility; a history created by the gentiles rather than willed by the Jewish people. He exhorts the Haganah leaders to wipe this humiliating and soiled record of a sorely tried people from the consciousness of the "new Jew." Jews of the past, he argues, wallowed in the tragedy of exile, they really did not wish to be redeemed. Traditional Judaism while praying for redemption was actually bent on preventing it. The story has many artistic flaws; on the first level it is clearly didactic and verbose. Another level, however, which gives the story dramatic impact, is created by the hero, a psychologically motivated round character, whose inner conflicts become apparent during his sermon; by the catcalls which his speech evokes; and by the network of imagery interwoven through the fabric of the story.

Hazaz' most comprehensive work, *Ya'ish* (4 vols., 1947–52), is set within an ethnological framework and traces the life of Ya'ish, a young Yemenite Jew. An ascetic and a dreamer, he abandons his mysticism upon his arrival in Ereẓ Israel. The work is a deep psychological probing into the inner recesses of Ya'ish's mind. Hazaz demonstrates an amazing familiarity with Yemenite culture and its rich religious heritage. These form a closely woven pattern within which the trials and conflicts of the protagonist are enacted. The emotional range and tension of the hero's struggles are filtered through the agonizing experience of a man whose fertile imagination and hallucinations are those of a kabbalist, whose perception is deep and penetrating, and whose inner struggles reveal a suffering divided soul. A network of symbols is woven through the fabric of the story highlighted by such fantasy scenes as Ya'ish's ascent to heaven where he converses with the angels. The Yemenite world with its local color and folklore is vividly and realistically conveyed and Ya'ish's life, steeped in mysticism, stands out in sharp relief against the backdrop of the humdrum life of the community. During the time that Hazaz wrote *Ya'ish*, he also published *Be-Keẓ ha-Yamim* ("At the End of Days," 1950) a play set in Germany (Ashkenaz) during the time of *Shabbetai Ẓevi; the theme of redemption not only creates the mood but is the motivating force of the dramatis personae. Despite the historical setting, the confrontation of ideas and concepts transcends time and place. The hero, a zealous advocate of messianism, faces a hostile public led by the rabbi who is the very embodiment of rationalist orthodoxy. The central theme of the drama is similar to that of *"Ha-Derashah"*: Jews suffer exile because they lack the courage to be redeemed. *Daltot Neḥoshet* (1956), an adapted and extended version of *"Pirkei Mahpekhah,"* was considerably revised stylistically. The author expanded the descriptive passages and restrained the expressionistic outbursts of the narrator whose personal feelings and attitude toward the revolution are now that of an outsider, the "objective observer." Instead of the earlier stormy fearful mood, the style is freighted with minute ironic descriptions. A retrospective tone weaves its way through the fabric of the story deflecting, and at times distorting, the narrator's angle of vision. *Ḥagorat Mazzalot* ("The Zodiac," 1958) is a collection of three stories: "*Ofek Natui*," "*Ḥuppah ve-Tabba'at*," and "*Nahar Shotef*." The plot of "*Ofek Natui*" ("Horizon") unfolds against the background of the Lachish region, an area developed for agricultural settlement in the 1950s; the theme is again the basic Jewish problem of Diaspora versus "redemption." The protagonist of "*Ḥuppah ve-Tabba'at*" ("Canopy and Wedding Ring") is an old Tel Avivian woman who lost all her sons in the Holocaust. She supports herself through peddling notions in cafes and donates her last penny toward the writing and consecration of a *Sefer Torah*. This symbolic act underlines her death which comes to her while she has a vision on the seashore. She leaves life, in which she was an alien, to go to a world where she belongs. *Nahar Shotef*, an adaptation of "*Mi-Zeh u-mi-Zeh*," shows similar stylistic changes as those effected in *Daltot ha-Neḥoshet*. *Be-Kolar Eḥad* ("In the One Collar," 1963; translated into French and Swedish) harks back to the struggle waged by the Jewish underground against the British in Palestine. The protagonists, young Jewish fighters condemned to death, cheat the hangman by committing suicide (the story is based on an actual occurrence). The question of Diaspora, redemption, and *Kiddush ha-Shem is also a major theme here. The concept of self-sacrifice as an ideal holy to man is present in all of Hazaz' works.

A revised edition of all his writings appeared in 1968. Hazaz more than once rewrote many of his works and while claiming that he remained faithful to the essence of his writings (*Moznayim*, 26 (1968), 261), he also insisted that whoever only read his early writings, without rereading them in the later editions, would not know him (*Ma'ariv*, Dec. 29, 1967). Hazaz' writings are extensive geographically, historically, and ethnographically. Geographically, he ranges over an area that extends from the far north of Russia to the south of Yemen, from Germany in the west to Ereẓ Israel in the east. Historically his creative imagination encompasses biblical times, prior to the revelation at Mount Sinai, extending to the Second Temple period before the destruction of the Temple, the messianic dreamers in Germany, the prerevolutionary period and the revolution years in Russia, the riots in the Diaspora and in Ereẓ Israel, the Holocaust generation and the one that has been resuscitated out of its own ashes, the fighters for Israel's freedom, and the new settlement in Israel. Ethnographically he roams over much of the Diaspora (from Russia to Yemen), probing into the life of different segments of the Jewish people and portraying them in their original dwellings and in their new homes. His themes form a network of fundamental ideas and phenomena of contemporary Jewish life, which he relates to the history of the nation. The modern Jewish period he sees as a link in the great chain of Jewish national history and of the different Jewish historical epochs: "These are multivariant parts of culture of one national personality which have been welded together" (*Hed ha-Ḥinnukh*, no. 37 (1968), 7). This concept of unity is also reflected in Hazaz' style and language, whose imagery and multiplicity of meaning are rooted in the ancient sources, thus encompassing and integrating simultaneously sources and originality. The wealth of his linguistic associations and his original imagery, at once real and fictitious, are the hallmarks of his style. Hazaz in his writings drew on his very wide knowledge of Talmud and Midrash to weave an intricate literary pattern. Thus many of his references and allusions are somewhat obscure to the average modern reader. In his revisions he has tended to minimize Arabic idioms which he had used extensively to create an effect of colloquial speech. He also deleted kabbalistic and *gematria* allusions and plays on cryptic words to arrive at a more limpid style. All his revisions thus have a sense of novelty and freshness. A movement from the tragic to the grotesque and satiric can be discerned in most of Hazaz' writings, especially in his later works. He uses different stylistic devices to achieve the tragic-comic. In his Russian tales the *shtetl* often rises to tragic stature, only to sink into caricature. A juxtaposition of sublime beliefs and the pettiness of those who profess them strikes the tragic-comic note in the Yemenite tales: thus the exalted redemptive theme of *Ha-Yoshevet ba-Gannim* is offset by parody; and the tragic moments in *Ya'ish* are undermined by the absurd. The play *Be-Keẓ ha-Yamim* borders on the tragic-grotesque. Hazaz was awarded the Israel Prize for literature in 1953.

[Jacob Bahat]

Hazaz was awarded the Bialik Prize for the second time in 1971 and the following year the Annual Prize of the American Academy for Jewish Research. In 1973 there appeared a collection of 16 short stories under the title *Even Sha'ot*, one of which, "*Otto ha-Ish*," has been translated into English, French, German, Spanish, Swedish, and Russian.

The first work published after his death by his wife, as his executor, was *Pa'amon ve-Rimon* (1975), consisting of 20 short stories written between 1969 and 1973. It was followed by *Mishpat ha-Ge'ulah* (1977), a collection of his essays and public addresses delivered on various occasions between 1950 and 1973, and in the same year a third printing of his 15 volumes was published in a paperback edition (Am Oved).

Hazaz was one of the initiators of Bet Ha-Sofer, the Hebrew Literary Center in the Old City of Jerusalem, and after his death the building was named in his honor.

An English translation of Hazaz's *Daltot Neḥoshet* (*Gates of Bronze*) was published in 1975. A French translation of *Be-Keẓ ha-Yamim* (*A la Fin des Temps*) was published in 1977 and an English translation entitled *The End of Days* 1982. "Raḥamim" appeared in G. Abramson (ed.), *The Oxford Book of Hebrew Short Stories* (1996). For English translations see: Goell, Bibliography, 2140–69, 2648, 2817; see also Spicehandler, in *Ariel* 1967. For further translations see ITHL at www.ithl.org.il. For a bibliography of Hazaz's works see R. Weiser (1992).

[Aviva Hazaz]

BIBLIOGRAPHY: M. Avishai, *Shorashim ba-Ẓammeret* (1969), 107–20; A. Ukhmani, *Le-Ever Adam* (1953), 248–82; J. Bahat, *S.Y. Agnon ve-Ḥ. Hazaz – Iyyunei Mikra* (1962), 175–257; idem, in: *Ha-Ḥinnukh*, 3–4 (1967), 121–7; idem, in: *Tarbiz*, 39 (1969/70), 390–414; idem, in: *Hasifrut*, 2 (1970), 538–64; A. Ben-Or, *Toledot ha-Sifrut ha-*

Ivrit be-Dorenu, 2 (1955), 97–131, includes bibliography; I. Halpern, *Ha-Mahpekhah ha-Yehudit* (1967), 518–45; I. Zmora, *Shenei Mesapperim – H. Hazaz ve-Ya'akov Horovitz* (1940), 9–32; I. Cohen, *Demut el Demut* (1949), 56–115; D. Kena'ani, *Beinam le-Vein Zemannam* (1955), 37–93; F. Lachower, *Rishonim va-Aḥaronim*, 2 (1935), 182–94; B.Y. Michali, *Ḥayyim Hazaz; Iyyunim bi-Yẓirato* (1968); D. Miron, *Ḥayyim Hazaz* (1959); D. Sadan, *Avnei Boḥan* (1951), 237–51; S.Y. Penueli, *Demuyyot be-Sifrutenu ha-Ḥ¦d¦sh¦ḥ* (1946), 131–43; idem, *Ḥulyot be-Sifrutenu ha-Ḥadashah* (1953), 171–85; idem, *Sifrut ki-Feshutah* (1963), 297–324; S. Kremer, *Re'alizm u-Shevirato* (1968), 149–73; Y. Keshet, *Havdalot* (1962), 170–232; E. Schweid, *Shalosh Ashmorot* (1964), 71–89. **ADD. BIBLIOGRAPHY:** Y. David, *H. Hazaz* (1965); W. Bargad, *Character, Idea and Myth in the Works of Hayim Hazaz* (1970); E.I. Morris, *Key Motifs in the Writings of H. Hazaz* (1974); I. Zimran, *Yeẓirato shel H. Hazaz: Ha-Shoah ben Shalosh Mahadurot Yeẓirah* (1974); I. Kalish, *Siḥot im Hazaz* (1976); S. Katz, *Nof Yerushalayim be-Yeẓirotehem shel Shenei Mesaperim: H. Hazaz ve-D. Shaḥar* (1978); D. Sadan and D. Laor (ed.), *Me,assef Mukdash li-Yeẓirat H. Hazaz* (1978); A.H. Elhanani, *Arba'ah she-Sippru: Burla, Agnon, Reuveni, Hazaz* (1978); R. Lee, *Masa al Rega ha-Ḥesed: Iyyunim bi-Yeẓiroteihem shel Agnon ve-Hazaz* (1978); H. Barzel (ed.), *H. Hazaz: Mivḥar Ma'amrei Bikoret al Yeẓirato* (1978); D. Laor, *H. Hazaz, ha-Ish vi-Yeẓirato* (1984); S. Werses, *Mi-Mendele ad Hazaz* (1987); H. Barzel, *Ḥazon ve-Ḥizayon* (1988).

HA-ẒEFIRAH (Heb. הַצְּפִירָה, "The Dawn"), a Hebrew paper appearing in Warsaw intermittently between 1862 and 1931. Founded as a weekly in 1862 by Ḥayyim Selig *Slonimski, *Ha-Ẓefirah* was devoted to science and technology, the only Hebrew paper of its kind during the 1860s and 1870s. The space devoted to news and Jewish scholarship was negligible. Slonimski, who had written scientific books in Hebrew from the 1830s, sought a regular forum for tracing the development of the sciences, which were expanding rapidly in those years. S. *Abramovitsh (Mendele Mokher Seforim), writing on science and technology, contributed regularly, but Slonimski was the principal contributor to most issues. The paper ceased publication after six months when the editor was appointed principal of the rabbinical school in Zhitomir. When that institution closed down in 1874, Slonimski revived *Ha-Ẓefirah*. Unable to obtain a permit in Russia, he published the paper in Berlin in the summer of 1874, with the aid of J.L. *Kantor. Although still mainly devoted to the sciences, Kantor introduced into the paper topical articles, political commentaries, and reports from Russia and other countries. Finally, Slonimski obtained his license and the paper again appeared in Warsaw from September 1875 until it ceased publication.

In Warsaw, too, Slonimski devoted the bulk of the paper to science and the rest to sections then common in the Hebrew press. In 1876, however, when Nahum *Sokolow began writing for the paper, its character changed as he increasingly supplemented scientific writing with topical articles and surveys of current affairs. Originally only a regular contributor, Sokolow became acting editor, then chief editor, and finally the author of almost all articles appearing in the paper. In the early 1880s he gradually reduced the size of the science section and made the paper more like its contemporaries, only more vibrant. Thanks to his introduction of variety into the paper's content, *Ha-Ẓefirah* enjoyed a wide circulation. Sokolow's name became synonymous with *Ha-Ẓefirah* and his articles on various subjects attracted many readers both among the *maskilim* and the Ḥasidim. Following *Ha-Yom's* lead, *Ha-Ẓefirah* became a daily in 1886, and began to provide an opportunity for new writers. Because Sokolow was deeply rooted in Polish Jewry, the paper served as the principal organ of Polish Jewry for almost two generations. *Ha-Ẓefirah* also printed reports from most of the Jewish centers throughout the world, particularly Ereẓ Israel and the United States. Sokolow realized the importance of innovation and novelty in journalism. Accordingly, he periodically changed the paper's format and writing style, to meet changing tastes. The attitude of Sokolow and the paper toward the Ḥibbat Zion movement and political Zionism was at first reserved, but after the First Zionist Congress *Ha-Ẓefirah* was faithful to Herzl.

Ha-Ẓefirah ceased publication early in 1906 when Sokolow became secretary of the World Zionist Organization. In 1910 the paper was revived with Sokolow as a regular contributor but edited by several of his disciples. During World War I the paper again ceased publication, but was reissued as a weekly in 1917 and as a daily in 1920. It did not appear from 1921 to 1926, when it was revived only to be discontinued again in 1928. *Ha-Ẓefirah* appeared for the last time in 1931, the year it permanently ceased publication. Among the paper's later editors were Isaac *Nissenbaum, Yiẓḥak *Gruenbaum, Joseph Heftman, and A.A. *Akaviah.

BIBLIOGRAPHY: Kressel, Leksikon, 2 (1967), 481–7, 504–7.

[Getzel Kressel]

ḤAẒER, ḤAẒERIM (Heb. חָצֵר, חֲצֵרִים).

(1) a biblical term for seminomadic settlements on the edge of the Negev that were fenced in but not walled. The *ḥaẓerim* occupy an intermediate position between nomadic encampments and settled towns (Josh. 21:12, where it is translated as "villages"), but in the course of time some of them developed into towns (cf. Hazar-Gaddah, Hazar-Shual, Josh. 15:27–28, etc.). A similar meaning is apparently expressed by the term *ḥagar* (from the root meaning "to fence in"). Place names combined with *ḥagar* are frequently mentioned in the Negev in the lists of *Shishak's conquests; in later sources the term refers to the Roman *limes*. The Avvim, who were absorbed by the invading Caphtorim (Philistines), also lived in *ḥaẓerim* in the south as far as Gaza (Deut. 2:23). In the Targum Yerushalmi, *Ḥaẓerim* is considered a locality and is identified with Rafah.

[Michael Avi-Yonah]

(2) ḤAẒERIM (Heb. חֲצֵרִים), kibbutz in the northern Negev, Israel, 4½ mi. (7 km.) W. of Beersheba, affiliated with Iḥud ha-Kevuẓot ve-ha-Kibbutzim, founded by graduates of Ha-Ẓofim, among them "Teheran Children" and Israeli-born youth on the night of Oct. 6, 1946, on which 10 other new settlements were simultaneously set up in the South and Negev. In the first 10 years of its existence, Ḥaẓerim sought ways to

treat its desert loess soils and overcame isolation and siege in the *War of Independence (1948). The kibbutz economy was based on field crops (mostly irrigated), fruit orchards, cattle, and an industrial enterprise, Netafim, for drip irrigation equipment, which became its economic mainstay with sales in over 100 countries, 24 subsidiaries and plants (including facilities in Cuba and China), and sales of $230 million in 2002. The population of the kibbutz in 2002 was 791.

[Efraim Orni / Shaked Gilboa (2nd ed.)]

BIBLIOGRAPHY: (1) Maisler, in: *Sefer…, J.N. Epstein* (1950), 317ff.; J. Braslavsky, *Le-Ḥeker Arẓenu* (1954), 255ff.

HAZEROTH (Heb. חֲצֵרוֹת, *ḥazerot*). (1) The second station of the Israelites on their journey eastward from Mount Sinai to Ezion-Geber between Kibroth-Hattaavah and Rithmah in the wilderness of Paran (Num. 11:35; 33:17–18). At Hazeroth, Miriam and Aaron "spoke against" Moses because he had married "a Cushite woman," and in punishment Miriam was "shut up" for seven days, during which the people waited there (*ibid.* 12:16). Hazeroth is also mentioned in the Bible together with Di-Zahab (Deut. 1:1). Its identification is dependent on the location of Mount Sinai. Those scholars who accept the traditional view of Mount Sinai at Jebel Musa identify Hazeroth with the oasis of ʿAyn al-Ḥaḍra, northwest of Dhahab (Di-Zahab?). Others who identify Mount Sinai with Jebel Ḥilāl locate Hazeroth at another ʿAyn al-Ḥaḍra in its vicinity.

(2) A Hazeroth is mentioned on the Samaria ostraca among the places paying tribute of wine and oil to Samaria in the time of the Israelite kingdom. It is possibly identical with ʿAṣīra al-Shamāliyya, 3 mi. (5 km.) north of Shechem.

BIBLIOGRAPHY: (1) Ms. W.M.F. Petrie, *Researches in Sinai* (1906), 262; Abel, Geog, 2 (1938), 214, 344; C.S. Jarvis, *Yesterday and Today in Sinai* (1931), 161, 171f.; (2) Ms. G.A. Reisner, et al., *Harvard Excavations at Samaria*, 1 (1924), 228ff.

[Michael Avi-Yonah]

ḤAẒEVAH (Heb. חֲצֵבָה), moshav in the central Aravah Valley, southern Israel, about 23 mi. (38 km.) S. of Sodom, affiliated with Tenu'at ha-Moshavim. It was founded in 1965 as a *Naḥal border outpost settlement. The moshav lies about 3 mi. (5 km.) southeast of the spring, oasis, and ancient site by that name (*Notitia Dignitatum*, ed. by O. Seeck (1876) gives *Eisiba*, ʿAyn Ḥuṣub in Arabic), where Iron Age sherds were found. Under Roman rule, Ḥaẓevah was a border castle at an important road junction, and a military unit, the second cohort of the Gratiana Legion, was stationed there. Under the British Mandate, a police station was set up near the spring, which is the most abundant in the Israeli part of the Aravah Valley. In November 1948, the occupation of Ḥaẓevah by Israel forces lifted the siege of Sodom and led to the conquest of the whole Negev. In the early 1950s an experimental station, mainly for the propagation of forest trees, was established at the oasis. In the 1960s, the existence of rich groundwater reserves in the area was confirmed. Two small settlements exist nearer the spring, a village of private farmers and a group of immigrants, mainly from North America. The moshav economy was based on farming, mainly vegetables and hothouse flowers. In addition, fruit plantations, vineyards, and ornamental fish were cultivated. Tourism was another source of income, including guest rooms, catering, guided tours, and jeep treks. In the mid-1990s, the moshav's population was approximately 520, dropping to 420 in 2002.

[Efraim Orni / Shaked Gilboa (2nd ed.)]

HAZKARAT NESHAMOT (Heb. הַזְכָּרַת נְשָׁמוֹת; "mentioning of the souls"), memorial prayer. In the Ashkenazi ritual, it is said after the reading of the Torah, during the morning service of the last day of Passover, Shavuot, and Sukkot (the three pilgrimage festivals), and on the Day of Atonement. In the Sephardi rite it is recited also on the Day of Atonement eve before *Ma'ariv.*

The prayer is divided into three sections; the principal part opens the prayer with the words, "*Yizkor Elohim*" ("May God remember… the soul…"). In common language the prayer has therefore become known as *Yizkor* or *Mazkir. Hazkarat Neshamot* expresses the fervent hope that the departed souls will enjoy eternal life in God's presence. There is evidence that this custom dates back to the period of the Hasmonean wars (c. 165 B.C.E.) when *Judah Maccabee and his men prayed for the souls of their fallen comrades and brought offerings to the Temple in Jerusalem as atonement for the sins of the dead (II Macc. 22:39–45). The belief that the meritorious deeds of descendants can atone for the departed appears frequently in aggadic literature (Hor. 6a; TJ, Sanh. 10:4, 29c; Sif. Deut. 210; Tanh. Berakhah 1; et al.). However, *Hai Gaon and his pupil *Nissim b. Jacob (c. 1000 C.E.) opposed the custom of praying for the departed on festivals and on the Day of Atonement, and of donating to charity on their behalf. They believed that only the actual deeds performed by a person during his lifetime count before God. Nevertheless, the memorial prayer became one of the most popular and cherished customs, especially in the *Ashkenazi ritual. Historically, it gained its significance through the *Crusades and through the severe persecutions that took place in Eastern Europe during the 17th century when thousands of Jews died as martyrs. They were all inscribed in the death rolls (called *kunteres or memorbuch*, or *yizker-bukh*) of their communities and commemorated in the memorial prayers held on the three festivals, on the Day of Atonement and, in some congregations, on the Sabbaths during the *Omer period (between Passover and Shavuot). In time, the death rolls came to include names not only of martyrs, but also of other members of the community, and the custom of memorial prayers for individuals evolved. After the memorial prayer for relatives, in the Ashkenazic rite the prayer *El Male Raḥamim is recited for those who have died. Nowadays, a special prayer is frequently added for the victims of the Nazi Holocaust and for the Jewish soldiers who died in wars, particularly in Israel. The traditional memorial service concludes with the recital of *Av ha-Raḥamim. The Torah Scroll(s) which had been taken out for the Reading of the Law is (are) returned to the Ark and the *musaf* service follows. In the Sephardi ritual, instead of reciting the *Hazkarat Neshamot* after the Torah service, everyone who is called to the Torah, after blessing it, recites a memorial prayer for his relatives. *Hazkarat Neshamot* mentions charitable offerings "for the repose of the departed souls" (Sh. Ar., OḤ 621:6) and in Orthodox synagogues, it is customary to promise donations during the service. It is also customary that those whose parents are still alive leave the synagogue during the entire *Hazkarat Neshamot* prayer. In the Conservative ritual, several introductory readings and appropriate Psalm verses in Hebrew and in the vernacular, as well as sections for meditation and special responsive readings in that language, were added to the traditional text of *Hazkarat Neshamot*. In the Reform ritual, the memorial service is held only on the last day of Passover and on the Day of Atonement as part of the late afternoon service before *Ne'ilah. This service consists of a shortened version of the traditional text, the recital of Psalm 23 and of selected poems by Ibn *Gabirol, *Judah Halevi, and *Baḥya b. Joseph, and of readings and meditations expressing the transience and evanescence of life and the merits of those who have lived an exemplary life. Solemn music accompanies this *Hazkarat Neshamot* service which concludes with the entire congregation reciting the *Kaddish. Synagogues are usually well attended by both men and women on the days that *Hazkarat Neshamot* is said; in some congregations these days have become occasions for major sermons by the rabbi.

BIBLIOGRAPHY: ET, 8 (1957), 603–9; S. Hurwitz (ed.), *Maḥzor Vitry* (1923^2), 392; Eisenstein, Yisrael, 96f.; M. Silverman, *High Holiday Prayer Book (Conservative)* (1939), 321–31; idem, *Sabbath and Festival Prayer Book (Conservative)* (1946), 221–7; *Union Prayer Book (Reform)*, 1 (1959), 268–73; 2 (1945^3), 306–24; Hertz, Prayer, 1106–08; P. Birnbaum, *High Holiday Prayer Book* (1951), 727–34; Petuchowski, *Prayerbook Reform in Europe* (1968), index.

[Meir Ydit]

ḤAZKUNI, ABRAHAM (b. 1627), rabbi and kabbalist. Ḥazkuni, who was born in Cracow, was a disciple of Yom Tov Lipmann *Heller. He published a summary of Isaac *Luria's *Sefer ha-Kavvanot* under the title *Zot Ḥukkat ha-Torah* (Venice, 1659). His commentary on the *Zohar, *Shetei Yadot* consisting of two parts, *Yad Ramah* and *Yad Adonai*, was lost through the negligence of the printer, with the exception of eight pages which are preserved in Oxford and New York (JTS). Ḥazkuni's son Jacob later published his father's commentary on the Pentateuch under this same title (Amsterdam, 1726). Ḥazkuni also wrote *Zera Avraham*, a two-part work containing casuistic *derashot* on the Torah; *Yode'a Binah*, of unknown content; and novellae to the tractates *Beẓah* and *Mo'ed Katan*. He died in Tripoli.

BIBLIOGRAPHY: Fuenn, Keneset, 24; Michael, Or, no. 92; P.H. Wetstein, in: *Ha-Eshkol* 7 (1913), 173–4; Neubauer, Cat, no. 1729, 6.

[Samuel Abba Horodezky]

HA-ẒOFEH (Heb. הַצּוֹפֶה).

(1) Daily Hebrew newspaper, published in Warsaw from 1903 to 1905. Following the journalistic tradition of **Ha-Yom*, *Ha-Ẓofeh* was well-balanced in its presentation of items of both Jewish and general interest, and upheld a Zionist point of view. Published daily, without interruption, the paper was managed by Y.A. Eliashov who also provided substantial financial support. Its first editor, A. *Ludvipol, was succeeded by H.D. *Nomberg. Ludvipol's regular staff included Simon *Bernfeld, Reuben *Brainin, A.L. Levinsky, I.L. *Peretz, and J. *Klausner, each of whom contributed material in his own field, e.g., stories, critical essays on Hebrew, Jewish and general literature, articles of political content, and feuilletons. Among the many other contributors to *Ha-Ẓofeh* were Hillel *Zeitlin, Mendele Mokher *Seforim, S. *Asch, Ḥ.N. *Bialik, S. *Ben-Zion, Y.D. *Berkowitz, I. *Bershadski, Y. *Gruenbaum, S. *Tchernichowsky, Ya'akov *Cahan, S.A. *Horodezky, V.Z. *Jabotinsky (he began his Hebrew writing here), M.L. *Lilienblum, J. *Fichmann, Itzhak *Katzenelson, Yaakov *Rabinowitz, Judah *Steinberg, Jacob *Steinberg, and Moshe *Smilansky.

Ha-Ẓofeh was bitterly opposed to the *Uganda Scheme. During the Sixth *Zionist Congress (1903), it reached the peak of its circulation (almost 15,000 subscribers), because of its reporting of Herzl's opening remarks on Uganda in a telegram (something hitherto unheard of in the Hebrew press), and also because of its representation at the Congress by Brainin, Bernfeld, Ludvipol, and Ḥermoni. A free copy of all of Bialik's poems was presented to its subscribers while subscribers to **Ha-Shilo'aḥ* were granted a substantial discount. The newspaper was discontinued in 1905, during the first Russian revolution, mainly because members of the *Bund struck against the publishing house in which the paper was published.

Ha-Ẓofeh conducted the first short-story contest in Hebrew literature. Y.D. Berkowitz won first prize, and his story was published, together with other worthy entries and the opinions of the judges, in *Koveẓ Sippurim* (1904).

[Getzel Kressel]

(2) Daily paper published in Tel Aviv. Established in August 1937 as the organ of the World Mizrachi Movement, it initially published three times a week and was edited by *Rabbi Benjamin (Yehoshua Redler-Feldman), and from December it was published daily and edited by Mordekhai *Lipson. The paper's editor-in-chief was Rabbi Meir *Bar-Ilan. Lipson was succeeded by Yeshayahu Bernstein.

Under Shabbetai Don-Yaḥia's (S. Daniel)'s editorship (1951–80) the newspaper generated support and understanding for the modern Orthodox outlook that the establishment of the State of Israel was the beginning of the messianic redemption, and that modern Orthodoxy should become an integral part both of the state's institutions such as the armed forces, and of the general population.

During the 1948–67 period key subjects the newspaper's op-ed and editorial columns dealt with at length were the relationship between religion and state, with particular attention to the budgetary needs of the state religious eductation sector, and to strengthening the chief rabbinate insttution – which was in effect a creation of the modern Orthodox sector. In 1961 Ben-Gurion criticized the paper, after the paper criticized him for a speech attacking the modern Orthodox community.

The newspaper gave expression to different shades of party opinion between Po'alei Mizrachi and Mizrachi. When Daniel was elected to the Knesset on the National Religious Party list, he resigned after only a month, preferring his work as *Ha-Ẓofeh's* editor. The newspaper led a hand-to-mouth existence, and several times faced closure. Its lack of resources limited news coverage. Though many rabbis and religious educators were among its readers it failed to widen its readership to the larger modern Orthodox public. The newspaper had a highly regarded weekly literary supplement mostly including Torani literature and edited by Yehoshua Shemesh, who became the paper's deputy editor.

The change in agenda of the NRP's Young Guard after the 1967 war found expression editorially inside *Ha-Ẓofeh*, which embraced the right of Jewish settlement in a Greater Land of Israel. Moshe Ishon, who was editor from 1980 to 1997, produced skilled polemics on the subject. After the 1993 Oslo accords, the newspaper found itself in direct conflict with the Likud government. Statements of leading Zionist rabbis castigating withdrawal from biblical territory were given prominence – raising afresh the question of the relationship between modern Orthodoxy and contemporary state institutions like the army. With the modern Orthodox dividing into three strata: the moderate veterans, the *ḥaredi le'ummi*, and the right the newspaper found itself having to appeal to all.

When Ishon retired in 1997 at the request of the paper's directors, facing ever-dwindling ciruclation as readers transferred their loyalties to the general press with its superior news coverage, the newspaper changed direction with the appointment of Gonen Ginat, a journalist who turned the paper into a bold tabloid with racy headlines. In revamping the news coverage, he recruited younger journalists. Chayuta Deutsch was appointed literary editor, widening the scope from Torah literature to the broad range of Israeli literature. Haggai Huberman was the settlements correspondent. The paper investigated the relationship between Shin Bet agent Avishai Raviv and Yigal Amir, Rabin's assassin. It also played an important part in generating opposition among the modern Orthodox camp to the Sharon government's withdrawl from *Gush Katif in 2005. At times the paper became so scurrilous – such as accusing ḥaredi girls' seminary students of engaging in prostitution – that Ginat on several occasions was forced to apologize in the paper's pages.

Circulation in 2005 was 12,000 daily and 18,000 on Sabbath and holiday eves. In 2005 the National Religious Party sold the paper to Shlomo Ben Zvi, a religious newspaper tycoon, owner of *Mekor Rishon*, a nationalist quality weekly, Radio Kol Chai, a ḥaredi-orientated radio station, and founder of Techelet, an expermental Jewish tradition television channel. The newspaper maintains a website.

[Yoel Cohen (2nd ed.)]

BIBLIOGRAPHY: (1) E.E. Friedman, *Sefer ha-Zikhronot* (1926), 275–314; J. Klausner, in: *Ha-Boker* (Jan. 2, 1953); Y. Rabinowitz, in: *Davar* (Jun. 1, 1945). (2) *Ha-Ẓofeh* (Jan. 20, 1939); (Jan. 6, 1948); (June 6, 1954); (Sept. 18, 1963); S. Daniel, in: *Sefer ha-Shanah shel ha-Ittona'im* (1963), 36–39; G. Kressel, *Toledot ha-Ittonut ha-Ivrit be-Ereẓ Yisrael* (1964), 166–72. **ADD. BIBLIOGRAPHY:** O. Tzarfati, "*Mi Mashpi'a al Emdot ha-Ẓiyyonut ha-Datit?*" in: *Kivvunim*, 12 (2005).

HAZOR (Heb. חָצוֹר), a large Canaanite and Israelite city in Upper Galilee. It is identified with Tell al-Qidāḥ (also called Tell Waqqāṣ), 8¾ mi. (14 km.) north of the Sea of Galilee and 5 mi. (8 km.) southwest of Lake *Ḥuleh. The city was strategically located in ancient times and dominates the main branches of the Via Maris ("Way of the Sea") leading from Egypt to Mesopotamia, Syria, and Anatolia.

Canaanite Hazor is mentioned in the Egyptian Execration Texts (19th or 18th century B.C.E.) and is the only Palestinian town mentioned (together with Laish) in the Mari documents (18th century B.C.E.) where it appears as a major commercial center of the Fertile Crescent with caravans traveling between it and Babylon. It is also frequently mentioned in Egyptian documents of the New Kingdom, in the city lists of Thutmoses III (where it appears together with Laish (*Dan), *Pella, and *Kinnereth), and of Amenhotep II and Seti I. In the *el-Amarna letters, the kings of Ashtaroth and Tyre accuse Abdi-Tirshi, king of Hazor, of taking several of their cities. The king of Tyre furthermore states that the king of Hazor left his city to join the *Habiru. In other letters, however, Abdi-Tirshi – one of the few Canaanite rulers to call himself king proclaims his loyalty to Egypt. Hazor is also referred to in the Papyrus Anastasi I (probably from the time of Ramses II).

The Bible contains a direct reference to the role of Hazor at the time of Joshua's conquests. *Jabin, king of Hazor, headed a league of several Canaanite cities against Joshua in the battle at the waters of *Merom: "And Joshua turned back at that time, and took Hazor, and smote the king thereof with the sword. For Hazor beforetime was the head of all those kingdoms… and he burnt Hazor with fire… But as for the cities that stood on their mounds, Israel burned none of them, save Hazor only – that did Joshua burn" (Josh. 11:10–13). Hazor is also indirectly mentioned in the prose account of *Deborah's wars (Judg. 4) in contrast to the "Song of Deborah" (Judg. 5) which deals with a battle in the Jezreel Valley and does not mention Hazor. According to I Kings 9:15, the city was rebuilt by Solomon together with *Megiddo and *Gezer. The last biblical reference to Hazor records its conquest, with other Galilean cities, by *Tiglath-Pileser III in 732 B.C.E. (II Kings 15:29). In Hasmonean times, Jonathan and his army, marching northward from the Ginnosar (Gennesar) Valley during his wars against Demetrius, camped on the plain of Hazor near *Kedesh (I Macc. 11:76). Josephus locates the city above Lake Semachonitis (Ant. 5:199).

Hazor was first identified with Tell al-Qidāḥ by J.L. Porter in 1875 and again by J. Garstang in 1926. The latter conducted soundings at the site in 1928. Four large campaigns of excavations – the James A. de Rothschild Expedition – took place between 1955 and 1958, under the direction of Y. Yadin on behalf of the Hebrew University, with the aid of PICA, the Anglo-Israel Exploration Society, and the Israel government. A fifth campaign took place in 1968.

The site of Hazor is composed of two separate areas – the tell proper covering some 30 acres (120 dunams) and rising some 130 ft. (40 m.) above the surrounding plain, and a large rectangular plateau, about 175 acres (700 dunams) in area, north of the tell. The latter is protected on its western side by a huge rampart of beaten earth and a deep fosse, on the north by a rampart and on the other sides by its natural steep slopes reinforced by glacis and walls.

Lower City

Garstang had concluded from his soundings that the large plateau (enclosure) was a camp site for infantry and chariots and since he found no Mycenean pottery (which first appears in the area after 1400 B.C.E.), he dated Hazor's final destruction to about 1400, the date he ascribed to Joshua's conquest. The excavations, however, revealed that the enclosure was not a camp site but that the entire area was occupied by a city with five levels of occupation. It was first settled in the mid-18th century B.C.E. (Middle Bronze Age II), to which the fortifications date, and was finally destroyed sometime before the end of the 13th century B.C.E. The discovery of Mycenean and local ware from the 13th century helped to disprove Garstang's date of its fall. Seven areas in different parts of the lower city were excavated and the same chronology was found in all. The first city (stratum 4) was followed by a settlement (stratum 3) from the end of the Middle Bronze Age II (17th–16th centuries) which was razed by fire. The city was rebuilt in the Late Bronze Age I (stratum 2, 15th century). This stratum represents the peak of Hazor's prosperity together with the 14th-century city (stratum Ib) in which time Hazor was the largest city in the area in the land of Canaan; City 1b suffered destruction in undetermined circumstances. The last settlement in the lower city (stratum 1a) was a reconstruction of the previous one and with its fall, before the end of the 13th century, occupation ceased in the lower city. Its destruction, both here and in the contemporary city on the tell, is to be ascribed to the conquering Israelite tribes, as is related in detail in the Book of Joshua.

In the southwestern corner of the lower city (area C) a small sanctuary was found on the foot of the inner slope of the rampart. It dates from stratum 1b and was rebuilt in 1a. A number of basalt steles and statuettes were found in a niche in one of the walls, one with two hands raised toward a divine lunar symbol – a crescent and a circle, and a statuette of a seated male figure with its head intentionally broken off. Benches for offerings line the walls of the temple. A pottery cult mask was found in a potter's workshop nearby as well as a bronze standard plated with silver and bearing a relief of a snake goddess.

Rock-cut tombs with an elaborate network of tunnels connecting them were found in the eastern sector of the lower city (area F), dating from the earliest stratum. A large building (probably a temple) with thick walls was constructed there in the next city which used the older tunnels for a drainage system. In the next stratum (stratum II) a temple was built. In stratum 1b the area assumed a definite cultic character and a large monolithic altar with depressions for draining the sacrificial blood stood there.

In several areas, a large number of infant burials in jars were found beneath the floors of houses from stratum III.

Four superimposed temples were found in area H, at the northern edge of the lower city. The earliest (stratum III) consisted of a broad hall with a small niche – a sort of holy of holies. South of the hall was a raised platform reached by several finely dressed basalt steps. The next temple was substantially the same in plan but a closed court was added and an open courtyard south of it. The court was entered through a broad propyleum. The courtyard contained a large rectangular *bamah* ("high place") and several altars. A clay model of a liver, inscribed in Akkadian, found in a pile of debris nearby, was intended for use by the priest-diviners and mentioned various evil omens. A bronze plaque of a Canaanite dignitary wrapped in a long robe was also found. In stratum 1b, the temple was composed of three chambers built on a single axis from south to north: a porch, a main hall, and a broad holy of holies with a rectangular niche in its northern wall. In its general plan it resembles several temples found at Alalakh in northern Syria as well as the temple of Solomon. A row of basalt orthostats (which may have belonged originally to the previous temple) forming a dado around the interior of the porch and the holy of holies which is very similar to some found at Alalakh and other sites, shows distinct evidence of northern influence. On either side of the entrance to the porch stood a basalt orthostat with a lion in relief (only one was found, buried in a pit). The following temple (stratum 1a) shows only minor alterations. Two round bases found in front of the entrance to the hall are apparently similar to the Jachin and *Boaz of Solomon's temple. The many ritual vessels (probably reused from the previous temple) include a basalt incense altar, with the emblem of the storm god in relief – a circle with a cross in the center, ritual tables and bowls, a statuette of a seated figure, cylinder seals and a scarab bearing the name of Amenhotep III. Outside the sanctuary were found fragments of a statue of a deity with the symbol of the storm god on its chest. The god had stood on a bull-shaped base.

A succession of city gates and walls ranging in date from the founding of the city to its final end was found in area K on the northeastern edge of the lower city. The gate from stratum III was strongly fortified, with towers on either side and three pairs of pilasters in the passage. A casemate wall adjoining it is the earliest example of this type found thus far in Ereẓ Israel. A similar series of gates was found in the 1968 season on the eastern edge of the lower city.

Upper City

Five areas were excavated on the tell proper where 21 levels (with additional sub-phases) of occupation were uncovered.

Settlement began here in the 27th century B.C.E. (end of the Early Bronze Age II), and, after a gap between the 24th and 22nd centuries, it was resettled in the Middle Bronze Age I (stratum XVIII). From the period of Hazor's zenith (15th century) parts of a large palace (the residence of the king?) and temple were uncovered which contained part of an orthostat with a lioness in relief similar to the lion orthostat from the contemporary temple in the lower city. Stratum XIII, the last Late Bronze Age city on the tell, shows the same signs of destruction in the 13th century as were found in the lower city. The upper city, however, in contrast, was resettled after a short interruption, but not in the form of a true city. Most of its constructions are still of a seminomadic character – silos, hearths, and foundations for tents and huts. These remains are essentially identical with those of the Israelite settlements in Galilee in the 12th century and indicate that the majority of this settlement occurred only after the fall of the cities and provinces of Canaan.

Stratum XI is an 11th-century, unfortified Israelite settlement, with a small high place. Only from the time of Solomon onward did Hazor return to its former splendor, though on a smaller scale than in Canaanite times. Solomon rebuilt and fortified the upper city (stratum X) with a casemate wall and a large gate with three chambers on either side and two towers flanking the passage. These are identical with the fortifications he constructed at Gezer and Megiddo (cf. I Kings 9:15). The following city was destroyed by fire and rebuilt by the House of *Omri in the ninth century (stratum VIII) which erected a strong citadel covering most of the western part of the tell (area B). The citadel is symmetrical in plan with two long halls running from east to west and surrounded on three sides by chambers. The entrance was ornamented with proto-Aeolic capitals and a monolithic lintel. Near the citadel were a number of public buildings. The citadel was strengthened in the eighth century and continued in use until Hazor's conquest by Tiglath-Pileser III in 732 B.C.E.

A large storehouse with two rows of pillars in the center (mistakenly interpreted as Solomon's stables by Garstang) also dates to stratum VIII (House of Omri). Stratum VI (eighth century) was destroyed by an earthquake, possibly the one which occurred in the days of *Jeroboam II, mentioned in the Book of Amos. The last fortified city at Hazor is represented by stratum V, and after its destruction by the Assyrians the city remained uninhabited except for a temporary unfortified settlement (stratum IV). A large citadel in stratum III was evidently constructed by the Assyrians and continued in use in the Persian period. Another citadel, from stratum I, is attributed to the second century, i.e., the Hellenistic period.

In the 1968 season a large underground water system was discovered at the center of the southern edge of the mound facing the natural spring below. It has the same plan (although on a much larger scale) as the famous one at Megiddo, and was hewn out of the rock at the same period, i.e., the ninth century B.C.E. (Hazor stratum VIII).

[Yigael Yadin]

Later Excavations and Chronology

Since 1990 excavations have been conducted at the site by A. Ben-Tor. Limited remains from the Early Bronze period were found in deep soundings (Strata XXI–XIX), mainly from the EB II and EB III with a fine assemblage of Khirbet Kerak ware. Only a handful of shards are known from the Intermediate Bronze Age (Stratum XVIII). Hazor flourished in the Middle Bronze Age II (Strata pre-XVII, XVII, XVI and post-XVI in the upper city; Strata 3–4 in the lower city) with the lower city being settled for the first time with impressive defense systems (earthen rampart and moat, and gateways) and the corner of a palace. Cuneiform tablets date from this period: a clay liver model, a bilingual Sumero-Akkadian text, a legal document, and an economic text and a fragment of a royal letter. The Late Bronze Age strata (upper city: Strata XV–XIII; lower city: Strata 2–1A) were separated from the preceding Middle Bronze Age city by a substantial destruction layer (Stratum post-XVI). The Late Bronze Age city included a number of major architectural monuments such as the earthen ramparts, the city gates, and the temples (the Stelae Temple in Area C; Orthostat Temple in Area H). Stratum XIV was destroyed in a fire and this may have been at the time of Seti I (end of the 14th century B.C.E.). The final phase of occupation in the Late Bronze Age was also destroyed. Yadin attributed this to the Israelites as described in Joshua 11:10. The exact date of this destruction is still unclear. The settlement in the Iron Age I (Strata XII–XI) was not very impressive, consisting mainly of storage pits and foundations of temporary structures. Monumental structures belong to the Iron Age II–III (Strata X–IV) and these include the fortifications: a six-chambered city gate and casemate walls. They were dated by Yadin to the 10th century (following I Kgs. 9:15), but attempts have recently been made to lower this date. Later works include the construction of a wall around the acropolis and the hewing of a water supply system. Hazor was conquered and destroyed in 732 B.C.E. An Assyrian citadel and palace are known (Stratum III), as well as a few remains from the Persian and Hellenistic periods (Strata II–I).

[Shimon Gibson (2nd ed.)]

BIBLIOGRAPHY: Y. Yadin et al., *Hazor*, 4 vols. (Eng., 1959–64); Y. Yadin, in: D.W. Thomas (ed.), *Archaeology and Old Testament Study* (1967), 245 ff. (includes bibl.); Y. Yadin, *The Biblical Archaeologist*, vol. 32 no. 3, 50 ff.

ḤAẒOR (ha-Gelilit; Heb. (חָצוֹר (הַגְּלִילִית)), development town with municipal council status in eastern Upper Galilee, N.E. of Rosh Pinnah and 2½ mi. (4 km.) S. of the mound of ancient Hazor. The site was chosen in 1950 and its first housing schemes were ready in 1953, taking in immigrants from the Rosh Pinnah *ma'barah* and newcomers and having a population of 895 by the end of that year. Large numbers of immigrants, principally from Middle East and North African countries, were housed at Ḥaẓor, but many of them left after a short interval, due to poor local conditions. Later, when economic opportunities improved, the population grew again and reached 5,250 at the end of 1969. In the mid-1990s, it was approximately 8,190, and at the end of 2002 it reached 8,550, on a municipal area of 2 sq. mi. (5.2 sq. km.). Ḥaẓor's assets have been a favorable location for communications, a rich farming hinterland in the Ḥuleh Valley, an ample water supply, and the availability of level ground for industrial enterprises. A drawback has been the proximity of two other towns – Safed and Kiryat Shemonah. Income has been considerably below the national average.

[Shlomo Hasson / Shaked Gilboa (2nd ed.)]

ḤAẒOR ASHDOD (Heb. חֲצוֹר אַשְׁדּוֹד), kibbutz in the southern Coastal Plain of Israel, affiliated with Kibbutz Arẓi Ha-Shomer ha-Ẓa'ir. It was founded together with 10 other settlements in the south and the Negev on Oct. 6, 1946, by a group which had previously founded *Gevulot as a Negev outpost. The members were joined by pioneer youth from the U.S., Bulgaria, and other countries. Ḥaẓor Ashdod had a population of 535 in 1968 and 560 in 2002. The kibbutz engaged in farming based on field crops and poultry and a number of successful enterprises, including Solbar Industries, manufacturing soy protein concentrates with sales in 45 countries, Danor, specializing in soy phytochemicals, and SafePlace, specializing in safety accreditation. The name Ḥaẓor is assumed to be historical as it is mentioned by Eusebius (Onom. 20:1; 30:22, et al.). The name of the nearest city, *Ashdod, was later added to distinguish between the kibbutz and the development town *Ḥaẓor, situated in Galilee.

WEBSITE: come.to/hatzor.

[Efraim Orni / Shaked Gilboa (2nd ed.)]

HA-ZORE'A (Heb. הַזּוֹרֵעַ; "the Sower"), kibbutz on the western outskirts of the Jezreel Valley, Israel, affiliated with Kibbutz Arẓi Ha-Shomer ha-Ẓa'ir. It was founded in 1936, during the Arab riots, by a group of the Zionist pioneer Werkleute movement from Germany. Later, immigrants from Bulgaria, Syria, and other countries joined the settlement, which in 1968 had 610 inhabitants. The population rose to approximately 1,030 in the mid-1990s but declined to 915 in 2002. Its economy has been based on highly intensive farming, including the breeding of ornamental fish and water lilies, a Quality Control Center with a laboratory for calibration tests, and a factory for polyethylene packaging material. Its well-known furniture factory was closed down. The Manasseh Forest, one of Israel's largest forests, is located nearby. Ha-Zore'a has an art and antiquities museum, Bet Wilfred Israel, housing inter alia Wilfred *Israel's Far Eastern art treasure collection.

WEBSITE: www.hazorea.org.il.

[Efraim Orni / Shaked Gilboa (2nd ed.)]

HA-ZORE'IM (Heb. הַזּוֹרְעִים), religious moshav in eastern Lower Galilee, Israel, affiliated with the Ha-Po'el ha-Mizrachi moshav association. It was founded in 1939 on land provided by the Palestine *Jewish Colonization Association. The settlers, who came from several countries, engaged mainly in raising field crops, livestock, and orchards. In the course of the years farming failed to support the settlers and today only a few still earn their livelihoods in agriculture (poultry, dairy cattle, and vegetables), with most working outside the moshav. Remnants of an ancient village assumed to be Serungiya (or Sirgunya) in the talmudic period (Gen. R. 1:6) were found here. The present settlement initially bore this name but the name of the founding group ("the Sowers") was later officially recognized. In 1968 its population was 300, rising to 400 in 2002, with expansion underway.

WEBSITE: www.hazorim.co.il

[Efraim Orni / Shaked Gilboa (2nd ed.)]

ḤAZZAN (Hazan), Turkish family, apparently of Spanish origin. Many of its members were scholars. In addition to Israel Moses b. Eliezer *Ḥazzan, the following members of the family may be mentioned. JOSEPH BEN ELIJAH ḤAZZAN (d. after 1694) was a pupil of Joseph *Trani, colleague of Ḥayyim *Benveniste in Constantinople, and the teacher of Abraham Israel Ze'evi. From Constantinople he proceeded to Smyrna, and from there to Jerusalem, where he died. He was the author of *Ein Yehosef* (Smyrna 1735), on *Bava Meẓia*, and some responsa – most of his responsa were destroyed in a fire together with other manuscripts; *Ein Yosef* (Smyrna, 1675), homilies on the weekly readings of the Bible; and a commentary on the *Ein Ya'akov*, to which he refers in the preface to the *Ein Yosef*. A commentary on the Pentateuch has also remained in manuscript. ḤAYYIM (d. 1712), his son, was one of the rabbis of Smyrna. He later served as a rabbi in *Egypt and then proceeded to Jerusalem. Queries were addressed to him from different countries. During 1704–7, together with Abraham Rovigo, he traveled in Western Europe as an emissary of the Jerusalem community. He continued alone to Eastern Europe and died in Mir, Lithuania. He was the author of *Shenot Ḥayyim* (Venice, 1693), sermons on the Pentateuch, as well as novellae and responsa left in manuscript. His son DAVID (18th century) was one of the scholars of Jerusalem, where he had been born. In the 1720s he traveled in Western Europe as an emissary of the Jerusalem community, then proceeded to Smyrna, where he established a printing press. David was the author of *Ḥozeh David* (Amsterdam, 1724), a commentary on the Psalms; *Kohelet Ben David* (Salonika, 1748), on Ecclesiastes; *Agan ha-Sahar* (Salonika, 1750), on Proverbs; and other works.

Jacob Ḥazzan (d. 1802), a Jerusalem scholar, was also an emissary of the Jerusalem community from 1770 to 1775 in Turkey, Western Europe, and Poland. JOSEPH RAPHAEL BEN ḤAYYIM JOSEPH (1741–1820), known as *ha-Yare'aḥ* from the first letters of his name (Y-osef R-aphael b. Ḥ-ayyim), was a rabbi in Smyrna. In 1811 he proceeded to Hebron and after two years went to Jerusalem where he was appointed *rishon le-Zion*. He was the author of *Ḥikrei Lev* (7 vols., Salonika-Leghorn, 1787–1832), novellae on the four parts of the Shulḥan Arukh, and *Ma'arekhei Lev* (Salonika, 1821–22) in two parts, homilies. His sons were Eliezer, Elijah Raḥamim, Isaac, and ḤAYYIM DAVID; Ḥayyim *Palaggi was his grandson. ELIEZER (d. 1823) was a rabbi in Jerusalem, where he died. His works, *Ḥakor Davar, 'Ammudei ha-Arazim*, on the *Sefer Yere'im* of Eliezer of Metz, and kabbalistic novellae have remained in manuscript. He was the father of Israel Moses *Ḥazzan. ELIJAH RAḤAMIM (d. 1840) was a rabbi of Smyrna and the author of *Oraḥ Mishpat* (Salonika, 1858), on the Shulḥan Arukh *Ḥoshen Mishpat*. He left in manuscript responsa, sermons for Sabbaths and festivals, and *Even ha-Mikkaḥ*, on the *Mikkaḥ u-Mimkar* of *Hai Gaon. A number of his responsa are contained in the *Ḥikrei Lev* of his father. ḤAYYIM DAVID (1790–1869) was born in Smyrna. At the age of 20 he went to Constantinople and in 1840 he was appointed rabbi in Smyrna. He settled in Jerusalem in 1855 and in 1861, succeeding Ḥayyim Nissim Abulafia, was appointed *rishon le-Zion*. He was the author of *Torat Zevaḥ* (Salonika, 1852), on the law of *sheḥitah; Nediv Lev* (2 pts. Salonika-Jerusalem, 1862–66), responsa; *Yitav Lev* (Smyrna, 1868), homilies; *Yishrei Lev* (*ibid.*, 1870), various novellae; and other works in manuscript. SOLOMON ḤAZZAN (d. 1856) was rabbi of *Alexandria and died in Malta. He was the author of *Sefer ha-Ma'alot li-Shelomo* (1894), a compilation of biographies of scholars not included in the *Shem ha-Gedolim* of Ḥ.J.D. Azulai. ELIJAH BEKHOR BEN ABRAHAM (d. 1908), grandson of Ḥayyim David, was born in Smyrna. In 1872–74 he went to North Africa as an emissary of the Jerusalem community. In 1874 he was appointed rabbi of *Tripoli and from there went to Alexandria, where he died. He was the author of *Ta'alumot Lev* (Leghorn-Alexandria, 1879–1902), responsa in four parts; *Neveh Shalom* (Alexandria, 1894), on the customs of Alexandria; *Zikhron Yerushalayim* (Leghorn, 1874), on love of the Holy Land; and other works.

BIBLIOGRAPHY: Frumkin-Rivlin, index; M.D. Gaon, *Yehudei ha-Mizraḥ be-Ereẓ Yisrael*, 2 (1937), 245–53; Rosanes, Togarmah, vols. 4 and 5, passim; A. Galante, *Les Juifs d'Izmir* (1937), passim; Yaari, Sheluḥei, index; idem, in: *Aresheth*, 1 (1958), 218 (index); M. Benayahu, *Rabbi Ḥayyim Yosef David Azulai* (1959), index; B. Taragan, *Les communautés israélites d'Alexandrie* (1932), 51–2, 54–8.

[Simon Marcus]

ḤAZZAN (pl. **Ḥazzanim**) (Heb. חַזָּן, חַזָּנִים), cantor officiating in a synagogue; used in this specific sense since the Middle Ages.

History of Role and Function

The word frequently occurs in talmudic sources, where it denotes various types of communal officials, most prominently the *ḥazzan ha-keneset*. This official performed certain duties in the synagogue, such as bringing out the Torah scrolls for readings (Sotah 7:7–8) and blowing a trumpet to announce the commencement of the Sabbath and festivals (Tosef., Suk. 4:12). He was not, however, regularly required to chant the synagogue service but could do so by request (TJ, Ber. 9:1, 12d); in talmudic times there was no permanent cantor and any member of the congregation might be asked to act as *sheli'aḥ ẓibbur* (TJ, Ber. 5:3, 9c). It was during the period of the *geonim* that the *ḥazzan* became the permanent *sheli'aḥ ẓibbur*. Among the factors which contributed to this change were the increasing complexity of the liturgy and the decline in the knowledge of Hebrew, together with a desire to enhance the beauty of the service through its musical content. The *ḥazzan ha-keneset*, who traditionally guarded the correct texts and selected new prayers, was a natural choice. When **piyyutim* began to take an important place in the liturgy of the synagogue, it was the *ḥazzan* who would recite them and provide suitable melodies. Some of the *paytanim* were themselves *ḥazzanim*. The recitation of the *piyyutim* was called *ḥizana* (*ḥizanatun*) by the Arabic-speaking *paytanim* and the Hebrew equivalent *ḥazzanut* (*ḥazzaniyyah* among Sephardi communities) came to refer to the traditional form of chanting the whole service, and later to the profession of cantor also.

During the Middle Ages the status of the *ḥazzanim* rose, and they were given better salaries, longer tenure of office, and more communal tax exemptions. The post of *ḥazzan* was "the most permanent and continuous synagogue office, one which underwent relatively few changes after the early Middle Ages" (Baron, Community, 2 (1942), 100). In Northern Europe eminent rabbis served as *ḥazzanim*, among them Jacob *Moellin ha-Levi (Maharil) of Mainz (c. 1360–1427), who established strict norms for Ashkenazi *ḥazzanim* and some of whose chants are still in use. Gradually, the qualifications demanded of a *ḥazzan* became fixed. He was required to have a pleasant voice and appearance, to be married, to have a beard, to be fully familiar with the liturgy, to be of blameless character, and to be acceptable in all other respects to the members of the community (Sh. Ar., OḤ 53:4ff.). These strict requirements were modified occasionally, but were rigorously enforced on the High Holy Days. Ironically, the growing popularity of the *ḥazzan* made him the most controversial communal official. His dual role of religious representative and artistic performer inevitably gave rise to tensions (which persist in modern times). In many communities priority was given to a beautiful voice and musical skill over the traditional requirements of learning and piety. Leading rabbis castigated the *ḥazzanim* for needless repetition of words and for extending their chanting of the prayers with the sole purpose of displaying the beauty of their voices.

The emancipation of European Jewry led to important changes in the style and content of synagogue music. Traditional melodies were now set down in musical notation with harmonies to be sung by *ḥazzan* and choir. New melodies were composed under the influence of modern European musical trends and techniques. The pioneer in this field was Solomon *Sulzer, chief *ḥazzan* in Vienna from 1825 to 1890; he was closely followed by Samuel *Naumbourg of Paris, Louis *Lewandowski of Berlin, Hirsch *Weintraub of Koenigsberg, Moritz *Deutsch of Breslau, Abraham *Baer of Goteborg, Sweden, and many others. The ḥasidic movement, where the rabbi recited the prayers, and parts of the Reform movement which substituted the plain reading of the liturgy for the office of *ḥazzan*, remained outside this development. Indeed the joyful tunes of the Ḥasidim gradually became popular with many Orthodox communities. The use of the organ and mixed choirs introduced by the *Reform movement radically changed cantorial music. Hebrew and German prayer texts were chanted to German chorale tunes; these replaced the traditional prayer music. Rabbi Isaac M. Wise, architect of American Jewish Reform, substituted the plain reading of liturgy for the office of *ḥazzan*. Only a few houses of worship retained *ḥazzanim* (e.g., Alois Kaiser) who tried to develop a tradition of American synagogue music. Classical reform in the U.S. was modified under the impact of the Zionist movement and East European immigration, and pressure grew to restore traditional forms of worship. Two *ḥazzanim* who became professors, A.W. Binder at the *Jewish Institute of Religion and A.Z. Idelsohn at the *Hebrew Union College, reintroduced traditional liturgy and music into Reform rabbinical studies.

The period from the end of the 19th century until World War II is described as the "Golden Era of *Ḥazzanut*." Cantorial music had a singular appeal to the Jewish masses, who would fill their synagogues to overflowing in order to hear an outstanding *ḥazzan*. Improved communications enabled leading *ḥazzanim* to tour Jewish communities on a far greater scale than previously, thus increasing their reputations, sometimes to legendary proportions. They were equated with the great operatic tenors of the time, whose style they grew to imitate. Even non-Jews were attracted to the synagogues to hear famous *ḥazzanim* and Gershon *Sirota was invited annually to sing for the czar. Following the mass emigration of Jews from Eastern Europe to the U.S., great *ḥazzanim* like Sirota, Josef *Rosenblatt, Mordechai *Herschman, and Zavel *Kwartin gave concert tours in America, where all of them, except Sirota, remained. They were able to command enormous salaries and fees for concerts and High Holy Day services.

A major factor in building up the reputations and perpetuating the fame of the great *ḥazzanim* was the development of sound recordings, beginning with the first cantorial disk made by Sirota in 1903. Furthermore, lesser *ḥazzanim* adopted the style and melodies of the great cantors which they learnt from the records, and the singing of famous musical compositions became a chief attraction of synagogue services. In the postwar period prominent *ḥazzanim* included Moshe *Koussevitzky and his brothers Jacob, Simchah, and David, Leib *Glanz, Israel Alter, Moshe Ganchoff, Pierre Pinchik, Leibele Waldman, Sholom Katz, and, in the younger generation, Moshe Stern. Some, such as Richard *Tucker and Jan *Peerce, achieved international fame as operatic tenors, but retained their contact with the synagogue through recordings and High Holiday and Passover services. In Israel the development of *ḥazzanut* lagged behind the U.S. However, the regular radio programs devoted to both Ashkenazi and Sephardi *ḥazzanut* had a large following. Many of the world's leading *ḥazzanim* sang in Israel and a cantorial conference was held there in 1968. *Ḥazzanim* served in the chaplaincy corps of the Israel army, but only the large towns employed *ḥazzanim* on a regular basis. A number of successful *ḥazzanim* were attracted to the U.S., Great Britain, and South Africa, where the financial rewards were much greater. Most major Jewish communities in the world had professional associations of *ḥazzanim* and several bulletins and journals were regularly published. An important factor in assuring the future development of *ḥazzanut* was the growth of cantorial training schools, in the U.S. (at Yeshiva University, the Jewish Theological Seminary, and the Hebrew Union College), in Great Britain (at Jews' College), and in Israel (at the Selah Seminary in Tel Aviv, and elsewhere).

[Hyman Kublin]

Later Developments

ISRAEL. In the 1970s the growing shortage of qualified *ḥazzanim* in the Diaspora was partly met by the increasing tendency on the part of Israeli *ḥazzanim* to officiate in communities in the Diaspora on the High Holy Days. A number of Diaspora *ḥazzanim* who immigrated to Israel, on retirement devoted themselves to the training of *ḥazzanim* (among them was Shelomoh Mandel of Johannesburg). In 1979, the Israel Institute for Religious Music in Jerusalem issued *Ve-Shinantam Le-Vonecha* for the teaching of the cantillation of the Bible according to the various traditions, Ashkenazi, Sephardi, Moroccan, and Yemenite, edited by its director Judah Kadaki, with the expert advice of Prof. I. Yeivin and Dr. Avigdor Herzog. In 1980 it issued two records of the traditional liturgy recordings of the prayers of the Jews of Salonika and Libya.

The First World Conference on Jewish Music, held in Jerusalem in 1978, included various aspects of *ḥazzanut*.

From 1977, an annual "*Ḥazzanut* Week" was held in Tel Aviv with the regular participation of David Koussevitzky. In 1978, the *ḥazzan* Shelomoh Ravitz, who has been in Tel Aviv since 1932, was appointed a "Yakir Tel Aviv" (Distinguished Citizen of Tel Aviv). Synagogue choirs are rare in Israel, but that of the Central Synagogue of Haifa, established by the *ḥazzan* Leon Kornitzer, was regarded as one of the best in the world, and celebrated its 40th anniversary in 1979. From 1950 it was conducted by Isaac Heilman.

The 1980s saw the gradual disappearance of *ḥazzanut* from synagogues in Israel, with only a few synagogues employing professional cantors. The only synagogue in the country with a permanent choir for Sabbaths and holidays was the Great Synagogue in Jerusalem, led by Eli Jaffe. Concert *ḥazzanut* was replacing synagogue *ḥazzanut* as the number of well-attended cantorial concerts continued to grow. In 1986, Dr. Mordecai Sobol established the Yuval Ensemble, composed of cantors, singers, and instrumentalists. The ensemble appeared in liturgical music concerts throughout Israel; it also took part in the Israel Festival in 1991. Cantorial training schools were founded in Tel Aviv, Bat Yam, Petaḥ Tikvah, and Jerusalem. The Renanot Institute, directed by Ezra Barnea, continued the dissemination of the melodies of the various Jewish communities. Tape recordings were produced for the High Holy Day, Festival, and Sabbath prayers and for the Passover *Seder* in the style of the different Jewish communities.

The series of books edited by Yehuda Kadari, *Ve-Shinantem le-Vanekha*, for the study of Torah cantillation in the tradition of the various Jewish communities, was completed. Renanot published *Mi-Zimrat Kedem*, edited by Edwin Seroussi, on the life of the Turkish cantor and Rabbi Isaac Algazi, one of the greatest Sephardi cantors.

The Tel Aviv Beth Hatefutsoth Museum's Center for Jewish Music, under the direction of Dr. Avner Bahat, began operations in 1982 and among other things has produced tapes of prayers in the traditions of the Jewish communities of Koenigsberg and Danzig sung by Cantor Naftaly Herstik as well as of works by the composer Alberto Hamzi. Tel Aviv University's music department marked the 80th birthday of Prof. Ḥanoch Avenary, an outstanding contemporary scholar of Jewish music and *ḥazzanut*, with a special edition of its journal, *Orbis Musica*. Two books by Akiva Zimmerman appeared in Tel Aviv, *Be-Ron Yaḥad* (1988), on the world of liturgical and Jewish music, and *Sha'arei Ron* (1992), on *ḥazzanut* in responsa literature and Jewish law. In 1992, upon the 50th anniversary of the death of the singer and cantor Joseph Schmidt, there was established in Tel Aviv a public committee to perpetuate his memory. Thus far there has appeared a memorial tape with selections of prayers and songs from Joseph Schmidt's repertoire sung by Cantor Moshe Stern. This tape was produced by the curator of the Jewish museum in Augsburg, Ayala-Helga Deutsch.

Prof. Isaac Bacon of Beersheba and Bar-Ilan universities published a book in 1991 containing the tunes of his father, Cantor Hirsch Leib Bacon. This is the first time the melodies of this cantor, who was extremely well known in Galicia, have appeared in print. Worthy of note is the book of melodies published by Dr. Zvi Talmon, *Pa'amei ha-Heikhal* (1992), which offers tunes for Sabbath and Festival prayers and is a continuation of his first book, *Rinat ha-Heikhal* which appeared in 1965.

EUROPE. England was the only country in Europe which had organized *ḥazzanut* activity. The Cantors Association organized concerts on Ḥanukkah and Lag Ba-Omer and published an annual *Cantors Review*, edited by Elie Delieb. In Belgium, Pinḥas Khallenberg, who for 43 years had served as *ḥazzan* of the Central Synagogue in Brussels, died. He had also served as the senior Jewish chaplain of the Belgian army and was known as a painter and writer.

Leo Rosenblatt, for close to half a century *ḥazzan* in the Central Synagogue of Stockholm, retired. His *Ha-Shirim asher le-Yehudah* was published by the Cantors Assembly of New York in 1979.

The memorial day in honor of Salomon *Sulzer in commemoration of 100 years since his death was marked in his city of birth, Hohenems, with the naming of a street after him. In 1990, the Austrian government produced a special postage stamp in his honor. In 1985 Prof. Ḥanoch Avenary published a book devoted to Sulzer and his times. An important work for the field of *ḥazzanut, Hebrew Notated Manuscript Sources up to circa 1840*, written by Prof. Israel Adler, head of Jerusalem's Center for Jewish Music, appeared in 1985.

Three works treating liturgical traditions of Amsterdam Jewish communities appeared; *Shirei Ḥazzanei Amsterdam*, edited by Cantor Hans Blumenthal, is devoted to the prayer services of the Amsterdam Ashkenazi congregation, while *Tenu Shevaḥ ve-Shirah* and *Mi-Yagon le-Simḥah* edited by Cantor Abraham Lopes Cardozo, addresses itself to the tunes of Amsterdam's Portuguese community.

In England the status of *ḥazzanut* declined and the London synagogues were forced to reduce cantors' salaries. In 1988 a concert including cantorial music was given in commemoration of the 50th anniversary of *Kristallnacht*.

Soon after the collapse of the Communist regime in Eastern Europe, concerts of cantorial music were held in Poland, Hungary, Romania, and the area of the former U.S.S.R. with the participation of cantors from Israel and the United States. An academy for Jewish music and *ḥazzanut* was established in Moscow with the support of the Joint Distribution Committee and Cantor Joseph Malovany, its director.

The chief cantor of the Vienna Jewish community, Abraham Adler, who retired in 1992 after holding the position for 17 years, published two volumes of his works as *Zeluta de-Avraham*.

The final stamp minted by East Germany prior to its reunification with West Germany in 1991 featured the composer Louis Lewandowski, who had been the choir conductor at the Oranienburgerstrasse synagogue in Berlin, a synagogue destroyed on *Kristallnacht* and now being restored.

In 1985 a Joseph Schmidt Archive was established in Rueti near Zurich. The collection contains recordings, documents, announcements, and much other material on the life history of the singer and cantor Joseph Schmidt. The initiator of the archive and its director is Alfred Fassbind, who in commemoration of the 50th anniversary of Schmidt's death published a biography on him. The book, *"Ein Lied geht um die Welt" – Spuren einer Legende, Eine Biographie – Joseph Schmidt* (1992), includes the first discography of Schmidt's recordings.

UNITED STATES. The various cantors' associations continued to conduct schools for *ḥazzanut*, and in addition they existed in conjunction with Yeshiva University (Orthodox), the Jewish Theological Seminary (Conservative), and the Hebrew Union College (Reform).

The Cantors Assembly of the United States, the largest of its kind in the world, published a quarterly *Journal of Synagogue Music*, as well as compositions by individual outstanding *ḥazzanim*, both past and present day, many of them hitherto unknown.

The oldest association of *ḥazzanim* in the United States, "the Jewish Ministers'" Cantors' Association of America expanded its activities and for the first time in many years held a conference in Atlantic City in 1980, on Ḥazzanut in the Eighties.

The largest center in the world for cantorial music is the United States, where great changes took place in the field of *ḥazzanut* in the 1980s and 1990s. Orthodox synagogues hardly employ any professional cantors, and in Conservative and Reform synagogues the main function of the cantor is that of musical director. Most of the Orthodox cantors belong to the Cantorial Council of America which holds a convention yearly and publishes an annual volume.

The Cantors Assembly held two conventions in Israel, one in 1987, marking 20 years of a united Jerusalem, and the second in 1992, noting 25 years of a united city. In addition, in 1991, during the Gulf War, a delegation of its members went to Israel and gave concerts as a sign of identification with the State of Israel. A special committee, led by Cantor Sol Mendelson, was set up to maintain links with Israel.

Among cantorial activities of note in the U.S. were Special Sabbaths organized by Park Synagogue in New York City devoted to the works of cantors and composers of earlier generations as well as contemporary ones. In charge of music activities in Park Synagogue was the cantor David Lefkowitz and the conductor Abraham Kaplan.

In commemoration of 100 years since the death of Solomon Sulzer a symposium was held in his memory sponsored by the Hebrew Union College, the Jewish Theological Seminary of America, the Leo Baeck Institute, and the Austrian Cultural Institute. Selections of prayers set to his music were aired and a special exhibit was mounted in his memory. The director of the event was Dr. Neil Levin.

Among the most famous U.S. cantors of this generation were Shlomo Katz (d. 1982), David Koussevitzky (d. 1985), Samuel Malovsky (d. 1985), and Ẓevi Aharoni (d. 1990). In Aharoni's honor, the University of Florida at Boca Raton established a memorial room which houses the important books in the fields of cantorial and Jewish music.

Books of notes in the sphere of cantorial music which appeared in the U.S. include *Chosen Voices* (1989) by Mark Slobin, surveying the history of *ḥazzanut* in the U.S.; *Synagogue Song in America* (1989) by Joseph A. Levin; and *The Golden Age of Cantors* (1992), edited by Velvel Pasternak and Noah Schall, which contains works by cantors of the "Golden Age" in America, biographies, an introduction by Irene Heskes, and cassettes tapes of the cantors performing their works.

Compact discs containing cantorial music have begun to appear; some feature contemporary cantors, others are recordings of music which previously appeared on phonograph records. There are also now video tapes of cantors. Of particular interest is a video made in 1990 by the National Center for Jewish Film of Brandeis University and produced by Sharon Puker Rivo and Cantor Murray E. Simon. It is of a film originally made in 1931 with the cantors Yossele Rosenblatt, Mordechai Herschman, Adolf Katchko, David Roitman, and Joseph Shlisky. Added to the film now are explanatory comments by the cantor, Prof. Max Wohlberg.

[Akiva Zimmerman]

Women in the Cantorate

Throughout most of Jewish history the cantor, or *ḥazzan*, was male. Ordination of women as cantors began in the United States in the 1970s. Between 1975 and 2000, several hundred female cantors were ordained. The major Jewish legal (halakhic) issue to be overcome was that of a woman fulfilling the obligation (*ḥiyyuv*) of public prayer for men who would say "Amen" to her blessing (*berakhah*). This ability and responsibility of the representative of the congregation (*shali'aḥ ẓibbur*) to fulfill the obligation (*le-hoẓi et ha-kahal*) for the community is central to the cantorial role. Because of this representative role, many traditional legal scholars believe that it is more complex to invest women as cantors than it is to ordain them as rabbis.

The Reform movement was the first to ordain women as cantors. As of 2005, three-quarters of all graduates from Hebrew Union College's (HUC) School of Sacred Music in New York were women. Worldwide, more than half of Reform cantors are women and there is some concern that the role of cantor in the Reform movement will be redefined into a female profession.

In the Conservative movement, the number of female cantors grew from zero to 30 percent between 1985 and 2005. Unlike the protracted national process that preceded the acceptance of women into the Rabbinical Assembly and as students in the rabbinical school, the 1984 admission of women to the cantorial program of the Cantors Institute of the Jewish Theological Seminary (JTS), where women had always been admitted as students of Jewish music, was accomplished by the decision of JTS chancellor Ismar *Schorsch. This led to some resentment among cantors in the field. Although JTS first ordained women cantors in 1986, the professional association of Conservative cantors (Cantors Assembly) did not admit them to membership until 1990.

By 2005, U.S. Reform (Hebrew Union College), Conservative (Jewish Theological Seminary), and Reconstructionist (Reconstructionist Rabbinical College) movements, as well as trans-denominational programs at Gratz College in Philadelphia and Hebrew College in Boston had formal training programs for cantors which ordained women. These *ḥazzanim* not only led services and educational programs; they also presided at life-cycle events, such as weddings and funerals.

[Rela M. Geffen (2nd ed.)]

BIBLIOGRAPHY: Baron, Community, index; Baron, Social[2], index; Idelsohn, Music; Sendrey, Music, 65–66, 75–80, 91–97, 201–7, 211ff., 336–7; Jewish Ministers Cantors' Association of America, *Di Geshikhte fun Khazzones* (Yid. and Eng., 1924); idem, *Khazzones* (Yid. and Eng., 1937); idem, *50 Yoriger Yovl Zhurnal* (Yid. and Eng., 1947); P. Gradenwitz, *Music of Israel* (1949); H.H. Harris, *Toledot ha-Neginah ve-ha-Hazzanut be-Yisrael* (1950); I. Rabinovitch, *Of Jewish Music* (1952); N. Stolnitz, *Negine in Yidishn Lebn* (Yid. and Eng., 1957); I. Shalita, *Ha-Musikah ha-Yehudit ve-Yozereha* (1960); I. Heskes (ed.), *The Cantorial Art* (1966); A.M. Rothmueller, *Music of the Jews* (1967[2]).

ḤAZZAN, ISRAEL MOSES BEN ELIEZER (1808–1863), rabbi and author. Ḥazzan was born in Smyrna, and in 1811 went with his father to *Jerusalem, where he studied in the yeshivah of his grandfather Joseph Raphael *Ḥazzan. In 1842 Israel was appointed a member of the *bet din* in Jerusalem and in 1844 journeyed to London as an emissary of the Jerusalem community. During his stay in London he wrote a pamphlet, *Divrei Shalom ve-Emet*, against a pamphlet issued by the recently established Reform movement in England; and another pamphlet against the decisions of the Rabbinical Synod at Brunswick under the title *Kinat Ẓiyyon* (Amsterdam, 1846). The same year he joined a group established for the purpose of fighting the Reform movement. He later went to Rome, where he was appointed rabbi (1847–54), and interceded on behalf of the Jews of Italy in the court of Pope Pius IX. From Rome he proceeded to Corfu, where he was rabbi for five years. He was then invited to *Alexandria, serving as rabbi and *av bet din* there until the end of 1862. He then settled in *Haifa but died in *Beirut, where he had gone on account of ill-health. His remains were taken for burial to Sidon since it was regarded as being within the borders of Ereẓ Israel. Ḥazzan also wrote *Naḥalah le-Yisrael* (Vienna, 1851), on the obligation of deciding laws of inheritance according to Torah; *Kedushat Yom Tov (ibid.*, 1855), against the attempt in Italy to abolish the second day of the festivals; and *She'-erit ha-Naḥalah* (Alexandria, 1862), a dispute between a merchant and two emissaries of Ereẓ Israel. It was later combined with the *Naḥalah le-Yisrael* (1862) but is part of a work *Neẓaḥ Yisrael*, which has remained in manuscript and is an attack on the *Vikku'aḥ al Ḥokhmat ha-Kabbalah* of S.D. *Luzzatto. Other works are *Iyyei 'ha-Yam*, in two parts (pt. 1 Leghorn, 1869; pt. 2 is still in manuscript), a commentary on the responsa of the *geonim*, and *Kerakh shel Romi* (Leghorn, 1876), responsa. Still in manuscript are *Ḥoker Lev*, responsa, and *Yismaḥ Lev*, sermons preached in Jerusalem and during his activity as an emissary.

BIBLIOGRAPHY: Frumkin-Rivlin, 3 (1929), 303; A. Galanté, *Les Juifs d'Izmir* (1937), 74f.; M.D. Gaon, *Yehudei ha-Mizraḥ be-Ereẓ Yisrael*, 2 (1938), 251f.; Yaari, Sheluhei, 176f., 729–32.

[Simon Marcus]

HE (Heb. ה; הֵא) the fifth letter of the Hebrew alphabet; its numerical value is therefore 5; pronounced as a fricative laryngeal. The earliest Proto-Canaanite form of the *he* is a pictograph of a calling (or praying) man. This developed in South Arabic into and in the Phoenician script into . Variants of the latter form survived in the Hebrew , Samaritan , and Greek (and Latin) "E", where it became the vowel *epsilon*. The Aramaic *he* unified the two lower horizontal bars into one vertical . This form was adopted by the Jewish script, but later the left vertical separated from the upper horizontal stroke . The Natatean *he* joined the two downstrokes and thus the Arabic developed. ה' is used as an abbreviation for the Divine Name. It is also frequently found on *amulets where it signifies the five fingers of the hand. See *Alphabet, Hebrew.

[Joseph Naveh]

HEAD, COVERING OF THE. Jewish tradition requires men to cover the head as a sign of humility before God, and women, as evidence of modesty before men, although the Bible does not explicitly command either men or women to cover the head.

Men

According to the description of the priestly garb in Exodus (28:4, 37, 40), the high priest wore a miter (*miẓnefet*), and the ordinary priests a hat (*migba'at*). It was generally considered a sign of mourning to cover the head and face (II Sam. 15:30, 19:5; Jer. 14:3–4; Esth. 6:12). In talmudic times, too, men expressed their sense of grief while mourning by covering their heads, as did *Bar Kappara after the death of *Judah ha-Nasi (TJ, Kil. 9:4, 32b; TJ, Ket. 12:3, 35a). A mourner, one on whom a ban (**ḥerem*) had been pronounced, and a leper, were, in fact, obliged to cover their heads (MK 15a), as was anyone who fasted in times of drought (Ta'an. 14b). These people had to muffle their heads and faces. It was considered an expression of awe before the Divine Presence to conceal the head and face, especially while praying or engaged in the study of mysticism (Ḥag. 14b; RH 17b; Ta'an. 20a). The headgear of scholars was an indication of their elevated position (Pes. 11b); some of them claimed that they never walked more than four cubits (about six feet) without a head covering (Shab. 118b; Kid. 31a; also Maim. Yad, De'ot 5:6, and Guide 3:52). The custom was, however, restricted to dignified personages; bachelors doing so were considered presumptuous (Kid. 29b). Artistic representation, such as Egyptian and Babylonian tablets or the synagogue at Dura Europos, generally depict Israelites, (and later Jews) without head covering. On the other hand, some rabbis believed that covering a child's head would ensure his piety and prevent his becoming a thief (Shab. 156b).

According to the Talmud (Ned. 30b), it was optional and a matter of custom for men to cover their heads. Palestinian custom, moreover, did not insist that the head be covered during the priestly benediction (see J. Mueller, *Ḥilluf Minhagim she-bein Benei Bavel u-Venei Ereẓ Yisrael* (1878), 39f., no. 42). French and Spanish rabbinical authorities during the Middle Ages followed this ruling, and regarded the covering of the head during prayer and the study of the Torah merely as a custom. Some of them prayed with a bare head themselves (Abraham b. Nathan of Lunel, *Ha-Manhig* (Berlin, 1855), 15b, no. 45; *Or Zaru'a*, Hilkhot Shabbat 43). Tractate *Soferim* (14:15), however, rules that a person who is improperly dressed and has no headgear may not act as the *ḥazzan* or as the reader of the Torah in the synagogue, and may not invoke the priestly benediction upon the congregation. Moreover, the covering of the head, as an expression of the "fear of God" (*yirat shamayim*), and as a continuation of the practice of the Babylonian scholars (Kid. 31a), was gradually endorsed by the Ashkenazi rabbis. Even they stated, however, that it was merely a worthy custom, and that there was no injunction against praying without a head cover (Maharshal,

Resp. no. 7; *Be'ur ha-Gra* to Sh. Ar., OḤ 8:2). The opinion of David Halevy of Ostrog (17th century) is an exception. He declared that since Christians generally pray bareheaded, the Jewish prohibition to do so was based on the biblical injunction not to imitate the heathen custom (*ḥukkat ha-goi; Magen David* to OḤ 8:2). Traditional Jewry came to equate bareheadedness with unseemly lightmindedness and frivolity (*kallut rosh*), and therefore forbids it (Maim. Yad, De'ot 5:6).

The covering of the head has become one of the most hotly debated points of controversy between Reform and Orthodox Jewry. The latter regards the covering of the head, both outside and inside the synagogue, as a sign of allegiance to Jewish tradition, and demands that at least a skullcap (Heb. *kippah*, Yid. *yarmulka*) be worn. Worship with covered heads is also the accepted rule in Conservative synagogues. In Reform congregations, however, it is optional.

[Meir Ydit]

Women

It was customary for most women in the ancient Near East, Mesopotamia, and the Greco-Roman world to cover their hair when they went outside the home. In biblical times, women covered their heads with veils or scarves. The unveiling of a woman's hair was considered a humiliation and punishment (Isa. 3:17; cf. Num. 5:18 on the loosening of the hair of a woman suspected of adultery; III Macc. 4:6; and Sus. 32).

In talmudic times, too, married women were enjoined to cover their hair in communal spaces (e.g., Ned. 30b; Num. R. 9:16). In a society so highly conscious of sexuality and its dangers, veiling was considered an absolute necessity to maintain modesty and chastity. If a woman walked bareheaded in the street, her husband could divorce her without repaying her dowry (Ket. 7:6). Some rabbis compared the exposure of a married woman's hair to the exposure of her private parts (Ber. 24a), and forbade the recitation of any blessing in the presence of a bareheaded woman (*ibid.*). The rabbis praised pious women such as Kimhit, the mother of several high priests, who took care not to uncover their hair even in the house (Yoma 47a; Lev. R. 20:11). Nevertheless, covering the head was a personal imposition and restriction from which men were glad to be exempt. According to Sotah 3:8, men differ from women in that they may appear in public "with hair unbound and in torn garments." In Eruvin 100b, one of the disadvantages or "curses" that is cited as an inevitable part of being female includes being "wrapped up like a mourner." Some aggadic sources interpret this custom as a sign of woman's shame and feeling of guilt for Eve's sin (Gen. R. 17:8; ARN² 9; Er. 100b and Rashi ad loc.; cf., also, the opinion of Paul in I Cor. 11:1–16). Girls did not have to cover their hair until the wedding ceremony (Ket. 2:1). It gradually became the accepted traditional custom for all Jewish women to cover their hair (see Sh. Ar., EH 21:2).

In the early modern period the practice of a woman's shaving off all her hair upon marriage and covering her head with a kerchief (*tichal*) became widespread in Hungarian, Galician, and Ukrainian Jewish communities. Justifications for this stringency were to ensure that a married woman's hair would never be exposed and to eliminate the possibility of a woman's hair rising to the surface during her ritual immersion in the *mikveh*, rendering it invalid. Opponents argued that shaving the head would make a woman unattractive to her husband. Toward the end of the 18th century some circles of women began to wear a wig (*shaytl*). This "innovation" was opposed by certain Orthodox authorities such as Moses *Sofer (see A.J. Schlesinger, *Lev ha-Ivri*, 2 (1928³), 109, 189) but continued to be widely practiced. In the early 21st century, a diverse range of customs connected with hair covering are followed by Orthodox Jewish women. Among some modern Orthodox women, there has been renewed interest in various modes of covering the hair after marriage. Many women who are not Orthodox continue the custom of covering their hair in synagogue.

[Judith R. Baskin (2nd ed.)]

BIBLIOGRAPHY: L. Loew, in: *Ben Chananja*, 6 (1863), 102–27, reprinted with alterations in his: *Gesammelte Schriften*, 2 (1890), 311–28; Buechler, in: WZKM, 19 (1905), 91–138; S. Carlebach, in: *Festschrift… D. Hoffmann* (1914), 454–9, and Heb. part, 218–47; Krauss, in: MGWJ, 67 (1923), 189–92; and Aptowitzer's reply *ibid.*, 195–9, 200–2; Goldziher, in: *Der Islam*, 6 (1915), 301–16; Lauterpach, in: CCARY, 38 (1928), 589–603; L.M. Epstein, *Sex Laws and Customs in Judaism* (1948), 46–55. **ADD. BIBLIOGRAPHY:** L.L. Bronner, "From Veil to Wig: Jewish Women's Hair Covering," in: *Judaism*, 42:4 (1993), 465–77; N.B. Joseph, "Hair Distractions: Women and Worship in the Responsa of Rabbi Moshe Feinstein," in: M.D. Halpern and C. Safrai (eds.), *Jewish Legal Writings by Women* (1998); M.M. Levine, "The Gendered Grammar of Ancient Mediterranean Hair," in: H. Eilberg-Schwartz and W. Doniger (eds.), *Off with Her Head! The Denial of Women's Identity in Myth, Religion, and Culture* (1995), 76–130; L. Schreiber (ed.), *Hide and Seek: Jewish Women and Hair Covering* (2003); M. Schiller, "The Obligation of Married Women to Cover their Hair," in: *The Journal of Halacha*, 30 (1995), 81–108.

HEAD, EDITH (1897–1981), U.S. costume designer. Head was born Edith Claire Posener to Max and Anna Posener (née Levy) in San Bernardino, California. When her mother divorced and remarried, Edith took her stepfather's surname, Spare, and adopted his Roman Catholic faith. The family moved to Los Angeles when Head was 12. She received an undergraduate degree from the University of California at Berkeley and a master's degree in French from Stanford University in 1920. She returned to Southern California to teach at the Hollywood School for Girls. When asked to teach an art course at the school, Head signed up for night classes at the Otis Art Institute and then the Chouinard School of Art. In 1923, she married Charles Head, but the couple divorced in 1938; however, Head would use his surname for the rest of her life. Head responded to an advertisement from Paramount for a costume design artist in 1923 and won the position by borrowing designs from art school students at Chouinard. In 1927, she was appointed assistant to Travis Banton, Paramounts chief costume designer. Her first film credit as a costume designer was for the Mae West film *She Done Him Wrong* (1933). In 1938, Head became the first woman to lead a studio's costume department. Barabara Stanwyck even had Head written into her contract after her deft handling of the numerous costume changes in *The Lady Eve* (1941). In 1945 she started making regular appearances on Art Linkletter's *House Party* to give fashion advice to women, which was followed by her advice books *The Dress Doctor* (1959) and *How to Dress for Success* (1967) and later a syndicated advice column. In 1946, she worked on the film *Notorious*, which began a 30-year collaboration with director Alfred Hitchcock. Head received her first Oscar nomination for costume design in 1948 for *The Emperor Waltz*; she was nominated a total of 34 times in her career, winning Oscars for *The Heiress* (1949), *Samson and Delilah* (1949), *All About Eve* (1950), *A Place in the Sun* (1951), *Roman Holiday* (1953), *Sabrina* (1954), *The Facts of Life* (1960), and *The Sting* (1973). When Paramount failed to renew her contract in 1967, Head went to Universal, where her six-decade career finally came to an end in 1981 with her 1,131st film, the Steve Martin comedy noir *Dead Men Don't Wear Plaid* (1982).

[Adam Wills (2nd ed.)]

HEAPS, ABRAHAM ALBERT (1885–1954), Canadian Labour leader, politician. Heaps was born in Leeds, England and attended school until 13, when he went to work to help support his family. He apprenticed as an upholsterer, and opened his own workshop and managed a large furniture store before he immigrated to Canada in 1911.

Once in Winnipeg, Heaps worked as an upholsterer for the Canadian Pacific Railway and became active in the local labor movement. He also joined the English branch of the Social Democratic Party of Canada, and was a pacifist in World War I. After two failed attempts to secure a seat as alderman, Heaps was elected in a 1917 by-election and subsequently won his seat easily.

Heaps was one of the main leaders of the Winnipeg General Strike, heading the strikers' Relief Committee. He was charged with seditious conspiracy and, after his release on bail, traveled to various Canadian cities to raise support and funds for the defense of the strikers. His conducted his own defense at his 1920 trial, and was the only one acquitted of the eight charged with seditious conspiracy.

After several years in the insurance business, Heaps was elected in 1925 to the federal House of Commons. He served as a Member of Parliament representing the heavily Jewish riding of Winnipeg North until 1940, first for the Independent Labour Party and then for the Co-operative Commonwealth Federation (CCF). He served as parliamentary whip for the CCF after 1935, and with the head of the CCF, J.S. Woodsworth, he strongly advocated the passage of social legislation, such as the federal old age pension and unemployment insurance.

Heaps' greatest sense of failure was his inability to convey the threat of the totalitarian regimes in Russia, Italy, and especially Germany. Resorting first to quiet diplomacy, he tried in vain to convince the federal government to open Canada up to desperate Jewish refugees from Hitler's Germany. He was no more successful with the public condemnation of the government of Mackenzie King. Despite Heaps' often-stated belief in the complete and vigorous prosecution of the Canadian war effort in World War II, Woodsworth's opposition to the declaration of war in September 1939 made Heaps suspect as well, and he was defeated in the federal election of 1940. Heaps subsequently held several government jobs, before moving to Montreal, where he briefly worked in the dress industry and as an arbitrator of labor disputes before his retirement.

Heaps married Bessie Morris (d. 1938) in 1913, and they had two sons, David and Leo, both of whom earned the Military Cross for distinguished wartime records. Leo also served with the Israeli army during the War of Independence. Heaps remarried in 1947, to Fanny Almond.

BIBLIOGRAPHY: H. and M. Gutkin, *Profiles in Dissent: The Shaping of Radical Thought in the Canadian West* (1997); L. Heaps, *Rebel in the House: The Life and Times of A.A. Heaps, M.P.* (rev. ed., 1984).

[Henry Trachtenberg (2nd ed.)]

HEART (Heb. לֵב, *lev*, pl. לִבּוֹת, *libbot*; לֵבָב, *levav*, pl. לְבָבוֹת, *levavot*). The corresponding Hebrew words only sometimes have the meanings in question but many translators and writers on Bible are, or act as if they were, largely unaware of the fact.

STRICTLY ANATOMICAL SENSES OF LEV AND LEVAV

Senses That Do Not Include the Heart

BREAST. The current English translations reveal an awareness that in Nahum 2:8 [7] *levav* means not heart but breast and rightly represent the women as "beating their breasts"; but breast is no less certainly the meaning of *lev* in Exodus 28:29–30 (three times in all). Again, in II Samuel 18:14–15, since it is only the attack of 10 of Joab's henchmen that finishes Absalom off after their leader has stuck three darts into the victim's *lev*, those darts must have been stuck, not into his heart, but into his breast. Somewhat similar is the case of II Kings 9:23–24. Jehoram is trying to flee from Jehu in his chariot, but an arrow from Jehu's bow overtakes him and strikes him "between the arms." Now, the rendering of some recent Bible translations (most recently NEB), "between the shoulders," is perhaps too free, but it is historically correct, since it can be seen on contemporary Assyrian reliefs that the lowness of the chariot floor compelled the charioteer to extend his arms horizontally when, like Jehoram here (verse 23), he held the reins in his hands. Add to this that the ground was level (Jezreel), and Jehu only a short distance behind Jehoram, and one must wonder what view of the course of the arrow through the hapless Omrid's chest was adopted by the same translators to account for the statement that "the arrow pierced his heart." What the words *va-yeẓe* (*wa-yeẓe'*) *ha-ḥeẓi mi-libbo* do mean is – word for word – "and the arrow emerged from his breast." Probably Jeremiah 17:1 is still another instance. This sense of *lev*, by the way, is not confined to biblical Hebrew (see Sot. 1:5; Mak. 3:12). The word *ḥazeh* ("breast"), unlike its Aramaic etymon, seems to have been used only of animals so long as Hebrew was a living language.

THROAT. This is what *lev* means in Isaiah 33:18; Psalms 19:15; 49:4; Job 8:10; Ecclesiastes 5:1. *Lev* is either parallel to *peh* ("mouth") or associated with the root *hgy* (which always denotes audible sounds, including the coo of the dove (Isa. 38:14; 59:11), the growl of the lion (Isa. 31:4), and the twang of the lyre (Ps. 92:4), and never silent meditation), or both, with the exception of Job 8:10, in which *lev* alternates with the *peh* of the otherwise identical phrase in 15:13. In fact, *lev* is the proper word for "throat" in biblical Hebrew, *garon* taking its place only where the former would be misunderstood (as where *lo' yehgu be-libbam* would have meant not, "They cannot utter sounds with their throats," but "They do not speak sincerely," see Hos. 7:14).

Senses that Include the Heart

Even where the word *lev* clearly refers to something inside the body cavity, it does not always mean specifically the heart. It doubtless does when it is paired with "kidneys" (Jer. 11:20; 17:10; Ps. 7:10; 73:21), but probably more often it merely conveys the general idea of "the insides, the interior of the body"; and from this sense derives its use with *yam(mim)* ("sea(s)") and *ha-shamayim* ("the air" or "space") to express the notions "(far) out at sea" and "(high) up in the air (in space)" (Ex. 15:8; Ezek. 27:4, 25–27; 28:2, 8; Ps. 46:3; Prov. 23:34).

NOT STRICTLY ANATOMICAL SENSES OF LEV AND LEVAV

The interior of the body is conceived of as the seat of the inner life, of feeling and thought. Strong feeling is conceived of as a stirring or heating of the intestines (*me'ayim*) – Isaiah 16:11; Jeremiah 4:19 [20]; Lamentations 1:20 – as well as of the heart – Deuteronomy 19:6; Jeremiah 48:36; Psalms 39:4. Gladness is a function not only of the heart (e.g., Prov. 23:15) but also of the kidneys (Prov. 23:16; cf. Jer. 12:2b), which also urge a certain course on a man. But it is the *lev(av)* that figures most often in references to the inner life, both emotional and – and this is its special sphere – intellectual. That is why when *lev(av)* is mentioned alone it is often hard to decide whether the underlying physical concept is specifically the heart or the inwards generally. At any rate, the Bible never mentions about the *lev(av)* anything that is literally physical, such as a heartbeat; nor does it ever mention any literal pain or ailment of it. That somebody's "heart" is sick means that he is grieving; that Israel's "heart" is obstructed (older translations, regrettably, "uncircumcised") signifies that it is religiously stubborn and intractable – cutting away the obstruction of Israel's "heart" of course means making it religiously reasonable. So, too, that a man says something "in his heart" means that he says it to himself, or thinks it; that he is "wise of heart" means that he is intelligent or skillful. One who has no "heart" is a dolt. A faithful English translation is precisely one that in most cases does not contain the word "heart," but either substitutes "mind," or sometimes "spirit," or – quite often – does not render the noun at all; for it is often hard to feel, let alone express, the differences between such pairs as "gladness of 'heart'" and plain "gladness," "he rejoiced 'in his heart'" and the bare "he rejoiced," etc. On the other hand, in the interests of both aesthetics and usefulness, "heart" should be substituted in English for the emotional kidneys and intestines of biblical Hebrew: the King James "my bowels were moved for him" (Song 5:4) is not either more beautiful or more enlightening than something like "my heart yearned for him." Finally, on the one hand the word *levav* illustrates biblical Hebrew's lack of a terminology for distinguishing clearly between mind (or "soul") and body; for when Psalms 104:15 says that bread fortifies a man's *levav* while wine cheers a man's *levav*, the first *levav* means "insides" if not actually "body," but the second one means "spirit." Nevertheless, the words *lev* and *levav* enable the language to come close to distinguishing between the two, the former by juxtaposition with *basar* (בָּשָׂר) the latter by juxtaposition with *she'er* (שְׁאֵר), two words meaning "body" (lit. "flesh"; see Ps. 73:26; 84:3; Eccles 2:3; 11:10). Psalms 73:26 helps us to detect the fact that the word ראש (*ro'sh*; "head") in Isaiah 1:5 is a corruption, due to contamination by the *ro'sh* in the following verse, of an original *she'er*, the restoration of which yields for Isaiah 1:5b the sense, "Every body (not just the head but the entire body, see verse 6) is sore and every spirit is anguished."

[Harold Louis Ginsberg]

IN THE TALMUD AND AGGADAH

The rabbis adopted the biblical view that the heart is the seat of the emotions, and they applied this notion to every sphere of human action and thought. It is doubtful if they were aware of the circulation of the blood and the part played in this by the heart, but they did state that "all the organs of the body are dependent on the heart" (TJ, Ter. 8:10, 46b). In the list of ailments and maladies which render an animal *terefah* – defects from which they cannot recover – is the perforation of the heart (Ḥul. 3:1).

However, most of the references to the heart in talmudic literature belong to the sphere of ethics. When each of the five disciples of *Johanan b. Zakkai was asked to express his view on "the good way to which a man should cleave and the evil way which he should shun," Johanan gave his approval to the answers of R. Eleazer b. Arakh, "a good heart" and an "evil heart," since "the answers of all the others are included in his" (Avot 2:9). The heart is the seat of all emotions, both good and bad, and commenting on the fact that the longer form *levav* is used in Deuteronomy 6:5 "thou shalt love the Lord thy God with all thy heart," the Talmud emphasizes that even the evil inclination can be impressed into the service of

God, "with both thy inclinations" (the good and the bad; Ber. 54a). The frequently quoted statement, "the All Merciful requires [only] the heart" is not found in that form in the Talmud, but is stated by Rashi (to Sanh. 106b) on the basis of an assertion of similar content.

Prayer is referred to as "the service of the heart" (TJ, Ber. 4:1, 7a). The word **kavvanah* ("intention," "direction") is found in its fuller and in its verbal form as "the direction of the heart." Thus a person who in the course of reading reaches the **Shema* at the time for the obligatory reading of that passage as part of the liturgy: "If he directed his heart he had fulfilled [this obligation]" (Ber. 2:1). The **etrog*, which is regarded as the fruit of perfection, is compared on the basis of its shape to the heart (Lev. R. 30:14). The hypocrite is described as he who is "one thing in the mouth and another in the heart" (BM 49a). On the verse "I communed with my own heart" (Eccles. 1:16) the Midrash (Eccles. R. 1:16) enumerates over 60 emotions of the heart, "the heart sees, hears, speaks, falls, stands, rejoices, weeps, comforts, sorrows, can be arrogant, can be broken, etc.," each one demonstrated by an appropriate verse from Scripture.

For the halakhic problems connected with heart transplants, see *Transplants.

[Louis Isaac Rabinowitz]

BIBLIOGRAPHY: Y.S. Licht, in: EM, 4 (1962), 411–5 (incl. bibl.); H.L. Ginsberg, in: VT, supplement, 16 (1967), 80.

HEARTFIELD, JOHN (1891–1968), German photographer, graphic artist, and caricaturist; pioneer of artistic photomontage and collage. Born in Berlin as Helmut Herzfeld, he enrolled at the Munich Arts and Crafts School in 1908 and at the Berlin Arts and Crafts School to continue his studies in 1913. In 1916, as a protest against German hostilities against England he changed his name to John Heartfield. At the end of World War I, in 1918, he joined the German Communist party (KPD) together with his friend George Grosz. In 1917 they founded the satirical journal *Die Pleite* ("The Crash") together with John's brother Wieland, for which he created his first political and satirical posters directed against Fascism by using the technique of photomontage. In 1929, at the International Werkbund exhibition in Stuttgart, he showed several of his collages and photomontages in journals and as book covers under the heading *Benuetze Foto als Waffe* ("Make Use of Photography as a Weapon"). He also illustrated *Deutschland, Deutschland ueber alles*, a satirical book written by Kurt Tucholsky. As a member of the Communist Party and on the staff of the *Arbeiter-Illustrierten-Zeitung*, a weekly newspaper for working people, he published satirical attacks and was already a thorn in the side of the Nazis and had to flee after their rise to power in 1933. He was able to continue his activities first from Prague and later from Paris, where he met Walter *Benjamin in 1935. In 1938, he settled in London and received permission to work as a freelance cartoonist in 1943. After the war, he returned to East Berlin, became a much-honored professor there at the Academy of Fine Arts, and had many exhibitions in Communist Berlin, Warsaw, Moscow, and Prague. Most of Heartfield's montages foreshadow the catastrophe of World War II, such as the cover of a journal under the title *Italy in Chains* (1928). Among his most famous posters was the one called *As in the Middle Ages... So in the Third Reich* (1934), featuring a dead body braided onto the swastika.

BIBLIOGRAPHY: P. Pachnicke and K. Honnef: *John Heartfield* (1992).

[Philipp Zschommler (2nd ed.)]

HEBER (Heb. חֶבֶר and חֵבֶר; "community").

(1) Heber son of Beriah son of *Asher son of Jacob (Num. 26:45) was among those who accompanied Jacob to Egypt (Gen. 46:17). He is the eponymous ancestor of the Asherite clan Heber (Num. 26:45). The importance of the clan is evident from the centrality of the genealogical listing of the sons of Heber among the Asherites (I Chron. 7:32–39).

(2) Heber the *Kenite, a descendant of Hobab, the father-in-law of Moses (Judg. 4:11), and the husband of *Jael (Judg. 4:17, 21; 5:24), who slew *Sisera. Heber had previously separated himself from the Kenites, the descendants of Hobab who dwelt in the Negev among the *Amalekites, and pitched his tents near Elon-Bezaanannim (Judg. 4:11; cf. I Sam. 15:6).

BIBLIOGRAPHY: W.F. Albright, *Yahweh and the Gods of Canaan* (1968), 36.

HEBRAISTS, CHRISTIAN (1100–1890). Factors governing gentile enterprises in Hebrew scholarship prior to the latest phase of more widespread secular attitudes may be distinguished as (1) motivation; (2) scholarly facilities; and (3) occasion; appreciation and assessment of these ought to suffice to set the achievements of gentile Hebraists in the context of the cultural background, including economics, geography, and politico-religious history relevant in each case. Such considerations ought to precede the arbitrary division into chronological periods. Since, however, time and place cannot be ignored, the section numbers that follow will be used for reference back.

(1) **Motivation**. (a) Study of the "Old" Testament and of New Testament origins and presuppositions. It was generally assumed that the Latin Bible (in whatever textform lay before the scholar) corresponded exactly, or at least virtually, with the Hebrew original; but (aa) in the later Middle Ages it was occasionally glimpsed, and from Erasmus' time more frequently appreciated, that the Hebrew Bible and its primary versions each have their own internal text history. (b) Christian commitment to self-identification with the religious experience of Jesus, the apostles and the early Church, which had been formed by reaction to the Hebrew Bible, the institutions, and at first also the language of the Synagogue. This sometimes led to (bb) interest in post-biblical Jewish institutions and their

exploration through verbal contacts with Jews and later from literary sources. The synchronistic assumptions of traditional Judaism regarding the coevality from Sinai of the Pentateuch and the institutional elaboration of Jewish life at its contemporary phase of development (as the modern scholar would consider it) were not questioned, except insofar as the Gospels may obliquely query them. The Christian student thus regarded his Jewish informants as an organically living, though theologically fossilized specimen of the personal, domestic, social, jurisprudential, ethical, and speculative realities of ancient Ereẓ Israel. Curiosity was often aroused by the presence of a vigorous Jewish life as an enclave within Christendom and in part independent of its presuppositions. This also acted as a spur to (c) missionary activity toward the Jews, expressed not only in preaching but (cc) by engagement in controversial disputations. This could easily slip into (d) antisemitism, and the unscrupulous exploitation of rabbinic literature for purposes of anti-Jewish propaganda. (e) The revival of learning in the West, and a religious humanism, discovered anew the notion of the classical language and its literature, and as explained more fully below could accommodate Hebrew within the same intellectual approach. Finally, there is (f) incipient Orientalism, and the exploitation of the Semitic versions of the Bible both as a bridge to the vocabulary, etc., of the cognate languages and as themselves affording tools for the understanding of biblical and post-biblical Hebrew and Aramaic. Archaeological interest, which arose only recently, belongs in this category; its predecessor, the antiquarianism of pilgrim and traveler, falls properly within (b).

(2) **Facilities for Scholarship**. (a) The availability of sources of information regarding Hebrew, Jews, and Judaism of a traditional, approved, and so scholastically recognized caliber, either scattered through the patristic writings, the greatest of which were read and reread throughout the western Church, or encyclopedically arranged. (aa) The invention of printing affected not only the availability of these but also the diffusion of post-scholastic tools – grammars and dictionaries of Hebrew – that could supersede them. (b) The availability of teachers of Hebrew, locally or through migration or invitation: either Jews (who, though unsystematic, were mostly learned in their "lore"), or apostate Jews, or gentiles who had achieved a real competence. (c) Finally, institutions with libraries and endowments: originally the monasteries and the mendicant orders, and later the colleges and universities, *ex hypothesi* institutions for professed Christians, but at the latest stage sometimes modified so as to accept Jews as students and as teachers *de jure*.

(3) **Occasion**, i.e., individual or mass movement and its consequences in interaction. (a) Medieval Christian scholars migrated from northern Europe, especially to Italy and Spain, in search of learning. (b) Jewish scholars and informants moved on, driven by persecution, expulsion, or economic stress, but (bb) sometimes for less urgent causes, and occasionally with a preparedness to accept Christian baptism. (c) Conquests, treaties, revolutions, ecclesiastical settlement or realignment, or liberalizing reform, frequently forced (and occasionally attracted) large-scale movements of Jews. (d) A common language for Jewish tutor and gentile pupil (e.g., Norman French, or English), or mutual intelligibility through closeness of their respective dialects (e.g., Judeo-German and High German, or (Judeo-)Spanish and Latin).

The 12th Century

During the first Christian millennium the Church produced two substantial Hebraists, *Origen and *Jerome (i.e., Hieronymus), whose biblical commentaries were widely read. These, together with *Philo and *Josephus, constituted the basic sources of information on Hebrew and Jewish matters, their data often being taken over unacknowledged. Of the two streams of transmission one was encyclopedic and the other exegetical. Isidore of Seville (seventh century) drew heavily on Jerome in his *Etymologies*, which became the standard work of reference, being utilized in particular by Bede (d. 735) and successively by Hrabanus Maurus and the latter's pupil Walafrid Strabo (c. 808–49). The exegetical tradition is likewise one of plagiarization of the standard Christian commentaries on each book of the Bible.

By the early 12th century this material was being digested, often so succinctly as to reach almost catchword proportions, in the gloss that was becoming a marginal and interlinear accompaniment to manuscripts of the Latin Bible. The gloss also incorporated some matter taken from the encyclopedic stream, and was itself a literary undertaking suggested by the glossation of the standard Western authorities in medicine and law. It seems highly probable that this Christian technique of dealing with voluminous material reckoned to give the "approved" interpretation of an authoritative text was deliberately adopted by *Rashi (1030–1105) as the model for his own succinct running commentaries on the Hebrew Bible and the Talmud.

Rashi's commentaries, which spread rapidly and with acclaim from the Rhineland over Jewish Europe, constitute the first important occasion for a fresh advance in gentile Hebraism. They were not pitched at a specialist rabbinic readership, but were meant for the ordinary educated Jew, and it was generally the latter (or his apostate mutation) rather than the professional rabbi to whom the Christian student turned for help. Northern France, particularly Paris and its environs, formed the locale, and "Romance" the *lingua franca*, as testified by the Cistercian Stephen Harding (d. 1134). Motivation (1, a) was central, but (1, cc) was also operative; for religious controversy with the Synagogue, actively prosecuted by the early Church, had revived in Carolingian times. It stimulated a Jewish apologetic in the commentaries of Rashi and his successors, but little of substance is known about the Christian side in these early public disputations.

Christian initiative came from the abbey of St. Victor, 1110, and its daughter house in England, Wigmore. Hugh of St. Victor, who taught in Paris from about 1125 until 1141, set himself the task of rehabilitating the literal-historical sense of Scripture that had traditionally in Christian exegesis been reckoned the mere handmaid of allegory. His endeavor brought him to the Jews, and to the fallacious assumption – shared by his successors – that all interpretation deriving immediately from Jewish sources must, *ex hypothesi*, be "literal," including midrashic assertions which the Jews themselves would not have regarded too seriously as "facts": for the bare "letter" of Scripture was all that the Jews were deemed to possess. Hugh consulted them regarding their understanding of the Prophets; he also learned some Hebrew, sometimes preferring a literal Latin translation to the established Vulgate reading. Deriving his knowledge from oral informants, he quoted matter found in Rashi, Joseph *Kara, and *Samuel b. Meir (Rashbam). Hugh's pupil *Andrew, an Englishman, was likewise dependent on oral sources, whereas the latter's own pupil, Herbert of Bosham, who was still using oral informants, could clearly read Rashi for himself. But Bosham's commentary on Psalms never circulated. Andrew's extensive works, which cover the Pentateuch and utilized matter from his contemporary Joseph *Bekhor Shor, were widely read in monastic libraries in England and France. They were not only exploited by *Nicholas de Lyre (see below), but were plagiarized by Peter the Digester, author of the standard medieval *Historia Scholastica*, and by preachers (e.g., Archbishop Stephen Langton) whose sermons circulated widely in written form.

During the 12th and 13th centuries Christian scholars were prosecuting their search for the philosophical and scientific texts of Greek antiquity and late antiquity in Italy, Sicily, southern France, and Spain. This sometimes brought them to Jewish interpreters, or to Hebrew versions of Aristotle and others made from the Arabic; but their concern with the intermediate Hebrew was incidental only, except insofar as it related to *Maimonides and – later on – other philosophers of Judaism who had written in Arabic and had been translated into Hebrew. It is a fair assumption – but no more – that the Latin-speaking translators of these Arabic texts, such as Gundissalinus, would have acquired some Hebrew alongside their study of Arabic. But in those cases where they were either dependent on a Hebrew version, or were collating one with its antecedent Arabic, they may very well have relied entirely on a Jewish collaborator.

The Rise of the Mendicant Orders

The year 1210 saw the foundation of the Franciscans, whose Hebrew interests were mainly motivated by (1, b), and 1215 that of the Dominicans or Preachers, who, responding primarily to (1, c) and (1, cc), sited their houses when possible near Jewish quarters or actually within them, as at Oxford. Their missionary zeal was directed also toward Muslims, and consequently to Spain where many Jews spoke Arabic, and led a few Dominicans to study Arabic and others Hebrew; they may have established a Hebrew school at Paris in about 1236. The efforts of the Franciscans have left more trace in England, due largely to the encouragement of Robert Grosseteste (d. 1253), bishop of Lincoln, and to the pioneering endeavors of Roger *Bacon, himself an author of Greek and Hebrew grammars, who grasped the cognate nature of Hebrew, Aramaic, and Arabic. An interlinear glossation of the Hebrew Bible (*superscriptio Lincolniensis*) reflects in its name Grosseteste's encouragement: it follows the Hebrew word order with syllabically literal faithfulness, and often reflects Rashi's exegesis and develops his Norman-French glosses. The Psalms version survives complete, and fragments of other parts of the Bible, but coverage was probably not completed; and Henry of Cossey, a Cambridge Franciscan (d. 1336), in saying that the Church had "not yet" authorized the version, may imply domestic aspiration or a serious project. The collaboration of Jews, possibly reluctant and still faithful rather than apostates, has been proved. Thus facility (2, b) was apparently available preeminently in France and England, and the English expulsion of 1290 (occasion type 2, b) may have increased potential consultants in Paris and elsewhere.

The result of this (and doubtless other unrecorded) interest, alongside motive (1, aa; see below) was the enactment of the ecclesiastical Council of Vienne (1312) – thanks to the efforts of the Arabist Raymond Lull – that two teaching posts each for Greek, Hebrew, Syriac, and Arabic should be established at Paris, Oxford, Bologna, and Salamanca respectively. In Oxford the converted Jew John of Bristol taught Hebrew and Greek for a few years from 1321, and in Paris and Salamanca the Hebrew chair was staffed for about a century, but that of Paris certainly thereafter lapsed. The *superscriptio* was forgotten, possibly being overshadowed by the commentary of the Franciscan Nicholas de Lyre to the entire Bible. Leaning on Andrew and heavily impregnated by independent use of Rashi, it was later supplemented by the apostate Paul of Burgos (see Pablo de Santa *Maria) (d. 1435) from *Ibn Ezra and *Kimḥi. The Christian student apparently now felt that he could skip the Hebrew text, and its linguistic study hibernated until the late 15th century. Lyre's supplemented "*Postillae*" became, alongside the *Historia Scholastica* (see above), the standard source for Jewish exegetical matter; Lyre's work was the first Christian commentary to reach print (1471–72), long retaining its place.

The other contributory stimulus (1, a; 1, aa) was the endeavor to correct and standardize the text of the Latin Vulgate, initiative here lying with the Dominicans, although the Franciscan *correctoria*, profiting from their predecessors' experience, were more influential. The general effect, however (in default of print), was to leave confusion worse confounded, as Bacon (criticizing the Dominican *correctoria*) pointed out with great emphasis; the reason partly being failure to separate the task of establishing the "best" Vulgate text (i.e., the purest or the fullest, according to standpoint), from that of collating the current (let alone the most primitive) Latin text with the current Hebrew, whose uncompromised originality was presupposed. Such Hebrew expertise as is evinced in this work is associated with the Dominican Hugh of St. Cher (d. 1263) of Paris, and with the Franciscan William of Mara (fl. 1280), whose Hebrew scholarship was enthusiastically acclaimed by Bacon. The only permanent effect of this activity was a unified chapter division since adopted (with slight exceptions) by Jews in the Hebrew text as well.

Missionary activity in Spain also led the Dominicans to investigate post-biblical Jewish literature, with a view to the refutation of matter therein allegedly incompatible with Christianity. In Raymond *Martini the Dominicans produced a scholar unusually versed in rabbinic literature, whose controversialist *collectaneum* (*Pugio fidei*) contains some extracts – now considered genuine – from Jewish sources which are no longer extant. A similar 13th-century enterprise, by French Dominicans led by Theobald, excerpted a number of allegedly objectionable *extractiones de Talmude* (including some from Rashi's commentary), the continued influence of which even into the age of print is only now becoming clearer. The *Pugio Fidei* remained a standard source for anti-Jewish polemic, which hovered between motives (1, cc) and (1, d). In the public *Disputations (1, cc) forced on the Jews, initiative came largely from apostates and from the Dominicans; and since most of the apostates (e.g., Pablo *Christiani, or Gerónimo de Santa Fé, alias Joshua (al-) *Lorki) were at best amateur rabbinists of inferior competence to their Jewish respondents, the Hebrew scholarship adduced on the Christian side was largely repetitive. After the Reformation, Protestant tractarians were able somewhat to enlarge the repertoire (see e.g., Johann *Eisenmenger).

Jewish Scientific Writings

In addition to Christian concern in the Hebrew Bible and messianic and similar passages in talmudic literature, there sometimes was an interest in Hebrew texts which were recognized as being both Jewish, and also creatively new, in a way that Talmud and Midrash were not: namely, scientific writings. This does not refer to the recovery of the older Greek texts through Arabic and Hebrew versions as described above, but rather to the near contemporary works – medical, mathematical, astronomical, etc. – of Abraham Ibn Ezra, *Abraham b. Ḥayya (Savasorda), Maimonides, and others. In Jewish philosophy the most significant production, Maimonides' *Guide of the Perplexed*, early became available in a Latin translation that relieved aspirant students of learning Hebrew. The same applies to the older medical writings of Jews, especially Isaac *Israeli, while the Jewish authorship of the *Fons Vitae* by Ibn *Gabirol (Avicebron) was apparently early forgotten. But by the 13th–14th centuries the scientific writings of Jews (mainly of Spain) were being sought by Christians in southern Europe, and occasionally (via these southern countries) further north; thus, Kepler was to put himself to trouble to see astronomical matter included in works of *Levi b. Gershom (Gersonides).

The presence, from 1391 onward, of many converted Jews in Spain, and after 1492 of many crypto-Jews, facilitated such studies (2, b; 2, c): not only because Hebrew teachers were relatively easy to find, and to employ (as being professedly Christians) *de jure* in the universities, but also because these "converts" had often carried with them into their Christian conformity an interest in, and familiarity with, earlier Jewish science, and themselves maintained the tradition in Latin (or Spanish), alongside the contemporary work (up until 1492) of their still faithful kinsfolk.

The Kabbalah, Italy, and the Renaissance

Spain was also the birthplace of the Zoharic Kabbalah, the wider impact of which was first felt in the communities of Italy and Provence, where (as in Spain) Jewish instructors could easily be found. Italy stands out, already in the 15th century, for Christian kabbalistic interests. Motivation was ambivalent (1, bb; 1, c; 1, cc). The *Zohar's ascription to R. *Simeon b. Yoḥai in late antiquity being presupposed, it was reckoned authentically Jewish, and consequently not open to repudiation by Jews if adduced controversially by Christians. Moreover, features of the kabbalistic system were deemed to be not merely coherent with Christian trinitarianism but indeed potentially to underwrite it. By the end of the 15th century, Kabbalah had become a significant discipline of study for a few Christian humanists – e.g., *Pico della Mirandola and *Egidio da Viterbo – who were really competent in Hebrew and Jewish Aramaic. Such names mark the crowning achievement of medieval Christian Hebraism, which is marked off (though still a continuity) from modern Hebrew studies by the work of Johann *Reuchlin and the age of print. Five outstanding 16th-century scholars in the field were Pietro Columna *Galatinus, Francesco *Giorgio, Guillaume *Postel, Guy Le *Fèvre de la Boderie, and Benito *Arias Montano. This Hebrew interest, as the outcome of the religious humanism of the Renaissance, is linked by the same parent to the Hebrew scholarship of the Reformation, in which the same atmosphere largely prevailed – and the Christian kabbalists could never have made such remarkable progress but for the encouragement of Hebrew in Italy by prince and prelate during the earlier part of the 15th century. A revised attitude (1, e) toward Greek and Roman antiquity, as having discovered the vehicle for certain permanent values in a linguistic meticulousness that could consequently be considered "classical," easily set the language of the Hebrew Bible alongside them: since biblical values (as read with a Christian glossation) were considered permanent, biblical Hebrew, no less than Plato's Greek or Virgil's Latin, must be acknowledged to be "classical." Post-biblical Hebrew might, as a corollary, have been scorned as debased and post-classical, but it was not; perhaps because, inarticulately and paradoxically, the Christian humanists sensed a continuity of a sort between post-biblical Judaism and Christianity, unlike the discontinuity with paganism. Consequently, despite the conviction that the Church had displaced the Synagogue as the authentic embodiment of the message of the "Old" Testament, the supposedly obsolete institutions and theology of Judaism – presumed still to be those of apostolic times – remained worth investigating.

Such academic motivations were reinforced by (1, c) conversionism, and led not merely to the study of Hebrew – occasionally even as a spoken language, with Jewish or apostate assistance – it also stimulated the collection of Hebrew manuscripts, not as curiosities but as appropriate to any humanist's library that purported to be well equipped. Typical of the enterprise may be considered Giannozzo *Manetti, who at the encouragement of Nicholas v laid the foundations of the Vatican Hebrew collection. At the turn of the 15th–16th centuries such interest flourished sufficiently to lead to the foundation of a few "trilingual" colleges – in Alcala (Spain), thanks to the patronage of Cardinal *Ximenes (Cisneros), in Paris (College de France), at Oxford (Corpus Christi College), at Louvain, Vienna, and conceivably elsewhere. In some cases these arrangements were absorbed in, or replaced by professorships (see below); elsewhere they may have petered out. But in England the tradition of "trilinguality" (to be carried further, in ideal, by Robert Wakefield's tract (1524) on the *laus et utilitas* of Arabic, Aramaic, and Hebrew) passed into some of the grammar schools then being founded, e.g., Colet's refounded St. Paul's (London) – there to survive, admittedly in an attenuated form, except in the case of Merchant Taylors' School, where it was prosecuted vigorously into the 20th century.

The Reformation and the Age of Printing

For approximately 50 years (1490–1540) the following three independent factors invigorated each other: (A) The emergence of a cadre of near-modern type scholars, preeminently J. Reuchlin and C. *Pellicanus, capable of training successors on the basis of comprehensive and categorically articulated grammars of at least biblical Hebrew accidence, which they themselves composed. These grammars were substantially influenced by David Kimḥi's. (B) The spread of the *printing press, and the demands of Christian Hebraists for Hebrew type – a need met in northern Europe at first by blockcutting for each word. Pride of place again belongs to Italy, where movable Hebrew type-font had already been well developed by Jewish printers; the enterprise of the Christian printer Daniel Bomberg of Venice stands out. Enjoying the patronage of Leo x, and availing himself of the editorial services of really expert rabbinists (including the convert Jacob b. Ḥayyim of Tunis, and Elijah *Levita) Bomberg gave Europe both its first "rabbinic" bibles (i.e., Hebrew texts with parallel Jewish commentaries), and the first complete edition of both Talmuds. The presence of these volumes, often from an early date, in academic libraries across Europe may be a significant pointer to Hebrew interest locally. Pellicanus' Hebrew grammar was the first to be printed (Strasbourg, 1504); Reuchlin's (Pforzheim, 1506) also contained a vocabulary. With these basic tools, which were rapidly improved, the modern foundations of western academic Hebrew may be considered laid. (C) The movement toward ecclesiastical reform that ended in the emergence of nation-centered Protestant churches independent of Rome owed much to the claim – ultimately a quasi-dogma – that authority lay not in the tradition of the western Church controlled by the papal curia, which had encrusted the Bible with its own interpretation (parallel to the procedure of rabbinic Judaism), but in the unadulterated text of the Bible itself. Hence the need for study of the biblical languages, and for producing improved translations – soon into the vernaculars of Europe, but also into Latin (e.g., that by Xanctes (Santes) *Pagnini, 1528). Pagnini's was a Catholic enterprise and when the Council of Trent asserted the "authenticity" of the Latin Vulgate, this was on grounds of its embodying of and linkage with "officially" endorsed patristic exegesis (analogous to the position of Targum Onkelos within Judaism), and not by way of depreciation of the greater accuracy of the new translations. But the result was that, until recent times, Catholic vernacular versions have continued to be made from the Latin, with the significant exception of the Spanish Bible, which was a Jewish production made in Italy, and accepted by the curia through (ex-) Marrano channels.

Together, these trends brought about the establishment of professorships of Hebrew in the universities, both in Catholic countries and under the reformed churches, in part as an item of governmental policy; the "Regius" chairs at Oxford and Cambridge, for example, being founded by Henry VIII in 1540. Henceforth, however, gentile Hebraism in Europe flows along divided streams – one Catholic, and the other in the countries of the Reform.

Post-Reformation Catholic Hebraism

The Counter-Reformation focused Catholic Hebrew scholarship almost exclusively on the Hebrew Bible, Jewish interests that had engaged men like Pico della Mirandola being left for Protestants. The major achievements were consequently the polyglot editions of the Bible (Antwerp, 1569–72, and Paris, 1628–45). But paradoxically it was an Italian Cistercian, *Bartolocci, and his successor Imbonati, whose *Bibliotheca Magna Rabbinica* (Rome, 1675–93) laid the foundations of Jewish bibliography, thereby adding to Hebrew scholarship a dimension from which Jewish no less than gentile Hebraists have benefited. In the late 18th century G.B. de *Rossi in Parma likewise set himself to widen Hebrew academic horizons once again.

The Protestant Countries

In the reformed countries, most Hebraists were members of the nationally established church concerned; but ecclesiastical and political frontiers break down in the case of Hungary, where a preponderant number of the Hebrew scholars were Calvinists, many of them having studied abroad. Protestant masoretic studies produced in the 17th century some notable editions of the Bible, particularly those of the Dutchmen Leusden and van der Hooght; but the crowning achievement was the publication in London (1657) of the most elaborate polyglot Bible ever produced, by a scholarly team led by B. *Walton. But during the later 16th and early 17th centuries the making of vernacular bible versions was earnestly prosecuted, having begun with Luther's German from 1523 and *Tyndale's English from 1530, both made direct from the Hebrew. The names of those responsible for the English "Authorised" Version (King James', 1611) are all known, and included some of the best contemporary Hebraists and Orientalists (see *Bible, Versions, English). The high frequency with which from 1504 onward Hebrew grammars were published (and reprinted) must imply a student market greatly outnumbering the names of those Christian Hebraists known to us as such from their publications; many others, theologians and lawyers, etc., from, e.g., Wittenberg, Jena, Leipzig, or Basle – place-names that occur time and again on the title pages of grammars – must have carried away an ability to read the Hebrew Bible, and their casual use of it in their writings can often be traced from the indexes, or the occurrence of Hebrew typeface, in their collected works.

Two Hebrew presses – at Basle and Leiden – stand out as academically adventurous. Sebastian *Muenster who published (1542) a post-biblical Hebrew grammar, issued from Basle a number of rabbinic texts, some with Latin translations, in which he enjoyed the cooperation of Paulus Fagius. The *Buxtorf dynasty carried on and extended the same editorial activity, producing translations of several of the classical texts of medieval Judaism, including *Judah Halevi's *Kuzari* and Maimonides' *Guide*, as well as the first large-scale *Lexicon Chaldaicum Talmudicum et Rabbinicum* (1639). The Leiden and Amsterdam presses, especially the former (as also to a lesser degree those of Lund and Uppsala) printed many Hebrew publications including the doctoral dissertations of students of Jewish texts, as presided over by their teachers. The typical set task, from the later 16th century until toward the end of the 18th, was to translate into Latin a tractate of the Mishnah, or a section of Maimonides' Code, or the commentary of Rashi, Ibn Ezra, or *Abrabanel, to part or all of one of the biblical books (Rashi to the whole Hebrew Bible was published in Latin by J.F. *Breithauft (1710–13)). Although any system will presumably have depended on a teacher's own interests and assignments to his pupils, probably with little attention to work being done elsewhere, the amount of rabbinic literature thus haphazardly placed in the hands of readers of Latin is impressive.

Other enterprises rank as fresh groundbreaking, such as *Scaliger's communication with the Samaritans of Nablus. Dutch and (even more so) English trading connections with the Levant gave some scholars opportunity to visit Turkey as chaplains, the preeminent example being Edward *Pococke, whose Hebrew scholarship won genuine acclaim from contemporary levantine rabbis. John *Selden, as a lawyer, developed remarkable insight into the workings of *halakhah*, and the body of rabbinic learning applied to the exegesis of the New Testament (an enterprise that had continental parallels) by J.B. *Lightfoot was highly considered indeed. Chrestomathies for introducing students were also being produced, e.g., *Reland's *Analecta Rabbinica* (Utrecht, 1702). Reland's pupil A. *Schultens (d. 1756) first systematically exploited Arabic for the elucidation of Hebrew vocabulary. Among the Puritans of New England, the *Mayflower* had included one or two with a knowledge of Hebrew in its passenger list, and H. *Ainsworth is to be reckoned a "professional"; otherwise, through the 18th century American Hebraism was an affair of amateurs, some of them by no means negligible in competence, typified by Ezra *Stiles of Yale.

The Nineteenth Century

After approximately 1800 two new factors reduced the spate of rabbinic dissertations. One was the growth, after J.D. Michaelis' study of the Mosaic Law (1770–75), of the modern source-analytical study of the Hebrew Bible, largely elaborated regarding the Pentateuch by K.H. *Graf, and classically stated by J. *Wellhausen in 1889. This diverted the attention of Hebraists in the reformed countries back toward the Bible, especially since the decipherment of cuneiform yielded, from the middle of the century onward, an increasing body of highly relevant new source material. The other factor was Jewish emancipation, which produced a few Jews of the type of *Zunz and *Steinschneider who were academically trained in the Western sense and eager to apply modern scholarly techniques and categories to Jewish material, to whose attentions contemporary Christian Hebraists were apparently content to resign it. Conceivably the change of attitude in Germany, where hitherto much rabbinic scholarship had been prosecuted by gentiles, may be linkable to reaction against the liberalism that had produced Jewish emancipation. The net result was that what had hitherto counted as Hebrew scholarship split into two quasi-independent disciplines, namely, Old Testament scholarship, which maintained a nodding acquaintance with the newly recognized discipline of Oriental or Semitic studies; both largely ignoring "Jewish" scholarship as having little more to contribute to their respective disciplines, and as falling in an academic no-man's-land between East and West. There was thus a gap of approximately a century in the cultivation by Christian scholars of rabbinics as a tool for New Testament and other late-antique studies, until its relevance was rediscovered in the 20th century, and enhanced in importance when the Dead Sea Scrolls began to be investigated.

The history of gentile Hebrew scholarship cannot be properly written until the careers and achievements of its practitioners have been not only assessed but also correlated. The list of names which follows makes no claim to completeness. (See Table: Christian Hebraists.) The Hebrew competence of those listed prior to about 1500 may prove, on investigation, sometimes to have been less than repute has credited to the individual concerned, but these early students have been given the benefit of the doubt. After about 1500 minimal qualifications for inclusion are tenure of an official academic or para-academic teaching post for Hebrew, or defense of a thesis on a rabbinic subject, or the publication of a Hebrew grammar (authors of the multitudinous manuscript Hebrew grammars extant in libraries have not been included, unless otherwise qualified). So far as is known, the list includes no name whose bearer was of Jewish parentage but who himself apostatized. With one or two readily intelligible exceptions, it excludes all who died after 1890. This year – that of the death of F. *Delitzsch, and following that of the publication of Wellhausen's documentary hypothesis – may be taken as the division between post-Reformation Hebrew scholarship and the accommodation of Hebrew and Jewish subjects within Semitics, the Hebrew Bible nevertheless sometimes still being felt to be a preserve of the Christian theologian, which prevails in the modern secular university and some of its confessional counterparts.

BIBLIOGRAPHY:

(The abbreviations in the right-hand column are used in the Christian Hebraists list following the bibliography).

GENERAL:

M. Steinschneider, in: ZHB, 1–5 (1896–1901), cited by serial numbers; **St.**

idem, Cat. Bod.; **Bodl. Cat.**

idem, *Die europaeischen Uebersetzungen aus dem Arabischen bis Mitte des 17. Jahrhunderts (1849);* **Europ. Uebers.**

idem, *Die hebraeischen Uebersetzungen des Mittelalters* (1893); **Hebr. Uebers.**

B. Ugolinus, *Thesaurus Antiquitatum Sacrarum…*, 34 vols. (Venice, 1774–69); **Ugolini**

M. Kayserling, in: REJ, 20 (1890), 261–8; idem, in: JQR, 9 (1896/97), 509–14;

D. Kauffmann, in: MGWJ, 39 (1895), 145–67;

B. Pick, in: *Bibliotheca Sacra*, 42 (1886);

H. Rashdall, *Universities of Europe in the Middle Ages*, ed. By F.M. Powicke and A.B. Emden, 3 vols. (19362);

P.S. Allen, in: *Erasmus* (1934), 138f.;

C. Singer and G.H. Box, in: E.R. Bevan and C. Singer (eds.), *Legacy of Israel* (1928^2), 238f., 315f.;

J. Parkes, in: SBB, 6 (1962), 11–28; **Parkes**

New Schaff-Herzog Encyclopedia of Religious Knowledge, 13 vols. (1949–50); **Enc. Rel. Kn.**

B. Blumenkranz, *Les Auteurs chrétiens latins du Moyen Age sur les juifs et le judaïsme* (1963);

F. Secret, *Le Zôhar chez les kabbalistes chrétiens de la Renaissance* (1964^2);

idem, *Les kabbalistes chrétiens de la Renaissance* (1964);

H. Hailperin, *Rashi and the Christian Scholars* (1963);

H.J. Schoeps, *Philosemitismus im Barock* (1952);

B. Smalley, *Study of the Bible in the Middle Ages* (1952^2);

R. Loewe, in: G.H.W. Lampe (ed.), *Cambridge History of the Bible*, 2 (1969), 148f.;

Allgemeine Deutsche Biographie; **ADB**

Nouvelle Biographie Générale; **NBU**

M. Michaud (ed.), *Biographie Universelle ancienne et moderne*, 45 vols. ($1854–65^2$); **Biogr. Univ.**

Encyclopaedia Brittanica (1911^{11}); **Enc. Br.11**

Jewish Encyclopaedia, 12 vols. (1901–05); **JE**

Catholic Encyclopaedia, 15 vols. (1907–15; 1967^2);

Hebraeische Bibliographie (1858–82); **Heb. Bibl.**

Zeitschrift fuer Hebraeische Bibliographie (1896–1920);

J. Zedner, *Catalogue of the Hebrew Books in the… British Museum* (1867). **Zedner**

RELIGIOUS ORDERS:

Franciscans: L. Wadding (ed.), *Scriptores Ordinis Minorum* (Rome, 1650; repr. 1967); **Wadding**

J.H. Sbaralea, *Supplementum…ad Scriptores trium ordinum…*, 3 pts. (1908–36); **Sbaralea Supple.**

Dominicans: J. Quétif and J. Echard, *Scriptores Ordinis Praedicatorum*, 2 vols. (Paris, 1719–23; repr., 2 vols. in 4, 1959);

Jesuits: A. and A. de Backer, *Bibliothèque de la Compagnie de Jésus*, ed. by C. Sommervogel, 11 vols. (1890–1932); **Bibl. Comp. de Jésus**

L. Polgár, *Bibliography of the History of the Society of Jesus* (1967).

COUNTRIES:

AMERICA:

W. Rosenau, *Semitic Studies in American Colleges* (1896);

D. de Sola Pool, in: AJHSP, 20 (1911), 31–83;

A. Johnson (ed.), *Dictionary of American Biography* (1928–37). **D. Am. B.**

AUSTRIA:

W.A. Neumann, *Ueber die orientalischen Sprachenstudien seit dem XIII. Jahrhunderte, mit besonderer Ruecksicht auf Wien* (1899);

C. von Wurzbach, *Biographisches Lexicon des Kaiserthums Oesterreich*, 60 vols. (1856–91); **BLK Oest**

L. Santifaller (ed.), *Oesterreichisches Biographisches Lexicon 1815–1950* (1954–). **OBL**

BELGIUM:

Biographie Nationale de Belgique (1866–); **BN Belg.**

J. Duverger, *Nationaal Biografisch Woordenboek* (in progress). **NBW**

BOHEMIA:

Czech Academy of Sciences, Oriental Institute, Moscow, *Asian and African Studies in Czechoslovakia* (1967);

See also HUNGARY, J. Janko.

DENMARK:

C.F. Bricka, P. Engelstoft, and S. Dahl (eds.), *Dansk Biografisk Leksikon*, 27 vols. (1933–44). **Dansk**

FRANCE:

S. Berger, *Quam notitiam linguae hebraicae habuerint christiani medii aevi temporibus in Gallia* (1893);
P. Colomiès, *Gallia Orientalis* (The Hague, 1665);
F. Secret, in: REJ, 126 (1967), 417–33;
idem, *Les kabbalistes chrétiens de la Renaissance* (1964), 151–217;
J. Batteau, M. Barroux, and M. Prévost (eds.), *Dictionnaire de Biographie Française* (1933–); **DBF**
See also above NBU.

GERMANY:

L. Geiger, *Das Studium der hebraeischen Sprache in Deutschland vom Ende des XV. bis zur Mitte des XVI. Jahrhunderts* (1870); **Geiger**
E. Sachau, *Die deutschen Universitaeten* (1893), 520;
B. Walde, *Christliche Hebraisten Deutschlands am Ausgang des Mittelalters* (1916); **Walde**
G. Bauch, in: MGWJ, 48 (1904);
C.F. Schnurrer, *Biographische und litterarische Nachrichten von ehmaligen Lehren der hebraeischen Litteratur in Tuebingen* (Ulm, 1792); *Zeitschrift der Deutschen Morgenlaendischen Gesellschaft* (1846–); **ZDMG**
G. Behrmann, *Hamburgs Orientalisten* (1902);
Neue Deutsche Biographie (1953–);
See also above ADB.

GREAT BRITAIN:

S.A. Hirsch, in: JQR, 12 (1900), 34–88;
S. Levy, in: JHSEM, 4 (1942), 61–84; **JHS Misc.**
R. Loewe, in: JHSET, 17 (1953), 225–49;
idem, in: J.M. Shaftesley (ed.), *Remember the Days* (1966), 23–48;
L. Roth, in: JSS, 6 (1961), 204–21;
Dictionary of National Biography (1885–); **DNB**
A.B. Emden, *Biographical Register of the University of Oxford to A.D. 1500*, 3 vols. (1957–59);
J. Foster (ed.), *Alumni Oxonienses*, 8 vols. (1888–92); **Foster**
idem, *Index Ecclesiasticus* (1890); **Index Eccles.**
J. and J.A. Venn (eds.), *Alumni Cantabrigienses* (1922–). **Venn**

HOLLAND:

D. Friedman, in: A.J. Barnhouw and B. Landheer (eds.), *Contribution of Holland to the Sciences* (1943), 219–49;
P.C. Molhuysen and P.J. Blok, *Nieuw Nederlandsch Biografisch Woordenboek*, 10 vols. (1911–37); **NNBW**
J.P. de Bie and J. Loosjes (eds.), *Biographisch Woordenboek van Protestantsche Godgeleerden in Nederland*, 6 vols. (1919–49). **BWPGN**

HUNGARY:

S. Kohn, *A Szombatosok* (1889); **Kohn**
A. Marmorstein, in: ZMB, 8–9 (1904–05); **Marm.**
L. Pap, *Die Wissenschaft vom Alten Testament* (1940); **Pap.**
L. Venetianer, in: IMIT (1898), 136f.; **Venet.**
J. Zovanyi, *Cikkei a Theológiai Lexikon számára* (1940); **Zov.**
R. Dan, in: *Magyar Könyvszemle*, 81 (1965), 284f.; **Dan**
K. Beranek, in: *Studia semitica philologica… Ioani Bakos dicata* (1965), 29f.;
J. Janko, *ibid.*, 33f.;
J. Szinnyei, *Magyar irok*, 6 vols. (1891–1914; repr. 1939–44). **Szin.**

ITALY:

D. Kaufmann, in: REJ, 27 (1893);
idem, in: JQR, 9 (1896/97), 500–8;
P. Colomiès, *Italia et Hispania Orientalis* (Hamburg, 1730);
A. de Gubernatis, *Matériaux pour servir à l'histoire des études orientales en Italie* (1876);
C. Roth, *Jews in the Renaissance* (1959), 137f.;
idem, in: *Jewish Studies… Israel Abrahams* (1927), 384–401;
Dizionario Biografico degli Italiani (1960–); **DBI**
Enciclopedia Biografica e Bibliografica Italiana (1936–); **Enc. Biogr. Ital**
Enciclopedia Italiana, 36 vols. (1929–39). **Enc. It.**

POLAND:

Polski Słownik Biograficzny (1935–). **Polski Slownik Biogr.**

SPAIN:

See above: P. Colomiès (Italy);
Enciclopedia Universal Ilustrada Europeo-Americana, 70 vols. in 71 (1905–30);

SWEDEN:

K.U. Nylander, in: *Ny Svensk Tidskrift* (1889);
E.L. Hydren, *Specimen historico-literarum de fatis literaturae Orientalis in Suecia* (Uppsala, 1775);
Svenska män och kvinnor (1942–) **Svensk**
B. Boethius, et al. (eds.), *Svenskt Biografiskt Lexicon* (1918–); **SBL**
See also GENERAL, H.J. Schoeps.

SWITZERLAND:

A.B. Staehelin, *Geschichte der Universitaet Basel 1632–1818* (1957);
E. Bonjour, *Die Universitaet Basel… 1460–1960* (1960);
J. Prijs, *Die Basler hebraeischen Drucke 1492–1866*, ed. by B. Prijs (1964);- **DHBS**
Dictionnaire Historique et Biographique de la Suisse, 7 vols. (1921–34);
Historisch-Biographisches Lexicon der Schweiz, 7 vols. (1921–34). **Hist. Biogr. Lex. Schweiz**

[Raphael Loewe]

Christian Hebraists

Name	Country-(ies)	Dates	Religious Confession	References
Aarhus, Peter Sim.	Denmark	fl.1711	Calvinist	**St. 57**
Abicht, Johann Georg	Germany	1672–1740	Lutheran	
Abram (Abrahamus), Nicolaus	France	1589–1645	Jesuit	**DBF**
Abresch, Petrus	Holland	1736–1812	Reformed Ch.	**NNBW; BWPGN; NBW**
Abundachus, Joseph Barbatus Memphiticus	Egypt, England, Flanders	1st half of 17th c.	Jesuit	**NBU**
Ackermann, Leopold	Austria	1771–1831	Catholic	**BLK Oest; OBL; ADB**
Acoluthus, Andreas	Germany	1654–1704	Lutheran	**ADB**
Addison, Lancelot	England	1632–1703	Anglican	**St. 59; DNB**
Adler, Jacob Georg Christian	Denmark	?1756–1834		**St. 60; Dansk; NBU; ADB**
Aegidius da Viterbo, *see* Viterbo, Aegidius da				
Agelli, Antonio	Italy	1532–1608	Theatine	**DBI; Enc. It; NBU**
Ainsworth, Henry	England, Holland	?1569–?1623	Brownist	
Ajtai, A.Mihály	Hungary	1704–1776	Calvinist	**Marm; Szin.**
Akai, Krisóf	Hungary	1706–1766	Catholic	**Marm; Szin.**
Alabaster, William	England	1567–1640	Anglican, then Catholic, then Anglican	**DNB**
Alber, Johann	Hungary	1753–1830	Catholic	**Marm; Szin.**
Alberti, Paul Martin	Germany	17th–18th c.	Protestant	**NBU**
Albert(in)a Katherina	Bohemia	late 17th c.		**Heb. Bibl. 20, 66.**
Allen, John	England	1771–1839		**DNB**
Allix, Peter	France, England	1641–1717	Huguenot	**St. 62; DNB; NBU; Enc. Br.[11]; DBF**
Alstedius, Johann Henr.	Hungary	1588–1638	Calvinist	**Marm; Szin; Zov.**
Alting, Jacobus	Holland	1618–1679	Calvinist	
Alting, Johann Heinrich	Holland	1583–1644	Calvinist	**NNBW; NBU; ADB; Enc. Br.[11]**
Amama, Sixtinus	Holland	1593–1629	Calvinist	
Amandus van Zieriksee	Belgium	c.1450–1524 (34)	Franciscan	**NBU; NNBW; ADB.**
Ambrogio, Teseo	Italy	1469–1540		
Amersfoordt, Petrus	Holland	1786–1824		**NNBW; NBW; BWPGN; NBU**
Amman (Ammonius), Kaspar	Germany, Belgium	c. 1450–post 1524	Augustinian	**ADB; NDB; NBW; Walde; Geiger**
Amoena Amalia of Anhalt	Germany	d. 1625		**Heb. Bibl. 20, 66**
Ancherson, Matth.	Denmark	1682–1741		**St. 88; Dansk**
Andala, Ruard	Holland	1665–1727	Reformed Ch.	**NNBW; NBU**
Andreas de León, *see* Zamora, Andreas de León				
Andrew of St. Victor	England	12th c.	Victorine	
Andrew, James	Scotland, England	1774(?)–1833		**Venn; Index Eccles.**
Andrewes, Lancelot	England	1555–1626	Anglican	**DNB**
Andrewes, Roger	England	c.1590–1635	Anglican	**DNB**
Andrews, Benjamin	England	1785–1868	Wesleyan	**JHS Misc. 4, 75**
Anna Sophia of Hessen	Germany	c. 1658	Catholic	**Heb. Bibl. 20, 66**
Anna Urban, *née* Weissbrucker, *see* Urban, Anna Weissbrucker				
Ansgarius, *see* Anchersen, Matth.				
Anslus, Gerebrard		*fl.* 1640		**St. 89**
Antonia, Princess of Wuerttemberg	Germany	d. 1679		**Heb. Bibl. 20, 67; JQR, 9 (1896/97), 509-14**
Apáczai, Csere János	Hungary	1625–1659	Calvinist	**Marm; Szin; Zov.**
Apáti, Miklós	Hungary	1662–1724	Calvinist	**Marm; Szin; Pap.**
Aretius (= Marti), Benedictus	Switzerland	?1505–1574		**DHBS; NBU; ADB**
Arias Montano, Benito	Spain, Low Countries	1527–1598	(nominal) Catholic	
Armengaud, Blasius	France	d. 1314		**St. 18; Europ. Ubers. 6, 19**
Arnd, Carol	Germany	1673–1721		**NBU**
Arnd(ius), Joshua	Germany	1626–1686		**St. 91; NBU**
Arnold of Villanova	Spain, France, Sicily	c.1230–1313		**St. 18; Europ. Ubers 6, 20; DBF**

Christian Hebraists (continued)

Name	Country-(ies)	Dates	Religious Confession	References
Arnoldi, Michael	Holland	1658–1738	Calvinist	**St. 92; NNBW; NBW; BWPGN**
Artoæpus (Bekker), Petrus	Germany	d. 1563	Protestant	**NBU**
Ashworth, Caleb	England	1722–1775	Dissenter	**DNB**
Aslakssen, Cort (Conrad Aslacus)	Norway Denmark	1564–1624	Lutheran	
Asp, Matthias	Sweden	1696–1763		**SBL**
Assemani, Joseph Simeon	Lebanon, Italy	1687–1768	Maronite	
Aubry, Esaias	?France, Germany	c. 1730		**St. 95**
Audran, Prosper Gabriel	France	1744–1819	Jansenist	**DBF**
Aurivillius, Carl	Sweden	1717–1786		**Svensk; NBU**
Aurogallus (Goldhahn), Matth.	Germany	c.1490–1543		**ADB; NBU**
Avenarius, *see* Haber- mann, Johannes				
Bacon, Roger	England	c. 1214–1292	Franciscan	
Bahrdt, Carl Friedrich	Germany	1741–1792	Lapsed Lutheran	**ADB; NBU; EB**
Baillie, William	Ireland	b. 1795		**Heb. Grammar, Dublin, 1840**
Baldi, Bernardino	Italy	1553–1617	Augustinian	**St. 96; DBI**
Baldovius, Jo.		*fl.* 1636		**Heb. Grammar, Leipzig, 1636**
Balduin, Dorothea	Hungary	1685–1739	?	**Marm; Szin.**
Bang, Thomas	Denmark	1600–1661	Lutheran	**Dansk; NBU**
Baratier(us), Johann Philip	Germany	1721–1740	Reformed Ch.	**St. 97; NBU; EB**
Barbatus, Joseph, *see* Abundachus, Joseph Barbatus Memphiticus				
Barker, Samuel	England	1686–1759		**DNB**
Barker, William Higgs	England	1744–1815		**DNB**
Barnard, Samuel	U.S.A.	*fl.* 1825		**Heb. & Aramaic Grammar, Philadelphia, 1825**
Barozzi (Barocius) Francesco	Italy	1537–1604		**St. 98; DBI; NBU**
Bartolocci, Giulio	Italy	1613–1687	Cistercian	
Bashuysen, Heinrich Jakob van	(Holland), Germany	1679–1738	Reformed Ch.	
Basnage, Jacques de Beauval	France, Holland	1653–1723	Reformed Ch.	
Bate, Julius	England	1711–1771	Hutchinsonian	**DNB; NBU**
Báthori, G. Mihály	Hungary	1631–1669	Calvinist	**Szin; Zov; Dan**
Bayley, Cornelius	England	1751–1812	Methodist, later Anglican	**DNB**
Bayly, Anselm	England	1719–1794		**DNB**
Baynes, Ralph	England, France	c.1504–1559	Catholic	**St. 101; DNB**
Beck(ius), Matthias Friedrich	Germany	1649–1701	Lutheran	**St. 102; ADB**
Beck, Michael	Germany	1653–1712	Lutheran	**ADB; NBU**
Beckmann, Jo. Christ.	Germany	*fl.* 1677		**St. 103**
Bedwell, William	England	1561 or 62–1632	Anglican	**St. 104; DNB; NBU**
Beekman, Jacob	Holland	17th c.		
Beelen, Jo. Theodor	Holland	*fl.* 1841		**St. 105**
Beeston, William	England	b. 1798		**Pre-masoretic ("Hieronymean") Heb. grammar, London, 1843**
Beke, Matth.	Holland	*fl.* 1708		**St. 106**
Békés, János	Hungary	17th c.	Calvinist	**Dan**
Bekker, Georges Joseph	Germany, Belgium	1792–1837		**BN Belg.**
Bekker, Petrus, *see* Artopæus (Bekker), Petrus				
Bél, Mátyás	Hungary	1684–1749	Lutheran	**Szin.**
Bellarmino, Roberto Francesco Romolo	Italy	1542–1621	Jesuit, Cardinal	**Enc. It.; Enc. Br. [11]; NBU**
Bellerman, Jo. Joachim	Germany	1754–1842		**ADB; NBU**
Benedicti, Jean	France	*fl.* 1584	Catholic	
Benivieni, Girolamo	Italy	1453–1542	Catholic	**Enc. It.; NBU; Roth, Renaissance, p. 146**

Christian Hebraists (continued)

Name	Country-(ies)	Dates	Religious Confession	References
Bennett, Thomas	England	1673–1728	Anglican	**DNB; NBU**
Benoit, J., *see* Benedict; Jean				
Benzelin	France	*fl.* 1826		**Heb. grammar, Paris, 1826**
Benzelius, Ericus	Sweden	1675–1743		**St. 312; Svensk; SBL; NBU**
Beregszászi, Pál	Hungary	18th c.	Calvinist	**Venet.**
Berkeley, George	Ireland	1685–1753	Anglican	**DNB**
Bernard, Edward	England	1638–1696/7		**St. 107; DNB; NBU**
Bernard, Hermann Hedwig	Austria, England	1785–1857		
Beronius, Magnus Olai	Sweden	1692–1775		**St. 137; Svensk; SBL**
Besange, Hieronymus von	Austria	1726–1764 (?)	Benedictine	**BLK Oest.**
Besnyei, György	Hungary	1730–70	Calvinist	**Marm; Szin.**
Bialloblotzky, Christoph Heinrich Friedrich	Germany, England	d. 1869	Lutheran	**ADB**
Bibliander (Buchmann), Theodore	Switzerland	1504–1564	Reformed Ch.	**DHBS; NBU; ADB**
Bidermann, Jo. Gottlieb	Germany	1705–1772		**ADB**
Binans, Jean François de	France?	?		
Bindrim, Johann Georg				**Parkes n. 57; Ugolini 26, 332**
Bircherod, Jan. (Jacob Jensen?)	Denmark	1624–1688		**St. 109; Dansk**
Biscioni(us), Antonio Maria	Italy	1674–1756		
Blancaccius, Benedictus	Italy	*fl.* 1608		**Heb. grammar, Rome, 1608**
Blankenburg(ius), Fridericus	? Germany	*fl.* 1625		**Heb. grammar, Strasbourg, 1625**
Blayney, Benjamin	England	1728–1801		**DNB; NBU**
Blebelius, Thom.	Germany	*fl.* 1587		**Heb. grammar, Wittenberg, 1587**
Blech, Wilhelm Philipp	Germany	*fl.* 1864		**Heb. grammar, Danzig, 1864**
Bloch, Søren Niklas Johan	Denmark	1772–1862		**Dansk**
Boberg, Andreas	Sweden	1678–1756		**SBL**
Bochart, Samuel	France	1599–1667	Calvinist	**NBF; EB; JE; ERK**
Bode(c)ker (Bodiker), Stephan	Germany	1384–1489	Praemonstratensian	**St. 52; Walde; A. Hauck, Kirchengesichte Deutschlands, v, 1177.**
Bodley, Thomas	England	1545–1613	Protestant	
Boeckel, Ernst Gottfr. Adolf	Germany	1783–1854		**ADB**
Boehm, Johann	Germany	d. 1535		**Walde**
Bohemus, Johann (?identical with foregoing)				**Heb. grammar, Wittenberg, 1636**
Boeschenstein, Johann	Germany	1472–1540		
Boettcher, Julius Friedrich	Germany	1801–1863	ADB	
Bogáthi, Fazekas Miklós	Hungary	1548–c 1590	Unitarian	**Marm; Szin; Kohn; Zov.**
Bohlius, Samuel	Germany	d. 1639	Lutheran	**St. 113**
Bois (Boys), John	England	1561–1644	DNB; Enc. Rel. Kn.	
Bo(u)lduc, Jacques	France	d. 1646	Capuchin	**DBF; NBU**
Bongetius, Jo.	? Italy	*fl.* 1717		**Heb. grammar, Rome, 1717**
Boote (Boate, Botius, etc.), Arnold (Arnt)	Holland, Ireland	1600– 1653 (?)	Reformed Ch.	**DNB; NNBW 4**
Boré, Eugene	France	1809–1878	Lazarite	**St. 114; DBF; NBU**
Bore(e)l, Adam (junior)	Holland	1603–1666 or 67	St. 115; NNBW 6.	
Borgwall, Andr.	Sweden	18th c.		**St. 269**
Borrha(us), Martin, *see* Cellarius, Martin				
Bosch, Jacobus	Holland	d.c. 1771		**NNBW 7**
Bosham, Herbert of	England, France	d. after 1190		
Bouget, Jean	France, Italy	1692–1775		**DBF; NBU**
Boulaese, Jean	France	1530– 1579 (?)	(nominal) Catholic	
Bouquett, Philip	France, England	1699–1748	Huguenot (?)	**DNB**
Bourdelot, Jean	France	d. 1638		**St. 116; DBF; NBU**

Christian Hebraists (continued)

Name	Country-(ies)	Dates	Religious Confession	References
Bowman, Thomas	England, Ireland	1819–c.1882		**Heb. grammar, Edinburgh, 1879–82 (completed by A. H. Bowman)**
Braemsonius, Anders Henriksen, *see* Brunchmann (Braemsonius), Anders Henriksen				
Braun, Johannes	Germany, Holland	1628–1708	Reformed Ch.	**Ugolini; NNBW 6**
Brecht, Jo. Reinhart	?	?	Lutheran	**Parkes (from Meuschen)**
Breithaupt, Johann Friedrich	Germany	1639–1713	Lutheran	
Brett, Richard	England	1567(?)– 1637		**DNB**
Brighenti, Giovann Antonio	Italy	d. 1702		**St. 118; MGWJ 1895–6, 458**
Brodaeus (Broad), Thomas	England	c.1577–1635		**St. 119; A. Wood, Ant. Oxon. ii, 593**
Brodberg, Nicholas	Sweden	18th c.		**St. 269**
Broughton, Hugh	England, Holland	1549–1612	Puritan	
Brown, William	Scotland	1766–1835	Presbyterian	**DNB**
Bruerne, Richard	England	1519(?)–1565		**DNB**
Brunchmann (Braemsonius), Anders Henriksen	Denmark	1690–1761		**Dansk**
Brunnerus, Jos.	Germany (?)	*fl.* 1585		**Heb. grammar, Freiburg, 1585**
Buchanan, Claudius	Scotland, India	1766–1815	Anglican	**DNB; EB; NBU**
Bucher, Samuel Friedrich	Germany	d. 1765		**Ugolini; NBU**
Buchmann, Theodore, *see* Bibliander (Buchmann), Theodore				
Budde (Buddeus), Joh, Franz	Germany	1667–1729	Lutheran	**St.122; ADB; NBU; EB**
Budny (Budnée, Budnaeus), Szymon	Poland	d. 1595	Socinian	**Polski Slownik Biogr.; NBU**
Buercklin, Georgius Christianus	Germany (?)	17th–18th c.		**Heb. grammar, Frankfurt, 1699**
Buettner, Christoph Andreas	Germany	1708–1774		**ADB**
Bullman, E.	England	*fl.* 1795		**Heb. grammar, London, 1795**
Burger, Nicol.	Denmark	?		**Heb.-Chald. Lexicon, Copenhagen, 1733**
Burgh, William (de)	Ireland	1800–1858		**Heb. grammar, Dublin, 1847**
Burgonovo, Archangelus de (Angiolo Pozzi)	Italy	*fl.* 1564	Franciscan	**St. 123; Wadding i, 13, Sbaralea Suppl. i, 101**
Burleigh (Burley), Francis	England	d. 1619		**Venn**
Burman, Frans	Holland	1628–1679	Reformed Ch.	**NNBW 4; ADB; NBU**
Burrell, Andrew	England	*fl.* 1739		**Heb. grammar, London, 1739**
Bush, George	U.S.A.	1796–1859	Presbyterian, later Swedenborgian	**D Am. B**
Buxtorf, Johann I	Switzerland	1564–1629	Calvinist	
Buxtorf, Johann II	Switzerland	1599–1664	Calvinist	
Buxtorf, Johann Jacob I	Switzerland	1645–1704	Calvinist	
Buxtorf, Johann (Jacob) III	Switzerland	1663–1732	Calvinist	
Bynaeus, Antonius	Holland	1654–1698	Reformed Ch.	**NNBW 6; NBU**
Byng (Bing(e)), Andrew	England	1574–1651/2		**DNB**
Bythner (Buttner), Victorinus	Poland, England	1605(?)–1670(?)		**DNB; NBU**
Caddick, Richard	England	1740–1819		**DNB**
Cademannus, Jos. Rud.	Austria	d. 1720		**St. 128**
Calasio(-ius), Mario di	Italy	c. 1550– 1620	Franciscan	**NBU; Enc. Br.[11]**
Calcio, Ignazio	Italy		*fl.* 1753	**Heb. grammar, Naples, 1753**
Calepinus, Ambrosius	Italy	1455–1511		**Biog. Univ. 6, 392**
Caligniis, Alanus Reffaut de		*fl.* 1541		**Heb. grammar, Paris, 1541**
Callenberg, Joh. Heinr.	Germany	1694–1760	Protestant	
Calonges, Madame de	?	?		**St. Z. f.H.B. xx, 67**
Calov(-ius) (Kalau), Abr.	Germany	1612–1686	Lutheran	**ADB; NBU; Enc. Br.[11]**
Calvert, James	England	d. 1698	Nonconformist	**NBU**

Christian Hebraists (continued)

Name	Country-(ies)	Dates	Religious Confession	References
Calvoer (Calvor), Kaspar	Germany	1650–1725	Lutheran	**ADB; NBU**
Calvert, Thomas	England	1606–1679	Puritan	**DNB**
Calvin, Jean	France, Switzerland	1509–1564	Reformer	
Caminero, Francisco Xavier	Spain	?		
Campen(-sis), Jan (Johannes) van	Holland, Germany	c. 1490–1538		**St. 129; NNBW vi, 259; NBU**
Campoi, János	Hungary	17th c.	Calvinist	**Kohn; Marm.**
Canini(us), Angelo	Italy, Greece, France	1521–1557		**St. 130; NBU**
Capito(Koepfel) Wolfgang Fabricius	Alsace, Switzerland	1478–1541	Benedictine, turned Reformer	
Capnio, *see* Reuchlin, Johann				
Cappellanus, Claude	France	d. 1667		**St. 131**
Cappel(le), Jacques	France	1570–1624	Huguenot	**NBU; Enc. Rel. Kn.**
Cappel[le](-lus), Louis	France	1585–1658	Huguenot	**NBU; Enc. Br. [11]**
Carpzov, Joh. Ben. II	Germany	1639–1699	Lutheran	**St. 132; NBU; ADB**
Carpzov, Joh. Gottlob	Germany	1679–1767	Lutheran	**St. 132; NBU; ADB**
Cartwright, Christopher	England	1602–1658	Anglican	**St. 133; DNB**
Castell, Edmund	England	1606–1685/6	Anglican	
Castro, Joh. (? José) Rodriguez de	Spain	1739–1796 (?)		**St. 135; NBU**
Castronovate, Jos. de	?	16th c. (?)		**St. 241**
Cate, Gerhardusten	Holland	1699–1749		**NNBW 4, 403**
Cayet, Pierre Victor Palma	France	1525–1610	Protestant, then Catholic	
Cellada, Diego (Didacus) de	Spain	1586–1661	Jesuit	**Bibl. Comp. De Jèsus, ii, 936**
Cellarius, Christ.	Germany	(?) 1638– 1707		**NBU; ADB**
Cellarius, Joh.	Germany	*fl.* 1518		**St. 136; L. Geiger Ztschr. Gesch. Jud. Deutschl. iv, 116**
Cellarius (Borrha(us)), Martin	Switzerland	1499–1564		**B. Riggenbach, M.B., 1900; E. Bonjour, Univers. Basel, 1960**
Celsius, Olaus, Sen.	Sweden	1670–1756		**St. 137; Svensk; NBU**
Ceporinus (von Wisendangen) Jakob	Switzerland	1499–1526 (?)		**Hist. Biogr. Lex. Schweiz, vii, 523**
Cevallerius (Chevalier), Petrus	Switzerland	*fl.* 1578– 1594		**Hist. Biogr. Lex. Schweiz, ii, 560**
Chatterton (Chaderton), Laurence	England	*fl.* 1611		**DNB**
Chenery, Thomas	England	1826–1884		**DNB**
Cher, *see* Hugh of St. Cher				
Chéradame, Jean	France	*fl.* 1537		
Chevalier (Cevallerius), Ant. Rud.	France, England	1507–1572	Huguenot	**St. 138; DNB; NBU**
Chiarini, Luigi	Italy, Poland (?)	1789–1832	Catholic	**St. 139; NBU**
Chilius, Andr.	Low Countries	?		**St. 140**
Christmann, Jacob	Germany	1554–1613		**St. 141; ADB; NBU**
Chrysococca, Georgios, *see* Georgios Chrysococca				
Chytraeus, Andr.	Sweden	*fl.* 1706		**St. (S.V. Lundius)**
Chytraeus (Kochhaff), David	Germany	1530–1610	Protestant	**St. 141; NBU; Geiger, Zeitschr. Gesch. Jud. Deutschl. iv, 107**
Cibo, Wife of Jo. Duke of Camerino	?	*fl.* 1550		**Zeitschr. f. Heb. Bibl. xx, 67**
Cinqarbres, Jean, *see* Quinquarboreus, Johannes				
Ciselius, Phil. (?)	Holland	*fl.* 1696		**St. 142**
Cisneros, Francisco, *see* Ximénez (Jiménez) de Cisneros, Francisco				
Clajus (Klai), Johannes	Germany	1535(?)–1592		**ADB; NBU**
Clanner, J.G. (?)	?	*fl.* c. 1726		**St. 143**
Clark (Clerke), Richard	England	*fl.* 1611		**DNB**
Clark (Clericus), Samuel	England	*fl.* 1667		**St. 145; Bodl. Cat. 847**
Clavering, Robert	England	1671–1747	Anglican	**St. 144; Bodl. Cat. 847; DNB**

Christian Hebraists (continued)

Name	Country-(ies)	Dates	Religious Confession	References
Claymond, John	England	1457(?)–1537		**DNB; R. Loewe, Heb. Union Coll. Ann. 28, 1957**
Clenardus (Cleynaerts), Nicolaus	Flanders	(?)1495– 1542		**NNBW; BN Belg; ADB; Enc. Br. [11]**
Clerc (Le Clerc), Jean-Thomas	Switzerland (French)	1657–1736	Huguenot (Remonstrant)	**NNBW; NBU; Enc. Br. [11]**
Clericus (Le Clerc), David	Switzerland	1591–1654		**Hist. Biogr. Lex. Schweiz, iv, 639**
Clericus, Samuel, *see* Clark, Samuel				
Clodius, David	Germany	1644–1684	Lutheran	**ADB**
Clodius, Jo. Chr.	Germany	1676–1745		**St. 146; ADB; NBU**
Cluverus, Jo.	?	17th c.		**St. 147**
Cnollen, Adam Andreas	Germany	1674–1714		**St. 148; M. Brann, D. Kaufmann Mem. Vol., p. 392**
Cnollen, Jos. Nicol.	Germany	17th c.		**St. 148**
Cocceius, Johannes, *see* Koch, Joh.				
Codde (Coddaeus), Guilh. van der	Holland	1575–1625 (?30)	Reformed Ch.	**St. 150; Bodl. Cat. 848; NNBW**
Collier, William	England	1742–1790		**Venn**
Collin, C.E.	Germany	*fl.* 1705		**St. 151**
Colomils, Paul	France, England	1638–1692	Huguenot- Anglican	**DNB; NBU**
Colvill, Abr.	Germany	*fl.* 1670		**St. (after 151)**
Conant, Thomas Jefferson	U.S.A.	1802–1891		**D. Am. B. Enc. Br. [11]**
Connelly, Thaddeus	Ireland	*fl.* 1823		**Proverbs, Irish-Engl. Heb., Dublin 1823**
Cornaro–Piscopia, Cornelia (?Eleonora), Lucr. Helena	Italy	1646–1684		**NBU; Zeitschr. f. Heb. Bibl. xx, 67**
Cossey (Costessey), Henry of	England	d. 1336	Franciscan	**Loewe, Heb. Union Coll. Ann. 28, 1957, 212**
Costus, Petrus	France	*fl.* 1554		**St. 152, Bodl. Cat. 849**
Cotta, Jo.Fr.	Germany	1701–1779		**St. 153; NBU; ADB; Enc. Br. [11]**
Covell, John	England	1638–1722		**DNB; NBU**
Cramer, Anna Maria	Germany	1613–1627		**Zeitschr. f. Heb. Bibl. xx, 67**
Cramer, Dan	Germany	1568–1637	Lutheran	**ADB; NBU**
Cramer, Gabriel (Elisée)	Switzerland	1822–1888		**B. Prijs, Basl. Heb. Drucke, 1964, 470, 318**
Cramer, Joh. Jacob	Switzerland	1673–1702		**St. 154, Bodl. Cat. 213; Hist. Biogr. Lex. Schweiz, ii, 642; NBU; ADB**
Cramer, Joh. Rudolph	Switzerland	1678–1737		**St. 155, Bodl. Cat. 849; Hist. Biogr. Lex Schweiz ii, 642; ADB; NBU**
Crawford, Francis	Ireland	*fl.* 1855		**Trans. Royal Ir. Acad. xxii (1855), 371 f.**
Cregut(us), Ant.	Switzerland (?)	*fl.* 1660		**NBU**
Crenius, Thom.	Germany	1648–1728		**St. 156, Bodl. Cat. 850; NBU**
Crocius, Lud. Mich.	Germany	*fl.* 1673		**St. 157**
Croius, Jo.	England	18th c.		**St. 158**
Cross, Walter	England	17th c.		**Br. Mus. Cat.**
Csécsi, János	Hungary	1689–1769	Calvinist	**Marm; Szin; Pap.**
Csekei, Pál	Hungary	18th c.	Calvinist	**Dan**
Csepregi, Ferenc	Hungary	1700–1758	Calvinist	**Marm; Szin; Zovanyi**
Csomos, János	Hungary	1730–1768	Calvinist	**Szin; Zovanyi**
Cudworth, Ralph	England	1617–1688	Anglican	
Cun(aeus), Peter van der	Holland	1586–1638	Reformed Ch.	**NNBW; ADB; NBU**
Cunitzen (Cunitia), Maria	?	?		**Zeitsch. f. Heb. Bibl. xx, 67**
Curtius, Sebastian	?	*fl.* 1645 (?)		**Heb. grammar, Geismar, 1645**
Czuppon, György	Hungary	1755–1820	Catholic	**Szin.**
Dachs, Friedr. Bernh.	Holland	*fl.* 1726		**St. 159; Bodl. Cat. 833**

Christian Hebraists (continued)

Name	Country-(ies)	Dates	Religious Confession	References
D'Allemand, J.D.	Germany	*fl.* 1837		**Heb. grammar, Munich, 1837**
Dailing (Deyling), Sal.	Germany	1665(?77)– 1755	Lutheran	**ADB; NBU**
Dalmaki, Laurentius	Hungary	*fl.* 1643		**St. 124b, Nachtrag p. 120**
Danz, Joh. Andr.	Germany	1654–1727		
Dassow(-vius), Th.	Germany	d. 1721		**St. 161; ADB**
Dávid, Ferenc	Hungary	1520–1579	Unitarian, Sabbatarian (Davidist)	**Kohn; Szin; Zov; E. Kiss, 1912**
Davies, Benjamin	Welsh-Canadian	1814–1875		**DNB**
Davis, Johan.	England	(?)1625– 1693		**DNB**
Debreczeni, Petkó János	Hungary	17th c.	Calvinist	**Dan**
Debreczeni, Szücs János	Hungary	1630–1671	Calvinist	**Zov; Dan**
de Dieu, Louis	Holland	1590–1642	Calvinist	**NNBW 8, 395; B.N. Belg; NBU; ADB**
Delitzsch, Franz Julius	Germany	1813–1890		**ADB; Enc. Br. [11]**
del Rio, Martin Ant.	Flanders, Spain	1551–1608	Jesuit	**B.N. Belg; NBU; ADB; Cath. Enc.**
Densing, Herman	Holland	1654–1722		**NNBW 8; NBU**
Dereser, Thadd. Ant.	Germany	1757–1827		**ADB; NBU**
Dertsik, János	Hungary	19th c.	Calvinist	**Szin.**
d'Espence, Claude, *see* Espencaeus, Claude				
Diederichs, Jo. Christ. Wilh.	Germany	1750–1781		**NBU**
Diest, Henr. van	Holland	b. 1595		**NNBW 4, 504**
Diest, Samuel van	Holland	d. 1694		**NNBW 4, 505**
Dieterich, Joh. Con.	?	?		**Ugolini 30, 1278**
Dietrich, Franz Ed. Chr.	Germany	1810–1883		**ADB**
Dilherr, Joh. Mich.	Germany	1604–1669	Lutheran	**ADB**
Dillingham, Francis	England	d. 1625	Anglican	**DNB**
Dindorf, Th. Imm.	Germany	?		**Heb. & Chald. Grammar, Leipzig, 1801**
Diószegi, KalmFr PFI	Hungary	1628–1669	Calvinist	**Szin; Zov; Dan**
Disma, P.	Italy	*fl.* 1757		**St. 162; Zedner, 198**
Disney, William	England	1751–1807		**DNB**
Dithmar, Justus Christ.	Germany	1677–1737		**St. 163; ADB; NBU**
Doederlein, Jo. Chr.	Germany	18th c.		**St. 295**
Doeleke, W.H.	Germany	*fl.* 1822		**Heb. Grammar, Leipzig, 1822**
Donatus, Franc.	Italy	c.1598–1635	Dominican	**St. 165, Nachtrag p. 121**
Dorothea Maria, wife of John, Duke of Saxe-Weimar	Germany	17th c.		**Zeitschr. f. Heb. Bibl. xx, 67**
Dove, John	England	*fl.* 1746		**St. 165 note, Bodl. Cat. 894**
Dowling, Ed. Dowman	England	*fl.* 1797		**Heb. Grammar, London, 1797**
Drusius (Driesche), Joh. van den I	Holland	1550–1616	Calvinist	**St. 166, Nachtrag p.121; NBU; ADB; Enc. Br. [11]**
Drusius (Driesche), Joh II	England	1588–1609		**St. 167, Bodl. Cat. 895**
Dufour, Thom.	France	*fl.* 1642	Benedictine	**Heb. Grammar, Paris, 1642**
Du Monin, Jean Edouard	France	1557–1586		
Duncan, William Wallace	England	*fl.* 1841		**Heb. Lexicon, London 1841**
Duns Scotus, Joh.	Scotland	1265(?)– 1308 (?)	Franciscan	**St. 1, 50; DNB; NBU**
Dunster, Henry	New England (U.S.A.)	1609–1659		**DNB**
Du Plessis–Mornay, *see* Mornay, Philippe de				
Easton, Adam	England	d. 1397	Benedictine	**St. 1; DNB**
Eath, Augustinus	?	?		**G. Meuschen, Nov. Test. ex Talmude Illustr. 197, 17**
Ebert(-us), Jac.	Germany	1549–1614		**St. 168; Bodl. Cat. 901; NBU**
Ebert(us), Theod.	Germany	d. 1630		**St. 169; Bodl. Cat. 901; NBU**
Edzardus, Esdras	Germany	1629–1708	Lutheran	**ADB; NBU**

Christian Hebraists (continued)

Name	Country-(ies)	Dates	Religious Confession	References
Eggers, Jo.	Switzerland	*fl.* 1719		**St. 170**
Egidio da Viterbo, *see* Viterbo, Aegidius da				
Einem, Joh. Justus von	Germany	*fl.* 1714– 1736		**St. 171; NBU**
Einsiedel, Marg. Sybilla, widow of Conrad Loeser	Germany	*fl.* 1670		**Zeitschr. f. Heb. Bibl. xx, 67**
Eisenmenger, Joh. Andr.	Germany	1654–1704	Lutheran	
Eisentraut, Alex., *see* Sancto Aquilino (Eisentraut), Alexius				
Elisabeth, Abbess of Pfalz	Germany	d. 1680		**Zeitschr. f. Heb. Bibl. xx, 67**
Elius, Matth. (? apostate Jew)	Germany	?		**St. 173**
Eloise, wife of Abelard	France	d.c. 1163		**Zeitschr. f. Heb. Bibl. xx, 68**
Elwert, Chr. Gottlieb	Germany	*fl.* 1822		**Heb. Lexicon, Reutlingen, 1822**
Engestroem, Jo.	Sweden	*fl.* 1733		**Heb. Grammar, Lund, 1733**
Engotler, Jos.	Austria	*fl.* 1758		**Heb. Grammar, Gratz 1758**
Ens, Petrus	Holland	18th c.		**NNBW 8, 487**
Ercsei, Daniel	Hungary	1754–1809	Calvinist	**Marm; Szin; Zov.**
Erdósi, Sylvester JFnos	Hungary	1504–155?	Catholic	**Marm; Szin; Zov; János Balazs, E.S. Budapest, 1961**
Erpen(-ius), Thom. van	Holland	1584–1624	Calvinist	**NNBW; ADB; NBU; Enc. Br. [11]**
Ertel, János	Hungary	1710(?)– 1757	Lutheran	**Venet.; Marm; Szin; Zov.**
Esenwein, M.	Germany	17th c.		**JQR, 9 (1896/97), 509–4**
Esgers, Jo.	Holland	18th c.		**St. 175**
Espencaeus (d'Espence), Claude	France	1511–1571	Catholic	**NBU**
Etheridge, John Wesley	England	1804–1866	Methodist	**DNB**
Eugubinus, *see* Steuco (Steuchus Eugubinus), Agostino				
Ewald, Geo. Heinr. Aug.von	Germany	1803–1875		**ADB; NBU**
Faber, George	Germany	17th c.		**Heb. Grammar, Nuremberg, 1626**
Faber Boderianus, *see* Le Fèvre de la Boderie, Guy and Nicolas				
Faber Stapulensis, *see* Le Fèvre d'Etaples, Jacques				
Fabricius, Ern. Christ.	Germany	*fl.* 1792		**St. 176. Bodl. Cat. 977**
Fabricius, Friedr.	Germany	1642–1703		**St. 177; NBU**
Fabricius, Guido, *see* Le Fèvre de la Boderie, Guy				
Fabricius, János	Hungary	1678–1734	Lutheran	**Marm; Szin.**
Fabricius, Laurentius	Germany	1555–1629	Lutheran (?)	**R. Dan, Journ. Jew. Stud. 19 (1968) 72**
Fabricius, Phil. Jac.	Germany	17th c.		**St. 177, note; Bodl. Cat. 977**
Fabricius, Theod.	Germany	1501–1570		**NBU**
Fagius (Buchlein), Paulus	France, England	1504–1549	Anglican	**St. 178; Bodl. Cat. 977, 3080; DNB; ADB; NBU**
Fahländer, Jo.	Sweden	18th c.		**St. 269 (Lundius)**
Fairclough, Richard	England	1553–1630		**Foster; Venn**
Farkas, György	Hungary	171?–1776	Lutheran	**Marm; Szin; Zov.**
Farkas, Jakab	Hungary	1630–167?	Calvinist	**Szin; Dan**
Faust(-ius), Joh. Friedr.	Germany	*fl.* 1706		**St. 180**
Feilmoser, Adr. Benedict	Austria	1777–1831		**ADB**
Fekler, Ignaz Aurel	Austria	1756–1839	Lutheran	**B.L.K. Oest.**
Fell, John	England	1625–1686		**DNB**
Fell, Margaret	England	1614–1702	Quaker	**L. Roth, Journ. Sem. Stud. 6 (1961), p. 210**
Ferenczi, Tobias	Hungary	1701–1767	Catholic	**Marm; Szin.**
Ferrand, Louis	France	1645–1699		**St. 181; NBU**

Christian Hebraists (continued)

Name	Country-(ies)	Dates	Religious Confession	References
Fessler, Ign. Aurelius	Germany	1756–1839		**ADB; Enc. Br.** [11]
Feuardent, Francois	France	1539–1610	Franciscan	
Ficino, Marsiglio	Italy	1433–1499	Catholic	**St.A. 35b; J. Perles, Rev. Etudes Juives, 12, 244–57**
Field, Frederick	England	1801–1885		**DNB**
Figueiro, Petrus	?Flanders	*fl.* 1615		**St. 182, Bodl. Cat. 981**
Fitz–Gerald, Gerald	Ireland	*fl.* 1799		**Heb. Grammar, Dublin 1799**
Flavigny, Valérian de	France	d. 1674		**NBU**
Floravanti, Gerónimo	Italy	1554–1630	Jesuit	**Bibl. Comp. de Jèsus 3, 791**
Fockens, Herman Fr. Th.	Holland	1794–1868		**NNBW 8, 552**
Foecklerus, Jo.	Holland	*fl.* 1658		**Heb. Grammar, Amsterdam, 1658**
Fontanella, Franc.	Italy	*fl.* 1824		**Heb. Lexicon, Venice, 1824**
Foreiro, Francisco	Portugal	1510–1581	Dominican	**NBU; Grande Enc. Port. e Brasil. 11 (1940), 623**
Forster (Föster, Forsthemius, or Vorstheimer), Johann	Switzerland	1496–1558	Lutheran	**Heb. Lexicon, Basle, 1557**
Fourmont, Etienne (sen.)	France	1683–1745		**St. 183; NBU; Enc. Br.** [11]
Fox, George	England	1624–1691	Quaker	**DNB; L. Roth, Journ. Sem. Stud. 6 (1961), 208**
Franciscus, Maria	?	?	Capuchin	**St. 183b, Nachtrag p.121**
Franck, Sebastian	Germany	1499–1542		**St. 184; ADB; Enc. Br.** [11]
Franke (Francus), Gregorius	Germany	*fl.* 1634		**Heb. Lexicon, Hanover, 1634**
Franz, Wolfgang	Germany	1564–1628	Lutheran	**ADB**
Frey, Jo. Ludw.	Switzerland	1682–1759		**St. 185; ADB; NBU**
Freytag, Geo. Wilh. Friedr.	Germany	1788–1861		**ADB; NBU; Enc. Br.** [11]
Friedrichson, D.	Germany	*fl.* 1871		**Heb. Grammar, Mainz, 1871**
Frischlin, Nicodemus	France	(?)1547– 1590		**NBU; ADB; Enc. Br.** [11]
Frischmuth, Joh.	Germany	1619–1687	Lutheran	**ADB; NBU**
Fritsch, Ernst Aug.	Germany	*fl.* 1838		**Kritik of grammar, Frankfurt, 1838**
Frommann(-us), Erhard Andr.	Germany	1722–1774	Catholic (?)	**St. 186; ADB; NBU**
Fronmueller, Conrad	Germany	*fl.* 1679		**St. 186 (bis)**
Fullenius, Bernardus	Holland	1602–1657		**NNBW 3, 426**
Fuller, Nicholas	England	1557(?)– 1626	Anglican	**St. 187; DNB; NBU**
Gaffarel(lus), Jacques	France	1601–1681	Catholic	**St. 188, Nachtrag p.121; NBU**
Gagnier, John	France, England	1670(?)– 1740		**St. 189; DNB; NBU**
Galatinus, Petrus Columna	Italy	1460–1540	Franciscan	**St. 190, Nachtrag p. 121**
Gallicciolli, Joh. Baptist	(Austria), Italy	1733–1806	Catholic	**B.L.K. Oest.**
Garcia Blanco, Antonio	Spain	?		
Garzias, Dominicus	Spain	*fl.* 1598	Catholic	
Gastabled, Franciscus, *see* Vatable, François				
Gataker, Thomas	England	1574–1654		**DNB; NBU**
Gaudia, Barthol. Valverdio	Spain	?		**St. 192**
Gaulmin, Gilbert	France	1585–1665	Catholic	**St. 193; NBU**
Gebhard, Brandanus Heinr.	Germany	1657–1729	Lutheran	**ADB**
Geitlin, Gabriel	?	*fl.* 1856		**Heb. Grammar, Helsingfors, 1856**
Gejerus, Martin	Germany	1614–1680		**St. 194, Nachtrag p.121; ADB**
Gelbe, H.	Germany	?		**Heb. Grammar, Leipzig, 1868**
Génébrard, Gilbert	France	1537–1597	Catholic	**St. 195, Nachtrag p.121, Bodl. Cat. 1026, Add; NBU**
Gennaro, Sisti	Italy	*fl.* 1747		**Heb. Grammar, Venice 1747**
Gentius (Gentz), Georg	(Germany), Holland	1618–1687	Lutheran	**St. 196, Nachtrag p.121; NNBW ix, 277; NBU**
Georgios, Chrysococca	Greece	1340– 1356 (?)		**St. A. 24, Heb. Übers 629**
Gerard of Cremona	Italy	c. 1114– 1187		**Enc. Br.** [11]

Christian Hebraists (continued)

Name	Country-(ies)	Dates	Religious Confession	References
Gerhard, Jo. Ernest G.	Germany	1621–1668		
Gerhard, Jo. G.	Germany	1582–1637	Lutheran	**ADB; NBU; Enc. Br.** [11]
Germber, Hermann	Germany	*fl.* 1604		**St. 197, Bodl. Cat. 1009; ADB**
Gerrans, R.	England	*fl.*1784		**St. 197 (with reservations)**
Gersdorff, Henrietta Kath. Friesen	Germany	17th c.		**Zeitschr. f. Heb. Bibl. xx,68**
Gesenius, Fr. Heinr. Wilh.	Germany	1786–1842		**ADB; NBU; Enc. Br.**[11]
Geyer (Geier), Martin	Germany	1614–1680	Lutheran	**St. 194; ADB**
Gezelius, Jo.	Lithuania	1615–1690		**NBU**
Gibelius, Abr.	?	*fl.* 1603		**Heb. Grammar, Wittenberg, 1603**
Giggeius (Giggeo), Ant.	Italy	d. 1632		**St. 198, Bodl. Cat. 1018; NBU**
Gill, John	England	1697–1771	Baptist	**St. 199; DNB; NBU**
Giorgio (Zorzi), Francesco	Italy	1460–1540	Franciscan	**Meuschen, Nov. Test. ex Talmude Illustr., 173, 17**
Giraud, l'Abbé	France, Poland	*fl.* 1825		**Heb. Fr. Vocab., Vilna, 1825**
Gireandeau, Bonar	France	*fl.* 1758–1778		**Heb. Grammar & Lex., Paris, 1758, 1778**
Giustiniani (Justinianus), Agostino	Italy, France	c. 1470–1536	Dominican	
Glaeser, Jos.	Germany (?)	*fl.* 1832		**Heb. Grammar, Ratisbon, 1832**
Glaire, Jean Baptiste	France	b. 1798		**Heb. & Aramaic Grammar, Paris, 1832**
Glass(-ius), Solomon	Germany	1593–1656	Lutheran	**ADB; Enc. Br.** [11]
Gleichgross, György	Hungary	1669–1712	Lutheran	**Marm; Szin; Zov.**
Godwyn, Thomas	England	1587–1642	Anglican	**DNB; Trans. Jew. Hist. Soc. Eng. vi (1912), 58**
Goez, Georg	?	?		**Ugolini, 30, 1160**
Goldhahn, Matth., *see* Aurogallus, Matth.				
Golius (Gohl), Jac.	Holland	1596–1667	Calvinist	**NNBW; ADB; NBU**
Gomarus	Holland	17th c.		**Prof. Groningen in 1630s**
Gousset (Gusset), Jacques	France, Holland	1635–1704	Protestant	**NNBW; NBU**
Graf, Karl Heinr.	Germany	1815–1869		**Enc. Br.**[11]
Grajal, Gaspar	Spain	16th c.		**Enc. Univ. Illustr. Eur.-Amer. 26, 967**
Granberg, Nic.	Sweden	*fl.* 1723		**St. 357 (S.V. Schulten)**
Grapo (Grappius), Zach.	Germany	1671–1713	Lutheran	**ADB; NBU**
Graser, Conrad	Germany	d. 1613		**St. 200**
Green, William	England	1714(?)– 1794		**DNB**
Gregori, Greg.	?	?	Lutheran	**Meuschen, Nov. Test. ex Talmude Illustr., 215, 18**
Greissing, Bálint	Hungary	1653–1701	Lutheran	**Marm; Szin; Zov.**
Greve (Greeve), Egbert van	Holland	1754–1811		**NBU**
Grey, Lady Jane	England	1537–1554		**Zeitschr. f. Heb. Bibl. xx, 68**
Grey, Richard	England	1694–1771		**DNB; NBU**
Groddeck, Gabr.	Germany	1672–1709		**St. 201, Bodl. Cat. 1022; NBU**
Groenewoud, Jacob Cornelis Swijghuisen	Holland	1784–1859		**Heb. Grammar, Utrecht, 1834**
Groll, Adolf	Hungary	1681–1743	Catholic	**Marm; Szin; Zov.**
Grotius (de Groot), Hugo	Holland	1583–1645	Remonstrant	**NNBW; NBU; ADB; Enc. Br.**[11]
Gualtperius, Otto	Germany	*fl.* 1590		**Heb. Grammar, Wittenberg, 1590**
Guarin, Pierre	France	1678–1729		**NBU**
Guevas, Aloysa Sigaea de	Spain	d. 1569		**Zeitschr. f. Heb. Bibl. xx, 69**
Guidacerio(-ius), Agathius	Italy	1477–1540	Catholic	**St. 202, Bodl. Cat. 1022; NBU**
Guise, William	England	1653(?)– 1683		**St. 203, Bodl. Cat. 1022; DNB**
Gundissalinus (Gundisalvo, Gundusalvi) Dominicus	Spain	*fl.* 1150		**Enc. Univ. Euro-Americana 27, 323; J.T. Muckle, De Anima of D.G., Toronto, 1940**

Christian Hebraists (continued)

Name	Country-(ies)	Dates	Religious Confession	References
Guertler, Nic.	Germany, Holland	1653/4–1711	Calvinist	**NNBW 6, 654; ADB; NBU**
Guete, Heinr. Ernst				
Gusset, Jacques, *see* Gousset, Jacques	Germany	*fl.* 1782		**Heb. Grammar, Halle, 1782**
Guyenne, Madame de	France	c. 1625		**Zeitschr. f. Heb. Bibl. xx, 68**
Gyarmathi, Samuel	Hungary	1751–1830	Calvinist	**Venet., Zov.**
Gyarmazi, István	Hungary	17th c.	Calvinist	**Dan**
Gyles, J.F.	England	*fl.* 1814		**Heb. Grammar, London, 1814–1816**
Gyöngyösi de Heteny, Paul	Hungary, Russia	1707–1769	Lutheran	**B.L.K. Oest.**
Haarbrccker, Theod.	Germany	19th c.		**Continued (Halle, 1843) Schnurrer's Tanhum Yerushalmi on Judges.**
Haas (Hasse), Jo. Gottfried	Germany	1737–1815		**ADB; NBU**
Habeler, Jakab	Hungary	1722–1793	Catholic	**Marm; Szin**
Habermann (Avenarius), Johannes	Germany	1520–1590		**Heb. Grammar, Wittenberg, 1562; Neu. Deutch. Biogr. 1, 467**
Habert, Susanna	France	d. 1633		**Zeitschr. f. Heb. Bibl. xx, 68**
Hackspan, Theodoric	Germany	1607–1659		**St. 204, Bodl. Cat. 1025; ADB; NBU**
Haener, Joh. Henr.	?	1682–1701	Lutheran	**Br. Mus. Cat.**
Halenius, Engelbert	Sweden	1700–1767		**St. 205, Bodl. Cat. 1877; no. 45; Svensk**
Haller, Albrecht von	Switzerland	1708–1777		**St. 206; ADB; NBU; Enc. Br.[11]**
Hamaker, Hendrik Arent	Holland	1789–1835		**NNBW; NBU**
Hambraeus, Jonas	Sweden, France	1588–1671		**Svensk; NBU**
Hamelsveld, Ysbrand van	Holland	1743–1812		**NBU**
Hamius, Jac.	Germany	*fl.* 1624		**Heb. Grammar, Hamburg 1624**
Hanel, Melchior	Bohemia	*fl.* 1661		**St. 207; Bodl. Cat. 796**
Haner, György	Hungary	1672–1740	Calvinist	**Marm; Szin; Pap.**
Hanewinkel, Gerhardus	Germany	*fl.* 1636		**Heb. Grammar, Bremen, 1636**
Hanne(c)ken, Meno (Memnon)	Germany	1595–1671		**St. 208; ADB**
Hannes, Edward	England	d. 1710		**DNB**
Happelius, Wigand	Switzerland	*fl.* 1561		**Heb. Grammar, Basle, 1561**
Harding, John	England	d. 1610		**Foster**
Harding, Stephen	England, France	1060(?)–1134	Cistercian	**Trans. Jew. Hist. Soc. Eng. 17(1953) 233; DNB; NBU**
Hardt, Anton Jul. van der	Germany	1707–1785		**St. 209, Bodl. Cat. 1094**
Hardt, Hermann van der	Germany	1660–1746	Lutheran	**St. 210, Bodl. Cat. 1032; ADB; NBU**
Hare, Francis	England	1671–1740	Anglican	**DNB; NBU**
Harrison, Thomas	England	1555–1631		**DNB**
Harrison, Thomas	England	1716–1753		**Venn**
Hart, John	England	?		**C. Roth, Bodl. Lib. Record, 7 (1966), 244**
Hartmann, Ant. Theodor	Germany	1774–1838	Protestant	**St. 213, Nachtrag p.121; ADB; NBU**
Hartmann, Joh. Melchior	Germany	1764–1827		**ADB; NBU**
Hartmann, Jo. Phil.	Germany	*fl.* 1708		**St. 211**
Hase, Christ. Gottfr.	Germany	*fl.* 1750		**Heb. Linguistic Study, Halle, 1750**
Haselbauer, Franz	Austria	1677–1756	Catholic	**B.L.K. Oest.**
Hasse, Jo. Gottfried, *see* Haas, Jo. Gottfried				
Hautecourt, Hen. Philipponneau de	France, Holland	1646–1715	Huguenot	**NNBW**
Havemann, Christoph.	Germany	17th c.		**St. 214**

Christian Hebraists (continued)

Name	Country-(ies)	Dates	Religious Confession	References
Havemann, Michael	Germany	1597–1672	Lutheran	**ADB**
Hebenstreit, Joh. Chr.	Germany	1686–1756	Protestant	**St. 215, Bodl. Cat. 1033; NBU**
Hedmann, Cl.	Sweden	18th c.		**St. 216, Bodl. Cat. 682**
Heeser, Johann.	? Germany	*fl.* 1716		**Heb. & Chald. Lex., Harderov, 1716**
Heidegger, Joh. Heinr.	Switzerland	1633–1698	Reformed Ch.	**ADB; NBU; Enc. Br.[11]**
Heilbronn, Anna	Hungary	18th c.	Calvinist	**Marm; Szin.**
Heinsius (Heinzs), Dan	Flanders, Holland	1580(?)–1655	Reformed Ch.	**NNBW; B.N. Belg.; ADB; NBU; Enc. Br.[11]**
Helen, John	England	d. 1839		**inf. from C. Roth; his Modern Judaism untraced; Gentleman's Magazine**
Hellmann, Laur.	Sweden	18th c.		**St. 137, Bodl. Cat. 1877**
Helman, Andr.	Sweden	18th c.		**St. 357 (sv. Schulten)**
Helmont, Joh. Baptist van	Holland	1577–1644	Protestant	**(untraced)**
Helner, Samuel	Hungary	18th c.	Calvinist	**St. 243, Bodl. Cat. 1582; Marm; Szin.**
Heltai, Gáspár	Hungary	1520–1574	Calvinist	**Szin; Zov; Erzsébet Székely, H.G., Budapest, 1957**
Helvicus, Christophorus	Germany	1581–1616	Lutheran	
Helwig (Helvicus)	Germany	1581–1617	Lutheran	**St. 220, Nachtrag p.121, Bodl. Cat. 1038; ADB**
Hempel, Ernst Wilh.	Germany	*fl.* 1776		**Heb. Grammar, Leipzig, 1776**
Henry of Hessen (Langenstein)	Germany	1340–1397		**NBU**
Hepburn, (Jas.) Bonaventura	Scotland, Italy	1573–1620	Minim	**St. 221, Bodl. Cat. 1382; DNB; NBU**
Hertel, W. Chr.	Austria	*fl.* 1735		**Heb. Grammar, Gratz, 1735**
Hesse, Anna Sophia von	Germany	*fl.* 1658	Catholic	**Zeitschr. f. Heb. Bibl. xx, 66**
Hetzel (Hezel), Joh. Wilh. Friedr.	Germany	1754–1829		**NBU**
Heyman, Johannes	Holland	18th c.		
Hiller(-us), Matth.	Germany	1646–1725	Protestant	**ADB; NBU**
Hilliger, Joh. Wilh.	Germany	1667–1701	Lutheran	**Br. Mus. Cat.**
Hilpert, Jo.	Germany	*fl.* 1651		**St. 222, Bodl. Cat. 1875**
Hilvai, János	Hungary	1720(?)–1769	Calvinist	**Marm; Szin; Zov.**
Hincks, Edward	Ireland	1792–1866		**DNB**
Hinkelmann, Abr.	Germany	1652–1695		**St. 223; ADB; NBU**
Hinlopen, Jelmer	Holland	18th c.		**NNBW 8, 777**
Hirth (Hirtius), Joh. Friedr.	Germany	1719–1784		**St. 224, Bodl. Cat. 1043; ADB; NBU**
Hochstet(t)er, Andreas Adam	Germany	1668–1717	Protestant	**St. 225; ADB**
Hody, Humphrey	England	1659–1707		**DNB; NBU**
Hoffmann, Jo. Ge.	Germany	*fl.* 1767		**Heb. Grammar, Giessen, 1767**
Holland, Thomas	England	d. 1612		**DNB; C. Roth, Bodl. Lib. Record, 6 (1966), 245**
Hollenberg, W.	Germany	*fl.* 1861		**Heb. Grammar, Berlin 1861**
Holten, Albert	Germany	*fl.* 1675		**St. 226**
Hombergk, Joh. Friedr.	Germany	1673–1748	Reformed Ch.	**ADB**
Hommel, Karl Ferd.	Germany	1722–1781		**St. 227, Bodl. Cat. 1046; ADB; NBU**
Honert, Taco Hajo van den	Holland	1666–1740		**NNBW**
Honorius	Scotland	*fl.* 1452	Cistercian (?)	**St. A. 27**
Hooght, Everardus van der	Holland	*fl.* 1686		**Heb. Grammar, Amsterdam 1686**
Hoornbeck, Joh.	Holland	1617–1666	Dutch Ref.	**NNBW; ADB**
Horche, Heinr.	Germany	1652–1729	Separatist	**ADB**
Horne, Robert	England	1519(?)–1580		**DNB; L. Roth, Journ. Sem. Stud. 6 (1961), 206**

Christian Hebraists (continued)

Name	Country-(ies)	Dates	Religious Confession	References
Hottinger, Joh. Heinr.	Switzerland	1620–1667	Swiss Ref.	**St. 228, Nachtrag p.121, Bodl. Cat. 1038; ADB; NBU; Enc. Br.[11]**
Hottinger, Joh. Heinr. II	Germany	1681–1750	Swiss Ref.	**St. 229, Bodl. Cat. 1048; ADB; NBU**
Hottinger, Joh. Jakob	Switzerland	1652–1735		
Houbigant(-ius), Chas. Franc.	France	1686–1783		**NBU**
Houting, Hendrik	Holland	*fl.* 1695	Calvinist	**St. 230, Bodl. Cat. 1048**
Hrabski, János	Hungary	1625–1678	Calvinist	**Szin; Zov.**
Hubschmann, I. Matth.	Germany	*fl.* 1751		**Heb. Grammar (Geschwinder Hebraer), Eisenach, 1751**
Huerga, Cipriano de la	Spain	?		**Colomils, Ital. et Hisp. Orientalis, index (only).**
Huet, Pierre Daniel	France	1630–1721	Jesuit	**NBU; Enc. Br.[11]**
Hufnagel, G.F.	Germany	*fl.* 1795		**St. 231, Bodl. Cat. 2720, Add. 1049**
Hugh of St. Cher	France	1200(?)–1263	Dominican	**Enc. Br.[11]; Smalley, Study of Bible in M. Ages[2], 398**
Hugh of St. Victor	Flanders, France	1078(?)–1141	Victorine	**NBU; Enc. Br.[11]; Smalley, op. cit., 398**
Hugo Insulanus, T.				**St. 232**
Huldrich(-icus), Joh. Jac.	Switzerland	1683–1731		**St. 233, Bodl. Cat. 1049; NBU**
Hulse(-ius), Ant.	Holland	1615–1685	Calvinist	**St. 234, Bodl. Cat. 1049; NNBW**
Hulsius, Paul	Holland	1653–1712	Dutch Ref.	**NNBW**
Hunt, Thomas	England	1696–1774		**DNB; NBU**
Hupfeld, Hermann Chr. Karl Friedr.	Germany	1796–1866		**ADB; NBU; Enc. Br.[11]**
Huré (Hureus), Car.	France	1639–1717	Jansenist	**NBU**
Husen, Franc. van	Holland	*fl.* 1676		**St. 235, Bodl. Cat. 1050**
Hussgen, Johannes, *see* Oecolampadius, Johannes				
Huszi, György	Hungary	1710–1768	Calvinist	**Marm; Szin; Zov.**
Hutter(-us), Elias	Germany	1553– 1607(?)		**ADB**
Hyde (H(e)ydius), Thomas	England	1636–1703		**St. 236, Bodl. Cat. 1050; DNB; NBU; Trans. Jew. Hist. Soc. Engl., Index**
Iken(ius), Conrad	Germany	1689–1753		**St. 237, Bodl. Cat. 1054; ADB; NBU**
Imbonati(-tus), Carlo Guiseppe	Italy	1650(?)–1696	Cistercian	**St. 238, Bodl. Cat. 1052; NBU**
Jacobi, J. Ad.	Germany	*fl.* 1797		**Heb. Grammar, Jena, 1797**
Jacob(s)(-bius), Henry	England	1608–1652		**St. 239; Foster**
Jahn, Joh.	Austria	1750–1816		**ADB; NBU; Enc. Br.[11]**
Janvier (Januarius), René	France	1613–1682	Benedictine	**St. 240, Bodl. Cat. 1249; NBU**
Jarrett, Thomas	England	1805–1882		**DNB**
Jean François de Binans, *see* Binans, Jean François de				
Jehne, Lebr. H.S.	Germany	*fl.* 1790		**Heb. Grammar, Altona, 1790**
Jenei, György	Hungary	17th c.	Calvinist	**Dan**
Jennings, David	England	1691–1762	Dissenter	**DNB; NBU**
Jetzius, Paul	Germany	*fl.* 1729		**Heb. Grammar, Stettin, 1729**
Jiménez de Cisneros, Francisco, *see* Ximénez de Cisneros, Francisco				
Johannes Luccae	Italy	*fl.* 1406		**St. A. 31, 254, Nachtrag p. 87, Heb. Bibliog. xv, 39; Z.D.M.G. 25, 404**
Johannson, Th. Carl	Denmark	*fl.* 1835		**Heb. Grammar, Copehagen, 1835**
Jones, William	England	1746–1794		**DNB; NBU**

Christian Hebraists (continued)

Name	Country-(ies)	Dates	Religious Confession	References
Jong, P. de	Holland	1832–1890		**NNBW 1, 1227**
Jud(ä), Leo	Germany, Switzerland	1482–1542	Reformer	**ADB; NBU; Enc. Br.[11]**
Junius (Du Jon), Franc.	France, Holland	1545–1602	Huguenot	**NNBW**
Jurieu, Pierre	France, Holland	1639–1713	Huguenot	**NNBW; NBU; Enc. Br.[11]**
Justinianus, Aug., *see* Giustiniani, Agostino				
Juynboll, Dietrich Will. (Joh.?) van	Holland	1802–1861		**NNBW**
Kalau, Abr., *see* Calov(ius), Abr.				
Kallai, Kopis János	Hungary	1645–1681	Calvinist	**Zov; Dan**
Kalmár, György	Hungary	1726–178?	Calvinist	**Marm; Szin; Zov; Pap.**
Kals, Joh. Guil.	Holland	b. 1702		**NNBW**
Kalthoff, J.A.	Germany	*fl.* 1837		**Heb. Grammar, Ratisbon, 1837**
Kamarási, Pal	Hungary	1693–1735	Calvinist	**Szin; Zov; Pap.**
Kampen, Jan van, *see* Campen(-sis), Jan van				
Kaposi, Samuel	Hungary	1660–1713	Calvinist	**Marm; Szin; Zov.**
Károlyi, Gáspár	Hungary	1529–1592	Calvinist	**Marm; Szin; Zov; K.G. Budapest, 1958**
Kaszaniczky, Ádám (de Nagy Selmecz)	Hungary	1748–1804	Catholic	**Marm; Szin**
Katona Gelei, István	Hungary	1589–1649	Calvinist	**Marm; Szin; Zov; Károly Brassay, G.K.I. Hajdunanas, 1903**
Kehe, G.J.	Russia	?		**Meuschen, Nov. Test. ex Talmude Illustr. 264, 23**
Kekkermannus, Balth.	Germany	*fl.* 1625		**Heb. Grammar, Hanau, 1625**
Keller, Gottl. Wilh.	Germany	17th c.		**St. 243, Bold. Cat. 1582**
Kelp, Márton	Hungary, (Germany?)	1659–1694		**Szin; Zov; ADB**
Kemink, H.H.	Holland	1817–1861		**NNBW 3, 676**
Kemmel, János	Hungary	1636–1685	Calvinist	**Marm; Szin; Dan**
Kennicott, Benjamin	England	1718–1783		**DNB; NBU**
Keresztes, József	Hungary	1846–1888	Calvinist	**Szin; Zov.**
Keresztesi, Pál	Hungary	1711–1734	Calvinist	**Marm; Szin.**
Kereszturi, Bálint	Hungary	1634–1680	Calvinist	**Marm; Szin; Zov.**
Kern, Mihály	Hungary	1731–1795	Calvinist	**Marm; Szin; Zov.**
Kerssenbroich, Hermanus	Germany	*fl.* 1560		**Heb. Grammar, Cologne, 1560**
Kesler (Chesselius, Ahenarius), Joh. Conrad	Switzerland	1502–1574	Lutheran	**Ugolini 28, 766; Enc. Rel Kn.**
Keyworth, Thomas	England	1782–1852		**DNB**
Kiber, David, *see* Kyber, David				
Kihn, H.	Germany	*fl.* 1885		**Heb. Grammar (with D. Shilling), Freiburg, 1885**
Kilbye, Richard	England	1561(?)–1620		**DNB; NBU**
King, Geoffrey	England	c.1567–1630		**Venn**
Kingsmill, Thos. Reg.	England	*fl.* 1605		**DNB**
Kircher, Athanasius	Germany, France, Italy	1602–1680	Jesuit	**St. 244, Nachtrag p.121, Bodl. Cat. 1584; ADB; NBU**
Kirschner, Conrad, *see* Pellicanus, Conrad				
Kismarjai Weszelin, PFI	Hungary	1600–1645	Calvinist	**Marm; Szin; Pap; Dan**
Klai, Joh., *see* Clajus, Johannes				
Klemm, Jac. Friedr.	Germany	*fl.* 1783		**Heb. Grammar, Tübingen, 1783**
Klemm, Joh. Christ.	Germany	*fl.* 1745		**Heb. Lex., Tübingen, 1745**
Kloppenburgh, Joh.	Holland	1592–1652		**NNBW; NBU**
Knipe, Thomas	England	1638–1711		**DNB**
Knollys, Manserd	England	1599(?)–1691	Baptist	**DNB**

Christian Hebraists (continued)

Name	Country-(ies)	Dates	Religious Confession	References
Knorr von Rosenroth, Christian	Germany	1636–1689	Lutheran	**St. 245, Bodl. Cat. 1586; ADB; NBU**
Knowlles, Richard	England	*fl.* 1600		**Grk. & Heb. Grammar, London, 1600**
Koch, Friedr. Christ.	Germany	*fl.* 1740		**Heb. Grammar, Jena, 1740**
Koch (Cocceius), Johannes	Holland	1603–1669	Calvinist	**St. 149, Bodl. Cat. 847; NNBW; ADB; NBU; Enc. Br.[11]**
Kochhaff, David, *see* Chytraeus, David				
Kocsi Csergö, István	Hungary	1700–1726	Calvinist	**Marm; Szin; Zov.**
Kocsi Major, Ferenc	Hungary	1680–1743	Calvinist	**Marm; Szin**
Kocsi Sebestyén, István	Hungary	1761–1841	Calvinist	**Marm; Szin; Zov.**
Koecher, Herm. Friedr.	Germany	*fl.* 1783		**St. 246, Bodl. Cat. 1586**
Koenig, Gu.	Germany	*fl.* 1847		**St. 348**
Koenig, Sam.	Switzerland	1670–1750		**St. 248, 332, Bodl. Cat. 245–6**
Koepfel, Wolfgang Fabricius, *see* Capito, Wolfgang Fabricius				
Koeppen, Nic.	Germany	*fl.* 1709		**St. 249, Bodl. Cat. 2372**
Koeppen, Nic.	?	*fl.* 1720–1730	Lutheran	**St. 249**
Köleséri, Samuel	Hungary	1634–1683	Calvinist	**Marm; Szin; Zov.**
Komáromi, Csipkes György	Hungary	1628–1678	Calvinist	**Károlyi Gáspár, K.C.G. Budapest, 1940**
Koolhaas, Jo. Christoph.	Germany	*fl.* 1670		**Heb. Grammar, Coburg, 1670**
Koolhaas, Willem	Holland	1709–1773		**Br. Mus. Cat.**
Körösi, Mihály	Hungary	1706–1775	Calvinist	**Marm; Szin; Zov.**
Körösi, Uri János	Hungary	1724–1796	Calvinist	**Marm; Szin; Zov.; I. Goldziher, K.U.J., Budapest, 1908**
Kosegarten, Joh. Gottfr. Ludw.	Germany	1792–1860		**St. 250, Bodl. Cat. 720; ADB; NBU**
Krafft, Karl	Germany	*fl.* 1839		**St. 251, Bodl. Cat. 1589**
Kraut, Paul	Sweden	*fl.* 1703		**St. 252**
Kromayer, Jo.	Germany	1576–1643		**NBU**
Kuemmel, Caspar	Germany	*fl.* 1688		**Heb. Grammar, Würtzburg, 1688**
Kyber (Kiber), David	Alsace	16th c.		**St. 253, Bodl. Cat. 1950**
Kypke, Georg David	Germany	1724–1779		**NBU**
Lakemacher, Joh. Gottf.	Germany	1695–1736		**St. 254, Bodl. Cat. 1593**
Lamy, Bernhard	France	1646–1715	Catholic	**Ugolini 32, 572; Enc. Rel. Kn.**
Landrianij, Ignazió	Italy	1579–1642	Catholic	
Lang, Kristóf	Hungary	164?–170?	Calvinist	**Marm; Szin; Zov.**
Lange, J. Christian	Germany	1669(?)–1756	Lutheran	**St. 255, Bodl. Cat. 1596; ADB; NBU**
Lange(-ius), W.	Germany, Italy	*fl.* 1710		**St. 256, Bodl. Cat. 1596**
Langenes, Henr.	Holland	*fl.* 1720		**St. 257, Bodl. Cat. 1887**
Langenstein, Heinr. von, *see* Henry of Hessen				
Langier, Jo. Jac	?	?		**St. 258**
Lapide, Cornelius B (van den Steen)	Flanders	1566–1637	Jesuit	**B.N. Belg; Enc. Br.[11]**
Laskai, Matko János	Hungary	1605–1663	Calvinist	**Szin; Dan**
Latouche, Auguste	France	*fl.* 1836		**Heb. Grammar, Paris, 1836**
Laurence, Richard	England	1760–1838		**DNB**
L'Avocat, Jean Bapt.	France	*fl.* 1755		**Heb. Grammar, Paris, 1755**
Layfield, John	England	d. 1617		**DNB**
Lazzarelli, Lodovico	Italy	1450–1500		
Le Clerc, Jean Thomas, *see* Clerc, Jean Thomas				
Lederlin, Joh. Heinr.	Alsace	1672–1737		**St. 259; ADB; NBU**

Christian Hebraists (continued)

Name	Country-(ies)	Dates	Religious Confession	References
Lee, Edward	England	1482(?)–1544		**DNB; NBU; F. Perez Castro, Alfonso de Zamora, 1vii**
Lee, Samuel	England	1625–1691	Puritan	**DNB**
Lee, Samuel	England	1783–1852		**DNB; NBU**
Le Fèvre (Fabèr Boderianus) de la Boderie, Guy	France, Flanders	1541–1598	Catholic	**NBU; Colomiès, Gallia Orient.; F. Secret, Le Zôhar chez… chrétiens, 139**
Le Fèvre de la Boderie, Nicolas	France, Flanders	1550–1613	Catholic	**F. Secret, ibid.**
Lefèvre d'Etaples (Faber Stapulensis), Jacques	France	1455(?)–1537(?)	Evangelical	**NBU; Enc. Br.[11]**
Lehmann, Ge. Heinr.	Germany	1619–1699		**St. 259b, Nachtrag p.121, Bodl. Cat. 233**
Leib, Chilian	Germany	1471–1548		**St. 260, Berlin Cat. i, 53, ii, v (MS 77)**
Leigh, Edward	England	1602–1671	Puritan	**DNB; NBU**
LeLong, Jac.	France	1665–1721		**St. 261, Bodl. Cat. 1599, Addenda; NBU; Enc. Br.[11]**
Lemoine, Henry	England	1766–1812		**DNB**
L'Empereur, Constantin van Oppyck	Holland	1591–1648		**St. 174, Nachtrag p.121, Bodl. Cat. 971 NNBW 8, 1031; ADB (S.V. Emp.)**
Lent, Joh. B	Germany	*fl.* late 17th c.	Reformed Ch.	**Ugolini 23, 1020**
Lenz, Jo. Leonh.	Germany	*fl.* 1700		**St. 262**
Leo, Christopher	England	*fl.* 1836		**Heb. Grammar, Cambridge, 1836**
León, Andrés, *see* Zamora, Andreas de León				
Leön, Luis de	Spain	1527–1591	Catholic	**NBU; Enc. Br.[11]**
Leopold, Em. Friedr.	Germany	*fl.* 1832		**Heb. & Chald. Grammar, Leipzig, 1832**
Lepusculus, Sebastian	Switzerland	1501–1576		**St. 263, Bodl. Cat. 1604**
Le Tartrier, Adrien	France	*fl.* 1586		
Lethenyei, János	Hungary	1723–1804	Catholic	**Marm; Szin.**
Lette, G.J.	Holland	1724–1760		**NNBW 10, 515**
Leusden, Joh.	Holland	1624–1699	Calvinist	**St. 264, Leiden Cat. 3; NNBW 9, 601; NBU**
Lewis, Thomas	England	1689– 1749 (?)		**DNB**
Leydekker (Leid-), Melchior	Holland	1642–1721/2	Calvinist	**St. 265, Bodl. Cat. 1622; NNBW; NBU**
Liebentanz, Mich.	Germany	before 1701	Lutheran	**Ugolini 7, 1034**
Lightfoot, John	England	1602–1675		**St. 266; DNB; NBU**
Lindberg, Jac. Christian	Denmark	b. 1797		**Heb. Grammar, Copenhagen, 1822; NBU**
Lippomani, Marco	Italy	*fl.* 1440		**St. A. 33, Heb. Übers. 320 A. 411; MS Bodl. Neubauer 2174**
Lischovini, János	Hungary	166?–172?	Calvinist	**Marm; Szin.**
Lisznyai, K. Pál	Hungary	1630–1695	Calvinist	**Marm; Szin; Zov.**
Lively, Edward	England	1545(?)– 1605		**DNB; E. Rosenthal, Essays…S.A. Cook (ed. D.W. Thomas), 1950**
Lizel, Geo.	Germany	1694–1761		**Heb. Grammar, Speyer, 1739; ADB**
Lloyd, Henry	England	1795–1831		**Venn**
Loescher, Valentin Ernst	Germany	1672/3–1749	Lutheran	**ADB; NBU**
Loeser, Margaret Sybilla, *see* Einsiedel, Margaret Sybilla				
Losa, Isabella	Spain	1491–1564		**Zeitschr. f. Heb. Bibl. xx, 68**
Loscan, Joh. Friedr.	Germany	*fl.* 1710		**St. 266a**

Christian Hebraists (continued)

Name	Country-(ies)	Dates	Religious Confession	References
Losius, Joh. Justus	?	18th c.		**St. 267, Bodl. Cat. 675**
Losontzi Hányoki, István	Hungary	1709–1780	Calvinist	**Marm; Szin; Zov.**
Louis de Valois, of Alais	France	*fl.* 1646		**F. Secret, Rev. Et. Juives 126 (1967), 423**
Louise Amoena	Germany	17th c.		**Zeitschr. f. Heb. Bibl. xx, 68**
Lowndes, Is.	?	*fl.* 1837		**Heb. Grammar in Greek, Malta, 1837**
Lowth (Louth), Robert	England	1710–1787		**DNB; NBU**
Lucca, John of, *see* Johannes Luccae				
Lucrecius, *see* Widmanstetter, Johann Albrecht				
Ludolf, Susanna Magdalena	Germany	*fl.* 1700		**Zeitschr. f. Heb. Bibl. xx, 68**
Ludovicus Sancti Francisci, *see* São Francisco, Luiz de				
Ludwig (Ludovicus,-ci), Christ. L.	Germany	1663–1732		**St. 268, Bodl. Cat. 1632**
Lull(-ius) (Lully), Raimon	Spain	1235(?)–1315		**St. A. 33, Hebr. Übers. 475; NBU; Enc. Br.[11]**
Lund, David	Sweden	1666–1747	Lutheran	**St. 269, Bodl. Cat. 274; NBU**
Lund, John	Denmark	1638–1684	Lutheran	**ADB**
Luther, Martin	Germany	1483–1546	Reformer	**ADB; NBU; Enc. Br.[11]**
Lyre (Lyra), Nicholas de, *see* Nicholas de Lyre (Lyranus)				
McCaul, Alexander	Ireland, England	c. 1799–1863	Anglican	**St. 270, Bodl. Cat. 871, 1844; DNB**
Macha, Joh.	Austria	1798–1845 (?)	Catholic	**B.L.K. Oest.**
Mádi, János	Hungary	1705–1772	Calvinist	**Marm; Szin; Zov.**
Madrigal, Alfonso Tostado, *see* Tostado, Alfonso de Madrigal				
Magnus, György	Hungary	1645–171?	Calvinist	**Marm; Szin; Zov.**
Mai, Joh. Heinr. (jun.)	Germany	1688–1732		**St. 271, Hamburg Cat. vi**
Major, József	Hungary	1739–1790	Lutheran	**Szin.**
Makai, Gergely	Hungary	17th c.	Calvinist	**Marm; Szin; Zov.**
Malamina, Caesar	Italy	*fl.* 1774		**St. 272 (+293 suppl.)**
Maldonado, Juan de	Spain	1533–1583	Jesuit	**Enc. Univ. Illustr. Eur.-Amer. 32, 498**
Mall, Sebastian	Germany	*fl.* 1808		**Heb. Grammar, Landshut, 1808**
Manetti, Gianozzo	Italy	1396–1459		**St. A. 35, Nachtrag p. 87; NBU**
Manfred Hohenstaufen, King of Sicily	Italy	1233–1266		**St. A. 34, Heb. Übers, 268; NBU; Enc. Br.[11]**
Manger, Samuel Hendrik	Holland	1735–1791		**NNBW 9, 644**
Manjacoria, Nicholas	Italy	*fl.* 1145	Cistercian	**R. Loewe, Cambr. Hist. of Bible, ii, ed. G. Lampe, 1969, 144 f.**
Mansperger, Joseph Julian	Austria	1724–1788	Catholic	**B.L.K. Oest.**
Mara (Mare), William de (la)	England, France	*fl.* 1280	Franciscan	**DNB; R. Loewe, op. cit., 149f.**
Marchina, Maria	Italy	d. 1646		**Zeitschr. f. Heb. Bibl. xx, 68**
Marck, Joh. van	Holland	1655/6–1731	Calvinist	**NNBW**
Maria Eleonore, wife of Ludwig Philipp of Pfalz	Germany	*fl.* 1669		**Zeitschr. f. Heb. Bibl. xx, 68**
Maria Elizabeth, daughter of Christian Albrecht	Germany	(?)1680–1741		**Zeitschr. f. Heb. Bibl. xx, 68 +B.N. Belg. (M.E. Theresa Josephine)**
Mariana, Juan de	Spain	1536–1624	Jesuit	**NBU; Enc. Br.[11]**
Marini, Marco	Italy	1541–1594	Augustinian	**St. 273**
Marlorat(-us) du Pasquier, Augustin	France	c. 1506–1562 (? 3)	Reformer, (Calvinist)	**NBU**
Marperger, Bernhard W.	Germany	1682–1746	Lutheran	**ADB**
Marsham, John	England	1602–1685		**DNB; NBU**

Christian Hebraists (continued)

Name	Country-(ies)	Dates	Religious Confession	References
Marsilius Ficinus, *see* Ficino, Marsiglio				
Marti, Benedictus, *see* Aretius, Benedictus				
Martinet, A.	Germany	*fl.* 1873		**Heb. Grammar (with G. Rigeler), Bamberg, 1873**
Martinez, Martinus	France	*fl.* 1548		**Heb. & Aramaic Grammar, Paris, 1548**
Martinez Cantalapiedra, Martin	Spain	?		**untraced**
Martini, Christoph. Sam.	? Germany	?	Lutheran	**Meuschen, Novum Test. ex Talmude Illustr., 212, 18**
Martini, Jo. Benjamin	Germany	*fl.* 1710		**Meuschen, 266, 25; Br. Mus. Cat.**
Martini, Raimundo (Raymond)	Spain	d. 1282	Dominican	
Martinius, Petrus	France	*fl.* 1568	Protestant	**Heb. Grammar, Paris, 1568**
Martinus, Dirck (Theodoricus) Martens	Flanders	*fl.* c. 1520		**Heb. Lex., Louvain, c.1520**
Mártonfalvi, Tóth György	Hungary	1635–1681	Calvinist	**Szin; Zov; Dan.**
Martyr, Peter (Pietro Martire Vermigli)	Italy, Alsace, England, Switzerland	1500–1562	Augustinian, turned Reformer	**DNB; NBU**
Masclefius, Franc.	France	1662–1728		**NBU**
Masius (Maes), Andreas	Flanders, Italy	1514/5–1573	(nominal) Catholic	**B.N. Belg.; ADB**
Matthias Aquarius	?	*fl.* 1581		**St. 274, Nachtrag p. 121**
Matthias, Elias Germanus	Germany	?		**St. 275; Monats. Gesch. u. Wiss. Jud., 1895/6, 280**
Maurer, Fr. J.V.D.	Germany	*fl.* 1851		**Heb. & Chal. Lex., Stuttgart, 1851**
Mayr, George	Germany	1565–1623		**NBU; Heb. Grammar, Ausburg, 1616**
Medgyesi, PFl	Hungary	1605–1663	Calvinist	**Venet.; Szin; Zov; Dan**
Meelfuehrer Joh. M.	Germany	1570–1640		**St. 276, Nachtrag p.122; D. Kaufmann Mem. Vol., 462**
Meetkerke, Edward	England	1590–1657		**DNB**
Megerlin, David Fr.	Germany	d. 1778		**St. 277**
Meier, Ernst Hein.	Germany	1813–1866		**Heb. Lex. Mannheim, 1845**
Meinhart, Geo. Friedr.	Germany	1651–1718	Lutheran	**Ugolini, 23, 812**
Meinigius, Christ. Gottl.	Germany	*fl.* 1712		**Heb. Lex., Leipzig, 1712**
Melanchthon (Schwarzerd), Philipp	Germany	1497–1560	Reformer	
Melchior, Alb. Wilh.	Germany	1685–1738		**NNBW**
Melchior, Joh.	Germany	1646–1689		**ADB**
Melius, Juhász Péter	Hungary	1536–1572	Calvinist	**Kohn; Marm; Szin; Zov.**
Mellissander, Casparus	Flanders	*fl.* 1586		**Heb. Grammar, Antwerp, 1586**
Menochio, Giovanni Stefano	Italy	1575/6–1655	Jesuit	**NBU**
Menschen, Gerhard, *see* Meuschen, Gerhard				
Merc(i)er (Mercerus), Jean	France	d. 1570		**St. 278, Bodl. Cat. 1748; NBU**
Metcalfe, Robert	England	1590(?)–1652		**DNB**
Metzlar	Holland	19th c.		**untraced**
Meuschen (Menschen, Musculus), Gerhard	Germany	1680–1743		**NBU**
Meyer (Meier), Joh.	Holland	(?)1651–1725 (?)	Calvinist	**St. 279, Bodl. Cat. 1753; NNBW**
Meyer (Mayer), Joh. Fr.	Germany	1650–1712	Lutheran	**ADB; Ugolini, 1, 378, 23, 792**
Michaelis, Joh. David	Germany	1717–1791		**ADB; NBU; Enc. Br.[11]**
Michaelis, Joh. Heinr.	Germany	1668–1738		**St. 280; ADB; NBU**
Midhorp, Joh.	?	*fl.* 1562		**St. 281, Bodl. Cat. 552 (no. 3562a)**
Mieg, Joh. Fried.	Germany	1642–1691 (?)		**St. 282; Rev. Et. Juives 20, 266; ADB**
Mill, David	Holland	1692–1756	Calvinist	**St. 283, Bodl. Cat. 1756; NNBW**

Christian Hebraists (continued)

Name	Country-(ies)	Dates	Religious Confession	References
Mill, Joh.	England	1645–1707		DNB; NBU; Ugolini 6, 1145
Mill, William Hodge	England	1792–1853		DNB
Milner, John	England	1628–1702	Non-juror	DNB; NBU
Milton, John	England	1608–1674	Puritan	DNB; L. Roth, Journ. Sem. Stud. 6 (1961), 213
Mirandola, Giovanni Pico della	Italy	1463–1494		
Misztótfalusi, Kis Miklós	Hungary	1650–1702	Calvinist	Marm; Szin; Zov; Zador Tordai, M.K.M., Budapest, 1965
Mitternacht, Jo. Seb.	Germany	*fl.* 1645		Heb. Grammar, Jena, 1645
Moeller,Helena Sybilla Wagenseil	Germany	*fl.* 1700		Zeitschr. f. Heb. Bibl. xx, 69
Molinaea, Maria	?	17th c.		Zeitschr. f. Heb. Bibl. xx, 68
Molitor, Christoph.	Germany	*fl.* 1659		St. 285
Moller, Daniel	Germany, Hungary	1642–1712	Calvinist	Marm; Szin; NBU; ADB
Molnar, János	Hungary	1757–1819	Calvinist	Venet; Szin; Zov.
Molza–Porrino, Tarquinia	Italy	(?)1542–1617		Zeitschr. f. Heb. Bibl. xx, 68; NBU
Montagnana, Petrus	Italy	*fl.* 1478		St. A. 40
Montaldi, Jos.	Italy	*fl.* 1789		Heb. & Chald. Lex., Rome, 1789
Montano, Benito Arias, *see* Arias Montano, Benito				
Montfalcon(-ius), Bern. de	France, Italy	1655–1741		St. 286, Bodl. Cat. 1758; NBU; Enc. Br.[11]
Moonen, Arnold	Holland	1644–1711	Reformed Ch.	NNBW
More, Alexander	Scotland	1616–1670	Calvinist	DNB; NBU
Moré, Eugéne	France	*fl.* 1837		
More, Henry	England	1614–1687		St. 288, Bodl. Cat. 2804, no. 6409b; DNB; NBU
Morgan, Robert	England	1665–1745		S. Levy, Jew. Hist. Soc. Engl. Misc. 4 (1942)
Morgan, William	Wales	1540(?)–1604		DNB
Morin, Jean	France	1591–1659	Protestant, converted to Catholicism	St. 287; NBU
Morini, Stephanus	France, Holland	1624/5–1700	Catholic (?)	NNBW 10, 651; NBU
Mornay, Philippe de (Du Plessis–Mornay)	France	1549–1623	Huguenot	NBU; NNBW; Enc. Br.[11]
Moser, Ph. N.	Germany	*fl.* 1795		Heb. & Chald. Lex., Ulm, 795
Mosheim, Joh. Lorenz von	Germany	c. 1694–1755	Lutheran	ADB; NBU; Enc. Br.[11]
Mott, John	England	*fl.* 1740		?=J.M. (Thurston, 1699-1776); Venn
Moyne, Etienne le	France, Holland	1624–1689	Huguenot	NNBW 10, 634
Mudge, Zachary	England	1694–1769		DNB
Muenden, Christian	Germany	1684–1741		ADB
Muenster, Sebastian	Germany, Switzerland	1489–1552	Franciscan, turned Lutheran	St. 292, Nachtrag p.122, Bodl. Cat. 2012 f; NBU; Enc. Br.[11]
Muhl, Jos.	Germany	?		St. 290
Muhle(-ius), Hein.	Germany	1666–1730/2	Lutheran	St. 289, Bodl. Cat. 2004; ADB
Muis, Simon Marotte de	France	1587–1644		St. 291, Bodl. Cat. 2009; NBU
Muller, August	Germany	*fl.* 1878		Heb. Grammar, Halle, 1878
Muller, Joh. Mart.	Germany	1722–1781	Lutheran	ADB; NBU
Muller, Ludw. Christian	Germany	1734–1804 (?)		ADB; NBU; Heb. Grammar in Danish, Copenhagen, 1834
Muntinge, Herman	Holland	1752–1824		NNBW
Murner, Thomas	Alsace	1475–1537 (?)	Franciscan	St. 293, Bodl. Cat. 2017; NBU; ADB; Enc. Br.[11]
Musculus, *see* Meuschen, Gerhard				
Myerlin, David Fr.	Germany	d. 1778		untraced
Mylius, Andreas	Germany	*fl.* 1639		Heb. Syntax, Königsberg, 1639

Christian Hebraists (continued)

Name	Country-(ies)	Dates	Religious Confession	References
N. (G.N.), *see* Norwich, William				
Naegelsbach, Carl W.E.	Germany	(?)1806–1859		**ADB; Heb. Grammar, Leipzig, 1856.**
Nagel, Joh. Andr. Mich.	Germany	1710–1788		**St. 295, Nachtrag p. 122, Bodl. Cat. 2030; ADB**
Nagy, János	Hungary	19th c.	Calvinist	**Szin.**
Nánási, Lovász József	Hungary	1701–1757	Calvinist	**Marm; Szin; Zov; Dan**
Neale (Nelus), Thomas	England	1519–1590 (?)		**St. 296; Bodl. Cat. 2059; DNB**
Neander, Conradus Burgens.	Germany	*fl.* 1589		**Heb. Grammar, Wittenberg, 1589**
Nebrija, Antonio de	Spain	15th–16th c.		**B. Hall, in Studies in Church Hist. 5 (ed. G.J. Cuming), 1969, 125, 134**
Neckam (Nequam), Alexander	England, France	1157–1217	Benedictine	**Loewe, Med. & Renaissance St., 4, 1958, 17f.**
Nerrelter, David	Germany	*fl.* 1700		**Meuschen, Nov. Test. ex Talmude Illustr., 221, 18**
Newcome, Henry	Ireland, England	1729–1800		**DNB; NBU**
Newton, James William	England	*fl.* 1808		**Heb. Grammar, London, 1808**
Nicholas de Lyre (Lyranus)	France	(?)1270–1340	Franciscan	
Nicholas of Manjacoria, *see* Manjacoria, Nicholas				
Nicholson, I.	England	*fl.* 1836		**tr. Ewald's Heb. Grammar, London, 1836**
Nicolai, Jo. Fried.	Germany	1639–1683		**ADB**
Nifanius, Christian	Germany	1629–1689	Lutheran	**ADB**
Niger (Nigri), Peter, *see* Schwarz, Peter				
Niger, Radulphus	England	13th c.		**St. A. 46**
Niloe, Jac.	?	?	Reformed Ch.	**Meuschen, Nov. Test. ex Talmude Illustr., 252, 19 Noble, James**
Nolde, Christian	Denmark, Holland	*fl.* 1650–1680	Lutheran	**Meuschen, op. cit. 202, 18**
Norberg, Olav	Sweden	*fl.* 1708		**St. 269, Bodl. Cat. 2372**
Norrellius, Andr.	Sweden	1677–1749		**St. 298, Bodl. Cat. 2804; Svensk**
Norwich, William (=G.N.)	England	d. 1675		**St. 294, Bodl. Cat. 1875, no. 28**
Novarini, Aloysius	Italy	1594–1650		**NBU**
Novenianus, Phil.	Germany (?), France	*fl.* 1520		**St. 299; Heb. Grammar, Paris, 1520**
Oberleitner, Franz Xavier	Austria	1789–1832	Benedictine	**B.L.K. Oest.**
O'Byrne	England	c. 1800		**"Prof." Heb., Swansea**
Occitanus, Andreas Real, *see* Realis Occitanus, Andreas				
Ockley, Simon	England	1678–1720		**DNB; NBU**
Odhelius, Laur.	Sweden	(?)1664–1721 (?)		**St. 300**
Oecolampadius (Hussgen, Husschein) Johannes	Switzerland	1482–1531	Reformer	
Offerhaus, Christiaan Gerhard	Holland	18th c.		**untraced**
Offredus, Ludovica Saracena	France	*fl.* 1606		**Zeitschr. f. Heb. Bibl. xx, 69**
Olearius (Oelschlaeger), Gothofred	Germany	1604/5–1685	Lutheran	**ADB; NBU**
Olearius (Oelschlaeger), Johannes	Germany	1546–1623	Lutheran	**ADB**
Olshausen, Justus	Germany	1800–1882		**ADB**
Onderliczka, János	Hungary	18th c.	Calvinist	**Marm; Szin.**
Opfergeld, Friedr.	Germany	1668–1746		**St. 301, Bodl. Cat. 2078; ADB**
Opitz, Heinr.	Germany	1642–1712	Lutheran	**ADB; NBU**
Opitz, Joshua Heinr.	Germany	1542–1585	Lutheran	**Meuschen, Nov. Test. ex Talmude Illustr. 18, 15; ADB**
Opitz (Opitius), Paul Friedr.	Germany	1684–1745		**St. 302; ADB; NBU**
Orchell, Francisco	Spain	?		**untraced**

Christian Hebraists (continued)

Name	Country-(ies)	Dates	Religious Confession	References
Osborn, William	England	*fl.*1845		**Heb. Lex., London, 1845**
Osiander, Luc.	Germany	1534–1604		**ADB; Heb. Grammar, Wittenberg, 1569**
Osterbröck, Aggaeus	?	?		**St. 303**
Otho (Otto), Joh. Heinr.	Switzerland	d. 1719		**St. 304, Bodl. Cat. 2080**
Otrokócsi, Fóris Ferenc	Hungary	1648–1718	Catholic	**Venet.; Szin; Zov; Pap; Ferenc Fallenbuechl O.F.F., Esztergom, 1899**
Otto, Gottlieb	Germany	*fl.* 1788		**Heb. Grammar, Leipzig, 1788**
Ouatablé, Franciscus, *see* Vatable, François				
Ouseel (Oisel, Loisel), Phil.	Germany	1671–1724		**St. 305; NBU**
Outhuijs, Gerrit	Holland	*fl.* 1822		**trs. J. Lelong on Polyglot**
Outram (Owtram), William	England	1626–1679		**DNB**
Outrein, Johan. d'	Holland	1662–1722		**NNBW**
Overall, John	England	1560–1619		**DNB**
Owmann, Mart. Jac.	Germany	*fl.* 1705		**St. 306**
Paggi, Angiolo	Italy	*fl.* 1863		**Heb. Grammar, Florence, 1863**
Pagnini(-nus, -no), Santes (Xanctes)	Italy, France	c.1470–1536	Dominican	**St. 307; NBU**
Palkovic, Georg	Austria	1769–1850	Lutheran	**B.L.K. Oest.**
Palm, Joh. Henricus van der	Holland	1763–1840		**NNBW**
Palmroot, Johan.	Sweden	1659–1728		**St. 308, Bodl. Cat. 2083; Svensk**
Pareau, Jean Henri	Holland	1761–1833		**NNBW**
Parkhurst, John	England	1728–1797		**DNB; NBU**
Parschitius, Daniel	Germany	*fl.* 1662		**Heb. Grammar, Rostock, 1662**
Pasini(-nus), Giuseppe Luca	Italy	1687–1770		**St. 309; NBU**
Pasor, Matthias	Holland, England	1599–1658		**NNBW; DNB; ADB; NBU**
Pastritius, Joh.	?	?		**St. 310**
Pataki, István	Hungary	1640–1693	Calvinist	**Szin; Dan.**
Patzschius, H.D.	Germany	*fl.* 1778		**Heb. Grammar, Lcneburg, 1778**
Paul (Paolo)	Sicily	*fl.* 1475	Dominican?	**St. after 310, Nachtrag, p. 87**
Paulinus, Simon	Sweden (?)	*fl.* 1692		**Heb. Grammar, Abo, 1692**
Pause, Jean de la, *see* Plantavit(ius) de la Pause, Jean				
Péchi, Simon	Hungary	c.1565–1642	Sabbatarian (Unitarian)	
Pedro, Dom, Emperor of Brazil	Portugal	I 1798–1834 II 1825– 1891		**NBU; Enc. Br.[11]**
Pellican(-us Rubeaquensis; Kirschner, Kürsner), Conrad	Alsace, Switzerland	1478–1556	Franciscan, later Zwinglian	**St. 311, Nachtrag p. 122; ADB; Enc. Br.[11]**
Penaforte, Raymundo of	Spain	c.1180–1275	Dominican	**NBU**
Penne, Jacobus	France	*fl.* 1699		**F. Secret, Rev. Ét. Juives 126(1967), 429**
Pepercorne, James Watts	England	*fl.* 1840		**S. Levy, Misc. Jew. Hist. Soc. Engl. 4, 1942, 78**
Pereszlényi, Pál	Hungary	17th c.	Catholic	**Venet.; Szin.**
Perez Bayer, Franc.	Spain	1711–1794		**Enc. Univ. Illustr. Eur.-Amer. 43, 665**
Peringer, Gustav	Sweden	1651–1710		**St. 312; Svensk**
Peritz, Ismar	U.S.A.	19th c.		**untraced**
Pertsch, W.H.F.	Germany	*fl.* 1720	Lutheran	**St. 313, Bodl. Cat. 2095**
Peter of Alexandria	Italy (?)	1342	Augustinian	**St. A. 38**
Peter Niger (Nigri), *see* Schwarz, Peter (Nigri)				
Peter of St. Omer	France	*fl.* 1296		**St. A. 42, Heb. Übers. 610**
Petermann, H.	Germany	*fl.* 1868		**Heb. Formenlehre nach... Samaritaner, Leipzig, 1868**

Christian Hebraists (continued)

Name	Country-(ies)	Dates	Religious Confession	References
Petit, Pietro Giovanni de	Italy	d. 1740		**St. 314**
Petit, Sam.	France	1594–1643		**Colomils, Gallia Orient. 169f; NBUColomils, Gallia Orient. 169f; NBU**
Petraeus, Nic.	Denmark	*fl.* 1627		**Heb. Grammar, Copenhagen, 1627**
Petraeus, Severus	Denmark	*fl.* 1642		**Heb. Grammar, Copenhagen, 1642**
Pettersson, J.	Sweden	*fl.* 1829		**Heb. Grammar, Lund, 1829**
Pfalz, Elisabeth of, *see* Elisabeth, Abbess of Pfalz				
Pfeiffer, Augustus	Germany	1640–1698	Lutheran	**St. 315, Bodl. Cat. 2098; ADB; NBU**
Pfeiffer, Aug. Fr.	Germany	1748–1817		**ADB; NBU**
Philippe, E.	France	*fl.* 1884		**Heb. Grammar, Paris, 1884**
Philipps, Will. Thos.	England	*fl.* 1830		**Heb. Grammar, Bristol, 1830**
Picinello, Felipe	Spain (?), Italy	?		**Meuschen, Nov. Test. ex Talmude Illustr., 196, 18**
Pico della Mirandola, Giovanni, *see* Mirandola, Giovanni Pico della				
Picques, L.	France	*fl.* 1670		**St. 316**
Pike, Samuel	Scotland	*fl.* 1802		**Heb. Lex., Glasgow, 1802**
Pilarik, Andrés	Hungary	1640–1702	Calvinist	**Szin; Zov; Dan**
Pilarik, Esaias	Germany (?)	*fl.* 1677		**Heb. Grammar, Wittenberg, 1677**
Pilarik, István	Hungary	1644–1717	Calvinist	**Szin; Zov; Dan**
Piscator (Fischer), Johan.	Germany	1546–1625		**ADB**
Pistorius (de Nida), Joannes Nidanus	Germany	1546–1608	Protestant, later Catholic	**St. 317, Bodl. Cat. 2406; ADB; NBU**
Placus, Andreas	Austria	*fl.* 1552		**Heb. Grammar, Vienna, 1552**
Plantavit(ius) de la Pause, Jean	France	1576–1651	Protestant, later Catholic	
Plato of Tivoli (Tiburtinus)	Spain	*fl.* 1116		**St. A. 44, Heb. Übers. 971; NBU**
Pocock(e), Edward	England	1604–1691		**DNB; Jew. Hist. Soc. Engl. index, s.v.**
Pocock(e), Edward	England	1648–1727		**DNB**
Pontack(-ous), Arnold	France	d. 1605		**St. 319, Bodl. Cat. 2110**
Pontack	England	(?)1638–1720 (?)		**DNB**
Pontus de Tyard, *see* Tyard, Pontus de				
Po(o)le, Matthew	England	1624–1679		**DNB; NBU**
Porter, Joh.	Ireland, England	1751–1819		**Venn**
Porter, John Scott	Ireland, England	1801–1880	Unitarian	**DNB**
Postel(-lus), Guillaume	France, Italy	1510–1581	(expelled) Jesuit, later heretic	**St. 320, Bodl. Cat. 2111; F. Secret, Le Zôhar chez... Kabbalistes chrétiens, 1958, 140; NBU**
Prache, Hilaric	Germany, England	1614–1679		**St. 321**
Prado, Laur. Ramirez de	Spain	?		**Colomiés, It. et Hisp. Orientalis, index (only)**
Praetorius, Abdias (Gottschalk Schultz)	Germany	1524–1575		**ADB; Heb. Grammar, Basle, 1558**
Preiswerk, S.	Switzerland (?)	*fl.* 1838		**Heb. Grammar, Geneva, 1838**
Prideaux, Humphrey	England	1648–1724		**St. 322, Bodl. Cat. 2112; DNB; NBU**
Prosser, James	England	*fl.* 1838		**Heb. Grammar, London, 1838**
Pruckner, Andr.	Germany	1650–1680		**Meuschen, Nov. Test. ex Talmude Illustr., 201, 18**

Christian Hebraists (continued)

Name	Country-(ies)	Dates	Religious Confession	References
Prufer, K.E.	Germany	*fl.* 1847		**Kritik of Heb. Grammatology, Leipzig, 1847**
Pusey, Edw. Bouverie	England	1800–1882		**DNB**
Puteus, Archangelus Burgonovo, *see* Burgonovo, Archangelus de				
Quadros, Diego (Didacus) de	Spain, Italy	*fl.* 1733		**Heb. Grammar, Rome, 1733**
Quenstedt, Joh. Andreas	Germany	1617–1688	Lutheran	**ADB; NBU**
Quinquarboreus (Cinqarbres), Johannes	France	d. 1587	Catholic	**St. 323, Bodl. Cat. 2127; NBU**
Quirinus, Laurus	?	*fl.* 1462–1471		**St. A. 45**
Quistorp, Johann. (sen.)	Germany	1584–1648		**ADB**
Rabe, Joh. Jac.	Germany	1710–1798		**St. 324; ADB**
Rachelius, Joach.	Germany	(?)1618–1669		**Heb. Grammar, Rostock, 1615; ADB; NBU**
Ráczböszörményi, János	Hungary	1649–1677	Calvinist	**Szin; Zov; Dan**
Raedt, Al(h)art de	Holland	(?)1645–1699 (?)		**NNBW**
Rainolds (Reynolds), John	England	1549–1607		**DNB; NBU**
Ransom, Samuel	England	*fl.* 1843		**Heb. Grammar, London, 1843**
Raphelengius, Franciscus	Netherlands	1539–1597	Catholic, later Calvinist	**St. 325, Heb. Übers. 653, Bodl. Cat. 2130, 3084; B.N. Belg; ADB**
Rau (Ravis, Ravius), Christian	Germany, England, Sweden	1613–1677		**DNB; NBU; NNBW**
Rau, Joach. Just.	Germany	*fl.* 1739		**Heb. Grammar, Königsberg, 1739**
Rau, Seebald	Germany, Holland	1721–1818		**NNBW; NBU; ADB**
Rau, Seebald Fulco Johan.	Holland	1765–1807		**NNBW; NBU**
Ravelingen, François van, *see* Raphelengius, Franciscus				
Raymund Martini, *see* Martini, Raimundo				
Raymund de Penaforte, *see* Penaforte, Raimundo of				
Real(-is) Occitanus, Andreas	France, Holland	*fl.* 1646	Franciscan	**F. Secret, Rev. Ét. Juives, 126, 423**
Reimann, Jacob. Friedr.	Germany	1668–1743		**ADB**
Reina, Casidoro de la	Spain	?		**Bible translator**
Reineccius, Chr.	Germany	1668–1752		**St. 326; ADB**
Reinke, Laurent	Germany	1797–1879	Catholic	**Heb. Grammar, Munster, 1861; ADB**
Reiske, Johann	Germany	(?)1641–1701	Lutheran	**ADB; NBU**
Reiske, Joh. Jacob	Germany	1716–1774		**St. 327; ADB; NBU; Enc. Br.[11]**
Reland, Adrian	Holland	1676–1718	Calvinist	**St. 328, Bodl. Cat. 2137; NNBW; NBU; Enc. Br.[11]**
Renan, Joseph Ernest	France	1823–1892	Lapsed Catholic	
Rendtorf, Joh.	Germany	?		**St. 329**
Reuchlin, Antonius	Germany	*fl.* 1554		**St., Bodl. Cat. 1142, no. 2**
Reuchlin (Capnio), Johann	Germany	1455–1522		
Reudenius, Ambr.	Germany	*fl.* 1586		**Heb. Grammar, Wittenberg, 1586**
Révai, Miklós	Hungary	1740–1807	Calvinist	**Szin; Zov; Jòzsef Melich, R.M., Budapest, 1908**
Reyher, C.	Germany	*fl.* 1825		**Heb. Grammar, Gotha, 1825**
Reynolds, John, *see* Rainolds (Reynolds), John				
Rezzonius, Franc. (sen.)	Italy	1731–1780		**St. 331; Assemani, Cat. Vat. xivii**
Rhenferd. Jac.	Holland	1654–1712	Lutheran	**St. 332, Bodl. Cat. 2140; NNBW; NBU**

Christian Hebraists (continued)

Name	Country-(ies)	Dates	Religious Confession	References
Ribera, Francisco de	?	1537–1591	Jesuit	
Richard of St. Victor	Scotland, France	12th c.	Victorine	**B. Smalley, Study of Bible in Mid. Ages.², 1952, 106f.**
Richardson, John	England	c.1564–1625		**DNB**
Richart	?	*fl.* 1335	Dominican	**St. A. 49**
Riegler, G.	Germany	*fl.* 1835		**Heb. Grammar, Bamberg, 1835**
Ries, Dan. Christ.	Germany	*fl.* 1787		**Heb. Grammar, Mainz, 1787**
Riesser, Joh.	Germany	*fl.* 1692		**Heb. Grammar, Marburg, 1692**
Rigelet, G.	Germany	*fl.* 1873		**Heb. Grammar (with A. Martinet), Bamberg, 1873**
Ritmeier, Chr. Hen.	Germany	*fl.* 1697		**St. 333, Bodl. Cat. 2312, 2146**
Rivet, André	France, Holland	1573–1651	Calvinist	**NNBW; ADB; NBU**
Rivinus, Tileman Andreas	Germany	1601–1656		**St. 334, Bodl. Cat. 2148**
Ro(h)an, Anna Princess of	France	(?)1584–1646	Reformed Ch.	**Zeitschr. f. Heb. Bibl. xx, 69; NBU**
Robertson, James	Scotland	1714–1795		**DNB**
Robertson, William	England	d.c. 1680		**DNB**
Roblik, Elias	Austria	1689–1765	Catholic (secular priest)	**B.L.K. Oest.**
Robustellus, Jos. W.	Italy	*fl.* 1655		**St. 335**
Rodriguez de Castro, José	Spain	1730–1799		**Enc. Univ. Illustr. Eur.-Amer. 51, 1282**
Rogers, John	England	1778–1856		**DNB**
Rohrbacher, René Franc.	France	(?)1789–1846		**Heb. Grammar, Metz, 1843; NBU**
Roht, Eberhard Rudolf	Germany	?	Lutheran	**Ugolini 29, 568**
Rolle (Rooles, Roales), Robert	England	*fl.* 1555–1585		**Roth, Bodl. Lib. Record, 7, 1966, 243; Foster**
Romaine, William	England	1714–1795		**DNB; NBU**
Römer, Maria Barbara Lehmann von	Germany	*fl.* 1700		**Zeitschr. f. Heb. Bibl. xx, 68**
Ron, Joh.	England	*fl.* 1637		**Heb. Grammar, London, 1637**
Ronnow, Magn.	Holland (?)	*fl.* 1690		**St. 336, Bodl. Cat. 239**
Roorda, Taco	Holland	b. 1801		**Heb. Grammar, Leiden, 1831**
Rosenbergius	Germany	*fl.* 1590		**Heb. Grammar, Wittenberg, 1590**
Rosenmuller, E.F.C.	Germany	*fl.* 1822		**Heb. & Chald. Lex., Halle, 1822**
Rosenroth, Chr. Knorr von, *see* Knorr von Rosenroth, Christian				
Röser, Jakab	Hungary	1641–1689	Calvinist	**Marm; Szin; Zov**
Rosselius, Paul	Germany	*fl.* 1618		**Heb. Grammar, Wittenberg, 1618**
Rossi, Giovanni Bern. de	Italy	1742–1831		**St. 337, Bodl. Cat. 2151, Add.; NBU; Filippo-Ugoni, Della Litteratura Ital., appendix**
Rota, Orazio	Italy	*fl.* 1775		
Row, John	Scotland	(?)1598–1672 (?)		**DNB**
Rowley, Alexander	England	*fl.* 1648		**Haber la-talmidim, London, 1648**
Roy, ?	U.S.A.	*fl.* 183?		**Heb. Lex., N.Y., 183?**
Rubeaquensis, Pellicanus, *see* Pellican, Conrad				
Ruckersfelder	Holland	18th c.		**untraced**
Rumelinas, Ge. Burchard	Germany	*fl.* 1716		**Lex. Biblicus, Frankfurt, 1716**
Rus, Johann Reichard	Germany	1679–1738	Lutheran	**Meuschen, Nov. Test. ex Talmude Illustr. 94, 15, 18**
Ruschat, Abr.	Holland	*fl.* 1707		**Heb. Grammar, Leiden, 1707**
Rutgers, Antonie	Holland	1805–1884		**NNBW 2, 1244**
Sa, Manoel de	Portugal, Italy	1530–1596	Jesuit	**NBU**
Sacy, Antoine-Isaac Sylvestre de	France	1758–1838		**St. 33, Bodl. Cat. 2257; NBU**
Sadler, John	England	1615–1674	Puritan	**DNB**
St. Cher, Hugh of, *see* Hugh of St. Cher				
Salchli, Joh. Jac.	Switzerland	1694–1774		**St. 339; ADB**

Christian Hebraists (continued)

Name	Country-(ies)	Dates	Religious Confession	References
Salmeron, Alfonso	Spain, Ireland	1515–1585	Jesuit	**NBU; Enc. Br.[11]**
Salome, S.C.	England	*fl.* 1825		**Heb. Grammar, London, 1825**
Sanden, Bernh. von (sen.)	Germany	1636–1703	Lutheran	**ADB**
Sanden, Bernhard von (jun.)	Germany	1666–1721	Lutheran	**ADB**
Sanctius (Sanches), Caspar	Spain	1553–1620	Jesuit	**Meuschen, Nov. Test. ex Talmude Illustr. 181, 17**
Sancto Aquilino (Eisentraut), Alexius	Germany	1732–1785	Carmelite	**Heb. Grammar, Heidelberg, 1776; ADB**
Sandbichler, Alois	Austria	1751–1820	Augustinian	**B.L.K. Oest.**
São Francisco, Luiz de	Portugal	*fl.* 1586	Franciscan	
Saravia, Hadrian a	France, Holland, England	1531–1613	Huguenot	**DNB; NNBW; B.N. Belg; NBU**
Sarchi, Philip	Austria, England	*fl.* 1824		**Essay on Heb. Poetry, London, 1824**
Sartorius, Joh.	Holland	1500–1570 (?)		**NNBW; ADB**
Sartorius, Joh.	Hungary	1656–1729 (?)	Calvinist (?)	**St. 340; Dan; ADB**
Saubert, Johann	Germany	(?)1638–1688 (?)	Lutheran	**St. 341, Bodl. Cat. 2505; ADB**
Saurin, Jacques	Holland, England	1677–1730	Huguenot	**NNBW; NBU**
Scaliger, Joseph Justus	France, Holland	1540–1609	Calvinist	**S. Reinach, Rev. Ét Juives 88, 1929, 171 f; NNBW; ADB; Enc. Br.[11]**
Scerbo	Italy	*fl.* 1888		**Heb. Grammar, Florence, 1888**
Schaaf, Carolus	Germany, Holland	1646–1729		**Heb. Grammar, Leiden, 1716; NNBW**
Schach (Scacchi), Fortunato(-tus)	Italy	1570–1640	Augustinian	**Ugolini 32, 806**
Schadaeus, Elias	Alsace	*fl.* 1591		**Heb. Grammar, Strasbourg, 1591**
Schaefer, Lud. Christoph.	Germany	*fl.* 1720		**Heb. Lex., Berburg, 1720**
Schauffler, Wilh. Gottl.	Germany, U.S.A.	1798–1883		**Heb. Grammar in Span., Smyrna, 1852; D Am. B**
Scheidt (Scheidius), Balth.	Alsace	1614–1670	Lutheran	**St. 342; ADB**
Scheidt (Scheidius?), Everard	Holland	1742–1794		**Heb. Grammar, Harderwick, 1792; NNBW**
Scheltinga, Theodorus	Holland	1703–1780		**NNBW 9, 975**
Scherlogus, Paul	?	?	Catholic	**Meuschen, Nov. Test. ex Talmude Illustr., 24, 14–17**
Scherping, Jacob	Sweden	*fl.* 1737		**St. 343**
Scher(t)zer(-us), Joh. Adam	Germany	1628–1683		**St. 344, Bodl. Cat. 2563; ADB**
Schi(c)k(h)ard(us), Wilhelm	Germany	1592–1635	Lutheran	**St. 345, Bodl. Cat. 2564; ADB; NBU**
Schindler, Valentin	Germany	d. 1604		**St. 346, Bodl. Cat. 2566; ADB**
Schleidan (Sleidanus), Joh.	Germany	1506/7–1556	Catholic, later Lutheran	**ADB; NBU; B.N. Belg; Enc. Br.[11]**
Schleusner, Joh. Friedr.	Germany	1759–1831		**ADB**
Schlevogt (Slevogt), Paul	Germany	1596–1655	Lutheran	**ADB (Slevogt)**
Schmid, Anton	Austria	1765–1855	Catholic	**B.L.K. Oest.**
Schmidt, Joach. Friedr.	Germany	*fl.* 1708		**Heb. Grammar, Frankfurt, 1708**
Schmidt, Johan. Andr.	Germany	1652–1726	Lutheran	**ADB; Meuschen, Nov. Test. ex Talmude Ilustr., 73, 15**
Schmidt, Karl Benjamin	Germany	*fl.* 1789		**Heb. Grammar, Lemgo, 1789**
Schmied(t), Sebast.	Alsace	*fl.* 1656	Lutheran	**St. 347, Bodl. Cat. 2568**
Schnabel, Hieronymus Wilh.	?	?		**Meuschen, op. cit. 255, 19**
Schnelle(-lius), Sebald	Germany	1621–1651		**St. 348, Bodl. Cat. 2569**
Schnurrer, Christ. Friedr.	Germany, England	1724–1822		**St., Bodl. Cat. 2668; ADB**
Schoettgen, Johan. Christian	Germany	1687–1751	Lutheran	**St. 350**
Scholl(-ius), J.C.F.	Germany	?		**Hebr. Laut. u. Formenlehre, Leipzig, 1867**
Scholz, Hermann	Germany	*fl.* 1867		**St. 351; NNBW B.N. Belg; ADB; NBU**

Christian Hebraists (continued)

Name	Country-(ies)	Dates	Religious Confession	References
Schotanus, Christ.	Holland	1603–1671	Reformed Ch.	
Schottanus, Andr.	Flanders, Spain, France, Italy	1552–1629	Jesuit	**St. 349, Bodl. Cat. 2572; ADB**
Schramm, David (Agricola)	?	*fl.* 1615		**Heb. Grammar, c. 1615 (?Place)**
Schreckenfuchs, Erasmus Oswald	Germany	1511–1575		**St. 353, Bodl. Cat. 673, no. 3**
Schreier, Norbert	Hungary	1744–1811	Catholic	**Szin; Zov**
Schroeder, Johan. Friedr.	Germany	*fl.* 1823		**Heb. Lex., Leipzig, 1823**
Schroeder, Jo. Joachim	Germany	1680–1756		**St. 354, cf. Bodl. Cat. 2574; ADB**
Schroeder, Nicolaus Wilh.	Hungary, Holland	1721–1798	(?) Calvinist	**NNBW; ADB**
Schubert, Heinr. Fr. W.	Germany	*fl.* 1830		**Heb. Grammar, Schneeberg, 1830**
Schudt, Johan. Jacob	Germany	1664–1722	Lutheran	**St. 355; ADB**
Schuenemann, Chr. Heinr.	Germany	*fl.* 1709		**Heb. Grammar, Leipzig, 1709**
Schult, Johan.	?	*fl.* 1696		**St. 356, 308**
Schulten, Carl	Sweden	*fl.* 1725		**St. 357, Bodl. Cat. 2574; Svensk**
Schulten(s), Albrecht	Holland	1686–1756		**NNBW; NBU; Enc. Br.[11]**
Schultens, Heinrich Albert	Holland	1749–1793		**NNBW; NBU; Enc. Br.[11]**
Schultens, Johan. Jac.	Holland	1716–1778		**NNBW; NBU; Enc. Br.[11]**
Schultz, Gottschalk, *see* Praetorius, Abdias				
Schul(t)z, Johan. Chr. Friedr.	Germany (?)	*fl.* 1785		**Heb. Lex.**
Schupart, Johan. Geo. (? Gottfried)	Germany	1677–1730	Lutheran	**ADB; Heb. Grammar, Leipzig, 1709**
Schurman(n), Anna Maria	Holland	1607–1678		**Zeitschr. f. Heb. Bibl. xx, 69; ADB; NBU**
Schwab, Johan. P.	Germany	*fl.* 1745		**St. 358, Bodl. Cat. 2030, no.7**
Schwarz, Johan. Conr.	Germany	1677–1747	Lutheran	**ADB**
Schwarz (Nigri), Peter	Germany, Spain	c. 1435– c. 1483	Dominican	**St. A. 41; NBU**
Schwenter, Daniel	Germany	1585–1636		**St. 359, Bodl. Cat. 2575; ADB**
Scio, P.	Spain	?		**Bible translator**
Scot(t), Michael	Scotland, Italy	(?)1175–1234		**DNB**
Scots, David	Scotland	(?)1770–1834		**DNB**
Sebastianus, Aug. Nouzanus(enus)	Germany	*fl.* 1530		**St. 360, Bodl. Cat. 2576**
Sebutia, Caccelia	Italy	*fl.* 1683		**Zeitschr. f. Heb. Bibl. xx, 69**
Securius, PFI	Hungary	1659–1721	Calvinist	**Szin; Pap**
Seffer, G.A.	Germany	*fl.* 1845		**Heb. Grammar, Leipzig, 1845**
Seidel(-ius), Casp.	Germany	*fl.* 1638		**St. 361, Bodl. Cat. 2579**
Seidenstuecker, Johan. Heinr. Phil.	Germany	1765–1817		**ADB; Heb. Grammar, Helmstedt 1791**
Seidenstuecker, W.F.F.	Germany	*fl.* 1836		**Heb. Grammar, Soest, 1836**
Seiferheld, Jos. Laur.	Germany	*fl.* 1763		**St. 362, Bodl. Cat. 2031, no. 11; S. Back, Jcd. Literaturbl., 1892, 2**
Seineccerius, Nicolaus	Germany	*fl.* 1584		**Heb. Grammar, Leipzig, 1584**
Selden, John	England	1584–1654	Puritan	
Senepin	France (?)	*fl.* 1888		**Heb. Grammar in Fr., Freiburg, 1888**
Serarius, Nicolaus	Germany	1555–1609	Jesuit	**Ugolini, 24, 898; ADB**
Setiers, L.P.	France	*fl.* 1814		**Heb. Grammar, Paris, 1814**
Seyfried, Christ.	Sweden	*fl.* 1664		**St. 363, Bodl. Cat. 1079, 2594**
Seyfried, Henr.	Germany	*fl.* 1663		**St. 364**
Sgambati(us), Scipio	Italy	1595–1652		**St. 365**
Sharp, Granville	England	1735–1813		**DNB**
Sharp, Thomas	England	1693–1758		**DNB; NBU**
Shaw, Thomas	England	1694–1751		**DNB; NBU**
Sheringham, Robert	England, Holland	1602–1678		**St. 366, Bodl. Cat. 2594**

Christian Hebraists (continued)

Name	Country-(ies)	Dates	Religious Confession	References
Shilling, D.(?)	France	*fl.* 1883		**Heb. Grammar, Lyons, 1883**
Sigebert of Gembloux	Flanders	d. 1113		**St. A. 51; Sitzungsber. Wiener Akad, 1859, 29, 309; R.Loewe, Cambridge Hist. Bible, 2, ed. G. Lampe, 1969, 141–3**
Sigonio, Carlo	Italy	(?)1520– 1584		**Enc. Biogr. Ital; NBU; Enc. Br.[11]**
Sike (Sykes), Henry	England	d. 1712		**Venn**
Simon, Richard	France	1638–1712	(expelled) Oratorian	**NBU; Enc. Br.[11]**
Simonis, Johan.	Germany	*fl.* 1741		**Onomasticon Vet. Test., H. Halle, 1741**
Sjöbring, P.	Sweden	*fl.* 1836		**Heb. Grammar, Uppsala, 1836**
Skinner, Ralph	England	16th–17th c.		**St. 367; Jew. Hist. Soc. Engl. Misc. 4, 1942, 62f.**
Slaughter, Edward	England,	1655–1729	Jesuit	**DNB; B.N. Belg.**
Sleidanus, Johan., *see* Schleidan, Johan.				
Slevogt, Paul, *see* Schlevogt, Paul				
Slonkovic, Martinus	Poland	*fl.* 1651		**Heb. Grammar, Cracow, 1651**
Smal(l)ridge, George	England	1663–1719		**DNB**
Smith, Frederick	England	*fl.* 1870		**Tr. Ewald's Heb. Grammar, London, 1870**
Smith, John	U.S.A.	*fl.* 1803		**Heb. Grammar, Boston, 1803**
Smith, Miles	England	1568–1624		**DNB**
Smith, Thomas	England	1638–1710		**St. 368, Bodl. Cat. 2646; DNB; NBU**
Sőlősi, Pál	Hungary	166?–1688	Calvinist	**Dan**
Sommer, Gottfr. Christ.	Germany	*fl.* 1734		**St. 369; Scholem, Bibliography. Kabbalistica, no. 1081; Monats. Gesch. u. Wiss. Jud., 1895/6, 423**
Somosi, P. János	Hungary	1625–1681	Calvinist	**Szin; Dan**
Somossi, János	Hungary	1783–1855	Calvinist	**Szin; Zov; Dan; János Erdélyi, S.J., Sárospatak, 1864**
Sonneschmid, Johan. Justus	Germany	*fl.* 1720–1770	Lutheran	**St. 370**
Sonntag, Christoph.	Germany	1654–1717	Evangelical Lutheran	**ADB**
Spalding, Geo. Ludw.	Germany	1762–1811		**St. 371; ADB**
Spalding, Robert	England	d. 1626		**Venn**
Spannheim, Friedr. (sen.)	Holland, Switzerland	1600–1649		**ADB; NNBW; NBU**
Spannheim, Friedr. (jun.)	Holland	1632–1701		**NNBW; ADB**
Speidelius, Johan. Chr.	Germany	*fl.* 1731		**Heb. Grammar, Tübingen, 1731**
Spelman, Henry	England	(?)1564–1641		**DNB; NBU; R. Loewe, Heb. Union Coll. Annual, 28, 1957, 221 n.74**
Spencer, John	England	1630–1693		**DNB; NBU; Trans. Jew. Hist. Soc. Engl. 8, 100f.**
Spencer, Philip Jacob	England (?), Germany	17th c.		**JQR, 9 (18–96/97), 510**
Sprecher, Johan. Died.	Germany	*fl.* 1703		**St. 372, Bodl. Cat. 1079, no. 25**
Springer, Daniel	Germany	1656–1708		**St. 373, Bodl. Cat. 2651**
Squier (Squire, Squyer), Adam	England	d. before 1588		**Roth, Bodl. Library Record, 7, 1966, p. 243; Foster**
Stadler, Johan. Ev.	Germany	*fl.* 1831		**Heb. Lex., Munich, 1831**
Staemmer, Christoph van	Holland (?)	*fl.* 1661		**St. 374, Bodl. Cat. 1445, 2651**
Stancaro(-rus), Franciscus	Italy	1501–1574	Reformer	**ADB; NBU; Heb. Grammar, Basle, 1547**
Stapleton, Thomas	England	1535–1598	Catholic	

Christian Hebraists (continued)

Name	Country-(ies)	Dates	Religious Confession	References
Starck (Starke), Heinr. Bened.	Germany	1672–1740	Lutheran	**Heb. Grammar, Leipzig, 1705; ADB**
Starckius (Starke), Sebast. Gottfr.	Germany	d. 1710		**St. 375; ADB**
Steen, Cornelius van den, *see* Lapide, Cornelius B (van den Steen)				
Steenbach, Joh.	?	?		**St. 376**
Steiner, Johan.	?	*fl.* 1600		**St. 376, n. 1**
Steinersdorff, Johan. Christ.	Germany	*fl.* 1747		**Heb. Grammar, Halle, 1747**
Steinmetz, Joh. Andr. (? Adam)	Poland (?)	1689–1762		**St. 377, Bodl. Cat. 1391, no. 3; Zeitschr. f. Heb. Bibl. 1, 112; ADB**
Steinweg, Geo. Friedr.	Germany	*fl.* 1753		**Heb. Grammar, Halle, 1753**
Stengel, Lib.	Germany	*fl.* 1841		**Heb. Grammar, Freiburg, 1841**
Stenhagen, G.	Sweden	*fl.* 1705		**St. 269, Bodl. Cat. 682, no. 29**
Steuco (Augustinus Steuchus Eugubinus), Agostino (Steuco de Gubbio)	Italy	1496–1549	Augustinian	**NBU; Enc. Br.[11]**
Stier, Ewald Rud.	Germany	1800–1862		**Heb. Grammar, Leipzig, 1833; ADB; Enc. Br.[11]**
Stier, G.	Germany	*fl.* 1857		**Heb. Lex. Leipzig, 1857**
Stiles, Ezra	New England (U.S.)	1727–1795	Congregationalist	**D. Am. B.; Enc. Br.[11]**
Stock, Joseph	Ireland	1740–1813		**DNB**
Stolberg, Balthasar	Germany	?	Lutheran	**Meuschen, Nov. Test. ex Talmude Illustr., 52, 15**
Stolle, Johan. Henr.	Germany (?)	*fl.* 1691		**St. 328**
Strauch, Aegidius (Giles)	Germany	1632–1682	Lutheran	**ADB**
Stridzberg, Nic. H.	Sweden	*fl.* 1731		**St. 380**
Struvius, Johan. Julius	Germany	*fl.* 1697		**St. 381**
Stuart, Moses	U.S.A.	1780–1852		**Heb. Grammar, Andover, New Hants, 1821; D. Am B. Enc. Br.[11]**
Stubbs, Wolfran	England	d. 1719		**Venn**
Stuckuis, Joannes Guilhelmus	Holland (?), France, Switzerland	1542–1607	Protestant	
Suetonio, Agostino	Italy	?		**St. 383, Heb. Übers. xxvii, line 7**
Summenhardt, Konrad	Germany	(?)1466–1502		**St. A. 23; ADB**
Sur(r)enhusius(-huis, -huysen), Wil.	Holland	1666–1729	Calvinist	**St. 382, Bodl. Cat. 2663; NNBW; NBU**
Sussex, Augustus Fred. Duke of	England	1773–1843		**DNB; NBU**
Swan, G.	Sweden	*fl.* 1706		**St. 269, cf. 384, Bodl. Cat. 682, no. 29**
Sykes, Arthur, Ashley	England	(?)1684–1756		**DNB**
Sykes, Henry, *see* Sike, Henry				
Sylvester, Johannes	Hungary	16th c.		**"Grammatica Hungarolatina"; Robert Dan, S.J., Magyar Könyvszemle 1969, 2**
Sypkens, Hendrik	Holland	19th c.		**NNBW 9, 1097**
Szántó, István	Hungary	1541–1612	Catholic	**Szin**
Szatmári, Ötvös István	Hungary	1620–1665	Calvinist	**Szin; Zov; Dan**
Szatmár–Némethi, Mihály	Hungary	1638–1689	Calvinist	**Szin; Zov**
Szatmárnémeti, Mihály	Hungary, Holland (?)	1667–1709	Calvinist	**Szin; Zov**
Szatmárnémeti, Samuel	Hungary	1658–1717	Calvinist	**Marm; Szin; Pap**
Szatmáry, Orban Samuel	Hungary	1711–1757	Calvinist	**Marm; Szin**
Szatmáry, P. Daniel	Hungary	1769–1818	Calvinist	**Marm; Szin**
Szegedi, István	Hungary	1505–1572	Calvinist	**Kohn; Szin; Marm**

Christian Hebraists (continued)

Name	Country-(ies)	Dates	Religious Confession	References
Székely, István	Hungary	151?–156?	Calvinist	**Szin; Pap; Károly Mohácsy, Károlyi Gáspár, Budapest, 1948**
Szemiot, Alexander	Austria, Poland	1800–1835	Catholic	**B.L.K. Oest.**
Szenczi, Molnár Albert	Hungary	1574–1634	Calvinist	**Venet; Szin; Zov**
Szentiványi, Márton	Hungary	1653–1705	Catholic	**Marm; Szin**
Szigmondy, Samuel	Austria	*fl.* 1828	Heb. Grammar, Vienna, 1828	
Szilágyi, Péter	Hungary	167?–1723	Calvinist	**Szin; Zov; Dan**
Tailor, Francis *see* Tayler, Francis				
Talbot, James	England	1665–1708		**Venn**
Tanfield, Elisabeth	England	1579–1639		**Zeitschr. f. Heb. Bibliography. xx, 69**
Tarnóczi, Márton	Hungary	1620–1685	Lutheran	**Marm; Szin; Zov**
Tarnow, Johan.	Germany	1586–1629	Lutheran	**ADB**
Tayler (Tailor, etc.), Francis England		*fl.* 1630–1660		**St. 385, Bodl. Cat. 2670**
Taylor, Edward	New England (U.S.A.)	d. 1729	Puritan	**American Nat. Biogr.; Norman S. Grabo, E.T.**
Taylor, Jacob	Pennsylvania (U.S.A.)	18th c.		**Inf. From C. Roth;? = author of almanac for 1745, Philadelphia**
Taylor, Jeremy	England	1613–1667		**DNB; L. Roth, Journ. Sem. Stud. 6, 1961, 204**
Taylor, John	England	1694–1761	Dissenter	**DNB**
Teigh, Robert	England	*fl.* 1611		**trs. Gen.-Kings, King James' Bible**
Tena, Luis de	Spain	d. 1622		**Enc. Univ. Illustr. Eur. Amer., 60, 848**
Terentius, Johan. Gerhardi	Holland	b. 1639		**St. 385 n. 1, Bodl. Cat. 169, no. 1133**
Theobald (Therebald)	France	*fl.* 1250 (?)		**St. A. 53**
Theunitz, Johan. Antonii	Holland	1569–1637 (?)		**NNBW**
Thiele, E.E.	Germany	*fl.* 1795		**Heb. Grammar, Jena, 1795**
Thiersch, H. Wilh. Josias	Germany	1817–1885		**ADB; Heb. Grammar, Erlangen, 1842**
T(h)irsch, Leopold (O.?)	Austria	1733–1788	Jesuit	**B.L.K. Oest. Heb. Grammar, Prague, 1784**
Thomason, George	England	d. 1666		**DNB; Trans. Jew. Hist. Soc. Engl. 8, 1918, 63f.**
Thompson, Richard	Holland, England	d. 1612/3		**DNB**
Thorndike, Herbert	England	1598–1672		**DNB**
Thorne, William	England	(?)1568–1630		**DNB; Roth, Bodl. Lib. Record, 7, 1966, 246 n.1**
Thuri, György	Hungary	157?–160?	Calvinist	**Marm; Szin; R. Dan, Journ. Jew. Stud., 19, 1968, 71f.**
Thysius, Antonius	Flanders, Holland	1565–1640		**B.N. Belg; NNBW; ADB**
Til, Sal. Van	Holland	1643–1713	Calvinist	**NNBW; NBU**
Tingstadius, Johan. Adam	Sweden	1748–1827		**Svensk**
Tissard(us), François	France	*fl.* 1508		**Heb. & Greek Grammar, Paris, 1508**
Tofeus Dobos, Mihály	Hungary	1624–1684	Calvinist	**Szin; Zov; Dan; József Koncz, T.M., Budapest, 1893**
Top, Alexander	England	*fl.* 1629		**Read Sephardic cursive letter from David Reubeni; trs. Psalms, 1629**
Torriano, Car.	England	1727–1778		**Venn**

Christian Hebraists (continued)

Name	Country-(ies)	Dates	Religious Confession	References
Tostado (Tostatus), alfonso de Madrigal	Spain	c.1400–1455		**NBU**
Townley, James	England	1774–1833	Methodist	**DNB; Misc. Jew. Hist. Soc. Engl., 4, 1942, 75**
Traegard, E.	Germany	*fl.* 1755		**Heb. Grammar, Greifswald, 1755**
Transisalanus, Johann., *see* Campen, Jan (Johannes) van				
Trigland, Jac. (nepos)	Holland	1583–1654	Calvinist	**St. 386, Bodl. Cat. 2686; NNBW**
Trilles, Vincentius	Spain	*fl.* 1606		**Heb. Grammar, Valencia, 1606**
Trithemius (Johann Heidenberg of Tritheim), Johannes	Germany	1462–1516	Benedictine	**ADB; NBU; Enc. Br.[11]**
Trivet(h) (Trevet), Nicholas	England	(?)1258–1328	Dominican	**DNB; B. Smalley, Study of Bible in Mid. Ages[2], 400; R. Leowe (ed. V.D. Lipman), 3 Cent. Anglo- Jew. Hist., 1961, 136, 141**
Trost(-ius), Martinus	Germany (? Syrian)	1588–1636		**ADB; Heb. Grammar, Copenhagen, 1627**
Tullberg, Hamp. Kr.	Sweden	*fl.* 1834		**Heb. Grammar, Lund. 1834**
Tyard, Pontus de	France	1521–1605	Catholic	
Tychsen, Oluf Gerard	Denmark, Germany	1734–1815		**St. 387, Bodl. Cat. 2687; ADB; NBU; Enc. Br.[11]**
Tydeman, B.F.	Holland	1784–1829		**NNBW 2, 1461**
Tympe, Johann Gottfr.	Germany	(?)1697–1768	Lutheran	**ADB**
Tyndale, William	England, Flanders	c.1490–1536	Zwinlian	
Uchtmann, Alard	France	*fl.* 1650		**St. 388, Bodl. Cat. 2659**
Udall (Uvedale), John	England	(?)1560–1592		**DNB**
Ugolino(-ini), Blasio	Italy	(?)1700–1770	Catholic (Jewish apostate?)	
Uhlemann, Friedr. Gottl.	Germany	1792–1864		**Heb. Grammar, Berlin, 1827; ADB**
Ulmann, Johan.	Alsace	*fl.* 1663		**St. 389, Bodl. Cat. 2691**
Uranius, Henricus	Switzerland	*fl.* 1541		**Heb. Grammar, Basle, 1541; B. Prijs, Basl. Heb. Drucke, 1964, pp. 97, 126**
Urban, Anna Weissbrucker	Germany	16th c.		**Zeitchr. f. Heb. Bibl. xx, 66; Heb. Bibl., 20, 66**
Urbanus, Rhegius Henr.	Germany	*fl.* 1535		**St. 390; L. Geiger, Zeitschr. f. Gesch. d. Juden in Deutschl. 3, 105**
Uri (Ury), Johan.	Hungary, England	1726–1796		**St. 391, Bodl. Cat. 2695; DNB**
Ursinus, Johan. Heinr.	Germany	1608–1667		**ADB; NBU; Ugolini, 21, 766**
Ussermann, Aemilian	Germany	1737–1798	Benedictine	**ADB; Heb. syntax, Salisbury, 1764**
Ussher, James	Ireland	1581–1656		**DNB; NBU**
Uythage, Cn. Cor.	Holland	*fl.* 1680		**St. 392, Bodl. Cat. 2696**
Valckenier, Johan.	Holland	b. 1617		**NNBW 10, 1071**
Valera, Cipriano de	Spain, England	b. 1531		**Foster; Venn**
Valensis, Theoph.	Germany	*fl.* 1631		**Heb. Grammar, Leipzig, 1631**
Valeton, J.P.P.	Holland	19th c.		**untraced**
Vallensis, Joannes	France	*fl.* 1545		**Heb. Grammar, Paris, c. 1545**
Valois, Louis de, *see* Louis de Valois				
Valperga, Tommaso di Caluso	Italy	1737–1815		**Heb. Grammar, Turin, 1805; NBU**
Valverdius, Bartholomaeus	Spain, Italy	*fl.* 1581		**St. 393**
Varenius, August	Germany	1620–1684	Lutheran	**St. 394; ADB**
Vásárhelyi, K. Péter	Hungary	160?–1660	Lutheran	**Szin**
Vasseur, Joshua le	France	*fl.* 1646		**Heb. Grammar, Sedan, 1646**

Christian Hebraists (continued)

Name	Country-(ies)	Dates	Religious Confession	References
Vatable(-blé, -blus, Ouatablé, Gastabled), François	France	c.1490–1547		**St. 395, Bodl. Cat. 2699; NBU**
Vater, Johan. Severin	Germany	1771–1826		**Heb. Grammar, Leipzig, 1798; ADB; NBU**
Vedelius, Nicolaus	Germany, Holland	1592–1642		**NNBW**
Vehe, Matth. (? Mich.)	Germany	*fl.* 1581		**St. 396; ADB**
Venema, Herman	Holland	1697–1787		**NNBW**
Venetus, Franc Geo. (Zorzi), *see* Giorgio (Zorzi), Francesco				
Venusi, Johann Bernhard	Austria	1751–1823	Cisterian	**B.L.K. Oest.**
Verbrugge, Otho	Holland	1670–1745		**NNBW 9, 1186**
Verestói, György	Hungary	1698–1764	Calvinist	**Marm; Szin; Zov**
Vermigli, Pietro Martire, *see* Martyr, Peter				
Verschuir, Johannes Hendrik	Holland	1735–1803		**NNBW**
Verseghy, Ferenc	Hungary	1757–1822	Catholic	**Marm; Szin; S. Krauss, Egy. Phil. Közl.,1899, 214–32**
Vesey, Gergely	Hungary	18th c.	Calvinist	**Marm; Szin**
Veszelin, Pál Kismariai	Hungary, Holland	d. 1645		**Szin**
Veszprémi, B. István	Hungary	1637–1713	Calvinist	**Szin; Zov; Dan**
Viccars, John	England	1604–1660		**DNB**
Vicinus, Jos. de, *see* Voisin, Joseph de				
Vieira, Eman.	Holland (?)	*fl.* 1728		**Heb. Grammar, Leiden, 1728**
Vigenlre, Blaise de	France	1523–1596	(nominal) Catholic	
Vignal(-ius), Pierre	France	*fl.* 1562–1612		**P. Colomils, Gallia Orientalis, p. 146**
Villalpando, Juan Bautista	Spain	1552–1608	Jesuit	**NBU**
Villanova, Arnaldo de	Spain	(?)1230–1313		**NBU; Enc. Br.[11]**
Vinding, Johan. Paul	Holland	*fl.* 1633		**St. 397, Bodl. Cat. 1837, note.**
Viterbo, Aegidius (Egidio) da	Italy, France	1465–1532	Augustinian (cardinal)	
Vitringa, Campegius	Holland	1659–1722	Calvinist	**NNBW 10, 1122; NBU; Enc. Br.[11]**
Viweg, Chr.	Germany	*fl.* 1685		**Heb. Grammar, Jena, 1685**
Vizaknai, U. Mihály	Hungary	1654–169?	Calvinist	**Szin; Zov; Dan**
Vloten, Willem van	Holland	1780–1829		**NNBW 8, 1304**
Voetius, Gysbertus	Holland	1589–1676		**NNBW; NBU; Enc.Br.[11]**
Vogel, Geo. Johan. Ludw.	Germany	1742–1776		**Heb. Grammar, Halle, 1769; ADB**
Vogelsangh, Reinerus	Holland	1610–1679		**NNBW 10, 1128**
Voisin (Vicinus), Joseph de	France	c.1610–1685		**St. 398, Bodl. Cat. 2269**
Volborth, Jo. Karl	Germany	1748–1796		**Heb. Grammar, Leipzig, 1788; ADB**
Vonck, Cornelis Hugo (? Valerius)	Holland	1724–1768		**NNBW**
Vorst(-ius), Will. Hen- drik van der	Holland	d. 1652	Remonstrant	**St. 399, Bodl. Cat. 2709**
Vorstheimer, Joh., *see* Forster, Johann				
Vosen, Christ. Hermann	Germany	1815–1871	Catholic	**Heb. Grammar, Freiburg, 1854; ADB**
Voss(-ius), Dionysius	Holland	1612– 1633(?)		**St. 400, Bodl. Cat. 2710; NNBW; NBU**
Vossius, Gerhard Jan	Holland, England	1577–1649	Reformed Ch.	**DNB; ADB; NBU**
Vossius, Isaac	Holland, Sweden, England	1618–1689	Anglican	**DNB; NNBW; ADB; NBU**
Vriemont, Emo Lucius	Holland	1699–1760		**NNBW; NBU**
Wachner, Andr. Geo.	Germany	*fl.* 1735		**Heb. Grammar, Göttingen, 1735**
Wachter, Johan. Geo.	Germany	1663–1757		**Scholem, Bibl. Kabbalistica, no. 1164; ADB; NBU**
Waeijen, Johan van der	Holland	1639–1701		**NNBW 10, 1148**
Wagenseil, Helena Sybilla Möller, *see* Moeller, Helena Sybilla Wagenseil				

Christian Hebraists (continued)

Name	Country-(ies)	Dates	Religious Confession	References
Wagenseil, Johann Christoph	Germany	(?)1633–1705 (?)		**St. 401, Nachtrag, p. 122, Bodl. Cat. 189, Add. p. 1xxv; ADB; NBU; Enc. Br.[11]**
Wagner, Christian	?	?		**St. 402**
Wakefield (Wakfeldus), Robert	England	d. 1537		**St. 403, Bodl. Cat. 2713; DNB**
Wakefield, Thomas	England	d. 1575		**DNB**
Wallin, Geo (jun.)	Germany	*fl.* 1722		**St. 404**
Walreven, Didericus Adrianus	Holland	1732–1804		**NNBW 9, 1276**
Walther, Johan.	?	*fl.* 1710		**St. 405**
Walther(-us), Christ.	Germany	*fl.* 1705		**St. 406, Bodl. Cat. 1875 no.30**
Walther, F.	Germany	*fl.* 1884		**Heb. Formlehre, Potsdam, 1884**
Walther(-us), Michael	Germany	1638–1692		**Heb. Grammar, Nuremberg, 1643; ADB**
Walton, Bryan	England	1600–1661		**DNB**
Warner, Levinius	Germany, Holland	1619–1665		**St. 407, Bodl. Cat. 2714, Leiden Cat. ix; NNBW**
Wartha, Johann Paul	Austria	1714–before 1800		**Heb. lexicon & grammar, Styria, 1756, Prague, 1743; B.L.K. Oest.**
Waser(us), Kaspar	Switzerland	1565–1625		**Heb. Grammar, Basle, 1600; ADB**
Wasmuth, Matth.	Germany	1625–1688	Lutheran	**Heb. Grammar, Kiel, 1666; ADB; NBU**
Weckerlin, Chr. Ferd.	Germany	*fl.* 1797		**Heb. Grammar, Stuttgart, 1797**
Weemes, John, *see* Wemyss, John				
Wegner, (?) Gottfr.	Germany	1644–1709		**ADB**
Weidmann (? Wiedemann), J.	Germany	?		**St. 295, 408**
Weiganmei(e)r, Georg	Germany	1555–1599		**St. 409, Bodl. Cat. 2715**
Weinmann, Johan.	Germany	1599–1672		**ADB**
Weissbrucker, Anna Urban, *see* Urban, Anna Weissbrucker				
Weitenauer, Ignaz	Austria	1709–1783	Jesuit	**B.L.K. Oest.**
Wemyss (Weemes), John	Scotland	c.1579–1636	Presbyterian	**DNB; J. Bowman, Jew. Quart. Rev., 39 (1949), 379f.**
Wenrik, Johann Geo.	Austria	1787–1847	Catholic	**B.L.K. Oest.**
Wessel, Johan.	Holland, Germany, Switzerland	1419–1489		**St. A. 35; ADB; NBU; Enc. Br.[11]**
W(eszelin), Kismariai Paulus, *see* Veszelin, PFI Kismariai				
Wet(t)stein, Johan. Jakob	Switzerland, Holland	1693–1754	Remonstrant	**NNBW; ADB; NBU; Enc. Br.[11]**
Wetzel, Joh. Chr. Friedr.	Germany	1762–1810		**Heb. Grammar, Berlin, 1796; ADB**
Weyers, Hendrik Engelinus	Holland	1805–1844		**NNBW 10, 1191**
Weymar, Daniel	Germany	*fl.* 1677	Lutheran	**Ugolini, 11, 646**
Wheeler, H.M.	England	*fl.* 1850		**Heb. Grammar, London, 1850**
Wheelocke, Abr.	England	1593–1653		**DNB**
Whittaker, John William	England	(?)1790– 1854		**DNB**
Wichmannshausen, Johan. Christoph.	Germany	1663–1727	Lutheran	**ADB**
Widmanstetter(-stadt, -stadius), Johann Albrecht or Lucrecius	Austria	1506–1557	Catholic	**St. 410; ADB; NBU**
Widmarius, Abdias	Holland	1591–1668		**NNBW 7, 1319**
Wiedemann, J., *see* Weidmann (? Wiedemann), J.				
Wiesendanger, Jakob, *see* Ceporinus, Jakob				
Wilkins, David	England	1685–1745 (?)		**St. 411, Nachtrag, p.122, Bodl. Cat. 2726; DNB**
Willard, ?	U.S.A.	*fl.* 1817		**Heb. Grammar, Harvard, 1817**

Christian Hebraists (continued)

Name	Country-(ies)	Dates	Religious Confession	References
Willemer, Johann	Germany	?	Lutheran	**Meuschen, Nov. Test. ex Talmude Illustr., 58, 15**
Willet, Andrew	England	1562–1621		**DNB**
Willis, Arthur	England	*fl.* 1834		**Heb. Grammar, London, 1834**
Willmet, Joannes	Holland	1750–1835		**NNBW 10, 1222**
Wilson, Charles	England	*fl.* 1782		**Heb. Grammar, London, 1782**
Wilson, Daniel	England, India	1778–1858		**DNB**
Wilson, John	Scotland, India	1804–1875		**Heb. Grammar in Marathi, Bombay, 1832; DNB**
Win(c)kler, Johan. Friedr.	Germany	1679–1738		**St. 412, Bodl. Cat. 1081, no. 37; ADB**
Winer, Johan. Geo. Bened.	Germany	1789–1858		**St. 413, Bodl. Cat. 2726; ADB; Enc. Br.[11]**
Winkler, ?	Germany (?)	18th c.		**St. 412; J.C. Wolf, Bibl. Hebr. ii, 1264, no. 69**
Wisendangen, Jakob von, *see* Ceporinus, Jakob				
Witter, Henr. Bernh.	Germany	*fl.* 1703		**St. 414, Bodl. Cat. 2726**
Wittig, Johan. Sigmund	Germany	*fl.* 1802		**Heb. Grammar, Wittenberg, 1802**
Witzius, Hermann	Holland	1636–1708		**NNBW 3, 1445**
Woeldicke, Marcus	Denmark	1699–1750		**St. 415, Bodl. Cat. 1877, no. 43**
Wolder(-us), David	Germany	d. 1604		**Heb. Grammar, Hamburg, 591; ADB (?)**
Wolf(f), Geo.	Germany	*fl.* 1557		**St. 416**
Wolf(f)(-ius), Johann Christian	Germany	1683–1739		**St. 417, Bodl. Cat. 2730, Add., Introd. xxxiv; ADB; NBU**
Wolf(-ph), Johan. Jac.	Switzerland	(?)1521–1571 (?)		**St. 419; ADB (?)**
Wolf, Johann W.	?	d. 1751		**untraced**
Wolfe, J. Robert	England	*fl.* 1860		**Heb. Grammar, London, 1860**
Wolfer(d)us, Michael	Holland	1627–1664		**NNBW 10, 1234**
Wolff, Johann Henr.	?	*fl.* 1726		**St. 418**
Wollaston, William	England	1659/60–1724	Deist	**DNB; NBU; A. Altmann, Trans. Jew. Hist. Soc. Engl., 16, 1949, 184f.**
Wolters, Ludovicus	Germany	*fl.* 1718		**Selecta e Sohar et Rabboth, Bremen, 1718**
Worm, Christian	?	?		**St. 420**
Wotton, William	England	1666–1726 (?)		**St. 421, Bodl. Cat. 2734; DNB; NBU**
Wuelf(f)er, Johan.	Germany	1651–1724	Lutheran	**St. 422, Bodl. Cat. 2734; ADB (s.v. Daniel W.)**
Wuerttemberg, Antonia, Princess of, *see* Antonia, Princess of Wuerttemberg				
Ximénez de Cisneros, Francisco	Spain	1436–1517	Franciscan	
Yeates, Thomas	England	1768–1839		**DNB**
Young, Robert	Scotland	1822–1888		**DNB; Jew. Hist. Soc. Engl., Misc. 4, 1942, 79**
Zabler, Jób	Hungary	1628–1664	Lutheran	**Szin; Zov; Dan**
Zamora, Andreas de León	Spain	?		**St. 64; J.C. Wolf, Bibl. Hebr. 2, 1167, 1180**
Zanolini, Antonio	Italy	*fl.* 1747		**St. 423**
Zasio, Andrés	Hungary	1740–1816	Calvinist	**Szin**
Zeleny, Franc.	Bohemia	*fl.* 1756		**Heb. Grammar, Prague, 1756**
Zeller, Andr. Christoph.	Germany	*fl.* 1711		**St. 424, Bodl. Cat. 1878, 2760**

Christian Hebraists (continued)

Name	Country-(ies)	Dates	Religious Confession	References
Zeltner, Geo. Gust.	Germany	1672–1738		**St. 425, Bodl. Cat. 2761, Add; ADB; NBU**
Zieriksee, Amandus van, *see* Amandus van Zieriksee				
Zorzi, Francesco Georgio (Franciscus Venetus), *see* Giorgio, Francesco				
Zsigmondi, Samuel	Hungary	1788–1833	Lutheran	**Szin**
Zwingli, Ulrich (Huldreich)	Switzerland	1484–1531	Reformer	**NBU; ADB; Enc. Br.**[11]

HEBREW BOOK TITLES.

Bible

A number of book titles are mentioned in the Bible, i.e., "Book of the Generations of Man" (Gen. 5:1), "*Book of the *Covenant" (Ex. 24:7 etc.), "Book of the Wars of the Lord" (Num. 21:14), "Book of Jashar" (Josh. 10:13; II Sam. 1:18), and "Book of Chronicles of the Kings of Judah and Israel." The Pentateuch itself is variously named as the "Book of the Law of Moses" (Josh. 8:31) or the "Law of God" (Josh. 24:26), later becoming the *Torah in short, or *Ḥamishah Ḥumshei Torah* ("Five Books of the Torah") or *Ḥummash*. Together with Prophets and Hagiographa this became in due course the Bible (Gr. Βιβλία lit. "Books") or in Hebrew *Kitvei ha-Kodesh* ("Holy Scriptures"). A term like *Ketuvim* originally described the Hagiographa only, but then was extended to the entire biblical canon. Still later, the title *Esrim ve-Arba'ah*, the 24 books (of the Bible) occurs. The *abbreviation תנ"ך (*Tanakh*), the first letters of the three sections in the Hebrew Bible – *Torah, Nevi'im, Ketuvim* – is now the most popular term. The term *Mikra* (or *Kera*) is also used in the Mishnah and Talmud for the Bible (or a verse thereof; Ned. 4:3; Shab. 63a; Ta'an 5a; TJ, Ket 35:3). For the titles of individual books in the Bible, in particular of the Pentateuch, it is necessary to go back to the Septuagint where they appear as Genesis, Exodus, Leviticus, Numbers, Deuteronomy, terms describing, more or less, the contents of the books. In later Hebrew usage, the first or one of the first words of each book (*Bereshit, Shemot, Va-Yikra, Ba-Midbar,* and *Devarim*) was adopted as a title, which was a widespread practice among Greeks as well. Titles in Apocrypha and Pseudepigrapha describe putative authors and/or contents (e.g., Wisdom of Ben Sira).

Talmudic Era

In the Mishnah and Talmud the names of orders and tractates reflect contents rather than authorship, but the unwieldy size of tractate *Nezikin*, homonymous with the entire order, led to its being divided into *Bava Kamma, Bava Meẓia*, and *Bava Batra* ("the first, middle, and last gate"). Chapters, which were not numbered, are quoted by one or several initial words. Alternatives to the title Talmud ("study") are *Gemara* ("learning"), or the abbreviation ש"ס (*shas*), for *Shishah Sedarim*, the six orders of the Mishnah and Talmud, a title which resulted from the Church's banning of the Talmud and the consequent censorship. The oldest Midrashim, like the commentaries on the books of the Pentateuch, take their titles either from these books (e.g., *Torat Kohanim* "priestly law" but later **Sifra*), from their use as textbooks (e.g., *Sifrei de-vei-Rav*, "schoolbooks"), or from their hermeneutic character (**Mekhilta*). Aggadic Midrashim bear either the generic name of Midrash added to that of the biblical book (e.g., *Midrash Shemu'el* or *Midrash Tehillim*) – sometimes with the word *Rabbah* ("great") added (*Midrash Bereshit Rabbah*, see *Genesis Rabbah etc.) or that of a talmudic teacher reputed to be its compiler (e.g., *Midrash Tanḥuma*, which is also called *Yelammedenu* from the characteristic opening phrase of each chapter, and the *Pesikta de-Rav Kahana*). Later Midrashim have more fanciful titles (see below) such as *Lekaḥ Tov* ("Good Teaching," Prov. 4:2), *Shoḥer Tov* ("Seeker of Good," Prov. 11:27), etc. Midrash אבכיר (*Avkir*) derived its name from the initials of the concluding peroration. אמן בימינו כן יהי רצון ("Amen, in our days, may it be [His] will").

In geonic literature titles express the general nature of their compilations, such as *Halakhot Gedolot* or *Halakhot Pesukot* ("Great Rules"; "Decided Rules") or these together with the author's name (e.g., *She'iltot* – ritual questions (and answers) – of Aḥai Gaon; the *seder* of Rav Amram, or of Saadiah Gaon).

Middle Ages

In the Middle Ages, with the great increase in Hebrew literature of all sorts, there was a proliferation of titles, which may be roughly classified as follows:

NAMES AS TITLES. The names or abbreviations of names of the leading exegetic or halakhic authors are now used to describe their works, such as Rashi (whose Talmud commentary was also called by the generic name *Kunteres*, from *commentarius*), RaSHBA (R. Solomon b. Abraham Adret), RoSH (R. Asher b. Jehiel), Mordecai (b. Hillel), etc. often the particular nature of the work (*tosafot*, "glosses"; *ḥiddushim*, "novellae"; *she'elot u-teshuvot*, "responsa") is indicated in the name. Later the names of authors appear as part of titles taken from a biblical phrase such as *Ein Ya'akov* (Deut. 33:28) by Jacob ibn Ḥabib; *Kaftor va-Feraḥ* (Ex. 25:33) by Estori Farḥi; *Paḥad Yiẓḥak* (Gen. 31:53) by Isaac Lampronti or *Magen Avraham* by

Abraham Gombiner. Combinations of names with the word *beit* ("house of"), *sha'ar* or *sha'arei* ("gate" or "gates of"), *minḥat* and *korban* ("offering of"), *derekh* ("way of"), *even* ("stone of"), *yad* ("hand of"), etc. are very frequent. While almost all titles in medieval (and post-medieval) religious literature began with the word *sefer* ("book of") in some cases the word *maḥberet* or *maḥbarot* ("composition of") was used in combination with the author's name, e.g., *Maḥbarot Menaḥem* (b. Saruk, a dictionary); *Maḥbarot Immanu'el* (of Rome, poems). The author's desire for anonymity, stemming from a genuine or assumed modesty, was in constant conflict with that of perpetuating his or his father's name; the result was devious titles, both concealing and revealing. Thus Joseph ibn Kaspi ("silver," of L'Argentière, 13th–14th centuries) incorporated this byname in all his works: *Adnei Kesef* ("Sockets of Silver," Ex. 26:19), *Ḥaẓoẓerot Kesef* ("Silver Trumpets," Num. 10:2), *Kesef Sigim* ("Silver Drops," Prov. 26:23), etc.

TITLES REFLECTING CONTENTS. In the Middle Ages this way of titling books was widely adopted. Saadiah Gaon called his treatise the *Book of Beliefs and Opinions*, and the title of Judah Halevi's philosophic dialogues, *Kuzari* ("The Khazars") reflects their imaginary framework. Similarly, titles such as Ibn Gabirol's *Mekor Ḥayyim* ("Source of Life"), Maimonides' *Guide of the Perplexed*, and Albo's *Ikkarim* ("Principles") express the basic idea or purpose of the works in question. In the same vein Maimonides called his code *Mishneh Torah* ("Repetition of the Torah" alluding both to Deut. 17:18 and to Judah ha-Nasi's Mishnah), though it was later called the *Yad ha-Ḥazakah* ("The Strong Hand," Deut. 34:12), since the numerical value of *yad* is 14, the number of books into which the code is divided. There are several works called "Book of Precepts" (*Sefer Mitzvot*), one by Maimonides (originally in Arabic), one by *Moses of Coucy, and the *Sefer Mitzvot Katan* of *Isaac b. Joseph of Corbeil. Israel Najara wrote a short manual of *sheḥitah* for youngsters, to which he gave the equivocal title of *Shoḥatei ha-Yeladim* ("Slaughterers of Children").

METAPHORICAL TITLES. These occasionally overlap with the previous categories, as can be seen from examples mentioned above. However, most of these fanciful appellations do not provide the uninformed reader with any clue to the true contents of the work. Jacob b. Asher called his code *Arba'ah Turim* ("Four Rows") from the four rows of precious stones on the high priest's breastplate (Ex. 28:17); Joseph Caro named his code Shulḥan Arukh ("Prepared Table"; Ezek. 23:41); and Moses Isserles titled his annotations to it *Mappah* ("Tablecloth"). Early halakhic compendia bore such titles as *Eshkol* ("Cluster of Grapes"), and *Shibbolei ha-Leket* ("Gleanings of Corn"). In his work *Levushim* ("Garments"), Mordecai Jaffe named each of the 10 sections with one of the epithets of the biblical Mordecai's attire (Esth. 8:15). Solomon ibn Gabirol called his astronomic treatise *Keter Malkhut* ("The Royal Crown"); the kabbalistic classic is known as the *Sefer ha-Zohar* ("Book of Splendor") and kabbalistic literature in general indulged in euphuistic titles which usually expressed some mystical idea as well; e.g., *Eẓ ha-Ḥayyim* ("Tree of Life") by Ḥayyim Vital and *Tomer Devorah* ("Palm Tree of Deborah") by Moses Cordovero.

The *gematria system of using the numerical value of letters and words also played a great part. Thus the responsa of Simeon b. Ẓemaḥ Duran were named *Tashbeẓ* – this was not only the abbreviation of *Teshuvot Shimon ben Ẓemaḥ* and the biblical term "chequer-work" (Ex. 28:4), but also its numerical value was 792, the number of responsa included in the work. In some cases an abbreviation based on initials displaced the title in common parlance: a typical example (apart from the classic case of Rashi) is *Shelah* (for *Shenei Luḥot ha-Berit*). The author, Isaiah Horowitz, became generally known as Ba'al ha-Shelah, and sometimes by paradoxical rebound the book was popularly called by this latter title. Similarly the Pentateuch commentary ascribed to Jacob b. Asher, author of the *Arba'ah Turim*, is known as the *Ba'al ha-Turim* (cf. Zerahiah ha-Levi's commentary *Me'orot* on Alfasi, known as *Ba'al ha-Ma'or*).

The importance the Jews attached to a man's literary or scholarly work caused authors like those mentioned above to be known almost exclusively by the titles or abbreviations of titles of their books, such as the SHeLaH just mentioned, or the Ḥatam Sofer (title of Moses Sofer's works: responsa, novellae etc.), the Ḥafeẓ Ḥayyim (Israel ha-Kohen of Radun, after his ethical treatise of that name), the Ḥazon Ish (Abraham Isaiah Karelitz, after the title of his novellae).

Some titles seemingly chosen simply from biblical personal or place names – e.g., *Avi'ezer* (by Eliezer b. Joel ha-Levi); *Taḥkemoni* (by Judah Al-Ḥarizi); *Tishbi* (by Elijah Levita) – usually contained an allusion to the author's name.

INITIAL WORDS AS TITLES. As with biblical and midrashic literature, medieval works were also occasionally called by their initial word or words, e.g., *Tanya*, the title of a 14th-century ritual and one popularly given to Shneur Zalman's *Likkutei Amarim*.

"FOLLOW-UP" TITLES. These were often used for commentaries, like the previously mentioned *Mappah* for the Shulḥan Arukh. Shem Tov Falaquera gave his commentary to Maimonides' *Moreh Nevukhim* the title *Moreh ha-Moreh* ("Guide to the Guide"), and N. Krochmal wrote a *Moreh Nevukhei ha-Zeman* ("Guide for the Perplexed of the Time"). Solomon b. Abraham Adret's *Torat ha-Bayit* ("Law of the House," Isa. 30:9) was criticized by Aaron ha-Levi in his *Bedek ha-Bayit* ("Repair of the House," II Kings 12:6) and this was countered by Adret by his *Mishmeret ha-Bayit* ("Guard of the House," *ibid.*, 11:6). Samuel b. David ha-Levi's *Turei Zahav* ("Circlets of Gold") prompted Shabbetai Kohen to write *Nekuddot ha-Kesef* ("Studs of Silver," cf. Songs 1:11). Further classifications and subclassifications can and have been made. For translators the older Hebrew book titles sometimes present a problem.

MODERN TIMES. While the medieval manner of entitling rabbinic books has continued into modern times, as exemplified by Rabbi A.I. (Ha-Kohen) Kook's responsa (*Da'at Kohen, Ezrat*

Kohen, Mishpat Kohen) and other writings (*Iggerot Ra'ayyah, Olat Ra'ayyah*, etc. – *Ra'ayyah* (**R**av **A**braham **Y**iẓhaq **H**a-Cohen) being an abbreviation of his name), modern writers in Hebrew follow the prevailing standards in Western literature and scholarship, without abandoning recourse to the former Hebrew tradition. Examples are the titles of some of S.Y. Agnon's novels and short stories (such as *A Guest Who Stays Overnight*, Jer. 14:18) and M. Shamir's *King of Flesh and Blood*, a frequent midrashic phrase.

HEBREW COLLEGE, transdenominational institution of Jewish higher education located in Newton Centre, Massachusetts. Founded in 1921 and first located in Roxbury, then the center of Boston Jewish life, through its several generations the college has followed the dynamism of the Boston Jewish community, relocating with post-World War II Jews to suburban Brookline in 1953, then to Newton in 2001.

At one time locally based and focused mainly on the Boston and New England Jewish community, the contemporary Hebrew College serves the American and worldwide Jewish community, via an array of degree and other educational programs designed for the entire gamut of the life cycle. That includes training for early childhood educators, day school and Hebrew school educators, a Prozdor for middle and high school students, Camp Yavneh, a summer camp for Jewish youth, degree programs ranging from bachelor's and master's degrees to rabbinic and cantorial ordinations, Hebrew language intensive Ulpan, and a host of adult learning opportunities including the two-year course known as *Me'ah*. Its mission has always been to provide a link between the world of higher education, academic Jewish studies, and the Jewish community.

Its birth in 1921 reflected several trends in American, American Jewish, and modern Jewish history. The rise of new ideologies in the wake of the breakdown of Jewish communal and cultural life meant a new approach to the question of a new culture and new identity for Jews. This involved centrally new approaches to education, as the vehicle for cultural transmission. The college, founded primarily by Hebraists, Zionists, legatees of the East European Haskalah, along with its sister institutions in other American cities like Philadelphia, Baltimore, Cleveland, and Chicago, to name a few, expressed these trends in its commitment to Hebrew language and culture. Its first location, Roxbury, lay at the heart of the burgeoning Jewish ethnic and religious community of Boston.

Its founding also stemmed from a particular moment in American Jewish life. The considerable energy that the immigrants expended in integration and acculturation, and the host of ethnic social welfare institutions created by them, (such as burial societies, free loan networks, *landsmenschaften*, synagogues), had not been matched by equal investment in Jewish educational institutions. This stemmed from lack of funds, the paucity of resources such as trained educators and few rabbinic immigrants, and some degree of disinterest and disagreement about what Jewish education should be. After World War I, there arose a series of Bureaus of Jewish Education, centralized institutions that began to create a momentum for routinizing and standardizing Jewish education, which would include the building of modern *talmud torahs* and the training of teachers to staff those new sorts of congregational and community schools.

These developments suggest the importance of the American context, particularly ideas of cultural pluralism on the one hand, and Progressivism on the other. Cultural pluralism, as articulated by figures like Randolph Bourne and Horace Kallen, saw America as a republic of nationalities, a symphony with distinctive parts contributing to a greater whole, an entity dependent upon those parts for their enduring existence. No matter the internal debates about what Jewish culture should be, Jews as an ethnic group had a right to exist, and should maintain group cohesion, so went this worldview. The college, with its de-emphasis of religious ideology and its embrace of the Jewish cultural heritage, dovetailed beautifully with such pluralism.

So too with Progressivism, which saw organization as a key to solving the myriad challenges of modern life. The increasing professionalization of modernity, the belief in rationalism and rational methods for creating organizations to problem solve, found expression in American higher education. The early part of the 20th century witnessed young Jews at institutions like Columbia's Teacher's College, where they imbibed the ideas of thinkers such as John Dewey. The head of the New York City Jewish *Kehillah*'s Bureau of Jewish Education, Samson *Benderly, inspired a whole generation of such future Jewish educational leaders. These men and women went on to found schools and summer camps like Yavneh; they played key roles in the emerging Hebrew College movement. Yavneh in particular signaled the belief that culture must be actualized through living experience, in formal and informal contexts. They also believed that modernized culture required intellectual deliberation. Method was necessary to rethink and re-engineer teacher training, the writing of new textbooks, the building of new schools.

Trends in postwar America contributed to the college's reformulation of its program, if not its larger purpose. The founding of the State of Israel, and declining interest in intensive Jewish supplementary education, led to the weakening of Hebraism as an ideology and as an approach to Jewish education. For a considerable time, the college was the one place where Jewishly interested intellectuals could seriously pursue advanced academic Judaic studies. The list of prominent alumni includes the journalist Theodore White, and academics such as Walter Ackerman, Arnold Band, Ben Halpern, Paula Hyman, Frank Manuel, and Isadore Twersky, men and women of diverse religious and Jewish ideological perspectives who went on to prominent academic careers at UCLA, Brandeis, Harvard, and Yale.

The explosion of academic Jewish studies challenged the college's mission in that regard. In its place has come the new emphasis upon adult Jewish learning, as the baby boom has created a new adult culture of interest in education throughout the broader American middle class, particularly in the areas of religion and spirituality. The College, together with the local Jewish Federation, created *Me'ah* in 1994, to meet this need. The program features a curriculum-based two-year program of academically taught adult Jewish learning, bridging the gap between classical Jewish texts, history and ideas, and the cognitive and affective needs of adults. Today the program reaches dozens of communities throughout Boston, New York, and elsewhere in America, with an enrollment in the thousands.

In its most recent phase it has truly become a national institution, recruiting students literally from around the globe, who may also study from around the globe via the Internet and the college's online offerings, including an M.A. degree.

Hebrew College represents the twin modern dynamics of building and subverting in Jewish cultural life. It maintains Jewish life while it changes it, incorporating the modern tensions between ethnicity and religion. It accepts classical notions of what constitutes Jewish culture, for example biblical and rabbinic texts, even as it experiments with new genres such as modern Hebrew literature that serve to expand our notion of the Jewish cultural canon. In recent years this has taken on programmatic form as the college embraced rabbinic and cantorial training, and moved – albeit transdenominationally – to a greater degree of openness to trends in contemporary spiritual life such as neo-mysticism.

Similarly, the College embodies interesting structural tensions of being Jewish in America. It espouses the virtue of Jewish community, and sees itself as among the vanguard of institutions training Jewish leaders, albeit in an American context much more comfortable with individualism and liberalism. Its physical place, situated alongside of the Andover Newton Theological School, the oldest Protestant seminary in America, symbolizes the college's increasing receptivity to participating in the larger American realm of higher religious education. It remains both communally based as well as academically elitist, striving to maintain the standards American Jews associate with academic excellence. Nowhere is this more in emphasis than in the college's commitment to adult learning, which attempts to bridge the distance between the folk and the elite as bulwarks of contemporary Jewish life.

[David Benjamin Starr (2nd ed.)]

HEBREW GRAMMAR.

The following entry is divided into two sections: (I) an Introduction for the non-specialist and (II) a detailed survey.

(I) HEBREW GRAMMAR: AN INTRODUCTION

There are four main phases in the history of the Hebrew language: the biblical or classical, the post-biblical or neo-classical and rabbinic (which includes medieval scholarly writings and continued until the latter part of the 19th century), and the modern. In biblical times Hebrew was a living, spoken language but, from the centuries immediately preceding the Christian era, it ceased to be the vernacular. Nevertheless, biblical Hebrew persisted as the language of the Scriptures and as a model for compositions of a devotional nature. Because it was transmitted from one generation to the next, over many centuries, as a written language which found oral expression only in pious recital, its structure became artificially fixed.

It is remarkable, however, that the basic structure of the language has remained constant throughout all its stages of development. In the post-biblical and modern phases there was a progressive accretion in vocabulary by the creation of new words in accordance with the inherent laws of the language and by borrowing. Yet, divergencies in grammar were, for the most part, not fundamental, but peripheral. Thus a general introduction to the Hebrew language would best be served by confining it to the biblical phase and, where relevant, by pointing out divergencies which appeared in the later stages. The scheme of biblical Hebrew grammar is derived from the literature of the Hebrew Bible, known as Masoretic (from מְסֹרָה (*massorâ*) "tradition").

Understanding the Patterns of Biblical Hebrew Grammar

An understanding of the patterns of biblical Hebrew grammar, as opposed to the mechanical learning of a catalogue of seemingly irrational rules, may be achieved by recognizing that the formulation of these rules rests on three main principles:

1. the adoption of agreed conventional signs in writing to represent the spoken word, as it was traditionally transmitted and articulated;

2. deliberate adjustments in spelling, in conformity with any spontaneous modification in the articulation of the spoken word, due to natural fluctuations caused by inflection;

3. statements, in concise but adequate terms, of forms of Hebrew thinking, as expressed in speech.

The aim of this article is not to present a comprehensive scheme of Hebrew grammar, but to demonstrate that there is a rationality underlying it. To achieve this end, items of grammar will be selected to illustrate how the above three principles are translated into formal Hebrew grammar. Occasional analogies from other languages will be cited to show that, in other languages also, elements of grammar reflect articulated speech and thought processes.

The Hebrew alphabet consists of consonants only. The reader of a Hebrew consonantal text – if he was proficient in the language – automatically supplied the appropriate vowels, as determined by the context. Anyone familiar with English would know automatically whether the context of a sentence requires him to read the consonantal word r-d as "red," "rid," or "rod." Similarly, anyone who knows Hebrew well would immediately recognize from the context whether אם (*'m*) is to be read as אִם (*'im*, "if") or אֵם (*'ēm*, "a mother"), or whether דבר (*dbr*) is to be read דָּבָר (*dāḇār*, "a word"), דֶּבֶר (*deḇer*, "a plague"), דִּבֵּר (*dibbēr*, "he spoke"), or דֹּבֵר (*doḇēr*, "speaking").

When Hebrew ceased to be a spoken language, the uninitiated were unable to supply the relevant vowels to a consonantal text. It was realized that some apparatus had to be devised to indicate vowel-sounds as aids to reading. There were two stages in the development of such an apparatus. The first was the employment of the weak letters ה, ו, י (*h, w, y*) to serve also as vowel indicators. ו (*w*) represented both the o and u sounds, so that מות (*mwt*) could be read as either מוֹת (*môt*, "death of") or מוּת (*mût*, "dying"). י (*y*) indicated both the i and e sounds; מי (*my*) could be read as either מִי (*mî*, "who?") or מֵי (*mê*, "waters of"). The terminal silent ה (*h*) generally indicated the a vowel-sound, but sometimes also the e sound, so that מה (*mh*) could be read as either מָה (*mâ*) or מֶה (*meh*), both meaning "what." This device was employed in the texts of the so-called Dead Sea Scrolls and is maintained even today in modern Hebrew writing.

Though this system reduced the area of possible error, it was clearly unsatisfactory, because it was not exact. In the eighth century C.E. the Tiberian system of vowel-points was devised to represent all the vowel-sounds, as traditionally held. This apparatus was generally adopted and is still in use.

Among Jews of European origin, the influence of their vernaculars on the articulation of Hebrew consonants led to the coalescing of several pairs of consonants. א and ע are both silent, כ and ק are both pronounced as the same *k* sound, ב and ו are both articulated as *v*, ס, שׂ, and also ת among Ashkenazi Jews are pronounced as *s*, while in Israel the ת and ת are both pronounced as *t*. However, it should be realized that, in biblical times, each Hebrew consonant had its own particular phonetic value, as is still the case among Oriental Jews in the recital of their sacred Hebrew texts. In ancient Israel there was a clear difference in sound between, for example, the word אִם (*ʾim*, "if"), and עִם (*ʿim*, "with"), the latter being articulated with a back-throated guttural sound. Similarly one could distinguish between אַתָּה (*ʾattâ*, "you," masc. sing.) and עַתָּה (*ʿattâ*, "now"). There was a clear distinction in sound between the words כֹּל (*kōl*, "all") and קוֹל (*ḳôl*, "a voice"), for the latter was articulated as a distinctive back-throated *k*.

The operation of the three above principles in the formulation of rules of Hebrew grammar can now be dealt with.

1a. When a vowelless letter stands at the beginning or in the middle of a word, the convention is to place two dots, vertically arranged (:), under it, as שְׁמוּאֵל (*šmûʾēl*, "Samuel") and יִצְחָק (*yiṣḥāk*, "Isaac"). This sign is known as שְׁוָא (*šwāʾ*, probably meaning "speed"), which for convenience is spelled *shewa*. It indicates that the letter under which it appears has no full vowel. It was found that, when articulating a syllable beginning with a vowelless letter, a quick, vowel-like sound was involuntarily induced (something like the quick *e* in the word "because"). The *shewa* under such a letter is known as *vocal* and is represented in transcription by a diminutive *e;* thus the first example is transcribed *šεmûʾēl*. At the end of a syllable in the middle of a word, as in יִצְ/חָק (*yiṣ/ḥāk*), the *shewa* under the vowelless letter is a silent ("quiescent") one.

The peculiarity of speech indicated by the vocal *shewa* suggests that the ancient Israelite could not articulate a word beginning with two consonants without involuntarily giving the first (i.e., the vowelless) letter a quick vowel-like sound. He would have pronounced the word *black* as *bεlack*. This peculiarity is shared by the Arabs, who would pronounce this word as either *balack* or *iblack*. In modern Hebrew, however, owing to the influence of European languages, there is no difficulty in articulating a word beginning with two consonants. The first example would be articulated as *shmuel*.

b. In the Hebrew alphabet there are six letters which under certain conditions are pronounced hard (*b, g, d, k, p, t*) and, in other situations, are pronounced *soft* (*ḇ, g̱, ḏ, ḵ, p̱, ṯ*). When such a letter is hard in speech, the convention in writing is to place a dot in it, called by grammarians דָּגֵשׁ (*dageš*, "piercing") *lene*, or *light dageš* (בּ, גּ, דּ, כּ, פּ, תּ). When such a letter is soft in the spoken word, it is left without any dot in it (ב, ג, ד, כ, פ, ת).

To the question as to when these letters are pronounced hard and when soft, the answer may be given that it seems that the vocal organs of the ancient Israelites were so conditioned that, when one of these letters began a syllable, and no vowel immediately preceded, they pronounced it hard, as פָּרַשׂ (*pāraš*, "he spread") and יִסְ/פֹּר (*yis/pōr*, "he will count"). It follows, then, that when one of these letters was at the end of a syllable, as יִפְ/רֹשׂ (*yip̱/rōś*, "he will spread"), or in the middle of a syllable, as בְּכֹל (*bεḵōl*), or at the beginning of a syllable but with a vowel immediately preceding, as סָ/פַר (*sā/p̱ar*, "he counted"), the letter was pronounced soft. When the word פָּרָה (*pārâ*, "cow"), whose initial letter is hard, receives the prefixed conjunction, it becomes וּפָרָה (*ûp̱ārâ*, "a cow"); the speaker automatically softens the letter after the vowel sound. In modern Hebrew, however, this rule is not always observed in fluent speech.

c. If a letter in the middle of a word is doubled in articulation, the convention is to write a single letter only, but with a dot in it. The word for "thief" is גַּנָּב and represents the spoken גַּנְנָב (*gannāḇ*). This dot, indicating a doubled letter, is known as *dageš forte*, or *strong dageš*, to distinguish it from the other *dageš*, the light one, which indicates the hard letter, as the גּ in this example. However, the six letters (*b, g, d, k, p, t*), when hard, may be doubled in the middle of a word, as שַׁבָּת, representing שַׁבְּבָּת (*šabbāt*), in which case the *dageš* is theoretically both *lene* and *forte*. It should be noted here that the guttural letters (א, ה, ח, ע), by their very nature of being either weak (inaudible) or throat letters, cannot be doubled in articulation, so that, in writing, they do not receive a *dageš forte*. Strangely enough, this also applies to the letter ר (*r*).

The doubling of a letter is by no means arbitrary; it is usually due to some natural phenomenon in speech. In anticipation an English composite word may be quoted, derived from Latin, with the negative prefix in-. The combination *inlegal* is articulated *illegal* and actually spelt phonetically. This is exactly what happens in Hebrew. When, for example, the two words מִן (*min*, "from") and שָׁם (*šām*, "there") are spoken together in the natural flow of speech, they become a composite word. The combination מִנְשָׁם (*minšām*) is articulated as מִשְׁשָׁם (*miššām*) but written מִשָּׁם, with the *dageš forte* indicating the double letter. This phenomenon of speech is described in the following rule of grammar: "When a vowelless נ (*n*) stands between two vowelled consonants, it is assimilated to the consonant immediately after it, giving rise to the doubling of the latter."

2. In many English words the spelling has not kept pace with changes in pronunciation. The word *daughter* is pronounced *dauter,* but the persistence of the medial *gh* in the spelling suggests that originally it must have been articulated with a guttural-like sound, as in the parent German word *tochter.* The American spelling of some words shows an arrested attempt towards writing words phonetically: *plough* is spelled *plow* and though is sometimes written as *tho,* but the trend did not develop consistently. In Hebrew, however, every modification in the articulation of words, usually due to the effect of inflection or the presence of a peculiar letter, is faithfully reproduced in writing by corresponding adjustments in spelling.

a. The first example is the two-syllabled word דָּבָר (*dāḇār,* "word, matter, thing"), which begins with an open syllable (i.e., one ending in a vowel) and has the stress on the second syllable. The plural is formed by attaching the ending ־ִים (*-îm*) and the stress moves on to this new syllable at the end. The speaker, hurrying on to the stressed syllable at the end, quite naturally elides the vowel ָ (*ā*) in the first (*open*) syllable. It becomes דְּבָרִים (*dǝḇārîm*), and not דָּבָרִים (*dāḇārîm*); the first syllable, now vowelless, is written with the vocal *shewa.* The modification in articulation is paralleled by the corresponding adjustment in the spelling. (An analogy of this phenomenon in speech is the English word *médicine*, which, with an accession at the end and the moving forward of the stress, becomes *medicinal* – almost *mdícinal.*)

b. The next example introduces a characteristic usage in Hebrew. In an expression such as "(the) word of Moses," דָּבָר (*dāḇār,* "word") and מֹשֶׁה (*mōšeh,* "Moses") are so closely associated that they become one compound idea; in fluent speech they are virtually one composite word and the stress is mainly on the second half of the composite word. The effect is similar to that in the example just quoted. That is, דָּבָר (*dāḇār*) has received an accession at the end and the stress has moved forward, so that the vowel in the first (open) syllable is elided and a secondary effect is that the vowel in the second (closed) syllable is shortened. The combination is pronounced דְּבַר־מֹשֶׁה (*dǝḇar-mōšeh*) and written as such. The first noun is so dependent upon the second one that it is said to be in the construct state. This natural shortening of the vowel in the closed syllable of a word in the construct state is seen also in the combination of יָד (*yāḏ,* " hand") with מֹשֶׁה (*mōšeh*) in the expression "(the) hand of Moses" – יַד־מֹשֶׁה (*yaḏ-mōšeh*).

c. It was noted earlier that a vowelless נ (*n*) between two vowelled consonants is assimilated to the following letter which, in consequence, is doubled and that, in writing, this doubling is represented by a *dageš forte* – מִנְשָׁם (*minšām*) becoming מִשָּׁם (*miššām*). When, however, the letter following the vowelless נ (*n*) is a guttural (א, ה, ח, ע) or ר which cannot be doubled in articulation, a natural adjustment is made. When the phrase "from a man" – מִן אָדָם (*min ʾāḏām*) – becomes a composite word in the flow of speech (hypothetically מִנְאָדָם, *minʾāḏām*), the vowelless נ (*n*) is assimilated, but the following letter cannot be doubled. The resultant form מִאָדָם, (*miʾāḏām*) leaves the first syllable open, i.e., ending in a vowel. Since the natural tendency was to pronounce an open syllable with a long vowel (unless that syllable was stressed, in which case the effect was the same), the short vowel (*i*) in the first syllable is automatically prolonged by the speaker to ...(*ē*) and the combination becomes מֵאָדָם (*mēʾāḏām*), the spelling being adjusted to conform with the modification in speech.

d. The following example of a rule of grammar appears superficially to be irrational and yet, on examination, it reflects a normal fluctuation in speech which is represented phonetically by the written word. The possessives are expressed by particles suffixed to the noun as "a house is old," "my house is old." The feminine singular noun, such as תּוֹרָה (*tôrâ,* "Torah") with a suffix ("my Torah") becomes תּוֹרָתִי (*tôrāṯi*). How can one account for the apparent insertion of the letter ת (*t*) before the suffix? Arabic provides the perfect analogy.

In classical (literary) Arabic, nouns have three case endings. The feminine singular noun "city" is *madīnat*un (nominative), *madīnat*in (genitive), and *madīnat*an (accusative). In colloquial Arabic, however, the case-endings are dropped, leaving the form *madīnat* for all cases, but it is actually pronounced *madīna* (or *medīna*). The final *t* is not articulated (like the tendency in America to pronounce the word *breakfast* as *breakfas*). However, when this *t* is in the middle of a word and it has a vowel, as with a possessive suffix attached ("my city" being *madīnatī*) it is, of course, clearly articulated.

Scholars have pointed to the same phenomenon appearing in the transition from pre-biblical to biblical Hebrew. There are indications that, originally, Hebrew nouns had case-endings, like Arabic: the word for Torah was *tôrāṯ*u (nom.), *tôrāṯ*i (gen.), and *tôrāṯ*a (acc.). The case-endings were dropped and the resultant form תּוֹרַת (*tôrāṯ*) was pronounced תּוֹרָה (*tôrâ*) and spelled that way. As with Arabic, it was the final ת (*t*) which was not articulated but, when it is medial with a vowel, it is, of course, clearly articulated – "my Torah" could only be תּוֹרָתִי (*tôrāṯî*). Because the final ת (*t*) was not articulated, it was dropped in spelling; when it is medial and audible, it is present in the spelling.

The tendency to drop a final *t* sound is present in other languages. In Ireland the well-known surname *McGrath* is actually pronounced *McGra.* The French say *il est* ("he is") pronounced *il-ē* but as a question it is *est-il?* ("is he?" – pronounced *ēt-il*), the medial vowelled *t* being quite naturally articulated. More striking still, and akin to the situation in Hebrew, is the French *il a* ("he has"), which, as a question, is *a-t-il?* ("has he?"), with the medial vowelled *t* articulated and reappearing in the spelling.

3. In biblical Hebrew the main idea of an expression is stated first and it is then qualified, limited in application or

modified by what immediately follows. "My word" is, in Hebrew thinking, something like "word, mine" – דְּבָרִי (*dεḇārî*), the main idea being "word," which is first expressed and then limited to "mine" by the following particle י (*î*). "A big house" is, in the Hebrew order of thought, "a house (the main idea), a big (one)" (qualifying it) – בַּיִת גָּדוֹל (*bayiṯ gāḏôl*). It follows logically that the phrase "the big house" is, in Hebrew thinking, "*the* house, *the* big (one)"– הַבַּיִת הַגָּדוֹל (*habbayiṯ haggāḏôl*) and "my big house" will be "house, mine, *the* big (one)" בֵּיתִי הַגָּדוֹל (*bêṯî haggāḏôl*). The rule which is then enunciated is "the adjective follows the noun it qualifies (and agrees with it in gender and number), and if the noun is specific (as indicated by the definite article or the possessive suffix) the adjective following the noun has the definite article." In the same pattern of thought the adverb follows the noun it modifies; "exceedingly good" is "good, exceedingly" – טוֹב מְאֹד (*tōḇ mε'ōd*).

THE VERB. In the structure of the Hebrew verbal system one again detects characteristic thought processes. Whereas medieval and modern Hebrew adopted the European concept of past, present, and future tenses, in biblical Hebrew no such notion was formulated. Instead acts or states of being were viewed as either completed or incompleted. The completed state, referring to something finished or done, generally corresponds to the notion of the past tense but, with certain verbs, it may indicate a European present tense. The form זָכַרְתָּ (*zāḵartā*) could mean "you remembered" but, since the basic sense is "our state of remembering is completed," it could imply "you remember." The incompleted state, indicating something not yet finished or not yet done, generally refers to the future but with a few verbs it could imply a continuing present. תִּזְכֹּר (*tizkōr*) could mean "you will remember" but, since the basic notion is "our state of remembering is incompleted," i.e., it is still going on, the derived sense could be "you keep on remembering," that is "you are mindful of." Unhappily, grammarians have adopted the terms perfect and imperfect – as used for Latin and Greek conjugations of verbs – but these do not accurately represent the biblical Hebrew concept.

It is to be noted that in the completed state, it is the act or state of being which is regarded as the main idea. Thus the verbal element is expressed first and is limited or applied to the person (in the example given the particle תָּ – (*tā*) for אַתָּה – *'attâ*, "you," masc. sing.) which immediately follows. In the incompleted state, however, what seems to be more prominent in the mind of the speaker is the person who is about to do, or is in the process of doing, something. Thus the element representing the person (in the example the ת, *t*) is stated first and the verbal element follows.

The Western notion of the present tense is represented in Hebrew by the participle, e.g., זֹכֵר (*zōḵēr*, "remembering"), preceded by the appropriate personal pronoun. "You remember" is, in Hebrew, אַתָּה זֹכֵר (*'attâ zōḵēr*). Since the Hebrew participle is virtually a verbal adjective, the thought underlying that expression is "you (are) a remembering (person)."

There are seven forms in the Hebrew verbal system. The first may be regarded as basic and the other six as derived forms, as in the following scheme:

I. SIMPLE ACTIVE: שָׁבַר (*šāḇar*, "he broke"). This is the completed state. It has also the incompleted state, participle, imperative, etc., and all these are conjugated with persons, numbers, and genders.

II. SIMPLE PASSIVE, but, with some verbs, the passive has also something of a reflexive effect. Its form is נִשְׁבַּר (*nišbar*), meaning "he (or "it") was broken." However, from the simple active רָאָה (*rā'â*, "he saw") the derived form of this category נִרְאָה (*nir'â*) means "he was seen," but this produces the extended sense "he showed himself," that is, "he appeared."

III. INTENSIVE ACTIVE. Derived from the simple active שָׁבַר (*šāḇar*, "he broke") is the intensive form שִׁבֵּר (*šibbēr*) (with the middle root-letter doubled to express intensity) and the derived sense is "he smashed," "he shattered." It will be realized that a derived form in this category must produce a new idea by extension, so that only such verbs which lend themselves to such an extension, by which a new idea is derived, can be included in it.

IV. INTENSIVE PASSIVE. This is simply the passive of III and its form is שֻׁבַּר (*šubbar*, "he (or "it") was smashed/shattered."

V. CAUSATIVE ACTIVE. The notion of *causative* is present in a few English verbs. "To seat" is the causative of "to sit" and "to fell" is the causative of "to fall." Since only a limited number of simple active verbs can be extended with a causative effect which produces a new idea, the verb גָּדַל (*gāḏal*, "he was great") is selected, of which the derived causative is הִגְדִּיל (*higdîl*, "he caused to be great," i.e., "he enlarged"). Of the verb רָאָה (*rā'â*, "he saw") the derived causative is הֶרְאָה (*her'â*, "he caused to see," "he let one see," "he showed"). Of the (weak) verb בָּא (*bā'*, "he came") the derived causative הֵבִיא (*hēḇi'*, "he caused to come") produces the sense "he brought."

VI. CAUSATIVE PASSIVE. This is the passive of V and its form is הָגְדַּל (*hogdal*), meaning "he (or "it") was made great," i.e., was enlarged.

VII. REFLEXIVE. Again, for the sake of clarity, another verb is taken as the parent of this derived form. From the simple active נָשָׂא (*nāśā'*, "he lifted up," "he raised up"), the derived reflexive is הִתְנַשֵּׂא (*hiṯnassē'*, "he raised himself up") and this, in turn, produces the sense "he boasted."

The terminology devised by the early Jewish grammarians to designate the above seven verbal forms has been universally accepted. They firstly considered the simple active to be קַל (*ḳal*, "light"), while the other six were said to be כְּבֵדִים (*kεḇēdīm*, "heavy"), since each one of them received additional letters or syllables. These six *heavy* forms were subdivided into the following categories. Taking as their basis the verb פָּעַל (*pā'al*, "he did"), they designated the simple passive as a נִפְעַל (*nip'al*), i.e., a "was done" form. The intensive active was called a פִּעֵל (*pi'ēl*), i.e, a "did intensively" form and its passive a פֻּעַל (*pu'al*) i.e, "was done intensively" form. The causative was designated a הִפְעִיל (*hip'il*)*i*, i.e., a "caused (one) to do" form and its passive a הָפְעַל (*hop̄ʿēl*), i.e., a "was caused to be done" form. The reflexive became the הִתְפַּעֵל (*hitpaʿēl*), i.e., a "did to oneself" form. Though this system may appear to be clumsy and cumbersome, its adoption as the standard, universal terminology has avoided the multiplicity of terminologies in different languages.

THE WEAK VERB. Hebrew has very few examples of irregular verbs, in which a complete conjugation is made up of two different roots. One such example is the verb שָׁתָה (*šāṯâ*, "he drank"), of which the derived causative form, with the meaning "he caused to drink," "he gave to drink," "he watered, irrigated," is not הִשְׁתָּה (*hištâ*) but הִשְׁקָה (*hiškâ*), from a different root, namely שָׁקָה (*šāḳâ*). There are, however, many verbs which, because of a peculiar letter in the stem, diverge from the normal or regular and these are known as *weak*. The reader will now be familiar with the categories of peculiar letters which bring about modifications in the articulated word. Examples of these as they affect the verb are given below:

a. The letter נ (*n*). The incompleted state of the normal verb שָׁמַר (*šāmar*, "he kept, watched") is יִשְׁמֹר (*yišmōr*, "he will keep, watch"). However, of the verb נָטַר (*nāṭar*) (which has the same meaning) the incompleted state is not יִנְטֹר (*yinṭōr*), for the medial, vowelless נ (*n*) standing between two vowelled consonants is assimilated to the next letter, which is thereby doubled, so that the resultant form of this word is יִטֹּר (*yiṭṭōr*) – a divergence from the normal.

b. Guttural letters (א, ה, ח, ע) and ר. It was noted above that the characteristic of the *piʿēl* (intensive) form is the doubling of the middle root-letter, as שִׁבֵּר (*šibbēr*, "he smashed"). When this medial letter is a guttural or ר, which cannot be doubled in articulation, the preceding vowel is prolonged. "He glorified" is not פִּאֵר (*piʾēr*) but פֵּאֵר (*pēʾēr*), "he refused" is not מִאֵן (*miʾēn*) but מֵאֵן (*mēʾēn*), thus producing a deviation from the normal. (Note: This always happens with the weak gutturals א and ע. With the harsh guttural ה and ח, no doubling takes place but, because of their harsh nature, the preceding vowel seems to merge with the letter (נִחַם – *niḥam*, "he comforted") and so the prolongation of that vowel is arrested.)

c. The weak letters (א, ה, ו, י). Taking again as the standard the verb שָׁמַר (*šāmar*, "he kept"), one with a medial weak letter ו (*w*) will deviate from the normal in the following way. "He arose," which one might have expected to be קָוַם (*ḳāwam*) deteriorates into קָם (*ḳām*); the weak ו melts into the vowel-sounds in which it is placed. The spelling is adjusted to the modified form. A verbal root with a terminal silent א also induces a deviation from the normal. "He found" is not מָצַא (*māṣaʾ*), for the terminal א is silent, so that, in actual sound, the syllable is open, i.e., ending in a vowel. Since the open syllable was usually pronounced with a long vowel, the speaker automatically prolonged it and the resultant form became מָצָא (*māṣāʾ*).

In this instance also the early Jewish grammarians devised a rather cumbersome terminology to denote categories of weak verbs, which has been universally adopted. It was based on the word פֹּעַל (*pōʿal*) which was their term for "verb." If the first root-letter was weak, they referred to it as the פ (*pe*) of the root, the second root-letter as the ע (*ʿayin*) of the verb and the third root-letter as its ל (*lameḏ*). For example, the verb נָטַר (*nāṭar*) was designated as a פ"ן (*pe nun*), i.e., initial נ, verb; the verb פֵּאֵר (*pēʾēr*) was described as an ע"א (*ʿayin ʾaleḇ*), i.e., medial guttural, verb; the verb קָם (*ḳām*), whose root-letters are קום, was designated as an ע"ו (*ʿayin waw*), i.e., medial ו, verb; the verb מָצָא (*māṣā*) became known as a ל"א (*lameḏ aleḇ*), i.e., terminal א, verb.

The structure of Hebrew grammar, of which a partial sketch has been given here, has not changed appreciably through the centuries, from biblical times to the present day. It manifests itself even in the highly evolved spoken and written Hebrew of contemporary Israel. The realization that Hebrew grammar reflects natural phenomena in speech and characteristic forms of thought leads to an understanding and appreciation of the genius of the language.

For a different view of Hebrew morphology in general and of the verbal system in particular, see U. Ornan, *Ha-Millah ha-Aḥaronah – Mangenon ha-Ẓurah shel ha-Millah ha-Ivrit* (2003).

[Jacob Weingreen]

(II) HEBREW GRAMMAR: DETAILED SURVEY

PHONOLOGY

Introduction

1. DEFINITION OF TOPIC. The Hebrew language is very old; but even in the oldest portions of the Bible, written more than three thousand years ago, it is a fully formed literary vehicle. No language, however, can remain unchanged over so long a period. Hebrew was subject to change, though for almost half its existence it was preserved only in writing, as a literary language. Nevertheless, an intelligent Hebrew speaker, of

the level of an Israeli high school graduate, can read and understand literature written in Hebrew from the very earliest times to the most modern. Furthermore he will find in the Hebrew language of each of the periods many elements actively used in modern speech. Many highly civilized societies from time to time rewrite the literary products of past generations to make them more comprehensible to the modern reader, sometimes wholly translating, at others, merely replacing the obsolete by more modern terms. By contrast, Hebrew literature such as the Bible, Mishnah, Midrashim, medieval poetry, etc., are today taught in schools in their original form, and may be read by the community at large. Hebrew thus appears to have maintained its original uniformity; yet linguistic analysis reveals that this uniformity is in fact limited and in part imaginary. The relative uniformity of Hebrew results primarily from two factors: the graphic representation of the language, and its morphology. Hebrew today is written, as it was in the past, in an alphabet in which all the letters represent consonants. Although several of these letters may, in specific circumstances, also indicate vowels (and in modern times even more so than in the past), this does not alter the general character of Hebrew writing, in which only a part of the total sounds are fully expressed: the part represented consists of those sounds which are naturally more stable and not given to radical change, while those sounds given more naturally to change are not represented by the writing. The employment of vowel points to express these sounds is very limited, and even nowadays does not determine the form of the written Hebrew word. This retention of the relatively constant element, and elimination of the element given to change, are great aids in understanding the written Hebrew word regardless of its date of origin. However, the factor primarily responsible for the uniformity of the language is Hebrew morphology. In the accepted vocalization of the Bible, the morphology of biblical Hebrew was fashioned in accordance with one tradition, the Tiberian. This tradition was not only accepted as the norm, but in the eyes of many even became sanctified. The morphology of biblical Hebrew in the Tiberian tradition determines the nature of the grammar of written Hebrew in general, and even new elements, whether taken from other periods or traditions of the language, or originally foreign elements, are adjusted to comply with the regulations of Hebrew morphology. In contrast to the relative stability of morphology and writing, the meaning and the function of grammatical forms and vocabulary and pronunciation have been variable. The particular pronunciation reflected by the accepted vocalization tradition of the Bible (even now mandatory for a vocalized word), is still heard today, but not all of its details are together represented in any one tradition. Closest to the pronunciation of the original vocalizers is that of the Yemenite and Babylonian communities (cf. below, Table 3: Consonants as Pronounced by Various Communities). The grammatical description given below refers to the language as it is written in modern times; a description of the various periods of the Hebrew language is given in the entry *Hebrew Language; and the distinctive traits of the various living traditions are discussed in the article *Pronunciations of Hebrew.

2. WRITING AND SPELLING. Hebrew is written in two sets of symbols, letters and vowel points; the first is, of course, mandatory, while the latter is reserved, primarily for the areas of education, poetry, prayer books and, to a limited extent, publications intended to reach a very wide audience. The basic alphabet consists of 22 letters; to these one must add five (ך, ם, ן, ף, ץ) used in final word position only, another seven (בּ, גּ, דּ, כּ, פּ, תּ, שׁ/שׂ), whose individual pronunciation is re-

Table 1:
The Letters

	A	B	C
א	ʾ (?)	ʾ	'*
בּ	b	b	b
ב	ḇ (bh)	v	v
גּ	g	g	g
ג	ḡ (gh)	ḡ	g
דּ	d	d	d
ד	ḏ (dh)	ḏ	d
ה	h	h	h
ו	w	w	w
ז	z	z	z
ח	ḥ	ḥ	ẖ
ט	ṭ	ṭ	t
י	y	y	y
כּ ךּ	k	k	k
כ ך	ḵ (kh)	ḵ	kh
ל	l	l	l
מ ם	m	m	m
נ ן	n	n	n
ס	s	s	s
ע	ʿ (?)	ʿ	'*
פּ	p	p	p
פ ף	f ; p̄	f	f
צ ץ	ṣ	ẕ	ẕ
ק	ḳ ; q	q	q
ר	r	r	r
שׁ	š (sh)	š	sh
שׂ	ś	ś	s
תּ	t	t	t
ת	ṯ (th)	ṯ	t
ג׳	–	ğ	ğ
ז׳	–	ž	ž
צ׳ ץ׳	–	č	č

* Generally this Hebrew letter is not represented and the sign is used only in special circumstances.

Punctuation[1]

		A[2]	B	C
Ḥireq	ִ	i	i	i
Ṣere	ֵ	e (ẹ)	é	é
Segol	ֶ	ae (ä, ẹ)	e	e
Pathaḥ	ַ	a	a	a
Qameṣ (long)	ָ	å ā	a	a
Qameṣ (short)	ָ	å ; o (ọ, ɔ)	o	o
Ḥolem	וֹ	o	o	o
Qibbuṣ	ֻ	u	u	u
Šureq	וּ	u	u	u
Šewa[3]	ְ	e	e	e
Ḥaṭef Segol	ֱ	æ	ĕ	e
Ḥaṭef Pathaḥ	ֲ	a	ă	a
Ḥaṭef Qameṣ	ֳ	o	ŏ	o
Dageš as מּ[4]		mm	mm	mm

1) Some of the vowel signs are accompanied by letters (*matres lectionis*) which are not part of the system of vocalization e.g., ִי , ֵי , ָא .
2) In A the length (or absence of it) in the vowels is represented in accordance with linguistic considerations.
3) The term *šewa* indicates both a reduced vowel and the absence of any vowel after the consonant; in the latter case it is not transliterated.
4) The *dageš* is also a double valued sign. In the letters בג"ד כפ"ת it indicates a different phonetic character and not necessarily gemination. Whether these letters, when pointed with *dageš*, also indicate geminated consonants depends on syllable structure; thus the correct transliteration of בּ – by b or by bb – for example demands a knowledge of Hebrew grammar. The *dageš* is placed in the letter הּ at the end of a word when the letter is pronounced consonantal h, and does not indicate gemination. In accordance with its function the *dageš* is variously called *forte* (for gemination), *lene*, and *mappiq*. Similarly a dot above ש indicates a pronunciation difference between š and ś.

flected only in vocalized writing, and three (ג׳, ז׳, צ׳) used in words of foreign origin only. All but four of the letters represent consonants only, while א, ה, ו, and י are used at times to indicate the presence of specific vowels. These letters, when not representing consonants, are called *matres lectionis*. Of the 13 vocalization signs, 12 are intended to represent vowels, and one represents changes in consonants. The various systems used to transliterate Hebrew into Roman script generally reflect two different approaches. The first transliterates the Hebrew alphabet into graphemes of the particular language in accordance with the spelling conventions of that language. This gives rise to a plethora of conventions according to the languages concerned. The other system attempts to transliterate Hebrew so that the letters and vowels will be perfectly or nearly perfectly represented. This system demands the addition of diacritic signs to the Roman alphabet. Table 1: Hebrew Letters and Punctuation is a synoptic table of three methods of transliteration.

The "A" system is used largely in linguistics or when an early Hebrew text is being transliterated. "B" and "C" were established by the Academy for Hebrew Language in 1957 in order to represent living Hebrew. "B" is used in catalogs, title pages, and maps. The sole difference between "B" and "A" is in the letters ב and צ where "B" represents the official modern pronunciation; this is also true with regard to the long *qameṣ* which is not differentiated from the *pathaḥ*. "C," on the other hand, intended for popular use, as in road and street signs, eliminates most of the diacritic signs, and simplifies the vocalization. The appearance of the unvocalized Hebrew word is likely to be different from the vocalized word even in its letters. This is due to the tendency to add *matres lectionis* in non-vocalized writing, in positions where they would be unacceptable in vocalized writing. For this reason it is also called "full spelling."

Phonology and Morphophonology

3. CONSONANTS. Table 2: Point and Way of Articulation summarizes the inventory of consonants in modern Hebrew, but they are not all at once present in any one of the varied pronunciation systems. The consonants are listed in accord with their general phonetic value, though some have more than one realization (כ, ל, ר). This variety is of a wider scale in Hebrew than in most other languages because the speakers of Hebrew are of diverse language backgrounds, and this background is apparent even in the generation whose mother tongue is Hebrew and who are, themselves, monolingual. The range of differences within each consonant is not represented in the table. Those consonants in squares are part of the Tiberian pronunciation (see *Masorah), and are therefore represented in modern writing; they are, however, normally not differentiated in the general or official pronunciation. They can still be heard in liturgy and worship (on ש see below) in some communities, and even in the speech of the older generation. The consonants in circles are not pronounced by a large part of the general populace and have been assimilated to בּ, כ, תּ. Their independence is maintained in the language in so far as their influence is felt in inflection and declension of words. Those consonants in dotted squares can be heard at times in originally Hebrew words in special situations, or in careless speech, as *ḥežbon* (חשבון), but are not independent except in words of foreign origin, as in *žargòn* (jargon), *žurnal* (journal); they do not determine the character of the Hebrew language in any area of grammar. Therefore, they will be referred to as "foreign," as distinct from "inherited."

If the foreign consonants and those which appear in squares are subtracted, it will be found that the total of inherited consonants in official modern Hebrew is 25, and the incidence of three, circled in the table, is very limited. In other words, the total varies between 22 and 25. This state of affairs changes in regard to the inventory of the consonantal phonemes. The phoneme, by definition, is that unit which only in distinction to another in the same position, performs the function of distinguishing between two words. The phoneme can be of more than one sound (ideally this is always the case), and all these sounds are related to each other as allophones (= variants). Not everyone is agreed as to the number of phonemes in the language, a problem which exists not only in Hebrew. It depends on how we evaluate sounds in foreign words, personal names, or rare words. For example, פּ, פ hardly ever occur in identical surroundings in Hebrew; where the one is

Table 2: Point and Way of Articulation

Point of Articulation	Way of Articulation										
	Plosive		Nasal	Lateral	Rolled	Affricate		Fricative		Semi-Vowel	
	Unvoiced	Voiced		Voiced		Unvoiced	Voiced	Unvoiced	Voiced		
bilabial	p פּ	b בּ	m מ							(w ו)	4
labiodental								f פֿ	v בֿ		2
interdental								[ṯ(θ)תֿ]	[ḏ(δ)דֿ]		2
dental (tongue tip and upper teeth)	t תּ	d ד	n נ	l ל	r ר	ẕ צ (ts,c)		s ס	z ז		(8)6
alveolar (tongue tip or blade and teeth ridge)			n נ	l ל		č צ׳	ğ ג׳	š שׁ	ž ז׳		4(6)
alveolo-palatal (tongue blade and teeth ridge)								[ś שׂ]			1
velarized alveolar (tongue blade and back, and teeth ridge)	(ṭ ט)							[ṣ צ]			2
palatal										y י	1
velar	k כּ	g גּ						ḵ(χ)כֿ	[ḡ(γ)גֿ]		4
uvular	(q ק)										1
pharyngal								ḥ ח	ʿ(ʕ)ע		2
glottal	ʾ(ʔ)א							h ה			2
	6	3	2	1	1	2	1	9	6	2	33

found the other is not (as וּפָנִים/פָּנִים and not וּפְּנִים/פָנִים); they are, therefore, allophones of the same phoneme. When, on certain rare occasions each sound may be heard in the same environment, there will be no difference in the meanings of the words. Generally, one of the forms of the word is considered incorrect in proper speech, as קִצְבָּה opposed to קִצְבָה. However, if foreign words are considered, the difference between p and f proves to be distinctive as in the words פּוּנקציה (*punkcya* = puncture) opposed to פונקציה (*funkcya* = function). To the extent to which such words enter the language of less educated persons there is more likely to be created a split between the p (פּ) and f (פ), and each is liable to appear in the same conditions. With regard to the written language, these rare phenomena are to be ignored, and the count will include 22 consonantal phonemes of the 25 consonants mentioned above, since פֿ בֿ כֿ are allophones of פּ בּ כּ and together are three phonemes. The consonantal phonemes can be divided into nine groups in accordance with their point of articulation:

bilabials	ו ,מ ,ב ,פ	4
dental	זסצ רלנ דת	8
alveolar	שׁ	1
velarized alveolar	ט	1
palatal	י	1
velar	ג ,כ	2
uvular	ק	1
pharyngeal	ח,ע	2
glottal	ה ,א	2 (= 22)

A pronunciation different from the one described above would show some slight differences in the localization of the phonemes. Ignoring the "foreign" consonants, the difference between the consonants in Hebrew and those (estimated) in proto-Semitic is in the number of fricative and affricative sounds only. Some of these sounds originate in Hebrew and did not exist in proto-Semitic (labio and dental fricatives), some palatals existed but were phonemes in proto-Semitic, while they are allophones in Hebrew (as כֿ). Similarly, all those proto-Semitic consonants which have disappeared from Hebrew are fricatives and were assimilated to other Hebrew fricatives, while in Aramaic, for example, the proto-Semitic fricatives were assimilated to the plosives (דֿכר in proto-Semitic became זכר in Hebrew and דכר in Aramaic). There are three types of articulation which determine phonemic contrasts in the consonants: voice, emphasis, and nasality. The voiced/unvoiced distinction has five pairs: ב, ד, ג, ז, ע opposed to ח, ס, כ, ת, פ; the emphatic/non-emphatic pairs are ט, ק opposed to ת, כ; and nasality affects six consonants: ב, פ (together an archiphoneme) opposed to מ; and נ (dental and not alveolar), ת opposed to ד. Voice and nasality are phonetic qualities, whereas emphasis does not denote a clearly defined common phonetic quality of the relevant phonemes. The most that can be said is that these sounds are produced partially with the back portion of the mouth. The plosive/fricative quality which in our arrangement does not determine the phonematicity of ב, כ, פ, is the determining difference between א and ה. There are those who are of the opinion that א is a voiced consonant, but this results from a desire to produce a symmetrical phonological scheme and has no foundation in actual articulation. Only if it is assumed that the ה is voiced (as in Arabic) is the difference between א and ה not one of plosive/fricative, but one of voice. The determining features do not necessarily have to rule all consonantal oppositions; for example, voice is a determining quality in ten (or at the most twelve) sounds only, and there are voiced consonants (ל, נ, ר) which do not have unvoiced pairs, and unvoiced consonants (ט, ק, צ, שׁ) which do not have voiced pairs.

4. CONSONANTS AS PRONOUNCED BY VARIOUS COMMUNITIES. The official, model, most careful pronunciation of Hebrew, used, for example, by radio announcers, especially in reading selections from the Bible (and sometimes called "Semitic," or "Eastern"), is the result of a mixture of different systems of pronunciation used for generations in the various communities. This mixture is not precisely the result hoped for by those who were instrumental in the rejuvenation of Hebrew speech; generally, it can be said that, of those sounds which were distinctive to only one community, more were omitted from the official and general pronunciations than were accepted. The consonants of the official pronunciation are reviewed in the section entitled Consonants above according to their general phonetic value; therefore, it will be instructive to review synoptically the consonants as they were articulated in the past in the different Jewish communities (still occasionally used in prayer and liturgy), from which the sounds of modern Hebrew were extracted. Such a review will indicate what shades of pronunciation are likely to be heard, primarily in the speech of the older generation in official Hebrew.

Table 3: Hebrew Consonants indicates that some consonants were retained in all pronunciations while others were lost or assimilated to other similar sounds. If we arrange them next to the 29 consonants of the vocalizers of the Bible, the following picture emerges: 11 stable consonants (ב, ד, י, כ, כ֗, ל, מ, נ, פ, פ֗, ת) are preserved in all traditions (nine, if we omit כ֗ and פ which developed in a unique manner in the Samaritan tradition); eight consonants א, ג, ה, ז, ס, ר, שׁ, שׂ are retained by most of the pronunciations and changed in a few; and ten consonants ב֗, ג֗, ד֗, ו, ח, ט, ע, צ, ק, ת֗ are changed in most of the pronunciations. It emerges that differences in pronunciation are mainly in two groups: five consonants ח, ט, ע, צ, ק which are "semitic" (gutturals and emphatics) and five others ב֗, ג֗, ד֗, ו, ת֗; of which at least four ב֗, ג֗, ד֗, ת֗; tend to lose their fricativeness.

5. בגדכפ"ת. As already pointed out, in the official language only ב, כ, פ are pronounced in two ways – hard and soft (spiranted) – but in vocalized spelling ג, ד, ת are similar to them in every way. The distribution of hard and soft allophones is not given to simple phonologic definition, and there are exceptions in both directions. However, since the distribution of the soft allophone is greater than the hard one, finding it in positions which contradict the rules is not a radical deviation. On the other hand, a hard allophone where it would be expected to find the soft constitutes a clear exception and, in proper modern speech, is even less common than in biblical Hebrew. The following are the rules for their distribution:

A) The hard consonant always appears when (1) there is gemination, as שַׁבָּת, סֻכָּה, סַכָּה, סַפָּר and (2) even when ungeminated, if it is not preceded directly by a vowel, as: מִסְפָּר, פֶּה, מִכְתָּב, כֶּסֶף; הַשְׁבָּתָה, בַּיִת.

B) The spiranted consonant appears (1) when ungeminated and preceded directly by a vowel, as: סוֹפֵר, סִיכָה, שָׁבַת; (2) when it is the second part of a cluster in one syllable, either at the beginning or the middle but not at the end of the word, as עִזְבוֹנוֹת (= עִזְ־בוֹנוֹת); מַרְ־כְּבוֹתָיו, רְ־כָבָה, צְ־רֵפַת; כְּפָר, כְּבִישׁ, דְּבַשׁ. Opposed to these are: יֵבְךְּ, יֵשְׁבְּ (rare forms likely to appear in poetry) נֵרְדְּ, שָׁמַרְתְּ and (3) when it is the second part of a cluster which divides into two syllables (opposed to rule A 2) in the following morphological types:

(i) *Nouns*: (a) In the plural forms of nouns of the type פְּעָלִים, פְּעָלוֹת as: מַלְ־כֵי, דַּרְ־כֵיהֶם, אַסְ־פֵיהֶם; מַלְ־כוֹת (construct) נִדְ־בוֹתֵיכֶם, כַּנְ־פוֹתֵיהֶם, בִּרְ־כוֹתָיו. (b) In declension of פְּעָלָה forms even in the singular, as: עֶרְ־בַת, נִדְ־בָתוֹ. (c) In the declension of פְּעָלָה, פָּעֵל forms in singular and plural even in those words where the *ṣere* is not retained, as: חֶשְׁ־כַת, חַנְ־פֵי. (d) In פַּעֲלָן and derived forms, as צַרְ־כָנוּת, עַגְ־בָנִיָּה, חַנְ־פָן; the same is true for פַּעַלְתָן forms, where the spirant is expressed in writing only, as רַעַבְתָּן, גַּאַוְתָן. (e) In פַּעֲלוּת forms, such as מַלְ־כוּת, עַצְ־בוּת. (ii) *Verbs*: (f) In the conjugation of the infinitive *qal*, as: בְּמָלְ־כוֹ, כָּתְ־בִי. (g) In the conjugation of the imperative *qal*, as כִּתְ־בָה, כִּתְ־בוּ, כִּתְ־בִי.

Generally: (h) In all forms of verbs and nouns when the syllable preceding בגדכפ"ת is closed in declension, as: נֶאֱסְ־פוּ – נֶאֱסַף, יַעַרְ־בוּ – יֶעֱרַב, מַעַרְ־כוֹת – מַעֲרָכָה, מַאַרְ־בֵי – מַאֲרָב. (i) In all forms of words after a closed syllable to which is prefixed one of the servile letters בוכ"ל with the exception of the *qal* infinitive with ל, as: לִזְ־בּוֹב, לְלִ־בָּבוֹ, כְּסְ־פֹּר, כִּזְ־בוּב, וְנִ־פֹּל, לִשְׁ־בֹּת, לִסְ־פֹּר, לִשְׁ־כַּב, but וְרִ־כַב, וְרִ־כַבְתֶּם, וּלְ־בָנְךָ, בִּנְ־פֹל, בִּלְ־בָבוֹ. Two exceptions worthy of note due to their frequency in the language are: שְׁתַּיִם, and the second person fem. perfect ending תְּ – as in שָׁמַעַתְּ, לָקַחַתְּ, in which a hard ת is retained contrary to the above rules.

Note: The distribution of the plosive and spiranted allophones of בגדכפ"ת is quite complicated, but can be ordered in accordance with the above rules with regard to the official language and the speech of intellectuals. In other social strata, and in the speech of children, these rules are not maintained, however; at times the plosive allophone dominates and at times the spirant (for example: יִתְפֹּס by analogy to the perfect תָּפַס; כִּבֵּס from the imperfect יְכַבֵּס). A further weakening of these rules is due to the foreign words in Hebrew which contain a p or f which is not in accordance with the aforementioned rules (cf. section on Consonants above).

6. אהח"ע. These consonants are similar in that (1) they cannot be geminated; (2) they do not usually close a syllable;

Table 3: Hebrew Consonants as Pronounced by Various Communities

	IRANIAN					Babylonian	Yemenite	Moroccan	Sephardi	Portuguese	ITALIAN				ASHKENAZI			SAMARITAN
	Persia	Western Persia	"Little" Persia	Bukhara	Dagestan (Mountains)						South	Central	North-east	North-west	Lithuania	Poland	Germany	
א	ʔ , –	ʔ , –	ʔ , –	ʔ , –	ʔ , –	ʔ	ʔ	ʔ	ʔ	ʔ	–	–	–	–	ʔ , –	ʔ , (h), –	ʔ , –	ʔ , –
ב	b	b	b	b	b	b	b	b	b	b	b	b	b	b	b	b	b, (p)	b
בֿ	v , (β) , w	v , (β) , w	v , (β) , w	v , (β) , w	v , (β) , w	(β) , b	v , (β) , b	w , b	b, v	b	v	v , (b)	v	v , (w)	v	v	v	b, (f)
ג	g	g	g	g	g	g	ğ	g	g	g	g	g	g	g	g	g	g	g
גֿ	γ	γ	γ	γ	γ	γ	γ	γ	g; γ	χ	g	g	g	g	g	g	g	g
ד	d	d	d	d	d	d	d	d	d	d	d	d	d	d	d	d	d , t	d
דֿ	d	d	d	d	d	d , (δ)	δ	d	d , δ	d	d	d	d	d	d	d	d , t	d
ה	h	h	h	h	h	h	h	h	h , ʔ	h	–	–	–	–	h	h	h	ʔ , –
ו	v , (β) , w	v , (β) , w	v , (β) , w	v , (β) , w	v , (β) , w	w	w	w	w , v	w	v	v , (w)	v , w	v , w	v	v	v	w , b
ז	z	z	z	z	z	z	z	z	z	z	dz	dz	z	z	z	z	z	z
ח	h	ḥ	h	ḥ , (h)	ḥ	ḥ	ḥ	ḥ	ḥ , χ	χ , (ʁ)	χ	χ	χ	χ	χ	χ	χ	ʔ , ʕ , –
ט	t	t	t	t	d	ṭ	ṭ	ṭ	ṭ , t	t	t	t	t	t	t	t	t	ṭ
י	y	y	y	y	y	y	y	y	y	y	y	y	y	y	y	y	y	y
כ	k	k	k	k	k	k	k	k	k	k	k	k	k	k	k	k	k	k
כֿ	χ	χ	χ	χ	χ	χ	χ	χ	χ	χ	χ	χ	χ	χ	χ	χ	χ	k
ל	l	l	l	l	l	l	l	l	l	l	l	l	l	l	l	l	l	l
מ	m	m	m	m	m	m	m	m	m	m	m	m	m	m	m	m	m	m
נ	n	n	n	n	n	n	n	n	n	n	n	n	n	n	n	n	n	n
ס	s	s	s	s	s	s	s	ś	s	s	s	s, (z)	s	s	s , ś , (š)	s	s	s
ע	ʔ , –	ʕ	ʔ	ʔ , ʕ	ʕ	ʕ	ʕ	ʕ	ʔ , ʕ	ʔ , ŋ	ŋ	ŋ	ŋ	ŋ	ʔ , ŋ , y	ʔ , y	ʔ	ʔ , ʕ , –
פ	p	p	p	p	p	p	p	p	p	p	p	p	p	p	p	p	p	f , (bb)
פֿ	f	f	f	f	f	f	f	f	f	f	f	f	f	f	f	f	f	f
צ	s	s	s	s	s	ṣ	ṣ	ṣ	ṣ , c	c	c	c	c , (s)	c , (s)	c	c	c	ṣ
ק	G , (k) , ʁ	G, (k)	G	G , (k) , ʁ	G, ʁ	q	q	q	q , k	k	k	k	k	k	k	k	k	q , (ʔ)
ר	r	r	r	r	r	r	r	r	r	r	r	r	r	r	r , γ	r , γ	r , γ	r
שׁ	š	š	š	š	š	š	š	ś	š	š	s (š)	s , (ž) , (š)	s , (š)	s , (š)	s , š , (ś)	š , ś	š	š
שׂ	s	s	s	s	s	s	s	ś	s	s	s	s	s	s	s , š , (ś)	s	s	š
ת	t	t	t	t	t	t	t	t , (c)	t	t	t	t	t	t	t	t	t	t
תֿ	t	t	t	t	t	θ	θ	c , t	t , θ	tʰ	d	d	d	d	s , š , (ś)	s	s	t

Notes: (1) Research into the various traditional pronunciations is still far from able to present all the information clearly tabulated; in fact it is only just beginning. Therefore, the table contains only those sounds described in the scientific literature, and it must be noted that the quality of these descriptions is not uniform, nor do they all attain the same level of precision. Still the table reflects the situation generally. It should be noted that the term "Sephardi" does not represent a homogenous community but one spread over Europe and Asia. This accounts for the high number of variants. (2) The horizontal line next to *'alef, heh, ḥet, 'ayin*, indicates that this consonant is not pronounced at all; when this line appears with a consonant it indicates that in certain environments it is not articulated, or that part of the community does not pronounce this consonant. (3) A consonant in parentheses is a less common variant or is limited to certain instances (as f, bb in the Samaritan tradition). (4) The consonants are listed in accordance with the rules of the International Phonetic Association. (5) For further details of pronunciation of the various communities see *Pronunciations of Hebrew.

(3) they generally influence the vowel which precedes them either in quality, or by creating a vowel similar to that with which the syllable is or should have been, closed; (4) they are vocalized with *ḥaṭefs* when they are not in syllable final position as: (1 and 3) (בֵּאֵר) instead of ‡ בְּאֵר; מְטֹהָר instead of ‡ מְטְהְהָר (2, 3, and 4); נֶאְדָּר instead of ‡ נְאְדָּר; נֶחְמָד instead of ‡ נְחְמָד; מַעֲבָרָה opposed to מִשְׁטָרָה; רוּחַ instead of ‡ רוּחְ; רֵיחַ instead of רֵיחְ; גָּבֹהַּ instead of ‡ גָּבֹהְ; נִצַּח opposed to נִסַּךְ; מַעֲלִית opposed to מַרְבִּית; פָּעֳלוֹ opposed to קָדְ־שׁוֹ. As a result of these qualities, they are classified under the heading of 'gutturals,' a name which has been accepted even though it does not accurately describe all of them from the point of view of their articulation.

א.

In modern speech, this consonant never closes a syllable. Still, there are some who, in certain words such as מַאְפֵּלְיָה, יַאְדִּים, נֶאְדָּר, are careful to close the syllable with the א because they are so vocalized in the Bible, a fact which is also exploited in writing poetry. On the other hand, (1) א always disappears at the end of a word, as וַיַּרְא, שָׁוְא, חֵטְא, נָשׂוֹא, מָבוֹא, מָלֵא, צֵא, מָצָא (compare נֵרְדְּ, וַיַּשְׁקְ); (2) within the word it sometimes disappears, and at other times receives a *ḥaṭef* vowel. This situation is not the result of precise phonological conditioning, but differs in different morphological situations, as תֹּאמַר, תְּבוּאָנָה, לֵאלוֹהִים, מְצָאתִי; but תַּאַךְ, נְשׂוּאֲכֶם, בּוֹאֲכֶם, מְצָאֲךָ, and not בּוֹאכֶם, תַּאךְ, מְצָאךְ, etc.; (3) unlike the biblical norm the א rarely disappears between a *šewa* and a vowel, but in several forms this is always the case: רָאשִׁים (from ‡ רְאָשִׁים), מָאתַיִם opposed to מְאַת. (When not pronounced it sometimes does not appear in the written word, and this is the rule in the imperfect of פ"א verbs in first person singular, as: אֹמַר from אֹאמַר, לוֹמַר, כְּלוֹמַר (from the root אמר). In the Bible this elision is more common.

ה.

(1) Feature number (3) of א is the rule with respect to ה: (a) when used as the definite article and coming after ב, כ, ל. For example: לַדָּבָר, כַּדָּבָר, בַּדָּבָר (but וְהַדָּבָר!);

(b) In the imperfect and participial forms of *hifʿil* and *hufʿal*, as מוּשָׁב, נוֹדִיעַ, מַפְקִיד, יַפְקִיד from ‡יְהַפְקִיד, מְהַפְקִיד, ‡מְהוּשָׁב, ‡נְהוֹדִיעַ, but in the infinitive the ה is retained: כְּהוֹדִיעוֹ, לְהַפְקִיד, etc. It is also retained in a number of personal names, as: יְהוֹנָתָן, יְהוֹרָם alongside יוֹנָתָן, יוֹרָם and יהודה alongside יודה.

Note: Some generations ago there was a tendency to retain the definite article and forms like להדבר, כהדבר were common. Today this is maintained in the words לְהַבָּא כְּהַיּוֹם, but the form כַּיּוֹם is also used.

(2) The ה tends to be assimilated to the preceding consonant when it is part of a pronomial suffix הוּ–, הָ–; שְׁמָרַתּוּ (rare form שְׁמָרַתְהוּ), יִשְׁמְרֶנּוּ (rare form יִשְׁמְרֶנְהוּ), שְׁמָרַתָּה, יִשְׁמְרֶנָּה (rare form יִשְׁמְרֶנְהָ).

(3) It tends to be elided in the pronomial suffix הו after –ִי as שְׁמַרְתִּיו, אָבִיו, פִּיו (the rare forms שְׁמַרְתִּיהוּ, אָבִיהוּ, פִּיהוּ, etc., are found mainly in poetry) and almost always is elided after –ָ: שְׁמָרוֹ (from שְׁמָרָהוּ).

ח.

Even in pronunciations in which there is no difference between this consonant and the spiranted כ, it maintains its independence in that it acts as a guttural and not as one of the בגדכפ"ת. It does not become a כּ and prefers those vowels preferred by gutturals, as: נִצַּח opposed to נִסַּךְ (only uneducated speakers, if they pronounce the כ as a ח are likely to equate them, for example saying סוֹמַכַת instead of סוֹמֶכֶת and vice versa).

ע.

Even in the pronunciation which identifies this sound with the א, the ע is kept separate in different phonetic contexts. In this way it is similar to that pronunciation which maintains the ע as an independent sound. For example, it tends to be pronounced with the furtive *pathaḥ* (נוֹסֵעַ opposed to נוֹשֵׂא) and often demands a vowel different from the vowel used for א as: יַעֲבֹר opposed to יֶאֱסֹף, and לַעֲבֹד opposed to לֶאֱבֹד. This independence is further realized in various morphological situations.

7. OTHER CONSONANTS. נ followed directly by another consonant is usually assimilated to it; only the נ which is part of the root is not usually assimilated to אהח"ע; in some roots and other forms this is also the case (perfect נָפַל, imperfect יִפֹּל; perfect נָהַג, imperfect יִנְהַג; perfect נָדוֹן, imperfect יָדוֹן; perfect נָעוֹר, imperfect יֵעוֹר; infinitive לִפֹּל but לִנְגֹּעַ, etc.).

צ pronounced as ẓ (= c) is a compound sound and can be heard in speech when ס and ת are contiguous, as, for example, in בית־ספר (a common spelling mistake among children is ביצפר!). It still acts in Hebrew as one sound (monophonematic), and it is impossible to demonstrate oppositions in meaning which depend on the opposition (ẓ/ts); the fact that ẓ can be only one of the elements of a root is itself proof of this assumption.

שצסז.

The clusters תס, תש, טצ, דז where the ת (ד or ט) is the t of the *hitpaʿel*, are impossible and the order is reversed to סת, שת, צט, זד. Also rare are the clusters תס etc., when the ת (or ד or ט) are elements of the root. In fact, in the words or forms derived from these roots a vowel usually appears between them – תשש, תסס. However, since the Middle Ages these combinations have appeared in a few words where the t is part of the root, as מַתְסִים, הִתְשִׁיר.

Note: It is possible to prove that the שׂ was an independent sound in biblical times and was so considered by the vocalizers of the Bible. Still, here and there, there are examples of the merging of this consonant with the ס in the Bible as in כעש alongside כעס, and in rabbinic Hebrew many of the words and roots with שׂ in the Bible appear with ס, as: סִיחָה instead of: שִׂיחָה etc. Hundreds of years have passed since שׂ ceased to exist as an independent sound and became ס in all Jewish pronunciations and שׁ in the Samaritan pronunciation. Only the spelling recognizes the differences between שׂ and ס, and in certain instances this is an aid in differentiating homonyms, as: שָׂרַר = rule / סָרַר = rebel, שָׂכַר = hired / סָכַר = closed, סְמִיכָה = diploma / שְׂמִיכָה = a blanket. The medieval *paytanim* used to put a word beginning with שׂ between נ and ע in their acrostics even though the biblical poets put it together with שׁ (Psalms 118); similarly there were lexicographers in the Middle Ages who placed words beginning with שׂ with those beginning with ס that is, according to their pronunciation rather than their graphic form.

ו"י.

These two sounds (if the ו is pronounced bilabially) are to be classified as being between a consonant and a vowel, also in their function in the language. Unlike other consonants, they interchange with vowels in specific instances and they are geminated like consonants. The ו at the beginning of a word or as the first element in a root was rare and was generally replaced by י; thus even in modern Hebrew there are very few words which begin with ו. [In the pronunciations of most of the communities which contain the spiranted ב, there is a tendency to pronounce the ב and ו identically, the ב at times being pronounced as a ו (bilabially) and vice versa. But even in this case only the ו retains the above relationship to the vowels, never geminated into a בּ. Only in the Samaritan pronunciation did the ו become a בּ in most positions, after the soft ב was entirely lost.]

8. GEMINATION AND CLUSTERS. Besides the gemination of a consonant caused, in Hebrew as in other languages, by the occasional immediate sequence of that consonant namely when a root consonant comes into contact with an affixed formative (for example הִתַּמֵּם > הִתְ־תַּמֵּם ,כָּרַתָּ > כָּרַתְתָּ ,נָתַנּוּ > נָתַנְ־נוּ), gemination is very common in Hebrew and serves to create nominal and verbal forms. Some call a geminated consonant in Hebrew a "long consonant" parallel to a "long vowel," but this comparison is justified neither by the phonetic process which takes place (the syllable boundary is within the consonant; a difference is felt, for example, between lengthened ז in תִּזְכְּרוּ and the regular geminated pronunciation of the ז in תִּזָּכְרוּ), nor by the function in the language which it fulfills.

(1) Every form which has a geminated consonant, can have that consonant replaced by a cluster of two consonants but never by one alone, and thus פִּלְפֵּל ,פִּרְנֵס ,פִּקֵּד are all of the same verbal type, and דַּיָּן and פַּרְנָס are considered to be of the same nominal type; (2) A cluster of two consonants at times becomes a geminated consonant, and the two forms may even exist side by side (לִפֹּל ,לִנְפֹּל). (3) A geminated consonant may split into a cluster of two consonants (common in Aramaic, rare in Hebrew), and in some of the words which have a two consonant cluster in Hebrew today there was originally a geminated consonant, as: גַּלְמוּד (from גַּמּוּד), שַׁרְבִיט (from ‡שַׁבִּיט). (4) The limitations regarding the vowel before the last consonant in the syllable, are also in force for the vowels which precede a geminated consonant. Therefore, a geminated consonant functions just like a cluster of different consonants, being more limited only in that it cannot come at the end of the word (compare צֵל (< צִלְּךָ) opposed to כָּרַתְּ ,נֶפֶט (< כָּרַתְתְּ, opposed to שָׁמַרְתְּ)). At the beginning of a word a geminated consonant can be found only when the first consonant is not part of the root but a formative element, as: תְּתַרְגֵּם ,מְמֻכָּן (see below); or when the word comes after the interrogative מַה (מַה־זֶּה), thus constituting a phonetic unit (in the Bible this is common in various combinations of words and vowels). In addition to geminated consonants, there are times in modern Hebrew, especially in the speech of young girls, when, as an expression of emotion, a consonant is lengthened, as *yof-f-f-fi* (יופי), but this has no grammatical function.

There is a tendency to eliminate gemination, especially when the geminated consonant is vocalized with a *šewa*; and thus the gemination is usually eliminated in י with *šewa* and in the מ of the participle after the definite article, as הַמְסִבּוֹת ,הַיְקָבִים (= they are causing; but הַמְּסִבּוֹת (= parties)). However, this tendency is overruled by morphological considerations (הַמְּסַפְּרִים and not הַמְסַפְּרִים; but in the Bible הַמְבַקְשִׁים). The tendency to eliminate becomes the rule when the consonant involved is either אהחע"ר or the spiranted allophones of בגדכפ"ת which are never geminated. In other words, five phonemes cannot be geminated. (In the Samaritan pronunciation the ר is geminated just as any other consonant, and this was also the case in the Hebrew of Septuagint times.) Many Hebrew speakers today do not commonly geminate consonants in their speech, but they maintain those conditions which derive from gemination and determine the form of the word, as the hard פּ in סַפָּר (a barber) and the spirant in סִפֵּר (counted) etc. According to the rule, a cluster of more than two consonants is impossible in Hebrew. A cluster at the beginning of a syllable is realized generally by a *šewa* inserted between them. Clusters of more than two consonants are found only in international words used in Hebrew, for example סטראטגיה (alongside אס־טראטגיה). In the middle of a word a cluster of three consonants is conceivable. This is especially true when the first element in the cluster is a geminated consonant as, שַׁבְּלוּל (<‡ שַׁבְּבְלוּל), שִׁמְרוּ (<‡ שִׁמְמְרוּ), which is usually articulated with the addition of a *šewa* between the geminated consonant and the one following it. In "inherited" words a cluster at the end of a word is possible if it ends in a plosive (for example יֵבְךְּ ,נֵרְדְּ ,קֹשְׁטְ, but תֶּפֶן). In international words this rule does not always apply (פִּילְם ,סוֹצְיָאלִזְם), but modern pronunciation tends to insert a *šewa* in such cases.

9. VOWELS. There is no essential difference between the two types of sounds – vowel and consonant – the difference being rather one of degree; in fact, the semi-vowels ו and י are proof that it is possible to pass from one category to the other. The consonants are classified above according to three criteria: point of articulation, method of articulation (open or closed), and the action of the vocal chords (voiced or unvoiced). Since the vowels are all voiced and articulated in the open position, we are left only with the criterion of point of articulation, that is, the relative closeness of the organs of articulation to each other. In articulating the vowels, actual contact is not conceivable; the basis for classification is, therefore, the movement of the tongue and the working of the lips (the traditional Hebrew names for the vowels, *pathaḥ, qameṣ*, etc., are an attempt to

describe the opening of the mouth and the activity of the lips). Following the direction in which the tongue is raised during the articulation of the vowels, we may divide them into "front," "central," and "back." Generally, a rounding of the lips is an accompanying feature of back vowels, and spreading the lips an accompanying feature of front vowels, but rounding and spreading of the lips are possible in all the types of vowels. The section on consonants above mentioned the great variety of consonants heard from the Hebrew speaker and the reasons for them. The vowels, by their very nature, are even more variegated. For the consonants it is at least possible to establish ideal standards for official speech, but there are no set standards applicable to the vowels. There have been no studies to date which can supply information as to the exact phonetic makeup of the vowels in modern Hebrew, but this deficiency does not prevent a phonemic description, since the variations in the vowels are not distinctive and do not affect the meanings of words. Therefore, it will be sufficient to classify the vowels generally into: front: *i, é, e*, represented in writing by ִ *ḥireq*, ֵ *ṣere*, ֶ *segol*, and ֱ *ḥatef segol*; central; *a*, represented by ַ *pathaḥ*, ָ *qameṣ (gadol)*, and ֲ *ḥatef pathaḥ*, and *ĕ*, represented by the *šewa*; back: *o* represented by ֹ *ḥolem*, ָ *qameṣ qaṭan*, and ֳ *ḥatef qameṣ*, and *u* represented by וּ *šureq* and ֻ *qibbuṣ*. By using average measurements the relationship among the vowels can be graphically described in the following way:

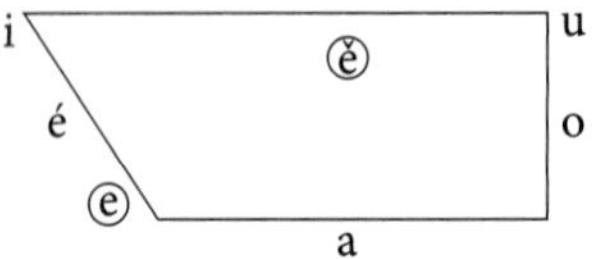

Since only the general values of the vowels have been mentioned, it emerges that the number of vowels is close to the number of vowel phonemes, which are all the above, save the two circled, i.e., the *segol* and the *šewa*. Regarding the phonemic value of a sound there are likely to be differences of opinion (see section 3, Consonants, above), and the doubts which might be raised about this classification will, therefore, be discussed in sections 12 and 13, on The Phonological Status of the Vowels and The *Šewa* and *Ḥaṭefs*, below. Many Hebrew speakers do not differentiate between e and é, and even those who do differentiate do not always apply the *ṣere* and the *segol* respectively where demanded by the rules of vocalization. Even among those who do differentiate, there are some who articulate the *ṣere* almost as a dipthong *ey*. Note that *ḥaṭefs* differ phonetically from the *šewa*, and do not represent independent qualities but are identical to full vowels.

10. VOWEL QUANTITY. In the common pronunciation the vowels are not differentiated as to length, only the *šewa* being of shorter duration than the other vowels. Experimental methods have proved that the vowel in an accented syllable is slightly longer than the vowel in an unaccented syllable, but this difference is not discernible by the ear, since no semantic difference depends on a vowel length. (In English, by contrast, this is a distinguishing feature, cf. [it] (it), opposed to [i:t] (eat).) In fact it may be said that the vowels in Hebrew are isochrons (of equal length). However, since there is long standing tradition in Hebrew of dividing the vowels into "long" (lit. big) and "short" (lit. small), an aspect which is also relevant to the rules of punctuation, this division will now be considered. The differentiation originated in an attempt to divide the vowels according to length (compare O-mega and O-mikron in Greek), that is: long and short. The Spanish grammarians of the Middle Ages felt that the *qameṣ* (pronounced "a"), the *ṣere, ḥolem, šureq*, and full *ḥireq* (with *yod*) were long vowels, while the *pathaḥ, segol, qameṣ* (pronounced "o"), *qibbuṣ* and *ḥireq* (without *yod*) were short vowels. They considered that there were five qualities of vowels (a, i, e, o, u) and that these were either long or short. This division is a reflection of the "Sephardi" pronunciation, but it must be recognized that in that pronunciation the accent also caused a lengthening of the vowel, and so the "short" vowels in accented syllables were long (for example פֶּה is pronounced with a long vowel even though it is a *segol*; the same is true for the *pathaḥ* of שָׁמַרְתִּי). The opposite is true for "long" vowels which are next to the accented syllable and are pronounced short (an exact description was given by R. Joseph Kimḥi in the 12th century). In the 19th century, which was interested in comparative historical study, this principle of division was accepted by Hebrew linguistics with one change: the symbol representing a vowel (excluding the *šewa* and *ḥaṭefs*) represents only quality, and that quality can be either long or short. The length is not determined by the symbol or by its place in the word (contrary to Kimḥi, above), but rather in accordance with comparative grammar. As a result of these considerations long vowels are those which generally remained unchanged in the declension of the word, while those which change are either short or lengthened in special phonetic conditions. Thus, for example, the *ṣere* of מֵת (dead) is always long while that of שֵׁן (tooth) is short (except for biblical pausal forms); similarly, the *ḥolem* of חוֹל is always long, while that in חֹל is short (except in pausal forms). This differentiation between originally long vowels and secondarily lengthened vowels gave rise to a threefold distinction: "long" vowels (that is originally long), "middle" (that is lengthened), and "short." However, the term "middle" never achieved wide acceptance. This division, unlike that proposed by Kimḥi, is not rooted in any real tradition of Hebrew pronunciation, but is entirely based on theoretical considerations, which assume a Hebrew pronunciation among the Masoretes, when they determined the vocalization of the Bible. Early evidence, such as Greek transliterations and well-based considerations, tends to justify the assumption that in early Hebrew there was a difference in the length of vowels, and that the behavior of the vowels as it appears in the vocalization of the Bible reflects the ancient division as to length. There is, however, no proof that these differences of length existed at the time of the vocalization of the text. In any case the vowel signs are indicative of seven qualities only (excluding the *šewa* and *ḥaṭefs*).

Phonematic investigation does not indicate any semantic differences dependent on vowel length. Such proofs as חוֹל (*ḥōl*) = sand opposed to חֹל (*ḥol*) = secular or profane, or עֵד (*ʿēḏ*) = witness, opposed to עֵד (*ʿéḏ*) = a piece of cloth, are misleading, since according to the traditional division the vowels are "long" in both pairs of words and the assumption that the vocalizers differentiated is completely unproven. According to the traditional pronunciation two pairs of homonyms can be seen, each of which arose in specific situations. The difference between the vocalization of official Hebrew today and that which is the assumed basis of the rules of vocalization – which are obligatory even today – lies not (at least from the phonemic point of view) in quantity, but in the change of quality of several vowels. Though it is claimed that Hebrew vowels are isochronic phonemes, this does not mean that in Hebrew speech all *a* vowels, for example, are of the same length in all situations. But on the other hand, the difference between מִן (*min*) = from, and מִין (*mīn*) = type, does not indicate that the vowel system is to be divided into long and short. The truth is that confronting such pairs is artificial since the two words differ in their syntax and linguistic position.

11. VOWELS AS PART OF THE SYLLABLE. From the discussion above it is clear that a description of vowel distribution should be on two levels: (1) the vowels as pronounced today; (2) the use of the vowel signs. In describing the written language it is impossible to ignore the distribution of the vowel signs, since it is not only an important part of Hebrew spelling, but helps to understand the morphophonemic relationships. Table 4: Syllables reflects the distribution of the vowels which are listed according to type of syllable and place of accent in the word.

12. THE PHONOLOGICAL STATUS OF THE VOWELS. From the above it is clear that there are altogether five phonemic vowels – *i, e, a, o, u*. This can be ascertained from a consideration of the possible oppositions, ten in all $(\frac{5 \times (5-1)}{2})$. We also see that all possible oppositions are utilized only in (a) open syllable, whether accented or not and in a (b) closed accented syllable; in an (c) unaccented closed syllable many oppositions neutralized, as the examples below will show.

In syllables of the types (a) and (b) *i* is defined by its opposition:

1) to é in נֵר/נִיר; שְׁכֵנָה/שְׁכִינָה;
2) to *a* in דָּן/דִּין; רַק/רִיק; פָּעַל/פָּעִיל; שָׂרָה/שִׁירָה; רַחֵם/רִחֵם;
3) to *o* in שׁוֹר/שִׁיר; בְּכוֹרָה/בְּכִירָה;
4) to *u* in צוּר/צִיר; אֲמוּרָה/אֲמִירָה; נֶחָמוּ/נִחֲמוּ;

é is defined by its opposition to *i* (see above);

5) to *a* in גָּר/גֵּר; עַד/עֵד; צָדָה/צֵדָה;
6) to *o* in קוֹץ/קֵץ; כָּבוֹד/כָּבֵד; גְּדוֹלָה/גְּדֵלָה;
7) to *u* in גּוּר/גֵּר; שְׁכוּנָה/שְׁכֵנָה;

a is defined by its oppositions to *i* and é (see above);

8) to *o* in שׁוֹר/שָׁר; אָמוֹר/אָמַר; קוֹרָה/קָרָה;
9) to *u* in שׁוּר/שָׁר; אָמוּר/אָמַר; צוּרָה/צָרָה;

o is defined by its opposition to *i, é, a* (see above);

Table 4: Hebrew Syllables

	open syllable		closed syllable	
vowel	Accented	Non-Accented	Accented	Non-Accented
i – ḥireq	יִפֶּן, שִׁימוּ; חֲנִינוּ; רַבִּי	רִחֵם, כִּישּׁוֹר; אֲבִירוּת; קוּמִי	מִן, מִין; –; תַּבְשִׁיל	גְּבַרְתִּי, שִׂמְחָה; אוֹיִבְךָ; –
é – ṣere	סֵפֶר; הוֹצֵאנוּ; צֵא, הַקְנֵה	עֵנָב, מֵיטָב; מַקְהֵלָה; –	אֵלֶּה; הֵסֵבּוּ; לֵב, לֵיל, מֵסֵב	–; –; –
e – segol	מֶלַח; סוּסֶיךָ; מִרְעֶה	נֶאֶמְרוּ, יֶחֱזַק; –; דֶּשֶׁא, הֶגֶה	נֶגְבָּה; –; אֶמֶת, בַּרְזֶל	נֶגְדּוֹ; מַקֶּלְכֶם; קֹדֶשׁ
pataḥ a – and qameṣ	קָמוּ, נַחַל; עָשָׂהוּ, שְׁמָרַנִי; שִׁמְךָ, מַלְכָּה	שָׁמַר, יַעַבְרוּ, נַחֲלָה; מִשְׁמָרוֹ; –	גַּג; הוֹרַדְנוּ; עוֹלָם, דּוֹנַג	מַלְכּוֹ; הוֹרַדְתֶּם; רוּחַ, בַּחַל
ḥolem o – and qameṣ qaṭan	קֹדֶשׁ; נָדוֹנוּ; פֹּה, מַלְכּוֹ	צָהֳרַיִם, גֹּרֶשׁ, קוֹנֶה; אַרְצוֹתֵיהֶם	קָמְנָה, תְּשׁוּבְנָה; קָטֹנְתִּי; אָדָם, כָּבוֹד	כְּתַבְתִּי, קָרְבַּנְכֶם; כְּתָנְתָּם; –
šureq u – and qibbuṣ	קוּמוּ; תָּקוּמוּ; בָּנוּ	רֻחַם, סוּגַר; מַלְבּוּשִׁים; אָחוּ	–; –; יַלְקוּט, מַלְבּוּשׁ	וּלְקַחְתֶּם, חֻלְצָה; מַשְׂכֻּרְתּוֹ; –
šewa and ḥaṭefs	–; –; –	אֳנִיָּה, חֲמוֹר, גְּבוּל; נוֹחֲלִים, שׁוֹמְרִים; –	–; –; –	–; –; –

* Accented syllables are marked by a single quote. Notes to Table 4:

(1) The examples show the vowels (a) in an opening syllable, (b) in a medial syllable (c) in the word final syllable; between each type there is a semicolon. Although there is no real difference between the first two categories, examples are cited for the sake of completeness. This enables us to see whether a certain vowel cannot appear in one of the syllables of the word, which situation is indicated by a dash.

(2) In each type examples are given for orthographical reasons. A comma is placed between them. This gives us a view of the distribution of the vowel signs. It may be concluded that each of the six vowels, except for *é*, can appear in all positions of the word. *é* alone does not appear in a closed unaccented syllable. The *šewa*, is – phonemically – the realization of a cluster, but from the phonetic point of view it is a syllable peak, and appears only in an unaccented syllable. The *ḥatefs* are to be classed with the šewa, and even those who pronounce the *ḥatefs* as full vowels do not produce any change in the above distribution picture. However, if the uses of the vowel signs and their relationship to the vowels which they represent are investigated, it will be seen that, unlike the vowels themselves, their use is limited and conditioned by the type of syllable in which they appear, and the rule is as follows: (1) *šere, ḥolem, qameṣ gadol*, and *šureq* do not appear in unaccented closed syllables; (2) *qameṣ qaṭan* and *qibbuṣ* do not appear in closed or open accented syllables. This shows that there is a connection between the distribution of vowel signs and accentuation. This relationship cannot be explained if only the accepted Hebrew pronunciation is considered; but must be seen against the phonetic values of the signs in the pronunciation of the Tiberian vocalizers. Similarly there is apparently a relationship between the type of syllable and the use of the full vowel signs (with ו and י), cf. the use of the *ḥolem* without a ו in קָטֹנְתִּי. This relationship is also not comprehensible given the modern pronunciation, but only on the basis of Hebrew pronunciation in the ancient past, when two important factors were in force: quantitative differences of vowels and a tendency to express that quantitative difference in the writing, as, for example, עוֹלָם opposed to אָמַר. This presents one of the greatest problems in teaching proper vocalization, for without the clear presentation of the historic background it is, of necessity, a mechanical process.

10) to *u* in שׁוּק/שׁוֹק; אָמוּר/אָמוֹר;

u is defined by its oppositions to the other vowels (see above).

In syllables of type (c) only the following oppositions are found:

i (1) to *a* in דַּבֵּר/דִּבֵּר; (2) to *o* as הָפְקַדְנוּ/הִפְקַדְנוּ; (3) to *u* in פִּנָּה/פֻּנָּה; חִיַּבְנוּ/חֻיַּבְנוּ; *a* opposed to *i* (see above); (4) to *o* in עָצְמוֹ/עִצְמוֹ; (5) to *u* as הִקְשׁ/הֻקְשׁ; חִפָּה/חֻפָּה. It will be seen, therefore, that *é* is not opposed to any vowel in this position and that *o*/*u* are not opposed; however, variants like אָמְנָם/אֻמְנָם and הָפְקַד/הֻפְקַד are found in Hebrew. In fact, most of the oppositions are derived from the conjugations of the verb, where *o*/*u* indicates the passive and *a*/*i* the active forms, and even in this area the oppositions are limited. This is the result of a process in ancient Hebrew, during which oppositions of short vowels in closed syllables were eliminated; and when the use of the internal passive in post-biblical Hebrew was minimized the scope of these oppositions was, automatically, greatly reduced.

In the above description the *e* (*segol*) was not included in the phonemes although there are cases where a difference of meaning between a pair of words is reflected in the relationship between the *segol* and some other vowel, as: אַרְאֶה/אֶרְאֶה; עֵרֶב/עֶרֶב; לֵחֶם/לֶחֶם (= solder). Though the *segol* is a very common vowel, such cases are quite rare and we cannot therefore assume the opposition *segol* to another vowel in the structure of the language. It is correct to see the *segol* as an allophone of the *ṣere*. If the forms אַרְאֶה/אֶרְאֶה through the whole of their paradigms, are investigated, it will be seen that the opposition in all conjugated forms is *a*/*i*, as, for example תַּרְאֶה/תִּרְאֶה; only in the first person singular is this *i* represented by a *segol*, since the *i* does not appear after an *alef* in a closed syllable (when not geminated). The *é* should have taken the place of the *i* but *é* cannot appear in an unaccented closed syllable. This complimentary relationship between *é* and *e* is common in all forms of the conjugation and declension of ל״י roots, as: מִקְנֵה/מִקְנֶה (construct state); לֵב/לֶב; מִקְנֶיהָ/מִקְנֵהוּ, מִקְנֵינוּ (possible in construct state); בֶּן/בֵּן (construct); and others. On the other hand *e* is found at times in the same environment as *é* in פֵּתַח/פֶּתַח; בֵּהֶן/בָּהֶן; שֵׂכֶל/שֶׂכֶל; יֵתֶר/יֶתֶר; נֵצַח/נֶצַח; נֵדֶר/נֶדֶר and others without any distinction. It may, therefore, be concluded that at times *e* is a conditioned allophone which becomes mandatory in certain environments, and at times – under different conditions – it is (in very limited scope), an optional allophone (cf. N.S. Trubetzkoy, *Grundzuege der Phonologie*, p. 46, regarding *d*/*t*). Examples such as עֶרֶב (evening)/עָרֹב (wasp) which both contain the phoneme *é* should be considered homonyms as are their plural forms עֲרָבִים and as is עָרֵב (pleasant/guarantor) etc. (The fact that the *segol* appears only with the א and is a conditioned vowel, and not independent, is also seen clearly in the forms אַעֲלֶה/אֶעֱלֶה; the *segol* does not appear in the rest of the *qal* paradigm, as תַּעֲלֶה/תֶּעֱלֶה‡, but all the forms save the first remain homonymous.)

Note: Although in modern Hebrew the *segol* must be considered to be an allophone of the *ṣere*, it is possible to prove that in ancient Hebrew the *segol* is a reflex, in all cases, of an original *a* and was an allophone of *a*.

13. THE ŠEWA AND ḤAṬEFS. A) The grapheme known as the *šewa* (ְ) represents two independent phonetic values: the absence of a vowel, and a very short vowel, which can be described as central and vague. In grammatical terminology the former is called *šewa quiescens* (שווא נח) and the latter *šewa mobile* (שווא נע). Only the second type interests us in our study of the behavior of the language. Indeed this term, *šewa*, has become accepted in general linguistics as describing a vowel of this quality. In Hebrew the *šewa* cannot rightfully be listed with the phonemes, since no difference in meaning depends on the *šewa* (the same applies to *ḥaṭefs*). The *šewa* must be regarded as a conditioned vowel which appears in clusters of consonants, whether, historically, the *šewa* comes in place of a full vowel (גָּדוֹל<גְּדוֹל) or the absence of a vowel (מַעְבָּר<מַעֲבָר compare מַעְבָּרָה). Therefore, phonetic differences such as פָּסוּל–פְּסוּל or זְרוֹעַ–זָרוֹעַ have the following phonologic makeup: /pasul/:/psul/, /zaroʿ/:/zroʿ/. In Hebrew the *šewa* is never accented and is always found between two consonants.

B) Since there is one grapheme, the *šewa*, for two values, the grammarians established rules indicating when the *šewa* was to be pronounced as mobile (נע); however, the pronunciation of the vocalizers who instituted the *šewa* sign differs from the Sephardic pronunciation, whose rules are accepted in the pronunciation of official Hebrew today. In common speech, different groups of speakers pronounce the *šewa* differently, or do not sound it at all. The following are the rules for educated speech: the *šewa* is pronounced (a) at the beginning of a word (קְנֵה, בְּדִיל, גְּבוּל); (b) when it is the second of two *šewas* (יִשְׁמְרוּ); c) when it comes with a *dagešed* consonant (יְפַלּוּ); d) after a vowel in an open syllable (יִי־רְאוּ, שִׁי־רְכֶם). Since the ability to distinguish the length of vowels has been largely lost, only a trained ear can determine which is an open syllable followed by a consonant plus *šewa* mobile, and which a syllable closed by the first of a cluster of consonants. Only when the cluster consists of a geminated consonant is the difference clear: סָבְרוּ, גָּדְלוּ are at times pronounced (*sav-ru*) (*gadlu*), but not סָבְבוּ, גָּלְלוּ (*savĕvu*) (*ga-lĕlu*). This differentiation was passed by analogy to words like קְ־לָלַת, קְ־לָלוֹ, whose first syllable is – historically – closed. In this way a differentiation developed between רִנַּת and רְ־נָנַת which was apparently unknown to early Hebrew, where both were pronounced simply (*rin-nat*); only in certain prosodic situations could רננת be pronounced (*ri-nĕnat*).

C) There are those who, in addition to the two types of *šewa* mentioned, find in Hebrew a third type which they call *šewa* medium בֵּינוֹנִי or מְרַחֵף. This is a *šewa* which comes after a "small" vowel (see above Vowel Quantity): (1) if the following consonant is a spirantized בגדכפ״ת, as מַלְכֵי, מִרְבָּד (see section on בגדכפ״ת above); (2) with an originally geminated consonant, as אִלְּמִים (compare singular אִלֵּם), הַמְקִימִים (sing. הַמֵּקִים); (3) with the first consonant of a cluster as רִנְנַת (see above). This *šewa* medium is not a separate phonetic entity, but in types (1) and (2) the *šewa* is quiescent, that is, it does not represent any vowel in pronunciation, and in type (3) may be pronounced as a *šewa* mobile, as pointed out above. Phonetically there is no such thing as a *šewa* medium which is between the quiescent and mobile; it is a fiction created to explain certain phonetic developments which are not uniform. There are some grammarians (Bergstraesser and others) who tend to see in the *šewa* medium an independent historical entity, i.e., a *šewa quiescens* where once there was a vowel, while others see in it an independent phoneme (Birkeland, p. 55). However, a sound which is not an independent part of the order of sounds (since it is either *quiescens* or *mobile*) cannot be considered a phoneme. It must be remembered that both the *šewa* and *ḥaṭefs*, as well as the absence of any vowel, are likely to appear in Hebrew in a position where once there was a vowel (שָׁ־מְרוּ, in pause שָׁמָרוּ; שִׁמְ־רוּ, in pause, שְׁמֹרוּ) or where there was no vowel at all (נֶ־אֱמָן opposed to נִשְׁ־מַר, זַעְ־פּוֹ, כַּעְ־סוֹ but נַ־עֲרוֹ).

D) In the official language the grapheme *šewa* reflects one sound (ĕ) in all phonetic situations where it is pronounced. In ancient Hebrew this sound varied between ă and ĕ, and tended to assume the sound of the neighboring vowels. This fact is reflected in personal names which have been transmitted in their Greek or Latin pronunciations as: סְדוֹם Sodom, שְׁלֹמֹה Solomon, נְתַנְאֵל Nathanael, גְּדֵרָה Gedera. In the pronunciation of the vocalizers the *šewa* was generally ă (this caused it to be interchanged with the *ḥaṭef-pathaḥ*), and it changed, according to ancient rules, toward the sound of the neighboring vowel when the *šewa* is next to אהח"ע. This feature can still be heard in the pronunciations of several communities where כְּמוֹ and נְקִיָּה are pronounced *kămo, năqiyya* and not *kĕmo, nĕqiyya*. The different nuances of the *šewa* in official Hebrew are the *ḥaṭefs* (if pronounced quickly), and these sounds are interrelated with the consonants א, ה, ח, and ע; only rarely is a *ḥaṭef* found with a different consonant, as דֲּמִי, כְּתֳנוֹת, צִפֳּרִים. In the Hebrew of the vocalizers the *šewa* and *ḥaṭef-pathaḥ* represented one quality; in the official pronunciation today the *šewa* and *ḥaṭef-segol* are equal, the latter with a guttural.

As opposed to what has been said above, on the relationship between the *šewa* and the *ḥaṭefs*, it is possible to claim, that semantic differences are dependent on the *ḥaṭefs*, unlike the *šewa*, and as a result the *ḥaṭefs* are phonemes. The differences are of the type אֲנִי/אֳנִי, חֲדָשִׁים/חֳדָשִׁים, עֲלִי/עֱלִי, חֲלִי/חֳלִי. However, as pointed out above regarding the *segol* (in section 12, The Phonological Status of the Vowels, above), it may be said that the *ḥaṭefs* are reflexes of the *šewa* – the result of a cluster of consonants – while the choice as to which nuance of the *šewa* is used in a particular instance depends, to a great extent (at least with regard to the *ḥaṭef-qameṣ*), on the quality of the full vowel found in the same position in other forms of the word; thus חֲדָשִׁים follows חָדָשׁ and חֳדָשִׁים follows חֹדֶשׁ. The oppositions of the *ḥaṭefs* are only apparent; the real oppositions being between the full vowels; there is thus the possibility of *ḥaṭef* interchanges within the very same word, as in שִׁבֲּלֵי– שִׁבֳּלִים, דְּמִי–דֳּמִי, אֲמָרְכֶם–אֱמָרְכֶם–אֱמֹר, אֲכָלְךָ–אֱכֹל.

Note: Diachronically, and also from the phonologic synchronic point of view, the furtive *pathaḥ* must be considered the same as a *ḥaṭef* which is pronounced *before* the guttural. However, unlike the *ḥaṭef*, the furtive *pathaḥ* is always pronounced as a full *a* vowel.

14. THE ACCENT. The accent in Hebrew falls on one of the last two syllables of the word. On the ultimate syllable it is called מלרע (*milraʿ*) and on the penultimate מלעיל (*milʿel*). It is impossible to determine clear phonological rules for each type of accentuation since the situation in Hebrew is the result of a complicated development, not all of which is clear today. One may say that in Hebrew the ultimate accentuation is dominant, while the penultimate is found:

A) in the noun:

1) in segolate forms, i.e., when preceding the final consonant there is

a) a *segol* (מֶלֶךְ, סֵפֶר, כֹּתֶל, שׁוֹמֶרֶת, כֹּתֶבֶת, מְסַפֶּרֶת, תִּלְבֹּשֶׁת);

b) a *pathaḥ* – if the last consonant is ה, ח, or ע (קֶבַע, מֶלַח, גֹּבַהּ, תֵּמַהּ) or if the consonant before the last is א, ה, ח, or ע (נַעַל, נַחַל, רַהַב, שֹׁהַם, תֹּאַר);

c) *ḥireq* if the consonant before the last is י (לַיִל, בַּיִת). In all of these forms the common feature is that the unaccented vowel is lost in declension. To this category belong also those nouns ending in an open syllable with *segol, ḥiriq*, or *šureq*, which when declined place a consonant for this vowel, as אַחְוֵי–אָחוּ, יָפְיוֹ–יֹפִי, דִּשְׁאוֹ–דֶּשֶׁא; this is also the case for the demonstrative אֵלֶּה;

2) nouns (and other words) to which are suffixed locative ־ָה or the dual ending ־ַיִם (אַרְצָה, מִצְרַיְמָה, שָׁמָּה; מַיִם, מִסְפָּרַיִם similarly לַיְלָה, הֵמָּה, הֵנָּה = הֵן);

3) nouns (and other words) to which are suffixed the possessive pronouns: ־ֶךָ, ־ַיִךְ, ־הוּ, ־הָ, ־נוּ (סוּסֶיךָ, עָלֶיךָ, עֵינַיִךְ, מַטֵּהוּ, אוֹתָנוּ, אָחִינוּ, מַלְכֵּנוּ, חָזֶהָ, אָבִיהָ); similarly ־מוֹ, which today is only found in poetry (בָּתֵּימוֹ, עָלֵימוֹ).

B) in the verb:

4) in the perfect: before the suffixes ־תִּי, ־תָּ, ־נוּ (הִשְׁכַּמְנוּ, שִׁבַּרְתָּ, שָׁמַרְתִּי);

5) in the imperative and the imperfect: before ־נָה (תְּשַׁבֵּרְנָה, שְׁמֹרְנָה);

6) in addition to those instances mentioned in (4) and (5): in *hifʿil* of all forms, excluding ל"י forms, and in עו"י and ע"ע forms in *qal* and *nifʿal*, and in ע"ע forms even in *hufʿal*, in forms ending ־ָה, ־ִי, ־וּ (הוּסַבָּה, יָסֵבּוּ, טוֹבוּ, בֹּאִי, קָמוּ, הִגִּידוּ, הַגִּידָה);

7) in verbs with suffixed object ־נִי, ־הוּ, ־נּוּ, ־הָ, ־נָּה, ־נוּ (יִמְצָאֻנוּ, יִשְׁמְרֶנָּה, יִשְׁמְרוּהָ, יֹאכְלֶנּוּ, יֹאכְלֵהוּ, קָנָהוּ, יֹאחֲזֵנִי, שְׁמָרַנִי).

C) in certain forms which today appear only in poetry, such as the pausal forms (יִשְׁמֹרוּ, שָׁמָרוּ, אָנֹכִי, אָנִי) or the inversive tenses (וַתָּגֶד, וַיָּשֶׂם, וַיָּקָם).

There are exceptions to the above rules: the accent is on the penultimate in the third person fem. sing. perfect with pronominal suffixes שְׁמָרַתַן, שְׁמָרַתַם, אֲהֵבָתֶךְ, אֲהֵבַתְךָ, the accent is on the ultima in the inversive perfect tense וְשָׁמַרְתָּ, וְשָׁמַרְתִּי.

If for the moment the segolate nouns and the forms appearing in inverted tenses are excluded, it may be concluded that the penultimate accent appears in Hebrew only when the word ends in an open syllable; this, to a certain degree, reflects the early division of ultimate and penultimate accents in Hebrew.

In the Bible the accent is given to change from penultimate to ultimate (as in עוּרִי in Judg. 5:2) and especially from ultimate to penultimate in word groups, but there are no cases of enclisis, only proclisis. In modern Hebrew, however, enclitic forms are common not only in speech but also in poetry; as opposed to אֱמָר־לִי, בּוֹא־נָא, שְׁמַע־נָא we find אֱמוֹר־לִי, בּוֹא־נָא, שְׁמַע־נָא; however, this is not considered the norm. Proclitic forms are common in construct. In speech there are certain tendencies to penultimate accentuation which differ from the rules given here, but they are not considered correct (as שְׁמַרְתֶּם). The accentuation of foreign and borrowed words and personal names must be considered separately. The rules of accentuation in the original languages have affected the accentuation of the borrowed words, so that at times even syllables before the penultimate are accented. In personal names the emotional factor cannot be ignored, and feelings such as love and indulgence affect the accentuation. However, the standard which is demanded by the Academy for Hebrew Language and used in broadcasting is the ultimate accentuation, and so the norm is אוּנִיבֶרְסִיטָה and not אוניברסיטה or אוניברסיטה, and similarly רָחֵל and not רָחֵל. On the other hand, foreign words with Hebrew suffixes are usually accented in keeping with the norm, as ליגאליותה, אוניברסיטאות. The tendency to penultimate accentuation is found in the pronunciations of many communities, and in Samaritan Hebrew has become the rule.

Accentuation has phonemic value in Hebrew, since it is a distinguishing feature between certain pairs of words – בָּנוּ (in us) / בָּנוּ (they built), בָּאָה (she is coming) / בָּאָה (she came), קוּמִי (imp. fem. sing.) / קוּמִי (infinitive with pron. suf.). Hebrew accentuation is "stress" type (dynamic accent) and by its nature is likely to affect the vocalization. In fact it causes changes in the vowels of a word depending on their nearness to the accent (see section 16. Interchange and Elision of Vowels, below).

15. THE DIPHTHONGS. The diphthong is – by definition – the combination of two vowels within one syllable. The diphthong is created when the point of articulation glides from place to place within the one breath. More precisely it is a combination of a series of vowels, but it is sufficient to indicate the extreme vowels, i.e., the opening and the concluding (or the intended conclusion). Thus instead of the sign *a..e..é..i*, the sign *ai* (or *ay, ai̯*) is used. By its very nature one of the parts of the diphthong is primary, and the other secondary, or accompanying. If the diphthong begins with the accompanying element it is called rising (as *u̯a*); if it ends with this element it is called falling (*au̯*).

In Hebrew grammar, combinations such as וּ, יְו, יו־ַ, יְ, ־ַי, וי are called diphthongs. However, in Hebrew it is the falling diphthongs that are of significance because of the morphological changes they cause. The use of the term diphthong in Hebrew is therefore limited to cases of a vowel with "semi-vowel," ו or י (see section 7. Other Consonants, above). A combination of two vowels in one syllable, whether caused by the splitting of one vowel into two (as in the frequent pronunciation of the *ṣere, ey*), or by the proximity of a certain vowel to ה, ח, or ע (furtive *pathaḥ*) – which is realized phonetically by being split into two syllables – concerns Hebrew grammar only as far as establishing the phonetic facts. In fact the term diphthong does not accurately describe the combination of a vowel and ו in the regular pronunciation of modern Hebrew, where it is a combination of a full consonant (v) and vowel. However, this combination can be regarded as a diphthong because in the pronunciation of some communities it is actually articulated as such, and because it interchanges morpho-phonemically with vowels, unlike the combination of vowel plus spiranted ב which is phonetically its equal. In the interchanges the early history of this combination is still apparent. (The fate of the early *aw, ew*, etc., in modern Hebrew is similar to that of the same diphthongs in late Greek.) From the point of view of function it is clear that the Hebrew diphthongs are syllables with a consonant; not a phoneme in the precise meaning of the word, but a bi-phonematic element. The only interchange within the provenance of the rising diphthong is the וי"ו החיבור (*waw copulative*) becoming וּ (*u*) before a cluster of consonants and before ב, ו, מ and פ as וְשֵׁם but וּשְׁ־מִי; וְנָתַן but וּמָשַׁךְ; וְיֶלֶד but וּוֶרֶד. In all other changes of vowel the *waw copulative* acts in the same way as the consonants ב, כ, and ל. The total of diphthongs is eight, that is ו with *i,e,a,u*, and י with *i,a,o,u*. The falling diphthongs which are always maintained and do not interchange are *iw, ew, uw* (אָחִיו, עִוְרִים; כִּסְלֵו, גֵּו; וּוְ־לָדוֹת); *oy, uy* (גָּלוּי, גּוֹי) while the other diphthongs are replaced in the paradigm of the word by vowels, or are split into two syllables. Even though there are no absolute rules, there is great consistency, especially with regard to the diphthongs *aw, ay*. The main points are as follows:

A) *iy. iy* is used only when the accompanying element is geminated, as סִיּוּם, עִבְרִיָּה, עִבְרִיִּים, קִיֵּם. The combination *iyyi* is at times interchanged with *i* as עִבְרִיִּים = עִבְרִים, צִיִּים = צִים.

i appears in all other situations, such as: מִימִינוֹ, בִּירוּשָׁלַיִם, לִיהוּדִים (in poetry there is sometimes to be found מִימִינוֹ, בִּירוּשָׁלַיִם, לִיהוּדִים). The morphological variant ־ִיָּה (feminine ending) / ־ִית is connected with this phenomenon.

B) *aw. aw* is found (a) within the word (1) when the accompanying element is geminated, and (2) in the syllable preceding the *heh locale*; and (b) at the end of a word when it concludes that word.

o is found within the word in an unaccented syllable; as far as this rule is concerned "within the word" includes the end of the word in construct, provided that the syllable is closed.

awe is found at the end of a word, when, after the diphthong that should rightfully appear, there is a consonant and an accented syllable, that is always in the absolute state.

Note: "End of the word" includes monosyllabic words. Examples for the interchange *awe/aw/o* are: מוֹת־/מוֹתוֹ/הַמָּוְתָה/

עָנָו, סְתָיו; צַו/צַוֵּה; כְּגוֹן/גּוֹנוֹ/גָּוֶן; חֲצַרְמוֹתִי/חֲצַרְמָוְתָה/חֲצַרְמָוֶת; מָוֶת בָּנָיו.

c) *ay. ay* is found (a) within the word (1) when the accompanying element is geminated, and (2) in the syllable preceding the *heh locale,* and (b) at the end of a word when the syllable ends with it and is not a construct form.

é is found within the word in an unaccented syllable (and here "within the word" includes the end of the word in construct forms); *e* is found in the same positions as é, and in place of it before the pronomial suffixes ךָ–, הָ–; *ayi* comes at the end of a word, when, after the diphthong that should be there, there is a consonant and the syllable is accented. Examples for the interchange *ayi/ay/é/e* are סוּסֶיךָ/סוּסֵיכֶם, סוּסֵינוּ/סוּסַי סוּסַיִךְ, סוּסֶיהָ; בַּיִת/הַבַּיְתָה/בֵּיתוֹ/בֵּית־; הַמַּיְמָה/מֵי־/מַיִם; לַיִל/לַיְלָה/לֵיל־; דֵּי־ מָתַי; חַי/חֵי־; דַּי/דַּיּוֹ/. Exceptions to the above rules are found in both directions, and in modern Hebrew more so than in the past. The important exceptions are the following:

The diphthong is found (a) where gemination has disappeared (see 8. Gemination and Clusters) as: וַיְחִי (see וַיְּחִי), הַיְהוּדִים; (b) in words where the accompanying element is felt to be essential for maintaining the paradigmatic connection, as in רַוְחָה, שַׁוְעָה, עַוְלָה (which are connected etymologically to רֶוַח, שֶׁוַע, עָוֶל), מַוְרִידִים, הַיְשַׁר, מַיְמִינִים, שַׁלְוָתִי (but מוֹרִידִים from יָרַד!). A vowel is at times found alongside a split diphthong, as: לֵיל alongside לַיִל, אֵין alongside אַיִן, און alongside אָוֶן (with a semantic difference), צִים alongside צִיִּים, עִבְרִים alongside עִבְרִיִּים. Today the tendency (apparently also in other areas) is to exploit the phonetic variants יִּים– ים– for semantic distinctions. Comparative grammar teaches that in various words which today have a vowel, there was originally a diphthong (for example יוֹם, סוּף) and in several instances this fact is reflected in the plural forms, as שְׁוָרִים from שׁוֹר, שְׁוָקִים from שׁוּק, דְּוָדִים from דוד (also דּוֹדִים), לְוָחִים from לוּחַ (alongside לוּחוֹת). At times – completely exceptional – a vowel other than the ones listed in the rules above interchanges with a diphthong; for example *i* in the already archaic form, in the Bible, עירה (ass; Gen. 49:11) and in the common word עִיר (town), where not only the archaic plural עֲיָרִים (Judg. 10:4) hints at an original diphthong, but even the derivative word עֲיָרָה (small town) (through עֲיָרוֹת) retains this connection; *e* is found alongside é in גֵּיא.

Generally it can be said:

1) finding a vowel in a position where a diphthong is expected is part of a general tendency of early Hebrew, and in many words and forms there is no remnant of this original diphthong;

2) finding a diphthong in a position where a vowel is expected is an increasing tendency of later and modern Hebrew, due to the morphological considerations stated above, and thus there is to be heard not only שָׁמַיְמָה but also שָׁמַיְמִי (not considered a literary form), דַּוְקָא, כַּוֵּן, דַּיְסָה (and cf. Bialik in *Ha-Berékhah;* גַּוְנֵי גְוָנִים). Variants such as עַוְלָה/עוֹלָה (cf. Job. 5:16; עַוְלָתָה/עֹלָתָה Ps. 92:16) שׁוֹעַ/שֹׁוַע (Isa. 22:5) are not produced in modern Hebrew.

The expansion of the diphthong and even its splitting into two syllables occurs in late Hebrew even more than in modern official speech: it is found in medieval Mss. and in modern Samaritan Hebrew. The special relationship between the diphthong and vowel affects the spirantization of the בגדכפ"ת (see section 5. בגדכפ"ת above) when near a diphthong. Within the word the diphthong usually acts as a vowel and causes the spirantization of בגדכפ"ת, as in הַיְבָמָה, הַיְבוּל, בַּיְתָה, מָוְתָה, but שַׁלְוָתִי.

Examining the diphthong and its interchanges, we learn that:

a) *ay, aw* display almost (cf. above *aw* (a) 2: *ay* (a) 2) identical traits: this is not the case in, for example, biblical Aramaic and later Jewish Aramaic, where *ay* is still found without gemination, whereas *aw* is always interchanged with a vowel. In an effort to limit the occurrences of the diphthong (which is common in Canaanite) by interchanging it with a vowel, Samaritan Hebrew went much further than classical Hebrew (although there are parallels in Jewish traditions); the original *aw* diphthong has disappeared completely while the *ay* diphthong appears only rarely;

b) the type of syllable – open or closed – and the place of accentuation affect the diphthongs and their interchanges. Still, it is impossible to establish pure phonological criteria for the above rules, since the phonological rules which governed biblical Hebrew with great regularity have long ceased to operate with respect to the quantity of the vowels and the structure of the syllable, and a new situation has developed in which the morphological factor has become dominant. This new situation, reflected in the vocalization of the Bible, continues to spread. Mention should be made not only of interchanges of the diphthong but to all vowel changes, to be discussed below, and accentuation discussed above. In these it is possible to discern morphophonemic phenomena and in fact morphophonemics plays an important role in Hebrew grammar. This may explain the large number of exceptions to phonological rules, especially in matters of the vowel system. These exceptions can be grouped into morphological rules (cf. above *aw* b); *ay* b); cf. also section 5. בגדכפ"ת above and the *Historical Note* in section 16 on Interchange and Elision of Vowels, below).

The dominance of morphological principles over phonological is one of the features of a literary language which continues to be used many generations after certain phonological rules have ceased to be operative and are exchanged for other rules.

16. INTERCHANGE AND ELISION OF VOWELS. In the light of the above-mentioned assumptions that vowel quantity is not a distinguishing feature in Hebrew (see section 10. Vowel Quantity, above), and that almost any vowel quality can appear in every type of syllable (see section 11. Vowels as Part of the Syllable, above), the fact that a given vowel is maintained in all the forms of a paradigm but interchanged with another vowel in a different paradigm is rather surprising. This is a complicated aspect of Hebrew grammar which cannot be understood without resort to its historical background. Con-

sideration will be given first to the phenomena themselves, excluding those interchanges caused by א, ה, ח, and ע (see section 6. אהח"ע above).

A) Interchange of Vowel with Vowel.

1) *é* is interchanged

(a) with *i*, as מֵסַב/מְסִבִּים, מָגֵן/מְגִנִּים, יָקֵל/יְקִלֶּנִי, עֵנָב/עִנְבֵי־, סֵפֶר/סִפְרֵי, לֵב/לִבּוֹ, קֵן/קִנִּים, הֵן/הִנֵּם;

(b) with *e*, as בֵּן/בֶּן (construct), מַקֵּל/מַקֶּלְךָ, יִתֵּן/יִתֶּנְךָ, יוֹצֵר/יוֹצֶרְכֶם; and in biblical forms used today only in poetry, as: יָקֵם/וַיָּקֶם, יֵלֵךְ/וַיֵּלֶךְ;

(c) with *a*, as: זָקֵן/זְקַן־ (construct), תִּשָּׁמֵר/תִּשָּׁמַרְנָה, קֵן/קַן, יָשֵׁן/יָשַׁנְתִּי, כֵּן/כַּנּוֹ, מַקֵּל/מַקַּל־, תֵּלֵד/תֵּלַדְנָה (construct). But: *é* is retained in תִּשָּׁמֵרְנָה :תִּשָּׁמֵר, חֵיק :חֵיק (construct), עַד :עֵדְךָ, מֵת :מִתוֹ, הֵיכָל :הֵיכְלֵי; in certain construct forms *é* is retained alongside *e* as: לֵב :לֶב, אֵשׁ :אֶשׁ; *i* is not interchanged in: נִחַם :נִחֲמוּ, בַּיִת :בֵּיתָנִי, נִיצוֹץ :נִיצוֹצֵי, שִׁיר :שִׁירוֹ.

2) *e* is interchanged

(a) with *i*, as in יְפֵהפֶה/יְפֵהפִיָּה, פֵּה/פִּיּוֹת, כַּרְמֶל/כַּרְמִלּוֹ, גֹּרֶן/גָּרְנוֹ, בַּרְזֶל/בַּרְזִלָּם, כֶּבֶשׂ/כִּבְשָׂה, צֶדֶק/צִדְקוֹ;

(b) with *a*, as in מַפְסֶלֶת/מַפְסַלְתְּךָ, שׁוֹמֶרֶת/שׁוֹמַרְתּוֹ, מֶלֶךְ/מַלְכּוֹ; in biblical forms such as: וַיֹּאמַר/וַיֹּאמֶר (pausal), וַיֵּלַךְ/וַיֵּלֶךְ;

(c) with *e*, as in: קוֹנֶה/קוֹנֵהוּ, שָׂדֶה/שְׂדֵה־, יִקְנֶה/יִקְנֵהוּ.

3) *a* is interchanged with *i*, as in: מַס, מִסִּים, סַף/סִפִּים, חַג/חַגִּי־, עַם/עַמִּים, גַּת/גִּתִּים, בַּת/בִּתָּם, פַּת/פִּתָּה, but maintained in גַּל/גַּלֵּי, גַּג/גַּגּוֹת.

There are forms where both possibilities exist: e.g., סַנְסִנִּים, זַלְזַלִּים, but even in modern Hebrew סַנְסִנָּיו is also found, and the same is true for גַּלְגַּלִּים, גַּלְגַּלֵּי, גִּלְגַּלִּים and גִּלְגְּלֵי.

4) *o* is interchanged with *u*, as in: רֹב/רֻבָּם, חֹל/חֻלּוֹ, מְעֻ־, נְסוּגוֹתִי/נָסוֹג, מְנוּסִי, מְנוּסָה/מָנוֹס, מְתוּקָה/מָתוֹק, יְסֻבֶּנִי/יָסֹב, זָם/מָעֹז, but is retained in: שׁוֹר :שׁוֹרָם, חוֹל :חוֹלוֹ, מָלוֹן :מְלוֹנוֹת. But there is also עֻזִּי :עֹז.

5) *u* is interchanged with *o*, as in: קוּם, תְּקוֹמְנָה, וַיָּקָם/יָקוּם (infinitive).

B) Elision of Vowels.

Here we refer both to *šewa quiescens*, which is phonetically a zero vowel, and to the *šewa mobile*, which is a zero vowel from the phonemic aspect, but realized as an ĕ vowel in a cluster of consonants. In fact the distribution of the *šewas* depends solely on the type of syllable, and each can replace the other.

1) *é* / *šewa* as in: מֵסַב/בְּמְ־ מִס־בִּים; סֵפֶר/סְפָ־רִים, לִס־פָרִים; כִּסְ־ מַק־דְּחוֹ/מַקְדֵּחַ; נִבְ־לָתוֹ/נְבֵלָה; חָבֵר/חֲבֵ־רִי; עֵנָב/עִנָ־בִים; סְבִים; חָפֵץ :חֲפֵצִי; הֵיכָל :הֵיכְלוֹת; (יִתְּ־תְנוּ=) יִתְּנוּ/יִתֵּן; יוֹצֵר/יוֹ־צְרוֹ; כִּסֵּא/אוֹת; בִּרְכָתָם :בְּרֵכָה; מַקְדֵּחַ/מַק־דְּחוֹ; שָׂמֵחַ/לִשְׂ־מֵחֵי, שְׂמֵחֵי.

2) *e* / *šewa*, as in: יוֹצֶרֶת/יוֹ־צְרוֹת; מֶלֶךְ/מַל־כִים/לִמְ־לָכִים.

3) *a* / *šewa*, as in: זָקֵן/זְקַ־נִים, זִקְ־נֵי־, לִז־קְנֵי־; דָּבָר/דְּבָ־רִי, דִּבְ־רֵיהֶם; בְּרָכָה/בִּרְ־כַּת; דְּבַשׁ/דִּבְ־שָׁהּ; כְּתָב/כְּתָ־בִי; שָׂמֵחַ/שְׂמֵ־חַי; זְקֵ־נֵיכֶם, ם חַטְאֵיהֶם; יִלְבַּשׁ/יִלְ־בְּשׁוּ; חָרָשׁ :חָרָשֵׁי; and others but: בִּרְ־כוֹתֵיהֶם יִלְבָּשׁוּם; עִירָה :עֲיָרוֹתֶיהָ; חֲטָאִים and others.

4) *o* / *šewa*: שִׁבֹּלֶת/שִׁבֳּלִים (= שִׁבְּ־בֳלִים); קָדְקֹד/קָדְ־קֳדִים; יִשְׁ־מְרוּ, יִשְׁ־מְרֵם/יִשְׁ־מֹר; מַחְלֹקֶת/מַחְ־לְקוֹת; (צִפְּ־פֳּרִים =) צִפֳּרִים/צִפֹּר; מִשְׁכֹּרֶת :מַשְׂכּוּרוֹת; כְּתֻבָּה :כְּתוּבּוֹתֵיהֶם, כְּתוּבּוֹת but יָכֹל/יְ־כָלָה and many others; some people retain the *o* even in the nouns מַחְלֹקֶת, צִפֹּר and שִׁבֹּלֶת.

The phenomena listed above present a many-faceted and complicated picture of vowel changes. The main points are as follows:

A) The vowels *e, a, o* in an open syllable or in an accented closed syllable tend to be interchanged or elided when the word is declined (the same is true when the word serves as the basis for a derivation; as סֵפֶר :סִפְרוֹן). However, in a closed unaccented syllable, they are always retained in all declensions and conjugations of the word: (N.B. In this regard the imperfect verbal forms are independent "words," and we are not to treat their vowels in connection with the perfect).

B) In *e* vowels the phenomena is limited to that morphological type called "segolate nouns." Since *e* is an allophone of /*é*/ (see sections 2. Writing and Spelling; 12. The Phonological Status of the Vowels, above), the interchange *e* / *é* is not of the type under discussion, and in fact its conditions and results are different from the other changes. Phonemically, there are no *e* interchanges, but these are part of *é* changes. The interchanges of *u* vowels are common only in a few forms and this vowel is not elided. In fact the historic basis for this change differs from that of the other vowel changes, and the only factor they have in common is that of accent.

C) The conditions for the interchange of *e, a, o*, and their elisions are clear: the place of the accent and the structure of the syllable. When an accented closed syllable becomes unaccented the above vowels tend to interchange; in an open syllable whose accent has been removed the vowel tends to be elided.

D) With regard to elision the noun acts differently from the verb, while the verb itself acts differently according to whether or not it has a pronomial suffix. A verb without pronomial suffixes elides the vowel next to the accent; a noun elides the vowel penultimate to the accent, the verb with suffixes acts at times like the noun (especially in the *qal* perfect) and at times like a verb without suffixes.

For example, in the verb (without suffixes): *šamar, šamĕra; yašén, yašĕnu; yišmor, yišmĕru; yišan, yišĕnu; yittén, yittĕnu*; with suffixes; *yišmĕréni; yittĕnennu*;

In the noun: *lévav, lĕvavi, bilvavi; bĕlivvotékem; zaqan; zĕqéni, lizqeno*;

In the verb with suffixes *šamar, šĕmarani, ušmaro; šakal* (in pause *šaḵé'aḥ*), *šĕḵéḥuhu; yilbaš, yilbašéni*;

E) As regards the very consistency of elision, the verb differs from the noun, and the behavior of the *o, é*, vowels differ from that of the *a* vowel.

1) In a verb without suffixes the elision is consistent;

2) In the noun, *é* and *o* tend to be maintained while *a* tends to be elided.

3) In the verb with suffixes *e* and *o* are elided while in the same position *a* is maintained as: *yišmor: yišmĕréni, yittén yittĕnéni*: but *yilbaš, yilbašéni*.

F) Although the phonetic conditions – accentuation and syllable structure – are determining factors, it is impossible to classify – phonologically – all the various vowel changes without involving the morphological factor. In fact, it is only possible to depict the vowel system by listing the various morphological types in which one or the other situation occurs. Even within the morphological types there are variations which confuse the Hebrew speakers. As far as the official language is concerned, the Academy for Hebrew Language determines what is correct in each type.

G) *Historical Note*: This complicated situation, full of phonological inconsistencies, is the result of the change which took place in early Hebrew when there were still quantitative differences in vowels (see section Vowel Quantity). When quantity ceased to be free and phonemic – that is, when the language no longer accepted short vowels in open syllables – it lengthened or elided such vowels (depending on their relationship to the accent). In this way there developed either long syllables (that is, consonant plus long vowel, or consonant plus short vowel plus consonant) or syllables with *šewas* (or *ḥaṭefs*). As a result, in the paradigm of a given word which contained an original short vowel there were forms with long vowels (that is the vowel was lengthened because of the accent and this in turn caused a change in quality) alongside forms with short vowels (in a closed syllable), or elided vowels. At the same time, there are words with original long vowels which are maintained in all the declensions of the word, for example:

1) עֵדָה (= assembly): *ʿēḏā* (<*ʿidat*): *ʿăḏāṯi: ʿēḏot: ʿāḏōṯēḵā*: עֵדָה (= feminine witness): *ʿēḏā: ʿēḏātī: ʿēḏōṯ: ʿēḏōtēḵā*;

2) גִּבּוֹר: *gibbōr* (<*gibbār*): *gibbōrĕḵem*: *gibbōrīm*: צִפּוֹר *ṣippor* (<*ṣippur*): *ṣippurḵem: ṣippŏrīm*.

Since a short vowel in Hebrew has become mechanically lengthened or elided by the stress, the basis for interchange and elision of originally short vowels has been lost. As a result of reciprocal influences, originally short vowels have begun to act as long vowels and vice versa. *é* and *o* were originally both long and short, and as long vowels played a key role in maintaining what were originally short vowels in declension and conjugation (compare כְּתוּבּוֹת, צִפֹּרָה, לֵדַת, זֵעַת). *a*, which was originally a short vowel (the original long vowel was *ō*), affected originally long *ā* which in certain instances (as in the words כְּתָב, קָרְבָּן) did not become *ō*, and so was later elided in positions where other *a* vowels would normally be elided; therefore, one can find כִּתְבֵי, קָרְבְּנֵיהֶם, etc. Beginning in mishnaic Hebrew, many words entered Hebrew from Aramaic with what was originally a long *ā*, and these maintained the *ā* in their declension; in this manner the relative symmetry of biblical Hebrew, which maintained ā only in few morphological types, was disturbed. Another factor disturbed the vowel *šewa* relationship: the existence of vowels (originally short) in syllables that became open after the cancellation of gemination (see section on Gemination and Clusters above) in all the declensions of the word. So, for example, פָּרָשׁ (<פַּרְרָשׁ) meaning "horseman," caused פָּרָשׁ meaning "horse" (II Sam. 1:6, Ez. 27:14) to retain the *a* vowel after the פּ, and not elide it in the manner that the *a* vowel was elided after the ג of גָּמָל. The verb (without suffixes) in Hebrew is less given to change than the noun and to a greater extent reflects the early relationships (and not only in this regard). The noun, however, is subject to the influence of analogy; there are thus, from the phonologic point of view, many more contradictions in the paradigm of the noun. The great confusion with regard to interchanges made it necessary for the Academy for the Hebrew Language to establish the rules for maintaining or eliding a vowel. The Academy based these rules on morphological and semantic principles, i.e., principles which are at variance with precise phonetic processes.

17. INTERCHANGES DUE TO SOUND COMBINATIONS. In addition to the changes already discussed, there are changes in Hebrew caused by the chance sequence of sounds in the word. The natural tendency of the speaker is to conserve effort in his speech, and to try to minimize sharp changes in the use of one or the other of the organs of speech. In fact, speech is full of the assimilation of one sound to the other. Only when this assimilation is particularly sharp is the change felt. Since the consonants are more stable than the vowels, they tend to change less; cf. the changes due to assimilation, e.g., the נ to the neighboring consonant, the exchange of ת with ט or ד when close to צ or ז (see section 7. Other Consonants, above). At other times, a sequence of similar sounds demands a greater effort from the speaker and he tends to dissimilate them, as: displacement of ו by י in the plural form עֲרָיוֹת (from עֶרְוָה, but קְצָווֹת!) or י by א in עַרְבִיאִים alongside עַרְבִיִּים (but there is no יְהוּדִיאִים!) or הַגָּאִים alongside הַגָּיִים. Many variants in Hebrew comparable to הַשְׁקָאָה/הַשְׁקָיָה are occasionally used to distinguish differences of meaning, as הַלְוָאָה/הַלְוָיָה, הוֹרָאָה/הוֹרָיָה. In this class of variants is the plural ending ־ָאוֹת/־ָיוֹת found commonly in loan words from the period of mishnaic Hebrew. Another type of change, called metathesis, is found in Hebrew in words like שַׂלְמָה/שִׂמְלָה, כֶּשֶׂב/כֶּבֶשׂ. More common are the vowel changes due to environment. This causes the *šewa/ḥaṭef* change after א, ה, ח and ע; *a* is preferred over é in שִׂמַּח (opposed to שִׁמֵּר) and over *i* in יַעֲמֹד opposed to יִשְׁמֹר, אֶשְׁמֹר against יִשְׁמֹר (but אִשָּׁמֵר is found alongside אֶשָּׁמֵר). Medieval manuscripts contain many more changes than are common in the official language, and some of the common forms in modern Hebrew can be explained as a result of this practice. So the common plural of מֵסַב is מְסִבִּים, but the plural מְסֻבִּים (מְסֻבִּין) is simply a variant of מְסִבִּים, which assumed one of the meanings of the word. Among the changes whose origin is the desire to dissimilate the following are noteworthy:

1) A change which is active to a certain extent and noticeable in modern Hebrew: – *u* or *o* in a syllable next to a syllable with *u* or *o* is interchanged with *i* or *é*. This is found not so much in the inflection of words as in the derived forms. In inflection: נִכְחוֹ from נֹכַח; in derived forms חִיצוֹן, תִּיכוֹן, רִאשׁוֹן from רֹאשׁ, תּוֹךְ, חוּץ, and חִלּוֹנִי instead of ‡חֻלּוֹנִי (from חֹל); in this way the *i* of שִׁלְטוֹן can be understood as opposed to שָׁלְטָן; similarly in all *paʿul* participles with the suffix ־וּת the *u* tends to be changed to *i*, פְּעִילוּת; in a combination of words לוּלֵא from לוּ לֹא.

2) The exchange of *a* by *e* is found in the definite article (also in the word מַה), given certain conditions in the word;

this change is not properly maintained in the spoken language.

MORPHOLOGY

Introduction

1. DEFINITION OF THE SUBJECT. There is considerable disagreement as to which linguistic features are to be included in the area of morphology. Generally, semiticists have commonly included the discussion of parts of speech and the changes which they undergo as a result of their declension, as well as word-formation, in discussions of morphology. This is usually from the "form" aspect alone, without entering into investigations of the uses of these forms in speech. This latter problem is included in the study of syntax. The exceptions to this rule are Gesenius' Hebrew Grammar (29th edition) which was written by Bergsträsser (incomplete) and the Mishnaic Grammar by M.Z. Segal, which include the functions of the forms in their discussion of morphology. Another problem is, what is to be included in the term "form": a part of a word which does not have an independent existence? A word? A combination of words with a specific meaning or a particular structure (compound)? Or a feature such as the word order in the sentence which in some languages is morphological? Those who take morphology in its simplest, most straightforward meaning, include the linguistic form and exclude meaning, and distinguish between Lexical Morphology and Syntactic Morphology on the one hand, and, parallel to these, between Lexical Semantics and Syntactic Semantics, on the other hand (cf. S. Ullman, *Principles of Semantics* (1957), 33ff.). The preceding statement has not discussed all the methods of systematization but has merely alluded to the wide gulf which separates the different systems. The following description includes in the term "form": a form which is not in itself an independent word; an independent word; and to a limited extent the unit which supersedes a single word, if it is a lexical unit. This discussion of the structure of a linguistic form also includes its functions in the expression.

2. THE ROOT AND THE STEM (גזרה). A study of series of Hebrew words which are related semantically, such as:

a) שָׁמַר, שְׁמוּרִים; שְׁמוּרָה, מִשְׁמֶרֶת, מִשְׁמָר, שְׁמִירָה, שׁוֹמֵר, נִשְׁמַר, שִׁמֵּר, etc., and

b) פִּקֵּד, פָּקַד, פִּקָּדוֹן; תַּפְקִיד, מִפְקָדָה, פָּקַד, פִּקּוּד, פְּקִידָה, פּוֹקֵד, הִתְפַּקֵּד, הִפְקִיד, etc., will immediately demonstrate that there are a number of consonants in each of the words, which contain the common semantic element (even if only in a general way) and a number of vowels or vowels plus consonants which serve to qualify the meaning which is common to the entire family, to the particular, specific meanings of the various words or forms. The group of consonants found in each word of the above examples (a) שמר (b) פקד is called the root while the rest is called the formative (see section Phonology: 4. Consonants as Pronounced by Various Communities above). In Hebrew as in the other Semitic languages the root is always made up of a group of consonants. This is not the case in English, for example (and other Indo-European languages), where the roots also include vowels, as: "cut," "boy," "love." Only in certain cases are there those who call the consonants common to a group of words the root, as: s-ng, in the words, song, sing, sung, while others will choose one of these words and refer to it as the root, the other forms which differ from it being called the derivatives of that root. Clearly, the Hebrew root is only the abstract basis of a family of words used in the language, and does not denote the origin from which these words are derived, as it is hard to assume any level of the language in which the speaker was able to pronounce consonants alone as words. However, the fact that it is an abstraction is not to say that it is a grammatical fiction and merely a technical tool for the analysis of linguistic forms; it is in fact a living reality, an integral part of the structure of the language, which every Hebrew speaker feels. The root is not simply a prehistoric residual or an inherited element but a reality which is continually being produced in the language, and to a certain extent modern Hebrew suffers from a hypertrophy of root production. The reality of the root in Hebrew is seen from the modern roots נטרל, אכלס, טלפן, דוח which are derived from the abbreviation דו"ח (דין וחשבון) through the verb דִּוֵּחַ, and from the words "telephone," אוכלוס ("population"), and "neutral," by eliding the vowels. This is done even though the vowels in these foreign words are an intrinsic part of the word, without which they would not retain the meaning they have as a Hebrew root. In slang and children's talk new roots are formed more easily – whether from Hebrew words such as צברח in the word מְצֻבְרָח from the phrase מצב רוח, or from foreign words such as בלף from bluff. However, only a small number of these words enter more educated speech. This is adequate proof of the reality and vitality of this phenomenon.

The norm for a root is three consonants, and this is in any event the minimum needed for formation of a verb. Hebrew, however, still recognizes roots of one consonant (especially in particles and pronouns) such as ז (in the words זֶה, זוֹ, זוּ), פ (in the words פֹּה, פֶּה), כ (in the word כֹּה); two letter roots, such as: חַם, אָב, עֵץ, בֵּן, יָד, but these are doubtless vestiges from an ancient period, when Hebrew had not yet separated from other Semitic languages. However, this is no longer a productive method for producing new roots in Hebrew. The standardization of the root to three consonants took place in the proto-Semitic period. Hebrew also contains a number of roots with four or more consonants. In the earlier stages of the language they are few, but today they have been greatly expanded, as for example תפקד from the noun תַּפְקִיד, which is in turn derived from פקד, or מספר from מִסְפָּר originally from ספר. The verb, however, needs a minimum of three consonants and whenever a verb is created, a root (at least of three consonants) is implied, even from a one-consonant root like זהי (in זִהוּי, זִהָה) from ז, or from a two-consonant root like אחי (אִחוּי, אִחָה) from אח, דמם (דִּמּוּם, דִּמֵּם) from דם. There is still no conclusive proof whether עו"י (see section 23. Paradigm of Mute Forms, below) verbs and ע"ע verbs are derived primarily from original two-consonant roots or from three-consonant roots one of whose consonants is elided under specific phonetic situations (cf. Biblical Hebrew). However, it is important to note that structurally in the historical period these verbs are integrated into the three consonantal root system and follow its rules, so that verbs of the form קָם, דָּן in the perfect, generate nouns and other forms like קִיּוּם, דַּיָּן. Theoretically, in all words which can be analyzed to a root, all the consonants of the root are present. These consonants of the root usually appear in all the forms, but as a result of phonetic processes, some of which took place in the earliest stage of Hebrew, there are cases where one (and occasionally even two) of the root consonants was weakened and does not appear in all of the derived forms of the root. For example, as a result of the tendency of the *nun* to be assimilated to the following consonant (cf. section Phonology: 7. Other Consonants) one finds forms such as מַפָּלָה, יִפֹּל, from נפל, and as a result of the elimination of the diphthong (see section Phonology: 15. Diphthongs) we find in Hebrew יִבְנֶה from the root בני against בָּנַאי, בִּנְיָן and others. In systematization of the Hebrew forms, and in categorizing the words grammatically, one must consider this feature which affects the external forms of words without necessarily weakening its association with the other forms and words derived from the same root. In accordance with the structure, it is customary to divide the Hebrew roots into two main groups (stems) called Strong Verbs and Weak (Hollow) Verbs. The three consonants פעל are used as the symbol of the root and in accord with the place of elision the weak verbs are divided into the following stems: פ"א (that is, the weakening takes place in the first consonant of the root and is the consonant *alef*, and similarly) ל"י, ל"א, ע"י, ע"ו, פ"נ, פ"י, פ"ו (usually called ל"ה because of the spelling of the perfect form like קָנָה). A separate category is assigned to the roots with duplication or the ע"ע which stand between the strong and weak verbs.

3. THE "BASIC ELEMENT." There are, however, a considerable number of Hebrew words – excluding verbs – in which morphological analysis does not yield a root in the form described above but a combination of consonants and vowels, whether (a) the word is an independent form (a "free" form, as in the Indo-European root discussed above) or (b) it does not appear as an independent form (a "bound" form) or (c) it is a loan word or (d) it is an old inherited part of the language. Thus a group of related words such as פִּנְקָס, פִּנְקְסָן, פִּנְקְסָנוּת, פִּנְקָסוֹן, does not yield a Hebrew root פנקס, just as the words טֶלֶפוֹן, טֶלֶפוֹנַאי, טֶלֶפוֹנָאוּת, although there is a Hebrew root טלפן, cannot be derived from that root since the formatives *é-é-o, é-é-o-ay* do not exist in Hebrew. In both these groups of words the "elements" פִּנְקָס and טֶלֶפוֹן, being independent words in the language, are not susceptible to further morphological analysis. The same is true for original Hebrew words such as אֶצְבְּעוֹנִי and מְחִירוֹן, which semantically have no connection to צבע, and מחר, but retain their connection to אֶצְבַּע, מְחִיר which are independent words. This phenomenon is especially noticeable in those cases where the "elements" do not serve, or, because of their makeup, are unable to serve, as independent words, such as מדיניות (the independent word is מדינה), צורני (the independent word is צורה), ירושלמי (the word is ירושלים), רשימון (the word is רשימה and not רשים), תברואן (the word is תברואה), בַּקָּשְׁנֵת (the word is בקשה: familiar usage). A "basic element" of this type is parallel to a root insofar as the derived forms and their semantic content are directly related to it and not its root, even if it can be analyzed further into a root. For the concept "basic element" which we have introduced into the morphological analysis of Hebrew we use, in Hebrew, the term נטע (plant) which is found in a grammatical text of the Middle Ages.

Note: Attention should be paid to the difference between the concepts "basic element" as used here and "base" which is used by some scholars in morphological analysis. They refer to a specific form of a noun or verb which is itself a combination of a root plus pattern. It is the base to which other morphemes or suffixes are added, thus שָׁמַר is the base of שָׁמַרְתִּי etc. or כֶּלֶב is the base for כְּלָבוֹ, כַּלְבָּם, כַּלְבּוֹן. The base is an historical genetic concept (cf. Brockelman, *Grundriss*, 1, 287; Bauer & Leander, 246). The term "basic element," however, refers to a structure parallel to the root and of the same level, in that it cannot be further analyzed without losing its semantic relation to the word which is based upon it.

In biblical Hebrew the formation basic element + formative was rare and found mainly in nouns with the ending

ִי- (denoting belonging in the widest sense; cf. section 9. Suffixes); in modern Hebrew this formation is much more common, and in fact it was already in wider use in tannaitic Hebrew, with the adaptation of many foreign words. At times, when there is no clear-cut morphological analysis as with רִשְׁימוֹן, or as with words such as קָרְבָּן, סַלְחָן, אֻמְדָּן there is some doubt as to which type of formation it is. Words like קרבן can be analyzed *qorb+an* or *QRB+.o..an* (QoRBan). In such instances one must fall back on semantic analysis. If there is a semantic connection between the word and the root, and this formative is found in the Hebrew language and forms are built up in this way – then one is dealing with a root, but if there is no semantic connection with the root or such a morpheme is not known in the language (cf. above טֶלְפוֹן) then this form is the result of a "basic element" plus a formative. So רַגְזָן is easily analyzed: a root plus the morpheme *a.an.*, while מרגיזן (in children's language) must be analyzed as a basic element (מרגיז) plus the formative *an*, for if this were not the case the causative quality, which is not expressed in the root but in the *hif'il* formative included in the "basic element" which is the *hif'il* participle, would be lost.

4. THE FORMATIVE AND THE MORPHEME. The formative is that element – a phoneme or group of phonemes – with which a word is created, whether from a root or a "basic element." In Hebrew morphology it is possible to speak of two types of formatives: one which is combined with the root and in Hebrew linguistics is traditionally called the משקל (pattern); and one added to the "basic element" and is either a prefix or a suffix. The formative called משקל is always an infix, because it comes within the root, but can also be a prefix and infix at one and the same time as in: mišMaR, or an infix and a suffix as: KiŠRon; or a prefix, infix and suffix as with mišBeẓet. This formant is always discontinuous while the one which comes with the "basic element" is always continuous. The group of patterns which make up one verbal paradigm is called a conjugation (בנין) as: šaMarti, šaMaRta, šaMaR. (In the early days of Hebrew linguistics in the Middle Ages the terms משקל and בנין were used interchangeably.) In the common spoken language there is also a "minus formative" discernible, where a word is developed by removing a part of the word which serves the basis of the derivation (this is called a back-formation), as the elision of the ִי- in the words אנטיפאטי, פסיכי: resulting in אנטיפאט, פסיך. In this way a differentiation is achieved between the description of the quality (adjective) and its subject (substantive). Literary language includes non-accentuation (the accentuation which has phonemic value in Hebrew, cf. Phonology: 14. The Accent) of one of the elements of a compound and so a difference is achieved between the preposition עַל יַד and עַל יָד when both words are given their full meaning. Formations such as מגדל אור>מגדלור, יכול אני>יכולני (in this last word the plural מִגְדְּלוֹרִים as against מִגְדְּלֵי אוֹר is proof for that formation) come into being by eliding part of the compound. In the section on "Basic Element" it was stated that the "basic element" could be a word in itself used in Hebrew or something different or less than a word. In the formation of "basic element" plus formative, attention should be paid to the third category, where the formative plays a special role. While Hebrew can absorb foreign words easily, Hebrew grammar does not absorb elements which are foreign to its structure. It has already been seen that it is impossible to form a Hebrew verb from a foreign word if a root is not abstracted from its consonants (cf. טלפן). Similarly, Hebrew has difficulty in absorbing words which are adjectives or adverbs without first giving them a Hebrew form. This is not the case with other nouns. Words like טנק, ריאליזם, אידיאליזם, אידיאליסט, כלור, בנק and many others were assimilated into Hebrew without any serious attempt to exchange them for Hebrew innovations. This is not the case with words such as banker, chloric, realistic, psychic, and clerical; if they appear in Hebrew whether in their English, French, German, or other form, they remain foreign. In order to derive Hebrew forms two methods are used: either the Hebrew formative is added to the foreign word like קלריקלי (clerical+*i*), ריאליסטי, etc., or the corresponding foreign formative is exchanged for a Hebrew one, like: בנקאי (אִי in place of -er), כלורי (ִי- in place of -ic), טרגיקון (Tragik + er), היסטוריון (histor + ion), etc. In each instance the grammatical element which determines the category of the word in the original language is replaced by a Hebrew element. Were it not for this process the word could not be assimilated into Hebrew, and would certainly not be able to serve as the basis for other derived forms. A similar situation is the addition of the feminine ending ָה- to words which are borrowed from a language in which they are feminine even though they do not have a special feminine ending or are not used as the feminine at all. The Hebrew feminine form lends to the borrowed word a Hebrew form which makes its declension simpler, as אוניברסיטה (plural אוניברסיטאות), פונימה (phoneme). A special function of the Hebrew formative is, therefore, to adapt foreign words to a Hebrew form. This type of formation has not yet been thoroughly investigated, nor has it been described.

Unlike the roots and "basic elements" which develop in modern times, the formatives (not only the pattern formatives) are mostly inherited from earlier times and fixed. They change as to their function and semantic value, which at times differ in modern Hebrew from what they were in biblical or earlier Hebrew. Still, it cannot be said absolutely that no new formatives are being created in Hebrew. The history of different languages shows that formatives generally originate from independent words whose meaning has become blurred as a result of the wide use of a particular compound, or by transferring an element from a word which already exists in the language (the so-called metanalysis). Thus in post-biblical and modern Hebrew the compound היה + participle is used to express continuous (durative) and repeated (iterative) action, and so there is a difference between הוא היה אומר and הוא אמר.

In biblical Hebrew היה, even when found in a similar syntactical frame, is not the formative element (auxiliary word) it is in modern Hebrew. Still, even in modern Hebrew היה has not become fixed as a formative only in the strict sense. However, in literary Arabic, for example, of the compound *sawfa yaḫruğu* (סופו לצאת in rabbinic Hebrew, "He will go out") only *sa* remains from the first word (*sayaḫruğu*) and this becomes the formative for expressing the future. Spoken Arabic knows of other such formatives. An investigation of modern Hebrew is likely to reveal several other candidates for new formatives, one of which is ש with the imperfect verbal form to express desire: ילך (נא) = שילך. In the literary language this formative developed from a certain syntactic combination. By analogy a new formative was created in modern Hebrew (probably as a result of a sarcastic expression), טרון– from the word תיאטרון, and it serves to refer to a place where performances are presented, as: זירהטרון (circus), צ׳יזבאטרון (a satirical theater), and בובהטרון (puppet theater). In literary Hebrew נֶת– is used as a diminutive form (as טִפֹּנֶת, קְטַנְטֹנֶת). This is a new formative. Some centuries ago וֹנִית– was used (cf. עַלְמוֹנִית, נַעֲרוֹנִית) coined in accordance with אֲדוֹנִית (fem. counterpart of אדון) or חִיצוֹנִית (fem. of חִיצוֹן). The attempts to reestablish the *šafel* (שכנע, שכתב, שכפל, שקם), which in ancient Hebrew had no position and certainly no fixed function (words of this form are always borrowed), are all parts of this process. To summarize: not even the area of the formative is completely closed to new addition or limited to its original complement. The root, "basic element," and formative are the three components to which the Hebrew word can be analyzed, and each, individually, is the minimal meaningful morphologic unit which cannot be divided further and which has semantic content, in other words: morphemes.

Note: Some modern linguists use the term morpheme as the basis of their morphologic analysis of the Hebrew language and do not see any need for the term formative. But even they cannot ignore the traditional concept, the root, completely (nor do they eliminate the concept of pattern); instead they speak of a root morpheme. But it seems that in a language such as Hebrew, where the root is a vital and living element (see section 2. The Root and the Stem), one must relate to the fundamental difference between the abstract "root" and the "formative," which is the element that generates a real word, a noteworthy stage in any morphologic analysis, even though both elements are similar in that they are minimal units – morphemes. The morpheme is a concept in morphology which includes inflection and derivation, while the formative is reserved for the process of derivation. Inflection is generally an automatic process, depending on the type of word (noun, verb, etc.); derivation is always a new process.

5. PARTS OF SPEECH. The elements discussed above combine to make words. It is common to sort the words into categories called "parts of speech." Traditionally, Hebrew grammar differentiates (as did Aristotle) between three types only: noun, verb, participle. However, for several generations, under the influence of the grammar of various European languages, the division into nine parts of speech has become part of Hebrew grammar. There is no area of modern linguistics where the differences between scholars are more pronounced than in the division into parts of speech. It has been correctly claimed that the criterion for the accepted division is not consistent; at times it is the form and at times the content, or a mixture of the two. The logical demand to categorize the words based on differences in form leads to the conclusion: "every language has its own scheme. Everything depends on the formal demarcations which it recognizes" (E. Sapir, *Language*, 1949, 119). It must be admitted that it is not easy to fulfill this prerequisite. In our opinion it is better to analyze Hebrew in accordance with the traditional division into three parts of speech since it is thus possible to include the formal criterion more precisely. A sharp distinction exists between the noun and the verb. The verbal nouns, the participle, and the infinitive belong morphologically to the category of nouns, although syntactically there are features common to them and the verb. Regarding particles, there is not always a sharp distinction between them and the noun; some are inflected like the noun (עִמְּךָ like יָדְךָ) or have other qualities which are like the noun, while only the conjunctions and the interjections are entirely different from the noun and the verb. But there are particles (prepositions) which can, in accord with their morphological behavior, be classified as "nouns" (תַּחַת, אחור־אחורֵי, אַיִן־אֵין, בַּיִן). Also from a syntactical point of view the only clear division is between the noun and the verb (a "verbal sentence" has a verb as a predicate; a "nominal sentence" has a noun or particle as a predicate). The division into nine parts of speech confuses, since it confounds meaning (substantive, adjective, number) with the criterion of form and does not necessarily follow from an analysis of Hebrew speech.

Noun Formation

PATTERNS. To the problem of how many patterns there are in Hebrew and what they are, there is apparently a simple answer; if the word is analyzed to its root then the pattern is left after eliding the root consonants. But, surprisingly enough, there is a great divergence between what is commonly presented in the grammars and scientific literature (particularly that not written in Hebrew during the last generations) and the practical grammars (especially those written in Hebrew) based on the long internal Jewish tradition. Suffice it to point out that a standard work such as Bauer and Leander's Hebrew Grammar lists about 80 patterns for the noun while the "traditional" count (since David *Kimḥi) is about 290. It is not in the nature of the language observed that the difference between these two systems lies, since few new patterns have been added to biblical Hebrew. The critical difference is the method of observation. The traditional method depends on a descriptive approach, in which each form is considered to be another pattern, while the accepted scientific system is based on a historical-diachronic approach, in which are classified together all nouns even if they appear in different forms if they were the same in the early (sometimes even prehistoric) stages of the language; that is, the criteria come from outside the linguistic stage being described. Following are some examples of different types of classification.

a) The nouns: גַּן ,גְּדִי ,עִיר ,לֵיל ,לַיִל ,תַּיִשׁ ,נַחַל ,מֶלֶךְ

"Traditional" system	*"Scientific" system*
1. פֶּעֶל pat: נחל ,מלך	these are all part of the *qatl* pattern because their original forms were: ‡*malk*, ‡*naḥl*, ‡*tayš*, ‡*layl*, ‡*ʿayr*, ‡*gady*, ‡*gann*
2. פַּיִל pat: ליל ,תיש	
3. פֵּיל pat: לֵיל	
4. פִּיל pat: עיר	
5. פְּעִי pat: גדי	
6. פַּל pat: גן	

b) The nouns: גָּב(ו)הַּ ,עָבֹת ,אָדֹם ,גָּדוֹל ,רָחוֹק ,כָּבוֹד ,שָׁלוֹם, קְרָב ,כְּתָב ,כָּרוֹז ,עָשׁוֹק are classified:

"Traditional" system	*"Scientific" system*
1. פָּעוֹל pattern: All nouns till כתב (but some point to the differences in declension)	1. *qatāl*: קרב ,כתב ,כבוד ,שלום.
a) elimination of the *qameṣ* שלום, etc., b) maintaining the qames כרוז etc., c) gemination of the 3rd radical אדם.	2. *qatul*: a) גבה ,עבת ,אדם b) רחוק ,גדול 3. *qatūl* (?) *qatāl* (?): עשוק ,כרוז.
2. פְּעָל pat: קרב ,כתב.	

c) The nouns: רַכָּב ,קַשָּׁת ,קַנָּא ,צִפֹּר ,גִּבּוֹר ,שִׁכּוֹר ,קַנּוֹא ,רַתּוּק, אַיָּל are classified:

"Traditional" system	*"Scientific" system*
1. פַּעוֹל pat: קַנּוֹא ,רתוק	1. *qattāl* pat: all except צפר ,איל
2. פִּעוֹל pat: צִפּוֹר ,גִּבּוֹר ,שִׁכּוֹר	2. *qattal* pat: איל
3. פַּעָל pat: איל ,קנא	3. *quttul* pat: צפר

(Another less acceptable division in the scientific system:
qattāl: קַנּוֹא ,רתוק   *quttol*: צפור ,שכור
qattal: איל ,קנא).

A further difference: the nouns with the addition ־ָה as: אַיָּלָה ,נְחָמָה ,גַּנָּה are independent patterns in the "traditional" system, *qatl, qattāl, qattal* in the "scientific" grammar. The examples show that none of the methods is entirely consistent. Traditional grammar does not distinguish between מֶלֶךְ with two *segols* and נַחַל with two *pathaḥs* and מֶלַח with a *pathaḥ* and a *segol*, while historical grammar is at times confused about the original form, and forced to establish patterns such as קְטִיל ,קְטוּל (with *šewa*!). The criteria upon which we should base the different patterns in Hebrew from a descriptive structural point of view, will be given below with examples.

Note: In confronting the "traditional" and "scientific" methods of classification two typical forms of classification have been used, but it should be remembered that in each there are differences (especially in the "traditional") which affect the final count of patterns. While David Kimḥi (12th cent.) counted 290 patterns, Jonah ibn Janāḥ (11th cent.) counted about 80 (if one eliminates about 60 which are patterns of personal names). He already classified diverse forms such as נֵרְךְ ,פֶּתִי ,עֲיָרִים עִיר ,אֶרֶץ under the same pattern.

7. PRINCIPLES OF PATTERN ANALYSIS. It is clear from the above that the "scientific" methods describe the way the Hebrew word was created from its proto-semitic form and are essentially interested in prehistory and not the historical reality. On the other hand, the "traditional" system is found to describe the external appearance of the noun, even if that appearance is unique among the forms which make up the paradigm of that noun, and due entirely to chance as a result of the coincidence of certain sounds in the word. For example, בַּיִת ,נַחַל ,מֶלֶךְ have two syllables in these forms only, while in other forms of the declension of the singular, the base is of one syllable: ־בֵּית ־נַחַל ־מַלְכְּ as in the nouns עם ,ליל ,יום. The analysis of patterns must be done on two levels: first the nouns must be analyzed as they appear: that is the root and the formative element must be distinguished; then the common features in appearance must be investigated in relation to the structure of the root ("stem") and each group will yield its pattern. Just as every group of words with a basic common meaning will yield a "root," so too from a group having common formation features the "pattern" will emerge. On both levels of the analysis the process is only descriptive and refers to the language in the given circumstances. It may be said that the relationship of the "appearance" to the "pattern" is as the phone to the phoneme or the morph to the morpheme. In the process of the analysis the following rules will be carefully considered:

1) The need to distinguish between nouns derived from roots by patterns and nouns derived from a basic element + formative. For example: לַהֲטוּטָן ,כַּרְטִיסָן, though there is a root כרטס (note: כַּרְטֶסֶת) להט, are to be analyzed כרטיס + ־ָן, להטוט + ־ָן as סמרטוט + ־ָר = סמרטוטר (see section 3. The Basic Element). These are not of concern here. One must be especially wary of nouns ending in the feminine as: יַבָּשָׁה ,אַיָּלָה: אילה is to be analyzed אַיָּל + ־ָה, יבשה however, is to be analyzed יבש + *a..a-a*.

2) Pattern formations are (primarily) the result of the relationship between the consonants of the root and the vowels and consonants which are not part of the root. The relationships between the root consonants themselves, such as the hollowness of certain roots (see the section: 2. The Root and the Stem) or the repetition of one or two of the consonants, do not affect the concept of pattern, nor the declensions which are connected to the structure. Pattern is an abstraction and the appearance of the word is its realization. This principle is not properly reflected even in scientific grammar books where the patterns *qattīl* and *qatlīl*, for example, are separated as are others, although from the point of view of the number of root consonants there is no difference between them (see Phonology: 8. Gemination and Clusters) nor is there a difference in the way they are declined. Repetition of a root consonant can have an expressive function, but is not a matter of the pattern. From this point of view, רַכֶּבֶת (= רככבת) ,כַּרְטֶסֶת ,טַפְטֶפֶת ,דַּפְדֶּפֶת are of the same form, as are סְבוּב (= סבבוב) ,נִדְנוּד ,סִדּוּר (= סדדור), and אִלֵּם (= אללם) ,פִּלְפֵּל and דַּיָּן (= דיין) ,פַּרְנָס.

3) As a result of vowel interchanges (cf. Phonology: 15. The Diphtongs; 16. Interchange and Elision of Vowels) a dif-

ferentiation must be made between those changes which affect the meaning of a word and those conditioned changes which do not. For example the vowels which follow the formative מ in the nouns מִזְמוֹר :מַעֲצוֹר, מִזְבֵּחַ :מַסְמֵר do not indicate a pattern change (although they produce different appearances!) whereas the three respective vowels after the צ in מַעֲצֹר מַעֲצֵר מַעֲצָר determine three different patterns. The same is true for the vowels of the formative in מִפְקָד :מְפֻקָּד or in מַעֲמָד :מָעֳמָד which determine different patterns, while the change מָעֳמָד :מְעֻמָּד does not determine different patterns.

4) As to the "appearance" one must consider its connection to the root, and in all the declensions of the noun in a specific paradigm, a form may be picked out and established as representative of the pattern, as long as the form chosen serves to clarify the others in accord with the rules of the language. The linguist is liable to discover that in Hebrew very often the declined form and not the dictionary form ("*casus rectus*" or absolute form) is the one which is most representative of the pattern. This is a result of certain developments in the language which caused change in the absolute form of the word. So from *qullo, qullot*, the form *qol* (lightness, easiness) could easily be understood according to the rules of vowel interchange (see section Phonology: 16. Interchange and Elision of Vowels) but not the opposite (the absolute *qull* is not possible!); there is, indeed, the homonym *qol* (voice) in the absolute which declines as *qolo, qolot*. Clearly one appearance (as *qol*) is liable to produce more than one pattern and vice versa. At times this method of analysis is likely to agree (although without intention) with the historical method, but very often it will yield different results. If the decision that *qull* is of the *qutl* pattern is in agreement with the historical position, the decision that *qol* is not of the *qatl* pattern (*qawl* in Arabic) or the *qal* pattern (*qāla* in Aramaic, and so in the Silwan inscription) but of the *qol* pattern, is opposed to the accepted historical point of view. Any agreement with the historical position is indicative of the fact that here and there the early state is still reflected in the modern makeup of the language.

5) From the above (4) it is clear that the patterns as they are determined by the structure of modern Hebrew must be arrived at not from the vocalized forms but from the pronunciation which does not recognize quantitative differences, recognizing instead a total of five vowel phonemes (see section Phonology: 12. The Phonological Status of the Vowels).

8. DETERMINING THE PATTERNS. In accord with the above principles the various stages in determining the patterns of the noun can be described: Example I: (1) מֶלֶךְ, (2) צֶדֶק, (3) סֶגֶל, (4) סֵפֶר, (5) אֶבֶן, (6) עֵדֶר, (7) יֶרַח, (8) נֶצַח, (9) צַד, (10) גַּן, (11) עַיִר, (12) גָּוֶן, (13) בְּכִי, (14) חֲצִי, (15) חֵטְא, (16) דֶּשֶׁא, (17) בֶּכֶה, (18) עֵד, (19) לֵיל, (20) שׁוֹר, (21) אוֹן. In almost all of them the three root-consonants are immediately recognizable, and in some of them when they are declined in singular or plural (חֲטָאִים, צְדָדִים, בִּכְיוֹ). In many there is an obvious connection with other nouns (צַדִּיק, מְלוּכָה, מְאֻבָּן, etc.), or to a verb (בָּכָה, גִּוֵּן) – indicating that these forms are derived from roots and not from a basic element. They can be divided, based on appearance, as follows:

פֶּעֶל: 1, 2, 3, 5, 7, 8, 16, 17
פֵּעֶל: 4, 6
פַּל: 9, 10
פֵּל: 15, 18, 19
פַּיִל: 11
פָּוֶל: (or פָּעֶל): 12
פּוֹל: 20, 21
פְּעִי: 13, 14

In all there are at least eight different appearances (some differentiate between פֵּל and פֵּיל [לֵיל]). Checking the structure of the roots (= "stems") we find five types: (a) strong (1–8), (b) ע״ו/ע״י (11, 12, 18, 19, 20, 21), (c) ל״א (15, 16), (d) ל״י (13, 14, 17), (e) ע״ע (9, 10). Since the types of consonants in the roots do not determine the pattern (cf. principle 2) it is fundamentally possible for all the words to be variations of one pattern, if it can be shown that with regard to the vocalizations attached to the root (the formative) there is no difference between them. In accordance with the declension of the following (a) מַלְכִּי, יַרְחִי, גַּנּוֹ, אַבְנֵיכֶם, etc. (b) צִדְקוֹ, סִפְרוֹ, עֶדְרוֹ, בִּכְיוֹ, צִדּוֹ the diachronic approach is likely to distinguish two patterns *qitl* and *qatl*, and, based generally on comparative reasoning, these nouns will be included in one of the two patterns, especially recognizable in the ע״ו/ע״י stems since some of the nouns have a diphthong and others a simple vowel (cf. section on Phonology: 15. The Diphtongs). On the other hand, the descriptive grammar of Hebrew in its historical setting will abstract from these forms three patterns:

a) *pi/a'l* 1–17, (20?)
b) *pel* 18, 19
c) *pol* 21, (20?)

Since for many generations (a fact which is already evident in the vocalization of the Bible) the form פעל is declined with an *i* after the first root-consonant, while *a* appears only if the first or second root-consonant is אהח״ע, and in a number of ancient words (as מַלְכּוֹ), therefore the interchange *a/i* is conditioned and this pattern may be called *paʿl* or *piʿl*; both have been absorbed in historical Hebrew to one pattern. On the other hand the ancient group which included 11, 18, 19, has been broken up and there is no longer any similarity in their behavior; this leads to the need for a *pel* pattern; the same is true for 12, and 20 is more properly placed in (a) because of its plural שְׁוָרִים.

Example II: (1) מִשְׁמָר, (2) מַעֲמָד, (3) מַחְמָד, (4) מַסָּע, (5) מַדָּע, (6) מֵידָע, (7) מוֹדָע, (8) מָקוֹם, (9) מָדוֹן, (10) מִמְצָא, (11) מִבְנֶה, (12) מַעֲשֶׂה, (13) מָסָךְ, (14) מֵסַב, (15) מַשָּׁק.

They are commonly divided into:

מִפְעָל: 1, 2, 3, 10
מִפְעֶה: 11, 12
מַפָּל: 4, 5, 15
מֵיפָל: 6
מוֹפָל: 7
מָפוֹל: 8, 9

מַפָּל: 13
מֵפַל: 14

An investigation of the structures yields seven types: (a) strong 1–3; (b) פ״נ 4, 15 (מַשָּׁק meaning touch, is related to the root נשק); (c) פ״ו/פ״י 5–7 (there is no root נדע to which מַדָּע may be related); (d) ע״ו/ע״י 8–9; (e) ל״א 10; (f) ל״י 11–12; ע״ע 13 (compare the verb סכך), 14, 15 (מַשָּׁק meaning noise is related to the root שקק). The diachronic approach will establish for these 15 nouns of eight appearances two patterns *maqtal* and *miqtal*. The last is indicated only in 14, just as the first is derived from the rest except for 1–3, 10–12; these cannot be historically included with certainty in either of the two patterns. But in accordance with principles no. 2 and 3 above one pattern, *mafʿal,* can be determined whose first vowel is easily distinguished in all the nouns except for 14 and for that reason a better symbol would be *ma/ifʿal*.

It must be noted that there is no permanence in the language; relationships to roots are constantly being eliminated and new relationships develop. A word which cannot be analyzed into a root and pattern is a basic element. The two words אִישׁ, שִׁיר are similar in their appearance, the second is related to the root שיר (שָׁר, מְשׁוֹרֵר, שִׁירָה) and so is analyzed according to the pattern *pi/aʿl* while the first was not related until modern times to any family of words, and when the root איש was created (מְאֻיָּשׁ, אִיֵּשׁ) its morphological status was changed. Consistency demands that we analyze words with fewer than three root-consonants such as יָד, שָׂפָה, פֶּה (which are actually relics of a period which preceded the three-root system!) as "basic elements," until there will be a family of words which will relate them to a root. In this way the 290 appearances in the "traditional" grammar will be reduced to about 90. About 50 of these are infix types, and the rest are prefix-infix-suffix types. The consonantal elements which precede the root are (in alphabetical order) א (אַזְכָּרָה), ה (הֶבְדֵּל), י (יַלְקוּט), מ (מַאֲכָל, מַלְבּוּשׁ, מוּסָד), נ (נַפְתּוּלִים), ת (תַּלְמוּד). The elements of the pattern which follow the root are: ־ָה (קַבָּלָה, פִּשְׁרָה), ־ֶת (מִשְׁקֶלֶת, מִסְגֶּרֶת), וֹן (עִקָּרוֹן), ־ָן (אָמְדָן). From this great number of possible patterns in Hebrew there are today no more than 25 which are productive (this is a general impression and not the result of an exact statistical investigation). If one ignores the patterns used for participles and infinitives (*nomina actionis*), which are automatically formed with the verb, then the infixed *pi/aʿl* is especially productive for concrete and abstract nouns, such as: מֶנַע, קֶצֶר, פֶּסֶל, מֶרֶק, כֶּבֶל; *po/uʿl* mainly for abstract nouns: אֹדֶם, קֹצֶר, אֹרֶךְ but also, טֹפֶס, עֹתֶק; while *paʿal* is used to indicate profession or permanent character: נַגָּח, שַׁדָּר, נַגָּן, סַפָּן. The prefixed and suffixed patterns which are productive are the ones with מ before the root and a "feminine" ending such as מַזְמֵרָה, מִסְפָּרָה, מִנְהָלָה, מִקְטֶרֶת, מִכְפֶּלֶת, etc.

9. SUFFIXES. Although the creation of forms through patterns is dominant in Hebrew (verb patterns should be added to noun patterns), ancient Hebrew once created forms from the basic element + suffix. The changeover from one type of word formation to the other can be illustrated by two examples.

(1) basic element + formative > pattern. The nouns רְעָבוֹן, רָעָב are differentiated by the suffix ־וֹן and it is likely that this was added to the basic element רָעָב, just as ־וֹן was added to ראש (there is no such root) and ראשון was formed. However, in various nouns which are formed in this way, a syllable + an open vowel which in antiquity must have become lengthened, are changed to a closed syllable by gemination of the next consonant. According to the accepted rule: לְבָנִים :לָבָן is equivalent to קְטַנִּים :קָטָן and which was *qatal+on* could develop into *qattalon* leading to פִּעָלוֹן. In historical Hebrew while רעבון can still be analyzed as basic element רָעָב + suffix ־וֹן, צִמָּאוֹן is a *piʿʿalon* pattern, and cannot be analyzed as צָמֵא +־וֹן. The same word in the Samaritan pronunciation, however, *ṣåmåm'on* enables us to see the older stage and can be analyzed as צָמֵא +־וֹן parallel to רעבון.

(2) Noun pattern > basic element + formative. The words מַלְכוּת, גַּבְהוּת, עַמְקוּת, גַּדְלוּת, יַהֲדוּת are each made up of two morphemes which are obtained through the analysis: roots מלכ, עמק etc. and the formative *.a..ut,* and cannot be analyzed into the stems מֶלֶךְ (note מַלְכוּת and not מֶלְכוּת!), עָמֹק or עמוק, יהודי and the suffix וּת, but in אֱנוֹשׁוּת the analysis is necessarily אֱנוֹשׁ + וּת. At times both types of creation function alongside each other as in the synonyms אֲדֻנּוּת (אדנ + the pattern *.a..ut*), אֲדוֹנוּת (the basic element אָדוֹן + the suffix *ut*). Though it is possible that the pattern containing וּת was formed from a basic element and a formative as in example (1) (since the element וּת was probably created as a result of metanalysis from ל״ו), historically one first finds in Hebrew words with וּת which are analyzed by patterns and only later those which are analyzed "basic element" + formative. Note that this type of formative is common in names of people and places.

The suffixes can be divided into two groups: those which have fallen into disuse (obsolete) and those still used. The suffixes which are no longer in use and are not productive, are at times not recognized even by the expert as formative elements. Still, they should not be ignored, and should be included in a descriptive grammar, since there is still a relationship between a noun with such a suffix and a noun without it. Furthermore, the availability of the early classical sources creates new forms through formatives which have been considered unproductive and long dead (cf. (ת)נִי = below). Of the suffixes in common use, some are very productive.

Obsolete suffixes:

a) vowels: ־ה, ־ו, are found mainly in personal names, as שלמה, עדו, מגדו, but also חיתו (= חית), בנו (= בן; perhaps the ו of בשעתו, בזמנו which was originally the third person suffix whose value was weakened because of the weakening of the syntactic connection, also belongs to this category). ־ֶה, ־ָה: אִשֶּׁה (fire-offering), לְבֵנָה (in this way the singular of בְּטְנִים :בָּטְנָה was formed several decades ago. Today this form is considered incorrect.), אריה (from ארי cf. אֲרָיוֹת). ־ָה ≤: so-called "*he* locale," found originally and mainly in adverbs denoting places as in שָׁמָּה, הָלְאָה, לְמַטָּה. See also ־ָתָה below.

b) vowels and consonants: ־ב in the place name שעלבים

which includes שעלב (תַּעלב in Arabic) = fox. ג-ָ: the name אבישג, in use even today as opposed to אבישי, the ג is considered to be a formative element regardless of its origin. יָה: כְּנוּפְיָה, מֶרְחַבְיָה, מַאְפֵּלְיָה; also to be analyzed in this way אַסְפַּקְלַרְיָה (from *specularium*), as there is the basic element אַסְפַּקְלָר. -יָן: עֶבְרָיָן the basic element עֶבֶר, connected with the noun עֲבֵרָה (cf. the noun, ירושלמי, no 3). ל: כַּרְמֶל, עֲרָפֶל, סְפֶל (the biblical word סף is found in poetry, as Bialik's לבי סף דמעה), עַרְסָל (basic element עֶרֶס), גבעול. ם-: רֵיקָם, אָמְנָם, חִנָּם, סֻלָּעָם, פִּתְאוֹם and in personal names like מִרְיָם. ן-: צִפּוֹרֶן, יְשׁוּרוּן, כְּנַעַן, גַּרְזֶן, זְבוּלוּן (this analysis is arrived at from comparative grammar).

-נִית(ת): קַדְמוֹנִית, קְדוֹרַנִּית, אֲחוֹרַנִּית. The new words: קְדוֹרַנִּי, קַדְמוֹנִי have been created analogically. ת-ֶ: Primarily in personal names (including those recently created) such as בָּשְׂמַת, אָסְנַת, יוֹנַת, רִנַּת. The nouns מְנָת (= מנה) and שְׁנָת (= שָׁנָה) can be so analyzed. This suffix is also found in place names: נָצֶרֶת, דּוֹבְרַת, שְׁמֶרֶת. ָתה: Originally this is the so-called "*he* locale" suffix which is added to nouns with feminine endings, but when this function disappeared (as in the noun לַיְלָה = ליל) it became a suffix which is used particularly in poetic language עֶזְרָתָה (= עֶזְרָה), ישועתָה (= ישועה) and others.

Common suffixes:

a) Vowels:

ה-ָ: Common feminine suffix in declension, and used to indicate: (1) collectives such as גּוֹלָה, "all those exiled," דָּגָה = "all the fish." As to the nouns חִטִּים: חִטָּה, שִׁקְמִים: שִׁקְמָה, etc. the plural always indicates the collective, while the form with the ה-ָ suffix indicates the collectives or one of the items in it, according to context; (2) an artificial as opposed to the natural limb בִּטְנָה, מִצְחָה.

י: also called the "relation suffix," since it relates the noun with this suffix to another by attributing to the new noun some quality of the noun serving as its "basic element." יְרוּשַׁלְמִי = of Jerusalem, רַגְלִי = on foot, יְמָנִי = on the right side, רָאשִׁי of the head (in the concrete and borrowed senses; see above, section 4. The Formative and the Morpheme).

b) Vowels and consonants:

(א)י-ַ: It may be that this was originally two suffixes which were consolidated. One, which is used in personal names such as יַנַּאי (< יוחנן), זַכַּאי (< זכריה), etc., and one parallel in function to י-ָ (and used in Aramaic parallel to Hebrew י-ִ). Usually it indicates a professional such as עִתּוֹנַאי, חַשְׁמַלַּאי, חַקְלַאי. (This form should not be confused with the ל״י verbal form זַכַּאי, "innocent" derived from the root זכי in the פַּעָל pattern; the name זַכַּאי is אי + זכ(ריה!)

-וֹן (-וֹנִי): Its modern use is preeminent (1) to create diminutives: סִפְלוֹן, דֻּבּוֹן, גַּנּוֹן; (2) to indicate publications which appear at regular intervals such as עִתּוֹן, שְׁבוּעוֹן, שְׁנָתוֹן, יַרְחוֹן and lists of similar items such as מִלּוֹן, שִׁירוֹן, חִידוֹן, תַּקְנוֹן. But there are other nouns derived in this way and the formative fulfills other functions. The combination י + -ונ becomes -וֹנִי in words like צְהַבּוֹנִי, צִמְחוֹנִי.

-וּת: Used primarily for abstraction (see above in this section).

-וֹת: Common suffix for feminine plural used (1) adverbially רַבּוֹת, ישירות, and (2) for collective and abstract nouns such as: מִסְכָּמוֹת, מפורסמות, נסתרות.

-ִית, ִיָּה: Combinations of the relation suffix י- and the feminine suffix, are used (1) for diminutive: כַּפִּית, יָדִית, מַצִּיָּה, עוּגִיָּה; (2) a workshop or gathering place סַנְדְּלָרִיָּה, כְּרִיכִיָּה, פְּנִימִיָּה, כְּנֵסִיָּה; (3) a collection of things צִמְחִיָּה, תַּקְלִיטִיָּה, סִפְרִיָּה.

-ִים, -ִין: Originally the plural suffix, they are used (1) with adverbs (plus the preposition) such as לסירוגין, במישרין, לחלוטין; (2) for abstract nouns such as נעורים, ניחומים.

ן-ָ: Today mainly used to indicate the subject of an action as רַפְתָּן, תַּכְסִיסָן, לַהֲטוּטָן (see above section 3. "The Basic Element").

-תָן: Functions as ן-ָ and originates in nouns which end in ה-ָ as גאותן (conceited) and through metanalysis תָן as opposed to ן-ָ became more expressive: רַעַבְתָן a very hungry person, כרסתן = one having a large stomach.

ר-ָ: Loaned from Latin-*arius* and is found in original Hebrew words such as סְמַרְטוּטָר, נַחְתּוֹמָר, עוּגָבָר, serves the same function as ן-ָ.

-נֶת: For diminution (see section 4. The Formative and the Morpheme).

The above survey indicates that the suffixes, like the noun patterns, are morphemes, every one of which has more than one semantic function, and at times these functions are quite dissimilar and it is difficult to find a logical connection between them (cf. for example -וֹן). The reason is that Hebrew is a very old language and in the course of time the formatives changed their functions, or new functions were added to them, without eliminating the words which were derived from them when their prime function was different.

10. PREFIXES AND COMPOUNDS. Words formed by the addition of prefixes ("secondary derivatives") as are common in Indo-European languages such as the English print, offprint, reprint, imprint and come, income, outcome, overcome, become, are unknown in Hebrew, which expresses these different notions by different noun patterns or by compounding words, or by different roots, as in (1) דפוס, תדפיס, הדפסה חוזרת, מִטְבָּע; (2) בוא, הכנסה, הוצאה, התגברות, היות or היעשות. Nevertheless, there are already compounds in biblical Hebrew which might be taken to be a prefix + a "basic element" when the prefix is a word of negation, as in: לא־אל, לא־עם (Deut. 32:21), אל־מות (Prov. 12:28): no-god, no-nation, no-death.

This is in fact the common way for analyzing compounds in modern Hebrew not only of the אי־צדק (injustice), אי־שימוש (disuse) type but also בין־לאומי (international), חד־צדדי (unilateral, one-sided), חד־שיח (monologue), דו־שיח (dialogue), על־אנושי (super-human), תת־עורי (hypodermic), אין־סופי (infinite), קדם־מקצועי (prevocational), בתר־מקראי (post-biblical), חוץ־לשוני (extra-lingual), and others. It is true that these and similar compounds were developed under the influence of Indo-European equivalents and indeed a deliberate attempt was made to achieve Hebrew equivalents for idioms which are basically technical terms. Such compounds gradually became assimilated into the common language and generated compounds like חד־סטרי (one-way) and חד־פעמי (unique) which are not entirely parallel to the English forms (but compare the German *einmalig* = unique). The fact that such foreign words are analyzed as including prefixes, cannot dictate that the Hebrew analysis be done in the same way; that must be done in accordance with the manner in which these words are integrated into the Hebrew system. It will be demonstrated that there is really no difference between this form and the existing compounds in Hebrew. A compound of two or more words which become one indivisible word, so that at times the original elements are no longer recognizable, is almost unknown in classical Hebrew; of this form are the early words בליעל, בלימה, כלום (כל מה), משהויין (plural of משהו> מה שהוא) and the modern words כדורגל, דחפור, רמזור, מַגְדָּלוֹר; in slang and affected speech compounds such as ארחיפרחיטורה (טורה + ארחי פרחי) "a student parade from the school of architecture," are formed.

There are, however, many combinations of more than one word in Hebrew, which due to their wide use have become fixed formally with fixed semantic values; they can be called compounds. The compound is usually the necessary condition and the first step toward merging the separate elements into one word. Various types and levels of construction can be differentiated:

1) Where one is in construct state; two nouns are joined, the first ("*nomen regens*") is qualified by the second ("*nomen rectum*"). This is the reverse of the situation in Indo-European languages: for example מלאכת־יד = hand-work, the same order is common in a compound of a noun and its adjective מלאכה קשה = hard work. The opposite order is possible, as in English, if the first part is a noun of quantity or vague, and therefore of wider meaning than the second part, which limits scope of the first word, as in: שלש קלשון (I Sam. 13:21) – trident, משנה כסף (Gen. 43:12; but Gen. 43:15 כסף משנה!) = double money, דרום אפריקה South Africa, צפון אמריקה North America (but קוטב הצפון = North Pole). There is no clear formal criterion to establish when a combination is a regular construct or when it is a fixed compound; the semantic content may help but it is not an absolute criterion. Still it may be pointed out that deviation from the normative grammatical rule which demands that the article be placed before the second word (*nomen rectum*) (בית הספר and not הבית ספר) does, to some degree, indicate that the combination is felt to be a fixed compound, and so we find התל אביבי, הבר מצוה (in the Bible בית הלחמי), המגן דוד, הבעל קורא. Indeed, this rule is obligatory with numerals: השבע עשרה (and never שבע העשרה) and is also the case for names of books such as השולחן ערוך, הבית יוסף. Another indication found in the older sources is the addition of the plural to the *nomen rectum* בית המבשלים (Ezek. 46:24), בית פרסות (שלושה) (Oholot 8:12), similarly the addition of the feminine ending to the *nomen rectum* as in Phoenician רבת הכהנים = רבכהנת. Still these possibilities have not become integrated into literary Hebrew, though they are found in slang as the plural of טוב מאד (the grade "Excellent") = טובמאודים. There are, however, some compounds, such as ברנש: plur. ברנשים, ברווז (> בר אוז): plur. ברווזים, fem. ברווזה, which reveal this formation principle. There is, therefore, no absolute formal differentiation between a fixed compound and the construct state of two nouns.

2) Where the form of the compound is two words joined by *waw* and at times even without it, as in: דין וחשבון, משא ומתן, יום יום (יום יומי). This last is the rule in the second decade (11–19) of the numerals as שבעה עשר (but שבעה ועשרים or עשרים ושבעה!). Regarding this type there is a syntactic test which indicates if it is a compound: if the adjective and the predicate are in the singular: המשא ו(ה)מתן נמשך, דין וחשבון מקיף. Already in the medieval Hebrew grammars we find עמם מסורה (segol =) שלש נקודות.

3) Another type is the compound of noun with an adjective as קרן־הקיימת, לבד(ה)גס, יום טוב, לשון (ה)רע. Here a possible formal test is the use of the article with the second word only.

In short, there is in Hebrew a basis for compound words becoming fixed lexical units, but the limits of the construction are not sharp. It is not difficult, therefore, to include in this category the formation which some see as second derivatives: such as בין לאומי. Since the two qualities which are commonly used to distinguish it from a compound, (a) the order in agreement with English and (b) the definite article being placed normally before the first term as הדו־תנועה (the "deviate" form due to hyper-correction דו־התנועה is also heard!), are not unique to this formation at all. It must also be noted that while in English most of the prefixes are not independent words the situation in Hebrew is the opposite. Only very few elements, foreign or loan words like ארכי, אנטי, do not function as independent words. The fact that most of the compounds have the relation suffix ־ִי, that is, they are used as adjectives, is a statistical fact, but is not grammatically meaningful, since forms which do not serve as adjectives such as תת־לשון (hypoglossus), תת־תזונה (undernutrition), are also found, though not as frequently.

In the discussion of compounds two types should not be excluded: (1) the derivation of words from commonly used abbreviations, עכו"ם (עובד כוכבים ומזלות) and thus עכומי; סכו"ם (= סכין כף ומזלג); להד"ם (לא היו דברים מעולם) and thus להדמי (a word used in poetry); this form is especially common in military jargon, and mention need only be made that this was how the word סַמָּל (sergeant) was created (= סגן מחוץ למניין), and many names of weapons, as תּוֹלָר (= תותח ללא רתע); and (2) blending two elements taken from two different words and making one word out of them, as in דחפור (דחף + חפר) מדחן (=מד + חניה). Early examples are פלמני (>פלוני + אלמוני) and זוטר (>זוט + זעיר).

11. THE DECLENSION OF THE NOUN. *Gender.* In nouns as in most pronouns and most of the verbal forms there are two genders, masculine and feminine, but only the feminine is normally marked. This mark in the singular establishes the gender whereas the feminine or masculine plural marks are not decisive. There are a number of nouns both for feminine

forms of living things and inanimate objects which are feminine although they do not have the usual grammatical symbol and there are also nouns which are grammatically bisexual.

The feminine endings are

1) ָה as טובה (masc. טוב), מלכה (masc. מלך), פקידה (masc. פקיד), שומרה (masc. שומר), יולדה;

2) ֶת, ַת, as גְּבֶרֶת (<גבירְת but used as fem. of גֶּבֶר, not of גְּבִיר), שומרת (masc. שומר), נוסעת (masc. נוסע);

3) ִית as טַבָּחִית (masc. טַבָּח), עתונאית (masc. עתונאי);

4) וּת–, the abstracting formative (see no. 9) which also implies the feminine mark;

5) It is common for the ending including ת to signify the feminine and at times ת as a root consonant is so taken by the speaker, thus פת, שבת (the root is פתת and the pattern is *pi/aʿl*) are feminine, and on the other hand the ending וּת- was not considered, especially in medieval Hebrew, a feminine mark.

All these suffixes are derived under different conditions from the primitive ending *-at* which still exist in the inflected forms. There are feminine nouns which do not have a feminine suffix such as אֶרֶץ, גֶּפֶן, בְּאֵר, אֶצְבַּע, עַיִן, יָד, שֵׁן, אָתוֹן, רָחֵל, עֵז, אֵם, and especially geographical names like לונדון, מצרים, בני־ברק, תל־אביב, ירושלים. There are even nouns which are used both as masculine and feminine like כּוֹס, לָשׁוֹן, שֶׁמֶשׁ, דֶּרֶךְ. In the course of time some nouns changed gender; an example is שדה which is masculine in biblical Hebrew and (commonly) today, but is feminine in tannaitic Hebrew. In some nouns which do not have a feminine ending there are even today ambivalences regarding the gender: the word שלד is feminine in literary language and masculine in the spoken, while the opposite is true regarding גֶּרֶב. Feminine nouns with no feminine symbol are a reflection of the division in the very early (prehistoric) period of Hebrew, when the criterion of sex was not the determining factor which was a different scale of values, probably one with many grades.

Number. There are three numbers: singular, dual, and plural, but the dual is found only in nouns. Only the dual and plural are marked by special suffixes indicating their number. The suffixes are:

ִים (ִין) for plural: generally used with nouns without the feminine suffix such as מלכים (sing. מלך), נופים (sing. נוף) but it is sometimes also found in nouns with the feminine ending such as: שָׁנִים (sing. שָׁנָה), תְּאֵנִים (sing. תְּאֵנָה), שְׂעוֹרִים (sing. שְׂעוֹרָה). The suffix ִין, very common in talmudic and rabbinic literature, is also found elsewhere, but is uncommon in simple language. In that literature the suffix ים (ין) appears with nouns that have a feminine ending such as שמיטין (sing. שמיטה) more so than in present-day literature.

ָות, ־אוֹת (ָיוֹת) for plural: is used generally with names that have a feminine ending but is also found with masculine nouns (and so used is considered florid) and so there is not only מְלָכוֹת (sing. מלכה), חידות (sing. חִידָה) but also קוֹלוֹת (sing. קוֹל), אָבוֹת (sing. אב), חובות, which only the context can indicate if it is the plural of חובה or of חוב. It should be noted that many nouns can be made plural in two ways, such as מדרשים, מדרשות. At times homonyms are differentiated by their plural forms as עֶצֶם: עֲצָמִים (substance), עצמוֹת (bones). The suffixes ָאוֹת (ָיוֹת) have been used since tannaitic times and are common in words dating from then. However, they are also used in new words (by analogy or to simplify the declension) and so we find not only the old words פרפראות (sing. פרפרת), מקואות (sing. מקוה), תיאטראות (sing, תיאטרון), מרחצאות (sing. מרחץ) but also the new גְּמְלָאוֹת (sing. גמלה), אוניברסיטאות (sing. אוניברסיטה), פקולטאות (sing. פקולטה).

ַיִם originally indicated duality, as in יָדַיִם, שְׂפָתַיִם, כְּנָפַיִם, רַגְלַיִם but those nouns which have this suffix maintain it even for the ordinary plural such as ארבע ידַיִם, שש כנָפַיִם. However, the function of this suffix to indicate the dual exclusively is retained in several nouns as we see from שלש שנים/שנתַיִם, ארבע פעמִים/פעמַיִם, and חמשה שבועות/שבועַיִם. Similarly there is a difference between גלגלַיִם (a tool) and שלשה גַּלְגַּלִּים, as there is between אוֹפַנַּיִם (an apparatus) and אוֹפַנִּים, among others. This suffix is very productive in technical nomenclature. Basically the suffix ַיִם is added to the singular noun (in its inflected form) as רֶגֶל: רַגְלַיִם, שָׁנָה: שְׁנָתַיִם, but at times it is added to the plural form of the noun as in דּוֹר: דּוֹרוֹתַיִם.

In addition to the numbers mentioned above, there is in Hebrew a list of collective nouns and abstract nouns which appear with all of the suffixes mentioned but do not have a singular form (*pluralia tantum*), such as קִדּוּשִׁים, בְּתוּלִים, נְעוּרִים (the singular קדוש has a different meaning), גירושין (sing. גירוש has a different meaning), שָׁמַיִם, מַיִם, פיפיות, כְּלוּלוֹת, מִפְּרְסָמוֹת.

State. Every noun can appear in one of three states: absolute, construct, and with pronominal suffixes. Everything stated above regarding the gender and number refers to the absolute state. From the morphologic point of view the absolute includes nouns with a preposition or article (היום, למחר) since these only affect their syntax and not their form (their vocalism is not influenced). When the noun is in the construct or has pronominal suffixes its form usually changes; the feminine ending ָה changes to ַת and ִים(ִין), ַיִם to ֵי (the plural and dual are the same). Only a relatively small number of nouns do not change in declension (that is when in construct or with pronominal suffixes) while the majority change in accordance with the rules for vowel changes (See Phonology, 15. The Diphthongs and 16. The Interchange and Elision of Vowels). There is no fixed system in the grammar books to arrange the different ways of declining the nouns into a set number of classes as is the case for Greek or Latin. But at least 11 declensions can be identified and some scholars determine 14. A description of their qualities has no place in this review but belongs in a grammar.

Often the form of the noun in construct is the same as its form with pronominal suffixes as in דבר: דְּבַר־הנביא, דְּבַרְכֶם and שמחות: שמחות־הילדים, שמחותינו but at times it is the same as the absolute form as in כֶּלֶב: כֶּלֶב־בית, כַּלְבִּי and שׁוֹמֶרֶת: שׁוֹמֶרֶת־לילה, שׁוֹמַרְתֵּנוּ. The pronoun which is added to the noun expresses the concept of ownership – in its widest sense – relative to the subject of the pronoun. The form of the pronoun differs when in the singular, the plural, or the dual. This feature is not logical since the subject of the pronoun does not change if the noun is plural. It is the result of internal phonetic development and metanalysis (part of the noun in masculine plural is merged together with the pronoun), and is not paralleled in classical Arabic or in ancient Aramaic (in later Aramaic a similar situation developed); in biblical Hebrew there are still remnants of the early situation (אֲבוֹתֵיהֶם = אֲבוֹתָם). Following is the list of pronouns with examples of the declension of the noun קול.

Pronominal Suffix

Singular Noun

־ִי	my voice קוֹלִי	1st Person Sing.
־ְךָ	your voice קוֹלְךָ	2nd Person Sing. Masc.
־ֵךְ	your voice קוֹלֵךְ	2nd Person Sing. Fem.
־וֹ	his voice קוֹלוֹ	3rd Person Sing. Masc.
־ָהּ	her voice קוֹלָהּ	3rd Person Sing. Fem.
־ֵנוּ	our voice קוֹלֵנוּ	1st Person Plural
־כֶם	your voice קוֹלְכֶם	2nd Person Plural Masc.
־כֶן	your voice קוֹלְכֶן	2nd Person Plural Fem.
־ָם	their voice קוֹלָם	3rd Person Plural Masc.
־ָן	their voice קוֹלָן	3rd Person Plural Fem.

Plural Noun

־ַי	my voices קוֹלוֹתַי	1st Person Sing.
־ֶיךָ	your voices קוֹלוֹתֶיךָ	2nd Person Sing. Masc.
־ַיִךְ	your voices קוֹלוֹתַיִךְ	2nd Person Sing. Fem.
־ָיו	his voices קוֹלוֹתָיו	3rd Person Sing. Masc.
־ֶיהָ	her voices קוֹלוֹתֶיהָ	3rd Person Sing. Fem.
־ֵינוּ	our voices קוֹלוֹתֵינוּ	1st Person Plural
־ֵיכֶם	your voices קוֹלוֹתֵיכֶם	2nd Person Plural Masc.
־ֵיכֶן	your voices קוֹלוֹתֵיכֶן	2nd Person Plural Fem.
־ֵיהֶם	their voices קוֹלוֹתֵיהֶם	3rd Person Plural Masc.
־ֵיהֶן	their voices קוֹלוֹתֵיהֶן	3rd Person Plural Fem.

These are the standard forms of the pronouns, but in poetry and in flowery style in general there are several variations found, especially in biblical Hebrew. The above pronouns are used also with the prepositions such as עם, את, מן, על; some with the pronominal suffixes usual for the singular nouns (as אִתּוֹ, עִמִּי) and some with those used for the plural noun (as תחתיו, עָלַי). It should be noted that in prepositions ־ְךָ as opposed to ־ְךָ in nouns is found (לְךָ, עִמְּךָ) and ־ָנוּ in place of ־ֵנוּ; this latter being also used in the noun כל to form כֻּלָּנוּ.

Besides this, the synthetic, method for indicating possession, there exists an analytic method, by the use of the word של. Expressions such as קוֹלִי, קוֹלָם and הקול שלי, הקול שלהם, are of equal value. For this reason there are those who call של a "separated pronoun." Actually, however, this is a syntactic method, since של originates (already in the earliest stages of the language) from the relative clause in which the relative particle is attached to the preposition. Thus the expression הקול שלי is to be analyzed as "the voice which I have" exactly the same as הקול שצועק "the voice which is crying," and in certain instances the preposition ב fills the same function as the preposition ל, for example הַפַּחַד שֶׁבִּי = הפחד שֶׁלִּי = פַּחְדִּי, but the compound... של, since it is so common, became one word parallel to a pronoun and competed with the pronoun successfully in common speech and in those cases where there is a morphological difficulty in declining the noun (as in foreign words or words with the definite article, which cannot be joined to a pronoun) and personal names or where there is a semantic difficulty. Fundamentally, the preference for one way over the other is a matter of style and not of grammar.

12. PRONOUNS. *Personal Pronouns.* When the person is not expressed through pronouns which are attached to the noun (see section 11. Declension of Nouns) or the verbs (see section 20. Inflection of Objective Pronouns), they are independent words whose forms are as follows:

Singular		**Plural**
אני, אנוכי	1st Person	אנחנו, אנו
אתה	2nd Person Masc.	אתם
את	2nd Person Fem.	אתן
הוא	3rd Person Masc.	הם, המה
היא	3rd Person Fem.	הן, הנה

There are also several variations in form and usage in the ancient language which are no longer used. The first person singular אנוכי whose use declined and completely disappeared by the end of the biblical period, is now found in modern Hebrew not only in poetry but also in general use, for emphasis. The pronouns הֵמָּה and הֵנָּה are considered archaic forms, and are only used in poetic writing. These personal pronouns are used only as subjects in the sentence; the pronominal object is expressed by the pronominal element suffixed to the verb or the preposition, or to the word אות (absolute אֶת) as אוֹתְךָ, אוֹתָם. It should be noted that the double forms for first person in singular and plural, is a distinctive feature of Hebrew among the other Semitic languages, and only in Ugaritic is there a duplication in the first person singular pronoun.

Demonstrative Pronouns. These pronouns are used to indicate something before the speaker, whether close-by or far off (deictic use), or something which has already been mentioned in the discussion (anaphorically). Today the distinction between the near and far demonstrative is more precise then it was in the ancient language. For that which is near, זה (masc.), זו ,זאת (fem.) = this (sing.) and אלו ,אלה ,הללו (poetry also אל(ה)) = these (pl.); for that which is far: ההוא (masc.), ההיא (fem.), הַלָּזֶה ,הַלָּה (masc.), הַלָּז (masc. and fem.), הַלֵּזוּ (fem.) = that (sing.), and ההם (masc.) ההן (fem.) = those (pl.). אותו, אותה, אותם, אותן can be substituted for the above but also express intense identification, "that same." The fact that in the past there was no differentiation between near and far, is seen from expressions like זה לזה and מזה ומזה (not: מזה ומההוא, זה לההוא). In certain instances the demonstrative force of the definite article has been maintained, as in היום, הלילה and in literary style it is used more frequently not only in these fixed forms. The use of the definite article in a direct address as: !הדוד is basically demonstrative. The third person singular pronoun is used as a demonstrative in expressions such as הוא שאמרתי: "that is what I said" and היא שעמדה לאבותינו: "it is that which stood for our fathers." When compounded with the interrogative pronoun like מי זה, מה זה, or such words as עתה זה the demonstrative force of the pronoun is weakened and it becomes an element of the emphasis.

Interrogative Pronouns. מי = "who," מה = "what," are not declinable, nor are איזה, איזו, אלו (אי) = "which." There is a variation of מַה: מֶה the use of which is subject to the same rules as the definite article, but which is found unconditionally with the interrogative pronoun בַּמֶּה. איזה is actually the demonstrative, with the addition of the interrogative אי, found also in the words איפה, איכן (= היכן). In plural the forms אי אלה, אי אלו were shortened for phonetic reasons to אילו(ה) and became identical to the demonstrative. Due to ambiguity the singular forms איזה and איזו are also commonly used in the plural (איזה אנשים היו שם) and it should be noted that the demonstrative element זה which can come to strengthen the interrogative מי as stated above, appears in tannaitic literature also with איזה as: ?אי זו? איזו זה and this is positive evidence for the crystallization of the compound איזה (which appears in the Bible as two words, and in which זה is used to strengthen the interrogative אי), into the interrogative pronoun.

Indefinite Pronouns. Except for the words פלוני (פלונית) אלמוני (אלמונים, אלמונית) ="somebody" and כלום, מאומה "nothing, something," there are no special words in Hebrew to express indefiniteness, and the interrogative words are used for that purpose as in מי לחיים, מי למות = "some for life – some for death," דבר־מה = "something" and especially in relative expressions such as עשה מי שעשה = "somebody did it." The words איש, אדם (בן) are also used to indicate the indefinite as is the pronoun אתה. (The indefiniteness of the subject is often indicated by use of the plural verb without a pronoun, as in: בעבר עשו את הדבר כך וכך היום עושים בדרך אחרת = "in the past they used to do it so; nowadays they do it differently.")

Relative Pronouns. The relative in as far as it is expressed syndetically (cf. Syntax) is made up of אשר or ש plus the pronoun (generally the personal pronoun) but in certain syntactic situations the pronoun is not explicitly stated: האיש שיושב (= האיש שהוא יושב), "the man who is sitting," המקום שהייתי (= המקום שהייתי בו), "the place in which I was." In verbal sentences the relative is ש, אשר, while in nominal sentences the definite article has that function, as in האיש היושב = האיש אשר יושב (in biblical Hebrew the demonstrative is also used in this way (cf. Job 19:19) as is the definite article before the verb as in ההרימו (Ezra 8:25). A relative pronoun can be a subject or an object and come directly after a preposition as: את שראה "whom he saw," לשכמותו = "to one such as him," לשעבר = "in the past," על ידי שנתן = "by his having given," but generally the use of correlatives is preferred, as: על ידי העובדה שנתן, על ידי כך שנתן, לאיש כמותו, את מי שראה. Sophisticated style prefers to forego the use of the modern correlatives such as עובדה and כך.

Reflexive and Reciprocal Pronouns. Reflexivity can be expressed synthetically, by verbal conjugations or analytically; since the tannaitic period the analytic method is preferred over the synthetic. In this construction the possessive pronoun suffixed to the prepositions is used, עשיתי דבר זה בי ולא בו = "I did it to myself and not to him"; הוא ניסה את הנסיון עליו ולא על חברו = "he experimented on himself and not on his friend," or suffixed to certain nouns such as the limbs of the body, ראש (דמו בראשו = "his blood is on his head"; "it's his own fault"), נפש (שומר נפשו = "he looks after himself"), גוף (הוא גופו אמר לי = "he himself said to me") and others especially with the noun עצם: איבד עצמו לדעת ("he deliberately destroyed himself" – suicide), בא בעצמו ("he himself came"), etc. The noun איל, as in מאליו, מאליהם, is also used in this way. From this last noun Aramaic produced the word ממילא, which was borrowed in Hebrew, and is a word whose sole purpose is to express reflexivity.

In early Hebrew reciprocity was also expressed synthetically, as נדברו = "they spoke with each other," התראו = "they saw each other," שניהם מצטרפים = "they join each other," but in the post-biblical period this method was abandoned and reciprocity was expressed analytically by repeating the demonstrative, as זה לזה, זה עם זה, or by expressions like, איש... חברו, איש... רעהו, אישה... אחותה; e.g., דברו איש אל רעהו, דברו זה עם זה, etc.

This review of the various pronouns indicates that this part of speech in Hebrew has unique aspects not only from the formal point of view (one and two consonant roots; no differentiation of gender and number as in מי and איזה) but also in function, i.e., the lack of clear demarcation between demonstratives, relatives, interrogatives, and indefinitives. In other words even in modern Hebrew the early situation is clearly reflected; one pronoun can be used freely for all the above functions. The differentiation of function (which is not new) is the result of a long process and can be compared to the exchange, in Hebrew, of paratactic structures, common in ancient Hebrew, for hypotactic structures using well-defined conjunctions for different purposes.

13. PARTICLES. In this category are to be classified all those words which are not nouns or verbs and whose common function is to indicate grammatical relationships. There are the following types:

Prepositions. Prepositions, which appear only with nouns, such as ב (in), ל (to), על (on), מן (from), על־פי (by).

Adverbs. Adverbs such as מאוד, במאוד (very), חנם (gratis), ישירות (directly), בעקיפין (indirectly), לא (not), אמנם (certainly).

(The term adverb, however, does not accurately describe the situation in a language like Hebrew since this type of word can qualify a noun as well, גדול מאוד = "very big," גבור מאוד = "very strong," or זה אמנם שלחן = "this (is) surely a table.")

Conjunctions. Conjunctions which join words and sentences such as ו, אף, גם, and those which join only sentences like אם, כי, ...מפני ש, ...בשביל ש, (ש) עד. The examples indicate that different layers are immediately recognizable. Primary words (i.e., whose origin is not obvious) such as: בוכ"ל which exist as proclitics, לא, אם; words whose origin is obvious, such as חנם (< חן), בעקיפין, and words which are derived from sentences, such as כיצד, whose original form כאיזה צד is still found, יען (shortened imperfect form from יענה). Synchronically, two kinds can be recognized: (a) those which formally behave like nouns – having suffixed pronouns (על פיו, לו, בי) – and those which do not behave like nouns or verbs, and (b) those which are syntactically nouns and can serve as the predicate of a nominal sentence, such as ראובן פה, דבר זה כיצד? and those which are unable to be used in this way (conjunctions). The above examples indicate how easy it is to form prepositions in Hebrew, and in fact the development in this area is great (many examples being influenced by foreign constructions), as in: ...הודות ל (older: בזכות, בגלל), ...בהתאם ל (older: לפי), למרות (older: עם, ...עם ש), which are considered less elegant than the older forms. Actually every noun can be used as an adverb, the criterion for the noun being not morphological but its syntactic use. In the sentence בשוגג ראובן עשה דבר זה ("Reuben did this thing unwittingly"), the word בשוגג can mean "as an unwitting person," but in שרה עשתה דבר זה בשוגג ("Sarah did this thing unwittingly"), it must be an adverb because there is no accord in gender between שוגג and שרה. So, too ראובן עשה ביודעים as opposed to עשה ביודע. The limited ability of the language to express adverbs as a special formal category is compensated by the syntactic devices mentioned as well as others.

14. NUMERALS. The numeral in Hebrew is a unique phenomenon and extremely complicated, both morphologically and syntactically. In part there are parallels in the other Semitic languages, and it is presumably a common residue from proto-Semitic. The numerals are expressed in Hebrew (a) by words which indicate units אֶחָד (1), שְׁנַיִם (2), שָׁלוֹשׁ (3), אַרְבַּע (4), חמש (5), שש (6), שבע (7), שמונה (8), תשע (9), עשר (10); (b) by the suffix ים– which is added to the numerals שלוש־תשע (30 = שלשים, 90 = תשעים) and עשר (20 = עשרים) and; (c) by the words 100 = מאה, 1000 = אלף, 10,000 = רבוא (archaic form and rarely used today). These basic words are compounded in different ways and from them are derived the various forms for particular use. There are different forms for the cardinal numerals, ordinal numerals, and fractions, but the ordinals and fractions exist only for the first ten, and must be expressed syntactically for the rest of the numerals.

Cardinal Numbers. There are two forms, the masculine: אחד, שנים, שלש, ...ארבע, and the feminine: אחת (אחד+ת), שתים (< שְׁנְתַּיִם), שלשה, ...ארבעה, but it is exceedingly strange that in Hebrew, as in Semitic languages in general (for a discussion see Robert Hetzron, *Journal of Semitic Studies*, 12 (1967), 180 ff.), there is no syntactic agreement between the cardinals (and any derived numerals) from 3–10 and their referents; the masculine numeral is used as an adjective or predicate for a feminine noun and the feminine numeral for a masculine noun; as in שלשה בנים (or בנים שלושה), שלש בנות (בנות שלש). When the object counted is not referred to, the masculine or feminine numerals can be used. The numerals 1–10, 100, 1000 have both absolute and construct forms, but are used with the counted object in either form, not according to any grammatical rule, as in: שלושה אנשים, שלושת אנשים, עשרה אלפים, עשרת אלפים אנשים, אלפי אנשים. The feminine construct form is also commonly used in the first decade for feminine nouns as in שלושת נשים, which is always the case with pronouns, and so not only שְׁלָשְׁתָּם but also שְׁלָשְׁתָּן (not, שלשן!). Pronominal suffixes are not used with the numerals 11–99; only in the early literature do we find חֲמִשֶּׁיהֶם (II Kings 1:14). On the other hand, pronominal suffixes are used for 100 and 1000 as in באלפיהם, במאתנו ("in our century") as is the dual and plural. For the second decade of numerals two constructions are used; construct in the feminine numeral as שלוש עשרה, and the connection of the two terms without the *waw* in the masculine numeral as שלושה עשר (cf. no. 10). Note, too, that the second part of the numeral in the second decade has a different form than it has in the first decade, thus: עָשָׂר (not עֶשֶׂר) masc., עֶשְׂרֵה (not עֲשָׂרָה) fem. For 20–90 the connection with *waw* is common today as: עשרים ושלשה with the ten first followed by the unit but also the reverse order שלשה ועשרים which was common in different periods, and is not very uncommon in literature. However, in the second decade such a construction is considered exceptional (cf. Ez. 45:12 חמשה ועשרים שקלים, עשרה וחמשה שקל; it is the rule in the Aramaic of Elephantine), just as the compound by construct in the masculine חֲמֵשֶׁת עָשָׂר אֶלֶף (Judg. 8:10) or שְׁמֹנַת עָשָׂר אֶלֶף (Judg. 20:25) would be considered exceptional today.

Numerals from 2–10 demand plural nouns only (חמישה איש for example, is considered to be incorrect), from ten upward the noun can be either singular or plural (שלשים איש, שלשים אנשים) and it should be noted that the Academy of the Hebrew Language has suggested that the plural be used to prevent mistakes in the first decade as mentioned above. Combinations of numbers above 100 can be made in different forms (in addition to the possibility of a different order for the tens and units as pointed out above). 3755 can be שלושת אלפים ושבע מאות וחמשים וחמישה or שלשת אלפים שבע מאות חמשים וחמישה or שלשת אלפים שבע מאות וחמשים וחמישה. The last seems to be the most common. It should be noted that a number like 3715 is rendered generally שלשת אלפים שבע מאות וחמשה עשר so that the ו is in the last possible place in the compound.

Ordinal Numbers. There are two types: masculine and feminine. From 3–10 its form appears to be derived from a basic element whose pattern is *paʿil*, as שלישי, רביעי, חמישית, etc. For 1 both the numeral ראשון (from ראש) and אחד serve. The fact that the number "one" has an ordinal form which is not connected etymologically to the cardinals is common to other Semitic languages. From 11 on the ordinal does not have an independent form and the cardinal fulfills that function also: הבית העשרים וחמישה, השנה השלוש עשרה. The common use of the singular of the ordinal (from the third ten and up) הבית העשרים וחמישי (as in Arabic) is considered incorrect. Ordinality can also be syntactically expressed, by using the cardinal as a *nomen rectum* in the construct state: השנה העשרים וחמש = שנת עשרים וחמש, שנה חמישית = שנת חמש. Just as in the construct the numeral is always the *nomen rectum* so when it is an adjective it also comes after the noun, as, האיש השלישי and not the opposite.

Fractions. For ½ the noun חצי is usually used. But, מחצה, מחצית, are also used; for ⅓, ¼, ⅕ on, the feminine ordinal form שלישית, רביעית, חמישית is used, but שליש, רביע or רבע (also רֹבע), חֹמש are also possible. From ⅙ to ⅒ only the form with ־ִית is used. Note that while the suffixes ־ית, ־יה are elsewhere similar in origin and function (cf. section 9. Suffixes), in the numerals there is a differentiation: עשירית = ⅒, עשיריה = group of ten, חמישית = ⅕, חמישיה = a group of 5.

Multiples. Multiples are often expressed by ־ַיִם; שבעתיים = ×7 (not 7×2).

Distributives. Expressed by repeating the number as in שנים שנים.

In summation it may be said that there is nothing in Hebrew morphology to compare with the numeral for different forms and types of usages and syntax, and that the numeral best reflects the special nature of Hebrew morphology which includes, side by side, the very old with the new. "The uniqueness of Hebrew in our day and the source of its problems is that nothing in it has died and so there exist – and are in use – different chronological layers side by side, not on top of one another as in languages with a historic continuity" (Z. Ben-Ḥayyim, "An Ancient Language in a New Reality," *Lešonenu La'am*, Jerusalem, 1953, 43–44).

[Zeev Ben-Hayyim]

Verb Formation

15. WHAT IS TO BE CLASSED AS THE VERB. The verb, a part of speech easily identifiable according to all theories and in all languages (including, of course, Hebrew), can be characterized from three points of view: semantically, the verb denotes an action or a change of state or the existence of a state; morphologically, it is usually accompanied by an indication of its grammatical subject, whether as a separate word or as an affix or as both; and syntactically, it functions as the main part of the predicate (see Syntax).

Forms of the Hebrew verb that never (or only sometimes) include an explicit reference to the subject, such as the infinitives and the verbal noun, are considered borderline cases between verb and noun. There are two extreme views on what is to be included in the paradigm of a Hebrew verb. According to one view, the paradigm comprises only such forms as distinguish persons and tenses, and hence each בִּנְיָן ("conjugation") is taken to be a separate verb. For others, however, the paradigm of the verb includes also the conjugations, which are regarded as belonging to one verb if they have a common root. There are also some who treat two or more of the conjugations (but not all) as part of the same paradigm, for example פִּעֵל – פֻּעַל – הִתְפַּעֵל or פָּעַל – נִפְעַל. The best English translation for בִּנְיָן would be "verb pattern," not "conjugation." The latter term is however kept in the following, since it is commonly used in English works dealing with Hebrew morphology.

16. THE CONJUGATIONS. The verb paradigms are treated almost identically in all accounts, whether traditional or modern, scholarly or pedagogic. There is unanimity on the existence of seven principal conjugations, to which most verbs are related, and also of certain other patterns that have only rare and partial exemplification.

The most acceptable names for the conjugations are based on the form of the third person singular masculine past of a regular root, i.e., of a root having all its consonants in all forms of the paradigm. From the very beginning of Hebrew grammar in the Middle Ages the root פ'ע'ל' has been used for this purpose, under the influence of Arabic grammar. Accordingly, the names of the conjugations are פָּעַל, נִפְעַל, פִּעֵל, פֻּעַל, הִתְפַּעֵל, הִפְעִיל, הָפְעַל (or הֻפְעַל). However, because of the peculiarity of the consonant ע in Hebrew (see Phonology 6), this root has disadvantages which do not apply to the corresponding root in Arabic:

(1) ע cannot be doubled and therefore the names of the conjugations פִּעֵל, פֻּעַל, הִתְפַּעֵל lack the principal formal characteristics of these conjugations, namely, the doubling of the middle radical, e.g., ב in דִּבֵּר (*dibber*), ל in שֻׁלַּח (*šullaḥ*), ג in הִתְרַגֵּל (*hitraggel*).

(2) When the ע is the first in a consonantal cluster, it is separated from the following consonant by a semi-vowel חטף (see above, §13), i.e., *ă*, *ĕ*, or *ŏ*. This type of vowel is not found, however, in corresponding verbs that do not have ע in that position. Contrast דָּרְשׁוּ (*darĕšu*) with פָּעֲלוּ (*paʿălu*), גְּדִי (*gĕdi*) with עֲדִי (*ʿădi*).

(3) The ע generally does not close a non-final syllable. When it does according to its pattern, it must be followed by a חטף. Contrast שִׁמְרִי (*šimri*) with גַּעֲרִי (*gaʿări*).

(4) The ע sometimes causes changes in preceding vowels, as in the last example (see below §22).

In the 19th century, scholars began to look for another root that would serve to denote the conjugations and decided on ק'ט'ל'. This root has two advantages:

(1) none of its consonants has any peculiarities; and

(2) it is found (sometimes in certain variations) in almost all Semitic languages. On the other hand, Hebrew grammarians have pointed out that this root had a serious disadvantage from the educational point of view: its meaning ("to kill") is unpleasant.

Recently, it has been recognized that it is in fact possible to use the root פ'ע'ל', provided that it is transcribed phonemically without reference to the phonetic properties of the ע. For this purpose, we have repeated (i.e., doubled) the consonant in the Hebrew representation as well as in the transcription. The names of the seven conjugations, according to this approach are: *paʿal* (פָּעַל), *nipʿal* (נִפְעַל), *piʿʿel* (פִּעֵעל), *puʿʿal* (פֻּעֲעל), *hitpaʿʿel* (הִתְפַּעֲעל), *hipʿil* (הִפְעִיל), *hupʿal* (הֻפְעַל). Since the transcription in Latin symbols is phonemic and not phonetic, the פ is always symbolized by /p/, even when phonetically it has the value [f]; likewise there is no need to distinguish between פַּתַח and קָמָץ, both being symbolized by /a/.

Other names have been proposed for the conjugations, which identify them semantically (see below), in particular קַל ("light") and כָּבֵד ("heavy"). Originally, these names covered all seven conjugations: קַל for פָּעַל and נִפְעַל; כָּבֵד for פִּעֵל, פֻּעַל, and הִתְפַּעֵל and כָּבֵד נוֹסָף ("supplemented heavy") or גּוֹרֵם ("causative") for הִפְעִיל and הֻפְעַל. However, the original application was later forgotten. In popular usage and in most textbooks, קַל alone has been retained, but it is restricted to the פָּעַל conjugation. Occasionally, הַבִּנְיָן הַגּוֹרֵם ("the causative conjugation") is used for הִפְעִיל and הַבִּנְיָן הַכָּבֵד ("the heavy conjugation") for פִּעֵל. The decision whether or not conjugations with a common root are to be treated as part of the same verb has great practical significance, not only grammatically but also lexicographically. Dictionaries of modern Hebrew list nouns according to their initial consonants, disregarding whether the consonants are radicals or not, so that, e.g., מִקְרָא appears under מ and תִּלְבֹּשֶׁת under ת. However, many follow the practice of dictionaries of biblical Hebrew in listing verbs, regardless of conjugation, according to the first radical, e.g., הִלְבִּישׁ under ל next to לָבַשׁ, and נִכְנַס under כ, next to כָּנַס, and sometimes, in the same way, even verbs without a corresponding form in פָּעַל, e.g., הִתְכּוֹנֵן under כ, because of its root כ'ו'נ'. Some modern popular dictionaries, on the other hand, enter the form of the third person masculine singular past for each conjugation, e.g., הִתְרוֹמֵם under ה and נִכְנַס under נ, thus following (though probably unconsciously) the view that verbs from the same root in different conjugations are to be treated as independent verbs. (For the advantages of this view for grammar and semantics, see below.)

17. A CONSIDERATION OF EARLIER VIEWS ON THE RELATIONSHIP BETWEEN THE CONJUGATIONS. Those adopting the view (traditional for all Semitic languages) that conjugations of verbs from the same root constitute one paradigm must consider the semantic relationship between the various conjugations. In the extreme formulation of this view, every conjugation is said to have a particular meaning in relation to the "basic form" of the verb, the form פָּעַל. An attempt along these lines has been made, in particular, for biblical Hebrew (see Biblical Hebrew 9). It has resulted in the fabrication of imaginary forms that do not appear in the Bible, and also in the neglect of some forms that do, for example, the נִפְעַל conjugation.

A similar, though less extreme, position is generally taken in textbooks. These also treat the פָּעַל conjugation as the basic form, said to be semantically "simple," but they attempt to establish a semantic relationship for each root between the פָּעַל conjugation and other conjugations, it being assumed that each of these makes some addition to the basic meaning of the פָּעַל. The principal additional meanings, expressed synthetically by a change in the form of the verb, are said to be passive, reflexive, reciprocal, strengthening, durative, iterative, causative, change in state, declarative, and deprivative. Thus, for example, the נִפְעַל is said to express the passive when the active agent is found with the פָּעַל, e.g., שָׁבַר ("he broke") – נִשְׁבַּר ("it was broken") or הִפְעִיל, e.g., הִרְגִּיעַ ("he soothed") – נִרְגַּע ("he was soothed"); reflexive, e.g., נִשְׁמַר, נִזְהַר ("he took care of himself"); or reciprocal, e.g., נִדְבְּרוּ ("they spoke to one another"). The פִּעֵל is said to express the strengthening, e.g., שָׁבַר ("he broke") – שִׁבֵּר ("he smashed"); the durative, e.g., רָקַד ("he danced") – רִקֵּד ("he danced for a long time"); repetitive, e.g., קָבַר ("he buried") – קִבֵּר ("he buried many"); causative, e.g., לָמַד ("he learned") – לִמֵּד ("he taught"); or deprivative, e.g., שֵׁרֵשׁ ("he uprooted"). The פֻּעַל is said to be the passive equivalent of verbs with the same root in פִּעֵל. The הִתְפַּעֵל is explained as denoting the reflexive, e.g., הִתְרַחֵץ ("he washed himself"); reciprocal, e.g., הִתְלַחֲשׁוּ ("they whispered to each other"); passive chiefly when the active is in the פִּעֵל, e.g., בִּשֵּׁל ("he cooked") – הִתְבַּשֵּׁל ("it was cooked"); or strengthening, e.g., הִתְנַשֵּׁם ("he breathed strongly"). The הִפְעִיל is said to denote the causative, chiefly when the active is in the פָּעַל, e.g., מָלַךְ ("he reigned") – הִמְלִיךְ ("he made [him] a king"), and consequently changes the verb from intransitive to transitive, e.g., יָשַׁב ("he sat") – הוֹשִׁיב ("he caused to sit," "he set"), or from unitransitive to ditransitive, e.g., אָכַל ("he ate") – הֶאֱכִיל ("he fed"); a change of state, e.g., הֶעֱשִׁיר ("he became rich"), especially a change of color, e.g., הִלְבִּין ("it became white"); or declarative, e.g., צַדִּיק ("righteous") – הִצְדִּיק ("he declared as righteous," "he justified"). The הֻפְעַל is considered the passive equivalent of the הִפְעִיל. In addition, some verbs with a "simple" meaning like that of the פָּעַל appear in other conjugations, e.g., נִכְנַס ("he entered"), רִחֵף ("he hovered"), הִתְנַגֵּד ("he opposed"), הִמְתִּין ("he waited").

However, this view of the semantic relationships of the conjugations, with the פָּעַל taken as the basic conjugation, does not sufficiently fit the facts. Even a partial examination of Hebrew verbs shows that, except for פֻּעַל and הֻפְעַל (which almost always have a predictable relationship with פִּעֵל and הִפְעִיל respectively), we cannot automatically predict the meaning of a root in one conjugation from that of the same root in another conjugation. Though there are many instances of predictable semantic relationships between the conjugations, like those given above, in many instances verbs of the same root have no relationship at all or have an unpredictable relationship, e.g., דִּבֵּר ("he spoke") – הִדְבִּיר ("he subdued"); מָהַר ("he bought a wife") – מִהֵר ("he hastened"); בָּצַר ("he gathered grapes") – נִבְצַר ("it was withheld") – בִּצֵּר ("he fortified"); סָפַר ("he counted") – סִפֵּר ("he told") – הִסְתַּפֵּר ("he had his hair cut"); סָפַק ("he clapped hands") – סִפֵּק ("he supplied") – הִסְפִּיק ("he made enough") – הִסְתַּפֵּק ("he had sufficient"); הֶאֱמִין ("he believed") – הִתְאַמֵּן ("he trained himself"). It may well be that at an early period of the language, the conjugations constituted a paradigm of predictable semantic relationships similar to the paradigm of changes of person and tense within a conjugation, but as a consequence of the development of meanings of verbs throughout the history of the language, the conjugations cannot now be recognized as belonging to one paradigm.

Similarly, there was once a fixed semantic relationship between nouns of different patterns belonging to the same root. Indeed, even in contemporary Hebrew there are such relationships, e.g., between nouns denoting people with particular occupation such as סַפָּר ("barber") and the corresponding noun for the place of work, מִסְפָּרָה ("barber shop"). In general, new nouns have been formed in recent times on the appropriate patterns, e.g., קָטִיף ("season for picking fruit growing on trees") and תָּלִישׁ ("season for picking fruit growing on low bushes") for the seasons of agricultural work; מִרְפָּאָה ("clinic") and מִכְבָּסָה ("laundry") for places of work. Nevertheless, each noun is treated as an entirely independent noun; the semantic relationship between nouns of the same root has not resulted in their being considered one noun with various patterns.

18. THE EXTENT TO WHICH A PREDICTABLE RELATIONSHIP EXISTS BETWEEN THE CONJUGATIONS. Two forms have predictable relations when they fulfill two conditions: (1) if one of them exists, it follows that the other exists too; (2) when the meaning of one of them is known, the meaning of the other one is self-explanatory. Only forms having predictable relationships with other forms can be considered as belonging to the same paradigm, since only these can be freely used by a speaker though he has never heard them before and are unambiguous to the hearer though he has never encountered them before. For example, within one conjugation there are predictable relationships between forms varying only in person or tense, such as שָׁמַרְתִּי–שָׁמַרְתָּ–שָׁמַרְתִּי or אֶשְׁמֹר–. Similarly, the relationships between verbs in פִּעֵל and הִפְעִיל and verbs of the same root in פֻּעַל and הָפְעַל, respectively, are virtually predictable. There is not complete predictability because some intransitive verbs in פִּעֵל, e.g., טִיֵּל ("he went for a walk") and רִחֵף ("he hovered"), and in הִפְעִיל, e.g., הִסְמִיק ("he became red") and הֶחְלִיד ("he [it] became rusty") either do not have corresponding forms in פֻּעַל or הָפְעַל or, if they do, these do not express a passive meaning.

Predictable relationships between פָּעַל and נִפְעַל (with respect either to the existence of one form if the other exists or to the stipulated semantic relationship) apply only to some verbs. Thus, there is no corresponding form in the other conjugation for יָרַד ("he descended"), נִבְהַל ("he was alarmed"), or נִשְׁבַּע ("he swore"), and a predictable active-passive relationship is lacking between יָשַׁב ("he sat") – נוֹשַׁב ("it was inhabited"); כָּנַס ("he assembled") – נִכְנַס ("he entered"); or יָשַׁן ("he slept") – נוֹשַׁן ("he was old"). Even less predictable are the relationships between פָּעַל and פִּעֵל. It is impossible to know whether the change from פָּעַל to פִּעֵל will entail strengthening, lengthening, repetition, causation, or some other meaning, which might be completely different from that of פָּעַל, e.g., שִׂחֵק ("he played") – שָׂחַק ("he laughed"), חִנֵּךְ ("he educated") – חָנַךְ ("he inaugurated"), בִּשֵּׁל ("he cooked") – בָּשַׁל ("it ripened"). Moreover, there are many verbs in פִּעֵל that have no corresponding forms in פָּעַל, e.g., טִיֵּל ("he went for a walk"), זִנֵּב ("he routed the rear"), חִדֵּשׁ ("he renewed"), חִיֵּךְ ("he smiled"), צִוָּה ("he commanded").

Similarly, it is impossible to be confident that the הִפְעִיל will express the causative of the פָּעַל, since many verbs in הִפְעִיל do not have any semantic connection with the same root in the פָּעַל, or have an unpredictable relationship, e.g., יָרַק ("he spat") – הוֹרִיק ("it became green"); סָרַט ("he scratched") – הִסְרִיט ("he filmed"); רָצָה ("he wanted") – הִרְצָה ("he lectured"). Furthermore, there are some verbs in הִפְעִיל whose passive is in נִפְעַל as well as in הָפְעַל (occasionally with some difference in nuance), e.g., הִרְתִּיעַ ("he deterred") – נִרְתַּע, הִדְפִּיס ("he published") – נִדְפַּס, and these somewhat disturb the predictability in relationship between הִפְעִיל and הָפְעַל.

There is certainly no predictable relationship between פָּעַל and הִתְפַּעֵל. Not only are there two large categories of semantic relationships, exemplified, on the one hand, by רָחַץ ("he washed") – הִתְרַחֵץ ("he washed himself"), and on the other, by כָּתַב ("he wrote") – הִתְכַּתֵּב ("he had a correspondence with [someone]"), but there are also many verbs appearing in only one of these conjugations, e.g., גָּזַל ("he robbed") and הִתְקָרֵר ("he caught a cold"), or which have independent meanings in the two conjugations, e.g., סָפַר ("he counted") – הִסְתַּפֵּר ("he had his hair cut"). The semantic relationships between other conjugations, such as הִתְפַּעֵל – פִּעֵל or הִפְעִיל – פִּעֵל are also unpredictable in similar respects.

An awareness of this situation requires a consideration of the conjugations not as an inflection of one verb but as a set of different verb patterns related by derivation. The relationships between פִּעֵל and פֻּעַל and between הִפְעִיל and הָפְעַל may perhaps be an exception to this generalization.

19. THE INFLECTION OF THE VERB. The inflection of a verb includes all forms of the verb that vary in pronominal subject or object, e.g., יִשְׁמֹר ("he will guard") – יִשְׁמְרֵהוּ ("he will guard him"), gender, number, tense, and modality. In traditional literary language, modal differences are chiefly expressed synthetically in the verb itself by certain additions to the normal forms, e.g., אֶשְׁמְרָה – אֶשְׁמֹר, but sometimes auxiliary verbs have this function (see Syntax). Differences in tense include not only the distinctions between past, present, and future, but also forms having a modal character, e.g., the imperative, and those that lack a time distinction, e.g., the construct infinitive, the absolute infinitive, and the action noun. These last three can be used in nonverbal functions as well as the present form which can also function as a noun in all respects. The affixed pronominal forms, which by their characteristics and by their place in the verb determine not only the

subject and object but also the tense, are the inflectional morphemes, and are attached to the basic form, the inflectional base. The relationship between the inflectional base and the inflectional morphemes is similar to that between basic element and formative (see above 3. The Basic Element; 4. The Formative and the Morpheme), except that the combination of the latter results in a new word with a separate entry in the dictionary, since it is a derivational process and lacks the completely predictable semantic relationship of an inflectional process. In the פִּעֵל, הִפְעִיל, and הִתְפַּעֵל conjugations, the same base serves for all the tenses, but in the other conjugations different bases are used, as can be seen in the table below. The existence of more than one inflectional base in a paradigm is not unique to the conjugations: there are some noun patterns with the same feature.

Inflectional Bases in the Conjugations. (In phonemic transcription, in which *šewa* is not marked; see Phonology: 13. The *Šewa* and *Ḥaṭefs*.) (See Table: Hebrew Grammar 1.)

The same inflectional morphemes are used for the same tense in the various bases, though between base and affixed morpheme there may develop sometimes transitional phones and other phonetic phenomena that can be described precisely in a few rules. The inflectional morphemes of past and imperative are suffixes, while those of future are prefixes, except that in the second and third person plural, and in the second person feminine singular there are also suffixes identical with those of the imperative. The inflectional morphemes of the participle are those for gender and number in nouns (see 11. The Declension of the Nouns) and do not vary with change of person. In addition, the forms of the participle in all the conjugations except פָּעַל and נִפְעַל are prefixed by the morpheme *m* (sometimes a vowel is inserted after the *m*, see below). The inflectional morphemes of the construct infinitive resemble the inflectional morphemes of nouns (see above 11. The Declension of the Nouns). Every verb which can be followed by an object (usually only a direct object) can take, after the inflectional morphemes already mentioned, an additional inflectional morpheme, the objective pronoun (for details, see below 21. Inflections of Weak Verbs).

Table: Hebrew Grammar 1

	Past	Participle	Future	Imp.	Inf.
Paʿal	*šamár*	*šomér*	*šmór*		šmór
		lebéš	*lbáš*		
Nipʿal	*nišmár*		*hiššamér*		
Piʿʿel	*dibbér*		*dabbér*		
Puʿʿal		*dubbár*			
Hitpaʿʿel			*hitgabbér*		
Hipʿil	*hitḥíl*		*hatḥíl*		
Hupʿal		*huḥláṭ*			

Note: The following changes affect the inflectional base of the הִתְפַּעֵל:
(1) When the first radical is ז, ס, צ, שׂ, or שׁ it precedes the *t* (see Phonology 6, 17). This change is optional if the first radical is ד or ט.
(2) The *t* is changed to *d* after ד and ז, and to ṭ after ט and צ.

The following are the affixed pronominal inflectional morphemes denoting the subject:

To the inflectional base (= –) of the Past

Singular:	1st Person	Common	– *ti*
	2nd Person	Masculine	– *ta*
		Feminine	– *t*
	3rd Person	Masculine	– *ø*
		Feminine	– *a*
Plural:	1st Person	Common	– *nu*
	2nd Person	Masculine	– *tem*
		Feminine	– *ten*
	3rd Person	Common	– *u*

To the inflectional base (= –) of the Future

Singular:	1st Person	Common	ʾ –
	2nd Person	Masculine	*t* –
		Feminine	*t* – *i*
	3rd Person	Masculine	*y* –
		Feminine	*t* –
Plural:	1st Person	Common	*n* –
	2nd Person	Masculine	*t* – *u*
		Feminine	*(*t* – *na*)
	3rd Person	Masculine	*y* – *u*
		Feminine	*(*t* – *na*)

To the inflectional base (= –) of the Imperative

Singular:	2nd Person	Masculine	– *ø*
		Feminine	– *i*
Plural:	2nd Person	Masculine	– *u*
		Feminine	– *(*na*)

*The masculine forms of the same person are usually used instead of these. The form given in parentheses is the prevailing one in biblical Hebrew, but nowadays it is considered a possible variant only. To some extent, especially in the colloquial language, the masculine form of the second person plural in the past is also used for feminine. See also note 8 of the following section.

20. CHANGES IN THE BASE. The following rules describe the principal changes affecting the form of the verb when the inflectional morpheme is affixed to the base:

(A) Prefix.

(1) *h* at the beginning of the base is omitted after future and participle prefixes (but not when ב, כ, or ל come before the construct infinitive).

t + *hiššamér* → *thiššamér* → *tiššamer*
y + *hatḥíl* → *yatḥíl*
but *l* + *hitgabbér* → *lhitgabbér*

(2) When by adding a consonant before a base, the result is a form with a cluster of three consonants at the beginning, a vowel (generally *i*) is inserted between the first two consonants, namely between the prefix and the first conso-

nant of the base. (This is a general rule which applies to the future and infinitive of *paʿal*, as well as to many other forms, e.g., below 7).

n + šmór → nšmór → nišmór

(3) After the prefix ʾ, the vowel *e* instead of *i* is used in rule 2 and when a preceding *h* is omitted (rule 1). See also the beginning of 22. Inflections of Weak Verbs.

ʾ + šmór → ʾšmór → ʾešmór

ʾ + hitgabbér → ʾhitgabbér → ʾitgabbér → ʾetgabbér

There are a few exceptions, chiefly in biblical Hebrew, where *i* follows the prefix ʾ.

(B) Suffix.

(4) The vowel before the last consonant of the past base, whether *é* or *í*, changes to *á* before any suffix beginning with a consonant.

dibbér + ti → dibbárti; hitḥíl + ta → hitḥálta

(5) When the suffix is a vowel, the vowels *é, ó,* and *á* before the last consonant of the base generally remain only in forms used in classical Hebrew, especially at the end of a sentence. ("Pausal forms.")

huggáš + a → huggáša

hadál + i → ḥadáli

šamár + u → šamáru

However, they disappear (become *šewa*) in the regular form of the verb, when the accent is on the syllable of the suffix.

šamár + á → šamrá (or *šamᵊrá*)

dibbér + u → dibbrú (= *dibbᵊru*)

See below for some uses of pausal forms in contemporary Hebrew. However, the vowel *i* does not disappear:

hitḥíl → hitḥílu

(6) The vowel *í* in the imperative and future base of הִפְעִיל changes to *é* before the suffix *–na*.

t + hatḥil + na → tatḥélna

And in the imperative before the suffix *ø*, *í* changes to *é*:

hathíl + ø → hatḥél

(7) If through the disappearance of *é, ó,* or *á* (according to 5) a cluster of three consonants is created at the beginning of the word, a vowel is inserted between the first two (as in 2). When the third consonant is *b, k, p* – it is realized as the corresponding fricative variant, i.e., *v, x, f.*

šmór + i → šmóri → šmrí → šimrí (imperative of פָּעַל), and similarly with construct infinitive, e.g.,

l + šmór + ó → l + šmró → l + šomró → lšomró.

(8) The vowels *a* and *e* in an open syllable before the accent disappear when the accent moves to the end of the bases:

labéš + im → labešim → lbešim

šamár + tém → šamartém → šmartém

In colloquial language, the suffix – *tem* is unaccented. It is used for both masculine and feminine. Since the accent does not shift, *a* and *e* do not disappear:

šamár + tem → šamártem (col.)

(9) The vowel *é* in the last syllable of the participle base (except for the base *labéš*) disappears when a suffix beginning with a vowel is attached to the base. (Such a suffix attached to a participle, which is a nominal suffix, is always accented. But see the next rule.)

mdabbér + ím → mdabbrím

šomér + á → šomrá

(10) If the suffix *–t* (but not *–át*) is attached to the participle base as the feminine inflectional morpheme, the result is a form ending in two consonants, which is treated like the segholates (see above 6).

nišmár + t → nišmárt → nišmáret → nišméret

mdabbér + t → mdabbért → mdabbéret

Notes:

(1) The attachment of the suffix ø to the base usually does not affect the form of the base, except for phonetic changes, e.g., the change of קָמָץ to פַּתָּח in the last syllable of the base (but see rule 6, above).

šamár (= שָׁמָר) + *ø → šamár* (= שָׁמַר).

(2) The theoretical form of the base is also the form that is realized at the end of a sentence. In general, the "pausal forms" of all the persons are the forms from which it is possible to produce the regular forms by the rules of inflection detailed above. It should be further noted that some "pausal forms" are sometimes used in ordinary speech, and not necessarily at the ends of sentences, e.g., הַהַצָּעָה לֹא הוּבָנָה כָּרָאוּי, הָבוּ לָנוּ.

21. THE INFLECTION OF OBJECTIVE PRONOUNS. (1) For the objective inflection the forms of the verb containing the subjective pronoun serve as the inflectional base (see 19, 20). The inflectional morphemes denoting objective pronouns are as follows:

Singular:	1st Person	Common	*ni*
	2nd Person	Masculine	*ka*
		Feminine	*k*
	3rd Person	Masculine	*hu, w, o*
		Feminine	*ha, h*
Plural:	1st Person	Common	*nu*
	2nd Person	Masculine	*kém*
		Feminine	*kén*
	3rd Person	Masculine	*m*
		Feminine	*n*

These inflectional morphemes are, in the main, attached to all the bases of the verb, but there is not always free variation in the inflectional morphemes of the third person singular, the choice of which sometimes depends on the nature of the base. Thus, the morphemes *h* and *o* are not affixed to the base *šamárti*, and others like it. The inflectional morphemes affixed to participle bases are generally the possessive inflectional morphemes of the noun (see above, 11).

(2) Changes in the Base. These inflectional morphemes generally cause changes in the vowels of the base, because the accent of the base usually moves forward when the inflectional morpheme is attached. As a result of the movement of the accent, vowels disappear, mainly according to regular phonetic principles (see Phonology 16).

šamárti + kém → šmartikém

(see above 20, rule 8.)

šamáru + ni → šmarúní

tišmóri + m → tišmrím

(the base vowels *á, ó* disappear, see above 20. Changes in the Base, paragraph no. 5.)

A striking change in the past form ending in *tém* or *tén* is the change of this suffix to *tú* when this form serves as the base for the objective inflection.

šmartém + ni → šmartún

(3) Transitional Phones. In several bases transitional phones are created between the base and the inflectional morpheme:

(1) The vowel *í* is added to the base of the second person feminine singular past:

šamárt + hu → šmartíhu

šamárt + nu → šmartínu

(2) *t* is added to the base of the third person feminine singular past with shift of accent:

šamára + ni → šmarátni

šamára + kém → šmaratkém

(3) The vowel *á* is added to the base of the third person masculine singular past:

šamár + nu → šmaránu

šamár + m → šmáram

But before the morpheme *k* (second person feminine singular) the inserted vowel is *é*:

šamár + k → šmarék

(4) The vowel *é* is added to the future bases ending in a consonant:

tišmór + ni → tišmréni

yilbaš + m → yilbašém

The vowel *á* of the future and imperative base of *lbáš* pattern does not disappear, unlike *é* and *ó* in other future and imperative bases. (See Phonology 16:2, 4.) Contrast future bases ending in a vowel, e.g.,

tišmóri + ni → tišmríni

yišmóru + m → yišmrúm

yilbášu + n → yilbašún

The transitional vowel *á* (and sometimes *é*) is affixed to the infinitive base:

lišmór + ni → lšmoréni (cf. 20.2)

laqáḥat + m → lqaḥtám

22. INFLECTIONS OF WEAK VERBS. This concept is first discussed above in 2 (end), where it is stated that because of a phonetic characteristic of one of the radicals it may sometimes happen that two realizations of the same pattern may be different. The simplest change is that resulting from the peculiar phonetic characteristics of the gutturals א, ה, ח, and ע (see Phonology 6, Morphology 16). Their presence sometimes necessitates a vowel not found in the corresponding form without a guttural, e.g.,

yišmór/yaḥboṭ; yilbaš/yeḥdal

In these cases, the high vowel *i* is replaced by a lower vowel, *e* or *a*, next to a guttural. (See also rule 3 in 20.) In addition, between a non-final guttural and the following consonant a vowel חטף is sometimes inserted, usually corresponding to the preceding vowel, e.g., *yaḥămol, yeḥəzaq, yoʿŏmad,* but also *muʿămad.* In the case of ה, ח, and ע if as the third radical it ends the word, and there is no vowel *a* preceding it, then a preceding *a* is inserted, e.g., *niẓẓéaḥ, yaškíaḥ*. With respect to א in this situation, see below 24.4. The impossibility of doubling the gutturals and ר (Phonology 8, Morphology 16) causes changes in preceding vowels when doubling is required in corresponding forms. The changes are from short vowels to long vowels, and are known in grammar as "compensation for the *dageš*." Sometimes, the change is expressed merely orthographically, e.g., in the pattern *ydabber*:

יְפָאֵר, יְפָרֵשׁ instead of ‡יְפַאֵר, ‡יְפַרֵשׁ

but sometimes it is also audible in modern pronunciation, e.g., in the pattern *mdubbar*:

מְיֹעָר, מְגֹהָץ instead of ‡מְיֻעָר, ‡מְגֻהָץ

תֵּאֵר, פֵּרֵשׁ instead of ‡תִּאֵר, ‡פִּרֵשׁ

Apart from the gutturals and ר, there are two characteristics that cause changes in the forms:

(1) Assimilation, when one consonant completely assimilates another consonant, usually regressive assimilation.

‡yinpol → yippol; ‡yilqaḥ → yiqqaḥ

(2) Elision, when one of the radicals is א, ו, or י:

qarʾú, but *qratém*

yašanta, but *tišán* (‡ *tiyšán*)

šaléw, but *šalíti*

The conditions for these changes are that, for assimilation, the assimilated consonant be at the end of a non-final syllable, and for elision, the elided consonant be at the end of any syllable. (See below, in this connection, forms of verbs with identical second and third radicals, e.g., נסב, סב.)

23. PARADIGMS OF ASSIMILATED FORMS. Typical of paradigms of assimilated forms is the presence of duplication of consonants in the middle of the verb. These paradigms are more often known as paradigms of defective verbs. This term derives from a study of the written language, since in the Hebrew script duplication is indicated by only one letter (with a point, "*dageš forte*," inserted in it). As a result, when a consonant is assimilated to its neighbor, one letter is missing from the script, that of the assimilated consonant. The term *assimilated* derives from a study of the phonetic characteristics of the language and an observation of the phonetic processes of assimilation as the principal characteristic typifying the membership of the root in this paradigm. However, there are a few instances in these paradigms of omission of a consonant and not its assimilation.

1. Defective פ״נ and Defective פ״י (Better: assimilated פ״נ and assimilated פ״י). The paradigm of this type with most roots is known as defective פ״נ (see Phonology 7), which comprises roots whose first radical is נ. This נ is assimilated to the second consonant of the root in certain circumstances, e.g.,

‡ *yinpol (//yišmor) → yippol*

‡ *ninẓal (//nišmar) → niẓẓal*

As stated at the end of 22, this assimilation occurs only when the assimilated consonant comes at the end of a non-final syllable. Most roots with נ as the first radical belong to this paradigm, but not all: sometimes the נ appears even when the condition exists for its assimilation. This is so when the second radical is a guttural, e.g:, *yinham, yanʿim.* (There are only two or three roots where the נ is assimilated to a guttural in some forms.) And it is so in a sizeable number of other roots, e.g., *yanziḥu, yinbor,* especially in verbs or forms that have been coined in recent times. It is worth pointing out that the facility for assimilating the נ has become a means of distinguishing between different meanings, e.g., *yanbiṭ* ("will cause to bud") versus *yabbiṭ* ("will look"), *yangid* ("will put contradictory items") versus *yaggid* ("will tell"), including meanings of verbal nouns, e.g., *hangada* versus *haggada, hankara* ("alienation") versus *hakkara* ("consciousness"). The root 'ל'ק'ח is generally included in this paradigm because of the assimilation of its first radical, even though it is ל and not נ.

A parallel paradigm is that of defective פ״י, which comprises roots whose first radical –י– assimilates to the second. There are only six or seven roots in this paradigm, e.g., *yẓb* (*yaẓẓib, hiẓẓib*), *yẓq* (*niẓẓaq, niẓẓoq*). The bases of verbs that are defective פ״נ and פ״י hardly differ from those of regular paradigms, which are detailed in 20, and the same changes of base occur, which are included in those rules. The exception is that the imperative bases in פעל (*lbaš, šmor*) tend in the פ״נ and פ״י paradigms to lose the first radical without any substitution, e.g., *pol* (for *npol*), *gaʿ* (for *ngaʿ*). In these imperative forms there is therefore a true loss and not an assimilation (see Biblical Hebrew 10). With the root נתנ the last נ is assimilated to the following consonants in cases like *natánti* → *nattáti* and in לָתֵת. This last form is to be understood as a development of a feminine infinitive, in which *t* is added to the radicals. Other infinitives like this occur mainly in biblical Hebrew, e.g., לְאַהֲבָה ,יְכֹלֶת. This construction as an infinitive is not productive nowadays, and most instances that are still used belong to the פ״נ or פ״י paradigms, e.g., לָדַעַת ,לָרֶדֶת ,לָטַעַת ,לָגֶשֶׁת. A similar process has occurred with the biblical form לָלַת for the root 'י'ל'ד, which must be understood as *laladt* → *lalatt* → *lalat.*

2. Verbs with duplicated second radical or geminates are usually included among the defective paradigms. This can be justified not because in certain forms one letter is written symbolizing both the second and third radicals, e.g., סַבּוּ, but because in other cases the last radical is entirely omitted, e.g., נָסַב ,סַב. But two points must be made clear: (a) In the inflections of roots in this paradigm, assimilation does not take place, since the two neighboring consonants written with gemination are identical; there is nothing unique in their being symbolized by one letter, since all gemination is symbolized in Hebrew script by one letter. Gemination is similarly symbolized by one letter in words like *natánnu* (נתנו), *karátti* (כרתי). (b) The omission of the third radical in forms like נָסַב ,סַב is only a realization rule, a phonetic rule, and does not convey anything about the theoretical structure of the word. The omission occurs, therefore, on the final level of the language, since there is a general rule in Hebrew that gemination of consonants does not occur at the end of a word, one consonant alone remaining instead. A theoretical form like *sabb* changes, therefore, to *sab* without any assimilation, just as with words like לֵב ,דֹּב ,חֹק, in all of which gemination occurs with the last radical when it appears in the middle of the word, e.g.,לִבִּי ,דֻּבִּים ,חֻקּוֹ. (See Table: Hebrew Grammar 2.)

Table: Hebrew Grammar 2

	Past Participle	Future Imp. Inf.
Paʿal	*sább*	*sóbb*
		qáll
Nipʿal	*nasább*	*hissább*
Piʿʿel	*sobéb*	
Puʿʿal	*sobáb*	
Hitpaʿʿel	*hitsobéb*	
Hipʿil	*hesébb*	*hasébb*
Hupʿal	*husább*	

The regular inflectional morphemes (19) are attached also to the bases of this paradigm, and rules 1, 3–5, 8–10 set out in 20 apply also to these bases, e.g.,

t + *hitsobéb* → *thistobeb* → *tistobeb* (20.1)

ʾ + *hitsobéb* → *ʾestobeb* (20.3)

sobéb + *ti* → *sobábti* (20.4)

sobáb + *u* → *sobábu* (pausal form) → *sobᵊbu* (20.5)

nasább + *á* → *nasabbá* → *nsabbá* (20.8)

m + *sobéb* + *ím* = *msobᵊbím* (20.9)

m + *sobéb* + *t* → *msobébt* → *msobébet* (20.10)

The principal phenomena that are peculiar to the rules for affixation of inflectional morphemes to bases of geminates are as follows:

Prefixed Morpheme: (1) a transitional vowel appears between the prefixed morpheme and the future bases of פָּעַל if the accent is on the base. Before the base *sobb* the transitional vowel is *a*, while before the *qall* it is *e:*

y + *sóbb* → *y* + *a* + *sóbb* → *yasóbb* → *yasób*

y + *sóbb* + *u* → *y* + *a* + *sóbb* + *u* → *yasóbbu*

y + *qáll* + *u* → *y* + *e* + *qáll* + *u* → *yeqállu*

The same applies when ל is affixed to the infinitive base:

l + *sóbb* → *lasóbb* → *lasób*

Suffixed Morpheme: (2) when a suffix beginning with a consonant is attached to a base ending with gemination, the transitional vowel *o* is generally inserted between them, with *e* instead of *o* preceding – *na:*

sább + *ti* + *sább* + *ó* + *ti* → *sabbótii*

sább + *tém* → *sább* + *o* + *tém* → *sabbotém*

hissább + *na* → *hissább* + *é* + *na* → *hissabbéna*

(3) However, there are forms lacking this transitional vowel which lose the gemination of the base before a suffix beginning with a consonant, as if it was at the end of the word:

hissább + *na* → *hissábna* = [*hissávna*]

hussább + *ta* → *husábta* = [*husávta*]

hesébb + *nu* → *hesábnnu* = [*hesávnu*]

(4) The vowel *e* before gemination of the base is changed to *i*, and *o* to *u* when the accent is after the gemination:

sóbb + *na* → *sóbb* + *é* + *na* → *subbéna*

m + *hesébb* + *ím* → *mesébbím* → *msibbím*

(5) As usual with a consonant cluster whose first consonant is *h*, a half-vowel appears in this situation:

hasébb + *nu* → *hasébb* + *ó* + *nu* → *hsibbónu* → [*hăsibbónu*]

24. PARADIGMS OF MUTE FORMS. The term "mute" refers to the phonetic process occurring to various inflectional forms in which the consonants א, ו and י of the root cease to be pronounced, becoming mute. (With respect to ה, see below.) Subclassification of these paradigms is based on the identity of the mute consonant and on its place in the root: mute פ״א; mute פ״י; mute ע״ו; mute ע״י; mute ל״א; mute ל״י. There are very few instances of mute פ״ו and mute ל״ו; these are therefore usually not treated separately, but are included under mute פ״י and mute ל״י respectively.

1. Mute פ״א. There are only five roots in this paradigm. א is mute chiefly in future forms of פָּעַל, e.g., יֹאכַל, יֹאבַד, יֹאפֶה. There are a few instances of other forms with mute א, e.g., נֹאחֲזוּ. The vowel *o* appears in a syllable in which א is mute.

2. Mute פ״י. This paradigm comprises two subclasses, distinguished by the vowel of the syllable in which י is muted: חִירִיק, e.g., יִינַק, יִישַׁן; or צֵירֶה, e.g., יֵדַע, יֵשֵׁב. This latter subclass is assigned by many grammarians to defective פ״י paradigm, chiefly because the letter י is not written in many of the forms. It is true that in the inflectional base of future, imperative, and infinitive of פָּעַל the first radical is omitted (see below in the table of bases in this paradigm: *réd*). However, the defective paradigms are characterized not by omissions, but by the assimilation of a consonant to its neighbor, and in this paradigm there is no such assimilation (compare above, 23:1). Consequently, this subclass belongs to the mute paradigms. Historically, only forms with חִירִיק as vowel of prefix give convincing proof of an original י as first radical, while those with צֵירֶה suggest an original ו. The difference is not apparent in the future forms of פָּעַל, but it is very clear in the הִפְעִיל: הֵינִיק, הֵישִׁיר as opposed to הוֹרִיד, הוֹשִׁיב. The vowel *o* following the ה is the result of monophthongization of *aw*, the original forms probably being ‡*hawrid*, ‡*hawšib* (see Phonology 15), while הֵינִיק, הֵישִׁיר result from the monophthongization of ‡*hayniq*, ‡*hayšir*. (Evidence of this is also to be found in forms like מֵימִינִים, מֵישִׁירִים, where monophthongization has not taken place.)

Inflectional Bases of Mute פ״י *Paradigm.* The bases of פָּעַל, פִּעֵל, and הִתְפַּעֵל are identical to those of regular verbs, see 19. (See Table: Hebrew Grammar 3.) The rules for inflection given in 20 apply to all inflections in this paradigm. Special attention should be paid to the following:

(1) The first radical י is mute when by rule 20.2 it is preceded by the vowel *i*:

Table: Hebrew Grammar 3

	Past	Participle	Future	Imperative	Infinitive
Paʿal	*yarad*	*yoréd*	*réd*		*redt*
		yašen	*yšan*		*yšon*
Nipʿal		*nolád*		*hiwwaléd*	
Hipʿʿil			*holíd*		
			heníq		
Hupʿal		*hurád*			

t + *yšán* → *tiyšán* → *tišán* (rule 20.3 does not apply);

(2) Before the base for future, imperative, and infinitive of פָּעַל *réd*, the transitional vowel *e* is inserted:

t + *réd* → *t* + *e* + *réd* → *teréd*

(3) The infinitive base of פָּעַל given in parentheses follows a development characteristic of the segholates, e.g., *rédt* → *rédet*, and the transitional vowel *a* is inserted before it and after the prefix *l*, e.g., *l* + *rédet* → *l* + *a* + *rédet* → *larédet* (when the infinitive is in the construct state, no transitional vowel is inserted).

3. Mute ע״ו–ע״י. The distinction between ע״ו and ע״י is evident only in the inflectional base for the future, imperative, and infinitive of פָּעַל, exemplified by *qum* in ע״ו and *šir* in ע״י.

Since this description is res tricted to contemporary Hebrew, there is no discussion of the difficult problem, still disputed, as to whether the roots of this paradigm were originally bilateral and at a later stage ו or י developed between the two consonants, or whether they were originally trilateral and subsequently the middle consonant, ו or י, was muted (see Biblical Hebrew 10, Morphology 2). For our purpose it is sufficient to point out that the name of this paradigm is based on the second possibility. On the other hand, there is evidence of the formation of regular trilateral roots (19) through the development into a consonant of a medial ו or י e.g., תִּוֵּךְ from תוך, בִּיֵּן from ב׳י׳נ׳. However, it should be mentioned that most of the creations are in פִּעֵל (as in the above examples) or in פֻּעַל and הִתְפַּעֵל (e.g., הִתְגַּיֵּר, מְגֻוָּן), that is to say in patterns where the middle radical should be doubled and hence greater attention is paid to it. When the development of a medial ו or י does not take place, the inflection for פִּעֵל, פֻּעַל, and הִתְפַּעֵל in this paradigm is identical to that of geminates described in the preceding section.

Inflectional Bases of Mute ע״ו–ע״י *Paradigm.* The inflectional morphemes detailed in 20 are affixed to these bases according to rules 1, 3, 4, 5 (but rule 5 does not apply to the bases *qám*, *nakón*), 6, 8, 10 listed in 20. (See Table: Hebrew Grammar 4.) In addition, transitional vowels are formed according to rules 1 and 2 stated for the geminates (see section on verbs with duplicated radicals in Paradigms of Assimilated Forms above), with only a slight difference: the transitional vowel of the prefix is always *a* (except for the base of the verb בוש – which serves both past and future – where it is *e*). The following rules are peculiar to this paradigm:

Table: Hebrew Grammar 4

	Past and Participle	Future Imp. Inf.
Paʿal	*qám*	*qúm*
		šír
Nipʿal	*nakón*	*hikkón*
Hipʿil	*heqím*	*haqím*
Hupʿal	*huqám*	

(1) The vowel *ú* of *qúm* changes to *o* before the suffix –*na*:

qúm + *na* → *qómna*

(2) The vowel *ó* generally changes to *u* before the transitional vowel *ó*:

nakón + *t* → *nakón* + *ó* + *t* → *nkunót*

Here are some additional examples of the production of forms:

(1) (rule 1) *t* + *haqím* → *taqím*

(2) (rule 3) ʾ + *hikkón* → *ʾikkon* → *ʾekkón*

(3) (rule 4) *heqím* + *ta* → *heqámta*

(4) (rule 5) *huqám* + *u* → *huqámu* (pausal form) → *huqmú*,

but

qám + *u* → *qámu*

nakón + *a* → *nakóna*

(5) (rule 6) *haqím* + *na* → *haqémna*

(6) *heqámtém* (rule 4) → *hqamtém* (rule 8) → [*hăqamtém*] (by rule 5 in the geminate paradigm)

(7) *m* + *huqám* + *t*→ *muqámt* (rule 1) → *muqámet* → *muqémet* (rule 10).

Examples of the rules for transitional vowels:

(8) *t* + *qúm* → *t* + *a* + *qúm* → *taqúm* (geminates – 1) but *n* + *boš* → *nebóš*

(9) *heqim* + *ta* → *heqím* + *ó* + *ta* (geminates – 2) → *hqimóta* (rule 8) → [*hăqimóta*] (geminates – 5)

For an example where a transitional vowel is not formed, see (3) geminates.

4. Mute Third Radical. With respect to the roots in this paradigm too, it can be argued that they were originally bilateral with a third consonant developing in the final position. Indeed, there is evidence in several cases of such a development (see above, Morphology 2: 'א'ח'י, 'ז'ה'י). However, the more common view is that these roots were originally trilateral and the final consonant was muted in certain circumstances. This view finds support in the history of Hebrew and other Semitic languages. It is worth pointing out that Hebrew has only a few instances of the existence of ו as a third radical (as in שָׁלַוְתִּי), apparently because already at an early stage the ו in such roots was changed to י. It should also be mentioned that the popular name ל״ה is based on the written language and not the spoken, since while the third person masculine singular past forms of these roots are indeed written with final ה, a consideration of the whole of the inflection shows that the final consonant is really י, e.g., in forms like the passive participle רָצוּי or verbal noun in פָּעַל, רְצִיָּה *rẓiya* (like *šmira*); verbal noun in פִּעֵל *niqquy* (like *dibbur*); and in various noun forms, e.g., *niqqayon*. Finally, it may be noted that in many instances there is an overlap between roots in the paradigms ל״א and ל״י, e.g., הַשְׁקָאָה (as well as הַשְׁקָיָה) from 'ש'ק'י, הַרְצָאָה from 'ר'צ'י. The reverse phenomenon is especially common: forms with a root from the paradigm ל״א but with their inflection following that of ל״י, e.g., בִּטּוּי ('ב'ט'א). In mishnaic Hebrew this was the general practice, which was apparently reinforced through the influence of contemporary Aramaic, in which the ל״א paradigm was completely lost and its forms became identical to those of ל״י. However, it would not be correct to argue that this is a phenomenon restricted to mishnaic Hebrew: the transition is reflected in the pointing of the biblical text, and most of the instances can be explained as deriving from an internal phonetic development, namely, the elision of א when it is second in a consonantal cluster, e.g., חוֹטְאִים ← חוֹטאים. Forms common in mishnaic Hebrew, e.g., מָצִינוּ, יָצְתָה serve nowadays merely as stylistic variants.

Inflectional Bases of Mute ל״א *Paradigm.* The inflectional morphemes listed in 19 are affixed to the bases of this paradigm and the rules detailed in 20 apply (with the reservations stated immediately below for rules 4 and 10). (See Table: Hebrew Grammar 5.) The following rules are specific to this paradigm:

(1) ʾ is mute at the end of a word, and in the middle of a word before a suffix beginning with a consonant:

qoréʾ → *qoré*

qaráʾ + *ti* → *qaráti*

milléʾ + *ta* → *milléta*

Similarly:

m + *hitmalléʾ* + *t* → *mitmallét*

i.e., rule 10 of 20 does not apply to this paradigm, because the elision of ʾ prevents the creation of a segholate form.

(2) Instead of rule 4 of 20 the following rule applies to this paradigm: *a* and *i* in past bases (except of פָּעַל) change to *e* before suffixes beginning with a consonant:

niqráʾ + *ti* → *niqráti* (rule 1) → *niqréti*

hiqríʾ + *nu* → *hiqrínu* (rule 1) → *hiqrénu*

Note: In a small number of roots in the past base of פָּעַל the second vowel is always *é*, e.g., *ẓaméʾ*, *maléʾ*.

5. Mute ל״י.

Table: Hebrew Grammar 5

	Past	Participle	Future Imp.	Inf.
Paʿal	*qaráʾ*	*qoreʾ*	*qraʾ*	*qroʾ*
Nipʿal	*niqráʾ*		*hiqqareʾ*	
Piʿʿel	*milléʾ*		*malléʾ*	
Puʿʿal		*mulláʾ*		
Hitpaʿʿel		*hitmalléʾ*		
Hipʿil	*hiqríʾ*		*haqriʾ*	
Hupʿal	*huqráʾ*			

Inflectional Bases of Mute ל״י *Paradigm.* (See Table: Hebrew Grammar 6.) It is easy to see that the distinction between the past bases and the other bases in this paradigm lies primarily in the final vowel, which is *á* in the past and *é* in the other bases. The following rules specify what is characteristic of this paradigm:

(1) The suffix *a* of the third person feminine singular past changes into *ta* (and is then classed with suffixes beginning with a consonant).

(2) The infinitive is formed by the affixation of a special suffix *ót* to the base (and this is then classed with suffixes beginning with a vowel).

(3) The final vowel of all the bases is omitted before a suffix beginning with a vowel, and in such a case the accent is on the vowel of the suffix (this rule replaces rule 5 in 20):

baná + u → banú
haqné + i → haqní
l + naqqé + ót → lnaqqót

Note: To take account of "pausal forms," ancient inflectional bases must be considered, e.g., *bakáy + u → bakáyu* (rule 5 in 20).

(4) The vowel *á* in past bases changes to *i* when a suffix beginning with a consonant is added in bases of פָּעַל, פִּעֵל, and הִפְעִיל, and to *e* in other bases and occasionally in bases of פִּעֵל and הִפְעִיל:

baná + nu → banínu
niqqá + ti → niqqíti (or *niqqéti*)
hiqná + ta → hiqnéta (or *hiqníta*)
nibná + tém → nibnetém

In addition rules 1, 2, 3, 8 detailed in 20 apply to the inflection of this paradigm:

t + hibbané → tibbané (20, rule 1)
t + bné → tibné (20, rule 2)
ʾ + bné →ʾebné (20, rule 3)
ʾ + hibbané → ʾebbane (20, rule 3)
baná + tém → banitém (rule 4 of this paradigm) → *bnitém* (20, rule 8)

but *l + hibbané + ót + m* (objective pronoun) → *lhibbanotám* (without change of the vowel *a* of the base).

Table: Hebrew Grammar 6

<table>
<tr><th></th><th>Past</th><th>Participle</th><th>Future Imp. Inf.</th></tr>
<tr><td>Paʿal</td><td>baná</td><td>boné</td><td>bné</td></tr>
<tr><td>Nipʿal</td><td>nibná</td><td>nibné</td><td>hibbané</td></tr>
<tr><td>Piʿʿel</td><td>niqqá</td><td colspan="2">naqqé</td></tr>
<tr><td>Puʿʿal</td><td>nuqqá</td><td colspan="2">nuqqé</td></tr>
<tr><td>Hitpaʿel</td><td>hitnaqqá</td><td colspan="2">hitnaqqé</td></tr>
<tr><td>Hipʿil</td><td>hiqná</td><td colspan="2">haqné</td></tr>
<tr><td>Hupʿal</td><td>huqná</td><td colspan="2">huqné</td></tr>
</table>

[Uzzi Ornan]

SYNTAX

SYNTAX

1: THE INFLUENCE OF FOREIGN WORKS ON HEBREW SYNTAX

1.1: The Traditional Grammars

The first Hebrew grammarians devoted their attention chiefly to phonology and morphology, generally omitting special, ordered chapters on syntax. Some study was, however, made into the syntactical connections between adjacent or related words. This usually appears in traditional grammars when they deal with the system of accents. Many centuries passed before syntactic questions such as agreement of gender and number between different words in a sentence were first discussed comprehensively in a Hebrew grammar (*Miqne Avram* by Abraham de *Balmes, 1523).

1.2: Neglect of Syntax

This neglect seems to be due to the influence of the treatment of syntax in languages such as Latin, Greek, or Arabic, where the function of a word is generally shown by its form, and especially by the suffixes attached to it. The grammarian might therefore suppose that syntax essentially consists of such case suffixes, so that Hebrew, which lacks these suffixes, "has no syntax," or at least its syntax is not central to the language. The grammarian might therefore persuade himself that he should rather devote his energies to phonology and morphology. This conception of syntax continued to influence the treatment of Hebrew syntax even in the period of "scientific grammar," when philologists included a separate chapter on syntax in their Hebrew grammars. Until very recently, syntax was considered a study which attempted to reveal the logic behind language and thus external reality. For several centuries Latin was thought to be the most complete expression of logic and reality. Hence, while grammarians such as Gesenius, Ewald, or König and their modern counterparts such as Pereẓ and Segal treat Hebrew syntactic phenomena in great detail, their approach is not based on linguistic formal criteria derived from a study of Hebrew, but on categories of "reality" as reflected in Latin and as "laid bare" in Latin syntax.

1.3: Conventional Syntax in Other Languages

It is well known that this defect has affected the treatment of syntax in other modern languages, including English. For example, grammarians have continued even recently to discuss the distinction between dative and accusative in English, as if the formal differences between them – noticeable in Latin but hardly at all in English – reflect relationships in external reality, and as if these relationships need to be considered in the syntax of every language, even where no distinction between them is made in the language.

1.4: Conventional Hebrew Syntax

Hebrew grammarians likewise saw Hebrew syntax as reflecting reality and the relationships existing in it, rather than as a formal study of the way words are linked and sentences are linked. For example, the Latin distinction between "direct object" and "indirect object" (see section Object below) is based upon the difference between a word that was an obligatory complement to a verb and was linked to it directly, i.e., without the word being preceded by a preposition, and a word which, while being an obligatory complement to a verb, needed a preposition before it. But in Hebrew what was called a "direct object" is under certain clear (and very frequent) conditions preceded by the preposition אֶת. "Direct object" in Hebrew, then, was applied not to a word with a certain status (or function) in the sentence, but to a word that designated a substance. That substance had a certain status in "reality" and had a certain relationship with another substance existing in the world. This relationship is realized by an action passed from this second substance to the one designated by the word which is "direct object." In other words, this syntax deals not with the grammatical relationships between words but with the relationships in the real world between what the words signify. A good illustration of this treatment of syntax appears in the comment usually quoted in the section dealing with the "direct object": "Sometimes the preposition לְ appears before the direct object instead of the preposition אֶת (for example in the biblical verse הָרְגוּ לְאַבְנֵר, II Samuel 4:30)." In this comment "direct object" is stated by the fact that a person is directly affected by the action, that is to say it is a person existing in the world that makes it "direct object" and not a linguistic relation existing in the sentence.

2: THE PARTS OF SPEECH

2.1: The Parts of Speech and External Reality

This conception of the word as reflecting reality is evident in what is traditionally the opening chapter of books on syntax: the chapter dealing with the "parts of speech." Since the early grammarians believed that reality was reflected best in Latin, it is precisely here that there is the greatest influence of Latin (and Greek) syntax. In these languages the function of a word can be recognized through its form, largely because of the many case suffixes that these languages have; hence, it was natural for the forms to serve as a basis for the treatment of functions. But in Hebrew it is exceptional for form and syntactic function to correspond, as in הַבַּיְתָה contrasting with הַבַּיִת. Only in the verb is there a regular correspondence, since it has merely one function, namely, to be the predicator of the sentence. It is reasonable to suppose that without the influence of foreign works on syntax the chapter on the "parts of speech" would have been the introduction to a treatment of morphology rather than of syntax. Indeed, the earliest medieval grammarians did include a discussion of the "parts of speech," which they then divided into three only: noun, verb, and particle (מִלָּה – literally "word"). They defined "noun" and "verb" semantically (for example, "a word denoting a substance or concept," "a word denoting an action or state"), while "particle" (comprising whatever was not regarded as "noun" or "verb") was defined by the function it had of linking other words. But, particles were also termed "sense words," since they supplied sense to the sentence. (See above 5. Parts of Speech in section Morphology above.)

2.2: The Classification into Parts of Speech

The division into three parts of speech was preserved in Hebrew grammar even when the division into nine parts of speech, traditional in Greek and Latin (and also in modern languages), entered Hebrew grammar. The nine were grouped under the three earlier parts as follows:

A. *noun*: 1. noun (substantive) 2. adjective 3. numeral 4. pronoun

B. *verb*: 5. verb

C. *particle*: 6. conjunction 7. preposition 8. adverb 9. interjection

2.3: A Criticism of the Conventional Classification

The division into nine parts of speech is also largely based on the meaning of words. That is to say, the assignment of a word to a particular part of speech is generally decided not by its formal features nor by its function, but by the concept it denotes. As a result, the classification suffers from several defects:

(1) Not every word denotes a concept. For example, conjunctions merely denote that words are linked to each other. In practice, therefore, grammarians define different parts according to different criteria: meaning, function, and sometimes even form.

(2) The meaning of a word depends on its context, and therefore the same word type is likely to be considered as belonging to several parts of speech, depending on the context of the particular word tokens. For example, in the sentence הַשּׁוֹמְרִים מְטַיְּלִים הַלַּיְלָה (The watchmen are walking around tonight) the first word is considered a noun and the second a verb, and the same applies to the sentence הַמְטַיְּלִים שׁוֹמְרִים הַלַּיְלָה (The hikers are on guard tonight). The third defect of this classification follows from the previous two:

(3) The division into parts of speech does not establish exclusive sets, since many words belong to more than one part of speech. It is this third defect in particular that has led some prominent linguists to deny any value to the classification into parts of speech. Yet this classification, virtually in its entirety, is generally accepted even in the most modern Hebrew textbooks, although it is clear that in many ways it does not fit the facts of the Hebrew language. Thus, many scholars claim that there is no basis for distinguishing in Hebrew between noun and adjective, since every adjective can be considered a noun (e.g., גִּבּוֹר, חָכָם), and clearly many nouns originally served as adjectives (e.g., חַמָּה, לְבָנָה). It is true that this claim is made particularly for biblical Hebrew, but it is true also for modern Hebrew. It applies to the forms of the participle, which can be taken as nouns, as adjectives, or as verbs. This last possibility is especially evident in modern Hebrew, where the forms of the participle are given in the verb paradigm, though formally they resemble nouns.

3: SENTENCE TYPES

A sentence is a syntactical unit built from a word or words of which each one (or a combination of them) fulfills a specific syntactical function as a "sentence-part." This unit can stand by itself, can sometimes be connected to other similar units – whether preceding it or following it, and whether they are articulated by the same speaker or by others – and it is intonated in a manner which members of that language-group recognize as a complete articulated unit which does not lack a continuation. The sentence has an additional typical attribute: it is recursive, i.e., this unit can include in it a further internal sentence or sentences, each one of which fills a function as a sentence-part (see below). Unlike many other languages, the Hebrew sentence – apparently also in its deep structure (see below 3.1: Structural Analysis) – does not have to include a verb (see below 4.23: Nominal Sentence and Verbal Sentence). On the other hand the Hebrew sentence may be a single word which is a verb, since the Hebrew verb includes a pronoun. Transformational rules (see below Structural Analysis) are likely to influence the sentence and reduce it to a single word which is not a verb; however, this attribute can be found in many languages.

3.1: Structural Analysis

Modern linguistic theory considers grammar to be a set of generative rules for the language. A central place is occupied by what are called transformational rules. Transformational rules are also generative rules, but they apply to sentences or parts of sentences derived from simpler generative rules. Transformational rules change the order of words in a sentence, produce conjoinings and dependencies within sentences or between sentences, replace words by other words or formatives by other formatives, delete sentences or parts of sentences, etc. According to this theory, one must distinguish between the surface structure of a language and its deep structure. The latter includes the generative and transformational rules and also most of the semantic links that appear "on the surface." So far, only a few works have been written on Hebrew grammar according to this theory or under its influence, and even these follow its earlier formulations. Consequently it is neither possible to describe here the "deep structure" of Hebrew, nor to survey the transformational rules that operate in the language, except in those areas where a few details have been discovered. The following description is therefore essentially a survey of surface structure, taking into account works written according to the classical method.

3.11: CLASSIFICATION OF SENTENCES. A classification of sentences according to their surface structure yields four types of sentences: (1) simple sentence, (2) multiple-unit sentence, (3) compound sentence, and (4) complex sentence.

This classification is usual in books on Hebrew syntax, except that some authors treat together the multiple-unit sentence and the compound sentence, while some do not treat the compound sentence at all, because "there is nothing to deal with in the compound sentence except what we find in its parts as separate sentences" (Segal).

3.12: THE SIMPLE SENTENCE. A simple sentence is a sentence in which each part is realized by one word. This seems the best definition, even though there are some problems with it. For example, several adjectives may be attached to one noun to form a noun phrase. At first sight each one might be considered adjectival to the same noun, and yet in most cases the sentence will be regarded as simple, e.g., הַמְּעִיל הַשָּׁחוֹר הֶחָדָשׁ שֶׁלִּי נִקְרַע (My new black coat was torn). Another problem is that sometimes the function of the predicator is realized by a verb phrase, one word of which is the main verb while the rest are auxiliaries, e.g., הַשִּׁיעוּר מַתְחִיל לְהֵרָאוֹת מְעַנְיֵן (The lesson begins to appear interesting). Here the three final verbs together realize the function of predicator. The problem of adjectives in a noun phrase can be solved by recognizing that sometimes an adjective is not attached directly to the noun, which forms the nucleus of the noun phrase, but to the whole of the preceding phrase – the phrase of noun + adjective. In the above example, the correct analysis for the constituency of the adjectives is נִקְרַע (3 שֶׁלִּי (2 הֶחָדָשׁ (1 הַמְּעִיל הַשָּׁחוֹר 1) 2) 3), compare the English equivalent (My (new (black coat))) was torn. First the words הַמְּעִיל הַשָּׁחוֹר (the black coat) form a phrase; then to this phrase as a unit the following adjective הֶחָדָשׁ is attached, forming the phrase הֶחָדָשׁ (הַמְּעִיל הַשָּׁחוֹר); finally שֶׁלִּי is added, relating to the whole of the preceding phrase שֶׁלִּי (הֶחָדָשׁ (הַמְּעִיל הַשָּׁחוֹר)).This explanation is based on one of the important principles of structural linguistics, "the theory of immediate constituents" (IC). A close examination reveals that each of the adjectives belongs to a different adjectival category, i.e., has a different function within the sentence. There are indeed many more parts of the sentence than is traditionally supposed (see below). The problem with auxiliaries is solved by considering them morphemes attached to the center of the predicator ("the main verb") to give it some modal or aspectual nuance (see below 4.45 Infinitive as Object). The auxiliaries also vary in their function. If they are regarded as realizing certain parts of the sentence, then they too are additional parts of the sentence.

3.13: THE MULTIPLE-UNIT SENTENCE. The multiple-unit sentence is a sentence in which one of the parts is realized by several words linked to each other by parataxis (sometimes expressed by a conjunction), e.g., "אָבִיךָ וְאִמְּךָ דּוֹאֲגִים לְךָ" (Your father and mother are anxious about you), "הָבֵא כַּפּוֹת וּמַזְלְגוֹת" (Bring spoons and forks). Some exclude from this type such sentences as have verbs that are linked paratactically, e.g., "הוּא הִתְרַחֵץ, הִתְלַבֵּשׁ וְיָצָא לַעֲבוֹדָה" (He washed, dressed, and went out to work); "וַיֹּאכַל וַיֵּשְׁתְּ וַיָּקָם וַיֵּלַךְ וַיִּבֶז" ("and he did eat and drink, and rose up, and went his way. So Esau despised his birthright," Gen. 25:34), maintaining that such a structure should be classed as a compound sentence (see 3.14: The Compound Sentence). The motivation for this view is that a construction containing a subject and a predicator is considered to be a sentence, and this definition applies to the verb, every form of which contains a subject-pronoun. Since a group of consecutive sentences linked paratactically is termed a compound sentence, the sentences in the above example should be considered compound sentences. In an analysis of the sentence (to be more precise, an analysis of the surface structure of the sentence) this approach is advantageous.

3.14: THE COMPOUND SENTENCE. The compound sentence is traditionally subclassified according to the type of linking: addition, contrast, choice, or result. It is obvious that this classification is essentially semantic. Though there is a practical need for it, it is doubtful whether it has a place in a theoretical treatment in syntax, at least as long as syntax is concerned only with surface structure (but see below 6.31: Coordination in section Links beyond the Sentence).

3.15: THE COMPLEX SENTENCE. The complex sentence is defined as a sentence one or more of whose parts is realized by a sentence (rather than by a word or a phrase). In every complex sentence there is therefore an embedded sentence. Since the embedded sentence performs, as a sentence, a function within the complex sentence, one can say that it is subordinate in the complex sentence. Some therefore define a complex sentence as follows: It is a sentence consisting of at least two sentences, which are linked by the subordination of one sentence to another. According to this view, the subordinated sentence is termed the dependent sentence, and the subordinating one the main sentence. But one should rather say that one sentence is a part of the other, and, in the same way as a sentence-element expressed by one word, it generally relates to one of the parts of the sentence as an independent unit. For example, if its function is that of adjunct, it is linked to the noun (irrespective of the noun's function), as in הַיֶּלֶד שֶׁרָאִינוּ אֶתְמוֹל חָזַר כְּבָר לְבֵיתוֹ (The boy, whom we saw yesterday, has already returned to his home) or רָאִיתִי אֶת הַיֶּלֶד שֶׁבָּא מִן הַכְּפָר (I saw the boy who came from the village). Similarly "וְשָׁמְמוּ עָלֶיהָ אוֹיְבֵיכֶם הַיּוֹשְׁבִים בָּהּ" ("and your enemies that dwell therein shall be astonished at it," Lev. 26:32) as opposed to "כָּכָה יַעֲשֶׂה ה׳ לְכָל אוֹיְבֵיכֶם אֲשֶׁר אַתֶּם נִלְחָמִים אוֹתָם" ("for thus shall the Lord do to all your enemies against whom ye fight," Josh. 10:25). Adjunct sentences are divided into relative clauses, as in the above examples, and adjunct-content sentences to be discussed below, in 4.38: Relative Clause. If adverbial, such a sentence is linked to the verb-predicator, e.g., חָזַרְנוּ מִן הַטִּיּוּל לִפְנֵי שֶׁשָּׁקְעָה הַשֶּׁמֶשׁ (We returned from the hike before the sun set). Even when the subordinated part is subject, it can be said to be chiefly linked to the predicator, e.g., מִי שֶׁטָּרַח בְּעֶרֶב שַׁבָּת יֹאכַל בְּשַׁבָּת (Whoever exerts himself on the Sabbath eve will eat on the Sabbath). The last example demonstrates the inappropriateness of the term "dependent" for the subordinated sentence, since it can realize one of the main functions of the sentence, that of subject, and hence "main" is likewise inappropriate for the subordinating part of the complex sentence. For other types of sentence structure, see 4.23: Nominal and Verbal Sentences, 4.24: Identifying Sentence, 4.25: Attributive Sentence, 4.26: Focusing Sentence, and 4.27: Indefinite Sentence.

3.2: Pragmatic Classification

Other analyses of sentences may be made according to the speaker's commitment to what is being said or according to his attitude to what is being said.

3.21: THE SPEAKER'S COMMITMENT. The speaker's commitment is discernible from the form of the sentence: declarative, exclamatory (or optative), and interrogative ("yes-no" question or "specific" question, i.e., question specifying type of information required). In modern Hebrew "yes-no" questions generally differ from declarative sentences merely in intonation, though sometimes – particularly in the written language – a question may be prefaced by a word indicating that the sentence is a question, e.g., הַאִם or כְּלוּם. In any event, the structure of the sentence remains the same when it serves as a "yes-no" question. In a specific question the sentence is introduced by the appropriate interrogative word, e.g., מָתַי (when), אֵיךְ (how), מַדּוּעַ (why). See below for the order of words in such questions. The same applies to the exclamatory sentence. Any declarative or interrogative sentence can be considered an exclamatory sentence when rendered by an exclamatory intonation. Investigation into Hebrew syntax must include intonation to allow for such a classification of sentences. But so far no research in this field has been published. We must therefore be content with the general observation that for a Hebrew sentence to be interpreted as a question it must be said with a rising tone, particularly toward the end, and in any case the last syllable must be heard as being on a higher pitch than the penultimate. On the other hand, in a declarative sentence the last syllable is lower in pitch than the penultimate. Specific questions vary and it is difficult to state what their characteristic intonation patterns are. However, it is important to point out that specific questions can function exactly as they are, as embedded (subordinated) sentences in a complex sentence, and then obviously they do not have an interrogative intonation.

3.22: THE SPEAKER'S ATTITUDE. The attitude of the speaker toward what is said in the sentence or toward one of the details in it, and the extent of his belief in what is said, can be expressed in three ways: (1) parenthetically, e.g., הַסּוּס, יִמַּח שְׁמוֹ, מִתְגָּרֶה בִּי (The horse – damn it – is annoying me);

(2) by a verb, by a subordinating expression, or by a sentence, the sentence transmitting the main content being subordinated to them, e.g., יִתָּכֵן שֶׁמָּחָר יֵרֵד שֶׁלֶג (It is possible that tomorrow snow will fall), יְהִי רָצוֹן שֶׁתֵּלֵד אִשְׁתִּי זָכָר ("May it be [God's] will that my wife bear a male child"), or מִי יִתֵּן (וְ) תָבוֹא שְׁאֵלָתִי ("Would (lit. who will give) that my desire be fulfilled"). See also Subordinators in 6.321: Links beyond the Sentence – אֲשֶׁר; (3) through certain auxiliaries (modal auxiliaries) that are attached to the nucleus of the predicator, e.g., מִסְפַּר הַמּוֹרְדִים עָלוּל לִגְדֹּל (The number of rebels may increase). See 4.45: Infinitive as Object.

4: THE PARTS OF THE SENTENCE

4.0: A Syntactic Framework

A syntactic analysis of surface structure means the identification of a string of words as a sentence and the identification of the function in the sentence of each word or group of words. The process of identification and analysis will be better understood if the sentence is compared to an elastic frame that can be expanded as required. The frame contains a string of words and each word or group of words appears within an inner frame, a frame symbolizing a part of the sentence. This conceptual framework underlies the definitions given above of types of sentences. Identification of a word's function in a sentence means determining in which inner frame to put the word; identification of sentence type means recognizing the composition of the inner frames in the external, sentence frame. The structure of the sentence is illustrated as follows with each term designating a frame making up a part of the sentence:

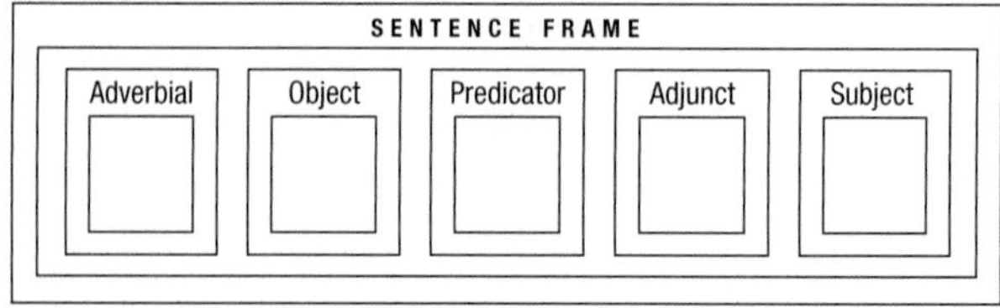

Note: The order of the parts of the sentence given from right to left is not intended to represent their actual order. On this, see below.

The frames shown here are filled with words. They are "elastic," that is to say they can "stretch" and contain more than one word. When one or more frames of the parts of the sentence is filled by a sentence, the sentence frame covering all the frames is termed a "complex sentence" and the sentence filling one of the parts of the sentence is termed an "embedded sentence." The features of an "embedded sentence" are generally the same as those of other sentences. An embedded sentence can itself contain within one of its internal frames another embedded sentence. This feature of the sentence – its recursiveness – allows for the possibility, at least theoretically, of expanding it to an infinite length.

4.1: The Division into the Primary Five Parts

Traditionally, Hebrew syntax distinguishes five parts of the sentence: (1) subject, (2) predicator, (3) adjunct, (4) object, (5) adverbial. It should be noted that this does not correspond to the division into subject and predicate, which is traditional in the grammars of many languages. On this, see 4.2: Subject and Predicator; 4.21: Predicator and Predicate. The first two parts are called the principal parts of the sentence, and the other three the subsidiary parts of the sentence or complements. The adjunct is complement to any noun whatever its function may be; the object and adverbial are complements to the predicator, but see 4.53: Sentence Adverbial. Some parts of the sentence are traditionally subclassified. A distinction must be made between two types of subclassification: (1) a part of the sentence is designated variously according to the nature of the words realizing it, e.g., the usual distinction between different kinds of adverbial: place, time, cause, result, etc.; (2) a part of the sentence is itself divided into two parts, each of which denotes a different syntactic functions, e.g., a predicator can be said to be composed of two parts: copula and predicator. (Some designate as extended predicator the part of the sentence comprising both of these.) The first type of classification is generally based on non-syntactic surface-structure features. For example, the distinction between place adverbial and time adverbial is determined merely by the meaning of the word filling the frame adverbial. A frame complementing a verb and filled by אֶתְמוֹל (yesterday) or אַחֲרֵי אַרְבָּעִים יוֹם (after 40 days) is called time adverbial, whereas if it is filled by כָּאן (here) or by בִּרְחוֹב פְּלוֹנִי (at X Street) it is called place adverbial. It is doubtful whether such a classification is relevant to the surface structure analysis, though obviously there are many occasions even here when it is necessary to make such distinctions (cf. 4.5: Adverbial). On the other hand, the classification of a part of the sentence into different internal parts is clearly relevant to all levels of syntax, since each part fulfills a different syntactic function and is distinct from the other parts of the sentence. For example, it is not enough to say that the phrase מַתְחִיל לְהֵרָאוֹת מְעַנְיֵן (begins to seem interesting) is the predicator in the sentence הַשִּׁעוּר מַתְחִיל לְהֵרָאוֹת מְעַנְיֵן (The lesson begins to seem interesting). To describe the internal composition of this part of speech: one part functions as predicator-nucleus (מְעַנְיֵן – interesting), while the others are attached to it, their function being to express the aspect (מַתְחִיל – begins) or the modality (לְהֵרָאוֹת – to seem) of the predicator-nucleus. These deserve attention from writers on syntax and an appropriate term, such as predicator-auxiliaries. Generative rules are needed for the ways in which the predicator-auxiliaries combine with the predicator-nucleus. Unfortunately, this area has not yet been sufficiently investigated in Hebrew. In the literature on Hebrew syntax there are only a few scattered remarks on such distinctions. In what follows each of the traditional parts of the sentence is surveyed in turn, with comments where possible on any subclassification.

4.2: Subject and Predicator

In syntax it is usual to define these two parts of the sentence in relationship to each other. The justification for doing so is that what determines whether a word fulfills the function of subject is the existence of a relationship between that word and another word with the function of predicator in the sentence. This relationship called Nexus by Jespersen – whether it exists between words actually appearing in the sentence or whether it exists only in the deep structure of the sentence – is a necessary condition for sentence status. It is not, however, a sufficient condition, since some types of Nexus appear in a frame which is not a "sentence," though it is the consequence of a transformation applied to a sentence, e.g., הֲלִיכַת הָרוֹפֵא (the doctor's walk) derived from הָרוֹפֵא הָלַךְ (the doctor walked) or אֲנִי חוֹשֵׁב אוֹתוֹ לְחָכָם (I consider him wise) the last two words of which are derived from הוּא חָכָם (He is wise). It is usual to define subject and predicator semantically, e.g., "The subject is the word denoting the substance spoken about in the sentence, the predicator is what is said about this substance." However, the question that the speaker is posing is not always amenable to an unequivocal answer. Moreover, sometimes it is clear that what is being spoken about in the sentence is not denoted by the word that is subject, but by a word with a different syntactic function. For example, in the sentence חַם לָהּ (She is warm, literally, Warm is to her) the topic of the sentence is third person singular feminine, but the corresponding pronoun is not the subject of the sentence. As elsewhere in syntax, one ought to use formal rather than semantic criteria to define "subject," "predicator," and the other parts of the sentence. If a straight definition (such as "The subject is…") seems too difficult, we can define the parts of the sentence operationally. The following is an example of such an operational definition of subject and predicator (following Ornan, *The Syntax of Modern Hebrew*): If one has a word that by itself constitutes a sentence, and if (1) the word is a verb, and one can substitute for it a combination of that verb and a subjective pronoun – הוּא (he), הִיא (she), etc., agreeing with it in gender and number, and this combination is likewise a sentence, then in this new sentence-frame the function of the subjective pronoun is termed "subject" and that of the verb is termed "predicator"; or if (2) the word is a noun, and one can substitute for it a combination of that noun and the verb הָיָה (be) agreeing with the noun in gender and number, and this combination is likewise a sentence, then in this sentence-frame the function of the noun is termed "subject" and that of the verb is termed "predicator." (On concord, see 5.11: Concord Between Subject and Predicator.) Substitution is an important factor in this definition. Indeed, it is a central principle in structural linguistics. According to this principle, words, phrases, or parts of words that are substitutable within a given frame, form a grammatical class. The above definition can be extended by the method of substitution to include all the words or phrases filling the function of subject in the given frame and all those filling the function of predicate. For that purpose the above definition must be supplemented: "Any word, or group of words, that can replace a word filling the function of subject, likewise fills the function of subject, provided that the resultant sentence does not thereby become deviant." A corresponding addition can be made for the definition of the predicator.

4.21: PREDICATOR AND PREDICATE. As noted above the division of the sentence usual in Hebrew syntax differs from that usual in the grammars of many languages, though Hebrew grammarians have not sufficiently considered the difference. In particular, a distinction should be made between the Hebrew concept נָשׂוּא (predicator) and the general concept "predicate." The parts of the sentence in the predicate are the predicator, the object, the adverbial, and any adjunct to these parts. The predicator is the nucleus of the predicate, with all the other parts in the predicate the complements of the predicator.

4.22: THE COPULA. The predicator itself can be expressed by more than one word. Modal or aspectual predicator-auxiliaries were mentioned above (in 4.1: The Division into the Primary Five Parts, cf. 4.5: Adverbial). To these should be added the past and future forms of the verb הָיָה (be), since when the predicator is expressed by a noun or participle these may be combined with it to denote time, e.g., וְקַיִן הָיָה עוֹבֵד אֲדָמָה (Cain was a tiller of the earth). In this use the verb הָיָה fills the function of copula, which is also considered a predicator-auxiliary. Similarly, the forms of the third person pronoun – הוּא, הִיא, הֵם, הֵן – are used as copulas. This type of copula is used for emphasis (but 5.23: Copula Concord). Some consider the negative word אֵין as a copula, since "like the third person pronouns" it can be combined only with a noun or a participle (see below). However, it is more correct to consider as copula only the pronominal attached to this negative word. Thus, it is true that there is a copula in the sentence אֶסְתֵּר אֵינָהּ מַגֶּדֶת (Esther does not tell), but it is the pronominal suffix in אֵינָהּ (literally she-not), while in אֵין אֶסְתֵּר מַגֶּדֶת there is no copula. It should also be noted that הוּא, הִיא, הֵם, הֵן can be combined with the predicator even when it is a verb in the past or future, e.g., עֲצַת יְהוָה הִיא תָקוּם (see 4.25: Attributive Sentence; 4.26: Focusing Sentence; 5.23: Copula Concord).

4.23: NOMINAL SENTENCE AND VERBAL SENTENCE. It is usual in Hebrew syntax to distinguish between nominal sentences and verbal sentences according to whether the predicator is a noun or verb. This distinction was borrowed from Arabic syntax, but in Arabic it depends on the first word of the sentence: if it is a noun, the sentence is nominal; if it is a verb, the sentence is verbal. Opinions differ when the predicator in Hebrew is a participle. In earlier Hebrew the participle was regarded as a noun and hence a sentence whose predicator was a participle was considered a nominal sentence. However, in modern Hebrew the status of a participle having the function of a predicator is identical with that of a verb, and consequently it is doubtful whether it is correct to consider such a sentence in modern Hebrew as a nominal sentence. Opinions also differ when the predicator consists only of a prepositional phrase, as in הַיֶּלֶד בַּבַּיִת (The boy [is] in the house). Generally, books on Hebrew syntax assign such sentences to the class of nominal sentences. Some maintain that a sentence whose predicate is a prepositional phrase has no predicator and therefore it cannot be a nominal sentence, but instead should be termed a verbal sentence without a predicator. The presence or absence of predicator (expressed by a verb) is the sole difference, according to this view, between these sentences and sentences such as הַיֶּלֶד יָשַׁב בַּבַּיִת (The boy sat in the house), הַיֶּלֶד הָיָה בַּבַּיִת (The boy was in the house). The word בַּבַּיִת (in the house) serves in the sentences exactly the same function of complement to the predicator (in this instance, adverbial).

4.24: IDENTIFYING SENTENCE. Nominal sentences (in the restricted meaning of the term) where the state of determination of the subject and predicator is the same – whether they are both determined or both undetermined – are called equative or identifying sentences. With such sentences, e.g., מִלְחָמָה הִיא מָוֶת (War is death), it is sometimes impossible to decide which is subject and which is predicator except by the context. At all events, each of the parts identifies the other, the predicator being called the identifying predicator. Of particular interest are cases where the second part of the sentence is realized by a subordinate sentence, e.g., יְהוָה אֱלֹהֵיכֶם הוּא הַנִּלְחָם לָכֶם (The Lord your God is the one who fights for you). There is no basis for the view that in such a structure the first part יְהוָה אֱלֹהֵיכֶם is always the subject and the second part הַנִּלְחָם לָכֶם is the predicator. On the contrary, the first part usually has the function of predicator.

4.25: ATTRIBUTIVE SENTENCE. When the subject is determined and the predicator is undetermined, the predicator's function is to attribute what is denoted in the subject to the class possessing the characteristic denoted by the predicator, e.g., in יוֹסֵף הוּא פָּקִיד (Joseph is an official) the attribution is to the class of officials. Such a predicator is termed an attributive predicator.

4.26: FOCUSING SENTENCE (EXTRA-POSITION). This last structure formally belongs to the focusing sentence structures, but this term is usually assigned to sentences such as הַוָּתִיקִים – אִישׁ אֵינוֹ שָׂם לֵב אֲלֵיהֶם (The veterans – nobody pays any attention to them) or סַבָּא – הוּא אֵינוֹ מִתְעַיֵּף לְעוֹלָם (Grandpa – he is never tired). The structure of such a sentence is explained in current syntax as the result of a transformation from another sentence in which the first word of the focusing sentence appears in the second part of the sentence in place of the pronoun that agrees with it in gender and number: אִישׁ אֵינוֹ שָׂם לֵב אֶל הַוָּתִיקִים (Nobody pays any attention to the veterans), סַבָּא אֵינוֹ מִתְעַיֵּף לְעוֹלָם (Grandpa is never tired). With a focusing sentence (in the restricted sense of the term) the first word, or first endocentric phrase, is always to be considered the subject of the sentence, while whatever comes after it is the predicate. The predicate itself is an embedded sentence, and hence the focusing sentence is always a complex sentence. Others maintain that the focusing sentence is merely a simple sentence with a change in the order of the words. In any case, all agree that the noun appearing initially in a focusing sentence is very much more emphasized than it would be in a simple sentence.

4.27: INDEFINITE SENTENCE. It is worth noting that there are sentences without a subject, in particular where the predicator-nucleus is realized by an infinitive linked to a modal auxiliary, e.g., אֶפְשָׁר לְהַבְחִין בְּכָךְ מִיָּד ([It is] possible to discern it immediately), cf. 4.45: Infinitive as Object. However, many will argue that אֶפְשָׁר (possible) alone is predicator, and the string of all the other words in the sentence is the subject. In any case, this sentence is an indefinite sentence, that is to say a sentence whose understood subject is any man or men in general.

4.3: Adjunct

The adjunct differs from the other parts of the sentence in that by definition it cannot serve as nucleus for another part of the sentence, nor can it be linked to any part except a noun, irrespective of what function the noun fills in the sentence. Any word to which an adjunct serves as a nucleus, is considered in Hebrew syntax also as an adjunct.

4.31: MORPHOLOGICAL CLASSIFICATION OF ADJUNCTS. From a morphological point of view, seven types of adjunct can be distinguished:

(1) attributive adjunct; (2) possessive pronoun adjunct (whether affixed or independent); (3) adjunct in the construct case; (4) prepositional phrase adjunct; (5) adjunct before nucleus; (6) appositive; (7) embedded sentence. These types are exemplified as follows:

(1) הָאִישׁ הַזָּקֵן הֶאֱזִין בְּסַבְלָנוּת (The old man listened patiently);

(2) הַכּוֹבַע שֶׁלִּי נָפַל לַמַּיִם (My hat fell into the water);

(3) קִירוֹת הַבַּיִת מְכֻסִּים אֵזוֹב (The walls of the house are covered with moss);

(4) הַזָּקֵן מִנַּהֲרַיִם הֵקִים אֶת הַמִּפְעָל (The old man from Nahrayim set up the enterprise);

(5) שְׁלוֹשָׁה סוּסִים דּוֹהֲרִים (Three horses are galloping);

(6) רְאוּבֵן, הַבְּכוֹר, יָרַד לְמִצְרַיִם (Reuben, the firstborn, went down to Egypt);

(7) הַנַּעַר, שֶׁלֹּא יָדַע בֵּין יְמִינוֹ לִשְׂמֹאלוֹ, הִסְכִּים בְּרָצוֹן (The lad, who could not distinguish between his right and left, agreed willingly).

All these types of adjunct appear to be transformed from other structures. With uncertainty as to the source of adjuncts of type (5), all have their source in the predicator (cf. 5.12: Predicator Transformed into Adjunct) or, in some cases, in another part of the predicate. Thus, the following set of sentences can be seen as the source of the adjuncts in the above examples:

(1) הָאִישׁ זָקֵן; הוּא הֶאֱזִין בְּסַבְלָנוּת (The man is old; he listened patiently);

(2) יֵשׁ לִי כּוֹבַע; הוּא נָפַל לַמַּיִם (I have a hat; it fell into the water);

(3) לַבַּיִת יֵשׁ קִירוֹת; הֵם מְכֻסִּים אֵזוֹב (The house has walls; they are covered with moss);

(4) הַזָּקֵן גָּר בְּנַהֲרַיִם (קָשׁוּר בְּנַהֲרַיִם); הוּא הֵקִים אֶת הַמִּפְעָל (The old man lived in Nahrayim (he is connected with Nahrayim); he set up the enterprise);

(6) ראוּבֵן הוּא הַבְּכוֹר; הוּא יָרַד לְמִצְרַיִם (Reuben is the firstborn; he went down to Egypt);

(7) הַנַּעַר לֹא יָדַע בֵּין יְמִינוֹ לִשְׂמֹאלוֹ; הוּא הִסְכִּים בְּרָצוֹן (The lad could not distinguish between his right and left; he agreed willingly). At present it is not clear what the source is for an adjunct denoting quantity. On concord with the adjunct, see 5.12: Predicator Transformed into Adjunct, and 5.3: Determiner Concord.

4.32: RESTRICTIVE AND NONRESTRICTIVE ADJUNCT. Only a few works dealing with Hebrew syntax mention the distinction between restrictive adjunct and nonrestrictive adjunct, sometimes merely to indicate that a nonrestrictive adjunct "is not an adjunct." An example of a restrictive adjunct would be if a man having three sons and wanting to say something about the eldest says בְּנִי הַגָּדוֹל לוֹמֵד כְּבָר בָּאוּנִיבֶרְסִיטָה (My grown-up son is already studying at the university). The function of the word הַגָּדוֹל (grown-up) is that of restrictive adjunct, distinguishing this son from the others. An example of a nonrestrictive adjunct would be if a man with one son wants to say something about him and wants incidentally to mention that he is grown-up; he says בְּנִי הַגָּדוֹל לוֹמֵד כְּבָר בָּאוּנִיבֶרְסִיטָה (My grown-up son is already studying at the university). The function of the word הַגָּדוֹל (grown-up) is then that of nonrestrictive adjunct. This distinction is important, and in practice has also a formal expression, particularly in intonation, but sometimes also in punctuation. There is no pause between the nucleus and a restrictive adjunct: the pitch of the latter rises slightly, and it has greater stress. On the other hand, there is a slight pause between the nucleus and a nonrestrictive adjunct: the pitch of the latter falls slightly, and it has a lighter stress. If the nonrestrictive adjunct is long, it is usual to put a comma before it. Usually there is no comma before a restrictive adjunct, even when it is a subordinate embedded sentence (despite the official rules for punctuation, which require a comma before every adjunct that is a sentence).

The structural ambiguity of the adjunct can be explained in transformational grammar. The adjunct is transformed from the predicate of another sentence, this sentence being the continuation of a preceding sentence. The same subject serves these two sentences, both of which are deleted by a deletion transformation and hence do not appear in the text. But the subject of the second sentence does not always refer to the same quantity of substances or material that the subject of the first sentence refers to. When it refers to a lesser quantity, the adjunct in the transformed sentence is a restrictive adjunct; when it refers to the same quantity, the adjunct is nonrestrictive. The sources of the above examples are therefore in the following two sets of sentences:

(a) He has three sons. יֵשׁ לוֹ שְׁלוֹשָׁה בָּנִים

One of them is grown-up. אֶחָד מֵהֶם גָּדוֹל

He is studying at the university. הוּא לוֹמֵד בָּאוּנִיבֶרְסִיטָה

His grown-up son is studying at the university (restrictive adjunct). בְּנוֹ הַגָּדוֹל לוֹמֵד בָּאוּנִיבֶרְסִיטָה

(b) He has one son. יֵשׁ לוֹ בֵּן אֶחָד

He is grown-up. הוּא גָּדוֹל

He is studying at the university. הוּא לוֹמֵד בָּאוּנִיבֶרְסִיטָה

His grown-up son is studying at the university (nonrestrictive adjunct). בְּנוֹ הַגָּדוֹל לוֹמֵד בָּאוּנִיבֶרְסִיטָה

4.33: POSSESSIVE PRONOUN AS ADJUNCT. Some explanatory comments on several of the types of adjuncts enumerated above are called for. The possessive pronoun as adjunct: in "deep grammar" its source is in a sentence denoting possession, e.g., יֵשׁ לוֹ אָח (He has a brother) → אָחִיו or הָאָח שֶׁלּוֹ (his brother). The possessive pronoun affix, e.g., in אָחִיו, and the independent possessive pronoun, e.g., שֶׁלּוֹ, are not entirely free variants, but sometimes the appearance of one or the other is conditioned (see below). It is worth noting that in written Hebrew the use of the affix is between ten and fifteen times more frequent than the use of the independent form. As far as can be ascertained from the few studies in this area, the use of the affix is greater in spoken Hebrew, but more substantial studies are required before one can establish the relative frequency with any certainty.

The most obvious conditions favoring the appearance of the independent form of the possessive pronoun are the following:

(1) when a second possessive pronoun is used to emphasize an affixed possessive pronoun, e.g., כַּרְמִי שֶׁלִּי לֹא נָטָרְתִּי (I did not tend my own vineyard);

(2) when the nucleus is a proper noun, e.g., לֹא יַעֲזֹב וְלֹא יִטֹּשׁ אֶת מֶנְדְּלֶי שֶׁלּוֹ (He will not desert his Mendele);

(3) generally with a foreign or borrowed word, e.g., הַטֶּלֶפוֹן שֶׁלּוֹ מְצַלְצֵל (His telephone is ringing);

(4) with a noun-numeral, e.g., בִּשְׁנוֹת הַשְּׁלוֹשִׁים שֶׁלּוֹ (In his thirties);

(5) with a noun in the construct state, e.g., דִּירַת הַשְּׂרָד שֶׁלּוֹ (His official residence);

(6) with a word that was not originally a noun, e.g., אַתָּה מוּכָן לְהָפֵר אֶת הַ"בְּרֹגֶז" שֶׁלְּךָ? (Are you ready to cancel your anger?);

(7) with a phrase that is used metaphorically, e.g., גַּם בְּאַרְבַּע אַמּוֹת שֶׁלָּנוּ (Even within our "four cubits");

(8) when the nucleus has two meanings and the rarer meaning is intended, e.g., הָעִיר הִתְפַּרְסְמָה בַּצַּדִּיקִים שֶׁלָּהּ (= בָּאַדְמוֹרִים) (The city was famous for its "pious men" = ḥasidic rabbis);

(9) when the nucleus is used euphemistically, e.g., זֹאת מַצִּיעִים לִי הַ"יְּדִידִים" שֶׁלִּי! (My "friends" suggest it to me!). Haim Rosén (see bibliography) has argued that the difference in usage between the two forms corresponds to the difference between inalienable possession (e.g., the family relationship or the parts of the body) and alienable possession. This proposal seems dubious.

4.34: THE CONSTRUCT STRUCTURE. An endocentric phrase consisting of nouns, or words that have nominal function, the order of which cannot be changed without changing the meaning of the phrase, is said to be in the construct state. This phrase may be in three structures:

(1) Close construct state, when two nouns are linked without interruption (except for the definite article), e.g., בֵּית הָאִישׁ (The man's house). On the changes in form of the first noun, see above, Morphology. The second noun does not change.

(2) Loose construct state when the word שֶׁל interrupts between the two nouns, e.g., הַבַּיִת שֶׁל הָאִישׁ (The house of the man).

(3) Reduplicated construct state, when a possessive pronominal affix agreeing in gender and number with the second noun is attached to the first noun, and the word שֶׁל is put between the nouns, e.g., בֵּיתוֹ שֶׁל הָאִישׁ (The (his) house of the man). The two last structures are termed dismembered construct states. There are other ways as well of making the construct state discontinuous, for example by the preposition לְ or מִן, e.g., צִנְצֶנֶת מִזְּכוּכִית (A glass container). It is difficult to say under what conditions the three types of construct states are in free variation and when one of them must be used. But it is clear that there are certain phrases that can only be used in one type of construct state, e.g., חֲנֻכַּת הַבַּיִת (the inauguration of the home), זוּטוֹ שֶׁל יָם (the floor of the sea). With other phrases, the meaning changes if a different type is used, e.g., זֶה דְּבַר הַמְּפַקֵּד (This is the message of the commander), זֶה דָּבָר שֶׁל הַמְּפַקֵּד (This item belongs to the commander); בֶּן עֶשְׂרִים (twenty years old), בְּנָם שֶׁל עֶשְׂרִים (the son of twenty). In a construct state consisting of two words the nucleus is usually the first word, while the second word is the adjunct, e.g., עֲבוֹדַת אֱלִילִים (the worship of idols). For other possibilities, see 4.36: Adjunct before the "Head." If it consists of three or more words, usually the second and later words are each adjunct to the immediately preceding word, and the combination is in turn adjunct to the immediately preceding word. For example in the phrase עֲבוֹדַת אֱלִילֵי זָהָב (the worship of idols of gold), זָהָב (gold) is adjunct to אֱלִילִים (idols) and אֱלִילֵי זָהָב (idols of gold) is adjunct to עֲבוֹדָה (worship):

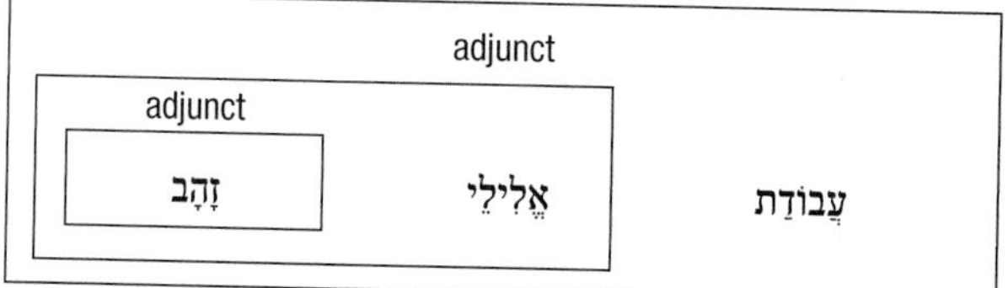

In an analysis of surface structure, the words in construct state are classified semantically; in deep grammar they can be classified according to the function they perform in the underlying structure from which the construct state has been transformed.

4.341: Classification of Types of Construct Structure. The following are the chief meanings attributed to the *nomen rectum* (the last noun of the construct phrase; following Pereẓ): (1) the owner of what is denoted by the *nomen regens* (the last but one of the phrase), e.g., גַּן הָאִכָּר (the farmer's garden); (2) the material from which is made what is denoted by the *nomen regens*, e.g., כְּלֵי כֶסֶף (vessels of silver); (3) the genus of what is denoted by the *nomen regens*, e.g., עֲצֵי שִׁטִּים (trees of acacia wood); (4) the characteristic of the *nomen regens*, e.g., לְשׁוֹן שֶׁקֶר (an expression of falsehood); (5) the limit of application for the characteristic expressed in the *nomen regens*, e.g., נְקִי כַּפַּיִם (clean of hands); (6) the content of the *nomen regens*, e.g., סִפְרֵי מוּסָר (books of ethics); (7) the agent of the action expressed as a verbal noun in the *nomen regens*, e.g., נְשִׁיכַת שׁוּעָל (the bite of a fox); (8) the object of the action expressed as a verbal noun in the *nomen regens*, e.g., הַדְלָקַת נֵר (the lighting of a candle); (9) the instrument used for the result expressed in the *nomen regens*, e.g., שְׂרוּפוֹת אֵשׁ (burnt by fire); (10) the place of the *nomen regens*, e.g., אַרְזֵי לְבָנוֹן (cedars of Lebanon); (11) the time of the *nomen regens*, e.g., חֲזוֹן לַיְלָה (the vision at night); (12) the cause for the fact in the *nomen regens*, e.g., חוֹלַת אַהֲבָה (sick through love); (13) the result of the *nomen regens*, e.g., גִּשְׁמֵי בְּרָכָה (rains of blessing); (14) the purpose of the *nomen regens*, e.g., מִזְבַּח קְטֹרֶת (altar of incense). In addition, sometimes the *nomen rectum* denotes the name of the *nomen regens*, e.g., נְהַר פְּרָת (the river of Euphrates), and sometimes it emphasizes the *nomen regens* or its quantity by repetition of the same word in the plural, e.g., עֶבֶד עֲבָדִים (slave of slaves). When the *nomen regens* is בַּעַל (master) or אָדוֹן (lord) the *rectum* is its property (the converse of 1 above). According to transformational theory every phrase in the construct state is a transformation from another structure, for example (cf. Ornan):

(The farmer has cows) לָאִכָּר יֵשׁ פָּרוֹת → פָּרוֹת־הָאִכָּר
(The fish has a sword – its characteristic) לַדָּג יֵשׁ חֶרֶב → דַּג־הַחֶרֶב
(The pen is made of iron) הָעֵט עָשׂוּי מִבַּרְזֶל → עֵט־בַּרְזֶל
(The moon is in the form of a sickle) הַיָּרֵחַ הוּא בְּצוּרַת חֶרְמֵשׁ → חֶרְמֵשׁ־הַיָּרֵחַ
(The land is called "Canaan") הָאָרֶץ נִקְרֵאת "כְּנַעַן" → אֶרֶץ כְּנַעַן
(The Jordan flows through the valley) הַיַּרְדֵּן זוֹרֵם בְּתוֹךְ בִּקְעָה → בִּקְעַת־הַיַּרְדֵּן
(The child is healthy) הַיֶּלֶד בָּרִיא → בְּרִיאוּת הַיֶּלֶד
(Jackals howl) תַּנִּים מְיַלְלִים → יִלְלַת תַּנִּים
(The dog (habitually) guards the flock) הַכֶּלֶב שׁוֹמֵר אֶת הַצֹּאן → כֶּלֶב צֹאן
(The old man walks in the morning) הַזָּקֵן מְטַיֵּל בַּבֹּקֶר → טִיּוּל הַבֹּקֶר (שֶׁל הַזָּקֵן)

Since the structure of the construct state can be transformed from a large number of different sources, it is clear that it has a large number of possible meanings. However, in practice many meanings are ruled out, since the speaker knows the meanings of the words and the context in which the structure appears. There is in fact no ambiguity in a construction such as פָּרוֹת הָאִכָּר (the farmer's cows) since the meaning of the words allows only one possible interpretation, namely that the farmer is owner of the cows (and not the reverse, for example). Nevertheless, there are instances where the construct state is ambiguous. This might arise, e.g., when the *nomen regens* is a verbal noun derived from a transitive verb, since the *rectum* can then be agent of the action (subject in a background sentence) or recipient of the action (object in a background sentence). For example, בְּחִירַת הַנָּשִׂיא (the choice of the president) could be interpreted as a transform of הַנָּשִׂיא בָּחַר (The president chose) or (מִישֶׁהוּ) בָּחַר אֶת הַנָּשִׂיא (X chose the president). It has been claimed that in such cases the close construct state is selected for one meaning and the loose one for the other, בְּחִירַת הַנָּשִׂיא being interpreted solely as "X chose the president" while the transform of "the president chose" would be הַבְּחִירָה שֶׁל הַנָּשִׂיא (cf. Haim Rosén in the bibliography). An examination of considerable material drawn from newspapers and modern literature does not support the claim.

4.35: PREPOSITIONAL PHRASE ADJUNCT. An adjunct realized as a prepositional phrase is the result of one or the other of two transformations:

4.351: Prepositional Phrase Adjunct as Sentence Remnant. (1) It may be a remnant of a sentence in which it functioned as an adverbial. When the sentence is embedded in another sentence, the subject and predicator are deleted and the adverbial becomes an adjunct to the subject of the other sentence. This is illustrated in the following example:

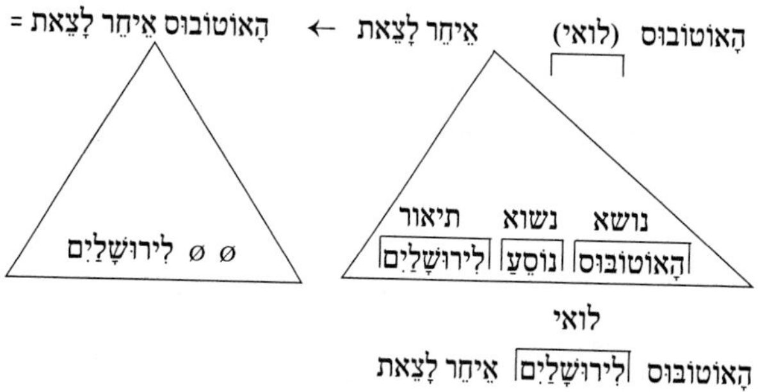

It is worth demonstrating how this explanation appears in the usual formulation of the generative-transformationalists. The two sentences are first placed one after the other:

Representation of הָאוֹטוֹבּוּס יְאַחֵר לָצֵאת
(The bus will leave late): $NP_i + VP_j$
Representation of הָאוֹטוֹבּוּס נוֹסֵעַ לִירוּשָׁלַיִם:
(The bus travels to Jerusalem): $NP_i + VP_k + PP$

$NP_i + VP_j + NP_i + VP_k + PP$
(1) (2) (3) (4) (5)

However, under certain conditions (e.g., when the subjects of the two sentences are two instances of the same nominal structure, if the referent of the subject is identical in both sentences), a transformation applies which changes the order of the words. In place of the order given above (left to right) the words are ordered (1) (3) (4) (5) (2), i.e:

$NP_i + NP_i + VP_k + PP + VP_j$

The second sentence is parenthetically included, as it was, in the first: הָאוֹטוֹבּוּס (הָאוֹטוֹבּוּס נוֹסֵעַ לִירוּשָׁלַיִם) אֵחֵר לָצֵאת. Now an obligatory transformation applies, which deletes the second instance of NP, and adds instead a relative (אֲשֶׁר, שֶׁ, or הַ). The result is $NP_i + \check{s}e + VP_k + PP + VP_j$, i.e., הָאוֹטוֹבּוּס שֶׁנּוֹסֵעַ לִירוּשָׁלַיִם אֵחֵר לָצֵאת. However, this sentence can again be transformed as follows:

Structural Description: $NP_i + \check{s}e + VP + PP + VP_j$
Structural Change: (1) (2) (3) (4) (5)
(1) Ø Ø (4) (5)

The relative ש and the internal predicator VP are deleted, leaving only $NP_i + PP + VP_j$: הָאוֹטוֹבּוּס לִירוּשָׁלַיִם אֵחֵר לָצֵאת

4.352: Prepositional Phrase with Verb Transformed to Noun. (2) The prepositional phrase is a remnant as before. However, the verb which is complemented is not deleted, but transformed into a noun, the phrase changing from complement of a verb to complement of a noun, that is to say an adjunct. For example:

adverbial *adjunct*
הֲלִיכָתוֹ לְבֵית הַסֵּפֶר ← הוּא הָלַךְ לְבֵית הַסֵּפֶר
הַטִּיּוּל בַּבֹּקֶר ← הַיְלָדִים טִיְּלוּ בַּבֹּקֶר

We should treat as a special case prepositional phrase adjuncts introduced by מִן (= מִ) (from) when they designate the place of origin or of action of what is denoted by the noun serving as nucleus, e.g., הַזָּקֵן מִנַּהֲרַיִם (the old man from Naharayim), הַמְכַשֵּׁפָה מִפָּרִיס (the witch from Paris). It is not clear what is the source sentence from which these adjuncts are transformed.

4.36: ADJUNCT BEFORE THE "HEAD" (CENTER, NUCLEUS). A pre-nucleus adjunct generally denotes quantity, and it comprises cardinals, dividers, measures, and words such as הַרְבֵּה (much), רֹב (the majority of), שְׁאָר (the rest of), קְצָת (a little), מִבְחַר (the best of).

Cardinals agree with the nucleus in gender, and in the case of units of measurement, also in number, e.g., חֲמִשָּׁה אֲנָשִׁים (five men), חָמֵשׁ אַמּוֹת בַּד (five cubits linen), שְׁנֵים עָשָׂר דוּנָם אֲדָמָה (twelve dunams of land). The numbers 3–10 are likely to be in the construct state before the nucleus, especially when the latter is determined, number 2 generally so, while number 1 appears after the nucleus when the latter is singular (אִישׁ אֶחָד), and in the construct state before the nucleus when it is determined and plural (אַחַד הָאֲנָשִׁים).

Nouns for containers, such as בַּקְבּוּק (bottle), פַּח (can), may serve as measuring units for liquids or for bulk solids such as קֶמַח (flour), or פֵּרוֹת (fruit), provided the reference is to mass-produced vessels of fixed size, e.g., הֶחָבִית מְכִילָה שְׁלוֹשָׁה פַּחִים (The barrel contains three cans), אַרְבַּע תֵּבוֹת תַּפּוּזִים (four boxes of oranges). It has not yet been established whether there is in modern Hebrew a systematic semantic difference (as Haim Rosén has claimed) between measures appearing in a close construct state, e.g., שְׁנֵי שַׂקֵּי קֶמַח (two sacks of flour), in a loose construct state, e.g., שְׁנֵי שַׂקִּים שֶׁל קֶמַח, or in apposition, e.g., שְׁנֵי שַׂקִּים קֶמַח. Similarly nouns for shapes, provided reference is to shapes with a more or less fixed size, can serve as measures for solids, e.g., שְׁנֵי כִּכְּרוֹת לֶחֶם (two loaves of bread).

4.37: APPOSITION. Two nouns one of which has the function of adjunct to the other, but without their being in the construct state relationship, are said to be in apposition. An appositive is transformed from a noun predicator. If the predicator from which it is transformed functioned as identifier in an identifying sentence (cf. 4.24: Identifying Sentence), the appositive also functions as an identifying appositive, e.g., מִרְיָם הִיא הָאָחוֹת הָרָאשִׁית (Miriam is the matron). הִיא נִמְצֵאת בְּחֻפְשָׁה (She is on leave) → מִרְיָם, הָאָחוֹת הָרָאשִׁית, נִמְצֵאת בְּחֻפְשָׁה (Miriam, the matron, is on leave). When the predicator is attributive (cf. 4.25: Attributive Sentence), the appositive is an attributive appositive, e.g., לֵוִי הוּא ד"ר לְמִשְׁפָּטִים (Levi is a doctor of law). הוּא הִתְמַנָּה לְמַרְצֶה (He has been appointed lecturer) → לֵוִי, ד"ר לְמִשְׁפָּטִים, הִתְמַנָּה לְמַרְצֶה (Levi, a doctor of law, has been appointed lecturer). Books on syntax generally note that the appositive follows the nucleus. Hence, in שְׁלֹמֹה הַמֶּלֶךְ (Solomon the king), הַמֶּלֶךְ is said to be appositive, while in הַמֶּלֶךְ שְׁלֹמֹה (King Solomon), the proper noun שְׁלֹמֹה is said to be appositive. But on the basis of the semantic identity of the two phrases, it has been proposed that an attributive noun denoting status, occupation, or title that is attached to a proper noun should be considered an appositive even when it precedes the proper noun, e.g., הד"ר לְמִשְׁפָּטִים לֵוִי הִתְמַנָּה לְמַרְצֶה (Doctor of Law Levi has been appointed lecturer). In such cases the appositive has a determiner.

As with the adjectival adjunct, all appositives can be divided into restrictive and nonrestrictive. Other types of appositives are appositional compounds, e.g., כֻּרְסָה = מִטָּה (divan bed) and quantifying apposition, e.g., שְׁלוֹשָׁה אֲנָשִׁים (three men). Certain introductory expressions appear before identifying appositives, e.g., כְּלוֹמַר (that is to say), דְּהַיְנוּ (that is), בְּיִחוּד (especially). Another characteristic of the identifying appositive is that the preposition before the nucleus is sometimes repeated before the following appositive. It seems that this only applies when the appositive is nonrestrictive. Such a repetition is obligatory when the nucleus is a pronoun and the following appositive is a noun, e.g., אָמְרוּ עָלָיו עַל רַבִּי עֲקִיבָא (They said about him, about Rabbi Akiva).

4.38: RELATIVE CLAUSE. An adjunct sentence is a transformation of a complete predicate and not just of a predicator, e.g., הַמַּחֲזֶה הֻעֲלָה אֶמֶשׁ לָרִאשׁוֹנָה (The play was put on last night for the first time). הוּא וַדַּאי יִזְכֶּה לְהַצְלָחָה (It will certainly meet with success) → הַמַּחֲזֶה שֶׁהֻעֲלָה אֶמֶשׁ לָרִאשׁוֹנָה וַדַּאי יִזְכֶּה לְהַצְלָחָה (The play which was put on last night for the first time will certainly succeed). The condition for this transformation is that the noun appearing in one sentence will also appear in the other sentence. In the transformed adjunct sentence this noun is deleted and is replaced by a pronoun agreeing with it in gender and in number. However, if the noun functioned as subject of the sentence before its transformation, then generally gender and number concord with the predicator is sufficient and a pronoun is not inserted. See further on this, 5.22: Pronoun Concord in a Relative Clause. The indicators of the subordination of the adjunct are שֶׁ and אֲשֶׁר (virtually in free variation), and ה under certain conditions (cf. 6.32: Subordinators in Links beyond the Sentence). Adjunct sentences may also be asyndetic, cf. 6.322: Word Order in Links Beyond the Sentence. Another category of adjunct sentence must also be distinguished, namely the adjunct content-sentence, e.g., הַהַשְׁעָרָה שֶׁיֵּשׁ חַיִּים עַל הַמַּאְדִּים נִתְבַּדְּתָה (The supposition that there is life on Mars has been proved false). The source for the content-adjunct is not in the predicate of a preceding sentence but in the object sentence of a preceding sentence. It is formed when the verb complemented by the object is converted into a noun. The source of the content-adjunct in the above example is in the object of the following sentence. שִׁעֲרוּ שֶׁיֵּשׁ חַיִּים עַל הַמַּאְדִּים (It was supposed that there is life on Mars) → הַהַשְׁעָרָה שֶׁיֵּשׁ חַיִּים עַל הַמַּאְדִּים (The supposition that there is life on Mars…), cf. the similar phenomenon in 4.35: Prepositional Phrase Adjunct and 4.352: Prepositional Phrase with Verb Transformed to Noun, a prepositional phrase as adjunct. There is no element in a content-adjunct which agrees in gender and number with the noun to which the adjunct is attached. Introducing words of the subordination of the content-adjunct are שֶׁ or כִּי. If the content-adjunct is transformed from a question, the interrogative word serves as an introducing word of subordination, e.g., הוּא דָאַג: מַה יַּעֲשֶׂה בָּעִיר הַגְּדוֹלָה? זֶה לֹא נָתַן לוֹ מָנוֹחַ (He worried: What would he do in the big city? This gave him no rest) → הַדְּאָגָה מַה יַּעֲשֶׂה בָּעִיר הַגְּדוֹלָה לֹא נָתְנָה לוֹ מָנוֹחַ (The anxiety about what he would do in the big city gave him no rest). When the content-adjunct begins with an infinitive there is no other introductory word of subordination, e.g., נִכַּר אֶצְלָם הָרָצוֹן לְהִתְבַּלֵּט (In them could be seen the desire to excel).

4.4: Object

Grammars of European languages and of Arabic, also accepted in Hebrew grammars, have long defined the object semantically (e.g., "The word denoting the substance to which the action expressed in the predicator passes is called the direct object. If the action is merely connected with it, the word is called the indirect object").

4.41: OBLIGATORY COMPLEMENT AND OBLIGATORY PREPOSITION. The syntactic definition of an object is based on its being obligatory, or "close," complements of the verb-predicator. Optional complements are adverbials (cf. 4.5: Adverbial). In many instances it is possible to distinguish sharply between an obligatory complement, e.g., the prepositional phrase consisting of ב and a following noun as complement to the verb הִשְׁתַּמֵּשׁ (use) and an optional complement, e.g., the same phrase as complement to the verb הָלַךְ (walk). הִשְׁתַּמֵּשׁ בַּחֶדֶר (He used the room), as opposed to הָלַךְ בַּחֶדֶר (He walked in the room). Usually the preposition introducing an obligatory complement cannot be changed, for example, we cannot replace the preposition ב linked to the verb הִשְׁתַּמֵּשׁ by another preposition. Sometimes there is a restricted range of permissible substitutions though generally only one additional preposition is allowed, e.g, נִתְמַנָּה כ... = נִתְמַנָּה ל... (He was appointed as…). Sometimes a change of preposition effects the meaning of the verb, e.g., קִנֵּא ב... (He envied) … ≠ קִנֵּא ל... (He suspected). A preposition introducing an obligatory complement is called an obligatory preposition. It can be considered a part of the lexical entry for the verb. Although at first sight the obligatory preposition must always accompany its verb, there are certain conditions, apparently varying with particular items, under which it can be omitted. In all probability one should speak of varying degrees of obligatoriness in Hebrew (cf. 5.5: Obligatoriness). Moreover, the same verb may appear also without requiring a particular preposition. Since the obligatory preposition is part of the verb's lexical entry, it must be concluded that such a verb should be given two separate lexical entries, one when the obligatory preposition is a part of it, and the other when the verb appears without an obligatory preposition. Generally the two entries will have different meanings, e.g., עָבַד (He worked) – עָבַד עַל (He worked upon); הִתְגַּלְגֵּל (He wandered around) – הִתְגַּלְגֵּל ל... (He was transformed into); הִשְׁתַּגֵּעַ (He became mad) – הִשְׁתַּגֵּעַ אַחֲרֵי (He longed desperately for). The difference can cause ambiguities since a particular preposition not required by the verb in a certain occurrence can nevertheless be attached to it as an optional complement. Hence, the combination of the same verb and preposition can be followed by either an object or by an adverbial. In such instances, of course, the distinction is not so easy to make. At all events, dictionaries do not adequately distinguish between prepositions that are obligatory to a certain degree, and optional prepositions.

4.42: DIRECT AND INDIRECT OBJECT. The terms "direct object" and "indirect object" derive from European or Arabic grammars. They were originally intended to distinguish between objects preceded by a preposition and those linked directly to a verb without an intervening preposition. Hebrew, however, has a preposition – אֶת – which appears before a direct object. Thus, the use of this term in Hebrew does not correspond to its original use. On the other hand, אֶת generally appears only before an object which is a determined noun, and many writers point to this as justification for the use of the term in Hebrew. It has also been argued that אֶת should not be regarded as a preposition at all, but merely as an indicator of determination. In practice there is no essential syntactic distinction between direct object and indirect object, since all objects are obligatory complements. A subclassification of obligatory complements based on the nature of the obligatory preposition should include אֶת, even though אֶת can be replaced under certain conditions by Ø, which is merely a variant of אֶת. It seems that here too the influence of foreign grammars has been excessive.

4.43: TRANSITIVE AND INTRANSITIVE VERB. These terms are entailed by the preceding terms. Generally, those defining object semantically will define "intransitive verb" and "transitive verb" semantically, e.g., "a verb whose action passes to another body is a transitive verb," while an intransitive verb is a verb "whose action does not pass to others, but affects only the actor." It is obvious that in such definitions "verb" means the lexical entry of the verb, comprising all its forms in all its occurrences. A moment's thought will show, as Jespersen has shown, that the action of many transitive verbs does not pass to another body. The syntactic approach should be applied here too and each verb classified in the sentence in which it appears. That is to say, one should not refer to a verb in this respect as a concept comprising all the possible forms distinguished in the grammar, but as a given form appearing in a given sentence. The tokens of the verbs and not their entries or their types should be classified as transitive and intransitive. In the sentence הַמַּלָּח מְעַשֵּׁן סִיגָר (The sailor is smoking a cigar), מְעַשֵּׁן is considered a transitive verb since it has an obligatory (close) complement, while in the sentence הַמַּלָּח מְעַשֵּׁן (The sailor is smoking) or הַמַּלָּח מְעַשֵּׁן בַּלְּהִיטוּת (The sailor is smoking eagerly) it is an intransitive verb since it does not have a complement or it has an optional complement.

4.44: FIRST AND SECOND OBJECT. When in the same sentence there are two objects with the relationship between them of subject-predicator, i.e., nexus (cf. 4.2: Subject and Predicator), it is usual to call them first object (the object performing the function of subject in that relationship) and second object (performing the function of predicator), e.g., הָרוֹפֵא חָשַׁב אֶת הַחוֹלֶה לְבַדַּאי (The doctor considered the patient an impostor), underlying which is the sentence הַחוֹלֶה בַּדַּאי (The patient is an impostor). Only certain verbs can appear in such a sentence, verbs denoting the attitude or opinion of the person designated in the subject to what is designated in the first object. This attitude, or an action resulting from this attitude, is expressed in the second object. Thus, in the above the attitude of the doctor to the patient is expressed in בַּדַּאי (an impostor). Similarly, מוֹצֵא אֲנִי מַר מִמָּוֶת אֶת הָאִשָּׁה (I find woman more bitter than death) – הָאִשָּׁה (woman) is first object, מַר מִמָּוֶת (more bitter than death) second object. Here another structure should be mentioned, namely sentences in which the object is a subordinate sentence beginning with a subordinator, e.g., הָרוֹפֵא חָשַׁב שֶׁהַחוֹלֶה בַּדַּאי (The doctor thought that the patient was an impostor). In biblical Hebrew the word הִנֵּה (behold) often opens the subordinate sentence, e.g., וּפַרְעֹה חֹלֵם...וְהִנֵּה מִן הַיְאֹר עֹלֹת שֶׁבַע פָּרוֹת ("and Pharoah dreamed… and, behold, there came up out of the river seven kine," Genesis 41:1, 2) and וַיַּרְא וְהִנֵּה חָרְבוּ פְּנֵי הָאֲדָמָה ("and he looked, and behold, the face of the ground was dried," Genesis 8:13). See also 4.51: Circumstance Adverbial.

4.45: INFINITIVE AS OBJECT. A complex sentence whose predicator is a verb denoting saying or thinking and whose object is an inner sentence, e.g., הִבְטַחְתִּי שֶׁאָבוֹא (I promised that I would come) with שֶׁאָבוֹא (that I would come) as object, can be expressed also as הִבְטַחְתִּי לָבוֹא (I promised to come) with לָבוֹא (to come) as object. The infinitive לָבוֹא is transformed in this case from אֲנִי אָבוֹא (I will come), containing subject and predicator. Sometimes the infinitive has its own complements, e.g., in the sentence הַמְּפַקֵּד דָּרַשׁ מִן הַחַיָּלִים לְהִשָּׁמַע לוֹ (The officer required the soldiers to obey him), לוֹ is object, obligatory complement to לְהִשָּׁמַע (to obey) while לְהִשָּׁמַע לוֹ (to obey him) is object of דָּרַשׁ (required). However, sometimes an identical surface structure should not be treated in this way because the first verb in such a combination is an auxiliary verb while the infinitive is the nucleus of the phrase with the function of predicator. "Auxiliary verb" has a wider range in this sense than is accepted for some languages, including English. These verbs complementing the nucleus of the predicator comprise modals and aspectual verbs, viz. verbs denoting the speaker's attitude toward the content of the sentence, the attitude of the person designated as subject toward the content of the rest of the sentence, or the point of time in the action, its duration, its recurrence, etc. For example: הַגֶּשֶׁר עָלוּל לְהִשָּׁבֵר (The bridge is likely to break), הַמְּפַקֵּד נֶאֱלַץ לְהַמְתִּין (The officer was forced to wait), הַגֶּשֶׁר מַתְחִיל לְהִשָּׁבֵר (The bridge is starting to break), הַגֶּשֶׁם מוֹסִיף לָרֶדֶת (The rain continues to fall), הָאִכָּר נוֹהֵג לִשְׁתּוֹת (The farmer is accustomed to drink). It ought to be added that besides the infinitive (the most usual form), the nucleus in such combinations may also take on such forms as participle, e.g., הִתְחִיל מְפַקְפֵּק (He began doubting); verbal noun preceded by the preposition ב, e.g., הִרְבָּה בָּאֲכִילָה (He ate a lot, literally: He increased in eating); or finite verb identical in person and tense to the auxiliary, the two verbs being coordinated by the conjunction ו, e.g., חָזַר וְקָרָא (He again read, literally: He returned and read); another aspect is expressed by repeating the same verb itself: הֵם הָלְכוּ וְהָלְכוּ (They walked for a long time). There have been hardly any studies in this area of Hebrew, and there is still no complete list or categorization of these auxiliaries.

4.46: INTERNAL OBJECT. An internal object is the term applied to a verbal noun functioning as object to a verb of the same root. The internal object is usually not an obligatory complement. It has one of two functions: (1) to emphasize the verb serving as predicator, e.g. לִגְזֹל גְּזֵלָה, לִמְעֹל מְעִילָה, לִגְנֹב גְּנֵבָה וּלְהִסְתַּלֵּק (To embezzle (misuse), to rob, to steal – and to disappear). This use is a modern counterpart of the use of the infinitive absolute in biblical Hebrew, e.g., הָלוֹךְ הָלְכוּ הָעֵצִים (The trees have surely gone); (2) to serve as nucleus to an adjunct when the combination of nucleus and adjunct functions as adverbial to a predicator, e.g., the phrase יְשִׁיבָה כְּבֵדָה וּמְאֻשֶּׁשֶׁת (a heavy and firm sitting) in the sentence יָשַׁב הַכַּפְרִי יְשִׁיבָה כְּבֵדָה וּמְאֻשֶּׁשֶׁת (The villager sat heavily and firmly). A direct object is usually not determined, and therefore the preposition אֶת rarely precedes it.

4.5: Adverbial

The adverbial is an optional complement of the predicator (or of the sentence as a whole, cf. 4.53: Sentence Adverbial). Adverbials generally begin with a preposition, if we exclude a few words considered adverbs, e.g., פֹּה (here), אֶתְמוֹל (yesterday), יַחְדָּו (together), הֵיטֵב (well), or temporal words, e.g., יוֹם (day), which in this function generally appear without anything added before them (though two adjacent instances of such words may appear, e.g., יוֹם יוֹם (every day), שָׁנָה בְּשָׁנָה (year by year), similarly טִפִּין טִפִּין (drop by drop)) and if we exclude the locative expressed by a noun to which is added an unstressed *a*, e.g., צָפוֹנָה (northwards), הַבַּיְתָה (home(wards)). The prepositions used for this purpose are the same prepositions introducing obligatory complements, except for אֶת. (See 4.51: Circumstance Adverbial.) In Hebrew syntax, as in the syntax of other languages without cases, it is usual to classify adverbials not formally – a method used in languages with cases – but according to content. Thus, often the following adverbials are distinguished, or at least some of them: place, time, cause, purpose, manner, measure, circumstance, condition, concession, and result. Not all of these appear in every book, nor do the authors agree on the ascription of a phrase to the same adverbial. Thus, there are differences with respect to phrases denoting duration of time, e.g., עָבַד שָׁלוֹשׁ שָׁעוֹת (He worked three hours). Different authors designate such a phrase as time adverbial, measure adverbial, or manner adverbial. Studies on the deep structure of adverbials have scarcely been written, apart from some work on the circumstance adverbial, which is recognized as a transformation of a predicator under certain conditions, e.g., הַיַּלְדָּה חָזְרָה עֲיֵפָה (The girl returned tired) ← הַיַּלְדָּה חָזְרָה (The girl returned); הִיא הָיְתָה עֲיֵפָה בְּאוֹתוֹ זְמַן (She was tired at that time). It may be supposed that research in this area will show that the traditional categories of adverbials, now based on semantic distinctions in surface structure, derive from deep structure.

4.51: CIRCUMSTANCE ADVERBIAL. The circumstance adverbial is also called "circumstance adjunct," since like adjuncts it agrees in gender and number with subject or object, e.g., הַיְלָדִים יָצְאוּ שְׂמֵחִים (The children went out happy), פָּגַשְׁתִּי אוֹתָם מְאֻשָּׁרִים (I met them happy). In both instances the agreement derives from the same source. The adjunct is transformed from a predicator – an adjective or participle – and so is the circumstance adverbial, except that with the latter the predicator denotes not a permanent phenomenon, but one that is contemporaneous with the action expressed by the predicator in our sentence. Thus, in the sentence הַיַּלְדָּה חָזְרָה עֲיֵפָה (The girl returned tired) the girl is said to be tired at that time. If tiredness was a permanent characteristic, the adverbial עֲיֵפָה would have been changed into an adjunct: הַיַּלְדָּה הָעֲיֵפָה חָזְרָה (The tired girl returned). On the other hand, the circumstance adverbial does not have to be attached to a subject or object, and these do not function as nucleuses to it. Moreover, the circumstance adverbial is not determined, even when the noun it is related to is determined. This adverbial can be expressed by a participle form preceded by the preposition ב, e.g., הוּא נִכְנַס לָעִנְיָן בְּמִתְכַּוֵּן (He entered into the affair intentionally). The adverbial differs in these features from the adjunct. (For the difference between circumstance adverbial related to the object and second object, cf. 4.44: First and Second Object.) Since the predicator is the source for both circumstance adverbial and adjunct, we cannot accept the suggestion that the circumstance adverbial be termed "circumstance predicator." The transformation of the predicator does not necessarily produce a circumstance adverbial. Furthermore, terms for the parts of the sentence in surface grammar are not generally based on their transformations from deep structure. A circumstance adverbial can be realized by a complete sentence. This sentence, considered a subordinate sentence, is linked to the independent part by the conjunctions כְּשֶׁ, בְּלִי שֶׁ, בְּלֹא שֶׁ, and ו, or it is juxtaposed to the independent sentence without a conjunction, e.g., הַיַּלְדָּה הִצְבִּיעָה עַל הַשּׁוֹדֵד כְּשֶׁהִיא רוֹעֶדֶת מִפַּחַד (The girl pointed to the robber while she was trembling with fright), הוֹלֵךְ לוֹ יְדִידֵנוּ בַּדֶּרֶךְ, הַשָּׁמַיִם הַכְּחֻלִּים מֵעַל רֹאשׁוֹ וְהַנַּחַל לִימִינוֹ (Our friend walks along, the blue skies above his head and the brook on his right). In circumstance sentences, the predicator is realized by a participle form (or the sentence lacks a predicator, cf. 4.23: Nominal Sentence and Verbal Sentence). See also 5.13: Predicator Transformed into Circumstance Adverbial.

4.52: TYPES OF CONDITIONAL ADVERBIAL. The conditional adverbial is unique among the adverbials. In the rare instances when it is realized as a nominal phrase in a simple sentence it will normally begin with… בְּמִקְרֶה שֶׁל (in case of), but it is chiefly realized as a subordinate sentence in a complex sentence. The conditional adverbial is called רֵישָׁה (protasis) whether it appears at the beginning or end of the sentence, while the rest of the sentence is called סֵיפָה (apodosis). The conditional adverbial can be distinguished grammatically, and not just semantically. Moreover, the two chief categories – real condition and hypothetical condition – are also formally distinguishable. Conditional sentences also have their own intonation patterns.

A "real condition" denotes something that has happened, is happening, or will happen and whose existence entails a result expressed in the apodosis part of the sentence. The chief signs of an adverbial of real condition are (1) special subordinating conjunctions – אִם, כְּשֶׁ־, כַּאֲשֶׁר; (2) the word order in the protasis; (3) the place of the protasis in the sentence; (4) the dependence of the tense of the verb in the superordinate part on that of the verb in the conditional part. Sometimes several of these signs come together, cf. 6.322: Word Order as Indication of Subordination in section Links beyond the Sentence.

A "hypothetical condition" is one which at the time it is said is known not to be fulfilled. The speaker speculates as to the possible results if the condition had been fulfilled.

The traditional conjunctions for a hypothetical condition are אִלּוּ, לוּ, and in the negative אִלּוּלֵא, לוּלֵא. The introductory אִלְמָלֵא (אִלְמָלֵי), used mainly in literature, is sometimes interpreted as positive and sometimes as negative. In modern Hebrew (also in some places in biblical Hebrew) אִם is used also for a hypothetical condition. This use is accompanied by a verb form consisting of הָיָה (verb "be") plus participle, e.g., אִם הָיִיתָ אוֹמֵר לוֹ (If you had said to him), which is usually interpreted as a hypothetical condition indicating that the speaker knew the other had not said it. On the other hand, אִם אָמַרְתָּ לוֹ (If you said to him) is interpreted as a real condition, denoting that the speaker does not know whether the other had said it or not, but it is certainly possible that he said it. The sign of an unreal condition here is not a special conjunction (אִלּוּלֵא, לוּלֵא, לוּ as opposed to אִם) but the form of the verb (הָיָה + participle as opposed to past tense). The verb in the apodosis of a hypothetical condition also has the form הָיָה plus participle, irrespective of the verb in the protasis.

A double condition is one in which the speaker sets out both the result of the fulfillment of the condition and the result of its lack of fulfillment. This structure is also known as תְּנַאי בְּנֵי גָד וּבְנֵי רְאוּבֵן (a condition of the children of Gad and the children of Reuven), cf. Numbers 32:29–30.

An emphatic condition with negative followed by positive (see below), is apparently related to the double condition and is derived from it by a deletion transformation. For example, לֹא יִכָּנֵס אָדָם לְמַחֲנֶה צְבָאִי אֶלָּא אִם (כֵּן) הֻרְשָׁה לְכָךְ (A person may not enter a military camp unless he is expressly permitted), which is presumably before the transformation לֹא יִכָּנֵס אָדָם לְמַחֲנֶה צְבָאִי אִם לֹא הֻרְשָׁה לְכָךְ; יִכָּנֵס אָדָם לְמַחֲנֶה צְבָאִי אִם (כֵּן) הֻרְשָׁה לְכָךְ (A person may not enter a military camp if he is not expressly permitted; a person may enter a military camp if he is expressly permitted).

A concessive sentence is a conditional sentence the content of whose apodosis is reversed as far as can be determined from its presumed protasis and the subject matter of the whole sentence. It also appears to be derived from a double condition, where neither the fulfillment nor the lack of fulfillment of the condition can change the result. For example, the sentence אִם לֹא תַּעֲמֹד עַל שֶׁלְּךָ – לֹא תְּקַבֵּל, וְגַם אִם תַּעֲמֹד עַל שֶׁלְּךָ – לֹא תְּקַבֵּל (If you don't defend your own, you will not receive anything, and even if you defend you own you will not receive anything) can be contracted to אִם לֹא תַּעֲמֹד עַל שֶׁלְּךָ וְגַם אִם תַּעֲמֹד עַל שֶׁלְּךָ – לֹא תְּקַבֵּל (If you don't defend your own and even if you defend your own, you will not receive anything). (The introductory formula for such a structure can be ,"אִם...אוֹ אִם..." "בֵּין שֶׁ...וּבֵין שֶׁ...", "גַּם אִם...(וְ)גַם אִם"). If from such a structure the condition which is more probable in the context is deleted, the result is a concessive sentence: גַּם אִם תַּעֲמֹד עַל שֶׁלְּךָ – לֹא תְּקַבֵּל (Even if you defend your own you will not receive anything). A concessive sentence can also come from a series of conditional sentences in which one element is changed every time until the series comprises a wide range of topics the last of which is the converse of the first. When only the last is expressed, the rest of the possibilities are understood, deduced *a fortiori*. For example, in אֲפִילּוּ אִם יִקְרְאוּ לִי אֶבּוֹלִיצְיוֹנִיסְט, לֹא אַסְגִּיר אֶת הַכּוּשִׁי (Even if they call me an abolitionist, I shall not hand over the Negro), what is also clear is that עַל אַחַת כַּמָּה וְכַמָּה לֹא אַסְגִּיר אֶת הַכּוּשִׁי אִם יִקְרְאוּ לִי בְּשֵׁמוֹת גְּנַאי פָּחוֹת חֲרִיפִים, אִם לֹא יִקְרְאוּ לִי כְּלָל בְּשֵׁמוֹת גְּנַאי, אוֹ אִם יְשַׁבְּחוּנִי עַל כָּךְ (All the more so, I will not hand over the Negro if they call me names that are less derogatory, if they do not use any derogatory names against me, or they praise me for it).

4.53: SENTENCE ADVERBIAL. Some adverbials do not complement the predicator, but are comments adding details to what is said in the sentence as a whole, e.g., בְּמַקְלִי עָבַרְתִּי אֶת הַיַּרְדֵּן (With my staff I crossed the Jordan), דַּרְכָּם נִמְשְׁכָה בִּשְׁתִיקָה (Their journey continued in silence). These are not predicator adverbials but sentence adverbials or situation adverbials. A subordinate clause can also realize this function, e.g., הוּא נִכְנַס לְעֶצֶם הָעִנְיָן בְּלֹא שֶׁנִּתְכַּוֵּן לְכָךְ (He went into the heart of the matter though he did not intend to do so). Following N. Chomsky's works on transformational grammar, it has been claimed by some authors, that in many cases place and time adverbials, as well as some other adverbials, should be considered as sentence adverbials, e.g., פֹּה הַנְּעָרוֹת נָאוֹת (Here the girls are nice) (see Rubinstein, *Lešonenu*, 35).

4.54: PREPOSITIONS AS INTRODUCERS OF ADVERBIALS. Grammars do not give a complete list of prepositions introducing classes of adverbials, but a large number can be extracted from the examples they give. A fuller list is provided of conjunctions introducing subordinate sentences functioning as adverbials. Below is a list of the main prepositions and conjunctions serving as introducers to adverbials:

Place Adverbial: prepositions – בְּ, לְ, מִ, אֶל, אֵצֶל, מִמַּעַל לְ, בְּמָקוֹם, עַל פְּנֵי, עַל יַד, עַל גַּבֵּי, עַל, מִתַּחַת לְ; conjunctions – בְּמָקוֹם אֲשֶׁר, מָקוֹם שֶׁ, בְּמָקוֹם שֶׁ (and other prepositions preceding מָקוֹם שֶׁ, or מָקוֹם אֲשֶׁר, eg. אֶל מָקוֹם שֶׁ, מִמָּקוֹם אֲשֶׁר).

Time Adverbial: prepositions – בְּ, כְּ, לְ, מִ, אַחַר, אַחֲרֵי, לִפְנֵי, עַד; conjunctions – קֹדֶם שֶׁ, טֶרֶם שֶׁ, טֶרֶם, מֵאָז, אַךְ, לְאַחַר שֶׁ, מֵעֵת שֶׁ, מִשָּׁעָה שֶׁ, מִדֵּי, כָּל עוֹד, בְּעוֹד, כֵּיוָן שֶׁ, כָּל אֵימַת שֶׁ, בְּעֵת שֶׁ, כָּל זְמַן שֶׁ, בְּשָׁעָה שֶׁ, לִכְשֶׁ, and also the above prepositions (except בְּ, לְ) in combination with שֶׁ, e.g., לִפְנֵי שֶׁ, אַחֲרֵי שֶׁ, מִשֶּׁ, כְּשֶׁ, or (except בְּ, לְ, מִ) in combination with אֲשֶׁר, e.g., עַד אֲשֶׁר, לִפְנֵי אֲשֶׁר, אַחֲרֵי אֲשֶׁר, כַּאֲשֶׁר.

Manner Adverbials: prepositions – בְּ, כְּ, לְ, מִ, מִתּוֹךְ, כְּמוֹ, יוֹתֵר מִ.

Measure Adverbials: prepositions – כְּ, עַד.

Cause Adverbials: prepositions – הוֹדוֹת לְ, מֵחֲמַת, בִּשְׁבִיל, בְּ, מִ, בִּגְלַל, מִפְּנֵי, לְרֶגֶל, בְּשֶׁל; conjunctions – הוֹאִיל וְ..., מִשּׁוּם שֶׁ, עַל שֶׁ, מֵאַחַר שֶׁ, לְפִי שֶׁ, מִכֵּיוָן שֶׁ, שֶׁכֵּן, כִּי בַּאֲשֶׁר, עֵקֶב, יַעַן כִּי, יַעַן, and several of the above prepositions followed by שֶׁ, e.g., בִּשְׁבִיל שׁ, מִפְּנֵי שֶׁ.

Purpose Adverbials: prepositions – לְ, לְמַעַן, לְשֵׁם, בִּשְׁבִיל, כְּדֵי; conjunctions – כְּדֵי שֶׁ, בִּשְׁבִיל שֶׁ, לְמַעַן אֲשֶׁר, לְמַעַן.

Conditional Adverbials: prepositions – בְּמִקְרֶה שֶׁל; conjunctions – אִם, כִּי, כְּשֶׁ, בִּזְמַן שֶׁ, לִכְשֶׁ (and other introducers of time adverbials) כָּל מִי שֶׁ, מִי שֶׁ.

Concessive Adverbials: prepositions – לַמְרוֹת, עַל אַף; conjunctions – עִם כָּל, בְּכָל, אִם כִּי, אַף אִם, אַף שֶׁ, אַף עַל פִּי שֶׁ, אֲפִילוּ, אַף כִּי, גַּם כִּי, גַּם אִם.

Result Adverbials: prepositions – עַד, עַד לְ, עַד כְּדֵי, וְ (in a negative sentence or in a rhetorical question); conjunctions – עַד כִּי, שֶׁ, עַד שֶׁ, עַד אֲשֶׁר.

Equative Adverbials: prepositions – כְּאִלּוּ, כְּמוֹ, כְּ, בְּ; conjunctions – בְּמִדָּה שֶׁ, כָּל כַּמָּה שֶׁ, כְּכֹל אֲשֶׁר, כְּמוֹ שֶׁ, כִּלְעֻמַּת שֶׁ, כְּדֶרֶךְ שֶׁ, כְּשֵׁם שֶׁ, כְּמוֹ שֶׁ, כְּשֶׁ, כַּאֲשֶׁר.

The independent part of the sentence is introduced by correlative conjunctions, e.g., אַף, כָּךְ, כָּכָה, כֵּן.

Comparative Adverbials: preposition – מִ; conjunctions – יוֹתֵר מִמַּה שֶּׁ, יוֹתֵר מִשֶּׁ, מֵאֲשֶׁר, מִשֶּׁ. Sometimes the whole sentence is a rhetorical question: the comparative adverbial opens with a conjunction such as הֲלֹא, הִנֵּה, אִם, וּמַה, הֵן while the independent part is introduced by a correlative conjunction, e.g., כָּל שֶׁכֵּן, עַל אַחַת כַּמָּה וְכַמָּה, קַל וָחֹמֶר, וְאֵיךְ.

Below are examples of other uses:

Instrumental Adverbial: בְּ (colloquially also עִם) – הִכָּה בְּפַטִּישׁ (He hit with a hammer).

Price Adverbial: בְּ (also בְּעַד) – קָנוּ בְּכֶסֶף רַב (They bought with a great deal of money).

Concomitant Adverbial: בְּ (also עִם) – יָצְאוּ בִּרְכוּשׁ גָּדוֹל (They went out with a lot of property).

Coordinate Adverbial: עִם – הָלַךְ עִם חֲבֵרוֹ (He went with his friend).

Material Adverbial: מִ – הַקִּיר בָּנוּי מִלְּבֵנִים (The wall is built of bricks).

Oath or Promise Adverbial: e.g., שֶׁכֹּה אָמוּת אִם, חֵי נַפְשִׁי שֶׁ, בְּחַיַּי שֶׁ.

5: DEPENDENCY WITHIN THE SENTENCE

In Hebrew, as in other languages, sometimes a word or a form involves the appearance of another word or form in the same sentence or in a neighboring sentence. The reciprocal relationship between the words is called "dependency." Dependencies within the sentence are classified as (1) concord in gender and number (5.11–5.23), (2) concord of determination (5.3–5.4), (3) obligatory appearance (5.5), and (4) order of parts of sentence (5.6).

5.11: CONCORD BETWEEN SUBJECT AND PREDICATOR. The basic concord rule in Hebrew is the rule requiring that as far as possible the predicator should agree in gender and number with the subject. When the predicator is a verb, participle, or adjective, it always appears in a form agreeing in gender and number with the subject (see below 5.14: Lack of Concord between Subject and Predicator; 5.25: Lack of Concord in Adjunct Sentences on instances of lack of concord), e.g. הַזְּמַן קָצֵר, הַמְּלָאכָה מְרֻבָּה, בַּעֲלֵי הַבַּיִת דּוֹחֲקִים וְהַפּוֹעֲלוֹת עֲצֵלוֹת (The time is short, the work is great, the masters of the house are pressing, the female workers are lazy). When the predicator is an adjective or participle, agreement of gender between subject and predicator in the plural is always determined by the singular form of the subject. That is to say, it is irrelevant whether the plural suffix of the noun is ־ִים or ־וֹת. If the noun is masculine, the plural suffix of the adjective predicator is always ־ִים, e.g., הָאָבוֹת זְקֵנִים (The fathers are old), since in the singular we have הָאָב זָקֵן, and of course הַבָּנִים חָרוּצִים (The sons are diligent) with a singular הַבֵּן חָרוּץ. Similarly, with a feminine noun the plural suffix of the adjective is always ־וֹת, e.g., הַתְּאֵנִים יְבֵשׁוֹת (The figs are dry), since the singular is הַתְּאֵנָה יְבֵשָׁה, and obviously הַבָּנוֹת חָרוּצוֹת (The daughters are diligent) with a singular הַבַּת חָרוּצָה.

It is different when the predicator is a noun. Nouns do not always have gender inflection, nor is the meaning of the plural form always the same as that of the singular. Therefore, when such a noun realizes the function of predicator, it is sometimes impossible for the predicator and subject to agree in gender or number, e.g., הַשָּׁלוֹם הוּא תִּקְוָתֵנוּ (Peace is our hope), מִלְחָמָה הִיא מָוֶת (War is death), הַמַּחְסָנִים הֵם הַמִּכְשׁוֹל הָאַחֲרוֹן (The stores are the last obstacle). Nevertheless, sometimes a noun that normally is not inflected for gender did receive gender inflection when used in new ways. For example, the noun כּוֹכָב (star) was used as predicator for both male and female when it was first applied to an actor, e.g., גְּרֶטָה גַּרְבּוֹ הִיא כּוֹכָב גָּדוֹל (Greta Garbo is a great star). But after a time the form כּוֹכֶבֶת was created, e.g., דָּלְיָה לָבִיא הִיא כּוֹכֶבֶת יִשְׂרְאֵלִית (Dalia Lavi is an Israel star).

5.12: PREDICATOR TRANSFORMED INTO ADJUNCT. When the predicator is transformed to the function of adjunct (see 4.31: Morphological Classification of Adjuncts), the agreement with subject is preserved, i.e., when the predicator in the source construction agrees with the subject, the adjunct transformed from it agrees in gender and number with its nucleus, e.g., הַזְּמַן הַקָּצָר לֹא הִסְפִּיק (The short time was not sufficient), הַפּוֹעֲלוֹת הָעֲצֵלוֹת פִּטְפְּטוּ (The lazy female workers chattered),אֶסְתֵּר הַמַּלְכָּה הָיְתָה יָפָה (Esther the queen was beautiful). But if the predicator in the source construction is a noun that cannot be inflected, then the appositive, which is the result of the transformation, does not necessarily agree in gender and number with its nucleus, e.g., הַשָּׁלוֹם, תִּקְוָתֵנוּ, עוֹדֶנּוּ רָחוֹק (Peace, our hope, is still far off), הַקַּרְקַע, סְלָעִים, לֹא תֵּעָבֵד (The ground, rocks, will not be tilled). When a predicate containing a verb as predicator is transformed into a subordinate sentence with the function of adjunct (see 4.38: Relative Clause), the predicator continues to agree with the nucleus in gender and number, e.g., הַיְלָדִים [הַיְלָדִים שִׂחֲקוּ בֶּחָצֵר] לֹא הִרְגִּישׁוּ בַּמִּתְרַחֵשׁ (The children [The children played in the courtyard] did not notice what was happening), הַיְלָדִים שֶׁשִּׂחֲקוּ בֶּחָצֵר, לֹא הִרְגִּישׁוּ בַּמִּתְרַחֵשׁ (The children, who played in the courtyard, did not notice what was happening).

5.13: PREDICATOR TRANSFORMED INTO CIRCUMSTANCE ADVERBIAL. Similarly, the circumstance adverbial also agrees in gender and number with the subject or object, since it is also a transform of the predicator (cf. 4.51: Circumstance Adverbial). There is also a requirement of concord between a circumstance sentence and one of the parts of the independent sentence in which it appears, e.g., הִיא דִּבְּרָה וְעֵינֶיהָ מַבְרִיקוֹת

(She spoke, as her eyes were flashing). In many circumstance clauses, however, no concord exists, at least in the surface structure, e.g., וַיַּעֲמֹד בְּמִשְׁעוֹל הַכְּרָמִים, גָּדֵר מִזֶּה וְגָדֵר מִזֶּה (And he stood in the path of the vineyard, a fence here and a fence here = between two fences).

5.14: LACK OF CONCORD BETWEEN SUBJECT AND PREDICATOR. In some instances there is no concord between subject and predicator. Usually, this results from a difference between the grammatical gender or number of the noun and the natural gender or number of the person or entity denoted by the noun (Hebrew has no neutral), as in the following cases:

(1) *Collective noun.* When the noun denotes a group of individuals, its form is singular, but its predicator can be in the plural, agreeing with the content rather than the form, e.g., הַחֶבְרָה רָצוּ לָלֶכֶת (The group wanted to go. Colloquial). The number of collective nouns with this usage seems to be fewer in modern Hebrew than in earlier periods of the language.

(2) Proper nouns that have the plural or dual form are always combined with a predicator in the singular and take the grammatical gender corresponding to the natural gender of the person, e.g., רַחֲמִים הָלַךְ (Raḥamim went off), תָּמָר חָזְרָה (Tamar returned), יוֹנָה הָלַךְ (Jonah went off (when the reference is to a male)), יוֹנָה הָלְכָה (Jonah went off (when the reference is to a female)).

(3) Names of countries are always in the feminine, whatever the form of the noun, e.g., וַתִּכָּנַע מוֹאָב בַּיּוֹם הַהוּא (Moab surrendered on that day), מִצְרַיִם שָׁלְחָה צָבָא לְתֵימָן (Egypt sent an army to Yemen), יַרְדֵּן הִכְרִיזָה עַל מַצַּב חֵרוּם (Jordan proclaimed a state of emergency), אַרְצוֹת־הַבְּרִית יָזְמָה וְעִידַת שָׁלוֹם (The United States initiated a peace conference).

(4) *Pluralis majestatis.* The noun is in the plural not to indicate plurality but out of respect to the person designated. Modern Hebrew includes in this category אֱלֹהִים (God) and also בְּעָלִים (owner), e.g., לֹא נִמְצָא בְּעָלָיו שֶׁל הַכֶּלֶב (The owner of the dog was not found).

5.21: PRONOUN CONCORD IN A FOCUSING SENTENCE (EXTRA-POSITION). Gender and number concord in a sentence is sometimes not the basic concord between subject and predicator (5.11–5.13), but the result of a transformation deleting a noun and replacing it with a pronoun. The substituted pronoun always agrees in gender and number with the deleted noun. Since there is usually another instance of the same noun elsewhere in the sentence, the pronoun agrees in gender and number to this other instance, as in the example given in 4.26: the sentence אִישׁ לֹא שָׂם לֵב אֶל הַוָּתִיקִים (Nobody paid any attention to the veterans) is transformed into a focusing sentence when the noun הַוָּתִיקִים (the veterans) is taken from its place and put initially while in its place is introduced a third person masculine plural pronoun, agreeing with it. Since the deleted noun followed a preposition, the substituted pronoun also follows the preposition and hence is attached to it. The resulting sentence is הַוָּתִיקִים – אִישׁ לֹא שָׂם לֵב אֲלֵיהֶם (The veterans, nobody paid any attention to them). The same applies when the focused part functioned as subject in the source sentence, e.g., סָבָא אֵינוֹ מִתְעַיֵּף אַף פַּעַם (Grandfather never gets tired). When the subject is extracted from this sentence and placed initially, a third person masculine singular pronoun is introduced in its place, agreeing with סָבָא (Grandfather). Since the noun is not preceded by a preposition, neither is the pronoun. The resulting sentence is סָבָא – הוּא אֵינוֹ מִתְעַיֵּף אַף פַּעַם (Grandfather, he never gets tired). The pronoun agreeing with the focused part is called referring pronoun or "binder". As explained in 4.26: Focusing Sentence, the first noun in a focusing sentence is the subject and the rest of the sentence is the predicate. Consequently, the basic concord rule between subject and predicate applies here too; the element in the predicate agreeing with the subject is the referring pronoun.

5.22: PRONOUN CONCORD IN A RELATIVE CLAUSE. When the predicate of a focusing sentence is transformed into an adjunct sentence (4.38: Relative Clause), the concord between subject and predicate is transformed into concord between the noun nucleus and the adjunct sentence: – הַוָּתִיקִים [הַוָּתִיקִים אִישׁ לֹא שָׂם לֵב אֲלֵיהֶם] הֵחֵלּוּ לְהִתְאַרְגֵּן בְּאִרְגּוּנִים נִפְרָדִים (The veterans [The veterans, nobody paid any attention to them] began to organize themselves in separate organizations → ,הַוָּתִיקִים שֶׁאִישׁ לֹא שָׂם לֵב אֲלֵיהֶם, הֵחֵלּוּ לְהִתְאַרְגֵּן בְּאִרְגּוּנִים נִפְרָדִים (The veterans, to whom nobody paid any attention, began to organize themselves in separate organizations). Even when the focused part was subject in the source sentence, e.g., סָבָא – הוּא אֵינוֹ מִתְעַיֵּף אַף פַּעַם (Grandfather, he never gets tired), the whole of the predicate can be transformed into an adjunct sentence. However, if there is already subject-predicator concord in this sentence, for example when the predicator is a verb or there is a copula in the predicate, then this concord is usually sufficient. In this case, the adjunct sentence does not contain the subject pronoun, e.g., סָבָא, שֶׁאֵינוֹ מִתְעַיֵּף אַף פַּעַם, חִיֵּךְ בְּסַלְחָנוּת (Grandfather, who never gets tired, smiled forgivingly) and not... ‡סָבָא, שֶׁהוּא אֵינוֹ מִתְעַיֵּף אַף פַּעַם, חִיֵּךְ בְּסַלְחָנוּת, or הָאִישׁ שֶׁהָלַךְ בַּדֶּרֶךְ, לֹא חָזַר (The man, who went off on a journey, did not return), and not ‡ הָאִישׁ, שֶׁהוּא הָלַךְ בַּדֶּרֶךְ ,לֹא חָזַר. This does not apply to a nominal sentence that does not have subject-predicator concord, e.g., הַמַּחְסָנִים הֵם הַמִּכְשׁוֹל הָאַחֲרוֹן (The stores[they] are the last obstacle), the source of which is in the identifying sentence הַמַּחְסָנִים – הַמִּכְשׁוֹל הָאַחֲרוֹן (The stores – the last obstacle), cf. 4.24: Identifying Sentence. The relative clause formed from the predicate includes the pronoun הֵם, which agrees with the subject: הַמַּחְסָנִים שֶׁהֵם הַמִּכְשׁוֹל הָאַחֲרוֹן עוֹלִים בָּאֵשׁ (The stores, which are the last obstacle, are going up in fire). On whether the subject pronoun (הוּא, הִיא, הֵם, הֵן) is copula or referring pronoun of a focused part, see below 5.23: Copula Concord.

5.23: COPULA CONCORD. The source of the copula (see 4.22: The Copula) is a referring pronoun in a subject-focusing sentence, cf. the examples in 5.21: Pronoun Concord in a Focusing Sentence and 5.22: Pronoun Concord in a Relative Clause. However, the subject pronoun is also used in sentences where the focused part is not felt to be emphasized in any way (4.24:

Identifying Sentence). This appears to have happened for two reasons:

(1) Subject-focusing sentences became common in nominal sentences in the present tense by analogy with nominal sentences in the past and future tenses, that is speakers tended to insert a word agreeing with subject in gender and number between subject and predicator, or more precisely, to link such a word to the predicator (not necessarily putting it before the predicator) as they do with sentences in the past or future. Since this word (an inflected form of הָיָה (be)) does not introduce any emphasis to the sentence in the past or future, the emphasis is also lost in sentences with subject pronouns in the present tense.

(2) In certain constructions that lack subject-predicate concord, and particularly in sentences without a predicator the desire for "leveling" activates speakers, i.e., the need is felt to add something that will produce subject-predicate concord, in order that such constructions can enter the regular framework of Hebrew sentences, in which there is subject-predicator concord. We can explain in this way the obligatory appearance of the pronoun as a copula in sentences such as הַפִּגּוּר הוּא בְּיִצּוּר דְּשָׁנִים (The delay is in the production of fertilizers), הָעֲלִיָּה הִיא בַּשָּׂכָר (The rise is in salary), which are transformed from sentences פְּלוֹנִי מְפַגֵּר בְּיִצּוּר דְּשָׁנִים (X is lagging in the production of fertilizers), הַשָּׂכָר עָלָה (The salary rose) respectively. (See E. Rubinstein, for another explanation.) Usually the copula agrees with the subject. However, there are cases where the copula agrees with the predicator, when several words separate the subject from the copula and the copula is next to the predicator. In the colloquial language, and sometimes in writing, some use זאת, זֶה, זֶהוּ, זְהִי (or זאתִי) as copula. There is also quite frequent use of הִנּוֹ or הִנֵּהוּ and other inflected forms of הִנֵּה as copula.

5.24: OTHER CASES OF CONCORD. (1) A possessive pronoun agreeing with a noun mentioned after it is to be found in the double construct state: בֵּיתוֹ שֶׁל הָאִישׁ (the man's house), חֶרְדָּתָם שֶׁל הַהוֹרִים (the parents' dread), cf. 4.34: The Construct Structure.

(2) A pronoun attached to a preposition and referring to a noun mentioned after it is to be found in the apposition structure אָמְרוּ עָלָיו עַל רַבִּי עֲקִיבָא (They said about him, about Rabbi Akiva), cf. 4.37: Apposition.

(3) A demonstrative pronoun introducing an identifying sentence agrees in gender and number with the noun appearing as part of the complement in the identifying sentence, and not with the noun in the preceding sentence to which the pronoun refers, e.g., הַשְּׁאֵלָה יְדוּעָה, אֲבָל זֶה עִנְיָן אַחֵר (The question is well-known, but this is a different matter); זוֹ פִּסְקָה חֲדָשָׁה (… this is a new paragraph); אֵלֶּה דְּבָרִים נְדוֹשִׁים (… these are matters that are well-known), cf. also 6.12: Demonstrative Pronouns. The same applies if the reference is to something mentioned after the identifying sentence, e.g., זאת הַתּוֹרָה (This is the law) or אֵלֶּה הַחֻקִּים (These are the statutes), when the details come after such a sentence.

The demonstrative pronoun זֶה can be attached to an undetermined noun or to an undetermined construct state. The noun or construct state then becomes determined. That is to say, בַּיִת זֶה is equivalent to הַבַּיִת זֶה and בֵּית אֲבָנִים זֶה to בֵּית הָאֲבָנִים. Agreement in gender and number between pronoun and preceding noun is obligatory.

5.25: LACK OF CONCORD IN ADJUNCT SENTENCES. (1) Adjunct content-sentences (see 4.38: Relative Clause), which are not transformed from a predicate but from an object sentence (on which there is no obligatory concord in gender and number with anything outside the sentence), do not require concord with the noun nucleus transformed from the verb-predicator in the source sentence.

(2) Introductory expressions, especially for adverbial sentences (see 4.54: Prepositions as Introducers of Adverbials), e.g., בְּאֹפֶן שֶׁ, שָׁעָה שֶׁ, מָקוֹם שֶׁ. The sentence subordinated by such an expression does not include a referring pronoun agreeing with מָקוֹם, שָׁעָה, אֹפֶן, etc., e.g., כָּל פַּעַם שֶׁנַּפְשׁוֹ הָיְתָה מָרָה עָלָיו (every time that he felt depressed). It means that the noun in the introductory expression loses its semantic force, in whole or in part, and becomes entirely or virtually a grammatical word. Its "adjunct sentence" is not really an adjunct sentence. The introductory expression can also subordinate a sentence with a different function, for example as subject, e.g., הַאִם לֹא הִגִּיעָה הַשָּׁעָה שֶׁתִּתְאַחֵד חָכְמַת יִשְׂרָאֵל עִם שְׂפַת יִשְׂרָאֵל? (Has the time when the wisdom of Israel will be united with the language of Israel not come?).

(3) Pronoun substitute. In some adjunct sentences the place adverbial שָׁם (there) replaces a pronoun attached to a preceding preposition, e.g., ...הַחַלּוֹן שֶׁהִצְטוֹפְפוּ שָׁם יוֹנִים (the window where the doves crowded, literally the window which doves crowded there). The substitution of שָׁם for an inflected preposition is found in the Bible, e.g., אֶרֶץ כְּנַעַן, אֲשֶׁר אֲנִי מֵבִיא אֶתְכֶם שָׁמָּה (the land of Canaan, where I shall bring you).

(4) If in the source the nucleus was the object of אֶת in the adjunct sentence, the appearance of אֶת with an inflected pronoun agreeing in gender and number with the nucleus is not obligatory. For stylistic reasons it is normally omitted, unless the omission will lead to ambiguity. For example, חֹמֶר שֶׁשָּׁמַע מִפִּי מוֹרָיו אוֹ קָרָא בֶּעָבָר (material that he heard from his teachers or read in the past) and not חֹמֶר שֶׁשָּׁמַע אוֹתוֹ מִפִּי מוֹרָיו אוֹ קָרָא אוֹתוֹ בֶּעָבָר (literally, material that he heard it from his teachers or read it in the past). It is normally possible to add in any such adjunct sentence the preposition אֶת inflected to agree with the nucleus.

(5) When the nucleus is a verbal noun or abstract noun with the same root as the predicator in the adjunct sentence. In such a case there is no referring pronoun in the adjunct sentence, e.g., הָאֵבֶל שֶׁמִּתְאַבֶּלֶת עַל בְּנָהּ (the mourning which she mourns for her son). This phenomenon is presumably connected with the characteristics of the internal object.

(6) "Space words." When the nucleus is only required for grammatical purposes, namely for the attachment of an ad-

junct sentence, words devoid of semantic content, such as indefinite pronouns or demonstrative pronouns, e.g., מַה, כָּךְ, זֶה, or words with a very general semantic content, e.g., דָּבָר (thing), עֻבְדָּה (fact) are used. Such a nucleus does not require the presence of a referring pronoun in the adjunct sentence that is attached to it, whether the nucleus sums up what is said before or whether it comes after an obligatory preposition as introduction to what is to follow. For example: לְאַבָּא אָמְרָה כִּי אֶת אֲרוּחַת הַצָּהֳרַיִם הוּא אוֹכֵל הַיּוֹם בְּמִסְעָדָה, מַה שֶּׁהוּא שָׁמַע מִתּוֹךְ שְׁתִיקַת הַכְּנָעָה (She told Father that he is eating lunch today at a restaurant, which he heard in submissive silence). However, sometimes the "space words" are not entirely devoid of semantic content and denote something more than a word like דָּבָר or עֻבְדָּה, e.g., בִּמְלֹאת שִׁבְעִים שָׁנָה לְהַדָּחַת בֵּית הַמְּלוּכָה הַפּוֹרְטוּגָלִי, תַּאֲרִיךְ שֶׁחָל אֶתְמוֹל (At the end of seventy years following the dethronement of the Portuguese monarchy, a date which fell yesterday…) or הוּא נֶחְבַּשׁ בְּמַחֲנֶה רִכּוּז, מָקוֹם שֶׁמֵּת אוֹ נֶהֱרַג בֵּין 1939 ל־1941 (He was imprisoned in a concentration camp, a place where he died or was killed between 1939 and 1941).

5.3: Determiner Concord

Determination is not recursive. It follows that the four methods of determination exclude each other: (1) the definite article; (2) a proper name; (3) a noun in combination with a possessive pronoun; (4) a *nomen regens* in the construct state. Determiner concord exists between a nucleus-noun and an adjective serving as its adjunct, i.e., either both words are determined or neither are determined: נְיָר חָלָק (smooth paper), הַנְּיָר הֶחָלָק (the smooth paper). In mishnaic Hebrew and to some extent in biblical Hebrew it is possible for the adjunct to be determined while its nucleus is not determined, e.g., מַיִם הָרָעִים (the evil waters), יָם הַתִּיכוֹן (the Mediterranean Sea), יוֹם הַשִּׁשִּׁי (the sixth day). This phenomenon is seldom found in modern Hebrew. Determiner concord does not have its source in the deep grammar. It is a surface phenomenon: the adjunct adjective receives determination even though the predicator, which served as its source, was not determined. The cause of determination is attraction: determination of the noun attracts determination of the adjunct adjective attached to it. The attraction of the definite article from the noun to the adjunct applies even to a demonstrative pronoun following a noun with the definite article (see section 5.24: Other Cases of Concord), since corresponding to בַּיִת זֶה (this house) we can have הַבַּיִת הַזֶּה without a difference in meaning being felt between these phrases. The same applies to the construct state relationship. Here too if the noun is determined by the definite article and the pronoun זֶה follows, the article is also attached to the pronoun בֵּית אֲבָנִים זֶה – בֵּית הָאֲבָנִים הַזֶּה (this house of stone). In the phrase הַבַּיִת הַזֶּה there is therefore a double determination. This is a clear example of redundancy, unique in determination, since determination is not recursive, i.e., a noun that is already determined cannot accept additional determination.

5.4: Restrictions on Determination

The non-recursiveness means that the definite article cannot be combined with a proper name, nor with a noun with an inflected possessive, nor with a *nomen regens*; a proper name cannot be combined with the definite article (unless the name has been changed into a common name, or if the definite article is part of the name, e.g., הַיַּרְדֵּן, הַלְּבָנוֹן (the Jordan, the Lebanon)) nor with a possessive pronoun and it cannot be a *nomen regens*; a noun inflected for the possessive cannot be a proper name (unless it became an independent item, not connected with the common noun), cannot be combined with the definite article, and cannot be a *nomen regens*; a *nomen regens* cannot be a proper name unless it is a shortened name, e.g., רִאשׁוֹן for רִאשׁוֹן לְצִיּוֹן, נַחֲלַת for נַחֲלַת יְהוּדָה; it cannot be combined with the definite article or with a possessive pronoun, but if the construct state is taken to be a compound the definite article can precede it, e.g., הַכַּדּוּרֶגֶל (the football). It should be added, however, that two (or more) people with the same name may be referred to with a definite article preceding the name in plural "שְׁתֵּי הַשִּׁפְרוֹת." Determination by the demonstrative pronoun זֶה, which may precede or follow the noun, does not come under this rule: זֶה can come in addition to the above four methods. But if זֶה follows a noun with the definite article or the construct state with the definite article, the definite article must precede: הַזֶּה (see 5.3: Determiner Concord). When זֶה follows a noun determined by another method, the definite article is not obligatory but optional: כּוֹבָעִי זֶה (or, כּוֹבָעִי הַזֶּה) (my hat), אַבְרָהָם זֶה, אַבְרָהָם הַזֶּה (this Abraham), but בַּיִת זֶה (this house) – הַבַּיִת הַזֶּה, בֵּית אֲבָנִים זֶה (this house of stone) – בֵּית הָאֲבָנִים הַזֶּה.

5.5: Obligatoriness

Obligatoriness in the widest sense refers to the obligatory appearance of a word or form as a result of the existence of another word or form in the same sentence. It signifies roughly what is signified by "dependency" in the sentence but from the standpoint of one element in the dependency, either the active element or the passive one. For example, when the word אֶתְמוֹל (yesterday) appears in a verbal sentence the verb normally is in the past. Here, what has been made obligatory is the element signifying that the verb is in the past form, while what made it obligatory is the word אֶתְמוֹל. A further instance is the infinitive following certain auxiliaries, e.g., הִתְאַמֵּץ, מֻכְרָח, עָשׂוּי, עָלוּל (cf. 4.45: Infinitive as Object). Other auxiliaries require either an infinitive or a certain form of the verb, i.e., a participle, or a verbal noun, e.g., הִתְחִילוּ לְהָבִין (they began to understand), הִתְחִילוּ מְבִינִים (they began understanding), הִמְעִיט לְדַבֵּר (he spoke less, literally: he lessened to speak), הִמְעִיט בְּדִבּוּר (literally: he lessened in speech). In a narrow and more usual sense, obligatoriness is used to denote the obligatory appearance of a particular preposition when there is in the same sentence a particular verb requiring the preposition. For example, the appearance of the preposition בְּ is required by the verb הִשְׁתַּמֵּשׁ (cf. 4.41: Obligatory Complement and Obligatory Preposition). Compared with English, the rules are less stringent in this respect, since there are various cases when certain "obligatory" prepositions can be omitted without affecting the meaning of the verb. In most cases when an obligatory preposition is retained, the meaning of the verb without the preposition differs discernibly from its meaning with the preposition, e.g., דָּלַק (burn) – דָּלַק אַחֲרֵי (pursue after); הִתְגַּלְגֵּל (roll) – הִתְגַּלְגֵּל לְ (change to). When the verb does not have another meaning, then under certain conditions the obligatory preposition can be omitted, e.g., לְ after הִתְכַּוֵּן (intend) can be omitted before a subordinate sentence beginning with שֶׁ, e.g., הִתְכַּוַּנְתִּי שֶׁתָּבוֹאוּ (I intended you to come). It is also possible to retain the preposition לְ here, but it would then be necessary to add a space-word between לְ and שֶׁ, e.g., הִתְכַּוַּנְתִּי לְכָךְ שֶׁתָּבוֹאוּ, cf. 5.25, (6): Lack of Concord in Adjunct Sentences – "Space Words." This area of degrees of obligatoriness, i.e., when the obligatory preposition can be omitted, has not been sufficiently investigated in Hebrew. The preposition אֶת is required (after certain verbs) only before a determined noun (it may be omitted, however, for stylistic reasons) but if an undetermined noun follows, its omission is obligatory. Some phrase the rule differently: "Before an undetermined noun the obligatory preposition אֶת is changed to the obligatory preposition Ø." Obligatory prepositions are retained in many cases when the verb is converted into a verbal noun, e.g., הָרְדִיפָה אַחֲרֵי הֲנָאוֹת הַחַיִּים (the pursuit after the pleasures of life), הַזִּלְזוּל בַּסַּכָּנָה (the contempt for danger). This area too requires further investigation.

5.6: The Order of the Parts of the Sentence

Concord between different parts of the sentence in gender, number, and person; marking of the subject pronoun in the verb form (Morphology – 19. The Inflection of the Verb); presence of prepositions, particularly presence of אֶת to mark the "direct object" – all these allow a reduction in Hebrew of restrictions on the order of the parts of the sentence. While comprehensive investigations have not been undertaken into the order of parts of the sentence in modern Hebrew, it is possible to say in general that word order is fairly free, and usually what the speaker wishes to emphasize he says at the beginning of the sentence. Below is given a list of restrictions (more or less accepted by all) on the order of the parts of the sentence. Nevertheless, in some instances the strict observance of them is more a matter of style than of syntax. The influence of word order in other languages can sometimes be discerned.

(1) When the sentence begins with an object or adverbial and the predicator is a verb, the predicator follows the object or adverbial and the subject comes after the predicator. The rule applies particularly when the verb is in the past or future, e.g., אֶתְמוֹל הִפְלִיגָה הָאֳנִיָּה – (Yesterday sailed the boat) הָאֳנִיָּה הִפְלִיגָה אֶתְמוֹל – (The boat sailed yesterday). In colloquial Hebrew, sometimes in writing also, there are cases where this rule is not kept.

When two complements of the predicator occur in the sentence, for example two different objects or an object and an adverbial, the speaker is free to give them in any order. But if one of them is an inflected preposition, i.e., the complement includes a personal pronoun, the inflected preposition precedes the second complement. If both of them are inflected prepositions, the order is free, unless one of the words is אֶת with a pronominal inflection, in which cases it comes first. For example: רָאִיתִי אֶת הַיֶּלֶד אֶתְמוֹל (I saw the child yesterday); רָאִיתִי אֶתְמוֹל אֶת הַיֶּלֶד (I saw yesterday the child) – but: רָאִיתִי אוֹתוֹ אֶתְמוֹל (I saw him yesterday) and not ‡רָאִיתִי אֶתְמוֹל אוֹתוֹ (literally: I saw yesterday him). לָקַחְתִּי אֶת הַסֵּפֶר מֵאֲחוֹתִי (I took the book from my sister); לָקַחְתִּי מֵאֲחוֹתִי אֶת הַסֵּפֶר (I took from my sister the book) – לָקַחְתִּי אוֹתוֹ מִמֶּנָּה (I took it from her) and not ‡לָקַחְתִּי מִמֶּנָּה אוֹתוֹ (literally I took from her it).

(3) Interrogative words, coordinating conjunctions, and the various subordinating conjunctions appear at the beginning of the sentence, whether the sentence is independent or subordinate. But a few subordinating words such as אִם כֵּן, עַל כֵּן, לָכֵן, sometimes occur not at the beginning of the sentence they are connecting but within it, e.g., לָכֵן שָׁאַלְתִּי אוֹתוֹ מַדּוּעַ לֹא בָּא (Therefore I asked him why he did not come), שָׁאַלְתִּי אוֹתוֹ, עַל כֵּן, מַדּוּעַ לֹא בָּא (I asked him, therefore, why he did not come). The coordinating word גַּם (also) links the word after it to one of the words preceding it in that sentence or in a preceding sentence. Hence, גַּם can appear in various places in the sentence. In speech גַּם sometimes occurs after the word it is linking (undoubtedly under the influence of foreign languages). For example: גַּם שָׁתִיתִי [וְ]אָכַלְתִּי (I ate [and] also I drank); הָיָה שָׁם גַּם הַנָּשִׂיא (Also the president was there). The latter sentence implies a previous statement that others were there.

(4) There is still no adequate investigation in modern Hebrew of the order of the parts of the noun phrase, i.e., the order of the various adjuncts relative to the nucleus. But if there is no special reason for changes, the order seems to be as given below (the degree of confidence in this order is sufficiently high for the first five parts, though in the rest it is less; the parentheses denote that it is possible to omit that part and pass on to the next, and still preserve a noun phrase): (quantity adjunct +) noun phrase nucleus (+ *nomen rectum* adjunct) (+adjective adjunct) (+separate possessive pronoun adjunct) (+demonstrative pronoun) (+prepositional phrase adjunct) (+appositional adjunct) (+subordinate sentence adjunct). For example: שְׁנֵי מְעִילֵי הַצֶּמֶר הַחֲדָשִׁים שֶׁלִּי הָהֵם מֵאַנְגְּלִיָּה, מַתְּנַת דּוֹדִי, שֶׁהִגִּיעוּ בְּדִיּוּק לִפְנֵי שָׁבוּעַ, נֶעֶלְמוּ. (Those two new woolen coats of mine from England, my uncle's gift, which arrived exactly a week ago, have disappeared; literally: Two coats of wool – new – mine – those – from England – the gift of my uncle – which arrived exactly a week ago – have disappeared). "A special reason for change" (above) includes the wish for emphasis, an afterthought, and the length of the adjunct, particularly when it is a subordinate sentence. An attached possessive pronoun may accompany any noun.

(5) Any noun can be placed initially as a focused part (cf. 4.26: Focusing Sentence). Though as a result the general word order is changed, within the source sentence now serving as predicate the word order remains as it was, with the referring pronoun taking the place of the focused noun, cf. also 6.322: Word Order as Indication of Subordination.

6: LINKS BEYOND THE SENTENCE

Although speech consists not only of the combination of words, but also of the combination of sentences, the links between sentences in the same discourse have not been described in books on syntax, and in fact have not been given a linguistic description at all. Those dealing with the combination of sentences do so within theories of rhetoric or composition and pay attention not to grammatical questions but to literary and logical structure. In this respect some changes occurred in the early 1950s, when Z.S. Harris began linguistic analyses of a whole discourse, which can include much more than one sentence and can sometimes consist of a dialogue between two or more speakers. In doing so, even though some previous scholars had already dealt with this topic, he laid the foundations for the development of modern linguistic views on deep structure. As stated in the section 3.1: Structural Analysis above, there are few descriptions in Hebrew as yet which are based on those assumptions, still there are works in Hebrew that describe some of the material related to the problem of links beyond the sentence, for example the uses of the various subordinating conjunctions. The following survey covers these topics: (1) anaphoric references in sequentially related sentences; (2) elliptical sentences related to previous sentences; (3) ways of combining sentences.

6.1: Anaphoric Reference in Sequentially Related Sentences

6.11: PERSONAL PRONOUNS. Those rules of pronoun concord applying within the sentence, e.g., in a focusing sentence or in a relative clause, apply also when the pronoun is in a different sentence, which follows the one with the noun, even though the two sentences do not have any other grammatical links. Moreover, the pronoun in the new sentence (if indeed the second instance of the noun has been deleted and a pronoun has replaced the noun) normally cannot be omitted as happens under certain conditions in adjunct sentences. Thus, the deletion of the second instance of a noun and its replacement by a personal pronoun happens not only in a focusing sentence or in a relative clause but in general, whether the first noun is in the same sentence (in surface structure) or in a preceding sentence. The personal pronoun therefore agrees in gender and number with the noun, even though only the first instance of the noun remains. For example: רָאִיתִי אֶת הַיֶּלֶד. הַיֶּלֶד חָזַר לְבֵית הַסֵּפֶר (I saw the child. The child returned to school), רָאִיתִי אֶת הַיֶּלֶד. הוּא חָזַר לְבֵית הַסֵּפֶר (I saw the child. He returned to school).

6.12: DEMONSTRATIVE PRONOUNS. (1) A demonstrative appearing in a sequentially related sentence but not functioning as adjunct sometimes refers back to a noun in a previous sentence. However, if its function in the sequentially related sentence is that of subject or predicator, it must agree in gender and number with the predicator or subject respectively of the sequentially related sentence and not with the noun in the preceding sentence to which it refers (cf. 5.24, (3): Other Cases of Concord). For example: הֵבֵאתִי אוֹתוֹ אֶל הַדִּירָה; "זֶה יִהְיֶה בֵּיתְךָ" אָמַרְתִּי (I brought him to the apartment. "This will be your home," I said). The same applies to the demonstrative כָּזֶה and its inflectional variants, e.g., יֵשׁ לִי עֲשָׂרָה פְּקִידִים גְּרוּעִים; אֵינֶנִּי רוֹצֶה עוֹד פָּקִיד כָּזֶה (I have ten rotten clerks; I don't want another clerk like that). (See H. Rosén, *'Ivrit Tova*, for another explanation.)

(2) Sometimes the demonstrative does not refer to a noun in the preceding sentence, but to the whole of the content of the sentence or to a part of it. In such a case there is no requirement for concord with a particular element in the preceding sentence. Generally the demonstrative is then זֶה, e.g., הַיְלָדִים שָׁכְבוּ לִישׁוֹן. זֶה הָיָה בְּשָׁעָה עֶשֶׂר (The children went to bed. That was at ten). A sequentially related sentence with such a structure can introduce stories, e.g., ...זֶה הָיָה בַּחֲנֻכָּה (It happened at Ḥanukkah). By doing so, the narrator plunges the reader straight into the story, making him feel that he is not at the beginning of the story. Another possible explanation: זֶה refers in these cases to something unknown which is to be explained later, so that the reader becomes anxious to know what is coming.

(3) The definite article should also be mentioned here, since its appearance before a noun indicates a reference to the previous appearance of the noun and confirms that the two instances of the noun have the same referent, e.g., אִישׁ הָיָה בְּאֶרֶץ עוּץ, אִיּוֹב שְׁמוֹ. וְהָיָה הָאִישׁ הַהוּא תָּם וְיָשָׁר (There was a man in the land of Uz, whose name was Job. And that man was perfect and upright). The fact that sometimes the definite article appears before the first appearance (in surface structure) of a noun does not invalidate this claim, since in such a case it may be supposed that a previous sentence containing a non-determined instance of the noun has been deleted as a result of a transformation. Here belong also various adjuncts, restrictive and nonrestrictive alike (4.32: Restrictive and Nonrestrictive Adjunct). There is no doubt that the sentences in which these appear are linked to preceding sentences, whether they are retained or deleted.

6.2: Fragmentary Sentences

Usually every sentence has two parts, a subject and a predicate. However, in Hebrew, as in other languages, there are short sentences that cannot be divided in this way. Some have called them single-element sentences, analyzing them according to their surface structure. But from the point of view of deep grammar they should be considered as remnants of normal sentences, with subject and predicate, from which some parts (subject and/or predicate or parts of the latter) have been deleted. Here belong expressions of agreement with or opposition to a preceding sentence (usually said by another speaker), e.g., כֵּן (Yes!), לֹא (No!), אוּלַי (Perhaps!), these being remnants of the predicate. Sentences such as רוּחַ. שֶׁמֶשׁ. חַם (Wind. Sun. Warm.) are used in literature and not necessarily in sequentially related sentences. The part that would complete them and make them into proper sentences has been omitted, because it can be understood or because it is unimportant, and not because it has been mentioned previously.

6.3: Sentence Connection
Two juxtaposed and linked sentences may be related in one of two ways: (1) The two sentences have equal status syntactically and are linked by coordination (see 3.14: The Compound Sentence above); (2) The two sentences have a different syntactic status, one of them being subordinate to the other (see 3.15: The Complex Sentence above).

6.31: COORDINATION. It is customary to classify the kind of relations between two coordinated sentences by the relation of the content of the sequentially related sentence to that of the preceding sentence. The relation may be (1) addition; (2) contrast; (3) alternative; (4) explanation or conclusion; (5) result.

Coordinated sentences may be juxtaposed without a coordinating marker between them (asyndetic coordination), but generally in modern Hebrew the coordination is marked by a coordinator (syndetic coordination). Some coordinators mark only one of the above types of coordination, others mark more than one kind. Coordinations of types (1) and (3) can comprise more than two consecutive sentences. In that case the coordinator can come merely between the last sentence and the one preceding it. When the coordination is expressed without a coordinator, it generally requires a special intonation, particularly for coordinations of explanation and result, and a significant pause before the sequentially related sentence suggests the content-type of the coordination. Sometimes the coordination is marked by a coordinator before the first sentence. Every such coordinator has available a correlative between that sentence and the sequentially related sentence, e.g., לֹא רַק..., כִּי אִם גַּם... (Not only… but also…). Sometimes, however, the correlative is omitted, the speaker being content with the appropriate intonation.

The coordinators:

(1) coordination of addition: לֹא דַי... אֶלָּא ; ...וְ... ; ... גַּם ... ; לֹא רַק... אֶלָּא גַּם ; ...אַף... ; ...וְלֹא עוֹד אֶלָּא שֶׁ... ; (וְ) גַּם ; גַּם... ; שֶׁ... ; לֹא זוּ בִּלְבַד... אֶלָּא שֶׁ ; לֹא רַק... (כִּי אִם) גַּם... ;

(2) coordination of contrast: אֶלָּא... ; ...וְ... ; ...אֲבָל... ; לֹא... כִּי אִם... ; אֵין... אֶלָּא... ; אוּלָם... ; ...אַךְ... ; רַק... ; ...אֶפֶס...

(3) coordination of alternative: אוֹ שֶׁ... אוֹ... ; אוֹ שֶׁ... אוֹ שֶׁ... ; ...אוֹ...

(4) coordination of reason or conclusion: ...מִכָּאן שֶׁ...; כְּלוֹמַר... ; ...שֶׁהֲרֵי...

(5) coordination of result: לָכֵן... ; ...עַל כֵּן... ; ...לְפִיכָךְ...

6.32: SUBORDINATION. A subordinated sentence realizes a function within another sentence (see 3.15: The Complex Sentence above). From the point of view of the other sentence "a link outside the sentence" does not apply, but from the point of view of the subordinated sentence that is the nature of the link.

Subordination is chiefly marked in Hebrew by words exclusively used to mark subordination, by words that mark either coordination or subordination, and by the order of the sentence elements, whether within the subordinated sentence or in the place of the subordinated sentence within the superordinate sentence. Intonation is also criterial for the nature of the sentence, but since descriptions of Hebrew intonation have not yet been published there will merely be occasional comments in this area. The following survey will cover only (1) words marking subordination; (2) the order of the sentence elements.

6.321: Subordinators. שֶׁ is the most general subordinator. It can introduce an adjunct sentence and an object sentence (after verbs of saying), and can combine with other words to introduce various adverbial sentences (cf. 4.54: Prepositions as Introducers of Adverbials). In historical grammar שֶׁ is considered to have evolved from an ancient demonstrative pronoun, the ancient subordination marker זוּ (found in biblical Hebrew) being pointed to as a transitional form between demonstrative pronoun and subordination marker. But even if this claim can be proved right historically, it should not be taken into account in a consideration of the function of שֶׁ in modern Hebrew. It now serves solely as a subordination marker and there is no trace in it of an ancient demonstrative pronoun. No concord of any kind applies between it and what precedes it, and therefore it does not serve as "substitute for the subject," as some authors have alleged.

אֲשֶׁר. Although this word is typical of biblical Hebrew (where שֶׁ appears only in late passages), modern Hebrew uses it too. Indeed, אֲשֶׁר is found in all levels of the contemporary language, particularly as a stylistic variant for שֶׁ, when the latter occurs too often for the speaker's taste. This variation is restricted, since שֶׁ cannot be replaced in all its uses by אֲשֶׁר, this being one of the reasons for the relative infrequency of אֲשֶׁר as compared with שֶׁ in literary modern Hebrew. אֲשֶׁר cannot introduce the following structures which are related in deep structure and can be transformed from one another: (1) adjunct content-sentences (see 4.38: Relative Clause); (2) object sentences which can be transformed into adjunct content-sentences; (3) subject sentences derived from such object sentences by the change of the predicator verb from active to passive, or by its replacement by modal predicators such as טוֹב (good), יָפֶה (fine), הַלְוַאי (would that), חֲבָל (a pity), which express the attitude of the speaker to what is said in the subordinated part. The following are examples:

Object content-sentence	*Adjunct content-sentence*
יָדַעְתִּי שֶׁרוּת עוֹבֶדֶת	הַיְדִיעָה שֶׁרוּת עוֹבֶדֶת
(I knew that Ruth works)	(the knowledge that Ruth works)
Subject content-sentence	*Subject content-sentence*
טוֹב שֶׁרוּת עוֹבֶדֶת	נוֹדַע לִי שֶׁרוּת עוֹבֶדֶת
(It's good that Ruth works)	(It became known to me that Ruth works)

In such sentences אֲשֶׁר can only be used exceptionally, in highly rhetorical language. Likewise, אֲשֶׁר does not introduce indirect speech, and generally it does not precede the participle.

כִּי introduces indirect speech, adjunct content-sentences, object sentences from which adjunct content-sentences can be transformed, and subject sentences derived from these object sentences by a change of the verb-predicator from active to passive. כִּי therefore is used in all structures not open to אֲשֶׁר. However, כִּי cannot introduce a subject sentence when the predicator is an initial modal expression such as הַלְוַאי (would that), חֲבָל (a pity), הַלְוַאי שֶׁיֵּרֵד שֶׁלֶג (would that snow will fall), but not הַלְוַאי כִּי יֵרֵד שֶׁלֶג ‡. Similarly, כִּי cannot introduce relative clauses. Another function of כִּי is to introduce adverbial sentences of cause (and in biblical Hebrew, also time and condition adverbials).

הַ introduces relative clauses that begin with the participle form of the verb, which agrees in gender and number with the nucleus.

ו mostly marks coordination rather than subordination. However sometimes, and especially in literature, it introduces a sentence that is or seems to be subordinated to the preceding sentence, when the subordinate sentence is one of circumstance, comparison, result, or purpose, e.g., הַנַּעַר יָצָא לַדֶּרֶךְ וְיָדָיו רֵיקוֹת (The lad went out and his hands were empty) – circumstance; הַשֶּׁמֶשׁ זָרְחָה, הַשִּׁטָּה פָּרְחָה, וְהַשּׁוֹחֵט שָׁחַט (The sun shone, the acacia blossomed, and the slaughterer slaughtered) – comparison; בַּקֵּשׁ רַחֲמִים וְיִסָּלַח לְךָ (Seek mercy and you will be forgiven) – result; מַה נַּעֲשֶׂה וְנִנָּצֵל? (What shall we do and we shall be saved?) – purpose. See also 4.54: Prepositions as Introducers of Adverbials.

6.322: Word Order as Indication of Subordination. Generally, the order of the parts of the sentence in a subordinated sentence does not differ from that in an independent sentence (5.6: The Order of the Parts of the Sentence). But word order in relative clauses and conditional sentences may influence the nature of the link between them and the sentences in which they appear. In conditional sentences the place of the subordinated sentence may determine the nature of the link, usually together with other factors, such as intonation.

(1) A relative clause beginning with an inflected preposition that agrees in gender and number with the nucleus (see 5.21: Pronoun Concord in Focusing Sentence; 5.22: Pronoun Concord in a Relative Clause) can occur without the initial subordinator שֶׁ (or אֲשֶׁר) e.g., רָאִיתִי אֶת הַבַּיִת בּוֹ גָּר אָחִיךָ (I saw the house in which your brother lives), as opposed to רָאִיתִי אֶת הַבַּיִת שֶׁאָחִיךָ גָּר בּוֹ. It is usual to term such a relative clause as an asyndetic relative clause, since it lacks an initial conjunction. It may be argued that a marker of subordination is present, though not the usual שֶׁ, the inflected preposition filling also that function besides its function within the relative clause. In biblical Hebrew an asyndetic relative clause may occur also without this condition e.g., יֹאבַד יוֹם אִוָּלֶד בּוֹ. A relative clause without an inflected preposition may appear without a marker of subordination if it has a verb in the future agreeing with the nucleus and preceded by the negative participle בַּל, e.g., אֱמוּנָה בַּל־תְּעֹרְעַר (a faith that cannot be uprooted). It is impossible to add the subordinator שֶׁ or some other subordinator in initial position here. In such a structure the negative participle לֹא can replace בַּל but it is then possible to add שֶׁ or אֲשֶׁר, e.g., כֹּבֶד שֶׁלֹּא יְתֹאַר (weight that cannot be described) or כֹּבֶד לֹא־יְתֹאַר.

(2) Conditional sentences (see 4.52: Types of Conditional Adverbial) can be expressed without an initial conditional word under certain restrictions: (a) the protasis must come first, (b) the predicator must come first in the protasis. The absence of the conditional word is usual in legal language, e.g., מָצָא אָדָם חֵפֶץ, יְבִיאֶנּוּ לְתַחֲנַת הַמִּשְׁטָרָה הַסְּמוּכָה (A man has found an object, he shall bring it to the nearest police station). The future form of the second verb expresses not the condition, but the intention of the whole sentence to serve as a permanent instruction in all cases to which the condition applies. Similar conditional sentences are found in literature. However, they are not instructions, but refer to recurring events. In these the second verb may also be in the past, e.g., מָצָא כַּפְתּוֹרִים – הֱבִיאָם לְאִמּוֹ; מָצָא מַסְמְרִים – הֱבִיאָם לְאָבִיו (He found buttons – he brought them to his mother; he found nails – he brought them to his father). Proverbs may likewise have this form, e.g., in biblical Hebrew, מָצָא אִשָּׁה – מָצָא טוֹב (He found a wife – he found a good thing). When such sentences are said orally, the conditional sentences have characteristic intonation patterns. In the colloquial language, too, there may occur conditional sentences without an introductory conditional word. Only sentence order, word order, and intonation show them to be conditional, e.g., יִרְצוּ – יֹאכְלוּ, לֹא יִרְצוּ – לֹא יֹאכְלוּ (They will want – they will eat; they won't want – they won't eat). A change of sentence order, of word order, or of intonation will necessitate a conditional word, e.g., יֹאכְלוּ, אִם יִרְצוּ; לֹא יֹאכְלוּ, אִם לֹא יִרְצוּ (They will eat if they want; they will not eat if they don't want).

[Uzzi Ornan]

The following is not intended to serve as an exhaustive bibliography, but rather as an aid to the interested reader seeking additional information. It includes entries of three types:

(1) General research works on Hebrew linguistics and contemporary language problems.

(2) Publications containing particularly extensive bibliographical material.

(3) Publications presenting a wide variety of approaches.

BIBLIOGRAPHY: A. GENERAL WORKS: F.E. Koenig, *Historischkritisches Lehrgebaeude der hebraeischen Sprache und historisch-comparative Syntax der hebraeischen Sprache*, 3 vols. (1881–97); E. Kautzsch (trans. A.E. Cowley), *Gesenius' Hebrew Grammar* (1910[28]); H. Bauer and P. Leander, *Historische Grammatik der hebraeischen Sprache des Alten Testaments*, 3 vols. (1918–22); G. Bergstraesser, *Wilhelm Gesenius' hebraeische Grammatik*, 3 vols. (1918–29); M.B. Sznejder, *Torat ha-Lašon běhitpattěḥutah*, 2 vols. (1923–40); Š.Š. Kantoroviẓ, *Diqduq ha-Śafa ha-ʿivrit lě-ḵol Signoneha*, 2 vols. (1928); M.H. Segal, *A Grammar of Mishnaic Hebrew* (1927); idem, *Diqduq lěšon ha-Mišna* (1936); M. Lambert, *Traité de grammaire hebraïque* (1938); Y. Avinery, *Heḵal Rashi*, 4 vols. (1940–49); D. Yellin, *Diqduq ha-Lašon ha-ʿivrit* (1942); P. Joüon, *Grammaire de l'hébreu biblique*

(1947[2]); P. Joüon-T. Muraoka, Ẓ. Har-Zahav, *Diqduq ha-Lašon ha-ʿivrit*, 6 vols. (1951–55); N.H. Ṭur-Sinai, *ha-Lašon wĕ-ha-Sefer*, 3 vols. (1954–59); B. Klar, *Meḥqarim wĕ-ʿiyyunim ba-Lašon, ba-Šira u-va-Sifrut* (1954); W. Chomsky, *Hebrew the Eternal Language* (1952; Heb., 1967); R. Meyer, *Die hebraeische Grammatik* (1955[2], 1966[3]), adaption of G. Beer's Grammar; E.Y. Kutscher, *Ha-Lašon wĕ-ha-Reqaʿ ha-Lĕšoni šel mĕgillat Yĕšaʿyahu* (1959); A. Sperber, *A Historical Grammar of Biblical Hebrew* (1966); A. Kašer (ed.), *Balšanut Ḥiššuvit* (1969); R. Macuch, *Grammatik des Samaritanischen Hebraeisch* (1969, see Z. Ben-Ḥayyim, in: *Biblica*, 52 (1971)); C. Rabin, in: *Current Trends in Linguistics*, vol. 6 (1971), 304–46. **ADD. BIBLIOGRAPHY:** M. Mishor, "The Tense System in Tannaitic Hebrew" (dissertation, Heb. Univ., 1983); N. Braverman, "*Ha-Milliyot ve-To'arei ha-Po'al Bilšon ha-Tanna'im*" ("Particles and Adverbs in Tannaitic Hebrew (Mishnah and Tosefta)," dissertation, Heb. Univ. Jerusalem (1995); P. Joüon, *A Grammar of Biblical Hebrew*, trans. and rev. by T. Muraoka, 2 vols. (1993). B. PROBLEMS OF MODERN HEBREW: E.M. Lipschuetz, *Vom lebendigen Hebraeisch* (1920); I. Garbell, *Fremdsprachliche Einfluesse im modernen Hebraeisch* (1930); Ẓ. Har-Zahav, *Lĕšon Dorenu* (1930); Y. Klausner, *Diqduq Qaẓar šel ha-ʿivrit ha-Ḥădaša* (1935); Y. Avineri, *Kibbuš ha-ʿivrit bĕ-Dorenu* (1946); Y. Epstein, *Hegyone Lašon* (1947); Y. Klausner, *Ha-Lašon ha-ʿivrit Lašon Ḥayya* (1949[2]); E.M. Lipschuetz, *Kĕtavim*, vol. 2 (1949); A. Avrunin, *Meḥqarim bi-lĕšon Bialik wĕ-Yalag* (1953); Z. Ben-Ḥayyim, "*Lašon ʿattiqa bi-Mĕẓi'ut Ḥădaša*," in: *Lešonenu Laʿam*, nos. 35–37 (1953); Ḥ. Rosén, *Ha-ʿivrit Šellanu* (1956); Y. Klausner, *Ha-ʿivrit ha-Ḥădaša u-vĕʿayoteha* (1957); Y. Livni, *Lašon Kĕ-Hilkatah* (1957); A. Bar-Adon, *Lĕšonam ha-Mĕdubberet šel ha-Yĕladim bĕ-Yiśra'el* (1959); Y. Pereẓ, *ʿivrit ka-Hālaka* (1961[2]); R. Sivan, *Ẓurot u-Mĕgammot bĕ-Ḥidduš ha-Lašon ha-ʿivrit bi-Tĕqufat Tĕḥiyyatah* (1963); A. Bendavid, *Lĕšon Miqra' u-Lĕšon Ḥakamin* (1967–69[2]); M. Ben-Asher, *Hitgabbĕrut ha-Diqduq ha-Normaṭivi* (1969). **ADD. BIBLIOGRAPHY:** M. Bar-Asher, *L'Hébreu Mishnique, études linguistiques* (1999). C. PHONOLOGY AND MORPHOLOGY: E.A. Speiser, in: JQR, 16 (1925/26), 343–82; 23 (1932/33), 233–65; 24 (1933/34), 9–46; M. Segal, *Yĕsode ha-Fonetiqa ha-ʿivrit* (1928); J. Cantineau, in: *Bulletin d'études orientales*, 1 (1931), 81–98; L. Gulkowitsch, *Die Bildung von Abstraktbegriffen in der hebraeischen Sprachgeschichte* (1931); E. Porat, *Lĕšon Ḥăkamim* (1938); C. Sarauw, *Ueber Akzent und Silbenbildung in den aelteren semitischen Sprachen* (1939); H. Birkeland, *Akzent und Vokalismus im Althebraeischen* (1940); C. Brockelmann, in: ZDMG, 94 (1940), 332–71; G. Lisowski, *Die Transkription der hebraeischen Eigennamen des Pentateuch in der Septuaginta* (1940); Z. Ben-Ḥayyim; in: *Lešonenu*, 11 (1941), 83–93; E. Brønno, *Studien ueber hebraeische Morphologie und Vokalismus der Hexapla* (1943); D. Yellin, *Tolĕdot Hitpattĕḥut ha-Diqduq ha-ʿIvri* (1945); Y. Cantineau, in: *Bulletin de la Société de Linguistique*, 46 (1950), 82–122; R.W. Weiman, *Native and Foreign Elements in a Language* (1950); G.J. Botterweck, *Der Triliterismus im Semitischen* (1952); Ẓ. Elner, *ʿAl Ḥuqqeha ha-Naʿălamim šel ha-Nĕgina ha-ʿivrit* (1952); V. Christian, *Untersuchungen zur Laut- und Formenlehre des Hebraeischen* (1953); Y.G.P. Gumpertz, *Mivṭĕʾe Śĕfatenu* (1953); Z. Ben-Ḥayyim, *Studies in the Traditions of the Hebrew Language* (1954); I. Garbell, in: *Homenaje a Millás-Vallicrosa*, 1 (1954), 647–96; S. Moscati, *Preistoria e storia del consonantismo ebraico antico* (1954); Z. Ben-Ḥayyim, *ʿivrit wa-aʾramit Nosaḥ Šomĕron*, 5 vols. (1957–77); Ḥ. Rabin, in: *Sefer Ṭur-Sinai* (1960), 169–206; idem, in: *Tarbiẓ*, 30 (1960/61), 99–111; Š. Morag, *Ha-ʿivrit še-bĕ-Fi Yĕhude Teman* (1963); Ḥ. Yalon, *Mavoʾ lĕ-Niqqud ha-Mišna* (1964); K. Koskinen, in: ZDMG, 114 (1964), 16–58; K. Aartun, *ibid.*, 117 (1967), 247–65; E. Jenni, *Das hebraeische Piʿel* (1968); R. Mirkin, in: *Lešonenu*, 32 (1968), 140–52; Y. Kutscher, in: *Sefer Zikkaron l-Vinyamin de-Vries* (1969), 218–51; W. Weinberg, in: HUCA, 40–41 (1969–70), 1–32; E. Brønno, *Die Aussprache der hebraeischen Laryngale nach Zeugnissen des Hieronymus* (1970); J. Blau, *On Pseudo-Corrections in Some Semitic Languages* (1970), 23–42, 114–25. **ADD. BIBLIOGRAPHY:** Y. Yeivin, *Masoret ha-Lašon ha-Ivrit ha-Mištakkefet ba-Nikkud ha-Bavli* (1985); O. (Rodrig) Schwartzwald, *Dikduk u-Metzi'ut ba-Po'al ha-Ivri* (1981); *ibid.*, *Perakim be-Morfologi'ah ivrit* (2002); U. Ornan, *Ha-millah ha-Aḥaronah: Mangenon ha-Tezurah shel ha-Millah ha-Ivrit* (2003). D. SYNTAX AND STYLE: S.R. Driver, *A Treatise on the Use of the Tenses in Hebrew* (1892[3]); E. Koenig, *Stilistik, Rhetorik, Poetik in Bezug auf die biblische Literatur* (1900); Y.Ḥ. Ṭaviov, *More ha-Signon* (1902[2]); J. Nodel, *Der zusammengesetzte Satz im Neuhebraeischen, auf Grund der Mischna, der Tosefta und Midraschim* (1928); G.R. Driver, *Problems of the Hebrew Verbal System* (1936); Y. Pereẓ, *Taḥbir ha-Lašon ha-ʿivrit* (1942); F.R. Blake, *A Resurvey of Hebrew Tenses* (1951); M. Gottstein, *Taḥbirah u-Millonah šel ha-Lašon ha-ʿivrit še-bi-Tĕḥum Hašpaʿatah šel haʿaravit* (1951); E. Lemoine, *Theorie de l'emphase hebraïque* (1951); M.M. Bravmann, *Studies in Arabic and General Syntax* (1953); C. Brockelmann, *Hebraeische Syntax* (1956); ʿU. Ornan, in: *Lešonenu*, 25 (1961), 35–51; F. Rundgren, *Das althebraeische Verbum, Abriss der Aspektlehre* (1961): E.J. Revell, *A Structural Analysis of the Grammar of the Manual of Discipline* (1962); U. Ornan, *Ha-Ẓerufim ha-Šemaniyim bi-Lĕšon ha-Sifrut ha-ʿivrit ha-Ḥădaša* (1964); Y. Pereẓ, *Mišpaṭ ha-Ziqqa ba-ʿivrit lĕ-Kol Tĕqufoteha* (1967); Ḥ.B. Rosén, *ʿivrit Ṭova* (1967[2]); E. Rubinstein, *Ha-Mišpat ha-Šemani* (1969); Y. Hayon, *Relativization in Hebrew* (1969); U. Takamitsu, *Emphasis in Biblical Hebrew* (1969); I.F. Anderson, *The Hebrew Verbless Clause in the Pentateuch* (1970); E. Rubinstein, *Ha-Ẓeruf ha-Poʿoli* (1971). **ADD. BIBLIOGRAPHY:** A. Abbadi, *Taḥbir ha-Siyaḥ shel ha-Ivrit ha-Ḥadashah* (1988); S. Fassberg, *Sugi'ot be-Taḥbir ha-Mikra* (1994); M.Z. Kaddari, *Taḥbir ve-Semantikah be-Ivrit she-le-aḥar ha-Mikra*, 2 vols. (1991–95). E. LEXICON AND SEMANTICS: J. Levy, *Woerterbuch ueber die Talmudim und Midraschim*, 4 vols. (1876–89); Ḥ.Y. Kohut, *Sefer he-ʿaruk ha-Šalem me'et Natan Ben-Yeḥi'el*, 8 vols. (1878–92); S. Krauss, *Griechische und lateinische Lehnwoerter im Talmud, Midrasch und Targum*, 2 vols. (1898–99); M. Jastrow, *A Dictionary of the Targumim etc.*, 2 vols. (1903); F. Brown, S.R. Driver, and C.A. Briggs, *A Hebrew and English Lexicon of the OT, Based on… Gesenius* (1907); E. Ben-Yehuda, *Millon ha-Lašon ha-ʿivrit ha-Yešana ve-ha-Ḥadašah*, 16 vols. (1908–50); W. Gesenius, *Hebraeisches und aramaeisches Handwoerterbuch ueber das AT* (ed. by Buhl; 1921[17]); Y. Klatzkin, *Oẓar ha-Munnaḥim ha-Pilosofiyim*, 4 vols. (1928–33); S. Krauss, *Tosefot he-ʾarukh ha-Šalem* (1937); Y. Kenaʿani, *Oẓar ha-Lašon ha-ʿivrit*, 1–11 vols. (1948–71); L. Koehler, W. Baumgartner, *Lexicon in Veteris Testamenti libros & Supplementum* (1953, 1958, 1967[3]); F. Zorell, *Lexicon Hebraicum et Aramaicum Veteris Testamenti* (1954); D. Sedan, *ʾAvne Śafa* (1967); Š.E. Loewenstamm, Y. Blau, *Oẓar Lashon ha-Miqraʾ* (א-ט), 3 vols. (1957–60); J. Barr, *Semantics of Biblical Language* (1961); Y.Y. Kutscher, *Millim ve-Toldotehen* (1961); R. Sappan, *Darke ha-Sleng* (1963); idem, *Millon ha-Sleng ha-Yiśrĕ'eli* (1965); Ẓ. Scharfstein, *Oẓar ha-Millim wĕ-ha-Nivim* (1964[3]); Y. Avineri, *Yad ha-Lašon* (1965); A. Even-Šošan, *Millon Ḥadaša*, 5 vols. (1949–52); idem, *Ha-Millon he-Ḥadaš*, 7 vols. (1966–1970); Ḥ. Yalon, *Mĕgillot Midbar Yĕhuda, Divre Lašon* (1967); Y. Avineri, *Gĕnazim Mĕgullim* (1968); N. Stutchkoff, *Oẓar ha-Safá ha-ʿIvrit* (1968); M.Ẓ. Qaddari, *Ha-Ḥiyyuv bi-Lĕšon ha-Mĕgillot ha-Gĕnuzot* (1968); idem, *Mi-Yrušat Yĕme ha-Benayim* (1970); Ḥ. Rabin and Ẓ. Radday, *ʾOẓar ha-Millim* (1970). **ADD. BIBLIOGRAPHY:** J. Schweka, *Rav Millim, Ha-Millon ha-Shalem Ivri-Ivri*, 6 vols. (also on CD and updated version at: www.cet.ac.il/ravmilim) (1997); A. Even-Shoshan, *Millon Even-Shoshan: Meḥuddash u-Me'udkan Lishnot ha-Alpayim* (ed. Moshe Azar), 6 vols. (2003). F. PERIODICALS: *Lešonenu* (1929–); *Lešonenu La-ʿam* (1949–);

Qunteresim le-ʿinyene ha-Lašon ha-ʿivrit (1937–8, ed. Ḥ. Yalon); *ʿInyene Lašon* (1942–3, ed. Ḥ. Yalon); *Balšanut Ivrit Ḥofšit* (1969–). **ADD. BIBLIOGRAPHY:** *Meḥkarim be-Lashon* (1985–).

HEBREW IMMIGRANT AID SOCIETY (HIAS), international immigrant and refugee service. HIAS was founded in New York City in 1881, when the Russian Emigrant Relief Committee, a temporary body established to help Jews escaping Czarist Russia, formed the Hebrew Emigrant Aid Society. The new organization provided meals, transportation, and employment counseling to arrivals at New York's Castle Garden, the main immigrant-processing center of that time. In 1882 the first Jewish shelter was established on the Lower East Side. In 1889 the shelter adopted the name Hebrew Sheltering House Association and was reorganized by East European Jewish immigrants under the Hebrew name, Hachnosas Orchim. In 1909 the Hebrew Sheltering House Association (1884) and the Hebrew Immigrant Aid Society (1902) merged. Responding to the growing needs of Jewish immigrants from Eastern Europe, the organization soon grew to national dimensions, providing help in legal entry, basic subsistence, employment, citizenship instruction, and locating of relatives for nearly half a million newcomers to the United States during the organization's first decade. Under President John L. Bernstein (1917–26), HIAS offices were opened in Eastern Europe and the Far East.

In 1927 HIAS joined the Jewish Colonization Association (ICA) and the European Emigdirect to form the collectively run HICEM. Although the economic depression of the 1930s resulted in demands for additional domestic services to Jewish communities all over the world, most of HICEM's efforts were devoted toward financing and assisting emigration from Nazi Germany and finding outlets for refugees from Eastern and Central Europe in Western Europe and South America. HIAS continued its European activities throughout World War II, while imploring Western governments to open their gates wider to Jewish war refugees. In 1945 HIAS dissolved its partnership with HICEM, and in 1949 it cooperated with the *American Jewish Joint Distribution Committee (JDC) in forming the Displaced Persons Coordinating Committee. As in previous years, HIAS continued to fight against restrictive U.S. immigration laws following World War II, and worked with Israel and with other Jewish immigrant services.

In 1954 HIAS merged with the United Service for New Americans and the JDC Migration Department into the United HIAS Service, a single international agency which helped thousands of East European and North African immigrants – especially following the Hungarian revolt of 1956 and the Middle East crises of 1956 and 1967 – to find new homes, mainly in Western Europe, the United States, and South America. Today about 30 percent of HIAS's budget comes from the U.S. Department of State; the remainder comes from private donations.

During the 1980s there were tensions between HIAS, representing the American Jewish community along with some of the Soviet Jewry movement's agencies, and the Israeli government over whether and how to aid Soviet Jews seeking freedom in countries other than Israel. The Israeli government felt that the Soviet Jewry movement was a Zionist movement and that since it had issued the visas under which Soviet Jews were able to leave, all Soviet Jews should go to Israel and emigrate, if they so chose, from Israel to other countries. HIAS, some local federations, and the Union of Councils felt that the Soviet Jewry movement was a human rights and human freedom issue and therefore, they were prepared to assist Soviet Jews just as they assisted Jews leaving other lands of oppression. The divisions were deep. Each side was faithful to the truth of their experience. In the end HIAS helped those Soviet Jews who wished to come to the United States directly and local federations assisted in the resettlement.

In addition to its world headquarters in New York City, HIAS maintains offices in Buenos Aires, Charlotte, N.C., Djabal and Goz Amir, Chad, Kiev, Moscow, Nairobi, Quito, Ecuador, Tel Aviv, Vienna, and Washington, D.C. Since its beginnings in 1881, HIAS has helped more than 4.5 million people to immigrate to the United States and other countries of safe haven around the world.

[Morris Ardoin (2nd ed.)]

HEBREW LANGUAGE. This entry is arranged according to the following scheme:

PRE-BIBLICAL
BIBLICAL
THE DEAD SEA SCROLLS
MISHNAIC
MEDIEVAL
MODERN PERIOD

A detailed table of contents precedes each section.

PRE-BIBLICAL

Nature of the Evidence
The Sources
Phonology
Morphology

Pre-biblical Hebrew, for the purposes of this article, refers to the Hebrew language as reflected in written documents up to and including the 12th century B.C.E. (Taanach, cf. below). This study is limited to an analysis of the written evidence which reflects the Hebrew spoken in Palestine during the pre-biblical period. (No attempt will be made to reconstruct Proto-Hebrew (‡) forms based on the masoretic Hebrew found in the Bible). Evidence of this type exists for the period from the mid-20th to the 13th centuries B.C.E.

Nature of the Evidence

There is no corpus of texts written in pre-biblical Hebrew, but only toponyms and single words transcribed into syllabaries which were not able to render accurately the consonants and vowel patterns of Hebrew. This material is written in the Egyptian and Akkadian syllabaries and care must be exercised in reconstructing the language upon which these transcripts are based.

The Akkadian syllabary (as a result of Sumerian influence) was unable to represent gutturals except for *ḫ*. Therefore, these transcriptions cannot help to determine which of the Proto-Semitic gutturals were still in use in pre-biblical Hebrew. However, whenever a guttural was pronounced it was usually rendered by an *ḫ*, e.g.,

נְחֹשֶׁת *nu-ḫu-uš-tum* (EA 69:28)
עָפָר *ḫa-pa-ru* (EA 141:4; also *a-pa-ru*, EA 143:11)
זְרוֹעַ *zu-ru-uḫ* (EA 287:27)
צֹהַר *zu-uḫ-ru-ma* (EA 232:11)

The Egyptian material, while more faithfully representative of the consonantal system, did not have a clearly defined vowel system. As far as the vocalization of the Egyptian material is concerned, this study bases itself on W.F. Albright's *Vocalization of the Egyptian Syllabic Orthography* (VESO).

In discussing the verbal scheme of pre-biblical Hebrew, it must be carefully determined if a particular form is pure Canaanite, or whether it is in fact simply poor Akkadian, or the result of contamination – a combination of Akkadian and Hebrew elements (cf. the discussion on *yaqattal* forms, Morphology no. 5 below). When assessing place names, it is necessary to remember that they are conservative by nature, and do not always undergo the same linguistic changes as other words (e.g., *Ak-ka* Phonology no. 5). It is important, too, to remember that place names are often lexically difficult and may at times be non-Semitic in origin (cf. Hazor Phonology no. 5). Naturally, such words are expected to behave differently than the norm of pre-biblical Hebrew. Finally, it must be remembered that Canaanite itself was probably under the strong influence of Amorite, and that some forms found in the transcriptions may be directly due to this influence.

Keeping these factors in mind, and remembering that there is no corpus of pre-biblical Hebrew as such, but words or groups of words written in non-Hebrew syllabaries, it is surprising how much can actually be said about the phonology and morphology of the earliest stage of Hebrew.

The Sources

(1) The Egyptian material consists of lists of Canaanite personal and place names. In 1909, Burchardt published all the words and Hebrew parallels known at that time. Much more important are the Execration texts, published first by Sethe, and supplemented by Posener. These are texts inscribed on vases and contain the names of potential rivals; it was assumed that with the smashing of the vase, the opponent would also be destroyed. These texts date from the mid-20th to the late 19th centuries B.C.E. The Egyptian material is completed by an 18th-century list of Egyptian slaves (The Hayes List) which contains more than 30 North-West Semitic names, and was published by Albright. In all, there are 150 names from the period between 1900 and 1750 B.C.E.

(2) At Taanach (5 mi. (8 km.) south of Megiddo), some important cuneiform material was unearthed by the archaeologist E. Sellin in 1903–04. It contains six letters written in cuneiform Akkadian, which date from the 16th–15th-century B.C.E. period and were edited by the Assyriologist F. Hrozny in 1904. The letters appear to have been written by Canaanite scribes (especially the first two), and in several instances their native speech is clearly reflected in the strange Akkadian forms found in the letters. This material was supplemented by another letter found at Taanach and published originally by D.R. Hillers in 1964; it is written in alphabetic cuneiform and dates from the 12th century B.C.E. (cf. F.M. Cross's republication of this letter).

(3) It has long been recognized that many of the Ur III and Old Babylonian names found in Akkadian sources do not reflect standard Akkadian, but a distinct dialect or language. The traditional division of Semitic languages sets Akkadian off as East Semitic, and it was naturally agreed that these names, if they are not Akkadian, must be West Semitic. In 1926, Th. Bauer collected and analyzed about 700 names of this type in his work *Die Ostkanaanaeer* and argued (following Landsberger) that these names were Canaanite (but originated east of the Tigris, hence were East Canaanite). Since many of these names were prefaced by the Sumerian ideogram *MAR. TU*, which is equivalent to the Akkadian *amurru* ("west"), the people who bore these names came to be known as Amorites. Other scholars (Albright) have suggested that the language was a dialect (eastern) of Canaanite, while some (Goetze) feel that Amorite and Ugaritic make up a separate division within North-West Semitic. Since Bauer's publication, the number of known Amorite names has virtually tripled; a more up-to-date study can be found in Huffmon's *Amorite Personal Names in the Mari Texts* (with a complete bibliography of the problems of Amorite). It is not clear whether the designations *MAR. TU* (Sumerian) and *amurru* (Akkadian) were originally independent terms or linguistic equivalents. In the older (Ur III) period, persons described as *MAR. TU* have names which are often not Semitic, while in the later (Old Babylonian) period, many persons with West Semitic names are not designated in this way. This fact has prompted scholars to distinguish two linguistic strains: one called Amorite (Ur III) and the other East Canaanite. It seems clear today that the relationship between these two groups is much closer than originally thought and both may be referred to as Amorite (cf. Gelb, in JAOS, 88 (1968), 39–47).

The similarity between many Amorite names and names found in the Egyptian Execration texts, points to the importance of this material for the study of pre-biblical Hebrew. There undoubtedly were many points of similarity between the Amorite West Semitic dialect and the language of Canaan; Amorite, however, is not Canaanite as seen clearly from the fact that *ā* does not go to *ō* (the Amorite *s* = the Canaanite š is also significant).

(4) Possibly the most important source which has direct bearing on the language spoken in Canaan in pre-biblical times are the *Tell el-Amarna letters (EA). Discovered in 1887 at Tell el-Amarna, in Egypt, these letters contain the

correspondence between the ruling Egyptian court and their vassal princes in Canaan. The letters are ostensibly written in Akkadian, which was at that time (14th century B.C.E.), the lingua franca of the Near East. However, the Canaanite scribes were not fully conversant with the Babylonian language they attempted to write, and constantly substitute Canaanite forms and idioms for the Babylonian, producing a real "*Mischsprache*" which, when analyzed, yields much information about the scribes' native tongue. There is, in fact, at least one Canaanite proverb written entirely in the language of the scribe: *ki-i na-am-lu tu-um-ḫa-zu la-a ta-ka-bi-lu u ta-an-si-ku qa-ti amelim ša yi-ma-ḫa-aṣ-ṣi*: (meaning, "If ants are smitten, they do not accept [the smiting quietly], but they bite the hand of the man who smites them") (EA 252:16–19; cf. Albright, in BASOR, 89 (1943), 29–32).

More important than the native influence on the Akkadian in these letters are the Canaanite glosses which the scribe wrote in the margins of the text (in the Akkadian syllabary) as the equivalents to Akkadian words in the body of the letter. For example, in a letter from Jerusalem (EA 287:27), the Akkadian *qat* has the gloss *zu-ru-uḫ* is equivalent to the Hebrew *zəroaʿ* (זרוע, "hand"). In the Akkadian syllabary ʿ = *ḫ*; and ō, which was non-existent, was transcribed as a *u*; therefore, *zu-ru-uḫ* is the exact equivalent to the Hebrew זרוע.

The reasons for writing these glosses are unclear. The scribe may have written the Canaanite gloss for an Akkadian word he was not sure of, and filled in the proper form later. This explanation is the most likely since the gloss is always the exact equivalent of the Akkadian word in the text, and the scribe surely did not expect the gloss to clarify the text for the Egyptian reader. Still, whatever the reason, these glosses remain the most direct evidence of pre-biblical Hebrew.

The letters were given an excellent edition by Knudtzon (with some help by Weber and Ebeling) in 1915. Further texts were published by Dossin, Gordon, Schroeder, and Thureau-Dangin (for complete references cf. R. Borger, *Handbuch der Keilschriftliteratur*, 1 (1967), 238). This was supplemented by fine grammatical studies by Boehl, Ebeling, Dhorme, Albright, and Moran (cf. bibliography).

The material is presented under two headings: Phonology and Morphology. Each grammatical point is given separate treatment with the appropriate title preceding the evidence. When necessary, any differences between the earlier (Egyptian) and the later (cuneiform) material are noted and explained.

Phonology

(1) *ḥ* AND *ḫ*. These two Proto-Semitic consonants are not distinguished in the Hebrew script. The Phoenician-Canaanite alphabet contains only one grapheme for these two consonants indicating that the language for which this alphabet was developed did not differentiate between these two sounds. The Tiberian vocalization shows that the reading tradition also did not distinguish between the two sounds, as a diacritic was not used to differentiate between them (as opposed to *š* and *ś*). Greek material indicates some differences in transcribing the ח, but this seems to be rooted in secondary and dialectical developments. It is, therefore, necessary to look elsewhere to determine whether Hebrew ever differentiated between the *ḥ* and *ḫ*. The material written in cuneiform (Taanach, Amorite, Amarna) is of no help here since the Akkadian syllabary only recognizes the consonant *ḫ*; thus the distinction, if it did exist, could not be represented in that syllabary. The Egyptian material, however, is of crucial importance.

The early Egyptian material clearly distinguishes between *ḥ* and *ḫ*:

ḥa-ar-pu in Canaanite ‡*ḥarbu*, Hebrew *ḥereb* (VESO XII, A, 4); while

ḫu-ru in Canaanite ‡*ḫurru*, Hebrew *ḥor* (VESO XIII, A, 5).

In the later Shoshenq list (c. 950), the etymological *ḫ* seems to have merged with *ḥ*, as: *bt ḥ(w)rn* (Beth-Horon) (which etymologically is probably *ḫ*). This indicates that the Egyptian (Amarna) documents reflect the state where the assimilation of *ḫ* to *ḥ* was becoming finalized, and that this later state is reflected in the Shoshenq list.

It is difficult to accept the position (Goetze) that where these consonants are differentiated, it is as a result of Amorite (!) influence. Amorite was written in the cuneiform syllabary which could not differentiate between *ḫ* and *ḥ*, so there are no objective grounds for assuming that Amorite made this distinction. This position can only be justified by the assumption that Ugaritic and Amorite form a subgroup within North-West Semitic, and that the Ugaritic differentiation was maintained in Amorite. But there is no real evidence that this distinction was maintained in Amorite, and it is more reasonable to assume that cuneiform writing limited the Amorite pronunciation of gutturals just as it did the Akkadian. While there was clearly an Amorite influence in Canaan, there is no reason to assume that some early stage of Hebrew could not have differentiated between *ḫ* and *ḥ* as in the early Egyptian material.

(2) INDEPENDENCE OF THE *Ś* PHONEME IN PRE-BIBLICAL HEBREW. The fact that only two graphemes are used in biblical Hebrew to distinguish the three sounds *s*, *ś*, *š*, (*ś* and *š* are distinguished by means of a diacritic) reflects the situation in the language from which the alphabet was borrowed, and not directly on Hebrew. The fact that Greek and Latin transcriptions were unable, at a much later date, to distinguish between the three sounds is not relevant, since there is only one Greek-Latin grapheme *s* (σ) which parallels the early Hebrew sibilants.

In biblical Hebrew the three phonemes *s*, *ś*, and *š* are kept distinct. This is also the case in Epigraphic South Arabic, while in the other Semitic languages these three phonemes have coalesced into two. This indicates that the situation reflected in biblical Hebrew is primary, and not the result of a late innovation.

In the pre-biblical cuneiform material, this distinction is difficult to recognize (where only *s* and *š* are distinguished), while the Egyptian material seems clearly to indicate that the distinction between these three phonemes was carefully maintained. Here *š* and *ṯ* were transcribed by the sign for *s*, while *ś* was represented by *š*, so that etymological *ś* and *š* were kept distinct:

Ya-si-r-ʾi-ra, in Hebrew ‡Yasirʾel (ישראל, "Israel") (VESO III B3);

sa-ʿa-ra-ta, in Canaanite ‡*śaʿar(a)t(a)*, in Hebrew *saʿara* (שערה, "hair") (VESO V A 13); while,

ša-ʿa-ra, in Hebrew *šaʿar* (שער, "gate") (VESO XV A 4).

(3) *ṯ* AND *š*. The Hebrew-Phoenician alphabet has only one grapheme for these two Proto-Semitic consonants, and they both seem to have coalesced into *š*.

The early Egyptian material seems to indicate that the distinction between these two phonemes was still maintained. In these transcriptions both *ṯ* and *ś* are written with an *s*:

ʾa-ṯi-ra, in Canaanite *ʾasira(a)*, in Amarna *asiru*, in Hebrew *ʾasir* (אסיר);

ṯu-pi-ir, in Canaanite *soper*, in Hebrew *sofer* (סופר), but *ʿstrt* (*ʿaṯtartu*) = Astarte (Burchardt 285);

ḥa-da-sa-t (*hadaṯatu*), in Canaanite *hadaš(a)t(a)*, in Hebrew *ḥadaša* (חֲדָשָׁה, "new") (VESO XII, A, 6).

But *š* is transcribed as *š* in the word *qa-di-š*, in Hebrew *qadoš* (קדש) (VESO XC9).

However the same lists mention *ša-ʿa-ra*, in Canaanite ‡*ša-ar*, in Hebrew *šaʿar* (שער, "gate") (VESO V, A, 14) (from *ṯaʿaru*), indicating that the *ṯ* was unstable even here and that it tended to merge into *š*. In the Shoshenq list, the *š* and *ṯ* are undifferentiated: *šbrt* = *šibbolet* (from *ṯibbolet*?). In short, the *ṯ* was already on its way to coalescing with the *š* in the period of the early material, and by the time of the Shoshenq list and biblical Hebrew, it had disappeared as a separate phoneme.

The Amarna evidence is difficult to interpret. On the one hand, the difference in spelling between La-ki-si (EA 288:43) and Ša-ak-mi (EA 289:23) in the Jerusalem letters indicates that in that area *š* and *ṯ* were kept etymologically distinct (*š* in Ša-ak-mi must be from *ṯ*, cf. Ugaritic *ṯkm*, as well as the fact that it is written with an *s* in the Egyptian transcriptions (VESO XIV A 15); and *š* in masoretic Hebrew). However, it has been noted (Goetze) that the spelling La-ki-ši also appears in the Jerusalem letters (EA 289:13) and that the cuneiform signs for *sa, si, su*, serve as scribal variants for *ša, ši, šu*.

(4) *ʿayin* and *ǧyin*. These two phonemes, which have coalesced into *ʿayin* in biblical Hebrew, are still distinguished in the Egyptian material.

ʿn-qn-ʿa-m(a), in Canaanite En-qne-ʿ-am(ma), in Hebrew Yoqnĕʿam (יקנעם) (VESO V, A, 6), while

ʿa-ḏa-ta, in Canaanite ‡Ǧazzat(a), in Amarna, Azzati, Hazati, in Hebrew Azzah (עזה, Gr. Γαζα) (VESO XVI, A, 11).

However, we also find *ša-ʿa-ru*, in Hebrew שער ("gate") < *ṯaεru* (VESO V, A, 14), which would indicate that *ǧ* > ʿ, as it has in biblical Hebrew. Here too, it must be pointed out that while the transcriptions prove that the distinction between the two phonemes still existed in early Hebrew, the distinction was fast disappearing. The cuneiform material can be of no help as the syllabary does not (generally) distinguish between these consonants.

In a published letter from Taanach (BASOR, 173 (1969), p. 45–50), dated the late 13th or early 12th century B.C.E., the name *pʿm* (*puʿm*) appears. If this name is related to the Ugarit *pǧm*, this would indicate that *ǧ* < ʿ. (This letter is written in an alphabetic orthography (related to Ugaritic?), and it may be assumed that if the *ǧ* = ʿ distinction still existed in Canaanite, it would have been represented in this way).

(5) LONG *a* (*ā*) BECOMES LONG *o* (*ō*). All the relevant material indicates that this shift, which is considered unique in Canaanite (of the classical Semitic languages), took place as early as the 15th century B.C.E. An instance from Amorite is especially interesting. The name of a northern city appears as Ḫaṣura (Hazor). Since the *ā* > *ō* shift did not take place in Amorite at all, this seems to indicate that the situation in Canaan in the 15th century B.C.E. was already post shift. (However, care must be taken in this case since the name is etymologically unclear and its vocalization may reflect a non-Semitic pronunciation.) All other relevant material indicates that when the Amarna period started the shift had already taken place in Canaanite.

(a) *Egyptian Material. Bi-ʾa-ru-ta*, in Canaanite *beʾrot*, in Hebrew באר (VESO X, C, 4)

(b) *Amarna Canaanite (Many Examples). a-nu-ki* (EA 287:66, 69), in Hebrew אנכי; *ṣu-un-nu* (EA 263:12), in Hebrew צאן; *ru-šu-nu* (EA 264:18), in Hebrew ראשנו. The place name Ak-ka, in Hebrew עכו reflects a conservative pronunciation.

(c) *Taanach*. Interestingly enough the only indication for this shift in Taanach is the name Gu-li which may be derived from the Canaanite Goʾeli, Hebrew גואל (I 3) (but cf. below). However, other place names, such as Ra-ḫa-bi (IV 22), Hebrew רחוב, and Ma-gi-id-da (V 15), Hebrew מגדו, seem to indicate that this shift had not yet taken place. (Another possible reading for the name in IV 22 is Elu-ra-pi-i, Hebrew רפא.)

Unfortunately, all the Taanach evidence is in the form of personal and place names, and it may be that although the shift had taken place generally, these names had preserved an older pronunciation. It is also possible that the shift had not yet taken place in the pre-Amarna period, or, at any event, not in the south of Canaan. The only evidence to the contrary is the name Gu-li which may be part of the Canaanite Gu-li-Adad (Albright), or the Hurrian Guli-Tešub (Maisler (Mazar)), in which case it is not relevant to the problem. The sum of the evidence seems to indicate that in Taanach, in the period preceding Amarna (16th–15th century) the shift *ā* > *ō* had not yet taken place.

(6) THE PROTO-SEMITIC *n* IS ASSIMILATED TO THE FOLLOWING CONSONANT. In biblical Hebrew, the ProtoSemitic *n* is assimilated to the following consonant. The pre-biblical material shows that this process was in a state of flux and that in the early period the *n* was not as consistently assimilated as later on.

The Egyptian *Bi-in-ti-ʿ-n-t* is in Canaanite ‡*Bint(i)-ʿanat* ("daughter of Anat"; Canaanite *bint* = Hebrew בת). In other words the *n* of בת remained unassimilated (VESO VI B 12).

In Amarna there is both *gitti* < *ginti* as well as *ginti* (Hebrew *gat*), indicating that the tendency to assimilate the *n* did exist, but had not yet reached the proportions of biblical Hebrew where it is the norm in these circumstances. *La-bi-tu* < *labintu* (EA 296:17) is also found in Amarna.

(7) *aʾ* > (*ā*) > *ō*. The Amarna material indicates that this change had already taken place in Hebrew:

(a) *ru-šu-nu* (EA 264:18), *roš* (ראש, "head") reflects the following development: *rōš* < *rāš* < ‡*raʾš*.

(b) *zu-u-nu* (EA 263:12); *ẓon* (צאן, "sheep") here too we assume *zōn* < *zān* < *zaʾn*.

The Egyptian material generally reflects the later stage, as in the name *ršqdš* (*rš* = ראש) (VESO X, C, 9), but *ru-ʾu-š (a)* is also found (VESO X, C, 7). Ru-ʾu-š(a)-qdš, in Canaanite ‡Roš-qids, is explained by Albright as being a Canaanite back formation of *roʾ(o)š* from *rōš*, on the analogy of the plural *raʾšim* (ראשים) which was probably dialectic (VESO III, E, 6). Another possible interpretation is that this name preserved the earlier pronunciation (cf. the name Ak-ka (עכו) in Amarna Hebrew (Phonology, no. 5).

(8) MIMMATION. Mimmation, known in early Akkadian, is almost unknown in biblical Hebrew, except for a few fixed forms like אמנם, יומם, חנם. The earlier material preserves several interesting examples. In the Execration texts, the city of Jerusalem is transcribed as ȝwsȝmm (= Urusalimum). Similarly, the Taanach letters indicate a high rate of mimmation, especially in the Canaanite letters. (In Amarna there is a marked decrease in the use of mimmation, an indirect indication that the Taanach letters precede the Amarna letters).

Morphology

(1) CASE ENDINGS. The Semitic languages had originally three basic cases: nominative, accusative, and genitive, which were differentiated by suffixes (in singular *-u,-a,-i*). Especially prominent in the early history of the language, they generally fell into disuse. In biblical Hebrew, the nominal case endings have generally been lost, except for certain compound names like מתושלח, and possibly poetic forms like בנו בעור, and חיתו ארץ. The *heh localis*, long thought to be a preserved accusative in biblical Hebrew, has to be reevaluated in the light of the Ugaritic evidence. In Ugaritic, which does not generally employ the *mater lectionis*, there is the word *šmmh* which would indicate that the *h* has consonantal force (cf. Speiser, in: *Israel Exploration Journal*, 4 (1954), 108–115).

Both the Egyptian material and the cuneiform material from Amarna indicate that case endings were still in use at that time. In the earlier Egyptian lists, place names usually end with *-u*, but the tendency was for *-a* to replace *-u* in later material, e.g., Ayaluna, Ašqaluna, Ṣiduna, and Ḫaṣura. This indicates that before the case endings were completely dropped, there was a period where these final short vowels were confused and the cases were no longer grammatically distinguished.

Boehl has shown (see also Dhorme, in: RB, 23 (1914), 347–8 = *Recueil E. Dhorme* (1951), 460–1) that the case endings in Canaanite are by and large not confused and the distinction between the different cases is maintained. Examples of the use of the nominative *-u*:

a-pa-ru (עפר) EA 141:4
ru-šu-nu (ראשנו) EA 264:18
The genitive *-i*:
sa-aḫ-ri (שער) EA 244:16
a-na-yi (אֳנִי) EA 245:28
The accusative *-a*:
ḫa-an-pa (חנף) EA 288:7
mu-ur-ra (מֹר) EA 269:16

These case endings were elided in Hebrew after the Amarna period and are very rare in biblical Hebrew.

(2) THE FIRST PERSON SINGULAR INDEPENDENT PRONOUN: *ʾanoki*. The *ʾanoki* form is found in Amarna Hebrew (*a-nu-ki* EA 287:66, 69). In late biblical Hebrew, this form becomes rare and is almost always replaced by *ʾani*.

(3) THE DUAL ENDING: *-ay(m)a*. In Amarna, the dual ending is known from the word *hi-na-ia* ("my (two) eyes" (nom.)) (EA 144:17). A similar form is known from Taanach *iṣma-ga-re-ma* (II, 8) ("two Chariot wheels"), with the Canaanite dual endings.

(4) FIRST PERSON POSSESSIVE SUFFIX: *-nu* (OUR). *Ti-mi-tu-na-nu* ((and you) "killed us"), in Amarna (EA 238:33).

THE VERB (1) CAUSATIVE PREFIX *ha-*. The Hebrew causative prefix *ha-* appears in Amarna as *ḫi-* (attenuation). The example is from EA 256:7, *ḫi-iḫ-bi-e*; it is clearly a Hebrew form which is impossible in Akkadian. The scribe used the Hebrew החביא for the common Akkadian verb of the same meaning, *puzzuru*.

(2) THE ENDING OF THE FIRST PERSON SINGULAR OF THE QATALA FORM: *-ti, qatalti*. In Amarna, *qatalti* forms appear, e.g., *ba-ni-ti* "I built" (EA 292:29).

TENSES. The Hebrew verbal scheme, which consists (primarily, cf. below) of two tenses, differs radically from the Proto-Semitic system. The two tenses: a prefixed one indicating incompleted action (imperfect), and the suffixed one indicating completed action (perfect), are secondary. It is possible to give approximate dates for the introduction of these verbal forms from the cuneiform evidence for early Hebrew.

(3) QATALA PRETERITE FORM. The *qatal(a)* form, which in Akkadian is the basis of the stative form (a nominal not a verbal form in Akkadian), is found in Amarna serving also as the Hebrew preterite form. For example:

la-ma-ad ("he has learned") (EA 196:30).
ša-al ("he questioned") (EA 289:10).

(4) YAQTUL IMPERFECT FORMS. The Amarna evidence points clearly to the fact that the *yaqtul* imperfect form had already been developed in Canaan. However, as Moran has pointed out, this function was not exclusive with this form. His work on the Amarna letters from Byblos led him to the conclusion that the imperfect indicative had two functions:

(a) present future; (b) past iterative. The passage EA 104:17–36, which Moran quotes, is instructive. The verb *lequ* ("take") appears three times in the prefixed form *tilquna*, once as a present, once as a future, and once as a past.

> *miya mārū Abd-aširta ardi kalbi šar māt Kašši u šar māt Mitanni šunu u tilqûna māt šarri ana šāšuna panânu tilqûna ālāni ḫazānīka u qâlāta annû inanna dubbirū rābiṣaka u laqû ālānišu ana šāšunu anumma laqû al Ullaza šumma kīamma qâlāta adi tilqûnu āl Ṣumuru u tidûkūna rābiṣa u ṣāb tillati ša ina Ṣumura.*
>
> Who are the sons of Abd-aširta the slave and dog? Are they king of the Kassites or the king of the Mittani that they take the royal land for themselves? Previously they used to take the cities of your governors, and you were negligent. Behold! now they have driven out your commissioner and have taken his cities for themselves. Indeed, they have taken Ullaza. If you are negligent this way they will take Simyra besides, and they will kill the commissioner and the auxiliary force which is in Simyra.

(5) YAQATTALU FORM OF THE VERB. The *yaqattal* form of the verb, attested to in the Akkadian present and the Ethiopic indicative, is generally thought to be missing from North-West Semitic. There are, however, certain forms found both in Amorite and in Amarna Hebrew which seem to indicate that an independent *yaqattal* form may have existed in North-West Semitic.

In Amarna Hebrew, the forms which seem to be of the *yaqattalu* pattern are, e.g., *tidabbibu* (EA 138:49)("they speak") and *i-paṭ-ṭar* (EA 2:46) ("he loosens"). However, the situation is not so simple. Even if the gemination in these forms is accepted as being genuine, they can be explained as Akkadian present forms with the Amarna Canaanite *i-* prefix in place of the Akkadian *a-*. In other words, these would not be genuine Canaanite forms but blends of Akkadian stems with Canaanite prefixes which were produced when speakers of Canaanite tried to write Akkadian.

In Amorite there are also certain names which give the impression of being *yaqattal* forms: e.g., the names *yabanni* (Akkadian: *ibanni*) and *yanabbi* (Akkadian: *inabbi*). Huffmon feels that these names can be properly compared to Ugaritic (cf. *piʿel* of *bāna* in post-biblical Hebrew), and do not necessarily reflect North-West Semitic *yaqattal* forms. Personal names, such as I-ba-as-si-ir and Ya-ba-an-ni-AN, are in his opinion clearly *piʿel* forms. There is therefore, in his opinion, no unambiguous evidence which indicates that there were in fact *yaqattal* forms of the verb in early North-West Semitic.

However, it has been pointed out (Von Soden, in: *Die Welt des Orients*, 3 (1964), 180) that the situation in Amorite is not at all clear:

(a) It is noteworthy that all the *yaqattal* forms that have been found in Amorite are derived from three weak verbs (excepting *ibassir* which may not even be Canaanite);

(b) Some of the roots, like *yanabbi* ("he calls") and *yabanni* ("he builds, makes") are not found as *piʿel* forms in Akkadian. The obvious conclusion is that these are not *piʿel* forms at all but the present of a true *yaqattal* form. (Some of the other names which appear in Amorite: *yabassi, yaḫatt/ṭṭi, yamatt/ṭṭi*, and *yasaṭṭi* are lexically unclear, and cannot be used as evidence.)

The fact that this form is clearly found in a North-West Semitic dialect (Amorite) may indicate that the Amarna Canaanite material should be reassessed. It may be that those forms which appeared to be Canaanite-Akkadian contaminations are true Canaanite Hebrew forms.

(6) YAQATULA (SUBJUNCTIVE) FORM OF THE CANAANITE VERB. In biblical Hebrew, the moods of the imperfect stem have a limited use (opposed, for example, to classical Arabic). The situation in pre-biblical Hebrew is more difficult to determine. Since Akkadian has a homophonous morpheme, known as the *ventive* (a modal suffix in Akkadian which indicates motion toward the speaker or focus of attention; e.g., *illik* ("he came"), *illikam* ("he came here")), a large number of relevant occurrences of the suffix *-a* (with *ya/i/u/qtal* forms) are readily explained, at least at first glance as examples of the *ventive*.

Moran has proposed that true *yaqatula* forms are identifiable by semantic means and that they are specifically used in two instances (*Orientalia*, 29 (1960), 1–19):

(a) to express a wish, request, or command – *yi-sa* LUGAL ("may the king come forth").

(b) in clauses of purpose or intended result – *ib-lu-ṭa* ("so that I may live").

The fact that the biblical Hebrew form, known as the cohortative, has the same functions as the Byblian Amarna (a group of Amarna letters from Byblos) *yaqtula*, indicates that the Hebrew cohortative is a continuation of this "subjunctive" (H. Bauer and P. Leander, *Historische Grammatik der hebraeischen Sprache* (1922), 273; P. Joüon, *Grammaire de l'Hébreu Biblique* (1923), 315 n. 1).

(7) TAQTALU(NA) THIRD PERSON MASCULINE PLURAL FORM. There seems to be some evidence from Amarna which points to the fact that a *taqtalu(na)* third person masculine plural form existed in pre-biblical Hebrew, as in Ugaritic (cf. Boehl, p. 53 and Moran, in: *Journal of Cuneiform Studies*, 5 (1951), 33–35). Hints of this form are also found in biblical Hebrew: e.g., ותקרבו in Ezekiel (37:7) as well as ותקרבון and ותאמרו in Deuteronomy (5:21).

(8) INFINITIVE ABSOLUTE USED AS A FINITE VERB. In biblical Hebrew there are a few clear cases of the use of the infinitive absolute form of the verb with finite force. ושבח אני (Eccles. 4:2) ונהפוך הוא (Esth. 9:1) are the clearest examples of this phenomenon, paralleled by the *qtl/yqtl ʾnk* construction found especially at Karatepe. The fact that this was a fairly regular construction in Early Hebrew (and North-West Semitic in general) is shown by the many examples in the Amarna letters: e.g., (from Amarna), *u ma-ti-ma šu-ut* ("and when he died truly") where the form *matima* is an infinitive absolute followed by the independent pronoun with the force of an independent verb (cf. Moran, in *Journal of Cuneiform Studies*, 4 (1950), 169–72).

[Chaim Brovender]

BIBLICAL

The Names

Biblical Hebrew is also called early Hebrew in contradistinction to living middle Hebrew, as reflected in the Mishnah, the older portions of the Talmud and early Midrash; to written middle Hebrew, as it was used after its extinction as a living language; and to modern Hebrew. It is known mainly from the Hebrew portions of the Bible (i.e., the whole Bible with the exceptions of its quite restricted *Aramaic parts, i.e., two words in Gen. 31:47; Jer. 10:11; Dan. 2:4–7:28; Ezra 4:8–6:18), which constitutes a rather limited corpus. The name "Hebrew Language" itself does not occur in the Bible; instead, it is called the "language of Canaan" (Isa. 19:18) and "Judean" (II Kings 18:26, 28; Isa. 36:11, 13; Neh. 13:24, in the last passage already in accordance with the late, post-exilic usage, which extended the term "Judean" to the nation). Not until about 130 B.C.E. (in the prologue to Ben Sira) does εβραϊστι – occur to denote old Hebrew. Josephus and the New Testament, however, use this term both of Hebrew and Aramaic (in contradistinction to Greek).

Ancient Evidence (Inscriptions and Transcriptions)

Only slight additional material can be adduced from inscriptions and transcriptions, which is not only due to their limited extent. The most important old Hebrew inscriptions are the calendar of *Gezer (c. 10th century B.C.E.), ostraca of *Samaria (from the eighth (?) century B.C.E.), the inscription of *Siloam (c. 700 B.C.E.), the *Lachish and Tel *Arad letters (sixth century B.C.E.). Their linguistic evaluation is impeded by their consonantal script, even the vowel letters being less frequent than in the Masoretic Bible Text. Thus î and *ú* in a medial position are often unmarked (as *ʾš* Siloam 2 = *ʾîš* ("man"), *ṣr* Siloam 3; 6 = *ṣûr* ("rock"). Nevertheless, some new, grammatical material may be derived from them, as the monophthongization of diphthongs even in stressed syllables outside Judah (cf. *qṣ* Gezer 7, *qayiṣ* ("summer"); cf. the pun of the prophet Amos (8:2) of this word with *qēṣ* ("end"); *yn* in the Samaria ostraca, *yáyin* ("wine") or the ending-*ô*, which is considered by some scholars as dual nominative ending in *status constructus* (*yrḥw* ("two months"), Gezer passim), and even the attestation of forms occurring exceptionally in the Bible (as *hyt* Siloam 3 = *hayâṯ* ("she was"), a rare form of the third person feminine perfect of *verba tertiae yôd*, instead of the usual *hâyṯâ*) is of help. Moreover, they often contain additions to the limited vocabulary of Biblical Hebrew.

Akkadian, Greek, and Latin transcriptions, on the other hand, mark the vowels as well, thus making the recognition of grammatical structure possible. Yet the special conditions of both the transcribed and the transcribing language has to be taken into account, besides the intricacies of transcription itself. Disregard of these pitfalls inevitably results in misinterpretations, as when P. Kahle regarded the double pronunciation of *b, g, d, k, p,* and *t* as artificial, *inter alia* because Origen (185–204 C.E.) and Jerome (342–420 C.E.) deviate in their transcriptions. Kahle did not take into account the fact that Greek and Latin at that time had no means of differentiating between aspirates and spirants (cf. e.g., the use of χ for Arabic *k* in the Greek papyri of Nessanah, because *k* was at least slightly aspirated; see Blanc in *To Honor R. Jacobson* (1967), 298). Moreover, with the exception of Origen's transcription of coherent texts, and words quoted by Jerome, these transcriptions are limited to proper names and thus make an insight into the lingual structure rather difficult. Nevertheless, they are by no means unimportant. Sometimes they exhibit Aramaized forms as against the Hebrew feature according to the Masorah (as Akkadian *sa-me-ri-na-ai*, Septuagint Σεμερων, Σαεμηρών; cf. Ezra 4:10, 17 *šâmráyin*, as against masoretic *šômrôn*), and vice versa (as masoretic *Bnê ḇraq*, cf. modern *Ibn ibraq*, as against Akkadian *ba-na-a-a-bar-qa*, Septuagint Βαναιβακάτ [!]). In some cases the noun formation is different (as Akkadian *am-qa-ru-na*, Septuagint ʾάκκάρώύ, exhibiting *qaṭṭâlôn* (masoretic *qiṭṭâlôn*), as against masoretic *ʿeqrôn*, reflecting the parallel *qiṭlôn*; or masoretic ʾέrεκ corresponding to Septuagint ʾΟπέχ, Akkadian *Uruk* (also *Arku?*)). Septuagint ʾΑμμάυ and Akkadian (*Bīt-*) *Ammānu* exhibit the stage preceding masoretic *ʿammōn* (cf. Septuagint variant lecture ʾΑμμών). Even more important are transcriptions exhibiting features preceding the masoretic vocalizations, as Akkadian *a-u-si* (Hosea) presumably still containing the diphthong, or Akkadian *ḫa-za-ki-a-a-a*, which, as against masoretic *Ḥizqiyyâ*, perhaps still exhibits the preservation of *a* in the second and first syllables (cf. also Septuagint ʾΕζεκίας). Since Greek may distinguish between long and short *e/o* by using η, ω and ε, ο, respectively, Greek transcriptions may even be very important for the recognition of grammatical structures (forms like Septuagint Ησαν = masoretic *ʿêśâw*, exhibit, it seems, the oldest attestations of the lengthening of vowels in pretonic open syllables). This situation may sometimes be complicated by later sources exhibiting forms that are considered to be earlier, as when the masoretic so-called *segolata* (as *zéḵεr* – "remembrance"), similarly transcribed in the Septuagint (as Γαθερ – *geṯer*), still appear *apud* Origen as monosyllables (as ζεχρ = *zeḵεr*).

The Masoretic Text

The Masoretic Text is also not easy to evaluate. It is made up of three historically distinct elements, viz. (in order of their antiquity and stability) the consonantal text, the vowel letters, and the system of diacritical marks for vowels and cantillation.

In the course of time, even the consonantal text underwent changes – an altering in pronunciation led to a change in spelling (since *śin* was pronounced as *samek̲*, the latter was rarely substituted for it, as *stâw* ("winter"), Song of Songs 2:11 instead of the original ‡*śtâw*). Similarly, antiquated forms were replaced by more usual ones (cf. e.g., II Sam. 22:37, 40, 48 *taḥatẹnî* ("under me"), as against *taḥtây*, Ps. 18:37, 40, 48, representing the more usual and, presumably, later form), and synonyms replaced obsolete words (cf. parallel passages occurring, e.g., in Chronicles as against Kings, or readings exhibited by "vulgar" Qumran biblical texts). It is even possible that puristic redactions expurgated usages still alive, in favor of literarily preferred features (as Bergstraesser, in: ZATW, 29 (1909), 40ff. assumed for *šɛ* being superseded by *ʾăšɛr*). On the other hand, the differences between Masoretic manuscripts (in contradistinction to the Samaritan version) are so few that this uniformity has to be explained according to the "one-recension" (or even the "archetype") theory.

More conspicuous are differences in the usage of the vowel letters *ʾ, h, w, and y*: in the Masoretic Text, as a rule, but not always, etymologically long vowels, with the exception of medial *â*, are marked by one of these letters. The spelling, however, was more defective than in available texts (cf. also the spelling of inscriptions discussed *supra*), at least at the time of the Septuagint, and there are some differences between the Tiberian and other traditions. Nevertheless, the uniformity mentioned above obtains, as a rule, also in the sphere of the vowel letters. However it has to be assumed that changes affected vowel letters (just as the consonantal text) as obsolete forms were superseded by later ones, and this is exhibited by variant readings occurring in "vulgar" biblical passages found in Qumran. In the Masoretic Text this development is reflected by the so-called *ktîv*, ("what is written") and *qrê* ("what is to be read"), two variant readings of which the *ktîv*, occurring unvocalized in the text, is rejected in favor of the *qrê*, adduced vocalized on the margin (in many Bibles, however, the *ktîv* is adduced in the text with the *qrê's* vocalization, thus causing confusion). Sometimes the *ktîv* exhibits an older feature, given up in favor of the later *qrê* (and in many manuscripts what is adduced as *qrê* in other manuscripts, has already penetrated into the text as a single reading). Thus, it seems that the archaic perfect third person plural feminine *-h*, to be read *-â*, as exhibited by *ktîv*, was superseded by the ending *-û* in *qrê*. Moreover, the pronominal suffix *-ô* of the third person singular masculine, after nouns terminating in a consonant, is still sometimes archaically spelled with *h* in *ktîv*, as against the more usual spelling with *w* in *qrê*. (Sometimes, however, the spelling with *-h* is the only spelling transmitted.) In other cases the *ktîv* exhibits the later feature. Thus *ʾty*, representing *ʾattî* ("you") (feminine singular), presumably due to Aramaic influence (cf. the Samaritan version and DSIa), sometimes occurs as *ktiv*, the *qrê* being *ʾatt*. The same applies to the perfect second person singular ending *-ty*, to be read *-tî*, which was superseded by *-t*.

The latest stage is exhibited by the vowel and cantillation marks, which developed between c. 600 C.E. (the date of the final redaction of the Talmud, in which they did not yet occur) and the beginning of the 10th century (from which period dated manuscripts have been discovered), but is based on a much older tradition. The only vocalization and cantillation system in use is the so-called Tiberian vocalization. It represents the most elaborate system and is the only one completely preserved. Therefore, it serves as the main base for the grammatical investigation of biblical Hebrew. In principle, however, the other vocalization systems are equally important, i.e., the Babylonian system, which includes several sub-species, and the so-called Palestinian. One has also to take into consideration the Samaritan tradition of pronunciation, and important linguistic features may also be elicited from the Dead Sea Scrolls. The most important innovation, differentiating Tiberian (and one subsystem of Palestinian) vocalization from the others is change of *â* to *å*, thus coinciding with *å* < *u*. (This feature seems to be very late, however, not after Jerome's time.) There are also other divergences, such as less attenuation of *a* to *i* in closed unstressed syllables according to the Babylonian vocalization (as *šäb̲ʿâ* = Tiberian *šIb̲ʿâ*, which, *obiter dictum*, already penetrated into Babylonian), a wider supersession of the perfect *paʿil* by *paʿäl*, and the preservation of *ä* in the perfect, imperfect, imperative, and infinitive of *hitpaʿel*. Yet even the Tiberian system exhibits inconsistencies, and it is difficult to establish whether they are due to the mixture of readings of different subschools (cf. those of *Ben Asher, whose readings have been accepted, and *Ben Naphtali), to chance, or to the desire to be over-accurate. Yet, in spite of all these difficulties in proper linguistic evaluation, the main features of biblical grammar are quite clear.

Despite the multilayered character of the linguistic tradition, the Bible, though stretching over many hundreds of years and emanating from different parts of Palestine, exhibits a surprisingly uniform language. This is due to its being a standardized literary language, on the one hand, and the later changes the text underwent (see *supra*) on the other. Nothing is known from the Bible even about dialectal differences, with the exception of the fact that the Ephraimites pronounced *sibbólɛt̲*, rather than *šibbólɛt̲* (cf. also *supra* for more far-reaching monophthongization outside Judah). Post-Exilic books, however, exhibit certain special features which are also found in Middle Hebrew (and sometimes in Aramaic), such as the prevalent use of *ʾăni* for *ʾânôk̲î*, and of *ʾet* with pronominal suffixes rather than their direct annexation to the verb, and the usage of the participle becomes more frequent. Moreover, these books evince a penchant for *scriptio plena*. On the other hand, poetry, in contradistinction to prose, exhibits certain peculiarities, as the longer forms of the prepositions *ʾelê*, ‡*ʿalẹ*,

ʿadẹ ("to, on, till") as against prosaic ʾel ʿal ʿad respectively, the less frequent use of the definite article, of the object marker ʾet and the relative pronoun, further the use of endings -î /-ô in the noun in *status constructus* (-î in additional cases as well), the pronominal suffix *-mô* ("their/them"), the use of *status constructus* when preceding prepositions, and the extended use of the shortened imperfect.

CONSONANTS. Biblical Hebrew uses the following letters to mark consonants (four of which may also serve as vowel letters, *v. supra*): א = ʾ, ב = *b*, ג = *g*, ד = *d*, ה = *h*, ו = *w*, ז = *z*, ח = *ḥ*, ט = *ṭ*, י = *y*, כ = *k*, ל = *l*, מ = *m*, נ = *n*, ס = *s*, ע = ʿ, פ = *p*, צ = *ṣ*, ק = *q*, ר = *r*, שׁ (or שׂ) = *š* (*ś*), ת = *t*. The letters *k, m, n, ṣ*, and *p* have special forms in final position. The inventory of Hebrew consonantal phonemes, as marked by these letters, is reduced as against the Proto-Semitic one, Hebrew *z* representing Proto-Semitic *z* and δ, Hebrew *ḥ* Proto-Semitic *ḥ* and *ḫ*, Hebrew *ṣ* Proto-Semitic *ṣ*, *ḍ*, and *ẓ*, Hebrew ʿ Proto-Semitic ʿ and *ġ*, and Hebrew *š* Proto-Semitic *š* and *ṯ*. On the other hand, some of the letters in the early period might have been polyphonic, as no doubt was ש, marking, in the Judean dialect at least, both *š* and *ś* (differentiated in Tiberian vocalization, e.g., by a point above the letter on its right or left side respectively). It has been claimed that ח and ע were polyphonic as well, exhibiting *ḥ* /*ḫ* and ʿ /*ġ* respectively, and that reminiscences of this feature were still alive at the time of the Septuagint, which transcribes ח and ע by *zero* /χ and *zero* /γ respectively, χ and γ roughly corresponding to *ḫ* and *ġ* respectively. On the other hand, these transcriptions may be due to difficulties of transcribing sounds lacking in Greek (cf., *mutatis mutandis*, the transcription of Arabic ʿ by Greek γ; see Violet, in: OLZ, 4 (1901), 384ff., and the papyri of Nessana, transcribing Arabic *ḫ* and *ḥ* as a rule by *zero*, once Χαλέδ, Χομαης] by χ; *ġ* by γ, but once by *zero* [ʾΑζαλής]. *B, g, d, k, p*, and *t* after vowels developed into spirants (even in juncture; differentiated in Tiberian vocalization by the absence of a point, the so-called *dageš lene*, in them, as against the point in stops), thus entailing the polyphonic use of them in writing. Yet, at first at least, these stops and spirants did not represent different phonemes, and even *if* they did so later (cf. *perhaps* ʾ*alpē* – "thousands," *status constructus* as against ‡ʾ*alpē* – "2,000" *status constructus*), their phonemical load was very small: this, however, depends on the moot question of the phonemic status of *šewa*, *v. infra*. It was in the later biblical Hebrew as well that *ś* coalesced with *s*, and this entailed rare cases of mixing them up in spelling (cf. *supra*). Other important sound shifts, affecting consonants in certain positions, are initial *w* very early becoming *y* (with the notable exception of *w* – "and"), which then often analogically penetrates into medial position as well; the dropping of intervocalic *h* (as ‡sûsahu becoming *sûsô*); and *w* and *y* dropping in many positions (as ‡*yiʿnawu* > *yaʿănɛ*, – "he will be humble," ‡*galaya* > *gala* – "he went into exile") and ʾ in some positions (ʾ*aʾkilu* > ʾ*ôḵẹl* [pause] – "I shall eat"). *N* preceding a consonant is assimilated to it. At a later phase, the laryngals and pharyngals became weakened and were no longer apt to be doubled (this applies to *r* as well); as compensation, the vowel preceding them is often lengthened in this situation. Moreover, ə following them appears in the Tiberian vocalization as ă, ẹ ɛ, and å, and these sounds usually develop after pharyngals and laryngals not followed by a vowel in the middle of the word. Moreover, these consonants often change *i* / *u* into *a* (*i* at least into ɛ). Doubling of final consonants is given up (as ‡*sall* > *sal* ("basket")) (with the partial exception of *tt* occurring e.g., in ʾ*att* ("you," feminine singular)), and this occurs even in medial position when followed by a consonant (as *tâsoḇnâ* ("they will turn," feminine)), and also when the originally following ə has become *zero*, (as ‡*wayyəhî* > *wayhî* ("it was")).

VOWELS. The vowels according to the various vocalization systems differ: mention has already been made that in Tiberian vocalization (and in one subsystem of Palestinian) *â* shifted to *å*. Babylonian vocalization does not differentiate between *a* and ɛ. Whereas the consonantal script is phonemic (and in some cases even polyphonemic), the vowel marks, especially according to the Tiberian system, can designate auxiliary vowels as well (cf., e.g., the so-called furtive *pattaḥ*, automatically developing before final *h, ḥ*, and ʿ after vowels other than *a* and *å*). On the other hand, the Tiberian vocalization is polyphonic as well, since absence of vowel, and ə are marked by same sign ְ, *šewa* (but in other vocalization systems absence of vowel is not marked at all, this being also the case with final letters in the Tiberian system, with the exception of *k, t* as stop, and final consonant clusters); it is perhaps the most important moot question of Hebrew vocalization, whether ְ has or has not to be analyzed as a phoneme, since, e.g., the phonemic status of spirantic *b, g, d, k, p*, and *t* largely depends on it (cf. *supra* ‡ʾ*alpê* as against ʾ*alpê*; if ְ has to be accorded a phonemic static, ʾ*alpê* has presumably to be phonemicized as ʾ*aləpê*, and then the spirantization would merely result from the preceding vowel). At any rate, historical ə may develop into *zero*, and vice versa. The Tiberian vocalization (and at least a part of the others) denotes (with the exception of *šewa* and its allophones ă, ĕ, and ẹ) quality rather than quantity: this is demonstrated mainly by the use of the same sign (ָ = *å*) to mark both historical *â* and *u*, as well as by the parallel occurrence of *a*/ɛ, accounted to be short, and *ẹ*/*o*, regarded as long, in certain paradigms (as the verbal paradigms *pâʿal, pâʿẹl, pâʿol*, the nominal paradigms *qáṭal* (*ṭ* being *h, ḥ*, or ʿ), *qẹ́ṭél* as against *qẹ́ṭel, qóṭel*; for the usage of *pʿl, qṭl v. infra*); therefore, length as marked in this article rests on historical reconstruction of a linguistic stage preceding that of the Tiberian vocalization (another change as against Tiberian vocalization, as used in this article, is that, as a rule, vowels were transcribed in accordance with the Sephardi pronunciation, ָ, as a rule, transliterated by *â* rather than by *å*).

The vowels of the Tiberian system (with the exception of *šewa* and its allophones mentioned above) are (the Tiberian vowel signs, are, as a rule, sublinear, whereas the other systems use superlinear vocalization): ַ = *a*, ָ = å, ֶ = ɛ, ֵ = *ẹ*, ִ = *i*, ֹ or וֹ = *o*, ֻ or וּ = *u*. Since no quantitative distinctions exist, there is no difference whether or not a vowel sign is followed by a vowel letter (as between ֶ and ֵ; ֶי and ֵי, or ֹ and וֹ respectively) and even ֻ and וּ are identical: their respective use depends only on whether or not the consonantal text exhibited vowel letters. Whereas the inventory of Hebrew consonants is restricted against the Proto-Semitic one (see *supra*), that of the Hebrew vowels is extended: Proto-Semitic had, it seems, a system of three short (*a:i:u*, at an earlier stage presumably *a:i /u*) and three long vowel phonemes (*â:î:û*) only, which, of course, were differently actualized. Tiberian *a* mainly stems from Proto-Semitic *a*, and also from *i* in closed stressed syllables (*lex Philippi*, as ‡*ḥafiṣtâ* > *ḥafaṣtâ* ("you wanted")), Tiberian *å* from Proto-Semitic *a, â*, and *u* (in the last case, pronounced according to Sephardi pronunciation *o*, as against *â* in the other cases), Tiberian *ɛ* from Proto-Semitic *a, i*, and *ay* (when preceding *å*), Tiberian *ẹ* from Proto-Semitic *i* and *ay*, Tiberian *i* from Proto-Semitic *i, î*, and *a* (in unstressed, closed syllables, see *supra*), Tiberian *o* from Proto-Semitic *u, â* (in formerly stressed syllables, then often analogically spreading to other positions as well), and *aw*, and Tiberian *u* from Proto-Semitic *u* and *û*. As shown, the diphthongs *aw* and *ay* were monophthongized, becoming *o* and *e* respectively. Sometimes, they are preserved, as normally before double *w* and *y*, e.g., *gawwḵâ* ("your back"), *ḥayyîm* ("life"), and in other conditions, like *mnūḥayḵî* ("your rest," Ps. 116:7) and *ʿawlâ* ("wickedness"). In closed syllables bearing the main stress *aw* and *ay* were split into two syllables, as ‡*tawk* = *táwɛḵ* ("middle"), ‡*bayt* >< *báyiṯ* ("house"), *iy* often becomes î, especially after prepositions (as ‡*liyhûḏâ* > ‡*lîhûḏâ* ("to Judah"); so also ‡*miyyəḏê* > ‡*miydê* > < *mîḏê* ("from the hands of…"). In Babylonian vocalization *yə*, especially in initial position, is graphically represented by *yi*, which, according to some scholars, is intended for the pronunciation of *ī* (as *yirâ* ("be afraid!"), as against *yərâ*), and similarly in Tiberian vocalization *w-* ("and") before labials, and consonants followed by ə, becomes *u* (as *umɛ́lɛḵ* ("and king")). Moreover, according to the Ben Naphtali school of the Tiberian system, medial *əyi* is apt to shift to *i. ə* (marked by *šewa*) developed from original short vowels in open syllables two or four syllables before the stress (as ‡*ladabaraykúmu* > *ləḏibərẹḵém* later *ləḏIḇrẹḵém*, ("to your things");sometimes short vowels in open pretonic syllables are reduced (as ‡*masmẹrîm* > *masmrîm* ("nails"); so always in *status constructus* and prepositions, bearing only secondary stress or no stress at all, as ‡*dabar-* > *dəḇar-*); in other cases again the following consonant is doubled, thus enabling the retention of the short vowel, as *qṭannâ* ("small," feminine); as a rule, however, pretonic short vowels (especially *a*) in open syllables are lengthened (as ‡*dabar* > *dâḇâr* ("thing"), ‡*ʿinab* > *ʿẹnâḇ* ("grape"), as well as in open stressed final syllables. In closed stressed final syllables vowels are lengthened, as a rule, in nouns in *status absolutus* (as *yâḏ* ("hand")), but not in *status constructus* (as *yaḏ-*) and in verbs (as *kâṯaḇ* ("he wrote")), presumably because the latter lost their short final letters earlier, thus terminating in closed syllables. Eventually, however, short final vowels were generally omitted.

STRESS. The stress is transmitted by the cantillation marks: it falls on the last or the penultimate syllable. Because oxytones are more frequent, in this article, as a rule, only paroxytones are marked as such. Since, as a rule, the penultimate syllable is stressed when no final syllable was lost, whereas the last syllable bears the stress, when the word terminated in a short final vowel at an earlier stage, a stage of general paroxytone accent may be reconstructed. The few exceptions, as *kâṯḇ'â* ("she wrote"), *kâṯḇû* ("they wrote"), and similar perfect, imperfect, and imperative forms, further e.g., *yâḏḵ'ā* ("your (masculine singular) hand"), also exhibiting exceptional reduction of the vowel in the syllable preceding the stress (see *supra*), have to be regarded as later forms, the original syllable pattern being preserved in the pausal forms *kâṯ'âḇâ, kâṯ'âḇû*, and *yâḏ'ĕḵâ*. An even later stage of stress is exhibited by the so-called *segolata*, in which the cluster was split at a very late stage (as ‡*sipr* > *sepɛr* ("book"); cf. *supra* for the transcription of these forms). An early stage of Proto-Hebrew stress may tentatively be reconstructed by the assumption (cf. *supra*) that it was *stressed â* that shifted to *ô*.

PRONOUNS. Hebrew (as Semitic) word formation exhibits, as a rule, tri-radical structure: the main meaning is carried by the (generally three) radical consonants, while the vowels only add shades to it. Yet particles (as much as not of nominal origin) and pronouns deviate from this structure, pronouns also allowing word composition, a feature alien to Semitic linguistic system (as *hallâzĕ* ("this"), compounded from the demonstrative that serves as definite article as well+*lâ*+*zĕ*).

"I" is expressed by *ʾănî* and *ʾânôḵî*, both occurring in pause as *ʾ'ânî* / *ʾân'ôḵî*, exhibiting a more original stress structure (as in the case in pause in most cases, cf. *supra*; for *ʾân'ôḵî* being the original form; cf. also the preservation of *â*, as well as *ô* < ‡*â* peculiar to stressed syllables, *v. supra*). The same is the case for pausal *ʾ'âttâ* (also *ʾ'attâ*) as against the context form *ʾattâ* ("you," masculine singular). In some rare cases *ʾattâ* is spelled defectively without the usual final *h*, i.e., *ʾt* (e.g., 1 Sam. 24:18), always as *ktîv*, in others again *ʾt* is vocalized *ʾatt* (e.g., Num. 11:15). For *ʾ'áttî* (*ktiv*) occurring for *ʾatt* ("you," feminine singular), *v. supra*. For *hi*(ʾ) ("she"), *hû* (ʾ) ("he") is substituted as *ktîv* in the Pentateuch, for which, as *qrê perpetuum, hî*(ʾ) is read. היאה, הואה ("he, she"), as occurring in the Qumran scrolls, exhibiting long forms with final vowels, are, it seems, due to secondary analogical formation. For the regular *ʾănáḥnû* ("we") *náḥnû* occurs rarely, and once (Jer. 42:6) the *ktîv ʾnw*, identical, it seems, with mishnaic *ʾ'ânû*. Whereas *hem* and *hémmâ* (Babylonian *häm* and *hämmâ*; "they"), *ʾattẹn* (once, Ezek. 13:20) and *ʾattẹna* (Babylonian *ʾattän* and *ʾatt'ännâ*, "you," feminine plural) alternate, *he'nna* (Babylonian *hẹ'nnâ*; "they," feminine plural) is the only existing form, rather than ‡*hẹn*. *ʾattɛm* ("you," masculine plural) is the only existing form in the masoretic text, *ʾtmh* (*ʾattémâ* or perhaps *ʾattẹ'mmâ*) occurring only in "vulgar" versions found in Qumrân, presumably exhibiting (as does *hẹmmâ*) a late analogical formation. For marking possession, etc., and direct object, identical pronominal suffixes attached to nouns, prepositions and verbs respectively are used in Hebrew (and in Proto-Semitic), the only difference between them being in first person singular, -î denoting "my" (and, as a rule, attached to prepositions) and *-nî* "me." If the word to which the pronominal suffixes are attached terminates in a consonant, it is, as a rule, preceded by a "connecting" vowel, *a* being the favorite vowel after perfect, *ẹ* after imperfect and imperative. Yet before *-ḵεm /ḵεn* the "connecting" vowel is missing (as *yεḏḵεm* ("your hand") as against, e.g., *yâḏẹ'nû* ("our hand")). The absence of the "connecting" vowel before the pronominal suffix of the second person singular masculine (as *yâḏḵâ* ("your hand")), however, is secondary, see *supra*. On the other hand, pausal forms such as *lâḵ* ("to you," masculine singular) display the omission of the final syllable. *-ḵâ* is sometimes spelled with a final *h*, and this spelling becomes more frequent in the Qumran scrolls. After nouns, prepositions, and imperfect forms terminating in consonants the pronominal suffix of the second person feminine singular is *-ẹḵ*, rarely *-âḵ* (*kullâḵ* ("you in your entirety"), presumably influenced by *lâḵ* ("to you" where the *â* belongs to the particle) or *-ẹḵî*. *-ô* ("his"), spelled archaically also with *-h, v. supra*, is sometimes superseded by *-ẹhû-*, which is the regular suffix only after imperfect, imperative, and nouns terminating in ε, but becomes more frequent in the Qumran scrolls. After perfect forms, *-ô* and *-âhû* alternate. *Tagmúl'ôhî* ("his benefits," Ps. 116:12), instead of ordinary *tagmûlâw* (*-âw* being the usual suffix after plurals), exhibits Aramaic influence. For *-âh* ("her"), also used after perfect (the consonantal value of the *h* being marked by a point in it, the so-called *mappîq*), quite often *-â* occurs (without *mappîq*, the *h* used as vowel letter only). For *-ḵεn* (second person plural feminine), *-hεm, -hεn* (third person plural masculine and feminine respectively), forms with final *-â* rarely occur: *-ḵεnâ, -hĕmâ*, and *hεnâ* respectively, and even *ḵεm* (second person plural masculine) is attested in the Qumran scrolls with final*-â*, where this ending is especially frequent. For*-hεm* the archaic poetical *-mô* occurs. For*-ân* (which together with*-âm* replaces *-hεn* and*-hεm* respectively after nouns and perfect forms terminating in consonants, whereas*-êm* is used after imperfect forms for the masculine) after nouns *'ânâ* is rarely attested. In nouns terminating in the plural ending*-ôṯ*, for *ôṯẹhεm /-ôṯẹhεn* (*"their," masculine/feminine*) *-ôṯâm / -ôṯân* occurs. Suffixes after imperfect and imperative forms, as well as after certain particles, are sometimes preceded by *-εn*, the so-called *nûn energicum*, as *yḇârăḵεnhû* ("he will bless him"), generally assimilated to the following consonant, as *yakkεkkâ*, ("he will smite you"), or assimilating a following *h*, as *yišmrεnnû* ("he will keep him").

The demonstrative pronouns *zẹ* (masculine singular), *zôṯ* (feminine singular, rarely *zô*),"*ẹll* ε (plural, rarely *'ẹl*) ("this"), exhibiting the alternation of δ -root in singular and *l* -root in plural, well known from other Semitic languages, are, if used attributively, preceded by the definite article, in analogy to the usage of attributive adjectives (as *hayyôm hazzε*, "this day"). This construction is to be regarded as later than that occurring in Middle Hebrew, exhibiting both the noun and the attributive demonstrative pronoun without the definite article (as *yôm zε*). Accordingly, a phrase like *ballaylâ hû* (instead of the regular *ballaylâ hahû*, exhibiting the use of the third person of the personal pronoun as "that" – demonstrative), in which the definite article is attached to the noun, rather than to the demonstrative, is, it seems, the intermediary stage. The definite article *ha-* (with doubling of the following consonant) has still retained its demonstrative force in phrases like *hayyôm* ("this day, today"). On the other hand, *zε* is sometimes used as presentative, or as relative pronoun (as is also *zû*). *Mâ/mε* ("what"), spelled *mh*, with doubling of the following consonant (this doubling is a real one, not like that called *dḥîq* or *'âṯê mẹraḥîq*), has presumably, partly at least, to be derived from *‡mah/ ‡mεh*. "Who" is *mî*.

TENSE SYSTEM. The Hebrew tense system, besides the imperative (in second person only, in form closely related to the imperfect), consists of four finite forms, *viz.* the perfect and the consecutive (the so-called conversive) perfect, the imperfect and the consecutive (conversive) imperfect. The consecutive tenses are preceded by *w-* ("and"), which before the imperfect has the basic form *wa* (with doubling of the following consonant). It is a moot question whether this system marks aspects (without any notion of time) or rather time. At any rate, in biblical prose at least, these forms seem to denote time, since the difference between perfect and consecutive imperfect, referring to the past, and imperfect and consecutive perfect, referring to the future/present respectively, depends, it would seem, on the syntactical environment only: as a rule, whenever it makes the use of *w-*, etc. ("and") possible, the consecutive forms are used, in accordance with the demanded time, otherwise simple imperfect/perfect are applied. Besides the indicative, the imperfect has a cohortative (especially in the first person), formed by the ending *-â*, (also occurring after consecutive imperfect and the singular masculine of the imperative), and a jussive. The latter, though often coinciding with the indicative, even more resembles the consecutive imperfect, both being formed from the apocopate; the main difference between them is the paroxyton stress of the consecutive form (presumably an archaic feature, reflecting the stage in which, see *supra*, general paroxyton stress obtained, the indicative being *‡yaf'álu > yaf'ál*, the apocopate *‡yáf'al*. The jussive was then more fully adjusted to the stress pattern of the indicative than the consecutive imperfect). In *verba tertiae y*, apocopate forms of the imperative occur as well. As to the consecutive perfect, it often exhibits oxyton stress, as against the paroxyton stress of the perfect. Yet this oxyton stress is, it seems, secondary, since syllable structure is in accordance with the paroxyton stress (as *wə'âḵalt'â* ("and you shall eat"), parallel to *'âḵáltâ* ("you ate"), rather than *‡wa'ăḵalt'â*).

The perfect is formed by afformatives, which in the first and second persons resemble the endings of the personal pronouns (but first person singular terminates in *-tî*). The third person singular masculine has the ending *zero*, the feminine *-â*, the plural-û.

Less clear are the formatives of the imperfect, which uses the prefixes *ʾv* (*v* marking any vowel) for first person singular, *tv* for second person, and third person feminine, *yv* for third person masculine, and *nv* for first person plural. Other persons are indicated, apart from the mentioned prefixes, by suffixes as well: *-î* (rarely *-în*) in second person feminine singular (as *tišmʿî* "you will hear"), *-û* (rarely *-ûn*, which, very seldom, penetrates into the third person plural of the perfect as well) in second and third person masculine plural (as *tišmʿû /yišmʿû* ("you/they will hear")), and *-nâ* in second and third person feminine plural (as *tišmaʿnâ* ("you/they (feminine) will hear"); rare is the *yv* prefix in third person feminine, as *yʿaămodnâ* ("they (feminine) will stand," Dan. 8:22)). The imperative has no prefixes, but the same suffixes; for-*nâ* very rarely ‡*-n* occurs: *šmáʿan* (< ‡*šmáʿn*) ("hear (feminine plural)!," Gen. 4:23) (in most cases forms of the imperfect and imperative terminating in *n* are considered as *scriptio defectiva*, and vocalized *-nâ*).

Among infinite forms, the Hebrew verbal system possesses a participle, which may behave as a noun (it may, e.g., stand in *status constructus* and be negated by *ʾẹn*, the negation of nominal sentences), on the one hand, and as a finite verbal form, on the other (it may, e.g., govern direct object and be continued by a consecutive finite form, as *makkẹ ʾiš wâmẹṯ* ("if one smites a man and he dies"), although the participle stands in *status constructus*). Among the two infinitive forms, the so-called *infinitivus constructus* has usual infinitive functions, as *mẹṭiḇ naggẹn* ("he who excels in playing," Ezek. 33:32); *wayyẹrɛḏ*... lirʾôṯ ("and He descended... to see," Gen. 11:5). Very often the *l-* form is used even when not in final sense, exhibiting the coalescence of *l* with the infinitive, as *ḥâfẹṣ*... *lahămîṯẹnû* ("He wanted... to kill us," Judg. 13:23; in Middle Hebrew this form becomes the only existent infinitive form). It is also used as gerund, as *bârâ*... *laʿăśôṯ* ("he created... in making," Gen. 2:3). The so-called *infinitivus absolutus*, so called, because it does not stand in *status constructus* nor is it governed by preposition, is a peculiar blend between verbal noun and verbal interjection. It is, besides its rare infinitive functions, mainly used as internal object (as *bêraktâ ḇârêḵ* ("surely you have blessed," Num. 23:11), as a rule preceding the finite verb (as *môṯ yûmâṯ* ("surely he will be killed," Gen. 26:11); also replacing modal adverbs (as *wayyẹlɛḵ hâlôḵ wəʾâḵôl* ("he went while eating," Judg. 14:9), and as substitution of finite verbal forms (as *zraʿtɛm harbẹ whâbẹ mʿâṭ ʾâḵól wʾẹn-lśoḇʿâ*, "you have sown much, but brought home few, you have eaten, but not to satiety," Hag. 1:6), mainly of the imperative (as *zâḵôr ʾɛt-yôm haššabbâṯ* ("be mindful of Sabbath")).

VERB PATTERNS. Of all word classes it is the verb that has the most conspicuous patterns, although patterns as such are one of the main characteristics of Semitic languages in general and of Hebrew in particular. These patterns are characterized by a certain vowel sequence, which, interwoven with the trilateral root, together with the repetition or doubling of radical consonants, as well as the addition of certain formative consonants, reflects various modifications of the root connected with specific meanings. It is customary to denote the verbal themes by the root *pʿl* (which, however, has the disadvantage of not being able to denote the doubling of the second radical, since ʿ cannot be doubled) in accordance with the vocalization of the third person masculine singular of the perfect. The usual verbal patterns in biblical Hebrew are the ground theme *pâʿal* (also called *qal*); its reflexive-passive *nifʿal; piʿẹl*, exhibiting doubling of the second radical and denoting intensive and factitive action, its passive *puʿal* and reflexive-reciprocal theme *hitpʿaẹl*, the causative *hifʿîl* and its passive *hofʿal*. Beyond these themes a stage may be reconstructed which, with the exclusion of *nifʿal*, exhibits a well-balanced system:

	Ground pattern	Double pattern	Causative pattern
	pâʿal	*pʿiel*	*hifʿîl*
internal passive	‡*puʿal*	*puʿal*	*hofʿal*
t-form (reflexive reciprocal)	‡*hiṯpâʿal*	*hiṯpaʿẹl*	‡*hiṯafʿẹl*

From the patterns marked by a double dagger (‡) only remnants exist. The inner passive of *paʿal* disappeared because of its resemblance to the inner passive of perfect *píʿẹl* and imperfect *hifʿîl*, being superseded by *nifʿal*, which, besides its original reflexive meaning, acquired passive functions as well; it can only be recognized by its perfect being identical with *puʿal*, the passive of *piʿẹl*, its imperfect with *hofʿal*, without a corresponding *piʿẹl /hifʿîl*. *Hiṯpáʿal* subsisted in *hiṯpâqḏû* ("they were counted") only (which is mixed up with its passive *hoṯpâqḏu*) whereas the very existence of *hiṯafʿẹl* is dubious, depending on the analysis of forms like *təṯaḥărê* ("you will compete"), *watteṯaṣṣaḇ* ("and she stood").

In *pâʿal*, the neutral perfect forms *pâʿẹl* and especially *pâʿol* are being superseded by *pâʿal*. In the imperfect and imperative *yafʿol /pʿol* and *yafʿal /pʿal* respectively are alive, *yafʿil /pʿil* being absorbed by *hifʿîl* and not really subsisting but in some "weak" roots. From vestiges a stage may be reconstructed exhibiting the imperfect forms *yafʿol* (and *yafʿil*) as against *yifʿal*, cf. *yɛḥɛlaš* as against *yaḥălоš; yêḇôš* as against *yâqûm; yêqal* as against *yâsoḇ*. The only living *infinitivus constructus* is *pʿol, pʿal* (as *liškaḇ* ("to lie"); the stop *k*, as against *ḵ* in *šḵaḇ*, is due to the coalescence of *l* – with the infinitive, *v. supra*) being marginal and *pʿil* existing in some "weak" verbs only. Feminine forms of the *infinitivus constructus* are attested as well, as *ʾahăḇâ* ("to love"). The *infinitivus absolutus* has the form *pâʿôl, ô* in the second syllable also occurring in other themes. The active participle, originally belonging to *pâʿal*, is *pôʿẹl*, whereas *pâʿẹl* and *pâʿôl* are the original participles of *pâʿẹl* and *pâʿol* respectively, yet losing ground against *pôʿẹl*. The passive participle is *pâʿûl* (whereas the participle of the internal passive of *pâʿal* is *puʿâl* and *piʿol*, with redoubling of the second radical, as *ʾukkâl* ("eaten"), *yillôḏ* ("born")).

Nifʿal, exhibiting attenuated *i* in its first syllable, still preserves *a* in some "weak" roots. In the imperfect, the imperative and the infinitive (the two latter forms have a *hi-* prefix), the *n*, immediately preceding the first radical, is assimilated to it; the last radical of these forms is, as a rule, preceded by Tiberian *ẹ*, but Babylonian *ä*. In contradistinction to all the other themes, with the exception of the ground theme, the participle is not formed with the prefix *m-*, but in accordance with the perfect (*nifʿâl*).

Piʿel exhibits *a* in perfect in the second syllable about as often as *ẹ*; in the Babylonian vocalization *ä* (corresponding to *a* /ɛ) prevails, and some few verbs (as *dibbɛr*, "he spoke") exhibit ɛ according to Tiberian vocalization as well. In the imperfect, etc., the first radical is followed by *a*, the second by *ẹ* in the Babylonian system sometimes by *ä*).

Hiṯpaʿẹl sometimes exhibits *a* in its third syllable in all forms (with the exception of the participle), especially in pause, and in the Babylonian vocalization the corresponding *ä* prevails. If the first radical is a sibilant, it precedes the *t* (as *hištappẹk* ("to be poured")). Sometimes, the *t* is assimilated to the first radical (as *hiṭṭammẹ* /*hiṣṭaddẹq* ("to be defiled/to clear himself")).

In *hifʿîl* the vowel of the prefix is *i* in the perfect (*a* occurring in "weak" verbs only), *a* in the other forms; that of the second syllable, as a rule, stressed î, before consonantal afformatives in the perfect *a*, in the imperfect, etc.*ẹ*, which is exhibited also by *infinitivus absolutus* and those forms of the imperative and jussive which lack conjugation endings and pronominal suffixes. The *h* of the prefix is, as a rule, dropped in the imperfect.

Puʿal and *hofʿal* have the vowel sequence *u* /*o-a*, characteristic of the internal passive.

WEAK VERBS. Verbs are that class of words in which triliteralism is most strictly carried out. Nevertheless, some verbal classes, *viz. mediae infirmae* and *geminatae*, cannot be explained on the assumption of sound shifts operating on triliteral roots only: they have to be considered as partly emerging from biliteral roots, blending with forms of triliteral roots, which underwent changes because of "weak" letters; and this may apply to other "weak" verb classes as well.

Verba primae n assimilate the *n* to the immediately following second radical, this being in accordance with the general behavior of *n* (see *supra*). Moreover, those having the imperative *pʿal* in the ground theme, drop the *n* in it (as *gaš* ("approach")), as well as in the *infinitivus constructus*, which terminates in the feminine ending *-t* (as ‡*gašt* > *gɛšɛṯ*). The same is the case with *nâṯan* ("to give"), which is the only verb *primae n* having an *i* – imperfect (*yittẹn*): *tẹn*, ‡*tint* > *tẹṯ*. It is also the only verb *tertiae n* which assimilates this *n* to consonantal suffixes, as *nâṯattî* (as against e.g., *sâḵantî*, where the *n* is analogically restored). It may be due to the influence of *nâṯan*, that its antonym *lâqaḥ* ("to take") treats its *l* like an *n: yiqqaḥ*, *qaḥ*, *qáḥaṯ*. Also some *verba primae y* (especially those having *ṣ* as their second radical, as *niṣṣaḇ* ("he stood") as against *hiṯyaṣṣẹḇ*) and *mediae infirmae* (as *massîg* ("removing") as against *nâsôg*) behave like *primae n*.

Verbae primae y form *yafʿil* imperfect, its imperative and its infinitive omitting the *y: yâšaḇ* ("to seat"), *têšẹḇ* (with assimilation of the prefix vowel to the following one), *šẹḇ*, *šɛḇɛṯ* (< ‡šibṯ, ə with feminine ending); *yâḏaʿ* ("to know"), *têḏaʿ* (< *tədẹăʿ*, cf. the infinitive-noun *dêʿâ*), *daʿ*, *dáʿaṯ*. *Hâlaḵ* ("to go") behaves similarly: *têlẹḵ*, *lẹḵ*, *lɛḵɛṯ*. *Yâḵol* ("can") has the solitary imperfect *yûḵal*. *Nifʿal* has in perfect and participle *ô* (*nôlaḏ* ("was born"), *nôlâḏ*, exhibiting the prefix vowel *a*, cf. *supra*, as does the whole paradigm of *hifʿîl*, as *hôlîḏ*), the other forms, as a rule, exhibit *w* as first radical. *Hofʿal* has û (as *hûḇal*, "he was brought").

In *verba tertiae infirmae*, *y* has superseded *w*. Forms without suffixes have the same endings in all themes: *-â* in perfect (and *əṯâ* in feminine singular third person), *-ɛ* in imperfect and participle, *-ẹ* in imperative, *-ôṯ* in construct infinitive. Consonantal afformatives are preceded in perfect by *-ẹ* or *î* in unstable distribution, *î* only being used in *pâʿal* (as if continuing *pâʿil*); *ˆɛnâ* (ˆɛ < *ẹ* [< *ay* due to assimilation to the following *â*, pronounced *å*]) is the suffix of imperfect second and third person, and imperative second person, plural feminine. Before vocalic afformatives *y* and the preceding vowel drop (as *ʿâśû-* ("they did"), *ʿăśî* ("do," feminine singular)). In jussive and the consecutive imperfect the second radical syllable is omitted (as *têʿâś*, "let it be done"); final double consonants thus arising are simplified (as *wayman* ("and he appointed"); so also in the shortened form of the imperative: *ṣaw* ("order!")). Final consonant cluster may be preserved, if the second consonant is a stop (as *wayyeḇk* ("and he wept")), or as a rule, broken up (as *yîrɛḇ* < ‡*yîrb* ("let it multiply")).

In *verba tertiae* ʾ, the ʾ is dropped (preserved as vowel letter only) in final position and a preceding short vowel lengthened (as ‡*mâṣaʾ* < *mâṣâ*, ("he found")). Before consonantal afformatives of the perfect ʾ is dropped, *â* (אָ) being the preceding vowel in *pâʿal* (as *mâṣâṯî*) and, it seems, in *puʿal* and *hofʿal* (the only instance being *hûḇâṯâ* ("you have been brought, Ezek. 40:4)). *ê* (אֵ) in the other perfect forms (as *yârẹṯî* ("I feared," *pâʿẹl* form of the ground theme), *niqrẹṯî* ("I was called")), as well as in the feminine singular of the participle (as *mûṣẹṯ* ("being brought out")). The suffix of imperfect second and third person and imperative second person, plural feminine, ends, as in *tertiae y*, in *-ˆɛnâ*, yet exhibiting ʾ as vowel letter, rather than *y* as in *tertiae y*.

Verba mediae infirmae exhibiting in the first and second persons of the perfect of the ground theme short vowels (as *qamtî*, "I stood up"), but long ones in the third (as *qâm*, corresponding to the *pâʿẹl-* form *mẹṯ* ("he died") and the (synchronically) *pâʿol*-form *bôš* ("he was ashamed")). In the (regular, jussive, and consecutive) imperfect, the imperative and *infinitivus constructus* of the ground theme, *verba mediae w* exhibit û, etc., as *yâqûm*, *yâqóm*, *wayyâqom* (with *qâmâṣ qâṭân* in the last syllable), *qûm*, *qûm* (but second/third person feminine plural *tâšoḇnâ*, along with *təmûṯˆɛnâ*, exhibiting, as do *mediae geminatae*, the same ending as *tertiae y*); *mediae y* î, etc., as *yâśîm* ("he will put"), *yaśẹm*, *wayyâśɛm* (these forms being identical with the corresponding *hifʿîl* forms; therefore ground themes of *mediae y* are apt to pass to *hif'îl*, as *bántâ* ("you understood") to *hẹḇîn*), śîm, *śîm*. The old *yif'al* imperfect is preserved in *yẹḇôš*. The active participle is identical with the perfect, but in contradiction to it is always oxyton (this applies to the other themes and to *mediae geminatae* as well), even before vocalic afformatives: perfect *qâm, q'âmâ, q'âmû, 'mêṯ, m'ẹṯâ, m'ẹṯû, bôš, b'ôšâ, b'ôšû*, as against participle *qâm, qâm'â, qâm'îm, qâm'ôṯ, mêṯ'â, bôš'â*, etc. The imperfect and imperative too have paroxyton stress before vocalic afformatives, and this applies to perfect, imperfect, and imperative *nif'al* and *hif'îl* and *mediae geminatae pâ'al, nif'al, hif'îl* and *hof'al* as well. Perfect and participle *nif'al* is like *nâsôg* ("to retreat"), *hif'îl* like *hêqîm, mêqîm* (where the preformative has the same vowel as that of the perfect); the perfect consonantal afformatives of these two themes as well as of *pâ'al, nif'al*, and *hif'îl* of *mediae geminatae* are preceded by *ô*, as *nəsûgôṯî* (exhibiting *û* rather than *ô* in the radical syllable), *hăḇî'ôṯîw* ("I brought him," along with *hẹḇ'ẹṯî*; rarely also forms like *wahăqẹmônû* with *ẹ* occur). *Nif'al* imperfect, etc., exhibits *ô* (as *yissôg*). *Hof'al* (as also that of *mediae geminatae*) is formed on the analogy of primae *y*. For *pi'ẹl, pu'al*, and *hitpa'ẹl*, in classical language *polẹl*, etc., is used: *qômẹm, qômam, hiṯqômẹm* (externally identical with the *pô'ẹl*, etc., forms of *mediae geminatae*, in which (along with forms like *sibbẹḇ, gullal, hiṯhammem*) forms like *sôḇẹḇ, gôlal, hiṯgôlẹl* are used for *pi'ẹl*, etc. From both verb groups *pilpẹl*, etc., themes may be derived, as *gilgẹl* from *gll* or *ṭiltẹl* from *ṭwl*).

Besides "strong" forms, *verba mediae geminatae*, as a rule, exhibit forms containing one radical syllable with doubling of the second (= third) radical (which, however, is simplified when not followed by a vowel, as *pâ'al raḇ* ("was much"), *nif'al timmaqnâ* ("they will be consumed")). Along with them forms with reduplication of the first radical occur, the so-called Aramaic formation, together with the doubling of the second radical (as *hoššammâ* ("its being desolate")), and without it (as *wayyiqqdû* ("and they bowed")). Forms without any reduplication are also attested (as *yâzmû*, ("they will plan")). In the imperfect of the ground theme, *yaf'ol* (as *yâsoḇ*, consecutive imperfect *wayy'âsọḇ*) corresponds to a perfect (when without ending or with vocalic afformatives) and participle built according to the "strong" pattern (as *sâḇaḇ, sâḇəḇû, sôḇẹḇ*), whereas *yi'fal* (derived from adjectives exhibiting *a* in their sole syllable, the final consonant being doubled when followed by afformatives, as *yẹqal* ("he will be easy") from *qal* ("easy")) has them in the "one radical syllable" form (as *qal, qállâ, qállû, qal, qallâ, qallîm, qallôṯ*). From the *yaf'il* imperfect only remnants exist (as *yâgẹn*, "he will defend"). Perfect/participle *nif'al* have two forms: *násaḇ/nâsâḇ* (also participle *nâgẹl) and nâḇoz/nâḇôz*, and the same applies to imperfect/imperative: *yiddam* and *yissoḇ*. *Hif'îl* perfect has *a* (as *hêqal*) or *ẹ* (as *hẹḥẹl*; the Babylonian system *ä* only), the imperfect *ẹ* (as *yâqẹl*; the Babylonian has sometimes *ä*), the participle *ˆẹ* in both the radical and prefix syllable: *m ˆẹs ˆẹḥ* (as have some perfect forms, *v. supra*).

SUBSTANTIVES. Both triliteralism and the development of patterns is less conspicuous in nouns than in verbs. There exists a set of biradical substantives with a fixed vowel, which, by their meanings, demonstrate that they belong to the oldest stratum of the language: *yâḏ* ("hand"), *dâm* ("blood"), *dâg* ("fish"), *b ˆẹn* ("son"), *š ˆẹm* ("name"), *'êṣ* ("tree"), *šânâ* ("year"), *śâpâ* ("lip," in plural transferred to triradical scheme by the inclusion of the feminine ending: *sipṯô'ṯ ˆɛḵâ*), etc. The notion of patterns is best developed in verbal nouns, in participles and infinitives, as *qiṭṭûl* (*q, ṭ, l* denoting the three radical letters respectively) belonging to *pi'ẹl*, moreover in nouns with *m*-prefix, especially in *nomina instrumenti* exhibiting *maqṭel*, less in those with *t*-prefix. The suffixes include *-ôn* and *-ûṯ* (containing the feminine ending as well). Among nouns without affixes *qâṭîl, qaṭṭîl* are frequent in adjectives, *qâṭôl*, plural *qṭullîm*, denotes color adjectives, *qiṭṭẹl* bodily or mental faults, *qaṭṭâl* intense qualities and occupations. One-syllabic nouns, terminating in a consonant cluster, open the cluster, mostly by *ɛ* (*segol*, the so-called *segolata*, see *supra*), as *yɛleḏ* ("child") ‡*yald, šɛḇɛṯ* ("to sit") < ‡*šibt* (in pause *yâleḏ; š'âbeṯ*, yet *mɛlɛḵ* and most nouns having original *qiṭl* pattern do not change in pause).

Substantives are used in different *status*:, in *status absolutus*, when standing alone; in *status constructus*, when closely attached to a following noun (the so-called *nomen rectum*, historically a genitive; the *nomen rectum* defines and, when itself determinate, determines the noun in *status constructus*); and *status pronominalis*, when attached to a pronominal suffix, which stands in the same relation to the noun as the *nomen rectum* does. The feminine ending is either *-â* (in *status constructus* and *pronominalis -at*, etc., exhibiting an earlier stage), or *-t*; sometimes these feminine endings alternate, as when *-â* used in *status absolutus* and *t* in *status constructus* and *pronominalis*, as *mɛrkâḇâ* ("chariot"), *mirkɛḇɛṯ-* (< ‡*mirkaḇt*, exhibiting the opening of the final cluster, as in the *segolata*), *mɛrkaḇtô*. The dual is rather reduced, being as a rule used with "two," "two hundred," some nouns denoting time and mainly with objects which naturally occur in pairs, especially the double members of the body. Its ending is *-áyim*, that of the masculine plural *-îm*, the *status constructus* and *pronominalis* of both *-ˆẹ* (historically to be derived from the dual), which is also added to the *status pronominalis* of the feminine plural ending *-ôt*. The so-called *segolata*, including one-syllabic nouns with feminine ending, as *yaldâ* ("girl"), form their plural from bisyllabic stems, exhibiting *â* after the second radical: *ylâḏîm* ("children"), *ylâḏôṯ* ("girls"). Mention must also be made of the unstressed locative ending *-â* (spelled *-h*, < ‡*ah*, as intimated by Ugaritic), as *ṣâ'pônâ* ("northward"), also occurring between *status constructus* and its *nomen rectum*, as *midbárâ dammɛśɛq* ("to the wilderness of Damascus").

ADJECTIVES. The boundaries between substantives and adjectives are rather blurred. There are relatively few patterns exclusive to one of these word classes (as *segolata* mainly for substantives, *qâṭôl*, plural *qṭullîm* for color adjectives). Adjectives invariably have feminine forms ending in-*â/t*, masculine plural terminating in-*îm* and feminine plural in-*ôt*; substantives, on the contrary, need not have special feminine forms and also feminines without endings occur (as *ʾâṯôn* ("she-ass")). Moreover, in the substantives *singularia/pluralia tantum* occur, and the plural ending-*îm* may be attached to feminine substantives (as *ʾiššâ* ("woman"), plural *nâšîm*), and even more often *vice versa* (as *ʾâḇ* ("father"), plural *ʾâḇôṯ*). Yet some substantives exactly behave as adjectives in this respect (as *yɛlɛḏ, yaldâ, ylâḏîm, ylâḏôṯ*). Adjectives proper do not have *status pronominalis*, yet substantival usage of adjectives (and sometimes also *vice versa*) is frequent. Sometimes adjectives may occur in *status constructus*, yet their usage is very special (as *nqî ḵappáyim* ("clean as regards hands")), and it may not be substituted by *status pronominalis* (as if ‡*nqîhɛn*; but this may apply sometimes to substantives in *status constructus* as well). Some syntactical usages, however, seem to be possible for adjectives only, rather than for substantives, as the use of modifiers like *məʾôḏ* ("very"), *yôṯẹr* ("more"). The simplest solution would perhaps be to set up three different classes: substantives, adjectives, and finally nouns, which would then include both word classes, as far as their special character cannot be defined by formal criteria. Adjectives used as attributes are preceded by the governing noun.

NUMERALS. As to the cardinal numbers, *ʾɛḥâḏ*, feminine *ʾaḥáṯ* ("one") is mainly used as adjective, *šnáyim*, feminine *štáyim* (sic! with *t* as stop, exhibiting a quite exceptional initial cluster) "two," as substantive, governing the counted noun in *status constructus: šnẹ-*, feminine *štẹ-*, or following it in *status absolutus*. As to the numbers three to ten, those with zero-ending refer to feminine nouns, whereas those with *-â* (*in status constructus -at/-t*) to masculine ones, a common Semitic feature, in opposition to the other noun classes. They precede or follow the counted nouns in *status absolutus*, but they may precede them in *status constructus* as well (historically an archaic feature): this is the rule with definite nouns, as well as with *yôm*, etc. The "ten" in the numbers 11–19 is *ʿâśâr* for masculine, *ʿɛśrẹ* for feminine, spelled *ʿśrh*; it is uncertain whether it exhibits an alleged feminine ending *-ẹ*, since in Ugaritic it is spelled with final *h*, thus intimating a consonantal ending. The ordinal numbers have special forms only from one to ten, exhibiting the theme *qtîlî*, with the exception of *šiššî* ("sixth"), and perhaps *šênî* ("second"). "First" is *rîšôn*, a relatively late form, as it is customary in Semitic language, the older usage being the use of the cardinal number "one," still persisting in biblical Hebrew.

PREPOSITIONS. Prepositions, as far as etymologically transparent, are as a rule nouns in *status constructus/pronominalis*, as *ʾẹṣɛl* ("near, by"), *ʾẹṣlḵâ; ʿal-*, poetical *ʿălẹ* ("on"), *ʿălẹḵɛm*, the suffix *-ẹḵɛm* originally exhibiting the final *-y* root, rather than a plural suffix. Through the influence of prepositions like *ʿălɛḵɛm*, other prepositions too govern plural suffixes, as *táḥaṯ* ("under"), *taḥtệḵɛm*. Among the three uni-consonantal prepositions, only *l-* ("to"), and *b-* ("in, by") govern pronominal suffixes (as *lḵâ, lâḵ, lâḵɛm*), but *k-*, originally a demonstrative element, governs pronominal suffixes mainly by means of *-mô-*: *kâmʾôḵá, kmôḵɛm*. *Min* ("from") as a rule assimilates its *n* to the following consonant (as *mibbnô* ("from his son"), *mikkɛm*, cf. also *mẹhɛm*, with lengthening of the vowel preceding the pharyngal not capable of doubling); before some suffixes *min* is doubled, as *mimménnî* < ‡*minminî* ("from me"), along with poetical *minnî*. There are two prepositions *ʾẹṯ*; one denoting "with," has the form *ʾittô*, etc., before pronominal suffixes, the other, used as optional mark of determinate direct objects, the forms *ʾôṯô, ʾɛṯḵém*; sometimes, however, these two sets become mixed up. Since the impersonal passive may govern objects (as indirect object, e.g., *yḇullaʿ lammɛ́lɛ́ḵ* ("the king will be afflicted," II Sam. 17:16)) or a direct one, e.g., *maṣṣôṯ yẹʾâḵẹl* ("unleavened bread shall be eaten," Ex. 13:7), it may govern *ʾẹṯ* preceding the definite object as well, e.g., *ʾɛ́ṯ-kol-dḡê hayyăm yẹʾâsẹp̄ lâhɛm* ("shall all the fishes of the seas be collected for them?" Num. 11:22).

NEGATION. As word negation and in verbal clauses *lô* is used, in nominal clauses *ʾẹn*, in prohibition *ʾal* with the imperfect (jussive; but, as in Semitic languages in general, never with the imperative).

CLAUSE FORMATION. It is in the domain of clause formation that Hebrew has best preserved the ancient Semitic character. In contradistinction to Arabic, it has not relinquished free sentence structure in favor of systematization. Yet, although it has lost, like Aramaic, the case and mood endings, it has not been affected by a similar syntactic formlessness. The boundary lines between main and subordinate clauses are blurred, since *w-* ("and") may precede the main clause following the subordinate one; cf. also *w-* introducing the main clause after phrases like *wayhî ʾim…, w-…* ("and it happened, when…, then…"). Circumstantial clauses resemble main clauses even more, mainly differentiated by the use of different tenses. Moreover, the number of subordinate conjunctions is relatively small, the most important ones being the relative pronoun *ʾăšɛr*, also used as introducing substantive clauses, *kî* introducing substantive and causal ones, conditional *ʾim* and hypothetical *lû*. Very frequent is the presentative *hinnẹ*, often followed by a participle marking the future.

VOCABULARY. The vocabulary of biblical Hebrew is, in accordance with the limited size of the Bible, restricted, exhibiting many words from the field of religion, morals, and emotion. Loan words include those borrowed from Akkadian, as a rule through the intermediary of Aramaic, the influence of which becomes strong in later language.

[Joshua Blau]

THE DEAD SEA SCROLLS

DISCOVERY

The discovery of the *Dead Sea Scrolls (= DSS, 1947) provided an important missing link in the development of Hebrew (= *H): a period which spans biblical Hebrew (= BH) and mishnaic Hebrew (= MH), extending from about the middle of the second half of the first century B.C.E. to 200 C.E. Before this discovery the only extant text dating back to this period (BH to MH) were fragments of the Book of *Ben Sira found in the Cairo *Genizah. Fragments found in the excavations at *Masada, however, indicate that the language used in the *Genizah* fragments is corrupt and does not faithfully represent the original text.

During the last centuries B.C.E., BH ceased to be a spoken language. Insofar as H was spoken, it was apparently, more or less, of the type that later emerged as MH. The literary language, which is represented by the DSS language, tried to hew as closely as possible to late biblical Hebrew (= LBH), as represented, for example, by the Books of Chronicles, which originated during the first centuries of the Second Temple period. Thus the language of the DSS should be considered as the last offshoot of LBH.

MAIN ELEMENTS OF THE LANGUAGE OF THE DSS

The DSS language, which apparently served only as a literary vehicle, is composed of the following elements: (1) BH; (2) Official Aramaic; since Aramaic (= A) had become, even before the destruction of the First Temple (586 B.C.E.), the lingua franca of the Near East and apparently also the vernacular of (nearly?) the whole of Syria-Palestine, it influenced the development of H; (3) vernacular H (the later MH) which increasingly infiltrated literary H.

The above three elements were the most important in the shaping of the language of the DSS which, however, also reveals novel traits, especially in spelling and phonology. These elements, apparently reflecting the linguistic situation in Palestine during the period in question, stem from the fact that (4) the educated classes apparently spoke Greek; (5) the vernacular of the common people was (apparently) an A dialect (or dialects) slightly different from literary A, Official Aramaic, the so-called A of the empire; (6) neither BH as transmitted, nor vernacular MH, was uniform (there being mainly two traditions: the Tiberian and the Babylonian, each with its own vocalization; sometimes the Babylonian forms emerge in the DSS); (7) there are many elements of Samaritan Hebrew (= SH) in the language of the DSS; (8) the possibility that archaic forms survived in the language of the DSS that had disappeared from H (known from the vocalization of the Jews and the reading traditions of the Samaritans) cannot be excluded.

Negative factors were also decisive in the formation of the DSS language: (9) an ever-decreasing knowledge of BH, resulting in a situation where archaic and rare words and forms of BH became obscure to the average literate Jews. In his writing, which in intention was to be BH, the literate Jew was inclined to replace obsolete words and forms with common and familiar ones. Thus a kind of basic BH, which included the above elements, came into being; (10) certain biblical words in the vocabulary of the DSS, whose meaning had become obscure (known today through modern research), not used in their original meaning but according to the interpretation given to the words by the members of the sect and their contemporaries; (11) the scrolls contain words that might have been taken over from other languages or dialects of Palestine or the neighboring territories, but have since disappeared entirely (e.g., the language of the Edomites, living in southern Judea); (12) it is possible that some new words in the DSS were common in the H or A vernacular(s) and by mere chance are not in the transmitted H and A sources.

The elements that compose the language of the DSS might have varied with the different writers. There are, for example, sources in which the role played by MH is much more prominent (e.g., the *Copper Scroll) than in other sources. The complexity of the picture that emerges from the DSS is the reason why there is as yet no solution for many of the linguistic problems in the DSS, and the outline of this language, given below, can only be tentative.

SOURCES

Biblical Texts

The complete *Isaiah* (1QIsa[a]) is one of the most important scrolls of the DSS. The language, which is "vulgar" (i.e., the intention was not to render the text exactly as transmitted), is a "modernization" of the original Isaiah, as represented by the Isaiah type of the Masoretic Text (= MT) whose language was modified so that the contemporary reader might more easily understand the text. As has been noted above, the average reader was scarcely able to understand the MT properly, and often unable to read it correctly. Therefore, copyists often substituted the contemporaneous forms for the original ones even in the case of proper nouns. For example, the form עוזיה, ישעיה, representing the type that became common mainly after 586 B.C.E. (the destruction of the First Temple), is used instead of the original ישעיהו, עוזיהו which represents the dominant type during the previous period.

Most of the biblical texts of the DSS are practically identical with those of the masoretic Bible. Fragments of "vulgar" texts from other books of the Bible, such as Exodus and Psalms, were, however, also found. The linguistic differences between these texts and the masoretic Bible are more or less to be attributed to the tendency to "modernize."

Non-Biblical Texts

The most extensive non-biblical texts are the Manual of *Discipline; the *Thanksgiving Psalms; the *Pesher Habakkuk, a commentary on the Book of Habakkuk; and the *War Scroll. These texts originated with a certain sect (generally identified with the *Essenes). A few fragments of non-canonical writings were also found, such as, The Book of *Jubilees and *Ben Sira* whose Hebrew version had until that time been practically unknown (see above Discovery). The *Zadokite* documents, as represented by the fragments found in the *Genizah*, do not reflect the original language of the DSS. (As with the Book of Ben Sira found in the *Genizah*, their language was also changed by the copyists of the Middle Ages.)

LANGUAGE OF THE DSS

Isaiah is the only DSS text which has been extensively dealt with from the linguistic point of view. The following survey, therefore, will be based mainly on the language of this scroll.

Spelling

The DSS employ the *scriptio plena* to make reading easier (there existed as yet no vowel signs) and to eliminate, as far as possible, A pronunciation. For example, לא ("not") was spelled לוא, otherwise the reader might have read it as לָא (*lā*) as in A (indeed, the Samaritans in their Bible substitute the A form for the H). Plene spelling with ו abound to indicate the phones (*u, o*), not only where these vowels represent an original dipthong (*aw*) that turned into an (*ō*), e.g., יום ("day"; a spelling common also in the MT), or an original long vowel, e.g., שלוש ("three"; which is fairly common in MT), but also for originally short, later lengthened, vowels, e.g., עול ("yoke"; this type of spelling is rare in MT), and short vowels that were not lengthened, e.g., אוזנים ("ears"; very rare in MT), and even half vowels, e.g., חולי ("illness": = חֳלִי; extremely rare in MT). To a lesser extent, the same applies to the use of י, e.g., מית ("dead"; = מֵת in MT), אבניטך (= אַבְנֵטְךָ, "your girdle"). א was also used as a vowel letter to indicate the vowel (*a*), e.g., יאתום ("orphan"; the spelling is extremely rare in MT). As a word final י might be used instead of ה indicating an (*e*) type vowel, e.g., יעני ("he will answer"). Generally there is no real consistency in the spelling. The word "head," for example, has different spellings: ראש, ראוש, רואש, רוש. The DSS share these types of plene spellings with MH, especially as preserved in the manuscripts.

The DSS, mainly, in the *Isaiah Scroll* and only sporadically elsewhere, developed another type of plene spelling where a digraph (two letters) indicates one vowel (like the English *ea* ("beat") as against *i* ("bit")). This type of spelling is exemplified at the end of words: וא indicated (*ō*), יא indicating (*i*), e.g., in the above mentioned לוא ("not," the א is original and the ו is added); בוא ("in it," the ו is original and the א is added); כיא ("because," the א is added). These spellings appear also in the middle of words, e.g., ראוש, רואש ("head"), but in this case the א is practically always original, while the ו (and י) are added. As to consonant spelling, שׂ at that period turned into ס, thus the spelling סאי (= שאי "lift up") is found. There is, however, also the inverse where through a hypercorrection מאס ("to despise, reject") is spelled מאש.

Phonetics and Phonology

An outstanding feature of the language of the DSS is that the laryngeals ה, א and the pharyngeals ע, ח, which became weakened, are sometimes dropped and sometimes confused with each other. For instance, תנתו (= תאנתו "his fig"), יבור (= יעבור "he will pass"), מנחל (= מנהל "leader"), סלה (= סלע "rock"). These pronunciations are a characteristic of SH and Samaritan Aramaic (= SA). According to both Talmuds, the Jews of Beth-Shean and Haifa, probably influenced by the Greek vernacular, could not pronounce these phones properly. (The same applies to European immigrants in Israel, since European languages also lack these phones. They do, however, exist in Arabic and the Yemenites, therefore, pronounce them properly.) It is then possible that the weakening of these phones in the DSS occurred under the impact of Greek.

Morphology

PRONOUNS. *Independent Personal Pronouns.* Instead of את ("you" fem.), אתי is sometimes found. This form (rare in masoretic BH), which at first sight seems to be archaic, is probably an Aramaism (the same happened in SH). Instead of הוא ("he") and היא ("she") very often הואה and היאה are employed in the DSS. These spellings might reflect archaic forms that disappeared from masoretic BH (see above, Main Elements of… DSS, 8), but the possibility of an analogous new formation cannot be excluded. אתמה = אתם ("you" plural) is no doubt a late form parallel with the form transmitted by the Samaritans orally in reading their Bible (despite the spelling אתם pronounced אתמה). אנו ("we") appears several times in the non-biblical scrolls (MH), in BH only once as *ketib*.

Personal Suffix Pronouns. The type ךָ (דְּבָרְךָ) ("your word") is very often spelled plene דבריכה/דברכה (plural). The spelling disproved the theory of P. Kahle who believed that the vocalization of the Masoretic Text came into being under Arabic influence (after the seventh century C.E.!). The type ידו ("his hand") is sometimes spelled ידיו, since apparently, as in SH, יו was pronounced (*o*) and both ו and יו could be used indiscriminately. The type בניה ("her sons") is sometimes spelled plene בניהא/ה; the type דברכם ("your word") is often spelled דברכמה (as in SH); the type דברם ("their (masc.) word") is often spelled דברמה (by analogy); and the feminine suffix הן is sometimes spelled הנה (original? or a new formation by analogy). There is a strong tendency to use forms like רוחהו (= רוחו "his spirit"), a BH poetic form, while forms like עלוהי (= עליו "upon him") are A.

The Verb

PERSONAL SUFFIXES. Instead of the type שמרתְּ ("you (fem.) watched"), the type שמרתי is sometimes used; it appears in the Song of Deborah (Judg. 5:7) whose language is archaic. The type apparently died out in BH but reentered the language under A influence, mainly in the late books of Jeremiah and Ezekiel (mostly as *ketib*, but not as *qeri*). It seems obvious, therefore, that the same influence is responsible for its emergence in the DSS (and in the Samaritan *Pentateuch). This is not the only known case where an archaic form disappeared from H and reentered the language through A, thus creating the impression of an archaic survival. As to the type שמרתמה (MT שמרתם "you (plur.) watched") it also parallels the Samaritan oral transmission (but spelled שמרתם) and is, as אתם < אתמה (see Morphology, Independent Personal Pronouns), a later development.

OTHER FEATURES. Instead of מסיר ("is taking away") (*hifʿil*) there is מהסיר, which again reflects the impact of A. Spellings like ישפול (= יִשְׁפַּל, "he will be degraded") indicate that an original (*a*) imperfect might turn into an (*o*) imperfect; such spellings are prevalent in MH and A dialects.

PAUSAL FORMS. Instead of the imperative form דִּרְשׁוּ ("seek"), there is דרושו, which is either an A form, or an H pausal, occurring also in BH according to the Babylonian vocalization. There seems to be little doubt that the forms of the type תזכורי ("you will remember") and אתמוכה (see below; pausal forms in the context) penetrated the DSS from MH. These forms are still found in the manuscripts (see Mishnaic Hebrew Language) and even entered the Christian Palestinian Aramaic (= ChPA) dialect from MH. The long imperfect forms of the type אתמוכה ("I would like to uphold") (expressing wish, etc.), which often take the place of the normal imperfect אתמוך, continue a trait fairly common in LBH (e.g., Ezra). The assumption of R. Meyer that the DSS employed a tense not found in masoretic BH, the so-called present future (as in Akkadian), is unfounded. However there is as yet no clear-cut solution to forms like ישופטני (= יִשְׁפְּטֵנִי).

Among the new noun patterns one especially worth mentioning is *quṭl* (= *qoṭel* in masoretic H) which sometimes appears as *qoṭol*, e.g., אוהול ("tent") = אֹהֶל; cf., masoretic מֹלֶךְ = "Moloch" in the Septuagint; kindred forms also appear in ChPA.

SYNTAX

Although very little research has been done in the field of syntax, a few characteristics can be mentioned. Biblical syntax is employed, including the use of the conversive ו(*waw*), yet the copyist of *Isaiah* (see above Sources) occasionally substitutes a form belonging to the contemporaneous spoken idiom, e.g., instead of ואת כל אלה ידי עשתה ויהיו כל אלה ("All these (things) my hand has made") he used… והיו כל אלה ("and so all these things came to be (mine).") (Isa. 66:2). Biblical syntax requires here the imperfect plus the conversive ו. In MH the perfect is followed by the perfect plus ו; it is then the MH construction substituted for the BH one. Asyndetic relative clauses (= without the relative pronoun אשר) are still found in BH. Since they disappeared from MH and A, the writer is inclined to add the "missing" relative pronoun אשר and instead of בדרך תלך ("the way you should go") (Isa. 48:17) he creates the normal clause: בדרך אשר תלך. Sometimes he employs other means to evade the problem: in Isaiah 62:1 וישועתה כלפיד יבער ("and her salvation is as a burning torch") where there is no אשר after כלפיד he turned יבער into תבער; לפיד thus is no longer the subject of יבער but ישועתה becomes the subject of תבער. The translation now is "and her salvation will burn like a torch."

אשר לוא plus the imperfect seems to be employed as a prohibitive in the non-biblical scrolls, e.g., אשר לוא ילך איש ("no one shall walk") which might have its parallel in MH and in the H and A letters of Bar Kokhba. The infinitive plus ל is sometimes used as a command, e.g., לשלח הואה מאתם ("They shall banish him") (LBH) and mainly negated by לוא as a prohibition, e.g., ולוא לסור ("and not to turn aside") also with אין, e.g., ואין לצעוד ("not to walk"). The same use is found in A inscriptions in Jerusalem: לא למפתח (lit., "not to open"), practically unknown in BH; it is also found in Punic (a Canaanite dialect of the Northern African coast); and it perhaps has its parallel in a certain Greek usage (found also in a Greek inscription in Jerusalem). It is impossible to pinpoint the origin of this use.

In the Book of Chronicles (LBH) the use of the accusative particle את with the pronominal suffix is generally avoided as in the *Manual of Discipline* (see above Sources). This is also the case in MH (as represented by the language of the *tannaim* only) which in this respect is a direct offshoot of the DSS.

Note אבית (= בבית "in the house"), and kindred forms, as in MH and Punic. Types like לאין שרית ("without a remnant") is to be found in LBH.

STYLE

In this area, too, more research is required. One point certainly deserves to be mentioned. The non-biblical scrolls are full of either biblical quotations, most of which are slightly different from the original, or of biblical allusions where the meaning is often not quite clear but the reference of the allusion is known, for instance, כי בשררות לבי אלך למען ספות הרוה את הצמאה "I follow my own willful heart – to the utter ruin of moist and dry alike" (i.e., everything) (Deut. 29:18) is alluded to by וילך בדרכי הרויה למען ספות את הצמאה out of which sense can hardly be made.

VOCABULARY

The vocabulary of the DSS consists of native and foreign elements (loans and loan translations).

Native Elements.

These comprise BH, MH, and H of undefinable origin that does not occur in any other H source, but might be original (or a loan? see above Main Elements of… DSS, 8 and 12).

BIBLICAL HEBREW. BH has to be subdivided according to its sources: (1) archaic BH (= ABH); (2) standard BH (= SBH); (3) LBH. BH should also be divided into: (a) words that survived unchanged; (b) words that are used in a morphologically changed form; (c) words whose meaning changed; (d) words whose meaning changed owing to a certain interpretation of their original meaning which had been forgotten; (e) words which are new morphologically and semantically, but which arise "legitimately" from BH.

ABH. אדיר ("mighty"), האזן ("to listen"), מעון ("dwelling place").

SBH. SBH is very much in evidence. אדון ("lord"), חלק ("to divide"), מערכה ("line of battle"), עת ("time"). Thanks to the DSS, MH, and SA it has been shown that the BH מסר means "to count" (> "to hand over").

LBH. Since the Hebrew of the DSS is the last offshoot of LBH (above Discovery), the presence of LBH words is not surprising, e.g., זוע ("to move") (intransitive), מדע ("knowledge?" "opinion?"), מדרש ("interpretation, study"), עמד ("to get up") instead of קום, פשר ("explanation"),שר ("prince" (= "angel")), כוהן הרואש ("high priest"). The case of קץ ("time, epoch") is striking. Its proper meaning in LBH, "time" (and not only "end"), was (re)discovered mainly because of its usage in the DSS. These instances represent words that have survived unchanged (type a.)

BH מָשְׁזָר (participle of *hof'al*) (= "twisted thread") appears as משוזר (obviously a participle of *pu"al*); the root נדב is used as *nif'al* (with the meaning of *hitpa"el* = "to volunteer"); לַהַב ("flame, blade (of sword)") is found as לוהב. The plural of איש ("man") sometimes appears as אנושים (as if it were the plural of אנוש "man," which does not occur in BH). These instances represent words that are used in a morphological changed form (type b).

גורל ("lot") is also used for "group" and עצה ("counsel") as "council." מבקר ("inspector") goes back to the BH root בקר ("to visit" > inspect). דשא (מועד) "spring (time)" (like Akkadian and Epigraphic South Arabic) in BH is "herbage"; זרק ("javelin, dart"). These instances represent words whose meaning changed (type c).

חרישית (= "stormy wind") apparently goes back to the interpretation of Jonah 4:8, but the meaning is obviously not the original (an instance of type d).

MISHNAIC HEBREW. גודל ("thumb") = גּוּדָל (אָ) in MH; כנסת ("assembly"); תלמוד ("learning"); מועט ("little"); מלאה ("pregnant woman" – this word occurs in the *Temple Scroll*); גבל ("to knead"); זעטוט ("youth (young man)"); ממון ("wealth"); נחשול ("wave"); and הלכה ("rule"?) might be MA or A. But בית משפט ("court") is perhaps a loan translation of the MH בית דין. Several technical terms of the sect also are found in mishnaic sources, e.g., קרב ("admission," lit., "to bring near"), or רבים (= "the many") which seems to be one of the names of the sect. However, רוב apparently means "many" (only?) as in BH, but not "majority" as in MH.

HEBREW OF UNKNOWN ORIGIN. (א)בדן (a kind of brocade?) whose root does not occur in BH. The roots מזז and תחם are as yet unexplained.

Foreign Elements

These are (1) A loans and loan translations; (2) Persian loans; (3) Greek and Latin loan translations.

ARAMAIC LOANS AND LOAN TRANSLATIONS. (MH vocabulary itself derives from A) דוכי ("purification") = the H root זכה. Typical for the language of the DSS is the root סרך used as a verb ("to draw up in battle order") and as a noun (meaning "order, battle order, ordinance, prescription"). It seems to be a loan word from A, but the meanings mentioned above are nearly unknown in A. The meaning of the root סדר (verb and noun), employed as a military term, is close to סרך and is apparently also A; אוחזי אבות ("intercessors") is a loan translation from A, going back to Akkadian.

PERSIAN LOANS. רז ("secret") and נחשיר ("battered") should be mentioned here. The latter shows the impact of the life at the court of the Persian governor.

GREEK AND LATIN LOAN TRANSLATIONS. Since there are no Greek and Latin loans in the DSS, it seems to be dangerous to hazard any suggestion concerning loan translations. However, if מגדל ("tower, turret") denotes a military structure and if the same holds true for the Greek πύργος and the Latin *turris*, there is reason to believe that some kind of connection exists between Indo-European words and Hebrew words. Even if it is assumed that the term יחד ("community") goes back to BH, the fact that the sect chose this term might have been influenced by the Greek κοινωνία. But כנפים ("wings") as a military term cannot be taken as a sign of Latin influence.

PROBLEMATIC ELEMENTS. Several words, among them תעודה, are not entirely clear, both with regard to their meaning and with regard to their development.

THE INFLUENCE OF THE DSS UPON CHRISTIAN GREEK

Scholars found a number of terms in the DSS which parallel Greek terms in the New Testament, e.g., "sons of light" (Luke 16:8). There is reason to believe that the Greek ἐπίσκοπος, a technical term of early Christianity (> "bishop"), reflects the term מבקר ("overseer") of the sect. The Greek τάγμα found in *Josephus, designating the sect of the Essenes, seems to be a loan translation of the term סרך which, as in the compound word סרך (היחד), was employed by the sectarians as the name of their sect.

Words and phrases quoted can be traced with the help of concordances and E.Y. Kutscher's indexes.

[Eduard Yecheskel Kutscher]

MISHNAIC

INTRODUCTION

The destruction of the Second Temple probably brought the continuous development of biblical Hebrew (= BH) (together with its last branch, the Hebrew of the Dead Sea Scrolls) to an end. With the destruction of the religious and spiritual center, the standard literary language disappeared, and its place was taken by the vernacular, namely mishnaic Hebrew (= MH). The recent discovery of the Bar Kokhba letters, some of which are in MH, supports this view. It is, however, most likely that MH had already existed previously for hundreds of years as a vernacular. Its influence can be detected in the later books of the Bible, e.g., the Chronicles and Esther, but it was not employed as a literary language until after the destruction of the Second Temple.

TYPES OF MISHNAIC HEBREW

Two main types of MH should be distinguished: (1) The language of the *tannaim*, i.e., the Hebrew (= H) of the Mishnah, the Tosefta, the halakhic Midrashim, and the *baraitot* in the two Talmuds. (It seems, however, that the *baraitot* of the Babylonian Talmud were influenced by the language of the *amoraim*, see (2)). It may be assumed that these literary works go back to a time when MH was still spoken, most probably until the end of the second century C.E. (see below). The language of the *tannaim* is known (a) in the form as used in Palestine (often vocalized with the Tiberian vocalization); (b) in the form it was transmitted in Babylonia, sometimes vocalized with the Babylonian vocalization. (2) The language of the *amoraim*. A distinction, however, must also be made between (a) the language of the Palestinian *amoraim* (the Hebrew in the Palestinian Talmud and the aggadic Midrashim); (b) the language of the Babylonian *amoraim* (the Hebrew in the Babylonian Talmud). Since at this period (third–fifth centuries C.E.), MH was probably no longer a spoken language in Palestine – certainly not in Babylonia – it may be assumed that, as in modern H, this dialect was mixed with BH, as well as with Aramaic (= A) of the respective areas (more than tannaitic H). As a result, the H of the *amoraim* cannot be employed as a trustworthy basis for the study of MH (on further difficulties, see infra second drawback of Segal – The Problem of the Sources of MH).

Besides the above three categories, mention should be made of the language of prayer and benediction which also in the language of the *tannaim* contains elements from BH. Even in general prose the BH elements in tannaitic sources might in a few cases be quotations or allusions from the Bible rather than living elements.

GEOGRAPHICAL PROVENANCE OF MISHNAIC HEBREW

It may be assumed that MH was the vernacular only in Judea which was resettled by the Babylonian exiles in the sixth and fifth centuries B.C.E. In the rest of Palestine, especially in Galilee which had been conquered by the Maccabees (second century B.C.E.), A was apparently the only vernacular. The few A words in the New Testament also point to this conclusion, since the major New Testament figures came from Galilee. After the Bar Kokhba revolt (132–135 C.E.), however, when the Romans had nearly annihilated the whole population or sold them into slavery, the number of settlements in Judea was greatly diminished. The rabbis and their disciples moved to Galilee bringing with them their language and the tannaitic literature written in it, i.e., MH. On the other hand, their children, born in an Aramaic-speaking environment, did not continue to speak H. As R. Meir (a contemporary of R. Judah ha-Nasi) states: כל הדר בארץ ישראל וקורא קרית (קריאת) שמע שחרית ערבית ומדבר בלשון הקודש הריהו בן העולם הבא. ("Anyone who dwells in Ereẓ Israel, recites the *Šema*ʿ morning and evening, and speaks in the 'Holy Tongue' is assured a place in the world to come," Sif. Deut. 333 and parallels). While there were still Jews who spoke MH, its position was already shaky and was in need of some kind of strengthening. The statement of R. Judah ha-Nasi: בארץ ישראל לשון סורסי למה? או לשון הקודש או לשון יונית ("In Ereẓ Israel why Syriac (i.e., Aramaic)? Either the 'Holy Tongue' or Greek," BB 82a) shows that the language of his contemporaries was mainly A.

The few Jews who continued to live in Judea possibly still spoke H. An indication of this may perhaps be found in the statement of R. Jonathan (fourth century C.E.) from Eleutheropolis, southern Palestine, who recommended עברי לדיבור ("Hebrew as the vernacular," TJ, Meg. 71b, bot.). This indicates that MH had not completely died out in this area, but in Galilee it was nonexistent. R. Johanan (the first Palestinian *amora* who was still a disciple of R. Judah ha-Nasi) had to emphasize that in MH the correct plural of רָחֵל ("ewe") is in a certain case (Epstein) רְחֵלוֹת and not רְחֵלִים as in BH. (His maxim was לשון תורה לעצמה ולשון חכמים לעצמן ("The language of the Torah is a language by itself and the language of the sages is a language by itself" (Hul. 137b)). The assumption that MH died out because the *tannaim* moved to Galilee explains why the disciples of R. Judah ha-Nasi had to ask his maidservant the meaning of such H words as מַטְאֲטֵא ("broom") (occurring in the Bible) and חֲלַגְלוֹגוֹת ("purslane") which were unclear to them (Meg. 11a). It may be assumed that the (old?) maidservant had moved from Judea to Galilee with R. Judah's household, and, therefore, spoke H. On the other hand, the (young?) disciples, who may have been born in Galilee, did not know the meaning of these words.

THE PROBLEM OF MISHNAIC HEBREW

The religious reformer A. Geiger, who was the first to write a scientific grammar of MH, thought that MH had never been a spoken language, but had been artificially created by the rabbis to facilitate their halakhic discussions. He was not the first to hold the opinion that MH was not a "normal" H dialect; some medieval Jewish scholars considered it to be a "corrupt" BH to a large extent. Since the concept of linguistic development was unknown in the Middle Ages, medieval scholars could see the reason for the differences between BH and MH only as deliberately wrought changes. Geiger, however, lived at a time when the historical study of languages and their development was taken for granted. H. Graetz, S.D. Luzzatto, and J. Levy, contemporaries of Geiger, strongly opposed his views. However, they, like Geiger, did not substantiate their arguments with tangible proofs and Geiger's view came to be accepted by all contemporary non-Jewish and some Jewish scholars until Segal refuted it convincingly.

In an article published at the beginning of the 20th century (JQR 1908), M.H. Segal showed Geiger's views to be unfounded. He demonstrated that MH was a natural outgrowth of BH (by BH is meant, besides the archaic poetic H and the standard prose, also late biblical Hebrew (= LBH) such as the language of the Books of Chronicles and the Book of Esther) and the natural link coming after LBH. As an example, consider the independent first person singular pronouns אָנֹכִי – אֲנִי (= I) both of which are found in BH. In LBH there is a distinct trend toward the use of אֲנִי. Moreover in the Books of Chronicles, which parallel the Books of Samuel and Kings to a great extent, אָנֹכִי is replaced by אֲנִי (e.g., I Chron. 21:10 = II Sam. 24:12). In MH only אֲנִי survived. Were MH an artificial language, it would be impossible to understand how the rabbis, not being modern linguists, were able to choose only the elements which belong to LBH. The situation is understandable, however, if it is assumed that MH was the natural continuation of LBH.

MH also has forms which are to be found neither in BH nor in A. Were Geiger correct in assuming that MH was an artificial creation, representing a mixture of BH and A, these novel forms in MH could not be explained, for example, where did MH get the pronoun אָנוּ ("we," found once in the Bible (Jer. 42:4) as *ketib*)? Clearly Geiger's opinion is in this form totally unfounded (see following par.).

The recent discoveries in the Judean Desert, especially the letters of Bar Kokhba and his contemporaries, some of which are written in MH, have dispelled all doubts as to Segal's conclusions. These letters show – as was rightly pointed out by Milik – that MH was a living natural language. As a matter of fact, however, both Segal and Geiger were right. MH was a living language in Palestine only until about 200 C.E., the time of the *tannaim*, but a dead language during the time of the *amoraim*.

THE PROBLEM OF THE SOURCES OF MISHNAIC HEBREW

Segal committed two methodical errors in his study which he repeated in the grammars of MH composed later: (1) he tried to minimize the extent of the influence of A on MH; (2) he based his work on the printed texts of MH rather than on manuscripts, which was an especially grave scholarly misjudgment.

The studies over the past decades of J.N. Epstein, H. Yalon, and S. Lieberman have shown that the printed texts are unreliable. This does not refer only to normal scribal errors, but it can be shown that during the Middle Ages the copyists, and later the printers, tried to harmonize MH with BH because they considered departures from BH in MH as mistakes. This "correcting" tendency led to a complete distortion of the linguistic structure of MH.

The following examples will prove this point. A glance at any dictionary of MH will show that the word "man" occurs in the BH form אָדָם. Since Segal's works appeared, however, hundreds of examples of the spelling אָדָן have been discovered in manuscripts of the Mishnah, Tosefta, the Palestinian Talmud, and the aggadic Midrashim (Epstein). It was corrected out of existence in printed versions, and in manuscripts where the form אָדָן does appear the beginnings of correction can already be observed (see, e.g., Ms. Kaufmann to Ber. 1:8). This phenomenon may be taken as clear proof of the widespread tampering with the printed text: the form אָדָן has completely disappeared from the printed texts on which the existing dictionaries of MH are based.

The following is another example: Segal states in his grammar that the second person singular masculine possessive (and objective) pronoun in MH is identical with the biblical form ךָ e.g., דְּבָרְךָ ("your word"). Mainly on the basis of vocalized manuscripts of mishnaic literature, as well as the oral reading tradition especially of Yemenite Jews, H. Yalon has shown that the correct form in MH is ־ָךְ, i.e., דְּבָרָךְ. The form was still known to be MH by the disciples of the medieval grammarian *Menahem b. Jacob ibn Saruq and is preserved until this day in the prayer book of the Sephardi (and Yemenite) ritual, e.g., נַקְדִּישָׁךְ וְנַעֲרִיצָךְ ("Let us sanctify you and glorify you"). In the prayer book of the Ashkenazi ritual, however, these forms have been "corrected" by the grammarians. Only in *piyyutim* are traces of the form still to be found, e.g., in the *piyyut* for *Hoshanah Rabba: (הושע נא למען) אֲמִתָּךְ (למען) בְּרִיתָךְ ("Your truth and your covenant"). Early transcriptions on the Hexapla (third century C.E.) and in the writings of *Jerome (fourth and fifth centuries C.E.) lead to the same conclusion. They superimposed it, however, on the biblical text (Ben-Ḥayyim). In the Sephardi communities there were also disputes as to whether this ending should be retained or dropped because the grammarians demanded the eradication of the "error." Recently, it has been shown that the second person singular feminine possessive pronoun suffered a similar fate. In manuscripts the ending ־ִיךְ is found; thus דְּבָרִיךְ and not דְּבָרֵךְ. Both these suffixes go back to A.

Having come to the conclusion that MH, as it appears in the printed texts, is unreliable, the problem arises: On what uncorrupted source can a description of MH be based? It can also be shown that even manuscripts of the Mishnah, the Tosefta, and the halakhic Midrashim are linguistically unreliable. The problem is to find a manuscript which the copyists have changed only to a minimal extent. The same problem exists with regard to the A of the Palestinian and Babylonian Talmuds. As to the Palestinian Talmud, the problem was solved mainly by comparing its A portions to the language of the contemporary Galilean inscriptions composed in A. Those manuscripts which were linguistically the closest to the Galilean inscriptions were thus linguistically most reliable. Concerning MH, this procedure was more difficult since inscriptions or parchments written in MH, such as the Bar Kokhba letters, are quite rare.

With the aid of reliable manuscripts of the Palestinian Talmud, it is possible, however, to identify good manuscripts of MH. It may be assumed that if the A portions of the text were not corrupted by the copyists, then the H portions are also reliable. With the help of these manuscripts, the few existing H inscriptions, transcriptions of Hebrew–Aramaic words in the New Testament, in Greek inscriptions, and in the writing (transcriptions) of certain Church Fathers, it was possible to establish the most salient criteria for determining how to identify uncorrupted manuscripts. In general, the copyists harmonized the spelling conventions of MH with those of the Bible and the Babylonian Talmud. Thus, if it were possible to show that the words in a particular manuscript had spellings and forms which differed from those found in the Bible and in the Babylonian Talmud, but were parallel to forms found in inscriptions and in the Greek transcriptions from Palestine, then it would be proved that the manuscript represented Palestinian MH close to its original form.

The following are a few examples to illustrate the above methodology:

(1) In good manuscripts of MH there is the form לעזר instead of the biblical אֶלְעָזָר. This form is found in contemporary Palestinian inscriptions and in the New Testament. On the other hand, it is nonexistent in Babylonian manuscripts and sources. This shows that manuscripts with the form לעזר represent a Palestinian version.

(2) The name Shammai is always spelled שמאי in the Babylonian Talmud. In good manuscripts of the Mishnah it is spelled שַׁמַּי or שַׁמַּיי. It can be demonstrated that the orthography ־י, ־יי is the Palestinian representation of the final diphthong *ay*. (The problem of the final *ḥiriq* (*e*) remains as yet unsolved.) On the other hand the Babylonian orthography is ־אי.

With the aid of several other distinguishing features, it was possible to identify several good manuscripts, in particular the following: the Kaufmann manuscript of the Mishnah (entirely vocalized), the Parma manuscript of the Mishnah (partially vocalized), the Cambridge manuscript published by W.H. Lowe (unvocalized), and fragments from the Cairo *Genizah*. The first two manuscripts mentioned above are vocalized with Tiberian signs, though in a vulgar manner since the punctuator, who had a "Sephardi" pronunciation, interchanged *qameṣ* with *pattaḥ*, *ṣere* with *segol* (and *qameṣ qaṭon* with *ḥolem*). The above sources represent, more or less, Palestinian tannaitic H. On the other hand, the Sifra manuscript (which is good) and certain Mishnah fragments from the Cairo *Genizah*, both with Babylonian vocalization, reflect tannaitic H as preserved in Babylonia.

With regard to the language of the Palestinian *amoraim*, the Vatican Ms. Ebr. 30 of Bereshit Rabbah, as well as the *Genizah* fragments of the Palestinian Talmud, were found to be reliable. Reliable sources for the H of the Babylonian *amoraim* have as yet to be determined.

The following description of MH is based, in the main, on the Kaufmann manuscript. Occasionally, reference will be made to Babylonian vocalized forms known mainly from the Sifra (see previous par.) and from *Genizah* fragments of the Mishnah (published mainly by P. Kahle and studied by E. Porath and recently by I. Yeivin).

Spelling

The spelling is more plene than that of BH. Not only the so-called long vowels (*ū, ō*) are spelled with ו (*waw*) e.g., שׁוֹמֵר ("guard"), but also short and even half vowels are indicated by ו, e.g., עֳוֹמָרִים ("sheaves") (the punctuator crossed out the ו). The same applies, more or less, to the different varieties of *i-e-ε* (long and short) being spelled with י (*yod*), e.g., לִיקְרוֹת ("to read"). Even א (*ʾalep*) is (rarely) used to indicate (*a*), e.g., שְׁיָארָה ("caravan") (also, cf., the following par.). ו and י, used as consonants, are often doubled, thus: וו, יי. The vowels *e, ε* as word finals might be indicated by י, cf., יווני = Yavne (see the following par.). Sometimes even spellings reminiscent of the Dead Sea Scrolls are found, like לִיקְרָאוֹת ("to read"); the etymological א plus the ו indicating (*o*). As the above-mentioned שְׁיָארָה indicates, א could be used as a vowel letter for *a*.

Phonetics

CONSONANTS. The consonantal inventory of MH is identical with that of BH. Though, undoubtedly, some change took place in their realization (= pronunciation) during the period under discussion, there is no foundation whatsoever for Kahle's assumption that the laryngeals and pharyngeals were completely lost. Nevertheless, some interchanges of these phonemes are found. It is known that in Tivon, Haifa, Beth-Shean, and in the academy of Eliezer b. Jacob ע (*ʿayin*) and א (*ʾalep*) were interchanged. According to the Babylonian Talmud, the Galileans were unable to distinguish between א (*ʾalep*), ה (*he*), ח (*ḥet*), and ע (*ʿayin*) in their A vernacular, a statement which, however, seems exaggerated. The laryngeals and pharyngeals were apparently confused mainly in the large urban centers, as a result of Greek influence. MH, as transmitted, has only been slightly influenced by this confusion and there are only a few places in the Mishnah where the *amoraim* are in doubt as to whether the correct reading is with א or ע, e.g., אֵיד or עֵיד ("festival") (Mishnah Av. Zar. 1:1).

It is quite possible, however, that the linguistic change ע < ח (*ḥet* > *ʿayin*) took place (as in Galilean Aramaic), e.g., עָג עוּגָה ("he made a circle") (Mishnah Ta'an.3:8). Final *mem* in non-declined words very often turns into *nun* אָדָן < אָדָם or הֵם > הֵן (see above the Problem of the Sources of MH). ב̱ (*ḇet* = ב without *dageš*) and ו (*waw*) merged. Thus they were interchanged in manuscripts, e.g., יַבְנֶה (place name) is spelled יווני. Interchanges between ק (*qop*) and כ (*kap*) are very infrequent. More common is the interchange ב (*bet*) and פ (*pe*), e.g., שְׁעָרִים = לְהַפְקִיעַ שְׁעָרִים (= לְהַבְקִיַע לְהַבְקִיעַ ("to raise prices arbitrarily") (Ta'an. 2:9). Initial א (when followed by a half vowel?) is sometimes dropped (+ its vowel) cf. above לעזר אלעזר (The Problem of the Sources).

VOWELS. The vowels of MH at first glance also seem identical with those of BH. There is, however, reason to assume that some change took place, thus instead of *ḥiriq qaton* a type of ε (*segol*) was pronounced, and instead of *qibbuẓ* a type of *o* (*qameṣ qaṭon* – *ḥolem*). However, even in manuscripts, very few examples of this pronunciation have survived, apparently as a result of the "corrections" of copyists under the influence of BH, e.g., הֶלֵּיל, חוּצְפָּה etc. = הִלֵּל (proper noun), חוּצְפָּה ("ḥuẓpa"). This type of pronunciation parallels that known from the transcriptions of the Septuagint and from vocalized texts of Galilean Aramaic.

ASSIMILATION AND DISSIMILATION. Assimilation of consonants in MH occurs more or less under the same circumstances as in BH. Vowels, as in Galilean Aramaic, preceding labials tended to be realized as *o* (*u*) e.g., מְסַבִּין < מְסֻבִּין (in the *Haggadah* of Passover "reclining") (Ben-Ḥayyim). ר (*reš*) seems to have had the same effect on vowels as labials. This accounts for forms like קַרְדֹּם < ‡ קוֹרְדּוֹם (BH) ("spade"), etc. (also cf. the Greek name of the river יַרְדֵּן = *Yordan(ēs)*). A long ī apparently could turn a preceding half vowel (*šewa* (:)) into an *i*, e.g., בִּיסִיד (instead of בְּסִיד) ("with lime").

Dissimilation of a consonant occurs in the word מַרְגָּלִית μαργαρίτις ("pearl") and of a vowel in the Greek word נִימוֹס (from Greek νόμος ("law") (on the pattern of תִּיכוֹן (תוֹכוֹן) – תּוֹךְ ‡ > ("inside," "central").

Metathesis occurs in נמיל (("port"), לִמֵן in the Palestinian form), the Babylonian form of the Greek λιμήν.

Morphology

PRONOUNS. *Independent Personal Pronouns*

Comparative Table

(not all the vocalizations of MH are documented)

Mishnaic Hebrew		Biblical Hebrew	
	אֲנִי		אֲנִי,אָנֹכִי
אַתְּ	אַתָּה,אַתְּ	(אתי) אַתְּ	אַתָּה
הִיא	הוּא	הִיא	הוּא
	אָנוּ		אֲנַחְנוּ, נַחְנוּ
אַתֶּן (?),אַתֶּם	אַתֶּם, אַתֶּן	אַתֵּנָה, אַתֶּן	אַתֶּם
הֵם,הֵן	הֵם,הֵן	הֵנָּה	הֵם,הֵמָּה

In MH (and already in LBH) אָנֹכִי had disappeared. אַתְּ as a masculine pronoun is apparently a borrowing from A. אָנוּ is an internal H development. The vocalic endings of הֵמָּה and הֵנָּה disappeared. Final ם (*mem*) was apt to appear as ן(*nun*) (see above Phonetics, consonants), therefore in both the pronoun and the verb the plural masculine and feminine forms merged (see following pars. on possessive pronouns and verb (the conjugation)).

The independent personal pronouns furnish a good example for the elements which make up MH: (1) BH; (2) A; (3) internal H development.

Possessive Suffixes
(not all the vocalizations of MH are documented)

Mishnaic Hebrew		Biblical Hebrew	
דְּבָרִי		דְּבָרִי	
דְּבָרַיִךְ	דְּבָרָךְ	דְּבָרֵךְ	דְּבָרְךָ
דְּבָרָהּ	דְּבָרוֹ	דְּבָרָהּ	דְּבָרוֹ
דְּבָרֵנוּ		דְּבָרֵנוּ	
דְּבַרְכֶן,-ם	דְּבַרְכֶם,-ן	דְּבַרְכֶן	דְּבַרְכֶם
דְּבָרָם,-ן	דְּבָרָם,-ן	דְּבָרָם	דְּבָרָם

Note: Instead of the ending ָן-, ָם- there occurs also an ending ים-, generally corrected to ן-, the י being crossed out (Epstein, Kutscher). It is found also as an object suffix of the perfect. The second person singular masculine (Yalon) and feminine (Kutscher) forms are the result of A influence. (On the interchange מ (*mem*) > נ (*nun*), see above Phonetics.)

Independent Possessive Pronouns. MH developed an independent possessive pronoun – שֶׁל (geminated ל), e.g., שֶׁלִּי ("mine"). The distribution between this pronoun and the suffixed forms is still unclear as are the rules governing the use of the definite article in this case. The beginning of this development is to be found in the biblical form אֲשֶׁר לְ- (= MH שֶׁ-), e.g., בְּמִרְכֶּבֶת הַמִּשְׁנֶה אֲשֶׁר לוֹ ("in the chariot of his second-in-command," Gen. 41:43).

Demonstrative Pronouns. *Near Deictic Pronouns.*

Mishnaic Hebrew		Biblical	
זוֹ	זֶה	(זֹה,זוֹ) זֹאת	זֶה
אֵלּוּ		אֵלֶּה	

Instead of זֹאת which predominates in the Bible, זוֹ, found mainly in LBH, occurs in MH. It is possible that this word entered MH from another dialect. (If it is assumed that the form developed in MH from the BH זֹאת, it is impossible to explain the loss of the final ת (*taw*). The form אֵלּוּ perhaps developed under the influence of plural verbal forms, such as כָּתְבוּ, etc. It is unclear under what conditions the definite article is employed with the noun and the demonstrative pronoun.

Far Deictic Pronouns. Alongside the forms הַהִיא, הַהוּא, etc., there are the following forms in MH: הַלָּה, הַלָּז for the masculine and the feminine, (הַלֵּילוּ) הָאֵילוּ־הַלָּלוּ for the plural. The particle אֵת with suffixed pronouns acts as a demonstrative pronoun (preceding the noun), e.g., אוֹתוֹ הַיּוֹם ("that day"). The reflexive pronoun is created by using עֶצֶם ("bone") (very much like the English "(my) self," e.g., קוֹנֶה אֶת עַצְמוֹ "he acquires himself (= his freedom)"); הוּא עַצְמוֹ ("he himself"). The relative pronoun is שֶׁ-, which appears both in archaic BH and in LBH.

Since שֶׁ- can scarcely go back to אֲשֶׁר of BH and besides is paralleled by the Akkadian *ša*, here too (see Near Deictic Pronouns) an H dialect different from BH may be assumed as its origin.

VERB. *Verbal Roots.* The verbal root pattern *xyx*, e.g., כָּרוֹךְ ("to wrap") only emerges in MH while four radicals, e.g., from ע"ו roots of the type לְנַעְנֵעַ ("to shake"), or by duplicating the last radical, e.g., עַרְבֵּב ("to mix") already appear in BH.

Conjugations. The *pu*‘‘*al* has practically disappeared (the participle excepted). The perfect of *hitpa‘‘el* practically disappeared and the form *nitpa‘al* (corrupted in the printed editions to *nitpa‘‘el*) occurs instead (only twice in the Bible). It is apparently a blend of *nitpa‘‘al* and *hitpa‘‘el*. In the פ"י verb an *ʾettap‘‘al* conjugation (borrowed from A) exists (extremely rare).

In addition to the *hip‘il* there is also a *šap‘el* conjugation (assumed to be borrowed from Akkadian through A) which is conjugated like the *pa‘‘el*, e.g., שִׁחְרֵר ("to liberate"). Traces of the passive *qal* are found in the פ"נ verbs, e.g., ‡נוּטַּל ("taken"), etc., however it might be a recreation in MH as in modern Hebrew נְשַׁכְתִּי ("I was bitten") and not נִשַּׁכְתִּי which is identical with the *pi‘‘el* (here an active form). This usage was extended to other verbs, e.g., נוּצַּר(??) ("saved").

The exact meanings of the various conjugations still remain to be clarified. The following is a tentative description:

The *qal* is generally identical with the *qal* of BH, i.e., it can indicate a simple action (transitive or intransitive) and it can serve as a denominative even in a case like פָּרָה חוֹלֶבֶת (lit., "a milking cow"). There is, however, a conspicuous difference in the intransitive verbs. While in BH a form like גָּדַלְתָּ can mean both "you were great" and "you became great" (even "you are great"), in MH only the second meaning occurs, e.g. גָּדְלָה ("grew" < "she became great"); the first meaning has to be expressed by means of the auxiliary הָיָה, plus the participle or adjective, e.g., הָיָה גָּדוֹל.

Nip‘al also seems generally to be identical with BH, i.e., it can be a reflexive נִטְמַן ("he hid himself") and also נִשְׁאַל ("he asked for himself"), apparently in a reciprocal meaning נֶחְלְקוּ ("they disputed"), but generally a passive, e.g., נֶאֱכַל ("it was eaten up"), and perhaps also with a new meaning to express perfectivity (inchoation), e.g., זָכוּר אֲנִי ("I am remembering") but אֲנִי נִזְכָּר ("it comes to my mind"). In BH *qal* זכר is employed in both meanings. Maybe נִכְנַס ("he entered") has to be explained the same way (cf., וַיֵּאָסֵף "he entered," Num. 11:30).

Pi‘el, as in BH, expresses intensive action, meaning repeated action, or an action performed on many objects (Yalon) (cf., BH וַיְבַתֵּר (*pi‘el*) אֹתָם בַּתָּוֶךְ... וְאֶת הַצִּפֹּר לֹא בָתָר (*qal*) ("and cut them in two… but he did not cut up the bird," Gen. 15:10)); or when the work is performed by many actors, e.g., הָיוּ מְתַלְּשִׁין ("they were plucking"); also as a denominative, e.g., מְעַשְּׁנִין ("to fumigate"); even in a privative sense מְיַבְּלִין ("to remove wens"), and as a causative מְיַלְּדִין ("to help in childbearing"). The *pi‘el* also can serve in an intransitive meaning as an inchoative בִּיכֵּירוּ ("began to ripen"). A few cases of this last meaning already appear in BH, e.g., פִּתְּחָה ("has been opened," lit., "has opened"). In some cases the *pi‘el* seems to have dislodged the *qal* without change of meaning, e.g., עִיבֵּר ("he passed") (Pes. 3:8), but whether it is a general feature of MH (Ben-Hayyim) has still to be established (cf., BH דֹּבֵר ("speaking") *qal*, but generally the *pi'el* is employed).

Hi'pil, as in BH, serves as a causative מַשְׁחִיטִין ("cause to slaughter"), as a denominative הִגְרִיל ("he cast lots") as in the *pi'el* (also *nip'al* and *qal* to a certain extent). It also serves as an inchoative הֶעֱשִׁיר ("he grew rich").

The *hop'al* served as a passive of the *hip'il*.

The *hitpa''el-nitpa''al* is mainly employed, as in BH, as a reflexive, e.g., נִסְתַּפֵּג ("he dried himself"), also as an inchoative, e.g., נִשְׁתַּטָּה ("he went mad"), a reciprocal נִשְׁתַּתְּפוּ ("they became partners"), and very often as a passive נִתְגַּלָּה ("it became uncovered"), rare in BH. In contrast to BH where it serves as a denominative very often meaning "to pretend to," e.g., מִתְעַשֵּׁר ("he pretends to be rich"), in MH this meaning does not occur and in the *hitpa''el* it means "to become rich" (cf. *Hip'il*). The *šap'el* is a causative (but conjugated as a *pi'el*).

Prefixes and Suffixes of The Tenses. As with personal pronouns, the masculine and feminine forms in the perfect of the verb also coalesced as a result of the phonological development of final ם (*mem*) > ן (*nun*), thus כתבתן – כתבתם. The loss of the feminine plural forms in the imperfect is the result of a different process. All the archaic forms of BH, e.g., imperfect forms with the ending *n* (ן) such as תִּשְׁמְרוּן ("you (plur.) will guard") disappeared from MH (in spite of the fact that some of them were identical with the parallel A forms).

	Perfect	
	כָּתַבְתִּי	
כָּתַבְתְּ		כָּתַבְתָּה
כָּתְבָה		כָּתַב
	כָּתַבְנוּ	
	כְּתַבְתֶּן,-ם	
	כָּתְבוּ	

(Note the full spelling of כתבתה). It should be noted that MH (as in the Dead Sea Scrolls) very often uses the pausal forms also instead of the contextual form. This is always the case in the *hop'al*, e.g., הוּקְדָּשׁוּ לַמִּשְׁכָּן ("they were dedicated to the Tabernacle," Zev. 14:10).

	Imperfect	
	אֶכְתֹּב	
תִּכְתְּבִי		תִּכְתֹּב
תִּכְתֹּב		יִכְתֹּב
	נִכְתֹּב	
	תִּכְתְּבוּ	
	יִכְתְּבוּ	

Participle (Imperative and Infinitive). The main changes in the participle are in the feminine singular only the ־ֶת ending is used: שׁוֹמֶרֶת ("guarding") (except for the ע"ו, and ל"י (ל"א) verbs to a certain extent), while the plural masculine employs, besides the ending ־ים also ־ִין (A). In the imperative, the feminine plural is replaced by the masculine plural (cf., imperfect above). The participle can be negated by לֹא and not only by אין, while the infinitive is negated by שֶׁלֹּא ל, e.g., שֶׁלֹּא לַחְתּוֹם אֵינוֹ רַשַּׁאי (= רַשַּׁיי) ("it is not permitted not to seal").

Verb Classes. Strong Verb. In the *qal* perfect only the patterns קָטַל and קָטֵל (חָשֵׁיכָה "it became dark") have survived, while in the participle all three forms, attested in BH; קוֹטֵל, קָטֵל, (e.g., דָּלֵק "burning") and the only case of קָטֹל = יָכוֹל (("he) can," "is able") appear. (Incidentally, the feminine and the plurals, not attested in BH Hebrew, are יְכוֹלָה, יְכוֹלִין, יְכוֹלוֹת.) In the "imperfect" there seems to be a tendency to turn (*a*) forms (of the intransitive verb) into (*o*) forms, cf., יִקְרוֹשׁ ("it should congeal"). The spelling indicates an (*o*) imperfect; the punctuator of the manuscript, however, crossed out the ו (*waw*) and vocalized יִקְרַשׁ (also see verbs ע"ח). In the *hitpa''el* imperfect there appear, though rarely, also forms like תִּתְחַבֵּר ("consort") (Avot 1:7).

Weak Verb. פ"א verbs: the infinite of *qal* is patterned after the 'imperfect'; לוֹמַר ("to say") etc. (cf., Spelling above), לוֹכַל ("to eat").

פ"ע verbs: note the form נֶעֱשָׂה ("it was done") (= נַעֲשָׂה in BH).

ע"ח verbs: in the imperfect and imperative the (*a*) turns (always?) into (*o*), e.g., יִשְׁחוֹט ("he shall slaughter") שְׁחוֹט ("slaughter") (see above the strong verb).

ל"א and ל"י verbs: The ל"א verbs generally turned (as in A) into ל"י verbs: sometimes, however, the former spelling is retained, e.g., קָרִינוּ ("we have read"), but יִקְרָא ("he shall read"), לִקְרוֹת ("to read"); in לִקְרֹאות ("to read") the original א appears, in spite of the ל"י form (see above Spelling); in the perfect the ending of the third person singular feminine is often ־ָת, e.g., הָיָת ("she was"). This ending, found also in BH (rarely) in the strong verb, is in BH considered mainly an archaic survival. Its emergence in the ל"י verb in MH cannot be attributed to A influence since it does not occur in the other verbal classes. It seems that this form entered MH from a non-biblical Hebrew dialect in which the original הָיָת ‡ had not become הָיְתָה. The ending ת (*taw*) is also found in the other conjugations but in the *nip'al* there are, besides forms like נִיכְוֵות ("she burnt herself"), such forms as נִיטְמֵת ("she became unclean") where the form of the original ל"א verb is identical with the feminine singular of the present. But the same form can also occur in an original ל"י form נִישְׁבֵּית ("she was taken prisoner"). Naturally, the biblical forms with the ending ־תָה also occur. In the participle *qal* there are two forms, e.g., קוֹנֶה ("he buys") and זָכֶה ("he takes possession," "he gains," "he obtains a privilege").

פ"י verbs: the infinitive of the *qal* is patterned after the imperfect, e.g., לֵירֵד ("to go down"). The same applies to פ"נ verbs: לִיתֵּן ("to give"); note forms like לִיטּוֹל ("to take") where the נ is assimilated (which is not the case in BH).

ע"ו verbs: *qal*, there are also participle forms like חוּלוֹת (rare in BH) ("they (fem.) dance"); in the infinitive and in the "imperfect" also forms like לָדוּן (also לָדוֹן and לָדִין) are found (cf., ע״י verbs). There are in BH perfect *qal* forms like קָם ("he got up"), טוֹב ("he was good"), and מֵת ("he died"), paralleling similar forms in the strong verbs. From the second pattern only בּוֹשׁ survived ("he was ashamed"), as did מֵת. In the perfect of *nip'al* forms like נָדוֹן and נִידוֹן ("he (it) was judged or he (it) was discussed"), in the participle נִידוֹן, are employed. There is also נָמוּךְ ("low, short") but in the Babylonian vocalization נָמוֹךְ. In the *hip'il* there are forms like הוֹבִיר ("he left (the field) fallow") (patterned after פ״ו). In the geminated conjugations (*pi''el, pu''al, hitpa''el*) the forms derived by doubling of the third radical (practically) disappeared; forms like הִתְכּוֹנֵן ("he intended" (from כון)) are replaced (practically always) by the נִתְכַּוֵּן type, the second radical being geminated, as in the strong verb.

ע״י verbs: they disappeared almost entirely by (1) turning into ע״ו; דִּין mostly appears (in the "imperfect") as דּוּן; (2) or by being transferred to the *hip'il* (since the "imperfects" are identical); participle *qal;* שָׂם ("putting" via imperfect יָשִׂים) > מֵשִׂים (participle of *hip'il*), only once in BH.

Geminate Verb. There is a tendency in the *qal* perfect and participle to employ the intransitive verbs with the transitive forms, i.e., they are patterned after the strong verb: e.g., גּוֹשֶׁשֶׁת ("(ship) touches (the ground)" – in Hebrew it is intransitive), but רַבּוּ ("they multiplied") (intransitive form). In the imperfect the so-called A forms do not seem to occur (יִיצַּנּוּ ("to keep it cool," Shab. 22:4) is not a clear-cut case). In the *nip'al* the geminate verbs are generally treated as strong verbs, e.g., נִימְדַּד ("was measured"), נִימְדָּד ("is being measured"), תִּיקָּצֵץ ("let it be cut off"). There seem to be very rare cases of forms like נִימוֹקוּ ("they were defeated") patterned after ע״ו verbs. In the geminated conjugations *pi''el, pu''al, hitpa''el* (as in the ע״ו verbs, see above) only the strong verb forms appear.

With the verbs הָיָה and חָיָה short form יְהֵא (= יִהְיֶה) is employed in the imperfect, while in the imperative the root הוה (A) is used often even in the A form הֱוִי (= H הֱוֵה) ("be" sing.); הֱווֹ (= H הֱווּ) ("be" plur.). The root חי sometimes appears in the participle *qal* as a geminate חי (חיי) ("he lives"), like קַל ("he is easy"), but according to spelling חיה, obviously to be vocalized חָיָה‡ (like זָכָה above) but corrected in the manuscripts to חי.

Tenses. The tense system of BH underwent a radical change in MH. The following forms disappeared: the long imperfect of the type אֶשְׁמְרָה ("I will guard"); the short imperfect of the type יַעַל ("he shall go up"); the forms with the consecutive ו (*waw*) (וַיִּשְׁמֹר, וְשָׁמַר) the absolute infinitive שָׁמוֹר. The infinitive construct only survived with the preposition ל, e.g., לִשְׁמוֹר ("to guard"), sometimes even when the preceding verb governs the preposition מִן, e.g., אָסוּר מִלִּרְחוֹץ ("(he) is forbidden to wash"). The new system comprises: (1) the perfect (which also serves as a preterit);

(2) a practically new periphrastic form: היה ("be") (mainly used for the past but also for the future and imperative) plus the active and passive participle to indicate repeated, usual, concurrent, etc., action (rare in LBH).

The participle is employed as present and future. A new periphrastic form (mainly employed when the future needs a clear-cut indication, especially when in contrast to the present) came into being: infinitive ל + דַּע מֵאַיִן בָּאתָה וּלְאַיִן אַתָּה הוֹלֵךְ וְלִפְנֵי מִי אַתָּה עָתִיד לִיתֵּן דִּין וְחֶשְׁבּוֹן, עָתִיד ("Know whence thou art come, whither thou art going, and before whom thou art designed to give an account and reckoning"). Contrary to BH the imperfect does not denote future anymore: it turned into a modal form expressing wish or intention (in the first person) or command (in the third person). It is also used after an imperative, as שְׁמוֹר לִי וְאֶשְׁמוֹר לָךְ ("guard for me and I shall (will) guard for you") and as a subjunctive, after the relative pronoun – שֶׁ. The imperative survived apparently unchanged. The passive participle, mainly the *qal* of intransitive verbs, is employed with certain verbs as a kind of present perfect-present אֲנִי יָשׁוּב ("I am sitting (seated)"). מְקוּבָּל אֲנִי ("I have received") (rare in BH).

It should be noted that MH, as A, very often uses the proleptic suffix with verbs, e.g., the common expression y לרבי x אָמַר לוֹ רבי (instead of y לרבי x אמר רבי).

NOUN. The noun forms are generally the same as those in BH, though some became more widespread, especially some of the verbal nouns of the *qal*. About 15 different noun forms are used as verbal nouns of the *qal*, among them the noun pattern קְטִילָה should be especially noted, e.g., אֲנִינָה ("grief"). This noun pattern in BH as a verbal noun (e.g., אֲכִילָה ("eating")) is rare, in the Mishnah, however, there are 130 examples. Its influence was so great that it was able to change the biblical form of שְׂרֵפָה ("conflagration") to שְׂרִיפָה. In the ל״י (and ל״א) verbs this form may appear in the קְטִיָה. pattern, e.g., בְּרִיָּה ("creature, creation"), קְרִיָה. ("reading"), etc. Though rare, the form קְטֵילָה is also found, such as כְּנִיסָה ("entrance"). The form קְטָלָה is also rare (though common with verbs that denote sound), e.g., צְוָוחָה ("shouting"). A new form is גָּזֵל ("robbery"), חֲנֵק ("strangulation"). Verbal nouns with suffixes are also found, e.g., פִּדְיוֹן ("redemption"). (The word does not occur in the absolute state in the Bible.) The number of A patterns is relatively small, e.g., כְּלָל ("general rule"), פְּרָט ("specification"); with the prefix מ (*mem*): מִכְנָס ("bringing in"), showing that A had a minor influence in this field.

The verbal noun of the *pi''el* is קִטּוּל. or קַטָּלָה (both BH but the latter is a borrowing from A). In the *hip'il* also the A form הַקְטָלָה (already in the Bible) predominates along with הֶקְטֵל, e.g., הֶקְטֵר ("burning" ("of offering")). In the ל״י verbs, the form in Babylonian sources is, e.g., הוֹרָאָה ("instruction"); whereas in Palestinian sources it is הוֹרָיָה. The form הֶקְטֵל, e.g., הֶקְטֵר, is, in fact, identical with the absolute infinitive in BH. (As in BH, the *segol* is an allophone of *pattaḥ*). In the Babylonian vocalization it may appear both as הֶקְטֵל and הֵיקְטֵל (in certain cases). The passive and reflexive conjugations do not have their own verbal nouns and employ the verbal nouns of the corresponding active conjugations, e.g., וִידּוּי ("confession of sin") from לְהִתְוַדּוֹת. It should be noted, however, that the *nip'al* infinitive הִכָּרֵת, occurring in the Mishnah also as

כָּרֵת ("extermination"), serves as a verbal noun; even a plural form occurs כָּרֵתוֹת.

The form with the ending ־ָן (*-ān*) is a *nomen agentis* (the agent) noun pattern which is peculiar to MH. In Palestinian manuscripts, these appear mainly as גּוֹזְלָן ("robber"), רוֹצְחָן ("murderer"), etc. (The vocalization is not uniform.) In Babylonian sources mainly the forms גזלן and רצחן occur. The origin of this form is still unclear. The *nomen agentis* for *qal* of the קָטוֹל pattern, e.g., לָקוֹחַ ("buyer") might be of A origin. It should be noted that MH tried to develop a special form to represent the result of an action, namely קְטִילָה (practically nonexistent in BH). The only example of this form is חֲתִיכָה ("a piece") alongside the verbal noun חֲתִיכָה ("cutting").

Alongside of the construct there is the paraphrastic (the circumlocuted) construct state which uses the particle של. As Yalon has demonstrated, this word was attached to the *nomen rectum* (if this was determined) and contained the definite article, e.g., ‡רִבּוֹנוֹ שֶׁלָּעוֹלָם = רִבּוֹנוֹ שֶׁל הָעוֹלָם ("master of the world"). How and when של was separated from the noun and ceased to contain the definite article is not entirely clear. In the Bar Kokhba letters של is separated from the following word, which, however, has the definite article. This shows that the dialect of the Bar Kokhba letters is not identical with MH as it is known today.

In the של phrase there are four types. In three of them של includes the definite article:

(a) הַיַּיִן וְהַחוֹמֶץ שֶׁלַּגּוֹיִם ("wine or the vinegar of Gentiles") (Av. Zar. 2:3). (b) with the prolectic suffix אֵידֵיהֶן שֶׁלַּגּוֹיִם "the festivals of the Gentiles"). The difference in meaning of these two constructions is not entirely clear. In each phrase both nouns are determined. (c) שֶׁלַּזָּהָב (= נברשת) נִבְרֶשֶׁת ("a golden candlestick") (Yoma 3:10). (d) לָשׁוֹן שֶׁלְּזְהוֹרִית ("a thread of crimson wool"). In each of these phrases both nouns are undetermined. The reason for the difference between the two last constructions is not clear.

Plural. Besides the plural with ־ִים, ־ִין, and ־וֹת, a plural with the ending ־ָאוֹת in Babylonian sources, ־ָיוֹת in Palestinian sources occurs, e.g., מֶרְחֲצָאוֹת = מֶרְחֲצָיוֹת ("bathhouses"). The plural of nouns ending in ־וּת is not ־ָיוֹת, as in the Bible, but ־ִיּוֹת, e.g., מַלְכִיּוֹת ("kingdoms"). A double plural of compound nouns, such as, רָאשֵׁי שָׁנִים ("new years") occurs (cf., for example, the form אַנְשֵׁי שֵׁמוֹת, found in Chronicles, to אַנְשֵׁי שֵׁם ("famous men") which appears in Genesis).

The rules governing the use of the definite articles are still not entirely clear. It should, however, be pointed out that a noun with an accompanying adjective generally does not take the definite article, e.g., לַיְלָה הָרִאשׁוֹן ("the first night"). Other usages, such as, הַכֹּהֲנִים גְּדוֹלִים ("the high priests") which appear to be exceptions to the rule require further investigation (cf., הכהן גדול in the Dead Sea Scrolls).

PARTICLES. While there are many new adverbs and conjunctions, such as, בֵּינְתַיִם ("meanwhile"), כְּדֵי ("in order to"), עַכְשָׁיו ("now"), כֵּיצַד ("how"), noteworthy is אבית instead of בְּבֵית. It seems that the biblical prepositions have remained to a greater extent than the other particles, as in the case of the language of the Dead Sea Scrolls and Punic. Some usages which should be especially noted are the following: ־ל is used to a great extent for ־ב, e.g., הָיְתָה תְרוּמָה לְתוֹךְ פִּיו ("the *terumah* was in his mouth"). Many verbs take either one of the following prepositions: ב or ל. ל also indicates the accusative (rare in BH but common in A). The prepositions על – עד interchange (as they do in Galilean and Samaritan Aramaic). The copulative ו (*waw*) sometimes acts as an explicative ו (*waw*), e.g., מְבָרֵךְ עַל הַטּוֹבָה וּמֵעֵין עַל הָרָעָה ("A man should say the benediction for good fortune regardless of any consequent evil") (in German: *und zwar*).

In particles of negation besides אֵין ("not"), employed in nominal sentences including participles (note the declension: אֵינִי, etc. אֵינָהּ / אֵינוֹ – "he/she is not"), also לא is used to negate participles. The A loan לָאו is used mainly in the phrase אם לאו ("if not"). אֵי ("אין") occurs apparently only before א, e.g., אֵי אַתֶּם ("don't you"). The expression "yes," which is absent in BH, in MH appears as הין (from A).

SYNTAX. Owing to the radical changes that occurred in the tense system of MH (see above), the syntax of MH looks very different from that of BH. However, since research in syntax has to be based on good manuscripts (see The Problem of MH), the picture is as yet not entirely clear.

The following may more or less be stated: in the verbal sentence generally the verb seems to precede the subject but not always. A verb can take a verbal complement in three ways: (a) infinitive plus ל (as in BH); (b) the participle הִתְחִיל בּוֹכֶה ("he started weeping") (rare in BH);

(c) a relative clause, צָרִיךְ שֶׁיֹּאמַר ("he must say"). In the past conditional the construction participle plus הָיָה is preferred, אִלּוּ (negative לוּלֵא) opening the sentence, e.g., אִילּוּ הָיִיתִי יוֹדֵעַ לֹא הָיִיתִי נוֹדֵר ("Had I known (that this was so) I would not have made my vow"). Interrogative sentences which expect a negative (?) answer begin with כְּלוּם. Relative sentences are more numerous than in BH since in MH subordinate clauses are used instead of the biblical infinitive plus ב or כ (not occurring in MH).

In the comparative sentence often יוֹתֵר is added, e.g., רַע יוֹתֵר מִסּוֹדוֹמִיִּין ("worse than the Sodomites") (Tos. Shab. 7:23).

While in BH the passive is used almost only if the agent is unknown (with very few exceptions), in MH it seems to be employed even if the agent is known, e.g., הַנּוֹלָדִים מִן הַסּוּס ("all offspring from a horse," lit., "born by a horse"). The agent is expressed by מִן and by ל, e.g., נֶאֱכָלִים לַכֹּהֲנִים ("are eaten by the priests"). As noted, the syntax of MH has to be restudied on the basis of good manuscripts.

VOCABULARY. A great part of BH vocabulary disappeared from MH including even words indicating close relation, דוד ("uncle") or parts of the body, such as, בֶּטֶן ("belly"), בֹּהֶן ("thumb") was replaced by גּוּדָל (אגודל). As is well known these two fields are the most resistant to change in every language. Less amazing is the fact that vocabulary used only in the poetic parts of BH did not generally survive in MH, e.g, חָרוּץ ("gold"). The vocabulary of MH is composed of the following elements: (1) Hebrew; (2) loanwords from Persian, Akkadian, Greek, Latin, and Aramaic.

Hebrew. The Hebrew element has many facets:
(a) BH whose meaning remained the same, such as, יָד ("hand"), רֶגֶל ("foot"), בַּיִת ("house"), מַטֶּה ("staff"), יָצָא ("to go out"), שָׁמַע ("to hear"), רָאָה ("to see").

(b) BH words which took on a different form (in the following examples the first word is the biblical form and the second the mishnaic): מַשּׂוּאָה – מַשְׂאֵת ("flares," "fire signs"), לְהַכְשִׁיל – לְכַשֵּׁל ("to cause to stumble"), יָמִין – יַמִּין ("right hand") (Aramaic?), זָג – זוֹג ("grape-peel"), חֵיל – חַיִל ("surrounding wall"). Some words found in the Bible are only in the singular whereas in MH they occur also in the plural, e.g., שְׁמִטָּה – שְׁמִיטִים ("sabbatical year"). In particular this is the case with collective nouns, such as פְּרִי – פֵּרוֹת ("fruit"), יָרָק – יְרָקוֹת ("vegetable"). Some words found only in the plural in the Bible occur in MH in the singular. such as, בָּטְנִים – בּוֹטְנָה (= בָּטְנָה "pistachio"). Verbs, such as תרם (רום > תרומה > תרם), from the BH root רום, in *hip'il* לְהָרִים ("to raise"), with the preformative ת (*taw*) formed the noun תְּרוּמָה ("heave offering"). MH derived from תְּרוּמָה a new root תרם which is now used instead of BH לְהָרִים. Nouns were formed from verbs, e.g., וַעַד ("meeting place") < הִוָּעֵד ("to meet"), וִדּוּי ("confession of sin") < הִתְוַדּוֹת ("to confess") where the biblical aversion to *waw* as the first radical did not apply anymore.

(c) Some nouns which apparently changed their gender under A influence, e.g., כּוֹס ("goblet") which became masculine while שָׂדֶה ("field") became feminine.

(d) A biblical element which changed semantically but not morphologically. Some words are concrete in the Bible and abstract in MH, e.g., נָהוֹג "to lead," in MH "to behave." Similarly גָּזוֹר in MH means only "to decide" and not "to cut." עוֹלָם in the Bible means "eternity," but in MH "world." Some words were semantically restricted, e.g., צְדָקָה "righteousness" and "charity," in MH means only "charity." חַג ("holiday") refers only to "Sukkot" in MH and עֲצֶרֶת ("assemblage") only to "Shavuot." It is sometimes difficult to decide whether a particular biblical root changed its meaning or the root in MH is simply homophonic, for example, פָּסוֹל in the Bible means "to hew," with the derived noun פְּסוֹלֶת ("refuse") (cf., נְעוֹרֶת "tow"). From פְּסוֹלֶת a denominative *qal* verb was formed ("to declare unfit"); there may, however, be a different root here (as found in Arabic). But the root לְהִתְחַטֵּא ("to ingratiate himself") is certainly not identical with the Hebrew root חטא ("to sin"), but is an A root.

(e) Non-biblical Hebrew elements. It is certain that the Bible does not contain the whole vocabulary of the biblical period, as shown by personal names and inscriptions (cf., the word זדה in the Siloam inscription (as yet unexplained) and נצף appearing on weights (meaning apparently "half," cf., Arabic). Therefore at least some of those roots which cannot be proven to be foreign loans are probably survivals from the biblical period and only incidentally did not appear in the Bible. This is, of course, impossible to prove in most cases. Sometimes, it cannot be determined whether the form originated in H (or in a Hebrew-Canaanite dialect) or in a neighboring dialect (such as Edomite (?)). It seems probable that most of these words are of H (or Hebrew-Canaanite) origin. Consider, for example, the root חָזוֹר ("to return") (in Eastern Aramaic הדר – חדר; in Western Aramaic חזר, apparently a borrowing from Hebrew). This root may have reached H through one of the Canaanite dialects. On the other hand, the root of לְהִתְעַכֵּב ("to be delayed") is less certain. (There is no certain parallel in the other Semitic languages.) The certainty is greater for agricultural terms or for parts of the body, e.g., סָרָף (שָׂרָף) ("resin"), which do not occur in other Semitic languages. The form of the word טְחוֹל ("spleen") shows its Hebrew-Canaanite origin. Since the Arabic cognate is *ṭiḥāl* and *ā* appears here as *ō*, as in Hebrew-Canaanite (a change which did not occur in A loanwords), the H origin of the word seems more or less to be certain. The root מסוק ("to harvest olives") is probably Hebrew since it has no cognate in the other Semitic languages. It was only by chance that these roots did not occur in the Bible, or maybe they were current in a different H dialect (regarding מסוק compare the biblical root נקוף with a similar meaning) but not in BH. In order to clarify the relationship between MH and BH, and especially A, the vocabulary of the former should be studied thoroughly on the basis of excellent manuscripts and according to different fields in semantics.

Loanwords. Persian. The Persian hegemony in Palestine lasted only 200 years and Persian consequently did not leave a strong mark. Administrative terms such as גִּזְבָּר ("treasurer"), already found in the Bible, occur, but not מַרְכּוֹל (the Palestinian form) – אמרכל (the Babylonian form) ("a high official"). The word וֶרֶד ("rose") seems to be Iranian. The fact that the word begins with ו (*waw*) points to its non-Hebrew origin (but see above Vocabulary (b)).

Akkadian. Most Akkadian words in MH were borrowed through an A intermediary. Some words, however, do not appear in A. The Akkadian-Sumerian אַפַּר ("meadow") is hardly found in the A dialects. On the other hand אֶמָּתַי ("when"), parallel to BH מָתַי, is found in several A dialects. Many Akkadian mercantile terms, such as, שְׁטָר ("writ"), גֵּט ("writ (of divorce)"), תַּגָּר ("merchant"), אָרִיס ("tenant farmer") from the Akkadian root *erēšu* ("to plough") have entered MH, as have terms from the material culture, such as, דַּף ("page") (of Sumerian origin). The root זוז ("to move") is also of Akkadian origin. It is possible that the meaning of לָקוֹחַ ("to purchase"), found mainly in MH, is an Akkadian calque (loan translation). That is apparently why when לָקוֹחַ ("to take") also acquired the new meaning "to purchase," the BH לָקַח אִשָּׁה ("to take a wife," i.e., "to marry") changed in LBH to נָשָׂא אִשָּׁה.

Greek. Many administrative, religious, mercantile, material culture (excluding agriculture), and even everyday words were borrowed from Greek. From the Greek word זוֹג ("yoke") a denominative verb was formed; similarly אֲוִיר (אויר?) ("air") and הֶדְיוֹט ("simple person") are Greek. There are mercantile terms: פִּינְקָס ("account book") and סיטון ("wholesale provision dealer"): household terms: קָתֶדְרָה ("chair with a back"), and פְּרוֹזְדוֹר (corrupted in the printed versions פְּרוֹזְדוֹר) ("vestibule"): administrative terms: סַנְהֶדְרִין (Greek "assembly"), and לְקַלֵּס ("to praise," mainly a king or a high official); urban terminology: מטרופולין ("city"), פלטין ("palace"), and לְמֵן (נמל in Babylonian sources of MH ("port")); food terms: כְּרוּב ("cabbage"). The expression יָפֶה (דָּרַשְׁתָּ) ("you have (well) explained") (in BH יָפֶה = beautiful) seems to be a calque, as is apparently הִשְׁלִים ("he did") (Lieberman).

Latin. The few Latin loanwords are from the administrative and military spheres, e.g., לִיבְלָר ("scribe"), לִגְיוֹן ‡ ("legion"), נוּמְרוֹן ("troop of soldiers") אסתרטה – סרטה ("street"), קָרוֹן ("wagon"), סַפְסָל ("bench"), and טַבְלָה ("table").

Other Languages. Assuming that the language of the Edomites who settled in Palestine was closer to Arabic than to H (there is, however, no proof of this), it may be hypothesized that the word שׁוֹבָךְ ("dovecote"), Arabic *šubbak* ("window"), was borrowed from Edomite. The Arabic *š* was taken into Hebrew without the linguistic change to שׂ. According to an opinion in the Talmud, the expression יוֹנֵי הוֹרדסיות (the second word appears in various forms) in the Mishnah means "doves of the king Herod," which (according to Josephus) he raised in his home. חוֹטֶם ("nose"), from a rare biblical root, brings to mind the nose ring (חָטָם) of the camel. This word may have come into Hebrew from the language of a people that still employed camels (from Edomite?); the assumption is, of course, purely speculative.

Influence of Aramaic. Unlike the above languages whose influence on MH was felt mainly in the vocabulary, A had a far-reaching impact and left its mark on all facets of the language, namely, orthography, phonetics and phonology, morphology including inflection, syntax, and vocabulary. There is room for investigation as to whether MH was a Hebrew-Aramaic mixed language. This question may be posed owing to the fact that A had a pervading influence in all spheres of the language, including inflection, which is generally considered to be impenetrable to foreign influence. It is possible, however, that because of the symbiosis of A and Hebrew-Canaanite the two exerted a mutual influence (see especially phonology).

Orthography. All of the peculiarities mentioned above as being in MH are found, more or less, in the Palestinian Aramaic dialects as well, especially Galilean and Christian-Palestinian Aramaic, and even in the eastern dialects.

Phonetics and Phonology. The fact that the consonantal phonemes (according to biblical A also the vocalic phonemes) are from a synchronic point of view identical in both languages – a phenomenon without parallel often even in different dialects of the same language – is noteworthy. There is reason to believe that this is due to Hebrew-Canaanite: from A inscriptions it is known that there were several phonemes in A which did not exist in Hebrew-Canaanite. Common to H and A are the double realization בג"ד כפ"ת (*b g d k p t*); the weakening of the gutturals to a greater or lesser extent in most of the A dialects; and common assimilation and dissimilation phenomena (with regard to ר (*reš*), especially in Galilean Aramaic).

Inflection. The independent personal pronoun אַתְּ ("you" masc.) and the possessive pronouns ־ָךְ, ־ִיךְ (see above Pronouns) are clear indications of A influence. With regard to the verb, the influence was weaker. The A root הוה appears maybe even with an A vocalization (see above). The loss of the *puʿʿal* is paralleled in A, whereas the *hopʿal* still exists as opposed to the A dialects where it disappeared (with the exception of the early dialects). The rare occurrence of the *ʾettapʿal*, the development of the *nitpaʿʿal*, and the rejection of forms such as תִּשְׁמְרוּן (see above conjugations) point to an anti-Aramaic trend. A influence was less felt in the noun patterns.

Tenses and Syntax. The tense system completely parallels that of Galilean Aramaic and is close to that of Christian-Palestinian and Samaritan Aramaic. It is also similar to that of Eastern Aramaic. The assumption that the whole tense system is influenced by A seems to be inescapable. Note, however, that biblical Aramaic and the old A inscriptions show that this system is not original with A. Even though there still is no real comprehensive study on the syntax of MH and the Western Aramaic dialects, there seems to be a far-reaching parallelism between them.

Vocabulary. It is clear that A influence is considerable in this category. Absolute proof is provided by loanwords having an A root consonant which differs diachronically from the Hebrew cognates (ד, ט, ע, ת), or by loanwords in which a difference arises because of the Hebrew Canaanite vowel shift $\bar{a} > \bar{o}$. Thus, for example, הִתְחַטֵּא ("to ingratiate"), אירַע ("to occur") < A ערע, Hebrew-Canaanite ערץ ‡ are all A; similarly, אֵילָא ("but") אם לא = אֶן לָא in BH, שָׁעָה ("hour"). Even in the numerals there are A elements, e.g., שְׁתוּת ("a sixth") and תּוֹמֶן ("an eighth"). As is well known also the numerals are most resistant to penetration of foreign elements.

In other cases the decision may be in favor of an A influence, e.g., אֶמְצַע ("middle"), מָמוֹן (?) ("money"), and many more. There is still no up-to-date work on this subject. All the studies published in this field are unreliable.

There are also many calques, such as, אָחַז = סָגַר ("he closed"). Similarly the fact that in MH כּוֹס ("goblet") is masculine and שָׂדֶה ("field") is feminine goes back to A influence.

Due to A influence there are occasionally in MH words which are archaic in the Bible (but in general such words disappeared from MH), e.g., עוֹנָה ("time"), – יְמוֹת ("days") as in the phrase יְמוֹת הַחַמָּה ("the sunny season").

A biblical word might change in form because of A influence, e.g., גֵּיא (בֶן) הִנֹּם in the Bible, but גֵּיהִנָּם ("Gehenna") in MH (with a different meaning). This is the traditional pronunciation in several Jewish communities.

DIALECTS OF MISHNAIC HEBREW

The early state of affairs as represented by the manuscripts will be discussed here and not the differences between the living traditions of the different Jewish communities (mainly the Yemenite, Sephardi, and Ashkenazi). It is certain that there were differences between the Babylonian and Palestinian traditions. It is even possible to assume that archaic forms which later changed in the Palestinian tradition occasionally remained in the Babylonian tradition. Consider the following example: according to the transcription of the New Testament it is known that the old form of רבי ("rabbi") was רַבִּי. This form was preserved in the Babylonian vocalization tradition, but in Palestinian manuscripts the vocalization is רְבִּי (רִבִּי) and even רַבִּי. Greek transcriptions from Palestine, and later transcriptions in Italy, prove that the first two forms are correct Palestinian forms. They were also preserved in the traditions of various communities. The form מוּעָט ("small part") is found mainly in Babylonian sources. The normal form מְמוּעָט is found mainly in Palestinian manuscripts (also מועט). However in the Dead Sea Scrolls the Babylonian form מועט occurs. A clear difference between Palestine and Babylonia is indicated by such forms as הוֹדָאָה ("thanks") (Babylonian) as opposed to הוֹדָיָה (Palestinian). Similarly גזלן (Babylonian) and גּוֹזְלָן (Palestinian).

It seems that even in Palestine there were dialectical differences and though the indications are few concerning the vocabulary, the evidence of the Talmud on certain points may be accepted. רְפָפוֹת ("shutters") were called by one *tanna* רְעָדוֹת. Besides this, it is difficult at the moment to find other differences, such as, the interchange א – ע (*ʿayin*) – (*alep*) attributed to the academy of Eliezer b. Jacob. The MH of the Bar Kokhba letters is slightly different from that which has been transmitted. של is not connected to the word following it. The *nomen rectum*, however, has the definite article (as opposed to the situation in the printed editions of MH texts). Instead of את, there is (as in Punic) ת, e.g., תכבלים = אֶת הַכְּבָלִים ("the chains") (perhaps this form will be discovered in good manuscripts). The word אזי ("then") found in these letters is not present in normal MH.

There seem to be traces of an H dialect which was not identical with BH. If this is not assumed, then it is difficult to explain the exclusive use of זו instead of זאת (*zō + t*) since there is no way of explaining the loss of the ת (*taw*). It is preferable to assume that זו came to predominate in MH from another H dialect in which this archaic form existed. (זו already occurs in the Bible.) The forms הָיָה ("she was") and קָנָה ("she bought") are even more to the point (see above weak verb). The regular biblical form הָיְתָה and קָנְתָה developed from קָנַת ‡ + *ā* which was taken over from the other verbal classes. It is impossible to understand how a retrogression would occur in MH; these forms are thus better explained as intrusions from a dialect in which the process קנת < קָנְתָה did not take place. (Survivals of the archaic form occur in the Bible and in the Siloam inscription.)

MISHNAIC HEBREW OF THE PALESTINIAN AMORAIM

This dialect has been studied on the basis of Vat. Ms. Ebr. 30 of Bereshit Rabbah. On the one hand it has been found to have a considerable mixture of BH and on the other to contain independent forms that are found in MH but not in tannaitic sources. (They occur in very few cases and must have been corruptions). Thus, זאת occurs as an adjective, e.g., הלבנה הזאת ("this moon"). The far deictic pronouns הַלָּה ("that") and הַלָּז ("that one") disappeared and were replaced by אוֹתוֹ ("him"), etc. These changes are to be regarded as internal H developments, though the last was perhaps influenced by A. The ending ת is sometimes found in the third person feminine perfect in verb classes other than ל"ה (A influence). In the imperfect first person singular, the first person plural form is sometimes employed (as in Galilean Aramaic). This usage is found only once in the Mishnah. As in BH the construct infinitive without -ל occurs, e.g., מִבּוֹא (מִן + בּוֹא). As opposed to MH the following differences should be noted: (1) internal H development; (2) admixture of BH; (3) increased A influence.

MISHNAIC HEBREW OF THE BABYLONIAN AMORAIM

This dialect has not yet been studied (see below). The word אשפה ("trash") as against אַשְׁפּוֹת (in the tannaitic Hebrew) may point to independent development.

[Eduard Yecheskel Kutscher]

Kutcher's description is still valid in its main features. However, since the 1970s research in MH has made considerable progress. While the description above is based on the Mishnah according to Ms. Kaufmann, in recent years other MSS of the Mishnah have been described, such as Paris, Parma 497, Deinard, Maimonides' Autograph, and Genizah fragments. Haneman's description of the verb system in Ms. Parma 138 can serve as a model for the "classic" MH verb system. Other tannaitic as well as amoraic sources were investigated, such as the Tosefta, Sifra, Palestinian and Babylonian Talmuds. Traditions contained in old sources and oral traditions were described, such as Yemen, Aleppo, Tunisia, Italy, early and late Ashkenazi traditions, the Karaite tradition, and others. The Babylonian Punctuation tradition is presented in detail in Yeivin's monumental work. Syntax is described according to Ms. Kaufmann of the Mishnah and there is a full description of the tense system.

In these descriptions many features were recognized to be typical of MH. The following are a few examples: It was proved that a doubling of ר was common in certain traditions of MH. The relative pronoun ש is vocalized with *sheva* in some circumstances, such as שְׁהוּא (these two phenomena are very rare in the Masoretic Vocalization of the Bible). Some conjugations of the verb (or modifications of old conjugations) were established: *nufʿal* as a variant of *nifʿal* in verbs I-y and I-n, e.g. נֻטַּל (instead of the common נִטַּל); *pŒ > el* and *nitpŒ > al* (instead of *paʿʿel* and *nitpaʿʿal*), e.g., מְזֻמָּן; *nitpaʿʿal* in participle can take the form נִתְפַּעֵל (instead of the common

מִתְפַּעֵל). For the meaning of the conjugations, it was claimed that the *hif'il* can serve for the same meaning as the *qal* (as it is claimed of the *pi''el*).

In the field of vocabulary, Moreshet's lexicon lists and discusses all the verbs in MH not found in the Bible. According to his findings, there are about 500 new verbs in MH, of which two-thirds can be attributed to Aramaic influence. In this field mention should also be made of the Historical Dictionary Project of the Academy of the Hebrew Language, which produced a full concordance of tannaitic and amoraic literature according to reliable MSS (of other periods). This concordance gives an accurate list of the vocabulary of MH and serves as a fundamental tool of research in this field.

The richness and variety revealed in so many reliable sources enabled Bar-Asher to sort and arrange MH sources according to two criteria (he deals exclusively with the Mishnah, but in fact his observations are valid for all tannaitic and amoraic sources): (1) Palestinian vs. Babylonian branches, e.g., while in Palestinian sources (such as Ms. Kaufmann of the Mishnah) we find the verb נתאלמנה, in Babylonian sources (such as quotations from the Mishnah in the Babylonian Talmud) the verb is נתארמלה. Although the last verb was probably borrowed from A, it is an ancient borrowing, as it occurs already in the Hebrew of the Dead Sea Scrolls. (2) Western vs. Eastern traditions, which differ mainly in the realization of written texts; e.g. while in the Western traditions a doubling of ר is almost nonexistent, it is quite common in the Eastern traditions of MH. Many of these differences seem to go back to ancient times and may have existed when MH was still a living tongue.

[Yochanan Breuer (2nd ed.)]

MEDIEVAL

INTRODUCTION
THE LANGUAGE OF PIYYUṬ
SAADIAH GAON
- Arabic Influence

SPANISH HEBREW POETRY
- Influence of Arabic on the Language of Secular Poetry

ORIGINAL PROSE WORKS AND TRANSLATIONS
- The Components of Arabic-Influenced Hebrew
  - LEXICON
  - NOUN MORPHOLOGY
  - VERB
  - SYNTAX

MAIMONIDES
ITALY
THE KARAITES
- Samaritans

PROVENCE AND NORTHERN FRANCE
ASHKENAZIC AND RABBINIC HEBREW
- The Influence of German on the Hebrew of the Jews of Ashkenaz and the Influence of Yiddish on Hebrew in Poland
- The Role of Mishnaic Hebrew in Ashkenazic Hebrew
- The Role of Biblical Hebrew
- The Role of Aramaic
- The Link With Arab-Influenced Hebrew
- Influence of Hebrew on Yiddish
- Haskalah and Medieval Hebrew

INTRODUCTION

After Hebrew as a spoken language was replaced by Aramaic, it became a written language whose history is from and for books alone. The principal sources for the writers were Biblical Hebrew and Mishnaic Hebrew and these met the needs of all forms of written expression: religious and secular poetry, letters, books on science, and philosophy.

Hebrew became a second language, existing side by side with the vernacular languages spoken by Jews wherever they happened to be. Such a duality was quite normal in the Middle Ages; spoken Arabic existed alongside classical Arabic, other languages were spoken where Latin was the literary medium. Although it became a written language, Hebrew did not remain petrified, limited to passages quoted in their original form and meaning, but lived "an active life" in written texts. New topics, whether in original writings or in translations, necessitated an expansion of the language, especially in the coining of new terms for concepts and subjects not found in the Bible, the Mishnah, or the Midrashim, e.g., philosophy, medicine, etc. Responsa which had to deal with everyday subjects, not found in earlier halakhic responsa, also led to linguistic innovation, especially in vocabulary. Since it was a written language, many new forms were invented for literary purposes: rhetorical language and stylistic embellishment, especially in poetry. It is difficult to evaluate the changes on linguistic grounds alone, particularly in poetry; the language was, as it were, raw material for stylistic variation.

In a living language which serves as a natural means of spoken communication, an innovation is any new form which carries a specific meaning (morphological-semantic innovation). Innovation of this kind occurred in the written language in books of science, especially as translations of new concepts which had previously been unknown to the Hebraic world and had no equivalents in Hebrew, e.g., *agron* (more correctly *egron*; "a dictionary"), *mahut* ("essence"). New meanings were added to existing words; this is a common feature of poetry as a means to enrich the language. In *piyyuṭ*, though not only there, use was made of the system of "alternate forms," whereby existing words could change their form – according to regular patterns of analogical formation, and also irregularly – without any change in meaning. These are morphological-stylistic changes, but not semantic. This technique is generally foreign to the spoken language where every form has its own specific meaning.

The linguistic changes of the written language, unlike those of the spoken tongue, do not take place of their own accord, through the operation of analogy, leveling, attraction, etc. They owe their existence to the needs of artistic and stylistic embellishment and are premeditated rather than spontaneous (as will be explained below). They include changes in frequency – rare words become common – sometimes because of the different frequency in the language of influence, sometimes because of a deliberate choice of words felt to beautify the language. Some innovations rose from a linguistic understanding of the processes of analogical word formation (הֶיקֵּשׁ) available in the language of their execution; others arose from the contact between written Hebrew and the spoken vernacular, or from the influence of a source language upon its Hebrew translation. A description of written Hebrew should include the different periods, places, and styles in which it was written. Each had its own attitude to the original sources; some were sparing in innovation, others rich in additions; some preserved words as they found them, others changed both form and meaning (whether intentionally or not). The different languages with which Hebrew came in contact must also be discussed: the Aramaic of the Midrashim and the Talmud which at the beginning of the period wielded its influence as a spoken vernacular and at the end of the period as a written language which stayed alive as the vehicle for study of the Babylonian Talmud (and to some extent of the Zohar); Arabic, from the period of the *ge'onim*; Middle High German which had considerable influence on the language of the Jews of Germany; there are even signs of French influence (e.g., in the language of Rashi) and Italian (a little in *Megillat Aḥima'aẓ*, 1504, and rather more in the language of *Immanuel of Rome). There is a strong connection between the form which written Hebrew took and the nature of the culture and society which supported it. The language of poetry in Spain flourished against the background of the Golden Age of Spanish culture, in imitation of the craft of Arabic poetry. The Midrashic folk language in Germany, unaffected by the rigors of syntax and grammatical rules, is well explained by the humble character of this Jewish community which was influenced by the liturgy and the *halakhah* of Ereẓ Israel, took hardly any interest in science and grammar, and lacked any social or cultural environment advanced enough to provide a model for literary creation.

The Hebrew language will be described mainly, but not solely, by reference to the language of prominent figures in the world of literature or Jewish intellectual life. An account will also be given of the link between the ideas of the grammarians and the writing of good Hebrew. Nothing will be said of the pronunciations of Hebrew (for phonological developments, see *Pronunciations of Hebrew).

THE LANGUAGE OF PIYYUṬ

The first revival of Hebrew after its extinction as a spoken vernacular was in the *piyyuṭ* in Ereẓ Israel, where there was a considerable return to written Hebrew, not only as a language from which to quote but as a linguistic activity aimed at increasing the vocabulary with newly derived nouns and verbs. The *piyyuṭim* were religious poems used as prayers in public worship. Some scholars have placed the beginning of liturgical poetry as early as the third or fourth century (J. Schirmann); others have put forward later dates. The generally accepted opinion is that they date from the fifth–sixth century, in Ereẓ Israel, and were written against a background of Midrashim and spoken Aramaic. The *piyyuṭim* are a blend of Biblical Hebrew, eminently suitable for ceremonial religious poetry of a national character, and Mishnaic Hebrew, without which it would have been impossible to give them the homiletic, midrashic content which is their main characteristic. Zunz seems to have been the first to name the *piyyuṭim* "Midrashim in the guise of poetry," and it is customary nowadays to emphasize that they are versified homilies (e.g., Mirsky). The linguistic blend is apparent not only in the choice of vocabulary but also in the grammar. The extensive revival of verbs in *binyan pu'al*, the co-occurrence of short and long tense forms, the use of the absolute infinitive and to a limited extent of the conversive *waw* are typical of Biblical Hebrew; the use of *binyan nitpa'al*, and complex infinitive forms like מלקטל, etc., derive from Mishnaic Hebrew.

The unique feature of the language of the *piyyuṭim*, however is not the blend of Biblical and Mishnaic Hebrew but its particular variety of linguistic innovation. Though the verse of the earliest known *payṭanim*, *Yose b. Yose and *Yannai, was not overcharged with difficult words in unusual declensions, the language of all the *payṭanim* was customarily referred to as *'aẓ qoẓeẓ* after the *piyyuṭ* read on Purim (a *qerobah to Parshat Zakhor* by Eleazar *Kallir):

אָץ קוֹצֵץ בֶּן קוֹצֵץ   קְצוּצַי לְקַצֵּץ
בְּדִבּוּר מְפוֹצֵץ   רְצוּצַי לְרַצֵּץ
לֵץ בְּבוֹא לְלוֹצֵץ   פְּלַץ וְנִתְלוֹצֵץ
כְּעָץ מְחַצְּצִים לְחַצֵּץ   כְּנֵץ עַל צִפּוֹר לְנַצֵּץ

The evil man, son of an evil man, ran
to cut down my persecuted ones;
With slander my broken ones to destroy;
The evil one when he came to do evil
was destroyed and the evil was done to him,
When he advised to shoot the shooters
like a hawk upon a bird to prey.

i.e., Haman, son of Hamdata, ran to cut down the Jews, to destroy them with slander. When the evil man came to do his evil deed he himself was destroyed and the evil was done to him; when he gave counsel that Israel be shot with arrows.

Many typical features of the *piyyuṭim* are indeed to be found in this poem: allusive phrases (קוֹצֵץ בֶּן קוֹצֵץ, also in the Midrash, מְחַצְּצִים), innovations in verb forms (פְּלַץ) and forms like כְּעָץ which has both עָץ for יָעַץ and כְּ before an inflected verb. The poem demands explication, not only linguistically but as a riddle, with its reminiscences of the Bible and the Midrashim, its brevity, and its wealth of allusive phrases. *Saadiah Gaon, whose language has much in common with the writings of the liturgical poets, was aware that the language of some of the *piyyuṭim* was faulty (see his introduction to the *Agron* (more correctly *Egron*) and his note to his *siddur*, p. 225). The main critic was Abraham *Ibn Ezra who described the language of Kallir as "a breached city, with no walls" (commentary to Eccles. 5:1) and said of the liturgical poets in general that "they do not know how to speak correctly, they strive to use hard words, and say תַּחַן instead of תְּחִנָּה" (in his book *Safah Berurah*). There were also many other harsh critics.

The following were the characteristic features of liturgical poetry:

(a) The method of creating verb forms; what has been called "one rule for all conjugations, defective and reduplicative." This was the most highly criticized feature (Zulai, *The Liturgical School of Poetry of Saadia Gaon*, p. 7, bibl.). Examples are עָשׂ for עָשָׂה (conjugating a ל"ה verb as though it were ע"ו), סָע for נָסַע (ע"ו for פ"נ), עָץ for יָעַץ (ע"ו for פ"י) and so on. However, this mixture is only found in the perfect. Forms like יָעוּשׁ (the imperfect of עוש if it were an ע"ו verb) and יָסוּעַ do not occur. Even in the perfect most of the forms can be explained simply as deletion of the first (סַע from נָסַע) or last (עָשׂ from עָשָׂה) letter; only a few isolated forms show a real conversion to a different conjugation, usually to ע"ו, in other forms of the perfect, e.g. חַזְתָּה, פַּצְתָּה. A more plausible approach, therefore, is to describe this method of conjugating verbs (which was not explained by the liturgical poets themselves) in the terms used by Saadiah Gaon in the second chapter of his *Sefer Ẓaḥot*, as deletion of the initial or final letter of a particular form, and not necessarily of the root consonants, by analogy with certain biblical forms: סָע after יִסַּע, עָשׂ after וַיַּעַשׂ and so on. The deletion of the *nun* is thus not conditioned by *šewa naḥ*, nor is the deletion of the *he* by the shortened imperfect form. Forms such as מַעַשׂ, תֶּחִי, and תַּאוּ can similarly be explained as deletion, by analogy with מַעַל־מַעְלָה in the Bible. With the recognition of the tri-consonantal basis of the Hebrew root (by *Ḥayyuj) such forms were strongly criticized by grammarians and poets in Spain, and this technique, much used by Saadiah Gaon, almost disappeared from secular poetry after the period of the *payṭanim*. (N.B. such forms as בָּט, פָּץ, etc. are not evidence that the weak roots were considered biconsonantal. Menahem and Dunash, who were unaware of the tri-consonantal nature of such conjugations, established the root שב for verb forms like שׁוּב, יָשַׁב and נָשַׁב, yet did not mix the conjugations in their writings, and derived the forms in accordance with biblical use. They never substituted קמית for קַמְתָּ for example).

(b) The liturgical poets created many new words by conjugating roots in all the *binyanim*; for them the *binyan* was part of the automatic inflectional system, like tense and person. The later poets of Spain saw the *binyan* as non-automatic, not subject to unrestricted analogical extension, confined to forms found in biblical Hebrew and mishnaic Hebrew. Not so the writers of the *piyyuṭim*. They derived many words from nouns: סִמְדֵּר (from סְמָדַר), זִלְעֵף (from זַלְעָפָה), הִבְטִין (from בֶּטֶן), and even from adverbs and particles: טֵרְמַנִי from טֶרֶם and לְבַלְעֵד from בִּלְעֲדֵי. They also incorporated derivational affixes and suffixes as root letters: לְהַתְשִׁיר from תְּשׁוּרָה by analogy with mishnaic לְהַתְרִים from תְּרוּמָה. This abundance of morphological variation is the hallmark of liturgical poetry, and has been vilified as bizarre by its critics. The grammarians and some of the poets in Spain rejected the alternate forms because they "changed the holy writ" (Dunash ben Labrat's reply to Saadiah Gaon, 95), stating "we shall read every word in the form in which we found it" (*ibid.*). Abraham Ibn Ezra declares: "a man must use a word in the form in which it is found" (*Moznayim*, 33). (A similar statement was made by Moses Ibn Ezra in *Širat Yisrael*, 148). Both Abraham and Moses Ibn Ezra criticized the use of given verbs in *binyanim* in which they did not occur in the Bible. Dunash denounced a change in noun forms but allowed the use of different *binyanim*. The early critics rejected these changes because they wanted to preserve biblical Hebrew; later critics deprecated poets who adopted different forms and made innovations which did not contribute to the sense of the poem.

Criticism of the language of *piyyuṭ* is intrinsically criticism of its style. Abraham Ibn Ezra mentions four flaws – two concerning the language and the other two content and poetic devices: the *piyyuṭ* is (1) influenced by a foreign tongue, i.e., the Aramaic of the Talmud; full of (2) grammatical errors; (3) riddles and fables obscure in meaning; and (4) homilies. In comparison to the prayers, the *piyyuṭ* is obscure in language and style and is unfit to be used in liturgy (Comm. Eccles. 5:1). Basically, however, the language of the *piyyut* is difficult because of its many allusions: עֲמוּסִים ("the encumbered") standing for "the Children of Israel," אֵיתָן ("the strong") for "Abraham," etc. Many of the forms, drawn from the Midrashim, were more difficult for the Jews of Spain than those of Ereẓ Israel who knew the Midrashim well. Graetz sharply criticized the *piyyuṭ*, while Samuel David Luzzatto explicitly defended Ha-Kallir: "not because of ignorance and duress did he write it so, but to embellish the style," (introd. to *Maḥzor Roma*, 1861), "Eleazar Kallir was not tongue-tied but for his wisdom and of his own will did he write it" (Letter to S.J. Rapaport, 1884). Zunz described the language of the *piyyuṭ* with great understanding and he knew that it was written for the taste of that generation (*Ha-Derašot be-Yisra'el*, pp. 184–5). In his opinion the plenitude of vocabulary serves as an ornament of style, and many forms are simply "nonce words," not meant to be established as part of the language (see bibl.).

The liturgical poets left nothing in writing which would inform us of their view of language and style, but it is clear that they regarded an active, prolific use of derivational inflections as one of the glories of the language. The wealth of forms is similar to the technique of listing synonyms (the liturgical poets liked to fill a line with a long list of synonyms or near-synonyms), the use of word play, and the use of a recurrent rhyme word. The invention of new forms which do not carry new meanings creates both a richness of sound and a degree of synonymy which are among the rhetorical techniques of liturgical poetry. For Bialik also, criticism of the literary value of the *piyyuṭim* is inseparable from criticism of their language: "the period of Ha Kallir and his disciples was a time of infatuation with liturgical poetry, which became more and more sentimental" (*Širatenu ha-Ẓeʿira*). He condemned the "makers of acrostics" and the "tasteless stammerers" whose language was "like the gravel (אבני חצץ) of *aẓ qoẓeẓ*."

(c) The letter *kap* (-כ standing for כַּאֲשֶׁר as well as -כ for כְּמוֹ) can be prefixed to an inflected verb: גֵּר צֶדֶק נִצַּחְתּוֹ כְּנֶחֱלַק לוֹ לַיְלָה "you made the righteous proselyte prevail at midnight" (Yannai in "*Wa-Yehi ba-Ḥaẓi ha-Laylah*"). So also כְּיֵלֵךְ, כְּדִבַּרְתָּ, כְּהָלְכוּ. This is a characteristic feature of liturgical poetry in Ereẓ Israel. Dunash regarded the prefixing of כ to verbs in the perfect tense as a rule of analogy from biblical practice (הֶהָלְכוּא, Josh. 10:24 – replies to Saadiah Gaon, 114). In his poem against *Menahem ibn Saruq he uses the form כְּשָׁקַט. Although Ibn Janaḥ permitted the use of *kap* before a perfect tense for reasons of scansion (to provide an iamb (Harikma 45–46)) it was not used in secular poetry in Spain, undoubtedly due to the influence of the grammarians. Saadiah Gaon used *kap* before perfect tenses, but in *Sefer Ẓaḥot*, written late in life, he denounced its usage. Examples of *kap* before perfect tenses are also to be found in the writings of Hai Gaon. However, in those communities which drew their inspiration from the Midrashim, the halakhah and the liturgical poetry of Ereẓ Israel, this linguistic feature continues to occur, and not only in acrostics. In *Megillat Aḥimaʿaẓ* (Italy, 1054) we find כְּבָאוּ, כְּשָׁמְעוּ, and in the German elegies and poems written about the horrors of the Crusades we find כְּהָלַךְ and כְּפָחֲזוּ.

From the Spanish period until the Enlightenment, the liturgical poets were charged with ignorance of grammar. It would be going too far to say that they had no understanding of language; their view of word creation is not in line with accepted grammar. A realization of the motives which led to such abundance of morphological-stylistic innovation can bring us closer to understanding the liturgical poet as a deliberate, if inartistic, manipulator of language. In recent years new light has been thrown on the language of the *piyyuṭim* as a linguistic and not merely a stylistic phenomenon. Study of Palestinian Aramaic and the language of Hebrew Midrashim written in Ereẓ Israel has revealed that the language of the *piyyuṭim* is based on "Palestinian idiom" (Zulai). Words thought to be arbitrary innovations invented by the liturgical poets have been shown to be rooted in the language of the Midrashim and the Targum. Yallon has pointed out words which passed from the Midrashim to the *piyyuṭim* (גהר meaning reproof, פנה meaning look, יאש meaning weak, לִבֵּב meaning shout, ברור meaning strong and existing, and others). Expressions from the Hebrew spoken in Ereẓ Israel survived in the *piyyuṭim*: קְפִידַת רוּחַ – severity – and זְרִיקַת תְּפִלּוֹת – prayer (noted by Zulai), or מוֹדַע for תְּעוּדָה document, and מַסְפֵּק – danger (Shalom Spiegel). S. Lieberman has also pointed out the affinity to midrashic language (see bibl.). The language of Ereẓ Israel can elucidate difficult passages in liturgical poetry, and makes it clear how the creation of the poets was natural and not artificial. A comprehensive description of the language of the *piyyuṭim* against the background of the languages of Palestine and the attitudes to grammar out of which it took shape would contribute greatly to a clearer understanding of this first important manifestation of written Hebrew.

SAADIAH GAON

It was Saadiah Gaon who brought about the great revival of Hebrew writing in Babylon. Actually, even before his time the use of Hebrew in writing had not been set aside completely. In Ereẓ Israel there had been liturgical poetry, Midrashim and collections of legal decisions, the best known, *Sefer ha-Maʿasim* ("The Book of Court Cases" or "Judgments"), was collected at the beginning of the geonic period.

After the period of Saadiah Gaon the Palestinian *geonim* continued to write a good Hebrew, and Ibn Janaḥ affirms that "the men of Tiberias excelled all others in the purity of their Hebrew." In the talmudic academy of Damascus, which took over from that of Ereẓ Israel, *halakhah* and metrical, rhymed prose were written in Hebrew (in the 11th century). The same kind of thing occurred in Babylon. In the Talmud short extracts from the *amoraim*, consisting of a presentation of the problem and a brief discussion, are written in Hebrew; detailed discussion in Aramaic comes later. At the end of the eighth century Pirkoi ben Baboi wrote chapters of *halakhah* in good Hebrew. The collections of halakhic decisions, *Halakhot Pesukot* of Yehudai Gaon and *Halakhot Gedolot* of Simeon Kayyara both contain sections in Hebrew. Needless to say they derive from Palestinian literature, but they do bear witness to the fact that even in Babylon, Hebrew had not given way completely to Aramaic, and was used for special purposes, e.g., for halakhic decisions. Several Aramaic books on *halakhah* were translated, or translated and edited in Hebrew, notably *Halakhot Re'u to Halakhot Pesukot* and the book *We-Hizhir* to the responsa of Aḥai of Shabḥa. Conventional opinion (Poznansky, Epstein, Assaf, and Ginzberg) holds that the translations were done in Ereẓ Israel, or at the very least in Greece and Italy, since Hebrew translation could only have been carried out where Babylonian Aramaic was unknown. Nevertheless, according to S. Abramson it is quite possible that they were written in Babylon when Aramaic had given way to Arabic. Therefore the *Halakhot Pesukot*, for instance, was translated into Arabic too. Linguistic features regarded as typically Palestinian – אָדָן for אָדָם, לוֹכַל as the infinitive of אכל – cannot therefore be taken as evidence of the place of composition; the translators in Babylon could well have considered language of Ereẓ Israel a fitting model for good Hebrew. If they were written in Babylon, it could not have been earlier than the time of Saadiah Gaon.

Saadiah Gaon introduced the writing of liturgical poetry in Hebrew into Babylon. He was followed by *Hai Gaon, whose language is generally simple, but very similar in its techniques of word creation, patterns, and usage to Saadiah's language. Saadiah Gaon brought a consciousness of the need for beauty to the writing of Hebrew. In the introduction to his dictionary, the *Agron*, he writes of Hebrew as a woman who had been slighted when the Children of Israel preferred the imperfect foreign tongues of exile to her own beauty of expression. The *Agron* was designed to fashion Hebrew into a proper instrument for the writing of poetry. It is commonly held that the language of Saadiah Gaon is a link in the chain connecting the language of the *piyyuṭim* and the language of Spanish Jewish poetry; this view is expressed primarily in "The Liturgical School of Poets of Saadiah Gaon" by Menahem Zulai. The language of Saadiah Gaon is far removed from the biblical purism of Spanish Jewish poetry, as we shall see. However, though it is true that it shares features with the language of the *piyyuṭim*, and continues this tradition, it also foreshadows in several ways the approach to language of the Spanish poets. Saadiah Gaon wrote *piyyuṭim* in Hebrew as well as polemical literature *Essa Meshali, Sefer ha-Galuy* and *halakhah* (*Sefer ha-Moʿadim*). He wrote an introduction to his *Agron*, his grammar of Hebrew (*Sefer Ẓaḥot*), philosophy (*Emunot ve-Deʿot*) and responsa in Arabic. It was he who initiated this duality in Jewish writing in the Middle Ages: Hebrew for poetry, and Arabic for prose, even for those who honored Hebrew, the mistress, more than Arabic, the serving maid (expression of Al-Ḥarizi in his book *Taḥkemoni* and Solomon ibn Gabirol in *Ha-ʿAnaq*).

It was Saadiah Gaon who introduced the concept of "pure" language – *zaḥot ha-lašon* – to Hebrew writings and grammar (on the basis of Isa. 32:4), thereby creating a Hebrew cognate of the Arabic *faṣāḥa* which is also etymologically related to the Arabic term *taṣḥīḥ*. "Pure" language for Saadiah Gaon is a linguistic ideal, beautiful, clear, and correct, with all forms derived according to proper rules of analogical formation, free from errors of irregular word formation. Analogy (הֶיקֵּשׁ) is permitted to operate according to biblical patterns which, in his opinion, were "fertile" but not according to infertile patterns. This view of purity of language matches the primary concept of *faṣāḥa*. Later, "purity" will be able to express various linguistic and stylistic qualitative features that affect poetic ornamentation and rhetorical figures (such as plays upon words and synonyms). According to Saadiah "purity" of language is not just the passive use of received vocabulary; it welcomes innovation, since it is linguistic activity that shows knowledge of the language and makes it beautiful. Thus Saadiah Gaon used Hebrew like the liturgical poets who preceded him. He created new verbs by using existing roots in all the *binyanim*, each with its special meaning, e.g., מַקְוֶה – giving hope, הַנְפִּישׁ gave rest (נֹפֶשׁ), לְהַחְדִּיל (from חָדַל) and so on. He formed verbs from nouns: הִתְהִים (from תְּהוֹם), הִמְעִין (from מָעוֹן).

In deverbal derivation Saadiah used the various nominal patterns which he regarded as nouns of action (infinitives), though not other noun-forms: לַעַט, טְפִיפָה, דִּרְשׁוֹן, שִׂטְמָה (hatred) these are the commonest types – and also מִדְבָּק (for דְּבִיקָה), מִגְלַעַת ("quarrel"), מַחֲמֹרֶת ("restriction" for חוּמְרָה). Like the liturgical poets he changed the form of extant words without changing the meaning, as he himself stated explicitly (with respect to word expansion and deletion in the second section of *Sefer Ẓaḥot*, and with respect to the variations in the form of nouns derived from verbs, see replies of Dunash, 122): *wa al-maʿnā wāḥid* "the meaning is one," i.e., the different forms are "equivalent in meaning," differing only in "articulation."

(a) He used expanded forms of words in accordance with techniques which he explained in his grammatical writings (he referred to expansion as *tafḵim*): סִדְסֵד for יָסַד, דּוֹתֵת (from דָּת), לְדוֹגֵג for לָדוּג, תִּלְתֵּל for תָּלָה, סתסת for סתת, אימימה for אימים ("horror"). Lengthened forms of the imperative and the imperfect like those of the infinitives are used without any implications of modality: יָבִיאָה, יוֹצִיאָה, יַעֲלֹזָה, לְנַשְּׂאָה.

(b) He omitted letters in various word forms, on the model of contractions found in the Bible: עָט, בָּט, פָּץ, סָע – shortened perfects; לְהַעַל – shortened infinitive; מַעַל for מַעֲלֶה – shortened present participle; תְּחִיָּה – תֶּחִי, חֵזֶה – חֵז, מַעֲשֶׂה – מַעַשׂ – shortened verbal nouns; and of course many shortened imperfects – תַּהַג, (תִּ)תְאוֹ – since this form does not carry any jussive meanings and can be used to form further shortened forms without any effect at all on the shade of meaning.

(c) He used alternative forms of words by analogy with doublets found in the Bible: עֲרִיס for עֲרִיסָה ("dough" like גָּלִיל – גְּלִילָה); כפור – כפורת, יסוד – יסודת (like יבוש – יְבֹשֶׁת); חֶפְצוֹן (from חֵפֶץ, like חרבון from חֹרב) and so on. The explanations given earlier for the word creation of the liturgical poets are made explicit in the writings of Saadiah Gaon. All these derived forms, he says, come easily to the language; they are mere changes in form which do not necessitate any special shade of meaning. In Saadiah Gaon's opinion, the principal source for Hebrew writing is the Bible, though he also made no small use of mishnaic Hebrew. Choice was dictated by the needs of style. He did not think of biblical Hebrew and mishnaic Hebrew as separate entities; the latter simply completed the documentation of the words in the former. Like the Arab grammarians of his time, he lacked any historical sense of earlier and later periods in the development of the language. He thought that all the words in the Bible were fit for use, including the rarest and oddest; further words could only be created by the operation of analogy on this vocabulary. He continued the tradition of the liturgical poets in his use of allusive phrases: בְּנֵי אֶלְעָד ("children of eternity") for the Children of Israel and פְּרִיזָה for the Temple and many others. Liturgical poetry was a source of literary inspiration for Saadiah Gaon in many ways: specific usages, nonce-words, allusive phrases, rhyme and alphabetical arrangement, and such words and expressions as גַּיְא, נֶשֶׁם, פֶּצָה, צָרָה ("valley," i.e., land), יָחִיד ("unique," i.e., Isaac), גַּבְנֹן ("peak," i.e., Mt. Sinai). Liturgical poetry was a source of style and thematic material, but not of linguistic innovation *per se*; he would not accept any new forms which did not satisfy his own linguistic principles. Such words, he thought, could be invented by anyone who knew the language and had the inclination. The main features he shares with the liturgical poets is his constant use of derivation without change of meaning. In the following respects he foreshadows the language of Jewish poetry in Spain

(1) There was a close relation between his linguistic inventiveness and his views on language; like the poets of Spain he remained faithful to the rules of grammar (though since his conception of the language was different, the results are also different).

(2) It was he who initiated the criticism of the language of the *piyyutim* (in the Arabic introduction of the *Agron*, and *Siddur* p. 225).

(3) Though he continued to use the techniques of the liturgical poets, he did so with reservations. He derived nouns according to the patterns of verbal nouns only, and placed restrictions of the freedom to create new words by analogy. (In Spain also, *vide infra*, innovations were more frequent with verbs than with nouns). Therefore like the Spanish poets he made considerable use of participles, active and passive, as adjectives (פּוֹתֵל – "crooked," כָּחוּד – "hidden").

(4) He used short and long tense forms freely, without any distinctive modal significance, and this lack of specific meaning facilitated morphological innovation by analogy. The Spanish poets did the same (*vide infra*).

(5) The rules of analogy are binding as far as the derivational inflections are concerned, but a word may have many different shades of meanings. Saadiah Gaon did not always use a word in the sense in which he translated it in his translation of the Bible. He translated תֶּבֶל as "punishment" (in Ar. *Dāhiya*) and then uses תַּבְלִית – by analogy with חֶרֶס – חַרְסִית (*Siddur Sa'adyah Ga'on* p. 198) – in the sense of "abomination." He translates אֲרֶשֶׁת שְׂפָתַיִם in Psalms 21:3, as "permission" (Ar. *isti'dhāna*) and explains this interpretation by reference to Ezra 3:7; in his poetry he uses אוֹרֵשׁ and רוֹשֶׁה as synonyms, with the meaning "say." The technique of allusive phrases also depends on the view of language that a word may have many meanings, all available for use.

(6) Saadiah Gaon had his own opinions as to which were the proper patterns for analogical word formation, and the frequency of a word had no relevance. A typically mishnaic word which occurs only once in the Bible is considered biblical. The Spanish poets took the same stand.

A conventional explanation of the language of liturgical poetry holds that it was not difficult for its audience, who were learned in the Midrashim. Saadiah Gaon certainly thought the *piyyuṭim* difficult to understand, and regretted that most people had a scanty knowledge of the language. He thought that people liked *piyyuṭim* even though they did not understand them (*Siddur Sa'adyah Ga'on* p. 156). Prayers and entreaties (בַּקָּשׁוֹת), by which a man might draw near to his Creator, were written by Saadiah Gaon in language devoid of allusions and morphological innovations, lest the language mar the prayers and therefore were praised by Abraham Ibn Ezra (commentary to Eccles. 5.1.). True innovations are scarce in the language of Saadiah Gaon, and occur not in his poetry but when he needs to coin technical terms; for these, like the Spanish writers (*infra*) he uses the method of loan-translation. He borrows both the concept and the way of expressing it: אגרון (lit., "hoard") for dictionary, a loan-translation of the Arabic *ğamhara*, (a verbal noun). There are other synonyms for dictionary in Arabic from the roots *ğml*, *ğm*ʿ and *'iḥatawā*, all meaning "hoard" or "collect" יסוד, from Ar. *'aṣl* (root).

Arabic Influence

The influence of Arabic is more strongly felt in his views on language than in his actual grammatical innovations. His grammatical theory is strongly influenced by the opinions of Arab grammarians on analogy, e.g., in his abundant use of the קֶטֶל pattern (as most fertile *fiʿl*, *faʿl*, and *fuʿl* in Arabic) in not differentiating between what would now be called the infinitive (קְטוֹל) and the verbal noun (קְטִילָה). There are very few Arabicisms in his language, even fewer than in the poetry of Spain (*infra*): צרחת בה – the root צרח is common in liturgical poetry, but the meaning "declare" and the use of the preposition ב are from Arabic עֵץ נִגְדַּעַת (in *Tešubot ʿal-Ḥiwwi* 4) where for reasons of rhyme the word עֵץ ("tree") is construed as feminine, as in Arabic. In his translation into Arabic he preferred words which were alike in sound to the Hebrew, and sometimes did the same in his own writing. In the introduction to the *Agron* he uses the expression חוֹדֶרֶת for "woman," from the expression יוֹשֶׁבֶת פְּנִימָה בַּחֲדָרִים. This is close to נָוָה which means "wife" in the writings of Saadiah Gaon and is etymologically similar to the Arabic *al-Mukdara* (girl kept indoors).

SPANISH HEBREW POETRY

Spanish Jewry followed the spiritual center that was in Babylonia as far as the *halakhah* was concerned; however in literary writing an important innovation took place there in comparison to both Ereẓ Israel and Babylonia. The duality – Hebrew for poetry and Arabic for prose – which started with Saadiah Gaon was fulfilled to a large extent in the literary activity of the Jews of Spain. Arabic replaced Aramaic as the vehicle for non-poetic expression (mainly *halakhah*) and became the language for prose writing (grammar, medicine, philosophy, exegesis, etc.) although there were still scientific books written in Hebrew (see below). Hebrew was used for poetry although some secular poetry was written in Arabic and Aramaic.

The Hebrew of poetry in Spain underwent a fundamental change when secular poetry became a separate and respectable literary genre. The beginnings of secular poetry are to be found in the polemic writings of Saadiah Gaon (which are the forerunners of poems of personal quarrels and denigration) and secular poetry became an accepted art – important and widespread in Spain – starting with the wine and war poems of Samuel ha-Nagid (d. 1055).

The earliest liturgical poets in Spain (especially Isaac ibn Ghayyat, Ibn Abitur, and Ibn Khalfon) drew their linguistic and stylistic inspiration from the *piyyutim*; they wrote mainly sacred poetry, in the same style and language as other liturgical poets, uninfluenced by the Arabs as the Arabs had no religious poetry. But secular poetry, a personal art (unlike religious poetry which was designed for public worship), was the product of Arab culture, and took shape in the image of Arabic poetry with which it competed by imitation. Liturgical poetry could not provide suitable vehicles for the writing of secular poetry. Linguistic change actually crystallized in secular poetry, under the influence of Arabic; iambic meter was taken over, and there is a close tie between the meter and the formation of words and verbal conjugations. In religious poetry it was used only sparingly; *Keter Malkut* by Solomon ibn Gabriol, for example, is written in one of the meters of liturgical poetry, with a fixed number of syllables per line. The move towards biblical purism, as understood by the poets of the Middle Ages, began in secular poetry.

The choice of Hebrew for poetry and Arabic for prose is closely interlinked with the move towards a biblical Hebrew. The writing of secular poetry in Hebrew was supported by the continued writing of religious poetry in Hebrew (which there was no cause to write in Arabic). The linguistic duality had its counterparts in the surrounding culture: old Spanish for speech and Latin for writing in Christian Spain, Andalusian Arabic for speech and the Classical Arabic of the Koran for poetry in Muslim Spain. The Jewish poet would rather make a careful, diligent, accurate study of the language of the Bible than learn how to write the language of the Koran. He had to choose between two languages which both required considerable study. (Prose was written in Middle Arabic, which did not need special study.) Perhaps, however, the fact that it suited his background is of little account compared with the national and religious feeling that biblical Hebrew had a special status, was a "superior language," a "very choice tongue" (Solomon ibn Gabirol in *Sefer ha ʿAnaq*) and "a wondrous language" the best of all the languages, and of course richer and more beautiful than Arabic (Al-Ḥarizi in the first chapter of *Taḥkemoni*). See also the speech of the companion in Judah Halevi's *Sefer ha-Kuzari*, Part 2, 68.

Biblical Hebrew was extolled as a "pure" language by no means inferior and indeed superior to the "pure Arabic" which was used for poetry. It was eminently suitable for the writing of verse comparable with Arabic verse, since it had similar virtues: (a) The similes, metaphors, and other figures of speech in the Bible were well suited to poetic style. In the last chapters of his book *Širat Yisraʾel*, Moses Ibn Ezra quotes examples from the Bible for every one of the rhetorical figures used in Arabic poetry. (b) The tradition of a fixed vocalization could serve as a basis for the iambic measures introduced from Arabic poetry. (c) The study of the grammar of biblical Hebrew was highly developed in the Middle Ages; there were few references to features of mishnaic Hebrew and the Hebrew of the period in grammar books. Arabic poetic language was also subjected to perpetual scrutiny by Arab scholars. (d) Biblical commentary added to the vocabulary a wealth of meanings and shades of meaning which were essential to a richness for poetic expression.

The introduction of a wide range of subjects – passion and wine, war, dispute, lampoon and jest, elegy, panegyric and self-aggrandizement, love, friendship and marriage – was accompanied by the use of iambic meters. Instead of every line containing a fixed number of syllables, there was a regular alternation of full vowels and *šewa naʿ*, i.e., reduced vowels. Dunash ben Labrat is usually considered the first to introduce iambic meters into Hebrew poetry. He used "well-scanned newly invented distinguished metrically constrained poetic forms" (Replies of Dunash to Menahem 4, 19). And this view is confirmed by the accusations leveled against Dunash by the disciples of Menahem, that he abused the forms of the language: "our holy tongue destroyed and left it null and void, because he had employed a foreign measure" (Replies of the disciples of Menahem 7, 44.) Menahem's disciples themselves phrased their replies in iambic measures, to show that their condemnation did not stem from poetic incompetence. The iamb was soon accepted by all poets as the proper measure for secular poetry. In the beginning it was difficult to adjust to the new meter; Al-Ḥarizi said of the language of the period when the iamb was first introduced that "the writers of the time wrote bad measures." It was the meter which usually determined the choice of words: שֶׁ or אֲשֶׁר, אָז or, אֲזַי, אֲנִי or אָנֹכִי, depending on the needs of the rhythm. Sometimes it even led to a change in the basic form of the word (e.g., קְרָב, with a *šewa*, for קֶרֶב); Ibn Janaḥ realized that the exigencies of meter could open the way to deviations from proper inflection (*Ha-Riqma*, 226–7). Many long and short tense forms were chosen to fit the meter (imperfect forms ending in וּן, e.g., יְרִיבוּן for יָרִיבוּ, were very useful) and rare words became common because they could provide iambs. לְמַעַן (from Neh. 6:13) or בְּיַעַן (which occurs only once in the Bible, in the combination יַעַן בְּיַעַן) were regularly used in place of יַעַן. The letter *he* with a *šewa* at the beginning of a word for emphasis (הֲכִי, "indeed"; הֲלִי, "indeed to me") fitted the meter and was grammatically acceptable (Ibn Janaḥ, *Ha-Riqma*, 68: "*he* to establish or verify a fact").

"Pure" language is, above all, grammatically accurate, and Spanish Hebrew poetry, especially secular poetry, is characterized by the poet's strict adherence to the rules of grammar (an approach which, as has been pointed out above, begins with Saadiah Gaon). In his *Sefer ha-Riqma* Ibn Janaḥ notes linguistic usages of the poets and affirms that a poet should not be blamed for linguistic deviations necessitated by the requirements of poetic forms (pp. 226–7 and p. 275); it even happened that poems were corrected by their readers according to the rules of grammar (*Ha-Riqma*, p. 275). In his book *Širat Yisraʾel*, Moses Ibn Ezra teaches the art of writing poetry. Matters of grammar, which "add salt to the food," are explained first, before any discussion of decorative figures, and the poet is told which grammar books are worthy of study before he is referred to any books on prosody (p. 100). Poets who "did not follow the grammarians" are condemned (p. 65) see also Al-Ḥarizi in *Taḥkemoni* ch. 18). The ideal form of poetic language is given full expression in *Širat Yisraʾel* from which the above are quotations. Essentially it is a matter of adherence to all the rules of the grammar of biblical Hebrew, with no innovations in form due to analogy, since "the language must be imitated, but without creating new words" (147). Verbs must not be used except in the *binyanim* in which they occur in the Bible (148). The given form of a word must not be changed. Care must be taken not to turn masculine into feminine or singular into plural, or vice versa. However, according to his system it is permissible to create new forms in the infinitive, קטול (149), and it follows from the general trend of his remarks (though he does not say so explicitly) that a verb could be inflected in all the forms of the given *binyan*: short and long tense forms, and *hip̄ʿil* on the model of יָהֵכִין, which was convenient for iambic meter. The ban on analogical word formation is a reaction against the copious use of such forms by the liturgical poets. (A similar opinion to Moses Ibn Ezra's can be seen in Abraham Ibn Ezra's *Ẓaḥut*, 26, with reference to the ban on analogy for nouns, by contrast with verbs and in the replies of Dunash to Saadiah Gaon, no. 95). However, there was not a single poet who abstained completely from morphological innovation, and even Moses Ibn Ezra allowed himself a few new forms, as he himself admitted (p. 156–7). In his opinion, his language was tainted with error because of human weakness, and lack of skill in his early poetry.

Moses Ibn Ezra's deviation into analogy are few: תְּבוּנָיו (the Bible has the form תְּבוּנוֹת), עֲלוּמוֹתַי (for עֲלוּמַי), מִגְדָּנַי (for מִגְדְּנוֹתַי), מַעֲצָב (for מַעֲצֵבָה or עֶצֶב in the Bible), and גַּחַל ,אַהַב singular forms derived from גֶּחָלֵי ,אֲהָבִים – though incorrectly since the correct singular forms occurring in the Bible are גַּחֶלֶת and אַהֲבָה. Moses Ibn Ezra's purity – *ẓaḥot* – of biblical language and abstention from morphological innovation are maintained to a fairly similar extent by Judah Halevi and Abraham Ibn Ezra. However in their work there are also exceptions, giving every secular poem a flavor of liturgical language. A further feature the secular lyrics share with the *piyyuṭim* is the use of allusive phrases: יְחִידָה (unique) for soul, צִיר (messenger) for Moses, יְקוּתִיאֵל for Moses, and so on. Considerable use of word derivation is made by Samuel ha-Nagid, who wrote when the language of Spanish poetry was just beginning to take shape (שְׁבָרָה חֲרִיזָה, אקדחה (גֶּוַע אקדח) ("hope"), and innovations in the *binyanim*. Indeed in his own time he was censured for his use of analogical word formation, especially in the creation of nouns (*Širat Yisrael*, 67). Solomon ibn Gabirol also has many new forms not found in the Bible (David Yellin counted 1,500), and though most are found in his sacred works, there are some in his secular poetry: חֶפְשׁוֹן בְּהִיקָה, תַּחַן, etc. The most serious offense in the eyes of Moses Ibn Ezra was the creation of verbs and adjectives from nouns; no wonder he criticized Solomon ibn Gabirol for such forms as מִשְׁהָמָה ,מְיֻשָּׁפָה and פְּנִינְיָה (*Širat Yisraʾel* 151).

Most violations of the ban on analogy are to be found in the *binyanim*; it is more difficult to avoid using verbs in active and passive conjugations than to refrain from inventing new noun forms. The use of passive conjugations – *puʿal* and *hop̄ʿal* – is particularly common in the language of poetry, partly under the influence of Arabic. Various forms of verbal nouns were fashioned – חֶפְצוֹן, גֶּוַע, בְּהִיקָה, – and many participles, active and passive, since this was the only way of creating adjectives (none of the adjectival patterns were productive). Singular forms were derived from plurals to a degree exceeding the limits prescribed by Moses Ibn Ezra (Al-Ḥarizi has סַנְוֵר from סַנְוֵרִים, and Ibn Ezra has פָּלִיל from פְּלִילִים used in the sense of "judge"). Even more frequent are plurals for singular: אַחְלָמוֹת ,לְשָׁמִים ,נְרָדִים and רְפָשִׁים (plural forms are much used in rhyming). Nevertheless, fundamentally and in comparison to liturgical poetry and to poetry of Saadiah Gaon on the one hand and to Hebrew prose literature on the other, secular poetry should be regarded as faithful to the given forms of biblical vocabulary. Innovations of language are of course far commoner in religious poetry. Certain of the techniques found in the *piyyuṭim*, anathema to those believers in "pure" language who hearkened to the grammarians, do occur in religious poetry: כְּ plus perfect tense (in Ibn Khalfon and quite frequently in Solomon ibn *Gabirol) and the use of "shortened perfects" such as עָט (for עָטָה) and סָט (for סָטָה) in Solomon ibn Gabirol.

Moses Ibn Ezra believed that analogical innovation marred the purity of biblical Hebrew, but sparing use of mishnaic Hebrew did no harm: "If we avail ourselves sometimes of the language of the Mishnah, this is acceptable, since its words are pure Hebrew" (p. 59). The language of secular poetry, unlike sacred poetry is free of forms typical of the *piyyuṭim*. Not only literary motives and content-words from the Mishnah are used, אִסּוּר ,תְּנַאי מִדְרָשׁ etc., – but also form-words such as צָרִיךְ, פְּרַט לְ- ,כָּאן. The word כְּאִלּוּ is popular, and the structure לִקְטֹל + מ (*yaday kebedim mi-lesapper* – Judah Halevi) is quite common. *Binyan nitpaʿal* appears sporadically (Abraham Ibn Ezra *niṭrapeʾta*), and not because of acrostic composition; Moses Ibn Ezra writes יִשְׁתַּבַּח in place of the biblical יְהֻלַּל. Samuel Ha-Nagid, a great talmudic scholar, especially introduced Mishnaic-Hebrew usage. At the end of the period, from the 13th century onwards, the adherence to biblical Hebrew weakened; Meshullam di Farra, for example, has more usages from the Midrash and even from the languages of his time, סְפִירָה from the kabbalists, בַּהֲמִי, etc. It should be recalled that it was not frequency and provenance of a word which determined its value. Not merely were rare words acceptable in poetry, but a word that occurred only once or twice in the Bible and regularly in the Mishnah was nevertheless regarded as biblical; it was used as commonly as a biblical word, and not sparingly like the mishnaic vocabulary. The alternation between שֶׁ and אֲשֶׁר is thus between two biblical words, and words of the קְטִילָה pattern (very common in the poetry of Samuel ha-Nagid for example), though regarded by present-day linguistic research as typically mishnaic, are treated as biblical on the strength of חֲנִינָה ,אֲכִילָה, and other biblical examples.

Despite the restraints on analogy, there were ways of diversifying the vocabulary; any *binyan* could be used in the long forms (לְכַפְּרָה ,יְרִיבוּן) and in the short forms (תְּשׁוּ ,יִתְעַל) in exact conformity with the conventions for adding or subtracting letters found in the Bible. In consequence, and by contrast with the language of liturgical poetry, forms like עָט for עָטָה and מַחַן for מַחֲנֶה are scarcely found in Spanish poetry. The free use of lengthened and contracted imperfect forms, which are useful for rhyming and scansion, derives from the writer's belief that such changes of form, unlike changes of *binyan*, had no effect upon the meaning. Medieval grammarians did not interpret the lengthened imperfect as cohortative, or the shortened imperfect as jussive (see Ibn Janaḥ, *Ha-Riqma* p. 96). Hence the license to use such forms freely accorded with the grammatical theory of the period. And there was similar freedom to meet the stylistic demands of poetry by using the *waw* conversive, pausal forms, possessive suffixes on the model of מְנוּחָיְכִי ,עָלֵימוֹ, and the imperfect *hipʿil* forms like יַהְכִין ,יַהְפְרִיד (even Moses Ibn Ezra, though not to excess). The restrictions on analogy reduced the abundance of forms, but the language of secular poetry is rich in means of expression, since the poets gave the biblical vocabulary a wealth of meanings. The formal, grammatical features of a biblical word were binding, but not the semantic. (Once the tri-consonantal form of the root was fully established, changes in the interpretation of a word – as revealed by the dictionaries – exceed changes in the formal analysis of root and declension – as revealed in the grammar books.) Abraham Ibn Ezra and Moses Ibn Ezra, for example, insisted on the correct use of a word, in accordance with its meaning in context, and were aware that a word might have different meanings, related and quite unrelated.

The poets were well aware that a particular word had been interpreted in different ways by the lexicographers, the commentators, and the translators, and this enabled them to choose whichever meanings they required for their poetry. They used duality of meaning to rhyme a word with itself, (צמוד שָׁלֵם). *Al-Ḥarizi does this in *Ha-ʿAnaq* and Moses Ibn Ezra in his poem *Ha-ʿAnaq*, also known as *Taršish*. The latter rhymes אֵיד ("misfortune") with אֵד ("mist"), and צִיר ("pain") with צִיר ("messenger") and צִיר ("door"). Judah Halevi writes דְּלָקוּנִי אֲהָבֶיךָ וְאַחֲרֶיךָ דָּלַקְתִּי ("my love inflamed me and I pursued thee"), using דלק in two different senses. אַגְמוֹן (Isa. 9:30) is used by Al-Ḥarizi with the meaning "fortress" (as interpreted by *Ibn Janaḥ) and by Samuel ha-Nagid with the meaning "branch" (as translated by Saadiah Gaon). Many words may be interpreted with the aid of the medieval dictionaries, and these interpretations are supported by the biblical commentators and the translators. Moses Ibn Ezra combines שִׁוָּה ("placed") with שִׁוָּה ("straightened") and שִׁוָּה ("lied-deceived"), in accordance with Ibn Janaḥ's interpretation of the word *yešawwe* in Hosea 10:1 as "will lie." For Solomon ibn Gabirol *qol ha-tor* is "the voice of salvation," as in the translation of Targum Jonathan. Moses Ibn Ezra, Samuel ha-Nagid, Al-Ḥarizi and others used the word אֲשִׁישָׁה with the meaning "chalice," an interpretation given to this biblical word by a few commentators. Moreover, the poets could add meanings at their own discretion, as their poetic talents dictated. Since the range of meanings was quite open, the influence of Arabic on poetic language, though on the whole restricted, was felt mainly in the meanings of existing words and not in the creation of new ones.

Influence of Arabic on the Language of Secular Poetry

Whereas the Hebrew of scientific works was deeply influenced by Arabic, the language of poetry was not greatly affected by Arabic other than in the meanings of words and the frequency of rare words. Some words took over the functions of their Arabic cognates but, in addition to the Arabic usage, a source could usually be found for this new meaning in the Bible, sanction was given by the grammarians, and further incentive for the use was provided by the demands of scansion: לְ is used to mean "because," as in Arabic, and as found by Ibn Janaḥ in the Bible (*Ha-Riqma* 55:13), וְאִם to mean "nevertheless," ostensibly like the Arabic *wa'in* but actually found in the Bible (Num. 36:4; Jer. 5:4).

The process of loan-translation, which so enriched the technical vocabulary of Hebrew in the Middle Ages was restricted in poetic language to literary symbols (in literature these are similar to technical terms): עֹפֶר ("doe"), צְבִי ("deer") for "beloved" – *ǧazal* in Arabic; זמן ("time"), *yamim* ("days") for "hostile fate" – *dahr, zamān* in Arabic; *gan* ("garden") for "paradise," Arabic *ǧanna; perud* for "a parting of lovers" – Arabic *tafriqa*, contrasting with *perida*, which expressed the separation of death; מוּסָר *musar* ("right conduct") for "erudition" – Arabic *adāb* (as in Saadiah Gaon's translation to Prov. 1:2); the expression *aḥi musar* derives from Arabic, and means "a learned man." *Midbar* ("desert") for "graveyard," and a few other expressions are reminiscences of similar Hebrew figures of speech to be found in the Bible or the Midrashim. Sometimes a word acquires a new meaning from the range of meanings carried by its Arabic cognate; even in these cases there is usually a biblical source, with Arabic influencing the preference for a particular usage and turning rare expressions into common ones: שָׁב meaning "became" (Ar. *ʿāda*) – וְשָׁבָה הָאַהֲבָה אֵיבָה ("and love turned to hate"; Al-Ḥarizi). The source of this usage is Isaiah 29:17. עַד for "even" (Ar. *ḥattā*) הֶבְגְּדוּ בִי עֲדֵי אָבִי וְאִמִּי "they betrayed me, even my father and my mother" – Moses Ibn Ezra, with authority for the usage in Judg. 4:16; מַעֲנֶה for "meaning" (Ar. *maʿnā* as in the Targum version of Prov. 1:1); עַם for "people" (Ar. *qawm*) – as in Judges 9:36 – אהב for "want" (Ar. *ahabba*).

Words acquire the meaning of their phonetic (and sometimes etymological) counterparts, even when there is basically no identity of meaning. אֲבָל, in addition to its usual meaning of "but," often signifies "and even more," as Ar. *bal* and authority can be found in Genesis 17:19. The usual synonym for אֲבָל, i.e., אולם also acquired the same meaning: כּוֹכָבָיו צִצִּים וְאוּלָם בִּסְתָיו פָּרְחוּ "his stars were flowers, moreover, in winter they bloomed" (Solomon ibn Gabirol). פֶּלֶךְ is regularly used to mean "the wheel of heaven" (Ar. *falak*), גִּיל is "generation" (Ar. *gˇil*), יעד means "promise" (Ar. *waʿda*), שָׁם means "afterward" (Ar. *thumma*). שׁוֹעֵר for Shem Tov *Falaquera means מְשׁוֹרֵר ("poet"; Ar. *šaʿir*), not the usual medieval interpretations for שׁוֹעֵר in the Bible. יָרֵחַ בְּהִלּוֹ (Al-Ḥarizi) is "a new moon" – Arabic *hilāl. Iggeret haqura* (Samuel ha-Nagid) is a "despised letter" – Arabic *haqira*. Whereas דְּפוֹק means "hasten" in the poetry of Khalfon, in the language of Samuel ha-Nagid and Judah Halevi the root דפק means "flow" (At. *dafaqa*) and is used as in Arabic figures of speech to describe the flow of tears. חֵשֶׁק is frequently used as love due to its similarity to Arabic *ʿašaqa*; נַעֲמָה is "an ostrich" (Arab. *naʿāma*), מְמוּלָּח is "beautiful" (Ar. *maliḥ*), and רָכַב אֳנִיּוֹת ("traveled on a ship") is also coined after an Arabic expression and הֵנָּה for "here" (Ar. *hunā*).

In translations the prepositions which follow a verb are much influenced by the source language, especially if it is a spoken tongue (see below on the language of the translations).

In the "pure" Hebrew of secular poetry, however, the prescriptions of the grammarians were preserved and the usage of the Bible was followed for most prepositions. Arabic influence explains נָטָה בִּי for "moved me" (Judah Halevi), נָסַע בְּ- for "transported," עָבַר בְּ- "transferred" (Moses Ibn Ezra); in Biblical Hebrew, however, one can find quite similar usages (יָצָא בְּמָחוֹל, נִבָּא בִּדְבָרִים). Solomon ibn Gabirol wrote וָאֶתְמַהּ מִשְּׁלֹמֹה for "surprised at," apparently as in Arabic *taʿağaba min* and was criticized for it by Moses Ibn Ezra (*Širat Yisrael* 154). There are also characteristic features of poetic language which have no clear links with Arabic: טוּר for "a line of poetry," תֵּבֵל for "the world below," פֶּגֶר for "a body," not a corpse. Features of medieval Hebrew which are common in the language of medieval translations are found only sparingly in poetry: nouns ending in -וּת which were regularly masculine in prose, are treated on a few occasions as masculine in poetry: דְּמוּת נִמְשָׁל (Judah Halevi) הָיָה פְּתַיּוּת (Al-Ḥarizi) לְבָבוֹת גְּדוֹלוֹת (Al-Ḥarizi) – this phenomenon is explained below in the section on the translations.

ORIGINAL PROSE WORKS AND TRANSLATIONS

Those poets who disparaged the writers of Arabic as "guarding the vineyards of others" themselves wrote scientific works in Arabic – on philosophy, *halakhah*, science, poetics, geography, etc. They include Saadiah Gaon, Ibn Gabirol, Judah Halevi, Moses Ibn Ezra and Al-Ḥarizi. Ḥayyuj, Ibn Janaḥ and others even wrote studies of Hebrew grammar in Arabic.

Just as various factors combined to produce a secular poetry in Hebrew, and in biblical Hebrew at that, so the writing of prose and the kind of Hebrew used for translations and original works were interconnected. The Arabs wrote prose in Middle Arabic, with none of the ideal "purity" of the language of the Koran reserved for poetry. And the Jews knew how to write this kind of Arabic (by contrast with the language of the Koran, which required special study). For prose writings they had hardly any linguistic tools to hand, unlike the language of sacred verse which provided a beginning for the writing of secular verse. There was the mishnaic tradition of prose writings on *halakhah* but Arabic had taken over the function of talmudic Aramaic, and was judged appropriate for writings on *halakhah*, especially where everyday matters were concerned. Since there was no need to set up a form of Hebrew which should rival the unrhymed Arabic of scientific writings in beauty they could write either in Arabic or in a different Hebrew from that of poetry, with no obligation to observe the rules of "purity" described above. The proportion of mishnaic Hebrew and biblical Hebrew varies from writer to writer. Abraham Ibn Ezra and Abraham b. Ḥiyya (d. c. 1136) both wrote original Hebrew. The former – a grammarian, poet, and biblical commentator – tended to write a biblical Hebrew and preferred forms like לֹא רַק to אַף כִּי, אֵין...אֶלָּא to כָּל שֶׁכֵּן and so on; the latter used many talmudic expressions: אַגַּב גְּרָרָא, לְהַלָּן, סְפֵקָא, כְּדַאי. The language of prose is mixed, though the writers could write a more biblical Hebrew close to the style of the *maqāma*, when they chose to, and this applies not only to the poetry of the translators – Abraham Ibn Ezra, Al-Ḥarizi, Ibn Ḥasdai but to passages of rhymed prose interspersed among the testamentary injunctions of Judah ibn *Tibbon to his son or in the letters of Abraham son of Maimonides etc. In his introduction to the translation of *Ḥoḇot ha-Leḇaḇot* ("Duties of the Hearts") Judah ibn Tibbon explains that he used biblical or mishnaic Hebrew, "whichever seemed closer, and as occurred to me at the time of translation." (It was, for example, convenient for him to translate *min ḥaythu* by the biblical word בַּאֲשֶׁר which is close to it, but the expression *lā illā* becomes mishnaic לֹא אֶלָּא.) In its syntax the language of prose is close to mishnaic Hebrew – there are no conversions of tense, no long or short verb forms – but the repertoire of conjunctions is considerably mixed (אַף עַל פִּי שֶׁ-, לְפִי שֶׁ-, כֵּיוָן שֶׁ-, טֶרֶם, לְמַעַן, יַעַן, etc.).

The language of the hundreds of translations carried out from the 11th to the 15th century, and the language of original works written in Hebrew in the style of the translations (e.g., the works of Albo, Crescas, and Levi b. Gershom) is sometimes called Tibbonian Hebrew, after the five generations of Ibn Tibbons who translated into Hebrew innumerable books written in Arabic by Jews and Arabs. Samuel ibn Tibbon called his father Judah "the father of translators," though there had been earlier translations for almost a hundred years. The "translatorese" in original writing derives from the general influence of Arabic, from imitations of language patterns created by the translators, and from the strong attraction of Arabic literature which, though not translated literally, was summarized, with a flavor of the original remaining in the summary. Of course, in kabbalistic literature in original Hebrew there is no more Arabic than sentence patterns derived from the translators, and some terminology, but these traces of Arabic are clearly discernible, both in Kabbalah and in Maimonides' *Mishneh Torah*.

Though there are nearly as many styles as there are writers or families of writers, it is possible to give a general description of the language of prose that came under Arabic influence. Since it contains many deviations from the forms described by the medieval Hebrew grammarians, Tibbonian Hebrew was sometimes used as a pejorative term for poor, inelegant Hebrew. But it was not usually the result of deliberate carelessness, or lack of respect for the grammarians. Judah ibn Tibbon in the introductions to his translations of *Ḥoḇot ha-Leḇaḇot* and *Sefer ha-Riqma*, and his son Samuel in his introduction to his translation of Maimonides' *Moreh Neḇukhim* ("Guide of the Perplexed") explained the difficulties arising from the tendency of the translator to adhere closely to the source language text (and they both realized that the similarity of the two languages actually strengthened this tendency). Hebrew was inadequate, they thought, to express the full richness of Arabic, and they asked readers to correct mistakes of language.

From the "explanations of strange words" which Samuel ibn Tibbon appended to his translation of the *Guide of the Perplexed*, we learn that after he had completed the translation he changed several Arabic-influenced words to better, more Hebrew equivalents: *kihun*, a borrowing from the Arabic *kihāna* (though with a Hebrew declension!) was replaced by קסם; the expression עַל דַּעְתִּי modeled on the Arabic *ʿalā raʾyī*, even though it can be given biblical authority (Job 10:7), was replaced by כְּפִי דַעְתִּי, since the greater frequency of the latter expression gives a more Hebrew flavor to the language. In his testamentary injunction to his son Samuel, Judah ibn Tibbon implored him to preserve "the purity (*ẓaḥut*) of the language," and to beware of Arabisms.

As the language of Spanish poetry should be judged by its appropriateness to prosody and poetic style, so the language of prose should be judged by its suitability to translation and for the skill of the writer as a translator. The principal writers who concerned themselves with the problems of translations were Al-Ḥarizi (*Taḥkemoni* ch. 18, and his preface to his translation of Maimonides' introduction to the Mishnah), Moses Ibn Ezra (*Širat Yisrael* p. 112), Judah and Samuel ibn Tibbon in the introductions quoted, and Abraham b. Ḥasdai in his introduction to his translation of Isaac Israeli's *Sefer ha-Yesodot*. The last three explained that there were "places which were liable to bring the translator into error," and the Ibn Tibbons listed the mistakes that were liable to be caused by too close an adherence to the source language text: confusion of masculine and feminine genders, prepositions, meanings of words, etc. They all described the mistakes as stemming from the "translator's bother." "Translatorese" is evident even in the *Maḥberot Iti'el* which Al-Ḥarizi translated from the *maqāmāt* of Al-Ḥariri. Despite their poetic style, with biblical interpolations, Arabic influence is more noticeable in them than in *Taḥkemoni*, which he wrote in original Hebrew. The latter has also more Arabic usages than his other poetry, since even though not actually a translation it is based on Arab sources.

For a full understanding of the language of prose, the degree of adherence to biblical and mishnaic Hebrew, the scope of Arab influence in all its aspects, and the particular Arabic patterns which affected the Hebrew, it is necessary to classify all the features of the language, distinguishing those which were deliberate innovations (mainly terminology) and those which were accidental, caused by too close an adherence to the source. There are some features which are hardly found outside translations, e.g., a singular verb preceding a plural subject (excluding the verb הָיָה, which was quite commonly found in the singular before a plural). Samuel ibn Tibbon tried to avoid this Arab grammatical rule of concord, as he explains in the introduction to his translation of *Moreh Nebukhim*. Features of common occurrence include -לְ to denote cause and שָׁב in the sense of "become." The Hebrew language of the beginning of the period, before it became a language of translation, can be judged as a separate entity, capable of influencing those who were faithful to it in their writings (e.g., Abraham Ibn Ezra and Abraham bar Ḥiyya), by contrast with the source language which had all the tools of expression for translation ready to hand. It is worth examining the language of those who did not know Arabic and wrote in the style of the translators, and the language of those who did know Arabic but who did not draw much upon Arabic cultural sources for content, e.g., the kabbalists and writers on *halakhah*.

It is not surprising that Al-Ḥarizi, who wrote in the first chapter of *Taḥkemoni* that Hebrew "is narrow but may turn broad to us, short but will suffice for all of us," strove to enrich it from its own sources, avoiding Arab loan-words. But Judah ibn Tibbon, who felt that "Hebrew is insufficient for all purposes of speech" (in the introduction to his translations of *Ḥobot ha-Lebabot*), since biblical and mishnaic Hebrew did not contain the wherewithal for handling new topics, took over many features of Arabic, a richer language in his eyes. However, though it is customary to describe the language of Al-Ḥarizi as simple, correct, elegant, and more biblical (Baneth, Mirsky), it is also full of all kinds of features showing Arabic influence, though not to excess. On the other hand, the Ibn Tibbons also used many specifically Hebrew expressions, out of opposition to Arabic, sometimes consistently and sometimes replacing expressions that showed Arabic influence.

Abraham Ibn Ezra criticized the language of the liturgical poets (in his commentary on Eccles. 5:1) but in the self-same critical passage he wrote that Kallir, as it were, "described the rose *on* fear," תֵּאֵר אֶת הַשּׁוֹשַׁנָּה בְּאֵימָה (as in Ar. *waṣafa bi*) and that he was "surprised *from* him" תָּמַהּ מִמֶּנּוּ (Ar. *taʿağab minhu*) and that he fled *off* the passage," בָּרַח מִן הַפָּסוּק (Ar. *haraba min*). None of these traces of Arabic are to be found in the *poetry* of Abraham Ibn Ezra.

Notwithstanding his decision to write a good Hebrew, Judah ibn Tibbon made a rule of preferring to impart the idea with precision rather than "use as good a style as he would prefer" (introduction to *Ḥovot ha-Levavot*). This method proved its worth; his translation of *Ḥobot ha-Lebabot* superseded that of Joseph Kimḥi, which was more grammatical but less accurate and his son's translation of the *Guide of the Perplexed* replaced that of Al-Ḥarizi, which aimed at a greater beauty of language at the expense of accuracy.

The Components of Arabic-Influenced Hebrew

LEXICON. (a) With all the abundance of innovation and wealth of terminology that accompanied the new ideas, the number of words borrowed with their original form and usage is extremely small; most of the borrowings take the form of loan-translations. Most of the terms in philosophic works were translated into Hebrew (one of the Arabic loans is מַשָּׁאִיִּים for "peripatetic," though Al-Ḥarizi translates it הַהוֹלְכִים). The Arabs themselves translated almost all the Latin and Greek terms into Arabic. It was actually in the natural sciences and allied subjects that more words were borrowed. This is immediately apparent if we compare Moses ibn Tibbon's translation of *Millot ha-Higgayon* ("Words of Logic") where he translated all the technical terms, with his translation of Maimonides' *Hanhagat ha-Beri'ut* ("Management of Health") where foreign words like אשרוב ("syrup"), names of plants, and foods remain untranslated, as they do in other translations of books on medicine in the Middle Ages. The borrowed words are all in forms and patterns which can easily be adapted into Hebrew and thus absorbed in the language and inflected just like any other word: לַחַן ("melody"), קֹטֶר ("caliber"), קֹטֶב ("pole"), מֶרְכָּז ("center"), אוֹפֶק ("horizon") הַנְדָּסָה ("geometry"), תַּאֲרִיךְ ("history"), עִלָּה ("disease"), אַקְלִים ("region"), חֹקֶן ("enema"), עָצָל ("muscle"). Some of them came into general use and became thoroughly Hebraized – אֹפֶק, תַּאֲרִיךְ – while others were in limited use like עָצָל in the works of Nathan ha-Me'ati ("the Italian Tibbon"), or נוע ("type"), which was rare, and used by Nahum ha-Ma'arabi in the translation of *Iggeret Teiman* in place of the more usual סוג and מין.

Samuel ibn Tibbon regarded borrowings as the major class of "strange words" and preferred native Hebrew words, changing כְּהוּן to קֶסֶם, and giving to גֶּשֶׁם, in the sense of "body," biblical authority – Isaiah 44:14 – though this is not the usual meaning attributed to this verse in the medieval dictionaries. Al-Ḥarizi who as we have seen wished to widen Hebrew from within, suggested נְקֻדָּה and עַמּוּד instead of מַסְמֵר, מֶרְכָּז instead of קֹטֶב, אֲלַכְסוֹן instead of קֹטֶר, and חֹמֶר רִאשׁוֹן instead of הַיּוּלִי. However, in his explanation of foreign words he also includes קֹטֶר and קֹטֶב. He uses two terms for one thing and this suggests that he was unaware of the importance of preserving uniformity of terminology. Other translators also tried to find Hebrew alternatives for loan-words: Nahum ha-Ma'arabi used עַמּוּד in place of קֹטֶב, whilst Abraham Ibn Ezra prefers סַדָּן. Abraham b. Ḥiyya who composed original scientific works before the language of translation had become fixed, quoted Arabic words as such, e.g., "the center of the circle, which in Arabic is called *markaz*." He uses the term תִּשְׁבֹּרֶת ("geometry," "plane," a loan-translation of Ar. *taksīr*) and prefers בְּרִיחַ to קֹטֶר, though occasionally he uses קֹטֶב.

(b) Words are sometimes introduced that are similar in *sound* to their Arabic counterparts, and generally any similarity in meaning or etymological connection is either lacking or very slight. "Grammatical inflection" (in Ar. *taṣrīf*) is translated by Dunash צֵרוּף, though נְטִיָּה would be more appropriate as a loan-translation (see (c) below).

Judah ibn Tibbon calls apical consonants אוֹתִיּוֹת הַדְּלִיקָה after al-Mudalaqa, which should etymologically be הַזְּלִיקָה. The waw consecutive is called ו"ו עוֹטֶפֶת, from the Arabic *ʿaṭafa*, מָחוּל means "absurd," like *muhāl*, פֶּרֶק means "difference" (Ar. *farq*), גֶּדֶר means the mathematical "to the fourth power" (Ar. *ǧadr*), לָכֵן is used with the meaning "but" (Ar. *lākin*) and נִצָּב is both "accusative case" and the vowel "*a*" (Ar. *naṣb*). Sometimes a biblical word which bears a phonetic resemblance to an Arabic word is used as a translation and the new meaning is given authority by biblical commentary, which was also influenced by the comparison with Arabic. חִידָה is translated as "talk" (Ar. *ḥadīth*), the translation used by Saadiah Gaon for this word in Proverbs 6:16 and the explanation given by Ibn Janaḥ in his book of roots, under חוד. The Arabic *ʿurūq* is sometimes translated גִּדִים דּוֹפְקִים, i.e., arteries, and a biblical parallel is found in the word עֹרְקַי (*ʿoreqay*; Job 30;17), which most medieval commentators interpreted in accordance with the Arabic. It should be pointed out that this kind of innovation is very close to borrowing; the borrowed word, however, is taken over with a change of form to a Hebrew declension, or is attached to an existing Hebrew word.

(c) The most prolific source of word creation was loan-translation. Among the new words created were אֵיכוּת (Ar. *kayfiyya*), מַהוּת (Ar. *mahiyya*), כַּמּוּת (Ar. *kamiyya*), and many other verbal nouns with suffix -וּת, which was used to express abstractions. However, Arabic words were mainly translated by existing Hebrew words. Most of the deliberate innovations used by translators for the enrichment of the means of expression and for accuracy, are in the realm of terminology: בִּנְיָן ("conjugation"; Ar. *mabniyya*), מִשְׁקָל ("declension"; Ar. *wazn*), שִׁמּוּשׁ הַלָּשׁוֹן ("language usage") and עֲשִׂיַּת הַלָּשׁוֹן ("language manipulation"; Ar. *istiʿmāl*), גָּזַר, also קָצַב, חָצַב, כָּרַת all meaning "inflect" (Ar. *ištaqqa*), מִלִּים נִרְדָּפוֹת ("synonyms"; *mutarādifāt*) מִלִּים מִשְׁתַּתְּפוֹת ("homonyms"; Ar. *muštaraka*), מָקוֹר ("infinitive"; Ar. *maṣdar*), מִקְרֶה ("Abstract noun"; Ar. *ḥadaṯ*). נָשׂוּא ("predicate" of a verbal sentence; Ar. *maḥmul*), הַגָּדָה ("predicate" of a nominal sentence; Ar. *ḫabar*), בְּחִינָה ("aspect"; Ar. *iʿtibār*), מֻפְשָׁט ("abstract"; Ar. *muǧarrad*), בְּכֹחַ ("potential") and בְּפֹעַל ("actual"; Ar. *bi al-quwwa* and *bi al-fiʿl*;), מַצְפּוּן ("conscience"; Ar. *ḍamir*), חִבּוּר ("a book"; Ar. *taʾlif*), הַתְחָלָה ("principle"; Ar. *mabdaʾ*), הַכָּה ("duplicate"; Ar. *ḍaraba*). There are also loan-translations which did not provide any technical terminology: בְּשִׁלּוּחַ ("absolutely"; Ar. *biʾiṭlāq*), חָבַר עַל ("agreed"; Ar. *uǧmiʿa ʿalā*), הִסְכִּים לְ-, נָאוֹת לְ- ("matched," "fit"; Ar. *wāfaqa*) בִּקְצַת הַיָּמִים ("one day," adv., Ar. *fi baʿḍi al-ayyām*). Since every loan-translation that makes use of an existing word also involves extending the meaning of that word in accordance with the range of meanings of its Arabic counterpart, it is difficult to distinguish between loan-translation and semantic borrowing. Perhaps the fundamental difference between them is the degree of intention. When the motivation is the need to translate an existing Arabic technical term (it is mainly technical vocabulary that is at issue, though non-technical expressions also occur) we speak of loan-translation; when it is the unintended effect of adherence to the Arabic text that leads to certain lexical associations, we speak of semantic borrowing.

(d) The following are examples of extension of meaning by semantic borrowing: עִנְיָן ("meaning"; Ar. *maʿnā*), לָקַח ("begin"; Ar. *ʾaḫada*), אִגֶּרֶת ("essay"; Ar. *risāla*), בֵּאוּר ("proof," "lecture"; Ar. *bayān*), גּוֹבֵר ("common"; Ar. *ġālib*), רָמַז ("advise"; Ar. *ʾišāra*), דִּין ("religion"; Ar. *dīn*), כְּמוֹ ("approximately"; Ar. *naḥwa*), רוֹצֶה ("mean"; as in רוֹצֶה לוֹמַר ("mean to say; Ar. *yurīd*), בְּחֹק ("concerning"; Ar. *bi ḥaqq*), אֶצְלִי ("in my opinion"; Ar. *ʿindi*). Sometimes an extension of meaning derives wholly or mainly from a similarity in sound, with or without any etymological connection: זִיֵּף acquires the meaning "deny" from Arabic *zayyafa*; זִיֵּן ("decorate"), חַג ("pilgrimage"), things which are מְפִיקִים are "suitable" (Ar. *muwāfiq*).

(e) A feeling for the Arabic language governed the choice of particular Hebrew words, and affected the frequency of words whose use in Hebrew was restricted; this gives a distinctly Arabic flavor to the language. רָאָה ("see") means "think," a use found in mishnaic Hebrew, אָמַר ("say") means "order," חָשַׁק ("love"), חוּשׁ ("feeling") and not רֶגֶשׁ (because of Ar.

ḥassa), חִלּוּף ("difference"; Ar. *Iḵtilāf*) and not שִׁנּוּי or חִדּוּשׁ, הֶבְדֵּל ("accident") more common than מִקְרֶה or מְאוֹרָע (Arab. *ḥadat*). What is a borrowing with one writer may be recognized as a legitimate Hebrew usage by another. Samuel ibn Tibbon, for example, quotes from the introduction to Maimonides' *Sefer ha-Madda*ʿ the expression לֵידַע שֶׁיֵּשׁ שָׁם מָצוּי רִאשׁוֹן to know that there is a God – as clear proof of Arabic usage in the original Hebrew writings of Maimonides, and understandable therefore in a translated text (Introduction to his translation *Moreh Nebukhim* – this is a usage of type (b) as analyzed above). Yet since there are rare examples in mishnaic Hebrew of שם used to mean "in reality" and not as a locative, it may well be that Maimonides had found this Hebrew source in rabbinic literature for himself. Samuel Ibn Tibbon's father-in-law, Jacob Anatoli, thought that Maimonides found a source for this non-locative use of שָׁם in Ezekiel (in his book *Malmad ha-Talmidim* p. 113a) as illustrated by S. Abramson, which would make it an example of class (e). Expressions of the form תַּכְלִית הַשְּׁלֵמוּת ("the peak of perfection") a literal translation of Arabic *Ġāyat al-Kimāl* – were widely used, and a source was found for them in Psalms 139:22 – תַּכְלִית שִׂנְאָה. Typical words include זוּלַת (as a translation for *ġayr* and *duna* in their various meanings) and בִּלְתִּי (to translate *ġayr* and *ʿadam*). Samuel ibn Tibbon acknowledged that his innovations led to new homonymy when he himself added new meanings to existing words (the fifth class of "strange words").

The following are the new kinds of homonymy created: 1. In addition to its usual meaning in the language, the word received a new technical sense: שֶׁבֶר is a term for the Hebrew vowel *ḥireq*; and, not particularly technical: *ḥida* means "talk" (Ar. *ḥadat*, see above) but also retained the meaning of the *ḥidot* of the Queen of Sheba, and thus also signifies "allegory" in kabbalistic literature and Maimonides' *Mishneh Torah*. Sometimes homonymy is transferred from Arabic to Hebrew; *bāb* in Arabic means "rule," "chapter of a book," and "explanation," and all these meanings were taken over by the Hebrew שַׁעַר. Arabic *ḥarf* means both "letter of the alphabet" and "particle," and both meanings were transferred to the Hebrew אוֹת. הֶעְתֵּק translates *naqala* both in the meaning "translate" and also "hand down (by tradition)," though "tradition" is just as commonly rendered by קַבָּלָה. 2. A Hebrew homonym is paralleled by different Arabic words, in different *binyanim* or patterns: מַאֲמָר is both "essay" (Ar. *maqāla*) and "category" (Ar. *maqūla*); הִשִּׂיג means both "add," a loan-translation of Arabic *alḥaqa* (fourth *binyan*), and "appeal," like the Arabic verb *lāḥaqa ʿalā* (third *binyan*). 3. The Hebrew homonyms translate two different Arabic words: עוֹבֵר means "possible" – (Ar. *ǧaʾiz*) and "past" – (Ar. *māḍi*); מְדַבֵּר is "logical" – (Ar. *nāṭiq* – "believer" in the philosophy of *al-kalām*) and also the grammatical term "first person," – (Ar. *mutakallim*). הִשִּׂיג means "understood" (Ar. *adraka*) and "added" (Ar. *alḥaqa*). העתקה is "translation" (Ar. *naql*), one of the types of metaphor (Ar. *maǧāz*), and "transmigration of souls" (Ar. *tanāsuḥ*). 4. The homonymy derives from the falling together of a loan-translation and a phonetic equivalent; גֶּדֶר is both "definition," loan-translation of *ḥadd*, and "to the fourth power" Arabic *ǧadr*. As regards the principles whereby the vocabulary could be expanded, there are equivalences between the language of scientific prose and the language of Spanish poetry, though the degree of expansion in prose is far greater, due to the needs of writing on new topics rich in new terms and concepts. The case is different with morphology and syntax, where derivations in general and those derived from Arabic in particular abound in prose yet are hardly found at all in poetry. Since the language of prose was not subject to the principles of *ẓaḥut* ("purity") which mainly affect the formal aspects of grammar, and since its counterpart was an intermediate variety of Arabic, which had a different degree of adherence to the strict rules of classical Arabic, it even deviated from the rules of grammar established in the grammatical writings of the period. It was not an elegant language, and its foreign features were conspicuous, but its freedom to innovate helped to fashion it into a precise language of scholarship, capable of expressing abstract, scientific ideas.

The following are the salient features of the language of prose:

NOUN MORPHOLOGY. The use of the suffix morpheme ־ִי (called in Ar. *nisba*) to turn a noun into an adjective meaning "possessing, related to, having the quality of" was productive, almost automatic: גַּשְׁמִי, שִׁמּוּשִׁי, דִּבְרִי; Arabic gave new life to this suffix (found in the Bible), which most frequently occurred as in Arabic without the infixed *nun* after short words or words ending in a vowel: גּוּפִי, חוּשִׁי, צוּרִי, תּוֹרִי, רוּחִי (for גּוּפָנִי, צוּרָנִי, etc.). This morpheme does not feature in the linguistic innovations of Saadiah Gaon and was rare in poetry, which used participles instead: מְדַבֵּר for דִּבְרִי ("logical"), or phrases like בַּעַל גֶּשֶׁם for גַּשְׁמִי and אֲחִי מוּסָר for מוּסָרִי etc. Moses Ibn Ezra also considered this kind of innovation contrary to analogy (unproductive) for the morphology of "pure" poetic language (*Širat Yisrael*, 151, apropos the derivation of פְּנִינִיָּה from פְּנִינָה, which is "mere cleverness").

In varieties of Hebrew which were closer to mishnaic Hebrew, and more restrained in their enthusiasm for Arabic, this derivation was replaced by the typically mishnaic pattern: קַטְלָן e.g., in the writings of Abraham bar Ḥiyya – שַׁקְרָן for שִׁקְרִי ("something containing lies" not "one who lies"), עַמְלָן for מַעֲשִׂי, "practical" (contrasted with שִׂכְלִי "intellectual"), דַּבְּרָן for דִּבְרִי ("logical"). The morpheme-*uṯ* creates abstract nouns and can be combined with nouns: נֶצַח נִצְחוּת "eternity," רֵיקוּת – רֵיק "vacuum," רְגִילוּת – רָגִיל "regularity," גַּשְׁמִיּוּת – גַּשְׁמִי "corporeality," and with verbal nouns: הִתְרַשְּׁמוּת, הֵאָצְלוּת, הִפָּעֲלוּת. Sparing use had been made of this device by the liturgical poets (דַּכְאוּת, וַתִּיקוּת), apparently under the influence of the infinitive with the suffixed definite article in Aramaic (אִתְעֲרוּתָא), but in the language of Saadiah Gaon it is not used at all and it is extremely rare in Spanish poetry. In prose it became indispensable, one of the preferred productive morphemes, even in the prose writings of the poets (Abraham Ibn Ezra uses דַּקּוּת and דַּיְקוּת). In Arabic the suffixed morpheme

-*ut* was borrowed from Aramaic, and is quite limited in distribution; this is not an example of Arabic influence.

The use of the masculine gender for nouns formed with ות- is characteristic, and though Samuel ibn Tibbon found authority for this in the Bible (אָחֵז בְּשָׂרִי פַּלָּצוּת "a shudder seized me" in the introduction to his translation of *The Guide for the Perplexed*, quoting Job 21:6) the abundance of these forms in the masculine clearly derives from Arabic: Nouns ending in ות- are masculine in Arabic, and a considerable number of the new words formed in Hebrew with this morpheme derive from Arabic infinitives which are also masculine: גַּשְׁמוּת (Ar. *tağsīm*), נַצְחוּת (Ar. *taʾbīd*), הִשְׁתַּדְּלוּת (Ar. *iğtihād*), and many more. Use of the masculine gender also spread to those words, few in number, where the suffix corresponds with the feminine abstract noun suffix in Arabic: אֵיכוּת כַּמּוּת, מַהוּת, though these words were also used in the feminine. Words with the suffix ית- were also used in the masculine and Samuel ibn Tibbon found authority for this usage also in the Bible (וְאַחֲרִיתְךָ יִשְׂגֶּא; Job 8:7). Sometimes words are used in the grammatical gender of their Arabic counterparts: אֱמֶת is masculine – אֱמֶת גָּמוּר (Arab. *ḥaqq*); דַּעַת is also masculine דַּעַת בָּרוּר (Arab. *ʿalm*). Words used in the feminine include טֶבַע, אִי (Ar. *ğazīra*), כֹּחַ (Ar. *quwwa*), מִנְהָג (Ar. *ʿāda*), כַּדּוּר (Ar. *kurra*), and סִפּוּר (Ar. *qiṣṣa*). They are of course also used in the masculine, in accordance with the tradition of the language, and the proportion of Arabic or Hebrew usages varies with the writer's talent and grammatical knowledge. In addition to the masculine use of אֱמֶת the form אֲמִתָּה is very common, due to Arabic *ḥaqiqah*. When a masculine plural is formed by adding -*oṯ*, attributive adjectives characteristically take the same ending: גְּדוֹלוֹת, מְקוֹמוֹת יְדוּעוֹת, סוֹדוֹת עֲצוּמוֹת, סְפֵקוֹת, (but שֵׁמוֹת מִשְׁתַּתְּפִים). This formal correspondence may have been helped by the rule in Arabic that inanimate plurals take adjectives in the feminine singular. When the translator was faced with *asrār ʿaṣima*, the adjective was drawn towards the feminine, though not feminine singular; since there was no precedent in Hebrew for a structure like "סודות גדולה" such a form was naturally rejected. Middle Arabic had also begun to challenge the rules of congruence in Classical Arabic, and tended toward greater uniformity. Since Arabic had only one form and syntactic usage for what are usually described nowadays as the infinitive (קָטוֹל) and the verbal noun (קְטִילָה), both these forms are used interchangeably in the language of prose, e.g., הַרְחָקַת הַגַּשְׁמוּת וְהַעֲמִיד הָאַחְדוּת "removal of corporeality and establishment of uniformity." Arabic *Ġāyat al-Taḥaffuẓ* is translated both תַּכְלִית הַשְּׁמוֹר and תַּכְלִית הַשְּׁמִירָה and this is the reason that the use of the infinitive with the definite article is common: הַהֵעָשׂוֹת, הַהִתְעַצֵּל (Saadiah Gaon also makes no distinction between these forms. The inability of the infinitive to take the definite article begins with Samuel ha-Nagid, and in the language of poetry neither the absolute nor the construct infinitive is used as verbal nouns.) The abundant use of fused construct forms (i.e., without *šel*) can be attributed to the influence of Arabic construct forms, as can the use of the definite article before an adjective in the construct form: הֶחָזֵק הַלֵּבָן, הַמְחֻיַּב הַמְּצִיאוּת and especially before the comparative הַיּוֹתֵר חָשׁוּב. This is the Arabic feature of marking as definite any construct form which is not a noun, the so-called "unreal construct." The tendency to use two construct forms with a single dependent noun – פּוֹשְׁעֵי וְרִשְׁעֵי יִשְׂרָאֵל ("the evil and wicked of Israel") – may be due to the influence of Middle Arabic.

VERB. In the introduction to his translation of *Guide of the Perplexed*, Samuel ibn Tibbon acknowledges the tendency of a translator to be drawn towards the קֶשֶׁר (his term for preposition) used with the verb in Arabic, e.g., *qibbel le-* instead of *qibbel min*. Arabic prepositional usages, infrequent in the language of poetry, are quite common in prose:

מִתְפַּלֵּא מִן, נִפְלָא מִן (Ar. *taʿağaba min*); מתרעם מִן (Ar. *ġaḍaba min*); חקר עַל (Ar. *fataša ʿan*); מקיף ב (Ar. *ʾaḥāta bi*), הבטיח ב (*waʿada bi*); חסר אל (Ar. *iftaqara ilā*); and so are התנגד עַל, קרוב מִן, גינה מִן, לא יתכן מִן, etc.

Sometimes the preposition adds a specific meaning as in Arabic: אָמַר בְּ- = הֶאֱמִין for "believe in" (Ar. *qāla bi*). Intransitive verbs of motion are made transitive by the "causative *bet*" like in Arabic; this usage is also found in poetry, but to a much greater extent in prose; הִתְגַּלְגֵּל בְּ- ("rolled"). עָף בְּ- ("set flying"), etc.

Judah and Samuel ibn Tibbon were aware of the influence of the Arabic *binyanim* on the Hebrew verb, but apparently did not consider this such a serious defect as the influence of the prepositions; in poetry too the amount of analogical formation and innovation in the verb was greater than in the noun and the particles. The main development was the increase in the use of the *hitpaʿel*, which translated three Arabic *binyanim: tafāʿala* (as הִתְחַסֵּר, Ar. *tanāqasa*); *tafaʿʿla* (פֹּעַל מִתְעַבֵּר "transitive verb," Ar. *mutaʿadd*, הִזְדַּכֵּר "remember," Ar. *tazakkara*, הִסְתַּפֵּק "be in doubt," Ar. *tašakkaka*); *iftaʿala* (שֵׁמוֹת מִשְׁתַּתְּפִים "homonyms," Ar. *muštaraka*, מִתְחַלְּפִים "different," Ar. *muḫtalifa*, הִסְתַּכֵּם "agree," Ar. *ittafaqa*, מִתְאַחֵר "later, following," e.g. הַגְּאוֹנִים הַמִּתְאַחֲרִים, Ar. *mutaʾaḫḫir*).

In Middle Arabic, these *binyanim* had largely supplanted the "internal passives," hence: הִתְבָּאֵר (Ar. *tabayyana*) instead of בֹּאַר (Ar. *buyyina*), הִתְיַלֵּד "was created" (said of rainbow, water, etc., Ar. *tawallada*), etc.

The use of *hitpaʿel* as a passive in place of passives with internal vowel modification is not simply continuation of mishnaic practice, since the Ibn Tibbons also introduced many forms of "internal" passives. The increase in the use of passive conjugations, in prose and in poetry, is attributed to the influence of Arabic. The "internal" passives – *puʿal*, and *nipʿal* – were used mostly in impersonal structures: יְחֻיַּב, יְסֻפַּק, יְעֻיַּן, יְזֻיַּן, יְכֻסַּף, יֵרָצֶה. New auxiliary verbs were created שָׁב, חָזַר in the sense of "become" (Ar. *ʿāda, rağaʿa*), לֹא זָז, לֹא סָר meaning "keep (doing something)" (Ar. *mā zāla*) and עָשָׂה, שָׂם, "make," with an objective complement – עָשָׂה הַסָּפֵק בָּרוּר ("make doubt clear, clarify doubt"; Ar. *ğaʿala*). Tenses converted by *waw* were almost no longer employed. The modal forms of the verb, jussive and cohortative, were scarcely used in medieval Hebrew prose. In poetry the long and short forms of the imperfect were used simply as morphological variants, not expressing modal ways as they were understood by Hebrew grammarians to appear in the Bible, without any influence from verbal patterns found in Classical Arabic. The language of prose dispensed with these forms, since it had no need of a multiplicity of forms for embellishment. Middle Arabic, which had lost some verb forms, may also have contributed to the general picture and helped to eliminate long imperfects in ון since in North Africa and Spain it was the short forms which were used in the plural. A Past Continuous or a Past Habitual, like the Arabic *kāna yafʿal* occurs: *hava yabo* (a usage also found in Saadiah Gaon and in the *maqāmāt* of Al-Ḥarizi). The combination of כְּבָר and the imperfect is used to express possibility, by analogy with Arabic *qad*; in fact, כְּבָר as an equivalent for *qad* is increasingly used, both in the language and in grammatical description. Ibn Janaḥ (*Sefer ha-Šorashim*, s.v. כְּבָר) explained that כְּבָר was like Arabic *qad*, and expressed "the existence of a thing." By using כְּבָר as an equivalent of *qad* the following tenses were formed: pluperfect: הָיָה כְּבָר עָשָׂה; future perfect: יִהְיֶה כְּבָר עָשָׂה. This pattern is found mainly in the language of translation, but also occurs elsewhere (e.g., in the writings of Crescas, 14th century). However, it had already begun to fade from the grammatical stock of medieval Hebrew a few generations after the end of the period of the translations. But the use of כְּבָר plus the perfect to signify time and for emphasis כְּבָר יָדַעְתָּ, כְּבָר נִתְבָּאֵר equivalent to the Arabic *qad*, was much more in line with the spirit of the language, and Arabic accounts merely for its widespread distribution. As in Arabic כְּבָר was placed before the verb, as in mishnaic Hebrew where this usage originates, and not after the verb, as occurred occasionally in mishnaic Hebrew and quite commonly in varieties of Hebrew influenced by languages where the equivalent of כְּבָר (*schon, déjà*) come after the verb. There are, however, examples of כְּבָר occurring after a verb, mainly when the verb is in a subordinate clause: מַה שֶּׁשָּׁמַעְתִּי כְּבָר מִטַּעֲנוֹת הֶחָבֵר ("… those statements of the companion which I have already heard"; beginning of the *Kuzari*).

SYNTAX. The use of the demonstrative without *he* (the definite article) before a noun with *he* is very common: אֵלּוּ הַדְּבָרִים, זֶה הָאִישׁ. The structure with the demonstrative before the noun and no *he* – אוֹתוֹ הָאִישׁ, as in mishnaic Hebrew – is preferred to הָאִישׁ הַהוּא, the biblical form. Though there are a few examples in the Bible to serve as precedents (זֶה הַיּוֹם Ps. 105), and an equivalent structure in late Aramaic (הָדֵין עָלְמָא), Arabic was certainly the major factor: *hādhā al-walad, dhalika al-walad*. This usage is not found at all in the writings of Saadiah Gaon and hardly in poetry, but occurs frequently in the original prose writings of Abraham b. Ḥiyya, Maimonides, and Al-Ḥarizi. However, there are many places where the Ibn Tibbons used forms like הַדְּבָרִים הָהֵם, הָאִישׁ הַהוּא in their translations, even when this meant deviating from the word order that confronted them in the Arabic text: *ḏalika al-rağul*. The use of relative clauses with no conjunction after an indefinite antecedent (-אִישׁ עַיִן בְּ for -אִישׁ שֶׁעַיִן בְּ, מְלָאכָה צְרִיכָה נִסָּיוֹן for מְלָאכָה שֶׁצְּרִיכָה נִסָּיוֹן) is also the exact counterpart of an Arabic structure (*sifa*). This structure can also be given biblical authority (שָׂרִים זָהָב לָהֶם) but comes in prose much more than in poetry. Elegant translators added the definite article, in places where it did not occur in Arabic, in order to bring the structure closer to the form prevalent in mishnaic Hebrew and to a considerable extent also in biblical Hebrew (compare Aḥiṭub's translation of *Millot ha-Higgayon* with Moses ibn Tibbon's). Moreover, the Ibn Tibbons added quite a few relative clause markers (שֶׁ, אֲשֶׁר, -הַ) where none existed in Arabic, and translators like Al-Ḥarizi and Aḥiṭub are not free from asyndetic relative clauses. Such clauses are also found in original texts which were influenced by the language of the translations, e.g., *Beit ha-Beḥira* by Ha-Me'iri, written in Provence at the end of the 13th century.

Relative clauses were also formed, on the modal of the Arabic *naʿt sababī*, in which the adjective or participle is predicative to a following noun, and agrees with it in number and gender, but preserves an indirect link with the antecedent with which it shares the same category of deixis, definite or indefinite: הַמִּדּוֹת הַמְסֻפָּר בָּהֶן הַבּוֹרֵא ("the qualities (feminine plural) attributed (masculine singular) to the Creator (masculine singular)"). This structure occurs most frequently when the predicate in the relative clause is a passive participle and impersonal: צֹרֶךְ הַלָּשׁוֹן הַמֶּעְתָּק אֵלָיו (Judah ibn Tibbon's introduction to Ḥobot ha-Lebabot) הַדְּבָרִים הַמֻּזְהָר מֵהֶם וְהַמְצֻוֶּה בָּהֶם ("things (masculine plural) warned against (masculine singular) and commanded (masculine singular)" (Moses ibn Tibbon's translation of *Sefer ha-Mizwot*). Also based on Arabic is the common structure with מַה...מִן, מִי...מִן (and similar structures with other words replacing מַה and מִן), where the first part of the sentence functions restrictively: מַה שֶּׁיֵּשׁ אִתִּי מִן הַטְּעָנוֹת וְהַתְּשׁוּבוֹת (the beginning of Ibn Tibbon's translation of the Kuzari; "what I have of claims and answers," i.e., those claims and answers that I have). Similarly מַה שֶּׁעָשׂוּ לָנוּ הַמִּצְרִים מֵעָוֶל וְחָמָס, מַה שֶּׁהִתְאַמֵּת וְהִתְבָּרֵר מִמַּאַמְרֵי הַתּוֹרָה, etc. This structure, modeled on Arabic, survived at least until the 18th century. Gershon b. Solomon composed his *Šaʿar ha-Šamayim* in the second half of the 13th century. All scholars are agreed that he did not know Arabic. His book, "a breviary of the wisdom of nature," was based on scientific works translated from Arabic. He picked up this structure, new to Hebrew, from the books he studied and he understood how to use it correctly. He writes for example: חוּשׁ הָרְאוּת לְכַוֵּן הַנָּאוֹת לוֹ מִמַּאֲכָל וּמַשְׁקֶה ("the appropriate from food and drink," i.e., those foods and drinks which are appropriate). In the spirit of Arabic are the many object-noun clauses in place of infinitives: נִרְצֶה שֶׁנֵּדַע ("we shall want that we shall know"; instead of נִרְצֶה לָדַעַת "we shall want to know"; compare the Arabic *nurīdu an naʿrifa*; נִצְטַוֵּינוּ שֶׁנַּעֲנִישֵׁהוּ ("we were ordered that we should punish him") instead of נִצְטַוֵּינוּ לְהַעֲנִישׁ אוֹתוֹ ("we were ordered to punish him"), רָאִיתִי גַּם כֵּן שֶׁאֲחַבֵּר חִבּוּר ("I decided to compose….") Subordinate clauses are also common after words such as רָאוּי, צָרִיךְ, etc. and are modeled on Arabic *ʾan* clauses introduced after such verbs e.g., צָרִיךְ שֶׁנִּתְבּוֹנֵן ("it is necessary that we look") for אָנוּ צְרִיכִים לְהִתְבּוֹנֵן ("we must look"; compare the Ar. *yağibu ʾan*).

By contrast, infinitives are frequent in place of subordinate adverbial clauses of time, purpose, reason, and comparison: אַחֲרֵי בָּאֲרִי for "after I had explained" (Ar. *baʿad tabayyuni*); לִהְיוֹתוֹ for "because he is" (Ar. *likawnihi*); כְּאָמְרוֹ ("as he says" or "as it says in the text"; Ar. *kaqawlihi*). Under the influence of Arabic the use of אֶת before a direct object diminished and the use of cognate objects increased e.g., תָּמַהּ תְּמִיהָה. The circumstantial use of participles is common אָמַר הַנָּבִיא מִתְחַנֵּן ("the prophet said, imploring"; Ar. *qāla al nabī mutašafiʿan*). The use of the objective complement is also frequent: יָשִׂים הַסָּפֵק בָּרוּר ("he will make the uncertainty clear," i.e., will clarify it.).

Literal translation produces structures which are the exact image of the original Arabic text: וּתְחִלַּת מִי שֶׁמָּצָא זֶה הַדַּעַת i.e., the first who found… (Ar. *awwal man ʿamada ʿalā*). The use of the prefix מִי – for listing details and explanations (called in Ar. the *mīm al-mubayyina*) was transferred from Arabic, when it was not translated by such words as כְּגוֹן, כְּמוֹ ("such as") which is the usual method. Though not mentioned by grammarians like Ibn Jannaḥ, it is found in untranslated Hebrew, even in thoroughly Hebrew contexts such as Maimonides' Mishneh Torah: כָּל הַבְּרוּאִים מִמַּלְאָךְ וְגַלְגַּל ("all created things, such as, angels…" *Yesodei Torah* 4, 1).

In the Bible the word אָמְנָם adds emphasis and by virtue of this usage is employed to translate typically Arabic structures. Due to its phonetic similarity to Arabic *ammā* it is used to emphasize the subject: וְאָמְנָם הָרִאשׁוֹנוֹת צְרִיכוֹת בֵּאוּר ("as for the first ones, they need proof"). And because of its phonetic similarity to Arabic *innamā* it can emphasize a following predicate. Other words are also used to translate *ammā* and *innamā* – אֲבָל, אִם, אוּלָם, אֲשֶׁר לְ- – even by the Ibn Tibbons. Al-Ḥarizi, who to some extent preferred אֲבָל, very often tried to side-step such structures altogether. However, the use of אָמְנָם to emphasize what follows, a structure modeled on Arabic syntax, is very common in works which drew their Arabic inspiration from the translations written in the 13th and 14th centuries: they occur frequently, for example, in the writings of Cordovero, who lived in the 16th century.

Translators who were nearly always led to render the Arabic *lā ilā* by לֹא...אֶלָּא very seldom managed to use לֹא אֶלָּא to translate the Arabic *innamā*. The merits of original, untranslated texts are noteworthy by comparison with the language of the translations. Samuel ibn Tibbon translated the words of Maimonides (*Guide of the Perplexed* 2, 44): הַנְּבוּאָה אָמְנָם תִּהְיֶה בְּמַרְאָה אוֹ בַחֲלוֹם ("prophecy will only be in a vision or a dream"; in Ar. the word *innamā* comes after the word for prophecy). But Maimonides himself wrote (*Hilkhot Yesodei Torah* 7, 2) אֵין רוֹאִין מַרְאָה בִּנְבוּאָה אֶלָּא בַחֲלוֹם ("no vision of prophecy is seen except in dream…").

MAIMONIDES

This example from Maimonides of a Hebraic structure, לֹא... אֶלָּא rather than the use of אָמְנָם in imitation of an Arabic pattern, is not unique. Asyndetic relative clauses are rare in the *Mishneh Torah*, and many of the laws begin after the fashion of mishnaic Hebrew: צוּרוֹת שֶׁעֲשָׂאוּם ("shapes that have been made"), אֶפְרֹחִים שֶׁקִּנְּנָה בָּהֶם ("chicks for whom a nest has been made"). נָבִיא שֶׁיַּעֲמֹד לָנוּ ("a prophet who shall represent us") etc. Subordinate clauses are preferred to infinitives, and particularly worthy of comparison are the many occasions where Maimonides uses בְּעִנְיָן שֶׁנֶּאֱמַר or כְּמוֹ שֶׁנֶּאֱמַר as against כְּאָמְרוֹ, which Moses ibn Tibbon uses in his translation of Maimonides' *Sefer ha-Mizwot*.

In vocabulary also, the Hebrew of Maimonides tends to be free from Arabic influence. Whereas Samuel ibn Tibbon writes of קֹטֶב הַתּוֹרָה ("the pole of the Law"; in his translation of *Guide of the Perplexed*), in line with the Arabic figure of speech, Maimonides himself wrote עַמּוּד הַחָכְמוֹת – "the pillar of wisdom" (introduction to *Sefer ha-Maddʿa*) – see above on the respective uses of עַמּוּד and קֹטֶב. He wrote גֹּלֶם וְצוּרָה and not גֶּשֶׁם וְצוּרָה ("matter and form"), נִתְבָּרֵר and not נִתְבָּאֵר (explained), which is a loan translation of *tabayyana*, מְאֹרָע and not חִדּוּשׁ (event; Ar. *ḥadaṯ*) though he did also use the words נִתְבָּאֵר (meaning "explained and proved") and יִתְחַדֵּשׁ (meaning "take place"). Maimonides took great care with the language of *Mishneh Torah*; he wanted it to be "clear and precise" (as he wrote in the introduction) and chose to use not the language of prophecy or the language of the Talmud (i.e., Aramaic) but "the language of the *Mishnah* so that it will be easy for the majority" (as he wrote concerning the *Mishneh Torah* in his introduction to *Sefer ha-Mizwot*). In fact, he used typically mishnaic forms more than was usual in the language of the translations: הֵיאַךְ, לֵילֵךְ, לֵידַע – and particularly the use of a proleptic pronoun נְתָנוֹ לוֹ לְמֹשֶׁה, which is not a feature of Arabic-influenced medieval Hebrew.

For all his conscious preference for "the language of the Mishnah," Maimonides interlarded his prose with many biblical expressions, not just vocabulary items but whole phrases in a rhetorical style replete with biblical quotations: מָרֵי נֶפֶשׁ ("bitter of soul," Prov. 31:6), מְפֻזָּר וּמְפֹרָד ("dispersed and scattered," Esth. 3:8) בְּלוֹיֵי סְחָבוֹת ("cast off remnants," Jer. 38:11), כְּמַר מִדְּלִי ("a drop in the bucket," Isa. 40:15), etc. There are undoubtedly traces of Arabic influence in the language of Maimonides, but they nearly all derive from Arabic features in Hebrew texts written by his predecessors, and most of them have their roots in Hebrew: prefixed לְ – to indicate cause, prefixed מ – for exemplification (see above), עִנְיָנוֹת רְחוֹקוֹת instead of עִנְיָנִים רְחוֹקִים in the masculine, דַּעַת; אֲמִתָּה for אֱמֶת; מִסְתַּפֵּק מִן meaning "be doubtful about…"; הָעוֹבְדֵי אֱלִילִים ("idol worshippers") with the definite article preceding the construct form; הִשִּׂיג meaning "understand"; הֶעְתִּיק meaning "hand down by tradition" (Ar. *naqala*); the technical terms עִקָּר "principle," צוּרָה ("form"); עִלָּה וְעָלוּל ("cause and effect"); מְצוּי רִאשׁוֹן ("first entity" – a term for God). A typical feature of his prose is the translation into Hebrew of most of the Aramaic expressions in the Talmud: שָׁלֵם הָעִנְיָן for סְלִיק עִנְיָנָא ("the matter is complete"); כָּל הַמִּתְגַּבֵּר זָכָה for כָּל דְּאַלִּים גְּבַר ("whoever is in power wins");בֶּן מֶצֶר for בַּר מִצְרָא (an immediate neighbor); and many more. Maimonides' language is closest to the style of learned medieval Hebrew in passages of philosophical reflection (especially in Yad, *Yesodei ha-Torah*), and it is these sections which best show how superior and "Hebraic" his style is by comparison with the language of the Ibn Tibbons.

ITALY

In the year 1054, in Italy, Ahimaaz b. Paltiel, descendant of a line of liturgical poets, wrote his *Megillat Aḥimaʿaz*, the genealogical record of his family. The language of his book is naturally akin to that of the liturgical poets. There are many features of mishnaic Hebrew (*binyan nitpaʿal*, proleptic use of pronouns as in יֶשׁ לוֹ לְאָדָם, demonstratives as in אוֹתָם הַיָּמִים, words such as שֶׁכֵּן, צָרִיךְ, סָבוּר etc.), enriched by biblical Hebrew in the form of interlarded quotations, morphology, syntax and vocabulary: *waw* conversive, infinitival phrases as in בְּבוֹא, בְּהַגִּיעַ, lack of innovation in *puʿal* and so on. A form like לֵילְכָה, with a mišnaic infinitive – לֵילֵךְ – and a biblical lengthening, testifies to the blend of language varieties! Like the liturgical poets that preceded him, he combined -כְּ with a perfect tense – כְּבָט, כְּרָאוּ, made much use of allusive phrases (שׁוֹשַׁנָּה, "rose" = Israel), and employed the typically liturgical vocabulary: רָשָׁה (for "said, command"), בְּכֵן, גֶּשֶׁם, פְּצִיחָה (for "then") etc. Traces of Italian influence on the language are slight but well defined (פִּרְקוֹן for "fork," and see below with respect to the use of טֶרֶם). The initial use of a demonstrative (זוֹ הַמְּדִינָה) in the language of Aḥimaʿaẓ may derive from late Aramaic, or from the occasional use of the structure in mishnaic Hebrew, or possibly even from Italian or Arabic, as in the case of מִזֶּה הָעִנְיָן in the writings of Shabbetai Donnolo, who preceded him by almost 100 years. This book was written before the language of Spanish poetry had taken definite shape, but Immanuel of Rome, who lived in the middle of the 13th century, and who wrote a clearly biblical Hebrew, studded with quotations, though enriched with mishnaic features and even references to the Mishnah, was well versed in Spanish poetry, as he himself bears witness. Since he followed the trend of Spanish poetry and drew upon its language as a source of inspiration, he makes use of innovations and words whose frequency has risen under the influence of Arabic: סָר meaning "stop," שָׁב for "become," אִנּוּן for "grief" (Ar. *ʾanna*), כְּמוֹ for "approximately," תִּשְׁבֹּרֶת ("geometry"), גֶּשֶׁם ("body"), אֱלוֹהִי ("theological"), לִמּוּדִי ("mathematical"), the pattern מִן...מַה (see above, p. 1631f.) and so on. The imprint of Italian is inestimably greater on his style than on that of Ahimaaz; he wrote poems in Italian and introduced the sonnet into Hebrew poetry. Italian accounts for the use of the following words in the masculine: תֵּבֵל, בֶּטֶן, רֶגֶל, צִפּוֹר, אֶצְבַּע, and of the following in the feminine: זָקָן, שֵׂעָר, חֶסֶד, etc. פֶּרַח, a name of a coin, is a loan translation of the Italian "florin" and the pattern הַשֶּׁלּוֹ is a reflection of *il suo*.

Shabbetai Donnolo, a physician who lived in the 10th century in southern Italy, also wrote in a style blended of mishnaic and biblical Hebrew, and the result is entirely different from the language of the Ibn Tibbons. In addition to technical terms borrowed from Latin and Greek, his language also shows Italian influence: בֶּטֶן in the masculine (like *il ventre*), טֶרֶם and מִטֶּרֶם take on the meanings of Italian *avanti* i.e., first of all, better: נָאֶה לָרוֹפְאִים לֵידַע טֶרֶם הַבְּשָׂמִים ("it is good for doctors, *first of all* to know perfumes"). Ahimaaz too uses *terem* in the sense of "before anything else."

Obadiah of Bartinoro wrote his letters from Ereẓ Israel (in the middle of the 15th century) in a language basically biblical but enriched with mishnaic features, and showing signs of Italian influence, apart from a few usages, mainly in loan words – *cottimo* for "piece work," *capitano* for "captain" etc.

THE KARAITES

The Hebrew of the Karaites has not yet been described as a distinct variety. For the moment it must suffice to say that the rhymed polemical writings resemble those of Saadiah Gaon and the language used by the *geʾonim* in their liturgical poetry. The writings of Daniel al-Qūmisī (ninth century), Sahl b. Maẓliʾaḥ, and Solomon b. Jeroham (10th century), for example, are largely biblical in style, and richly studded with quotations, but also contain freely derived verb forms, in all the *binyanim*, and noun declensions of which the most productive are קִטְלוֹן, קְטִילָה and קֶטֶל. The Karaites fought against the oral tradition, and Saadiah Gaon countered their arguments by pointing out the indispensability of mishnaic Hebrew for understanding the Bible (in his *Perush Shivʿim Millim*); their language, however, is not a pure biblical Hebrew. None of them abstained completely from mishnaic usage, not merely as regards such content words as were vital in the debate on oral law (הֶתֵּר, אִסּוּר, גְּזֵרָה, תַּקָּנָה, מִדְרָשׁ, etc.) but also structures and form words characteristic of the Mishnah: *binyan nitpaʿal*, אוֹתָהּ הַשָּׁנָה, רָאוּי לְ-, צָרִיךְ שֶׁ-, etc. And their vocabulary included words typical of liturgical poetry: רָשָׁה ("say, command"), צָרַח, פְּצִיחָה, etc.

The Karaites were much influenced by Arabic culture, and their prose style is therefore marked by the influence of Arabic; it is very close to the language of the Ibn Tibbons (see *Eškol ha-Kofer* by Hadassi, written in Istanbul in the 12th century). But its specific features are worth special study. There are certain terms characteristic of Karaite Hebrew, some of which occur nowhere else: נִזְכָּרִי and נְקֵבָתִי ("masculine" and "feminine"), עַדְפָנוּת ("advantage"), כֶּתֶם ("impression"), אֶפַע ("event"), הֱיוֹתוּת ("existence"), and so on.

For recent studies of Karaite Hebrew see Maman in Bibliography.

Samaritans

From the 13th and 14th centuries onwards the Samaritans composed prayers and other works in Hebrew influenced by Arabic. A full description has not yet been made; Cowley has offered initial research as has Z. Ben Ḥayyim (*Tarbiz* 10). A necessary line of investigation will have to be how this Hebrew could exist independent of extra-biblical Hebrew (Ben Ḥayyim, *Lešonenu Laʿam*, 1969).

See also Ben Hayyim, *Ivrit va-Aramit Nusaḥ Shomron*, vols. 1–5 (1957–77).

PROVENCE AND NORTHERN FRANCE

The Jews of Provence came under the influence of Spanish Jewry; it was in the towns of Provence (mainly Narbonne and Lunel) that the work of the Ibn Tibbons and the Kimḥis in translation was carried out. It is not surprising, therefore, that Menahem ha-Me'iri from Provence (14th century) wrote his book *Beit ha-Beḥira* in a style containing all the typical features of "Tibbonian" Hebrew. The influence of Arabic is marked, especially in the introduction, and not in the body of the work, which is a summary of halakhic judgments. Nevertheless, even the actual discussion of *halakhah* shows far more Arabic influence than the Hebrew of Maimonides' *Mishneh Torah*.

Unlike the Jews of Provence, the Jews of northern and eastern France had strong cultural and social ties with the Jews of western Germany – "Ashkenaz" – and it was in the towns of Champagne, the Rhine Valley and Lorraine that Ashkenazi Hebrew was fashioned. The Hebrew of Rashi and the French authors of Tosafot (talmudic commentary) is close to Ashkenazi Hebrew, as regards its sources and constituent elements, but the language of influence is Old French, not Middle High German; the influence is much smaller than the corresponding influence of German on Ashkenazi Hebrew.

The influence of French accounts for the increased use of the verb *ʿasa* in the Hebrew of Rashi, by analogy with "*faire*," e.g., עָשָׂה בְּרָכָה, though such forms do occur in mishnaic Hebrew. Also from French is the use of בַּיִת and בָּשָׂר in the feminine. But the French background is most marked in the direct quotation of Old French words in order to explain the Hebrew: "רֹשֶׁם, in French *cogneau*," etc. The language of Rashi is generally excellent, accurate Hebrew; it is largely mishnaic, enriched with biblical words and forms, even his commentary on the Talmud, e.g., תִּפְעַלְנָה, infinitival clauses like בְּבוֹא, בְּשׁוּבִי, the lengthened imperfect, and figurative expressions such as לִבּוֹ דָוֶה עָלָיו ("his heart grew faint" – see Lam. 5:17), הוֹן עָתֵק מְאֹד ("very great riches" – see Prov. 8:18), though on a modest scale compared with the rhetorical figures in the rabbinical style. In his commentary on the Bible he made sparing use of Aramaic, and only in fixed expressions: כְּמָה, דְּאִיתְמַר דִּכְתִיב, and a wide use of the Aramaic prefix *de-* but in his commentary on the Talmud and in *Siddur Rashi* he did use Aramaic and not only technical terms; his language in this respect can be described in the same terms as we shall use for the language of rabbinical Hebrew in general. Rashi created new words and patterns; his understanding of Hebrew grammar and his ability as a stylist give him a special place among the writers of Hebrew in Ashkenaz.

ASHKENAZIC AND RABBINIC HEBREW

The Jews of Ashkenaz (western Germany and eastern France) had close ties with Ereẓ Israel, and this relationship is very evident in their *piyyutim* (Gershom ben Judah Me'or ha-Golah, Jacob Tam, Meir of Rothenburg etc.), which continued the language and grammar of Palestinian liturgical poetry, though on a more modest scale. However, in the responsa, in the books on ritual, in community records, and to some extent, also in books dealing with their trials and tribulations, there is apparent, already from the 11th century, the beginnings of the blended style known as rabbinical Hebrew, found in its most characteristic form in the responsa written in Poland, mainly from the 16th century. It is composed of mishnaic Hebrew, biblical Hebrew, Aramaic (largely from the Babylonian Talmud), a certain amount of Arabic-influenced Hebrew, the influence of Middle High German in Ashkenaz, and once the center of Ashkenazi Jewry had moved to Poland the influence of Yiddish, whose German component was the same kind of German as that spoken by the Jews of Ashkenaz.

The Influence of German on the Hebrew of the Jews of Ashkenaz and the Influence of Yiddish on Hebrew in Poland

The status of Hebrew in Ashkenaz as compared with Middle High German was different from its status in Spain compared with its sister-tongue Arabic. In Germany the two languages in contact were from different families and far apart in form and structure. It is the strangeness of the effect of the influencing language that is most marked, though the very distance can also tone down the influence. The Ibn Tibbons were well aware that it was the closeness of Arabic to Hebrew which secured it such huge influence. From Arabic Hebrew borrowed a few words in Hebrew declensions; from German, at the beginning of the period, no words were borrowed at all, and they were quoted as foreign whenever they were needed in explanation: "כְּוִיָּה or in German *brennt*" (Eleazar b. Nathan, 11th century). Loan words begin to appear in Hebrew in Poland from the 16th century, more in the questions that were posed than in the responsa of the rabbis, and almost all of them dealing with everyday life, hardly any concerned with matters of ritual. They include names of colors and clothes, food, and diseases. Words were also borrowed for which Hebrew equivalents existed: *Diamant* (יַהֲלֹם), *Juwelen* (תַּכְשִׁיטִים) etc. It is the language of the Ḥasidim and the *Mitnaggedim* in the 18th century which is most full of loan words.

Whereas Spanish Jewry was bilingual as far as writing was concerned (Hebrew and Arabic), in Ashkenaz Hebrew served as the sole written language. The literary language of the surrounding culture was mainly Latin, though Middle High German was also beginning to be used in writing for epic poetry, courtly lyrics and sermons. The Middle High German used in sermons to bring people to confession, repentance and fear of sin could well have influenced Ḥasidim of Germany by virtue of the subjects themselves but only as a literary language heard in sermons out of doors, not as a written language. Its influence should therefore be considered as that of a spoken vernacular not as a vehicle for literary expression. The Jew did not regard it as an enlightened, respectable language, worthy of competition with such an excellent tongue as Hebrew. They did not imitate it, they did not translate from it, and they had very little occasion to adopt from it terms and concepts that needed a Hebrew guise. The main effect is felt in passages dealing with everyday life: the account books of the religious congregations, responsa dealing with everyday affairs, accounts of troubles and persecutions.

When Polish Jewry replaced German Jewry as the spiritual center, a change began to take place in the status of Yiddish, transferred to a Slavic environment (though there had been earlier written documents in Yiddish); it became henceforth a normal second written language. Among the responsa written by Moses Isserles, Solomon Luria and others in Poland in the 16th century there are also some written in Yiddish. No study has yet been made on the relation of Hebrew and Middle High German in Germany as compared with that of Hebrew and Yiddish in Poland. Generally speaking, the German element in the Hebrew of Ashkenaz is close to that in the Hebrew of Poland; it is only in the language of the Ḥasidim and the *Mitnaggedim* in the 18th century that the influence of Yiddish is far more profoundly felt.

In the history of Ashkenazi Hebrew, a special place is reserved for the language of *Sefer Ḥasidim*, a collection of tales and customs attributed to *Judah he-Ḥasid from Regensburg and written or collected by his disciples in the 12th and 13th centuries. The spirit of modesty and humility typical of those ascetic God-fearing Ḥasidim permeated not only the subject-matter but also the language, which was very close to the spoken variety, abounding in anacolouthon, unstylized, without interlarded quotations or figurative embellishment. The vocabulary of the book is small, sufficient for the needs of the subject-matter, with no concern for the needs of style, and the influence of Middle High German is quite strongly felt. The influence of Middle High German and the German element in Yiddish is best described by reference to the *Sefer Ḥasidim* and the responsa written in Germany and Poland. The following are some of the most noteworthy features: there is considerable use of prepositions in the German manner, though Hebrew prepositional usages were not rejected completely; they are also used, the proportion depending on the writer, the translator or the context (as already noted, the influence of German is more marked in passages dealing with everyday affairs: גָּנַב לְ- instead of גָּנַב מִן, ... מתגאה מִן ("proud of"") as in *sich rühmen von*; יָדַע מִן as in *wissen von*. The preposition אַחֲרֵי takes on the uses of *nach* – שָׁלַח אַחֲרָיו ("send for him"), and so on. The preposition עַל is used like *auf*: קָנָה עַל הַשּׁוּק ("bought in the market") *auf den Market*; הָיָה עַל הָרְחוֹב ("was in the street") – *auf der Strasse*; הִמְתִּין עַל פְּלוֹנִי ("wait for someone") – *auf jemand*; and even more in the language of the Ḥasidim in the 18th century: נָסַע עַל שַׁבָּת, קֶמַח עַל פֶּסַח etc. Though the possessive construct pattern found in the Bible is commoner than the prepositional structure with *šel* found in mishnaic Hebrew, there are exceptional cases where a prepositional structure with *min* is used, in imitation of *von*: גַּבַּאי מִן הַצְּדָקָה ("a collector of charity"). There are a few loan translations, mainly for the purpose of expressing concepts from daily life: בֵּית הָעֵצָה (*Rathaus*); בֵּית עֲנִיִּים ("poorhouse"); בֵּית יְתוֹמִים ("orphanage"). Much commoner is the extension of the meaning of the Hebrew word in accordance with the meanings of its Middle High German equivalent: נֶגֶד or כְּנֶגֶד means "approximately," a secondary meaning of *gegen*, and in later Hebrew סָבִיב לְ- is used in this sense, like *um*. יָדַע means "be able" as well as "know," since *koennen* has both meanings; הַפָּסוּק עוֹמֵד כָּתוּב (as in Ger. *steht*), תּוֹפֵס means "hurry" (*chappen*), עָזַב means "let" (*lassen*), אֵיזֶה means "some" as well as "which," both meanings of *welche*; לְהוֹזִיל means "agree" (from *billigen*); חוֹלֶה אֵצֶל הַקֹּר "sick because of the cold," a secondary meaning of Middle High German *bi* (the similarity between אֵצֶל and עַל יְדֵי may have helped). In the responsa, the phrase הָיָה לוֹ expresses duty and obligation, not permission and ability as in mishnaic Hebrew and Aramaic; this is the meaning of Middle High German *hân ze*. Very common is the use of מַה as a relative pronoun – מַעֲשִׂים מַה שֶּׁחָפֵץ שֶׁיַּעֲשֶׂה "deeds that he wants to perform" (*Sefer Ḥasidim*) – like Middle High German *was*. One new sentence structure came from Middle High German: a subjective clause whose predicator was a modal adjective (אָסוּר "forbidden," צָרִיךְ "necessary," טוֹב "good") could begin with the word אִם, which gave it the force of a conditional clause – יֵשׁ דְּבָרִים שֶׁאָסוּר אִם יְלַמֵּד לַאֲחֵרִים "there are things which it is forbidden that (or "if") he teaches (them) to others." A similar structure with *ob* is found under such conditions in Middle High German.

German also produced a marked increase in the use of features which already existed in Hebrew though less conspicuously. רַק in the prepositional sense of "but" is found in the Bible אֲשֶׁר לֹא תְדַבֵּר אֵלַי רַק אֱמֶת ("tell me nothing but the truth"; I Kings 22:16) – and this biblical stylistic feature occurs in Spanish Jewish poetry. In Ashkenazic Hebrew רַק is also used as a conjunction in the sense of "but, however," before a verbal clause; it also occurs in the form רַק שֶׁ presumably under the influence of Middle High German *nur*, which means both 'but' and 'only.' An example is חַס לִי לִרְאוֹת כָּזֶה וְלֹא לִמְחוֹת וְרַק כָּל זֶה עֲדַיִן הוּא שׁוֹרֶשׁ רֹאשׁ וְלַעֲנָה "God forbid I should see such a thing and not protest, *but* all this is still a source of evil and corruption" (from the 17th century *Shenei Luḥot ha-Berit*). עַד occurs with the meaning "as long as," found in biblical and mishnaic Hebrew, and assisted by the fact that *bis* carries this meaning. In the Bible אָז sometimes comes at the beginning of the apodosis in a conditional sentence: לוּלֵי תוֹרָתְךָ שַׁעֲשֻׁעָי אָז אָבַדְתִּי בְעָנְיִי (Ps. 119:92) "if thy law had not been my delight *then* I should have perished in my troubles." In Ashkenazic Hebrew the high frequency of אָז after a conditional or temporal clause can be attributed to the corresponding use in German of *denn*, e.g., in the language of Berthold from Regensburg, a preacher at the time of the *Sefer Ḥasidim*. The normal pattern is thus אִם יִהְיֶה בְּהַגְרָמָתוֹ אָז כָּל הַקָּהָל פְּטוּרִים "if he is the cause, *then* the whole congregation is exempt."

The large number of expressions in German with *machen* is matched in Ashkenazic Hebrew by the number of expressions with עָשָׂה, though a few such phrases can be found in the Midrashim: עָשָׂה חֲרָפָה, עָשָׂה נְזִיפָה, עָשָׂה עוֹלָה, עָשָׂה עֲבֵרָה, עָשָׂה רְצִיחָה, etc. The influence of German also explains the number of expressions like הָיָה לוֹ עָוֶל, הָיָה לוֹ בּוּשָׁה, הָיָה לוֹ צַעַר. Here it is the frequency which is affected, since they are not a complete innovation in Hebrew. The use of *sich* as a reflexive object leads to the use of inflected עֶצֶם in Hebrew translation – equivalents; to the few examples found in mishnaic Hebrew are added מְסַגֵּל עַצְמוֹ ("adjust oneself"), מַחֲזִיק עַצְמוֹ ("hold oneself," i.e., avoid, as in Ger.) תּוֹפֵס עַצְמוֹ ("consider oneself"). It was also used with verbs in *binyan hitpa'el*, which in such cases lost reflexive meaning: מִתְקַשֵּׁט עַצְמוֹ ("adorn oneself"), מִתְלַבֶּשֶׁת עַצְמָהּ כְּכוֹמֶרֶת ("dresses herself as a priestess" – *Sefer Ḥasidim*), etc.

German could also lead to a diminution in frequency of occurrence: the relative infrequency of אֶת as compared with biblical and mishnaic Hebrew can be explained by the absence of any corresponding particle in German. Similarly the reduction in the use of the definite article corresponds with its reduced use in Middle High German; נָטְלוּ כֹּל and not… הַכֹּל is modeled on the use of *alles*.

No new tense forms were created in Ashkenazic Hebrew, but to some extent the systemic relationships of existing forms were reorganized (see Rabin in bibl.). In *Sefer Ḥasidim* the use of the participle for both present and future indicative is well marked: לֶעָתִיד לָבוֹא מִתְפַּלְּלִים. The imperfect יִקְטֹל serves as present and future subjunctive, expressing doubt, possibility etc.: הַזֶּרַע שֶׁל גֵּר יִהְיֶה צַדִּיקִים "the seed of a proselyte may produce righteous men." And this systemic relationship between קוֹטֵל and יִקְטֹל corresponds with the opposition between present-future indicative and present-future subjunctive in Middle High German, where the expression of futurity by means of modal auxilliaries – *will, soll* – was still rare. Moreover, since there is a firm foundation for this division of function between קוֹטֵל and יִקְטֹל in mishnaic Hebrew and Aramaic, the novelty is felt more strongly in the use of the pattern הָיָה פּוֹעֵל not only as a past continuous (a usage inherited from mishnaic Hebrew) but also as a functional, though not formal, equivalent of the past subjunctive in Middle High German: וְהָרַב לֹא הָיָה מְלַמְּדוֹ בְּחִנָּם "the rabbi *would not* teach him for nothing" (*Sefer Ḥasidim*, section 585). This use is also not a complete innovation, since it resembles the combination הָיָה and present participle in unfulfilled conditions in Aramaic and in mishnaic Hebrew (אִלּוּ הָיִיתִי יוֹדֵעַ "if I had known," הֲוָא אמינא); what is new is the systemic relationship between קָטַל and הָיָה קוֹטֵל, corresponding to the past indicative and past subjunctive in Middle High German. There are examples in Ashkenazic Hebrew of the sequence of tenses found in German: רָאָה בַּחֲלוֹם שֶׁהָיָה רוֹכֵב עַל סוּס אָדֹם "he saw in a dream that he was riding on a red horse" (in *Sefer Ḥasidim*); the tense in the subordinate clause is marked as past, like the main clause, and not present, which is normal in Hebrew.

The Role of Mishnaic Hebrew in Ashkenazic Hebrew

The language of Jews who studied Talmud naturally made great use of mishnaic Hebrew. It should be noted that *Sefer Ḥasidim* actually uses forms that are not particularly common, e.g., *binyan nuf'al* – נֻצַּל ("was saved"), נֻטַּל ("was taken" – and the pattern הַקְטִילָה as verbal noun for *binyan hif'il* – הַרְעִיבָה, הַפְסִידָה. The most productive derivational pattern by far was קַטְלָן from mishnaic Hebrew; the innovations include שַׁדְּכָן, עַוְלָן, שַׂמְחָן, עַצְרָן ("miser"), שְׁתַדְּלָן, מַטְבְּעָן ("coiner"), פַּשְׁרָן, etc.

The Role of Biblical Hebrew

Ashkenazic Hebrew took from all varieties known to its writers; the Hebrew of the Bible was absorbed from the stratum of biblical Hebrew in the liturgy, from the weekly readings of the law and from the *hafṭara*. Hence the use of אָז, יַתְכֵן, לְמַעַן, יַעַן, טֶרֶם, and so on. And unlike Arabic-influenced prose, Ashkenazic Hebrew also made use of lengthened tense forms: אֶכְתְּבָה, יִשְׁמְרוּן and the future with *waw* conversive. This tense is seldom found in *Sefer Ḥasidim* and relatively infrequently in the prose of Rashi, but it began to occur with increasing frequency until it became a distinguishing mark of rabbinic Hebrew. The increasing use of rhetorical figures from the Bible may have helped to establish it in the language; fragments of verses which contained a *waw* conversive were directly quoted as part of the rhetorical figure, and thus made their way into rabbinic Hebrew. Biblical figures of speech are absent from the humble style of *Sefer Ḥasidim*, and used with taste and moderation by Rashi; in the language of Jacob Tam they are widespread (their flavor of *piyyut* derives from his being a liturgical poet), and they are quite common in the writings of Rabbi Meir of Rothenburg (end of the 14th century), for example. They are very common in the salutations, at the beginning of many of the responsa from Germany and Poland, though not only there. Some writers use them more, some less, depending on their individual taste and ability. Though most rhetorical figures derive from verses in the Bible, there are also some from mishnaic Hebrew, and even from Aramaic, all for the rhetorical adornment of the opening section of the letter, with no conception of the principle of purity of biblical language as a rhetorical virtue. The writers of the responsa begin שָׁמַעְתִּי וַתִּרְגַּז בִּטְנִי ("I heard and my stomach quaked"; Meir of Rothenburg); or צָלַלְתִּי בְּמַיִם אַדִּירִים וְהֶעֱלֵיתִי חֶרֶס (see Ex. 15:6, "I plunged into deep water and brought up nothing"; Moses Isserles); or וָאֶתֵּן אֶת לִבִּי לִדְרֹשׁ וְלָתוּר סִבּוֹתָיו בִּסְפָרִים (see Eccles. 1:13, "I gave my heart to seek and search out its reasons in books" (a frequent figure)). They begin with a rhymed eulogy: (see Ps. 18:30, אִמְרָתְךָ צְרוּפָה וּמַחְשְׁבֹתֶיךָ עֲמֻקָּה וְצָפָה "thy word is perfect and thy feelings are deep…"; Meir of Rothenburg)). Sometimes the point of the quotation distorts the original meaning of the verse quoted: Simeon accuses Reuben in the words בִּפְלַגּוֹת רְאוּבֵן גְּדוֹלִים חִקְרֵי לֵב (see Judg. 5:16, "in the divisions of Reuben there were great heart-searchings" (a question addressed to Jacob Tam). Sometimes the form is changed: the Rabbi replies הַקּוֹל קוֹל עָקֹב (not עִרְעוּרִים וְקוֹל – יַעֲקֹב) "the voice is the voice of the deceit." Sometimes the spelling of the word is changed: הָאֶרֶז אֲשֶׁר בַּלְּבָנוֹן בְּאֵר ("the cedar of Lebanon is proof") the reference is to Isaiah 40:16 where the form is actually בָּעֵר ("burns"; a quip from the responsa of *Ša'ar Efrayim*, 17th century).

The Role of Aramaic

In *Sefer Ḥasidim* there are slight touches of Aramaic – דִּכְתִיב, כִּדְבָעֵי, – and they are fairly restricted in Rashi's commentary on the Bible. However, in Rashi's commentary on the Talmud, in the responsa of Jacob Tam, or in *Sefer ha-Rokeaḥ* of Eleazar of Worms, the amount of Aramaic acquires a status comparable to that of mishnaic Hebrew, since both constitute the language of the Talmud and the writers may not always have realized when they had moved from Hebrew to Aramaic.

The extensive use of Aramaic is not confined to the Aramaic *halakhah* under discussion, nor even to the technical terms alone (קַיְימָא לָן, אַלְמָא, טַעֲמַיְהוּ, צְרִיכָא, פְּלִיגֵי, etc.). -דְּ is used instead of שֶׁ in an otherwise completely Hebrew context, to mean "of" – הַפֶּרֶק דְּהַמַּסֶּכֶת (the chapter of the tractate); הָרַב דְּשְׁפֵּירָא; פִּנְקָס דְּוַעַד אַרְבַּע אֲרָצוֹת – and also to mean "that" – נִרְאֶה לִי דְּ- ("it seems to me that…"); אָמַרְתִּי דְּאָסוּר ("I said that it was forbidden"). Whereas as Rashi commenting on the Bible writes מִשּׁוּם שֶׁ-; כֵּיוָן שֶׁ-; אַף עַל פִּי שֶׁ- when he comments on the Talmud he writes מִשּׁוּם דְּ-; כֵּיוָן דְּ-; אַף עַל גַּב דְּ-. The verb forms מַיְירֵי and מַיְיתֵי are much used in Hebrew contexts, and sometimes complete clauses in Aramaic are interpolated. Generally the Aramaic phrases are quoted freely in new Hebrew contexts, though in the form and with the inflections found in the Talmud. The Hebrew most thoroughly mixed with Aramaic was written in Poland during the 17th and 18th centuries.

The Link With Arab-Influenced Hebrew

The Jews of Ashkenaz and the Jews of Spain maintained cultural ties, whether by means of responsa (e.g., when Asher ben Jeḥiel moved from Germany to Spain) or by reading each other's books. The kabbalists of Spain were interested in the Ḥasidism of Ashkenaz, in Germany they read the writings of Maimonides, Saadiah Gaon, and the *musar* book, *Ḥobot ha-Lebabot*. In Poland several of the scientific works, all written in "Tibbonian" Hebrew, were well known.

Since Ashkenazic Hebrew reflects all the varieties of literature known to its writers, and since in principal there was no form of the language whose use was banned on stylistic and grammatical grounds, it is not surprising that several features of Arab-influenced Hebrew also occurred. The use of nouns ending with the suffixes -ִית and -וּת in the masculine is characteristic of rabbinic Hebrew (פְּרִישׁוּת רַבָּנִי, תַּכְלִית אַחֲרוֹן), and similarly plural concord of the form סוֹדוֹת גְּדוֹלוֹת (instead of גְּדוֹלִים). It is not clear whether this usage derives from Spanish Hebrew or whether it is an aspect of the general weakening of strict grammatical rules (it is possible that this is due to the fact that words ending in *-ut* and *-it* in Yiddish entered the neuter gender). Sometimes Arabic and German/Yiddish tended to produce the same result, e.g., the demonstrative without the article before the noun, reduced use of אֶת, the preposition מִן in סֵפֶר מִן, דָּבָר מִן and the comparative form יוֹתֵר נָאֶה, יוֹתֵר טוֹב, where the frequency and the order of words can be attributed to German (*mehr…*) and French (*plus…*), though Arab-influenced Hebrew also uses this structure as a translation of Arabic.

A deliberate, quite marked use of the Hebrew which took shape in Spain and Provence is found in Poland, mainly from the 16th and 17th centuries. Moses Isserles was a man of philosophic bent and apart from his responsa on matters of *halakhah* he also used the language of the *Guide of the Perlexed*: עִיּוּנִי, אֱלֹהִי, אַקְלִים ("region"), מַסְכִּים ("match, fit"), מֻשְׂכָּל, בָּרַח מִלַּעֲסֹק ("refrain from doing"…), עַל צַד הַשֵּׂכֶל and so on.

Forty years after the expulsion from Spain 16th-century Safed became a center for Jewish learning and Kabbalah whose greatest scholars generally wrote a Hebrew close to the Arabic-influenced variety of Spain and Provence, especially in Kabbalistic works where a style of writing had already been established in Spain (see, for example, the language of Moses Cordovero). In Safed, too, the use of lengthened tense forms and the *waw* conversive were introduced into the language of prose. Isaiah Horowitz, author of *Shenei Luḥot ha-Berit,* was educated in Poland and wrote an Ashkenazic Hebrew, but his style contained many of the distinguishing marks of Arabic-influenced Hebrew: the definite article before an infinitive e.g., הַהִשְׁתַּמֵּשׁ, רֹשֶׁם for "influence," מֻשְׂכָּל, מַסְכִּים meaning "match," אֱמֶת in the masculine, עַצְמוּת, מַהוּת and so on; after all, he was a kabbalist, immigrated to Ereẓ Israel, and wrote his book there.

The extreme case of the encounter between Spanish Hebrew and Ashkenazic Hebrew is the language of the 18th century Ḥasidim. Besides being stamped with the imprint of Yiddish to a greater extent than any preceding variety of Hebrew, it also continues the traditional prose style of Ashkenazic Hebrew (as exemplified in the responsa, in the *musar* books and especially in the well-loved *Sefer Ḥasidim*). But whereas stories of the *ẓaddikim* and passages dealing with everyday life are written mainly in Ashkenazic, rabbinic Hebrew, the philosophic literature of Ḥasidim is strongly marked by Spanish Hebrew; the ḥasidic writers continued the kabbalistic tradition of Isaac Luria, and took over the terms and expressions from kabbalistic literature and Spanish books of ethics such as *Ḥobot ha-Lebabot*; רוּחָנִיּוּת ("spirituality"), אַחְדוּת ("unity"), גַּשְׁמִיּוּת ("corporeality"), בְּחִינָה, סְגֻלָּה, דְּבֵקוּת, בְּתַכְלִית, etc. (see M.Z. Kaddari in bibl.).

Influence of Hebrew on Yiddish

It was through rabbinic Hebrew, with its blend of all varieties, that Hebrew words found their way into Yiddish. From biblical Hebrew – עַוְלָה, אָז יִתָּכֵן; from mishnaic – אֶפְשָׁר, אֲפִלּוּ; from Aramaic – פְּשִׁיטָא, סְתָמָא, and even from Arab-influenced Hebrew, mainly via ḥasidic literature: שְׁלִילָה, מֻגְשָׁם, גַּשְׁמִיּוּת, הֶעְדֵּר, etc. Many of the high frequency words most characteristic of Ashkenazic Hebrew, words occurring already in *Sefer Ḥasidim*, came into Yiddish: מֵאוּס ("obnoxious"), עוֹלָם (with the meaning "people," as in Aramaic כְּלֵי עָלְמָא), קָהָל ("an urban Jewish community"), מַעֲשֶׂה, מַמָּשׁ (in the language of the *Sefer Ḥasidim* it already has the meaning "story" as well as "deed"), אָז, אוֹדוֹת, תָּדִיר. The Hebrew derivational pattern most characteristically Yiddish – קַטְלָן – (in words like יַשְׁרָן, יַקְרָן, בַּלְעָן, בַּטְלָן, etc.) is also the pattern most vital to Ashkenazic Hebrew.

Haskalah and Medieval Hebrew

The stylistic uniqueness of rabbinic Hebrew lies in its blend of different varieties of the language: only a few new words were coined, to meet the needs of writing about everyday life. By contrast, Spanish Hebrew was a professional tool, a necessary instrument for all kinds of scientific, philosophic and scholarly writing. The writers of the Haskalah turned their backs on rabbinic Hebrew for its careless grammar and because it represented the Judaism of the Talmud. For poetry and to a considerable extent for stories they adopted biblical Hebrew; however, for serious prose works some of the *maskilim* chose the Arabic-influenced language of Spain, especially for technical terms and expressions (see for example the extensive use of Tibbonian Hebrew made by Naḥman Krochmal in *Moreh Nebukhei ha-Zeman*).

The Hebrew language was a major concern of Haskalah writers. They were keenly aware of normative problems in writing and the need for linguistic research in Hebrew. Writers and grammarians like Naphtali Herz *Wessely, Judah Leib *Ben Ze'ev, and those who collected ancient texts made a decisive contribution toward the molding of the language and its modernization. The Haskalah may be seen as a preparatory period for the revival of Hebrew (see Modern *Hebrew Literature).

[Esther Goldenberg]

MODERN PERIOD

The growth of Hebrew as a modern language, spoken by masses and gradually used in all areas of life and thought, may be divided into three stages corresponding to periods in the history of modern Palestine: (1) 1881–1918 initiated by Eliezer *Ben-Yehuda's arrival in the country. He and his followers developed and propagated Hebrew in everyday life. (2) 1918–1948; under British rule when Hebrew was first considered a language of Palestine, and later (1922) one of the three official languages. During this time the Hebrew-speaking population increased rapidly, established many cultural institutions, including its own educational system up to university level, in all of which Hebrew, with few initial exceptions, became the only language used. (3) 1948– marked by the foundation of the State of Israel. Hebrew became the predominant language of the state, and was used in all branches of its activities: government departments, the army, etc., were integrated into the life of the Hebrew-speaking population. Gradually Hebrew was also spoken by non-Jewish citizens. Each of these three periods, characterized by the cultural background and the linguistic past of the immigrants who adopted Hebrew as their new language, has influenced its revolution.

[Eli Eytan]

At the time of the revival of Hebrew for everyday speech, the languages most current in the old *yishuv* (Jewish population) were *Yiddish, *Ladino, and *Arabic, while French and German formed the main channels to European culture. The immigrants of the first period, mostly from Eastern Europe, spoke Yiddish; many of them also spoke Russian or Polish and at least understood German. These languages influenced Hebrew but their effect, noticeable in new aspects of Hebrew, gradually decreased, and the impact of English grew. Since the end of World War I English had a marked influence on Hebrew because of the influx of British and other English-speaking government and army personnel and their closer contacts with the *yishuv*. The fact that the establishment of the State of Israel did not diminish this influence is due to a wide knowledge of English among the Israeli population through higher education and close acquaintance with English and American culture to which immigration from English-speaking countries contributed substantially.

Period of Revival (1881–1918)

Hebrew was spoken in Palestine even before the revival movement, but only as a *lingua franca* among Jews who had no other common language. This phenomenon also existed among Jews in many other countries in earlier periods. The revival, in contrast to early periods, however, saw the establishment of Hebrew as the sole or at least the principal language, i.e., a transformation from a language used only occasionally for special purposes by speakers of other languages to a language used by a community for all their communication needs – speaking, reading, and writing.

The revival took place in Palestine. When the British conquered the country, Hebrew was already one of the languages of Palestine. In General Allenby's published proclamation about martial law in Jerusalem, Hebrew was published on top, while Arabic was the second, before Russian and Greek, all considered languages used by the local population. On the other side of the sheet, the proclamation was published in (1) English, (2) French and (3) Italian, languages of the allies. Only toward the end of this period, Hebrew also began to be studied in the Diaspora to a limited extent.

Eliezer Ben-Yehuda's pioneer work for the revival of Hebrew would have failed had there not been at that time three conditions which proved essential to the process of revival: (1) There was no national language in Palestine. The inhabitants did not belong to a "nation" (in the Western sense), but were divided into religious-ethnic communities ("millets") that used a number of languages. Literary Arabic was the language of prayer, worship, and study for all Muslims including government workers and members of the Turkish army and, to some degree, for several Christian denominations. But millions of Muslims outside Palestine also used literary Arabic in a similar fashion, thus preventing it from being an exclusive national language. Turkish was used for political, governmental, and military matters all over the Ottoman Empire. The most common spoken language was local colloquial Arabic, which was used only as a spoken vernacular and thus deemed unworthy to be a national language. Other languages, such as French, Russian, Italian, Greek, and Armenian were used by certain millets, or as cultural languages. None of them, however, could be taken as a national language. (2) European nationalist thought, together with a yearning for a Hebrew renaissance, reached Palestine in the middle of the 19th century. Already in the 1860s young people in the Jewish communities of Palestine attempted to change the static way of life there. Newspapers, printing houses, and various workshops were founded, and settlements were established "outside the walls" (i.e., of the old *yishuv*). The lack of a national language in Palestine created the need for a common language for the developing society, and it was natural that Hebrew be considered worthy of this role; all the more so that Hebrew (in the Sephardi pronunciation) even before this had been the common language of different Jewish communities. (3) The fact that the original language of the country had been Hebrew provided a solid ideological basis for the revival of the language, and gave it an advantage which no other language had. Publication of such ancient Hebrew inscriptions or engravings as the Siloam inscription (1880) and the Mesha inscription (1868) made a deep impression upon the people of that generation and emphasized the connection between Hebrew and Palestine. The revival of the language symbolized the "Golden Age" of ancient Israel which was about to be renewed.

The major difficulty encountered in making Hebrew the sole (or principal) language of the country was in the area of vocabulary. There were few difficulties, if any, in the field of grammar. In Hebrew phonology the need for marking such new sounds as č, ž, ğ (to accommodate foreign words and non-Hebraic personal names) was met without difficulty by adapting the letters ג', ז', צ'. (These sounds had previously been marked by combinations of letters such as טש, זש, דזש. ז' had been indicated for some time also by the letter י', undoubtedly through the influence of the French pronunciation of the letter *j*.) The problems of orthography were solved at once: "defective" orthography (כתיב חסר) was introduced. There were, certainly, difficulties in this area, and it is relevant to mention Ben-Yehuda's short-lived experiment in the use of "capital" letters for personal names (as in English and French). Morphology was not expanded, but newly invented words were usually styled according to existing morphological patterns. It is often possible to distinguish tendencies to use a certain pattern or a specific suffix, such as Ithamar *Ben-Avi's predilection for the suffix of relation (יהודה מיידית, עמדה זכותית). Although Hebrew syntax changed considerably during the days of the revival of the language, these changes were generally brought about unintentionally and without premeditation. (However, an apparent example of an intentional syntactical change is to begin sentences with a verb, like in Arabic, as was done for a time in newspapers.) In contrast, the need for new words was recognized from the start. Ben-Yehuda illustrates this in the following statement: "Have any of the readers (of Smolenskin) ever felt that in all of the circumstances of the different events that this very capable author brought into his stories, he never mentioned for example, the simple, common act, of tickling? This act which we meet often in every story in a living language we will never meet in the stories of Smolenskin, simply because he did not have a word for it. In spite of this his stories are well written. But whoever wishes to write something of wisdom and science, and especially someone like myself, who speaks Hebrew at home with the children, about everything in life, feels every moment a lack of words without which living speech cannot take place" (the Large Introduction," 12–13). Most of the efforts of those who revived the language were dedicated to answering this need.

The End of the Revival Period

The period of revival was characterized by reviving existing words, creating new ones, and enriching the language with words from Semitic sources (in the main) cast in the Hebrew mold. However, a large number of these words (several thousand) were rejected and have fallen into disuse. The pressing need to remedy the critical lack of words often led to hasty innovations. Those educated in literary Hebrew, especially the last generation of *maskilim* in Eastern Europe, did not readily accept this "manufacturing of words" in Palestine. They tended to be more careful in making innovations, preferring to adopt foreign words, especially "international" terms, the majority of which were of a Latin or Greek origin. This school of thought began to make its influence felt in Palestine from 1905 onward, with the Second Aliyah. The coming of the Third Aliyah from Eastern Europe, immediately after World War I, strengthened this view until in the late 1920s the influence of the "language of the revival" could hardly be recognized since many of its words were forgotten. The late books and journalism of Ithamar *Ben-Avi were a kind of "swan song" of the revival period, but even his language greatly reflected the abovementioned changes. The end of the Ottoman Empire and the recognition of Hebrew as an official language in Palestine is therefore only one reason for fixing the end of World War I as the close of the "revival period." The other reason is that at this time the influence of those who demanded great caution in the formation of new words grew, and they were tolerant to foreign words as long as proper Hebrew terms had not been created with careful consideration.

See also Y.M. *Pines, Z. *Jawitz, the *Academy of the Hebrew Language.

[Uzzi Ornan]

Linguistic Problems of Modern Hebrew

PRONUNCIATION. Reviewing the first 22 years of the Va'ad ha-Lashon (*Zihkronot Va'ad ha-Lashon* I, 2nd ed. p. 4), Ben-Yehuda recalls the days when all the various pronunciations of Hebrew were heard in Jerusalem "from the Lithuanian to the Sephardi, from the Volhynian to the Yemenite and the Persian." The necessity to establish a standard pronunciation was under discussion for some time. At a meeting of teachers in 1885, for example, it was decided to teach Ashkenazi Hebrew for the first two years in Ashkenazi schools and then switch to Sephardi pronunciation, while in Sephardi schools the opposite should be done – in "order that they know both." By 1912, however, Ben-Yehuda continues, "by the nature of things the Oriental pronunciation, the one living among the Sephardim, had become dominant, and from Jerusalem it spread to all speakers of Hebrew in the country." This statement was a rough summary of the position which had developed in a relatively short time, but which, in fact, was – and is to this day – only a limited fulfillment of the original wish to adopt the Sephardi pronunciation. The phonetic inventory of the Ashkenazim, both of the old *yishuv* and new immigrants whose number rapidly grew, could not easily be replaced by the whole range of sounds found in genuine Sephardi speech. To give one example, any Ashkenazi could easily learn to pronounce both vowels of the verb עָצַר ("he restrained," etc.) as *a* and to stress its last syllable, instead of pronouncing the first vowel as *o* (as according to his Ashkenazi dialect), and stressing the first syllable. It proved, however, impossible for the vast majority of Ashkenazi Jews – except by sustained conscious effort to – pronounce the Sephardi (like Arabic) consonants ע [ʿ] and צ [ṣ]. עָצַר and אָצַר ("he stored up"), as well as many other pairs of linguistic forms, thus became homophonous, creating new problems in teaching orthography and grammar. This process of different phonemes coinciding in actualization even led to certain restrictions in the use of the existing vocabulary and in the possibilities of its enlargement. אָצַר, e.g., is hardly ever used in everyday speech, and a possible new noun מַאֲצָר ‡ would be rejected owing to its homophonous rival מַעֲצָר ("retention, arrest"). The difficulties, stemming from the homophony of originally distinctive features, constituted, and still do, one of the main arguments to continue trying to propagate a purer Oriental pronunciation. On the other hand, the common "Sephardi" pronunciation had meanwhile acquired a certain value of social superiority, since most of the leaders of the new *yishuv* came from Ashkenazi circles, and many Oriental Jews, whose original speech did contain the sounds in question, abandoned that part of their native phonetic inventory in order to imitate the speech of their social superiors.

At the first convention of the Hebrew Teachers' Association in 1903, the pronunciation issue was discussed, but no decision was taken, mainly because Eliezer Ben-Yehuda and David Yellin, members of the Va'ad ha-Lashon, held different views on the desirability and feasibility of one or the other feature of genuine Oriental pronunciation being adopted as standard. The debate went on until, in 1923, the Va'ad ha-Lashon decided to demand the following reform in the pronunciation of the Hebrew letters in question: ב without *dageš* = English *v*; ו = Arabic *wāw* and English *w*; ח = Arabic *ḥā* as distinct from כ without *dageš* = Arabic *ḫā* and German *ch* (as in "Bach"); ט = Arabic *ṭāʿ* emphatic *t*; ע = Arabic *ʿayn*; צ = German *z* (*tz*); ק = Arabic *qāf* (emphatic velar); ת without *dageš* = Arabic *ṯā* and English unvoiced *th* (as in "thin").

It is noteworthy that this ruling does not follow the Sephardi tradition in all details. Here, both alternants of *bet*, one written with *dageš* (בּ) and the other without (ב), were pronounced by some Sephardi communities as *b*, and the settlers of Galilee, following their Sephardi teachers, had already adopted this pronunciation. The Sephardim also pronounced צ as emphatic unvoiced ṣ, like Arabic *ṣād*, while the pronunciation *tz* provided for in the ruling is Ashkenazi. Furthermore, nothing was said about the vowel *segol* (ֶ), which in Sephardi speech is not distinguished from *ṣere* ֵ), i.e., closed *ẹ*, while Ashkenazim and some Israeli speakers to this day distinguish *segol* from *ṣere*. The Va'ad ha-Lashon in this decision also omitted mentioning the difference in pronouncing *qameṣ* preceding *ḥaṭaf-qameṣ*, as in נָעֳמִי, which the Sephardim pronounce *Naʿomi* and the Ashkenazim (and most Israelis) *Noʿomi*.

The authority of the Va'ad ha-Lashon was not sufficient to enforce this reform in the face of already-established speech habits. Consequently, current Hebrew pronunciation differs from that of the Ashkenazim in the following details only: (1) *qameṣ-gadol* (ָ) = *a*; (2) *ḥolem* (וֹ) = *o*; (3) *taw* without *dageš* (ת) = *t*; (4) ultimate stress of most words, while penultimate stress is confined to some classes of words, as in classical Hebrew.

In the matter of stress, however, the Ashkenazi way has led to some more deviations from the Sephardi and classical Hebrew system. Many proper names of persons and places have penultimate stress in everyday speech: ('Raḥel; 'Moshe, 'Shlomo, 'Ḥẹfa, etc.), and the retracted accent has become, particularly in childrens' speech, a mark for names of things charged with some affective value: *'glida* ("ice cream"), *buba* ("doll"), etc. Penultimate and antepenultimate stresses are also characteristics of foreign borrowings: *komu'nisti* ("communist"), *rele'vanti* ("relevant") etc., notwithstanding their Hebrew suffix *-i; integ'raẓya* ("integration"), *uni'versita* or *univer'sita*; ("university"), etc.

Efforts to propagate a diction based on classical grammar and Sephardi pronunciation were especially made among broadcasters. The question, however, as to what this desirable correct diction entails and what can be attained was debated up to the late 1960s. Up to that time, the *Academy of the Hebrew Language had recommended to the Israel Broadcasting Service to observe the Oriental pronunciation of *ḥet* and *ʿayin*, the gemination of consonants with *dageš-ḥazaq*, as in *hassefer* (הַסֵּפֶר); *dibber* (דִּבֵּר); and the *šewa-naʿ*, as in *devarim* (דְּבָרִים), *katevu* (כָּתְבוּ), *dibberu* (דִּבְּרוּ). This recommendation was followed to some extent. It is doubtful whether the Oriental diction, though preserved by some Jews of the Oriental communities and applied to Hebrew by Arab citizens, can still contribute to a reform in the speech of wider circles. On opposite trends see Bentolila in Bibliography.

SPELLING. In 1929 when the Va'ad ha-Lashon first published its quarterly *Leshonenu*, the editors stated in their programmatic introduction: "The problem of spelling has not yet been solved.... Some advocate grammatical spelling, others insist on 'full' spelling. This is why the editors have decided to use, for the present, the accepted grammatical spelling and add complete punctuation wherever the reading is doubtful... Thus, we have attained uniformity of spelling without deciding upon the problem itself." What is meant by "full spelling" (כְּתִיב מָלֵא) here is the method of employing, instead of vowel punctuation, vowel letters to supplement the letters admitted in the "accepted grammatical spelling" which, in turn, is a standardized biblical orthography. This system had been proposed by David Yellin and adopted in the summer of 1905 at the teachers' convention at Gederah. Although it has been taught in schools ever since, the debate on the problem never ceased, and actual usage outside, and partly inside, schools went its own way.

According to this system, every word is spelled in one way only, whether vocalization for vowels etc. is added or left out, e.g., בֹּקֶר ("morning"), בָּקָר ("cattle"), בִּקֵּר ("he visited"), and other words having the same three consonants all have the same written form in unvocalized spelling. Their intended reading is revealed by the context only, unless one or more significant vowel points are added to hint at it, e.g., בֹקר, בָקר, בִקר. Yellin's system of unvocalized spelling was based on the orthography that, as far as is known, had first been used by the writers of the Haskalah who tried to follow the Bible in all respects. But since the spelling of the words of the masoretic Bible is not uniform, i.e., the same or analogous forms are sometimes written *plene* and sometimes defectively (without vowel letters), orthography complying with biblical grammar had to be standardized. While the spelling with few vowel letters in fact causes the reader, who knows Hebrew, less difficulty than the inexperienced may expect, it has been under constant attack for other reasons: (1) It is taught in schools, but most writers and printers continue to insert the available vowel letters in the consonantal skeleton of the word in the same way in which Hebrew has been written for many centuries starting even before the rise of vocalization and continuing side by side with vocalized writing down to the present time. (2) It made the language hard to learn for new immigrants, etc., and occasionally caused even fluent readers to stumble. (3) It demanded of everyone a considerable knowledge of grammar or a rare accuracy in diction that would distinguish between long and short vowels, between geminated and ungeminated consonants, etc.

The advocates of "grammatical" unvocalized spelling, mainly teachers and grammarians, also have some weighty arguments to adduce: (1) Their system nowhere contradicts pointed "grammatical" spelling as preponderantly found in the Bible, prayer books, poetry, etc., and taught in schools in conjunction with grammar from which, in their view, it cannot be divorced. (2) They insist upon the ease with which a learner can pass from vocalized spelling to reading and writing texts with the same allowed vowel letters, but without vocalization. (3) They maintain that supplementary vowel letters obstruct the recognition of word roots and thus hamper learners of the language. (4) They emphasize the educational and cultural disadvantage of the simultaneous currency of two contradictory systems. (5) They stress the absence of generally accepted rules for, and the prevailing confusion in the use of, supplementary vowel letters.

This last point is aimed at the fact that many writers add, whenever they see fit, י for *i* or *e*; ו for *u* or *o*; and – particularly in foreign words – א for *a*; and use וו for consonantal ו and יי for consonantal י or the diphthong *ay*. Thus, סָבָה may be found spelled סבה or סיבה; שְׂרֵפָה – שרפה or שריפה; קֹדֶשׁ – קדש or קודש; שֻׁלְחָן – שלחן or שולחן; אֲקָדֵמִי – אקדמי or אקאדמי or אקאדימי; בִּנְיָן – בנין, בניין or ביניין; עִוֵּר – עור, עוור, עיור or עיוור; דַי – די, דיי or דאי.

When the Va'ad ha-Lashon published, in 1948, its "Rules for Unvocalized Spelling" (*Lěšonénu* 16, 82ff.), this was the outcome of over 30 years of deliberations in general meetings of the Va'ad, in committees, and in subcommittees, where frequently also teachers and scholars from outside took part. The various proposals submitted and discussed included suggestions to equip the Hebrew alphabet for the representation of the vowel *a* and *e* by creating new letters. The use of Latin script for Hebrew was also advocated, as had been done earlier by Ithamar Ben-Avi and Ze'ev V. Jabotinsky. The principles underlying the rules are set forth in the introduction to the draft rules published in 1943 (*Lěšonénu* 11, 232ff.) and will be summarized here:

> The rules must be founded upon the literary sources and the grammar of Hebrew, adapted to modern pedagogical and practical needs, and be acceptable to the public. Therefore, extreme innovations such as the use of א or ע or new letters as vowel signs are to be avoided. The aim is to regularize the spelling actually current and direct it in line with the general tendency of linguistic and cultural developments. For many generations two spelling systems, the vocalized and unvocalized, have existed side by side, and each has its domain of function. But while punctuation by now has fairly well-established rules, in unpointed spelling two contradictory systems compete, one with and the other without supplementary vowel letters; both of them sometimes intermingle in the same text. The evolution of orthography from its beginning to our days tends toward supplemented spelling; unvocalized orthography must therefore be based on it. This is by no means incompatible with grammar and correct pronunciation, for nowadays Hebrew, like any other living language, is naturally learnt by hearing, not from writing. The aim is to facilitate reading, and that is why, whenever supplemented spelling is liable to mislead, it must be dispensed with. Complete consistency is not sought, but this does not mean giving up the formulation of systematic and scientifically founded rules, it rather explains the exceptions recommended by the committee.

The rules themselves submitted for discussion and decision were substantially the same that were later adopted by the Va'ad ha-Lashon in 1948 and again confirmed, with few amendments, by the Academy of the Hebrew Language in 1969. The following words, each spelled without vocalization in accordance with the rules, followed by unvocalized grammatical spelling, and then again fully vocalized will illustrate the principal rules:

השולחנות כולם = השלחנות כלם = הַשֻּׁלְחָנוֹת כֻּלָּם; חולצה אדומה; חלצה אדמה = חֻלְצָה אֲדֻמָּה; בוקר = בקר = בֹּקֶר; מוח = מח = מֹחַ; תשמורנה = תשמרנה = תִּשְׁמֹרְנָה; עיקר = עקר = עִקָּר; זימן = זמן = זִמֵּן; ניתן = נתן = נִתַּן; עלייה = עליה = עֲלִיָּה; זיכרון = זכרון = זִכָּרוֹן; עירבון = ערבון = עֵרָבוֹן; פירש = פרש = פֵּרַשׁ; קירוב = קרוב = קֵרוּב; ייראה = יראה = יֵרָאֶה; ריאתה = ראתה = רֵאָתָהּ; עניין = ענין = עִנְיָן; הצייר צייר = הציר ציר = הַצַּיָּר צִיֵּר; בניי = בני = בָּנַי; חודשיים = חדשים = חָדְשַׁיִם.

Exceptions to the main rules, i.e., classes of words and letter combinations where no addition of vowel letters is allowed, are shown in these examples: קנה = קָנָה; תאמר = תֹּאמַר (in these verb forms with quiescent א and ה, there is no ו for *o*); טהרה = טָהֳרָה; אנייה = אֳנִיָּה; חכמה = חָכְמָה; אמנם = אָמְנָם (*qameṣ-qaṭan* and *ḥaṭaf-qameṣ* are normally not rendered by ו); נטיות = נְטִיּוֹת; דיון = דִּיּוּן (*i* left unmarked when preceding -יוֹ- or -יוּ-).

It will have been noticed that this supplemented unpointed orthography still uses the following diacritical points: dots in וּ and וֹ to distinguish them from each other and from consonantal ו; in בּ, כּ, פּ to distinguish them from ב, כ, פ; and in הּ to mark this letter as the final consonantal *h*. While recommending this method, the Va'ad ha-Lashon had made it optional considering that the necessary printing types may not be available. The result could have been foreseen: almost nobody used the dotted letters, but wrote ו for both *o* and *u* and used וו to mark the consonant *w* (*v*), taking advantage of the alternative allowed by the Va'ad. Thus, in fact, בֹּקֶר was (and still is) written בוקר; שֻׁלְחָן – שולחן; דִּבּוּר – דיבור, etc., and עִוֵּר – עיוור; הַוַּעַד – הוועד, etc. When the Academy of the Hebrew Language adopted the rules of the Va'ad ha-Lashon in 1969, this alternative was abrogated and the basic ruling alone maintained.

The resolution of the Academy was submitted to the Ministry of Education and Culture and published with the minister's signature. A committee appointed by the ministry started consultations to decide at what stage and by what didactic methods supplemented unvocalized spelling should be taught in schools.

Since that time, the Academy revised the spelling rules once again. The decisions made in 1994 can be consulted in R. Gadish (ed.), *Kelalei ha-Pissuk, Kelalei ha-Ketiv Hasar ha-Nikud, Leshonenu La-Am*, special issue, 4th edition (2002).

VOCABULARY. How the vocabulary of the "dead" language was adapted to the requirements of expression in all fields of life and thought is taken by many as the most outstanding achievement of the revival period. True, in less than two generations, thousands of new words and new uses of words have become part of the Hebrew lexicon. However, in this respect at least, Hebrew never was really dead; in literature and occasionally in speech, new words were being coined continually, and while these activities did not cover all domains of life, contents were not restricted to religion, philosophy, poetry and the like. Medieval literature comprises works on medicine, mathematics, astronomy, and other sciences. Matters of daily life were dealt with, for example, in the vast *responsa literature, in itineraries, etc. and new impulses of modernization further widened their scope. To adduce only two examples, one of a more comprehensive character and the other one particular word: (1) many names of animals used today are not words invented by Ben-Yehuda or after him, but first appeared around 1870 in *Mendele Mokher Seforim's "Natural History"; (2) if the Hebrew word for "passport" occurring in medieval literature – תִּיּוּר (*tiyyur*) or כְּתַב־תִּיּוּר (*kètav tiyyur*) – had not been overlooked, there would have been no need for the recent use of the ancient word דַּרְכּוֹן (*darkon*, a coin) in this sense.

As the last example shows, new words have been formed for concepts that had already been expressed by other words in the past. *Bialik's idea (in his essay "*Ḥevlé Lašon,*" 1891) that total acquaintance with the store of the language ought to precede coining new words could not be followed, let alone his wish that a complete dictionary of all Hebrew writing should be the source for new word creations. In *Aḥad Ha-Am's view (put forward in his essay *Ha-Lašon we-Sifrutah*, 1909), the vocabulary could only be expanded by creative artists and thinkers who would be guided by the genius of the language. Bialik, though he agreed with him with regard to genuine autonomous creation, insisted upon the necessity to supply, even by designed regular activity, all the words needed, particularly those that had their semantic counterparts in other languages.

Bialik thus approved of, and later participated in, the work undertaken by Ben-Yehuda and the Va'ad ha-Lashon. While many words were, and are, to an ever-increasing degree, invented by writers and experts in their special fields, the principles and methods that guided Ben-Yehuda and his circle were followed by almost all authors of words, if not through conscious abidance, then by imitation and analogy.

The sources and ways for extending the vocabulary were expounded in *Zikronot Waʿad ha-Lašon* I (p. 7f.): (1) The best method to glean lexical items for modern use was "to search all departments of Hebrew literature and gather from them words…" If the meaning of an ancient word in its original context is doubtful, efforts should be made to clarify its interpretation; if, however, no decision can be reached, coining a new word is preferable to using a contested word. Thus, even today a biblical or later word may be submitted to the Academy for inclusion in a dictionary, but may be opposed by some members, or rejected by the majority, because commentators disagree on its meaning at its source. (2) As far as necessary, Aramaic words may be accepted, but these, unless they are already well known in their original form, are to be reshaped to fit Hebrew pattern and grammar, as happened to the Aramaic עוֹבָדָא (*ʿovada*) which became עֻבְדָּה (*ʿuvda*) ("fact"), changing both its vocalization and gender.

Ben-Yehuda's design to exploit freely the abundant vocabulary of Arabic has been accomplished to a limited extent only. Most of the words from an Arabic source found in literary and higher colloquial language are either medieval borrowings: אֹפֶק (*ʿofeq*), קֹטֶב (*qoṭev*), קֹטֶר (*qoter*), מֶרְכָּז (*merkaz*), and more, or are due to Ben-Yehuda himself: הֲגִירָה (*hagira*), הַצְהָרָה (*haṣhara*), זִבְדָּה (*zivda*), אָדִיב (*adiv*), לְטִיפָה (*leṭifa*), etc. Later, few new words entered standard Hebrew from Arabic, presumably because the creators of the new vocabulary came in the main from circles who knew no Arabic. When borrowing from foreign languages, they preferred the European, often international, word to the Arabic one, e.g., נֵיטְרָלִיּוּת

(*neṭraliyyut*; "neutrality") to the suggested חִיּוּד (*ḥiyyud*: from the Arabic *ḥiyâd*). It is all the more remarkable that substandard speech has a high proportion of Arabic words and phrases.

In earlier years, borrowing from non-Semitic languages was firmly rejected with the exception of words with a Hebrew-like form or already in frequent use, but this attitude was later abandoned. Yet, many speakers of Hebrew even today frown upon words taken from European languages, such as, אֲקָדֶמְיָה (*aqademya*) and אוּנִיבֶרְסִיטָה (*universita*) proving that such words are felt to be foreign unwieldy elements and that the prior general attitude in this respect did not merely stem from the extremism of a few. On the whole, however, international technical terms are now widely adopted not only in specialized publications but in newspapers and books for the general public. Colloquial speech, too, comprises many foreign words, partly perhaps due to a passing snobbish fashion. *Even-Shoshan's seven-volume "New Dictionary" (1966–1970) contains 3,448 foreign, mainly international, words among its 33,549 basic items, and in the "Dictionary of Terms in Photography," published by the Academy in 1966, there are 53 borrowed international words among its 700 items. An important restriction on the borrowing of words of non-Semitic origin is the structure of the Hebrew verb which is formed according to severe rules, e.g., that certain vowels must appear in certain positions in verb forms; that only a limited number of consonants can constitute a verb-root, etc. As a matter of course, the necessary coining of an original Hebrew verb often also leads to the replacement of the corresponding foreign noun.

According to the principles of the Va'ad ha-Lashon, words should be created "in agreement with the rules of grammar and analogy." As far as possible, they are to be derived from roots found in biblical and talmudic literature and, in the second place, from Aramaic and other Semitic, especially Arabic, roots. To establish new scientific terms, one should aim at the essential signification, not the literal meaning, of the words of other languages. Newly coined words have not only to be grammatically correct, but pleasing to the ear and appropriate to the spirit of the language.

Contrary to the intention to avoid expressing only the literal and etymological meaning of the foreign word, loan-shifts and loan-translations have been and are an ever-growing source for new uses of existing Hebrew words. As in every language throughout the ages, Hebrew words also contract new meanings under the influence of particular applications of corresponding words in other languages, and foreign compound words and phrases are rendered in Hebrew by literally translating their components. English "crane," for the hoisting machine, French "grue," etc. have brought about the Hebrew עֲגוּרָן (*ʿaguran*) derived from the name of the bird; and German "Kindergarten" has engendered גַּן־יְלָדִים (*gan-yeladim*; "garden" (of) "children"). Nowadays, the principle of such semantic borrowings is seldom debated; only innovations that are felt to be too farfetched and removed from prevailing usage are rejected. In word formation, modern Hebrew, for the most part, follows the methods inherited from former stages of the language. The available noun and verb patterns are used to the full for innovations. Yet, some possibilities of derivation and combination that in older Hebrew were realized in relatively small measure are now put to use more extensively and, as some maintain, even excessively. The following deserve special mention and exemplification:

(1) Many nouns and adjectives are derived from noun bases by adding suffixes:

(a) *-an*, fem. *-anit* for nouns, as in: חֲצוֹצְרָן (*ḥaṣṣeran*, "trumpeter"); תּוֹתְחָן (*totaḥan*, "artilleryman"); דּוֹדָן (*dodan*), fem. דּוֹדָנִית (*dodanit*, "cousin"); מַהְפְּכָן (*mahpěḵan*, "revolutionary," n.); תִּיקָן (*tiqan*, "cockroach,"), from תִּיק (*tiq*, "envelope," i.e., the protective shell of the insect's eggs).

(b) *-ay*, fem. *-aʾit* for nouns, as in: עִתּוֹנַאי (*ʿittonay*, fem. עִתּוֹנָאִית *ʿittonaʾit*, "journalist"); בּוּלַאי (*bulay*, "philatelist"); אֲוִירַאי (*awiray*, "airman"); מְכוֹנַאי (*měḵonay*, "machinist"); טֶלֶפוֹנַאי (*ṭelefonay*, fem. טֶלֶפוֹנָאִית (*ṭelefonaʾit*), "telephone operator"); סְטָטִיסְטִיקַאי (*staṭisṭiqay*, "statistician").

(c) *-on*, fem. *-ónet*, often for diminutive nouns: דֻּבּוֹן (*dubbon*, "young bear, teddy bear"); יַלְדוֹן (*yaldon*, "small boy"), יַלְדֹּנֶת (*yaldonet*, "small girl"); שֵׁדוֹן (*šedon*, "sprite").

(d) *-i*, fem. *-it*, mainly for adjectives: צְבָאִי (*ṣevaʾi*, "military"); גַּמָּדִי (*gammadi*, "dwarfish"); אַפְסִי (*afsi*, "amounting to nothing"); תְּהוֹמִי (*těhomi*, "abysmal"), עֲנָקִי (*ʿanaqi*, "colossal"). The suffix *-i* is also widely used to derive adjectives from compounded pairs of nouns, as in צְפוֹן־מִזְרָחִי (*ṣěfon-mizraḥi*, "north-eastern"), from צְפוֹן־מִזְרָח (*sěfon-mizraḥ*, northeast); גַּב־לְשׁוֹנִי (*gav-lěšoni*, "dorsal," in phonetics), from גַּב־לָשׁוֹן (*gav-lašon*, "dorsal surface of the tongue"); כְּלַל־אֱנוֹשִׁי (*kělal-ěnoši*, "all-human, universal"). This mode of derivation, found in the Bible in gentilitial names, like בֶּן־יְמִינִי (*Ben-Yěmini*, "Benjaminite") and בֵּית־הַלַּחְמִי (*Bet-Hallaḥmi*, "Bethlehemite"), has also been extended to compounds whose first member is a quantifier, as in חַד־כִּוּוּנִי (*ḥad-kiwwuni*, "unidirectional"); דּוּ־לְשׁוֹנִי (*du-lěšoni*, "bilingual"); רַב־צְדָדִי (*rav-ṣědadi*, "many-sided"); or a preposition, as in בֵּין־לְאֻמִּי (*ben-lěʾummi*, "international"); קְדַם־מִקְצוֹעִי (*qědam-miqṣoʿi*, "pre-professional"): עַל־אנוֹשִׁי (*ʿal-ěnoši*, "superhuman").

(e) *-it*, for nouns, some diminutive (besides being the feminine form of *-i*): מְכוֹנִית (*měḵonit*, "automobile"); מוֹנִית (*monit*, "taxi"); יָדִית (*yadit*, "handle"); מַפִּית (*mappit*, "napkin"); תָּוִית (*tawit*, "label").

(f) *-ut*, for abstract or collective nouns: בּוֹרְרוּת (*borěrut*, "arbitration"): צִיּוֹנוּת (*ṣiyyonut*, "Zionism"); רוֹקְחוּת (*roqeḥut*, "pharmacology"); מְיַלְּדוּת (*meyallědut*, "obstetrics"); עִתּוֹנוּת (*ʿittonut*, "press").

(g) Several of the foregoing suffixes may combine to form new derivations, such as: מַהְפְּכָנִי (*mahpěḵani*, "revolutionary," adj.); מַהְפְּכָנוּת (*mahpěḵanut*, "revolutionism"); תּוֹתְחָנוּת (*totěḥanut*, "artillery"); עִתּוֹנָאוּת (*ʿittonaʾut*, "journalism"); גַּמָּדִיּוּת (*gammadiyyut*, "dwarfishness"); אַפְסִיּוּת (*afsiyyut*, "worthlessness").

(2) New nouns are built by joining elements of two other words, particularly when this is suggested or facilitated

by both words having one or more consonants in common or by the second word beginning with a glottal stop (*ʾalef*) which can easily be omitted. קולנוֹע (*qolnoaʿ*, "cinema") is but a simple joining of קוֹל (*qol*, "sound") and נוֹעַ (*noaʿ*, "movement"), while אוֹפַנּוֹע (*ʾofannoaʿ*, "motorcycle") joins אוֹפַן (*ʾofan*, "wheel") and נוֹעַ (*noaʿ*). Two original consonants are omitted in דַּחְפּוֹר (*daḥpor*), a blending of the verbal roots דחף (*d.ḥ.f.*) and חפר (*ḥ.f(p).r*); with the recurring pair ח (*ḥ*) and פ (*f(p)*) inserted only once, the sequence דחפר (*d.ḥ.f(p).r*) is left and shaped into a noun with the vowel sequence *a.o* frequent in nouns. On the same vowel pattern רַמְזוֹר (*ramzor*, "traffic light") is formed from the verbal root רמז (*r.m.z*, "to indicate") and the noun אוֹר (*ʾor*, "light") whose initial א *ʾalef* is elided. The popular creation שְׁמַרְטַף (*šĕmarṭaf*, "babysitter") is compounded from שמר (*š.m.r.*, "to watch") and טַף (*ṭaf*, "children"), but the Academy prefers שׁוֹמֵר-טַף (*šomer-ṭaf*) modeled after the biblical שׁוֹמֵר־סַף (*šomer-saf*, "keeper of the door").

(3) Among verbal innovations the amount of denominative verbs is significant: רִשֵּׁת (*riššet*, "to cover with a net") comes from רֶשֶׁת (*rešet*, "net"); קִרְקַע (*qirqʿa*, "to ground [an aircraft]") from קַרְקַע (*qarqaʿ*, "ground"): נִתֵּב (*nittev*, "to pilot") from נָתִיב (*nativ*, "path"), and numerous others, especially scientific, technological, and military terminology. For such new active verbs, the pattern *piʿel* is preferred with *hifʿil* left far behind and *paʿal* (*qal*) almost entirely neglected.

(4) Many of these new denominative verbs are derived from nouns with prefixed or suffixed formatives. Thereby, new roots, mostly quadriliteral, have entered the language: מִרְכֵּז (*mirkez*, "to centralize"), with it the passive participle מְמֻרְכָּז (*mĕmurkaz*), and the action noun מִרְכּוּז (*mirkuz*) have been derived from מֶרְכָּז (*merkaz*, "center") to differentiate from the former verb רִכֵּז (*rikkez*, "to concentrate") which shows the original root רכז (*r.k.z*) מִסְפֵּר (*misper*, "to number") contains in its secondary root מספר (*m.s.p.r*) the consonants of מִסְפָּר (*mispar*, "number"), a noun derived from the primary root ספר (*s.f(p).r*). The relation between תִּזְמֵר (*tizmer*, "to orchestrate"), תִּזְמֹרֶת (*tizmóret*, "orchestra"), and the primary root זמר (*z.m.r*) is similar. In a *piyyuṭ* by Eleazar *Kallir (of the early Middle Ages) there is the verb הִתְמִיר (*hitmir*) originating from תְּמוּרָה (*tĕmura*, "change") which in turn is based on the primary root מור (*m.w.r*); the verb הִתְמִיר (*hitmir*) has now passed from its remote literary source into modern use in the meaning "to substitute" in chemistry. From the primary root חמץ (*ḥ.m.ẓ*) Ben-Yehuda formed the noun חַמְצָן (*ḥamẓan*, "oxygen"), and this served as a base for the new verb חִמְצֵן (*ḥimṣen*, "to oxydize").

(5) Another way to form denominative verbs is to derive new roots from contractions or acrostics of compound words. Thus, from דִּין־וְחֶשְׁבּוֹן (*din-wĕ-ḥešbon*, "account, report") first the acrostic דו"חַ (*duaḥ*, "report") came into use, and then the verb דִּוֵּחַ (*diwwaḥ*, "to report") was formed with the artificial root דוח (*d.w.ḥ.*). In order to obtain a Hebrew verb for "to internationalize," to which בֵּין־לְאֻמִּי (*ben-lĕʾummi*, "international") did not lend itself, a contracted root בנאם(*b.n.ʾ.m*) had to be presumed to arrive at the desired verb בִּנְאֵם (*binʾem*) and its action noun בִּנְאוּם (*binʾum*, "internationalization"). However, this presumption is not so farfetched, since there is a Hebrew noun אֻמָּה (*umma*), besides לְאֹם (*lĕʾom*) for "nation."

(6) In analogy to several verbs of the *šafʿel* formation inherited from biblical and later Aramaic and Hebrew, some new causative verbs and action nouns with the prefixed š- have been created from existing roots, mainly where other verb formations had already been exploited for the same root. To these innovations, some of which have been sanctioned by the Academy, belong שִׁחְזֵר (*šiḥzer*, "to restore"), root חזר (*ḥ-z-r*, "to return"), and its action noun שִׁחְזוּר (*šiḥzur*); שִׁקֵּם (*šiqqem*, "to rehabilitate") with שִׁקּוּם (*šiqqum*) as action noun, root קום (*q-w-m*, "to rise"); שִׁפְרֵט (*šifreṭ*, "to elaborate") derived from פְּרָט (*pĕraṭ*, "detail"); שִׁכְפֵּל (*šikpel*, "to duplicate, multiply (written matter)"), etc. Among the first and most widely used of these new words were שִׁחְזוּר (*šiḥzur*) with the meaning of restoration of a previous condition inherent in its root חזר (*ḥ-z-r*), and שִׁקּוּם (*šiqqum*), which intrinsically only means "causing to rise, erecting," but was used in contexts entailing the connotation of "again." Many speakers, therefore, came to attribute this meaning of remaking or redoing to the *šafʿel* formation, and by way of vindicating this semantic shift, some even interpreted the prefixed š- as an abbreviated שׁוּב (*šuv*, "again"). On this assumption, more verbs and action nouns with initial š-, corresponding to English *re-*, have been formed and in part accepted: שִׁחְלֵף (*šiḥlef*, "to re-exchange"), root חלף (*ḥ-l-f*) – in another sense שִׁחְלֵף > שַׁלְחֵף (*šalḥef* < *šaḥlef*) is already found in the Aramaic of the Targum and Talmud; שִׁעֲרוּךְ (*šiʿiaruḵ*, "reassessment"), root ערך (*ʿ-r-ḵ*); שִׁזְרַע (*šizraʿ*, "to resow"), root זרע (*z-r-ʿ*), שִׁגְזוּר (*šigzur*, "back formation" in linguistics), root גזר (*g-z-r-* "to derive"), etc.

(7) A considerable number of passive verbal adjectives has been adopted with the vowel sequence *a-i* inserted in the root and corresponding in meaning to French and English adjectives in *-able, -ible*. The first of these probably was שָׁבִיר (*šavir*, "breakable"), followed by קָרִיא, (*qari*, "readable," "legible"), סָבִיר (*savir*, "reasonable"), כָּבִיס (*kavis*, "washable"), חָדִיר (*ḥadir*, "penetrable"), דָּחִיס (*daḥis*, "compressible"), and more. However, this pattern has at all times served in the formation of other adjectives (as the biblical *ʿašir* "rich") and of nouns (as the biblical *qaṣir* "harvest"). Its application to defective roots meets with difficulties; its use is limited to derivations from *paʿal* (*qal*) verbs, and its corresponding abstract noun is ambiguous (e.g., דְּחִיסוּת *dĕḥisut* may be understood as "compressibility" and as "[state of] compression," from *daḥus*, "compressed"). Words of this semantic category are, therefore, also formed in other ways, either with the suffix *-i* appended to an action noun, as in שִׁמּוּשִׁי (*šimmuši*, "practical"), from שִׁמּוּשׁ (šimmuš, "practice, use"), or, as in classical Hebrew, either by the use of passive participles, such as, מִתְקַפֵּל (*mitqappel*, "collapsible," "folding"); נֶאֱכַל (*neʾĕkal*, "edible"); מִטַּלְטֵל (*miṭṭalṭel*, "portable"), etc., or by compounding בֶּן־ *ben-* or בַּר־ *bar-* with abstract nouns, mostly action nouns, as in בֶּן־סֶמֶךְ (*ben semeḵ*; "reliable"), בֶּן־בּוּז (*ben-buz* [Bialik],

"contemptible"); בַּר־בִּצּוּעַ (*bar-biṣṣua*" "executable"); בַּר־בִּטּוּל *bar-biṭṭul*, "abolishable"), etc.

GRAMMAR. In 1905, the teachers' convention agreed to Yellin's proposal for a standardized orthography based on the biblical vocalization system. This, to a large extent, led to the acceptance of biblical Hebrew grammar for modern Hebrew. The spelling and vocalization adopted determined the form of words and their inflection, though in this sphere, too, usage had to be normalized to eliminate variations and prosodic peculiarities of the Bible text.

In 1910, this topic was discussed in a meeting of the Va'ad ha-Lashon in which Eliezer Ben-Yehuda, Yisrael Eitan, David Yellin, Aharon Masie, and Yosef Meyuḥas took part. The summary of this debate, published in *Zikronot Wa'ad ha-Lašon* II (2nd ed., 1929, p. 17ff.) has lost little of its import; many of the arguments set forth then are still heard whenever there is doubt about the preferable form and inflection of a word or a class of words. The discussion then originated from one particular question, i.e., the correct plural for the mishnaic אֹגֶן (*'ogen*, "rim, brim"), whether it should be אֲגָנִים (*o'ganim*) according to grammar based on the Bible, or (אָגְנִים אוגנים) (*'ognim*) as found in mishnaic Hebrew. Many aspects of modern grammar were treated in the light of ancient literary sources during this debate.

In conclusion, the following resolution was proposed by D. Yellin and adopted: "We take from talmudic and midrashic literature words and expressions which we need and new grammatical forms supplementing those found in the Bible. Talmudic words accepted are to be given a Hebrew form whenever possible. For verbs no new forms are needed if in the Bible there are corresponding forms." The significant words in this resolution provide that neither in vocabulary nor in grammar should anything available in the Bible be replaced by elements from later literature. Regarding the special problem of the plural of nouns, such as אֹגֶן (*'ogen*), both forms were admitted, but later the "Dictionary of Technical Terms," published in 1929 by the Va'ad with Ḥ.N. Bialik as one of its editors, contained only the plural form אֲגָנִים (*'oganim*) in conformity with biblical grammar.

The principles adopted by the Va'ad ha-Lashon were observed, with few exceptions, by teachers and in textbooks. According to these norms, the teaching of grammar, on the whole, not only excluded the divergent traditions of Hebrew and the innovations found in post-biblical literature, but also disregarded the language in which Hebrew literature had been written since the end of the Haskalah. It was to the principles of the Haskalah that normative grammarians now reverted. The literature before the revival of Hebrew speech in Palestine, especially since Mendele Mokher Seforim, had not submitted to the restrictions imposed by the Haskalah, but had freely blended biblical elements with talmudic and later grammatical forms as well as with words and phrases from all periods and even borrowings from modern European languages. However, as modern literature and speech have continued to grow, grammar based on the Bible has proved inadequate for all the new material.

The strict adherence to what was known and held in biblical grammar is well exemplified by A.Y. Shapiro in his *More Nevuké ha-Lašon* (Warsaw, 1909). The author corrects about 140 words and grammatical forms found in the writings and speech of his contemporaries, naturally according to his views on the Bible text and to the conclusions he draws from it. Thus, he rejects נֶאֱבַד for אָבַד; הִתְאַנֵּח for נֶאֱנַח; אֲרוּכָה for אֲרֻכָּה (fem. of אָרֹךְ, "long"), the infinitives לֵידַע, לֵישֵׁב, לֵילֵךְ, etc., for the biblical forms לָדַעַת, לָשֶׁבֶת, לָלֶכֶת, etc.; infinitives such as לִקְרוֹת for לִקְרֹא; יֹפִי both in the absolute and construct case for יְפִי; the imperfect אֶלְמוֹד for אֶלְמַד; עָמוּס for עוֹמֵס ("carrying, burdened"): ...לְ...הֶרְאָה אֶת for ...אֶת...הֶרְאָה אֶת; etc. Although the author, in an appendix, shows that some of these and other non-biblical forms are found in talmudic literature, he does not approve of their use in modern language. However, these forms and many more have in fact existed in the literature, or in certain traditions of Hebrew, for centuries and are accepted by some of the best modern writers, their selection being but a matter of personal style.

As Hebrew is the paramount unifying factor of modern national culture in Israel, a distinction had of necessity to be made between the standard language taught in schools and used in public addresses, broadcasting, and the like, and the individual idiom of creative writers and the traditions of the various Jewish communities in reading religious and other texts that naturally also influence their everyday speech. The work of establishing a normative grammar of modern Hebrew – one of the chief tasks of the Va'ad ha-Lashon and the Academy of the Hebrew Language – will understandably take a long time and, in fact, imposes itself constantly anew in response to cultural developments. However, once the foundations have been laid and become general usage, much can be left to natural growth without interference of any linguistic authority. Even today the greater part of new words and word forms used spontaneously by individuals already conforms to grammar rules.

The new, Hebrew grammar is gradually being built by two separate activities: by comprehensive discussion and decision on systematic divisions of grammar and by ad hoc instructions on particular problems submitted by writers, teachers, journalists, and other members of the public or arising from the work of terminological committees. The former course is naturally preferred, yet it is lengthy and cannot answer urgent needs; therefore, the latter is unavoidable, although its ad hoc directives have occasionally to be amended to agree with a subsequent comprehensive ruling.

The foremost aim of the Va'ad ha-Lashon in its systematic treatment of grammar was to decide on words for which the biblical text does not provide sufficient exemplary evidence or offers several divergent forms of one word, e.g., for the noun לְטָאָה ("lizard"), found only in this form once in Leviticus, two forms with pronominal suffixes may be inferred: לְטָאָתִי or לְטָאָתִי; by analogy, two forms for the post-biblical

מְחָאָה ("protest") would be possible; אֲגַם ("pool," "pond") has two inflected forms belonging to different paradigms: אֲגַמִּים and אַגְמֵיהֶם, both in Exodus. Whenever there was no doubt about the biblical form of a word, the Va'ad accepted this precept and allowed only very few exceptions dictated by firmly established usage, e.g., permitting כִּתְבֵי הַקֹּדֶשׁ ("Holy Scriptures") besides the form based on the Bible כְּתָבֵי הַקֹּדֶשׁ from כְּתָב with an unchangeable *qameṣ*. This principle inevitably led to a twofold treatment of words of one and the same morphological pattern: Words taken from the Bible went one way, and those coming from later sources or coined recently went another. Thus, the rule for nouns of the pattern *qĕṭal* to which כְּתָב belongs, lists the biblical words whose *qameṣ* is to be unchangeable, and provides for the change of *qameṣ* to *pattaḥ* or *šewa* only in words from later sources, such as שְׁטָר ("writ, note") – שְׁטַר־חוֹב ("note of debt," sing. construct state) – שִׁטְרֵי־חוֹב (plur. construct state).

When the Academy continued this work of the Va'ad ha-Lashon, the renewed debate led to a fundamental change. Now, the rules are to deal with modern Hebrew as a whole, and the dichotomy of its vocabulary by reason of its sources, whether biblical or post-biblical, has been abandoned. It is no longer a matter of course that for each biblical word its biblical inflection be accepted in the modern language. If this is to be done, and, in general, it is, the issue is open to discussion and subject to decision in accordance with the tendency to allow well-established traditions and usages their proper place, and to make each new rule as comprehensive as possible. Most of the rules still have their exceptions, of course, but these are few, and they sometimes include biblical forms or state their existence without recommending their use.

So far, only the rules for the inflection of nouns have been systematically discussed and partly established. The arrangement of the rules follows the alteration of the vowels in each class of nouns, this being the prominent feature in Hebrew inflection. Each rule is the outcome of a thorough examination of the ways in which the various sources of the language treated the vowels in inflection. The rules for *qameṣ gadol* and *pattaḥ* have been published (*Zikronot* 7–8, 1962, p. 91ff and 13, 1967, p. 7f.), and the rules for the other vowels were decided upon and issued by the Academy in later sessions, the most recent publication being in *Leshonenu La-Am*, 51–52 (2000–1), pp. 153–98.

As an example, paragraph 8 of section 2 in chapter I will be given here with some added remarks:

The *qameṣ gadol* is stable in the endings ־ָר, ־תָן, ־ָן in nouns denoting occupations and qualities, such as לַמְדָן – לַמְדָנֵיכֶם; בִּימָר – בִּימָרֵי; לַבְלָר – לַבְלָרֵיכֶם; גַּאַוְתָן – גַּאַוְתָנֵי; קַבְּלָן – קַבְּלָנֵי; סַנְדְּלָר – סַנְדְּלָרֵיכֶם; סְמַרְטוּטָר – סְמַרְטוּטָרֵי.

The *qameṣ* is stable in the nouns אֵיתָן – אֵיתָנֵי, סִימָן – סִימָנֵי, and in loanwords, such as גְּרָמוֹפוֹן, רוֹמָן, etc.

In other nouns, the *qameṣ* changes in inflection: שֻׁלְחָן – שֻׁלְחַן (constr.); שֻׁלְחָנוֹת; בִּנְיָן – בִּנְיְנֵי; עִנְיָן – עִנְיְנֵיכֶם; אָמְדָּן – אָמְדְּנֵי; פֻּלְחָן – פֻּלְחֲנֵי; סוֹדָר – סוֹדְרֵי; טִפְסָר – טִפְסְרֵי; קָרְבָּן – קָרְבְּנוֹתֵי; עַכְבָּר – עַכְבְּרֵי; קוֹלָר – קוֹלְרֵיכֶם.

This paragraph presupposes paragraph 1 of section 1 which provides that "every *qameṣ gadol*, occurring in the absolute state in a stressed syllable, changes to *pattaḥ* in the singular construct state and before the pronominal suffixes ־כֶם, ־כֶן." Therefore, שֻׁלְחָן, e.g., in these two contexts becomes שֻׁלְחַן and שֻׁלְחַנְכֶם respectively.

Of the 21 words adduced as examples in this rule, only seven are biblical: אֵיתָן, שֻׁלְחָן, קָרְבָּן, בִּנְיָן, עִנְיָן, עַכְבָּר, טִפְסָר. (The last word, of Sumerian-Accadian origin, occurs twice in the Bible, once with *ḥireq* and once with *pattaḥ* in the first syllable.) Another nine words, partly Greek or Latin borrowings, are found in talmudic-midrashic literature: סוּדָר, קוֹלָר, סַנְדְּלָר, לַבְלָר, סִימָן, אָמְדָּן, פֻּלְחָן, גַּאַוְתָן, קַבְּלָן, and one, לַמְדָן is found in medieval writings (and also in Yiddish), but there are many newly created words of the same formation. Two words are modern derivations from older ones: סְמַרְטוּטָר ("rag picker") from the talmudic סְמַרְטוּט ("rag") and בִּימָר ("stage technician") from the originally Greek בִּימָה ("stage"). The remaining two, גְּרָמוֹפוֹן, רוֹמָן, are contemporary loans from European languages.

The salient point here is that, without regard to their history, all these words are integrated in the modern vocabulary and divided with respect to their inflection not necessarily in conformity to biblical grammar. The fact that they do not behave uniformly in inflection has historical reasons. The group with changing *qameṣ* follows three of its members – שֻׁלְחָן, עַכְבָּר, קָרְבָּן – for which the Bible text has *šewa*, or *šĕwa compositum*, replacing *qameṣ* in the relevant inflected forms. The other group, with stable *qameṣ*, complies with the usual pronunciation of most of its members.

Outside of the systematic treatment of grammatical and other problems by the Academy, ad hoc solutions of specific questions deal not only with morphology, but with syntax and style as well. A few examples must suffice here. In the field of morphology it is often necessary to fix the exact spelling and vocalization of old words that have been handed down in several forms. The vowels of the talmudic noun גופן ("character of script") are uncertain; thus of the forms גֹּפֶן, גּוּפָן, גּוֹפָן which are found, the first has been chosen. Even for the verb הזיע ("to sweat," in the *hifʿil*, two vocalizations have been in use: הֵזִיעַ and הִזִּיעַ; the choice fell on הֵזִיעַ because it agrees with the root suggested by the inflection of the biblical noun זֵעָה ("sweat") which alone is in common use today (not יֶזַע). Committees on terminology, when proposing a new word, are often in doubt about its grammatical form. Thus, מְכָל ("container") has been selected instead of מֵכָל previously chosen by the Va'ad ha-Lashon. Foreign words admitted into the language require their Hebrew plural to be determined. Thus for the plural of מַקְסִימוּם ("maximum") the form מַקְסִימָאוֹת has been proposed in the same way as mishnaic Hebrew dealt with similar Greek and Latin nouns (וִילוֹן – Latin "vellum" – plural וִילָאוֹת).

Syntactic structure in translated literature and in journalistic writing has been greatly influenced by European languages (now mainly English). One of the results, for example, is the frequent appearance of non-restrictive, continuative relative clauses, such as, הַשּׁוֹטְרִים רָדְפוּ אַחֲרֵי הַגַּנָּב שֶׁנִּמְלַט לְתוֹךְ הַבַּיִת

הַקָּרוֹב. ("The police pursued the thief, who escaped into the nearest house"). Although this use is found neither in the colloquial language nor in that of writers whose Hebrew is considered exemplary, it is frequent in journalese and officialese. Some linguists do not condemn it on this level of the language, and the same applies to other syntactic structures, equally foreign to more elevated and conservative style.

Modern Hebrew as a Semitic language, with an ancient literary heritage still cherished and studied, was already exposed to the impact of the modern world and of modern non-Semitic languages when it only was the vehicle of literary revival and before it became a fully living language. Whoever took part in the revival of the language, in writing or in speech, was aware of this position, its requirements and consequences. But for the past 80 years at least, Ben-Yehuda and his collaborators and their successors have made a conscious effort to develop Hebrew and adapt it to modern use on the lines on which, in their view, it would have developed if its natural life had continued without interruption into the 20th century. In fact many other languages which have not passed a period of suspended animation now face problems quite similar to those of modern Hebrew. What Hebrew experienced now has happened to it before, for example, in the talmudic period and in the later Middle Ages, when not only new words were formed or borrowed and old words were used to refer to new objects, but the morphological, syntactic, and conceptual structure of the language changed in part, both by direct imitation of other languages and under the influence of their manner to organize the relation between words and concepts.

One of the characteristics of modern Hebrew is the speed of the changes in all respects. Thus it offers much interesting material to the linguist to show the trends of its evolution and to discover general linguistic facts and processes in it. Two phenomena: "Westernization" and "re-Hebraization" (much discussed in treatises on language policy, especially by Rosén, Ben-Ḥayyim, and Bendavid), in the recent development of the language are obvious to all observers. The "ancient language being in a new reality" absorbs concepts and forms of Western languages through cultural contacts, through more or less apt translation, immigration, and bilinguism, etc. The wish to strengthen the inherited Hebrew component is obvious and may be realized through extended Hebrew education, more intense study of classical writings, the growth of modern literature imbued with old language tradition and the increased number of its readers, competent guidance of language development and by adapting old forms to modern contents.

[Eli Eytan]

BIBLIOGRAPHY: PRE-BIBLICAL GENERAL: C. Brockelmann, in: *Handbuch der Orientalistik*, vol. 3, *Semitistik*, Abschnitt 1 (1953), 40–58 (Canaanite dialects and Ugaritic), 59–70 (Hebrew); G. Garbini, *Il Semitico di Nord-ovest* (1961): Gelb, in: *Journal of Cuneiform Studies*, 15 (1961), 27–47; A. Goetze, in: *Language*, 17 (1941), 127–38; Greenberg, in: JAOS, 72 (1952), 1–9; Z.S. Harris, *Development of the Canaanite Dialects* (1939); Moran, in: Wright, Bible, 59–85; Polotsky, in: *A World History of the Jewish People* 1st series, 1 (1964), 104–11; Roessler, in: ZDMG, 100 (1950), 461–514; Von Soden, in: WZKM, 56 (1960), 177–91. EGYPTIAN MATERIAL: W.F. Albright, *The Vocalization of the Egyptian Syllabic Orthography* (1934); idem, in: JPOS, 8 (1928), 223–56; idem, in: JAOS, 74 (1954), 222–33; Borée, M. Burchardt, *Die altkanaanaeischen Fremdwoerter und Eigennamen im Aegyptischen* (1909–10); Moran, in: *Orientalia*, 26 (1957), 339–45; K. Sethe, *Die Aechtung feindlicher Fuersten, Voelker und Dinge auf altaegyptischen Tongefaesscherben des mittleren Reiches* (1926); J. Simons, *Handbook for the Study of Egyptian Topographical Lists Relating to Western Asia* (1937); G. Posener, *Princes et Pays d'Asie et de Nubie* (1940). CUNEIFORM MATERIAL FROM TAANACH: Albright, in: BASOR, 94 (1944), 12–27; Gross, *ibid.*, 190 (1968), 41–46; Hillers, *ibid.*, 173 (1964), 45–50: F. Hrozny, in: E. Sellin, *Tell Ta'annek, Bericht ueber eine... Ausgrabung in Palaestina* (1904), 113–22. CUNEIFORM MATERIAL FROM EL-AMARNA: Albright, in: BASOR, 89 (1943), 7–17; F.M.T.Boehl, *Die Sprache der Amarnabriefe* (1909); E. Dhorme, in: RB, 22 (1913),369–93; 23 (1914), 37–59, 344–72; Ebeling, in: *Beitraege zur Assyriologie und semitischen Sprachwissenschaft*, vol. 8, pp. 39–70; J.A. Knudtzon, *Die El-Amarna Tafeln* (1915); Moran, in: *Orientalia*, 29 (1960), 1–19; idem, in: *Journal Of Cuneiform Studies*, 4 (1950), 169–72; A.F. Rainey, *El-Amarna Tablets* 359–379, suppl. to J.A. Knudtzon's *Die El-Amarna Tafeln* (1970); For primary references see: R. Borger, *Handbuch der Keilschriftliteratur*, 1 (1967), 237f. AMORITE CUNEIFORM MATERIAL: G. Buccellati, *The Amorites of the Ur III Period* (1966): T. Bauer, *Die Ostkanaanaeer* (1926); A. Finet, *L'Accadien des Lettres de Mari* (1956); E. Dhorme, in: RB, 37 (1928), 63–79, 161–180; 39 (1930), 161–78; 40 (1931), 161–84; Gelb, in: *Atti della Accademia Nazionale dei Lincei, Rendiconti, Classe di scienze morali, storiche e filologiche*, serie 8, 13 (1958), 143–64; idem, in: JAOS, 88 (1968), 39–47; H.B. Huffmon, *Amorite Personal Names in the Mari Texts* (1965). **ADD. BIBLIOGRAPHY:** ONOMASTICS: S.C. Layton, *Archaic Features of Canaanite Personal Names in the Hebrew Bible* (1990); Y. Muchiki, *Egyptian Proper Names and Loanwords in North-West Semitic* (1999). EL-AMARNA: D. Sivan, *Grammatical Analysis and Glossary of the North-West Semitic Vocables in Akkadian Texts of the 15th–13th C.B.C. from Canaan and Syria* (1984); A.F. Rainey, *Cannanite in the Amarna Tablets*, 4 vols. (1996); W.L. Moran, *The Amarna Letters* (1992); idem, *Amarna Studies: Collected Writings* (2003). AMORITE: I.J. Gelb, *Computer-aided Analysis of Amorite* (1980); C.H. Gordon, "Amorite and Eblaite," in R. Hetzron (ed.), *The Semitic Languages* (1997), 1001–13; M.P. Streck, *Die Amurriter, die onomastische Forschung, Orthographie und Phonologie, Nominalmorphologie* (2000). BIBLICAL. The best grammar is still that of G. Bergstraesser, *Hebraeische Grammatik* (1918–29), which, though a torso, is an impressive piece of scholarship in the field of phonetics and the verb. An excellent short account is contained in G. Bergstraesser's *Einfuehrung in die semitischen Sprachen* (1928, repr. 1963), 36–46. For the development of stress see M. Lambert, REJ (1890), 73–77; J. Cantineau, in: *Bulletin d'Études Orientales de l'Institut Français de Damas* (1931), 81–98. Important grammars are: H. Bauer and P. Leander, *Historische Grammatik der hebraeischen Sprache des Alten Testaments* (1922; does not contain syntax); W. Gesenius, E. Kautzsch and A.E. Cowley, *Hebrew Grammar* (1913² and many reprints; translated from the 28th German edition of 1909); P. Joüon, *Grammaire de l'Hébreu Biblique* (1923). Important material is contained in E. Koenig, *Historisch-kritisches Lehrgebaeude der hebraeischen Sprache* (1881–97). Biblical Hebrew against its general Semitic background is described in C. Brockelmann, *Grundriss der vergleichenden Grammatik der semitischen Sprachen* (1907–13); yet his *Hebraeische Syntax* (1956), mostly taken from the masterly syntax contained in the second volume of his *Grundriss*, is less good, since it lacks the general Semitic background. Good is the syntax of A.B. Davidson, *Introductory Hebrew Grammar; Hebrew Syntax* (1912[3]), and even today one will often consult the masterly syntax contained in H. Ewald, *Ausfuehrliches Lehrbuch der hebraeischen Sprache des Alten Bundes* (1870[8]) which was translated into English by James Kennedy as *Syntax of the Hebrew Language of the Old Testament* (1879). The new work of (G. Beer-) R. Meyer, *Hebraeische Grammatik* (1952–55[2]) is only important because of the new material adduced; the same applies to A. Sperber, *A Historical Grammar of Biblical Hebrew* (1966), where, e.g., material of Jerome's transcriptions is to be found. For the language of the Qumran scrolls see E.Y. Kutscher, *Ha-Lašon wĕ-ha-Reqaʿ ha-Lĕšoni šel Mĕğillat Yĕšaʿyahu ha-Šĕléma* (1959; with English summary). For Hebrew inscriptions cf. S. Moscati, *Stato e problemi dell'epigrafia ebraica antica* (1952) where additional literature is adduced; also Aharoni and Amiran, in: IEF, 14 (1964), 138–43; Aharoni, in: IEF, 16 (1966), 1–7. For transcriptions of Palestinian place names see W. Borée, *Die alten Ortsnamen Palaestinas* (1930); for transcriptions of the Septuagint, G. Lisowsky, *Die Transkription der hebraeischen Eigennamen des Pentateuch in der Septuaginta* (1940); for those of Origen, E. Bronno, *Studien ueber hebraeische Morphologie und Vokalismus auf Grund der Mercatischen Fragmente der zweiten Kolumne der Hexapla des Origines* (1943). For the transcription of Arabic names in Nessana see the index of Arabic names by F.E. Day, in: C.J. Kraer (Jr.), *Excavations of Nessana*, 3 (1958), 352–5. For the Bible text see D. Ginsburg, *Tora Nĕvi'im Kĕtuvim* (1926[2]); R. Kittel and P. Kahle, *Biblia Hebraica* (1962[13]). One sample of the edition of the Hebrew University Bible Project has also appeared: M.H. Goshen-Gottstein, *The Book of Isaiah*, sample edition (1965). For an example of P. Kahle's views on the work of the masoretes see his *Cairo Geniza* (1959[2]). The best biblical dictionaries are still F. Brown, S.R. Driver, and A. Briggs, *A Hebrew and English Lexicon of the Old Testament* (1906, etc.); W. Gesenius and F. Buhl, *Hebraeisches und aramaeisches Handwoerterbuch ueber das Alte Testament* (1915[16]); W. Gesenius, *Hebrew and Chaldee Lexicon to the Old Testament* (1857, repr. 1957); and L. Koehler and W. Baumgartner, *Lexicon in Veteris Testamenti libros* (1953, Supplement 1958) – only the Aramaic part is up to the high standards of its predecessors. A new edition of this dictionary by W. Baumgartner, B. Hartmann and E.Y. Kutscher is appearing: *Hebraeisches und Aramaeisches Lexikon zum AltenTestament*, 1 (1967). For further literature see Steinschneider, Handbuch. **ADD. BIBLIOGRAPHY:** GRAMMAR: R.J. Williams, *Hebrew Syntax: An Outline* (1976[2]); J. Blau, *A Grammar of Biblical Hebrew* (1976); idem, *Studies on Biblical Hebrew* (1995); idem, *Studies in Hebrew Linguistics* (1996); idem, *Topics in Hebrew and Semitic Linguistics* (1998); B.K. Waltke & M. O'Connor, *An Introduction to Biblical Hebrew Syntax* (1990); P. Joüon and T. Muraoka, *A Grammar of Biblical Hebrew* (1991), a translation and updating of Joüon's 1923 French grammar; J. Hoftijzer, *The Function and Use of the Imperfect Forms with Nun Paragogicum in Classical Hebrew* (1985); T. Muraoka, *Emphatic Words and Structures in Biblical Hebrew* (1985); J.C.L. Gibson, *Davidson's Introductory Hebrew Grammar – Syntax* (1994); S.E. Fassberg, *Studies in Biblical Syntax* (1994); I. Ben-David, *Contextual and Pausal Forms in Biblical Hebrew* (1995); C.L. Miller, *The Representation of Speech in Biblical Hebrew Narrative* (1996); idem (ed.), *The Verbless Clause in Biblical Hebrew* (1999); T. Zewi, *A Syntactical Study of Verbal Forms Affixed by -n(n) Endings* (1999). DICTIONARIES AND LEXICONS: D.J.A. Clines et al., *The Dictionary of Classical Hebrew* (1993–); L. Koehler and W. Baumgartner, *The Hebrew and Aramaic Lexicon of the Old Testament* (2001); P. Mankowski, *Akkadian Loanwords in Biblical Hebrew* (2000). VERBAL SYSTEM: L. McFall, *The Enigma of the Hebrew Verbal System* (1982); E.J. Revell, "The System of the Verb in Standard Biblical Prose," in: HUCA, 60 (1989), 1–37; G. Hatav, *The Semantics of Aspect and Modality: Evidence from English and Biblical Hebrew* (1997); W. Randall Garr, "Driver's *Treatise* and the Study of Hebrew: Then and Now," in: S.R. Driver, *A Treatise on the Use of the Tenses in Hebrew and Some Other Syntactical Questions* (1998), xviii–lxxxvi; P. Gentry, "The System of the Finite Verb in Classical Biblical Hebrew," in: HS 39 (1998), 7–39; Z. Zevit, *The Anterior Construction in Biblical Hebrew* (1998); J. Cook, "The Hebrew Verb: A Grammaticalization Approach," in: ZAH, 14 (2001), 117–43. LATE BIBLICAL HEBREW: A. Hurvitz, *The Transition Period in Biblical Hebrew* (1972); R. Polzin, *Late Biblical Hebrew: Toward an Historical Typology of Biblical Hebrew Prose* (1976). TRANSCRIPTIONS: G. Janssens, *Studies in Hebrew Historical Linguistics Based on Origen's Secunda* (1982); DEAD SEA SCROLLS. General: Up to 1965: C. Burchard, *Bibliographie zu den Handschriften vom Toten Meer*, 2 vols. (1957–65). 1965 TO 1970: Bibliographies in: *Revue de Qumran*, 1–6 (1958–69); J.A. Sanders, "Palestine Manuscripts 1947–1967," in: JBL, 86 (1967), 431–40 (includes a bibl. of the text-publications of Mss. discovered in Palestine from 1947 to Aug. 1, 1967). CONCORDANCES: K.G. Kuhn, *Konkordanz zu den Qumrantexten* (1960); idem, "Nachtraege zur 'Konkordanz zu den Qumrantexten,'" in: *Revue de Qumran*, 4 (1963), 163–234; A.M. Habermann, *Mĕgillot̲ Mid̲bar Yĕhuda* (1959), 3–175. WORKS: WAR SCROLL: J.P.M. van der Ploeg (ed. and tr.), *Le Rouleau de la guerre* (1959); Y. Yadin (ed.), *Scroll of the War of the Sons of Light Against the Sons of Darkness*, tr. by B. and C. Rabin (1962). THANKSGIVING PSALMS: M. Mansoor (ed. and tr.), *Thanksgiving Hymns* (1961); J. Licht, "Thanksgiving Scroll," in: *Peruš Mĕgillat ha-Hodayot* (1957); E. Kimron, "Language of the Psalms Scroll," in: *Lĕšonénu*, 35 (1971/72), 99–116. PEŠER ḤABAQQUQ: K. Elliger, *Studien zum Habakuk-Kommentar vom Toten Meer* (1953). MANUAL OF DISCIPLINE: P. Wernberg-Møller (ed. and tr.), *Manual of Discipline* (1957); J. Licht (ed.), *Mĕgillat ha-Sĕrak̲im* (1965; "Rule Scroll"); J. Maier (ed.), *Texte vom Toten Meer…* 2 vols. (1960), includes all the above scrolls. ZADOKITE DOCUMENTS: C. Rabin (ed. and tr.), *Zadokite Documents* (1954, 1958[2]). STUDIES ON THE GRAMMAR IN THE DSS: E.Y. Kutscher, *Ha-Lašon we-ha-Reqaʿ ha-Lĕšoni šel Mĕğillat Yĕšʿayahu ha-Šĕléma* (1959; "The Language and the Linguistic Background of the Isaiah Scroll"), includes summary in English; Ḥ. Yalon, *Mĕğillot̲ Mid̲bar Yĕhuda; Divré Lašon…* (1967; "Studies in the Dead Sea Scrolls, Philological Essay"), includes summary in English; M.Z. Qaddari, *Ha-Ḥiyyuv bi-Lĕšon ha-Mĕgillot ha-Gĕnuzot* (1968; "Semantic Fields in the Language of the DSS"), includes summary in English. SELECTED ARTICLES: B. Jongeling, "Les formes QTWL dans l'hébreu des manuscrits de Qumrân," in: *Revue de Qumran*, 1 (1958/59), 483–94; F.W. Bush, "Evidence from Milḥamah and the Masoretic Text for a Penultimate Accent in Hebrew Verbal Forms," *ibid.*, 2 (1959/60), 501–14 (against his conclusions see: E.Y. Kutscher above, 254–61); M.H. Goshen-Gottstein, "Philologische Miszellen zu den Qumrantexten," *ibid.*, 2 (1959/60), 44–46; J.C. Greenfield, "The Root GBL in Mishnaic Hebrew and in the Hymnic Literature from Qumran," *ibid.*, 2 (1959/60), 155–62; E.J. Revell, "The Order of the Elements in the Verbal Statement Clause in 1Q Sereq," *ibid.*, 3 (1961/62), 559–69; S.J. de Vries, "Syntax of Tenses and Interpretation in the Hodayoth," *ibid.*, 5 (1964/66), 375–414; S. Lieberman, "The Discipline in the so-called Dead Sea Manual of Discipline," in: JBL, 71 (1952), 199–206; von N. Adler, "Die Bedeutung der Qumran Texte fuer die neutestamentliche Wissenschaft," in: *Muenchener theologische Zeitschrift*, 6 (1955), 286–301; J.P. de Menasce, "Iranien Naxcir," in: VT, 6 (1956), 213–4; W. Nauck, "Probleme des fruehchristlichen Amtsverstaendnisses," in: ZNW, 48 (1957), 200–20; Z. Ben-Ḥayyim, "Traditions in the Hebrew Language, with Special Reference to the Dead Sea Scrolls," in: *Scripta Hierosolymitana*, 4 (1958), 200–14; R. Meyer, "Spuren eines westsemitischen Praesens-Futur in den Texten von Chirbet Qumran," in: *Gottes ist der Orient. Festschrift... O. Eissfeldt ...* (1959), 118–28; T. Leahy, "Studies in the Syntax of DSS," in: *Biblica*, 41 (1960), 135–57; A. Bendavid, *Lěšon Miqra u-Lěsson Ḥakamim* (1967^2), 80–94 (deals mainly with mutual influences of Aramaic, Greek, etc. and Qumran Hebrew). COPPER SCROLL: The language of the *Copper Scroll*, first published by J.M. Allegro (1960, 1964^2), which is close to Mishnaic Hebrew, was not dealt with in this article because the readings are not sure; see, however, B. Lurie, *Měgillat ha-Něḥošet mi-Midbar Yěhuda* (1963); H. Braun, *Qumran und das Neue Testament*, 2 vols. (1966); this important work systematically goes through the New Testament and compares it with the Qumran scrolls also in linguistic respects (lone translation); An index *verborum* of Qumran Hebrew only a *Stellenregister*, 368–83. See also bibliography at end of Dead Sea Scrolls article. **ADD. BIBLIOGRAPHY:** EDITIONS OF TEXTS: Y. Yadin, *The Temple Scroll, Three Volumes and Supplement* (1983); J.H. Charlesworth, ed., *The Dead Sea Scrolls* (1994–); F. García Martínez and E.J.C. Tigchelaar (eds.), *The Dead Sea Scrolls Study Edition* (1997); E. Qimron, *The Damascus Document Reconsidered* (1992); idem, *The Temple Scroll: A Critical Edition with Extensive Reconstructions* (1996); idem and J. Strugnell, *Miqsat Ma'ase Ha-Torah* (DJD 10; 1994); idem & D.W. Parry, *The Great Isaiah Scroll (1QIsaa): A New Edition* (1999); J.K. Lefkovits, *The Copper Scroll (3Q15): A Reevaluation* (2000). GRAMMAR: E.Y. Kutscher, *The Language and Linguistic Background of the Isaiah Scroll (1QIsaa)* (1974), Eng. transl. of 1959 Heb. work; E. Qimron, *The Hebrew of the Dead Sea Scrolls* (1986); idem, "Observations on the History of Early Hebrew (1000 B.C.E.–200 C.E.) in the Light of the Dead Sea Documents," in: D. Diamant and U. Rappaport (eds.), *The Dead Sea Scrolls: Forty Years of Research* (1992), 349–62; S. Morag, "Qumran Hebrew: Some Typological Observations," in VT, 38 (1988), 148–64; M.S. Smith, *The Origins and Development of the Waw-Consecutive* (1991); T. Muraoka and J.F. Elwolde (eds.), *The Hebrew of the Dead Sea Scrolls & Ben Sira* (1997); idem, *Sirach, Scrolls, & Sages* (1999); idem, *Diggers at the Well* (2000); W.M. Schniedewind, "Qumran Hebrew as an Antilanguage," in: JBL, 118 (1999), 235–52; S. Weitzman, "Why Did the Qumran Community Write in Hebrew?" in: JAOS, 119 (1999), 35–45. CONCORDANCE: M.G. Abegg et al., *The Dead Sea Scrolls Concordance: The Non-Biblical Texts* (2002). MISHNAIC SPELLING: A. Bendavid, Lěšon Miqra u-Lěšon Ḥakamim, 1 (1967^2; to be used critically); E.Y. Kutscher, "Maẓẓav ha-Meḥqar šel Lešon Ḥazal," in: ʿEré ha-Millon he-Ḥadaš šel Sifrut Ḥazal (1971); idem, "Mi-Bě'ayot ha-Millon he-Ḥadaš le-Sifrut Ḥazal," ibid,; (both articles contain many bibl. refs.); idem, "Mischnaisches Hebraeisch," in: Rocznik Orientalistyczny, 28 (1964), 35–48; idem, "Mittelhebraeisch und Juedisch-Aramaeisch imneuen Koehler-Baumgartner," in: B. Hartmann et al. (eds.), Hebraeische Wortforschung (1967), 158–75; idem, "Lěšonan šel ha-ʾIggerot ha-ʿIvriyyot wě-ha-ʾAramiyyot šel Bar Kosbaʾ u-Věné Doro," in: Lěšonénu, 26 (1962), 7–23; M.H. Segal, Mishnaic Hebrew and its Relation to Biblical Hebrew and to Aramaic (1909; repr. from JQR, 20 (1908), 647–737); Much material is to be found dispersed in the works of J.N. Epstein (below) especially in his Mavo lě-Sifrut ha-Tanna'im (1957); of S. Lieberman (below), especially in his Hellenism in Jewish Palestine (1950); and of H. Yalon (below). GRAMMAR: A. Bendavid (above); Z. Ben-Ḥayyim, "Traditions in the Hebrew Language with Special Reference to the Dead Sea Scrolls," in: Scripta Hierosolymitana, 4 (1958), 200–14; J.N. Epstein, Mavo lě-Sifrut ha-Tanna'im (1957), especially 1050, 1207–67; E.Y. Kutscher, "Bişşuaʿ Tēnuʿot u, i be-Taʿtiqé ha-ʿIvrit ha-Miqraʾit ba-ʾAramit ha-Gelilit u-vi-Lěšon Ḥazal," in: E.Z. Melamed (ed.), Séfer Zikkaron lě-Binyamin De-Vries (1968), 218–51 (many printing errors corrected in rev. ed. (1971), idem, "Lěšon Ḥazal," in: S. Lieberman et al. (eds.), Séfer Hanoch Yalon (1963), 246–80; idem, "Meḥqarim bě-Diqduq Lěšon Ḥazal (lě-fi Kětav Yad Kaufmann)," in: Séfer Bar-Ilan, Qoveṣ he-ʿAsor 1956–1968, 2 (1968), 51–77; E. Porath, Lěšon Ḥakamim lě-fi Masorot Bavliyyot u-vě-ktivé Yad Yěšanim (1938); I. Yeivin, "Ha-Niqqud ha-Bavli u-Masoret ha-Lašon hamištaqqefet mimmenno" (1968; Typescript, unpublished Ph.D. dissertation Hebrew University, Jerusalem. Important); M.H. Segal, A Grammar of Mishnaic Hebrew (1927); M.Z. Segal, Diqduq Lěšon ha-Mišna (1936) includes bibliography (both outdated); Ḥ. Yalon, Mavo lě-Niqqud ha-Mišna (1964; very important work); idem, Pirqé Lašon (1971). Some material contained in this chapter is as yet unpublished. VOCABULARY: Ḥ. Albeck, Mavo la-Mišna (1959), 128–215; A. Bendavid (above). J.N. Epstein, Mavo lě-Sifrut ha-Tanna'im (1957); idem, Introduction to Amoraitic Literature (1962); idem, Mavo lě-Nusaḥ ha-Mišna (1964); (idem, many other works and articles published mainly in Tarbiẓ are very important); S. Lieberman, Ha-Yěrušalmi ki-Fěšuto (1934); idem, Greek in Jewish Palestine (1942); idem, Hellenism in Jewish Palestine (1950); idem, Tosefta (1970); idem, Tosefta ki-Fěšuta, 10 vols. (1955–67); idem, Tosefet Rišonim, 4 vols. (1937–39); idem, ʿAl ha-Yěrušalmi (1929); idem, "Roman Legal Institutions in early Rabbinics and in the Acta Martyrum," in: JQR, 35 (1944/45), 1–57; idem, "Palestine in the Third and Fourth Centuries," ibid., 36 (1945/46), 329–70; idem, many other articles (see T. Preschel, "Bibliografya šel Kitvé R. Šaul Lieberman," in: Hadoar, 42 (1963), 381–4); Ḥ. Yalon (above). DICTIONARIES: s.v. Aramaic; Ben Yehuda, Millon (contains the material of mishnaic Hebrew). Some material in this chapter is as yet unpublished. **ADD. BIBLIOGRAPHY:** Two collections of papers on MH are very useful and contain rich bibliography: M. Bar-Asher (ed.), Koveẓ Ma'amarim bi-Leshon Ḥazal, 1–2 (Jerusalem, 1972–80); M. Bar-Asher and S.E. Fassberg (eds.), Scripta Hierosolymitana 37: Studies in Mishnaic Hebrew (Jerusalem, 1988). A list of bibliography can also be found in M. Bar-Asher, "The Study of Mishnaic Hebrew Grammar – Achievements, Problems and Goals," in: Proceedings of the Ninth World Congress of Jewish Studies, Panel Sessions: Hebrew and Aramaic (Jerusalem, 1988), 30–37. GENERAL: M. Bar-Asher, "The Different Traditions of Mishnaic Hebrew," in: D.M. Golomb (ed.), "Working with No Data," Semitic and Egyptian Studies Presented to Thomas O. Lambdin (1987). MSS OF THE MISHNAH: M. Bar-Asher, The Traditions of Mishnaic Hebrew in the Communities of Italy: According to Ms. Paris 328–329, Eda Ve-Lashon, 6 (Jerusalem, 1980); Y. Bentolila, A French-Italian Tradition of Post-Biblical Hebrew, Eda Ve-Lashon, 14 (Jerusalem, 1989); G. Birnbaum, "Studies in the Phonology and Morphology of Mishnaic Hebrew According to Geniza Fragments," Ph.D. Thesis, Bar-Ilan University (1994); G. Haneman, The Morphology of Mishnaic Hebrew According to the Tradition of MS Parma (de Rossi 138) (1980); T. Zurawel, Maimonides' Tradition of Mishnaic Hebrew as Reflected in his Autograph Commentary to the Mishnah, Eda Ve-Lashon 25 (2004). OTHER TANNAITIC SOURCES: S. Naeh, "The Tannaic Hebrew in the Sifre according to Codex Vatican 66," Ph.D. Thesis, Hebrew University of Jerusalem (1989); H. Nathan, "The Linguistic Tradition of Codex Erfurt of the Tosefta," Ph.D. Thesis, Hebrew University of Jerusalem, Publication of the Faculty of Humanities, School of Advanced Studies (1984). AMORAIC HEBREW: Y. Breuer, The Hebrew in the Babylonian Talmud according to the Manuscripts of Tractate Pesahim (2002); E. Netanel, "Morphological Description of the Hebrew Verb in Jerusalem Talmud," Ph.D. Thesis, Hebrew University of Jerusalem (1995). OLD TRADITIONS: I. Eldar, The Hebrew Language Tradition in Medieval Ashkenaz (ca. 950–1350 C.E.), 1: Phonology and Vocalization; 2: Morphology, Eda ve-Lashon 4–5 (Jerusalem, 1978–79; Y. Kara, "Yemenite Traditions in Mishnaic Hebrew According to a 16th Century Manuscript," in: Leshonenu, 44:24–42;

M. Ryzhik, "Italian Jewry's Traditions of Mishnaic Hebrew in the MSS of Mahzorim in the 14th–15th Centuries," Ph.D. Thesis, Hebrew University of Jerusalem (2001); O. Tirosh-Becker, "Rabbinic Hebrew Handed Down in Karaite Literature," Ph.D. Thesis, Hebrew University of Jerusalem (1999); I. Yeivin, The Hebrew Language Tradition as Reflected in the Babylonian Vocalization, 1–2 (1985). ORAL TRADITIONS: Y. Henshke, "The Hebrew Component in the Judeo-Arabic of Tunisia," Ph.D. Thesis, Hebrew University of Jerusalem (2000); K. Katz, The Hebrew Language Tradition of the Community of Djerba (Tunisia): The Phonology and the Morphology of the Verb, Eda ve-Lashon 2 (Jerusalem, 1977); idem, The Hebrew Language Tradition of the Aleppo Community: The Phonology, Eda ve-Lashon, 7 (Jerusalem, 1981); T. Kessar, Oral and Written Traditions of the Mishnah: Morphology of the Noun in the Yemenite Tradition, Eda ve-Lashon, 23 (Jerusalem, 2001); M. Mishor, "Ashkenazi Tradition – Toward a Method of Research," in: Massorot 3–4 (1989):87–128. SYNTAX: M. Azar, The Syntax of Mishnaic Hebrew (1995); N. Braverman, "Particles and Adverbs in Tannaitic Hebrew (Mishnah and Tosefta): A Syntactic Analysis," Ph.D. Thesis, Hebrew University of Jerusalem (1995); M. Mishor, "The Tense System in Tannaitic Hebrew," Ph.D. Thesis, Hebrew University of Jerusalem (1983). VOCABULARY: M. Moreshet, A Lexicon of the New Verbs in Tannaitic Hebrew (1980); Academy of the Hebrew Language, Ma'agarim (databases) CD-ROM (Jerusalem, 1998). ARAMAIC: I. Gluska, "The Influence of Aramaic on Mishnaic Hebrew," Ph.D. Thesis, Bar-Ilan University (1988). MEDIEVAL. THE LANGUAGE OF THE PIYYUT: Zunz, Lit. Poesie, 29–41; N. Chomsky, in: JQR, 75 (1967), 121; I. Davidson, in: *Qoveṣ Maddaʿe ha-Yahadut* (1926), 187–95; S. Lieberman, in: *Sinai*, 4 (1939), 221–50; M. Zulay in: YMḤSI, 6 (1945), 161–248; idem, in: H. Yalon (ed.), *Qunṭĕresim lĕ-ʿInyĕné Lašon* (1942–43), 1–4; idem, in: *Moznayim*, 16 (1943), 217–23; H. Yalon (ed.), *Qunṭĕresim lĕ-ʿInyĕné Lašon* (1942), 3–7, 51–55; S. Spiegel, in: *Hadoar*, 42 (1963), no. 23, 397–400; A. Mirsky, in: *Zikronot ha-ʾAqademya la-Lašon ha-ʿIvrit* (1956–57), 41–45; idem, in *Lĕšonénu*, (1966), 296–304; Y. Kena'ani, *Millon Qonqordanṣyoni li-Lešon ha-Piyyuṭim* (1936); K. Levias, in: *Hadoar*, 11 (1932), no. 33. SAADIAH GAON'S LANGUAGE: A. Ben Ezra, in: *Séfer Alfenbein* (1967), 33–43; idem, in: *Horeb*, 8 (1944), 135–7; 9 (1946), 176–85; 10 (1948), 295–318; M. Zulay, *Ha-ʾAskola ha-Payyĕtanit šel Rav Sĕʿadya Gaʾon* (1964), 13–40; S. Abramson, in: Y.L. Eishman (ed.), *Qoveṣ Rasag* (1943), 677–88; idem, in; *Sinai*, 49 (1966), 133–245; C. Rabin, in: *Saadya Studies* (1943), 127–38. LANGUAGE OF THE HEBREW POETRY IN SPAIN: Schirmann, Sefarad, 2 (1956), 27–34; M. Medan, in: *Lĕšonénu*, 17 (1951), 110–14; B. Klar, in: *Meḥqarim wĕ-ʿIyyunim* (1954), 174–9; S. Abramson, in: *Ha-Kinnus ha-ʿOlami lĕ-Maddaʿé ha-Yahadut* (1947–52), 274–8; A. Mirsky, in: *Lĕšonénu*, 18 (1952–53), 97–103; S. Abramson, *ibid.*, 11 (1941–43), 54–57; Y. Ratzaby, ibid., 21 (1957), 22–32; idem, in: *ʾOṣar Yĕhudé Sĕfarad*, 8 (1965), 11–16; in: *Lĕšonénu la-ʿAm*, 2 (1969), no. 3–6; N. Allony, in: *Lĕšnénu*, 11 (1941–43), 161–4; idem, in: *ʾOṣar Yĕhudé Sĕfarad*, 3 (1960), 15–48; idem, in: *Sinai*, 44 (1959), 152–69; 64 (1969), 12–35, 155–73; idem, in: *Lĕšonénu*, 15 (1944), 161–72; D. Yarden, *Diwan Šĕmuʾel ha-Nagid* (1966), 14–27; D. Yellin, in: JQR, 16 (1925/26), 272ff.; A. Mirsky, *Širé Yiṣḥaq kalfon* (1961), 40–44; D. Yellin, *Ketavim Nivḥarim*, 2 (1939), 319–30; idem, in: *Tarbiz*, 7 (1936), 314–19; Y. Ratzaby, in: *Lĕšonénu la-ʿAm* (1959), 18. PROSE AND TRANSLATIONS WITH ARABIC INFLUENCE: A.S. Halkin, "The Medieval Jewish Attitude toward Hebrew," in: A. Altmann, *Biblical and Other Studies* (1963), 233–48; M. Gottstein, *Taḥbirah u-Millonah šel ha-Lašon ha-ʿIvrit še-bi-Tĕḥum Hašpaʿatah šel ha-ʿArvit* (1951); idem, in: *Lešonenu* 16 (1948–9), 156–163; B. Klar, in: *Meḥqarim wĕ-ʿIyyunim* (1954), 31–41; C. Rabin, in: *Metsudah*, 3–5 (1945), 158–70; J. Klatzkin, *Oṣar ha-Munnaḥim ha-Pilosofiyyim* 4 vols., (1928); I. Efros, in: JQR, 17 (1926/27), 129–64, 323–68; 20 (1929/30), 113–38; idem, *Philosophical Terms in the Moreh Nebukim* (1924); D.Z. Baneth, in: *Tarbiz*, 6 (1935), 10–40; G. Zarfati, *Munnĕḥé ha-Matémaṭiqa ba-Sifrut ha-Maddaʿt ha-ʿIvrit šel Yĕmé ha-Bénayim* (1969); Z. Bacher (ed.), *Séfer ha Šorašim* (1896), 562–6; M. Wilensky (ed.), *Sefer ha-Riqma*, 2 (1964²) 710–29; Z. Ben-Ḥayyim, in: *Lĕšonénu*, 16 (1948–49), 156–63; M. Goshen, in: *Tarbiz*, 30 (1961), 385–95; D.Z. Baneth, *ibid.*, 11 (1939/40), 260–70; 23 (1952), 111–76; N. Shapira, *Lešonenu* (26), 209; E.M. Lipschuetz, *Ketabim* 1 (1947), 203–209. **ADD. BIBLIOGRAPHY:** KARAITE HEBREW: A. Maman, "*Ha-Ivrit shel Toviah b. Moses ha-Kara'i*," M.A. Thesis, Hebrew University of Jerusalem) (1979); idem, "Karaites and Mishnaic Hebrew: Quotations and Usage," in: *Leshonenu* (1991), 221–68 (Heb.); idem, "Karaites and Mishnaic Hebrew: Quotations and Usage," in: M. Bar-Asher and S.E. Fassberg (eds.): *Studies in Mishnaic Hebrew, Scripta Hyerosolomitana* 37 (1998), 264–83; idem, "Karaite Hebrew, in: M. Polliack (ed.), *Karaite Judaism, A Guide to Its History and Literary Sources* (2003), 485–503. MAIMONIDES' LANGUAGE: B. Z, Bacher, in: *ʿErké Midraš* (1927), 324–36; P. Birnbaum, in: *Hadoar*, 21 (1942) 721f.; I.A. Zeidman, in: *Sinai*, 12 (1943), 428–38; 13 (1943), 96–101; M.Z. Qadari, *Mi-Yrušat Lĕšon Yĕmé ha-Bénayim* (1970). HEBREW IN FRANCE, GERMANY, AND POLAND: Y. Avineri, *Ḥékal Raši*, (1949); 3 (1956); 4 (1960); C. Rabin, in: *Fourth World Congress of Jewish Studies, Papers*, 2 (1968); S. Nobel, in: *Lĕšonénu*, 23 (1959), 172–84, 216–69; S. Eidelberg, in: *Lĕšonénu la-ʿAm*, 20 (1969), 120–7; Y. Avineri in: *Metsudah*, 2–4 (1945), 229–48. MODERN PERIOD *Zikronot Waʿad ha-Lašon*, 1–6 (1912–28); *Lešonénu* 1–35 (1913–71), (index volume, 1969); E.M. Lipschuetz, *Vom lebendigen Hebraeisch* (1920); idem, *Kĕtavim*, 2 (1949 50); Z. Har-Zahav, *Lĕšon Dorénu* (1930), G. Bergstraesser, *Einfuehrung in die semitischen Sprachen* (1928), 47, 57ff.; S. Spiegel, *Hebrew Reborn* (1930); Y. Avineri, *Millon Hiddušé Ḥ.N. Bialik* (1936); idem, *Ḥékal Raši*, 1–4 (1940–60); idem, *Kibbušé ha-ʿIvrit bĕ-Yaménu* (1946); Y. Epstein, *Meḥqarim ba-Psikologya šel ha-Lašon wĕ-ha-Ḥinnuk ha-ʿIvri* (1947); idem, *Hegyoné Lašon* (1947); Y. Klausner, *Ha-Lašon ha-ʿIvrit Lašon Ḥayya* (1949); R.W. Weiman, *Native and Foreign Elements in a Language, a Study in Linguistics Applied to Modern Hebrew* (1950); E. Rieger, *Modern Hebrew* (1953); Z. Ben-Ḥayyim, in: *Lĕšonénu la-ʿAm*, (1953/54), 35–37; *Zikronot ha-ʾAqademya la-Lašon ha-ʿIvrit*, 1–17 (1954–71); A. Avrunin, *Meḥqarim bi-Lĕšon Bialik wĕ-Yalag* (1954); Ḥ. Blanc in: *Middle Eastern Affairs*, vol. 5, pp. 385ff.; Ḥ. Rosén, *Ha-ʿIvrit Šellanu* (1956); R. Bachi, in: *Scripta Hierosolymitana*, 3 (1956); Y. Livni, *Lašon ke-Hilkatah* (1957); W. Chomsky, *Hebrew – The Eternal Language* (1957); idem, *Ha-Lašon ha-ʿIvrit bĕ-Darké Hitpatteḥutah* (1967); C. Rabin, in: *Jewish Frontier* (Sept. 1958), 11ff.; E.Y. Kutscher, *Millim wĕ Tolĕdotéhen* (1961); S. Morag, in: *Lĕšonénu la-ʿAm* (1959/60), no. 95; C. Rabin, in: *Jewish Frontier* (June 1961); Z. Ben-Ḥayyim et al, in: *Lĕšonénu la-ʿAm* (1960), no. 104; Ḥ.B. Rosen, *A Textbook of Israeli Hebrew* (1962); R. Sivan, *Ṣurot u-Mĕgammot bĕ-Ḥiddušé ha-Lašon ha-ʿIvrit bi-Tequfat Teḥiyyatah* (1964/65); Y. Avineri, *Yad ha-Lašon* (1964); R. Sappan, *Darké ha-Sleng* (1964); Z. Iggeret, *Biʿur Koṣim mi-Kerem Lĕšonénu* (1964/65); R. Sappan, *Millon ha-Sleng ha-Yisrĕʾéli* (1965); A. Bendavid, *Lĕšon Miqra u-Lĕšon Hakamim* (I, 1967; II 1971); Ḥ. Rosén, *ʿIvrit Ṭova* (1967); M. Goshen-Gottstein, *Mavo la-Millonaʾut šel ha-ʿIvrit ha-Hadaša* (1969); M. Ben-Asher, *Hitgabbĕšut ha-Diqduq ha-Normaṭivi* (1969), S. Yeivin et al, in: *Ariʾel*, 25 (1969); *Leqeṭ Teʿudot lĕ-Toledot Waʿad ha-Lašon we-ha-ʾAqademya la-Lašon ha-ʿIvrit – 5650–5730 – u-lĕ-Ḥiddušé ha-Dibbur ha-ʾIvri* (1969/ 70); R. Sivan, in: *Lĕšonénu la-ʿAm* (1970), 204–25; *Munnaḥim ʿIvriyyim le-Miqṣoʿotehem* (published by the Academy of the Hebrew Language, 1970). **ADD. BIBLIOGRAPHY:** Y. Bentolila, *The Sociophonology of Hebrew as Spoken in a Rural Settlement of Moroccan Jews in the Negev* (Hebrew University of Jerusalem, 1984)

HEBREW LITERATURE, MODERN.

The entry is arranged according to the following outline:

DEFINITION AND SCOPE

For the purposes of this article the term modern Hebrew literature designates belles lettres written in Hebrew during the modern period of Jewish history.

The definition is more limited than the generally accepted notion that modern Hebrew literature includes everything written in Hebrew during the modern period (e.g., Y.F. Lachower, *Toledot ha-Sifrut ha-Ivrit ha-Ḥadashah* (1928–48); J. Klausner, *Historyah shel ha-Sifrut ha-Ivrit ha-Ḥadashah* (1930–1950) and others). This view has some validity concerning Hebrew letters written before 1914 when most Hebrew authors, in addition to belles lettres, wrote historical or philosophical works, journalistic articles, and even popular science, all of which were generally held to be "literature." Dov Sadan has suggested that a history of modern Hebrew literature should also include rabbinic literature written in the modern period, literature composed in other Jewish languages (particularly Yiddish), and even works of Jewish content composed in European languages (*Al Sifrutenu*, 1950). However while the influence of these types of literary endeavors in modern Hebrew literature must be taken into account by the historian, they are not in themselves an integral part of it.

The development of modern Hebrew literature represents an almost unique phenomenon in world literature. It is now generally assumed that Hebrew ceased being the spoken language of most Palestinian Jews even before the close of the biblical period, albeit evidence exists that small pockets of Hebrew speakers persisted even in the mishnaic period. In the Middle Ages, it became *leshon ha-kodesh* ("the sacred tongue") and the overwhelming number of books written in Hebrew were of a religious nature. Side by side with these religious works a secular or quasi-secular literature also developed – in Spain, Provence, and Italy. By the time modern Hebrew literature began, however, this literature was on the wane, even in Italy, its last stronghold. Moreover, modern Hebrew is, on the whole, the work of Ashkenazi Jewry and among them secular literature rarely appeared before modern times.

Hebrew was not only the literary language of medieval Jewry but also served as its *lingua franca*. Nevertheless, it had to be rendered flexible before it could adequately be used as a language to depict modern life. The literary problem created by the radical difference between Hebrew and Yiddish, which most of the Hebrew writers and readers spoke, became crucial with the rise of realism on the Hebrew literary scene. It was difficult to write in Hebrew realistic dialogue which was spoken in another tongue.

To some degree, too, the command of Hebrew was a class phenomenon. Large segments of the Jewish working class never attained sufficient competence in the language. It is therefore no accident that as Yiddish literature developed at the close of the 19th century, it not only enjoyed greater popularity but politically tended to be more radical than Hebrew literature. Moreover, it was natural that Hebrew would become the vehicle of the Zionist movement, while Yiddish, the language of the Diaspora, was that of Jewish movements which were Diaspora orientated. On the other hand, it would be oversimplifying matters to claim that the Yiddish-speaking masses were capable of understanding many of the sophisticated modernist poets and writers of fiction who were the proponents of Yiddish literature in its heyday. In any society most significant literature has always been and is still produced and read by the educated segment.

Unlike the authors of many "folk" literatures which developed in Europe during the nationalist period (19th century), Hebrew writers had the advantage of possessing a rich tradition and a large corpus of "classical" literature: the Bible, the Talmud, the Midrashim, the prayer book, medieval religious and secular poetry and prose, and the prose works of various pietistic groups. As modern Hebrew literature developed, the classical tradition proved to be a mixed blessing. Writers were overwhelmed particularly by the literary excellence of the Bible and often became discouraged in the face of its achievement. It is, however, to the credit of contemporary Hebrew writers that this is no longer a major problem. Without abandoning its classics, Hebrew writing is no longer frustrated by them.

From a statistical point of view Hebrew is a minor literature. It is currently estimated that there are approximately seven million people who speak Hebrew, of whom the large majority are either children or semiliterates in the language (including both poorly educated Israel natives and the very large number of immigrants who are highly educated but read European languages). Hebrew bestsellers have a circulation of 10,000–50,000. Hebrew poetry on the other hand is read by a comparatively large group of Israelis and dozens of volumes of verse are published annually. Being a "small" literature, written and read by a society whose intellectuals belong to a variety of language cultures, Hebrew literature is strongly subject to multifarious European literary influences. The interplay of Russian, Polish, English, French, and German literatures with Hebrew literature has greatly enriched the Hebrew literary scope and has given it its special flavor.

BEGINNINGS

Scholars disagree as to when modern Hebrew literature actually began. There are generally two schools of thought:

(1) those who adhere to Gershom *Scholem's views and consider the disruption of the medieval authority of the Jewish community in the wake of the Shabbatean debacle at the close of the 17th century the starting point of the modern age (Simon Halkin, *Modern Hebrew Literature* (1950), 29–32);

(2) those who hold that the German Haskalah (see below) of the latter half of the 18th century marks the beginning (J. Klausner; *Historyah* etc.; B. Kurzweil, *Sifrutenu ha-Ḥadashah: Hemshekh o Mahpekhah*?, 1959; Ḥ.N. Shapiro, *Toledot ha-Sifrut ha-Ivrit ha-Ḥadashah*, 1940). *Lachower, without reference to Scholem's thesis, opens his history with Moses Ḥayyim *Luzzatto (1707–1746) contending that not only was he the cultural heir to the Italian-Hebrew humanists of the 16th and 17th centuries, but was influenced by modern non-Jewish writers and by their secularist ideas (a view held by Ḥ.N. Bialik, Shalom Streit, N. Slouschz, and Avraham Shaanan). Scholem's thesis explains the inner causes which ultimately led to the development of the "anti-establishment" movements of the late 18th and early 19th centuries (Ḥasidism and Haskalah) and points out that proto-Haskalah ideas were current among the disillusioned Frankists in Prague during the 18th century (*"Mitzvah ha-Ba'ah ba-Averah"* in: *Keneset*, 2 (1937) see also *Commentary*, 51 (Jan. 1971), 41–70). However, the secularism which clearly identifies the modern period first received significant literary expression in Germany during the Enlightenment (for contrary opinions see B. Kurzweil, *Ba-Ma'avak al Erkhei ha-Yahadut* (1970), and Ḥ.N. Shapiro, *Toledot ha-Sifrut ha-Ivrit ha-Ḥadashah*).

Those who would begin modern Hebrew literature with Moses Ḥayyim Luzzatto agree that its basic characteristic is its secularism but assert that Luzzatto's plays were products of the "new spirit" and that these in turn affected subsequent modern Hebrew literature. Luzzatto's world view however was not modern. He was a kabbalist and the bulk of his works were religious and mystical. His poetics too are clearly based on medieval notions; *Leshon Limmudim* (1927) draws heavily on Quintilian. Moreover, while he influenced David *Franco-Mendes during his stay in Holland, his plays were not known to the early German Hebrew authors.

PERIODIZATION

Historians also disagree as to the periodization of modern Hebrew literature. Lachower follows a geographical-chronological pattern in the first two volumes of his history: (1) "From the Growth of the New Literature in Italy until the Decline of the Haskalah in the West" – Italy, Holland, and Germany (1750–1830); (2) "The Early Days of the Haskalah in the East until the Close of the Haskalah Period" – Austria, Galicia, and Russia (1820–1880). In volume 3 he shifts to a conceptual definition: "From the Beginnings of the Jewish National Idea until our Times" – Russia (1860–1920). *Klausner, proposing a more "literary" scheme, limits his history to the Haskalah (1781–1881) dividing it into three periods which are also defined conceptually and geographically: (1) the rationalist, pseudoclassical period (1781–1830) – the defense of the Enlightenment in Germany against the attack of the traditionalists; (2) the romantic period (1830–1860) – the reconciliation between religion and the Haskalah in Galicia; (3) the realistic period (1860–1881) – the attack of the Haskalah on religion in Russia and Poland.

B. *Kurzweil prefers a cultural-historical scheme distinguishing between (1) the "naïve Haskalah" which attempts to reconcile modernism with religion (1781–1830); (2) the militant reformist Haskalah (1830–1881) with its humanist-European orientation; (3) the period of disillusionment with European humanism (1881–1948). He argues unconvincingly that a fourth period, characterized by an apocalyptic vision of national sovereignty, begins with Uri Ẓevi *Greenberg. The schemes of Klausner and Lachower are faulty because they treat early modern Hebrew literature as a mature literature when in reality it possessed little aesthetic value prior to 1881. Most of the authors were provincial, used a cumbersome language, and hardly had acquired the European education and the standards of judgment which they were avidly seeking. Their works must therefore be considered as precursors of a literature which was to reach maturity only at the close of the 19th century.

The following scheme reflects more accurately the periodization of modern Hebrew literature:

I. The European Period (1781–1921)

(1) Haskalah Literature: the beginnings of modern Hebrew literature in Europe (1781–1881): (a) The German Haskalah (1781–1830); (b) The Galician Haskalah (1820–1860); (c) The Russian Haskalah (1840–1881)

(2) Modern Hebrew Literature in Europe: in Russia and Poland (1881–1920)

II. The Palestinian-Ḥalutzic Period (1905–1948)

(1) The Ottoman period (1905–1917)

(2) The Mandate period (1920–1948)

III. The Israel Period (1948 to the present)

THE EUROPEAN PERIOD (1781–1917)

Haskalah Literature: The Beginnings of Modern Hebrew Literature in Europe (1781–1881)

THE GERMAN HASKALAH (1781–1830). The first center of modern Hebrew literature developed in Prussia (particularly in the cities of Berlin and Koenigsberg) among the new Jewish merchant and managerial class, which had risen to social and economic prominence during the latter half of the 18th century. This new class discovered in the ideology of the German *Aufklaerung* ("Enlightenment"), with its emphasis on "reason," "good taste," and "the rights of man," a rationale that would justify their abandonment of many Jewish religious practices which had hindered their access to gentile society. It would also support their demand for social and political rights in a society which judged a man's worth by his ability and not by his origins. They believed that the realization of this ideology would transform the Jews into productive and enlightened citizens of the emerging modern state. When the Hebrew writers of Germany began propagating the "new philosophy" they selected the Hebrew word *haskalah* as the equivalent for the German *Aufklaerung*. Etymologically *haskalah* is derived from the root שכל denoting understanding, reason, or intelligence. *Haskalah* meant a commitment to reason rather than to revelation as the source of all truth, or, perhaps more correctly, the identification of revelation with reason. The *maskilim* averred that the practices, beliefs, and mores of Judaism and Jews must be in consonance with reason and that those which were not were basically not Jewish but distortions of the lofty purposes of Judaism.

The *maskilim* chose as a model the enlightened gentile merchant class which had accepted good taste and reason as its two social criteria. Their world view included not only the realms of science and philosophy but also the whole area of social behavior and aesthetics. Jews must not only abandon their medieval patterns of thought but also their outlandish manners, dress, and taste and adopt those which are in accord with the new order of things. The task of the *maskil* was *lehaskil* ("to be enlightened" and "to enlighten others"). For the *maskil*, education was not only the tool for the dissemination of the new truth but formed the very basis of his aesthetic theory. The prime purpose of literature was to educate the reader morally, socially, and aesthetically. Haskalah literature was therefore didactic and propagandist, aiming at bringing enlightenment to the "benighted" and backward Jewish communities of Germany and Eastern Europe.

It was natural for the Haskalah to choose Hebrew as its linguistic vehicle. The Yiddish dialects had no literary prestige at the time and were especially repugnant to *maskilim* who considered Yiddish to be a vulgar and ungrammatical corruption of German. Yiddish identified and isolated Jews from the general culture and underscored their cultural inferiority. On the other hand, Hebrew was not only the classical language of Judaism and the written language of its educated classes, but it also enjoyed enormous prestige in the non-Jewish world as the language of the Bible. Since educated and intelligent Jews of the old school could not read German, Hebrew served as the medium through which not only ideas of the Haskalah were disseminated but also, by means of appropriate translations and textbooks, as a vehicle to acquire German, the modern language most accessible to them. A major literary enterprise of the German Haskalah was the *Biur* (publ. 1780–1783), a German translation in Hebrew characters of the Pentateuch which was supplemented with a modern commentary in Hebrew (see Translations of *Bible). Thousands of Jews learned German through the *Biur.*

Moses Mendelssohn. The most significant personage of the German Haskalah, Moses *Mendelssohn, wrote mainly in German. In his literary and philosophical works he attempted to harmonize traditional Judaism with the new rationalist-deistic philosophy of his times. Mendelssohn also dealt with general philosophical problems and was accepted as a cultural, if not a social, equal in gentile circles – a symbol of the new type of Jew for both gentiles and Jews. Though he wrote very little Hebrew, he was the unchallenged leader of the German Haskalah and the initiator (or at least the one who encouraged) its main literary projects: the *Biur* and *Ha-Me'assef* (see **Me'assef*), the first Hebrew periodical. The *Biur* was at first favorably received by Western European traditional Jewry but soon, for fear that it would lead to cultural assimilation, was denounced as heretical. On the other hand, enlightened Jews hailed it as a major achievement. It served as a textbook to generations of East European Jews in the study of literary German, which in turn was a means to obtain secular knowledge. *Ha-Me'assef*, a Hebrew monthly magazine, modeled after the *Berliner Monatsschrift*, was founded in 1783 in Koenigsberg by a group of young *maskilim*. It appeared intermittently until 1829. All of the leading figures of the early Haskalah contributed to *Ha-Me'assef* including Moses Mendelssohn, Naphtali Herz *Wessely, Solomon *Maimon, David Franco-Mendes, Isaac Abraham *Euchel, Isaac *Satanow, and Shalom b. Jacob *Cohen. Its influence during the earlier years of the German Haskalah was great, but with the Germanization of Jewish intellectual life its circulation dropped off. Readers of German were unable to abide its lower literary and critical standards. From a purely literary point of view *Ha-Me'asef* was not very important. It is significant only as a pioneering project of modern Hebrew literature.

Naphtali Herz (Hartwig) Wessely. The leading Hebrew author of the German Haskalah, Naphtali Hartwig Wessely (Naphtali Hirsch Weisel), wrote only in Hebrew although he knew several European languages, including German. Through his pamphlet *Divrei Shalom ve-Emet* (1782), an impassioned plea in support of the edict of toleration (1781), he won renown as the foremost apologist of the Haskalah. In it he urged the adoption of modern educational methods and the need for "human" knowledge (science, history, and social ethics) as well as "religious" knowledge.

Wessely's main contribution to modern Hebrew literature however is *Shirei Tiferet* ("Poems of Splendor"), a long epic poem on the life of Moses; it is the major literary work of the German Haskalah (pts. 1–5, 1789–92; pt. 6 posthumously 1829). Judged by modern standards, the poem has small literary merit; while it is written in an almost purely biblical style, it is imitative and lacks the conciseness and concreteness of the original biblical account. Moses is cast in the rationalist image of the Haskalah and the entire work is permeated with Haskalah preachments. From a formal point of view, Wessely introduces the alexandrine (the 12-syllable heroic line prevailing in the French poetry of his day) which was to dominate early modern Hebrew poetry for half a century. Of particular interest are his prose introductions to the "books" of the poem which, although written in a period in which sentimentalism already predominates in German literature, still express earlier neoclassical views.

Types of Literature. The German Haskalah produced several epic poems besides the work of Wessely; most significant among them were Shalom b. Jacob Cohen's *Nir David* ("The Splendor of David," Vienna, 1834); Issachar Schlesinger's *Ha-Ḥashmona'im* ("The Hasmoneans," 1817); *Ḥayyei Shimshon* ("The Life of Samson") by Sueskind Raschkow (d. 1836); and Moses Frankfurt *Mendelsohn's *Toledot Avraham* and *Toledot Yosef.* Other poets influenced by the Italian Hebrew school of the 17th and 18th centuries composed closet dramas in verse which were either allegories imitating Moses Ḥayyim Luzzatto's *La-Yesharim Tehillah* ("Praise to the Upright," Amsterdam, 1743), or based on biblical themes: Shalom Cohen's *Amel ve-Tirẓah* (1862); *Gemul Atalyah* ("Athaliah's Retaliation," Amsterdam, 1770), by David Franco-Mendes (1713–1792), adapted from Racine's *Athalie*; and Joseph *Ha-Efrati's (Troppolowitz) *Melukhat Sha'ul* ("Saul's Reign," Vienna, 1794). A third genre was the Hebrew proverb or maxim in which Isaac Satanow excelled. He published *Mishlei Asaf* ("The Fables of Asaf") and its sequel *Gam Elleh Mishlei Asaf* ("Also These Are the Fables of Asaf"). Related to this genre are the *mikhtamim* (maxims in rhymed quatrain form) and the fable (Joel (Brill) *Loewe, Baruch *Jeiteles, and Judah Leib *Ben-Zeev). Except for the verse of Ephraim *Luzzatto, a contemporary of the German Haskalah who lived in Italy and later in London, no lyrical poetry of any merit was produced. Most of the poetry in this genre was a feeble imitation of contemporary German verse and moralistic or didactic in tone. Two poems worthy of mention are *Aggadat Arba Kosot* ("The Legend of the Four Goblets," Berlin, 1790), by the talented poet Solomon *Pappenheim, which after Wessely's epic is the most important poem of the period, and Solomon *Loewisohn's ode to the Hebrew language which he composed as a preface to his book *Meliẓat Yeshurun* ("The Poesy of Jeshurun," 1816).

The German Haskalah produced no remarkable narrative prose. The few pieces in *Ha-Me'assef* are merely sentimental prose poems. Mention should be made, however, of Aaron *Wolfsohn-Halle's *Siḥah be-Ereẓ ha-Ḥayyim* ("A Conversation in the Land of the Living"), a biting satirical sketch directed against the rabbis of his day, and Moses Frankfurt Mendelsohn's article on the history of the German Haskalah (in *Penei Tevel*, published posthumously in 1872). Solomon Maimon's contribution to Hebrew literature was insignificant compared to his role as a German post-Kantian philosopher and to his literary contribution as the author of an autobiography in German which influenced later autobiographical writing in Hebrew. He also wrote a number of works in Hebrew, almost all in philosophy, the physical sciences, and mathematics. His best Hebrew work, *Givat ha-Moreh* (Berlin, 1791), is a commentary on Maimonides' *Guide of the Perplexed*.

Ancillary Centers of the Early Haskalah. Besides the German authors, a number of *maskilim* continued the tradition of Hebrew writing in Italy. Foremost among them were Ephraim Luzzatto, whose *Elleh Benei ha-Ne'urim* ("These Young Men," London, 1768) contain the best lyrical poetry of the period, and Samuel *Romanelli. In Amsterdam a group of writers appeared who were influenced by Moses Ḥayyim Luzzatto or his disciples. In Alsace several poets wrote patriotic Hebrew poetry, the most notable being Elie Ḥalfan *Halevy. Not all "German" *maskilim* were natives of Germany. Solomon Maimon and Solomon b. Joel *Dubino were born in Lithuania, Isaac Satanow in Podolia, and Judah Leib Ben-Zeev in Poland. In Lithuania a subcenter of the Haskalah developed in the town of Shklov and from there moved to St. Petersburg where a number of Shklov's wealthy merchants settled (Joshua *Zeitlin, Nathan *Notkin, and Abraham *Peretz; for a short time the Galician author Menahem Mendel *Levin (Lefin) was a tutor in Peretz's home). The most important St. Petersburg *maskil*, Judah Leib *Nevakhovitch (Ben Noah), published a pamphlet in Russian that he had originally composed in Hebrew, in which he urged the emancipation of Jews.

The End of the German Haskalah. The rapid Germanization of German Jewry led to the displacement of Hebrew as the language of the enlightened Jewish middle classes in Prussia. Between 1794 and 1797 one issue of *Ha-Me'assef* was published annually. By 1797 only 120 subscribers remained. In the meantime a Jewish literature in German, including a literary journal, began to develop. It is no accident that it was reported that Aaron Wolfsohn-Halle, one of the editors of *Ha-Me'assef*, was unable to write Hebrew in his old age.

THE GALICIAN HASKALAH (1820–1860). From Prussia, the Haskalah movement spread to Polish Galicia. Prosperous Jewish merchants from Galicia involved in the export-import trade (exporting agricultural products to Germany and importing manufactured goods) often frequented the great trade fair at Leipzig where they met the new, enlightened German Jewish merchants. German-Jewish salesmen in turn came to the larger cities of Galicia bearing the new way of life with their wares. Centers of the Haskalah were soon established in Brody, Tarnopol, Lemberg, and Cracow in the early 19th century.

Demographically the Jewish population of Galicia was larger and more concentrated than that of Prussia. Intellectually, however, it was uninfluenced by the indigenous Slavic communities of the area whose cultural level was on the whole inferior to that of the Jews. Galician *maskilim* looked to German as the language of European culture. Politically, it was in the interest of the Austro-Hungarian monarchy to encourage Jewish, pro-Austrian elements as a separatist counterforce to Polish nationalism. Consequently, the assimilationist factors which affected Prussian Jewry were far less felt in Galicia.

The first Haskalah leader to come to Galicia was Naphtali Herz *Homberg who, in 1787, upon Mendelssohn's recommendation, was appointed chief inspector of German Jewish schools in Galicia by Joseph II. Despite the vigorous opposition of rabbinic and ḥasidic leaders, he established over a hundred modern Jewish schools in Galicia and Bukovina and opened a teachers seminary in Lemberg. Homberg's arrogance toward Jews and his subservience to the government earned him the hatred of Galician Jewry. They blamed him not only for the "heretical" views and practices taught at his schools but even more for his part in the imposition of the notorious and discriminatory candle tax from which he personally and illegally profited. Homberg also served as censor of Hebrew books. His critical and caustic reports about the backward social situation of the Jews and their inferior morals reinforced the antisemitic views of his patrons. In the wake of growing protests and accusations by the Jews, he was finally removed from his office in 1806 and the schools he established were gradually closed.

Far more significant for the development of the Haskalah in Galicia was M.M. *Levin (Lefin) who, like Homberg, came to Berlin in the 1780s and for a time was a member of Mendelssohn's circle. Mendel Levin ultimately returned to Galicia, living most of the time in Brody. There he became a leader of the first generation of the Galician Haskalah and a friend of N. *Krochmal, S. *Rapoport, Josef *Perl, and Jakob Samuel *Bick. Levin's major contribution to modern Hebrew literature, the development of a Hebrew prose style based on mishnaic Hebrew, was to affect subsequent prose writing. He is also one of the early writers of modern Yiddish.

A key literary figure of this early period is the poet Shalom Cohen. Polish born, he too came to Berlin in the 1780s joining N.H. Wessely's circle. After *Ha-Me'assef* ceased publication in 1797, he succeeded in reviving it in 1808 for a short time. In 1810, he was invited by Anton von *Schmidt, the Viennese gentile publisher of Hebrew books, to serve as editor of his publishing house. In Vienna he launched **Bikkurei ha-Ittim*, the first Hebrew periodical in the Austro-Hungarian Empire (Vienna). The journal was in the form of an almanac and at first served as a vehicle for the reprint of an anthology of *Ha-Me'assef*, but later included original articles. Anton von

Schmidt's publishing house played a major role in encouraging the new Hebrew literature. He employed leading *maskilim* as editors and proofreaders, published many of their books, and printed the two periodicals which were to serve as the forum of the Galician Haskalah, *Bikkurei ha-Ittim* (1820–1831) and *Kerem Ḥemed* (1833–1856).

The major contribution of the Galician Haskalah was in the area of Jewish studies. The first generation of German *maskilim* had attempted studies in this field but, except for some grammatical works, their achievements were awkwardly unprofessional. Only after the succeeding generation had shifted to German as their medium of expression did the golden age of *Wissenschaft des Judenthums dawn in Germany. In Galicia, however, Hebrew remained the language of modern Jewish scholarship. Foremost in the ranks of its scholars was Nachman Krochmal, the mentor of an entire generation. His *Moreh Nevukhei ha-Zeman* ("Guide of the Perplexed of the Time," 1851) is considered to be the philosophical statement of the period. An amorphous work, unfinished by its author and put together and published posthumously in 1851 by Leopold Zunz, it attempts to reconcile Judaism with the post-Kantian (mainly Hegelian) idealism, the prevailing philosophy of the age. Krochmal is the first to outline a scheme for Jewish history which not only explains the survival of Jewry in time but attributes to it an eternal existence because of the special relationship of God (The Absolute Spirit) to the Jewish people. With great erudition and intelligence he discusses almost all of the major problems of Jewish historiography, thus laying the groundwork for future historical research.

Less profound but still significant are the monographs of Krochmal's disciple Solomon Judah Rapoport which, in the main, constitute scholarly biographies of leading Jewish scholars in the medieval period (the series *Toledot Anshei Shem* which was published in *Bikkurei ha-Ittim* and *Kerem Ḥemed*). Although Samuel David *Luzzatto lived in Italy, his works also belong to the Galician Haskalah in whose journals he published and with whose scholars he was intimately involved. Luzzatto was a prolific writer who was involved in almost every scholarly, theological, and communal problem of his times (see his voluminous correspondence, *Iggerot Shadal* (1882–94)). His best work was in the areas of Hebrew and Aramaic grammar, biblical exegesis, and medieval Hebrew poetry.

From a purely literary point of view, the Galician Hebrew authors are to be credited for evolving the Hebrew prose satire. They not only influenced Hebrew style but introduced character types which would receive more sophisticated development in subsequent Hebrew fiction.

Galicia's most important satirist Josef Perl was a communal leader involved in educational reform who used his connections with the monarchy to foster the Haskalah. Perl's two satires *Megalleh Temirin* ("The Revealer of Secrets," 1819) and *Boḥen Ẓaddik* ("The Ẓaddik on Trial," 1838) were primarily directed against the new ḥasidic movement which had captured the imagination of the lower classes of Galician Jewry during the first half of the 19th century. Perl evinced a profound, if hostile, interest in Ḥasidism, studied its sources diligently, wrote the article on Ḥasidism in Peter *Beer's book on Jewish sects, and is said to have completed a book on Ḥasidism in German which was never published. *Megalleh Temirin*, written in an epistolary style, parodies the folkish ungrammatical Hebrew of the Ḥasidim. In keeping with the rationalist-modernist prejudices of a *maskil* Perl draws a grotesque picture of the ignorance, superstition, and gullibility of the Ḥasidim and the cunning of their leaders. Unwittingly, he creates a Hebrew prose style which imitates the Yiddish speech of his characters. In *Boḥen Ẓaddik*, he widens his satiric scope to include other classes of Galician Jewish society, even the *maskilim* themselves. Despite the satirical distortion, Perl's is the first attempt to depict the social context in Hebrew fiction and his cast of types often served as prototypes for the more sophisticated characters of later East European fiction.

Stylistically, Isaac *Erter chose a different path than Perl's. The high style of biblical Hebrew in which his satires are written seems to Hebrew readers of today to be out of keeping with his subject matter. He uses dream sequences or imaginary visions as vehicles for his satires. He spares no one: impoverished Ḥasidim, enlightened physicians, corrupt tax farmers who exploit the poor. In *Gilgul Nefesh* ("Transmigration of Souls," 1845) he uses a bestiary to satirize his characters. Although Erter is less basic to the development of Hebrew prose than Perl, his influence, even on as late a writer as S.Y. *Agnon, is discernible. The Galician Haskalah did not produce great poetry. *Maskilim* continued the tradition of adapting European poetic drama to fit the taste of their Hebrew reading contemporaries. Rapoport, whose poetic talent was decidedly limited, adapted Racine's *Esther* and *Athalie*, justifying his choice in terms of the importance of historical themes for the restoration of Jewish pride. Meir *Letteris adapted Goethe's *Faust*; he eliminated Christological references, set it in the mishnaic period, and identified Faust with the heretical *tanna* *Elisha b. Avuyah.

Letteris and Samuel David Luzzatto were the best of a number of poets who wrote lyrical, meditative, and eulogistic poetry. Other poets deserving mention are Aryeh Leib Kinderfreund (1788–1837), Baruch Shenfield (1787–1852), and Dov Ginzberg (1776–1811).

THE RUSSIAN HASKALAH (1840–1881). The Haskalah in Russia developed in two geographical centers – Lithuania (Vilna) and Belorussia (Kremenets Podolski). Vilna was influenced by the tradition of rationalist Orthodoxy developed among the disciples of *Elijah b. Solomon the Gaon of Vilna and by the German Haskalah. Haskalah came to Belorussia by way of Galicia with many of its earliest authors actually having lived in Galicia at various times.

Early Period. Historians of the Russian Haskalah aver that already during the German period proto-*maskilim* were to be found in Vilna, Shklov, and St. Petersburg, but it is generally agreed that the first Russian *maskil* of major significance was Isaac Dov (Baer) *Levinsohn of Kremenets Podolski. Levinsohn came into contact with almost all the leaders of the Galician Haskalah during his long stay in that province (1813–24). Following his return to Volhynia, he began a period of prolific publication primarily in the area of Jewish history, theology, and philology. His first major work, *Te'udah be-Yisrael* (1828), attempts to justify the Haskalah in terms of traditions and urges a reformation of the *ḥeder* system and the introduction of Hebrew grammar and German translation as aids to the understanding of the Bible. More significant are his apologetic-theological works: *Beit Yehudah* (1839), *Zerubbavel* (1863–64), and *Aḥiyyah ha-Shilloni ha-Ḥozeh* (1863). Levinsohn lacks historical and scientific methodology and he was only vaguely aware of current philosophical views about religion in general, and Judaism and Christianity in particular. The works are a defense of Judaism, especially the Talmud; he contends that the latter is a great encyclopedic work, full of wisdom and deep faith, and Judaism is a liberal religion – far more rational, liberal, and comprehensive than Christianity. Jesus he saw as a rabbinic Jew who never intended to found a new religion and whose moral teachings are all to be found in the Talmud. Jews rejected Jesus' political views, not his ethical program. Levinsohn also wrote a book refuting blood libels (*Efes Damin*, 1837) and published works on Hebrew philology.

In the field of belles lettres, Levinsohn composed two satires against Ḥasidism which were clearly influenced by Josef Perl's and Isaac Erter's works, but are inferior to them. He also wrote a volume of verse comprised of epigrams, satires, and occasional poetry of no literary merit whatsoever.

Poetry. Greater strides were made in the development of Hebrew poetry and prose fiction in Lithuania. Four important writers appeared at the close of the century who paved the way for the great Hebrew writers: Adam ha-Kohen *Lebensohn, his son Micah Joseph *Lebensohn, Judah Leib *Gordon, and the novelist Abraham *Mapu. Adam ha-Kohen Lebensohn is the first of a long line of Russian Hebrew poets. Essentially cerebral, his poetry is the product of the mental world of a Vilna *maskil* who viewed life as a somber enterprise and literature as having a serious ethical purpose. Lebensohn's personal life, beset as it was with economic difficulties in his early adult years and the untimely deaths of several of his sons, reinforced his basically tragic view of life. Restrained by the literary conventions of the times, his long poems, written in a pseudo-biblical style, were marred by verbosity, a penchant for punning, and an exaggerated tendency to intellectualize.

The emotional fire lacking in Adam ha-Kohen Lebensohn's intellectualized verse animates the poetry of his son Micah Joseph Lebensohn (Mikhal). Mikhal's talents were encouraged and nurtured by his father, who afforded him every opportunity to gain the European education which he, the father, lacked. Mikhal studied at German universities and was strongly influenced by the German Romantics. Although his style remains biblical, his Hebrew attains a remarkable flexibility and he does not hesitate to introduce neologisms. The poetry of his Berlin days is urban, with allusions to city parks, gas lamps, and carriages. He is also one of the first modern Hebrew poets to write love poetry. Many of his longer poems are on biblical themes but his attitude to biblical heroes often differs from the traditional view. For example, he is able to empathize with Sisera in *Ya'el ve-Sisra* ("Yael and Sisera"); the hero of *Nikmat Shimshon* ("Samson's Revenge") becomes a symbol of revolutionary ardor; and he identifies with Moses, in *Moshe al Har ha-Avarim* ("Moses on Mt. Abarim," all published in Mikhal's collection of poems *Shirei Bat Ẓiyyon* (1851)). Mikhal, sick with tuberculosis, like Moses will not reach the Promised Land. In *Ḥag ha-Aviv* ("Spring Holiday"), one of his most moving poems, the young poet bewails his tragic inability to relate to nature and to society because he is aware of his imminent death. In contrast to all his predecessors, Mikhal wrote genuine lyrical poetry. Unfortunately, he appeared too early on the Hebrew literary scene to attain the literary level to which his talents might have carried him had the language and the literature in which he wrote reached the maturity it was to gain half a century later.

The greatest literary figure of the Russian Haskalah, Judah Leib Gordon, was a poet, short-story writer, and militant journalist who dominated the literary scene until the 1880s. Emerging in the 1860s as a younger member of the Vilna Haskalah and a disciple of Lebensohn the elder, he was committed to what has been described as the realistic Haskalah. Although his poetry was written in biblical Hebrew and was often hampered by the bombast of biblical rhetoric, it reached beyond the limitations of its period. Most of it was also dominated by the reformist thrust of the Haskalah. Gordon, unlike his predecessors, not only questioned the "spirituality" of the traditional Jewish values of the rabbinic period but also those of the Bible. He demanded a more vital materialistic commitment to life. His rejection of the "impractical and overspiritualized" Jewish world of his childhood led him to depict traditional "villains" of the Bible in more positive terms. Thus in his long poem *Ẓidkiyyahu be-Veit ha-Pekuddot* ("Zedekiah in Prison," 1879), he justified Zedekiah's criticism of Jeremiah's unrealistic stress on the spiritual at a time of national crisis. Soldiers and statesmen, realistic men of affairs, and not prophets and scholars were needed to save the country. Gordon's poems frequently struck out against the unreasonable legalism of the rabbis and called vigorously for the improvement of the woman's status ("*Koẓo shel Yod*," 1869). A genuine lyricism pervades his poetic fables which, although drawn from the Midrash, Aesop, La Fontaine, and particularly Krylov, are original works. More than any of his predecessors, Gordon had an uncanny ear for the biblical idiom and was able to forge new phrases which retained the biblical cadences. Bialik was to acknowledge the debt which he and his generation owed to Gordon.

Prose. Abraham Mapu, the first modern Hebrew novelist, chose the historical novel (*Ahavat Ẓiyyon* (1853) and *Ashmat*

Shomeron (1865)) as his genre and in keeping with the general tendency of Hebrew writers preferred biblical themes to current topics. The difficulties in writing a contemporary social novel in Hebrew became manifest when Mapu himself tried to do so later in his career. Mapu, who knew French, was clearly influenced by both Eugène Sue and Alexandre Dumas *père*, whose long, involved, historical and social novels enjoyed great popularity during the period. *Ahavat Ẓiyyon* ("Love of Zion), set in the days of the kings of Judah, was also influenced by Moses Ḥayyim Luzzatto's two works *Migdal Oz* and *La-Yesharim Tehillah* even to the point that there exists evidence that the names of its two main characters were initially to be the same as those in *Migdal Oz*. The pastoral quality of the novel reflects not only the Haskalah's attitude toward agriculture but Luzzatto's as well. *Ahavat Ẓiyyon* became the first "best seller" of modern Hebrew literature. More ambitious, but less successful artistically, was Mapu's social novel *Ayit Ẓavu'a* ("The Painted Eagle," 3 vols., 1857–64). For all its structural faults, long-windedness, and inability to go beyond typology in its characterization, it constitutes the first attempt at depicting contemporary Jewish life in fiction. The characters are types that Mapu transposed from historical novels into the social context of the day; he also drew upon the satires of Erter and Perl. The infant state of modern Hebrew literature, the yet undeveloped Hebrew prose idiom, and the social and cultural situation of Russian Jewry hampered Mapu's effort. Nevertheless, his was a daring attempt to extend the new literature, thus paving the way for the next generation of Hebrew novelists who were to draw upon his typology.

In the generation following Mapu, Peretz *Smolenskin and Reuben Asher *Braudes contributed to the development of the Hebrew novel. Smolenskin, by far the more influential of the two, founded **Ha-Shaḥar* (1869–84), a journal which he was forced to publish outside of Russia to circumvent censorship restrictions. Abandoning his initial Haskalah assimilationism he embraced a fiery brand of Jewish nationalism which called for an ultimate return to Zion. Smolenskin's *Ha-To'eh be-Darkhei-Ḥayyim* ("Who Wanders in the Ways of Life," 3 vols. (1868–70)) became the novel of the generation. A character novel like *Ayit Ẓavu'a, Ha-To'eh be-Darkhei ha-Ḥayyim* is structured more competently than Mapu's work because it centers around the main protagonist (Joseph) who roams the Jewish Pale of Settlement in search of the meaning of life. The novel contains elements of the picaresque: Joseph wanders into the world of Jewish beggars, sees life in a yeshivah and the court of a ḥasidic rabbi, and travels as far as London, Paris, and Berlin. Smolenskin thus attempted to draw a panorama of Jewish life not only as it was lived inside Russia but also in Western Europe. Far more realistic than Mapu's, his fictional world is still considerably removed from life. The novel remained a rambling, poorly constructed work, full of Haskalah speculations about life, European culture and society, and the meaning of Jewish history. Although many of its characters were derived from Mapu and, like the latter's, are flat and drawn in black and white, Smolenskin extended their range.

More realistic and written with greater discipline were the novels of Reuben Asher Braudes. The plot of his unfinished novel *Ha-Dat ve-ha-Ḥayyim* ("Religion and Life," 1885) revolves around the struggle of a young *maskil* to liberate himself from the narrow world of his childhood town and become a European; it is, in part, drawn from the biography of Moses Leib Lilienblum. In *Shetei ha-Keẓavot* ("Two Extremes," 1888), the protagonist has liberated himself from tradition only to discover that the new secularism lacks the certainty and peace of mind afforded by the old Orthodoxy. Although Braudes was unable to free himself from the one-sided view of the Haskalah and often lapsed into ideological preachments, he came closer to the reality he attempted to depict than any other novelist of the period.

The Modern Period (1881–1917)

RUSSIA AND POLAND. By the 1880s, literary and political factors earmarked a new period in modern Hebrew literature. Almost a century of literary endeavor had been completed by then. Writers had a large corpus of literature to fall back on, a literature which had struggled with language, genre, and motifs and was ready for real artistic achievement. The cultural situation of East European Jewry had also undergone a radical change. A generation of writers had emerged that expressed its awareness of the secular-scientific orientated European culture through Hebrew literature. Although few writers could be called totally "European" in their point of view, a degree of sophistication had been attained that had been lacking in the previous generations. In the meantime European Romanticism, intimately bound to idealist philosophy, had given way to naturalism and realism – literary movements which were rooted in a more materialistic view of the universe. Influential Russian literary critics, like Pisarev and Chernyshevski, called for a more realistic form of writing and demanded a literature of social criticism. These attitudes were quickly picked up by some of the younger Hebrew critics who began publishing in the journals of the Russian Haskalah. Abraham Uri *Kovner, well versed in Russian positivist criticism, called for a realistic literature which would mirror the true character of the nation and lead to economic and social reform. He attacked the artificial biblicism which dominated much of Hebrew literature and commended the satires of Erter and Perl and Mapu's *Ayit Ẓavu'a*. A more realistic-materialistic literature was also advocated by Abraham Jacob *Paperna. Moses Leib Lilienblum in his *Olam ha-Tohu* ("Desolate World," 1873) attacked the idealistic Haskalah; he ascribed its use of romantic and unrealistic subject matter and theme to an escapism nurtured by the tragic and hopeless reality of Jewish life. Critics of the 1870s attacked the *batlanut* ("the impracticability") of Hebrew literature and denigrated most of its achievements.

Political and social events reinforced these new views. The rise of Russian reaction during the reign of Nicholas II, and particularly the pogroms of the early 1880s, which were either instigated by the czarist regime or at least actively encouraged by its political police, disillusioned the vast majority of the *maskilim*. The whole reformist program, grounded on the naïve belief that the only deterrent to the emancipation of Russian Jewry was its own religious obscurantism and its own economic and social backwardness, was thus put into question. A new empathy for the people, its way of life, and its aspirations now replaced the bitter sarcasm of the realistic Haskalah. The prejudice against the older way was softened by a more balanced evaluation of its significance. While Hebrew writers did not abandon their criticism of the old way, they were capable of greater artistic objectivity.

The new nationalism did not reject modernization; on the contrary, it defined Jewish life in terms of the values of European nationalism. A national literature must aim at an objective depiction of the condition of the people and it must use European aesthetic standards in the working out of its themes. The shift from universalism to particularism led also to the discovery of the individual. In the Haskalah period fiction and poetry tended to depict types. The literary type stood somewhere between the allegorical hero and the individualized character. With the new period a more individualized characterization manifested itself in fiction and poetry.

The literary activity of Moses Leib *Lilienblum serves as a paradigm of this transvaluation of values. Raised in an obscurantist ḥasidic environment, he began his literary career as a polemist advocating religious and social reforms. His autobiography *Ḥatot Ne'urim* ("Sins of Youth," 1876–99), a classic work of the period, eloquently describes his struggle toward freedom. Lilienblum, influenced by Joshua Heschel *Schorr, a radical Galician *maskil*, argues against the "divine authority" of the Talmud and the Shulḥan Arukh contending that although the halakhic laws had validity in their time, they should not be accepted uncritically by modern Jews. In the 1860s, he and J.L. Gordon were the leading proponents of reform. During the 1870s, he seems to have lost hope in theological solutions and turns to positivism, and even socialism, as the new alternative. After the 1880s, he despaired of Russian liberalism and embraced the Zionist nationalism of the Ḥibbat Zion movement, stressing the "Oriental" quality of Jewish life. He never lost his pragmatic view of the world and therefore rejected Aḥad Ha-Am's cultural nationalism as being unrealistic and vapid.

The Age of Aḥad Ha-Am. The most influential intellectual figure of the European period was *Aḥad Ha-Am (Asher Ginzberg), a brilliant essayist, who attempted to develop an integrated philosophy for the new nationalist movement. He was not an original thinker but was able to articulate an ideology out of contemporary ideas with which to meet the needs of many Hebrew intellectuals of his day. Aḥad Ha-Am had indicated, at various times in his career, that he planned to write a systematic exposition of his philosophy, but he did not carry out his program. Unfortunately the essay form, which was his medium, hardly lends itself to a systematic presentation of ideas.

Aḥad Ha-Am drew heavily on positivist, utilitarian ideas current in his days and on the then newly developed science of sociology. At the center of his philosophy he placed the nation, which he equated with society. Judaism was the system of ideas, laws, and mores which the Jewish nation had developed in order to preserve itself. Individuals are merely limbs of the nation. The nation is the constant factor in human history. The success and prosperity of the nation is the only reward which is vouchsafed to the ephemeral individual.

In times of national crisis or degeneracy, Judaism was forced to express itself in terms of the individual. Biblical Judaism was national and communal, but after the destruction of the Second Temple and the loss of national sovereignty, rabbinic Judaism was compelled to direct its appeal to the individual, and only then was the doctrine of individual salvation propounded. Natural redemption will follow when the center of gravity will shift from the selfish concern for individual prosperity, spiritual or material, to the broader concern for the welfare of the people as a whole.

In his system society, i.e. the nation, replaced God as the source of authority. Yet Aḥad Ha-Am was careful not to tamper with the *sancta* of Judaism. The traditional Jewish customs were justified in terms of the national culture and its values. At the center of the national culture he placed the prophetic ethic, its peculiar expression. "There is almost a general consensus about the moral genius of the Jewish people and that in this area the Jewish people stand above all other nations. It makes no difference as to how the Jewish people attained this talent or how it evolved among them" (in *Shinui Arakhim*). Aḥad Ha-Am obviously avoided a metaphysical explanation for the uniqueness of the Jew and yet at the same time asserted its existence. His definition of the national character, or as he called it the national spirit, saved him from a biological definition of nationality and lent a universalistic humanist dimension to his nationalism. The universal ethic finds its expression in the particularist culture of the Jew. Jewish cosmopolitanism was for Aḥad Ha-Am an inauthentic expression of the Jewish ethical idea. Universal values must be rooted in the concrete experiences of the people and within its culture, otherwise they will remain vapid generalities. Translated in terms of a specific culture, they must be properly assimilated so as to become a part of it.

The nation-society, an organic fact, has a will and a life of its own in his system. Nationhood is axiomatic and must be accepted on faith. The Jew who asked why he was a Jew was already inauthentic. In his past history, the Jew taught theology and played a central role in preserving the nation, but with the breakdown of religious authority the national idea became the rallying point of Judaism. Aḥad Ha-Am saw in Zionism the return to the national idea. The very effort to establish a Jewish settlement in Palestine would serve as a focal point around which the national "will" could rally. He did not believe that a mass return to the national homeland was possible; instead he conceived of the homeland as the future spiritual (cultural) center of the Jewish people wherever it resided. The spiritual center would not only preserve the people but would bring about a national cultural renaissance.

The national revival, however, cannot occur merely because of the practical needs of the nation for migration or for a refuge. Ereẓ Israel was a poor and underdeveloped country and settlement must be preceded by a renewal of the national will. The task of the nationalist intellectuals must be to educate the people toward the difficult struggle for national renewal. For the Jewish intellectuals who had lost their faith in traditional Judaism, Aḥad Ha-Am's cultural-humanist nationalism offered itself as a welcome solution. One could preserve not only one's group loyalty but a great part of Jewish mores and customs by shifting the source of authority from God to history and from community to nation. One could likewise retain the old ethical goals of Judaism by identifying them with the national culture. It is no small wonder that the majority of Hebrew authors rallied to Aḥad Ha-Am's banner.

Aḥad Ha-Am's role in modern Hebrew literature went beyond his ideology. From a literary point of view he is the father of the modern Hebrew essay. His Hebrew style, which draws a great deal on Maimonides' Hebrew, is lucid and well constructed. Moreover, as the editor (1897–1903) of the most influential Hebrew journal of the period, **Ha-Shilo'aḥ*, he set a high standard of literary taste for an entire generation of Hebrew writers. His conservative literary views, however, discouraged radical experimentation. He also insisted that writers of Hebrew belles letters should confine themselves to Jewish subjects. These two attitudes ultimately led to a revolt against his literary domination and he finally resigned his editorship of *Ha-Shilo'aḥ*.

The career of Sholem Yankev *Abramovitsh (Mendele Mokher Seforim) stands at the crossroads between the Haskalah and the nationalist period. Sociologically he still belonged to the Russian Haskalah, but aesthetically he was the harbinger of the new period with its stress on realism and artistic discipline. To Mendele belongs the double crown as the father of the new Hebrew literary style and the first serious writer in Yiddish. He began writing in the biblically orientated Hebrew style of the Haskalah, although even then his work *Ha-Avot ve-ha-Banim* ("The Fathers and the Sons," 1865) was influenced by Turgenev and is cast in a realistic mode. Mendele's penchant for realism led him in 1864 to abandon the inflexible and literary Hebrew of the Haskalah for the more vivid and folk-like Yiddish. He returned to Hebrew in 1886, writing original fiction or translating and recasting his Yiddish works. The style of these later works are a landmark in the development of modern Hebrew literature. The more simple Hebrew prose of mishnaic and talmudic literature and of the Hebrew prayer book replaced the high biblical Haskalah style that had characterized his earlier works, and with it he forged an idiom more akin to the realism which had become dominant in Hebrew fiction. Mendele's long short stories and novels were better structured than any of the prose works of his predecessors. He drew on the modern Hebrew literary tradition for his characters but added a new, realistic subtlety. The picaresque *Sefer ha-Kabẓanim* (1909; *Fishke the Lame*, 1960), for example, recalls Smolenskin's description of the society of beggars in *Ha-To'eh be-Darkhei ha-Ḥayyim*, but the prose and the characterization are infinitely more sophisticated. Mendele satirized the Jewish life of Eastern Europe so mercilessly that later patriotic critics have urged to expunge his works from school curricula because they "desecrate the memory of European Jewry." His portrayal, however, is not one-sided and he often depicts the folk piety and warmth of the Jews of the townlet with deep sympathy. Despite his emphasis upon the grotesque, the world he describes has a Jewish unity which even pervades the natural world; he "Judaizes" nature. Mendele's characters rarely develop beyond typology. Yisrulik, for example, in "*Susati*" (1911; *The Nag*, 1949) is a typical Jewish external student preparing for state examinations, and Binyamin in *Masot Binyamin ha-Shelishi* (1911; "The Travels of Benjamin the Third") is a typical impoverished and impractical member of the scholarly lower middle class. Mendele never became an active Zionist but his later works reflect the disillusionment with Russian liberalism ("*Susati*"). His meticulous devotion to the craft of writing became a model for the disciples of his Odessa school. Two of them, Ḥayyim Naḥman *Bialik and Shalom *Aleichem, were to become major literary figures in Hebrew and Yiddish literature respectively.

In contrast to the realism of Mendele's Odessa school, a neoromantic, impressionist center developed in Warsaw whose leading authors are David *Frischmann, I.L. *Peretz, and Micha Josef *Berdyczewski. The Polish Haskalah was far less practical and doctrinaire than that of Odessa. It tended to stress form and beauty rather than a central idea. Poland, moreover, if not completely removed from the literary influences of the Russian utilitarians, was drawn to the continent and was more sensitive to the new aestheticism which in the 1880s had captured the European literary imagination. David Frischmann laid great stress on style and form. He was the self-declared European of Hebrew letters, but for him Europeanism had little to do with a materialist view of the universe or even scientism but was a matter of aesthetic values and literary taste. His Hebrew prose has a limpid and almost lyrical quality; his plots are carefully rounded although not devoid of impressionistic lapses. In keeping with his aestheticism, he no longer describes the struggle of the generations in Jewish life as a clash between reason and tradition but as a struggle between beauty and life on the one hand and an unrelenting tradition on the other (*Be-Yom ha-Kippurim* (1881)). Frischmann's characters are often individuals whose irrational passion leads them to break with their tradition. He can also sympathize with the rigid traditionalism of the older generation and at the same time poke fun at the rationalist absurdities of half-baked *maskilim*. His secularist lyrical, biblical "legends" are one of his original contributions to Hebrew literature. Frischmann, through his knowledge of folklore and myth, created stories almost devoid of biblical ethos but which attempt to reconstruct the passionate world of the primitive quasi-pagan Hebrews ("*Meḥolot*" = Dances). The mythical-pagan setting contrasts strongly with the biblical stories and poems produced by such writers as Mapu or even Micah Joseph Lebensohn.

I.L. Peretz continues the Polish tradition. Unlike Frischmann, he shifted to Yiddish (in which language he wrote most of his works) in the middle of his career and became the proponent of Yiddishism after the revolution of 1905. His contribution to modern Hebrew literature, however, is also of great significance. Like Frischmann he attacks the realism of the Odessa school, dubbing it anachronistic. "In the world of general literature the sun of realism has set. It has been followed by materialism and then the decadents have raised their banner, but among us, so removed from the battlefield, realism is the new slogan which excites the heart" (*Ha-Ḥeẓ*, 1884). Peretz earned his place in Hebrew literature primarily as a prose writer of the 1880s and 1890s. His earlier short stories: "*Ha-Dibbuk ve-ha-Meshugga*" ("The Dibbuk and the Madman") and "*Hiẓtaddekut ha-Ne'esham*" ("The Alibi") were influenced by the sentimentalism of German-Jewish authors who wrote about East European Jewish life. The stories emphasize the individual rebellion of young Jews against the traditionalistic puritanism of their environment. His stories often took a psychological turn: *Be-Leil Zeva'ah* ("Nightmare") and "*Mi Anokhi*" ("Who Am I"), whose characters display a split personality. Peretz's ḥasidic tales, in the main, represent a humanistic-secularist, and especially romantic, reading of ḥasidic themes. Although they have been described as ḥasid-like, rather then authentically ḥasidic, Peretz is nevertheless one of the earliest Hebrew writers to portray Ḥasidism in a positive rather than a critical light. In his folk ḥasidic tales he uses an impressionistic sentimental style in an attempt to capture the pious rapture of his characters (kabbalists) and he often resorts to lyrical monologues or dialogues – "*Ha-Mekubbalim*" ("The Kabbalists"), "*Gilgulo shel Niggun*" ("Metamorphosis of a Melody"), and "*Bein Shenei Harim*" ("Between Two Mountains"). One of his best short stories, "*Oseh Nifla'ot*" ("The Magician"), is a folktale in which Elijah the Prophet appears as a magician who miraculously provides a *seder* for an impoverished pious family. (All of I.L. Peretz's were published in *Kol Kitvei I.L. Peretz* (1947).)

Perhaps the most skillful proponent of the Polish neoromantic style was Micha Josef Berdyczewski, whose work reflects the Nietzschean demand for a transvaluation of values. He put into question the entire value system of traditional Judaism with its stress on communal discipline and religious conformism at the expense of individualism. Challenging Aḥad Ha-Am's contention that there exists a mainstream in Judaism and arguing that there is no unified Jewish culture, he advanced the concept of a heterodoxy of Jewish experience. There is no rational evolution of a tradition but rather a series of miraculous and irrational revelations. Tradition always strove toward discipline, it controlled the outbursts of the spirit but was never able to contain them for long. During these periods of restraint Judaism lost its vitality. Berdyczewski insisted that the Judaism of his day was stagnant and must free itself of its restraining legalism and its intellectualism. He opposed Aḥad Ha-Am's attempt to provide a utilitarian-nationalist apology for tradition and to reconstruct a unified nationalist culture. Only the creative spark of the individual and the individualist dissent can lead to a national renaissance. The call for individualism and the individualist rebellion against the yoke of tradition and society also form the core of Berdyczewski's fiction. His characters often are Jews who try to escape the narrow world of their childhood but are psychologically incapable of making the break. They are lost souls moving in a limbo between traditional puritanism and modern libertinism, impotent physically and psychologically to live the life they desire. The impotence is often accentuated, not only by feelings of guilt toward their former system of values, but also by their deep group loyalty and their feelings of familial love (e.g., Nathaniel in "*Me-Ever la-Nahar*" ("Across the River" in *Kitvei M.Y. Bin-Gorion* (1960)). In Ḥasidism Berdyczewski discovered a dissenting, individualist movement which had broken with the loyalism and conformism of rabbinism. Stylistically, his Hebrew bears affinities to Frischmann's impressionist lyricism, but unlike the latter, he often cuts the flow of his prose either with impassioned outbursts or to indicate moments of doubt and despair.

The writings of M.Z. *Feuerberg also mirror the tragedy of loss of faith but, unlike the Berdyczewskian hero, the Feuerbergian protagonist, although he rejects the simple faith of his fathers, never crosses the line into the secular world which remains beyond his grasp. Feuerberg's hero lives in an irresolvable crisis. Naḥman in *Le'an* ("Whither," 1927), having lost the living God of Israel (tradition), finds no solace in the God of Aristotle (reason) who to him is lifeless and impotent. His anxieties, resulting from his loss of faith, ultimately drive him mad.

Most of Feuerberg's stories are autobiographical in which the basic concept is a variation of the same theme: the world of childhood secure in its faith is disrupted as the child or young hero experiences life. The process is inevitable. In a letter to Aḥad Ha-Am he wrote: "The new life extends its domain among us without the consent of literature. The old life is disappearing despite its sanctity and sublimity." Feuerberg's outlook, however, was not devoid of hope. He saw his disrupted world in a state of crisis but believed in the ultimate revival of the spirit of man: "Europe is sick now, everyone senses that society is collapsing and that its very foundations are rotten. Human society is weary and yearns for the word of God. The minor prophets who arise, Kant and others, last for only a century. We need a great prophet and lawgiver… Not only do we turn our face eastward, the entire West is journeying to the East. The greatest enemy of Judaism is the West… Therefore when you journey to the East, my brothers, do not go as the enemies of the East but as its sons and lovers" (*Le'an*).

The Age of Bialik. The achievement of Ḥayyim Naḥman *Bialik marks the high point in form and content of the European period in Hebrew literature. Most of Bialik's poetry was written between 1892 and 1917, the turbulent years which immediately preceded the Russian Revolution and the decline of the East European Jewish community. At the brink of catastrophe, Russian Jewry produced its greatest poet. In the genius of Bialik, a delicate balance is attained between the old traditionalistic culture nurtured on sacred books and on a medieval religiosity and the new European culture to which the products of the old culture now turned.

Bialik consciously accepted the Aḥad Ha-Am view that through cultural nationalism a synthesis between these two polar cultures could be established (*"Al Saf Beit ha-Midrash,"* 1894; *"Le-Aḥad Ha-Am,"* 1905). Baruch Kurzweil and others, however, have demonstrated that Bialik often unconsciously rejected the all-too-pat Aḥad Ha-Am solution and gave vent to the tragic despair that the lost paradise of faith cannot be regained (*"Levadi"* ("Alone)" 1910) *"Lifnei Aron ha-Sefarim"* ("In Front of the Bookcase," 1910)). He also writes about the clash between traditional Jewish puritanism, with its religious ethical imperatives, and the hedonistic-aesthetical orientation of the secularized Jews (*Ha-Matmid*, 1894–95). In his Zionist poems *"El ha-Ẓippor"* ("To the Bird") and *"La-Mitnaddevim be-Am"* ("To the Volunteers") he castigates both the people and its leaders for their shortcomings and in *Ha-Matmid* nostalgically reflects upon the piety and devotion of the past. The desperate struggle to discover the link between the past and the present is central to Bialik's poetry.

From the very outset of his career Bialik was totally committed to the national revival. His is therefore a poetry of involvement in his people's quest for a national identity and it expresses its tragic experience of persecution and massacre: *"Be-Ir ha-Haregah"* ("In the City of Slaughter"), 1904; *"Al ha-Sheḥitah"* ("On the Slaughter"), 1903. These nationalist poems earned him the title of *ha-meshorer ha-le'ummi* ("the national poet"). It would be a mistake, however, to limit Bialik's achievement to his nationalist themes, as profound as his involvement in them, and expression of them, might be. He was also a great lyric poet whose thematic scope embraced love and nature poems, folk poetry, and even children's verse. Even these poems, because they could be read on several levels – personal, nationalistic, and universalistic – were often interpreted as nationalistic by the one-sided criticism of his generation. Contemporary criticism has corrected this imbalance.

No modern Hebrew poet possesses Bialik's command of the vast resources of Hebrew literature. His vocabulary and symbols are drawn from a literary tradition that spans the entire literature of his people from the biblical period to the latest works written by his contemporaries. Bialik's knowledge served him not simply as a means to reproduce old phrases but to forge a new idiom capable of meeting the literary needs of a modern literature. He freed Hebrew poetry from the bonds of the Haskalah rhetoric and yet his poetry style remained essentially biblical. Unlike his predecessors, his line is not a composite of biblical phrases and half verses. Mastering the source from the inside, he creates his phrasing in the image of the biblical diction. Although he was not a great innovator structurally, and generally preferred the more traditional patterns of meter and rhyme, he developed the Hebrew prose poem, *"Megillat ha-Esh"* ("The Scroll of Fire," 1905) and his occasional experiments with symbol and myth (*"Megillat ha-Esh," "Metei Midbar"* ("The Dead in the Desert," 1902) extended the frontier of modern Hebrew poetry.

Bialik's impact on Hebrew literature was not altogether positive. His literary genius cast an entire generation into the shadow; its writers were dominated by Bialik's style and themes. Yet a number of significant Hebrew poets of the period were able to maintain a great degree of artistic independence. Foremost among them was Saul *Tchernichowsky, who by education and temperament was much more "European" than many of his contemporaries. Thematically and structurally he strove to introduce a more European poetry and therefore utilizes a large variety of European poetic structures (sonnets, idylls, ballads) and rhyme patterns. His poetry also expresses revolt against the puritanism of the Jewish tradition and its shunning of the plastic and the physical. Like Berdyczewski, he stresses the individualism of his characters and the revolt of healthy passion against the suppressive puritanism of the Jewish society. More radical than Frischmann, he sought to bring to the fore the pagan undercurrent which he believed had flourished in the biblical period. He found it embodied not only in the erotic passion of the biblical woman (*Ashtorti Li*), but in the suppressed prophecies of the "false prophets." Yet it would be a mistake to stress only this aspect of Tchernichowsky's work. As a humanist, he remained committed to the universalist goals of European culture despite the tragedy of terror and war (*"La-Shemesh,"* "To the Sun," 1919). He rejected, however, the traditionalistic belief that nature, passion, and physical prowess are antithetical to morality. Unlike Bialik, Tchernichowsky wrote extensively after his migration to Ereẓ Israel in 1931. Some of his landscape poems are among the finest composed in Israel (*"Ayit, Ayit"* 1936, "Eagle! Eagle!"). The Ereẓ Israel experience is also reflected in his patriotic verse (*"Re'i Adamah"* ("See Earth") 1938) and in his profound long poem *"Amma de-Dahavah"* ("People of Gold," 1937–40).

A third and less significant poet of Bialik's generation, Zalman *Shneour, expressed a rebellious and individualistic disillusionment with conventional mores. His poetry is often permeated with a pessimistic view of the future of European civilization as in *Yemei ha-Beinayim Mitkarevim* ("The Middle Ages are Approaching," 1915). In a literature which was in his day extremely puritanical, his verses are marked at times by a comparative erotic boldness. Shneour had a gift for descriptive poetry (*"Be-Harim,"* "In the Mountains," 1908), but his diction often took on an immature and extravagant tone. His world is one of unbridled passion and instincts experienced by a sensitive poet who would have preferred a more idealist view of man but discovered that such a view is an illusion. Against this backdrop of blood and instinct, he describes the massacres of Jews in the Ukraine following the Russian Revolution and later in World War II. Erotic motifs also appear in his later work, the less successful series of poems on the theme of Israel's false prophets in biblical times (*Luḥot Genuzim*, "Hidden Tablets," 1941).

A very prolific poet of Bialik's school, Ya'akov Cahan, wrote verse in keeping with the great European Romantics. His poems are highly nationalistic. He frequently wrote closet drama dealing with historical Jewish themes. Bialik's school also produced two poets whose meditative lyrical poems have elicited renewed enthusiasm of contemporary Israel students of literature. Jacob *Fichmann wrote impressive landscape poetry in a terse but simple verse and Jacob *Steinberg, elliptic philosophical poetry. Deeply personal and pessimistic, Steinberg's poetry is almost devoid of the social and nationalist idea which were the earmark of his generation.

THE PALESTINIAN- ḤALUTZIC PERIOD (1905–1948)

The Ottoman Period (1905–1917)

The Second Aliyah brought an increasing number of Hebrew authors to Palestine; they settled mainly in the Jewish part of Jaffa. Among the major writers were: Shlomo *Ẓemach (1904); S. *Ben-Zion (1905); Yosef *Aharonovitch (1906); Mordecai ben Hillel *Hacohen, Rabbi *Binyamin (Radler), Uri Nissan *Gnessin, David *Shimoni (1907; Gnessin and Shimoni returned to Russia in 1908); S.Y. Agnon, J.Ḥ. *Brenner, *Raḥel (Bluwstein; 1909); Ya'akov *Rabinowitz, Ẓevi *Schatz (1910); Devorah *Baron, Yeshurun *Keshet (1911); and Asher *Barash, Jacob Steinberg (1914). They were preceded by several Hebrew writers who had settled in Ereẓ Israel during the 1880s (First Aliyah); the foremost among them, Eliezer *Ben-Yehuda, arrived in Jerusalem in 1881. Ben-Yehuda was not only the great advocate of the revival of spoken Hebrew but an important lexicographer who coined hundreds of new Hebrew words, many of which were absorbed by the revived language. He also was the father of modern Palestinian journalism. After serving on the editorial staff of I.D. *Frumkin's **Ḥavaẓẓelet*, he founded his own weekly, *Ha-Ẓevi*, in 1885 and in 1909 converted it into a daily. The paper often appeared under different names to avoid censorship restrictions. As editor, Ben-Yehuda adopted the sensational journalistic style then current in Paris. The historian and essayist Ze'ev (Wolf) *Jawitz lived in Ereẓ Israel between 1888 and 1897 and published romantic stories about the early agricultural settlements in the Sharon. Moshe *Smilansky, who arrived in 1891, wrote slightly more realistic stories about Palestinian life. He was the first to write Hebrew fiction about Arab life, using the pseudonym "Ḥawajah Musa."

Hebrew literature in Palestine acquired significance during the Second Aliyah, particularly after the founding of **Ha-Po'el ha-Ẓa'ir* (1907), the literary-political organ of the younger pioneers. The Palestinian short story grew out of the landscape of the old-new homeland. Jawitz's romantic picture of God-fearing, observant farmers who tilled their soil peacefully like their biblical ancestors gave way to the more realistic depiction of the hardships of pioneering, the life of disillusioned immigrants in Jaffa or Jerusalem (Brenner, Ẓevi Schatz, S. Ẓemach). Stylistically, the development of spoken Hebrew and its extension from the classroom, the library, and the study to the farm and the workshop not only lent a new flexibility to the language but also broadened its active vocabulary. Thus the poetry of Raḥel strives to capture the rhythms of new speech and, in contrast to the poetry of European Hebrew poets, scans in the Sephardi accent.

The most significant prose writer of the period is J.Ḥ. Brenner who began his literary career in Russia. Brenner was influenced by the Russian psychological school, particularly Dostoevski (he translated *Crime and Punishment* into Hebrew). His main characters are "underground" men, Jewish intellectuals who are unable to free themselves of the society against which they revolt because psychologically they have been thwarted by its restrictions. Brenner's writing, brutally honest, eschews sham or pretense; his sentences, clipped, often broken, and rarely polished, convey the hesitancy and the tension of his neurotic characters. The world he depicts is tragic and helpless, pervaded by a gloomy pessimism which holds no promise for a way out. His Palestinian stories followed those of his Russian period and except for the change of venue, the dark mood is hardly altered. His later works, however, point to a maturing of style and a greater concern for structure. Undoubtedly *Shekhol ve-Khishalon* ("Bereavement and Failure," 1920) is the best of his works.

Brenner's close friend, Uri Nissan Gnessin, spent only one year in Palestine and therefore geographically belongs to the European period of Hebrew literature. His experiments in style, particularly his use of the long, meditative, almost lyrical sentence to express the *Angst* ("anxiety") of his characters, his individual use of the interior monologue, and his psychological insight mark him as a forerunner of the Palestinian school.

S.Y. Agnon, who began writing in his native Galicia, arrived in Palestine in 1909, and at this time published his first mature works, including *Agunot* ("Forsaken Wives," 1909, in: *Ha-Omer*), under the pseudonym Agnon, which in 1924 became his official name. His best works which made such a great impact on Hebrew literature were, however, written after World War I.

The Mandate Period (1917–1948)

The upheavals which racked Russian Jewry in the wake of World War I and the Russian Revolution all but spelled the end of the Hebrew literary center in Russia. Following the revolution there was some attempt to start a Communist Hebrew literature in Russia but Hebrew was soon declared a counter-revolutionary language. Hebrew publications were banned, and many Hebrew writers, including Bialik, were thrown into prison. At the request of Maxim *Gorki, Lenin ordered their release. For a few years the exiled writers established a center in Berlin. In Poland and Lithuania a few writers maintained small subcenters. Some also migrated to New York where they reinforced the already existing U.S. Hebrew press (*Ha-Toren* and later *Hadoar*) and maintained a small center (see below, Hebrew Literature in the U.S.). But a seemingly inevitable process was propelling the majority of Hebrew writers to Palestine.

The pioneers of the Second Aliyah had begun to develop an indigenous Palestinian literature – the so-called "Ereẓ Israel genre." Their numbers, however, were small and they remained an annex of the European center. With the destruction of the old center, the Hebrew writers of Palestine came into their own. Bialik arrived in Tel Aviv in 1924 and shortly thereafter organized the Dvir Publishing House and the Hebrew Writers Association, and became the undisputed leader of the literary community. However, his contact with the new homeland left little impact upon his writing and the little poetry he wrote in the last decade of his life, which he spent in Palestine, was generally in the mode of his Odessa period. The writers of the Second Aliyah and the older immigrant authors who arrived after World War I formed a cohesive community. The younger writers of the Third Aliyah (1920–24) soon, however, began to question their literary leadership and gave expression to the radical changes in the social, political, and literary views which grew out of the trauma of World War I and the Russian Revolution.

Politically and socially, the younger writers were far more radical than their elders. While their Zionist commitment led them to reject the Leninist denial of Jewish nationalism (at least in the Zionist sense), they embraced the socialist ideal and its call for a radical change of the class structure of Jewish society. Whether Marxists or voluntarist socialists, they dreamt of a new social order often in terms of farm or city communes. Almost all of them were *ḥalutzim* who had come to build a new society. The Ukrainian pogroms and the general breakup of their home communities in Russia found expression in a somber pessimism which often led them to question the ideology they had embraced. Their youthful exuberance and a leap of faith which grew out of the camaraderie of fellow *ḥalutzim,* however, redeemed their idealism. Yiẓḥak *Lamdan's poem *Massadah* (1927), for all its expressionist rhetoric, is an honest document of the period.

POETRY. From a literary point of view, the well-rounded, learned phrasing of Bialik's school and its preoccupation with classical structure and clarity of expression was hardly in consonance with the mood of the younger writers and of European letters. Russian revolutionary writers had broken with classicism: the rhythms and wild images of poets like Aleksandr Blok and Sergei Esenin more aptly expressed the psychological world of these younger writers. At the same time, the new poetic diction of the Russian symbolists, the acmeists, and the German neoromantics (Stefan George, Rainer Maria Rilke, and Hugo von Hoffmannsthal) also left its mark on Hebrew poetry. The latter trends made their appearance in such poets as Avraham ben Yiẓḥak *Sonne, David *Vogel, and Yehudah *Karni.

The new literary views found expression in *Ketuvim,* a magazine founded by the Hebrew Writers Association in 1926, but soon taken over by the younger generation. Under the editorship of Eliezer *Steinman, who was soon joined by the poet Abraham *Shlonsky, it became the organ of the modernist group and disassociated itself from the sponsorship of its founders. Among the new writers who published in *Ketuvim* were: Ya'akov *Horowitz, Yiẓḥak Norman, Yisrael *Zmora, and later Nathan *Alterman, Lea *Goldberg, and Ezra *Sussman.

Abraham Shlonsky, Nathan Alterman, Uri Ẓevi Greenberg, and Lea Goldberg were the leading poets of the Palestinian period. From the very beginning of his career Shlonsky was the staunch advocate of modernism. As coeditor of *Ketuvim,* and the editor of *Turim* (1933–38), he openly challenged Bialik's literary authority, calling for a modern, individualistic, "de-theologized" Hebrew poetry and rejecting both the "logical" rationalist poetry of Bialik's school as well as its collective-nationalist orientation. He demanded the acceptance of spoken Hebrew and even slang usage as a legitimate form of poetic diction. Under the influence of the Russian revolutionary poets, Blok, Esenin, Mayakovski, and the French symbolists (Shlonsky lived in Paris between 1924 and 1925), he wrote poems which gave expression to the ennui and despair of his generation, particularly of the Jew who has suffered so much from war, revolution, and pogroms. "*Devai*" (1923–24), the title poem of his first volume of verse, is a long symbol-laden poem which takes up the malaise and the horror of modern secularized urban life and offers little hope for the future. In other poems Shlonsky returns again and again to the sheltered world of childhood, contrasting it with the lonely, desperate life of the *ḥalutz* torn between his dream of rebirth and the reality of his pioneering hardships ("*Le-Abba Imma*" (1927), *Ba-Galgal* (1927)). In his later works these themes receive a more mature treatment; Shlonsky somehow strikes a balance between the low-key symbolist influences and the more blatant surrealistic and even expressionist imagery. His urban hell now also embraces the fascist threat. At the same time, he continuously harks back to the primordial themes of soil and agriculture with their blessings of fertility and security.

Nathan Alterman and Lea Goldberg may be considered Shlonsky's disciples. Both were discovered by him and he encouraged their writing during their crucial years as beginners. Alterman continued and extended Shlonsky's experiments with new rhythms and the syntax of the spoken idiom. Simultaneous with his serious poetry, he wrote light verse not only for the musical comedy theaters which staged political satires and enjoyed popularity in the 1920s and 1930s, but especially for his weekly verse column *Ha-Tur ha-Shevi'i* ("The Seventh Column"), which enjoyed great popularity during the struggle against the British. From a stylistic point of view these media enabled him to develop a saucy, slangy diction. In retrospect, like Shlonsky, he did not stray too far from classical Hebrew, perhaps because in the 1920s and 1930s a literal language was needed to fill the lacuna left by the yet inadequate spoken tongue. Alterman's serious poetry was punctuated with wild expressionist metaphors and slangy or slang-like neologism. At his best he produced a score of impressive modernist poems which in their day had a major impact on the works of his younger contemporaries. Many of his poems have a ballad-like quality and have as themes: the love and death motifs of the romantic agony with the recurring figure of the dead lover returning to haunt his living mate; the poet as a wandering troubadour for whom the world is an inn; the urban ennui of the European city dweller; The raw vitality of Tel Aviv in which the new city is projected against a background of the horror of the European catastrophe and the desperate hope of the reborn homeland.

Lea Goldberg was influenced by the Russian acmeists and the symbolist German poets. She shunned the verbal extravagance of the expressionist, preferring calmer tones. Like the acmeists, she aimed at simple conversational diction and gave preference to more conventional poetic forms. Her themes were modern, however, and her verse expresses the sad wisdom of an urbane and mature artist who, despite her sophistication, was able to experience and give voice to the miracle of the poetry which lies behind the ordinary phenomena of nature and life.

Perhaps the most talented poet of the age, and far less accessible to schematic definition, is Uri Ẓevi Greenberg. Unlike his contemporaries, Greenberg rejected the humanist socialist ideologies of his contemporaries, positing bold gigantic strokes, a mystic, anti-rational, and quasi-racial conception of the destiny of the Jewish people. He draws the Jew with bold gigantic strokes, a God-elected figure living outside history. His tragedy grows out of his great refusal to fulfill his historic destiny as the bearer of the holy seed. European civilization is a satanic fraud which beguiles him and leads to his massacre. Only by accepting his historic vocation with all the horror and the glory its fulfillment calls into being will the Jew survive. From a formal point of view Greenberg's rejection of Europe leads him to seek poetic forms and cadences which are historically Jewish. His language and metaphors are drawn not only from biblical sources but also from later Hebrew literature, frequently from the Kabbalah. Although he is also capable of writing terse lyrical verse, he prefers the expressive cadences of biblical rhetoric. He, himself, acknowledges his stylistic debt to Walt Whitman.

In his poetry Shin *Shalom wedded a strong nationalist commitment with a mystical individualistic experience which often showed a deep psychoanalytic insight into the world of the self. The increasing momentum of his nationalist enthusiasm in his later poetry overshadows his personal experience and much of his lyrical force is lost. Yonathan *Ratosh successfully endeavors to give formal expression to the cult of Canaanite primitivism and paganism whose first signs appear in the prose of Frischmann and the poetry of Tchernichowsky. Ratosh strove to revive ancient poetic forms and metaphors by reconstructing mythical remnants preserved in biblical narratives and by drawing upon ancient Ugaritic poetry. Ratosh's preoccupation with Canaanite myth is related to his Canaanite political ideology that views Israel as a new nation which is no longer Jewish and must reintegrate itself into the Middle Eastern culture of the Fertile Crescent. This he believes can be done by picking up those strands of ancient Near Eastern myths which were abandoned after the Jews forsook the Middle East and became Europeans.

PROSE. The two leading prose writers of the period are S.Y. Agnon and Ḥayyim *Hazaz. Agnon's literary achievement is second only to Bailik's and his work encompasses large areas of the Jewish experience: Jewish Galicia of the remote past; the Galicia of his childhood; the Palestine of the Second Aliyah; the Jerusalem of the older traditionalistic settlement; Austria, Germany, and Galicia of the interbellum period; and Jerusalem of the British Mandate. His career marks the high point of the Polish-Galician strain in modern Hebrew literature with its stress on the emotional and nonrational experience of its protagonists. The influence of ḥasidic and Jewish pietistic folk literature are integrated in Agnon with the psychological, symbolistic, and existential mode of Scandinavian and Austro-Hungarian literature. His style is based, in the main, on the rabbinic-ḥasidic prose of the period immediately preceding the development of modern Hebrew but it also owes much to such early Galician Hebrew writers as Menahem Mendel Levin (Lefin) and Josef Perl and in its biblical tone (*Bi-Demi Yamehah* ("In the Prime of Life") for example) even to Erter. To the contemporary Hebrew reader it has a manneristic obsolescence deliberately reinforced by the Yiddish spelling of certain European words (*zuker* instead of the accepted *sukar* or *kahve* instead of *kafe*). Some critics see in his style an attempt to point up the paradox of writing modernistic stories in an ancient sacred tongue. Others explain it as an attempt to preserve the flavor of the Yiddish idiom used by many of his characters in his Galician stories.

Agnon's novels are landmarks in modern Hebrew literature. *Hakhnasat Kallah* (second rev. 1929; *Bridal Canopy*, 1937) is an attempt to depict the spiritual world of 18th-century Galician Jewry. From a structural point of view Agnon develops an indigenous Jewish literary form built around cyclical motifs drawn from pietistic literature (marriage, hospitality, wandering, etc.). It is essentially a character novel, and the hero R. Yidel is a quixotic personality who confronts life with a world view which is nurtured in the past. Traditional folk themes, the treasure and the cock, are imbued with modern symbolic significance. *Ore'aḥ Nata Lalun* ("A Guest for the Night," 1939), Agnon's attempt to describe the decline of East European Jewry after World War I, has for its hero a hesitant Palestinian Jew who returns to his native Galicia to seek the key to the forsaken synagogue. He is confounded by the realization that after the key turned up, it is he alone who is charged with the responsibility of keeping the synagogue open. *Temol Shilshom* ("The Days Before," 1945), probably the best modern Hebrew novel, is set in Ottoman Palestine and is a tale of two cities – Jaffa (Tel Aviv), symbolizing the new secular *yishuv*, and Jerusalem, representing the traditional Holy Land. Isaac Kummer ("he who comes" or "grief and sorrow") is torn between the two civilizations; unable to orientate himself toward either, he goes mad. The story within the story, that of Balak the dog, is one of the profoundest animal symbolistic fables in world literature. Agnon's use of fable (also the cock in *Hakhnasat Kallah*) has its roots in medieval Jewish literature and in early modern Hebrew literature (Erter and later in Mendele's "*Susati*"; "The Nag"). Agnon's range is wide and varied. Side by side with his pietistic fiction, there are modern existential love stories, such as: *Panim Aḥerot* ("Metamorphosis"), *Givat ha-Ḥol, Ha-Rofe u-Gerushato* ("The Doctor and his Divorcee"), and his posthumously published *Shirah* (1971). They are all animated by a profound understanding of the existential tragedy of modern man. Ḥayyim Hazaz's realism harks back to the Odessa school but is relieved by a penchant for the grotesque. His early works describe the milieu of Ukrainian Jewry during the period of the Russian Revolution (*Pirkei Mahpekhah* ("Chapters of the Revolution") and *Shemu'el Frankfurter*). Ukraine at the brink of the revolution forms the background of *Be-Yishuv shel Ya'ar* ("Forest Settlement"). After his migration to Palestine, Hazaz shifted to ḥalutzic themes and later to the depiction of the life of Israel's Yemenite Jews both in Israel (*Ha-Yoshevet ba-Gannim* and *Mori Sa'id*) and in Yemen before their migration (*Ya'ish*). Central to Hazaz's works is his insistence that Jewish redemption (Messianism and later Zionism) was not realized because the Diaspora Jew and Diaspora Judaism lacked the courage to risk everything for its fulfillment. Some of his characters also express the belief that redemption means the end of Judaism, others declare Zionism to be the negation of Diaspora Judaism: *Ha-Derashah* ("The Sermon") and *Be-Keẓ ha-Yamim* ("At the End of Days"), a play set in Poland during the time of Shabbetai Ẓevi (stories of Hazaz in *Kol Kitvei Ḥayyim Hazaz*, 1968). Like Agnon's, Hazaz's style is literary and its vocabulary and syntax differ from contemporary Israeli Hebrew. Unlike Agnon, he prefers the mishnaic, talmudic style developed by the Odessans which he, however, stamped with his own mark. To convey the speech of his various characters, he distorts his Hebrew, "Ukrainizing" it to record the speech of Ukrainian peasants, or Arabicizing it to convey that of Yemenite Jews.

Other leading prose writers of the Mandate period are Yehuda *Burla, one of the early modern writers of Sephardi descent, who wrote stories depicting Sephardi life in his native Jerusalem and in the Middle East; Asher Barash, a prolific short-story writer and novelist who wrote of Jewish life in his native Galicia and in Palestine; Devorah Baron whose short stories sensitively describe life in her native Belorussia; Gershon *Shofman whose psychological-lyrical short stories and sketches are an original type of narrative.

[Ezra Spicehandler]

WOMEN'S WRITING

The Genesis of Women's Hebrew Literature

Only recently has it become known that the history of women's writing in Hebrew literature starts in the mid-19th century, during the Haskalah period. Hitherto, it was generally assumed that as a result of women's ignorance of Hebrew and the canonical texts, the Hebrew Haskalah was a male movement. The very few women who dared to compose poetry or fiction were never considered to have initiated women's literature. That picture has changed as a result of the discovery of Hebrew writings by some 25 women in manuscript archives and Hebrew-language literary periodicals of the Haskalah period. The few known women writers now appear to have been part of a wider phenomenon. Even in this early period, several others not only read Hebrew but also put their knowledge of the language, their ability to express themselves, and their creativity to active use in writing.

Women gained a significant place in Hebrew enlightenment circles only in the latter half of the 19th century, mainly in Russia and Lithuania. Most of them expressed themselves in non-literary genres: various kinds of correspondence, social essays, and translations (of which the best known example is Miriam Markel-Mosessohn's Hebrew translation of a German-language work of history, which she called *Ha-Yehudim be-Angliyah*, 1869).

The only extant complete archive of a woman's correspondence is that of Miriam Markel-Mosessohn (1839–1920). However, other letters have survived in men's archives, such as those of Judah Leib Gordon (which contains letters by Rivka Rottner, Sheyne Wolf, Sarah Shapira, Nehama Feinstein, and others), Dr. Judah Loeb Landau, Perez Smolenskin, and Shneur Sachs. Other letters (for example by Sarah Cohen Nevinsky, Bertha Kreidman, and Shifra Alchin) were published in Hebrew Haskalah periodicals or collections of correspondence. Most of the letters demonstrate an excellent knowledge of Hebrew and a strong commitment to Haskalah ideas.

Another way in which *maskilot* sought to participate in maskilic creative endeavor was to publish feminine social essays in Haskalah Hebrew periodicals. Some of these essays (for example Sara Feiga Foner Meinkin's "*Ha-Aviv*," 1876, and Marka Altschuler's "Thoughts on the Ninth of Av, My Birthday," 1880) focused on conventional maskilic "male" ideological themes. Others (like Taube Segal's "The Woman Question," 1879) expressed specifically female protests and a demand to improve girls' education.

Prior to the end of the Haskalah period, very few women published conventional literary works; we know of only three poets and one significant prose writer. Two of the poets wrote only two poems each: Hanna Blume Sulz of Vilna ("The Play," 1882, and "The Valley of Revelation," 1883) and Sara Shapira ("Remember the One Caught by a Horn," 1886, and "Zion," 1888). These poems display good knowledge of Hebrew and familiarity with canonical texts and Haskalah poetry. However, Sulz's poems are an example of the woman poet's failure when she surrendered to the masculine tastes of the time, losing her feminine authenticity. Shapira's poems are more authentic and therefore more successful, but her writing never developed into mature poetry.

A first poetic expression in Hebrew of the woman's world and her problems may be found in the writings of the Jewish-Italian poet Rachel *Morpurgo (1790–1879), whose works were collected in book form only after her death (*Rachel's Or-*

gan, 1890). Morpurgo's main achievements are in her poems of personal contemplation (including "See, This Is New," "Lament of My Soul," "Why, Lord, So Many Cries," "O Troubled Valley," "Until I Am Old"). A careful reading of these poems reveals a hidden, subtle level of significance, formed by the contrast between the canonical texts to which the poem refers and the poem itself. At this level we hear the voice of a woman describing her suffering and protesting her inferior status in Jewish society and culture.

Only one woman dared to write novels during the 1880s, Sarah Feiga Foner Meinkin, who published four Hebrew books, three of them works of fiction: *A Righteous Love, or The Pursued Family* (first volume 1881; the second was never published) *The Treachery of Traitors* (1891), and a children's didactic story, *Children's Way or A Story From Jerusalem* (1886). The fourth book was her memoirs (*Memories of My Childhood, or A Memoir of Dvinsk*, 1903). *A Righteous Love* is the first Hebrew novel by a woman. Although it seems merely to imitate male Haskalah novel-writing conventions, the author did not abandon her authentic female voice (from which she retreats in her later works). It comes out in the lively, persuasive, and colorful descriptions of the character and world of the heroine, Finnalia, her relationships (especially with other women), and her domestic life. Feminist criticism of her society also finds expression: When describing arranged marriages in Galicia, the narrator critically comments on fathers who use their daughters for business deals, "like horses and donkeys."

Sarah Feiga Foner Meinkin, however, was a unique phenomenon in her own times. Further Hebrew short stories by women were not published in Russia until the first decade of the 20th century. Thus, in 1902 the first stories by Devorah *Baron appeared in *Hamelitz* and in 1909 a small collection of short stories (*Kovez Ẓiyyurim*) by Chava Shapira (1871–1943) was published. Both writers (Shapira wrote only a few more stories but Baron became a dominant writer) centered their stories around women's lives and thus mark the beginning of conscious female writing within a tradition of Hebrew women's writing.

[Tova Cohen (2nd ed.)]

Women's Prose Writing in the Period of the Yishuv (1882–1948)

From the very outset of the Zionist settlement movement, at the end of the 19th and the beginning of the 20th centuries, a smattering of writings by women, setting out their own vision of Ereẓ Israel, can be seen in the pages of the Hebrew-language periodicals of the time. In the Jewish communities of Europe, despite the increasing acquisition of culture and learning by women, very few of them had made so bold as to make their writings public. A woman writer was seen as deviating from accepted social norms, compromising the natural occupations of women as homemakers and mothers, and invading, by way of her creative activity, a realm that was reserved exclusively for men. Those women who nevertheless had the courage to publish their writings were received with derision and criticism so harsh as to deter others (see Sarah Feiga Foner Meinkin). However, things were different in Ereẓ Israel. Here, too, the creative efforts of women writers were either roundly criticized or ignored, but this no longer put them off writing. To be sure, if the Zionist revolution, particularly in its socialist stripe, had declared its pioneering endeavor to be an equal partnership of men and women, it had retreated from this declaration on the practical level from the moment the settlement effort got underway. In keeping with the traditional conceptions characteristic of the Diaspora, women were kept in the margins of public and nationalist activity and were expected to serve as "helpmeets" rather than equal partners in the leadership of the *yishuv*. However, the women did not keep quiet. Unlike their Diaspora predecessors, they were cognizant of their roles and contributions in advancing the Zionist endeavor, and they set out to fight for their rightful place in both the public and the literary arenas. For the women who took part in that endeavor, as settlers, laborers, or pioneers, the national revival was also a women's revival, and so also a women's literary revival. Women insisted on making their voices heard in the male-dominated public sphere of the *yishuv* and on continuing to publish their creative work, even if they met with rejection.

On the other hand, a perusal of anthologies, historiographies, and Hebrew literary studies concerned with the period of the *yishuv* reveals very little in the way of prose writing by women. Their literary output, it would seem, was largely confined to poetry, including that of *Raḥel Blaustein, Esther Raab, Lea *Goldberg, Elisheva Bichovsky, Anda Pinkerfeld-*Amir, and others. These poets, too, never received the support and encouragement they deserved from contemporary male poets and critics, but their poems nevertheless made their way into the public consciousness and became an inseparable part of the literary repertoire of the period. This fortune was not shared by the women prose writers, notwithstanding their literary productivity, which enriched the Hebrew bookshelf with dozens of novels, novellas, short stories, plays, stories for children and young adults, non-fictional works, essays, memoirs, and biographies. Only the fiction of Devorah Baron attracted the interest of literary critics and scholars. Baron's works certainly were outstanding in their aesthetic quality, but the exclusive focus upon them gave rise to the unfounded historiographical thesis that there was nothing much in the way of women's prose writing from Devorah Baron until Amalia *Kahana-Carmon, who began publishing her work in the 1950s. The impression was of a void during the period of the *yishuv* that began to be filled only in the early period of the state.

Who were the "unknown" women prose writers, and what did they write? They began arriving in Ereẓ Israel with the first waves of settlers, with aspirations not only to give vent to their creative impulses but first and foremost to fulfill their Zionist, or socialist-Zionist, commitment to building the Jewish national homeland. They were working women – their writing always emerged as a secondary occupation – who engaged in public and ideological activity within the rural or urban frameworks in which they lived: in the kibbutzim (Emma Levine Talmi, Ruhamah Hazanov, Rivkah Gurfein, Yehudit Mensch); in the moshavot (Yehudit Harari, Shoshanah Shababo); in Jerusalem (Shulamit Kelugai); and in Tel Aviv (Rachel Feingenberg, Shoshanah Sherira). Some of them started out in rural communities and later moved on to the city (Batyah Kahana, Sarah Gluzman, Rivkah Alper). In the rural settings, they were usually employed in agriculture or in education, while in the cities, aside from school and kindergarten teaching (Shulamit Flaum, Sarah Levy), they worked as journalists (Bracha Habas, Shoshanah Sherira, Miriam Tal), in the theater (Miriam Bernstein Cohen), or as laborers (Rachel Adiv and Pnina Caspi were factory workers). Devorah Baron was the only woman writer of the period to devote all her time to writing, after becoming a recluse in her home, which she did not leave for over 30 years (1922–56).

Taken together, these writers do not present a uniform typological visage; rather, they represented a multicultural cross-section of the various sectors of the *yishuv*. If most of them were secular, there were those who were religiously observant (Malka Shapira); and if the majority originated in Eastern Europe, there were those who hailed from Western Europe (Hannah Trager) and several from the Yemenite (Sarah Levy, Yonah Wahab) and Sephardi (Shoshanah Shababo) communities. Politically, they belonged to several different streams in the Zionist movement, some to the labor sector (Rivkah Alper belonged to the moderate wing, Emma Levine Talmi to the radicals), and some to the "civil" sector (Ira Yan, Shoshanah Sherira). Most were new immigrants, but a few were born in the country (Hannah Lunz Bolotin, Shoshanah Shababo).

The women prose writers of the *yishuv* can be grouped into three generations. Those of the first generation, born in the second half of the 19th century, immigrated to Ereẓ Israel with the first and second *aliyot*, in the years immediately before and after the turn of the 20th century, and began publishing their works from this period onward (Nehamah Pukhachevsky, Hemdah *Ben-Yehuda, Devorah Baron). Those of the second generation, born in the first decade of the 20th century, immigrated to the country and began publishing their works in the period between the two world wars (1918–1939 – Batyah Kahana, Rivkah Gurfein, and the native-born Shoshanah Shababo). Those of the third generation, born during the second two decades of the 20th century and brought to the country as young children, grew up for all intents and purposes as native Israelis (Sarah Gluzman, Pnina Caspi, Shoshanah Sherira, Yehudit Hendel) and began publishing their works in the 1930s and 1940s.

This diverse community of writers naturally produced a spectrum of women's narratives that varied in their social, political, and cultural perspectives. The plots ranged around two principal foci: (1) women's experience qua women: their self-awareness, motherhood, male–female relations, sexuality, relationships among women, the exploitation and oppression of women, and so on; and (2) women's experience as a function of their situation in Ereẓ Israel: their encounter with the land, the transition from conservative ways of living to freer ones, the absence of the older generation, women's isolation within the "united" collective, their struggle for a place in public life, their critique of the masculine character of the Zionist endeavor, and so on. These women's themes contributed to the creation of a unique female narrative, an integral part of which was a female version of the national narrative that had a distinctly different character from the dominant masculine one. If the latter was one of dramatic struggle, danger, and heroic death, the female narrative was one of gray, ongoing struggle for survival. If the masculine national narrative presented itself as the collective subject, giving every plot the power of a statement of historic vision, the female national narrative focused on the private and the everyday, which it treated in a restrained but critical tone.

A further distinctive quality of the female narrative was the presence, to varying degrees, of critical "feminist" tendencies. From the very outset of women's prose writing in the *yishuv*, two principal feminist positions may be discerned in it: a constructivist trend, trail-blazed by Hemdah Ben-Yehuda, and a melancholic one, whose first representative was Nehamah Pukhachevsky. According to the constructivist stance, women were destined, with time, to emerge from their marginal position in the society of the *yishuv*. Their increasing acquisition of learning and culture, particularly their reeducation to Hebrew culture and national consciousness, would surely advance their equality and centrality in the evolving national community. Ben-Yehuda spoke primarily of the centrality of women as mothers in constructing the new generation and emphasized how the quality of their mothering conditioned that of the entire nation. This optimistic feminism emerged in a variety of fictional narratives in which alternatives to the conventional portrayal of women posed models of strong-willed, self-confident women, able to stand their ground against patriarchal men (as in the works of Batyah Kahana, Sarah Gluzman, and Shoshanah Sherira).

The melancholic position took the shape of a more critical type of feminism. It excoriated the masculine Zionist activity that in practice replicated all the ills of the past, so that instead of realizing the liberal-nationalist rebirth of the people and of humanity, it rebuilt a reactionary society characterized by overweening hegemonies, new class hierarchies, and indifference to the weaker members of society, such as laborers, members of the Oriental Jewish communities, "others," and, of course, women. The writers who took this position sought to recount, from the perspective of women, the national narrative of those who stood in the margins of Zionism and the society it was creating and to expose the oppressive situation in which they found themselves. However, this critical protest was not voiced aggressively or stridently. On the contrary; it was muted and introverted, fluctuating between anguish and melancholy in a kind of drawn-out lament (as may be seen in the works of Ruhamah Hazanov, Pnina Caspi, Yehudit Mensch, and Miriam Tal).

These and other features led to the coalescence of a female meta-poetics. Although the writers emerged from different sectors and were informed by different ideological and literary worldviews, they may be seen as belonging to an "imagined community" – one that worked and created, consciously or unconsciously, according to a shared meta-poetics with several distinctive qualities. (1) Unlike contemporary male writers, who devoted little space to representations of women in their pioneering narratives, the women writers completed the missing half of the map by filling that void with their own creations. Moreover, they endowed women in the *yishuv* with a more powerful presence, allowed them to articulate themselves, and gave voice to all those representations of silent or silenced women. (2) Prose-writing in the *yishuv* devoted much discussion to the development of the "new Hebrew," while continuing to represent the "Hebrew woman" according to men's traditional conceptions, represented by just two archetypal contrasts: that between Eve and the she-demon Lilith, and that between the lover and the wife-mother. But women's prose was different; it endeavored to mold a new woman with a female Israeli character, in possession of a female Hebrew culture (anticipating the appearance of the native-born *sabra*). (3) The "literature of the homeland," as written by men, developed two primary genres: novels on the theme of settling the land, and documentary novels. Women writers, too, dealt in their own way with these genres, but they narrated them along the lines of romance, or "national romance," interweaving them with elements of legend and fantasy.

It is perhaps because of these gendered differences in poetics that the male literary community showed little understanding for and interest in women's prose, to the point of excluding and banishing it from the collective memory. That exclusion was not entirely all-encompassing; here and there a few male writers and critics encouraged women writers, particular in the early stages of their careers. Thus, Joseph Klausner read and commented upon the writings of Batyah Kahana; Yitzhak Lamdan, editor of the literary periodical *Gilyonot*, published the work of Shoshanah Sherira; Avigdor Hameiri facilitated the publication of Miriam Tal's first book; and Asher Barash, as editor of the Mitzpeh publishing house, published works by Rivkah Alper, Shoshanah Shababo, and Miriam Bernstein Cohen. However, this kind of partial, fleeting recognition did not lead to the public embrace of their work, nor were women's journals like *Ha-Ishah* (1926–29), *Devar ha-Po'elet* (1934–70), and *Olam ha-Ishah* (1940–48) successful at keeping the women prose writers of the *yishuv* in the public eye.

Only in the 1980s, when literary scholarship began to take an interest in feminist and gender theory and so also to take up the status of women writers as a topic of study, were these nearly forgotten writers rediscovered, as works by Yaffah Berlovitz, Orly Lubin, Avivah Ufaz, Tamar Hess, and others began restoring their writings to the collective memory of contemporary Israeli culture.

[Yaffah Berlovitz (2nd ed.)]

THE ISRAEL PERIOD (1948–2005)

The year of the establishment of the State of Israel, 1948, is a convenient date to mark the onset of the Israel period of modern Hebrew literature, although it actually began earlier. One of its leading literary figures, S. *Yizhar, published his first short story, *Efrayim Ḥozer la-Aspeset*, as early as 1938. Most of the younger generation of writers on the literary scene in 1948 were either native Palestinians or had come to Palestine in their childhood. The few who came in their youth or later had been so deeply involved in Zionist or Hebrew youth movements in the Diaspora that they too were culturally Palestinians. Hebrew was the mother tongue of these writers or at least their childhood language. The earlier Palestinian generation had by now forged a spoken language which had rid Hebrew of its somewhat pedantic character and the Hebrew of the new school was a natural language alive with colloquialisms and the echoes of childhood speech. Born into the Palestinian landscape, the younger authors viewed it more realistically than the older generation with its tendency to idealize the land of their Zionist dreams, on the one hand, and to recollect nostalgically the northern climes of their childhood on the other. For the new generation, the East European landscape existed only in the memory of childhood stories which they had read or heard from their parents. The change of geographic locus also affected their Hebrew style. The new secular Hebrew school de-emphasized rabbinic and medieval Hebrew studies and gave primacy to biblical and modern literature. The Hebrew of the new writers was more flexible than that of the older generation but not as learned. Yiddish language and literature hardly affected their style or choice of themes. While the older writers were generally influenced by Eastern or Central European literature, the new school, whose second language was usually English, was affected by British and, especially, American literature. Moreover, unlike many of their predecessors, whose knowledge of a European literature was intimate and acquired in the country in which it was spoken, most Israel writers knew European literature through translations or criticism in Hebrew. Many learned a European language only after they began to publish.

The more "natural" approach of the Israel writers often expressed itself in its questioning of the Zionist-Socialist ideology of the parent generation. This trend was discernible in the earliest of their works. S. Yizhar in *Efrayim Ḥozer la-Aspeset* questions the kibbutz ideology and whether it really succeeded in establishing an egalitarian society. Uri, the hero of M. *Shamir's *Hu Halakh ba-Sadot* ("He Walked Through the Fields," 1947), for all his sense of duty, is hardly representative of the new type of Jew which the kibbutz movement apparently intended to produce. The ideology crisis and its subsequent existential anxiety, already dominant in post-World War II European literature, was delayed in the first phase of Israel literature by the struggle for national independence.

Many of the younger writers were members of kibbutzim and associated with various left-wing movements. They served in the Palmaḥ, the crack army units of the War of Liberation, and subscribed to a Socialist-Zionist ideology. During this early phase, they embraced Andrei Zhdanov's doctrine of socialist realism which called upon writers to preach socialism but at the same time point out aberrations within the system. They favored an ideological literature with its stress on the collective we rather than on the introspective I. But even in this early phase the rise of existential dissent is discernible. Poets like *Gilboa and *Gouri, for example, speak of the darker side of personal experience found already in their early "life affirming" period.

By the 1950s the ideology crisis had set in: "Utopia" realized came to be seen as "utopia" lost. The enthusiasm of the War of Liberation and its victory gave way to the harsh reality of building the new state. Mass immigration, the unresolved conflict with the Arabs, the shift of Russian foreign policy, the necessity to compromise ideals in order that the state might survive militarily and economically, and the rise of careerism tended to erode the utopian ideals of the soldier-writer. National independence and the creation of the state had not resolved all problems. During the national struggle egoisms had been harnessed, following it, they seemed to burst forth. After the War of Independence some of the idealism that had led to the creation of the state paled and people began to pursue their own private ends. On the literary scene, the writer, his finger on the pulse of the nation, aesthetically expressed what the man in the street unconsciously felt. He chose to no longer subordinate his talent to a national cause to which he had often in the past consciously sacrificed his originality. Writers began to question the possibility of any ideology except subjective expression of their inner world. The prose and poetry in the late 1950s therefore took on an individualistic, existentialist, and even surrealistic tone expressing the anxieties of a generation disillusioned with ideologies. Their central theme is the alienation of modern man; their world that of the secularized, non-ideological urbanite. Rarely, except for their cultural or geographical context, does their writing deal with parochial Jewish topics. Yet, even when the Israel writer had rejected ideologies, he could not entirely escape the ethical imperatives of his Jewish tradition. Even before the Six-Day War his conscience had been disturbed by the Arab problem: the plight of the refugees whose solution could endanger the survival of the nation. After the war, which had come as a natural consequence of a long-term conflict, while accepting its harsh reality, he was perturbed by the military atmosphere. Perhaps the crisis following the war had already shifted the pendulum back to ideology.

Poetry

The leading poets of the early Israel period, Ḥaim Gouri, Amir Gilboa, Abba *Kovner, and T. *Carmi are connected in one way or another with the Palmaḥ. Gouri's early verse, *Pirḥei Esh* ("Flowers of Fire," 1949), perhaps more than any other poem, expresses the revolutionary Zionist ideology of his generation which "spoke in the first person plural." While throughout his career he retained his commitment to his youthful ideology (this was reinforced by the experience of the Six-Day War) his later poetry took on a more personal tone. His anguish, however, is often rooted in the lonely feeling of a man who has retained a truth that others have abandoned: "But I guard the walls of a city that died years ago." Amir Gilboa, unlike Gouri, was born in Europe and his poetry, even during the earliest phases, is permeated by the tragedy of the Holocaust in which his family perished. Gilboa also confronted the horror of the Holocaust when as a soldier in the Jewish brigade he encountered the remnants of European Jewry after World War II. Breaking with the Shlonsky-Alterman tradition, he not only introduces his particular individual blend of traditional and colloquial elements but a surrealistic atmosphere pervaded by dream sequences and childish memories. In his later phase these characteristics became more pronounced and he added to them a remarkable experimentation with Hebrew sounds, extracting from them poetic implications. Abba Kovner, like Gilboa, is a product of the European Zionist left. Unlike Gilboa, who had arrived in Ereẓ Israel in 1937 and had experienced the Holocaust indirectly, Kovner was in Eastern Europe during the Nazi period. He was the partisan leader of the Vilna ghetto and later became a high-ranking resistance commander. His is a modernist poetry in which he fuses themes of the national struggle and the anti-Nazi resistance with the personal tragedy of the partisan or Palmaḥ fighter. Surrealistic symbols and visions which recur throughout his work project a complex image of the war and the Holocaust.

T. Carmi, an American by birth, was one of the earliest new poets to draw upon modernist American and French techniques for his verse. (Simon Halkin had preceded him.) He combines a deep knowledge of European and American poetry with a mastery of traditional sources. Although his earliest volumes deal with "national" themes, the Holocaust, and the war even they, like his later works, have a subjective, existentialist perspective. In the 1950s he moved completely to a personal poetry which is intelligent, playful, and commands all the skills of the trade.

The second phase of Israel poetry is dominated by the work of Yehudah *Amichai in which are integrated the author's German Jewish Orthodox heritage and his Ereẓ Israel experience (arrived in Palestine in 1936). His use of daily speech, irony, metaphysical metaphors, and existentialist *Angst* have become the hallmarks of much of the poetry written by his younger contemporaries, who freely acknowledge their debt to him. These younger writers formed a literary group called *Akhshav* ("Now") which proclaimed the end of ideological poetry and broke with the Alterman-Shlonsky tradition. In later years Amichai personally disassociated himself from the group. Among the many talented poets of this generation are Nathan *Zach, Tuvyah *Ruebner, Dan Pagis, David Avidan, Dalia *Ravikovitch, and David *Rokeaḥ. At the same time, a new generation of poets began publishing; among the most promising are Meir Wieseltier, Mordecai Geldman, Ya'ir Hourvitz, Aryeh Sivan, and Israel Pincas.

Prose

The Palmaḥ generation produced realistic literature dealing in the main with their kibbutz experience and with their experiences during the War of Liberation. Prominent among them is Moshe Shamir, who in his novel *Hu Halakh ba-Sadot*, a best seller set during the War of Liberation, gives a realistic description of a Palmaḥ commander whose sense of duty seemed greater than his ideological commitment. *Pirkei Elik* (1952; *With his Own Hands*, 1970), a quasi-biographical work, is artistically the more interesting. Shamir's historical novel *Melekh Basar va-Dam* (1954; *A King of Flesh and Blood*, 1958) was very popular, while his later works are somewhat more experimental and have not enjoyed the popularity of his earlier novels.

S. Yizhar writes a more lyrical prose and his long novel *Yemei Ẓiklag* ("The Days of Ziklag," 1958) is undoubtedly the most important novel of the Palmaḥ generation. Despite its amorphous style, its lyrical repetitions, and its rather limited range of characterization, it expresses more than any other work the crisis of belief which shook the entire generation in the wake of the establishment of the State. S. Yizhar is one of the earliest authors who dealt honestly with the Arab question and expressed certain moral reservations with regard to handling the Arab refugee problem (*"Ha-Shavui"* "The Prisoner," 1949) and *"Sippur Ḥirbet Ḥizeh,"* 1949).

Aharon *Megged began his literary career by writing seafaring short stories (*Ru'aḥ Yamim*, "Sea Wind," 1950) but turned to humor in his popular work *Ḥedvah va-Ani* ("Hedvah and I," 1954) and later to existentialist short stories and novels, such as *Yisrael Ḥaverim* (1955), *Mikreh ha-Kesil* (1960; *Fortunes of a Fool*, 1962); and *Ha-Ḥai al ha-Met* ("Living off the Dead," 1965). His characters, foiled by their own human weaknesses, are unable to adhere to the ideals (humanist-Zionist-socialist value system) they advocate and are therefore in a constant state of conflict.

Hanoch *Bartov, like Megged, depicts the challenge of the value system of the native Israeli confronted by a state he helped to create in which the new immigrants are not ideologically orientated and natives have become careerists: *Ha-Ḥeshbon ve-ha-Nefesh* ("The Reckoning and the Soul," 1953) and *Shesh Kenafayim le-Eḥad* ("Each Has Six Wings," 1954). He, too, writes about the Nazi catastrophe, as seen through the eyes of a Jewish Brigade soldier from Israel *Piẓei Bagrut* (1965; *The Brigade*, 1968). In his novel *Shel Mi Attah Yeled* ("Whose Are You, Boy," 1969), he returns to his childhood in Petaḥ Tikvah.

Poets like Amichai and Gouri have also written serious fiction. Amichai's *Lo me-Akhshav Lo mi-Kan* ("Not from Now nor Here," 1963), set in Jerusalem and in Germany, plumbs the Nazi Holocaust in an attempt to find meaning in it. He also wrote a volume of surrealist stories. Gouri's *Iskat ha-Shokolad* (1965; *The Chocolate Deal*, 1968) approaches the Holocaust theme through the relationship of two refugees. Of the younger prose writers, the more significant are Amos Oz (1939–), whose *Mikha'el Shelli* (1968) also alludes to the Arab problem; and Nissim *Aloni who writes brilliantly about his childhood in the Jaffa slums and is by far the most original Israel playwright. He combines a superb sense of the theater with a talent for the absurd. Benjamin *Tammuz writes nostalgically about his childhood in Tel Aviv (*Ḥolot ha-Zahav*, 1950; *Sands of Gold*, 1953); he has published a trilogy which centers around a picaresque hero, Eliyakum. Avraham B. *Yehoshua, published three volumes of short stories: *Mot ha-Zaken* ("Death of the Old Man," 1963); *Mul ha-Ye'arot* ("Facing the Forests," 1968); and *Tishah Sippurim* ("Nine Stories," 1970); *Three Days and a Child* (1970) is a collection of five short stories.

Aharon *Appelfeld delves into the inner world of his characters, who, like himself, are victims of the Holocaust. His central theme is the psychological residue of the Holocaust experienced by the characters years later. Thus he approaches the tragedy obliquely, writing in a lyrical prose which is simple, but freighted with nightmarish symbols. The deep religious mysticism which dominates Pinḥas *Sadeh's prose and poetry is not orthodox and at times takes on Christological overtones. Amaliah Cahana-Carmon's sensitive short stories deal with her childhood.

[Ezra Spicehandler]

The 1970s

The 1970s marked the passing of most of the prolific writers of this generation: S.Y. *Agnon (d. 1970) and Ḥayyim *Hazaz (d. 1973), two outstanding writers of prose fiction, and Nathan *Alterman (d. 1970), Lea *Goldberg (d. 1970), and Abraham *Shlonsky (d. 1973), three eminent poets. Only Uri Ẓevi *Greenberg, in his eighties, continued to write his exceedingly powerful, expressionist-mystical verse until his death in 1981.

Collected works of these authors appeared either shortly before or soon after their deaths. Most significant were the posthumously published works of Agnon, which were edited by his daughter, Emunah Yaron. These include the novels *Shirah* (1971), depicting Jerusalem's intellectual community of the 1930s and 1940s, and *Be-Ḥanuto shel Mar Lublin* ("In Mr. Lublin's Shop," 1974), set in Leipzig during World War I, *Ir U-Meloah* ("A City and its Fullness"), a monumental portrayal of Agnon's home town and for that matter of 1,000 years of Jewish life in Poland (1973), and *Sofer, Sippur ve-Sefer* ("Writer, Story and Book," 1978), a collection of traditional vignettes relating to the art of writing. Despite their sometimes incomplete form, these works reinforce the generally accepted view that Agnon was the greatest fiction writer of modern Hebrew literature.

Older poets, like Sh. *Shalom (*Ki Panah ha-Yom* – "The Day is Setting"; *Shai Lavan* – *"White Gift,"* 1974) and Avraham *Broides (*Kol Od Odi* – "While I Still Am"), continued to publish poetry whose very titles reflect their stage of life. Yehoshua Tan Pai (1975) and Yonatan *Ratosh (d. 1981), who 30 years ago were looked upon as innovating trailblazers, published their collected works. Ezra *Sussman's (d. 1973) reflective prose poems *Keshet Nisan* ("April Rainbow," 1976) were extolled by the critics. The collected verse of Simon *Halkin appeared in 1977 (*Shirim*). Halkin has also rendered a learned translation of George Seferis' early verse. Gabriel *Preil, the only Hebrew poet of distinction living in the United States who chronologically belongs to this generation, continued to create highly lyrical, subjective poetry. Ephraim *Broido's long awaited translation of Shakespeare's sonnets won critical acclaim (1977).

Writers associated with the "Generation of 1948," such as Ḥaim *Gouri, T. *Carmi, Abba *Kovner, and Amir *Gilboa, were active. In *Mar'ot Geḥazi* ("Visions of Geḥazi," 1973), Gouri seemed to be reliving vicariously the fears, anxieties and the glory of the War of Independence in poems reflecting the Yom Kippur War. Carmi's selected poems *Davar Aḥer* appeared in 1973. In *Hitnaẓlut ha-Meḥaber* ("The Author's Apology," 1974), he too reacts movingly to the trauma of the Yom Kippur War, and his *El Ereẓ Aḥeret* ("To Another Land," 1977), contains highly sophisticated, ironic lyric poetry reflecting his two-year stay at Oxford. In *Raẓiti Likhtov Siftei Yeshenim* ("I Wish to Write Sleeping Lips," 1968) and *Ayalah Eshlaḥ Otakh* ("Gazelle, I Dispatch You," 1972). Amir Gilboa moved away from his originally surrealistic poetry to a more realistic and concrete world. There is a thinning out of metaphor, yet at the same time a dazzling display of aural experimentalism. With *Moaḥ* ("Brain," 1975). Dan Pagis moved from a Rilkesque poetry to a more economical and cerebral idiom. Ozer Rabin, a poet who writes comparatively few poems, produced an impressive volume of delicately meditative verse (*Be-Terem Ta'avor*, 1976). *Zelda surprised Israeli readers with moving religious poetry (*Al Tirḥak*, "Do Not Go Far," 1975).

Fiction writers were equally productive. Moshe *Shamir's *Yonah Be-Ḥaẓer Zarah* ("Pigeon in a Strange Yard," 1975) is part of a trilogy written in a realistic vein which attempts to depict the saga of several generations of Israeli settlers. Aharon *Megged has made a more courageous effort to vary his themes and style. In *Al Eẓim ve-Avanim* ("Just About Everything," 1974), he tries to portray the ugly Israeli without the usual stereotyping. His anti-hero turns out be a frustrated human torn between the moral values he inherited from his Zionist past and a crass, almost self-destructive realism. Megged explores the theme of disillusionment with Zionist leaders rather than ideology in *Maḥberot Evyatar* ("Evyatar's Notebooks").

Benjamin Tammuz's *Requiem le-Na'aman* ("A Requiem for Na'aman," 1978) also deals with the failure of the Zionist dream to transform Jews into an earth-bound "normal" people. Like many contemporary novelists, Tammuz examines the naive ideals of the early settlers of Israel and the disillusionment of their descendants.

Aharon *Appelfeld's *Badenheim, 1939* (English: Boston, 1981) recaptures the eerie inevitability of the approaching Holocaust as viewed through the eyes of alienated middle-class Jews vacationing at an Austrian summer resort. His novel *Tor ha-Pelaot* ("The Time of Wonders," 1978) tells the story of an assimilated Austrian-Jewish family before, during and after the Nazi period.

Interesting is the *Seneds' (Alexander and Yonat) experimentation with new techniques of novel writing, influenced by the modern anti-novel writers like Natalie Serraut (*Tandu* – "*Tandem*," 1974).

THE NEW WAVE. The New Wave is a term coined by the Israeli critic Gershon Shaked for the generation of prose writers which began publishing in the late 1950s and the 1960s but is equally applicable to the poets of this period as well. The movement expressed itself not only in its rejection of the earlier Zionist Socialist certainties but in its proclaimed indifference toward all ideologies. In the words of Shimon Sandbank, there was a "Withdrawal to a no man's land of existential *angst.*" The New Wave not only questioned the patriotic rhetoric which characterized some of the writing of the pre-State period, but called for a written idiom which was more concrete and closer to the spoken language. Their ideology was articulated in the *avant garde* magazines which were founded in the 1950s and 1960s, *Li-Kerat* ("Towards," 1953–54), *Akhshav* ("Now," 1957–to date) and *Yokhani* (1961–67).

Among the ideologists of the New Wave were the poet Nathan *Zach and the critic Gavriel Moked. Zach's iconoclastic criticism of poets like Alterman cleared the ground for the new poetry. Zach objected to Alterman's strict and regular metrics and what he called his high-blown diction and advocated the writing of more concrete, low-key poetry.

Zach, together with Yehuda *Amichai who chronologically belong to the 1948 group, and David *Avidan, wrote poetry which reflected the new poetics. When from time to time they had recourse to the phrasing of classical literature they would yank words and phrases out of their original context and give them an ironic twist. As is frequently the case the new style either influenced or was influenced by some of the more sensitive older poets such as Amir Gilboa and Abba Kovner. By the 1970s however, the poetry of the New Wave assumed an "after the battle" air. Nathan Zach almost ceased publishing poetry or criticism. Amichai appeared to be restating completely what he already had said (*Ve-lo al Menat Lizkor* – "So as Not to Remember," 1971; and *Me'aḥorei Kol Zeh Mistater Osher Gadol* – "Behind all This is Concealed Great Joy," 1974). David Avidan's troubador pyrotechnics, previously permeated by an air of youthful exuberance, have lost their verve.

The prose writers of the New Wave, on the other hand, played a leading role in Hebrew letters. A.B. *Yehoshua and Amos *Oz, whose short stories have been described by Hillel Barzel as meta-realistic, without entirely abandoning their symbolistic proclivities, moved closer to realism. This is evidenced in Yehoshua's bestselling novel *Ha-Me'ahev* (*The Lover*, 1976) and in Oz's *Har ha-Eẓah ha-Ra'ah* (*The Hill of Evil Counsel*, 1976). In *The Lover* the symbolic referents are less concealed. Although universal themes such as loss of innocence and aging underlie the story, it has specific Israeli-Zionist dimensions. There is not only veiled criticism of the failure of the post-1948 society to realize the Zionist-socialist ideologies of the past but an assertion of its inability to comprehend the present in terms of any ideology. Amos Oz's world is in a constant state of siege. The kibbutz, the fortified towns, are encircled by a primitive, vital and animal-like world which is ready to break in and destroy it. The state of siege is a hidden allegory pointing to the condition of modern man. In the end it is not Jews against Arabs but the clash between the destructive vital forces of the ego breaking against the ethical barriers of the id. In their quest for romantic fulfillment his female characters seem ready to surrender to the vitality of animal passion.

Amalia *Kahana-Carmon's work has greater affinity to that of the post-1948 generation. Her first collection of short stories appeared in 1966, *Bi-Khefifah Aḥat* ("Under One Roof"), and includes stories written in the late 1950s. With her novel *Ve-Yare'aḥ be-Emek Ayalon* ("And the Moon in the Valley of Ayalon," 1971) and her collection of three novellas, *Sadot Magneti'im* ("Magnetic Fields," 1977), she emerged as one of Israel's leading writers of fiction. Unlike Yehoshua and Oz, she uses a stream of consciousness technique influenced by Virginia Woolf. Kahana-Carmon's handling of narrative time is not chronological but psychological. Her major theme is the impossibility of sustained human relations, since such relationship means a surrender of that independence which alone can redeem one from the tragedy of the human condition. In the best short story in her latest book *Ḥadar ha-Ḥadashot* ("News Room"), Kahana-Carmon's style is elliptical, manneristic, elusive and freighted with all the ambivalences which mark an in-depth probing of the psychology of modern men and women.

Yiẓḥak *Orpaz, like Amaliah Kahana-Carmon, belongs to the 1948 age group but his writing is closer to that of the New Wave. While his earlier stories still retain a great deal of the realism of the 1948 group, his writing moves toward the more elliptical, involuted style of the psychological school. This is increasingly apparent in his post Six-Day War novels. *Masa Daniel* ("Daniel's Odyssey," 1969) describes how Daniel, a war-weary veteran, discovers the meaning of life through a mystical encounter with the well-springs of existence on an abandoned beach. His novel *Bayit le-Adam Eḥad* ("A House for One," 1975) is existentially religious in tone.

In *Sus Eẓ* (*Rockinghorse*, 1973) Yoram Kaniuk continues to explore the alienated Israeli. His hero Aminadav Sus Eẓ, an emigré living in New York, returns to his native Tel Aviv in the wake of the Six-Day War and proposes to make a film about the Tel Aviv of his childhood as an uncommercial exercise in self-examination. Kaniuk is at his best when he evokes the Israel of the 1930s. His artistic control of the spoken idiom and his masterful use of the stream of consciousness technique place him among the more effective writers of his generation. His story concludes with an ironic note; the film was a commercial success.

The achievement of the younger generation was mainly in poetry. The writers of prose have veered away from the fundamentally symbolist bias of their predecessors to a more realistic vein. Yitzḥak Ben-Ner, in *Shekiah Kafrit* ("Village Sunset," 1976), and Y. Koren, in *Levayah ba-Ẓohorayim* ("Funeral at Noon," 1976), set their stories in the more established communities of rural Israel.

Revolting against the anti-romantic, new-criticism type of poetry of the New Wave, the younger poets strive for a more decorative idiom. In part they take their cue from Amir Gilboa's experiments with sound and syntax. Many evoke a personal mythology in which beauty, music and free association are given free rein thus creating what Aharon Shabbetai called "the new sweet style," in which the logic of words gives way to the harmony of sound. Ya'ir Hourvitz speaks of his preferring "sea time" to "land time."

Yonah Wallach's *Shirah* ("Poetry," 1976) tinkers with the subconscious mechanisms of feeling pushing boldly against the very borders which divide sanity from madness. In contrast, Moshe Sartal takes up the apocalyptical, mystical cadences of Uri Ẓevi Greenberg in *Basar al Gabei Geḥalim ve-Shirim Aḥerim* ("Meat Over the Coals & Other Poems," 1976). Aharon Shabbetai's *Kibbutz* (1974) was written when he was still much under the influence of the New Wave and is almost devoid of adjectives. His *Ha-Po'ema ha-Beitit* ("Domestic Poem," *Siman Kriah*, 6, 1974) is rich with images.

On the other hand, Mordecai Geldman, whose earlier poetry was suffused with pictorial opulence, began writing a sparser verse, without sacrificing musicality. "I want to say it still more/still more simply." Meir Wieseltier's approach to poetry is eclectic. He criticizes Zach for being "romantic" and "uncommitted." Zach took the "self" to be an autonomous being. Wieseltier considers his "self" exposed in all directions and susceptible to constant charges, to the direct impact of "things." In the title poem of his collected works *Kaḥ* ("Take," 1975), he takes on an anti-poetic, quasi-Mayakovskiesque tone.

Anti-romanticism carried to grotesque parody was characteristic of Hebrew playwright Ḥanoch Levin. His brutal exposé of the banality of urban living, its ugly loneliness, its cruel division between people "who make it" and "the slobs" excludes the slightest ray of hope in his society of the damned. Other playwrights who represent the New Wave in Hebrew drama of the 1970s are Hillel Mittlepunkt and Yehoshua Sobol.

[Avner Holtzman]

The 1980s and After

PROSE. Intense activity characterizes Hebrew prose since the 1980s, with members of various literary generations writing at the same time: From the "Palmaḥ Generation," which marked 60 years at the turn of the century since its appearance on the literary scene, to writers who were born in the 1960s and 1970s and made their debut in the 1980s and 1990s. The prose of this period is many-sided in theme and approach, enterprising and innovative in style and in its use of diverse literary techniques. Ideologically, this prose follows for the most part the long-established tradition which considered Hebrew literature to be a means for examining and grappling with the basic questions of Jewish-Israeli existence by exposing the collective tensions in individual characters and fates. Among the major concerns repeatedly treated are the making of Israeli identity and its relation to Jewish roots and Diaspora experience; the legitimacy and validity of the Zionist vision and the discrepancy between the initial Zionist project and its implementation; the recurrence of war and acts of terror and the inability to solve the more than 100-year old Arab/Palestinian-Israeli conflict in non-violent ways; the changes in the system of political, social, and moral values and in the mentality of the Israelis; the long shadow of the Holocaust, the inner world of the survivors as well as the duty and need to remember; problems of absorption, socio-ethnic differences and discrimination; and last, but not least, gender issues, primarily the status of women in Jewish/Israeli life and culture, and homoerotic proclivities. Grappling with these issues, writers turned to various genres and narrative modes such as the historical novel, the family saga, realistic allegories, expressionist and surrealist narratives or, more recently, to postmodernist narrative. Moreover, some authors, like Aharon *Megged, Moshe *Shamir, Abraham B. *Yehoshua, Amos *Oz, David *Grossman, Yoram *Kaniuk, and Gadi Taub, went beyond fiction and published collections of essays on social and political topics.

One of the striking phenomena is the astounding creative energy and tremendous output of the older writers, those commonly referred to as the "Palmaḥ Generation" or "Dor Ba-Areẓ." Moshe Shamir, one of the seminal voices of that group, completed his historical trilogy *Raḥok Mi-Peninim* in 1992, the saga of Zionist settlement and at the same time a sweeping epic following the various stages in the life of Leah Berman, a model type of the idealistic Jewish pioneer. During the last decade of his life, Shamir (d. 2004) published a book of poetry, a collection of stories, and a biographical novel on Avraham "Yair" Stern (2001), the legendary figure of the Leḥi underground organization, who in many respects personifies Shamir's national and political ideal. "The Jewish people faces a new Holocaust, initiated by the Muslim Arab world," Shamir warned, maintaining further that "the Arab terror has one goal: to annihilate the State of Israel."

Shamir's contemporary S. *Yizhar surprised Israeli readers in 1992: After 30 years of self-imposed silence, he published *Mikdamot* ("Foretellings"). This is a lyrical, impressionistic novel reconstructing the author's early childhood in pre-state Ereẓ Israel. The novel was followed by stories and novellas (*Ẓalhavim*, 1993, *Malkomiyah Yefefiyah*, 1998) in which the doyen of modern Hebrew prose displays his unparalleled art of storytelling, rich in sensual vivid images.

Two of the leading figures of the veteran generation passed away during the period. David *Shahar, who died in Paris in 1997, added further volumes to his monumental work *Heikhal ha-Kelim ha-Shevurim* ("The Palace of Shattered Vessels") and left behind a fragment *Har ha-Zeytim* ("The Mount of Olives"). Like Shahar, the other master of the modern Hebrew picaresque, Benjamin *Tammuz (d. 1989), also tried in his later works to view Zionism within the larger context of Jewish history, and to examine Zionist accomplishments and failings while reevaluating the Jewish heritage (e.g., *Requiem le-Na'aman*; 1987; *Requiem for Na'aman*, 1982). In his last work, *Ha-Zikkit ve-ha-Zamir* ("Chameleon and Nightingale," 1989), Tammuz presents the chronicles of a Jewish family over 1,300 years, integrating fiction, letters, diaries, and wills from the family archive. Ironically, the generation that celebrated the New Jew, the mythological Sabra, seems to have rediscovered the riches of the Jewish past. Tammuz, once committed to Canaanite ideology, was later fascinated by the mysteries of Diaspora existence. The belated encounter with Jewish life underlies also the works of Aharon Megged, Hanoch *Bartov, Nathan *Shaham, and other representatives of the "Palmaḥ Generation." Megged depicts the tensions between Hebrew and Jewish culture in his novel *Foigelman* (1987; *Foiglman*, 2003); deals with early idealists traveling to the Holy Land in *Duda'im min ha-Areẓ ha-Kedoshah* (1998; *Mandrakes from the Holy Land*, 2005); describes intrigues in the local literary scene in *Ha-Gamal ha-Me'ofef ve-Dabeshet ha-Zahav* (1982; "The Flying Camel and the Golden Hump"); recounts the joys and agonies of creative writing with humor and a touch of satire that verges on the grotesque in *Ga'agu'im le-Olgah* (1994) and *Nikmat Yotam* (2003). Bartov recollects the past in a realistic style, mingling humor with nostalgic longing (*Be-Emẓa ha-Roman*, 1988). He writes about loneliness in the big city of Tel Aviv (*Lev Shafukh*, 2001; "A Heart Poured Out"), and outlines the professional as well as personal frustrations of an aging Israeli (*Zeh Ishel Medaber*, 1990; "This is Ishel Speaking"). In 1987, Nathan Shaham published a story about four musicians and a writer in pre-State Israel, *Rosendorf Kevartet* (*The Rosendorf Quartet*, 1991), which many saw as his most accomplished work of fiction. Music figures in the novel as a metaphor for universal understanding and cosmopolitan identity, transcending nationalism and language. In the wake of the novel's success, both in Israel and abroad, Shaham followed up the adventures of the protagonists in the far less successful *Ẓilo shel Rosendorf* (2001; "Rosendorf's Shadow").

The writers known as "Dor ha-Medinah" (writers born in Ereẓ Israel in the 1930s) were equally prolific as was the movement known as the "New Wave" (G. Shaked) of the 1950s and 1960s. Yaakov *Shabtai's impressive final work, *Sof Davar* (*Past Perfect*), a masterpiece of Hebrew style and the stream-of-consciousness technique, appeared three years after his death in 1981. In her later works, Shulamit *Hareven (d. 2003) confronted seminal moments in Jewish history, going back to biblical times (*Soneh ha-Nissim*, 1983). Yehudit *Hendel was remarkably successful. Her early novels *Reḥov ha-Madregot* (1955; *Street of Steps*, 1963) and *Ha-Ḥaẓer shel Momo ha-Gedolah* ("The Yard of Momo the Great," 1969) were reissued (1998 and 1993, respectively) as was her first collection of stories *Anashim Aḥerim Hem* (2000; "They are Different"), one of the early literary attempts (1950) to confront the Holocaust. Hendel's trip to her native Poland resulted in a moving, perturbing book, *Leyad Kefarim Sheketim* (1987; "Near Quiet Places"). The death of her husband, painter Zvi Mairovitch, led to her extraordinary, lyrical memoir *Ha-Ko'aḥ ha-Aḥer* (1984;

"The Other Power"). Love, betrayal, loss, and bereavement are recurring themes in her prose, as in *Kesef Katan* (1988; *Small Change*, 2002), *Har Ha-To'im* (1991), and the novella *Terufo shel Rofe ha-Nefesh* (2002; "Crack-Up"). Another female writer, Ruth *Almog, published novels and stories giving prominence to the fate and the concerns of women, elderly people, and immigrants (*Shorshei Avir*, 1987; *Me'il Katon*, 1993). Together with Esther Ettinger, Almog published two bestsellers (*Me'ahev Mushlam*, 1995, and *Estelinah Ahuvati*, 2002).

The vigorous and versatile author Yoram *Kaniuk, published numerous novels and stories such as the family portrait *Post Mortem* (1992), *Od Sippur Ahavah* (1996; "Another Love Story"); the delightful *Hamalka ve-Ani* (2001; "The Queen and I"); recollections of time spent in New York (*Ḥayyim al Neyar Zekhukhit*, 2003; "I Did It My Way"); a fictitious account of a perturbing journey through Germany (*Ha-Berlinai ha-Aḥaron*, 2004; "The Last Berliner"); and books for children (*Wasserman*, 1988). Dan *Tsalka published the monumental epic mosaic *Elef Levavot* (1991). Yossel *Birstein (1920–2003), a Yiddish author hailed by some critics as the Hebrew Shalom Aleichem, published the novel *Panim ba-Anan* (1991), among others. Yitzhak *Orpaz, David Schütz, Naomi *Frankel, Ehud Ben Ezer and Amos *Kenan came out with new novels and collections of stories, as did Yitzhak *Ben-Ner with his realistic, often somber portraits of decadent contemporary Israeli society (*Protokol*, 1982; *Boker shel Shotim*, 1992; *Ir Miklat*, 2000).

Special attention was paid by critics and readers to new works by Abraham B. Yehoshua, Amos Oz, Yehoshua *Kenaz, Meir *Shalev and David *Grossman. Yehoshua continued to explore and modify the realistic-psychological family novel and the narrative of mono-dialogues, while constructing parallel plots and playing with hidden ideas and allegories. *Molcho* (1987; *Five Seasons*, 1989) depicts the tumultuous first year in the life of the widower Molcho and the mental process he undergoes in his pursuit of a new life. Jewish history and Zionist dreams underlie the novel *Mar Mani* (1990; *Mr. Mani*, 1992), the story of a Sephardi family over five generations. Jewish history in Spain and in Ashkenaz is featured in *Mas'a el Tom ha-Elef* (1997; *A Journey to the End of the Millennium*, 1999). The physical journey as a voyage into the subconscious is a leitmotif in Yehoshua's prose as in *Ha-Shivah mi-Hodu* (1994; *Open Heart*, 1996). In his latest novels, Yehoshua has returned to the political scene: In *Ha-Kalah ha-Meshaḥreret* (2001; *The Liberated Bride*, 2003) the Orientalist Yohanan Rivlin confronts the traditions and hardships of Israeli Arabs living in Galilee and of Palestinians in the West Bank; in *Sheliḥuto shel ha-Memuneh le-Mashabei Enosh* (2004) he tells the story of a Russian worker who is killed in a terror attack in Jerusalem as a kind of modern Passion, at times comic, at others serene.

The many shades of the collective Israeli experience are present in the prose works which Amos Oz, the best-known Israeli author abroad, has published over the past two decades. Oz addressed the changes in the political climate in Israel (e.g., *Menuḥah Nekhonah*, 1982; *A Perfect Peace*, 1985; *Kufsah Sheḥorah*, 1987; *Black Box*, 1989) as well as the relationships between Ashekanzi and Sephardi Israelis (e.g., *Kufsah Sheḥorah*); His landscapes vary from the Negev desert (*Al Tagidi Laylah*, 1994; *Don't Call It Night*, 1995) to the unappealing cityscapes of Bat Yam (*Oto ha-Yam*, 1998; *The Same Sea*, 2001). In his later novels (*Lada'at Ishah*, 1989, *To Know a Woman*, 1991; *Ha-Maẓav ha-Shelishi*, 1991, *Fima*, 1993; *Oto ha-Yam*) he gives prominence to trials and dreams of antiheroes, men like Fima or Albert Danon. Moving away from his highly symbolical early stories, Oz experimented with narrative modes: He turned to the epistolary novel (*Kufsah Sheḥorah* or the story "*Ga'agu'im*"), structured his novel *Oto Ha-Yam* as poetic prose fragments which at times even rhyme, and merged the autobiographical with the fictional in his universally acclaimed work, *Sippur al Ahavah ve-Ḥoshekh* (2002; *A Tale of Love and Darkness*, 2004) which he defined as an "autobiographical novel".

David Grossman, the outstanding author to emerge during the 1980s, is equally innovative. His wide-ranging works deal with the Arab-Israeli conflict (e.g., *Ḥiyukh ha-Gedi*, 1983; *The Smile of the Lamb*, 1990) as well as the inadequacy of language to confront the Holocaust (in the highly ambitious *Ayen Erekh Ahavah*, 1986; *See Under Love*, 1989). Grossman also revisits his youth in Jerusalem in the 1960s (*Sefer ha-Dikduk ha-Penimi*, 1991; *The Book of Intimate Grammar*, 1994) and depicts the peculiar love relationship, an affair in writing, between Miriam, a married woman, and the younger Yair in *She-Tihiyi li Sakkin* (1998; *Be My Knife*, 2001), an epistolary novel containing intertextual allusions to Kafka's *Letters to Milena*. Time and again Grossman tests the power of language to convey meaning and emotions, and reflects on his own métier, the world of fiction. In 2002 he published *Ba-Guf Ani Mevinah*.

Exceptionally popular among Israeli readers is Meir Shalev, who made his literary début with *Roman Russi* (1988; *The Blue Mountain*, 1991), the chronicle of pioneering settlers in the Jezreel Valley. Shalev's novels (*Esav*, 1991; *Be-Veyto ba-Midbar*, 1998; *Fontanella*, 2002) combine realistic and fantastic elements, and his multi-layered narrative teems with biblical and mythic associations.

Yehoshua Kenaz is one of two prominent Israeli authors who shun publicity, declining interviews as well as all forms of public relations. But this has in no way affected the success and high reputation which he and Yoel *Hoffman have enjoyed. Kenaz, whose first novel, *Aḥarei ha-Ḥagim*, appeared in 1964 (*After the Holidays*, 1987), published remarkable novels dealing with the frailty of human relations, the loneliness of individuals in urban society (*Maḥzir Ahavot Kodmot*, 1997; *Returning Old Loves*, 2001), physical and mental decline (*Ha-Derekh el ha-Ḥatulim*, 1991; *The Way to the Cats*, 1994), or the disruption of adolescence and rites of manhood (*Moment Musikali*, 1980; *Musical Moment*, 1995). One of his finest accomplishments is the novel *Hitganvut Yeḥidim* (*Heart Murmur*, 2003), a book which has been compared to Yizhar's seminal *Yemei*

Ziklag: The story of a group of recruits in an Israeli army base in the 1950s presents individual lives and at the same time a kaleidoscope of Israeli society.

Like Kenaz, Yoel Hoffman was born in 1937, but unlike him – Kenaz is a Sabra who grew up in the "Moshava" – Hoffman's first year of life was spent in Hungary. He presents a world of uprooted Jews, Europeans who escaped the Holocaust by the skin of their teeth, yet remain strangers in Israeli society. They remain German Jews, their acquired Hebrew interspersed with German expressions, their dreams filled with longings for the culture they had to leave behind (*Bernhart, Kristus shel Daggim*). While Kenaz is a virtuoso of realistic style, Hoffman's prose is postmodern: instead of a traditional, linear plot, he writes an idiosyncratic narrative made up of enigmatic fragments in a private, Joyce-like language. Anecdotes, recollections, and observations both humorous and melancholy form a unique prose texture which poses a challenge to the reader.

The European world left behind and primarily the cataclysm of the Holocaust seem to engross the imagination of Israeli writers the more they recede in time. An attempt to map out the many prose works relating to the Shoah discloses various groups. The first comprises the survivors themselves. Innumerable books recollecting the traumatic years of humiliation, hunger, constant fear, brutal persecution, and above all the loss of family members, have appeared over the last 25 years. Quite a number of these "nonprofessional" authors, such as psychologist Shlomo Bresnitz (*Sedot ha-Zikaron*, 1993), Ruth Segal (*Goyah im Nemashim*, 2002), or Esther Eisen (*Imi Tafrah Kokhavim*, 2003), to name but a few, display remarkable literary subtlety. Established authors such as Uri *Orlev recounted their shattering experiences in the ghetto and the concentration camps in books for adults and young readers. Among the survivor-writers, however, Aharon *Appelfeld is unique in his obsessive descriptions of a world lost forever. In spare, unsentimental yet powerful prose, Appelfeld describes a prewar Jewish community that shut its eyes to reality; men and women who wander alone or in small groups across Europe, hoping to be saved; others who fail to escape death; antisemites, oppressors, and occasionally warm-hearted Christians who empathize with the victims and help them (*Katarina*). It is notable, however, that Appelfeld's survivors remain strangers in their new home, Israel. They cannot start a new life. Instead they are haunted by the past, or consciously indulge in memories of earlier days. Some even reject any hope for a new beginning, glorifying instead their years in the forests or in the camps, which they consider to have been their finest "heroic" hour.

Israeli writers born in Israel before the war, such as Yoram Kaniuk or Nathan Shaham, focused mainly on the emotional scars of the survivors while European-born authors who came to Palestine before the Holocaust – such as Naomi Frankel, Yehudit Hendel, or Shulamith Hareven – wrote about a childhood world left behind and the "otherness" of the survivors. David Schütz, born in Berlin in 1941, wrote compelling semi-autobiographical novels, such as *Ha-Esev ve-ha-Ḥol* (1978; "The Grass and the Sand"). Most impressive, however, is the prose written by the so-called "Second Generation": Israeli writers born after the Shoah who nonetheless felt the need to confront that unique chapter in Jewish history. David Grossman's novel *Ayen Erekh Ahavah* (1986) is a milestone in the works of Sabra authors on the Holocaust. Savyon *Liebrecht (b. 1948; *Tapuḥim min ha-Midbar*, 1986; *Apples from the Desert*, 1998; *Susim al Kevish Gehah*, 1988), Nava Semel (b. 1954; *Kova Zekhukhit*, 1985, "Hat of Glass"; *Ẓeḥok shel Akhbarosh*, 2001, "The Rat Laughs"), Ya'akov Buchan (b. 1946; *Yeled Shakuf*, 1998), Eleonora Lev (*Sug Mesuyam shel Yatmut*, 1999, "A Certain Kind of Orphanhood"), Hannah Herzig (*Temunot Meḥapessot Koteret*, 1997), Lizzie Doron (b. 1953; *Lamah lo B'at lifnei ha-Milḥamah*, 1998; *Hayetah Po Pa'am Mishpaḥah*, 2002), Lili Perry (b. 1953; *Golem ba-Ma'agal*, 1987, "Golem in the Circle"), Rachel Talshir (b.1957; *Ha-Ahavah Meshaḥreret*, 2001, "Love Macht frei"; *Pegishah bi-Keẓeh ha-Erev*, 2003, "Meeting at the Edge of the Evening"), Amir Gutfreund (b. 1963; *Shoah Shelanu*, 2000; "Our Holocaust"), to name but a few, depict the sufferings of the victims and the effect of the parents' traumatic experiences on their children who were often brought up amidst secrets and untold tales, and had to discover the truth for themselves years later.

The relationship between German persecutors and their Jewish victims is yet another aspect of the complex Holocaust theme, especially in the works of Savyon Liebrecht, Itamar Levy (b. 1956; *Agadat ha-Agamim ha-Aẓuvim*, 1990, "The Legend of the Sad Lakes") or Rivka Keren (b. 1946; *Anatomiyah shel Nekamah*, 1993, "Anatomy of Revenge").

Confronting the Holocaust inevitably sensitized the authors to the "otherness" of the survivors, who could not or would not conform to the model of the New Jew, the self-confident Sabra. The literature of the past decades shows that the survivors were only one group of outsiders who drew the attention of Israeli authors. Another group was the Oriental Jews, who immigrated to Israel from various Arab countries in the 1950s. Among the older generation (Sami *Michael, Shimon *Ballas, Amon Shamosh, Dan Benaya *Seri, Yitzhak Gormezano-Goren, Eli *Amir), recent years have seen many works on the hardships of and discrimination against immigrants and their children in overcrowded transit camp (*"ma'barot"*), in development towns or destitute city suburbs (such as south Tel Aviv). Among these are novels by Albert Suissa (b. 1951; *Akud*, "Bound,"1990), Sami Bardugo (b. 1970; *Yaldah Sheḥorah*, "Black Girl," 1999), Dudu Busi (b. 1969; *Ha-Yare'aḥ Yarok ba-Vadi*, "The Moon Goes Green in the Wadi," 2000; *Pere Aẓil*, "A Noble Savage," 2003), and Yossi Sucary (b. 1959; *Emiliyah ve-Melakh ha-Areẓ*, "Emilia," 2002). In fact, the growing self-awareness of the so-called Oriental writers combined with a feeling of long-suffering injustice have led to the founding of a press (Kedem) as well as a magazine (*Ha-Kivvun Mizraḥ*) promoting this literature.

Another social group which did not conform to the ideal of the secular, heroic Israeli and was thus ignored, occasionally even denounced by the dominant Zionist narrative, was that of religious and ultra-Orthodox Jews, who have recently become the subject of a growing number of novels and stories. Haim *Be'er (*Nozot, Et ha-Zamir, Ḥavalim*), wrote partly autobiographical novels, often marked by biting criticism, about the ultra-Orthodox Jerusalem milieu in which he grew up. The hermetic world of religious Jews is also depicted by Dov Elbaum (b. 1970; *Zeman Elul*, 1997; *Ḥayyai im ha-Avot*, 2001), Yisrael Segal (*Ne'ilah*, 1990; *Vekhi Naḥash Memit?*, 2004), and by a significant number of women writers, who turned their back on the restrictive ḥaredi milieu in which they grew up. Among these are Yehudit Rotem, Yochi Brandes, Mira Magen (with novels like *Al Take ba-Kir*, 1997), Haya Esther (Godlevsky), and Hanna Bat-Shahar (a nom de plume for an Orthodox woman writer).

Indeed, the "other" in his various configurations has ousted the mythologized, self-confident Israeli from his dominant position and moved from the margins of Hebrew literature to center stage. Along with stories about various ethnic minorities (Sephardi, Bukhari, Iraqi Jews, or "yekkes"), the voice of new immigrants from the Soviet Union has made itself heard. Writers like Alona Kimhi, who was born in Lvov in 1966 (*Ani, Anastasia*, 1996, *I, Anastasia*, 2000; *Suzannah Bokhiyah*, 1999, *Weeping Susannah*, 2001), Marina Groslerner, who came to Israel at the age of six (*Lalya*, 2001), or Suzane Adam (*Kevisah*, "Laundry," 2000; *Maymia*, 2002), who was born in Transylvania and came to Israel at the age of 10, have written about their native country and their experience as immigrants in Israel, particularly in their earlier works. Born in Leningrad, Alex Epstein (b. 1971) came to Israel in 1980 and is one of the younger original writers who experiment with various narrative techniques, as in *Ahuvato shel Metapes Harim* ("The Mountaineer's Beloved," 1999) or in his dictionary-like novel *Milon Mahapakh* ("Honey Dictionary," 2000).

Beside these religious and ethnic minorities, women have made a sweeping entrance into male-dominated Hebrew literature, both as fictional figures and as writers. Cynical observers of the contemporary Israeli scene maintain that being a woman and writing about female concerns guarantee the publication and commercial success of a novel. The list of female writers who started publishing over the past three decades is impressive, especially in view of the few women writers in previous generations and the fact that the main issues of Israeli life – war, army life, professional success, political involvement etc. – were almost always represented by male characters. Along with established women such as Amalia Kahana-Carmon – one of the first and most vehement champions of gender issues – and Yehudit Hendel, many new names have joined the literary scene. Among these are Dorit Abusch (1955–), Leah Eini (1962–), Marit Ben Israel, Gail Hareven (1959–), Esty G. Haim (1963–), Yael Hedaya (1964–), Shifra Horn, Avirama Golan, Judith *Katzir (1963–), Ronit *Matalon (1959–), Dorit Rabinyan (1972–), Zeruyah *Shalev (1959–), and Shoham Smith (1966–). Their fiction addresses political and historical issues, social and ethnic themes as well as "typically" feminine concerns such as love, sexuality, betrayal and abandonment, menstruation, pregnancy, motherhood and female friendship, or the status and role of women in Israeli society.

The new gender-oriented literature also deals with homoerotic love. Yossi Avni (a pseudonym) published stories (*Gan ha-Eẓim ha-Metim*, "The Garden of the Dead Trees," 1995) and novels (*Arba'ah Aḥim*, "Four Brothers," 1998; *Doda Farhumah lo Hayetah Zonah*, "Auntie Farhuma Wasn't a Whore After All," 2002) depicting homosexual relations, as have Ilan Schoenfeld (*Rak Attah*, "Only You," 1998), Motti Auerbuch (*Elohim Nekheh Me'ah Aḥuz*, "God Is One Hundred Percent Disabled," 2003), Yossi Waxman (*Alexandria Yakirati*, "Dear Alexandria," 1988; *Liebchen*, 2004) and Dan Shavit (*Pitom Ra'iti Oto*, "Suddenly I Saw Him," 2004). Yehudit Katzir recounts a lesbian relationship between a young woman and her teacher in her novel *Hineh Ani Mathilah* ("Here I Begin," 2003).

While the majority of Israeli writers cling to the realistic modes of expression and traditional conventions of characterization, some of the younger writers explore postmodernist techniques. No doubt the most outstanding of these (apart from Yoel Hoffman, mentioned above) is Orly *Castel-Bloom (b. 1960; *Doli Siti, Ḥalakim Enoshiyim*). Particularly popular among younger readers is Etgar Keret (1967–), who has published collections of mini-narratives and comics that shift between the funny and the serious, the real and the imaginary. These and other postmodernist writers are eager to debunk prevailing myths, to experiment and to shock; they play with language, probe metaphors and clichés, and underscore the inadequacy of words while creating their own vocabulary.

Other original voices in contemporary Hebrew literature include Gabriela *Avigur-Rotem (b. 1946; *Mozart Lo Hayah Yehudi*; "Mozart Was Not a Jew"; *Ḥamsin ve-Ẓipporim Meshuga'ot*, "Heatwave and Crazy Birds"); Yitzhak *Laor (1948–), Youval *Shimoni (b. 1955; *Me'of ha-Yonah*; "The Flight of the Dove," 1990; *Ḥeder*, "Room," 1999); Dror Burstein (b. 1970; *Avner Brenner*, 2003); Yoav Alvin (b. 1962; *Marak*, "Soup," 2002); Benny Barbash (b. 1951; *My First Sony*, 1994; *Hilukh Ḥozer*, "Rerun," 2003) Uzi Weill (b. 1964; *Le'an Holekh ha-Zikaron ke-she-Anu Metim*, 1996); Alon Ḥilu (with the historical-fictional novel *Mot ha-Nazir*, "Death of a Monk," 2004); Eran Bar-Gil (b. 1969, with his lyrical, reflective novel about identical twins handed over for adoption soon after their birth, titled *Parsah ve-Kinor*, "Horseshoe and Violin," 2005) and Eshkol Nevo (1971–) with the novel *Arba'ah Batim ve-Ga'agu'a* ("Osmosis," 2004), a fine example of the way collective Israeli experience and questions concerning the Zionist narrative are intertwined with the experience of individual protagonists.

The reproach sometimes voiced is that the new writers are a "private generation," less preoccupied with collective national and political themes than with selfish concerns, materialistic gratification, and immediate pleasure, but this is inaccurate. In some prose writers, the political is clearly present between the lines; others, like Etgar Keret, handle it with less pathos than previous generations, but with equal urgency. Troubled by recent political developments, Itamar Levy published *Otiyot ha-Shemesh, Otiyot ha-Yare'aḥ* ("Letters of the Sun, Letters of the Moon," 1991), Semadar Herzfeld recounts a Romeo-and-Juliet love affair between a Palestinian and an Israeli woman in *Inta Omari* (1994). Yitzhak Laor published *Am, Ma'akhal Melakhim* (1993) and *Ve-Im Ruḥi Geviyati*, and Boaz Neuman (1971–) wrote an autobiographical account with the ironic title *Ḥayal Tov* ("Good Soldier," 2001). Asher Kravitz (1969–) wrote a disturbing, albeit funny novel about an Israeli soldier disguised as a Palestinian (*Ani, Mustafah Rabinovitch,* 2004) and Gilad Evron (1955–) published a prose collection titled *Mareh Makom* (2003).

As the discussion on the literary canon continues and critics vary in their opinion of which prose works "qualify" as canonical, there has been a continuous expansion of so-called "popular literature." The weekly list of bestsellers features many writers who are often commercially more successful and popular than the leading canonical ones; their novels (e.g., Irit Linor, *Shirat ha-Sirenah, Benot Braun*) set up a mirror to the prevailing Israeli mentality and create a literary vogue that is later imitated by others (Michal Shalev, *Shevua'at Rachel*, 1997; Sheli Yechimowitz, *Eshet Ish*, 2001; Rakefet Zohar, *Ha-Ahayot Schuster Nikhnasot le-Herayon*, 2002; Semadar Shir, *Roman Amiti*, 2002). Among the reasons for the proliferation of this inferior, titillating prose, is no doubt the ever-growing number of new publishing houses that are willing to take commercial risks and publish unknown young writers, as well as the dictates of a market that is dependent on ratings. Beside the long-standing publishing houses (Schocken, Am Oved Ha-Kibbuẓ ha-Me'uḥad and the associated Ha-Sifriah ha-Ḥadashah), new publishing enterprises have shot up like mushrooms. Among these are Keter, Zemorah-Bitan, Sifriat Maariv, Yedioth Ahronoth, Miskal, Kinneret and Kedem, Bavel, Ḥargol, Gevanim, Astrolog and Carmel. Mention should also be made of Keshet, Ram *Oren's privately owned press, which began by publishing its owner's commercially successful thrillers and later published also "pop"-literature (Kobi Oz) as well as bestsellers of considerable literary quality such as the novels of Avigur-Rotem and Zeruyah Shalev. Keshet is a major promoter of Israeli detective novels (Ram Oren), though others have followed suit. Amnon *Dankner has published a detective novel set against the emergence of Zionism, *Ha-Ish le-Lo Aẓamot*, "The Man without Bones," 2002; see also *Malkodet ha-Devash*, 1994). On the whole, the sophisticated Israeli thriller, a relatively new genre in Israeli fiction, has had tremendous success and includes writers of international repute such as Batya *Gur, Uri *Adelman, Shulamith Lapid, Amnon Jackont, and Agur Schiff.

Finally, at the initiative of publishers, editors, and literary scholars, major books by earlier generations have been reissued and some forgotten classics of early Hebrew literature rediscovered. These include the prose of David *Vogel, David Kimchi's family saga *Beit Ḥefeẓ* ("House of Hefetz"), Aharon *Reuveni's trilogy *Ad Yerushalayim*, as well as prose works by Y.H. *Brenner, M.Y. *Berdyczewski, D. *Frischmann, and A. *Hameiri, S. Yizhar, M. Shamir, H. Bartov, B. Tammuz, and others.

POETRY Over the past 25 years Israeli poets have alternated between politically oriented and meditative, personal poetry. The Lebanon War of 1982–83 as well as the First and Second Intifadas produced an impressive protest poetry. Two collections were published following the Lebanon War: *Ḥaẓiyyat Gevul* ("Crossing the Border") and *Ve-Eyn Tikhlah li-Keravot u-le-Hereg* ("Fighting and Killing No End"). The poetry that emerged in the wake of the Lebanon War and the uprisings of the Palestinians was written by established poets like Nathan *Zach, Yehuda *Amichai, Meir *Wieseltier, Moshe *Dor, Aryeh *Sivan, and Aharon *Shabtai as well as by newcomers to the literary scene: Maja *Bejerano (1949–), Rami Ditzany, Yitzhak *Laor (1948–), and Rami Sa'ari (1963–). Poets expressed shame, fear, rage, and helplessness. The political poems of Dalia *Ravikovitch were particularly impressive (see: *Ima im Yeled,* "Mother with Child"), and focused on the sufferings of the individual victim, especially the agony of mothers and children. The impact of the Gulf War was reflected almost immediately in Hebrew poetry; see, for example, the collections published by David *Avidan and Ilan Schoenfeld.

The tendency of contemporary Hebrew poets to reflect on their own medium – language – was seen in two anthologies edited by Ruth Kartun-Blum: *Shirah bi-Rei Aẓmah* ("Poetry in its own Mirror," 1982) and *Yad Kotevet Yad* ("Self-Reflexive Hebrew Poetry," 1989). Kartun-Blum also edited the volume *Me'ayin Naḥalti et Shiri* ("Writers and Poets on Sources of Inspiration," 2002).

The past two decades have also seen the passing of prominent poets of the older generation like S. *Halkin, A. *Yeshurun, Z. *Gilead, K.A. *Bertini and * Zelda, as well as of poets belonging to the "Palmah Generation" and the "Generation of the State" such as A. *Gilboa, A. *Hillel (Hillel Omer), Y. *Shalev, A. *Kovner, D. *Pagis, A. Sachs, and, in 2000, the internationally famous Yehuda *Amichai. The "Tel Aviv Circle," which dominated the scene in the 1960s and 1970s, lost two of its seminal figures: Yona *Wallach (d. 1985) and Yair *Hourvitz (d. 1988). Meir *Wieseltier, who belonged to that group, published a number of collections which gave impressive expression to intimate experiences, childhood memories, and current events (*Mikhtavim ve-Shirim Aḥerim, Maḥsan*).

Artistic maturity and a tendency to reflect on time, old age, and transience characterize the writing of veteran poets of the "Palmaḥ Generation" and the "Generation of the State," with new collections coming out as well as the publication of the collected works of H. *Gouri, N. *Zach, M. *Dor, A. *Sivan, Moshe Ben Shaul (1930–) and Ya'akov Besser (1934–). A tone of maturity and sobriety prevails also in the poems of Ori *Bernstein (who also published a sensitive, melancholy autobiographical novel in the genre of the *Bildungsroman*, *Safek Ḥayyim*, 2002). Asher *Reich, Tuvia

*Rübner, and Israel Pincas (b. 1935; *Geneologia*, 1997) published new books of poetry that tended to avoid abstraction and sentimentality. Instead, subtle reflection is expressed in a poetic language whose deeper connotations are masked by a simple, spoken style.

Blending together the world of scientific thought with recollections and immediate experiences scientist-poet Avner Treinin (1928–) published a number of original collections (*Euclidium*, 1985; *Zikhron ha-Mayim*, 1991). One of the consequences of abandoning the "high" diction used by previous generations was a more intimate access to the psyche and the observation of mental processes and crises. Among the first to turn inward was Yona Wallach, followed by poets like Leah Ayalon (*Daniel, Daniel*, 1988; *Yehudiyot ve-Yehudim*, 2001), Maja Bejerano (1949– ; *Bat Ya'anah*, 1978; *Anaseh Laga'at be-Tabur Bitni*, 1998), and others. Instead of romantic love, male poets (e.g., Aharon Shabtai in *Zivah*) and, more importantly, a considerable number of women depicted the sexual experience, celebrating the authentic erotic element and occasionally transforming their poetry into a manifesto for transsexuality. Indeed, bisexuality as well as homoeroticism figure prominently in contemporary Hebrew poetry as in the writing of Hezy Leskli (1952–1994; *Leah Goldberg ve-ha-Akhbarim*) and in poems by Ilan Schoenfeld (1960– ; *Leta'ah Mekhushefet*, 1981) or in the lesbian poetess known as Shez.

Others who made their debut during the past three decades and publish regularly are M. *Geldman (1946–);Yosef Sharon (1952– ; *Dibbur*, 1978; *Sippur Iti*, 1994), Zali Gurevitch (1949– ; *Shurah Pesukah*, 1984; *Sefer Yare'aḥ*, 1998), Ronny *Someck (1951– ; *Goleh*, 1976; *Bloody Mary*, 1994), Pereẓ Dror Banay (1947– ; *Ḥamẓan*, 1980; *Turkiz*, 1993; *Gevul Aḥaron le-Yofi*, 1999), Erez Biton (1942– ; *Minḥah Marokait*, 1976; *Ẓippor bein Yabashot*, 1989), Zvi Azmon (1948– ; *Kortekst*, 1993), Leah Ayalon, Sabina Messeg (1942– ; *Zeh ha-Yam ha-Zeh, Yam Kinneret*, 1998); Hava Pincas-Gan (1955–); Miron C. Izakson (1956–), Yonadav Kaploun (1963– ; *Ha-Keter ha-Afor*, 1987; *Bat Shelomo*, 1994); and Admiel Kosman (1957– ; *Higanu le-Elohim*, 1998), the last two coming from a religious background. Some poets, like Rami Sa'ari (1963– ; *Hineh Maẓati et Beiti*, 1988; *Kamah ve-Khama Miḥamah*, 2002), Dori Manor (*Bariton*, 2005; notably poetry which reverts to traditional forms and rhymed verse), and Amir Or (1956–) have also translated world poetry into Hebrew. An unusual voice is that of Maya Arad (1971–), a linguist living in Stanford, Calif., in the United States, who published a novel in rhymed verse (*Makom Aḥer Ir Zarah*, 2003), which tells the story of Orit, a soldier who has been asked to write a leaflet about Israeli identity and to help a lonely soldier who has just immigrated from Canada to feel at home. Inspired by Pushkin's *Eugene Onegin*, she spices her unusual poetic text, written in a seemingly old-fashioned rhyme scheme, with wit and humor. The poetry of Agi *Mishol (1947–) has attracted a great deal of attention from literary critics such as Dan Miron and from the media; as a result, she has advanced to the forefront of the contemporary scene. On the whole, however, Hebrew poetry arouses far less interest than prose. It is read by a coterie of loyal devotees, many of whom write and publish their own poetry. Poems are usually published in the literary supplements of the bigger newspapers, in literary journals such as *Moznayim*, *Iton 77*, *Siman Keriah*, *Keshet ha-Ḥadashah*, *Akhsahv*, *Dimmu'i*, *Ho!*, and *Mita'am*, or in special journals promoting poetry, such as *Ḥadarim* and *Helikon*. Publishers are reluctant to take the risk of publishing poetry; among the few who do so are Keshev, Eked, and Ha-Kibbuẓha-Me'uḥad, Tag, Even Ḥoshen, and Shufra. An important contribution to the dissemination of Hebrew poetry abroad is no doubt the English-language periodical *Modern Hebrew Literature*, published by the Institute for the Translation of Hebrew Literature, the *Tel Aviv Review*, and the magazine *Ariel*, which has been published intermittently for many years in various languages, including English, German, and French, and is sponsored by the Ministry for Foreign Affairs. Along with the translation of individual poems in various foreign periodicals and anthologies (e.g., T. Carmi's *Hebrew Verse*), a number of poets have had books of poetry published in foreign languages (Amichai, Dor, Reich). The new and updated edition of *The Modern Hebrew Poem Itself* (edited by Stanley Burnshaw, T. Carmi, S. Glassman, Ariel Hirschfeld, and Ezra Spicehandler; Wayne University Press, 2003) is highly recommended. It includes translations, interpretations of individual poems, and general articles on Hebrew poetry and prosody.

Finally, one should mention new editions as well as the collected works of leading poets of previous generations. The two main projects, both directed by Dan Miron, were the scholarly edition of Ḥ.N. Bialik's poetry (two volumes: 1983, 1990) and the complete work of U.Z. *Greenberg. Avner Holtzman is responsible for a new edition of Bialik's poems (Devir Publishing House, 2005) marking the 70th anniversary of his death. There has been a new edition of *Kol Kitvei Tschernichovsky* (1990–98), a collection of Lea Goldberg's poems (1989) and a new edition of *Shirei Raḥel* (1997). Yehuda Amichai's collected poems were published in five volumes shortly after his death (2002–04). A previously unknown book of David Vogel's poetry, *Le'ever ha-Demamah*, was published by Menaḥem Peri in 1983. Other poets whose work was collected after their death are Y. *Katzenelson, A. *Ben-Yitzhak, Y. *Karni, E. *Raab, A. Chalfi, A. *Gilboa, D. *Pagis, and Y. *Hourvitz. A selection of poems by Y. *Orland appeared in 1997.

[Anat Feinberg (2nd ed.)]

DRAMA

Introduction

The drama is one of the least developed forms of literary expressions in Hebrew literature. Some have attributed its modest achievements to the inherent contradiction between the monotheistic spirit of the Jewish religion and the dualism implicit in drama (A.J. *Paperna, I. *Zinberg, and others). Others have stressed the objection of the sages to the ritualistic and "heretical" aspects of the drama (J.H. *Schirmann) which emerged in the Western World (e.g., the medieval mystery, morality, miracle, and passion plays). Jewish tradition undoubtedly inhibited the development of the drama since the art of the theater was incompatible with the traditional way of life. The secularization of Jewish life, a process which started in the 18th century and stimulated the development of secular literature, did not, however, in its initial phases, mark a rise in dramatic art, nor lead to the establishment of independent Jewish theaters. The revival of spoken Hebrew lagged behind the revival of the written language, impeding the development of the Hebrew drama, a genre primarily dependent on the spoken idiom. Thus until Hebrew became a living tongue, there was little prospect that a vital Hebrew theater might flourish. The Jewish theatergoer, introduced to his secular foreign environment, found satisfaction for his dramatic needs beyond the limits of the Jewish pale.

Amateur and professional Hebrew troupes emerged in Eastern Europe and in Ereẓ Israel only at the close of the 19th century. The amateur Hebrew groups of Brody and Lodz and itinerant troupes, like I. *Katzenelson's, were the harbingers of the Hebrew theater in the Diaspora, where since Abraham *Goldfaden (1840–1906) the Yiddish theater had greatly flourished. The amateur theatrical troupe in Jaffa, on the other hand, was the precursor of the theater in Israel. By the 1920s there already existed in Ereẓ Israel a professional theater while in the Diaspora, *Habimah, the first professional Hebrew theatrical company (established 1917, premiere in 1918) gained a great reputation in Russia. It established itself in Tel Aviv in 1931.

The development of the Hebrew theater in the 20th century is linked with the Zionist movement, the revival of Hebrew as a spoken language, and the Jewish claim for cultural national autonomy. The linguistic and sociocultural reorientation in the attitude of the public to the theater gave new impetus to the Hebrew drama (intended for the stage) and brought about its continuous development in Hebrew literature.

Early Beginnings

Dramatic elements and dialogue are already found in the Book of Job and, at a later period, in the *piyyut* (the Hebrew liturgical hymn), for example "*Ozlat Yokheved*"; or in some of the polemical verse of Abraham *Ibn Ezra depicting the conflict between body and soul, summer and winter, water and wine. Hebrew drama as such was, however, written occasionally mainly in Italy and Holland as early as the end of the 16th century and during the 17th and 18th centuries. This period in the Hebrew drama is mainly characterized by sporadic isolated plays which failed to lead to a continuous development and by a "literary," nontheatrical structure of the play.

Judah Leone b. Isaac *Sommo's *Ẓaḥut Bediḥuta de-Kiddushin* ("An Eloquent Marriage Farce"), the first Hebrew play, was written in Italy under the influence of the 16th-century Italian comedy. Though first printed in 1618, it had apparently been written a few years earlier. Schirmann assumes that it was probably staged in connection with Purim. Unlike Jewish playwrights of the 17th and 18th centuries, Sommo was well versed in theatrical technique (his essay *Trattato sul arte rappresentativa* points to this fact); his language is not purely biblical but contains later Hebrew phrasing and idioms lending the play not merely a visual but also an auditory dimension. The plot, characters, and structure are borrowed from the *commedia dell'arte* and only the Jewish comic subject (related to halakhic problems) and the cultural atmosphere in the play are original.

Most Hebrew playwrights of the 17th and 18th centuries (from Sommo to Moses Ḥayyim *Luzzatto) were unable to free themselves from the influence of the "Mediterranean" culture. They tried to transpose the Italian and Spanish live theater into the Jewish cultural milieu. In their adaptation of dramatic elements to a language and themes remote from the theater, they forfeited the structural authenticity of the play.

Moses *Zacuto in *Yesod Olam* (Altona, 1874), a dramatization of the story of Abraham and Nimrod, imitates the Spanish auto, and in *Tofteh Arukh* (Venice, 1715, 1881[2]), whose plot is the journey of the dead to hell, he follows the structure and content of medieval Christian allegorical plays. *Asirei ha-Tikvah* ("Prisoners of Hope," Amsterdam, 1673, Leghorn, 1771[2]), by Joseph Penso de la Vega, is patterned according to the Spanish *commedia*. Both Zacuto and Penso published their plays in Amsterdam, which was then enjoying a late renaissance of Judeo-Spanish culture.

Plays written in Hebrew in Italy during this period drew on their foreign cultural environment for their dramatic form and style without reference to contemporary Hebrew drama, thus failing to create a continuous link. Immanuel *Frances wrote a few occasional plays for festivals, a dramatic dialogue on woman (1670), and a Purim play. The most significant playwright of the Italian school, Moses Ḥayyim *Luzzatto, had a definite effect on the development of the Hebrew drama. He wrote three different types of plays which had been influenced by the Italian allegorical and pastoral drama. *Ma'aseh Shimshon* ("The Story of Samson," 1724) serves as a paradigm to illustrate the dramatic genre in his work on literary theory, *Leshon Limmudim* (Mantua, 1727). The play, a monologue interspersed with a chorus and fragmentary dialogue, is not a genuine drama. His other two plays, *Migdal Oz* ("The Mighty Tower," 1837) and *La-Yesharim Tehillah* ("Praise to the Upright," Amsterdam 1743, 1954[25]), show the influence of Guarini's pastoral drama, *Pastor Fido.* Luzzatto attempted to impose on Jewish moral themes and ethical language the Italian dramatic structure. (It has been suggested that these plays also allude to kabbalistic themes.) *Migdal Oz*, the story of young lovers who prevail over antagonists scheming against them, is an allegorical-pastoral drama. It is the earlier of the two plays and had no decisive influence on the Hebrew dramatic genre. Conversely, Luzzatto's *La-Yesharim Tehillah* greatly influenced the development of the Hebrew play in the 18th and 19th centuries. It is an allegorical drama in which the characters are personifications of positive and negative moral qualities. The theme is the victory of good over evil and the plot – the story of lovers who separate and then are reunited – represents the struggle of the forces of good to be united as one, and to have their virtue universally acknowledged. "Yosher" (uprighteousness) claims and finally wins "Tehillah" (praise). In his contest against "Tarmit" (deceit) and "Rahav" (conceit), he is helped by "Sekhel" (reason).

Haskalah Drama

La-Yesharim Tehillah was the first Hebrew play which exerted direct influence upon the subsequent Hebrew drama. Its dramatic and didactic elements affected Hebrew authors caught up in the *Haskalah movement as it moved from Western to Eastern Europe. Unrighteousness was viewed as a symbol of the Haskalah – the rational good which struggles against evil – seen as the anti-Haskalah forces. Plays written in this tradition were *Yaldut u-Vaḥarut* (Berlin, 1786) by the bookseller Mendel b. Ḥayyim Judah Bresslau (d. 1829); *Ha-Kolot Yeḥdalun o Mishpat Shalom* (Berlin, 1791) by S.A. *Romanelli; *Amal ve-Tirẓah* (Roedelheim, 1812, 1862[3]) by Shalom b. Jacob *Cohen; *Tiferet li-Venei Binah* (Zhitomir, 1867) by A.B. *Gottlober; *Emet ve-Emunah* (Vilna, 1867) by Abraham Dov *Lebensohn; and *Mashal u-Meliẓah* (Paris 1867) by Meir Leib *Malbim. While in these plays the *maskilim* were usually the protagonists, Malbim used the genre in order to attack them. All the plays lack real characters, genuine dramatic dialogue, and a proper plot, but were a means through which the Hebrew writer, to whom the dramatic art was still foreign, was initiated into writing dialogue. The Haskalah literature was nontheatrical, even nondramatic, yet it heralded the beginning of a genuine drama.

Another important trend in Haskalah dramatic literature was the translation and adaptation of European plays on biblical themes into Hebrew and the composing of original biblical drama. The first author to develop the technique of adapted translation was the 18th century writer David *Franco-Mendes. In *Gemul Atalyah* (first printed in Amsterdam 1770, 1860[3]), an adaptation based on Racine and Pietro Metastasio, Franco-Mendes altered the plot and structure of his neoclassic sources but did not write an original play. *Melukhat Sha'ul ha-Melekh ha-Rishon al Yeshurun* (Vienna, 1794), by Joseph *Ha-Efrati, though influenced by the German *Sturm und Drang* movement, Shakespeare, and Albrecht von Haller, is an original work with an ingenious and imaginative structure. The dramatis personae (David, Saul, Michal, and Jonathan), characters in their own right, are protagonists in a dramatic action which is not a struggle between good and evil but between noble heroes who are invested with moral qualities. The structure is defective, yet designed for the stage, and while the text includes "literary" passages unrelated to the plot (e.g., the play ends with Haller's poem "On Honor") which detract from the play, it nevertheless (as Paperna, one of the earliest Hebrew drama critics, asserted) paved the way for original Hebrew theatrical works on biblical themes.

Most playwrights, however, followed in the footsteps of Franco-Mendes – translating and adapting into Hebrew European plays on biblical themes. They were incapable of producing an original viable drama during this early phase of Hebrew literature. Not steeped in a dramatic tradition and lacking experience in the genre, they could not go beyond rhetorical writing. Plays written or adapted during this period were *Ma'asei Navot ha-Yizre'eli* (Roedelheim, 1807) by Shalom b. Jacob Cohen; *On Ben Pelet* and *Ḥananyah Misha'el va-Azaryah* (in *Kinnor Na'im*, Vienna, 1825), by Samuel David *Luzzatto; *She'erit Yehudah* (Vienna, 1827), an adaptation and translation of Racine's *Esther*, by S.J. *Rapoport; and *Shelom Ester* (Vienna, 1843), another rendition of the same play and a translation of Racine's *Athalie* (1835), both by Meir ha-Levi *Letteris. Basically, all these plays are dramatic failures. In his translation and adaptation of Goethe's *Faust*, which he called *Elisha ben Avuyah* (Vienna, 1865), Letteris deviated somewhat from the accepted practice of adapting neoclassic plays. He judaized the text, renamed the dramatis personae ("Faust" becomes "Elisha b. Avuyah,") and introduced character changes. Yet he remained faithful to the original dialogue, the general structure and even to certain key ideas, thus aborting his own attempt at genuine Hebrew dramatic creation.

The two didactic biblical plays by Naḥman Isaac *Fischman: *Mappelet Sisera* (Lemberg, 1841) and *Kesher Shevna* (Lemberg, 1870), though original in theme, do not differ in structure and didactic purpose from the allegorical dramas of the period.

The Haskalah period did not produce any real dramatists. It is the *Ḥibbat Zion generation which first prepared the ground for genuine Hebrew theater.

National Renaissance Period (1880–1947)

HISTORICAL MELODRAMA. Some of the trends of the Haskalah continued through the period of the national renaissance. Allegorical plays were still being written (cf. S. Zweibel's *Milḥemet ha-Ḥokhmah im ha-Sikhlut*, 1895) in the 1890s and some of the later historical and topical dramas also contain allegorical elements. The most common characteristic of the period was, however, the historical melodrama which had evolved from the Haskalah. Among the significant playwrights of the period is Judah Loeb *Landau, whose poetic dramas developed Haskalah themes and were written in the same ornate style. The theme is either the relationship of gentiles and Jews during crises in Jewish history, or the plays are permeated with the ideology of Ḥibbat Zion, as *Yesh Tikvah* (1893) and *Lefanim o Le'aḥor* (1923, 19442). *Bar Kokhva* (1884), and *Aḥarit Yerushalayim* (1886) are historical plays whose protagonists Rabbi Akiva and Rabbi Johanan b. Zakkai expound ideas about freedom and the glory of Israel which were drawn from Nachman *Krochmal. F. Hebbel's *Herodes und Mariamne* served as a model for Landau's *Hordos* which is an attempt at a historical justification of Herod; it takes up his defense against the Jewish historical tradition which Landau felt had unjustly vilified him. The lofty spiritual values propounded by the *raisonneur* characters in the monologues of all three historical plays are neither complemented by the actual episodes in the play nor realized in the action. The plays are simple, not sophisticated, and their style and structure are as yet unsuited for the theater. His other two historical plays, written in prose, *Don Yiẓḥak Abrabanel* (1919) and *Yisrael Besht* (1923), are patterned on the historical "chronicle" drama. Thus the Hebrew historical play of that period is very much a "melodrama of ideas"; the playwrights were unable to create dramatic action that derived naturally from the cultural milieu it was supposed to represent.

One of the playwrights of the period was Meir Poner (1854–1936), whose *Joseph della Reina* (1904) is a dramatic adaptation of the story of this legendary character. The play is on two levels: the relationship of Jews and gentiles; and the relationship of man and God (in the manner of *Faust*). His other plays *Beit Eli* (1902), *Yemei Hordos ha-Aḥaronim* (1913), *Mot ha-Melekh Hordos* (1928), *Yehudah ben Yeḥizkiyyahu ha-Gelili* (1921), and others have as their main theme the freedom of the people of Israel; the plot, however, does not dramatically realize the rich texture of ideas. Poner's prose style, unlike Landau's uninspired, florid language, is quite original.

Hebrew writers of the 1930s and 1940s continued to write "melodramas of ideas," e.g., A.A. *Kabak's *Be-Himmot Mamlakhah* (1929) and *Bat Sanballat* (1934); and S. *Tchernichowsky's *Bar Kokhva* (1930). *Bar Kokhva* is replete with monologues on liberty by Rabbi Akiva and his wife Rachel; but the action of the plot centers around Bar Kokhba's betrayal of his people because of Havivah, the Samaritan. Tchernichowsky, however, failed to integrate the conceptual and melodramatic planes in the play. The ideas of the play are not realized in the action and therefore lack dramatic validity.

Most of Ya'akov *Cahan's plays are marked by a gap between a high view of existence and sentimental melodrama. In the King Solomon trilogy, *Shelomo u-Vat Shelomo* (1924, 1928), *Shelomo ve-Shulammit* (1942), *Malkat Sheva* (1945), the sentimental melodrama centers around Solomon's love for Shulamit, Ido's love for Solomon's daughter, and Solomon's love for the Queen of Sheba. Its ideological interpretation has a "Faustian" *Weltanschauung*. These plays are also marred by Cahan's inability to activate his ideas; his characters never gain the stature their positions demand, and the tone never rises above the sentimental. Most of his other plays are poetic drama but whether they are biblical like *Hoshe'a* (1956), *David Melekh Yisrael* (1921), *Ha-Nefilim* (1939–40), and *Leyad ha-Piramidot* (1939), or post-biblical plays: *Aḥer* (1950), *Rabbi Me'ir u-Veruryah* (1952) and *Yannai u-Shelomit* (1955); or nonhistorical prose plays: *Ken ha-Nesher* (1932), *Ha-Shali'aḥ* (1937), and *Terufo shel Ben Adar* (1939), they are mostly of the same caliber and texture. The style is very conventional and Cahan tends to embellish concrete dramatic reality with very ornate metaphors which are not always in keeping with the subject or theme. Some of Cahan's plays are, however, genuine melodrama: in *Yiftaḥ* (1945) no attempt is made to impose ideas on the plot and in *Be-Luz* (1940) they develop out of the action.

An earlier playwright, I.L. Mekler, in *Pilegesh ba-Givah* (1899), a dramatization of a biblical story, also stressed the drama of the play rather than its ideas. Yet most of the playwrights of "the melodrama of ideas" (S.D. Goitein, E.L. Jaffe, S. *Zemach, and others) created either stock characters or personifications of ideas which they failed to realize into fully developed dramatis personae. The American Jewish playwright Harry *Sackler made a significant contribution to the Jewish theater. Sackler wrote in Hebrew, in Yiddish, and in English. He was familiar with the theater and with stagecraft. *Yosi min Yokrat* (written in Yiddish, 1917, and translated into Hebrew by Sackler in 1921) is tragic in form. The plot revolves around the conflict between Yosi and his wife Yalta over the conduct of their daughter Ursilla, whose great beauty arouses men to passionate rivalry and ultimately to murder. The tragedy culminates in Ursilla's death. Yosi, prompted by rigid stringent moral convictions, kills his daughter because he believes that her beauty is an evil which spells disaster for all men. Although the play has dramatic impact, the dialogue fails to sustain the tragic intensity of the plot. In a number of other Hebrew plays (e.g., *Raḥav* (1934), *Ha-Derekh l-Elohim* (1964), *Yizkor* (1964)), which were printed in Yiddish before they were translated into Hebrew, the effect is basically melodramatic; Sackler fails to involve the characters in deep dramatic conflict. A mixture of humor and melodrama characterizes his Hebrew ḥasidic plays and playlets: *Nesi'at ha-Ẓaddik* (1936), *Ha-Ḥozeh Ro'eh et Kallato* (1932), *Kelappei Mizraḥ* (1933). Other works by Sackler resemble the chronicle play *Orot me-Ofel* (1936), a historical canvas of the persecution of Jews during the *Fettmilch riots in Frankfurt on the Main and alluding to Hitler's rise to power, and *Mashi'aḥ – Nosaḥ Amerikah* (Hebrew, 1933), a comic treatment of Mordecai Manuel *Noah's plan to found a Jewish state in the United States. Sackler's plays are well structured, the dialogue is simple and functional, and the stock characters find their actualization in social circumstances and historical garb. Some of them (*Yosi min Yokrat* and *Raḥav*) have been produced in the United States and in Israel.

The most frequently staged playwright of the 1930s and 1940s, Aharon *Ashman, began as a "ḥalutzic" writer (e.g., *Min ha-Meẓar* (1932); and *Ha-Adamah ha-Zot* (1942, which was successfully staged by Habimah) whose pioneering themes reflect the problems of his generation. He later wrote historical plays: the trilogy *Mikhal Bat Sha'ul* (first part printed in 1941), two parts of which were performed by Habimah; *Aleksandrah ha-Ḥashmona'it* (1947), used as a libretto for an opera by *Avidom; and *Ha-Ḥomah* (1938), written in the manner of the chronicle play. Most of Ashman's dramas have intricate plot structures in which simple characters become entangled in intrigues. The biblical or historical setting has little significance and serves only as an exotic background to the love story of the dramatis personae. While the melodramatic effects have a strong histrionic impact, his themes are superficial and trivial.

POETIC DRAMA. In contrast to the historical plays in which preference was given to the theatrical aspects over and against the poetic, dramatists like I. *Katzenelson, who is one of the finest Hebrew lyrical dramatists, stressed the lyricism of playwriting. Katzenelson, a prolific and versatile writer, wrote in a number of literary genres, both in Hebrew and Yiddish. Among the various types of plays he composed are *Tarshish* (1921), a realistic drama, produced in New York; *Ha-Ḥammah! Ha-Ḥammah!* (1907), a poetic, impressionistic one-act play performed at the gala opening of Habimah in Moscow (it later formed part of the trilogy *Anu Ḥayyim u-Metim*, 1913); *Ha-Ma'gal* (1911), a bedroom farce performed in Lodz; *Istharah* (1933); the biographical playlets *Ha-Matmid ve-Ẓillo* (1935) and *Mendele im ha-Kabẓanim* (1936); and plays for children about holidays and festivals. Katzenelson's most significant contribution to the Hebrew drama are his verse plays, poetic prose drama, and a number of lyrical dramatic fragments: *Ha-Navi* (*Ha-olam* 1912 – Act I; *Ha-Ẓefirah* 1918 – Act II; published in book form 1922); *Gilgal* (1911–13); *Amnon* (1938); and *Ḥanniba'al* (1947). While his plays in prose are dramatically effective, their themes and structures are conventional. Katzenelson's value as a dramatist lies in the high literary quality of his impressionistic plays, which are written in poetic prose. Intense dramatic situations are rendered lyrically, though in no way detracting from the interaction of dialogue and plot. His original interpretations of biblical and post-biblical historical themes and their poetic dramatic rendering are most expressive of Katzenelson's dramatic genius. In *Ha-Navi* the relationship between *Elisha and *Gehazi is the inescapable bond existing between a man and his shadow; in *Amnon*, Katzenelson characterizes Amnon, the heir-apparent to David, as a weakling, unfit to be king because he is incapable of rebelling against his father; in *Ḥanniba'al*, Hannibal, who is called upon to revenge the heinous crimes the Aryans committed against the Semites (the play was written in a German concentration camp), recoils from meting out vengeance. Katzenelson's verse plays have great literary merit from the point of view of language, but they are not theatrically effective.

Mattityahu *Shoham, a major figure in Hebrew literature, composed four biblical plays in verse which, because of their original style and structure and imaginative conception of historical events, are landmarks in Hebrew drama. *Yeriḥo* (1924), a dramatization of the fall of Jericho, has for its main characters Achan and Rahab, whose love for each other is symbolic of the attraction between the decadent culture of Jericho and the rigorous, vital Hebrew culture of the desert. In *Bilam* (1925–29), the subplot which portrays the tension between Balaam and Moses embodies the dramatic theme of conflict between the forces of darkness (Balaam) and the forces of light (Moses). The tension is resolved in Balaam's regeneration. *Ẓor vi-Yerushalayim* (1933) presents the theme of culture polarity through the characters of Jezebel, Elijah, and Elisha. Elisha's dissociation from Jezebel indicates a subtle change from Shoham's earlier view on the attraction between the Jewish culture and a foreign culture. In *Elohei Barzel Lo Ta'aseh Lakh* (1937) Gog, who personifies Aryanism, and Abraham, who represents Judaism, are locked in a relentless struggle which forms an allegorical superstructure to a plot that revolves around Sarah, Hagar, and Lot's daughters. Shoham through the power of his poetry endows language with a dimension of its own which is revealed in the dramatic tension between his symbols. While the dramatic content is embodied in symbols of fire and water (*Yeriḥo*), light and darkness (*Bilam*), and the vine and the lion (*Ẓor vi-Yerushalayim*), it is actualized not in the plot, or in the characters who remain mostly symbolic or allegoric, or in the dialogue. Shoham's dramas fall short as theater primarily because his "literary," idiosyncratic language is completely unsuited for the stage. Thus while his literary dramatic achievement is undisputed, his plays are theatrically not successful. Shoham's dramaturgical problems reflect those of contemporaneous Hebrew drama.

EXPRESSIONIST-HISTORICAL DRAMA. Among the writers who attempted to write expressionist-historical drama were Nathan *Agmon, Sh. *Shalom, and Ḥayyim *Hazaz. Agmon broke with the tradition of the conventional plot and in the plays *Yehudah Ish Kerayot* (1930), *Shabbetai Ẓevi* (1931), and *Be-Leil Zeh* (1934) emotional tension rather than coherent sequence is the cohesive factor. The dialogue is fragmentary and rhetorical; the characters tend to be symbolic and episodes grotesque. The structure of the plays, however, renders them unsuitable for the stage. Years later Agmon rewrote two of these plays: *Shabbetai Ẓevi* (1936) and *Be-Leil Zeh*, renamed *Leil Yerushalayim* (1953), trying to tone down the expressionistic effects. Although the adaptations are much closer to the realistic school, they lack the verve, spontaneity, and originality of the earlier plays. All three dramas have for theme crisis in Jewish history as manifest in the struggle between traditional conservatism, which acquiesces to exile, and the demand for messianic redemption. *Yerushalayim ve-Romi* (1939), a dramatization of *Josephus, and the Herzl trilogy, *Ḥevlei Gilgul* (appeared in complete form in 1960), are two of his plays which were originally written in a realistic style. Some later plays, *Maḥlefot Avshalom, Harostrat*, and *Don Quixote* (1960), while original and interesting in their approach and interpretation of the subject matter, fall short of their theatrical realization.

*Shin Shalom gave full vent to his expressionistic dramatic tendencies in the two poetic playlets *Shabbat ha-Olam* (1945, first appeared as *Elisha ve-ha-Shabbat*, 1932) and *Me'arat Yosef* (1934) which are not intended for the stage but are dialogues giving voice to the *Schrei* (the famous expressionist cry). *Elisha b. Avuyah, the protagonist of *Shabbat ha-Olam*, revolts against tradition and in *Me'arat Yosef* Josephus attempts to return to the primordial forces of life after the destruction of civilization. Shalom's characters are projections of the poet's "I" rather than genuine portrayals of the "I" of the personae of his plays. His characters are never fully rendered as independent human beings. His "ḥalutzic" plays *Yeriyyot el ha-Kibbutz* (1940) and *Adamah* (1942) are less expressionistic.

Ḥayyim Hazaz's play *Be-Keẓ ha-Yamim* (different versions: 1934, 1950, 1968), probably one of the outstanding achievements of contemporary Hebrew drama, is an expressionist play in which the author has carefully kept to the thematic and structural framework. Set in the time of Shabbetai Ẓevi, the theme of the drama is the tension between the polar concepts of exile and redemption. Yozfa, the "hero of redemption," attacks the smugness of the community, represented on the one hand by Yost and his friends who prefer the safety of the status quo to the disruptive and revolutionary challenge that redemption offers, and on the other hand by the beggars who misinterpret the significance of the deliverance. While the dramatis personae are infused with an exaggerated intensity, they fulfill their dramatic function as characters. Hazaz is original in his rhetoric style which remains within the confines of the language of the theater.

Hebrew historical drama during the national revival can point to a number of important literary works (e.g., the plays of Shoham). The discrepancy between the ideas of the playwright and his ability to realize them in a theatrical context is the reason why there were no major dramatic achievements during this period. Hebrew historical drama was also affected by a variety of Western literatures. Dramatists were eclectic and were influenced by many schools, plays, and a wide range of dramatic genres extending from French neoclassicism, to German classicism (Goethe), to Polish expressionism (S. Wyspiański).

ZIONIST MELODRAMA. The period of national revival (1880–1947) also saw the development of the play that dramatizes different facets of contemporary Jewish life. This type of play was a vehicle of expression in contemporary Yiddish literature as well, and some playwrights wrote in both languages.

The Zionist melodrama follows the tradition of the didactic Haskalah allegory and the historical "conceptual melodrama." J.L. Landau's *Yesh Tikvah* ("There is Hope," performed in Brody and published in 1893) is an early example. Shulamit, the heroine, is the daughter of the rich man of the town who must decide between Binyamin Ish Nadiv, the Zionist whom she likes, and Max Bilam, the assimilationist whom her father favors. In the end love and Zionism triumph. The play is a Zionist reading of allegories like M.Ḥ. Luzzatto's *La-Yesharim Tehillah*. *Lefanim Le'aḥor* (1923), another play by J.L. Landau, is much more complex. Its theme is an ideological struggle between Zionism and assimilationism for the souls of the youth and the whole community. The conflict is embodied in the dramatis personae: the rabbi of the community De Shneour Michal, a spiritual Zionist, and the aristocrat Steinbach, the man who wields power in the small town and whose daughter converts to Christianity at his instigation. In two other melodramas: *Ha-Sorer be-Veito* (printed in 1900) by I.H. *Tawiow and *Ba't ha-Rav o Giyyoret ha-Ẓiyyonut* (1904) by Jacob Gordon, Zionism serves as the criterion of the good. The Zionists are the positive characters and good overcomes evil. The structure of the Zionist melodrama thus follows the pattern of the Haskalah allegory where enlightened "nationalists" are juxtaposed with the "enlightened *maskilim*" and the assimilationists take the place of the religious reactionaries.

NATURALISM. Many of the plays of the national renaissance period bear affinity to the trends and forms prevalent in modern European drama, showing the influences of Ibsen's drama, Maeterlinck's symbolistic plays, and Hauptmann's social naturalism. Some of Peretz *Hirschbein's plays are markedly naturalistic while others are symbolistic. He wrote mostly in Yiddish but translated his own works into Hebrew. *Miryam* (1905), a conventional social melodrama about a poor and simple country girl, is a prime example of the influence of naturalism in Hebrew drama. She is seduced by the "landlord's" son and ends up in a brothel. The protagonist of the naturalistic play *Nevelah* ("Carrion," printed in 1905), Mendel Nevelah, is also a victim of society, here represented by his forefathers. Driven by suffering, he murders his own father and sinks into madness. *Bein Yaldei ha-Sadeh* (original Yiddish *Grine Felder;* Hebrew 1922), a comedy staged in Hebrew by Habimah, describes the comic confrontation between country Jews and Levi Yiẓḥak, a scholar from town.

Jacob *Steinberg, primarily a poet and short story writer, also wrote naturalistic social drama. The heroine of *Ḥankah* (1907), a play in the pattern of *Miryam*, is a pathetic girl who, persecuted by her stepmother, finally commits suicide. In *R. Leib Goldman u-Vitto* (1907), Steinberg dramatizes the eternal conflict of the generations as manifest in his time. *Bayit mul Bayit* (1908) by Zalman *Shneour, who is also mainly known for his poetry and prose rather than his plays, is a social drama in which prostitution is exposed by means of contrast with bourgeois life. Shneour's *Adam* (1926) is a lyrical dramatization of the story of Adam and Eve. Joseph Hayyim *Brenner's *Me-Ever la-Gevulin* (1907), a play comprised of a series of dialogue fragments, marks a chapter in the history of Hebrew drama and dialogue. Brenner's dramas, which he termed "plays and fragmentations of plays," use the dramatic fragmentation technique, a literary device also found in many of his prose works. Not well structured, the play is nevertheless interesting from the point of view of style, technique in dramatic dialogue, and theme. Its setting is the London of Jewish-Russian emigrants whose social customs and ideological struggles form the dramatic tension in the play. The protagonists, Yoḥanan and Ḥezkoni, despair of all socialist theories and regard suffering as the ultimate truth. Brenner, attempting to recreate the spoken word, evolved a kind of Hebrew-English dialect which was meant to be analogous to the Yiddish-English dialect in actual use. He thus brought the "language of the theater" closer to the "language of life." The playlets *Le-Et Attah* (1905) and *Erev u-Voker* (1908), written in a similar style, evince a better control of the medium and dramatically are realized more fully.

REALISTIC HEBREW DRAMA. One of the first exponents of realism in Hebrew drama is Yitzḥak Dov *Berkowitz who wrote a number of important plays, among them *Oto ve-et Beno* (1928 and performed by Habimah). The play follows a realistic Ibsenian technique and is a landmark in contemporary Hebrew drama. The theme, the relationship between an apostate father who wishes to return to Judaism and his son who has become a Jew hater, is comprehended within an analytical design and set against the bloody landscape of Russian pogroms during the Bolshevik Revolution. Two minor realistic plays by Berkowitz are *Ba-arazot ha-Reḥokot* (1928), a comedy on the life of Jewish immigrants in the United States whose lives are thrown into comic confusion through the arrival of Anton, a non-Jewish Russian farmer; and the social drama *Mirah* (1934), also set in the United States, and strongly influenced by Ibsen's *A Doll's House.*

Yitzḥak *Shenhar also wrote realistic drama, though of a different type. *Al ha-Gevul* ("On the Border," 1943) is about a group of pioneers who attempt to immigrate to Ereẓ Israel. Their efforts lead to a momentary reorientation in the life of a degenerating family; no real change, however, is effected. Chekhov's *Three Sisters* served the author as model. His protagonists are three brothers and the ideal and yearning for Ereẓ Israel replace the nostalgic longing for Moscow. To some extent Shenhar writes in the earlier tradition of translation and adaptation of European themes, topics, and literary structures to a Jewish milieu, ambiance, and cultural ideal. Some of the best authors of Hebrew literature tried their hand at naturalistic-realistic plays, a parallel school of which developed in Yiddish drama. This affinity between Hebrew and Yiddish drama is still more evident in the symbolistic and expressionistic techniques of I.L. *Peretz, H. *Leivick, and D. *Pinski, who wrote mostly in Yiddish.

SYMBOLISM AND EXPRESSIONISM. Isaac Leib Peretz (1852–1915) was one of the first symbolists and expressionists in Hebrew and Yiddish drama. *Ḥurban Beit Zaddik* (1903, had a number of versions, one in Hebrew) is a mystical play which dramatizes the decline of a ḥasidic *ẓaddik's* dynasty. Germinated in doubt, the degenerative process takes its full course, ending finally in heresy. The symbolistic technique is typical of Peretz's Yiddish plays. His social playlets are written in a naturalistic style, e.g., *Seḥufei Zerem* (1912) and *Ba-Shefel* (1924). P. Hirschbein also wrote symbolic plays: *Olamot Bodedim* ("Lonely Worlds," 1905) is set in a cellar where a group of wretched and oppressed people live in close proximity without talking to each other but "next to each other." In technique and atmosphere the play resembles M. Maeterlinck's *Les Aveugles* (translated into Hebrew in the same year). *Teki'at Kaf* (*Ha-Shiloaḥ* 18, 1908) bears similarity to S. *An-ski's *Dybbuk.* Its theme of innocent pure love, culminating in a blood bond between the young lovers, is enacted against the background of a contract sealed by their parents which, however, they later break. The breach leads to disaster and the young hero's death. The technique is symbolistic, as in the historical drama *Be-Ẓel ha-Dorot* (1922) and in the playlets *Al Yad ha-Derekh* (1907) and *Pirḥei Sedeh ha-Kevarim* (1907). Hirschbein's drama is thus marked by two distinct literary trends in European literature – naturalism and symbolism. A number of less important Hebrew playwrights also experimented with symbolism; none however attained the artistic level of the Yiddish dramatists. Their contribution to the Hebrew drama was the development of natural Hebrew style.

THE "ḤALUTZ" PLAY. Developed mainly in Ereẓ Israel, the "ḥalutz" play (or "*Maḥaze ha-Hityashvut,*" "the Settlement Drama") is defined by its subject matter: the story of the settlers in Ereẓ Israel, their problems, and their struggles. The underlying theme of the "ḥalutz" drama is to praise the pioneers and their efforts and to denounce all their opponents. Most of these plays were insignificant melodramas which at best were well constructed. The characters were drawn from the social milieu of Ereẓ Israel. Yehoshua Barzilai in *Ha-Baḥlan* ("The Disdainer" 1919: special edition), one of the early plays in the genre, transposed Molière's *Misanthrope* to the Ereẓ Israel landscape and its problems. "Ha-Baḥlan," the protagonist, hates his urban environment (Jerusalem) but when he comes face to face with the new settlement he has a change of heart. *Allah Karim* (1912), by L.A. Orloff-Arieli (1886–1943), has a more complex plot and is enacted within a pattern of intricate human relationships. The central character, Naomi Shatz, immigrates to Ereẓ Israel during the Second Aliyah and becomes engaged to one of the pioneers. She is, however, disappointed by the Jewish "pioneering" intellectuals and prefers the native Arabs (Ali, the pastry vendor) whom she sees as really belonging to the land. Set against the Arab-Jewish conflict, the play ends with Naomi's hope for a new Jewish generation whose character will be shaped by the native soil. *Allah Karim* heralds the development of "*Maḥaze ha-Safek,*" "the Doubt play," a sub-genre of the "Settlement Drama" that accentuates the impotence of European newcomers in overcoming the hardships with which the physical and human reality in the Land of Israel confronts them. Although diminishing in number in course of the 1930s, in which the "positive," "optimistic" Settlement plays flourished due to the numerous anniversaries of veteran Jewish settlements and the establishment of new ones, the "Doubt play" prevailed until the ideological "earthquake" following the *Yom Kippur War* in 1973. David *Shimoni is another playwright of the "ḥalutzic" trend who extols the pioneering spirit (*Laylah ba-Kerem*, 1911) as does Haim *Shurer, whose dramatic canvas unfolds against the social problems of the pioneers. *La-Rishonah* (1920) dramatizes the conflict between the viticulturists of the village and their workers and the tension generated by the contradictory social and national views of the laborers themselves. Structured as a family melodrama, the viticulturist's daughter Michal falls in love with a laborer, David, her father's social antagonist. Shurer exposes the unreasonable extremism of the young people as they rebel against their parents. Only as the play draws to a close do the young come to acknowledge the right of existence of their opponents. Various "ḥalutz" plays continue to be written over a long period. *Roḥaleh* (1933) by Moshe *Smilansky is but a new version of an old subject. *Ha-Adamah ha-Zot*, by A. Ashman, has also for theme the pioneering spirit, acted out in a confrontation between father and son. Yoel Yoshpeh, a pioneer, opposes his son who seeks to escape from the village and to take Ḥannah, his beloved, with him. Ḥannah, however, loves Ya'akov, a worker on the moshav; *ḥalutziyyut* ("pioneering") wins out in the end and overcomes all obstacles. Though the melodramatic structure of the play is different, the class division of characters and concepts is the same, and the basic theme, the triumph of pioneering, remains the focal issue. Other plays written in this vein are *Bein Iyyim* (1928), by Mordekhai *Avi-Shaul, a drama of pathos in which the labor movement values of the protagonist, Yehoshua Ne'eman, are paramount; *Yeriyot el ha-Kibbutz* (1940) and *Adamah* (1942) by Sh. Shalom; *Ḥayyim* (1942) by Menaḥem Bader which also glorify the value of labor; and *Ha-Zaken* (1942) by Yehoshua *Bar Yosef, a realistic playwright, who draws on the prototype of A.D. *Gordon. In *Medurot* ("Bonfires") Alexander Karmon contrasts the martyr spirit of the hero to the values of his opponents and extols the role he takes in illegal immigration. While many of these pioneering plays are melodramas, some comedies on the subject were also written, e.g., A. Ashman's *Min ha-Meẓar* ("Out of Distress," 1932). The comic action revolves around the contention between two parties over the hand of Ellah, a pioneer. She has to choose between the temptation offered by the American family Stevens and the journalist Brown and the pioneering idealism of Yehudah. Ellah, of course, chooses the "good." The comedies *Banim li-Gevulam* ("Sons Return to their Border," 1945, performed by Habimah) by Asher *Beilin and *I Like Mike* by Aharon *Megged (1956) are constructed along similar lines.

Not all plays about Ereẓ Israel have for theme the problems of pioneering. Some dramatize other aspects and problems arising from life in Ereẓ Israel. A central theme is the conflict between generations and the struggle between tradition and those who rebel against it. M. Avi-Shaul in his dramatization of the conflict in *Ha-Maḥarozet* ("The Necklace," 1928) pits the old values of the Diaspora represented by Raphael Ḥai, a member of the Jerusalem Moghrabi (Moroccan) Jewish community, against the new life in Ereẓ Israel to which his daughter Mas'udah is dedicated. Bar Yosef's *Ya'akov ha-Zoḥek* ("Laughing Jacob," 1939) and *Be-Simta'ot Yerushalayim* ("In Jerusalem Alleys," 1941, performed by the *Ohel Theater) have similar themes. The dramatic tension is between the values of traditional Jewry of Safed and Jerusalem, and their children who rebel against the suppression of eroticism in their society. The conflict is not resolved but has its tragic "dissolution" in madness to which some of the characters are ultimately driven. Ithamar Ben-Hur's *Ha-Soreret* (1942) and M. Berger's *Me'ah She'arim* (1943) are similar. A different aspect of Ereẓ Israel was probed by A. Karmon who, in *Ba-Sevakh* ("Entanglement," 1926) and *Neginat ha-Em* ("Mother's Melody," 1928), dramatizes various intricate human relationships in kibbutz life (e.g., incest between a brother and a sister, family and education problems in a collective settlement). Only toward the end of the 1940s were some attempts made at introducing into Hebrew drama contemporaneous Western dramatic elements. Thus Ya'akov *Horowitz, who had earlier written an expressionistic play (*Gesher ha-Leẓim*, 1929), wrote in 1956 *Ani Roẓeh Lishlot* ("I Want to Rule"), a social-universal play which broke with the conventional "ḥalutz" drama, a trend that had continued into the early period of the state, though in a different garb.

Drama in Israel

Hebrew drama gained considerable impetus after the War of Independence. The establishment of the state accelerated the development of the Hebrew theater. The *Cameri (Chamber) Theater, established in 1944, promoted the realistic school. In the wake of the War of Independence a youth cult developed to which the stage also tended to cater. Most of the plays were a continuation of the "ḥalutz" play in theme and form, with the young fighters of the War of Independence replacing the young *ḥalutzim*. Two plays belonging to this category are Yigal *Mossinsohn's *Be-Arvot ha-Negev* ("In the Negev Desert," 1949, performed by Habimah), a melodrama about the defense of a besieged Jewish settlement during the War of Independence; and Moshe *Shamir's *Hu Halakh ba-Sadot* ("He Walked in the Fields," 1947, an adaptation of a novel by the same name), a love story set in a kibbutz. The two lovers are Uri, born on the kibbutz and now a soldier, and Mika, a survivor of the Holocaust. Both plays end in the death of the heroes. Similar plays are *Kilometer 56* (1949) and *Beit Hillel* (1951) by M. Shamir. The only exception to this wave of mythical self-glorification was Nathan *Shaham's *Hem Yagi'u Maḥar* ("They Will Arrive Tomorrow," 1949). In this realistic morality play, Jonah, the commander of an Israeli platoon, sends his comrades and two Arabs to their certain death on a landmined hill. Through this morally dubious act, fiercely condemned by his second in command, Avi (named after Abraham, the first legislator of the monotheist ethos), Jonah liberates himself and the remaining soldiers. The play is thus an early paradigm of the constant vacillation in Israeli drama (reflected even as late as 2005 in Yehoshua *Sobol's *Zeman Emet* ("The Moment of Truth") and in Yael Ronen's *Plonter* ("The Gordian Knot")) between vindication for any atrocities committed by Israelis against Arabs for survival's sake and fidelity to the humane tradition of Jewish morality.

Most of the plays of the 1950s are social dramas – distinguished by realistic-documentary or satirical-grotesque styles – in which the new developing society in Israel is criticized in the light of the values of the labor movement, e.g., A. Megged's *Ḥedvah va-Ani* ("Ḥedvah and I," 1964) and N. Shaham's *Kera Li Syomka* ("Call Me Syomka," 1950). The young dramatists of Israel's formative era (early 1950s) were primarily enraged by the "counter-revolutionary" symptoms of the new society. Corruption, bureaucracy, careerism, social inequality, and racial discrimination are criticized in realistic works which are all too often shallow: the new generation had ceased to uphold the cooperative and rural values of the prestate Jewish population and had instead become bourgeois, trying to achieve its selfish ends at the expense of the young state, while the state on its part has been ungrateful to that part of the young generation that fought for its establishment.

The following list of topical plays shows that many of the best of Israel's writers tried through social drama to grapple with the problems that beset the decade: M. Shamir's *Sof ha-Olam* and *Aggadot Lod* (1958), Ḥ. *Bartov's *Shesh Kenafayim le-Eḥad* (1954), and N. Shaham's *Ḥeshbon Ḥadash* deal with the absorption of immigrants; Y. Mosinsohn's *Kazablan* (1958) and Judith *Hendel's *Reḥov ha-Madregot* (1955) describe the discrimination of the Oriental community by the hegemonic Ashkenazi veterans; and Ephraim *Kishon's *Shemo Holekh Lefanav* (1953) satirizes the new bureaucracy; Y. Mosinsohn's *Eldorado* depicts prostitution and crime among the socially deprived and stigmatized Oriental sectors (1963), Yosh's *Ani Rav ha-Ḥovel* deals with the big seamen's strike, and Yoram Matmor's fine Pirandellian play *Maḥazeh Ragil* (reminiscent in content and style of *Six Characters in Search of an Author*) denounces society's betrayal of the freedom fighters. The protagonists are usually conventional, typical, and local, representing only their way of life and the immediate situation in which circumstance has cast them. They therefore lack any kind of universality. They are either clerks, new immigrants, or Oriental Jews. The playwrights tried to draw Oriental types but in actuality they only imitated their manner of speech and customs, and not always successfully. The language of these plays comes close to slang and though it is more flexible than the dramatic language of earlier generations, it lacks "style." The episodes are in the form of "reporting" and the playwrights make no attempt at stamping on the world they had created their personal "literary" seal. The plays of the humorist E. *Kishon, *Shaḥor al-gabei Lavan, Af Millah le-Morgenstern, Shemo Holekh Lefanav,* and *Ha-Ketubbah* created a new type of comedy. In a way they were a continuation of the comedy staged by Matateh ("Broom"), a satirical theater founded in the late 1920s.

An outstanding play in its superior aesthetic quality is *Tura*, a psychological-mythical drama by Y. Bar-Yosef (1933–). It is set in the traditional Oriental Jewish community, and depicts the horrendous results of the devaluation of the patriarchal family and its codes in Israel's "melting pot" of the 1950s. The situation is aggravated by the fact that the protagonists become pawns within the tenacious grips of the codes of the traditional community, so that their violation by the young heroine sweeps the dramatic action to a climax which culminates in her "ritual" murder.

New developments in contemporary Hebrew drama were nevertheless apparent, even in the 1950s. Biblical and historical drama is manipulated as a religiously connoted prism for critique of political and moral problems. It gained fresh impetus with *Akhzar mi-Kol-ha-Melekh* (1955) by Nissim *Aloni; *Milḥemet Benei Or* (1956) and *Ha-Laylah le-Ish* by M. Shamir; *Tamar Eshet Er* (1947) by Y. Mosinsohn; *Yoḥanan Bar-Ḥama* (1952) by N. Shaham; *Bereshit* by A. Megged; *Ha-Dov* and *Shalosh Nashim be-Ẓahov* (both 1966) by Y. Eliraz; *Uriyyah ha-Ḥitti* and *Sedom Siti* (1959) by B. *Galai; *Massa le-Nineveh* (1963) by Y. *Amichai; and *Keter ba-Rosh* (1969) by Y. Shabtai. These plays are not cast in one mold: some, like Shamir's, are politically topical drama in which contemporary social problems (revolution, mixed marriages) are projected into the past. Others try to dramatize the past but the protagonists are motivated psychologically (*Tamar Eshet Er*). *Akhzar mi-Kol-ha-Melekh* ("Most Cruel of All – the King") is an interesting social-poetic interpretation of the period of division between the kingdoms of Judah and Israel. Replete with allusions to contemporaneous problems, warning against the dangers of separatism and internal *Kulturkampf*, the play has nevertheless an independent existence as a psychological-poetic drama which is bound neither by time nor place. Some brilliant and pungent parodies on the past were written by modern Israel authors. They follow either the comic-parodic style of contemporary French drama (Eliraz), or are modern poetic reinterpretations of biblical themes which shed a new light on the rather untended facets of the ancient myth (such as the depiction of the old, impotent, and unstable King David, who is nevertheless reluctant to retire and deal with the question of his political legacy in Shabtai's *Keter ba-Rosh*). Playwrights have also tried to achieve comic effects through the treatment of a lofty subject with bathos (Megged, Galai, Eliraz). All these dramatists show a certain originality of expression, form, and approach to the material. Among the finest and most problematic modern Hebrew dramatists is N. *Alterman. Nathan Alterman, primarily a poet, wrote very diverse plays: *Kinneret Kinneret* (1962), a kitsch-nostalgic new "settlement play" devised to idealize the courage of the pioneers; *Pundak ha-Ruḥot* (1963), a drama which, through obvious analogies with Goethe's *Faust* and Ibsen's *Peer Gynt*, deals with the dilemma confronting every great artist of having to choose between life, love, and familial happiness, on the one hand, and artistic success, glory, and loneliness on the other; Among Alterman's other dramatic work one should mention *Malkat Ester* (1968), a Purim farce, and *Mishpat Pythagoras* (1966), an allegorical-topical play. The predominant strength of Alterman's plays is their rich and multi-layered poetic language that thrives at the expense of a convincing and gripping dramatic plot and conflict.

The so-called "Holocaust Dramaturgy" is one of the main genres of the Hebrew-Israeli play. It rarely focuses on commemorating the historical catastrophe, but rather contemplates the Shoah's shifting repercussions on Israeli society or uses it as a socio-political metaphor. The Holocaust is presented in the plays written during the 1940s and 1950s as an image of impotence, and is juxtaposed with the sublime convention of the *Sabra*. This is the underlying premise of plays such as the above-mentioned *Hu Halakh ba-Sadot* ("He Walked in the Fields," 1947) by Moshe Shamir, in which Holocaust survivor Mika has to sacrifice her private dream of leading a normal life with her boyfriend, Uri, for the sake of fighting for the establishment of the state. So too in Nathan Shaham's *Ḥeshbon Ḥadash* ("A New Account," 1952), or Aharon Megged's *Hanna Senesh* (1958) which glorifies the bravery of the woman paratrooper who was executed in Nazi occupied Hungary in her attempt to save Jews, those weaklings who went to their death like "cattle to the slaughter." The only exception to this orientation is *Ba'alat ha-Armon* ("Lady of the Manor," 1956), by the poet Lea *Goldberg, who focuses on the juxtaposition between European culture and modern civilization (including Zionism). It is acted out against the background of the rescue of European Jewish children from forced conversion. The protagonists are an old Polish nobleman, who represents the declining European culture, and an Israeli woman, who embodies the new civilization. The author's obviously romantic sympathies tend toward the old gentleman and the fading world he embodies. The poetic realistic and allegorical plays of the 1960s manifest a shift in the Israeli attitude toward the Holocaust. They belie the recognition that a society cannot forgo its past, and present the world of the victims and Nazi accomplices as the analogous alter ego of the rootless cult of the mythologized *Sabra*. The foremost accomplishments in this category include Moshe Shamir's *Ha-Yoresh* ("The Heir," 1963), Yehuda Amichai's *Pa'amonim ve-Rakavot* ("Bells and Trains"), as well as Ben Zion Tomer's *Yaldei ha-Ẓel* ("Children of the Shadow," 1963). This interesting play deals with Holocaust children who do not become rooted in the new reality of Israel, though on the surface they seem to have adapted. The drama is enacted in the garb of a symbolic relationship between the young protagonist Yosef-Yoram and his uncle, Dr. Sigmund Rabinovicz, who had been a *Judenrat* member and a Kapo guilty of the extermination of his own family.

THE SIX-DAY (1967) AND YOM KIPPUR (1973) WARS AS TURNING POINTS. The turning point in the Hebrew drama's attitude to society was the euphoric mentality that overtook Israel after the sweeping victory in the Six-Day War (1967). This was followed by a period of collective self-reckoning, soul searching, and myth shattering in the wake of the humiliating surprise of the Yom-Kippur War (1973). Whereas Israeli drama before 1967 was basically positive toward the ideal of the "New Jew," post-1967 protest plays adopted an asocial, agnostic, and deconstructive position in order to warn society against the dangers of a militarist power-cult and the moral deterioration inextricably connected with the occupation of the Palestinians and the subordination of human values to the imperative of territorial expansion. In fact, one may argue that from 1967 to Rabin's murder in 1995 the core of Hebrew drama was politically mobilized, rhetorically militant, and ideologically leftist. This thematic and stylistic watershed was also accompanied by a higher degree of ripeness and professionalism in Hebrew dramatic writing thanks primarily to the efforts of Oded Kotler as the artistic director of the Haifa Municipal Theater to promote young dramatists.

Hanoch *Levin's satirical revues *At va-Ani ve-Hamilḥamah Haba'ah* ("You and I and the Next War," 1968), *Ketchup* (1969, performed in fringe theaters), *Malkat ha-Ambatiyah* ("Queen of the Bathtub"), staged in 1970 by the establishment Cameri Theater and swiftly closed due to public outcry, and Levin's censored *Ha-Patriyot* ("The Patriot," Neveh-Ẓedek Theater 1982), denouncing the Lebanon War, did not shrink from resorting to profane and provocative devices in order to slaughter the most sacred cows of Israel's collective value system: the ideal of the "justified war"; the cult of the fallen hero; bereavement and the admiration for the military; the avoidance of any chance for peace; the sanctification of land at the expense of life and ethics; and the ingrained racist attitude to Arabs. A.B. *Yehoshua (1936–), one of the foremost young authors of the 1960s, heralded in *Laylah be-Mai* ("A Night in May," 1969) the falling apart of Israeli society through the metaphor of the psychological disintegration of a complex Jerusalem family during the period preceding the Six-Day War. One of the most vehement adversaries of Israel's belligerent orientation, provinciality, and disdain for culture was Yosef Mundy, who, as a deliberate rhetorical provocation, proclaimed his Diaspora-cosmopolitan *Weltanschauung* and anti-Zionist disposition. Mundy's most accomplished play, *Zeh Mistovev* ("It Turns," 1970) takes place in a madhouse (a common dramatic metaphor for Israel): the allegorical megalomaniac Herzl, representative of political and expansionist Zionism, torments the humanist, individualistic Kafka. In the symbolist-surreal play *Moshel Yeriḥo* ("The Governor of Jericho," 1975), written after the Yom Kippur War, Mundy depicts the racist and demeaning side of Israeli conduct towards the Palestinians through the vulgar, sexist, and despotic figure of the governor of Jericho, the first biblical town to be conquered by the Hebrew tribes as they invaded the Land of Canaan. One of the major genres in which the Israeli reality has been effectively examined and criticized is the docudrama. The most notable dramatists who continuously work in this genre are Yitzhak Laor, Motti Lerner, Edna Mazya, Ilan Hatzor, Daniela Carmi, Hillel Mittelpunkt, Matti Golan, Amnon Levy and Rami Danon, Shmuel Hasfari, Miriam Kainy, and Yael Ronen. They employ the strategy of undermining the accepted "photographic" conventions from within, thereby upsetting the positive self-image of Israeli society traditionally reasserted by the theater. Docudrama was inaugurated in the early 1970s by the American-born Nola Chilton, who created a succession of "living paper" documentaries promoting a spectrum of social causes in "the other Israel." Her partner in these ventures was Yehoshua Sobol, one of Israel's most prolific, politically engaged, and internationally successful dramatists. Sobol was also one of the major dramatists who developed – in the wake of the 1973 War – the mode of soul-searching plays that dissect the national myths and explore their false nature. Sobol's *Leyl ha-Esrim* ("The Night of the Twentieth," 1976), based on a historical episode, analyzes the mistakes of the Zionist founding fathers through the narrative of a group of young pioneers in 1920, engaged in a profound and merciless process of soul searching about their motives and purposes before descending from a Galilean hill to a new settlement where they expect to exchange "murderous blows with the Arab occupants of the Land." Sobol employs and develops similar docudramatic strategies in a number of plays, most notably in *Nefesh Yehudi* ("The Soul of a Jew," 1982), which deals with Jewish self-hatred and reconstructs the biography of Otto Weininger, the misogynist and genial Viennese Jewish philosopher, and in *Palestinait* ("The Palestinian Woman," 1985). In the latter, Sobol delineates the ordeals of Samira/Magda, a fictional TV-drama character who is the alter-ego of its author. She tries "to crystallize the borders and meeting points between the Israeli Jewish and the Israeli Arab/Palestinian cultural, ethnic, and national identities" (F. Rokem). A relatively late achievement in the docudramatic revisionist vogue is Hillel Mittelpunkt's *Gorodish, o ha-Yom ha-Shevi'i* ("Gorodish, or The Seventh Day," 1993), a chronicle of the rise and fall of General Shmuel Gonen, a hero of the Six-Day War who became the scapegoat of the "defeat" in the Yom Kippur War, thus symbolizing the ideological bankruptcy of all of Israeli society.

Yet although mainly realistic, the trend of post-Zionist drama that began in the mid-1970s did not preclude stylized and fantastic plays. Yaakov Shabtai's *Namer Ḥavarburot* ("The Spotted Tiger," 1974) tells the story of Fink, half dreamer half charlatan, who at the end of the 1920s comes to the tiny township of Tel Aviv, a provincial resort of embittered, materialist, and desperate ex-pioneers. Fink brings with him a whiff of the wide world, hoping to establish an international circus in Israel with all its trimmings, including a spotted tiger, the symbol of speed, courage, and unearthly beauty. Being unable to live up to the imaginary dimensions of Fink's utopian dream, the petty, dystopian settlers of Tel Aviv bring about his death in a duel. In *Shitz* (1975) Hanoch Levin provides a biting satirical grotesque about the cynical Israeli philistines who are transformed by greed into warmongers who thrive on blood. Danny Horowitz's *Cherli Ka-Cherli* (1977) – a parody on the Israeli *Massekhet*- genre in the form of an oratorio for speaking voices and chorus – reflects the spirit of soul searching by offering an ironic dissection of the once sacred *Sabra* myth. The tradition of post-Zionist, non-realistic parables on the shattered ideals of the morally corrupt Israeli society is pursued on the threshold of the third millennium by several dramatists (Yehonatan Geffen, Eldad Ziv, Shlomi Moskovitch). They are, however, surpassed by the theatrical texts of the director and playwright Michael Gurevitch, whose phantasmagorias *Mila Aḥat shel Ahavah* ("One Word of Love"), *Ḥeyl Parashim Anu* ("We Are a Unit of Cavaliers") and *Osher* ("Happiness") constitute poetic stage legends that lend themselves to a plethora of interpretations.

THE MOBILIZATION OF HISTORICAL AND BIBLICAL DRAMA. The process of mobilizing the stage for political ends left its mark also on historical and biblical drama. Historical as well as biblical materials have served since 1967 for a critical illumination of local political and existential problems. Aharon Megged's *Ha-Onah ha-Bo'eret* ("The Burning Season," 1967) takes up the theme of Job in order to warn against the hazards of forgiving the Germans by accepting compensation and establishing diplomatic relations with Germany. Instead of being loyal to the biblical characterization of Job as a righteous and God-fearing patriarch who rightfully lives to see a happy end to his various ordeals, Megged presents him as a blind, "Holocaust-denying" person who deserves the recurrence of his tragic fate. The same biblical myth acquires a radically existential and agnostic interpretation in Hanoch Levin's *Yissurei Iyov* ("The Sorrows of Job," 1981). In the first part of this "Passion"-play we witness the descent and fall of Job presented as a catastrophic succession of episodic events, corresponding to the biblical narrative (apart from the omission of the prologue in Heaven); yet, in contrast to the Scriptures, the chain of events in Levin's play is the result of both human short-sightedness and selfishness as well as of Job's own moral corruption. In the second part we witness the increasing agony of Job on the verge of dying, having been speared on a pole by the Romans for refusing to renounce God. Becoming part of a circus spectacle, without being granted the sanctification of a martyr's death, Job's anti-heroic suffering is rendered as the epitome of the purposelessness of human existence, of the relativity of human happiness, not even an existential gesture of protest against a metaphysical void. Yaakov Shabtai's *Okhlim* ("Eating," 1979) is an updated version of the theft of Naboth's vineyard by Jezebel and Ahab. This canonical parable is directed against the apparently "legal" dispossession of the occupied Palestinian land, while *Jehu* by Gilad Evron (1992) – the story of a ruthless army commander who escapes the death sentence for disobedience, overthrows the reigning monarch, commits hideous crimes, and drives his chief supporter, Ziph, to commit suicide – has been interpreted as a parable on the man who pulls the strings, Ariel Sharon's cynical manipulations of Prime Minister Menachem Begin, which led to the war in Lebanon in the beginning of the 1980s. Rina Yerushalmi's *Bible Project* – consisting of two parts, *Va-Yomer Va-Yelekh* ("And he said and he went," 1996) and *Va-Yishtaḥu Va-Yar* ("And he bowed and he saw," 1998) – harnesses the biblical text itself to its peculiar political ends. Even a harmless biblical musical such as *Shelomo ha-Melekh ve-Shalmai ha-Sandlar* ("King Solomon and Shalmai the Cobbler") by Sammy Groenemann and Nathan Alterman has been deciphered in its Habimah revival in 2005 as an allegory on social exploitation.

THE HOLOCAUST AS SOCIO-POLITICAL METAPHOR. The 1973 Yom Kippur War, which shattered the invincible image of Israel, resulted in a growing awareness that the Holocaust and Israeli experiences are metonymical and interchangeable. The best-known play of the period is Yehoshua Sobol's *Ghetto* (1984). The play dared for the first time to present – through an alienating "German" epic style and a "profane" image of a theater company in the Vilna Ghetto – the symbiotic relations and reversible roles of the Nazi victimizer and the Jewish victim, thereby reflecting on Israel's belligerency against Lebanon and the occupied territories. Similar political attitudes were advocated by Motti Lerner in his docudramatary *Kasztner* (1985), acquitting the hero, Rezso Kasztner, of collaborating with the Nazis in liquidating Hungarian Jewry, and in Shmuel Hasfari's family plays *Kiddush* (1985) and *Ḥameẓ* (1995). The Acre Theater Center's stunning theatrical event *Arbeit macht frei mi-Toitland Europa* ("Work Liberates from the Dead Land Europe," 1991) marked the beginning of the fourth stage of Holocaust dramaturgy, with the second and third generations exposing and reacting to the deforming influence of the Holocaust experience on the collective psyche, on the socio-political *Weltanschauung* and the ethical norms of Israeli society. The fifth phase of Holocaust dramaturgy denotes a "normalization" in the Israeli attitude to the Holocaust, by either employing the Shoah as a relatively indifferent background for soap operas, as in Edna Mazya's *Sippur Mishpaḥti* ("A Family Story," 1996) and Savyon Liebrecht's *Sonya Mushkat* (1997) and *Sinit Ani Medaberet Elekha* ("Chinese I'm Talking to You," 2003), or by the complete role reversal between former victims and victimizers, thus disinheriting the Jews of their moral superiority, as in Aliza Ulmert's *Sonata Lifsanter* ("A Piano Sonata," 1994) and Hillel Mittelpunkt's *Madrikh la-Metayel be-Varsha* ("A Warsaw Tourist Guide," 1999) – both preoccupied with the sadistic *vendetta* of Israelis against partly innocent Polish citizens and their property.

ALONI AND LEVIN. The unrivaled poets laureate of Hebrew drama are Nissim Aloni (1926–1998) and Hanoch Levin (1943–1999). Even though their plays are saturated with references and allusions to the local milieu, both Aloni and Levin tend to "distance the evidence" of their theatrical, self-referential phantasmagorias to mythical, literary, and legendary regions, thus serving as vanguards of the universal-existential trend in Hebrew drama. Aloni's signature play *Ha-Nessikhah ha-Amerika'it* ("The American Princess," 1962) delineates, through the detached narrative of a dethroned monarch, murdered by his opportunistic son, the cultural and normative deformation of Israeli society. This small lyrical-ironic masterpiece, strongly affiliated with the French Drama of the Absurd in the 1950s, and some of Aloni's other plays from an opus of 11 plays altogether (for example, *Bigdei ha-Melekh*, 1961; *Ha-Kallah ve-Ẓayyad ha-Parparim*, 1966; *Ha-Dodah Lizah*, 1969; and *Eddie King*, 1975) mark the playwright's ongoing influence on Israeli drama and theater, as an antidote to the prevailing flat journalistic dramaturgy.

Dramatist and director Hanoch Levin was undoubtedly the most prominent and prolific (60 works) theater practitioner to emerge from the aftermath of the Six-Day War. In the domestic neighborhood comedies that followed his first satirical revues, e. g., *Ya'akobi and Leidenthal* (1972); *Ne'urei Vardaleh* ("Vardaleh's Youth," 1974); *Krum* (1975); *Popper* (1976); *Soḥarei Gummi* ("Rubber Merchants," 1978); *Halvayah Ḥorpit* ("A Winter Funeral," 1978); *Orezei Mizevadot* ("Suitcase Packers," 1983); *Melekhet ha-Ḥayyim* ("The Labor of Life," 1989), Levin unravels the Diaspora myths underlying the apotheosized Jewish-Israeli family, and develops his image of humankind as a beastly hierarchy of humiliater and humiliated, motivated exclusively by their basest drives and thanatopsic fears. Levin's final cycle comprises legendary-universal phantasmagorias or "Spectacles of Doom," as, for example *Hoẓa'ah La-Horeg* ("Execution," 1979); *Ha-Zonah ha-Gedolah mi-Bavel* ("The Big Babylonian Whore," 1982); *Ha-Nashim ha-Avudot mi-Troya* ("The Lost Women of Troy," 1984); *Kulam Roẓim Liḥyot* ("Everybody Wants to Live," 1985); *Ha-Yeled Ḥolem* ("The Child Dreams," 1993); *Pe'urei Peh* ("Open-Mouthed," 1985); *Kritat Rosh* ("Beheading," 1996); *Ha-Holkhim ba-Ḥoshekh* (1998). In *Ashkavah* ("Requiem," 1999) he composed his own funeral oration, and *Ha-Bakhyanim* ("The Weepers," 2000), based on the Agamemnon narrative, was conceived on his deathbed.

THE PRIVATIZED ERA. The second substantial reversal in Israeli drama took place in the 1990s and characterizes plays written and performed at the beginning of the third millennium. The interconnected historical and theatrical developments (from the Oslo Peace Accord to Rabin's murder and the second Intifada) produce a complete renunciation of communal ideals along with their formal objective correlatives. The personal, cosmopolitan, and humane note is most clearly evident in the upsurge of women's – not necessarily feminist or gender-conscious – dramaturgy and directing. Most of the female dramatists work in the more established, well-made pattern. Shulamit Lapid's *Rekhush Natush* ("Abandoned Property," 1988) relates the story of an aging, half-blind and bitter mother who was long ago abandoned by her husband, and now tyrannizes her daughters under the pretext of wishing to protect them. Playwright and director Edna Mazia presents provocative, mentally unstable, and attractive heroines, and also directed several of Anat Gov's plays, of which the best and most popular is *Ha-Ḥaverot Hakhi Tovot* (1999), which takes for its theme the inextricable bonds among girlfriends. The opposite pole consists of stylized, poetic dramatic and theatrical texts, such as Yossefa Even-Shoshan's *Ha-Betulah mi-Ludmir* ("The Virgin of Ludmir," 1997), and Ravid Davara's *Ha-Sirpad shel ha-Shakhen* ("The Neighbor's Thistle," 1999).

The idealistic, committed, and selfless Hebrew plays of the early settlement period in Ereẓ Israel have thus reached the extreme opposite pole, as has indeed the entire Zionist ideology which generated them. However, both drama and theater are still engaged in the same quest for social identity.

[Gershon Shaked / Gad Kaynar (2nd ed.)]

CRITICISM

Introduction – Beginnings of Literary Criticism

Hebrew literary criticism as a discipline has existed for the past 200 years only, but the rudiments of literary appreciation can be traced to medieval works on normative poetics and rhetoric. In *Shirat Yisrael* (written in Arabic (*Kitāb al Muḥadara wa-al-Mudhākara*), Heb. ed. (1924) by B. Halper), Moses *Ibn Ezra lays down the rules for writing excellent poetry, which he applies to his criticism on the Spanish poets, and discusses the problems of artistic creation. Critical evaluations of the Spanish poets are also found in Judah *Alḥarizi's *Taḥkemoni* (Constantinople, 1578; Tel Aviv, 1952) and *Immanuel of Rome, in *Maḥberot Immanu'el* (critical edition, Tel Aviv, 1950), devotes a section to poetry. He is either profuse in his praise of poetry or he deprecates it. The prevalent tradition of distinguished personalities prefacing books with *haskamot* ("agreements," i.e., favorable recommendations) can also be considered a forerunner of literary criticism although the *haskamot* were mainly apologetic and couched in a formal conventional style. Often, the authors themselves wrote introductions to their works describing their aims and motives. It was, however, in the 18th century that Hebrew literary criticism as a school began to evolve, growing out of a cultural atmosphere which was able to appreciate Hebrew literature not only for ethical and didactic values but also for its own sake. The centers of Hebrew literary criticism correspond geographically and chronologically to centers of modern Hebrew literature – they shifted from Italy and Germany in the 18th century to Austria-Hungary and Russia in the 19th century. Hebrew literary criticism developed significantly in Russia (including Poland and Lithuania) from 1860 to 1918, and in Ereẓ Israel from the beginning of the century to this day. Literary criticism also evolved in the United States, where, in the main, it dealt with Hebrew literature written in that country between the world wars. Although critical activity usually reflects the development of other literary forms, modern Hebrew criticism in its beginnings lagged far behind the development of the different genres in modern Hebrew literature. The situation, however, began to change with the rise of the Hebrew press, which became the main vehicle of critical expression, in Russia, in the 1860s.

18th Century – Normative-Aesthetic Approach

The development of aesthetic literary appreciation is primarily linked with the study of the Bible. Moses Ḥayyim *Luzzatto in his works on poetics and rhetoric draws mainly on the Bible for the many examples with which he illustrates his theories. His poetic methods and theories, however, are mostly influenced by medieval and contemporary Italian rhetoricians. In the *Bi'ur* (1780–83) project, a translation and exposition of the Bible in German, edited by Moses *Mendelssohn and his circle, aesthetic appreciation of the scriptural text formed an integral part of the exegesis. Influenced by 18th century German aesthetic thought, the introductions and commentaries are often an eclectic combination of neoclassical and sentimentalist views. Sometimes a psychological moralistic approach is in evidence and aesthetic distinctions are made, mainly in the poetical sections of the Bible. The discussion on rhyme and structure in Mendelssohn's commentary on "The Song of Deliverance" adheres to Robert *Lowth's aesthetic distinctions (*De Sacra Poesi Hebraeorum Praelechones…*, 1753; trans. from Latin by G. Gregory, London, 1787) in its emphasis on the connection between rhetoric and emotion. In Joel *Brill's preface to the book of Psalms (2 vols., Berlin, 1787–88) the influence of the author's mentor, Moses Mendelssohn, and that of Johann Gottfried von *Herder (*Vom Geiste der hebraeischen Poesie*, 1782; trans. by J. Marsh, *The Spirit of Hebrew Poetry*, 1833) can be discerned. Despite Brill's declared adherence to the Haskalah, he devotes much attention to the effects of poetry and rhetoric on man's senses and emotions. These are achieved through repetition, deliberate shifts in syntax, and the frequent use of similes and metaphors. Enumerating the qualities of the ideal poet, he distinguishes delicacy of feeling, imagination, wit, and psychological insight. Naphtali Herz (Hartwig) *Wessely in the introductions to sections of his epic composition "*Shirei Tiferet*" (5 vols., 1789–1802) on the Exodus from Egypt discusses the power of poetry and its characteristics. His view on the universality of poetry, the earliest literary form, is in the spirit of neoclassical thought which attempted to harmonize between reason and emotion. Temperate and cautious in his biblical exegesis, Wessely believes, however, that modern poetic interpretation of biblical themes is obviously superior to the biblical source itself, especially in the portrayal of the inner motivation of events and their causal connection. His many attempts at expounding in detail the relationship of his poetry to biblical and midrashic sources indicate his predilection for criticism.

In his discussion on the theory of literature, Isaac ha-Levi *Satanow in *Sefer ha-Ḥizzayon* (Berlin, 1785) confuses the elements of poetics, rhetoric forms, and general definitions of the essence of poetry. Stressing the didactic significance of poetry in some of the formulations, Satanow, a leading representative of the Haskalah, also points out the sensual and ecstatic elements of poetry which affect the reader. The emotional characteristics of the Sturm und Drang, already discernible in some of the works of Mendelssohn's disciples, became more prominent at the beginning of the 19th century and are given a distinctly personal expression in Solomon Lewisohn's *Meliẓat Yeshurun* (Vienna, 1816). Lewisohn integrates these elements with Longinus' concepts, gleaned from reading *On the Sublime* which enjoyed widespread popularity in the Germany and England of his day. *Meliẓat Yeshurun*, a book of normative poetics illustrated with examples from the Bible, but also from Wessely and Lewisohn himself, attempts to define poetic forms. The poet's personal emotional confession, written with dramatic pathos, intrudes on some of the explanations and definitions which are of an apparently prescriptive nature. Poetry, according to Lewisohn, is a phenomenon existing in and of itself and affecting the entire universe. He thus freed himself of the neoclassical distinctions which tried to create a balance between reason and sentiment, and to harmonize between aesthetic experience for its own sake and the didactic objective of the work, the latter, according to neoclassicism, having to guide poetry. Using biblical rhetoric, Lewisohn posits a normative order, in which he demonstrates how the sublime scriptural effects were designed to arouse reactions of wonder and amazement in the reader.

19th Century

CRITICAL REVIEWS. Parallel to normative aesthetic studies, reviews of new books began to appear in *Ha-Me'assef*

(1784–1811), the Haskalah journal in Germany. Its anonymous "News of Books" column was, at times, little more than disguised publicity by the author. On rare occasions, the criticism went into a more detailed discussion of the work, quoting excerpts either for the sake of a polemic argument or for purposes of apologetic praise. Although the annual **Bikkurei ha-Ittim* (1821–1832) published in Vienna was in the spirit of *Ha-Me'assef*, it did not cultivate literary criticism. Two articles in *Bikkurei ha-Ittim* (1832, p. 175–181) and in **Kerem Ḥemed*, 1839, 45–57, on the satirical writings of Joseph *Perl, by Solomon Judah *Rapoport, a major figure of the Galician Haskalah, are of significance. Despite the anti-ḥasidic undertone, Rapoport presents a discerning literary evaluation of the work itself, its relationship to reality, and alludes to the general tradition of satirical literature in Europe. Samuel Joseph *Fuenn's review of the poetry of Abraham Dov *Lebensohn in *Pirḥei Ẓafon* (Vilna, 1844, pp. 90–103) is one of the early important critical works to come from the literary center of Vilna. Fuenn is a precursor of the genetic chronological literary review which considers the background of the author as essential to the understanding of the actual work, thus anticipating later critics, e.g., A.J. *Paperna, M.L. *Lilienblum, and Ḥ.N. *Bialik, who also followed the method. Like his Haskalah contemporaries Fuenn advocated the *meliẓah* style (ornate biblical syntax) as ideal, but was, at the same time, aware of the tension between content and linguistic patterns in poetry. He considered the different stages of Lebensohn's work from the aspect of the poet's personal development – tracing his growth from his lyrical subjective period to his more universal meditative poetry. This detailed evaluation led to a well-reasoned textual reading of each poem. Nonetheless Fuenn's criticism tends toward undiscriminating generalizations and superlatives which were unsupported by a proper theoretical aesthetic foundation.

ENCOMIASTIC AND EPISTOLARY CRITICISM. Besides the satirical parodizing approach to book reviewing by Haskalah writers (mainly Perl and *Erter), literary appreciation also took the form of ornate encomiastic verse which praised the author and his work. This was in fact a continuation of the traditional *haskamah*. S.D. *Luzzato, A.D. Lebensohn, and J.L. *Gordon included such eulogies in their collected works and notwithstanding their florid style, these helped shape public opinion concerning the merit of certain works and authors.

While the value of this type of poetry was transitory, critical comments found in literary letters, written often for publication, helped shape contemporary taste. Among these are the letters of Samuel David Luzzatto and Judah Leib Gordon containing relevant critical remarks on their own works and that of their contemporaries. The normative approach to contemporary literature was also prevalent and Luzzatto for one, in discussing A.D. Lebensohn and Meir ha-Levi *Letteris, expressed strong views on the meter, rhyme, and ideas in their poetry.

"POSITIVIST SCHOOL." An important step in the development of literary criticism was the proliferation of the Hebrew press in Russia in the early 1860s. More liberal censorship regulations led to weekly publications. The unsigned short editorial review was very common in such periodicals as **Ha-Karmel* (1861–1879), **Ha-Ẓefirah* (1862–1931), and **Ha-Meliẓ* (1860–1904; and also in the **Ha-Maggid* 1856–1892), as was the topical article which related Hebrew literature to contemporaneous needs. The Hebrew press was also instrumental in disseminating the ideas of Russian positivist criticism of Vissarion G. Belinski and Dmitri I. Pisarev. Iconoclastic in character (major exponents were S.Y. *Abramovitsh (Mendel Mokher Seforim), A.U. *Kovner, A.J. Paperna), Hebrew criticism of the 1860s had revolted against the accepted aesthetic values of German neoclassicism and sentimentalism and had taken on more radical social orientation. Qualitatively (i.e., in the development of analytic and stylistic tools) it achieved little. Common to it was the polemical-sarcastic style, whose dominant feature was its concentration of inimical quotations, and the journalistic tendency to associate sociological matters with literary phenomena. Conversely, however, some critics of the group developed a distinctive personal approach.

UTILITARIAN-SOCIOLOGICAL TREND. With the appearance of A.U. Kovner (*Ḥeker Davar*, 1865 (first edition), *Ẓeror Peruḥim*, 1868) on the Jewish social and literary scene, a utilitarian-sociological trend developed whose aim was not only the evaluation of literature as such, but a social reformation of Russian Jewish life. The new ideas affected the choice of literary genres and critics began to express their reservations regarding poetry on biblical themes, preferring and encouraging literary vehicles such as social satire or the novel. Kovner developed the utilitarian tendency already formulated by some Haskalah authors. Challenging the accepted aesthetic concepts in Hebrew literature and rejecting its neoclassicist hypotheses, he distinguished between "idealist" and "realist" poets, as did his favorite Russian critic Pisarev. He strongly objected to the lofty and ornate style which he claimed had no real content, and called for the use of simple and natural language which would be intelligible to a wide reading public. As for the function of criticism, it should make bold demands, be unbiased, and not submit to conventional authority.

A.J. Paperna, Kovner's contemporary, was an even more fiery advocate of the didactic and theoretical approach to criticism. While fighting the uninspired and ornate conventions of the *meliẓah* poetry and condemning allegorical drama as obsolete (in his essays "*Kankan Ḥadash Male Yashan*," 1867; and "*Ha-Drama bi-Khelal ve-ha-Ivrit bi-Ferat*," 1868), he took great pains to enunciate the principles of literary theory to the Hebrew reader, and to define literary genres: epic, drama, and novel. His views were inspired mainly by the aesthetic theories of the Russian critic Belinski, but they were also rooted in classical aesthetics. Thus his demands for realism in Hebrew literature are aesthetically rather than socially motivated, forming criteria by which to measure the writer's creative talents.

M.L. Lilienblum's critical essays of the 1870s (and even of his Zionist period in the 1880s) were grounded in superficial positivism and utilitarianism in which ideological considerations led him to confuse literature with social pamphleteering. Reality was for him the sole criterion by which to arrive at "the truth of life." He judged Abraham *Mapu's novels accordingly and in his nationalist period criticized Judah Leib Gordon's poetry in the light of the "real" demands of the Ḥibbat Zion ideology as he understood them.

CULTURAL-HISTORICAL PERSPECTIVE. Simultaneously, the short newspaper article was also extensively cultivated. Its principal exponents were P. *Smolenskin, editor of **Ha-Shaḥar* (Vienna, 1869–1884), and J.L. Gordon, writing for the weekly *Ha-Meliẓ* (mainly in the 1880s). These reviews, not exclusively on belles lettres, reveal not only a great sensitivity to questions of language and style, but also a more balanced cultural-historical perspective regarding contemporary Hebrew literature. Neither Smolenskin nor Gordon spared those authors whom they considered undeserving. Smolenskin is sometimes apologetic as regards the achievement of the Hebrew language which he considers fundamental to the Jewish national culture. His literary tools are rather superficial, and his comparison of Hebrew works with world classics are sometimes unrealistic. His principles of literary criticism are expressed in his definition: "The ability to describe scenes which are real to life and a style both beautiful and vigorous."

Late 19th Century – The Limits of Hebrew Literature

During the sudden growth of Hebrew criticism in the 1890s, attention focused on the basic problems of Hebrew literature rather than on practical and detailed criticism of individual works. On the one hand, there was a call for a Hebrew artistic revival which would be close to European literature and on the other a hesitancy and a conservatism arising out of a concern for authenticity and for the national objectives of Hebrew literature.

AESTHETIC APPRECIATION FOR ITS OWN SAKE. Two principal figures of this trend were D. *Frischmann and R. *Brainin. David Frischmann declared his criterion to be personal talent and the refinement of aesthetic taste. He tried to realize his goals through a criticism which was essentially negative, resorting not only to irony but even to controversy. Discussing works which he liked, he took on a lyrical pathetic tone, however, which, at times, became even hackneyed. His preference for the feuilleton form (an aesthetically orientated literary column) affected his critical writing since the feuilleton by definition must be playful and humorous, maintaining contact with the reader and underscoring the presence of the author's personality. Frischmann's egocentric tendency was given further free play in his "Letters about Literature" which he wrote at various times. He was particularly skillful in portraying authors and in depicting characteristic elements in their works. The aesthetic notions which he so profusely advocated were, however, rarely implemented in his own articles.

Reuben Brainin, like Frischmann, based his call for a literary revival on criteria drawn from Western literature. But while his tone was egocentric, he lacked the lyrical sentimental and ironic refinement so characteristic of Frischmann. His essays, particularly those written toward the end of the 19th century under the influence of G. Brandes and J.A. Taine, stressed biographical detail and the impact which environment and background have on the literary work. Brainin, rooted in the spirit of European literature, drew his examples and metaphors from the natural sciences. Comparing Hebrew literature with world literature, he was pessimistic as to its possibilities. Like Frischmann, Brainin had a propensity for sketching portraits, interlacing these with memoirs and anecdotes designed to interest readers of Hebrew dailies which began to appear in 1886. Brainin, however, lacked the analytic ability of the practical critic who discusses and relates to the specific work. He was interested in the writer's personal image rather than the literary work under discussion. His detailed article on Mendele Mokher Seforim's works, written at the turn of the century, is illustrated by ample citations from Mendele's writings. Brainin pointed out that Mendele's recording of Jewish life in Russia was of documentary import. (Frischmann used the same approach when writing about Mendele some years later.)

This orientation toward world literature is more clearly manifest in the criticism of Nahum *Sokolow despite the fact that he wrote in a more traditional "Jewish" style. His article (written in the 1890s) on experiments in naturalism in the Hebrew short story is a case in point. Sokolow's discussion of Zola's literary method bears witness to his knowledge of contemporary world literature and his ability to apply it to his own criticism. He makes few pronunciamentos which call for the cultivation of ties with world literature; instead, he maintains these ties in reality.

THE AHAD HA-AM AND BERDYCZEWSKI CONTROVERSY. While the debate on the orientation of Hebrew literature toward universal culture appears in Frischmann's and Brainin's essays, it takes a more serious turn in the controversy between *Aḥad Ha-Am and the Ha-Ẓe'irim (The Young Writers) group, headed by Micha Josef *Berdyczewski, which was conducted mainly in the monthly *Ha-Shilo'aḥ* (1897–1926) at the end of the 19th century. Though the discussions did not contribute directly to the criticism of specific works, they gave it impetus and inspiration. Aḥad Ha-Am's utilitarian approach, which denies literature its autonomous status, was in consonance with a trend already existing in Hebrew criticism. He considered speculative writing of prime importance. In his view of the historical continuity of Jewish literature, literary form was the product of a nation's conceptual framework. Aḥad Ha-Am, striving "to unite poetry and thought," saw it as a medium through which the existential problems of the Jewish people could be expressed. Yet he did not disregard the quality of a work of art: Literary description, he felt, contributed to animation of thought and to fostering national consciousness.

The purpose of literary criticism was to examine the relation of man's spirit to truth, goodness, and beauty. Aḥad Ha-Am aimed at a harmony between the logical moral elements in literature and its aesthetic quality. Yet he arrived at the paradoxical conclusion that it was not necessary to fulfill aesthetic needs within the sphere of Hebrew literature. These standards he declared in defining the program of *Ha-Shilo'aḥ*, the literary journal he founded in 1896. Aḥad Ha-Am's preference for a literature of ideas rather than belles lettres reflects the doubts and the reservation of that epoch. Endowing his view of literature with a historic dimension, he claimed that the Jewish people was naturally inclined to ideas. His views were not superficially utilitarian and in fact he recognized the "beautiful" as a value in itself. He tended, however, to limit somewhat the space allocated to creative literature in *Ha-Shilo'aḥ*. Pointing to the pressing human needs of the Jewish people, Aḥad Ha-Am's antagonist, Berdyczewski, warned against the danger of separating Jewish and universal values in literature. He believed that the time had come for creating a literature which would also fulfill a historical need. In calling for the autonomy of all literature, which he groups under the title "poetry," his views also tend toward the idealistic-romantic. For a literary work to affect reality, the writer does not necessarily have to be inspired by contemporaneous social and historical problems; it is rather the work created in isolation and through the individual author's own motivation that influences. He negates the genetic approach in analyzing an author and his work. The appearance of an author on the literary scene he saw not as the result of development, but as a miracle and he attributed to chance the fact that writers exist in the same environment, creating side by side. Berdyczewski left his mark on Hebrew literary criticism also in his short reviews. Using primarily the illustrative method, he quotes extensively in order to stress and exemplify the essential elements in a work. His criticism, basically subjective, reflects his own spiritual and aesthetic world. While giving striking and concise definitions, Berdyczewski also tends toward biased exaggeration.

SYNTHETIC APPROACH. J. Klausner's approach to the relationship between Hebrew and world literatures is simplistic-synthetic and his comparisons between the works of Hebrew writers and other poets are superficial. He firmly advocated the harmonization of Jewish and universal values and propagated his philosophical principles in his literary criticism. Biographical information is one of the basic elements in his criticism and his critical remarks are substantiated by many textual examples. Though Klausner, unlike Aḥad Ha-Am, stressed the special place of modern Hebrew literature in the life of the people, his evaluations are of a didactic and pedagogic nature. They tend to appraise literary works – of the Haskalah and his own period – in terms of their contribution to the national Zionist movement. Occasional normative ideological demands on contemporary literature can also be found in his criticism.

Early 20th Century – Aesthetic and Ideological Concepts

Among the young critics at the turn of the century M.M. *Feitelson deserves mention. Influenced by Russian 19th-century criticism, his aesthetic criterion was the relationship of fiction to life itself, but he also represents the trend which called for the freeing of Hebrew literature from its conceptual relationship to social ideas. His contemporary I.E. Lubetzki (in his essays as yet not collected) took an even more extreme stand on this issue. He claimed that the critical discipline should not be governed by actual ideological demands and aesthetic criticism should not be concerned with the conceptual and moral aspect of the work. He spoke of the need for "artistic documents" and not for "human documents." In contrast to Frischmann's aesthetic demands characterized by the critic's subjective sentimental attitude, Lubetzki proposed objectivity and pertinent criteria, advocating what he called a "science of literature" as a critical criterion. Lubetzki, however, did not implement his own ideas in his critical writings; instead, like his predecessors, he drew superficial comparisons either between literary works or between authors. He elucidated details but was unable to evolve an analytical system. To clarify literary concepts, he drew on the terminology of painting and music, a method which could not lead him to the realization of his scientific ideal.

CRITICISM BY POETS AND WRITERS. Criticism written by poets and authors at the end of the 19th and beginning of the 20th centuries bears a special stamp. Subjective in its approach, it reflects the private world of the creative writer and his aesthetic concepts, and is lyrical and descriptive in style. The significance of this criticism lies in the fact that it is the product of the creative writer. To this category belong Berdyczewski's short, critical reviews mentioned above. *Bialik in his discussion on the development of Hebrew style and the essence of language points to the significant role played by Mendele Mokher Seforim and his successors in forging a new Hebrew prose. His treatment of the development of Hebrew poetry is not merely genetic but shows contemporary Hebrew literature to be an antithesis to earlier trends. In his article "*Shiratenu ha-Ẓe'irah*" ("On Our Young Poetry," in *Ha-Shilo'aḥ*, 16 (1906), 66–76), Bialik rebelled against the poetic and linguistic traditions of Hebrew poetry and hailed the generation of national renaissance. He acclaimed its outlook which sought to fuse the subjective and individualistic aims of the artist with the literary traditions and ideals of the nation. His many allusions to biblical and rabbinic sources often have a rhetorical reversal of meaning. They testify to his profound knowledge of tradition and to his fertile poetic imagination. Bialik also devotes special attention to the problems of literary creation, often projecting his own predicament as a poet. The relationship between author and language he sees as a dramatic struggle of the creative artist with formless matter. J. *Steinberg's literary essays, written in Ereẓ Israel mainly between the two world wars, sometimes appear similar to those written by Bialik. They, too, are highly sensitive to the problems of language and style, and insist upon verbal purism and idiomatic refinement. According to Steinberg, the essence of a work is to be found in the single syntactical unit which must be carefully scrutinized by the critic. While describing the atmosphere and the essence of the language of literature in general terms, Steinberg fails to deal with any specific work or text. At the same time, in his essays, he focuses mainly on the comprehensive phenomenon of contemporary Jewish culture and its historic roots. An interpenetration of literary criticism and fiction is reflected in Joseph Ḥayyim *Brenner's works. Literary criticism relevant to the actual situation sometimes motivates the plot of a story and in some of the introductions to his works, Brenner is ironically critical of his own literary manner but even more so of that of his contemporaries. Conversely, some of his critical and journalistic articles are written in fictional dialogue, thus expressing the author-critic's split personality, his inner conflicts and his fluctuation between hope and despair. Brenner's criticism is expressed in a variety of literary vehicles: the general review, criticism of one specific work, a general overview of all the aspects of an author's writings, and the lecture form. All of them are motivated by the wish to combine the social vision of the revival of the Jewish people and the normative aims of literature. In his attempt to remain faithful to his artistic ideals, Brenner seeks to establish a certain link between literary genres and historical and social conditions. Thus the truth of a work of art depends on the artistic integration of purpose and stylistic expression. His criticism encompasses both the moral teacher and the art critic, moralistic pathos and keen analytical ability which is expressed in an ironical-polemic style. Literature has socio-historical significance and reflects the changes taking place in Jewish society in modern times, but concurrently Brenner strives to uncover the aesthetic forces which go into creative art. This aim of reviving the Jewish people through literature did not always achieve full integration with the artistic ideal.

BEGINNINGS OF CRITICISM IN EREẒ ISRAEL. Brenner's literary activity is typical of the literary shift that occurred with the transfer of the literary center from Russia to Ereẓ Israel as far back as the Second Aliyah (prior to World War I). It served as a main link between the literary centers in the Diaspora and the new center evolving in Ereẓ Israel. This process is also reflected in the critical endeavors of Jacob *Rabinowitz, Jacob Steinberg, Shlomo *Zemach; and following World War I – Jacob *Fichmann, Fishel *Lachower, Joseph Klausner, and others. The immigration of authors and critics to Ereẓ Israel gave Hebrew criticism a special socio-national quality, though many of the critics preserved their individual character in their aesthetic and stylistic perceptions. The publication of critical articles (among them articles by Klausner, Lachower, and Fichmann) which had originally appeared in Russia were now presented to a new public in a new land and in a different historical context.

CRITICISM IN THE UNITED STATES. Parallel to the evolvement of the Ereẓ Israel center since the Third Aliyah (from the 1920s), a literary center evolved in the United States. Inspired by the national movement, the American critics followed the explanatory descriptive critical school (e.g., M. *Ribalow's and A. *Epstein's articles) reminiscent of Klausner, but they lacked his special personal and public pathos. At the same time, however, it introduced criticism of a more individualistic poetic nature by poets and writers (e.g., S. *Halkin and A. *Regelson during their American period and E. *Silberschlag and Y. Rabinowits). American Hebrew literary criticism, thematic in content, focused mainly on the specific manifestations and problems of Hebrew literature in the United States. This critical attitude was rooted in a wish to encourage the development of Hebrew literature in a foreign cultural environment. Concurrently, interest in world literature, hitherto hardly touched upon by Hebrew criticism, increased. Hebrew critics in the United States did not generally assimilate the methods of modern American criticism, but described in essay form Anglo-American artists, poets, and writers. World literature was analyzed and criticized for its own sake, and not only discussed by way of pronunciamentos and statements of principles.

EREẒ ISRAEL AFTER WORLD WAR I – OLD AND NEW CRITERIA. Hebrew criticism in Ereẓ Israel since the end of World War I in its method has been a continuation of the trends evolved at the beginning of the century, mainly because the same critics continued writing in the new center. Nevertheless, the critical essay has developed as a result of a further crystallization of the Hebrew language which allowed it to lend itself to the tools of modern study. Conversely, as a result of the remarkable growth of the Hebrew press, which served as a forum for the best critics, the brief critical article flourished. Research study of modern Hebrew literature, including different intermediate stages, ranging from the critical review to scholarly research, began in the 1930s. The polarity between the two domains reached its peak in the 1960s with the expansion of academic teaching of Hebrew literature and the persistent impetus of literary scholarly research in the world. Impressionist criticism continues to be one of the main trends, as does the tendency to regard the artistic creation as a continuation of the artist's life. The lines between poetic reality and actual reality are thus blurred and documentary elements are constantly looked for in the work of art under discussion. Accurate depiction thus becomes the artistic criterion. In contrast to this superficial realism there is conceptual criticism which seeks a common denominator for all the components in a work of art, while paying little attention to the influence of genre and style. As to method, there is on the one hand a tendency to deal with various literary components: characterization, description of nature, and conceptual goals, without exhaustively studying any one of them, and on the other hand use is made of examples, the choice of which is completely subjective, being in consonance with the critic's personal reading. Contrary to the above eclectic method, there is also a tendency to isolate each problem and discuss it without functional relation to the totality of the work. But even when discussing a single defined problem, the critic tends to arrive at a general evaluation of the work, thus reducing all the components to one essence. These trends are parallel, the critics stressing various aspects according to their inclinations, personal talents, and their ability to give their presentation and phrasing original expression. The critic's own personality counterweights the methodic weakness. The poet Jacob Fichmann, spanning the two periods and the two centers of Hebrew literature, was impressionistic in his criticism. He relates to works of art and authors not only by personal association, but also by examining the work in the light of its general significance. He usually describes the work as a whole, showing both sympathy and approval, and refrains from giving the author normative advice. In his essays, Fichmann developed a distinctive style, rich in description and lyrical metaphor, though lacking Bialik's force. Informative biographical elements and a general review of the work are woven into his personal impression of it. Fichmann's essays also possess a certain historical evolutionary dimension and include treatments of poets and novelists of the Haskalah period. He seeks to familiarize the reader with the authors' writings and their poetical value which extends beyond chronological and conceptual criteria. Fichmann's interpretations are generally impressionistic, derived at times from personal experience. He points out the mutual relationship between the critic-scholar and the critic-artist, thus advocating a synthesis between "scholarship and art." Impressionist criticism of this type is also to be found in the critical essays of Fichmann's contemporaries and disciples, but they lack his personal quality and status.

Mid-20th Century – New Perspectives

Hebrew criticism had a strong impetus in Ereẓ Israel in the 1940s. Critics who had started to write before World War I (e.g., S. Zemach, E. *Steinman, Y. *Keshet) had now attained original insight and had cultivated their own style. A number of new influential critics also appeared. D. *Sadan's analytical approach probed the hidden inner world of the author and of his work. He also underlined the recent tendency of extending the domain of Hebrew literature. At the same time, however, he emphasized its various ideological trends and the phenomenon of bilingualism as manifest in the mutual relation of Hebrew and Yiddish literatures. B. *Kurzweil sought to synthesize the intellectual sensitivity to the crisis of Judaism and to the shattering of the Jew's religious tradition in modern times with the artist's aesthetic formulation of this crisis through poetical and fictional symbols and motifs. S. Halkin continued to stress the significance of the secular-humanistic character of modern Hebrew literature. While discussing the author's individual poetical values, he pointed out their relation to trends and values current in Jewish society and emphasized their national pathos which formed a stimulating vehicle in Hebrew literature. A. *Kariv demanded a reevaluation of the literary heritage of European Hebrew literature, accusing its writers and proponents of having distorted in their writings East European Jewish life.

The increasing activity in criticism from the 1950s (after the War of Independence and the establishment of the State of Israel) underlines the tension between personal criticism in essay form and criticism based on scholarly criteria. Demands are made for the autonomous status of criticism as a special creative branch with its own distinctive characteristics extending beyond its interpretative task of "mediating" between the literary work and the reader (S. Zemach, I. *Cohen, and I. *Zmora). On the other hand, there are also normative trends attempting to direct literature from a spiritual and social point of view both as a creation of the contemporaneous generation and as the individual creation of the writer (A.Y. Kariv, A. *Ukhmani). Critics are also seeking to integrate the individualistic essay form, based on creative intuition, and literary analytical methods for examining the formal and literary qualities of a text. The search for such a methodical synthesis is variously approached in the critical works of S. Halkin, D. Sadan, and B. Kurzweil, who taught modern Hebrew literature at universities in Israel from the 1950s. The polarity between essay criticism and literary critical scholarship has intensified among the new generation of critics, most of whom have studied literature at the Hebrew University of Jerusalem. At first they had been influenced by the essay tradition and by the normative-existential trends which they had adopted in their debates on the literature of the post-War of Independence period. At the same time, however, they evinced a certain sensitivity to the social and cultural processes that formed the background to the development of Hebrew literature during the last few generations. But mainly they assimilated methods of textual explication of the New Criticism school current in English-speaking countries and adapted the interpretation systems of the postwar Swiss and German schools. There are also slight traces of the Russian formalism of the 1920s and the 1930s to be found in modern Hebrew literary criticism. These influences led to a special sensitivity to problems of form, rhetoric, and structure, and to the development of genres, while the conceptual and historic aspects have become secondary and marginal. At the same time, there is a tendency to consider exhaustively every problem through maximum use of the textual data.

The tendencies to break completely with traditional literary criticism are growing. At the same time two diverse domains – literary criticism and literary research or study – each based on different principles, are still crystallizing. The process has found expression in *Ha-Sifrut*, a periodical (edited by B. Hrushovsky) which by its own stated purposes, and in fact, is a "Quarterly for the Study of Literature."

[Samuel Werses]

The 1970s and After

In the late 1960s and early 1970s, Hebrew literary criticism was transformed by the inauguration of two new academic journals: *Ha-Sifrut* ("Literature"), which was founded in 1968–69 and published by Tel Aviv University under the editorship of Benjamin Hrushovsky, and *Bikoret u-Parshanut* ("Criticism and Interpretation"), published from 1970 on by Bar-Ilan University, originally under the editorship of Baruch Kurzweil. If literary criticism until then had appeared alongside poetry and short fiction in literary journals such as *Moznayim*, *Likrat*, and *Akhshav*, it was now upgraded to an academic discipline, empowered and sustained by the use of theoretical literary models and critical tools borrowed from other text-oriented disciplines. Not for naught did Hrushovsky introduce his journal as "the first of its kind in Hebrew," in that its role was to be "entirely of a scholarly nature." As he wrote: "The science of literature, as a systematic discipline that has developed a methodology and theory of its own, accumulated clusters of knowledge in various and distinct areas, and generated methods of academic research and instruction, is a relatively young discipline."

This conceptualization of criticism as a "science" and a "young discipline" stirred up a controversy within the literary and academic communities, of which Kurzweil was the most vocal mouthpiece. In the introduction to his own journal, Kurzweil attacked Hrushovsky for proclaiming innovation where there was none. "Critical reading" and "the art of reading" (as Kurzweil called it) had always employed the methods and the poetic, aesthetic, and interdisciplinary theories that the "innovative" terminology was claiming for the "literary theory" and "scientific writing" of the new discipline. Moreover, if, by speaking of the "scientific" nature of "literary theory," Hrushovsky was referring to objectivity in the interpretation, and hence to the evaluation of literary texts, this too was deceptive, since objectivity was not "within the confines of what is attainable in the humanities." This does not mean that there are no restraints to subjectivity in the scholarly study of literature, but they are set by other disciplines in the humanities.

This debate signaled the beginning of a "new age" in the history of Hebrew literary criticism in the State of Israel. From here on, Hebrew literary criticism took three parallel courses, aimed at different types of audiences or consumers of criticism. The first, as discussed above, was that of academic literary journals published by the literature departments of various universities. Their aim was initially to provide a publication venue for their own scholars, though other scholars of Hebrew literature were invited to contribute as well. Thus, for example, Ezra Fleischer, editor of *Meḥkarei Yerushalayim be-Sifrut Ivrit* ("Jerusalem Studies of Hebrew Literature"), addressed the readers of the first issue (1981) with the following words:

> This first volume ... contains articles written by academic staff members of the Department of Hebrew Literature at the Hebrew University of Jerusalem ... Its gates will be open to all those engaged in the study of Hebrew literature, in Israel and abroad.

The same year saw the founding of *Meḥkarei Yerushalayim be-Folklor Yehudi* ("Jerusalem Studies in Jewish Folklore") and *Meḥkarei Yerushalayim be-Maḥshevet Yisrael* ("Jerusalem Studies in Jewish Thought"). *Dappim le-Meḥkar be-Sifrut* ("Papers in Literary Research"), published by Haifa University, was launched in 1984; *Sadan: Meḥkarim be-Sifrut Ivrit* ("Anvil: Studies in Hebrew Literature"), published by the School of Jewish Studies and the Katz Institute at Tel Aviv University, in 1996; and *Mikan: Ketav Et le-Ḥeker ha-Sifrut ha-Ivrit* ("From Here: A Journal for the Study of Hebrew Literature"), published by Ben-Gurion University of the Negev, in 2000.

Along with these purely academic journals, a number of "mixed" periodicals, publishing both theoretical articles and literary works, began to appear. Some of these were issued with the assistance of educational institutions (universities or research institutes) or were edited by scholars. Among these are *Siman Keriah*: *Rivon Me'orav le- Sifrut* ("Bookmark, a Mixed Literary Quarterly," 1972); *Alei Si'aḥ*: *Ha-Ḥugim le-Sifrut Brit Tenu'at ha-Kibbuẓim* ("Leaves of Discourse of the Literary Circles of the Kibbutz Movement," New Series, 1974); *Zehut: Ketav-Et le-Yeẓirah Yehudit* ("Identity: A Journal of Jewish Creativity," 1981), later reconstituted as *Mahut* ("Essence, 1989); *Efes Shetayim: Ketav-Et le-Sifrut* ("02 [the Jerusalem Area Code]: A Journal of Literature," 1992); and *Reḥov: Ketav-Et le-Sifrut* ("Street: A Journal of Literature," 1994).

A further context that began to be associated with literary criticism in the mid-1980s was that of broader cultural critique. This association was indicative of an effort to break out of the ivory tower of solipsistic intra-disciplinary discussion and open up, by means of critical, theoretical tools, to the multicultural representations of contemporary reality. A prime example of this development is the journal *Te'oriyah u-Vikoret: Bamah Yisrelit* ("Theory and Criticism: An Israeli Forum"), published from 1991 by the Van Leer Institute in Jerusalem. The journal is devoted to reflexive, "interdisciplinary, systematic, and ongoing" discourse among scholars and writers within the academic world and outside of it, focusing on subjects from the realms of the "locale, society, and culture." Other such journals, with varying percentages of academic content, include *Alpayim le-Iyyun, Hagut ve-Sifrut* ("2000: A Journal of Inquiry, Thought, and Literature," 1989); *Dimu'i: le-Sifrut, Omanut, Bikoret ve-Tarbut Yehudit* ("Image: A Journal of Literature, Art, Criticism, and Jewish Culture," 1990); *Mikarov: le-Sifrut u-le-Tarbut* ("Close Up: A Journal of Literature and Culture," 1997); *Ha-Kivvun Mizraḥ: le-Tarbut u-le-Sifrut* ("Eastward: A Journal of Culture and Literature," 2000); *Keshet ha-Ḥadashah: le-Sifrut, Iyyun u-Vikoret* ("New Rainbow: A Journal of Literature, Inquiry, and Criticism," 2002); and *Mita'am: Ketav-Et le-Sifrut u-le-Maḥshavah Radikalit* ("On Behalf: A Journal of Radical Literature and Thought," 2005).

Meanwhile, non-scholarly literary criticism continued to be published in the weekend literary supplements of the daily newspapers and in the periodicals that carried on the tradition of the literary magazine, such as *Iton 77*: *Yarḥon le-Sifrut u-le-Tarbut* ("Journal 77: Monthly of Literature and Culture," 1977); *Apirion: le-Inyanei Sifrut, Tarbut ve-Ḥevrah* ("Canopy: A Journal of Literary, Cultural, and Social Affairs," 1983); *Pesifas: Itton le-Shirah u-le-Meida* ("Mosaic: A Journal of Poetry and Information," 1987); *Ẓafon* ("North"), published by the Association of Hebrew Writers, Haifa (1989); and *Gag* ("Roof"), published by the General Association of Writers in Israel (1998).

The third direction was the publication of reviews in the literary or cultural sections of weekday editions of the daily newspapers. Here critics do not necessarily seek to evaluate or judge a literary work, but rather to share with readers the experience of reading and the impressions a book leaves. This kind of personal critique ultimately became accepted as legitimate, and it contributed, among other things, to the introduction of the bestseller list in the back pages of *Sefarim Haaretz*, the weekly book review supplement (launched in 1994) of the daily newspaper *Haaretz*.

Mention should also be made of the Hebrew-language websites devoted to literary criticism which began cropping up in the mid-1990s. A plethora of articles and essays of varying levels of quality may be found on these sites, some of them run by individuals and others by discussion forums. In some, the articles undergo selection and editing, in others not. These sites are open to a wide range of writers who wish to share their impressions and evaluations of literary works, including scholars seeking a wider audience for their writings.

This array of critical writing with its multiple aspects and directions marks the last three decades of the 20th century, during which it has absorbed the deconstructivist trends as well as the postmodernist theories. The encounter of Israeli literary scholarship with postmodernist theories (drawn from the fields of history, political science, sociology, and cultural studies), and even more so with post-colonialist and post-Zionist theories, shook the hegemonic community of literary critics. It led to new, subversive readings of foundational literary texts, and also to the unearthing and examination of "other" texts, which the critical elite had for years pushed to the literary margins for lack of interest or appreciation. Moreover, together with its gradual permeation by postmodernist critical tools, Hebrew literary scholarship continued to surprise its readers with a steady stream of innovative interpretations arrived at by means of modernist scholarly approaches, in which discussion of the classics of modern Hebrew writing remained a central concern.

Thus, new critiques were written of works by those writers who had heralded the rebirth of modern Hebrew: Ḥ.N. Bialik (by Shmuel Werses, Dan Miron, Hillel Barzel, Menahem Perry, Adi Tzemach, Yitshak Bakon, Zvi Luz, Reuven Tzur, Ziva Shamir, Uzi Shavit); Shaul Tchernikhowsky (Yosef Haefrati, Boaz Arpaly, Uzi Shavit, Reuven Tzur, Haim Shoham); Micha Joseph Berdyczewsky (Shmuel Werses, Tzipora Kagan, Joseph Even, Avner Holtzman, Yitzhak Ben-Mordehai); Y.H. Brenner (Yitzhak Bakon, Menahem Brinker, Boaz Arpaly, Nurit Govrin, Ariel Hirschfeld, Adir Cohen); U.N. Gnessin (Dan Miron, Zvi Luz, Dan Laor, Hamutal Bar-Yosef); Gershon Shofman (Nurit Govrin); S.Y. Agnon (Shmuel Werses, Gershon Shaked, Hillel Barzel, Hillel Weiss, Dov Landau, Yitshak Bakon, Dan Miron, Aliza Shenhar, Dan Laor, Nitza Ben-Dov, Yehudith Zweig Halevi); and Devorah Baron (Nurit Govrin).

There were also new treatments of writers active in the period of the *Yishuv* between the two world wars: Uri Zvi Greenberg (Dan Miron, Yehudah Friedlander, Benjamin Hrushovsky, Hillel Barzel, Shalom Lindenbaum, Reuven Shoham, Dov Landau, Ortsion Bartana, Lilian Guri, Hannan Hever); Avraham Shlonsky (Israel Levin, Hagit Halperin, Aviezer Weiss, Abraham Hagorni-Green, Shlomo Yaniv); Nathan Alterman (Dan Miron, Uzi Shavit, Ziva Shamir, Aharon Komem, Ruth Kartun-Blum, Dan Laor, Haya Shaham, Shoshana Zimmerman); Lea Goldberg (Tuvia Rivner, Abraham B. Yaffe, Ruth Kartun-Blum, Ofra Yaglin); and Yonathan Ratosh (Ziva Shamir, Dan Laor). The works of writers who came of age in the 1940s, 1950s, and 1960s (known collectively as "Dor ba-Areẓ" and "Dor ha-Medinah") are nowadays also considered as classics and therefore are subjected to scholarly discussion and research: Yehuda Amiḥai (Boaz Arpaly, Nili Gold-Scharf, Yehudit Zweig-Halevi, Yosef Milman, Yair Mazor); Amalia Kahana-Carmon (Abraham Balaban, Lily Ratok, Yael Feldman); Aharon Appelfeld (Lily Ratok, Yigal Schwartz, Yitzhak Ben-Mordehai); Amos Oz (Nurit Gertz, Abraham Balaban, Yair Mazor); Abraham B. Yehoshua (Nili Sadan-Levenstein, Yedidiah Yitzhaki, Nitza Ben-Dov).

Israeli literary research has also been broadened by its extension to several genres (satire, drama, epistle), thematic and prosodic structures of the Hebrew literature of the Haskalah, the 18th and 19th century Jewish Enlightenment (Shmuel Werses, Yehudah Friedlander, Dan Miron, Uzi Shavit, Ben-Ami Feingold, Tovah Cohen, Yehudit Zweig-Halevi, Menuhah Gilboa, Reuven Shoham, Naomi Zohar, Iris Parush).

As mentioned above, suggestions emerged for culturally and politically subversive ways of reading. At the beginning of the 1970s, semiotic reading was in fashion (Itamar Even-Zohar, Nurit Gertz, Zohar Shavit, Ziva Ben-Porat), while from the end of the 1980s political reading was in the ascendant. The latter can be seen in Ḥannan Ḥever's analyses of Hebrew poetry between the two world wars, particularly of the work of Uri Zvi Greenberg. Other examples include Nissim Calderon's studies of writings from the 1950s and 1960s (by Natan Zach, Yaakov Shabtai, David Avidan, Dalia Ravikovich, Hanoch Levin, and others); Yohai Oppenheimer's post-colonial readings of several classic works of prose and poetry (by Moshe Smilansky, Avot Yeshurun, and Yehuda Amichai); and Michael Gluzman's political reading of the male national body in the writings of Moshe Shamir and Benjamin Ze'ev Herzl.

A further innovative form of scholarly inquiry impelled by these anti-hierarchical trends was that of feminist and gender critique. The steady flow of new writing by women was accompanied by a burst of feminist and gender research, which undertook the reevaluation of works written by women since the establishment of the state (Lily Ratok, Pnina Shirav, Yael Feldman) and also rediscovered forgotten troves of writings by women in Hebrew. These new studies made it clear that literary women had played their part in the rise of modern Hebrew literature, from the Enlightenment, through the period of *Ha-Teḥiyah* (in the late 19th and early 20th centuries), and in the pre-state period (Iris Parush, Tovah Cohen, Yaffah Berlovitz, Dan Miron), and had conceived poetic alternatives of their own. Further scholarly inquiries examined the themes and poetics of women's writings, as expressed in modernist and postmodernist poetry and prose (Lily Ratok, Hannah Naveh, Haya Shaham, Orly Lubin).

Various dates were celebrated during the 1980s and 1990s to mark a centennial of Zionist endeavor. Thus, 1982 represented "a century of settlement" from the beginning of the first wave of Zionist settlement in 1882, while 1997 concluded "a century of Zionism," recalling the First Zionist Congress (1897). Likewise, literary critics commemorated a century of Hebrew literature in transition from the Diaspora to the homeland of the Jewish people. This anniversary fueled the attempt to mark the borders of Israel's cumulative written creative activity, with the aim of summing up its literary manifestations and expressions. These interim assessments were meant to systematize and categorize what was known about the past and to offer some insight into the present. The period of summation opened with Gershon Shaked's comprehensive five-volume historiographical work, *Ha-Sipporet ha-Ivrit 1880–1980* ("Hebrew Prose from 1880 to 1980"). Hillel Barzel undertook a history of modern Hebrew poetry, from the period of Ḥibbat Zion to the present, of which six volumes have thus far appeared. A third representative of this effort, Hannan Hever's *Sifrut she-Nikhtevet Mikan: Kiẓẓur ha-Sifrut ha-Yisraelit* ("Literature Written from Here: A Compendium of Israeli Literature") offers a historical-cultural survey of 50 years of literary life in the State of Israel.

Alongside these monumental works, there have been several partial historiographies which have endeavored to chart literary developments, processes, and trends, particularly since the establishment of the State, in the realms of drama (Haim Shoham, Gideon Shunami, Ben-Ami Feingold, Gideon Ofrat, Shimon Levi, Abraham Oz, Dan Oryan), poetry (Benjamin Hrushovsky, Dan Miron, Dov Landau, Aharon Komem, Yair Mazor, Reuven Shoham, Yehudith Bar-El, Rachel Weissbord), and prose (Shmuel Werses, Dan Miron, Hillel Barzel, Hannah Herzig, Hillel Weiss). The same has been done for the country's literary and cultural life, in the 50 years preceding the establishment of the state (Itamar Even-Zohar, Yaffah Berlovitz), in the first few decades of the 20th century (Zohar Shavit, Nurit Gertz, Avidov Lipsker), and in literary circles (in the 1940s, 1950s) like the Dor Ba-Areẓ group (Nurit Graetz, Hillel Weiss, Reuven Kritz) and the "Canaanites" (Nurit Gertz, Dan Laor).

This process of collection and discovery also posed the challenge of examining the writings of hitherto neglected literary schools, such as Ha-Mahalakh ha-Ḥadash ("New Course"; Joseph Even, Menuhah Gilboa) and the literature of the First Aliyah (Nurit Govrin, Yaffah Berlovitz).

The effort to summarize and categorize a century of modern Hebrew literature also brought forth the publication of numerous monographs on writers of both the early and later periods. Zvi Luz issued a series of monographs on poets, including half-forgotten ones from the pre-state period (Yosef Zvi Rimon, Jacob Fichman, Jacob Steinberg) and others from the periods of Dor Ba-Areẓ (Pinchas Sadeh, Ayin Hillel, Natan Yonatan, Ozer Rabin) and Dor ha-Medinah (Uri Bernstein). Additional monographs worth mentioning in this context are those of Aharon Komem (on David Fogel and Jacob Steinberg), Hannan Hever (on Avraham Ben-Yitzhak Sonne), Ruth Kartun-Blum (on Yocheved Bat-Miriam), Hamutal Bar-Yoseph (on Zelda), Reuven Shoham (on Esther Raab and Abba Kovner), Rachel Frankel Madan (on Jacob Horowitz), and Reuven Kritz (on Rachel Blaustein).

Special mention must be made here of the colossal opus of Dan Miron. Though he has not organized his studies as an ordered historiography, there is no period of modern Hebrew literature, from the Enlightenment through post-modernity, in poetry and in prose, to which he has not turned his scholarly attention (see his studies of such writers as Abraham Mapu, Mendele Mokher Seforim (Shalom Jacob Abramowitsch), Ḥayyim Naḥman Bialik, Uri Nissan Gnessin, Shmuel Yosef Agnon, Ḥayyim Hazaz, Nathan Alterman). Miron has also collected and edited the writings of a number of authors from different periods, adding his own comprehensive introductions and afterwords (as he has done for the writings of Yehudah Karni, Uri Zvi Greenberg, Abraham Halfi, Menashe Levine, K. Aharon Bertini, Ya'akov Orland, and Abba Kovner).

Most of these efforts to collect and summarize, on the one hand, and to open new avenues of research, on the other, were the initiatives of lecturers and scholars of literature at various institutions of higher education in Israel, made for the purpose of preparing textbooks and further reading materials for their students. These instructional aims led them to issue studies of foundational issues, such as genres (the ballad, by Shlomo Yaniv; fantasy, by Ortsion Bartana; the allegory, by Uri Shoam; utopia, by Leah Hadomi; the confession, by Hannah Naveh; the historical novel, by Ruth Sheinfeld; the idyll, by Joseph Ha'efrati, Hamutal Bar-Yosef, Rachel Frankel-Madan); literary schools (the neo-romantics, by Ortsion Bartana; decadence, by Hamutal Bar-Yosef); and prosody (Bejamin Hrushovsky, Uzi Shavit, Dov Landau, Reuven Tsur, Zvi Luz, Ziva Ben-Porat).

Further concerns of theme and genre that came in for scholarly attention at the end of the century include the literature of the Holocaust (Hannah Yaoz-Kest, Hillel Barzel, Dov Landau, Nurit Graetz, Ben-Ami Feingold, Ruth Sheinfeld, Avner Holtzman, Yitzhak Ben-Mordechai, Yigal Schwartz) and that of the labor and kibbutz movements (Leah Hadomi, Shula Keshet, Pinhas Genosar, Aviva Ufaz). Research on literature for children and young people also developed during this period, with the opening of departments at several universities and colleges and the work of various scholars (Adir Cohen, Aliza Shenhar, Zohar Shavit, Miri Baruch, Maya Fruchtman, Menahem Regev, Shlomo Harel, Menuhah Gilboa, Leah Hovav, Aviva Krinsky, Meira Karmi-Laniado, Ben-Ami Feingold, Bosmat Even-Zohar, Yael Dar). New journals focusing on the study of literature for young readers include:

Sifrut Yeladim va-No'ar ("Literature for Children and Youth"); *Be'emet?* ("Really?"); *Olam Katan: Le-Ḥeker Sifrut Yeladim ve-No'ar* ("Small World: A Journal for the Study of Literature for Children and Youth").

The publication of anthologies was also on the increase towards the end of the century. These include anthologies of critical articles and studies of Hebrew literature based on conference papers and edited by faculty members of literature departments; and collections devoted to the critique of single literary works, such as Shaul Tchernikhowsky's corona of sonnets, *La-Shemesh* ("To the Sun"); the short story *Ve-Haya he-Akov le-Mishor* ("The Crooked Shall Be Made Straight") by Shmuel Yosef Agnon; and Abraham B. Yehoshua's novel *Mar Mani*.

[Yaffah Berlovitz (2nd ed.)]

TRANSLATIONS OF HEBREW LITERATURE

The translation of Hebrew literature into foreign languages involves a number of unique problems; some are specific to the art of translation while others concern the publishing, marketing, and diffusion of a translated work. Translation from one European language to another is no small task, despite common linguistic and cultural features. Translation from Hebrew – a Semitic language – into a European language is even more difficult: the entire range of literary associations and cultural realia that in fact provide the literary flavor of the original work can rarely be rendered as is. Echoes of biblical or mishnaic Hebrew, or from the wealth of Jewish liturgy, can hardly be captured, and significant details of the Israeli everyday scene often require footnotes or clumsy explanations. Given these obstacles, literary translations from Hebrew sometimes reflect a variety of compromises and conflicting solutions. It is even difficult to evaluate the quality of a translation, and a number of experts checking a translation for its accuracy and literary value in the target language will generate an equal number of different views. Even so, an excellent translation is considered one that is as close to the original Hebrew as possible, while reading smoothly in the target language and conveying as much as possible of the original texture, music, and diverse layers of linguistic and cultural sources. In recent years, an excellent team of literary translators from Hebrew has crystallized and their highly professional work is the main reason for the outstanding reception of Hebrew literature in translation since the 1990s, mainly in European languages.

The international publishing marketplace provides another angle to the difficulty of introducing Hebrew literature to world readership. Given the limited audience in the writers' mother tongue – Israel has a population of 6.8 million – they naturally seek to expand it. And while authors in general want to be translated into foreign languages, for authors writing in Hebrew it is a must. On the other hand, whereas foreign colleagues writing in a widely known language may submit their work to a publisher in the original, Israeli authors are unable to do so because of the lack of competent readers in Hebrew at the disposal of foreign publishing firms. Even when a Hebrew title is highly recommended by Hebrew lectors or attracts international attention, the publisher – especially in English-speaking countries – will generally refrain from a commitment to publish before he receives a complete English translation of the work. Synopses and translated extracts may draw his attention to the book, but it will not necessarily generate a decision to publish. This applies primarily to authors who have already made their reputation in Israel but have yet to make their mark on the international scene. Thus a Hebrew author has to find a qualified translator into English, pay his fee, and prepare a synopsis – without any guarantee that the English translation will arouse genuine interest, and without even knowing whether his efforts will result in an offer to publish the translation.

Publication of translations in other languages is more complicated as the publisher must invest considerable sums in a translation, hence the decision process becomes longer and more complicated. The Institute for the Translation of Hebrew Literature, a non-profit organization founded in 1962, has been entrusted by the Israeli government with the task of promoting Hebrew literature in translation worldwide. It is responsible for a wide range of activities, such as commissioning translations of selected Hebrew literary works, publishing professional catalogues which introduce the titles, providing financial aid to foreign publishers who initiate publication of Hebrew works in translation, publishing a literary journal in English – *Modern Hebrew Literature* – which keeps the foreign reader abreast of the literary scene in Israel, building and maintaining an attractive website, initiating international translation conferences, participating in selected international book fairs. The Institute also maintains a unique Bibliographic Center. Established in 1972, its database lists all translations of Hebrew literature in 66 languages (over 45,000 bibliographic entries).

In recent years, the Institute for the Translation of Hebrew Literature has become more attentive to the buzz of the marketplace, hence a significant rise in the number of Hebrew authors and works in translation, and in the variety of languages in which Hebrew literature has become available.

Facts and Figures

From 1874 to 1974 (100 years), some 500 Hebrew books were published in translation. From 1975 to 2004 (30 years), we see this number increased to about 3,460. Today, the total number of books published in translation exceeds 4,000. The first Hebrew novel in translation was *The Love of Zion* by Abraham Mapu, published in Yiddish in 1874. From then until 1960, an average of five books were published per year. As of the 1960s, figures increased to 27 books per year. During the 1970s, Hebrew literature was translated into 25 languages, and this grew to 40 languages during the 1980s. Today, the number stands at 66 languages. If we compare the figures in the decade 1983–93 to those in the following decade, 1994–2004, we see that the number of books in translation increased from 956 to 1,743.

Furthermore, in certain languages the number of books has increased very significantly. Taking the same two 10-year periods: English increased from 346 books to 396 (+12%); German increased from 185 to 405 (+116%); Italian increased from 39 to 165 books (+350%); French from 107 to 158 (+40%); Spanish from 49 to 87 (+70%); Dutch from 63 to 98 (+50%). Today, nearly 60 Hebrew authors have been published in book form in more than five foreign languages – 20 authors have been published in more than 10 languages, and among these, three have been published in over 30 languages: Amos Oz, Ephraim Kishon, and Uri Orlev.

Translations of Books for Children and Youth

Hebrew literature for children and youth started appearing in translation only in the 1930s: English and German in 1936, French in 1946, Spanish in 1949, Italian in 1958. Translations into Arabic started to be published only in 1966. The largest number of children's books is now being translated into German, with 129 books to date, followed by English with 76, Italian with 50, Spanish with 38, Dutch with 30, Arabic with 29. One tends to assume that interest in adult fiction in a certain foreign market will arouse interest in children's books as well, that a writer of adult fiction who does well in a certain market will have his children's books published there too and that this will bring about more and more translations of other authors. But this is not entirely the case. If we compare the number of adult versus children's books translated over the past two 10-year periods (1983–93 and 1994–2004) we get the following results: In English, in the first 10-year period, children's books made up 6% of the total number of translated books; in the second, the percentage rises to 15%. In German, the percentage has not changed over the past 20 years, and stands at a steady 21%. Spanish increased from 6% to 29%, and Italian from 12% to 27%. As a point of reference, in Israel today, Hebrew books for children and youth constitute about 5% of the total published per year. Hebrew literature for children is now available in book form in 42 languages, 34 of which have been added since 1975. To the earlier eight languages (English, German, Dutch, French, Spanish, Italian, Polish, and Arabic), the following have been added: Afrikaans, Albanian, Asamiya, Bangla, Catalan, Chinese, Czech, Danish, Estonian, Finnish, Greek, Guajarati, Hindi, Hungarian, Japanese, Kannada, Korean, Malayalam, Marathi, Norwegian, Portuguese, Punjabi, Romanian, Russian, Serbian, Slovak, Slovene, Swedish, Tamil, Thai, Telugu, Turkish, Ukrainian, Urdu.

Translations into Arabic

Although literary translation activity from Hebrew into Arabic has developed over the years, it has been overshadowed by the political conflict in the Middle East. This conflict has influenced translation policy in the Arab countries as well as in Israel. The first novel translated from Hebrew into Arabic was Abraham Mapu's *The Love of Zion* (1899). A limited number of translations followed, until 1948. Between 1948 and 1967, translations were mostly published in newspapers and periodicals but a few books were published too, such as Yehuda Burla's novel, *In Darkness Striving*, an anthology of short stories, and a collection of works by Ḥ.N. Bialik. Publication of literary research and translated literary texts emerged in Arab countries only towards the end of the 1960s. A significant increase in number and frequency can be detected from 1967 up to the present. Records reflect some 80 translated books and 21 anthologies published during this period in Israel and Arab countries (mainly Egypt, Jordan, Lebanon, and Syria).

Translation into Special Languages

With the general flourishing of Hebrew literature abroad in the 1990s, new markets have opened up for Hebrew literature, and newly added languages have reflected the growing interest. Since 1990, 57 literary works have been published in Chinese, 63 in Japanese, 25 in Korean, and a few in each of the following: Georgian, Azeri, Armenian, Thai, Assamiya, Bongla, Gujarati, Marathi, Malayalam, Punjabi, Tamil, Telugu, Hindi, Kannada, Urdu. This wave of interest is still developing.

Anthologies and Special Journal Issues on Hebrew Literature

Anthologies and special issues of literary journals are considered to be the best way to enter a new market. Anthologies provide a taste of Hebrew literature and are bound, in the longer term, to generate interest in publishing whole books by the authors introduced in the general anthology. Special literary issues have an even better marketing effect as they usually have their own subscription system and the print run – normally a few thousand – can reach a focused readership which is a priori interested in quality foreign literature. Records show that some 428 anthologies of Hebrew literature are available in 40 languages. Among them, 162 volumes in English, 41 in French, 30 in Spanish, 28 in German, 26 in Russian, 25 in Italian. 105 anthologies were published between 1983 and 1993; in the 1994–2004 period, the number increased to 163 volumes.

All the above statistical data is from the Bibliographic Database of the Institute for the Translation of Hebrew Literature. Figures include whole books and anthologies only; individual poems and stories are not included.

[Nilli Cohen (2nd ed.)]

HEBREW LITERATURE IN THE UNITED STATES

Hebrew writing began in the United States shortly after the arrival of the first Jews in New Amsterdam (1654), but the period of modern Hebrew literature only starts after 1870 when Hebrew writers came to America during the mass immigration from Eastern Europe. They settled mainly in New York and between 1918 and 1940 the city served as a subcenter for modern Hebrew literature. Despite their efforts, the immigrant writers were unable to raise a generation of native American Hebrew authors and the older writers are not being replaced. The rapidly growing center in Israel likewise attracted several of the more talented authors. At present a small, diminishing group of aging Hebrew writers are living in the United States.

Hebrew writing in the United States may be divided into three periods:

I. 1654–1870 – the period of sporadic publication and literary curiosities

II. 1870–1918 – the early modern period

III. 1918–to the present – the modern period

Sporadic Publication and Literary Curiosities (1654–1870)

During the first two centuries of Jewish settlement in North America no major contribution was made to Hebrew letters. The Jewish population was small and unlearned in Hebrew. Sporadic attempts were, however, made to write and publish Hebrew works; and mention must be made of literary curiosities which have survived, such as the unpublished nomenclature by Judah *Monis, a converted Jew who taught Hebrew at Harvard College, and tombstone inscriptions: the elegy to Walter J. Judah who died in 1798 at the age of 20, or the rhymed epitaph on the grave of Samuel Zanvill Levy of New York City. Hebrew language and literature were also kept alive through publications of the Bible and works on Hebrew grammar. The latter were written both by Jews and by gentiles. A publication of the Bible, initiated by Jonathan P. *Horwitz of Philadelphia and continued by Thomas Dobson, appeared in 1814 and a Hebrew-English edition of the Pentateuch by Isaac *Leeser in 1845. Among the works on grammar there is John Smith's *A Hebrew Grammar Without Points* (Boston, 1803), Moses Stuart's *A Grammar of the Hebrew Language* (1835), and Isaac Nordheimer's *A Critical Grammar of the Hebrew Language* (New York, 1838; 1842).

Certain congregations showed a deep concern for the preservation of Hebrew as a language among Jews and for a sound Hebrew education. The New York synagogue Shearith Israel as early as 1731 "maintained some sort of Jewish schooling," and its constitution (1805) provides that "the fixed prayers shall forever be read in the Hebrew language." In 1830, Dr. Daniel L. Maduro Peixotto (1799–1843), a physician who favored the establishment of a Pestalozzi school, recommended that Hebrew should be taught there. These, however, can only be seen as isolated efforts which did not greatly influence the general Jewish cultural atmosphere in colonial America and in the early years of independence. Hebrew was so little known in the community at large that in Newport, toward the end of the 18th century, the Torah was read from a printed, vocalized text and not from a scroll.

Joshua Falk's *Avnei Yehoshu'a* ("Book of the Stones of Joshua," 1860), the first original work in Hebrew published in the United States, is a homiletic commentary on *Pirkei Avot* which also includes the classical text.

The Early Modern Period (1870–1918)

With the coming of large numbers of East European Jews to America, the influence of European Hebrew writing began to be felt. A small group of Hebraists who wanted to spread Hebrew culture made efforts to establish a Hebrew press. In a period of less than 30 years, 20 Hebrew journals appeared, most of which, however, were short lived, mainly because there was no receptive readership. The number of Jews conversant in Hebrew was limited despite the large waves of immigrants from Eastern Europe. The first independent Hebrew periodical, *Ha-Ẓofeh ba-Areẓ ha-Ḥadashah*, edited by Zvi Hirsch *Bernstein, appeared from 1871 to 1872. It slavishly followed the style and tone of contemporaneous East European Hebrew journals and, to a certain extent, the Anglo-Jewish press in America which had much earlier beginnings (1823). Unfortunately, no complete set of its issues has survived. Other major Hebrew periodicals during that period were *Ner Ma'aravi* (1895–97) and *Ha-Pisgah* (1889–1899 intermittently), which were of a high literary and journalistic standard, aroused hopes for a Hebrew renascence in America. *Ner Ma'aravi* in its first issue published a poem expressing the ardent longing for the development of Hebrew learning and Hebrew literature. *Ha-Pisgah*, edited by Zeev Wolf Schorr, an ardent lover of Zion, firmly tried to stimulate interest in Hebrew culture, and writers of the caliber of Saul *Tchernichowsky contributed to its literary columns.

Most of the periodicals of the early 20th century, like *Ha-Yom* (1909–13) and *Ha-Le'om* (1901–08), were close in style and character to their predecessors. Not until the appearance of *Ha-Toren* (as a monthly June, 1913–December, 1915; as a weekly March 3, 1916–March 18, 1921; as a monthly again May 1921–December 1925) did a real literary organ appear on the North American scene. But even *ha-Toren* did not rise to its full stature before the end of World War I, for there were not many good Hebrew writers, readers were not numerous, and libraries of Judaica and Hebraica were meager and, with few exceptions, insignificant.

Many of the American Hebrew writers were of East European origin and they were intensely patriotic about their new country. Judah David *Eisenstein translated the Declaration of Independence and the Constitution of the United States into Hebrew. Moses Aaron Schreiber, cantor of the Congregation Shaarey Tefila in New York, wrote a long poem, *Minḥat Yehudah* ("Offering of Judah"), for the centennial of American Independence (1876). The poem is a historical account of the American people and describes the mass of stricken humanity that surged to the shores of America. Abraham Luria dedicated a poem to President McKinley.

The fabric of traditional Jewish life changed under the impact of America; rabbinic responsa are flooded with names of towns in the United States. Questions on ritual from Kalamazoo and Leavenworth found their erudite answers in a halakhic work by Shalom Elḥanan Joffe, *Sho'el ka-Inyan* ("Asking to the Point"), which was published in Jerusalem in 1895.

Early American Hebrew writers were not uncritical of the American milieu: its vulgarism, optimism, its predilection for shallow panacea. Their denunciation of internal squabbles and communal ills was particularly keen. They were conscious of the effects of the democratization of society, the attendant ills of the leveling process, and they deplored the organized chaos in Jewish organizations. They could not reconcile themselves to the fact that stature and status were no longer coincidental.

The Jewish *Kulturkampf* was fought out with an intense bitterness in the United States. The war between the Reform and the Orthodox aroused Mayer Rabinowitz to publish *Ha-Maḥanayim* ("The Two Camps," 1888). Abraham Moses Shershevsky, rabbi in Portland, Maine, at the turn of the century lashed out against American Jewry:

"Just as our forefathers… crossed the sea and made the Golden Calf, so do their sons after them in this country; after they crossed the Atlantic, they bowed and prostrated themselves before the Golden Calf."

The Golden Calf became a standard metaphor. The poet Menahem Mendel *Dolitzki used it in his introduction to *Shirei Menaḥem* (1900), while another early author complains: "The basis of all things in America is the dollar… it's the method, it's the aim, it's the glory, it's the power…" Most Hebrew writers earned a precarious living. They were rabbis, teachers, or cantors. Some who were not fortunate enough to gain a livelihood as religious functionaries became peddlers. They never acquired wealth or even economic security.

Though American Hebrew literature cannot boast of a single drama or a single novel of importance at the beginning of the 20th century, two writers, Naphtali Herz *Imber and Gerson *Rosenzweig, exhibit a marked individuality. Imber, who became immortalized with the composition of *Ha-Tikvah*, the anthem of the Zionist movement and of the State of Israel, made an impact with his delicate lyricism. A note of mordant wit was injected into Hebrew literature by Rosenzweig with his merciless castigation of Jewish professions and occupations in the United States.

After World War I

The end of World War I marked an important milestone in the development of Hebrew literature. Eastern Europe, the center of creative efforts in the Hebrew language for over a century, relinquished its hegemony: The Communist Revolution had relegated Hebrew literature in Russia into insignificance and with the rise of the Nazis to power the splinter center of Hebrew literature which flourished in Germany after the end of World War I was destroyed. The Nazi occupation of Poland almost obliterated creative Hebrew writing there. The previously insignificant foci of Hebrew literature in Palestine and in the United States thus emerged to new significance.

Anglo-American literature which had exerted a negligible influence before World War I now became a potent factor in Hebrew literature. Hebrew poets in America – B. *Silkiner, E.E. *Lisitzky, H. *Bavli, S. *Ginzburg, S. *Halkin, A. *Regelson, M. *Feinstein, H.A. *Friedland, R. *Avinoam (Grossman), A.S. *Schwartz, and Noah *Stern – were not only stimulated by the literary environment of the United States but translated English and American poetry, and even prose and drama, into Hebrew. They translated several plays by Shakespeare; Walt Whitman's *Leaves of Grass* (transl. by S. Halkin *Alei Esev* (1952)); and many poems by Keats, Shelley, Yeats, and Frost.

The Hebrew poets in America led their European colleagues in critical appraisal of English and American literature, thus opening new vistas for modern Hebrew literature. Their subject matter was also drawn from the American milieu. Benjamin Silkiner (1882–1933) turned to Indian lore for his inspiration in *Mul Ohel Timmorah* ("Opposite the Tent of Timorah," 1910). He was followed by other poets. Israel *Efros devoted an entire book, *Vigvammim Shotekim* ("Silent Wigwams," 1933), to a love story of a white man and a half-Indian girl. Ephraim E. Lisitzky wrote his *Medurot Do'akhot* ("Dying Campfires," 1937) on the basis of Indian legends. Like Silkiner, he struggled with the theme of Indian civilization before its destruction, and like the older poet he tended to idealize the noble savage. Unlike Silkiner, he successfully adapted the unrhymed trochaic tetrameter of *The Song of Hiawatha* to his story of the warring sons of the vulture and sons of the serpent.

The greatest impact on Hebrew writers in America was, however, made by the Afro-American civilization: spirituals, folk songs, sermons, and the Afro-American sense of rhythm and flair for music. Hillel Bavli, in his critical article which included translations from Afro-American poetry, pioneered in the field of critical appreciation of the Afro-American. He was followed by Avinoam (Grossman), Simon Ginzburg, and, especially, by Lisitzky, who published a cycle of poems on Afro-American themes: *Be-Oholei Kush* ("In African Tents," 1953). Not only the exotic minorities but the American Anglo-Saxon caught the imagination of Hebrew writers in the U.S. Hillel Bavli's idyll *Mrs. Woods* (1937) is an American version of the idealized country folk. Israel Efros in his narrative poem "*Zahav*" ("Gold") created an American character, Ezra Lunt, against the background of the gold rush of 1849. Stories about Jewish immigrants and American gentiles were written by such writers as Y.D. *Berkowitz, H. *Sackler, H.A. Friedland, A. Soyer, S.L. *Blank, Y. *Twersky, S. Halkin, and R. *Wallenrod. Yitzḥak Dov Berkowitz in his stories about American Jewish life wrote almost exclusively about immigrants. *Ben Ereẓ ve-Shamayim* ("Between Earth and Heaven," 1924), a novel by Harry Sackler, traces the history of an immigrant family from the time it planned to come to the United States to its painful years of adjustment. He also wrote historical novels which depict the struggles of early Judaism against a Canaanite milieu, the conflicts of rabbinic and ḥasidic Jewry, and the strife of early American Jewry with its new environment. Like Sackler, Yoḥanan Twersky culled from the past and present material for his stories and novels. Among these are historical personalities such as Rashi, Uriel da Costa, Alfred Dreyfus, and Aḥad Ha-Am. Simon Halkin, on the other hand, tends to be introspective. The two novels, *Yeḥiel ha-Hagri* (1928) and *Ad Mashber* ("On the Brink of Crisis," 1945), set in a New York immigrant milieu, are essentially religious novels whose theme is the quest of modern man for faith in a society which has lost its God. Reuben Wallenrod deliberately abandoned the old themes and consciously and realistically explored the life of the first- and second-generation Jew in

America. Daniel *Persky, who for many years wrote a weekly humorous column in *Hadoar*, promoted Hebrew language and literature in the U.S.

Among the more significant literary critics of the older generation are A.A. *Epstein, whose *Soferim Ivrim ba-Amerikah* ("Hebrew Writers in America," 1953) is still a standard work, Menachem *Ribalow, and S. Halkin. Three periodicals of the 20th century fostered high-level essays and critiques of Hebrew and non-Hebrew writing: *Miklat* (1920–21), *Ha-Toren* (1917–25), and *Ha-Tekufah* (1930–31). They became defunct, but periodicals like *Hadoar* and *Bitzaron*, which began to appear in 1922 and 1940 respectively, still publish criticism. *Hadoar* owes its original impetus to Ribalow, an excellent journalist and a serious critic, who was succeeded by M. *Maisels; and *Bitzaron* to the learned and dynamic Rav Tzair (Ḥayyim *Tchernowitz). These periodicals, particularly *Hadoar*, were supported by a small group of enthusiastic Hebraists. Hebrew journalism in the U.S. is greatly indebted to Reuben *Brainin and Y.D. Berkowitz, the editors of *Ha-Toren* and *Miklat* respectively. The future historian will, perhaps, recognize the Berkowitz/Brainin/Silkiner triad as the fathers of Hebrew literature in the U.S.: Berkowitz as the Hebrew stylist and realist, Brainin as the champion of catholicity and literary tastes, and Silkiner as the author who introduced American themes and motifs into Hebrew literature.

On the whole, Hebrew literature in America became less potent. Gabriel *Preil, a modernist lyric poet influenced by American imagists, also won acclaim in Israel. Isaiah *Rabinovich continued to write serious criticism which questions the growing tendency of some Israeli critics to apply the methods of New Criticism to Hebrew literature. Arnold (Avraham) Band (1929–) published a major work on S.Y. Agnon. Aaron *Zeitlin, who arrived in the Unites States in 1939, expressed himself with equal ease in Hebrew and in Yiddish in a number of genres. His poetry is reflective and marked by mystical insights.

A number of American-Hebrew writers settled in Israel. S. Halkin and A. Regelson, although born in Eastern Europe, were educated in the United States and their poetry and criticism reflected their American experience. M. Maisels was an essayist and editor of considerable talent. Reuven Avinoam and T. Carmi were native Americans who spent most of their lives in Israel.

There seems to be little prospect that Hebrew writing in America will recover the force it had in its heyday. A small center, however, mainly nurtured by Israelis living in America and a limited American audience will probably survive.

For English translations of Hebrew works, see Goell, Bibliography.

[Eisig Silberschlag]

BIBLIOGRAPHY: Klausner: *Sifrut;* B. Kurzweil, *Sifrutenu ha-Ḥadashah: Hemshekh o Mahapekha?* (1959), Lachower, *Sifrut*; A. Shaanan, *Ha-Sifrut ha-'Ivrit*, 4 vols. (1962–1967); D. Sadan, *'Al Sifrutenu (*1950); H.N. Shapiro, *Toledot ha-Sifrut ha'Ivrit ha-Ḥadashah* (1940); S. Halkin, *Modern Hebrew Literature* (1950); Idem, *Derakhim ve-Ẓide Derakhim be-Sifrut*, 3 vols. (1969); S. Spiegel, *Hebrew Reborn* (1962); Waxman, *Literature*, 3–5 (1960); R. Wallenrod, *Literature of Modern Israel* (1956), inc. Bibl; N. Slouschz, *Renascence of Hebrew Literature* (1909). **ADD. BIBLIOGRAPHY:** D. Miron, *Modern Hebrew Literature: Zionist Perspectives and Israeli Realities*, in: *Prooftexts* 4, 1 (1984), 46–69; A.J. Band, "The Beginnings of modern Hebrew Literature," in: *AJS Review*, 13:1–2 (1988), 1–26; L.Yudkin, "The Specific Character of Modern Hebrew Literature," in: *Modern Hebrew Literature in English Translation* (1987), 97–118; D. Patterson, "The Emergence of Modern Hebrew Literature," in: *A Phoenix in Fetters* (1988), 1–20; G. Shaked, "Breaking the Mould: The Maturing of Hebrew Literature," in: *Terms of Survival* (1995), 385–411; Amos Oz, "Contemporary Hebrew Literature," in: *Partisan Review*, 49:1 (1982), 16–22; G. Shaked, *Ha-Sipporet ha-Ivrit*, 5 vols. (1977–1998); idem, "Through many small windows: An Introduction to Postrealistic Hebrew Literature 1950–1980," in: *Prooftexts*, 16:3 (1996), 271–91; idem, *Modern Hebrew Fiction* (2000); H. Bar Yosef, "De-romanticized Zionism in Modern Hebrew Literature," in: *Modern Judaism*, 16:1 (1996), 67–79; D. Miron, "Depictions in Modern Hebrew Literature," in: N. Rosovsky (ed.), *City of the Great King* (1996), 241–87; 515–16; W. Bargad, *From Agnon to Oz: Studies in Modern Hebrew Literature* (1996); R. Kartun-Blum, *Profane Scriptures* (1999); Y. Oren, *An Unconventional Attitude towards Israeli Literature* (2002); H. Hever, *Producing the Modern Hebrew Canon* (2002); G. Abramson, "Modern Hebrew Literature," in: *The Oxford Handbook of Jewish Studies* (2002), 515–40; J. Bar Ilan, "Modern Hebrew Literature on the Web: A Content Analysis," in: *Online Information Review*, 27:2 (2003), 77–86; R. Shoham, *Poetry and Prophecy* (2003); I. Milner, "Holocaust Survivors and their Children: The Dialogue between the Generations in Modern Hebrew Literature," in: *Erinnerte Shoah* (2003), 437–44; M. Gluzman, *The Politics of Canonicity: Lines of Resistance in Modern Hebrew Literature* (2003); A. Band, *Studies in Modern Jewish Literature* (2003); D. Patterson, "Against all Odds: Hebrew Literature in Our Times," in: *The Solomon Goldman Lectures*, 8 (2003), 85–102. WOMEN'S WRITING: C.B. Balin: *To Reveal Our Hearts: Jewish Women Writers in Tzarist Russia* (2001); T. Cohen, "From the Private Sphere to the Public Sphere: The Writings of Hebrew Maskilot in the Nineteenth Century," in: D. Assaf et al. (ed.), *Studies in East European History and Culture in Honour of Professor Shmuel Werses* (Heb., 2002), 235–38; S.F. Foner-Meinkin, *A Righteous Love, or The Pursued Family* (Heb., 1881); idem, *A Story from the Days of Shimon the High Priest* (Heb., 1891); idem, *Children's Way or A Story From Jerusalem* (Heb., 1886); idem, *The Days of My Youth, or A Memoir of Dvinsk* (Heb., 1903); R. Morpurgo, *Ugav Raḥel* (Heb., 1890). DRAMA: M. Kohansky, *The Hebrew Theatre* (1969); L. Ben-Zvi (ed.), *Theater in Israel* (1996); F. Rokem, *ibid.*, 51–84; Kaynar, *ibid.*, 285–301; N. Yaari, *ibid.*, 151–171; S. Levy and K. Shoef, *Israeli Drama: Synopses* (2000); A. Yaari, *Ha-Maḥazeh ha-Ivri ha-Mekori ve-ha-Meturgam me-Reshito ve-ad ha-Yom* (1956), incl. bibl.; Shunami, Bibl, 1207–1211; Ḥ.N. Bialik, in: *Bamah*, no. 2 (1933), 3–12; G. Hanoch, *ibid.*, no. 1 (1945), 32–38; J. Fichmann, *ibid.*, no. 6 (1941), 3–4; L. Goldberg, in: *Bamot*, 1 (1951), 7–15; H. Gamzu, in: *Me'assef*, 1 (1960); M. Silberthal, in: *Orlogin*, 2 (1951), 28ff.; 10 (1954), 122ff.; A. Paperna, *Ha-Drama bi-Khelal ve-ha-Ivrit bi-Ferat* (1868); J. Schirmann, in: *Gilyonot*, 22 (1948), 217–67; idem, in: *Keneset*, 1 (1936), 430–42; idem, in: *Moznayim*, 4 (1935), 623–45; G. Shaked, *Ha-Maḥazeh ha-Ivri ha-Histori bi-Tekufat ha-Teḥiyyah* (1970); idem, in: *Bamah*, no. 6 (1960), 9–17; Waxman, Literature, index, s.v. *Dramas;* S. Levy (ed.), *The Bible as Theatre* (2000); H. Barzel, *Drama of Extreme Situations: War and Holocaust* (1995); H.S. Joseph (ed.), *Modern Israeli Drama: An Anthology* (1983); D. Urian, *Demut ha-Arvi ba-Teatron ha-Yisraeli* (1996); idem, *Yahaduto shel ha-Teatron ha-Yisraeli* (1998); G. Abramson, *Drama and Ideology in Modern Israel*

(1998); B.-A. Feingold, *Tashakh ba-Teatron* (2001); M. Nathan, *Kishuf neged Mavet* (1996); H. Nagid, *Ẓeḥok u-Ẓemarmoret* (1998); G. Kaynar, F. Rokem, E. Rozik (eds.), *The Cameri: A Theatre of Time and Place*. CRITICISM: GENERAL CRITICAL WORKS: S. Halkin, *Modern Hebrew Literature* (1970²); idem, *Mekorot le-Toledot ha-Bikkoret ha-Ivrit bi-Tekufat ha-Haskalah* (1960); Y. Beker and S. Span (eds.), *Mivḥar ha-Massah ha-Ivrit* (1962); S. Werses, *Ha-Bikkoret ha-Ivrit ba-Me'ah ha-Esrim, Tekhanim ve-Ẓurot* (1966); Kressel, Leksikon, 2 vols. (1965–68), incl. bibl.; Shunami, Bibl, index, s.v. *Brainin, Brenner, Fichmann, Frischmann, Lachower* and *Klausner*; G. Shaked, *Mivḥar Bibliografi shel ha-Maḥashavah ha-Sifrutit ha-Ḥadashah* (1958). SPECIFIC CRITICAL WORKS: D. Pagis, *Shirat ha-Ḥol ve-Torat ha-Shir le-Moshe Ibn Ezra* (1970); Klausner, Sifrut, 4 (1953), on Korner and Paperna; Averbuch, *Horetah ve-Ledatah shel ha-Bikkoret ha-Re'alistit ha-Ivrit*, in: Orlogin, 9 (1953), 166–87; idem, "*A.U. Kovner, ha-Ish, ha-Mevakker u-Morashto*," in: *ibid.*, 11 (1955), 94–122; Breiman, "*A.U. Kovner u-Mekomo be-Toledot ha-Bikkoret ha-Ivrit*," in: *Meẓudah*, 7 (1954), 416–57; Kuenstler, "*Reshit Bikkoret ha-Dramah ha-Ivrit*," in: *Molad*, 2 (1969), 379–90; Elkoshi, "*J.L. Gordon ha-Mevakker*," in: *Meẓudah*, 7 (1954), 458–89; N. Gruenblatt, *Mevakkerim be-Sifrutenu* (1944); Lachower, Sifrut, 3 (1963), on Frischmann, Aḥad Ha-Am, Klausner and Berdyczewski; Y. Keshet, *M.J. Berdyczewski, Ḥayyav u-Fo'alo* (1958); F. Lachower, *Shirah u-Maḥashavah* (1953), 200–26 (on Brainin); Kramer, "*Re'uven Brainin ki-Mevakker Sifruti*," in: *Me'assef Soferei Ereẓ Yisrael* (1940), 368–76; A.A. Rivlin, *Aḥad Ha-Am u-Mitnaggedav ve-Hashkafotehem al ha-Sifrut ha-Ivrit be-Doram* (1955); Werses, "*J. Klausner be-Vikkoret u-ve-Ḥeker ha-Sifrut*," in: *Molad*, 16 (1958), 616–21; idem, "*Al Demutah shel 'Shiratenu ha-Ẓe'irah*'" (Bialik's Essay), in: *Me'assef le-Divrei Sifrut, Bikkoret ve-Hagut*, 4 (1964), 381–92; N. Rotenstreich, *Al "Gillui ve-Khissui ba-Lashon" le-Ḥ.N. Bialik* (1951); Averbuch, "*Frishmann, ha-Ish, ha-Mevakker ve-Doro*," in: *Orlogin*, 8 (1953), 77–89; Kariv, "*Frishmann ha-Mevakker ve-Ḥozeh ha-De'ot*," in: *Atarah le-Yoshnah* (1956), 199–236; Lachower, "*Brenner ha-Mevakker*," in: *Rishonim va-Aḥaronim* (1966²), 321–7; Kartun-Blum, "*Al Mishnato ha-Sifrutit shel Brenner*," in: *Molad*, 1 (1968), 687–93; Halkin, "*F. Lachower*," in: *Bitzaron*, 16 (1947), 80–93; Kramer, "*Netivot ba-Bikkoret ha-Ivrit*," in: *Me'assef le-Divrei Sifrut, Bikkoret ve-Hagut*, 5–6 (1965–66), 348–76; A. Shanan, *Ha-Sifrut ha-Ivrit ha-Ḥadashah li-Zeramehah* (1962–); Waxman, Literature, 3, 313ff.; *ibid.*, 4, 339ff.; *ibid.*, 5, 52ff. TRANSLATIONS: Y. Goell, *Bibliography of Modern Hebrew Literature in English Translation* (1968); Y. Goell, *Bibliography of Modern Hebrew Literature in Translation* (1975); I. Goldberg, Y. Goell, A. Zipin, *Bibliography of Modern Hebrew Literature in Translation*. The Institute for the Translation of Hebrew Literature, vols. 1–7, 1979–1985; new series. ed. I. Goldberg, N. Raz, A. Zipin, E. Kandelshein and N. Duchovni, v. 1–10, 1988–1998; I. Goldberg and N. Duchovni, *S. Agnon: A Bibliography of His Work in Translation Including Selected Publications about Agnon and his Writing* (1996); E. Lapon-Kandelshein and N. Duchovni, *Yehuda Amichai: A Bibliography of his Work in Translation* (1994); M. Kayyal, *Bibliography of Arabic Translations and Studies about Modern Hebrew Literature in Israel and the Arab World* (2003); A. Feinberg, "Bibliography of Modern Hebrew Literature in German Translation," in: A. Feinberg, *Moderne hebraeische Literatur* (2005).

HEBREW THEOLOGICAL COLLEGE (Beis HaMidrash LaTorah), Orthodox rabbinical school and institute of higher Jewish education; founded in Chicago, Illinois, in 1922, by Rabbis Saul Silber, Ephraim Epstein, Abraham Cardon, and Chaim Zvi Rubinstein. It was an outgrowth of the Hebrew high school, Yeshiva Etz Chaim, organized in 1899 and was the first Orthodox rabbinical institution in America to require courses in Bible, Jewish philosophy, and history, etc., in addition to Talmud and Codes. In 1970, about half of those ordained at the Hebrew Theological College were in the practicing rabbinate. Others served as teachers in yeshivot and religious high schools. Requirements for admission to the rabbinical school include a college degree and extensive preparation in Talmud and related Jewish subjects. Graduates receive a Bachelor's degree, as well as rabbinical ordination. Among its non-talmudic faculty was Eliezer Berkovits, professor of Jewish Philosophy. Its first president was Rabbi Saul Silber. In 1966 Simon Kramer, who was then president, brought Rabbi Aaron Soloveichik to serve as *rosh ha-yeshivah*. The rabbinical program was extended from two to three years and the course of talmudic study somewhat reorganized.

As of the 1990s the Hebrew Theological College has seen significant growth and development under the leadership of Rabbi Shlomo Morgenstern, *rosh ha-yeshivah*, and Rabbi Dr. Jerold Isenberg, chancellor. As of 2005 the yeshivah had ordained 391 rabbis. The 17 members of the Sam & Nina Bellows Kollel pursue advanced Torah learning, while serving as study partners (*ḥavrutot*) and role models to younger students.

Since 1997 the college has been affiliated with the Higher Learning Commission of the North Central Association of Colleges as an accredited institution. Hebrew Theological College houses two main collegiate divisions on separate campuses: the Beis Midrash (for men) and the Blitstein Institute (for women) with a combined enrollment of 214. Graduates receive a B.A. degree through its department of Talmud and Rabbinics (men only), the Bressler School of Advanced Hebrew Studies, and the Kanter School of Liberal Arts and Sciences. Additional majors are offered in: Accounting, Business, Computer and Information Sciences, Education (both Elementary Education and Special Education are recognized Illinois State Certification programs), English, and Psychology. An expanded science curriculum prepares students for graduate and professional studies in allied health sciences. Students enrolled in the college have the option of participating in a year abroad in Israel through HTC's Israel Experience Program. Hebrew Theological College also supports an Adult Degree Completion Program that provides accelerated degree programs.

The college's Saul Silber Memorial Library is the largest rabbinic library in the Midwest with over 75,000 books and manuscripts. The library's Lazar Holocaust Memorial Wing has significant holdings in Holocaust studies. The college regularly publishes several publications including the *Or Shmuel Torah Journal*, and the *HTC Academic Journal*.

Other programs of the college include a preparatory division, the Rabbi Oscar Z. Fasman Yeshiva High School for young men, whose 2005 enrollment was 173 and two summer camps: *Yeshivas HaKayitz*, a residential summer camp for boys in grades 7–12 and *Midreshet HaKayitz*, a program for girls in grades 9–12. The Community Services division provides annual lectures on campus as well as variety of classes throughout the community including the Chicago Jewish Medical Forum and an annual Medical Ethics *Yarchei Kallah.* A vibrant alumni association serves the institution's alumni throughout the year.

HTC's 10-acre Skokie campus, constructed in the late 1950s, includes a spacious Beis Midrash, modern classrooms and computer and science laboratories for both the college and high school programs. The campus also houses libraries, dormitory facilities, auditoriums, dining halls, apartments for faculty and married students, computer centers, fitness center, and Memorial Hall. The new, separate Chicago campus for the Anne M. Blitstein Teachers Institute for Women consists of classrooms, computer and science laboratories, library facilities, a student lounge, offices and student residences.

Hebrew Theological College's annual budget for 2004 was $6,000,000.

BIBLIOGRAPHY: *The Hebrew Theological College Dedication Journal* (1939); Hebrew Theological College, *Select Research and Publication Activities of the Faculty* (1963).

[Michael Berenbaum (2nd ed.)]

HEBREW UNION COLLEGE-JEWISH INSTITUTE OF RELIGION (HUC-JIR) is the oldest rabbinical seminary in the United States. Dedicated to Jewish scholarship and the training of religious leadership for the Reform movement, it has campuses in Cincinnati, New York, Los Angeles, and Jerusalem. The school was founded in Cincinnati, Ohio, in 1875, by Isaac M. *Wise to offer "general rabbinical instruction … for the Jewish ministry." Wise was convinced that "Judaism would have no future in America unless … it would become reconciled with the spirit of the age" and the Jewish community found it possible to "educate American rabbis for the American pulpit." After a 25-year struggle, Wise succeeded in establishing a Union of American Hebrew Congregations (today: Union for Reform Judaism) whose primary object was the founding of HUC. President until his death (1900), Wise was succeeded by Kaufmann *Kohler (1903–21), Julian *Morgenstern (1921–47), Nelson *Glueck (1947–71), Alfred Gottschalk (1971–96), Sheldon Zimmerman (1996–2000) and David Ellenson (2001–). Initially intended as a rabbinical school for all American Jews, following adoption of the radical Pittsburgh Platform by Reform rabbis in 1885, it took on the character of a Reform denominational institution.

In 1922 Stephen S. *Wise founded the Jewish Institute of Religion (JIR) in New York to provide training "for the Jewish ministry, research, and community service." Students were to serve either Reform or traditional pulpits. Wise remained president until 1948. Housing JIR next to his Free Synagogue on West 68th Street, he hoped that its graduates would generate other Free Synagogues "animated by the same spirit of free inquiry, of warm Jewish feeling, and of devotion to the cause of social regeneration." JIR from the start inclined to Zionism, in contrast to HUC, which at the time did not favor Jewish nationalism. Motivated largely by budgetary difficulties, Wise accepted the prospect of JIR's merger with HUC once the biblical archaeologist Nelson Glueck assumed the presidency. Negotiations were completed in 1948 and in 1950 the two schools merged. In 1954 a school in Los Angeles was chartered and, in 1963, primarily as a result of Glueck's efforts, a Jerusalem campus, initially devoted to archaeology, was opened.

All rabbinical and cantorial students spend the first year of their studies at the Jerusalem campus, which also houses a rabbinical program for Israelis as well as a school and museum of biblical archaeology. The Cincinnati, New York, and Los Angeles campuses all offer a rabbinical program leading to ordination. The Cincinnati campus also has a graduate school for Jews and Christians, which is especially strong in studies focusing on Bible and the Ancient Near East. The Hebrew Union College Annual (founded in 1924) and the Hebrew Union College Press are also located in Cincinnati. The New York campus includes a School of Sacred Music, which trains cantors for the Reform movement, and a doctor of ministries program, whereas the principal School of Education and the School of Jewish Communal Service are both located in Los Angeles. The HUC-Skirball Museum in Los Angeles possesses a very rich collection of archaeological artifacts and general Judaica.

Situated on the 18-acre Clifton Avenue campus, the Cincinnati school also houses the *American Jewish Archives, which publishes its own journal, the American Jewish Periodical Center, a small museum of Judaica, the Center for Holocaust and Humanity Education, and, in conjunction with the University of Cincinnati, an Ethics Center. The Cincinnati Library and Rare Book Building contain some 450,000 volumes, 160 incunabula and 6,200 manuscripts, including the Eduard Birnbaum Manuscript Collection in Jewish Music, making it one of the foremost libraries of Judaica in the world. Smaller, but significant collections are housed at the other campuses.

The HUC-JIR faculty, which has included some of the most notable American and European scholars, has over 60 ranked members, many of them Reform rabbis. Among the scholars of international renown who taught at HUC-JIR in earlier years are the talmudists Moses Mielziner and Jacob Lauterbach, the philosopher David Neumark, the historians Jacob Mann, Guido Kisch, and Jacob Rader Marcus, the semiticist Julius Lewy, the musicologist Abraham Z. Idelsohn, and the biblical scholar Harry M. Orlinsky.

In 1972 Hebrew Union College became the first rabbinical seminary to ordain women as rabbis, and it regularly admits students regardless of sexual orientation. In the early 21st century the school was strongly oriented toward Zionism and to high academic standards. In recent years its curriculum has placed greater emphasis on practically oriented clinical pastoral education. It remains the only institution within the American Reform movement that prepares men and women for the various roles of spiritual, intellectual, educational, and communal leadership.

Although within Reform Jewry the congregational Union for Reform Judaism and the Central Conference of American

Rabbis are the more activist in taking stands on contemporary American and Jewish issues, HUC-JIR serves as the principal intellectual resource of the movement. By the year 2005 it had ordained more than 2,500 rabbis (of whom about 400 are women), invested 400 cantors, and graduated over 500 communal service workers and 300 educators.

BIBLIOGRAPHY: M.A. Meyer, *Hebrew Union College-Jewish Institute of Religion: A Centennial History, 1875–1975* (rev. ed. 1992); *Response to Modernity: A History of the Reform Movement in Judaism* (1988).

[Stanley F. Chyet / Michael A. Meyer (2nd ed.)]

HEBREW UNIVERSITY OF JERUSALEM. The first university established in Israel. The establishment of an institute of higher learning in Ereẓ Israel was first proposed by Hermann *Schapira in 1884 at the Kattowitz Conference of the Ḥovevei Zion, and again at the first Zionist Congress in 1897. A few years later, a group of young Zionists were inspired by Chaim *Weizmann, then a teacher at the University of Geneva, to make the foundation of such an institution a primary aim of the Zionist movement. The group, which included Martin *Buber and Berthold *Feiwel, brought the question before the Congress of 1901, and Herzl submitted a petition to the Ottoman sultan for permission to establish a university in Jerusalem.

The Congress of 1913 appointed a committee, including Weizmann and Judah L. *Magnes of America, to execute the project, but the outbreak of World War I prevented action. While the war with the Turks was still being waged, Weizmann, who had come to Ereẓ Israel as head of the *Zionist Commission after the issue of the *Balfour Declaration, initiated the establishment of the university. On July 24, 1918, 12 foundation stones of the university were laid on Mount Scopus, north of the Old City of Jerusalem. This site, incomparable in beauty and impressiveness, had been acquired before the war by Isaac *Goldberg from the estate of an English lawyer, Sir John Gray-Hill. The view commanded on one side the Holy City and Bethlehem, and on the other the rugged landscape of the Wilderness of Judea, the Jordan Valley, the Dead Sea, and the Mountains of Moab. Weizmann, the only speaker at the ceremony, concluded: "Here, out of the misery and the desolation of war, is being created the first germ of a new life.… In this university we have gone beyond restoration; we are creating during the war something which is to serve as symbol of a better future. In the university the wandering soul of Israel will reach its haven."

There was an interval of seven years before any faculty of the university could be opened. The first lecture was given in 1923 by Albert *Einstein on his theory of relativity, and he spoke the first sentences in Hebrew, which was to be the language of teaching. He was dedicated to the university, and had accompanied Weizmann to the United States in 1921 to apprise American Jewry of its significance. It was decided that, before undergraduate teaching was initiated, work should be in postgraduate studies and scientific research. Three tiny institutes of research were opened, in Jewish studies, chemistry, and microbiology. The university was to develop in two directions: on the one hand, it should be the center where the Hebrew tradition would be molded in its original language and in the light of general humanities; on the other, it should be a center of research in the natural and medical sciences, which would help the regeneration of the land. The former development was the work of Magnes, who settled in Jerusalem in 1923, and devoted himself to bringing the university into being. Weizmann and committees in England and the United States launched the effort for scientific research. The university was opened on April 1, 1925, by Arthur *Balfour, at an impressive ceremony attended by the High Commissioner, Sir Herbert *Samuel, General Allenby, Chaim Weizmann, Ḥ.N. *Bialik, *Aḥad Ha-Am, and Chief Rabbi *Kook.

The university did not at that time receive any grant from the Government of Palestine; it was the financial responsibility of the Jews of the world. The supreme governing body included Jews eminent in public or academic life in many countries. Weizmann was chairman of the board, and Magnes chancellor – later president. The university grew quickly. Following the inauguration, new institutions were added: Jewish studies (1924); Oriental studies (1926); mathematics (1927); general humanities (1928): philosophy and history, geography and archaeology, classical literature, English, and other languages; physics (1930); and biological sciences (1931). Demand grew for regular courses of postgraduate studies, leading to a Master's degree. Two faculties were constituted: humanities, and science and mathematics. The first degrees were awarded in 1931. At this stage, however, the authorities were opposed to the opening of professional schools for doctors or lawyers: learning should be acquired for its own sake, and research was the main objective. About half the students were from Palestine, and half from abroad. Some of the teachers now appointed were graduates of the university.

The Nazi persecution of Jews in Germany and their exclusion from institutions of higher learning gave fresh importance to the Hebrew University. It could take its part in the battle for academic freedom, and be a principal place in which exiled scholars and scientists could find a haven. Hebrew remained the language of instruction, and was rapidly adapted to the needs of modern learning and science. Vocabulary, based on biblical and rabbinical Hebrew, multiplied. The library, which was also the Jewish National *Library, grew to half a million books, housed in the principal building on Mount Scopus and containing one of the most valuable collections of Hebraica and Judaica. Before the outbreak of World War II, medical research was developed in laboratories attached to the university hospital, itself a gift of the *Hadassah Women's Zionist Organization. The hospital and medical center did valuable work for the Allies and the civilian population of the Middle East throughout the war. A school of agriculture at Reḥovot was added in 1940. At the end of the war, plans were made for large extensions, and new buildings were started on Mount Scopus.

The years between 1945 and 1948 were troubled. Both Jews and Arabs were in revolt and university progress was halted. The outbreak of riots and fighting at the end of November 1947, which followed the United Nations decision to partition Palestine into Jewish and Arab states, caused temporary suspension of academic work. Teachers and students were engaged in the defense of the National Home; and, in April 1948, an Arab mob attack which murdered a convoy of doctors, nurses, and students to Scopus compelled the evacuation of the Hadassah Hospital and Medical Center, in order to avoid further losses and bloodshed. The fighting during and after the War of Independence involved the university. The buildings were held against Arab attacks, but grave damage was done. During the first cease-fire, the United Nations mediator contrived to obtain agreement for demilitarization of Mount Scopus and the Mount of Olives. The university buildings were to remain an Israel enclave, surrounded by Arab land, and were occupied by a small body of Jewish police and caretakers.

The Israel-Jordan *Armistice Agreement, concluded in April 1949, included "an agreement in principle for restoration of the normal functioning of the cultural and humanitarian institutions on Mount Scopus, and free access thereto." An Arab-Jewish committee was to work out details. That, however, was not done, as Jordan refused to nominate representatives to the committee, and the enclave remained inaccessible to teachers and students.

In the summer of 1949 the university resumed its work in western Jerusalem, housed in a number of improvised and unsuitable buildings scattered over the town. The rooms for lectures were bare; there were no laboratories or equipment and very few books. At the same time, the creation of the State of Israel required intensified expansion of the university departments to provide the civil servants, teachers, doctors and lawyers, scientists and agronomists for building rapidly. The pre-faculty of medicine was transformed into a faculty (opened in 1949) for both undergraduate and postgraduate studies. A law faculty was opened in the same year, while the school of agriculture (later, renamed the Levi Eshkol Faculty of Agriculture) and the department of economic and social sciences also became faculties in 1952 and 1953 respectively, and the school of education was opened in 1952. An extensive new campus was dedicated at Givat Ram on a ridge of the Judean Hills in the west of the city. A department of business administration and a school of social work (1958/59) were added; the Institute of Oriental Studies (1926) was developed into a department of Asian and African studies (1962) and the Ben-Zvi Institute for research on the Jewish Communities in the Middle East (founded 1947) was affiliated. Other new departments were the Institute for Contemporary Jewry (1959/60), the institute for research in Jewish Law (1963), and the Library School. A bigger Hadassah University hospital (opened in 1961), a medical school for 500 students, and a dental school for 250 students were built on another site, at Ein Kerem on the outskirts of Jerusalem. Since 1929, the Hebrew University has had its own publishing house, the Magnes Press, which publishes significant work done at the university and produces two important series, *Scripta Hierosolymitana* and *Textus*, the latter devoted to Bible studies. The number of students rose from 1,000 in 1947/48 to 5,000 in 1958/59 and over 15,000 in 1969/70. During this period the academic staff increased from 200 to 1,430, many themselves graduates of the university. The National and University Library in 1970 contained 1¾ million books and numerous periodicals.

At Givat Ram, 150 acres of eroded limestone have been transformed into a new university campus with more than 50 buildings. This phoenix-like resurgence was made possible by the combined financial help of the state and of Jewish communities and individuals abroad. Government and Jewish Agency grants cover nearly two-thirds of the maintenance budget, and societies of friends of the university have given the funds for new buildings. The university has not, however, become a state institution. The government attaches no conditions to its contribution, has no administrative control, and nominates only a few lay members to the executive council. The university is open to all students without discrimination of sex, creed, color, or nationality. The number of students from abroad steadily mounted, and there was a large influx of Jewish students, most of them American, after the Six-Day War. In 1970, foreign students totaled 3,200, of whom some 1,200 came from the United States and some 50 were Asian or African. In addition, 205 were Arabs or Druze (45) including some from east Jerusalem and the Israel-held territories in Judea and Samaria.

The board of governors, meeting annually in Jerusalem, elects the president for a four-year term, approves the budget, and decides major issues of policy. Half the board consists of members resident in Israel. The control of the university is maintained by a senate, an academic body presided over by an elected rector, and an executive council, composed of a majority of lay members together with some academics. After Magnes, the presidents were: Selig *Brodetsky (1949–51), Benjamin *Mazar (1953–61), Giulio *Racah (acting; 1961–62), Eliahu *Elath (1962–68), and Avraham *Harman (from 1968). As a result of the Six-Day War, the university's original home on Mount Scopus was recovered, and the former building of the humanities faculty was put to immediate use. Studies were restarted in the Rosenbloom building, dormitories designed for 2,500 students, and a residential center for pre-academic studies opened. The original Hadassah-University hospital was rehabilitated and the Harry S. Truman Research Center, endowed by American Friends of the Hebrew University, has been erected on Scopus as part of the university. The faculty of law was transferred in 1969 to Mount Scopus. The university now has four campuses: Scopus, Givat Ram, and Ein Kerem in Jerusalem, and Reḥovot. It was invited to set the academic standards for the University College in Haifa, and, together with the Weizmann Institute of Science and the Haifa Technion, to do the same for the University of the Negev in Beersheba. In 1958, the Hebrew University opened branches of its law and social sciences faculties in Tel Aviv; but between 1966 and 1969 these were transferred to the University of Tel Aviv. The high quality of research done in Jewish Studies, the humanities and social sciences on one hand, and the natural, physical, and medical sciences on the other, has won encouragement and financial subsidies from U.S. government departments and private foundations in various countries, and has brought the Hebrew University worldwide recognition. It becomes more and more the university of the whole Jewish people.

[Norman Bentwich]

1970s

The decade of the 1970s was marked by expansion and consolidation. Prior to the Yom Kippur War of 1973, the university's student enrollment climbed to a peak of some 18,000 at the height of a period of growth in tertiary education. At the same time, the academic staff was enriched by the immigration to Israel of many scholars from the Western world as well as from the U.S.S.R.

Concurrently, the rebuilding of the campus on Mount Scopus proceeded apace both with regard to premises to house the academic work of the university and student accommodation, in particular that set aside for married students with young children.

Noteworthy in this period of expansion was the growth in the School for Overseas Students, where enrollment climbed to 1,000, with approximately another 1,000 attending the annual summer courses. The school offered courses varying in duration from one to four years, with teaching in English, French, Spanish and Russian, in addition to Hebrew. It now played a key role in strengthening Israel's ties with the younger generation of Diaspora Jewry.

A number of new research institutes came into being in response to fresh needs and possibilities; these were within the areas of Jewish studies, and those for the history and traditions of Jews in the Eastern and Western Diasporas, Slavic language and literature, international affairs, European studies, Soviet and East European research, Israeli society, economics and politics, energy resources; environmental sciences, lasers, marine sciences, agriculture, medicine, and dental medicine.

In line with the university's policy of serving Israel's needs for trained manpower, it also established, in conjunction with Hadassah, the Henrietta Szold-Hadassah-Hebrew University School of Nursing, the Hadassah-Hebrew University School of Occupational Therapy (both granting a bachelor's degree) and the Hebrew University-Hadassah School of Community Medicine and Public Health, which gives a master's degree. In 1975, the Institute of Advanced Studies was set up to provide a framework for the encouragement of scientific and scholarly leadership and the advancement of top level research. The institute offers fellowships to Israeli and overseas scholars, initially in the areas of mathematics, Jewish studies and economics.

The 1973 war was a turning point which marked profound changes within Israel, including severe cuts in public spending for tertiary education, and they affected the Hebrew University, where the stress was on consolidating the growth of past years. The Mount Scopus campus became a residential university city, providing accommodation for over 3,000 students and premises for the Faculty of Law, the School for Overseas Students, the Institute of Archaeology, the School of Education, first-year science studies for all the experimental faculties, the Harry S. Truman Research Institute, the Martin Buber Center for Adult Education and the Joseph Saltiel Center for Pre-Academic Studies. There were new buildings for the Faculty of Social Sciences, for the Faculty of Humanities and an undergraduate library for these faculties. These units moved from Givat Ram to Mount Scopus in the fall of 1981 as scheduled. The physical development of the university was thus virtually completed on all four campuses. Enrollment stood at over 15,000, of whom more than a third were engaged in post-graduate work. This latter figure marked the latest phase in the development of the university, making it the Jewish world's foremost center of advanced study. In addition, university extension courses, both on-campus and throughout the country, brought faculty members to the service of a further 12,000 people each year; while under special arrangements with a number of leading universities, notably in North and South America, the university also aided Jewish studies abroad in staffing and curriculum design and planning. With the growth of local universities in other Israeli cities, the Hebrew University, which had 70% of its student body coming from outside Jerusalem, increasingly served as a national institution.

The university's Authority for Research and Development coordinated the work of some 2,500 research projects underway at the university with funding received from over 500 different granting agencies. Much of this work and of the more than 3,000 books and papers issuing annually from the academic community were of direct practical importance to the State of Israel and its economic, scientific, and social development. Taken as a whole, the research record made the university an international center of scholarship which attracted hundreds of visiting academics from all parts of the world.

At the meeting of the board of governors held in May 1980, it was decided, despite the financial stringency prevailing, to proceed with the completion of the rebuilding of the Mount Scopus campus, in order to carry out the move of the Social Sciences and Humanities Faculties from Givat Ram in the spring and summer of 1981. The transfer from Givat Ram to Mount Scopus was completed in the summer of 1981 as scheduled.

[Devorah Getzler]

Developments from 1982

As the university re-established itself in the renovated and greatly expanded campus on Mount Scopus in the early 1980s, the consolidation of units that had been scattered in temporary quarters throughout Jerusalem during the 1948–67 "exile" from Mount Scopus enabled the Givat Ram campus to become primarily the university's science campus, incorporating lecture rooms and laboratories that had been in other locations. As part of this development, the Avraham Harman Science Library was opened at Givat Ram. At Mount Scopus, the Bloomfield Library for Humanities and Social Sciences opened its doors.

As enrollment continued to expand from the early 1980s level of some 16,000 students to close to 23,000 by the mid-1990s, the university sought ways to provide expanded dormitory facilities. This became a matter of high priority not only because of the natural growth in the number of Israeli students, but also because of the influx of immigrant students, particularly from the Soviet Union. The total number of dormitory accommodations has reached approximately 6,500.

A major development project initiated in 1995 was a new home for the Rothberg School for Overseas Students on Mount Scopus. The school had been located since 1971 in the Goldschmidt building on Mount Scopus, a facility which was unable to answer all the needs of a school that is now serving some 4,200 students a year in a multitude of programs geared to meet the specific needs of students from various countries.

In the Faculty of Science, the Belmonte Science Laboratory for Youth, opened in 1990, provides state-of-the-art facilities for use by high school science classes and their teachers – the only such laboratory in Israel built and operated exclusively for this purpose. The laboratory provides science enrichment for youngsters beyond that which would normally be available to them in their own schools.

At the Ein Kerem medical campus, a full story was added to the existing School of Dental Medicine in the mid-1990s. Besides providing needed additional space for the training of a new generation of dental practitioners and researchers, the new story will also contain the world's most advanced laboratory for experimentation and documentation involving dental implantations.

Also at Ein Kerem, the Faculty of Medicine proceeded with plans for a significant expansion of its facilities. A new building, the National and International Institute of Health, provided an improved infrastructure, enabling the faculty to increase its intake of new students and provide them with optimal learning conditions. It also provided more opportunities in teaching and research for talented Israeli scientists who have been compelled to seek adequate conditions abroad.

A major addition to the cultural life of Jerusalem took place on the Givat Ram campus with the development in the 1980s of the Jerusalem and University Botanical Garden, a facility open to the general public which provides a showcase of plant life from all over the world. The garden also included a Visitors Center in the Hank Greenspan Plaza. Another public attraction in Givat Ram are the windows by the artist Mordecai Ardon, dedicated in 1984. The windows, located in the Jewish National and University Library, conceptualize the prophet Isaiah's vision of peace.

Another development project was the opening in 1987 of the Astrid and Henry Montor Outdoor Sports and Recreation Center of the Mount Scopus campus. The first phase of this center is tennis courts. A soccer field, swimming pool, and track and field facilities were also planned.

NEW ACADEMIC PROGRAMS. An innovation in Israeli higher education was taken in 1985 with the opening of the Koret School of Veterinary Medicine at the Faculty of Agriculture in Rehovot – the country's first-ever school in this discipline. The school, along with the university's Veterinary Teaching Hospital in Rishon Lezion – the largest facility of its type in the Middle East – provide an opportunity for students who formerly were forced to go abroad to study this branch of medical science.

Another innovation in Israeli higher education came in the 1990s with the establishment of Israel's first B.A. programs in communications and journalism and in hotel studies. Israel's first Institute for European Studies was also established during this decade at the university.

Rapid expansion took place, in terms of equipment and numbers of students and faculty, in computer science. This trend was given further impetus due to the large influx of talented students from the former Soviet Union. The growth resulted in the creation of a separate Institute of Computer Science.

East Asian studies gained greatly in popularity among students at the university, bringing with it an expansion of staff and subject matter. In addition to Japanese and Chinese, the study of other East Asian languages and cultures was initiated, including courses in the Vietnamese, Thai, and Mongol languages.

In the area of programs for students from abroad, the Rothberg School for Overseas Students made great efforts to respond to the wave of immigration from the former Soviet Union. Besides offering courses taught in Russian, the school also initiated a special training program for Hebrew Ulpan teachers to provide a cadre of instructors to the large influx of new immigrants both within the university and elsewhere. Another service to the community was the formation of a special training program to prepare immigrant scientists as teachers of mathematics and science in Israeli high schools.

The Rothberg School for Overseas Students, in cooperation with the faculties of Humanities and Social Sciences, began offering in the mid-1990s new programs taught in English for graduate students around the world. An M.A. degree can now be earned in this manner.

An outreach to the public is the university program of adult education. This program offers a wide range of courses, taught in Hebrew, English, and Arabic, to those who find themselves with increasing leisure hours and a desire to expand their educational/cultural scope of knowledge.

Interdisciplinary study gained impetus throughout the 1980s and 1990s as the pursuit of knowledge and the development of new technologies began to erase old, increasingly artificial definitions of areas of expertise. A prominent example of this was the decision by the university to open a Department of Biotechnology in 1984, a unit jointly administered by the faculties of Science, Medicine, and Agriculture. Another area of interdisciplinary studies and research that gained increasing emphasis in the 1990s was that of environmental studies.

As an institution which has always stressed research (approximately one-third of the total student body is in graduate studies), the university began in the mid-1980s to institute programs designed to attract the most outstanding students and young researchers to its rolls. This was accomplished though the institution of special scholarships and individualized programs of study. One especially significant vehicle for furthering this goal was the establishment of the Golda Meir Fellowship Fund which, since 1984, has granted many hundreds of fellowships to outstanding graduate students, post-graduates, and young lecturers from Israel and abroad.

Close to 40 percent of all civilian research carried out in the country is conducted at the Hebrew University of Jerusalem. In the closing decades of the 20th century, the university placed increasing emphasis on its role in the development of the Israel high-tech industry. The university's Yissum Research Development Company has grown over the years. The university is also a partner in the encouragement of new high-tech firms through a "scientific incubator" company.

The university was a pioneer in establishing contacts with Palestinian scholars as well as researchers from Arab countries even before the political movement towards peace began in the early 1990s. University units such as the Harry S. Truman Research Institute for the Advancement of Peace, the Sanford F. Kuvin Center for the Study of Infectious and Tropical Diseases and the Faculty of Agriculture were leaders in contacts with their Arab counterparts, much of which earned the financial support of Western governments and institutions. These contacts focused on joint research projects involving such topics as regional economics, water usage, environmental quality, education for tolerance, political solutions, and the overcoming of animal and human diseases endemic to the region.

In 2005 the university included eight faculties: Humanities, Natural Sciences, Social Sciences, Medicine, Dental Medicine, Law, Agriculture, Food and Environmental Sciences. The university had 15 schools: Applied Science, Business Administration, Dental Medicine, Education, Engineering and Computer Sciences, the Rothberg School for Overseas Students, Librarianship, Archive and Information Administration, the Medical School, the Nursing School, Food Sciences, Occupational Therapy, Pharmacy, Public and Community Medicine, Social Work, and Veterinary Medicine. Around 1,200 faculty members teach over 24,000 students, of which about half study in postgraduate programs. University alumni number about 90,000. On the university campuses there are 11 professional libraries in addition to the National Library. The university has 100 research centers. In 2001 university research facilities had sales of $12 million to industry. In 2005 the president of the university was Menahem Megidor and the chancellor was Haim D. Rabinowich.

[Jerry Barasch / Shaked Gilboa (2nd ed.)]

BIBLIOGRAPHY: N. Bentwich, *Hebrew University of Jerusalem 1918–1960* (1961); L. Levenson, *Vision and Fulfillment* (1950); C. Weizmann, *Trial and Error* (1966), index; H. Parzen in JSS (July 1970), 187–213; Hebrew University, *Calendar* (1925–68), *Scopus – a periodical magazine* (1946–). *Research Reports* (1965–69), *Report by the President* (1953–). **WEBSITE:** www.huji.ac.il.

HEBRON (Heb. חֶבְרוֹן; Ar. **al-Khalīl**), city in Ereẓ Israel, 19 mi. (32 km.) S. of Jerusalem in the Judean Hills, 3,050 ft. (930 m.) above sea level. The name Hebron is explained as deriving from the root *ḥbr* (friend), the name *Ḫabiru, or the Arabic word *ḥaber* ("granary"). In the Bible, Hebron is also referred to as Kiriath-Arba: "Now the name of Hebron formerly was Kiriath-Arba; this Arba was the greatest among the Anakim…" (Josh. 14:15; see Anak, *Anakim; Ahiman, Sheshai, *Talmai). B. Mazar maintains that the name Kiriath-Arba implies that the city was a member of four (*arba*) neighboring confederated settlements in which the families of Aner, Eshkol, and *Mamre resided around the citadel of Hebron.

Biblical Period

Canaanite Hebron was located to the south of modern Hebron, on the strategic hill known as Jebel al-Rumayda, which was also the site of the later Israelite city. Numbers 13:22 states that Hebron was founded seven years before *Zoan, the capital of the Hyksos which was founded in about 1720 B.C.E. (cf. Jos., Wars, 4:530). Artifacts from this period – the middle Bronze Age – were found in a tomb in Wādī al-Tutāḥ; these included pottery, alabaster objects, and personal articles. At this time the name Hebron is connected with the Patriarchs, especially the purchase of the Cave of *Machpelah by Abraham from *Ephron the Hittite. Hebron, however, remained a Canaanite city; it was one of the important localities visited by the 12 spies (Num. 13:22). Hoham, the king of Hebron (Josh. 10:3), participated in the Battle of Aijalon against Joshua and was defeated there together with the other kings of Canaan. His city was conquered by Caleb son of Jephunneh (Josh. 15:13; Judg. 1:20).

After the death of Saul, David chose Hebron as his royal city and was anointed there as king over Judah (II Sam. 2:1–4). In addition, Abner was buried there (3:32) – his traditional tomb is still standing. The assassins of *Ish-Bosheth, the son of Saul, brought Ish-Bosheth's head to David in Hebron, and he ordered that they be hanged next to the pool in the town (4:12). Eventually David was anointed king over all Israel in Hebron (5:1–3). The city was also one of the *levitical cities and a *city of refuge (Josh. 21:13; I Chron. 6:42); it was an important administrative center and this was the reason why Rehoboam fortified it (II Chron. 11:10). In the division of Judah into districts during the Monarchy (cf. Josh. 15:54) Hebron was a city of the mountain district.

Post-Biblical Period

After the destruction of the First Temple the Jewish inhabitants of Hebron were exiled and their place was taken by Edomites, whose border extended to Beth-Zur. According to

Nehemiah 11:25, however, there were still some Jewish families living in the town; nevertheless, the Jews of Hebron did not participate in the construction of the walls of Jerusalem.

In I Maccabees 5:65 it is stated that Edomite Hebron was attacked by Judah Maccabee and its towers set on fire; the incorporation of the town into Judah, however, only took place after the conquest of Idumea by John Hyrcanus at the end of the second century B.C.E. With the conversion of the Idumeans, Hebron again became a Jewish city. King Herod built the wall which still surrounds the Cave of Machpelah. During the first war against the Romans, Hebron was conquered by Simeon Bar Giora, the leader of the Zealots (Jos., Wars, 4:529), and the city was plundered; it was later burned down by the Roman commander Cerealius (Jos., Wars, 4:554), but the Jews continued to live there. It appears that the population did not suffer during the Bar Kochba revolt. There are remains in the city of a synagogue from the Byzantine period. It was during this period that a church was erected over the Cave of Machpelah: the "very large village" of Hebron then formed part (together with the Botna fortress to the north) of the fortified southern border of the country.

[Michael Avi-Yonah]

Arab Conquest

It appears that Hebron fell to the Arabs without offering resistance. The Arabs, who honored the memory of Abraham, named the city Khalīl al-Raḥmān ("the beloved [i.e., Abraham] of [God] the Merciful"), or simply al-Khalīl; however, the name Ḥabrā or Ḥabrān is also found in Arabic sources. The first period of Arab conquest (638–1100) was a relief for the Jews of Hebron, as for the other Jews of Palestine, after the cruel Byzantine rule. There is, however, not much evidence about this period, but as more evidence is uncovered it becomes increasingly more probable that there was a permanent settlement in Hebron at that time. The testimony of historians from an earlier period and documents discovered in the course of time in the **Genizah* give a fairly clear picture of the continuity of the Jewish settlement in Hebron. The first evidence is provided by the story which appears in several versions in both Muslim and Christian sources, which tells of the permission *Omar gave to the Jews to build a synagogue near the cave of Machpelah, as well as a cemetery. The popularity of this story indicates that it has a nucleus of historical truth at least. The Arabs converted the Byzantine church over the cave into a mosque. Under their rule the town grew, and the Arabs traded with the bedouin in the Negev and the people to the east of the Dead Sea. According to the tenth-century Arab geographer Al-Muqaddasī they also conducted a far-reaching trade in fresh fruit.

There is no real evidence about the nature and situation of the Jewish settlement in Hebron in the eighth, ninth, and tenth centuries. However, there is evidence of the existence of a *Karaite community there at the beginning of the 11th century (1001), and tangible evidence from later in that century about continuing Jewish settlement. From inscriptions and fragments of documents from the *Genizah* it is possible to formulate a genealogical reconstruction for four to six generations of two Hebron families, from which it can be seen that the Jewish population was concentrated around the cave of Machpelah and that the synagogue was built near the cave. One of these two families held the inherited title *he-ḥaver le-kivrei avot*, or *anshei kivrei avot*, and was in charge of maintaining the holy place. This even included the burying of the dead brought by Jews from near and far for burial close to the cave of Machpelah.

Crusader Rule

The Crusader rule (1100–1260) brought a temporary end to the Jewish settlement in Hebron. In 1100 the Crusaders captured the city, turned the mosque and the adjoining synagogue into a church and monastery, and expelled the Jews. There was probably no Jewish settlement in Hebron after that time – at any rate, there is no mention of the existence of Jews in Hebron. *Maimonides, who visited Hebron (1166), as well as *Benjamin of Tudela (c. 1171), *Pethahiah of Regensburg (1176), and Jacob b. Nethanel (second half of 12th century) make no mention of a Jewish settlement or of the existence of Jews in Hebron. It is possible that Jews began to settle again in Hebron toward the end of the period of Crusader rule, and by the beginning of the 13th century (1210) mention is made of a Jewish dyer "and his group" in Hebron (cf. A. Yaari, *Iggerot Ereẓ Yisrael* (1943), 7–83).

Mamluk Rule

The *Mamluks (1260–1517), who expelled the Crusaders finally from Palestine, made Hebron their district capital (c. 1260), at which time the Jewish settlement apparently began to be perceptibly renewed. *Naḥmanides, who immigrated to Palestine in 1267, wrote to his son that he could "go to Hebron to dig a grave for himself there" (Yaari, op. cit., 84). Such an action would have been unthinkable had there not been a Jewish settlement in Hebron.

It appears that the tolerant Muslim attitude toward the Jews which had existed in pre-Crusader times did not continue with the return of the Muslims to Palestine. In 1266 it was decreed that the Jews were not to enter the Cave of Machpelah, and this decree was strictly enforced until the 20th century. A Christian traveler who visited Hebron in the first half of the 14th century reported that "Christian and Jewish people are regarded by them [by the Muslims] as dogs, and they do not allow them to enter such a holy place" (cf. M. Ish-Shalom, *Masei Noẓerim le-Ereẓ Yisrael* (1965), 230). The prohibition is mentioned by both Meshullam of Volterra (1481) and Obadiah of Bertinoro (1488), who visited Hebron. They both recount that the Muslims "built a wall at the entrance of the cave, in which they made a small window through which the Jews pray." The number of the Jews was also small at that time – 20 households according to Meshullam and Obadiah of Bertinoro (A. Yaari, *Masot Ereẓ Yisrael*, (1946) 68–69). Nevertheless, although the Jewish settlement in Hebron was small, it was considered as very important by the Jews. This is seen in evidence found in both Christian and Jewish sources. At the end of the 15th century Christian pilgrims report about a Jewish pilgrimage to Hebron: "The Jews recognize them [the graves of the Patriarchs] and hold them in great esteem... and make pilgrimage there [to Hebron] from Jerusalem and even from other countries ..." (the traveler Martin Kabatnik (1492), in M. Ish-Shalom, op. cit., 242). Obadiah of Bertinoro wrote in one of his letters that "there is a tradition among all the people of the land that burial in Hebron is better than in Jerusalem" (Yaari, *ibid.*).

The first evidence about spiritual and economic activity by the Jews of Hebron during the Mamluk period appears in the 14th century, but this is fragmentary, is derived from a single source, and is doubtful. R. Isaac Ḥilo from Larissa (Greece) reported in 1333 that the Jews were engaged in a prosperous trade in cotton, which they themselves wove and spun, and that they were also engaged in all types of glasswork. Some scholars maintain that the Venetian Jews who emigrated to Palestine after the Crusades introduced the art of glasswork to Hebron, but this is not certain (O. Avisar (ed.), *Sefer Ḥevron*, (1970), 89). R. Isaac Ḥilo of Larissa also reported about the spiritual activity of the Jews of Hebron, mentioning "an ancient synagogue [in Hebron] in which they prayed day and night." Some scholars doubt, however, whether this description stems from contemporary testimony or from hearsay.

Ottoman Rule

A definite turn for the better in the situation of the Jews of Hebron occurred during the Ottoman period (1517–1917), which began in Palestine in 1517. However, the Jews of Hebron did suffer misfortune and in this very year a great calamity befell the Jewish population of the town. In a parchment document, written at approximately the time of the event (1518), a man named Japheth b. Manasseh from Corfu tells about the attack by "Murad Bey, the deputy of the king and ruler in Jerusalem," on the Jews of Hebron. The results were very grave. Many were killed, their property was plundered, and the remainder fled for their lives to "the land of *Beirut." This same document also attests the stable situation of the Hebron community at that time. The very fact that the sultan's deputy took the trouble to have his armies plunder and loot Hebron in the hope of gaining wealth proves that the Jews of Hebron had considerable property. Furthermore, from the words in the same document "and they killed many people," it may be deduced that many Jews were there. The growth of the Jewish population of Hebron at the beginning of the 16th century is explained by the fact that some of those Jews who were expelled from Spain went to Hebron, probably contributing by their strength and wealth to the spiritual and material enrichment of the settlement.

In the course of the 16th century the influence of the Spanish *megorashim* (expellees) began to make its mark, especially in the realm of spiritual leadership. This stems from the emergence of two phenomena of note in the second half of the 16th century: the rising power of the Hebron settlement, on the one hand, and the decline of *Safed as a spiritual and economic center, on the other. The consolidation of the Hebron settlement took place in 1540 when Malkiel *Ashkenazi settled in the town. This multifaceted personality, who combined spiritual and practical greatness, organized communal life in Hebron both practically and spiritually. Ashkenazi's first act was to buy the courtyard in which the Jews of Hebron lived. This courtyard, which was surrounded by the stone walls of tall buildings, provided the Jewish community of Hebron with a degree of security. Ashkenazi built some additional buildings in the same location as the well-known synagogue, which was named for *Abraham the Patriarch. He also served as Hebron's first rabbi, and his legal decisions and customs were regarded by the Hebron community as irrevocable *halakhot* not only in his time but in subsequent generations as well. Toward the end of the 16th and at the beginning of the 17th centuries some of the most important kabbalists of Safed moved to Hebron. The most famous among these was Elijah de *Vidas, author of the well-known moralistic work *Reshit Ḥokhmah* and a student of Moses Cordovero and Isaac Luria, as well as Isaac Arḥa and Menahem b. Moses ha-Bavli, also disciples of Luria.

The teachings of the *Kabbalah and mysticism made a deep impression on the spiritual life of Hebron, and a spirit of asceticism was widespread. Isaiah Horowitz tells about the custom in Hebron of castigation and flagellation (*Ammud ha-Teshuvah*, a commentary on the tractate Yoma), which is an eyewitness description of castigations and a process of atonement which includes lashing, wearing sackcloth, being dragged, and the symbolic performance of the four judicial executions. Kabbalah and asceticism were prevalent in Hebron for approximately 300 years, until the settlement of the *Chabad Ḥasidim in the 19th century. Thus, the settlement in Hebron grew and became stabilized, although not from an economic aspect. The great majority of the population was economically dependent on continuous outside assistance, in the form of donations and contributions from abroad. The money came in two ways: donations which were sent directly to Palestine from abroad and contributions which were collected by emissaries who went abroad specifically for this purpose. Until the middle of the 17th century Hebron did not have its own emissaries; since the community was small and poor, it could not afford the large investment required for sending such an emissary abroad. Hebron was thus dependent on chance contributions from the Diaspora and on the general *ḥalukkah* among the four holy cities (*Jerusalem, Hebron, Safed, and Tiberias), from which Hebron received the smallest share (three parts out of 24). In the 16th century the charitable organization known as *Yaḥaẓ* was established. This was a kind of united fund whose name was a combination of the first letters of Jerusalem, Hebron, and Safed. It seems, however, that all these attempts did not greatly alleviate Hebron's difficult economic situation. This can be seen in "*Kol Kore*" (1616), which proclaimed to the Diaspora the difficult situation of Hebron's Jews. A central factor in their troubles was the huge debt owed by the community to the ruling authorities as a result of various decrees. Characteristic of the situation is the legend which tells about a tyrannical governor who forced the community to pay him thousands of grushim (coins whose value was equivalent to the German thaler) by threatening to burn half of the town and sell the other half into slavery (A.M. Luncz, in O. Avisar (ed.), *Sefer Ḥevron*, 306).

Nevertheless, in spite of the heavy tribulations, which included a plague, locusts, and harsh decrees by the authorities during the 17th century, the Jews of Hebron did not surrender their desire for spiritual survival. In the middle of the 17th century (1659) the famous philanthropist from Amsterdam, R. Abraham Pereira, established the yeshivah Ḥesed le-Avraham in Hebron. Distinguished rabbis and *ḥakhamim* lived in Hebron at that time. The yeshivah Ḥesed le-Avraham was a primary factor in the creation of this spiritual prominence of Hebron.

A difficult crisis befell the spiritual leadership of the town in the second half of the 17th century, after the visit of *Shabbetai Ẓevi in 1663 on his way to *Egypt. His visit made a great impression on the community. His disciples related that the people of Hebron stayed awake the entire night in order to see his wondrous deeds. He gained the adulation of the most important rabbis of Hebron, some of whom, as well as their descendants, maintained their faith in him even after his conversion. People like the kabbalist Abraham Conki and the emissary Meir ha-Rofe, and especially Nehemiah Ḥayon, devoted themselves to Shabbateanism.

The Shabbatean crisis had a very adverse effect on Hebron and led to both its spiritual and economic decline. There was no improvement during the 18th century, which was marked by disease, decrees of expulsion, a blood libel, and upheavals during the rebellion of Ali Bey and the Russo-Turkish War. Despite these troubles, there was a certain increase in population as a result of the breakdown of the Jewish settlement of Jerusalem in 1721 and the immigration of Abraham Gershon of Kutow (Kuty), the brother-in-law of Israel Baal Shem Tov. Abraham Gershon relates that in the single Jewish courtyard there was so little room that they could not even let him bring his family.

In the beginning of the 19th century the Hebron settlement gained some relief. In 1807 and 1811 the Jews bought and leased over 800 dunams of land. Nor was there stagnation in the spiritual life. First and foremost among the *ḥakhamim* of Hebron in the second half of the 18th and the beginning of the 19th centuries was Ḥayyim Joseph David *Azulai (called Ḥida). Mention should also be made of R. Mordecai *Rubio, the rabbi of Hebron and *rosh yeshivah* of Ḥesed le-Avraham, and Raphael Ḥazzan, author of halakhic works. There was a distinct improvement from a financial point of view as well, notwithstanding the robbery and oppression perpetrated by the authorities. Financial help came from several sources. The philanthropist Simon Wertheimer established a large fund which regularly supported the poor of Jerusalem, Hebron, and Safed. In 1814 Ḥayyim Baruch of Ostrava was appointed as the emissary of Hebron and he succeeded in organizing a network of funds which regularly provided Hebron with considerable amounts (O. Avisar op. cit., 131, 219). Sir Moses Montefiore, who visited Hebron in 1839 and was impressed with its beauty, also made generous contributions to the town. There is even evidence of independent economic progress made by the Jews of Hebron toward the second half of the 19th century. There were Jews who dealt in wine (1838), crafts, and trade (1876 and after).

The most significant development in the history of the Hebron settlement in the 19th century, however, was brought about by Chabad *Ḥasidim. The community was headed by R. Simon Menahem Ḥaikin who moved from Safed in 1840. Internal life was well organized; an agreement was signed between the Sephardi and Ashkenazi communities (in 1830 and 1842), and a close relationship was maintained between them. In the middle of the 19th century Elijah *Mani founded several public institutions, including the *bet ha-midrash* Bet Yaakov, and reorganized the Sephardi **kolel* in Hebron, freeing it from the administration of the Sephardi *kolel* of Jerusalem. He also revolutionized communal life by instituting a *takkanah* which stated that the *kolel* could subsidize only those actually engaged in studying the Torah. This step encouraged many of the inhabitants to begin to work, thus leading to a greater productivity in Hebron's economic life. There was even a hospital in Hebron by 1895, and the Jewish population reached 1,500 by the late 19th century.

An important contribution to Hebron's spiritual life was made by Ḥayyim Hezekiah *Medini, who founded a yeshivah for young people in Hebron. Four years previously (1900) R. Shalom Baer of Lubavich had established the yeshivah Torat Emet. Together with the religious education system, which reached the height of its development at the beginning of the 20th century, there was a parallel development in secular education, and in 1907 the German Hilfsverein set up the first school that included secular studies in its curriculum. Nevertheless, due to limited economic possibilities the Jewish population fell to 700 by 1910.

World War I and British Rule (1917–1948)

The flourishing period of the Jewish settlement in Hebron came to an end in 1914, with the outbreak of World War I. The young men were conscripted into the Turkish army, the channels of financial assistance were blocked, hunger and plagues created havoc among the populace, and the ghetto of Hebron was almost entirely emptied of its inhabitants after the closing of the *kolelim* in the town – except for the Sephardi *kolel*. The Hebron settlement underwent a grave depression. In 1918, however, when Hebron was captured by the British and World War I ended, the Jewish settlement began to recover. The education department of the Zionist organization established schools for boys and girls, as well as a kindergarten. The number of inhabitants was smaller than before the war (430 out of a total population of 16,000 in 1922) but their economic situation was stable. The spiritual situation, on the other hand, was poor – the yeshivot were impoverished and there were only 17 students. In 1925 the *Slobodka Yeshivah from Lithuania was established under the leadership of Rabbi M.M. Epstein, and the Jewish population rose to 700 in 1929 (out of a population of 18,000).

The year 1929 dealt a heavy blow to the Jewish settlement with the killing of many of Hebron's Jews by Arab rioters. The assault was well planned and its aim was well defined: the elimination of the Jewish settlement of Hebron. The rioters did not spare women, children, or the aged; the British remained passive. Sixty-seven were killed, 60 wounded, the community was destroyed, synagogues razed, and Torah scrolls burned. However, those who remained did not surrender and 35 families went to resettle in 1931. The community slowly began to rebuild itself, but everything was again destroyed in the upheavals of 1936. On the night of April 23, 1936, the British authorities evacuated the Jewish inhabitants of Hebron. The Jewish settlement of Hebron thus ended and only one inhabitant remained there until 1947.

After 1948

In 1948 Hebron was incorporated into the kingdom of Jordan. It was captured by the Israel army in the Six-Day War of June 1967, and Jews again returned to visit Hebron. The old Jewish quarter was found destroyed and the Jewish cemetery almost obliterated. According to the 1967 census, conducted by Israel, Hebron had 38,309 inhabitants, all of whom (excepting 106 Christians) were Muslim. In 1997 the city's population numbered 119,093 inhabitants, 18% of them refugees. Hebron has a smaller percentage of Palestinian Arab refugees than most other places of the West Bank.

On the eve of Passover 1968 a group of religious settlers went to reestablish the Jewish settlement. This new settlement encountered opposition both from the local Arabs and from official Israel sources as their move had not been authorized. The settlers had to fight for official recognition and the right to build a Jewish township in Hebron. In May 1968 the settlers were moved from their temporary quarters to the area occupied by the military government, thus acquiring the protection of the government but not the right to engage freely in economic activity. In 1970 the government decided to permit Jewish settlement in the town of Hebron and to build 250 housing units there. Through the influence of Hebron's mayor Muhammed Ali al-Jaʿbarī, the town remained relatively quiet under the Israel military government, although in 1968 and 1969 attacks repeatedly occurred on Israel soldiers, visitors, and settlers. There were several attacks on Jews who came to pray at the cave of Machpelah, as well as arguments about the right to pray there.

[Moshe Shapira]

Throughout most of its history Hebron's economy has been characterized by its position on the border of two regions – the farming area and the desert. Therefore, it has served as a marketplace for the exchange of goods between the peasants and the Bedouin shepherds. Even in the 1970s its economy was based principally on retail trade and on handicrafts such as pottery, glass blowing, and leather tanning. Hebron's built-up area, which expanded after 1948, extends mainly northward along the road leading to Bethlehem and Jerusalem and approaches the village of *Halhul.

[Efraim Orni]

Developments through 1972 and After

The new Jewish quarter adjacent to Hebron continued to develop. The building of the first 250 dwellings was completed and the quarter named Kiryat Arba, a former biblical name for Hebron. Government approval was given for the building of an additional 100 dwellings and at the end of 1972 Kiryat Arba had a population of almost 1,000, and a large industrial zone was under construction. Kiryat Arba was administered by an officer belonging to the military government, with an advisory committee of the inhabitants, under the provisions of the local (Jordanian) municipal law, though as Israel citizens individual residents were subject to Israel law. However, not all the settlers agreed to move to Kiryat Arba, and in 1981 they moved to the old Jewish quarter, which had been abandoned during the 1929 riots, taking possession of Bet Hadassah and the adjacent buildings.

Most of the residents were religious, and there were some disagreements between them and the government as a result of their demand for autonomous municipal status and the right to approve new candidates for housing in the quarter. Another important issue was the question of services at the Tomb of the Patriarchs (Cave of *Machpelah), which had served for centuries as a Muslim mosque. They objected to the agreement between Defense Minister Moshe Dayan and Muhammad Ali al-Jaʿbarī, the mayor of Hebron, on the scheduling of prayer services and other arrangements between Jews and Muslims, particularly at the Solemn Festivals.

Many Israelis regarded the re-establishment of a Jewish presence in Hebron, one of the Land of Israel's four holy cities, where Abraham had lived and David ruled, as an act of historic justice. There were complaints that the development of Kiryat Arba was too slow, and that it was being held up for political reasons. However, the new quarter was the target of criticism from left-wing and pacifist circles, who feared that its existence might prove an obstacle to an eventual peace settlement. The Jewish presence in the city created tensions between Arabs and Jews. During the first Intifada, Palestinian fire-bombing and rock-throwing attacks on Jews in and around the city were incessant, The tension reached its peak on Purim, February 25, 1994, when Baruch Goldstein, Kiryat Arba's medical doctor, entered the Cave of Machpelah during Muslim prayers and opened fire with an automatic weapon, killing 29 and wounding 100.

[Daniel Rubinstein]

As part of the Oslo Agreements, the majority of the territory of Hebron was handed over to the Palestinian Authority on January 17, 1997, with only some 35 Jewish families and

200 yeshivah students remaining in the city proper. There were some 5,600 Jewish residents in Kiryat Arba. However, the tension between both sides continued and was exacerbated from 2000 with the coming of the second Intifada. At the end of 2002 Kiryat Arba had 6,580 inhabitants and the Jewish settlement in Hebron numbered 500 residents. (See also *Israel, State of: Historical Survey.)

BIBLIOGRAPHY: O. Avisar (ed.), *Sefer Ḥevron* (1970); I.S. Horowitz, *Ereẓ-Yisrael u-Shekhenoteha* (1923), 248–63; Z. Vilnay, *Maẓẓevot ha-Kodesh be-Ereẓ-Yisrael* (1963), 71–98; A.M. Luncz (ed.), *Yerushalayim*, 10 (1914), 304–10; I. Kaplan, *Ir ha-Avot* (1924); Ha-Va'ad le-Vinyan Ḥevron, *Tazkir la-Congress ha-Ẓiyyoni…* (1931); Y.E. Levanon, *Yalkut Ḥevron* (1937); M. Mani, *Ḥevron ve-Gibboreha* (1963); J. Braslavsky, in: *Eretz Israel*, 5 (1958), 221–3; idem, in: YMHEY, 10 (1943), 66–70; idem, *Le-Ḥeker Arẓenu* (1954), index; B.Z. Dinaburg, in: *Zion (Me'assef)*, 2 (1927), 54–55; J. Pinkerfeld, in: YMHEY, 6 (1939), 61–65; A.Y. Shaḥrai, *Ḥevron* (1930); *Sefer ha-Yishuv*, 1 (1939), 40–42; 2 (1944), 6–9; S. Assaf, *Mekorot u-Meḥkarim be-Toledot Yisrael* (1946), 43–49; A. Yaari, *Masot Ereẓ Yisrael* (1945), index; idem, *Iggerot Ereẓ Israel*, index; idem, Sheluḥei, index; idem, in: *Yerushalayim: Meḥkerei Ereẓ Yisrael*, 4 (1953), 185–202; idem, in: *Maḥanayim*, no. 72 (1962), 84–96; N.H. Torczyner, in: E.L. Sukenik and I. Press (eds.), *Yerushalayim:… Le-Zekher Avraham Moshe Luncz* (1928), 109–10; M. Ish-Shalom, *Masei Noẓerim le-Ereẓ Yisrael* (1965), index; Press, Ereẓ, 2 (1948), 244–6; M. Benayahu, in: *Sura*, 2 (1955–56), 219–23; N. Fried, in: *Sinai*, 53 (1963), 108–111; Prawer, Ẓalbanim, 2 (1963), index; M.D. Gaon, *Yehudei ha-Mizraḥ be-Ereẓ Yisrael*, 1 (1928), 177–94; I. Ben Zvi, *She'ar Yashuv* (1966), index; idem, *Ereẓ-Yisrael ve-Yishuvah…* (1967), index; idem, in: YMHEY, 5 (1937), 119–23; B. Meisler, in: *Sefer Dinaburg* (1949), 310–25; L.H. Vincent, E.J.H. Mackay and F.M. Abel, *Hebron. Le Haram el-Khalîl* (1923); Abel, Geog, 2 (1938), 345–7; G.L. Strange, *Palestine under the Moslems* (1890), 309 ff.

°HECATAEUS OF ABDERA (fourth century B.C.E.), Greek historian and ethnographer. He evidently visited Jerusalem and was the first pagan who wrote extensively on the history of the Jews, incorporating it into his account of Egypt. A summary of it has been preserved in Diodorus, the first-century C.E. historian (60:3), via the ninth-century Photius (*Bibliotheca*, 224). The following is a summary of Hecataeus' report.

> From time immemorial there lived minorities in Egypt whose manner of sacrificing differed from that of the general population. When a plague occurred, the Egyptians expelled them. Some found refuge in Greece; the majority fled to Judea, then uninhabited. Their leader, Moses, founded Hierosolyma and its Temple, establishing a cult and a constitution which differed completely from any other. Because he believed that God is the master of the universe, Moses prohibited the presentation of the divine in a human form. The laws of marriage and burial differed from those among other groups of men, to whom the Jews adopted a hostile attitude. The Jews never had a king, but Moses assigned a prominent role to the priests, the chief of whom is said to receive messages from God. When he teaches the divine commandments, the assembled Jews prostrate themselves until the high priest concludes with these words: "Moses heard these words from God and he spoke them to the Jews." During the Persian and Macedonian occupations, Hecataeus concludes, many of their ancient institutions were modified.

Hecataeus' account, like those of Megasthenes and Theophrastus, is on the whole sympathetic to the Jews. He stressed the humaneness of such enactments as Moses' prohibition of infant exposure and his equal distribution of the land. His apparently high regard for the Mosaic constitution explains the popularity of pseudonymous books under his name. Hecataeus, according to the Letter of *Aristeas (v. 31), wrote to *Ptolemy II of Egypt asking him to invite 72 priests from Jerusalem to translate the Torah. This passage probably apppeared in Pseudo-Hecataeus' book called "On the Jews," from which Josephus has preserved extensive excerpts. The work treated conditions in Palestine during the period of Alexander's successors, the Diadochi, mentioning the high priest *Hezekiah (not elsewhere mentioned) recording the extent of Judea, and describing Jerusalem's Temple and cult. Many scholars, including H. Lewy, Tcherikover, and Guttmann, attribute this work to the genuine Hecataeus. They point, for example, to the statement that the Persians deported the Jews to Babylon, a slip a Jewish forger was unlikely to have made. There is no question, however, that Josephus' *Contra Apionem*, 1, 183–204, is the work of a pseudographer. Hecataeus indirectly criticized the Jews for not mixing with other nations; Pseudo-Hecataeus displays the fervor of an ardent Jew. The suspicion of forgery was already raised in the second century C.E. by Philo of Byblos, who wondered whether Hecataeus had become a Jewish convert. The author of this work may be labeled "Pseudo-Hecataeus I." Also forged, though by a different hand ("Pseudo-Hecataeus II"), is the book "On the Time of Abramus and the Egyptians" to which there are two known allusions. Josephus (Ant., 1:159) states that Hecataeus wrote a work about the patriarch, Abraham. Clement of Alexandria (*Stromateis*, 5:113) quotes nine lines from a drama attributed to Hecataeus, portraying the patriarch's smashing of the idols. The quotation was taken from a Jewish anthology of Greek poets and philosophers who purportedly subscribed to the truth or antiquity of biblical tenets. Scholarly opinion is divided over Pseudo-Hecataeus I, but there is a general consensus that Pseudo-Hecataeus II is a forgery. Pseudo-Hecataeus I is certainly earlier than the Letter of Aristeas, and was possibly written in the first half of the second century B.C.E. Pseudo-Hecataeus II antedates Josephus, and is perhaps as early as or even earlier than *Aristobulus.

BIBLIOGRAPHY: F. Jacoby, *Fragmente der griechischen Historiker*, 3a (1940), no. 264; Jaeger, in: JR, 18 (1938), 127–43; Klausner, Bayit Sheni, 2 (1951^2), 17, 26, 106; N. Walther, *Thoraausleger Aristobulos* (1964).

[Ben Zion Wacholder]

HECHAL SHLOMO, the former official seat of the Chief Rabbinate of Israel in Jerusalem, opened in 1958, Hechal Shlomo was built largely through the munificence of Sir Isaac *Wolfson, who named it in memory of his father.

Hechal Shlomo housed a number of institutions and organizations. The interior of its synagogue was brought from the synagogue of Padua, Italy. It also housed the Central Rabbinical Library and a Museum of Religious Art. Among the organizations under the aegis of Hechal Shlomo were the Union of Israeli Synagogues and the World Conference of Synagogues. Among its other activities Hechal Shlomo published an annual, *Shanah be-Shanah*. Today the building houses several religious Zionism organizations.

°**HECHLER, WILLIAM HENRY** (1845–1931), Christian Zionist. Hechler was born in Benares, India, where his father served as a missionary of the Evangelical Church. His father was of German origin and his mother was English, and as a result Hechler spoke both languages equally well. In 1871 he served as a missionary in Lagos, Nigeria, and in 1874 became the tutor of the children of *Frederick the grand duke of Baden, an uncle of Kaiser William II. When he failed in his attempts to be appointed Anglican bishop in Jerusalem, he became the chaplain of the British embassy in Vienna and served in that post from 1885 to 1910. He spent the rest of his life in London. Throughout his life, Hechler was engaged in mystical and messianic calculations, and when he became interested in the Jewish problem he sought its solution by calculating the date of the return of the Jewish people to Ereẓ Israel. After the pogroms in Russia in the early 1880s, he visited Odessa, where he met L. *Pinsker. From there he proceeded to Constantinople, bearing a letter to the sultan from Queen Victoria, in which the queen entreated the sultan to grant Russian Jews asylum in the Holy Land. The British embassy, however, refused to submit the letter. In his book *Restoration of Jews* (1884) Hechler traced the link between his mystical calculations and the Return of the Jews; his conclusion was that the redemption of the Jewish people would occur in the years 1897–98. When Theodor *Herzl's *Der Judenstaat* was published, Hechler dispatched a letter to the grand duke of Baden, dated March 26, 1896, to draw his attention to Herzl's work, "the first serious, quiet and practical attempt to show the Jews how they can reunite and form a nation of their own in the Land of Promise, given them by God." Thereafter Hechler devoted his efforts to establishing a close relationship between the grand duke and Herzl, and, through the help of the grand duke, between Herzl and William II. Until recently, these efforts were known only from Herzl's diaries and letters and statements made by contemporaries; their full scope came to light, however, with the discovery of the original correspondence involving Hechler, the grand duke of Baden, Herzl, and the kaiser.

In the second issue of *Die Welt*, Hechler published a comprehensive article containing his conclusion that the time of redemption had come and stating his conviction that Zionism was the ultimate solution. He attended the First Zionist Congress (1897), for which Herzl expressed his public appreciation. Hechler accompanied Herzl on his trip to Ereẓ Israel in 1898, when he was to meet the kaiser, and it was he who welcomed the Jewish delegation that presented the kaiser with an album of photographs depicting scenes from the new Jewish settlements. Another noteworthy effort made by Hechler was his attempt to arrange a meeting between Herzl and the czar through the czar's brother-in-law, the grand duke of Hesse. He visited Herzl on his deathbed, and it was to him that Herzl whispered the words: "Give my regards to all of them and tell that I gave my heart's blood to my people." Hechler retained his interest in Zionism throughout his life and also met Martin *Buber. He had a museum in his house, which included Montefiore's famous carriage. In his last will, he left it to the "Ereẓ Israel Museum" (the carriage was restored and is displayed in Jerusalem, next to Montefiore's windmill). In 1928 Hechler published his memories of Herzl in *Theodor Herzl, A Memorial* (ed. by M. Weisgal (1929), 51–52). Herzl depicted Hechler in *Altneuland*, under the name of Rev. Hopkins.

BIBLIOGRAPHY: *Herzl Year Book*, 4 (1962), 207–70; T. Herzl, *Complete Diaries*, 5 vols. (1960), index; S.R. Landau, *Sturm und Drang im Zionismus* (1937), 60–65, 193, 198–9; D. Pardo, *Prêtres, rois et diplomates au service du sionisme politique* (1933); H. and B. Ellern, *Herzl, Hechler, The Grand Duke of Baden and The German Emperor* (1961).

[Getzel Kressel]

HECHT, BEN (1893–1964), U.S. novelist and playwright. Born in New York City, Hecht was brought up in Racine, Wisconsin. He rebelled against a college education and after a variety of jobs became a reporter first on the *Chicago Journal* then on the *Chicago Daily News*. The year he spent in Berlin as a foreign correspondent inspired his first novel, *Erik Dorn* (1921), while *1001 Afternoons in Chicago* (1922) and *Broken Necks* (1924) included pieces originally published in the Chicago press. Hecht first came to prominence as coauthor with Charles MacArthur of *The Front Page* (1928), a tough play about newspaper life. The two writers continued their partnership with a number of very successful film scripts throughout the 1930s and 1940s.

Hecht's portrayal of Jews in his earlier works, such as *A Jew in Love* (1931), was unsympathetic and sometimes even grotesque, but the rise of Nazism, which inspired his antifascist play *To Quito and Back* (1937), resulted in a sensational change in his attitude. In 1941 Hecht publicly proclaimed his Jewish nationalism and became a leading advocate of the dissident underground organization *Irgun Ẓeva'i Le'ummi, whose activities he championed in the American League for a Free Palestine and the Hebrew Committee of National Liberation. His sympathies were made clear in *A Guide for the Bedevilled* (1944), a controversial analysis of antisemitism, and in *A Flag is Born* (1946). The "illegal" immigrant ship bought by IẒL after World War II was called *Ben Hecht*. When during the War of Independence the Israel government ordered the sinking of the *Altalena*, an Irgun ship loaded with arms which arrived off Tel Aviv and refused to surrender them unconditionally to the Israel government, Hecht, who was one of the organizers of its dispatch, withdrew from further Zionist activity. He nevertheless maintained his sentimental attachment to the Revisionist cause, and manifested his partisanship in *Perfidy* (1961), a vitriolic attack on David *Ben-Gurion and the Israel "establishment" and an examination of the *Kasztner affair.

In the course of a 40-year career, Hecht enjoyed success as a controversial writer on many issues. His autobiography, *A Child of the Century* (1954), was a best seller. His other works include *Count Bruga* (1926); *20th Century* (1932); *A Book of Miracles* (1939); *The Sensualists* (1959); *Gaily, Gaily* (1963); and a book of recollections, *Letters from Bohemia* (1964).

BIBLIOGRAPHY: J. Mersand, *Traditions in American Literature…* (1939), 112–7; O. Cargill, *Intellectual America* (1941), 503–6; S. Liptzin, *Jew in American Literature* (1966), 188–90. **ADD. BIBLIOGRAPHY:** G. Fetherling, *The Five Lives of Ben Hecht* (1977); W. MacAdams, *Ben Hecht* (1995).

[Joseph Mersand]

HECHT, REUBEN (1909–1993). Israeli industrialist and Zionist activist. Hecht, the son of Jacob *Hecht, was born in Antwerp but grew up in Basle, and studied at the University of Heidelberg, receiving his doctorate in political science in 1933. Hecht was engaged in transport and shipping before emigrating to Ereẓ Israel in 1936. An active Revisionist from his student days, Hecht cooperated with Ze'ev Jabotinsky during his stay in Paris in 1933–34, joined the Irgun Ẓeva'i Le'ummi, and was sent by David Raziel to Europe in 1939 to organize "illegal" immigration. In 1941 he escaped with his wife from German-occupied Yugoslavia to Switzerland, where he intensively continued his political and rescue work as representative of the Irgun and the Hebrew Committee of National Liberation. After World War II he joined the family shipping combine, Neptun-Rhenania, of which he was president from 1963 to 1970. In Israel he obtained the first concession granted in the state for the erection of port grain silos and in 1951 established the Dagon Silo Company in Haifa. Among his other activities are the foundation of the Shikmona publishing company and the unique Dagon Archaeological Museum, devoted to the means of cultivation and storage of grain since the most ancient times.

Hecht served on numerous governmental, civic, cultural, and educational bodies, including membership in the Archaeological Council attached to the Ministry of Education and Culture, the International Council of Museums, Paris, the Bezalel Academy, the Israel Museum and the Israel Board of the American-Israel Cultural Foundation, of whose subcommittee for art, archaeology, and museums he was chairman until 1976. He was among the founders of Haifa University and a member in its board from 1971 until the day he died. In 1981 he established the Hecht Museum, located inside the university, and donated his private collections. In 1984 he was the first to receive an honorary doctorate from Haifa University.

He was awarded the Kaplan Prize for efficiency in 1960, in 1970 he was made an honorary citizen of Haifa, and in 1977 he was appointed personal advisor to the prime minister. In 1986 he was awarded a special humanitarian prize from the international *B'nai B'rith organization. He was awarded the Israel Prize in 1988 for exemplary lifelong service to society and the state.

HECHT, SELIG (1892–1947), U.S. biophysicist. Hecht was born in Glogau, Austria, and was taken to the United States as a child. He carried out extensive research in physical chemistry and physiology, both in the United States and elsewhere. He taught biophysics at Columbia University in New York from 1926 until his death. Hecht was a pioneer in the physiology of vision and propounded the photochemical theory of vision. His experiments showed that minute quantities of light are sufficient to cause a reaction by the human retina. Measuring the visual properties of insects, he proved that in terms of light sensitivity these are much the same as for creatures with eyes. He was also an exponent of popular science; in particular his *Explaining the Atom* was widely read.

[J. Edwin Holmstrom]

HECKERLING, AMY (1954–), U.S. writer, director, producer. Heckerling grew up in New York City. She attended the High School of Art and Design and though she studied photography during her time there, she opted to pursue a different path upon completing high school, and went to NYU's prestigious Tisch School of Arts to study film. Based on the short films she made as an undergraduate student, one of which starred her NYU classmate and future mega-producer Joel Silver, Heckerling was accepted to the American Film Institute's directorial program, from which she received a master's degree. Despite a slow start at breaking into the movie industry after completing her graduate work, Heckerling's feature film debut was wildly successful. This was *Fast Times at Ridgemont High* (1982), a comic look at modern, suburban teenagers that included such up-and-coming stars as Sean Penn and Jennifer Jason Leigh in its young cast. After *Fast Times*, Heckerling went on to make several consecutive box office duds, including *Johnny Dangerously* (1984) and *National Lampoon's European Vacation* (1985). Following these movies, Heckerling came up with the idea for her next project while pregnant with her daughter Mollie Israel. Heckerling turned her inspiration into *Look Who's Talking* (1987), the box-office smash in which an infant's internal monologue is conveyed by the voice of Bruce Willis. She also wrote and directed the cultural touchstone *Clueless* (1995), which launched the career of Alicia Silverstone. Besides her many career achievements, Heckerling is a politically active liberal and devoted environmentalist.

[Casey Schwartz (2nd ed.)]

HECKSCHER, ELI FILIP (1879–1952), Swedish economic historian. Heckscher was born in Stockholm, where he taught from 1909 to 1944 at the University College of Commerce. His books, which were translated into many languages, were the *Kontinentalsystemet* (1918; *The Continental System, an Economic Interpretation*, 1923), and *Merkantilismen* (1931; *Mercantilism*, 1935). Based largely on new sources, *Mercantilism* presents an analysis of the intellectual world of the mercantile system. The study which occupied the last years of Heckscher's life was *Sveriges ekonomiska historia från Gustav Vasa* (begun in 1935; *Economic History of Sweden Since Gustavus Vasa*, 1954). The author's death prevented him from continuing the study beyond 1815. Heckscher is regarded as one of the most important Swedish historians of his time.

BIBLIOGRAPHY: Montgomery, in: *Ekonomisk Tidskrift* (1953); *Svenska män och kvinnor*, 3 (1946).

[Hugo Mauritz Valentin]

°HEDEGÅRD, OSKAR DAVID LEONARD (1891–1971), Swedish theologian. Hedegård edited and translated *Seder R. Amram Gaon* for his doctoral dissertation (1951). He held various educational posts in the Swedish church and wrote a series of popular publications and handbooks on sacred history and New Testament theology. He co-edited (with A. Saarisalo) a Swedish interpreter's dictionary of the Bible, *Biblisk uppslagsbok, en handbok för bibelläsare* (1939, 1958[3]). His two-volume *Nya Testamentet på vår tids språk* (1964–65), consists of several New Testament books translated into modern idiom.

[Ignacy Yizhak Schiper]

ḤEDER (Heb. חֶדֶר; lit. "room"), the common name for the old-fashioned elementary school for the teaching of Judaism. The name first occurs in the 13th century. The *ḥeder* was distinct from the *talmud torah*. Whereas the latter was a communal institution maintained by the community for poor children whose parents could not afford tuition fees, the *ḥeder* was a privately run institution, the teacher receiving his fees from the parents. It was generally housed in a room in the private house of the teacher, called the *rebbe* (Yiddish form of "rabbi") or *melammed*. Usually three classes were held concurrently; while the teacher taught one the children in the others went over their lessons. The age groups were from 3–5, 6–7, and 8–13. The teacher ruled with an iron hand and freely wielded his cane (*kanchik*). No secular studies were taught, the subjects for the three classes being, respectively, reading in the prayer book, the Pentateuch with Rashi, and Talmud. To the *rebbe* was sometimes added an assistant, called the *belfer* ("behelfer"). The *ḥeder* came under the withering attacks of the *maskilim*, who criticized the primitive methods and the restricted nature of the curriculum (cf. P. Smolenskin, *Ha-To'eh be-Darkhei ha-Ḥayyim*, 1 (1868), 4; J.L. Gordon, *Kol Kitvei…* (1899), 112–3) and toward the end of the 19th century attempts were made to introduce a "reformed *ḥeder*" (*ḥeder metukkan*) but without solid results. From the *ḥeder* the pupil proceeded to the yeshivah.

BIBLIOGRAPHY: E.M. Lipschitz, *Ketavim*, 1 (1947), 305–80.

[Louis Isaac Rabinowitz]

HEEGER, ALAN J. (1936–), U.S. physicist and material scientist and Nobel laureate. Heeger was born in Iowa. He was the first of his family to continue his education beyond high school and graduated from the University of Nebraska with a dual major in physics and mathematics. He received his Ph.D. in physics at Berkeley in 1961 while working part time for the Lockheed Space and Missile Division in Palo Alto, California. He joined the Physics Department at the University of Pennsylvania as an assistant professor in 1962 and was made full professor in 1967. At Penn he served as laboratory director and vice provost for research. In 1982 Heeger moved to the University of California, Santa Barbara, where he held the Presidential Chair and served as professor of physics and professor of materials. He headed a research group at the University's Center for Polymers and Organic Solids. Heeger holds approximately 50 patents, which have broad commercial potential for use in polymer electronics ("plastic" electronics) with applications in areas ranging from electroluminescent displays (for cell phones, PDAs, and laptops) to solar cells and integrated electronic circuits. In 1990 he founded UNIAX, which played a leading role in developing the science and technology of conducting polymers with many important contributions. UNIAX was acquired by DuPont in 2000. Heeger served on the board of directors of Konarka Technologies, Inc., SBA Materials, and RitDisplay (Taiwan), and was a venture partner in NGen Partners. His research efforts continued to focus on the science and technology of semiconducting and metallic polymers. Later interests included biosensors and the detection of specific targeted sequences on DNA.

Heeger is the recipient of numerous awards, including the Nobel Prize in chemistry in 2000, the Oliver E. Buckley Prize for Condensed Matter Physics, and the Balzan Prize for the Science of New Materials. He is a member of the U.S. National Academy of Sciences and National Academy of Engineering. Heeger has more than 700 publications in scientific journals.

BIBLIOGRAPHY: *Les Prix Nobel* (2000).

[(Gali Rotstein (2nd ed.)]

HEFER (Feiner), ḤAYIM (1925–), Israeli writer of light verse and song lyrics. Born in Poland, Hefer went to Palestine in 1936, served in the *Palmaḥ from 1943, and was one of the founders of Chizbatron, the army's popular entertainment troupe. His verse appeared widely in the Hebrew press, and he also wrote lyrics for satirical works for various theater groups and for literary programs in cabarets which he established together with Dahn *Ben-Amotz. Collections of his verse appeared in *Taḥmoshet Kallah* (1956), *Millim le-Manginot* (1962), and *Sefer ha-Pizmonim* (1981). Many Israeli composers, such as Alexander (Sacha) *Argov, Dov Seltzer, Moshe *Vilensky, Nurit *Hirsch, Mordechai *Zeira and Yoḥanan Zarai set his songs to music and they became quite popular. A series of poems on the *Six-Day War, including those he wrote for his weekly column in *Yedioth Aḥaronoth*, appeared in *Misdar ha-Loḥamim* (1968). He also wrote the lyrics for two original Hebrew musicals *Kazablan* (1966) and *I Like Mike* (1968). He was awarded the Israel Prize for Israeli song in 1983.

[Getzel Kressel]

ḤEFER PLAIN (Heb. עֵמֶק חֵפֶר), the central part of the Sharon Plain between the *Ḥaderah sand dunes in the north and

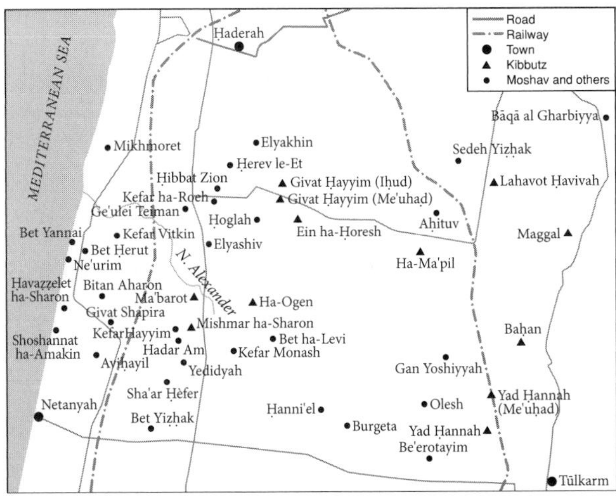

The Hefer Plain.

the *Netanyah-Tul-Karm road in the south. In 1928–29, the *Jewish National Fund (JNF) acquired the Wadi Hawārith lands initially comprising an area of some 8,000 acres. This purchase, one of the largest at the time, was made through aid extended by Canadian Zionists. A continuous chain of Jewish holdings was now created throughout the length of the Sharon to form the backbone of the Jewish settlement network. The first settlers, members of the moshav group "Irgun Vitkin," who arrived in the Ḥefer Plain in 1929, drained the swamps of the Alexander River which flows through the region from east to west, and planted trees to prevent the shifting of sand dunes. The legal land transfer was finalized and arrangements made with Bedouin who claimed tenant rights, while obstacles placed in the way by Arab nationalists and British Mandatory officials were dealt with. From 1931, permanent villages were set up, and in 1939–40, a further portion of the Ḥefer Plain ("Wadi Kabāni") was acquired, where additional settlements were later founded, partly by veterans of World War II. After the *War of Independence (1948), the settlement bloc was extended also eastward, in the direction of Tul-Karm. The Ḥefer Plain became one of Israel's most thoroughly developed and densely settled rural districts, with 32 villages (44, including the newer villages in the east). Farming is highly intensive throughout, with citrus groves and dairy cattle breeding as prominent features. Midrashiyyat Ruppin (named after A. *Ruppin), maintained by the *Histadrut and other bodies, was for a time a center of agricultural study and research. Numerous industrial enterprises were founded in its kibbutzim, and its seaside villages developed as bathing resorts.

[Efraim Orni]

ḤEFEẒ BEN YAẒLI'AḤ (ha-Ashuri, "the Assyrian"; probably second half of 10th century), Babylonian talmudic scholar. Few personal details are known about him save that he was a native of Mosul, was blind, and bore the identical titles of *alluf* and *resh kallah*, evidence of his high standing in the Babylonian academies. The claim that Ḥefeẓ lived in Kairouan, North Africa, has not been substantiated. The exact dates of his activity are unknown, but it is clear he was already recognized as a scholar at the beginning of the 11th century. Jonah *Ibn Janaḥ, for one, held him in great esteem. Ḥefeẓ was renowned among the scholars of Spain and Egypt as a grammarian and talmudic scholar, and is cited by such luminaries as *Alfasi, *Maimonides, *Judah b. Barzillai, *Baḥya ibn Pakuda, *Nathan b. Jehiel, and the lexicographers, Salomon ibn *Parḥon and Judah *Ibn Balaam. Maimonides specifically acknowledges that he was guided by him in his commentary on the Mishnah (*Maimonides' Letters*, ed. by Baneth (1944), 78). Because he wrote in Arabic, Ḥefeẓ's teachings were not known to French and German scholars.

His most important work is his *Sefer ha-Mitzvot* ("Book of Commandments"), probably the first comprehensive book of laws in Hebrew literature, including laws which no longer had practical application. Only fragments of this book are extant (see bibliography). Unlike the earlier *Halakhot Gedolot which follows the order of the Talmud, his book was arranged according to an inner logical system. His numeration of the precepts differed too from that of the *Halakhot Gedolot*. His method was to embark upon an extensive interpretation of each precept as treated in talmudic literature, including in the process many quotations from the Babylonian and Jerusalem Talmuds and the Tosefta with important variant readings, reflecting his closeness to the geonic sources. Statements of *Samuel b. Hophni are to be found in the book, though lack of exact chronological data leaves open the question as to who borrowed from whom. A work attributed to Ḥefeẓ is a lexicon of the *Halakhot Gedolot* (mentioned in lists of books from the *Genizah), a few quotations of which are to be found in the works of the *rishonim*.

French and German scholars alone refer to a certain *Sefer Ḥefeẓ*. It is first mentioned by *Eliezer b. Nathan, and later by his pupils and followers: *Eliezer b. Joel ha-Levi, *Isaac b. Abba Mari in his *Ittur*, *Isaac b. Moses of Vienna in his *Or Zaru'a*, *Mordecai b. Hillel in his *Sefer Mordekhai*, and others. All that is known of it is that it was a book of decisions written in Hebrew and including the orders *Nashim, Nezikin*, and *Mo'ed*. The great similarity – mostly as a result of copying – between this *Sefer Ḥefeẓ* and the anonymous *Metivot*, one of *Alfasi's sources, led various scholars to regard the *Sefer Ḥefeẓ* as identical with the book of Ḥefeẓ b. Yaẓli'aḥ. Subsequent study has shown, however, that they have nothing in common but the title. Fragments of the anonymous book have been collected by B.M. Lewin (see bibliography).

BIBLIOGRAPHY: Aptowitzer, in: *Tarbiz*, 4 (1932/33), 127–52; B. Lewin (ed.), *Sefer Metivot… ve-Sefer Hefez* (1933), I–XLVI; Assaf, in KS, 11 (1935), 161–6; Assaf, Ge'onim, 206f.; M. Zucker, in: PAAJR, 29 (1961), 1–68 (Heb. section; idem, in: *Hadoar*, 42 (1962/63), 385–8.

[Israel Moses Ta-Shma]

HEFKER (Heb. הֶפְקֵר), ownerless property and renunciation of ownership. *Hefker* is property that is ownerless and can therefore be legally acquired by the person who first takes possession of it. There are two categories of ownerless property: (1) property that has never been owned before – such as wild animals and birds, fish of the river and ocean, and wild or forest plants (Maim. Yad, Zekhi'ah, 1:1–2); and (2) property that has ceased to belong to its former owner.

Property becomes *hefker* in two different ways, just as *ownership can generally cease in the same two ways:

(1) When it is clear that the property can no more return permanently to an individual's possession – for example, birds which have escaped (Ran on Rif, Ḥul. beginning of Ch. 11) – provided that no other person has acquired it. Similarly, the property of a proselyte who leaves no Jewish heirs becomes *hefker*, since his gentile relatives do not inherit from him.

(2) When the owner decides not to have it again in his possession, i.e., if he renounces it or if he gives up hope of recovering *lost property. As in all other instances of termination of ownership, such as **ye'ush*, the only formality required in the case of renunciation is the manifestation of the owner's intention, whether by word or conduct, as when he declares "this is renounced in favor of anyone who wants it" (Ned. 43a) or by any conduct to this effect. Thus, for instance, if a Jew purchases land from a non-Jew, the latter may vacate it on receipt of the purchase money, whereas the purchaser may not wish to acquire the land except in the prescribed manner in which it would be acquired from another Jew, i.e., by *shetar* or *ḥazakah* (see *Acquisition). It is thus possible that in the interval the field becomes ownerless and may be acquired by anyone taking possession of it (BB 54b), although in practice the secular law of the land would usually prevail to make the transfer effective. Similarly, the circumstances in which property is found may indicate that ownership thereof has been renounced, as in the case of "intentional loss" (*avedah mi-da'at*), i.e., when the owner knowingly leaves the property in a place where he is likely to lose it, such as produce scattered on the threshing-floor (BM 21a), or open jars of wine or oil in a public domain (BM 23b). The fact that ownership is relinquished by mental decision means that minors, having no "mind" in law, cannot dispose of their property by renunciation (BM 22b). For the same reason *hefker* created through a mistake of fact (see *Samson b. Abraham of Sens, Comm. Pe'ah, 6:1), or under duress (TJ, Suk. 4:2, 54b) is void.

There is a difference of opinion with regard to *hefker* between the schools of Shammai and Hillel. The former hold that a renunciation in favor of the poor only is valid, comparing it to **pe'ah* ("the corner of the field," Lev. 23:22), while the latter maintain that to be valid the renunciation must apply to rich and poor alike, as is the case with regard to *shemittah* ("the sabbatical year," Lev. 25:1–7). In R. Johanan's view both schools agree that renunciation in favor of all human beings, but excluding animals, or to all Jews, but not non-Jews, is valid, while Simeon b. Lakish maintains that the school of Hillel would regard it as invalid (TJ, Pe'ah 6:1, 19b). It is possible that the difference of opinion centers around the principle that where the renunciation is not of universal application, the renouncer, by preventing the property from being acquired by certain categories excluded from the renunciation, thereby retains some possession of it which is a bar to renunciation. However, where the owner disregards the possibility of it being acquired by those whom he excludes, he thereupon ceases to guard it and it passes out of his possession. The school of Shammai opines that the owner who renounces his property in favor of the poor has no fear that the rich may take possession of it, while the school of Hillel disagrees.

Ownership of property that has been lost ceases from the moment the owner gives expression to his despair of recovering it (see **ye'ush*). In the case of *hefker* there is a dispute as to whether it takes effect immediately upon renunciation, in which case the owner cannot retract, or upon the acquisition of the property by another (Ned. 43a; TJ, Pe'ah 6:1, 19b). A person may renounce his property for a fixed period, and if it is acquired by another within the stated period it becomes the latter's permanently. At the end of the stated period the renunciation is automatically annulled if the property has not so been acquired (Ned. 44a).

Hefker property is exempt from a number of commandments. It is free from the obligations of the gifts due to priests and levites, as from *terumah* ("heave offering"), tithes, and the giving of the firstborn of animals to the priest. Advantage was sometimes taken of this law to evade these obligations. The owners would renounce their property to evade their liability, subsequently reacquiring it before others could take possession of it. To prevent this an enactment was made restricting the ability to withdraw a renunciation to three days from the time it was made (Ned. 43b); within this period a renounced field remains subject to the various imposts, and owners would be afraid to make the renunciation apply for a longer period lest the field be acquired by someone else. However, there are different opinions as to the details of this enactment. Similarly, it was enacted that renunciation had to be made before three persons (Ned. 45a), so that it could be made public and people would be able to take advantage of it. Some scholars hold that the requirement of three witnesses is based on biblical law; others hold that in biblical law two witnesses suffice for this purpose, and that the need for three is a rabbinical enactment.

In the State of Israel, ownerless property belongs to the State, in accordance with the "State Property Law, 5711/1951." For acquisition of ownerless property, see *Acquisition. For *hefker bet din hefker*, see *Confiscation and Expropriation, **Takkanot*.

[Shalom Albeck]

Shemittah and Hefker

It has recently been proposed that the law of *hefker* be applied to solve the problem of *shemittah* (the Sabbatical year) in the State of Israel. The approach thus far adopted to solve this problem in practice has been that of the *heter mekhirah*, i.e., the temporary sale of the property on which the produce grows to a non-Jew, so that the law of *shemittah* does not apply. Rabbi Naphtali Ẓevi Judah Berlin (the *Neẓiv*, Resp. Meshiv Davar II.56) ruled that the prohibitions of the *shem-*

ittah year do not apply to property that has been made *hefker* by its owner, much like the rule that the prohibition of *ḥameẓ* on Passover does not apply to property that has been made *hefker* by its owner. Soon after the establishment of the State of Israel, it was suggested that the Neẓiv's ruling be used to obviate the application of *shemittah* prohibitions, by making the property *hefker*.This suggestion raises a number of issues, such as whether property can be made *hefker* for only a limited period of time, and whether it is possible to prevent another person from receiving ownership of property that has been made *hefker;* a number of responses were offered to these questions. At the time, the Chief Rabbinate discussed the suggestion but did not issue any ruling. Recently, the suggestion has again been raised.

[Menachem Elon (2nd ed.)]

BIBLIOGRAPHY: Gulak, Yesodei, 1 (1922), 97 n. 1 and 4, 138–40; 3 (1922), 76 n. 8, 78 n. 4, 85f.; J.M. Guttmann, in: *Ve-Zot li-Yhudah… Aryeh Blau* (1926), 77–82; Herzog, Instit, 1 (1936), 287–96; S.S. Zeitlin, in: *Sefer ha-Yovel… Louis Ginzberg* (1945), 365–80; B. Cohen, in: *Israel* (Heb., 1950), 89–101; reprinted in his *Jewish and Roman Law* (1966), 10–22 (Hebrew part); ET, 10 (1961), 49–95; S. Albeck, in: *Sefer ha-Shanah… Bar Ilan*, 7–8 (1970), 94–116. **ADD. BIBLIOGRAPHY:** M. Elon, *Ha-Mishpat ha-Ivri* (1988), 1:282, 415, 490, 564; idem, *Jewish Law* (1994), 1:333; 2:507, 596, 685; I. Warhaftig, "The Seventh Year in Land Which is Hefker," in: *Teḥumin*, 13 (1993), 76–88 (Heb.).

HEFTER, ALFRED (Hidalgo; 1892–1957), Romanian editor, journalist, and author. Born in Jassy and influenced by Marxism, Hefter published a pamphlet in this spirit in 1908 together with his brother, the Socialist journalist Jean Hefter (1887–1974). Alfred Hefter edited the symbolist magazine *Versuri şi Proză* in Jassy (1912–14), the paper *Arena* in 1918 (suspended by censor), and then *Lumea*, which appeared until 1924. Moving to Bucharest, he edited two papers there, but incurred government opposition and left for France, later moving to Geneva, Switzerland (1931), where he edited the French-language journal *Le Moment*. Having returned to Bucharest he had to leave again in 1941, settling in Jerusalem. In 1948 he left for France, and went to Italy, where he went into business. He died in Rome. His published works include *Cuvinte despre oameni* ("Some Words on People," 1913), *Din umbră* ("From the Shadow," 1913), and two dramatic works, *Ariana* (1915) and *Miros de iarbă* ("Smell of Grass," 1915).

BIBLIOGRAPHY: I. Marcus (M. Miricu), *Tot sapte momente* (1983), 159–68.

[Lucian-Zeev Herscovici (2nd ed.)]

ḤEFẒI BAH (Heb. חֶפְצִי־בָּהּ), kibbutz at the foot of Mt. Gilboa, Israel, affiliated with Ha-Kibbutz ha-Me'uḥad. It was founded in 1922 by pioneer youth from Germany and Czechoslovakia, who were soon joined by immigrants from Romania, and later from other countries. On the grounds of the kibbutz, the mosaic floor of the ancient *Bet Alfa synagogue was uncovered and is protected by a hall built over it. Ḥefẓi Bah's economy was based on intensive farming (field crops, fishery, dairy cattle, and poultry), and factories for water meters and plastic duct installations. The kibbutz also had guest rooms and a fish restaurant. In 1968, Ḥefẓi Bah had 500 inhabitants, dropping to 400 in 2002. The name, Ḥefẓi Bah, biblical in origin (Isa. 62:4), was taken over by the kibbutz from the name of the Ḥaderah suburb where its first members had their transit camp.

WEBSITE: www.hefzi.org.il.

[Efraim Orni / Shaked Gilboa (2nd ed.)]

HEGEDÜS, ARMIN (1869–1945), **SEBESTYÉN, ARTUR** (1868–1943), and **STERK, IZIDOR** (1860–1935), winners of a competition for the design of Hotel Gellért (1909–1918), an eye-catching example of Secessionist architecture. Its thermal bath and swimming pool were planned later (1927) by Sebestyén whose projects also included buildings outside Hungary, such as cinemas in Odessa and Sofia. He was baptized. Among the main works of Hegedüs was the reconstruction of the Central Municipality building in Budapest, originally serving as barracks for invalid soldiers. Sterk designed factories, apartment houses, and department stores.

[Eva Kondor]

°HEGEL, GEORG WILHELM FRIEDRICH (1770–1831), German philosopher and culminating figure of German Idealism. After studies in philosophy (1788–90) and theology (1790–1793) at the Tuebingen seminary, he served as lecturer and professor at Jena (1801–07), Heidelberg (1816–18), and Berlin (1818–31). Hegel is important for Jewish history for two reasons: first, for his attitude to Judaism, which, because of his importance, was of major interest for many Jews throughout the first half of the 19th century; second, for his philosophy of history and religion in general, which influenced Jewish and other thinkers for an even longer period. Unfortunately most of his statements on these subjects were published only after his death, and were compiled based on his lecture notes and notes taken by his students. This circumstance, as well as the complexities of his language and his extraordinarily systematic thinking, makes his thought on Judaism and the philosophy of history and religion difficult to understand. Thus Hegel has become one of the most controversial figures in the history of philosophy.

Initially marked by anti-Judaic bias (in part inherited from Kant), Hegel changed his views on Judaism considerably during the course of his life. In his early writings, never intended for publication, he contrasted Greek folk religion, in which Divinity is immanent as beauty, with Jewish and, to some extent, Christian book religion consisting of positive, externally imposed law (in Christianity, sacred fact). This dichotomy is later abandoned as Hegel, rejecting his youthful romanticism, develops his dialectical method. Greek beauty and Jewish holiness are now on a par. There is truth in the Greek worship of man-made statues, for Divinity is in their beautiful making; yet, being man-made, their infinity is partly false, despite their beauty. Hence they are doubly demythologized – by the Roman Empire in life (the pantheon assembles and destroys all the pagan gods), and by ancient philosophy in thought. Judaism, in contrast, demythologizes from the start. Its infinite God, transcendent of and over against nature and man, reduces both to nondivine creatures. This achievement too, however, is bought at a price. Recognizing divine human nonunion, the Jew cannot in love be united with, but only in fear serve, a distant, holy Lord. Hence the place of reconciliation is taken by obedience to the law and confidence in the promised reward. Hence too, unlike the Greek-Roman world which universalizes its truth, the Jewish people most stubbornly remain in their particularity, despite the universality of their God, because of His unyielding transcendence. Obviously even Hegel's mature thought repeats once again the traditional Christian opinion since Paul, and fails to do justice to Judaism – to the divine-human union manifest, e.g., in the love of God, the messianic expectation and, perhaps above all, the covenant. This failure is partly due to the Christian component of his thought, partly to his doctrine of total reconciliation, antipathetic, e.g., to Judaism's absolute opposition to idolatry; partly to the restriction of his thought to an idealized biblical Judaism, and to his neglect and ignorance of rabbinic Judaism.

Methodically he developed as a system the "absolute" Idealism by which he tried to explain and reconcile the contradictions and tensions of his time. He saw these processes as part of a comprehensive and rational unity, which evolved through and manifested itself in a steady and dynamic process of contradictions, negations, and (preliminary) syntheses (Hegel himself did not use the term "synthesis," but rather the "Whole"). He applied this system of dialectics to explain the totality of science, art, history, and religion. In his system, religion and revelation are the same, for God – the "Absolute" – is perceptible only to the thinking mind, so that there is no contradiction between what religion believes and what reason sees.

These ideas had a wide impact, which did not cease with Hegel's death. The subsequent history of philosophy has recognized two opposing camps of successors, the so-called Right Hegelians and the more revolutionary Left Hegelians (the latter, also known as the Young Hegelians, include Bruno Bauer, David Friedrich Strauss, and the young Karl Marx, among others). Among Jewish circles it was the notion of development and progressive perfection of humanity that aroused particular interest, providing a basis for assigning to Israel a particular mission. Hegel thus affected such various Jewish thinkers as Samson Raphael *Hirsch, Heinrich *Graetz, Samuel *Hirsch, and Moses *Hess, a fact testifying to the many-sidedness and adaptability of his thought. These thinkers' critiques of Hegel's attitude toward Judaism, including Samuel Hirsch's profound, full-scale, Jewish critique, have, however, been ignored by all except Jewish scholars.

BIBLIOGRAPHY: H. Liebeschuetz, *Judentum im deutschen Geschichtsbild von Hegel bis Max Weber* (1967); E.L. Fackenheim, *The Religious Dimension in Hegel's Thought* (1968). **ADD. BIBLIOGRAPHY:** C. Taylor, *Hegel* (1975); Q. Lauer, in: *Encyclopedia of Religion*, vol. 6 (2005²), 3892–95; Y. Yovel, *Dark Riddle* (1998); G. Hentges, *Schattenseiten der Aufklaerung* (1999); M. Brumlik, *Deutscher Geist und Judenhass* (2000); F. Tomasoni, *Modernity and the Final Aim of History* (2003).

[Emil Ludwig Fackenheim / Marcus Pyka (2nd ed.)]

HEGENHEIM, town in the Haut-Rhin department, E. France, 3 mi. (5 km.) W. of Basle. Fourteen Jewish families were recorded here in the census of 1689; the community increased steadily until in 1784, with 409 persons, it was one of the three largest in Alsace. From then onward, however, the numbers rapidly declined, and in 1936 only 36 Jews remained. The community had owned a cemetery from 1672, which served many other Jewish communities in Upper Alsace and from the 19th century was also used by the Jews of Switzerland. A monument has been erected in this cemetery in memory of the victims of the Nazi persecution.

BIBLIOGRAPHY: A. Nordmann, *Der israelitische Friedhof in Hegenheim* (1910); *Société d'Histoire et du Musée d'Huningue*, no. 4 (1955), 20ff.

[Bernhard Blumenkranz]

HE-ḤALUTZ (Heb. הֶחָלוּץ; "the pioneer"), an association of Jewish youth whose aim was to train its members to settle on the land in Israel. The original meaning of the Hebrew word is the vanguard that leads the host on its advance (Josh. 6:13).

Origin of the Movement

The idea of He-Ḥalutz was conceived during the crisis that overtook Russian Jewry in the aftermath of the 1881 pogroms. This awakening was influenced indirectly by the Russian revolutionary movement, which called upon the intelligentsia to "go out to the people." Two of the societies that were formed at this time – *Bilu, which called for settlement in Ereẓ Israel, and *Am Olam, which advocated settlement in the United States – were pioneer movements that imposed the concepts of "self-fulfillment" upon their members and planned for collective or cooperative settlement. At the beginning of the 20th century, a Jewish youth movement made up of small groups gradually came into being. Menaḥem *Ussishkin gave impetus to this development in 1904, when he called for the establishment of "a general Jewish workers' organization made up of unmarried young people of sound body and spirit. Each member would be committed to settle for a period of three years in Ereẓ Israel, where he would render army service for the Jewish people, his weapons being not the sword and the rifle, but the spade and the plow" (in *Our Program*). Such movements arose under different names in various countries: in America He-Ḥalutz, founded by Eliezer *Joffe in 1905 (see below); in Russia, a number of societies, among them Bilu'im Ḥadashim (new Bilu'im) and He-Ḥalutz. They were encouraged by the Ereẓ Israel workers, who called for the settlement of *ḥalutzim* (A.D. Gordon in 1904, Joseph *Vitkin in 1905, the Ha-Po'el ha-Ẓa'ir in 1908, etc.) and sent emissaries abroad to urge young Jews to settle in Ereẓ Israel.

The *Ẓe'irei Zion movement included in its platform "the organization of *ḥalutzim* and their training for *aliyah*."

In the summer of 1906 the Ẓe'irei Zion held a conference of *ḥalutzim* (the Bilu'im Ḥadashim) that decided to impose upon the members of the movement the goal of settling in Ereẓ Israel and engaging in manual or intellectual labor in groups or as individuals, as well as studying Hebrew and Arabic. During the 11th Zionist Congress in Vienna (1913), Ẓe'irei Zion decided to establish a center for Russia and Poland and to include among its tasks "the training of *ḥalutzim* who are contemplating settlement in Ereẓ Israel." At the conference of Ẓe'irei Zion in Russia (Vilna, April 1914), Eliahu Munchik, an emissary from Ereẓ Israel, spoke on *aliyah* (immigration) and *ḥalutziyyut* (pioneering), and the conference decided to organize groups and establish a mutual aid fund for them. During World War I the movement came to a standstill except in Russia and the United States. In the U.S. David *Ben-Gurion and Izhak *Ben-Zvi attempted to establish a pioneering movement. In their Yiddish pamphlet, "*Printcipen un Oyfgaben*" ("Principles and Tasks," 1917), the guidelines were formulated as follows: "To create and organize the first workers' army for Ereẓ Israel" and to impose upon each member the obligation of "settling in Ereẓ Israel when the need arises." A few hundred youngsters joined the organization. At the end of 1917, when the call came to join the *Jewish Legion, these members of He-Ḥalutz in the U.S. volunteered for military service and went to Ereẓ Israel together with the other volunteers.

Russia

The February Revolution of 1917 opened up new possibilities for Zionist activities in Russia. An article on He-Ḥalutz by Ben-Zvi, published in *Yevreyskaya Zhizn* in April 1917, made a profound impression upon Jewish youth. The second conference of Ẓe'irei Zion, which convened in Petrograd in May 1917, adopted a resolution calling for "the education of the youth to the ideas of *ḥalutziyyut* and the organization of He-Ḥalutz groups to serve as the basis of Jewish national life in Ereẓ Israel." The *Balfour Declaration, issued in November 1917, greatly accelerated the process, and groups of *ḥalutzim* developed in Russia, Poland, Lithuania, Latvia, Galicia, Bessarabia, etc. At first the various groups had no connection with one another, but gradually they became part of a national organization and eventually a worldwide movement. In January 1918, the founding convention of the Russian He-Ḥalutz met in Kharkov. At this conference, a controversy, which dominated the movement for a number of years, arose between the "idealists," who argued that He-Ḥalutz should serve as a vanguard and assume tasks of outstanding importance for the Zionist movement, and the "materialists," who saw the movement simply as the organization of Jewish workers planning to settle in Ereẓ Israel.

In the spring of 1918, Joseph *Trumpeldor joined the organization of He-Ḥalutz. In July and September 1918, conferences of Zionist organizations and of He-Ḥalutz groups were held, and it was decided that the movement would be Zionist but nonpartisan and would accept for membership Jewish youth over 18 who recognized Hebrew as their national language and were preparing for settlement in Ereẓ Israel. Trumpeldor formulated these decisions in a Russian-language pamphlet titled *He-Ḥalutz*, which was widely distributed in Russia. On Jan. 6, 1919, the first conference of the movement, in which representatives of 23 groups in central Russia and Belorussia took part, took place in Moscow. Trumpeldor, who had lost hope of creating a Jewish army of 100,000 men in Russia that would march to Ereẓ Israel through the Caucasus, called for the establishment of a "military He-Ḥalutz" of 10,000 men to replace the British garrison in Ereẓ Israel. The conference decided upon a series of general principles: He-Ḥalutz is a nonpartisan association of workers who have resolved to settle in Ereẓ Israel in order to live by their own labor, rejecting exploitation of others' work; it will train its members for life in Ereẓ Israel, transport them there, and facilitate their absorption in the country; its final goal is the establishment of a sovereign Jewish nation in Ereẓ Israel; it accepts the authority of the Zionist Congress. Trumpeldor was elected president and asked to go to Ereẓ Israel to prepare the ground for the absorption of *ḥalutzim*. An executive body was elected and took up its seat in Minsk. In spite of the chaotic conditions prevailing in Russia during the civil war, He-Ḥalutz entered upon a period of rapid development. A wave of unorganized emigration began; it was made up of various groups of *ḥalutzim* who set out on the way to Ereẓ Israel along different routes – across the Romanian, Polish, Lithuanian, and Latvian borders and by way of the Black Sea and the Caucasian Mountains. The number of groups associated with the center grew to 120. When Trumpeldor fell at *Tel Ḥai (March 1920) the movement lost its natural leader, but he became the symbol of its ideals, as he had realized the aims of He-Ḥalutz – settling in Ereẓ Israel, working there, and being prepared to give one's life in its defense.

For He-Ḥalutz, the consolidation of the Soviet regime meant the beginning of a process that was to end in the total suppression of the movement. The *Yevsektsiya* (the Jewish "section" in the Communist Party) played a role in this process. When the He-Ḥalutz center, then in Moscow, applied to the authorities for official approval of its activities, it received the reply (March 18, 1918) that there was no need for official approval as long as the activities of He-Ḥalutz conformed to the laws of the Soviet Union. This rather equivocal reply (which at the time did not apply to the Ukraine and Belorussia) provided a basis, however uncertain, for the continued existence of the movement. In many places, its training farms dovetailed with the official efforts of "productivization" of those Jews who had lost their source of livelihood, and sometimes He-Ḥalutz was even officially encouraged to continue these training activities. The hasty and unorganized *aliyah* of *ḥalutzim*, however, adversely affected the development of the movement. In October 1920 another conference of He-Ḥalutz, which took place at Kharkov, emphasized the need for training *ḥalutzim* before their move to Ereẓ Israel. During the following years while the Jewish *shtetl* was rapidly being destroyed, the movement continued to develop, even though many branches, as well as entire areas, were out of touch with the center. In Odessa, for example, a special center for the Ukraine functioned independently. One group that had a considerable influence upon training of *ḥalutzim* in the early 1920s was the Volga Guard at Saratov, which later moved to Yartsevo, near Moscow, and established the J.Ḥ. *Brenner Work Battalion. In January 1922, the third He-Ḥalutz conference was held at Kharkov and was attended by delegates from Russia, the Ukraine, and Belorussia. Its participants were arrested and continued their deliberations in jail, but He-Ḥalutz continued its work. At the end of the year a training farm named Tel Ḥai was opened up in the Crimea.

At this juncture, the first signs of a split in the ranks of He-Ḥalutz made their appearance. Some of its members decided to adapt "He-Ḥalutz" to the state ideology in order to achieve official approval of its activities; others, however, felt that He-Ḥalutz should retain its nonpartisan character and disassociate itself from Communism. In April 1923 the Council of He-Ḥalutz met in Moscow and decided upon program guidelines, which included a paragraph defining He-Ḥalutz as an organic part of the Jewish and international working class and, recognizing the inevitability of the class war, declaring that the movement would fight against capitalism in all its forms. Another paragraph stipulated that members who "oppose the idea of the *kevuẓah* and who wish to plan their lives as members of a moshav ovedim would not be admitted to the training groups." These resolutions caused an uproar in He-Ḥalutz and a bitter controversy broke out. Ben-Gurion, who was in the Soviet Union at the time visiting its agricultural exhibition as a delegate of the *Histadrut, made an unsuccessful attempt to settle the dispute. In August 1923, when the He-Ḥalutz statute was given official sanction, the movement split into two factions: the "legal" faction, advocating class warfare and a collective way of life, and the "illegal" faction, which regarded itself as a national Jewish workers' movement.

The legal He-Ḥalutz strove to utilize the limited possibilities deriving from its status. Official branches were opened in various places (excluding, however, the Ukraine and Belorussia, where the official approval did not apply); a struggle was conducted, in public, with the Jewish Communist activists, and permission was obtained for the publication of a journal (*He-Ḥalutz*), which printed 3,000 copies and contained news from Ereẓ Israel. Members of He-Ḥalutz participated in official celebrations and holidays (May Day, the anniversary of the Revolution), displaying Zionist slogans and singing Zionist songs. He-Ḥalutz also joined the organizations designed to encourage the agricultural settlement of Jews in Russia (Ozet) and struggled inside these organizations against the design to turn them into instruments against *aliyah*. More training farms such as Ma'yan in the Crimea and Zangen near Moscow were established. The illegal faction of He-Ḥalutz carried on its activities underground and also succeeded in establishing training farms of its own, such as Mishmar in the Crimea (1924) and Bilu in Belorussia (1925). At the end of 1925 the factions had a total membership of 14,000.

The year 1926, however, was a turning point for the worse. News of the economic crisis in Palestine had a depressing effect, and many *ḥalutzim* – including some who had been members of the Work Battalion – returned from Palestine as disappointed men. At the same time the settlement of Jews on the land in the U.S.S.R. boasted considerable achievements, and it seemed to many that this was the proper way to the large-scale "productivization" of Russian Jewry. The Soviet authorities now persecuted both factions of He-Ḥalutz. No aid was forthcoming from the Zionist movement or the He-Ḥalutz movement abroad. In March 1928 the government canceled the approval it had given to one faction, and both were now illegal. The training farms of He-Ḥalutz were disbanded and their members had only one course left – to go to Ereẓ Israel after first spending years in jail and exile. Even this course was fraught with difficulties and eventually came to an end. Slowly the movement was suppressed, although efforts to keep it alive continued until 1934. Those members of He-Ḥalutz who had not succeeded in leaving for Ereẓ Israel remained in prison or exile, some to be liquidated during the mass purges (among them Shemu'el Schneurson, one of the leaders of the underground He-Ḥalutz who had returned from Ereẓ Israel in 1926 to take part in the underground work of the movement).

The He-Ḥalutz movement in Russia affected the development of the movement far beyond the confines of the country. Hundreds of *ḥalutzim* from Soviet Russia who passed through Poland, Romania, Lithuania, Latvia, etc., on their way to Ereẓ Israel were of significant help to the movement in those countries. The final severance of the He-Ḥalutz movement in Russia from the outside world and from Ereẓ Israel was one of the severest blows dealt to the Zionist Movement.

Poland

At the same time, the movement spread all over Europe, as well as overseas. In 1921 He-Ḥalutz conferences took place in no fewer than 25 countries in Eastern, Central, and Western Europe, the countries of North Africa and the Middle East, North and South America, and South Africa. With the suppression of all Zionist activities in the Soviet Union, the center of the movement was resituated in Poland. During the 12th Zionist Congress (Carlsbad 1921), the He-Ḥalutz organizations held their first world conference and decided to establish a world federation with headquarters in Warsaw. The movement in Poland began at the same time as in Russia (at the beginning of the century), but only at the end of the war did it become a mass movement. The growth of He-Ḥalutz in Poland was greatly encouraged by the Balfour Declaration and the renewal of ties with Ereẓ Israel, particularly with the workers' parties, as well as by the pauperization of the Jewish masses and the appearance of a young and inspired leadership that searched for a way to Jewish national freedom and the creation of a new Jewish society.

The program of He-Ḥalutz consisted of three basic, interdependent points: organization, training (*hakhsharah*), and *aliyah*. The last was the most difficult to achieve, as the British military authorities in Palestine were largely anti-Zionist and discouraged Jewish immigration. It was also deemed impossible to enter the country illegally by eluding the border control, since peace had not yet been restored and there were no land or sea communications. In spite of these obstacles, individual immigrants and small groups succeeded in entering the country; the groups grew in size and eventually the road of *aliyah* lay open. The first group to enter Ereẓ Israel in this manner was the "Bendin" group, consisting of six *ḥalutzim*. They left Poland in the summer of 1918 and made their way through Odessa and Constantinople, finally reaching Jaffa on Dec. 5, 1918, after they had risked their lives in a daring and arduous trip. A second group left Radom in November 1918. Originally numbering 15 persons, they were joined en route by 90 *ḥalutzim*. Their trip entered Zionist history as "The 105." Without passports and visas they passed through Czechoslovakia, Austria, Serbia, Croatia, and Italy, and time and again they were arrested, imprisoned, and beaten. Finally they reached Naples, where, lacking entry visas, they were unable to board a ship for Palestine. It was only after great efforts were made in their behalf (in which the author Axel Munthe, then a resident of Capri, also took part) that London authorized the issue of visas. When they landed in Egypt, they were imprisoned by the British military authorities, who suspected them of being "Bolsheviks." Finally, after six months of hardship, they reached Palestine. On their arrival by train from Egypt during Passover 1919, they were welcomed by almost the entire population of Tel Aviv. "The 105" had in fact inaugurated a new wave of immigration – the Third *Aliyah.

The reports of the arrival of the "Bendin" and Radom groups gave new encouragement to the movement in Poland. Branches were organized and training programs instituted in hundreds of towns and cities. Training was divided into two parts: ideological training (Zionism and social sciences, history and geography of Ereẓ Israel, and Hebrew) and practical training (vocational education, primarily in agriculture). Many *ḥalutzim* were employed by Jewish and gentile landowners (especially in Galicia) as individuals or in groups; but in the main the training was conducted on farms established and maintained by He-Ḥalutz. The largest and best known of the dozens of such farms were at Grochow (near Warsaw), Czestochowa, Grodno, Suwalki, and Bendzin. There were also training facilities in quarries (the best known of them, in Klosow, Volhynia), sawmills, textile factories, etc. The expansion of the training program was followed by an increase in *aliyah*.

In 1918 Russian *ḥalutzim* on their way to Palestine began entering Poland illegally. At first they came in small groups, but in the period 1919–23 the flow took on considerable proportions. The *ḥalutzim* came mostly from Podolia, the Ukraine, Volhynia, and Belorussia, and they converged on Vilna, Baranovichi, Rovno, Pinsk, and Warsaw. In the initial phase the Polish authorities tolerated their illegal entry on the basis of documents furnished by the Palestine Office of the Zionist Movement and provided the *ḥalutzim* with emigrants' passports on the assumption that their stay in Poland would be short. When immigration to Palestine was stopped in 1921, however, the Polish authorities took severe measures against the *ḥalutzim*, arresting and deporting them back to the Soviet border. It was only after the Zionist institutions had undertaken to speed up the departure of the *ḥalutzim* for Ereẓ Israel that the situation was alleviated. The Russian *ḥalutzim* established an organization of Russian and Ukrainian *ḥalutzim* in Poland, many of whom were placed in the Polish He-Ḥalutz training farms, while others were in *ḥalutzim* hostels and private employment. These refugees from Russia left an indelible imprint upon the Polish movement. Eventually the Russian *ḥalutzim* were able to go to Palestine, and the last transport of 400 arrived in Jaffa on May 3, 1923.

The Polish He-Ḥalutz movement established within its ranks He-Ḥalutz ha-Ẓa'ir, which maintained close relations with various Zionist youth movements, such as Dror (Freiheit), *Gordonia, *Ha-Shomer ha-Ẓa'ir, etc. The Polish He-Ḥalutz reached the height of its development during the Fourth and Fifth *aliyot*. In 1924, He-Ḥalutz in Poland had a membership of 1,700; in 1925 – 4,600; 1930 – 11,600; 1933 – 41,000. Members enrolled in the training program numbered 712 in 1925, 2,450 in 1926, 2,230 in 1932, 4,450 in 1933, 7,915 in 1935. The Polish movement also published a number of periodicals: *He-Ḥalutz*, *He-Atid*, *He-Ḥalutz ha-Ẓa'ir*, etc. In 1934 He-Ḥalutz inaugurated the "illegal" *immigration movement by dispatching the boat *Velos* with *ḥalutzim* from Poland and the Baltic states. In the late 1930s He-Ḥalutz cooperated with the *Haganah in organizing the *ḥalutzim* as "illegal" immigrants, in their transportation to Palestine, and in the struggle for opening the gates of Palestine. During World War II He-Ḥalutz members were among the most active resistance fighters against the Nazis.

Lithuania

He-Ḥalutz in Lithuania was established after World War I and based itself initially upon cooperative societies (in carpentry, tailoring, food processing, etc.). Due to lack of capital and experience, these cooperative societies did not last long, and they were replaced by agricultural training facilities. The main center of agricultural training was a farm run solely by He-Ḥalutz known as Kibbush. Memel, the German port annexed by Lithuania, was also a center of He-Ḥalutz activities; it had an urban cooperative, the members of which were engaged in a variety of activities, including marine and port operations. Memel was also known in the movement for its outstanding He-Ḥalutz House. Other urban He-Ḥalutz cooperatives existed at Kaunas, Siauliai, Vilkaviskis, Poniviez, etc. The membership of He-Ḥalutz in Lithuania ranged from 1,000 to 1,500.

Latvia

In Latvia, the He-Ḥalutz movement's main training farm was located at Altasmuza, near Riga. Originally the property of *OZE, it was transferred to He-Ḥalutz and also served as a school, with the teachers receiving their salaries from the state.

Other cooperatives existed at Dvinsk, Tukum, and Libau. In the period 1920–21, 150 *ḥalutzim* settled in Palestine and were followed by many more in the subsequent years.

Romania

He-Ḥalutz came into existence in Romania in 1918, when Bessarabia, Bukovina, and Transylvania were incorporated into the country. It was started by *ḥalutzim* who had fled from Russia and the Ukraine and had to spend periods of varying length in Romania before they were able to proceed to Ereẓ Israel. These *ḥalutzim*-in-transit established cooperatives of their own and also worked in the fields and forests. As a first step, the Romanian He-Ḥalutz acquired two training farms: one was later sold and replaced by the Massadah farm near Beltsy, and the other was near Jassy. Other farms were established near Galati and Bucharest. The capital for the acquisition of the farms and their maintenance was provided by a Friends of He-Ḥalutz Society. Most Zionist youth movements (Ha-Shomer ha-Ẓa'ir, Gordonia, Dror, *Ha-No'ar ha-Ẓiyyoni, *Bnei Akiva, etc.) participated in the activities of He-Ḥalutz. During the 1930s, when the antisemitic *Iron Guard rampaged the country, the He-Ḥalutz movement grew at a rapid pace, assisted by emissaries from Palestine. An important role was played by the Romanian ports, mainly Constanţa, which were used by *olim* from all over Europe on their way to Ereẓ Israel. The passage of many thousands of *ḥalutzim* through the country served to accelerate the *aliyah* of Romanian *ḥalutzim* as well. During the war the Romanian ports made history when no fewer then 40,000 "illegal" immigrants to Palestine, using dozens of boats, set out from them. Romanian *ḥalutzim* functioning under Nazi rule as an underground organization fulfilled a vital task in organizing and safeguarding the "illegal" immigration, often at the risk of their lives.

Central Europe

Early manifestations of interest in *ḥaluziyyut* among a part of the Jewish youth in Germany, Austria, and what was later to become Czechoslovakia came to the fore during World War I. Officially, He-Ḥalutz was established in Germany at the end of 1918, and, as a first step, hundreds of *ḥalutzim* (calling themselves *Praktikanten* and organized in a *Praktikantenbund*) went out to work on farm estates in order to train for life in Ereẓ Israel. This experiment, however, did not last long, and He-Ḥalutz established a number of training farms of its own. The movement's farms were not successful either, and only one ("Ha-Mahpekhah" – "the Revolution") was able to maintain itself for any period of time. The lack of Zionist education and of a sizable working class among Central European Jewry prevented the development of He-Ḥalutz along East European lines. There were differences between the members of *Blau-Weiss and the *ḥalutzim* who had not been affiliated with this youth movement; the former had their roots in the German youth movement (e.g., the *Wandervogel*), and the revolutionary spirit of He-Ḥalutz in Eastern Europe was alien to them. This created difficulties in the merger of the two elements in one organization, which was technically achieved by the efforts of leaders on both sides. The differences between them, however, were never entirely overcome. Czechoslovakia was the country in which He-Ḥalutz was the closest in spirit and methods to the movement in Lithuania and Poland. The movement in Western Europe developed along lines similar to Central Europe.

United States

The first He-Ḥalutz organization in the U.S. was established in 1905, at the same time that a similar organization was formed in Odessa (Crimea). Its founders were a group of Zionist youth, most of whom were Russian immigrants from rural communities, who met in the Ha-Teḥiyah offices in New York and formed He-Ḥalutz to serve as the nucleus of a world movement to revive Jewish settlement in Ereẓ Israel. Anchored in *Po'alei Zion, the organization was led by Eliezer Joffe who wrote articles in several newspapers to enlist the participation of youth in settling in Palestine as pioneers. In 1906 Joffe published an article titled "The People's Road to Its Land," in which he staked the rebirth of the Jewish people on the dedication of young pioneers. Meanwhile, in 1905, Ḥalutzei Po'alei Zion was formed within Po'alei Zion, with branches in New York, Philadelphia, Montreal, Baltimore, and elsewhere. In 1908 the New York He-Ḥalutz group was absorbed into a new organization, Ha-Ikkar ha-Ẓa'ir, whose program remained nearly identical with that of He-Ḥalutz. During World War I, the U.S. He-Ḥalutz movement received a tremendous impetus from the presence of Ben-Gurion and Ben-Zvi, who tried to establish a He-Ḥalutz organization in the U.S. with the help of the Po'alei Zion party and published a Yiddish pamphlet, "*Printsipen un Oyfgaben*" (Sifriyyat He-Ḥalutz, 1917). Several hundred Jewish youth responded to its call for pioneers to rebuild a Jewish homeland through practical settlement rather than political or other means. The original goal of the movement was to settle pioneers at the earliest opportunity. However, when immigration to Palestine was restricted in 1926, the world He-Ḥalutz movement began to focus its emphasis on *hakhsharah* ("preparation" or "training") for potential pioneer youth.

Many Jewish youths were aroused by the Arab riots in Palestine and the subsequent British White Paper in 1929, and in 1932 the He-Ḥalutz Organization of America was formed with headquarters in New York and 20 city and rural branches across the U.S. and in Canada. In 1933 He-Ḥalutz rented its first *hakhsharah* farm, and it subsequently purchased farms at Creamridge, N.J. (1936); Heightstown, N.J. (1940); Poughkeepsie, N.Y.; Smithville, Ont.; and Colton, Calif. (1948) to train its members for agricultural work in Palestine. In 1935 Young Po'alei Zion embarked on a training program within the He-Ḥalutz framework, and in 1939 Ha-Shomer ha-Ẓa'ir joined He-Ḥalutz after nearly a decade of negotiations. By 1940 the He-Ḥalutz Organization of America included nearly all Zionist youth of the Labor and General Zionist wings. After the outbreak of World War II, He-Ḥalutz initiated industrial, aviation, nursing, and other technical training programs, while continuing its agricultural training. By 1948 He-Ḥalutz had grown from a few hundred members to 1,600, and since its inception several hundred members had emigrated to Ereẓ Israel. When the *hakhsharah* farms were liquidated in the mid-1950s, the activities of He-Ḥalutz were assumed by Ha-Shomer ha-Ẓa'ir, which had always maintained a large degree of autonomy. Nominally, however, the He-Ḥalutz Organization of America still exists. The only American group to support He-Ḥalutz financially was the American Fund for Palestinian Institutions.

Summary

When World War II broke out, He-Ḥalutz had a membership of 100,000. In 1927, according to statistics published by the Histadrut, 43% of all workers in Ereẓ Israel and 80% of the members of kibbutzim had been trained by He-Ḥalutz before settling in Ereẓ Israel. After the war, the world movement of He-Ḥalutz ceased to exist, although the activities that it had conducted were renewed on a smaller scale in Europe, the United States, and other countries. Pioneering youth movements, like all Zionist youth movements, now conduct their work under the auspices of the Youth and He-Ḥalutz Department of the World Zionist Organization.

BIBLIOGRAPHY: M. Basok (ed.), *Sefer He-Ḥalutz* (1939); He-Ḥalutz, *Me'assef li-Tenu'at He-Ḥalutz* (Warsaw, 1930); *HeḤalutz be Rusyah* (1932); D. Pines, *He-Ḥalutz be-Khur ha-Mahpekhah* (1938);); Y. Ereẓ (ed.), *Sefer ha-Aliyyah ha-Shelishit*, 2 vols. (1964); idem, *Sefer Z.S.* (1963); Z. Liberman (Livneh), *Pirkei ha-Aliyyah ha-Shelishit* (1958); I. Ritov, *Perakim be-Toledot Ẓe'irei-Ẓiyyon* (1964); Asufot, 6 (1959), 98–110; L. Spiezman, *Khalutsim in Poyln*, 3 vols. (1959–1962); M. Braslavsky, *Toledot Tenu'at ha-Po'alim ha-Arẓisre'elit*, 4 vols. (1955–1962), index. **ADD. BIBLIOGRAPHY:** Y. Utiker, *Tenu'at he-Ḥaluẓ be-Polin 1932–1935*; Y. Oppenheim, *Tenu'at he-Ḥaluẓ be-Polin*, 2 vols. (1982, 1993); L.A. Sarid, *He-Ḥaluẓ u-Tenu'ot ha-No'ar be-Polin 1917–1939* (1979); R. Perlis, *Tenu'ot ha-No'ar va-Ḥaluẓiyyot be-Polin ha-Kevushah* (1987); S. Nashmith, *Hayu Ḥaluẓim be-Lita 1916–1941* (1983); I. Oppenheimer, "'Hehalutz' in Eastern Europe between the Two World Wars," in: *Zionist Youth Movements during the Shoa* (1996), 33–116; idem, "The Ideological Background of the 'Hehalutz' Movement in Russia and Poland in the 1920s," in: *Polin* 5 (1999), 131–55, C. Schatzker, "The Jewish Youth Movement in Germany in the Holocaust Period," in: LBIYB, 32 (1987), 157–81; 33 (1988), 301–25.

[Israel Ritov / Yehuda Slutsky]

HE-ḤALUTZ (Heb. "the Pioneer"), periodical of Jewish scholarship, edited by Joshua (Osias) Heschel *Schorr, which appeared in Lemberg, Breslau, Prague, Frankfurt on the Main, and Vienna from 1852 to 1889. Schorr, a second generation Galician *maskil*, devoted the periodical principally to incisive and radical criticism of the Talmud, attempting to prove by a series of studies that the talmudists had adapted Jewish tradition to their time and that later generations were therefore also permitted to do the same. Accordingly, Schorr argued that the words of the talmudists need not be accepted as necessarily applicable to modern times. Such pointed and bold criticism had almost never before been voiced in the Hebrew language. For his radical stand and the wit of his expression, Schorr was called the "Voltaire of Galicia." Publishing *He-Ḥalutz* with his own funds, Schorr, a man of wealth, could be independent. At first others who held similar views, such as Abraham *Geiger and Abraham *Krochmal, contributed to the periodical. Later, however, Schorr himself wrote all the material which included satires directed against the rabbis and topical articles, written in a critical, sarcastic vein, directed against the rabbinic-talmudic tradition. *He-Ḥalutz*, in turn, was denounced by all those it criticized. But this only served to increase the wit and sharpness of Schorr's writing. The scholarly research that appeared in *He-Ḥalutz* had the effect of supporting radical reform, although that was not the editor's intention. *He-Ḥalutz* greatly influenced M.L. Lilienblum and J.L. Gordon, the advocates of religious reform in Russia.

BIBLIOGRAPHY: G. Kressel, Leksikon, 2 (1967), 896f.; Spicehandler, in: HUCA, 40–41 (1969–70), 503–22.

[Getzel Kressel]

HE-ḤAVER, Zionist student organization established in 1912. Its membership consisted mainly of Zionist students from Russia who were attending universities in Western Europe, and the organization engaged in Zionist propaganda and led the struggle against assimilationist Jewish students. In Russia itself underground branches of He-Ḥaver existed in various cities, and upper classmen of the high schools also participated in them. In April 1917, when He-Ḥaver had a total of 100 branches, it held its first open conference in Petrograd, but after the October Revolution it had to revert to clandestine activity. The organization had its own organs: the Russian-language *Yevreyskiy student* ("Jewish Student") which appeared in Berlin from 1912 to 1914, in Petrograd from 1915 to 1918, and in Moscow in 1922 and 1923; and the Hebrew-language *He-Ḥaver*, of which two issues appeared in 1914. It sought to spread the knowledge of Hebrew, Jewish history, and of Ereẓ Israel among its members. In March 1924 the organization merged with the Zionist Students' Organization in the Ukraine and Kadimah in Belorussia to form the United Federation of Zionist Youth in Russia (or EVOSM, the initials of its name in Russian).

BIBLIOGRAPHY: A. Refaeli, *Pa'amei ha-Ge'ullah* (1951), 194–5, 198–200; idem, *Ba-Ma'avak li-Ge'ullah* (1956), 25, 89–92, 142.

[Yehuda Slutsky]

HEICHELHEIM, FRITZ MORITZ (1901–1968), ancient history scholar. He taught at the university of his native Giessen in Germany from 1929, but was dismissed in 1933 during the Nazi purge. Heichelheim then became a research scholar at Cambridge, England (1933–42), and later lectured at Nottingham (1942–48). From 1948 he taught Greek and Roman history at the University of Toronto. He was elected fellow of the Royal Society of Canada in 1966.

Heichelheim produced over 600 publications in economic history, numismatics, archaeology, and papyrology. His major work is *Wirtschaftsgeschichte des Altertums* (2 vols., 1938; translated and revised as *An Ancient Economic History from the Palaeolithic Age*, 3 vols., 1958–70). Other important publications include *Auswaertige Bevoelkerung im Ptolemaerreich* (1925); *Wirtschaftliche Schwankungen der Zeit von Alexander bis Augustus* (1930); "Roman Syria" (in: T. Frank (ed.), *An Economic Survey of Ancient Rome*, 4 (1938), 121–257); *The Adler Papyri* (with E.N. Adler et al., 1939); *Sylloge Nummorum Graecorum*, vol. 4 (1940–65); and *History of the Roman People*, with C.A. Yeo (1962). Heichelheim also wrote extensively on classical Judaism. From 1951 he contributed a column, "Mind and Spade," to the *Jewish Standard* of Toronto and Montreal. He was president of the Jewish Historical Society of Toronto (1951–53), trustee of the Liberal Jewish Congregation "Habonim" (1956–61), and a member of the cultural commission of the Canadian Jewish Congress (1950–54).

[Sydney Eisen]

HEIDELBERG, city in Baden, Germany. Heidelberg is mentioned in the will of Judah b. Samuel he-Ḥasid (d. 1217), but the reference may be a later addition. The first reliable evidence for the presence of Jews in the town dates from 1275. In the years thereafter numerous Jews lived in Heidelberg until the community was decimated during the *Black Death (1349). However, soon afterward the elector Rupert I admitted Jewish refugees from Worms and Speyer in the face of local opposition, in return for a considerable payment. There is evidence that a well-organized community began functioning again, at the latest in 1357. Its development was halted abruptly, however, through the expulsion by elector Rupert II in 1391 of all the Jews in his domain, including those of Heidelberg. Among the 12 families driven out of their homes was Israel of Heidelberg, the copyist of the Darmstadt *Haggadah. Their houses, synagogue, bath, cemetery, and manuscripts were given to the university. From then till the mid-17th century only isolated settlements of individual Jews occurred. In 1660 the *Oppenheimer family arrived; Joseph Suess Oppenheimer, the powerful Court Jew, was born there in 1698. In 1700 11 Jewish families lived in Heidelberg, which was the seat of the chief rabbi of the Palatinate. Their number increased during the 18th century in spite of local opposition, and they were granted full civil liberty by the edict of 1808. They suffered during the Hep! Hep! riots of 1819 and during the revolution of 1848. The Reform movement had little success in introducing prayer in the vernacular into the Heidelberg synagogue. A Jewish elementary school was founded. Heidelberg University was among the first in Germany to accept Jews as students. At the end of the 19th century and beginning of the 20th, some illustrious Jews from Russia studied at the university including S. Tchernichowsky and J. Klausner. Among its professors were H. Schapira and E. Taeubler. The university was also traditionally a center of strong antisemitic agitation, and after 1933 Jewish students and professors were harassed and driven away.

In 1933 there were 1,100 Jews in the city (1.3% of the total population). The April 7 expulsion of Jews from the civil services resulted in the dismissal of 34 Jewish professors. By 1935 there was only one "full" Jewish student at the University, the remaining "Jewish" students were of mixed ancestry. Fourteen Polish Jews were expelled in October 1938. The synagogues were demolished on Nov. 10, 1938; its religious objects were confiscated and destroyed by university students. One hundred and fifty Jewish men were deported to Dachau, but later released. On Oct. 22, 1940, 339 Jews were transported to Gurs. One hundred Jews were saved from deportation by Protestant Evangelical Pastor Hermann Maas, who got them out of the country. He was subsequently recognized by Yad Vashem as a Righteous Gentile. From 1942 to 1945 a further 103 were deported, mainly to Theresienstadt. Eighteen returned after the war and joined the 50, of mixed marriages, who had outlived the war at Heidelberg. A new community came into being after World War II, numbering 139 persons in 1967. A new synagogue was consecrated in 1958. In 1979 the Central Council of Jews in Germany (Zentralrat der Juden in Deutschland) opened the Hochschule fuer Juedische Studien (University for Jewish Studies) in Heidelberg. From 2001 it offered a program for rabbinical training in cooperation with Orthodox, Conservative, and Liberal rabbinical seminaries in Jerusalem, New York, and London. In 1987 the Central Council of Jews in Germany established the Central Archives for research on the history of the Jews in Germany, which collects documents from Jewish communities, associations, organizations, and individuals. The Jewish community numbered 188 in 1989 and 550 in 2005. The membership increased due to the immigration of Jews from the former Soviet Union. A new community center was opened in 1994.

BIBLIOGRAPHY: L. Loewenstein, *Geschichte der Juden in der Kurpfalz* (1895); Germ Jud, 2 (1968), 344–5; M. Ludwig (ed.), *Aus dem Tagebuch des Hans O.: Dokumente… ueber… den Untergang der Heidelberger Juden* (1965); PK Germanyah; Rieger, in: *Beitraege zur Geschichte der deutschen Juden: Festschrift… Martin Philipsons* (1916), 178–83; F. Hundsnurscher and G. Taddey, *Die juedischen Gemeinden in Baden* (1968), 121–9 and index; M. Lowenthal, *The Jews of Germany* (1936), 231–3. **ADD. BIBLIOGRAPHY:** N. Giovannini and F. Moraw, *Erinnertes Leben. Autobiographische Texte zur juedischen Geschichte Heidelbergs* (1998); A. Cser et al., *Geschichte der Juden in Heidelberg* (1996; Buchreihe der Stadt Heidelberg, volume 6); N. Giovannini, J.-H. Bauer, and H.M. Mumm (eds.), *Juedisches Leben in Heidelberg. Studien zu einer ununterbrochenen Geschichte* (1992); A. Weckbecker, *Die Judenverfolgung in Heidelberg 1933–1945* (1985; Motive – Texte – Materialien, volume 29); idem, "Die Judenverfolgung in Heidelberg 1933–1945," in: J. Schadt and M. Caroli (eds.), *Heidelberg unter dem Nationalsozialismus. Studien zu Verfolgung, Widerstand und Anpassung* (1985), 399–467; idem, *Gedenkbuch an die ehemaligen Heidelberger Buerger juedischer Herkunft. Dokumentation ihrer Namen und Schicksale 1933–1945* (1983).

[Zvi Avneri / Larissa Daemmig (2nd ed.)]

HEIDELBERGER, MICHAEL (1888–1991), U.S. biochemist and immunologist. Born in New York, he completed his undergraduate and graduate education at Columbia University. After earning his Ph.D. in chemistry in 1911, he joined the faculty of the Rockefeller Institute, where he worked from 1912 to 1927. In 1928 he joined the College of Physicians and Surgeons of Columbia University, where he became first professor of immunochemistry. After his retirement in 1955 he was visiting professor at Rutgers University until 1964, and subsequently adjunct professor of pathology at New York University. Heidelberger's research dealt with immunological reactions and a wide range of subjects in bio- and organic chemistry. His publications included *Advanced Laboratory Manual of Organic Chemistry* (1923) and *Lectures in Immunochemistry* (1956). Heidelberger was president of the American Association of Immunologists and of the Harvey Society. Heidlelberger was also a strong supporter of human rights. He won numerous honors throughout his life, including two Lasker awards in 1953 and 1978, for his work in the development of methods for the quantitative analysis of antibodies.

[Samuel Aaron Miller / Bracha Rager (2nd ed.)]

HEIDENHAIN, RUDOLF (1834–1897), German physiologist. Heidenhain, who was born in Marienwerder, was a convert to Christianity. He was appointed professor of physiology and histology at Breslau University in 1859. Heidenhain was considered one of the greatest of 19th-century physiologists; he laid the foundations for the recognition of the secretory mechanism as a system of intercellular physical and chemical processes. He described the active role of the kidney cells in the secretion of urine and proved that secretions, especially saliva, are products of the glands. This conception was based on his description of the cell structure of the salivary, mammary, gastric, intestinal, pancreatic glands, and in particular, of the histological changes in the glands while functioning. For this, he perfected histological methods, including one for staining the kidney cells, by the injection of indigo-carmine into the bloodstream. He started research into the mechanism of muscle contraction from the point of view of energetics and metabolism, paving the path for muscular physiology in later generations. His books include *Mechanische Leistung, Waermeentwicklung und Stoffumsatz bei der Muskeltaetigkeit* (1864) and *Physiologie der Absonderungsvorgaenge* (1880). His son MARTIN (1864–1949) was professor of anatomy at Tuebingen University and made important contributions to histology; he was one of the first cytologists.

BIBLIOGRAPHY: *Bibliographisches Lexikon der hervorragenden Aerzte*, 3 (1931), s.v.

[Joshua O. Leibowitz]

HEIDENHEIM, WOLF (Benjamin Ze'ev; 1757–1832), Hebrew grammarian, masoretic scholar, exegete, and commentator on the liturgy. Born in Heidenheim, Germany, he studied with Rabbi Nathan Adler in Frankfurt. In 1788 he established himself in Offenbach, where he subsequently published Abraham ibn Ezra's grammatical work *Moznayim* (1791), with commentary and notes and part of an edition of the Pentateuch (up to Gen. 43:16) with a carefully corrected text of the Targum and several commentaries, together with explanations and a detailed commentary on Rashi by Heidenheim (*Torat Elohim Meforash*). He was obliged to abandon the project for financial reasons.

In 1798 he received a license to establish a German and Hebrew press in partnership with Baruch Baschwitz. In 1800 Heidenheim began the publication of his most famous work, the nine-volume edition of the *maḥzor, Sefer Kerovot* (Roedelheim, 1800–02), which went through numerous printings. The work included the first pure German translation (in Hebrew characters) of the liturgical poems for the festivals (individual pieces were translated by his friends Wolf Breidenbach and Baer Bing), a Hebrew commentary and a literary historical introduction, and an alphabetical summary of the liturgical poets. Heidenheim devoted great care to typographical setup as well as to the restoration of the correct text of the prayers. With this objective, he drew on manuscripts and occasionally on old printed texts. The prominent rabbis of his time approved of Heidenheim's work and also contributed notes and comments to many *piyyutim*. Despite the *haskamot* of these rabbis prohibiting the reprinting of Heidenheim's *maḥzor*, many pirated editions appeared in the 19th century.

His other works in the field of liturgy include a small edition of the daily prayers, *Sefat Emet* (Roedelheim, 1806), distinguished for its correctness and typographical beauty, which went through more than 150 printings; a larger prayer book, *Safah Berurah* (1825), with German translation in Hebrew characters; the ritual for Passover eve (Roedelheim, 1822–23); for Purim (1825); for the month of Av (1826); for the night of Shavu'ot and Hoshana Rabba (1830); and penitential prayers (Roedelheim, 1823). In the edition of the prayer book *Siddur li-Venei Yisrael* (1831), which presented his translation in German letters for the first time, Heidenheim made many concessions to efforts for reform in that he omitted individual prayers and printed a preface by Michael D. Creizenach on the prayers. In Orthodox circles, Heidenheim was very much blamed for this, just as his approval of the innovations of the Kassel Consistory (in his foreword to Menachem Mendel Steinhardt's *Divrei Iggeret*, Roedelheim, 1812) had shocked them. Heidenheim also made major contributions to the field of masoretic studies. He published the *Mishpetei ha-Te'amim* (Roedelheim, 1808) on biblical accents; and an edition of the Pentateuch in four different forms, all containing material important to the masoretic text and commentaries, as well as the editions of medieval masoretic texts. Works of later scholars heavily relied on Heidenheim's materials, both printed and manuscripts. Many of Heidenheim's works remained unpublished and most of his manuscripts were acquired by the Bodleian Library in Oxford.

BIBLIOGRAPHY: I. Rosenthaler, in: MGWJ, 49 (1905), 107–12; L. Lewin, *Heidenheimiana* (1924); S. Baer, in: ADB, S.V. **ADD. BIBLIOGRAPHY:** I.M. Levinger, "Die deutschen Gebetsbücher und Chumaschim: 150. Jahrzeitstag von Wolf Heidenheim," in: *Udim*, 11/12 (1981/82), 69–82; M. Garel, "The Rediscovery of the Wolf Haggadah," in: JJA, 2 (1974), 22–27.

[Sefton D. Temkin]

HEIDINGSFELD, town in Bavaria, Germany. The name of a Jewish woman who perished there during the *Rindfleisch persecutions (1298) is recorded, perhaps reflecting the existence of a Jewish community at that time. In 1391 King Wenceslaus canceled all debts to the Jews, thereby impoverishing the local community. The privilege of *de non tolerandis Judaeis*, granted to the town in 1423, was rescinded eight years later when the Jews were granted residence rights along with the civil and economic privileges enjoyed by their coreligionists in other German cities. In 1498 only seven families lived in the town, but the community grew in numbers and importance in the following centuries. When in 1565 the Jews of the nearby bishopric of Wuerzburg were expelled, many settled in Heidingsfeld, which was excepted from the decree although it was then also under the jurisdiction of the bishop of Wuerzburg. In 1652 there were 19 Jewish households in Heidingsfeld. A year later the community's *pinkas* ("minute-book") was begun, a significant source for Jewish history in Germany from 1653 to 1774, as well as an important source for the community's continuing relationship with Ereẓ Israel in that period. In 1669 the second synagogue was built; a third, erected around 1780, was renovated in 1929. A cemetery was consecrated only in 1810. In the early 17th century Heidingsfeld became the seat of the chief rabbinate for Lower Franconia. However, in 1813 the office was discontinued and Abraham *Bing, then chief rabbi, obtained permission to move to Wuerzburg together with other Heidingsfeld Jews. The community declined from around 600 persons (20% of the total population) in 1805, the second largest community in Bavaria, to 150 (4%) in 1890. Anti-Jewish acts were a source of continuing concern in the early 19th century; riots took place in 1801, while during the *Hep! Hep! disturbances of 1819 homes were burned. In 1930 the town and community were incorporated into Wuerzburg. The synagogue was burned down on Nov. 10, 1938, and the eight Jewish families molested; all left the town soon after. After World War II, the U.S. occupation forces ordered the population to renovate the desecrated Jewish cemetery.

BIBLIOGRAPHY: B. Brilling, in: *Yerushalayim* (1953), 220–31; E. Toeplitz, in: *Notizblatt der Gesellschaft zur Erforschung juedischer Kunstdenkmaeler*, no. 16 (1926), 2–13; idem, in: *Menorah*, 3 (1925), 203–6; A. Wolf, in: HUCA, 18 (1943/44), 247–78; Salfeld, Martyrol, 233; L. Heffner, *Die Juden in Franken* (1855), 59–60; PK.

HEIFETZ, JASCHA (1901–1987), U.S. violinist. Born in Vilna, Lithuania, Heifetz started playing at the age of three under his father's tuition, and later studied at the Vilna music school. At seven he played the Mendelssohn violin concerto in public and at 10 entered the St. Petersburg Conservatory, where his teacher was Leopold *Auer. In 1912 he played with the Berlin Philharmonic Orchestra under Nikisch. At the outbreak of the Russian Revolution, the family decided to emigrate and reached America via Siberia and Japan. Heifetz ultimately made his home in Beverly Hills, California. His playing early reached perfection, never relied on excessive display, and was marked by aristocratic restraint. It set a new style in violin mastery. He was acclaimed in the United States, toured abroad with triumphant success, and was received with enthusiasm in Russia in 1934. He appeared in Ereẓ Israel in 1925, and donated his fees for the promotion of music in Tel Aviv. He first played with the Israel Philharmonic Orchestra in 1950, and again in 1953, when his inclusion of a work by Richard Strauss (whose works were not played publicly in Israel because of his association with Nazism) in his programs provoked a bodily attack on him by an extremist youth, in which Heifetz was slightly injured. In later years he lived in semi-retirement. He was also an accomplished pianist, and made many transcriptions for violin and piano. Composers dedicated violin concertos to him, among them Sir William Walton, Erich *Korngold, Louis *Gruenberg, Joseph *Achron, and Mario *Castelnuovo-Tedesco.

BIBLIOGRAPHY: A. Holde, *Jews in Music* (1959), index.

[Uri (Erich) Toeplitz]

HEIJERMANS, HERMAN (1864–1924), Dutch playwright and novelist. Heijermans grew up in Rotterdam, the eldest son of a prominent journalist, and started writing after an unsuccessful time in the rag business. In 1893 he became a theater critic for the Amsterdam-based daily *De Telegraaf*, while exploring the latest fashions in naturalism and symbolism in his plays and stories. After his dramatic encounter with the woman who would become his first wife, he intensified this exploration. He established a periodical called *De Jonge Gids* (1897–1903), largely filled by himself under a dozen pseudonyms and in the most divergent styles, and turned the encounter with his wife into the novel *Kamertjeszonde* ("Little Room Sins," 1898). He also turned to socialism, to which he would remain loyal for the rest of his life.

Heijermans' early works show both his interest in social questions and his struggle with Jewish identity. His concern for the fate of Jewry first manifested itself in *Ahasverus* (1893), a play about a Russian pogrom. A Hebrew version of this drama, *Ha-Noded ha-Niẓḥi*, appeared in 1917. In two novels, *Sabbath* (1903) and *Diamantstad* ("Diamond City," 1904), and in the play *Ghetto* (1898), Heijermans denounced the backwardness of traditional Jewry in the Amsterdam ghetto. A more compassionate attitude is apparent in the serials he published in newspapers under the pseudonym Samuel Falkland between 1894 and 1915. These stories, more than 800, were collected in 18 volumes.

After 1900 Heijermans slowly moved away from Jewish subject matter and concentrated on writing drama. *Op hoop van zegen* ("The Good Hope," 1900) movingly described the miseries of Dutch fishermen. *Schakels* ("Links," 1903) offered an ironic portrayal of domestic strife. Other plays include *Uitkomst* ("Outlet," 1907), *Eva Bonheur* (1917), and the satirical *De wijze kater* ("The Wise Cat," 1918).

Heijermans became the most important Dutch dramatist of his time, winning international acclaim. *Op Hoop van Zegen* was performed all over Europe. A Hebrew version, *Dayyagim* (1927), by Abraham *Shlonsky, was staged by the *Ohel company. Heijermans cooperated with directors like Konstantin Stanislavski, Max Reinhardt, and Otto Brahm. But after 1910 his international reputation faded and his national successes also decreased. In his last years he returned to the genre of the novel. *Droomkoninkje* ("King of Dreams," 1924) and its sequel, *Vuurvlindertje* ("Firefly," 1925) appeared posthumously.

BIBLIOGRAPHY: S.L. Flaxman, *Herman Heijermans and His Dramas* (1954); B. Hunningher, *Toneel en werkelijkheid* (1947); H. Goedkoop, *Geluk. Het leven van Herman Heijermans* (1996).

[Hans Goedkoop (2nd ed.)]

HEILBORN, ERNST (1867–1942), German author and literary historian. Born and educated in Berlin, Heilborn became the Berlin drama critic of the *Frankfurter Zeitung* in 1901. From 1911 he edited *Das literarische Echo*, a fortnightly of international character which, in 1924, changed its name to *Die Literatur*. He wrote realistic short stories and novels mostly set in the middle-class society of Berlin. The best known of these were *Die steile Stufe* (1910) and *Die kupferne Stadt* (1918). In *Zwischen zwei Revolutionen* (2 vols., 1929), Heilborn dealt with the social and artistic history of the German capital. The first volume, *Der Geist der Schinkelzeit*, surveyed the years from 1789 to 1848, while the second, *Der Geist der Bismarckzeit*, covered the period from 1848 to 1918. Heilborn's other works include *Novalis der Romantiker* (1901), *Das Tier Jehovahs* (1905), *Josua Kersten* (1908), and *E.T.A. Hoffman: der Kuenstler und die Kunst* (1926). He published a critical edition of the 18th-century German romantic poet Novalis' works: *Novalis: Schriften; Kritische Neuausgabe auf Grund des handschriftlichen Nachlasses* (1901). In 1936 he was forbidden to continue to write. In 1937, after a trip to Palestine, he returned to Germany. In 1942 he attempted to flee to Switzerland but was arrested and died in Nazi "protective custody."

ADD. BIBLIOGRAPHY: B. Wegener, *Bibliographie Ernst Heilborn*, (1994); A. Hartmann, in: W. Killy (ed.), *Literaturlexikon* 5 (1990), 121.

[Rudolf Kayser / Konrad Feilchenfeldt (2nd ed.)]

HEILBRON, SIR IAN MORRIS (1886–1959), British organic chemist. Born in Glasgow, he joined the staff of the Royal Technical College there. In World War I he was assistant director of supplies in Salonika. In 1920 he was appointed to the chair of organic chemistry at Liverpool University. In 1933 he became professor at Manchester University, and in 1937 professor of organic chemistry at Imperial College, London. In World War II he acted as scientific adviser to the Ministries of Supply and Production. In 1949 he resigned his chair to become the first director of the research association of the brewing industry. Heilbron's original publications deal mainly with a broad range of natural product chemistry. He was a pioneer in the steroid field, cholesterol, ergosterol, fucosterol, and others. He elucidated the structure of Vitamin A, isolated vitamin A^2 and worked on Vitamin D^2 and the synthesis of Vitamin A. He also worked on the chemistry of penicillin. His studies extended to polyenes and to acetylenic compounds and other fields of organic chemistry. With H.M. Bunbury he produced the monumental *Dictionary of Organic Compounds*. He was a Fellow of the Royal Society, a recipient of its Royal Medal, and president of the Chemical Society, 1948–50.

[Samuel Aaron Miller]

HEILBRON, DAME ROSE (1914–2005), English lawyer. Born in Liverpool, Rose Heilbron was admitted to the bar in 1939 and rapidly established a reputation as a criminal advocate of exceptional ability. In 1949, she was made a king's counsel and in 1956 she was made recorder (chief criminal judge) of Burnley, the first woman to be appointed a recorder in Britain. Vice president of the British Federation of Business and Professional Women, she was frequently cited as an example of the professional advance of women in a man's world. From 1974 until her retirement in 1988 she served as a Judge of the High Court (Family Division), the second British woman to be appointed to the High Court. She was created a dame in 1974.

[Israel Finestein]

HEILBRONN, city in Baden-Wuerttemberg, Germany. There apparently were Jews living in Heilbronn in the second half of the 11th century, as attested by an inscription found in an old synagogue mentioning Nathan ha-Parnas. By the end of the 13th century, their number must have been significant because on Oct. 19, 1298, the followers of *Rindfleisch massacred 143 Jews at Heilbronn. Jewish learning evidently flourished as the names of scholars and teachers are recorded among the martyrs. Jews had reestablished themselves in Heilbronn by 1316. They possessed a synagogue and a cemetery, and lived on a *Judengasse*, where non-Jews also resided. During the *Black Death persecutions between February and April 1349 the community was expelled and their property transferred to the city. Some returned in 1357 and in 1361 obtained royal protection. After 1411 King Sigismund granted the Jews of Heilbronn protection of life and property, limited taxation, freedom of movement, and judicial autonomy in Jewish lawsuits; a Jewish oath was to apply in cases tried before the city court. The Jews were expelled from Heilbronn three times during the 15th century, the last in 1490 when the synagogue and the cemetery were confiscated.

Subsequently, until the 19th century, there was no organized Jewish community in the city. Individual Jews were allowed into the city during the daytime on payment of a body-toll. Seven Jewish families settled in nearby Sontheim, where they built a synagogue in 1702.

After the grant of civil emancipation to the Jews in Wuerttemberg by the edict of 1828 a number of Jews settled in Heilbronn and became citizens there. The Jewish lawyer, Moritz Kallmann, was active in the revolution of 1848 and became a city councilor. The community, established officially in 1851, numbered 65 persons in 1858, 137 in 1862, 994 in 1885 (3.5% of the total population), 815 in 1900, and 900 in 1925 (2%). In Sontheim there were 88 Jews in 1822 (8.8%), 45 in 1855, 72 in 1870, and 59 in 1880. The Heilbronn community was liberal in its religious affiliation. Jewish children attended the general schools and received additional religious education in schools sponsored by the community. A large synagogue was built in 1877. A separate Orthodox community was established in 1911. At Sontheim a Jewish old-age home was established in 1907 and cared for 78 persons in 1937. During the Weimar period antisemitism was at a low ebb. There was even an attempt on Hitler's life in Heilbronn in 1926.

After the Nazi rise to power in 1933 the 790 Jews then living at Heilbronn were subjected to restrictions and discrimination, boycott of Jewish goods, vicious agitation in the press, and occasionally physical attacks. In 1936 the community was forced to establish its own elementary school. In October 1938, all Jews of Polish citizenship were deported back to Poland. On Nov. 10–11, 1938, the synagogue was set on fire, the windows of Jewish stores were smashed, and Jewish homes destroyed. Many Jews from Heilbronn were sent to Dachau. In August 1939 the community was officially dissolved. By 1941, around 600 Jews had emigrated. The others were deported to the East, along with 88 Heilbronn Jews who had found refuge in other localities. There were 10 Jews living in Heilbronn in 1967. In 2004 there were about 65 Jews living in Heilbronn who officially belong to the Jewish community of Wuerttemberg in Stuttgart. About 80% of them were immigrants from the former Soviet Union who came to Germany after 1990.

BIBLIOGRAPHY: H. Franke, *Geschichte und Schicksal der Juden in Heilbronn* (1963), incl. bibl.; P. Sauer, *Die juedischen Gemeinden in Wuerttemberg und Hohenzollern* (1966), 95–100; O. Mayer, *Die Geschichte der Juden in Heilbronn* (1927); Germ Jud, 2 (1968), 346–50. **ADD. BIBLIOGRAPHY:** W. Angerbauer, "Heilbronn," in: W. Angerbauer and H.G. Frank, *Juedische Gemeinden in Kreis und Stadt Heilbronn. Geschichte, Schicksale, Dokumente* (1986; Schriftenreihe des Landkreises Heilbronn, vol. 1), 81–101; H.G. Frank, *"Und unser Glaube ist Sieg." Die Judentaufe in Heilbronn – Wie aus dem Juden Hirsch anno 1717 Georg Heinrich Siegfried wurde*, 249–255.

[Ze'ev Wilhem Falk]

HEILBRONN, JACOB BEN ELHANAN (16th century), rabbi and mathematician. Born in Italy, Heilbronn studied in Prague and traveled through various German and Italian cities, earning his livelihood from teaching. For some time he was employed as a tutor to the children of Nehemiah Luzzatto in Venice. He finally settled in Padua, where he was appointed rabbi. Many scholars of renown addressed their halakhic queries to him, including Samuel *Archivolti, Simone *Luzzatto, Abraham Menahem *Porto, and Avigdor Cividal. Heilbronn is the author of *Seder Meliḥah* in Judeo-German, on the precept of salting meat, based on Moses *Isserles' *Torat Ḥattat* (Cracow, c. 1570), issued with a memorial address on the death of Avigdor Cividal (Venice, 1602); *Shoshannat Ya'akov* (Venice, 1623), mathematical riddles and elementary arithmetic, edited as a supplement to the *Orḥot Ḥayyim* (Prague, 1521) of R. Eliezer ha-Gadol; *Naḥalat Ya'akov* (Padua, 1623), responsa and halakhic novellae, dedicated to his benefactor Simḥah Luzzatto. In his approbation, R. Isaiah *Horowitz praises Heilbronn for his erudition, as did others in their exchange of responsa with him. Other responsa of Heilbronn are included in the *Mashbit Milḥamot* (Venice, 1606). He also translated into Italian *Seder Mitzvot Nashim* on women's religious obligations by Benjamin *Slonik of Grodno (Venice, 1606).

BIBLIOGRAPHY: Ghirondi-Neppi, 173; Fuenn, Keneset, 544.

[Jacob Hirsch Haberman]

HEILBRONN, JOSEPH BEN DAVID OF ESCHWEGE (d. 1771), masoretic scholar. He was a private tutor in Frankfurt and later moved to The Hague. He is the author of *Mevin Ḥidot* (Amsterdam, 1765), on the masorah. It contains a lengthy four-part prologue and is arranged according to the weekly portions of the Pentateuch. The book received the endorsements of the Ashkenazi and Sephardi chief rabbis of Amsterdam. In reply to an accusation by Asher Worms, author of *Seyag la-Torah*, that Heilbronn had either plagiarized his own work or was negligent in textual research, Heilbronn issued a pamphlet in defense of his position. Heilbronn also composed a prayer book on the liturgy of Simḥat Torah (Amsterdam, 1769). He died in Amsterdam.

BIBLIOGRAPHY: Fuenn, Keneset, 491; S. Seeligman, *Het geestelijk leven der Hoogduitsche Joodsche Gemeente te's Gravenhage* (1914).

[Marvin Tokayer]

HEILBRUN, CAROLYN G. (1926–2003), U.S. academic, literary critic, and feminist writer; president of the Modern Language Association (1984). Born in New Jersey, the only child of Archibald and Estelle Roemer Gold, Heilbrun moved to New York City with her family in 1932 and lived there for the rest of her life. Privately schooled in childhood, she received her B.A. from Wellesley College in 1947. She married James Heilbrun in 1945, during her sophomore year. The couple had three children, born while Carolyn worked toward a Ph.D. in English at Columbia University. Heilbrun taught briefly at Brooklyn College, then at the Columbia School of General Studies, moving eventually onto the Graduate Faculty where she taught as a full professor until her resignation in 1992.

While still at Wellesley, Heilbrun published a prize-winning short story in the *Atlantic Monthly* that opened the vexed question of her sense of herself as a Jew. As a result of her parents' rejection of their Jewish identity, Heilbrun had grown up without any attachment to the Jewish community or knowledge of its heritage, observances, and beliefs. She was entirely unaware of the antisemitism endemic at Wellesley in the postwar period until she began to question, years later, her college's indifference to her achievements. In *Reinventing Womanhood* (1979) she wrote of her realization that "Wellesley had ignored me because I was a Jew." Eventually she would turn this new sense of herself toward the development of her feminism: "To be a feminist," she said, "one had to have had the experience of being an outsider."

Between 1961 and 2002, Heilbrun published nine works of non-fiction crucial to the development of feminist thought, including *Toward A Recognition Of Androgyny* (1973); *Reinventing Womanhood* (1979); *Writing A Woman's Life* (1988); *Hamlet's Mother And Other Women* (1990); *The Education Of*

A Woman: The Life Of Gloria Steinem (1995); *The Last Gift Of Time* (1997); and *Women's Lives: The View From The Threshold* (1999). In these works she taught women to recognize the possibilities latent in androgyny, to reinvent themselves as women, to appreciate the distinctive shape of women's lives, to seize control of the boundaries of life, and to reconsider the ambivalent power of male mentors on women's lives (*When Men Were the Only Models We Had* (2002)).

Heilbrun also published more than a dozen popular novels under the pseudonym "Amanda Cross," in which a beautiful academic, a Protestant detective named Kate Fansler, dazzles the world by solving its mysteries. These include *In the Last Analysis* (1964); *The James Joyce Murder* (1967); *Death in a Tenured Position* (1981); and *An Imperfect Spy* (1995).

Although the tensions for women within academic life were always comfortably resolved for Kate Fansler, her fictional alter ego, Heilbrun left Columbia in bitterness in 1992, over a fight to tenure several women in her department. She committed suicide at 77, in 2003.

BIBLIOGRAPHY: S. Kress, *Carolyn G. Heilbrun: Feminism in A Tenured Position* (1997).

[Janet Burstein (2nd ed.)]

HEILBUT, ELEAZAR LAZI BEN JOSEPH BEN LAZI (1740–1814), rabbi and author. Heilbut was born in Berlin. He was first a *dayyan* in Posen and then succeeded Raphael b. Jekuthiel Susskind *Kohen as rabbi of the combined community of Hamburg, Altona, and Wandsbeck. He was the teacher of the literary historian and bibliographer, Heimann Joseph *Michael, who married his daughter. Heilbut compiled a work on the Shulḥan Arukh *Ḥoshen Mishpat*, the first part of which was published by his son Moses under the title *Mishnah de-Rabbi Eli'ezer ve-hu Dammesek Eli'ezer* (Altona 1815). He wrote a polemic against the *Mizpeh Yokte'el* of Saul *Berlin which was published without a title or the name of the author (*ibid.*, 1789). A large number of his works remain in manuscript. They include a work on the Shulḥan Arukh *Even ha-Ezer*, the manuscript of which was stolen from him; novellae and glosses to the Talmud, as well as commentaries on the minor tractates of the Talmud; an exegetical homiletical work on the Pentateuch with expositions of Rashi's commentary; and an alphabetical composition of all the rules of blessings with sources. His glosses to Joseph b. Wolf Heilbut's homiletical commentary to the Pentateuch, *Beitah Yosef*, are still extant (Neubauer, Cat. no. 1387/2).

[Samuel Abba Horodezky]

HEILMANN, YITZHAK (1906–1997), *ḥazzan* and choirmaster. Heilmann, was born in Lvov to a family of Belzer ḥasidim. He sang in the temple choir in Lvov with Cantor Yehoshua Moshe Saitz. Afterwards he was appointed assistant to the choir conductor Yisrael Faiwishis, with whom he learned to read and play music. When Faiwishis moved to Lodz, Heilmann was appointed choir conductor at the Lvov and the Gilead Synagogue. He was conductor of the Polish military orchestra and teacher at the Lvov Conservatory. In 1935 he moved to Belgium where he conducted the choir at the Central Synagogue of the *Shomre Hadass* community in Antwerp. He performed with his choir on the Belgian radio. During World War II he was in a refugee camp in Switzerland. He immigrated to Israel in 1949, and from 1950 was choir conductor in the Central Synagogue of Haifa for over 45 years.The choir was famous for the old Warsaw-style approach to choral music and performed frequently on *Kol Israel*. At first it was mixed (boys and men) but in the later years it was an adult male choir. He trained many cantors from among the choristers, including David *Ullmann, Moshe *Shavit, Mordekhai Ronen, Dov Keren, and Naḥum Malik, and composed hundreds of melodies for sections of the prayer service. In 1997, under the auspices of the Toronto Council of *ḥazzanim*, a three-volume set of Heilmann's compositions were published under the title *Shirat Itzḥak*.

[Akiva Zimmerman / Raymond Goldstein (2nd ed.)]

HEILPERIN, FALK (1876–1945), educator and Yiddish writer. Born in Nieswiez, Belorussia, Heilperin began his teaching career in Minsk in 1904. He first rose to prominence during World War I as director of a Yiddish secular school for refugee children. In 1916 he helped to organize a Jewish teachers' conference at Tambov, which proclaimed Yiddish as the basic language of the Jewish child at the elementary school level, but which also recommended Hebrew as a prescribed language. The Zionists attacked him violently for giving priority to Yiddish, the struggle between the Hebraists and Yiddishists reaching a climax at the first all-Russian conference of Jewish teachers, convoked in St. Petersburg during June 1917. There Heilperin appeared as the spokesman of secular Yiddish schools, maintaining that the mother tongue of the children should be the natural, normal language of instruction, that the government should be urged to provide compulsory elementary education for all children, and that Hebrew should be included in the curriculum for all Jewish classes. In 1918 he served as educational adviser to the Jewish ministry of the short-lived government of the Ukraine. In 1921 he joined the Jewish Teachers' Seminary in Vilna as a teacher of Hebrew and Yiddish and was active in YIVO during its early Vilna period. From 1900 onwards he published his writings in Hebrew and Russian and from 1906 also in Yiddish. He prepared readers, story books, and educational texts in both Hebrew and Yiddish, as well as simplified translations of world literature into Hebrew. He edited the first Yiddish magazine for children, *Grininke Beymelekh* ("Green Trees") and founded a publishing house for children's literature in Jekaterinoslaw. He translated the fairy tales of Andersen and the Grimm brothers into Yiddish as well as novels by Disraeli, Hamsun, Gogol, Twain, Chekhov, Schiller, and Tolstoy. With Max *Weinreich he published a widely used Yiddish grammar (1928), joined the literary circle of "Yung Vilne," and published several volumes of short stories and plays: *Ertseylungen* ("Tales," 1910), *Yidishe Mayses* ("Jewish Tales," 1917), *Oyfn Shvel* ("On the Threshold," 1918), *Mayses fun Fartsaytn* ("Ancient Tales," 1929), *Fun Opgruntn* ("From the Abyss," 1930). In 1938 he settled in Palestine, where the Ohel Theater produced a Hebrew version of his drama "Hordos" ("Herod," in: *Fun Opgruntn*).

BIBLIOGRAPHY: Rejzen, Leksikon, 1 (1926), 829–32; M. Ravitch, *Mayn Leksikon* (1945); LNYL, 3 (1960), 128–31; Kressel, Leksikon, 1 (1965), 615–6.

[Sol Liptzin / Tamar Lewinsky (2nd ed.)]

HEILPERIN, MICHAEL ANGELO (1909–), Swiss economist. Heilperin was born in Warsaw and educated in Geneva where he settled. He was appointed professor at the Graduate Institute of International Studies in Geneva. His main fields were money, banking, and international economics and he became prominent through his analysis of international monetary crises. His publications include *Trade of Nations* (1947, 1952^2); *Studies in Economic Nationalism* (1960); and *Gold and Monetary Order* (1962).

[Joachim O. Ronall]

HEILPERN (Raphael), YOM TOV LIPMAN BEN ISRAEL (1816–1879), rabbi and author. Heilpern was born in Rozan where his father was rabbi, and was appointed rabbi of Krewo in 1836. He later served in Kieidany, Ciechanowiec, Mezhirech, and finally in Bialystok (1859), where he died. His collection of responsa, *Oneg Yom Tov* (2 parts, 1880), was highly regarded in rabbinical circles. He also wrote a homiletical work under the same title (1906). Heilpern played an active role in communal affairs. Because of his opposition to certain communal notables who discriminated against the children of the poor in favor of the rich with regard to the selection for military service, he was accused of disloyalty to the Russian government, tried, and sentenced to several months of imprisonment.

BIBLIOGRAPHY: I.T. Eisenstadt and S. Wiener (eds.), *Da'at Kedoshim*, 1 (1897), 29 (first pagination); *Yahadut Lita*, 3 (1967), 44.

[Samuel Abba Horodezky]

HEILPRIN, U.S. family in 19th and early 20th centuries. MICHAEL HEILPRIN (1823–1888), who was born in Piotrkow, Poland, was a linguist, scholar, encyclopedist, and author. In 1842 Heilprin and his family went to Hungary, where he joined the Hungarian liberal movement soon after his arrival, and became well known as a writer and revolutionary poet during the Revolution of 1848. After the suppression of the uprising, Heilprin went into hiding and then fled to Paris for some months. He emigrated to the U.S. in 1856 and taught in Hebrew Education Society schools in Philadelphia until 1858, when he moved to Brooklyn to become an editor and contributor to *Appleton's New American Cyclopaedia* (1858–63). He later worked as an associate editor on the revised work (1872–76). He also wrote for the New York *Tribune* and contributed articles to E.L. Godkin's *Nation* from 1865 until his death, and was considered one of the foremost writers in the U.S. on European literature and politics. In the 1880s Heilprin was active in the work of the Emigrant Aid Society and advocated the establishment of colonies for Russo-Jewish refugees in Oregon, the Dakotas, and New Jersey (see *Am Olam). He wrote the two-volume *Historical Poetry of the Ancient Hebrews* (1879–80), of which a third volume was begun, but not completed.

Heilprin's elder son, ANGELO HEILPRIN (1853–1907), was a geologist, explorer, and author. He made several trips of exploration including one to the erupting volcano Mt. Pelée. He also went to the Arctic on a mission to bring relief to Peary (1892). His younger son, LOUIS HEILPRIN (1856–1912), who was born in Miskolc, Hungary, was an encyclopedist, too. He assisted his father in the revision of the *American Cyclopaedia* (1872–76), wrote the *Historical Reference Book* (1884), was an editor of *Nelson's Encyclopaedia*, an associate editor of the *New International Encyclopaedia*, and co-edited *Lippincott's New Gazetteer* (1905) with Angelo Heilprin.

BIBLIOGRAPHY: G. Pollak, *Michael Heilprin and his Sons* (1912).

HEILPRIN, JEHIEL BEN SOLOMON (1660–1746), Lithuanian talmudic scholar and historian. Heilprin, the son of the rabbi of Sokolov, studied Kabbalah and, according to legend, performed miracles. He served as rabbi first in Glussk (Bobruisk district), where his compilation of rules and regulations for the *ḥevra kaddisha* were preserved in his own manuscript for several generations. In 1711 he was appointed head of the yeshivah in Minsk. His method of teaching the Talmud, contrary to *pilpul*, caused friction between him and Aryeh Leib b. Asher *Gunzberg, who was also a *rosh yeshivah* in Minsk. Aryeh Leib later left Minsk, and Heilprin was able to continue in his own yeshivah, unhampered, and with the affection of his pupils.

Heilprin became famous mainly for his historical-chronological book *Seder ha-Dorot* (Karlsruhe, 1769), which is divided into three parts: (a) chronology of events and personages dated from the Creation to 1696; (b) the biographies and chronologies of the *tannaim* and *amoraim* in alphabetical order; (c) the names of Hebrew authors and books, listed alphabetically, up to Heilprin's period. In the first part of this work he made use of stories from the **Sefer ha-Yashar* and the earlier chronological books, including *Ẓemaḥ David* by David *Gans, *Sefer Yuḥasin* by Abraham Zacuto, and *Shalsft ha-Kabbalah* by Gedaliah ibn Yaḥya. In the third part he used *Siftei Yeshenim* by Shabbetai Bass; Heilprin copied the list of books from this work with all its errors. The second part, devoted to the history of the *tannaim* and *amoraim*, is of utmost importance. Although Heilprin followed *Sefer Yuḥasin* in compiling the list of individuals, the history he wrote was the first modern-type biography of the *tannaim* and *amoraim*, being based on original research of the talmudic sources. In the introduction to his book Heilprin discussed the importance of the history of the *tannaim* to halakhic decisions.

Seder ha-Dorot was published a second time (Lemberg, 1858) with comments by Joseph Saul Nathanson, the rabbi of Lemberg. An improved edition of the book with a preface was later published by Naphtali Maskil le-Eitan (Maskileison; Warsaw, 1878). Heilprin also published annotations to the Babylonian Talmud (Vilna, 1880); *Erkhei Kinnuyim* (Dyhernfurth, 1806), a work similar to a concordance, listing the nouns and verbs in the Bible and Talmud: a new edition entitled *Kav Shalom* with notes and comments (letters (A–Ḥ) was published by S.Ẓ. Adler (Satu Mare, 1939).

BIBLIOGRAPHY: N. Maskileison, in: Heilprin, Dorot (1882^2, repr. 1956), preface; B.Z. Eisenstadt, *Rabbanei Minsk va-Ḥakhameha* (1898), 14–16; B.Z. Katz, *Rabbanut, Ḥasidut ve-Haskalah* (1957), 141.

[Zvi Meir Rabinowitz]

HEILPRIN, PHINEHAS MENAHEM (1801–1863), Hebrew scholar and anti-Reform polemicist. Born in Lublin, Poland, he moved to Hungary in 1842 and, in 1859, emigrated to the U.S. Heilprin was opposed to reforms in Judaism and the moderation of his critical views on talmudic literature stemmed from a loyalty to Jewish tradition. In 1845 he wrote a sharp polemical work, *Teshuvot be-Anshei Aven* (signed S.M.N., the last letters of his names), directed against Samuel *Holdheim and his school, in which he expressed the view that Jews have a right to exist as a nation, and not merely as a religious community. Heilprin's second work *Even Boḥan* (1846), signed "Peli," contains a penetrating criticism of Abraham *Geiger's *Melo Ḥofnayim*, and a critical edition of Profiat *Duran's *Al Tehi ka-Avotekha*. An article on methods of talmudic textual criticism, *"Kevod Ḥakhamim Yinḥalu,"* was published posthumously in *Bikkurim* (vol. 2, 1865).

BIBLIOGRAPHY: G. Pollak, *Michael Heilprin and his Sons* (1912); A. Ginzig, in: *Oẓar ha-Sifrut*, 3 (1889–90), 11–12 (fourth pagin.).

[Gedalyah Elkoshi]

HEILPRIN, SAMUEL HELMANN BEN ISRAEL (1675–1765), rabbi of Bohemia. Heilprin was born in Krotoszyn, and studied under Abraham b. Saul *Broda of Prague. He was rabbi of Kremsier (Kromeriz) in Moravia from 1720 to 1726 and from 1726 to 1751 of Mannheim, where he devoted himself particularly to strengthening the education system and established a yeshivah. In 1751 he succeeded Jonathan *Eybeschuetz as rabbi of Metz, remaining there for the rest of his life. While rabbi of Kremsier he was a firm opponent of Shabbateanism, and when in Mannheim he began to take an active part in the controversy against Eybeschuetz. He intensified his battle against him when in Metz as a result of the discovery of five amulets written by Eybeschuetz which increased his suspicion that Eybeschuetz did indeed belong to the Shabbatean sect. In 1752 Heilprin, together with the rabbis of Frankfurt, Amsterdam, and Hanover, excommunicated Eybeschuetz. Only a few of Heilprin's glosses to the Talmud have been published. These are to be found in the *Kol Yehudah* (Amsterdam, 1729) of Judah b. Ḥanina Selig of Glogau (5a, 15c, 52d) and there is a responsum by him in *Shav Ya'akov* of Jacob b. Benjamin Katz of Prague (pt. 2 (Frankfurt, 1742), no. 20). The eulogy on him delivered by Ezekiel *Landau, author of the *Noda bi-Yhudah*, is published in Landau's *Ahavat Ẓiyyon* (vol. 1 (Prague, 1827), sermon 6). His son, URI SHRAGA PHOEBUS, who died while on a visit to his father's grave in Metz in 1770, served as rabbi of the towns of Hanau, Lissa, and Bonn.

BIBLIOGRAPHY: Cahen, in: REJ, 12 (1886), 289–94; I.T. Eisenstadt and S. Wiener, *Da'at Kedoshim* (1898), 59f.; D. Kahana, *Toledot ha-Mekubbalim, ha-Shabbeta'im, ve-ha-Ḥasidim*, 2 (1914), 30–34; L. Lewin, *Geschichte der Juden in Lissa* (1904), 190–2; L. Loewenstein, *Geschichte der Juden in der Kurpfalz* (1895), 198–201; N. Netter, *Vingt siècles d'histoire d'une communauté juive* (1938), 113–5, 132–231.

[Yehoshua Horowitz]

HEILPRUN, ELIEZER LEIZER BEN MORDECAI (1648–1700), Galician rabbi. Heilprun was born in Jaroslaw (Galicia), and studied in Pinczow at the yeshivah of Saul Katzenellenbogen, father of his son-in-law, Moses Katzenellenbogen. His dialectical ability gained him the sobriquet of "R. Leizer Ḥarif" ("the sharp-witted"). He served as rabbi of Mezhirech and of Tomaszow, and in 1700 moved to Fuerth where he died. He left in manuscript glosses to the Talmud, sermons, responsa, rulings, and *hadranim* on tractates of the Talmud entitled *Si'aḥ ha-Se'udah* ("Conversations at Meals"), the *hadran* being delivered at a festive banquet held on the completion of the study of a tractate.

BIBLIOGRAPHY: Brann, in: *Gedenkbuch… D. Kaufmann* (1900), 397f., 408; I.T. Eisenstein and S. Wiener (eds.), *Da'at Kedoshim* (1897–98), 63; Loewenstein, in: JJLG, 6 (1908), 172f.; Michael, Or, no. 446; Neubauer, Cat, nos. 469, 470, 523, 960, 1019.

[Yehoshua Horowitz]

HEIMANN, MORITZ (1868–1925), German author and essayist. Heimann was born into an Orthodox family in Werder. He received his Jewish education at home since his was the only Jewish family in the village. Despite Heimann's devotion to German culture and language, he appreciated Zionist and national Jewish thought. In his essay *Zionismus und Politik* (1917), written under the impression of World War I, he described the Jewish longing for a homeland as mainly a political issue, which should find its pragmatic solution apart from religious visions.

Heimann worked as the chief literary adviser to the Berlin publishing house of S. *Fischer between the years 1895 and 1923. There he had a profound influence on German literature during the first quarter of the 20th century. In those years he discovered and encouraged many talented young writers. His aphorisms, short stories, and psychological novellas were collected and edited by Oskar Loerke as *Prosaische Schriften* (5 vols., 1918–26). Of Heimann's plays, only *Armand Carrel* (1920) was moderately successful. Heimann's poems on Jewish themes include "Der Rabbi und der Fluss," a reworking of the talmudic legend about R. Phinehas ben Jair (Ḥul. 7a). His essays include an appreciation of his friend M.J. *Berdyczewski and a defense of the right of a Jew, Walter *Rathenau, to become a German cabinet minister. Heimann's drama *Das Weib des Akiba* (1922) idealized Jewish womanhood, personified in the wife of the heroic sage R. *Akiva, and was largely based on talmudic sources. Two posthumous volumes were *Die Spindel* (ed. I. Bin Gorion, 1937) and *Die Wahrheit liegt nicht in der Mitte* (1966), a collection of essays edited by Heimann's biographer, Wilhelm Lehmann.

BIBLIOGRAPHY: Bab, in: G. Krojanker (ed.), *Juden in der deutschen Literatur* (1922), 260–392; W. Lehmann, *Moritz Heimann, eine Einfuehrung in sein Werk* (1960). **ADD. BIBLIOGRAPHY:** D. Rodewald, in: *Juedische Intellektuelle und die Philologien in Deutschland, 1871–1933* (2001), 41–51.

[Sol Liptzin / Noam Zadoff and Mirjam Triendl (2nd ed.)]

HEIMWEHR (Ger. "home defense"), a paramilitary organization, closely connected with the *Christian Social Party in Austria. Founded in 1919 on a stridently anti-Marxist platform, its energies were directed mainly against its social democratic counterpart, the *Schutzbund. For this reason it enjoyed the support of such baptized Jews as Rudolf von Sieghardt, the governor of the national bank, and the arms manufacturer Fritz Mandel. There was even a Jewish unit in the late 1920s. In December 1929 Jewish group leaders declared that they could no longer participate because of growing antisemitism which the organization identified with anti-Marxism. In the Korneuburger Program (1930) the organization proclaimed its affiliation to fascism against democracy and parliamentarianism. The Heimwehr became the decisive factor in Austrian politics after the outlawing of the Social Democratic Party (1934). After the collapse of the "Pfrimer coup" in 1931 the Styrian branch of the Heimwehr formed a common front with the National Socialists against the Jews. The Heimwehr was responsible for many of the anti-Jewish riots of the period.

BIBLIOGRAPHY: A. Diamant, *Austrian Catholics and the First Republic* (1960), index; P.G.J. Pulzer, in: J. Fraenkel (ed.), *The Jews of Austria* (1967), 439–42; L. Jedlicka, in: *Journal of Contemporary History*, 1 (1966), 127–44. **ADD. BIBLIOGRAPHY:** C.E. Edmondson, *The Heimwehr and Austrian Politics* (1978); G.R. Bell, *The Austrian Heimwehr and the Diplomacy of Reaction in Central Euorpe 1930–1934* (1996); W. Wiltschegg, *Die Heimwehr – Eine unwiderstehliche Volksbewegung?* (1985); W. Chraska, *Die Heimwehr und die Erste Republik Österreich* (1981).

[Meir Lamed / Bjoern Siegel (2nd ed.)]

HEINE, HEINRICH (originally **Ḥayyim** or **Harry**; 1797–1856), German poet and writer. Though a celebrated romantic poet and a political writer, whose works provoked passionate discussion, Heine produced some of the greatest Jewish verse outside Hebrew or Yiddish. Heine's way of thinking was shaped by the contradictions between his Jewish origin and the intellectual tradition of the enlightenment and is characterized by a specific Jewish perspective on the significance and tradition of Scripture. During his early years his birthplace, Duesseldorf, was part of the Napoleonic Empire (1806–14). The rights of citizenship and equality before the law that the Jews enjoyed under French rule later found expression in works idealizing Napoleon and the achievements of the French Revolution. Although Heine, in childhood and later in his life, was spared the experience of direct persecution, he remained aware of the stigma of Jewishness. The disappointments that affected German liberalism and Rhenish Jewry after Napoleon's overthrow partly account for the conflicts and paradoxes that mark Heine's career.

The German Years (1797–1831)

Heine's ancestors on his father's side, long settled in northern Germany, included prosperous merchants and bankers. His mother came from a respected family of bankers and scholars who had lived in Duesseldorf since the mid-17th century. Heine's father, Samson Heine, was raised traditionally, but his family life was dominated by the secularized Judaism of his wife, Betty Heine (née Peira van Geldern). Heine received a religious education from a private Jewish school and after attending the regular school (1803–7), he was sent to the first Duesseldorf *lycée*. The founding principal of this institution, which had been established by the French government, Aegidius Jakob Schallmeyer, was an exponent of the late enlightenment in the Rhineland. In his early years Heine experienced the benefits of the assimilated status of the Jews under the French government. Although he was impressed and stimulated by what he heard about the Jewish tradition by his mother's late uncle, the traveler and adventurer Simon van *Geldern, who had visited the Holy Land, his knowledge of Judaism was fragmentary and superimposed on the ideas of the Enlightenment. In 1815 he left school and was sent first to Frankfurt and then later to Hamburg for training in business. In Hamburg he made further acquaintance with his father's family. His uncle Salomon *Heine was one of the wealthiest bankers in northern Germany. Some of Heine's early poems were inspired by a frustrated passion for Salomon's daughter Amalie. Some years later when he fell in love with her sister Therese, Salomon Heine again thwarted his nephew's aspirations. In 1818, after two years in his uncle's business, Harry Heine & Co was established as a branch of his father's Duesseldorf company. The business failed one year later, when his father went into bankruptcy because of the illness that eventually caused his death in 1828. Salomon Heine felt responsible for his nephew's further development and paid for his studies at the universities of Bonn, Berlin, and Goettingen (1819–25). In one way or another he helped him remain financially solvent for many years. In Berlin Heine became a disciple of the philosopher G.W.F. *Hegel, met some of the leading German writers and philosophers at the salons of Rahel (Levin) *Varnhagen von Ense and Elise von Hohenhausen, and published a well-received first verse collection, *Gedichte* (1822). He also joined the reformist *Verein fuer Cultur und Wissenschaft der Juden, becoming its secretary in 1822 and enjoying the friendship of such cultured German Jews as Eduard *Gans, Moses *Moser, Leopold *Zunz, Immanuel *Wohlwill, and Ludwig *Markus. The wider Jewish knowledge that Heine gained in their company was later reflected in works like the fragmentary *Der Rabbi von Bacharach* (1840), which he began in 1824. Berlin Jewry's indifference to the cultural aims and activities of the Verein led to its collapse, and Heine was incensed and disillusioned by the subsequent apostasy of some of the leading members. After abandoning plans for a journalistic career in Paris, he finally surrendered to the pressure of his environment. He was baptized as a Lutheran in 1825, adopting the Christian name of Johann Christian Heinrich. Heine soon became ashamed of his conversion, which was solely intended to facilitate the gaining of his doctorate of law at Goettingen and the pursuit of his career as a civil servant or academic. He was mistaken, for the doors remained closed: to Jews he was a renegade, to Christians an insincere turncoat or dangerous radical. Although Heine spoke of the baptismal certificate as an "admission ticket (*entrée billet*) to European culture," it gave him no advantages and for the rest of his life he suffered from the stigma of a convert.

With the *Reisebilder*, published in four volumes (1826–31), Heine, at the end of the romantic period, introduced into German literature a new and sometimes alarming style, which made him a much acclaimed but at the same time controversial writer. These travel sketches combined the characteristic tone of the German Romantic Movement with the ideas that arose from the French Revolution. He satirized religious bigotry and political reaction and pointed to the necessity of constitutions that would provide for parliamentary government and civil liberty. Their publication led to numerous discussions and a ban on the four volumes in several German states. The most incisive disputes arose with the poet August Graf von Platen (1829) and the writer and critic Wolfgang Menzel (1836), both of whom resorted to antisemitic polemics, which were to prove persistent in public opinion and literary criticism up to the first half of the 20th century. It is an irony that Heine found himself a target of massive antisemitic attacks for the first time in public after his conversion. Besides the *Reisebilder*, the collection of his early lyrical works, the *Buch der Lieder*, which was published in 1827, made him one of the most celebrated lyrical poets of the time.

Failing to obtain a chair at the University of Munich in 1828, and fearing sterner police action and a boycott of his works, Heine left Germany. He settled in Paris in 1831, after the liberal July Revolution in France. Four years later, the publication of his works was temporarily suspended by the parliament of the German confederation. Except for two short visits to his family in 1843 and 1844, he never returned to his native country.

The French Years (1831–1856)

In Paris, during the 1830s and 1840s a place of exile for writers and intellectuals from various European countries, Heine found a more congenial atmosphere. He admired the achievements of the 1830 revolution and praised the French capital as a "New Jerusalem." Through his journalistic contributions to the Augsburg *Allgemeine Zeitung*, the *Morgenblatt fuer gebildete Staende*, *L'Europe littéraire*, and the *Revue des deux mondes* during his first French decade, Heine became an intermediary between the cultural traditions of France and Germany. His writings on France (*Ueber die franzoesische Buehne*, *Franzoesische Maler*) and Germany (*Die romantische Schule*, *Zur Geschichte der Religion und Philosophie in Deutschland*) were later collected in the four volumes of the *Salon* (1834–40). These works show that his view of German literature and philosophy was influenced not only by the thinking of Hegel and of Jewish emancipation but also by ideas derived from the Saint-Simonian movement, with which Heine came into contact during his early Paris years.

In the course of the 1830s he became the leading figure of a group of young German writers who were to be known in the history of German literature as *Junges Deutschland* ("Young Germany"). Yet he fell out with Ludwig *Boerne, the other prominent liberal German writer in Paris, who regarded him as a lukewarm revolutionary. Heine's views of his fellow exile, expressed after Boerne's death in *Ludwig Boerne. Eine Denkschrift* (1840), provoked enraged reactions by the liberal Germans writers of the time, for whom Boerne was an exponent of the republican idea. It is one of the paradoxical characteristics of antisemitism in 19th century Germany that in the course of the controversy even the conservative and nationalistic press, while rejecting Boerne's liberal ideas, accused Heine of being unprincipled and unscrupulous. The spreading of antisemitic stereotypes was thus employed to play off the two exponents of Jewish-German literature in the first half of the 19th century against each other. In response, Heine satirized the younger generation of political writers in the mock epic *Atta Troll. Ein Sommernachtstraum* (1843). His second mock epic, *Deutschland. Ein Wintermaerchen*, written in 1843 after a visit to Hamburg and satirizing reactionary German monarchies, made Heine again a target for nationalistic critics who decried him as frivolous and unpatriotic.

Heine's circle during his French years included numerous well-known writers and intellectuals of the time, such as Honoré Balzac, Alexandre Dumas, Théophile Gautier, Ferdinand *Lassalle, George Sand, Alexandre *Weill, and Karl *Marx. Another of his acquaintances was James Mayer de *Rothschild. In 1841 he married a non-Jewess, Augustine Crescence Mirat ("Mathilde"), an illiterate Paris shop assistant he had been living with for seven years. Following the death of Salomon Heine in 1844, the poet experienced a serious struggle for a promised annuity, and obtained it only on condition that he refrain from publishing critical memoirs on the Heine family. From 1848 up to his death in 1856 Heine was confined to his "mattress-grave." He himself believed that he suffered from a spinal disease. As no contemporary diagnosis has been handed down, recent research speculates most frequently about venereal infection. In spite of his condition he continued to work as a writer. The late works – *Romanzero* (1851), *Gedichte 1853 und 1854* (1854), *Gestaendnisse* (1854), *Lutezia* (1854) – poems, autobiographical reflections, and a compilation of his journalistic writings once more show the characteristic features of this style: they combine irony with pathetic metaphors emphasizing the tradition of German romanticism and the necessity of political and religious emancipation.

Heine and Jewish Tradition

Heine's Judaism has been a matter of controversial discussion. From a biographical point of view, one of the questions has been to what extent he saw himself as a Jew and as an exponent of Jewish culture in Germany. The problematic nature of this issue is due mainly to Heine's technique of blending biographical information and fictitious sketches in his works. Confronted with antisemitic attacks after the short period of Jewish emancipation under the French government, he began playing in his writing a confounding though fascinating game of hide-and-seek concerning his Jewish origin, which reveals his attempt to achieve a synthesis of European culture and Jewish tradition and in retrospect exposes the impossibility of his effort to become part of a Christian-dominated society.

The early tragedy *Almansor* (1823) is set in Grenada in medieval Spain and emphasizes the persecution of the Jews and Muslims under the reestablished reign of the Catholic kings. Within the historical setting of a drama, which refers to G.E. *Lessing's *Nathan der Weise* as well as to Heine's own situation in the early 1820s, the author reflected on the problem of Jewish identity within the Diaspora and the conflicts of apostasy. In the fragmentary novel *Der Rabbi von Bacherach*, which was drafted during his time as a member of the Verein fuer Cultur und Wissenschaft der Juden in Berlin, and published in 1840 as a reaction to the *Damascus Affair, he identified himself quite obviously with the cynical, freethinking Don Isaac *Abrabanel, though at the same time stressing the beauty of traditional Jewish ceremonies. He fiercely condemned both French diplomatic intrigues in Syria and the passivity of many French Jews in his "Damascus Letters" for the Augsburg *Allgemeine Zeitung*, but his articles were published anonymously. His book about Ludwig Boerne was not only a justification of his own political ideas; it was also a polyphonic attempt to show his life in Paris, his suffering abroad in the tradition of the exile of Babylon. In the late *Romanzero* he included the *Hebraeische Melodien*, a title consciously borrowed from Lord *Byron's *Hebrew Melodies*; *Prinzessin Sabbat*, a fairy-tale evocation of the Jew's transformation on the day of rest; *Jehuda ben Halevy*, in praise of the great Jewish-Spanish poet and philosopher, and the tragicomic *Disputation*. *Romanzero* also contained other poems reflecting Jewish themes, as did his earlier collections of verse.

Not only the works that obviously refer to Jewish topics deal with the problem of Jewish identity. Almost every piece of Heine's prose or verse reflects in one way or another the conflict of his Jewish origin. His modernist view of Judaism is poised between identification with the history of the Jewish people, the Jewish tradition of Scripture, and a feeling of strangeness and exclusion. In some of his writings he stressed the curse of Judaism: the Flying Dutchman in the fragmentary picaresque novel *Aus den Memoiren des Herrn von Schnabelewobski* (1834) is but a figuration of Ahasuerus, the Wandering Jew. His early travel sketch *Ideen. Das Buch Le Grand*, which can be seen mainly as an attempt to rewrite romantic themes, plays with the Judaism of its author. Reflecting about the female figures in Shakespeare's dramatic works (*Shakespeares Maedchen und Frauen*, 1839), he gives Shylock, the Jew, a prominent position. Whereas in his early years Lessing, Shakespeare, Homer, and Cervantes became figurations of his own identity as a writer, in his last years Heine wrote a fragmentary poem, *Jehuda ben Halevy*, which points to the great Jewish poet as one of the ancestors of his writing.

One of the most controversial issues of Heine's Judaism has been the question of whether, in the years of the "mattress-grave," he returned to Jewish belief. When he published the epilogue to the *Romancero*, in which he quite frankly announced his return to a personal god, the reading public and the critics were shocked. Taking into consideration that the reproach of atheism has a long tradition within German literature and philosophy (Moses *Mendelssohn) and furthermore that one of the main features of Heine's writing is the idea of an emancipation of thought through an ironic and provoking style, and looking at his writings, which paradoxically stress the ideas of continuity and tradition rather than change, it seems as if Heine was always a man of faith – but faith without confession.

Reception

Up to the second half of the 20th century Heine remained one of the best-known and most controversial writers in German literature. In the first decades following his death the reading public, the critics, and the scholars emphasized the romantic tone of his early lyrical works and ignored his attempts to renew German romanticism by superimposing the poetical ideas of the romantics on the enlightened conceptions of political and religious emancipation. More than 13,000 recognized musical settings of his poetry supported this attempt. In the course of the decline of nationalism and chauvinism in the late 19th century, Heine's critics emphasized his Jewish descent and his sympathy for the achievements of the French revolution. Resorting to antisemitic stereotypes, critics like Heinrich von Treitschke and Adolf Bartels reviled him as a "*Vaterlandsverraeter*" (betrayer of his native country), both unprincipled and frivolous. One of the most influential voices in the early reception of his works was Karl *Kraus. In his essay *Heine und die Folgen* (1910) he pointed to the contrast between the depth of German thought and the frivolous French style, which in his view was introduced into German literature by Heine. It is one of the ironies of the reception of Heine's works that another Jewish writer perpetuated the stereotypes of earlier antisemitic judgments. Nevertheless Heine became one of the most influential German poets and writers. His works influenced Richard Wagner's *Flying Dutchman* and *Tannhaeuser* and inspired countless writers, including Matthew Arnold, George *Eliot, George B. Shaw, Charles Baudelaire, Friedrich *Nietzsche, Thomas *Mann, Giorgio *Bassani, Jorge Luis Borges, and Paul *Celan. Heine's influence has been traced in practically all of Western literature, and his poems have been translated into most languages, including English (by Humbert *Wolfe, Louis *Untermeyer, Hal Draper, and Terence J. Reed) and Hebrew (by David *Frishman and Yiẓhak *Katznelson). Much of Heine's prose work has been translated into Hebrew by S. *Perlman. Outstanding among the works based on Heine's life is Israel *Zangwill's sketch "From a Mattress Grave" (in *Dreamers of the Ghetto*, 1898).

During the era of National Socialism in Germany (1933–45) Heine's writings were excluded from anthologies and schoolbooks, the publication of his works was suppressed, and on May 10, 1933, his works were burned together with the writings of many other Jewish-German writers and liberal thinkers. After the liberation of Germany in 1945 the East Germans proclaimed Heine an early socialist writer, whereas the West German reception stressed his works as part of the heritage of German culture that had not been abused for the ideological purposes of the Hitler regime.

As numerous editions and translations of his works, congresses, exhibitions, and monuments in Germany and many other countries throughout the world show, Heine has, 150 years after his death, been acknowledged not only as an outstanding poet and writer, but as the founding father of Jewish-German literature.

ADD. BIBLIOGRAPHY: K. Briegleb, *Bei den Wassern Babels* (1997); K. Briegleb and I. Shedletzky (eds.), *Das Jerusalemer Heine-Symposium* (2001); R.F. Cook, *By the Rivers of Babylon* (1998); L. Feuchtwanger, *Heinrich Heine's Rabbi von Bacherach* (1907); M.H. Gelber (ed.), *The Jewish Reception of Heinrich Heine* (1992); W. Goetschel and N. Roemer (eds.), *The Germanic Review: Heine's Judaism and Its Reception*, 74:4 (1999); J. Hessing, *Der Traum und der Tod* (2005); G. Hoehn, *Heine-Handbuch* (2004); R.C. Holub, "Heine and the Dialectic of Jewish Emancipation," in: B. Kortlaender and S. Singh (eds.), *Heinrich Heines dialektisches Denken* (2004); H. Kircher, *Heinrich Heine und das Judentum* (1973); J.A. Kruse, *Heines Hamburger Zeit* (1972); E. Lutz, *Der Verein fuer Cultur und Wissenschaft der Juden* (1997); M. Perraudin, "Irrationalismus und juedisches Schicksal," in: J.A. Kruse (ed.), *Aufklaerung und Skepsis* (1999); P. Peters (ed.), *Prinzessin Sabbat. Ueber Juden und Judentum* (1997); P. Peters, *Heinrich Heine "Dichterjude"* (1990); S.S. Prawer, *Heine's Jewish Comedy* (1983); I. Shedletzky (ed.), *Heinrich Heine in Jerusalem* (2005); S. Singh, *Heinrich Heines Werk im Urteil seiner Zeitgenossen* (2006); M. Werner and J.C. Hauschild, *"Der Zweck des Lebens ist das Leben selbst"* (1997); B. Witte, "Der Ursprung der deutsch-juedischen Literatur in Heinrich Heines *Der Rabbi von Bacherach*," in: E.G.L. Schrijver and F. Wiesemann (eds.), *Die von Geldern Haggadah* (1997).

[Godfrey Edmond Silverman / Sikander Singh (2nd ed.)]

HEINE, SOLOMON (1766–1844), German banker and philanthropist. Heine was born in Hanover, but moved to Hamburg where he opened a successful banking house. After the crisis of 1825 and the great fire of 1842 Heine, the only banker in Hamburg, continued to discount legitimate bills at the usual rate of 4% thus saving the credit of the city's trading community. Despite this public service, a substantial subscription to the city's rehabilitation loan, and numerous charitable contributions, including the establishment of Hamburg's Jewish hospital, he was refused citizenship and denied admission to the Chamber of Commerce. Heine made a provision that gentiles could use the hospital when civil rights were granted to the Jews of Hamburg, a condition fulfilled in 1864. His heirs moved the bank to Paris where it became one of the leading financial institutions. He was the uncle of Heinrich *Heine, whom he supported with an annual subsidy in his Paris period.

BIBLIOGRAPHY: E. Lueth, *Der Bankier und der Dichter…* (1964); A. Landsberg, in: YLBI, 1 (1956), 360–9; G. Wilhelm (ed.), *Heine Bibliographie*, 2 (1960), index; F. Kramer and E. Lueth, *Salomon Heine und seine Zeit* (1968).

[Joachim O. Ronall]

HEINE, THOMAS THEODOR (1867–1947), German graphic artist and cartoonist. Born in Leipzig of a Jewish father and a non-Jewish mother as David Theodor Heine, he studied art at Duesseldorf, and later made his home in Munich. Though he started as a painter, he became known as a poster designer and illustrator. He worked for *Fliegende Blaetter* and *Jugend*, Munich magazines, developing a varied technique and acuteness of expression. He was one of the founders of the satirical review *Simplicissimus* (1896) and its best known political caricaturist for 37 years. His biting caricatures satirizing the Prussian officer class, the German student corps and officialdom, spared no one. A cartoon satirizing Kaiser William II led to Heine's detention for a term. In 1926 Heine published his autobiography as a collection of essays, *Randbemerkungen zu meinem Leben*, in the monthly *Uhu* published in Berlin. When *Simplicissimus* aligned itself with the Nazis in 1933, Heine fled to Prague, where he published *Das spannende Buch* in 1935, a collection of his non-political drawings. Later Heine escaped to Oslo, where he remained in hiding for nine months. Finally he reached Stockholm and settled there. In addition to collections of his drawings, he published a short satirical novel *Ich warte auf Wunder* (1945; *I Wait for Miracles*, 1947). In 1947 the National Museum of Stockholm organized a comprehensive retrospective of the work that Heine had created during emigration.

ADD. BIBLIOGRAPHY: T.W. Hiles, *Thomas Theodor Heine. Fin-de-siècle Munich and the Origins of Simplicissimus* (1996); M. Peschken-Eilsberger, T. Raff, *Thomas Theodor Heine. Das künstlerlische Werk und Biographie*, 2 Bde. Exhibition catalogue (Helmut Friedel ed.) Städtische Galerie im Lenbachhaus und Kunstbau München (2000); E. Stüwe, *Der "Simplicissimus" – Karikaturist Thomas Theodor Heine als Maler. Aspekte seiner Malerei. Mit einem kritischen Katalog der Gemälde* (1978).

HEINE-HEIMOWITZ, MORRIS (1853–1943), theatrical organizer. An early member of the *Goldfaden troupe in Romania, he later formed his own company in Warsaw, touring Poland and Russia. In 1883, the czar's ban on Yiddish theater obliged him to leave for London, where the Jewish community helped him to migrate to the U.S. Subsequently Heine-Heimowitz leased theaters in New York and Chicago and managed movie houses. He also produced plays in Italian and Chinese.

HEINEMANN, FRITZ (1889–1970), German philosopher. Born in Lueneburg, he was a student of Hermann *Cohen and

Paul Natorp. He became a lecturer in philosophy at the University of Frankfurt on the Main in 1922 and served as professor there from 1930 to 1933. He was then forced to leave Germany, and taught philosophy at Oxford. His most important earlier works are *Der Aufbau von Kants Kritik der reinen Vernunft und das Problem der Zeit* (1913), *Plotinus* (1921), and *Titian* (1928). Of particular importance was his *Neue Wege der Philosophie: Geist, Leben, Existenz* (1929). In it Heinemann presented the first summary of the development of the philosophical schools, including existentialism, which became prominent after World War I. When he left Germany, he wrote *Odysseus, oder die Zukunft der Philosophie* (1939), and in the same year his book on the foundation of aesthetics appeared. This was followed by *David Hume, the Man and his Science of Man* (1940) and *Existentialism and the Modern Predicament* (1953). In *Odysseus* Heinemann developed a program for present-day philosophy. Contemporary philosophers, he argues, are being tested by experiences unique in the history of mankind. The philosopher has become an Odysseus. Heinemann demands of philosophers that they take advantage of these trials in order to enlarge the range and the tasks of philosophy. Hitherto philosophy has looked backward; now it must look forward. "We are the pioneers of the pioneers." In 1959 Heinemann edited *Jenseits des Existentialismus* (1957) and *Die Philosophie im 20. Jahrhundert* (1959), an encyclopaedic survey of contemporary philosophy for which he wrote some of the main articles. Heinemann holds that the various philosophical systems constitute "alternatives," not in the sense that the one negates the other but rather that it complements the other; they are different perspectives of the one truth which is not given to man directly. In remembrance the city of Lueneburg founded the Heinemann Archive in 1972.

[Samuel Hugo Bergman]

HEINEMANN, JEREMIAH (1778–1855), German writer, educator, and communal leader. From 1808 to 1813 he was a member of the Jewish consistory of Westphalia and from 1825 to 1831 was principal of a school in Berlin. Heinemann was one of the last of the German *maskilim* (see *Haskalah) in the tradition of the *Me'assefim and Moses *Mendelssohn, who sought to adapt Jewish life in Germany to modern times. In 1817 he founded and edited the eight volumes of *Jedidja*, a periodical of Jewish studies in German (1817–31), which appeared in a new series in 1839–41 and later as *Allgemeines Archiv des Judenthums* (1842–43). His Hebrew commentary to the Torah, *Be'ur la-Talmid*, was published in a new edition of the Pentateuch along with Mendelssohn's translation (1831–33). His publications include a collection of articles and letters written by and to Mendelssohn, books on Judaism and Jewish education, a German translation of Isaiah, and essays on the legal and cultural status of the Jews of Prussia.

BIBLIOGRAPHY: EJ, s.v. (incl. bibl.); M. Eliav, *Ha-Ḥinnukh ha-Yehudi be-Germanyah* (1960), index.

[Zvi Avneri]

HEINEMANN, YIẒḤAK (**Isaac**; 1876–1957), Israel humanist and philosopher. Born in Frankfurt, Heinemann studied at German universities, and at the Berlin Rabbinical Seminary. In the years 1919–38, he lectured in Jewish philosophy and literature at the Jewish Theological Seminary in Breslau, where he reached the rank of professor, and, from 1920 was editor of the *Monatsschrift fuer Geschichte und Wissenschaft des Judentums. In 1939, he settled in Jerusalem, where he continued to pursue his studies of Jewish philosophy. He was awarded the Israel Prize for Jewish studies in 1955.

Heinemann's works, which deal with Hellenistic and medieval Jewish philosophy, as well as with *aggadah*, include: *Poseidonios' metaphysische Schriften* (1921–28); *Die griechische Quelle der "Weisheit Salomos"* (1921); *Die Lehre von der Zweckbestimmung des Menschen im griechisch-roemischen Altertum und im juedischen Mittelalter* (1926); *Philons griechische und juedische Bildung* (1931–32); and *Altjuedische Allegoristik* (1936). Two of his works were published in Hebrew: *Ta'amei ha-Mitzvot be-Sifrut Yisrael* (dealing with the reasons for the commandments, 1942–57), and *Darkhei ha-Aggadah* (on talmudic methodology in creating the *aggadah*, 1950). He contributed articles to various journals. He also published an abridged edition in English of Judah Halevi's *Kuzari* with introduction and commentary (1947).

Heinemann's clear and well-founded investigations were the result of his facing the problems of contemporary Judaism and standing up to the influences of European culture as well as German nationalistic hatred. He expounded his ideas in lectures, in German, *Zeitfragen im Lichte juedischer Lebensanschauung* (published in 1921), as well as in series of essays, such as *Die geschichtlichen Wurzeln des neuzeitlichen Humanitaetsgedankens* (1930), in which he discusses topical problems like militarism or pacifism, by analyzing historical attitudes which stem from either Greek or Germanic thought, or from Christianity, and comparing them with the Jewish viewpoint as reflected in Scripture. The Jewish attitude, he concluded, is the correct one, and the Jew should refer back to his own sources and find his place in world culture, not by refuting his faith, but rather by adhering to it. This motif recurs especially in his work on *Die Lehre von der Zweckbestimmung des Menschen*, where he attempts to show that while originally Jewish philosophy did accept ideas from Greek sources, this was done only after Aristotle and neoplatonism had been interpreted in a spirit close to Judaism and Christianity, and imbued with eschatological content. Moreover, Greek influence, in spite of creating a conflict, led to the emergence, in Judaism, of original thought which, in its turn, was imparted to European culture. Thus, Jewish thought in the Middle Ages constituted an essential link in the history of philosophy.

BIBLIOGRAPHY: H. Emmrich, in: MGWJ, 80 (1936), 294ff.; A. Jospe, in: G. Kisch (ed.), *Das Breslauer Seminar* (1963), 395ff.; E.E. Urbach, in: S. Federbush (ed.), *Ḥokhmat Yisrael be-Ma'arav Eiropah*, 1 (1958), 219ff.; H. Schwab, *Chachme Ashkenaz* (Eng., 1964), 48; Kressel, Leksikon, 1 (1965), 601.

[Eliezer Schweid]

HEJAZ (Ar. Ḥijāz), a region N.W. of present-day *Saudi Arabia, from the Gulf of 'Aqabah in the north to 'Asir in the south along the Red Sea. The narrow coastal stripe (*Tihāmah*) is a dry, barren land, while the mountain chain (2100–2400 m and peaks topping 3000 m) is fertile due to plenty of precipitations. Because of its being the site of *Islam's holy cities *Mecca and *Medinah, it is significant in the Arab and Islamic historical and political landscape. The name *Hijāz* means sequestration, impoundment, signifying the mountain bar between the sea and the hinterland. Scattered oases, drawing water from springs and wells in the vicinity of the wadis, permit some settled agriculture. Of these oases, the largest and most important are Medinah and *Khaybar. According to a legend of Jewish source, but kept in Muslim writings, the first Jews arrived at the *Hijāz* when Moses dispatched an army to expel the Amalekites from the land of Yathrib (in time: Medinah). According to another legend, the second Jewish immigration took place in 587 B.C.E. with the destruction of the First Temple. Jews settled then in Wādī al-Qurā', Taymā, Yathrib, and Khaybar. However, from epigraphic evidence recently excavated, the earliest Jewish settlement in the Ḥijāz dates from the reign of Nabonidus, son of Nebuchadnezzar of Babylon (6th century B.C.E). Nothing is known about later times, but Aramaic and Judeo-Arabic inscriptions at 'Ullā (biblical Dedan) and Madā'in Ṣāliḥ (Ḥijrah) from the late third and early fourth centuries C.E. attest to the existence of Jewish settlements in the Ḥijāz at that time. Jewish sages such as 'Anan b. Ḥiyya of Ḥijrah are cited in the Talmud (Yev. 116a). These communities strictly observed Jewish practical commandments and were even much more meticulous in questions of purity and impurity.

At the beginning of the seventh century C.E., there were three Jewish tribes living in Yathrib: Banū *Qaynuqa',*Banū Naḍīr, and Banū *Qurayẓa. All three tribes were rich and powerful, and, also, were more civilized than the Arabs. Whereas the Arabs were all farmers, the Jews were the entrepreneurs of industry, business and commerce in Arabia, and they controlled the economic life of Yathrib. The two Arab tribes – Aws and Khazraj – were debt-ridden to the Jews perennially. Besides Yathrib, the strong centers of the Jews in Ḥijāz were Khaybar, Fadak, and Wādī al-Qurā' (Aylah, Maqnā, Tabūk). The lands in these valleys were the most fertile in all Arabia, and their Jewish cultivators were the best farmers in the country. Moreover, Arabs settling among the populous Jewish communities of Medinah, Taymā, and Khaybar often adopted Judaism.

The rise of Islam gradually resulted in the complete disappearance of Jews from the Ḥijāz. Already in *Muhammad's time the three Jewish tribes in Yathrib were destroyed, forcefully converted to Islam or expelled. The Jewish settlement in Khaybar and Wādī al-Qurā', whom Muhammad recognized as protected people, existed as agricultural centers at least until the 11th century, as attested by letters sent by them to a *gaon* in Iraq regarding religious issues of agriculture. Since then there has not been any Jewish settlement in the Ḥijāz. Islamic tradition even invented a **ḥadīth* ascribed to Muhammad, who said to his wife before his death: "There shall not be two religions in the Ḥijāz". In days to come, the 16th to the 18th century, that saying would be the main religious argument for expelling the Jews of *Yemen, based on the claim that in this matter Yemen should be referred to like the Ḥijāz.

BIBLIOGRAPHY: Baron, Social², 3 (1957), 60–80; H.Z. Hirschberg, *Yisrael be-Arav* (1946), index; I. Ben-Zvi, *The Exiled and the Redeemed* (1958), index; EIS², 3 (1969), 362–4; Y. Tobi, in: *Ben 'Ever La-'Arav*, 2 (2001), 17–60; idem., "The Orthography of the Pre-Saadianic Judaeo-Arabic Compared with the Orthography of the Inscriptions of Pre-Islamic Arabia," in: *Proceedings of the Seminar for Arabian Studies*, 34 (2004), 343–49; G.D. Newby in JQR, 61, 214–21; idem., *A History of the Jews in Arabia* (1988); M. Lecker, *Jews and Arabs in Pre- and Early Islamic Arabia* (1998).

[Yosef Tobi (2nd ed.)]

HEKDESH (Heb. הֶקְדֵּשׁ), consecrated property, property dedicated to the needs of the *Temple; in post-talmudic times the term *hekdesh* without qualification (*setam hekdesh*) came to mean property set aside for charitable purposes or for the fulfillment of any other **mitzvah*.

Consecration for the Temple Needs

The consecration of property was the means of providing for the upkeep of the Temple and the sacrificial services as detailed in Scripture (Lev. 2:7; II Kings 12:5–17, et al.). In the Temple period a person could consecrate property to either (1) the Temple treasury (*hekdesh bedek ha-Bayit*) that was utilized for maintaining and repairing the Temple buildings; or (2) the altar (*hekdesh Mizbe'aḥ*) for the purchase of sacrifices, namely the animals, and meal- and drink-offerings brought to the Temple altar. If a man simply consecrated his property without specifying which of these two purposes he intended and such property included animals fit for sacrifice at the altar, the animals would be sold for sacrifice and the proceeds allocated to the Temple treasury; i.e., "simple consecration to the Temple treasury" (Tem. 7:2; Shek. 4:7, opinion of R. Eliezer; Maim. Yad, Arakhin 5:7).

IRREDEEMABLE AND REDEEMABLE. Consecration (Kedushat ha-Guf and Kedushat Damim)

Property could be consecrated with different degrees of sanctity: i.e., intrinsic sancitity (kedushat ha-guf), embracing all objects consecrated to the altar and fit for sacrificial purposes, such as animals, doves and pigeons, flour, incense, wine and oil; or monetary sanctity (kedushat damim), embracing objects consecrated to the Temple treasury, as well as objects consecrated to the altar that were not fit for sacrifice or disqualified because of blemish from use at the altar. Consecrated property of the former kind could not be redeemed, whereas the latter could and the redemption money applied to the purpose for which the property was consecrated. Redeemed property ceased to be sacred and was relegated to its former secular status; but objects fit for the altar could be redeemed solely for the purpose of sacrifice there, since "anything which is fit for the altar, is never released from the altar" (Men. 101a; Maim. Yad, Arakhin 5).

CREATION OF CONSECRATED PROPERTY. Contrary to the general principle of Jewish law that the transfer of ownership cannot be effected in a merely oral manner but requires the performance of a symbolic act such as *mesirah, meshikhah,* or *ḥazakah* (see *Acquisition), the rule is that simply an oral statement suffices to transfer the ownership of property from the common man (*hedyot*) to *hekdesh* ("Dedication to the Temple by word of mouth is equal to the act of delivery to a common person even if the property is situated at the world's end"; Kid. 1:6; TB, Kid. 28b–29a). This reference introduces the concept that consecrated property is in the ownership of God (*bi-reshut Gavoha*), and therefore can be transferred to Him by mere oral declaration, since "His is the earth and the fullness thereof" and "the earth is as a courtyard which acquires for Him" (TJ, Kid. 1:6, 61a; *Beit ha-Beḥirah*, Kid. 28b).

LEGAL IMPLICATIONS OF CONSECRATED PROPERTY. The principle that consecrated property is *bi-reshut Gavoha* and not in the ownership of a neighbor or the common man (*bi-reshut re'ehu* or *hedyot*) had the effect of placing such property to a large extent beyond customary legal relationships. Thus, neither the law of **ona'ah* was applicable to it, "even if a man sold a thousand dinars' worth for one dinar or one dinar's worth for a thousand" (BM 4:9; Tosef. BK 4:3; Maim. Yad, Mekhirah, 13:8; Tur and Sh. Ar., ḤM 227:29), nor the prohibition against *usury (BM 57b; Tur, YD 160). Similarly, no compensation was recoverable in *tort under any of the recognized heads of tort (see **Avot Nezikin*), in respect of damage caused by or to consecrated property – in terms of the rule that "there is tort in respect of the commmon man, but not in respect of consecrated property" (i.e., *Gavoha*; BK 4:3; TB, BK 37b; Tosef. BK 4:1; TJ, Git. 5:1, 46c; Rashi and Tos. BK 6b; Maim. Yad, Nizkei Mamon 8:1). Furthermore a man who stole consecrated property was not liable to pay double compensation and whoever slaughtered or sold it was only required to make good the capital value and was exempted from the four- or five-fold penalty (BM 4:9; Maim. Yad, Genevah 2:1; see also *theft and robbery).

So, too, the law on the different degrees of liability for damage or loss attaching to the four categories of bailees (see **shomerim*) did not apply to consecrated property, a bailee being exempted from taking the judicial oath or from paying compensation in respect of such property (BM 4:9; Shev. 6:5; Maim. Yad, Sekhirut, 2:1; Tur and Sh. Ar., ḤM 301:9). In strict law (*din Torah*) a man was exempt from the need to take the different forms of *oath (BM 4:9, Shev. 6:5; Maim. Yad, To'en 5:1; Tur and Sh. Ar. ḤM 95:1), but the scholars (BM 58a) prescribed that the oath, including the bailees' oath, was required even in respect of consecrated property in order that such property should not be lightly dealt with; the rabbinical decision on taking the oath had to be regarded – according to some of the **posekim* – as having the severity of biblical law (Maim. Yad, To'en 5:1). Consecrated property was also distinguished from other property in relation to its modes of acquisition. Thus, *hekdesh* could acquire from the common man and the common man from *hekdesh* by way of money (*kinyan kesef*), whereas one person could only acquire from another in one of the prescribed manners, such as by way of the formality of "drawing" (*meshikhah*; Kid. 1:6; Tosef. Kid. 1:9).

The institution of *hekdesh* bears a certain resemblance to the concept of a legal "*persona*" found in other legal systems. The two are nevertheless distinguishable because of the notion that consecrated property is in the ownership of God and does not belong to any legally created *persona*, as well as by the fact that to a large extent such property is not circumscribed by or subject to the customary legal relationships. Ishmael's opinion that *hekdesh* funds could be used to purchase wines, oils, and flours, in order that these could be sold to those requiring them for sacrificial purposes and the profits set aside for the sacred funds, was disputed by Akiva, who stated that there could be no trading for profit with the sacred funds (Shek. 4:3) – since "there must be no poverty where there is wealth" (Ket. 106b; see also Rashi (*mahadura kamma*) *Shitah Mekubbeẓet*, Ket. 106b and "lest loss be caused to the sanctuary" (Maim. Yad., Ar. 6:5)). The custodian of *hekdesh* was the treasurer of the temple (*gizbar*). It was his task to collect all consecrated property, supervise it, buy and sell according to the needs of the sacred funds, represent *hekdesh* at law, and "all *Melekhet ha-Kodesh* was done by him" (Tosef. Shek. 2:15; Maim. Yad, Kelei ha-Mikdash 4:18).

CONSECRATION AS A MITZVAH. Although it was considered a *mitzvah* for a man to contribute part of his assets for *hekdesh* purposes "in order to subdue his inclination to be parsimonious" (Maim. Yad, Arakhin 8:12, with ref. to Prov. 3:9), failure to do so involved no blame, in accordance with the biblical injunction, "But, if thou shalt forbear to vow, it shall be no sin in thee" (Deut. 23:23; Yad, Arakhin 8:12). Moreover, according to Maimonides, it was forbidden for a man to consecrate all his property, and "whoever did so acted contrary to the requirements of the law and committed a foolish rather than a pious act … placing himself at the mercy of his fellow beings …" (Yad, Arakhin 8:13). If a person nevertheless did so, the clothing of his wife and children would be excluded by law from the effect of his consecration (Ar. 6:5; Yad. Arakhin 3:14). Similarly, it was a *mitzvah* to fulfill an undertaking to consecrate by not later than the first festival after such an undertaking had been given and failure to do so after three festivals had passed was a transgression against the negative precept of "thou shalt not be slack to pay it" (Deut. 23:22; Yad, Ma'aseh ha-Korbanot 14:13).

MISAPPROPRIATION OF CONSECRATED PROPERTY (I.E., SACRILEGE, ME'ILAH BE-HEKDESH). Deriving a benefit from consecrated property – of either degree of sanctity – was forbidden for as long as it retained its sanctity, the enjoyment of such benefit being considered sacrilege (*me'ilah*; Me'il. 15a; Yad, Me'ilah 1:1). The inadvertent misappropriation of consecrated property of "monetary" sanctity (see above) by its transfer to another as *ḥullin* ("secular property") put an end to its sanctity and rendered it *ḥullin*; consecrated property of "intrinsic" sanctity (see above) retained its sanctity, however, and did not become secular (Kid. 55a; Me'il. 20a; Maim. Yad, *Me'ilah*, ch. 6).

Hekdesh after the Destruction of the Temple

After the destruction of the Temple the *tannaim* laid down that a man must no longer consecrate his property as this could give rise to complications if someone were to derive benefit from it, resulting in *me'ilah*. If a man did this, however, the property would be duly consecrated, but certain precautions would be taken: "if an animal – the door should be locked before it, so that it die of itself; if fruits, garments, or vessels – they should be left to rot; if coins or metal vessels – they should be thrown into the Dead Sea or the ocean so as to lose them" (Av. Zar. 13a and Rashi *ibid.*; Yad, Arakhin, 8:8). The Talmud records an incident from amoraic times where people ceased to frequent a bathhouse that had been consecrated, for fear of committing possible *me'ilah* (BM 6a–b).

CONSECRATION FOR THE POOR, OR FOR THE PURPOSE OF ANY OTHER MITZVAH. In post-talmudic times the term *hekdesh* was principally used, theoretically and in practice, to signify the dedication of property for a charitable purpose or for the fulfillment of some other *mitzvah*: "Since we no longer have the Temple, the unqualified consecration of property means consecration for synagogues or the poor" (Nov. Ri, Migash, BB 102b; see also Resp. Rashba vol. 5 no. 135; *Sefer ha-Terumot*, 46:4 and 8; *Beit ha-Beḥirah Av. Zar.* 13b); "... even if he said 'consecration to heaven,' his intention is for charity" (Duran, Solomon b. Simeon, *Sefer ha-Rashbash*, no. 361). Only if a person stated that he intended consecration proper to the altar or the Temple funds would the sanctity of *hekdesh* apply to the property concerned, as well as the prohibition against benefiting from it (Nov. Ri Migash, BB 102b. *Rama*, YD 258:1). Other scholars expressed the opinion that even in the post-Temple period the law was that if a man simply stated that he was consecrating property, without specifying for what purpose, the sanctity of *hekdesh* with the prohibition against deriving any benefit it would still be applicable – even if such a person in his heart envisaged an appropriation for the needs of *talmud torah* and the like. In the 13th century the example was quoted of a book found in Russia bearing the inscription that it had been given to *hekdesh* by a certain individual, and therefore studying from it was prohibited lest a benefit be derived from consecrated property (*Or Zaru'a*, Av. Zar., nos. 128 and 129). It was held that the proper way to overcome the prohibition was to approach a scholar with a request for the property to be "released" from its consecration on the grounds that the consecrator had repented of his undertaking – as in the case of a *vow (see Sh. Ar., YD, 258:1).

COMPARISON BETWEEN CONSECRATION FOR THE TEMPLE NEEDS AND CONSECRATION FOR THE POOR. The special rules laid down for consecration for the needs of the Temple did not generally apply to consecration for the poor or for the purposes of some other *mitzvah*; the latter were subject to the same laws as those governing the property of the common man (Tur ḤM, 95, in the name of R. Isaiah; see also Resp. Rosh 13:1) and "certainly there can be no question" of the law of *me'ilah* applying to consecration for the poor (Resp. Maharashdam, YD 208). In certain matters, however, the law of consecration for the Temple needs was extended to consecrations of the other kind. In the opinion of most halakhic scholars, the rule that "a mere declaration to the sanctuary is equivalent to transfer to the common man," was applicable also to *ẓedakah* (see *charity) and "whoever states 'I give such and such an object to charity'... may not retract" (Rif, *Halakhot*, BK 36b; Ran. Nov. Ned. 29b; Resp. Radbaz, no. 802; Sh. Ar., YD 258:13). Similarly, the laws of *ẓedakah* were applied in the case of consecration for the poor or for some other *mitzvah*, and in several respects these laws are similar to those of *hekdesh*; for example, the negative precept, "thou shalt not be slack to pay it" applies also to *ẓedakah*, with certain variations (RH 6a and Codes). It was also decided that the act of consecration would be effective even if couched in the language of *asmakhta* – since "the law of *asmakhta* does not apply to vows and consecrations" (Resp. Rif, no. 247; *Sefer Teshuvot ha-Rashba ha-Meyuḥasot le-ha-Ramban*, no. 255; see also Sh. Ar., YD 258:10).

LOANS AT INTEREST FROM HEKDESH FUNDS. The analogy between consecration for charitable purposes and consecration for the Temple needs – despite their substantial difference – provided the halakhic scholars with a solution to the problem of the permissibility of deriving profit from *ḥekdesh* monies (*ma'ot*), namely, the consecration (by endowment) of a capital fund whose income was to be set aside for the consecratory purpose. The customary and virtually the only means of deriving income from such monies, was by their loan against interest; however, if this was permissible with regard to consecration for the Temple, funds consecrated for the poor (i.e., *ẓedakah*) were regarded as property of the "common man" (see e.g., BK 93a) and could not therefore be lent at interest (Raviah, quoted in *Or Zaru'a*, Hilkhot Ẓedakah, sec. 30 and in Resp. of Meir of Rothenburg, ed. Lemberg, no. 478). At the beginning of the 14th century *Isaac b. Moses of Vienna, a pupil of Eliezer b. Joel ha-Levi (Raviah), decided that only such *ẓedakah* money as had already been allocated for distribution to a particular individual fell within the prohibition since thereafter it was as if the money already belonged to this individual; until such allocation, however, "the law of *hekdesh* applies [to *ẓedakah*] and there is no prohibition against earning interest. Accordingly, when people contribute money and stipulate that the capital is to be preserved but the income distributed to the poor, the law of *hekdesh* certainly applies to such capital and it may be lent against fixed interest which is prohibited by biblical law [*ribbit keẓuẓah de-oraita*] since it is not about to be distributed ..." (*Or Zaru'a, ibid.*: the author at first states that this was his opinion prior to knowing that Raviah had laid down a prohibition on the same matter, but he gives no hint at all that he subsequently retracted). This problem, a vexatious one for medieval scholars and communal leaders, was also resolved by Solomon b. Abraham *Adret along similar lines, but on the basis of a different halakhic distinction. In reply to the question whether it was permissible to "lend at interest money contributed for the poor and held by treasurers" – which was customary at that time (Resp. Rashba, vol. 1, no. 669) – Solomon b. Abraham Adret replied that "the Law has only prohibited interest coming directly from the borrower to the lender," and here there is no lender since these monies have no specific owners and there is no specific share that any poor individual may recover from the treasurers, who distribute as they see fit – much, little, or none at all; hence lending at interest was prohibited only in respect of money consecrated for the specified poor, but "in the consecrations customary in our areas the poor are not specified and interest is permissible" (*Sefer Teshuvot ha-Rashba ha-Meyuḥasot le-ha-Ramban* no. 222). Solomon b. Abraham Adret added, however, that he instructed thus in theory only but not in practice, and "it is not desirable that this be done, lest the fence be breached" (*ibid*; but cf. idem, Resp. vol. 5, no. 249).

The far-reaching innovation contained in the two above-mentioned decisions was not accepted by other scholars. *Meir of Rothenburg took the view that the lending of *ẓedakah* money at fixed interest was a *mitzvah* stemming from a transgression, but in view of the prevailing custom he refrained from instructing the *hekdesh* trustee to act in any other way: "By reason of our sins, the matter has spread to become permissible throughout the kingdom, and the *gabba'im* sin but not for their own sake, because it is the sin of the whole community; I have not the power to protest and it is better that it be done by them inadvertently and not intentionally" (Resp. Meir of Rothenburg, ed. Lemberg, no. 479.) However, he wrote to questioners that thenceforth they were to refrain from the practice (cf. *ibid.*, secs. 234 and 425) and in his opinion money consecrated for the poor could only be lent at interest when the prohibition stemmed solely from rabbinical law, as was the law with regard to orphan money (*ibid.*, see also BM 70a). The same opinion was expressed by the latter's pupil, *Asher b. Jehiel, who added that this was "plain law requiring no proof" (Rosh 13:17, and 8 and also 10). This view was also accepted as the law in the Tur and Shulḥan Arukh (YD 160:18). It may be surmised that after the rabbis had prescribed a *hetter iska*; i.e., permission to take interest on loans of money given from any source whatever (see *"Shetar Iska"* in: Samuel b. Moses David ha-Levi, *Naḥalat Shivah*, no. 40; see also *Usury); this general permission reduced the need for the special permission innovated by Isaac b. Moses and Solomon b. Abraham Adret in respect of funds for the poor.

PURPOSES OF HEKDESH FUNDS. From the geonic period onward, the term *hekdesh* came to be widely used to denote the dedication of property for public or communal needs, for the benefit of the poor or the fulfillment of other *mitzvot*. The purposes for which such funds were endowed were many and diverse, as can be gathered from the responsa of the *geonim* and later scholars, and included such beneficiaries as: "the poor in general" (as early as the time of the *geonim*, Hai and Sherira, see S. Assaf, *Teshuvot ha-Ge'onim* (1927), 69, no. 59); "the poor relatives of the donor"; "synagogal needs" (Scrolls of Law, cantor's salary, etc.); "the ransom of captives" (e.g., Resp. Rif, no. 6); *"talmud torah"* and "those who cling to *Torat ha-Shem*" (presumably the same, Resp. Rashba, vol. 1, no. 1100); "the burial of the dead"; "dowries for orphans about to be married"; and many others. In various places it was laid down in *takkanot* that a portion of the fine imposed on a person convicted of a criminal offense was to go to *hekdesh* (see e.g., *Zikhron Yehudah*, 36). Many funds took their names from their particular localities, such as *Hekdesh Kahal Tortosa* (Resp. Rashba, vol. 1 no. 656), *Hekdesh le-Aniyyei Saragosa (ibid.* 617), *Hekdesh Ashkelona* (Resp. Rosh 3:13), etc. Testamentary bequests were also commonly expressed in wills in terms of *hekdesh*. The term was further used to describe particular institutions which served as *talmudei torah*, homes for the poor or the aged, hospitals, hospices for travelers, etc. (see e.g., Resp. Ranaḥ, no. 84, giving a detailed description of such *hekdesh* institutions in Constantinople). Halakhic literature, *takkanot* collections, and Jewish communal documents of the Middle Ages are richly studded with varied references to matters of *hekdesh* and its different purposes, offering material of much historical interest.

CHANGING THE PURPOSE OF HEKDESH FUNDS. A frequent question concerned the permissibility of changing the original purpose for which the *hekdesh* funds and the fruits thereof were designated. With regard to *ẓedakah* monies it was laid down that "the townsmen may convert the soup kitchen to a charity box and vice versa, and to divert their use to any purpose they think fit" (BB 8b, and Codes); in the opinion of Jacob b. Meir *Tam, the townsmen were at liberty to divert the funds even toward a purpose that was permissible but not obligatory (*devar ha-reshut*) such as the maintenance of the town guard (Tos. to BB 8b). On the other hand, it was decided that funds explicitly contributed for a specified purpose could not be diverted (Resp. Rambam, ed. Blau, no. 206; Resp. Ritba no. 206); a standing local custom relied on by the communal leaders for the diversion of funds from their stated purpose justified the assumption that a contribution was given subject to the said custom (S. Assaf, *Teshuvot ha-Ge'onim* (1927), 69, no. 59; *Sefer Teshuvot ha-Rashba ha-Meyuḥasot le-ha-Rambam*, no. 268), unless the contrary had been expressly stipulated (Resp. Rambam no. 206; Rema YD 259:2). In the discussions on this question, the nature of the charitable purpose played an important role and the principle was accepted that there could only be a change in charitable objects from a less to a more important one: e.g., funds for the synagogue or cemetery could be applied to the needs of a house of study or those of *talmud torah*, but not vice versa (Sh. Ar., YD 259:2). The same principle applied in the case of a field contributed for the purpose of the annual distribution of its produce to the poor, even when seven prominent townsmen agreed to a change of purpose, since the contributor had declared his intention that the field be used for this particular purpose only and any change would amount to "robbing the poor" (Resp. Rashba, vol 5, no. 269; in this case the change was prohibited even for the purpose of *talmud torah*, Sh. Ar., YD 259:2; see also PDR 1:359f.). However, diverting funds was held to be permissible even of those destined for *talmud torah* or the support of the poor, for the purpose of redeeming captives, since this amounted to saving life and took precedence over all other charitable purposes (Sh. Ar., YD 251:14; 252:1).

ADMINISTRATION AND LEGAL PROCEDURE. *Hekdesh* is administered by an **apotropos* ("guardian" or "trustee") or *gizbar* ("treasurer") appointed by the benefactor or the court; the court is the higher guardian of *hekdesh* and in the administration the *apotropos* is subject to the court's supervision (*Sha'arei Uziel*, 1 (1944), 108–15; PDR, 2:34). The trustee must be godfearing, trustworthy, and experienced in negotiating transactions (Resp. Rambam no. 54), his task being to guard the *hekdesh* assets from all loss and to administer them faithfully in accordance with the purposes for which they were endowed and the instructions of the court (PDR 1:359f.) If there is a strong suspicion concerning the good faith of his administration of the assets, the court is obliged to dismiss him from his position (PDR *ibid.*) but if he was appointed by the benefactor himself, he cannot be dismissed unless proved to have been derelict in his duties (PDR 2:27ff.). In many places it was customary to appoint special supervisors, called *avi yetomim* ("father of orphans"), as a board of control over trustees, and this has been considered appropriate also for *hekdesh* assets (*Taz* to Sh. Ar., YD, 258:5; PDR loc. cit.).

Contrary to the rule evolved from talmudic law, that a three-year period of undisputed possession does not confer the title of *ḥazakah* ("presumptive ownership") in respect of *hekdesh* for public needs – because there is no one to protest on its behalf – it was decided by Solomon b. Abraham Adret that in his time *hekdesh* assets were so organized as to make it possible for them to be acquired by *ḥazakah*, "since here there are known owners and appointed treasurers, who have a part in such property and buy, sell, and barter with the knowledge of the *ḥavurah*" (i.e., society or corporate body; Resp. Rashba, quoted in *Beit Yosef*, ḤM 149, n. 37). It was also thus decided in respect of all *hekdesh* property supervised by treasurers (Sh. Ar., ḤM 149:31 and see Isserles' gloss thereto). On the question of the extent to which a charitable fund of such kind could be regarded as having a separate legal identity, see *Legal Person.

EVIDENCE IN MATTERS OF HEKDESH. In the post-talmudic period *hekdesh* was associated with an interesting development in the rules of evidence in Jewish law. In talmudic times the law was that persons connected with or having an interest in the matter under dispute were disqualified from testifying in regard to it (see *Witness) and a townsman could not therefore testify in a matter concerning the property of his town, unless he had renounced all benefit from such property (BB 43a and Codes). In terms of this halakhic ruling it was decided, as late as the beginning of the 11th century, that those who worshiped in a particular synagogue were disqualified from testifying in regard to *hekdesh* contributed for the benefit of that synagogue (Resp. Rif nos. 163 and 247). With the proliferation of public institutions and particularly as far as the community was concerned, the observance of the prohibition in matters involving the interests of such bodies represented an ever-increasing burden, with the result that new customs and **takkanot* established and confirmed the competency of such witnesses, "in all public matters, including *hekdeshot*, for if it were not to be so, who would there be to testify?… there would be no remedy where public needs are concerned … if competent witnesses have to be brought from outside … there would be found but one in a thousand" (Resp. Rashba, vol. 1, no. 680). This custom became the decided law enshrined in the Shulḥan Arukh (ḤM, 37:22; see also **takkanot ha-kahal*; taxation).

The concept of *hekdesh* in its later meaning was a creation of the post-talmudic historico-social situation, and was accompanied by a number of legal developments corresponding to the changes in the social fabric of Jewish life. The phenomenon of a term bearing two different meanings, of which *hekdesh* is an interesting example, offers evidence of one of the paths along which Jewish law has developed. Adherence to a common appellation for a concept with alternative meanings, despite the substantial difference between them, permitted the application of laws pertaining to the concept within one of its meanings – *hekdesh* or consecration for the Temple needs – to the concept within its alternative meaning – *hekdesh* or endowment for charitable purposes – for the purpose of solving certain problems emanating from the changing realities of everyday life.

In the State of Israel

In Israel *hekdesh* exists in two forms. First is endowment of property as approved by a religious court and administered in terms of religious law. Originally, Muslim law was applied, even in respect of non-Muslim endowments of this kind. In terms of the Palestine Order-in-Council, 1922, the Jewish community, as well as several Christian communities, were empowered to found *Wakf* or religious endowments and to administer them according to the religious law of the community in question. The second is the endowment of property for charitable purposes according to the civil, as opposed to the religious law, namely in terms of the "Charitable Trusts Ordinance." The ordinance subjects the charitable trust and the trustee administering it to the supervision of the courts and defines "charitable trusts" as "including all purposes for the benefit of the public or any section of the public within or without Palestine [now to be read "the State of Israel"], of any of the following categories:

(1) for the relief of poverty;

(2) for the advancement of education or knowledge;

(3) for the advancement of religion or the maintenance of religious rites or practices;

(4) for any other purpose beneficial, or of interest to, mankind.

[Menachem Elon]

In the Middle Ages the *hekdesh* was a communal shelter and infirmary for the poor, transient, and the sick. The term does not appear until the late Middle Ages, though Jewish *hospitals are found much earlier. By the 17th century every important community in Central and Eastern Europe had a *hekdesh* for the sick and the poor. The institution persisted into the 19th century. The size of the hospice ranged from a rented room to a house or group of small buildings. Most often it was located out of town near the cemetery. The *hekdesh* was administered by a local **ḥevrah*, usually named *bikkur ḥolim*, and supervised by the *kahal*. The **gabbai* of the association, often a local merchant, was expected to visit the hospice as often as several times a day and to supervise the work of the beadle, the physician, the surgeon, and the *hekdeshleyt* ("attendants"). The *hekdesh* was usually so unsanitary and dirty that a person would view with horror the prospect of staying there. The patients in Altona, about 1764, described themselves thus: "We the poor, fathers with children, lying-in women with their offspring, nursing mothers with their sucklings, old men and young men, all of whom are cast upon the bed of sickness, enduring our ailments, crushed, wasted; also we who are insane and distraught…" A British missionary who visited Minsk in the early 19th century writes: "In the Jewish Hospital we saw 45 young and old of both sexes, seemingly without any classification of disease, placed in several small rooms. They certainly presented one of the most appalling scenes of wretchedness I ever witnessed; filth, rags, and pestilential effluvia pervaded the whole place." Thus in Yiddish *hekdesh* became synonymous with disorder and disarray in the home, in a room, or concerning a person. Not until the modern hospital came into its own did the situation improve.

[Isaac Levitats]

BIBLIOGRAPHY: J. Lampronti, *Paḥad Yiẓḥak*, s.v. *Hekdesh* and *Beit Hekdesh*; Gulak, Yesodei, 1 (1922), 50–54, 98f.; Gulak, Oẓar, 112, 128–31, 347f.; Herzog, Instit, 1 (1936), 288–91, 295; 2 (1939), 17, 30, 68 n. 1, 189; B.Z.M.Ḥ. Ouziel, *Sha'arei Uziel*, 1 (1944), 93–107; ET, 2 (1949), 40–42, 201f.; 5 (1953), 51–65; 10 (1961), 352–442. IN THE MIDDLE AGES: J. Marcus, *Communal Sick-Care* (1947); I. Levitats, *Jewish Community in Russia* (1943).

HEKHSHER (Heb. הֶכְשֵׁר; "approbation" or "attestation"), certificate issued by the rabbinate or by individual rabbis certifying that a certain food product has been prepared under their supervision and in accordance with the traditional dietary *laws, hence declaring it *kasher*. Such an attestation is also required for all foodstuff prepared for consumption on *Passover in which case it must also be free from all leaven (*ḥameẓ). The *hekhsher* certificate is now usually printed on the package of the product. Restaurants which are under the supervision of a rabbinate need a *hekhsher* (which is displayed on the premises), testifying that the food served by them is prepared in accordance with the traditional dietary laws and that a **mashgi'aḥ* oversees the kitchen. In some countries specific symbols have been adopted to indicate that the product is under supervision. The Union of Orthodox Hebrew Congregations in the U.S. uses Ⓤ (a "u" inside an "O" – **U**nion of **O**rthodox) and in that country there is also widespread use of various other *kashrut* supervising bodies that employ the letter "K", alone or in combination with other communally recognized symbols. In England the seal of the *bet din* is used. In certain states of America it is illegal to declare a product *kasher* if it is not, but for observant Jews that does not obviate the need for a rabbinic *hekhsher*.

ḤELBO (third–early fourth century C.E.), *amora*. Ḥelbo was apparently a Babylonian who migrated to Ereẓ Israel. In Babylon he studied under Huna (Ber. 6b, et al.) and under Ḥama b. Gurya, the pupil of Rav, in whose name he transmits Rav's statements (Shab. 37a, et al). In Ereẓ Israel he studied under Samuel b. Naḥman (TJ, Meg. 1:1, 70b, et al.) and transmitted sayings in his name (Gen. R. 78:1; Theodor-Albeck, 916 note). He was an associate of *Ammi (TJ, Kil. 9:4, 32c), Ulla Biraah (Meg. 4a), and Isaac Nappaḥa (Git. 59b–60a), and among his colleagues was apparently also the *nasi* Yudan (TJ, Ta'an. 2:1, 65a). Ḥelbo was childless and lived a lonely life (Yev. 64b; Ned. 39b–40a). His pupil was Berechiah (Gen. R. 78:1, et al.) who frequently transmitted his sayings, particularly in *aggadah* (TJ, Ber. 1:1, 2d, et al.). Among his noteworthy sayings are the following: "One must always be regardful of the honor due to one's wife, because blessings rest on a man's house only on account of his wife" (BM 59a); "whosoever partakes of the wedding meal of a bridegroom and does not cause him to rejoice transgresses the five voices mentioned in Jeremiah 33:11" (Ber. 6b); and "Proselytes are as injurious to Israel as a scab" (Kid. 70b) – an individual opinion presumably reflecting contemporary conditions which nevertheless in future generations influenced the attitude with regard to the acceptance of proselytes.

BIBLIOGRAPHY: Bacher, Pal Amor; Hyman, Toledot, 451–2; Ḥ. Albeck, *Mavo la-Talmudim* (1969), 325–7.

[Zvi Kaplan]

HELD, ADOLPH (1885–1969), U.S. communal and labor leader and Yiddish journalist. Held, who was born in Borislav, Poland, was taken to the United States in 1892. He joined the staff of the Yiddish-language *Jewish Daily Forward, where he served as news editor from 1907 to 1912 and then as business manager from 1912 to 1917. From 1917 to 1919 he was a Socialist member of New York City's Board of Aldermen. In 1920 he was appointed European director of the Hebrew Immigrant Aid Society (HIAS), in which capacity he assisted hundreds of thousands of Jewish immigrants to the United States. Returning to America in 1924, he became president of the Forward Association, the paper's governing body, and of the Amalgamated Bank, whose main function it was to provide financial aid to the garment industry. In 1938 he was chosen national chairman of the Jewish Labor Committee. Held resigned his presidency of the bank in 1945 in order to become welfare director of the International Ladies Garment Workers Union. He was made general manager of the *Jewish Daily Forward* in 1962. In the years before his death he was also active in senior citizens' groups and took part in the campaign for the extension of Social Security benefits and the establishment of Medicare.

[Hillel Halkin]

HELD, ANNA (1873–1918), French actress. Born in Paris, Anna Held made her debut at the Folies Manguay, Paris, in 1895, and soon afterward was engaged by Florenz Ziegfeld for his first New York production. Later the two were married and she appeared in many plays, including Jean Richepin's *Mam'selle Napoleon* (1903). She toured the U.S. in 1903 in the title role of *The Little Duchess.*

HELD, MOSHE (1924–1984), Bible scholar. Held was born in Poland, brought to Mandatory Palestine in 1935 and raised in Tel Aviv. He entered the Hebrew University of Jerusalem in 1943. His studies, interrupted by service in the British army in World War II, were resumed in 1946, but delayed once again by Israel's War of Independence. He completed his M.A. in Hebrew literature at the Hebrew University, studying Hebrew and Arabic with D. Baneth, S.D. *Goitein, and H. Polotsky, studies which he later described as "sins of his youth." His academic direction took a new turn thanks to Umberto Moshe David *Cassuto, an Italian Jewish scholar, and a pioneer in the study of the *Ugaritic tablets of the second millennium B.C.E. unearthed in 1929. Cassuto urged Held to study Ugaritic at Johns Hopkins with W.F. *Albright. Albright, in turn, sent Held to study Akkadian (Assyro-Babylonian) at the University of Chicago under the great Assyriologist Benno *Landsberger, himself a German Jewish émigré of the Hitler years. After completing his Ph.D. at Hopkins (1957), Held came to Dropsie replacing Cyrus *Gordon who had moved to Brandeis. In 1959 Held began his visits to the Jewish Theological Seminary, where he was to continue as adjunct professor of Bible for 25 years. The JTS connection brought Held under the tutelage of H.L.*Ginsberg, to whom Held always referred as "my mentor." In 1966 Held came to the Middle East Department at Columbia, where he taught until his death. The two positions enabled Held to concentrate on the study of the Bible in its larger Near Eastern context. Held was a superb comparative philologist who, in accord with his teachers Albright and Landsberger, insisted that etymological comparisons had to take a backseat to contextual comparisons, or better, "interdialectal distributions." A passionate teacher, Held's Columbia position enabled him to train Jewish students at JTS and Christians at Union Theological Seminary in the serious reading of biblical texts against the background of the ancient Near East.

BIBLIOGRAPHY: S. Lieberman, in: JQR, 76 (1985), 1–3; E. Greenstein and D. Marcus, in: JANES, 19 (1989), 1–2; bibliography; ibid., 7–8; C. Cohen, ibid., 9–23; S.D. Sperling, *Students of the Covenant* (1992), 101–3.

[S. David Sperling (2nd ed.)]

HELDMAN, GLADYS MEDALIE (1922–2003), leader in women's tennis and sports media and founder of the professional women's tennis tour. Heldman was born in New York City, daughter of well-known New York attorney and judge George Z. Medalie. She married Julius Heldman, a 1936 U.S. junior tennis champion, in 1942 and later her whole family became involved in tennis. Heldman, who earned a B.A. from Stanford University in 1942 with Phi Beta Kappa honors, and an M.A. in medieval history from the University of California, Berkeley in 1943, started playing tennis after her two daughters were born. She achieved No.1 amateur ranking in Texas and No. 2 in the Southwest in 1954; she competed at Wimbledon in 1954 and participated in the U.S. Championships at Forest Hills. In 1951, Heldman received the Service Bowl awarded to "the player who yearly makes the most notable contribution to the sportsmanship, fellowship and service of tennis." She founded *World Tennis* magazine in 1953, serving as the publisher and editor-in-chief, and as a writer. She sold the magazine in the 1970s.

Heldman championed the founding of the women's professional tennis tour to provide more equity in prize money for women in a male-dominated sport. In 1970, nine top players, including Heldman's daughter JULIE (1945–), played in the first Virginia Slims Circuit tournament in Houston in 1970. The Virginia Slims Circuit later merged with the U.S. Tennis Association (USTA). Legendary tennis champion Billie Jean King wrote that, "With the invaluable help, support and guidance of Gladys Heldman" women tennis players were able to revolutionize their sport by establishing their own tennis tour.

Heldman and her family maintained an active role in tennis. In recognition of her tremendous contributions to the world of tennis, Gladys Heldman was inducted into the International Tennis Hall of Fame and the International Jewish Sports Hall of Fame. Julie Heldman won medals in singles and doubles tennis exhibition events at the 1968 Olympics and also won three gold medals in the 1969 Maccabiah Games. She was inducted into the International Jewish Sports Hall of Fame in 2002.

BIBLIOGRAPHY: L.J. Borish, "American Jewish Women in Sports," in: S.H. Norwood and E.G. Pollack, *Encyclopedia of American Jewish History* (2005); B.J. King, "Challenges in Keeping Women's Tennis Growing," in: *New York Times* (Feb. 26, 1984); B. Postal, J. Silver, and R. Silver, "Heldman Family," in: *Encyclopedia of Jews in Sports* (1965), 447–48.

[Linda J. Borish (2nd ed.)]

HELENA (first century C.E.), sister and wife of *Monobazus I, king of *Adiabene (cf. Jos., Ant., 20:17–96). Helena and her son *Izates became converts to Judaism in about 30 C.E. through the influence of Ananias, a Jewish merchant. When her husband died, she appointed Izates as king in accordance with his expressed wish. As was customary in the East, the other sons of Monobazus were imprisoned and were in danger of being put to death, but Helena and Izates sent them to Rome – a humane act probably dictated by their new religion. Only her son Monobazus II, who ruled for a short time after his father's death, remained in Adiabene. Helena spent the latter part of her life in Jerusalem, where she built herself a palace (Jos., Wars, 5:252; 6:355). When a famine raged in Judea at the time of Claudius (Ant., 20:51), she bought grain and figs in Egypt and Cyprus for the starving people. Echoes of this are found in the Talmud (BB 11a; TJ, Pe'ah 1:1, 15b; Tosef., *ibid.*, 4:18). Helena also made gifts to the Temple (Yoma 3:10), and was meticulous in the observance of the precepts of Judaism (Naz. 3:6). She died in Adiabene but her remains and those of Izates were transferred to Jerusalem by Monobazus, and interred in the mausoleum she had built at a distance of three stadia to the north of the city, known today as "the Tombs of the Kings" (Jos., Ant., 20:95; Jos., Wars, 5:55, 119, 147). Pausanius (*Graec. Descrip.* VIII, 16:4–5 (358)) provides a description of the Tomb of Helena and refers to a special mechanism that kept the door of the tomb closed. The inscription on the sarcophagus found by De Saulcy in the Tomb of the Kings was of great value in identifying Helena's tomb. The first line has the words מלכתא צדן and the second line מלכת א צדה. The language of both lines is Aramaic, but the script of the first line is Syrian and of the second, Hebrew. This proves that at least the second queen mentioned was Jewish and that she came from a Syrian royal family.

BIBLIOGRAPHY: J. Derenbourg, *Essai sur l'histoire et la géographie de la Palestine* (1867), 223ff.; Graetz, Hist, 2 (1893), 216–9; Schuerer, Gesch, 3 (1909[4]), 169ff.; M. Kon, *Kivrei ha-Melakhim* (1947); Klausner, Bayit Sheni, 5 (1951), 13, 44ff. **ADD. BIBLIOGRAPHY:** N.C. Debevoise, *A Political History of Parthia* (1938); N. Kokkinos, *The Herodian Dynasty: Origins, Role in Society and Eclipse* (1998), 250; M. Stern, *Greek and Latin Authors on Jews and Judaism*, vol. 2 (1980), 196–97; T. Ilan, *Lexicon of Jewish Names in Late Antiquity. Part 1: Palestine 330 BCE–200 CE* (2002), 317–18, s.v. "Helene."

[Abraham Schalit / Shimon Gibson (2nd ed.)]

HELENA AUGUSTA (c. 255–329 C.E.), mother of the Emperor Constantine and a pious convert to Christianity. In the writings of Geoffrey of Monmouth (c. 1100–1154) she is described as the daughter of the British King Coel of Colchester ("Old King Cole"), but this seems highly unlikely. Having originated from a modest background, serving for a while in Diocletian's court at Nicomedia, Helena was later at Constantine's side at the imperial court in Trier and was accorded great honor there. In the aftermath of Constantine's defeat of Licinius in September 324 C.E., Helena, who was about 80 years of age, made a journey to the Holy Land (between c. 325 and 327) to offer prayers at the holy places (described in Eusebius' *Vita Constantini*), and is said to have founded churches on the Mount of Olives (the Eleona Church) and at Bethlehem. Although not mentioned by Eusebius as having played any part in the building operations next to the Tomb of Jesus at Golgotha, it is difficult to make a sharp division between churches ascribed to Constantine and those attributed to his mother. Helena is also credited with the discovery of the true cross (*lignum crucis*) on which Jesus was crucified in a cistern not far from the place of his tomb, but scholars have questioned the authenticity of this tradition. Indeed, Eusebius does not mention the discovery at all and his absolute silence on this matter is quite telling (20 or so years later the first references appear mentioning the relics of the cross, e.g. Cyril of Jerusalem in 350 C.E.). Ambrose of Milan, however, in c. 395 C.E., is the first to mention Helena as the discoverer of the cross (*De Ob. Theod.* 46–48). According to Ambrose, Helena "…opened up the earth, scattered the dust, and discovered three crosses in disarray (*confusa*)." The holy cross still retained the inscription (*titulus*) and nails were also found. Thereafter, various embellished versions of the story exist, with faith rapidly ousting the facts from the tradition. Some versions refer to the holy cross being found lying between two crosses with an inscription (John Chrysostom, *Hom. In Joh.* 75:1, PG 59, 461) and others to the authenticity of the cross being verified by its ability to cure a sick woman (e.g., Rufinus, *Hist. Eccles.* 10:7–8). None of these early sources provide information regarding the exact find-spot of the cross. Recent archaeological researches show that the traditional place where the cross was supposed to have been found, at the Cave of the Invention of the Cross in the Church of the Holy Sepulchre, was a subterranean cavity that was converted into a cistern no earlier than the 11th century. Helena died soon after her return to court. In the fifth and sixth centuries C.E. Helena was highly praised by Church historians and pilgrims for her discovery of the true cross and for her part in the Christian rebuilding of Jerusalem. In later tradition Helena was said to have been responsible for the foundation of most of the important churches in the Holy Land, notwithstanding the fact that some were built centuries after her death.

BIBLIOGRAPHY: E.D. Hunt, *Holy Land Pilgrimage in the Later Roman Empire AD 312–460* (1984); S. Borgehammar, *How the Holy Cross was Found: From Event to Medieval Legend* (1991); J.W. Drijvers, *Helena Augusta: the Mother of Constantine the Great and the Legend of Her Finding the True Cross* (1991); J.E. Taylor, "Helena and the Finding of the Cross," in: *Bulletin of the Anglo-Israel Archaeological Society*, 12 (1992–93), 52–60; C.P. Thiede and M. D'Ancona, *The Quest for the True Cross* (2000); "On the 'Cave of the Invention of the Cross,'" in: S. Gibson and J.E. Taylor, *Beneath the Church of the Holy Sepulchre, Jerusalem. The Archaeology and Early History of Traditional Golgotha* (1994), 83–84.

[Shimon Gibson (2nd ed.)]

ḤELEẒ (Heb. חֶלֶץ), site of Israel's first oil field, which exploits oil-bearing strata discovered in 1955. It is located near a moshav of the same name in the southern Coastal Plain of Israel, 7½ mi. (12 km.) S.E. of *Ashkelon. In the later stages of the *War of Independence (1948), a hard battle was won there against the invading Egyptian army. The moshav, affiliated with Tenuat ha-Moshavim, was founded in 1950. Its first settlers came from Yemen, but later immigrants from Tunisia took over. In 1968, the moshav Ḥeleẓ had 510 inhabitants. Its economy was based on intensive field crops, vegetables, citrus, and dairy farming. The name Ḥeleẓ – connected with the Hebrew root meaning "to extricate" or "to pioneer" – was regarded as similar to that of the nearby abandoned Arab village Ḥulayqāt. After a drop in population, the moshav began to expand, its population rising from around 340 in the mid-1990s to 433 in 2002.

[Efraim Orni / Shaked Gilboa (2nd ed.)]

HELFMAN, ELḤANAN (1946–), Israel economist. Born in the U.S.S.R., he lived in Poland until the age of 11, when his family moved to Israel. He studied economics and statistics at Tel Aviv University. He received his doctorate from Harvard in 1974 and became a professor at Tel Aviv University, holding the chair in International Economic Relations. In 1988 he was elected a member of the Israel Academy of Sciences. In 1989–91 he was the president of the Israeli Economic Association. In 1991 he was awarded the Israel Prize for social sciences. In 1995 he was awarded the Feher Prize from the Jerusalem Institute for the Study of Israel and in 1998 he was awarded the Bernhard-Harms Prize from the Kiel Institute for World Economics. In 2000 he was the president of the Econometric Society. In 2002 he was awarded the EMET Prize from the AMN Foundation for the Advancement of Science, Art and Culture and the Rothschild Prize from the Yad Hanadiv Foundation.

HELFMAN, HESSIA MEYEROVNA (1855–1882), Russian revolutionary. Born in Mozyr near Minsk (Belorussia) into a rich family, Hessia Helfman left home at the age of 16 and joined the revolutionary movement in Kiev. In 1875 she was arrested and was one of the accused in the "Trial of Fifty." She was sentenced to two years imprisonment and on her release was banished to Staraya Russa. She escaped, however, and joined the terrorist Narodnaya Volya party in St. Petersburg where she helped to run a clandestine press and distributed propaganda among students and workers. In 1881 Hessia Helfman was sentenced to death, together with five other revolutionaries, for complicity in the assassination of Czar Alexander II. Because she was pregnant at the time, her execution was delayed, and as a result of protests from abroad, the sentence was commuted to life imprisonment. She died in the Peter-and-Paul Fortress in St. Petersburg shortly after the birth of the child, which was taken from her. Hessia Helfman did not take part in the assassination itself and was the only Jewish person among the six condemned. Nevertheless antisemitic groups blamed the Jews for the murder of the Czar.

°**HELIODORUS** of Antioch, chancellor of *Seleucus IV Philopator (187–175 B.C.E.). The official title of chancellor (ὁ ἐπί τῶν πραγμάτων), by which he is described in II Maccabees 3:7, is also found in an official inscription (W. Dittenberger (ed.), *Orientis Graeci inscriptiones selectae*, 1 (1903), no. 247). When Simeon, "head of the Temple" in Jerusalem, denounced the Jews before Apollonius, commander of the Syrian army, claiming that there were treasures in the Temple which belonged to the king, Heliodorus was sent to Jerusalem to remove these treasures. Attempting to break into the Temple, he was suddenly smitten by two angels (II Macc. 3:7–40). It is probable that in fact Heliodorus was driven from the Temple by force. In 176 B.C.E. Heliodorus murdered Seleucus IV, and placed the king's young son upon the throne. Subsequently he had him removed also in order to obtain the throne for himself. However, Antiochus Epiphanes put an end to his rule. These events are perhaps reflected in *Daniel 7:7–8 and 11:20.

BIBLIOGRAPHY: V. Tcherikover, *Hellenistic Civilization and the Jews* (1959), index; B. Niese, *Geschichte der griechischen und makedonischen Staaten*, 3 (1903), 91–92; W. Otto, in: Pauly-Wissowa, 15 (1912), 12ff.; E. Bickerman, in: *Annuaire de l'Institut de Philologie et d'Histoire Orientales et Slaves*, 7 (1939–44), 5–40; W.R. Farmer, *Maccabees, Zealots and Josephus* (1956), 93–96.

[Abraham Schalit]

HELIOPOLIS (Gr., meaning "city of the sun"; Egyptian, **Iunu**; Heb., **On**), ancient city of lower Egypt situated about six miles N. of Cairo on the site of the modern village of El Matariyah. From earliest times Heliopolis was the cult center for the worship of the sun god, usually in his manifestation as Re, but also as Re-Horakhty and Atum. Although some form of sun worship existed from the beginning of recorded Egyptian history, it was not until the Fifth Dynasty (c. 2480–2340 B.C.E.) that the Helipolitan cult of Re achieved its preeminent position in the cosmogony of the Egyptians, a position which it retained well into the third century B.C.E.

Heliopolis is specifically mentioned four times in the Bible: Genesis 41:45, 45:50 and 46:20, where Joseph is given as wife Asenath, the daughter of Poti-Phera, the priest of On (who must have been the high priest of Re of Heliopolis); and Ezekiel 30:17, where the prophet foretells the destruction of Egypt by the hand of Nebuchadnezzar, the Babylonian king, and mentions Heliopolis among the great cities to be destroyed. The prediction of the destruction of Beth-Shemesh, "the House of the Sungod," in Jeremiah 43:13 is also probably a reference to Heliopolis. Another possible reference to the city is Isaiah 19:18, where, in view of the Egyptian context of the passage, the reading *ir ha-ḥeres*, or "city of the sun," as attested by Symmachus and Vulgate, is preferred by many scholars to the present masoretic text *ir ha-heres*, or "city of destruction."

BIBLIOGRAPHY: A.H. Gardiner, *Ancient Egyptian Onomastica*, 2 (1947), 144–6 (texts).

[Alan Richard Schulman]

°**HELLADIUS OF ANTINOUPOLIS** (fl. c. 310 C.E.), Greek grammarian, who notes, in a passage derived from the Alexandrian antisemitic Exodus tradition, as do *Nicarchus and *Ptolemy of Chennos, that Moses was called "Alpha" because of his leprous spots (alphoi), but cites Philo as a source (in no extant work, however).

[Louis Harry Feldman]

HELLENISM, term generally used by historians to refer to the period from the death of Alexander the Great (323 B.C.E.) to the death of Cleopatra and the incorporation of Egypt in the Roman Empire in 30 B.C.E. Egypt was the last important survivor of the political system which had developed as a consequence both of the victories of Alexander and of his premature death. The word Hellenism is also used to indicate more generically the cultural tradition of the Greek-speaking part of the Roman Empire between Augustus and Justinian and/or the influence of Greek civilization on Rome, Carthage, India, and other regions which were never part of the empire of Alexander. Finally, Hellenization is used with reference to Judea, Persia, etc. to indicate the penetration of elements of Greek civilization into territories which, though subject to Greco-Macedonian rule for a certain period of time, preserved their national culture with conspicuous success.

The words Hellenism and Hellenistic have a long history in which the text of the Acts of the Apostles 6:1 plays a central part because it opposes *Hebraioi* to *Hellenistai*. At least from the 16th century onward (J. Scaliger) this text was interpreted to imply a contrast between Jews who used Hebrew and Jews who used Greek in the synagogue service. D. Heinsius developed the notion that Jewish *Hellenistai* used a special Greek dialect *(lingua hellenistica)*, which is reflected in the Septuagint translation of the Bible. C. Salmasius denied the existence of such a special dialect (1643), but the notion of a special *lingua hellenistica* to indicate the Greek of the Old and New Testaments remained in circulation until the middle of the 19th century. In the 18th century in Germany, J.G. Herder used *Hellenismus* to indicate the way of thinking of Jews and other Orientals who spoke Greek. In 1820 in France J. Matter specifically connected the word *Hellénisme* with the thought of the Greek-speaking Jews of Egypt. J.G. Droysen stretched the meaning of the word to signify the period of transition from the pagan to the Christian world which started with Alexander. In 1833 he published a volume on Alexander the Great; and in 1836 and 1843 he published two volumes of *Geschichte des Hellenismus* embracing the century 323–222 B.C.E. He intended to continue his work in further volumes, but never did so, and it is not quite clear from what he says whether his original intention was to reach the age of Muhammad or to stop with Augustus. In 1877–78 he published a second (considerably modified) edition of these three volumes under the title of *Geschichte des Hellenismus* (which now included the reign of Alexander). The second edition, both in the German text and in the French translation by A. Bouché-Leclercq, became authoritative, and consolidated the notion of Hellenism as a special period of the history of antiquity characterized by a mixture of Greek and Oriental elements. Since Droysen, many historians have reexamined the political and constitutional history of this period; they include B. Niese, K.J. Beloch, A. Bouché-Leclercq, J. Kaerst, W.W. Tarn, E. Bickerman, and E. Will. But research has been particularly intense and productive in the field of economic and social history (U. Wilcken, M. Rostovtzeff, W. Otto, C. Préaux, and C. Schneider) and in the field of the history of religions (F. Cumont, R. Reitzenstein, H. Usener, P. Wendland, W. Bousset, A.D. Nock, and M.P. Nilsson). Droysen's notion of Hellenism has also deeply influenced the work of literary historians such as U. Wilamowitz-Moellendorff, F. Susemihl, F. Leo, E. Norden, and R. Pfeiffer.

The study of Greek influence on Judaism has developed into a special branch of research on which E. Bickerman, H. Lewy, S. Lieberman, V. Tcherikover, and M. Hengel, among others, have written with distinction. Research on Hellenism has been helped by archaeological discoveries, new inscriptions, and the constitution of a new branch of research, papyrology, since the beginning of the 20th century. Papyrology is especially relevant to the study of the Hellenistic period because a considerable portion of the papyri discovered in Egypt belongs to the last three centuries B.C.E.

However, a knowledge of the political history of Hellenism is hampered by the fragmentary nature of the surviving sources. The works of the great historians of the Hellenistic age (Hieronymus of Cardia, Duris, Timaeus, Agatharchidas, Phylarchus, and Posidonius) are all lost, with the exception of Polybius, and only fragments of his work remain. The only continuous account of the Hellenistic age is found in the short summary of the *Historiae Philippicae* by *Pompeius Trogus (end of the first century B.C.E.) written by Justinus in the second century C.E. Plutarch's *Lives* of some Hellenistic kings and politicians are of the utmost importance. Books I, II, and III of Maccabees are invaluable for Jewish history and must be supplemented by the relevant sections of Josephus' *Jewish Antiquities*. Strabo, Pliny the Elder, Pausanias, Galen, Athenaeus, and Diogenes Laertius, though all writing in the Roman Empire, provide essential information on Hellenistic science, social life, and customs.

The empire of Alexander the Great was the result of the military and intellectual cooperation of Greeks and Macedonians, who constituted the ruling class in the states emerging from the struggles of Alexander's successors. This collaboration was precarious in Greece alone, where consequently there was no political stability. The rivalries between Greek cities and the interference of the great Hellenistic states in Greek affairs led to Roman intervention at the end of the third century and ultimately contributed to the transformation of Greece into a direct Roman dependency in 146 B.C.E. The great Hellenistic states – Macedonia, Syria, Egypt, Thrace (for the brief period until 281 B.C.E.), Pergamum (at least after 240 B.C.E.) – though much stronger, had other sources of difficulty: they were faced by dynastic struggles in their midst, by frequent wars with their neighbors, and above all they had large native populations to control. The third century was the period of the greatest power and prosperity of these kingdoms. Almost everywhere during the second century B.C.E. the increasing inability of the Greco-Macedonian ruling class to prevent internal dissolution is noticeable. The Romans took full advantage of the difficulties of the Hellenistic states, played on the fear of social revolution among the wealthy Greeks, and exploited rivalries and native rebellions, with the result that they defeated and ultimately absorbed all the Hellenistic states. Macedonia, first defeated in 197, was reduced to impotence in 168 and transformed into a province in 149. Syria (the Seleucid state) was first deprived of some of its best Oriental regions by native rebellions (such as those leading to the creation of the Parthian and Bactrian states about 250 B.C.E.). Later it was defeated and mutilated by the Romans (188). The Jewish rebellion of the Maccabees contributed to the further decline of the Seleucid state, which was transformed into a Roman province in 64 B.C.E. Pergamum became a Roman province (province of Asia) in 129 B.C.E., Bithynia in 74. Egypt (the kingdom of the Ptolemies), as already noted, was incorporated by the Romans in 30 B.C.E. The last strong resistance of the Macedonian-Greek elements against the Romans was provoked and supported by Mithridates VI Eupator about 80 B.C.E. and ended in violent repression by the Romans. The last act of resistance against the Romans during the Hellenistic period in the East was not Greek, but Jewish.

In all the Hellenistic states Greek was the language of the aristocracy and the administration. The foundation of new cities (especially in the Seleucid kingdom) and of new villages (particularly in Egypt) contributed to the spread of Greek, but the peasants and the native priests kept the indigenous languages alive. Except in Judea, which had an original literature in Hebrew and Aramaic even under Greek rule, the important developments in literature were all in Greek. Even natives of Egypt and Babylonia wrote their histories in Greek (Manetho, Berossus; cf. Fabius Pictor in Rome). The schools and the gymnasia were organized according to Greek tradition: Homer, the tragedians of the fifth century (especially Euripides), and the orators and historians of the fourth century were the models of the new classicism. Erudition developed for its own sake and, notably in Alexandria and Pergamum, was under royal protection. The libraries of Alexandria were centers of research, besides containing extraordinary collections of manuscripts (apparently not confined to texts in Greek). Classicism notwithstanding, literature and art developed new styles, characterized by realism of detail and a tendency toward the idyllic and the pathetic. Modern scholars have recognized local trends not only in literature but also in art. They are, however, not so important as the essential unity of Hellenistic culture. Philosophy remained centered in Athens, but the great philosophic schools of the academy (Platonists), Peripatos (Aristotelians), Stoa (disciples of Zeno), and Porch (Epicureans) spread everywhere. There was also a revival (perhaps a transformation) of Pythagorean groups, which began to look like a religious sect. Natural sciences made enormous progress, and so did mathematics. Euclid, Apollonius of Perge, and Archimedes represent the culmination of Greek research in geometry and mechanics. Eratosthenes applied mathematics to geography and Aristarchus developed the heliocentric theory, but Hipparchus (who made fundamental discoveries in astronomy) persuaded the succeeding generations with his new version of the geocentric system. Scientific medicine flourished in Alexandria and elsewhere: The advances in anatomy (Herophilus), physiology (Erasistratus), etc., remained unsurpassed until the Renaissance. Pytheas explored new regions in the north. The philosopher Posidonius explained the tides.

Everywhere the new literature and art interested large strata of the Greek-speaking public, which was predominantly middle-class. If some poets were obscure and full of subtle allusions to the literature of the past (Callimachus, Lycophron, Euphorion, and to a certain extent Theocritus), others were easily comprehensible (Menander, Herodas, and perhaps Apollonius Rhodius). New prose genres, such as the erotic novel, were meant to appeal to a large public. There are signs that much of the literature now lost was fairly popular in character. Figurative art certainly had a wide appeal, as can be deduced from the amount of cheap, but graceful, figurines of this period. Improved techniques of work affected the lives of the many, and town-planning together with the easier economic conditions of private persons produced better housing in many places. But neither philosophy nor science meant much even to the middle class in the Greek-speaking cities. In religion the stronger influences came from the native populations, not from the upper (Greek or Hellenized) stratum. There was no sign that the gods of the Greek Olympus were dying: they went on performing miracles and acquiring new festivals and new sanctuaries. However, a progressive transformation of the old city cults was noticeable, with a new emphasis on free associations of devotees of a specific god, on mysteries, on spiritual notions such as philanthropy and purification. Dionysus became distinctly popular. At the same time Oriental gods – either with their original names (Osiris, Isis) or by identification with Greek gods (Hermes – Thot; Jupiter – Dolichenus) – were widely worshiped outside their original countries, with appropriate modifications of their cults. A curious case of a new god with old Egyptian roots was Serapis. Babylonian astrology gained many believers, even among philosophically educated Greeks. The Greek idea of Fortune (*Tyche*) increased in importance and was worshiped as a goddess, partly owing to Oriental influences. No doubt there were educated people who cared little for gods, either Greek or Oriental. Epicurus preached the indifference of gods to human events and Euhemerus reduced the gods to ancient human benefactors; yet the climate of the age was religious.

With all its regional and chronological differences, Hellenism is a cultural unity which corresponds to the existence of a uniform upper stratum of society and is reflected in the remarkable uniformity of the Greek language (the so-called *koiné*) from India to Gaul, wherever there was a Greek settlement. International trade both favored, and was favored by, this uniform upper stratum; Greek-speaking traders moved round the world. They were joined by more or less Hellenized Orientals and later by Italians. The slaves, the native peasants, and the Greek proletariat neither contributed much to, nor enjoyed the advantages of, this civilization.

It is much more difficult to speak of Hellenism as a political and institutional phenomenon, because conditions varied so profoundly from region to region. Monarchy was the unifying institutional fact. The king was supposed to own his own state by right of conquest (patrimonial monarchy). He was surrounded by a hierarchy of officials with specific functions. Monarchy was connected with religion by a dynastic cult. The army in each country was modeled on the Macedonian prototype which had ensured Alexander's victories. New military features included the use of elephants, the improvement of siege-engines, and the construction of bigger ships. The fact remains, however, that the political organization of Egypt was different from that of Syria, and both Egypt and Syria were of course different from Pergamum (where the king was much more the head of a Greek community) and from Macedonia, not to speak of the Greek city-states and leagues (Aetolia, Achaea, etc). Economic production, taxation, relations between natives and Greeks, and religious institutions varied greatly from state to state. The Ptolemies organized a state-controlled economy in Egypt which had no parallel elsewhere and slowed down urbanization. The Seleucid state included territories which differed from each other economically and socially. They were kept together (when they were kept together) by the royal army and the militarized Greco-Macedonian colonies. The Seleucids never made any serious attempt at central control of the economic affairs of their state.

The great paradox of the Hellenistic age is that a Greek-speaking man could move easily from country to country with a reasonable expectation of finding work and being well received everywhere – and yet he would not find himself at home anywhere outside his native city. Furthermore, from the end of the third century onward any Greek would also increasingly feel the presence of a new intimidating power – Rome. The structure of Hellenistic civilization was not weak, for it survived the defeat of Hellenistic states, but daily life seemed dangerous; and indeed wars and rebellions were frequent and increasingly catastrophic. Philosophy and religion both provided escape from worldly commitments and consolation for disappointments.

Here the Jews presented a remarkable exception. Confronted with Greek ideas, some attempted to combine Greek intellectual values with Hebrew ones; such efforts were more successful in Egypt than in Judea. However, even in Judea the Hellenizing movement under Antiochus IV came near to prevailing. Ultimately the Jews organized their culture and their political life on their own terms, as witnessed by the rise of the Essenes and Pharisees. The independence of Jewish intellectual life in the Hellenistic age is partly explained by the fact that while Jews took a great interest in Greek ideas, the outside world took relatively little interest in Hebrew ideas. The translation of the Bible into Greek did not mean that the Greeks read the Bible. The isolation in which the Jews lived, especially in Judea, was conducive to the creation of a style of thought and life which can be (and was) considered competitive with Hellenistic civilization.

[Arnaldo Dante Momigliano]

Hellenism and the Jews

Contact between Greeks and Semites, probably including Jews, seems likely to have occurred in Mycenaean times, as remains of Greek pottery in Palestine and Syria testify. Several interesting parallels between early Greek, especially that of Homer, and biblical vocabulary have been suggested, such as Homeric *amumōn* ("without blemish") and biblical *mum* ("blemish"), Homeric *machaira* ("sword") and biblical *mekherah* (Gen. 49:5), Homeric *erebos* ("darkness") and biblical *erev* ("evening") and *ma'ariv* ("west"), and Greek *kados* ("pitcher," in Archilochus) and Hebrew *kad* ("pitcher"). Parallels between Homeric and biblical motifs are generally less striking. The possibility of a link between the even earlier Minoan civilization and Jews, or at any rate Semites, suggested by the presence of Minoan pottery at Ugarit and supported by bilingual (Greek and Northwest Semitic) inscriptions in Crete dating from 600 to 300 B.C.E., awaits the decipherment of Linear A.

It was not until the time of *Alexander the Great, however, that the contacts between Greeks and Jews were revived and intensified. The fact that for two centuries Palestine was part of Hellenistic kingdoms, first of Ptolemaic Egypt and then of Seleucid Syria, made Greek influence on Jewish thought and life inevitable. In the first third of the second century B.C.E., a group of Hellenizing Jews came to power in Jerusalem. They were led by wealthy Jewish aristocrats such as Joseph son of Tobiah, and his son Hyrcanus, who were apparently attracted to the externals of Hellenism; their Hellenization was, at first, primarily social rather than cultural and religious. *Jason the high priest carried his Hellenizing to the extent of establishing Greek educational institutions, the gymnasium and *ephebeion*, and of founding Jerusalem as a Greek city, Antioch-at-Jerusalem. But Jason was only a moderate Hellenizer compared with *Menelaus, whose succession as high priest occasioned a civil war between their factions, with the *Tobiads supporting Menelaus and the masses of the people standing behind Jason. As the scholars Bickermann, Tcherikover, and Hengel have shown, it was the Hellenizers, notably Menelaus and his followers, who influenced Antiochus Epiphanes to undertake his persecutions of Judaism so as to put down the rebellion of the *Hassideans, who were supported by the masses of Jerusalem and who rebelled against the Hellenizers. Perhaps the account in the *Dead Sea Scrolls of the war between the sons of light and the sons of darkness reflects this struggle.

In the following year the fight of the Maccabees against the Hellenizers began. This struggle highlights the antagonism between the rich and highborn in the towns, who believed in finding a modus vivendi with Hellenism, and the peasants and urban masses, who could brook no compromise with their religious traditions. In victory the Maccabees were particularly ruthless toward the Greek cities of Palestine (of which there were 30) and their inhabitants, but their struggle was against the Greek cities as a political rather than as a cultural force. It is a mistake to regard the Hellenization of the Palestinian Jews as so deep that they would have been absorbed had not

Antiochus' persecution aroused a fanatic reaction. Similarly it is a mistake to look upon the Maccabees as despisers of Greek culture. In point of fact, Jonathan the Hasmonean, far from hating Greek culture, renewed the treaty of friendship with Sparta (Jos., Ant., 13:164–170) that the high priest *Onias I is said to have negotiated about 300 B.C.E. Alexander Yannai employed Greek mercenaries in his army (*ibid.*, 13:387), and from his time onward coins are inscribed with Greek as well as with Hebrew. The very Aristobulus who forced the Itureans to become Jews called himself "philhellene" (*ibid.*, 13:318). The rise of the Pharisees may be seen, to some degree, as a reaction against the Greco-Roman culture favored by the Sadducees, who were allied with the phil-Hellenic Hasmoneans. The Hellenic influence increased under Herod, who built a Greek theater, an amphitheater where Jews wrestled naked with Greeks, and a hippodrome in or near Jerusalem. Even Agrippa I, who is so highly regarded in rabbinic sources (Bik. 2:4, etc.), built a theater and amphitheater at Berytus (Jos., Ant., 19:335) and himself attended the theater at Caesarea (*ibid.*, 19:332–4).

Jews came to Egypt just before the end of the kingdom of Judah in the sixth century B.C.E. and fought as mercenaries, in all probability side by side with Greeks who had come for the same purpose. But large-scale emigration began with *Ptolemy I after the death of Alexander. Philo (*In Flaccum*, 43) reports that in his day the Jews in Egypt numbered a million. By that time there were large Jewish communities in Syria, especially Antioch (Jos., Wars, 7:43), Greece proper (Philo, *Legatio ad Gaium*, 281–2), Asia Minor (Jos., Ant., 14:213, 255–64; Philo, op. cit., 245), Cyprus (Jos., Ant., 13:284), Rome (Cicero, *Pro Flacco*,67), and Cyrene (Jos., Ant., 14:115), all of which were primarily Greek speaking.

The Hellenization of the Jews, both in Palestine and the Diaspora, consists in the substitution of the Greek language for Hebrew and Aramaic, the adoption of Greek personal names, the adoption of Greek educational institutions, the growth of a Jewish Hellenistic literature and philosophy, and religious deviation and syncretism as seen in legal institutions and in art (see *Diaspora). In Palestine, the predominance of Greek in ossuary inscriptions (the dates vary) so that of 168, 114 are in Greek only, the discovery of Greek papyri in the Dead Sea caves, and of Greek letters from leaders of the Bar Kokhba rebellion, and the presence of perhaps as many as 2,500–3,000 Greek words in the talmudic corpus, especially in the homiletic Midrashim composed for popular consumption, testify to what degree the Greek language had gained currency (see Rabbinical Knowledge of *Greek and Latin). The contact with Greek influenced, moreover, a number of developments in Hebrew phonology and syntax and led to the establishment of a number of Hebrew roots derived from Greek. Simeon b. Gamaliel went so far as to praise Greek as the only language into which the Torah could be perfectly translated (Esth. R. 4:12). Judah ha-Nasi remarked, "Why talk Syriac in Palestine? Talk either Hebrew or Greek" (Sot. 49b). It was said (Ḥag. 19b) of the second-century rabbi Elisha ben Avuyah, that he never ceased reciting Greek poetry. In the next century R. Abbahu knew Greek so well that he was able to pun in it (Gen. R. 14:2), and justified teaching his daughters Greek since it served as an ornament (TJ, Pe'ah 1:1, 15c). The fact that the Mishnah (Sot. end) records that during the war of Lusius *Quietus (117 C.E.) a decree was passed banning the teaching of Greek to one's son indicates that the rabbis regarded the use of Greek as a real danger, but the language continued in vogue.

It can hardly be maintained that Greek was used only by the upper classes and was restricted to commerce, or that it was restricted to those who needed it to communicate with the governing authorities; the Christian Hellenizers (Acts, 6:1), who apparently spoke Greek only and were thus more deeply affected by Hellenization, were not restricted to the higher classes. Josephus (Ant., 20:264) clearly indicates that ordinary freemen and even slaves in Palestine had learned many languages. However, his statement (*ibid.*, 20:263) that it had proven difficult for him to master Greek, especially the pronunciation, and the faulty Greek in many inscriptions indicate that the level of knowledge of Greek was not high. Even Josephus (Apion, 1:50) had to employ assistants to polish the Greek of his *De Bello Judaico.* The knowledge of Greek possessed by Jewish Christians in Palestine, however, because of their closer contact with Diaspora Jews and with non-Jews outside Palestine, must have been better; and recent scholarship has concluded that it is probable that Jesus himself sometimes spoke Greek.

In the Diaspora, the earliest Jewish inhabitants of Alexandria in the fourth century B.C.E., to judge from the papyri, spoke Aramaic; but so thoroughgoing was the victory of the Greek over the Hebrew language that after the third century B.C.E., with the exception of the Nash Papyrus, until 400 C.E., all papyri from Egypt pertaining to the Jews are in Greek. Similarly, of the 116 Jewish inscriptions from Egypt only five are in Hebrew, and they are, it appears, of late date (see *Alexandria; *Egypt, Hellenistic Period; *Zeno Papyri). Even in the Jewish community of Rome, which seems to have had a stronger identification with Judaism, only five of the 534 inscriptions are in Hebrew or Aramaic. Because the *Septuagint was regarded as divinely inspired, there appeared to be no need to learn Hebrew. Indeed, there is a very real question as to whether Philo, by far the greatest of the Alexandrian Jewish writers, knew more than a modicum of Hebrew; it is surely significant that whereas he tells so much of his Greek education he tells nothing about his Hebrew education.

Another aspect of Hellenization is the choice of Greek personal names. In Palestine the percentage is much lower than in the Diaspora, but the names of rabbis such as Abtolemus, Alexander, Antigonus, Symmachus, and Theodosius indicate that the process was at work even there. The fact that at least three-fourths of the personal names of the Jews of Hellenistic Egypt are of Greek origin is striking. The Jews often tried to choose Greek names similar in meaning or sound to their Hebrew names, but names derived from those of Greek or Egyptian deities are common. In Rome about half of the names of the Jews in inscriptions are of Latin origin, about a third are of Greek origin, and only about a sixth are derived from Hebrew or Aramaic.

Education was a key area of Greek impact. After the establishment of the gymnasium and *ephebeion* by Jason the high priest in pre-Maccabean times, there is no further information on Greek educational institutions established by Jews. However, in the first century Rabban Gamaliel had 500 students of Greek wisdom in addition to 500 students of Torah (Sot. 49b, et al.), although this permission to study Greek was granted to the house of Rabban Gamaliel only because of their special relationship with the Roman government. In Egypt the only known schools with Jewish content were the Sabbath schools, intended for adults, which, according to Philo (Spec., 1:62), taught the traditional Greek four cardinal virtues. On the other hand, there is mention of the eagerness of Jews to enroll their children of secondary school age in Greek gymnasia; and apparently, until they were excluded by the Emperor *Claudius in 41, they had succeeded in their efforts. Such an education initiated youths into the Greek way of life, especially athletics, its most characteristic feature. No Jew could have attended a Greek gymnasium without making serious compromises with his religion, for the gymnasia had numerous busts of deities, held religious processions, sponsored sacrifices, and participated in the athletic games associated with the festivals. Similarly, the fact that the 72 translators recommended that King Ptolemy watch plays (Letter of Aristeas, 284) and that Philo himself often attended the theater (Ebr., 177) shows that Hellenization had made deep inroads. It is not surprising that the rabbis (Av. Zar. 18b) forbade attendance at theaters, for ancient dramas were performed only at festivals of the gods in the presence of the altar and priests of the gods.

The most obvious instances of Greek influence are to be seen in Jewish literature of the Hellenistic period. In Palestine, even *Ben Sira, whose opposition to Hellenism before the Maccabean rebellion is manifest, has a number of aphorisms which seem to be derived from Aesop, Theognis, and Euripides. The *Testament of Joseph and the Book of *Judith show Greek influence in the introduction of erotic motifs found in Greek romances. Similarly, the Book of *Tobit, composed either in Palestine or Antioch in the second century B.C.E., shows Hellenistic influence in the form of its romance. Aside from Justus of Tiberias and Josephus, no Palestinian author is known who definitely wrote in Greek, and indeed there is no apparent Greek influence in the first century B.C.E. "Biblical Antiquities" of Pseudo-Philo. But in his paraphrase of the Bible, Josephus, in his eagerness to answer antisemitic charges, makes numerous changes. Thus his Abraham is presented as worthy of Greek political and philosophical ideals: he possesses skill in persuasion, the power of logical deduction, and scientific knowledge, and, in a show of liberalism, he offers to be converted by the Egyptians if he fails to convince them. Samson is an Aristotelian-like *megalopsychos* ("great-souled man"); Saul is a kind of Jewish Achilles; and Solomon a kind of Jewish Oedipus. Finally, Josephus' portraits of Moses and of Esther are in the tradition of Hellenistic romance, with emphasis on erotic elements. Indeed, the life of Moses used by Artapanus, Philo, and Josephus contained details borrowed from the legendary life of Pythagoras.

There has been much debate on the degree of Hellenic influence on the rabbis themselves. A number of tales about Hillel recall Socratic and Cynic anecdotes. Joshua b. Hananiah's discussions with Athenians, Alexandrians, and Roman philosophers (Bek. 8b; Nid. 69b; Sanh. 90b), Meir's reported disputations with the Cynic *Oenomaus of Gadara (Gen. R. 68:20) – a city a little east of the Jordan which also produced three other famous ancient Greek writers, Menippus the satirist, Meleager the poet, and Philodemus the Epicurean philosopher and poet – as well as Judah ha-Nasi's discussions with "*Antoninus"; Av. Zar. 10a–11a, etc.) and rabbinic condemnation of Epicureanism (Mish. Sanh. 11:1; Avot, 1:3; etc.), all reflect rabbinic interest in and concern about Hellenism (see Classical *Greek Literature). We know of only one rabbi, however, *Elisha b. Avuyah, upon whom Greek influence was so great that he actually became a Gnostic heretic.

It has been suggested that *Platonism influenced the rabbis with its theory of ideas, the notion that the soul possesses perfect knowledge before birth, and, above all, the method of dialectic. Moreover, a number of striking parallels in content and form between the Epicureans and the rabbis have been noted. The *Stoic ideal of the sage, as well as Stoic techniques of allegorizing and expounding law, influenced Philo, but it is doubtful to what extent they influenced the rabbis. The rabbis mention only two philosophers – Epicurus and Oenomaus – by name, and they do not use any Greek philosophical terms. The fact that they never mention Plato, Aristotle, or Philo would indicate that their information was probably drawn second-hand. Similarly the proverbs in rabbinic literature which have classical parallels probably represent contact not with Greek literature but with Greek speakers. The alleged influence of Hellenistic rhetoric upon rabbinic methods of interpretation is in the realm of terminology rather than of substance. The "fence" which the rabbis created around the Torah (see Avot 1:1) succeeded, on the whole, in keeping the masses of the Jews from succumbing to Greek culture, as the complaints about Jewish religious and social separateness (cf., e.g., Tacitus, *Histories*, 5:4) indicate. As to sectarian groups, it has been argued, with some degree of probability, that the communal organization and the strict rules for the administration of the Essenes and the Dead Sea brotherhood were directly influenced by Pythagoreanism and its revival, neo-Pythagoreanism. Josephus (Ant., 15:371), in any case, remarks that the Essenes followed the Pythagorean way of life.

The influence of Greek thought on Diaspora Jews starts with the Septuagint (the alleged meeting of a Jew with *Aristotle (Jos., Apion, 1:176–82) is fictitious). Recent investigators, on the whole, agree that there is no systematic pattern of Hellenizing, and that the Greek elements tend to be superficial and decorative rather than deep-seated and significant. Again, it was formerly thought that the language of the Septuagint was a kind of Jewish Greek which would be unintelligible to non-Jews; but the papyri show that the language is that of Hellenistic Egypt. Yet the fact that, for example, "Torah" was translated as *nomos* ("law"), *emunah* as *pistis* ("belief"), and *ẓedakah* as *dikaiosynē* ("justice") brought the connotations, especially Platonic, of these words to the Greek reader ignorant of the original. Hence Paul could preach antinomianism to an audience that looked upon the Torah as a law which could be repealed rather than as a way of life, and when the injunction *Elohim lo tekalel* (Ex. 22:24) was interpreted to mean "Thou shalt not curse the gods," it became a text for Philo (*De Vita Mosis*, 2:205; Spec., 1:53) and Josephus (Apion, 2:237; Ant., 4:207) to preach liberalism toward other religions. Apparently because they saw the danger in the adulation of the Septuagint by the Hellenistic Jews, the rabbis changed their initially favorable reaction to the translation (Meg. 9b) to a bitter comment (Sof. 1:7) comparing the completion of the Septuagint with the making of the golden calf. The stature of the Septuagint is obvious in the fragments of the Greco-Jewish historian *Demetrius, who already in the latter part of the third century B.C.E. followed the Septuagint's patriarchal chronology rather than that of the Hebrew text, though his Septuagint was not quite identical with any of our versions.

The Letter of *Aristeas, supposedly written in the third century B.C.E., but more probably about 100 B.C.E., apparently by an Alexandrian Jew who was a propagandist for the cooperation of Hellenism and Judaism, is addressed not merely or even primarily to non-Jews but rather to fellow Jews. The 72 elders to whom the translation of the Torah was entrusted are depicted as having had a good Greek education, and engage with the king in a symposium on ethics and politics reminiscent of those described by Plato, Xenophon, Athenaeus, Plutarch, and Macrobius. "Aristeas" (16) even goes so far as to identify Zeus with God. Social isolation is not a corollary of Judaism in his view. Among his contemporaries only the author of III Maccabees opposed the drive for citizenship of the Alexandrian Jews.

Other Alexandrian Jewish writers attempted to show that the Greeks had borrowed from the Jews. Thus the Jewish Peripatetic philosopher Aristobulus, in the second century B.C.E., asserts (in Eusebius, *Praeparatio Evangelica*, 13:12, 1–16) that Homer, Hesiod, Pythagoras, Socrates, and Plato were all acquainted with a translation of the Torah into Greek which had been made before the Persian conquest of Egypt (525 B.C.E.). The historian Eupolemus (c. 150 B.C.E.), perhaps a Palestinian, reports that Moses taught the alphabet to the Jews, who in turn passed it on to the Phoenicians, who transmitted it to the Greeks. The historian Artapanus (c. 100 B.C.E.) identifies Moses with the semilegendary Greek poet Musaeus and with Hermes-Thoth, and makes him the founder of navigation, architecture, strategy, and philosophy; Moses thus, far from hating mankind, as antisemites had charged, is a benefactor in the Hellenistic sense. Cleodemus (or Malchus), perhaps a Jewish historian, boasts that two of the sons of Abraham accompanied Heracles in his campaign against Libya and that Heracles married the daughter of one of them (Jos., Ant., 1:240–1).

Among the most obvious instances of Greek influence on Jewish writers are *Philo the Elder's epic poem *On Jerusalem* (c. 100 B.C.E.) in Homeric hexameters, and that of his presumed contemporary *Theodotus, a Samaritan, on the rape of Dinah. Ezekiel the poet, at about the same time, composed tragedies, of which a portion of one, *The Exodus*, is extant, a veritable exercise in Euripidean trimeters. Among Apocryphal books the Wisdom of Ben Sira, dating from perhaps the second century B.C.E., uses a number of technical terms drawn from Platonic and Stoic philosophy; and such a view as the preexistence of the soul is apparently drawn from Plato. It and its presumed contemporary, IV *Maccabees, are reminiscent of Cynic-Stoic diatribes. Furthermore, the latter shows Greek influence in its presentation of the Torah as teaching the four cardinal virtues; the arguments are pervasively Stoic, and the form of the disputation is modeled on Plato's *Gorgias*. Of Philo it was said already by Jerome (*De Viris Illustribus*, 11), "Either Plato philonizes or Philo platonizes." That his Hellenization transcends mere language can be seen in his description of Moses' education, which is presumably held up as an ideal. His Egyptian instructors are said to have taught him arithmetic, geometry, harmonics, and philosophy (*De Vita Mosis*, 1:23–24), the very subjects which constitute the higher education of Plato's philosopher-king (*Republic*, 521c–535a), while his Greek teachers are said to have taught him the rest of the regular school course – presumably, grammar, rhetoric, and logic. In his profound debt to Platonism Philo is similar to the author of IV Maccabees, his presumed contemporary.

Evidence of Greek influence on Jews of the middle and lower classes is largely dependent upon *papyri and art objects that have been discovered. The papyri show many instances of Jews using common Hellenistic law in their business life. The documents are drawn up as Hellenistic documents in a government notary's office. The most obvious violations of *halakhah* are seen in the loan documents: of the 11 that have come down only two do not charge direct interest. One of them is in a highly fragmentary condition and the other is subject to the interest of 24% if not repaid within a year. The one divorce document follows non-Jewish formulas completely; and, in direct violation of *halakhah*, there is no statement that it is the husband who is divorcing the wife.

Greek influence, as Goodenough has amply shown, is clearly to be seen in Hellenistic Jewish art and architecture. Thus Josephus tells that the courts and colonnades of the Temple built by Herod in Jerusalem were in the Greek style. Pagan and syncretistic art has been discovered in the synagogues of both Palestine and the Diaspora (especially at *Dura-Europos in Mesopotamia), in direct violation of stringent biblical and rabbinic prohibitions. It cannot be argued that these motifs were merely decorative, since they were employed in a similar way by earlier and contemporary pagans and by contemporary and later Christians. Goodenough has concluded that these figures had meaning as symbols; that these symbols constituted a sub-rational lingua franca among Jews and non-Jews alike, just as the Greek language provided a rational bond among them; and that they represented a kind of allegorization through art, of the sort that Philo had attempted through philosophy. Additional evidence that some Jews adopted certain pagan elements can be seen in the charms (that is, verbal incantations) and apotropaic amulets (or the material objects themselves containing graphic symbols used to ward off evil) which Goodenough has collected.

It is not surprising that contact with Hellenism should have produced deviations from Jewish observance. Philo (*Post.*, 35–40) mentions the extreme allegorists, who insisted on interpreting the ceremonial laws as only a parable: these are undoubtedly forerunners of Pauline antinomianism. Others relaxed their Jewish observance in order to become citizens of Alexandria, an act that involved worship of the city gods. Actual apostasy was apparently rare, though there is mention of the case of Philo's nephew, *Tiberius Julius Alexander, as well as those of Dositheos and Helicon, all of whom pursued careers at the imperial court. Philo on one occasion (Spec., 3:29) does attack intermarriage, but the virulent *antisemitism in Alexandria must have served as a deterrent. A more common reaction to the challenge of secularism was for Jews to cease religious observance except on the Day of Atonement (Philo, Spec. 1:186). Finally, there is some evidence that the one city where Christianity seems to have made real inroads in converting Jews was the one most deeply influenced by Hellenism, Alexandria.

See also *Bible (in Hellenistic Judaism); *Hellenistic Jewish Literature; *Cynics and Cynicism.

[Louis Harry Feldman]

Spiritual Resistance

One aspect of the contact between Hellenism (and Rome) and Judaism deserves special treatment, the spiritual resistance against their rule. The struggle of the Jewish people against Greek and Roman domination was accompanied by a literature which encouraged and intensified resistance. After military defeat it became frequently the only weapon, an important instrument of hope and survival. A significant trend in recent scholarship considers much of Jewish literature between Alexander the Great and the conquest of Islam as spiritual or religious resistance.

Resistance of this type was found among all the larger nations of the ancient Near East: the Babylonians and Egyptians under the Persians and the Egyptians and Persians under the Greeks who, in turn, developed a preponderantly cultural resistance under the Romans. The eastern pattern, however, was religious: foreign conquest destroys the sacred and just world order by which native king, cult, nature, and people function under the ruling god, a belief which was strengthened by the frequent misrule of the conqueror. A future cataclysmic reestablishment under a kingly redeemer must therefore right all wrongs. Meanwhile, a hereafter would punish or reward the individual. This apocalyptic scheme existed throughout the Near East: e.g., the *Oracle of Hystaspes* and the later *Bahman Yasht* (Persian), Sesostris and Ramses legends, *Demotic Chronicle*, *Oracle of the Potter* (Egyptian), *Babylonian Chronicle*, Ninos-Semiramis legend (Babylonian). Archaizing styles (e.g., script and literature, cf. *Coins, *Dead Sea Scrolls), clerical organization, and proselytism were also aspects of resistance.

Jewish spiritual resistance differed in some respects from this general pattern; here it was the weapon of a small people lacking the glory of an imperial past. It differed, further, in its intensity and perpetuity, its monotheism (though dangerously attenuated in the apocalypse) and, at times, its appeal to all classes from aristocracy to peasantry. It differed in a stronger stress on social justice inherited from biblical prophecy and the constant reference to past liberations in sacred scriptures. In his glorification of the Augustan restoration *Virgil may have combined classical concepts with eastern "Empire" apocalyptic ones (*Eclogue* 4; cf. Horace, *Epode* 16; Dan. 2 and 7). Oppression created obscure allusions (to Antiochus, Pompey, Nero, etc.) and secret code words in both *apocalypse and Talmud (e.g., Edom or Babylon for Rome adopted from here by Christian apocalyptic writers (Rev. 16:5) and perhaps in the Dead Sea Scrolls ("*Kittim*" in the Habakkuk Pesher)). Finally, Jewish resistance created an incomparably greater variety of literary sources and forms. Alongside the detailed apocalypse, with its violent cosmic vision, the psalm remained popular as a vehicle of resistance (Dan. 9:4–19; II Macc. 1:24–29; Psalms of Solomon, perhaps the heading of Ps. 30, et al.). Martyrology emerged, and many of its features were borrowed by emerging Christianity (II Macc.; IV Macc.; talmudic examples collected in *Midrash Elleh Ezkerah*, cf. H.A. Fischel, in JQR, 37 (1946/47), 265–80, 363–86). Alongside Diaspora historiographies, Palestinian works treated both biblical and contemporary history in the spirit of religious resistance (I Macc.; Jub.; *Pseudo-Philo*). Many talmudic dialogues ("Antoninus" versus Rabbi Hadrian and the Athenian wise men versus Joshua b. Hananiah), Alexander legends (Tam. 31b.ff., et al.), parables, and fables (Akiva, fox and fishes, Ber. 61b) have resistance aspects. Spiritual resistance is also manifest in the Hebrew examples of the erotic Greco-Oriental romance (Esth., Judith, Testament of Joseph, III Macc., Moses Romance). The talmudic sermon interpreted biblical passages, such as those of the unclean animals, as referring to Greece and Rome (Lev. R. 13, 5, et al.). The resistance aspects of liturgy, still little explored, may be considerable. Resistance is obvious and probably intentional in the symposiastic *seder* ritual (cf. S. Stein, in JJS, 8 [1957], 13–44).

The resistant writer freely added materials from foreign literature. Judith, some details of the Greek Lindus chronicle and Daniel and the Sibylline Oracle (Oriental prophecies) are among prominent examples. Similarly, the Midrash seems to have been acquainted with the Hellenistic critique of Rome's materialism and cruelty (cf. Shab. 33b and Cicero, *Academica* 21, 137; Meg. 6b; Pes. 119b, et al., and Dio. 13, 16, 31, 41ff., 121) and its "scandalous" foundation legend (Shab. 56b; Esth. R. 3, 5 and Justin 28:2, 8ff.; Horace, *Epode*, 16). Occasionally, resistance consisted in quietism, and the talmudic sage resembled (and was acquainted with) the Greco-Roman philosopher-rhetor who also often had to choose between martyrdom and withdrawal. The rabbis created much *halakhah of decisive resistance value, especially legislation against emperor worship, later used by Tertullian among others. Naturally, resistance never excluded periods of accommodation, objective insights into the virtues of Greece and Rome (Avot 3, 2; Av. Zar. 2b; 18a; Gen. R. 9 end, 16, 4, et al.), and useful borrowings. Strangely enough, much earlier non-Jewish scholarship condemns Jewish resistance, totally oblivious to the fact that without it there would be no Western civilization as we know it.

[Henry Albert Fischel]

BIBLIOGRAPHY: W.W. Tarn, *Hellenistic Civilization* (1952[3]); M. Hadas, *Hellenistic Culture* (1959); V.A. Tcherikover, *Die hellenistischen Staedtegruendungen von Alexander dem Grossen bis auf die Roemerzeit* (1927); idem, *Hellenistic Civilization and the Jews* (1959); M. Hengel, *Judentum und Hellenismus* (1969); N. Bentwich, *Hellenism* (1919). HELLENISM AND THE JEWS: Schuerer, Gesch; Baron, Social[2]; Goodenough, Symbols; Tcherikover, Corpus; S. Lieberman, *Greek in Jewish Palestine* (1942); idem, *Hellenism in Jewish Palestine* (1962[2]); idem, in: *Studies and Texts*, 1 (1963), 123–41; CH Dodd, *The Bible and the Greeks* (1954); J.N. Sevenster, *Do You Know Greek?* (1968); Y. Baer, *Yisrael ba-Ammim* (1955); E. Bickermann, *Der Gott der Makkabaeer* (1937); R. Marcus, in: PAAJR, 16 (1946–47), 97–181; CH Gordon, in: HUCA, 26 (1955), 43–108; M. Smith, in: BJRL, 40 (1958), 473–512; L.H. Feldman, in: JSOS, 22 (1960), 215–37; H.A. Fischel, in: *American Oriental Society Middle West Branch Semi-Centennial Volume* (1969), 59–88. SPIRITUAL RESISTANCE AGAINST GREEK AND ROMAN RULE: M. Radin, *The Jews among the Greeks and Romans* (1915); M. Braun, *History and Romance in Graeco-oriental Literature* (1938); H.L. Ginsberg, *Studies in Daniel* (1948); S.K. Eddy, *The King Is Dead* (1961); V.A. Tcherikover, *Ha-Yehudim ba-Olam ha-Yevani ve-ha-Romi* (1961); M. Avi-Yonah, *Bi-Ymei Roma u-Bizantiyyon* (19522); H. Fuchs, *Geistige Widerstand gegen Rom…* (1938); R. MacMullen, *Enemies of the Roman Order* (1966); E. Bickerman, *Four Strange Books of the Bible* (1967), sections *Daniel* and *Esther*. **ADD. BIBLIOGRAPHY:** E. Bickermann, *The Jews in the Greek Age* (1988); J.J. Collins, *Between Athens and Jerusalem* (2002); L.L. Grabbe, *Judaism from Cyrus to Hadrian*, 2 vols. (1992); M. Hengel, *Judaism and Hellenism*, 2 vols. (1974); L.I. Levine, *Judaism and Hellenism in Antiquity* (1998); A. Momigliano, *Alien Wisdom: The Limits of Hellenization* (1975); E.S. Gruen, "Hellenistic Judaism," in: D. Biale (ed.), *Cultures of the Jews* (2002), idem, *Diaspora: Jews amidst Greeks and Romans* (2002).

HELLENISTIC JEWISH LITERATURE. To a general historian the term "Hellenistic" describes the literature of the period from the death of Alexander the Great (323 B.C.E.) until Rome's predominance in the Mediterranean (c. 30 B.C.E.). Sometimes the same general term is used to refer to Jewish material as well; thus, the Book of Ecclesiastes, early rabbinic literature, and the *Dead Sea Scrolls are sometimes referred to as "Hellenistic." More precisely, however, the term Hellenistic Jewish literature does not describe a historical period – nor even characterize a movement – but rather applies to a specific body of literature that was written in the Greek language; was transmitted only in the Greek language; or was preserved in one or more secondary versions derived from the Greek (though a number of these works have now been found in the original). Its two main centers were Palestine and Alexandria (Egypt), although other localities of the Diaspora may have contributed (see *Jason of Cyrene). Its temporal limits extend into the second century C.E., for the educated classes of the major cities of the Roman period continued to use Greek rather than Latin as the language of culture. Since the term Hellenistic Jewish literature refers to a subclass of the literature of a period, it is difficult to discuss it historically or in terms of genres in isolation from the rest of the literature of the same period. Traditionally, the material of this literature has been divided into Apocrypha, *Pseudepigrapha, and individual authors. Schuerer presents the material as either Palestinian or as Diaspora literature. Only recently, in the works of Joshua Gutmann, has there been an attempt at a systematic historical presentation.

The fundamental book of this literature is the Greek translation of the Bible, the *Septuagint. Although the story of its origin as told in the Letter of *Aristeas is probably propaganda, in fact an early date for this translation, at least of the Pentateuch, is very probable (the reign of *Ptolemy Philadelphus, 285–246 B.C.E.), testifying to the rapid loss of knowledge of the Hebrew language by the Alexandria Jewish community. The rest of the literature is greatly dependent on this text. In historical writing, for example, retelling of biblical history is found in the fragments of *Demetrius, *Eupolemus, *Artapanus, Aristeas, *Cleodemus, and *Thallus, in Pseudo-Philo's *Biblical Antiquities*, and in the first half of the *Antiquities* of *Josephus, all couched in the language of the Greek translation with little or no reference to the Hebrew original. In more contemporaneous histories, such as I and II *Maccabees, *Philo's *Embassy to Gaius*, and Josephus' *Jewish War*, there is an obvious debt to the models of Thucydides and Polybius. With the exception of I Maccabees (probably), Pseudo-Philo, and the original of Josephus' *Jewish War*, all these histories were composed in Greek. The folkloristic elaborations on the biblical text found in this literature are more often translations from a Semitic original. Some are insertions into the biblical text, perhaps stemming from the original copy, such as the story of the three youths in I *Esdras 3:1–5:6 or the insertions in the Greek *Esther; others are additions, such as **Susanna or Bel and the Dragon, to the biblical Book of Daniel; still others, separate books in themselves, such as *Jubilees, *Tobit, *Judith, and the Ascension of *Isaiah, are further examples of stories told in a biblical manner. Artapanus and II and III Maccabees come closer to the dramatic manner of a Greek romance.

Books such as the Wisdom of *Ben Sira (Ecclesiasticus) continue the tradition of biblical wisdom literature. Little or no direct influence of Greek philosophy can be discerned in them; but in books like the Wisdom of *Solomon, especially in the latter half, and in IV Maccabees, Platonic and Stoic terminology and ideas are present. *Aristobulus and Philo explain Mosaic law as an anticipation of Greek philosophy, and they employ the Greek technique of allegory to reconcile these two traditions. Apocalyptic literature, as found in *Enoch, the Assumption of *Moses, IV Esdras, the Syrian and Greek *Baruch, and the Testaments of the *Twelve Patriarchs, owes much to the prophetic tradition, as well as to Greek popular lore, Stoicism, and Platonism. The Testament of Abraham, for example, is reminiscent of Plato's vision of Er at the end of the *Republic*. In poetry, at least in form, the Greek and the Semitic elements can be clearly distinguished. Semitic poetry uses parallelism; Greek poetry uses syllabic metrics. The Psalms of *Solomon and parts of the Wisdom of Ben Sira represent a continuation of the tradition of Psalms; the writings of *Philo the Elder and those of *Theodotus are in Homeric hexameters; *Ezekiel the poet writes in iambics. The Prayer of *Manasseh, however, shows how the Greek and Hebrew elements are not always clearly delineated, for this book, although probably written in Greek, is more akin to biblical poetry.

Finally, there is the question of the extent to which this literature was addressed to a pagan audience. Most of these books are too deeply steeped in Jewish tradition to have been meaningful except to either traditional or partially Hellenized Jews. Some books, such as Josephus' *Contra Apionem*, seem to be addressed specifically to non-Jewish audiences. The Pseudepigrapha which are ascribed to pagan authors, such as the *Sibylline Oracles, Pseudo-Hecataeus, or Pseudo-Phocylides, also belong to this category.

See also *Greek Literature, Classical; *Hellenism.

BIBLIOGRAPHY: Charles, Apocrypha; Schuerer, Gesch, 3 (1909[4]), 420ff.; N. Bentwich, *Hellenism* (1919), 197–249; J. Gutmann, *Ha-Sifrut ha-Yehudit ha-Hellenistit*, 2 vols. (1958–63).

[Marshall S. Hurwitz]

HELLER, U.S. Reform rabbinical family. MAXIMILIAN HELLER (1860–1929) was born in Prague and lived in the heart of the ghetto. He came to the United States in 1879, two years after his parents. Heller was ordained by Hebrew Union College in 1884, the second class of ordainees. After two years in Chicago, where he was assistant to Rabbi Bernhard *Felsenthal, and then Houston, Texas, for a year, he was named to the pulpit of Temple Sinai, New Orleans, and remained there for the rest of his life. Firmly grounded in Jewish scholarship, Heller was an able preacher and a felicitous writer. Though identified with the Reform movement, he took a position independent of the majority of his contemporaries, and in particular was an early adherent of Zionism. Out of respect for Rabbi Isaac Mayer *Wise, who was a mentor, Heller did not declare his Zionism until after Wise's death in 1900. Heller was active in furthering social causes in Louisiana and was a prolific writer for the Jewish press. During 1909–11 he was president of the Central Conference of American Rabbis, a position that was almost denied him because of his Zionism. He sought to reconcile Reform Judaism and Zionism at a time when most Reform rabbis were strongly anti-Zionist. He stressed that Zionism was the fulfillment of the prophetic vision and that the people and Zionism were "one and inseparable." His position, widely unpopular at the time, gained adherents over time. In 1912 he became professor of Hebrew at Tulane University.

His son, JAMES GUTHEIM HELLER (1892–1971), was born in New Orleans, receiving his B.A. from Tulane and his M.A. from the University of Cincinnati (1914); he was ordained at Hebrew Union College in 1916. His first position, interrupted by war service as an army chaplain, was as assistant rabbi at Congregation Keneseth Israel in Philadelphia. In 1919 he went to Little Rock, Arkansas, and in 1920 to the Isaac M. Wise Temple in Cincinnati, where he remained until his career in the pulpit came to an end in 1952. Like his father he was a devoted disciple and later a biographer of Wise, but also like his father his adherence to Zionism was strong. Heller was active in the Central Conference of American Rabbis, serving as president during 1941–43. At the 1942 convention he helped secure the adoption of a resolution favoring the creation of a Jewish division to fight in World War II, which brought about a crystallization of the anti-Zionist element that established the American Council for Judaism. A graduate of the Cincinnati Conservatory of Music, Heller was a keen musician and his compositions include several pieces for the synagogue. He received a prize from the Society for the Publication of America Music for a string quartet that he composed. Upon retirement he became president of the Labor Zionist Organization of America, and then joined the Israel Bonds organization as executive director. In 1965 he published *Isaac Mayer Wise, His Life, Work and Thought*.

ADD. BIBLIOGRAPHY: J.G. Heller, *As If It Were Yesterday: A History of Isaac M. Wise Temple K.K. B'nai Yeshurun 1842–1942* (1942); idem, *Isaac M. Wise: His Life, Work and Thought* (1965).

[Sefton D. Temkin / Michael Berenbaum (2nd ed.)]

HELLER, ARYEH LEIB BEN JOSEPH HA-KOHEN OF STRY (1745?–1813), Galician rabbi, a descendant of Yom Tov Lipmann *Heller. Heller was born in Kalisz, and studied under Meshullam Igra of Pressburg. In his youth he served as rabbi of the small town of Rozhnyatov, Galicia, where he lived in poverty, and there he wrote his works. He went from there to Lemberg where he was a teacher of Talmud. The publication of his *Keẓot ha-Ḥoshen* brought him fame, and in 1788 he was elected rabbi of Stry (Pol. Stryi), where he established a large yeshivah. Stry was a center of Ḥasidism, and although Heller violently opposed the Ḥasidim, the ḥasidic rabbis themselves held him in great esteem and referred to him as a "prince of the Torah." The *dayyan* David ha-Kohen attacked him and even published a work *Ahavat David vi-Yhonatan* in criticism of the *Keẓot ha-Ḥoshen* but the work had no repercussions.

Heller's *Keẓot ha-Ḥoshen* (2 pts., Lemberg, 1788–96), on the Shulḥan Arukh, *Ḥoshen Mishpat*, was acclaimed by scholars and students of yeshivot with unusual enthusiasm as soon as it appeared and to the present day is regarded as a classic work of halakhic *pilpul*. Jacob Lorbeerbaum, one of the important *posekim* of his generation, devoted a considerable portion of his *Netivot ha-Mishpat* (Zolkiew, 1809–16) to a polemic with Heller. Heller replied to the criticisms in a special work, *Meshovev Netivot*. Heller died before he completed the work, which covers only chapters 1–133 of the *Ḥoshen Mishpat*. As a result of this profound work Lorberbaum made considerable changes and additions to his work, even though he does not mention the name of his opponent. Beside Lorberbaum many other well-known contemporary rabbis discussed the *Keẓot* in their own works, which in itself is an unusual phenomenon. Heller's other works were also enthusiastically received by scholars: *Avnei Millu'im* (Lemberg, 1816) on the Shulḥan Arukh, *Even ha-Ezer*, and the *Shev Shemateta* (*ibid.*, 1804), an examination and clarification of the laws concerning cases which involve doubt. All his works have gone through many editions and all still serve as a cornerstone of the method of Torah learning in the yeshivot, despite the radical changes in method effected in the Lithuanian yeshivot by Ḥayyim *Soloveichik. These three works may therefore be regarded as classics in the accepted sense of the word. It is worthy of note that his method of study gained adherents both in Poland and Lithuania despite the difference in method in both places. The *Keẓot* combines great acumen with logical reasoning, and is distinguished by its scintillating analysis, and its emphasis on the inner logic of the *halakhah*. Specially worthy of note are the introductions which Heller wrote to his works, particularly that to his *Shev Shematata*. It freely combines sound logic, extensive erudition, and a profound acumen in its explanation of aggadic topics and ideas and morals. Heller had three sons: DAVID, who published the *Shev Shematata*; JOSEPH DOV, rabbi of Weicislaw; and HIRSCH, who was rabbi of Uzhgorod. His son-in-law Solomon Judah *Rapoport (Shir), edited Heller's later works, prepared them for publication, provided them with indices, and attached his own comments. Heller's brothers, whom he mentions frequently in his works, were also outstanding talmudists. His brother Judah *Heller appended to the *Keẓot ha-Ḥoshen* his *Kunteres ha-Sefekot*.

BIBLIOGRAPHY: A. Stern, *Meliẓei Esh al Ḥodshei Tishri u-Marḥeshvan* (1933), 95b, no. 235; H. Tchernowitz, *Toledot ha-Posekim*, 3 (1947), 246–52; J.A. Kamelhar, *Dor De'ah* (1953[2]), 126–9; *Sefer Stry* (1962), 32, 111; S. Raz, in: *Shanah be-Shanah* (1963), 515–9; N. Ben-Menahem, *Mi-Sifrut Yisrael be-Ungaryah* (1958), 295–329.

HELLER, BERNARD (1897–1976), rabbi, teacher, author. Heller was born near Kishinev, Russia, and shortly after the pogrom there in 1903, came to South Philadelphia. He received a B.A. degree at the University of Pennsylvania in 1916, an M.A. degree in 1917 from Columbia University, and was ordained at Hebrew Union College in Cincinnati in 1920. After ordination Rabbi Heller served in Scranton, Pennsylvania, from 1920 to 1930 and became widely known for his religious, civic, and communal work. From the Scranton pulpit, he went to serve the B'nai B'rith Hillel Foundation at the University of Michigan, where he was awarded a Ph.D. degree in 1932. He was also awarded an honorary Litt.D. degree from the Jewish Theological Seminary of America.

In 1943 Heller was appointed to a commission established to eliminate prejudicial references to Jews in Catholic and Protestant textbooks. In 1949 he was named director of Restitution of Jewish Cultural Reconstruction, Inc., the agency charged with restoration of cultural property seized by the Nazis from Jewish people and institutions. From headquarters in Frankfurt-am-Main, Heller handled the distribution of the more than 30,000 confiscated volumes, many of them rare and valuable, which the Nazis had assembled for use in antisemitic institutes they hoped to establish after their victory.

In the early 1950s Heller traveled to India, where he served as rabbi of the liberal community of Bombay and then to Australia, and other parts of the world, where he lectured on Jewish topics and established Jewish study groups. From 1952 until his retirement he taught Jewish ethics and religion at the Hebrew Union College-Jewish Institute of Religion and lived in New York in close association with students and faculty of this institution and of the Jewish Theological Seminary, where he was awarded an honorary D.D. degree.

Heller published a number of works. His *Epistle to an Apostate* (1951) was an answer to the attempts of apostates to belittle and even defame Judaism, emphasizing, however, that it was not to be regarded as an attack on Christianity but only as an attempt to enlighten without counter-proselytizing. In his *Dawn of Dusk?* (1961) Heller showed how the antisemitic ideas of medieval Europe had prepared the ground for Nazism, but he avoided blaming all Germans for the Holocaust. His best-known work, however, is *The Odyssey of a Faith* (1942).

After years of rabbinic service, Dr. Heller pursued his interests in business as one of the founders of the predecessor to the United Brands Corporation and also of the West Indies Investment Company in the U.S. Virgin Islands.

Dr. Heller was deeply concerned with the survival of the Jewish people and with the transmission of Jewish religious and cultural heritage. His life reflected his abiding interest in philosophy, in Jewish thought, and in scholarship. By the terms of his Last Will and Testament, Dr. Heller established the Dr. Bernard Heller Foundation for the benefit of Jewish education and for the welfare of the Jewish people in Israel. To date, the Foundation has distributed close to $10 million for these purposes. Dr. Heller frequently referred to himself as a trustee of his wealth for Israel.

BIBLIOGRAPHY: *Yearbook Central Conference of American Rabbis.*

[Milton Ridvas Konvitz / Michael Berenbaum (2nd ed.)]

HELLER, BERNÁT (1871–1943), Hungarian scholar, Arabist, folklorist, and literary historian. Heller was born in Nagybicse, Hungary. He was ordained at the rabbinical seminary in Budapest, in 1896. From 1896 to 1919 he taught French and German and sometimes also Hungarian literature in a non-Jewish high school in Budapest. In 1919 he was appointed director of a newly established Jewish high school in Budapest. From 1922 to 1931 he taught Bible at the rabbinical seminary in Budapest, and thereafter he became superintendent of the Jewish schools in Budapest. Heller was a member of the ethnographical and Oriental societies of the Hungarian Academy of Sciences. Deeply influenced by his teachers W. *Bacher and I. *Goldziher, Heller devoted his life to the study of *aggadah* and

Islam. He tried to interpret aggadic literature by comparing its themes, motifs, and sources to the literatures of other peoples. He was particularly interested in tracing themes common to *aggadah* and early Christian literature and *aggadah* and Islamic legendary literature. As a folklorist and general literary historian, he also wrote comparative studies on Western European literature, particularly on Jewish influences on Western European and Hungarian novelists and poets. Heller was the author of most of the articles on the legends of Islam and the legends surrounding biblical personalities for the *Encyclopaedia of Islam* (4 vols., 1913–36) and for the German *Encyclopaedia Judaica* (10 vols., 1928–34). During the last years of his life Heller devoted himself to the study of the Apocrypha. He translated the Book of Tobias and the Additions to Daniel for A. Kahana's *Ha-Sefarim ha-Ḥiẓonim* (1947). Among Heller's works are *Die Bedeutung des arabischen Antar-Romans fuer die vergleichende Literaturkunde* (1931) and "Das hebraeische und arabische Maerchen" (in J. Bolte and G. Polivka's *Anmerkungen zu den Kinder-und Hausmaerchen der Brueder Grimm*, 4 (1930), 315–418). He was a frequent contributor to the *Revue des Etudes Juives*, the *Jewish Quarterly Review*, and the *Monatsschrift fuer die Geschichte und Wissenschaft des Judentums*. His devotion to his teacher I. Goldziher is reflected by his editing a volume in honor of his 60th birthday entitled *Keleti tanulmányok* ("Oriental Studies," 1910). He translated Goldziher's *Vorlesungen ueber den Islam* into Hungarian as *Előadások az iszlámról* (1912), and prepared a bibliography of Goldziher's works, *Bibliographie des oeuvres de Ignace Goldziher* (1927).

A gentle person, Heller greatly influenced many Hungarian rabbis. On his 70th birthday he was honored by a multilingual jubilee volume edited by A. Scheiber, *Jubilee Volume in Honour of Bernat Heller* (1941), which contains a bibliography of his writings.

BIBLIOGRAPHY: Budai Izraelita Hitközség, *Heller Bernát jubileuma* (1941); *A. Scheiber, in: S. Federbush (ed.), Ḥokhmat Yisrael be-Ma'arav Eiropah*, 1 (1959), 223–31.

[David Samuel Loewinger]

HELLER, BUNIM (1908–1998), Yiddish poet. Born in Warsaw to a ḥasidic family, Heller became a devoted communist and was forced to flee Poland for Paris in 1937 because of his political activities, returning to Warsaw in 1939. After the Blitzkrieg, Heller fled to Bialystok, where he lived for two years before escaping to the interior of Russia, living for the balance of the war in Alma-Ata, Kazakhstan, before moving to Moscow for a brief period. In 1947, Heller returned to Poland, where he lived in Lodz and Warsaw and became active in several Yiddish literary organizations. In 1956, he left Poland for Brussels and, in 1957, settled in Tel Aviv where he lived the remainder of his life. A life-long committed communist, Heller contributed his poems, essays, and translations to the radical Yiddish press in France, Poland, America, Argentina, Uruguay, Brazil, and Israel. Heller is perhaps best known for his poems of his hometown Jewish community, including "In Varshaver Geto Iz Khoydesh Nisn" ("It Is the Month of Nissan in the Warsaw Ghetto," 1948).

BIBLIOGRAPHY: LNYL, 3 (1960), 185ff; M. Ravitch, *Mayn Leksikon*, 3 (1958), 165–8; M. Gross-Zimmerman, *Intimer Videranand* (1964), 281–6. **ADD. BIBLIOGRAPHY:** D. Sfard, *Shrayber un Bikher* (1949), 65–75.

[Josef Schawinski / Marc Miller (2nd ed.)]

HELLER, ḤAYYIM (1878–1960), rabbinical and biblical scholar. Heller was born in Bialystok. From 1910 Heller served as rabbi in Lomza, Poland. In 1917 he settled in Berlin, where in 1922 he established a new type of yeshivah (Bet ha-Midrash ha-Elyon) for research in Bible and Talmud; his yeshivah attracted a number of graduates of Eastern European yeshivot, such as Samuel *Bialobocki and J.B. *Soloveitchik. In 1929 he joined the faculty of the Isaac Elchanan Theological Seminary, New York. After a short sojourn in Palestine, he returned to the United States, living first in Chicago and then New York. He published several volumes of novellae, including: the two-volume *Le-Ḥikrei Halakhot* (1924–1932); *Peri Ḥayyim* (Schulsinger edition of Maimonides' Yad, 1947); and *Kunteres be-Hilkhot Loveh u-Malveh* (1946). Other works, which are of great scholarly value, are: his critical edition of Maimonides' *Sefer ha-Mitzvot* (1914, 1946²), based on two different translations (Mss. Munich 213, and Margoliouth, Cat, 2 (1904), nos. 503–5), the Arabic original, early editions, and others; an annotated edition of the *Peshitta* version of Genesis and Exodus in Hebrew characters (1927–29); the Samaritan Pentateuch (1923); a critical essay on the Palestinian Targum (*Al ha-Targum ha-Yerushalmi la-Torah*, 1921); and on the Septuagint, critical annotations to Mandelkern's Bible Concordance *Al Targum ha-Shivim ba-Konkordanzyah Heikhal ha-Kodesh* (1944), with an introduction in English. In German, Heller published *Untersuchungen ueber die Peshitta*, 1 (1911) and *Untersuchungen zur Septuaginta*, 1 (1932). Heller was one of the very few modern scholars who combined a vast and deep talmudic erudition of the traditional type with a thorough competence in the methods of textual research. He defended the traditional masoretic text against the Bible critics.

BIBLIOGRAPHY: *H. Seidman, in: S. Federbush (ed.), Ḥokhmat Yisrael be-Ma'arav Eiropah* (1963), 96ff.; J.L. Soloveitchik, in: *Hadoar*, 40 (1961), 400ff.; T. Preschel, in: *Or ha-Mizraḥ*, 9 (1962), 74–76; 10 (1963), 52 (bibl.).

HELLER, HERMANN (1891–1933), German political scientist. Born in Austria he was active in the Socialist movement, and contributed to a non-Marxian social democratic theory, believing that it would more easily fit the framework of national traditions. He warned against the danger of Fascism and dictatorship and had to leave Germany early in 1933. He died that year in Madrid where he had been offered a professorship. Heller was one of the small group who revived political science in Germany in the 1920s, after it had stagnated through legal positivism and normativism from the middle of the 19th century. He was regarded as one of the leading political scientists of his time; as such he contributed the article on political science for the *Encyclopedia of Social Sciences* (1934). He placed political science firmly among the social sciences, stressed social power relationships as one of its major focuses, while denying the contention that political science is necessarily devoid of moral content. His major work, *Staatslehre*, was published posthumously and unfinished (1934).

BIBLIOGRAPHY: IESS, S.V.

[Edwin Emanuel Gutmann]

HELLER, JEHIEL BEN AARON (1814–1863), Lithuanian author and preacher. Heller was rabbi of Glusk (district of Volkovisk) before he became rabbi of Plungian where he remained until his death. Like his brother Joshua, Heller was a disciple of R. Israel *Salanter to whose journal, *Tevunah*, he contributed. He became a popular preacher of the *Musar movement, on various occasions delivering his sermons in German. His published works are *Shenei Perakim*, or *Kevod Melekh* (St. Petersburg, 1852), "published by order of the Russian government" and translated into German by Leon *Mandelstamm, dealing with the duty of loyalty to the ruler and obedience to the laws of the country, as laid down in the Bible and Talmud; *Ammudei Or* (1855), responsa, in his introduction to which Heller deplores the general neglect of Talmud study and expresses his apprehension of the attacks on Jewish beliefs by the protagonists of the *Haskalah; *Or Yesharim* (1857), a commentary on the *Haggadah* of Passover; and *Oteh Or* (1865), a commentary on the Song of Songs.

BIBLIOGRAPHY: Fuenn, Keneset, 521f.; *Yahadut Lita* (1967), 46.

[Jacob Hirsch Haberman]

HELLER, JOSEPH (1923–1999), U.S. novelist and dramatist. Heller was born in Brooklyn, New York, and during World War II joined the Air Force. He attended college after the war and received a Fulbright to study at Oxford. He later worked as an advertising writer and manager for leading magazines and published short stories before turning seriously to literature. His bestselling novel *Catch-22* (1961, and later made into a film) was an outstanding satire on the military mind, based on World War II experiences. It was – and is – so popular that the phrase "catch-22" won a place in the English language. (Heller returned to the characters of Catch-22 with *Closing Time* [1994]). He also wrote the play *We Bombed in New Haven* (1968). His memorable dark novel about business culture, *Something Happened* (1974), was comically offset by his satirical portrait of an American-Jewish English professor in *Good as Gold* (1979). *God Knows* (1984) is the imaginary death-bed autobiography of King David, whose voice is shrewd, world-weary, as well as flamboyant. A recovery from illness led to Heller's *No Laughing Matter* (with Speed Vogel, 1986). His posthumous novel, *Portrait of an Artist as an Old Man* (2000), a mixture of large and often biting humor, traces the struggles of Eugene Pota to find his commanding theme before his reputation diminishes. Heller's own autobiography is *Now and Then: From Coney Island to Here* (1998).

BIBLIOGRAPHY: M.J. Bruccoli, *Joseph Heller: A Descriptive Bibliography* (2002); D. Craig, *Tilting at Mortality: Narrative Strategies in Joseph Heller's Fiction* (1997); S. Pinsker, *Understanding Joseph Heller* (1991); A. Sorkin, *Conversations with Joseph Heller* (1993).

[Lewis Fried (2nd ed.)]

HELLER, JOSEPH ELIJAH (1888–1957), Hebrew writer. Born in Ponivezh, Lithuania, Heller was a graduate of Berlin University, and lived in Russia and Germany, where he was one of the editors of the *Encyclopaedia Judaica* (German) and of the *Enziklopedyah Yisre'elit "Eshkol"* (1929–32). In 1938 he moved to London, where he taught and edited the Zionist Organization's journal, *Tarbut*. Heller published studies of Jewish and general philosophy in German, English, and Hebrew, and was a contributor to various Hebrew periodicals including *Haolam, Hadoar*, and others. His analysis of Aḥad Ha-Am's philosophy was published in *Aḥad Ha-Am, ha-Ish, Po'alo ve-Torato* (ed. by L. Simon, 1955). He also wrote *The Zionist Idea* (1947), *Ḥ.N. Bialik* (1944), and translated several of Plato's works into Hebrew.

[Getzel Kressel]

HELLER, JOSHUA BEN AARON (1814–80), Lithuanian rabbi and author. Heller was a preacher in Grodno and became successively rabbi of Polangen and of Telschi. He was a disciple of Israel *Salanter and played an important role in the *Musar movement. Heller fought against the inroads of secularism menacing Jewish religious life in Russia. He emphasized that teaching methods at the yeshivah must imbue the students with strong religious convictions. Heller contributed to the Hebrew periodical *Ha-Levanon* and published the following works: *Divrei Yehoshu'a* (1865), on Jewish ethics and philosophy outlining a full ethical "training program"; *Toledot Yehoshu'a* (1866), a commentary on *Avot*; *Ma'oz ha-Dat* (1873), a defense, in dialogue form, of the oral tradition extolling the wisdom of the talmudic rabbis; *Ḥosen Yehoshu'a* (1872), a guide to Torah study.

BIBLIOGRAPHY: D. Katz, *Tenu'at ha-Musar*, 2 (1954^2), 349–64; Fuenn, Keneset, 429.

[Jacob Hirsch Haberman]

HELLER, JUDAH (d. 1819), Hungarian talmudist. Heller was born in Kalisch, Galicia. He was a publican in one of the nearby villages but after losing his wealth and facing starvation, he moved to Lemberg, where he acted as tutor to the children of well-to-do parents. He met Joseph Teomim, author of the *Peri Megadim*, who was also a tutor in Lemberg. There Heller compiled his *Kunteres ha-Sefekot* and was in frequent contact with his brother, Aryeh Leib *Heller, author of the *Kezot ha-Ḥoshen*, who at the time lived in Rozhnyatov near Lemberg. The brothers decided to publish the *Kezot ha-Ḥoshen* pt. 1 (Lemberg, 1788) and to attach to it the *Kunteres ha-Sefekot*. The appearance of the work brought fame to the brothers, and as a result Judah was appointed rabbi in Hungary, first in Munkacs and then in Nagyszollos. In 1802 he was appointed rabbi of Sziget. In 1805 he refused an invitation to become rabbi of Grosswardein since, although it was a smaller community, he was unwilling to leave Sziget, where he remained for the rest of his life. Heller was an intimate of Moses *Sofer. Apart from his *Kunteres ha-Sefekot*, his *Terumat ha-Keri*, on the Tur and the Shulḥan Arukh, *Ḥoshen Mishpat*, has also been published (1858). He is also known to have compiled a work on the Bible, but the manuscript appears to have been lost.

BIBLIOGRAPHY: P.Z. Schwartz, *Shem ha-Gedolim me-Ereẓ Hagar*, 1 (1914), 376 no. 12; A. Stern, *Meliẓei Esh al Ḥodshei Nisan ve-Iyyar* (1930), 129–33; N. Ben-Menahem, *Mi-Sifrut Yisrael be-Ungaryah* (1958), 295–329.

[Naphtali Ben-Menahem]

HELLER, STEPHEN (1813–1888), Austrian pianist and composer. His first name originally was Jacob; he was baptized when his parents converted to Catholicism. Heller, who was born in Budapest, studied in Vienna, and became a virtuoso pianist. When illness interrupted his career, he accepted a post as a music teacher in Augsburg and turned to composing. In 1838 he settled in Paris, where he earned the respect of his contemporaries, especially Schumann. Heller wrote for the piano in a subtle, romantic, and evocative mood, and produced more than 150 short compositions. These were frequently played by pianists of his day, but since they were not suited for concert halls they were later rarely played.

BIBLIOGRAPHY: Grove's Dict; Riemann-Gurlitt; MGG.

[Claude Abravanel]

HELLER, THEODOR (1869–1935), Austrian psychologist. Heller, who was born in Vienna, was among the pioneers of *Heilpaedagogik*, a form of clinical psychology devoted to the application of therapeutic techniques in an educational framework, operating generally under Freudian thought and theory. He founded the Heilpaedagogische Anstalt in Vienna, and wrote *Grundriss der Heilpaedagogik* (1904; 1925[3]). His research covered the fields of child, adolescent, abnormal, and educational psychology. His published works include *Studien zur Blindenpsychologie* (1904), *Paedagogische Therapie fuer praktische Aerzte* (1914), and *Ueber Psychologie und Psychopathologie des Kindes* (1911; 1925[2]). He was coeditor of *Enzyklopaedisches Handbuch des Kinderschutzes und der Jugendfuersorge* (2 vols., 1911).

BIBLIOGRAPHY: A. Grinstein, *Index of Psychoanalytic Writings*, 2 (1957), 860–1.

[Aaron Lichtenstein]

HELLER, YOM TOV LIPMANN BEN NATHAN HA-LEVI (1579–1654), Moravian rabbi, commentator on the Mishnah. Heller was born in Wallerstein, Bavaria. He received his education in the home of his grandfather, Moses Wallerstein, as well as, among others, from *Judah Loew b. Bezalel (the Maharal) of Prague. Besides his great talmudic knowledge, he engaged in the study of Kabbalah, religious philosophy, and Hebrew grammar and also acquired an extensive general knowledge, particularly of mathematics, astronomy, and natural sciences. In 1597, when only 18 years of age, he was appointed *dayyan* in Prague, and served in this office for 28 years, during which period he acquired renown for his profound knowledge and for his integrity. In 1625 he was appointed rabbi of Nikolsburg (Moravia) but in that same year moved to Vienna where he was elected *av bet din*. Through his endeavor the suburb of Leopoldstadt (at that time still outside the boundaries of Vienna) was confirmed as a special residential quarter for Jews. Heller saw to its communal organization and orderly administration, until the settlement became "a city filled with the qualities of wisdom, wealth, and honor" (*Megillat Eivah*). In 1627 he returned to Prague.

When, during the Thirty Years' War (1618–48), it was decreed that the Jews of Bohemia must pay a heavy tax to the government, the leaders of the Prague community, including Heller, imposed taxes upon its members to repay the loan which the community had borrowed to pay the impost. Several of the poor who opposed the assessment accused Heller of favoring the wealthy and, when their plot to remove him from office failed, slandered him to the emperor Ferdinand II, accusing him of contempt of the state and of insulting Christianity. He was imprisoned on June 25, 1629, and transferred to Vienna. When during the investigation he was asked how he dare defend the Talmud since it had been ordered to be burned by the pope, he replied: "Jews are obliged to obey the Talmud which is the main Oral Law." The sentence of death passed upon him by a court of Catholic priests was, "by grace of the emperor," commuted to a large monetary fine. Through the efforts of the Jews of Prague the other heavy penalties imposed were partly reduced. Instead of his books being banned, only the fragments on which he was condemned were erased, and the prohibition imposed on his serving in the rabbinate throughout the Austrian Empire was limited to the district of Prague. After spending 40 days in prison he returned to Prague in August 1629. He appointed the fifth of Tammuz, the day on which the order for his arrest was issued, as a fast day for all the members of his family. The details were described by Heller in his autobiography, *Megillat Eivah*.

In 1631 he removed to Poland, living first in Lublin and subsequently in Brest-Litovsk and Nemirov (among other things he composed a eulogy on the destruction of Nemirov in the *Chmielnicki massacres). From 1634 to 1643 he served as rabbi of Vladimir-Volynski. Heller took part in the rabbinical activities of the *Council of Four Lands and was one of the members of the permanent *battei-din* and one of the chief speakers at the conventions during the fairs in Lublin, Jaroslaw, and other places. He demanded that the **takkanot* and bans of 1587 prohibiting the purchase of rabbinic office be renewed and strengthened. This incited against him the anger of "those that hate without cause, and mendacious enemies." As a result of a calumny, a decree of expulsion from

Vladimir was issued against him, but this decree too was rescinded through the efforts of his influential friends in Warsaw. In 1643 he was called to serve in the Cracow rabbinate and after the death in 1648 of *Joshua b. Joseph, author of the *Meginnei Shelomo*, he also headed the Cracow yeshivah. During his residence in Cracow, Heller prepared a second edition of his *Tosefot Yom Tov* (Prague, 1614–17; Cracow 1643–44^{2}). Following the persecutions of 1648–49 he concerned himself with the amelioration of the lot of *agunot*. On his death Zelig Margulies testified of him that "he did not leave the wherewithal to purchase shrouds even though he was the *av bet din* of Cracow… all this, because he never took dishonest money" (Introd. *Ḥibburei Likkutim* (Amsterdam, 1715)). Contrary to popular belief, Heller was married only once. His wife's name was Rachel. In his commentary *Tosefot Yom Tov*, Heller mentions in various places his four sons, Moses, Samuel, Abraham, and Levi.

Heller's attitude toward non-Jews was very different from that of his teacher the Maharal of Prague. According to the Maharal, the election of the Jewish people by God reduced the divine image and innate spirituality of non-Jews. Heller disagreed, asserting that everyone, Jew and gentile, is judged by God according to his deeds. In addition, Heller did not believe that the talmudic proscription against "Greek wisdom" included all secular knowledge. He was particularly inclined toward all knowledge that increases the understanding of the world, including natural sciences and astronomy.

Along with his success as a rabbi, Heller failed at a number of his endeavors, which speak volumes concerning his character. He failed to expand the educational curriculum of Ashkenazi Jewry. He attempted but later abandoned his efforts to block the acceptance of Joseph *Caro's *Shulḥan Arukh*. His demand to prohibit the purchase of rabbinic office led to his arrest (see above), and he failed to pass on to the next generation his love of philosophy, astronomy, and science.

Of Heller's many works, which testify to his diversified scholarship, his commentary to the Mishnah is the most famous. He named this *Tosefot Yom Tov* because its purpose was to serve as an addition (*tosefet*) and exposition, supplement and work of source reference to the Mishnah commentary of Obadiah of *Bertinoro. Heller traced the sources of the Bertinoro commentary, explained obscurities, examined and also criticized its conclusions in the sphere of *halakhah*, and made linguistic comments. He explained the words grammatically, noted the *halakhah* on the basis of the Talmud and the *rishonim* and *aḥaronim* and took care to establish accurate readings, most of which he added to the second edition of his commentary, through clarification and elucidation of the text on the basis of various manuscripts and earlier published works. Heller endeavored to reconcile the contradictions between one Mishnah and another by means of straightforward and logical rationalization. All his comments are formulated with the utmost simplicity – and here he follows in the footsteps of his teacher Judah Loew b. Bezalel, who opposed the method of *pilpul*. Despite his positive attitude to Kabbalah, he refrained from relying upon it in deciding the *halakhah*, since "in explaining the Talmud, we have no dealings at all with esoteric matters" (*Ma'adanei Yom Tov*; Ber. 1). Heller even tried at one point to prevent the publication of kabbalistic works. When making halakhic decisions, he refrained from relying on kabbalistic leniencies or stringencies that ran counter to the plain sense of the Talmud. In his opinion the Mishnah might be interpreted differently from the explanation given in the Talmud, "providing no decisions which contradict the view of the authors of the *Gemara* are given" (*Tosefot Yom Tov* to Naz. 5:5). In his introduction he formulated his attitude to the commentary of Bertinoro: "My task, however, is to examine carefully in the Mishnah in order to see whether anything requires explanation that has not been explained in the commentary of the Rav [Bertinoro], or whether there is a contradiction from some other Mishnah to which he has not drawn attention, and also whether there is anything in his commentary for which an explanation and reason has to be given, as well as if there be any contradiction in the commentary itself, and more so from the Mishnah."

In his interpretation of the Mishnah, Heller endeavored to put into effect what Judah Loew impressed upon him in investigating the *halakhah*: the deduction of the halakhic ruling in the Mishnah. Through his examination of the text of the Mishnah he arrived at halakhic decisions since he was of the opinion that the Mishnah was to be accepted as the basis of the *halakhah*, while *Asher b. Jehiel (the Rosh) was to be regarded as a general decisor. He stressed this view in his *Ma'adanei Melekh ve-Leḥem Ḥamudot* (pts. 1 and 4, Prague, 1628, 1619; pts. 2 and 3 still in Ms., also entitled *Ma'adanei Yom Tov*). In his introduction to part 4 (entitled *Ma'adanei Melekh u-Filpula Ḥarifta*) he summarizes the development of the *halakhah* and deals especially with the importance of Isaac Alfasi, Maimonides, Asher b. Jehiel, and the latter's son Jacob, author of the *Turim*. After differentiating between the method of those who amplify, like Alfasi, and those who curtail, like Maimonides, he summarizes the contribution of Asher b. Jehiel and Jacob b. Asher and remarks that it is fitting that the work of the Rosh should be a guide for halakhic decision. In his exposition he seeks to supplement Asher b. Jehiel, to explain the contents of his writing, and to add new laws to them so that "all the children of Israel will turn to listen to Rabbenu Asher." A digest of the commentary, entitled *Ikkar Tosefot Yom Tov*, was published by Meshullam b. Joel Katz (Lemberg, 1790).

Of his other works, all of which are distinguished by their clarity of language and outstanding style, the following of his expository works should be mentioned: (1) a commentary on the *Beḥinat Olam* of Jedaiah ha-Penini (Prague, 1598); (2) *Ẓurat Beit ha-Mikdash* (*ibid.*, 1602) on the plan of the Temple according to the prophecy of Ezekiel; (3) glosses to the *Givat ha-Moreh* of Joseph b. Isaac ha-Levi (*ibid.*, 1611); (4) *Malbushei Yom Tov* (1895–97), *hassagot and novellae on Mordecai Jaffe's *Levush* on *Oraḥ Ḥayyim* in two parts.

The following works have remained in manuscript: (5) *Tuv Ta'am*, a commentary on the kabbalistic part of Ḥiyya

b. Asher's commentary on the Pentateuch; (6) expositions on Abraham ibn Ezra's Pentateuch commentary; (7) *Leket Shoshannim* on the *Arugat ha-Bosem* of S. *Archivolti, who sent Heller the book for examination (*Tosefot Yom Tov*, to Tam. 7, end); (8) *Torat ha-Asham* on the *Torat Ḥattat* of Moses *Isserles; (9) *Parashat ha-Ḥodesh* on the laws of the new moon in Maimonides' *Mishneh Torah*; (10) *haggahot* to the *Kaftor va-Feraḥ* of Estori ha-Farḥi.

Beside his responsa (published in collections: *Ge'onei Batra'ei* (Turka, 1764), *Bayit Ḥadash ha-Ḥadashot* (Koretz, 1785), and *Ẓemaḥ Ẓedek* (Amsterdam, 1675)), a sermon (Prague, 1626), and approbations given in connection with his activities in the Council of Four Lands, Heller compiled various *piyyutim* and *seliḥot*, in connection with the massacres of 1618–20 in Prague and of 1648 in the Ukraine, which express with great fidelity the worries and sufferings of the Jews during the persecution in his lifetime. Exceptionally well-known is his autobiography *Megillat Eivah* (Breslau, 1818) which appeared in many editions (among others, with a German translation by Seligmann Kisch, Prague, 1849, with Yiddish translations, 1864, 1880, and with an English translation, 1991; see bibliography). This work, containing vivid descriptions of events in Heller's life and also of the communities of his time, serves as a valuable source for Jewish history in the first half of the 17th century. Of his Yiddish works intended for "the common people and women," his *Berit Melaḥ* (Prague, 1552?; Cracow, 1665) on the laws of salting and rinsing meat, and the Yiddish translation of Asher b. Jehiel's *Orḥot Ḥayyim* (Prague, 1626) should be noted. A letter of 1619 in Yiddish from Heller to a female relative, dealing with family matters, was published in 1911.

BIBLIOGRAPHY: Davidson, Oẓar, 4 (1933), 398; Zunz, Gesch, index; Zunz, Lit Poesie, 426f.; Zunz, Poesie, 342, 362; G. Wolf, *Ferdinand II und die Juden* (1859), 16f.; idem, *Die Juden in der Leopoldstadt* (1864), 7, 8, 11, 18; Perles, in: MGWJ, 16 (1867), 306f.; D. Kaufmann, *ibid.*, 37 (1893), 380; Graetz-Rabbinowitz, (1899), 46–50, 112–4; Steinschneider, in: MGWJ, 47 (1903), 285; 49 (1905), 490; S.M. Chones, *Toledot ha-Posekim* (1911), 167–72; A. Landau and B. Wachstein (ed.), *Juedische Privatbriefe aus dem Jahre 1619* (1911), 49, no. 20a; A.Z. Schwartz, in: *Festschrift… D.S. Simonsen* (1923), 206–12; G. Kisch, in: JGGJČ, 1 (1929), 421–47; I. Halpern, in: KS, 7 (1930/31), 140–8, 482; idem, *Pinkas Va'ad Arba Araẓot* (1945), index; M. Grunwald, *Vienna* (1936), 86–87; Zahavi-Goldhammer, in: *Arim ve-Immahot be-Yisrael*, 1 (1946), 211f.; 4 (1950), 264; Pograbinsky, *ibid.*, 2 (1948), 271, 280–2; H. Tchernowitz, *Toledot ha-Posekim*, 3 (1947), 127–37; Klemperer, in: HJ, 12 (1950), 51–66; I.D. Beth-Halevy, *Rabbi Yom Tov Lipmann Heller* (Heb., 1954); J.L. Maimon (ed.), *Li-Khevod Yom Tov* (1956); B. Katz, *Rabbanut, Ḥasidut, Haskalah*, 1 (1956), 91–97; J. Fraenkel, *Jews of Austria* (1967), 320–1. **ADD. BIBLIOGRAPHY:** Yom Tov Lippmann Heller, *A Chronicle of Hardship and Hope: An Autobiographical Account* (1991); J.M. Davis, in: *Science in Context*, 10:4 (1997); M. Herskovics, *Two Guardians of the Faith: The History and Distinguished Lineage of Rabbi Yom Tov Lipmann Heller and Rabbi Aryeh Leib Heller* (2000); J.M. Davis, *Yom-Tov Lipmann Heller: A Portrait of a Seventeenth Century Rabbi* (2004); Y. Ben Hayyim, in: *Koveẓ Beit Aharon ve-Yisra'el*, 10:1 1995), 131–35.

[Josef Horovitz / David Derovan (2nd ed.)]

HELLER, ẒEVI HIRSCH (1776–1834), Galician and Hungarian rabbi. Born in Zamoscz, Galicia, Heller was already noted for his acumen in his youth and was designated "Hirsch Ḥarif" ("Hirsch, the sharp-witted"). His first rabbinate was in Brugl, Silesia, and in 1817 he was appointed head of the yeshivah in Brody, Galicia, and many of his students later became renowned talmudists, among them Ẓevi Hirsch *Chajes. Because of a calumny he was expelled from Brody and moved to Hungary. He first became rabbi in Ungvar, and c. 1820 was appointed rabbi of Bonyhad, where he served for 13 years. During this period the Reform controversy began, and its adherents in the town fought against him. As a result he accepted the invitation of the Ungvar community to return there in 1833, but later that year he was elected rabbi and *av bet din* of the community of Obuda (= Old Buda); however, after seven months there, he fell ill and died. Responsa to him are found in Moses *Sofer's *Ḥatam Sofer* (*Even ha-Ezer*, 1:94, 2:30).

BIBLIOGRAPHY: P.Z. Schwartz, *Shem ha-Gedolim me-Ereẓ Hagar*, 1 (1913), 215–6; *Arim ve-Immahot be-Yisrael*, 4 (1950), 7–8; 6 (1955), 79, 201; A. Buechler, *A zsidók története Budapesten* (1901), 324–5.

[Samuel Weingarten-Hakohen]

HELLERSTEIN, ALVIN K. (1933–), U.S. federal judge. Hellerstein was born in New York City in 1933. He received his B.A. from Columbia College in 1954. After graduating from Columbia Law School in 1956, he clerked for the Hon. Edmund Palmieri of the U.S. District Court for the Southern District of New York, and served in the Judge Advocate General's Corps of the U.S. Army from 1957 to 1960. He practiced law with the firm of Strook and Strook and Lavan in New York City for nearly four decades.

In 1998 President William J. Clinton nominated him to serve on the U.S. District Court for the Southern District of New York. In less than a decade on the federal bench, Hellerstein demonstrated skill in resolving complex issues. For example, he sustained the regulations issued by the administrator of the fund to compensate victims of the attack of terrorists on the World Trade Center in New York City on September 11, 2001.

Judge Hellerstein also displayed a strong commitment to the independence of the judiciary. He presided over the 2005 case in which, under the Freedom of Information Act (FOIA), the American Civil Liberties Union (ACLU) requested all the photos and videos that touched off the prisoner abuse scandal at Abu Gharib prison in Iraq. The government argued against disclosure on two grounds: national security and human rights, stating that publication of the photos would have the effect of causing American military personnel in Iraq to die and that "releasing the photos would reveal the prisoner's identities, a violation of their rights under the Geneva Conventions." After viewing eight of the photos, Judge Hellerstein concluded that civilians and detainees could be protected against insults and public curiosity by blocking facial characteristics, and ordered the production of the 144 pictures and videos in this redacted form. Judge Hellerstein wrote: "No one is above the law.... my task is not to defer to our worst fears, but to interpret and apply the law, in this case, the Freedom of Information Act, which advances values important to our society, transparency and accountability in government.... they are at the very heart of the values for which we fight in Afghanistan and Iraq. There is a risk that the enemy will seize upon the publicity of the photographs and seek to use such publicity as a pretext for enlistments and violent acts. But the education and debate that such publicity will foster will strengthen our purpose and, by enabling such deficiencies as may be perceived to be debated and corrected, show our strength as a vibrant and functioning democracy to be emulated.... "

Judge Hellerstein also rendered strong opinions on the First Amendment. In 2000 he ruled that postal employees may post political messages on a union bulletin board. In 2002 Hellerstein joined Judge Harold Baer of the federal court in Brooklyn in an opinion requiring the City of New York to allow the Ku Klux Klan to demonstrate, wearing their masks, in lower Manhattan. The two judges were of the view that the New York Anti-Mask law violated the First Amendment rights of Klan members to anonymous speech and that the city had engaged in discrimination on the basis of the viewpoint of the speakers, by enforcing the statute selectively. The appellate court reversed this view, and the Supreme Court declined to hear the case.

BIBLIOGRAPHY: Cases: *ACLU v. Department of Defense*, F. Supp. 2d (SDNY 2005); *Burrus v. Vegliante*, 247 F. Supp. 2d 372 (SDNY 2000); *Church of American Knights of Ku Klux Klan v. Kerik*, 232 F. Supp. 2d 205 (SDNY 2002).

[Edward McGlynn Gaffney, Jr. (2nd ed.)]

HELLINGER, MARK (1903–1947), U.S. columnist and playwright. A reporter for the *New York Daily News*, in 1923 Hellinger became the first columnist to write regularly about Broadway. In 1930 he moved to the *New York Daily Mirror*. He wrote musicals, plays, film scripts, and novels, and the last *Ziegfeld Follies* to be produced by Ziegfeld himself in 1930.

In 1937 he went to Hollywood as a producer and became known as a master of screen violence. Some of the films he produced include *They Drive by Night* (starring George Raft, 1940); *Torrid Zone* (James Cagney, 1940); *High Sierra* (Humphrey Bogart, 1941); the comedy *Affectionately Yours* (Rita Hayworth, 1941); *Manpower* (Edward G. Robinson, 1941); the musical *Thank Your Lucky Stars* (Eddie Cantor, 1943); *Between Two Worlds* (John Garfield, 1944); *The Killers* (Burt Lancaster, 1946), which won the Edgar Alan Poe Award for Best Motion Picture; *Brute Force* (Lancaster, 1947); *The Two Mrs. Carrolls* (Bogart, 1947); and *The Naked City* (Howard Duff, 1948).

In 1931 *Moon over Broadway*, a collection of his short stories, was published. To find material and to add verisimilitude to the articles and stories he wrote, Hellinger researched real-life crimes, with the aid of such friends as gangsters Al Capone, Lucky Luciano, Bugsy Siegel, and Dutch Schultz.

In 1944 he worked as a war correspondent for Hearst newspapers.

In 1949 a theater on Broadway that had been built in 1930 was renamed in his honor. The Mark Hellinger Theater showcased such Broadway classics as *Two on the Aisle*, *My Fair Lady*, *The Sound of Music*, *On a Clear Day You Can See Forever*, *Sugar Babies*, *Merlin*, and *Tango Argentino*.

BIBLIOGRAPHY: J. Bishop, *The Mark Hellinger Story: A Biography of Broadway and Hollywood* (1952).

[Ruth Beloff (2nd ed.)]

HELLMAN, CLARISSE DORIS (1910–1973), U.S. historian of science. Hellman was born and raised in New York City. She studied astronomy and mathematics at Vassar College, received an M.A. in the history of science from Radcliffe College in 1931, and her Ph.D. from Columbia University in 1943. Her dissertation, *The Comet of 1577: Its Place in the History of Astronomy*, was published by Columbia University Press in 1944 (rev. ed., AMS Press, 1971). Hellman taught as an adjunct professor of history of science at the Pratt Institute from 1951 to 1966 and also briefly at New York University from 1964 to 1966. From 1966 until her death she was professor of history at Queens College and the CUNY Graduate Center. A specialist in the history of Renaissance science, particularly astronomers and astronomy, Hellman edited and translated Max Caspar's biography *Johannes Kepler* (1959) and published articles and reviews on Tycho Brahe and Georg Samuel Doerffel, as well as Kepler. She was a fellow of the Royal Astronomical Society and the American Association for the Advancement of Science. As secretary of the U.S. National Committee of the International Union of History and Philosophy of Science (1958–60), she served as a delegate to the Ninth International Congress of the History of Science in Barcelona, Spain, in 1959, representing the National Academy of Sciences and the National Research Council. Her papers are found in the Columbia University Rare Book and Manuscript Library.

BIBLIOGRAPHY: P.E. Hyman and D. Dash Moore (eds.), *Jewish Women in America*, 1 (1997), 617–18; Obituary, *New York Times* (March 29, 1973).

[Harriet Pass Freidenreich (2nd ed.)]

HELLMAN, ISAIAS WOLF (1842–1920), U.S. banker. Hellman was born in Rickendorf, Bavaria. He immigrated to Los Angeles in 1859 with his younger brother, Herman. For six years he clerked in a cousin's dry goods store until in 1865 he bought a dry goods and shoe store of his own. Hellman early began to buy real estate, ultimately dealing in city lots, subdivision property, and ranch lands, and in time he became the largest single owner of property in Los Angeles. Allowing friends to keep gold dust and other valuables in his safe, he soon established the Hellman Temple and Company Bank (1868), which he sold to his partners a few years later. Hellman founded the Farmers and Merchants Bank of Los Angeles in 1871, beginning a career in banking which was to make him president or leading stockholder of a large number of banking enterprises in the Los Angeles area. Because of his staunch conservatism and unquestioned probity, Hellman was able to maintain the soundness of his banks in depressions and panics. He single-handedly brought an end to the boom of 1887 by restricting credit on speculative real estate, thus saving the city from serious potential damage. Hellman founded the Main Street Railway trolley line in Los Angeles, which he later merged into the Huntington and the Pacific Electric Street Railway Systems. In 1900 he moved to San Francisco to become president of the Nevada National Bank of San Francisco, later consolidated with the Wells Fargo Bank (1905), then with the Union Trust Company (1924), which was founded by Hellman in 1893.

A major philanthropist of his era, Hellman founded the first synagogue of Congregation B'nai B'rith in 1872, serving as its president (1871–82). In 1865, together with a Catholic and a Protestant associate, he contributed land for the establishment of the University of Southern California. He was especially generous in contributions to orphanages in the Los Angeles and San Francisco areas. Hellman served on the Board of Regents of the University of California (1881–1918). He was president of the Los Angeles Clearing House Association (1887–1900).

HERMAN WOLF (1843–1906) was the brother of Isaias, with whom he immigrated to Los Angeles. Like his brother, Herman was a pioneer in the economic development of Los Angeles. After working in a grocery business, he served as cashier in his brother's Farmers and Merchants Bank, then established the Merchants National Bank. It became one of the principal banks of southern California, later managed by his sons MARCO (b. 1878) and IRVING (b. 1883) until it closed in the depression of the 1930s.

BIBLIOGRAPHY: H. Newmark (ed.), *Sixty Years in Southern California, 1853–1913* (1916), passim; R.G. Cleland and F.B. Putnam, *Isais W. Hellman and the Farmers and Merchants Bank* (1965); L.P. Gartner and M. Vorspan, *History of the Jews of Los Angeles* (1970).

[Max Vorspan]

HELLMAN, JACOB (1880–1950), labor Zionist leader and editor. Born in Talson, Latvia, Hellman studied at yeshivot, and from 1897 at Frankfurt and the University of Marburg (where he was a pupil of Hermann *Cohen), completing his studies at the University of Berne in 1910. He took part in Zionist activities from his early youth, after having displayed some interest in the Territorialist movement and the Social Revolutionaries. He lived in Berlin and Riga and during the war years in Russia, where he became one of the founders of the *Ẓe'irei Zion movement. When he settled in Riga in 1919, he became one of the prominent leaders of Latvian Jewry, especially of the Zionist Socialist movement, and in 1920 was elected to the Latvian parliament. He edited various periodicals in Riga, including the Yiddish daily *Frimorgen* and as one of the founders of *Hitaḥadut he traveled on its behalf in various countries and became a member of the central body of the World Union of Po'alei Zion. In 1933 Hellman served as editor in chief of *Dos Naye Vort*, the Po'alei Zion organ in Warsaw, and remained in that post until 1936. After attending the 21st Zionist Congress (1939), he went to Argentina as the representative of the *World Jewish Congress. There he also became active in Zionist and general Jewish affairs and was a regular contributor to the press. His book *Yerusholaim* (in Yiddish) was published posthumously (1951; Hebrew translation, 1957). In 1952 his remains were transferred from Argentina and he was reinterred in Jerusalem.

BIBLIOGRAPHY: M. Gertz, *25 Yor Yidishe Presse in Letland* (1933), 30–38, 43–49; Y. Uri, *Ketavim Nivḥarim*, 2 (1967), 79–83; G. Ḥanokh, *Bi-Demi ha-Sa'ar* (1962), 209–10; *Yahadut Latvia* (1953), 421–3.

[Getzel Kressel]

HELLMAN, LILLIAN FLORENCE (1905–1984), U.S. playwright. Sources vary about the year of her birth. The Library of Congress lists it as 1906. The *New York Times*, the newspaper of record, in its obituary for her in 1984, listed her age as 79. She first worked for a publishing house and wrote short stories. Turning to the theater, she won instant fame with *The Children's Hour* (1934), a psychological tragedy about a schoolgirl's accusation of lesbianism against two of her teachers. The play ran for 691 performances in New York and was later made into a movie; it was banned in England. Her reputation was enhanced by *The Little Foxes* (1939), which portrayed a reactionary Southern family striving to maintain its position in face of social change. The play was adapted for the screen two years later and made into a successful opera, *Regina*, by Marc *Blitzstein (1949). She wrote an outspokenly anti-Nazi drama, *Watch on the Rhine* (1941), partly inspired by her experiences in Spain during the Spanish Civil War. Hellman's gift for dialogue and her remarkable stage technique were allied to a skill in handling strong, even unpleasant, themes. After *The Searching Wing* (1944), set in pre-World War II Europe and wartime America, came *Another Part of the Forest* (1946), a sequel to *The Little Foxes*. In the 1950s Hellman's career was arrested as a result of her refusal to incriminate fellow artists when called before the U.S. Congress's House Committee on Un-American Activities in 1952, at the height of the McCarthy era. Declaring that "I cannot and will not cut up my conscience to fit this year's fashions," she thereby resigned herself to several years of relative anonymity. *Toys in the Attic* (1960) dealt with problems of race and sex in her native New Orleans. Together with Richard Wilbur and Leonard *Bernstein, she also wrote *Candide* (1957), a comic opera based on Voltaire's satirical classic. Her own interpretation of her political history – which was and is controversial – is easily found in her memoirs: *An Unfinished Woman* (1969), *Pentimento* (1973), *Scoundrel Time* (1976), and her meditation, *Maybe, A Story* (1980). (In 1979, Mary McCarthy called Hellman "dishonest" as a writer and in 1980, Martha Gellhorn argued that *An Unfinished Woman* was, in the main, fiction.) Hellman's life and personality enjoyed renewed interest when her semi-autobiographical story of the wartime relationship between two women was made into a film, *Julia*, with Jane Fonda playing the part of Hellman.

For years, the great love of her life was Dashiell Hammett, a writer of classic crime novels such as *The Maltese Falcon* (1930) and *The Thin Man* (1934).

ADD. BIBLIOGRAPHY: M. Estrin (ed.), *Critical Essays on Lillian Hellman* (1989); P. Feibleman, *Lily: Reminiscences of Lily* (1988); B.Horn, *Lillian Hellman: A Research and Production Sourcebook* (1998); C. Rollyson, *Lillian Hellman: Her Legend and Her Legacy* (1988). Anon., "Lillian Hellman ... Dies at 79," *New York Times* (July 1, 1984), 1.

[Joseph Mersand / Rohan Saxena and Lewis Fried (2nd ed.)]

HELMSLEY, LEONA (1920–), U.S. hotel operator and real estate investor. Leona Mindy Rosenthal Helmsley was born in Marbletown, N.Y. A high-school dropout, she was a model as a young woman under the name Leni Roberts, and a successful real-estate saleswoman. She was a real-estate agent when she met and began her involvement with Harry Helmsley (who would become her third husband), a then-married multimillionare real-estate investor who amassed his fortune as sole owner or in partnership with others in real estate worth about $5 billion. At his zenith, he held or controlled some of the most famous and admired office buildings in New York, including the Empire State Building; the Helmsley Building at 230 Park Avenue; the Lincoln Building at 60 East 42d Street; the Graybar Building at 420 Lexington Avenue; 1350 Broadway; the Flatiron Building; the Toy Center; and the Fisk Building at 250 West 57th Street. There were also large residential developments: Tudor City and Park West Village in Manhattan, Parkchester in the Bronx, and Fresh Meadows in Queens. He also had a stake in such major industrial properties as the Bush Terminal in Brooklyn and the Starrett-Lehigh Building in Manhattan. By 1989 he had become just as well-known for his hotels, particularly the Helmsley Palace on Madison Avenue. Leona was featured in many advertisements for the hotel as its demanding "queen," standing guard over the welfare of her guests. Other Helmsley hotels included the Park Lane on Central Park South and the Helmsley Windsor on West 58th Street. A supremely self-made man, Helmsley began his career in 1925 as a $12 a week office boy and ended it with great wealth as the head of far-flung Helmsley Enterprises but in the shadow of his forceful second wife, Leona, whom he married in 1972. Both were indicted for income tax evasion but Harry was found mentally unfit to stand trial. After legal moves to avoid prison failed, Leona began serving a four-year prison term in April 1992; she spent 18 months in a Federal prison in Danbury, Conn., before being transferred to a halfway house in Manhattan. She completed her sentence under curfew in the Helmsley apartment in the Park Lane. Harry died in 1997. He had no children and he left Leona his vast fortune.

With Leona in charge, Helmsley Enterprises began to divest itself of some non-hotel investments, including Brown, Harris, Stevens, Inc., a residential brokerage that Helmsley bought in the early 1960s. In 2002 she was sued by Charles Bell, a former employee, who said he was discharged solely for being homosexual. A jury agreed and ordered her to pay Bell $11.7 million in damages; a judge reduced this amount to $554,000. The story of her adult life was dramatized in the 1990 TV movie *Leona Helmsley: The Queen of Mean.*

[Stewart Kampel (2nd ed.)]

HELPERN (Halperin), MICHAEL (Mikhl; 1860–1919), socialist Zionist in Russia and pioneer in Ereẓ Israel. Born in Vilna, Helpern received a large legacy from his wealthy father and decided to devote it to the welfare of the Jews. He joined the Ḥovevei Zion after the pogroms in southern Russia (1881) and visited Ereẓ Israel in 1885. He traveled the length and breadth of the country on foot, and upon his return to Russia (1886) he suggested that the Ḥovevei Zion use his financial resources to establish an industrial enterprise in Ereẓ Israel. The suggestion was rejected, but Helpern accepted Judah Leib Pinsker's idea that he donate a large sum of money to purchase the lands of Yesud ha-Ma'alah. In 1886 he returned to Ereẓ Israel and settled in Rishon le-Zion, where he supported the workers' struggle against Baron Edmond de Rothschild's management, which resulted in the resignation of the chief official, Y. Osovitzky. After a visit to Russia at the end of 1890, he made a substantial contribution toward the purchase of land near Wadi Hanin in order to found a workers' settlement, Nes Ẓiyyonah.

In Russia he promoted Labor Zionism among Jewish youth. His major preoccupation, however, was the plan to organize a Jewish military force to conquer Ereẓ Israel and establish a Jewish government there. After the *Kishinev pogrom (1903), he played an important role in organizing Jewish self-defense in Russia. He collected money, gathered arms, and organized and headed fighting groups in Vilna and other towns. Helpern returned to Ereẓ Israel at the end of 1905, fought for the rights of Jewish labor in Jewish villages, and joined the small group founded by Joseph *Trumpeldor to establish a collective settlement. From his return until his death, he was a laborer and defense guard in various localities. He was wounded by Arabs one night when on guard duty in Tel Aviv.

Helpern continued to deliver speeches, devise plans, and compose memoranda to the Zionist movement on the political redemption of Ereẓ Israel by military means. Although he was admired by young people in Russia for his romantic idealism, he became increasingly alienated from the pioneers who had to face the struggles of existence in Ereẓ Israel at the beginning of the Second Aliyah period, so that in his last years he was almost completely isolated. He wrote several unpublished poems and plays in Yiddish on the theme of the destiny of the Jews. Givat Mikhael, a moshav near Nes Ẓiyyonah, is named after him. His colorful personality was the subject of a musical play "Days of Gold" by Shlomo Shva, presented by the Haifa Municipal Theater in 1965.

[Shlomo Breiman]

His son YERMIYAHU (Irma; 1901–1962), seaman and *Betar leader, was born in Smolensk, Russia, and was taken to Ereẓ Israel in 1913. In the late 1920s he joined Betar and became head of its school for instructors, leading it as a defense unit in Tel Aviv during the Arab riots in 1929. He later became a member of the world leadership (*shilton*) of Betar, organizing self-defense courses throughout Europe that trained thousands of Betar members. In 1934 he organized and headed Betar's naval training school at Civitavecchia, Italy. After the establishment of the State of Israel Helpern founded the marine museum in Eilat. He wrote pamphlets on military training, short stories, and several books: *Avi Michael Helpern* ("My Father Michael Helpern," 1964); *Via Dolorosa* (Heb., 1960); *Teḥiyyat Ha-Yamma'ut ha-Ivrit* ("The Jewish Maritime Revival," 1961).

[David Niv]

BIBLIOGRAPHY: S. Tchernowitz, *Im Shaḥar* (1935), 86, 358, 424–5; B. Ḥabas (ed.), *Sefer ha-Aliyyah ha-Sheniyyah* (1947), index; M. Smilansky, *Mishpaḥat ha-Adamah*, 2 (1954²), 57–60; Dinur, Haganah, 1 pt. 1 (1954), 194–7; 1 pt. 2 (1956), 812–3; M. Singer, *Be-Reshit ha-Ẓiyyonut ha-Sozyalistit* (n.d.), 198–222; Y. Helpern, *Avi Michael Helpern* (1964); Tidhar, 6 (1955), 2572–74; Dinur Haganah, 2 (1963), index.

HELPERN, MILTON (1902–1977), U.S. forensic pathologist. Helpern was born in East Harlem, New York, and educated in New York City public schools. He received his B.Sc. from City College in 1922 and M.D. from Cornell University Medical College in 1926. From 1954, he served as chief medical examiner of the City of New York and professor and chairman of the Department of Forensic Medicine at the New York University School of Medicine (1954–74) and was on the Faculty of Cornell University Medical College. He was co-founder of the American Academy of Forensic Sciences and the National Association of Medical Examiners.

Helpern was consultant in forensic pathology to many governmental agencies and lectured extensively. He brought attention to public health issues such as malaria among drug users, carbon monoxide poisoning, and Sudden Infant Death Syndrome. From 1968 he was president of the National Association of Medical Examiners, editor of the *International Microfilm Journal of Legal Medicine* from 1965, and coauthor of *Legal Medicine, Pathology and Toxicology* (1954²). The Milton Helpern Library of Legal Medicine, established in 1962, was one of the finest of its kind. Helpern's basic philosophy held that forensic pathology cannot cure socioeconomic ills but it may be able to help society understand and prevent their tragic effects.

BIBLIOGRAPHY: M. Houts, *Where Death Delights: the Story of Dr. Milton Helpern and Forensic Medicine* (1967).

[Fred Rosner / Bracha Rager (2nd ed.)]

HELSINGFORS PROGRAM, a system of Zionist policy and activities in Russia and other Diaspora countries adopted at the third conference of Russian Zionists, which took place in Helsingfors (Helsinki) on Dec. 4–10, 1906. The Finnish capital was chosen as the site of the conference because conditions in Russia proper restricted meetings and the exercise of free speech. The conference dealt with fundamental problems of Zionism in general, and Russian Zionism in particular, as they appeared after *Herzl's death and the fading of his "diplomatic" Zionism and in view of the upheavals and constitutional changes in czarist Russia after the 1905 Revolution. The conference, which was meticulously prepared by meetings of Russian Zionist editors and journalists, formulated the idea of "synthetic Zionism," which stood for the simultaneous integration of parallel political and practical work in Zionism. It postulated the principle that the achievement of international recognition for a Jewish Ereẓ Israel would be the end, not the precondition, of systematic *aliyah* and settlement work. It was, however, the conference's resolution on "work in the present," i.e., among the Jewish masses in the Diaspora, that became famous both because of the innovation that it represented in Zionism and its practical consequences, particularly in Eastern Europe. The principal speaker on this subject was Isaac *Gruenbaum, who, with the experience of Jewish and Zionist work in Poland behind him, submitted the following formulation: Zionism opposes the Exile (*galut*), but does not oppose the Diaspora (*golah*). This principle was of particular importance for the Jews of Russia, who were then exposed to a variety of ideological influences besides Zionism. Other speakers on this subject included Vladimir *Jabotinsky and Leo *Motzkin. The "work in the present" resolution was based on Paragraph Two of the *Basle Program ("The organization and binding together of the whole of Jewry by means of appropriate institutions, both local and international, in accordance with laws of each country"), interpreting it as a directive to Zionists to organize the Jewish masses in the Diaspora as a national minority and lead them, in the Zionist spirit, in their daily life. The conference felt that such activity would "strengthen Diaspora Jewry and provide it with new cultural, material, and political means in its struggle for the creation of a sound national life in Ereẓ Israel." It envisaged a liberalized, democratic Russia with wide, autonomous rights for its non-Russian peoples, including the Jewish nation, which, through a comprehensive organizational framework, would exercise its political rights and its cultural, educational, and, in certain respects, even administrative autonomy both in Hebrew and Yiddish. The implementation of this program would transform Zionism from an activity remote from the Jewish masses – confined in the "diplomatic" and pioneering sphere – into a dynamic movement concerned with the actual needs of the Jews, particularly in Russia, as one national-cultural entity among many others. The spirit of the Helsingfors Program engendered and fostered new forms of Zionist activity, as, e.g., the wide network of modernized *ḥadarim* and secular Hebrew schools, active participation in the political life of the country wherever possible, etc.

In Russia, the Zionist movement was able to apply the political aspect of the new program only after the overthrow of the czar (1917), and then only for a short period, until the

Soviet regime liquidated the Russian Zionist movement. Unsuccessful attempts were made to apply this program in Galicia in the parliamentary elections during the period 1907–11. It was, however, implemented in Poland and the Baltic states after World War I. "Work in the present" remained a controversial program in Zionism. Its opponents contended that it caused a waste of effort in the Zionist movement, and that instead of being a means to an end – the creation of a Jewish nation in Ereẓ Israel – it could, in the course of time, become an end in itself.

BIBLIOGRAPHY: B. Halpern, *The Idea of the Jewish State* (1961), index; N.M. Gelber, in: *Gesher*, 2 no. 4 (1956), 33–41; A. Boehm, *Die zionistische Bewegung*, 1 (1935), index; *Sefer Tchlenow* (1937), 339–53; *Sefer Motzkin* (1939), 74–81; Gepstein, in: *Sefer Idelsohn* (1946), 31–39; Jabotinsky, *ibid.*, 83–88; idem, *Ne'umim 1905–1926* (1958), 23–53; Y. Gruenbaum, in: *He-Avar*, 5 (1957), 11–17; A. Zenziper, in: *Kaẓir* (1964), 67–102.

[Getzel Kressel]

HELTAI, JENŐ (originally **Herzl**; 1871–1957), Hungarian poet, playwright, and novelist. A cousin of Theodor *Herzl, Heltai studied law in his native Budapest but became a journalist. Between 1914 and 1918 he was the director of a Budapest theater and from 1916 was chairman of the Association of Hungarian Playwrights. A leading figure on the Hungarian literary scene during the first half of the 20th century, Heltai (who converted to Christianity) published his first verse anthology *Modern dalok* ("Modern Poems") in 1892. His themes were taken from urban life – an innovation in Hungarian poetry, which until then had been a rustic, folk type – and his poetry is a synthesis of the French chanson and Hungarian folk poetry. Heltai's plays include the comedy *A néma levente* (1936; English adaptation by Humbert *Wolfe, *The Silent Knight*, 1937) and *Egy fillér* ("One Penny," 1940), based on the life of Ferenc *Molnár. Heltai voiced his criticism of contemporary Hungarian society in a number of humorous plays and short stories. Several of his works, including the novel *Csárdás*, have been translated into English, Hebrew, and other languages.

BIBLIOGRAPHY: *Magyar Irodalmi Lexikon*, 1 (1963).

[Baruch Yaron]

HEMAN (Heb. הֵימָן), orchestral leader in Israel in biblical times. According to the Book of Chronicles, Heman was related, through the prophet Samuel, to the levite family of Korah and Kohath (I Chron. 6:18). The affiliation of Heman with Samuel indicates the increasing prestige of Heman's house. At first he worshiped together with Jeduthun (*ibid.* 16:41–42; cf. II Chron. 29:14–15) on the high places of Gibeon where the remains of the *Tabernacle were preserved. In taking the Ark up to Jerusalem (I Chron. 15:2–3), David participated together with the two families of singers, Asaph and Ethan; when the Temple was built by Solomon (*ibid.* 6:16ff.), David had already arranged to transfer Heman to Jerusalem (*ibid.* 25:1), where, together with the families mentioned, he could make music in the Temple, directing his sons (cf. *ibid.* 25:4–6). Heman and his sons, dressed in linen, made music (II Chron. 5:12), and performed their rites at the east of the altar. In one instance (I Chron. 25:5) Heman is called "the king's [David's] seer." I Chronicles 25 reflects the rise of the Hemanites at the expense of the Asaphites during Second Temple times.

Heman the Ezrahite

In the superscription of Psalm 88 the name Heman the Ezrahite is mentioned (similarly, the singer of Psalm 89 is called: Ethan the Ezrahite). "Ezrathite," the native, may indicate continuity with older Canaanite psalmody. According to this genealogy, which relates Heman to "sons of Korah," it appears that the writer establishes a relationship between Heman the Ezrahite and "the sons of Korah," such as exists between them and Heman in Chronicles (see above). But contrary to this I Kings 5:11 mentions Ethan the Ezrahite as well as Heman, Calcol, and Darda, "the sons of Mahol," as great sages who were surpassed in wisdom only by Solomon; and in I Chronicles 2:6 these four are taken as belonging to the family of Zerah b. Judah ("the sons of Zerah: Zimri, and Ethan, and Heman, and Calcol, and Dara"). Various theories have been advanced to reconcile these discrepancies, but it seems that the most probable view is that Ezrahite is identical with Zarhi (agreeing with I Chron. 2:6); Heman the Ezrahite is to be regarded as the father of the singers and related to the "sons of Korah." In ancient Israel singing and wisdom were associated. See, e.g., Psalm 49:4–5.

The Sons of Heman

According to I Chronicles 25:5 Heman had "fourteen sons," all of whom assisted "their father in song in the house of the Lord, with cymbals, psalteries, and harps." Since I Chronicles 6:18 establishes Heman's relationship to Korah, the sons of Heman are to be identified (see Abraham ibn Ezra to Ps. 42:1) with the sons of Korah, to whom Psalms 42–49 and 84–88 have been ascribed and who also are described as singers in the war chronicle dating from the days of Jehoshaphat (II Chron. 20:18). The sons of Heman are spoken of in the days of Hezekiah (II Chron. 29:12); they are not mentioned in the days of Josiah (ibid. 35:15); nor is anything said of them (and "the sons of Korah") in the genealogical lists of Ezra and Nehemiah. Perhaps this reflects a tradition that they were removed from office during the days of Josiah.

ADD. BIBLIOGRAPHY: S. Japhet, *I & II Chronicles* (1993), 156–58.

[Yehoshua M. Grintz]

HEMAR (Hescheles), MARIAN (1901–1972), Polish author, satirist, and writer for the stage and screen. Born in Lemberg, Hemar began his career around 1920 as a poet and writer of revues. He wrote material for several Warsaw theaters and cabarets, among them the Quid Pro Quo, where he worked in collaboration with Julian *Tuwim. Together with such outstanding poets as Tuwim, Antoni *Slonimski, Jan Lechón, and Konstanty Galczyński, Hemar – who wrote under several other pseudonyms – produced many famous political skits and trenchant satires. He also wrote two comedies and a number of screenplays.

In 1939 Hemar left Poland and settled in London where, during World War II, he worked for the BBC's European Service and the Polish exile press and ran a Polish cabaret, the Bialy Orzel (White Eagle). In 1967, like many other uncommitted Jews, he felt the impact of the *Six-Day War and publicly affirmed his Jewishness and support for Israel and wrote the poem *"Sciana płaczu"* ("The Wailing Wall").

Hemar's verse collections include *Dwie ziemie świete* (Two Holy Lands, 1942), *Lata londyńskie* (The London Years, 1946), *Pisanki* (Ornamented [Easter] Eggs, 1946), and *Satyry patetyczne* (Pathetic Satires, 1947). Other works are *Adolf Wielki* (1943; *Adolf the Great*, 1943); a satirical diary, *Marchewka* (The Carrot, 1943); and a translation of Shakespeare's sonnets, *Sonety Szekspira* (1968).

[Stanislaw Wygodzki]

ḤEMDAT YAMIM (Heb. חֶמְדַּת יָמִים; "The Best of Days"), a major 18th-century Hebrew work of homiletics and ethics, comprising three volumes in the first four editions and four in the last two editions. Its impact on Jewish life and letters, first among the Ashkenazim, and later among the Orientals and Sephardim, has been very great. In modern Hebrew literature, the writings of S.Y. *Agnon have been especially influenced by the work's language and ideas. As it has come down, *Ḥemdat Yamim* is probably incomplete. The extant part deals with the halakhic observances and ethical behavior of a pious Jew who tries to attain the maximum religious elevation during the various holidays, fasts, and special days of the year. It is possible that a part of the work treating the ordinary days was lost because it was never printed.

Each section of the work is a homily in which the author substantiates his ideas by interpreting biblical verses and talmudic and midrashic sayings in homiletical sequences. The writings offer examples of some of the best rhetoric in Jewish homiletics, and the beauty of the sermons helped to endear the work to all readers. Although the author frequently raises halakhic problems, he does not deal with them in a purely halakhic manner – his main objective being to instruct the reader in the ḥasidic or pious way of life. A product of ethical kabbalistic literature, *Ḥemdat Yamim* was especially influenced by the Lurianic Kabbalah (see *Kabbalah, *Ethical Literature), which flourished in both Eastern and Western Judaism from the beginning of the 17th century. Accordingly, each chapter of the work stresses the mystically symbolic significance of the 613 commandments and of every custom and tradition carried out within the framework of Jewish religious life. The deeds performed in this world are seen as a reflection of mystical processes in the divine world. Through his religious acts the pious, observant Jew participates in a mythical drama of war between the mystical powers of good and evil. In a Jewry which accepted the Lurianic Kabbalah almost without exception, *Ḥemdat Yamim* had literary and practical value – people enjoyed both reading it and following its teachings.

The work was first printed by Israel Jacob b. Yom Tov *Algazi in Smyrna in 1731–32 (and subsequently five more times in the next generation). Although a major work and written only a few years before its publication, the author is unknown and the question of authorship remains one of the great mysteries in Jewish bibliography. That the work was written in the early 18th century and studied in depth by many of the best Jewish scholars and bibliographers heightens the irony of its anonymity. One fact seems clear, though some scholars have contested it in recent years, namely that the author was a *Shabbatean. Scholars have detected many Shabbatean ideas and allusions hidden in the work; the most obvious, pointed out in the 18th century by R. Jacob *Emden, the fanatic enemy of Shabbateanism, are the *notarikons* of *Nathan of Gaza, the prophet of Shabbetai Ẓevi, included in some of the work's *piyyutim*. This fact gave rise to the belief, accepted especially in the East, that Nathan of Gaza was the author of the entire work. Accordingly, Nathan is sometimes known as *Ha-Rav Ḥemdat Yamim* because of the common practice of calling an author by the name of his major work.

Although the book was written by a Shabbatean, it has been proved that Nathan of Gaza was not the author. First to disprove Nathan's authorship was Menahem Heilperin in *Kevod Ḥakhamim* (Jerusalem, 1896). Heilperin went even further, though unsuccessfully, in trying to demonstrate that the author had no connection with the Shabbatean movement. A recent effort to discover the author was made by Avraham Yaari in *Ta'alumat Sefer*, where he tried to prove that the author was Rabbi Benjamin ha-Levi, one of the major kabbalists in 17th-century Safed, who, according to Yaari, wrote the work during his old age in 1671–72. G. Scholem, in a thorough analysis, cited – among the many bibliographical and historical facts making Yaari's thesis unacceptable – the fact that *Ḥemdat Yamim* was written after R. Benjamin died.

Further insight into the work was provided by I. Tishby, who proved conclusively that the author of *Ḥemdat Yamim* made extensive use of works published in the beginning of the 18th century. Thus, the book could not have been written before the second, or even the third decade of that century, a time approximating the date of its publication. The comparison between *Ḥemdat Yamim* and the sources on which it is based reveals that many chapters of the work are in fact anthologies gleaned from many books. But by changing numerous details and transforming the special character of the individual sources, the author integrated his diverse sources into a new whole. The author quoted ancient and medieval sources faithfully, but used the subject matter of contemporary sources in any way which suited the literary character of his work. Many "personal" experiences reported by the author were in fact taken from other works and adapted to the demands of his style and purpose.

BIBLIOGRAPHY: A. Yaari, *Ta'alumat Sefer* (1954), incl. bibl.; G. Scholem, in: *Beḥinot be-Vikkoret ha-Sifrut*, 8 (1955), 79–95; A. Yaari, *ibid.*, 9 (1956), 71–79; G. Scholem, *ibid.*, 80–84; I. Tishby, *Netivei Emunah u-Minut* (1964), 108–68.

[Joseph Dan]

HEMLOCK, the plant *Conium maculatum*, probably the Heb. ראש or רוש (*rosh*) of the Bible. *Rosh* is mentioned 11 times in the Bible, five together with *la'anah* ("wormwood"), as a simile for wickedness and for something evil and poisonous. The Authorized Version renders *rosh* as "gall," i.e., snake venom, but the Bible explicitly refers to it as a plant that puts out roots (Deut. 29:17) and flourishes in the fields (Hos. 10:4). Its poisonous fruits are called "grapes of *rosh*" (Deut. 32:32; which by transference was applied there to snake venom). It is a tall plant with which the elegist of the Book of Lamentations (3:5) sees himself surrounded and whose poison he fears. From this plant a poisonous potion was prepared (Jer. 8:14, 9:14). On occasion it was eaten, the psalmist (Ps. 69:21–22) describing the wicked surrounding him as coming to comfort him in his mourning and, instead of the mourner's meal, giving him *rosh* to eat. There is no exegetical or philological evidence by which to identify the scriptural *rosh*. A number of poisonous plants have been suggested for it as, for example, the colocynth. Among those deserving consideration, is the poppy (*Papaver somniferum*; see *Spices), for whose round seeds the name *rosh* ("head") is apt, and from the juice of which opium is prepared. This is mentioned in the Jerusalem Talmud (Av. Zar. 2:2, 40d) as a dangerous substance. Others have identified *rosh* with the plant *Hyoscyamus aureus*, which contains a poisonous and intoxicating juice. In Aramaic it is called *shikhrona* ("intoxicator"), a term also found in Josephus (Ant. 3:172ff.). The latter compares the crown above the gold plate of the high priest (Ex. 28:36) to its calyx, describing this plant in all its detail, the first morphological description of a plant in ancient Jewish literature.

Of all those proposed identifications the most reasonable is hemlock (*Conium*), a plant of the family of Umbelliferae, with a large inflorescence like an umbrella for which the name *rosh* ("head") is apt. It grows wild in fields and on the roadside in various parts of Israel. It contains a powerful poison.

BIBLIOGRAPHY: Loew, Flora, 2 (1924), 364–70; 3 (1924), 48; J. Feliks, *Olam ha-Ẓome'ah ha-Mikra'i* (1968[2]), 197–201. **ADD. BIBLIOGRAPHY:** I. Jacob and W. Jacob, in: ABD, 2:816; J. Tigay, *JPS Torah Commentary Deuteronomy* (1996), 398, n. 35.

[Jehuda Feliks]

HEMP, the plant *Cannabis sativa* called *kanbus* in talmudic literature. The Mishnah speaks of its fibers as being woven with or without linen (Kil. 9:1). The prohibition of *sha'atnez* ("the mixture of wool and linen") did not apply to coarse garments and felt shoes, the products of overseas lands, the presumption being that they were sewn with hempen thread (Kil. 9:7). The Jerusalem Talmud (Kil. 9:5, 32d) notes that while in mishnaic times hemp was an important commodity because of the difficulty of cultivating linen, in the days of the *amoraim* linen replaced it. An interesting comment on the cultivation of linen and hemp in Europe at the end of the 12th century is given by Samson of Sens in his comment on the Mishnah in *Kilayim* (*ibid.*) that in his region linen was more expensive than hemp, whereas in Normandy and England it was very cheap. From another strain of hemp (*Cannabis sativa var. Indica*), grown in southern Asia, hashish is extracted. The use of hemp as a narcotic is extremely old. Herodotus (*Historia*, 4:75) mentions that the Scythians scattered hemp seeds on heated stones and inhaled the fumes. Hashish is not mentioned however in Jewish sources.

BIBLIOGRAPHY: Loew, Flora, 1 (1928), 255–63; J. Feliks, *Kilei Zera'im ve-Harkavah* (1967), 220f. **ADD BIBLIOGRAPHY:** Feliks, Ha-Ẓome'aḥ, 145.

[Jehuda Feliks]

HEMSI, ALBERTO (1897–1975), composer, ethnomusicologist, and music publisher. Born in Turgutlu (Cassaba), *Turkey, he attended l'Alliance Israélite Universelle (AIU) school and the local yeshivah. In 1907, he attended the Societé Musicale Israélite (SMI) in Izmir, studying composition with Shemtov Shikayar and cantorial music with Isaac *Algazi. In 1913, he won a scholarship to the Royal Conservatory of Music (Milan), where, from 1914 to 1915 and from 1917 to 1919, he studied piano with Guglielmo Andreoti, theory and composition with Renzo Bossi and Ettore Pozzoli, and musicology with Giusto Zampieri. In those intervening years, while serving in the Italian Army, he was wounded during a battle in northeastern Italy. In 1919, he returned to Izmir to teach piano and vocal music at the AIU and directed a youth orchestra at the SMI. From 1920, he became intensely interested in the traditional secular and liturgical music of the Sephardim, which he began to collect in Turkey, and from 1923 more intensively in Rhodes, where his family settled after the great fire in Izmir. In 1927, he moved to *Alexandria, where he founded Édition Orientale de Musique, the first Egyptian music-publishing house, and published a booklet, *La Musique Oriental en Egypte* (1930). He also founded a conservatory to propagate his ideas about Middle-Eastern music, served as music director of the Grand Eliahu ha-Navi Synagogue (1927–57), established the Alexandria Philharmonic Orchestra (1928–40), and continued his fieldwork (publishing the first-five fascicles of his *Coplas sefardies*). In 1957, fearing Nasser's political policies, he left for Paris to teach at the Séminaire Israélite de France. From 1958 he simultaneously assumed the music directorships of the Berith Shalom and Isaac Abravanel Synagogues. He studied ethnomusicology under Claudie Marcel-Dubois (1961–65) and was also active in French radio. His musical manuscripts and unpublished works are deposited in the Music Department of the Jewish National and University Library in Jerusalem. These works include *Coplas sefardíes, 10 fascicles* (Alexandria-Paris, 1932–1973); *Cancionero sefardi* published posthumously, edited by E. Seroussi et al. (Jerusalem, 1995), and *Maḥzor sefardi*, an edited collection of 200 liturgical melodies).

BIBLIOGRAPHY: Grove Music Online.

[Israel J. Katz (2nd ed.)]

HENDEL, NEḤAMA (Helena; 1936–1998), Israeli folk singer. Born in Jerusalem, Neḥama Hendel started her career as a singer in *Lehakat ha-Naḥal,* the military entertainment troupe.

After her army service, she went to Paris for singing and acting studies. In 1957 she returned to Israel and was a member of the *Batzal Yarok* (Green Onion) entertainment troupe. A year later she participated as an actor in the American movie *Amud ha-Esh* and formed one of the first Israeli folk-style duos with Ran Eliran ("Ran and Nama"). She was known especially as a performer of old folk songs (Israeli and others in several languages), the first Israeli singer to evolve a soprano folk-style intonation, breaking a convention established by the "Yemenite altos" such as Bracha *Zefirah and Shoshana *Damari. In 1969 she left Israel for Germany with her husband and from 1984 she lived in Australia until her return to Israel in 1994. Among her recordings are songs of Ḥ.N. *Bialik, *Outside the Storm* (1997). A collection of most of her recordings was published in two CDs in 1998.

[Israela Stein (2nd ed.)]

HENDEL, YEHUDIT (1926–), Hebrew writer. Born in Warsaw to a rabbinic family, Hendel came to Palestine as an infant. The family settled in Haifa, the setting of many of Hendel's prose works. Hendel's stories were first published in *Mi-Bifnim* (1942), and subsequently appeared in various Israeli literary journals. Her first collection of stories, entitled *Anashim Aḥerim Hem* ("They are Different") appeared in 1950, followed by her first novel *Reḥov ha-Maderegot* (1956; reissued 1998; *Street of Steps*, English translation 1963), a social novel, depicting the disparity between two classes in the new Jewish state: the poverty-stricken, disadvantaged Oriental Israelis, living in downtown Haifa, and the established, influential Ashkenazi elite, living on Mount Carmel. Hapless Oriental characters, traumatized Holocaust survivors, and weary immigrants are the anti-heroes in Hendel's second novel, *Ha-Ḥazer shel Momo ha-Gedolah* ("The Yard of Momo the Great," 1969; reissued as *Ha-Ḥamsin ha-Aḥaron*, "The Last Hamsin" in 1993) which is set again in downtown Haifa shortly before the Six-Day War. Hendel, commonly associated with the "New Wave" in Hebrew literature, was one of the first Israeli novelists to foreground the fate and sufferings of ethnic minorities and of women in Israeli society. The novel *Ha-Koaḥ ha-Akher* ("The Other Power," 1984) is a lyrical elegy to her late husband, the painter Zvi Mairovitch, in which Hendel describes and contemplates on the nature and meaning of the creative process. No less personal is her next work, *Le-yad Kefarim Sheketim* ("Near Quiet Places," 1987), a moving account of a voyage she undertook to Poland, juxtaposing pastoral landscapes and the awareness of the shattering past, the concentration camps and a Jewish world lost forever: "One cannot avoid the feeling that Poland is a great cemetery," she writes. Sickness, death, loss and bereavement became major themes in Hendel's works. In the collection *Kesef Katan* (1988; *Small Change*, 2002) she tells of a woman dying of cancer ("My Friend B's Feast," included also in R. Domb (ed.), *New Women's Writing from Israel*) and of a man twice widowed; in *Har ha-To'im* ("The Mountain of Losses," 1991) she critically reflects on the state-organized ceremonies in military cemeteries, pleading for a genuine and heartfelt private ritual of mourning. Following the collection of stories *Aruḥat Boker Temimah* ("An Innocent Breakfast," 1996), Hendel published the novel *Terufo shel Rofe ha-Nefesh* ("Crack Up," 2002), a skillfully narrated psychological novel describing the disintegration of a man who marries the wife of his deceased best friend, the woman he had always loved. The marriage is marred by hallucinations and guilt feelings, overshadowed by the imaginary presence of the dead.

Some of Hendel's prose works have been adapted for stage, screen, and television. She was awarded the Jerusalem Prize and the Bialik Prize and is one of the few women writers to be awarded the prestigious Israel Prize for literature (2003). "A Story with No Address" is included in G. Abramson (ed.), *The Oxford Book of Hebrew Short Stories* (1996); "Small Change" is included in G. Shaked (ed.), *Six Israeli Novellas* (1999). For further information concerning the translation of Hendel's prose into various languages see the ITHL website at www.ithl.org.il.

BIBLIOGRAPHY: R. Wallenrod, *The Literature of Modern Israel* (1956), index; S. Kremer, *Ḥillufei Mishmarot be-Sifrutenu* (1958), 300–6; G. Schoffmann, *Kol Kitvei* (1960), 124–5; L. Rattok, "*Kol Ishah Makirah et Zeh*," in: *Apiryon*, 15 (1989), 10–17; L. Rattok, "*Al 'Kesef Katan*,'" in: *Siman Keriah*, 20 (1990), 428–437; G. Steindler Moscati, "Memoria e storia: Viaggio in Polonia di Y. Hendel," in: *Viaggiatori ebrei* (1992), 119–128; R. Litwin, "*Ha-Text ha-Samui shel ha-Ḥayyim ha-Shakulim*," in: *'Iton 77*,' 144–145 (1992), 44–45; D. Miron, "*Ha-Har she-Heḥemiẓu ha-To'im*," in: *Alpayim*, 14 (1997), 232–256; P. Shirav, *Ketivah Lo Tamah* (1998); H. Nave, "*Al ha-Ovdan, al ha-Shekhol ve-al ha-Evel ba-Ḥevrah ha-Yisra'elit*," in: *Alpayim*, 16 (1998), 85–120; N. Gertz, "'I Am Other,' the Holocaust Survivor's Point of View in Y. Hendel's Short Story 'They Are Others,'" in: *Divergent Jewish Culture* (2001), 217–237; D. Miron, *Ha-Ko'aḥ ha-Ḥalash: Iyunim ba-Sifrut shel Y. Hendel* (2003); D. Miron, *Ha-Rofe ha-Medumeh veha-Marah ha-Shevurah*, in: *Alei Siaḥ*, 50 (2003), 12–33; D. Miron, *Bein Ofek la-Anakh: Al Reḥov ha-Maderegot*, in: *Ẓafon*, 7 (2004), 19–36.

[Anat Feinberg (2nd ed.)]

HENDRICKS, U.S. family. URIAH HENDRICKS (1737–1798), who was born in Amsterdam, Holland, emigrated from London to New York in 1755. In 1764 he established a metals business there which his grandson Uriah continued as Hendricks Bros., the oldest Jewish business concern in America. He was one of the Tories who in 1776 signed a Loyalist address to the British general William Howe. Hendricks was a president of the Sephardi congregation Shearith Israel, in which his family was active for generations. Uriah's only son, HARMON (1771–1838), was born in New York and graduated from Columbia College. In 1812 he established one of the first copper-rolling mills in the United States in Soho, New Jersey, with his brother-in-law, Solomon I. Isaacs. This firm developed metal parts for warships, which were useful in the War of 1812. When the government issued war bonds in 1813, Hendricks subscribed $40,000. Hendricks was the leading New York Jewish philanthropist of his time, and he was president of Congregation Shearith Israel from 1824 to 1827. His sons, URIAH (1802–1869), HENRY (1804–1861), and MONTAGUE (1811–1884), carried on the copper firm, which then was handed down to Uriah's four sons, including JOSHUA HENDRICKS (1831–1893). Joshua's son HENRY HARMON HENDRICKS (1860–1904) was born in New York City. After some years as a practical chemist, he joined Hendricks Bros. and remained an active partner. A trustee of Congregation Shearith Israel, Hendricks belonged to many Jewish and secular organizations, including the National Arts Club and the American Association for the Advancement of Science. Another of Joshua's sons, EDGAR (d. 1894), married Lilian Henry. Their son HENRY S. HENDRICKS (1892–1959), born in New York City, associated himself with the law firm of Cardozo and Nathan. From 1926 to 1938 he practiced privately, then joined Hendricks, Robbins & Buttenweiser; he resumed private practice in 1947. Active in the Jewish Historical Society, for 25 years he presided over Congregation Shearith Israel, later becoming its honorary president.

BIBLIOGRAPHY: M. Bortman, in: AJHSP, 43 (1954), 199–214.

[Edward L. Greenstein]

°HENGSTENBERG, ERNST WILHELM (1802–1869), German Bible scholar. He earned his Ph.D. at Bonn (1823) after studying Hebrew and Arabic with G. Freytag, the prominent Orientalist. As editor of the *Evangelische Kirchenzeitung* (1827–69) he led an anti-rationalistic crusade which upheld the doctrine of infallibility in regard to the fundamental beliefs of Protestant Christianity. Hengstenberg belonged to the group of orthodox Christian scholars known as "Confessionalists," because of their adherence to such formularies as the Augsburg Confession. He is remembered principally for his *Christologie des Alten Testaments* (1829–35; *The Christology of the Old Testament*, 1854–58), a strictly Christian orthodox presentation of the Bible, which views the messianic prophecies on a spiritual plane and totally ignores their original historical setting. Adaptations of the hermeneutical principles of the Reformation are found throughout his biblical commentaries which include *Kommentar über die Psalmen* (4 vols., 1842–47; *Commentary on the Psalms*, 3 vols., 1845–48); *Prediger Salomo* (1858; *Commentary on the Book of Ecclesiastes*, 1860); *Weissagungen des Propheten Ezechiels* (1867–68; *The Prophecies of Ezekiel*, 1869); and *Beiträge zur Einleitung ins Alte Testament* (1831; *Genuineness of the Pentateuch*, 2 vols., 18547), a defense of the unity of the Pentateuch. He also wrote *Geschichte des Reiches Gottes unter dem Alten Bunde* (2 vols., 1869–71; *History of the Kingdom of God under the Old Testament*, 2 vols., 1871–72), *Die Opfer der heiligen Schrift* (1859), and *Egypt and the Books of Moses* (1843). Twelve of his books were translated into English to combat the inroads that critical scholarship was making among English readers.

BIBLIOGRAPHY: A. Mueller, *Hengstenberg und die evangelische Kirchenzeitung* (1857); P. Schaff, *Germany, its Universities, Theology and Religion* (1857), 300–20; J. Bachmann, *Hengstenberg, sein Leben und Wirken*, 2 vols. (1876–79); H.J. Kraus, *Geschichte der historisch-kritischen Erforschung des Alten Testaments* (1956), 203–7. **ADD. BIBLIOGRAPHY:** J. Rogerson, in: DBI, I, 494–95.

[Zev Garber / S. David Sperling (2nd ed.)]

HENKIN, JOSEPH ELIJAH (1880–1973), rabbi. Henkin was born in Klimovichi, Belorussia, where his father Rabbi Eliezer Henkin was head of the yeshivah. Leaving his native town, he studied for six years at the yeshivah of Slutsk under Isser-Zalman *Meltzer, who together with Baruch Baer *Leibowitz and Jechiel Michael *Epstein ordained him. After serving as rabbi in Kavkazskaya and as head of the yeshivah in Sokolov, Henkin immigrated to the United States in 1922 and settled in New York City. In 1925 he was appointed director of Ezras Torah, an organization founded in 1915 by the Union of Orthodox Rabbis to provide assistance to rabbinical scholars in war-torn Europe. Under his direction, Ezras Torah expanded into a general charity distributing hundreds of thousands of dollars annually to thousands of needy persons, raising funds honorably, and disbursing funds fairly. Paid a modest salary, he insisted that when he aged and cut down his hours of work, his salary be reduced accordingly. His stature derived from his person and not from the positions he held. Henkin was one of the leading authorities on Jewish law and was continually called upon to decide points of Jewish law. He was particularly authoritative on divorce procedure and on laws of Sabbath as they relate to the new technology. His writings also include such issues as the Holocaust, Zionism, and Jewish communal life. Originally opposed to the State of Israel, once it was established he gave it support. His published responsa appear in Chaim Bloch's *Even me-Kir Tiẓak* (1953) and in his own *Perushei Lev Ivra* (c. 1925). His son LOUIS HENKIN (1917–) became professor of international law and diplomacy at Columbia University.

BIBLIOGRAPHY: A. Shurin, *Keshet Gibborim* (1964), 77–82; O. Rand (ed.), *Toledot Anshei Shem* (1950), 38; *Kitvei ha-Gaon Rabbi Yosef Eliyahu Henkin* (1980).

[Aaron Lichtenstein / Michael Berenbaum (2nd ed.)]

HENLE, ELKAN (1761–1833), an early advocate of emancipation in Bavaria. Son of a wealthy Fuerth court agent, Jacob Buttenwies(en) Henle, he published a number of books and pamphlets demanding the spread of education and enlightenment (Haskalah) among his coreligionists and opposing the view that the Jews were not ready for emancipation. His writings include *Ueber die Verbesserung des Judenthums* (Frankfurt, 1803); *Ueber die Verfassung der Juden im Koenigreiche Baiern und die Verbesserung derselben zum Nutzen des Staates* (Munich, 1811); *Die Stimme der Wahrheit in Beziehung auf den Kultus der Israeliten* (3 vols., Fuerth, 1827). His last work sharply criticized the reformist catechism of Alexander *Behr and opposed the formulation of a secular consistory in Bavaria.

BIBLIOGRAPHY: F. Babinger, in: MGWSJ, 62 (1918), 223–30.

HENLE, JACOB (Friedrich Gustav; 1809–1885), German anatomist and pathologist. Henle, who is considered one of the outstanding histologists of his time, was a member of a well-known family in Bavaria and the grandson of the rabbi of Fuerth. He was baptized at the age of 11 by his parents. He studied medicine at Bonn, and was the outstanding pupil, and later assistant, of Johannes Mueller. He moved with the latter to Berlin, where he was appointed lecturer of anatomy in 1837. From 1840 he served as professor of anatomy and physiology at Zurich, from 1844 at Heidelberg, and from 1852 at Goettingen.

Henle was a great anatomist and one of the founders of modern medicine. The scope of his research work, from his first study of the cornea of the eye (1832) until the final one on the growth of man's nail and the horse's hoof (1884), was astonishing in its variety. His book, *Allgemeine Anatomie* (1841), was the first in which the study of the cell was presented as a professional branch, thus taking a definite step forward in medicine. While at Zurich, he founded the *Zeitschrift fuer rationelle Medizin*, in opposition to the obscure romantic medicine of his day.

His anatomical discoveries were numerous and at least a dozen microscopic structures in anatomy were named after him. He summed up his life's work on anatomy in his great book *Handbuch der systematischen Anatomie* (1855–71). He also made contributions to pathology. His book, *Pathologische Untersuchungen* (1840) included, among others, a chapter on miasmas and infections, in which he first expressed (long before ways were found to stain and identify microbes) the theory that infectious diseases were caused by specific microorganisms, a contention that was to be proved 40 years later by his pupil Robert Koch.

BIBLIOGRAPHY: V. Robinson, *Life of Jacob Henle* (1921); S.R. Kagan, *Jewish Medicine* (1952), 147; R.H. Major, *A History of Medicine* (1954), 797–9.

[Joshua O. Leibowitz]

HENLE, MORITZ (1850–1925), cantor and composer. Born in Laupheim (Wuerttemburg), Germany, Henle became cantor and choral conductor and worked in various cities. In 1879, he was appointed chief cantor in the reformed Israelitischer Tempelverband of Hamburg, where he reintroduced biblical cantillation and Ashkenazi pronunciation. In 1905 he was among the founders of the Standesverein der juedischen Kantoren in Deutschland, which later became the Allgemeiner Deutscher Kantorenverband. His works include *Liturgische Synagogen-Gesaenge* (1900), for solo, mixed choir, and organ; a revised edition of the *Gesangbuch* of the Hamburg Synagogue (1887); and a setting of Byron's *Hebrew Melodies*. His leaning toward the East European style is discernible in the settings of prayers *Halokh ve-Karata, U-Netanneh Tokef*, and *Adonai Mah Adam*. Henle wrote articles on synagogue music, the training of cantors, and similar subjects, and was an advocate of moderate Reform.

BIBLIOGRAPHY: Sendrey, Music, indices; A. Friedmann, *Lebensbilder beruehmter Kantoren*, 2 (1921), 152–6; E. Zaludkowski, *Kultur Treger fun der Yidisher Liturgie* (1930), 274–5; Idelsohn, Music, 240, 292.

[Joshua Leib Ne'eman]

HENNA (Heb. כֹּפֶר, *kofer*), the plant *Lawsonia alba* whose leaves yield a much-used dye. Its English name is derived from Arabic. Henna is included among the spices growing in the garden of tropical spices to which the beloved maiden is compared in Song of Songs (4:12–13), while she compares her beloved to "a cluster of henna in the vineyards of En-Gedi" (*ibid.* 1:14). The Mishnah mentions henna alongside the rose among the aromatic plants that grow in Ereẓ Israel (Shev. 7:6). The henna of "Ashkelon in Judea" was praised by Pliny (*Historia Naturalis*, 12:51) and Dioscorides (*De materia medica*, 1:117). According to Josephus (Wars 1:181), the name of Herod's mother was Cypros (Κύπρος), that is *kofer*, and he called a fortress which he built "Cypros" after her. Henna is a shrub which is grown in various places in the Jordan Valley and in the Shephelah. Its aromatic flowers are arranged in clusters (hence the "cluster of henna"). From its root or leaves a powder is prepared which is soluble in water and produces a reddish-orange dye. Throughout the ages the peoples of the East prized this beautiful, fast dye which was used for dying the hair, the palms of the hand, the nails, and even the teeth. With it the Egyptians dyed mummies. The Talmud (TJ, Git. 69b) mentions henna as a remedy for a disease of the urinary organs. In Yemen, Jews smeared a bride's body with henna dye (the person doing it pays for the privilege with a wedding gift) and hence the name "henna night" given by them to a marriage. The custom is still maintained by several communities in Israel.

BIBLIOGRAPHY: Loew, Flora, 2 (1924), 218–25; H.N. and A.L. Moldenke, *Plants of the Bible* (1952), index; J. Feliks, *Olam ha-Ẓome'aḥ ha-Mikra'i* (1968²), 270–1. **ADD BIBLIOGRAPHY:** Feliks, Ha-Ẓome'aḥ, 84.

[Jehuda Feliks]

HENOCHSBERG, EDGAR SAMUEL (1894–1966), South African Supreme Court judge. Born in Durban, he became king's counsel in 1939, and was raised to the bench in 1955. Maintaining a constant interest in Jewish affairs, Henochsberg was a founder, executive officer, and president of the Durban Jewish Club, Durban Hebrew Congregation, and Council of Natal Jewry. Active on behalf of many undenominational and humanitarian causes, he was emeritus commissioner of the South African Scout Council, a chairman of Adams College Educational Trust (for non-whites), and president of the Durban Bantu Children's Welfare Society. He served in Egypt during World War I. In World War II he was judge advocate with the South African forces, and later senior law adviser with the rank of lieutenant colonel.

[Lewis Sowden]

HENRIQUES (Quixano Henriques), Anglo-Jewish family. The family progenitor was MOSES HENRIQUES of Kingston, Jamaica, who married Abigail Quixano in 1768. The eldest son of this marriage, ABRAHAM QUIXANO HENRIQUES (18/19th cent.), immigrated to London, where he established himself as a West India merchant. His sons DAVID (1804–1870) and JACOB (1811–1898) were prominent communal workers and were among the founders of the Reform congregation in London in 1840.

Later members of the family include: HENRY STRAUS QUIXANO HENRIQUES K.C. (1864–1925), lawyer, communal worker, historian, president of the Board of Deputies of British Jews (1922–25), and author of the standard works *The Jews and the English Law* (1908) and *Jewish Marriages and the English Law* (1909). CYRIL QUIXANO HENRIQUES (1880–1976) was a civil engineer. He served in the Indian Civil Service before going to Palestine, where he was engineer for the Zionist Executive from 1925 to 1928. Returning to England he was active in Zionist affairs and a leader of the Nazi boycott movement of the 1930s.

SIR BASIL LUCAS QUIXANO HENRIQUES (1890–1961) was a social worker, a leading authority on juvenile delinquency, and an advocate of progressive Judaism. Born in London, Basil Henriques was educated at Harrow and Oxford, where he helped to edit a prayer book for the synagogue services conducted by the undergraduates. An officer during World War I, he wrote sermons and prayers, later issued in booklet form, for Jewish troops. Henriques devoted his principal efforts to helping underprivileged and delinquent youth in the East End of London. In 1915 he founded his first boys club. After World War I, Henriques and his wife established the St. George's Jewish Settlement. A gift of £65,000 from Bernhard *Baron enabled them to build more spacious premises, and they made their home there so that they could be close to the Settlement's members, who numbered in the thousands. As a magistrate and later chairman of the East London Juvenile Court, Basil Henriques' chief purpose was to understand the causes of juvenile delinquency and develop preventive social action. He visited boys' homes and prisons, suggested reforms, and took a great interest in the care of young Jewish offenders after their discharge. He made lecture tours throughout the world to spread his views on the prevention of juvenile delinquency and to advance the cause of progressive Judaism. After World War II he headed the anti-Zionist "Jewish Fellowship" which however dissolved on the establishment of the State of Israel. Basil Henriques was knighted in 1955 for his services as social worker and magistrate. He described his career in *The Indiscretions of a Warden* (1937) and *The Indiscretions of a Magistrate* (1950). He also wrote *The Home Menders* (1955). Sir Basil's wife LADY ROSA LOUISE HENRIQUES (1889–1972), a sister of Herbert Loewe, was a gifted artist and herself a noted social worker. She was chairwoman of the British *OSE, vice president of English *ORT, and chairwoman of the German section for Jewish Relief Abroad.

ROBERT DAVID QUIXANO HENRIQUES (1905–1967) was an author and soldier, who devoted his most productive years to writing, farming, and Anglo-Jewish affairs. Robert Henriques joined the British regular army, retiring in 1933. His first important novel, *No Arms, No Armour* (1939), was awarded various prizes. He returned to the army on the outbreak of World War II and served in the artillery and the commandos before reaching the rank of colonel as a planning officer on the combined operation staff of Field Marshal Montgomery. His awards included the U.S. Silver Star. His novel *Through the Valley* (1950), published in the U.S. as *Too Little Love*, was awarded the James Tait Black Memorial Prize. A member of the London Reform Synagogue and originally a vigorous opponent of political Zionism, Henriques underwent a "conversion" to Zionism at the time of Israel's *Sinai Campaign of 1956, which he recorded in his *100 Hours to Suez* (1957). He subsequently built himself a cottage in kibbutz Kefar ha-Nasi and paid annual visits to Israel. In his later years, he was president of The Bridge in Britain, an organization established to promote friendship between Britain and Israel. Robert Henriques' autobiographical novel, *The Commander* (published in 1967), deals with his commando career in World War II. Henriques' biographic fragments appeared in 1969 in *From a Biography of Myself.*

His other works include biographies of two Anglo-Jewish oil tycoons, *Marcus Samuel, First Viscount Bearsted* (1960) and *Sir Robert Waley-Cohen, 1877–1952* (1966).

Members of the Kingston, Jamaica, branch of the Henriques family, distinguished themselves in the development of Jamaica's industry and by their activity in civic affairs.

BIBLIOGRAPHY: *Times* (Nov. 13, 1925), 14; *ibid.* (Dec. 4, 1961), 15; *ibid.* (Jan. 24, 1967); Montefiore, in: *Jewish Monthly*, 1 (Nov. 1947), 9–11; A.M. Hyamson, *Sephardim of England* (1951), 63, 280. **ADD. BIBLIOGRAPHY:** ODNB for Sir Basil Henriques; L. Loewe, *Basil Henriques: A Portrait* (1976); C. Bermant, *The Cousinhood*, 377–93, index; R. Miller, *Divided Against Zion: Anti-Zionist Opposition to a Jewish State in Palestine, 1945–1948* (2000), index.

[Zvi Hermon / Harold Harel Fisch]

°**HENRY IV** (1056–1106), German emperor. His measures defined the status of the Jews in Germany, sometimes in opposition to canon law (e.g., he allowed them to employ Christian wet nurses, and from 1097 permitted baptized Jews to revert to Judaism). In 1074 he exempted the Jews of *Worms from custom dues in imperial towns. His charters granted in 1090 to the Jews of *Speyer and later to those of Worms gave them far-reaching privileges, including the right to travel and trade throughout the empire. In the Worms charter Henry specifically stated that the Jews should come under no jurisdiction but his own, since "they belong to Our chamber." While in Italy during the First Crusade (1096), he urged the German princes to protect the Jews and begged the bishop of Speyer to shelter the survivors of the massacres; later he opened investigation on the theft of Jewish property during the riots. In 1103 Jews were included for the first time in a *Landfrieden* ("peace proclamation") of Mainz – along with clerics, women, and merchants – in which the emperor and his lords pledged to protect certain classes of people for a specified period of time.

BIBLIOGRAPHY: Aronius, Regesten, index; Germ Jud, index; Kisch, Germany, index; G. Kisch, *Forschungen zur Rechts-und Sozialgeschichte der Juden in Deutschland waehrend des Mittelalters* (1955), index; S. Schiffmann, in: ZGJD, 3 (1931), 39–58; S.W. Baron, in: *Sefer… Y.F. Baer* (1961), 112–5.

[Meir Lamed]

HENRY, BUCK (**Zuckerman**; 1930–), U.S. screenwriter and actor. Born in New York, Henry began his career at age 16 in the cast of the long-running Broadway production *Life with Father*. Henry saw military service with the army during the Korean War and afterwards found work writing jokes for the Steve Allen and Garry Moore television shows. Although he gained national attention as a writer/performer on the TV satire *That Was the Week That Was* (1964–65), his first big success was as co-writer with Mel Brooks of the hit comedy series *Get Smart* (1965–70). Henry became a member of the screenwriters' elite when he shared credit for the script of the feature film *The Graduate* (1967), and subsequently wrote the screenplays for such films as *Candy* (1968), *Catch-22* (1970), *The Owl and the Pussycat* (1970), *Is There Sex after Death?* (1971), *What's Up, Doc?* (1972), *The Day of the Dolphin* (1973), *Protocol* (1984), *To Die For* (1995), and *Town and Country* (2001).

In 1978 he co-produced and co-directed *Heaven Can Wait* with Warren Beatty, and in 1980 he directed *First Family*, which he also wrote. As an actor, Henry appeared in many of his films, as well as making cameo appearances in a long string of other movies. Films in which he played a significant role include *Taking Off* (1971), *The Man Who Fell to Earth* (1976), *The Absent-Minded Waiter* (1977), *Strong Medicine* (1979), and *Curtain Call* (1999).

[Jonathan Licht / Ruth Beloff (2nd ed.)]

HENRY (Lyon), EMMA (1788–1870), English poet. The daughter of the Rev. S. Lyon, who opened at Cambridge England's first Jewish boarding school, Henry was one of the first English Jews to attract attention as a writer. Her *Miscellaneous Poems* (Oxford, 1812), dedicated to the Princess of Wales, carried a subscription list headed by the Prince Regent. Her son, Michael Henry, was an early editor of *The Jewish Chronicle*.

HENRY, JACOB (c. 1775–1847), North Carolinian of Bavarian parentage. Henry represented Carteret County in the state's lower chamber in 1808 and 1809, despite constitutional restrictions against non-Protestants. In December 1809, a motion denying him his seat on religious grounds was countered by Henry in an eloquent letter, possibly inspired by Judge John L. Taylor, asserting that "man ought to suffer civil disqualification for what he does… not for what he thinks." Holding that non-Protestants could make the laws, though not interpret or execute them, the House let Henry retain his seat. He later moved to Charleston, South Carolina.

BIBLIOGRAPHY: H. Simonhoff, *Jewish Notables in America, 1776–1865* (1956), 137–40; L. Huehner, AJHSP, 16 (1907), 46–52, 68–71; M. Schappes (ed.), *Documentary History of the Jews in the United States* (1950), 122–5, 597–8.

[Stanley F. Chyet]

HENRY, JULES (1904–1969), U.S. anthropologist. Henry taught at various institutions in the United States and Mexico and from 1947 taught at Washington University, St. Louis, Missouri. He served in various governmental agencies, such as U.S. Department of Agriculture and Office of War Information. As research associate and consultant he also served various national and international organizations, e.g., the World Health Organization and the National Institute of Mental Health. His special interests were in the interrelations of personality and culture; the anthropological approach to the study of education; the analysis of social structure and function; and the emotional problems of children and adolescents. He wrote *Culture Against Man* (1963), and *Jungle People…* (1964).

BIBLIOGRAPHY: B. Kaplan, *Studying Personality Cross Culturally* (1961), index.

[Ephraim Fischoff]

HENRY, MICHAEL (1830–1875), British journalist. Born in London, son of the poet Emma *Henry (Lyon), he worked in a Paris bank. Later he was a patent agent in London and then assistant to Abraham *Benisch, editor of the *Jewish Chronicle*. On Benisch's retirement in 1868, he succeeded him as editor and held the position until his death. Interested in Jewish education, he was secretary to the Stepney Jewish Schools. His collected essays, *Life Thoughts*, appeared in 1875.

HENRY OF WINCHESTER (13th century), the most notorious convert to Christianity in the medieval Jewish community of England. King Henry III was involved in the conversion of Henry of Winchester and ensured that he received at baptism his own name Henry. The king then also knighted him. In 1252 Henry was granted an allowance of 12 pence a day for life at the Exchequer and appointed king's notary at the Exchequer of Jews, apparently with responsibility for compiling the Hebrew plea roll, but this appointment was short-lived or wholly ineffective. His wife, Clarice, was also a convert. From the mid-1250s he was involved in buying and selling Jewish bonds in partnership with Moses of Clare and in 1261 commissioned to inventory bonds in six chests on behalf of the King. In 1278–79 he played an important part in a secret, but officially-approved, scheme for the purchase of silver made from coin-clippings, in order to accumulate evidence against those involved in this illegal activity to be used at their trials. He was subsequently allowed to purchase some of the forfeited property of those executed in the trials for resale at a profit in England and abroad.

BIBLIOGRAPHY: R.C. Stacey, "The Conversion of Jews to Christianity in Thirteenth-Century England," in: *Speculum*, 67 (1992), 276–77; P. Brand, "Jews and the Law in England, 1275–1290," in: *English Historical Review*, 115 (2000), 1138–58.

[Paul Brand (2nd ed.)]

HENSCHEL, SIR GEORGE (**Isidor Georg**; 1850–1934), conductor, singer, and teacher. He was born in Breslau and was active until shortly before his death as a conductor and singer. He was successively during his career a tenor, baritone, basso, and basso profundo. Henschel was the first conductor of the Boston Symphony Orchestra (1881–84), founded the

London Symphony Concerts (1886–97), conducted the Scottish Symphony Orchestra (1893–95), and taught singing at the Royal College of Music and the Institute of Musical Art in New York. He composed an opera, a requiem mass, and songs, and wrote *Personal Recollections of Johannes Brahms* (1907) and the autobiography *Musings and Memories of a Musician* (1918). He converted to Christianity in his youth. He was knighted in 1914.

HENSCHEL BROTHERS. Four artist brothers – AUGUST (d.1829), FRIEDRICH (d. 1837), MORITZ (d. 1862), and WILHELM (d. 1865) – who went from Breslau, Germany, and worked in Berlin from c. 1806 to 1829, when August committed suicide. They worked as a team, signing their work "the brothers Henschel," producing portraits in pastel and miniatures and also engravings which won them popularity. The subjects of their engravings included famous personalities, such as Fichte, scenes from the theater, patriotic illustrations, and "Scenes from the Life of Goethe." When August committed suicide, his brothers returned to Breslau where they lived in obscurity.

HENSEL, KURT (1861–1941), German mathematician. Professor of mathematics at Marburg from 1901, Hensel wrote on number theory and algebra. He edited *Crelle's Journal fuer Mathematik* (1901–36) and wrote the authoritative article "Arithmetische Theorie der algebraischen Funktionen" for *Encyklopaedie der mathematischen Wissenschaften* (1921).

HENSHEL, HARRY D. (1890–1961), U.S. industrialist and sports administrator. He was born in Rochester, New York, joined the Bulova Watch Company in Flushing, New York, in 1918, and by 1930 was one of its principal executives. Henshel devoted his spare time to sports administration; in 1911 he became chairman of the basketball committee of the Metropolitan Association of the Amateur Athletic Union. Henshel served as chairman of the United States Olympic Basketball Committee from 1952 to 1956. In World War II Henshel was a colonel with the U.S. Army in Europe. Henshel organized the U.S. Committee Sports for Israel and was a zealous worker on its behalf. He established a school of watchmaking for paraplegic war veterans. His son HARRY B. HENSHEL (1919–), who became president of Bulova, introduced the first successful phototimer for sporting events.

BIBLIOGRAPHY: B. Postal et al. (eds.), *Encyclopedia of Jews in Sports* (1965), 85f., 466.

[Jesse Harold Silver]

HENTOFF, NAT (1925–), U.S. music critic, journalist, novelist, author. The roots of Hentoff's dazzlingly variegated career are to be found in his boyhood in Depression-era Boston. The son of Russian Jewish immigrants, he grew up in the predominately Catholic city in the era of Father Coughlin, the virulently antisemitic "radio priest," whose broadcasts were followed avidly by Hentoff's neighbors. As a result, he was exposed early and often to antisemitism. Yet at the same time, commuting from the Jewish enclave of Roxbury to school at the famous Boston Latin, he heard and fell in love with jazz and was equally intoxicated by the city's fabulous libraries. This combination would lead him to a lifelong passion for social justice, a deep commitment to freedom of expression and the wonders of the written word, and a profound attachment to the music of America's dispossessed, both black and white.

By his own amused recollection, Hentoff was much too young for admission to the city's liquor-serving jazz clubs, but managed to sneak in anyway to hear the music. It was the beginning of a much-requited love affair, as jazz criticism became the launching pad for his writing career. He would work variously as a critic, disk jockey and columnist (later New York editor) for *Down Beat*. He was, typically, fired by the magazine in 1957 after he lobbied aggressively for them to hire African-American writers. He then wound up at the nascent *Village Voice*, where he agreed to work for free if they would let him write about anything but jazz. He remained at the weekly from then on, writing on education, race, and civil liberties. He also wrote regular columns on civil liberties for publications as radically different as *The Progressive* and the *Wall Street Journal*.

Hentoff's interest in race and jazz led him to yet another career path as a frequently honored author of books for young adults. In 1960 he wrote his first YA novel, *Jazz Country*, and followed it with several more, including *This School Is Driving Me Crazy* (1976) and *The Day They Came to Arrest the Book* (1982). He also wrote adult fiction, non-fiction, and a charming memoir, *Boston Boy* (1986).

BIBLIOGRAPHY: Biography Resource Center, "Nat Hentoff," at: www.galenet.com.

[George Robinson (2nd ed.)]

HEP! HEP!, a derogatory rallying cry against the Jews, common in Germany; also the name given to a series of anti-Jewish riots that broke out in August 1819 in Germany and spread to several neighboring countries. Opinions differ as to the origin of the slogan. Some believe that it was the crusaders' rallying cry, derived from the initials of *Hierosolyma est perdita* ("Jerusalem is lost"). However, more likely it was originally an exhortatory cry for driving domestic animals, particularly goats, in Franconia.

The causes of the 1819 riots are highly complex and are rooted in the social and economic condition of Germany in the early 19th century. The Jewish demand for civil rights at the Congress of *Vienna aroused vicious opposition in academic circles. The antisemitic fulminations of J. *Fries were read aloud in the beerhouses and the anti-Jewish extremism of F. *Ruehs was vigorously supported by the nationalistic *Burschenschaften* (see *Students Associations). Romantic writers and liberal nationalist politicians such as H. *Hundt-Radowsky, E.M. *Arndt, Father Jahn, etc., identified the Jews with the conservative, anti-nationalist policies of *Metternich,

Sites of major Hep! Hep! riots in 1819. Shaded area denotes disturbances in rural districts of Bavaria, Baden, Hesse, and Wuettemberg.

who was accused of being in the pay of Jewish financiers. The bitterness of the population toward the new "upstart" class of Jewish financiers and bankers was expressed by K.B.A. *Sessa in a popular play, *Unser Verkehr* ("Our Crowd," 1815). The situation was further complicated in the rural areas of Baden, Hesse, and Bavaria by the indebtedness of the peasants to Jewish livestock traders and moneylenders. 1816 had been a year of severe famine, and serious unemployment plagued German factories. An entire series of postwar economic misfortunes was blamed on Jewish financiers and entrepreneurs.

The first anti-Jewish outburst occurred on Aug. 2, 1819, in Wuerzburg, after a period of tension between Jews and Christians over commercial and civil rights, and was initiated by students. The Jews fled as window smashing and looting continued, and returned only after troops had restored order. The riots spread to Bamberg, Bayreuth, and other localities in Bavaria. In Frankfurt, where the dispute over civil rights had been particularly bitter, the houses of the Rothschilds became a special object of attack. The senate with difficulty restored order by means of police and troops. Troops had to be called in at Leipzig, Dresden, and Darmstadt; riots occurred in Mannheim, Pforzheim, and the rural areas of Baden. In Heidelberg a volunteer contingent of students restored order. Danzig (Gdansk) was the only place in autocratic Prussia where riots took place; they were also rare in Austria. Anti-Jewish disturbances also took place in Riga, Cracow, and Prague. The serious riots in Hamburg on September 1 spread to Copenhagen, where rioters were sailors and burghers, and to the neighboring villages. They had to be suppressed by troops.

The authorities utilized the riots to argue that emancipation must be withheld from the Jews because of the obvious ill-will this aroused among the people. At the same time they did their best to suppress all details on the course of the riots. Jews also sought to suppress the details, and the significance of the riots was belittled in Jewish Enlightenment and Reform circles, the periodical *Sulamith barely taking note that they occurred lest this "weaken our coreligionists' love for our Christian fellow citizens." However, Jewish banks refused to do business with Christian merchants suspected of participating in the riots, and large numbers of Jews stayed away from the September fair in Frankfurt. Even more forceful had been the threat of the Rothschilds to leave both Frankfurt and Germany if the riots did not cease. The riots were a factor in speeding the process of assimilation and conversion among some Jews. Conversely, they influenced the foundation of the Verein fuer Kultur und Wissenschaft der Juden.

The Hep! Hep! cry was raised a few more times in Germany in the following decades and was again heard during the revolution of 1830. A. *Stoecker's antisemitic movement tried to revive the rallying cry but it was outdated, having been replaced by more virulent slogans.

BIBLIOGRAPHY: E. Sterling, *Judenhass* (1969), passim; idem, in: YLBI, 3 (1958), 103–21; idem, in: HJ, 12 (1950), 105–42; H. Bender, *Der Kampf um die Judenemanzipation im Spiegel der Flugschriften, 1815–1820* (1939); S. Stern, in: MGWJ, 83 (1963), 645–66; M. Kohler, in: AJHSP, 26 (1918), 33–81; E.C. Corti, *The Rise of the House of Rothschild* (1928), 208–14; Lifschits, in: *YIVO Bleter*, 14 (1939), 26–45; U. Jeggle, *Judendoerfer in Wittenberg* (1969), 90ff.

[Henry Wasserman]

HEPHER (Heb. חֵפֶר). (1) A royal Canaanite city mentioned in the list of kings defeated by Joshua (12:17); it appears between Tappuah (Sheikh Abu Zarad in the hill country of Ephraim) and Aphek (Ras al-ʿAyn at the sources of the Yarkon). The "land of Hepher" is included in one of Solomon's administrative districts together with Aruboth and Socoh (Ra's al-Shuwayka near Tulkarm; I Kings 4:10). On the basis of these topographical details, most scholars locate Hepher in the northern Sharon, in the area formerly known as the Wadi Ḥawārith, a region sparsely populated in antiquity, containing mostly swamps and woods. The Israelites were apparently unable to subdue the few Canaanite cities in this area until the time of David. The appearance of the name Hepher in the genealogies of Manasseh (Num. 26:33; 27:1; Josh. 17:2) has led various scholars to assume that some of the former Canaanite population had become integrated into the Israelite clans. Since Zelophehad, son of Hepher, had no male descendants (Num. 27:1; Josh. 17:3), and the names of some of his daughters correspond to known localities in the vicinity of Samaria, it has been suggested that these families were grafted onto the Israelite tribal system. The exact location of the city of Hepher is uncertain. Alt has proposed al-Ṭayyiba (Ophrah) south of Tūl Karm, and Mazar has suggested Tell al-Ifshār in the western Sharon, where pottery from the 16th century B.C.E. to the Roman period has been found. Others, however, locate Hepher in the northern part of the hills of Samaria on the assumption that all the clans of Manasseh were settled in this region.

(2) A city mentioned in the Talmud as the home of Tanḥum b. Ḥiyya, a pupil of Manna (TJ, Shev. 6:1, 36c). It was some 12 mi. (19 km.) from Sepphoris. The city has been identified with *Gath-Hepher, the traditional home of Jonah (II Kings 14:25) whose tomb is still venerated in the nearby village of Mashhad. Jerome (*Praefatio in Jonam*) and Benjamin of Tudela also locate the tomb in this vicinity (cf. Gen. R. 98:11).

BIBLIOGRAPHY: (1) Albright, in: JPOS, 11 (1931), 249ff.; Alt, in: PJB, 22 (1926), 68–9; 28 (1932), 27ff.; idem, in: ZDPV, 70 (1954), 48, 59–60; Maisler, in: ZDPV, 58 (1935), 82; Abel, Geog, 2 (1938), 23, 81, 348; Press, Ereẓ, 2 (1948), 268–9; Aharoni, Land, index; Wright, in: *Ereẓ Yisrael*, 8 (1967), 63 (English section). (2) Neubauer, Géogr, 200–1; Albright, in: BASOR, 35 (1929), 8; Avi-Yonah, in: QDAP, 5 (1936), 32, s.v. *Gath Ofer*; idem, Geog, 134.

[Michael Avi-Yonah]

HEPPNER, ARON (1865–1938), German rabbi, historian, and archivist. Born in Pleschen, Posen province, Heppner served as rabbi at Koschmin from 1890, also at Jarotschin from 1906, administering both rabbinates until 1920 when Posen became Polish once more. Heppner settled in Breslau, where he continued to act as rabbi and teacher, but also founded and directed the archives of the community (from 1924). His scholarly interest was devoted to local Jewish history, first of his native province and later of Breslau. His main publications, apart from contributions on the history of Jewish families to periodicals and newspapers, were *Aus Vergangenheit und Gegenwart der Juden und der juedischen Gemeinden in den Posener Landen* (with I.J. Herzberg, 1909–29) and *Juedische Persoenlichkeiten in und aus Breslau* (1931). Between 1900 and 1926 he published a "Jewish-Literary Calendar."

BIBLIOGRAPHY: O. Marcus, *A. Heppner* (Ger., 1965).

ABBREVIATIONS

GENERAL ABBREVIATIONS

This list contains abbreviations used in the Encyclopaedia (apart from the standard ones, such as geographical abbreviations, points of compass, etc.). For names of organizations, institutions, etc., in abbreviation, see Index. For bibliographical abbreviations of books and authors in Rabbinical literature, see following lists.

*	Cross reference; i.e., an article is to be found under the word(s) immediately following the asterisk (*).
°	Before the title of an entry, indicates a non-Jew (post-biblical times).
‡	Indicates reconstructed forms.
>	The word following this sign is derived from the preceding one.
<	The word preceding this sign is derived from the following one.

ad loc.	*ad locum*, “at the place”; used in quotations of commentaries.
A.H.	*Anno Hegirae*, “in the year of Hegira,” i.e., according to the Muslim calendar.
Akk.	Addadian.
A.M.	*anno mundi*, “in the year (from the creation) of the world.”
anon.	anonymous.
Ar.	Arabic.
Aram.	Aramaic.
Ass.	Assyrian.
b.	born; *ben, bar.*
Bab.	Babylonian.
B.C.E.	Before Common Era (= B.C.).
bibl.	bibliography.
Bul.	Bulgarian.
c., ca.	Circa.
C.E.	Common Era (= A.D.).
cf.	*confer*, “compare.”
ch., chs.	chapter, chapters.
comp.	compiler, compiled by.
Cz.	Czech.
D	according to the documentary theory, the Deuteronomy document.
d.	died.
Dan.	Danish.
diss., dissert,	dissertation, thesis.
Du.	Dutch.
E.	according to the documentary theory, the Elohist document (i.e., using Elohim as the name of God) of the first five (or six) books of the Bible.
ed.	editor, edited, edition.
eds.	editors.
e.g.	*exempli gratia*, “for example.”
Eng.	English.
et al.	*et alibi*, “and elsewhere”; or *et alii*, “and others”; “others.”
f., ff.	and following page(s).
fig.	figure.
fl.	flourished.
fol., fols	folio(s).
Fr.	French.
Ger.	German.
Gr.	Greek.
Heb.	Hebrew.
Hg., Hung	Hungarian.
ibid	*Ibidem*, “in the same place.”
incl. bibl.	includes bibliography.
introd.	introduction.
It.	Italian.
J	according to the documentary theory, the Jahwist document (i.e., using YHWH as the name of God) of the first five (or six) books of the Bible.
Lat.	Latin.
lit.	literally.
Lith.	Lithuanian.
loc. cit.	*loco citato*, “in the [already] cited place.”
Ms., Mss.	Manuscript(s).
n.	note.
n.d.	no date (of publication).
no., nos	number(s).
Nov.	Novellae (Heb. *Ḥiddushim*).
n.p.	place of publication unknown.
op. cit.	*opere citato*, “in the previously mentioned work.”
P.	according to the documentary theory, the Priestly document of the first five (or six) books of the Bible.
p., pp.	page(s).
Pers.	Persian.
pl., pls.	plate(s).
Pol.	Polish.
Port.	Potuguese.
pt., pts.	part(s).
publ.	published.
R.	Rabbi or Rav (before names); in Midrash (after an abbreviation) – *Rabbah*.
r.	recto, the first side of a manuscript page.
Resp.	Responsa (Latin “answers,” Hebrew *She'elot u-Teshuvot* or *Teshuvot*), collections of rabbinic decisions.
rev.	revised.

Rom.	Romanian.
Rus(s).	Russian.
Slov.	Slovak.
Sp.	Spanish.
s.v.	*sub verbo, sub voce*, "under the (key) word."
Sum	Sumerian.
summ.	Summary.
suppl.	supplement.
Swed.	Swedish.
tr., trans(l).	translator, translated, translation.
Turk.	Turkish.
Ukr.	Ukrainian.
v., vv.	*verso*. The second side of a manuscript page; also verse(s).
Yid.	Yiddish.

ABBREVIATIONS USED IN RABBINICAL LITERATURE

Adderet Eliyahu, Karaite treatise by Elijah b. Moses *Bashyazi.
Admat Kodesh, Resp. by Nissim Ḥayyim Moses b. Joseph |Mizraḥi.
Aguddah, Sefer ha-, Nov. by *Alexander Suslin ha-Kohen.
Ahavat Ḥesed, compilation by *Israel Meir ha-Kohen.
Aliyyot de-Rabbenu Yonah, Nov. by *Jonah b. Avraham Gerondi.
Arukh ha-Shulḥan, codification by Jehiel Michel *Epstein.
Asayin (= positive precepts), subdivision of: (1) *Maimonides, *Sefer ha-Mitzvot;* (2) *Moses b. Jacob of Coucy, *Semag.*
Asefat Dinim, subdivision of *Sedei Ḥemed* by Ḥayyim Hezekiah *Medini, an encyclopaedia of precepts and responsa.
Asheri = *Asher b. Jehiel.
Aeret Ḥakhamim, by Baruch *Frankel-Teomim; pt, 1: Resp. to Sh. Ar.; pt2: Nov. to Talmud.
Ateret Zahav, subdivision of the *Levush*, a codification by Mordecai b. Abraham (Levush) *Jaffe; *Ateret Zahav* parallels Tur. YD.
Ateret Ẓevi, Comm. To Sh. Ar. by Ẓevi Hirsch b. Azriel.
Avir Ya'akov, Resp. by Jacob Avigdor.
Avkat Rokhel, Resp. by Joseph b. Ephraim *Caro.
Avnei Millu'im, Comm. to Sh. Ar., EH, by *Aryeh Loeb b. Joseph ha-Kohen.
Avnei Nezer, Resp. on Sh. Ar. by Abraham b. Ze'ev Nahum Bornstein of *Sochaczew.
Avodat Massa, Compilation of Tax Law by Yoasha Abraham Judah.
Azei ha-Levanon, Resp. by Judah Leib *Zirelson.

Ba'al ha-Tanya – *Shneur Zalman of Lyady.
Ba'ei Ḥayyei, Resp. by Ḥayyim b. Israel *Benveniste.
Ba'er Heitev, Comm. To Sh. Ar. The parts on OḤ and EH are by Judah b. Simeon *Ashkenazi, the parts on YD AND ḤM by *Zechariah Mendel b. Aryeh Leib. Printed in most editions of Sh. Ar.
Baḥ = Joel *Sirkes.
Baḥ, usual abbreviation for *Bayit Ḥadash*, a commentary on Tur by Joel *Sirkes; printed in most editions of Tur.
Bayit Ḥadash, see *Baḥ*.
Berab = Jacob Berab, also called Ri Berav.
Bedek ha-Bayit, by Joseph b. Ephraim *Caro, additions to his *Beit Yosef* (a comm. to Tur). Printed sometimes inside *Beit Yosef*, in smaller type. Appears in most editions of Tur.
Be'er ha-Golah, Commentary to Sh. Ar. By Moses b. Naphtali Hirsch *Rivkes; printed in most editions of Sh. Ar.
Be'er Mayim, Resp. by Raphael b. Abraham Manasseh Jacob.
Be'er Mayim Ḥayyim, Resp. by Samuel b. Ḥayyim *Vital.
Be'er Yizḥak, Resp. by Isaac Elhanan *Spector.
Beit ha-Beḥirah, Comm. to Talmud by Menahem b. Solomon *Meiri.
Beit Me'ir, Nov. on Sh. Ar. by Meir b. Judah Leib Posner.
Beit Shelomo, Resp. by Solomon b. Aaron Ḥason (the younger).
Beit Shemu'el, Comm. to Sh. Ar., EH, by *Samuel b. Uri Shraga Phoebus.
Beit Ya'akov, by Jacob b. Jacob Moses *Lorberbaum; pt.1: Nov. to Ket.; pt.2: Comm. to EH.
Beit Yisrael, collective name for the commentaries *Derishah*, *Perishah*, and *Be'urim* by Joshua b. Alexander ha-Kohen *Falk. See under the names of the commentaries.
Beit Yizḥak, Resp. by Isaac *Schmelkes.
Beit Yosef: (1) Comm. on Tur by Joseph b. Ephraim *Caro; printed in most editions of Tur; (2) Resp. by the same.
Ben Yehudah, Resp. by Abraham b. Judah Litsch (ליטש) Rosenbaum.
Bertinoro, Standard commentary to Mishnah by Obadiah *Bertinoro. Printed in most editions of the Mishnah.
[Be'urei] Ha-Gra, Comm. to Bible, Talmud, and Sh. Ar. By *Elijah b. Solomon Zalmon (Gaon of Vilna); printed in major editions of the mentioned works.
Be'urim, Glosses to Isserles *Darkhei Moshe* (a comm. on Tur) by Joshua b. Alexander ha-Kohen *Falk; printed in many editions of Tur.
Binyamin Ze'ev, Resp. by *Benjamin Ze'ev b. Mattathias of Arta.
Birkei Yosef, Nov. by Ḥayyim Joseph David *Azulai.
Ha-Buẓ ve-ha-Argaman, subdivision of the *Levush* (a codification by Mordecai b. Abraham (Levush) *Jaffe); *Ha-Buẓ ve-ha-Argaman* parallels Tur, EH.

Comm. = Commentary

Da'at Kohen, Resp. by Abraham Isaac ha-Kohen. *Kook.
Darkhei Moshe, Comm. on Tur Moses b. Israel *Isserles; printed in most editions of Tur.
Darkhei No'am, Resp. by *Mordecai b. Judah ha-Levi.
Darkhei Teshuvah, Nov. by Ẓevi *Shapiro; printed in the major editions of Sh. Ar.
De'ah ve-Haskel, Resp. by Obadiah Hadaya (see *Yaskil Avdi).*

Derashot Ran, Sermons by *Nissim b. Reuben Gerondi.
Derekh Ḥayyim, Comm. to *Avot* by *Judah Loew (Lob., Liwa) b. Bezalel (Maharal) of Prague.
Derishah, by Joshua b. Alexander ha-Kohen *Falk; additions to his *Perishah* (comm. on Tur); printed in many editions of Tur.
Derushei ha-Ẓelaḥ, Sermons, by Ezekiel b. Judah Halevi *Landau.
Devar Avraham, Resp. by Abraham *Shapira.
Devar Shemu'el, Resp. by Samuel *Aboab.
Devar Yehoshu'a, Resp. by Joshua Menahem b. Isaac Aryeh Ehrenberg.
Dikdukei Soferim, variae lections of the talmudic text by Raphael Nathan*Rabbinowicz.
Divrei Emet, Resp. by Isaac Bekhor David.
Divrei Ge'onim, Digest of responsa by Ḥayyim Aryeh b. Jeḥiel Ẓevi *Kahana.
Divrei Ḥamudot, Comm. on *Piskei ha-Rosh* by Yom Tov Lipmann b. Nathan ha-Levi *Heller; printed in major editions of the Talmud.
Divrei Ḥayyim several works by Ḥayyim *Halberstamm; if quoted alone refers to his Responsa.
Divrei Malkhi'el, Resp. by Malchiel Tenebaum.
Divrei Rivot, Resp. by Isaac b. Samuel *Adarbi.
Divrei Shemu'el, Resp. by Samuel Raphael Arditi.

Edut be-Ya'akov, Resp. by Jacob b. Abraham *Boton.
Edut bi-Yhosef, Resp. by Joseph b. Isaac *Almosnino.
Ein Ya'akov, Digest of talmudic *aggadot* by Jacob (Ibn) *Habib.
Ein Yiẓḥak, Resp. by Isaac Elhanan *Spector.
Ephraim of Lentshitz = Solomon *Luntschitz.
Erekh Leḥem, Nov. and glosses to Sh. Ar. by Jacob b. Abraham *Castro.
Eshkol, Sefer ha-, Digest of *halakhot* by *Abraham b. Isaac of Narbonne.
Et Sofer, Treatise on Law Court documents by Abraham b. Mordecai *Ankawa, in the 2nd vol. of his Resp. *Kerem Ḥamar.*
Etan ha-Ezraḥi, Resp. by Abraham b. Israel Jehiel (Shrenzl) *Rapaport.
Even ha-Ezel, Nov. to Maimonides' *Yad Ḥazakah* by Isser Zalman *Meltzer.
Even ha-Ezer, also called *Raban* of *Ẓafenat Pa'ne'aḥ,* rabbinical work with varied contents by *Eliezer b. Nathan of Mainz; not identical with the subdivision of Tur, Shulḥan Arukh, etc.
Ezrat Yehudah, Resp. by *Isaar Judah b. Nechemiah of Brisk.

Gan Eden, Karaite treatise by *Aaron b. Elijah of Nicomedia.
Gersonides = *Levi b. Gershom, also called Leo Hebraecus, or Ralbag.
Ginnat Veradim, Resp. by *Abraham b. Mordecai ha-Levi.

Haggahot, another name for *Rema.*
Haggahot Asheri, glosses to *Piskei ha-Rosh* by *Israel of Krems; printed in most Talmud editions.
Haggahot Maimuniyyot, Comm,. to Maimonides' Yad Ḥazakah by *Meir ha-Kohen; printed in most eds. of Yad.
Haggahot Mordekhai, glosses to *Mordekhai* by Samuel *Schlettstadt; printed in most editions of the Talmud after *Mordekhai.*
Haggahot ha-Rashash on Tosafot, annotations of Samuel *Strashun on the Tosafot (printed in major editions of the Talmud).
Ha-Gra = *Elijah b. Solomon Zalman (Gaon of Vilna).
Ha-Gra, Commentaries on Bible, Talmud, and Sh. Ar. respectively, by *Elijah b. Solomon Zalman (Gaon of Vilna); printed in major editions of the mentioned works.
Hai Gaon, Comm. = his comm. on Mishnah.
Ḥakham Ẓevi, Resp. by Ẓevi Hirsch b. Jacob *Ashkenazi.
Halakhot = Rif, *Halakhot.* Compilation and abstract of the Talmud by Isaac b. Jacob ha-Kohen *Alfasi; printed in most editions of the Talmud.
Halakhot Gedolot, compilation of *halakhot* from the Geonic period, arranged acc. to the Talmud. Here cited acc. to ed. Warsaw (1874). Author probably *Simeon Kayyara of Basra.
Halakhot Pesukot le-Rav Yehudai Ga'on compilation of *halakhot.*
Halakhot Pesukot min ha-Ge'onim, compilation of *halakhot* from the geonic period by different authors.
Ḥananel, Comm. to Talmud by *Hananel b. Ḥushi'el; printed in some editions of the Talmud.
Harei Besamim, Resp. by Aryeh Leib b. Isaac *Horowitz.
Ḥassidim, Sefer, Ethical maxims by *Judah b. Samuel he-Ḥasid.
Hassagot Rabad on Rif, Glosses on Rif, *Halakhot,* by *Abraham b. David of Posquières.
Hassagot Rabad [on Yad], Glosses on Maimonides, *Yad Ḥazakah,* by *Abraham b. David of Posquières.
Hassagot Ramban, Glosses by Naḥmanides on Maimonides' *Sefer ha-Mitzvot;* usually printed together with *Sefer ha-Mitzvot.*
Ḥatam Sofer = Moses *Sofer.
Ḥavvot Ya'ir, Resp. and varia by Jair Ḥayyim *Bacharach
Ḥayyim Or Zaru'a = *Ḥayyim (Eliezer) b. Isaac.
Ḥazon Ish = Abraham Isaiah *Karelitz.
Ḥazon Ish, Nov. by Abraham Isaiah *Karelitz
Ḥedvat Ya'akov, Resp. by Aryeh Judah Jacob b. David Dov Meisels (article under his father's name).
Heikhal Yiẓḥak, Resp. by Isaac ha-Levi *Herzog.
Ḥelkat Meḥokek, Comm. to Sh. Ar., by Moses b. Isaac Judah *Lima.
Ḥelkat Ya'akov, Resp. by Mordecai Jacob Breisch.
Ḥemdah Genuzah, , Resp. from the geonic period by different authors.
Ḥemdat Shelomo, Resp. by Solomon Zalman *Lipschitz.
Ḥida = Ḥayyim Joseph David *Azulai.
Ḥiddushei Halakhot ve-Aggadot, Nov. by Samuel Eliezer b. Judah ha-Levi *Edels.
Ḥikekei Lev, Resp. by Ḥayyim *Palaggi.
Ḥikrei Lev, Nov. to Sh. Ar. by Joseph Raphael b. Ḥayyim Joseph Ḥazzan (see article *Ḥazzan Family).
Hil. = Hilkhot … (e.g. *Hilkhot Shabbat).*
Ḥinnukh, Sefer ha-, List and explanation of precepts attributed (probably erroneously) to Aaron ha-Levi of Barcelona (see article *Ha-Ḥinnukh*).
Ḥok Ya'akov, Comm. to Hil. Pesaḥ in Sh. Ar., OḤ, by Jacob b. Joseph *Reicher.
Ḥokhmat Sehlomo (1), Glosses to Talmud, *Rashi* and Tosafot by Solomon b. Jehiel "Maharshal") *Luria; printed in many editions of the Talmud.
Ḥokhmat Sehlomo (2), Glosses and Nov. to Sh. Ar. by Solomon b. Judah Aaron *Kluger printed in many editions of Sh. Ar.
Ḥur, subdivision of the *Levush,* a codification by Mordecai b. Abraham (Levush) *Jaffe; *Hur* (or *Levush ha-Hur)* parallels Tur, OḤ, 242–697.
Ḥut ha-Meshullash, fourth part of the *Tashbeẓ* (Resp.), by Simeon b. Zemaḥ *Duran.

Ibn Ezra, Comm. to the Bible by Abraham *Ibn Ezra; printed in the major editions of the Bible *("Mikra'ot Gedolot").*
Imrei Yosher, Resp. by Meir b. Aaron Judah *Arik.
Ir Shushan, Subdivision of the *Levush,* a codification by Mordecai b. Abraham (Levush) *Jaffe; *Ir Shushan* parallels Tur, ḤM.
Israel of Bruna = Israel b. Ḥayyim *Bruna.
Ittur. Treatise on precepts by *Isaac b. Abba Mari of Marseilles.

Jacob Be Rab = *Be Rab.
Jacob b. Jacob Moses of Lissa = Jacob b. Jacob Moses *Lorberbaum.
Judah B. Simeon = Judah b. Simeon *Ashkenazi.
Judah Minz = Judah b. Eliezer ha-Levi *Minz.

Kappei Aharon, Resp. by Aaron Azriel.
Kehillat Ya'akov, Talmudic methodology, definitions etc. by Israel Jacob b. Yom Tov *Algazi.
Kelei Ḥemdah, Nov. and *pilpulim* by Meir Dan *Plotzki of Ostrova, arranged acc. to the Torah.
Keli Yakar, Annotations to the Torah by Solomon *Luntschitz.
Keneh Ḥokhmah, Sermons by Judah Loeb *Pochwitzer.
Keneset ha-Gedolah, Digest of *halakhot* by Ḥayyim b. Israel *Benveniste; subdivided into annotations to *Beit Yosef* and annotations to Tur.
Keneset Yisrael, Resp. by Ezekiel b. Abraham Katzenellenbogen (see article *Katzenellenbogen Family).
Kerem Ḥamar, Resp. and varia by Abraham b. Mordecai *Ankawa.
Kerem Shelmo. Resp. by Solomon b. Joseph *Amarillo.
Keritut, [Sefer], Methodology of the Talmud by *Samson b. Isaac of Chinon.
Kesef ha-Kedoshim, Comm. to Sh. Ar., ḤM, by Abraham *Wahrmann; printed in major editions of Sh. Ar.
Kesef Mishneh, Comm. to Maimonides, *Yad Ḥazakah,* by Joseph b. Ephraim *Caro; printed in most editions of *Yad Ḥazakah.*
Keẓot ha-Ḥoshen, Comm. to Sh. Ar., ḤM, by *Aryeh Loeb b. Joseph ha-Kohen; printed in major editions of Sh. Ar.
Kol Bo [*Sefer*], Anonymous collection of ritual rules; also called *Sefer ha-Likkutim.*
Kol Mevasser, Resp. by Meshullam *Rath.
Korban Aharon, Comm. to *Sifra* by Aaron b. Abraham *Ibn Ḥayyim; pt. 1 is called: *Middot Aharon.*
Korban Edah, Comm. to Jer. Talmud by David *Fraenkel; with additions: *Shiyyurei Korban;* printed in most editions of Jer. Talmud.
Kunteres ha-Kelalim, subdivision of *Sedei Ḥemed,* an encyclopaedia of precepts and responsa by Ḥayyim Hezekiah *Medini.
Kunteres ha-Semikhah, a treatise by *Levi b. Ḥabib; printed at the end of his responsa.
Kunteres Tikkun Olam, part of *Mispat Shalom* (Nov. by Shalom Mordecai b. Moses *Schwadron).

Lavin (negative precepts), subdivision of: (1) *Maimonides, *Sefer ha-Mitzvot;* (2) *Moses b. Jacob of Coucy, *Semag.*
Leḥem Mishneh, Comm. to Maimonides, *Yad Ḥazakah,* by Abraham [Ḥiyya] b. Moses *Boton; printed in most editions of *Yad Ḥazakah.*
Leḥem Rav, Resp. by Abraham [Ḥiyya] b. Moses *Boton.
Leket Yosher, Resp and varia by Israel b. Pethahiah *Isserlein, collected by *Joseph (Joselein) b. Moses.
Leo Hebraeus = *Levi b. Gershom, also called Ralbag or Gersonides.
Levush = Mordecai b. Abraham *Jaffe.
Levush [Malkhut], Codification by Mordecai b. Abraham (Levush) *Jaffe, with subdivisions: [*Levush ha-*] *Tekhelet* (parallels Tur OḤ 1–241); [*Levush ha-*] *Ḥur* (parallels Tur OḤ 242–697); [*Levush*] *Ateret Zahav* (parallels Tur YD); [*Levush ha-Buẓ ve-ha-Argaman* (parallels Tur EH); [*Levush*] *Ir Shushan* (parallels Tur ḤM); under the name *Levush* the author wrote also other works.
Li-Leshonot ha-Rambam, fifth part (nos. 1374–1700) of Resp. by *David b. Solomon ibn Abi Zimra (Radbaz).
Likkutim, Sefer ha-, another name for [*Sefer*] *Kol Bo.*

Ma'adanei Yom Tov, Comm. on *Piskei ha-Rosh* by Yom Tov Lipmann b. Nathan ha-Levi *Heller; printed in many editions of the Talmud.
Mabit = Moses b. Joseph *Trani.
Magen Avot, Comm. to *Avot* by Simeon b. Ẓemaḥ *Duran.
Magen Avraham, Comm. to Sh. Ar., OḤ, by Abraham Abele b. Ḥayyim ha-Levi *Gombiner; printed in many editions of Sh. Ar., OḤ.
Maggid Mishneh, Comm. to Maimonides, *Yad Ḥazakah,* by *Vidal Yom Tov of Tolosa; printed in most editions of the *Yad Ḥazakah.*
Maḥaneh Efrayim, Resp. and Nov., arranged acc. to Maimonides' *Yad Ḥazakah* , by Ephraim b. Aaron *Navon.
Maharai = Israel b. Pethahiah *Isserlein.
Maharal of Prague = *Judah Loew (Lob, Liwa), b. Bezalel.
Maharalbaḥ = *Levi b. Ḥabib.
Maharam Alashkar = Moses b. Isaac *Alashkar.
Maharam Alshekh = Moses b. Ḥayyim *Alashekh.
Maharam Mintz = Moses *Mintz.
Maharam of Lublin = *Meir b. Gedaliah of Lublin.
Maharam of Padua = Meir *Katzenellenbogen.
Maharam of Rothenburg = *Meir b. Baruch of Rothenburg.
Maharam Shik = Moses b. Joseph Schick.
Maharash Engel = Samuel b. Ze'ev Wolf Engel.
Maharashdam = Samuel b. Moses *Medina.
Maharḥash = Ḥayyim (ben) Shabbetai.
Mahari Basan = Jehiel b. Ḥayyim Basan.
Mahari b. Lev = Joseph ibn Lev.
Mahari'az = Jekuthiel Asher Zalman Ensil Zusmir.
Maharibal = *Joseph ibn Lev.
Mahariḥ = Jacob (Israel) *Ḥagiz.
Maharik = Joseph b. Solomon *Colon.
Maharikash = Jacob b. Abraham *Castro.
Maharil = Jacob b. Moses *Moellin.
Maharimat = Joseph b. Moses di Trani (not identical with the Maharit).
Maharit = Joseph b. Moses *Trani.
Maharitaẓ = Yom Tov b. Akiva Ẓahalon. (See article *Ẓahalon Family).
Maharsha = Samuel Eliezer b. Judah ha-Levi *Edels.
Maharshag = Simeon b. Judah Gruenfeld.
Maharshak = Samson b. Isaac of Chinon.
Maharshakh = *Solomon b. Abraham.
Maharshal = Solomon b. Jeḥiel *Luria.
Mahasham = Shalom Mordecai b. Moses *Sschwadron.
Maharyu = Jacob b. Judah *Weil.
Maḥazeh Avraham, Resp. by Abraham Nebagen v. Meir ha-Levi Steinberg.
Maḥazik Berakhah, Nov. by Ḥayyim Joseph David *Azulai.

*Maimonides = Moses b. Maimon, or Rambam.
*Malbim = Meir Loeb b. Jehiel Michael.
Malbim = Malbim's comm. to the Bible; printed in the major editions.
Malbushei Yom Tov, Nov. on *Levush*, OḤ, by Yom Tov Lipmann b. Nathan ha-Levi *Heller.
Mappah, another name for *Rema.*
Mareh ha-Panim, Comm. to Jer. Talmud by Moses b. Simeon *Margolies; printed in most editions of Jer. Talmud.
Margaliyyot ha-Yam, Nov. by Reuben *Margoliot.
Masat Binyamin, Resp. by Benjamin Aaron b. Abraham *Slonik
Mashbir, Ha- = *Joseph Samuel b. Isaac Rodi.
Massa Ḥayyim, Tax *halakhot* by Ḥayyim *Palaggi, with the subdivisions *Missim ve-Arnomiyyot* and *Torat ha-Minhagot.*
Massa Melekh, Compilation of Tax Law by Joseph b. Isaac *Ibn Ezra with concluding part *Ne'ilat She'arim.*
Matteh Asher, Resp. by Asher b. Emanuel Shalem.
Matteh Shimon, Digest of Resp. and Nov. to Tur and *Beit Yosef,* ḤM, by Mordecai Simeon b. Solomon.
Matteh Yosef, Resp. by Joseph b. Moses ha-Levi Nazir (see article under his father's name).
Mayim Amukkim, Resp. by Elijah b. Abraham *Mizraḥi.
Mayim Ḥayyim, Resp. by Ḥayyim b. Dov Beresh Rapaport.
Mayim Rabbim, , Resp. by Raphael *Meldola.
Me-Emek ha-Bakha, , Resp. by Simeon b. Jekuthiel Ephrati.
Me'irat Einayim, usual abbreviation: *Sma* (from: *Sefer Me'irat Einayim*); comm. to Sh. Ar. By Joshua b. Alexander ha-Kohen *Falk; printed in most editions of the Sh. Ar.
Melammed le-Ho'il, Resp. by David Ẓevi *Hoffmann.
Meisharim, [*Sefer*], Rabbinical treatise by *Jeroham b. Meshullam.
Meshiv Davar, Resp. by Naphtali Ẓevi Judah *Berlin.
Mi-Gei ha-Haregah, Resp. by Simeon b. Jekuthiel Ephrati.
Mi-Ma'amakim, Resp. by Ephraim Oshry.
Middot Aharon, first part of *Korban Aharon,* a comm. to *Sifra* by Aaron b. Abraham *Ibn Ḥayyim.
Migdal Oz, Comm. to Maimonides, *Yad Ḥazakah,* by *Ibn Gaon Shem Tov b. Abraham; printed in most editions of the *Yad Ḥazakah.*
Mikhtam le-David, Resp. by David Samuel b. Jacob *Pardo.
Mikkaḥ ve-ha-Mimkar, Sefer ha-, Rabbinical treatise by *Hai Gaon.
Milḥamot ha-Shem, Glosses to Rif, *Halakhot,* by *Naḥmanides.
Minḥat Ḥinnukh, Comm. to *Sefer ha-Ḥinnukh,* by Joseph b. Moses *Babad.
Minḥat Yiẓḥak, Resp. by Isaac Jacob b. Joseph Judah Weiss.
Misgeret ha-Shulḥan, Comm. to Sh. Ar., ḤM, by Benjamin Ze'ev Wolf b. Shabbetai; printed in most editions of Sh. Ar.
Mishkenot ha-Ro'im, Halakhot in alphabetical order by Uzziel Alshekh.
Mishnah Berurah, Comm. to Sh. Ar., OḤ, by *Israel Meir ha-Kohen.
Mishneh le-Melekh, Comm. to Maimonides, *Yad Ḥazakah,* by Judah *Rosanes; printed in most editions of *Yad Ḥazakah.*
Mishpat ha-Kohanim, Nov. to Sh. Ar., ḤM, by Jacob Moses *Lorberbaum, part of his *Netivot ha-Mishpat;* printed in major editions of Sh. Ar.
Mishpat Kohen, Resp. by Abraham Isaac ha-Kohen *Kook.
Mishpat Shalom, Nov. by Shalom Mordecai b. Moses *Schwadron; contains: *Kunteres Tikkun Olam.*
Mishpat u-Ẓedakah be-Ya'akov, Resp. by Jacob b. Reuben *Ibn Ẓur.
Mishpat ha-Urim, Comm. to Sh. Ar., ḤM by Jacob b. Jacob Moses *Lorberbaum, part of his *Netivot ha-Mishpat*; printed in major editons of Sh. Ar.
Mishpat Ẓedek, Resp. by *Melammed Meir b. Shem Tov.
Mishpatim Yesharim, Resp. by Raphael b. Mordecai *Berdugo.
Mishpetei Shemu'el, Resp. by Samuel b. Moses *Kalai (Kal'i).
Mishpetei ha-Tanna'im, Kunteres, Nov on *Levush,* OḤ by Yom Tov Lipmann b. Nathan ha-Levi *Heller.
Mishpetei Uzzi'el (Uziel), Resp. by Ben-Zion Meir Hai *Ouziel.
Missim ve-Arnoniyyot, Tax *halakhot* by Ḥayyim *Palaggi, a subdivision of his work *Massa Ḥayyim* on the same subject.
Mitzvot, Sefer ha-, Elucidation of precepts by *Maimonides; subdivided into *Lavin* (negative precepts) and *Asayin* (positive precepts).
Mitzvot Gadol, Sefer, Elucidation of precepts by *Moses b. Jacob of Coucy, subdivided into *Lavin* (negative precepts) and *Asayin* (positive precepts); the usual abbreviation is *Semag.*
Mitzvot Katan, Sefer, Elucidation of precepts by *Isaac b. Joseph of Corbeil; the usual, abbreviation is *Semak.*
Mo'adim u-Zemannim, Rabbinical treatises by Moses Sternbuch.
Modigliano, Joseph Samuel = *Joseph Samuel b. Isaac, Rodi (Ha-Mashbir).
Mordekhai (Mordecai), halakhic compilation by *Mordecai b. Hillel; printed in most editions of the Talmud after the texts.
Moses b. Maimon = *Maimonides, also called Rambam.
Moses b. Naḥman = Naḥmanides, also called Ramban.
Muram = Isaiah Menahem b. Isaac (from: Morenu R. Mendel).

Naḥal Yiẓḥak, Comm. on Sh. Ar., ḤM, by Isaac Elhanan *Spector.
Naḥalah li-Yhoshu'a, Resp. by Joshua Ẓunẓin.
Naḥalat Shivah, collection of legal forms by *Samuel b. David Moses ha-Levi.
*Naḥmanides = Moses b. Naḥman, also called Ramban.
Naẓiv = Naphtali Ẓevi Judah *Berlin.
Ne'eman Shemu'el, Resp. by Samuel Isaac *Modigilano.
Ne'ilat She'arim, concluding part of *Massa Melekh* (a work on Tax Law) by Joseph b. Isaac *Ibn Ezra, containing an exposition of customary law and subdivided into *Minhagei Issur* and *Minhagei Mamon.*
Ner Ma'aravi, Resp. by Jacob b. Malka.
Netivot ha-Mishpat, by Jacob b. Jacob Moses *Lorberbaum; subdivided into *Mishpat ha-Kohanim,* Nov. to Sh. Ar., ḤM, and *Mishpat ha-Urim,* a comm. on the same; printed in major editions of Sh. Ar.
Netivot Olam, Saying of the Sages by *Judah Loew (Lob, Liwa) b. Bezalel.
Nimmukei Menaḥem of Merseburg, Tax *halakhot* by the same, printed at the end of Resp. Maharyu.
Nimmukei Yosef, Comm. to Rif. *Halakhot,* by Joseph *Ḥabib (Ḥabiba); printed in many editions of the Talmud.
Noda bi-Yhudah, Resp. by Ezekiel b. Judah ha-Levi *Landau; there is a first collection *(Mahadura Kamma)* and a second collection *(Mahadura Tinyana).*
Nov. = Novellae, Ḥiddushim.

Ohel Moshe (1), Notes to Talmud, *Midrash Rabbah,* Yad, *Sifrei* and to several Resp., by Eleazar *Horowitz.

Ohel Moshe (2), Resp. by Moses Jonah Zweig.
Oholei Tam. Resp. by *Tam ibn Yaḥya Jacob b. David; printed in the rabbinical collection *Tummat Yesharim.*
Oholei Ya'akov, Resp. by Jacob de *Castro.
Or ha-Me'ir Resp by Judah Meir b. Jacob Samson Shapiro.
Or Same'aḥ, Comm. to Maimonides, *Yad Ḥazakah,* by *Meir Simḥah ha-Kohen of Dvinsk; printed in many editions of the *Yad Ḥazakah.*
Or Zaru'a [the father] = *Isaac b. Moses of Vienna.
Or Zaru'a [the son] = *Ḥayyim (Eliezer) b. Isaac.
Or Zaru'a, Nov. by *Isaac b. Moses of Vienna.
Orah, Sefer ha-, Compilation of ritual precepts by *Rashi.
Oraḥ la-Ẓaddik, Resp. by Abraham Ḥayyim Rodrigues.
Oẓar ha-Posekim, Digest of Responsa.

Paḥad Yiẓḥak, Rabbinical encyclopaedia by Isaac *Lampronti.
Panim Me'irot, Resp. by Meir b. Isaac *Eisenstadt.
Parashat Mordekhai, Resp. by Mordecai b. Abraham Naphtali *Banet.
Pe'at ha-Sadeh la-Dinim and Pe'at ha-Sadeh la-Kelalim, subdivisions of the *Sedei Ḥemed,* an encyclopaedia of precepts and responsa, by Ḥayyim Hezekaih *Medini.
Penei Moshe (1), Resp. by Moses *Benveniste.
Penei Moshe (2), Comm. to Jer. Talmud by Moses b. Simeon *Margolies; printed in most editions of the Jer. Talmud.
Penei Moshe (3), Comm. on the aggadic passages of 18 treatises of the Bab. and Jer. Talmud, by Moses b. Isaiah Katz.
Penei Yehoshu'a, Nov. by Jacob Joshua b. Ẓevi Hirsch *Falk.
Peri Ḥadash, Comm. on Sh. Ar. By Hezekiah da *Silva.
Perishah, Comm. on Tur by Joshua b. Alexander ha-Kohen *Falk; printed in major edition of Tur; forms together with *Derishah* and *Be'urim* (by the same author) the *Beit Yisrael.*
Pesakim u-Khetavim, 2nd part of the *Terumat ha-Deshen* by Israel b. Pethahiah *Isserlein' also called *Piskei Maharai.*
Pilpula Ḥarifta, Comm. to *Piskei ha-Rosh, Seder Nezikin,* by Yom Tov Lipmann b. Nathan ha-Levi *Heller; printed in major editions of the Talmud.
Piskei Maharai, see *Terumat ha-Deshen,* 2nd part; also called *Pesakim u-Khetavim.*
Piskei ha-Rosh, a compilation of *halakhot,* arranged on the Talmud, by *Asher b. Jehiel (Rosh); printed in major Talmud editions.
Pitḥei Teshuvah, Comm. to Sh. Ar. by Abraham Hirsch b. Jacob *Eisenstadt; printed in major editions of the Sh. Ar.

Rabad = *Abraham b. David of Posquières (Rabad III.).
Raban = *Eliezer b. Nathan of Mainz.
Raban, also called *Ẓafenat Pa'ne'aḥ* or *Even ha-Ezer,* see under the last name.
Rabi Abad = *Abraham b. Isaac of Narbonne.
Radad = David Dov. b. Aryeh Judah Jacob *Meisels.
Radam = Dov Berush b. Isaac Meisels.
Radbaz = *David b Solomon ibn Abi Ziumra.
Radbaz, Comm. to Maimonides, *Yad Ḥazakah,* by *David b. Solomon ibn Abi Zimra.
Ralbag = *Levi b. Gershom, also called Gersonides, or Leo Hebraeus.
Ralbag, Bible comm. by *Levi b. Gershon.
Rama [da Fano] = Menaḥem Azariah *Fano.
Ramah = Meir b. Todros [ha-Levi] *Abulafia.
Ramam = *Menaham of Merseburg.
Rambam = *Maimonides; real name: Moses b. Maimon.
Ramban = *Naḥmanides; real name Moses b. Naḥman.
Ramban, Comm. to Torah by *Naḥmanides; printed in major editions. ("Mikra'ot Gedolot").
Ran = *Nissim b. Reuben Gerondi.
Ran of Rif, Comm. on Rif, *Halakhot,* by Nissim b. Reuben Gerondi.
Ranaḥ = *Elijah b. Ḥayyim.
Rash = *Samson b. Abraham of Sens.
Rash, Comm. to Mishnah, by *Samson b. Abraham of Sens; printed in major Talmud editions.
Rashash = Samuel *Strashun.
Rashba = Solomon b. Abraham *Adret.
Rashba, Resp., see also; *Sefer Teshuvot ha-Rashba ha-Meyuḥasot le-ha-Ramban,* by Solomon b. Abraham *Adret.
Rashbad = Samuel b. David.
Rashbam = *Samuel b. Meir.
Rashbam = Comm. on Bible and Talmud by *Samuel b. Meir; printed in major editions of Bible and most editions of Talmud.
Rashbash = Solomon b. Simeon *Duran.
*Rashi = Solomon b. Isaac of Troyes.
Rashi, Comm. on Bible and Talmud by *Rashi; printed in almost all Bible and Talmud editions.
Raviah = Eliezer b. Joel ha-Levi.
Redak = David *Kimḥi.
Redak, Comm. to Bible by David *Kimḥi.
Redakh = *David b. Ḥayyim ha-Kohen of Corfu.
Re'em = Elijah b. Abraham *Mizraḥi.
Rema = Moses b. Israel *Isserles.
Rema, Glosses to Sh. Ar. by Moses b. Israel *Isserles; printed in almost all editions of the Sh. Ar. inside the text in Rashi type; also called *Mappah* or *Haggahot.*
Remek = Moses Kimḥi.
Remakh = Moses ha-Kohen mi-Lunel.
Reshakh = *Solomon b. Abraham; also called Maharshakh.
Resp. = Responsa, *She'elot u-Teshuvot.*
Ri Berav = *Berab.
Ri Escapa = Joseph b. Saul *Escapa.
Ri Migash = Joseph b. Meir ha-Levi *Ibn Migash.
Riba = Isaac b. Asher ha-Levi; Riba II (Riba ha-Baḥur) = his grandson with the same name.
Ribam = Isaac b. Mordecai (or: Isaac b. Meir).
Ribash = *Isaac b. Sheshet Perfet (or: Barfat).
Rid= *Isaiah b. Mali di Trani the Elder.
Ridbaz = Jacob David b. Ze'ev *Willowski.
Rif = Isaac b. Jacob ha-Kohen *Alfasi.
Rif, *Halakhot*, Compilation and abstract of the Talmud by Isaac b. Jacob ha-Kohen *Alfasi.
Ritba = Yom Tov b. Abraham *Ishbili.
Riẓbam = Isaac b. Mordecai.
Rosh = *Asher b. Jehiel, also called Asheri.
Rosh Mashbir, Resp. by *Joseph Samuel b. Isaac, Rodi.

Sedei Ḥemed, Encyclopaedia of precepts and responsa by Ḥayyim Ḥezekiah *Medini; subdivisions: *Asefat Dinim, Kunteres ha-Kelalim, Pe'at ha-Sadeh la-Dinim, Pe'at ha-Sadeh la-Kelalim.*
Semag, Usual abbreviation of *Sefer Mitzvot Gadol,* elucidation of precepts by *Moses b. Jacob of Coucy; subdivided into *Lavin* (negative precepts) *Asayin* (positive precepts).
Semak, Usual abbreviation of *Sefer Mitzvot Katan,* elucidation of precepts by *Isaac b. Joseph of Corbeil.

Sh. Ar. = *Shulḥan Arukh*, code by Joseph b. Ephraim *Caro.

Sha'ar Mishpat, Comm. to Sh. Ar., ḤM. By Israel Isser b. Ze'ev Wolf.

Sha'arei Shevu'ot, Treatise on the law of oaths by *David b. Saadiah; usually printed together with Rif, *Halakhot;* also called: *She'arim of R. Alfasi.*

Sha'arei Teshuvah, Collection of resp. from Geonic period, by different authors.

Sha'arei Uzzi'el, Rabbinical treatise by Ben-Zion Meir Ha *Ouziel.

Sha'arei Ẓedek, Collection of resp. from Geonic period, by different authors.

Shadal [or Shedal] = Samuel David *Luzzatto.

Shai la-Moreh, Resp. by Shabbetai Jonah.

Shakh, Usual abbreviation of *Siftei Kohen*, a comm. to Sh. Ar., YD and ḤM by *Shabbetai b. Meir ha-Kohen; printed in most editions of Sh. Ar.

Sha'ot-de-Rabbanan, Resp. by *Solomon b. Judah ha-Kohen.

She'arim of R. Alfasi see *Sha'arei Shevu'ot.*

Shedal, see Shadal.

She'elot u-Teshuvot ha-Ge'onim, Collection of resp. by different authors.

She'erit Yisrael, Resp. by Israel Ze'ev Mintzberg.

She'erit Yosef, Resp. by *Joseph b. Mordecai Gershon ha-Kohen.

She'ilat Yaveẓ, Resp. by Jacob *Emden (Yaveẓ).

She'iltot, Compilation arranged acc. to the Torah by *Aḥa (Aḥai) of Shabḥa.

Shem Aryeh, Resp. by Aryeh Leib *Lipschutz.

Shemesh Ẓedakah, Resp. by Samson *Morpurgo.

Shenei ha-Me'orot ha-Gedolim, Resp. by Elijah *Covo.

Shetarot, Sefer ha-, Collection of legal forms by *Judah b. Barzillai al-Bargeloni.

Shevut Ya'akov, Resp. by Jacob b. Joseph Reicher.

Shibbolei ha-Leket Compilation on ritual by Zedekiah b. Avraham *Anav.

Shiltei Gibborim, Comm. to Rif, *Halakhot*, by *Joshua Boaz b. Simeon; printed in major editions of the Talmud.

Shittah Mekubbeẓet, Compilation of talmudical commentaries by Bezalel *Ashkenazi.

Shivat Ẓiyyon, Resp. by Samuel b. Ezekiel *Landau.

Shiyyurei Korban, by David *Fraenkel; additions to his comm. to Jer. Talmud *Korban Edah;* both printed in most editions of Jer. Talmud.

Sho'el u-Meshiv, Resp. by Joseph Saul ha-Levi *Nathanson.

Sh[ulḥan] Ar[ukh] [of Ba'al ha-Tanyal], Code by *Shneur Zalman of Lyady; not identical with the code by Joseph Caro.

Siftei Kohen, Comm. to Sh. Ar., YD and ḤM by *Shabbetai b. Meir ha-Kohen; printed in most editions of Sh. Ar.; usual abbreviation: *Shakh.*

Simḥat Yom Tov, Resp. by Tom Tov b. Jacob *Algazi.

Simlah Ḥadashah, Treatise on *Sheḥitah* by Alexander Sender b. Ephraim Zalman *Schor; see also *Tevu'ot Shor.*

Simeon b. Ẓemaḥ = Simeon b. Ẓemaḥ *Duran.

Sma, Comm. to Sh. Ar. by Joshua b. Alexander ha-Kohen *Falk; the full title is: *Sefer Me'irat Einayim;* printed in most editions of Sh. Ar.

Solomon b. Isaac ha-Levi = Solomon b. Isaac *Levy.

Solomon b. Isaac of Troyes = *Rashi.

Tal Orot, Rabbinical work with various contents, by Joseph ibn Gioia.

Tam, Rabbenu = *Tam Jacob b. Meir.

Tashbaẓ = Samson b. Zadok.

Tashbeẓ = Simeon b. Zemaḥ *Duran, sometimes also abbreviation for Samson b. Zadok, usually known as Tashbaẓ.

Tashbeẓ [Sefer ha-], Resp. by Simeon b. Ẓemaḥ *Duran; the fourth part of this work is called: *Ḥut ha-Meshullash.*

Taz, Usual abbreviation of *Turei Zahav*, comm., to Sh. Ar. by *David b. Samnuel ha-Levi; printed in most editions of Sh. Ar.

(Ha)-Tekhelet, subdivision of the *Levush* (a codification by Mordecai b. Abraham (Levush) *Jaffe); *Ha-Tekhelet* parallels Tur, OḤ 1-241.

Terumat ha-Deshen, by Israel b. Pethahiah *Isserlein; subdivided into a part containing responsa, and a second part called *Pesakim u-Khetavim* or *Piskei Maharai.*

Terumot, Sefer ha-, Compilation of *halakhot* by Samuel b. Isaac *Sardi.

Teshuvot Ba'alei ha-Tosafot, Collection of responsa by the Tosafists.

Teshjvot Ge'onei Mizraḥ u-Ma'aav, Collection of responsa.

Teshuvot ha-Geonim, Collection of responsa from Geonic period.

Teshuvot Ḥakhmei Provinẓyah, Collection of responsa by different Provencal authors.

Teshuvot Ḥakhmei Ẓarefat ve-Loter, Collection of responsa by different French authors.

Teshuvot Maimuniyyot, Resp. pertaining to Maimonides' *Yad Ḥazakah;* printed in major editions of this work after the text; authorship uncertain.

Tevu'ot Shor, by Alexander Sender b. Ephraim Zalman *Schor, a comm. to his *Simlah Ḥadashah*, a work on *Sheḥitah.*

Tiferet Ẓevi, Resp. by Ẓevi Hirsch of the "AHW" Communities (Altona, Hamburg, Wandsbeck).

Tiktin, Judah b. Simeon = Judah b. Simeon *Ashkenazi.

Toledot Adam ve-Ḥavvah, Codification by *Jeroham b. Meshullam.

Torat Emet, Resp. by Aaron b. Joseph *Sasson.

Torat Ḥayyim, , Resp. by Ḥayyim (ben) Shabbetai.

Torat ha-Minhagot, subdivision of the *Massa Ḥayyim* (a work on tax law) by Ḥayyim *Palaggi, containing an exposition of customary law.

Tosafot Rid, Explanations to the Talmud and decisions by *Isaiah b. Mali di Trani the Elder.

Tosefot Yom Tov, comm. to Mishnah by Yom Tov Lipmann b. Nathan ha-Levi *Heller; printed in most editions of the Mishnah.

Tummim, subdivision of the comm. to Sh. Ar., ḤM, *Urim ve-Tummim* by Jonathan *Eybeschuetz; printed in the major editions of Sh. Ar.

Tur, usual abbreviation for the *Arba'ah Turim* of *Jacob b. Asher.

Turei Zahav, Comm. to Sh. Ar. by *David b. Samuel ha-Levi; printed in most editions of Sh. Ar.; usual abbreviation: *Taz.*

Urim, subdivision of the following.

Urim ve-Tummim, Comm. to Sh. Ar., ḤM, by Jonathan *Eybeschuetz; printed in the major editions of Sh. Ar.; subdivided in places into *Urim* and *Tummim.*

Vikku'aḥ Mayim Ḥayyim, Polemics against Isserles and Caro by Ḥayyim b. Bezalel.

Yad Malakhi, Methodological treatise by *Malachi b. Jacob ha-Kohen.

Yad Ramah, Nov. by Meir b. Todros [ha-Levi] *Abulafia.
Yakhin u-Vo'az, Resp. by Ẓemaḥ b. Solomon *Duran.
Yam ha-Gadol, Resp. by Jacob Moses *Toledano.
Yam shel Shelomo, Compilation arranged acc. to Talmud by Solomon b. Jehiel (Maharshal) *Luria.
Yashar, Sefer ha-, by *Tam, Jacob b. Meir (Rabbenu Tam); 1st pt.: Resp.; 2nd pt.: Nov.
Yaskil Avdi, Resp. by Obadiah Hadaya (printed together with his Resp. *De'ah ve-Haskel).*
Yaveẓ = Jacob *Emden.
Yehudah Ya'aleh, Resp. by Judah b. Israel *Aszod.
Yekar Tiferet, Comm. to Maimonides' *Yad Ḥazakah,*by David b. Solomon ibn Zimra, printed in most editions of *Yad Ḥazakah.*
Yere'im [*ha-Shalem*], [*Sefer*], Treatise on precepts by *Eliezer b. Samuel of Metz.
Yeshu'ot Ya'akov, Resp. by Jacob Meshullam b. Mordecai Ze'ev *Ornstein.
Yiẓhak Rei'aḥ, Resp. by Isaac b. Samuel Abendanan (see article *Abendanam Family).
Ẓafenat Pa'ne'aḥ (1), also called *Raban* or *Even ha-Ezer,* see under the last name.
Ẓafenat Pa'ne'aḥ (2), Resp. by Joseph *Rozin.
Zayit Ra'anan, Resp. by Moses Judah Leib b. Benjamin Auerbach.
Ẓeidah la-Derekh, Codification by *Menahem b. Aaron ibn Zerah.
Ẓedakah u-Mishpat, Resp. by Ẓedakah b. Saadiah Huẓin.
Zekan Aharon, Resp. by Elijah b. Benjamin ha-Levi.
Zekher Ẓaddik, Sermons by Eliezer *Katzenellenbogen.
Ẓemaḥ Ẓedek (1) Resp. by Menaham Mendel Shneersohn (see under *Shneersohn Family).
Zera Avraham, Resp. by Abraham b. David *Yiẓḥaki.
Zera Emet Resp. by *Ishmael b. Abaham Isaac ha-Kohen.
Ẓevi la-Ẓaddik, Resp. by Ẓevi Elimelech b. David Shapira.
Zikhron Yehudah, Resp. by *Judah b. Asher
Zikhron Yosef, Resp. by Joseph b. Menahem *Steinhardt.
Zikhronot, Sefer ha-, Sermons on several precepts by Samuel *Aboab.
Zikkaron la-Rishonim . . ., by Albert (Abraham Elijah) *Harkavy; contains in vol. 1 pt. 4 (1887) a collection of Geonic responsa.
Ẓiẓ Eliezer, Resp. by Eliezer Judah b. Jacob Gedaliah Waldenberg.

BIBLIOGRAPHICAL ABBREVIATIONS

Bibliographies in English and other languages have been extensively updated, with English translations cited where available. In order to help the reader, the language of books or articles is given where not obvious from titles of books or names of periodicals. Titles of books and periodicals in languages with alphabets other than Latin, are given in transliteration, even where there is a title page in English. Titles of articles in periodicals are not given. Names of Hebrew and Yiddish periodicals well known in English-speaking countries or in Israel under their masthead in Latin characters are given in this form, even when contrary to transliteration rules. Names of authors writing in languages with non-Latin alphabets are given in their Latin alphabet form wherever known; otherwise the names are transliterated. Initials are generally not given for authors of articles in periodicals, except to avoid confusion. Non-abbreviated book titles and names of periodicals are printed in *italics.* Abbreviations are given in the list below.

AASOR	*Annual of the American School of Oriental Research* (1919ff.).
AB	*Analecta Biblica* (1952ff.).
Abel, Géog	F.-M. Abel, *Géographie de la Palestine,* 2 vols. (1933-38).
ABR	*Australian Biblical Review* (1951ff.).
Abr.	Philo, *De Abrahamo.*
Abrahams, Companion	I. Abrahams, *Companion to the Authorised Daily Prayer Book* (rev. ed. 1922).
Abramson, Merkazim	S. Abramson, *Ba-Merkazim u-va-Tefuẓot bi-Tekufat ha-Ge'onim* (1965).
Acts	Acts of the Apostles (New Testament).
ACUM	*Who is who in ACUM* [*Aguddat Kompozitorim u-Meḥabbrim*].
ADAJ	*Annual of the Department of Antiquities, Jordan* (1951ff.).
Adam	Adam and Eve (Pseudepigrapha).
ADB	*Allgemeine Deutsche Biographie,* 56 vols. (1875–1912).
Add. Esth.	The Addition to Esther (Apocrypha).
Adler, Prat Mus	1. Adler, *La pratique musicale savante dans quelques communautés juives en Europe au XVIIe et XVIIIe siècles,* 2 vols. (1966).
Adler-Davis	H.M. Adler and A. Davis (ed. and tr.), *Service of the Synagogue, a New Edition of the Festival Prayers with an English Translation in Prose and Verse,* 6 vols. (1905–06).
Aet.	Philo, *De Aeternitate Mundi.*
AFO	*Archiv fuer Orientforschung* (first two volumes under the name *Archiv fuer Keilschriftforschung)* (1923ff.).
Ag. Ber	*Aggadat Bereshit* (ed. Buber, 1902*).*
Agr.	Philo, *De Agricultura.*
Ag. Sam.	*Aggadat Samuel.*
Ag. Song	*Aggadat Shir ha-Shirim* (Schechter ed., 1896).
Aharoni, Ereẓ	Y. Aharoni, *Ereẓ Yisrael bi-Tekufat ha-Mikra: Geografyah Historit* (1962).
Aharoni, Land	Y. Aharoni, *Land of the Bible* (1966).

Ahikar	Ahikar (Pseudepigrapha).
AI	*Archives Israélites de France* (1840–1936).
AJA	*American Jewish Archives* (1948ff.).
AJHSP	*American Jewish Historical Society – Publications* (after vol. 50 = AJHSQ).
AJHSQ	*American Jewish Historical (*Society) *Quarterly* (before vol. 50 =AJHSP).
AJSLL	*American Journal of Semitic Languages and Literature* (1884–95 under the title *Hebraica*, since 1942 JNES).
AJYB	*American Jewish Year Book* (1899ff.).
AKM	Abhandlungen fuer die Kunde des Morgenlandes (series).
Albright, Arch	W.F. Albright, *Archaeology of Palestine* (rev. ed. 1960).
Albright, Arch Bib	W.F. Albright, *Archaeology of Palestine and the Bible* (1935^{3}*).*
Albright, Arch Rel	W.F. Albright, *Archaeology and the Religion of Israel* (1953^{3}*).*
Albright, Stone	W.F. Albright, *From the Stone Age to Christianity* (1957^{2}*).*
Alon, Meḥkarim	G. Alon, *Meḥkarim be-Toledot Yisrael bi-Ymei Bayit Sheni u-vi-Tekufat ha-Mishnah ve-ha Talmud,* 2 vols. (1957–58).
Alon, Toledot	G. Alon, *Toledot ha-Yehudim be-Ereẓ Yisrael bi-Tekufat ha-Mishnah ve-ha-Talmud,* I (1958^{3}), (1961^{2}).
ALOR	Alter Orient (series).
Alt, Kl Schr	A. Alt, *Kleine Schriften zur Geschichte des Volkes Israel,* 3 vols. (1953–59).
Alt, Landnahme	A. Alt, *Landnahme der Israeliten in Palaestina* (1925); also in Alt, Kl Schr, 1 (1953), 89–125.
Ant.	Josephus, *Jewish Antiquities* (Loeb Classics ed.).
AO	*Acta Orientalia* (1922ff.).
AOR	*Analecta Orientalia* (1931ff.).
AOS	American Oriental Series.
Apion	Josephus, *Against Apion* (Loeb Classics ed.).
Aq.	Aquila's Greek translation of the Bible.
Ar.	*Arakhin* (talmudic tractate).
Artist.	Letter of Aristeas (Pseudepigrapha).
ARN^{1}	*Avot de-Rabbi Nathan,* version (1) ed. Schechter, 1887.
ARN^{2}	*Avot de-Rabbi Nathan,* version (2) ed. Schechter, 1945^{2}.
Aronius, Regesten	I. Aronius, *Regesten zur Geschichte der Juden im fraenkischen und deutschen Reiche bis zum Jahre 1273* (1902).
ARW	*Archiv fuer Religionswissenschaft* (1898–1941/42).
AS	*Assyrological Studies* (1931ff.).
Ashtor, Korot	E. Ashtor (Strauss), *Korot ha-Yehudim bi-Sefarad ha-Muslemit,* 1(1966^{2}), 2(1966).
Ashtor, Toledot	E. Ashtor (Strauss), *Toledot ha-Yehudim be-Miẓrayim ve-Suryah Taḥat Shilton ha-Mamlukim,* 3 vols. (1944–70).
Assaf, Ge'onim	S. Assaf, *Tekufat ha-Ge'onim ve-Sifrutah* (1955).
Assaf, Mekorot	S. Assaf, *Mekorot le-Toledot ha-Ḥinnukh be-Yisrael,* 4 vols. (1925–43).
Ass. Mos.	Assumption of Moses (Pseudepigrapha).
ATA	Alttestamentliche Abhandlungen (series).
ATANT	Abhandlungen zur Theologie des Alten und Neuen Testaments (series).
AUJW	*Allgemeine unabhaengige juedische Wochenzeitung* (till 1966 = AWJD).
AV	Authorized Version of the Bible.
Avad.	*Avadim* (post-talmudic tractate).
Avi-Yonah, Geog	M. Avi-Yonah, *Geografyah Historit shel Ereẓ Yisrael* (1962^{3}).
Avi-Yonah, Land	M. Avi-Yonah, *The Holy Land from the Persian to the Arab conquest (536 B.C. to A.D. 640)* (1960).
Avot	*Avot* (talmudic tractate).
Av. Zar.	*Avodah Zarah* (talmudic tractate).
AWJD	*Allgemeine Wochenzeitung der Juden in Deutschland* (since 1967 = AUJW).
AZDJ	*Allgemeine Zeitung des Judentums.*
Azulai	Ḥ.Y.D. Azulai, *Shem ha-Gedolim,* ed. by I.E. Benjacob, 2 pts. (1852) (and other editions).
BA	*Biblical Archaeologist* (1938ff.).
Bacher, Bab Amor	W. Bacher, *Agada der babylonischen Amoraeer* (1913^{2}).
Bacher, Pal Amor	W. Bacher, *Agada der palaestinensischen Amoraeer* (Heb. ed. *Aggadat Amora'ei Ereẓ Yisrael),* 2 vols. (1892–99).
Bacher, Tann	W. Bacher, *Agada der Tannaiten* (Heb. ed. *Aggadot ha-Tanna'im,* vol. 1, pt. 1 and 2 (1903); vol. 2 (1890).
Bacher, Trad	W. Bacher, *Tradition und Tradenten in den Schulen Palaestinas und Babyloniens* (1914).
Baer, Spain	Yitzhak (Fritz) Baer, *History of the Jews in Christian Spain,* 2 vols. (1961–66).
Baer, Studien	Yitzhak (Fritz) Baer, *Studien zur Geschichte der Juden im Koenigreich Aragonien waehrend des 13. und 14. Jahrhunderts* (1913).
Baer, Toledot	Yitzhak (Fritz) Baer, *Toledot ha-Yehudim bi-Sefarad ha-Noẓerit mi-Teḥillatan shel ha-Kehillot ad ha-Gerush,* 2 vols. (1959^{2}).
Baer, Urkunden	Yitzhak (Fritz) Baer, *Die Juden im christlichen Spanien,* 2 vols. (1929–36).
Baer S., Seder	S.I. Baer, *Seder Avodat Yisrael* (1868 and reprints*).*
BAIU	*Bulletin de l'Alliance Israélite Universelle* (1861–1913*).*
Baker, Biog Dict	*Baker's Biographical Dictionary of Musicians,* revised by N. Slonimsky (1958^{5}; with Supplement 1965).
I Bar.	I Baruch (Apocrypha).
II Bar.	II Baruch (Pseudepigrapha).
III Bar.	III Baruch (Pseudepigrapha).
BAR	*Biblical Archaeology Review.*
Baron, Community	S.W. Baron, *The Jewish Community, its History and Structure to the American Revolution,* 3 vols. (1942).

Baron, Social	S.W. Baron, *Social and Religious History of the Jews,* 3 vols. (1937); enlarged, 1-2(1952²), 3-14 (1957–69).
Barthélemy-Milik	D. Barthélemy and J.T. Milik, *Dead Sea Scrolls: Discoveries in the Judean Desert,* vol. 1 *Qumram Cave* I (1955).
BASOR	*Bulletin of the American School of Oriental Research.*
Bauer-Leander	H. Bauer and P. Leander, *Grammatik des Biblisch-Aramaeischen* (1927; repr. 1962).
BB	(1) *Bava Batra* (talmudic tractate). (2) *Biblische Beitraege* (1943ff.).
BBB	Bonner biblische Beitraege (series).
BBLA	*Beitraege zur biblischen Landes- und Altertumskunde* (until 1949–ZDPV).
BBSAJ	*Bulletin,* British School of Archaeology, Jerusalem (1922–25; after 1927 included in PEFQS).
BDASI	*Alon* (since 1948) or *Hadashot Arkheʾologiyyot* (since 1961), bulletin of the Department of Antiquities of the State of Israel.
Begrich, Chronologie	J. Begrich, *Chronologie der Koenige von Israel und Juda* (1929).
Bek.	*Bekhorot* (talmudic tractate).
Bel	Bel and the Dragon (Apocrypha).
Benjacob, Oẓar	I.E. Benjacob, *Oẓar ha-Sefarim* (1880; repr. 1956).
Ben Sira	see Ecclus.
Ben-Yehuda, Millon	E. Ben-Yedhuda, *Millon ha-Lashon ha-Ivrit,* 16 vols (1908–59; repr. in 8 vols., 1959).
Benzinger, Archaeologie	I. Benzinger, *Hebraeische Archaeologie* (1927³).
Ben Zvi, Eretz Israel	I. Ben-Zvi, *Eretz Israel under Ottoman Rule* (1960; offprint from L. Finkelstein (ed.), *The Jews, their History, Culture and Religion* (vol. 1).
Ben Zvi, Ereẓ Israel	I. Ben-Zvi, *Ereẓ Israel bi-Ymei ha-Shilton ha-Ottomani (1955).*
Ber.	*Berakhot* (talmudic tractate).
Beẓah	*Beẓah* (talmudic tractate).
BIES	Bulletin of the Israel Exploration Society, see below BJPES.
Bik.	*Bikkurim* (talmudic tractate).
BJCE	Bibliography of Jewish Communities in Europe, catalog at General Archives for the History of the Jewish People, Jerusalem.
BJPES	Bulletin of the Jewish Palestine Exploration Society – English name of the Hebrew periodical known as: 1. *Yediʾot ha-Ḥevrah ha-Ivrit la-Ḥakirat Ereẓ Yisrael va-Attikoteha* (1933–1954); 2. *Yediʾot ha-Ḥevrah la-Ḥakirat Ereẓ Yisrael va-Attikoteha* (1954–1962); 3. *Yediʾot ba-Ḥakirat Ereẓ Yisrael va-Attikoteha* (1962ff.).
BJRL	*Bulletin of the John Rylands Library* (1914ff.).
BK	*Bava Kamma* (talmudic tractate).
BLBI	*Bulletin of the Leo Baeck Institute* (1957ff.).
BM	(1) *Bava Meẓia* (talmudic tractate). (2) *Beit Mikra* (1955/56ff.). (3) British Museum.
BO	*Bibbia e Oriente* (1959ff.).
Bondy-Dworský	G. Bondy and F. Dworský, *Regesten zur Geschichte der Juden in Boehmen, Maehren und Schlesien von 906 bis 1620,* 2 vols. (1906).
BOR	*Bibliotheca Orientalis* (1943ff.).
Borée, Ortsnamen	W. Borée *Die alten Ortsnamen Palaestinas* (1930).
Bousset, Religion	W. Bousset, *Die Religion des Judentums im neutestamentlichen Zeitalter* (1906²).
Bousset-Gressmann	W. Bousset, *Die Religion des Judentums im spaethellenistischen Zeitalter* (1966³).
BR	*Biblical Review* (1916–25).
BRCI	*Bulletin of the Research Council of Israel* (1951/52–1954/55; then divided).
BRE	*Biblical Research* (1956ff.).
BRF	*Bulletin of the Rabinowitz Fund for the Exploration of Ancient Synagogues* (1949ff.).
Briggs, Psalms	Ch. A. and E.G. Briggs, *Critical and Exegetical Commentary on the Book of Psalms,* 2 vols. (ICC, 1906–07).
Bright, Hist	J. Bright, *A History of Israel* (1959).
Brockelmann, Arab Lit	K. Brockelmann, *Geschichte der arabischen Literatur,* 2 vols. 1898–1902), supplement, 3 vols. (1937–42).
Bruell, Jahrbuecher	*Jahrbuecher fuer juedische Geschichte und Litteratur,* ed. by N. Bruell, Frankfurt (1874–90).
Brugmans-Frank	H. Brugmans and A. Frank (eds.), *Geschiedenis der Joden in Nederland* (1940).
BTS	*Bible et Terre Sainte* (1958ff.).
Bull, Index	S. Bull, *Index to Biographies of Contemporary Composers* (1964).
BW	*Biblical World* (1882–1920).
BWANT	*Beitraege zur Wissenschaft vom Alten und Neuen Testament* (1926ff.).
BZ	*Biblische Zeitschrift* (1903ff.).
BZAW	*Beihefte zur Zeitschrift fuer die alttestamentliche Wissenschaft,* supplement to ZAW (1896ff.).
BŻIH	*Biuletyn Zydowskiego Instytutu Historycznego* (1950ff.).
CAB	*Cahiers d'archéologie biblique* (1953ff.).
CAD	*The* [*Chicago*] *Assyrian Dictionary* (1956ff.).
CAH	*Cambridge Ancient History*, 12 vols. (1923–39)
CAH²	*Cambridge Ancient History,* second edition, 14 vols. (1962–2005).
Calwer, Lexikon	*Calwer, Bibellexikon.*
Cant.	Canticles, usually given as Song (= Song of Songs).

Cantera-Millás, Inscripciones	F. Cantera and J.M. Millás, *Las Inscripciones Hebraicas de España* (1956).
CBQ	*Catholic Biblical Quarterly* (1939ff.).
CCARY	Central Conference of American Rabbis, *Yearbook* (1890/91ff.).
CD	*Damascus Document* from the Cairo *Genizah* (published by S. Schechter, *Fragments of a Zadokite Work*, 1910).
Charles, Apocrypha	R.H. Charles, *Apocrypha and Pseudepigrapha . . .*, 2 vols. (1913; repr. 1963–66).
Cher.	Philo, *De Cherubim.*
I (or II) Chron.	Chronicles, book I and II (Bible).
CIG	*Corpus Inscriptionum Graecarum.*
CIJ	*Corpus Inscriptionum Judaicarum,* 2 vols. (1936–52).
CIL	*Corpus Inscriptionum Latinarum.*
CIS	*Corpus Inscriptionum Semiticarum* (1881ff.).
C.J.	Codex Justinianus.
Clermont-Ganneau, Arch	Ch. Clermont-Ganneau, *Archaeological Researches in Palestine*, 2 vols. (1896–99).
CNFI	*Christian News from Israel* (1949ff.).
Cod. Just.	Codex Justinianus.
Cod. Theod.	Codex Theodosinanus.
Col.	Epistle to the Colosssians (New Testament).
Conder, Survey	Palestine Exploration Fund, *Survey of Eastern Palestine*, vol. 1, pt. I (1889) = C.R. Conder, *Memoirs of the . . . Survey.*
Conder-Kitchener	Palestine Exploration Fund, *Survey of Western Palestine*, vol. 1, pts. 1-3 (1881–83) = C.R. Conder and H.H. Kitchener, *Memoirs.*
Conf.	Philo, *De Confusione Linguarum.*
Conforte, Kore	D. Conforte, *Kore ha-Dorot* (1842²).
Cong.	Philo, *De Congressu Quaerendae Eruditionis Gratia.*
Cont.	Philo, *De Vita Contemplativa.*
I (or II) Cor.	Epistles to the Corinthians (New Testament).
Cowley, Aramic	A. Cowley, *Aramaic Papyri of the Fifth Century B.C.* (1923).
Colwey, Cat	A.E. Cowley, *A Concise Catalogue of the Hebrew Printed Books in the Bodleian Library* (1929).
CRB	*Cahiers de la Revue Biblique* (1964ff.).
Crowfoot-Kenyon	J.W. Crowfoot, K.M. Kenyon and E.L. Sukenik, *Buildings of Samaria* (1942).
C.T.	Codex Theodosianus.
DAB	*Dictionary of American Biography* (1928–58).
Daiches, Jews	S. Daiches, *Jews in Babylonia* (1910).
Dalman, Arbeit	G. Dalman, *Arbeit und Sitte in Palaestina*, 7 vols.in 8 (1928–42 repr. 1964).
Dan	Daniel (Bible).
Davidson, Oẓar	I. Davidson, *Oẓar ha-Shirah ve-ha-Piyyut*, 4 vols. (1924–33); Supplement in: HUCA, 12–13 (1937/38), 715–823.
DB	J. Hastings, *Dictionary of the Bible,* 4 vols. (1963²).
DBI	F.G. Vigoureaux et al. (eds.), *Dictionnaire de la Bible,* 5 vols. in 10 (1912); Supplement, 8 vols. (1928–66)
Decal.	Philo, *De Decalogo.*
Dem.	*Demai* (talmudic tractate).
DER	*Derekh Ereẓ Rabbah* (post-talmudic tractate).
Derenbourg, Hist	J. Derenbourg *Essai sur l'histoire et la géographie de la Palestine* (1867).
Det.	Philo, *Quod deterius potiori insidiari solet.*
Deus	Philo, *Quod Deus immutabilis sit.*
Deut.	Deuteronomy (Bible).
Deut. R.	*Deuteronomy Rabbah.*
DEZ	*Derekh Ereẓ Zuta* (post-talmudic tractate).
DHGE	*Dictionnaire d'histoire et de géographie ecclésiastiques,* ed. by A. Baudrillart et al., 17 vols (1912–68).
Dik. Sof	*Dikdukei Soferim,* variae lections of the talmudic text by Raphael Nathan Rabbinovitz (16 vols., 1867–97).
Dinur, Golah	B. Dinur (Dinaburg), *Yisrael ba-Golah,* 2 vols. in 7 (1959–68) = vols. 5 and 6 of his *Toledot Yisrael,* second series.
Dinur, Haganah	B. Dinur (ed.), *Sefer Toledot ha-Haganah* (1954ff.).
Diringer, Iscr	D. Diringer, *Iscrizioni antico-ebraiche palestinesi* (1934).
Discoveries	*Discoveries in the Judean Desert* (1955ff.).
DNB	*Dictionary of National Biography,* 66 vols. (1921–222) with Supplements.
Dubnow, Divrei	S. Dubnow, *Divrei Yemei Am Olam,* 11 vols (1923–38 and further editions).
Dubnow, Ḥasidut	S. Dubnow, *Toledot ha-Ḥasidut* (1960²).
Dubnow, Hist	S. Dubnow, *History of the Jews* (1967).
Dubnow, Hist Russ	S. Dubnow, *History of the Jews in Russia and Poland,* 3 vols. (1916 20).
Dubnow, Outline	S. Dubnow, *An Outline of Jewish History,* 3 vols. (1925–29).
Dubnow, Weltgesch	S. Dubnow, *Weltgeschichte des juedischen Volkes* 10 vols. (1925–29).
Dukes, Poesie	L. Dukes, *Zur Kenntnis der neuhebraeischen religioesen Poesie* (1842).
Dunlop, Khazars	D. H. Dunlop, *History of the Jewish Khazars* (1954).
EA	El Amarna Letters (edited by J.A. Knudtzon), *Die El-Amarna Tafel,* 2 vols. (1907 14).
EB	*Encyclopaedia Britannica.*
EBI	*Estudios biblicos* (1941ff.).
EBIB	T.K. Cheyne and J.S. Black, *Encyclopaedia Biblica,* 4 vols. (1899–1903).
Ebr.	Philo, *De Ebrietate.*
Eccles.	Ecclesiastes (Bible).
Eccles. R.	*Ecclesiastes Rabbah.*
Ecclus.	Ecclesiasticus or Wisdom of Ben Sira (or Sirach; Apocrypha).
Eduy.	*Eduyyot* (mishanic tractate).

EG	*Enziklopedyah shel Galuyyot* (1953ff.).
EH	*Even ha-Ezer.*
EHA	*Enziklopedyah la-Ḥafirot Arkheologiyyot be-Ereẓ Yisrael*, 2 vols. (1970).
EI	*Enzyklopaedie des Islams*, 4 vols. (1905–14). Supplement vol. (1938).
EIS	*Encyclopaedia of Islam*, 4 vols. (1913–36; repr. 1954–68).
EIS²	*Encyclopaedia of Islam, second edition (1960–2000).*
Eisenstein, Dinim	J.D. Eisenstein, *Oẓar Dinim u-Minhagim* (1917; several reprints).
Eisenstein, Yisrael	J.D. Eisenstein, *Oẓar Yisrael* (10 vols, 1907–13; repr. with several additions 1951).
EIV	*Enziklopedyah Ivrit* (1949ff.).
EJ	*Encyclopaedia Judaica* (German, A-L only), 10 vols. (1928–34).
EJC	*Enciclopedia Judaica Castellana*, 10 vols. (1948–51).
Elbogen, Century	I Elbogen, *A Century of Jewish Life* (1960²).
Elbogen, Gottesdienst	I Elbogen, *Der juedische Gottesdienst ...* (1931³, repr. 1962).
Elon, Mafte'aḥ	M. Elon (ed.), *Mafte'aḥ ha-She'elot ve-ha-Teshuvot ha-Rosh* (1965).
EM	*Enziklopedyah Mikra'it* (1950ff.).
I (or II) En.	I and II Enoch (Pseudepigrapha).
EncRel	*Encyclopedia of Religion*, 15 vols. (1987, 2005²).
Eph.	Epistle to the Ephesians (New Testament).
Ephros, Cant	G. Ephros, *Cantorial Anthology*, 5 vols. (1929–57).
Ep. Jer.	Epistle of Jeremy (Apocrypha).
Epstein, Amora'im	J N. Epstein, *Mevo'ot le-Sifrut ha-Amora'im* (1962).
Epstein, Marriage	L M. Epstein, *Marriage Laws in the Bible and the Talmud* (1942).
Epstein, Mishnah	J. N. Epstein, *Mavo le-Nusaḥ ha-Mishnah*, 2 vols. (1964²).
Epstein, Tanna'im	J. N. Epstein, *Mavo le-Sifruth ha-Tanna'im.* (1947).
ER	*Ecumenical Review.*
Er.	*Eruvin* (talmudic tractate).
ERE	*Encyclopaedia of Religion and Ethics*, 13 vols. (1908–26); reprinted.
ErIsr	*Eretz-Israel*, Israel Exploration Society.
I Esd.	I Esdras (Apocrypha) (= III Ezra).
II Esd.	II Esdras (Apocrypha) (= IV Ezra).
ESE	*Ephemeris fuer semitische Epigraphik*, ed. by M. Lidzbarski.
ESN	*Encyclopaedia Sefaradica Neerlandica*, 2 pts. (1949).
ESS	*Encyclopaedia of the Social Sciences*, 15 vols. (1930–35); reprinted in 8 vols. (1948–49).
Esth.	Esther (Bible).
Est. R.	*Esther Rabbah.*
ET	*Enziklopedyah Talmudit* (1947ff.).
Eusebius, Onom.	E. Klostermann (ed.), *Das Onomastikon* (1904), Greek with Hieronymus' Latin translation.
Ex.	Exodus (Bible).
Ex. R.	*Exodus Rabbah.*
Exs	Philo, *De Exsecrationibus.*
EẒD	*Enziklopeday shel ha-Ẓiyyonut ha-Datit* (1951ff.).
Ezek.	Ezekiel (Bible).
Ezra	Ezra (Bible).
III Ezra	III Ezra (Pseudepigrapha).
IV Ezra	IV Ezra (Pseudepigrapha).
Feliks, Ha-Ẓome'aḥ	*J. Feliks, Ha-Ẓome'aḥ ve-ha-Ḥai ba-Mishnah* (1983).
Finkelstein, Middle Ages	L. Finkelstein, *Jewish Self-Government in the Middle Ages* (1924).
Fischel, Islam	W.J. Fischel, *Jews in the Economic and Political Life of Mediaeval Islam* (1937; reprint with introduction "The Court Jew in the Islamic World," 1969).
FJW	*Fuehrer durch die juedische Gemeindeverwaltung und Wohlfahrtspflege in Deutschland* (1927/28).
Frankel, Mevo	Z. Frankel, *Mevo ha-Yerushalmi* (1870; reprint 1967).
Frankel, Mishnah	Z. Frankel, *Darkhei ha-Mishnah* (1959²; reprint 1959²).
Frazer, Folk-Lore	J.G. Frazer, *Folk-Lore in the Old Testament*, 3 vols. (1918–19).
Frey, Corpus	J.-B. Frey, *Corpus Inscriptionum Iudaicarum*, 2 vols. (1936–52).
Friedmann, Lebensbilder	A. Friedmann, *Lebensbilder beruehmter Kantoren*, 3 vols. (1918–27).
FRLT	*Forschungen zur Religion und Literatur des Alten und Neuen Testaments* (series) (1950ff.).
Frumkin-Rivlin	A.L. Frumkin and E. Rivlin, *Toledot Ḥakhmei Yerushalayim*, 3 vols. (1928–30), Supplement vol. (1930).
Fuenn, Keneset	S.J. Fuenn, *Keneset Yisrael*, 4 vols. (1887–90).
Fuerst, Bibliotheca	J. Fuerst, *Bibliotheca Judaica*, 2 vols. (1863; repr. 1960).
Fuerst, Karaeertum	J. Fuerst, *Geschichte des Karaeertums*, 3 vols. (1862–69).
Fug.	Philo, *De Fuga et Inventione.*
Gal.	Epistle to the Galatians (New Testament).
Galling, Reallexikon	K. Galling, *Biblisches Reallexikon* (1937).
Gardiner, Onomastica	A.H. Gardiner, *Ancient Egyptian Onomastica*, 3 vols. (1947).
Geiger, Mikra	A. Geiger, *Ha-Mikra ve-Targumav*, tr. by J.L. Baruch (1949).
Geiger, Urschrift	A. Geiger, *Urschrift und Uebersetzungen der Bibel* 1928²).
Gen.	Genesis (Bible).
Gen. R.	*Genesis Rabbah.*
Ger.	*Gerim* (post-talmudic tractate).
Germ Jud	M. Brann, I. Elbogen, A. Freimann, and H. Tykocinski (eds.), *Germania Judaica*, vol. 1 (1917; repr. 1934 and 1963); vol. 2, in 2 pts. (1917–68), ed. by Z. Avneri.

GHAT — *Goettinger Handkommentar zum Alten Testament* (1917–22).
Ghirondi-Neppi — M.S. Ghirondi and G.H. Neppi, *Toledot Gedolei Yisrael u-Ge'onei Italyah ... u-Ve'urim al Sefer Zekher Ẓaddikim li-Verakhah* . . .(1853), index in ZHB, 17 (1914), 171–83.
Gig. — Philo, *De Gigantibus.*
Ginzberg, Legends — L. Ginzberg, *Legends of the Jews,* 7 vols. (1909–38; and many reprints).
Git. — *Gittin* (talmudic tractate).
Glueck, Explorations — N. Glueck, *Explorations in Eastern Palestine,* 2 vols. (1951).
Goell, Bibliography — Y. Goell, *Bibliography of Modern Hebrew Literature in English Translation* (1968).
Goodenough, Symbols — E.R. Goodenough, *Jewish Symbols in the Greco-Roman Period,* 13 vols. (1953–68).
Gordon, Textbook — C.H. Gordon, *Ugaritic Textbook* (1965; repr. 1967).
Graetz, Gesch — H. Graetz, *Geschichte der Juden* (last edition 1874–1908).
Graetz, Hist — H. Graetz, *History of the Jews,* 6 vols. (1891–1902).
Graetz, Psalmen — H. Graetz, *Kritischer Commentar zu den Psalmen,* 2 vols. in 1 (1882–83).
Graetz, Rabbinowitz — H. Graetz, *Divrei Yemei Yisrael,* tr. by S.P. Rabbinowitz. (1928 1929[2]).
Gray, Names — G.B. Gray, *Studies in Hebrew Proper Names* (1896).
Gressmann, Bilder — H. Gressmann, *Altorientalische Bilder zum Alten Testament* (1927[2]).
Gressmann, Texte — H. Gressmann, *Altorientalische Texte zum Alten Testament* (1926[2]).
Gross, Gal Jud — H. Gross, *Gallia Judaica* (1897; repr. with add. 1969).
Grove, Dict — *Grove's Dictionary of Music and Musicians,* ed. by E. Blum 9 vols. (1954[5]) and suppl. (1961[5]).
Guedemann, Gesch Erz — M. Guedemann, *Geschichte des Erziehungswesens und der Cultur der abendlaendischen Juden,* 3 vols. (1880–88).
Guedemann, Quellenschr — M. Guedemann, *Quellenschriften zur Geschichte des Unterrichts und der Erziehung bei den deutschen Juden* (1873, 1891).
Guide — Maimonides, *Guide of the Perplexed.*
Gulak, Oẓar — A. Gulak, *Oẓar ha-Shetarot ha-Nehugim be-Yisrael* (1926).
Gulak, Yesodei — A. Gulak, *Yesodei ha-Mishpat ha-Ivri, Seder Dinei Mamonot be-Yisrael, al pi Mekorot ha-Talmud ve-ha-Posekim,* 4 vols. (1922; repr. 1967).
Guttmann, Mafte'aḥ — M. Guttmann, *Mafte'aḥ ha-Talmud,* 3 vols. (1906–30).
Guttmann, Philosophies — J. Guttmann, *Philosophies of Judaism* (1964).
Hab. — *Habakkuk* (Bible).
Ḥag. — *Ḥagigah* (talmudic tractate).
Haggai — *Haggai* (Bible).
Ḥal. — *Ḥallah* (talmudic tractate).
Halevy, Dorot — I. Halevy, *Dorot ha-Rishonim,* 6 vols. (1897–1939).
Halpern, Pinkas — I. Halpern (Halperin), *Pinkas Va'ad Arba Araẓot* (1945).
Hananel-Eškenazi — A. Hananel and Eškenazi (eds.), *Fontes Hebraici ad res oeconomicas socialesque terrarum balcanicarum saeculo XVI pertinentes,* 2 vols, (1958–60; in Bulgarian).
HB — *Hebraeische Bibliographie* (1858–82).
Heb. — Epistle to the Hebrews (New Testament).
Heilprin, Dorot — J. Heilprin (Heilperin), *Seder ha-Dorot,* 3 vols. (1882; repr. 1956).
Her. — Philo, *Quis Rerum Divinarum Heres.*
Hertz, Prayer — J.H. Hertz (ed.), *Authorised Daily Prayer Book* (rev. ed. 1948; repr. 1963).
Herzog, Instit — I. Herzog, *The Main Institutions of Jewish Law,* 2 vols. (1936–39; repr. 1967).
Herzog-Hauck — J.J. Herzog and A. Hauch (eds.), *Real-encyklopaedie fuer protestantische Theologie* (1896–1913[3]).
HḤY — *Ha-Ẓofeh le-Ḥokhmat Yisrael* (first four volumes under the title *Ha-Ẓofeh me-Ereẓ Hagar)* (1910/11–13).
Hirschberg, Afrikah — H.Z. Hirschberg, *Toledot ha-Yehudim be-Afrikah ha-Zofonit,* 2 vols. (1965).
HJ — *Historia Judaica* (1938–61).
HL — *Das Heilige Land* (1857ff.)
ḤM — *Ḥoshen Mishpat.*
Hommel, Ueberliefer. — F. Hommel, *Die altisraelitische Ueberlieferung in inschriftlicher Beleuchtung* (1897).
Hor. — *Horayot* (talmudic tractate).
Horodezky, Ḥasidut — S.A. Horodezky, *Ha-Ḥasidut ve-ha-Ḥasidim,* 4 vols. (1923).
Horowitz, Ereẓ Yis — I.W. Horowitz, *Ereẓ Yisrael u-Shekhenoteha* (1923).
Hos. — Hosea (Bible).
HTR — *Harvard Theological Review* (1908ff.).
HUCA — *Hebrew Union College Annual* (1904; 1924ff.)
Ḥul. — *Ḥullin* (talmudic tractate).
Husik, Philosophy — I. Husik, *History of Medieval Jewish Philosophy* (1932[2]).
Hyman, Toledot — A. Hyman, *Toledot Tanna'im ve-Amora'im* (1910; repr. 1964).
Ibn Daud, Tradition — Abraham Ibn Daud, *Sefer ha-Qabbalah – The Book of Tradition,* ed. and tr. By G.D. Cohen (1967).
ICC — International Critical Commentary on the Holy Scriptures of the Old and New Testaments (series, 1908ff.).
IDB — *Interpreter's Dictionary of the Bible,* 4 vols. (1962).
Idelsohn, Litugy — A. Z. Idelsohn, *Jewish Liturgy and its Development* (1932; paperback repr. 1967)
Idelsohn, Melodien — A. Z. Idelsohn, *Hebraeisch-orientalischer Melodienschatz,* 10 vols. (1914 32).
Idelsohn, Music — A. Z. Idelsohn, *Jewish Music in its Historical Development* (1929; paperback repr. 1967).

IEJ *Israel Exploration Journal* (1950ff.).
IESS *International Encyclopedia of the Social Sciences* (various eds.).
IG *Inscriptiones Graecae*, ed. by the Prussian Academy.
IGYB *Israel Government Year Book* (1949/50ff.).
ILR *Israel Law Review* (1966ff.).
IMIT *Izraelita Magyar Irodalmi Társulat Évkönyv* (1895 1948).
IMT International Military Tribunal.
INB *Israel Numismatic Bulletin* (1962–63).
INJ *Israel Numismatic Journal* (1963ff.).
Ios Philo, *De Iosepho.*
Isa. Isaiah (Bible).
ITHL Institute for the Translation of Hebrew Literature.
IZBG *Internationale Zeitschriftenschau fuer Bibelwissenschaft und Grenzgebiete* (1951ff.).

JA *Journal asiatique* (1822ff.).
James Epistle of James (New Testament).
JAOS *Journal of the American Oriental Society* (c. 1850ff.)
Jastrow, Dict M. Jastrow, *Dictionary of the Targumim, the Talmud Babli and Yerushalmi, and the Midrashic literature*, 2 vols. (1886 1902 and reprints).
JBA *Jewish Book Annual* (19242ff.).
JBL *Journal of Biblical Literature* (1881ff.).
JBR *Journal of Bible and Religion* (1933ff.).
JC *Jewish Chronicle* (1841ff.).
JCS *Journal of Cuneiform Studies* (1947ff.).
JE *Jewish Encyclopedia*, 12 vols. (1901–05 several reprints).
Jer. Jeremiah (Bible).
Jeremias, Alte Test A. Jeremias, *Das Alte Testament im Lichte des alten Orients* 1930[4]).
JGGJČ *Jahrbuch der Gesellschaft fuer Geschichte der Juden in der Čechoslovakischen Republik* (1929–38).
JHSEM Jewish Historical Society of England, *Miscellanies* (1925ff.).
JHSET Jewish Historical Society of England, *Transactions* (1893ff.).
JJGL *Jahrbuch fuer juedische Geschichte und Literatur* (Berlin) (1898–1938).
JJLG *Jahrbuch der juedische-literarischen Gesellschaft* (Frankfurt) (1903–32).
JJS *Journal of Jewish Studies* (1948ff.).
JJSO *Jewish Journal of Sociology* (1959ff.).
JJV *Jahrbuch fuer juedische Volkskunde* (1898–1924).
JL *Juedisches Lexikon*, 5 vols. (1927–30).
JMES *Journal of the Middle East Society* (1947ff.).
JNES *Journal of Near Eastern Studies* (continuation of AJSLL) (1942ff.).
J.N.U.L. Jewish National and University Library.
Job Job (Bible).
Joel Joel (Bible).
John Gospel according to John (New Testament).
I, II and III John Epistles of John (New Testament).
Jos., Ant Josephus, *Jewish Antiquities* (Loeb Classics ed.).
Jos. Apion Josephus, *Against Apion* (Loeb Classics ed.).
Jos., index *Josephus Works*, Loeb Classics ed., index of names.
Jos., Life Josephus, *Life* (ed. Loeb Classics).
Jos, Wars Josephus, *The Jewish Wars* (Loeb Classics ed.).
Josh. Joshua (Bible).
JPESB Jewish Palestine Exploration Society Bulletin, see BJPES.
JPESJ Jewish Palestine Exploration Society Journal – Eng. Title of the Hebrew periodical *Kovez ha-Ḥevrah ha-Ivrit la-Ḥakirat Erez Yisrael va-Attikoteha.*
JPOS *Journal of the Palestine Oriental Society* (1920–48).
JPS Jewish Publication Society of America, *The Torah* (1962, 1967[2]); *The Holy Scriptures* (1917).
JQR *Jewish Quarterly Review* (1889ff.).
JR *Journal of Religion* (1921ff.).
JRAS *Journal of the Royal Asiatic Society* (1838ff.).
JHR *Journal of Religious History* (1960/61ff.).
JSOS *Jewish Social Studies* (1939ff.).
JSS *Journal of Semitic Studies* (1956ff.).
JTS *Journal of Theological Studies* (1900ff.).
JTSA Jewish Theological Seminary of America (also abbreviated as JTS).
Jub. Jubilees (Pseudepigrapha).
Judg. Judges (Bible).
Judith Book of Judith (Apocrypha).
Juster, Juifs J. Juster, *Les Juifs dans l'Empire Romain*, 2 vols. (1914).
JYB *Jewish Year Book* (1896ff.).
JZWL *Juedische Zeitschift fuer Wissenschaft und Leben* (1862–75).

Kal. *Kallah* (post-talmudic tractate).
Kal. R. *Kallah Rabbati* (post-talmudic tractate).
Katz, England *The Jews in the History of England, 1485-1850 (1994).*
Kaufmann, Schriften D. Kaufmann, *Gesammelte Schriften*, 3 vols. (1908 15).
Kaufmann Y., Religion Y. Kaufmann, *The Religion of Israel* (1960), abridged tr. of his *Toledot.*
Kaufmann Y., Toledot Y. Kaufmann, *Toledot ha-Emunah ha-Yisre'elit*, 4 vols. (1937 57).
KAWJ *Korrespondenzblatt des Vereins zur Gruendung und Erhaltung der Akademie fuer die Wissenschaft des Judentums* (1920 30).
Kayserling, Bibl M. Kayserling, *Biblioteca Española-Portugueza-Judaica* (1880; repr. 1961).
Kelim *Kelim* (mishnaic tractate).
Ker. *Keritot* (talmudic tractate).
Ket. *Ketubbot* (talmudic tractate).

Kid.	*Kiddushim* (talmudic tractate).
Kil.	*Kilayim* (talmudic tractate).
Kin.	*Kinnim* (mishnaic tractate).
Kisch, Germany	G. Kisch, *Jews in Medieval Germany* (1949).
Kittel, Gesch	R. Kittel, *Geschichte des Volkes Israel,* 3 vols. (1922–28).
Klausner, Bayit Sheni	J. Klausner, *Historyah shel ha-Bayit ha-Sheni,* 5 vols. (1950/512).
Klausner, Sifrut	J. Klausner, *Historyah shel haSifrut ha-Ivrit ha-Ḥadashah,* 6 vols. (1952–582).
Klein, corpus	S. Klein (ed.), *Juedisch-palaestinisches Corpus Inscriptionum* (1920).
Koehler-Baumgartner	L. Koehler and W. Baumgartner, *Lexicon in Veteris Testamenti libros* (1953).
Kohut, Arukh	H.J.A. Kohut (ed.), *Sefer he-Arukh ha-Shalem,* by Nathan b. Jehiel of Rome, 8 vols. (1876–92; Supplement by S. Krauss et al., 1936; repr. 1955).
Krauss, Tal Arch	S. Krauss, *Talmudische Archaeologie,* 3 vols. (1910–12; repr. 1966).
Kressel, Leksikon	G. Kressel, *Leksikon ha-Sifrut ha-Ivrit ba-Dorot ha-Aḥaronim,* 2 vols. (1965–67).
KS	*Kirjath Sepher* (1923/4ff.).
Kut.	*Kuttim* (post-talmudic tractate).
LA	Studium Biblicum Franciscanum, *Liber Annuus* (1951ff.).
L.A.	Philo, *Legum allegoriae.*
Lachower, Sifrut	F. Lachower, *Toledot ha-Sifrut ha-Ivrit ha-Ḥadashah,* 4 vols. (1947–48; several reprints).
Lam.	Lamentations (Bible).
Lam. R.	*Lamentations Rabbah.*
Landshuth, Ammudei	L. Landshuth, *Ammudei ha-Avodah* (1857–62; repr. with index, 1965).
Legat.	Philo, *De Legatione ad Caium.*
Lehmann, Nova Bibl	R.P. Lehmann, *Nova Bibliotheca Anglo-Judaica* (1961).
Lev.	Leviticus (Bible).
Lev. R.	*Leviticus Rabbah.*
Levy, Antologia	I. Levy, *Antologia de liturgia judeo-española* (1965ff.).
Levy J., Chald Targ	J. Levy, *Chaldaeisches Woerterbuch ueber die Targumim,* 2 vols. (1967–68; repr. 1959).
Levy J., Nuehebr Tal	J. Levy, *Neuhebraeisches und chaldaeisches Woerterbuch ueber die Talmudim . . .,* 4 vols. (1875–89; repr. 1963).
Lewin, Oẓar	Lewin, *Oẓar ha-Ge'onim,* 12 vols. (1928–43).
Lewysohn, Zool	L. Lewysohn, *Zoologie des Talmuds* (1858).
Lidzbarski, Handbuch	M. Lidzbarski, *Handbuch der nordsemitischen Epigraphik,* 2 vols (1898).
Life	Josephus, *Life* (Loeb Classis ed.).
LNYL	*Leksikon fun der Nayer Yidisher Literatur* (1956ff.).
Loew, Flora	I. Loew, *Die Flora der Juden,* 4 vols. (1924 34; repr. 1967).
LSI	*Laws of the State of Israel* (1948ff.).
Luckenbill, Records	D.D. Luckenbill, *Ancient Records of Assyria and Babylonia,* 2 vols. (1926).
Luke	Gospel according to Luke (New Testament)
LXX	Septuagint (Greek translation of the Bible).
Ma'as.	*Ma'aserot* (talmudic tractate).
Ma'as. Sh.	*Ma'ase Sheni* (talmudic tractate).
I, II, III, and IVMacc.	Maccabees, I, II, III (Apocrypha), IV (Pseudepigrapha).
Maimonides, Guide	Maimonides, *Guide of the Perplexed.*
Maim., Yad	Maimonides, *Mishneh Torah (Yad Ḥazakah).*
Maisler, Untersuchungen	B. Maisler (Mazar), *Untersuchungen zur alten Geschichte und Ethnographie Syriens und Palaestinas,* 1 (1930).
Mak.	*Makkot* (talmudic tractate).
Makhsh.	*Makhshrin* (mishnaic tractate).
Mal.	Malachi (Bible).
Mann, Egypt	J. Mann, *Jews in Egypt in Palestine under the Fatimid Caliphs,* 2 vols. (1920–22).
Mann, Texts	J. Mann, *Texts and Studies,* 2 vols (1931–35).
Mansi	G.D. Mansi, *Sacrorum Conciliorum nova et amplissima collectio,* 53 vols. in 60 (1901–27; repr. 1960).
Margalioth, Gedolei	M. Margalioth, *Enẓiklopedyah le-Toledot Gedolei Yisrael,* 4 vols. (1946–50).
Margalioth, Ḥakhmei	M. Margalioth, *Enẓiklopedyah le-Ḥakhmei ha-Talmud ve-ha-Ge'onim,* 2 vols. (1945).
Margalioth, Cat	G. Margalioth, *Catalogue of the Hebrew and Samaritan Manuscripts in the British Museum,* 4 vols. (1899–1935).
Mark	Gospel according to Mark (New Testament).
Mart. Isa.	Martyrdom of Isaiah (Pseudepigrapha).
Mas.	Masorah.
Matt.	Gospel according to Matthew (New Testament).
Mayer, Art	L.A. Mayer, *Bibliography of Jewish Art* (1967).
MB	*Wochenzeitung* (formerly *Mitteilungsblatt*) *des Irgun Olej Merkas Europa* (1933ff.).
MEAH	*Miscelánea de estudios drabes y hebraicos* (1952ff.).
Meg.	Megillah (talmudic tractate).
Meg. Ta'an.	*Megillat Ta'anit* (in HUCA, 8 9 (1931–32), 318–51).
Me'il	*Me'ilah* (mishnaic tractate).
MEJ	*Middle East Journal* (1947ff.).
Mehk.	*Mekhilta de-R. Ishmael.*
Mekh. SbY	*Mekhilta de-R. Simeon bar Yoḥai.*
Men.	*Menaḥot* (talmudic tractate).
MER	*Middle East Record* (1960ff.).
Meyer, Gesch	E. Meyer, *Geschichte des Alterums,* 5 vols. in 9 (1925–58).
Meyer, Ursp	E. Meyer, *Urspring und Anfaenge des Christentums* (1921).
Mez.	*Mezuzah* (post-talmudic tractate).
MGADJ	*Mitteilungen des Gesamtarchivs der deutschen Juden* (1909–12).
MGG	*Die Musik in Geschichte und Gegenwart,* 14 vols. (1949–68).

MGG² *Die Musik in Geschichte und Gegenwart, 2nd edition (1994)*
MGH *Monumenta Germaniae Historica* (1826ff.).
MGJV *Mitteilungen der Gesellschaft fuer juedische Volkskunde* (1898–1929); title varies, see also JJV.
MGWJ *Monatsschrift fuer Geschichte und Wissenschaft des Judentums* (1851–1939).
MHJ *Monumenta Hungariae Judaica,* 11 vols. (1903–67).
Michael, Or H.Ḥ. Michael, *Or ha-Ḥayyim: Ḥakhmei Yisrael ve-Sifreihem,* ed. by S.Z. Ḥ. Halberstam and N. Ben-Menahem (1965²).
Mid. *Middot* (mishnaic tractate).
Mid. Ag. *Midrash Aggadah.*
Mid. Hag. *Midrash ha-Gadol.*
Mid. Job. *Midrash Job.*
Mid. Jonah *Midrash Jonah.*
Mid. Lek. Tov *Midrash Lekaḥ Tov.*
Mid. Prov. *Midrash Proverbs.*
Mid. Ps. *Midrash Tehillim* (Eng tr. *The Midrash on Psalms* (JPS, 1959).
Mid. Sam. *Midrash Samuel.*
Mid. Song *Midrash Shir ha-Shirim.*
Mid. Tan. *Midrash Tanna'im* on Deuteronomy.
Miége, Maroc J.L. Miège, *Le Maroc et l'Europe,* 3 vols. (1961 62).
Mig. Philo, *De Migratione Abrahami.*
Mik. *Mikva'ot* (mishnaic tractate).
Milano, Bibliotheca A. Milano, *Bibliotheca Historica Italo-Judaica* (1954); supplement for 1954–63 (1964); supplement for 1964–66 in RMI, 32 (1966).
Milano, Italia A. Milano, *Storia degli Ebrei in Italia* (1963).
MIO *Mitteilungen des Instituts fuer Orientforschung* 1953ff.).
Mish. Mishnah.
MJ *Le Monde Juif* (1946ff.).
MJC see Neubauer, Chronicles.
MK *Mo'ed Katan* (talmudic tractate).
MNDPV *Mitteilungen und Nachrichten des deutschen Palaestinavereins* (1895–1912).
Mortara, Indice M. Mortara, *Indice Alfabetico dei Rabbini e Scrittori Israeliti ... in Italia ...* (1886).
Mos Philo, *De Vita Mosis.*
Moscati, Epig S, Moscati, *Epigrafia ebraica antica* 1935–1950 (1951).
MT Masoretic Text of the Bible.
Mueller, Musiker [E.H. Mueller], *Deutisches Musiker-Lexikon* (1929)
Munk, Mélanges S. Munk, *Mélanges de philosophie juive et arabe* (1859; repr. 1955).
Mut. Philo, *De Mutatione Nominum.*
MWJ *Magazin fuer die Wissenshaft des Judentums* (18745 93).

Nah. Nahum (Bible).
Naz. *Nazir* (talmudic tractate).
NDB *Neue Deutsche Biographie* (1953ff.).
Ned. *Nedarim* (talmudic tractate).
Neg. *Nega'im* (mishnaic tractate).
Neh. Nehemiah (Bible).
NG² *New Grove Dictionary of Music and Musicians* (2001).
Nuebauer, Cat A. Neubauer, *Catalogue of the Hebrew Manuscripts in the Bodleian Library ...,* 2 vols. (1886–1906).
Neubauer, Chronicles A. Neubauer, *Mediaeval Jewish Chronicles,* 2 vols. (Heb., 1887–95; repr. 1965), Eng. title of *Seder ha-Ḥakhamim ve-Korot ha-Yamim.*
Neubauer, Géogr A. Neubauer, *La géographie du Talmud* (1868).
Neuman, Spain A.A. Neuman, *The Jews in Spain, their Social, Political, and Cultural Life During the Middle Ages,* 2 vols. (1942).
Neusner, Babylonia J. Neusner, *History of the Jews in Babylonia,* 5 vols. 1965–70), 2nd revised printing 1969ff.).
Nid. *Niddah* (talmudic tractate).
Noah Fragment of Book of Noah (Pseudepigrapha).
Noth, Hist Isr M. Noth, *History of Israel* (1958).
Noth, Personennamen M. Noth, *Die israelitischen Personennamen. ...* (1928).
Noth, Ueberlief M. Noth, *Ueberlieferungsgeschichte des Pentateuchs* (1949).
Noth, Welt M. Noth, *Die Welt des Alten Testaments* (1957³).
Nowack, Lehrbuch W. Nowack, *Lehrbuch der hebraeischen Archaeologie,* 2 vols (1894).
NT New Testament.
Num. Numbers (Bible).
Num R. *Numbers Rabbah.*

Obad. Obadiah (Bible).
ODNB online *Oxford Dictionary of National Biography.*
OḤ *Oraḥ Ḥayyim.*
Oho. *Oholot* (mishnaic tractate).
Olmstead H.T. Olmstead, *History of Palestine and Syria* (1931; repr. 1965).
OLZ *Orientalistische Literaturzeitung* (1898ff.)
Onom. Eusebius, *Onomasticon.*
Op. Philo, *De Opificio Mundi.*
OPD *Osef Piskei Din shel ha-Rabbanut ha-Rashit le-Ereẓ Yisrael, Bet ha-Din ha-Gadol le-Irurim* (1950).
Or. *Orlah* (talmudic tractate).
Or. Sibyll. Sibylline Oracles (Pseudepigrapha).
OS *L'Orient Syrien* (1956ff.)
OTS *Oudtestamentische Studien* (1942ff.).

PAAJR *Proceedings of the American Academy for Jewish Research* (1930ff.)
Pap 4QSᵉ A papyrus exemplar of IQS.
Par. *Parah* (mishnaic tractate).
Pauly-Wissowa A.F. Pauly, *Realencyklopaedie der klassichen Alertumswissenschaft,* ed. by G. Wissowa et al. (1864ff.)

PD — *Piskei Din shel Bet ha-Mishpat ha-Elyon le-Yisrael* (1948ff.)
PDR — *Piskei Din shel Battei ha-Din ha-Rabbaniyyim be-Yisrael.*
PdRE — *Pirkei de-R. Eliezer* (Eng. tr. 1916. (1965[2]).
PdRK — *Pesikta de-Rav Kahana.*
Pe'ah — *Pe'ah* (talmudic tractate).
Peake, Commentary — A.J. Peake (ed.), *Commentary on the Bible* (1919; rev. 1962).
Pedersen, Israel — J. Pedersen, *Israel, Its Life and Culture,* 4 vols. in 2 (1926–40).
PEFQS — *Palestine Exploration Fund Quarterly Statement* (1869–1937; since 1938–PEQ).
PEQ — *Palestine Exploration Quarterly* (until 1937 PEFQS; after 1927 includes BBSAJ).
Perles, Beitaege — J. Perles, *Beitraege zur rabbinischen Sprach- und Alterthumskunde* (1893).
Pes. — *Pesaḥim* (talmudic tractate).
Pesh. — Peshitta (Syriac translation of the Bible).
Pesher Hab. — Commentary to Habakkuk from Qumran; see 1Qp Hab.
I and II Pet. — Epistles of Peter (New Testament).
Pfeiffer, Introd — R.H. Pfeiffer, *Introduction to the Old Testament* (1948).
PG — J.P. Migne (ed.), *Patrologia Graeca,* 161 vols. (1866–86).
Phil. — Epistle to the Philippians (New Testament).
Philem. — Epistle to the Philemon (New Testament).
PIASH — *Proceedings of the Israel Academy of Sciences and Humanities* (1963/7ff.).
PJB — *Palaestinajahrbuch des deutschen evangelischen Institutes fuer Altertumswissenschaft,* Jerusalem (1905–1933).
PK — *Pinkas ha-Kehillot,* encyclopedia of Jewish communities, published in over 30 volumes by Yad Vashem from 1970 and arranged by countries, regions and localities. For 3-vol. English edition see Spector, *Jewish Life.*
PL — J.P. Migne (ed.), *Patrologia Latina* 221 vols. (1844–64).
Plant — Philo, *De Plantatione.*
PO — R. Graffin and F. Nau (eds.), *Patrologia Orientalis* (1903ff.)
Pool, Prayer — D. de Sola Pool, *Traditional Prayer Book for Sabbath and Festivals* (1960).
Post — Philo, *De Posteritate Caini.*
PR — *Pesikta Rabbati.*
Praem. — Philo, *De Praemiis et Poenis.*
Prawer, Ẓalbanim — J. Prawer, *Toledot Mamlekhet ha-Ẓalbanim be-Ereẓ Yisrael,* 2 vols. (1963).
Press, Ereẓ — I. Press, *Ereẓ-Yisrael, Enẓiklopedyah Topografit-Historit,* 4 vols. (1951–55).
Pritchard, Pictures — J.B. Pritchard (ed.), *Ancient Near East in Pictures* (1954, 1970).
Pritchard, Texts — J.B. Pritchard (ed.), *Ancient Near East Texts* ... (1970[3]).
Pr. Man. — Prayer of Manasses (Apocrypha).
Prob. — Philo, *Quod Omnis Probus Liber Sit.*
Prov. — Proverbs (Bible).
PS — *Palestinsky Sbornik* (Russ. (1881 1916, 1954ff).
Ps. — Psalms (Bible).
PSBA — *Proceedings of the Society of Biblical Archaeology* (1878–1918).
Ps. of Sol — Psalms of Solomon (Pseudepigrapha).

IQ Apoc — The *Genesis Apocryphon* from Qumran, cave one, ed. by N. Avigad and Y. Yadin (1956).
6QD — *Damascus Document* or *Sefer Berit Dammesk* from Qumran, cave six, ed. by M. Baillet, in RB, 63 (1956), 513–23 (see also CD).
QDAP — *Quarterly of the Department of Antiquities in Palestine* (1932ff.).
4QDeut. 32 — Manuscript of Deuteronomy 32 from Qumran, cave four (ed. by P.W. Skehan, in BASOR, 136 (1954), 12–15).
4QEx[a] — Exodus manuscript in Jewish script from Qumran, cave four.
4QEx[α] — Exodus manuscript in Paleo-Hebrew script from Qumran, cave four (partially ed. by P.W. Skehan, in JBL, 74 (1955), 182–7).
4QFlor — *Florilegium,* a miscellany from Qumran, cave four (ed. by J.M. Allegro, in JBL, 75 (1956), 176–77 and 77 (1958), 350–54).).
QGJD — *Quellen zur Geschichte der Juden in Deutschland* 1888–98).
IQH — *Thanksgiving Psalms* of *Hodayot* from Qumran, cave one (ed. by E.L. Sukenik and N. Avigad, *Oẓar ha-Megillot ha-Genuzot* (1954).
IQIs[a] — Scroll of Isaiah from Qumran, cave one (ed. by N. Burrows et al., *Dead Sea Scrolls* ..., 1 (1950).
IQIs[b] — Scroll of Isaiah from Qumran, cave one (ed. E.L. Sukenik and N. Avigad, *Oẓar ha-Megillot ha-Genuzot* (1954).
IQM — The *War Scroll* or *Serekh ha-Milḥamah* (ed. by E.L. Sukenik and N. Avigad, *Oẓar ha-Megillot ha-Genuzot* (1954).
4QpNah — Commentary on Nahum from Qumran, cave four (partially ed. by J.M. Allegro, in JBL, 75 (1956), 89–95).
IQphyl — Phylacteries *(tefillin)* from Qumran, cave one (ed. by Y. Yadin, in *Eretz Israel,* 9 (1969), 60–85).
4Q Prayer of Nabonidus — A document from Qumran, cave four, belonging to a lost Daniel literature (ed. by J.T. Milik, in RB, 63 (1956), 407–15).
IQS — *Manual of Discipline* or *Serekh ha-Yaḥad* from Qumran, cave one (ed. by M. Burrows et al., *Dead Sea Scrolls* ..., 2, pt. 2 (1951).

IQS[a] — The *Rule of the Congregation or Serekh ha-Edah* from Qumran, cave one (ed. by Burrows et al., *Dead Sea Scrolls* ..., 1 (1950), under the abbreviation IQ28a).
IQS[b] — *Blessings* or *Divrei Berakhot* from Qumran, cave one (ed. by Burrows et al., *Dead Sea Scrolls* ..., 1 (1950), under the abbreviation IQ28b).
4QSam[a] — Manuscript of I and II Samuel from Qumran, cave four (partially ed. by F.M. Cross, in BASOR, 132 (1953), 15–26).
4QSam[b] — Manuscript of I and II Samuel from Qumran, cave four (partially ed. by F.M. Cross, in JBL, 74 (1955), 147–72).
4QTestimonia — Sheet of Testimony from Qumran, cave four (ed. by J.M. Allegro, in JBL, 75 (1956), 174–87).).
4QT.Levi — *Testament of Levi* from Qumran, cave four (partially ed. by J.T. Milik, in RB, 62 (1955), 398–406).

Rabinovitz, Dik Sof — See Dik Sof.
RB — *Revue biblique* (1892ff.)
RBI — *Recherches bibliques* (1954ff.)
RCB — *Revista de cultura biblica* (São Paulo) (1957ff.)
Régné, Cat — J. Régné, *Catalogue des actes . . . des rois d'Aragon, concernant les Juifs* (1213–1327), in: REJ, vols. 60 70, 73, 75–78 (1910–24).
Reinach, Textes — T. Reinach, *Textes d'auteurs Grecs et Romains relatifs au Judaïsme* (1895; repr. 1963).
REJ — *Revue des études juives* (1880ff.).
Rejzen, Leksikon — Z. Rejzen, *Leksikon fun der Yidisher Literature,* 4 vols. (1927–29).
Renan, Ecrivains — A. Neubauer and E. Renan, *Les écrivains juifs français* ... (1893).
Renan, Rabbins — A. Neubauer and E. Renan, *Les rabbins français* (1877).
RES — *Revue des étude sémitiques et Babyloniaca* (1934–45).
Rev. — Revelation (New Testament).
RGG[3] — *Die Religion in Geschichte und Gegenwart,* 7 vols. (1957–65[3]).
RH — *Rosh Ha-Shanah* (talmudic tractate).
RHJE — *Revue de l'histoire juive en Egypte* (1947ff.).
RHMH — *Revue d'histoire de la médecine hébraïque* (1948ff.).
RHPR — *Revue d'histoire et de philosophie religieuses* (1921ff.).
RHR — *Revue d'histoire des religions* (1880ff.).
RI — *Rivista Israelitica* (1904–12).
Riemann-Einstein — *Hugo Riemanns Musiklexikon,* ed. by A. Einstein (1929[11]).
Riemann-Gurlitt — *Hugo Riemanns Musiklexikon,* ed. by W. Gurlitt (1959–67[12]), Personenteil.
Rigg-Jenkinson, Exchequer — J.M. Rigg, H. Jenkinson and H.G. Richardson (eds.), *Calendar of the Pleas Rolls of the Exchequer of the Jews,* 4 vols. (1905–1970); cf. in each instance also J.M. Rigg (ed.), *Select Pleas* ... (1902).
RMI — *Rassegna Mensile di Israel* (1925ff.).
Rom. — Epistle to the Romans (New Testament).
Rosanes, Togarmah — S.A. Rosanes, *Divrei Yemei Yisrael be-Togarmah,* 6 vols. (1907–45), and in 3 vols. (1930–38[2]).
Rosenbloom, Biogr Dict — J.R. Rosenbloom, *Biographical Dictionary of Early American Jews* (1960).
Roth, Art — C. Roth, *Jewish Art* (1961).
Roth, Dark Ages — C. Roth (ed.), *World History of the Jewish People,* second series, vol. 2, *Dark Ages* (1966).
Roth, England — C. Roth, *History of the Jews in England* (1964[3]).
Roth, Italy — C. Roth, *History of the Jews in Italy* (1946).
Roth, Mag Bibl — C. Roth, *Magna Bibliotheca Anglo-Judaica* (1937).
Roth, Marranos — C. Roth, *History of the Marranos* (2nd rev. ed 1959; reprint 1966).
Rowley, Old Test — H.H. Rowley, *Old Testament and Modern Study* (1951; repr. 1961).
RS — *Revue sémitiques d'épigraphie et d'histoire ancienne* (1893/94ff.).
RSO — *Rivista degli studi orientali* (1907ff.).
RSV — Revised Standard Version of the Bible.
Rubinstein, Australia I — *H.L. Rubinstein, The Jews in Australia, A Thematic History, Vol. I (1991).*
Rubinstein, Australia II — *W.D. Rubinstein, The Jews in Australia, A Thematic History, Vol. II (1991).*
Ruth — Ruth (Bible).
Ruth R. — *Ruth Rabbah.*
RV — Revised Version of the Bible.

Sac. — Philo, *De Sacrificiis Abelis et Caini.*
Salfeld, Martyrol — S. Salfeld, *Martyrologium des Nuernberger Memorbuches* (1898).
I and II Sam. — Samuel, book I and II (Bible).
Sanh. — *Sanhedrin* (talmudic tractate).
SBA — Society of Biblical Archaeology.
SBB — *Studies in Bibliography and Booklore* (1953ff.).
SBE — *Semana Biblica Española.*
SBT — *Studies in Biblical Theology* (1951ff.).
SBU — *Svenkst Bibliskt Uppslogsvesk,* 2 vols. (1962–63[2]).
Schirmann, Italyah — J.Ḥ. Schirmann, *Ha-Shirah ha-Ivrit be-Italyah* (1934).
Schirmann, Sefarad — J.Ḥ. Schirmann, *Ha-Shirah ha-Ivrit bi-Sefarad u-vi-Provence,* 2 vols. (1954–56).
Scholem, Mysticism — G. Scholem, *Major Trends in Jewish Mysticism* (rev. ed. 1946; paperback ed. with additional bibliography 1961).
Scholem, Shabbetai Ẓevi — G. Scholem, *Shabbetai Ẓevi ve-ha-Tenu'ah ha-Shabbeta'it bi-Ymei Ḥayyav,* 2 vols. (1967).
Schrader, Keilinschr — E. Schrader, *Keilinschriften und das Alte Testament* (1903[3]).
Schuerer, Gesch — E. Schuerer, *Geschichte des juedischen Volkes im Zeitalter Jesu Christi,* 3 vols. and index-vol. (1901–11[4]).

Schuerer, Hist — E. Schuerer, *History of the Jewish People in the Time of Jesus*, ed. by N.N. Glatzer, abridged paperback edition (1961).
Set. T. — *Sefer Torah* (post-talmudic tractate).
Sem. — *Semaḥot* (post-talmudic tractate).
Sendrey, Music — A. Sendrey, *Bibliography of Jewish Music* (1951).
SER — *Seder Eliyahu Rabbah.*
SEZ — *Seder Eliyahu Zuta.*
Shab — *Shabbat* (talmudic tractate).
Sh. Ar. — J. Caro Shulḥan Arukh.
OḤ – *Oraḥ Ḥayyim*
YD – *Yoreh De'ah*
EH – *Even ha-Ezer*
ḤM – *Ḥoshen Mishpat.*
Shek. — *Shekalim* (talmudic tractate).
Shev. — *Shevi'it* (talmudic tractate).
Shevu. — *Shevu'ot* (talmudic tractate).
Shunami, Bibl — S. Shunami, *Bibliography of Jewish Bibliographies* (1965^2).
Sif. — *Sifrei Deuteronomy.*
Sif. Num. — *Sifrei Numbers.*
Sifra — *Sifra* on Leviticus.
Sif. Zut. — *Sifrei Zuta.*
SIHM — Sources inédites de l'histoire du Maroc (series).
Silverman, Prayer — M. Silverman (ed.), *Sabbath and Festival Prayer Book* (1946).
Singer, Prayer — S. Singer *Authorised Daily Prayer Book* (1943^{17}).
Sob. — Philo, *De Sobrietate.*
Sof. — *Soferim* (post-talmudic tractate).
Som. — Philo, *De Somniis.*
Song — Song of Songs (Bible).
Song. Ch. — Song of the Three Children (Apocrypha).
Song R. — *Song of Songs Rabbah.*
SOR — *Seder Olam Rabbah.*
Sot. — *Sotah* (talmudic tractate).
SOZ — *Seder Olam Zuta.*
Spec. — Philo, *De Specialibus Legibus.*
Spector, Jewish Life — *S. Spector (ed.), Encyclopedia of Jewish Life Before and After the Holocaust (2001).*
Steinschneider, Arab lit — M. Steinschneider, *Die arabische Literatur der Juden* (1902).
Steinschneider, Cat Bod — M. Steinschneider, *Catalogus Librorum Hebraeorum in Bibliotheca Bodleiana*, 3 vols. (1852–60; reprints 1931 and 1964).
Steinschneider, Hanbuch — M. Steinschneider, *Bibliographisches Handbuch ueber die . . . Literatur fuer hebraeische Sprachkunde* (1859; repr. with additions 1937).
Steinschneider, Uebersetzungen — M. Steinschneider, *Die hebraeischen Uebersetzungen des Mittelalters* (1893).
Stern, Americans — M.H. Stern, *Americans of Jewish Descent* (1960).
van Straalen, Cat — S. van Straalen, *Catalogue of Hebrew Books in the British Museum Acquired During the Years 1868–1892* (1894).
Suárez Fernández, Docmentos — L. Suárez Fernández, *Documentos acerca de la expulsion de los Judios de España* (1964).
Suk. — *Sukkah* (talmudic tractate).
Sus. — Susanna (Apocrypha).
SY — *Sefer Yeẓirah.*
Sym. — Symmachus' Greek translation of the Bible.
SZNG — *Studien zur neueren Geschichte.*

Ta'an. — *Ta'anit* (talmudic tractate).
Tam. — *Tamid* (mishnaic tractate).
Tanḥ. — *Tanḥuma.*
Tanḥ. B. — *Tanḥuma.* Buber ed (1885).
Targ. Jon — Targum Jonathan (Aramaic version of the Prophets).
Targ. Onk. — Targum Onkelos (Aramaic version of the Pentateuch).
Targ. Yer. — Targum Yerushalmi.
TB — Babylonian Talmud or Talmud Bavli.
Tcherikover, Corpus — V. Tcherikover, A. Fuks, and M. Stern, *Corpus Papyrorum Judaicorum*, 3 vols. (1957–60).
Tef. — *Tefillin* (post-talmudic tractate).
Tem. — *Temurah* (mishnaic tractate).
Ter. — *Terumah* (talmudic tractate).
Test. Patr. — Testament of the Twelve Patriarchs (Pseudepigrapha).
Ash. – Asher
Ben. – Benjamin
Dan – Dan
Gad – Gad
Iss. – Issachar
Joseph – Joseph
Judah – Judah
Levi – Levi
Naph. – Naphtali
Reu. – Reuben
Sim. – Simeon
Zeb. – Zebulun.
I and II — Epistle to the Thessalonians (New Testament).
Thieme-Becker — U. Thieme and F. Becker (eds.), *Allgemeines Lexikon der bildenden Kuenstler von der Antike bis zur Gegenwart*, 37 vols. (1907–50).
Tidhar — D. Tidhar (ed.), *Enẓiklopedyah la-Ḥalutẓei ha-Yishuv u-Vonav* (1947ff.).
I and II Timothy — Epistles to Timothy (New Testament).
Tit. — Epistle to Titus (New Testament).
TJ — Jerusalem Talmud or Talmud Yerushalmi.
Tob. — Tobit (Apocrypha).
Toh. — *Tohorot* (mishnaic tractate).
Torczyner, Bundeslade — H. Torczyner, *Die Bundeslade und die Anfaenge der Religion Israels* (1930^3).
Tos. — *Tosafot.*
Tosef. — Tosefta.
Tristram, Nat Hist — H.B. Tristram, *Natural History of the Bible* (1877^5).
Tristram, Survey — Palestine Exploration Fund, *Survey of Western Palestine*, vol. 4 (1884) = *Fauna and Flora* by H.B. Tristram.
TS — *Terra Santa* (1943ff.).

TSBA	*Transactions of the Society of Biblical Archaeology* (1872–93).
TY	*Tevul Yom* (mishnaic tractate).
UBSB	United Bible Society, *Bulletin.*
UJE	*Universal Jewish Encyclopedia,* 10 vols. (1939–43).
Uk.	*Ukẓin* (mishnaic tractate).
Urbach, Tosafot	E.E. Urbach, *Ba'alei ha-Tosafot* (1957^2).
de Vaux, Anc Isr	R. de Vaux, *Ancient Israel: its Life and Institutions* (1961; paperback 1965).
de Vaux, Instit	R. de Vaux, *Institutions de l'Ancien Testament,* 2 vols. (1958 60).
Virt.	Philo, *De Virtutibus.*
Vogelstein, Chronology	M. Volgelstein, *Biblical Chronology (1944).*
Vogelstein-Rieger	H. Vogelstein and P. Rieger, *Geschichte der Juden in Rom,* 2 vols. (1895–96).
VT	*Vetus Testamentum* (1951ff.).
VTS	*Vetus Testamentum* Supplements (1953ff.).
Vulg.	Vulgate (Latin translation of the Bible).
Wars	Josephus, *The Jewish Wars.*
Watzinger, Denkmaeler	K. Watzinger, *Denkmaeler Palaestinas,* 2 vols. (1933–35).
Waxman, Literature	M. Waxman, *History of Jewish Literature,* 5 vols. (1960^2).
Weiss, Dor	I.H. Weiss, *Dor, Dor ve-Doreshav,* 5 vols. (1904^4).
Wellhausen, Proleg	J. Wellhausen, *Prolegomena zur Geschichte Israels* (1927^6).
WI	*Die Welt des Islams* (1913ff.).
Winniger, Biog	S. Wininger, *Grosse juedische National-Biographie ...,* 7 vols. (1925–36).
Wisd.	Wisdom of Solomon (Apocrypha)
WLB	*Wiener Library Bulletin* (1958ff.).
Wolf, Bibliotheca	J.C. Wolf, *Bibliotheca Hebraea,* 4 vols. (1715–33).
Wright, Bible	G.E. Wright, *Westminster Historical Atlas to the Bible* (1945).
Wright, Atlas	G.E. Wright, *The Bible and the Ancient Near East* (1961).
WWWJ	*Who's Who in the World Jewry* (New York, 1955, 1965^2).
WZJT	*Wissenschaftliche Zeitschrift fuer juedische Theologie* (1835–37).
WZKM	*Wiener Zeitschrift fuer die Kunde des Morgenlandes* (1887ff.).
Yaari, Sheluḥei	A. Yaari, *Sheluḥei Ereẓ Yisrael* (1951).
Yad	Maimonides, *Mishneh Torah (Yad Ḥazakah).*
Yad	*Yadayim* (mishnaic tractate).
Yal.	*Yalkut Shimoni.*
Yal. Mak.	*Yalkut Makhiri.*
Yal. Reub.	*Yalkut Reubeni.*
YD	*Yoreh De'ah.*
YE	*Yevreyskaya Entsiklopediya,* 14 vols. (c. 1910).
Yev.	*Yevamot* (talmudic tractate).
YIVOA	*YIVO Annual of Jewish Social Studies* (1946ff.).
YLBI	*Year Book of the Leo Baeck Institute* (1956ff.).
YMḤEY	See BJPES.
YMḤSI	*Yedi'ot ha-Makhon le-Ḥeker ha-Shirah ha-Ivrit* (1935/36ff.).
YMMY	*Yedi'ot ha-Makhon le-Madda'ei ha-Yahadut* (1924/25ff.).
Yoma	*Yoma* (talmudic tractate).
ZA	*Zeitschrift fuer Assyriologie* (1886/87ff.).
Zav.	*Zavim* (mishnaic tractate).
ZAW	*Zeitschrift fuer die alttestamentliche Wissenschaft und die Kunde des nachbiblishchen Judentums* (1881ff.).
ZAWB	*Beihefte* (supplements) to ZAW.
ZDMG	*Zeitschrift der Deutschen Morgenlaendischen Gesellschaft* (1846ff.).
ZDPV	*Zeitschrift des Deutschen Palaestina-Vereins* (1878–1949; from 1949 = BBLA).
Zech.	Zechariah (Bible).
Zedner, Cat	J. Zedner, *Catalogue of Hebrew Books in the Library of the British Museum* (1867; repr. 1964).
Zeitlin, Bibliotheca	W. Zeitlin, *Bibliotheca Hebraica Post-Mendelssohniana* (1891–95).
Zeph.	Zephaniah (Bible).
Zev.	*Zevaḥim* (talmudic tractate).
ZGGJT	*Zeitschrift der Gesellschaft fuer die Geschichte der Juden in der Tschechoslowakei* (1930–38).
ZGJD	*Zeitschrift fuer die Geschichte der Juden in Deutschland* (1887–92).
ZHB	*Zeitschrift fuer hebraeische Bibliographie* (1896–1920).
Zinberg, Sifrut	I. Zinberg, *Toledot Sifrut Yisrael,* 6 vols. (1955–60).
Ẓiẓ.	*Ẓiẓit* (post-talmudic tractate).
ZNW	*Zeitschrift fuer die neutestamentliche Wissenschaft* (1901ff.).
ZS	*Zeitschrift fuer Semitistik und verwandte Gebiete* (1922ff.).
Zunz, Gesch	L. Zunz, *Zur Geschichte und Literatur* (1845).
Zunz, Gesch	L. Zunz, *Literaturgeschichte der synagogalen Poesie* (1865; Supplement, 1867; repr. 1966).
Zunz, Poesie	L. Zunz, *Synogogale Posie des Mittelalters,* ed. by Freimann (1920^2; repr. 1967).
Zunz, Ritus	L. Zunz, *Ritus des synagogalen Gottesdienstes* (1859; repr. 1967).
Zunz, Schr	L. Zunz, *Gesammelte Schriften,* 3 vols. (1875–76).
Zunz, Vortraege	L. Zunz, *Gottesdienstliche vortraege der Juden ...* 1892^2; repr. 1966).
Zunz-Albeck, Derashot	L. Zunz, *Ha-Derashot be-Yisrael,* Heb. Tr. of Zunz Vortraege by H. Albeck (1954^2).

TRANSLITERATION RULES

HEBREW AND SEMITIC LANGUAGES:

	General	*Scientific*
א	not transliterated[1]	ʾ
בּ	b	b
ב	v	v, ḇ
גּ	g	g
ג		ḡ
דּ	d	d
ד		ḏ
ה	h	h
ו	v – when not a vowel	w
ז	z	z
ח	ḥ	ḥ
ט	t	ṭ, t
י	y – when vowel and at end of words – i	y
כּ	k	k
כ, ך	kh	kh, ḵ
ל	l	ḻ
מ, ם	m	m
נ, ן	n	n
ס	s	s
ע	not transliterated[1]	ʿ
פּ	p	p
פ, ף	f	p, f, ph
צ, ץ	ẓ	ṣ, ẓ
ק	k	q, k
ר	r	r
שׁ	sh[2]	š
שׂ	s	ś, s
תּ	t	t
ת		ṯ
ג׳	dzh, J	ğ
ז׳	zh, J	ž
צ׳	ch	č
◌ָ		å, o, ŏ (short) â, ā (long)
◌ַ	a	a
◌ֲ		a, ^{a}
◌ֵ		e, ẹ, ē
◌ֶ	e	æ, ä, ę
◌ֱ		œ, ĕ, ^{e}
◌ְ	only *sheva na* is transliterated	ə, ĕ, e; only *sheva na* transliterated
◌ִ, ◌ִי	i	i
◌ֹ, וֹ	o	o, o, o
◌ֻ, וּ	u	u, ŭ û, ū
◌ֵי	ei; biblical e	
‡		reconstructed forms of words

1. The letters א and ע are not transliterated.
   An apostrophe (') between vowels indicates that they do not form a diphthong and are to be pronounced separately.
2. *Dagesh ḥazak* (forte) is indicated by doubling of the letter, except for the letter שׁ.
3. Names. Biblical names and biblical place names are rendered according to the Bible translation of the Jewish Publication Society of America. Post-biblical Hebrew names are transliterated; contemporary names are transliterated or rendered as used by the person. Place names are transliterated or rendered by the accepted spelling. Names and some words with an accepted English form are usually not transliterated.

YIDDISH

א	not transliterated
אַ	a
אָ	o
בּ	b
בֿ	v
ג	g
ד	d
ה	h
ו, וּ	u
וו	v
וי	oy
ז	z
זש	zh
ח	kh
ט	t
טש	tsh, ch
י	(consonant) y (vowel) i
יִ	i
יי	ey
ײַ	ay
כּ	k
כ, ך	kh
ל	l
מ, ם	m
נ, ן	n
ס	s
ע	e
פּ	p
פֿ, ף	f
צ, ץ	ts
ק	k
ר	r
שׁ	sh
שׂ	s
תּ	t
ת	s

1. Yiddish transliteration rendered according to U. Weinreich's Modern *English-Yiddish Yiddish-English* Dictionary.
2. Hebrew words in Yiddish are usually transliterated according to standard Yiddish pronunciation, e.g., חזנות = *khazones*.

LADINO

Ladino and Judeo-Spanish words written in Hebrew characters are transliterated phonetically, following the General Rules of Hebrew transliteration (see above) whenever the accepted spelling in Latin characters could not be ascertained.

ARABIC

ا ء	a[1]	ض	ḍ
ب	b	ط	ṭ
ت	t	ظ	ẓ
ث	th	ع	c
ج	j	غ	gh
ح	ḥ	ف	f
خ	kh	ق	q
د	d	ك	k
ذ	dh	ل	l
ر	r	م	m
ز	z	ن	n
س	s	ه	h
ش	sh	و	w
ص	ṣ	ي	y
ـَ	a	ـَا ى	ā
ـِ	i	ـِي	ī
ـُ	u	ـُو	ū
ـَو	aw	ـِيّ	iyy[2]
ـَي	ay	ـُوّ	uww[2]

1. not indicated when initial
2. see note (f)

a) The EJ follows the *Columbia Lippincott Gazetteer* and the *Times Atlas* in transliteration of Arabic place names. Sites that appear in neither are transliterated according to the table above, and subject to the following notes.

b) The EJ follows the *Columbia Encyclopedia* in transliteration of Arabic names. Personal names that do not therein appear are transliterated according to the table above and subject to the following notes (e.g., Ali rather than ʿAlī, Suleiman rather than Sulayman).

c) The EJ follows the *Webster's Third International Dictionary, Unabridged* in transliteration of Arabic terms that have been integrated into the English language.

d) The term "Abu" will thus appear, usually in disregard of inflection.

e) Nunnation (end vowels, *tanwīn*) are dropped in transliteration.

f) Gemination (*tashdīd*) is indicated by the doubling of the geminated letter, unless an end letter, in which case the gemination is dropped.

g) The definitive article *al-* will always be thus transliterated, unless subject to one of the modifying notes (e.g., El-Arish rather than al-ʿArīsh; modification according to note (a)).

h) The Arabic transliteration disregards the Sun Letters (the antero-palatals (*al-Ḥurūf al-Shamsiyya*).

i) The *tā-marbūṭa* (o) is omitted in transliteration, unless in construct-stage (e.g., *Khirba* but *Khirbat Mishmish*).

These modifying notes may lead to various inconsistencies in the Arabic transliteration, but this policy has deliberately been adopted to gain smoother reading of Arabic terms and names.

GREEK

Ancient Greek	*Modern Greek*	*Greek Letters*
a	a	*Α; α; ᾳ*
b	v	*Β; β*
g	gh; g	*Γ; γ*
d	dh	*Δ; δ*
e	e	*Ε; ε*
z	z	*Ζ; ζ*
e; e	i	*Η; η; ῃ*
th	th	*Θ; θ*
i	i	*Ι; ι*
k	k; ky	*Κ; κ*
l	l	*Λ; λ*
m	m	*Μ; μ*
n	n	*Ν; ν*
x	x	*Ξ; ξ*
o	o	*Ο; ο*
p	p	*Π; π*
r; rh	r	*Ρ; ρ; ῥ*
s	s	*Σ; σ; ς*
t	t	*Τ; τ*
u; y	i	*Υ; υ*
ph	f	*Φ; φ*
ch	kh	*Χ; χ*
ps	ps	*Ψ; ψ*
o; ō	o	*Ω; ω; ῳ*
ai	e	*αι*
ei	i	*ει*
oi	i	*οι*
ui	i	*υι*
ou	ou	*ου*
eu	ev	*ευ*
eu; ēu	iv	*ηυ*
–	j	*τζ*
nt	d; nd	*ντ*
mp	b; mb	*μπ*
ngk	g	*γκ*
ng	ng	*νγ*
h	–	‘
–	–	’
w	–	*Ϝ*

RUSSIAN

А	A
Б	B
В	V
Г	G
Д	D
Е	E, Ye[1]
Ё	Yo, O[2]
Ж	Zh
З	Z
И	I
Й	Y[3]
К	K
Л	L
М	M
Н	N
О	O
П	P
Р	R
С	S
Т	T
У	U
Ф	F
Х	Kh
Ц	Ts
Ч	Ch
Ш	Sh
Щ	Shch
Ъ	omitted; see note [1]
Ы	Y
Ь	omitted; see note [1]
Э	E
Ю	Yu
Я	Ya

1. Ye at the beginning of a word; after all vowels except ***Ы***; and after ***Ъ*** and ***Ь***.
2. O after ***Ч***, ***Ш*** and ***Щ***.
3. Omitted after ***Ы***, and in names of people after ***И***.

A. Many first names have an accepted English or quasi-English form which has been preferred to transliteration.
B. Place names have been given according to the *Columbia Lippincott Gazeteer*.
C. Pre-revolutionary spelling has been ignored.
D. Other languages using the Cyrillic alphabet (e.g., Bulgarian, Ukrainian), inasmuch as they appear, have been phonetically transliterated in conformity with the principles of this table.

GLOSSARY

Asterisked terms have separate entries in the Encyclopaedia.

Actions Committee, early name of the Zionist General Council, the supreme institution of the World Zionist Organization in the interim between Congresses. The Zionist Executive's name was then the "Small Actions Committee."

***Adar**, twelfth month of the Jewish religious year, sixth of the civil, approximating to February–March.

***Aggadah**, name given to those sections of Talmud and Midrash containing homiletic expositions of the Bible, stories, legends, folklore, anecdotes, or maxims. In contradistinction to **halakhah.*

***Agunah**, woman unable to remarry according to Jewish law, because of desertion by her husband or inability to accept presumption of death.

***Aharonim**, later rabbinic authorities. In contradistinction to **rishonim* ("early ones").

Ahavah, liturgical poem inserted in the second benediction of the morning prayer *(*Ahavah Rabbah)* of the festivals and/or special Sabbaths.

Aktion (Ger.), operation involving the mass assembly, deportation, and murder of Jews by the Nazis during the *Holocaust.

***Aliyah**, (1) being called to Reading of the Law in synagogue; (2) immigration to Ereẓ Israel; (3) one of the waves of immigration to Ereẓ Israel from the early 1880s.

***Amidah**, main prayer recited at all services; also known as *Shemoneh Esreh* and *Tefillah.*

***Amora** (pl. **amoraim**), title given to the Jewish scholars in Ereẓ Israel and Babylonia in the third to sixth centuries who were responsible for the **Gemara.*

Aravah, the *willow; one of the *Four Species used on *Sukkot ("festival of Tabernacles") together with the **etrog, hadas,* and **lulav.*

***Arvit**, evening prayer.

Asarah be-Tevet, fast on the 10th of Tevet commemorating the commencement of the siege of Jerusalem by Nebuchadnezzar.

Asefat ha-Nivḥarim, representative assembly elected by Jews in Palestine during the period of the British Mandate (1920–48).

***Ashkenaz**, name applied generally in medieval rabbinical literature to Germany.

***Ashkenazi** (pl. **Ashkenazim**), German or West-, Central-, or East-European Jew(s), as contrasted with *Sephardi(m).

***Av**, fifth month of the Jewish religious year, eleventh of the civil, approximating to July–August.

***Av bet din**, vice president of the supreme court (*bet din ha-gadol*) in Jerusalem during the Second Temple period; later, title given to communal rabbis as heads of the religious courts (see **bet din*).

***Badḥan**, jester, particularly at traditional Jewish weddings in Eastern Europe.

***Bakkashah** (Heb. "supplication"), type of petitionary prayer, mainly recited in the Sephardi rite on Rosh Ha-Shanah and the Day of Atonement.

Bar, "son of . . . "; frequently appearing in personal names.

***Baraita** (pl. **beraitot**), statement of **tanna* not found in *Mishnah.

***Bar mitzvah**, ceremony marking the initiation of a boy at the age of 13 into the Jewish religious community.

Ben, "son of . . . ", frequently appearing in personal names.

Berakhah (pl. **berakhot**), *benediction, blessing; formula of praise and thanksgiving.

***Bet din** (pl. **battei din**), rabbinic court of law.

***Bet ha-midrash**, school for higher rabbinic learning; often attached to or serving as a synagogue.

***Bilu**, first modern movement for pioneering and agricultural settlement in Ereẓ Israel, founded in 1882 at Kharkov, Russia.

***Bund**, Jewish socialist party founded in Vilna in 1897, supporting Jewish national rights; Yiddishist, and anti-Zionist.

Cohen (pl. **Cohanim**), see Kohen.

***Conservative Judaism**, trend in Judaism developed in the United States in the 20th century which, while opposing extreme changes in traditional observances, permits certain modifications of *halakhah* in response to the changing needs of the Jewish people.

***Consistory** (Fr. *consistoire*), governing body of a Jewish communal district in France and certain other countries.

***Converso(s)**, term applied in Spain and Portugal to converted Jew(s), and sometimes more loosely to their descendants.

***Crypto-Jew**, term applied to a person who although observing outwardly Christianity (or some other religion) was at heart a Jew and maintained Jewish observances as far as possible (see Converso; Marrano; Neofiti; New Christian; Jadīd al-Islām).

***Dayyan**, member of rabbinic court.

Decisor, equivalent to the Hebrew *posek* (pl. **posekim*), the rabbi who gives the decision (*halakhah*) in Jewish law or practice.

***Devekut**, "devotion"; attachment or adhesion to God; communion with God.

***Diaspora**, Jews living in the "dispersion" outside Ereẓ Israel; area of Jewish settlement outside Ereẓ Israel.

Din, a law (both secular and religious), legal decision, or lawsuit.

Divan, diwan, collection of poems, especially in Hebrew, Arabic, or Persian.

Dunam, unit of land area (1,000 sq. m., c. ¼ acre), used in Israel.

Einsatzgruppen, mobile units of Nazi S.S. and S.D.; in U.S.S.R. and Serbia, mobile killing units.

***Ein-Sof**, "without end"; "the infinite"; hidden, impersonal aspect of God; also used as a Divine Name.

***Elul**, sixth month of the Jewish religious calendar, 12th of the civil, precedes the High Holiday season in the fall.

Endloesung, see *Final Solution.

***Ereẓ Israel**, Land of Israel; Palestine.

***Eruv**, technical term for rabbinical provision permitting the alleviation of certain restrictions.

***Etrog**, citron; one of the *Four Species used on *Sukkot together with the **lulav, hadas,* and *aravah.*

Even ha-Ezer, see Shulḥan Arukh.

***Exilarch**, lay head of Jewish community in Babylonia (see also *resh galuta*), and elsewhere.

***Final Solution** (Ger. *Endloesung*), in Nazi terminology, the Nazi-planned mass murder and total annihilation of the Jews.

***Gabbai**, official of a Jewish congregation; originally a charity collector.

***Galut**, "exile"; the condition of the Jewish people in dispersion.

***Gaon** (pl. **geonim**), head of academy in post-talmudic period, especially in Babylonia.

Gaonate, office of *gaon.

***Gemara**, traditions, discussions, and rulings of the **amoraim*, commenting on and supplementing the *Mishnah, and forming part of the Babylonian and Palestinian Talmuds (see Talmud).

***Gematria**, interpretation of Hebrew word according to the numerical value of its letters.

General Government, territory in Poland administered by a German civilian governor-general with headquarters in Cracow after the German occupation in World War II.

***Genizah**, depository for sacred books. The best known was discovered in the synagogue of Fostat (old Cairo).

Get, bill of *divorce.

***Ge'ullah**, hymn inserted after the **Shema* into the benediction of the morning prayer of the festivals and special Sabbaths.

***Gilgul**, metempsychosis; transmigration of souls.

***Golem**, automaton, especially in human form, created by magical means and endowed with life.

***Ḥabad**, initials of *ḥokhmah, binah, da'at*: "wisdom, understanding, knowledge"; ḥasidic movement founded in Belorussia by *Shneur Zalman of Lyady.

Hadas, *myrtle; one of the *Four Species used on Sukkot together with the **etrog, *lulav*, and *aravah*.

***Haftarah** (pl. **haftarot**), designation of the portion from the prophetical books of the Bible recited after the synagogue reading from the Pentateuch on Sabbaths and holidays.

***Haganah**, clandestine Jewish organization for armed self-defense in Ereẓ Israel under the British Mandate, which eventually evolved into a people's militia and became the basis for the Israel army.

***Haggadah**, ritual recited in the home on *Passover eve at seder table.

Haham, title of chief rabbi of the Spanish and Portuguese congregations in London, England.

***Hakham**, title of rabbi of *Sephardi congregation.

***Hakham bashi**, title in the 15th century and modern times of the chief rabbi in the Ottoman Empire, residing in Constantinople (Istanbul), also applied to principal rabbis in provincial towns.

Hakhsharah ("preparation"), organized training in the Diaspora of pioneers for agricultural settlement in Ereẓ Israel.

***Halakhah** (pl. **halakhot**), an accepted decision in rabbinic law. Also refers to those parts of the *Talmud concerned with legal matters. In contradistinction to **aggadah*.

Ḥaliẓah, biblically prescribed ceremony (Deut. 25:9–10) performed when a man refuses to marry his brother's childless widow, enabling her to remarry.

***Hallel**, term referring to Psalms 113-18 in liturgical use.

***Ḥalukkah**, system of financing the maintenance of Jewish communities in the holy cities of Ereẓ Israel by collections made abroad, mainly in the pre-Zionist era (see *kolel*).

Ḥalutz (pl. **ḥalutzim**), pioneer, especially in agriculture, in Ereẓ Israel.

Ḥalutziyyut, pioneering.

***Ḥanukkah**, eight-day celebration commemorating the victory of *Judah Maccabee over the Syrian king *Antiochus Epiphanes and the subsequent rededication of the Temple.

Ḥasid, adherent of *Ḥasidism.

***Ḥasidei Ashkenaz**, medieval pietist movement among the Jews of Germany.

***Ḥasidism**, (1) religious revivalist movement of popular mysticism among Jews of Germany in the Middle Ages; (2) religious movement founded by *Israel ben Eliezer Ba'al Shem Tov in the first half of the 18th century.

***Haskalah**, "enlightenment"; movement for spreading modern European culture among Jews c. 1750–1880. See *maskil*.

***Havdalah**, ceremony marking the end of Sabbath or festival.

***Ḥazzan**, precentor who intones the liturgy and leads the prayers in synagogue; in earlier times a synagogue official.

***Ḥeder** (lit. "room"), school for teaching children Jewish religious observance.

Heikhalot, "palaces"; tradition in Jewish mysticism centering on mystical journeys through the heavenly spheres and palaces to the Divine Chariot (see Merkabah).

***Ḥerem**, excommunication, imposed by rabbinical authorities for purposes of religious and/or communal discipline; originally, in biblical times, that which is separated from common use either because it was an abomination or because it was consecrated to God.

Ḥeshvan, see Marḥeshvan.

***Ḥevra kaddisha**, title applied to charitable confraternity (**ḥevrah*), now generally limited to associations for burial of the dead.

***Ḥibbat Zion**, see Ḥovevei Zion.

***Histadrut** (abbr. For Heb. **Ha-Histadrut ha-Kelalit shel ha-Ovedim ha-Ivriyyim be-Ereẓ Israel**). Ereẓ Israel Jewish Labor Federation, founded in 1920; subsequently renamed Histadrut ha-Ovedim be-Ereẓ Israel.

***Holocaust**, the organized mass persecution and annihilation of European Jewry by the Nazis (1933–1945).

***Hoshana Rabba**, the seventh day of *Sukkot on which special observances are held.

Ḥoshen Mishpat, see Shulḥan Arukh.

Ḥovevei Zion, federation of *Ḥibbat Zion, early (pre-*Herzl) Zionist movement in Russia.

Illui, outstanding scholar or genius, especially a young prodigy in talmudic learning.

***Iyyar**, second month of the Jewish religious year, eighth of the civil, approximating to April-May.

I.Ẓ.L. (initials of Heb. ***Irgun Ẓeva'i Le'ummi**; "National Military Organization"), underground Jewish organization in Ereẓ Israel founded in 1931, which engaged from 1937 in retaliatory acts against Arab attacks and later against the British mandatory authorities.

***Jadīd al-Islām** (Ar.), a person practicing the Jewish religion in secret although outwardly observing Islām.

***Jewish Legion**, Jewish units in British army during World War I.

***Jihād** (Ar.), in Muslim religious law, holy war waged against infidels.

***Judenrat** (Ger. "Jewish council"), council set up in Jewish communities and ghettos under the Nazis to execute their instructions.

***Judenrein** (Ger. "clean of Jews"), in Nazi terminology the condition of a locality from which all Jews had been eliminated.

***Kabbalah**, the Jewish mystical tradition:
  Kabbala iyyunit, speculative Kabbalah;
  Kabbala ma'asit, practical Kabbalah;
  Kabbala nevu'it, prophetic Kabbalah.

Kabbalist, student of Kabbalah.

***Kaddish**, liturgical doxology.

Kahal, Jewish congregation; among Ashkenazim, *kehillah*.

***Kalām** (Ar.), science of Muslim theology; adherents of the Kalām are called *mutakallimūn*.

***Karaite**, member of a Jewish sect originating in the eighth century which rejected rabbinic (*Rabbanite) Judaism and claimed to accept only Scripture as authoritative.

***Kasher**, ritually permissible food.

Kashrut, Jewish *dietary laws.

***Kavvanah**, "intention"; term denoting the spiritual concentration accompanying prayer and the performance of ritual or of a commandment.

***Kedushah**, main addition to the third blessing in the reader's repetition of the *Amidah* in which the public responds to the precentor's introduction.

Kefar, village; first part of name of many settlements in Israel.

Kehillah, congregation; see *kahal.*

Kelippah (pl. **kelippot**), "husk(s)"; mystical term denoting force(s) of evil.

***Keneset Yisrael**, comprehensive communal organization of the Jews in Palestine during the British Mandate.

Keri, variants in the masoretic (*masorah) text of the Bible between the spelling (*ketiv*) and its pronunciation (*keri*).

***Kerovah** (collective plural (corrupted) from **kerovez̦**), poem(s) incorporated into the **Amidah.*

Ketiv, see *keri.*

***Ketubbah**, marriage contract, stipulating husband's obligations to wife.

Kevuz̦ah, small commune of pioneers constituting an agricultural settlement in Erez̦ Israel (evolved later into *kibbutz).

***Kibbutz** (pl. **kibbutzim**), larger-size commune constituting a settlement in Erez̦ Israel based mainly on agriculture but engaging also in industry.

***Kiddush**, prayer of sanctification, recited over wine or bread on eve of Sabbaths and festivals.

***Kiddush ha-Shem**, term connoting martyrdom or act of strict integrity in support of Judaic principles.

***Kinah** (pl. **kinot**), lamentation dirge(s) for the Ninth of Av and other fast days.

***Kislev**, ninth month of the Jewish religious year, third of the civil, approximating to November-December.

Klaus, name given in Central and Eastern Europe to an institution, usually with synagogue attached, where *Talmud was studied perpetually by adults; applied by Ḥasidim to their synagogue ("*kloyz*").

***Knesset**, parliament of the State of Israel.

K(c)ohen (pl. **K(c)ohanim**), Jew(s) of priestly (Aaronide) descent.

***Kolel**, (1) community in Erez̦ Israel of persons from a particular country or locality, often supported by their fellow countrymen in the Diaspora; (2) institution for higher Torah study.

Kosher, see *kasher.*

***Kristallnacht** (Ger. "crystal night," meaning "night of broken glass"), organized destruction of synagogues, Jewish houses, and shops, accompanied by mass arrests of Jews, which took place in Germany and Austria under the Nazis on the night of Nov. 9–10, 1938.

***Lag ba-Omer**, 33rd (Heb. **lag**) day of the **Omer* period falling on the 18th of *Iyyar; a semi-holiday.

Leḥi (abbr. For Heb. ***Loḥamei Ḥerut Israel**, "Fighters for the Freedom of Israel"), radically anti-British armed underground organization in Palestine, founded in 1940 by dissidents from *I.Z.L.

Levir, husband's brother.

***Levirate marriage** (Heb. *yibbum*), marriage of childless widow (*yevamah*) by brother (*yavam*) of the deceased husband (in accordance with Deut. 25:5); release from such an obligation is effected through *ḥaliz̦ah.*

LHY, see Leḥi.

***Lulav**, palm branch; one of the *Four Species used on *Sukkot together with the **etrog, hadas*, and *aravah.*

***Ma'aravot**, hymns inserted into the evening prayer of the three festivals, Passover, Shavuot, and Sukkot.

Ma'ariv, evening prayer; also called **arvit.*

***Ma'barah**, transition camp; temporary settlement for newcomers in Israel during the period of mass immigration following 1948.

***Maftir**, reader of the concluding portion of the Pentateuchal section on Sabbaths and holidays in synagogue; reader of the portion of the prophetical books of the Bible (**haftarah*).

***Maggid**, popular preacher.

***Maḥzor** (pl. **maḥzorim**), festival prayer book.

***Mamzer**, bastard; according to Jewish law, the offspring of an incestuous relationship.

***Mandate, Palestine**, responsibility for the administration of Palestine conferred on Britain by the League of Nations in 1922; mandatory government: the British administration of Palestine.

***Maqāma** (Ar. pl. **maqamāt**), poetic form (rhymed prose) which, in its classical arrangement, has rigid rules of form and content.

***Marḥeshvan**, popularly called Ḥeshvan; eighth month of the Jewish religious year, second of the civil, approximating to October–November.

***Marrano(s)**, descendant(s) of Jew(s) in Spain and Portugal whose ancestors had been converted to Christianity under pressure but who secretly observed Jewish rituals.

Maskil (pl. **maskilim**), adherent of *Haskalah ("Enlightenment") movement.

***Masorah**, body of traditions regarding the correct spelling, writing, and reading of the Hebrew Bible.

Masorete, scholar of the masoretic tradition.

Masoretic, in accordance with the masorah.

Meliz̦ah, in Middle Ages, elegant style; modern usage, florid style using biblical or talmudic phraseology.

Mellah, *Jewish quarter in North African towns.

***Menorah**, candelabrum; seven-branched oil lamp used in the Tabernacle and Temple; also eight-branched candelabrum used on *Ḥanukkah.

Me'orah, hymn inserted into the first benediction of the morning prayer (*Yoz̦er ha-Me'orot*).

***Merkabah**, *merkavah*, "chariot"; mystical discipline associated with Ezekiel's vision of the Divine Throne-Chariot (Ezek. 1).

Meshullaḥ, emissary sent to conduct propaganda or raise funds for rabbinical academies or charitable institutions.

***Mezuzah** (pl. **mezuzot**), parchment scroll with selected Torah verses placed in container and affixed to gates and doorposts of houses occupied by Jews.

***Midrash**, method of interpreting Scripture to elucidate legal points (*Midrash Halakhah*) or to bring out lessons by stories or homiletics (*Midrash Aggadah*). Also the name for a collection of such rabbinic interpretations.

***Mikveh**, ritual bath.

***Minhag** (pl. **minhagim**), ritual custom(s); synagogal rite(s); especially of a specific sector of Jewry.

***Minḥah**, afternoon prayer; originally meal offering in Temple.

*__Minyan__, group of ten male adult Jews, the minimum required for communal prayer.

*__Mishnah__, earliest codification of Jewish Oral Law.

Mishnah (pl. **mishnayot**), subdivision of tractates of the Mishnah.

Mitnagged (pl. ***Mitnaggedim**), originally, opponents of *Ḥasidism in Eastern Europe.

*__Mitzvah__, biblical or rabbinic injunction; applied also to good or charitable deeds.

Mohel, official performing circumcisions.

*__Moshav__, smallholders' cooperative agricultural settlement in Israel, see moshav ovedim.

Moshavah, earliest type of Jewish village in modern Ereẓ Israel in which farming is conducted on individual farms mostly on privately owned land.

Moshav ovedim ("workers' moshav"), agricultural village in Israel whose inhabitants possess individual homes and holdings but cooperate in the purchase of equipment, sale of produce, mutual aid, etc.

*__Moshav shittufi__ ("collective moshav"), agricultural village in Israel whose members possess individual homesteads but where the agriculture and economy are conducted as a collective unit.

Mostegab (Ar.), poem with biblical verse at beginning of each stanza.

*__Muqaddam__ (Ar., pl. **muqaddamūn**), "leader," "head of the community."

*__Musaf__, additional service on Sabbath and festivals; originally the additional sacrifice offered in the Temple.

Musar, traditional ethical literature.

*__Musar movement__, ethical movement developing in the latter part of the 19th century among Orthodox Jewish groups in Lithuania; founded by R. Israel *Lipkin (Salanter).

*__Nagid__ (pl. **negidim**), title applied in Muslim (and some Christian) countries in the Middle Ages to a leader recognized by the state as head of the Jewish community.

Nakdan (pl. **nakdanim**), "punctuator"; scholar of the 9th to 14th centuries who provided biblical manuscripts with masoretic apparatus, vowels, and accents.

*__Nasi__ (pl. **nesi'im**), talmudic term for president of the Sanhedrin, who was also the spiritual head and later, political representative of the Jewish people; from second century a descendant of Hillel recognized by the Roman authorities as patriarch of the Jews. Now applied to the president of the State of Israel.

*__Negev__, the southern, mostly arid, area of Israel.

*__Ne'ilah__, concluding service on the *Day of Atonement.

Neofiti, term applied in southern Italy to converts to Christianity from Judaism and their descendants who were suspected of maintaining secret allegiance to Judaism.

*__Neology__; **Neolog**; **Neologism**, trend of *Reform Judaism in Hungary forming separate congregations after 1868.

*__Nevelah__ (lit. "carcass"), meat forbidden by the *dietary laws on account of the absence of, or defect in, the act of **sheḥitah* (ritual slaughter).

*__New Christians__, term applied especially in Spain and Portugal to converts from Judaism (and from Islam) and their descendants; "Half New Christian" designated a person one of whose parents was of full Jewish blood.

*__Niddah__ ("menstruous woman"), woman during the period of menstruation.

*__Nisan__, first month of the Jewish religious year, seventh of the civil, approximating to March-April.

Niẓoẓot, "sparks"; mystical term for sparks of the holy light imprisoned in all matter.

Nosaḥ (**nusaḥ**) "version"; (1) textual variant; (2) term applied to distinguish the various prayer rites, e.g., *nosaḥ Ashkenaz*; (3) the accepted tradition of synagogue melody.

*__Notarikon__, method of abbreviating Hebrew works or phrases by acronym.

Novella(e) (Heb. **ḥiddush (im)*), commentary on talmudic and later rabbinic subjects that derives new facts or principles from the implications of the text.

*__Nuremberg Laws__, Nazi laws excluding Jews from German citizenship, and imposing other restrictions.

Ofan, hymns inserted into a passage of the morning prayer.

*__Omer__, first sheaf cut during the barley harvest, offered in the Temple on the second day of Passover.

Omer, Counting of (Heb. *Sefirat ha-Omer*), 49 days counted from the day on which the *omer* was first offered in the Temple (according to the rabbis the 16th of Nisan, i.e., the second day of Passover) until the festival of Shavuot; now a period of semi-mourning.

Oraḥ Ḥayyim, see Shulḥan Arukh.

*__Orthodoxy__ (Orthodox Judaism), modern term for the strictly traditional sector of Jewry.

*__Pale of Settlement__, 25 provinces of czarist Russia where Jews were permitted permanent residence.

*__Palmaḥ__ (abbr. for Heb. *peluggot maḥaẓ*; "shock companies"), striking arm of the *Haganah.

*__Pardes__, medieval biblical exegesis giving the literal, allegorical, homiletical, and esoteric interpretations.

*__Parnas__, chief synagogue functionary, originally vested with both religious and administrative functions; subsequently an elected lay leader.

Partition plan(s), proposals for dividing Ereẓ Israel into autonomous areas.

Paytan, composer of **piyyut* (liturgical poetry).

*__Peel Commission__, British Royal Commission appointed by the British government in 1936 to inquire into the Palestine problem and make recommendations for its solution.

Pesaḥ, *Passover.

*__Pilpul__, in talmudic and rabbinic literature, a sharp dialectic used particularly by talmudists in Poland from the 16th century.

*__Pinkas__, community register or minute-book.

*__Piyyut__, (pl. **piyyutim**), Hebrew liturgical poetry.

*__Pizmon__, poem with refrain.

Posek (pl. ***posekim**), decisor; codifier or rabbinic scholar who pronounces decisions in disputes and on questions of Jewish law.

*__Prosbul__, legal method of overcoming the cancelation of debts with the advent of the *sabbatical year.

*__Purim__, festival held on Adar 14 or 15 in commemoration of the delivery of the Jews of Persia in the time of *Esther.

Rabban, honorific title higher than that of rabbi, applied to heads of the *Sanhedrin in mishnaic times.

*__Rabbanite__, adherent of rabbinic Judaism. In contradistinction to *Karaite.

Reb, rebbe, Yiddish form for rabbi, applied generally to a teacher or ḥasidic rabbi.

*__Reconstructionism__, trend in Jewish thought originating in the United States.

*__Reform Judaism__, trend in Judaism advocating modification of *Orthodoxy in conformity with the exigencies of contemporary life and thought.

Resh galuta, lay head of Babylonian Jewry (see exilarch).

Responsum (pl. ***responsa**), written opinion (*teshuvah*) given to question (*she'elah*) on aspects of Jewish law by qualified authorities; pl. collection of such queries and opinions in book form (*she'elot u-teshuvot*).

***Rishonim**, older rabbinical authorities. Distinguished from later authorities (**aḥaronim*).

***Rishon le-Zion**, title given to Sephardi chief rabbi of Ereẓ Israel.

***Rosh Ha-Shanah**, two-day holiday (one day in biblical and early mishnaic times) at the beginning of the month of *Tishri (September–October), traditionally the New Year.

Rosh Hodesh, *New Moon, marking the beginning of the Hebrew month.

Rosh Yeshivah, see *Yeshivah.

***R.S.H.A.** (initials of Ger. *Reichssicherheitshauptamt*: "Reich Security Main Office"), the central security department of the German Reich, formed in 1939, and combining the security police (Gestapo and Kripo) and the S.D.

***Sanhedrin**, the assembly of ordained scholars which functioned both as a supreme court and as a legislature before 70 C.E. In modern times the name was given to the body of representative Jews convoked by Napoleon in 1807.

***Savora** (pl. **savoraim**), name given to the Babylonian scholars of the period between the **amoraim* and the **geonim*, approximately 500–700 C.E.

S.D. (initials of Ger. *Sicherheitsdienst*: "security service"), security service of the *S.S. formed in 1932 as the sole intelligence organization of the Nazi party.

Seder, ceremony observed in the Jewish home on the first night of Passover (outside Ereẓ Israel first two nights), when the *Haggadah is recited.

***Sefer Torah**, manuscript scroll of the Pentateuch for public reading in synagogue.

***Sefirot, the ten**, the ten "Numbers"; mystical term denoting the ten spheres or emanations through which the Divine manifests itself; elements of the world; dimensions, primordial numbers.

Selektion (Ger.), (1) in ghettos and other Jewish settlements, the drawing up by Nazis of lists of deportees; (2) separation of incoming victims to concentration camps into two categories – those destined for immediate killing and those to be sent for forced labor.

Seliḥah (pl. ***seliḥot**), penitential prayer.

***Semikhah**, ordination conferring the title "rabbi" and permission to give decisions in matters of ritual and law.

Sephardi (pl. ***Sephardim**), Jew(s) of Spain and Portugal and their descendants, wherever resident, as contrasted with *Ashkenazi(m).

Shabbatean, adherent of the pseudo-messiah *Shabbetai Ẓevi (17th century).

Shaddai, name of God found frequently in the Bible and commonly translated "Almighty."

***Shaḥarit**, morning service.

Shali'aḥ (pl. **sheliḥim**), in Jewish law, messenger, agent; in modern times, an emissary from Ereẓ Israel to Jewish communities or organizations abroad for the purpose of fund-raising, organizing pioneer immigrants, education, etc.

Shalmonit, poetic meter introduced by the liturgical poet *Solomon ha-Bavli.

***Shammash**, synagogue beadle.

***Shavuot**, Pentecost; Festival of Weeks; second of the three annual pilgrim festivals, commemorating the receiving of the Torah at Mt. Sinai.

***Sheḥitah**, ritual slaughtering of animals.

***Shekhinah**, Divine Presence.

Shelishit, poem with three-line stanzas.

***Sheluḥei Ereẓ Israel** (or **shadarim**), emissaries from Ereẓ Israel.

***Shema** ([Yisrael]; "hear... [O Israel]," Deut. 6:4), Judaism's confession of faith, proclaiming the absolute unity of God.

Shemini Aẓeret, final festal day (in the Diaspora, final two days) at the conclusion of *Sukkot.

Shemittah, *Sabbatical year.

Sheniyyah, poem with two-line stanzas.

***Shephelah**, southern part of the coastal plain of Ereẓ Israel.

***Shevat**, eleventh month of the Jewish religious year, fifth of the civil, approximating to January–February.

***Shi'ur Komah**, Hebrew mystical work (c. eighth century) containing a physical description of God's dimensions; term denoting enormous spacial measurement used in speculations concerning the body of the **Shekhinah*.

Shivah, the "seven days" of *mourning following burial of a relative.

***Shofar**, horn of the ram (or any other ritually clean animal excepting the cow) sounded for the memorial blowing on *Rosh Ha-Shanah, and other occasions.

Shoḥet, person qualified to perform **sheḥitah*.

Shomer, *Ha-Shomer, organization of Jewish workers in Ereẓ Israel founded in 1909 to defend Jewish settlements.

***Shtadlan**, Jewish representative or negotiator with access to dignitaries of state, active at royal courts, etc.

***Shtetl**, Jewish small-town community in Eastern Europe.

***Shulḥan Arukh**, Joseph *Caro's code of Jewish law in four parts:
Oraḥ Ḥayyim, laws relating to prayers, Sabbath, festivals, and fasts;
Yoreh De'ah, dietary laws, etc;
Even ha-Ezer, laws dealing with women, marriage, etc;
Ḥoshen Mishpat, civil, criminal law, court procedure, etc.

Siddur, among Ashkenazim, the volume containing the daily prayers (in distinction to the **maḥzor* containing those for the festivals).

***Simḥat Torah**, holiday marking the completion in the synagogue of the annual cycle of reading the Pentateuch; in Ereẓ Israel observed on Shemini Aẓeret (outside Ereẓ Israel on the following day).

***Sinai Campaign**, brief campaign in October–November 1956 when Israel army reacted to Egyptian terrorist attacks and blockade by occupying the Sinai peninsula.

Sitra aḥra, "the other side" (of God); left side; the demoniac and satanic powers.

***Sivan**, third month of the Jewish religious year, ninth of the civil, approximating to May–June.

***Six-Day War**, rapid war in June 1967 when Israel reacted to Arab threats and blockade by defeating the Egyptian, Jordanian, and Syrian armies.

***S.S.** (initials of Ger. *Schutzstaffel*: "protection detachment"), Nazi formation established in 1925 which later became the "elite" organization of the Nazi Party and carried out central tasks in the "Final Solution."

***Status quo ante** community, community in Hungary retaining the status it had held before the convention of the General Jewish Congress there in 1868 and the resultant split in Hungarian Jewry.

*Sukkah, booth or tabernacle erected for *Sukkot when, for seven days, religious Jews "dwell" or at least eat in the *sukkah* (Lev. 23:42).

*Sukkot, festival of Tabernacles; last of the three pilgrim festivals, beginning on the 15th of Tishri.

Sūra (Ar.), chapter of the Koran.

Ta'anit Esther (Fast of *Esther), fast on the 13th of Adar, the day preceding Purim.

Takkanah (pl. ***takkanot**), regulation supplementing the law of the Torah; regulations governing the internal life of communities and congregations.

***Tallit (gadol)**, four-cornered prayer shawl with fringes (*ẓiẓit*) at each corner.

***Tallit katan**, garment with fringes (*ẓiẓit*) appended, worn by observant male Jews under their outer garments.

***Talmud**, "teaching"; compendium of discussion on the Mishnah by generations of scholars and jurists in many academies over a period of several centuries. The Jerusalem (or Palestinian) Talmud mainly contains the discussions of the Palestinian sages. The Babylonian Talmud incorporates the parallel discussion in the Babylonian academies.

Talmud torah, term generally applied to Jewish religious (and ultimately to talmudic) study; also to traditional Jewish religious public schools.

***Tammuz**, fourth month of the Jewish religious year, tenth of the civil, approximating to June-July.

Tanna (pl. ***tannaim**), rabbinic teacher of mishnaic period.

***Targum**, Aramaic translation of the Bible.

***Tefillin**, phylacteries, small leather cases containing passages from Scripture and affixed on the forehead and arm by male Jews during the recital of morning prayers.

Tell (Ar. "mound," "hillock"), ancient mound in the Middle East composed of remains of successive settlements.

***Terefah**, food that is not **kasher*, owing to a defect on the animal.

***Territorialism**, 20th century movement supporting the creation of an autonomous territory for Jewish mass-settlement outside Ereẓ Israel.

***Tevet**, tenth month of the Jewish religious year, fourth of the civil, approximating to December–January.

Tikkun ("restitution," "reintegration"), (1) order of service for certain occasions, mostly recited at night; (2) mystical term denoting restoration of the right order and true unity after the spiritual "catastrophe" which occurred in the cosmos.

Tishah be-Av, Ninth of *Av, fast day commemorating the destruction of the First and Second Temples.

***Tishri**, seventh month of the Jewish religious year, first of the civil, approximating to September–October.

Tokheḥah, reproof sections of the Pentateuch (Lev. 26 and Deut. 28); poem of reproof.

***Torah**, Pentateuch or the Pentateuchal scroll for reading in synagogue; entire body of traditional Jewish teaching and literature.

Tosafist, talmudic glossator, mainly French (12–14th centuries), bringing additions to the commentary by *Rashi.

***Tosafot**, glosses supplied by tosafist.

***Tosefta**, a collection of teachings and traditions of the *tannaim*, closely related to the Mishnah.

Tradent, person who hands down a talmudic statement on the name of his teacher or other earlier authority.

***Tu bi-Shevat**, the 15th day of Shevat, the New Year for Trees; date marking a dividing line for fruit tithing; in modern Israel celebrated as arbor day.

***Uganda Scheme**, plan suggested by the British government in 1903 to establish an autonomous Jewish settlement area in East Africa.

***Va'ad Le'ummi**, national council of the Jewish community in Ereẓ Israel during the period of the British *Mandate.

***Wannsee Conference**, Nazi conference held on Jan. 20, 1942, at which the planned annihilation of European Jewry was endorsed.

Waqf (Ar.), (1) a Muslim charitable pious foundation; (2) state lands and other property passed to the Muslim community for public welfare.

***War of Independence**, war of 1947–49 when the Jews of Israel fought off Arab invading armies and ensured the establishment of the new State.

***White Paper(s)**, report(s) issued by British government, frequently statements of policy, as issued in connection with Palestine during the *Mandate period.

***Wissenschaft des Judentums** (Ger. "Science of Judaism"), movement in Europe beginning in the 19th century for scientific study of Jewish history, religion, and literature.

***Yad Vashem**, Israel official authority for commemorating the *Holocaust in the Nazi era and Jewish resistance and heroism at that time.

Yeshivah (pl. ***yeshivot**), Jewish traditional academy devoted primarily to study of rabbinic literature; *rosh yeshivah*, head of the yeshivah.

YHWH, the letters of the holy name of God, the Tetragrammaton.

Yibbum, see levirate marriage.

Yiḥud, "union"; mystical term for intention which causes the union of God with the **Shekhinah*.

Yishuv, settlement; more specifically, the Jewish community of Ereẓ Israel in the pre-State period. The pre-Zionist community is generally designated the "old yishuv" and the community evolving from 1880, the "new yishuv."

Yom Kippur, Yom ha-Kippurim, *Day of Atonement, solemn fast day observed on the 10th of Tishri.

Yoreh De'ah, see Shulḥan Arukh.

Yoẓer, hymns inserted in the first benediction (*Yoẓer Or*) of the morning **Shema*.

***Ẓaddik**, person outstanding for his faith and piety; especially a ḥasidic rabbi or leader.

Ẓimẓum, "contraction"; mystical term denoting the process whereby God withdraws or contracts within Himself so leaving a primordial vacuum in which creation can take place; primordial exile or self-limitation of God.

***Zionist Commission (1918)**, commission appointed in 1918 by the British government to advise the British military authorities in Palestine on the implementation of the *Balfour Declaration.

Ẓyyonei Zion, the organized opposition to Herzl in connection with the *Uganda Scheme.

***Ẓiẓit**, fringes attached to the **tallit* and **tallit katan*.

***Zohar**, mystical commentary on the Pentateuch; main textbook of *Kabbalah.

Zulat, hymn inserted after the **Shema* in the morning service.

ISBN-13: 978-0-02-865936-7
ISBN-10: 0-02-865936-8